The Right **School** = The Right **Job**

- As the leading media company for career information, Vault understands that your education is an integral part of your career path.

- You go to college or graduate school because you want to reach your career goals.

- In Vault's *Buzz Books*, we bring readers detailed, exclusive information about employment prospects at top schools.

- Each profile also includes exclusive information on admissions, academics, quality of life and social life at the schools.

- All information is based on exclusive Vault surveys of students and alumni at each school.

VAULT

> the most trusted name in career information™

DREXEL UNIVERSITY COLLEGE OF LAW

Scientia, Ars, Officium

The Drexel University College of Law is the first law school to be founded by a major research university in 30 years. The College builds on Drexel University's great strengths in the areas of engineering, science, business, and health care. Law students will be prepared for the challenges of 21st-century practice through:

- *Co-op opportunities providing valuable practice experience*

- *Small class sizes and accomplished faculty in all subject areas*

- *Initial specializations in health care, intellectual property, and entrepreneurial business*

- *A newly constructed law school building with wireless Internet access*

3141 Chestnut Street, Philadelphia PA   215.895.1LAW   www.drexel.edu/law

The Law School
Buzz Book

The Law School
Buzz Book

EDITED BY CAROLYN C. WISE
AND THE STAFF OF VAULT

For information about permission to reproduce selections from this book, contact Vault Inc.150 W. 22nd St. New York, New York 10011-1772, (212) 366-4212.

Library of Congress CIP Data is available.

ISBN 13: 978-1-58131-424-3

ISBN 10: 1-58131-424-8

Printed in the United States of America

Acknowledgments

Thanks to everyone who had a hand in making this book possible. We are also extremely grateful to Vault's entire staff for all their help in the editorial, production and marketing processes. Vault would also like to acknowledge the support of our investors, clients, employees, family and friends. Thank you!

Vault would also like to thank all of the public affairs and admissions officers at law schools who worked with us to ensure that the information provided by students and alumni is as accurate and placed within as much context as possible. Thanks for all of your patience and assistance with our editorial process!

Read all of Vault's Law School surveys at **www.vault.com/lawschool** — get complete surveys on 100s of law schools, expert advice on applicaton essays, LSAT prep and more.

VAULT CAREER LIBRARY   vii

Practice What We Teach

At **Western New England College School of Law**, you will gain practical lawyering skills through myriad experiential learning opportunities. In our collegial learning environment, you will be challenged to articulate persuasive legal arguments, and research and write thorough, precise, legal memoranda.

Our small class size sections encourage engagement and collaboration with faculty and fellow students, both in and out of the classroom. And we support experiential learning through our curricula and programs like our Public Interest Law scholarships.

Through clinics, simulation courses, moot court competitions, and externships you will put into practice what we teach.

To learn more about our law programs, call **800-782-6665** or **413-782-1406**.

WESTERN
NEW ENGLAND
COLLEGE
SCHOOL *of* LAW

Springfield, Massachusetts
www.law.wnec.edu

Table of Contents

Read all of Vault's Law School surveys at **www.vault.com/lawschool** — get complete surveys on 100s of law schools, expert advice on applicaton essays, LSAT prep and more.

VAULT CAREER LIBRARY   ix

Read all of Vault's Law School surveys at **www.vault.com/lawschool** — get complete surveys on 100s of law
schools, expert advice on applicaton essays, LSAT prep and more.

VAULT CAREER LIBRARY   xi

Read all of Vault's Law School surveys at **www.vault.com/lawschool** — get complete surveys on 100s of law
schools, expert advice on applicaton essays, LSAT prep and more.

VAULT CAREER LIBRARY   **xiii**

Advocate for your future.

Earn your degree from the law school ranked #1 in trial advocacy and #4 in legal writing by *U.S. News & World Report.*

STETSON UNIVERSITY
College of Law

www.law.stetson.edu • 727.562.7802 • lawadmit@law.stetson.edu

Read all of Vault's Law School surveys at www.vault.com/lawschool — get complete surveys on 100s of law schools, expert advice on applicaton essays, LSAT prep and more.

VAULT CAREER LIBRARY   xv

Read all of Vault's Law School surveys at **www.vault.com/lawschool** — get complete surveys on 100s of law schools, expert advice on applicaton essays, LSAT prep and more.

VAULT CAREER LIBRARY **xvii**

WHITTIER LAW SCHOOL

FOR FORTY YEARS, PREPARING STUDENTS FOR SUCCESS ON THE BAR EXAMINATION & IN PRACTICE

SUCCESS IN TAKING THE BAR EXAMINATION

The Institute for Student and Graduate Academic Support offers the necessary tools to pass the bar examination on the

first attempt:

- An Early Bar Preparation Program focusing on all three types of bar examination questions and all the bar examination subjects;
- A Supplemental Bar Preparation program with proven success on the Multistate Bar Examination;
- A first-year skills curriculum featuring small group sessions with individualized practice and feedback;
- An upper-level curriculum featuring bar examination essay and writing workshops; and
- Individual one-on-one counseling sessions for students in academic difficulty.

• 124 Whittier Law School graduates passed the California Bar Exam on their first attempt. This is 19 points higher than the July 2005 rate and 28 points higher than the rate just three years ago.

• Substantial participation in the Early Bar Preparation Program significantly increases the likelihood of passing the Bar Exam. Graduates that took 60% of the Early Bar Prep Program passed the July 2006 Bar Exam at 83%, higher than the state average of 74%.

SUCCESS IN THINKING AND WRITING AS A LAWYER

The Institute for Legal Writing and Professional Skills sponsors the most extensive program in the country with five required semesters covering all aspects of legal writing and analysis.
The legal writing program has:

- An in-house Writing Advisor who offers one-on-one assistance and numerous writing workshops;
- Small sections, allowing intensive focused individual attention; and
- A Certificate in Legal Writing, including a Legal Writing capstone course.

• Full-time and Part-time Day and Evening programs available • Concentrations in Business Law, Children's Rights, Criminal Law, Intellectual Property Law, and International & Comparative Law, • 5 Clinics • 200 Externships
• 5 Summer Abroad Programs in Amsterdam, China, France, Israel, and Spain • Network of over 4,000 graduates

WHITTIER LAW SCHOOL

In service of justice and enterprise ℠

3333 Harbor Boulevard • Costa Mesa, California 92626
(714) 444-4141 • www.law.whittier.edu

Whittier College — 1887 • Whittier Law School — 1966

Introduction

Welcome to the third edition of Vault's *Law School Buzz Book*. In this unique guide, we publish extended excerpts from surveys of students and alumni at more than 140 top law schools to bring you the inside scoop on the specific programs. The survey comments cover the following areas:

- Admissions
- Academics
- Employment prospects
- Quality of life
- Social life

The guide is intended to serve as a complement to other references to law schools currently available that utilize school-reported data. Unlike those guides, Vault's *Buzz Books* (which also include *The Business School Buzz Book* and *The College Buzz Book*) are composed almost entirely of information provided directly to Vault from students and alumni. (We asked schools to comment on the surveys after they were collected; this process is detailed later in this introduction.)

About this Vault *Buzz Book*

Founded in 1997, Vault—The Most Trusted Name in Career Information®—is the leading publisher for career information. We publish more than 100 guides to careers, and annually survey 10,000s of employees to bring readers the inside scoop on specific employers and industries. In the law field, we annually survey more than 15,000 attorneys at major law firms to produce our well-known *Vault Guide to the Top 100 Law Firms* (now in its 9th edition), and also annually survey attorneys for our regional law firm guides (*Vault Guide to the Top Mid-Atlantic Law Firms*, *Vault Guide to the Top Southeastern Law Firms*, etc.)

In the past two years, we've extended our surveys of employees to include students and alumni because we recognize that education—especially graduate education—is a vital component of our readers' career paths. In considering their career options, readers of our guides and visitors to our web site (www.vault.com) also consider law school and other graduate programs.

Law school and careers

The main reason for getting a law degree, of course, is to become a lawyer, for which there are ample career opportunities. The most immediately lucrative is what is known as BigLaw—working as an associate at one of the few hundred largest law firms in the country. At top firms in major legal markets like New York, Chicago, Washington, D.C. and Los Angeles, first-year associates just out of law school make $125,000 annually plus bonuses.

While many law school graduates take positions at large law firms upon graduation, newly-minted JDs have many other career opportunities available, including public interest work, work for the government in the district attorney's office, and careers with government agencies like the FBI, Department of Justice or Department of State, to name just a few. (For information on career opportunities for JDs, see the *Vault Guide to the Top 100 Law Firms*, the *Vault Guide to Government and Nonprofit Legal Employers* and other Vault guides at www.vault.com/law.)

Read all of Vault's Law School surveys at **www.vault.com/lawschool** — get complete surveys on 100s of law schools, expert advice on applicaton essays, LSAT prep and more.

VAULT CAREER LIBRARY 1

We're excited to bring our award-winning "insider" survey methodology to the beginning of this career path—law school. Knowing that law school students are pursuing their JDs specifically to enhance their career opportunities, we've made a special point of surveying students about employment prospects. Their comments in this area concern their perception of the relative prestige of the law school, the strength of on-campus recruiting (including what type of firms recruit at the school) and the alumni network, as well as other important considerations concerning employment prospects.

A Guide to this Guide

Vault's survey process

Vault collects all of its student and alumni surveys online through Vault's proprietary online form. We collect surveys from students and alumni primarily through Vault's network of members and readers at top law schools and law firms. This year, we also invited all of the law schools we cover to invite their students and alumni to take our survey online.

The designations of whether a survey entry was filled out by a "current student" or "alumnus/a" indicate the survey takers' status at the time their surveys were completed (i.e., if a student completed the survey in spring 2005, and graduated in May 2005, the entry would be designated as filled out by a current student, even though the student has since graduated). To provide additional context for our readers, we have also included the month that the survey was submitted. Vault began collecting student and alumni surveys in September 2003.

Survey questions

The survey asked students and alumni to comment on their experience at the law school in five areas: admissions, academics, employment prospects, quality of life, and social life. The exact questions asked are indicated below.

Admissions: Please provide a detailed account of the admissions process, including advice on getting in, interview, essays and selectivity.

Academics: Please provide a detailed account of the academic nature of the program, including quality of classes, ease of getting popular classes, grading, professors and workload.

Employment Prospects: Please provide a detailed assessment of employment prospects for graduates of your school, including prestige with employers, types of jobs graduates obtain, helpfulness of alumni network, and on-campus recruiting and internships.

Quality of Life: Please provide a detailed account of the program with respect to quality of life issues, including housing, campus, facilities, dining, neighborhood and crime and safety.

Social Life: Please provide a detailed account of the school's social life, including bars, restaurants, dating scene, events, clubs and Greek system. Please include specific student favorites if possible.

Editing the surveys

In producing this book, our Vault editors edited surveys to formalize the surveys for syntax and style, and to correct egregious grammatical errors (yes, law school students do make them). However, it was our intent to maintain the colloquial flavor of each respondent's survey comments, so we retained sentence fragments, slang, and other nonstandard language elements that we felt did not distract from the narratives.

School responses

After editing the surveys, we sent the edited profiles to each school for comment. We asked the schools to do the following:

- Indicate any instances where students or alumni had provided factually incorrect information (average test scores or GPAs, for example)

- Provide any information they felt would contribute necessary context to specific survey comments

- Provide a separate 500-word narrative to be published with the profile.

We received responses from virtually every school; comments came from either the public affairs/media relations office or the admissions office, depending on the school. We have included comments next to appropriate survey sections, offset with a different font and indented to be easily recognizable as school-provided comments. Corrections within the body of the comments are enclosed in brackets. In the cases where a school provided a separate narrative, we have included this at the end of the school's entry, under the heading "The School Says."

Also note that many law schools reviewed our survey profiles and indicated that they saw no factual errors and did not have any comments to add.

Read all of Vault's Law School surveys at **www.vault.com/lawschool** — get complete surveys on 100s of law schools, expert advice on applicaton essays, LSAT prep and more.

VAULT CAREER LIBRARY

3

Law School
Programs and
Services Directory

Read all of Vault's Law School surveys at **www.vault.com/lawschool** — get complete surveys on 100s of law schools, expert advice on applicaton essays, LSAT prep and more.

VAULT CAREER LIBRARY   7

Duke University School of Law

Science Drive and Towerview Road
Box 90393
Durham, NC 27707
Phone: 919-613-7020
Fax: 919-613-7257
www.admissions.law.duke.edu

Duke Law School offers a rigorous legal education in an exceptionally collegial and collaborative environment. Faculty members are top scholars who engage with students and involve them in their research and activities. Duke's curriculum and intellectual climate are enhanced by first-rate interdisciplinary centers in the areas of national security, public law, intellectual property, environmental law, international law, and business law, as well as student-led programs. Many students opt to pursue a joint-degree, and can earn both a law and masters degree in three years. Duke Law graduates are highly sought, taking positions in every major legal market nationally and internationally.

Contact:

admissions@law.duke.edu

Hofstra Law School

121 Hofstra University
Hempstead, NY 11549-1210
Phone: 516.463.5916
Fax: 516.463.6264
www.law.hofstra.edu

Hofstra Law School is committed to teaching students not just how to think like lawyers, but to become lawyers. Our curriculum, which evolves each year to address changes in the law, includes significant offerings in skills practice enabling students to integrate and master substance learned in the classroom through application to real-life situations. Our students benefit from an atmosphere of intellectual excitement, personal support and cooperative learning. The faculty at Hofstra Law, many of whom are renowned leaders in their field, are truly dedicated to student success.

Hofstra Law offers full-time and part-time programs as well as advanced law degree opportunities in Family Law, International Law and American Legal Studies. An LL.M. in Real Estate and Development Law is currently in development and will be offered in Spring 2007. Joint degree opportunities are also available including a J.D./M.B.A. with Hoftra's Zarb School of Business.

Contact:

Deborah M. Martin
Assistant Dean for Enrollment Management
516.463.5916
lawadmissions@hofstra.edu

Penn State Dickinson School of Law

150 South College Street
Carlisle, PA 17013-2899
100 Beam Building
University Park, PA 16802-1589
Phone: 1-800-840-1122
www.dsl.psu.edu

PENN STATE
The DICKINSON SCHOOL of LAW

The merger of Penn State University and The Dickinson School of Law has been transformative for the law school. Since the merger, applications for admission have increased by more than 100 percent, student body diversity has tripled, student body academic credentials have improved significantly, and our faculty has grown to include several of the world's top legal scholars.

The law school now operates as a unified enterprise with facilities on Penn State's flagship University Park campus in State College, PA, and in our original home of Carlisle, PA. The University is investing $100 million in new facilities for the law school in both locations (occupancy 2009) and has allocated an additional several million dollars to the law school on a recurring annual basis to support new faculty and programs. These initiatives represent the largest investment in an academic unit in the history of Penn State University.

Contact:
Janice Austin
Assistant Dean for Admissions & Financial Aid
dsladmit@psu.edu

Santa Clara University School of Law

Law Admissions & Financial Aid
500 El Camino Real
Santa Clara, CA 95053
Phone: (408) 554-5048
Fax: (408) 554-7897
www.scu.edu/law

Santa Clara University
School of Law

• **Expert Faculty**: At Santa Clara Law, you will study under a faculty of skilled and experienced educators and dedicated teachers. The faculty includes former U.S. Supreme Court law clerks, a Rhodes Scholar, Silicon Valley and Wall Street practitioners, and federal public defenders.

• **Dynamic Curriculum:** The curriculum at Santa Clara Law is rigorous and will prepare you to enter the practice of law .You can explore your interests in specialty areas such as social justice and public interest law, intellectual property law, trial and appellate advocacy and international and comparative law. You can learn about the roles that lawyers play in our society and in California's high tech Silicon Valley through the law school's many internships, clinical programs, summer international study programs, joint degree programs and certificate programs.

• **Admission Information:** Learn more about receiving your legal education at Santa Clara University at www.scu.edu/law or by contacting our Admissions professionals at (408) 554-4800.

Contact:
Jeanette J. Leach
Assistant Dean of Admissions & Financial Aid
(408) 554-5048
lawadmissions@scu.edu

Read all of Vault's Law School surveys at **www.vault.com/lawschool** — get complete surveys on 100s of law schools, expert advice on applicaton essays, LSAT prep and more.

VAULT CAREER LIBRARY   9

Stetson University College of Law

1401 61st Street South
Gulfport, FL 33707
Phone: 727-562-7800
www.law.stetson.edu

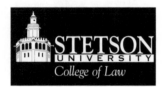

As Florida's first law school, Stetson University College of Law has educated outstanding lawyers, judges and community leaders since 1900. With campuses in Gulfport and Tampa, Stetson is consistently ranked among the top law schools in the nation for trial advocacy and legal writing. Stetson combines small classes, top-notch professors and state-of-the-art resources to prepare its students for exceptional legal careers. With approximately 1000 students, the College of Law is committed to diversity, professionalism, and community service. Stetson is fully accredited by the American Bar Association and has been a member of the Association of American Law Schools since 1931.

Contact:
Office of Admissions
727-562-7802
lawadmit@law.stetson.edu

Western New England College School of Law

1215 Wilbraham Road
Springfield, Massachusetts 01119-2684
Phone: 413-782-1406
Fax: 413-796-2067
www.law.wnec.edu

Western New England College School of Law offers full- or part-time programs. The School of Law offers three joint/combined degree programs: JD/MBA (Masters in Business Administration through Western New England College); JD/MSW (Masters in Social Work through Springfield College); JD/MRP (Masters in Regional Planning through the University of Massachusetts). Students may earn an advanced law degree in Elder Law and Estate Planning. Western New England College School of Law is the only Massachusetts law school outside the Boston area accredited by the American Bar Association and member of the AALS.

Contact:
Michael A. Johnson
Assistant Dean and Director of Admissions
413-782-1286
admissions@law.wnec.edu

Whittier College School of Law

3333 Harbor Boulevard
Costa Mesa, CA 92626
Phone: 714 444 4141
Fax: 714 444 0250
www.law.whittier.edu

The first ABA law school in Orange County, Whittier Law School offers a variety of programs and opportunities. The Law School has three Centers in Children's Advocacy, International and Comparative Law, and Intellectual Property; two Institutes in Legal Writing Skills and Graduate Academic Support; two certificate programs in Criminal and Business Law; and five summer abroad programs in China, Israel, France, Spain, and Netherlands.

Contact:
Office of Admissions
714 444 4141 ext 123
info@law.whittier.edu

Widener University School of Law

Delaware Campus
4601 Concord Pike
Wilmington, DE 19803-0474
Phone: 302-477-2100
Fax: 302-477-2224

Harrisburg Campus
3800 Vartan Way
Harrisburg, PA 17106-9381
Phone: 717-541-3900
www.law.widener.edu

Widener Law prepares students to practice law in the real world, combining education with experience in a dynamic learning environment. Widener Law students build their legal resumes while they earn their degrees. With one of the premier clinical programs in the region, Widener Law provides students ample opportunity to help people who need it, handling real cases in a variety of specialties. Widener Law students enjoy an exceptional externship program, and are often placed in highly sought-after government and public service law offices, earning credits while working alongside practicing attorneys and judges. For more information, visit www.law.widener.edu.

Contact:
Barbara Ayars
Assistant Dean for Admissions
302-477-2100
lawadmissions@mail.widener.edu

Read all of Vault's law school surveys at **www.vault.com/lawschool** – get complete surveys on more than a hundred law schools, get expert advice on applicaton essays and LSAT prep and more.

VAULT CAREER LIBRARY   11

Law School
Profiles

The University of Alabama School of Law

Admissions Office
Box 870382
Tuscaloosa, AL 35487-0382
Admissions phone: (205) 348-5440
Admissions e-mail: admissions@law.ua.edu
Admissions URL: http://www.law.ua.edu/prospective/

 Admissions

Status: Alumnus/a, full-time
Dates of Enrollment: 8/2002-5/2005
Survey Submitted: May 2006

Admissions is a fairly straightforward process. When I applied, two essays were required and they were both fairly short. Rarely are they the focus of the application. At the time of my enrollment, I do not think an interview was conducted on anyone, though this process may have changed. From my experience and those of other students, I do believe a high LSAT score trumps everything else. My GPA was a few tenths below that required for admission, but my LSAT score was a full 10 points higher than what was required and I had no problems. A fellow student graduated college with a C average but was still admitted based largely on his LSAT.

While I was in attendance, the school climbed in rank and became more and more selective, with GPA and LSAT requirements climbing. Because of the state's history, however, minority students are heavily recruited though overall minority representation is still lacking.

Status: Alumnus/a, full-time
Dates of Enrollment: 8/2001-5/2004
Survey Submitted: April 2006

I had to fill out an application, accompanied by a personal statement and essay about my "most character-building experience." I met with the assistant dean of admissions, visited a class, met with the dean and was taken to lunch by a student. I spoke with the assistant dean of admissions on several occasions, and she was a helpful resource for all my questions associated with the application and scholarship process.

Status: Alumnus/a, full-time JD/MBA
Dates of Enrollment: 8/1999-5/2004
Survey Submitted: April 2006

There was no interview on the law side and I believe that the LSAT score weighs heavily on admissions decisions. I don't remember getting penalized at UA for taking the LSAT more than once—they just took the highest score. There was an interview process for the MBA program. To get into the joint JD/MBA program, there was a separate application. The law school is fairly selective. I know a lot of friends that did not get in. Work experience was not necessary to get into MBA school, making it a little different from most B-schools.

Status: Alumnus/a, full-time
Dates of Enrollment: 8/2001-5/2004
Survey Submitted: April 2006

The chances of getting into Alabama's law school are apparently somewhat higher if you're from the state of Alabama. It is after all a state school. Median LSAT scores continue to rise, and a solid 160 is likely necessary to be competitive candidate these days. LSAT scores are far more important that GPA. The ratio of applicants to admittants was around 5:1 when I was accepted. The admission essays were easy, there was no interview. My law classmates were some of the most clever people I've ever met. Everyone that gets into law school is intensely competitive and used to getting perfect/near perfect grades.

> **The school says:** "The median LSAT for the 2006-07 first-year class is 163."

Status: Alumnus/a, full-time
Dates of Enrollment: 8/2002-5/2005
Survey Submitted: April 2006

The University of Alabama School of Law has a downloadable application available on its web site at www.law.ua.edu. I downloaded, printed and reviewed the application well in advance of the application deadline. There are several items which take additional time and thought to complete. These include, but are not limited to, questions regarding any misconduct in and out of school (which may, for some, require checking criminal records and school files in more than one state, which cannot be done overnight), having letters of reference completed by individuals who know you well and will speak highly of your character, intelligence and work ethic (it takes time to write a letter of reference that will really help a potential student, so be courteous and remember that this individual is doing you a huge favor—give them plenty of time to meet with you and several weeks to have the letter completed). You will need official transcripts from ALL universities and junior colleges you have attended, regardless of how long it has been since your last class or if you only attended for one class.

You will also need to complete several essay questions. Do not wait until the last minute to complete these. Come up with some possible responses to the questions, and do not be afraid to ask others close to you if they feel your response is true to your character. Also, most colleges have career services offices, and I strongly suggest making an appointment with such an office to go over your essay responses. You will also be required to submit a copy of your resume. Make sure that it is up to date, and it is also wise to take this with you to your meeting with your career services office for suggestions. Do not hesitate to compliment yourself for volunteer activities and unique experiences; law schools look to diversify each class with students from different backgrounds, with different beliefs and experiences.

Status: Current student, full-time
Dates of Enrollment: 7/2003-Submit Date
Survey Submitted: April 2006

Alabama has a very simple admissions process based upon a formula. The stated formula is a weighted average of the undergraduate GPA and your LSAT score. Essentially, if an applicant has a 3.0 undergraduate GPA combined with a 168 LSAT, then admissions is almost guaranteed. Further, if an applicant has a 3.8 undergraduate GPA and a LSAT score of 162, then the applicant will probably gain admission to the law school. Alabama is constantly improving itself in the *U.S. News & World Report* rankings. Because of such concentration on the rankings, Alabama tends to value both the LSAT and the undergraduate GPA highly.

There are a couple of downsides to the process. First and foremost, the law school does not concentrate on diversity, personal experiences, etc. Additionally, the law school does not do interviews for prospective students. However, there is a required essay that must be completed before admission is considered. This essay asks the applicant the question of what is the biggest obstacle that said individual has overcome. Alabama is fairly selective in its admission process. Because of the aforementioned *U.S. News & World Report* ranking obsession, Alabama wishes to recruit only the best and brightest in state, as well as out of state.

> **The school says:** "Admissions decisions are not based upon a formula or index. The Admissions Committee considers the entirety of each applicant's file. The Committee evaluates each applicant's contributions to the class, including diversity and personal experiences. The fall 2006 incoming class in nearly 20 percent minority."

Read all of Vault's Law School Surveys at www.vault.com/lawschool — get complete surveys on top law schools, expert advice on applicaton essays, LSAT prep and more.

VAULT CAREER LIBRARY   15

Status: Alumnus/a, full-time
Dates of Enrollment: 8/2002-5/2005
Survey Submitted: April 2006

UA Law uses "rolling admissions" so applying early may give you an advantage in getting accepted. The caliber of candidates who apply also seems to rise each year. A lot of people in the the classes ahead of me acknowledged that if they were competing against a newly arriving student, their grades and LSAT scores would likely pale in comparison to the new students'. There was no interview, but the application requires a personal statement. The personal statement should showcase to the school why you would provide something that other students can't. All the students are smart, you need something else, like diversity, hardship overcome, volunteer work, or leadership. Especially now that selectivity is so intense at UA law. The number of applications has probably doubled since I applied four years ago. The number of students accepted had remained the same. UA also awards "bonus" points for legacies of the school, giving preference to those applicants who have relatives that attended the school, much the way fraternities operate.

> **The school says:** "The admissions process does not involve a point or bonus system."

Status: Current student, full-time
Dates of Enrollment: 8/2003-Submit Date
Survey Submitted: April 2006

I just took the LSAT, and then filled out an application. I wrote the two essays required on the application and had a friend read them over. My grades were about average, but my LSAT score was well above Alabama's average. The school put me on a waiting list for about three weeks, then I received my acceptance letter. Based on that, I would say they were fairly selective. I, perhaps arrogantly, thought I would be accepted immediately, but as I said, that is not what happened.

Status: Current student, full-time
Dates of Enrollment: 8/2002-Submit Date
Survey Submitted: October 2003

Admission to Alabama is becoming more and more selective. This year [2002] only about 24 percent of applicants were admitted. It seems the key to getting accepted to Alabama is to score high enough on the LSAT. If you score a 161 or higher on the LSAT, then you are almost certainly guaranteed admission, even if your undergraduate GPA is mediocre or even abysmal. Conversely, if you have a really high GPA and you can't seem to make at least a 157 on the LSAT, then you probably will be denied admission. Additionally if you have a decent GPA and also are able to score really high on the LSAT (i.e., 165+), then you probably have a shot at getting a scholarship.

> **Regarding admissions, the school says:** "The admissions process, as with any law school, is competitive. The LSAT and UGPA are the two most significant factors in the admissions process. However, an applicant's file will be reviewed for other factors such as: unique work experience or community service; leadership roles; history of overcoming adversity; travel experience; demonstrated concern for the disadvantaged; exceptional talents; career achievements; trends in academic program; writing abilities; graduate school performance; and other qualities from an applicant's background. The committee typically does not conduct interviews. The Admissions Committee begins making some decisions as early as November. Thus, it is to an applicant's advantage to get his/her application in early in the process. However, it is also important to submit a competitive file. The committee usually offers admission only to candidates with exceptionally strong applications during the first several meetings."

Status: Alumnus/a, full-time
Dates of Enrollment: 8/2000-5/2003
Survey Submitted: September 2003

Two brief essays were required when I applied: a personal statement and a description of a life-altering moment. No interview is necessary, but I highly advise candidates to visit the campus if they are interested. I waited until after I was accepted to visit, and everyone was wonderful. The atmosphere was very inviting, and the reception I received from the students, faculty and staff was so welcoming—my visit ended up being the deciding factor in where I attended law school. I visited other campuses, but the people at Alabama were the most friendly. As a top-tier school, it has a pretty intense selection process. Most students are from within the state; I was one of very few students with no connection to Alabama.

 Academics

Status: Alumnus/a, full-time
Dates of Enrollment: 8/2002-12/2005
Survey Submitted: May 2006

Academics are good for the most part. There is a wide variety of classes although some are not offered very often. Most classes are easy to get into, although some clinical, seminars and trail advocacy spots are more difficult. Professors are generally very friendly and accessible outside of class. They will take the time to talk with you and answer questions. Workload is heavy, especially the first year. If you don't want to fall behind, expect to spend about seven to eight hours per day outside of class reading/studying/outlining during the week, and four to five hours total on the weekends. This, of course, will vary depending on your efficiency and tendency to procrastinate. I had friends who did the bare minimum until two weeks before finals, and then studied around the clock for two weeks and still did OK—however they did not excel. The workload during second and third years is significantly less—which is pretty much the case at all schools.

Status: Alumnus/a, full-time
Dates of Enrollment: 8/2002-5/2005
Survey Submitted: May 2006

Class quality was rarely an issue. The school pulls quality professors from both the professional and academic fields, creating a great mix of real-life and by-the-book studies. The only area that really suffered from professor quality was Legal Writing. Taught through the entire first year, this class teaches and corrects those skills needed for proper legal writing style, not only for the professional field but for school exams. Unfortunately this is where the school placed new professors for "trial runs" at teaching a class. These new professors sometimes did not have the skills needed to instruct and correct a student, which negatively impacted the student. In my case, I studied with a group of friends with knowledge similar to mine. They had one professor for Legal Writing, I had another. Their early drafts were corrected and conferences with their professor proved beneficial. My early drafts were simply graded, never corrected, and my professor would only tell me, "You're doing something wrong, but I can't tell you what it is." The majority of my study group performed a letter better than I did grade-wise throughout school.

> **The school says:** "The Legal Writing Program is not a training ground for new professors. In fact, the program has four full-time instructors. Currently, three instructors have taught legal writing for several years."

Status: Alumnus/a, full-time
Dates of Enrollment: 8/2001-5/2004
Survey Submitted: April 2006

The University of Alabama School of Law prides itself on its academic quality. UA boasts many great professors including a former dean who, literally, wrote the book on Evidence. I have heard stories where judges were persuaded on an evidence question simply because "Dean Gamble said so." On top of this, his entertaining teaching style makes his classes some of the most sought after. Still, in my entire time at UA, there was never a class I wanted that I didn't get. Alabama requires students to take at least one seminar where the student/teacher ratio is less than 10:1. The most popular of these fill up rather quickly, but I was able to get my first choice as were most other people. (Those who didn't simply waited and got them the next year when third-year students are given priority.)

Status: Alumnus/a, full-time
Dates of Enrollment: 8/2001-5/2004
Survey Submitted: April 2006

The Socratic Method of teaching law is alive and well at Alabama as with most American law schools. I'm skeptical that this is the ONLY method that should be employed, and it definitely doesn't help you learn the law itself. (The case method and Socratic presentation style does help you think like a lawyer, which is an important foundational skill.) First-year professors at Alabama are desperately trying to emulate *The Paper Chase*, and you'd be well advised to watch the movie before you try to attend law school. Ostensibly, challenging law students to defend every single thing they do and say prepares them for dealing with judges, opposing counsel, and senior partners; the reality is, most lawyers sit in an office all day writing, reading or talking to people on the phone.

Getting popular classes can be a challenge, especially Trial Ad. Grading is strictly curved for first-year courses and large courses thereafter. This will make or destroy your life: enjoy. After the first year, professors range from genial and terribly helpful to detached, total you-know-whats. First-year workload is horrendous, if you can survive it, you'll wonder what the other two years are for. You can pretty much tune out for the last two years if you aren't competing for a top ranking (at a certain point it becomes mathematically impossible to change your ranking much), you'll learn the ACTUAL law during the Bar/Bri course which I recommend for passing the bar exam.

> **The school says:** "The grading curve for first-year classes is recommended, but not required and not strictly enforced."

Status: Alumnus/a, full-time
Dates of Enrollment: 8/2002-5/2005
Survey Submitted: April 2006

The University of Alabama School of Law has a wonderfully diverse class offering. As most potential law students know, your schedule is pre-determined for your first year, and there are several classes that you are required to take during your second year. However, you are allowed flexibility in scheduling during your second year. I could not give one complaint about any professor, whether tenured or visited, which I experienced during law school. They are all available after classes and at their office hours for additional help and discussion, and I have even kept in touch with several of my professors who have given me guidance as I work through my first year of practice in a small firm.

The workload is less than what it will be when you are an attorney, so learn to manage your time in school. If you treat school like a job—go in around seven or eight and then stay until around six or seven, with a little extra work on the weekend, you can stay AHEAD of the game. Be sure not to fall behind in your reading, and always go to class prepared. The discussions in class mean much more and will be more valuable when you are prepared. Popular classes are easier to get during your third year, but I never had a problem getting into a class I wanted to take. Try to diversify your free choice classes and explore areas of law you may be interested in; do not limit yourself to classes that you "know" will be tested on the bar. There are bar preparation classes for those courses that will amply prepare you when the time comes.

Status: Current student, full-time
Dates of Enrollment: 7/2003-Submit Date
Survey Submitted: April 2006

Outside of first-year courses and the required Legal Profession course taken the second year, Alabama has a very lenient grading policy. Most upper level students take various clinics, seminars and courses of interest. The quality of the faculty is outstanding. The professors have a true interest in helping students succeed in class and in life. Many professors have clerked for the Supreme Court, as well as having graduated top of their class at Harvard, Yale, Stanford or Columbia. The average workload for a first-year student is typical of other law schools. There is much work to be done and much studying to partake. However, as a second-year and third-year a student sees a drastic drop in the workload required of them. All class registration is done through the Internet on a first come, first serve policy. The law school clinics are the most popular classes and 3Ls have first dibs on entrance into the clinics. Outside of the clinics, classes that students want to take are easy to register for.

Status: Current student, full-time
Dates of Enrollment: 8/2003-Submit Date
Survey Submitted: April 2006

The professors are great and extremely supportive—most are very involved in both academic affairs and student life issues. For example, professors regularly donate items like free lunches or happy hours to the Dorbin Charity Auction. And you can basically just wander around the third floor and pop into offices any time of the day. Grading is hard. There's a pretty strict curve first year that eases up so that by third year. A's are still hard to get—but you probably won't get a D either. It's difficult to get into clinical programs and certain seminars, but there are enough sections of most other electives that getting in isn't a problem. Right now, the biggest issue with classes is that too many of them are scheduled at overlapping times, but they're working on that, and should have more flexibility with the new building.

Status: Alumnus/a, full-time
Dates of Enrollment: 8/2002-5/2005
Survey Submitted: April 2006

The first year of law school at Alabama, your schedule is almost entirely chosen for you. The summer prior to the first semester, they offer a Contracts course. While it may seem like it is geared toward somewhat slower students, I think it is a benefit to have that class under your belt. It probably provided a nice orientation into law school classes, including an intimate introduction to some classmates and at least one or two professors. It never hurts to get your bearings in a place; and it could only help you to go ahead and realize what it's like to have your entire grade based on that one final exam.

> **The school says:** "The school no longer offers the summer Contracts class, but provides substantial academic support options during the school year."

Status: Alumnus/a, full-time
Dates of Enrollment: 8/2002-5/2005
Survey Submitted: April 2006

Many of the class are topnotch with great experienced professors. However, there are a substantial number of classes taught by "adjunct" professors. While they often have good practical experience, since they are in fact local practicing attorneys, they tend to lack effective teaching skills. I generally find their lectures to be more boring and less organized.

> **The school says:** "Practicing attorneys with significant litigation experience teach the Trail Advocacy classes. Other adjuncts may teach courses in their specialized areas. The law school employs only those adjuncts it believes will be the best 'teacher.'"

The workload is fairly substantial, especially case reading. It's pretty common to have approximately four or five hours of reading to do each night. This is something important to keep in mind when working out your schedule. It's often tempting to schedule classes so that you can have two or three days off each week, like selecting only courses on Tuesdays and Thursdays, but beware...you're going to kill yourself trying to read for six classes on every Monday and Wednesday night, or worse yet, you'll realize it's impossible and attend class unprepared. This is especially dangerous, because most of the professors at UA invoke random call to strike fear into the hearts of unprepared pupils. Nothing is worse that being randomly selected to recite a case that you haven't read in front of a room full of your peers. It's painful both to endure or observe.

Status: Current student, full-time
Dates of Enrollment: 8/2004-Submit Date
Survey Submitted: April 2006

The quality of academics is strong and getting stronger. The incoming crop of students seems to get better each year, making things more competitive. Even though your classmates will be bright and hard-working, the competition at UA is not unhealthy. UA law school does a great job of selecting intelligent and driven students without sacrificing the collegial spirit at the school. My classmates get along very well and I've never heard of anyone doing anything unfair or sneaky to try to gain an advantage here. The quality of the classes is excellent as well. There are excellent professors across the board and a wide variety

Read all of Vault's Law School Surveys at www.vault.com/lawschool — get complete surveys on top law schools, expert advice on applicaton essays, LSAT prep and more.

VAULT CAREER LIBRARY   17

of classes to suit a large number of interests. First-year grading is done on a B-curve, but it isn't too harsh and you have to really slack to get a failing grade.

Status: Current student, full-time
Dates of Enrollment: 8/2002-Submit Date
Survey Submitted: October 2003

I have overall been quite impressed with the quality of academics at Alabama. I did not know what to expect coming to a public school in Alabama, but they have attracted some great professors. Alabama has a great program called the Hugo Black Fellow Program, which attracts one former Supreme Court clerk to teach for a year at Alabama. My first year I had one of Justice Rehnquist's clerks teach Constitutional Law. He was quite young but an amazing professor. Furthermore, it was really neat to hear from someone who had really reached the pinnacle of success in the legal world.

It is quite easy to register for classes, and you typically are able to take any class that you wish to take. For a few classes that are extremely popular because of the professor teaching the class, priority is given to third-years, and there might be a waiting list to get a spot in the class. However, this is only a handful of classes, and the classes aren't ones that you would think would be so popular, it is the professor that draws people's attention to the class. For example, White-Collar Crime seems to be one of the most popular classes, which would likely not be the case if it were taught by any professor other then the one who typically teaches it.

Alabama does seem to have a pretty good range of class. There are plenty of classes to take for any practice group you would consider joining at a law firm. There are even a fair number of intellectual property classes, taught by a professor who was formerly an attorney with Morrison Foerster. Additionally there is a fair number of classes related to such esoteric areas as entertainment law and sports law.

 # Employment Prospects

Status: Alumnus/a, full-time
Dates of Enrollment: 8/2002-5/2005
Survey Submitted: May 2006

Employment prospects are great if you plan on working inside the state of Alabama and you are in the top 50 percent. If you are a C-student or plan on moving out of state (or worse, out of region), job prospects are few and far between. The on-campus recruiting was geared for the state, with few resources dedicated to finding work out of state. The one recommendation I received was: "Look up out-of-state alumni." Of the alumni I traced to the Pennsylvania area, only one responded to my initial contact. This contact couldn't help once they discovered I was not in the top 5 percent. In the months before and after graduation, resumes were rejected, if they were responded to at all, with a request to pass the bar. All this while students from lower ranked local schools were employed pending bar passage.

> **The school says:** "The law school enjoys a consistently high employment rate—nearly 100 percent. Thus, students, wherever they rank in the class and wherever they grew up, are obtaining employment. The on-campus interview process only accounts for 20 percent of the job success. The Career Services Office is active and has created several new out-of-state initiatives."

Status: Alumnus/a, full-time
Dates of Enrollment: 8/2001-5/2004
Survey Submitted: April 2006

The employment prospects are exceptional for UA graduates. As a top-tier law school, it is not difficult for students to obtain offers throughout the country. The Class of 2004 has graduates in New York, Washington, D.C., Chicago, Dallas, Houston, Atlanta and Miami. (There are probably others—these are just the ones of which I have heard.) I do think that a majority of graduates stay in the Southeast, but with the education you receive at UA, it is not required.

The employment office was wonderful when I was going through the on-campus interview process. Some students take advantage of this service more than

others. I got to know the staff on a first name basis during this time. They were never too busy to help me with any questions I might have. Most are still there when I go back for on-campus recruiting for my firm.

UA has many internships, both with judges and nonprofit organizations. It is possible to get actual court experience as a third-year in the state of Alabama. UA takes advantage of this law to allow students to represent underclassmen in minor disputes. I did not participate in these programs, but I know they are available.

Status: Alumnus/a, full-time
Dates of Enrollment: 8/2001-5/2004
Survey Submitted: April 2006

If you are not in the top 10 to 33 percent of your law school class, you will have very restricted options for the rest of your life, effectively. If you're in the bottom half of your class (and half of you will be...remember...everybody in law school is a great student, so it's a crapshoot to a certain extent) you will probably never be able to work as a non-criminal defense attorney. If you like criminal law, my best friend in Tuscaloosa would probably like you to know that Tuscaloosa County District Attorneys start around $35K and don't rise rapidly. Your best bet is to make a STRONG positive impact on a specific employer LONG before you graduate (even before starting law school), if you want a shot at a job you like. There are WAY too many lawyers everywhere, get used to this idea as soon as possible. It's supply and demand, people won't pay you good money or give you a fun job just because you're clever.

Status: Current student, full-time
Dates of Enrollment: 8/2005-Submit Date
Survey Submitted: April 2006

There are many internships and externships (for five credit hours) available through UA. Students may choose to intern for federal judges, federal prosecutors, AG's office, public defender, many different DA's offices, General Counsel to the University, Legal Services, a local domestic violence shelter, or even work with Katrina victims.

Whenever attorneys ask about my decision to attend Alabama, they always follow up with, "You made a wise choice." Now that I am finishing my first year, I know that this is true. The alumni network is vast, loyal and available to open doors. Aside from being first tier, Alabama has a strong tradition of producing leaders. Both of Alabama's Senators are alums, and the list goes on. Leadership is encouraged in the law school through a wide variety of generously funded student clubs.

Status: Current student, full-time
Dates of Enrollment: 8/2003-Submit Date
Survey Submitted: April 2006

Most people still stay in Alabama. The typical "dream job" is supposed to be one of the big firms in Birmingham, and that's what a lot of CSO efforts still focuses on. However, the alumni network is good, and they're making a concerted effort to bridge the out-of-state gap and branch out into more public service avenues. The CSO staff is very helpful and supportive. You should be aware that you may have to 'educate' out-of-state firms about the fact that Alabama is actually a top-tier law school. If you're from out of state, there is still a little bit of hostility from in-state firms.

Status: Alumnus/a, full-time
Dates of Enrollment: 8/2002-5/2005
Survey Submitted: April 2006

I've been told since applying to UA Law how wonderful their career placement is, but haven't really personally observed it. The career center personnel seems to rotate a bit. According to the numbers, apparently everyone who graduates gets hired within a couple of months, but I know several people from my class who still aren't employed or are underemployed. There are a good number of firms that do on-campus interviews and recruiting, but my experience has been that they are all predominantly fighting over the same top 10 percent of the class. The requirements that they post for candidates tend to whittle down the prospect pool to about 30 students they are really interested in talking to. UA is a well-respected law school. Especially within the state. People who attend other schools, especially unaccredited schools in the state envy those with degrees from UA. And whether they'll admit it or not, UA grads look down their noses at graduates from other schools. It's not that uncommon to hear someone point out that a judge or someone went to one of the "lesser" schools. It is not intended as a compliment.

Status: Current student, full-time
Dates of Enrollment: 8/2002-Submit Date
Survey Submitted: December 2004

Career services office does a nice job getting prestigious firms on campus to interview students but that also hurts students whose grades are in the middle to lower half of their class; the new dean of career services seems to be outstanding and excited to help students. There are programs throughout the year for 3Ls dedicated to finding a job; anyone who wants to clerk for a federal judge in the South would do well to attend Alabama. Excellent internship program with the DA offices throughout the state (if you can afford to go a summer without getting paychecks). Focus is generally only on in-state employers.

Because Alabama is so focused on academics rather than trial skills, it is very difficult to find a job with a plaintiff's firm. Slightly difficult to get a job in the Birmingham area due to Cumberland being located in Homewood; it is difficult to work during the school year due to the lack of large firms in Tuscaloosa and important classes are sometimes offered at odd times.

Status: Current student, full-time
Dates of Enrollment: 8/2002-Submit Date
Survey Submitted: October 2003

There is an externship program that gives you the opportunity to have an internship with places like the U.S. Attorney's Office or the District Attorney's Office, as a clerk for a judge, etc., while earning class credit. There is also a program that allows students to take classes in Australia or Switzerland that Alabama offers for a pretty affordable price.

 ## Quality of Life

Status: Current student, full-time
Dates of Enrollment: 8/2003-Submit Date
Survey Submitted: May 2006

The law school is in the midst of a building campaign, scheduled to be complete some time in the fall. After the renovation and added building, the facilities will be much improved. The University of Alabama campus is beautiful, but the law school sits on the outskirts of the university campus. Housing in Tuscaloosa ranges from apartments to houses; very few, if any, law students live on campus. Cost of living is reasonable; rent ranges from $550 to $900 per month, depending on the space. Also, some students live in apartments or houses in Northport, just outside of Tuscaloosa.

Fine dining in Tuscaloosa is somewhat limited (recommended: Yazoo Courtyard Grill, The Globe, Epiphany Cafe), but the city has some good casual restaurants (recommended: Cypress Inn, Cobblestone Cafe, Manna Grocery and Deli, Mugshots, DePalma's). Tuscaloosa is not the safest college town in the world. There were a couple of shootings on the Strip while I was in law school, and a few other incidents. However, I never encountered any dangerous situations. Northport is very safe, and parts of Tuscaloosa are safe as well. Simply be picky about where you live.

Status: Alumnus/a, full-time
Dates of Enrollment: 8/2002-5/2005
Survey Submitted: May 2006

While the university has a large on-campus housing system, I knew of no law student that resided there. Off-campus student housing was plentiful at all economic levels. The one drawback was school placement in relation to other neighborhoods. The law school sat away from the rest of the university as a self-contained unit, with the exception of clinic facilities. It was bordered by a housing project to one side and off-campus housing to the other.

There is no dining hall attached to the school itself, though the university has several dining areas around campus. The school was less than a mile from local and chain restaurants, and kitchen facilities and drink machines within the

school allowed for meals to be packed and brought in and for snacks to be purchased.

Status: Current student, full-time
Dates of Enrollment: 8/2004-Submit Date
Survey Submitted: April 2006

UA law school offers an excellent quality of life. Tuscaloosa is a nice college town which offers reasonably-priced nice places to live. Like any significantly populated area, Tuscaloosa has some higher-crime areas, but none where any law students live and none that are close enough to campus to be an issue. The law school itself has very nice facilities, high technology, and is adding a huge renovation that will include new classrooms and moot courtrooms, plus a nice new student lounge with big-screen TV and an on-site cafeteria exclusively for law students. The collegial nature of the law school greatly enhances the quality of life as well.

Status: Current student, full-time
Dates of Enrollment: 8/2005-Submit Date
Survey Submitted: April 2006

I love Alabama's campus and facilities. We have a new dining hall, coffee area, and student lounge in our building, and the parking is good at the law school. GET FOOTBALL TICKETS EARLY! Also, the housing is primarily undergraduate, so everyone I know has an apartment. They are cheaper farther away from campus, and they are nicer out there too. Look in Northport or Cottondale, or off of Skyland for the best value. There are some nice ones out towards Shelton State as well on Highway 69.

Status: Current student, full-time
Dates of Enrollment: 8/2004-Submit Date
Survey Submitted: April 2006

UA is building a brand new addition to the law school that will open next fall. This addition will have a new student lounge and some sort of dining hall in it. The UA campus is beautiful—big oaks, grassy lawns, and a bustling college scene. Crime is not a big problem and there are campus safety officers at the school most of the time just in case.

Status: Current student, full-time
Dates of Enrollment: 8/2003-Submit Date
Survey Submitted: April 2006

Quality of life in Tuscaloosa is pretty good. It isn't very expensive to live here, so people can afford apartments by themselves and don't have to have roommates. Almost all law students live off campus. The law school is on one side of campus, by itself, so we don't have much interaction with the undergrads. That is great when it comes to parking, as we have a big lot to ourselves. The student recreation facilities are incredible, nicer than any other gym I've been in (the new gym opened last year). There is a students-only water park, as well. I have always felt safe, though there have been a couple shootings outside nightclubs recently.

Status: Current student, full-time
Dates of Enrollment: 8/2003-Submit Date
Survey Submitted: April 2006

Can't beat the quality of life in Tuscaloosa, so long as you don't hate football. Rentals are plentiful and modestly priced—just make sure not to get in one of the undergrad party complexes off 15th St. or Hargrove Rd. Most accept pets. The town is small, fairly cute, and easy to get around, with everything you need for everyday living (a modest mall, a Super Target, a decent restaurant selection). For special occasions and weekends, Birmingham is about an hour away, with all the symphonies, shopping and "cuisine" you could want.

Status: Current student, full-time
Dates of Enrollment: 8/2002-Submit Date
Survey Submitted: October 2003

Housing in the Tuscaloosa area is quite cheap. A two-bedroom, two-bath apartment can be found near campus for around $550 per month. A one-bedroom, one-bath apartment would be right around $400 per month. There may be housing available for law students on campus, but I don't know anyone personally that lives in such housing. I would say almost everyone lives in off-campus apartments. Tuscaloosa is a big enough city that it does have quite a few good dining establishments. It has usual chain restaurants like Chili's, Outback,

Read all of Vault's Law School Surveys at www.vault.com/lawschool — get complete surveys on top law schools, expert advice on applicaton essays, LSAT prep and more.

VAULT CAREER LIBRARY   19

Applebee's, etc., but it also has some really good independent restaurants as well. These range from really cheap and really good fare (15th Street/Northport Diner, DePalma's, Cafe Venice, Tut's) to expensive (Arman's, The Globe, Kozy's).

Status: Alumnus/a, full-time
Dates of Enrollment: 8/2000-5/2003
Survey Submitted: September 2003

There are numerous places to live near the law school. One great thing about Alabama is that the law school has its own parking lot, so you can always find a place to park—this is not the case at so many schools. There are couches all over the law school, and it is not unusual to see people napping or just taking a break on the couches.

 ## Social Life

Status: Alumnus/a, full-time
Dates of Enrollment: 8/2002-5/2005
Survey Submitted: May 2006

Adjacent to the University of Alabama is a strip of bars and student-oriented shops known as The Strip. About two miles down this same street is another gathering spot of bars and restaurants known colloquially, and not surprisingly, as Downtown. We didn't really put a whole lot of thought into nicknames. The state alcohol board, along with local police and government, has really cracked down on underage drinking as well as overall conditions in these areas so students can enjoy a night out without any major drama. With all these nice bars, the law school has selected as its hang-out the only dirty, nasty, swing-shift bar in the area. Jackie's has been an established bar for decades, and only within the past three years have they decided to paint the cinder blocks that make up its walls and install carpeting...yet this is where the law school hangs out.

Status: Alumnus/a, full-time
Dates of Enrollment: 8/2001-5/2004
Survey Submitted: April 2006

Phil's is always a great place to eat, especially if the night will include hanging at the Strip. The Jupiter, on the Strip, has a huge dance/band area and usually has the best bands in town but will sometimes allow under 21 year olds in. The Houndstooth (named after Coach Bryant's famous hat) is a more laid-back place with a nice patio for people watching. While the Strip is fun, you will more often find more law students in the establishments in the recently renovated downtown. WilHagens' is an exceptional sports bar for both viewing sports or playing pool. The owner of WilHagens' reportedly recently opened a jazz bar, but it was not there when I was in Tuscaloosa. Another law school hangout is Inn is Free, an Irish bar that is always crowded. For a slightly older crowd downtown, there is Rhythm & Brews. There are many nice restaurants downtown such as Cafe Venice or DePalma's as well as the always friendly Mellow Mushroom.

There are numerous clubs to join at UA including Student Farrah (the alumni organization) and Phi Delta Phi. This latter is a legal fraternity (men and women are welcome). The Greek system at the law school is very weak but Phi Delta Phi takes on one charitable project a year and has a couple of pretty cool parties (one per semester).

Status: Alumnus/a, full-time
Dates of Enrollment: 8/2002-5/2005
Survey Submitted: April 2006

The law school hosts several events throughout the year—golf tournaments, pool tournaments, "races" to the courthouse, socials with the MBA program, formals, tailgate parties, etc. which offer a great opportunity to unwind, and all prospective students should become as involved as possible in these events. There are also a lot of volunteer opportunities with the law school, and they offer a special chance to give back to the community. There is a great YOGA studio, Yoga Bliss, which works wonders for relaxation (on top of utilizing the university's topnotch gym to unwind).

Status: Current student, full-time
Dates of Enrollment: 7/2003-Submit Date
Survey Submitted: April 2006

The social life of Tuscaloosa is briefly described as a common college town full of undergraduates. The Greek scene rules on the campus and testosterone fills the air. Such division between Greeks and non-Greeks also flows into the law school. It is apparent who was not Greek at his/her undergraduate school and who was Greek at his/her undergraduate institution.

The dating scene in Tuscaloosa is kind of dead for graduate/law students. There are 22,000 undergraduates ranging from ages 16 to 24. The average age is usually 19 years old. Compare that with the average age of 25 for a typical graduate student. There is little to no dating between the law school and other schools. However, there is much romance between law students. Various individuals have gotten engaged or married to another law student. There are cliques, just like high school. From the day of orientation on, individuals flock to those who are familiar. However, there is much collegiality amongst students.

Status: Current student, full-time
Dates of Enrollment: 8/2003-Submit Date
Survey Submitted: April 2006

Tuscaloosa's social life revolves around football in the fall. Homecoming is probably the most anticipated event of the year, with a parade (in which the law school always has three floats), parties and dances all week long. Law Week in the spring is also a big deal. Other than that, most people hang out with each other at houses or in the town's college bars. Clubs are plentiful and very active. The school is very supportive of student clubs and social events, which helps bond the school to gather. The student body is tight-knit. Although everybody is smart and competitive, it's more of a competition with one's self and with the material then with one's classmates, so everybody is very friendly and there's very little book-hiding, etc. that goes on.

Status: Alumnus/a, full-time
Dates of Enrollment: 8/2002-5/2005
Survey Submitted: April 2006

The law school Student Bar Association, does plan a good number of social events, including bowling parties each semester, Friday afternoon Bar Reviews, band parties, cocktail parties, semi-formals, and Barristers Ball (law prom). There are also week-long competitive events in the spring and fall that include golf, pool, flag football and other tournaments, with parties in between. It is difficult to get anything done during Law or Homecoming Weeks. One of the best events is our Res Judicata a.k.a., Race to the Courthouse, where students often pair running shorts with buttons downs and ties and chase an ambulance to the courthouse from the UA parking lot. It's a great tradition that people can enjoy in a town that is chock full of attorneys.

Status: Current student, full-time
Dates of Enrollment: 8/2004-Submit Date
Survey Submitted: April 2006

Tuscaloosa also attracts great local and nationally-known bands, making for enjoyable weekends on the Strip, which is the chain of bars and clubs close to campus. The Houndstooth was recently named by *Sports Illustrated* as the top sports bar in the country and is popular with students; as are Venue, the Booth, and Willhagen's. Being on a campus the size of UA's virtually guarantees that there will always be something fun going on each weekend and there are plenty of single students to create a good dating scene.

Status: Current student, full-time
Dates of Enrollment: 8/2002-Submit Date
Survey Submitted: October 2003

Before I started law school at Alabama, I heard rumors about the cutthroat competition. I have not seen that during my time at Alabama. Granted, law school students are competitive by nature because they know that good grades go a long way to landing you a good job, but not to the degree that they will step on somebody to get those good grades. When I have had to miss class, students have been more than helpful to give me the notes that I miss. I have also helped students with their job search, and others have helped me with mine. The atmosphere is quite collegial, and that bonding that is done during 1L leads to many close relationships.

The School Says

The University of Alabama School of Law is located in Tuscaloosa, Alabama, which is home of The University of Alabama. There are approximately 500 students at the law school—a student body large enough to have a diverse community, yet small enough to be nurturing and comfortable. The larger University campus also offers many athletic, music, theatre and museum opportunities, and as with any large university, a diverse cultural experience.

With a first-year class size of 170, law students are able to benefit from accessible faculty and administration and smaller course sizes. The average course size for the first year is 55 and the average course size for the second and third years is 25. The law school provides a significant number of electives and experiences for students. For example, typically there are more than 140 electives offered for second- and third-year students in the academic year. There are about 90 clinical positions available for each year, and students may choose to participate in Moot Court or a nationally recognized trial advocacy program.

The law school's employment rate within nine months of graduation for about 10 years has been 97 percent and higher. Our law students and graduates work in Alabama and other states. The school has a strong network of alumni; our graduates are located in 49 states. Our bar passage rate is high. In addition, the tuition at Alabama is reasonable—$19,902 a year for out-of-state students in 2006-07 and $9,736 a year for in-state students in 2006-07.

Please contact the Recruitment Office at creeves@law.ua.edu or (205) 348-2728 or the Admissions Office at admissions@law.ua.edu or (205) 348-5440 with questions or if you would like to schedule a visit.

Read all of Vault's Law School Surveys at www.vault.com/lawschool — get complete surveys on top law schools, expert advice on applicaton essays, LSAT prep and more.

VAULT CAREER LIBRARY   21

Arizona State University

Sandra Day O'Connor College of Law
McAllister & Orange Streets
P.O. Box 877906
Tempe, AZ 85287-7906
Phone: (480) 965-6181
Fax: (480) 965-2427
Admissions URL: http://www.law.asu.edu/Admissions

Note: The school has chosen not to comment on the student surveys submitted.

 Admissions

Status: Current student, full-time
Dates of Enrollment: 8/2004-Submit Date
Survey Submitted: June 2005

The ASU College of Law is focused on two things in the admissions process right now: increasing rankings by admitting candidates with top statistics and ensuring present and future revenue by admitting students connected to sources of financial support. Last year, the admissions process was overseen by a long-standing, outgoing professor who was not afraid to spend money to get top candidates and probably drew in better students than ASU would normally attract by so doing.

My LSAT and undergraduate GPA were towards the high end, so I received scholarship money, as did other students with high LSAT and undergraduate GPAs. If/when a scholarship offer is extended, NEGOTIATE. Be realistic, but don't be afraid to up-sell yourself based on the impact that you will have in the legal community, your GPA and LSATs and offers you have from other law schools.

ADVICE ON GETTING IN: Practice like mad for the LSAT and write an essay that stands out (assuming that you have already sealed your fate with regards to undergraduate GPA). Essays that stand out, according to conventional wisdom are those that tell a colorful, memorable story. If you've got it, flaunt it.

FORMAT FOR ADMISSIONS: ASU College of Law has not used interviews in the past. I highly recommend going to information sessions and speaking with the professors and staff that you meet at those sessions. They remember the people they meet. If you make a good impression, they remember you favorably.

Status: Current student, full-time
Dates of Enrollment: 9/2004-Submit Date
Survey Submitted: February 2005

Very selective. Quick to notify you. Helpful staff. Wonderful admissions dean who is great to talk with. Students are on the admissions committee, and help recruit future students with telephone calls, answering any and all questions one might have.

Status: Alumnus/a, full-time
Dates of Enrollment: 8/2007-5/2000
Survey Submitted: April 2005

The admissions process is similar to any other law school's, but I found it helpful to actually visit the school and call the admissions office with any questions I had about the school. The admissions personnel along with the school administration were very helpful and promptly responded to my calls. I also think that calling with my questions and visiting provided an opportunity for the faculty and admissions personnel to get to know me. The school doesn't conduct an interview as part of its admissions process, but I think visiting the school and meeting some of the faculty and administrators can substitute for an interview and provide some of the benefits that an interview normally provides in the admissions process.

Also, the school has specialized programs in information and technology and American Indian law. If you are interested in these programs, it is important to note that on your application. It is also important to contact the administrators and faculty involved with these programs as they can be beneficial in providing support for your application for admission to the admissions committee. The programs have great support from the dean and the overall school and university.

Status: Alumnus/a, full-time
Dates of Enrollment: 8/1988-5/1991
Survey Submitted: January 2005

The admissions process was pretty straightforward. From what I could tell, it was based almost entirely on undergraduate record and LSAT. I did well on the latter, not so well at the former. While my undergraduate GPA was low for most law schools (and I think was the lowest in my law school class), I did get it at a "prestigious" undergraduate college, so that probably counted for something.

Turnaround on the application was pretty quick; I think I applied some time in January, and got my acceptance letter in March. As far as selectivity is concerned, I suspect it's harder to get into now than it was then. We had a pretty good distribution of people from a variety of schools; there were a lot of ASU people there, of course, but also a lot of Big 10 people like myself, as well as a handful who went to the Ivies. From what I know, I think most did at least OK wherever they went to school.

 Academics

Status: Current student, full-time
Dates of Enrollment: 1/2003-Submit Date
Survey Submitted: October 2005

The school offers great IP-related classes. Profs call on students randomly but are very respectful of the students.

Status: Current student, full-time
Dates of Enrollment: 8/2004-Submit Date
Survey Submitted: June 2005

The first-year courses and sections are chosen for the student. Like in all schools, professors range from average to brilliant, malevolent to benevolent, but tend towards the benevolent side, with few but notable exceptions. Given that the choice of instructors in your first year is not up to you, not too much to worry about. If you have seen *The Paper Chase* you have seen everything that ASU is not about. The program is competitive and challenging, but the atmosphere is not the antagonistic, demeaning one depicted in the classic law school flick.

ASU College of Law boasts great clinical programs (hands-on lawyering for students), the premier law, science and technology faculty and program among law schools, and a world-renowned Indian Law Program. In addition, there are a number of new programs in the works and the integration with the MBA program gets better year over year. There is also a focus on health care and elder law, and many other areas of law. Generally, if you are interested in it, there is a faculty member here that can help you explore it. The faculty to student ratio is second in the country. Yeah, at little 'ole ASU. I believe it's Yale that beats us out, but you get the picture. Additionally, the faculty is growing as the administration is looking to add a leadership focus to the school, etc. For more info on the programs, check the law school web site.

Status: Alumnus/a, full-time
Dates of Enrollment: 8/2007-5/2000
Survey Submitted: April 2005

I found the quality of the classes to be very good. Most of the professors come from esteemed schools on the East Coast. I believe this is because many want the benefit of enjoying the nice weather that Arizona has to offer. I found the classes to be geared more towards a practitioner's viewpoint rather than purely academic theory. Most professors are easily accessible and willing to take the time to thoroughly answer your questions. I found this especially true after the first year, when I actually started having lunch with some professors.

Large classes are graded on a forced curve, with half the class having to be above a certain grade and the rest below. This results in many grades being near the average. Smaller classes have no forced curve and everyone can do good or bad. The workload was difficult your first year, but I think this mostly because you are getting used to law school. I found it very doable to work part-time and go to school full-time my second and third years, and still have a social life. Most of the time was spent reading and trying to understand the legal concepts.

Status: Alumnus/a, full-time
Dates of Enrollment: 8/1988-5/1991
Survey Submitted: January 2005

I can't compare the workload to anywhere else, of course, but having come from an undergraduate school where the workload was quite heavy, ASU Law was not a significant step up. You had to do several hours of reading a day, but there were no regular late nights until finals.

Quality of classes was mixed; some were excellent, especially in the areas of natural resources law and environmental law. I understand ASU also has excellent programs in American Indian law, although I did not take advantage of those. First year everyone took pretty much the same courseload, although there was one large section and one small section for each of these classes. Each first-year also had to take an elective small section seminar; mine was Law and Social Change, which was excellent.

Like the courses, some professors were better than others, and each had a different style. Most pretty much stuck to the old Socratic style, rather than just lecturing, but each had different methods of selecting who would get called on each day. Grading was done on a curve, so that a 78 was average. I think about half the class wound up with scores between 77 and 79; getting an 84 was considered very good, and anything above 88 was outstanding. There were maybe one or two 90s in each class (I got two in my three years).

Status: Current student, full-time
Dates of Enrollment: 9/2004-Submit Date
Survey Submitted: February 2005

The faculty is amazing, as is the dean of the law school. Most classes are small, and EVERYBODY ALWAYS GETS THE CLASSES THEY WANT. This school has one of the lowest student-to-faculty ratios out of any school in the country. Workload is substantial, but not overwhelming.

 # Employment Prospects

Status: Current student, full-time
Dates of Enrollment: 1/2003-Submit Date
Survey Submitted: October 2005

I am in the fall semester of my third year and have already received a job at a large law firm. The position is in another geographical area so graduates are not limited by geography when looking for work.

Status: Current student, full-time
Dates of Enrollment: 8/2004-Submit Date
Survey Submitted: June 2005

Overall, ASU alums generally stay in Arizona, because after living here for three years, most people just don't want to leave (hard to believe when it's 110 degrees, but easier to believe when swimming outdoors at Christmas). Generally, the fast-growing Phoenix legal market is split between the two law schools in the state, ASU and U of A. U of A is ranked higher and it seems that sometimes there is a preference for U of A students among some firms, but no one will admit to it.

Generally, the statistics are good. Unlike most schools, ASU reports its salary figures including public and private employment, so the numbers look low compared to those that start in the mid-six figures as a base, but there are a whole lot of people who choose those $30k/year public sector or nonprofit jobs that water

down the mean quickly. A scan of the medium-to-large firms in the area shows that starting salaries are generally in the low six figures.

Status: Alumnus/a, full-time
Dates of Enrollment: 8/2007-5/2000
Survey Submitted: April 2005

The school is great at assisting students in finding jobs, especially in Arizona and Southern California. The on-campus recruiting for these two states is very good. The school is also good at assisting students in finding federal jobs, especially for work in the natural resources area. The alumni network for the two specialty programs (information technology and American Indian law) are excellent, with alumni holding very prestigious positions. Internships are also plenty in Arizona and in federal offices.

Status: Alumnus/a, full-time
Dates of Enrollment: 8/1988-5/1991
Survey Submitted: January 2005

Hopefully better now than it was then. The placement office worked hard, but ASU is considered the Number Two school in Arizona. Most of the firms in Phoenix would interview on campus, but they really did not have many slots open for ASU students, and they were all after just the top 10 percent of the class. As someone just outside the top 10 percent, this was pretty frustrating.

Don't even bother trying to interview in Tucson with an ASU degree; it's very provincial down there, and they will only talk to U of A students. A handful of students were able to find jobs in other large western cities (L.A., SF, LV, Denver), but you either needed to beat the very top of the class, or have some connection. I don't know any that found work in Chicago or New York, and I'm one of the few that came this far east—although my old roommate found a spot with a big firm in Philly.

Status: Current student, full-time
Dates of Enrollment: 9/2004-Submit Date
Survey Submitted: February 2005

THE BEST ANYWHERE: There are only two law schools in AZ, and ASU is one of them. Most lawyers in Phoenix attended ASU Law, and probably had the same instructors you will have. Also, Phoenix is one of the fastest growing cities, and the AZ Bar is very tight on allowing out of state attorneys to practice in the state of AZ.

 # Quality of Life

Status: Current student, full-time
Dates of Enrollment: 1/2003-Submit Date
Survey Submitted: October 2005

Phoenix offers a nice quality of life. Great weather, good economy and reasonable housing prices.

Status: Current student, full-time
Dates of Enrollment: 8/2004-Submit Date
Survey Submitted: June 2005

Quality of life in general is good. The campus has a great rec center and is in the middle of a college town, with all of its perks, but located in a larger metro area, with all of its perks. However, some caveats—survival in Phoenix without a car is challenging. Think Southern California suburbs, if you have never been here before. Everything is a short drive away, but not in walking distance, unless you live right next to campus.

Apartments/housing right next to campus is typical university fair. Overpriced (but still cheap if you're coming from a big city) and ranging from nice and new to dumpy, with a lot on the mangy end.

One warning: PARKING SUCKS. Most 1Ls get assigned to a lot that is a mile or more away and have to ride infrequent and crowded shuttle busses from the satellite lots. When you spend your life on campus, that's a pain. Even worse if you have to scoot out to an internship or job in the middle of the day and return for classes. Also, the whole campus is under construction—that's a good thing

Read all of Vault's Law School Surveys at www.vault.com/lawschool — get complete surveys on top law schools, expert advice on applicaton essays, LSAT prep and more.

VAULT CAREER LIBRARY   23

because it means lots of new services, etc. coming in, but can be a hassle as streets and parking lots close, some temporarily and some permanently.

Status: Alumnus/a, full-time
Dates of Enrollment: 8/2007-5/2000
Survey Submitted: April 2005

The law school facilities are very high-tech and comfortable. The law library is very new with Westlaw and Nexis centers along with a computer lab and plenty of meeting rooms and individual tables that can accommodate laptops. Housing on campus is more geared towards undergrads, but it is easy to find decent housing within a few miles of campus.

However, it is almost necessary to have a car when living in Arizona, as public transportation is not a high priority yet. The campus dining and academic facilities are very nice, including the recreation center which has state-of-the-art workout facilities. The quality of life in the town is nice with crime being low.

Status: Alumnus/a, full-time
Dates of Enrollment: 8/1988-5/1991
Survey Submitted: January 2005

Tempe was pretty safe when I lived there. Plenty of student housing available, and not too expensive. As far as quality of life is concerned, ASU has to be at the very top of the list. A lot to do, every place has a pool, there's a lot of eye candy, and the weather is outstanding. Nothing beats jumping in the hot tub on a Saturday night in January and toasting those poor souls left behind in the frigid Midwest.

Status: Current student, full-time
Dates of Enrollment: 9/2004-Submit Date
Survey Submitted: February 2005

GREAT—no crime, good foods, great library, wireless Internet, cheap living, great weather (except the summer) and everyone is friendly.

 ## Social Life

Status: Current student, full-time
Dates of Enrollment: 1/2003-Submit Date
Survey Submitted: October 2005

The school social life seems very focused on drinking. Not very social for those that don't like to go to the bars every week.

Status: Current student, full-time
Dates of Enrollment: 8/2004-Submit Date
Survey Submitted: June 2005

Social life is what it is in law school. Plenty of activities, not enough time to do them all. If you want to play, there's always someone to play with and somewhere to do it. We have a good time and the atmosphere is much more collegial than at a lot of other law schools that I toured when I was making my choice. Don't get me wrong, there is competition come grades time, but I have yet to see the stupid stuff of law school lore like stolen books, destroyed computers, etc.

Generally, people just retreat into their cocoons and small inner-circles of friends around finals and emerge back to normal afterwards.

I have found that people adjust here the way they adjust in most places—if you hate new situations and new crowds and tend to have trouble making friends here, guess what, it's you and a new school won't change that. If you like meeting new people and experiencing new things, like exposure to the many cultures and beliefs represented here, bingo, it's a great place. Not to say you won't want to club some gunner over the head on a regular basis, but the good news is you won't be alone in feeling that way.

Status: Alumnus/a, full-time
Dates of Enrollment: 8/2007-5/2000
Survey Submitted: April 2005

The social life in Arizona generally is good. The nice weather creates an atmosphere of people wanting to be outside often. I got in the best shape of my life during law school. Also, because the undergraduate university is so large, there are always activities going on. The main sports stadium and downtown area are all within walking distance from the law school. The law school is located on campus, but in a corner. So it is somewhat isolated but close enough to the main campus center so that you can be focused on school yet get to the center of activity easily. Also, because the law school's alumni mostly stay and practice in-state, there are always events being hosted by local firms for law students.

Status: Alumnus/a, full-time
Dates of Enrollment: 8/1988-5/1991
Survey Submitted: January 2005

At least in my class, the social life was very good. Our first-year class was very close, and we did a lot socially together. Every Thursday night a large group (up to 30 or more) went to a bar across the street called the Vine, where we'd basically drink until they kicked us out. By second year, people started drifting their own ways a bit more, but we still did a lot together.

Not a lot of dating, because we were too busy and it could complicate things, although I did meet my eventual wife at one Thursday outing (at Sheperd's, "The Dog," which no longer exists). Other favorite hang-outs included the Dash (next door to the Vine), and Mill Avenue (which changes so much that I couldn't identify a place in business today except maybe McDuffy's). Sometimes we'd go to Scottsdale to be upscale; Downside Risk (is that still around?) and Anderson's Fifth Estate (which was still there the last time I was in town a few months ago).

Status: Current student, full-time
Dates of Enrollment: 9/2004-Submit Date
Survey Submitted: February 2005

Bar Review is available, but so are other non-alcoholic activities. There is always some famous speaker giving a small "talk" each week.

The University of Arizona

James E. Rogers College of Law
Admissions Office
1201 E. Speedway, Room 114
PO Box 210176
Tucson, AZ 85721
Admissions phone: (520) 621-3477
Admissions fax: (520) 621-9140
Admissions URL: http://www.law.arizona.edu/Admissions/

 ## Admissions

Status: Alumnus/a, full-time
Dates of Enrollment: 8/1997-12/2000
Survey Submitted: March 2006

Admissions process is fairly typical of top-tier law schools. The college is selective, particularly with non-residents. Strong weight appears to be given to the personal statement, and the dean of admissions very obviously reads the statement of all students who are selected.

Status: Alumnus/a, full-time
Dates of Enrollment: 8/1999-5/2002
Survey Submitted: April 2004

The University of Arizona makes very individualized admissions decisions. The dean of admissions knew my name and my background. The school is fairly selective but does pride itself on diversity and admitting non-traditional student (those who have had previous careers).

Status: Alumnus/a, full-time
Dates of Enrollment: 9/1995-5/1998
Survey Submitted: April 2004

Admissions was very good to me. They were responsive to my questions, financial aid issues, and since I had applied later in the process, they were prompt in their response.

Status: Current student, full-time
Dates of Enrollment: 1/2001-Submit Date
Survey Submitted: November 2003

You are required to send the standard information: transcripts of previous institutes attended, a personal letter, your resume, an application fee. Then the director calls you to talk with you about the program and possible financial options that you could be eligible for. There is a group of faculty and administration that reviews your application and select the candidates they feel will bring the most to the next incoming class.

> **The Rogers College of Law states:** "In addition, applicants have to submit a formal application and an LSDAS report with LSAT score. Our Admissions Committee is drawn from faculty, students and administration."

 ## Academics

Status: Alumnus/a, full-time
Dates of Enrollment: 8/1998-12/2000
Survey Submitted: March 2006

The program is rigorous. Professors are of exceptional quality and all are highly accessible. Grades are on a strict curve. The atmosphere is not overly competitive, but leans more toward the collegial amongst students and professors.

Status: Current student, full-time
Dates of Enrollment: 1/2001-Submit Date
Survey Submitted: November 2003

The program has prerequisites that teach the fundamentals of what you will need to go on. The faculty and style of teaching are excellent but varies from class to class, meaning some will be typical college classroom instruction, others more Socratic, and finally those that are presentation oriented or clinical. The workload is good, the grading more than fair and the professors are approachable and experienced.

Status: Alumnus/a, full-time
Dates of Enrollment: 8/1999-5/2002
Survey Submitted: April 2004

The professors are excellent and very talented teachers, not mere academics. I had little difficulty getting all of the classes that I desired. Nearly all professors would go out of their way to make exceptions to class size limitations if a student wanted to attend their class.

Status: Alumnus/a, full-time
Dates of Enrollment: 9/1995-5/1998
Survey Submitted: April 2004

I thought the academics were great. I was challenged, but I did not feel that the goal of the class was to fail a certain number of students. It was a chance to explore the philosophical background of law and why everything is the way it is.

Popular classes are hard to get, and you must be active in your selection of classes to avoid missing a program that is only held once or twice while you are in law school. For instance, you must look ahead to make sure that you can get the required prerequisites in order to take the popular classes. Many folks took evidence in the summer so that they could then take some of the more popular litigation classes (such as pre-trial and trial advocacy). Mauet is one of the most coveted teachers.

Workload is large, but unavoidable. Don't expect to breeze through unless your IQ is somewhere around 170. Also, folks need to understand that you will always have someone that will "book" all of the classes (i.e., read the books and not attend the lectures). You just have to realize that, if you are wistfully thinking you could maybe do that, you are not that smart, and you shouldn't even attempt it. Also, there are a few teachers that will take attendance, and when the attendance is low, they will give out "gems" that will likely be on the final. Let the folks "booking" the class beware!

 ## Employment Prospects

Status: Alumnus/a, full-time
Dates of Enrollment: 8/1998-12/2000
Survey Submitted: March 2006

West of the Mississippi you are in good shape for an excellent job. East of the Mississippi, things are a bit more challenging.

Status: Current student, full-time
Dates of Enrollment: 1/2001-Submit Date
Survey Submitted: November 2003

There is an on-site professional development office. They review your resumes and cover letters and help you set up interviews. They will also run seminars on interview skills and career opportunities throughout the year. Their advice is sometimes critical but always constructive.

Read all of Vault's Law School Surveys at www.vault.com/lawschool — get complete surveys on top law schools, expert advice on applicaton essays, LSAT prep and more.

VAULT CAREER LIBRARY   25

Status: Alumnus/a, full-time
Dates of Enrollment: 8/1999-5/2002
Survey Submitted: April 2004

Employers from throughout the West visit and hire from the U of A. I had little difficulty finding job opportunities and receiving job offers from every geographic location I was interested in. However, the U of A is particularly strong in Arizona, and students will have to work somewhat harder to get a job outside of the western United States.

Status: Alumnus/a, full-time
Dates of Enrollment: 9/1995-5/1998
Survey Submitted: April 2004

Career prospects in Arizona are excellent. U of A has a strong alumni following in Arizona. I am not familiar with outside of the state. Job opportunities are really for the upper 20 percent of the class, and internship/externships in the summer are an excellent way to use your skills and get to know people who might help you in the future.

Campus recruiting is also for the top 25 percent, except for the government positions, which are more open to experiences other than just grades. Since I was in the top 20 percent, I did not have any trouble with job placement, and the dean of career services was one of the most helpful people throughout my law career.

 ## Quality of Life

Status: Alumnus/a, full-time
Dates of Enrollment: 8/1998-12/2000
Survey Submitted: March 2006

Tucson is an excellent place to live and study. The weather is fantastic, allowing for lots of time outdoors. There are very few other places where you can get by without a winter coat (ever). The weather allows opportunities for any kind of outdoor activity from studying by the pool or lounging around the mall to intramural soccer. The mountains and parks allow for excellent hiking for the outdoor enthusiast. Spring training baseball makes a great diversion every March. Students at the main campus as well as the law school can always be found congregating at tables outdoors.

Status: Current student, full time
Dates of Enrollment: 1/2001-Submit Date
Survey Submitted: November 2003

The campus life is intense. It is as much as you make it. The athletic program is wonderful and the sports teams are considered some of the best in the nation. The weather is 300 or more days of sunshine a year. The student center is newly built with numerous restaurants and shops to choose from.

Housing is always an issue wherever you go, you never know what you want. Definitely a car or a bicycle is an asset as Tucson is spread out, although bicycles are stolen from campus. It is a [medium-sized] city at [800,000] and is spread out.

Status: Alumnus/a, full-time
Dates of Enrollment: 8/1999-5/2002
Survey Submitted: April 2004

Tucson is a great college town with ample housing options. This is probably the U of A's greatest strength and the reason I attended school there.

Status: Alumnus/a, full-time
Dates of Enrollment: 9/1995-5/1998
Survey Submitted: April 2004

Tucson is not a fabulous city with lots of culture, but law school does not give you too much time to explore your surroundings. I enjoyed Tucson for the outdoors, the college nightlife (which is to say it had good bars), and the proximity of all the resources that I needed to campus. Housing is ample (off campus), and you have many choices. Crime is typical for a college town; be sensible, and you should be fine.

 ## Social Life

Status: Alumnus/a, full-time
Dates of Enrollment: 8/1998-12/2000
Survey Submitted: March 2006

A favorite law school tradition is the Thursday night Bar Review. Typically organized by a 3L, the Bar Review is an opportunity to get great deals at a different bar each week. You can go alone or in a group because you can always count on a great crowd from the school.

Status: Current student, full-time
Dates of Enrollment: 1/2001-Submit Date
Survey Submitted: November 2003

There are a number of bars just off of campus that are always busy. There is a performance center in the middle of campus that attracts Broadway shows, international performers (ballet, jazz, circus, modern dance and so on) and celebrities. The bars are good places to meet people and the campus is large enough to have opportunities for a good social life. There are also a number of casinos around the city and it is surrounded by mountains.

Status: Alumnus/a, full-time
Dates of Enrollment: 8/1999-5/2002
Survey Submitted: April 2004

A great college town with a lively social scene.

Status: Alumnus/a, full-time
Dates of Enrollment: 9/1995-5/1998
Survey Submitted: April 2004

Bars are fun, and there are ones for every lifestyle. There were some great organized runs (for charity) that were fun (on the main campus), and both the intramural and intercollegiate teams allow graduate students. I had a very good time, but to be honest, much of it was in the library or the law school area.

 ## The School Says

The Rogers College of Law has a well-deserved reputation for serious scholarship and student support. Admission is very competitive, but applicants get the benefit of highly personalized review of their application materials. In the first year, students are divided into small sections with faculty who will work with them to resolve problems and maximize their opportunities.

This law school is an especially good choice for students considering interdisciplinary opportunities. We offer nine dual-degree programs in addition to the JD: a JD/PhD in Philosophy, Psychology or Economics; the JD/MA in Economics, Latin American Studies, American Indian Studies or Women's Studies; a JD/MPA; and the JD/MBA. We have two LLM programs in International Trade Law and in Indigenous Peoples Law and Policy. Other curriculum strengths include Intellectual Property and Business Law and Environmental Law.

We are also strong in clinical offerings, with seven legal clinics: Child Advocacy Law; Domestic Violence Law; Immigration Law; Indigenous Peoples Law; Tribal Law; Criminal Defense; and Criminal Prosecution. In addition to these programs, a very active Career and Placement Service Office helps students secure internships, clerkships and legal experience in other settings.

There are many student organizations and groups, including a nationally-recognized community service program, that helps them become involved in the life of the community and in the profession.

University of Arkansas School of Law

Dean of Admissions
Waterman Hall 107
Fayetteville, AR 72701
Admissions phone: (800) 377-8632
Admissions e-mail: uofa@uark.edu
Admissions URL: http://law.uark.edu/admissions/admissions.html

 ## Admissions

Status: Current student, full-time
Dates of Enrollment: 8/2002-Submit Date
Survey Submitted: January 2005

Very smooth process. No interview or essay.

Status: Alumnus/a, full-time
Dates of Enrollment: 9/1999-5/2003
Survey Submitted: December 2004

Standard paper application combined with a statement of interest essay. Admission standards tend to be a little bit lower in Arkansas compared to many of the big Ivy League schools.

 ## Academics

Status: Current student, full-time
Dates of Enrollment: 8/2002-Submit Date
Survey Submitted: January 2005

You will get a solid education. The professors are great and are easy to contact after class if there are any questions about lectures or assignments. The workload can be substantial but that is expected for law school.

Status: Alumnus/a, full-time
Dates of Enrollment: 9/1999-5/2003
Survey Submitted: December 2004

Most classes were of high quality. It really depended on the quality of the professor. There were several OUTSTANDING professors with impeccable credentials.

It was not difficult getting into popular classes at all. It all depended on scheduling rather than classes being maxed out.

Grading was difficult. The school was trying to set a high standard at the time when that Bill Clinton was in office. Clinton was a former professor at the law school.

The school was enjoying great success at the time, shooting up the ranks of law schools in the country. Part of this was due to Clinton being in office, but also, the school was investing substantial dollars and resources creating a first-class legal writing and research department.

 ## Employment Prospects

Status: Current student, full-time
Dates of Enrollment: 8/2002-Submit Date
Survey Submitted: January 2005

Most of the employers that conduct on-campus interviews are from Little Rock and a few from Tulsa, Springfield, Nashville and Memphis. I feel like we do not have as many employment opportunities as other schools maybe because of our location.

Status: Alumnus/a, full-time
Dates of Enrollment: 9/1999-5/2003
Survey Submitted: December 2004

Employment prospects were difficult for me, personally. I returned home to Ontario and my law degree from Arkansas was not considered prestigious. Employers in Ontario opted for a less impressive locally educated individual rather than risk employing someone with an Arkansas education.

Because I did not look for a career in Arkansas, I did not avail myself to any alumni network or on-campus recruiting.

 ## Quality of Life

Status: Current student, full-time
Dates of Enrollment: 8/2002-Submit Date
Survey Submitted: January 2005

They are starting construction on a brand new addition this year. It is going to be beautiful. Fayetteville is right in the middle of country and big city. Not too big and not too small.

Status: Alumnus/a, full-time
Dates of Enrollment: 9/1999-5/2003
Survey Submitted: December 2004

Excellent quality of life.

The campus was well-maintained and quite beautiful. Arkansas is referred to as the Nature State and it is clear why—the landscape is covered by lakes and forests. There are so many exciting outdoor activities that are available to students ranging from fishing to rock climbing and caving.

On-campus housing was adequate. I was fortunate enough to have landed a position as the custodian for the law programs building. As such, I was given free board. I did have duties such as opening and locking the building at night.

Dining was surprisingly above average. The school had an all-you-can-eat buffet-style presentation. Most days, the main dishes were good. Even when they were not to your tastes, there was always a soup, sandwich and salad bar so you were never out of luck. One of the most impressive things about the dining was the theme nights they had. For instance, each year, they have a Mardi Gras day. On this day, there is authentic Louisiana cooking. They bring in all kinds of seafood including JUMBO shrimp cooked in the most authentic Southern recipes. Delicious.

Meal plans were very reasonable and considering the fact that it was all you can eat, very economical.

No crime in Fayetteville, relatively speaking.

Status: Current student, full-time
Dates of Enrollment: 8/2004-Submit Date
Survey Submitted: April 2005

This law school offers a very comfortable and all inclusive environment so that all students have the opportunity to succeed.

Read all of Vault's Law School Surveys at www.vault.com/lawschool — get complete surveys on top law schools, expert advice on applicaton essays, LSAT prep and more.

VAULT CAREER LIBRARY   27

Social Life

Status: Current student, full-time
Dates of Enrollment: 8/2002-Submit Date
Survey Submitted: January 2005

There are lots of bars and clubs right near campus. Fayetteville is also really growing so many restaurants have emerged in the past year.

Status: Alumnus/a, full-time
Dates of Enrollment: 9/1999-5/2003
Survey Submitted: December 2004

Fayetteville is an amazing town for a student. There is a lot to do including some outstanding restaurants. Major cities such as Tulsa and Memphis are not that far away.

California Western School of Law

Admissions
225 Cedar Street
San Diego, CA 92101
Admissions phone: (619) 525-1401 or (800) 255-4252 ext. 1401
Admissions e-mail: admissions@cwsl.edu
Admissions URL:
http://www.CaliforniaWestern.edu/admissions

 ## Admissions

Status: Alumnus/a, full-time
Dates of Enrollment: 8/2000-5/2003
Survey Submitted: March 2006

I applied late after not getting into Cornell. The school was accommodating and personal; traits I enjoyed for all three years. This school cares about the individual person and is very receptive to minority/female and disadvantaged students. The trimester system gives applicants more options. Prior work experience is valued. As all schools today, it is selective; you can see the stats online. But don't be afraid to apply if you offer unique background and/or skills. Wanting to make a difference matters here. It is small enough to really see the individual.

Status: Current student, full-time
Dates of Enrollment: 8/2003-Submit Date
Survey Submitted: August 2004

The admissions process was very simple as the school does not appear to be overly selective in who it admits. Average LSAT scores (145 to 155 range) and average undergrad GPA (2.5 to 3.0 and higher) should get you in the door. It is unfortunate that the admission process is not more strict, and certainly seems to suggest that the school is more concerned with enhancing its financial base than increasing its academic reputation.

> **The school says:** "In the fall 2004 entering class the LSAT range was 152 (25th) to 157 (75th) and the GPA range was 2.97 (25th) to 3.48 (75th)."

Status: Alumnus/a, full-time
Dates of Enrollment: 8/1998-6/2001
Survey Submitted: April 2004

The application process was fairly easy. It included a standard application, including essay and three references letters. They have average standards on the selection process. There was no interview required for my admission and I didn't know anyone who had an interview. They offer scholarships based on LSAT scores.

> **California Western says:** "Candidates for top scholarships are required to visit the law school for interviews. California Western awards scholarships to a variety of worthy students, including those whose life experience or ethnic and cultural backgrounds enrich the campus experience."

Status: Current student, full-time
Dates of Enrollment: 8/2001-Submit Date
Survey Submitted: September 2003

Personal statement is important. Previous work experience, LSAT and undergraduate grades are not as important as with upper-tier law schools.

 ## Academics

Status: Alumnus/a, full-time
Dates of Enrollment: 8/2000-5/2003
Survey Submitted: March 2006

Basic academics were demanding but not impossible. Quality varied with some of the faculty. The most relevant courses were with adjunct faculty who practiced in the local bar and benches. It was usual to have federal judges teach each semester. As the school has grown, many unique opportunities for cross-training are available. Great clinical opportunities in the many state and federal courts in San Diego. There was never trouble getting into classes—you could approach individual profs and they cared so they let you in.

Status: Alumnus/a, full-time
Dates of Enrollment: 8/2000-5/2003
Survey Submitted: March 2006

There are several exceptional professors at CWSL. The curriculum tends to be focused on practical lawyering and not theory. CWSL is very competitive. The professors also tend to be very tough graders as approximately 20 percent of the first-year class "fails" out. Because CWSL is not a top-tier school, they tend to give an amazingly large amount of work in an effort to get their students up to the level of top-tier students.

Status: Alumnus/a, full-time
Dates of Enrollment: 9/2003-9/2005
Survey Submitted: September 2005

Grading was on the curve. Workload was heavy but I was in the two-year program, which made it more onerous. The quality of classes was very good. I never had any trouble getting a class I wanted. California Western School of Law has a very popular Sports Law Program and also had an excellent alternative dispute resolution program when that field was in its infancy.

Status: Current student, full-time
Dates of Enrollment: 8/2003-Submit Date
Survey Submitted: August 2004

Academics at Cal Western are as difficult as you make them. Although the top students in any given class are smart, hardworking individuals, the majority of each new 1L class seems to be filled with students who are more concerned with social life than academic achievement. Those students tend not to do well; in fact, many of them are gone after the first year.

The workload, particularly in the first year, is rather intense. It's pretty much equal to what you might get at any other ABA-accredited law school in your first year. Upper-level classes are more relaxed but the more popular classes can be difficult to get. The fact that the school is on a trimester schedule means that classes are only about 12 weeks long, which can lead to a stressful feeling of neverending final exam preparation.

Grading is fair but the school notifies you of your exact rank within your class, which can make for an extremely competitive environment, even among friends.

Probably the best thing about Cal Western (at least among the first-year classes) is the professors. A few of the professors are outstanding educators that could easily teach at a top law school. Many of the professors attended Harvard, USC or UCLA and have moved to San Diego at the twilight of their professional lives. Getting to know these professors outside of the classroom can aid tremendously in job leads over the coming years.

Status: Alumnus/a, full-time
Dates of Enrollment: 8/1998-6/2001
Survey Submitted: April 2004

The academic program was average. There wasn't enough focus on the practical application of the law and legal tactics. The professors tended to focus more on theory than what one actually does while practicing law. Classes were read-

Read all of Vault's Law School Surveys at www.vault.com/lawschool — get complete surveys on top law schools, expert advice on applicaton essays, LSAT prep and more.

VAULT CAREER LIBRARY   29

ily available for the most part, only negotiation and mediation were difficult classes to get. The grading system is still the antiquated curve system, only one student gets the highest grade, which encouraged competition between students rather than camaraderie. The workload was average depending on the professor. The professors were professional for the most part, only a select few still subscribed to the "rule the classroom by fear and intimidation" theory.

> **Regarding academics, the school says:** "Many opportunities at California Western allow our students to combine a strong traditional legal education with practical experience. Students participating in programs such as the California Innocence Project (www.CaliforniaInnocenceProject.org), the Bail Project and our Advanced Mediation course put their legal skills to work by writing briefs and investigating cases, representing clients at bail hearings and helping mediate problems at small claims court respectively. Approximately 75 percent of California Western's third-year students participate in the Clinical Internship Program, which gives students the opportunity to earn academic credit for legal work in private law offices, courts, corporations or government agencies."

Status: Current student, full-time
Dates of Enrollment: 8/2001-Submit Date
Survey Submitted: September 2003

Moderate to heavy workload. The professors are very approachable.

 # Employment Prospects

Status: Alumnus/a, full-time
Dates of Enrollment: 8/2000-5/2003
Survey Submitted: March 2006

If they are looking for Harvard grads, you will not get the job from Cal Western, but there are many more jobs than these. The bench, high-level corporate and government positions are all held by Cal Western grads. Many have been successful in development/real estate and corporate work. Alumni are close knit and supportive. Lots of federal practice opportunity because of proximity to the border. The Cal Bar is tough for everyone, but grads do well in other states also.

Status: Alumnus/a, full-time
Dates of Enrollment: 8/2003-5/2003
Survey Submitted: March 2006

It is very difficult to get a job from CWSL. The career services department is not very good. In addition, CWSL does not have good name recognition outside of San Diego so it is virtually impossible to get positions outside of the area. It is also exceedingly difficult to break into the "big firm" market as many of the big firms discriminate against CWSL because they view it as a sub-par school.

Status: Alumnus/a, full-time
Dates of Enrollment: 9/2003-9/2005
Survey Submitted: September 2005

The alumni network was nonexistent. It is better now. The internship program was very good. I served two different internships and had job offers from both of them.

Status: Current student, full-time
Dates of Enrollment: 8/2003-Submit Date
Survey Submitted: August 2004

Good luck. That's what you'll need to be blessed with in order to get an internship while attending Cal Western. You also need to be at the very top of your class to have a shot at a decent firm in San Diego. Outside of San Diego, the school is completely unknown with the exception of maybe Las Vegas where the reputation of the school is growing.

Be prepared to network independently and don't get your hopes up about getting a job with a top firm right out of law school. Most likely it will take a lateral move after a few years of practice to move into a top firm.

> **Cal Western notes:** "California Western has had students intern in a wide variety of legal settings and throughout the United

States as well as Argentina, England, Germany, Spain, Switzerland and the Philippines."

Status: Alumnus/a, full-time
Dates of Enrollment: 8/1998-6/2001
Survey Submitted: April 2004

Career prospects were limited from Cal Western because it is a fourth-tier school. While the career services people work hard to increase employment among students, like many other schools, unless you were in the top 10 percent your employment was hit or miss. The school didn't adequately prepare students for the bar exam and as such, employers were less likely to hire a graduate or summer associate from Cal Western.

Campus recruiting was difficult, because many firms weren't interested in hiring a Cal Western student unless he/she was in the top few students. Internships were scarce and tended to stay within government positions. Cal Western's reputation in the community is average.

> **The school says:** "California Western's Career Services Offices has a staff of eight, including five career advisors—who are attorneys—who arrange interview programs, provide career counseling and job search materials, help students find law clerk and attorney positions and much more. Visit our Career Services web site at www.CaliforniaWestern.edu then click on Career Services."

Status: Current student, full-time
Dates of Enrollment: 8/2001-Submit Date
Survey Submitted: September 2003

The career services has job fairs.

 # Quality of Life

Status: Alumnus/a, full-time
Dates of Enrollment: 8/2000-5/2003
Survey Submitted: March 2006

It's San Diego, quality of life is the best anywhere. Housing is available from the school and living at the beach is always an option. Many people stay in the area, everyone goes back to visit. The high cost of housing is not as big a problem for students and San Diego has many other students. You can have a real life and do well here. It is a very positive place where the facilities have become better and better. Being downtown is tough because of the parking; but there is public transportation

Status: Alumnus/a, full-time
Dates of Enrollment: 8/2003-5/2003
Survey Submitted: March 2006

CWSL is located in downtown San Diego. The facilities are very nice.

Status: Alumnus/a, full-time
Dates of Enrollment: 9/2003-9/2005
Survey Submitted: September 2005

There was no housing on campus but the downtown San Diego location was priceless. I used to study on the beach at La Jolla. It was difficult to find affordable housing. San Diego had a high rate of stealing cars but I never heard of anyone having their car stolen.

Status: Current student, full-time
Dates of Enrollment: 8/2003-Submit Date
Survey Submitted: August 2004

San Diego is a great town to be in. The school is right downtown and only minutes from the beach as well as world-class restaurants and bars. Parking is nonexistant, so be prepared to drive around for an hour to find a spot or pay over $10 per day to park.

A multimillion dollar renovation has transformed the school. The library is fantastic with brand-new facilities. The newer classrooms are state of the art but older rooms can be uncomfortable and crowded.

The school is right next to a homeless shelter and some students have been attacked walking late at night to their cars, although the school does have security guards that do a good job at keeping the campus clear of panhandlers.

It is the quality of the campus and professors that make this school more worthy than a tier four ranking. Improving the student body by increased selectivity in admissions would go along way towards getting the school into tier three or low tier two.

Cal Western Law says: "California Western works in close partnership with the San Diego police department and our local neighborhood association to monitor and prevent crime. In the past five years there have been two incidents involving members of the California Western community in proximity to our campus, both occurred prior to the opening of the referenced Rescue Mission. The mission is slightly more than a quarter-mile away from the school. Since the mission opened in Jan 2004, there have been no reports of incidents or problems involving our students, staff or faculty."

Status: Alumnus/a, full-time
Dates of Enrollment: 8/1998-6/2001
Survey Submitted: April 2004

There is no housing for students; this is a commuter school. At the time, there was a coffee cart and a deli for students to find lunch. The neighborhood is downtown San Diego and quite safe for the most part. Some car break-ins but no violence. The school works very hard to ensure the safety of the students by providing constant security.

Regarding housing, the school says: "California Western's Admissions Office assists students in finding housing through: apartment search, providing detailed information about various San Diego neighborhoods and helping them find roommates. California Western's urban campus is in close proximity to several housing options for students, in fact many opt to live within walking distance of the school. Our setting also puts us close to courts, major law firms, San Diego's beautiful bay and Petco Park."

Status: Current student, full-time
Dates of Enrollment: 8/2001-Submit Date
Survey Submitted: September 2003

Low crime. Lots of restaurants. Parking can be expensive.

 # Social Life

Status: Alumnus/a, full-time
Dates of Enrollment: 8/2000-5/2003
Survey Submitted: March 2006

A warm, caring environment with great diversity. Everything is available in the city and via public transportation. Enough social activity to keep people in touch without being a burden. There was always a lot to do and friendly students to go places with. Mexico is a trolley ride away and there are sports and theater in the park; and it is reasonably priced. It is small enough that everyone knows everyone and people are respected for their individual accomplishments.

Status: Alumnus/a, full-time
Dates of Enrollment: 8/2003-5/2003
Survey Submitted: March 2006

CWSL is only a law school so the number of students is far less than that of a university affiliated law school.

Status: Alumnus/a, full-time
Dates of Enrollment: 9/2003-Submit Date
Survey Submitted: September 2005

There was no Greek system. I was about 20 years older than most of the student body, so I was not part of their dating scene. However, I do know that they hung out at the Red Onion and the other bars at Pacific Beach. They also liked, as did

I, Rocky's Balboa, which was a sports bar. There were not many events or clubs. Most of the time we were too busy with classes, research and study.

San Diego also has the Gaslamp Quarter, which was just being revived at the time I was attending law school. The jazz clubs were very good and occasionally we would spend evenings at those clubs.

There was an annual picnic and an annual ball, which were held at various locations. One, I remember, was at Mission Bay; the picnic and the ball were held at the San Diego Zoo.

We also were able to attend the Parade of Lights on Mission Bay at Christmas Time, which was very beautiful.

There was also a singles sailing club, which was very helpful. Singles of all ages gathered. Owners of boats got crews and those who didn't own boats but wanted to sail got to go out. This was not a school-sponsored club but was available to anyone who was single and lived in the San Diego area.

Status: Current student, full-time
Dates of Enrollment: 8/2003-Submit Date
Survey Submitted: August 2004

Social life at any law school is pretty weak, although at Cal Western it's better than most, primarily because many first-year students care more about partying and than studying.

The school does put on some decent events and has a number of interesting speakers come to visit.

Status: Alumnus/a, full-time
Dates of Enrollment: 8/1998-6/2001
Survey Submitted: April 2004

The school's social life was fairly active. There were many social clubs that sponsored events for students which were usually well attended. Downtown San Diego is not far from the school and there is a plethora of bars and clubs for students to relax at. There was no Greek system to speak of, certainly nothing like undergraduate or larger schools.

Status: Current student, full-time
Dates of Enrollment: 8/2001-Submit Date
Survey Submitted: September 2003

Several clubs and social events.

Read all of Vault's Law School Surveys at www.vault.com/lawschool — get complete surveys on top law schools, expert advice on applicaton essays, LSAT prep and more.

VAULT CAREER LIBRARY   31

Chapman University School of Law

Law Admissions Office
One University Drive
Orange, CA 92866
Admissions phone: (714) 628-2500 or (877) CHAPLAW
Admissions fax: (714)628-2501
Admissions e-mail: lawadm@chapman.edu
Admissions URL:
http://www.chapman.edu/admission/law/admission.asp

 ## Admissions

Status: Alumnus/a, full-time
Dates of Enrollment: 8/1998-5/2001
Survey Submitted: August 2004

Pretty standard. Scores, grades and recommendations. The process was straightforward and the admissions people were friendly in answering questions.

Status: Current student, full-time
Dates of Enrollment: 8/2003-Submit Date
Survey Submitted: August 2004

The admissions process is pretty typical. Transcripts, LSAT score, letters of rec. Admissions is becoming more selective as the school becomes more established.

Status: Current student, full-time
Dates of Enrollment: 8/2003-Submit Date
Survey Submitted: June 2004

Chapman has a rolling admissions deadline. However, Chapman has A LOT of scholarships to give out, and if you want one, you should apply early. In the past, if you had above a 162 LSAT score you were given a full ride.

Status: Current student, full-time
Dates of Enrollment: 1/2002-Submit Date
Survey Submitted: April 2004

No strict deadline, but the earlier the better, especially if you want scholarship money.

Status: Current student, full-time
Dates of Enrollment: 8/2003-Submit Date
Survey Submitted: April 2004

Admissions are done on a rolling basis. If you are a blue chip, you should get your materials in early as you will be eligible to receive generous scholarships. Selectivity is increasing as it is a new law school and its location in Southern California means that it will get its fair share of applicants.

Status: Alumnus/a, full-time
Dates of Enrollment: 8/2000-5/2003
Survey Submitted: September 2003

Chapman has a rolling admissions process, but get your application in as soon as possible. A great LSAT score and GPA will be rewarded with a full scholarship and good LSAT scores will receive a partial scholarship.

> **The school says:** "GPA and LSAT are elements of the merit scholarship awards. Apply early as we are receiving increasingly competitive applications."

 ## Academics

Status: Alumnus/a, full-time
Dates of Enrollment: 8/1998-5/2001
Survey Submitted: August 2004

Challenging. I was one of those people who was always studying. It paid off, though. I really enjoyed most of my professors and still keep in touch with a few.

Status: Current student, full-time
Dates of Enrollment: 8/2003-Submit Date
Survey Submitted: August 2004

I really enjoyed my first-year professors for the most part. As with any school, there were some that I preferred over others, but they were all very respectful.

Status: Current student, full-time
Dates of Enrollment: 8/2003-5/2006
Survey Submitted: June 2004

First year is pretty standard: Contracts, Property, Civil Procedure, Torts, LRW, Criminal Law. Chapman specializes in tax law, corporate law and real estate law. However, they have an EXCELLENT Constitutional Law Clinic headed by John Eastman, as well as other clinics and classes.

Status: Current student, full-time
Dates of Enrollment: 1/2002-Submit Date
Survey Submitted: April 2004

Strong group of professors. Visiting professors have included Kenneth Starr, amongst other prominent names.

Status: Current student, full-time
Dates of Enrollment: 8/2003-Submit Date
Survey Submitted: April 2004

The professors are generally younger but have pretty good resumes. They are friendly and try to provide a fair and nurturing environment.

Status: Alumnus/a, full-time
Dates of Enrollment: 8/2000-5/2003
Survey Submitted: September 2003

The academic program is rigorous and there is a mandatory 2.8 median the first year and a mandatory 2.8 GPA the second and third years. The student to teacher ratio is 16:1, which is great. You have a wonderful opportunity to get to know your professors. Register early to get the classes that you want—especially trial practice with Hueston and Gross who are brilliant trial attorneys.

> **The school says:** "Our specialty areas include tax law, elder law, alternative dispute resolution, environmental, land use and real estate law, lawyering skills and an LLM in tax."

 ## Employment Prospects

Status: Alumnus/a, full-time
Dates of Enrollment: 8/1998-5/2001
Survey Submitted: August 2004

I started with a mid-size firm but made a lateral move to a firm with over 300 lawyers. Reputation is really growing and will eventually be very strong.

Status: Current student, full-time
Dates of Enrollment: 8/2003-Submit Date
Survey Submitted: August 2004

OCI added a couple more employers this year. Eventually, I think that Chapman will have a reputation in Southern California similar to that of Fordham in NY. However, that is probably still some years away.

Status: Current student, full-time
Dates of Enrollment: 8/2003-Submit Date
Survey Submitted: June 2004

Career services helps if you're in the top 20 percent of students. But they can only help you find a clerkship with a judge or a job with a government agency. Job prospects in the surrounding areas seem pretty good. However, if your life goal is to work in New York City, then Chapman may not be the right school for you.

Status: Current student, full-time
Dates of Enrollment: 1/2002-Submit Date
Survey Submitted: April 2004

Most major West Coast firms have offices in Orange County and Chapman is only about 35 miles from Los Angeles. There is also a federal courthouse within five miles of the school.

Status: Current student, full-time
Dates of Enrollment: 8/2003-Submit Date
Survey Submitted: April 2004

Strong areas include taxation, real estate and dispute resolution. However, ties with a superior film school should make the entertainment law area a real gem soon.

Reputation is really growing and Chapman is clearly the best school in Orange County. Will soon have a reputation similar to that of Fordham in NY.

Status: Alumnus/a, full-time
Dates of Enrollment: 8/2000-5/2003
Survey Submitted: September 2003

Externship opportunities are great with the Ninth Circuit, U.S. District Courts in Los Angeles and Orange County and the U.S. bankruptcy courts. The area also has exciting opportunities with the California Court of Appeals in Santa Ana and Orange County Superior Court. Upon graduation, students work as federal and state law clerks, associates in large law firms, district attorneys, public defenders and lawyers in state and federal agencies.

> **Chapman says:** Career Services is available to all students irrespective of where they rank. Firms, agencies and organizations may request to interview students with specific academic credentials.

 Quality of Life

Status: Alumnus/a, full-time
Dates of Enrollment: 8/1998-5/2001
Survey Submitted: August 2004

I loved it so much that I stayed in Orange County rather than moving back to where my family is from.

Status: Current student, full-time
Dates of Enrollment: 8/2003-Submit Date
Survey Submitted: August 2004

Very convenient with great weather. Perfect for the non-urbanite.

Status: Current student, full-time
Dates of Enrollment: 8/2003-5/2006
Survey Submitted: June 2004

The quality of life is exceptional. The cost of living isn't unbearable. Angels Stadium and Arrowhead Pond are visible from the parking structure (that's how close they are!). There is great shopping nearby and the beach is 20 minutes away. Olde Town Orange is within walking distance of the school.

Status: Current student, full-time
Dates of Enrollment: 1/2002-Submit Date
Survey Submitted: April 2004

Southern California but not as congested as L.A. If you are a little more laid-back, Orange County is a good place.

Status: Current student, full-time
Dates of Enrollment: 8/2003-Submit Date
Survey Submitted: April 2004

Orange County California. Perfect weather and all of the other amenities of Southern California. L.A. is a reasonable distance but far enough to not be considered an L.A. school.

Status: Alumnus/a, full-time
Dates of Enrollment: 8/2000-5/2003
Survey Submitted: September 2003

If you want to get good grades in law school during your first year at any school then you will have no social life. However, you should try to find a job or clerkship during your second year and try to relax a little. Chapman has a great quality of life and the students, although competitive, are always willing to help each other out.

 Social Life

Status: Alumnus/a, full-time
Dates of Enrollment: 8/1998-5/2001
Survey Submitted: August 2004

I made good friends and always had something to do if time permitted. The students were generally friendly when I attended, which is not always the case at all law schools from what I hear.

Status: Current student, full-time
Dates of Enrollment: 8/2003-Submit Date
Survey Submitted: August 2004

Most of the people are pretty down to earth and friendly. Not city life but there is plenty to do in Orange County. Plus, L.A. is only about 35 miles away.

Status: Current student, full-time
Dates of Enrollment: 8/2003-5/2006
Survey Submitted: June 2004

Because of the small size of the school, it can seem high school-ish with groups of huddled girls giggling in the hallways. Everyone knows everyone else, and everyone seems to revert in maturity. That said, every Thursday is Bar Review at a local bar.

Status: Alumnus/a, full-time
Dates of Enrollment: 8/2000-5/2003
Survey Submitted: September 2003

The social life at Chapman is great. Activities include Law Review, Nexus Journal of Opinion, Mock Trial, Moot Court, PILF, Christian Legal Society, American Bar Association, Law Students Division, Minority Law Students Association and Student Bar Association. There are fun bars on the Orange Circle and it is great to join your fellow classmates for a beer at Zito's Pizza, down the street from school.

 The School Says

Chapman University's ABA-accredited law school offers a dynamic approach to legal education, one that puts students first. Chapman University School of Law was established in 1995 and now resides in Kennedy Hall on the main campus. Completed in 1999, the law building houses state-of-the-art classrooms and two courtrooms, one appellate and one trial courtroom. These courtrooms provide fully equipped facilities for trial advocacy exercises, moot court competitions and for-

Read all of Vault's Law School Surveys at www.vault.com/lawschool — get complete surveys on top law schools, expert advice on application essays, LSAT prep and more.

VAULT CAREER LIBRARY   33

mal hearings by visiting courts. Adjacent to the trial courtroom is the jury deliberation room and judges' chambers.

The curriculum at Chapman balances the best of traditional educational practices with new technology and pedagogies to create a program designed to become a force in American legal education. The curriculum is rigorous and there is a mandatory 2.8 median GPA for all law students. The student to teacher ratio is 16:1, and the students value the accessibility and interaction with their professors. Chapman law school faculty are outstanding legal scholars with law degrees from prestigious schools such as Duke, Georgetown, Columbia, Boalt Hall, Stanford, UCLA, USC, Harvard and Yale.

Every application is given individual attention and is reviewed for scholarships upon review for admissions. Entering scholarships are merit based. Undergraduate GPA and the LSAT score are two factors utilized in the determination of a scholarship award. Other factors include, but are not limited to, major, undergraduate institution attended, etc.

The small entering class size provides an intimate setting for the students to get to know each other and form close relationships.

The Career Services Office provides many programs to all students and alumni including excellent externship and internship opportunities. An on-campus interview program is also available to provide the students with first-hand experience of not only the interview process, but also possible part-time employment with prestigious law firms. In 2004, 86 percent of Chapman Law students were employed nine months after graduation.

All 1L students take required courses the first year of law school. First-year students are automatically registered for these classes by the Registrar's Office; continuing students are encouraged to register early.

Chapman University School of Law offers three certificate programs: Tax Law, Environmental, Land Use & Real Estate Law (ENLURE) and Advocacy & Dispute Resolution, plus a joint JD/MBA program. Clinical programs include: Tax Law, Elder Law and Claremont Institute Center for Constitutional Jurispendence.

The Harry & Diane Rinker Law Library features seating for 300 with computer access at all stations. There are over 282,000 volumes and volume equivalents in the law library. The second floor has a number of group study rooms, a microfilm room and a periodical reading room. There are also numerous law journals, and a large treatise collection to support the research needs of faculty and students.

Concord Law School

Admissions Office
Concord Law School
10866 Wilshire Boulevard, Suite 1200
Los Angeles, CA 90024
Admissions phone: (800) 439-4794
Admissions fax: (888) 564-6745
Admissions e-mail: infoconcord@concordlawschool.edu
Admissions URL:
http://www.concordlawschool.edu/admissions.html

Note: Concord's Juris Doctor program is a four-year, part-time program. Most of its students are working professionals or caregivers; therefore, a designation between "part-time" and "full-time" is not relevant.

 ## Admissions

Status: Current student, part-time
Dates of Enrollment: 1/2003-Submit Date
Survey Submitted: March 2006

Concord requires that students complete a personal essay that details why they desire to attend law school. They do not require the potential student take the LSATs, but rather base a student's admission status on several factors including the personal statement, undergraduate grades, life experiences and current position. There are both written elements as well as interviews to make the determination.

Status: Alumnus/a, part-time
Dates of Enrollment: 1/2002-1/2006
Survey Submitted: March 2006

Admission is not as difficult as other law schools. There is no LSAT required. Instead, there is a 15-question quiz for which the student reads a passage from a hornbook and then answers the multiple choice questions. There are several essays as part of the admission process, but they are not difficult or complex.

Status: Alumnus/a, part-time
Dates of Enrollment: 1/2002-12/2005
Survey Submitted: March 2006

Admissions was selective in the beginning, as only three years have graduated thus far, but had become less so lately. The word from the deans is that the school is now as big as they want it to be, and they will be focusing on maintaining the quality of the students, to ensure good numbers of grads who can pass the bar, and students who will finish the program. The classes are very diverse, accomplished people, usually with careers ongoing in a wide range of disciplines, and are very atypical of fixed-facility schools, maybe more typical of better night schools

Status: Current student, part-time
Dates of Enrollment: 9/2002-Submit Date
Survey Submitted: March 2006

Concord had an online application which initiated a series of telephone calls from their admissions office. One of the calls was an interview and information session. They requested official transcripts. There was also an entrance exam that required reading and analysis skills, and passing a series of multiple choice questions. It was not a terribly difficult admission test.

Status: Current student, part-time
Dates of Enrollment: 9/2003-Submit Date
Survey Submitted: March 2006

The school seemed very selective about the type of person who can suceed in an online environment—highly driven and self-motivated. Indeed, there was an interview and an essay required. The goal of the new school and new format is to make legal education accessible to those who do not have the money, time or lofty academic pedigree required by many law schools. More access to legal education will promote diversity in the legal profession and increase the ability of the public, therefore to obtain justice.

Status: Current student, part-time
Dates of Enrollment: 1/2003-Submit Date
Survey Submitted: March 2006

Admission required an online exam similar to the reasoning portion of the LSAT. That was followed by a telephone interview to discuss the school, my motivation for seeking a JD degree, an evaluation of my potential for sucess in the online environment and a review of my academic history.

After getting a green light to proceed to the next step in the admissions process, I submitted a resume and an essay. The essay could be about anything and was meant to examine how well I could express myself in writing.

The results of all of the admissions materials were sent to an admissions committee comprised of faculty and staff at the law school.

Concord Law School appears to look for mature, highly motivated students who are interested in learning the law. It takes that type of person to work in an academically demanding curriculum while working full-time within their profession.

Status: Current student, part-time
Dates of Enrollment: 9/2005-Submit Date
Survey Submitted: March 2006

The school was not, at least when I enrolled, particularly selective. I spoke to an admissions rep, took a sample quiz after reading a few pages of material, wrote a personal essay and voila, I was in. Enrollment has grown notably, so they may or may not have gotten more selective since then. However, I strongly doubt that anyone with a reasonable IQ and a fair amount of attention to detail wouldn't be admitted.

Status: Current student, part-time
Dates of Enrollment: 8/2003-Submit Date
Survey Submitted: April 2005

The admissions process began with an interview with a counselor who evaluates how much time a prospective student might have in their day in order to be able to handle the workload of the JD program. This is an online program designed for people who work. It is a very challenging program, so the counselors ask many questions in regard to all the commitments the prospective student has (job, family, community, etc.) to see if the student has time. It also gives the prospective student an inkling of the kind of time required to complete this program.

Next, the student is required to take an online exam. It is a kind of reading comprehension where you are given a legal passage and have to answer questions on it. If you pass, you are admitted and asked to send in transcripts of the undergraduate degrees and other supporting material. The selection process was relatively easy, and no LSAT was required.

Status: Current student, part-time
Dates of Enrollment: 1/2002-Submit Date
Survey Submitted: April 2005

Concord's admissions process is a breeze compared to other law schools'. It is designed to give those who already have a profession or other obligations an opportunity to receive a high-quality legal education while located anywhere on Earth with Internet access. The admissions process consists of an online application, a 15-question online test, a 500+ word personal statement and a telephone interview. Concord currently does not require LSAT scores for admission.

Read all of Vault's Law School Surveys at www.vault.com/lawschool — get complete surveys on top law schools, expert advice on applicaton essays, LSAT prep and more.

VAULT CAREER LIBRARY   35

An admissions review board looks these over and makes a decision. Because Concord is designed for and appeals to those who may have been out of a formal academic environment for many years, its initial admission standards tend to be inclusive rather than exclusive. One should not be fooled by this broad standard. Gaining admission and completing Concord's rigorous four-year curriculum are two entirely different things. Concord's inclusive admissions standards do not detract from the quality of its curriculum or of its professors. Instead, such broad standards provide an opportunity where one would not exist otherwise.

Status: Current student, part-time
Dates of Enrollment: 8/2003-Submit Date
Survey Submitted: April 2005

The admission process at Concord was excellent. First, I completed an interest survey online followed by an short online assessment to determine if I was an appropriate candidate for distance education. After passing the assessment, I completed an extensive application that included information such as academic history and work history. I also was asked to prepare several essays, one of which was a personal statement explaining why I wanted to become an attorney and another that asked me to discuss my greatest accomplishment. Several weeks after my application was received, I had a phone interview that lasted about one hour and the interviewer made a recommendation regarding the chances for success in the online program. The selection committee reviewed each part of the process and made the final determination regarding admission. My best advice to a potential student is to be truthful and honest with every step of the application process. Law school is challenging and the student and school must be a comfortable fit so that the student has a greater chance for success.

Status: Current student, part-time
Dates of Enrollment: 4/2001-Submit Date
Survey Submitted: April 2005

Concord is an Internet-based law school, so all of my admission processes were either done via telephone or the computer. The recruiter was friendly and helpful, and didn't try to rush me into enrolling. I took a short quiz and provided a writing sample via a computer interface!

 **Academics**

Status: Current student, part-time
Dates of Enrollment: 4/2002-Submit Date
Survey Submitted: April 2006

The program is conducted entirely online. Students complete the various readings and receive lectures via the Web from noted professors in the field. Examples include Arthur Miller from Harvard who lectures in Civil Procedure and Raphael Guzman from Arkansas who lectures in Criminal Law, Criminal Procedure and Evidence. Students can watch the lecture any time they want to.

Students attend a live class via the Web conducted by a Concord professor. The professor questions, similar to the Socratic Method and students respond via keyboard.

Each course has one or more essay exams as well as a final exam and most courses (all MBE subjects) also have multiple choice quizzes.

Concord grades very strictly along the lines of how the Cal Bar grades the bar exam. This results in low grades for most students. As an example, I have just under a 3.3 GPA and I am in the top 10 percent of my class.

Status: Current student, part-time
Dates of Enrollment: 1/2003-Submit Date
Survey Submitted: March 2006

Concord excels in this area particularly for students who have full-time careers and cannot travel to a campus. With the distance learning structure, students learn in an environment that is condusive to their individual learning style. This means if you're traveling on business or stuck in the office late, you don't jeopardize your studies—you merely postpone them until later in the evening. The lectures are thorough and because they are offered online, you can go back and listen to portions of the lecture that you are experiencing difficulty with or even record them and listen to them in the car, as you exercise, etc.

The professors are particularly attentive to the needs of the student body. They are quick to respond to your e-mails and are even available for phone conferences when needed. It is a very supportive environment and one that is condusive for the rigors of the law. The faculty and administration have as much on the line as do the students.

Status: Alumnus/a, part-time
Dates of Enrollment: 1/2002-1/2006
Survey Submitted: March 2006

The rigor of the courses appears to be comparable to that of other law schools. The same and similar casebooks and hornbooks are used, and the quality of instruction is excellent. The lecture professors are famous law professors, including Arthur Miller and Mary Cheh. The workload is about 25 to 30 hours a week, which is quite a bit considering that virtually all the students are career professionals in other fields, working full-time and maintaining families as well. Grading follows the ABA format, where a 65 is the most common grade (C). Students are taught from the first how to write bar exam style essays, and there are many quizzes in each course that are made up of MBE-style questions. I felt well prepared for the bar exam.

Status: Current student, part-time
Dates of Enrollment: 1/2003-Submit Date
Survey Submitted: March 2006

The curriculm at Concord Law School centers on the subjects tested on the Californina bar exam, the state in which Concord is registered as an institution. The curriculum is challenging and the classes offered by the school are of extremely high quality and academic rigor.

The teachers are very professional in that they have a great deal of practical knowledge that is founded on a solid theoretical legal foundation. By that I mean, the professors do not simply teach for the bar exam, they teach for a long-term career in the law by helping students understand the principles contained within the law.

The classes, assignments and workload are demanding and tough. There appear to be no shortcuts to getting through the program since there are no short-cuts to the professional practice of the law. The first two years of the four-year Concord program are spent in required classes. Electives become available in the third and fourth years.

Before the end of the second year of study, Concord students must pass the First-Year Law Student Exam (FYLSE) administered by the California Bar. This exam is eight hours in duration and includes four essays in contracts, criminal law and torts (one subject repeated) and 100 multiple choice questions. The exam is no cake-walk and the overall success rate is about 25 percent with Concord success rates of about 38 percent. If you don't pass the exam, you can no longer continue in the JD program. The exam is a good expereince to get through because it prepares you for the environment of the full bar exam at the end of the fourth year of study. It also is a good reality check for your understanding of the law that is independent of Concord's grading system. On this last point, the Concord grading system is designed to mirror that of the CA Bar in that students are graded to reflect what they would receive by a bar examiner. This allows the student to know what kind of legal writing will allow them to pass the bar. The scores are then scaled to a typical academic shedule of grades.

I have a PhD and taught college for years and I have to admit that I was never the kind of professor that I find at Concord. I cared about my students but Concord faculty really care about their students by being available for helpful discussions about the law. No question is too unimportant for them to respond. Students communicate with faculty via e-mail and phone. Each e-mail question is logged in on the Concord web site, as well as each answer. Each e-mail usually gets a response within 24 to 48 hours. The student-faculty communication process is excellent.

Status: Current student, part-time
Dates of Enrollment: 9/2005-Submit Date
Survey Submitted: March 2006

In spite of seeming ease of admission, the academic program is outstanding but rigorous. As a law school, the vast majority of classes (including all in the first two years) are mandatory, so ease of getting classes is irrelevant. The classes are extremely challenging, but not unreasonably so; they can be handled with due diligence. However, law school is law school—it's extremely difficult, and those who fall behind pay a severe price for doing so.

There are a few layers of professors one deals with, and the vast majority are somewhere between very good and tremendous. First, there are video lecturers for the subjects—all are at least excellent; a few are true stars. Better still, taped video lectures may be shot and edited like a movie or TV show. Thus, there are no real rough spots in the lectures; however, they leave in enough coughing, throat-clearing, etc. to make the lectures feel human and relatively live.

Then, there are specialty lecturers, also primarily on tape. Not surprisingly, the handful of these (for example, one is an expert at breaking down essay questions) are very specialized and VERY good at what they do.

Finally, each class has a professor who: (1) leads online classes on the subject; (2) maintains constant e-mail contact with the student; and (3) grades and gives feedback on work. There is a ton of very personlized feedback with each grade, which is extremely useful. Of the 10 or so professors I've had, one was personally grating but very knowledgeable. Perhaps half have been extremely good, helping me a lot. The rest have been well beyond extremely good—two have been several levels beyond "as good as it gets," and I will never forget them.

The classes use traditional hornbooks and casebooks and the school provides student Westlaw accounts with enough support to allow you to use your account to supplement your work. (Prior, of course, to the classes that aim to make you an expert in this stuff.)

The workload is heavy, but again, this IS law school. The workload can be accomplished by anyone dedicated enough to the program. However, the student must realize that dedication to this program requires a daily commitment, every day. Out of 365 days of the year, I probably do schoolwork 340 of them, generally at an average of two hours per day.

Status: Current student, part-time
Dates of Enrollment: 8/2003-Submit Date
Survey Submitted: April 2005

Let me start with the workload! This is a very challenging program and I cannot seem to keep up with the work unless I put in 40+ hours of work every week. It is a Juris Doctor degree program where the successful candidates are eligible to take the California Bar Exam. The quality of the classes, which are all delivered on the Internet via video lectures, are EXCELLENT. The student has the added advantage of being able to replay the lectures, fast forward and rewind any number of times. You can pause and take notes as you go along. I sometimes also tape them and listen to the lectures while jogging. The program is a fixed curriculum for the first two years, after which there is the introduction of electives. I had no trouble getting into the elective class I chose to take (Federal Income Taxation), however there was one class that seemed quite popular, and the faculty was encouraging everyone to sign up early. To my knowledge, everyone who wanted to take that class got in as well, although I cannot be sure.

The chat professors have been extremely helpful and kind. The substantive lectures are delivered via video, but the chat lectures are where the professor discusses various aspects of the law and gives the students a chance to ask question (this is online as well). It is sort of like an Internet classroom, if you will. The chat professors are extremely helpful and if I e-mail them with a question, I usually get the answer the next day or two days after at the latest. I also have had classes where the professor has scheduled a telephone conference in order to give me telephone feedback.

The grading policy is quite harsh. The expectations are very high and the students have to work very hard in order to get a decent grade. I find it very hard to score higher than a B. For anything more, I have to put in a disproportionately higher amount of time. Most of the time, I end up with C's.

Status: Current student, part-time
Dates of Enrollment: 9/2003-Submit Date
Survey Submitted: April 2005

Your professors and classes are assigned to you; there are no electives until third year (but then, it's law school). That having been said, the professors as a whole, excellent, with more than one standout. The workload is nasty, but manageable as long as you don't slack off—and again, it's law school, what did you expect? Grading is a perpetual mind-[expletive deleted]. Again, this seems to be the law school way. It's frustrating, but you learn to deal with it. Overall, the education is excellent, and the workload is such that, if you are an established professional adult, you can accomplish your goal of becoming a lawyer while maintaining your professional, adult life. It's hard work, and you must make personal sacrifices on a daily basis, but that speaks to the challenges of living a part-time adult (non-student) life and learning the law; the school makes it possible to do both with a little (OK, a lot of) self-discipline.

 Employment Prospects

Status: Alumnus/a, part-time
Dates of Enrollment: 1/2002-1/2006
Survey Submitted: March 2006

Because Concord is not an ABA-approved school, there are only a few states where a graduate can take the state bar exam. California, of course, allows grads to take the bar. In addition, there are two or three other states that will allow Concord grads to take their state bar after passing the California bar. Since Concord is a fairly new school, the pool of graduates is still quite small, but growing rapidly. There are a number of Concord grads who are successfully practicing law in California, as well as several who are in practice in other areas of the country.

Status: Alumnus/a, part-time
Dates of Enrollment: 1/2002-12/2005
Survey Submitted: March 2006

Pass the CA Bar, and at least in CA, you are good to go. There hasn't been much time for word of mouth to spread in the world of "the firm," but Concord grads are out there, and the word on the street is that they can write a memo, they can see the issues. If the quality stays as high as it has been up to now, the relative uncertainty of where you came from will be pushed aside when they see what you can do. The ABA has a long way to go to realize this, as do most state bars, so you will have a problem with "state lock" until the attitude changes.

But you can practice in the federal system based on your CA Bar; you can do patents and the usual behind the scenes work without actually standing up and litigating. The school is very interested in helping to place grads, and remains connected as a resource. They also put a lot of effort into bar prep for the students, since that is the final measure of their success.

> **The school says:** "Concord's unique method of delivering instruction—via the Internet without a fixed classroom facility—places it in the correspondence school category under California law. While the State Bar of California and the American Bar Association (ABA) do not accredit correspondence schools, the Committee of Bar Examiners of the State Bar registers schools in this category. Concord Law School is registered as such and the Juris Doctor (JD) program is designed to meet the legal education requirements of the Committee of Bar Examiners so that graduates may apply for admission to the State Bar of California.
>
> "Prospective students, who are interested in state bar admission other than in California, should contact the bar admissions officials directly in the state of interest."

Status: Current student, part-time
Dates of Enrollment: 9/2005-Submit Date
Survey Submitted: March 2006

The school is just young enough that I don't think there's a set pattern. Moreover, the nature of the program (all online) makes it a school largely for

Read all of Vault's Law School Surveys at www.vault.com/lawschool — get complete surveys on top law schools, expert advice on applicaton essays, LSAT prep and more.

VAULT CAREER LIBRARY   37

mid-career professionals (who don't have time to attend a brick and mortar school). Consequently, students may continue in their general fields of work—in which they are often very experienced—but with a new bent on things. (For example, I work in the entertainment industry and intend on continuing in that field, representing entertainers and corporations in my specific area of performance.)

There is a growing alumni network and a strong internship program. While there is no campus to recruit on, the school offers twice-yearly career day seminars for upper division students that are designed to help us plan our careers. Further, as mid-career professionals, it's very easy for us to converse with professors and administrators on an even playing field about career choices and options.

Status: Current student, part-time
Dates of Enrollment: 9/2003-Submit Date
Survey Submitted: March 2006

Concord has a wonderful externship program (LEEP) headed by one of the country's most famous legal scholars, Dr. William Weston.

Status: Alumnus/a, part-time
Dates of Enrollment: 6/2000-12/2004
Survey Submitted: April 2005

This is a serious issue due to the accreditation issue as it is an online school. The positive side to the coin is that the school is working as hard as possible for its students, because anything that makes the school more respectable makes its students more respectable and vice versa. The tuition is affordable for those who would not attend law school otherwise. This was a deciding factor for me. I wanted to enter the nonprofit public interest law sector, and this is nearly impossible due to the enormous loans resulting from a regular law school education. Online education is about the only solution to the massive debt that prohibits the conventional law school graduate from entering the public interest sector.

Status: Current student, part-time
Dates of Enrollment: 1/2002-Submit Date
Survey Submitted: April 2005

Employment prospects for Concord students remain an open question. On the one hand, Concord has devoted considerable effort to providing students with all the tools they need to pursue jobs as lawyers. This is done through extensive career development forums given twice a year. On the other hand, several factors limit a Concord graduate's immediate acceptance into the legal community. One factor is the limited number of states currently allowing Concord graduates to sit for their bar exams. Another is the relatively small number of Concord graduates since the first graduating class in 2002, which makes assessing job prospects difficult. Finally, the market demand for lawyers also plays an important role.

From yet another perspective, the demand for lawyers or the ability to take a bar exam is irrelevant to many students. Students seek the kind of legal education Concord offers for a variety of reasons, not just to become practicing lawyers. A good legal education offers valuable skills to many executives and managers who have no intention of practicing law. Given the high quality of its program and increasing popularity, I can only predict that Concord's program represents the future of education and Concord graduates will soon establish themselves as valuable assets to the legal community and the community at large.

Status: Current student, part-time
Dates of Enrollment: 5/2002-Submit Date
Survey Submitted: April 2005

This school has been in existence only seven years, so we have only had three graduating classes. One graduate works for a county defendant's office; one set up her own family counseling practice; another works for a judge in Massachusetts; and another is the general counsel for his construction firm. In the fourth year, we have an opportunity to participate in an externship. Students have been placed with federal and county judges, legal aid services for abused women, law firms and the ABA office of professional responsibility.

 **Quality of Life**

Status: Current student, part-time
Dates of Enrollment: 1/2003-Submit Date
Survey Submitted: March 2006

This is by far the greatest benefit. With three children and a senior position in my company that requires extensive travel, I would never have been able to attend law school. However, because it is through distance learning, I can do it on my schedule for the most part, which means a higher quality of life because school fits into my schedule versus me into its schedule.

Status: Current student, part-time
Dates of Enrollment: 9/2005-Submit Date
Survey Submitted: March 2006

The school is online, so there is no brick and mortar campus. That having been said, I'll focus on a different "quality of life" issue.

Because the school is online, the full-time professional may maintain his or her quality of life by controlling when and where he does his work. Even live classes are archived for those who either miss them or want to review them again. I have done school work at home, in my office, and in the Caribbean. I've done school work at 4 a.m. and 4 p.m. For someone with a challenging career, this is a tremendous quality of life issue.

Because Concord is an online law school, technical problems affect the quality of one's experience. There are a few problems, but then I recall sitting in a few classrooms with broken air conditioning on a 100 degree day before too. Overall, major problems happen very rarely (the school web site has been down once for a few hours during my three years as a student). Minor, irritating problems do crop up from time to time, and no one should attempt this school without broadband, but they're pretty limited.

Status: Alumnus/a, part-time
Dates of Enrollment: 1/2002-1/2006
Survey Submitted: March 2006

Concord is an online law school, so there is no physical community where we all live. However, we have many opportunities to get together, and the relationships between students are very close and dynamic. We have easy access to our professors, administration and other students. Instead of competitiveness between students racing for the top spot, the students at Concord are more likely to work cooperatively and collegially with the professors and each other to bring the whole group to understanding.

Status: Alumnus/a, part-time
Dates of Enrollment: 1/2002-12/2005
Survey Submitted: March 2006

Not an issue. Take your current life. Add 18 hours/week of work- and deadline-related stress. Shake or stir, your preference.

Status: Current student, part-time
Dates of Enrollment: 9/2003-Submit Date
Survey Submitted: March 2006

Because Concord's program is wholly online, I enjoy the flexibility of keeping up with my family life and my studies at a reasonable pace. As a non-traditional student (started 1L at age 29), had it not been for Concord's program, I would never have been able to enroll in a JD program.

Additionally, I do not live in the vicinity of any law schools. The nearest would be approximately 120 miles away.

Status: Current student, full-time
Dates of Enrollment: 8/2003-Submit Date
Survey Submitted: April 2005

This is an online law school, so issues such as these are moot. We receive our lectures in our homes, or hotels if we're traveling so we don't have to worry about housing, crime, etc. The wonderful thing is that you never have to miss a class because you overslept or had to go out of town. You take your laptop with you when you travel or log on and receive the lecture whenever it is a good time (sometimes even the middle of the night!).

Status: Current student, part-time
Dates of Enrollment: 9/2002-Submit Date
Survey Submitted: April 2005

This is the ideal campus; it's your own study or computer den! No issues to deal with outside of network traffic!

Status: Current student, full-time
Dates of Enrollment: 8/2003-Submit Date
Survey Submitted: April 2005

Because Concord offers a flexible distance program utilizing the computer and Internet, the quality of life is excellent. I am able to study and learn in the comfort of my home and can fit my education into my busy work and family schedule. I am able to study when and where it is most convenient and I do not lose valuable hours traveling or sitting in traffic. I am able to eat with my family and do not have to rely on the quality of a restaurant; and I have no worries regarding driving at night or walking to my car in a dark parking lot after an evening class. I am safe in my home. In addition, I do not have the added expense associated with gas and tolls to get back and forth from a fixed-facility classroom. I have a great deal of time and money saved through this learning format.

 ## Social Life

Status: Alumnus/a, part-time
Dates of Enrollment: 1/2002-1/2006
Survey Submitted: March 2006

When we get together physically, we have a really good time. Friendships develop without the usual constraints of appearance, gender, social position and so on. We are also older than the average student body, so bars, dating and the Greek system are insiginifcant in our world. We are more interested in conversation around a coffee table than dance clubs!

Status: Alumnus/a, part-time
Dates of Enrollment: 1/2002-12/2005
Survey Submitted: March 2006

You can, and lots do, make study groups. I had one "buddy" throughout, with whom I compared notes and discussed both school life and "real" life. It can be what you want it to be. There is a Student Bar Association and a newsletter. A Law Review is surely in the future, and needs to be, just to get some quality writing by the best students into the public eye.

Status: Current student, part-time
Dates of Enrollment: 1/2003-Submit Date
Survey Submitted: March 2006

Concord Law School offers many opportunities for its students to socialize for fun and work. Students usually get together in person for local groups spread throughout the country; they get together for Concord regional law conferences; and they get together online if they wish. This is all in addition to once per week or often twice per week chat classes in which students meet with their professors online and students hear the professor's voice live and each student responds to questions by writing out answers. The environment is very interactive. Overall, Concord students don't feel isolated during their studies.

Status: Alumnus/a, part-time
Dates of Enrollment: 9/2001-2/2006
Survey Submitted: March 2006

There is no campus life as we are all over the world. However there are various very active e-mail chat rooms, bulletin boards and an active student body that contacts one another, keeps in touch and because for the most part are an older group are extremely supportive of one another's issues both at school and in life rather than competitive. Most if not all of the student body are already successful individuals in their previously chosen career. This allows them to bring a great source of outside experience in just dealing with life to the school and to the program. The student body is one of the most supportive and dedicated to success for all communities I have ever been a part of.

Status: Current student, part-time
Dates of Enrollment: 9/2005-Submit Date
Survey Submitted: March 2006

Again, as an Internet school, there's no bar near campus with $1 beers and a wet t-shirt contest on Wednesday nights. However, students do organize their own groups and do meet, study and socialize together. Further, there are numerous Yahoo groups that are open only to students and that serve as a conduit for a great deal of "public" interaction between those who wish to be involved.

Status: Alumnus/a, part-time
Dates of Enrollment: 6/2000-12/2004
Survey Submitted: April 2005

Students have bonded in study groups and list servers. For those who can be distracted by student life, like me, the privacy I have enjoyed has been perfect. My "social life" has been the working world, which has been enriched by my law school education. The adult student has different priorities, and I believe that everyone could benefit from a law education. An online school is a democratizing entity, as I am able to communicate what I learn to the wider world, which is not the insular law school student body.

Status: Current student, part-time
Dates of Enrollment: 1/2002-Submit Date
Survey Submitted: April 2005

Concord Law School has an active student body. My Concord friends and I pick a location to meet, such as L.A., then we all fly in for the weekend to visit with each other or to attend someone's graduation. The first time we met each other in person was amazing! We had been friends via the Internet for almost a year and we just picked up where we left off in our conversations. Three years later, our friendships have only grown stronger. There are many students groups that have formed at Concord Law School, including the first fully online Student Bar Association. The Concord Law School Student Bar Association (SBA) is the student government of the school. The SBA meets once a month in a chat room to discuss issues occurring at our school. The officers of the SBA meet have teleconferences once a month with the administration of Concord Law School, so discuss ways to make Concord a better school to attend. The previous SBA President was responsible for getting Supreme Court Justice Scalia to address our school, via the Internet. That was fantastic!

Status: Current student, part-time
Dates of Enrollment: 4/2001-Submit Date
Survey Submitted: April 2005

The average Concord student is 42 years old, has at least a master's degree and often a doctorate, and does not participate in the social scene of bars, dating and clubs. However, the students have formed very active virtual study groups, support groups and virtual student unions via Yahoo groups. The typical group consists of 200 to 400 people. Students do occasionally get together physically to study, but most interactions are through the Yahoo groups. As a result, the average Concord student makes 20 to 30 close friends, and is acquainted with about 200 to 300 fellow students. Concord offers school get-togethers a few times a year, and many students travel to attend those get-togethers. I live in Texas, but I have traveled to Los Angeles four times, and to Washington, D.C. once for Concord functions. Those meetings were nice, but not necessary. We have a close virtual community that is not seen in what we call "bricks and mortar" institutions.

 ## The School Says

Concord Law School is the first law school of its kind. As a wholly online, robust and interactive, part-time program, Concord is designed to meet the needs of a working adult student population. Our mission is to provide a high quality legal education at a reasonable cost for persons with professional and/or personal schedules or geographic constraints that make attendance at a "bricks and mortar" law school difficult or impossible. Concord's affordability and accessibility, as well as its method of delivering a legal education, are distinguishing characteristics of the program.

Read all of Vault's Law School Surveys at www.vault.com/lawschool — get complete surveys on top law schools, expert advice on applicaton essays, LSAT prep and more.

VAULT CAREER LIBRARY   39

Since opening its virtual doors in October of 1998, Concord has attracted a diverse student population. Our students' motivations for going to law school range from the desire to improve their skills and knowledge for their current work to starting a new career as a lawyer to the personal satisfaction of obtaining a life-long goal. Students reside in all 50 states and 12 other countries. The typical student is mid-career, with an average age of 43 and an undergraduate GPA of 3.0. More than 40 percent of the entering students already hold advanced degrees.

Concord's student-centered philosophy contributes to a learning environment that supports the student on many levels. There is an expectation that students will have to integrate their law school studies with other work and family responsibilities. Each student is assigned a Law Advisor who provides guidance on these issues as well as help with study techniques and basic skill development.

Concord's doors never close. The Law School curriculum is available to students 24 hours a day, seven days a week, from any part of the globe. The online curriculum allows for multiple methods of delivering course materials to accommodate a variety of learning styles. Students have access to video lectures, participate in synchronous discussion groups, and receive substantial feedback from their professors throughout the term. Many of the professors also work in public law offices, law firms or other legal settings and bring that practical knowledge to their teaching. Professors are accessible and are expected to respond to student e-mails within 24 to 48 hours—a standard they regularly beat.

Concord Law School is a leader in expanding the use and recognition of distance learning in legal education. It is part of Kaplan, Inc., which is a wholly owned subsidiary of The Washington Post Company. At present, since the ABA Standards for the Approval of Law Schools prohibit approval of programs that are fully or substantially delivered by distance education methodologies, without regard to the quality of those programs, Concord cannot qualify for ABA approval. This currently constrains bar-taking opportunities for Concord graduates. Concord is accredited by the Accrediting Commission of the Distance Education Training Council (DETC, www.detc.org), which is a national accrediting agency recognized by the U.S. Department of Education. It operates under the rules of the State Bar of California and its graduates may sit for the California Bar Examination.

The school is a leader in expanding the use and recognition of distance learning in legal education.

For information and a tour of the school, please visit www.concordlawschool.edu.

Golden Gate University School of Law

Office of Admissions and Financial Aid
536 Mission Street
San Francisco, CA 94105-2968
Admissions phone: (415) 442-6630 or (800) GGU-4YOU
Admissions fax: (415)442-6631
Admissions e-mail: lawadmit@qqu.edu
Admissions URL:
http://www.ggu.edu/school_of_law/law_admissions_finan-cial_aid

 ## Admissions

Status: Alumnus/a, full-time
Dates of Enrollment: 1/2000-12/2003
Survey Submitted: October 2005

Golden Gate University School of Law is considered one of the easier law schools to get admitted to. While this school's reputation is not as highly esteemed as the University of California, Hastings School of Law, Golden Gate University School of Law does its best to recruit students who will successfully complete the three years of law school or four years, if they are night-time students, and pass the California bar exam on the first try.

The school gives incentives like scholarship money and special honors programs to these stellar students. I knew of many classmates who were accepted to UC Hastings, but decided on Golden Gate University because of the financial support GGU provided them in scholarship money. There was no interview for the admissions process. There were a couple of essays that ask you why you would want to attend law school and Golden Gate in particular. I found the entire admissions process simple and straightforward. The admissions staff was kind, courteous and pretty fast in its reply. I found out whether I was accepted or rejected within one month of my submission. It should be noted that I was a mid-year admit student. That is what is so wonderful about GGU. I wanted to start my law studies in January and GGU offered such a program.

Status: Alumnus/a, full-time
Dates of Enrollment: 9/1989-5/1992
Survey Submitted: March 2006

I had excellent LSATs (top 10 percent) and mediocre grades from a great school. I was admitted.

Status: Alumnus/a, part-time
Dates of Enrollment: 8/1999-5/2003
Survey Submitted: March 2005

Admissions process was fairly easy. Admission is not very competitive. However, I was pleased that the dean of the school called me to see if I had any questions. That type of personal attention swayed my decision to attend this school.

 ## Academics

Status: Alumnus/a, full-time
Dates of Enrollment: 1/2000-12/2003
Survey Submitted: October 2005

I was a mid-year admit, where I started school in January as opposed to the rest of the class that started in August. Being in the mid-year class allowed me to have smaller classes, we only had 15 students in our class. We all got individualized attention from the professors and this was really important to all of us. We even had special legal studies classes to help us transition into the legal studies a lot faster than the rest of the law students in the country. It was really easy to

get the popular classes, because it is all about getting your courses selected as soon as possible. Additionally, the professors would always have waitlists, and these waitlists tend to move. Often times the professors would allow more students in the class as long as the professor gets a larger lecture hall. So, although the classes can be small, they can also be larger than you would want because the professor is so popular that the class is huge.

Grading is fair. Each professor has their own type of teaching and testing. The great thing about Golden Gate is that they have old tests of the professors in indexed bound books in the library on reserve. This is a great resource for those who want to ace their exams and get to know the professors a lot better. These are the golden orange books that all law students at Golden Gate should learn to love and adore.

The workload was relatively OK considering I still had time to play. I usually would review my class notes after class. I usually had a library break in between classes, so I would either prepare for class or review notes. I would study until 6 p.m. in the library and then go home. I would just relax when I got home. Sometimes when I really wanted to I would review the lessons and the class materials a bit more after dinner, but usually I would save that for the morning when I got to the library at 7:30 a.m. with my study group. Study groups are not for everyone, but I found that having a study group help ease off the pressure in preparing for the Socratic Method that most of the professors still apply at Golden Gate. This Socratic Method is the only thing that I detested while in law school, because I didn't think that this method really helped me in learning the material. Rather, I would be so afraid of getting called on and quizzed on the most bizarre theories that I over-prepared on the cases. I realized that this does not pertain to the bar exam that we all face after graduating from law school.

Status: Alumnus/a, full-time
Dates of Enrollment: 9/1989-5/1992
Survey Submitted: March 2006

I took a class at Boalt in addition to my classes at GGU. I honestly found no difference in the quality of instruction or of the students between the two schools' day programs. GGU is more student-friendly, however, in that it has a night-school program where people with day jobs and families have to fit in classes and study.

Status: Alumnus/a, part-time
Dates of Enrollment: 8/1999-5/2003
Survey Submitted: March 2005

Academics were adequate. I think the quality of classes was quite good. Many professors had practiced and could offer practical experience. In general, I think the experience at this school is very practical. I did not have any difficulty getting any class I wanted. Grading, for the most part, was fair. However, I have to admit that I found it insulting that many professors supposedly linked your final grade to your attendance and in a very formal way. For example, if you missed more than some number of classes with an "unexcused absence" your final grade would be lowered. I found this to be incredibly childish.

 ## Employment Prospects

Status: Alumnus/a, full-time
Dates of Enrollment: 1/2000-12/2003
Survey Submitted: October 2005

Employment is competitive as it is at any school. Golden Gate has on-campus interviews and I am happy to be one of the students that got my first job out of law school through OCI at GGU. I am very satisfied with the career services office. Of course, a lot of my satisfaction is my own making since I was the one with the resources. Many times the career services office just offers the rooms where interviews are to take place, but most of the contacts I created on my own. The staff is still very supportive and often times helps people calm down before the interview or after an interview.

Read all of Vault's Law School Surveys at www.vault.com/lawschool — get complete surveys on top law schools, expert advice on applicaton essays, LSAT prep and more.

VAULT CAREER LIBRARY   41

Alumni networking is great at GGU, as well as the professors. The great thing about GGU is that the professors are also practicing attorneys. Many times they come and teach at GGU after working a full day. I really love hearing real live cases that they are handling at any given time. Real live case studies make going to class and preparing for the future better than the other law schools.

Status: Alumnus/a, full-time
Dates of Enrollment: 9/1989-5/1992
Survey Submitted: March 2006

When I graduated GGU had no prestige among local employers except MoFo and Pillsbury (they were willing to hire the very top students, like top five). This has improved somewhat, but still not enough.

Status: Alumnus/a, part-time
Dates of Enrollment: 8/1999-5/2003
Survey Submitted: March 2005

I think this is one of the challenges this school will face in the future. In general, fellow graduates had a more difficult time getting jobs than graduates from other Bay Area schools. While I do think that most of my fellow graduates finally found jobs, they frequently had to wait a long time and many ended up with jobs they were not necessarily happy with.

Quality of Life

Status: Alumnus/a, full-time
Dates of Enrollment: 1/2000-12/2003
Survey Submitted: October 2005

There is no housing for GGU students. The campus is beautiful because it is in downtown San Francisco with all the new buildings that surround the campus. We get a discount for a fitness center if you decide to join (24-hour fitness) and there are lovely restaurants all around. Our campus is better than Hastings, where there tends to be a lot of drug addicts. We have a lot of business people, and that's pretty much it. We have security walk around and monitor the building's surroundings. They even have a security walker if you need to get to your car at night. There is a parking lot conveniently across the street.

Status: Alumnus/a, full-time
Dates of Enrollment: 9/1989-5/1992
Survey Submitted: March 2006

The school building is located in downtown San Francisco. I believe it still offers a discounted YMCA membership.

Status: Alumnus/a, part-time
Dates of Enrollment: 8/1999-5/2003
Survey Submitted: March 2005

This is a commuter school in the middle of San Francisco. I'm not aware of any student housing. Nor am I aware of any real campus life. Generally, students attend classes and leave. It is in a fairly safe neighborhood, but you still need to be careful after dark.

Social Life

Status: Alumnus/a, full-time
Dates of Enrollment: 1/2000-12/2003
Survey Submitted: October 2005

There is a great social life at GGU. Although we think that we study a lot, we also get to play a lot too. We have something called "bar review" where we go and visit a local bar and socialize with fellow classmates. Usually, the school reserves a private room at the bar or club and orders food and we get the drinks. It's a lot of fun. A lot of people start dating each other in law school, especially GGU. I know of at least 10 couples who met in GGU and are now engaged or married. GGU is at the heart of downtown, and is close enough to the trendy restaurants, clubs, bars and night spots.

Status: Alumnus/a, full-time
Dates of Enrollment: 9/1989-5/1992
Survey Submitted: March 2006

It's there and it's hopping.

Status: Alumnus/a, part-time
Dates of Enrollment: 8/1999-5/2003
Survey Submitted: March 2005

There are some bars in the vicinity of the school. I did not find that students socialized with each other all that much. I think the reason for this is that most students live far from school and many have other jobs. This school offers very flexible schedules so that people with jobs can still attend law school. While this makes it convenient to attend classes and maintain a job, it is not all that conducive to an active social life.

Loyola Law School Los Angeles

Admissions Office
919 Albany Street
Los Angeles, CA 90015-1211
Admissions phone: (213) 736-1074
Admissions fax: (213) 736-6523
Admissions e-mail: admissions@lls.edu
Admissions URL: http://www.lls.edu/admissions/

 Admissions

Status: Current student, full-time
Dates of Enrollment: 8/2004-Submit Date
Survey Submitted: February 2006

The application requires two essays: one general essay and one essay on why you want to attend Loyola. The *U.S. News* ranking stats on Loyola are pretty right on, so if your numbers fall into those ranges you will probably be OK. Transfer applications do not require any letters of recommendation. I transferred from a lower tier two to Loyola and I ranked in the top 25 percent of my class.

> **The school says:** "The school requires one essay—a personal statement. Addenda and resumes are welcome but not required."

Status: Alumnus/a, full-time
Dates of Enrollment: 8/2002-5/2005
Survey Submitted: April 2006

Loyola's admissions process was more welcoming than other schools'. They invited me to spend a day on campus visiting a class and tours were encouraged. They also threw a reception for admitted students and invited professors and current students to meet us. I was impressed.

Status: Alumnus/a, part-time
Dates of Enrollment: 8/1999-5/2003
Survey Submitted: March 2005

Appears to be getting more selective, as more people are learning of this school's great law program, and as the school moves up to the list of second-tier law schools.

Status: Alumnus/a, full-time
Dates of Enrollment: 8/1995-5/1998
Survey Submitted: March 2005

The admissions process is fairly standard. There is no interview. My perception was that the LSAT was heavily weighted.

Status: Alumnus/a, full-time
Dates of Enrollment: 8/2001-5/2004
Survey Submitted: March 2005

Nothing too different from other schools. I got a $15,000 scholarship for my first year. The school was making an effort to get top students to improve its rankings. I do remember there was a strange Scantron portion to the application.

Status: Alumnus/a, full-time
Dates of Enrollment: 1/2001-0/2004
Survey Submitted: March 2005

The admissions process required a detailed application, essay, writing sample and LSAT score. Additionally, students seeking public interest scholarship funding were required to fill out an additional application and essay. The process was fairly selective. And, sizeable scholarships were awarded to top applicants.

Status: Alumnus/a, full-time
Dates of Enrollment: 8/1999-5/2002
Survey Submitted: January 2004

Many law schools offer early admission to their fall semester's entering class. Generally, this requires submission of your application by the preceding November or December. Otherwise, applications are usually not due until mid-March. Though Loyola has an application deadline of February 2, highly qualified individuals who apply after expiration of the deadline are often admitted. However, these individuals usually must have far superior credentials to applicants who applied in a timely manner.

According to some rankings, Loyola is the third-best law school in the Los Angeles area (if not all of Southern California). As a result, it attracts a lot of really talented, smart individuals who could easily attend a number of top-tier schools located in other cities, but declined and attended Loyola in order to remain in L.A. Thus, the applicant pool is somewhat more competitive than Loyola's rank might imply.

There is no interview required for admission to Loyola Law School.

Status: Current student, full-time
Dates of Enrollment: 8/2003-Submit Date
Survey Submitted: April 2004

Pretty standard application package, including essay, grades, etc. Loyola does invite prospective students to visit the campus, attend a class and get a tour of the facilities.

Status: Current student, full-time
Dates of Enrollment: 8/2002-Submit Date
Survey Submitted: October 2003

Spend some time on your personal statement. Since law schools do not have an interview process, the personal statement is your only chance to express your personality and make the application more than just a numbers game.

Status: Alumnus/a, full-time
Dates of Enrollment: 8/1998-5/2001
Survey Submitted: April 2004

I applied at the very last minute to law school and may not have as clear of an understanding of the different options with respect to admissions. I simply took the LSAT and filled out an application, which included an essay. There was no interview process involved with respect to Loyola. In terms of selectivity, Loyola has, in the past, admitted more students than the other local law schools, including USC and UCLA. I'm not sure if this has changed at all, and Loyola's admissions department should be contacted about this. I do know, however, that Loyola does offer some great merit-based scholarships that an applicant definitely should inquire into.

Status: Alumnus/a, full-time
Dates of Enrollment: 9/1993-6/1996
Survey Submitted: April 2004

Application, essay, normal process. No interview. School has become significantly more selective over the last 10 years.

 Academics

Status: Current student, full-time
Dates of Enrollment: 8/2004-Submit Date
Survey Submitted: February 2006

Professors are great and most are approachable. Some classes are recorded, so there's no stress if you miss a class. You can just listen to the lecture off a link that is posted on the class web site. Professors are pretty straightforward here, they really want you to learn. There is less "hiding the ball" than at other

Read all of Vault's Law School Surveys at www.vault.com/lawschool — get complete surveys on top law schools, expert advice on applicaton essays, LSAT prep and more.

VAULT CAREER LIBRARY   43

schools. The school is very concerned with public service and there is a minimum pro bono hours requirement. Although this is a pain in the arse, it helps round out your resume! There are several different law journals on campus, thus your chances of getting on law review is greater! The three different law reviews are: *Loyola Law Review*, *Entertainment Law* and *International Law*. All three are great and look good on your resume. You only have to submit one essay to qualify for consideration for all three of the law journals. Transfer students get a chance to write one in the beginning of the year. First-year students write one at the end of spring semester.

Status: Alumnus/a, full-time
Dates of Enrollment: 8/2002-5/2005
Survey Submitted: April 2006

Loyola's professors are topnotch teachers. Students during the first year are assigned to a section and have no choice regarding the professors, but I did not find that to be a problem at all because I did not know anything about the professors when I got there. I enjoyed just about all of my professors and would recommend them to anyone. For 2Ls and 3Ls, Loyola offers all of the bar courses as well as several interesting electives and clinical classes. Class sizes range widely from five to over a hundred.

Status: Alumnus/a, full-time
Dates of Enrollment: 8/2001-5/2004
Survey Submitted: March 2005

Very rigorous with a huge emphasis on writing. LLS grads know how to write much better than grads from many higher ranked schools. Professors vary in effectiveness but on a whole are very effective. It can be tough to get classes but rarely does anyone never get to take a class, you have to be assertive. Significant drop-off in workload from 1L to 2L to 3L years. Professors are extremely accessible.

Status: Alumnus/a, full-time
Dates of Enrollment: 1/2001-0/2004
Survey Submitted: March 2005

The first-year program was standard for all students. The courseload in the first year was heavy, but manageable. Because students are graded on a strict curve (with numerical grading instead of letter grades; failing is below 75, highest possible grade is 100), it is very competitive. The quality of classes and instruction was excellent. In the second and third years, there is a wide variety of class offerings, and classes were fairly easy to get into (i.e., seldom waitlists for popular classes). There is a pro bono requirement for graduation, which I feel is an excellent requirement!

The professors are among the top in their fields, and the school brings in excellent adjuncts to teach classes like Advanced Trial Advocacy (course taught by two U.S. attorneys). The Byrne Trial Advocacy Team was another great opportunity available at the school. Students have to try out for the team in an extremely competitive process. Students on the team compete in national trial advocacy competitions, spend long hours practicing, and receive course credit. The trial advocacy program at Loyola is currently among the Top 10 in the nation. Overall, I had a great experience at Loyola, and feel that my education was excellent preparation for my current career at a large civil defense firm.

Status: Alumnus/a, full-time
Dates of Enrollment: 9/2003-Submit Date
Survey Submitted: March 2005

1Ls are assigned to a section and do not pick their professors. On the whole, the quality of classes and professors is exceptional. I never had trouble getting into any of the electives that drew my attention, though the District Attorney seminar is highly competitive. In addition, mainstream classes (like Ethics or Appellate Advocacy) taught by tenured faculty are also more difficult to get into. Students may have to settle for adjunct professors for such classes, and they can be hit or miss (rely on word of mouth from students who took the class before or peruse the adjunct's student reviews available in the library, don't fly blind!). Tenured faculty are outstanding. My experience with adjunct professors was very positive, though fellow students did not always feel the same.

Grading is on a curve. Nonetheless, this did not result in cut-throat competition and students were, by and large, very supportive of each other, willing to exchange outlines for classes, form study groups, etc. The environment amongst

the students is very positive. The workload was as one might expect: overwhelming the first year; leading to more time management and less outright panic the second year; very manageable the third year.

Status: Alumnus/a, full-time
Dates of Enrollment: 8/1998-5/2001
Survey Submitted: April 2004

Loyola's first-year class is divided into four sections. You see the members in your section all the time because you take the same core classes together. In years two and three, you choose different classes and no longer are wedded to your section. The professors are great, and the quality of classes is equally appealing. I never had a problem enrolling for any of the popular classes, which, when I was there, was a Trademark class taught by an adjunct professor.

Several of the more practical classes, which I believe is one of Loyola's selling points, are taught by practicing lawyers in the community with an incredible expertise in that area, which makes the education very rewarding. The grading, I thought, was pretty fair and the workload completely manageable. You can definitely participate in Law Review and/or a moot court while maintaining a challenging workload.

Status: Alumnus/a, full-time
Dates of Enrollment: 8/1999-5/2002
Survey Submitted: January 2004

I was consistently surprised by the quality of the education I received at Loyola. Many of my professors were not only extremely accomplished attorneys, but often fantastic educators. In addition, the adjunct professors taught classes, such as Trial Advocacy, that were some of the best courses I took in law school. These adjunct professors, who generally had full careers outside the law school, brought real-world experience, advice and theory to the classroom. I believe this is one of the primary reasons why Loyola has a reputation for turning out fantastic attorneys. When you graduate from Loyola, you not only have a solid educational background, you have some real-world legal experience and knowledge that few, if any, other law school graduates have when they enter the job force.

Because Loyola has a full night school, day students have ultimate flexibility. Classes begin at 8 a.m. and continue until 10 p.m. at night.

Status: Current student, full-time
Dates of Enrollment: 8/2002-Submit Date
Survey Submitted: October 2003

Loyola is a departure from the cutthroat mentality at most other law schools. I have found the classes to be more educational than torture, and the classmates more helpful than secretive. There are always your typical law school students, but the overall atmosphere is one of support, not backstabbing.

 Employment Prospects

Status: Current student, full-time
Dates of Enrollment: 8/2004-Submit Date
Survey Submitted: February 2006

Big firms usually interview the top 20 percent at Loyola, some are more selective. Most big firms look for Law Review and moot court. Loyola has such a great name in Los Angeles, it shouldn't be too difficult to get a job if you get decent grades. There is an OCI in the fall and one in the spring. The spring one is smaller with mid-size firms, government agencies, small firms and public interest organizations. Transfer students are usually accepted after the fall OCI deadlines and will probably not be able to participate.

Status: Alumnus/a, full-time
Dates of Enrollment: 8/2002-5/2005
Survey Submitted: April 2006

Loyola has a great network in Los Angeles. I met several alums who work in Los Angeles, both downtown and in Century City, and two of them helped me get the jobs that I got after 1L and 2L year. The alumni network was crucial to my job search, as was on-campus interviewing. OCI is especially helpful for students at the top of the class.

Status: Alumnus/a, full-time
Dates of Enrollment: 8/1998-5/2001
Survey Submitted: March 2005

If you want to practice in Southern California and you obtained good grades, you should have plenty of opportunities to work in a big law firm. If you got average grades, opportunities will still be out there because there are so many Loyola alumni in Southern California, but outside of California, things will be more difficult.

Status: Alumnus/a, full-time
Dates of Enrollment: 8/2001-5/2004
Survey Submitted: March 2005

Not too difficult to get a job in L.A. with a LLS degree. Top 10 percent can go to big firms, but who wants to work at a big firm anyway? Getting a job outside L.A. is quite difficult. Career services does a good job once you realize that it's not their job to GET you a job, it's their job to HELP you get a job. Excellent externship opportunities. LLS is very tied into the local government scene.

Status: Alumnus/a, full-time
Dates of Enrollment: 9/2003-Submit Date
Survey Submitted: March 2005

LLS is well-known and respected in the Los Angeles market. Students wishing to practice in other geographic areas may have a more difficult time securing employment. During my second year, LLS fell into the third tier of schools in the *U.S. News* survey, prompting the dean and faculty to commit themselves to gaining broader exposure for LLS beyond Southern California. The next year, LLS was back in the second tier. Particularly in Southern California, LLS is well-respected and employment prospects with top firms are very good if you finish in the top 20 percent. Graduates obtain jobs with large, prestigious firms (Skadden, O'Melveny, Jones Day, Paul Hastings, Irell, Orrick, etc.) and with solo practitioners and in the public sector. The sheer number of graduates ensures quite a variety. I obtained my job via on-campus recruiting. I've also noticed that other LLS alums in my firm are pretty proud of the fact and are willing to give fellow LLS grads the benefit of the doubt during the hiring process.

Status: Alumnus/a, full-time
Dates of Enrollment: 1/2001-0/2004
Survey Submitted: March 2005

Students near the top of the class have no problems finding employment at the top firms in the country. Students in the top 10-15 percent of the class can generally expect to have 25 or more on-campus interviews, and will finish the interviewing process with several prestigious job offers. Because of the large alumni base in Los Angeles, and Loyola's excellent reputation in the L.A. legal community, a wide variety of job opportunities are available to students as summer associates and for permanent employment upon graduation. Among the large national firms, Loyola has a reputation for producing attorneys with a wide range of practical skills, especially strong litigation skills. Though Loyola is arguably not as prestigious as a Top 10 law school, students who do well at Loyola are generally very well-received by the best firms in the country.

Status: Alumnus/a, full-time
Dates of Enrollment: 8/1999-5/2002
Survey Submitted: January 2004

Loyola has one of the strongest alumni in the Los Angeles legal community. The loyalty that Loyola engenders in its students has afforded a multitude of opportunities and connections. It is unfortunate that this strong alumni base does not extend far beyond the limits of Southern California. Also, the job database at Loyola was always richer than from other schools. I know that in future, I intend to give Loyola students preference and to continue to assist Loyola law school in achieving the status and recognition it rightfully deserves.

Status: Alumnus/a, full-time
Dates of Enrollment: 8/1998-5/2001
Survey Submitted: April 2004

Personally, I believe that in the past, Loyola did not have as much credibility as USC and UCLA with some of the big L.A. firms. However, I believe that is changing because of the quality of lawyers that Loyola produces. As a practicing attorney who has worked with junior associates from various law schools, I

must say that Loyola graduates have a more practical approach regarding law practice, which is great for client relations.

 ## Quality of Life

Status: Current student, full-time
Dates of Enrollment: 8/2004-Submit Date
Survey Submitted: February 2006

The school really makes an effort to take care of its students. The campus has wireless Internet everywhere, so that's nice. The library has free coffee during finals. Even though the school is not in the best part of L.A., there's plenty of security and the campus is pretty secure. The nice part about Loyola's location is that in your second and third year when you want to extern the courthouse—it is right down the street from campus. Thus you can get an externship working at the superior or federal courthouse and still get to class on time! It would be difficult for someone from Pepperdine or UCLA to extern during the day and get to an evening class on time (especially with Los Angeles traffic!)

Status: Alumnus/a, full-time
Dates of Enrollment: 8/2002-5/2005
Survey Submitted: April 2006

The campus is a commuter school. It is not located with the rest of the university campus. That said, it is in close proximity to downtown Los Angeles, making it easy to take field trips to courtrooms and to work part-time while going to school.

Status: Alumnus/a, full-time
Dates of Enrollment: 8/1998-5/2001
Survey Submitted: March 2005

Loyola is in the middle of Rampart, so it's dangerous outside of campus, but it's walking distance to the Staples Center, so you can go to a Laker's game after class. Also, it's close to Korea Town and some of the best restaurants in So. Cal. Facilities on campus are fine.

Status: Alumnus/a, full-time
Dates of Enrollment: 8/1999-5/2003
Survey Submitted: March 2005

Neighborhood is terrible, but the campus is like an oasis with good security and excellent facilities. Parking is a premium (and you pay for it) because everyone has to drive to get there.

Status: Alumnus/a, full-time
Dates of Enrollment: 1/2001-0/2004
Survey Submitted: March 2005

The campus is located near downtown Los Angeles. Because of the location (and lack of campus housing), most students commute to school from other parts of L.A. The campus itself is beautiful. It was designed by a noted architect, and is a very comfortable place to study with a large library and excellent computer facilities. There is a wireless network in all lecture halls. Additionally, there are two courtrooms on campus.

Status: Alumnus/a, full-time
Dates of Enrollment: 9/2003-Submit Date
Survey Submitted: March 2005

The LLS campus is fairly small and is not located in a very good part of downtown L.A. Even so, it is a closed, gated campus with 24-hour security and is very safe and secure. Given the surrounding neighborhood, most students will commute. Quality apartments close to campus are available, though the prices are fairly high. There is a movement to redevelop the downtown area, particularly around the Staples Center (less than a mile from campus). In addition, luxury lofts are popping up downtown and the area may be on the upswing. The campus itself is very well-kept, with modern facilities, an excellent computer lab, high speed Internet at every study table throughout the library and quality classrooms. The Girardi Advocacy Center, completed in 2003, provides state-of-the-art courtroom technology for Trial Advocacy classes (it's really quite something!). The on-campus cafeteria is good, particularly on specialty days when the staff provides BBQ meals outside. Sometimes the SBA pays for the In 'n Out Burger truck to stop by (once or twice a year).

Read all of Vault's Law School Surveys at www.vault.com/lawschool — get complete surveys on top law schools, expert advice on applicaton essays, LSAT prep and more.

VAULT CAREER LIBRARY   45

Status: Current student, full-time
Dates of Enrollment: 8/2003-Submit Date
Survey Submitted: April 2004

Facilities, classrooms and campus are amazing, and I doubt there is a better-looking law school in the U.S. Totally wired campus, with enough computers and printers for every student. Library is amazing. All around pleasant place to study, especially when combined with the Los Angeles weather.

Status: Alumnus/a, full-time
Dates of Enrollment: 8/1998-5/2001
Survey Submitted: April 2004

The campus is great. Unlike other local law schools, Loyola provides an entire campus just for law students. The dining is better than at most places, but is simply a cafeteria and could be improved with more variety. I am not too familiar with the housing situation, but there are several nice communities in the nearby area that are close enough for a decent commute. The neighborhood is probably not as ideal, but because the campus is so self-contained and the security is great, I never felt that security and safety were issues.

Status: Alumnus/a, full-time
Dates of Enrollment: 8/1999-5/2002
Survey Submitted: January 2004

LLS is located in downtown L.A., about half a mile from the Staples Center. While the surrounding environs are not the most desirable, I never felt unsafe or uncomfortable while at school. In fact, unlike USC, which is about five or 10 minutes away and has an open campus, LLS has a closed campus with round-the-clock security. Moreover, the law school is much larger and more self-contained than other law schools. You rarely needed to leave campus for anything (except to go home).

 ## Social Life

Status: Current student, full-time
Dates of Enrollment: 8/2004-Submit Date
Survey Submitted: February 2006

It's a commuter school, so it lacks a sense of community on campus but people are very friendly. There are lots of different clubs on campus and the student body is very diverse. There is plenty of opportunity to get involved and take leadership roles on campus. There are usually "bar reviews" every week put on by a different club at various venues in L.A. These are a great way to get out and meet people.

Status: Alumnus/a, full-time
Dates of Enrollment: 8/2002-5/2005
Survey Submitted: April 2006

There are events throughout the year that are worthwhile, and I know that the friends I met in law school will be friends for life. I especially enjoyed the Turf Club, a monthly social event on campus.

Status: Alumnus/a, full-time
Dates of Enrollment: 8/1998-5/2001
Survey Submitted: March 2005

Loyola has a lot of connections with the entertainment industry, and everyone seems to want to get involved in the industry. Lots of outgoing personalities and lots of temptations to party.

Status: Alumnus/a, part-time
Dates of Enrollment: 8/1999-5/2003
Survey Submitted: March 2005

Who has time for a social life if you work full-time and go to school at night? Better to study hard for the first two years and get a good job, rather than wait until the fourth year to see what prospects await you.

Status: Alumnus/a, full-time
Dates of Enrollment: 8/2001-5/2004
Survey Submitted: March 2005

Beer and pizza once a month. I always had at least one party per semester at an L.A. bar or club, which was always a good time. People tend to stick to their friends from their 1L section, which is not surprising.

Status: Alumnus/a, full-time
Dates of Enrollment: 1/2001-0/2004
Survey Submitted: March 2005

There are many student organizations on campus that host various student events. The Public Interest Law Foundation (PILF) hosts a large silent auction/casino night fundraiser every year, and almost all students attend. There are not many restaurants and bars nearby, however, a lot of students live in West L.A. and West Hollywood, so there are always social events for students in those areas of town. There is not a Greek system on campus. However, given the fact that it is a graduate school (and most of the students are more mature), a Greek system is really unnecessary.

Status: Current student, full-time
Dates of Enrollment: 8/2002-Submit Date
Survey Submitted: October 2003

Social life and happy hours are abundant, what with all of downtown L.A. at your fingertips. Student favorites include McCormick & Schmick's, The Standard, Morton's Steakhouse, the Pantry and The Eastside Bakery.

Status: Alumnus/a, full-time
Dates of Enrollment: 8/1998-5/2001
Survey Submitted: April 2004

Wonderful. Loyola law students work hard and play hard. There are constantly different social opportunities amongst the law students. In addition, there are various annual alumni events, which the law students are invited to attend. There is somewhat of a "Greek" system for students with topnotch grades. Lots of clubs and events.

Status: Alumnus/a, full-time
Dates of Enrollment: 8/1999-5/2002
Survey Submitted: January 2004

Because LLS campus houses only the law school (its mother campus, Loyola Marymount, is located approximately 30 minutes away in Westchester), the law school has a unique social environment. Every Thursday the law school hosts a happy hour with drinks, food and socializing for the students. Moreover, the LLS constituency is richly varied, largely thanks to its night program and aggressive affirmative action policies. It makes for a diverse group in which almost anyone would be hard pressed not to find a niche.

Pepperdine University School of Law

Office of Admissions and Records
24255 Pacific Coast Highway
Malibu, CA 90263
Admissions phone: (310) 506-4631
Admissions fax: (310) 506-7668
Admissions e-mail: soladmis@pepperdine.edu
Admissions URL: http://law.pepperdine.edu/admissions/

 ## Admissions

Status: Alumnus/a, full-time
Dates of Enrollment: 8/2002-5/2005
Survey Submitted: March 2006

The application for admission is standard as far as law school applications are concerned. The only additional thing that is required to apply to Pepperdine is an essay about how morality will factor into your career as a law student and future attorney. This might be a turn-off for some students who are not religious. However, I myself am not religious but was still able to write an honest essay about the role that integrity and honestly play in my life. Your essay doesn't have to mention God to guarantee you a spot at the school.

Status: Current student, full-time
Dates of Enrollment: 10/2002-Submit Date
Survey Submitted: May 2005

Regular law school admission process: good LSAT, letters of recommendation and good grades from undergrad. The main difference in application process is the "mission statement," a short essay in which the student describes the reasons why they would fit in with the school's emphasis on Christian education. Admission to Pepperdine law school is getting more and more competitive each year.

Status: Alumnus/a, full-time
Dates of Enrollment: 8/1997-5/2000
Survey Submitted: April 2005

The admissions process was very straightforward; you filled out an application that includes essays and letters of recommendation from previous professors or other employers. I do recall writing an mandatory essay either relating to religion or morality and how I would combine my education with the mission statement of the university. There is no interview required. At the time I applied, the school was moderately selective, but as I have watched the admissions process over the last four years it is becoming even more selective.

Status: Current student, full-time
Dates of Enrollment: 9/2002-Submit Date
Survey Submitted: April 2005

The easiest way to get into Pepperdine (or any law school) is to have a high GPA and LSAT scores. Most schools begin with those two as the major criteria. For Pepperdine, there are lengthy questions about public service on the application. As such, it helps if you have been involved in charity work, church work (all faiths are accepted), etc. There was no interview process to get accepted to the school. The best advice I can give to anyone is to pay the $1,000 for a Kaplan course on the LSAT and take that exam very seriously.

Status: Alumnus/a, full-time
Dates of Enrollment: 8/2001-5/2004
Survey Submitted: May 2005

The admissions process was simple. There is no interview unless you are in contention for the Faculty Scholars Program. Then the school will fly you to Malibu, wine and dine you and evaluate your candidacy. Since Pepperdine is a Church of Christ school, my advice would be to tailor your application to be honest, and make your essays reflect the conservative values that Pepperdine

views as important. With the rise of graduate school applications in the past couple of years, it is becoming harder to be admitted to Pepperdine. That being said, I do not think it is an insurmountable challenge. I know people from undergrad who did not have the best grades and got into Pepperdine. It is not one of the more selective schools in Southern California, like UCLA or USC.

Status: Alumnus/a, full-time
Dates of Enrollment: 8/2002-5/2004
Survey Submitted: January 2005

The process is relatively similar to that of other law schools. The one additional element that Pepperdine requires is a statement based on the missions of Pepperdine University. While the statement may seem a bit religious, the school does use the response as a part of the application process, so pay attention to it.

Status: Current student, full-time
Dates of Enrollment: 8/2003-Submit Date
Survey Submitted: January 2005

The admissions process was easy. The application experience for both the law school as well as the master's program (specifically, public policy) was simple. The Pepperdine staff (as a whole) are the most wonderful and helpful I've come across; happy and willing to help with any questions or concerns. Admissions was rolling and I received a decision within a few weeks.

Status: Current student, full-time
Dates of Enrollment: 8/2002-Submit Date
Survey Submitted: July 2004

I applied to Pepperdine because I had a good chance of getting a scholarship there based on my LSAT score and GPA. The admission process was easy; all necessary information was included in the catalog. I did not have to undergo an interview, but students are interviewed for faculty scholarships (I missed the application date for this). I think the deadlines were very fair. I took the LSAT in December and could still apply with plenty of time. Advice on getting into Pepperdine—especially with scholarships—is to do well on the LSAT (obviously) and be active in your community. Pepperdine is affiliated with the Church of Christ, so they appreciate religious or community involvement. But the school itself does not push religion on you. The curriculum does focus on ethics and morals a lot, but if you are not religious, you should not feel uncomfortable.

Status: Current student, full-time
Dates of Enrollment: 9/2000-Submit Date
Survey Submitted: September 2003

Pepperdine's selectivity is getting tighter. My class was the last before the crackdown on LSAT scores. Really, though, your prospects are pretty good so long as you are in the top 35 percent of LSAT takers. As for the process itself, it is a pretty standard application. With one exception: the morality statement. Yes, you must write about your moral character and, though not absolutely required, I am sure it is appreciated. I don't know how much weight this actually carries in the admissions process, but it has been the one thing that prevented many of my friends from applying.

Status: Current student, full-time
Dates of Enrollment: 5/2002-Submit Date
Survey Submitted: May 2004

Pepperdine's admission process was straightforward, with room for creativity on the essays. The law school has become much more selective in the past few years, since becoming number one in dispute resolution and in the Top 100 for law schools. I would focus on dispute resolution (arbitration or mediation) or other goals that are compatible with the university's mission, as well as personal integrity and ethics. All of these are top priorities at Pepperdine.

Read all of Vault's Law School Surveys at www.vault.com/lawschool — get complete surveys on top law schools, expert advice on applicaton essays, LSAT prep and more.

VAULT CAREER LIBRARY 47

 **Academics**

Status: Alumnus/a, full-time
Dates of Enrollment: 8/2002-5/2005
Survey Submitted: March 2006

The workload at Pepperdine is driven by personal preference. You can study in the library all day, or alternatively do the reading right before class and try to squeak by. Whichever route you choose depends on what you want to get out of the law school experience; though people with better grades get better jobs and more financial assistance. People who do not commit as much time to studying do have more freedom to engage in activities that they enjoy. It is a trade-off.

The range of classes that is offered at Pepperdine is really incredible—War Crimes, Constitutional Law, Art Law, a variety of trial preparation classes, etc. There is something for everyone's specialized interest. Many of these classes are small and fill up rapidly, but by the time you are a second- or third-year you should have no problem picking out the schedule you want.

By far, from what I have experienced personally and what I have heard from other law school graduates, the professors at Pepperdine are topnotch. They are phenomenal teachers and extremely knowledgeable in their subject areas, but they are also available on a personal level. With all the stress of law school, having the option to sit down with a professor and voice your concerns about your classes, your competition, your tensions in general, is unique in the graduate school setting.

Status: Alumnus/a, full-time
Dates of Enrollment: 8/1997-5/2000
Survey Submitted: April 2005

Pepperdine law provides the traditional first-year curriculum and second- and third-year electives. If you're doing it right, you are working like a maniac your first year. The classes generally top out at 75-80 students per section in the first year and many of the more specialized classes are very small—sometimes only 10-25 people. The faculty is wonderful; they have an open-door policy and keep very generous office hours. The professors really are dedicated to the success of the students. I rarely had difficulty getting into a class I wanted and if I missed a one semester I was almost guaranteed to get in the next time around.

Grading is a traditional bell curve. There are a few at the top and a few at the bottom and a lot in the middle. There is definitely competition, especially because of the rules to keep the generous scholarships Pepperdine gives as part of the admissions process. You can earn anywhere from 25 to 100 percent of you tuition through a dean's scholarship awarded based solely on LSAT and grades. To keep it, you must stay in the top third of your class. Overall, the competition was still friendly and not cutthroat or as nasty as in some larger Ivy League schools.

Status: Current student, full-time
Dates of Enrollment: 9/2003-Submit Date
Survey Submitted: April 2005

Classes that are popular and taught by good professors are generally easy to get into, as those class sizes are increased. The professors are, for the most part, exceptional. While there are a few that are boring like at most schools, Pepperdine professors are interesting, demanding and do a great job of preparing you for the bar and practice. They aren't just a bunch of Ivy League graduates concerned about publishing papers to look good, but they genuinely enjoy teaching, and all have an open-door policy, which makes the atmosphere at Pepperdine professional, demanding, yet enjoyable. If you just walk down the hall by all of the faculty offices, you will see doors open, showing students and professors talking. In fact, all of my professors know me by name, something none of my friends at Ivy League schools can say.

Status: Current student, full-time
Dates of Enrollment: 8/2002-Submit Date
Survey Submitted: April 2005

Our academic courseload is rigorous, especially the larger number of required classes that we carry. I never had trouble getting the classes I wanted or the favorite professors. In fact, special effort is made to open those classes up to students who really want them. My academic experience has been spectacular.

We are graded on a forced curves, so "grade inflation" isn't present. The work is intense, but the fairness and payoff is great. My professors are the best part of my experience. On day one several will give out home phone numbers and cell numbers in class. I have at least five professors on speed dial in my phone. Our open-door policy doesn't mean that there is a door somewhere on some hall open at some time. Rather, all of our professors encourage attendance at their regular office hours and all will work with your schedule to set up a meeting if that doesn't work. This goes not just for professors that I have for class, but all of them.

Status: Alumnus/a, full-time
Dates of Enrollment: 8/2001-5/2004
Survey Submitted: May 2005

The nice thing about Pepperdine is that it is a school focused on teaching. The professors are usually open to speaking with you during their office hours; however, if you haven't done your reading and are just looking for them to give you a second lecture, don't waste your time. If you have done your reading and you truly don't understand, that is when they will help you. The classes are good for the most part. I had some excellent professors; but I also had some brand-new professors who utterly confused me. First year, the workload is intense. You will take six classes per semester and have about 100 pages of reading per night. Second and third year it gets much easier because you get to choose the classes and times of the classes that you want to take. However, you will have upper-level required classes that are mandatory. But, these classes are great because most of them, except for tax, will be on the bar exam in California. But, tax is a very useful and practical class to take.

Status: Alumnus/a, full-time
Dates of Enrollment: 8/2002-5/2004
Survey Submitted: January 2005

The academics at Pepperdine are of the nature and caliber that you would find at a top-tier law school. The professors are knowledgeable, and similar to that of other schools, range in their availability. For the most part, all professors are available if you need to get a hold of them. The student body tends to be young, hence ending up with a popular grade somewhere close to the mean, requires only a diligent amount of work. The grading is fair, and top grades require a lot of work. The workload is reasonable if you are looking for popular grades, the school has their fair share of wannabe Wendel Holmes, but they are few and far between.

Status: Current student, full-time
Dates of Enrollment: 10/2002-Submit Date
Survey Submitted: May 2005

Pepperdine has a very rigorous workload. Compared to other law schools, Pepperdine has many more required classes. My experience has been that this creates much less schedule flexibility than students' at other law schools. The professors are exceptional. They are very bright and are interested in getting to know their law students on a personal level.

Status: Current student, full-time
Dates of Enrollment: 5/2002-Submit Date
Survey Submitted: May 2004

The workload seems about the same as at other law schools. Many Pepperdine students have gone on to win moot court competitions this year, and have been complimented for their oral advocacy skills by judges and other professionals. Academics focus on a wide area, though there is an obvious emphasis on international law, dispute resolution (negotiation, mediation and arbitration) and business law.

The quality of the courses and professors has been mostly excellent in the past two years. Pepperdine, unlike many schools, requires professors to have an open-door policy, and to maintain consistent office hours. I've always been successful at finding my professor and seeking help. I've even seen professors give out their home numbers and allowed students to call until 2 a.m. the night before finals.

Status: Current student, full-time
Dates of Enrollment: 8/2002-Submit Date
Survey Submitted: July 2004

Unfortunately, this is one area where Pepperdine's size is not an asset. Though first-year classes are all the same so there is no problem with registration, some upper-level classes can be hard to get. Also, due to the small size of the faculty (it seems), sometimes there does not seem to be a lot of variety in the class offerings, and sometimes classes are dropped that a few students find crucial to their futures. This school has a big focus on constitutional law, so we have some amazing professors in that area, but we are therefore weaker in more practical areas like tax and estate planning. Some professors prefer to teach small (16 to 20 students) classes, making the offerings very limited for those professors.

While I feel that I have definitely been challenged here, some of the first-year professors that I had seemed to focus a bit too much on those students in the bottom half of the class helping them move up and succeed. Therefore, if you were in the top half of the class, you may have felt left out or bored at times. But all the professors have great availability and are willing to help everyone. So if you are lost or just have a question, you can go to office hours and talk to your professor. This is invaluable, and I understand that most law schools do not work this way.

Grading is on a forced curve, which can be good or bad depending on the class size, the exam and lots of other factors. Though I don't really like it, I can see its good points. However, not all classes are equal, so someone could take all easier classes and get a higher GPA than someone who takes more challenging classes, but I've been told by my professors that employers take this into consideration.

Workload is manageable. Try to schedule your classes somewhat around the exam schedule. I had exams three days in a row last semester and it was awful. There is a lot of reading, and it's hard to catch up if you get behind, so don't get behind. And start outlining EARLY. It is nearly impossible to complete all your reading and do an entire, thorough outline if you wait until after midterm.

Employment Prospects

Status: Alumnus/a, full-time
Dates of Enrollment: 8/2002-5/2005
Survey Submitted: March 2006

Grads of Pepperdine can get any job they want. There are several people from my graduating class that have excellent jobs at Top 10 law firms all over the country. There are many with prestigious judicial clerkships. The only limit on employment prospects after graduation is the amount of effort put in by the student.

Status: Alumnus/a, full-time
Dates of Enrollment: 8/1997-5/2000
Survey Submitted: April 2005

I had very little trouble finding a job in my preferred field, criminal law. I wanted to work in a large DA's office and I was offered almost immediate employment in both Orange County and Riverside County. The people I interviewed with thought very highly of my credentials as a Pepperdine graduate. Prior to deciding on criminal law, I did some interviewing with civil firms in California, Oregon and Washington. I had an interesting experience in that the California civil firms were far less impressed with my credentials than the out-of-state firms. My stock rose automatically when I interviewed out of Southern California. It seems, likely due to the saturation of law schools in Southern California, that there is a preference (or bias, if you will) for USC and UCLA graduates, regardless of the overall qualifications of the individual applicants.

Status: Current student, full-time
Dates of Enrollment: 9/2002-Submit Date
Survey Submitted: April 2005

I got my job through the on-campus interviewing process at Pepperdine. I am working for one of the best firms in the Inland Empire, and the highest paying for a first-year associate. I have had an offer since August 2004, which made this a pretty relaxing year. For students that are ranked anywhere in the top 30-40 percent, getting a job at a great firm is pretty easy. Some of the top firms come to Pepperdine. Of course, one's own personality is the biggest factor in

actually getting a job. Pepperdine can get you in any door, but it is up to you to impress the partners.

Upon graduation, there are students clerking for federal circuit courts around the country, for federal district courts and state courts. There are students working for Latham and Watkins, Jones Day, Kirkland and Ellis, etc. There are students working for the government, such as the DA, JAG, SEC, CIA, FBI, etc. There are students working for medium-sized firms, small firms and corporations. The alumni are extremely helpful for both the on-campus interviewing process and for finding jobs on your own. Most alumni will go out of their way to help students find a job. Along with our regular OCI program, Pepperdine also hosts a public interest day and a small firm recruiting day. These are great opportunities for students who either don't want to work for large firms, or for students whose grades were not as high, to find work. Pepperdine has a wonderful internship program. I have friends working for Miramax, ESPN, judges, small law firms, homeless shelters, etc.

Status: Alumnus/a, full-time
Dates of Enrollment: 8/2001-5/2004
Survey Submitted: May 2005

Unless you're in the top 10 percent, it is going to probably be a challenge to get a great job. The alumni network is OK but not great. Many fellow graduates I know do not practice law, either because they couldn't find a job or never wanted to practice to begin with. They work in entertainment or business. On the West Coast, Pepperdine is not that prestigious but for some reason, in the South, it is considered almost Ivy League. So, it's easier to get a job in Texas than the East or West Coast. Pepperdine does have a good externship program where you can work while going to school for a government agency, judge, entertainment studio or agency or network. Many times, this provides invaluable experience and can pave the way to get a job later. I have seen several students get full-time jobs after graduation through this program. On-campus recruiting is getting better but again, if you're not in the top 10 percent, many firms won't even talk to you.

Status: Alumnus/a, full-time
Dates of Enrollment: 8/2002-5/2004
Survey Submitted: January 2005

The employment prospects are what you make of them. If you put the energy into finding the job that you want, then you'll find it. The revamping of the career services center at the school in 2003 put the school miles ahead of other programs in terms of helping students find internships and jobs upon graduation.

Quality of Life

Status: Alumnus/a, full-time
Dates of Enrollment: 8/2002-5/2005
Survey Submitted: March 2006

The on-campus housing for first-years is beautiful and convenient. There is basically no crime in the area. The weather can be a bit temperamental at times (fires, floods, rockslides), but for the most part it is a gorgeous place to go for three years.

Status: Alumnus/a, full-time
Dates of Enrollment: 8/1997-5/2000
Survey Submitted: April 2005

There is no more beautiful setting to attend law school than the Pepperdine campus in Malibu. It is absolute paradise. The campus itself is beautiful and exquisitely maintained. There is a gorgeous ocean view from every building. The campus sits nestled in the hillsides of the Santa Monica Mountains that back up against a state park and wildlife refuge. Campus housing for graduate students consists of very nice apartments and they continue to build more. You can also chose to rent a bungalow in Malibu or an apartment in Santa Monica or Brentwood, depending on your personal preferences. There is virtually NO crime.

Status: Current student, full-time
Dates of Enrollment: 9/2003-Submit Date
Survey Submitted: April 2005

Read all of Vault's Law School Surveys at www.vault.com/lawschool — get complete surveys on top law schools, expert advice on applicaton essays, LSAT prep and more.

VAULT CAREER LIBRARY   49

Malibu is gorgeous. Housing is pricey, so I live inland. Lots of my single friends live in Santa Monica and drive along the coast to get to school. The city life is good. I have two small children, so I live in Ventura County, which is reasonably priced and great for families. Pepperdine has both student and married housing, which are reasonably priced. Crime isn't an issue.

Status: Alumnus/a, full-time
Dates of Enrollment: 8/2001-12/2003
Survey Submitted: April 2005

For the most part, it is a good quality of life. While moral values are stressed, occasionally they are put on the back burner and malfeasances are not addressed properly or timely. The school should be updated with better furniture, web connections and safety.

Status: Alumnus/a, full-time
Dates of Enrollment: 8/2001-5/2004
Survey Submitted: May 2005

If you can afford it, Pepperdine is a great place to go because you will live in Malibu. It is very posh and a little snobby, but a beautiful place to go to school. The graduate housing on campus is expensive and you share an apartment with three other people. I would recommend getting a guest house or apartment in Malibu or Santa Monica. The campus facilities are decent, although it is very dorm-like. There is little to no crime in Malibu, except for an occasional celebrity getting arrested for drunk driving. Malibu plays host to some of the finest restaurants in all of Southern California, although, many of them come with a hefty price tag. On one side of campus you have the mountains and the other side is the ocean. It's a beautiful campus.

Status: Current student, full-time
Dates of Enrollment: 8/2003-Submit Date
Survey Submitted: January 2005

Malibu is a beautiful area and the graduate housing fits in with this theme. Housing is located in brand-new buildings across the street from the graduate campus. Students share apartments with three other students; each has a private bedroom and all utilities are included. Graduate student housing has full kitchens in each apartment and students take advantage of being able to shop and cook for themselves. Pepperdine's campus is very safe with on-campus security as well as local police officers keeping an eye out for any disturbances. Pepperdine is a dry campus and a Christian institution and, that being the case, there are rules. For example, there is a rule regarding overnight guests (no guests of the opposite sex). There are shuttles that run around campus and to the surrounding areas (grocery stores, shopping, banks, etc.) although most students have cars.

Status: Alumnus/a, full-time
Dates of Enrollment: 8/2000-5/2003
Survey Submitted: November 2003

The campus is absolutely beautiful, and the view from the cafeteria is breathtaking. However, student housing is limited and very expensive. Basically you pay $1,100 a month for a room. Also, in the graduate housing you cannot have alcohol, overnight visitors or HBO. The neighborhood is expensive, but being in Malibu, there are very few crime issues (although a couple of laptops were stolen from the library), and you can often have celebrity sightings in the town. Parking on campus was [difficult] during my final year, as they had an unusually large 1L class.

> **Regarding available TV channels, the school says:** "The cable provider does not allow students to get any premium channels unless the university insures against theft of equipment, so no premium channels (even sports channels) are available."

Social Life

Status: Alumnus/a, full-time
Dates of Enrollment: 8/2002-5/2005
Survey Submitted: March 2006

In Malibu itself, there are only one or two bars as far as nightlife. There is a variety of coffee shops to study at all day, complete with celebrity sighting opportunities. There is a large religious community at the undergraduate campus that many people are involved in as well.

Status: Alumnus/a, full-time
Dates of Enrollment: 8/1997-5/2000
Survey Submitted: April 2005

The social life of any law student in general is fairly limited due to the rigorous course of study, but there is a great bar scene in Santa Monica and Brentwood as well as the L.A./Hollywood club scene if that's what you're into. On Thursday nights, there has traditionally been a "bar review" with other local law schools to try out a new bar or club once a week. Malibu, itself is fairly low key, it is a typical beachside community with great restaurants and a couple of great beachside cantinas, perfect for watching the sunset over calamari and Corona.

Status: Current student, full-time
Dates of Enrollment: 9/2003-Submit Date
Survey Submitted: April 2005

Those students interested in an active evening scene (bars, clubs, etc.) have no problem finding it. Many students live in Santa Monica, which is exciting, and is also close to L.A., so enough said about the social life. It's good for single people, good for married people and good for married people with kids.

Status: Current student, full-time
Dates of Enrollment: 9/2002-Submit Date
Survey Submitted: April 2005

Malibu is known for being quiet and up-scale. For a great nightlife scene, Santa Monica is only 15 minutes north. Around half of the student body lives in Santa Monica for their second and third years. There are great clubs, bars and people in the area. Every Thursday [an anonymous group of students] hosts a bar review, in which students get together and hang out. As a married student, I cannot comment on the actual dating scene. As a person with eyes, I can say that Pepperdine has the best looking student body in the world. Whether it is the beach, sun or competition of living in Los Angeles, the effects are clear.

Status: Alumnus/a, full-time
Dates of Enrollment: 8/2001-5/2004
Survey Submitted: May 2005

When in law school, your social life should be put on the back burner. But, if you do want to go out, Malibu is not the place to be. It's really far from Hollywood, although you can go out in Santa Monica, which is about 25 minutes away. But, nightlife in Malibu is minimal. The restaurants are amazing, but again, many are expensive. Finding a mate in law school occurs more than you'd think. But, normally it happens because you are in the same classes or see them at school. You rarely meet them because they live in Malibu. There are campus organizations in which you can get involved, but many of them are not social. Rather, they are law societies or certain practice group clubs.

Status: Alumnus/a, full-time
Dates of Enrollment: 8/1998-5/2001
Survey Submitted: March 2005

The law school fosters an active social life. Each Thursday, the school sponsors a "bar review" at a local bar. Students from all three classes (1L, 2L and 3L) come out to let off steam and have a good time. People actively date, and often times meet their spouses among their classmates. There are wonderful restaurants in the area. The school also has intramural sport teams (soccer, football, basketball).

Santa Clara University School of Law

Office of Admissions
500 El Camino Real
Santa Clara, CA 95053
Admissions phone: (408) 554-5048
Admissions e-mail: lawadmissions@scu.edu
Admissions URL: http://www.scu.edu/law/admissions/

 ## Admissions

Status: Alumnus/a, full-time
Dates of Enrollment: 9/1996-5/1999
Survey Submitted: September 2005

The admissions process is like every other law school in that you have to fill out an application, provide transcripts, letters of recommendation (three) and take the LSAT. There was not an interview.

My advice on getting in is to request an interview and get face to face with the admissions people. Santa Clara has gotten more selective over the years and has increased its requirements. However, the school is run by the Jesuit Order of the Catholic Church. Therefore, play up your public interest work (i.e., community service) and this will go a long way.

Status: Current student, full-time
Dates of Enrollment: 9/2003-Submit Date
Survey Submitted: March 2005

The best part about the Santa Clara admissions process is that they let you apply for early admissions without making you commit to Santa Clara early if you are admitted. Santa Clara really takes a look at the type of undergrad degree that you have. They take into account that the average GPA in engineering isn't going to be as high as the average GPA in other disciplines. So don't worry about not making the cut if your GPA is lower if you have a technical degree and a high LSAT score.

Status: Current student, part-time
Dates of Enrollment: 8/2002-Submit Date
Survey Submitted: March 2005

No interviews. Essays. School is becoming increasingly competitive because it is particularly famous for its intellectual property specialization, and because it is located in the heart of Silicon Valley. Engineers and scientists who were either laid off or decide to switch careers and explore law as an option, increase the admissions competition to the school.

Status: Current student, full-time
Dates of Enrollment: 8/2001-Submit Date
Survey Submitted: March 2005

Santa Clara only required an application, transcripts and LSAT scores. There was no interview component. However, Santa Clara provided many pre-admissions information sessions that were extremely helpful. One session that stands out because the admissions staff invited graduates to discuss their jobs since graduation. It was eye-opening to see the wide variety of employment options available to law school grads. In terms of selectivity, Santa Clara has become tougher to get admitted in recent years. I am glad I got in when I did because I do not think I could get in to Santa Clara now with my LSAT scores.

Status: Current student, full-time
Dates of Enrollment: 8/2004-Submit Date
Survey Submitted: March 2005

Admission is fairly competitive and largely determined by GPA and LSAT scores. Additional factors are work and educational background and life experience, which is discussed in the essay. The law school generally does not conduct interviews. The school is one of the most diverse in the country and each class tries to have a wide variety of students.

Status: Current student, full-time
Dates of Enrollment: 9/2002-Submit Date
Survey Submitted: January 2004

After you take your LSAT, write an essay and have your letters of recommendation, the admissions process is simple. Unlike many other law schools, the actual application is relatively easy to fill out. The earlier you apply, the better off you are, because SCU operates on rolling admissions. Additionally, they have an early admissions program, which is great if you are impatient like me and want to have an answer soon. SCU is selective, but they really look beyond the numbers. If you have a story and unique life experience, write about it in the essay. There is an additional optional essay that you can write to stress your less-than-ideal opportunities in life and any other background information that puts you in a disadvantaged group. SCU always ranks high as far as diversity.

Status: Alumnus/a, full-time
Dates of Enrollment: 8/2000-5/2003
Survey Submitted: January 2004

The quickest response I received came from Santa Clara, and the best response time prior to admission when I left messages with admissions personnel. There was even a dedicated law counselor for financial aid issues, who helped navigate that quagmire of red tape.

Status: Alumnus/a, full-time
Dates of Enrollment: 8/2000-12/2003
Survey Submitted: December 2003

I think Santa Clara is pretty selective, but they will give students a second chance if their prior academic career was not glowing, if they had a good reason. I know people with much better stats than mine who did not get accepted, but I had some personal issues that I dealt with during undergrad, as I explained in my admissions essay. They seemed to put more weight on the LSAT, and I had a far better than their average admissions score on the LSAT.

 ## Academics

Status: Alumnus/a, full-time
Dates of Enrollment: 9/1996-5/1999
Survey Submitted: September 2005

I was very impressed with SCU Law's academic quality. Many of the professors at SCU also teach at Stanford, so the quality is quite impressive. The classes remain small. The first year is like other law schools in that you are in a section with about 50 other students who all take the same core classes together. This works out well, but if you are not the top student in one class, you definitely will not be in any other. The range of classes was impressive and there was not much difficulty in getting classes, just register early!

The workload is pretty significant the first semester. Going to law school requires you to think, study and learn very differently than undergraduate work. Once the first semester is over, it is easy to hold down a part-time job and take a full load of classes.

Status: Current student, full-time
Dates of Enrollment: 8/2002-Submit Date
Survey Submitted: April 2005

1L classes are year-long instead of semester-long, making it very difficult to transfer to another school and still graduate on time. Evening 1L courses often taught by visiting, not tenure-tracked professors. Research and writing instructors are often ill-equipped to handle student questions beyond those related to the specific assignments. Interesting elective courses listed in the catalog are not always offered every year, or even every other year, so do not rely on the course catalog to determine what you want to take, it may not be accurate. Required and bar courses are on a mandatory grade curve. Workload was reasonable, as were most professors.

Read all of Vault's Law School Surveys at www.vault.com/lawschool — get complete surveys on top law schools, expert advice on applicaton essays, LSAT prep and more.

VAULT CAREER LIBRARY   51

Status: Current student, full-time
Dates of Enrollment: 8/2003-Submit Date
Survey Submitted: April 2005

The mandatory grade curve is among the most strict of any ABA-accredited school; one half of the students in every class must receive a grade of C+ or lower. Grades of C+ and lower do not look good on a transcript especially when compared to candidates from schools who are not subject to the same grade distributions (this is most other schools). The mandatory grade curve, therefore, puts most students at a competitive disadvantage in the employment marketplace. This effect is in addition to the negative motivational impact that low grades have on many students.

With regard to bar preparation, there seems to be no acknowledgement that students will be taking the bar upon graduation. There is no emphasis on bar-specific knowledge or skills in any of the substantive course work. Likewise, the school does nothing in the way of preparing students by way of review course offerings, practice bar exams or any other such means. I am hoping that a commercial review course will supply me with the skills that SCU has not. GPA and bar passage statistics have a significant impact on the employability of graduates from any law school. The SCU Law administration seems disinclined to address either of these issues and is therefore handicapping its students in the job market. It is no wonder that the school is ranked in the lowest tier of all ABA-accredited schools.

Status: Current student, full-time
Dates of Enrollment: 8/2003-Submit Date
Survey Submitted: March 2005

This is a Black Letter law school. There are very few seminar or theoretical courses. You will come out prepared to take the California Bar and prepared to practice. The curve is tight in bar courses, which makes your life stressful since you are graded against your peers. Unlike many other "top" law schools, Santa Clara makes you work for each and every grade you get. Basically, you work really hard and will not be guaranteed an A, but if you don't work hard, you're guaranteed to do poorly. The professors are approachable, and most are good teachers. They have practical experience rather than just academic experience, which makes them incredible resources.

Status: Current student, full-time
Dates of Enrollment: 8/2004-Submit Date
Survey Submitted: March 2005

There is a substantially greater time commitment to studying compared to undergraduate coursework. It really is no longer possible to get solid grades without doing any reading or missing class occasionally. When you'd probably rather be doing something else, it is often a matter of psychological coercion to commit to sitting down and putting in the time necessary to sufficiently learn the material. Most of the professors are concerned with student-learning and are more or less helpful if approached. Your entire grade will be based on two exams, relative to your respective performance compared with the rest of the class. Virtually no one fails, but approximately half the students will earn a C or lower.

Status: Current student, full-time
Dates of Enrollment: 8/2004-Submit Date
Survey Submitted: March 2005

Every professor at Santa Clara comes from top-tier law schools, has a background in the classes taught, and conveys the material on a level that first-year students can comprehend. One difference between SCU and other law schools is that we take six classes our first semester. This may sound like quite a bit, and it is, but the diversity of the classes is important to your overall legal education, and perhaps more important for those competing for top-end jobs and clerkships, the six classes allow you to spread your GPA over more classes. By that, I mean a C in one class hurts a lot less if you have five other classes than if you only have three other classes. I won't lie, law school is a lot of work, but it's nothing backbreaking. I come home from class, take a break for a couple of hours, then study until I'm prepared for the next day (by the way, being prepared is not an option like in undergrad, it's a necessity). Sometimes that takes four, five, even six hours. But after the first few weeks that amount of work, which probably was how much you did in undergrad per week, if even that, will seem like nothing. And there is no doubt in my mind that you can take at least one day on the weekend off, if not both days, if you work hard during the week. So those in long distance relationships, don't fear.

Status: Alumnus/a, part-time
Dates of Enrollment: 8/2000-5/2003
Survey Submitted: April 2004

The quality of the classes at SCU is first-rate. There are more practical classes than at most schools, and these seem to be the most helpful after graduation. The best part of the school is the professors. Few schools have professors that get to know their students on a personal level, including inviting them over for dinner and the like. I personally have received phone calls from professors and kept in touch with several professors after graduation. I've yet to hear of another school at which the professors care so much about their students.

Class sizes vary from small sections of 10 to large lectures of 100. Most first-year classes have 30 to 40 students. Popular classes are not hard to get. The waiting list for enrollment in a class allows most students to get the classes they desire. The only downside is that some classes, especially specialized high-tech courses, are not offered often enough for some schedules.

Status: Current student, full-time
Dates of Enrollment: 9/2002-Submit Date
Survey Submitted: January 2004

SCU is very academic. Like all law schools, you have to do your work, and a lot of it (a couple of hours a night at minimum). Some professors use the Socratic Method to call on you at random; some assign you a date to be on-call. Regardless, you really have to keep up, or you can easily fall behind very fast. Students are very competitive, but they are in no way cutthroat. Books don't get stolen from the library. People are willing to share their notes with you if you missed class. It is a pleasant academic environment, and most people juggle life outside of studying. I have been impressed with all of my professors, and my classes have been topnotch. Sometimes popular classes get filled up, but there is usually another section. Grading can be tough; a strict curve is enforced for grading in mandatory and bar courses. However, you can choose to take bar courses Pass/No Pass. Seminars do not require a curve.

Status: Alumnus/a, full-time
Dates of Enrollment: 8/1999-5/2002
Survey Submitted: October 2003

Most classes were great. Some professors are better, and some are worse, as with all schools. But overall I would rate the professors, on a scale of one to five with five being best, a 3.5. Program was quite varied but with a very strong focus upon high-tech law and public interest law. If you are interested in a general legal education, it is not exactly easy to achieve. You must "create your own." Workload was as expected in law school. Those that can handle it make it, those that cannot, do not.

 ## Employment Prospects

Status: Alumnus/a, full-time
Dates of Enrollment: 9/1996-5/1999
Survey Submitted: September 2005

Unfortunately, Santa Clara must compete with Stanford, Boalt Hall and Hastings. Almost all of them are first-tier schools. Santa Clara bounces between second and third tier. The school is well known in the region, but outside of the region, nobody knows the school, which is definitely a hindrance in finding employment. The great majority of students go into private practice. The school is one of the top-ranked intellectual property schools in the nation and it is well deserved. There is no alumni network outside of California.

Status: Current student, full-time
Dates of Enrollment: 8/2004-Submit Date
Survey Submitted: April 2005

Competition for jobs is very tight, because we are close to many other very highly ranked law schools. The law career services staff is good. The best thing to do is to network as much as possible, and especially get involved with student organizations. The alumni are also great. There is a little bit of on-campus recruiting, but mostly this is for the top 10 percent of the class, so don't count on it.

Status: Current student, part-time
Dates of Enrollment: 8/2002-Submit Date
Survey Submitted: March 2005

Many law firms recruit from the school because of the reputation of the school locally. There are probably not as many NY firms or Midwest firms recruiting because we are not as famous as Berkeley or Stanford, but regionally, SCU has a great reputation. Alumni are often very helpful as are on-campus recruiting, internships and, in particular, the law career services group. The school provides ample opportunities to students, but students still need to be proactive to seek the right opportunities for themselves.

Status: Current student, full-time
Dates of Enrollment: 8/2001-Submit Date
Survey Submitted: March 2005

If you are interested in becoming a patent attorney or have a hard science background, it should be easy getting a job as a graduate of Santa Clara law school. Law firms and companies know Santa Clara produces great IP attorneys. Santa Clara also has a lot of graduates in the DA's and PD's office. We sometimes seem to have a tough time because of all the competition, including Stanford, Boalt and Hastings. However, I have noticed Santa Clara alums at all the big firms.

Status: Current student, full-time
Dates of Enrollment: 8/2002-Submit Date
Survey Submitted: March 2005

The school has excellent connections to the San Francisco Bay Area legal community. Some grads from prestigious schools on the East Coast who have come here to live have complained to me that the Bay Area legal community treats Santa Clara grads with more respect and is more eager to hire them than the grads of prestigious out-of-state schools. If you are interested in criminal law, I would caution that despite the ease of getting some kind of internship at a DA or PD around here, there are almost no jobs due to budget problems and a lack of retirement. From last year's grads there is rumored to be only one person who got a full-time job in the criminal arena. If patents and IP is your thing, then you could not go anywhere better. The school has great IP teachers and many connections to law firms and high-tech companies.

Status: Current student, full-time
Dates of Enrollment: 8/2004-Submit Date
Survey Submitted: March 2005

My experiences with career services at SCU have been great. My advisor has helped me with everything from creating my resume and cover letter to showing me how to use the school's job postings. I am looking for summer employment right now, and it's amazing that every day the school receives new postings from prospective employers all over not only California, but the country as well. The average salary out of SCU is very competitive, somewhere around $80k or $90k for the private sector, and a process called OCI (on-campus interviewing) brings employers to the campus to make your life easier when the time comes to find that second-year summer internship that normally leads to a job offer after school.

Status: Alumnus/a, part-time
Dates of Enrollment: 8/2000-5/2003
Survey Submitted: April 2004

SCU has an excellent reputation locally. Local firms and national firms with local offices know that SCU graduates have been well-trained. Students near the top of the class will have no problem finding jobs. There also is an excellent high-tech and civil internship program that provides internships for students at well-known companies. Unfortunately, this program is underused by students. Law career services provides a lot of assistance for those who look for it. On-campus interviews (OCIs) are the main method of finding qualified applicants for many larger firms, so students should take advantage of such on-campus events.

Quality of Life

Status: Alumnus/a, full-time
Dates of Enrollment: 9/1996-5/1999
Survey Submitted: September 2005

SCU Law is on a beautiful and safe campus. The school does provide graduate (law) housing and there are a lot of places to live around campus. The school has great facilities and really takes advantage of being in the middle of Silicon Valley. The entire school is extremely high tech. Besides the great academics, this is probably the number one reason to go to SCU Law.

Status: Current student, full-time
Dates of Enrollment: 8/2004-Submit Date
Survey Submitted: April 2005

The neighborhood at SCU is safe, has relatively low crime and the campus is gorgeous—palm trees, lots of green grass and roses everywhere. There is very little on-campus law housing so most students live off campus. The on-campus housing is in fact, off campus literally, and is about a 10-minute walk to the law building. As for the quality of life, I think the academic competitiveness creeps into the happiness of the students and leaves us feeling guarded, unsure and less willing to be generous, helpful or contribute to one another's educational experiences.

Status: Current student, full-time
Dates of Enrollment: 9/2003-Submit Date
Survey Submitted: March 2005

The atmosphere at Santa Clara is fantastic! Your classmates are willing to help you, and older students are always willing to give advice. There are a lot of student organizations, which bring in fantastic speakers from industry, for example the IPA (Intellectual Property Association) brings in a speaker every Tuesday for lunch to discuss some aspect of IP law. The campus itself is BEAUTIFUL! The campus is right near a Caltrain line, so a lot of students commute by Caltrain.

Status: Current student, full-time
Dates of Enrollment: 8/2004-Submit Date
Survey Submitted: March 2005

Student housing is available for 1Ls. I highly suggest the Villa Apartments over any of the other housing arrangements. The campus is absolutely beautiful, but being a law student doesn't allow for much time to enjoy it. When it is warm outside, there is a patio with a lot of tables and a water fountain where students hang out and study. The law school classes are fully equipped with wireless and state-of the-art technology. Food around campus isn't too great. Two Starbucks, Safeway and a Henry's Fresh Mexican Grill is the extent of the good food available. The neighborhood is residential and as far as I know, really safe.

> The school says: "There is on-campus housing for law students, especially those just entering."

Status: Current student, full-time
Dates of Enrollment: 8/2001-Submit Date
Survey Submitted: March 2005

Sometimes life at Santa Clara is a challenge because the rest of the university is on the quarter system. Also, the services are geared toward the undergrads. However, the administration and support staff of the law school are topnotch. The school is across the street from the main police station. I have never felt unsafe at Santa Clara. For those not familiar with the area, Silicon Valley is extremely expensive, especially compared to other states, so it might be shocking.

Status: Current student, full-time
Dates of Enrollment: 8/2002-Submit Date
Survey Submitted: March 2005

Great place to live if you like sitting in the sun, going to the beach or skiing. There's a lack of culture, though, if you like plays and classical music. A lack of good restaurants. Local towns just go to sleep at 8 p.m. The people in Silicon Valley are very strange, they work late then go home to watch TV; there is very little nightlife. Immigrant communities seem more fun than long-time California communities. Campus is very nice. Warm and sunny nearly all year. Safe.

Read all of Vault's Law School Surveys at www.vault.com/lawschool — get complete surveys on top law schools, expert advice on applicaton essays, LSAT prep and more.

V/\ULT CAREER LIBRARY   53

Status: Current student, full-time
Dates of Enrollment: 8/2004-Submit Date
Survey Submitted: March 2005

Housing at SCU is easy to find, comfortable, clean and safe. I live across the street from campus in a campus-owned apartment complex. The location is fantastic: seven-minute walk to classes, right next to Safeway, across the street from the gym and pool, etc. The campus is tiny compared to where I went to undergrad, but it is a nice change. You see familiar faces every day. There is only one dining hall, and I'll be honest, it's not five-star cuisine, but it gets the job done. You won't eat many meals there as a law student, anyway. If you are the type that likes to cook, I would suggest the University Square or Villas apartments over the Alameda South studio apartments, as both of those have larger kitchens. I can't say much about off-campus housing, but I know that many people do live off campus and like it. From what I hear there is plenty of housing available in the area. I have never heard of any crimes related to on-campus housing.

Status: Alumnus/a, full-time
Dates of Enrollment: 8/2000-5/2003
Survey Submitted: April 2004

There are great restaurants, shops and interesting nightlife near SCU for those who want it. The only complaint I've heard is that because tuition is high (as with all private schools), it is hard to find affordable housing. For those with stricter budgets, there are several campus-owned dwellings that are very affordable. I never heard of any problems with crime or safety during my time at SCU.

 ## Social Life

Status: Alumnus/a, full-time
Dates of Enrollment: 9/1996-5/1999
Survey Submitted: September 2005

There is not much a nightlife scene around the campus. However, the majority of students who do socialize go to Los Gatos, Palo Alto or San Francisco to get their entertainment.

Status: Current student, full-time
Dates of Enrollment: 8/2003-Submit Date
Survey Submitted: April 2005

Law school is like high school all over again and I think it is much the same at most law schools. However, I do appreciate the fact that the faculty participates in many school events such as the public interest fundraiser and other similar events by being auction items (dinners with professors) and participating in the students and professors basketball game.

Status: Current student, full-time
Dates of Enrollment: 8/2004-Submit Date
Survey Submitted: April 2005

The student organizations on campus are pretty good. They are really the social life and you should go to as many events of theirs as you can. This is also the best way to meet people and network. There is a local bar near campus, but I just don't recommend drinking during your first year. As for dating, most students don't have time. If you are in a relationship, the first year will be hard, but if it is worth it, you will be fine. As for restaurants, there are not many nearby. The events on campus and around campus are generally through the student organizations and are pretty good. There aren't any real Greek organizations. The fraternities that we have are more like student clubs.

Status: Current student, full-time
Dates of Enrollment: 8/2002-Submit Date
Survey Submitted: March 2005

As an adult student and a commuter, I do not engage in the social activities of the school. However, there are regularly scheduled events and plenty of networking activities with working professionals. Also, the Alumni Association has a comprehensive calendar of events.

Status: Alumnus/a, full-time
Dates of Enrollment: 8/2000-5/2003
Survey Submitted: April 2004

The social scene is what you make of it at SCU. There is a group of students who opt for Thursday nights at "The Hut," a so-close-it's-almost-on-campus bar. And alcohol is served at the Bronco (on-campus bar and restaurant) for those who want to party. On the other hand, many students are more concerned with their education and do not attend these events, yet do not feel like social outcasts. There are very few cliques among students, and most people find similarities between each other rather than differences.

Status: Alumnus/a, part-time
Dates of Enrollment: 8/2000-12/2003
Survey Submitted: December 2003

As a part-time student who worked full-time, I didn't have a social life. I don't remember what that was like. I think the full-time students went out, though. There's a local bar where we would meet up after class for study sessions my first year, and my section went out the last day of finals as a group too, which was pretty fun. The people in my study group are still some of my best friends, and one person even ended up being a bridesmaid in my wedding. So overall, I'd say the quality of people Santa Clara attracts is pretty high, and they are people you could be friends with for life.

Status: Alumnus/a, full-time
Dates of Enrollment: 8/1999-5/2002
Survey Submitted: December 2003

There is one bar just off campus, with another on campus but mostly utilized by the undergraduates. San Jose is close with bars and restaurants. Mostly students enjoy house parties or trips to the local bar.

The school says: "We offer many lunchtime activities, including a speaker series through our Center for Social Justice and Public Interest and also activities and speakers through High Technology and Intellectual Property Institute."

 ## The School Says

Dean's Welcome

Santa Clara University is the oldest university in California and was founded in 1851. The School of Law opened in 1912 and continues to educate men and women for careers in law, business and government and public service. The curriculum is designed to provide our graduates with the skills and values necessary for success in a variety of careers and the ability to serve their communities as competent and ethical counselors and problem-solvers. Moreover, the School of Law curriculum and its co-curricular and extracurricular programs provide opportunities for the development of lawyering skills and a deeper understanding of legal rules and policy in several cutting-edge areas of law.

The intellectual property program is nationally recognized for the excellence of its faculty and the pertinence of its wide range of technology and intellectual property courses. The international law program provides opportunities for students to understand the global world in which lawyers work and to study law and legal systems in other countries. The School of Law's public interest law program, which has been honored by national public interest law organizations, offers a variety of programs for law students, plus clinical programs on campus and at a community legal center.

If you attend Santa Clara University School of Law, you will have an opportunity to study law with a distinguished faculty of national and international reputation. The faculty is dedicated to excellence in teaching their students and to the production of legal and interdisciplinary scholarship that influences courts, policy-makers and law reform efforts.

I hope that you are impressed with the quality of the School of Law and with the opportunity to study law in the exciting Silicon Valley of California. Please let us know if you have questions about the School of Law or if you'd like to arrange a visit to the campus.

Sincerely,

Donald J. Polden

Read all of Vault's Law School Surveys at www.vault.com/lawschool — get complete surveys on top law schools, expert advice on applicaton essays, LSAT prep and more.

VAULT CAREER LIBRARY   55

Southwestern Law School

Admissions Office
3050 Wilshire Boulevard
Los Angeles, CA 90010-1106
Admissions phone: (213) 738-6834
Admissions fax: (213) 383-1688
Admissions e-mail: admissions@swlaw.edu
Admissions URL:
http://www.swlaw.edu/audience_prospect

 Admissions

Status: Current student, full-time
Dates of Enrollment: 8/2004-Submit Date
Survey Submitted: September 2005

Southwestern has an average (for the L.A. area) LSAT and GPA requirement and generally people who could not get into other higher ranked Los Angeles law schools CAN get into Southwestern.

Status: Current student, full-time
Dates of Enrollment: 8/2003-Submit Date
Survey Submitted: June 2004

The online application was relatively easy, but the form is unappealing and you can lose your information. I had better luck with e-mail than phone for getting answers to questions. Try to avoid the registrar's office if at all possible. The rest of the departments are generally good.

Status: Alumnus/a, full-time
Dates of Enrollment: 8/1993-5/1996
Survey Submitted: April 2005

Easy. I got in strictly on application, LSAT score and recommendations. No interview.

> **The school says:** "In 2005, Southwestern accepted less than 25 percent of its applicants. Among those who matriculated, the 75th percentile GPA was 3.6, and the 25th percentile GPA was 3.1. The 75th percentile LSAT was 158, and the 25th percentile LSAT was 153."

Status: Alumnus/a, full-time
Dates of Enrollment: 8/1996-5/2000
Survey Submitted: April 2005

There is very little to the admissions process—fill out the form and send in the supporting documents. I learned later that the school does not appear to be very selective as to whom it admits. I did not have to undergo any interviews. Be careful when SW offers you scholarships, because they do not always (at least in my case) deliver them in the end, even if you have given up admission to another school in expectation of the promised scholarship.

Status: Alumnus/a, full-time
Dates of Enrollment: 9/1991-5/1994
Survey Submitted: October 2003

Admissions seem mostly based on LSAT scores and grades, but it doesn't appear that they were terribly selective except for when it came to handing out scholarship money, as their strategy is to let in large numbers of students and weed them out by 25 to 33 percent before graduation. They required an essay but no interview.

> **The school says:** "Southwestern admits students with the hope and expectation that every one of them will graduate. The school does not have a policy of 'weeding out' students. For more on this issue, see the Academics section."

Status: Alumnus/a, full-time
Dates of Enrollment: 8/2001-5/2004
Survey Submitted: June 2005

At the time that I applied to Southwestern, it was more of a fallback law school, where you applied here, just in case you did not get in anywhere else. The application process was extremely easy because at the time Southwestern was one of only a few schools that had online application capabilities. Southwestern looks for diverse students, so try to showcase that in your essay.

Status: Current student, full-time
Dates of Enrollment: 8/2004-Submit Date
Survey Submitted: February 2005

Not very selective, but they do give out quite a bit of scholarship money if you have high GPA and high LSAT. I am on a full-ride, and I know of others who are also.

> **The school says:** "Southwestern takes pride in its commitment to providing students with financial aid. More than 30 percent of the full-time students who matriculated in 2005 received grants and/or scholarships. The median grant amount was $8,000."

Status: Alumnus/a, full-time
Dates of Enrollment: 1/2003-Submit Date
Survey Submitted: January 2005

To enter the school, it is somewhat competitive because there are so many applicants to California law schools. However, a 3.0 to 3.2 with a LSAT around 157 should be sufficient. The stress of getting in is not so bad.

Status: Current student, full-time
Dates of Enrollment: 8/2002-Submit Date
Survey Submitted: December 2004

The admissions office is extremely helpful in every aspect. I felt like they were one of the few schools that actually cared about my entire application not just my numbers. I went to one of their open houses and the staff was knowledgeable, warm and honest.

Status: Alumnus/a, full-time
Dates of Enrollment: 8/2002-7/2003
Survey Submitted: October 2004

The admissions process consists of writing an essay and filling out an application.

Status: Current student, full-time
Dates of Enrollment: 8/2004-Submit Date
Survey Submitted: September 2004

Of all of the law schools I applied to, SW seemed to have an intuitive appreciation for the concerns of a 1L. The process of notification was thoughtful and comprehensive.

> **Regarding admissions, the school says:** "Southwestern Law School selects its students from a diverse and accomplished pool of applicants from across the globe. Applicants' GPAs and LSAT scores are the primary factors considered, although academic work and areas of concentration, post-baccalaureate study and experience, motivation, recommendations and diversity are also evaluated."

Academics

Status: Current student, full-time
Dates of Enrollment: 8/2004-Submit Date
Survey Submitted: September 2005

Southwestern is a very good school. The professors are excellent, especially the first-year professors. The school has actively recruited many young brilliant legal scholars who graduated from Harvard, etc. These younger members of the faculty are the main reason Southwestern has became a better school, graduating higher quality students in recent years. Southwestern is INCREDIBLY competitive once you are in. The school makes up for its easy admission process with a very harsh curve that forces most student's first-year GPAs under a C +. Most students work very hard, and many are very cutthroat in their approach to class and studying. Workload during the first year is very heavy, but if students work hard and apply themselves, they can get a lot out of it.

> **The school says:** "The faculty approved a new, more liberal grading system in 2006."

Status: Current student, full-time
Dates of Enrollment: 8/2003-Submit Date
Survey Submitted: June 2004

The professors are extraordinary. Perhaps because the school isn't prestigious, the teachers are focused on teaching, not publishing. Office hours are extensive, and almost every professor is happy to go over practice exams one-on-one.

Most Southern California law students agree that Southwestern students work harder than anyone else. The curve is very harsh (the registrar's office had to start sending out a letter with transcripts explaining why our grades are so low) and about one-third of the first-year class is eliminated. This is fascinating, since virtually every other school in the area looks better on a resume, while they flunk almost no one out. Basically, Southwestern students are fighting for their lives, so the competition can be intense just to stay in a third or fourth tier school.

> **The school says:** "The current grading policy sets the median as a B, a GPA mean of 2.9 with a minimum of 15 percent of grades to be in the A- to A + range. Over the past few years, the typical attrition rate at Southwestern for 1Ls has been 11 to 17 percent; the rate for 2Ls, 3Ls and 4Ls has been 0 and 5 percent."

Status: Alumni, full-time
Dates of Enrollment: 8/1993-5/1996
Survey Submitted: April 2005

Southwestern is underrated for its very good, hands-on, practical education. In addition to teaching us how to think like an attorney and preparing us for the bar exam, Southwestern is big into giving its students practical, real-life experience. For example, it offered a class in California civil procedure, which has been much more helpful to me in my practice than my federal civil procedure class.

Status: Alumnus/a, full-time
Dates of Enrollment: 8/1996-5/2000
Survey Submitted: April 2005

The academic program is weak during the first year because the level of teaching is reduced to the lowest common denominator, which includes people who, in my judgment, should not have been admitted to begin with. Some teachers are great, while others are terrible. The grading is on a strict, mandated curve, which puts you at a disadvantage when your GPA is compared to those of the better schools that do not have a mandated curve. Also, a lot of the higher tiered schools that do impose a mandated curve, have a higher curve average than that of SW.

Status: Alumnus/a, full-time
Dates of Enrollment: 9/1991-5/1994
Survey Submitted: October 2003

They pride themselves on using the Socratic Method, but it seems more like the instructors don't know any Black Letter law than that they are trying to get students to think. The most common remark after a student question was, "Well, what do you think?" All grades are based on an arbitrarily made-up system that

is designed to flunk out the 25 to 33 percent mentioned above before graduation. The forced mean, median and mode is 2.3, which deflates all grades and causes most students who actually survive the "weeding out" to end up with less than a 3.0 at graduation (which automatically puts graduates at a disadvantage with employers who require transcripts).

Status: Alumnus/a, full-time
Dates of Enrollment: 8/2001-5/2004
Survey Submitted: June 2005

The workload and classes at Southwestern are very comparable to other law programs, however, Southwestern grades on a mandatory curve, and this was very different to me as compared to undergraduate classes. The professors must have a mean grade of 2.3, therefore your chances of graduating with a high GPA are low, and you have to be able to explain this in interviews when you are being compared to other students who did not have to endure this process. Furthermore, if at any time a student's GPA drops below a 2.0 for two consecutive semesters, that student is literally kicked out of the program, regardless of how far along he/she is.

Status: Current student, full-time
Dates of Enrollment: 8/2004-Submit Date
Survey Submitted: February 2005

Professors are pretty good, especially in the first year. Since there is a mandatory curve and drop-off percentage, it can be quite competitive and stressful at times. But, you get that at all law schools.

Status: Alumnus/a, full-time
Dates of Enrollment: 1/2003-Submit Date
Survey Submitted: January 2005

Quality of classes really depends on the professors, and the professors, overall, are not that helpful. A few of the professors are great and can teach the subject matter very well. On the other hand, the majority of the professors lack teaching ability, amiability and concern for the students. The professors seem to be very well-qualified due to their impressive resumes—however, on a closer examination, they don't care about the students, they do not attempt to teach the subject matter, and often times engage in preferential treatment. Furthermore, what little kindness and concern that the teachers do exhibit are nothing more than facades in order to maintain tenure or keep the non-assuming students happy.

The workload is fine. Approximately 50 to 80 pages of reading per week, which is the law school norm.

Getting popular classes is pretty easy unless the administration makes an error, which quite frequently happens. For example, my friend had all her classes dropped due to a clerical error; as a result, by the beginning of the school year, she had to re-apply for open classes, which were slim in number.

The grading is arbitrary, similar to most examinations regarding written essay answers. The key is to learn the erraticism of the professors; however, the problem is that the professors, themselves, are somewhat inconsistent and contradict themselves, making this puzzle-solving more difficult.

The first-year workload is by far the toughest.

Status: Current student, full-time
Dates of Enrollment: 8/2002-Submit Date
Survey Submitted: December 2004

The faculty at Southwestern surpassed my greatest expectations. They care about their students and it shows through everything from their open-door policy to their involvement with student organizations. The core classes are laid out to effectively teach subjects for the bar exam and there are many interesting electives to choose from. It is hard to get into some of the more popular seminar-type classes but other than that you can get into most classes with ease. The grading curve sucks, but in classes that are not core classes the curve is higher and the rumor that the school drops the bottom third is COMPLETELY false. The people that do get dropped probably shouldn't have been in law school in the first place.

Read all of Vault's Law School Surveys at www.vault.com/lawschool — get complete surveys on top law schools, expert advice on applicaton essays, LSAT prep and more.

VAULT CAREER LIBRARY   57

Status: Alumnus/a, full-time
Dates of Enrollment: 8/2002-7/2003
Survey Submitted: October 2004

These professors were so smart. They put a lot of effort into their programs, including high-tech things like computer graphics programs to make their points. The professors were very much at ease in answering questions, but also had no problem being animated in order to strongly make a point. They were very interesting. Not only did they challenge us, but they challenged the law itself to see how it would hold up to challenges. We watched them do it and felt more comfortable doing it ourselves afterwards. The professors are pleasant even on a friendship level.

Status: Current student, full-time
Dates of Enrollment: 8/2004-Submit Date
Survey Submitted: September 2004

I've sat in on lectures given by professors from Yale, Harvard, USC and University of Virginia. My professors at SW, every single one of them, is outstanding in comparison. I'm completely flabbergasted. There are times when I've sat back in the class, amazed at how these people are able to improvise efficient descriptions and analogies of very complex concepts with such grace. I've at times sat back and just looked at the professors standing there, thinking silently to myself: "This guy is on some completely other level." Only a very deep and enthusiastic experience with the subject matter, accumulated over a substantial period of time, could produce such a level of familiarity. My money has been well spent.

Know this: the reading load is significant. You WILL be challenged, in and out of class. When I first began, I was up until nearly midnight every night of the week, and still couldn't keep up with it all. My goal was to complete my studies two days before each class; this was not an efficient plan considering my particular distribution of classes. Once I realized this, I remixed my daily distribution of time spent on each class, and am relieved by the results. The moral of the story here is: don't be afraid to talk to your professors or upper levels about how you're spending your time. All the schools tell you this over and over again. My advice to you is: listen and obey. If you're getting burned out, it's probably because you've not properly organized your time. Ask somebody to take a look at your weekly routine and see what they have to say about it.

As a 1L, I can't offer any critique for grading or registering for popular classes.

 Employment Prospects

Status: Current student, full-time
Dates of Enrollment: 8/2004-Submit Date
Survey Submitted: September 2005

There are still problems with the reputation of Southwestern with larger law firms. Even though the school's employment rate and salary rate is pretty even with Loyola and Pepperdine, far less large firms participate in the Southwestern on-campus interview program. This being said, the students who are in the higher part of the top 10 percent of their class can still get access to some big firms during the fall recruiting season of their 2L year. If these students have some other connection with these firms (i.e., family, friend, alumni or job placement connection) then they can be even better off. The career services office works very hard on behalf of the students, especially the students within the top 10 percent. Students should really take advantage of the office more, and begin strategizing in the first year and first summer in order to best position themselves with the bigger firms. The help of alumni could be better and students do need to really seek it out in order to take advantage.

> **The school says:** "Career Services provides extensive programming and individualized counselling services to all students regardless of rank. It is to the school's advantage to have all their graduates employed and satisfied with their careers. Alumni networking is very strong with many on-campus opportunities, mock interviews conducted by alumni, and the Alumni Resource Network."

Status: Current student, full-time
Dates of Enrollment: 8/2003-Submit Date
Survey Submitted: June 2004

The highly motivated students do find good jobs. Several people in my first-year class got great internships for the summer. Also, a majority of judges in Los Angeles are Southwestern grads. This presumably leads to a large number of clerkships.

The career resource center puts on a multitude of workshops during the year. They offer a lot of help.

Status: Alumnus/a, full-time
Dates of Enrollment: 8/1993-5/1996
Survey Submitted: April 2005

Good if you're practicing in L.A. Poor outside of L.A.

> **The school says:** "Although the majority of alumni practice throughout Southern California, Southwestern graduates can be found in 48 states and 15 foreign countries, with large contingents particularly in Washington, Nevada, Arizona, Texas, Florida and New York."

Status: Alumnus/a, full-time
Dates of Enrollment: 8/1996-5/2000
Survey Submitted: April 2005

The key while in law school is to get a job through the on-campus interview process. The high-end employers do not even do on-campus interviews here because it is considered a fourth-tier school. As far as those employers that do interview there, it appeared that only those students in the top 10 percent got interviews (I was one of them, so I lucked out, but I had friends who were not, and they ended up with low-paying jobs or no jobs at all at graduation). Out of the top 10 percent who got interviews, not all got jobs. Many people graduated without having jobs already lined up.

> **The school says:** "Within in nine months of graduation, 90 percent of the class was employed or enrolled in graduate degree programs."

Status: Alumnus/a, full-time
Dates of Enrollment: 8/2001-5/2004
Survey Submitted: June 2005

Southwestern alumni seek recent Southwestern grads, because they know first hand how hard the program is. Many graduates go into nonprofit and/or government jobs, and also there is a large percentage of grads that go into entertainment legal positions.

Status: Current student, full-time
Dates of Enrollment: 8/2004-Submit Date
Survey Submitted: February 2005

Of the people in the 10 percent and on law review, only four got decent jobs through on-campus interviews. If you're not in the top 10 percent, good luck because chances are you won't get a very good job.

Status: Current student, full-time
Dates of Enrollment: 8/2002-Submit Date
Survey Submitted: December 2004

The on-campus interview program is extensive and helpful but really just for those with the top grades. However, a large majority of people are able to get jobs through alumni, who are always looking to help out Southwestern students. The career services office is extremely helpful when it comes to advice, reviewing resumes, and letting students know about networking type of events.

Status: Alumnus/a, full-time
Dates of Enrollment: 8/2002-7/2003
Survey Submitted: October 2004

They are very active in the area of employment. They have lots of books and the staff is knowledgeable, friendly and active.

> **Regarding employment prospects, the school says:** "Many students secure employment through Southwestern's extensive

alumni network. The law school's popular externship program also allows students to forge working relationships with law firms, corporations, government agencies and legal aid organizations, expanding their professional network."

Quality of Life

Status: Current student, full-time
Dates of Enrollment: 8/2004-Submit Date
Survey Submitted: September 2005

No housing. The campus is very nice, VERY safe with 24-hour guard presence. The library is the most gorgeous law library in Southern California. New building improvements, including new bathrooms, gym, and classrooms equipped with state-of-the-art technology make the campus very attractive.

Status: Current student, full-time
Dates of Enrollment: 8/2003-Submit Date
Survey Submitted: June 2004

The highlight of Southwestern is the Bullocks Wilshire Building. It used to be a fancy department store located next to the drab office building that housed the law school. When it closed down, Southwestern bought the building and restored it to its Art Deco glory. They filmed part of the new Howard Hughes biopic there. The library is on three floors, with plenty of wired study carrels and a good number of private study rooms. Most of the faculty offices are there now, too, and a few classrooms and the cafeteria.

The old building still houses most of the administration and classrooms. The classrooms have all been refurbished in Art Deco style. Most are wired with power plugs for laptops, and the campus just got wireless Internet. Last year, they installed a courtyard between the two buildings, with grass (rare in downtown L.A.), fountains and hotly contested cafe tables.

Southwestern has no housing. They finally have enough parking (paid) and campus security is vigilant and well-armed, probably since the L.A. riots occurred quite nearby. Still, I always feel safe on campus, even after leaving the library late, and security offers escorts. But don't ever leave your laptop unattended.

The on-campus cafeteria is small, but good. The campus is in Koreatown, so there's lots of great, cheap food nearby. Most people stay on campus, though.

Status: Alumnus/a, full-time
Dates of Enrollment: 8/1993-5/1996
Survey Submitted: April 2005

My quality of life during law school was good. There is no on-campus housing. While the neighborhood is a bit rough, the school has excellent security.

Status: Alumnus/a, full-time
Dates of Enrollment: 8/2001-5/2004
Survey Submitted: June 2005

This school does not provide housing, however, they do have a state-of-the-art gym that is available to all students, and the campus is now like a park, with volleyball, and park benches. The security is extremely tight on the campus, and there was never any concern for my safety.

Status: Current student, full-time
Dates of Enrollment: 8/2004-Submit Date
Survey Submitted: February 2005

Great food around the area, and great library to study in. What else do you need? Not a very safe neighborhood.

Status: Alumnus/a, full-time
Dates of Enrollment: 1/2003-Submit Date
Survey Submitted: January 2005

There is no provided housing, so housing will have to be found in the greater Los Angeles area.

The campus is a beautiful historic building in the middle of Los Angeles. It shines like an emerald in the mud.

Status: Current student, full-time
Dates of Enrollment: 8/2002-Submit Date
Survey Submitted: December 2004

It's law school—how great is your quality of life going to be anywhere? It is a small school so it is fun because everyone pretty much knows everyone and it is also a very supportive atmosphere.

Status: Alumnus/a, full-time
Dates of Enrollment: 8/2002-7/2003
Survey Submitted: October 2004

The school itself is very beautiful. Part of it is made out of an old, famous retail store that has been beautifully restored using an Art Deco theme. The cafeteria offered salad to eat and other nutritious food. It isn't in the best part of town, but it's right on the underground train, within short walking distance to at least one courthouse, and only a few blocks from the good part of town. Some people say it was the bad part of town, but I found it interesting.

Status: Current student, full-time
Dates of Enrollment: 8/2004-Submit Date
Survey Submitted: September 2004

The gym is great. Not a lot of people take advantage of it, so many times I have the whole place to myself. Everyone is very, very busy here; as I said, the reading load is significant.

The cafeteria food isn't four star, but it's clean and palatable. Staff and administration are friendly, and they will remember your name if you care to offer a smile in passing.

As the campus is ensconced in a former Art Deco department store, it is a STRANGE looking law school in comparison with more traditional campuses. But you get used to it.

> **The school says:** "Southwestern's campus is one block from the nearest Metro station, easily accessible by several major freeways, and centrally located within the city. Downtown (Walt Disney Concert Hall, Staples Center, etc.) is 10 minutes away; Hollywood (Sunset Strip, Griffith Park, restaurants, etc.) is 15; Santa Monica/Venice (beaches, boardwalk, shopping, etc.) is 20; Malibu (beaches, hiking) is half an hour."

Social Life

Status: Current student, full-time
Dates of Enrollment: 8/2004-Submit Date
Survey Submitted: September 2005

There is a restaurant on the fifth floor "tea room" of the Bullocks Wilshire building. The food is good, although during peak times the line is very long. All students in the know visit the corner "taco stand," which is fast, good, and best of all, CHEAP!

Status: Current student, full-time
Dates of Enrollment: 8/2003-Submit Date
Survey Submitted: June 2004

Bar review is active and popular, and not very clique-y. I was actually pretty impressed by how little stratification happened in my section. Unfortunately, most people go to bars in other areas, so there isn't a lot of casual hanging out— it's always pre-arranged. I really wished a few of the social events were not entirely alcoholic.

A few groups of students go out to eat every day, but most stay on campus and eat in the courtyard or in the lobbies outside the classrooms.

Some of the networking events are pretty cool, since Southwestern is an entertainment law school. Others are like a slow death.

Read all of Vault's Law School Surveys at www.vault.com/lawschool — get complete surveys on top law schools, expert advice on applicaton essays, LSAT prep and more.

VAULT CAREER LIBRARY   59

Status: Alumnus/a, full-time
Dates of Enrollment: 8/2001-5/2004
Survey Submitted: June 2005

People come here to get their degree, not to socialize. Although I left with a few good friends, there is not much of a social scene, as this is primarily a commuter school.

Status: Current student, full-time
Dates of Enrollment: 8/2004-Submit Date
Survey Submitted: February 2005

Lots of social events if you want to get involved.

Status: Alumnus/a, full-time
Dates of Enrollment: 1/2003-Submit Date
Survey Submitted: January 2005

For those who strive to do well academically, there is not much of a social life. On the other hand, for those who want to barely pass, there is much of a social life. This really depends on how well the person can juggle school and a social life.

Status: Current student, full-time
Dates of Enrollment: 8/2002-Submit Date
Survey Submitted: December 2004

Well, the Brass Monkey is a close karaoke place nearby. Otherwise, anywhere is fairly close: Hollywood, West Hollywood, Los Feliz, Beverly Hills, etc.

Status: Current student, full-time
Dates of Enrollment: 8/2004-Submit Date
Survey Submitted: September 2004

There is a very visible and active preponderance of student activities; everything that is available at any other law school is available here. I have time for absolutely none of it, though!

 # The School Says

Founded in 1911, Southwestern Law School is committed to providing an exceptional education that prepares students to excel as lawyers and leaders in the community. Students hail from virtually every state and over a dozen foreign countries. About two-thirds have prior work experience or have already completed advanced degrees in diverse disciplines from accounting to urban planning. Approximately 50 percent of the students are women and over 35 percent are minorities.

Southwestern is the only American Bar Association-approved law school in the country that offers four different programs of study leading to a JD degree that differ in scheduling and instructional approach. In addition to traditional full-time day and part-time evening programs, Southwestern has developed two unique options: SCALE®, the two-year alternative JD course of instruction; and PLEAS, one of the only part-time day programs in the country designed to meet the needs of students with child care responsibilities.

Southwestern's distinguished and highly accessible faculty includes nationally known legal experts in a wide variety of fields. The school's adjunct faculty includes prominent judicial officers and practicing lawyers. Southwestern alumni include public officials—from members of Congress to mayors, district attorneys, and over 200 judges—as well as founders of major law firms and general counsels of multinational corporations.

Solidifying its reputation as a center for the study of entertainment law, Southwestern in 2000 launched the Biederman Entertainment and Media Law Institute—which offers specialized courses on various topics in the field. The school also offers the first LLM degree in Entertainment and Media Law. Southwestern is known for leading innovation in three other burgeoning fields: international law, criminal law, and trial advocacy/litigation.

Southwestern recently completed an extensive, decade-long modernization project, bringing all of its facilities to the state-of-the-art level. The centerpiece of the campus is the Bullocks Wilshire building, an Art Deco landmark that was purchased by the school in 1994 and converted into a multi-purpose academic facility. The building includes the award-winning, 83,000-square-foot Taylor Law Library; the technologically-advanced Dixon Courtroom and Alternative Dispute Resolution Suite; multi-media classrooms; a penthouse cafeteria/dining room with city views; and a new gym. While the campus is situated amidst an urban backdrop, the green, park-like promenade and student commons create a decidedly tranquil environment.

Public interest work is at the core of Southwestern's mission, and the school offers several popular fellowships and grants that enable students to serve those in need while gaining vital professional experience. The law school's Moot Court and International Trial Advocacy programs have won national recognition. Other student activities include Law Review, the *Journal of Law and Trade in the Americas*, and the *International Media and Entertainment Law Journal*. Southwestern also sponsors summer law programs in London, England; Buenos Aires, Argentina; Vancouver, Canada; and Guanajuato, Mexico.

Stanford Law School

Office of Admissions
Crown Quadrangle
559 Nathan Abbott Way
Stanford, CA 94305-8610
Admissions phone: (650) 723-4985
Admissions e-mail: admissions@law.stanford.edu
Admissions URL:
http://www.law.stanford.edu/school/offices/admissions/

 ## Admissions

Status: Current student, full-time
Dates of Enrollment: 9/2004-Submit Date
Survey Submitted: October 2005

I think I can fairly share a few pointers based on the fact that the application process at Stanford is reasonably unique. First, LSAT is not all important. This is in stark contrast to Harvard, where the incoming 75/25 LSAT percentile divide for this year's incoming class was 176/170! At Stanford, if you can hit 169 or higher, emphasis will shift to other parts of your application (there are still lots of people in the 180 range, mind you).

In this regard, a super-high GPA from a prestigious undergrad is almost a pre-requisite. However, I believe that the single most important factor for gaining admission at Stanford (especially if your numbers are low) is to have a truly unique story/life experience to tell. My classmates are some of the most interesting people I've ever met—they have fought in wars, run international charities, been senior managers in Fortune 500 companies, have PhDs in interesting fields from the most prestigious universities worldwide, the list goes on.

In summary, and in contrast to Harvard where if you have (extremely) high numbers you will get in, admission to Stanford and Yale is unquestionably something of a crapshoot for all save the most qualified of applicants. Having said that, though, if Stanford is somewhere you'd like to go, I'd highly recommend applying.

One final thought: in your application, stress how much you want to attend Stanford specifically. The school undoubtedly cares about its yield ratio and I think averring to the fact that SLS is your top choice would be to such an applicant's advantage. Good luck!

Status: Current student, full-time
Dates of Enrollment: 9/2003-Submit Date
Survey Submitted: March 2006

Very hard to get in. No interviews, spend a lot of time on your essay, get top grades, do something interesting between college and law school, different law professors choose each class, so exactly what they are looking for might vary from year to year—the professor who chose my class was especially interested in an "intellectual" class, so he looked for students who'd written a thesis.

Status: Alumnus/a, full-time
Dates of Enrollment: 8/2001-5/2004
Survey Submitted: May 2005

The admissions process is fairly straightforward and standard. There are no interviews; just an essay (I wrote my essay about Chinese watercolor painting) and the application. I have heard the most important criteria are GPA and LSAT scores, though. It all boils down to numbers. You probably need to be an Olympic gold medalist to get in without the right grades and LSAT score.

The school says: "Stanford, of course, looks at the LSAT and the GPA in the admissions process, but (as the *U.S. News* data shows), Stanford places less importance on raw numbers than many of its peer institutions. Rather, the school prefers to focus on an applicant's overall accomplishments in order to bring quality and diversity to the entering class."

Status: Alumnus/a, full-time
Dates of Enrollment: 9/1999-5/2002
Survey Submitted: April 2005

Stanford values work coupled with academic experience and this makes your class extraordinarily interesting. Most of my class had work, grad school and/or international experience. A significant percentage had all three.

Status: Alumnus/a, full-time
Dates of Enrollment: 9/1998-6/2001
Survey Submitted: April 2005

LSATs. Application. LSATs. Letters of Rec. LSATs. No interview. Did I mention LSATs? LSATs (and GPA) seem to be the most important aspects of getting into a top law school.

Status: Alumnus/a, full-time
Dates of Enrollment: 9/2001-5/2004
Survey Submitted: March 2005

One of the most selective law schools in the country, Stanford Law is able to look past the numbers, since all applicants have great scores, and instead choose students based on other aspects of the backgrounds, leading to an extremely diverse and interesting class.

Status: Alumnus/a, full-time
Dates of Enrollment: 8/1997-5/2000
Survey Submitted: March 2005

Stanford is obviously highly selective, but it looks for more than high grades and LSATs. Stanford is interested in having a well-rounded class as a whole. Students often have significant accomplishments in areas unrelated to law, which adds to the class profile as a whole.

Leadership is highly valued. Your essay probably should emphasize what you would add to the class and link that to past accomplishments.

Status: Alumnus/a, full-time
Dates of Enrollment: 9/2000-5/2003
Survey Submitted: March 2005

The simplest way to get in—have a killer LSAT score and solid undergrad GPA. Other, more intangible factors seem to help, too. For instance, my class had three medical doctors and about five people who had already completed PhDs. Other classmates also had very interesting line-items on their resumes, i.e.: working on the Human Genome Project for a year after college, serving as an officer in the armed forces, and so on.

I applied right at the deadline. I went to an unimpressive undergrad institution, but graduated with a 4.0. Also, I scored a 173 on my LSAT and had co-authored several law review articles as an undergrad. I think that's why I got in.

Status: Alumnus/a, full-time
Dates of Enrollment: 9/2000-5/2003
Survey Submitted: March 2005

While most top-tier law schools place the vast majority of weight on LSAT scores and college GPA, I am convinced that Stanford takes a much more holistic approach. They look at work experience, extracurricular activities, and to some degree the application essay. In dealing with the school, everyone involved in the application and admissions process was friendly and professional. By far the most impressive aspect of the process was the fact that Stanford e-mailed me an answer on my application weeks before any other school!

It's true that, as a top two or three school in the nation, Stanford is selective. But you can improve your odds by emphasizing any activities or experiences you've had with the issue of "diversity." The school is currently under a big push for diversity. You can also be yourself and let a strong personality shine through in

Read all of Vault's Law School Surveys at www.vault.com/lawschool — get complete surveys on top law schools, expert advice on applicaton essays, LSAT prep and more.

VAULT CAREER LIBRARY   61

interviews and essays. I think they really like personality and it can tip the scale if your other stats are right on the fence.

In terms of the stats, you need to have about a 170 LSAT score. You can get in with a slightly lower score but need stellar grades and extracurriculars in order to compensate. A solid GPA of 3.7 or 3.8 at a good undergraduate school is usually adequate, but it'll need to be higher if your LSAT score is lower. The school also has a very good financial aid program, giving lots of money to subsidize student tuition. There are also plenty of opportunities to work as a research assistant or teaching assistant to a law professor, to get additional cash and tuition remission.

Status: Alumnus/a, full-time
Dates of Enrollment: 9/2000-5/2003
Survey Submitted: April 2004

Stanford Law has such a small class size and is in such an amazing location that it is incredibly competitive to get in. But once you're in, you're IN—it is an amazing network of gifted people, and I think it is less stressful and competitive than any other top law school.

Status: Alumnus/a, full-time
Dates of Enrollment: 9/1999-5/2002
Survey Submitted: April 2004

Stanford Law School's admittance philosophy has changed since I applied in 1998. The law school used to seek out "whole" students who had real-world experience and could bring more to the classroom than a drive to obtain a high grade. Sadly, my advice to today's applicant is to achieve a 170+ LSAT score and have a very high undergraduate GPA. Applicants should focus their essays on who they really are; winning essays give the selection committee a window into the applicant's soul.

Status: Current student, full-time
Dates of Enrollment: 1/2003-Submit Date
Survey Submitted: April 2004

The school is very selective. I believe it now has more of a focus on numbers, which I think is unfortunate. Our class was one of the most interesting groups of people I have ever met. Now the students are smart, but not as interesting. I think moving up in the rankings actually hurt us because people choose Stanford because of its rank, not because it offers something special in a law school.

 # Academics

Status: Current student, full-time
Dates of Enrollment: 9/2004-Submit Date
Survey Submitted: October 2005

It's hard to know where to begin! I absolutely love the academic experience here and I think most people at SLS would agree. The largest 1L class I studied in had less than 60 people in it and two of the first semester 1L classes had only 30. I doubt many other schools could match such a teacher-student ratio for the first year.

In addition, all of my professors have been excellent (though there are varying degrees of excellence) and most have written the book we study in class. There is little to say other than both the professors and students are incredible.

A beautiful feature of SLS—there is outrageous grade inflation. The median is a 3.4, with 3.5 constituting an A-! Given that the median applies only loosely in most 2L and 3L classes, you can expect to graduate with a highly respectable GPA, even if you're in the middle of the pack.

In addition, Stanford has the enticing 3K system where you can elect to take a course you don't like or are having difficulty with on a pass/fail basis. You can do this on EVERY class for your first semester of 1L, which really takes the heat off, and you can do it twice more for the rest of your time at the school. In addition, some classes, such as LRW (Legal Research and Writing) are mandatory 3K.

All in all, Stanford Law provides a rewarding, challenging, yet manageable academic experience.

Status: Alumnus/a, full-time
Dates of Enrollment: 8/2002-5/2005
Survey Submitted: March 2006

Some lottery classes are small and difficult to get if you are a 1L. Still, you should show up on the first day because most people shop classes and it's common to still get in the class despite being 60 on the waitlist. Blind grading with enforced mean is better for those who don't kiss up or oppose the professor. Off-mean writing or clinical classes are better for those who get along with the professor or kiss up. Major grade inflation can occur for people kissing up in off-mean classes. Be careful of teachers who play favorites in off-mean classes.

Professor Miguel Mendez is tremendous in class and as a mentor. Negotiations classes are not only an easy pass and units, but very practical and staffed with great professors. Professor Fogel's Psychology of Litigation class should be required for anyone at Stanford Law.

Status: Alumnus/a, full-time
Dates of Enrollment: 8/1997-8/2000
Survey Submitted: March 2006

Some small popular seminars are tough to get into—there's a lottery component, plus it helps if the professor teaching it knows somehow that the quality of your participation is good. Classes are AWESOME—the faculty are the very best of the very best.

The workload can be crushing—but it is also what you make it. People can figure out efficient ways to study and manage their time. I learned how to handle it and had a terrific experience, though the demands on my time could be pretty stressful. Grading for large classes is on the mean, which is not too informative. Off-mean grading in seminar classes gives you better feedback.

Status: Alumnus/a, full-time
Dates of Enrollment: 9/2000-5/2003
Survey Submitted: March 2005

Because Stanford is a very small law school (about 175 per class), it's pretty easy to get into whatever class you want. The size also makes the school able to provide many small seminar classes, where you sit with a professor and 10 or 15 other students in an intimate and personal environment, unlike other schools dominated by large lecture halls. You can also get significant one-on-one time with profs for the same reason, because there is no line to wait in when you go to visit them during their office hours.

Academically, Stanford is —needless to say—on the cutting edge. With a new dean who is stressing interdisciplinary partnerships with business schools and other fields of study, as well as the expansion of clinical education where students get to work on real-life matters, it's a terrific place to be. But if you are more interested in theoretical pondering, Stanford's legal theory professors abound. You can chat with them over coffee about the latest abstract legal notions. And they are the top scholars in their particular areas of law.

Profs and deans WANT their students to succeed, so unlike other schools where the Socratic Method brutally tries students' sanity, Stanford offers an atmosphere that is much more collegial than competitive. It is the opposite of Scott Turow's *One-L* and of *The Paper Chase*. If you miss a day of class, simply ask a friend for a copy of her notes. No big deal. In other schools, they tear pages out of library books just so competing classmates won't get the same answer. That's terrible, and Stanford fosters an environment that is far less stressful and far more positive.

We also have an excellent selection of seven or eight legal journals that students can work on. We also draw the cream of the crop from the field of actual practitioners. Our clinical profs are the best litigators, international lawyers, diplomats and appellate advocates in the nation. We offer a fun Moot Court Competition class and many other simulation courses. Clinics with real cases include an Environmental clinic, Educational clinic, a Supreme Court clinic, and others.

Stanford's course selection is also very strong. In addition to standard survey classes in the basic subjects, there are lots of choices in legal history and theory, international law, environmental law, securities, corporate law, litigation, and so on. They even have a clinic where you get to work on real Supreme Court petitions! One class meets at a prof's house around her kitchen table!

And if you want to build up your academic credentials with a stint on a law review staff, no problem. Stanford's Law Review, unlike other schools, does NOT consider your GPA when considering you for admission. You just have to do a competent job on a sample editing assignment and you're in! Alternatively, you can join one of a half-dozen other journals covering more specific subjects: a public policy journal, an environmental journal, a technology law journal and so on.

Status: Alumnus/a, full-time
Dates of Enrollment: 9/2000-6/2003
Survey Submitted: March 2005

SLS has among the strongest law programs in the country. Professors who emphasize legal theory (i.e., Kelman, Lessig) are rare elsewhere, so it's a good idea to take advantage of their extraordinary presence.

Status: Alumnus/a, full-time
Dates of Enrollment: 9/1999-5/2002
Survey Submitted: March 2005

Quality of classes is topnotch, teachers are world-class, workload is heavy but worth it. Getting into classes is not that hard and small class sizes make it a great learning experience.

Status: Alumnus/a, full-time
Dates of Enrollment: 9/1999-5/2002
Survey Submitted: April 2005

Access to professors is easy and open; professors are warm and generous with their time. Unlike most law schools, Stanford provides a large number of trans-action-related coursework, including solid finance classes. Although students are bright and work hard, pressure and competitiveness are minimal.

Status: Alumnus/a, full-time
Dates of Enrollment: 9/1998-6/2001
Survey Submitted: April 2005

Stanford is a wonderfully relaxed campus for a law school. Small class size (180 students per year, largest first-year class is 60 or so students). Talented, interesting and energetic professors and classmates. Any student can get into any class (even if class size is limited) with sufficient motivation. Difficult to fail courses, but also difficult to get high marks in normed courses. In second and third year, students have option to take grade-by-paper courses that are not tied to any mean.

> **The school says:** "Stanford raised its mandatory mean for exam-based classes to 3.4 (which translates to a B+) in autumn 2001. Classes that are not exam-based do not have a manda-tory mean."

Status: Alumnus/a, full-time
Dates of Enrollment: 9/2000-5/2003
Survey Submitted: March 2005

For the most part, all work at Stanford is optional. I graduated in the middle of my class having read maybe 50 percent of what was assigned. After first year, almost no professors will cold-call, and even during the first year, only about half will. Truth be told, I was disappointed by the quality of the classes, but that may be only because I had unreal expectations.

Stanford does not do a great job training you to be a practicing attorney. Nor are the classes really intellectually fulfilling. Instead, they're caught in limbo—not intellectually rich enough to stand on their own as an academic course of study, but too far divorced from the realities of practice to be effective as professional training.

The professors are almost all former Supreme Court clerks, and it seems that their main interest is in training the top 10 people in each class for their tempo-rary positions as appellate clerks for prestigious federal judges. Everyone else is just there to watch. If you're one of the top 10, you're welcome to talk to them during office hours. If you're not, then you had better have a good reason for going to see them; otherwise you're just interrupting their "more important" work.

Status: Alumnus/a, full-time
Dates of Enrollment: 8/1999-5/2002
Survey Submitted: April 2004

There are few opportunities as privileged as the chance to spend three years with some of the most amazing people you will ever know—both faculty and class-mates—discussing the most fundamental questions of our society. The workload is challenging, and just keeping up with your fellow students will push you to excel. Fortunately, because of Stanford's small class size (180) and solid repu-tation, students really don't have to compete against one another to land top jobs and judicial clerkships. This means that learning at Stanford Law is a much more collaborative than competitive experience. I never had a single incidence of not getting admitted to a class I wanted.

Status: Current student, full-time
Dates of Enrollment: 8/2003-Submit Date
Survey Submitted: October 2003

Classmates are amazingly bright. Exceptionally collegial. The perfect mix of non-nerdy and nerdy types. Some of the nicest people I have ever met. Professors care, and they look out for you. Grading is not really an issue. Students can elect to take classes pass/fail. The workload is probably the same as at other places. The only time people were stressed, though, was during finals week. The law school's current goals are to increase clinical programs, enhance international law concentration and send more people into academics.

 ## Employment Prospects

Status: Current student, full-time
Dates of Enrollment: 9/2004-Submit Date
Survey Submitted: October 2005

OK, this is a joke. Even someone who is last in the class will get a $125K job somewhere if he/she wants one. Practically every night during campus inter-view programs (CIP), a law firm has a reception with free food and drink to entice you into applying.I had good, though not the best, grades, and having interviewed with 14 firms on campus, I got 14 callbacks. That pretty much tells the story.

A common issue for Harvard and Yale Law admits relates to a desire to work on the East Coast. Harvard and Stanford were my options and I chose the latter despite wishing to work out east. From an employment standpoint, I don't think that decision has hurt me one bit and it may even be an advantage. The reason is simply because there are so few SLS grads, and even fewer wishing to work back east, that employers are happy to see you. Employers do want to have an eclectic group of summer associates, so going to Stanford may even be a plus.

At any rate, such a discussion is largely academic. Here at Stanford the world is your oyster and I'm sure the same is true at H and Y. If you want to hit the very top—Supreme Court clerkships or academia, for example—Yale may be mar-ginally better, though I firmly believe that at some point the prestige of the law school must give way to the actual academic performance of the student while there.

> **Regarding salaries, the school says:** "Not all students earn $125K at graduation. The median salary for graduates working in the private sector is $125,000. For those working in public interest organizations or the public sector, the median salary is $50,000."

Status: Alumnus/a, full-time
Dates of Enrollment: 8/1997-8/2000
Survey Submitted: March 2006

Stanford has tremendous prestige—I had over a dozen offers as a 1L, and again as a 2L. I could be selective about where to interview. Graduates I know got clerkships and law firm jobs, then about two years later got the public interest and law firm jobs they wanted (some firms do not take anyone straight out of school). Alumni have often been helpful to me, and I try to extend the favor to those who follow.

Read all of Vault's Law School Surveys at www.vault.com/lawschool — get complete surveys on top law schools, expert advice on applicaton essays, LSAT prep and more.

VAULT CAREER LIBRARY   63

Status: Alumnus/a, full-time
Dates of Enrollment: 9/1998-6/2001
Survey Submitted: April 2005

Any student that wants a firm job can get one coming out of Stanford (that's not to say such a job is for every student that does come out of Stanford). Same is true for clerkships. Motivated students can snag a U.S. Supreme Court clerkship, but students have to carve out their own path as their is no organized institutional process at Stanford, like there is at Yale.

Stanford Law says: "Stanford manages the entire application process, from providing Supreme Court clerkship workshops for students to coordinating production and mailing of application packets."

Status: Alumnus/a, full-time
Dates of Enrollment: 9/2000-5/2003
Survey Submitted: March 2005

Although Stanford's career services department does have a public interest section, it seems that the department's primary interest is in getting people to go to firms. Consequently, Stanford's fall interviewing process is overrun by law firms, and only a few public interest organizations show up.

In terms of prestige with law firms, Stanford is a great place to go. I got the impression during one of my summer associateships that they were so thrilled to have someone from SLS, that I could have belched loudly at a meeting and one of the partners would have thanked me for my insightful comment. Stanford's prestige within the judiciary community, though, seems to have slipped. Word on the street is that a lot of judges view SLS grads as slackers, and would prefer to hire clerks from the East Coast schools.

The school says: "OCI is not an accurate reflection of a school's commitment to public interest, as most public interest organizations choose not to recruit through on-campus programs. More reflective of Stanford's commitment is our funding of all students who choose to work in the public interest/public sector during the summer and post-graduation (Miles Rubin Loan Repayment Assistance Program), our development of an extensive clinical program with nine clinics to provide practical training, and our ability to obtain public interest fellowships for our students (Skadden, Equal Justice Works, in-house) and placement in the DOJ Honors Programs.

"Stanford's clerkship placement rate is one of the highest among law schools. Each year, for the last 10 years, Stanford has placed 24-33 percent of its graduates into federal judicial clerkships across the country."

Status: Alumnus/a, full-time
Dates of Enrollment: 9/2000-5/2003
Survey Submitted: March 2005

Bottom line: the old adage that the person who graduates at the bottom of his class in law school is still called "lawyer" rings all too true at Stanford. No matter where you are in the class rankings (which, by the way, are secret until the day you graduate!), your chances of finding a good job are excellent.

For most people, permanent job prospects are locked in by fall of the third year. Of course, the really prestigious experiences—like Supreme Court clerkships—are reserved for the top academics in the class. But otherwise, the market is pretty open to any Stanford grad. And the same holds true for summer jobs at very selective public interest organizations, firms, courts, and government agencies.

Status: Alumnus/a, full-time
Dates of Enrollment: 9/1999-5/2002
Survey Submitted: April 2004

The law degree from Stanford Law School is rightly coveted and imparts automatic credibility with the major firms. Firms are excited at the prospect of inviting Stanford Law students to join their summer programs; that will not change in any economy. As the economy continues to grow at a super-heated rate, the Stanford Law School graduate will have great opportunities and many choices on where to begin a career.

However, the wise student will not rely solely on career services as a firm search resource. Alumni are flattered to hear from current law students seeking advice. Students should take advantage of the lists of alumni who agree to make themselves available to answer career and career search questions from current students.

Status: Current student, full-time
Dates of Enrollment: 1/2003-Submit Date
Survey Submitted: April 2004

Everybody respects Stanford, but its cachet on the West Coast is much better than on the East. The career services program at the school is probably its weakest point—they figure that once you get in, you'll get a job. That's not helpful to finding the right firm or the right job.

The school says: "The Career Services Office offers extensive resources, programming and individual counseling aimed at helping students make educated choices and reach their career goals. Employment rates for our graduating classes rang from 97 to 99 percent. Over 45 percent obtain jobs somewhere other than the West Coast. While a significant percentage of our students begin their careers in jobs on the West Coast, this is not due to a lack of East Coast opportunities—over 65 percent of employers participating in on-campus interviews are interviewing for non-West Coast offices. Students stay on the West Coast because, having spent three years in California, they have decided that it is where they want to live.

"A substantial majority of students (over 90 percent) find positions throughout the United States and abroad through the relatively painless on-campus recruiting or judicial clerkship application processes. Students applying for fellowships, government honors programs or alternative careers inevitably invest more time and energy in the job search than those going through these on-campus programs, they also receive considerable one-on-one assistance from our career counselors."

 Quality of Life

Status: Current student, full-time
Dates of Enrollment: 9/2004-Submit Date
Survey Submitted: October 2005

You can't go wrong with the quality of life at Stanford—it's absolutely fantastic! I cycle from Palo Alto every morning and find myself cycling up Palm Drive with the sun in my face, 100 feet high palm trees flying past, a crazy number of squirrels running around the place, and Memorial Church ahead. The entrance to heaven may not be much better.

The weather for the first and last few months is always in the mid-70s during the day with little humidity and in the mid-50s at night. The "winter" involves drizzles every few days and such terrifyingly low daytime temperatures of 50. There is so much to love.

The campus itself is beautiful and enormous—8,000 acres I believe. Housing is quite expensive, but if one is willing to live three to five miles away and drive/cycle it's possible to find a place for less than $800 per month.

Status: Alumnus/a, full-time
Dates of Enrollment: 8/2002-5/2005
Survey Submitted: March 2006

Stanford West is the nicest apartment complex you can get through the housing lottery, with in-unit washer and dryer, nice atmosphere and gym right next to campus. I even got a connected garage. The law school is sparkling new. Stanford and Palo Alto are ultrasafe. Take advantage of the camping class open to all Stanford people through the geology department. Moderate California weather, less than an hour from San Francisco and San Jose.

Status: Alumnus/a, full-time
Dates of Enrollment: 8/1997-8/2000
Survey Submitted: March 2006

Housing is very nice—renovated or new, many studios for single students. We had a great loft apartment as a couple, right on campus. Rents in the area are high, but Stanford helps with subsidies. Campus ands its facilities are lovely and well kept.

Dining is great—wonderful markets, and good restaurants (fabulous restaurants up in San Francisco at any price range). Neighborhoods vary in their feel of safety—don't assume that it's a homogeneous feel near campus—talk to several people in each area you consider.

Status: Alumnus/a, full-time
Dates of Enrollment: 9/2000-5/2003
Survey Submitted: March 2005

Frequently, as my friends and I would drive down Palm Drive to return to campus from a night out, one of them would say, "Guys, in the game of life, we are the big winners." Palo Alto is not the most thrilling place to live, but it is very safe, and the campus is absolutely beautiful. Furthermore, you're close enough to San Francisco that you have access to great restaurants, clubs and concerts.

Students are not guaranteed to get housing, but the housing available runs from adequate to excellent (albeit a bit expensive). Living off campus isn't that bad of an option, either, but expect to shell out a few extra bucks if you go that route. As for facilities, the law building was recently remodeled. All the classrooms have wireless Internet access and more technological doohickies than the profs will ever be able to figure out. Throw in the Aeron chairs, and going to class doesn't seem like such a bad thing. Also, the recently remodeled library is spectacular.

On-campus eateries aren't the greatest, but they'll suffice. There's a small cafe in the law school where students can pick up something quick between classes. For a heartier meal, the student union is only a short walk from the law school. And for real food, Palo Alto has plenty to offer.

Status: Alumnus/a, full-time
Dates of Enrollment: 9/2000-5/2003
Survey Submitted: March 2005

For students who prefer to be immersed in an animated community of friends, at the expense of sacrificing quality infrastructure, I highly recommend the on-campus dorm. I developed many close friendships there. But I, unlike others, am willing to prioritize social interaction over things like personal bathrooms and kitchens.

In many ways, the law school dorm experience at Stanford was similar to the undergrad dorm experience for many students around the country. We threw wild parties, played absurd pranks on each other, and genuinely enjoyed the company of our friends. Also, we lived a mere two minutes from the law school, so we could sleep later than others. And we were a short walk from the heart of the larger Stanford campus—with its impressive architecture, libraries, artwork, coffee shops, etc. For the rest of you, there are nice on-campus suites and apartments, and overpriced apartments in the real estate black hole that is Palo Alto.

The neighborhood surrounding the campus is a virtual Shangri-la of scenic hillsides, decadent California mansions, manicured lawns and quaint shops. Palo Alto, the epicenter of Silicon Valley, houses many of the world's tech businesses right outside the school.

The campus itself is an Eden—replete with palm trees, ubiquitous flowers, tons of open space for lounging or playing sports, and gorgeous Southwestern architecture. Of course, the weather is almost always beautiful except for the occasional cloud cover and the three-week winter of rain. The state-of-the-art swimming pool is a terrific place to spend your hours.

Many of the newest facilities were completed just after I graduated, so I cannot speak about them, other than to say they sound like an excellent array of perks for students. The law library just underwent a multi-million dollar renovation; the university recently completed a brand-new alumni center; the rec center/gym for the law school dorms was updated; and plans are in the works for a brand-new luxury dorm exclusively for law students. The school itself has each class-

room and lecture hall equipped with the latest in wireless Internet, "smart" class-room technology, and Aeron chairs. The moot court room is also impressive with its dark wood and imposing bench.

A short drive away are some of the most beautiful and interesting places in America: San Francisco, with its renowned restaurants, stellar nightlife, and picturesque landmarks; Carmel; Sausalito; Napa and Sonoma Valleys (wine country); Monterey; San Jose; the giant redwoods; and the Berkeley head shops. Drive a couple more hours and you can spend a weekend in L.A. or in breath-taking Lake Tahoe for skiing and gambling or in Yosemite National Park. Hiking and biking trails abound near Stanford, and most folks are somewhat "outdoorsy."

I was mildly surprised by the lack of interaction with undergrads at Stanford, a fact that mattered more to me as a younger law student than to the other law students who already have their own families. It was particularly odd considering that the law school is smack dab in the middle of the undergrad campus.

Status: Alumnus/a, full-time
Dates of Enrollment: 9/1999-5/2002
Survey Submitted: April 2004

You have nothing to fear in Palo Alto unless you are a bicycle or car stereo. The graduate housing shortage and inflated off-campus rents may have abated as the tech bubble burst, but I still encourage independent-minded students to live off campus either in one of the nearby communities or in San Francisco. There is great comfort in knowing that you will leave campus at the end of every day.

Status: Current student, full-time
Dates of Enrollment: 9/2003-Submit Date
Survey Submitted: May 2004

Yes, Palo Alto is superficially "perfect"—clean, safe, good weather. But it can be horribly stifling—no culture, homogenous yuppy people, etc. Palo Alto itself contributed to much of my 1L misery. I ran away to San Francisco at every opportunity.

 ## Social Life

Status: Current student, full-time
Dates of Enrollment: 9/2004-Submit Date
Survey Submitted: October 2005

First of all, I should emphasize that I am a city person and was a little worried about Palo Alto for social life. However, I have been very pleasantly surprised! There is a new graduate student bar on campus, which is good fun and a lot of us tend to go there regularly during the week for late night munchies and/or chill-out beers. Palo Alto actually has quite a good number of bars, which I have come to enjoy and Thursday night bar review is always a great time. Add in weekly house parties and I'm happy.

Nevertheless, as Palo Alto is a little too small for my tastes, I try to make it up to San Francisco most weekends. It's very achievable—Caltrain takes only 45 minutes from P.A. to S.F. The class seems to be divided between people who stay in P.A. regularly at the weekends and those that do not. While I obviously belong in the latter category, I have never been short of company.

Status: Alumnus/a, full-time
Dates of Enrollment: 8/2002-5/2005
Survey Submitted: March 2006

Kan Zeman on University Avenue is the best affordable restaurant. Monday night free stand up comedy at Rose and Crown Bar is a must see. The law students are overall such unpleasant, competitive jerks. There are a few nice, genuine students in there, and it is worth the time to seek them out.

Status: Alumnus/a, full-time
Dates of Enrollment: 8/2000-5/2003
Survey Submitted: March 2006

Palo Alto is a college town, but with a layer of insane wealth laid over it. Mainly bars and restaurants in Palo Alto, but very close to San Francisco and the rest of the Bay Area, which offers more cosmopolitan variety.

Read all of Vault's Law School Surveys at www.vault.com/lawschool — get complete surveys on top law schools, expert advice on applicaton essays, LSAT prep and more.

VAULT CAREER LIBRARY   65

Status: Alumnus/a, full-time
Dates of Enrollment: 8/1997-8/2000
Survey Submitted: March 2006

I am married and was as a student, so I missed a lot of the main social scene—younger single students did what I did as a graduate student before law school, going out for drinks and dancing, hanging out at someone's place in the evening and taking trips together. I had single friends, but mostly saw them for coffee or walks rather than in the evening. Some wonderful couples became our fast friends, and we're now having children at the same time.

Status: Alumnus/a, full-time
Dates of Enrollment: 8/2001-5/2004
Survey Submitted: May 2005

It's a pretty close-knit student body because there are only 170 per class. I got to know pretty much everyone in my class and we were very congenial with each other. I had a great time at Stanford, and I definitely feel school pride and loyalty.

Status: Alumnus/a, full-time
Dates of Enrollment: 9/2001-5/2004
Survey Submitted: March 2005

Being a small law school, with only 180 students per class, students quickly come to know their peers. The law school bunch is fairly social with frequent parties. Many students take advantage of the proximity of San Francisco to hang out (or live—as frequently 3Ls do).

Status: Alumnus/a, full-time
Dates of Enrollment: 9/2000-5/2003
Survey Submitted: March 2005

The upside and downside of going to law school at Stanford is the class size. There are about 180 per class, so it's like high school—everyone knows everyone else's business. This also cuts down on the dating options. And for men going there hoping to meet an undergrad, good luck. The undergrads, for the most part, want nothing to do with students who are not undergrads. And the other grad students are mostly engineers, which means "mostly men." So the prospects for straight male students aren't all that wonderful.

The law school puts on a number of events each year, from public interest auctions, to students vs. faculty in the Battle of the Brains, to Cinco de Mayo parties, and so on. Additionally, every Thursday night, the law association puts on a bar review, where SLS students flock to a local bar for drink specials. The Palo Alto bars aren't the greatest in the world, but they get the job done.

Status: Alumnus/a, full-time
Dates of Enrollment: 9/2000-5/2003
Survey Submitted: March 2005

Here are recommendations: dive bars—Dutch Goose; Oasis. Nicer bars—Blue Chalk; Nola. Spectacles—late night sushi and sake bombs at Miyake. Bagels—Noah's. Weekend getaways—skiing in Lake Tahoe, winery tours in Napa or Sonoma, clubbing and dining in San Francisco.

Best spots on campus—the outdoor pool, the Thai Cafe, the Treehouse Restaurant, the top of Hoover Tower, the Oval, Crothers Hall. Best goofy activities—sneaking into the history building at night to watch a movie on the huge screen in a lecture hall, fountain hopping, streaking through the undergrad library during their finals week (the undergrads are on a quarter system while the law school is on a semester system), theme parties in the basement bar in Crothers Hall.

School events—the annual musical where law students ridicule professors, the annual charity "SPILF" auction, the "law school prom," keg parties at the Crothers and Rains dorms, Cinqo de Mayo party at the law school, "full moon on the quad" where students gather to kiss strangers every autumn

Status: Alumnus/a, full-time
Dates of Enrollment: 9/2000-5/2003
Survey Submitted: April 2004

The law school is so small that people sometimes joke that it feels regressively high-schoolish, in that we have lockers and that there are loose cliques of the "gunners," the "beautiful people," the "marrieds" and "public school kids." But the folks who choose Stanford are generally laid-back and unpretentious, and the social scene is a lot of fun and mixes most of the class together.

Thursday night bar review and the formals are a lot of fun, and the nightlife of San Francisco is a short drive or train ride away. Stanford is excellently situated for sports, and most students participate in some kind of outdoor activity. Ski mountains are a few hours' drive by car, surfing beaches can be reached in 30 minutes, and for equestrians there is an excellent riding stable on campus! Of the Top Three, this is definitely the law school to choose for the socially and athletically inclined.

 School Says

Stanford Law School is one of the nation's leading institutions for legal scholarship and education. Its alumni are among the most influential decision makers in law, politics, business and high technology. Faculty members argue before the Supreme Court, testify before Congress and write books and articles for academic audiences, as well as the popular press. Along with

Thomas Jefferson School of Law

Admissions Office
2121 San Diego Ave.
San Diego, CA 92110
Admissions phone: (619) 297-9700 or (800) 936-7529
Admissions e-mail: info@tjsl.edu
Admissions URL: http://www.tjsl.edu/admissions

 ## Admissions

Status: Current student, full-time
Dates of Enrollment: 8/2002-Submit Date
Survey Submitted: January 2005

The admission process is pretty straightforward. Submit LSAT scores, under-grad transcripts, application and essay. TJSL is very interested in a diverse campus. We have an extremely high number of mid-career professionals. Since they are a "newer" law school (recently fully accredited by the ABA) they are really looking for people who will make an impact in the public eye.

Status: Alumnus/a, full-time
Dates of Enrollment: 8/2002-5/2005
Survey Submitted: May 2006

The admission process at TJSL was a breeze. After graduating undergrad I had never heard of Thomas Jefferson School of Law—I thought it must have been located in Virginia or some uninteresting place. Instead I got a series of mailings and glossy brochures showing beautiful beaches, palm trees, great surf and a school that touted itself as a bastion for the "student's quality of life." I am, and was at the time, a "quality of life" kind of guy.

I immediately dropped an application in the mail and was contacted almost immediately by one of the reps. My only concern was that I had never heard of the school before. The admissions rep was very candid and explained that although TJ wasn't a top national school, it was known in the region and would provide me a quality education (and they'd throw a lot of scholarship money around to boot).

Shortly after my application was submitted I was contacted by one of the associate deans of the school. He was very enthusiastic about building TJSL's reputation and wanted me to be a part of that growth. I then interviewed at the school, checked out the campus, sat in on a class, etc. Once I saw it first-hand, my mind was made up. I was accepted at and toured a number of California law schools, including all of the schools in San Diego, however, there were certain intangibles at TJ that just felt right. At the end of the day, the candor, enthusiasm and graciousness of the admissions staff really sold me, and I have never regretted the decision I made.

Status: Alumnus/a, part-time
Dates of Enrollment: 8/2000-5/2004
Survey Submitted: May 2006

Admissions staff extremely helpful in answering all questions and providing tours of campus. They also do a great job of informing potential students of any potential scholarships offered by the school for which the student may qualify.

Status: Alumnus/a, full-time
Dates of Enrollment: 8/2001-5/2004
Survey Submitted: April 2006

The admission process is the same as it is for other law schools. An application with a personal statement is required. Letters of recommendation, LSAT scores, transcripts, etc. Most application materials are collected through the LSDAS. When I applied, no interview was needed, although a campus visit is recommended for any school you are seriously considering. I applied to several schools with higher rankings—and got in. But after visiting the schools, meet-ing with students and professors (and administrators), I felt the quality of my education would be best at Thomas Jefferson.

Status: Current student, full-time
Dates of Enrollment: 1/2005-Submit Date
Survey Submitted: April 2006

As with every law school—APPLY EARLY! The fact is that this as well as other ABA schools are becoming more and more selective. Writing a good essay about what you really want to do with your life is a good place to start.

Status: Alumnus/a, full-time
Dates of Enrollment: 8/2002-5/2005
Survey Submitted: April 2006

Based on my experience, the admissions process was quite tough. Like all other law schools, I had to submit a detailed application with references and a personal statement. I was at the very bottom of the statistics they generally accept, so I went through an interview process for them to better assess my anticipated performance at their law school. After a few novelas, I received my acceptance in the mail.

Once I received my acceptance letter and I accepted their offer, I received countless correspondences regarding tuition, financial assistance, housing, roommate options, locale of San Diego, and many more helpful programs. The staff and administration will extremely supportive in helping me move from Buffalo, New York to San Diego, California. As for the selectivity of the applicants, I am not aware of the statistics, but I do know that they have increased every year since I started. I know that it is likely I would not be able to attend TJSL if I applied today.

Status: Alumnus/a, part-time
Dates of Enrollment: 9/2000-12/2003
Survey Submitted: April 2006

I thought it was pretty straightforward. I completed an application and an essay. The only advice I can give is to be honest on both. If you don't think you will qualify as a full-time student because your grades or LSAT are high enough, consider a part-time program. You can transfer to a full-time program later.

Status: Current student, full-time
Dates of Enrollment: 8/2005-Submit Date
Survey Submitted: April 2006

The admissions process was relatively easy. It was not easier or more difficult than the other programs that I applied to. The admissions department is incredibly nice and helpful and are willing to work with students to make the process relatively painless.

Status: Current student, full-time
Dates of Enrollment: 8/2004-Submit Date
Survey Submitted: February 2006

This school is one of the easier law schools to get into. The application itself was simple and standard—no surprises here. TJ uses LSAT score-based scholarships to lure you into choosing TJ over other (probably better) schools. The catch is that if you're not in the top 10 percent of the class, you'll lose the scholarship. TJ uses 2.0 as a median grade, and requires a 3.0 to keep the scholarship.

The school says: "Thomas Jefferson School of Law offers a variety of need and merit-based aid, and uses its funds for both recruitment and retention. There is a broad array of scholarship funds and criteria available to students. LSAT scores are NOT the only criteria considered when awarding scholarships to students."

Read all of Vault's Law School Surveys at www.vault.com/lawschool — get complete surveys on top law schools, expert advice on applicaton essays, LSAT prep and more.

VAULT CAREER LIBRARY   67

Status: Current student, full-time
Dates of Enrollment: 1/2004-Submit Date
Survey Submitted: January 2005

First, I needed to register for and take the LSAT exam. To prepare for the exam, I took a preparatory course through the San Diego College of Extended Studies. I also needed to register for a database LSDAS. I then had to have my undergraduate transcripts sent to the schools that I was applying to. Then, I had to submit my application fee of $75. I strongly recommend taking a prep class for the LSAT because many schools, including Thomas Jefferson, award scholarships based on your LSAT score. Admission to the school is also based on your score combined with your GPA and one can help make up for the other.

Status: Current student, full-time
Dates of Enrollment: 8/2003-Submit Date
Survey Submitted: July 2004

There is an interview and essay process. Selectivity depends on when you apply but the school seems to accept a lot of people in order to increase numbers rather than have a huge dropout rate. They have a low retention rate.

Academics

Status: Alumnus/a, full-time
Dates of Enrollment: 8/2002-5/2005
Survey Submitted: May 2006

The course work at Thomas Jefferson was challenging and laid the groundwork for my success as a lawyer. All of the professors were not only experts in their respective fields, but most were experienced in real-world practice. This confluence of academic expertise and real-world know-how made each class that much more rewarding and valuable. Every professor had an open-door policy for questions, follow-ups, extra attention, etc., and that open-door policy continues for alumni.

When I recently got stuck with a Dormant Commerce Clause issue in practice (believe it or not, but it can happen) I called up my old Con Law prof. She immediately called me back and I spent a half-hour picking her brain about all those cases that I had forgotten from Con Law and all of the recent developments. Her insights were invaluable and my adversary was thrown for a loop when I was prepared to brief and argue those issues.

I never had any difficulty getting the classes I needed/wanted, and found the array of core classes and electives to be very diverse. I don't have a bad word to say about any prof I had. Of course, some were better than others, but all were committed to their craft and did their job to the best of their abilities. All in all, I don't believe I could have found a faculty more committed to making their students better lawyers and better people.

Status: Alumnus/a, part-time
Dates of Enrollment: 8/2000-5/2004
Survey Submitted: May 2006

Following the recommended schedule for students planning to take the California bar exam, the classes are readily available and conveniently scheduled. Getting the electives you want may be difficult. If there are specific classes you want, you may have to wait a year or two (as a part-time student) before that class fits in with the recommended program. Taking classes in the summer is highly recommended, as you have a better selection of electives with no set schedule to try to juggle.

Status: Alumnus/a, full-time
Dates of Enrollment: 8/2001-5/2004
Survey Submitted: April 2006

Academics are what you make of it. The workload was tolerable. I would not have been able to work a full-time job, but was able to intern throughout my years of attendance. Quality of classes and professors varied. Most were excellent. Some professors seemed more impressed with their titles than with their role as educators. By listening to my classmates about their experiences, I believe I was able to select some of the better classes/professors. But, as with everything, the academic program is only as valuable as you make it. The opportunities are there, but you need to reach for them.

Status: Alumnus/a, part-time
Dates of Enrollment: 1/2001-12/2004
Survey Submitted: April 2006

Although the JD program was difficult for a full-time employee, I truly enjoyed the academics, the challenge and the education I received. Most all of the professors were true professionals and I learned a great deal from them. The workload was arduous, but doable. I don't believe I was unable to enroll in any class I desired. The classes were meaningful.

Status: Alumnus/a, full-time
Dates of Enrollment: 8/2002-5/2005
Survey Submitted: April 2006

The academic nature of the program at TJSL is very law student friendly. They focus their attention to teaching the law and less on making it a competitive sport for who receives the highest grade. Socratic Method is, of course, the method of choice for all professors and in my opinion the only way to teach the law.

The classes start out larger in the beginning classes and then get progressively smaller as you complete semesters. The classes are very demanding and require a heavy workload, which is to be expected. Each class is taught by world-accredited professors in their respective areas of law, and each student is privy to some of the leading scholars for whatever elective he/she decides to pursue later in law school.

During my three years at TJSL, I never once had a problem getting into any class that I requested on my semester class schedule request. They generally try to accommodate everyone that wants to take that class during a specific semester.

Grading is always a shock for students who first come to law school because at TJSL there is generally a midterm worth 10 percent of your grade and a final worth 90 percent of your grade for the class. Some classes didn't have a midterm, so your final was worth 100 percent of your grade. Professors really did a good job of including everything covered in the class for inclusion in the final exam. Students who performed the best on the exam really knew their material and how to apply that material to the given fact pattern.

I am not exactly positive as to how much reading was required during the week per class, but I would say it was in the vicinity of 80 to 120 pages a week. Times that by four or five classes and you didn't have much free time.

All of the professors had plenty of office hours to ask them questions and even the dean himself had plenty of office hours to ask him questions. I really was surprised at that because the undergraduate university I came from had a law school and the dean was never seen by the student body, let alone made available to discuss questions.

Status: Alumnus/a, part-time
Dates of Enrollment: 9/2000-12/2003
Survey Submitted: April 2006

TJSL is a good school for many reasons. It isn't as impressive on the resume as better known schools. However, if you want hands-on attention from your professors, it is the place for you. I have a learning disability and I really believe that I would not have finished law school without the personal attention of the faculty and staff. I passed the bar on my first try. I feel like TJSL was a good foundation for my successful legal career.

Status: Current student, full-time
Dates of Enrollment: 8/2004-Submit Date
Survey Submitted: February 2006

Most of the professors are good teachers with impeccable credentials. Some of the classes are solid, while others seem to lack coherence—the adjuncts often don't know what they're doing. If you register early, you should get the classes you want. The workload is heavy as in any law school. The grading system is terrible, if you ask me. For some reason this school uses 2.0 as its median grade in utilizing their curve. Most law schools (which are ranked higher) have higher median grades which makes their grads look better on paper. TJ's reputation is nonexistent and the curve here makes the grads here look worse than grads at other law schools. Why? It's supposed to be better for us (?). Also, the bar passage rate at TJ is disappointing, to say the least.

Regarding grading, the school says: "Unlike many law schools, Thomas Jefferson School of Law does NOT have a fixed mean grading curve. On the contrary, the curve is quite flexible. The typical mean GPA for the law school is approximately 2.8. Grading policies certainly differ among law schools, and as a result, most legal employers now look to class rank in addition to GPA.

"During the past year, the law school instituted a new in-house bar preparation course. The most recent bar pass rate among Thomas Jefferson students who took that course was 67 percent, considerably higher than the state average for first-time bar takers."

Status: Current student, full-time
Dates of Enrollment: 1/2004-Submit Date
Survey Submitted: January 2005

The first year of law school, I had no choices in my schedule: Torts, Contracts, Legal Writing and Property. What I didn't like about law school was that most law schools grade on a curve, therefore, my grade never truly reflected my knowledge. The curve also created an extremely competitive learning environment where no one was willing to help anyone else.

The school says: "Thomas Jefferson School of Law faculty are dedicated educators who pride themselves on being accessible outside the classroom to help students. In fact, The Princeton Review recently ranked the law school in the Top 25 law schools for Professors Accessibility.

"The law school also has an extensive Academic Support Program, which provides assistance to students in all three years of law school, as well as its new Cognitive Academic Protocol program, an exciting innovation in legal education. CAP is the first program in the nation that helps law students gets the most out of their legal studies by effectively integrating cognitive science, cognitive psychology and learning theory into the law school curriculum. CAP is designed to maximize every student's learning potential. Through a series of individual diagnostics, one-on-one coaching sessions and collaborative learning experiences, CAP helps students to understand their own cognitive process and to use their own unique talents to excel in law school. CAP trains students how to achieve their best in law school regardless of their background, learning style or LSAT score."

 Employment Prospects

Status: Alumnus/a, full-time
Dates of Enrollment: 8/2002-5/2005
Survey Submitted: May 2006

I utilized the career/student services dept as best I could to get my foot in the door, and then pounded on the employers I was most interested in. Ultimately, the name of the school will only take you so far—the rest is up to you. So if TJSL doesn't go that far that simply means you may have to try a little harder. That's what I did. I landed a clerk position while in law school with the most prestigious plaintiff's firm in town and I worked my tail off. I knew I couldn't sit back on my laurels and wait for the job to come to me. That clerk position led to me being hired as an associate and I've been here ever since. I worked for it and I earned it, and the folks at Thomas Jefferson were behind me all the way.

Status: Alumnus/a, part-time
Dates of Enrollment: 8/2000-5/2004
Survey Submitted: May 2006

Historically, it has been difficult for a TJSL graduate to get a job at a prestigious firm. This has changed in the past couple of years, and more and more high profile firms are hiring TJSL graduates for competitive associate positions. Still, plan on having high grades to join that elite group.

Status: Alumnus/a, full-time
Dates of Enrollment: 8/2001-5/2004
Survey Submitted: April 2006

This is one area where I feel the school did not help at all. My key internship that I landed while in law school was more because of a work connection I had before law school. I was a top student at Thomas Jefferson (top 10 percent). I applied to over 400 jobs during my final year and after graduation, and received less than 10 positive responses. I do have a job now that I absolutely love. But it took me nearly 10 months after graduation and four months after passing the bar to get this job. The career services center does an excellent job in preparing individuals for careers in law. And I believe they have some excellent civil law connections. My goal was to enter the government/criminal field. That was a little tougher.

Status: Alumnus/a, full-time
Dates of Enrollment: 8/2002-5/2005
Survey Submitted: April 2006

TJSL has a great reputation throughout the State of California for the work ethic of TJSL graduates. Not only in CA, but all throughout the country as well. Jobs that students could apply for internships were in the 100s and most of them were paid positions. The various types of jobs graduates obtain are far reaching. Pretty much every area of law that you can think of, TJSL graduates receive jobs in.

The alumni network is amazing and extremely helpful. I am an active member of our alumni network and I still continue to use TJSL alumni to further my development as an attorney. On-campus recruiting and internship opportunities are so numerous that it is almost overwhelming. Whatever your niche may be, there will be an internship for you. I never had a problem getting internships and had several over my career at TJSL.

Status: Current student, full-time
Dates of Enrollment: 8/2003-Submit Date
Survey Submitted: July 2004

The career placement office has a very nice and helpful staff. However, the school is limited because of their reputation, which even in San Diego is limited due to other schools that have better ranking.

The school says: "Thomas Jefferson School of Law is one of three ABA-accredited law schools in San Diego. While Thomas Jefferson is the youngest of the three, only one other school is ranked in a higher tier. Our reputation grows stronger every day as evidenced by the accomplishments of our faculty, students and alumni, and the fact that typically about half of our entering class comes from outside California, making Thomas Jefferson a geographically diverse law school."

Status: Alumnus/a, full-time
Dates of Enrollment: 8/1999-5/2002
Survey Submitted: May 2004

Thomas Jefferson has gained prominence in Southern California in recent years. The current elected District Attorney of San Diego County is Bonnie Dumanis, a TJ grad. You will also find alums as Deputy DAs in Riverside and SD County. Many alums have acquired positions at Find Law as legal commentators, the U.S. Military as JAGs, as well as at top law firms as associates throughout the country.

The career services is in the business of providing you access to legal opportunities. With many of the faculty and alumni practicing in San Diego and Southern California, our network is strong and loyal. Recently, over 300 firms have conducted on-site interviews.

Read all of Vault's Law School Surveys at www.vault.com/lawschool — get complete surveys on top law schools, expert advice on applicaton essays, LSAT prep and more.

VAULT CAREER LIBRARY   69

Quality of Life

Status: Alumnus/a, full-time
Dates of Enrollment: 8/2002-5/2005
Survey Submitted: May 2006

Quality of life at TJ is second to none. The school is located smack-dab in the center of San Diego. Two minutes from Old Town (a great place for a taco or a shot of tequila), three minutes from downtown and five minutes from the beach. The school buildings are nestled into a hillside overlooking the bay and harbor and are surrounded by million-dollar homes on all sides. Not a bad place to go school every day. Parking could be a drag, but I believe they may have fixed that problem since my tenure there.

The campus was completely satisfactory—two buildings, one with a library and admin offices, the other with lecture halls, a nice courtyard and a mini-restaurant. Everything you needed was right there. The sprawling campus, quad, sports center, etc. of undergrad days gone by was no longer necessary. I didn't need it or want it. Rather I simply wanted a convenient place to pull up, go to class, study and go home. Thus, TJ's campus fit my needs perfectly.

Status: Alumnus/a, full-time
Dates of Enrollment: 8/2002-5/2005
Survey Submitted: April 2006

The quality of your life at TJSL is about as close to living in paradise for three years as you can get. The law school does not have a dorm house so you need to get general apartment in the San Diego area. The campus is set in Old Town, San Diego, which is one of the most beautiful areas in all of San Diego. Parking is free and there are plenty of spots.

The law school just purchased another building next to the existing campus, which has opened up so much more room that they are currently planning for what will be done with the new space. The facilities in general are very soothing and create a sense of ease when walking into the classrooms and common areas.

Status: Current student, full-time
Dates of Enrollment: 1/2005-Submit Date
Survey Submitted: April 2006

We just got a new cafeteria and the food is great, a little pricey though. The housing in San Diego is outrageously expensive though. I'm paying $800 a month for a one-bedroom cottage that would probably would be deemed unsuitable for human habitation in the northeast because there is no insulation and the walls are basically no thicker than cardboard. But other students pay closer to $1,100 a month and have much nicer places. Old Town itself is very safe but there are some rough parts of San Diego, so if you are looking for a place to live PLEASE consult the admissions office because there is someone there that can give you information about where you should and should not go apartment hunting.

Status: Current student, full-time
Dates of Enrollment: 8/2004-Submit Date
Survey Submitted: February 2006

San Diego is a really safe city. TJ has no housing—it's basically a commuter school in San Diego's Old Town area that consists of two crappy former office buildings. The buildings are ugly, parking is absolute hell, the library is tiny and a joke (it can't even accommodate the entire 2L class). There are a few places to eat near the school. Also San Diego is one of the most expensive cities in the U.S., which means you have to be rich or borrow A LOT to survive here.

Status: Current student, full-time
Dates of Enrollment: 1/2004-Submit Date
Survey Submitted: January 2005

The life of a law student is tough. I spent most nights studying and am constantly sleep-deprived. I don't have much spare money once my bills are met but it's for the greater good; at least that's what I've been telling myself.

Thomas Jefferson does not provide any assistance with housing but there are many rentals (apartments and houses) nearby campus and around San Diego in general. Different areas of San Diego have different costs of living so that is something very important to look at.

> **The school says:** "Our Student Services Office regularly assists students with a housing newsletter, housing mailings, a roommate program and personalized service. The office also maintains a strong relationship with local housing complexes to learn about available units as early as possible. Thomas Jefferson School of Law was the first law school in San Diego to have a formal housing assistance program."

Status: Alumnus/a, full-time
Dates of Enrollment: 8/1999-5/2002
Survey Submitted: May 2004

TJ is one of best places to complete your legal education. Why? For one, the staff is friendly, competent and devoted. The administration listens to student input. The student body, while I was attending, decided not to allow an attorney who represented convicted child killer David Westerfield to speak at our school on the anniversary of the victim's death. It was a matter of propriety. In any event, how many schools do you know of where the school bends to accommodate the wishes of its students? (This is but one example of many.) At TJ, you are treated as the professionals you will soon be. You are treated with respect and your opinions are given weight.

The facilities at TJ include: a library building with computer terminals, study rooms, classrooms and professors' offices. The courtyard building across the street includes: the student lounge, moot court, student deli, student mailboxes, admin offices, bookstore and open-air courtyard.

> **The school says:** "The library contains a combined book and microform collection of more than 250,000 volumes and volume equivalents in its more than 31,000 square feet of space, and also offers computer labs, private study rooms, study carrels and a variety of other types of seating on two floors. With more than 700 students who attend classes at varying times during the day and evening, the law school is not overcrowded. The number of parking spaces has increased with the purchase of properties adjacent to the law school."

Social Life

Status: Alumnus/a, full-time
Dates of Enrollment: 8/2002-5/2005
Survey Submitted: May 2006

Camaraderie and social life at Thomas Jefferson is great! The environment is such that every student wants to meet every other student. It is not cliquish or stratified in any way. Whether it was skipping classes together to go the beach, dropping into a local tequilaria after classes, or sneaking over to Kelly's Pub (about 50 yards from campus) for a mid-day frosty beverage, everyone was looking for a good time. I was married during my 1L year so I can't speak to the dating scene, but I can say that although I'm married—I'm not dead! The women at TJ, and San Diego in general, are beautiful!

Status: Current student, full-time
Dates of Enrollment: 1/2005-Submit Date
Survey Submitted: April 2006

Every weekend there is a Bar Review night at a local bar. The SBA holds a Barrister's Ball every year and it's very fancy. There's also a diversity picnic every year and that's always a blast. Hillcrest is just up the hill and there are tons of nice little restaurants that don't cost an arm and a leg. The local theatres (live) have really good student discounts. The movie theatre at Fashion Valley also has student discounts.

As for student clubs—there are a lot of them. If you have an interest then there is most likely a club for it. And if there isn't, the good thing is that you can form one relatively easy. Everything from intermural sports, the surf club, environmental club to the immigration society and moot court. Several of the groups on campus also get some big speakers to come in. I encourage all of the students to go to the speakers because they are sometimes more educational than the coursework—no offense to torts but it's just not my thing.

Status: Alumnus/a, full-time
Dates of Enrollment: 8/2002-5/2005
Survey Submitted: April 2006

The social life at TJSL cannot be beat! Between Student Bar Association-sponsored bar/nightclub events and general student organization events, there is always something to do on the weekend or even during the week. San Diego has some of the coolest and best clubs/bars that I've ever been too and they are all only five to 10 minutes away from the law school. Some of the favorite student places to go hang out or party at are: Henry's Pub, Kelly's Pub, Onyx, CJ's, PB Bar and Grill, Moondoggies, Silver Fox and Cafe Sevilla (this one is my personal favorite!).

Status: Current student, full-time
Dates of Enrollment: 8/2004-Submit Date
Survey Submitted: February 2006

There is a lot to do in San Diego—it's expensive, but you can always find cool restaurants, bars, etc. near the school in downtown. Some students party excessively but most can keep it under control. There are SBA events, and there is something of a dating scene. Again, the cost is high, but if you're willing to borrow you can enjoy yourself for three years while preparing for unemployment or being a legal secretary or paralegal who happens to have a JD.

Status: Alumnus/a, full-time
Dates of Enrollment: 8/1999-5/2002
Survey Submitted: May 2004

Are you kidding!! This is San Diego! Outside the school, activities are only limited by your imagination. Surfing, sailing, kayaking, hiking, biking, camping, gambling and so on. The renovated downtown area with new ballpark has increased the dining, bar and club opportunities tenfold. It was off the hook when I lived there during my 1L days. I cannot imagine the place now with more than eight square blocks of entertainment potential. There's something for everyone. I loved living by the beach and downtown.

The school sponsors many activities with alumni and among current students. We have also had the honor of having Justices Ginsburg and Scalia speak at our school to audiences of 200. Not many law schools can say they have ever seen, more less debated issues with the learned justices. The student clubs and activities are currently expanding. At TJ, we had a strong sense of community. We endeavor to serve San Diego community and look out for one another.

Having attended several large schools in my academic career, Thomas Jefferson provided me all that I needed to succeed. I am proud to be a Thomas Jefferson graduate and feel confident in saying our quality education rivals MANY of the tier one schools. However, don't come to TJ for that reason. Come for the sense of community. Come for the quality of education. Leave with the skills necessary to be successful on the bar, in practice and in life.

Status: Current student, full-time
Dates of Enrollment: 1/2004-Submit Date
Survey Submitted: January 2005

Many law students drink excessively. They go out to bars a lot and the school encourages this by having a "bar night" once a week when the school sponsors drink specials and sometimes even provides free drinks for the students. The class is also an incestuous dating pool. Students are always dating each other, which tends to create high school-type drama with he-said she-said stuff.

> **The school says:** "The law school does NOT encourage students to drink nor does it sponsor a 'bar night' with free or special drinks. School policy also forbids student organizations from using student activity fees to purchase alcohol."

The School Says

Thomas Jefferson School of Law is a private, nonprofit law school perched on a hillside in the historic community of Old Town that overlooks San Diego's scenic harbor. The law school's distinctive features include an experienced and caring faculty, quality classroom instruction, a curricular focus on emerging areas of law as well as traditional areas, and dedication to providing a personalized education in a collegial and supportive environment. Students may begin studies in August or January, enroll in the part-time or full-time programs, attend classes in the day or evening, and graduate in two-and-a-half to four years.

The faculty comprises 36 distinguished teachers and remarkably productive scholars from the nation's leading law schools and diverse practice areas. They have structured business transactions at both the international and domestic levels, and litigated before the World Court at The Hague and the U.S. Supreme Court as well as federal, state and appellate courts. Members of the faculty have written leading law books in use in the U.S., Canada, Europe, and South America. They have testified before Congress and legislatures, have appeared as experts in the media, and have served as legal consultants to our government, the United Nations, and several foreign governments. In addition to meeting individually with students, the faculty engage in all aspects of student life, from advising the more than 30 diverse student organizations on campus to playing on the student-faculty softball team to attending the annual Barrister's Ball.

Thomas Jefferson's balanced and comprehensive curriculum prepares students for practice in any area of the law and ensures that they will graduate with a strong, general legal education. The school offers a variety of forms of support to meet the individual needs of students, including an extensive Academic Success Program and a Preparing to Enter the Profession Program. A large number of electives allows students to tailor their studies to individual interests and career aspirations. The law school also has three academic centers to provide an institutional framework for the study of technological change and globalization and their effects on the law and how changes in society affect our core principles of liberty and equality. Our Moot Court, Mock Trial and Alternate Dispute Resolution teams, for which students may earn credit, have performed exceptionally well in regional and national competitions in the past several years.

Our highly qualified Career Services staff helps students define their career goals and market themselves effectively. Students gain valuable experience by participating in the Clinical Education Program and earn academic credit while working at select government agencies, corporations, law firms and public interest organizations. Qualifying students also can earn credit working for a federal or California state court judge through the Judicial Internship Program. An ever-growing number of students are being offered summer law clerk or summer associate positions as well as post-bar clerkship and post-graduate judicial clerkship positions.

Thomas Jefferson is committed to providing an admissions process that considers each applicant as an individual and seeks to admit students who, through their personal, intellectual or professional background and experience, will contribute to the diversity of the law school community. The school has a rolling admissions process and offers a variety of need- and merit-based aid.

Read all of Vault's Law School Surveys at www.vault.com/lawschool — get complete surveys on top law schools, expert advice on applicaton essays, LSAT prep and more.

VAULT CAREER LIBRARY   71

University of California, Berkeley

Boalt Hall School of Law
Admissions Office
5 Boalt Hall
Berkeley, CA 94720-7200
Admissions phone: (510) 642-2274
Admissions fax: (510) 643-6222
Admissions e-mail: admissions@law.berkeley.edu
Admissions URL: http://www.law.berkeley.edu/admissions/

 ## Admissions

Status: Alumnus/a, full-time
Dates of Enrollment: 8/2001-6/2004
Survey Submitted: March 2006

Grades and LSAT scores are still the primary factors. For the essay, put some thought into why you are going to law school. I didn't really have a good answer because I didn't really know and that hurt the quality of my essay (thankfully I had good grades and LSAT scores). Also, in the essay emphasize unique characteristics of any type. Admitted students typically had done fascinating and amazing things (other advanced degrees, foreign languages, living or being born in other countries, political experience, starting one's own business, Olympic training, etc.). Anything that makes you stand out should be included. I didn't have anything like that, but after two years of law school realized that my religion had been involved in several important First Amendment cases. Since then I've learned a lot about the role that legal advocacy plays in my religious faith and if I had it to do over, that is something I would emphasize (members of my religion are still pretty rare at law schools, particularly competitive ones).

> **Regarding admissions, UC Berkeley says:** "The law school uses an holistic review process in which no one factor is valued over another."

Status: Alumnus/a, full-time
Dates of Enrollment: 9/2002-5/2005
Survey Submitted: March 2006

No interview. Simply standard admissions application. Emphasis on good LSAT score and undergrad grades from good undergrad school. Essay is what makes you a "real" person and I think Boalt emphasizes this. Truly consider what you want to say, not merely what you think they want to hear. Don't be afraid to be vulnerable and expose past mistakes or challenges; I think that is the most courageous of all and Boalt admissions recognizes that.

Status: Alumnus/a, full-time
Dates of Enrollment: 8/2002-5/2005
Survey Submitted: March 2006

The admissions committee is comprised of faculty members, each paired with a student. The faculty member makes the final decision with input from the student. I served on the admissions committee in my second year, so I can speak to this.

While Berkeley does have numerical cut-offs, both for students who will be automatically admitted and those who will be automatically denied, it looks more carefully than most schools at those in the middle. So, unless your LSAT score and GPA are extremely high and you think you'll be an automatic admit, put a lot of time into your essay and choosing your references. As for your essay, make it personal and interesting. Keep in mind that human beings will be reading your essay, and that they see tons of them. Most of them are boring. Make sure yours isn't.

Status: Alumnus/a, full-time
Dates of Enrollment: 8/2000-5/2003
Survey Submitted: May 2006

Boalt has auto-admits, auto-denies and the bulk of the applicants go into the consideration pile where the personal essays set people apart. Everyone has good GPAs and LSATs. My LSAT was low 163 but my GPA was high (3.95) from a good school. My personal essay was about "overcoming adversity," which is a theme they love to see. They give a lot of credence to life and work experience. Boalt has the highest over-35 population of any top school.

Status: Alumnus/a, full-time
Dates of Enrollment: 8/2003-5/2005
Survey Submitted: March 2006

Edward Tom, the Head of Admissions, told me that he reads the personal essay before looking at any of the numbers. I did not score that well on the LSAT—I was below the 25 percent threshold—and I believe that I got in on the strength of my GPA and my essay. While there's not much that you can do to change your numbers, I think that Boalt is unique in terms of the weight it gives to the essay, and I would encourage applicants to focus on writing a good and unique essay.

Status: Alumnus/a, full-time
Dates of Enrollment: 8/2001-5/2004
Survey Submitted: March 2005

I had the advantage of being a California resident. Also, although competition was tight and Berkeley was Top 10 at the time of my application, I knew that certain traits would help me get in despite my good-but-not-great LSATs, average undergraduate grades and diverse but insubstantial and non-committal work experience. Fact is that UC schools need international students (I am a permanent resident and citizen of a "desirable" country) to diversify in more ways than race, creed and major.

Status: Alumnus/a, full-time
Dates of Enrollment: 8/1997-5/2000
Survey Submitted: March 2005

I was a resident of Georgia when I applied to Boalt Hall. Boalt is a very selective school for out-of-state students; my understanding is that they receive as many as 4,000 applications for 125 slots. You should have top grades and top LSAT scores. I don't remember any interview component of the process. The essay was the standard, "Why do you want to go to law school?" essay. Try not to write an essay that begins: "Ever since I watched [insert TV law program here], I have wanted to be a lawyer," or "I want to be a lawyer to make the world a better place." My impression during my time at Boalt is that the admissions committee best liked essays that said something concrete and different about the applicant.

Status: Current student, full-time
Dates of Enrollment: 8/2003-Submit Date
Survey Submitted: June 2004

I have extensive experience with the admissions process at Boalt Hall because I applied three times before (finally) getting in! That said, I am well-informed of the intricacies and details of the entire process.

I cannot emphasize enough that the essay is by far the most critical component of the entire process, particularly for the majority of applicants (those who are on the fence with regard to numbers—namely, LSAT scores and GPAs), and particularly at Boalt Hall. In the face of Proposition 209 in California, students, faculty and the administration have had to fight severe battles to admit students of color into every year's incoming class. Numbers are no longer enough. Boalt Hall takes its admissions process VERY seriously, and is truly committed to admitting a diverse class. I serve on BHSA (Boalt Hall Student Association), and am closely involved with the admissions process through the Student admissions committee. I can tell you that the amount of time, energy and passion an applicant pours into her personal statement is directly correlated to that applicant's likelihood of procuring an offer of admission into the school. Because

Boalt Hall is legally unable to set aside quotas or seats for minority students, the admissions committee is all the more focused on paying close attention to applicants' statements, extracurricular activities, public interest experience and more [than just numbers].

Like any law school, there is a select contingent of "spots" set aside for those applicants who "make the grade (the numbers)." For the rest, the majority of incoming applicants, WHO YOU ARE is what we look to see. Tell us about a life-changing experience you had working at a homeless shelter; share with us the challenges of growing up in a community with a different religious or ethnic composition from your own. Provide us insight into who you are as a person as opposed to what you do every day. The last two times I applied, nothing about my numbers changed. Of course I gained one more year of work experience, but ultimately, what truly secured me a seat in the incoming class was the amount of time and energy that I invested into the personal statement. Almost every school I applied to not only admitted me, but also wrote me a separate note to commend me on a well-written, thorough personal statement. At Boalt Hall, the admissions director recognized me on the first day because he put my face to a name on that statement. I cannot emphasize enough how crucial this is!

Status: Current student, full-time
Dates of Enrollment: 8/2001-Submit Date
Survey Submitted: October 2003

In most regards, Boalt is a typical Top 10 law school with respect to its admissions policies; that is, heavy emphasis is placed on an applicant's grades and LSAT score. My student contacts on the admissions committee tell me that any applicant with approximately a 3.8/170, or any reasonable facsimile thereof (i.e., 4.0/167), is automatically admitted. In such instances, an applicant may expect a positive response within two weeks of submitting his or her application. With that said, however, Boalt also differs significantly from most of its Top 10 brethren. The school has attempted to deal with California's Proposition [209], which, simply characterized, banned affirmative action programs of state-funded entities, by engaging in policies that may be characterized as either: (a) attempts to ensure an adequate level of diversity in each entering class; or (b) "backdoor" affirmative action. These policies are manifested in the school's treatment of a special optional section of the admissions application, as well as the admissions committee's treatment of an applicant's personal statement. In each instance, the school actively seeks out both "unique experiences" and evidence of various types of hardship, each of which tend to correlate highly with some racial and ethnic backgrounds. Of course, those from a "majority" ethnic background may also benefit from such special considerations in certain instances.

Another issue that is related (albeit only tangentially) to the school's diversity battles is its clear emphasis on candidates' undergraduate grade point averages as compared to their LSAT scores. Again, while this is merely an opinion of mine—one which I share with many others—this is another means by which the school justifies admitting candidates with LSAT scores that would not allow them to be admitted to other top JD programs. I do not mean to insinuate that this policy is only in effect for those of certain backgrounds, however; those I have spoken with who are "in the know" indicate that LSAT scores are de-emphasized, vis-a-vis GPA, for all candidates. Boalt's policy on this matter makes it a great choice for applicants who did very well as undergrads but had an uncharacteristically bad day on the day of the LSAT.

Other, perhaps less interesting ways in which Boalt differs from other schools are: (1) its reputation for making relatively quick admissions decisions; and (2) its heavy emphasis on personal recruiting. In an attempt to land top candidates, Boalt tends to get back to the most desirable candidates (among some 6,000 annual applicants) very quickly. Additionally, various alumni and student identity groups personally contact many applicants to convince them to attend Boalt over more prestigious schools in its peer group (i.e., Harvard, Stanford, Yale and perhaps NYU and Columbia). While this is not particularly unique, it is emphasized at Boalt to an extremely high degree, particularly for highly coveted members of minority groups and many East Coast students. Due to the issues presented above, I have actively encouraged my friends considering Boalt to compose application materials tailored specifically to the areas emphasized by the school. This, in my opinion, has helped them gain admission even though they were only borderline candidates.

Academics

Status: Alumnus/a, full-time
Dates of Enrollment: 9/1994-5/1998
Survey Submitted: November 2005

The professors are fabulous! They seem a lot more conscientious and interested in student learning than the professors I had as an undergrad. Other than common "core" coursework such as Criminal Law, Contracts or Civil Procedure, many of my Boalt classes were small seminars, with a lot of faculty-student interactions during and after class. The professors also just seemed like fantastic human beings. (The younger, single ones sometimes went out to party with us!)

Boalt Hall is much less of a pressure-cooker than most other schools. When I attended, Boalt and Yale were the only law schools to not really have letter grades, nor rank students. Boalt uses a system of HH (high honors, for the top 10 percent of students), H (honors, for the next 20 or 30 percent) and the remainder, which is the majority 60 or 70 percent, get P (pass). But at a GPA level (because some employers and grad schools require this) all HH's and H's are translated into A's, and P's are B's. So even the "worst" students can graduate with a 3.0. You see how irrelevant the grades are? Using the HH to P scale, I actually got decent "grades" from Boalt. But to this day I don't know what my GPA or class rank were. And while my first employer asked for a transcript, no one has ever asked my GPA or class ranking.

> **Regarding the grading system, the school says:** "We have five possible grades: High Honors (HH), which can be awarded to the top 10 percent in the class; Honors (H), to the next 30 percent; and Pass (P), to the remaining 60 percent. Then you can also have a PC (this is a passing grade, but it is below par, substandard) or an NC (No Credit—in other words, you fail the class)."

Status: Alumnus/a, full-time
Dates of Enrollment: 8/2001-6/2004
Survey Submitted: March 2006

I would say that the classes are rigorous, challenging, but doable. The more driven and consistent you can be in studying through all three years, the more opportunities and success you will have. Those that succeed during the first year are those who can maintain the grueling pace for the entire year without burning out. The time commitment is high and sometimes unexpected. The same is true of the whole three years. Grades from all three years will have an impact on clerkships, future employment and other opportunities. I was unable to maintain the necessary level of effort to achieve the same success in my second and third years as I did in my first. I regret that. Most classes are easy to get into, but popular professors' classes generally fill up quickly. So while guaranteed of getting Evidence, you might not get it with your first choice professor. Looking back, professors are the key to the entire experience. Taking classes from interesting professors, or professors you get along with makes all the difference. The best classes are the ones that engage you even when you're tired, stressed and bored. Those classes almost always have great professors. The quality of professors at Boalt is very high. Not all professors are great, but many of them are. There are rumors that grading at Boalt is somehow less rigorous or less competitive. It's true that there are minor differences, but you'll be better prepared if you just assume that it's exactly the same as everywhere else.

Status: Alumnus/a, full-time
Dates of Enrollment: 8/2001-5/2004
Survey Submitted: March 2006

I think the academics were great at Berkeley. There were always tons of different options available and after first semester, we had almost complete flexibility of schedule. Even if a class was full, there was almost always a way to get in—either through the dean or by attending the first day of class. Shopping around was pretty easy. I attended several classes on the first day and decided against them. Or I heard from a friend about a great class and came on the second day to sign up. The small classes (less than 15) are really the treasure of the school. I liked the array of classes that catered to specific topics. For instance, Tort Stories, which was in-depth look at famous torts cases. Brilliant! Very limited competition, happy people, and plenty of time to get involved in extracurricu-

Read all of Vault's Law School Surveys at www.vault.com/lawschool — get complete surveys on top law schools, expert advice on applicaton essays, LSAT prep and more.

VAULT CAREER LIBRARY   73

lars. LOVED IT! Similarly, workload was very light, especially compared with my friends at other schools.

Status: Alumnus/a, full-time
Dates of Enrollment: 9/2002-5/2005
Survey Submitted: March 2006

Getting into classes generally was not a problem. Classes ranged from large lecture style with 100+ students to small skills courses or seminars with fewer than 10 students. It greatly depended on your individual interests. As for professors, like at any teaching institution, some were brilliant teachers and others, although brilliant legal scholars, were terrible teachers. Most tried, some simply weren't as talented in teaching. Too much politics, though more often fueled by the students rather than the professors in the classroom.

Status: Alumnus/a, full-time
Dates of Enrollment: 8/2002-5/2005
Survey Submitted: March 2006

Berkeley is very strong academically, especially in intellectual property, environmental law, constitutional law and critical theories. The past few years, the law school has been using more adjunct professors to teach classes, which results in more practical knowledge but less academic depth. Popular classes are probably as difficult to get as at any other school. The professors at Berkeley are great, and they're getting better. The new dean has embarked on a capital campaign, and it has already yielded enough money to hire several more topnotch professors.

Status: Alumnus/a, full-time
Dates of Enrollment: 8/2001-5/2004
Survey Submitted: March 2005

Truth is, despite everyone's complaint about arbitrariness (due to blind grading in huge classes and paper options in more personal seminars), Boalt is as good as it gets with respect to grades. I may have been one of the few to receive a sub-pass grade, but I made up for it with many H's in my second and third years, with a lot less work. We should know this by now: do what people expect of you, play within the system and you'll do fine.

Professors are accessible, there aren't too many pure-Socratic profs anymore, and this is Berkeley, so many students tend to be more liberal than at Harvard or Yale. BUT the law school is NOT the undergrad campus, and some die-hard liberals are surprised to find that there is a sizeable conservative constituency here (part of which probably due to backlash against Berkeley politics). It's fun to play devil's advocate, and it challenges these liberals just a little. After all, the rest of the country sure ain't Berkeley.

Status: Alumnus/a, full-time
Dates of Enrollment: 8/2001-5/2004
Survey Submitted: March 2005

Berkeley's reputation for being laid-back is well-deserved. A handful of students were "gunners," those who sat in the front and always raised their hands, but most of us just took it easy, did 90 percent of the reading and went to class maybe 80 percent of the time. Extracurriculars were a huge part of my life as a JD student. I assistant taught a Moot Court class, worked as a research assistant to a professor, edited two journals and was a member of another journal. That made things more fun.

Status: Alumnus/a, full-time
Dates of Enrollment: 8/1998-5/2001
Survey Submitted: April 2004

Academics are topnotch, but don't expect the classes to fully prepare you for the bar. Boalt has the nation's top ranked IP law program, and features several up-and-coming IP law professor superstars. Boalt also offers numerous practice clinics and practical skills classes. I did not find it difficult to get into most of the classes I wanted, though the school had a practice of scheduling some of the most popular classes and professors at the same times so as to force students to prioritize. In general, I found Boalt professors to be helpful and easily approachable.

Boalt also does not officially rank its students; though Boalt will provide judges with ranking numbers for purposes of considering students for clerkships. (It is against school policy to use these numbers for any other purpose.) The only

other "ranking" the school does is recognize the top ranked student upon graduation, and award students membership in Order of the Coif (which requires student to be in the top 10 percent). Workload was heavy in the first year, but manageable (and self inflicted) in the second and third years.

Status: Current student, full-time
Dates of Enrollment: 8/2002-Submit Date
Survey Submitted: November 2003

If you are seeking a school to teach you how to be a lawyer, go to a third-tier law school. If you are looking for an intellectually stimulating and vivacious environment, Boalt is your school. The fall term tends to be much better in terms of class selection, but overall most substantive courses are available and open. The smaller seminars tend to go first come, first serve, but professors do make exceptions.

Status: Current student, full-time
Dates of Enrollment: 8/2001-Submit Date
Survey Submitted: October 2003

In any event, it is easy to learn of the "top instructors," along with other insider tips as to how to succeed at Boalt, in part because of the ease of which Boalt students may join journals and other student groups. Additionally, the school has several clinical opportunities, both inside and outside the Boalt environment. Indeed, these opportunities are more plentiful than at most top schools, and cover a broad range of subject areas. Clinical opportunities often, but not always spring from some of the academic "centers" (such as the Center for Social Justice and the Center for Law and Technology) that have become ingrained in the Boalt community.

Employment Prospects

Status: Alumnus/a, full-time
Dates of Enrollment: 8/2001-5/2004
Survey Submitted: March 2006

After going to Berkeley, the world is your oyster. I had a very easy time getting multiple offers in each city I was looking in. And by multiple, I mean almost 10 in both Chicago and LA. I was totally happy with my job search and I know all of my friends and classmates felt the same way. Berkeley has a fabulous reputation. Employers were impressed and were enthusiastic about learning more about my time in Berkeley. I know that my friends were able to get jobs at big firms, small firms, public interest organizations and in the government. On-campus recruiting was a very intense program, but I think Berkeley does a great job of helping you through the process. It was very easy for me to get through it and to do well.

Status: Alumnus/a, full-time
Dates of Enrollment: 8/2002-5/2005
Survey Submitted: March 2006

There are a wide variety of public sector, public interest and private sector jobs, with BigLaw firms and some government agencies recruiting on campus. Alumni tend to look out for one another. Any angst my classmates seemed to have was not due to concerns about finding good jobs, but rather due to concerns about finding the good job that each person wanted. This is always most difficult in public interest work.

Status: Alumnus/a, full-time
Dates of Enrollment: 8/2002-5/2005
Survey Submitted: March 2006

Berkeley is one of the most prestigious, if not the most prestigious, public law school in the country. Employers know that, and actively seek out Berkeley students. There is a coordinated on-campus recruiting program. In the spirit of Berkeley's egalitarian nature, students choose employers to interview with rather than vice versa. So everyone has the chance to interview, no matter what their grades are. Students can get jobs nationwide. I had friends go on to work in New York, San Francisco, Los Angeles, Chicago, Boston, Texas and other smaller markets. Alumni of Berkeley are proud to have gone there, and so there is a solid alumni program.

Status: Current student, full-time
Dates of Enrollment: 8/2003-Submit Date
Survey Submitted: November 2004

Terrific reputation with employers. Not a problem to get a law firm job with adjacent law firm, even if your grades are mediocre. I got poor grades but multiple offers. Most people in my class got multiple job offers. Usually law students have the honor of picking and choosing. On-campus recruiting is great—great access to firms and job of your dreams. Very helpful career counselors. I am very happy with the school and the access I got to employers of my choice. I don't know much about alumni, but they must be very good at what they do, because Boalt students are able to enjoy the respect and great reputation.

Status: Alumnus/a, full-time
Dates of Enrollment: 8/1999-12/2003
Survey Submitted: March 2005

The alumni network is improving, but is still nothing much compared to the top Ivies. With that as with everything else, you need to make an effort to go find alumni that are in the jobs in which you are interested. I find that the best alumni networks at Berkeley are the networks in clubs and fraternities. Always stay involved in extracurricular activities at Berkeley. There are thousands of things to choose from, and what you choose will no doubt help you with employment prospects afterwards.

Status: Alumnus/a, full-time
Dates of Enrollment: 8/2000-5/2003
Survey Submitted: March 2005

In California, Boalt and Stanford are regarded as the best schools by employers. With rare exceptions, any student that wants a job, in or outside of California, at a national firm can get one, regardless of grades. Clerkships are also common. Boalt is also a large feeder to the public interest and government sector jobs. Some students in my class were also offered professorships directly out of law school. This is not to say, though, that the ease at which Boalt students are given jobs has anything to do with career services. Boalt is a public school and when it comes to departments like career services, it shows. However, because of Boalt's reputation, firms line up to conduct on-campus interviews and most students have no problem landing the job they want.

Status: Alumnus/a, full-time
Dates of Enrollment: 8/2000-5/2003
Survey Submitted: April 2004

IP-related jobs are easy to come by. A lot of alumni contact. The technology law journal hosts weekly luncheon sponsored by firms. So you get an idea about a firm and its people from very early on and have a chance to meet practitioners whenever you want to.

Status: Current student, full-time
Dates of Enrollment: 8/2002-Submit Date
Survey Submitted: November 2003

Privates sector: with the exception of a few cities, Boalt attracts potential employers from all over the U.S. and the world. With over 300 employers coming to campus every year, if you want a job, there is probably an employer who will hire you.

Public interest/public sector: Boalt is keenly aware of its duties to its student body and actively participates in the PIPS (Public Interest Public Sector) day. The career office provides assistance with both private and public sector job searches and even helps you tailor your resume.

Intern/extern: Boalt is very flexible with internships and externships. Just go through the proper channels and you will have no problems.

Status: Current student, full-time
Dates of Enrollment: 8/2001-Submit Date
Survey Submitted: October 2003

The "gunners," many of whom are on the *California Law Review* and/or have several HH grades on their transcripts, have the same employment options as top students from Top Five *U.S. News & World Report* schools. Such students regularly secure summer and postgraduate positions at Top Five Vault law firms, and Boalt places many of its students into prestigious appellate clerkships. After that, however, the employment issue becomes more complicated.

One reason for the complication is, in a paradigmatic chicken-and-egg situation, Boalt has a great many students entirely disinterested in large firm practice. This is due both to Boalt's admission policies and some of the policies emphasized by the school's placement office (and many of its faculty members). Such students typically enjoy great success in landing highly competitive government positions and jobs doing public interest work. Boalt is a great choice for students interested in performing such work after graduation.

 **Quality of Life**

Status: Alumnus/a, full-time
Dates of Enrollment: 8/2001-6/2004
Survey Submitted: March 2006

The only negative is cost. Living in the Bay Area is expensive! Beyond that, the quality of life issues are some of the biggest reasons to consider Boalt Hall. The Bay Area has numerous options for entertainment, dining, politics, art, etc., that make it a great place to spend three years. Berkeley itself has great public transportation, great restaurants (both cheap and expensive), good local music, museums, etc. Boalt students usually have several intramural teams that compete against other Berkeley students (grad and undergrad) in sports such as soccer and softball. Housing can be a challenge, but it's gotten better. There is more on-campus housing for undergrad and grad students, which frees up more of the area apartments to rent. You have to accept less space for more money, but you get to live in a great place.

Status: Alumnus/a, full-time
Dates of Enrollment: 8/2001-5/2004
Survey Submitted: March 2006

Quality of life at Berkeley is great. You are living in a college town that is attached to a fabulous metropolis like San Francisco. I couldn't have asked for a better law school experience. My first and second year, I lived in Berkeley in a fabulous house in a quaint neighborhood 10-minute walk from the school. It was safe and quiet, with great restaurants, shops, etc. The campus is beautiful and green, with lots of grass and trees. Campus activism is present in full-force and there is always something going on. The gym was great, as was the library, where I spent a lot of time.

The law school is on the north side of campus, which is good because it is a little bit isolated from the hustle and bustle of a crazy college life. But all of that is just a couple of minutes walk away. Third year I moved to San Francisco, which was an amazing experience that I highly recommend. Berkeley made that move and commute very easy by allowing me to have a flexible schedule (class two or three days a week) and I got to take advantage of all that Northern California had to offer. I had enough free time to be able to travel around too, to Hawaii, Napa Valley, Lake Tahoe. It was perfect!

Status: Alumnus/a, full-time
Dates of Enrollment: 8/2000-5/2003
Survey Submitted: March 2006

The student body at Boalt is very supportive of each other. The faculty and staff are also supportive. The main campus is a lot of fun and exciting if you make yourself get down there. Many law students will TA on the undergraduate campus in their second and third years just to be a part of UC Berkeley if they did not attend undergraduate there. The housing is not cheap and the university housing is fair to middling. They do have a nice complex for married students with families.

The cafe at the law school is absolutely horrible but by the end of your first year, you will be eating your lunch at the Haas School of Business on a regular basis (they have the best cafe of the graduate schools) or going down the street to eat lunch. Everyone thinks that Cafe Zeb is terrible, but no one ever does anything about it. The neighborhoods are mostly safe but there is a smattering of crime in and around the city so be careful at night.

Read all of Vault's Law School Surveys at www.vault.com/lawschool — get complete surveys on top law schools, expert advice on applicaton essays, LSAT prep and more.

VAULT CAREER LIBRARY   75

Status: Alumnus/a, full-time
Dates of Enrollment: 9/2002-5/2005
Survey Submitted: March 2006

The students in general were very laid-back and non-competitive for a law school. In fact, the super type-A personalities were looked down upon, so they didn't dominate our school culture. Neighborhood is semi-urban so it has problems inherent in semi-urban areas, but nothing out of the ordinary. The campus is beautiful from the outside, but the interior facilities are considerably under-budgeted, but you should expect this at a state school.

Status: Alumnus/a, full-time
Dates of Enrollment: 8/1999-12/2003
Survey Submitted: March 2005

North Berkeley is quieter and safer than downtown/South Berkeley. However, there are night shuttles that drop you door to door and people to walk you home late at night, so there is really no danger if you take the right precautions. The food around Berkeley is fantastic. There is an incredible number of restaurants available and every kind of food you could want. Food in the dorms is of pretty low quality, unfortunately, but you can just eat out instead. Housing prices are improving in Berkeley, and quality has a very wide range—from dirty, dank holes to modern high-rise apartments. Berkeley has a good amount of tennis courts, pools, a large all weather track, an improving gym and Haas Pavilion, which is a fabulous basketball facility. All that said, Berkeley is a public institution that has been hit by funding costs, so don't expect lavish facilities.

Status: Alumnus/a, full-time
Dates of Enrollment: 8/1998-5/2001
Survey Submitted: April 2004

There are numerous areas to live in the greater Bay Area from which you could commute using BART or other public transit, which is great in the Bay Area. Berkeley is an urban campus, and the city and campus are unique. For someone who is not from Berkeley, I found it at once strange and fascinating. Outside of school there are a million things to do, like spend a lazy summer day visiting numerous festivals in San Francisco, catch an opera, drive a couple hours north and wine taste in Napa Valley. Visit numerous national parks within an hour or two driving distance. There is a fair amount of petty crime in Berkeley (e.g., bikes are stolen often), like any urban area.

Status: Current student, full-time
Dates of Enrollment: 8/2001-Submit Date
Survey Submitted: October 2003

Boalt Hall is no misnomer, but instead true in the literal sense; all the law classes are taught in aging, eclectically built, largely concrete Boalt Hall. The building is located in the southeast corner of the UC Berkeley campus, proximal to the Berkeley Hills and many of the university's sororities and fraternities. It is the product of various expansions over the years and, even for many 3Ls, generally unnavigable without a map. Despite all the expansions, however, space for professors, journals and even classes is lacking. Moreover, only a few of the moderate-sized classrooms contain outlets for laptops or other devices.

The campus itself is a hybrid of a college campus setting and an urban campus setting. Many of the streets surrounding the campus are full of typical university district proprietorships such as record shops, pipe shops, small eateries and so forth. Many of the campus buildings have outdated architecture and, like Boalt itself, resemble concrete bunkers. On the north side of campus, however, one can find large, beautiful college buildings with pillars, marble and the like, and various forested areas and park-like settings are also on the western side of the campus.

> **Regarding housing, the school says:** "A lot of the comments about housing are actually not accurate for this year (or last). There is a housing glut in Berkeley and the Bay Area. Apartments and houses are sitting unrented. Landlords have lowered rents to attract renters. So incoming students should have little or no problem finding housing."

 ## Social Life

Status: Alumnus/a, full-time
Dates of Enrollment: 9/1994-5/1998
Survey Submitted: November 2005

Social life is really great. There is a ton of student clubs and journals. Every week there is a "bar review" held at a different watering hole, and there are frequent off-campus private parties that through word-of-mouth, everyone goes to. There was a pretty big dating scene when I was there—lots of couples, short-term and long-term.

Because of the esteem of UC Berkeley, there are always a ton of famous speakers and cultural activities right on campus. (Some examples of what I did with my friends: seeing the Dalai Lama speak at the Greek Amphitheater, attending dance performances by the likes of Alvin Ailey and Merce Cunningham, right on campus at a large auditorium!) I also attended events offered by other departments, e.g., a talk with Terry Gross (of NPR's Fresh Air program) at Berkeley's Journalism School. To be entertained at Berkeley, you don't have to go anywhere, the best and the world-renowned come to you.

Status: Alumnus/a, full-time
Dates of Enrollment: 8/2001-6/2004
Survey Submitted: March 2006

The truth is that the law school social scene is a little bit schizophrenic. Many people are there to study, study, study. Many people are there for the extra-educational activities (e.g., Law Review or other journals, clubs and speakers, moot court competitions, etc.). There are still people who's primary goal seems to be drinking and partying, but at times it all feels overwhelming. Thus, applicants should expect a slightly more subdued social life than in college.

Status: Alumnus/a, full-time
Dates of Enrollment: 8/2001-5/2004
Survey Submitted: March 2006

By far the best attribute of Berkeley. I met some of the most amazing people, some of whom will be my friends for life. The best thing about Berkeley was that I met and became friends with people who are TOTALLY different from me. After being friends with people exactly like me in college, it was a great experience to meet all sorts of new people, from different races, countries, states, etc. There are TONS of bars in Berkeley, some quite close to the law school. Every Thursday night, everyone would meet up at a bar that was posted Thursday morning. It was a great way to meet people and connect with people who weren't necessarily in your classes. SO FUN! I wish I could do it all over again. There were also lots of parties and social events both in the school and out of the school. I already mentioned Berkeley's fabulous restaurants. We would go out to lunch every day and get some of the best cuisine around; Asian, Mexican, Vegan, hamburgers, hot dogs, salads. You name it, it is close to school. There are tons of clubs available in the law school. Minority groups are thoroughly represented, as are women, people with children, older law students, ecologists, techies, etc. There is truly a group for anyone. I absolutely loved the social life at Berkeley. I have never experienced anything like it!!

Status: Alumnus/a, full-time
Dates of Enrollment: 8/2002-5/2005
Survey Submitted: March 2006

The social life at Berkeley is as good as it can be, given that law students are usually a geeky bunch. I met some of my best friends there. There is a great, wide variety of student organizations. The public interest law foundation, called Berkeley Law Foundation, is very popular and holds an annual auction. The auction is one of the best social events of the year. Also, there is an event called AmJur Day where students who got the best grades in their 1L classes provide their outlines and other study tools to current 1Ls.

Status: Alumnus/a, full-time
Dates of Enrollment: 8/2001-5/2004
Survey Submitted: March 2005

Lots of stuff to do at Boalt. To tell you the truth, I never had this much free time even in college. I had a good time with *Women's Journal*, various keggers (really), etc. Although I took a few years off between undergrad and law school, even those my age and older seemed to regress once at school. It's understandable, and that kind of regression seems a lot more attractive than pretending to be grown-up with 18-hour days.

Status: Alumnus/a, full-time
Dates of Enrollment: 8/1999-12/2003
Survey Submitted: March 2005

Because there are so many organizations at Berkeley, there is always something to do. The city of Berkeley is also a hub for debuts in classical music and dance (Zellarbach), famous speakers (Clinton, Bill Bradley, to name the big political ones) and art. The proximity of San Francisco provides access to great clubs and lounges. Berkeley also has a good number of bars with personalities. As for the dating scene, you're in a school of 20,000 undergraduates. You will not lack for possibilities. The Greek system is strong but not a central part of life; I personally was not a part of it so I can't comment. I'm not going to name student favorites in terms or organizations because those will become obvious if you visit the campus during the school year. Those organizations are great, but make an effort to seek out smaller organizations, as well. You may find one that fits you better. And besides, the spirit of entrepreneurship at Berkeley is huge. Start your own thing, grow a small club into a big one, or be a big part of something already established. The great part about this school is that you have a choice.

Status: Alumnus/a, full-time
Dates of Enrollment: 8/2000-5/2003
Survey Submitted: March 2005

Boalt is a blast. Kegs in the courtyard at least once a week, Bar Review every Thursday night, and plenty of parties. The students are very social with one another and there is true camaraderie. Many of my best friends are people I met in law school. The dating scene is pretty vibrant. While perhaps not the most attractive school in the country, there are enough people that everyone seems to make do. Several of my friends have married people they met at Boalt. The gay scene at Boalt is also vibrant. On-campus mock weddings are held every year. As for bars and clubs, San Francisco is a 20-minute drive or subway ride and has as much of that to offer as any other major city, including a particularly good music scene.

Status: Alumnus/a, full-time
Dates of Enrollment: 8/1999-5/2002
Survey Submitted: April 2004

Lots of great places to eat, cafes to study in or hang out, and bars in Berkeley. Some favorites include Jupiter's, Cafe Strada, Cheeseboard, Yali's, Albatross. Dating is not great, although there were several couples within the law school. The BLF auction and the Barrister's Bash are the two big fancy social events each year.

Read all of Vault's Law School Surveys at www.vault.com/lawschool — get complete surveys on top law schools, expert advice on applicaton essays, LSAT prep and more.

VAULT CAREER LIBRARY   77

University of California, Davis School of Law

UC Davis School of Law
Admission Office
400 Mrak Hall Drive
Davis, CA 95616-5201
Admissions phone: (530) 752-6477
Admissions e-mail: lawadmissions@ucdavis.edu
Admissions URL: http://www.law.ucdavis.edu/admissions/admissions_wel.shtm

 ## Admissions

Status: Current student, full-time
Dates of Enrollment: 8/2004-Submit Date
Survey Submitted: June 2006

The admissions process was very smooth and the staff was very helpful. The school is quite selective, but promotes diversity in its selection process. There seems to be an appreciation of post undergrad, real-life experience that can help an applicant set him or herself apart.

Status: Alumnus/a, full-time
Dates of Enrollment: 9/1974-6/1977
Survey Submitted: May 2006

UCD had many more applicants than positions. It was distinguishing itself by admitting (not discriminating against) women in numbers nearing 50 percent of the class, which was unknown in 1974. It continues to have a very diverse student body.

Status: Alumnus/a, full-time
Dates of Enrollment: 8/1999-5/2002
Survey Submitted: March 2006

When I attended law school, the admissions committee was comprised of four faculty and two student evaluators. It was split into two three-person teams with two faculty and one student per team. The criteria each team evaluated was basically the same: undergraduate school, undergraduate GPA, LSAT score, letters of recommendation, and essay. If the candidate is reviewed by the committee in full then letters of recommendation and essay are reviewed and an admissions decision is made. Accordingly, the importance of an essay and letters of recommendation are important for the bulk of the applicants.

> **The school says:** "UC Davis School of Law index score is not affected by the undergraduate school attended; both the admissions staff and the Admissions Committee consider all factors before a decision is made."

Status: Current student, full-time
Dates of Enrollment: 9/2004-Submit Date
Survey Submitted: July 2005

The admissions process was typical of all law schools I would say. The majority of the students are from California but there are a fair number from other states, too. There are a lot of students from Bay Area schools such as UC Berkeley and Stanford. There were no interviews at Davis. I don't think any law schools request interviews. A unique thing about the admissions committee is that there is one student on it. I've also heard that the committee tends to weigh factors outside of GPA and LSAT greater than some schools also, but I'm not sure how accurate that info is. In general, it still seems like numbers are the first factor.

Status: Current student, full-time
Dates of Enrollment: 9/2002-Submit Date
Survey Submitted: November 2003

Davis Law was, in the not-so-distant past, a fallback school among the Top 30 law schools. Being in an obscure, rural locale didn't help it rise to the top of the list for most applicants. Not so now with 4,400 applications coming in for the Class of 2006; that works out to about 27 applicants for every seat. Admissions at Davis Law is now and will be in the future extremely competitive. The current 1L is chock full of students who attended undergrads such as Yale, Harvard, Berkeley, UCLA, Penn (the Ivy) and Stanford (there is a particularly high representation of Stanford alumni). Now that this high caliber of students has been achieved, it can be a safe bet that they are not about to settle for too much less.

Because Davis Law is not a strict GPA/LSAT ratio school, they tend to attract students who have done so much more than be a regular student: anything from chemistry PhDs from Princeton to former car salesmen. Best advice on admissions: sell your other points besides the basics. That will bring you in line with the current makeup of the student body. Get that application in as early as possible. Again with a school that now has its pick of the best potential students either from the academic or real world, you need to get the front of the line. There isn't an interview process, but the essay portion of the application should be used to answer the questions you know they would ask if they did have an interview process. Also, sell yourself in the same way you would if you were a product in a commercial—get the things out there that will get them to buy you.

Status: Current student, full-time
Dates of Enrollment: 8/2002-Submit Date
Survey Submitted: January 2004

It is getting tougher to get into UC Davis each year. UC Davis is unusual in that it allows for students to serve on the admissions committee. Named after Martin Luther King, Jr., King Hall (as it is known locally) prides itself on commitment to social justice and serving the community. While numbers remain part of the admissions game, applicants should distinguish themselves as well-rounded individuals, with activities demonstrating maturity and a commitment to justice.

Status: Alumnus/a, full-time
Dates of Enrollment: 8/2000-5/2003
Survey Submitted: September 2003

Most public schools—especially law schools—are extremely numbers-driven. However, the Davis admissions committee allows one's personal statement to get added weight where appropriate. To some extent the admissions process is still numbers-driven: based on GPAs, test scores and a few other factors, there are automatic admits and automatic rejects. But unlike many other schools, Davis has an unusually large possibly admit/reject area, where the admissions committee scrutinizes each application. There, the personal statement and particular background of a student may make a huge difference. Also of interest is the fact that there are students (usually two third-years) on the admissions committee. While Davis is certainly among the most selective schools, it is not arbitrarily selective in a purely statistical sense. It makes a great deal of sense to fine-tune one's application to UC Davis, because even nuances can carry a great deal of weight.

Status: Alumnus/a, full-time
Dates of Enrollment: 8/2001-5/2003
Survey Submitted: October 2003

Admissions process seemed straightforward. My LSAT and GPA were above average, but they were the last to actually offer me a spot, later than some higher rated schools. No interview.

 ## Academics

Status: Current student, full-time
Dates of Enrollment: 8/2004-Submit Date
Survey Submitted: June 2006

Classes tend to provide a good balance of traditional Socratic Method with techniques that encourage class discussion. Some second-year students may have a hard time getting into classes with the most popular professors, but the overall quality of the faculty is very strong. There are many great young professors that compliment the amazing older faculty. As with any law school workload is a difficult balance as a first-year, but it was surprisingly less than I expected after hearing horror stories about law school.

Status: Alumnus/a, full-time
Dates of Enrollment: 9/1974-6/1977
Survey Submitted: May 2006

We worked hard but were very collegial—helped each other succeed. Excellent professors. I still keep in touch with them and have engaged some as experts.

Status: Alumnus/a, full-time
Dates of Enrollment: 9/1972-5/1975
Survey Submitted: May 2006

UC Davis and the law school is a very intimate campus. All law school classes in one building. Very accessible professors who were animated, engaging and helpful. Small class sizes because the law school student population is small and no problem with getting into classes I desired.

Status: Alumnus/a, full-time
Dates of Enrollment: 8/1999-5/2002
Survey Submitted: March 2006

Davis has a strong academic reputation. First-year classes are graded on a strict curve. The professors are generally very good with a few exceptions. Popular classes are sometimes difficult to get because of the limited class sizes that the law school building can accommodate.

Status: Current student, full-time
Dates of Enrollment: 9/2004-Submit Date
Survey Submitted: July 2005

The nice thing about UC Davis is although the students are very smart and bright, the competition is not as grueling as other schools can be. My classmates were all very friendly and helpful. The sections are very small (30 or 60 students) so we got to know our professors very well. Torts, K, Civ Pro, and Property are year-long classes at Davis so by the end of the year all of the professors knew me by name.

Status: Current student, full-time
Dates of Enrollment: 9/2002-Submit Date
Survey Submitted: November 2003

Davis Law's academics are, in sum, precisely aimed at making you a great lawyer, and it does so with right and proper emphasis on the basics.

Davis is different from most law programs in that its first-year core classes last a year, and grades for four of the six do not become final until the spring. In one way that means you have an academic year to succeed, which cuts you more slack than having a mere semester. In another, however, it means that you have to stick with classes for a whole year where really a semester might do the trick. However it mostly balances out for the best to have it for a year, and the students probably prefer it like that after it is all over.

> **The school says:** "Beginning fall 2006, the curriculum at UC Davis School of Law will no longer include year-long courses; all grades will be final at the end of the semester."

Davis Law is a school with mainly one goal in mind: getting its students to pass the notoriously tough California bar. While there are certainly a variety of courses that you can take second and third year, the emphasis is definitely placed on bar classes rather than what will ultimately be just cosmetic courses. The quality of classes is superb: they are taught by some of the foremost experts in the fields. Your professor will more than likely have written THE universally regarded and used textbook in that field, particularly in the areas of property, civil procedure and criminal law.

The workload is like most law schools—brutal. Davis has a way of easing you into it, but then, in the end, it is a law school with high expectations of its students. Its grading is exacting; you pretty much understand why you got what you got, and the exams are almost always fair. As a second- and third-year you can get most classes that you want; there are certain classes that the third-years (who have registration priority) will gobble up over the second-years, but because you have to go to law school three years, you will get your turn.

Status: Alumnus/a, full-time
Dates of Enrollment: 8/2000-5/2003
Survey Submitted: September 2003

Like many law schools, Davis has a grueling first-year program. The remaining two years are not easy, either. However, the thing that really sets Davis apart and makes it all quite bearable is the fact that the distinguished faculty is accessible to and collegial with students. There is also a tutoring program where students can receive one-on-one guidance in first-year courses. Suffice it to say that getting in is the hardest part. Unlike other regional law schools (e.g., McGeorge), Davis does not purposely fail out any fraction of its entering class. Indeed with a retention rate in the high 90th percentile, the only reason for classmates to disappear is for reasons of compelling personal circumstances or to transfer to other, perhaps more lucrative schools. Classes can be gotten by all, and the workload is such that it will not kill someone to pull the extra weight required to get an A, but relaxing quite a bit does not necessarily force someone to get C's (provided one is strategic).

Status: Alumnus/a, full-time
Dates of Enrollment: 9/2000-5/2003
Survey Submitted: January 2004

Professors were excellent. Classes were thorough and interesting. Difficult to get popular classes. Grading was tough, but the curves have been changed to allow more A's and B's since my time. Workload was significant.

Status: Current student, full-time
Dates of Enrollment: 8/2002-Submit Date
Survey Submitted: June 2004

The first-year courses are rigorous, as they are at most law schools, and Socratic Method is widely used. Students are arranged into set groups with coursework in Contracts, Civil Procedure, Property, and Torts. Criminal Law is condensed into the first semester and Constitutional Law the second semester; Legal Research is a first-semester course, and Legal Writing is required the second semester. Professors are by and large excellent; there are a handful of extraordinarily brilliant teachers whose phrases resonate in your mind long after the course is over.

Popular classes are tough for 2Ls to get into, but not for 3Ls. The workload is how you choose it to be— you may push yourself, or you can take it easy if you want. The computer exam option has been implemented, which can greatly ease the test-taking experience.

Status: Alumnus/a, full-time
Dates of Enrollment: 8/2001-5/2003
Survey Submitted: October 2003

Not as grueling as expected. Most professors don't seem to mind if you are prepared or not. You might get a grumpy look. An attempt is made at the Socratic Method, but it is pretty noncommittal. First-year grades are on a predetermined curve. First-year classes are scheduled for you. After that it is often difficult to get a schedule that works well. Often classes have very odd schedules like Monday and Tuesday, 10 a.m. to 11:30 a.m., Thursday 2 p.m. to 3 p.m. This makes it hard to puzzle-fit a schedule together because of time conflicts. Once you have registered for classes, you may not get a physical seat. Classes are overscheduled, with the hope that enough drop out to fit everyone else in. Many classes are only offered every other year, so you have one shot to get it in your schedule.

Workload is moderate. Maintained a B+/A- without pulling too much hair out. Much of the academics reflect a left-leaning bias. There are a few well-known, distinguished faculty.

> **The school says:** "Course enrollment is limited to the number of students who can be seated in the classroom (and many classes are smaller, due to the law school's small size). While individual professors will sometimes allow students wishing to add a class to sit in on a full class during the 'add' period at the beginning of a semester, each registered student in every class has a physical seat. After the 'add' period expires, only registered students (and auditors with the permission of the professor) may attend classes. No audits are allowed unless there is sufficient space in the classroom.

Read all of Vault's Law School Surveys at www.vault.com/lawschool — get complete surveys on top law schools, expert advice on applicaton essays, LSAT prep and more.

VAULT CAREER LIBRARY   79

"Some highly specialized electives are offered every other year because student demand is insufficient to allow an annual offering. However, a large majority of the law school's classes, including specialized electives, are offered every year, and many classes are offered every semester."

Employment Prospects

Status: Current student, full-time
Dates of Enrollment: 8/2004-Submit Date
Survey Submitted: June 2006

King Hall has a great emphasis on work in the public sector. However, there are many opportunities for graduates at topnotch firms. Most students are presented with several options during on-campus recruiting. The alumni network could use improvement, but is not a hindrance. Similarly, some other schools may draw more employers to on-campus interviews, but most students are able to interview with several topnotch employers.

Status: Alumnus/a, full-time
Dates of Enrollment: 8/1999-5/2002
Survey Submitted: March 2006

For the top one-third to one-half of the class, employment prospects in the Bay Area, Sacramento, and Southern California are very good. Davis also has a reputation of producing excellent nonprofit lawyers and government lawyers.

Status: Alumnus/a, full-time
Dates of Enrollment: 8/1997-5/2000
Survey Submitted: May 2006

Many students at King Hall are public service or public interest minded. Nevertheless, the majority of graduates still enter private practice while others are successful at finding jobs with legal services, at other nonprofits and in the public sector. There are many opportunities for graduates of UC Davis School of Law. The Sacramento-area network is fantastic, and the alumni base is enthusiastic about helping students learn more about the field and helping them enter it. There are also many opportunities throughout the state and in many areas outside of the state as well. Because of its close proximity to Sacramento, there are wonderful opportunities for internships and clerkships—from working for a judge, at the Capitol or for a lobbyist, in private practice, DA's and PD's offices, or at the numerous nonprofits.

Status: Current student, full-time
Dates of Enrollment: 9/2004-Submit Date
Survey Submitted: July 2005

Most students end up working for the private sector although there are great employment prospects in government also, because the school is close to Sacramento. The professors and career services are also very supportive of public interest careers so it's a nice balance of the different career paths. In terms of location most students seem to stay in Northern California post-graduation namely, the Silicon Valley, SF, and Sacramento.

Status: Current student, full-time
Dates of Enrollment: 9/2002-Submit Date
Survey Submitted: November 2003

Because Davis Law brings in students who already have achieved more than just a BA or a BS, the career prospects of its students tend to match those of even the Top 10 law schools. Those who do well at Davis find themselves at no disadvantage when it comes to getting jobs at "biggie-biggie" firms such as Jones Day, MoFo, Arnold and Porter, even New York's finest. In the 2003 OCI season, Davis placed a high number of students in the Bay Area, which means they were able to compete successfully alongside such law school titans as Stanford and Boalt.

The campus recruiting is adequate if you are way above adequate. But if you are coming in with not much more than a BA, you will have to hustle more than a little to get the big break. Davis is well regarded among potential employers throughout the state, and it is believed that its profile will be raised on a national level once its alums branch out. Davis Law, not quite 40 years old as a law

school, is just now seeing its best and brightest shine. As more and more students make their mark, the name will be that much more marketable.

Status: Current student, full-time
Dates of Enrollment: 8/2002-Submit Date
Survey Submitted: January 2004

UC Davis is known statewide to be a good school that produces down-to-earth students who are highly qualified. Nationally, they are still building their reputation, but there are small presences on the East Coast. Most of the top 10 percent get the big-firm jobs that they want; some in the top third were disappointed not to land the big-firm job. By graduation, most students have located a clerkship or job that suits their interests.

Status: Alumnus/a, full-time
Dates of Enrollment: 8/2001-5/2003
Survey Submitted: October 2003

Career resources were adequate, with on-campus recruiting and workshops to assist in career searching and planning. Law school seems to have good reputation within California, but drops off quickly outside California.

Status: Alumnus/a, full-time
Dates of Enrollment: 8/2000-5/2003
Survey Submitted: September 2003

Davis is especially prestigious in Northern California, where most of its alumni are. However, it is well known throughout California and the U.S. because of its distinguished alumni. It is generally regarded as among the elite schools in California (mentioned in the same breath as Stanford, Berkeley, UCLA and USC), and generally regarded as better than Hastings. Other schools (such as San Diego, Loyola, McGeorge, Pepperdine, San Francisco, Golden Gate, Whitter, etc.) are widely consider to be far inferior, and tend to carry the tag "regional" by comparison.

Quality of Life

Status: Current student, full-time
Dates of Enrollment: 8/2004-Submit Date
Survey Submitted: June 2006

The quality of life is definitely what I like most about Davis. The King Hall community is amazing. People tend not to be ultra-competitive, but instead just focused on the curriculum and actually improving as human beings. Students readily share their outlines and there is a true sense of community. Nobody will be tearing pages out of books to gain a competitive edge, like many prospective law students are told. Faculty, students, and staff all endeavor to be very helpful and encouraging.

Davis is also a great town for graduate school. There are not a lot of distractions, but always enough to do to keep yourself busy. There are plenty of housing options. Having access to the greater UC campus gives law students ability to use top notch facilities. There is basically no significant crime except for a few bike thefts. If you didn't know Davis is the bike capital of California.

Status: Alumnus/a, full-time
Dates of Enrollment: 1/1970-6/1972
Survey Submitted: May 2006

Davis is not a large city. If you want the hustle and bustle of big city life, you may not be happy here. But if you want a moderately sized community that is close to the mountains, the ocean and the big city (all within a few hours drive) this will meet all your needs. I thoroughly enjoyed living in Davis. The community is a drawing card for many other residents because of its quality of life and good schools.

Status: Alumnus/a, full-time
Dates of Enrollment: 9/1972-5/1975
Survey Submitted: May 2006

Quality of life is probably UC Davis law school's strongest asset. It is a very small community, safe and easy to get around but very accessible to San Francisco and the Sierra/Lake Tahoe region.

Status: Current student, full-time
Dates of Enrollment: 8/2002-Submit Date
Survey Submitted: January 2004

Davis is an ideal location for your first year: There are very few distractions, and it is very easy to get around. It is extremely safe and small-town suburban. The Farmer's Market embodies the quaintness of the town. Dining is above average, but the San Francisco Bay Area is a little over an hour's drive away, if one has the resources. Sacramento is also about a 15-minute drive away and is not unlike a midsized East Coast city. You can find plenty to do if you look hard enough, and people are less assuming than those in larger cities. Housing is commensurate, slightly less than the Bay Area, but higher than the surrounding rural areas of Davis and Sacramento.

Status: Current student, full-time
Dates of Enrollment: 9/2002-Submit Date
Survey Submitted: November 2003

Life at Davis Law takes place in a tight self-contained universe: one building, two-and-a-half floors. Intimate isn't even the word. You will become very, very close to all schoolmates, so it is a relief that Davis Law is not nastily competitive at all. It is competitive in the sense that people want to succeed for themselves, and the only way they can really do that on a graded curve is to be better than someone else, but no one asserts that over another. The facilities are decent; again people come in with their own laptops and technology, so the basics are really enough. The best thing is that access to the law library is 24/7; each student has a key, and if the mood strikes, they can go in any time they want.

Status: Alumnus/a, full-time
Dates of Enrollment: 8/2001-5/2003
Survey Submitted: October 2003

City of Davis housing is outrageously expensive and getting worse. Real cost of housing is not reflected in financial aid calculations. Recent tuition hikes were implemented with no warning in mid-semester, then again in summer. Don't put it past California to raise tuition even more to balance the budget. Plan to get to Davis and find a place by March or April, or you'll be stuck and limited in what you can find. Davis landlords have the advantage and often use it. Get familiar with California landlord/tenant laws; you may need to refresh your landlord's memory of them. Pay particular attention to the amount they can ask for a deposit.

UC Davis campus is very nice: clean, well kept, with lots of plants and green space. The law school is on one end of campus, so you really don't see much of it in everyday life. There is no cafeteria at the law school, only a few vending machines. There is a small campus food court nearby with Carl's Jr, Taco Bell, Pizza Hut, and other odds and ends of food (espresso, crepes, deli sandwiches, sodas, chips, etc.). Law school has a small student lounge, shared with some of the administration staff. Small high school lockers are located two floors from most of the classrooms. Classrooms are in dire need of updating. Computers are present, but technology is rarely used in classes. Most information is still passed along by pushpins and cork bulletin board.

The city and UC Davis have an extensive bus system that reaches most residential areas of the city. Some of the routes can get crowded during school "rush hours" especially in bad weather. The city of Davis is bicycle capital of the world. More bikes than cars at some times, it seems. Biking can be quicker route to campus than driving, plus much of campus is off limits to cars. If you drive, watch out for bikes! They're everywhere, and if you don't keep a close eye out, you'll probably hit one.

Summers are HOT. Don't even think about living without air conditioning. Winters are mild, with some rain showers. Davis is generally a safe city. Many good neighborhoods, really no slums or scary places.

> **The school says:** "The number of rental housing units in Davis has grown substantially since 2003. Well into the school years, apartments have been offering special incentives for new tenants."

Status: Alumnus/a, full-time
Dates of Enrollment: 8/2000-5/2003
Survey Submitted: September 2003

The city is among the safest law school communities. Housing is comfortable and well maintained in general, although it is scattered throughout a city with a very low vacancy rate. There is no on-campus housing set aside for law students in particular, although there is married housing. The campus gym privileges are very popular among law students who want to work out. The very friendly and walkable downtown area is filled with popular restaurants of all sorts. The only drawback is generally said to be that the vast majority close early.

 ## Social Life

Status: Current student, full-time
Dates of Enrollment: 8/2004-Submit Date
Survey Submitted: June 2006

King Hall has a great social scene. The student body puts on several extremely fun events. These include among others: Over the Hump (a.k.a., law school prom), a law school talent show, a casino night, a great live auction, snow-boarding/skiing trips, and several other parties throughout the year. Also, every Thursday night law students can be found at one of the several local bars in Davis.

I truly feel that no other law school would match the balance that Davis gives a law student in terms of work and social opportunities. I have met lifelong friends here and have even seen a couple classmates get engaged.

Status: Alumnus/a, full-time
Dates of Enrollment: 9/1972-5/1975
Survey Submitted: May 2006

Law school social life at UC Davis law school is a reflection of the school and the community: a sense of intimacy and friendliness without the cutthroat conditions of many other law schools.

Status: Current student, full-time
Dates of Enrollment: 9/2004-Submit Date
Survey Submitted: July 2005

Since Davis is such a small town, the social life can be a bit bland. There are a few activities within the school like softball and bowling but other than that there's not much. The school does put on a few events throughout the year such as the law school prom, talent show, and legal foundation auction, which a lot of students attend. The upside is that San Francisco is only an hour drive away and since there's not much to do, it allows you to focus on your studies! There's also Sacramento although I wouldn't suggest going there for the social scene!

Status: Alumnus/a, full-time
Dates of Enrollment: 9/2000-5/2003
Survey Submitted: January 2004

Davis is not a big town, but there is great community within the law school. Lots of law school functions like softball and bowling leagues, and there is some life in town with all the other UC students.

Status: Current student, full-time
Dates of Enrollment: 8/2002-Submit Date
Survey Submitted: January 2004

Downtown Davis has a handful of bars and nightclubs; many law students pack the bar at Sophia's Thai Kitchen on Thursday nights. Sacramento offers more variety, from reggae clubs to more urban-like nightclubs. It is not an easy place to meet people if you are older, but if you are just out of college, you will feel right at home. King Hall has an annual semiformal, and there are mixers with the other professional schools, providing opportunities to meet different people.

Status: Current student, full-time
Dates of Enrollment: 9/2002-Submit Date
Survey Submitted: November 2003

No one is going to mistake Davis for Hollywood, but the fact of the matter is San Francisco is a mere hour away. You want social and nightlife of a big city, you can drive or hop a train and you've got it. The school is almost claustrophobic

Read all of Vault's Law School Surveys at www.vault.com/lawschool — get complete surveys on top law schools, expert advice on applicaton essays, LSAT prep and more.

VAULT CAREER LIBRARY   81

socially; this is how you are forced to know your fellow students. 99 percent of the people are extremely cool, well rounded and funny. Dating within the law school happens and to put it diplomatically, succeeds on a case-by-case basis. The law students all congregate at a local bar called Sophia's on Thursday night, yet again a small confined area where everyone runs into everyone. Life at Davis Law can be a law school version of *The OC*. If anyone were to do a *Real World* version of law school, they could do no better for Davis to achieve almost Shakespearean drama.

Status: Alumnus/a, full-time
Dates of Enrollment: 8/2000-5/2003
Survey Submitted: September 2003

There are not many bars in Davis, but they are always bursting with people. The social life, for better or for worse, revolves around parties and bars, because there is really nothing else open late at night, unless someone decides to make the short drive to Sacramento or the manageable drive to San Francisco or Berkeley. The favorite bar for dancing is Cantina, although it is primarily an undergraduate scene. The favorite bar among graduate students is Sophia's, which is the progeny of the Thai restaurant next door with the same name. This student favorite has extremely skilled bartenders who specialize in making exotic drinks, yet the prices are very reasonable. There are a few other haunts such as a local brewery, Sudwerk; there is a smaller bar with a country flavor called Froggy's; and finally the bar that routinely features seven drinks for the price of one (you get what you pay for, however), as well as salsa and line dancing, the Graduate.

 The School Says

UC Davis School of Law is one of the best, small public law schools in the United States and offers a three-year, full-time program leading to the juris doctor degree, as well as programs for LLM, MICL, and combined degrees. The school was founded in 1965 and is accredited by the American Bar Association and is a member of the Association of American Law Schools.

The school's academic program is progressive, with intellectual property programs, legislative and public interest offerings, bioethics law, and immigration and human rights law joining the school's established strengths in international law, environmental law, and corporate and public law. The distinguished faculty is nationally and internationally renowned, and the school's teaching methods combine the best features of traditional legal education with modern techniques for giving students practical legal experience.

UC Davis School of Law is also referred to as King Hall since its main building is named after Dr. Martin Luther King, Jr. in recognition of his efforts to bring social and political justice to disadvantaged peoples. The school continues its rich heritage of providing an excellent and comprehensive legal education marked by high ethical standards and is nationally recognized among the Top 15 law schools for its diverse faculty and students. All faculty offices, classrooms and the law library are housed in King Hall, which has a moot courtroom, a pretrial-skills laboratory, computer labs, study carrels, student journal offices, lounges, an infant care co-op, offices for student organizations, and is easily accessible to disabled students. Every law student is given a key to the building, allowing access to the facilities around the clock. The student body of King Hall is small compared to that of most law schools, which diminishes the excess competition among a highly qualified student body. Students on the whole work well with fellow students, faculty, administrators and staff. Cooperation and collegiality are the hallmark of student life at King Hall.

Students are recruited nationwide, and successful alumni are found in all of the diverse areas of the legal and business worlds. Each first-year section has less than 70 students, with at least one of the required first year courses taught in small sections of 25-35 students. Students can select upper-division

courses within broad areas of concentration, including criminal justice, business and taxation, civil litigation, estate planning and taxation, labor and employment law, environmental law, human rights and civil liberties law, immigration law, intellectual property, international law and public law. King Hall is renowned for its clinical programs in the areas of immigration, prison law, family law, and civil rights litigation. Virtually every student participates in one or more of the school's trial and appellate advocacy programs. The school also offers certificate programs in Public Service Law, Environment and Natural Resources Law, and Pro Bono Service.

The Davis campus is 20 minutes from the state capitol city of Sacramento, a little over an hour from San Francisco, and within easy reach of the major recreational areas of Lake Tahoe.

The admission committee seeks students of diverse backgrounds and interests. The entire application file is carefully reviewed with consideration given for many factors, including undergraduate grades, LSAT score, economic and other disadvantages, advanced studies, significant work experience, extracurricular and community activities, maturity and commitment to law study.

University of California, Hastings College of the Law

Admissions Office
200 McAllister Street
San Francisco, CA 94102-4978
Admissions phone: (415) 565-4623
Admissions fax: (415) 565-4863
Admissions e-mail: admiss@uchastings.edu
URL: http://www.uchastings.edu/

 Admissions

Status: Current student, full-time
Dates of Enrollment: 8/2004-Submit Date
Survey Submitted: May 2006

I was impressed with the admissions process. I appreciated the online system that allowed applicants to check the status of their applications. I received a call from a professor at Hastings who answered a lot of my questions. I thought the Admitted Students Day was good as well. I liked hearing from several professors and having the opportunity to speak to students.

Status: Current student, full-time
Dates of Enrollment: 8/2004-Submit Date
Survey Submitted: May 2006

The admissions process was rather easy and Hastings was fairly quick on the turn around given its size and number of applications. Well, actually since the class size is so large, it may actually be easier for them to make decisions. The essays and the application was comparable and standard to most law schools. It was neither more nor less labor-intensive than other schools.

Status: Current student, full-time
Dates of Enrollment: 8/2003-Submit Date
Survey Submitted: April 2006

I sent in my applications in January 2002 and got rejected from Hastings but accepted to Davis. I knew I wanted to live in the city of San Francisco because I wanted to experience living in a larger community and enjoy my spare time. So I worked another year and re-applied to Hastings in December 2002. The readers on the admissions committee likes to see well-rounded people who have experienced life and have altruistic and positive reasons for attending law school. LEOP is an excellent program and I wish I had applied because they provide the students with an instant support group and lots of motivation. I highly suggest you spend time working on your personal statement and get some feedback. Strong letters of recommendation will also be recognized.

Status: Current student, full-time
Dates of Enrollment: 8/2004-Submit Date
Survey Submitted: April 2006

I applied for early admission and enjoyed the experience. I was given a tour of the campus by a student who was both candid in giving warnings of upcoming construction and building closure, as well about positive experiences with students. Also, upon request, the general counsel made time to have lunch with me and tell me about the school from her point of view.

Status: Current student, full-time
Dates of Enrollment: 8/2004-Submit Date
Survey Submitted: April 2006

I applied to Hastings by mail the day they opened the admissions process. I was then fortunate enough to hear back from them in early January, so I would suggest that submitting early can help (especially in the rolling admissions process). They definitely like to have a balanced group of people here, and the student body is comprised of both people who have always harbored an interest in law

and those who are seeking a different career after years as a PhD, investment banker, etc. They seem to be pretty selective, although they also have a diversity admissions process that might not be as selective. There's no interview, and I recall the essays were pretty standard. Again, if you have a high LSAT, decent GPA, come from a good school, and can offer that little extra "umph," you should have no problem getting in.

Status: Current student, full-time
Dates of Enrollment: 8/2004-Submit Date
Survey Submitted: April 2006

The admissions process is just like any other, you send in the application, your LSAT scores, an essay and letters of recommendation. Although Hastings is selective when it comes to LSAT and GPA cutoffs, you can still get in by also applying through the Legal Education Opportunity Program. The LSAT and GPA requirements are slightly lower but the program is designed for students who are socioeconomically disadvantaged or had some other obstacle in their education.

Status: Current student, full-time
Dates of Enrollment: 8/2004-Submit Date
Survey Submitted: April 2006

I was placed on the waitlist for the Class of 2007. I was taken off the waitlist and offered a spot about two weeks before the start of the school year and about one week before I was going to fly out to Iowa to begin law school at the University of Iowa. I was actually shocked to have been placed on the waitlist at Hastings. I graduated summa cum laude from UC Davis in 2003 with a BA in Philosophy and Political Science, Public Service. I also had a minor in History, and my GPA was 3.81. I had been involved in a number of organizations and had done a number of internships. I was also Phi Beta Kappa. The first time I took the LSAT I received a 157. I re-took the LSAT and received a 163. I am a white male from a middle-class family (my father is a pharmacist and my mother is a middle school teacher). The only reasons I can think of for not getting in initially was my LSAT score, my lack of work experience (other than internships), and my lack of diversity. So is Hastings selective? Yes.

Status: Current student, full-time
Dates of Enrollment: 9/2003-Submit Date
Survey Submitted: April 2006

They seem to like people who have actually done something interesting. At least, we have a lot of people who are going into law as a second career. Life is better when your friends are former chefs, actors, dot-com-ers, athletes and at least one rock star (really!).

Status: Alumnus/a, full-time LLM
Dates of Enrollment: 8/2005-5/2006
Survey Submitted: May 2006

The program is tailored for non-U.S. lawyers and law graduates. The admissions process was not very burdensome. There was no admissions test. I just wrote a very chatty personal statement about my background, interests and why I wished to study at Hastings. I also filled in a short application form, requested that my academic transcripts be sent directly to admissions and organized a couple of letters from referees.

Status: Current student, full-time
Dates of Enrollment: 8/2003-Submit Date
Survey Submitted: March 2006

Wrote and essay, took the LSAT, submitted undergraduate transcript, and included two letters of recommendation: one from my employer, one from a former professor. My LSAT was at the high end of their 25 to 75 percentile and my grades were at the low end. I worked some with the admissions department while a student. They care about applicants' experience outside of their under-

Read all of Vault's Law School Surveys at www.vault.com/lawschool — get complete surveys on top law schools, expert advice on applicaton essays, LSAT prep and more.

VAULT CAREER LIBRARY 83

graduate study, especially post-undergraduate work experience. They also take their alternate admissions program for people with disadvantaged backgrounds seriously.

Status: Alumnus/a, full-time
Dates of Enrollment: 8/1999-5/2002
Survey Submitted: April 2005

Standard process—GPA, LSAT, essay and letters of recommendation. This school is selective (and getting more so). If you don't have scores in the median ranges for GPA and LSAT, your essay and (more importantly!) letters of recommendation need to be superb. Members of the admissions committee report that letters by people who know you well are much more important than letters from important/famous people who don't.

Status: Alumnus/a, full-time
Dates of Enrollment: 8/2000-5/2003
Survey Submitted: April 2004

Selectivity is moderately high, and getting higher as the number of applicants increases (as it has for the last three years). It is most likely based primarily on your undergraduate (and prior graduate) GPA and LSAT. Other factors certainly come into play, but the GPA/LSAT averages are the best indicator of your competition for admission. Prior work experience is highly valued, as reflected in the high number of returning (out of higher education for more than one year) students, as is a solid writing background. The school's LEOP program is meant for disadvantaged applicants, whether minority status or otherwise. It begins with the admissions process, so if you think you qualify (as demonstrated by your LEOP application essay), it is an excellent route to take. Additionally, if admitted through LEOP, you will receive additional tutoring and training, as needed, throughout your time at Hastings.

Status: Current student, full-time
Dates of Enrollment: 8/2001-Submit Date
Survey Submitted: December 2003

From comparing notes with my fellow classmates, Hastings is the destination for extremely talented individuals with good, but not stellar, LSATs and strong undergraduate performances. The breadth of undergraduate campuses represented is impressive! The best advice of getting in is take the admissions essay seriously. I know that those who OK over them are extremely unforgiving of spelling errors, grammatical errors, etc. Be sure to clearly articulate (and support) why you want to go to law school, and more importantly, what you will bring to the classroom to boost the learning experience of your classmates. As an aside, the campus and everyone it employs is liberal to very liberal on the political spectrum—be honest in your essay, but remember who your audience is!

The school says: "Hastings has several conservative organizations as well, including the Federalist Society and the Hastings Republicans, and its faculty and staff reflect a wide spectrum of views."

Status: Alumnus/a, full-time
Dates of Enrollment: 8/2000-5/2003
Survey Submitted: April 2004

Admissions are based almost exclusively on grades and GPA. Once you are accepted, be persistent about financial aid. They have a tendency to lose applications and not give financial aid packages. If they do that and run out of money for you, then it is too late. Also, make sure they list you as a California resident if you are one. They bill almost everyone as an out-of-state resident the first semester (even if you have only lived in California), and then you have to go through an annoying process of submitting tax returns, etc., to prove your residence status.

The school says: "More than 80 percent of each class receives a Hastings grant of $4,000 or more based on financial need. Additional scholarships not based on need are also available. Filing deadlines are strict, however."

 # Academics

Status: Current student, full-time
Dates of Enrollment: 8/2004-Submit Date
Survey Submitted: May 2006

The worst thing about Hastings is the class size. I believe that this creates a lot of competition because Hastings is not top tier and most of the students are not going to get the premier jobs. I believe this is a big problem and that Hastings should cut its class size. Currently, I believe it is about 420 per class. I think a better class size would be more like 300. This would also create more open spots in the best classes. Furthermore, I don't see how cutting down the student body would have any negative effect on the school itself, as I believe you can still achieve great diversity with 300 students per class.

Status: Current student, full-time
Dates of Enrollment: 8/2003-Submit Date
Survey Submitted: April 2006

Hastings professors are top of the line. I have been extremely impressed with the vast majority of my professors—many are at the top of their field. Many people feel that the tenured faculty is stronger than Boalt's. Due to its proximity to the San Francisco legal market, Hastings uses a lot of adjunct faculty, which I think is great because it allows me to take a lot of specialized classes (Election Law, IP Licensing) from the best attorneys in these fields. However, it is often difficult to get all the classes you want because way too many classes are scheduled to overlap with each other. Classes are not logically scheduled.

Status: Current student, full-time
Dates of Enrollment: 8/2004-Submit Date
Survey Submitted: April 2006

Hastings takes advantage of adjuncts, which I find to add an element of practicality into an otherwise over-theoretical experience. In that sense, I feel that I understand the system and politics of the law, and not just the law itself. I wish however, there would be a greater foundation for those who wish to practice business law, as we are somewhat ignored in terms of class offerings and available faculty.

Status: Current student, full-time
Dates of Enrollment: 8/2004-Submit Date
Survey Submitted: April 2006

The quality of the classes at Hastings is superb. My first-year professors collectively possessed more than 100 years of teaching experience, and all of them were masters in their field. There was not a question you could ask that they could not answer or quickly find an answer to. The same has proven true this year. While some might be more entertaining than others, there is no shortage of professors here who know what they are doing. The professors also seem to be quite collegial with one another, which I think trickles down to their good rapport with students. If you're willing to wait it's usually not too difficult to end up in popular classes—the waitlist system is quite efficient, and the school rotates by alphabet when you get the prime spots for registration.

Status: Current student, full-time
Dates of Enrollment: 8/2004-Submit Date
Survey Submitted: April 2006

The quality of my professors has run the gamut. I've had professors who are simply not effective in a classroom setting and professors who are amazingly effective speakers and simply wonderful persons. Overall, I would rate the quality of my professors quite high. But, then again, I do a good deal of research on professors before I take them, and usually stick with the ones that are good. I have had no problem enrolling in any of the courses I wanted (you just need to stick it out on the waitlist and you'll get in eventually). Hastings has a strict curve that always seems to be followed (approximately 10 to 20 percent A's). The finals are grueling and the amount of reading seems enormous. And, with all the extracurricular activities that spring up during your second year at Hastings, the first year (which is usually thought of as the worst at most schools) is a walk in the park. Lastly, Hastings has a ton of classes, and I've never had a problem finding classes I'm really interested in (of course, the professor can change that in a hurry).

Status: Alumnus/a, LLM

Dates of Enrollment: 8/2005-5/2006
Survey Submitted: May 2006

You study alongside U.S. juris doctor students. There is one research class solely for foreign LLMs. You are free to explore your interests and study what you want. There's also flexibility to become involved in law school clinics, do judicial externships, enter competitions, write journal articles, etc. The school makes a big effort to make you feel welcome. LLMs are given a preference in getting the classes they want. Professors are friendly and accommodating. The workload is comparable to the JD program—but you can work harder or on more challenging/demanding things if you want (depending on your interests and what you get involved, e.g., clinical work demands a lot of time and effort). Most classes are of a high quality. The IP, litigation, tax, nonprofit and clinical programs are particularly good.

Status: Alumnus/a, full-time
Dates of Enrollment: 9/2003-5/2005
Survey Submitted: October 2005

The professors for the most part are excellent and the variety of classes offered is greater than almost any other law school. The practical classes, including Legal Writing, Moot Court, Appellate Advocacy and Trial Advocacy are topnotch and greatly contributed to my ability to practice law independently after graduation. I graduated actually knowing how to be a lawyer.

Status: Alumnus/a, full-time
Dates of Enrollment: 8/2000-5/2003
Survey Submitted: April 2004

As do most law schools, Hastings has a pseudo-Socratic Method of teaching, some professors lecture more than others, but overall there is a lot of question-and-answer, especially in the first year. The faculty are very knowledgeable and mostly very approachable. I remain in contact with some of them; some adjunct professors do not do as well in the classroom. Hastings has high academic standards, and reflects that in a correspondingly low grade curve (which is forced).

If you have prior work experience, expect a full-time workload, plus a little overtime (more around finals). If you don't have work experience, imagine that you actually have to get those huge reading assignments done, and are expected to answer questions about them intelligently. The reading is shorter than your average liberal arts undergraduate assignments, but much more intellectually challenging. Each word is more important than in the average liberal arts curriculum, so it takes much longer per page to complete. The first year of classes is set in stone, except one elective (from among five options). After that, it's all elective, and you can get any class you want (through a lottery system), though not always when you want it.

Most students end up taking similar bar prep-type classes plus electives in the areas that excite them, though the faculty all discourage taking classes merely because they are on the bar. That said, many of the bar courses are important in the practice of law—not taking Con Law would be strange, even though it's not required. Only a few classes require prerequisites. The clinical programs do, and are the most difficult to get into (because of popularity and prerequisite), but also extremely worthwhile—almost everyone who takes them says they are the best thing going.

Finally, because of proximity to all levels of the state and federal courts (except the U.S. Supreme Court), many judicial externships, for classroom credit, are available and valuable. The workload generally increases in your second year, and decreases in your third (or at least, you do less of it). Hastings has a reputation for being cutthroat that is overstated. The curve does cause some angst and, as noted, some take it too seriously. Some people feel that big-firm on-campus interviewing directed at the top quarter to third of the class creates classes of "haves" and "have-nots," but that, too, seems overstated. That said, the overwhelming majority of students (and faculty) are very friendly and more than willing to help each other out.

> **The school says:** "Hastings has a suggested, not a mandatory, curve with 65 to 80 percent of grades B- or better and 10 to 20 percent of grades A- or better."

Status: Current student, full-time
Dates of Enrollment: 8/2001-Submit Date
Survey Submitted: December 2003

The professors are topnotch! Most of the professors have written the textbooks used by all of your peers on the East Coast and in So Cal. The quality of education has met every expectation. While the selection of classes offered has shifted with the economy (slightly away from transactional practice and more toward litigation), the academic dean has responded to students' requests and steered the curriculum back toward a balanced approach that meets the needs of those students who are praying for the "bullish economy of yester-year" to return. The school has been upgrading its technology infrastructure (which has not been easy given the California budget crisis).

Thank heavens Hastings has its own Board of Regents apart from the general UC system, because it means registering for classes is much smoother. Getting popular classes is usually easy, since there are at least two good profs per subject. Note: the school is massive! With one of the largest student bodies in the country, plenty of classes have 50 to 80 students. However, the stadium seating is great, all classrooms have Internet access via wireless networks, and if you don't like getting called on, great! There are plenty of intimate seminars that have 15 to 20 students in the second and third year. Don't let the size scare you away. Just think, that much more room for success in the grading curve!

Status: Alumnus/a, full-time
Dates of Enrollment: 5/1994-6/1998
Survey Submitted: April 2004

Traditional Socratic-focused law school program. The quality of classes is incredibly high. You will get as good a law school education as anywhere in the Top 10 law schools. I supervise enough Harvard, Stanford and Yale grads to know that to be true. The grading curve is very harsh, and consequently it is a very competitive school. But that will only make you a better lawyer in the long run. People do flunk out of this school, and most get below a B average, but you will graduate feeling you really earned your degree, and you will feel good about it.

> **The school says:** "75 percent of Hastings students graduate with a GPA of B- or better."

 ## Employment Prospects

Status: Current student, full-time
Dates of Enrollment: 8/2003-Submit Date
Survey Submitted: April 2006

Hastings graduates have an outstanding reputation in California, especially the Bay Area. With the largest alumni network west of the Mississippi, Hastings students can draw upon a slew of connections. Our graduates are judges, big-firm attorneys, civil servants, public interest advocates, CEOs and politicians. We really have a reputation for diligence and resolve that is unparalleled. Big firms come to our campus to recruit for summer associates, the alumni have gotten me my past two jobs, and every attorney on the West Coast knows about Hastings and our reputation.

Status: Current student, full-time
Dates of Enrollment: 8/2004-Submit Date
Survey Submitted: April 2006

I think that if you're within the top third of the class and you're not a rock in a chair during interviews, you shouldn't have a problem getting a job in BigLaw during OCI. In all honesty, everyone else shouldn't have trouble finding a job if they were willing to reduce their standards, but it seems that many feel like if their friends are getting BigLaw jobs, they should be getting BigLaw jobs, even if they don't have the grades to prove it. Employers seem very impressed with Hastings, and I think we have a reputation in the legal community of producing hard-working, competent attorneys. The OCI process was fantastic—it ran very smoothly, there was a great selection of top employers, and I felt like I was seriously considered for every position I applied for. I did not get the impression that the interviews were merely pro forma. There are also great opportunities for students in the upper tiers of the class for clerkships and other public interest positions after graduation. With respect to the alumni network, I haven't really

Read all of Vault's Law School Surveys at www.vault.com/lawschool — get complete surveys on top law schools, expert advice on applicaton essays, LSAT prep and more.

VAULT CAREER LIBRARY 85

had an experience first-hand, although I definitely got the impression that when I interviewed with Hastings attorneys they were always willing to go to bat for me, and I landed a considerable number of offers.

Status: Alumnus/a, full-time program
Dates of Enrollment: 9/1995-5/1998
Survey Submitted: April 2006

As a seven-year member of a recruiting committee at a major California law firm, we view those in the top 20 percent of the Hastings class as being very strong candidates whom we actively recruit. Most of the major law firms in the Bay Area and many from beyond participate in the on-campus interviews. The alumni network in the Bay Area is quite extensive and most of the large firms have many graduates who are interested in helping qualified contacts.

Status: Alumnus/a, full-time school
Dates of Enrollment: 9/2000-5/2003
Survey Submitted: March 2006

The career services office is helpful and always willing to answer questions, give guidance and advice, or help with any requests or concerns. If you are in the top 10 to 15 percent of your class, you should have no problem getting a job in a high-paying firm. However, most students prefer to work in mid-sized firms or do public sector work. Hastings on-campus recruiting and public interest fair provide opportunities to meet the right people to secure these job openings.

Status: Alumnus/a, full-time
Dates of Enrollment: 1/1994-6/1998
Survey Submitted: March 2005

If you want to work in the top law firms, Hastings can open that door for you if you are willing to work hard to get good grades. I am a senior associate for a Vault Top 10 law firm and on track to make equity partner. All the top firms in the country have Hastings grads. At my firm, over 85 percent of the associates come from Top 15 law schools, yet Hastings is one of the best regarded in terms of performance of its graduates here. I would say 60 percent of Hastings grads end up at law firms, with the remainder in public service or government work. All the top firms recruit on campus. If you end up in the top 10 percent, you will have the same job opportunities as the top third from Harvard—without question.

Status: Alumnus/a, full-time
Dates of Enrollment: 8/2000-5/2003
Survey Submitted: April 2004

Hastings provides excellent job prospects in Northern California. The career center is friendly, accessible and very helpful. Still, if you want a job outside of Northern California, you are going to have to do a little extra work. Some firms from Southern California do on-campus interviews, but not many. (Whereas ALL the big firms in Northern California do.) Some firms from New York also come. But if you want a job out of state, you will probably have to arrange an interview on your own. That can be tough. Out-of-state firms are also not as aware of Hastings. Despite its drop in the ratings, Hastings still has an excellent reputation with California law firms. Northern California firms hire almost exclusively from Hastings, Stanford, Boalt and Santa Clara.

Status: Alumnus/a, full-time
Dates of Enrollment: 8/2000-5/2003
Survey Submitted: April 2004

Hastings opens every door there is in the job market, just not as wide as at the very top law schools (Harvard, Stanford, Boalt, etc.). Generally, the top 25 percent of the Hastings class is very competitive nationally in the most selective job markets—and especially on the West Coast (big firms, Department of Justice Honors Program and judicial clerkships). On-campus interviewing in the fall of the second year determines most of the highly selective jobs, and unfortunately seems to occupy the majority of the career services department's time.

That said, the career services department is excellent at job placement, and can provide a lot of help finding any kind of job. Hastings has a huge number of lawyers and judges in practice in California, which never hurts in job interviews, although the alumni connections don't seem as strong as with some smaller, especially private, schools. Hastings has an excellent reputation as a law school for lawyers (as opposed to academics). The bar pass rate for Hastings is always high (around 80 percent, typically a touch lower than at Stanford and Boalt), and

if the bottom 10 percent of a Hastings class is removed from the statistics, the rate goes up dramatically (the top half of the class generally has a pass rate of around 98 or 99 percent).

Status: Current student, full-time
Dates of Enrollment: 8/2001-Submit Date
Survey Submitted: December 2003

One of the main reasons I chose Hastings was their career services office. They are incredible! They help with resume review, mock interviews with alumni and practitioners at all the major firms, and everyone gets at least several OCI interviews. Thanks to their support, I had a firm job for both my 1L and 2L summers. Go visit the CSO if you visit the campus.

Status: Alumnus/a, full-time
Dates of Enrollment: 8/1993-5/1996
Survey Submitted: June 2004

Hastings is great if you want to work in a big firm. If you are not on the traditional career path (i.e., small firm, government, nonprofit, outside the law), you are on your own. This is a large public school, so you are not paying for the individual attention that a private school can provide.

> **The school says:** "Hastings annually hosts one of the largest public interest/public sector job fairs in the country, as well as an annual small-firm event. The school offers workshops as well as written material for students targeting small firms and public interest employers and has a large number of alumni mentors from both areas with whom students can be matched."

Quality of Life

Status: Current student, full-time
Dates of Enrollment: 8/2004-Submit Date
Survey Submitted: May 2006

It is difficult to maintain a good quality of life at Hastings. I imagine that students who are not involved in any extracurricular activities have an easier time. I have spent quite a bit of energy on student organizations, and have felt overextended for my entire second year.

The campus is in a fantastic location—within walking distance from California state trial, appellate and Supreme Courts, the federal district courts and the Ninth Circuit. It is also interesting to be in the middle of a neighborhood like the Tenderloin, where students receive daily reminders of our duty as professionals to work towards a better society.

Status: Current student, full-time
Dates of Enrollment: 7/2005-Submit Date
Survey Submitted: May 2006

It's hard to judge since the library is currently being renovated. When the library wasn't under renovation the quality of life was good, there was plenty of room for facilities. Things seem a bit crowded now, but things should change by 2007. The law school is located in both the nicest and worst area of San Francisco. It is in the political and legal center of California, but in the poorest and most dangerous area of San Francisco. However, the school does provide security services. Plus, Hastings students have the option of living at UCSF housing in Mission Bay, which is a plus.

Status: Current student, full-time
Dates of Enrollment: 8/2003-Submit Date
Survey Submitted: April 2006

Housing in the on-campus Tower is incredibly convenient and provides you with the most affordable, beautiful view of San Francisco you will ever have. The pool table and gym downstairs provide a welcome respite from studying, and the restaurants nearby are cheap and delicious. We are located in the Tenderloin, so the indigent community is visible and safety is always a concern. Car break-ins are common so you don't want to leave anything in the car. However, I have found that living in this part of the city is only beneficial for us because there are more opportunities to get involved in various clinics, nonprofits and every major courthouse, which you would never think to join if you attended law school in a safe little bubble. The Tenderloin reminds us of why we came to law school and, I think, the chance to get practical experience with so many opportunities surrounding you. Also, being smack-dab in the Civic Center provides us with easy transportation options, BART and MUNI stops.

Status: Current student, full-time
Dates of Enrollment: 8/2004-Submit Date
Survey Submitted: April 2006

While some students who have never lived in San Francisco can be intimidated by the surrounding area (which is known for its crime/drugs), the campus is a very safe place to be, and getting to and from campus from anywhere in the city is easy and safe. With the recent building closures, study areas and food are hard to come by, but we know that the administration is busy making life better for those students who will come after us. However, the wireless they boast about has terribly low bandwidth and can't support the student's technology needs.

> **The school says:** "Hastings has expanded its bandwidth so that in 2006-07 it should meet all needs."

Status: Current student, full-time
Dates of Enrollment: 8/2004-Submit Date
Survey Submitted: April 2006

Housing is actually great at Hastings, because if you don't want to go to the trouble of finding a place in the city you can always live right down the street in the McAllister Tower. The campus is unique in that it is an urban campus, and I think the access we have to the nearby California Supreme Court, Court of Appeal, Ninth Circuit and Superior Court is unparalleled. Every semester since I've been at Hastings I've probably been given an assignment to observe a hearing, and the professors do a great job of integrated the nearby courts into the curriculum. All three buildings in the campus have or are currently undergoing a retrofit and remodel, and all in all it's a comfortable place to go to school. While there's a certain "shock factor" when you're first adjusting to the Tenderloin, once you're here a few weeks you get used to it and it doesn't even really bother you anymore. The school also has a great dining facility on campus, so if you want to avoid going out during the day there's little problem with staying in. The school also provides a San Francisco Police Officer at night who will escort anyone to nearby public transportation and other places, as well as a shuttle. We may be in the 'Loin, but the school does a good job of mitigating the impact that could have.

Status: Alumnus/a, full-time
Dates of Enrollment: 9/2000-5/2003
Survey Submitted: October 2005

The school is in the Tenderloin, which is certainly not the nicest neighborhood in the city. It is getting better with the re-opening of the Asian Art Museum and the public library, but it is still highly populated by homeless and there is plenty of drug dealing/using around the neighborhood. That being said, other than a little harassment, I was never the victim of crime nor were my friends. Because the neighborhood is not great, there are tons of cheap/good restaurants. Also, it is near all the courts, which is nice and should be taken advantage of. The work itself is no different than any other law school but if you are looking for an undergrad like experience don't go to Hastings. Its campus is two buildings and a dorm. While the dorm is cheap, I would not live there. At this point, the rents in the city are reasonably affordable (and even cheaper in the East Bay) so I would pick a nicer neighborhood to live in. Hayes Valley and the Haight are great places, reasonably cheap places with tons of character.

Status: Alumnus/a, full-time
Dates of Enrollment: 8/2000-5/2003
Survey Submitted: April 2005

Housing is not too much of a problem. I would recommend moving into the Tower for your first year. I did not and regretted it. The neighborhood is not great but not nearly as bad as it used to be—and better neighborhoods are only a short BART ride away.

Status: Current student, full-time
Dates of Enrollment: 8/2001-Submit Date
Survey Submitted: December 2003

This is really the only blemish Hastings has. Being in San Francisco is great—tons to do, great town, killer places to eat, party, etc. Campus housing is in the

old Hotel San Francisco (historic building 26 stories tall) and is very convenient. The area where the school is located, however, is quite poor (drugs, homelessness, etc.). Coming from UCLA (beautiful campus) I was quite disappointed. Additionally, I am married with two children (one born during law school!), and the city is a very difficult place to raise a family unless you have money. Many students, myself included, commute from the East Bay (Oakland, Berkeley, Walnut Creek, etc.) via BART (Bay Area Rapid Transit), which is incredibly reliable and allows for some great studying. In all fairness, after three years I have never had a problem personally with the neighborhood.

Status: Alumnus/a, full-time
Dates of Enrollment: 8/2000-5/2003
Survey Submitted: April 2004

The quality of life at Hastings is what you make it. The campus is essentially three buildings in one of San Francisco's rougher areas (although also nice to look at, with City Hall, the public library, newly finished Asian Art Museum, Opera House, etc., within a block). It's safe during daylight, and the school provides escorts after dark.

Students live all over the Bay Area, with some commuting as much as an hour each way to get to school—that is all personal preference. The school's apartment building includes a modest gym and basketball court, which are enough, given that the school only has about 1,000 students. Every classroom is wired for wireless Web and has electrical jacks for computers (a little more than half of the student body uses them). The school has a cafeteria that is open in the morning until 4 p.m. Many people use it, but San Francisco offers so much more, it's more for convenience.

 ## Social Life

Status: Current student, full-time
Dates of Enrollment: 8/2003-Submit Date
Survey Submitted: April 2006

Just a five-minute walk from Union Square, and numerous bars, theatres and restaurants within walking distance make for an exciting nightlife. Mr. Smith's at 34 Seventh Street is a favorite spot and we usually hold fundraiser parties there every month, in addition to our biweekly BOB (Beer-on-the-Beach), when we roll several kegs onto campus and enjoy some free entertainment or food booths on Thursday afternoon.

Restaurants nearby include Soluna and Lalita's Thai, both on the same block and with great happy hours. Jade on Gough St. has $2 drink specials every afternoon from 3 to 7 p.m. There are plenty of good eats, like Le Pettits Sourdough on Golden Gate, behind our school, and tons of good ethnic food such as Mangosteen and Saigon Sandwiches (Vietnamese) on Larkin St., Osha's Thai on Geary and Leavenworth, and Indian/Pakistani, such as Chutney and Naan & Curry on Leavenworth and Jones St., respectively. Dating scene is awesome, tons of parties in San Francisco every night, but mainly Thursday through Saturday nights.

Big clubs with DJs include Suite 181 on Eddy St. and the aforementioned Mr. Smith's. Lots of other spots in SOMA, North Beach and Russian Hill are only a short cab ride away. The dating scene within the law school is strong, one of the pluses of a large law school. The student organizations are also the most well-led and active groups I've ever witnesses. Every week, they are hosting panels, guest speakers, charity events, parties, poker tournaments, cultural activities, sport competitions, trivia tournaments and other annual traditions. Living in San Francisco is one of the best assets about Hastings and finding lifelong friends in law school with whom to enjoy the city has made it all worthwhile.

Status: Current student, full-time
Dates of Enrollment: 8/2004-Submit Date
Survey Submitted: April 2006

The best thing about Hastings is the people. Most of the students and professors are down-to-earth, common-sense folk. Perhaps I just got lucky, and sometimes I think I might have, but the people I've met and become friends with are laidback and normal individuals, and lord knows you need that in an environment like law school. Of course, there are still those "gunners" that get to class early,

Read all of Vault's Law School Surveys at www.vault.com/lawschool — get complete surveys on top law schools, expert advice on applicaton essays, LSAT prep and more.

VAULT CAREER LIBRARY   87

sit in front, talk incessantly, and stress you out just by being around them, but they seem to be farther and fewer in-between than what I've heard about and experienced at other schools. Being in San Francisco is an amazing experience. The city truly is European in the sense that there are a whole bunch of little areas, almost villages, that are different and unique. There is always something to do and somewhere to go. You name the type of people, type of food, type of bar, type of anything that you want, and you can get it in San Francisco. You'll always seem to run into Hastings people whenever and wherever you go out at night. And on one of those rare sunny days, nothing beats being in San Francisco.

Status: Current student, full-time
Dates of Enrollment: 8/2004-Submit Date
Survey Submitted: April 2006

Any discussion of student life has to start with the weekly Beer on the Beach. The Beach is a patio on the front of our primary academic building, and every Thursday a student organization hosts a social event with plenty of free beer, cider and typically some sort of food. This provides a great opportunity to get to know members of your section and other sections, as well as more senior members of the class. It also usually spins off into a night on the town. Student government also hosts a Bar Review, where they get a special deal for Hastings students at a nearby bar. While there was a limited amount of "section-cest," most people seemed to start Hastings with husbands/wives or serious girl-friends/boyfriends in tow (not actually at the school, they just were already involved in a committed relationship). We're in San Francisco, so you have some of the greatest restaurants, bars and nightlife in the country, and it's almost all available by mass transit. A few other fun events include the Barrister's Ball, and there's probably no event more fun that the Public Interest Law Foundation (PILF)'s Annual Auction.

Status: Alumnus/a, full-time
Dates of Enrollment: 8/1999-5/2002
Survey Submitted: April 2005

If you don't live on campus, I hear the school doesn't feel all that social. Living in the Tower, though, you'll get more of a college-like dorm feel, at least in your first year. One consistent social event is a bi-monthly keg party that takes place in front of the school called Beer on the Beach (because the area in front of the school has been nicknamed "the Beach"). The school also has a lot of great annual events—the HPILF auction, various ethnic nights and the Barrister's Ball. Popular student hangouts are Soluna, the Renoir and Lalita's.

Status: Alumnus/a, full-time
Dates of Enrollment: 1/1994-6/1998
Survey Submitted: March 2005

What social life? This is law school, not business school.

Status: Alumnus/a, full-time
Dates of Enrollment: 8/2000-5/2003
Survey Submitted: April 2004

Because the school is a stand-alone law school, it doesn't have the community feel that most universities do. However, it does have clubs for everything, polit-ical, racial and otherwise, from the National Lawyers Guild (lefties, probably aligned mostly with the Green Party) to the Federalist Society (conservatives), Black Law Students, South Asian Law Students, La Raza, surfing, soccer, ski-ing, you name it. The intramural basketball league is always lively and compet-itive (at the top). Also, because you spend almost all of your first year with the same set of about 85 people, you get to know them well. Law journals and moot court teams offer even more for bringing people together (in the second and third years).

There is a beer function sponsored by the student body every other Thursday, and the student services department sponsors several fun social events through-out the year. The dating scene is largely underground (I think, I was already mar-ried when I got there), but I'm told it flourishes. The social life is more about San Francisco and the Bay Area than about the school. San Francisco is a great town for eating out and has a lively nightlife. In addition, most outdoor adven-tures are nearby, with the farthest, skiing, only about three and a half hours away by car (and some of the best in the world, at that).

Status: Current student, full-time
Dates of Enrollment: 8/2001-Submit Date
Survey Submitted: December 2003

The social scene is there for those that are interested in it. Every week there is Beer on the Beach, sponsored by one of the many campus groups. It usually involves music, live entertainment, 200 people minimum and free beer, soda, water, etc. There really is something for everyone with respect to outside inter-ests. From the surfing club to the hockey club to power yoga and an intense bas-ketball tournament, there is plenty to do.

 The School Says

University of California Hastings College of the Law was found-ed in 1878 and named after Serranus Clinton Hastings, the first Chief Justice of the California Supreme Court. Hastings, the first-established law department of the University of California, is the oldest public law school in the western U.S.

The college's location in San Francisco's Civic Center puts stu-dents near all levels of state and federal government. Every aspect of the law—from a multimillion dollar antitrust action to a hearing on welfare benefits—is happening within a short walk.

Hastings is the third-largest public law school in America, enrolling some 1,200 students and granting about 400 law degrees each year. More than 6,100 applied for the 420 places in Hastings' 2005 entering class. The current student body is comprised of about half men and half women. One of every three students is from a minority group.

The Legal Education Opportunity Program was created more than 30 years ago to help equalize opportunities in the law, rec-ognizing that the traditional academic criteria used to determine admissions might not be the best indicators of academic poten-tial for students from non-traditional backgrounds. LEOP is an alternative means of evaluating an applicant's potential for the study of law, and it is an academic support program committed to the success of LEOP students in law school and in the legal profession. LEOP students have overcome significant obsta-cles—educational, economic, social or physical—that have restricted their access to traditional academic opportunities and resources generally considered an indicator of a successful law school career. Approximately 20 percent of each Hastings entering class is comprised of LEOP students.

Hastings has seven student-led scholarly journals, more than most law schools. Its clinical program is the most extensive in Northern California. Clinics in civil justice, criminal practice, immigrant rights, environmental law, workers' rights and medi-ation give students hands-on experience and enable them to confront professional, ethical and societal issues. Many stu-dents volunteer for public interest programs, such as those of the Public Interest Clearinghouse and the student-run General Assistance Advocacy Project. The campus also hosts the Center for State and Local Government Law, the Center for International Justice and Human Rights, the Center for Negotiation and Dispute Resolution, and the Center for Work-Life Law.

More than 300 employers interview annually on campus through one of the most comprehensive law career services pro-grams in the West. Some 80 percent of the college's 16,500 alumni live and work in California. More Hastings alumni sit as judges in the federal, state, county and municipal courts of California than from any other law school in the nation.

Class visits and student-guided tours are offered in spring and fall. Self-guided tours are offered year-round through the admis-sions office at (415) 565-4623.

University of California, Los Angeles School of Law

Office of Admissions
71 Dodd Hall
Box 951445
Los Angeles, CA 90095-1445
Admissions phone: (310) 825-2080
Admissions e-mail: admissions@law.ucla.edu
URL: http://www.law.ucla.edu/

 Admissions

Status: Current student, full-time
Dates of Enrollment: 8/2005-Submit Date
Survey Submitted: February 2006

Unlike many other schools, UCLA Law has a separate Program in Public Interest Law and Policy (PILP) for which there is a separate addendum application. To come in as a member of the PILP program, you need to submit an additional essay detailing your interest in/commitment to public interest. I didn't apply to the program, but I believe it is quite selective. PILP students attend classes with everybody else—the only difference is that they have a separate law skills class and additional weekly lectures.

The only complaint I had was with the difficulty I had contacting the school by phone with questions. The automated phone system is almost impossible to navigate.

Status: Alumnus/a, full-time
Dates of Enrollment: 8/2002-5/2005
Survey Submitted: March 2006

Quick and simple online applications process. Because UCLA is a state school, it's much more difficult for out-of-state students to be admitted. However, out-of-state students who are admitted may obtain in-state tuition after one year. And competitive out-of-staters may receive a tuition waiver that makes their first-year tuition equal to the in-state rate.

Status: Alumnus/a, full-time
Dates of Enrollment: 8/2002-5/2005
Survey Submitted: October 2005

The admissions process is pretty standard of most law schools—LSAT, undergrad degree, personal statement, resume, letters of recommendation, etc. Because the law school is ranked in the Top 20 law schools in the nation, it is quite difficult to get in. The school is especially selective and most are admitted based on raw numbers. A few are admitted based on their personal statement, resume, community service and/or employment background.

Status: Alumnus/a, full-time
Dates of Enrollment: 2000-2003
Survey Submitted: April 2005

UCLA law school is fairly selective. To give you an idea of the type of people who apply, the largest undergraduate "feeder" schools are UCLA and UC Berkeley, with a healthy dose of graduates from Stanford as well as the Ivies. The application process itself is fairly straightforward—application, references and personal statement. No interviews are granted, as far as I know. Do not underestimate the power of recommendations. I had a good GPA but only an OK LSAT. I am convinced to this day that I got into UCLA law school on the strength of my professor recommendations. I got my recommendations from professors in classes that were small, so that the professor actually got to know me personally, as well as my work product.

Status: Alumnus/a, full-time
Dates of Enrollment: 8/1998-12/2003
Survey Submitted: March 2005

The admissions process for UCLAW is pretty straightforward. With affirmative action gone from the public educational institutions, the primary difference between an application for UCLAW and other institutions is that no reference to your race is permitted. However, if race is important to you, you can attempt to indicate your own by highlighting ethnic-based community service or organizations that you belong to. Another tip is to DEFINITELY visit the campus and find out who the people are that will be making the decision on your application. Find out who is on the admissions committee and try and speak with them. That way, when your application comes across their desk, you become more than a piece of paper. I don't remember whether the admissions committee is a name-blind process but if you have the opportunity, make sure you use similar anecdotes in your conversations with the members of the committee that you will use in your essay; that way even without the name, the application should seem familiar to the reviewer.

Status: Current student, full-time
Dates of Enrollment: 9/2003-Submit Date
Survey Submitted: March 2005

UCLA is quite selective, but it is looking for a diverse student body. Of course, grades are important, but the essay is a real booster as well. They aren't just looking for the Mr. or Ms. Straight-A, so reveal your unique interests and passions in your essay and show how you can add to diversity here.

Status: Alumnus/a, full-time
Dates of Enrollment: 8/1999-5/2002
Survey Submitted: April 2004

Because it's a University of California school (public school with public school prices), competition will be very stiff with many, many applicants. Unfortunately, admissions appears numbers-driven because there are too many applicants to weed through. From what I remember, UCLA Law was within the Top Five or Six in terms of selectivity. Many people want to attend not just for the school, but also the location. The essays did not ask for anything out of the ordinary, and I would say that numbers would be looked at as priority over personal information that can be conveyed in an essay. If you are applying to the Public Interest Program, in almost all cases, you need to get accepted into the general law school first, then pass another hurdle that scrutinizes your past experience and match with a Public Interest Program. In rare occasions, a person would get admitted into the public interest program who didn't have the scores for general admission if the background and/or potential for public interest work was sufficient.

> **The school says:** "Every single file is read and, while academic numbers are important in that we want our students to be successful in law school, many other factors are considered in the admissions process. Everyone offered admission, including applicants to the public interest program, have academic criteria that qualifies them for admission. The applicants to the public interest program have the additional criteria of experience in, and commitment to, public service."

Status: Alumnus/a, full-time
Dates of Enrollment: 2000-2003
Survey Submitted: April 2004

It's not impossible, even if you don't have a 170+ LSAT (though that certainly helps). A detailed essay of how you will contribute in a positive way to the law school experience for other students goes a long way. Also, show them a detailed plan of: (1) What you plan to do with your law degree and why you're going there (too many students just go to grad school because they can't find a

Read all of Vault's Law School Surveys at www.vault.com/lawschool — get complete surveys on top law schools, expert advice on applicaton essays, LSAT prep and more.

VAULT CAREER LIBRARY   89

job they want); and (2) What steps you will take to mitigate the tough 1L experience. (I took research classes at the law library as an undergrad.) There are no interviews. Selectivity has become even more competitive in the last few years because the ROI is very favorable, compared to the relatively low tuition. UCLAW is getting Harvard, Yale, Stanford people who don't want the big debt they'd get if they stayed at their schools.

Status: Current student, full-time
Dates of Enrollment: 8/2001-Submit Date
Survey Submitted: February 2004

UCLA is a highly selective law school. At the time of my admission, it was ranked 15th in *U.S. News & World Report* professional school ranking. UCLA Law admits applicants on a rolling basis, so it is advisable to apply as soon as possible. That way, applicants can know their status (i.e., admitted, denied admission, waitlisted) relatively early and plan accordingly. The admissions process is streamlined. You are required to submit an official application by the deadline, including a personal statement. You may also submit any additional information you believe might help the admissions office get to know you. Here, you can submit a resume, curriculum vitae or other listing of personal accomplishments or training.

Status: Current student, full-time
Dates of Enrollment: 8/2001-Submit Date
Survey Submitted: September 2003

The admissions process for the UCLA School of Law is fairly standard; application, personal statement and a few supplements that vary depending on whether or not you wish to apply for a specific program (public interest law and policy, critical race studies, etc.). The application itself is fairly straightforward and relatively uncomplicated and short.

The school is very selective, normally accepting roughly [13 percent of] applicants. Admissions has experienced an influx in applications in recent years, likely due to the lagging economy. For example, UCLA Law experienced a 20 percent rise in applications between the Class of 2004 and the Class of 2005. The office is slightly understaffed and overworked, and makes the majority of its decisions by the numbers; namely undergrad GPA and LSAT scores.

The school will not demand an outrageous sum of money to hold your place in the class, which can work to your advantage if you are still considering multiple schools at the last minute. There is a helpful reception in April of every year, during which admitted students are invited to visit the campus and talk with professors and administrators.

Status: Current student, full-time
Dates of Enrollment: 8/2002-Submit Date
Survey Submitted: September 2003

I applied to 15 law schools in 2002. Every single law school I applied to, without exception, admitted me if my LSAT score was higher than their average LSAT score for the previous year, rejected me if my LSAT score was lower than their average LSAT score and waitlisted me if their average score was the same as mine. UCLA was no exception. I got a 165, I got in. It may be easier to get in if you apply to the public interest program or the critical race program.

> **The school says:** "Both of these programs are highly competitive. The Program in Public Interest Law and Policy admits approximately 10 percent of its applicants, and the Critical Race faculty committee recommends for admission less than 10 percent of applicants who express interest in that program."

 **Academics**

Status: Current student, full-time
Dates of Enrollment: 8/2005-Submit Date
Survey Submitted: February 2006

The academics here are excellent. Every professor I have had has been at the top of his/her particular field of expertise and/or has received teaching awards. The professors represent a wide variety of political, social and intellectual backgrounds, and there is a great amount of respect for differing viewpoints here.

There's a lot of reading for the first-year classes, but I don't think it's anything different from other schools. I'm only a first-year, so I can't say anything about the ease of getting into classes (we're assigned to a standard curriculum) or the workload in the advanced courses.

UCLA has an excellent system of academic support, including student mentoring, optional study skills classes for first semester 1Ls, and extra help for second semester 1Ls who didn't do well in the first semester. My professors have, by and large, been very accessible. They generally make themselves available to 1Ls in the second semester to discuss performance on first semester exams, which is nice.

Status: Alumnus/a, full-time
Dates of Enrollment: 8/2002-5/2005
Survey Submitted: March 2006

UCLA offers a lot of clinical classes, which is great. Students should take advantage of early registration slots to enroll in the clinicals or popular seminars. The school has a large student body and a lot of great faculty members. The student body is also quite diverse; you'll run across students from all over the country who went to just about every top school you can think of.

Status: Alumnus/a, full-time
Dates of Enrollment: 8/2002-5/2005
Survey Submitted: October 2005

The workload is particularly heavy during your first year. The weight of one's workload in the second or third year depends on the number of units, classes, professors and/or other activities to which one is involved in. UCLAW offers many innovative programs, such as the Critical Race Studies Program and a concentration in Business Law and Policy. The professors are excellent and most sincerely care about the students and the community. Right now, UCLAW is transitioning into a new grading policy, which will be interesting to see how it progresses.

Status: Alumnus/a, full-time
Dates of Enrollment: 2000-2003
Survey Submitted: April 2005

First-year students are broken up into sections for the core courses. Professors are overwhelmingly dedicated, intelligent and hardworking. There are some who use their position, however, to grind their political axe instead of actually teaching law. This is unfortunate, but is the rare exception. Students are, by and large, friendly and hardworking. It's the type of place that if you get sick and miss a day of class, people are generally friendly enough and will give you their notes.

Status: Alumnus/a, full-time
Dates of Enrollment: 9/1996-6/1999
Survey Submitted: March 2005

The law school has a tremendously gifted faculty with an emphasis on both the theoretical academic side of the law, as well as the actual practice of law. Of particular note are the law school's transactional and advocacy seminars as well as the certificate in business law, a courseload for those that know they want to practice corporate and/or restructuring law when they graduate. All grading is anonymous and done on a hard curve; there is no grade inflation at UCLA!

Status: Alumnus/a, full-time
Dates of Enrollment: 8/1999-5/2002
Survey Submitted: March 2005

The clinical classes are grade-A choice cuts, and UCLA has one of the largest breadth of clinical classes to choose from. But because they are limited in size, and the professor often gets to pick which students get in, you better get to know your professor before you try to take his clinical. Should you not like classes, there is always the option of taking independent projects with professors, where you will meet with a professor depending on his availability and write a paper. Using this method I only had class from 4 to 6 p.m. on Monday and 2 to 4 p.m. on Wednesday my entire last semester. You also have the option of taking a limited number of undergraduate classes for law school credit if you can convince the dean that the undergraduate class has some bearing on your future law school career. Taking a class in the undergrad public policy department was a popular choice.

Status: Alumnus/a, full-time
Dates of Enrollment: 8/1998-12/2003
Survey Submitted: March 2005

Obviously, this is law school so the academics are rigorous, as should be expected. One advantage that UCLAW has, though, is that students fill out evaluations of their class and professors toward the end of every semester. This information is kept inside the dean of students' office and is available to anyone who wants to look at it. This is the best way to get an idea of the workload and popularity of both the class and the professor.

Status: Current student, full-time
Dates of Enrollment: 9/2003-Submit Date
Survey Submitted: March 2005

No matter how interesting the subject matter, the quality of a class largely depends on the professor. Each professor's teaching style is different, but I would say most of them are superb. I got some of the best professors for my first-year classes, and that made a huge difference to the rest of my law school career. My professors encouraged class discussion and invited us to think critically about the policies behind the law, but they also clearly taught the Black Letter law, which is important both for law school finals and the bar exam. Though professors do call on students in class, this actually kept me from falling behind in reading, which was very helpful. Moreover, students could easily say "pass" if they did not know how to answer the question.

Status: Current student, full-time
Dates of Enrollment: 8/2003-Submit Date
Survey Submitted: January 2005

UCLAW employs a strict curve for all first-year classes, and any classes over 40 students require that an equal number of C's be given as A's. This is being reviewed by administration because given the grade inflation at other top tier schools, this is viewed as a potential disadvantage to UCLAW students. Grading aside, the nature of the classes is topnotch. Generally, professors are very accomplished and highly accessible. Furthermore, our new Dean Schill seems very dedicated to furthering UCLAW's reputation by continuing to invest in getting great professors and offering a wide array of classes. The workload is as you might expect, HEAVY. This is less so in second- and third-year courses, but it is my understanding that is the way law school is designed to be.

Status: Current student, full-time
Dates of Enrollment: 8/2001-Submit Date
Survey Submitted: February 2004

Overall, the quality of classes is excellent. Of course, you will find some classes unbelievably dull and others very engaging. If you are lucky, most of your classes will fall into the latter category. Professors approach the material differently. Some use a PowerPoint presentation (very helpful), others lecture and still some follow a modified Socratic Method where the professors ask students direct questions to elicit the answer.

During first year, school officials pick students' classes. Students show up during orientation and pick up their schedules. That is it. After first year, you may pick your own classes. However, it may be difficult to get into certain popular classes. To ensure fairness, UCLA has a pass system where students are randomly assigned a number (one through four) that determines when that particular student registers. For example, if X is assigned "one" first semester second year, X (along with other ones) will register first, followed by those assigned twos, threes and so on. Also, students can only be assigned each number once. For example, if X is assigned "one" first semester second year, he will not be assigned "one" again. He will be assigned two, three or four to correspond with his remaining semesters.

Status: Current student, full-time
Dates of Enrollment: 8/2001-Submit Date
Survey Submitted: April 2004

As with nearly every law school I am aware of, first-year students are assigned to a section, and all classes are assigned. They are the same courses generally offered by other law schools: Torts, Property, Criminal Law, Civil Procedure, Constitutional Law, Contracts, and a year-long Legal Writing course.

During the second and third year, students may choose all of their courses. The school requires upper-year students to take a course in Professional

Responsibility or write a paper relating to the subject for credit. The school strongly encourages students to take the course in Evidence, though there are no other requirements. Courses on subject matter covered by the bar exam are offered each semester, along with several other electives, usually related to the interests of the professors or their pet projects. Upper-year offerings tend to be heavy in business-related courses. The school is lagging in International Law offerings, though it is making an effort to rectify that.

The workload is the same as any law school. Expect not to have much time for anything but school during your first year. During second year, time is generally consumed by other activities, namely finding the next summer's job and participating in Law Review, moot court or other extracurricular activities. Third-year students are notorious for slacking off and there is a significant rate of absenteeism in classes.

Professors are generally very friendly and willing to assist students. There are a couple that seem to thrive on intimidating students, but they are not by any means the norm. I was surprised to discover how much UCLA Law professors were NOT like the intimidating professor in *Paper Chase*.

 Employment Prospects

Status: Alumnus/a, full-time
Dates of Enrollment: 8/1997-6/2000
Survey Submitted: March 2006

Very prestigious with employers. All of the large firms recruit from UCLA through the on-campus interview program (OCIP). Graduates can obtain any type of job they want—large firm, small firm, government, public interest.

Alumni network is not helpful or supportive. Very few alumni contacts were available through the career office, and the alumni in general were not very approachable at law school functions.

Status: Alumnus/a, full-time
Dates of Enrollment: 8/2002-5/2005
Survey Submitted: March 2006

Excellent career services; including a lengthy on-campus interviewing process. Most, if not all 3Ls, end up with jobs; not all big-firm jobs, but jobs. Only potential problem is that on-campus interview slots are awarded somewhat randomly, which helps students with lower GPAs, but sometimes is a detriment to employers and top students. For 1Ls, there is also an 1L on-campus interviewing process, but if you want a big-firm job, finding a backdoor or sending cover letters and resumes is probably a better strategy.

Status: Alumnus/a, full-time
Dates of Enrollment: 8/2002-5/2005
Survey Submitted: October 2005

Although UCLAW is a top law school, landing a job is not that easy. UCLAW grads are competing with other grads from top law schools that have a 3.4 GPA, whereas UCLAW is around 2.8 to 3.0. Indeed, most grads move on to work at top law firms in LA; however, their loyalty to UCLAW grads is not as strong as grads from private schools.

Status: Alumnus/a, full-time
Dates of Enrollment: 8/1999-5/2002
Survey Submitted: March 2005

UCLA is considered a great regional school and top national school. With a decent GPA—top 40 percent, maybe 30 percent—one can easily grab a large law firm job, especially in California. But colleagues of mine have taken jobs in New York, Chicago and D.C. without any problem. Generally, when looking at taking a job outside of California, the employers see UCLA on the resume, and then want to know why you possibly want to leave Southern California (it's good to have some type of family connection to the other region if applying outside of CA). The office of career services does an incredible job of trying to place students and about 350 firms do on-campus interviewing. (Well, with all the mergers, I'm not sure if it's still 350, but you get the idea.) I think the average is about 96 percent of students have a job within one year of graduating from law school.

Read all of Vault's Law School Surveys at www.vault.com/lawschool — get complete surveys on top law schools, expert advice on applicaton essays, LSAT prep and more.

VAULT CAREER LIBRARY   91

Status: Alumnus/a, full-time
Dates of Enrollment: 8/1998-12/2003
Survey Submitted: March 2005

UCLAW is a nationally recognized school and that makes it much easier when searching for jobs. This is especially so if one plans to practice within California or L.A. specifically, because every major law firm has multiple UCLAW alums. The process of searching for a job is not an easy one, however. But the career services staff is wonderful and they are an invaluable resource to all of those who take advantage of what they have to offer. Even in the difficult economic times that our country is facing, everyone finds a job within three to six months after graduation; although most get jobs by the end of their second summer.

Status: Current student, full-time
Dates of Enrollment: 9/2003-Submit Date
Survey Submitted: March 2005

UCLA is a top law school, and I think that employers keep that in mind. The on-campus interviewing here is hectic because it overlaps with classes. But there are many employers here for on-campus interviews, and that is good. I think most students here are in one of two categories: large law firms or public interest. I didn't find the alumni network very helpful.

Status: Current student, full-time
Dates of Enrollment: 8/2003-Submit Date
Survey Submitted: April 2005

If you want to work at a big firm, it's easy to find one on campus. If you don't, that's another story. The great thing is that the public interest office is one of the most helpful offices at the school, and they do an excellent job at placing people. The bad news is that the career services office doesn't seem to have a clue about how to find non-big firm jobs or clerkships.

Status: Current student, full-time
Dates of Enrollment: 8/2001-Submit Date
Survey Submitted: September 2003

UCLA is a prestigious law school, thus students have little difficulty finding a legal job after graduation. In recent years, after experiencing an inflation of law firm salaries in California (and elsewhere) as well as a shrinking economy, it has been harder for students to find employment in large law firms. Still, even in these hard times, a substantial portion (roughly one-third to one-half) will enter a large law firm immediately after graduation. Government, public interest and small law firm jobs tend to be rather easy to obtain.

The on-campus interviewing program (OCIP) is by far the most visible way that law students receive jobs. Employers participating in OCIP tend to be the larger, national law firms, with a few local mid-size firms also participating. There are also other job fairs during the year. Government employers come on campus during the fall, though that tends to be informational in nature rather than direct recruiting. In the spring, there is a public interest fair during which employers set up information tables and some interview students for summer and permanent positions. Many students find jobs outside of these on-campus recruitment fairs and programs, however.

Status: Alumnus/a, full-time
Dates of Enrollment: 8/1999-5/2002
Survey Submitted: April 2004

I did all of my job seeking on my own. UCLA offers the typical law school on-campus recruiting programs. The Public Interest Program is excellent in terms of connecting alumni and graduates with opportunities. The career services people are helpful if you approach them and develop a relationship. They will not hold your hand, though. They are also helpful once you've graduated.

Obviously, the best job prospects are in Southern California and Los Angeles, in particular. The prestige of the school carries more weight in California.

> **The school says:** "In addition to the fall and spring on-campus interview programs, the law school sponsors a range of events to help students learn about and find opportunities in a variety of practice settings. These activities include a government reception and information fair, a small/mid-size law firm reception, public interest career day and practice specialties day."

Quality of Life

Status: Current student, full-time
Dates of Enrollment: 8/2005-Submit Date
Survey Submitted: February 2006

My experience of the culture here is that it is friendly, relatively laid-back and very collegial. People do not rip pages out of required library reading, or refuse to give you the notes from class if you had to miss a day. It is becoming increasingly less of a "commuter school" so there are generally lots people around campus both during the week and on weekends.

I live in the new UCLA graduate student housing in Westwood, L.A. It is clean and comfortable, and you have a choice of living in a studio, a two-bedroom apartment or a two-bedroom townhouse. It is conveniently located about a mile away from school, and there's a free bus on weekdays. The main problem with the graduate housing is that they are completely disorganized, it took them months longer than they had projected to figure out their availability, and I didn't get confirmation that I had a spot until late July (just one month before I was supposed to start school!). Dealing with UCLA housing is a Kafka-esque nightmare. But having gotten housing, I am pretty happy with it.

Status: Alumnus/a, full-time
Dates of Enrollment: 8/1997-6/2000
Survey Submitted: March 2006

Los Angeles is a car culture, but obtaining parking on campus is a nightmare, there is a shortage of parking spaces and the cost of an annual parking permit is at least $500 (I think it has increased over the last several years). If you can't afford a car or lose in the parking lottery, you have to commute to the school by bus, which is not an appealing option for most people.

Status: Alumnus/a, full-time
Dates of Enrollment: 8/2002-5/2005
Survey Submitted: March 2006

Beautiful campus, lush and green, and the weather is perfect year-round. Students eat lunch and study outside in the courtyard year-round. The library is very large, and you can usually find a place to study.

Most students live off campus near Westwood, West Hollywood/Beverly Hills or West L.A./Santa Monica. If you live close to campus, parking on (and around) campus can be a problem for 1Ls and 2Ls, unless you're willing to carpool. Buses around UCLA are abundant and run frequently. Still you probably DO need a car to get around in L.A. If you choose to drive, then depending on where you live, traffic really isn't that bad once you learn the side streets and also the times to avoid the freeways.

Status: Alumnus/a, full-time
Dates of Enrollment: 8/2002-5/2005
Survey Submitted: October 2005

L.A. is expensive, but then again it's diverse and there are so many things to see in L.A. The restaurants are incomparable and the people are beautiful. Housing is expensive if you choose to live near the school. Living farther away from the school is a way to save some pennies but with gas prices, L.A. traffic and the stress of law school, you might be better off living in Westwood. UCLAW's facilities are better than decent. The law library is fairly new and especially comfortable—for some students, it's home. Westwood is fairly safe. In the three years that I attended UCLAW, there was only a handful of reported crimes.

Status: Current student, full-time
Dates of Enrollment: 8/2004-Submit Date
Survey Submitted: February 2005

UCLA is a beautiful campus in a great neighborhood. The biggest problem is lack of parking, but there are tolerable public transit options. The law library is relatively new and architecturally stunning. The classrooms are lackluster, and the law building overall is a bit jumbled since it used to be several separate buildings. UCLA is located in Westwood, which offers ample restaurants, bars and shopping. The campus and the neighborhood get pretty crowded, especially when the undergrads are here. Traffic can be astonishingly awful; typical for Los Angeles, though.

Status: Alumnus/a, full-time
Dates of Enrollment: 9/1998-5/2001
Survey Submitted: February 2005

Quality of life is pretty good, considering you are in law school. People are generally friendly and not bitter like they may be at other law schools. The law school campus is state of the art (i.e., Internet connections in most classrooms), the library is topnotch (opened in 1998) and you can't beat the neighborhood.

Status: Current student, full-time
Dates of Enrollment: 8/2002-5/2006
Survey Submitted: April 2005

Who wouldn't want to study the law in an environment where it's sunny and warm year-round? Students are serious about the law, yet study in the comfort of flip-flops and shorts. The quality of life at UCLA Law is second to none. Situated on the campus of UCLA, law students have access to the university's amenities, including its research libraries, gym, cultural, musical performances in world-class Royce Hall and UCLA sports, such as gazing on the 12 basketball championship banners in Pauley Pavilion.

Status: Current student, full-time
Dates of Enrollment: 8/2001-Submit Date
Survey Submitted: September 2003

The law school itself is a great building, very well kept-up and aesthetically pleasing. There is a courtyard in the center in which students socialize between classes and eat lunch. There is a student lounge, but it is quite small. When it rains, which is very infrequent, students often sit along the walls of the main hallway to enjoy lunch due to a lack of indoor common area seating. All of the desks in classrooms are equipped with Internet access, which allows for easy browsing and instant messaging while professors are droning on. The law library was recently expanded and is without question the nicest library on campus.

 ## Social Life

Status: Current student, full-time
Dates of Enrollment: 8/2005-Submit Date
Survey Submitted: February 2006

There isn't much of a social life, though a few dedicated law students try by having Bar Review nights every Thursday (they go to different bars each week, and all law students are invited). Basically, everybody I know just studies a lot. But that's law school.

A lot of students here are from the area originally, and have friends outside of school. So you don't necessarily get the intense bonding among students you might in other places.

Status: Alumnus/a, full-time
Dates of Enrollment: 8/2002-5/2005
Survey Submitted: March 2006

Like most schools, 1Ls will spend a lot of time in classes and the library, but it's a gorgeous campus to be stuck at. 2Ls and 3Ls have more free time to enjoy all that L.A. has to offer. The ocean at Santa Monica and Venice is only a couple of miles away if you like the beach; even better beaches at Malibu or closer to Orange County are also close. World-class shopping is all around and close, as is the nightlife of Hollywood and West Hollywood. L.A. offers TONS of live music. Plus, you will literally run into dozens of celebrities throughout the streets of L.A. and Hollywood.

Status: Current student, full-time
Dates of Enrollment: 8/2004-Submit Date
Survey Submitted: February 2005

There are weekly bar events for law students, which are pretty well attended. There are also some popular annual events, like the Barrister's Ball. Like many other law schools (I hear), people tend to make friends with their 1L sectionmates and it's a bit difficult to branch out during the first year. Los Angeles has everything you could possibly want to do in your spare time; it's a great place to be a distracted law student.

Status: Alumnus/a, full-time
Dates of Enrollment: 8/1999-5/2002
Survey Submitted: March 2005

UCLA is probably the most social of the top-tier schools. The Southern California weather just makes people happier. We regularly do parties with other graduate schools (the business school, the med school, the school of public policy, etc.). There is normally a social (keg in the courtyard) at least once a month, and plenty of "socializing" immediately after every final. Every Thursday is Bar Review (where the entire school is encouraged to meet up at the same bar) and about 60-100 people normally attend every week (less as finals approach). In short, if socializing is a big part of who you are, there could be no better place than UCLA. Westwood is a wonderful area to live and study in. You are also very close to Santa Monica, Venice Beach and Beverly Hills.

Status: Current student, full-time
Dates of Enrollment: 8/2002-5/2006
Survey Submitted: April 2005

Put down that *US Weekly* and experience the L.A. scene for yourself. Tired of hearing about Sunset Blvd. clubs mentioned in rap songs without any frame of reference? UCLA Law has Bar Reviews each Thursday for students to "de-stress" but only in the hippest bars and clubs in Hollywood, Santa Monica and Melrose. Law students don't have to look far for potential mates since Southern California boasts the best looking singles in the nation. Dating within sections is usually taboo but some have made it happen without too much gossip. Most law students have better luck with students from other programs like the UCLA business school.

Status: Current student, full-time
Dates of Enrollment: 8/2001-Submit Date
Survey Submitted: September 2003

The student bar association sponsors occasional social events in the courtyard after school, a weekly "bar review" where one local bar is designated as a meeting point for all UCLA Law students seeking to go out and spend time with friends that evening, and Barrister's Ball, a semi-formal dinner and dance in the spring. In addition, various extracurricular groups provide their members with additional social opportunities.

Law students tend not to socialize much with other members of the general university student body, but on occasion we have co-sponsored events with the medical and business schools. The graduate student association sponsors "Grad Bar" approximately once a month, and this offers the opportunity to socialize with other graduate students on campus.

Many law students choose to take UCLA-offered recreation courses. Recreation offerings tend to be plentiful and interesting. Among the offerings are: sailing, surfing, horseback riding, ballroom dancing and a smattering of aerobics classes.

Status: Alumnus/a, full-time
Dates of Enrollment: 8/1999-5/2002
Survey Submitted: April 2004

This depends on your age when you enter law school. The law school is located with the other schools, including the undergrad campus and other professional schools. The business school often invites law students for mixers. There are always sporting recreational events to participate in, both on campus and off.

The ethnic food in Los Angeles is some of the best. A favorite is a Cuban restaurant called Versailles located in the Palms area, about five miles south of UCLA. There is also great Japanese food on Sawtelle Boulevard, also just south of campus. The good bars are located down Wilshire Boulevard toward the ocean and also in the Third Street Promenade area closer to the beach. Bars and restaurants in California are smoke-free, so you can go to a bar without smelling afterwards.

Status: Current student, full-time
Dates of Enrollment: 8/2003-Submit Date
Survey Submitted: April 2004

The law student newspaper is popular. The Thursday keg of beer sponsored by SBA is always popular as well, especially with the 1Ls who are stuck on campus until midnight. Several bars and restaurants in Westwood Village that you can take a bus to. Law students date each other because who has the time to hang out at clubs/bars?

Read all of Vault's Law School Surveys at www.vault.com/lawschool — get complete surveys on top law schools, expert advice on applicaton essays, LSAT prep and more.

VAULT CAREER LIBRARY   93

University of the Pacific

McGeorge School of Law
Admissions Office
3200 Fifth Avenue
Sacramento, CA 95817
Admissions phone: (916) 739-7105
Admissions fax: (916) 739-7134
Admissions e-mail: admissionsmcgeorge@pacific.edu
Admissions URL: http://www.mcgeorge.edu/admissions/

 ## Admissions

Status: Current student, full-time
Dates of Enrollment: 8/2004-Submit Date
Survey Submitted: June 2005

The school makes a very strong effort to pursue applicants. More so than any other law school I applied to. The school is intent on recruiting higher caliber students and gives scholarships to a majority of incoming students. The application process is stress free. I was turned down by most schools but was offered a scholarship by McGeorge.

Status: Current student, full-time
Dates of Enrollment: 8/2004-Submit Date
Survey Submitted: August 2005

The admissions process is relatively standard as it all goes through LSAC. However, it was my experience that the administration was very efficient with handling paperwork, getting me information, and they had current students contact me so that I could ask questions and discuss law school. The standards are becoming more rigorous as McG was ranked second tier last year but the school does take all the applicant's life experience into account, in addition to academics, LSAT score, etc.

Status: Current student, full-time
Dates of Enrollment: 8/2002-Submit Date
Survey Submitted: July 2004

The admissions process for McGeorge is much like that of any other law school because LSAC handles most everything for all ABA schools. You need to send them letters of recommendation, transcripts and LSAT scores and then check off which school you are applying to. The rest is done with McGeorge's application. The school is quite good at looking for serious students and those with other relevant experiences that will show determination, such as job and military experience.

Status: Alumnus/a, full-time
Dates of Enrollment: 8/2000-5/2003
Survey Submitted: August 2004

I filled out an application and sent letters of reference.

Status: Current student, part-time
Dates of Enrollment: 8/2002-Submit Date
Survey Submitted: May 2004

The admissions process included taking the LSAT, subscribing to the law school admissions services, submitting two letters of recommendation, writing a personal statement, submitting a resume and an application directly to the school. Selection supposedly depended on GPA, LSAT score and personal statement, along with consideration of personal and professional factors.

 ## Academics

Status: Current student, full-time
Dates of Enrollment: 8/2004-Submit Date
Survey Submitted: June 2005

I can say with complete confidence that McGeorge's curriculum is as challenging and rigorous as any school in the country. Classes are very Socratic, there is no option to "pass" if called upon (instead, most teachers will lower your grade). Legal writing assignments are frequent and intense and not an excuse for not preparing for classes, and students, while friendly and courteous are certainly competitive (60 percent have scholarships but only the top third retains the scholarship after first year). As for the quality of the program, I have been very satisfied.

For a school outside of the top tier, the professors are very accomplished. Most have written and published extensively in their subjects and some have issued textbooks used by many other schools. All are experts. Also, there is a practical focus to everything that is done. From the beginning, the goal is clear and stated: students will be fully able to practice law immediately upon graduation and after the bar. Professors are also very accessible. Every professor is available after class and several times a week for a few hours at a time, and all professors provide phone numbers and e-mail info where they can be reached. They usually always respond. In class, most professors are intense and intimidating and won't accept anything other than an acceptable answer, but out of class, professors are encouraging and much more explanatory.

As far as grading, I am at a total loss for the method used. But it seems to work out. There are very few A's given; maybe two or three in a section of 80. The upside, though, is that if you make B's or B+'s, you have done quite well. I received four B+'s and two B's after my first year and finished top 20 percent. So it works out. Students must have a C+ average to continue on, so the sense among students is that C work is failing, which I suppose is true. As far as choosing classes, McGeorge has quite a few required upper level courses. All the subjects that the bar tests are required at McGeorge. Thus, most of the registration strategies center around getting the best teachers for those classes. But I'm not sure it makes that big of a difference.

McGeorge also offers a strong set of electives in some emerging areas. You won't find purely academic undergrad-type classes like "Dickens and the Law," but electives such as International Water Rights, Tax, and all the advocacy courses make for interesting options. There are also excellent clinical opportunities available that most students can choose to take part in. There are about seven including Business Litigation, Civil Practice (mostly landlord/tenant type stuff), Bankruptcy and a fairly new Parole Representation clinic where students argue before parole boards on behalf of life inmates. Because of the extensive elective options and the somewhat substantial load of required courses, most students' first choices for non-required courses are accommodated. One other thing about McGeorge: I think it inspires a somewhat rabid mind-set in most of its students. What I mean is that everyone understands the school is a virtual unknown nationally and that if anyone is going to notice us as lawyers, we are going to have to blow them away with our preparedness and skills. I think the mind-set of an underdog is a good one to have, and it certainly comes mostly from the school.

Status: Current student, full-time
Dates of Enrollment: 8/2004-Submit Date
Survey Submitted: August 2005

McGeorge has a rigorous program and trust me, you will work your butt off. However, the faculty is excellent and the school really does a lot to help students succeed. In addition, the school covers first-year basic classes (Torts, Property, Contracts, Civil Procedure) over a year rather than one semester like many law schools do. Personally, I think that this gives students a broader, more solid understanding of the law and better prepares them for the bar, which is, of course, kind of the whole point.

Status: Current student, full-time
Dates of Enrollment: 8/2002-Submit Date
Survey Submitted: July 2004

In academics, McGeorge does very well. Since the required classes are fairly standard thanks to the ABA, the differences in academic quality come from the electives and the professors. The school has a large variety of elective classes from Water Law to international courses on the law of the EU. The only problem is that some courses may be offered only once per year, so if that course is a prerequisite for others then you need to pay attention and sign up early. As for signing up for the classes, McGeorge is a bit behind the times. Where many schools are now offering registration online, McGeorge has just started a "mail-in" registration. Before 2004, you actually had a first come, first serve "in-person" registration.

The professors at McGeorge are generally a great bunch who really have the will to teach and are readily available with on-campus offices. There is always a variation between how much or how little a certain professor will grill students with the Socratic Method compared to another, but overall the professors are knowledgeable, well-published and generally have a lot of practical experience.

> **The school says:** "Pacific McGeorge now has online registration capabilities."

Status: Alumnus/a, full-time
Dates of Enrollment: 8/2000-5/2003
Survey Submitted: August 2004

Socratic Method of teaching.

Status: Current student, part-time
Dates of Enrollment: 8/2002-Submit Date
Survey Submitted: May 2004

I attended the evening program. The quality of the classes is quite rigorous and demanding—grading is stringent and exam taking can be stressful. My workload was extraordinarily heavy considering the program is intended for working professionals.

 Employment Prospects

Status: Current student, full-time
Dates of Enrollment: 8/2004-Submit Date
Survey Submitted: June 2005

McGeorge is certainly a regional school at this point, so outside of California (even Southern California is stretching McGeorge's reach) and some of the areas in the Pacific Northwest, the locales where people have actually heard of McGeorge is limited. In Northern California, however, the name is quite good, and McGeorge is known to produce some of the most well-prepared and hardest working graduates of any school in the region. I can't validate this for sure, but the talk around campus (which again may be only a nice-sounding rumor) is that McGeorge is consistently rated by employers as producing the best prepared young lawyers. Anyhow, despite the limited name recognition, if you do well and are active enough to pursue other options besides Nor. Cal., then I don't think there should be any problem in gaining employment outside the region. After my first year, I have a clerkship in D.C., and I plan to send out resumes to all sorts of different areas for next summer. I don't want to stay in Nor. Cal. (even though I like it), and I don't think I will be forced to just because of McGeorge's lack of name recognition. Graduates obtain all sorts of different jobs, including big firm, big salary associate positions. All that info is published on the web site.

The career services office is very active, and students are offered guidance beginning in Nov. of their first year. There are constant resume drops where the school will send out your materials to various employers, as well as workshops for improving job seeking skills. Each student is assigned to a career adviser who can help with any difficulties in the process. There is an established network in D.C., and quite a few students work in there each year. There is a D.C.

liaison who facilitates the process, and while in D.C. lunches with area alumni are organized to provide further networking advantages. In CA, the alumni network is very strong and it seems quite helpful. But I can't say for sure. As far as on-campus recruiting, there is some, but I think it is lacking a bit. Not many of the big firms recruit on campus, which is annoying.

Status: Current student, full-time
Dates of Enrollment: 8/2004-Submit Date
Survey Submitted: August 2005

The McGeorge career development office is very active in assisting students. Sometimes I felt like I was being bombarded with too much information. They do a good job of collaborating with student clubs to bring attorneys practicing various areas of the law to campus to speak with students. Personally, I secured two paid legal internships my first summer (both part-time), and expect to secure a valuable summer associate position this upcoming summer.

Status: Current student, full-time
Dates of Enrollment: 8/2002-Submit Date
Survey Submitted: July 2004

McGeorge has been working very hard to provide externships, clerkships and jobs in the local area and being in a government town there is quite a good list to choose from. Before I finish law school, I will have worked for four judges in three different courts. There are also plenty of opportunities with the local administrative agencies, DAs and firms. This really is one of the better towns for work experience being that there is just such a variety. The only drawback might be that as McGeorge is still climbing in the rankings—some of the largest firms might overlook its potential.

Status: Current student, full-time
Dates of Enrollment: 8/2002-Submit Date
Survey Submitted: May 2004

Career prospects primarily include: attorney, legal consultant, judge, hearing officer, arbitrator and mediator, among others. Internship opportunities consist of primarily the same, except under the supervision of an attorney or judge.

 **Quality of Life**

Status: Current student, full-time
Dates of Enrollment: 8/2004-Submit Date
Survey Submitted: June 2005

The campus is gorgeous. It isn't in the best neighborhood, but once on the campus, there are fir trees next to palm trees, open green spaces, benches, a small gym, a nice cafeteria/gathering area, swimming pool, etc. On-campus housing is a good option, with lots available. Some students like living on campus very much. While the neighborhood is run-down, I have never felt anything was dangerous. There are campus police who patrol the campus 24/7 and parking and walkways are well lit at night.

Status: Current student, full-time
Dates of Enrollment: 8/2004-Submit Date
Survey Submitted: August 2005

It's no secret that, being located in Oak Park, McGeorge is not in the greatest of neighborhoods. The neighborhood, however, is old and has a lot of heritage, and McGeorge adds to the attributes. Also, the school has an active security force, which provides information on crimes, preventative measures and is more than happy to escort students across campus at night.

Status: Current student, full-time
Dates of Enrollment: 8/2002-Submit Date
Survey Submitted: July 2004

This is probably the worst area for McGeorge, as it is located in Oak Park, Sacramento, which is known as one of the rougher neighborhoods. This has been tempered by the many city efforts and thanks to vigilant and ever-present campus cops, but it is still not a great neighborhood. I have lived on campus for a year and the accommodations are better than they were in college and are inexpensive. The school is very accessible by freeway though and so most people choose to get an apartment elsewhere. The campus is beautiful, almost a mini-

Read all of Vault's Law School Surveys at www.vault.com/lawschool — get complete surveys on top law schools, expert advice on applicaton essays, LSAT prep and more.

VAULT CAREER LIBRARY   95

Stanford, with great redwoods and green grass everywhere. Being solely a law school, McGeorge is always filled with aspiring students.

Status: Alumnus/a, full-time
Dates of Enrollment: 8/2000-5/2003
Survey Submitted: August 2004

Cost of living is cheap.

Status: Current student, part-time
Dates of Enrollment: 8/2002-Submit Date
Survey Submitted: May 2004

Quality of life depends primarily on your own finances, or the financing your family provides. If you have neither, then your quality of life may be quite poor depending on your circumstances.

Social Life

Status: Current student, full-time
Dates of Enrollment: 8/2004-Submit Date
Survey Submitted: August 2005

Most students favor Thursday night bar review; it's held at a different Sacramento bar/club every week. Sacramento has a great selection of cultural/ethnic restaurants, which many of the ethnic clubs on campus take advantage of. All in all, though, most students don't have a ton of time for a social life in the sense that a working professional or undergrad student does.

Status: Current student, full-time
Dates of Enrollment: 8/2004-Submit Date
Survey Submitted: June 2005

School doesn't leave much time for anything else, but some students seem to manage to get out most weekends. Every Thursday, there is an organized bar event that is quite popular. And a few different formal type things at various points during the year. I can't really speak to these things, because I never went. There are also all sorts of recreational opportunities close by (San Fran., Napa, Tahoe). I spent my free time travelling up to Tahoe to go snowboarding or mountain biking. It's a nice drive and if you're committed, you can get up there most weekends for a day or so without any trouble. Some people thought it was too far. I didn't at all, maybe a 90-minute drive.

Overall, students are friendly and everyone knows each other. By the time the year is over, the scene is very small..

Status: Current student, full-time
Dates of Enrollment: 8/2002-Submit Date
Survey Submitted: July 2004

McGeorge has all of Sacramento for a social scene and does a fairly good job taking it all in. The year begins with a campus-wide river rafting trip and has several school socials. Also, the clubs are numerous and range from the Federalist Society to the Married Students Club. They all put on events that are open to all students and some are full black and white balls. Also, the school has a Thursday night at the bars get together every week called the Bar Review.

Status: Alumnus/a, full-time
Dates of Enrollment: 8/2000-5/2003
Survey Submitted: August 2004

Social life in Sacramento is fun unless you come from a big city like San Francisco or Los Angeles.

Status: Current student, part-time
Dates of Enrollment: 8/2002-Submit Date
Survey Submitted: May 2004

Social life is diverse depending on what you're looking for. The students organize numerous activities, as do local law firms and legal organizations. Student favorites include Bar Review, which is a student-organized event, chalking chalkboards with the name of a local bar for Thursday night visits by the law students. It's a good time to get together and relax since most of the week is finished.

The School Says

Welcome to a community dedicated to your success as a leader and in the law.

University of the Pacific, McGeorge School of Law is focused on creating leaders for an increasingly "globalized" world. We involve you in a rigorous, purposeful education, and offer you countless opportunities to explore and excel in every area of legal study.

Pacific McGeorge is the only ABA-accredited law school in Sacramento, California—the country's most populous state and the sixth largest economy in the world. Our green and wooded 13-acre campus nestled amidst a bustling city is a law- and student-centered community.

Academic Programs: Ranked in the Top 20 for our international law programs, Pacific McGeorge has a growing national and international reputation. Our academic programs are organized under three distinctive centers focused on Global Business and Development, Advocacy and Dispute Resolution, and Government Law and Policy—one of few such programs in the nation. U.S. Supreme Court Justice Anthony Kennedy has been affiliated with Pacific McGeorge for more than 40 years and has taught in our summer program in Salzburg, Austria for each of the last 17 years.

Our faculty are great teachers, but they're also experts—they write the books used by many other law schools—and with a 16:1 student-to-faculty ratio, you can be sure they will know you by name and will be there to help you. You'll be encouraged to put classroom theory into practice in one of our six on-campus clinics: Victims of Crime, Business and Community Development, Landlord/Tenant, Bankruptcy, Parole Representation, and Immigration. By graduation, more than half of all our students have participated in one or more internships, externships or clerkships—more than 100 different options are offered annually. Additionally, Pacific McGeorge offers you opportunities to compete on our nationally recognized mock trial teams, or to engage with one of our academic journals, *The McGeorge Law Review*, *The Pacific McGeorge Global Business & Development Law Journal* or *The Journal of National Security Law & Policy*.

The Region: Recognized as the nation's most integrated city, (according to *Time*), one of America's Top 10 Cities (according to *Newsweek*) and one of the top places to start a career (according to *Forbes*), there are more than 2 million people in the Sacramento metro area, yet it is close to the natural beauty of Lake Tahoe and the Sierra Nevada mountains, Napa Valley, the San Francisco Bay Area and more.

Learn More: You may find yourself practicing across the country or around the world; you may be standing up for the rights of others in the courtroom or making an impact in government or public service; or you may be serving as a mentor and an educator. One thing is clear: your Pacific McGeorge degree enables you to make a difference, for yourself and others, wherever you choose to go. Visit Pacific McGeorge to see how well you will fit into our community, and how well we will prepare you for success in law school and beyond. Learn more at www.mcgeorge.edu.

University of San Diego School of Law

USD School of Law
Office of Admission
5998 Alcalá Park
San Diego, CA 92110-2492
Admissions phone: (619) 260-4528
Admissions fax: (619) 260-2218
Admissions e-mail: jdinfo@sandiego.edu
Admissions URL: http://sandiego.edu/usdlaw/finadm/

 Admissions

Status: Current student, full-time
Dates of Enrollment: 8/2004-Submit Date
Survey Submitted: September 2005

USD is actually a selective school, and becoming more so every year. I was at first admitted only to the evening division (as I had been a late applicant) and approximately two weeks later was admitted into the day program, which is by far the preferable program unless you really have other pressing commitments. The application itself was comparable to other, bigger schools. Although USD's web site is infinitely slow, the application was easy to download and send electronically. The process seemed well-run and my admission was smooth sailing. My biggest concern was that the admission notification came late in the summer, which made me string other back up schools along and led to more grief and uncertainty than necessary. But it was worth it.

Status: Current student, full-time
Dates of Enrollment: 8/2003-Submit Date
Survey Submitted: March 2006

Essentially, it is easy to get into University of San Diego School of Law (USD). Visits to campus consist entirely of walking around the law school building and the rest of campus. Here's where they suck you in. The campus really is gorgeous. Spanish architecture for all the buildings with views of the bays and oceans.

Status: Alumnus/a, part-time
Dates of Enrollment: 8/2001-5/2005
Survey Submitted: November 2005

I applied outside of the regular deadline but applied specifically for the evening program. While many students I talked to said getting into the day program was difficult and they sometimes found out at the last minute (i.e., a week before the semester began), I received my response only a month after I had applied. My grades from undergrad were above average but what I think the most important thing for getting into USD is to have a solid LSAT score. The school is very supportive after you have been accepted with helping you obtain financial aid. There was no interview process and so there was no need to ever step foot on the campus until orientation.

Status: Current student, full-time
Dates of Enrollment: 8/2003-Submit Date
Survey Submitted: November 2005

Having spoken with several members of the admissions committee, admission decisions are similar to other school. A certain portion is deemed admitted based on their GPA and LSAT scores as long as everything checks out. However, a good deal of applicants are accepted outside of this process. While everyone's applications are read, I can assure that that outliers' are read VERY carefully by several people, including professors, deans and administrators.

The personal statement and "explain why..." portions of the applications are essential for many applicants and form the make or break portion of the admissions process. They are great places to explain how you will contribute to diversity, the public interest and USD's mission of service. Also, they should be used to explain a bad semester, time spent away from school, etc. Providing a win-

dow into your challenges and successes helps form a bond with the interviewer and get a big envelope rather than a small one.

Admission is becoming increasing difficult, especially as the school gains a stronger reputation. The grading scale was changed last year to more accurately mirror the scales used by other top schools, with the goal of making USD students easier to compare "on paper."

Status: Current student, full-time
Dates of Enrollment: 8/2004-Submit Date
Survey Submitted: November 2004

Admissions process is typical of most law schools. The school is becoming more and more selective regarding applicants. In fact, during orientation, a famous alumni visited and informed us that he did not think he would be able to get into law school now because of the increase in standards. The school is becoming diverse by getting a lot of students from different states. There are a good amount of female law students and Asian-American students. However, the school could do a little better job with more diversity such as gaining a few more Hispanic students and African-American students. Overall, it is a great school with a lot of great students.

Status: Alumnus/a, full-time
Dates of Enrollment: 8/2001-5/2004
Survey Submitted: March 2005

The admissions process is rolling and requires the usual grades, LSAT, essay and application. The school is pretty selective, so probably the most helpful thing to applicants is to have a high GPA and LSAT. The culture of the school is pretty mellow, so an essay that shows your true personality is probably helpful; the school has a program for prospective students to meet with law school alumni and professors before and/or after they apply to determine if the school is really for them; take advantage of that.

Status: Alumnus/a, full-time
Dates of Enrollment: 8/1998-5/2001
Survey Submitted: March 2004

I had to complete an application and submit two letters of recommendation and a personal statement. The personal statement was more focused on me, my life and my interests than on why I wanted to go to USD. There is no interview. If you get your application in early (or before the deadline) and are a "presumptive admit," then they let you know early as well.

After I began law school there, I had the honor of serving on the admissions and financial aid committee, and I was one of three students for the year that had the responsibility of reviewing the admissions applications. The files were reviewed and rated by three students and two faculty members. They were dissected, and everything mattered. The student's choice of major matters (the harder the major, the lower the grades that were permissible), the personal statement was important (the more interesting the student, the higher the score on the file), and the letters of recommendation mattered (who they were from, what personal knowledge the recommending person seemed to have about the applicant and what they said). This process showed me that if you think you're going to be in the middle area for any school that you apply to, make sure that everything that you still have control over (your grades, major and LSAT scores are done, but your statement and letters are not), is done really well!

Status: Alumnus/a, full-time
Dates of Enrollment: 8/2000-5/2003
Survey Submitted: April 2004

Almost entirely dependent on LSAT scores, and to a much lesser degree, undergraduate GPA. If you do well on the LSAT, you will get in regardless. In fact, if you do really well, you can get substantial scholarships. I got a 165 and was given a 90 percent tuition scholarship. If you do well on the LSAT, you don't need a good undergrad GPA. On the other hand, however, if you do poorly on the LSAT, a good undergrad GPA will not save you.

Read all of Vault's Law School Surveys at www.vault.com/lawschool — get complete surveys on top law schools, expert advice on applicaton essays, LSAT prep and more.

VAULT CAREER LIBRARY   97

The school states: "The Admissions Committee reviews all aspects of the application, including the personal statement, LSAT score, and undergraduate GPA."

Status: Current student, part-time
Dates of Enrollment: 8/2002-Submit Date
Survey Submitted: March 2004

The admissions process was very straightforward and typical of most ABA law schools. Requirements include a four- to five-page application, personal statement, and registration with LSAC (Law School Admissions Council). LSAC maintains LSAT scores, transcripts, and letters of recommendations. No interview was conducted.

Status: Alumnus/a, full-time
Dates of Enrollment: 8/2000-5/2003
Survey Submitted: October 2003

The admissions process didn't seem that rigorous to me. There were no interviews, and I don't think personal statements factored in much, because I wrote a really bad one and still got accepted. The school uses a rolling admissions process, so the earlier you apply, the better your chances are. Also, if you have less than stellar grades and LSAT, the evening program is much easier to get into and allows you to transfer to full-time after the first year.

Status: Alumnus/a, JD/LLM program
Dates of Enrollment: 8/1995-6/1999
Survey Submitted: April 2004

Excellent admissions office. I had some initial problems related to my own record (i.e., I was placed on the hold list), but after some tenacity on my part and patience, of course, the admissions director phoned me himself to indicate that I had been accepted and walk me through the initial process. Outstanding personal service. All in all, a real easy process, and they'll take care of you. Demand personal attention and you'll get it. The squeaky wheel gets the oil!

 **Academics**

Status: Current student, full-time
Dates of Enrollment: 8/2004-Submit Date
Survey Submitted: September 2005

USD has impressed me beyond any expectations in terms of the quality of professors, the curriculum itself, and the overall nature of the academic environment. USD is competitive, but not cutthroat. Academic excellence is expected, fomented, and supported. Grading is better than it used to be—the average GPA has been adjusted to correspond to the Big 10 schools, whereas previously USD's averages appeared to skew low.

Getting the popular classes as a 2L is not impossible, although you are at the mercy of your luck of the draw. Class registration is done by lottery. Students rank their top seven class choices and the school does its best to make everyone happy. If that concerns you, know that third-year students are automatically given first priority for required courses, and maybe even some popular electives. The professors at USD are of the highest caliber—Harvard, Yale, Stanford, UMich, et al. They are all passionate about their subjects, and many are the pre-emanate scholars in their area. While USD is a hot place for professors who publish, they also keep their doors open and are interested in the pursuits and intellectual curiosities of their students. I couldn't ask for more in the academic area. Students who transferred into my class from other schools are highly impressed by the quality of our instruction. I will be prepared for the world after law school.

Status: Current student, full-time
Dates of Enrollment: 8/2003-Submit Date
Survey Submitted: March 2006

There is a complete lack of course offerings. The process often results in just taking the one class that has an opening so that you can graduate on time—not exactly a desirable place to be. The registration process is antiquated and nonsensical. Apparently the telephone and this "new thing," the Internet are just too complicated to be used by the registrar. Instead you register by hand, in triplicate, for every class. Then there is a lottery where your class year gives you no preferential standing for classes unless they are required and you are in your last semester of law school.

Status: Alumnus/a, part-time
Dates of Enrollment: 8/2001-5/2005
Survey Submitted: November 2005

The professors at USD are fabulous, however, I found my favorite classes were taught by adjunct professors who worked full time in the field they were teaching. This is a huge benefit of the evening program as most of the day classes are taught only by the full-time faculty. The grading curve is impossible to understand and extremely frustrating as an evening student who worked full time during the day. You are ultimately ranked against the day program and I could not put in the time it would have taken to achieve the grades needed to graduate in the top 10 percent while working full-time. However, while the workload was tough, it was not so overwhelming that I couldn't complete it and keep my day job at the same time.

Status: Current student, full-time
Dates of Enrollment: 8/2003-Submit Date
Survey Submitted: November 2005

Courses are rigorous. USD invests heavily in bringing top professors to the campus, lured both by money and the lure of better weather. Yale Kamisar, the father of the Miranda Decision is one example. Donald Dripps, one of the most published professors is also on that list. Judge McKeown of the Ninth Circuit is a notable adjunct professor.

Getting into classes can seem challenging, especially "easy" pass/fail courses. Some that are prerequisites—especially advocacy course—can be more than just a slight challenge to get. The registration process seems silly and is based on a priority pass system. No touch-tone phones or Internet-based registration—the school has person-to-person contact, which can be a relief if your undergraduate institution was large. Several of the records office employees know just about every student by name.

Workload is high, as with most law programs, and seems to get easier as you get closer to the end. Students should consider taking advantage of classes offered by talented visiting professors lured to the school for a year. USD offers an academic support program for at-risk students, providing small group work with a TA for first-year classes. TAs are also available for most first-year courses for general office hours. Professors remain very available for help outside the classroom (of course, some professors are more helpful than others, but, on the whole, they are quite approachable and helpful).

USD has a relationship with both Thomas Jefferson and Cal Western law schools to allow students to take courses from the other institutions. So, if an area school offers a course that you find interesting, you can generally enroll in the other school's class, with no additional fee.

Status: Current student, full-time
Dates of Enrollment: 8/2004-Submit Date
Survey Submitted: November 2004

Professors bring their unique points of view to most classes. A lot of professors are very well-published in their area of specialty and they have some interesting takes on subjects such as torts. Teachers make classes pretty fun, however, it is law school and concepts are not always the easiest to get down. Furthermore, grading is competitive because there are lots of good students. Supposedly, grading does get better after your first year of school.

Status: Current student, full-time
Dates of Enrollment: 8/2004-Submit Date
Survey Submitted: February 2005

First-year classes are mandatory so there is no problem getting classes. From what I understand, second- and third-year classes are harder to get and some are almost impossible. Also, from what I understand, the selection of classes offered has decreased substantially over the last few years. Nonetheless, the faculty is nationally recognized and superb. The school also has an extensive summer abroad program.

Status: Alumnus/a, full-time
Dates of Enrollment: 8/2000-5/2003
Survey Submitted: October 2003

The program was great academically. Lots of well-known, talented professors. The required courses are pretty standard; pretty much all the bar subjects are required with the exception of trusts and estates. The only potentially useless required course is tax, which the school makes you take because they're strong in that area. Popular classes are quite difficult to get.

Status: Alumnus/a, JD/LLM program
Dates of Enrollment: 8/1995-6/1999
Survey Submitted: April 2004

Challenging, but rewarding curricula and professors. USD law is a hidden gem in California, and its reputation is growing year after year. USD Law has professors that even are called upon to render congressional testimony periodically. Order of the Coif—got it. Excellent library—got it. Reputation—on the move upward. Be prepared, be prepared, be prepared. Rent *Paper Chase* well in advance of starting school and watch it several times. Then imagine it being 50 times worse than in the movie and a constant strain on your life (both personal and professional). However, keep in mind that you will reap rewards at the end of it all. Still, if you have the grades, background and aptitude and can stand the sight and smell of blood, you are probably much better going to medical school than any law school. The legal life isn't always what its chalked up to be, and remember, the bottom of the class in medical school is still called "doctor."

Status: Alumnus/a, full-time
Dates of Enrollment: 8/2000-5/2003
Survey Submitted: April 2004

Academics are pretty much standard. One caveat—if you got into better schools but choose USD because you think it will be easier to make law review, you are mistaken. I know several students who did this and failed to make law review.

Status: Alumnus/a, full-time
Dates of Enrollment: 8/1998-5/2001
Survey Submitted: March 2004

This school offers a very strong academic program. It is much more legal theory-based rather than being a "legal trade school," and I found that although I felt that I got a very good legal education, I did not feel very prepared to take the bar when it was time. I felt that the professors were very well qualified and accessible. The classes were interesting, and it was not difficult to get the classes that I was interested in.

Grading seemed fair (I never ranked really high so I was not as locked into the whole grading system as some other people were). I did feel that it was done fairly and that I was rewarded for communicating with the professors on a personal level even though the grading is done blind. The workload was heavy during the first and second years. The first year was heavy because you are just figuring out what to do and you are assigned your classes and times. The second year is heavy because you are not only responsible for the academics, but you should try to become involved in some sort of law school activity (journal, moot court, SBA). This really does serve as a resume booster and kind of rounds out your law school experience. At the very least, it give you something to talk about during your interviews. However, this extra activity is usually very time-consuming, and when added to your academics, it makes for a very heavy workload during your second year.

Status: Current student, part-time
Dates of Enrollment: 6/2001-Submit Date
Survey Submitted: December 2003

The professors are topnotch. After the first year, the classes offer a good balance between theory and practice-oriented instruction. Many professors still use the Socratic Method, even after the first year. The law review is very highly ranked in the nation—higher than the school itself. The school is rising quickly through the ranks to catch up, though.

 Employment Prospects

Status: Current student, full-time
Dates of Enrollment: 8/2004-Submit Date
Survey Submitted: September 2005

USD is by far the best law school in San Diego, and outranks any school in Orange County, Arizona, Nevada, New Mexico, etc. Law firms from all over the country recruit from USD. While it is more difficult to get a job at a big New York, Boston, Chicago or San Francisco firm coming from USD, if you want one of those jobs, you should know better than to go to school in Southern California unless you get into USC or UCLA. Even then, they still might not take you. But overall, law firms recognize that USD is a gem and has a rigorous curriculum. We may have to work harder to get the jobs, but we succeed. Part of our success comes from USD's career services. They are experienced, helpful and resourceful. Knowing what you want is the hardest part, but once you figure that out there are plenty of opportunities. On-campus interviewing is widely available, mostly for the top 15 percent, but not necessarily. There are also many networking events at the school and sponsored by the school. USD alums are very loyal and always eager to do what they can to help.

Status: Alumnus/a, part-time
Dates of Enrollment: 8/2001-5/2005
Survey Submitted: November 2005

Only the students who ranked at the top of the class and participated in law review seemed to walk away with the prestigious jobs. If you were not top of the class then your external experience becomes really important and I wish that someone had told me to quit my day job so that I could clerk and intern getting the "right" experience before graduation. San Diego is a small legal community and the job market is extremely competitive because it is such a wonderful place to live. I found my current job through the *San Diego Daily Transcript*. I do know a couple of students who did get jobs through on-campus recruiting but the jobs were located outside of San Diego.

Status: Current student, full-time
Dates of Enrollment: 8/2003-Submit Date
Survey Submitted: November 2005

Students below the top third often find themselves needing to work considerably harder to get a job. Most students secure jobs, though many do so after bar results are released (which is a common hiring practice for many smaller firms who can't gamble on a student passing the bar or afford to pay for the bar prep courses). Students seeking positions with the government sector fair quite well. Be ready to seek out and keep appraised of many of these deadlines on your own, as they are not generally broadcast to the student population.

Status: Current student, full-time
Dates of Enrollment: 8/2004-Submit Date
Survey Submitted: November 2004

School is getting better and better with recruiting. There are always law jobs in Southern California, however, a large group of schools are competing for these jobs. The alumni are strong and constantly growing as is the prestige of the school. In fact, last year this university had the fourth highest bar passage rate in California which is no small task with other great schools like USC, UCLA, Stanford, and Cal-Berkeley. Internships start at the end of second year and there are a few with some of the prestigious law firms, however, you better score high in your class to get these jobs. On-campus recruiting is doing a good job encouraging students to not be afraid to look at other avenues of law employment by looking into some accounting firms and major businesses that need in-house counsel.

Status: Alumnus/a, full-time
Dates of Enrollment: 8/2001-5/2004
Survey Submitted: March 2005

Our career center is better than most, but can only do so much. Our alumni base is very strong in San Diego, but not as strong outside of San Diego—but every day it gets better. Students who attend USD can get into top law firms if they are at the top of their class, but the hiring doesn't go very deep into the class. Almost everyone gets good jobs, however, at every single conceivable place of employment. I don't know anyone who didn't get a job they are happy with.

Read all of Vault's Law School Surveys at www.vault.com/lawschool — get complete surveys on top law schools, expert advice on applicaton essays, LSAT prep and more.

VAULT CAREER LIBRARY   99

Status: Alumnus/a, full-time
Dates of Enrollment: 8/1997-12/2000
Survey Submitted: March 2005

The top 5 percent of graduates can obtain a job most anywhere in the country, including judicial clerkships. Students in the top 15 percent are competitive for large law firm positions. Students should be encouraged to look outside of California, and especially to Washington, D.C. and New York, when considering job opportunities.

Status: Alumnus/a, full-time
Dates of Enrollment: 8/1998-5/2001
Survey Submitted: March 2004

I ranked just outside the bottom 10 percent, and I have had amazing opportunities. You have to face the reality that only a handful of people will rank in the top, and there are certainly firms that will only look at your grades and will not even speak to you if you are from a school at USD's level and not in the top 5 percent. There are definitely things you can do to make yourself more attractive to everyone else. I served as the managing editor on a journal during law school; I was a federal judicial extern during school and a federal judicial law clerk after graduation. I am currently employed at a small firm but am in the process of interviewing at a firm that has 1,000 attorneys nationwide.

At USD most of the big firms require that you rank in the top 5 or 10 percent in order for you to get an interview. You have to be creative and aggressive. I did not get a lot of interviews during on-campus interviews but I participated fully and did end up with one on-campus interview, one fly-back (in San Francisco) and one off-campus interview that resulted in an offer for the summer, which I turned down. I had absolutely no trouble getting an externship during school for credit with a federal judge.

USD's extern program is a well-kept secret, but if you can get the information and participate in the program, you will be rewarded. I got my federal clerkship partly because the federal judge that hired me as a judicial law clerk went to "judge school" with the judge that I was an extern for during law school. It's always a small world, so be sure to do an outstanding job and remember that sometimes it's not what you know but who you know and who they know.

Status: Alumnus/a, JD/LLM program
Dates of Enrollment: 8/1995-6/1999
Survey Submitted: April 2004

USD Law has what is probably one of the best career placement departments in Southern California. Honestly, they work with you as you need it and are very responsive. Job and internship opportunities are readily available to those who pursue them. They provide some outstanding opportunities to ALL students. Be prepared to work for them, as they won't be handed to you.

 **Quality of Life**

Status: Current student, full-time
Dates of Enrollment: 8/2004-Submit Date
Survey Submitted: September 2005

Quality of life at USD is excellent. The campus is beautiful—from location, to architecture, to upkeep. It is perfect. The legal research center is one of the very best in the country, and I am forever impressed by the reference librarians. I'm on law review, so that means a lot. The classrooms are not the most modern themselves, but there is wireless Internet everywhere. I wish classrooms didn't have air conditioning on so much, and the chairs are less than comfortable, but I'm usually so absorbed in class that it doesn't matter much.

Status: Current student, full-time
Dates of Enrollment: 8/2003-Submit Date
Survey Submitted: November 2005

Couldn't ask for more. The USD campus has to be one of the nicest pieces of property in the country, with sweeping views of the Pacific Ocean, Sea World and Mission Bay. The weather provides ample excuses to go surfing or enjoy a day in Balboa Park.

Students are decidedly friendly. The rumors of book stealing and page tearing that run rampant at other schools are not present at USD. Students tend to be helpful to one another, often collaborating on their studies. USD is a very safe campus according to its crime reports, and there is usually an armed guard at the front gate welcoming students and guests to campus. Parking can be a challenge, though there is ample parking if you arrive early, or are willing to walk from a parking structure.

Housing options abound. Few law students choose to live on campus. There are a number of neighborhoods close by. A number of students opt for a slightly longer commute from locations closer to the beach or bars. Pacific Beach, Mission Beach, Ocean Beach, Point Loma and Downtown are all popular options amongst students. Get on the school's "admitted students" housing list and seek out a roommate via e-mail. The school's housing office also maintains an online listing of places for rent and roommate seekers. (Don't forget Craigslist.) You can find housing in a neighborhood that suits your tastes. Consider a trip to check out the options.

Having access to the resources offered by an undergrad institution is also nice. The library system permits interlibrary loans from San Diego State, San Marcos and UC San Diego—usually delivered the next day. In addition, the Kroc Institute for Peace and Justice offers a wide array of speakers and programs for students.

There is an on-campus health center providing most basic medical care as part of a fee included with tuition. They refer out much of the lab work and refer a number of students to outside providers, but it's nice to have the resource on campus. (Note: Because of USD's Catholic underpinnings, do not expect to receive birth control prescriptions or resources from the health center!)

Status: Alumnus/a full-time
Dates of Enrollment: 8/2001-5/2004
Survey Submitted: March 2005

The campus is amazingly beautiful. It is serene and well-kept; it is an excellent example of how beautiful living in San Diego can be. Like almost all colleges I have seen, there is some parking shortages up close, but if you don't mind walking or taking a shuttle, there is plenty of parking for all. Food facilities are good, but there isn't a lot of variety. The school is in a pretty good neighborhood and I've always felt very safe there, using common sense.

Status: Current student, full-time
Dates of Enrollment: 8/2003-Submit Date
Survey Submitted: April 2004

Great quality of life. For all the hard work you do and the countless hours of studying, you are rewarded with fun in the sun. It is a pricey city, but there are many pockets of affordable living. Additionally, for those fleeting moments you do muster up some free time, you are guaranteed to have sunshine and 70 degrees. It's always there.

Status: Current student, part-time
Dates of Enrollment: 8/2002-Submit Date
Survey Submitted: March 2004

USD is a beautiful campus (from the outside). Inside, the classrooms could use some upgrading. The campus computer network is very unreliable, and copy machines on campus are very expensive (10 to 15 cents per copy). The law library is very good and considered the best in San Diego County. USD is located in a low-crime neighborhood, although, as with the rest of San Diego, housing is very expensive.

USD has a good workout facility open to both undergrad and law students, although their limited hours of operation can be a bit frustrating at times. Parking can be tough at times because of a lack of spots, and to top it off, USD charges $185 per year (in 2004-2005 it will be $215).

Status: Alumnus/a, full-time
Dates of Enrollment: 8/1998-5/2001
Survey Submitted: March 2004

I lived on campus buzz graduate housing. I loved it. The apartments are extremely limited, so apply for housing early. The cost was a little high, but I didn't have a car my first year and didn't need one living on campus. The graduate housing consists of private one-bedroom apartments that are small but fully furnished, comfortable and safe. This campus does service a very large undergraduate student body, and the law school is basically restricted to two buildings (the building where the classes are held and the LRC—Legal Research Center), which are separated by a parking lot. The food is all located across the street, and it is reasonably priced and tasty. It gets really busy around meal times but that's just how it is. The campus is well lit at night and very safe. There is a lot of on-campus housing for the undergrads, so the campus stays well occupied throughout the later evening. The campus is a huge part of why I would recommend this school. I got accepted to this school and one in Los Angeles, and after seeing both, it was absolutely no contest!

Status: Current student, part-time
Dates of Enrollment: 6/2001-Submit Date
Survey Submitted: December 2003

The campus is beautiful, and it seems like they're always building some new state-of-the-art facility. However, the law school classrooms are not state of the art. They need to wire them for better laptop accessibility and get some padded seats! The library is tops as far as references go, but they need some student comfort, such as padded seats and Internet access at all desks.

Status: Alumnus/a, full-time
Dates of Enrollment: 8/2000-5/2003
Survey Submitted: October 2003

Great quality of life. San Diego is a fun, laid-back city, and the campus is minutes from the beach and downtown San Diego. While San Diego is not a super-cosmopolitan city, it has its share of culture and nightlife, and L.A. is within easy driving distance. The campus and neighborhood are both very safe. Housing is getting pricey, but still isn't too bad, considering you can get places super close to the beach.

 ## Social Life

Status: Current student, full-time
Dates of Enrollment: 8/2004-Submit Date
Survey Submitted: September 2005

Social life in law school? There is a Bar Review every Thursday night, which means the school sponsors an event at a different bar each week offering reduced cover and drink prices. I hear they are fun, but I haven't had time for one in a year and a half. USD students, although not diverse enough, are well-rounded and friendly. An easy place to make friends.

Status: Current student, full-time
Dates of Enrollment: 8/2003-Submit Date
Survey Submitted: March 2006

Essentially, the best advice to anyone considering law school is to take a few years off in between college and law school. I know you don't want to and people try to scare you by saying if you take time off you'll never go back. That's not true. What is true is you'll get some experience and not just go to law school because you don't know what else to do. Additionally, working for a few years will probably help you get into a better law school. Finally, think long and hard if this is really what you want to do. It's a lot of money and I know no one who is happy during these three years (many describe it as the most unhappy time in their lives.)

Status: Alumnus/a, part-time
Dates of Enrollment: 8/2001-5/2005
Survey Submitted: November 2005

As an evening student there were very limited clubs or events that could be accommodated by the evening schedule. To even participate in a moot court competition, you would have to miss your regular classes. The only notable USD law school social event is the annual Halloween Party, which always promises to be a lot of fun and occasionally delivers.

Status: Current student, full-time
Dates of Enrollment: 8/2003-Submit Date
Survey Submitted: November 2005

San Diego offers a fantastic array of social opportunities, many of which are taken advantage of by law students. Weekly Bar Reviews offer chances (and

usually discounts) for student to attend a selected San Diego bar as a group. Often, the other area law schools attend as well.

Whether you're looking for a club, dive bar or something more trendy, San Diego has it. Extensive revitalization of the downtown area offers a number of great places to live, eat or play. The new PETCO ballpark remains a popular entertainment option.

Status: Current student, full-time
Dates of Enrollment: 8/2004-Submit Date
Survey Submitted: November 2004

Outstanding social life around San Diego, however, this is not always a good thing in law school. University of San Diego and San Diego State are within about 10 miles of one another so there are plenty of people into going out to the bars and restaurants. The dating scene is alive and very well. It is very distracting, but if you do have the time, there is always something fun to do.

Status: Alumnus/a, full-time
Dates of Enrollment: 8/2001-5/2004
Survey Submitted: March 2005

San Diego is a mellow place, and the school follows suit. There are some regular social events for barhoppers and clubbers. There is plenty to do here and many people surf or do other outdoor activities. We have law school softball teams. It is not a party school, however; in my opinion, it has the perfect mix of formal and informal social activities.

Status: Current student, full-time
Dates of Enrollment: 8/2003-Submit Date
Survey Submitted: April 2004

Social life is supported by the Student Bar Association. It is OK, but more social life exists in the beach bars and downtown bars for the young and single. There are many events in San Diego that range from Cinco de Mayo to sailing races. There is a lot to do, such as surfing, sailing, mountain biking, golfing and simply lying out in the sun. The community is an active community that stays in shape. You will never need a warm coat and can spend the whole summer in shorts if you so desire.

Status: Current student, part-time
Dates of Enrollment: 8/2002-Submit Date
Survey Submitted: March 2004

The USD Student Bar Association hosts several social events throughout the year. There are barbeques or bar reviews as often as two or three times a month. USD is central to many San Diego hotspots (five minutes from downtown or the beaches). Weather in San Diego is the best in the nation (averages 65 to 70 degrees, year-round).

Status: Alumnus/a, JD/LLM program
Dates of Enrollment: 8/1995-6/1999
Survey Submitted: April 2004

Social life is great. All sorts of activities take place both on and off campus and are both sponsored and non-sponsored. Take your pick, but don't get too crazy. Remember, you'll have to be ready for answering up if you are called on in class. You'll have a great time I am sure.

Status: Alumnus/a, full-time
Dates of Enrollment: 8/1998-5/2001
Survey Submitted: March 2004

There are a great deal of clubs available to join, and they all have their own social events throughout the year and in general. The student body is friendly, laid-back, helpful and cooperative. I really enjoyed going there, and even though it was expensive, I feel as though I got my money's worth and had an amazing experience. I would highly recommend USD School of Law!

Status: Alumnus/a, full-time
Dates of Enrollment: 8/2000-5/2003
Survey Submitted: October 2003

USD has an active Student Bar Association that plans many social events yearly, such as Halloween and Mardi Gras parties and weekly bar reviews at various bars and clubs around San Diego. There are also many clubs at the law school.

Read all of Vault's Law School Surveys at www.vault.com/lawschool — get complete surveys on top law schools, expert advice on applicaton essays, LSAT prep and more.

VAULT CAREER LIBRARY 101

University of San Francisco School of Law

2130 Fulton Street
San Francisco, CA 94117-1080
Admissions phone: (415) 422-6586
Admissions e-mail: lawadmissions@usfca.edu
Admissions URL:
http://www.usfca.edu/law/prospective/prospective.html

Note: The school has chosen not to comment on the student surveys submitted.

 ## Admissions

Status: Current student, full-time
Dates of Enrollment: 8/2004-Submit Date
Survey Submitted: September 2005

I was originally waitlisted for the day program at USF. However, I was quickly given the option of joining the night program in lieu of waiting for the chance of entry into the day program, and I am thankful that I took the opportunity. As it ended up, they did not go to the waitlist at all for further enrollment, and I joined an older and more diverse group of students. It really helped me by having friends who were current students that knew admissions officers. They went in every other day to mention how interested I was in coming to USF. That paid off, I was the first person they called to let in off of the waitlist.

Status: Current student, full-time
Dates of Enrollment: 9/2004-Submit Date
Survey Submitted: March 2005

The usual LSAC, essay, LSAT score and personal statement. Advice on getting in: have good grades and a high LSAT. Seriously, though, the school looks highly on volunteer work or previous work experience, even if not law related. The numbers are definitely going up. My GPA/LSAT were in the top 25 percent the year before I went and for my class they were the median, so that is quite a jump. USF is improving in terms of their *U.S. News* ranking and should rise 10 to 15 spots in my three years.

Status: Alumnus/a, full-time
Dates of Enrollment: 9/2000-5/2003
Survey Submitted: April 2005

Applying to USF is just like applying to any other law school. Grades and LSAT matter most.

Status: Current student, full-time
Dates of Enrollment: 8/2002-Submit Date
Survey Submitted: June 2004

Rolling admissions process, which means the earlier you apply, if you are a good candidate, the more scholarship money you receive. I applied the earliest they allowed, and got my acceptance back shortly thereafter, notifying me that I received a scholarship for two-thirds of the tuition.

There are no interviews, but they do require the usual generic essay.

In terms of selectivity, it goes up each year. Each year gets more competitive, and where, during my class's admission the average GPA was around 3.3 and the LSAT was around 155, now, the average GPA is probably 3.6 and the LSAT more like 162.

Status: Alumnus/a, full-time
Dates of Enrollment: 8/2000-5/2003
Survey Submitted: March 2004

School attempts to select mainly on GPA and LSATs if possible. The LSAT range is [going up], and it is possible to get considerable financial support if a student is above the LSAT range. The school also admits based on a diversity plan. Outside the standard admission procedure, personal interviews and interest may also be taken into account, especially if the student is on a waitlist.

 ## Academics

Status: Current student, full-time
Dates of Enrollment: 8/2004-Submit Date
Survey Submitted: September 2005

USF, unlike most law schools, does not value cutthroat competition. The congenial nature of school allows for friendships to prosper while encouraging teamwork and study groups. This is not to say that people here are not competitive, they are, as you have to be in this field, but they don't let it undermine their relationships with other students. I felt lucky my first year to have incredible professors, I have very little to complain about in terms of accessibility and experience. This year I expect the same to be true. As for grading, there is a very difficult curve here at USF, more so than other Bay Area schools. Some students say this hampers our job prospects, and they may be right. But it also makes us work that much harder in order to do well. The workload is admittedly heavy; 60 pages of contracts reading is not a fun way to spend an entire day. This year, I'm taking 16 credits and the reading level is even more demanding. I spend all day on campus reading and attending classes from 8 a.m. to 11 p.m. when the library closes. I have had very little difficulty getting the classes that I wanted. I expected to be disappointed with my schedule this year, but ended up with a good grouping of classes. The strongest asset USF has is its writing program. Students come away with a skill set which shines through later in their career. We are known to produce some of the top writers in the state.

Status: Current student, full-time
Dates of Enrollment: 9/2004-Submit Date
Survey Submitted: March 2005

First year (which I am in the second half of) has a fixed curriculum. The quality is hit and miss, mostly pretty decent, some very engaging while I thought that some profs should not be teaching (but that is the exception). I have heard that getting classes is not too difficult but the popular ones (meaning popular profs) fill up quickly. We are on a very fixed curve the first year, 10 to 15 percent is in the A range, 15 to 20 percent is in the B range, the rest is C+ or lower. Workload is what you make it, it is demanding but it should be. The profs are very approachable and it is not uncommon to have four or five students in the professors' office during office hours, every office hours. There is a great tutoring system that I understand most schools don't have. We have a 2L or 3L that has taken the course from the same professor sit in and take notes. The tutor holds tutorials every two weeks, all optional for the students, and some are very, very helpful. For law school, it is a great idea because law is such a different type of education than anyone has ever had.

Status: Alumnus/a, full-time
Dates of Enrollment: 9/2000-5/2003
Survey Submitted: April 2005

Generally speaking, I think the quality of the academic program is very good. However, there is definitely a difference from professor to professor, as I imagine is the case at most, if not all, law schools.

Status: Current student, full-time
Dates of Enrollment: 8/2002-Submit Date
Survey Submitted: June 2004

Academics are great, including the professors. We have the famed Osborn, who authored *The Paper Chase*, for you law genre afficionados. Other professors are wonderful, from all over, but mostly Ivy League schools. The profs and the school in general tend to lean to the left politically, so be aware. The popular classes are difficult to get into, but I always get in off the waitlist.

Grading is rough. We have a majorly tough curve. We are generally encouraged to put our class percentage on resume/applications because if we just put our GPAs it wouldn't look so good. Workload is tough, but I assume at all schools it is.

Status: Alumnus/a, full-time
Dates of Enrollment: 8/2000-5/2003
Survey Submitted: March 2004

Grading is tough, in accord with general second-tier law school practice. Contrary to popular wisdom, the school retains a C average leading to low GPAs and tremendous competition for high grades. A minimum 2.0 is required for graduation and those achieving exactly that after first year are put in a special "at risk" program. Tutoring is only available to those admitted under the special admissions program.

Getting classes is not difficult for the most part, although clinical opportunities tend to be very competitive. Only two major clinics are available—Criminal and Human Rights—and most students do not get a chance to participate. The Intellectual Property clinic is up-and-coming and not as difficult to achieve membership in as the other two.

Employment Prospects

Status: Current student, full-time
Dates of Enrollment: 8/2004-Submit Date
Survey Submitted: September 2005

USF has gone through a lot of employment and career office upheaval in the past year.

Status: Current student, full-time
Dates of Enrollment: 9/2004-Submit Date
Survey Submitted: March 2005

I am in the top 10 percent, which helps, and I want to practice corporate law so OCI is great for me. From what I hear, that is standard at most schools. However, unlike most schools, we are competing against Hastings, Boalt, Stanford, Davis and Santa Clara for the same jobs.

Status: Alumnus/a, full-time
Dates of Enrollment: 9/2000-5/2003
Survey Submitted: April 2005

If you graduate in the top 25 percent of the class, you will likely find a good job in the Bay Area before graduation. If you graduate between 25 and 50 percent, you will likely find a decent job in the Bay Area sometime between after you take the bar and when you receive your results. If you graduate between 50 and 75 percent, you might find a job in the Bay Area after you pass the bar. If you graduate below the 75 percentile, you're gonna need some connections or luck.

If you don't want a job in the Bay Area, don't go to school at USF. If you want a job in L.A., go to Loyola. If you want a job in San Diego, go to USD. If you want a job in Silicon Valley, go to Santa Clara. You get the picture.

There is an extremely good alumni network in San Francisco if you are willing to pursue it. And there are more judges on the CA bench from USF than any other law school.

Status: Current student, full-time
Dates of Enrollment: 8/2002-Submit Date
Survey Submitted: June 2004

The program with respect to career prospects is so-so. You really have to work to find yourself a good job. Our career services really helps you if you are top 5-10 percent and want to go big firm, or if you want to do nonprofits. If you aren't in one of those groups, you may have to work harder.

Interning and getting jobs in the area are pretty manageable. We are regarded relatively highly in the area (more judge alums than any other Bay Area school), but I am not sure how well known we are nationally. Also, getting jobs gets competitive with higher ranked Stanford, Berkeley and Hastings close by.

Quality of Life

Status: Current student, full-time
Dates of Enrollment: 8/2004-Submit Date
Survey Submitted: September 2005

The USF campus is beautiful, and readily accessible by bus. I am unfamiliar with the housing situation, as law students generally are not offered housing. I live in an apartment within walking distance, in a decent neighborhood. Crime rates are fairly low in the area, but as you near downtown, they increase exponentially as you run through the projects.

You can easily walk to Golden Gate Park or the Haight, and local bars are within walking distance as well. Food options are pretty limited, but there is a grocery store five blocks away. The school's facilities are decent. No cafeteria, just a little over-priced cantina with limited hours. The library is great, but again, its hours are very limited, a point of contention among many students and administrators.

Status: Current student, full-time
Dates of Enrollment: 9/2004-Submit Date
Survey Submitted: March 2005

USF has a great campus. Our library is amazing. For those that drive, parking is not too bad. It is very safe. Being across the street from an undergrad and MBA campus is great because there is a decent dining hall and a fantastic gym. Housing is expensive, but that is true anywhere in SF.

Status: Alumnus/a, full-time
Dates of Enrollment: 9/2000-5/2003
Survey Submitted: April 2005

You're on the top of a hill in San Francisco. It doesn't get much better than that.

Status: Current student, full-time
Dates of Enrollment: 8/2002-Submit Date
Survey Submitted: June 2004

This campus is phenomenal. It is a Jesuit school, and the undergrad campus is right across the street, along with the Catholic church. Tons of greenery and beautiful buildings. Our facilities are topnotch, with a newly refurbished multi-million dollar state-of-the-art library. Profs, students and alums come from all over the area to use the library. There's Internet access at every seat in the library.

The neighborhood is good and safe. Many people live close by, but be aware that parking is brutal so use public transportation. Food in our little cafe is lame, so most people eat out of the vending machine.

Status: Alumnus/a, full-time
Dates of Enrollment: 8/2000-5/2003
Survey Submitted: March 2004

As with most second-tier schools, life is competitive and grueling. First-year Legal Writing is both graded and curved to a C, with classes as small as 10 students per class, getting decent grades is more like playing musical chairs with the few available A's and B's.

Aside from academics, the school's location is central to San Francisco, close to downtown and the Civic Center. Though San Francisco has been reported as one of the fastest shrinking cities in the U.S., earlier on this location was an asset for the school's students, which occupies a decent regional reputation in the Bay Area.

Social Life

Status: Current student, full-time
Dates of Enrollment: 8/2004-Submit Date
Survey Submitted: September 2005

Quality of social life at USF is very high. It is hard not to be given the great city that the school is located in. I subscribe to the attitude that you need a little balance, and that all work and no play does not make me a happy person.

Read all of Vault's Law School Surveys at www.vault.com/lawschool — get complete surveys on top law schools, expert advice on applicaton essays, LSAT prep and more.

VAULT CAREER LIBRARY 103

Status: Current student, full-time
Dates of Enrollment: 9/2004-Submit Date
Survey Submitted: March 2005

The usual; every Thursday a different club puts on bar night at a bar in the city. There are occasional BBQ and baseball games, but that is run by the clubs not the school. San Francisco is such a great city, though, there is no real need for the school to organize much. As is typical, law students make friendships fast, bonding through the sheer volume of work.

Status: Alumnus/a, full-time
Dates of Enrollment: 9/2000-5/2003
Survey Submitted: April 2005

I studied my butt off, and still had a great time. If you want to stroll around a college campus, don't go to USF. If you want to meet cool people, make good friends and hang out at fun places in a city, USF is the place to be.

Status: Current student, full-time
Dates of Enrollment: 8/2002-Submit Date
Survey Submitted: June 2004

We have bar nights religiously every week and a decent amount of people go. We are in San Francisco, so the bars, clubs and restaurants are the best!

Status: Alumnus/a, full-time
Dates of Enrollment: 8/2000-5/2003
Survey Submitted: March 2004

Social life in San Francisco is excellent. There are bars restaurants and clubs; and Haight Street, downtown and Golden Gate Park are all within a short distance from school.

University of Southern California

Gould School of Law
Admissions
University of Southern California
Los Angeles, CA 90089-0074
Admissions phone: (213) 740-2523 or (213) 740-2503
(TTY/TTD)
Admissions e-mail: admissions@law.usc.edu
Admissions URL: http://law.usc.edu/admissions/

 ## Admissions

Status: Current student, full-time
Dates of Enrollment: 9/2004-Submit Date
Survey Submitted: October 2005

USC has a very standard admission process, but apply early to get merit-based aid. It is selective in terms of academics, and USC prides itself on its diversity.

Status: Current student, full-time
Dates of Enrollment: 8/2003-Submit Date
Survey Submitted: October 2005

The "Law Preview Day" was a wonderful opportunity to learn about the school prior to deciding which law school to attend.

Status: Current student, full-time
Dates of Enrollment: 8/2004-Submit Date
Survey Submitted: October 2005

Admissions responses came very late. I did not get an answer until about late May, informing me that I was on the waiting list. Considering that my LSAT score was considerably below the median, this was a surprise. I believe what pushed me over the edge was my excellent GPA and my personal statements. I also sent a letter to them during to summer to affirm my interest in the school. I was accepted from the waiting list a few days before classes began.

The school seems to be VERY selective, but from talking to fellow classmates, it seems that school is apt to take someone with an extremely high LSAT score and relatively low GPA.

Status: Current student, full-time
Dates of Enrollment: 8/2004-Submit Date
Survey Submitted: September 2005

The admissions process is fairly straightforward. There is no formal interview process; but it is possible to talk to the admissions people to leave a good impression on an informal basis. The admissions staff looks at the personal statement and the resume. And, they do have a tendency to admit many non-traditional applicants, such as older applicants. Other than that, they mostly look at undergraduate GPA, without much concern for the school or the major that that GPA was earned in. Also, there is an emphasis on LSAT score, like at most other top schools, but not to the same degree.

Status: Alumnus/a, full-time
Dates of Enrollment: 8/2000-5/2003
Survey Submitted: October 2005

My own experience suggests that in some instances, the admissions office is willing to look beyond the numbers. Based purely on the numbers, I should not have been admitted. While my LSAT score was in the 75 percent range for the school, my GPA was probably in the bottom 10 percent. Lucky for me, other factors definitely seemed to have come into play in the admissions process such as caliber of undergraduate institution, the personal statement, an addendum explaining the disparity between my GPA and LSAT and letters of reference. Geographic, ethnic, experiential and socioeconomic diversity probably also played a significant role. The school is highly committed to diversity, not just ethnic, and my diversity of experience is something I tried to highlight in my personal statement. The school is always seeking fresh perspectives in the classroom.

Status: Current student, full-time
Dates of Enrollment: 8/2004-Submit Date
Survey Submitted: April 2005

The USC application, at least when I applied, was one of the easiest and therefore, the first one that I sent. All you need is a personal statement. APPLY EARLY! Not only does this increase your chances of getting accepted, but it makes you eligible for more scholarship opportunities. The people in USC admissions are really friendly and helpful; feel free to call them with any questions. If you get in you get a really nice acceptance packet and they sponsor a lot of admitted students events that are amazing and informative. Admitted Students Day at USC is a ton of fun and a great opportunity to meet future classmates and learn about the school. I definitely recommend going.

Status: Alumnus/a, full-time
Dates of Enrollment: 8/2000-5/2003
Survey Submitted: June 2004

The admissions process was fairly brief. There's no interview because it's law school, just sending in LSAT scores, grades and the application, which wasn't that long either. There was an essay as well. Even though I took the December LSAT and sent in my applications the day I got my results about four weeks later, I think, I got my admission letter by the end of January so they were really on top of that. I also was offered a generous scholarship, and in my experience a lot of people get some money.

The school is definitely selective, but with an eye toward the value of diversity. There are only 200 students per class, unlike 400 or 500 at many Top 20 schools, so the admit rate is kind of low. I think the criteria is typical of a top-ranked law school—good grades and good LSAT scores with personality probably as a tiebreaker.

Status: Current student, full-time
Dates of Enrollment: 8/2003-Submit Date
Survey Submitted: October 2003

The process started out with a letter from a professor who concentrated in the same things that I did as an undergrad. It kept getting better. Other schools were cryptic at best and rude at worst, but USC's admissions committee was attentive and professional, just like a private school should be. Constant updates and information made the whole process easier.

Status: Current student, full-time
Dates of Enrollment: 8/2002-Submit Date
Survey Submitted: September 2003

Excellent admissions process. Everything goes smoothly, and you are constantly being updated on your status with nicely printed letters. The tours are great and definitely worth taking. As always, grades and LSAT are key so do your best to boost both.

Status: Current student, full-time
Dates of Enrollment: 8/2003-Submit Date
Survey Submitted: June 2004

The school is very selective. It's a bit more idiosyncratic than other schools, meaning that good numbers won't guarantee you entry (I know quite a few students rejected from places like Boalt) or bar you, either. The school tends to identify and lock in on the students it wants. Consequently, nearly all of my friends turned down comparable or higher prestige schools to be there. The name is getting better, and the students believe in the quality.

Read all of Vault's Law School Surveys at www.vault.com/lawschool — get complete surveys on top law schools, expert advice on applicaton essays, LSAT prep and more.

VAULT CAREER LIBRARY 105

Status: Alumnus/a, full-time
Dates of Enrollment: 8/2000-6/2003
Survey Submitted: April 2004

The USC staff was very helpful during the admissions process. They sent a package of information and gave me numbers of people to contact, including numbers of students. Students then followed up with a phone call to see if I had any questions. I was very impressed.

 Academics

Status: Current student, full-time
Dates of Enrollment: 9/2004-Submit Date
Survey Submitted: October 2005

It is easy to get into even the most popular classes. Grading is curved to a 3.2 1L year, which isn't so awful. The workload is heavy, but manageable. I was very grateful for the intensive 1L writing program once I started my first real legal job. I knew how to write circles around some of my friends from Top Five schools. There are some great professors, and the size of the school is small enough that you can actually get to know them.

Status: Current student, full-time
Dates of Enrollment: 8/2004-Submit Date
Survey Submitted: October 2005

Overall, I am satisfied with the quality of the classes that I have taken. There are some genius professors and some horrible ones, but I am not usually one to complain. Because registration is completely randomized, getting stuck registering at the end can mean that you will not be able to get into some classes you had planned on taking. The hardest class to get into is probably Lefcoe's Real Estate Transactions class. The workload is quite horrendous during the first year, taking 17 graded semester units. Second year, you are taking fewer classes, yet are still extremely busy with interviews and journal work.

Status: Current student, full-time
Dates of Enrollment: 8/2004-Submit Date
Survey Submitted: September 2005

Workload is heavy the first year, but most of the classes are of a high quality. Popular classes are difficult to get, but the registration process is a lottery system for order of selection after the first year. So there is usually a chance to get the classes you want. Grading is usually fair, but varies significantly based on the professor. Some professors, especially the older ones, still tend to use a pure check system that assigns scores mostly based on the length of the response, instead of looking at quality. Most of the younger professors have moved to a more qualitative, holistic grading system for exams.

Status: Alumnus/a, full-time
Dates of Enrollment: 7/1999-5/2002
Survey Submitted: March 2006

It is law school. The classes, particularly the first year, are quite challenging, as measured both by level of difficulty and by workload. Grading is on a strict curve, but interestingly that did not lead to fierce competition among my class. The full-time faculty is stellar and quite accessible—there were a couple of exceptions but overall very impressive. I had mixed results with adjunct faculty, some were outstanding and some should not be in the classroom. Getting into popular classes is not that difficult. Even if you don't get the class through normal registration, it is almost always possible to get permission from the faculty to join the class.

Status: Alumnus/a, full-time
Dates of Enrollment: 8/2000-5/2003
Survey Submitted: October 2005

The curriculum at USC was academically rigorous and demanding. There are lots of very bright students competing against each other, and the students that come in prepared are a step ahead of the game. It would behoove potential students to hone their typing, outlining, critical reading and general study skills prior to beginning school. It is difficult enough just keeping up with the coursework without having to develop these skills along the way as well. In order to

really succeed, you will have to dedicate yourself to your studies, probably more so than if you were working a full-time job.

It is always important to keep in mind the strict curve on which grading takes place. Not everybody can be top 10 percent. Thus, the measure of how tough grading is is how tough your competition is. Being a Top 20 law school, your competition at USC is pretty heavy.

The quality of the classes ranged from incredibly intellectually stimulating to incredibly boring. Overall, the classes were very good and in an environment where you are surrounded by very intelligent people from the professor to the students, you are bound to learn a thing or two. For the most part, the full-time faculty is highly competent, with some nationally renowned scholars in the midst (Susan Estrich, Elizabeth Garett, etc.), while classes taught by adjuncts are hit or miss. There seems to be a pull away from the Socratic Method in the classroom at least in its most strict, humiliation inducing sense. I found that most of the time you will know in advance and have ample time to prepare before you are called in front of your peers.

However, there is one drawback to this high degree of academic freedom. You are not forced to take the majority of the 14 subjects that are on the California bar exam. This combined with the highly theoretical, as opposed to Black Letter law, bent of the school results in a bar passage rate that is low relative to its peers (such as UCLA and Berkeley) in the Top 20.

Status: Current student, full-time
Dates of Enrollment: 8/2004-Submit Date
Survey Submitted: April 2005

Your first year, you do not get to pick your classes or your professors, but the school tries to be fair and equally distribute the great professors among the sections. Also, if you have early classes your first semester, then you will usually get afternoon classes your second. You take five classes each semester, all graded on a strict curve, so it is pretty intense. It also feels like six classes because technically, research and writing is one class, but you have separate assignments for both.

The class size is great; for research you are in small groups of six or seven students and your writing class is 17 (approximately). Even in the larger classes, (the largest will be 100, but most classes are around 65), professors still take the time to get to know you. A lot of professors will have lunch with their students every week and on the second day of class my contracts professor went around the classroom to make sure that she knew all of our names (she had them all memorized). I went to a large undergraduate school, so the small classroom environment is a big plus at USC.

Status: Alumnus/a, full-time
Dates of Enrollment: 8/1999-5/2002
Survey Submitted: March 2005

USC's academics exceed its reputation. It has an incredible faculty with a diversity of interests and expertise, from the intersection of religion and law to some solid law and economics types. These are balanced well by effective, meaningful work in clinical programs and active journals and pro bono opportunities. In general, the classes are of very high quality. While having academically accomplished professors, there is still great value placed on teaching. The professors are accessible, both to discuss class materials and to discuss outside interests or topics. There are occasional disappointments during second year getting into some popular classes or getting a popular professor. However, as a third-year, this can mostly be made up. I got into every class I wanted to by the time I graduated. Sometimes an interesting class that is in the handbook is not offered during a two-year period, which can be disappointing. I know there was a listed Bioethics class that had been used to recruit me that was never offered during my time there.

Status: Alumnus/a, full-time
Dates of Enrollment: 8/2000-6/2003
Survey Submitted: April 2004

Most classes are a very good size, ranging from 15 or 20 to about 35. The professors are very knowledgeable, and most are willing to help students in whatever way they can. I rarely went to office hours as an undergrad, but I often utilized the time at USC in law school. The workload for most classes was fair. Some didn't require much work, while others were a bit overwhelming.

Sometimes there is difficulty getting classes of interest, because they often fill up quickly, and you may have to take second choice classes.

Status: Current student, full-time
Dates of Enrollment: 8/2002-Submit Date
Survey Submitted: December 2003

The academics have a policy (rather than Black Letter) orientation. This is purposeful and makes classes both more interesting and more worthwhile. Black letter law can be found in books. The quality of classes is generally very good. Most professors are engaging and entertaining. Classes are generally not crowded.

Status: Current student, full-time
Dates of Enrollment: 8/2003-Submit Date
Survey Submitted: October 2003

Classes are like classes everywhere—tough. However, the quality of the student body is not just measured in the intellectual arena. Almost everyone is a genuinely nice person, no "gunners" here. You are taught by a superstar faculty that is fantastically accessible; in fact, we had an opening social at the house of my Torts professor! The analysis is rigorous but fair, and while you are expected to be prepared for class, I haven't once seen a professor abuse anyone. On the contrary, the professors are fantastically bright, and you see their names on CNN, Fox and *The L.A. Times* almost daily.

Status: Alumnus/a, full-time
Dates of Enrollment: 8/2000-5/2003
Survey Submitted: June 2004

First year is kind of nightmare with grading because of the set mean and the forced curve and a sense of powerlessness about the grading. I think you have to come to the conclusion it's not about what you know, but what you know relative to the rest of your class, which can be aggravating at first. My first semester I got the same grade in three classes—one I felt I bombed the final (I didn't finish the essay), one I felt extremely confident about and one had no idea what the final was about, but neither did anyone else. This really killed my faith in the grading, but probably kept me sane about the whole thing. Some professors go "Socratic" first semester, and I put it in quotes because some professors have different ideas about exactly what that means. Most abandon it by second semester of first year, but it depends. The professors aren't there to hassle you. There's very little cold calling after first year.

Status: Current student, full-time
Dates of Enrollment: 8/2002-Submit Date
Survey Submitted: September 2003

Very difficult; however, students are collegial, nice and team-oriented. No *Paper Chase* here, but you are surrounded by extremely bright students and professors. Attending school with the future leaders of the legal community and the world is also a perk.

 Employment Prospects

Status: Current student, full-time
Dates of Enrollment: 8/2004-Submit Date
Survey Submitted: October 2005

Those that are in the top 20 percent of the class seem to have a fairly easy time getting offers from some of the most prestigious law firms in the area. The Career Services Office is very helpful for students that want to practice in large law firms, but provides less guidance for those that would like find jobs with government or nonprofits.

Status: Alumnus/a, full-time
Dates of Enrollment: 8/2000-5/2003
Survey Submitted: October 2005

The majority of the top national and regional firms recruit on campus at USC. The downside is that only about 20 percent of the student body (generally those with stellar grades) find jobs through this process. The rest of the students need to embark on major letter writing campaigns and rely on networking to find employment. The career services office also leaves something to be desired. It seems that unless you are a star student, you are left to your own devices. Also,

the alumni network, while extremely strong in the business world, is less helpful when it comes to legal jobs because of the strict grade criteria that most law firms have.

The upside is that USC Law students are pretty highly regarded, particularly in the Los Angeles area and most students seem to find their way into cushy corporate law jobs, even though the process of getting there may be circuitous for some. Recent graduates may need to start out at smaller firms or take staff attorney positions as a stepping stone. A minority of students elect to enter government service, undertake clerkships or enter the business world.

> **USC says:** "USC Law's Career Services Office is dedicated to assisting all students and provides a full range of resources for those seeking employment, and has recently added a staff member who focuses in part on government and clerkship placements. In addition, the school's new Office of Public Service provides additional assistance to students who are interested in public service employment opportunities."

Status: Alumnus/a, full-time
Dates of Enrollment: 8/2000-5/2003
Survey Submitted: June 2004

If you want to get a job in L.A., you're in good shape. If you get a job through OCI (on-campus interviewing), you're golden. If you want to work outside of L.A., you've got to work a lot harder because they have fewer resources. This is not to say that it's impossible—people from my class are working in New York, San Francisco and Texas among other places. There are fewer choices at OCI, which makes sense because most lawyers stay in the region they went to law school in. Also, I know the school doesn't have the greatest resources for unemployed recent alumni, who are in a tough job seeking position as it is. The Career Services Office has helpful people.

> **The school says:** "USC Law recently hired a career counselor who works with alumni to help enhance career services for graduates."

Status: Alumnus/a, full-time
Dates of Enrollment: 8/1999-5/2002
Survey Submitted: April 2004

USC has a great reputation in California, and a good reputation nationally. Accordingly, the recruiting process for law firms is relatively successful. The on-campus recruiting gives you access to a lot of firms, though the policies governing first-round, screening interviews means sometimes the firms and qualified students are not directly matched. Occasionally, it is necessary to seek out the firm if you were not matched to in the draw. Interests in government and pro bono firms can be met, though they are generally more local to California, and it requires more student initiative.

Status: Alumnus/a, full-time
Dates of Enrollment: 8/2000-6/2003
Survey Submitted: April 2004

I found it was very easy to get a job coming out of USC. Employers are very impressed with the school, particularly employers in Los Angeles. I also interned for a public interest organization my first year and externed for a judge my third year. For both of these, coming from USC helped a lot, particularly with the judge who was a USC grad herself.

Status: Current student, full-time
Dates of Enrollment: 8/2003-Submit Date
Survey Submitted: October 2003

The school sponsors recruiting events in New York City, Boston, Chicago and D.C. if anyone is interested in getting jobs out there. Alumni come in, and you can get most of your interviews done in a day. While it's true that the USC name may not be as strong back east, out west it is golden. Lastly, if your numbers qualify you for a fellowship, you are set! These students get a great scholarship (no minimum GPA) and are guaranteed to work at a studio and big firm during that notoriously hard-to-navigate first summer. Not bad.

> **The school says:** "USC Law's unique Summer Fellowship Program provides scholarship funds and a guaranteed summer

Read all of Vault's Law School Surveys at www.vault.com/lawschool — get complete surveys on top law schools, expert advice on applicaton essays, LSAT prep and more.

VAULT CAREER LIBRARY 107

position with a law firm, company or public interest organization during the summer after the student's first year of law school."

Quality of Life

Status: Current student, full-time
Dates of Enrollment: 8/2004-Submit Date
Survey Submitted: October 2005

On-campus housing is provided for a limited number of first-year students, although most students prefer to live off campus, since the area around campus is not the most savory area of Los Angeles. However, the campus's Department of Public Safety does an excellent job of patrolling the area and responds quickly to any incidents.

Status: Alumnus/a, full-time
Dates of Enrollment: 7/1999-5/2002
Survey Submitted: March 2006

Incredibly good quality of life. The neighborhood just off campus is dicey but improving. Crime rate, however, is quite a bit lower than that cross-town school in a better neighborhood! USC's campus is beautiful, the law school building itself is not the most lovely architecture, but the facilities are comfortable and the place really becomes home. The greatest contributor to quality of life at USC law is the people. It sounds trite, but somehow USC manages to snag really impressive students and faculty with open minds, good hearts and widely ranging perspectives. Of course everyone is smart, talented, etc., but the real bonus is how everyone participates in making the law school such a challenging AND supportive environment. Your teachers and classmates will become lifelong friends and resources. Oh yeah, and we have postcard weather most of the time.

Status: Alumnus/a, full-time
Dates of Enrollment: 8/2000-5/2003
Survey Submitted: October 2005

The USC campus itself is beautiful (both the actual campus AND the people) and has topnotch facilities consistent with its standing as a top-ranked national university. Fortunately, law school students have access to all of the facilities that the university has to offer because the law school structure is somewhat underwhelming, particularly the library. The feel of the building is dark and cramped. A law school of USC's caliber should definitely have at the minimum bigger and more inviting library facilities, since that is where its students will spend a great deal of their three years at the school.

Although there is on-campus housing available, most law students choose to live off campus and commute to the school. With so many inviting neighborhoods in Los Angeles (Santa Monica, Manhattan Beach, Los Feliz, etc.) to choose from and easy freeway access to the school, it is no surprise that most students live outside of the school's general vicinity of South Central, a historically crime-ridden neighborhood that has actually improved significantly in recent years.

Status: Current student, full-time
Dates of Enrollment: 8/2004-Submit Date
Survey Submitted: April 2005

Only about 40 students live on campus. The rest live in L.A. L.A. is really unique because there are a lot of different neighborhoods; most students live in the Miracle Mile area or further west. The school helps you find housing because they send you a roommate referral book, which lists all the first-years looking for a place to live. This is how I found my roommate and it has worked out really well. USC's campus is beautiful and the law school is on campus, which is great. We aren't completely isolated either; we can go grab lunch where the rest of the students eat and we attend the football games. There is a ton of places to eat on campus and next year the law school will actually have a cafe, which is supposed to be nice. USC is not in the best neighborhood, but since law students don't really live there, I don't think that is a big deal. Also, you need a car in L.A.

Status: Alumnus/a, full-time
Dates of Enrollment: 9/2000-9/2003
Survey Submitted: April 2005

The neighborhood around USC is pretty terrible and there aren't a lot of useful amenities in the vicinity. I should have known better (being from Los Angeles) than to try to live near campus my first year, but I did it and was pretty disappointed. I lived in the "law dorm," which was actually a lot of fun—there are just not many interesting things to do in the area. Living in the Mid Wilshire area or Manhattan Beach puts you in a nice area with an acceptable commute. The USC campus itself is great and has all the amenities one would expect and more (a bar, for example). The law school building is a bit of a dump, but has everything one would need. Crime and safety are not big issues on campus, but is a very big issue if you venture a few blocks to the east, west or south—north is generally OK.

> **The school says:** "A brand-new cafe and renovated law library opened in August 2005, significantly enhancing the quality of the school's facilities."

Status: Current student, full-time
Dates of Enrollment: 8/2003-Submit Date
Survey Submitted: November 2004

Quality of life is good. It's sunny and warm all year; the people are good looking, and you can go to the beach whenever you're in the mood. The people who run the law school at USC are nice people, and they attract students who are pleasant to be with, as well. Competition your first year is intense, but the unpleasantness doesn't come from the other students but from the workload and the knowledge that everyone in your section is smart and working just as hard as you are. USC has a special dorm for law students. I didn't live there, but many of my friends did. It doesn't seem like that great place. It's near a lot of the fraternities and constant loud parties coupled with the stress of law school didn't seem like a great combination. I don't know anyone who chose to live there a second year. Living in L.A. is a lot different from living in a college town, and you might want to spend some time exploring living situations a little further away from the campus. USC as a school doesn't have the greatest amenities (the gym is tiny and there're no good places to eat within walking distance) so there's not much to be gained by living near the school. But the football team is Number One. Make sure you take advantage of the parking the law school reserves for first-year students. It's expensive, but it's very hard to find parking near the campus.

Status: Current student, full-time
Dates of Enrollment: 8/2002-Submit Date
Survey Submitted: September 2003

Housing on campus is great for 1Ls, but there is plenty of affordable housing in L.A. Crime is not too high in the area (not more than most cities), but added vigilance is smart when you are walking around alone. Campus itself boasts amazing facilities that you have full access to (tons of food, gyms, etc.). Excellent campus. The law school is in a nice but older building with full wireless Internet support and a built-in cafeteria. Very convenient and easy to get around.

Social Life

Status: Current student, full-time
Dates of Enrollment: 9/2004-Submit Date
Survey Submitted: October 2005

There is a great social scene. Lots of people go out together, and there is a weekly bar review at a different bar each week. There are a good number of "school couples." There are also plenty of people with lives outside of school who are fun to see at school, but don't really hang-out outside of school.

Status: Current student, full-time
Dates of Enrollment: 8/2004-Submit Date
Survey Submitted: September 2005

There are weakly Bar Reviews at local bars for law students. People are friendly and not cutthroat competitors in class. There is not much of a dating scene, as the class is very small. Some people in on-campus housing tend to to pair up for long-term relationships during the opening weeks of the first year. People tend to be very close to their sectionmates. Every first-year class is divided into sections of 20, and you have every class, including a small legal writing class, with these 20 people.

Status: Alumnus/a, full-time
Dates of Enrollment: 8/2000-5/2003
Survey Submitted: October 2005

While law school leaves limited time for social activities, USC law school does provide its students with various social outlets. One popular event seems to be the weekly bar review where law students gather at a different watering hole in Los Angeles each week. There are also yearly galas in which the faculty participates as well. Clubs also play a large role in the school's social scene, particularly the ethnic ones, which hold numerous events like first-year picnics and alumni dinners. Another popular social event is the yearly Public Interest Law Foundation Auction where students and alumni can bid on such items as a night on the town with a law professor.

Status: Current student, full-time
Dates of Enrollment: 8/2004-Submit Date
Survey Submitted: April 2005

USC gets an A+ for social life. The student body is just fantastic. People are really friendly, there is a great sense of camaraderie and everyone, for the most part, gets along. Every week we have Bar Review, which means the entire school goes to a different bar somewhere in L.A. A lot of students go, and it is a great way to get to know the city. Some dating goes on among classmates, but not a ton. The law school has every club you can imagine and if a club you want to be in does not exist you can start it. Because of the small size of the school, it is really easy to get involved, and if you want to have a leadership position in a group, it is not competitive. Everyone who wants to do something can. Also, almost every day at lunchtime there is something to do; a club meeting, club-sponsored lunch, speakers, etc. Almost all lunch events have free food. Students at USC Law have found a great balance between academics and social life.

Status: Current student, full-time
Dates of Enrollment: 8/2003-Submit Date
Survey Submitted: November 2004

There are many organizations and public service programs at the law school but, on the whole, the social life revolves around Bar Review, which is a weekly get-together at a bar somewhere in L.A. During the course of the semester you'll pretty much cycle through all the of the moment clubs in L.A., so at the end of the semester you'll have the satisfaction of knowing you've been to all the clubs

mentioned in the celebrity gossip magazines. Even if you never go to bar review, by the end of first year, you'll know most everyone in your section and even if you're still not quite sure of someone's name, you'll have bonded with him/her after having gone through such a stressful experience together. But that's only the USC law social life. Living in L.A., you'll have the second largest city in the country and the entertainment capital of the world to explore. You'll be young, single, and three short years from making truckloads of money.

Status: Alumnus/a, full-time
Dates of Enrollment: 8/2000-5/2003
Survey Submitted: June 2004

There's lots to do... off campus. There's like two Starbucks and a Jamba Juice on campus and that's the extent of it. You almost need a car or good friends or the desire to learn the bus system because the city is spread out and the activities law students arrange are too. There are a few chain fast-food restaurants near campus, but not much else.

In terms of fun things to do, several intramural sports teams are formed each year. There are several clubs and associations within the law school: Black Law Students Association (BLSA); La Raza, Asian Pacific American Law Student's Association (APALSA); Middle Eastern South Asian Law Association (MESALA); International Law Society; Sports, Music & Entertainment Law Society (SMELS); Intellectual Property Society; Phi Alpha Delta; and the Women's Law Association to name a few. Most clubs have a few meetings every year and have various other events and outings, and there are also public service opportunities.

Status: Alumnus/a, full-time
Dates of Enrollment: 8/1999-5/2002
Survey Submitted: April 2004

There are Bar Reviews every Thursday night for bar-hopping, they're pretty popular. There are also numerous student organizations meeting all sorts of interests and needs. The number of organizations far outstrips the number of students. The dating scene felt a bit sophomoric, it was a bit like being in high school again, except you could end up taking someone home.

Status: Current student, full-time
Dates of Enrollment: 8/2003-Submit Date
Survey Submitted: October 2003

It's L.A.; come on. Hollywood, the beaches, the Lakers, Clippers, Dodgers, Angels, Kings, Ducks, Santa Monica and San Diego. Trust me, there are things to do.

Read all of Vault's Law School Surveys at www.vault.com/lawschool — get complete surveys on top law schools, expert advice on applicaton essays, LSAT prep and more.

VAULT CAREER LIBRARY   109

University of Colorado at Boulder School of Law

Admissions Office
403 UCB
University of Colorado at Boulder
Boulder, CO 80309-0403
Admissions phone: (303) 492-7203
Admissions e-mail: Lawadmin@colorado.edu
Admissions URL: http://www.colorado.edu/law/admissions

 ## Admissions

Status: Alumnus/a, full-time
Dates of Enrollment: 8/1997-5/2000
Survey Submitted: March 2005

The admissions process included an application with a written essay. There was no interview. In the essay, it is important to describe what unique qualities you will bring to the law school community. The admissions committee is able to look at transcripts and test scores and make their own assessment of those items. So, the essay should really discuss the individual's character, motivation for attending the school and any other unique qualities.

Status: Alumnus/a, full-time
Dates of Enrollment: 8/1999-5/2002
Survey Submitted: March 2004

This school is fairly selective, especially among students from out of state. The admissions office is very friendly and helpful. No interview was required when I applied. In the essay, the admissions committee is looking for unusual life experiences and how those experiences could benefit a person in the study of law.

Status: Alumnus/a, full-time
Dates of Enrollment: 8/1998-5/2001
Survey Submitted: April 2004

Standard application process. Admissions office is very responsive and helpful. Very difficult to get in, however. Last I heard there were more than 6,000 applicants for 160 slots. It is notable that the admissions committee makes a distinct effort to admit at least a few students who do not perform well on the LSAT but whose resumes indicate they will perform well and add something to the class.

> **Regarding admissions, the school says:** "CU Law received 2,565 applications for the fall 2006 entering class. The entering class size was 172."

 ## Academics

Status: Alumnus/a, full-time
Dates of Enrollment: 8/1997-5/2000
Survey Submitted: March 2005

The academic nature of the program was rigorous but manageable. The class quality was largely dependent on the professor teaching the class. For the most part, professors were quite good, though I understand there has been considerable changes in the faculty since I have left. Average grades were B's and professors generally set the mean for the curve at 84. Popular classes were generally not difficult to get into because the total size of the student body is relatively small. Seminars were the only difficult classes to get into, because they were limited to 12 students.

Status: Alumnus/a, full-time
Dates of Enrollment: 8/1999-5/2002
Survey Submitted: March 2004

The quality of the classes was, for the most part, excellent. There are always a few exceptions, usually involving adjunct professors who don't know how to effectively present material. Classes are fairly demanding and it is tough to get good grades, since students are competitive. Popular classes are easy to get once you have some seniority. Professors are good about providing opportunities to see them outside of class. Workload is heavy; don't expect to have much of a social life!

Status: Alumnus/a, full-time
Dates of Enrollment: 8/1998-5/2001
Survey Submitted: April 2004

The class assignment system has changed since I attended, for the better. It's now completely automated. Not difficult to get popular classes. Quality of professors and courses is, by and large, excellent. Very few adjuncts. Like any other law school, workload is a function of what you decide to put in.

 ## Employment Prospects

Status: Alumnus/a, full-time
Dates of Enrollment: 8/1997-5/2000
Survey Submitted: March 2005

Employment prospects were generally good, but I would not say great. People who wanted jobs could get them.

Status: Alumnus/a, full-time
Dates of Enrollment: 8/1998-5/2001
Survey Submitted: April 2004

If you plan to stay in Colorado or work on the West Coast, it's a great school. More difficult to get traction with East Coast law firms.

Status: Alumnus/a, full-time
Dates of Enrollment: 8/1999-5/2002
Survey Submitted: March 2004

Summer clerkship opportunities are limited to the top people in the class. There is very little campus recruiting. Prestige with employers is high compared to the other law schools around the region. Expect to be responsible for finding your own job opportunity.

> **Regarding career opportunities, the school says:** "The mission of the Office of Career Development at the University of Colorado Law School is two-fold. We are here to provide our law students and alumni with individualized career counseling and professional development to help them identify and achieve their career goals. We also assist local, regional and national employers in meeting their employment needs by providing on-campus interview programs, resumes collections, job postings and opportunities to reach out to our students and graduates. The Office of Career Development offers an array of services and programs designed to assist our students and alumni in identifying and reaching their career goals."

Quality of Life

Status: Alumnus/a, full-time
Dates of Enrollment: 8/1997-5/2000
Survey Submitted: March 2005

Quality of life at Boulder is outstanding. Housing was somewhat expensive, but not too bad. The campus is very nice. The law school building itself was not the best, but a new facility is now under construction. The neighborhoods in and around campus are all quite nice and crime is not a large problem.

Status: Alumnus/a, full-time
Dates of Enrollment: 8/1998-5/2001
Survey Submitted: April 2004

The law school building isn't great, but one of the administration's key priorities is procuring funds to construct the already planned new building. Myriad of outdoor activities, including skiing, biking, hiking and so on. Most law students don't interact much with the rest of campus.

Status: Alumnus/a, full-time
Dates of Enrollment: 8/1999-5/2002
Survey Submitted: March 2004

Fixtures in campus apartments were old and dirty, although I hear that new housing just opened. Campus is beautiful, but the law school is kind of isolated from the main campus areas—it is a long walk to the student center, main library and bookstore. Facilities in the law building are definitely substandard, but a new law building is in the works at some point. There is plenty of fast food nearby. Boulder is extremely expensive to live in; therefore many students commute from surrounding areas. Campus is fairly safe and secure.

> **Regarding quality of life, the school says:** "The School of Law is now housed in the new 180,000 square foot Wolf Law Building, located on the southern edge of the CU Boulder campus. The Wolf Law Building features state-of-the-art classrooms, two high-tech courtrooms, 50 percent more space for law journal offices and law clinics, and the largest resource collection and most technologically advanced law library in the 12-state Rocky Mountain region. Colorado Law is also striving to make the Wolf Law Building the first Gold-certified public law school building in the country under the exacting standards of the U.S. Green Building Council's Leadership in Energy and Environmental Design Certificate."

Social Life

Status: Alumnus/a, full-time
Dates of Enrollment: 8/1997-5/2000
Survey Submitted: March 2005

Boulder social life is outstanding. Bars, restaurants and clubs are plentiful and offer a wide range of options and price points. Outdoor activities are plentiful both near campus and within short driving distances. Social events at the law school itself were also very common, with students often having Friday Afternoon Clubs (FACs) where they would provide snacks and drinks.

Status: Alumnus/a, full-time
Dates of Enrollment: 8/1998-5/2001
Survey Submitted: April 2004

Academic environment is incredibly collegial, not cutthroat at all. Not a party school by any definition, but by and large the students know how to have a good time. The SBA used to sponsor a keg party every Friday, which was usually well-attended.

Status: Alumnus/a, full-time
Dates of Enrollment: 8/1999-5/2002
Survey Submitted: March 2004

Social life mostly revolves around drinking. There are many good bars in Boulder, although they are very expensive. Most law school functions involve bars or kegs. Restaurants in Boulder are just average. Clubs tend to be cliqueish. The Dark Horse is a great bar near campus, and one of the least snobby establishments in Boulder. Social life has many, many more options if you drive down to Denver!

Read all of Vault's Law School Surveys at www.vault.com/lawschool — get complete surveys on top law schools, expert advice on applicaton essays, LSAT prep and more.

VAULT CAREER LIBRARY   111

University of Denver

Sturm College of Law
Admissions Office
2255 East Evans Avenue
Denver, CO 80208
Admissions phone: (303) 871-6135
Admissions fax: (303) 871-6992
Admissions e-mail: admissions@law.du.edu
Admissions URL: http://www.law.du.edu/ad/

 ## Admissions

Status: Alumnus/a, full-time
Dates of Enrollment: 9/2002-5/2005
Survey Submitted: March 2006

Very receptive to second-career or "non-conventional" law students (adults!). The admissions staff always seemed to have plenty of time to talk to me, and it was easy to schedule a personal meeting with the Dean of Admissions.

Status: Alumnus/a, full-time
Dates of Enrollment: 8/1980-5/1983
Survey Submitted: April 2005

The admissions process was relatively easy in that the admissions office was very helpful in suggesting what items of education, work history and desire to attend were the most likely get a student admitted. They also offered a program for entering students who the school felt might be at risk for failing. I ultimately attended those classes, which really benefitted me throughout law school.

Status: Current student, full-time
Dates of Enrollment: 9/2003-Submit Date
Survey Submitted: May 2004

The admissions process was fairly standard. LSATs, essays, recommendations and a transcript. The selectivity of DU is moderately lower than many schools simply because DU takes so many students each year. Overall, the admissions process was fairly simple if you know what you're getting into and start preparing early.

Status: Current student, full-time
Dates of Enrollment: 8/2002-Submit Date
Survey Submitted: May 2004

The admissions process is pretty similar to most law schools. There were no required interviews, and the essays were pretty much what you would expect. The selectivity has increased greatly since I applied. The LSAT scores and GPAs have gone up significantly, as has the number of applicants. In terms of getting in, DU is really committed to diversity in every form. Any experience you have that is unique or interesting should certainly be highlighted in you application.

Status: Current student, full-time
Dates of Enrollment: 8/2001-Submit Date
Survey Submitted: October 2003

The admissions process has become more grueling and challenging, given the increased rise of applications to the university. More and more attention is given to the whole person, and not just to grades and LSATs. The university, given its dedication to increased diversity, looks for individuals whose stories and life experiences can help bridge the gap between class and real life. Grades and high LSATs will help. There is no actual interview process, but a campus visit can always enhance your profile, showing your interest in the institution.

 ## Academics

Status: Alumnus/a, full-time
Dates of Enrollment: 9/2002-5/2005
Survey Submitted: March 2006

I was very pleased with the quality of the professors and developed friendships with several of them. The registrar and dean of academics were both very concerned that students had a positive experience. I developed a serious illness during my second year, and they worked with me to develop a plan to help me graduate with my class.

Status: Alumnus/a, full-time
Dates of Enrollment: 8/1980-5/1983
Survey Submitted: April 2005

The school held academics in high regard and offered many classes or tutorials from upperclassmen, as well as faculty to assist students in achieving the most out of their studies. The majority of classes were very well-prepared and there was much thoughtful discussion between the professor and students. The most well-received and acknowledged courses were in natural resources, environmental law and international law. It was not too challenging to get a class you wanted, although sometimes the more popular professors had their classes fill up more quickly than others and you would have to wait for the next semester to take the course with a particular professor.

Status: Current student, full-time
Dates of Enrollment: 8/2001-Submit Date
Survey Submitted: October 2003

Grading here works on a curve, which means that you should not expect to get an A in every class like you did in undergrad. Popular classes fill up fast, and the registrar will keep a cap on popular professors just to keep class sizes small. The quality of classes and selection of classes depend on what you are looking for. If you want to go on a corporate track, then you might be out of luck, given that the school focuses more and more on land use and water law. The professors here are excellent, and you'll find that they are knowledgeable in their subject to an extent. Several professors have clerked for judges as well, providing an untapped resource for career advisement. You'll also find professors who have worked in large firms or have had successful practices as well. The downside is that you'll find that most professors are focused more on their research for law review articles, and not on helping students find jobs for life after graduation.

Status: Current student, full-time
Dates of Enrollment: 9/2003-Submit Date
Survey Submitted: May 2004

The professors are great. They are very educated, and there are quite a few excellent professors. There is also the rare professor who has no business trying to teach but who is protected from his or her own folly by the colossal mistake that is the tenure system. Fortunately, this is rare at DU. Of course, the real trouble with DU is class size. Some of the classes have only 10 students. Others have up to 90. Anybody who has attended a state university knows the feeling of sitting in the seventh seat from the right on the 20th row and having the professor stare at a seating chart to figure out your name in the last week of class. You become a number. The classes have little or no interaction. Rather, the professor rambles through a tried and true two-hour speech on whatever, while you desperately struggle to pay attention.

Status: Current student, full-time
Dates of Enrollment: 8/2002-Submit Date
Survey Submitted: May 2004

The professors at DU are almost bar-none exceptional. They are amazingly approachable and helpful out of class. I have had many who have challenged the entire way I think about the world, not just the law. The workload is difficult but not overwhelming. The professors expect a lot from you, but if you are applyng to law school, you likely expect no less from yourself. Grading varies from professor to professor but, for the most part, it is fair. Like most law schools, grading is blind and there is a curve applied, so that affects grades some. In terms of getting into classes, you will get in, but you might have to wait a semester. Typically, you can get into any class that you did not get into online by showing up the first day. Professors are sympathetic to the online registration process and generally willing to help you out if they have room in the class.

Employment Prospects

Status: Alumnus/a, full-time
Dates of Enrollment: 9/2002-5/2005
Survey Submitted: March 2006

DU grads have a good reputation regionally and locally for being "practice-ready" attorneys, as DU focuses more than some other schools on the practical aspects of the legal profession, rather than just theory. What can I say? All my friends have good jobs.

Status: Alumnus/a, full-time
Dates of Enrollment: 8/1980-5/1983
Survey Submitted: April 2005

The employment prospects were very high when I attended DU. Many of the local law firms were particularly fond of hiring DU grads, as they felt the students were very well-qualified and understanding of the legal system in the Denver area. The university also had a very well-attended mentor program with alums throughout studies at the university. They were willing to meet with the students and help them decide on an area of law to emphasize during school, as well as helping the student devise a resume that would be acceptable to employers. Many of the local firms were very encouraging to students in hiring them as law clerks, too. I held three law clerk positions while in law school that I could easily go to between classes due to the proximity of the school and the downtown jobs.

Status: Current student, full-time
Dates of Enrollment: 9/2003-Submit Date
Survey Submitted: May 2004

Career and community involvement are shining stars of the DU law program. The school immediately attempts to immerse its law students in practical programs and offers numerous opportunities. The percentage of students getting employed within six months of graduation is very high, due in part to the practical programs offered for students and in part to the tight Denver legal community.

Status: Current student, full-time
Dates of Enrollment: 8/2002-Submit Date
Survey Submitted: May 2004

The job placement stuff at DU is ever changing. They are constantly trying to make it better in terms of both efficiency and prestige of jobs offered. Within Denver, DU students fare pretty well. Most of the attorneys in the Denver area went to DU, so they are always willing to help out the alma mater. If you are planning on practicing somewhere other than Colorado, you should look at law schools in that area. Although outside the state the University of Colorado seems to get more prestige than DU, within the state there is not the same disparity. Most Colorado firms hire equally from both, and do not particularly favor one over the other.

Status: Current student, full-time
Dates of Enrollment: 8/2001-Submit Date
Survey Submitted: October 2003

Career prospects are slim right now. 80 percent of all lawyers in the state of Colorado are DU graduates. This means that for those of us who want to leave the state of Colorado, chances are slim to none. Campus recruiting is limited to firms in the Colorado area. So if you want to move to another city, you are on your own. However, the internship office is extremely helpful in locating internships for students who want more clinical experience prior to joining the working ranks. They will go out of their way to make sure that your experience is worthwhile.

Quality of Life

Status: Alumnus/a, full-time
Dates of Enrollment: 9/2002-5/2005
Survey Submitted: March 2006

The DU campus is small and user-friendly. Nice location with plenty of restaurants and shops nearby, and downtown Denver just a few minutes north.

Status: Alumnus/a, full-time
Dates of Enrollment: 8/1980-5/1983
Survey Submitted: April 2005

The campus and facility, at the time I was in school, was downtown across from the courthouse. It was thus very convenient to courtroom observations as well as housing and dining opportunities. The bus system was very efficient at getting students around the downtown area, too. Although the law school was very close to the Denver jail and the neighborhood had many bail bonds offices near by, I always felt very safe and never heard of any criminal acts against the school, students or faculty. Parking could sometimes be a challenge with the courthouse so near but we always could count on a security guard or another student to walk us to our cars in a nearby parking lot if it was late.

Status: Current student, full-time
Dates of Enrollment: 9/2003-Submit Date
Survey Submitted: May 2004

DU has just finished construction of a brand-new law school building. The building is as high tech as it gets. Touch screens by the elevators notify visitors of each day's activities, times and locations. Every seat in every classroom is wired, as are most common-area seats. The building itself is beautiful. The woodwork alone provides one with a greater understanding of exactly where that $25,000 a year really went. The neighborhood is great, and there are plenty of nearby places to eat, as well as fantastic athletic facilities nearby.

Status: Current student, full-time
Dates of Enrollment: 8/2002-Submit Date
Survey Submitted: May 2004

Denver is a great city. The weather is phenomenal, and people are always doing outdoor activities. DU's neighborhood is a safe place with a lot of single-family homes. There are plenty of relatively inexpensive apartment and house rentals within walking distance of the school. The campus is amazing. The last seven or so years at DU have seen unbelievable transformation. The new law school building, which opened in the fall of 2003, is possibly unparalleled in the nation. To go into the specifics of it would take pages, but here is a glimpse: every seat in every classroom has its own plug and Internet connection. The teachers can use every technological teaching aid you can think of in every classroom. There are private study rooms on every floor, both inside and outside the library (obviously equipped with Internet, plugs and white boards). There are many public phones and computers throughout. Every publication and many other groups have their own offices. The faculty offices are all on one floor, so you can see (or avoid) many faculty in one area.

Status: Current student, full-time
Dates of Enrollment: 8/2001-Submit Date
Survey Submitted: October 2003

The campus is beautiful, with the university having completed its new law facility. The law school has raised the standard, with classrooms complete with computer/Internet hookups and wireless connections, allowing you to study anywhere on the campus. Furthermore, the neighborhood where the university is located is surrounded by affordable housing, and great restaurants and coffee shops. Crime is not a problem in the area.

Social Life

Status: Alumnus/a, full-time
Dates of Enrollment: 8/1980-5/1983
Survey Submitted: April 2005

We had a very collegial group of students in my division and often had FACs (Friday afternoon clubs) with professors and students at a local bar near the

Read all of Vault's Law School Surveys at www.vault.com/lawschool — get complete surveys on top law schools, expert advice on application essays, LSAT prep and more.

VAULT CAREER LIBRARY 113

school or study groups that met at local restaurants for dinner and study. I remember Dozens, Don's Mixed Drinks, the Library, Duffey's, The Pub, the White Spot, Wazee Supper Club and My Brother's Bar as being favorites. The Greek system was mainly on the main campus and didn't have an impact on the law school students. A group of my classmates and some others also formed a group while in law school that we carried on after we graduated and ultimately we put on an annual Halloween party raising money for a local children's charity.

Status: Current student, full-time
Dates of Enrollment: 9/2003-Submit Date
Survey Submitted: May 2004

Social life in law school consists of law students talking to other law students about law school. Though this is not what many would call thrilling, DU does what it can. There are numerous clubs, functions, lunches, auctions and so on, all of which provide free food drinks and the like. The one thing that can be said of private schools is that they can afford to feed you.

Status: Current student, full-time
Dates of Enrollment: 8/2002-Submit Date
Survey Submitted: May 2004

The bar scene around campus is fun. Because it is also an undergraduate campus, there are plenty of places that take you back to your college days. However, within a few blocks there are also more sophisticated restaurants and bars in a variety of price ranges. The new building and accompanying green space is ideal for meeting people and creating a social atmosphere within the law school. People can always be seen sitting on the porch chatting or grabbing a snack at the snack bar. Within walking distance of the school, there are two coffee shops, two Middle Eastern restaurants, two sandwich shops, three Asian restaurants, a burrito place, a Mexican place and about six bars, so there is a lot of foot traffic around.

Status: Current student, full-time
Dates of Enrollment: 8/2001-Submit Date
Survey Submitted: October 2003

We're in Denver, which means that most of us will shun the city on the weekends for a trek into the mountains.

Dating doesn't happen much around the class, as most of the students who attend have a significant other of some sort. You'll find your time taken up with other pursuits as well, hampering any chance you have to meet that special somebody. The school is clique-ish; most students with similar interests or pursuits will hang out with each other.

Quinnipiac University School of Law

Office of Admissions
275 Mount Carmel Avenue
Hamden, CT 06518-1908
Admissions phone: (203) 582-3400
Admissions e-mail: ladm@quinnipiac.edu
Admissions URL: http://law.quinnipiac.edu/x17.xml

 Admissions

Status: Alumnus/a, evening program
Dates of Enrollment: 1/2001-12/2003
Survey Submitted: March 2005

I took the LSATs and submitted an application. I was sent an acceptance by mail and an award of scholarship letter. A follow-up call from the admissions office would have been nice.

Status: Alumnus/a, full-time
Dates of Enrollment: 8/1999-5/2003
Survey Submitted: October 2004

There is a trend that the school is becoming more selective and competitive in its selection process. Middle tier grades and LSAT scores should assure you success in your acceptance.

Status: Current student, full-time
Dates of Enrollment: 8/2003-Submit Date
Survey Submitted: May 2004

The admissions process is very arbitrary. People with LSATs of 149 were admitted, and people with better records and LSATs were not. Also, admissions scholarships were small.

> **The school says:** "The admissions staff reviews the complete file of every applicant to determine which candidates have the greatest chance for success in law school. Additionally, the staff and Admissions Committee are looking for students who will add diversity, in the broadest sense, to the classroom. Diversity is defined in many ways, including ethnicity, age, life and work experience, geography, etc.

> "The average merit award for entering full-time students in fall 2006 was greater than $15,000."

Status: Current student, full-time
Dates of Enrollment: 8/2002-Submit Date
Survey Submitted: February 2004

Applications are easy to fill out. Decisions are based on LSAT scores and GPAs among other criteria and are made within four to six weeks of receiving the application. There is no interview. Personal statements are recommended to improve the quality of the application.

> **The school says:** Personal statements are a required part of the application.

Status: Current student, full-time
Dates of Enrollment: 9/2000-5/2005
Survey Submitted: September 2003

Not very selective. Rather undiverse student body. No interviews.

> **The school says:** "Admissions have become increasingly selective over the past several years. For fall 2006, only 24 percent of the applicant pool was offered admission. The median GPA and LSAT respectively were 3.4 and 158 for the full-time program. The middle 50 percent of the class had following credentials: GPA 3.00-3.60; LSAT 156-159.

"12 percent of the fall 2006 class identified themselves as persons of color. Interviews are available for admitted students."

 Academics

Status: Alumnus/a, evening program
Dates of Enrollment: 1/2001-12/2003
Survey Submitted: March 2005

Getting into day classes is not easy for night students. Most professors were competent—few seemed to have no interest in teaching. Workload was lighter than I had expected. They keep focusing on writing skills.

> **The school says:** "For the past three years, our evening students have had little difficulty enrolling in day classes."

Status: Alumnus/a, full-time
Dates of Enrollment: 8/1999-5/2003
Survey Submitted: October 2004

Aside from the C curve, which I think has changed, the classes were for the most part challenging and at the same time very interesting. Professors were topnotch considering the ranking of the school. As with most law schools, there is definitely a heavy workload, which decreases as you progress through the years.

Status: Current student, full-time
Dates of Enrollment: 8/2002-Submit Date
Survey Submitted: February 2004

The first-year program is uniform for all students, split into two to three sections. Contracts, civil procedure and legal skills are yearlong programs and the first-year curriculum also includes criminal law, torts, property and constitutional law. The professors are available in the nearby offices and make appointments when their office hours are not suitable. The second and third years offer a variety of classes in general legal areas with recommendations to take certain cores that will be tested on the bar exam.

 Employment Prospects

Status: Alumnus/a, evening program
Dates of Enrollment: 1/2001-12/2003
Survey Submitted: March 2005

Degree does not travel far from school. I made contact with some alumni on my own and got a summer associate and full-time position with a large NYC firm. Large firms generally do not hire 3Ls and that is when most students started to look for employment.

Status: Alumnus/a, full-time
Dates of Enrollment: 8/1999-5/2003
Survey Submitted: October 2004

Top students and locals should have a fairly easy time finding employment after graduation. However, middle of the road students trying to find work outside the region may have a difficult time finding employment.

Status: Current student, full-time
Dates of Enrollment: 8/2003-Submit Date
Survey Submitted: May 2004

The career office will help you with a resume, but you might be on your own after that.

> **The school says:** "Significant changes to improve career services for all students began in fall 2004. The placement rate for the Class of 2005 was 92 percent nine months after graduation."

Read all of Vault's Law School Surveys at www.vault.com/lawschool — get complete surveys on top law schools, expert advice on application essays, LSAT prep and more.

VAULT CAREER LIBRARY 115

Status: Current student, full-time
Dates of Enrollment: 8/2002-Submit Date
Survey Submitted: February 2004

Small- and medium-sized firms like the students who learn people skills through working in one of the three on-campus legal clinics, taking classes in representing clients and working in an externship for one to two semesters. Large firms are reluctant to interview anyone but the top 10 to 30 percent of the class.

Status: Current student, full-time
Dates of Enrollment: 9/2000-5/2005
Survey Submitted: September 2003

Career services seem tailored only for the top 10 percent of class.

 ## Quality of Life

Status: Alumnus/a, evening program
Dates of Enrollment: 1/2001-12/2003
Survey Submitted: March 2005

Campus and school are beautiful and very comfortable.

Status: Current student, full-time
Dates of Enrollment: 8/2002-Submit Date
Survey Submitted: February 2004

Nearby New Haven is a nice city and New York City is less than 90 minutes away. There is no on-campus housing for grad students. There is one cafe on the law school campus that has a variety of foods; and on the main campus, there is a large cafeteria offering everything. Security patrols every building 24 hours a day and the parking lot. The parking situation is not good, but a shuttle transports students from far parking lots to the law school.

Status: Current student, full-time
Dates of Enrollment: 9/2000-5/2005
Survey Submitted: September 2003

Off-campus housing. Very good facilities. Rarely any criminal activity.

 ## Social Life

Status: Current student, full-time
Dates of Enrollment: 8/2002-Submit Date
Survey Submitted: February 2004

The school has the Barrister's Ball once a year. On Thursdays, school clubs have TGITs.

Status: Current student, full-time
Dates of Enrollment: 9/2000-5/2005
Survey Submitted: September 2003

Unfortunately, the town of Hamden doesn't really accommodate very well. For decent bars and restaurants, one must travel to New Haven.

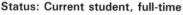 ## The School Says

Full-time day and part-time evening programs are offered beginning each fall. The academic program is designed to prepare students to be generalists or specialists. Quinnipiac provides a dynamic blend of traditional classroom instruction and extensive experiential learning opportunities. Students who wish to focus on a specific area of study may choose from six different concentrations: Civil Advocacy & Dispute Resolution, Criminal Law & Advocacy, Family & Juvenile Law, Health Law, Intellectual Property and Tax.

Quinnipiac is recognized as having one of the premier clinical and externship programs in the country and students often cite their experiences in these programs as one of the highlights of their law school experience. These experiential learning opportunities allow students to bridge the gap between theory and practice.

The seven clinical programs include Civil, Health Law, Tax, Advanced, Evening (for part-time students), Defense Appellate and Prosecution Appellate. The nine externship programs are Corporate Counsel, Criminal Justice, Family & Juvenile Law, Judicial, Legal Services, Legislative, Mediation, Public Interest and Field Placement II. The law school also offers a joint JD/MBA degree and a summer study abroad program with Trinity College in Dublin, Ireland.

Quinnipiac has established two centers in specialized fields of law—the Center for Health Law & Policy and the Center on Dispute Resolution—both of which draw on considerable academic strengths and resources within the law school community.

Student Group: Quinnipiac students often comment about the strong sense of community that permeates the law school. The sense of community is enhanced by the numerous and varied opportunities for students to participate in co-curricular activities, including a dynamic Student Bar Association, more than 30 different student organizations, a thriving Moot Court Society, an active Quinnipiac Law Review, and two law journals—the *Health Law Journal* and the *Probate Law Journal*.

Location: The Quinnipiac University School of Law is situated on the Quinnipiac University campus, a picturesque 500-acre site in Hamden, Connecticut. Close to New York, Boston, Hartford and New Haven, the law school is at the heart of one of the biggest concentrations of private law firms, corporate headquarters and financial institutions in the country. The beautiful, state-of-the-art law center, opened in 1995, with wireless computer access in all the classrooms and study areas, provides students with a modern, relaxed and safe environment for study.

Faculty: The fundamental strength of the law school lies in the faculty members' dedication to academic excellence. Faculty members come from a wide variety of distinguished backgrounds in law practice and teaching and have a commitment to excellence in education.

The faculty combines excellence in scholarship and teaching with exceptional accessibility. The care with which faculty members demonstrate their interest in each student's progress and success is a distinguishing characteristic of Quinnipiac Law. Most have an open-door policy and generously share of their expertise, insights and time. The low student-faculty ratio (15:1) allows students to work closely with faculty, and this translates into a different kind of law school experience.

University of Connecticut School of Law

Admissions Office
45 Elizabeth Street
Hartford, CT 06105-2290
Admissions phone: (860) 570-5100
Admissions e-mail: admit@law.uconn.edu
Admissions URL: http://law.uconn.edu/admissions

 ## Admissions

Status: Current student, full-time
Dates of Enrollment: 8/2005-Submit Date
Survey Submitted: April 2006

In comparison to most of the other schools I applied to, there was very little information from UConn. If I had questions, it was very easy to call and ask, and the staff was friendly. The web site was terrible at the time, but it has been updated. Decisions were made pretty early in the game—January, I think, but I know some other people were kept waiting into July. Also, if you are a CT resident, you can pre-apply (basically send them your demographic information) so they can open up a file for you in September, then wait for you to send your essay, transcript, references and all that good stuff. Pre-applying carries no obligation and a dropped price of $25.

Status: Current student, part-time
Dates of Enrollment: 8/2004-Submit Date
Survey Submitted: April 2006

This school's approach to admissions is to look at the "big picture" when considering an applicant. By that I mean that an applicant is not simply reduced to an LSAT score or a GPA. If you are one of those "borderline" applicants, or someone with a few years of experience between college and law school, I highly recommend answering all of the essay questions, not just the personal statement. There is no interview process, so this it the best way to let them see who you are.

Status: Current student, full-time
Dates of Enrollment: 9/2005-Submit Date
Survey Submitted: April 2006

The admissions process to get into UConn is pretty extensive. As the administration tells us regularly, "You got in, the hard part is over." They are generally referring to the rigorous admissions standards, but I think that also applies to the process itself. In addition to the application they require undergraduate transcripts (of course), a resume, your academic history and a good LSAT score (I believe the median for admission this year was 163). I persistently called the admissions and financial aid people, double-checked things and just generally obsessed, so things went pretty smoothly for the most part.

There were some problems with the financial aid people, which caused some headaches for me. There were some mistakes made clearing my financial aid and processing my awards; and I received misinformation about the availability and process for awarding grants. However, all my issues were eventually resolved and I have not had problems since then.

> **The school says:** The median for admission this year was actually 161.

Status: Current student, full-time
Dates of Enrollment: 8/2005-Submit Date
Survey Submitted: April 2006

Fairly quick and painless. Financial aid also runs fairly smoothly. No interview. They seem to appreciate a diversity of life and work experience. Fluency in another language also a big plus (clinics always looking for translators).

Status: Current student, full-time
Dates of Enrollment: 8/2004-Submit Date
Survey Submitted: April 2006

Getting into law school is tough, there are a lot of qualified people applying these days and most of the top tiered schools have the opportunity to pick and choose the ones they want. That being said, there are a few things that you can do to stand out above the rest and get into the schools you want to.

First, the LSAT, no matter what a school says about its "full candidate" admissions process the LSAT is important. It is an accepted indication about how you will do in law school and schools like higher numbers. Take a look at what the school's mean LSAT score is and where your score falls into that range. The best thing about the LSAT is that if you haven't taken it already then you have a clean slate and can take the time to prepare for it. If you have taken it already then the school will see your past scores and does not necessarily have to assume your highest score is "your score." That means the best was to have the LSAT work for you is to take it once and to ace it. There are a lot of LSAT training programs out there. They are good if you need the extra motivation to study—once you spend the money (and the money is considerable) you should feel the pull to to study. That being said, you can also get the same benefits from internal motivation and a couple of LSAT books from the library or bookstore.

Second, college GPA, not much you can do here if you are already out of college. The same "numbers" game applies here as it does in the LSAT score. If your college grades are low, you might want to consider offering an explanation. If your overall GPA is low but you had great grades in your major or in some field you think applies well to law school then feel free to offer an explanation for that.

Third, essay, law schools get thousands of applications. Is your application something that someone will remember reading? If not, start over. Once the school gets past the numbers and actually reads what you have sent them you had better make that reading interesting. Take your time writing your essay and make sure you enlist plenty of help to see if it is interesting. Something you find hilarious might not come off right to others and you want to make sure your essay is perfect.

Fourth and last, law schools want people that will succeed. There is nothing better for a school than an applicant who comes to campus guns blazing, does well, does it all, gets the best job and then send lots of money back to the school. That being said, let the school know that you know what you are getting into. That law school is where you want to be, not that you necessarily need to tell them you know where you want to be after law school, but at least that you have researched law school, are ready for the commitment, and will succeed. Along with this point, if you have the opportunity to get involved in the law after college and before law school then by all means get involved. Volunteer at a law center, go to the school you want to go to and see if they need anyone to do anything, read about the law, not only should the law school see that you know what you are getting into but YOU should know what you are getting into. If you make it a point to make the school know who you are then your application will stand out that much more.

Status: Current student, full-time
Dates of Enrollment: 8/2005-Submit Date
Survey Submitted: April 2006

In a group that seems fairly homogenous, after getting to know your fellow classmates it becomes increasingly clear that the admissions committee relies heavily on personal statements. The staff in the admissions office does a great job of admitting people with all kinds of different, interesting backgrounds, so play that up. The admissions staff is also really friendly and encouraging, not stuck up and elitist like a lot of other tier one schools

Read all of Vault's Law School Surveys at www.vault.com/lawschool — get complete surveys on top law schools, expert advice on applicaton essays, LSAT prep and more.

VAULT CAREER LIBRARY 117

Status: Current student, full-time
Dates of Enrollment: 8/2004-Submit Date
Survey Submitted: September 2005

The UConn admission process is very similar to most other law schools—I found it to be neither more nor less stressful. The admissions staff is very helpful in answering any and all questions, and very good at being available to applying students as well as to current students. I don't think that there is a real "trick" to getting in, other than good LSAT scores and a decent undergraduate GPA. UConn also seems to value previous work experience—even if not law related.

In the past few years UConn does seem to be getting more selective as it gains more recognition and more and more students are starting to see the benefit of a half-priced education (in-state tuition). Even for students who are not Connecticut residents, however, it is very easy to complete the steps to qualify for in-state tuition after their first year. So, even if you have to pay one year of full tuition, you still get two at half price!

Status: Current student, full-time
Dates of Enrollment: 8/2002-Submit Date
Survey Submitted: July 2004

From what I remember the admissions process wasn't difficult. No interview, just a number of forms, etc. The one item I will mention is that if you are admitted and choose to defer attending for a year, keep on top of the school for financial aid. I deferred and missed out on financial aid for my first year because the school never sent me additional forms or reminders and I didn't know any better.

 **Academics**

Status: Current student, full-time
Dates of Enrollment: 8/2003-Submit Date
Survey Submitted: April 2006

Classes at UConn Law are much smaller than many schools and, aside from the basic curriculum, there are a number of intimate survey courses available on topics ranging from insurance to Justice Jackson. This is a benefit, but its cost is that it can be a challenge finding the class you want. Conflicts was not offered for several semesters in a row, for instance.

There is a B median, which, unfortunately, is applied in wildly varied ways. One professor may give all B's, while another may give a number of grades lower. As a consequence, it is typically difficult to distinguish yourself if you are in the middle of the pack. Imagine the difference between the best and worst B's in a class when 30 students receive that mark. The best-performing B will look exactly the same to an employer as the student who just missed a C+.

Status: Current student, full-time
Dates of Enrollment: 8/2005-Submit Date
Survey Submitted: April 2006

Great professors—really, really accessible. The classes aren't that big, your large section in your first-year classes is about 70, in contrast to a lot of other schools that have about 120. You really feel like you get to know all of your professors, the staff is usually very laid-back. You get to choose one elective during your second semester and almost everyone got what they wanted. As far as choosing for second year there are some very popular classes that are hard to get into, but if you are high enough on the waiting list you'll usually make it in.

The Moot Court interim is intense but a great learning experience. It's a little over three weeks long, you have to write an appellate brief and do an appellate argument in front of three judges (sometimes lawyers sit in as judges, but my panel was composed of two Connecticut state judges and a district court judge). The first week of the course is fairly laid-back with a light workload but don't be fooled, it gets much more intense after that. Luckily that is the only class you have at the time so it is manageable and you get a lot of social time with your friends. The bonus is that everyone gets to practice public speaking and it forces those who normally wouldn't put themselves out there to do it and gain the valuable experience. I personally hate public speaking but after having done it several times in my Moot Court class I felt comfortable participating in the school's moot court competition.

Status: Current student, part-time
Dates of Enrollment: 9/2002-Submit Date
Survey Submitted: April 2006

Being a true evening student, working full-time during the day and going to school at night, is tough here. First, they allow anyone from the evening program to switch to the full-time day program after the first year. At least 50 percent do. This means that at least 50 percent of your classes your first year are students who do not work during the day and who are taking only a part-time academic program. They have way too much time to study. Since all first-year classes are graded on a B median (i.e., you are graded in comparison to the other students in the class), you're at a real disadvantage.

Status: Current student, full-time
Dates of Enrollment: 8/2004-Submit Date
Survey Submitted: April 2006

UConn is a practical law education. I mean that in a good way. The school gives you a chance to establish a career from your second semester. There are a ton of opportunities to work on real cases with real people, solving real problems. (Just not your first year.) There are about half a dozen or more clinics, there are special courses of instruction in Tax and Intellectual Property, there is an amazing insurance program, and other opportunities that a lot of schools don't offer.

Writing is KEY! Write well, grade well. You need to know the material but if you read for class and are prepared to discuss class material each day then you will know the material.

As to getting popular classes, this is not always easy. In any semester there are probable half a dozen really popular classes and there is NO WAY to get into all of them. You have to pick the one that you really want to take and run with that. The class selection system seems to be geared towards allowing everyone at least one favored class. The system of selection itself is relatively complicated. Make sure you know what you are doing well in advance of selection time or else you will not get any popular classes. Talk to upperclassmen to learn the tricks of the system and to all students to see where peoples preferences lie so you know what classes you will have to choose first to ensure enrollment. After the popular classes there are usually enough options to fill out schedules without taking classes you don't want, although they might not have been your first choices.

READ. READ. READ. Make sure you put in the hours outside of class so that class is worth it. Also, go to CLASS! Professors write the exams, professors talk about the material that interests them in class, students should know this. One of the most important things is to use your time wisely. If you have a morning class and then a few hours off before the afternoon class then use that time to work! That way at night, when there are tons of fun things going on, you can spend more time having fun. That's right, you are supposed to have fun. It's life, work hard so that you have the ability to play hard. That being said, don't fall into undergrad mode where your week is planned around the happy hour circuit. Take your fun in doses so that you do well and get a good job so that when you get out you can afford to have real, adult fun, instead of still planning your week around $1 pints and free chicken wings.

As to professors, there are good ones and bad ones. When it comes time to choose your own classes, take a look at the course evaluations in the library. They don't lie. Don't take them as the gospel though, talk to upperclassmen and to other professors as well. In general, the professors are very accessible; be an adult, though and establish a real relationship with them instead of e-mailing them questions out of the blue. Take the time to go to their offices, talk with them about their class but also get as much info about the law, about them in general, and about the school as you can. They are human and when it comes time to grade an exam the fact that you have a relationship with them will not get you an A from a B but it will give you benefit of the doubt in some situations and get that A from an A-.

Status: Current student, full-time LLM
Dates of Enrollment: 1/2005-Submit Date
Survey Submitted: April 2006

The Insurance Law LLM program offers a wide variety of courses that focus on specific aspects of insurance. For example, there are separate courses on Liability Insurance, Property Insurance, Surety Bonds, Executive and Professional Liability Insurance, Insurance Finance, Insurance Regulation, Principles of Insurance, Principles of Reinsurance, Health Insurance Law and Policy, and even a seminar on Religion, Risk and Responsibility.

Registration is done via the Internet. Upper-level students can choose to sign up for one course that they really want on the first day of registration, or they may instead take their chances and sign up for two classes on the second day. They can then fill in the rest of their schedule on the third day.

Status: Alumnus/a, full-time
Dates of Enrollment: 8/1994-6/1997
Survey Submitted: March 2005

UConn provides a rigorous legal education that prepares students to teach, practice law in the public or private sector, or return to school for additional education. The professors are first-rate experts in their respective fields of endeavor. The classes are relatively small which allows for dynamic classroom discussions as well as one-on-one interaction with the professors.

Status: Current student, full-time
Dates of Enrollment: 8/2002-Submit Date
Survey Submitted: July 2004

The classes are generally very good. All professors are knowledgeable, although few have practical experience in their fields. The classes are generally well taught, and students usually have a good experience in them. The workload varies greatly depending on the class type. For example, you will work a LOT more for a clinic than almost anything else, Federal Courts has a lot of reading, etc. Most times the workload is manageable and not overly oppressive.

Grading isn't too bad. There's a B median. Basically, it keeps some professors from handing out too many low grades and brings up the average GPA of the school. Unfortunately, this means that if you have a B average GPA, you'll be in the lowest quintile. After my first year, the border between the fifth quint (lowest one) and the fourth was around a 2.9. Between the fourth and the third was around a 3.1. Between the third and the second was around a 3.3/3.4. Amazingly enough, although the grading can feel arbitrary at times, it's not. It can't be when those who should be at the top of the class are at the top of the class. My year, no one doubted why the number one student was that rank nor that he/she deserved it.

One program I am familiar with (though am not in) is the Intellectual Property Certificate Program. It's rather competitive to get into and all you get out of it is an extra piece of paper. The price for that paper is a series of course requirements and a paper on an IP topic undertaken with one of the IP faculty. Considering everyone has to write a paper at some point (for the upperclass writing requirement, a.k.a., the UCWR), it's not a very onerous series of tasks. All in all, if you plan on taking the courses anyway and can manage to wrangle your way into the program, give it a shot. Otherwise, if you don't get in or choose not to try, it's no big deal at all.

Employment Prospects

Status: Current student, full-time LLM
Dates of Enrollment: 1/2005-Submit Date
Survey Submitted: April 2006

In the just-released *U.S. News & World Report* rankings, UConn has retained its status as a tier one law school. However, I can tell you that the law school that one attended is usually of far less importance to prospective employers than one might think. It is useful, however, if the student wishes to clerk for a federal judge, as they tend to be both more attentive to law school rankings and provincial in the sense of paying undue favoritism to graduates of their own alma mater.

Status: Current student, full-time
Dates of Enrollment: 9/2005-Submit Date
Survey Submitted: April 2006

There aren't many law schools in CT (just Yale and Quinnipiac), and UConn is the only one within 45 minutes of Hartford. UConn's obviously not as prestigious as Yale but it's way better than Quinnipiac, and it's very highly regarded in the area. UConn Law grads have no problem getting a job, and I think the average starting salary is somewhere around $100K. Hartford has a huge insurance industry, so there are also lots of lawyers around. The school has great relationships with the most prestigious law firms in the area, and it's not too hard to get internships (unless you work during the day, like me; then it's more complicated). Graduates often go into insurance law, trial law or public interest law.

> **The school says:** UConn is in Hartford. Hartford contains many large law firms as well as insurance agencies. Its graduates tend to enter into private practice and litigation.

Status: Current student, full-time
Dates of Enrollment: 8/2003-Submit Date
Survey Submitted: April 2006

Top-performing UConn Law students will have no problem joining one of Connecticut's top firms and many have met great success in the Boston and New York markets. I got an offer from Sullivan & Cromwell and friends have received them from Skadden, White & Case, Sidley Austin and others.

On-campus recruiting works well for top students looking to stay in New England. Folks going to New York, so far, have had to venture out on their own. The job search for students in the middle of the class can be difficult, though my understanding is that our placement rate is very good.

It appears that the alumni networking approach is one the school has only begun to employ recently. As the school continues to improve its alumni relations this should be an even better option. Moreover, as UConn students attain jobs at bigger and better firms, the network will improve as well.

There is a good deal of interest in judicial clerkships. Most students who clerk do so in the state courts. Several will go to the federal districts, and only the very top of the class will even be considered by the federal circuit courts of appeals. This is just a fact of life, due, I think, mostly to the fact that the judges at that tier are from the top echelon of schools and tend to hire their clerks from their alma maters. This is changing, and UConn Law students have managed to get circuit court clerkships in the less-competitive western circuits and/or with a few years of experience (say at a federal district court or in a state supreme court).

Status: Alumnus/a, full-time
Dates of Enrollment: 8/2001-5/2004
Survey Submitted: March 2006

I had no difficulty securing the job I wanted. I was able to secure an interview with all but one of the firms I wanted to speak to and the one that turned me down was the least prestigious firm I selected.

Status: Alumnus/a, full- and part-time
Dates of Enrollment: 8/2002-5/2005
Survey Submitted: March 2006

I did not have a problem at all finding a job. Indeed, I am working for the firm I have always wanted to work for since my first year in law school! The Career Services Office assists students in getting internships using the on-campus interview process and using non-traditional methods such as using the alumni network. The alumni I have contacted were always willing to speak with me, professing their love for the school as a reason they want to give back in time.

Status: Alumnus/a, full-time
Dates of Enrollment: 8/1994-5/1997
Survey Submitted: April 2004

The Career Services Office is very well networked with Connecticut employers and employers based in New England generally. Students may have more difficulty finding out-of-state jobs and internship opportunities.

Read all of Vault's Law School Surveys at www.vault.com/lawschool — get complete surveys on top law schools, expert advice on applicaton essays, LSAT prep and more.

VAULT CAREER LIBRARY   119

Status: Current student, full-time
Dates of Enrollment: 8/2002-Submit Date
Survey Submitted: July 2004

There is a program for on-campus interviews (OCI) for second-years on up (no first-years). Very few students get jobs from OCI so don't stress too much over it. As far as I can tell, job prospects aren't bad. Most of the students I know were able to find jobs if they were looking for them, so there you go.

 ## Quality of Life

Status: Current student, full-time
Dates of Enrollment: 8/2003-Submit Date
Survey Submitted: April 2006

Hartford is not the best place to live, but UConn makes a great effort to keep the campus and neighborhood safe. Many students live within walking distance of the school in the surrounding neighborhoods. UConn makes efforts to supply students with great places to rent that are UConn-friendly. Campus is beautiful and cafeteria services have been upgraded in the past year to answer student requests and needs.

Status: Current student, part-time
Dates of Enrollment: 8/2004-Submit Date
Survey Submitted: April 2006

There is no campus housing. The campus is kept safe by campus police. The food is good, but the food service is handled by restaurants who do catering. Every year it goes out to bid, so the quality of the food can change each year. So far, it has been decent. The campus will be gorgeous if they ever get the construction equipment out of there. The library is falling apart, but the dean assures us all that it will be fixed by summer. I am not holding my breath.

FYI, they closed the library early the weekend before the bar exam last year. What were they thinking? Frequently, certain offices will just shut down early for the day, making it more difficult for those of us with jobs or internships to get to campus to conduct business.

Status: Current student, full-time
Dates of Enrollment: 8/2003-Submit Date
Survey Submitted: April 2006

The quality of life at UConn Law is terrific. The neighborhood is wonderful and there are plenty of apartments available at pretty good rates. The students are very collegial, offering to share notes and/or talk through issues. Nobody hides books in the library. Nobody talks about grades. There are a few bars around campus, which typically cater to law students on particular nights. (Thursdays at the Spigot, for example.)

The faculty are very approachable and most, with only a few exceptions, are excellent teachers. It is also not unusual for faculty and students to socialize with each other. I often went to a wine bar with my Evidence professor (not while actually enrolled in his class, of course) and another friend goes out to eat with her Constitutional Law professor and his wife every now and again.

Status: Current student, full-time
Dates of Enrollment: 9/2005-Submit Date
Survey Submitted: April 2006

The campus itself is nice, but students do not live there. It's right on the edge of Hartford (rough), next to West Hartford (nicer). It's not exactly high-crime, but it's still close to downtown. There's a reason I live 45 minutes away. The campus is beautiful. It is an old stone former seminary, Gothic style. There is a brand-new stone library, which is state of the art and stunning. The only drawback to campus is they do not have wireless Internet yet, but they're working on it (for two years now!).

Status: Current student, full-time
Dates of Enrollment: 9/2005-Submit Date
Survey Submitted: April 2006

No on-campus housing is available, and most students end up commuting to school. The west end of Hartford is a nice place to live, and an increasing number of students choose to live there. The campus is beautiful. Gothic architec-

ture adorns the exterior walls, and high-tech multimedia devices grace several of the classroom interiors.

Status: Current student, full-time
Dates of Enrollment: 8/2004-Submit Date
Survey Submitted: September 2005

The campus is the most beautiful thing ever—and in fact, played a major role in my decision to come here (that and the in-state tuition)! Situated in the old Hartford Theological College campus, the buildings are reminiscent of Oxford or Cambridge in their architectural style and aura.

Hartford, itself is a growing city and in fact its slogan is "New England's Rising Star." In the last few years there have been dozens of new restaurants and bars opening up and there is significant revitalization going on in the downtown area. Because it is a small but extremely diverse city, as well as the state capital, it provides a plethora of opportunities to get involved at many levels of government as well as grassroots community based organizations.

Status: Alumnus/a, full-time
Dates of Enrollment: 9/1998-5/2001
Survey Submitted: March 2006

The law school is located in a very diverse and interesting neighborhood in Hartford. I enjoyed the atmosphere. Most law students lived in apartments within a few blocks of the law school, lending to a campus feel. There were also several local bars that were law school hangouts, and that was very enjoyable.

The law school buildings themselves are quite beautiful. The law school is located in an old seminary. The classroom facilities were slightly outdated at the time of my graduation, but I understand improvements have been made recently. The library is topnotch.

Status: Current student, full-time
Dates of Enrollment: 8/2002-Submit Date
Survey Submitted: July 2004

The campus is gorgeous! For a campus in Hartford, it's downright shocking. There's no on-campus or school-provided housing. The dining area is OK. Nothing exciting or spectacular, just decent food at moderately high prices. There's campus security although the library isn't that secure. (Don't leave your laptop or bag unattended.) The parking lots are lit. There isn't enough parking all the time (usually only in the mornings) but it's not a huge problem. All in all, a nice place with a beautiful library and a recently refurbished student lounge.

 ## Social Life

Status: Current student, full-time
Dates of Enrollment: 8/2003-Submit Date
Survey Submitted: April 2006

Hartford is "New England's Rising Star" and while folks from New York or Chicago may be disappointed, the city has a lot to offer. The Hartford Symphony is quite good and offers an incredible student discount. The Hartford Stage is an excellent regional theater company. There is also the Wadworth, the nation's oldest public art museum, and other cultural events like the annual Hartford Jazz Festival each summer.

The law school is in the city's best neighborhood, right on the border of West Hartford, one of the state's nicest—and wealthiest—communities. West Hartford Center offers an array of topnotch dining and Elizabeth Park, which straddles the Hartford-West Hartford border, is a charming place with a public rose garden and softball fields where law students often play.

The dating scene can be a bit like high school; it's a small school so there is lots of gossip. It is hard to mix and mingle outside the law school scene. The law school and medical school (which is in Farmington) facilitate would-be lawyer-doctor relationships through some joint events. I haven't heard of any lasting, however.

A favorite social event is the annual Public Interest Law Group (PILG) Auction to raise money to pay grants to students who take non-paying public interest jobs during their summer breaks. The organizers solicit contributions from the community, which range from iPods to vacation home rentals, and auction them off at a big event in the fall. Professors and students share the stage as auctioneers. Everybody goes and it is a wonderful time.

Status: Current student, full-time
Dates of Enrollment: 8/2005-Submit Date
Survey Submitted: April 2006

The social life at school is great, everyone is really open about inviting people everywhere and the students go out a lot. The law school bar is the Spigot, on the border of Hartford and West Hartford; the Half Door, located about one and a half blocks from the school, is also very popular. There are lots of bars in downtown Hartford and the SBA will frequently sponsor outings at specific bars. There are always a lot of parties, especially at the beginning of the year, and students basically send mass e-mails out to the entire law school community e-mail list inviting anyone and everyone to come to their party. It's a real tight-knit community.

There are also fun trips like skiing and this year we participated in a law school softball tournament at UVA for the first time. The SBA essentially covered all of the expenses for the weekend and the trip only cost students $40! There is also a law school ice hockey team called Capital Punishment (which men and women can join). The student e-mail list provides a connection for the community. Whenever anything is going on an e-mail is sent out about it. Since we have our own field there are frequently e-mails sent out to meet up for soccer or softball, football in the snow, kickball in the neighboring Elizabeth Park. It's a really friendly, inclusive social atmosphere.

Status: Current student, full-time
Dates of Enrollment: 9/2005-Submit Date
Survey Submitted: April 2006

The law school is blessed with a variety of student organizations, from the ACS and LAMBDA (LGBT club) to the Christian Legal Society and the Federalist Society. Clubs sponsor social events on a regular basis. There are a number of bars (which, in New England, means nice family-style sit-down restaurants that also contain a bar), which seem to be social hubs for out-of-class life.

Status: Current student, full-time
Dates of Enrollment: 8/2005-Submit Date
Survey Submitted: April 2006

Social life is what you make it. Active bar scene. Clubbing in Hartford is limited, but there. Older/married minority bond quickly. Campus groups/organiza-

tions are fairly active. Lots of good restaurants around. Most importantly, despite the stress and challenge, the atmosphere is VERY laid-back and supportive. No overly competitive crap. The few jerks (two or three per 70) really stand out, but are too oblivious to realize it.

Status: Current student, full-time
Dates of Enrollment: 8/2002-5/2005
Survey Submitted: July 2004

The actual school-based social life isn't much so to speak. The Student Bar Association has trouble funding alcohol-inclusive events, which is usually the main draw. There are a lot of school-based organizations but they're not much of a substitute for social activities.

The surrounding area is OK. There are two local bars. The Half Door is an awesome Irish Pub on Sisson, only a few blocks from the school. The Spigot is over on Prospect, very much a local, towny, seedy-type bar. There are some restaurants in the area—The Wood 'n Tap (another pub, only a few blocks down from the Half Door; excellent burgers and appetizers, serves until 10 or 11 p.m.), Braza, Monte Alban, South Whitney Pizza; moving further away there's Barb's Pizza, Lena's First & Last, AC Petersen, Lemongrass, C.O. Jones ("the Mexican Restaurant"), the Agave Grill; and downtown (West Hartford) there's the Elbow Room, Max's Oyster Bar, Puerto Vallarta and more. There's also some nightlife in downtown East Hartford—the Brickyard, the Standing Stone, Blue and more. Clubs, bars mostly. Right near the train station and Agave Grill if you're looking.

In the summertime, there are various festivals and other activities in and around Hartford. All in all, it's not the best place to be but it's got enough to offer that you shouldn't be too bored if you don't want to be.

Status: Alumnus/a, full-time
Dates of Enrollment: 8/1994-5/1997
Survey Submitted: April 2004

Hartford is a medium-sized city with plenty of restaurants, clubs and bars. Students have little difficulty finding ways to entertain themselves. Students have also been known to travel to NYC or Boston for the weekend given their close proximity to Hartford.

Read all of Vault's Law School Surveys at www.vault.com/lawschool — get complete surveys on top law schools, expert advice on applicaton essays, LSAT prep and more.

VAULT CAREER LIBRARY **121**

Yale Law School

Admissions Office
P.O. Box 208329
New Haven, CT 06520-8329
Admissions phone: 203 432-4995
Admissions e-mail: admissions.law@yale.edu
Admissions URL: http://www.law.yale.edu/admissions/

 ## Admissions

Status: Alumnus/a, full-time
Dates of Enrollment: 9/1998-4/2001
Survey Submitted: March 2006

The admissions process appears to focus heavily on LSAT, transcripts and the personal statement. Low LSATs or GPAs make it almost impossible to be admitted, but even applicants with near-perfect LSATs and GPAs are often turned away because of the small size of the class relative to the number of applications received. In my opinion, successful applicants are generally either: wealthy geniuses with undergraduate degrees from Harvard or Yale (who make up about half the class) or people of middle-class background from other parts of the country who create both geographic and socioeconomic diversity.

> **The school says:** "While the students he or she is referring to were obviously talented enough to gain admission to those schools, it is certainly true that you don't have to be wealthy to attend an Ivy League college."

Status: Alumnus/a, full-time
Dates of Enrollment: 9/2000-6/2003
Survey Submitted: March 2006

Candidates who pass the initial screening process have their applications circulated to three professors who evaluate the candidate on a scale of one to four. Candidates with total scores of 11 or 12 are admitted, those with lower scores may be waitlisted or rejected. Thus, one professor is able to "ding" a candidate by giving a very low score.

Status: Alumnus/a, full-time
Dates of Enrollment: 9/1992-5/1995
Survey Submitted: March 2006

Yale is one of the most selective law schools in the country. For most applicants, significant emphasis is put on having stellar undergraduate grades and a superlative LSAT score. The Law School does not necessarily focus, however, on the prestige of the applicant's undergraduate institution. For some unique individuals, whose academic record is less than perfect, having a compelling life story can also assist in obtaining admission. My classmates included some people who had amazing life experiences and brought a wealth of different perspectives to the classroom.

Status: Current student, full-time
Dates of Enrollment: 1/2003-Submit Date
Survey Submitted: January 2006

Yale Law School (YSL) wants future leaders in all walks of life. It sounds old, but it's true. Enough YLS graduates will go on to become law partners that the admissions process has a very informal, yet strong bias towards interesting, creative, risk-taking, wannabe world savers, artists, entrepreneurs, and aspiring politicians. I cannot stress this enough. The admissions committee realizes that the way to maintain their dominance and prestige is to produce senators, Pulitzer winners, etc. If your GPA and LSAT are not exceptional, then take a few years to decide what you want to do in life and work in a few jobs in that area, so when you apply to YLS you can make a convincing case that you will actually be successful in that same field after you graduate. It sounds odd, but they don't want everyone to practice law, so admitting it and being able to back up your desire to do X by demonstrating two to four years of jobs in the field of X is impressive and makes you more interesting than someone with a 180 straight out of undergrad. Why go to YLS if you aren't sure you want to practice law. The prestige (I'm just being realistic, you have to believe me when I say I only look in the mirror as much as the average busload of people—joke), the contacts, the intellectual practice, it's fun; and what else are you going to spend $150,000 on?

Finally, as with birthright and having Brad Pitt accidentally fall on your lap, luck is important, so please don't feel you didn't deserve an acceptance letter or be jealous of those who get in because they are just like everyone else (besides being luckier). Remember, if you are reading this, you are luckily not one of the 8.5 million people in the world who will starve to death this year (I'm not trying to be smug, just helpful).

Status: Alumnus/a, full-time
Dates of Enrollment: 8/1996-6/1999
Survey Submitted: February 2005

When I was a senior in Yale College, I hadn't applied to Yale Law and intended to go into consulting for two years and then defer a Chicago acceptance or maybe apply to Stanford the following year. Then I remembered that I wrote a news article where I interviewed the dean (now Judge Calabresi of the Second Circuit Court of Appeals)—and he wrote on his card to call him to talk if I was ever interested in law school. I made an appointment to see him to ask him for advice. He said to bring a sample application with me so he could know more about me. I handed it to him and he looked and me and said, "hold on a second." He left the room in the way only "Guido," as we called him and he preferred to be called, could, with a bounce. "I want you to come here. I was going to personally invite you, but I have no room. Apply again next year and come." Unusual story, yes. But true. I wouldn't try this at home—I think that he was off-put by my obstinacy about staying at Yale, but he sold me on Yale's law and econ offerings, and their new hires. Two years later, I matriculated—after two years of consulting. I would definitely say that people who waited two years or more had a better chance of getting in and probably still do.

The process remains the same at the law school for admissions. There's a big pile. A bunch of the apps go right to reject—low scores, low grades, etc. A small bunch go right to admit. You know them when you see them—but there aren't many. A large bunch get divided up and sent out to the craziest selection of random faculty members you can imagine. This is where luck comes in. I think three professors read each application and rate it on a scale. If you're a law and econ guy and Anne Alstott, tax prof, reads your app, she might like it more than the First Amendment guy. Or maybe the opposite. You need good fundamentals and damn good luck to get in.

Status: Alumnus/a, full-time
Dates of Enrollment: 8/1999-5/2002
Survey Submitted: March 2005

Applications are reviewed by rotating groups of faculty members. In general, they look for the very top scores (obviously) as well as people who have had very interesting life experiences, including prior careers, PhDs and other achievements. They also look for socially conscious people who demonstrate a thoughtful approach to using the law for the public good. The essay is extremely important.

Status: Alumnus/a, full-time
Dates of Enrollment: 8/1999-6/2002
Survey Submitted: April 2004

Given its selectivity it's more able to look to other things such as background or a compelling story. It requires an additional 250-word essay aside from the optional standard law school essay. Unlike elsewhere, the entire faculty reads applications—each application is read by three faculty members who grade it on a scale of two to four.

Status: Current student, full-time
Dates of Enrollment: 9/2003-Submit Date
Survey Submitted: February 2004

Like other schools, Yale relies heavily on GPA and LSAT. Having high numbers for those is the point of entry—then you worry about letters of recommendation and essays. Yale is special in that the professors all read a selection of student files and "rate" them, so in that respect, the intangibles are probably more important than at most schools. Perfect that personal statement.

Status: Current student, full-time
Dates of Enrollment: 8/2003-Submit Date
Survey Submitted: January 2004

Good grades and a good LSAT score are usually necessary but not sufficient for admission. Research, teaching activities and advanced degrees seem to make the admissions officers happy. Your 250-word essay can really help you. Spend as much time as you need to make it interesting so you stand out in a positive way, especially if your numbers are borderline.

> **Regarding admissions, Yale Law School states:** "Yale Law School seeks to enroll a diverse and talented student body with a variety of backgrounds, experiences and professional aspirations. The small size of the school—approximately 185 students in each entering class—requires an extremely selective admissions process. No one aspect of an application (such as the LSAT score or GPA) is determinative; we base our judgments on the entire application.

> "All applications are first read by the Dean of Admissions. She submits approximately 20 to 25 percent of the applications to the faculty, based on a holistic assessment of the applicant's academic and professional promise. Each application that is sent to the faculty is evaluated by three readers. The entire faculty, including academic faculty, clinical faculty, and associate deans, read applications. Faculty readers rate each file on a scale of two to four, based on criteria of the faculty reader's choosing. The scores from the three faculty readers are combined to determine which applicants are admitted. The Law School also maintains a small waitlist over the summer.

> "About a third of the Law School's student body comes directly from college, a third is one or two years out of college, and a third is three or more years out of college."

 Academics

Status: Alumnus/a, full-time
Dates of Enrollment: 9/2001-5/2004
Survey Submitted: March 2006

Former Dean Tony Kronman fairly summarized Yale's approach to law teaching when he described it as a law school with "its head in the clouds and its feet on the ground." Although its boundaries for academic exploration are virtually limitless, making it the closest thing to a utopian academic playground you could find in a U.S. law school, it also offers unparalleled clinical opportunities for students starting in the second semester of their first year, giving students vital real-world experience in wide-ranging areas of legal practice.

Status: Alumnus/a, full-time
Dates of Enrollment: 9/1992-5/1995
Survey Submitted: March 2006

Classes are academically challenging, though often theoretical in nature. Depending on the professor, some classes have very little to do with the day-to-day work of lawyering—in my opinion, however, this is not necessarily a criticism of the school. Grades are not emphasized in general. Nor is there a strict grading curve—so, as a result, different professors could have somewhat different grading policies. Most of the professors are fantastic teachers and wonderful people outside the classroom as well.

Status: Alumnus/a, full-time
Dates of Enrollment: 9/2000-6/2003
Survey Submitted: March 2006

First semester is credit/no credit, and remaining semesters are honors/pass. Low passes are virtually unheard of. The professors are world-class scholars but not necessarily world-class teachers. Many of the more famous profs are particularly poor lecturers, but classes are small, the students are brilliant, and there are incredible opportunities for any who choose to seek them out. Those who wish to keep their heads down and go unnoticed will also graduate with a law degree from the best school in the country, and may be able to do so without learning any law whatsoever.

Status: Alumnus/a, full-time
Dates of Enrollment: 9/1999-5/2001
Survey Submitted: March 2006

Getting in is the hardest part. The classes are fantastic. The professors are fantastic. I felt that the atmosphere was collegial and intellectually stimulating.

Status: Alumnus/a, full-time
Dates of Enrollment: 9/1998-4/2001
Survey Submitted: March 2006

The JD program is very unstructured; required classes comprise only the first semester, with one or two other classes required at some point prior to graduation. Students essentially have two and a half years to take whatever classes they choose, and there is little institution guidance on what to take leading to fairly haphazard coverage of legal topics. (For instance, property is not a required class, though it is an important part of the bar exam.) Classes generally don't close out, since the school tries to move more popular classes to larger spaces if the need arises. The school is very open to students taking courses from other graduate programs and using the credit toward their JD, if the student can make a reasonable case that the course is somehow related to their legal future.

Courses are graded pass/fail in the first semester and thereafter they are graded as High Pass/Pass/Low Pass/Fail. Urban legends about the length to which students must go to get any grade other than P or HP. Professors vary wildly in the timeframes in which they grade exams—with some students graduating without having grades from their first year on their transcript yet. Given the fairly lax grading standards, the workload can be very limited. However, professors who are making an effort to actually instruct students tend to assign a large amount of reading, which is necessary to understand the class discussion.

Writing is emphasized in the curriculum through two required papers of substantial length done in independent courses with professors or in connection with regular courses.

Status: Alumnus/a, full-time
Dates of Enrollment: 8/1999-5/2002
Survey Submitted: March 2005

Some classes, such as workshops or paper classes make it much easier to get honors and some students try to game the system by taking more of those classes (which are usually more interesting, anyway). You really do not need more than a "pass" average to get any job except a federal appellate clerkship.

The quality of teaching is mostly excellent, although it varies like any school. Almost all professors are very accessible, particularly if you want to bounce ideas off them. Workload is what you make it—you can either do very little work and get all passes, or you can push yourself to try to get all H's if you want a Supreme Court clerkship. It is really up to you. There were many people in my class who rarely, if ever, went to class, and still did fine. Of course, this is not the ideal academic experience, but you can still have a very rich and valuable experience just by interacting with your classmates.

Status: Alumnus/a, full-time
Dates of Enrollment: 8/1999-5/2002
Survey Submitted: March 2005

YLS changed the way I look at the world. I can't say enough about the academics, which go far beyond the rote memorization that sometimes typifies a law school experience. You are give great rein to explore and develop your own interests, and fabulous resources are available to you.

Read all of Vault's Law School Surveys at www.vault.com/lawschool — get complete surveys on top law schools, expert advice on applicaton essays, LSAT prep and more.

VAULT CAREER LIBRARY 123

Status: Alumnus/a, full-time
Dates of Enrollment: 9/2000-5/2003
Survey Submitted: April 2004

Yale's program is unique among top law schools in that we don't have grades. Officially, there's a system of honors, pass, low pass and fail, but three-quarters or more of the class gets a pass, and professors rarely give out low passes (you really have to anger a prof to get one). The number of honors a professor gives varies—it can be from one-quarter of the class to just two or three top students, depending on the professor's philosophy. And it's impossible to know how to get an honors in any given class, so you can't really aim for it. Given all that, there really aren't any grades to study for, so it's a completely different academic experience from high school or college. If you do all the reading, the workload is quite heavy—if you get by without doing it, your workload can be quite light. The work, and the learning, are all what you make of it.

Status: Current student, full-time
Dates of Enrollment: 9/2003-Submit Date
Survey Submitted: February 2004

Yale is an exceedingly laid-back academic world. There are no grades first semester, and a limited grading structure after that. Classes are more theoretical than most law schools (or so we're told) and there is a great proliferation of classes that begin "Law and X," as if classes that simply teach us the law are not worth our time. Class workload is entirely manageable, but Yale's students tend to keep VERY busy with a variety of extracurricular activities.

Status: Current student, full-time
Dates of Enrollment: 8/2003-Submit Date
Survey Submitted: January 2004

First semester, you get no choice and take all your classes with the other 17 or so people that make up your small group. One of these classes (out of Torts, Contracts, Con Law, and Procedure) will be taught in small group form around a large table. Most of the JD requirements are out of the way by January. You get to choose all your classes and can participate in clinics after first semester, which is a big bonus. Teaching quality can be pretty uneven, but you can work around this by researching professors before signing up for classes. Visiting professors are often a good bet.

Last but not least, the first semester is credit/fail, and all semesters after that are graded honors/pass/low pass/fail, the latter two categories being extremely rare. This grading system really takes the pressure off! Extracurriculars are plentiful and varied. You can participate in almost everything (including law journals) starting your first semester.

Status: Alumnus/a, full-time
Dates of Enrollment: 9/2000-5/2003
Survey Submitted: April 2004

The professors are there because they are the absolute top of their field, which is to say that they have written the most influential scholarship; it is not to say that they are the best teachers. Even so, the students are brilliant, several professors are devoted to their students, the curriculum is very flexible, and there are open-ended opportunities to participate in journals and clinics, or to opt out entirely and live in Italy for the duration of most of your law school career. It is entirely what you make of it.

Status: Alumnus/a, full-time
Dates of Enrollment: 9/1999-6/2002
Survey Submitted: April 2004

The beauty of Yale is your ability to shape your own education. You can take a lot of standard classes or a lot of independent studies. If you want to write a paper, you can find a professor to supervise.

Employment Prospects

Status: Alumnus/a, full-time
Dates of Enrollment: 9/1998-4/2001
Survey Submitted: March 2006

Yale Law School graduates have no trouble obtaining the jobs of their choice. Law firms are eager to hire us, in part because the supply is so small. A large percentage of students (over 50 percent) begin their legal careers by clerking for state or federal judges; a relatively large number remain in the public sector or go onto non-law firm professions (such as journalism or public policy).

Many firms recruit on campus in two or three weeks of structured interviews; and the school provides a convenient week-long fall break for students to travel to call-back interviews out of state. I personally found that firms that did not interview on campus were happy to fly me out for interviews on the basis of my résumé alone.

Status: Alumnus/a, full-time
Dates of Enrollment: 9/1992-5/1995
Survey Submitted: March 2006

Superlative employment prospects for both second-year summer positions and after graduation. Unparalleled connections with judicial clerkships and private law firms. Many graduates will choose to clerk for their first year after graduation before going to a firm. The alumni network is wonderful—I have found support and mentorship from Yale graduates at every single employer I have had.

Status: Alumnus/a, full-time
Dates of Enrollment: 8/1996-6/1999
Survey Submitted: February 2005

You can do anything you want, within reason. The alumni network is loyal and powerful and if they can't help you, they have a friend who will. The D.C./NY corridor is especially packed with powerful alums. Most grads do a judicial clerkship, some do two. After that, many try firms; a few try consulting. You'll find in my class that people are doing everything from running for Mayor of Cincinnati to running a camp for obese children!

Status: Alumnus/a, full-time
Dates of Enrollment: 8/1999-5/2002
Survey Submitted: March 2005

If you have any interview skills at all, it should not be a problem to get virtually any firm job you want. Clerkships are more competitive, but people with at least one or two H's should be assured at least a district court clerkship (federal appellate courts are usually more competitive). Most YLS graduates do clerkships for one or two years after law school and then move to a law firm, government or public interest. The best public interest jobs and fellowships are probably more competitive than clerkships, but getting those relies on demonstrating commitment to the cause. They are hard to get, but you have no better shot at one of those jobs than if you go to Yale and get involved in the public interest community.

Status: Alumnus/a, full-time
Dates of Enrollment: 8/1999-5/2002
Survey Submitted: March 2005

The greatest benefit of going to Yale over other top tier law schools is that it gives you a definite leg up in the law school teaching market.

Status: Current student, full-time
Dates of Enrollment: 8/2003-Submit Date
Survey Submitted: January 2004

The YLS name opens a lot of doors, and it doesn't hurt that the Career Development Office is terrific. Some of the programs they put on aren't helpful, but many are. CDO people are willing to meet with you to discuss strategy and improve your resume. They are generally enthusiastic and friendly. The CDO library is helpful and includes hundreds of summer job reviews by former and current students. On-campus interviews draw lots of big names, and employers aren't allowed to choose who they meet with. The office is said to be helpful when it comes to getting clerkships and academic positions as well.

Status: Current student, full-time
Dates of Enrollment: 9/2003-Submit Date
Survey Submitted: February 2004

Career prospects are probably better here than anywhere. The world is yours, seriously. Even with a below-average academic record, you are virtually guaranteed a job with a variety of big, prestigious firms. Yale is also a leader in placing government and public interest leaders. At Yale, "finding a job" is honestly the least of your concerns.

Status: Alumnus/a, full-time
Dates of Enrollment: 9/2000-5/2003
Survey Submitted: April 2004

Academia is probably the most common goal of most students. About half of each class clerks immediately after graduation, and after spending a few years penance at a law firm, most students end up either teaching or working in government or in public interest. BigLaw firms and Wall Street jobs are easy to come by, but often not the ultimate choice of most graduates.

Status: Alumnus/a, full-time
Dates of Enrollment: 9/2000-5/2003
Survey Submitted: April 2004

Yale is prestigious with employers, so getting a job is not a problem. You can't exactly write your own ticket, though—it's not as though each person can pick their top firm and get that job. The numbers just don't work out that way. But you are pretty much guaranteed to get a GREAT job (private or public) with a Yale degree.

Status: Alumnus/a, full-time
Dates of Enrollment: 9/2000-5/2003
Survey Submitted: April 2004

Career prospects are basically limitless. The challenge will be deciding which offer to accept.

Status: Alumnus/a, full-time
Dates of Enrollment: 9/1994-5/1997
Survey Submitted: April 2004

Yale has great prestige with employers. There is a tendency for the school to take advantage of this fact and to not help students develop good interviewing skills and career focus. Yale graduates seem to be fairly coveted at law firms in particular since there are relatively small graduating class sizes at Yale. Many students do clerkships or go into public service, and the student body is relatively geographically dispersed post-graduation.

Status: Alumnus/a, full-time
Dates of Enrollment: 8/1999-6/2002
Survey Submitted: April 2004

Scarcity breeds demand. There seems to be great appreciation for graduates of Yale Law School in the real world. Easy to get a job at most of the BigLaw firms. Yale is especially well-suited for sending its graduates on to judicial clerkships.

> **Regarding, employment prospects, the school says:** "The Law School's Career Development Office has published a guide to the different career paths of recent graduates. The guide is entitled *What Yale Law Students Do: A Summary of CDO's 5th Year Survey, Classes 1996-2000* and can be found at www.law.yale.edu/cdo."

 ## Quality of Life

Status: Alumnus/a, full-time
Dates of Enrollment: 9/1998-4/2001
Survey Submitted: March 2006

There is a dormitory at the Law School that was recently renovated, but only a small percentage of the students are able to live there. The dormitory life seems to be a continuation of (boarding) high school for many of its residents. Off-campus housing is readily available in New Haven, which has a large population of graduate students, although a car is helpful because the city itself has only one grocery store and few other retail establishments. Most students drive to North Haven or another suburb for groceries. The city's crime rate is not as bad as it once was, and expensive boutiques line the scenic streets around Yale, but New Haven is still a fairly blighted urban area with severe racial and economic segregation. A few blocks away from the boutiques are neighborhoods of very poor, desperate people. As a result, personal safety is always a concern for students and especially their parents.

Status: Alumnus/a, full-time
Dates of Enrollment: 9/2000-6/2003
Survey Submitted: March 2006

The school itself is beautiful. The library is a wonderful place to study filled with comfy chairs, big desks, smaller carrels—something for everybody. There's a reading room and a good cafeteria. The downside is New Haven. The good news is it's incredibly inexpensive, boasting wonderful apartments for as little as $400 a month that are easily within walking distance. But apart from the university, there's not much that's good about New Haven.

Status: Alumnus/a, full-time
Dates of Enrollment: 8/1996-6/1999
Survey Submitted: February 2005

The Law School has just been beautifully renovated. It is a Gothic Disneyland with computer access at every seat. It's a city block of new dorms and state-of-the-art classrooms, auditoriums and dining facilities. New Haven is a city with a crime problem—but a little self-awareness off campus at night (not walking alone long distances) will go a long way. The dining hall is mediocre in terms of food, spectacular in terms of setting. Most people live off campus after their first year (most first-years live off campus) in the graduate school area.

Status: Alumnus/a, full-time
Dates of Enrollment: 8/1999-5/2002
Survey Submitted: March 2005

The Law School itself is beautiful, and provides not only topnotch facilities, but a wonderful sense of community. Lots of people complain about New Haven, but I really liked it. It all depends on what neighborhood you live in. Some people live in graduate student housing or the Law School dorms (newly refurbished and very nice), but many people live off campus, either in apartments downtown (walking distance to restaurants, school, shopping, etc.) or in apartments farther away from campus, in the "grad student ghetto" (it is actually a beautiful, leafy, residential neighborhood where all the professors live) where apartments are usually a floor of a house, and are generally bigger, nicer and cheaper than downtown.

Status: Alumnus/a, full-time
Dates of Enrollment: 8/1999-5/2002
Survey Submitted: March 2005

New Haven is a comfortable place to live, and the fact that the city itself is somewhat small means that a lot of social life centers on the Law School (so you bond with your fellow students). YLS's facilities are all recently renovated, and the Yale campus is beautiful. The most important difference between YLS and almost every law school in the country is that because the class is not ranked and because it is so small, there is no sense of competition with your classmates. Which makes for a supportive, open atmosphere, and leads to the development of great friendships.

Status: Current student, full-time
Dates of Enrollment: 9/2003-Submit Date
Survey Submitted: February 2004

We have a pretty great quality of life, in that the classes are interesting, students encouraging, and we get to live in New Haven! OK, New Haven isn't great. But there are a lot of house parties, which limits the financial wreckage of our student lifestyle, and there is sort of a Stockholm syndrome going on here where our collective pain at existing in central Connecticut binds us together in a sort of kumbaya sort of way. Maybe.

Status: Current student, full-time
Dates of Enrollment: 8/2003-Submit Date
Survey Submitted: January 2004

Housing is abundant and (relatively) inexpensive. There's a supermarket several blocks from the Law School, and plenty of clothing and book stores within walking distance. The Law School's physical plant is beautiful and modern inside, and I love arriving there every morning. The library is pretty and usually has plenty of room to accommodate 1Ls who want to study there (2Ls and 3Ls get their own carrels). New Haven itself can sometimes be sketchy, but Yale offers an escort service and a shuttle service. Be cautious and alert and you should be fine. I personally find New Haven to be not as bad as people make it out to be, especially for people from larger cities.

Read all of Vault's Law School Surveys at www.vault.com/lawschool — get complete surveys on top law schools, expert advice on applicaton essays, LSAT prep and more.

VAULT CAREER LIBRARY 125

Status: Alumnus/a, full-time
Dates of Enrollment: 9/2000-5/2003
Survey Submitted: April 2004

The quality of life is fantastic! New Haven isn't the most fun place to spend three years, but you don't need to be in a fabulous town if you have great friends. And most people at the Law School do have great friends—it's an environment that's conducive to making strong friendships. My fellow students were undoubtedly the best part of my Yale experience—so smart, so motivated, and with such interesting life experiences. I really miss it.

 ## Social Life

Status: Alumnus/a, full-time
Dates of Enrollment: 9/1998-4/2001
Survey Submitted: March 2006

New Haven pizzerias are world famous and also popular with Yale Law students. Thai and Indian restaurants are everywhere, and I lived on $5.95 all-you-can-eat lunch buffets (which carry you through dinner). The student body tends to be fairly cliquish, with old pals from Choate or Exeter reuniting for good times in New Haven. Non-Old Guard (i.e., middle class) students tend to mingle together and take advantage of the offerings of the city. The Yale Repertory Theater has discount same-day tickets for students, which are popular. The Law School also hosts a dizzying array of guest speakers every week, so attending lectures and discussion groups (which generally provide free food!) is probably the single most common extracurricular activity. Who wouldn't want to hear a talk by the Foreign Minister of Israel the week after peace accords are reached?

For rock music lovers, New Haven is home to Toad's Club (directly across from the Law School) which is a small venue for huge bands. Well-known acts appear regularly as part of their North American tours.

Status: Alumnus/a, full-time
Dates of Enrollment: 9/2000-6/2003
Survey Submitted: March 2006

The students study a lot and take their work very seriously. There are always attempts at mixers, but you're more likely to find people studying in the library on a Friday night than at a bar. That said, there are small clusters of friends and, the advantage of a small school is that everyone knows each other. Most people are very friendly and chat over study breaks in the library and attend the few big bashes that are attended by all. There's plenty of dating for singles, but a lot of people have already paired off by third year.

Status: Alumnus/a, full-time
Dates of Enrollment: 8/1996-6/1999
Survey Submitted: February 2005

New Haven has a veritable variety of great restaurants. Louie's allegedly invented the hamburger or brought it to the United States. Pepe's makes the same claim about pizza on Wooster Street. Sally's, Pepe's twin (Sally was taught by Pepe), inspires debates about which is better. Pepe's, Sally's, or Modern A Pizza up on State Street—all brick oven pizza, all good.

As far as bars, they are always changing, but Toad's is a mainstay. They are across the street from the Law School and host a lot of fringe acts—but occasionally a tune-up will come through (the Stones came through in 1989, for example) or a recording will be done (Billy Joel). They Might Be Giants, Men at Work, Weird Al, Fishbone, Everclear and lots of others have come through and come through regularly.

Dating in Law School can be strange. I met my wife there, so did Bill Clinton, so did several of my friends. It's that time of life. You have to be aware that it's like junior high school. Everyone knows everyone's business, everyone has lockers, some people take the Yale bus into school and everyone has the same teachers!

Status: Alumnus/a, full-time
Dates of Enrollment: 8/1999-5/2002
Survey Submitted: March 2005

Because it is a smaller class, it tends to feel like high school—you have lockers, you hang out at school all day and go home at night, and you know everyone's business. The social life is generally what you'd expect from a bunch of over-achieving brainiacs; although if you make the effort to seek a group of like-minded people, you can make it whatever you want. The recent college grads tend to party more, while the older people tend to have dinner parties and sit around talking about politics. The people are in general great to be around, and some of the people I met in law school are still some of my best friends.

Status: Alumnus/a, full-time
Dates of Enrollment: 8/1999-5/2002
Survey Submitted: March 2005

New Haven is the perfect place to be a "poor" student, because there are so many $10 a plate restaurants with good food. My favorites were Archie Moore's (the Bar Burger), Naples (the pizza), Crown Pizza (the pizza), Louie's (the burgers), and Indochine (the Thai lunch buffet). The best bar is Rudy's, which has a great juke box and no pretensions.

Status: Current student, full-time
Dates of Enrollment: 9/2003-Submit Date
Survey Submitted: February 2004

To reiterate, New Haven is not nice, but the students are surprisingly social, given that we've all spent most of our lives as total dorks. There are enough bars to keep us inebriated several days a week, and house parties are common. It's a very welcoming social environment. And the dating, oh the dating. We have a prom, we have weekly happy hours, we have free burrito bars at a local place. Dating is incestuously rampant, and the rumors are even better. You can't go wrong here, particularly if you're coming from a bustling social hub like Fargo or Duluth.

Status: Current student, full-time
Dates of Enrollment: 8/2003-Submit Date
Survey Submitted: January 2004

There are plenty of bars and restaurants in New Haven, a handful of which are favored by YLS students. There is one movie house within walking distance, and while it doesn't always show first-run movies, it is cozy, and tickets are inexpensive. Other theaters are within driving distance. There's also an assortment of live theatre if that's your thing. Live music is also available at several local venues (i.e., Toad's). House (or, more accurately, apartment) parties are frequent, and it's not unusual for the whole class or school to be invited. All in all, Yale Law students get out and enjoy themselves often.

> The school says: The aforementioned movie house has been replaced by a new movie theatre that shows first-run films.

Status: Alumnus/a, full-time
Dates of Enrollment: 9/1994-5/1997
Survey Submitted: April 2004

The law students at Yale are rather social—living in New Haven requires people to center activities around the Law School. After first year, people tend to spend a bit less time around the school, but people are still very sociable and friendly. Singles may prefer being in a bigger city like Boston or New York.

Status: Alumnus/a, full-time
Dates of Enrollment: 9/2000-5/2003
Survey Submitted: April 2004

First semester, students are fairly social, but increasingly, students get preoccupied with their academic commitments. Those who don't get caught up in their schoolwork tend to opt out entirely and live their third year in another city (or even another country). There's some dating and certainly a fair number of parties on weekends, but most students are married or in committed relationships.

Widener University School of Law

Wilmington, DE location
4601 Concord Pike
Post Office Box 7474
Wilmington, DE 19803-0474
Admissions phone: (302) 477-2162

Harrisburg, PA location
3800 Vartan Way
Harrisburg, PA 17106
Admissions phone: (717) 541-3910

Admissions e-mail: lawadmissions@widener.edu
Admissions URL: www.law.widener.edu/admissions

 ## Admissions

Status: Alumnus/a, full-time
Dates of Enrollment: 8/1998-5/2001
Survey Submitted: March 2006

The admissions process was very simplistic; application, writing sample and an interview. No problem getting in.

> **The school says:** "There is no interview process. Applicants are strongly encouraged to submit the optional personal statement and letters of recommendation."

Status: Current student, full-time
Dates of Enrollment: 8/2005-Submit Date
Survey Submitted: December 2005

The admissions process is similar to the process used at other law schools. Key criteria are GPA, LSAT score and personal statement. Though Widener is less selective than many law schools, most applicants are denied admission. Thus applicants should exercise care when filling out the application and writing the personal statement.

> **Widener says:** "The law school is in the process of downsizing its enrollment, making admissions a much more selective process. Acceptance rates have become dramatically more selective in recent years, from 60 percent of applicants accepted in 2000 to 37 percent of applicants accepted in 2005."

Status: Current student, full-time
Dates of Enrollment: 8/2004-Submit Date
Survey Submitted: November 2004

The admissions process was very simple, straightforward and short. Also, my application fee was waived for applying online.

Status: Alumnus/a, full-time
Dates of Enrollment: 8/1983-5/1986
Survey Submitted: September 2004

There was no interview and I can't recall an essay. The main criteria for getting in were LSAT score and GPA. At the time, the school was not super-selective, as they had only recently become fully ABA-accredited.

Status: Alumnus/a, full-time
Dates of Enrollment: 1/2000-12/2003
Survey Submitted: April 2004

First, as a senior in college, I had to take the LSATs to even get into law school. Once I received those scores, I attained applications to law schools that I was interested in. In order to get admitted into Widener University School of Law, I had to answer an essay question pertaining to my desire to become a lawyer. In addition to the essay question, I had to answer general questions, such as the name of my college, my GPA, my LSAT scores and personal information. Once I mailed in the application, along with a check for $50, my college transcript and my resume, I waited approximately three months for a response. After about three months, I received my acceptance letter. Widener did not have a pre-acceptance interview requirement. My best advice that I would give to anyone attempting to gain admission to Widener, is to send your application out as early as possible after you get your LSAT results. I found out that those who applied earlier, had the best chances of getting in (assuming they met the other criteria that Widener was looking for).

> **The school says:** "The application fee has been $60 for at least the last 10 years. The fee is waived for those who apply online or before Dec. 31. Potential students may write an optional personal statement to accompany their application."

Status: Alumnus/a, part-time
Dates of Enrollment: 8/1989-5/1995
Survey Submitted: November 2003

As my father was a professor at the time I initially applied, my admission went slightly differently from that of other students. I took the LSAT and upon receiving the results, I went to Widener to see if I could be admitted believing at that time my score was not high enough for admission. My score and college grades were average for Widener admittees. I took a tour of the campus and when asked how I became interested in law I mentioned that my father was an attorney. I answered when asked his name. I was then introduced to the dean of the law school. I started law school about five weeks later after completing an application.

 ## Academics

Status: Alumnus/a, full-time
Dates of Enrollment: 8/1998-5/2001
Survey Submitted: March 2006

The first semester professors teaching the core courses were excellent.

The school frontloaded their best in order to have students satisfied with the teaching, and then they pulled the rug out from under us with a couple of the second semester professors.

Administration at the time did not know how to lead the student body, and time and time again failed miserably. This aided in schoolwide apathy.

Until third year, most of the classes were pre-selected, as the law school has hangups about passing the bar exam; see the state statistics for yourself, I do not blame them.

Grading was the worst. The 50th percentile was between a C+ to a B-. You can do fairly well there and still be under a 3.0. This was to prevent many solid students from transferring to Penn State Law, down the road. Good luck telling that to your prospective employer, as your resume is placed into the "do-not-hire" pile.

> **The school says:** "The majority of required courses are taught by full-time tenured or tenure-track faculty, noted for excellent teaching and writing abilities.
>
> "All law schools want students to pass the bar exam at the highest possible level and to that end the American Bar Association allows law schools to teach bar review courses for credit. Widener Law's Delaware campus had the highest bar pass rate of all Pennsylvania-area law schools on the February 2006 Pennsylvania Bar Exam."

Read all of Vault's Law School Surveys at www.vault.com/lawschool — get complete surveys on top law schools, expert advice on applicaton essays, LSAT prep and more.

VAULT CAREER LIBRARY 127

Status: Current student, full-time
Dates of Enrollment: 8/2005-Submit Date
Survey Submitted: December 2005

The professors are excellent teachers, and vary in style. Some of my professors rigidly follow the old Socratic Method. These professors ask questions, then follow-up questions, grilling a student for several minutes at a time. Other professors use a more relaxed approach.

The daily workload is manageable, but since law school is graded on a strict bell curve, some students feel the need to work very long hours. Preparation involves one to three hours of study per class, but progressive review takes additional time, and papers present a special problem of time management.

I was surprised at first by how sharp and prepared the students seemed to be. Because the school is not a top-tier school, I was expecting other students to be a few nachos short of a Mexican platter, maybe unprepared or kind of slow. The reality is that all students are hardworking and articulate. It's nothing like college.

Status: Current student, full-time
Dates of Enrollment: 8/2004-Submit Date
Survey Submitted: November 2004

I am just about to finish my first semester. The workload has been tough and my classmates have been very competitive due to the very strict curve. The exam at the end of the orientation period set a very serious and competitive tone for the rest of the semester. The professors have been very knowledgeable and approachable. The campus is nice and the security is good. The only bad thing is that a lot of people commute to school so there isn't a lot of community there. I do not live in the dorms so maybe that would make a difference. Everyone pretty much clears out on the weekends.

Status: Alumnus/a, full-time
Dates of Enrollment: 8/1983-5/1986
Survey Submitted: September 2004

The first year and a half of law school, any law school, is full of required classes so you are guaranteed admission. You'll always be able to, for example, take Contracts. The workload is a few hours of studying per night, depending how much you rely on study aids. Studying during the day is a good idea as that frees up some time later in the day; also, keeping up is really the best idea as it's easy to get behind. Later in law school, it is tougher to get the classes you want. Required courses are large, usually a few hundred people, but electives could contain as few as a dozen. Professor quality varied as it does everywhere.

> **According to Widener Law,** "Required courses typically have no more than 85 students per class. Many classes have even far fewer students than that."

Status: Alumnus/a, full-time
Dates of Enrollment: 1/2000-12/2003
Survey Submitted: April 2004

I was in a full-time law program in order to obtain my JD so that I could practice law. The program that I was in was intense and hard, yet very worthwhile. I learned a lot about the law, but more importantly, I learned how to "think like a lawyer." I even participated in mock trials and a clinic, where I was actually given real clients and got to argue in court. In Widener, it was easy to get the classes you wanted to get, because the school is fairly small—about 300 in your graduating class—and they routinely offered the same classes. So, in the event you were unable to get a class that you wanted one semester, it would always be offered the next semester. The grading was all done on a curve, which was bittersweet. At times, this curve really helped me. If, for example, there was a class that everyone did poorly in, the curve would be a tremendous help because my C would be turned into an A. Yet, on the flip-side, if there was a class that most students did well in, my A would be lowered to a B or C. So, as I said, the curve was bittersweet.

The professors there were GREAT. They were all law school graduates, and all had their LLMs. They were all very fair and understanding, not to mention extremely knowledgeable. In addition, ALL of them were more than happy to stay after class and clarify or explain something to us. The workload was usually heavy, but definitely manageable. It appeared to get lighter as the years

went by, but that might just be due to the fact that I got more familiar with the law and I could subsequently do my work faster.

Status: Alumnus/a, part-time
Dates of Enrollment: 8/1989-5/1995
Survey Submitted: November 2003

The first year was all required courses. As a night student, there were not that many convenient electives even after first year. However, I eventually registered for all the courses I wanted to take even if it was not the semester I wanted to take each course. Grading was from anonymous tests for the most part. There was a curve.

 Employment Prospects

Status: Current student, full-time
Dates of Enrollment: 8/2005-Submit Date
Survey Submitted: December 2005

Opportunities in government offices, including the Supreme Court of PA, are accessible because of the school's location in Harrisburg. Many students secure clerkships with state level judges or begin work with local prosecutors, etc. Elite firms are probably out of reach for most students at my school, but for students in the top half of the class, plenty of opportunities arise in local firms and government offices.

> **The school says:** "Widener Law has placed students in elite firms and clerkships, and excellent regional firms and government jobs."

Status: Current student, full-time
Dates of Enrollment: 8/2004-Submit Date
Survey Submitted: November 2004

Widener has a good reputation with employers in this region. They are aware that the school is small and still growing and that the curve is so severe, at least for the first-year students. Career services has had seminars with us to keep us on track for summer employment and to get us thinking about our ultimate career goals. We also were given alumni mentors to provide us with assistance. Basically, a graduate is going to do as well as any other law school graduate that may be higher ranked in this region, or it may just take the Widener grad a few more years to reach their dream jobs.

Status: Alumnus/a, full-time
Dates of Enrollment: 8/1983-5/1986
Survey Submitted: September 2004

Career placement is good if you want to stay in the area. I did not, and found it extraordinarily difficult to get my first law job out of school, as I have no relatives in the legal profession on the East Coast and the school did not offer practicums outside of Delaware, Pennsylvania and New Jersey. There was no placement and no assistance as I did not wish to remain in Delaware, Pennsylvania or New Jersey, and nearly no placement assistance for someone in my academic position (I was not on Law Review).

Status: Alumnus/a, full-time
Dates of Enrollment: 1/2000-12/2003
Survey Submitted: April 2004

Widener was a great school, and I do not regret going there. However, they are a fourth tier law school. As such, many employers looked down on Widener. They did not think that students at Widener possessed as much intelligence or potential as students from other schools. However, in my experience, that is completely inaccurate. I met some very intelligent people there, who all have gone on to have wonderful careers. Yet, still, in the eyes of many employers, Widener just isn't good enough. Widener DID have a campus recruiting program, but mostly only small firms were interested. Large and prestigious firms did not seem interested in students at Widener. However, despite this, I managed to get a great job after law school and after passing the bar exam. Widener had a great internship program, too. They had things known as clinics—there was a family law clinic, a criminal defense clinic and a civil clinic. These clinics were a semester long and were worth six credits. They were a great way to get some hands-on experience and they gave you an opportunity to really get a feel for what it would be like to be a lawyer. Only those students with exceptional grades were selected to participate in these programs. The reason for that was obvious—this was REAL. We were given REAL clients, and were required to interview them, research the law that pertained to their problems, write motions and briefs to the court on their behalf, and represent them in court. This was, by far, the best thing that I ever did in law school.

Status: Alumni, part-time
Dates of Enrollment: 8/1989-5/1995
Survey Submitted: November 2003

I did a term at the local court during one semester. That led to my first job. It also has led to the contract I recently signed to start next September. The graduates are now in the major local law firms, as well as on the courts. The graduates are respected. The first job is the hard one to get.

Quality of Life

Status: Alumnus/a, full-time
Dates of Enrollment: 8/1998-5/2001
Survey Submitted: March 2006

Nice local housing, LUSH campus, generic facilities, decent local Harrisburg food, residential neighborhood and low crime.

For environment (notwithstanding the apathy from most students realizing they should have strived better for grades and LSAT in college), it was one of the nicest and calming campuses I visited.

Status: Current student, full-time
Dates of Enrollment: 8/2005-Submit Date
Survey Submitted: December 2005

Harrisburg is affordable and Susquehanna township, where the school is located, is safe. The building is modern and the classrooms are high tech. I'd rather be in a major university environment, studying amidst masses of other graduate students in various fields, but the environment here is clean and comfortable.

Status: Current student, full-time
Dates of Enrollment: 8/2004-Submit Date
Survey Submitted: November 2004

Dining is abundant around the campus. However, the on-campus dining is atrocious. On good days, you can stomach the pizza, maybe. There are tons of hotels, malls, stores like Target and such, a movie theater right nearby and free membership to the gym that comes with admission. The JCC is not the finest of facilities, but it gets the job done. The dorms are sufficient, not the worst I've ever seen and not the best either. The rooms are very big and the desks are large. I would suggest trying to live in one of the on-campus apartments if possible. They are newer and nicer than the dorms.

Status: Alumnus/a, full-time
Dates of Enrollment: 8/1983-5/1986
Survey Submitted: September 2004

Delaware is beautiful and the city of Wilmington felt safe and accommodating. At the time, the school was strictly for commuters, but off-campus housing was cheap and plentiful, particularly if you ventured outside most students' basic comfort zone. The facilities were brand new.

Status: Alumnus/a, full-time
Dates of Enrollment: 1/2000-12/2003
Survey Submitted: April 2004

Widener's location and housing opportunities were great. It is on a beautiful campus surrounded by a beautiful environment. There are malls and restaurants surrounding the campus. On campus, Widener has two dorms in addition to an apartment complex. There was always plenty of parking, and the campus was kept safe and secure by public safety, who were present 24 hours a day. I felt very safe there. I cannot recall one crime or act of violence being committed on campus in any of the three years that I lived there. The facilities were always functioning and kept very clean. There was a dining hall but I rarely used it because I cooked at my apartment. From what I heard, the food was not bad at all, and it was fairly inexpensive.

Status: Alumnus/a, part-time
Dates of Enrollment: 8/1989-5/1995
Survey Submitted: November 2003

I lived at home with my husband and son while working 20-plus hours per week and doing volunteer work as well. It took careful scheduling of my time and use of my energy. The drive was less than 10 miles. There were convenient roads. Campus was well patrolled at night. There are restaurants nearby as well as a snack shop on campus. There is shopping nearby, as well as the campus bookstore. The neighborhood is safe.

Social Life

Status: Alumnus/a, full-time
Dates of Enrollment: 8/1998-5/2001
Survey Submitted: March 2006

Social life was great. Within two weeks at school, a couple of us realized grades were going to get us nowhere by speaking with the 3Ls who passed down "priceless and time-saving knowledge." With this, we went out and partied and socialized like we were in a frat at college.

Caveat: during this time, we interacted with as many 2Ls, 3Ls and local successful attorneys as we could to figure out how to succeed in our profession and in business. I was diligent while in class, and did what I had to do to understand as much as I could in terms of the work, but I had a great time doing MANY other things outside law school.

When you go to an educational center where it does not matter whether you get a 3.5, 3.0, 2.5 or a 2.0 (YES, really!), and if a student can make time and enjoy quality of life while just making sure they get out of THERE with a JD, then it really does not matter.

> **The school says:** "Grades really matter. A host of employers and recruiters focus intently on GPA as a criteria for success. Some recruiters openly have preferred minimum GPA standards."

Status: Current student, full-time
Dates of Enrollment: 8/2005-Submit Date
Survey Submitted: December 2005

There are numerous clubs and organizations at this school. In general, however, the social atmosphere is relatively dull. Harrisburg has some nice restaurants, but many students spend the majority of their time studying.

However, the school is within a few hours of several major cities. Some students go to New York, Philadelphia or even Atlantic City on occasion.

Status: Current student, full-time
Dates of Enrollment: 8/2004-Submit Date
Survey Submitted: November 2004

The social life at the school is basically nonexistent. Well, Wednesday night is the big night to go to the neighboring bar, Scrimmages. They have mugs that you return with every week and fill for $2. There are a few bars and clubs in the city of Wilmington. Trolley Square is a really young, fun place to go out for a bar atmosphere and they have cute apartments. Also, there is a riverfront area, which is more like clubs with club music and such. However, in law school, you don't really go out, so it doesn't really make that much of a difference, in fact, it probably helps.

Status: Alumnus/a, full-time
Dates of Enrollment: 8/1983-5/1986
Survey Submitted: September 2004

There was some social activity, but law school in general is extraordinarily time-consuming, so it wasn't enjoyed too much. Stanley's was a favorite bar of most, but I personally found it pedestrian. The dating scene was not great as a lot of the class was either married or in committed relationships, as the average age of the incoming class for my year was about 28. The school offered Greek life but it was unsatisfying, as there were only a few social events and, well, it was the same people all the time.

Read all of Vault's Law School Surveys at www.vault.com/lawschool — get complete surveys on top law schools, expert advice on applicaton essays, LSAT prep and more.

VAULT CAREER LIBRARY 129

Status: Alumnus/a, full-time
Dates of Enrollment: 1/2000-12/2003
Survey Submitted: April 2004

As previously stated, the campus was surrounded by restaurants and malls. In addition, there was a bar within walking distance. This bar was a favorite among students on Wednesday nights. The great thing about this bar was that you could just walk home, so no one ever had to worry about anyone driving drunk. The dating scene at Widener was all right. I personally did not date anyone from Widener, because I, like many others, was already involved in a committed relationship.

But I am aware of some students who dated each other. Widener also had some dances and parties that gave students the chance to mix and mingle. For example, Widener has an annual Halloween costume party that is always a hit with the students. In addition, Widener also has clubs, ranging from academic ones, such as Law Review and Moot Court Honor Society, to Greek ones, such as Phi Alpha Delta (a law fraternity that anyone can join.)

Status: Alumnus/a, part-time
Dates of Enrollment: 8/1989-5/1995
Survey Submitted: November 2003

I was not involved in the social life as a usual student might be. From the talk I overheard, there was plenty to do for those interested. Sometimes, the places needed to be researched but to me that is part of the fun.

 The School Says

The Widener University School of Law provides an ABA-accredited program, and operates on two campuses, one in Wilmington, DE and the other in Harrisburg, PA.

Widener provides an all-around comprehensive legal education program with special certificates available from the Health Law Institute, Institute of Delaware Corporate Law and Trial Advocacy Institute, all in Delaware, and the Law and Government Institute in Harrisburg. The Health Law Program is consistently ranked among the nation's 10 best.

Widener students get real-life, hands-on experience working on court cases through legal clinics that specialize in environmental law, criminal defense and civil law including bankruptcy, family law and legal assistance on veteran benefits cases. The Trial Advocacy Institute offers an eight-day, intensive training program that prepares students to become lawyers who can conduct themselves properly in a courtroom trial—from opening statement to closing argument.

Both campuses offer a variety of pro bono work opportunities through the Public Interest Initiative on the Harrisburg campus to the Public Interest Resource Center on the Delaware campus. Students also participate in wide range of extra- and co-curricular activities including moot court and Moe Levine Trial Advocacy Honor Societies and three law reviews.

Students earn degrees through regular day and part-time evening divisions. The ambitious faculty published more than 40 articles and books in the past year. The Delaware campus is an East Coast Center for the National Judicial College, hosting continuing legal education opportunities for the nation's judges.

The Delaware campus is located north of Wilmington, the nation's corporate law capital. Shopping, lodging, entertainment and recreation venues are just off campus, yet the leafy confines of the law school provide quiet tranquility for study. The Harrisburg campus is nestled in the Blue Mountains yet located only minutes from the Capitol Complex. Diverse cultural and recreational opportunities abound.

American University

Washington College of Law
Admissions Office
4801 Massachusetts Avenue, NW
Suite 507
Washington, D.C. 20016
Admissions phone: (202) 274-4101
Admissions fax: (202) 274-4107
Admissions e-mail: wcladmit@wcl.american.edu
Admissions URL: http://www.wcl.american.edu/admissions.cfm

Note: The school has chosen not to comment on the student surveys submitted.

 Admissions

Status: Alumnus/a, full-time
Dates of Enrollment: 9/2002-5/2005
Survey Submitted: April 2006

The law school looks for strong students with a well-balanced background. The law school puts tremendous emphasis on the individual accomplishments of the law student, which makes for a very interesting class. The law students have a wide array of interests from international law to corporate law, to government service, to community service.

Status: Alumnus/a, full- and part-time JD/LLM
Dates of Enrollment: 8/1999-5/2003
Survey Submitted: March 2006

The admissions process requires the usual LSAT scores, essay (there is a choice of topics), background information, etc. The school also seems to look for public interest backgrounds, as well as diversity candidates.

Status: Current student, full-time LLM
Dates of Enrollment: 1/2006-Submit Date
Survey Submitted: February 2006

I am a just a student so I can only add my personal observations. It seems the administration takes a whole person approach and not just grades. Unlike the JD programs, an LSAT is not required and, since many are foreigners, the students come from very diverse academic backgrounds. What this translates into is: write good statement of purpose essay and get quality recommendations. The school takes about 130 LLM students annually, of which only 10 to 30 are domestic (i.e., are American and have U.S. JDs), the rest are foreigners. Also, the quality of students is quite good, the school is currently host to five to 10 Humphrey Fellows each year and also has about 10 to 20 visiting scholars and SJDs. I would say about a third of the LLM students are topnotch students who could have gone to Harvard and the like. About another third are basically exchange students from various foreign law schools that WCL has alliances with. These students tend to be in their 20s. And the final third, an older crowd, come from the working world at various stages of their lives, hoping that the LLM would advance their careers. The school is not selective as Harvard, NYU, Columbia or Georgetown. In terms of selectivity, it is probably in the same ball park as George Washington, Cornell and Tulane. But this is just my guess.

Status: Alumnus/a, full-time
Dates of Enrollment: 8/1998-5/2001
Survey Submitted: December 2005

American's admissions aren't quite as rigorous as other law schools of its caliber, but this always seemed like an intentional policy. They look at essays, and at how the applicant will contribute to life at AU. Diversity—based on race, nationality, religion, sexual orientation, even something as simple as background and viewpoint—seem to be very important. That's not to say a high LSAT and GPA without much else will be a hurdle to your admission, but a well-crafted essay explaining why grades weren't as high, or detailing an unusual background, or challenges that have been overcome, will get the attention of the admissions office as well.

Status: Current student, full-time
Dates of Enrollment: 8/2004-Submit Date
Survey Submitted: January 2005

When looking at the numbers given out by the universities I applied to and the numbers given by *U.S. News & World Report*, I was certain that I would have gotten into four of the eight schools I applied to quite easily. However, this was not the case. Last year, some schools received 4,000 more applications than normal. The point being that you never can tell what the process is going to be like from year to year, so apply to as many schools as you are interested in within reason. Don't bother applying to schools you have no interest in, but make sure that you apply to a wide variety and in the regions that interest you the most. I have not heard of any law schools giving out interviews. However, you can try to get a backdoor interview by contacting the school for an informational meeting. Arrive with intelligent, thoughtful questions. Ask questions that you could not find the answers to online; for example, what criteria does the school use in hiring its professors (research vs. teaching). It is, of course, important to have a stellar essay. But as much as schools say they look at the whole picture, if you do not have a LSAT score and GPA any where near the range the school is looking for, they will most likely not even get to read your essay and see your resume. This is unfortunate, but with thousands of applicants, it seems to be a reality at most schools. So apply to schools that are a reach, but don't apply to schools that are out of the question. If you have a 150, forget Harvard, and focus on something reasonable, and put your heart into your essay.

Status: Alumnus/a, full-time
Dates of Enrollment: 8/2000-5/2003
Survey Submitted: October 2004

The admissions staff is approachable and helpful so feel free to contact them by telephone. I might suggest scheduling a campus visit to speak with current students, tour the law school, and solicit an interview or information session with the admissions staff. I'd recommend boning up some on legal periodicals or even the ABA web site or your home state's bar web site in order to get a baseline level of legal familiarity before you speak with admissions staff or prepare your personal statement just so you'll be able to ground your personal story into a real-life foundation.

Status: Alumnus/a, full-time
Dates of Enrollment: 8/2000-5/2003
Survey Submitted: March 2005

With thousands of law school applicants, your experience and your essay must make you memorable. If you are applying to law school directly after college and have no work experience, the essay is the opportunity to sell yourself. Use an interesting life story, trait, family background, etc. to explain your goals to the admissions committee.

Status: Alumnus/a, full-time
Dates of Enrollment: 8/2001-5/2004
Survey Submitted: April 2005

This is a school that will look at your complete package. Lots of attention is paid to your personal statement, especially since unlike most schools, American gives you an outline of information that they want on it. If you're a strong candidate, then your timing is not as crucial as someone that is barely making the minimal requirements. If you are one that needs to cross your fingers when you mail in your application, then I suggest you get it in early and really put in effort into the essay and recommendations.

Read all of Vault's Law School Surveys at www.vault.com/lawschool — get complete surveys on top law schools, expert advice on applicaton essays, LSAT prep and more.

VAULT CAREER LIBRARY   131

Status: Current student, full-time
Dates of Enrollment: 8/2002-Submit Date
Survey Submitted: June 2004

It is becoming more and more of a numbers game, but I think there is a genuine effort made to get well-rounded and interesting people with life experience. There is no interview. If you really do want to come to this school and not just because you didn't get into Georgetown, then make sure you really include that in the essay (they do read them), and you could even submit another letter during the process indicating your interest.

Status: Current student, full-time
Dates of Enrollment: 8/2002-Submit Date
Survey Submitted: May 2004

No interview was required for admission. I downloaded the online form using the LSDAS service. There was only one essay required for admission and then one optional essay asking you to describe something unique you would add to the university. I only completed the required essay. In terms of selectivity, my LSAT score was directly the median, but my GPA was at the 25th percentile, so I really do think my shining point was my essay. Emphasize your interest in the law program and why you want to go to law school. Go for the details. I believe I was accepted because of my sincere interest in the school and in the law.

 ## Academics

Status: Alumnus/a, full-time
Dates of Enrollment: 9/1996-5/1999
Survey Submitted: March 2006

Having been founded by woman, American has traditionally been a public interest law school. In recent years, American has developed a considerable reputation in international law, and for providing excellent clinical opportunities. I, myself, pursued more of a commercial litigator's curriculum, and took considerable advantage of the school's clinic program. For the most part, I found the quality of the professors at American to be of the highest caliber, very dedicated and completely accessible to students. Those of lesser quality don't last long at American. I don't recall experiencing any difficulties getting the courses that I wanted or in managing my time for school work. One unique feature at American is that many of the classes are graded on one open-book take-home final exaM. By virtue of being open book, these exams tend to be more difficult, time-consuming and, at times, agonizing.

Status: Alumnus/a, full-time
Dates of Enrollment: 8/1999-5/2002
Survey Submitted: March 2006

The integrated first-year curriculum is a great benefit AU. Students learn how different areas of the law intersect—this is how it works in the real world. The professors are very engaged with the students for the most part. There are a couple of classes that are difficult to get into, but you can always get in before you graduate. Grading is fair.

Status: Alumnus/a, full-time
Dates of Enrollment: 8/1995-5/1998
Survey Submitted: April 2006

Having served on both the curriculum and hiring faculty-student committees, I can say that the biggest problem in law school (in my opinion) seems to be the extreme disconnect in the nature of law school. The school seems divided between tenured professors who want the school to be an extension of a liberal arts education (a "graduate school"), and students and adjuncts who realize that school should be a preparation for the practice of law (a "trade school"). To that end, the school leans toward hiring professors who have researched and written extensively—but many have never even taken the bar exam. This is not to say they don't have interesting insights and excellent analytic minds. But graduating students have very little, if any, practical skills to fall back on during the scurrying, fear and adrenaline-enhanced first year of practice. This may well be the case for most, if not all, law schools. However, if all you are given upon graduation is the right to apply to positions under the title "attorney," but have no real skills in practice (particularly in civil and non-litigious areas of the law),

I would strongly recommend not paying for a private institution, where the drain of debt can determine your life decisions for the next 15 years.

Otherwise, you can get popular classes, and the professors tend to be extremely well-versed in the academic practice of their fields, if not the actual practice of their fields. There are a number of exceptions, and the criminal justice and international practices tend to have tenured professors and adjuncts who have actual experience in their field. I would say, however, that a number of their business, property and torts professors have little, if any, practical experience in the area. Also, several of the first-year professors clearly dislike teaching first-year students, and this tends to turn people off from entire practice areas. In addition, in the hiring committee, I noted that adjuncts with high student satisfaction ratings and excellent experience, though little research background and non-"glamorous" positions (i.e., trenchwork) were not hired on a tenure track, in favor of those with less practical experience, a (much) worse reputation as a professor, but with a more glorified academic and research background. It's quite astonishing to see it in action.

Status: Current student, full-time LLM
Dates of Enrollment: 1/2006-Submit Date
Survey Submitted: February 2006

The faculty is the strength of the school. The international law faculty is consistently ranked Top 10 in the nation and was ranked fifth, tied with Yale, in a recent survey in 2006 by *U.S. News & World Reports*. There is a consistent stream of esteemed academics and lawyers that come to speak at the free seminars and discussions panels that are given on a nearly weekly basis. The school has a clear international law focus so much of the seminars are in international law field; and food and drink are often served for free. The whole campus has an open wireless access and is housed in one giant building that gives the school a cozy feel to it.

Status: Alumnus/a, full-time
Dates of Enrollment: 8/1998-5/2001
Survey Submitted: December 2005

AU is a very, very high quality school. However, unlike many of the Ivy League and other first-tier schools, most of the professors value relationships with their students over a Socratic Method. Our Civil Procedure professor had memorized the facebook before the first day of class and knew each of us by name, he brought bagels and coffee in for the final. Another professor baked cookies. I've been to several of their homes for dinner, and went to a Washington Wizards game with still another.

Status: Current student, full-time
Dates of Enrollment: 8/2004-Submit Date
Survey Submitted: January 2005

American was the only school that I was accepted to, and I was extremely disappointed about the whole situation. When I arrived at the school, I felt no attachment to it and was ready to start my transfer applications that fall. But American is an amazing school. The attitude of the professors and the atmosphere of the law school is exceptional. Its focus on human rights and public service is inspiring even when you do not want to work in those areas. The international law programs and classes are varied and topnotch. All my professors have studied at Princeton, Harvard or Columbia. All of the professors were kind, encouraging, and available outside of class. Some professors were a little too nice, and tended to spoon feed the class a little. But they were always demanding and expected our full effort. The workload was intense, while the pressure was not repressive, leaving a wonderful atmosphere to learn.

Status: Alumnus/a, full-time
Dates of Enrollment: 8/2003-Submit Date
Survey Submitted: October 2004

The quality of legal education is excellent, and is unfortunately not adequately recognized by the schools top of tier two, bottom of tier one ranking; although the clinical education is consistently highly rated. The professors are approachable, the students are community-oriented, and the academic setting is conducive to the long hours of necessary studying! The journals offer a tremendous opportunity to supplement traditional coursework. The class grading seems typical of many law schools, but you will have to put the time into rank in the top 15 percent, where you'll really want to be. I strongly recommend participating in the writing competitions to compete for the Law Review or other journals.

Status: Alumnus/a, evening program
Dates of Enrollment: 9/1995-5/1999
Survey Submitted: March 2005

The thing I liked best about AU was that the entire law school had a culture of education. The professors were all teachers, and the atmosphere encouraged them to improve their teaching skills. Even the adjuncts, who taught one or two classes while working in their speciality, spent time to prepare lesson plans and made an effort to make the material understandable. Also, as a night student I appreciated the fact that the professors for the core classes all rotated through the night program. Thus, even though I never took a day class, I had the same teachers that the day students did. By nature, the number of night classes was limited, but there was plenty of variety. I never had to take a class that didn't interest me because it was the only one that "fit."

Status: Current student, full-time
Dates of Enrollment: 8/2002-Submit Date
Survey Submitted: June 2004

Coming from a large and impersonal college, I was bowled over by the friendliness, openness and helpfulness of the professors. Most of my professors know me by name and have a genuine interest in getting to know students (including weekly lunches, etc.) and helping them in their careers. Grading is still pretty professor-specific. I think that most grade on a B+ curve, whether they admit it or not. People complain about the legal writing program (legal rhetoric is mandatory for first-years), but from what I hear it is far better than most other law schools, and you really need those skills to get a good job and be a good lawyer.

The school has a great community feel, much more than any other law school where I have friends who hate everyone they're with all day long. There are definitely some administrative issues, but on the whole it is a great place and most of the people in the building genuinely care about the success of the school and its students. The academic programs like moot court and law review are very competitive. The clinic is the only thing where you are "guaranteed" a spot (if you make your selections correctly) and they do make a genuine effort to accommodate everyone who wants to participate.

Status: Current student, full-time
Dates of Enrollment: 8/2002-Submit Date
Survey Submitted: May 2004

My class is exceptionally large: over 600 students. However, most years total up to 400 students. I believe if your class size is relatively average in size, you should have no difficulty being accepted into the clinic program or in registering for classes. Each first-year class is divided into five or six sections determined by alphabetical order. Our first year is predetermined, and you have to take the requisite classes: Contracts, Property, Civil Procedure, Torts, Constitutional Law and Criminal Law. The other requisite class, legal writing, is also a year long, but the class size is about 12 to 15 students. American's legal writing program is one of the best! While intense and quite a lot of work (you write two or three memos per semester), you learn a great deal about legal writing but not as much about effective legal research. The downside to having a big class size is the need for adjunct writing professors, who differ in quality.

Status: Alumnus/a, part-time
Dates of Enrollment: 9/1995-5/1999
Survey Submitted: April 2004

I know I wanted to study international law upon graduation, and even though there are more prestigious schools that pretend to offer international law courses, AU is definitely the best school in the country in this area. Being in Washington, D.C., you not only have the luxury of learning the theory of the law, but also being exposed to real-life situations through the quality of faculty who often come directly from the government or international organizations. Although a lot of schools say it, AU really does have you ready to hit the ground running.

 Employment Prospects

Status: Alumnus/a, part-time
Dates of Enrollment: 8/1996-12/1999
Survey Submitted: March 2006

I worked in the Senate after graduating, but after an election loss I was out of a job and had to take a job as a contract attorney—I was shocked at the number of grads from WCL who were also contracting because they'd been unable to find jobs. There were five people out of 27 who were WCL grads—others came from schools outside the D.C. area. Prospects for George Washington and Georgetown grads are significantly higher in this area.

Status: Alumnus/a, full- and part-time JD/LLM
Dates of Enrollment: 8/1999-5/2003
Survey Submitted: March 2006

I have found that in Washington, D.C., the school is very well known and well respected. There are some employers who only look at Top 10 schools, and therefore it is hard to get a job with those employers, but for the most part law firm jobs, clerkships, government positions, and other competitive positions are available to WCL grads with strong academics. The alumni network is reasonably helpful, but should be stronger. On-campus recruiting and internships are widely available, but the career services office should do even more in this regard, particularly to take advantage of our Washington, D.C. location.

Status: Alumnus/a, full-time
Dates of Enrollment: 8/1995-5/1998
Survey Submitted: April 2006

The Office of Career Services on the main campus was helpful. It should be noted, however, that I am the only one of this group who is currently in a non-legal field (after many years of legal practice). The others gave up after it was too difficult to find a role. The school hires several of its graduates, which improves employment numbers but reduces the odds of such graduates gaining successful legal employment. The positions tend to be non-legal, and any and all years spent in non-legal employment tends to dramatically reduce an individual's hiring potential in traditional legal venues (e.g., nonprofit, government and law firms—particularly in the latter two venues) as compared to individuals who graduated from law school and were immediately hired as attorneys.

The prestige of employers includes the entire spectrum, and individuals wanting to interview with top-tier firms certainly have the opportunity to do so in on-campus recruiting (as well as post-graduation). I interviewed and was offered employment as an attorney beginning in law school, and continuing for many years afterward, in top firms and federal agencies. The opportunities are certainly there. I will say, however, that the alumni network is not particularly strong, and several never returned calls for informational interviews. On the other hand, if you happen to hit upon a hiring partner, senior attorney, or senior manager who has had American graduates before (or, better yet, is one), the likelihood that you will be hired seems to be exponentially higher.

Status: Alumnus/a, full-time
Dates of Enrollment: 8/2000-5/2003
Survey Submitted: October 2004

The office of career services could use some beefing up, but as long as a student achieves a high GPA he/she will not be lacking for interviews in the D.C., NY and Boston markets. Many of my colleagues were employed at big firms and most were employed by graduation. AU places very well in the D.C.-Maryland-Virginia region, but many students travel throughout the country. My class, likely typical, was comprised of a healthy mix of big firm, medium firm, government and public interest positions.

Status: Alumnus/a, full-time
Dates of Enrollment: 8/2000-5/2003
Survey Submitted: April 2005

My employment after law school depending solely on networking. Employers didn't have any interest in me during fall recruitment, so I worked a family connection to get a part-time job during school. The part-time job became a full-time job offer and the experience that got me a clerkship. I didn't have stellar grades and I didn't want to work for a public interest law organization. I had one good experience with alumni networking. I made an appointment with an alum-

Read all of Vault's Law School Surveys at www.vault.com/lawschool — get complete surveys on top law schools, expert advice on applicaton essays, LSAT prep and more.

VAULT CAREER LIBRARY   133

nus who is general counsel for a large MD-based corporation, and he was very interesting and helpful. Based on that experience, I would encourage other current AU students to contact AU alumni just to learn what life's like where they work.

Status: Current student, full-time
Dates of Enrollment: 8/2002-Submit Date
Survey Submitted: June 2004

The externship program is really good and bigger than most schools, (but you're paying to work, so it really shouldn't be that hard to get employers to sign up). Campus recruiting is so-so. They will tell you that only the top 10 percent of the class will get a job through fall recruitment. That is probably true for the most part, but I was in the bottom 50 percent and got a job through fall recruitment. Be smart about the jobs you apply for and do it right. Prestige is very dependent on location and type of law you're interested in. If you want to do international law or human rights law or anything nonprofit, the prestige is very high. Among those in the know, it is also very prestigious for IP law. WCL is not well-known on the West Coast. Many attorneys I spoke to in L.A. at most have "heard of it." I think that is improving slowly, but I do not think the school makes a big effort to increase its reputation and prestige outside of the D.C. metro area and beyond the practice of international human rights.

Status: Current student, full-time
Dates of Enrollment: 8/2002-Submit Date
Survey Submitted: May 2004

American manages to attract a fair number of recruiters, and the fall recruitment system works like clockwork. Be aware, American has to compete with the other law schools in D.C., so you really have to hustle in order to snag the best opportunities. Some people have reported that the large firms recruiting at American merely do it for show and don't really conduct serious interviews. Of course, this also depends largely on your GPA and work experience. The upside to the bidding process for fall recruitment (which starts the summer before your second year) is that we get to bid for up to 40 employers. In addition to direct bids, there are also direct drops in the career services office.

 Quality of Life

Status: Alumnus/a, full-time
Dates of Enrollment: 9/2002-5/2005
Survey Submitted: April 2006

The law school housing is where I lived for three years (i.e., all of law school). The housing is brand new with beautiful apartments, a study den with a lovely fireplace, a gym, aerobics room and a large living room with a massive television unit and plenty of room and comfortable furniture for social gatherings. There are study rooms and a prompt support staff. It was great! The law school students are collegial, but very motivated and strike a balance between enjoying D.C. and working very hard.

Status: Alumnus/a, full-time
Dates of Enrollment: 8/1999-5/2002
Survey Submitted: March 2006

The neighborhood around the law school is quite stifling. I would not recommend living near the law school, it is too suffocating to be that close. The neighborhood is perhaps too nice of an area—the residents look down on the law school and its presence. That was very frustrating. The campus is nice, well kept and very safe. Parking is frustrating, although I never had a car. Public transportation is very easy.

Status: Alumnus/a, full-time
Dates of Enrollment: 8/1998-5/2001
Survey Submitted: December 2005

Can't say enough about it. The school fosters a collegial atmosphere among the students, and for the most part, it succeeds. The programs they put on are excellent, and often broadcast on C-SPAN. Recently, two Supreme Court Justices spoke. There is animosity between the school and the wealthy neighbors who surround it, however.

Status: Alumnus/a, full- and part-time JD/LLM
Dates of Enrollment: 8/1999-5/2003
Survey Submitted: March 2006

I would give the law school fairly high marks on quality of life issues. It is a very friendly school, professors are accessible, and the students are not as "cutthroat" as at many schools. Students generally are very positive about the law school. The neighborhood is extremely safe, the facilities are good but a little cramped now that the class sizes have increased (parking is particularly a problem). There are only limited places to dine outside of the school, but there are a couple of good choices within walking distance.

Status: Current student, full-time
Dates of Enrollment: 8/2004-Submit Date
Survey Submitted: January 2005

The neighborhood is beautiful, many diplomats live near the law school and it is considered one of the safest areas of D.C. There are cafes and delis next door to the school, as well as a cafeteria on the sixth floor of the building. There is a grocery store right next door to the school, as well as a little restaurant bar within a few minutes walk. Eating is never a problem, and there is also a CVS pharmacy/drugstore, so running errands is so easy it's often a study break during the day.

D.C. is a dream city to live in. It has everything for your career, education, social life, shopping bug, cultural enlightenment and taste buds. The museums are free, you can study in some of the most amazing buildings in the country, and hear every language but English walking down the street at times. It can be a little rough around the edges, but that just takes common sense to avoid for the most part. It is an urban area, even though it does not always feel like it, so there is always a chance of something happening.

Status: Alumnus/a, full-time
Dates of Enrollment: 8/2000-5/2003
Survey Submitted: April 2005

I didn't live in school housing, but the apartments that I saw in Glover Tunlaw were very nice. The neighborhood around AU's law school is nice enough, but hard to get to. It's not near a Metro and for the first year I was there, the school didn't provide a direct to metro shuttle. There is city bus service, but it only runs twice an hour during non-peak hours. The building itself is nice—still relatively new and wired. The cafeteria seemed to be getting by the time I graduated. The school had awarded its contract to a new vendor. There are a few other dining options near the school, but they're relatively pricey. I recommend the salad bar at Wagshal's.

Status: Alumnus/a, full-time
Dates of Enrollment: 8/2000-5/2003
Survey Submitted: March 2005

Most people do live off campus and live in a variety of the suburban towns or in the city. Many local restaurants are within walking distance of the law school, and the law school itself has its own food service. The law school is located about a mile from the main campus of American, so law students rarely spend time there, unless to go to the gym. I, for one, enjoyed the separate locations.

Status: Alumnus/a, full-time
Dates of Enrollment: 8/2001-5/2004
Survey Submitted: April 2005

American is located in a really nice, residential neighborhood. The area is so suburban that is looks as if it were isolated from the rest of the city. Housing may vary. You can get an apartment within walking distance or even rent out a room in one of these enormous houses. The law school is about four blocks from the main campus. There is a shuttle bus that takes you to the main campus and the Metro station. It is a very clean, safe and quiet area.

Status: Current student, full-time
Dates of Enrollment: 8/2000-Submit Date
Survey Submitted: September 2003

We have interesting lectures and conferences almost every day. Very famous lawyers and policy makers come to speak at the law school. There is no on-campus housing. Food is good. Neighbors like to complain about noise and parking. The law school location is great; the school is located in a green and quiet residential area, which has a calming effect.

Social Life

Status: Alumnus/a, full-time
Dates of Enrollment: 9/2002-5/2005
Survey Submitted: April 2006

The law school has a weekly bar event, a theatrical group, intramural sports, an annual prom, incredible lectures from prominent politicians, justices and international figures. The law school is also integrated with the beautiful campus and many students enjoy social events at the business school and School of International Service.

Status: Current student, full-time LLM
Dates of Enrollment: 1/2006-Submit Date
Survey Submitted: February 2006

The student governing body, the LLM board, sets up social events, like road trips and Bar Review. Plus, there are enough people in the program that you can always find people to party with and let out some steam. As expected, people form clicks based on nationality but this is because people want to hang out with people they are comfortable with and not really out of xenophobia. WCL LLMs are generally friendly.

Status: Current student, full-time
Dates of Enrollment: 8/2004-Submit Date
Survey Submitted: January 2005

The law school holds a Bar Review every Thursday night, which is nice because we do not usually have class on Fridays. It is very popular and is a good outlet to see the city and spend a relaxing time with the other students. The student population is extremely talented, motivated and focused, but does enjoy a few drinks and getting out.

It is easy for things to get frenzied and competitive at any school. American seems very balanced and healthy. It obviously does get very quiet as the semester progresses, but it is not a school of students who spent their undergrad in their dorm rooms. I think it is more for students who sought out new experiences, and were concerned with their academics but also concerned about learning from their environment and the people around them.

Status: Alumnus/a, full-time
Dates of Enrollment: 8/2000-5/2003
Survey Submitted: April 2005

The social life is harder to get into if you don't live near school. I lived in Greenbelt, MD my first year and met very few people outside my small writing group because I had a tremendous commute. Living in the school-owned apartment building, Glover Tunlaw, would be a good idea for students looking for a more active social life. Dating among students was kind of gross—very high school-like and gossipy. Men seemed to date like women were in a batting order—done with the last one, on to the next.

Status: Alumnus/a, evening program
Dates of Enrollment: 9/1995-5/1999
Survey Submitted: March 2005

I went to law school nine years after graduating from college. I worked during the day and took classes at night. I already had a strong network of friends and family in the area that took up what little free time I had. I did not participate in the social life beyond hanging out in the student lounge, so I can't help you here.

Status: Alumnus/a, full-time
Dates of Enrollment: 8/2000-5/2003
Survey Submitted: March 2005

Although law school does become a full-time job (plus weekends), the social life is fantastic. The SBA sponsors Bar Reviews each week, and the individual first-year sections tends to be very social. I never approached law school as a dating scene, but I have several classmates that are now married to each other. I had a better social life at WCL than I did in college.

Status: Current student, full-time
Dates of Enrollment: 8/2003-Submit Date
Survey Submitted: November 2004

Students are all very laid back, welcoming, friendly, interesting people. This leads to a lot of "in-breeding," so I'd say the dating scene and social life, in that regard, are pretty healthy at WCL. But don't look for social activities near the school, since there's nothing in Spring Valley worth staying past 5 p.m. for.

Status: Current student, full-time
Dates of Enrollment: 8/2002-Submit Date
Survey Submitted: June 2004

D.C. is a great town for young professionals and grad students. The school is relatively social for law school. There are a ton of active student groups, so there are lots of opportunities to get involved and meet people outside of your section if you want to. The school also has tons of events all year long with distinguished legal scholars and political people. They can be very interesting and are worth making time for. They can really enrich the experience and there is nothing wrong with taking a break from studying, especially when it could provide useful insight into the law or a career in the law.

Melio's is the local bar, which is expensive and not too exciting but we all go there because it is right next to the law school. After a final the place is usually packed out the door. Cactus Cantina and Guapos are other WCL hangouts. I think people still go to Bar Review (at least the first-years go). What we are missing is the weekly happy hour or keg that other law schools have every Friday afternoon. It would be a great chance to mingle with profs, etc. and to feel part of the community Dating people in law school can be dangerous anywhere, so I won't comment on the dating scene!

Read all of Vault's Law School Surveys at www.vault.com/lawschool — get complete surveys on top law schools, expert advice on applicaton essays, LSAT prep and more.

VAULT CAREER LIBRARY 135

The Catholic University of America

Columbus School of Law
Office of Admissions
The Catholic University of America
Cardinal Station
Washington, D.C. 20064
Admissions phone: (202) 319-5151
Admissions e-mail: admissions@law.edu
Admissions URL: http://law.cua.edu/admissions

 Admissions

Status: Current student, full-time
Dates of Enrollment: 8/2003-Submit Date
Survey Submitted: May 2006

I didn't expect any difficulty getting admitted. I fit within or exceeded the numbers requirements, my application was well put together, and I emphasized my appreciation of the school's Catholic identity. I applied very early in the application season, and received an acceptance letter right around January 1. I didn't have an interview. My acceptance letter even included a handwritten note congratulating me on my undergraduate record. But I was very surprised that I wasn't offered scholarship money. However, I was doubly surprised by how liberal the school was with scholarship money; after the first year, I think everyone in the top 20 percent gets some money.

Status: Current student, full-time
Dates of Enrollment: 8/2005-Submit Date
Survey Submitted: April 2006

The admissions process was very simple when you used the LSAC database for applying to law schools. In regards to getting in, like any law school, LSAT scores play a large roll. However, I truly feel they evaluated by undergraduate experience fully and took into account my high GPA and extracurricular activities. It was nice to have everything I'd done since I entered college come into play, not just a test I took early on a Saturday morning for four hours.

I wrote my essay about my interests in law and how I would be a good addition to the law school community. It is important to let them know who you are and how you can set yourself apart from the hundreds of other students that are also interested in law school. Remember, they want people that want to be here and that are interested in law, so let them see that through your essay.

As far as selectivity for me I applied to a dozen law schools, but my first choice was Catholic. I wanted to be in D.C. and be in the Communications Institute, so I felt it was a match made in heaven.

Status: Current student, full-time
Dates of Enrollment: 8/2003-Submit Date
Survey Submitted: April 2006

I filled out an application, visited the school on accepted applicants day, and had a brief interview with the admissions director and a few professors. In my opinion, Catholic attempts to select students from a diversity of backgrounds.

I think that participation in some sort of community service activity is a plus, as the school is community oriented. Many students have taken time between college and law school.

Status: Current student, full-time
Dates of Enrollment: 8/2005-Submit Date
Survey Submitted: April 2006

I highly recommend speaking personally with the staff. They are EXCELLENT and were very helpful when I had a personal situation that demanded knowing whether I was accepted by a certain date. If you want to have a shot at a schol-

arship, apply BEFORE the December holidays. It is definitely harder to get admitted after January than it is before. Apply early!! It's the best tip I can give.

Status: Current student, full-time
Dates of Enrollment: 8/2003-Submit Date
Survey Submitted: April 2006

The admission process was very typical compared to the admission processes of the other nine schools I applied to. Despite its conservative reputation, I wrote a very liberal essay and the dean personally responded to it. When I came for a visiting day with other interested students, the dean read parts of each student's essay to demonstrate the diversity of applicants. I was offered a scholarship and was able to call the school and have the scholarship raised by an additional $4,000. The selectivity of the school varies year by year, but I think that, like everywhere else, having good test scores and grades is the most important.

Status: Current student, full-time
Dates of Enrollment: 8/2003-Submit Date
Survey Submitted: April 2006

After you receive your LSAT scores you will have a better idea of where you stand for admission. Catholic Law is not in the top tier of law schools, so it is a little easier to get into. However, each year the students apply with higher GPAs and higher LSAT scores. I had a 162 LSAT and 3.56 GPA and had no problem getting in. No interview (most law schools don't interview).

CUA Law is looking for people with interesting backgrounds, so the more you have done in college or between college and law school, the better off you'll be.

Status: Current student, full-time
Dates of Enrollment: 8/2005-Submit Date
Survey Submitted: April 2006

No interview, just an application and essay; similar to other schools. Fairly selective, but nearly on par with the other schools in Washington, D.C.

Apply before the deadline for consideration for scholarship money. If you are accepted early, there are two deadlines for down payments. If you are invited to an area reception or have a chance to meet alumni at an event, definitely go to get a real feel for the kinds of students and alumni that come from this school. Meeting a graduating student and alumni changed my perception of the school and made me want to attend.

Status: Current student, full-time
Dates of Enrollment: 8/2004-Submit Date
Survey Submitted: April 2006

Catholic's law school takes a "whole candidate" approach to admissions. The essay is not just an exercise. At Catholic, the admissions team carefully looks at the whole person: their life experiences and what perspective a person can add to an incoming class, in addition to the numbers (LSAT and GPA) that matter so much to other schools. If you want to get in, you need to present yourself as a well-rounded candidate with an unique voice.

Status: Current student, full-time
Dates of Enrollment: 8/2002-Submit Date
Survey Submitted: April 2005

The admissions process was very helpful. As there were a lot of decisions to make at that time, the staff at CUA were fantastic. Any time I had questions or concerns about anything from where to live when I moved to the area to how I was going to pay for school. The admissions staff was knowledgeable and helpful. Part of what helped me make my final decision and accept my offer was the energy and enthusiasm the staff had for the school.

Status: Current student, part-time
Dates of Enrollment: 8/2002-Submit Date
Survey Submitted: April 2005

I'd done reasonably well on the LSATs (162) and was admitted to the night programs of both Georgetown and CUA and chose to attend CUA for several reasons: [lower cost, better location, several professors whom I admired, including Helen Alvare and Douglas Kmeic (who has since departed for Pepperdine)]. I did not interview. I don't remember my essays. Selectivity increased the year I was admitted in a concerted attempt by the administration to improve the quality of the student body (and improve *U.S. News & World Report* ranking), so my sense is that it is now more difficult to get in than it had been previously.

Status: Current student, full-time
Dates of Enrollment: 8/2004-Submit Date
Survey Submitted: April 2005

I filled out the application through LSDAS. The application asked the basic questions, such as major, GPA and extracurricular activities. I also sent three letters of recommendation and my LSAT score. I included a personal statement on a topic of my choice. I talked about my experiences of participating in many forms of community service through my sorority. I also talked about my overall college experience and how it made me the person I am today.

 # Academics

Status: Current student, full-time
Dates of Enrollment: 8/2005-Submit Date
Survey Submitted: April 2006

The professors are very accessible and committed to teaching. I highly recommend Prof. Perez (Contracts; International Law), Prof. Elliott (Civil Procedure and Administrative Law), Prof. Rutledge (Criminal Procedure) and Prof. Kaplin (Education Law). I could go on and on. It is competitive to get into the "top choice" classes, but I was able to get all of my top choices on the first try. Classes are organized by the administration for the first year, and during the second and third years, it's up to the students to decide their schedule. CUA makes a great effort to ensure all bar courses are readily available. The school has invested in a writing and academic enhancement program that's well worth the time.

You cannot underestimate the workload. Every week, I invest 20 hours to class time (classes and tutorials) and another 40 or 50 to studying. I miss having a social life. Some people do an excellent job balancing personal and academic demands. If you're considering law school, know that it will demand all of your time. Few people can have a part-time job, class and a personal life.

CUA complies with the common bell curve that places all students on a mandatory curve (for example, in a class of 30 students, there would be three A's, two A-'s, two B+'s, six B's, 10 B-'s, three C+'s, three C's, and one D or F). I'm not a fan, but it is what it is. Class rank is determined at the end of the year, and is important for job opportunities in the fall.

Status: Current student, full-time
Dates of Enrollment: 8/2003-Submit Date
Survey Submitted: April 2006

The first-year classes are set up so you spend all of your classes with the same students, which is nice. The biggest problem is that we have some great teachers and some very bad teachers teaching the very important first-year classes, and it is luck of the draw as to who you get. For example, my first year there was a very pro-life professor who taught constitutional law and refused to teach *Row v. Wade* and *Texas v. Lawrence*. This teacher also taught Civil Procedure without talking about any of the rules of civil procedure. On the other hand, our Contracts and Property teachers are amazing.

Sometimes I feel like the first-year atmosphere here is controlled by the teachers who are bullies and like to intimidate students. Particularly the male faculty tend to take the hard-nose teacher act a little far. At times it felt as if I were back in middle school being scolded. The faculty often forgets most law students are already adults.

There is a wide variety of classes to choose from second and third year, but it can be very hard to get into the staple classes such with the teachers you want.

I think that I have learned a lot in my classes; and on the whole, despite personality conflicts the teachers are very smart and able to teach a great deal. There are a handful of teachers here, who are willing to do anything to help their stu-

dents. Finding one of those teachers can make up for anything the other teachers may be lacking. These teachers include Professor Wagner, Silechia, Kelly, Watson and Rutledge.

The grading curve is a little lower than other schools, with a B- curve your first year. Also, students can fail classes. The workload varies by the teacher but it is easy to find out about the workload from fellow students.

Status: Current student, full-time
Dates of Enrollment: 8/2003-Submit Date
Survey Submitted: April 2006

The professors here are great—a result, I think, of being located in D.C. (where many lawyers want to be). I feel I have received an excellent education here.

However, as CUA Law is not as big as Georgetown or American, the courses do not span as wide a selection as at those schools. If you are completely into a certain area (e.g., international law), I would recommend checking the course offerings before accepting a seat at any school.

I had no problem getting into the courses I wanted. Grading is tough—it is, after all, law school. They curve and rank, and your GPA is important in the overall job search. Workload is, I would assume, comparable to other law schools, i.e., you are going to work your butt off.

Status: Current student, full-time
Dates of Enrollment: 8/2005-Submit Date
Survey Submitted: April 2006

First-year classes are all assigned. Some professors are better at teaching than others, but they are all extremely knowledgeable about their subjects. Some professors use the Socratic Method while others lecture; it just depends on who your section is assigned to.

Professors are always easy to talk to and some are happy to take time to have coffee with students. Workload varies by class and professor. I have not yet registered for next semester, the first chance to select my own classes, but I have heard that it's difficult to get into the popular classes and to be ready to register online for those classes right when registration begins.

Status: Current student, full-time
Dates of Enrollment: 8/2005-Submit Date
Survey Submitted: April 2006

The school is on a B- curve, which is kind of a drag since the rest of the D.C. area schools are on B/B+ curves. I have been very impressed with the quality of professors, and the clinic program is great. Also, the possibilities of interning for credit during the school year are ample, as D.C. has tons of interest groups, government agencies and courts that are willing to hire year-round.

Status: Current student, full-time
Dates of Enrollment: 8/2004-Submit Date
Survey Submitted: April 2006

Academics at Catholic are unparalleled. They really seek to prepare you for the work you will encounter once you get out of law school and begin to practice law. Classes are generally pretty small, and class participation is highly encouraged, but in a very non-threatening way. Most professors no longer use the stand-and-recite Socratic Method, but students are still eager to participate.

Catholic has a couple of programs within the law school that are really unique—programs that you cannot find at any other law school in the country. Catholic has the top rated securities law program in the country. Catholic also has a top communications law program. In addition, the clinic program at Catholic, in which you take on clients under the supervision of a practicing attorney, is one of the top clinic programs in the nation.

Status: Current student, full-time
Dates of Enrollment: 8/2004-Submit Date
Survey Submitted: April 2006

CUA Law's academic program is rigorous. First-year classes are prescribed and include most of the major areas of law covered on all/most bar exams (e.g., Contracts, Property, Torts, Constitutional Law, Criminal Law, Civil Procedure).

Read all of Vault's Law School Surveys at www.vault.com/lawschool — get complete surveys on top law schools, expert advice on applicaton essays, LSAT prep and more.

VAULT CAREER LIBRARY   137

For the most part, class instruction is exceptional. Registration allows most people to get into the most popular classes, and several sections of popular second-year classes are offered every semester. Grading is done anonymously and adheres to a B- curve unless there are too few people in the class.

Workload is heavy but manageable. Most professors use a syllabus that covers the entire semester, so planning around big projects or extracurricular activities is easy.

Status: Current student, full-time
Dates of Enrollment: 8/2004-Submit Date
Survey Submitted: April 2006

Most professors are excellent. Because it's a smaller class size than other schools in the D.C. area, there is more contact with the profs. The clinic programs are recognized as among the best in the area, and were some of the first to be established. It's not that hard to get into popular classes with preferred professors, though you do have to register as early as possible. The registration system has a waitlist capability, so even if a class is full, students can put themselves on the waitlist and will be automatically added in a priority sequence (whoever lists themselves first) as people swap in and out of classes.

Status: Current student, full-time
Dates of Enrollment: 12/2003-Submit Date
Survey Submitted: April 2005

First year: courses were challenging, and the professors were FANTASTIC— motivated by an interest in ensuring we were "getting it," they were communicative, made themselves available after hours and on weekends to talk specifics or just talk. The workload was moderate; exams were challenging. Administration was amenable to changes in final exam scheduling on an individual basis as family and work issues dictated.

Second year: workload eased off of first-year challenges. Substantive courses yielding to electives and a reduced level of Socratically induced "pucker factor." Exams got easier. Professors became a little more spotty in regards to motivation and accessibility. One was downright unapproachable.

Status: Current student, full-time
Dates of Enrollment: 8/2004-Submit Date
Survey Submitted: April 2005

Oh, the joys of being a first-year! I would say the classwork is probably typical for any law school, with the one exception being our Legal Skills Program. It is a two-credit class each semester of your first year with a six-credit workload. Be prepared to do a lot of reading; the professors may be nice but if you are not prepared you will have to deal with your own embarrassment. Grading is on a mystical, statistical B curve that I have not quite figured out yet, but I do not think anyone fails, not without trying at least.

The professors vary. I have been lucky and had almost a perfect run with the exception of one professor that rivaled Ben Stein in *Ferris Beuller's Day Off*, and one who I think might have been a bit far gone. Expect a more conservative bend to most of the classes, but not hard core conservative. Hey, it is called "Catholic University." The popular classes are harder to get into, but you can usually talk a professor into letting you in once classes start (if it is a large class). Other popular classes are easier if you are part of the particular tract (public interest, communications). The clinics are fantastic and I think almost everyone has an opportunity if he/she wants to take one.

Status: Current student, full-time
Dates of Enrollment: 8/2002-5/2005
Survey Submitted: April 2005

Catholic is a great community environment. I feel that is necessary to mention here because it has a direct impact on the academics. The students and faculty build a community that fosters a great learning environment. Unlike many law schools, CUA is not tremendously competitive, no one ever rips pages out of books to get the edge and students genuinely want to help one another succeed. There are active student study groups and an academic success program that helps students become better test takers. Most of the professors are great, experienced and enthusiastic about their jobs and this school. I never had a problem getting into a class I needed and/or wanted, (I did always register as soon as the system would let me).

The curve here at Catholic is a B/B-, which is lower than other schools in the area. This is OK if you are job hunting here in D.C. where the employers understand that we have a lower curve, but may prove to be detrimental if you are hunting for a job some place else. The workload is tough—but it's law school and that's what is expected. There are several great clinic programs, such as D.C. Law Students in Court, Criminal Prosecution Clinic, Families and the Law Clinic and Trial Advocacy—these programs give students an opportunity to really begin practicing and get out of the classroom. CUA has some of the best clinic programs in the country and this adds tremendous value to the educational experience. The clinic programs also add a ton of work to your schedule but are well worth it.

Status: Current student, full-time
Dates of Enrollment: 9/2004-Submit Date
Survey Submitted: April 2005

Very friendly staff and students. The upper-level students are very helpful in helping you to decide which classes to take and which professors are best. The teachers are pretty good, especially for the upper-level courses. Beautiful campus that is right next to the Metro in Washington, D.C., Catholic University has one of the best law libraries in the country as well as one of the best support staff working there.

Status: Current student, full-time
Dates of Enrollment: 8/2002-Submit Date
Survey Submitted: June 2004

The professors and classes are excellent. Classes are offered enough so you'll get what you want. First-year classes run 30 to 60 per class (my first year) and second- and third-year classes can be as small as 16 (my largest was about 60). If you want a popular class, you'll most likely get it as a second-year, but may have to wait until third year. I have taken just about every class that interests me. The professors truly are amazing...some will be the best you've ever had.

Employment Prospects

Status: Current student, full-time
Dates of Enrollment: 8/2003-Submit Date
Survey Submitted: May 2006

I've been pretty pleased with my employment prospects. But if you're unsuccessful with fall recruiting your second year, you're pretty much locked out of big firm jobs after graduation. It's amazing that with the saturation of CUA Law alums in the area, there isn't a bigger network of employment support.

Faculty, on the other hand, are incredibly helpful. Just about every faculty member I broached employment options with either offered a lead or important support. As far as clerkships go, LCS is relying heavily (and wisely) on a former Supreme Court clerk to field clerkship questions. The results this year were very good.

Status: Current student, full-time
Dates of Enrollment: 8/2003-Submit Date
Survey Submitted: April 2006

I can only really speak for myself but I have had great employment opportunities at Catholic. I have worked for professors and on a presidential political campaign. I interned for a federal judge. Through on-campus recruiting, I received a job for my second-year summer at a large and prestigious D.C. law firm. I will return there when I graduate for a year and then I will be moving across the country for a federal appellate clerkship. I think any employment opportunity is available to a student who is willing to work hard.

Status: Current student, full-time
Dates of Enrollment: 8/2004-Submit Date
Survey Submitted: April 2006

25 percent of CUA grads go into the government to work in the public's service. The school is particularly proud of this aspect. A good number of us go into major firms, but it is important to be in the top of your class. On-campus recruiting is similar to any other school. I've had three internships so far: public interest org., DOJ, and a federal judge. Just being in D.C. opens doors.

Status: Current student, full-time
Dates of Enrollment: 8/2003-Submit Date
Survey Submitted: April 2006

There is an OCI (on-campus interviewing) program at CUA Law. However, it is not as expansive as those at Georgetown or Harvard (because all employers want students from those schools). That being said, I know a lot of people who got some great law firm jobs this way.

Legal career services will help you if you know what type of job you want (i.e., they have called people personally for some students). The internship ("externship") program is great—I did an externship every semester since first year. As a result, I have received a broad background in a variety of legal settings. And I think this ultimately helped me get my job. A lot of graduates go into government work, or judicial clerkships, so this is not one of those law schools where the pressure is on getting a big firm job.

The CUA alumni are very proud and usually want to employ CUA students, both in internships and jobs. The sense of community here is perhaps the reason this is so.

Status: Current student, full-time
Dates of Enrollment: 8/2004-Submit Date
Survey Submitted: April 2006

In the region in which it is located, Washington, D.C., Catholic grads are highly regarded as mature, well-prepared individuals that come out of school ready to practice in the real world. Around 40 percent of Catholic Law grads go into government work right after leaving school. The one area of employment that Catholic doesn't get many recruiters from is large, top-flight law firms, but that isn't as important to Catholic grads, because most seek to work in some sort of public service field upon graduation.

The opportunities for internships and externships in Washington, D.C. are really amazing. If you're interested in politics, you can get an internship in the United States Congress. You can choose from the various departments in the administration to search for a externship. From the Justice Department to the SEC to the Pentagon, Washington, D.C. is a great place to be to find a job.

Status: Current student, full-time
Dates of Enrollment: 8/2005-Submit Date
Survey Submitted: April 2006

According to our legal career services office, the six-month employment rate is somewhere between 92 and 94 percent. As a first-year, I was able to get a summer job relatively quickly, despite the NALP mandated guidelines.

LCS constantly has networking and informational interviews in addition to OCI. There are also two externship fairs and a mock interview program. It is not unusual for alumni to return to campus to speak or host networking coffees. According to legal career services, many Catholic students go into public service, next is private practice, and the fewest head to judicial clerkships.

Status: Alumni, full-time
Dates of Enrollment: 8/1996-5/1999
Survey Submitted: March 2006

Employment prospects is definitely one of the pluses of going to Catholic. Because it is located in Washington, D.C., a significant number of large firms do on-campus recruiting—and even if they don't, it's not much trouble going to their D.C. offices—even though it's not in the top tier. Internships and jobs in government agencies are also very accessible since Catholic is in D.C. The alumni network is strong, and a large number of alumni end up practicing in D.C. and its surrounding areas.

Status: Alumnus/a, full-time
Dates of Enrollment: 8/1994-5/1997
Survey Submitted: April 2004

Since the school is located in Washington, D.C., there are excellent opportunities for internships in the government and career placement with both the government and large and small law firms. The school enjoys an excellent reputation in and around Washington. The school's reputation in communications law and labor and employment law extends well beyond the Washington area. Prospective students who will not remain in Washington should consider the school's reputation in their desired location before attending. The school has a helpful and dedicated placement staff to assist with job seeking.

Status: Current student, full time
Dates of Enrollment: 8/2002-Submit Date
Survey Submitted: June 2004

Career prospects and internship opportunities in D.C. are endless; however, you must do things for yourself. While our legal career services helps you with your resume and cover letter, it is up to you to network and find your niche. Campus recruiting is not the way most get jobs. Good interviewing skills, internships and networking are the way to get in in Washington, D.C. If you want them, internships are plentiful—apply for many because they are tough to get.

 ## Quality of Life

Status: Current student, full-time
Dates of Enrollment: 8/2003-Submit Date
Survey Submitted: May 2006

Most law students commute, which can be a bit of a bummer given the traffic congestion in the area. Metro accessibility is pretty good and mostly reliable. Once students get to campus, the amenities are nice. The law school building and grounds are great (and even better in the sunshine and warm weather of spring and summer). Safety around the area is a concern, but the walk to the Metro is very short and well patrolled.

Status: Current student, full-time
Dates of Enrollment: 8/2005-Submit Date
Survey Submitted: April 2006

The quality of life at Catholic Law is very good. The school itself is Metro accessible and a short walk. Security, as in any city, can be a problem; you must remain smart and alert, just as if you went to any other city school.

Housing is largely off campus and in the suburbs, or Maryland, Virginia or downtown D.C. All places are Metro accessible and it is easy to find housing once you know where you would like to live. Living in the neighborhood around the school can be done, but due to safety reasons not many law students do it. That is more for undergraduates.

The facilities are great. A nice new building, locker space to store books and a dining hall in the law building, directly next to the student center, where the school store is. The food is good with a fairly wide variety right on campus including a standard all-you-can-eat dining hall.

Status: Current student, full-time
Dates of Enrollment: 8/2003-Submit Date
Survey Submitted: April 2006

The neighborhood isn't the best, but it is easy to get to and people come from all over the D.C. metro area. The campus itself, especially the law school, is beautiful. The quality of life here is amazing—everybody works together. There is a real sense of community and while law school is inherently competitive, I think that the students at Catholic are genuinely willing to help one another succeed. The faculty and staff are always approachable—one of the benefits of a smaller school.

Status: Current student, full-time
Dates of Enrollment: 9/2003-Submit Date
Survey Submitted: April 2006

The law building at CUA is less than 10 years old and is state of the art. Its modern architecture and cutting-edge technology do not detract from its reputation as a traditional school of law.

Safety issues have been on the forefront of the CUA's agenda. Situated in northeast Washington, D.C., CUA has challenges of any inner city neighborhood. The campus has manned stations to guard students' commute to the Metro. The law school houses a secure garage for those who drive.

Read all of Vault's Law School Surveys at www.vault.com/lawschool — get complete surveys on top law schools, expert advice on application essays, LSAT prep and more.

VAULT CAREER LIBRARY   139

Status: Current student, full-time
Dates of Enrollment: 8/2004-Submit Date
Survey Submitted: April 2006

The quality of life at Columbus School of Law is wonderful—community-building is encouraged and supported by the staff, administration and faculty. The very design of the law school encourages conversations among people.

Though there is no on-campus housing, the law school is only a two-minute walk from a Metro station. While some people live within walking distance, most live a few Metro stops away. The facilities on campus suit the school well. While seminar space is tight, the building has two courtrooms, a large atrium for dinners and receptions. The classrooms and library are hooked up for wireless Internet access.

The library is open virtually all the time (7 a.m. to midnight), and the collection is varied without sacrificing depth. The library also houses two computer labs with four printers. There are separate Lexis and Westlaw printers as well as printers for laptop users.

There is a small cafeteria in the law school that serves full meals daily during the week. Since the law school is located on the university's campus, there are also the dining halls used by the undergraduates a short distance away.

Though there is some crime in the neighborhood, few incidents take place on the law school's campus. The neighborhood also offers additional options for restaurants and bars.

Status: Current student, full-time
Dates of Enrollment: 8/2005-Submit Date
Survey Submitted: April 2006

CUA is in a lower-class neighborhood, but with a Metro stop right next to the campus, you could go to the school for three years without really noticing what surrounds the campus. The law school is new and beautiful, though its cafeteria services are pretty disappointing. There are athletic facilities nearby, and a better facility with showers about half a mile away.

The BIG failure of the school is in its LGBT policies. As an institution of the Vatican, CUA is not really gay-friendly, and gay students are pretty much expected to keep their mouths shut about it. The school's speaker policy is also disappointing since it basically says anybody who has every said they're pro-choice can't speak on campus.

Status: Current student, full-time
Dates of Enrollment: 8/2004-Submit Date
Survey Submitted: April 2006

I like to call Catholic the "kinder and gentler law school." There is a real sense of community here. People help each other out. Sure there are people who make the top grades and are at the top of the class, but those people never hesitate to share class notes, or help a fellow student. I always heard about cutthroat antics at other law schools, and knew that kind of scene just wasn't for me.

At Catholic, people compete for grades, but they don't compete at the expense of other students. Most Catholic students are in competition with themselves, to prove to themselves that they can make the grade, not with other students to try to cut another down to boost themselves up. Students at Catholic realize that life outside of law school is a cooperative group effort. We just start living that lifestyle earlier than students at other law schools.

Status: Current student, full-time
Dates of Enrollment: 8/2005-Submit Date
Survey Submitted: April 2006

The law school has a ton of programming and social events. There are receptions, speakers, symposiums and visits from Supreme Court Justices almost every week. The student organizations host happy hours, dances, festivals and the standard Bar Reviews as well.

Status: Current student, full-time
Dates of Enrollment: 8/2002-Submit Date
Survey Submitted: April 2005

We have a beautiful facility (built in 1994) and it contains everything we ever need. There are two wonderful courtrooms, a full legal clinic, and tremendous,

three-story library. There is also a cafe where we eat pretty much every day. The law school is located on Catholic University's campus, which sits next to the Basillica of the National Shrine of the Immaculate Conception. The main campus is beautiful, but we rarely leave the law school building. There is on-campus graduate housing but most students live in the suburbs of Northern Virginia, Maryland or in the D.C. area. The area around the university is not the best—but we are fairly safe and protected here on campus.

Status: Current student, full-time
Dates of Enrollment: 8/2002-Submit Date
Survey Submitted: April 2005

Safety is the number one concern at CUA. Crime rates are high and it is unadvisable for women to walk around campus at night unescorted. However, the school has made great strides to counter crime coming from the nearby community. Security has doubled since I started at CUA in 2002 and there is a shuttle from the law school to the Metro, which is approximately 500 yards from the law school.

The faculty and staff are highly accommodating of students with families. The editor-in-chief of one of our publications this year, *Communications Law Conspectus*, had a child during her tenure. The faculty, staff and other students were so supportive of her that not only did she complete her work with their help but she had many, many shower gifts before and upon the birth of her child.

Status: Current student, full-time
Dates of Enrollment: 8/2003-Submit Date
Survey Submitted: April 2005

There is on-campus housing but I can count on one hand how many people I know who live there. Nearly all law students live off campus. The neighborhood of CUA isn't great but some people live here. There were some crimes issues recently, but CUA has increased security and there are always ways to stay safe; e.g., you can get an escort to walk the 1,000 feet to the Metro). Most people live elsewhere. CUA is a Metro stop on D.C.'s red line, so it is very popular for law students to live at a different red line stop. We have dining in the law school building and backup campus dining available with only a two-minute walk out the back door.

Status: Alumnus/a, full-time
Dates of Enrollment: 8/1996-5/1999
Survey Submitted: April 2004

This is another factor that attracted me to Catholic University. The school has a beautiful facility close to Capitol Hill. There is a nice cafeteria where law students regularly eat breakfast, lunch and dinner together. The large library, with individual group study rooms and a computer room, is not a bad place to have to spend a good portion of three years. For those who do not know the area, there are dormitories available for incoming law students.

 Social Life

Status: Current student, full-time
Dates of Enrollment: 8/2003-Submit Date
Survey Submitted: April 2006

The law school has a vibrant social life. Different student organizations host lectures, events and happy hours all the time. There are several big events during the year including an auction, the Barristers Ball and a golf tournament. Being a 10-minute Metro ride from downtown D.C. means that there is always something to do.

Status: Current student, full-time
Dates of Enrollment: 8/2005-Submit Date
Survey Submitted: April 2006

The people at CUA are very ethically driven and are also very social. Weekly bar nights or restaurant reviews are common. If I had to list a student favorite, I'd go with any Irish pub within a half mile of a Metro stop: Dubliner, Four Peaks, etc. But there are also a lot of events on campus that are annual traditions: Crab Bake, SPIL auction and the Student Activities Fair come to mind.

The people of CUA are its greatest asset.

Status: Current student, full-time
Dates of Enrollment: 8/2003-Submit Date
Survey Submitted: April 2006

I think the students here are great. If you miss class, students will e-mail you the notes. There are a lot of activities, both on and off campus. There is a real sense of community here, some of my best friends in the world are my law school friends. We usually go to bars and restaurants in D.C., but not in the neighborhood of CUA. Which is fine, because a lot of students live elsewhere.

There are a variety of clubs, all easy to belong to if you are interested. There is no sense of cliqueishness (which is good seeing as this is a graduate program). I think that the students here at CUA Law made this experience what it was for me—they are supportive, fun, intelligent, and definitely the type of people I want to work with when I am out in the legal world.

Status: Current student, full-time
Dates of Enrollment: 8/2005-Submit Date
Survey Submitted: April 2006

Compared to what I've heard about other schools in the area, Catholic is the most collegial. Of course we are competitive, as law students and law school inherently are, but we are also very supportive of one another and no one tries to sabotage another student's work in order to move up in the rankings.

In addition to all the receptions and events that go on at school, people go out to area bars and also to bars mainly in Farragut Square, Foggy Bottom, Georgetown, Dupont Circle and Adams Morgan. It seems like there is always a speaker or panel going on at school, so much so that it's difficult to attend even half of them due to school work.

Status: Current student, full-time
Dates of Enrollment: 8/2005-Submit Date
Survey Submitted: April 2006

Being gay on campus tends to not be as much of an issue as I expected, so that was nice. The people are pretty typical to law school students. Overall a friendly group of people. Being in D.C. offers a lot of opportunities for social activities

Status: Current student, full-time
Dates of Enrollment: 8/2005-Submit Date
Survey Submitted: April 2006

D.C. has an amazing social scene, and is consistently rated by *Forbes Magazine* as one of the top cities in America for single people. There are enough bars in the city to go to a different one every night,although the students tend to stick to the Adams Morgan and Dupon Circle areas. In addition to this, there is a high female to male ratio both in the city and in the school, making it an attractive area for singles to meet.

Status: Current student, full-time
Dates of Enrollment: 8/2005-Submit Date
Survey Submitted: April 2006

I don't get out much, but a lot of people do on the weekends. There are some who are more interested in socializing than others, but I pretty much came to law school with a community established outside of school, so I am not as involved as others.

Irish Times is pretty much the bar that people go to. A lot of people live in Silver Springs or on the Hill, and go out to happy hours there. Not many people are dating within school (far fewer than in undergrad) but that is for age/time reasons.

Events are hit or miss, sometimes you show up and it is a boring panel. Sometimes you show up and get to chat with a Supreme Court Justice. The biggest event was Barristers Ball (a.k.a., law school prom), which was done well and widely attended with the appropriate amount of self-deprecation (e.g., can you believe we are at law school prom?).

Clubs tend to be strongly religious or at least influenced by religion, which is annoying. There is no cohesive representation whatsoever of a gay/lesbian community. Likewise, movements like pro-choice are strangely silent on campus.

Status: Current student, full-time
Dates of Enrollment: 8/2005-Submit Date
Survey Submitted: April 2006

This is a conservative, religious school. The dating scene is low key. Many people are married or in serious relationships, as many students here follow the Catholic faith.

There are two legal fraternities here: Phi Alpha Delta and Delta Theta Pi. Phi Alpha Delta, or PAD, is the largest and has the most programming, which includes happy hours, student sessions and parties.

Throughout the school year, there are several big social events: the grad student picnic, the Labor Day Crab Bake, the SPIL Auction, the Christmas tree lighting, Barristers Ball, Spring Festival, Halloween parties, an Easter egg hunt (with and for kids at a nearby orphanage), the pre-exam pancake dinner, coffees with the Dean and a number of other parties.

Status: Current student, full-time
Dates of Enrollment: 8/2002-Submit Date
Survey Submitted: April 2005

The school has a wonderful community environment. There is a very active SBA with nearly 40 student organizations and there is something planned pretty much every weekend. D.C. is a fun young city with amazing restaurants, bars, and social scene. The school helps add to a great social life by hosting events such as the annual Students for Public Interest (SPIL) Auction and the Barristers Ball, which is well attended. The SBA hosts parties at local pubs and bars—some local favorites are the Irish Times by Union Station and the Front Page in historic Dupont Circle.

Status: Current student, full-time
Dates of Enrollment: 8/2004-5/2007
Survey Submitted: April 2005

The school has social events throughout the year. These typically include BBQs or formal events (such as the Barrister's Ball or some alumni networking cocktails). All of these include alcohol. The bar scene is usually found at the Irish Times outside of Union Station, the Front Page in Dupont, Tom Tom's and the Angry Inch at Adams Morgan, Four Providences at Cleveland Park, and the Irish Channel at Gallery Place Chinatown. The rest is all somewhat moot. There are no popular restaurants that many go to, really. The dating scene is quiet given the size of sections and the gossipy nature of the school. Finally, there are "law" fraternities, which are basically for alumni networking and happy hours. Those happy hours are open to all students, however.

Read all of Vault's Law School Surveys at www.vault.com/lawschool — get complete surveys on top law schools, expert advice on applicaton essays, LSAT prep and more.

VAULT CAREER LIBRARY   141

The George Washington University Law School

JD Admissions Office
The George Washington University Law School
700 20th Street, NW, Lower Level
Washington, D.C. 20052
Admissions phone: (202) 994-7230
Admissions e-mail: jdadmit@law.gwu.edu
Admissions URL: http://www.law.gwu.edu/admissions/

 ## Admissions

Status: Current student, full-time
Dates of Enrollment: 8/2004-Submit Date
Survey Submitted: April 2006

By the time you read this, you have likely taken the LSAT and completed the majority of your undergraduate studies, so the rigid cut-off numbers are already in place. Now you need to concentrate on your resume, recommendations and personal statement.

George Washington University Law School draws a diverse crowd, but there is a single trait that runs throughout each incoming class. The students are courteous to each other. Your statement should reflect your personality. If you are pompous, it will likely come out in how you write and you will receive a big thumbs down from the GW board. This does not mean that your statement should explain how you once saved the world or how you spend weekends at the zoo feeding koala bears (unless you were a zookeeper, then I guess you would be justified in including the koala pitch). Be honest about yourself, because it will be reflected in your work.

Status: Current student, full-time
Dates of Enrollment: 8/2003-Submit Date
Survey Submitted: April 2006

The admissions process was straightforward and easy to follow. I submitted my application in early November, and heard back by the end of December. GW was also exceptional at contacting students to give advice and answer questions; the phone calls from current students were especially appreciated and informative. GW takes every part of the application seriously, including the LSAT essay and personal statement; as a result, I felt that my application was fairly and properly considered, and I appreciated the efficiency with which the financial aid office processed my FAFSA and GW financial aid application. They were easy to reach by phone and e-mail and answered many of my questions.

Status: Current student, full-time
Dates of Enrollment: 8/2005-Submit Date
Survey Submitted: April 2006

The admission process to law schools in general is very stressful. GW e-mailed me about my acceptance early on in the process and later followed up with a formal letter of admission. It's a very selective law school; however, once a student is selected, the school is very accommodating. Their preview day was enticing and over the summer the "Pre-L" portal (basically a blog monitored by the dean of student affairs) was very helpful in figuring out everything from where to live in Washington to what to expect from the first week of school.

Status: Current student, full-time
Dates of Enrollment: 8/2003-Submit Date
Survey Submitted: April 2006

Admissions was very difficult, but you appreciate that once you get in, as the student body is an excellent and diverse group. By nature of its location in D.C., GW Law attracts many people from around the U.S. and the world with unique backgrounds. There is a great mix of government/policy people, those interested in nonprofit work and students pursuing corporate and litigation work.

Status: Current student, full-time
Dates of Enrollment: 8/2004-Submit Date
Survey Submitted: April 2006

Applying to GW Law is similar to the admissions process for other top law schools. You must write a personal statement, submit three letters of recommendation, and provide LSAT and undergrad transcripts. GW gets among the highest number of applications in the entire country, so it is very competitive. They are looking for excellence in academics, but also a well-rounded individual. I think it is important to create a "package," that gives the admissions committee a good sense of what kind of a person you are. The admissions committee consists of five or so faculty, and they review each applicant individually. They give out a good number of merit scholarships, and are always available to discuss the admissions process with you.

> **The school says:** "GW Law encourages, but does not require, applicants to submit two letters of recommendation."

Status: Alumnus/a, full-time
Dates of Enrollment: 8/1999-5/2000
Survey Submitted: March 2006

I was admitted as a transfer student from the Chicago-Kent College of Law. When I was a student, it was well known, unofficially, that the admission formula was a basic formula based on LSAT score and undergraduate GPA. If those two scores cleared an established threshold, you got admitted. The admission statistics for GW keep increasing, so I cannot say if the admission process remains the same.

The transfer process is rather simple. You simply fill out the forms, get copies of your transcript, gather recommendation letters from professors at your first school, send in your money and wait. GW admits a healthy transfer class, at least in the past (16 in my year). Keep in the mind the class size is large (400+).

If you want to change schools, APPLY! You never know. The other transfers admitted with me were all from smaller "lesser" schools, but only like one of 16 was a top 5 percent student. If you get admitted, the process is insane. You have two weeks from when they notify you that you are admitted to when classes start. Be ready for the move, finding a place to live long before you get the letter on August 1.

Status: Current student, full-time
Dates of Enrollment: 8/2003-Submit Date
Survey Submitted: March 2005

Standard law school admissions process; no fluff or schmoozing. Just fill out your forms and I encourage students to submit them as early as possible. GW receives around 13,000 law school applications every year and accepts a fraction of those for admission. The earlier you submit you application, the earlier your application appears before the admissions committee, and the greater your chances of being accepted. And the added bonus of having your personal decision resolved early.

> **The school says:** "The Law School receives approximately 11,000 applications annually."

Status: Current student, full time
Dates of Enrollment: 9/2003-Submit Date
Survey Submitted: July 2004

Typical admissions process: essay, LSAT, undergrad GPA, resume. No interview. Just get good grades and good scores. Pretty selective, especially in the last few years the school has been getting more applicants and more acceptance

Read all of Vault's Law School Surveys at www.vault.com/lawschool — get complete surveys on top law schools, expert advice on applicaton essays, LSAT prep and more.

VAULT CAREER LIBRARY   143

from applicants. And this year the school broke into the Top 20 in the national rank, which means it will be even more selective.

 ## Academics

Status: Alumnus/a, full-time
Dates of Enrollment: 8/2000-5/2002
Survey Submitted: May 2006

As a transfer student, I had the opportunity to attend and compare two law schools. I believe the academic environment at GW Law School is generally excellent—and it was certainly far superior to the environment at the school I attended during my first year. The professors are enthusiastic and the students seem eager to engage in meaningful debate and discussion. Certain classes were unfavorably large; however, these were generally lectures that did not invite dialog. Students were able to develop relationships with professors by making a reasonable effort. Students are generally cooperative.

Status: Current student, full-time
Dates of Enrollment: 8/2004-Submit Date
Survey Submitted: April 2006

GW Law draws professors that are engaged in D.C.'s political and legal community. The school also fosters a friendly environment and this starts in the classroom with a pleasant professor from the first day. Granted the workload is heavy, but it is much more bearable with friendly professors who are willing to answer questions and classmates who aren't completely absorbed with themselves. On multiple occasions, I have heard students describe professors as "mother" or "father" types, instead of stoic *Paper Chase* bores (that definitely can't be said for every top-rated law school). There will always be some professors who are boring in class, but that is to be expected.

Status: Current student, full-time
Dates of Enrollment: 8/2003-Submit Date
Survey Submitted: April 2006

The academics at GW Law are structured to allow each student to create an environment that is most conducive for learning. First-year law students are placed in sections of approximately 80 to 100 students, and have all their classes together the first year. One of those fall classes will have students in that section broken down into three smaller sections of about 30 to 35 students each, and the legal research and writing seminar courses (which lasts all year) are 12 students. They are cotaught by a third-year law student, called a "Dean's Fellow," and an adjunct professor (who usually works at a government agency like the Dept. of Justice). Each class has a comprehensive student evaluation process, which is submitted anonymously online, and the Law School administration really takes students' feedback seriously. The workload is normal for first-year students; there will be a sharp increase in students' acclimation and ability to comprehend reading assignments, and students have freedom to select many different courses in the subsequent years of law school.

The grading system is also very fair. First-year grades are all standardized across sections and the entire class, and students in the top 1 to 15 percent are labeled George Washington Scholars, while those in the top 16 to 35 percent are Thurgood Marshall Scholars. After the first year, students can choose to take a few courses pass/fail only, rather than for a letter grade. Some classes have exams, which are currently on a fixed schedule each semester, and other classes have papers as the main grading criterion.

The professors at GW Law are all experts in the subject matter of the courses they teach, and they are accessible to students through office hours and social opportunities. I've found that the professors are very nice and always willing to take extra time to help students understand the material.

Status: Current student, full-time
Dates of Enrollment: 8/2003-Submit Date
Survey Submitted: April 2006

I found the class selection to be broad and varied. Students can take classes in everything from sports law to simulated negotiations, commercial transactions, international law, national security law and animal/environmental law, in addition to core courses. Each semester students get one "priority" class that they

are guaranteed, but in three years I never had a problem getting into any class I wanted. The workload is difficult but likely similar to many other law schools. The professors are EXCELLENT. I would encourage any interested students to sit in on a class.

Status: Current student, full-time
Dates of Enrollment: 5/2003-Submit Date
Survey Submitted: April 2006

It's a top law school, the workload is intense and the classes are demanding but if you are decent at time management it's completely doable. Most of my friends go out a few times a week and still manage to do well and be prepared for class. I've never had a problem getting a class I wanted, some classes fill up, but if you are a 3L you get priority and you have the ability to use a priority form for one class each semester (which means you will most likely get the class). For really popular classes they hold a lottery system.

Class discussion varies based on who is in your class, the smaller classes usually have better discussions even though some professors are really good about getting people involved in the big sections. Most professors don't love "gunners," so class is usually not dominated by one person.

The professors are awesome; they participate in events, they invite you to their homes and they will meet with you any time you want. First year, our section professors took our entire section out to a happy hour where they bought us food and gave us an open bar for two hours. In fact, I was able to coach one of the professor's kid's soccer team, which really enabled me to get to know the professor on a personal level. Furthermore, our adjunct faculty are all real-world experts that bring a lot of experience to the classroom. Some are great teachers, but as adjuncts they are not as good in the classroom as our full-time faculty.

Students are not super competitive with each other. There have been numerous occasions where I have done group outlines for class with friends, shared attack sheets and received notes if I missed a class without asking. The school is very collegial.

Status: Alumnus/a, full-time LLM
Dates of Enrollment: 8/1993-6/1994
Survey Submitted: April 2006

Being an International and Comparative Law LLM student at George Washington University is, to say the least, a highly inspirational experience led by a faculty of superior legal minds who, by virtue of their own personal and professional experiences, emphasize the human aspects of the science of law particularly in the context of cross-border relations between governments, entities or individuals. It is a combination of that level of commitment, and the diverse body of students, especially in the LLM program, that an LLM experience from start to finish is nothing short of a life changing ride and a true eye-opener.

Status: Current student, full-time
Dates of Enrollment: 8/2003-Submit Date
Survey Submitted: March 2005

The program is, of course, reading intensive, and your classmates are competitive, but not viciously so. You can usually get notes from someone if you miss a class. The professors are decent on average; however, some professors tend to teach their own little research universe. Avoid these professors, they will teach you their ideology and not the Black Letter Law. There are professor and class surveys filled out by students at the end of each semester that admitted students can read on the student portal. These will help you select professors and classes. Grading is done on a curve; you want to be on the right-hand side of the normal curve.

Status: Alumnus/a, full-time
Dates of Enrollment: 8/2001-5/2004
Survey Submitted: March 2005

The Intellectual Property Program is in the best in the nation. There are more classes offered in patent, copyright, trademark and IP licensing that most people would ever take. As an example, with respect to patent law, GW offers: Patent Law, Patent Enforcement, Patent Prosecution, Patent Appellate Practice (taught by Don Dunner, one of the most experienced practitioners before the Federal Circuit), the Federal Circuit (taught by Judge Rader who is a judge on the

Federal Circuit) and Licensing of Intellectual Property (which intensely addresses patent licensing).

Status: Current student, full time
Dates of Enrollment: 9/2003-Submit Date
Survey Submitted: July 2004

Lots of good professors, but definitely a few bad ones; make sure to read the professor evaluations on the portal. Not too hard to get popular classes, they give you a priority form that you can use for one top choice class. Grading is hard of course because of the curve, but they just bumped the curve up to a B+ curve, which puts it on par with other surrounding schools. Workload is very heavy but typical of law school.

First year you have 18 hours of class a week, but outside of that you have about one and a half to two hours of reading per class to prepare for the next day. You're easily doing 10 hours of school work per day, whether studying or attending class. When finals start approaching, about four to six weeks prior, you're working at least 12 hours a day outlining and studying, seven days a week, right up until the last day of finals.

 Employment Prospects

Status: Current student, full-time
Dates of Enrollment: 8/2003-Submit Date
Survey Submitted: April 2006

Almost all (95 percent or more) of graduates from GW Law have jobs upon graduation, usually with big firms, judicial clerkships or the federal government (such as the DOJ). GW Law alumni can be found all over Washington, D.C. and the country, especially in prestigious positions, and many students take advantage of these connections in seeking jobs with such employers. The on-campus interviewing through the fall interview program, which occurs in the fall of students' second and third years of law school, is comprehensive and brings employers from firms, public interest organizations and the government from across the country. Internships are also very popular among upperclassman law students at GW Law; I took advantage of the many clinical and outside placement opportunities and worked in various internships and externships during my second and third years at GW Law.

Status: Current student, full-time
Dates of Enrollment: 8/2003-Submit Date
Survey Submitted: April 2006

Employment prospects at GW Law are one of the primary draws. First, you are at the Number 19 law school in the country, located in Washington, D.C. If you want to work in D.C. and take the time to put together a resume, you will have no problem finding a job. Most of the class ends up in D.C., followed by New York and elsewhere on the East Coast, with a few in Chicago and other places.

As far as on-campus interviewing, all of the big firms come to GW to hire for their D.C./NY offices, and many for their offices in smaller cities as well. For people interested in ANY kind of government/nonprofit work, there are opportunities galore in D.C. Many students interested in these fields are working a couple of days a week by their third year, just to get some additional experience.

Status: Alumnus/a, full-time
Dates of Enrollment: 8/2002-5/2005
Survey Submitted: March 2006

I believe that GW has a strong reputation with employers. I was able to get several offers at major firms in a variety of cities for my 2L summer. My grades were near the bottom of the top third of my class, so they were solid, but certainly achievable by anybody. I ended up splitting my time between two firms in the city of my choice. After deciding not to return to that city after law school, I was still able to get a job at the top firm in the city I ended up in as a 3L, which tends to be difficult. So I think GW is no slouch when it comes to reputation—in fact, GW was the lowest "ranked" school of my fellow first-years at my new firm. So it's possible to get into the best firms out of GW.

On-campus recruiting is great. You pick who you want to interview with, and if they're interested, they'll pick you up.

Of my closest circle of friends, four are working for large, Top 100 law firms (including one person at a Top Three law firm in the world). Two are working for small firms. One went into JAG. One works in-house at a corporation. One didn't have a job at graduation, more due to lack of effort than anything else.

Status: Alumnus/a, full-time
Dates of Enrollment: 8/1999-5/2000
Survey Submitted: March 2006

If you want to work in Washington, D.C., New York, Los Angeles or San Francisco, you better be top 25 percent of the class or better. To the elite East and West Coast firms, a GW grad is a good recruit, but there are a lot better out there. Keep in mind the competition. GW is a good school, and compared to most out there, a great school, but GW hovers around Number 20 in the country, and most of the schools that are better are located either in Washington, D.C. or Virginia, New York or New England and California. If those are the markets you are interested in, you are just going to have to do well or have fabulous connections.

However, if you intend to work anywhere else in the country, the degree will swing the doors of law firms wide open. I have worked for big firms first in Cincinnati and now in Phoenix. I have never had a problem getting an interview. Your degree will be from a better school than just about anyone else the firm can recruit. You will be at the front of the line, even if your grades are in the top 25 percent.

GW grads get jobs in all fields from elite big firm jobs, to government positions, to public interest work. The school has an okay program for tuition reimbursement for public interest work. Unfortunately, GW's endowment is not sufficient for you to borrow your tuition funds directly from the school. You have to go through outside sources, which means the school cannot forgive debt directly like some other schools for those students interested in public interest work.

If you are interested in getting a job working for the federal government, seriously give GW a look. It does have fantastic connections to jobs with the government as well as good government contracting classes.

Status: Current student, full-time
Dates of Enrollment: 8/2003-Submit Date
Survey Submitted: March 2005

Employment prospects are very good, particularly for those wishing to stay in the D.C. metro area. There is a sizeable on-campus law firm recruitment program in addition to endless resources of securing a government or public interest position. I have not used the alumni network yet. There are lots of internship possibilities including the option of earning school credit through the externship possibility.

Status: Current student, full time
Dates of Enrollment: 9/2003-Submit Date
Survey Submitted: July 2004

Campus recruiting and career office are both pretty good. They send out a newsletter every week with job opportunities. There is also a career counselor for each section, who is useful for checking resumes and cover letters and general job search advice. They do a good job with giving people notice of jobs around D.C., but if you want something in another city, there is not much, and you have to do most of the searching on your own. This is particularly disappointing for big cities like New York City and Boston where the school should realize that lots of students want to go.

Status: Alumnus/a, full-time
Dates of Enrollment: 8/1998-5/2001
Survey Submitted: April 2004

This school does really well if you plan on working in Washington, D.C. or New York. If you plan on going to the Midwest or the West Coast you would probably be better served by going to a different school. Although I was in the top quarter, I noticed that the career development department really only helped people that were in the top quarter. If you were in the bottom half of the class, you probably had to do everything on your own (aside from help with drafting letters and resumes).

Read all of Vault's Law School Surveys at www.vault.com/lawschool — get complete surveys on top law schools, expert advice on applicaton essays, LSAT prep and more.

VAULT CAREER LIBRARY   145

Quality of Life

Status: Current student, full-time
Dates of Enrollment: 8/2004-Submit Date
Survey Submitted: April 2006

The quality of life is okay. It's a walking city. The university is the only thing in Foggy Bottom besides large law firms and businesses. This drives housing costs way up forcing anyone not on a trust fund to commute by Metro. Minimum commutes for people not in Foggy Bottom are probably around 30 minutes. Food in and around the university are also terrible. It's either $25/plate restaurants or take-out sandwich places and everything closes at 5 p.m. because it's essentially a business district. Other than that, the neighborhood is safe.

Status: Current student, full-time
Dates of Enrollment: 8/2004-Submit Date
Survey Submitted: April 2006

Housing is spread throughout MD, D.C. and VA. There are plenty of options to choose from and you can find the qualities in a neighborhood that you would like to have (quiet family-oriented neighborhood like Pentagon City or Ballston vs. downtown D.C. like McPherson Square). The Metro system makes most locations between 15- to 45-minute commutes. The prices are incredibly high for any purchase in D.C. But one variable to consider is rent drops as you move farther from the district, so apartments on the orange line west of Rosslyn, blue line south of Crystal City and red line in the northern neighborhoods will be the least expensive and are still accessible to public transportation. I would recommend living close to a subway station to cut out waiting time each day at a bus stop, but that's just me.

Status: Current student, full-time
Dates of Enrollment: 8/2003-Submit Date
Survey Submitted: April 2006

GW Law provides a good balance of work and life, and GW can provide subsidized housing just a few blocks away at Columbia Plaza, a very nice apartment complex in which GW has an ownership interest. The campus is centrally located on to the Metrorail (subway) and Metrobus, as well as nightlife and shopping in Georgetown and downtown. GW Law is only a few blocks away from the White House!

The facilities are also excellent, including a new health and wellness center on campus. There are so many dining options nearby, and GW Law is expanding over the next few years to include a deli/cafe/coffee shop inside the Law School! Plus, there are student organization events such as bake sales, speaker and panel events, and social gatherings at or near the Law School all the time.

The neighborhood of Foggy Bottom, where GW and the Law School are located, is one of the safest areas in all of D.C., and is right across the Potomac from Rosslyn and Arlington. The Law School's doors are locked every evening at 6:30 p.m., and law students swipe their ID cards to gain access to the buildings. There are also security guards on-site and around campus at all times, so the entire area feels very safe. Not only does the Metropolitan Police Dept. (D.C.'s main police) patrol the area, but the GW police patrol the area, and even have their headquarters adjacent to the Law School. The U.S. Park Police, Capitol Police and security at the World Bank/IMF next door and the State Dept. down the street all monitor the area. So it is quite safe!

Status: Current student, full-time
Dates of Enrollment: 5/2003-Submit Date
Survey Submitted: April 2006

There is no real campus housing you are better off finding your own living situation. The quality of life around campus is okay, there isn't all that much to do in Foggy Bottom. But D.C. as a city is great, there is plenty of stuff to keep you busy. The Law School facilities are beautiful, they've been renovating them over the last few years and it has made quite an improvement. The area around school is safe, but dining options immediately around campus are limited.

One quirk about the dining options around campus, we have a hot dog vendor who is permanently located right next to the Law School. The "Cart Lady," as she is affectionately known, is an institution in and of herself. She has a unique personality, doesn't speak much English, but the students love her. If you are short on cash she'll feed you if you promise to pay her back later.

Status: Alumnus/a, full-time
Dates of Enrollment: 8/1999-5/2000
Survey Submitted: March 2006

There is no on-campus housing for students. You will have to fend for yourself in the rental market. Rents are high but can be lowered depending on your tolerance for living in either less desirable (read: dangerous) areas or your tolerance for a lengthy commute. (If there are bars on the second story windows, it's a bad neighborhood and you probably want to reconsider.) The Law School is located between two Metro stations, so access is easy even if you do not want to drive or do not have a car.

Status: Current student, full-time
Dates of Enrollment: 8/2004-Submit Date
Survey Submitted: March 2005

D.C. is expensive, but I am very glad I live here. It's so fantastic living in the nation's capital. I have a tiny studio a block from campus for $800 per month. Other larger studios cost about $1,050 per month, and larger places go up in price fast. However there are some cheaper things in Northern Virginia and Maryland but I hate commutes (if you do the subway is pretty good). There is NO on-campus housing for law students, but my apartment is closer to school than some undergrad dorms. The neighborhood (unlike say Georgetown) is very safe, we're so close to the White House and World Bank, that there are federal and district cops on every other corner. However there are few bars, you have to take a 10-minute walk (or $7 cab ride) to get to some decent bars. The facilities at the school are great.

The school says: "Beginning in 2007, efficiency units in a nearby university residential building will be available to first-year law students. In addition, housing is available to graduate students in a campus residence hall, and GW facilitates the application process and lease arrangements for law students at a nearby privately-owned apartment complex (Columbia Plaza)."

Social Life

Status: Current student, full-time
Dates of Enrollment: 8/2004-Submit Date
Survey Submitted: April 2006

There are plenty of things to do. Everyone seems social the first semester. The second semester everyone becomes a library rat. There is always something going on (usually involving alcohol). If someone wants to have a well-balanced law school experience they have the option here if they try. George Washington tries to pride itself on the well-balanced students but it's mostly lip service. It's predominantly a visible group that tends to work hard and play hard. Most students fall into one category or the other but not both. When it is time to show everyone's true colors, it all boils down to getting the grades for the average student.

Status: Current student, full-time
Dates of Enrollment: 8/2004-Submit Date
Survey Submitted: April 2006

The District's resources are numerous. Federal courts, national monuments, restaurants, bars, shopping centers and law firms galore surround you.

The Law School is competitive, but not cutthroat. Students hang out in the lounge before and after class. Your small writing section and 1L class section will be a source of new friends. They won't be there merely for a study group opportunity either. My first year, a student had a personal emergency back home and everyone showed that they really did care about each other. Yes, you come for the education, but it is true that you can learn more from your classmates than a lecture. GW has proven just that for me. My discussions in the lounge with classmates about cases, current politics and their personal qualms have been priceless. Don't let law school turn you into a library rodent that constantly avoids any contact with classmates.

At GW, you'll learn and go to football/basketball games with your classmates, not hate them (except maybe for those select few that slipped through the "pompous" test during admissions, but that's a constant at any law school). One way to get a feel for the student body at any school is to wander off from the group tour and talk to the students in the hallways/lounges (and the GW students won't mind). Make the most out of your experience, it only lasts three years. Good luck with your search and I hope you find the right fit.

Status: Current student, full-time
Dates of Enrollment: 8/2005-Submit Date
Survey Submitted: April 2006

Thirsty Thursdays: Every Thursday a different student organization provides a couple of kegs and some snacks for students. It's a great time to hang out with your friends and your professors and share a drink. These organizations also sponsor an event at a different bar every Thursday night (Bar Review) where lots of students go out and have fun. The D.C. bar scene is great—very eclectic—there's something for everyone. The dating scene seems pretty healthy, not over-whelmingly couple-y but not like everyone's single. There have been some great events this year; the Equal Justice Fund's auction was a riot, basically we auc-tioned off things that professors had donated (lunch/dinner at fancy restau-rants/baseball games, etc.). They were the auctioneers and just took it to town. Also they had the first ever GW Law games here this year, basically a field day and cookout on the quad, the professors participated as well and it was just tons of fun. Felt like middle school, not like law school.

Status: Current student, full-time
Dates of Enrollment: 5/2003-Submit Date
Survey Submitted: April 2006

First year you will go to McFaddens way too many times for your own good. There aren't many bars in Foggy Bottom, most students go out to Dupont, Georgetown, U-Street, Adams Morgan or Northern Virginia. Some of our favorite spots include Tom Tom's, Clarendon Ballroom, Lucky Bar and The Guard's.

It seems like everyone on campus is involved in some student group or student government. Students really take ownership of the school. I know there is a Greek system at the undergrad level, but I've never heard of a law student being involved with it.

Status: Current student, full-time
Dates of Enrollment: 8/2003-Submit Date
Survey Submitted: April 2006

I met my wife in law school, so I may be biased when I say it is a great place to meet people. But the Law School does do a good job facilitating social events, right from the beginning of 1L orientation. Throughout the school year, there are Thirsty Thursdays in the lounge, where everyone gathers to socialize after a hard week and Bar Reviews at local bars once a week.

In addition, the SBA sponsors a law school prom, which generally sees about 1,000 people come out dressed in their finest. Other highlights include the annu-al Law Revue, dozens of intramural sporting events, the Equal Justice Foundation Auction and the Law School Olympics.

Status: Current student, full-time
Dates of Enrollment: 8/2004-Submit Date
Survey Submitted: April 2006

The social life at GW Law is about as good as it gets in law school! Everyone at the Law School is extremely friendly and most students are very involved in student-run organizations. People actually *enjoy* spending the day at school, hanging out in the lounges, eating lunch with friends and attending student-organized events. Because there are so many students organizations running the gamut of the political, religious and economic spectra, there is a place for every-one to meet people who share similar interests. There are many events happen-ing every day, whether put on by the faculty, outside organizations or students. The administration really supports and fosters this happy and non-competitive social environment.

Status: Alumnus/a, full-time
Dates of Enrollment: 8/2002-5/2005
Survey Submitted: March 2006

Now this where GW really shines. I'm a more social person than some, and I fit in perfectly at GW. I never encountered the backstabbing, rude behavior that you hear about so frequently at other Top 20 schools. The community is amaz-ing and I wouldn't hesitate to rank it the best in the nation.

GW students are fantastic. They're from all over the country so you don't find yourself having to integrate with a glut of locals. Making friends is very easy since most people there only know one or two other people. Or they're like me when I first got there and don't know anybody! After my first year, I had a very tight circle of about eight or nine friends. We played poker every week and hung out all the time. We were also buddies with a few other circles of about eight to 12 people. So nights at the bars could get pretty raucous, and my roommate and I threw parties that had as many as 50 GW Law students at them. No matter your personality type, you're likely to find yourself developing some of the strongest friendships you've ever known. I have no doubt that I will keep in touch with about five or six of my friends for the rest of my life, even though we're not all in the same city.

Join the softball team. Good times and a fun road trip to the University of Virginia's softball tourney. Huge tourney with about 50 other law schools and a great chance to meet tons of other students.

Status: Alumnus/a, full-time
Dates of Enrollment: 8/1999-5/2000
Survey Submitted: March 2006

The size of law school classes leads to some difficulties in school-sponsored events. But the school tries. In the end, participating in the school-sponsored event will be up to you. Unlike other schools, the sponsored event will be just one of the hundreds of things that people can do. Except for the end of semes-ter bashes with free food and drinks, the sponsored event will not be "THE" social event of the weekend. Instead, there are lots of more informal activities going on be it bar hopping, intramural sports, cultural events, etc. I think this is an issue because everyone does not know everyone else, even within your cohort. The class size is simply too big.

As a middle-class Midwestern kid coming from a public university, I was struck by the shear amount of wealth among the law student class. GW is an expen-sive, well-regarded private school. If you are from more limited means, keep this in mind. You won't be alone, but it is an element to be aware of. There will be people from backgrounds and experiences that are simply foreign to you. The school also attracts a significant number of students from New York and New Jersey and it is obvious on a day to day basis. To those reading this not from New York or New Jersey, you understand my point. Just be aware.

Status: Alumnus/a, full-time
Dates of Enrollment: 8/1999-5/2002
Survey Submitted: September 2003

GW Law School is right on their undergraduate campus, which is hopping. There are plenty of bars, and it is close to Adams Morgan (Madam's Organ, Heaven and Hell), Midtown (LuLu's, Mad Hatter, Sign of the Whale) and the Georgetown strip (The Guards, Mr. Smith's, Old Glory). And of course there is Lindy's Red Lion right on campus for a cold beer and good burger, though it's usually very crowded. The 1L sections usually have a happy hour once per week, and, weather permitting, there is usually beer on the quad every Thursday and two or three barbecues per semester. There is no Greek system to speak of, save for the undergrad. There is a new student gym that is topnotch, although the pool is a little small. GW law students can audit undergrad courses for free (save for course-specific fees), so you can brush up on languages or learn a new instrument, etc.

Read all of Vault's Law School Surveys at www.vault.com/lawschool — get complete surveys on top law schools, expert advice on applicaton essays, LSAT prep and more.

VAULT CAREER LIBRARY 147

The School Says

Located in the heart of downtown Washington, D.C., GW is the oldest law school in the District of Columbia. It is also one of the largest law schools in the country with a diverse student population of 1,875 JD and graduate law students who come from across the country and around the world.

Admission is competitive with approximately 11,000 prospective JD students applying each year. All admitted applicants are considered for merit scholarships, and an estimated 85 percent of students receive some form of financial aid. The Law School's commitment to supporting its students and alumni who wish to work in the public interest includes significant financial support programs, including the Loan Reimbursement Assistance Program (LRAP).

The Law School is widely recognized in the local, national and international legal communities for the strength of its academic program, particularly in areas such as intellectual property, international, environmental, clinical, government procurement and constitutional and administrative law. GW's distinguished full- and part-time faculty includes some of the most prolific scholars and recognized experts in the country. Their academic work, and that of the student body, is supported by the Jacob Burns Law Library, which is among the largest and most prestigious academic law libraries in the United States.

In fall 2007, the Law School will offer to its incoming 1L class an opportunity to live in Aston Hall, a university residential building with approximately 110 furnished efficiency units within walking distance of the Law School. Aston Hall, The Hall on Virginia Avenue (a graduate student residential hall) and Columbia Plaza (a private apartment complex with simplified application and lease processes for GW Law students) offer a variety of options for living on or near campus.

Applicants are invited to regularly visit www.law.gwu.edu to learn more about GW Law's exceptionally rich academic and community life.

Georgetown University Law Center

600 New Jersey Ave. N.W.
Washington, D.C. 20001
Admissions phone: (202) 662-9000
Admissions e-mail: admis@law.georgetown.edu
Admissions URL: http://law.georgetown.edu/admissions

 Admissions

Status: Current student, full-time
Dates of Enrollment: 8/2005-Submit Date
Survey Submitted: May 2006

The admissions process at Georgetown is welcoming. The school makes a strong effort to make this large law school into a community, and I think that effort comes across in the admissions process. From phone calls from current students to a personal note written by the dean of admissions on every admittance letter, the admissions department made me feel like I was becoming a part of a community. I did not feel like I was just another number to help them raise their statistics for a national magazine. Other schools either did not return my phone calls or answer my questions. Georgetown, on the other hand, always returned my phone calls promptly and was willing to spend the extra time it took to make sure that my questions were answered. Also, every admission even has a chocolate fountain, and you can't beat that!

Status: Current student, full-time
Dates of Enrollment: 8/2005-Submit Date
Survey Submitted: April 2006

Georgetown is in the most selective category of law schools, but one advantage of being the largest law school is that it admits a large number of students. Georgetown students are genuine and interesting, so be yourself throughout the application process! Be passionate about your previous experiences and your future aspirations, and don't be afraid to admit that you aren't sure what you want to be doing in 10 years—just be sincere about what interests you and why you want to dedicate the next three years of your life to pursuing a law degree.

Numbers are important but Georgetown doesn't use a magical formula to select its students, so put time into the other parts of your application to make yourself stand out and to show your interest in attending the school. Proofread everything you send in—every correspondence with the school is a potential writing sample. Take advantage of whatever resources your undergraduate school offers to give you feedback on your personal statement and resume. Also, choose your references very carefully—send them your resume and talk to them about why you want to go to Georgetown. Make sure some are academic, but if you can, find an employer or someone else to provide a more complete picture of who you are.

Georgetown doesn't offer many interviews so really put time into your essay to say something about yourself. Do not feel like you must have a Peace Corps experience in order to be interesting! Your essay should show the admissions committee who you are and why Georgetown would be lucky to have you as a student—don't tell them why Georgetown is great, they already know that. Also, don't tell them why you NEED to go to Georgetown—focus on who you are and what you've done and what you hope to do, and maybe if there's something unique that Georgetown has that matches your aspirations.

Status: Current student, part-time
Dates of Enrollment: 8/2005-Submit Date
Survey Submitted: April 2006

I have found that there are two groups of people. (1) People who have excelled in their college or recent graduate programs and want to go to law school; and (2) people who have excelled at something in the working world (especially politics). As far as advice on getting in, the best thing I could say is show them that you are interested and you love Georgetown and it is your first choice. No mat-

ter how smart you are, I guarantee your scores, grades and undergrad institution are a dime a dozen. Go beyond what is asked, write notes, meet alumni and visit the campus. Remember, Georgetown has a huge applicant pool so you have to differentiate yourself. Also, if I could give anyone advice, go work for a year before going to law school...you'd be surprised how much it helps.

Status: Current student, full-time
Dates of Enrollment: 8/2005-Submit Date
Survey Submitted: April 2006

I did not apply to law schools until the last minute, or at least pretty close to the last minute. It was mid-January before I turned all of my materials, and given that law schools practice rolling admission and my LSAT scores were not that impressive, I was sure I would be working at some fast-food joint after receiving my "Thanks for applying, but..." letters. This is before I knew about the culture of admissions at GU Law. Georgetown Law is VERY interested in YOU and what you have to offer the university and the classroom discussion. It is more important for you to have something interesting to say and something substantial to offer, than have an LSAT score above or within their mean range.

Status: Alumnus/a, full-time
Dates of Enrollment: 9/2004-5/2005
Survey Submitted: March 2006

The dean of admissions really does consider people individually. I worked in a student organization that helped recruit prospective students, and found that they put a great deal of careful thought into who they admit. They ensure that there is a wide range of talent and background. No question, you need to be sharp to gain admission, but the admission staff is not seeking clones—so be yourself.

I was a transfer student, so I was able to see the process from both sides. Georgetown treats its transfers almost like adopted family. The dean hand signs a note of welcome and congratulations on every admission approval, which may seem small, but when it was my second attempt to attend Georgetown, it meant a lot to me. Your essay is important. Again, be yourself, and try not to force yourself on the school. If you fit, they will admit you.

Status: Alumnus/a, full-time LLM
Dates of Enrollment: 7/2004-5/2005
Survey Submitted: March 2006

My application was submitted from Belgium, together with an extensive resume, recommendation letters and a personal motivation letter. I have the impression that the admissions department tries to build a complete image of the applicant's personality. Legal skills as well as personal experiences and abilities play an important role in admitting applicants. Cultural diversity seems another goal of the university, since they manage to compose a cultural heterogeneous group from different parts of the world.

It is very much appreciated that the director of the LLM program visits in person different countries to meet with applicants and accepted students. This meeting gives the application a more personal touch. However, it is common knowledge that a top ranked university is very selective. In this way, Georgetown University Law Center does not differ from other top universities. As mentioned above, this university differs from others by its personal approach towards the applicants, and, in particular, its accepted students.

Status: Current student, full-time
Dates of Enrollment: 8/2004-Submit Date
Survey Submitted: April 2005

Georgetown Law gets 13,000 applications a year so to get in you need, first, a very strong LSAT (generally in the 95-99 percentile). You also need good grades in CHALLENGING courses, preferably from a respected school (if you're coming from a lesser known school, you should show how you made your mark and why you went there—close to family, financial considerations, etc). Now the GPA/LSAT combination may seem obvious, but it is truly necessary. So, if you have a 172 and a 3.9, no worries, right? There's still more work to be done. Get strong letters of rec—while letters may not help people whose scores and grades

Read all of Vault's Law School Surveys at www.vault.com/lawschool — get complete surveys on top law schools, expert advice on applicaton essays, LSAT prep and more.

VAULT CAREER LIBRARY 149

are lacking, a lackluster letter can really hurt you. Of course, letters are confidential, but you can and should ask the recommender not only if they will give you a recommendation, but if they would be willing to give you a STRONG recommendation. I got three letters and focused each recommender on separate strengths. I wrote each recommender a customized letter stating my intent, experience, and some well-placed hints about what I would like them to emphasize. This might seem silly, but many professors have to write a lot of recommendations and will grasp at any reminder of what made you stand out. You don't want a recommendation that says: "I didn't really know him too well," or just recites your grades, and a little guidance helps a lot.

As for the personal statement, you must manage to be both innovative and show your strengths. This does not mean simply reciting your reasons for applying (the school already knows how good it is, and does not care that *CSI* is your favorite show, and certainly does not want to know that you just don't know what else to do). It sounds cliche, but you have to find your own voice and make yourself sound interesting. For me, I found a common theme that united several key things that made me both distinct and successful sounding, and that worked wonders. As for the resume—do not ignore it.

Status: Current student, full-time
Dates of Enrollment: 9/2003-Submit Date
Survey Submitted: March 2005

Play to your strengths and emphasize what makes you stand out from all of the other great academic records, because that isn't the only thing they consider. I highly advise coming to visit because you get a much better feel for the school, and the admissions officers are by far the best I worked with. They are genuinely friendly and always ready to discuss all of your options. Once you've been admitted, their goal really is to help you make the best decision, although of course persuading you that Georgetown is the best option!

Status: Current student, full-time
Dates of Enrollment: 8/2003-Submit Date
Survey Submitted: April 2004

GULC admissions is highly competitive—the year I was admitted, there were more than 12,000 applications for seats in the 600-member class. A top LSAT score and good undergraduate performance is essential, but to stand out in a crowd like that, the essay is extremely important. It helps if you have some experience or perspective you can articulate that separates you from the horde of other applicants. I worked for four years before going to law school. Almost everyone in my class took at least one year off before going to law school—some taught English overseas, pursued personal interests, gained skill in non-legal areas, or worked as assistants for law firms.

The admissions staff at Georgetown was very helpful throughout the process. They were willing to answer questions before the application was actually submitted, responded promptly to e-mails and phone messages, and provided excellent direction to other offices on campus that could be helpful in meeting my needs. The final decision in my particular case was made after only a month. The admissions office sends postcards and has an up-to-date web site to let the applicant know what stage the application is in—whether the application is complete, when it is being evaluated, when a decision has been made and finally a letter as to what the decision was. Georgetown sent the best stuff. I applied and was admitted to seven top-tier schools. Out of those, Georgetown's admissions packages were by far the best. The most memorable was a large box I got in late spring, after I let the school know I would be coming there. The package was like a care package from Georgetown—it was full of colorful, helpful information on everything from local radio stations to campus life to phone numbers for utility companies, cable companies and the department of motor vehicles for registering your car. Basically, all the information we needed to get situated in our new homes was provided by the school.

The school also provides a fabulous admitted students web site. The web site allows admitted students to interact through an active message board. Various departments on campus host live chats to help incoming students in areas like curriculum, career planning and housing. There is also a specific housing section of the web site to help students find housing in the D.C. area.

Status: Current student, full-time
Dates of Enrollment: 8/2003-Submit Date
Survey Submitted: May 2004

Very straightforward. It can (and should) be filled out online.

Georgetown is pretty selective. Even though it is not ranked in the Top 10 law schools nationally, many students who are accepted at Top 10 schools end up attending Georgetown. One major reason is that it is located in Washington, D.C., within walking distance of both the Supreme Court and the Capitol, in addition to numerous federal agencies. Another reason is the optional alternative first-year curriculum, called Curriculum B, which is chosen by about one quarter of the first-year class. Curriculum B is an interdisciplinary approach to the first year with an emphasis on legal theory, philosophy, and the history of American jurisprudence.

Academics

Status: Current student, part-time
Dates of Enrollment: 8/2005-Submit Date
Survey Submitted: April 2006

Classes are great. I have liked every professor except for one and even he wasn't that bad, he just wasn't a good communicator. It is called part-time but it is really full-time. The credit difference between full-time and part-time is only six credits at the end of the first year. The school was started as a part-time program and professors are rotated to teaching at night. Therefore, the quality of the night and day professors is the same.

The workload is high given that you are trying to balance a job and school, plus law school itself is time consuming. It is manageable but you have to have a plan. The first semester is nice because you get every other Friday off, whereas second semester you have class every night.

Status: Current student, full-time
Dates of Enrollment: 8/2005-Submit Date
Survey Submitted: April 2006

The Georgetown faculty is really topnotch. Georgetown's biggest criticism is its size—it is the largest law school and most first-year classes have 100-120 students in them. That can be frustrating, but there are benefits from the size that, in my opinion, outweigh the drawbacks. First, the number of course selections is incredible. Georgetown offers a wide variety of upper-level courses, a large number of which are small seminars, so it's easy to get second- and third-year schedules that are really tailored to your interests. Also, because Georgetown is located in Washington, D.C., Georgetown has an amazing adjunct faculty that comes in to teach upper-level courses in their areas of expertise. It's a really unique opportunity to learn from someone who is an expert in her field while she's practicing.

Just as an example, one of Georgetown's professors, Neal Katyal, argued the Hamdan case representing a Guantanamo detainee—next year, he's teaching Criminal Law and an upper-level course on terrorism. You couldn't ask for higher quality professors than the Georgetown faculty.

As for grading and workload, Georgetown is typical in that academics are very competitive. I've heard professors recommend spending four to eight hours of studying each day, in addition to as many as five hours of classes. First-year courses are graded on a curve with the average somewhere around a B. Unfortunately, they're pretty strict about that, so if you have a really bright section it's extremely difficult to place in the top 10 percent. But upper-level courses are graded on a different scale, so many students say their grades dramatically increase come second year of school.

Georgetown has a number of strong academic areas. The current dean is very focused on increasing Georgetown's reputation internationally. Because of Georgetown's location, it has a very strong program for those with political aspirations. Also, because of the number of practitioners who are adjunct faculty members, there's a very strong trial and appellate advocacy program. Finally, Georgetown has the Number One clinical education program of any school. Admission is selective, but a majority of students who want to do a clinic are able to. Imagine devoting an entire semester to representing someone seeking asylum in the United States—from the initial interview all the way to court! Other popular clinics deal with domestic violence, housing issues, appellate advocacy, international women's human rights, and teaching the law to D.C. high school students.

Status: Current student, full-time JD/MPP
Dates of Enrollment: 8/2005-Submit Date
Survey Submitted: April 2006

Law school is a lot of work, and GULC is certainly no exception. However, because your professors are all lawyers, they've all been through the law school experience and know how it feels. They still expect the students to be prepared for class and to answer questions, but most professors have a system to allow a student to get out of being called on if he/she is just overwhelmed a few times a semester .

Also, none of my professors ever sought to embarrass a student who was underprepared. They didn't let him/her off the hook, but they continued to ask questions to draw the answers out instead of ridiculing him/her for not knowing the "right" answers (of course, in law, there are very few right or wrong answers!).

1L courses are chosen for you, so you don't have to worry about scheduling until the end of your first year. When you do start working out your upper-class schedule, the school provides you with information on how rapidly the course has filled up in past years, and whether or not there is preference given to certain class levels.

The professors are all very smart, and they are required to have office hours, which they frequently expand if there's a heavy interest in asking questions. While a lot of the professors here lean left politically, they are willing to entertain opposing arguments and in fact embrace such debates because opposing views can help tease out issues and possible solutions.

GULC also offers 10 journals and 11 clinics, as well as several types of mock trial and moot court programs. This means there are a large number of academic extracurriculars to choose from and get some practical experience in practicing law before you graduate. The size of the school makes these programs pretty competitive, but because of the number of choices you can find something that will interest you.

Generally, people use their laptop computers to take notes, and all the buildings are equipped for wireless Internet access. Almost all of the classes have the appropriate electric plugs to accommodate this use. While finals don't have to be typed on a computer, it is definitely to your advantage to do so. GULC finals do not require a PC; in fact, often Apple computers work better with the wireless than some types of PC wireless cards.

Status: Current student, full-time
Dates of Enrollment: 8/2005-Submit Date
Survey Submitted: April 2006

Amazing. Great classes, great profs, no cutthroat mentality. In fact,when my hard drive failed and my note backups were a couple months old, I had many people in my class voluntarily give me their notes to help me fill the gaps. There are many classes in international human rights too. This is great for me since I want to practice in that field. There's also a certificate in refugee and humanitarian emergencies program that is great. The professors are all great people. They will invite you into their office and have open conversations with you.

Status: Current student, full-time
Dates of Enrollment: 8/2005-Submit Date
Survey Submitted: April 2006

Law school is tough. Don't neglect to prepare yourself for the challenge, as it is unlike anything you've ever done before academically. Most classes are taught in a Socratic Method, which basically means that the professors will "cold-call" you in a class of 100+ and expect you to give them the answers. If you have a question, they might just respond with a question to get you thinking. It's all about them asking the right questions to get you to the right answer. Don't let them stump you—just broaden your way of thinking.

Status: Current student, full-time
Dates of Enrollment: 9/2003-Submit Date
Survey Submitted: November 2005

The bidding system is a little strange, but somehow it all works. The number of courses Georgetown offers is staggering. Everything from Laws of Terrorism to Trial Practice to Mediation seminars. In addition, the chance to do clinical work in your second and third years is fantastic.

Professors here are amazing. You have your Ivory Tower guys, but you also have practitioners and judges who want to teach a class or two. For example, John Roberts was teaching a summer class in Georgetown's London program when he was nominated to the Supreme Court this year. Not bad!

Status: Alumnus/a, full-time
Dates of Enrollment: 9/2004-5/2005
Survey Submitted: March 2006

While many students groan about the "lottery" system for class admission, I found it to be very fair. Successive rounds of lottery selection nearly assured admission into all but the most popular classes (and even those usually admitted the majority of waitlisted students). The range of topics covered at Georgetown astounded me. Georgetown's best-kept secret is its adjunct professors, drawn from the vibrant D.C. legal community. For example, my Criminal Procedure class was taught by Michael Dreeben, the deputy solicitor general, who has argued more than 53 cases before the Supreme Court. Not only was he incredibly articulate and kind, but when I asked him why the Justices seemed to hang on a particular point, he stroked his chin, looked at the ceiling, and answered, "You know, in this case, I asked Justice Scalia that, and..." Amazing. As a student, I had that experience more than once.

The students are very capable, they work hard, and most importantly, they actually enjoy law—so lunch conversation is always entertaining. Between the two law schools I attended, I found the Georgetown students more engaged in what they studied, and a bit more passionate about practicing law.

Status: Current student, full-time
Dates of Enrollment: 9/2002-Submit Date
Survey Submitted: March 2005

The professors are wonderful! Such an extensive range of teaching styles and personalities. They are all approachable and more than willing to go out of their way to address your questions and concerns. The other week, I e-mailed my tax professor because I wanted to meet with him and talk about some issues relating to the course. He said he would be out of the office all week, but he gave me his home number and his cell phone number so that I could reach him any time I wanted to talk. When I called him on his cell phone, he was on his way to meet his son for lunch, but took the time to talk with me for a few minutes. Then he called me the next day to continue our conversation. Also, I've gone to have lunch or dinner at three of my professor's houses. Workload is pretty heavy first year (pretty much a given at any law school you go to). Then second year is a breeze!! You have time to have a life, and a really fun life too!

Status: Current student, full-time
Dates of Enrollment: 8/2004-Submit Date
Survey Submitted: March 2005

The program is a rigorous course of study, but not overly burdensome. You will learn the Black Letter Law, but you have options. There are two different first-year curriculums, but both result in an excellent grasp of first-year courses. The first year is broken down into five different sections and even smaller sections after that, so that students do not get lost in the crowd and actually get to know their classmates and professors. The legal writing class is broken down into an even smaller section, for more in-depth learning.

Read all of Vault's Law School Surveys at www.vault.com/lawschool — get complete surveys on top law schools, expert advice on applicaton essays, LSAT prep and more.

VAULT CAREER LIBRARY   151

Employment Prospects

Status: Current student, full-time
Dates of Enrollment: 8/2005-Submit Date
Survey Submitted: May 2006

Great. Every top firm has a Georgetown graduate. As a former Hill staffer, I can speak from experience that if a student wants to get a job in government or in Congress, there is no better place than Washington, D.C. You are in the middle of the action, and you can take advantage of employment opportunities in this city first. This summer I am working with the FCC. Everyone talks about the difficulty of getting a summer job after the first summer, but I can honestly say that every one of my friends has a job. Whether they are working as an assistant for a teacher doing research, working for a local judge, working in a major law firm in their home town, or working for a government agency, the breadth and quality of jobs is impressive.

Status: Current student, full-time
Dates of Enrollment: 8/2005-Submit Date
Survey Submitted: April 2006

Georgetown has an amazing on-campus interview program for all the best law firms in Washington, New York, and most other legal markets across the country—and even some abroad! An increasing number of Georgetown students are finding permanent employment in London—both at American firms and British firms. Georgetown also has the strongest government interview program—it really pays to be located down the street from their offices.

The most exciting employment program that's really unique to Georgetown is its international internship program. Over one hundred overseas employers offer to take Georgetown students for a summer internship, and the application process couldn't be simpler students submit resumes, employers choose between them, and away you go. If you're interested in an international career, I can't imagine any school would be more supportive of whatever regional and topical interests you might have. And finally, since Georgetown is a big school, it has a big alumni network, which is especially prominent in all of the major cities. Georgetown alumni are very proud of their school and while I wouldn't say the connection is an automatic job offer, I think the alums do pay special attention to Georgetown students.

Status: Alumnus/a, full-time
Dates of Enrollment: 8/2001-5/2004
Survey Submitted: April 2006

Graduates work for a variety of different employers ranging from private sector law firms, government, judicial clerks, to nonprofit organizations. On-campus interviewing was very convenient and easy for us, thankfully. The school could improve on its alumni network by creating some kind of list serve or searchable database to allow students to contact alums directly for networking/job purposes. Princeton does this and it works fantastically.

Status: Alumnus/a, full-time
Dates of Enrollment: 8/2002-5/2005
Survey Submitted: April 2006

I didn't have a problem finding both a law firm job and a clerkship after graduation, but I know many people who did. Georgetown is the top law school in D.C. (where there are many), and it is nationally recognized, so the "prestige" factor is on your side. That said, if you want to work in a top market (D.C., NYC, etc.) you still need to be closer to the top of the class than the middle, as you are competing with the top graduates of all the top schools. The office of career services is great about setting up multiple on-campus interview weeks (both with firms and public interest employers) and the clerkship coordinator is very helpful. Some people complain that the school isn't great about helping you find firm jobs outside of campus interviewing, but I don't know what more they could do (beyond setting up many interview schedules, organizing resume drops, and constantly posting and e-mailing job opportunities).

Status: Alumnus/a, full-time
Dates of Enrollment: 9/2004-5/2005
Survey Submitted: March 2006

On-campus interviews are amazing. They are not perfect for everyone, but there are more than 700 employers from across the country that come to one hotel for one week and interview you. You get 50 lottery entries for any employer you like. The most popular are difficult to gain access to, but they usually have hospitality suites where you can drop off a resume and set up alternative interview times. The process is much like speed-dating: you've got 20 minutes to convince them to call you back for a thorough interview. While I faced many rejections (who doesn't?), the on-campus interview process eventually yielded enough interviews for me to return to my home state (across the country) and practice with one of the best firms in town.

The staff at employment services works very hard for students who show some initiative to get the ball rolling. Georgetown is a large campus, so you need initiative for the system to work for you. Once I did the initial legwork, I found that my career advisor did hers. She called prospects, contacted networking alumni in my home city, and revised my resume countless times. The whole process was very helpful.

Because of its size, Georgetown has a large, connected alumni network. It is amazing how many alums I meet each week in my practice.

Georgetown also offers a great internship placement program. Again, due to its size, Georgetown has institutionalized many opportunities that folks at smaller schools must find for themselves. It can be overly competitive for the popular program, but there are so many opportunities in D.C. that internships abound.

Status: Alumnus/a, full-time
Dates of Enrollment: 8/1998-5/2001
Survey Submitted: March 2006

The very best firms flock to GULC to recruit. Judges hire scores of GULC students as clerks. The career services office keeps track of alumni in different professions and cities. Naturally, it is a bit harder for people seeking less traditional jobs, e.g., non-law firm jobs. Still, GULC does have a separate career services office for public interest work, and the Equal Justice Foundation raises money for stipends for most students who want to do nonprofit work in the summers instead of working at firms.

Status: Current student, full-time
Dates of Enrollment: 9/2004-Submit Date
Survey Submitted: September 2004

I have a job for next summer, so I give the office of career services a 10. The OCS has a huge staff and plenty of resources. As a transfer student, having transferred from another Top 20 law school, I can definitely say that I see an absolutely marked difference between the phenomenal career services resources offered at Georgetown and the slightly anemic OCS resources available at my old school, which was ranked well academically, but which is not quite as established as Georgetown.

Georgetown has definitely allocated a good deal of money to career development, and makes things like the Vault Career Library accessible to law students for free with a password. This is a great advantage (and money saver) to students researching employment options. Also, each student is assigned a particular career advisor. Unlike at many schools, Georgetown's OCS staff seems knowledgeable and are actually helpful when you ask for advice or information. Overall, as long as you have semi-decent grades coming from Georgetown, you're going to be making six-figures by graduation.

Status: Alumnus/a, part-time
Dates of Enrollment: 8/1997-5/2001
Survey Submitted: April 2004

If you want to work in a top-tier firm in Washington, D.C., or, to a lesser degree, New York City in the areas of white collar litigation, corporate transactions, or international or regulatory law (particularly antitrust), Georgetown is the place for you. In spite of talking the "public service" talk, 75 percent of the people who graduate from here work in big firms. They have to in order to pay off their debts. To mitigate this fact, Georgetown does have one of most generous programs in the country for debt repayment for those going into public service. It's a lot of money, but not enough to help more than a small fraction of the graduating class.

The school has one of the best clinic programs in the country, which allows students to develop their practical lawyering skills. Their Supreme Court clinic, for example, conducts moot court boards for actual litigants preparing to appear before the U.S. Supreme Court. That's a real resume booster.

Quality of Life

Status: Current student, full-time
Dates of Enrollment: 8/2005-Submit Date
Survey Submitted: May 2006

My father attended Georgetown and graduated in 1969. I took him around the campus recently, and he was amazed at the changes. In the past year, the school has opened a state-of-the-art fitness center and an international law library filled with the latest technology for research. Georgetown is located within blocks of the Capitol, and there is no other law school in the country where you can walk out of Constitutional Law and see the United States Capitol. Georgetown is located almost within the shadow of the Supreme Court, and, in my opinion, there is no better place to learn the law.

Status: Current student, part-time
Dates of Enrollment: 8/2005-Submit Date
Survey Submitted: April 2006

Housing on campus is available to all first-year students. It is a good idea for a part-timer to live there because it makes you part of the day student community.

Status: Current student, part-time
Dates of Enrollment: 8/2005-Submit Date
Survey Submitted: April 2006

GULC is separate from the main campus but we have a dorm right on campus. There is a new sports and fitness facility that offers free exercise classes M-F. You can find an informative program, lunch talk or reception on campus at least three days per week and we have the weekly Keg on the Quad every Wednesday with free snacks and beer. The campus is located between two Metro stations (Union Station and Judiciary Square) and is also walking distance to the U.S. Capital. Chinatown and MCI Center are walking distance from campus and the freeway runs alongside the backside of campus. While the area is not the safest it is typical of any neighborhood located in the heart of a major city.

Status: Current student, full-time
Dates of Enrollment: 8/2005-Submit Date
Survey Submitted: April 2006

Georgetown has a dorm right on campus that houses about one-half of the first-year class. For people who are new to D.C. it's a great option—it's really accommodating to a wide variety of lifestyles, from those right out of college to those who have been living on their own for years. They have several options with varying prices: a single with a bathroom and kitchen; two bedrooms with a shared bathroom and kitchen; and three bedrooms with a shared bathroom and kitchen; two bedrooms with a shared bathroom, kitchen and common room. There are also lounges and the beautiful new gym is right next door. In addition to the new gym, which has plenty of machines and extended hours, there's a new international library and cafe area. For an urban school where a majority of students do commute, Georgetown has an amazing campus which really contributes to a sense of community. The neighborhood is improving, with tons of luxury condos being built all around, but it's so close to Capitol Hill that it does still empty out a bit at night. There are some restaurants and bars nearby and it's easy to get to lively areas like Dupont Circle and Adams Morgan by Metro or cab.

Status: Current student, full-time JD/MPP
Dates of Enrollment: 8/2005-Submit Date
Survey Submitted: April 2006

GULC is fairly unique among law schools in that it is separate from the main Georgetown campus and has its own campus on Capitol Hill. But several recent expansions and improvements have made it a real campus,with two quad areas where, when the weather's nice, students can study or play frisbee, baseball, football, etc.

There is an apartment-style dorm on campus. Every student has his or her own room, and depending on the style of the apartment, you can have the apartment to yourself or share with one or two others (you share a bathroom, an extremely small kitchen, and some form of common living area). The living facilities can

be a bit cramped, and this year there were frequent problems with the water in the building. Still, it's extremely convenient for classes (the classroom building is right across the street and the library is a block away), and it is very nice to meet people and not have to worry about finding housing before you arrive.

The campus itself is very safe, but it is in the middle of an area that has historically not been good to be in alone after dark. However, you are on Capitol Hill, and there are police frequently in the area. Also, the area is undergoing some pretty big changes, and so the area is improving constantly. The general rule of thumb is just to remember you are in the heart of a major city, so you should be sensible when you are out walking around.

Status: Alumnus/a, full-time
Dates of Enrollment: 9/2004-5/2005
Survey Submitted: March 2006

All I have to say is "HOTUNG." Wow. Georgetown's new international law library/cafe/fitness extravaganza is incredible. Full basketball court, two racquetball courts, full weight/aerobic gym, whirlpools, and a lap pool make this a place to keep fit, socialize, and de-stress. I gained many friends on the racquetball court during my third year. Even the professors come by to play (Vladeck is an animal on the B-ball court).

Gewertz offers on-campus dorm housing, which is very convenient. The dorms are spacious and well-lit. The law library is huge, and the whole campus is wireless. I loved being three blocks from the U.S. Capitol and Supreme Court.

Quite honestly, the best part of attending Georgetown, is studying law in Washington, D.C. It is such a great place to watch the law unfold just across the street from your classroom. I constantly felt a sense of electricity through the campus due simply to all that was going on at any given moment. In short, I felt engaged.

Status: Current student, full-time
Dates of Enrollment: 9/2003-Submit Date
Survey Submitted: April 2005

The neighborhood is like any other urban environment. There are some sketchy areas near the campus, but they can be easily avoided by walking an extra block here and there. At night, the school offers a shuttle service to the D.C. Metro, so it's actually pretty easy to get about safely. The campus facilities are very secure with controlled access points at every exterior door. Security guards are posted at all the main entrances. The facilities are outstanding; Georgetown recently finished constructing a state-of-the-art fitness center. Dining options on campus are acceptable and reasonably priced. Union Station is a five-minute walk from campus if students would like more varied meal choices.

Social Life

Status: Current student, part-time
Dates of Enrollment: 8/2005-Submit Date
Survey Submitted: April 2006

GULC has a host of student-run organizations. My favorites are the Black Law Students Association and the Equal Justice Foundation (EJF). This year our EJF raised money to provide summer stipends for over 100 students who will be doing unpaid public interest work this summer. The campus is very collegial and the male female ratio is great!

The local pub is a campus favorite as is the bar located at the National Association of Realtors Building. One of our campus restaurants also serves beer and wine after 5 p.m. Union Station and Chinatown provide a host of restaurants as does all of D.C. The nightlife in D.C. is great and not only will you have a great time but you will meet young professionals from every culture who are either working on the Hill, attending law or graduate schools or working for the government. There is a party every night of the week in D.C. and students at GULC somehow find time to attend these events and also plan numerous Bar Review happy hours and social functions.

Read all of Vault's Law School Surveys at www.vault.com/lawschool — get complete surveys on top law schools, expert advice on applicaton essays, LSAT prep and more.

VAULT CAREER LIBRARY   153

Status: Current student, full-time
Dates of Enrollment: 8/2005-Submit Date
Survey Submitted: April 2006

Georgetown Law is across town from the main, undergraduate campus, and most students do not attend events on that campus, even though we do have full access. Georgetown is very much a city school, in that people are much more likely to go out to dinner or to a bar than to a party or school-sponsored weekend event. During the week there are an inordinate number of events sponsored by student groups, often with free food and alcohol. There's always too much to do on campus, too many interesting speakers, and too many friends to catch up with—but the atmosphere is much more academic or issue-focused than, for example, a large state school with football games and on-campus parties.

Status: Current student, full-time JD/MPP
Dates of Enrollment: 8/2005-Submit Date
Survey Submitted: April 2006

The law school campus is not in the heart of D.C.'s nightlife. However, the Metro system will get you pretty much wherever you need to go, and there are stops located just a few short blocks away. There are a few small bars in the area, including student favorites, Kelly's Irish Times and the Billy Goat. There are also shops like CVS and Starbucks moving closer to the school in the next few years.

The school is also only a 15-minute walk away from Chinatown. It has lost a lot of its Chinese stores, but there are still good restaurants, a movie theater, and chain stores (Bed, Bath and Beyond, Urban Outfitters, Colors of Benneton) right there.

The Student Bar Association organizes regular Bar Reviews—that is, nights when a D.C. bar offers drink specials for GULC students and guests. These are great chances to mix with your fellow students outside of class and unwind a bit from the tension of school. Students in the dorm have also been known to throw floor parties and social events to blow off steam, as well. GULC students work hard, but they really know how to party hard, too.

The school itself offers other opportunities for a social life. There are more student organizations than you can count, from the Black Law Students Association to Habitat for Humanity to the Georgetown Gilbert and Sullivan Society. These groups offer seminars, social events, community service opportunities and performances throughout the year. Several times during the year, there are other basketball, dodgeball or bowling tournaments available for participation. If there's not a student group you're interested in, there's always the option of creating one!

Finally, D.C. offers many many options for getting out. There are professional baseball, football, basketball, hockey and soccer teams that all offer fairly cheap tickets (or the Office of Student Affairs may have discounted group tickets). Many theaters in the area have student tickets for performances, and you can see everything from Shakespeare to the newest, hottest touring Broadway musical. The Smithsonian Museums offer free exhibits and events, including the zoo. In the spring is the Cherry Blossom Festival, complete with a parade and Japanese Street Fair. The National Opera has even simulcast a performance on the Mall, allowing thousands of people to watch for free. Of course, tourists get very plentiful in the spring and summer, but there are still a lot of different things to see and do in the city.

Status: Current student, full-time
Dates of Enrollment: 8/2004-Submit Date
Survey Submitted: March 2005

There are weekly Bar Reviews, lots of available people to date and people go out a lot. There are always events on campus. Irish Times, My Brother's Place (used to have $12 all-you-can-drink beer nights on the weekend, not sure if they still do). I found that it was tough to find time for a social life between homework and working. There are a lot of student groups (various religions, social causes, two legal fraternities, a singing group and a theater group, etc.) and a lot of journals, and of course there's a great deal of nightlife in the Baltimore-Washington area, as well as pro soccer, basketball, hockey, baseball, football. Also lots of museums and tourist attractions of all kinds, obviously. I'm not sure about student favs, but the cool places are all in Dupont Circle, Adams Morgan,

and downtown in Metro Center. There's a lot more to do in D.C. than there is time to do it.

It's important to note that the law campus isn't just separate from the main campus—it's really far away from it. The D.C. traffic is such that, because the Metro doesn't run under the Georgetown section of the city, it can easily take 45 minutes to an hour to get to the main campus from the law campus, so there's not a lot of hanging with undergrads going on.

 ## The School Says

Georgetown University Law Center is located in the heart of Washington, D.C., in the midst of the major legal institutions of the nation, including the Supreme Court, the U.S. Capitol and the Department of Justice. Georgetown nurtures the very highest standards of scholarly inquiry, intellectual rigor and ethical behavior, in a way that respects each student's individuality. The faculty encompasses an extraordinary range of professional and scholarly accomplishments in virtually every area of legal practice. The result is a dynamic intellectual community, in which students have an unprecedented range of academic opportunities both inside and outside the classroom.

Unlike many other law schools, Georgetown offers first-year students choices in their course of study. The first option, Curriculum "A," provides a thorough grounding in the foundations of subjects including civil procedure, constitutional law, criminal procedure, property and torts, while enabling students to select from a diverse menu of elective courses in the spring semester. Curriculum "B," covers the traditional subjects offered in Curriculum "A," but takes an interdisciplinary approach, placing emphasis on the public nature of law and sources of law in economics, philosophy and other social sciences.

Georgetown has recently introduced another exciting innovation to its first-year curriculum, Week One: Law in a Global Context. Drawing on Georgetown's unparalleled international law faculty, this new program engages all first-year students in an interdisciplinary study of cutting-edge transnational legal issues during the first week of the spring term. Addressing problems ranging from the extradition of criminals from foreign countries to global commerce in cyberspace, students participate in small-group discussions and lectures taught by full-time faculty and distinguished practitioners of international law from the D.C. legal community.

A pioneer in clinical legal education, Georgetown has developed a top-ranked program that now offers 13 clinical courses, including Appellate Litigation, Criminal and Juvenile Justice, Domestic Violence, Federal Legislation, International Women's Human Rights courses. Nearly 300 students participate in the clinic program each year, where they gain first-hand insight into the strategic and ethical dimensions of legal practice.

Not surprisingly, more Georgetown graduates go into public interest and government service each year than those of any other law school. Programs such as the Public Interest Law Scholars program and the Law Center's loan repayment assistance program (LRAP) provide financial and other support to students who demonstrate a commitment to spend most of their careers in public service.

Career counselors in the Office of Career Services are available throughout students' job search process. More than 800 employers from 115 cities in the U.S. and abroad come to the campus to interview Georgetown Law students each year. Upper-class students have the opportunity to interview with private sector employers through an intensive Early Interview Week.

Georgetown's long-term goal is to educate students to be superb lawyers who will promote justice and serve others in their legal practices and in their lives. That mission is fulfilled by offering students a welcoming, vibrant community, an accessible and talented faculty and an educational experience geared to the whole person.

Read all of Vault's Law School Surveys at www.vault.com/lawschool — get complete surveys on top law schools, expert advice on applicaton essays, LSAT prep and more.

VAULT CAREER LIBRARY 155

Howard University School of Law

Admissions Office
2900 Van Ness Street, NW
219 Holy Cross Hall
Washington, D.C. 20008
Admissions phone: (202) 806-8009
Admissions e-mail: admissions@law.howard.edu
Admissions URL:http://www.law.howard.edu/55

 Admissions

Status: Alumnus/a, full-time
Dates of Enrollment: 8/2002-5/2005
Survey Submitted: April 2006

The admissions criteria has gotten tougher in recent years. The application is not incredibly difficult, but the admissions committee is looking for top quality students in terms of undergraduate grades, LSAT scores and diversity. Though Howard is a historically black university, there is room for everyone, and the school takes creating a class of diverse students along the lines of race, ethnicity, nationality, geography, sex, sexual orientation and any other classification there is, very seriously. The goal is provide a quality legal education to all.

Status: Alumnus/a, full-time
Dates of Enrollment: 8/1997-5/2000
Survey Submitted: April 2006

Given the student is starting with the appropriate credentials (i.e.: LSAT score and undergrad GPA), the application process is easy if the student starts the process early. The later the student waits, the more hassle it will become. I found that doing everything earlier worked to my advantage because when other students were still waiting on decisions, I had my decision from Howard for a long time. I believe the application and essays are fairly standard. The trend I noticed in my law school classmates was that all were very active in undergrad. Thus, I believe the admissions office was placing a high value on extracurricular activities. I believe the school is extremely selective especially given increased applicants. I was not required to go through an interview process for admission.

Status: Alumnus/a, full-time
Dates of Enrollment: 8/2002-5/2005
Survey Submitted: March 2006

The office of admissions is extremely well run. The open house was helpful, and I recommend attending, if you can. Candidates should also schedule visits when possible; you get to meet current students, professors and staff (especially the library staff who are topnotch).

There are no interviews involved. With good LSATs, you might be in the running for a scholarship. Howard is good on making prompt admissions decisions.

Status: Current student, full-time
Dates of Enrollment: 7/2005-Submit Date
Survey Submitted: November 2005

I actually applied twice and was in close contact with admissions personnel. I applied the first time with average grades, an average LSAT score and solid letters of reference. My personal statement talked about diversity and the need of role models in my community. I had turned my application by late January. My first year I was put on a waitlist and later denied.

The second time I applied my application was completed by the middle of October. However, this time I had started a master's degree and was in the top 5 percent of my class. I had also put a lot more time and effort on making co-op/internship experiences on my resume stand out. I figured I was an average student, so I had to make my professional work experience stand out.

For anyone having trouble with a personal statement you can buy the *Princeton Review Guide to Law School Essays*. The key here is to write a different and memorable personal statement. Howard gets literally hundreds of personal statements with very general, "I should be a lawyer because—" essays. Write something more genuine, go out of your way to show the admissions council how you think, talk about your views on crucial issues or world events. Your essay has to stand out amongst hundreds, do something different.

I have taken a one-year deferment since my acceptance to save funds. If you are accepted turn your deposit information promptly. If you want to request a year off be prepared to pay the $500 deposit and a formal letter with your request. Request your letter of accepted deferment for your records.

If you are awarded any merit scholarships you will be told so upon your admission award. All other scholarships are only for students who have been in school for at least 30 days.

Admissions staff is very friendly and personable. They call you back promptly if you leave a voicemail and are more than happy to work with you and answer any questions you may have. If you ask for honest feedback on how to reapply, they will provide it for you.

Status: Alumnus/a, full-time
Dates of Enrollment: 8/2001-5/2004
Survey Submitted: May 2005

An interview is not required, but it doesn't hurt. Howard is looking for a well-rounded student just like any other law school. The good thing is that grades are more important than LAST scores, so if a person worked hard in in undergrad but didn't do so well on the LSAT, they still have a good chance of getting in.

Status: Alumnus/a, full-time
Dates of Enrollment: 8/1999-5/2002
Survey Submitted: April 2005

Usual admissions process for professional school. Emphasis on personal statement. Good idea to speak to the dean of admissions regularly if you are serious about getting in.

Status: Alumnus/a, full-time
Dates of Enrollment: 8/2000-5/2003
Survey Submitted: September 2004

I applied in January of 2003 and got my acceptance letter in March. However, there were a handful of people that didn't receive their letter until the summer time, yet applied earlier than I did. On the other hand, there are those that got a response even quicker than I did. There is no rhyme or reason to the way of the admissions process. However, now under a new dean, Howard's admissions process seems more efficient and selective. There was nothing arduous about completing the application. Moreover, there is nothing arduous about the process—at least not for me. Since Howard has a rolling admissions process, I suggest applying early because you may never know what may happen once they start your file.

Status: Alumnus/a, full-time
Dates of Enrollment: 9/2001-5/2003
Survey Submitted: June 2004

Application, plus application fee. You can find admissions information (and download application) at www.law.howard.edu. Howard Law is very competitive, receiving more than 1,500 applications each year, and enrolling approximately 150 in each fall class. The average LSAT is 152, the average GPA is at least a 3.0. Those with higher scores and GPAs are more likely to get in, though the school seeks a diverse student body (diverse in culture, life and academic experience). My advice would be to write a strong essay and highlight your personal enriching experiences.

The school says: "Currently we receive over 2,500 applications, our median (not average) LSAT for accepted students is a 154 and our median (not average) GPA is a 3.3 for accepted students. The rest is consistent with the law school's position on the matter."

Status: Alumnus/a, full-time
Dates of Enrollment: 8/1999-5/2002
Survey Submitted: April 2004

The admissions process was fairly simple. From what I remember, the application was straightforward, and they offered us the opportunity to visit the law school. In writing an essay, I indicated that I wanted an opportunity and that they would not be sorry if I was admitted. Once I was admitted, I was contacted by current students who were quite helpful in answering questions about school and places to live.

Status: Alumnus/a, full-time
Dates of Enrollment: 7/1991-5/1994
Survey Submitted: September 2003

The admissions process was surprisingly simple. The forms were easy to understand. There were two essays required: the typical "why do you want to go to law school?" and "why here?" This is a historically black university, and most people who apply want to go here; it is typically a first-choice school. They look for students who are well-rounded, have good grades and can offer something significant personally.

 ## Academics

Status: Alumnus/a, full-time
Dates of Enrollment: 8/2002-5/2005
Survey Submitted: April 2006

The academic program is rigorous. Many of the professors have been at the law school for a long time and believe in an "old school" manner of teaching and learning. Currently, exams are handwritten (as most, if not all, bar examinations are), and many professors use the Socratic Method. Popular classes and professors can be difficult to get, but it is doable. Grading style often depends on professor, but it is easy to get the skinny on that from older students.

Status: Alumnus/a, full-time
Dates of Enrollment: 8/1997-5/2000
Survey Submitted: April 2006

The academic nature of the program was respectable. There were classes for numerous areas of focus. For example, I was interested in litigation and took several classes which focused on that particular area. The class sizes were very small (after first year) and you get to know your professors very well. As with any school, there were several professors that I could have done without, however, the majority of the teachers were extremely qualified and more than willing to go the extra mile for you if asked.

I was always able to get the classes that I wanted. Sometimes you had to wait a semester but if you planned accordingly, you were able to get all of the classes you wanted. Grading, as with any law school, is always subjective. I did find that if I met with my professors before the exam, which they were all willing to do, I understood what they were looking for and fared much better on the exam. Grading was always fair, timely and confidential. The workload was manageable as long as the student worked all semester long. Waiting until the last minute was overwhelming but I was able to handle the law school workload, do well and still have fun.

Status: Alumnus/a, full-time
Dates of Enrollment: 8/2002-5/2005
Survey Submitted: March 2006

The 1L workload is brutal. Howard grades on a very steep curve. There are no easy grades, especially in the first year class. The first-year load is unevenly spread between the fall and spring semesters (nine credits in fall; 21 in spring!). Howard also will kick out under-performing students and place others on probation. I would say this is probably the most rigorous—if unnecessarily so—program there is in the country.

There are a few professors to avoid, but you don't get to choose as a 1L. You should try to take classes with Professors Dark, Gavil, Robinson and Taslitz; they are some of the most professional, smart, humane and prolific faculty at the HUSL.

Status: Alumnus/a, full-time
Dates of Enrollment: 8/2001-5/2004
Survey Submitted: May 2005

The program at Howard is rigorous, just as at any law school. The quality of the classes is generally very high. Some of the teachers are notorious for being harsh and others are easier. The Socratic Method is not used universally at Howard law, but some professor do employ it. Popular classes such as entertainment law or copyrights and trademarks, are not easy to get. If you don't register for the class within an hour or so after registration begins, you may not be able to get in.

Status: Alumnus/a, full-time
Dates of Enrollment: 8/2000-5/2003
Survey Submitted: September 2004

Well, the first year is taught in a very traditional Socratic Method. Not every professor teaches the same, but all of them, underlying their teaching style, practice that method. Some first-years like to study in the library. I did too, until I realized what a social haven it is. It's a beautiful library, but very distracting if you do not like to be surrounded by noise when you study. The workload is ample, but not impossible, except for one property professor whose name will not be mentioned. As long as the professor is organized, the class runs smoothly. If there is disorganization, just brace yourself and study on your own. As a 2L, I find the professors to be more relaxed with me and my classmates than in first year, which further proves their Socratic ways of first year. The classes are fine. I learn the law. As for getting into the classes, it's probably the most competitive time of the year. We have to register via Internet and it's a first come, first serve system with few classes to choose from and everyone desiring to take the same classes for the bar and their personal ambitions. It's a brief crazy period that only gets easier, when you have to deal with adding classes again at the beginning of the school semester because at the first go around, you didn't get the classes you need because they were filled at the time. Strange system, but at least the first week of classes aren't worth going to if you might switch out.

Howard is a social justice school with law firms constantly present on campus, so the interests in classes vary from IP, business classes, to social justice seminars to international law classes. Professor Rogers seems to be a favorite in the school, with his Corporations classes being the largest this semester.

Status: Alumnus/a, full-time
Dates of Enrollment: 9/2001-5/2003
Survey Submitted: June 2004

Classes at Howard Law are rigorous; the professors are tough and expect a lot from students. Workload in the first year is enormous, with students taking Legal Methods, Contracts I, Torts I, and Legal Reasoning, Research and Writing I (LRRW) in the fall; and LRRW II, Contracts II, Torts II, Property, Constitutional Law and Criminal Law in the spring. Contracts and LRRW are yearlong courses. Additional required courses to complete before graduation are: Constitutional Law II; Evidence; LRRW II (Appellate Advocacy); a Skills course; and a LRRW II (seminar paper) requirement.

All first-year classes are taught using the Socratic Method, with professors adhering to the method in varying degrees. It can be difficult to get more popular courses, but you may be surprised. A space may miraculously open up in Civil Rights Litigation or the Corporate and Commercial Lawyer as Social Engineer, or Advanced Intellectual Property. There is an amazing array of classes on a rotation, so you are likely to get into several interesting classes on a second try, if not the first. Clinic is also very popular, and students compete to get into the various clinics. Professors are generally very open with their time, and offer help through office hours and individual appointments. Some professors invite students to networking opportunities, locally and sometimes at their homes.

Read all of Vault's Law School Surveys at www.vault.com/lawschool — get complete surveys on top law schools, expert advice on applicaton essays, LSAT prep and more.

VAULT CAREER LIBRARY **157**

Status: Current student, full-time
Dates of Enrollment: 8/2003-Submit Date
Survey Submitted: October 2003

Classes are challenging and quite diverse. Students are friendly, and 2Ls and 3Ls are eager to help. Classes for 1Ls are predetermined, but I think this may be the trend at most law schools. Faculty is diverse, a good mix, [Asian, African American, Latino, European male and female].

Status: Alumnus/a, full-time
Dates of Enrollment: 8/1999-5/2002
Survey Submitted: April 2004

The academics are quite rigorous the first year. There was a lot to learn, and you were expected to be in class every day and know the subject of the day. The professors were easy to approach and were willing to spend time answering questions. I'd put my professors up against most of the law school in the country. During my summer internships, I quickly found that those students from premier law schools had not learned any more that I had at Howard. Getting the popular professor is fairly hard, but I eventually got the class I wanted and, 90 percent of the time, the professor I wanted. Depending on the professor, the workload for a class could vary from quite manageable to quite time consuming. Grading is fairly standard as that of any law school, although our grading scale is lower than at most law schools.

> **The school says:** "The law school uses grade normalization with a B curve."

Status: Alumnus/a, full-time
Dates of Enrollment: 7/1991-5/1994
Survey Submitted: September 2003

The quality of classes was excellent. I truly enjoyed my experience at HUSL and would recommend it to those who are interested in attending an academically challenging program in a friendly environment. I rarely encountered problems getting the classes of my choice. The grading process was slanted, working on a C curve when every other law school worked on a B curve. However, my understanding is that this has been corrected. The professors are engaging and intelligent. Most professors seem to express genuine interest in the well-being and success of the student body.

Workload: it's law school, what can you expect? Yes, the workload is heavy, but that is what it is.

 # Employment Prospects

Status: Alumnus/a, full-time
Dates of Enrollment: 8/2002-5/2005
Survey Submitted: April 2006

The Top 100 law firms recruit at Howard. Also, there are a ton of public interest and commercial opportunities for graduates. A new Center for Public Interest was created, and the firm takes providing a range of employment opportunities seriously. Many graduates go on to work in law firms, but some start their own practice. The alumni network is very strong. Because Howard is a smaller school, bonds are inevitably built and those who attend have a strong sense of responsibility to the school and helping younger graduates. Judicial internships and summer associateships at various law firms, public interest fellowships, and government positions are readily available during the academic year as well as during the summers.

Status: Alumnus/a, full-time
Dates of Enrollment: 8/1997-5/2000
Survey Submitted: April 2006

On-campus recruiting is great because most of the private employers are targeting minority candidates by coming to Howard. The drawback, however, is that the top firms are looking for the top four or five students, not top 5 or 10 percent. Thus, there are limited opportunities for those looking to go with the top law firms. Most students though are working for either small to medium law firms or in the public sector in between both their first and second, and second and third years. If I had to pinpoint a type of job graduates obtain, I would say

in the government. At the time that I was a student, there was not a strong alumni network. Our director of career services is GREAT!

Status: Alumnus/a, full-time
Dates of Enrollment: 8/2002-5/2005
Survey Submitted: March 2006

To stand a chance with the so-called top employers (read NYC behemoths), you need to place in the top quarter of your class, and preferably in the top 10 or 15 percent. Journal membership GREATLY accentuates your chances; but journal membership is also predicated on grades, so it all comes down to getting good grades your first year.

More than 200 employers participate in the fall OCI, a large number of which are prominent law firms in the major legal markets.

Status: Alumnus/a, full-time
Dates of Enrollment: 8/2001-5/2004
Survey Submitted: May 2005

Any legal employer that recruits at top-ranked schools generally recruits at Howard, as well. Although *U.S. News & World Reports* doesn't give the school the highest ranking, the reputation of the school with those who know speaks for itself. Howard graduates work for many top firms such as Sullivan & Cromwell, Covington & Burling and Paul Weis, just to name a few. Other graduates take government jobs as prosecutors or defense attorneys. Howard is renowned for the training it gives it students in trial work, which is evident from the constant first, second and other top placements in trial advocacy and moot court competitions. There are a very wide spectrum of jobs for the students readily available.

The alumni network is very helpful. There is an e-mail list that sends numerous job openings for alumni on a weekly basis. Many offers and opportunities are sent out to all interested alumni.

In addition, the on-campus recruiting environment is excellent. During interview season, dozens of legal employers come to Howard. A person can interview as often as they want, depending on how ambitious that person is. Of course, the better the grades one has, the more opportunities one has to interview.

Status: Alumnus/a, full-time
Dates of Enrollment: 9/2001-5/2003
Survey Submitted: June 2004

The career services office is absolutely the best feature at Howard Law. It is run smoothly, and with great concern for students' futures. Over 100 law firms (including the top firms in the country and world) participate in OCI, as well as numerous public interest career opportunities. The career services office offers several trainings, beginning in the late fall of the first year. Placement for the top 25 percent of the class is very high. Employers come to Howard expecting well-trained lawyers and respect the university's tradition. Students are urged to consider all opportunities, firms, clerkships, public interest jobs with the government, military, etc.

OCI is pretty intense in the fall, starting in August and ending in late November. OCI continues in the spring, where first-years get their first opportunity to interview with employers hiring first-years. Top first-year students are often placed in paying, summer positions.

Status: Alumnus/a, full-time
Dates of Enrollment: 8/1999-5/2002
Survey Submitted: April 2004

Howard does quite well in attracting top firms and clerkships. The office of career services is very helpful in providing information and advice in determining which internship to choose. Given Howard's location, many firms from New York, D.C., Chicago and Atlanta recruit from Howard. The prestige of the school will vary depending on the location of the organization, but it is very highly regarded by any organization in the Mid-Atlantic and Northeastern regions. Prestige is growing in the Midwest and West.

> **Regarding alumni, Howard Law says:** "Howard University School of Law's alumni are respected nationwide. We only produce 150 attorneys a year that return or move to various locations. There is a strong network of HU Law alum in every major market in this country."

Quality of Life

Status: Alumnus/a, full-time
Dates of Enrollment: 8/2002-5/2005
Survey Submitted: April 2006

There is no campus housing. There is housing which can be provided to graduate students on the main campus (the law school is located about 15 minutes from the main campus), but most students find housing elsewhere. The school is working diligently to upgrade its facilities and technology. There are areas which need improvement, but it does not impede a student's ability to learn. The school recently constructed a new library, which is fantastic. Law students from area schools often come to Howard to use it. The neighborhood in which the law school is located is wonderful. There are restaurants and stores within walking distance on one side and on the other is a residential community. The Metro system has a subway stop two blocks away and buses regularly run on the main street at the end of the block.

Status: Alumnus/a, full-time
Dates of Enrollment: 8/1997-5/2000
Survey Submitted: April 2006

Housing is nonexistent. There are apartments very close to the school but the majority of students do not live in them. Many students live in Maryland or Virginia while some live on Connecticut Avenue. The campus is small and very manageable. The law school is in Northwest D.C. while the main campus is in Northeast. This is a huge advantage because law students are not interrupted in any way by the undergrad activities. Facilities could be better but they work. Dining is not that great. I would expect to lose weight because the dining hall food is pretty bad and there are not that many nearby restaurants. Crime and safety is as good as you are going to get in D.C. given the fact that the school is in Northwest D.C.

Status: Current student, full-time
Dates of Enrollment: 7/2005-Submit Date
Survey Submitted: November 2005

One of the things that amazes me about Howard is how much people stereotype the school. I am not African American but many people assume that I would feel uncomfortable because the majority of the student body is. In my interaction I think people accept me for who I am and judge me by my effort to do well in the program, not any other factor.

Status: Alumnus/a, full-time
Dates of Enrollment: 8/2001-5/2004
Survey Submitted: May 2005

The quality of life at Howard is what you make of it. D.C. is a city with a lot of things to do and a lot of different types of neighborhoods. In terms of housing, the law school is located in one of the more expensive parts of the city. One should expect to pay around $1,500 a month or so to live close to the law school. There is graduate housing available at the undergrad campus as well, and it costs about $1,000. However, there are other parts of the city that cost a lot less. The problem is that some of those areas aren't considered to be the safest areas. Crime is a problem in D.C., so if one is really concerned about that, staying in a posh area is probably your best bet. That will hurt your pockets a bit though. But if you are use to inner cities, you can find a place for a for around $700 dollars. Of course, if you don't mind having a roommate, even in the expensive parts of town you can cut your costs in half.

Status: Current student, full-time
Dates of Enrollment: 8/2003-Submit Date
Survey Submitted: September 2004

The law school has no housing, so many students live in graduate apartment on the main campus, 15 minutes away from the law school. Some pay a pricey amount of rent to live next door to the school at the Consulate or one of the Van Ness Apartments. Some live along Connecticut Avenue. Everyone else is scattered in the D.C., Maryland and Virginia regions. There is little crime in the community and few places to eat, and the community around the school isn't problematic.

Status: Current student, full-time
Dates of Enrollment: 8/2003-Submit Date
Survey Submitted: October 2003

The law school cafeteria is just so-so, but is open late. There are a lot of weekly programs and receptions, and almost all have food. Living in D.C. is expensive; be prepared. The law school is away from main campus, and that is a plus. Free shuttle service is provided between law school and the main campus. Not enough on-campus parking: a lottery system for 2Ls and 3Ls only, street parking for 1Ls.

Status: Alumnus/a, full-time
Dates of Enrollment: 9/2001-5/2003
Survey Submitted: June 2004

Life is difficult, as in any law school, I presume. However, there is a wonderful community there. There is no housing on campus, particularly because the law school is not on Howard's main campus. Rather it is in great neighborhood (100 feet away from Connecticut Avenue) and on the Red Line (Van Ness stop). The school is a block away from Rock Creek Park. The new library is great to look at and study in. It is steadily building its circulation. There is 24-hour security, and a shuttle to main campus. There is a cafeteria, which is probably better than most cafeteria food, though the selection can get monotonous and seems pricey for a law student budget. The campus is easy to get to, and you can find a range of living arrangements in D.C., Virginia or Maryland. Parking is available on campus for third-year and second-year students (who participate in a lottery and pay a yearly fee). First-year students do not participate in the lottery and thus have no parking, unless special circumstances require it (e.g., disability status).

Status: Alumnus/a, full-time
Dates of Enrollment: 8/1999-5/2002
Survey Submitted: April 2004

The law school is not located on the main campus but rather in a popular part of D.C. Many embassies are located near the school. There are graduate dorms on the main campus, and a new apartment community is being built for students near the main campus, which is 10 minutes away. Many of the law students live in Silver Spring, which is about 15 minutes from the school. The facilities are improving; there is now a premier library, arguably the best of the law school libraries in D.C. Many of the classrooms have be renovated.

Status: Alumnus/a, full-time
Dates of Enrollment: 7/1991-5/1994
Survey Submitted: September 2003

The law school is located in scenic Washington, D.C, in the upper northwest area. This a safe and beautiful location. The campus itself is located on a hilltop with great views and close to Rock Creek park. Housing can be a problem, as Northwest D.C. is a high-rent area. However, feel free to live anywhere in the D.C. Metro area near a metro. There is a Metro (subway) stop one block from the campus. I commuted in from Virginia all three years and never felt it to be burdensome. HUSL is in a beautiful old building that really feels like "law school."

 # Social Life

Status: Alumnus/a, full-time
Dates of Enrollment: 8/2002-5/2005
Survey Submitted: April 2006

There is no official Greek system at the law school, however, there is a legal fraternity and legal sorority. Students regularly get together to go to bars and restaurants. There is definitely time to socialize. Various clubs often plan events for students to attend like date auctions, parties and speaker series. Many students date one another, and marriages have been known to result!

Read all of Vault's Law School Surveys at www.vault.com/lawschool — get complete surveys on top law schools, expert advice on applicaton essays, LSAT prep and more.

VAULT CAREER LIBRARY 159

Status: Alumnus/a, full-time
Dates of Enrollment: 8/1997-5/2000
Survey Submitted: April 2006

Social life is good. There are always parties, clubs, etc. to go to. Restaurants are plentiful in D.C. just not very close to the school. But since most students do not live by the school, it doesn't really affect the social life. The dating scene is heavy. Many students date each other. Specific student favorites change every year based on the bar scene in D.C. There is always a hot club though.

Status: Alumnus/a, full-time
Dates of Enrollment: 8/2001-5/2004
Survey Submitted: May 2005

The social life at Howard is definitely alive. If you are interested in studying often, which you should be interested in since you are in law school, you can, of course, busy yourself with that. But if partying is what you want, partying is what you will get. There are tons of bars in the D.C. area for all who are interested. And the Adams Morgan neighborhood is very active and it is filled with everything you want in terms of clubs and entertainment. In downtown D.C., there are many clubs to fit every taste.

Status: Current student, full-time
Dates of Enrollment: 8/2003-Submit Date
Survey Submitted: September 2004

The nightlife in D.C. is EXCELLENT. No matter where you are in D.C., albeit a bar or nightclub, you'll have a good time, especially if you like to dance. Dress to impress is the nightlife code of conduct.

Status: Alumnus/a, full-time
Dates of Enrollment: 9/2001-5/2003
Survey Submitted: June 2004

D.C. is a thriving city, with tons of things to do. I guess you could get involved in the social life on campus, but as a married student, I hardly ever participated in the numerous parties and events. There is some representation of Greek life. Passport, a small bar at the corner, is very popular.

Status: Alumnus/a, full-time
Dates of Enrollment: 8/1999-5/2002
Survey Submitted: April 2004

The social life at Howard is one of the best aspects of the law school in that there is a sense of family among the students and faculty. I can say that I personally knew most of the students in my class and a lot from the other classes. There are many hangout spots for students like Dream and spots in Adams Morgan. There are many clubs and Greek organizations.

Status: Alumnus/a, full-time
Dates of Enrollment: 7/1991-5/1994
Survey Submitted: September 2003

HUSL has many social organizations for students to take part in. The city (Washington, D.C.), itself provides many opportunities for those who want them. You really cannot say there is nothing to do, unless that is your choice.

Florida International University College of Law

Florida International University
College of Law
Office of Admissions, GL 475
Miami, FL 33199
Admissions phone: (305) 348-8006
Admissions fax: (305) 348-2965
Admissions e-mail: lawadmit@fiu.edu
Admissions URL: http://law.fiu.edu/admissions/index.htm

Note: The school has chosen not to comment on the student surveys submitted.

Admissions

Status: Current student, full-time
Dates of Enrollment: 9/2003-Submit Date
Survey Submitted: April 2006

Everything went smoothly. Admission was based on LSAT scores, GPA, writing samples and a personal statement. Much attention was given to individual traits in the selection for the 2003 entering class. A total of approximately 150 students were selected from 1,100. At the time, the College of Law was awaiting provisional accreditation, which it received in 2004. It is my understanding that the number of applicants has increased. Each entering class, since the College of Law's inception in 2002, has had higher scores than its preceding class. My acceptance letter contained an informal but gracious personal note on a post-it, saying that they would be honored to have me attend.

Status: Alumnus/a, part-time
Dates of Enrollment: 8/2002-12/2005
Survey Submitted: April 2006

FIU requires good grades and SAT scores to matriculate to the law school. Demand for public law school seats is strong in the Miami area.

Status: Current student, full-time
Dates of Enrollment: 8/2004-Submit Date
Survey Submitted: April 2006

You must provide three references. Know ALL of your employers from the last 10 years, including dates of employment, addresses, phone numbers, duties and why you left. Must write a letter explaining why you want to go to law school. Application is relatively simple as long as you have gathered your employment history. It helps to have a resume handy. Must send transcripts from all undergraduate or transfer institutions. Apply as early as possible (some schools only accept for fall so find out when you can apply for the semester you want to start).

Status: Current student, full-time
Dates of Enrollment: 8/2004-Submit Date
Survey Submitted: April 2006

I used the Internet site to obtain the application. I found it user-friendly and helpful. I had no difficulty understanding what I needed to submit for consideration to be admitted.

I followed up by phone. The admissions staff in the law office were both friendly and helpful and invited me to a campus tour. So I set up an appointment, had a private meeting with the admissions personnel and was given a tour of the campus portion relevant to the College of Law.

Status: Current student, full-time
Dates of Enrollment: 8/2003-Submit Date
Survey Submitted: April 2006

I have attended this university for my undergraduate, graduate and currently my JD program (law). The best advice regarding the admissions process deals with organization, timeliness and follow-up. Be certain to make yourself aware of any deadlines and required documents. Follow-up letters and phone calls to the various departments are also of the essence.

Status: Current student, full-time
Dates of Enrollment: 8/2003-Submit Date
Survey Submitted: April 2006

For FIU's law school, you'll need a good LSAT and strong GPA; the school is fast becoming the hottest law program in Florida and competition is tough. Your best bet is to aim for over 155 on the LSAT and well-above 3.0 undergraduate GPA.

Academics

Status: Current student, full-time
Dates of Enrollment: 9/2003-Submit Date
Survey Submitted: April 2006

The faculty is outstanding. Their academic credentials could not be any more impressive. The workload is appropriate for law school, perhaps even more rigorous as we are a new law school and everyone is eager, motivated and in pursuit of excellence. Grading method uses the bell curve, which is standard.

Status: Alumnus/a, part-time
Dates of Enrollment: 8/2002-12/2005
Survey Submitted: April 2006

Classes are demanding and attendance is counted toward grades. The workload is substantial.

Status: Current student, full-time
Dates of Enrollment: 8/2004-Submit Date
Survey Submitted: April 2006

Not very many criminal law classes. Very business and international law oriented. Great for those interested in business law, tax law, corporate law, immigration law and international law. Most professors are great, a few not so great. You will most likely get every class you choose. Grading is tough but on a curve. Sometimes the curve works to your benefit and sometimes not. Workload is reasonable but I suggest you don't work while in school and don't take more than 15 credits. That is even pushing it.

Status: Current student, full-time
Dates of Enrollment: 8/2004-Submit Date
Survey Submitted: April 2006

The professors are extremely well-versed in what they teach. The availability for help with questions and problems is well above average in my estimation. The class selection is excellent, given the size of the student body in this fairly new College of Law. The workload is demanding; but then again, it's law school, so a heavy workload is to be expected. I find the quality of the education I have received there so far to be exceptional in comparison to, for example, my social graduate degree from another Miami university.

Read all of Vault's Law School Surveys at www.vault.com/lawschool — get complete surveys on top law schools, expert advice on applicaton essays, LSAT prep and more.

VAULT CAREER LIBRARY **161**

Status: Current student, full-time
Dates of Enrollment: 8/2003-Submit Date
Survey Submitted: April 2006

The school has an illustrious group of law professors, including Harvard graduates, law textbook authors and even a Supreme Court justice's old law clerk. The courses are intense and intellectually challenging. It's easy to get classes, but it's slim pickings when it comes to variety.

 ## Employment Prospects

Status: Current student, full-time
Dates of Enrollment: 9/2003-Submit Date
Survey Submitted: April 2006

Although I am not personally familiar with these processes, there are numerous e-mails circulating and flyers constantly announcing seminars, fairs, employment opportunities, internship opportunities, etc. We have an office and administrator dedicated to career seeking. I have heard through the grape vine that FIU College of Law graduates are in demand as word and evidence of the program's caliber has circulated.

Status: Alumnus/a, part-time
Dates of Enrollment: 8/2002-12/2005
Survey Submitted: April 2006

The law market is weak, but FIU has a good reputation. You will need to find your own opportunities.

Status: Current student, full-time
Dates of Enrollment: 8/2004-Submit Date
Survey Submitted: April 2006

Great in Miami. Many employers in Miami give preference to FIU Law graduates. Career office is very helpful. On-campus interviewing available and internships are plentiful.

Status: Current student, full-time
Dates of Enrollment: 8/2004-Submit Date
Survey Submitted: April 2006

My experience is limited to the summer opportunities that I have sought as a law student. However, I applied at one place for a judicial clerkship, and was granted the summer position. Most of the contacts the College of Law has are in Miami, with a few exceptions. This is seconded by Broward. From Palm Beach County farther north, and in other areas the opportunities advertised are fairly poor.

However, this is a new College of Law (only in its fourth year). Hopefully, as the university grows, the dean of career placement will place more aggressive marketing efforts for students outside the Miami area.

Status: Current student, full-time
Dates of Enrollment: 8/2003-Submit Date
Survey Submitted: April 2006

FIU law school maintains a career office to help students find part-time work while in school, and permanent careers when they graduate. FIU grads are employed in nearly every sector of law, including government, community service and private law firms.

Status: Current student, full-time
Dates of Enrollment: 8/2003-Submit Date
Survey Submitted: April 2006

The career services department is extremely knowledgeable and eager to help.

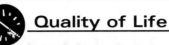 ## Quality of Life

Status: Current student, full-time
Dates of Enrollment: 9/2003-Submit Date
Survey Submitted: April 2006

As a commuter student, FIU is easily accessible from the FL turnpike and other major roads in the city of Miami. The campus is well lit and there are many restaurants in the neighborhood and on campus as well. I have not had any experience of crime in three years, nor have I heard any reports of such from classmates. Of course, Miami is a large city and one must always be cautious.

Status: Alumnus/a, part-time
Dates of Enrollment: 8/2002-12/2005
Survey Submitted: April 2006

FIU is an excellent facility and the law school is opening its own building this year.

Status: Current student, full-time
Dates of Enrollment: 8/2004-Submit Date
Survey Submitted: April 2006

Excellent! Brand new law building. Very safe.

Status: Current student, full-time
Dates of Enrollment: 8/2003-Submit Date
Survey Submitted: April 2006

The campus is constantly growing and offering more services to the students. Housing and campus facilities are excellent.

Status: Current student, full-time
Dates of Enrollment: 8/2003-Submit Date
Survey Submitted: April 2006

Most students do not live on campus, preferring to rent suitable quarters in the neighborhood. FIU Law facilities are adequate right now, but a brand new College of Law building is opening in fall 2006 and can only be described as enormous. Law students get plenty of opportunities to interact with other law students and lawyers in the Miami area.

 ## Social Life

Status: Current student, full-time
Dates of Enrollment: 9/2003-Submit Date
Survey Submitted: April 2006

Although I do not participate because I am an older student and live 80 miles away, there is a festive atmosphere on campus and there are always announcements of all kinds of events going on, on and off campus. Miami is a diverse city that never sleeps and there is a lot of spirit.

Status: Alumnus/a, part-time
Dates of Enrollment: 8/2002-12/2005
Survey Submitted: April 2006

Great social life if you can make the time to enjoy it.

Status: Current student, full-time
Dates of Enrollment: 8/2004-Submit Date
Survey Submitted: April 2006

Fantastic! Camaraderie is great. Very social and friendly. Lots of bars nearby campus. New Wave is a favorite.

Status: Current student, full-time
Dates of Enrollment: 8/2004-Submit Date
Survey Submitted: April 2006

Although I am not involved, the Greek life appears well and alive on campus. There are a lot of things to do right on campus, including an eating and drinking establishment that serves beer and wine (Gracie's). There is a cafeteria and a food court. I have not stayed in the housing, so cannot comment on it. The campus is just a little ways from downtown Miami (maybe 30 to 45 minutes) and the beach.

Status: Current student, full-time
Dates of Enrollment: 8/2003-Submit Date
Survey Submitted: April 2006

The Greek system is constantly growing. The school is located in Miami, which is a mecca for nightlife.

Status: Current student, full-time
Dates of Enrollment: 8/2003-Submit Date
Survey Submitted: April 2006

FIU has a varied and complex social life. There is an underlying Latin beat, as the school is located in the heart of Cuban Miami. The Latin American Restaurant, about a block from the campus, is a school favorite and Salsa and Merengue dancing at local clubs is enjoyed by most. The Greek system is well-developed and party-oriented as well. Look for an extensive on- and off-campus social life.

Read all of Vault's Law School Surveys at www.vault.com/lawschool — get complete surveys on top law schools, expert advice on applicaton essays, LSAT prep and more.

V/\ULT CAREER LIBRARY 163

Florida State University College of Law

Admissions Office
425 W. Jefferson Street
Tallahassee, FL 32306-1601
Admissions phone: (850) 644-3787
Admissions e-mail: admissions@law.fsu.edu
Admissions URL:
http://www.law.fsu.edu/prospective_students/admissions/

 Admissions

Status: Current student, full-time
Dates of Enrollment: 8/2002-Submit Date
Survey Submitted: April 2005

The admissions process at FSU is very unique in that the admissions office makes it a point to single out every prospective student and make their application process go smoothly. From the minute they receive the student's application they have not only someone from the admissions office contact the prospective student, but also a faculty member and current student. Also, the admissions office puts on several days throughout the year (Admitted Students Day, Scholar's Day) to assist the prospective students in making their choice to come to FSU.

Over the past several years that I have been at FSU, it has gotten considerably more competitive and we have jumped 11 spots in the national rankings and are in the Top 75 law schools in the nation. The best advice to give a prospective student is work hard to get a high GPA and study hard to get a high score on the LSAT. Our average GPA right now is about a 3.4 and LSAT is 159.

> **The school says:** FSU College of Law is currently ranked 53 in the Top 75 law schools in the nation, up 14 ranks in the last two years.

Status: Current student, full-time
Dates of Enrollment: 8/2003-Submit Date
Survey Submitted: April 2005

I was really thrilled with FSU's admissions office. They made me feel extremely welcome. I was working full-time, so I had to try to squeeze in campus visits. I was on my way home for Easter and e-mailed the week before to see if someone could show me around. Even though classes had already ended for the semester, they found someone willing to give me a tour. In addition, when I got accepted, they called me and told me, as well as e-mailed me before the letter got there. It's the small details like that that make you feel like you are coming to a school that tries hard to make the tough experience of law school better.

Status: Current student, full-time
Dates of Enrollment: 8/2003-Submit Date
Survey Submitted: October 2004

The admissions process is pretty typical for a law school. There is a standard application form and an essay requirement. The law school prefers that students submit their applications online, but it will not adversely affect you to apply using the standard paper form. Good grades and LSAT scores are the best way to get in. [The admissions committee looks at every application.] They also give considerable weight to work done after graduation and graduate education.

Florida State's administration is working very hard to improve the law school's reputation as a "national" law school, so it helps to come from an out-of-state college and/or be an out-of-state resident. In the alternative, it helps to make sure that your resume and personal statement reflect a unique aspect of your personality or background.

There is no interview, but the admissions office highly recommends its tours of the school. Prospective students may sit in on first-year classes, also. You may also set up an appointment with an admissions officer during your visit.

Status: Current student, full-time
Dates of Enrollment: 8/2003-Submit Date
Survey Submitted: October 2003

Admissions are based primarily on a combination of LSAT and GPA. Heavy focus on LSAT in recent years, as the school is pushing to improve the profile of its student body.

Status: Current student, full-time
Dates of Enrollment: 1/2002-Submit Date
Survey Submitted: May 2004

Almost completely based on your LSAT and GPA.

> **Regarding admissions, Florida State College of Law says:** "The College of Law receives over 3,300 applications for approximately 225 places in its entering class. This year's median LSAT score is 159 and the median GPA is 3.49. The current student body represents 34 states, 12 countries and 209 schools.
>
> "Admission to the College of Law is a competitive process and applications with the strongest record are given priority. The majority of admissions decisions are made primarily on the basis of combining LSAT scores with undergraduate grades. In addition, the personal statement, writing sample, recommendation letters and strength of undergraduate program are reviewed for all applicants. The admissions committee reviews all applications, and takes into consideration a number of other factors, including an applicant's graduate study, significant activities of leadership, unique work or service experience, history of overcoming economic or other social hardships, and contribution to a diverse academic environment in terms of life experiences."

 Academics

Status: Current student, full-time
Dates of Enrollment: 8/2002-Submit Date
Survey Submitted: April 2005

The program is great at FSU. All of the faculty at FSU have an open-door policy and it is easy to speak with them to get feedback or advice. The workload is what you make of it. What I tell every prospective student or new student is that from the first day of law school, you have one choice to make: what kind of student do you want to be? For example, if you want to be in the top 10 percent of your class then OK, but you're going to have to work hard and put in your hours. If you're not concerned about class rank and want to maintain a healthy social life then that's fine too, but it will make things a little bit more difficult when you are trying to get your first job.

People have different study habits and it's all about finding what suits you best. At law school, it's not like you have various projects throughout the semesters—instead, your grade for each class is determined on a single cumulative final exam at the end of each semester and possibly a midterm. Because of this, you probably won't know what study habits are best for you until after the first semester's grades are out or even the first year is finished. Some people study better with groups and others as individuals; it's all about finding what works best for you.

Status: Current student, full-time
Dates of Enrollment: 8/2003-Submit Date
Survey Submitted: April 2005

The 1L year is a bear everywhere, but FSU has great professors to ease your way in. The legal writing program is especially good, and many people still go to their legal writing professor for any questions they may have. It seems like you can always get into classes you want if you keep checking back with registration. There are some amazing and incredible professors here, as well as some who should probably stick to research. Upperclassmen are very helpful in course selection, and will steer you in the right direction. In addition, there is a great camaraderie like nothing else I have heard of in other law schools with sharing outlines from previous years, discussing study strategies, etc. People seem to really be willing to help each other out, especially the 2L and 3Ls you are not competing for grades with. We have an incredible study abroad program in Oxford that should not be missed. It's a wonderful chance to see England, take classes and get to know people better. (Of course, you are allowed to go on any ABA approved study abroad, but I am partial to Oxford. It was the best experience!)

Status: Current student, full-time
Dates of Enrollment: 8/2003-Submit Date
Survey Submitted: October 2004

FSU takes a "liberal arts" approach to legal education. The professors tend to approach subjects using general, national trends rather than Florida-specific ones. Most of the professors are involved in legal research that gets national recognition and several professors are members of prestigious national groups, such as the ALI. Overall, quality of classes is high. Teachers are very accessible for out-of-class questions, and there are plenty of courses in popular areas such as environmental, international and business law. There are certificate programs in international and environmental law. The environmental law program has perhaps the best national reputation.

There are several popular classes, and only one of them is what I'd term difficult to get into. That's evidence with Professor Ehrhardt, which can get up to 200 applications for a 100-seat class. However, the other evidence teachers are also popular and well-qualified. It is possible that you might not get into a class the first time you register, but people often drop during the first week, freeing up space for others. The law school has a lottery system for limited enrollment classes, and students get more "weight" in their lottery choices with each semester of attendance.

Grading is tough. There is a strict curve, allowing no more than 15 percent of the class to get an A. However, no more than 15 percent of the class can get a D or an F, too. Grades are given on a scale of 61 to 100. Most teachers do not give 100s. It is very hard to flunk out, though.

As I said before, professors tend to be well-regarded in their respective fields and fairly accessible. There are one or two "bad eggs," but it's easy to find out about them through word of mouth. The administration is also very sympathetic to students having difficulties with their personal lives and/or with professors; they can and do act as advocates for students. It's nice to know that you can get help from a dean when a professor is acting out of line or teaching poorly. There have been several new hires in the business law subjects, and so far they are getting good reviews from students.

The school says: "All grades at the College of Law are subject to grade normalization rules, which can be found on the College of Law's web site at www.law.fsu.edu."

Status: Current student, full-time
Dates of Enrollment: 8/2003-Submit Date
Survey Submitted: October 2003

Very smart, accessible professors. All but a handful are very good teachers. They put a real focus on scholarship, but it doesn't come at the cost of their classes. The curricular strengths are in administrative law, environmental law, international law and business law topics. Accessibility to law firms and courts in the state capitol of Florida is a plus.

Status: Current student, full-time
Dates of Enrollment: 1/2002-Submit Date
Survey Submitted: May 2004

Your first year is a bit of a load, but afterwards the classes get easier to handle. Even first-year teachers aren't really into the Socratic Method—you will get it a little, but not a lot. Sometimes getting into popular classes is difficult because the school is expanding so quickly.

According to the school: "Our faculty members are skilled and dedicated teachers, widely recognized for their contributions to legal scholarship and their profession. They take their students' education and professional growth seriously and want them to succeed. They encourage independent and creative thinking and a high level of interaction inside and outside of the classroom.

"The superior quality of our faculty is significant because it guarantees a first-class education for our students and illustrates the high regard in which our faculty members are held by peers at other law schools. Their reputation further enhances the perception among potential employers of the value of a degree from our law school, and helps to ensure that students find the jobs that they want."

 Employment Prospects

Status: Current student, full-time
Dates of Enrollment: 8/2002-Submit Date
Survey Submitted: April 2005

FSU and UF are probably the two strongest law schools in the state of Florida and remain competitive within the Southeastern region. We have an on-campus interviewing program that allows employers to contact the school if they are interested in recruiting specifically from FSU. Students then submit their resumes through the career placement office and then the employer can pre-select candidates for interviews to be conducted on campus. We also have an alumni-mentor program online where alumni who have volunteered to help out current students are categorized with contact information by location and area of practice. Tallahassee is a perfect place to go to law school because it is in the middle of everything—being in the capitol of Florida we have the State Legislature, State Supreme Court and First D.C.A. County Courthouse all within walking distance from the College of Law. Not to mention the number of state agencies and law firms.

Status: Current student, full-time
Dates of Enrollment: 8/2003-Submit Date
Survey Submitted: April 2005

FSU is doing a wonderful job of expanding their career placement options. While we have always had a great presence in Florida, they are now actively trying to expand to the Southeast region and nationwide. Our clinic programs are incredible and really allow us the opportunity to practice and hone our skills. In addition, those clinicals look amazing to future employers—they love it when you are a certified legal intern and can practice limitedly before finding out you passed the bar!

Status: Current student, full-time
Dates of Enrollment: 8/2003-Submit Date
Survey Submitted: October 2004

Employment prospects are best in the Florida and Atlanta markets, since alumni prefer to stay in the region (who wouldn't with such great weather?). Graduates obtain a range of jobs, from positions at large firms with big corporate practices to public defender positions. There's a 98 percent job placement rate (within one year of graduation). The alumni network is very helpful, especially in markets where there are not many FSU alumni (e.g., Chicago and New York). We get frequent e-mails from the administration regarding employment opportunities with alumni. Law students are also encouraged to attend alumni reception events around the country. We receive invitations to all of them.

On-campus recruiting tends to focus on the top quarter of the class. Among the top quarter, there are several on-campus interview opportunities all year long.

Internships are possible in almost every practice area. FSU is located in the state capital, and almost every major firm in the state has an office here. There is a very popular externship program with the state agencies, and opportunities to clerk in the county, state appellate and federal trial levels.

Read all of Vault's Law School Surveys at www.vault.com/lawschool — get complete surveys on top law schools, expert advice on applicaton essays, LSAT prep and more.

VAULT CAREER LIBRARY   165

Status: Current student, full-time
Dates of Enrollment: 1/2002-Submit Date
Survey Submitted: May 2004

If you are in the top 10 percent you won't have a problem—otherwise, you are pretty much on your own.

Status: Current student, full-time
Dates of Enrollment: 8/2003-Submit Date
Survey Submitted: October 2003

The placement office has good contacts in markets like Miami and Atlanta— with top 20 percent grades, you can get a job in these markets. There is a solid alumni network in Washington, D.C. Also, alumni in Richmond and Raleigh have been helpful to me.

> **Regarding employment prospects, the school says:** "FSU College of Law graduates are in demand by major law firms, government agencies and private businesses around the state, nation and the world. The placement rate for the Class of 2005, was 99 percent within nine months of graduation. FSU consistently ranks in the Top Three in the percentage of students placed, compared to other law schools in Florida. While most of our graduates choose to stay in Florida, other popular areas include Atlanta, Washington, D.C. and New York City.
>
> "The placement office's mission is to provide law students with the tools they will need to facilitate successful job searches and connect with employers. The office offers a full range of services to students, alumni and potential employers. These services include, but are not limited to:
>
> • Providing individual career counseling sessions for students and alumni
>
> • Hosting Fall and Spring Semester On-Campus Interviewing ("OCI") programs
>
> • Coordinating off-campus interviewing and resume collection/forwarding programs for employers who cannot come to campus
>
> • Posting job opportunities online for students and alumni
>
> • Sponsoring workshops on resume writing, interviewing techniques and networking lunches
>
> • Setting up reciprocity with other law school career services offices for students and alumni to use
>
> • Maintaining a resource room stocked with books, magazines and information files on law firms and governmental agencies
>
> • Updating the job placement software system (eCampusRecruiter)."

 Quality of Life

Status: Current student, full-time
Dates of Enrollment: 8/2002-Submit Date
Survey Submitted: April 2005

Tallahassee has an abundance of housing and is in the process of building several high-rise condominiums in the downtown area within walking distance to the law school.

Status: Current student, full-time
Dates of Enrollment: 8/2003-Submit Date
Survey Submitted: April 2005

I love that our school is so self-contained—everything we need is close together on our own little campus, from the law library to the house where the Children's Advocacy Center is placed. They also have a coffee shop in the student lounge, which is way helpful to wake up in the mornings AND you can catch the Otis Spunkmeyer cookies coming out of the oven—they cheer up

everyone's day! They also serve sushi, salads, sandwiches and soup if you want to grab a quick lunch. We do have a slight parking problem (as does every school I have heard of), but I know they are working hard to resolve it.

Status: Current student, full-time
Dates of Enrollment: 8/2003-Submit Date
Survey Submitted: October 2004

Quality of life is excellent. Housing in Tallahassee is very affordable, and there are several apartment complexes across the street from the law school. The law school campus is self-contained in three adjacent buildings. There is a cafe serving breakfast and lunch daily. The neighborhood is full of students, both graduate and undergraduate. Crime is low, and police have patrols in the area.

Status: Current student, full time
Dates of Enrollment: 1/2002-Submit Date
Survey Submitted: May 2004

Tallahassee is a safe town that really likes football.

Status: Current student, full-time
Dates of Enrollment: 8/2003-Submit Date
Survey Submitted: October 2003

Tallahassee is a very livable city; safe, no major transportation issues. The law school facility is nice, but a bit crowded. Parking can be a problem at times. Housing in the area is very affordable compared to Atlanta, where I lived before.

> **The school says:** "Both teaching and learning at FSU College of Law are strengthened by the diversity of our student body, which is of increasingly high quality. Their life and work experiences are as rich in diversity as they are. They are gifted and competitive, excelling in national moot court and mock trial competitions. They encourage each other, challenge each other and forge friendships that extend beyond their school years into their legal careers."

 Social Life

Status: Current student, full-time
Dates of Enrollment: 8/2002-Submit Date
Survey Submitted: April 2005

Because FSU has such a large undergraduate population, there is never a shortage of things to do. There are plenty of things going on in downtown area, within walking distance of the college. For example, on a nice, warm afternoon, many of us get together and walk to Andrew's for lunch or happy hour. The Student Bar Association also holds socials every week usually at one of the local cafes, bars or clubs. It is a chance for all the law students to get together and interact socially, as opposed to the classroom. As opposed to some law schools that are largely competitive, the student body at FSU is very friendly and social with one another both in and out of the classroom.

Status: Current student, full-time
Dates of Enrollment: 8/2003-Submit Date
Survey Submitted: April 2005

I have the best social life of anyone I know in law school. SBA does an awesome job of planning a social at a different bar around town every Thursday night, and tons of people go to them. In addition, SBA coordinates block seating for FSU football games, which are always a ball. Of course, I do have to study, but there are always great options for study breaks! Student organizations are very active on campus, and constantly bring in wonderful speakers to provide a wide range of topics. This year, the ACLU brought in a debate on gay marriage and public interest law students brought in state attorneys and public defenders to talk about their jobs, just to name a few. The organizations are a wonderful way to learn more about fields you are interested in and get connected to other people practicing in that field.

Status: Current student, full-time
Dates of Enrollment: 8/2003-Submit Date
Survey Submitted: October 2004

The social life is also excellent. There are three bars within walking distance of the law school. There are several bars in town. Law students get to benefit from FSU's undergraduate "party school" reputation. Football is the center of university life in the fall. Every Thursday night during the semester, the student bar association holds a "social" with free beer at a local bar. The dating scene is pretty good if you stay outside the law school. If you date someone in the law school, prepare for word to get around fast.

Status: Current student, full-time
Dates of Enrollment: 8/2003-Submit Date
Survey Submitted: October 2003

It is excellent. There are great looking students at FSU all around, who like to have a good time. There are things to do almost every night of the week. Student favorites include Sloppy Joe's, Potbellies, AJ's and Paradise.

Read all of Vault's Law School Surveys at www.vault.com/lawschool — get complete surveys on top law schools, expert advice on applicaton essays, LSAT prep and more.

VAULT CAREER LIBRARY 167

St. Thomas University School of Law

Office of Admissions
16401 NW 37th Avenue
Miami Gardens, FL 33054
Admissions phone: (800) 245-4569 or (305) 623-2310
Admissions fax: (305) 623-2357
Admissions e-mail: admitme@stu.edu
Admissions URL: http://www.stu.edu/lawschool

 Admissions

Status: Alumnus/a, full-time
Dates of Enrollment: 8/2000-5/2003
Survey Submitted: March 2005

The admissions department was courteous and professional. The school is looking for well-rounded students.

Status: Current student, full-time
Dates of Enrollment: 8/2003-Submit Date
Survey Submitted: March 2005

Short application that was processed and I received a timely acceptance.

Status: Alumnus/a, full-time
Dates of Enrollment: 8/2000-7/2003
Survey Submitted: March 2005

Perhaps the most user-friendly application process. The staff was very helpful and catered to my needs in a very professional and diligent manner.

Status: Alumnus/a, full-time
Dates of Enrollment: 9/2001-12/2003
Survey Submitted: April 2006

STU Law offered me a scholarship, and applying was simple. I was able to tour the school and meet with administrators before accepting the offer.

Status: Alumnus/a, full-time
Dates of Enrollment: 8/2002-12/2005
Survey Submitted: April 2006

The "Glimpse of St. Thomas" events are outstanding. Prospective students are able to meet with professors, administrators, current students and alumni, in some of the nicest locals in Miami. Always informative and a lot of fun.

Status: Alumnus/a, full-time
Dates of Enrollment: 8/2001-12/2003
Survey Submitted: March 2005

My experience was unique from other alumni probably. The recruiters called me because of high LSAT score and undergrad GPA, offered me a scholarship. I knew about St. Thomas, but unsure about a Catholic institution, but accepted the offer. The application was typical of other schools.

> **The school says:** "Consistently ranked one of the most diverse law schools in the nation, St. Thomas strives to make all of our prospective students, applicants and accepted students feel welcome and valued."

Status: Alumnus/a, full-time
Dates of Enrollment: 8/2000-5/2003
Survey Submitted: March 2005

The admissions process was very simple. People were usually available and friendly. More information prior to enrollment would have been helpful.

Status: Alumnus/a, full-time
Dates of Enrollment: 8/2003-8/2004
Survey Submitted: September 2004

Getting admitted to St. Thomas is really not that hard. They take students that no other school in the country will take. My advice is to go to the admissions office and meet the staff. They are very nice people, and they can tell you best what you need to do to get admitted.

> **STU says:** "The law school is dedicated to fulfilling its mission of being 'a school of opportunity' through our detailed application process, which takes into account not only academic credentials, but also work experience, life experience, community service and the personal statement."

 Academics

Status: Alumnus/a, full-time
Dates of Enrollment: 8/2002-12/2005
Survey Submitted: April 2006

The workload seems onerous at first and becomes more manageable as time goes on. There are more and more judges and practicing attorneys as professors, allowing for a greater "real world" picture of how the law really is.

Status: Alumnus/a, full-time
Dates of Enrollment: 9/2001-12/2003
Survey Submitted: April 2006

Just like any school you attend (I had similar experiences in undergrad), there are some professors with whom you feel a connection, some you don't feel as comfortable with. But I feel my education was as good as any Ivy League, I passed the bar exam on the first try (in two states), and the professors were very accessible.

Required courses are offered every semester, so scheduling was simple. Final exam schedules were also given out prior to registration so students could adjust their class schedules accordingly to exam preparation.

Status: Alumnus/a, full-time
Dates of Enrollment: 8/1999-5/2002
Survey Submitted: March 2005

Most of the professors were lackluster, most classes not memorable, pretty rote. Classes were structured on passing the bar.

Status: Alumnus/a, full-time
Dates of Enrollment: 8/2001-12/2003
Survey Submitted: March 2005

Since St. Thomas is a relatively small school, at times there was difficulty getting classes that you really wanted to take. One time a class was offered, and I showed up the first day to find it cancelled due to a conflict with the professor's schedule. I was dissapointed, but the administration allowed me first choice of any other class, even if the class was "full."

The classes were fairly standard, and the professors were excellent. Of course every school has professors that aren't exactly the best, but overall I feel I got an education equal to any other law school...when it came time to study for the bar exam, there were no surprises.

Status: Alumnus/a, full-time
Dates of Enrollment: 8/2000-7/2003
Survey Submitted: March 2005

At no time did I fail to register for a class for which I had an interest. Grading always seemed fair, and the professors and faculty were always very accessible. At St. Thomas, there was always an open-door policy.

Status: Alumnus/a, full-time
Dates of Enrollment: 8/2000-5/2003
Survey Submitted: March 2005

In general, my class learned as much as any other student at any other school. Most of the professors were competent, however, they were not monitored very well.

Status: Current student, full-time
Dates of Enrollment: 8/2003-Submit Date
Survey Submitted: March 2005

Professors are wonderful. Committed, qualified and enthusiastic to create a positive learning environment.

Status: Alumnus/a, full-time
Dates of Enrollment: 8/2000-5/2003
Survey Submitted: March 2005

The workload is intense. The professors are compatible with any law program. The classes are good quality and the ability to get into popular classes is not difficult.

Status: Alumnus/a, full-time
Dates of Enrollment: 8/2003-8/2004
Survey Submitted: September 2004

Quality classes/profs are hard to find at St. Thomas. I don't think I realized how much I was missing out on as a STU student. The faculty is much like the student body, very hit and miss. A couple great profs at the school, but for the most part they are a disappointment.

> **Regarding the professors, the school says:** "Our faculty members represent a strong mix of practitioners and academics who have earned their degrees from some of the nation's most prestigious institutions and who maintain an open-door polcy, enabling student to interact with them on a personal level."

Employment Prospects

Status: Alumnus/a, full-time
Dates of Enrollment: 8/2002-12/2005
Survey Submitted: April 2006

St. Thomas students tend to do well in the law field. Alumni go out of their way to help other St. Thomas students. Career services and alumni relations are fantastic at pairing current students and alumni for work.

Status: Alumnus/a, full-time
Dates of Enrollment: 9/2001-12/2003
Survey Submitted: April 2006

Alumni network is great, and because the STU Law is such a close-knit community, you are able to keep in touch with your classmates easier, and everyone is willing to help out.

Status: Alumnus/a, full-time
Dates of Enrollment: 8/1999-5/2002
Survey Submitted: March 2005

Any internships I obtained independently.

> **St. Thomas says:** "St. Thomas offers a comprehensive array of clinical and internship opportunities, including a prestigious Supreme Court internship program."

Status: Alumnus/a, full-time
Dates of Enrollment: 8/2000-5/2003
Survey Submitted: March 2005

Internships are a big plus, they provide a basis for your law career. St. Thomas does a great job providing intern opportunities for its students. As St. Thomas' alumni base grows the employers are hiring more and more graduates.

Status: Alumnus/a, full-time
Dates of Enrollment: 8/2001-12/2003
Survey Submitted: March 2005

The career services area always provided lunch and learn sessions on different legal topics, on-campus interviewing, and intership/job opportunities through various firms and alumni. I was not the typical law student, however, because I did not necessarily want to practice upon graduation. There was always a connection between career services, alumni and students.

Status: Alumnus/a, full-time
Dates of Enrollment: 8/2000-7/2003
Survey Submitted: March 2005

Others from my class went on to work at the most prestigious law firms in South Florida. I chose to work at the State Attorney's Office, and have found that the graduates from St. Thomas rank among the top lawyers there.

Status: Alumnus/a, full-time
Dates of Enrollment: 8/2000-5/2003
Survey Submitted: March 2005

We are seriously underrated as a school but excel as peers in the field. People are afraid that we won't be good simply because of the name of our school, however, we are some of the best in the state as well as the country.

Status: Current student, full-time
Dates of Enrollment: 8/2003-Submit Date
Survey Submitted: March 2005

I have interned for a federal judge as well as the Florida Supreme Court. This school has been a huge help to my career prospects and has gone out on a limb to provide adequate services and support staff on an individual basis.

Status: Alumnus/a, full-time
Dates of Enrollment: 8/2003-8/2004
Survey Submitted: September 2004

Career counselors are really, really nice and they try to help, but the academic reputation just isn't there and the opportunities are lacking. As a STU student you WILL get sick of answering the questions, St. Thomas is that a school in the Carribean?? Where is that? I didn't know there was another school in Miami. Why didn't you go to UM?

Quality of Life

Status: Alumnus/a, full-time
Dates of Enrollment: 8/2001-12/2003
Survey Submitted: March 2005

On-campus housing was limited, and I lived in an apartment off-campus. During the admissions process, I did not received much assistance in locating off-campus housing, but I was familiar with the area already. The classrooms were adequate, and since I have graduated they have been fully renovated.

A cafeteria and small bar and grill are located on campus, and the law school had a small cafe, too. Some would say St. Thomas is not located in the best of neighborhoods, but I always felt very safe there, very little crime (if any) on campus. Since graduating, the surrounding neighborhoods are starting to thrive. The campus has a great location, right in between Fort Lauderdale and Miami, so you have the best of both worlds.

Status: Alumnus/a, full-time
Dates of Enrollment: 8/2002-12/2005
Survey Submitted: April 2006

On-campus housing is not the best. The facilities have been recently renovated and look great. The surrounding neighborhood is not the best.

Status: Alumnus/a, full-time
Dates of Enrollment: 9/2001-12/2003
Survey Submitted: April 2006

I never lived on campus or utilized the dining facilities, except the on-campus pub. They had decent food, beer and recreation. The gym was nothing much to talk about, but for a school that size, it was sufficient. I never experienced any

Read all of Vault's Law School Surveys at www.vault.com/lawschool — get complete surveys on top law schools, expert advice on applicaton essays, LSAT prep and more.

VAULT CAREER LIBRARY   **169**

crime while at STU Law. I heard of one classmate whose car was broken into, but that was the only incident I am aware of.

Status: Alumnus/a, full-time
Dates of Enrollment: 8/2000-5/2003
Survey Submitted: March 2005

The on-campus housing isn't the best. Quality of life is OK on campus, I never feared for my safety.

> **The school says:** "On-campus housing is undergoing a complete renovation that will be completed in the fall of 2006."

Status: Current student, full-time
Dates of Enrollment: 8/2003-Submit Date
Survey Submitted: March 2005

I don't technically live on campus, although I am here all the time. The school has been improved vastly in the past two years and it's continuing to grow. The architectual additions planned look wonderful and state of the art. They are expected to begin in about two years.

Status: Alumnus/a, full-time
Dates of Enrollment: 8/2000-7/2003
Survey Submitted: March 2005

The campus is always undergoing renovations. It seems like they are always on the cutting edge of technology.

> **Regarding renovations, the school says:** "Recently, all of the classrooms and the moot court room underwent a renovation; a closed-circuit television system was installed to keep students updated on events and announcements; and a distance learning system was installed, enabling students to learn from leading experts in the country."

Status: Alumnus/a, full-time
Dates of Enrollment: 8/2000-5/2003
Survey Submitted: March 2005

The law school has gotten better. The campus is not as lush as it could be, but it is getting nicer. The classrooms are well kept and updated.

Status: Alumnus/a, full-time
Dates of Enrollment: 8/2003-8/2004
Survey Submitted: September 2004

Neighborhood is kind of scary. Miami is a great city, but STU isn't really in the heart of the action. Traffic is awful, so expect a nasty commute.

 ## Social Life

Status: Alumnus/a, full-time
Dates of Enrollment: 8/2002-12/2005
Survey Submitted: April 2006

Situated near both Ft. Lauderdale and South Beach, you have the best of both worlds. The students and faculty are very sociable and regularly go out together. There is a big emphasis on networking and social activities.

Status: Alumnus/a, full-time
Dates of Enrollment: 9/2001-12/2003
Survey Submitted: April 2006

Many student organizations were available for students. Again, because the school is small, there is a big sense of community. Students also had a breezeway area between the classrooms and the law library, and the breezeway was a big part of the law school experience. Everyone gathered to study and socialize there.

There was also a nearby community called Miami Lakes where many students lived in close proximity to each other. That community was self-sufficient in the fact that there were movie theatres, shopping, restaurants, bars, etc., all within a couple of miles of campus.

Status: Alumnus/a, full-time
Dates of Enrollment: 8/2001-12/2003
Survey Submitted: March 2005

Because St. Thomas is a small school (and the law school is a small part of that) the student social scene might be limited in some people's eyes. However, there are various clubs and organizations that I was involved in, and the SBA made a huge effort to keep students entertained outside of classes, whether it was an off-campus or on-campus happy hour, etc.

Like I said previously, the campus is in a GREAT location, so there are possibilities for students to hit Fort Lauderdale or Miami within about 15 minutes each. And one must not forget the BEACHES! If you head directly east about 10 minutes you are at the beach. And of course there is the famous South Beach.

Status: Alumnus/a, full-time
Dates of Enrollment: 8/2000-5/2003
Survey Submitted: March 2005

Social life in law school is slim. You spend most of your time studying. If you are looking for a good time try another graduate program.

Status: Alumnus/a, full-time
Dates of Enrollment: 8/2000-7/2003
Survey Submitted: March 2005

Miami is a great place for a social life ... not much more needs to be said.

Status: Alumnus/a, full-time
Dates of Enrollment: 8/2000-5/2003
Survey Submitted: March 2005

We had a great time. There was always an intellectual or social gathering. We always had fun.

Status: Current student, full-time
Dates of Enrollment: 8/2003-Submit Date
Survey Submitted: March 2005

The SBA goes a great job putting together happy hours and social events. Barrister's Ball was outstanding last year and I'm looking forward to another night at a five-star hotel with all my colleagues and professors.

Status: Alumnus/a, full-time
Dates of Enrollment: 8/2003-8/2004
Survey Submitted: September 2004

I didn't really have a social life at STU, but thats because I was studying so hard to get out of there! South Beach and Coconut Grove are both a good 30 minutes away, but if you are looking to party you won't find a better city than Miami. As for the students, most take school pretty lightly and expect the alcohol to be free flowing before, during and after finals!

 ## The School Says

St. Thomas University School of Law is a highly-diverse, student-centered law school where the Catholic heritage of ethical behavior and public service flourishes. Since its founding in 1984, St. Thomas has received national attention for its commitment to student and faculty diversity, and has maintained a special commitment to training lawyers who are members of South Florida's Hispanic and Black communities, which have been traditionally underserved by the legal profession. The School of Law offers the traditional JD degree program, as well as four joint degree programs, two LLM degree programs and a J.S.D. degree program.

Fundamental to our curriculum at St. Thomas University School of Law is the emphasis placed on the development of professional skills. The School of Law offers a wide array of opportunities to develop practical lawyering skills to ensure your success in the legal profession upon graduation. Through our extensive clinical, externship and internship offerings and our in-depth legal writing programs, students participate in a variety of substantive experiences in order to hone the skills necessary for the practice of law.

We've assembled a world-class faculty with international visibility that is readily accessible to students. We continue to push the boundaries of a quality legal education through the innovative use of technology in the classroom, and through cutting-edge programs that promote scholarship and research.

St. Thomas University School of Law's location in Miami, Florida provides an ideal setting for the study of law. Miami is a vibrant, thriving international community. A hub of domestic and international trade, an innovative center for performing and fine arts, and one of the world's most popular vacation spots, Miami is a dynamic place to live and study. As the gateway to Latin America and the Caribbean, Miami enjoys a rapidly expanding multinational legal community and is home to federal and state trial and appellate courts.

Our mission is to provide a personalized education that produces inquiring, ethical and productive lawyers. We are committed to developing within our students the ability to think clearly, to communicate effectively and to make informed and ethical judgments in an increasingly complex world. We believe this personalized education forms a strong foundation where students are offered an outstanding curriculum, where small classes guarantee access and personal guidance from a respected faculty of legal scholars, and where ideas are challenging and people are passionate about their beliefs.

We train our students to be excellent lawyers, equipped for any number of different careers, and committed to the values of hard work, integrity, personal responsibility, tolerance, respect and service.

Read all of Vault's Law School Surveys at www.vault.com/lawschool — get complete surveys on top law schools, expert advice on applicaton essays, LSAT prep and more.

VAULT CAREER LIBRARY 171

Stetson University College of Law

Admissions Office
1401 61st Street South
Gulfport, FL 33707-3299
Admissions phone: (727) 562-7800
Admissions e-mail: lawadmit@law.stetson.edu
Admissions URL: http://www.law.stetson.edu/admissions/

 ## Admissions

Status: Alumnus/a, full-time
Dates of Enrollment: 1/1996-5/1998
Survey Submitted: April 2006

Strong academics and LSAT score are important, but other factors are included, such as non-traditional students and minority status.

Status: Alumnus/a, full-time
Dates of Enrollment: 1/1996-12/1999
Survey Submitted: March 2005

From what I recall, the application asked for one essay. I did not interview with anyone and learned that—as with 90 percent of law schools—admission will depend almost solely on your undergrad GPA and your LSAT scores.

Status: Current student, part-time
Dates of Enrollment: 8/2004-Submit Date
Survey Submitted: March 2004

Register with LSDAS first. Request transcripts from all undergraduate and graduate schools you've attended. Request two letters of recommendation early and ask your recommender to mail them to LSDAS. Take the LSAT. I highly recommend a study course before taking the LSAT. You need to get a high score and you only want to take the test once. It is a real killer!

> **The school says:** "Admissions are based on a holistic review of the file by a faculty committee. Though LSAT scores and undergraduate GPA are considered, so are a number of other factors which may include, among others, work experience, personal statements, diversity, recommendations and post-college education."

 ## Academics

Status: Alumnus/a, full-time
Dates of Enrollment: 1/1996-5/1998
Survey Submitted: April 2006

The professors had a more practical approach to legal training, which I enjoyed. Grading is on a curve and the perception is that grading is tough. But employers typically look at class rank, rather than GPA.

Status: Alumnus/a, full-time
Dates of Enrollment: 1/1997-7/1999
Survey Submitted: March 2005

Stetson has a great academic environment due to its separation from the undergraduate campus. Law students form unique bond because they share a common existence and only interact with one another. The grading scale is tough. Stetson is a C standard school. This means that the average student has a 2.5 GPA at the end of their first year. The professors are extremely approachable and are very giving of their time. The workload is bearable. As with any law school, it becomes more manageable as time goes by.

> **The School Says:** Stetson is no longer a C-standard school.

Status: Alumnus/a, full-time
Dates of Enrollment: 1/1996-12/1999
Survey Submitted: March 2005

It paid to register early. Success is often hinged upon personality conflict and compatibility with your professors, as it is in many Socratic Method institutions. The workload was extreme, but manageable.

Status: Current student, part-time
Dates of Enrollment: 8/2004-Submit Date
Survey Submitted: March 2004

The part-time program is great for working adults who aspire to earn a law degree but can't go to school full-time. It's really convenient. You can go to school two or three nights a week during the first two years and also on weekends.

> **Regarding academics, Stetson says:** "Success in law school depends on many factors. While a student may prefer the teaching style of one professor over another, we do not generally find that to be the determining factor in a student's grade. First-year course averages typically fall between 2.7 and 2.9."

> Part-time students are expected to attend class three nights a week during the first two years. After that point, students may take elective courses offered throughout the week, including weekends.

 ## Employment Prospects

Status: Alumnus/a, full-time
Dates of Enrollment: 1/1996-5/1998
Survey Submitted: April 2006

Employers generally perceive a Stetson Law graduate as well-rounded and prepared to contribute to the firm or practice. One of the best advantages of Stetson is the internship program throughout the Tampa area and most of Florida.

Status: Alumnus/a, full-time
Dates of Enrollment: 1/1997-7/1999
Survey Submitted: March 2005

There is at least one Stetson graduate practicing in all the BigLaw firms in Florida. Because Stetson emphasizes advocacy, most graduates go into litigation. Stetson has been ranked in the Top Five of trial advocacy law schools in the nation for the past 10 years. The alumni network is enormous because Stetson was the first law School in Florida. Most of the large Florida firms interview at Stetson. Unfortunately, there are not many Stetson Alums that work outside the state of Florida, so not many out of state firms interview at Stetson.

Status: Alumnus/a, full-time
Dates of Enrollment: 1/1996-12/1999
Survey Submitted: March 2005

With a degree from Stetson you could interview with most firms, but not all (including the one at which I am currently employed—I am here as a lateral transfer). It is definitely not the top school in the state, but it is in the second tier.

Status: Current student, part-time
Dates of Enrollment: 8/2004-Submit Date
Survey Submitted: March 2004

You can open your own law firm. You can work for government agencies. You can join a law firm. You can work for a corporation. You can teach. Your choices are unlimited.

> **The school says:** "Though nearly 75 percent of our graduates live in Florida, Stetson law alumni practice in 48 states, the District of Columbia, two U.S. territories and 22 foreign coun-

tries. Stetson offers programs on how to conduct out-of-state job searches, and we routinely connect students with alumni working in the geographic areas where they wish to practice."

Quality of Life

Status: Alumnus/a, full-time
Dates of Enrollment: 1/1996-5/1998
Survey Submitted: April 2006

Each student's quality of life is a big focus of the college. An advantage of the college is its size and commitment to students. On-campus housing is decent and there are a number of college-owned houses for rent. The main campus is in Gulfport, which is a small town between St. Petersburg and St. Pete Beach. It is very near the ocean.

Status: Alumnus/a, full-time
Dates of Enrollment: 1/1997-7/1999
Survey Submitted: March 2005

Stetson is a beautiful campus. It's located about five miles from the St. Petersburg Beach. The campus has beautiful Spanish architecture and was once a resort. Campus housing ranges from on-campus dorm rooms to off-campus apartments and houses—all reasonably priced. The campus cafeteria has decent food at a good price.

Status: Alumnus/a, full-time
Dates of Enrollment: 1/1996-12/1999
Survey Submitted: March 2005

Quality of life at Stetson is good. They offer nice, affordable, off-campus housing, and the campus facilities are top-rate.

Status: Current student, part-time
Dates of Enrollment: 8/2004-Submit Date
Survey Submitted: March 2004

The campus is beautiful. The nearby beaches are relaxing and calming. Miami and Orlando are only a few hours away, as are Jamaica and the Bahamas. Palm trees, warm weather, scenic views, exotic birds and flowers. A beautiful place to live.

Social Life

Status: Alumnus/a, full-time
Dates of Enrollment: 1/1997-7/1999
Survey Submitted: March 2005

Stetson law school is a community in and of itself. Most of the students hang out with each other. There is no Greek system at the law school campus.

Status: Alumnus/a, full-time
Dates of Enrollment: 1/1996-12/1999
Survey Submitted: March 2005

Being that it is law school, the social life is what you make of it. St. Pete has a lot to offer, and St. Pete Beach is very close by.

Status: Current student, part-time
Dates of Enrollment: 8/2004-Submit Date
Survey Submitted: March 2004

The Tampa Bay area has it all. Have lunch along the bay while overlooking downtown Tampa. Restaurants, beaches, parks bars, it's all here.

The School Says

Stetson University College of Law was founded in 1900 as Florida's first law school. Originally located on the campus of Stetson University in DeLand, Fla., the College moved in 1954 to Gulfport/St. Petersburg. In 2004, Stetson opened the Tampa Law Center, designed for working professionals enrolled in the school's part-time program.

The College of Law is consistently ranked among the nation's top law schools for trial advocacy and legal writing. Stetson offers full-time and part-time programs for the JD, dual JD/MBA, and LLM degrees, combining small classes, top professors and state-of-the-art resources to prepare students for exceptional legal careers. Stetson's international programs include summer programs in Argentina, China, Germany, the Netherlands and Spain. Stetson is fully accredited by the American Bar Association and has been a member of the Association of American Law Schools since 1931.

In 2005, Stetson became the first U.S. law school since 1996 to win the world championship at the Vis International Arbitration Moot competition in Austria, and the Stetson team won a silver medal at the 2006 competition. Stetson is one of three law schools in the United States to share space with a working court, the Tampa branch of Florida's Second District Court of Appeal. Stetson is home to the National Conference of Law Reviews, three academic journals, and the National Clearinghouse for Science, Technology and the Law. Stetson also has Centers for Excellence in Advocacy, Elder Law, Higher Education Law and Policy, and International Law.

Read all of Vault's Law School Surveys at www.vault.com/lawschool — get complete surveys on top law schools, expert advice on applicaton essays, LSAT prep and more.

VAULT CAREER LIBRARY   173

University of Florida

Fredric G. Levin College of Law
Admissions Office
PO Box 117635
Gainesville, FL 32611-7635
Admissions phone: (352) 273-0890
Admissions fax: (352) 392-4087
Admissions e-mail: admissions@law.ufl.edu
Admissions URL: http://www.law.ufl.edu/admissions/

 ## Admissions

Status: Current student, full-time
Dates of Enrollment: 8/2003-Submit Date
Survey Submitted: October 2005

Admission is getting harder every semester. I transferred in after my first full year of law school. However, I was in the top 7 percent of my class, on moot court and Law Review at the school I transferred from.

Status: Alumnus/a, full-time
Dates of Enrollment: 8/2001-5/2004
Survey Submitted: April 2006

I applied in 2000 for the 2001 class...it seemed the economy had just taken a turn for the worse, and many students were looking to law school as a way of waiting out the bad times. Admissions was competitive, and I actually requested an interview with the dean of admissions, to try to get a jump on the competition. Otherwise, the application itself was simple and the cheapest one around.

Status: Alumnus/a, full-time
Dates of Enrollment: 1/2000-12/2003
Survey Submitted: March 2006

This was the only law school that I applied to so I cannot compare it to others. I was diligent with the application process, making sure that I crossed every "t" and dotted every "i."

Status: Alumnus/a, full-time
Dates of Enrollment: 8/2001-5/2004
Survey Submitted: March 2006

Admissions process was fairly simple and less detailed than the other institutions that I applied to for law school. I had FL residency, which I think helps with this state school. I also had an above average LSAT score and a great undergrad GPA with many undergrad extracurriculars. Application fee was also much less than many of the other schools that I applied to.

Status: Current student, full-time
Dates of Enrollment: 1/2004-Submit Date
Survey Submitted: April 2005

The admissions process is a simple application and a personal statement. No interview is required or allowed. The University of Florida is highly partial to in-state students. The main things considered are residency, GPA, and LSAT score. It is very difficult to get in from out of state. UF is the most competitive school in the state, and only takes the best and the brightest of Florida. Once you decide to apply, you can make an appointment to come see the school and check out the facilities and possibly meet the dean of admissions. The dean of admissions does not do a very good job recruiting and seems to think it is a privilege if you get into the school. That is the one downside of the admissions process.

> **The school says:** "The University of Florida College of Law uses identical standards for residents and nonresidents."

Status: Alumnus/a, full-time
Dates of Enrollment: 8/2001-5/2004
Survey Submitted: March 2005

The UF admissions process is relatively painless (unless you get rejected, of course). By far, the most important factors in admissions decisions are LSAT and undergrad GPA. If your numbers exceed the standards, you are an automatic admit (and you, thereby, qualify for numerous academic scholarships). The remainder of the pack go on to committee, and this is where your essays will be read, and more time will be spent determining what you bring to the table. Financial aid is easy to apply for as well, and easy to get. Note, however, the cost of attendance is so low, and the reputation of the school so high (at least in FL), that it makes the decision pretty easy for Florida's brightest

Status: Current student, full-time
Dates of Enrollment: 8/2002-Submit Date
Survey Submitted: January 2005

It is a pretty difficult school to get into. Make sure that you have a high GPA and do well on the LSAT. Every incoming class is getting more and more competitive. Make sure that you spend time on your essay. Be honest, but make sure that you show how you are different than every other applicant. Emphasize what makes you unique and what you can bring to the law school.

Status: Current student, full-time
Dates of Enrollment: 8/2004-Submit Date
Survey Submitted: September 2004

Getting admitted to UF is very difficult; I was rejected the first time I applied with a 157 LSAT, A- to B+ undergrad grades and excellent work experience and recommendations. I was able to transfer from another law school after my first year, as a student in the top 20 percent of my class. My only advice is not to give up, and if you get accepted you should be very proud!

Status: Current student, full-time
Dates of Enrollment: 8/2003-Submit Date
Survey Submitted: July 2004

The University of Florida Levin College of Law is a large state school. Accordingly, getting in is in large part a numbers game. And the average you need is getting higher for a number of reasons. It is the best law school in the state; it is a steal with respect to tuition (all three years are less than one semester in many other programs); and each semester, only 200 students are accepted (this will be changing soon).

Status: Alumnus/a, full-time
Dates of Enrollment: 1/2001-12/2003
Survey Submitted: April 2004

The UF College of Law is getting more and more competitive, especially given that the school has done away with its spring class. As a result, each semester it gets more and more difficult to get in. The admissions process is relatively straightforward, and one of the nicest things is that you can always call the admissions office at the school to get a status update. It may not always be personalized, but at least you can find out about where the administrators are in the process. There is no interview, but rumor has it that coming by to meet the dean(s) and sitting in on classes can help. This is a school that looks for overall good candidates, so realistically, you should have at least a solid LSAT score and above a 3.0 from a good school.

Status: Alumnus/a, full-time
Dates of Enrollment: 8/1999-5/2003
Survey Submitted: April 2004

The law school's admissions process is completely impersonal, but relatively straightforward.

Academics

Status: Current student, full-time
Dates of Enrollment: 8/2003-Submit Date
Survey Submitted: October 2005

Quality of classes depend a lot on your political viewpoint (i.e., very liberal or conservative minded). If one is very liberal, then the quality of classes will likely be seen as good. However, a conservative-minded individual that wants practical as opposed to theoretical classes will likely view the course offerings as sub-par. If you don't wait until the last minute, the popular classes are relatively easy to get. Grading at UF Law: high grading curve but very hard to get into the top 10 to 20 percent because everybody gets B's. Very few A's or C's given. Professors: from my experience, the majority of the professors are liberal minded individuals that do not want to teach practical information. They are happy just talking about theories rather than teaching helpful information. With that said, there are a number of professors that keep political viewpoints out of the class and really teach.

Status: Alumnus/a, full-time
Dates of Enrollment: 8/2001-5/2004
Survey Submitted: April 2006

UF tends to attract students who see themselves working in a corporate, mega-law firm environment, meaning the student seeking a more academic experience should look elsewhere; at UF, it's about Corporations, Accounting for Lawyers, etc. That being said, I was able to find like-minded professors and took over 10 seminars, which not only boosted by GPA (no final exams, just papers), but also made the whole experience less formulistic and boring.

Status: Alumnus/a, full-time
Dates of Enrollment: 1/2000-12/2003
Survey Submitted: March 2006

The workload in the first year is heavy. The professors are exceedingly well-qualified and most of them work hard at providing an excellent education for the students. It can be difficult to get popular classes, but if you stay on top of sign-up times and work with the administration, you can usually get what you want.

Status: Alumnus/a, full-time
Dates of Enrollment: 8/2001-5/2004
Survey Submitted: March 2006

Good programs, for the most part. School was very recently renovated (of course after I left!) and so is much nicer in physical appearance now. I was impressed with most of my teachers, although of course not with all of them. I felt like I usually got into most classes that I wanted. I did have a problem with the grading system with regards to some professors—not giving enough feedback regarding grades given, but that is a teacher-specific problem I believe. I will say that when I left many students were unhappy about the growth of many less academic classes, such as Gender and the Law, etc. over many solid law classes that give edges for the bar exam, such as UCC courses. That was disappointing, and I hope it won't affect UF's bar passage rates.

Status: Current student, full-time
Dates of Enrollment: 1/2003-Submit Date
Survey Submitted: September 2004

Amazing teachers for the most part. Just a tremendous group of instructors, by far the greatest part of the school. The school is very focused on continuing to attract the best instructors from around the nation; and its reputation reflects that commitment. Professors are willing to talk to students in and out of class. I had never met such brilliant people until coming to school here—it really is a gift to listen to some of the teachers instruct. The workload is consistent with most first tier universities. The first year is a considerable adjustment, but classes do become more routine after that. The school offers a good selection of courses and makes it relatively easy to get into those courses. The administration is certainly not focused on preparing students for the Florida Bar; but allows student to take classes that will assist in the bar examination—this is a national law school, which is a great thing. You should prepare for the bar when you graduate; while in school you can take some great courses that will do much more that just prep your for that test.

Status: Current student, full-time
Dates of Enrollment: 1/2004-Submit Date
Survey Submitted: April 2005

Academics are fairly difficult. The professors are hit or miss in my experience. Most are well-published and great, but there are a few who are not up to par. Registration gets easier as you gain more credit hours, because you get better registration times each semester you have completed. Grading is standard. There is a curve that all the professors must abide by. The workload is probably comparable to other law schools, as well. The average workload is about 15 hours of studying a week, and that probably triples or quadruples during finals time. The school is competitive if you want it to be. It all depends on whom you surround yourself with.

Status: Alumnus/a, full-time
Dates of Enrollment: 8/2001-5/2004
Survey Submitted: March 2005

Florida is a top-tier law school, and along with that ranking come the things you would expect. It is also a public law school, and along with that reality come the things you would expect. UF Law has some incredible professors and some duds, too. The class choices after the first year seem a bit limited, particularly given how large the school is, but it is character building to suffer through a few miserable classes (that's what I told myself while sitting in Secured Transactions, anyway). It is not easy to get into a popular class unless you have an early registration appointment, which can only be achieved by number of credit hours accumulated. That means, if you are smart, lucky, and bright enough to be employed your first summer, you are SCREWED, and I mean SCREWED, for the rest of your registration periods. The good news is that the school has a drop/add period that allows you to slide into some classes that were full at registration time; and of course, there is always the old, go-talk-to-the-professor tactic. Grading is on an enforced curve, the formula for which would boggle most statisticians' minds, but the workload is whatever you make it.

Status: Current student, full-time
Dates of Enrollment: 8/2002-Submit Date
Survey Submitted: January 2005

The first year is very demanding. The professors are great for the most part, but you will have a lot of reading and the Socratic Method will be a little intimidating at first. After your first year, professors loosen up a lot and many just lecture. There isn't a great selection of electives, but the ones that are offered are very interesting and well taught. Grading is fair overall, but many times has no relationship to the amount of time you study for a particular class. Some of my best grades have come from classes that I have put the least effort into, but that I understood naturally.

Status: Current student, full-time LLM
Dates of Enrollment: 1/2003-Submit Date
Survey Submitted: November 2004

UF Law's LLM program in Tax is second in the nation. 1L courses are pre-planned for all students. After your first year, there is variety of classes to choose from; getting into them is the hard part.

Status: Alumnus/a, full-time
Dates of Enrollment: 1/2001-12/2003
Survey Submitted: April 2004

Getting A's used to be very difficult, but UF finally caught up with the rest of the schools and raised its curve (it used to be a 2.65). The curve is strictly enforced. First-year courses are required, so there are no issues registering (which is a relief, trust me). And in later years, you are given priority registration for the courses which are suggested, based on your year. The electives are sometimes hard to get into, so usually the best way to deal with a booked class is by speaking with the professor or the assistant dean. You can always switch around during the first two weeks. This way, you can check everything out, and you almost always can get the classes you want during the add/drop period. Classes are good; some tougher than others, but overall the classes and the teachers get reputations, and they generally tend to be true to form.

Read all of Vault's Law School Surveys at www.vault.com/lawschool — get complete surveys on top law schools, expert advice on applicaton essays, LSAT prep and more.

VAULT CAREER LIBRARY 175

Status: Current student, full-time
Dates of Enrollment: 8/2003-Submit Date
Survey Submitted: July 2004

The University of Florida Levin College of Law is a large state school. So you will find a real mix. There are some very bright students and some who are just very hardworking. The student body is largely Floridian, and in fact almost 40 percent of the class finished their undergrad at the University of Florida. There was also a mix of professors. But I can say that each semester I had at least one or two who I know were world class, having studied at a number of schools. Like most programs your classes are selected for you the first year. After that you have free reign among those offered. The selection is limited to a good core offering but lacks breadth for those who fancy the bizarre or eccentric.

Status: Alumnus/a, full-time
Dates of Enrollment: 8/1999-5/2003
Survey Submitted: April 2004

The law school has placed too much emphasis on "fringe" classes, meaning that core classes can be harder to fit into a class schedule. If you want to take lots of classes on the various oppressed peoples in the U.S. and worldwide, then you should have no problem finding classes. Focusing on corporate and transactional classes is much more difficult. Additionally, more emphasis should be placed on research and writing, but I think that may be impossible, based on the current quality of instructors in those areas.

 # Employment Prospects

Status: Alumnus/a, full-time
Dates of Enrollment: 8/2001-5/2004
Survey Submitted: April 2006

UF, I would say, is primarily a regional law school, meaning that if you are wanting to practice in NYC or San Francisco, although possible, it is unlikely that a diploma from UF will help. On the other hand, for the student wanting to stay in Florida, UF is a great deal and has a great network of alumni situated in law firms of all sizes throughout the State of Florida and in the Southeast. On-campus recruiting tends to be for the top 25 percent only, and career services was not altogether very helpful.

> According the college's Center for Career Services, "38 percent of the eligible (second semester and above) JD students interviewed during fall 2004 on-campus interviews and almost 40 percent of the eligible JD students interviewed during fall 2005 OCI."

Status: Alumnus/a, full-time
Dates of Enrollment: 1/2000-12/2003
Survey Submitted: March 2006

I was a second-career law student. Because I was not a traditional student (older than most) it was maybe a little more difficult for me to get a job. On-campus recruiting is a lot of work and can be very frustrating, but you have to stick with it and put your best face forward. Internships are excellent at UF; I was selected for two of them (at the county attorney's office and as an intern for a federal judge) and they provided some of the best experience that I had while at law school.

Status: Alumnus/a, full-time
Dates of Enrollment: 8/2001-5/2004
Survey Submitted: March 2005

UF is the only truly top-tier law school in the state. Having said that, not everyone wants to practice in Florida, and sometimes it can be difficult to get a job in other states. I had a job well before graduation, as did most of my friends, and all of them were employed by graduation. Alumni are VERY loyal to their alma mater, and it seems that the UF network is strong throughout the state and in Georgia (for those students interested in Atlanta). On-campus recruiting is pretty solid, but difficult to manage sometimes with class schedules. Most professors seem to be understanding about missing a class for call backs, etc.

Status: Current student, full-time
Dates of Enrollment: 8/2003-Submit Date
Survey Submitted: July 2004

You eat what you kill, or you can end up working for the government. Most fine jobs, and many find jobs in Florida's top firms. Careers in law in other states is a stretch but feasible, especially in the Southeast. And the law degree will work for you in other fields quite nicely. There is a great network of dedicated "Gators," but you might have to talk football, even if you never left the library.

Status: Alumnus/a, full-time
Dates of Enrollment: 1/2001-12/2003
Survey Submitted: April 2004

UF is by far the most highly regarded law school in Florida. Hands down. That right there is a benefit. The people in the top 10 percent of the class are going to get jobs during school. Career services is excellent at UF for organizing the OCIs (big firms' on-campus interviewing process)—this typically caters mostly to the top 25 percent. There is a job bank of sorts online, and the office does provide resume assistance and some resources, but to be honest, if you are in the bottom 75 percent of the class, you're pretty much on your own. You had better hustle for a job, because people expect the top at Florida, and once those big-firm jobs are gone, that's it—the school does very little with the smaller firms in other cities.

Status: Alumnus/a, full-time
Dates of Enrollment: 8/1996-5/1999
Survey Submitted: April 2004

Good career services program and on-campus interviewing system (plenty of employers come to interview). Easy to get a job, especially in Florida. Plenty of prestige, especially in Florida. Everyone gets a job, including all major law firms, clerkships and government jobs. Again, harder if you want to work in New York, for example. If you want to work in New York, a New York employer would ask, why did you attend the University of Florida? If you are a Florida person who intends to live in Florida, as many are for many reasons (great weather), then UF is just fine as far as prestige and getting any job you want (assuming grades are OK and you have the right social skills, etc.).

 # Quality of Life

Status: Current student, full-time
Dates of Enrollment: 8/2003-Submit Date
Survey Submitted: October 2005

Parking drastically wears on your quality of life. I have to get to campus one or two hours before my classes start just to get a spot. Other than that, quality of life is good. However, if you do not like going to clubs and bars, Gainesville is a very, very bad place to live. The town's residents are a bunch of Woodstock generation hippies that protest everything. I personally hate the town and can't get away from here quick enough.

Status: Alumnus/a, full-time
Dates of Enrollment: 1/2000-12/2003
Survey Submitted: March 2006

Gainesville is a fun town. It's reasonably safe if you act responsibly. Housing can be a drag and expensive if you're renting. If you can afford it, purchase a condo, then sell it at graduation. The law school facilities have been significantly upgraded since I was there and they are terrific now. The classrooms are good, the library is wonderful, and the law school itself is clean and functional. Take advantage of the free gym, it's great.

Status: Current student, full-time
Dates of Enrollment: 1/2003-Submit Date
Survey Submitted: September 2004

Great quality! Biggest bang for your buck. Gainesville is your typical college town. New library and classrooms make this school a great choice. There are homes very close to campus that are unbelievably reasonable. Plenty of typical college-style apartments located near and farm from the law school. Gainesville is an extremely safe city. If you are into athletics, it is awesome. The university has an amazing recreation center—also, plenty of places to run and bike.

Status: Current student, full-time
Dates of Enrollment: 1/2004-Submit Date
Survey Submitted: April 2005

Quality of life is great. Gainesville is a cheap place to live and very conducive to student living. The campus and its facilities are also very nice. The law school will have a brand new library shortly, and brand new buildings. There is not that much crime. Gainesville has pretty much most chain restaurants and a few upscale restaurants. The campus has two gyms that are free for students, and a few other gyms surround campus. Gainesville is a fairly safe town, but depending on where you live, the crime rate could be higher.

Status: Current student, full-time
Dates of Enrollment: 8/2002-Submit Date
Survey Submitted: January 2005

The campus is beautiful and tranquil. The law school is finishing a complete remodeling and looks great. The new rooms are comfortable and set up for technology. During football season, it is the wildest place on earth! Gainesville is a college town and there is plenty to do any night of the week.

Status: Current student, full-time
Dates of Enrollment: 8/2003-Submit Date
Survey Submitted: July 2004

As the cheer goes, It is good to be a Florida Gator. Housing is plentiful around the law campus, which is connected to, but not near, the main campus. The school is under construction, which means the incoming classes will have brand-new facilities. Believe it or not, Gainesville has some great restaurants. And yes, you can eat a piece of the school mascot in a few of them. A few years back this college town was ranked the best place to live in America. I wouldn't go so far as to say that, because in Florida you should be on the coast, although St. Augustine is only an hour away. In the end I have found Gainesville a friendly place to live, despite my lack of interest in sports.

Status: Alumnus/a, full-time
Dates of Enrollment: 1/2001-12/2003
Survey Submitted: March 2005

Gainesville has the right mix of "not enough to do" (so you have time to study) and "plenty to do" (so you don't get bored). If you're into nature, you're in heaven. If you're into beer—you're in heaven. If you're into football—you're really in heaven. Shopping—not so much. But surprisingly, there are a ton of bands that come through Gainesville, pretty good theater. But it's still a small town. Safety around campus is very good. For a law student, living on campus is out of the question; living is pretty cheap anyway. There is very cheap housing for married students (with or without families), close to the campus. The biggest problem is the parking, so live within walking or biking distance!

Status: Alumnus/a, full-time
Dates of Enrollment: 8/1996-5/1999
Survey Submitted: April 2004

It is the University of Florida, a party school. If you want to have a ton of fun and not work too hard, you can do that. Go to ufl.edu to see all UF has to offer. If you are more serious-minded, you may want to consider a smaller school (if you are the type who gets annoyed that your law school classmates still act like frat boys). Now, if you want to consider benefits of the low cost of UF compared to most schools, and you are that serious type of person, you can do your thing and ignore the partying going on around you. Overall, it is what you make of it.

 ## Social Life

Status: Current student, full-time
Dates of Enrollment: 8/2003-Submit Date
Survey Submitted: October 2005

A LOT of bars, clubs and restaurants. Dating scene is decent but the law school is away from main campus so not a lot of contact with non-law students. School's social life is very clique-ish meaning several smaller groups that don't really associate with anyone outside of their little circle. Popular clubs: The Library (not the actual school library), The Bank (again, not an actual bank), The Grog House and Durty Nelly's.

Status: Alumnus/a, full-time
Dates of Enrollment: 8/2001-5/2004
Survey Submitted: April 2006

Gainesville is the prototypical college town, catering mostly to gastronomically-challenged undergraduates (pizza, wings, beer, etc.), and good restaurants are few and far between. The Hippodrome Theater shows good foreign films, and there are a few bars in downtown that cater to those over 23 (The Top, Speakeasy). Then there's UF Football, which is a blessing and a curse, but you'll find that out if you go there.

Status: Alumnus/a, full-time
Dates of Enrollment: 8/2001-5/2004
Survey Submitted: March 2006

Gainesville is a partyer's dream (not that I took advantage of that, of course!). If you like football games and big college communities, you will love Gainesville. Lots of things going on all of the time-cultural events, sports events, great dining as well as more affordable dining. Affordable bars and nightclubs, etc. Great gymnasiums available. A nice large mall. Gainesville is very hot though for all of you non-Floridians so be prepared!

Status: Current student, full-time
Dates of Enrollment: 1/2003-Submit Date
Survey Submitted: September 2004

UF lives up to its reputation as a party school. There is a great balance of work and play—I love it. Gainesville really does have a great selection of restaurants—in fact, the best sushi restaurant anywhere, Dragonfly. There is also a large and diverse selection of clubs and bars. The city is easy to navigate and cab fare is very cheap. The undergrad campus is clearly dominated by the Greek system. This somewhat pervades into the law school since many students came from undergrad at UF—this makes the school somewhat cliquey. However, the law school is a very sociable place and it is conducive to making new friends. Coming to the university without knowing anyone is not a problem. There are plenty of activities and groups to get involved in. As far as the dating scene, it is easy. Many law students find new love in the first year—in fact, some have even gotten married already.

Status: Current student, full-time
Dates of Enrollment: 1/2004-Submit Date
Survey Submitted: April 2005

The social life is great. Gainesville is a wonderful college town. It's a cheap town, as well. Amongst the favorites bars and restaurants are the Swamp, Market Street, Bank and Durty Nelly's. Gainesville is a typical college town with a Greek system, lots of events and clubs to join, and never a dull moment. Most people meet others at school or out at clubs or bars. Even in law school, there is still time to go out and have a good time.

Status: Alumnus/a, full-time
Dates of Enrollment: 8/2001-5/2004
Survey Submitted: March 2005

There are a variety of choices, socially speaking. Gainesville caters to a wide variety to people because of the huge undergraduate population. There are the earthy people places, the classic martini bars, the clubs, the pubs, etc. There is actually a decent variety of restaurants, given the size of the town. My experience at the law school included a mix of hitting the pubs and parties at students houses (of the, "bring your own bottle of wine" variety, not the "we got a keg!" variety). Either way, there shouldn't be a problem finding your niche, unless you are timid—a trait that would not work well for you at any large public school. Believe it or not, UF tends to breed very socially and politically savvy people. Get in the game or be pushed aside because this school is not for the timid, but it will definitely set you up for a big future in the state if you have the drive.

Status: Current student, full-time
Dates of Enrollment: 8/2003-Submit Date
Survey Submitted: July 2004

Bars abound. Salty Dog is great. Market Street Pub is a ritual. And beer courses through the streets during game days. Excellent restaurants are easily found. Chopstix is a superb pan-Asian spot tucked away on a lake. You can feed alligators from the deck and watch bald eagles soar and hunt the lake, Biven's Arm. Paramount Grill is cozy, the food is sublime, the chocolate ganoush leads one to

Read all of Vault's Law School Surveys at www.vault.com/lawschool — get complete surveys on top law schools, expert advice on applicaton essays, LSAT prep and more.

VAULT CAREER LIBRARY 177

nirvana, and the place is worthy of Michelin star rating. And one cannot leave town without a burrito from Burrito Bros. Great sushi can also be found "downtown" at Dragonfly. Maude's Cafe has jazz by Unsafe Sax on Fridays outside, which is nice. I highly recommend going out to see some of the local college bands performing around town. And, oh yeah, do go visit the Ginnie or Ichetucknee Springs. The water is crystal clear with manatees floating about. You can rent floats and drop a keg in one as you float down the pristine rivers.

The School Says

The University of Florida Levin College of Law is one of the nation's most comprehensive public law schools. Founded in 1909, the college is accredited by the American Bar Association and is a member of the Association of American Law Schools. Alumni of the college are leaders in law, business, government, public service and education at the state and national level. No other law school has produced as many presidents of the American Bar Association—four—in the past four decades.

The law school offers courses of study leading to the JD; LLM in Taxation; LLM in International Taxation; LLM in Comparative Law; and SJD in Taxation degrees. It also offers certificate programs in Environmental and Land Use Law, Estates and Trusts Practice, Family Law, Intellectual Property Law and International and Comparative Law. Joint JD/MA and JD/PhD degrees in a variety of disciplines also are available. The college's Graduate Tax Program regularly ranks in the nation's Top Two, and its Environmental and Land Use Law Program in the Top 20.

Students and faculty enjoy the benefits of a recent $25 million expansion project that created a legal learning setting second to none. Located on the wooded western border of the UF campus, the law school is housed in state-of-the-art facilities that include one of the largest law libraries in the southeast and two new education towers with modern, comfortable classrooms. Most classrooms offer advanced technology such as wireless Internet access, outlets for laptop computers, and "smart podia" for presentations. Computer services available to stu-

dents also include a personal computer lab, research areas and a multi-station computer hub in the library's reference area.

Levin College of Law is a distinctive part of a preeminent research university that also is one of the nation's most comprehensive, offering a wealth of opportunities for interdisciplinary research, teaching and learning. Founded in 1853, the University of Florida is one of only 30 public universities in the prestigious Association of American Universities, which recognizes outstanding North American graduate research universities. The University of Florida also offers a variety of social and extracurricular activities, ranging from world-famous performers to Gator football, basketball and other top-ranked athletic programs.

The university is located in Gainesville, a city of approximately 118,000 in North Central Florida. It is on the I-75 corridor halfway between Atlanta and Miami and between the Atlantic Ocean and Gulf of Mexico, less than two hours by car from either coast, as well as from major cities such as Orlando, Tampa and Jacksonville. Its moderate temperature averages 70 degrees. *Money* magazine and other publications consistently rate Gainesville as one of America's most livable cities, and *Outdoor Explorer* magazine identified Gainesville as one of the nation's Top 10 cities for outdoor recreation. The beauty of north central Florida's freshwater springs, the many rivers and coastal areas that offer opportunities for kayaking and canoeing, and its proximity to Florida's famed beaches attract many outdoor enthusiasts to Gainesville.

University of Miami School of Law

Office of Admissions and Student Recruiting
P.O. Box 248087
Coral Gables, FL 33124
Admissions phone: (305) 284-6746
Admissions e-mail: admissions@law.miami.edu
Admissions URL: http://www.law.miami.edu/admissions/

 ## Admissions

Status: Current student, full-time
Dates of Enrollment: 8/2004-Submit Date
Survey Submitted: April 2006

One of the first things I remember about coming for a campus tour, and as per usual, I was running late—this time because I was lost. So I called to say how sorry I was and that I was still coming to campus. Jane (from the admissions office) stayed on the phone with me the whole time, giving me step by step directions. Pretty sure I might still be roaming around Miami if she hadn't.

One of the best pieces of advice I heard while I was applying to UM was with regards to studying. Someone in my tour group asked if it's true that everyone just spends all their time in the library studying 24/7. The tour guide's answer was: you should only do that if that's what works for you. Obviously, whatever you've been doing up until now has been working pretty well if you're looking at law schools and at a school like this one. So don't go and change your habits drastically jut because it's what you think you're supposed to do. You may not be able to do everything you did up until now, but pick one or two things and keep doing them.

In other words, you're not likely to have time to hang out on South Beach, go to the gym, the football games, parties, movies, and plays, but if going to the gym is something you've always enjoyed, don't stop going just because you're in law school. Or if you've always been into sports, go to the games. Don't spread yourself too thin but don't forget to do things that will keep you sane and grounded while you study because if all you do is study all the time, especially if that's not your style, you're likely to burn yourself out real quick. That's something I still try to get across to prospective students when I give tours. Might sound cheesy, but the point of it is pretty clear, I think.

Status: Alumnus/a, full-time
Dates of Enrollment: 8/1998-5/2001
Survey Submitted: April 2006

As what is called a "non-traditional student" (i.e., "old lady"), I was hesitant to submit a lengthy application without an interview first. I was shocked when the red-carpet was rolled out to me, I was encouraged to apply and received admission. I was selected for a summer pre-law scholarship program, which was enormously helpful for a transitioning student who had not been in school for 35 years. Later I learned that we "non-trads" usually help to up the bar passage rate by many percentage points. I did my part!

Status: Alumnus/a, full-time
Dates of Enrollment: 8/1997-5/2000
Survey Submitted: April 2006

University of Miami works on somewhat of a rolling admissions standard, and considers who should receive scholarships fairly early on. If you think you are a scholarship candidate, get your application in before January because they will be setting up interviews. I interviewed with a professor and an alum: they were incredibly smart and knew a lot about both my undergraduate school and my major; I was impressed, given that both are not overly well known .

I think UM is pretty selective—it seems that the smartest students could have had their choice of law school and UM lures them with scholarships, a great faculty, a nice campus, and a great place to live. UM, while a definite home for

locals, is really interested in getting students from out of state, particularly competitive colleges. My incoming class had a lot of students from Ivies and small northeast schools, including me, though I was a Miami native.

Also, they are truly interested in having a diverse group—there are a lot of ethnic and special interest clubs, and a definite need to have students talented in something other than just studying. For example, one dean loves the theater and is always staging shows with law school students. Because of the weather and the law school's close proximity to the amazing health center and outdoor practice fields, we have pretty athletic students,which is great for the annual Dean's Cup competition with the medical school. So if you have interests or a talent that could serve the law school, make sure they know it.

Status: Current student, full-time
Dates of Enrollment: 1/2005-Submit Date
Survey Submitted: November 2005

The route I chose with the admissions process at the University of Miami was to first apply early. Many people want to study law in southern Florida so the earlier the better. I was not required to interview with an admissions officer but I did have to provide them with an essay. My essay was very forthright and honest about my prior experience as a student as well as my role in the private sector. Overall, I feel like the caliber of students at UM are bright and thus the selectivity is greater than one would expect. Many of my classmates and I have graduate degrees in a wide variety of subjects.

Status: Current student, full-time
Dates of Enrollment: 8/2004-Submit Date
Survey Submitted: March 2006

The admissions process seemed to actually be the smoothest out of the 10 schools I applied to. Most schools do not require you to write additional essays when applying, however the University of Miami application has several essays which take some time to complete. After submitting the application, I received an offer of admission in only three weeks. In that time frame I had went to visit the campus for a tour, and I asked a lot of questions and showed my interest towards becoming a student there. My advice to anyone applying to this program is to make sure the essays are of top quality, and book a visit to campus after applying.

Status: Alumnus/a, full-time
Dates of Enrollment: 8/1985-5/1988
Survey Submitted: April 2005

Work hard in undergraduate school. Grades matter. Your scholastic work with professors and mentors matters. Meet as many people as you can. You never know who can provide guidance to you. If you have a family member who is an alum of UM School of Law, tell the school in your application. Dress for success. You don't have the wear an Armani suit, but look the part. Your interview is not the time for off-the-wall individual fashion sense.

Spend time on your essays. Yes, they are read and they do matter. Although law schools tend to have a population heavy in the conservative arena, UM loves individuals who have a strong work ethic and care about the world.

Status: Alumnus/a, full-time
Dates of Enrollment: 8/1998-5/2001
Survey Submitted: April 2005

Very active and helpful admissions department. Had current students call and talk to you about the school. Provided contact names of alumni for questions and set up online chatroom meetings for same. Sends list of prospective students to arrange roommate situations. Apply early, as the school's requirements and average scores are jumping every year.

Read all of Vault's Law School Surveys at www.vault.com/lawschool — get complete surveys on top law schools, expert advice on applicaton essays, LSAT prep and more.

VAULT CAREER LIBRARY   179

Status: Alumnus/a, full-time
Dates of Enrollment: 8/1992-5/1995
Survey Submitted: April 2005

The admissions process was very smooth. The application arrived very quickly from the school and was easy to understand. The required essay was relatively easy to put together as we were permitted to choose the topic. I was notified fairly quickly of my acceptance and with plenty of time to evaluate the law schools where I was accepted to make a decision on my selection.

There was a standard application, and I took the school tour. They were very good in requiring several short essays (one or two paragraphs), and did not place a huge emphasis on LSATs, though they did count. I was admitted without UM having received my final recommendation, and the letter was accompanied by a personal note from the admissions director, which was a nice touch.

Status: Current student, full-time
Dates of Enrollment: 8/2001-Submit Date
Survey Submitted: September 2003

Miami's selectivity has risen since I applied. As a result of wanting to move up into the top tier of law schools, they want high-caliber students. LSAT scores have risen among our incoming classes. UM has a rolling admissions policy, so apply as early as possible. This is also true for scholarship consideration. I applied in October, and by January I had an offer and a scholarship. You can get excellent scholarships here, but it takes a lot of effort. Write, rewrite, proof and re-proof your essays. The university likes clear, concise writing that doesn't meander to the point. They want to know that you're in a good position to write like a lawyer. After all, the school prides itself on a strong alumni base, and it wants to keep the reputation.

Status: Alumnus/a, full-time
Dates of Enrollment: 9/1998-5/2001
Survey Submitted: September 2003

The admissions process used to be very easy. I would take the LSAT plenty of time in advance. It pays off to be one of the first applicants with a high LSAT score because they are willing to throw money at LSAT scores of 165 and above. Use the recruiting director there, she will help with any problems that you have.

 **Academics**

Status: Current student, full-time
Dates of Enrollment: 8/2004-Submit Date
Survey Submitted: April 2006

The quality of classes is good on the whole, though classes differ so much from professor to professor (and, in all fairness, depending on the material) that it's sometimes tough to compare one to the next. In terms of ease of getting popular classes, I don't know that I'd say there's much EASE, necessarily, but it's not impossible. Waitlists are pretty useful and often work out for the best plus when the faculty realizes how popular something is, I've seen them add another section of the class or would imagine they'd just offer it again the following semester for those who weren't able to take it the first time around. So even though getting in to the classes might not be that easy the first time around (registering is a hectic time of year and a complete toss-up because of times and class-status—1L, 2L, 3L, first semester, second semester, etc.), there's usually some way to ultimately have it all work out.

Grading is rough. The curve the first year is tough and having one exam per class per semester is no treat. The way I explain it is that I'd much rather have multiple chances to mess up than to put all of my eggs in one basket. It's rough having no idea what to expect, how to read or write an exam (the workshops help but it's still different when you're sitting in a room for the first time for a whole four hours with absolute silence, tension you could cut with a knife and all the weight of the class grade on your shoulders) or whether each particular professor will like what you have to offer in an answer.

Status: Current student, full-time JD/MBA
Dates of Enrollment: 8/2005-Submit Date
Survey Submitted: April 2006

The program is good. UM Law allows first-year students to take electives in the spring semester. I was able to get into my first choice for electives. Grading is based on a curve the first year and most professors inform students on their method of grading. The professors are very nice and helpful. Each has a very different way of teaching, but all are very knowledgeable. Law school is a lot of work. A lot of reading, analyzing and in some classes, working on projects. In fact, Legal Research and Writing is all research and writing, with minimal reading (as compared to the reading in other courses).

Status: Current student, full-time
Dates of Enrollment: 8/2003-Submit Date
Survey Submitted: April 2006

The classes offered were very good and that was probably mostly due to the strength of the faculty. Almost every popular class was attainable at some point during the three years—if you couldn't get in as a 2L you would most likely get in as a 3L. The professors were very knowledgeable beyond just simple textbook reading; however, grading at times seemed arbitrary and harsh. Some professors are reluctant to give out A's even after the first year where the school imposes a C+ mandatory class average (school has no A- or B- grades). The workload though is typically manageable.

Status: Alumnus/a, full-time
Dates of Enrollment: 8/1998-5/2005
Survey Submitted: April 2006

Workload is time consuming, but not enough that one doesn't have time for friends and family and hobbies. Each professor has his/her own way of conducting class, but each one is effective in its own way. Some professors provide the occasional quiz/test, while some provide two projects during the year, etc. In law school, for the most part, there is one final exam per class for the entire semester, however, that also depends on how the professor decides to assign the grades.

My only complaint is that UM is very expensive. Although law school is competitive, there are always people, whether they be the professors, administration, other students, deans, etc. People should definitely take advantage of the Writing Center, Dean's Fellows Programs and other academic programs.

Status: Alumnus/a, full-time
Dates of Enrollment: 8/2001-5/2004
Survey Submitted: April 2006

UM Law (as far as I understand) is pretty traditional and especially in the first year, the Socratic Method is widely used. Like the majority of other law schools, the classes for the first year are preset, with the exception of one elective in the second semester. I believe that the "required" classes are crucial and the caliber of the professors is very high.

In the second and third year, students are given a lot more liberty in choosing the classes they want to take, having to fulfill one "professional responsibility" class and otherwise filling general "categories" of classes. Although as a second-year student it was sometimes difficult to get a class some students considered "prime," by the third year it was rare that a student was not able to take a desired class.

Status: Alumnus/a, full-time
Dates of Enrollment: 8/1997-5/2000
Survey Submitted: April 2006

I found law school challenging but not ridiculously impossible. The professors are very cool and very accomplished—these are people who totally appreciate the weather and everything living in Miami has to offer. They are also incredibly accessible—with office hours, before and after class, hanging out at events on the Bricks or working out at the gym, and there are some really great professors who make class awesome. It can be difficult to get into some classes but they try to offer a lot of different sections of certain classes to accommodate the need.

UM is very big on having students be exposed to more than just academics—in my first year, my legal writing class was with a local trial and appellate attorney, and in my second year, my litigations skills class was with a judge who is now a federal judge, and my pre-litigation skills class was with a very successful and well-known local attorney. Some of my other classes were also taught by local attorneys—because of their practice, they are not as accessible as the professors but it is fun to have practicing attorneys teaching you the material.

The school encourages employment and the professors are pretty aware that most students are working so the workload is very reasonable, and the employers are really reasonable at exam time—there is mutual respect between the law school and the local law community.

Status: Current student, full-time
Dates of Enrollment: 8/2004-Submit Date
Survey Submitted: March 2006

There is some outstanding faculty at this institution, and I emphasize the word some. While the faculty has received much recognition on their publications in the legal world, the school is trying desperately to make up for the relatively low rankings the school receives in *U.S. News & World Report*, and they are doing so by overloading the students with work. One teacher whose class I had for 50 minutes three times a week recommended that we spend three hours a night preparing for each class.

The most horrific part about the academics is the C+ grading curve the school utilizes, where as every other law school to my knowledge has a B grading curve. The University of Miami has made some horrible choices when it comes to picking teachers. My civil procedure teacher has received hundreds of complaints from students year after year on the poor quality of teaching he provides and the school refuses remove this teacher because of his tenure. Not one of the other faculty members can help themselves from rolling their eyes each and every time this civil procedure teacher is mentioned.

The school says: "For first-year classes only, faculty must give a combined total of A and B+ grades to at least 20 percent of the class and a combined total of B, B+ and A grades to at least 45 percent of the class. Faculty are free to give more A, B+ and B grades. Faculty who teach first-year classes are required to give C- or below grades to at least 5 percent of the class, which would just be five in a class of 100 or three in class of 50. The reason for the latter rule is to ensure that students who are in serious academic difficulty are forced to confront the problem early in their law school career, rather than 'squeak by' in school and then find themselves unable to pass the bar and unprepared for practice. The standard advice regarding study time is that you should expect to prepare two to three hours for every hour in class, but you may find that some classes require more preparation time than others.

"Second, having high academic standards for students does nothing for our *U.S. News & World Report* ranking. While entry level LSAT scores play a role in the ranking, law school grades do not. One of the many anomalies of *U.S. News* ranking is that its selectivity measures are going to somewhat disadvantage schools with larger student bodies. Does that mean we should down-size classes in order to improve our *U.S. News* ranking? The answer is 'no.' Our larger size means that at UM a student can study with the leading expert on 'law of the sea,' the leading expert on how to detect whether someone is lying, as well as the leading expert on partnership tax. The point is that having a large school means having a large faculty and offering many many more opportunities for students. It also means that rather than going to school with other students who look just like you, at Miami classes are filled with people from different backgrounds, who come from all across the country and the world.

"Finally, as to the civil procedure teacher—what can we say? Different students have different learning styles. We do monitor teaching evaluations and counsel and sometimes reassign professors when there is good cause, but bear in mind that the teacher that one student believes to be 'horrible' another student believes to be 'tough, but fair.'"

Status: Alumnus/a, full-time
Dates of Enrollment: 8/2001-5/2004
Survey Submitted: April 2005

I selected the school because of the quality and credentials of their faculty and I was not disappointed. I think that the faculty at the UM law school compares favorably with that at any of the Top 10 schools—my friend attended one year at UM and transferred to Georgetown and reports that the faculty at UM sometimes surpassed that at Georgetown. The faculty is also very interested in the students and readily accessible.

The range of classes is amazing—being in a large city the school has access to some powerful and brilliant practitioners who serve as adjuncts in their field of expertise. There are classes in maritime law, Latin American law, trademark, copyright and some classes and programs are conducted completely in Spanish. Grading is tough—but on a blind basis, so pretty fair. Workload can be pretty intense first year but tappers off depending on the student's focus and objectives.

Status: Current student, full-time
Dates of Enrollment: 8/2001-Submit Date
Survey Submitted: September 2003

The variety of classes offered is amazing. One word of caution: the first-year curve is harsh. We have a highly recognized faculty who bring not only academics, but a lot of experience as well. The best classes—Evidence with Michael Graham (he wrote the *Nutshell*) and the Lit Skills Program. Both are hard to get into, but well worth the extra time and energy of waitlists and work.

> **The school says:** "There is no mandatory grading curve for upper-division courses taught by full-time members of the faculty. The curve in the first year is used to maintain parity among sections and functions mainly as a floor, not a ceiling. The vast majority of students are successful in their first year and go on to graduate with knowledge and skills that make them highly effective to employers.
>
> "Virtually everyone who comes to Miami has at least three semesters to try to take Litigation Skills. Third-year students are given preference in the fall semester. In the spring semester, priority is given to second-year students who commit to participating in a clinical placement."

Status: Alumnus/a, full-time
Dates of Enrollment: 8/1996-12/1998
Survey Submitted: September 2003

I really enjoyed most of my classes. There were a few that I couldn't stand, especially Elements, which is required of all 1Ls at UM. My second- and third-year classes were, of course, wonderful, mainly because I was able to choose them. I also spent the summers between year one and year two, and then year two and year three, in London on the school program. I was able to get a semester ahead and had a fabulous time.

I truly highly recommend the program. The workload was as expected, mostly a lot of reading, but if you keep up it isn't terrible. The grading was harder in some classes than others, but what law school is a cakewalk?

 Employment Prospects

Status: Current student, full-time
Dates of Enrollment: 8/2003-Submit Date
Survey Submitted: April 2006

The during and after school employment prospects were much better than I expected. There were always employers (from small to large firms, to judges and corporations) in the area looking for UM students for during school and after graduation. A number of students placed with big time law firms like White and Case, Sidley Austin, Greenberg Traurig, Holland and Knight, Carlton Fields, etc. Students also got federal clerkships, and placed with the State Attorney's and Public Defender's Offices in and out of Miami.

The career office is very helpful when it comes to placement. The only drawback is that the top 20 percent of the class eat up almost all of the OCI inter-

Read all of Vault's Law School Surveys at www.vault.com/lawschool — get complete surveys on top law schools, expert advice on applicaton essays, LSAT prep and more.

VAULT CAREER LIBRARY   181

views, so students outside of that must work fairly hard to get in on all the opportunities.

Status: Alumnus/a, full-time
Dates of Enrollment: 8/2001-5/2004
Survey Submitted: April 2006

One very positive aspect of UM Law is that I do not know one person that I graduated with who is unemployed (except that rare case where one is unemployed by choice). Personally, I have had a fabulous experience work-wise both as a student and as a graduate. I believe that UM Law is invaluable in the way it makes available so many contacts.

At the end of my first year, the school held a mini-job fair and a simple inquiry on my part with one of the "information tables" led to a paid internship with the General Counsel of the then INS, Dept. of Justice. Once my internship ended there in my third year, I browsed UM Law's career center's online clerk posting web site for another clerkship and I ended obtaining a position with the General Counsel of the largest international bank in Miami. As luck would have it, I was offered a job toward the end of my third year with the same bank and I am still currently there as an Associate General Counsel.

During law school, I believe that the UM Law career center was a tremendous help for me—from providing on-campus interviews, reviewing (and making suggestions to) my resume, doing a mock interview (so I might know what to expect in a real interview).

I consider myself lucky, but a lot of it has to do with the school. UM Law has tremendous respect in the S. Fla. community and many of my former schoolmates are also work with reputable firms, businesses and organizations.

Status: Alumnus/a, full-time
Dates of Enrollment: 8/2001-5/2004
Survey Submitted: April 2006

While I wouldn't say that people were tripping over themselves to hire me, the employers in South Florida know that graduates who did well at UM are the equals of graduates from any of the "better" law schools in the country. Outside Florida, it's harder to find a job. I know people who have moved to New York and passed the bar there and who are still struggling to find anything but temp work.

Status: Alumnus/a, full-time
Dates of Enrollment: 8/1997-5/2000
Survey Submitted: April 2006

You are probably not going to get a clerkship with the Supreme Court. Other than than, you can get a job anywhere, and the school will prepare you to be there. The school starts your first year with introducing you to local prominent attorneys through their Firm Night series where every first-year goes to a dinner hosted by a prominent firm. They push the summer abroad programs for the first summer, but also provide a lot of information on working for judges and the career placement office is a really hard-working bunch who will work with you on your interests.

For second-year and third-year students, the school has on-campus interviews where the big firms come to the school and conduct interviews, and the school also hosts a career fair every year for all students to attend with members of local firms in every practice area you can think of. If you want to stay in Miami, though plenty of people leave and have jobs, no one thinks more highly of a UM grad than a UM grad, and the big and small firms and judiciary are chock full of them wanting to hire fellow Hurricanes. The school totally understands that people get jobs through networking and gives students every opportunity to do so.

Status: Alumnus/a, full-time
Dates of Enrollment: 8/1996-5/1999
Survey Submitted: April 2005

Since graduation five years ago, I have worked at a top-tier law firm and as in-house counsel. I recently started my own business and I volunteer as an alumni it events in my local area. I had no problem getting a job and employers seemed generally impressed with my resume. During law school, the university assisted me with an internship with a local federal judge and with obtaining a summer associate position with a top law firm.

Status: Current student, full-time
Dates of Enrollment: 8/2001-Submit Date
Survey Submitted: September 2003

The career planning center knows its stuff. One caveat—you have to be a high-performing student to really get the jobs. However, the resources are there for everyone, and they help each student create a quality resume and prep them for interviews. On-campus recruiting is tedious at best, and obviously not random. They generally take law review members and a few phenomenal others.

> **Miami says:** "Top firms and governmental agencies want to interview top students; grades and law review status are measures of students' academic accomplishments. While the fall on-campus interviewing program is selective based on employers requirements, the Career Planning Center provides many other on- and off-campus opportunities for all students to interview and network with employers regionally and nationally. Students must be willing to take advantage of, and follow up on, opportunities that are offered through the CPC."

 **Quality of Life**

Status: Current student, full-time
Dates of Enrollment: 8/2003-Submit Date
Survey Submitted: April 2006

The law school is located in a very nice, beautiful, safe area located on the edge of the undergrad campus. Crime is generally not a probably since the area is patrolled by university police as well as Coral Gables and South Miami police. Parking is always a problem because the school shares a parking lot with the music school, and because almost all students have to drive to school since there is no graduate housing on campus.

But there is plenty of housing options, locations, and price ranges, for students to choose from—e.g., near the school, the beach, downtown Miami, Sunset, Cocowalk, etc. The dining facilities are comparable to a mall's dining area. Unfortunately it doesn't stay open much past the lunch hour, so students are stuck with the same small selection of places to eat in they want to stay on campus (Subway, Sbarro, Starbuck's, or the university's Rathskeller).

Status: Alumnus/a, full-time
Dates of Enrollment: 8/2001-5/2004
Survey Submitted: April 2006

Even though on-campus housing was not an option, the school did provide a lot of informational help. First, it "polled" current students about their living situation (information about where they're living, costs, neighborhood, etc.) and made the information available to prospective students. Additionally, the school has a "roommate" list where students and prospective students can find people who need a place to live or need a roommate.

Status: Alumnus/a, full-time
Dates of Enrollment: 8/1997-5/2000
Survey Submitted: April 2006

The worst thing about Miami is the traffic. Don't move to West Kendall or Cutler Ridge and think it will take 10 minutes to get to school. Get satellite radio or lots of friends with cell phones while you spend a lot of time in the car. Parking is also a pain at the law school—while there a million parking spaces, there are not that many right next to the law school and in Miami, we are very into immediate gratification—you do not want to wait five minutes in the heat for the shuttle to take you to the law school. It is a badge of honor for an upperclassman to snag a parking space (those classes start much later than first-year classes, the students who hog the spaces all day) and the parking lot is a veritable battlefield.

> **The school says:** "Students can use the Miami Metrorail, which is Miami's 22-mile elevated rapid transit system. The metrorail runs from the South Dade community of Kendall through Coral Gables, downtown Miami and UM's medical campus to the North-Dade community of Medley, with connections to Fort Lauderdale and West Palm Beach via Tri-Rail. Metrorail runs

from 5 a.m. until midnight seven days a week. You can hop on the Metrorail from the convenient University Station adjacent to the UM campus."

Status: Alumnus/a, full-time
Dates of Enrollment: 8/2001-5/2004
Survey Submitted: April 2006

The facilities are pretty decent, and the weather (outside hurricane season) is fantastic. Miami is a nice place—a little devoid of high culture like you get in New York or D.C., but it's growing. Be prepared, however, that you will run into people who really speak only Spanish or Haitian Creole, so it really is helpful to know some basic Spanish. Not a necessity, but you'll enjoy the experience more, as people will treat you more nicely.

Status: Current student, full-time
Dates of Enrollment: 1/2005-Submit Date
Survey Submitted: November 2005

The quality of life at UM is probably better than most but still worse than other professional degrees. There is no housing on campus for law students and apartments in Miami are very expensive for the quality offered. The campus is pretty and well kept, but the law school is in need of an extreme makeover. The library provides for printing and copies included with your tuition, but the services are crowded and limited.

Dining in the area is very expensive and can eat up a lot of your money. A major drawback for someone who is not supported by his or her family is that many of the students are wealthy and are therefore ignorant of the expenses that they incur. UM is a very expensive school and the decision to attend should not be undertaken without some thought. However, if you have the money to enjoy sunny FL then this is the place to be. Many of the areas that students live are safe and free from crime.

> **Miami Law says:** "Beginning fall 2006, limited on-campus housing became available to law students in the university's new Village Apartments. Assignments are made on a lottery basis. To assist students in finding off-campus housing, the Office of Student Recruiting provides an Apartment and Relocation Guide, connections to local realtors (who do not require a fee), a summer housing session, a housing message board, a roommate referral service, and individual assistance as needed."

Status: Current student, full-time
Dates of Enrollment: 8/2004-Submit Date
Survey Submitted: March 2006

The school does not make it convenient for their students to come to class every day. The parking lot by the law school is extremely small and the spots are so tight that even an economy car has trouble pulling into and out of spots. Unless you have an 8 a.m. class, you will not find a spot in the law school parking lot and you will be forced to park in a dirt lot somewhere around campus and you must take the shuttle bus to get to the law building. When I say the law school parking lot, that doesn't seem to stop just about every undergraduate student from parking in there as well. If you are lucky enough to get a parking spot, the fear of not getting another spot, should you want to go out or go home for lunch, prevents you from leaving campus for lunch.

Status: Alumnus/a, full-time
Dates of Enrollment: 8/1996-5/1999
Survey Submitted: April 2005

Law school is stressful, no matter what school you attend. I wanted to live in a city I could enjoy when I wasn't studying. There is no better quality of life than living in Miami/Coral Gables, Florida. The campus is beautiful, the environment surrounding the campus is safe and there are lots of activities for students. There is a Metrorail across the street from the school and plenty of shopping in walking distance. The weather is amazing and, of course, there is the beach when you are tired of studying in the library and need a more relaxing environment to read. I moved cross country and was able to find law school roommates and had no problem fitting in.

Status: Current student, full-time
Dates of Enrollment: 8/2004-Submit Date
Survey Submitted: March 2005

Miami is fabulous—great environment, almost a little too much fun at times. Housing can be a little expensive since this is a huge metro area. UM is in the process of building graduate student housing, though. What that means, however, is less parking for us now. Word of advice—don't park in the law school parking lot unless you don't mind getting a few dents in your car—the spaces are tiny and the aisles are very tight. Overall, safety is fine so long as you don't do stupid things. UM fosters a really close knit community through classroom interaction and social endeavors. The law school environment encourages people to get to know each other well both in and out of school.

Status: Alumnus/a, full-time
Dates of Enrollment: 8/1999-5/2002
Survey Submitted: May 2004

As a whole, the University of Miami has an incredibly beautiful campus. There is a small lake in the middle of campus with an illuminated fountain. The grounds on the entire campus are impeccably kept. The university's Wellness Center (gym) is also magnificent. It is relatively new and better than most private gyms. It has a large weight and exercise room, a large basketball gym, racquetball courts, a swimming pool, and an indoor track. Furthermore, a basketball stadium was recently built on campus, also an incredible building.

Relatively, Miami's law school facilities are poor. The classrooms have not been remodeled in years, if ever. One only needs to walk a little way across campus to the graduate business school, where there are hardwood floors, a marble staircase, leather chairs and conference rooms, to appreciate the relatively poor quality of the law facilities.

The law school courtyard, however, is very nice. The "Bricks," as it is referred, is a cobblestone courtyard with trees, benches and picnic tables. There is a Subway sub shop located within the law school complex, which is a convenient place to eat when studying late. Furthermore, there is a pizza place and a food court located a short walk from the law school. There is also the university's sports bar located across the street from the law school complex. Periodically, the student bar association sponsors what used to be called "Beer on the Bricks" at the sports bar. This is a great way to relax and drink some free beer while talking with classmates.

The law library is among the largest in the Southeast. It houses reporters from every state as well as books and information on various law topics. Reference librarians are very helpful in helping students with research issues.

 ## Social Life

Status: Current student, full-time
Dates of Enrollment: 8/2004-Submit Date
Survey Submitted: April 2006

There's no shortage of events, and I think it's great that the law school actually hosts so many social events/happy hours. It's a nice way for people to get motivated to get out and to meet other students/people. Plus, it's always fun to see professors and deans out at bars and clubs and what not. There's no shortage of bars, restaurants, and clubs for everyone and all tastes. Beer at the Rat every other week for the law students is a cool idea, and it'll be a bummer not to have a bar on campus when they get rid of the Rat and turn it into something else.

Status: Current student, full-time
Dates of Enrollment: 8/2003-Submit Date
Survey Submitted: April 2006

For Miami, the law school is relatively small (most high schools in the area are larger). So generally everyone is familiar with everyone, and that means plenty of law school dating. Also because the law school (unlike the med school) is next to the undergrad campus, there is also some law school-undergrad dating.

Every other Thursday, the law school hosts a Beer at the Rat(hskeller) happy hour. Since the drinks are free for law school students there is always a big turnout. Also on Thursdays a majority of the students that go out, go to Moe's

Read all of Vault's Law School Surveys at www.vault.com/lawschool — get complete surveys on top law schools, expert advice on applicaton essays, LSAT prep and more.

VAULT CAREER LIBRARY 183

in Cocowalk. Sunday to Wednesday a number of the students head to either Titanic (bar/eatery near campus) or Sunset Tavern (bar/eatery three-quarters of a mile away from campus). On the weekend, students either go to South Beach (Rok Bar, Delano, Shore Club, Pordy Lounge, Playwright) or Cocowalk (Sandbar, Moe's). Probably the favorite places for casual dining favorites is Moon (Thai/Japanese restaurant).

Status: Alumnus/a, full-time
Dates of Enrollment: 8/1997-5/2000
Survey Submitted: April 2006

Miami cuisine and nightlife is now, finally, on a par with New York, and, like New York, for budget-conscious students, there are plenty of places to grab a delicious and inexpensive or very expensive meal. Students are very social and hang out either at the bars where the law schools go or to the clubs on the Beach and in the Design District. Some law students live like law students but a lot are supplemented by wealthy parents and trust funds, so $20 for a martini at the Delano or $100 per person dinner at Barton G where you valet ($15) your Mercedes is just another Saturday night. The law school has a Beer on the Bricks every Thursday night and everyone, students and professors go. Students date and hook up but law school is a lot like junior high—whatever you do, people will know.

Status: Current student, full-time
Dates of Enrollment: 1/2005-Submit Date
Survey Submitted: November 2005

The social life at UM is above and beyond what you will find at most law schools. Many of the students are bright but not competitive to the point of sacrificing all of their spare time for school. Everyone is either getting together on the weekend and for drinks, food, or a movie. There are many clubs that one can become involved in and the dating scene is great. Most of the students come here because it is a great school and the students are very attractive. I guess that it has something to do with the weather.

Status: Current student, full-time
Dates of Enrollment: 8/2004-Submit Date
Survey Submitted: March 2006

The atmosphere at a private school is quite different from that of a public school. A lot of the students at this school seem very stuck up and clicky. No one has anything nice to say about anyone else. I can relate the scene at this school to *Beverly Hills 90210*. There is a big courtyard in the middle where everyone chooses to mingle on their lunch break and in between classes. The problem with doing so is it gets really hot and muggy in the courtyard, and it is impossible to get any work done with people continuously walking by and trying to socialize with you.

There are no good restaurants in the vicinity of the school. The closest night spot to the school is in Coconut Grove, but the bars in this scene are poor in quality and get old quick. If you are looking to have a good time or a good meal, the best bet is to head to South Beach which is a 15 to 50 minute drive from campus depending on traffic.

Status: Alumnus/a, full-time
Dates of Enrollment: 7/2000-7/2003
Survey Submitted: September 2004

South Miami and Coral Gables have a plethora of bars and shops. South Beach is about 20 minutes away. Brickell is about 10. As for school related—there were your standard SBA type activities. Word to the wise though—the average student age was 24 in 2003. The majority were right out of undergrad. People are generally pretty happy and laid back. Life is certainly easier in FL than elsewhere and the law school reflects that.

Status: Alumnus/a, full-time
Dates of Enrollment: 8/1999-5/2002
Survey Submitted: May 2004

There are basically two favorite areas of Miami students—Coconut Grove and South Beach. South Beach can be an adventure, but expect to pay big bucks for cover charges and drinks (a mixed drink can easily cost $14) in the clubs. If you are not into the "club scene," there are some other low-key places on the beach where you can have an equally good time. The Delano Hotel can be busy, yet low-key. However, drinks there are also very expensive. The Clevelander on Ocean Drive is a nice place to hang out. It is mostly outdoors, and drinks and food are reasonably priced.

Coconut Grove is an area closer to campus, which many students frequent. There are many bars and restaurants that are much cheaper than those on South Beach, yet students can have an equally good time. Favorites include Sandbar, the Tavern (which only serves beer), Barracuda, and Monty's. Monty's is a great place to go for happy hour, as it is outdoors and right on Biscayne Bay. Monty's also has an excellent indoor restaurant adjacent to its outdoor part. Fort Lauderdale's Los Olas Boulevard is also a great place to go out for a night. There are many restaurants and clubs located on the street. The only drawback is that it is located about 35 miles from campus, which equates to about a 45 minute to one-hour drive. Across the street from campus, there are many restaurants and some bars. Students should definitely check out Origin, a restaurant not far from campus (also located in South Beach). The food there is incredible and reasonably priced. There is also an outdoor shopping mall, "The Shops at Sunset Place," across the street from campus. There is always something to do or go see in South Florida.

Taking a drive down to Key West can be a great way to get away from studying and relax. Furthermore, all of the major cruise lines leave from Miami, and sometimes cruises to the Caribbean can be very reasonably priced. Since you already live in South Florida, airfare or other transportation costs are unnecessary. Also, going to a Hurricane athletic event, or a professional athletic event (Dolphins, Heat, Marlins, Panthers) can be a good time. There are also dog tracks and horse racing tracks located in South Florida.

Emory University School of Law

Admissions Office
1301 Clifton Road
Atlanta, GA 30322
Admissions phone: (404) 727-6802
URL: www.law.emory.edu

 Admissions

Status: Alumnus/a, full-time
Dates of Enrollment: 8/1999-5/2003
Survey Submitted: April 2006

The interview process was very standard for law school—GPA, LSAT and an essay. I did attend a tour of the campus, but did not have an interview. I believe that admissions is based greatly on a function of GPA and LSAT score (like most law schools).

Status: Alumnus/a, full-time
Dates of Enrollment: 1/2002-12/2004
Survey Submitted: April 2006

I was a mid-year transfer. The admission process is fairly routine, but one has to be rather vigilant to find out that Emory does in fact accept mid-year transfers. I was only able to do so after being instructed to write a letter to one of the academic deans and having him approve my application. Overall, getting admitted to Emory is much like getting admitted to most other top-tier law schools; strong undergrad grades as well as solid (though not Harvard/Yale/Stanford type) scores on the LSAT. Essay might be helpful, but I'm pretty sure the grades and LSATs are biggest factors.

Status: Current student, full-time
Dates of Enrollment: 9/2002-Submit Date
Survey Submitted: March 2005

The admissions department was very helpful in providing details and answering questions on the best dates to submit the application and most efficient way to fill out all materials. The event that stood out at Emory Law was an admitted students weekend in April that allowed accepted students to preview the Emory campus and the Emory law program

Status: Current student, full-time
Dates of Enrollment: 8/2002-Submit Date
Survey Submitted: March 2005

Standard law school admission process. Be sure to apply for the Woodruff scholarship.

Status: Current student, full-time
Dates of Enrollment: 8/2002-Submit Date
Survey Submitted: March 2005

The admissions process is very efficient and they usually get back to you within the stated period of time. The selectivity of the school has gone up in recent years as the number of applicants has increased.

Status: Current student, full-time
Dates of Enrollment: 7/2003-Submit Date
Survey Submitted: January 2005

The admissions faculty is very receptive to answering student's questions throughout the admissions process. Especially once you are accepted. If you attend one of the admitted students receptions, there will be plenty of faculty, current and former students, and other prospective students. It was the optimal place to address all of my pre-attendance questions. Furthermore, since the time I applied, the school web site has become 100 percent more informative and user friendly. Finally, during the actual application process, I asked an admissions counselor to speak with a current student and she put me in contact with a stu-

dent of similar background. who ultimately became my mentor and life long friend!

Status: Current student, full-time
Dates of Enrollment: 8/2003-Submit Date
Survey Submitted: May 2005

The admissions process was a breeze. The staff is responsive by phone or if you are a walk in. The essay should be personal. A lot of people think it is all about the grades and LSAT, but I think (know) a really good personal statement carries weight with admissions. LSAT and work experience also was given more weight than undergraduate GPA.

Status: Current student, full-time
Dates of Enrollment: 8/2002-Submit Date
Survey Submitted: February 2005

Emory Law is fairly easy to get into, compared with some other schools. They have a later application deadline for admission, but earlier deadlines for scholarships. Also, this school tends to be more interested in numbers and geographic distribution than interviews, essays, past disciplinary record, or past employment. However, the paperwork in regard to their admission process tends to be sort of lax—I never received my first acceptance letter. Nearly a month after the response date, I had to call the admissions office to find out if letters had been sent out and they told me over the phone that I had been admitted.

Status: Current student, full-time
Dates of Enrollment: 9/2003-Submit Date
Survey Submitted: October 2003

I had very average grades and pretty good LSAT's, but not high enough that I could get in on the LSAT alone. My GPA was nicely below Emory's 25 to 75 range, but it did come from an Ivy.

Status: Current student, full-time
Dates of Enrollment: 8/2002-Submit Date
Survey Submitted: March 2004

Grades and LSAT are the most important factors. Like it or not, this must be the focus for a school trying desperately to break into the Top 15.

 Academics

Status: Alumnus/a, full-time
Dates of Enrollment: 8/1999-5/2003
Survey Submitted: April 2006

I received an absolutely fabulous education. I thought that the faculty was top-notch—excellent teachers and leaders in their fields. Their doors were always open and they took an interest in the students. I always felt that I could pick up the phone, call a professor and he/she would know exactly who they were speaking with. This is a product of the community feel at Emory.

Status: Alumnus/a, full-time
Dates of Enrollment: 1/2002-12/2004
Survey Submitted: April 2006

Classes are routine; don't expect any high-brow intellectualism. While some seminar-type classes do offer study of law in a more esoteric manner, students should attend Yale (if they can get in) or Harvard or a Top 10 school to fully explore critical studies. Emory is essentially a pre-professional school, so rote memorization is still the norm; if one can figure our what the professor wants, then getting good grades is easy without really having to show any innate ability to think and analyze issues. Since this is probably the case at most law schools, I wouldn't necessarily say this is a negative about Emory.

Read all of Vault's Law School Surveys at www.vault.com/lawschool — get complete surveys on top law schools, expert advice on applicaton essays, LSAT prep and more.

VAULT CAREER LIBRARY   185

Status: Current student, full-time
Dates of Enrollment: 9/2002-Submit Date
Survey Submitted: March 2005

I have never had a problem getting the classes that I needed. For the most part, the professors are well prepared and well read in the current events relating to their respective fields. The biggest weakness would be the lack of experience in professors teaching transactional work; however, Emory Law has recently begun to bolster this area of interest.

Status: Current student, full-time
Dates of Enrollment: 8/2002-Submit Date
Survey Submitted: March 2005

The courseload is rigorous. Overall, the faculty is topnotch and the quality of class stellar. Great criminal law faculty. Easy to get into all classes. Grading would be better if we were on a 4.0 scale opposed to a 4.3 scale as many professors do not give out As. First-year courseload is a bit overwhelming, but that is pretty standard for law school in general.

Status: Current student, full-time
Dates of Enrollment: 8/2002-Submit Date
Survey Submitted: March 2005

The professors at Emory are some of the best in the field. Academically the school is Top 15 material. The courseload is difficult and the curve is strictly upheld first year. It is possible to find a handful of easy classes during your last two years, but most classes are still very challenging. It is possible to take two classes outside the law school, which most 3Ls do.

Status: Current student, full-time
Dates of Enrollment: 7/2003-Submit Date
Survey Submitted: January 2005

Emory's registrar uses a point system to assign classes which can be confusing, but as with everything at Emory, there are helpful people close by. Other than that, I have had no trouble getting the classes I wanted. Emory's program focuses on exceptional writing and trial advocacy skills. The professors are some of the most intelligent people I have ever met. They are extremely helpful and adhere closely to the "open door" policy. I have stopped a professor in the hall to ask a quick question and ended up chatting for hours! On the other hand, they also stick closely to the grading curve which actually fosters an environment where we realize that GRADES AREN'T EVERYTHING. The workload is HEAVY but what the hell, IT'S LAW SCHOOL!

Status: Current student, full-time
Dates of Enrollment: 8/2003-Submit Date
Survey Submitted: May 2005

The professors are great and you can do well even if you are not intense. If you are an over achiever, you will have to work very hard because it is a very tight curve and you are pretty evenly matched with your peers so it is difficult to get an A. I have never had a problem getting into the classes I wanted. The classes are usually decent in size and most professors know your name. Some professors are know for having crazy subjective criteria in grading and you are usually warned in advance so you can avoid the "kooky" grading if getting that A cannot be left to chance.

Status: Current student, full-time
Dates of Enrollment: 8/2002-Submit Date
Survey Submitted: February 2005

Emory Law is an excellent legal education, as long as you are interested in transactional or financial based law. The course offering and clinic opportunities in other areas tend to be very spotty and targeted toward a certain liberal elite point of view (they offer credit for ACLU internships but not for internships with corresponding conservative organizations). The grading is on an allegedly strict bell curve (with median set at 3.1) but it seems very arbitrary and allows for no feedback or true learning; no matter how hard you work or how well you know your material, it is almost impossible to get out of the B range. The professors vary a great deal, from young, ambitious and arrogant to older and kindly—it tends to be the luck of the draw. This school does not offer any particular legal concentrations and, due to the small number and limited scheduling of classes, leaves limited opportunities for practical legal experience outside the classroom. Also, Emory Law does not have strong ties to the Atlanta community and Emory

Law students tend to have little contact, context or experience in the city of Atlanta at large (it's like a little piece of New Jersey in Georgia).

Status: Current student, full-time
Dates of Enrollment: 8/2002-Submit Date
Survey Submitted: March 2004

Very strict grading curve. Quality of education depends on which first-year teachers you are assigned to. However, they make a sincere effort to have the star faculty teach first-year courses. Legal Methods is required first year, and it functions as an introductory Jurisprudence class that really sets the tone for an Emory legal education. It gives students the tools to engage in sophisticated policy arguments from the first week of school. Otherwise, the faculty at Emory is phenomenal. Most have open-door policies, and the Law and Religion Program is leading the way in the national scholarly discussion on that topic.

Status: Alumnus/a, full-time
Dates of Enrollment: 8/2000-5/2003
Survey Submitted: October 2003

Classes are very hit or miss. There are some amazing professors who are willing to go out of their way for students that express an interest, and others who should never have stepped foot in a classroom. Emory's bidding system makes it very difficult to get exactly that classes that you want. Each student gets 30 points to bid on the classes that they want, many of the more popular classes close out at 30 points, making it difficult to get into more than one popular class a semester. The workload depends more on the student body than the professors. Emory students are competitive, and students tend to work as hard as the best student, instead of simply working as hard as they need to.

Status: Alumnus/a, full-time
Dates of Enrollment: 9/1996-5/1999
Survey Submitted: April 2004

In general, the quality of academic instruction is high, and instructors, for the most part, seem genuinely interested in their teaching responsibilities. Required courses make up the first-year curriculum, with a few required courses (evidence, trial techniques) in the second year as well. Emory has a unique, intensive two-week practical course called "Trial Techniques" that is mandatory for second-year students. It is either an invaluable experience (if you plan to focus on litigation) or an extra $3,000 to $4,000 expense (if you plan never to set foot in a courtroom, as I did, and could not start your summer associate job for an extra two weeks).

Generally, it's possible to get most classes that you want to take, and Emory has a points bidding system to allocate spaces in some of the more popular seminar classes. Unfortunately, many small seminars are held only once every other year, so if you miss a class in your second year, you may not have an opportunity to take it the following year.

Workload was generally reasonable, provided that you kept up with reading and outlining during the year. Second-year workload could be trying during the fall semester given that interviewing, law review and moot court were all in full swing simultaneously. However, I should qualify this by saying I worked 50+ hours per week as a consultant prior to law school, so the whole experience seemed like a vacation to me.

Status: Alumnus/a, full-time
Dates of Enrollment: 8/1992-5/1995
Survey Submitted: April 2004

When I was there, Emory placed strong emphasis on its litigation training. As a corporate lawyer now, I realize how well Emory prepares its students to do litigation but not as much in other areas. Still, considering how the threat of litigation hangs over everything you do for a client, and how I sometimes assist litigators when corporate/business issues arise, it's good to know and understand the whole process of litigation. There was little intellectual property training when I was there, but I understand there is a lot more now.

Emory always had a good amount of classes involving international issues and professors from other jurisdictions in the U.S. and overseas to add different perspectives. Two of the tax professors were the most popular of any professors—Professors Doernberg and Abrams, both brilliant guys, but most of the professors were topnotch (there were a few exceptions). Virtually all of my classes were of high quality; the only ones that come to mind as exceptions were by new professors just starting off.

If I recall correctly, an average of 83 over three years was needed to graduate "with distinction." Emory law students don't graduate "with honors," they graduate "with distinction." There was no grade inflation; students actually had to work to get good grades.

 # Employment Prospects

Status: Alumnus/a, full-time
Dates of Enrollment: 8/1999-5/2003
Survey Submitted: April 2006

Emory students get the best jobs in Georgia, hands down, and are marketable at any job in the southeast. Strong alumni networks and interviewing programs in NY and Washington, D.C. are incredibly helpful in getting a job in either of those cities. There are additionally interview programs in Dallas and Chicago.

> **The school says:** "Emory also participates in regional interview programs in Southern California (for employers in Northern and Southern California, Arizona, New Mexico and Nevada) and New England (for employers throughout the six-state region)."

Status: Alumnus/a, full-time
Dates of Enrollment: 1/2002-12/2004
Survey Submitted: April 2006

Again, like most schools, the best students (top ranked) will get the best jobs. If one wants to work at the top firms in Atlanta, then Emory is very well regarded, but these firms also recruit nationally, so Emory students are competing with students from Harvard, Yale, Stanford, Michigan, etc. Still, if one wants to work in Atlanta, attending Emory is a good bet. The school does have the best reputation of all the regional schools and alumni are very active in recruiting. Speaking of recruiting, Emory's on-campus recruiting will generally have recruiters from all over the country—large, mid and small sized firms. Students ranked in the top 15 to 20 percent typically have better options, but lower ranked students are also successful in finding jobs. I particularly found the career center very helpful, although students with lower rankings typically argue that the center is more focused on students in the top 10 percent.

Status: Current student, full-time
Dates of Enrollment: 8/2002-Submit Date
Survey Submitted: March 2005

Great clerkship opportunities and if you are self-motivated, it's easy to find a job. The faculty is also great with assisting in the job hunt. The students wish we had more name recognition on the West Coast. The alumni network is easily accessible and very helpful.

Status: Current student, full-time
Dates of Enrollment: 8/2003-Submit Date
Survey Submitted: May 2005

If you are in the top 25 percent, your prospects are great. Career services and employers will welcome you and try their best to woo you. If you are the other 75 percent, then chances are you will still get a job, but you are going to work for it. The great thing is even if you don't get that prestigious summer internship at "Kaanwe, Cheatham, and Howe," you will still have plenty of opportunity to build your resume and experience with field placements and working for professors. There is plenty of opportunity for networking so you will get intimate with prominent attorneys at the big firms who will later be interviewing you.

Status: Current student, full-time
Dates of Enrollment: 8/2002-Submit Date
Survey Submitted: February 2005

The name of Emory Law carries some cachet with employers but it tends to be known mostly for corporate and transactional lawyers. I'm having a hell of a time finding a job in another sector, since I am only in the middle of my class—on-campus recruiting is targeted at the top 10 percent and career services, and while they try hard and mean well, are little help for the remaining 90 percent,

especially if they are interested in other areas of law. However, the alumni that I have contacted in the course of my job search have been extremely helpful and glad to do so.

Status: Current student, full-time
Dates of Enrollment: 8/2002-Submit Date
Survey Submitted: March 2004

As is well documented, this is really the only area of the law school that is not up to standards. Emory really struggles to break out of the Southeastern legal market, although it completely dominates the Atlanta and Nashville markets. We are still deanless in the career services office.

But make top grades and you write your ticket to any job in the country. However, I would like to offer a reason why Emory career services office staff may not be to blame. Emory is an up-and-coming school, so its graduates are becoming increasingly competitive for higher-profile jobs. But, its relative newfound prominence hampers Emory because of the lack of older alumni in the nation's top jobs (read: we have a lack of powerful grads making the hiring decisions for today's highly achieving grads). Frankly, this will just take time to correct.

> **The school says:** "The law school hired Laurie Hartman as assistant dean for career services in fall 2004." The school also notes that "our graduates are hiring partners at some of the nation's most prestigious law firms, including Kilpatrick Stockton, Alston & Bird and King & Spalding."

 # Quality of Life

Status: Alumnus/a, full-time
Dates of Enrollment: 8/1999-5/2003
Survey Submitted: April 2006

Atlanta is a very easy city to live in. There are tons of almost-new apartment complexes around Emory, and the university has recently opened very nice graduate housing. Law school is tough, but I think that there is a good quality of life at Emory, driven in part by the size of the school. The campus of Emory is fantastic—it is a very wealthy school (endowment) and the money is spent on facilities and faculty.

Status: Alumnus/a, full-time
Dates of Enrollment: 1/2002-12/2004
Survey Submitted: April 2006

Biggest problem at Emory is parking and traffic. While not in Atlanta proper, the Emory corridor is one of busiest in the area because of the concentration of students, hospitals and local residents. During peak times, it is an absolute nightmare, though students living on campus need not worry about it, particularly those living in the new graduate campus affectionally known as (the "Taj Majal"), a reference no doubt to the sheer lavishness of the compound—complete with fitness center, swimming pools, all kinds of amenities, and a dedicated, private restricted access road for use by the Emory Shuttle only to ferry students to and from the compound, located about 1/2 mile away from Emory's main campus. Food is good, Atlanta's climate cannot be beat, and the campus is beautiful.

Status: Current student, full-time
Dates of Enrollment: 9/2002-Submit Date
Survey Submitted: March 2005

The facilities at Emory Law are satisfactory, but should be renovated in the next 10 years because of normal wear and tear. The law school has shown a renewed commitment to the students by completing a new student lounge with new computers, a wide screen TV, and comfortable couches in which students can meet and discuss issues of the day.

Status: Current student, full-time
Dates of Enrollment: 8/2002-Submit Date
Survey Submitted: March 2005

Quality of life in Atlanta is incredible. Upscale housing is affordable and quality of life top, especially for a graduate student. A car is a must. The law school

Read all of Vault's Law School Surveys at www.vault.com/lawschool — get complete surveys on top law schools, expert advice on applicaton essays, LSAT prep and more.

VAULT CAREER LIBRARY 187

itself needs an uplift, but we have been assured that is coming over the next five years. Great restaurants. Atlanta looks like a suburb with the amenities of a city.

Status: Current student, full-time
Dates of Enrollment: 7/2003-Submit Date
Survey Submitted: January 2005

ATLANTA IS GREAT! Whether you are from the South is irrelevant. Atlanta is a world of its own. The law school housing, Clairmont Campus, is very new and very nice. Although it isn't within walking distance of the school, there are constant shuttles that can get you to main campus in minutes. Other than that, there are plenty of nice and affordable apartment complexes nearby. On the other hand, the entire city is not walker friendly, I would never recommend relocating to Atlanta or Emory without a car! Our campus is beautiful although it is in the city, is still has a campus feel. There is no substitute for Atlanta weather or culture. There is always something to do. This is also true for the law school itself. The weekly kegs are worth tuition alone—not to mention the Bar Reviews, lectures, and everything else. Crime within Atlanta is comparable to that of any major city but the law school is one of the safest places I have been. I feel safe studying and leaving campus by myself at all hours of the night. Also, I can leave all my stuff at any number of tables throughout the law school and library and it would be there in a week! And if someone ever moved it they would e-mail the entire school to find its owner!

Status: Current student, full-time
Dates of Enrollment: 8/2002-Submit Date
Survey Submitted: February 2005

Law school in general is not conducive to any sort of quality of life, but I feel Emory Law's is especially low—the grad student housing available is linked with undergraduate dorms, parking is difficult and expensive, the law school facility is designed in such a way that none of the classrooms or student areas have windows and the law school is generally alienated from the rest of the campus. Also the student health insurance and student health services access for grad students is expensive and largely inaccessible.

Status: Current student, full-time
Dates of Enrollment: 8/2002-Submit Date
Survey Submitted: March 2004

The neighborhood is beautiful, Emory is beautiful, the weather is beautiful. If you can't love the unique laid-back but hyper-urban Atlanta lifestyle, you need not even apply.

Status: Alumnus/a, full-time
Dates of Enrollment: 9/1996-5/1999
Survey Submitted: April 2004

Emory is located in a beautiful area of Atlanta, and off-campus garden apartments, where most students live, are plentiful and relatively inexpensive. Emory is in the process of building additional graduate student housing, which is currently inadequate for, and largely unavailable to, law students. Emory's facilities are modern and plentiful, though most of these seem targeted at undergraduates rather than graduate students. The two exceptions are the athletic center, which has facilities that rival the nicer health clubs in town, and the student ticket booth, which offers discounts to just about any cultural or music event (even movies) going on in Atlanta (and which few law students seem to know about or take advantage of).

Overall, the Emory area of Atlanta is convenient to downtown and other neighborhoods (10 minutes to just about anywhere in town), very safe and loaded with amenities such as a variety of restaurants and bars, and shopping. The campus also offers additional eating and shopping venues, though these are somewhat limited. Most law students spend the bulk of their free time off campus in the surrounding neighborhoods like Midtown, Virginia Highlands and Buckhead.

 # Social Life

Status: Alumnus/a, full-time
Dates of Enrollment: 8/1999-5/2003
Survey Submitted: April 2006

There are tons of places to go out in Atlanta. There is a scene for everyone. Clubs, bars, art houses, playhouses, art galleries, sporting events, you name it—it is the biggest city in the south and certainly keeps you busy. You will not get bored over the course of your three years.

Status: Current student, full-time
Dates of Enrollment: 9/2002-Submit Date
Survey Submitted: March 2005

While the social life on campus is rather mundane, Atlanta serves as a strong outline for law students to go out and have a great time.

Status: Current student, full-time
Dates of Enrollment: 8/2002-Submit Date
Survey Submitted: March 2005

There is no graduate Greek system. Bars in the Virginia Highlands are a hot spot for law school (especially Neighbors). Dining clubs have become very popular between the grad schools at Emory. Dating within the law school is quite common, but can turn into a nightmare overnight. It's like going back to high school. Overall, it's a fun place to be.

Status: Current student, full-time
Dates of Enrollment: 8/2002-Submit Date
Survey Submitted: March 2005

The law school community at Emory is lacking. Most people retain their loyalty to their undergraduate institution and have little to do with anything campus oriented. Being in Atlanta there is so much to do outside the school that the university ceases to be the center of social life.

Status: Current student, full-time
Dates of Enrollment: 8/2002-Submit Date
Survey Submitted: February 2005

The law school has a pretty active social life; there are Bar Reviews and law school events scheduled at regular intervals throughout the year, as well as frequent kegs and pizza events at the school itself. Due to the small and self-selecting student body and the strain and constraints of law student schedules, there is little dating within the student body—and lots of grade-school style gossip about student interactions. Also, many students find their pre-existing relationships deteriorating or changing due to the pressures of Emory Law as well, though a few of my classmates have married sweethearts they met in Atlanta while in law school. Generally, if you want more details, hit Neighbor's Bar on a Thursday or Whole Foods or Starbucks on Briarcliff at any time on any day...

Status: Alumnus/a, full-time
Dates of Enrollment: 9/1996-5/1999
Survey Submitted: April 2004

Two words: high school. Remember when you knew everyone at your school, you kept your books in lockers, and everyone ate together in one lunchroom? It's back! Life in the law school is like an ongoing soap opera, with a rumor mill that is off and flying fast and furious from the get-go (I never ceased to be amused, even when I was the grist). If you're observed having dinner with someone of the opposite sex, chances are you'll be "dating" (according to unnamed sources) by the next week. With a small class, everyone knows (or thinks they know) everyone else's business, but it's harmless chatter all in all.

Overall, Emory is a pretty fun and social place to go to law school, and the student bar association organizes frequent bar events (there is even a law school "prom" each spring). Favorite hangouts include Neighbors in Virginia Highlands (every Thursday night, still going strong) and Famous Pub for sports events. Since it's grad school, Greek life and clubs are less important to social life. And it's not unheard of for law students to mix and mingle outside of the law school (the business school is across the street, and the med school is down a block) or even outside of Emory. Atlanta has a great young professional community, and the opportunities to be involved in that community while a law student are ample for those who choose to take advantage of them.

Status: Alumnus/a, full-time
Dates of Enrollment: 8/1992-5/1995
Survey Submitted: April 2004

Students at the law school had virtually no interaction whatsoever with the rest of the university. The law school had some events of its own—beer bashes on the lawn, but students' social lives did not revolve around the school. Emory is in Atlanta; there is always something to do there—going shopping or to a club, museum, sporting event (Braves, Hawks or Falcons), concert, park, etc. There are tons of bars and restaurants nearby, especially in nearby Buckhead and Virginia Highlands. What more does one really need to say? As for the dating scene, some students dated and ended up marrying, others ended up breaking up, many of us already had significant others when we started—which is good, because for many of us, the law was our lives and we didn't have time to look around for that someone special.

Status: Alumnus/a, full-time
Dates of Enrollment: 8/2000-5/2003
Survey Submitted: October 2003

Social life? What social life? This is law school.

Read all of Vault's Law School Surveys at www.vault.com/lawschool — get complete surveys on top law schools, expert advice on applicaton essays, LSAT prep and more.

VAULT CAREER LIBRARY 189

Georgia State University College of Law

Urban Life Center
Suite 400 (4th Floor)
140 Decatur Street
Atlanta, GA 30303
Admissions phone: (404) 651-2048
Admissions fax: (404) 651-1244
Admissions e-mail: admissions@gsulaw.gsu.edu
Admissions URL: http://law.gsu.edu/admissions/

Note: The school has chosen not to comment on the student surveys submitted.

 Admissions

Status: Current student, full-time
Dates of Enrollment: 9/2003-Submit Date
Survey Submitted: January 2006

The school is relatively easy to get in to compared to higher ranked schools. Neither the average GPA nor LSAT is particularly high, although both have been moving higher in recent years. No interviews are available and the application form is short and straightforward. I applied early (it was my fall-back school) and was accepted within a couple of weeks.

Status: Alumnus/a, part-time
Dates of Enrollment: 8/2001-5/2005
Survey Submitted: March 2006

Georgia State has become highly selective. I did submit an essay, but there was no interview. Georgia State, especially in the part-time program, seems to look for students with a wide range of educational and work backgrounds. There is also a wide range in the ages of students.

Status: Alumnus/a, part-time
Dates of Enrollment: 8/1998-5/2001
Survey Submitted: November 2005

Admission to GSU law school has become increasingly competitive because the school is such a fantastic value for the quality of education provided. Fewer than one in five applicants is admitted to the full-time program, and the part-time program is, as I understand it, more selective than the full-time program. GSU is the only game in town if you must work while you attend law school. Admission is primarily a numbers game; your undergraduate GPA and your LSAT score place you in a specific square on the GSU admissions grid. The current average GPA is 3.3 and the current average LSAT score is 159. For prospective students who have taken the LSAT more than once, the average score from all test attempts will be used. If your stats are better on either measure, GPA or LSAT, the probability that you will be offered admission goes up accordingly. If your stats are lower than average on either measure, you should spend extra time crafting your personal statement. Tell your story in a compelling way so that you stand out as a potential asset to the school.

All students, full-time and part-time, must begin their study in the fall semester, and all applications materials must be received in March (usually March 15). If you have not yet taken the LSAT on the deadline date but your application is stellar, the admissions committee has the option of holding your file to allow you to take the LSAT in early summer. Depending on your LSAT results, the committee may offer you admission shortly before orientation begins. In such a case, you will be called directly by one of the professors on the committee. GSU law school charges a $50 application fee. The law school provides a handy web page that allows you to check the status of your specific application after your materials have been submitted.

Status: Current student, full-time
Dates of Enrollment: 8/2003-Submit Date
Survey Submitted: March 2005

The admissions process at GSU Law runs fairly smoothly. There are always people available to help. When I applied, I was easily able to meet with the director of admissions and took tours led by both a student and an administrator. Even though it's very difficult to get into law school these days, GSU was good about considering my personality and outside interests. GSU is truly looking for a well-rounded individual.

Status: Current student, full-time
Dates of Enrollment: 8/2004-Submit Date
Survey Submitted: March 2005

Our class had over 5,700 applicants, and only 234 were accepted. The admissions office is very personable, and I received many phone calls to assist me with the transition into law school once I was accepted. I would say that you have to make yourself really stand out on your essay. In law school, everyone has good grades and good test scores, so the essay is the place to make your mark. Georgia State does not conduct interviews, but encourages students to stop by or contact them throughout the process. In my experience, the people I spoke with remembered my file, and what was in it, so it was not like undergrad where you're just a number.

Status: Current student, full-time
Dates of Enrollment: 8/2002-Submit Date
Survey Submitted: March 2005

It is important that you have a solid LSAT score, as well as a strong GPA. You don't need a 4.0, but you need to demonstrate that you perform well academically. As for the essay, I believe that it is important to show: (1) why you want to come to law school; (2) a little background on yourself (any professional experience is a plus); (3) something that ties you to Georgia State (do you want to practice law in Georgia and if so why); and (4) something memorable to separate you from the other applicants.

Status: Current student, full-time
Dates of Enrollment: 8/2002-Submit Date
Survey Submitted: October 2003

The process is straightforward and comparatively short. As with other schools, the emphasis is on undergrad GPA and LSAT scores, with medians steadily moving up. GSU does seem to take other factors into account, especially for admissions into the highly competitive part-time slots. Substantial work experience, unusual histories and uncommon undergraduate studies all seem to play into the admit equation.

Status: Alumnus/a, full-time
Dates of Enrollment: 8/1994-6/1997
Survey Submitted: April 2004

I was fairly naïve about the admission process for law school. If I had known what I know now, I probably would have done things differently. I thought the GSU application was reasonable, and I did not tailor my essay specifically for the school. I had not done my research, and it is only in hindsight that I realized that admissions to GSU College of Law is very competitive. It is one of the few programs in the Southeast offering a part-time program in a major metropolitan area, which makes it very attractive to traditional and non-traditional students all over the country.

The year I was accepted, GSU had the seventh-lowest ratio of acceptances to applications in the country. Even with the large number of applications, the office of admissions staff was very friendly and helpful. Dr. Cheryl Jester Jackson was the utmost professional admissions administrator I have ever met. She offered tours of the school and advice with respect to timing of acceptances. The admissions office kept me posted about the status of my application (a postcard was sent with the status). When I called because my application was still on hold, I was told that the only reason a decision had not been made was because one of my references was missing, and if I could get the reference, a decision would be made within a week. I immediately contacted the reference, who sent in the letter. I received my acceptance the following week.

 ## Academics

Status: Current student, full-time
Dates of Enrollment: 9/2003-Submit Date
Survey Submitted: January 2006

The professors are almost all outstanding. The teaching style is largely Socratic in the first year and then more lecture or seminar-based after that. The faculty are experts in their fields and most spent a significant part of their career in practice. Since the school is also located in downtown Atlanta, it is able to further boost course offerings by hiring practicing adjuncts. I've had classes with current judges, SEC staff attorneys and nationally prominent trial attorneys. Several of my full-time faculty members taught from a text that they authored. It is relatively easy to get into the classes you want and because there is also a part-time program, the course offerings are essentially doubled when you include night classes.

Status: Alumnus/a, part-time
Dates of Enrollment: 8/2001-5/2005
Survey Submitted: March 2006

The classes are of very high quality. As a part-time student, I took most of my classes at night, However, this is not a disadvantage. Because teachers rotate teaching night classes, the quality level remains. Because part-time students get preference for night classes, I did not have many problems getting into the classes that I wanted to take. However, the variety of classes available at night can be limited.

Status: Alumnus/a, part-time
Dates of Enrollment: 8/1998-5/2001
Survey Submitted: November 2005

1Ls must take the usual array of killer courses—Civil Procedure, Contracts, Property, Torts, Criminal Law, and Research, Writing and Advocacy (RWA). The latter course is famously tough, and GSU law school has a reputation for producing the best legal writers of any Georgia law school, including Emory. Part-time 1Ls spread the required 1L courses out over two years, although they may take a couple of electives in the second year to fill out their schedules. A full-time student graduates after six semesters, while a part-time student may graduate after nine semesters. Until all required courses are taken, part-time students must take at least eight hours per semester and no more than 11 hours of credits per semester. Part-time students must certify that they are working full-time and full-time students must certify that they are working, if at all, only part-time.

Students who make the cut to participate in Law Review, the Moot Court Board and the Student Trial Lawyers Association can earn some limited course credit through those activities. In addition to the JD program, the school offers five joint degree programs, including a JD/MCRP in Law and Urban Planning, in which Georgia State partners with Georgia Tech.

Status: Current student, part-time
Dates of Enrollment: 8/2002-Submit Date
Survey Submitted: April 2005

Overall, the classes are very informative. Almost all classes are taught by Socratic Method, so preparation is important. Professors generally do a good job of answering reasonable questions and deflecting detailed, specific interest questions until outside of class. All classes are offered at night, and most classes are offered during the day, too. However, the night sessions seemed to be geared more towards people with some "real world" experience and the "day classes" have a majority of students who started law school immediately after college. This is a good division because the interests and experiences of these groups are different.

Status: Current student, full-time
Dates of Enrollment: 8/2001-Submit Date
Survey Submitted: March 2005

Georgia State College of Law has the highest bar pass rate in the state of Georgia. The academic program is very good, offering a wide variety of classes in many areas of legal study. The health law program is especially comprehensive, for anyone interested in that field. Many of the upper level classes have guest speakers ranging from the Georgia Supreme Court Chief Justice, to respected lawyers in any applicable field of study. Guest speakers are brought in from around the country for special workshops and conferences. The school is very flexible to work with the part-time students, offering any combination of classes to fit into the schedule of those of us who work and have families. I have been able to take a combination of day and night classes that work with my other life obligations.

The workload is what you make it; it is definitely doable. As I stated, I work, have a family, attend law school, and incidentally, I have a two-hour commute one way every time I attend class. You can do anything that you make it a priority to do. You can work and maintain a healthy family relationship, but you have to prioritize what is the most important, and be able to leave some unessential things undone. The professors are all willing to help in any way they can. They are available during office hours, or via phone or e-mail, or they will set up a mutually convenient time to meet with a student. I have been academically challenged at Georgia State, and feel that I will be prepared to step into the legal work force when I graduate in December.

Grading is done on a curve, which I do not like very well. About 80 percent of the class gets the set curved grade, and then those who do exceptionally well above that average make a few points higher, and a few students make a lower grade. I think each student should get the grade she earned, and not such a set curve. This applies mostly to the 1L classes with multiple sections, "to ensure fairness in grading." The upper level smaller classes allow for higher grades, and grades based on the individual's actual performance.

Status: Current student, full-time
Dates of Enrollment: 8/2002-Submit Date
Survey Submitted: March 2005

It is fairly easy to get in classes that you want because there is a variety offered. I never had any problems getting into a class that I wanted. I found my Corporations class, my Land-Use class and my Alternative Dispute Resolution class to be the most useful. As for grading, the curve is low as a first-year. You should be prepared that you might not make all A's and B's—like you are used to.

Status: Current student, full-time
Dates of Enrollment: 8/2002-Submit Date
Survey Submitted: March 2005

All of the classes offered are substantively very good. The registrar makes switching into classes that you want even if enrollment is full very easy—they are friendly and helpful and I have never been denied something that I wanted. The grading is like any other law school, you are graded on a curve. Unfortunately the curve is set lower than at other law schools, but you still have a rank that is ultimately what really matters to employers. The workload is heavy, but as is the case at any law school. The professors are phenomenal and very accessible outside of class.

Status: Current student, full-time
Dates of Enrollment: 8/2003-Submit Date
Survey Submitted: March 2005

The professors are outstanding! They are not hard to get hold of out of class, and in class they are always prepared to provide interesting and thought-provoking discussions. I wish we offered a wider selection of classes each semester because it seems like I need to wait a year or semester to get what I want. Maybe that is just the way it has to be. Having a full array of night classes is good for some, but it forces day students to take some night classes to get everything they want. That can be a big pain for commuters who like me, don't want to spend more time in the city at night.

Read all of Vault's Law School Surveys at www.vault.com/lawschool — get complete surveys on top law schools, expert advice on applicaton essays, LSAT prep and more.

VAULT CAREER LIBRARY **191**

Status: Current student, full-time
Dates of Enrollment: 8/2003-Submit Date
Survey Submitted: March 2005

The quality of classes is amazing. With a lower ranking than other schools I looked at, I expected the academic quality of Georgia State to be lower, but it has been the opposite. I cannot imagine that students at other schools are getting as good of an education as I am. The lower ranking must be attributed to Georgia State being a relatively new law school. Georgia State is known to be more of a practical school, academically, which is great for practice. Professors tend to be less philosophical, and more realistic. The professors here are amazing—their credentials are great and they are well-known in the community and beyond. Also, I never had a problem getting the classes or professors I wanted as long as I signed up as soon as I could. Another plus is that we offer night classes, and you can be a full-time student and opt to take those night classes. Like any other school, the workload can be overwhelming, but I knew that when I signed up. As for grading, that is a mystery to me. I've heard that one professor throws the essays down the stairs and whoever's lands the farthest gets an A.

Status: Current student, full-time
Dates of Enrollment: 8/2002-Submit Date
Survey Submitted: October 2003

Required classes are graded on a strict curve and are generally Socratic. The night sections [geared toward part-timers] are often more laid-back. Teaching quality varies (and is often dependent on the student's attitude), but there are quite a few superlative individuals, tops in research and teaching ability. The administration makes an effort to have multiple sections of the more popular electives, but registering as early as possible is still best. Workload is workload is workload. You're going to put in long hours in any program. But they are still probably less than some starting associate hours. Suck it up and realize that everyone else in the degree is putting them in as well (or won't be back next year).

Status: Alumnus/a, full-time
Dates of Enrollment: 8/1994-6/1997
Survey Submitted: April 2004

I find the quality of class increasingly competitive and thorough. GSU now offers perhaps the most comprehensive health care law (my practice area) classes of any school in Georgia. The school also is located in the heart of Atlanta, with access to the county, state and federal courts as well as federal offices, which allows the school to offer a substantial number of externships with these facilities. The strength of the academic program is its practical application of the law. There were a few classes that could not be entered because of popularity, but usually required a wait of only a semester. Grading is tough because it's on a 100-point scale with a strict 78 (C) average for first year. This somewhat handicaps students competing with schools on a four-point scale. Because of the 100-point scale, standing is hard to determine. In one class the top person may have a 92 average, in another class the top person could have an 88 average. Many students and firms find the grading confusing. The professors are accessible, and the workload is manageable.

Status: Alumnus/a, part-time
Dates of Enrollment: 8/1997-5/2001
Survey Submitted: September 2003

The part-time program is fairly rigid if you need to do night classes only. The first two years involve the classes that full-time students take in the first year, plus one or two electives. It can be difficult to schedule all electives you are interested in by taking only night classes. The school also offers a number of externship opportunities with various government agencies and nonprofit organizations, as well as the state appellate and supreme courts.

 Employment Prospects

Status: Alumnus/a, part-time
Dates of Enrollment: 8/2001-12/2004
Survey Submitted: March 2006

Very thorough Career Services Office. My estimate would be that most students joined law firms after graduation. The bar pass rate is very high. On-campus recruiting is comprehensive, but only for the top 20 or so students in each class. Internships are outstanding, as are clinic opportunities.

Status: Alumnus/a, part-time
Dates of Enrollment: 8/1998-5/2001
Survey Submitted: November 2005

GSU has a excellent reputation, particularly in the Greater Atlanta area, with BigLaw and with other employers. The fall recruiting season brings a large number of law firms and other legal employers onto campus, though students without Law Review or moot court credentials can be heard to complain that it's extremely difficult to get an interview with the big firms. The Career Services Office is reasonably competent, but the office is definitely geared more to helping full-time students with traditional placement than to helping part-time students who may not, for example, be able to leave their current jobs to take a summer clerkship as a means of trying out for a permanent job. After the first ranking, faculty members meet with students who place at the top of the class and encourage them to apply for federal judicial clerkships, describing their own experiences as clerks and answering questions. The 11th Circuit Court of Appeals sits just a mile from the campus, and a number of GSU grads have worked there as clerks. The Georgia Supreme Court sits a few blocks away in another direction, and that court also hires GSU grads regularly.

Status: Current student, full-time
Dates of Enrollment: 8/2001-Submit Date
Survey Submitted: March 2005

Georgia State is recognized in Atlanta for its high academic demands, and many prestigious law firms regularly hire Georgia State graduates. The Career Services Office has regularly scheduled on-campus interviews and opportunities to meet with many of the top law firms in Atlanta at hiring workshops. Graduates obtain jobs in a wide variety of settings all around the country. Most 3Ls already have jobs lined up for after graduation. There are many externship programs that also frequently lead to full-time employment post graduation. The on-campus recruiting and internship opportunities are endless.

Status: Current student, part-time
Dates of Enrollment: 8/2004-Submit Date
Survey Submitted: March 2005

I have not met nor talked with anyone who has had a problem finding a job after graduating from the school of law. Our Career Services Office is wonderful in that they set up so many recruiting fairs that I can't even keep up. They are also very helpful in assisting individual students. I went in to make a game plan, since I was working full-time in another field and wanted to know at what point did I need to consider getting into law full-time. They made suggestions to me about student research at a local firm and even had lists of small firms in the area. I called a firm and asked if they employed student researchers. They hired me in two days. I was able to quit my full-time job and now work in law research, which has helped me so much in school. I know so many people who have had similar experiences and now have summer internships.

Status: Current student, full-time
Dates of Enrollment: 8/2002-Submit Date
Survey Submitted: October 2003

The number of jobs is growing as the early alumni reach partner status. The first-time bar pass rate is [consistently at or near the top] in the state. The school offers an internship program with employers ranging from Supreme Court of Georgia Justices and U.S. District Judges to Indigent Service and a plethora of state and federal agencies. Participants receive three hours of credit and generally work 10 hours per week. The tax program also runs the Tax Clinic, which offers services to indigent clients.

Status: Alumnus/a, full-time
Dates of Enrollment: 8/1991-5/1994
Survey Submitted: April 2004

GSU's prestige extends beyond the borders of Georgia and continues to expand. GSU students are known for their strong foundation in the fundamentals of the law. Extracurricular activities can make a big difference in the number and quality of opportunities available to you.

Status: Alumnus/a, part-time
Dates of Enrollment: 8/1997-5/2001
Survey Submitted: September 2003

The GSU law school has been growing in prestige and is gaining a good reputation with local employers. The career office does a good job of facilitating the interview process and ensuring a wide variety of employer interviews on campus. Unfortunately, a number of the larger Atlanta firms only look at the top 10 percent because the school is not a top-tier school. However, there are a number of GSU alumni at all Atlanta firms!

Quality of Life

Status: Current student, full-time
Dates of Enrollment: 9/2003-Submit Date
Survey Submitted: January 2006

It is on an urban campus in the downtown of a city's whose metro population is about four and a half million. The actual facilities (e.g., library, building) are sub-par, despite the education being solid. The school does an excellent job incorporating technology into its classrooms. The courtrooms all are wired for video and have the latest software (e.g., Trial Director), flat-screen monitors and projection screens. The classrooms also all have overhead projectors and the tech staff is very helpful. The school is much more collaborative among students than many other schools. Whereas Emory across town has a reputation for being competitive, and even cutthroat, GSU is much less adversarial among students. Student housing is available, but most prefer to find off-campus apartments around the city. I know of at least one student who commutes from Chattanooga, TN. The school is an excellent value considering the strong education and relatively cheap tuition. Out-of-state students can gain in-state tuition relatively easy after one year.

Status: Alumnus/a, part-time
Dates of Enrollment: 8/2001-12/2004
Survey Submitted: March 2006

Virtually all law students live off campus, and many are non-traditional (older/second career) students. The law classes are all conducted in the same building. The building has an outstanding court room, excellent library and average food court. The campus itself is quite safe but it is located in the heart of downtown Atlanta, so if you stray off campus, you can expect panhandlers.

Status: Alumnus/a, part-time
Dates of Enrollment: 8/1998-5/2001
Survey Submitted: November 2005

GSU law school is located in downtown Atlanta, near Grady Memorial Hospital, the Georgia State Capitol, and Turner Field, home of the Atlanta Braves baseball team. Crime and safety have been an issue of concern in this neighborhood, but the area has steadily improved since the 1996 Olympics, when people began to move back into the heart of the city. Now, downtown Atlanta abounds in residential options, with apartments, lofts and condominiums located in both new and renovated buildings within walking distance of the law school. The university has some limited housing stock for graduate students in the GSU Village (formerly the Olympic Village), a mile or so from campus, and in the University Lofts, which are right on campus. The school is located near an interstate exit and has its own MARTA rapid-transit rail station. Students who drive in to classes may use parking decks near the law school for reduced (at least as compared to normal downtown parking fees) rates. The exterior of the law school building is showing its age, but the law classrooms have been retrofitted with the latest in technology. The moot courtroom is especially impressive. The law school facilities are generally kept clean if not always neat. The law library has a considerable holding of almost 300,000 volumes. In fact, the library is so chock full

of books that book shelves must be mechanically collapsed together to conserve floor space when someone is not accessing those shelves. GSU built a fantastic recreation center across from the law school about three years ago that is great for working off some stress or just hanging out and relaxing.

Status: Current student, full-time
Dates of Enrollment: 8/2002-Submit Date
Survey Submitted: March 2005

Georgia State is in downtown Atlanta, which is a very urban environment. Of course, people will differ on preference of an urban or more "college-town" environment. I believe that the location of our school within a mile of the Supreme Court building and the State Capitol gives our students a particular edge. Of course, there is more crime in the area of our school than a more suburban school would have but our school has done a great job of protecting its students. The university provides housing for law school students and graduate students at the university lofts, which is located only two blocks from the law school. It is extremely convenient with Internet access included, but many choose not to live there because it is pretty expensive. I have lived there all three years of law school and I could not see commuting to the law school like many other students do. I think it is worth the extra money. There are a lot of places to eat on campus, although the university has been trying to provide more options as both the law school and the college have become more popular in the state.

Status: Current student, full-time
Dates of Enrollment: 8/2002-Submit Date
Survey Submitted: March 2005

There is on-campus housing, though I did not live there. The campus is a bustling downtown campus without a lot of green space. There are several restaurants close by and students have the resources of the rest of the university available to them. The neighborhood is growing as urban revitalization is occurring. Crime and safety aren't too much of an issue, but being a public space I wouldn't leave my laptop without someone keeping an eye on it for me.

Status: Current student, full-time
Dates of Enrollment: 8/2003-Submit Date
Survey Submitted: March 2005

I really enjoy being in downtown Atlanta every day. You can see the capital from our building and it really is beautiful. Also, the setting offers many opportunities since it is so close to all of the courthouses and the law firms in town. Our urban life building that houses the law school is quite nice and is constantly being updated. There is a good cafeteria and plenty of cafes and restaurants a few blocks away. The only downside is that our school is right downtown, so past dark I don't feel as safe as I do outside of the city. But it is completely safe during operational hours, and parking is close by.

Status: Current student, full-time
Dates of Enrollment: 8/2002-Submit Date
Survey Submitted: October 2003

GSU is historically a commuter school, although it has recently added some graduate housing. These facilities are peppered with boisterous undergrads and are not recommended. Affordable housing is not a problem in Atlanta or the surrounding suburbs, especially in the current market.

Although in downtown Atlanta, the area is really quite safe if individuals take common-sense precautions like keeping valuables in car trunks and not on the seat. Campus police frequent the parking decks and surrounding streets and are always happy to serve as escorts during a late night walk from library to car. Theft of personal items was a big problem in years past, but has decreased with the addition of library security and cameras. The campus itself is a patchwork of buildings and something is always under renovation, but there are network and power connections in all of the classrooms and in the library study rooms and carrels. The school is also expanding a wireless network that will hopefully make its way to the law school soon.

Read all of Vault's Law School Surveys at www.vault.com/lawschool — get complete surveys on top law schools, expert advice on applicaton essays, LSAT prep and more.

VAULT CAREER LIBRARY 193

Social Life

Status: Current student, full-time
Dates of Enrollment: 9/2003-Submit Date
Survey Submitted: January 2006

All of the advantages of a major city are available to the students of GSU COL. The student body consists of students from around the country with a good deal, as you would expect, from Georgia. The students like to go out and drink like every other bunch of law students at any other school. Since about a third of the students are part time, there is some difference between those two groups though everyone seems to get along. The addition of the part-timers actually strengthens the experience because of the rich life and work experience they bring to the classroom. I've had everything from 21 year-old recent college grads to classmates in their late 50s in my classes.

Status: Alumnus/a, part-time
Dates of Enrollment: 8/2001-12/2004
Survey Submitted: March 2006

Restaurants and bars adjacent to campus are nonexistent, but the various law clubs do a solid job of organizing off-campus happy hours and social events. Since no one lives on campus and everyone drives there anyway, getting to locations a few miles away is no trouble. Many students are older and already married, but there were several "hook-ups" on campus. Smith's Olde Bar and Manuel's Tavern are a couple of the more popular locations for get-togethers.

Status: Alumnus/a, part-time
Dates of Enrollment: 8/1998-5/2001
Survey Submitted: November 2005

In addition to fast-food restaurants (Subway and the other usual suspects), students can find a number of good places to grab a sandwich, salad or stir-fry near campus—Loaf & Kettle, Jake's Flatiron, Mocha Delites, Pixels Cafe, even the Sweet Auburn Curb Market. Vegetarian options are consistently available. Atlantic Station has a movie complex and restaurants like Fox Sports Grill, too. Busy GSU law students do manage to find time to date, and the full-time students in particular seem fond of dating each other. Most part-time students are married, often married with children, and, as a rule, don't mix socially with the full-time students. However, when I was attending GSU, several marriages broke up while one spouse attended law school. One student was actually served with divorce papers as class began. For single law students, Buckhead is a perennial after-hours favorite, with its watering holes such as Andrews Upstairs, Babylon and The Tavern at Phipps. The Earl in East Atlanta is increasingly popular for law students. On campus, there is a fairly broad array of student organizations to choose from, including active chapters at both ends of the political spectrum of the Federalist Society and the American Constitution Society. There are organizations for African Americans, Asian Americans, Hispanic students, Jewish students, gays and lesbians, etc. There are also organizations for those interested in a particular area of the law—intellectual property, public interest law, environmental law, international law and so forth. Students are welcomed into these clubs and can generally be as active as they'd like.

Status: Current student, full-time
Dates of Enrollment: 8/2003-Submit Date
Survey Submitted: March 2005

Social life is very good. The classes seem to come together in a seemingly non-competitive spirit. We have a good time together and get very close to classmates. There are lots of places to go out—from The Irish Pub at Underground for weekday happy hours following class to Midtown, Buckhead or the Virginia Highlands from Thursday night on! There are tons of festivals, music and cultural, in Atlanta if you have time to break away from the books!

Status: Current student, full-time
Dates of Enrollment: 8/2002-Submit Date
Survey Submitted: March 2005

I would not call Georgia State a "party school" because I believe that the students are extremely dedicated to academics, but a large portion of our school would not turn down a chance to party or network and there are lots and lots of social events. PAD and SBA hold several events each year. We also have an annual Barrister's Ball and the PILA auction which is an event to raise money for stipends given to students who participate in unpaid public service positions during the summer. Furthermore, our school is in the heart of Atlanta, so there is always a place to go to chill out and study or party on the town.

Status: Current student, full-time
Dates of Enrollment: 8/2004-Submit Date
Survey Submitted: March 2005

Atlanta has a lot to offer in the way of social activities. There is a bar scene for the most liberal and conservative of people. My personal favorites are found in the midtown area, but many would argue that Buckhead is the place to be. The area is full of young professionals, so dating should not be a problem. There are more restaurants than one can eat in at in a year's time, if they chose a different one every day. GSU-COL has a very active student body with its clubs constantly providing out-of-school functions where students can gather and express ideas, or simply take a break form studies for a fun night.

Status: Alumnus/a, full-time
Dates of Enrollment: 8/1993-6/1996
Survey Submitted: March 2005

Because Atlanta is so diverse, it is difficult to pigeon hole something so big. Most bars were located in the Buckhead area and in Virginia Highlands. The clubs were in downtown, midtown and in Buckhead, including a number of clubs that are no longer in existence. There were too many to list. Events local to Georgia State included concerts both indoor and outdoor, sporting events. When I was in law school a student could see pro sports including the Braves for baseball, the Falcons for football, the Hawks for Basketball and the Knights for hockey.

Mercer University

Walter F. George School of Law
Office of Admissions
1021 Georgia Avenue
Macon, GA 31207
Admissions phone: (800) 637-2378 ext 2605
Admissions URL: http://www.law.mercer.edu/admissions/

 ## Admissions

Status: Alumnus/a, full-time
Dates of Enrollment: 8/1998-5/2001
Survey Submitted: March 2005

The admissions process was typical of any law school program. However, the admissions staff was very helpful whenever I called.

Status: Alumnus/a, full-time
Dates of Enrollment: 8/2000-5/2003
Survey Submitted: November 2004

The admissions process was competitive, but fair. I highly recommend getting your application in early, so that you qualify for ALL of the available scholarships. These are distributed on a combination of factors, and early application plays into that equation.

Status: Current student, full-time
Dates of Enrollment: 8/2003-Submit Date
Survey Submitted: June 2004

Mercer Law tends to place less emphasis on raw numbers (GPA, LSAT) than on the applicant as a whole person. Thus, unique experiences, strong character and positive academic trends can result in acceptance for students who, for instance, don't take standardized tests well or performed poorly their first year in college. The admissions process is otherwise fairly standard.

Mercer keeps in close contact with prospective students, admits students on a rolling basis and invites accepted students to take part in campus activities such as Law Day. Mercer is typically ranked as a mid-range law school, but such rankings are adversely affected by the law school's willingness to look beyond numbers, as described above. Mercer Law conducts interviews only for full-tuition scholarships, of which there are several (Woodruff Scholarship, Walter F. George Scholarship and others). The essays are pretty standard law school fare.

Status: Current student, full-time
Dates of Enrollment: 8/2001-Submit Date
Survey Submitted: April 2004

Applications were accepted as early as August prior to the year I wished to start my first year. I recommend having your application proofed and ready to be mailed (or better yet, sent through the Web) about one-and-a-half years prior to your preferred admittance date. Mercer officials often note that more than 1,000 applications are submitted each year for about 100 to 150 seats. The last thing you want to do is be in the remaining pile of applicants fighting it out for a seat when only a few seats remain. Right now, Mercer is in the second tier of law schools (out of five tiers) nationwide since the last *U.S. News & World Report* survey. Timing the application, letters of recommendation and scholarship applications to be completely submitted to the office of admissions by October greatly increases your chances for admittance.

Statistics/necessary numbers: the numbers may vary slightly and can be found at the school's web site, www.law.mercer.edu under "Prospective Students." In past years, the admissions committee (law professors, admissions staffers and so on) looked for LSAT scores between 151 to 157 combined with a 3.3 GPA or higher. One admissions officer explained how they looked at these in terms of how each score was weighted. Overall admittance score = LSAT + (GPA x 10).

Keep in mind that this weighting was given a few years back. So, a very high LSAT score or a very high GPA can really help.

For instance, my husband had a 3.0 GPA, so a GPA total of 30 points. However, he got a 165 LSAT score. He received a $15,000 scholarship renewed for each of his three years. I think this is due less to his combined score but because he really prepared for the LSAT. The higher LSAT can factor into the school's scores for *U.S. News & World Report* to boost the school's ranking.

A high GPA may also factor in to the decision for the same reason. I had a so-so LSAT score (154), but a fabulous GPA (3.954). The school generously gave me a full-tuition scholarship, plus a yearly stipend for living expenses.

The school is very generous with scholarships, giving at least $2 million away each year to entering students. The school is also introducing a public interest loan forgiveness program.

Letters of reference: I had 12 letters from employers, co-workers, professors and so on. Remember, schools often ask for a minimum of three letters of recommendation. Get extra. Another scholarship recipient in an early graduating class had nine letters. Ensure that they know you well.

 ## Academics

Status: Alumnus/a, full-time
Dates of Enrollment: 8/1998-5/2001
Survey Submitted: March 2005

The quality of instruction at Mercer Law was first-rate. The professors were very accessible. The grading was very fair. The workload was typical of any JD program.

Status: Alumnus/a, full-time
Dates of Enrollment: 8/2000-5/2003
Survey Submitted: November 2004

The Woodruff Curriculum is unique to Mercer, and encompasses a focus on legal research and writing. In addition to the required courses in writing, students have the opportunity to obtain a certificate in legal writing and hone their research and writing skills. Additionally, the structure of the curriculum provides ample opportunity to take classes which are of interest to the individual student. Class sizes are relatively small after the first-year courses are completed and are typically less than 30 students. Most students have little difficulty getting into the classes or sections that they want, and the faculty makes every effort to accommodate. The relatively small student body allows for access to the faculty and staff, and the professors maintain an open-door policy. The staff tends to know the students by name and are helpful and friendly. Many professors provide students with their home telephone numbers and personal e-mail so that access is never an issue. One unique aspect of the curriculum is that there are usually no final exams in the sixth semester. This allows students the opportunity to focus on the transition from student to career in an effective manner.

Status: Current student, full-time
Dates of Enrollment: 8/2003-Submit Date
Survey Submitted: June 2004

Most law school curricula are virtually identical to one another, including Mercer's. The most distinctive aspect of the Mercer curriculum is its emphasis on legal writing and reasoning. Mercer's legal writing faculty includes experienced, tenured professors, such as Linda Edwards, who is a national authority and prolific writer on legal writing. Additionally, Mercer offers one-week seminars before the second and third years in client counseling and mediation and arbitration.

The classes are generally good, with some variation between the best, most experienced professors and the youngest, least experienced professors. There

Read all of Vault's Law School Surveys at www.vault.com/lawschool — get complete surveys on top law schools, expert advice on applicaton essays, LSAT prep and more.

VAULT CAREER LIBRARY   195

are substantially more of the former than the latter. Because of the small class size (around 140 to 150), it is not usually too hard to get good professors. Grading, like at all law schools, is done on a curve; class rank is the only important number. The workload is probably similar to most law schools, too, but not so heavy it precludes all social activity.

Status: Current student, full-time
Dates of Enrollment: 8/2001-Submit Date
Survey Submitted: April 2004

The school is an ABA accredited law school that primarily uses the problem method and Socratic Method for teaching. The school is home to the Legal Writing Institute and the National College of Defense Counsel, in addition to the main law school. Between 84 and 93 percent of first-time bar takers from Mercer pass the bar. More than 95 percent of students are employed or going into an LLM program within the first six months after graduation.

If you want into a class, you are most likely to get into it, as many of the classes will go forward with as few as three students. Classes are limited to about 60 students. Every student will be assigned a required class if too many people register because they won't allow ability to get into a class be a factor in delaying graduation. Any class with more than 60 something students is lotteried by the registrar.

All classes with more than 15 students are graded on a curve. The mandatory average for first-year classes is 82.5 (+/- 5). Upperclassmen classes can go up to 83.5 (+/- 5). However, students can and often do get into classes with no curve in their subsequent years.

You can find biographies of all of the teachers on the school web site. And, the school only has 400 or so students. People will tell you everything and most upperclassmen will provide outlines to requesting students.

Workload can be atrocious at times, especially if you decide to do it all. Sometimes you just can't. Just manage your allotted "unprepareds" and absences, provided at the beginning of the semester by your professors. You will need them. Try to get yourself trained to read quickly and use different colors or symbols to quicken your writing.

 ## Employment Prospects

Status: Alumnus/a, full-time
Dates of Enrollment: 8/1998-5/2001
Survey Submitted: March 2005

As someone who wanted to remain in the Southeast United States, Mercer was very helpful on my resume. The alumni network is very active and supportive. I received more job offers that I ever imagined I would.

While the school is located in the heart of Georgia, the employment prospects are much more broad. The school enjoys great relationships with many Downtown Atlanta firms and regularly places students and graduates in the largest and most prestigious of these. Outside the state of Georgia, Mercer has a solid reputation for the quality of its education, and graduates have many opportunities available to them. Many Mercer grads clerk for federal judges and have the opportunity to place in "super-sized" firms around the country, but they also find success in small-and medium-sized firms in fields such as environmental law, public interest, corporate and corporate defense, as well as securities and criminal law. The diversity of the curriculum and that of the school's alumni allow for numerous opportunities in the employment arena. Many employers take comfort in the fact that Mercer graduates annually succeed on the bar and can contribute to the goals of the firm instantly.

Status: Current student, full-time
Dates of Enrollment: 8/2001-Submit Date
Survey Submitted: April 2004

The career prospects seem to correspond with your class ranking, chosen career path and location in which you wish to practice. The more urban your designated location, the more competition for a job you will have. King & Spalding (of Atlanta) only wishes to interview the top 10 percent of the class. Of course, if you want a job in a more medium-sized city, your skills at connecting with

clients may be more important than your analysis. Therefore, a ranking in the top half may be more acceptable. At our law school, 95 percent of people are employed within six months of graduation. Most go to small to medium private firms. Others go into government work. A few go into public interest or sign on as corporate counsel.

Status: Current student, full-time
Dates of Enrollment: 8/2003-Submit Date
Survey Submitted: June 2004

Mercer is well thought of in the South, and especially in Georgia. Outside the South, Mercer is not ill thought of; it's probably just not thought of at all. That said, campus recruiting and job opportunities are ample for students who want to remain in the South, particularly Georgia, Florida and the Carolinas. In the highly competitive and fairly lucrative Atlanta market, Mercer graduates are hired without any problem at all. Some of Atlanta's biggest firms actually prefer Mercer graduates, and show that preference with their hiring every year. The career services staff is very helpful and always eager to assist.

 ## Quality of Life

Status: Alumnus/a, full-time
Dates of Enrollment: 8/1998-5/2001
Survey Submitted: March 2005

The Mercer law community is very close. The campus is simply incredible. The law school facilities are second to none.

Status: Alumnus/a, full-time
Dates of Enrollment: 8/2000-5/2003
Survey Submitted: November 2004

While Macon offers very little in the way of nightlife, the environment is conducive to study and allows few distractions. However, for entertainment and relaxation, Atlanta is only an hour north and of course offers anything that a person could want or need. The cost of living in Macon is modest and there are plenty of low-cost housing opportunities a short distance from campus. There are on-campus opportunities as well, but I am not familiar with those. The campus facilities are very student-friendly. Students have access to the facilities 24/7 and there is usually personal assistance available in the library seven days a week during the semesters. Each classroom has computer and network connections at each seat, and are designed so that all students can hear and see the professors.

Status: Current student, full-time
Dates of Enrollment: 8/2003-Submit Date
Survey Submitted: June 2004

Most Mercer Law students live in the historic neighborhood around the law school in houses converted into apartments. As a result, crime is infrequent, and minor when it occurs. The law school itself is self-contained in a fairly majestic building overlooking downtown Macon. The law school was recently completely renovated, so the facilities are outstanding. The entire building is wired and wireless. Because the law school is a couple of miles away from the undergrad campus, few students have a meal plan. There is, however, an adequate lunch grill in the student lounge.

Status: Current student, full-time
Dates of Enrollment: 8/2001-Submit Date
Survey Submitted: April 2004

Many students live within walking distance in the historic district. You are surrounded by Antebellum homes and can walk to school. The downside is someone you know is likely to have their car vandalized before you graduate. Common sense can help. Forget the alarm. Get a club. Lock your car. Hide your CDs.

Social Life

Status: Current student, full-time
Dates of Enrollment: 8/2005-Submit Date
Survey Submitted: February 2006

The social life is actually quite refreshing.

Status: Alumnus/a, full-time
Dates of Enrollment: 8/1998-5/2001
Survey Submitted: March 2005

The social life at the law school was very good. It was better for married students than single students—Macon is not a very big city. However, the law students frequently met at local restaurants, bars or each other's houses for social events.

Status: Alumnus/a, full-time
Dates of Enrollment: 8/2000-5/2003
Survey Submitted: November 2004

As mentioned above, Macon offers a limited nightlife, but there are several clubs and dining opportunities in the downtown area (just a few blocks from the law school). The school offers many social functions, and the service organizations and clubs keep things busy as well. There are, of course, the national chains such as Outback, Carraba's and Chili's, as well as local flavor restaurants.

Status: Current student, full-time
Dates of Enrollment: 8/2003-Submit Date
Survey Submitted: June 2004

Macon is a nice enough city, but it's not bustling, nor is it a college town (despite the presence of several colleges). There's enough to keep a law student entertained, since law students don't have that much free time, but the real geographical selling point is that it's around an hour and 15 minutes to Atlanta and an hour and a half to Athens (for UGA grads and others interested in seeing the ideal college experience).

There are several bars and a few good restaurants around Macon, which is well known for its musical heritage (jazz and blues, think the Allman Brothers and Otis Redding). A lot of students hang out at the 550 Blues Club, Trio Jazz Bar, CJ's (a world-class beer joint) and Dea, which is Macon's attempt at a dance club.

The student bar association hosts Freaker's Ball (a very popular Halloween party) and Barrister's Ball. Ducks Unlimited and the Association of Women Law Students have well-attended banquets in the spring, and the Phi Delta Phi chapter has a golf tournament every April. In the fall, a lot of folks take Highway 129-N to Athens for UGA football games, or wherever their alma maters may be playing. Though it is a private school, Mercer is heavily populated by the products of Southern state schools—Georgia, Auburn, Alabama, South Carolina, etc.—and that mentality dictates a lot of the social scene.

Status: Current student, full-time
Dates of Enrollment: 8/2001-Submit Date
Survey Submitted: April 2004

Pizza: Jenoely's ($3 lunch deal with drink); Cafe Giambrone's (best garlic knots ever). Downtown fare: Bert's (garlic soup that is out of this world); Michael's (sandwiches, pasta, steak, wine and so on; very near the school); Adriana's (known for its Italian food and fabulous ice cream); Jeneane's and The Bear's Den (for home cookin'). A little further out: Ron's Kuntry Kitchen (soul food, catfish, dressin'). Southern cuisine that is not to be missed.

Bookstores: Barnes & Noble. Many students can be found in the cushiony chairs to study instead of the library. (Some of the first-years had tried to "claim" cubicles at B&N by decorating them. Not cool. People will laugh at you and suggest you pay rent.)

Read all of Vault's Law School Surveys at www.vault.com/lawschool — get complete surveys on top law schools, expert advice on applicaton essays, LSAT prep and more.

VAULT CAREER LIBRARY   197

University of Georgia School of Law

Admissions Office
School of Law
Harold Hirsch Hall
University of Georgia
Athens, GA 30602-6012
Admissions phone: (706) 542-7060
Admissions e-mail: ugajd@uga.edu
Admissions URL: http://www.lawsch.uga.edu/admissions/

 ## Admissions

Status: Current student, full-time
Dates of Enrollment: 8/2004-Submit Date
Survey Submitted: March 2005

Make sure your recommendations come from undergraduate professors and I recommend taking a class to help prepare for the LSAT.

Status: Alumnus/a, full-time
Dates of Enrollment: 8/2000-5/2003
Survey Submitted: May 2005

I had a 161 LSAT score, 3.8 undergrad GPA and three years prior work experience. I was quickly admitted. I never got feedback on what was most important. I had little interaction with admissions. Friends had great things to say about admissions. Lots of scholarships available. Short essay required. Very selective for a public school.

Status: Alumnus/a, full-time
Dates of Enrollment: 8/2000-5/2003
Survey Submitted: March 2005

UGA Law looks for commitment to community service in their applicants. Make sure any community service you've done is reflected in your application, personal statement and recommendation letters. They also look for leadership, not mere participation. The school appreciates letters of recommendation from professors more than employers, but if you took time off between college and law school, employer letters are important. Big names (e.g., governors or other figures) are not impressive to the admissions committee unless there is a solid, real relationship there. Just because you worked in the governor's office for a summer (with no real interaction with the governor) or your dad is a big contributor, don't think this will make the best recommendation letter than a letter from a professor or alumni that knows you well. UGA Law does not conduct interviews.

Status: Current student, full-time
Dates of Enrollment: 8/2003-Submit Date
Survey Submitted: January 2004

The admissions process was typical of most law schools. UGA is a top-tier school, so LSAT scores seemed to be very important. It also seemed that the standards are a bit higher for nonresidents than for Georgia residents. One bonus about UGA was that they told me online that I was admitted (at their online status check center), so I didn't have to wait for an envelope! Much better than schools who just tell you that a decision has been made, but not what that decision actually is!

Status: Current student, full-time
Dates of Enrollment: 8/2002-Submit Date
Survey Submitted: October 2003

Typical law school admissions process, involving GPA, LSAT, references and essays. No interview. UGA seems to give a little more weight to solid GPAs. But expect to score at least a 160 LSAT to have a shot. Expect admissions to be tighter than usual this year. More people than expected accepted offers last year. So the 1L class has about 40 or 50 more people than usual.

> **The school says:** "For the 2003 entering class, the LSAT range was 173-146, with a median of 162."

Status: Alumnus/a, full-time
Dates of Enrollment: 8/1997-6/2000
Survey Submitted: April 2004

The admission process in 1997 required a general essay (topic of applicant's choosing), and I think also some recommendations. UGA law is relatively selective, but has many applications, so numbers (LSAT and GPA) are probably important to at least get you past the initial screening process.

> **According to the school:** "For the last 20 years, all applicants have had to write an essay telling why they want a legal education."

Status: Alumnus/a, full-time JD/MBA
Dates of Enrollment: 8/1994-5/1999
Survey Submitted: April 2004

UGA is much more selective for out-of-state students than in-state. The process was pretty simple, involving a simple straightforward application for both schools (law and MBA).

 ## Academics

Status: Current student, full-time
Dates of Enrollment: 8/2004-Submit Date
Survey Submitted: March 2005

First-years all take the same classes, although it's good to confer with someone to make sure you get the types of professors you want. The workload is heavy, stressful and challenging, but all law schools are like that.

Status: Alumnus/a, full-time
Dates of Enrollment: 8/2000-5/2003
Survey Submitted: May 2005

Professor Ellington is a legend in civil procedure and professional responsibility, and kindest professor I have ever had, a true Southern gentleman. Every student loved him. No grades until after spring finals first year. The only grades in winter were the semester-long Criminal Law and Legal Writing. Students are competitive but the school has a very friendly atmosphere. Great clinics includes legal aid and prosecutors office. Great advocacy programs, moot court, mock trial. Three great journals, lots of opportunities to write on a journal or join the advocacy programs if grades are tops. Very collegial groups.

Status: Alumnus/a, full-time
Dates of Enrollment: 8/2000-5/2003
Survey Submitted: March 2005

The professors are great overall. Very distinguished and accomplished names in Georgia law. Not a lot of nationally known professors, but very bright folks that are thoughtful and really care about the development of the students. The professors are also helpful post-graduation. Several times, I've called or e-mailed a professor to ask legal questions and they are more than happy to discuss. The class offerings are good and it usually isn't difficult to get the classes you want. The school has a bidding point process. Each semester you have more points and you put a certain number of points on the classes you want and the class takes the highest bidders. Some smaller classes may be difficult, but you can certainly get the classes you want before you graduate. Grading is on the curve like most other law schools. I don't recall the median GPA that is set anymore, but I do know it has recently increased. Workload depends on the professors and their reputations are well-known around the school—older students are more than willing to share their knowledge of the professors.

Status: Current student, full-time
Dates of Enrollment: 8/2003-Submit Date
Survey Submitted: October 2003

So far, I am enjoying my classes. The first-year class is broken down into three sections. I am in section Y, which supposedly has the best teachers. All of our first-year classes are full-year classes, except for Criminal Law. This was nice, because our fall exams were midterms, not finals, and only counted for one-third of our final grade. First year we take Property, Torts, Contracts, Criminal Law, Civ Pro, and Legal Research and Writing. Second Semester Criminal Law drops out, and LRW only lasts until late February, which means only four classes for March and April.

We are graded on a strict curve, with the median being a B. Teachers are good about sticking to this system. Just like anywhere, we have some good professors, and some not so good. Laptops are not required, but most people take notes on them every day. All classrooms and the library have plugs and wireless access. I take notes by hand, but type my exams. I think typing your exams is the best way to go, because speed is a major factor. If you want to take exams on a laptop, you need an IBM-compatible computer; the software doesn't work on Apple.

Status: Current student, full-time
Dates of Enrollment: 8/2002-Submit Date
Survey Submitted: October 2003

First-years are divided into three sections of about 70 students. I have yet to have a professor who was not a great teacher. The excellent teachers outweigh the rest. Many are at the top of their fields, and their enthusiasm carries over into the classroom.

Grading is on a strict B curve. The gap between the top and bottom of the class is razor-thin. So be prepared to work very hard to make it. Workload varies from professor to professor. LSAT and GPA mean nothing once you get in the door, because so many great students come here. So whether you're on full scholarship or off the waitlist, you're going to have to earn your keep.

The 2L and 3L classes are awarded on a lottery system. Some of the more popular classes can be difficult to get into. There does need to be a few more faculty hired.

> **The school says:** "The size of our faculty has increased in recent years."

Status: Alumnus/a, full-time JD/MBA
Dates of Enrollment: 8/1994-5/1999
Survey Submitted: April 2004

Law school is on a pure curve. The median is 2.7 GPA; the top third of class is set at 3.0; 3.3 for the top 10 percent. It is a very difficult curve and highly competitive. Law firms look mainly at students in the top 20 percent of their class.

Status: Alumnus/a, full-time
Dates of Enrollment: 8/1997-6/2000
Survey Submitted: April 2004

UGA is challenging and stimulating academically. I received an excellent education and worked very hard. Because it is not a top-tier school, grades and class rank are important. So if you want to have many options upon graduation, come prepared to work very hard.

> **The school says:** "*U.S. News & World Report* currently identifies the Top 50 law schools as being in the top tier. The University of Georgia has been ranked in the Top 50 for over a decade."

Employment Prospects

Status: Alumnus/a, full-time
Dates of Enrollment: 8/2000-5/2003
Survey Submitted: May 2005

Tons of big firms from around the country come to campus and hire in droves. Lots of people opt for public interest and small firm careers. Everyone in the top 10 percent got federal clerkships if they wanted one. I summered with a big D.C. firm and easily got a job doing IP litigation. On-campus interviewing is all you can eat if you are in the top third of the class.

Status: Alumnus/a, full-time
Dates of Enrollment: 8/2000-5/2003
Survey Submitted: March 2005

If you want to work in Georgia, you could not pick a better school than UGA. The network of UGA alumni is terrific. It is harder to go outside of Georgia and even

harder to go outside the Southeast. We certainly have alumni in D.C. and NY but it is difficult. All the big Atlanta firms recruit on campus and many D.C. firms do as well. The career services office at UGA could stand lots of improvements. They don't do a good job of thinking outside the box. If you are looking for a non-firm job, you will have to rely on alumni contacts to help you seek out those opportunities.

Status: Current student, full-time
Dates of Enrollment: 8/2003-Submit Date
Survey Submitted: January 2004

The career office is spectacular and very willing to help anyone who asks! There are lots of recruiting events and opportunities for on-campus interviews and networking. Of course, it's a bit harder to get jobs out of state, but if you want one, the staff will do all they can to help you out.

Status: Current student, full-time
Dates of Enrollment: 8/2002-Submit Date
Survey Submitted: October 2003

If you're among the top 10 percent here, you'll have the pick of the litter in job prospects. Most of the top firms in the Southeast interview here. All of the Atlanta firms, big and small, looking to hire will make a stop. Because of the drop in the economy, job prospects have been thin for students not in the top third of the class. There is supposed to be a cap of 25 on-campus interviews per student. But unfortunately for the non-Law Review students, career services does not seem to be rigorously enforcing the limit.

> **The school says:** "The limit is enforced; however, waivers are granted on an individual basis."

Status: Alumnus/a, full-time
Dates of Enrollment: 8/1994-5/1999
Survey Submitted: April 2004

Career opportunities are perfect for any Atlanta law firm and any law firm in the state of Georgia. Students do go to Washington, D.C., South Carolina and North Carolina, but almost 90 percent of the students stay in state (because they want to be in Georgia).

> **The school states:** "Actual statistics confirm that around 80 percent of our students obtain work in the state of Georgia after graduation each year."

Status: Alumnus/a, full-time
Dates of Enrollment: 8/1997-6/2000
Survey Submitted: April 2004

UGA Law has an excellent record of placing students—somewhere in the high 90 percent of graduates are employed within a year. The school has an excellent reputation regionally, so finding a job in the South is usually not a problem. Nationwide, it may be a bit more difficult, but I got a job in one of Boston's biggest firms a year after I graduated, so we do have graduates nationwide.

Quality of Life

Status: Alumnus/a, full-time
Dates of Enrollment: 8/2000-5/2003
Survey Submitted: May 2005

Laid-back Southern life. Close to Atlanta, but still tucked away from the hustle. Cheap rent. $425 per month for a one-bedroom downtown, close to everything. I had many friends that paid less than $300 per month. Fantastic weather. Great hiking and whitewater kayaking nearby. Great places to study downtown. The law school library is fantastic with huge windows looking onto lush lawns and lots of trees. Library can be a little loud because everyone is so social. Can get in the way of studying. I was touring another law school and ran into two Georgia undergrads. They said that they didn't think they could go to Georgia for law school because Athens is too much fun. Right then, I knew I had to go check it out. They were right, it was a fun, fun town.

Read all of Vault's Law School Surveys at www.vault.com/lawschool — get complete surveys on top law schools, expert advice on applicaton essays, LSAT prep and more.

VAULT CAREER LIBRARY   199

Status: Alumnus/a, full-time

Dates of Enrollment: 8/2000-5/2003

Survey Submitted: March 2005

Athens is a terrific town! After you attend school there, Athens will certainly carry a special place in your heart and you will want to visit often. Great restaurants, great bars and great entertainment (lots of live music). It is a college town, so everything focuses around the school. The downtown area is just a short walk from the law school so it is easy to enjoy a nice lunch or happy hour downtown after class. Housing is cheap. The area is relatively safe—basic precaution is necessary.

Status: Current student, full-time

Dates of Enrollment: 8/2003-Submit Date

Survey Submitted: January 2004

The town has a lot of hills and requires a lot of walking, so be prepared to get in shape! The bus system is fantastic, and if you are up for public transportation, it is probably the best way to get to school. Buses stop at all the major apartment complexes in the area and drop you off closer to the law school than any parking lot is. If you do drive to school, the easiest place to park is the North Deck. It is currently $30 per month, but it is the easiest place to walk to, and with all the books you carry your first year, you will need an easy place to park. Some people park in the Hull Street lot, which is cheaper, $10 per month, but it is a huge hike to class every day. I made the mistake of parking there this year, and it is really bad, although I am not athletically inclined. First-years generally bring a lunch with them; we have classes from 9:30 a.m. to 3:30 p.m. daily, and while there are many restaurants close by, it gets expensive. We have lockers, refrigerators, microwaves and lounges.

Athens is a college town, so there is a bit of crime just because the average age is so low, and 18 to 25 year olds tend to commit the most crime.

Status: Current student, full-time

Dates of Enrollment: 8/2002-Submit Date

Survey Submitted: October 2003

Most Athens apartments are overpriced. Expect to pay $450 to $500 per month to live in an old one-bedroom apartment. If you're lucky enough to have a lot of money saved or funding from Daddy, you can get nicer apartments for around $600. Per capita, Athens has more public housing than just about any town in America. So if you're uncomfortable sharing neighborhoods and a town with the poor, think twice. This isn't suburbia or the country. Crime is surprising for a small town. There are car break-ins. So don't have a nice car stereo, and if you do, buy an alarm system. There aren't many serious crimes.

> **With regard to crime, the school says:** "For actual crime statistics, we would recommend prospective students visit www.uga.edu/safeandsecure/home.html."

Dining options are numerous. Downtown Athens has great food for very reasonable prices. Parking isn't bad here for a big school; most law students park within a three- to five-minute walk from class. UGA's campus is beautiful. Some of the law classrooms are older and haven't been remodeled in decades. But about half or more of the classrooms are state of the art. The law library has been a bit crowded this year because the 1L class is one of the largest ever.

> **The school says:** "All classrooms have been completely refurbished within the last five years."

Status: Alumnus/a, full-time

Dates of Enrollment: 8/1994-5/1999

Survey Submitted: April 2004

Athens is one of the greatest places on earth. Perfect college town. It's the right size, and you have Atlanta when you want to see major sporting events or concerts. Plus, the sports programs at UGA are topnotch. Sanford Stadium holds 90,000 people. UGA is one of the most beautiful campuses in the country.

Status: Alumnus/a, full-time

Dates of Enrollment: 8/1997-6/2000

Survey Submitted: April 2004

Athens is a great college town. Lots to do, but still a small-town feel. The cost of living is cheap.

 # Social Life

Status: Alumnus/a, full-time

Dates of Enrollment: 8/2000-5/2003

Survey Submitted: May 2005

Athens has to be one of the top college towns around. There are 40 or so bars of all kinds crammed within a few small blocks in downtown, right across from the law school. Everyone goes out and socializes. Great music scene—David Lowry of Cracker has his music label there and REM and the B-52s play a lot. Lots of up and coming bands. Always fantastic shows. The 40-Watt is legendary. Great sport teams. Great football tradition. Law school always has great tailgate parties before all of the home football games. Auburn weekends are nuts. Season football tickets are extremely cheap.

Status: Alumnus/a, full-time

Dates of Enrollment: 8/2000-5/2003

Survey Submitted: March 2005

The student body is great. In any law school, you will find competitive atmospheres, but UGA is not overtly cutthroat, though there is always "that guy" who is going to try to hide library books. Overall the students are friendly and supportive of each other. The students tend to socialize a lot outside of school. Many of the other graduate programs have mixer events so that there is always opportunity to meet other graduate students.

Status: Current student, full-time

Dates of Enrollment: 10/2003-Submit Date

Survey Submitted: November 2004

I lived off campus and did not have a social life at the time. I had no time to socialize. I did not have time for a social life as I was going to school full-time and working two jobs all at the same time. I got about two hours of sleep per 24 hours and really did not even have time to eat!

Status: Current student, full-time

Dates of Enrollment: 8/2002-Submit Date

Survey Submitted: October 2003

In terms of student life, UGA might be the best place to go to college (or law school) in the nation. Downtown Athens is the greatest. The workout facilities are among the top in the nation. UGA's football and basketball teams are improving. Most students are very friendly. However, many students come from suburban Atlanta. So there are some spoiled brats living off Mom and Dad and driving SUVs. But you just gotta look past those few.

Status: Alumnus/a, full-time

Dates of Enrollment: 8/1994-5/1999

Survey Submitted: April 2004

Great social life. The law school sponsors many functions. The bar scene in Athens is second to none. Great dating scene in Athens! Harry Bissett's, Boars' Head, East West Bistro and City Bar are all favorites!

Status: Current student, full-time

Dates of Enrollment: 8/2003-Submit Date

Survey Submitted: April 2004

Who has time for a social life in law school? But, if you do, Athens is a great place! Lots of bars, great food and great shopping, all right across from campus. Plus, if you get a parking permit, you can park in the North Deck for free on nights and weekends, which means easy access to downtown, and a relatively safe place to leave your car. Parking downtown can be difficult otherwise, unless you are willing to pay for one of the public parking decks. There are also lots of events on campus, and football is huge here. I think our stadium holds almost 100,000 people, and the whole town is dedicated to UGA sports. Each student has the opportunity to buy football tickets at the beginning of fall semester. I think it's about $8 a game. You can often resell tickets you don't use for a large profit. No matter what, you will never be bored in Athens!

Chicago-Kent College of Law

Illinois Institute of Technology
Office of Admissions
Chicago-Kent College of Law
565 West Adams Street
Chicago, IL 60661-3691
Admissions phone: (312) 906-5020
Admissions e-mail: admit@kentlaw.edu
Admissions URL: http://www.kentlaw.edu/adm/

 Admissions

Status: Current student, full-time
Dates of Enrollment: 8/2005-Submit Date
Survey Submitted: May 2006

Chicago-Kent has great opportunities for students interested in going to law school. In the fall (sometime in October usually) they hold a program about how to get into law school. Although they tell you specifics about the CK process, it was very helpful just for overall knowledge of the law school application process. They continue to hold programs for prospective students throughout the year, which I found to be very helpful because the best way to know if you want to attend a school is to visit it. Chicago-Kent does not require interviews, but the admissions staff is willing and available to speak with any time.

Status: Current student, full-time
Dates of Enrollment: 8/2003-Submit Date
Survey Submitted: May 2006

The admissions process was very simple. The school required a standard application form. The admissions staff was very accessible. At the time, Mike Burns (Former Chicago-Kent head of admissions and current DePaul head of admissions) took me on a tour, and introduced me to key figures in the Intellectual Property Law Program. The school does not require and interview, but does require an essay. I would note that selectivity increased substantially since I applied. I jokingly note that I probably wouldn't be admitted to Chicago-Kent if I were to apply today...but that may be true.

Status: Current student, full-time
Dates of Enrollment: 8/2004-Submit Date
Survey Submitted: May 2006

Chicago-Kent sent me more information than the rest of the schools combined. It seemed like every other week I was getting something new from them that would help me in my decisions. The process did take longer than I expected. Chicago-Kent was my top choice, so that was my first application in the mail. It was also the last acceptance I received. But they also gave me the most money...so I figured the delay was worth it if they were considering me for scholarships. Overall, I was very pleased with the admissions process.

Status: Current student, full-time
Dates of Enrollment: 8/2003-Submit Date
Survey Submitted: April 2006

The school genuinely creates a very diverse student body, not just race, gender, religion, ethnicity, but people who come from different backgrounds. Few people in the class even came to school with the same undergraduate majors. As a result, the personal essay is an important part of the process.

Status: Current student, part-time
Dates of Enrollment: 8/2005-Submit Date
Survey Submitted: April 2006

I feel that the admissions process is pretty selective here, as it is at most schools since so many people are applying. I think that Kent is very good at giving students whose statistics (GPA, LSAT score) might be lower than the school's average a chance to go to an excellent school. They also admit some students to the part-time evening program and then allow them to switch to the day division, which is a great opportunity to go to a good school even if your LSAT score didn't turn out as you'd hoped. I didn't have an interview, but I did really like my essay (about Feminism, traveling, and the law) and I think it helped me get accepted.

Status: Current student, full-time
Dates of Enrollment: 8/2003-Submit Date
Survey Submitted: April 2006

I recommend that students score well on the LSAT. To score well they should practice, practice, practice. Get involved in organizations, the community, something to make a name for yourself and make yourself stick out from everyone else. For your personal statement, make it just that: personal. Try to avoid some cookie cutter speech that sounds like a blurb from an election campaign and just be a genuine and honest, even if that honesty means saying "I am not sure what I want to do after law school." Grades are not everything. You can have a 4.0 and if you have done NOTHING but study, someone with a 3.0 could get in over you.

Status: Current student, full-time
Dates of Enrollment: 8/2003-Submit Date
Survey Submitted: November 2005

I had an undergraduate 3.0 along with a 165 on the LSAT and some work experience and I was offered a partial scholarship, which surprised me a bit. The school has increased its selectivity with the increase in applicants in recent years. But, you should be able to get accepted as long as you have decent grades, do better than the norm on the LSAT and write a decent essay. For my essay, I selected some interesting themes from my life and I put them all together in a story that would stick in the mind of the applications committee. You're much better off doing this than trying to write the usual "This is where I grew up, this is what I want to do with my life" essay. As far as interviews, Chicago-Kent does not interview applicants (except maybe in extreme circumstances).

Status: Alumnus/a, full-time
Dates of Enrollment: 9/2001-5/2004
Survey Submitted: April 2005

Kent is steadily moving up the ranks and its admissions process reflects its rising reputation. Be prepared to show the admissions committee how you are unique and how you will add to the eclectic student body. The typical Kent student is a strong individual with a unique background and a diverse set of life experiences—which is to say that there is no typical Kent student. The professors are looking for the next unique voice in the class. They want the students who will ask the interesting questions. It isn't enough to have the grades—everyone has the grades in this market. Take a good look at yourself and ask "what makes me interesting?" If you can't come up with a good answer—look elsewhere.

Status: Alumnus/a, full-time
Dates of Enrollment: 8/2000-5/2003
Survey Submitted: September 2003

Essentially, I filled out an application that included an essay portion and had to submit my LSAT score as well as transcripts from undergraduate institutions and three letters of recommendation. There wasn't an interview, but I was invited to various programs to take a look at the school and hear about the views of the school and the programs available with emphasis on the legal writing program and the legal clinic program.

Currently, the school is attempting to have smaller classes and raise the LSAT scores and therefore the ranking of the school, which started the year before I was applying. Therefore, it has become more selective and students that would have gotten in five years ago are being waitlisted. My advice to students attempting to get into Chicago-Kent College of Law would be to attend the various events available at the school and make an attempt to meet with the deans and other administrators both to learn more about the school currently and

Read all of Vault's Law School Surveys at www.vault.com/lawschool — get complete surveys on top law schools, expert advice on applicaton essays, LSAT prep and more.

VAULT CAREER LIBRARY 201

the direction the school is taking and to establish yourself as an individual rather than as a GPA or an LSAT score.

 ## Academics

Status: Current student, full-time
Dates of Enrollment: 8/2005-Submit Date
Survey Submitted: May 2006

Chicago-Kent has a very friendly environment. For the first year, students are broken into sections and have all the courses that year with the same group of people. This allows for a great learning environment. The first-year courses are Legal Research and Writing, torts, Contracts, Criminal Law, Civil Procedure, Property, and Legislative Process. All the courses, except Legal Writing, are graded on a mandatory curve, but grading is done anonymously. Some professors will use participation as a deciding factor for a grade if it is on the border. Based on the professor, they will cold call on students, or take volunteers, or never have student involvement. Although the workload is heavy, especially with the writing assignments, it is not completely overwhelming. The majority of professors are amazing, incredibly dedicated to teaching, and very approachable and helpful.

Status: Alumnus/a, full-time
Dates of Enrollment: 8/1995-12/1998
Survey Submitted: May 2006

The program features a good mix of traditional classwork and practical skills training. Legal writing is heavily emphasized, and the program is excellent. I was very pleased with all of my instructors, who I found to be accessible in and out of class. In addition, the school offered practical opportunities such as judicial externships with the state and federal judiciary that I found to be invaluable.

Status: Current student, full-time
Dates of Enrollment: 8/2003-Submit Date
Survey Submitted: May 2006

Classes are fantastic. As most schools, you have your "good teachers" and "mediocre teachers." Even the best teachers are accessible. These teachers often teach two classes a semester, allowing students to be exposed to their area of expertise. I focused on the Intellectual Property program. Almost half of the Chicago-Kent students take an IP class in one form or another. I am attaining a certificate in intellectual property law, which gave me priority to register for IP classes.

Some of the finest professors, including those that wrote the text books, treatises, and casebooks for the classes taught them as well. Workloads were as expected, and professors were phenomenal. Frankly, I think that Chicago-Kent has amazing professors that go under-recognized by the larger community through rankings.

Status: Current student, full-time
Dates of Enrollment: 8/2004-Submit Date
Survey Submitted: May 2006

The academics of Chicago-Kent have been fantastic. I have been particularly pleased with the Legal Writing Program. This program is definitely one of the strengths of Chicago-Kent. The program is intense and requires a lot of work, but the reward is worth it. The program is thorough, requiring five semesters of legal writing. The program is very effective. It is very feedback oriented, and so instead of making the same mistakes over and over again, a student can learn from their mistakes and implement those lessons to progress their skills in the next assignment.

I have been especially pleased with has been the faculty. Like most schools, I have had a variety of professors with a variety of styles. Some have been harder than others, some more theory based than others, some more Socratic than others. But I have never had a professor who I felt was out to make students feel small. I have never that a professor was out to build up his or her own ego by making some student look foolish. I have felt that each and every one of my professors has had my best interest and that of my fellow students at the top of their list of priorities. They are friendly, and personable, they are real people you

joke with in class and out. They are helpful and always available for questions, discussions, or general advice on how to survive law school or how to get a good job afterwards.

Status: Current student, full-time
Dates of Enrollment: 8/2003-Submit Date
Survey Submitted: April 2006

The professors are not just intellectuals but are incredible teachers as well. Unlike many law schools, the professors care that the students learn and understand the information. Also, getting classes and teachers are relatively easy. Some professors and classes are competitive to get into, but most classes are offered again.

Status: Current student, full-time
Dates of Enrollment: 8/2004-Submit Date
Survey Submitted: April 2006

Chicago-Kent has a highly talented and dedicated faculty and continues to draw a diverse array of the top professors in their field. The area in which Chicago-Kent gets the most accolades is its three-year legal writing program. Lawyers from Chicago and beyond note that associates from Chicago-Kent always enter the workforce with superior writing skills. As one lawyer recently told me, "Kent graduates just 'get it.'" Chicago-Kent also has a particularly strong Intellectual Property department which continues to distinguish itself among its peers in Chicago and across the country. A public interest certificate was just created this year to help focus students interested in pursuing a public interest career after they graduate.

Status: Current student, part-time
Dates of Enrollment: 8/2005-Submit Date
Survey Submitted: April 2006

Since I'm a 1L I really only am able to talk about first year classes thus far-which are quite large (about 90 people). This was hard for me to get used to since I went to a very small school with several classes as small as four to five people. However, the Legal Writing Classes (mine had about 17 people) are much smaller and give you a chance to meet more people in your class as well as interact with the Professor on an everyday basis.

The workload is quite heavy, especially with the Legal Writing Program here, which works you to death. We are just registering (late, I might add) for next years classes now, so I'm not sure how easy it is to get popular classes. I did get accepted (through a lottery) to the very popular immigration clinic, which I am very excited about because it's supposed to be an invaluable opportunity.

The professors have been pretty accessible (esp. by e-mail) for the most part. Grading is curved so students are competing against each other for grades (unlike some other schools in the area).

Status: Current student, full-time
Dates of Enrollment: 8/2003-Submit Date
Survey Submitted: November 2005

Reinforcing what you've read about law school, your first-year grades are the most important. What they will tell you is that it helps you get the job interviews and, theoretically, a better job. What they will not tell you is that the students with good grades in the first year are more likely to continue to get good grades throughout. Professors talk to one another and want to know who "should" be their best students coming into second-year classes.

The first-year workload was the most demanding.

Status: Alumnus/a, full-time
Dates of Enrollment: 9/2001-5/2004
Survey Submitted: April 2005

The classes are pretty much all topnotch. There is obviously the occasional dog, but by and large, the courses are excellent. Professors tend to have a more practically-based experience level than you would expect from a full-time program. These are actual lawyers who have actual war stories. This is not a "beard stroking" faculty. Granted, there is the occasional stuffed shirt who has never seen the real world of the legal profession, the overall faculty is seasoned and accessible. This is not to say that the faculty is in any way unqualified. On the contrary, the professors at Kent are among the brightest scholars in their fields. A search will reveal that most of the faculty have published voluminously.

There was never a problem getting into a class, and if a class were "full," a quick trip to the assistant dean was usually sufficient to cure the problem without any complications. There really was no theme to grading at Kent, it totally depends on the professor. Some are easy, some are tough, some toe the line. One thing that was true of every professor and every class was that the professors were available. Not once did I hear that they were too busy.

Status: Alumnus/a, full-time
Dates of Enrollment: 8/2000-5/2003
Survey Submitted: September 2003

There are certain core classes that every law student is required to take prior to graduation. In addition, the faculty and administration comes up with a list of recommended classes to take and suggests that students take certain classes which almost always appear on the bar exam in Illinois. Although there are times when a student cannot get into a class with a certain section or certain professor, it only happened to me once as a second-year and I was able to get into the class the next year, so still had the opportunity to take the class. Additionally, many professors will allow students who haven't gotten into a class to sit in the class from the beginning. Then, they may add them if there are only a few such students, or they may have them wait to see whether another student will drop and a space will become available.

The best professors at Kent are brought in to teach a class in their area of specialty. They have the real-world experience that many other law professors do not have. However, all of the professors that I had at Chicago-Kent were involved in their field in some way outside of the classes they were teaching at the law school. This made the classes more interesting and allowed the professors to show how the material being discussed in class related to real-world situations they had experienced.

The workload at Kent is reasonable. There is always reading for class, and a student must be prepared to discuss the cases they have read. There is definitely more reading in law school than in undergrad and some of the material is dry since many of the cases in things like property law are old cases. One of the important things is to figure out how each professor wants students to be able to discuss a case. Some want a student to be able to tell the class every minute detail, and others merely want students to be able to glean both the issue and the law from the case without any reference to the minute details.

At Kent, grades are curved for classes that are mandatory and classes that exceed a certain modest number of students. Additionally in most classes there is a component of the grade that is for participation. I have heard of situations where students have felt that this was merely a way for the professor to raise students grades that he or she like while lowering the grades of students that he or she did not. It does give a professor some wiggle room.

On a final note, I would suggest that one cannot fully appreciate the Chicago-Kent experience without taking at least one class from Michael Spak and one from Richard Conviser.

 Employment Prospects

Status: Current student, full-time
Dates of Enrollment: 8/2005-Submit Date
Survey Submitted: May 2006

Chicago-Kent is very well known in the Chicagoland area. The school provides many opportunities to network by offering panels and other such events. The main thing that is said about Chicago-Kent students looking for jobs is that employers know they have an excellent writing background based on our program. Also, Chicago-Kent students are very involved and one legal aid clinic in town said that over half of their student volunteers were from Chicago-Kent despite the number of law schools in the city.

Status: Alumnus/a, full-time
Dates of Enrollment: 8/1995-12/1998
Survey Submitted: May 2006

Kent grads are known in the Chicago market as being good writers, hard workers, and lawyers who think well on their feet. The law school's reputation has continued to rise every year since I graduated in 1999. I had a job immediately after passing the Bar exam at an 80-lawyer law firm, and I landed that job through alumni contacts I had made while in law school. The alumni network is good and continuing to get better, both in Chicago and in the major legal markets around the country.

Status: Current student, full-time
Dates of Enrollment: 8/2003-Submit Date
Survey Submitted: May 2006

The traditional top 20 percent students that had summer associate positions while they were 2Ls were offered jobs when they graduate. The rest of the 80 percent is a mix. Chicago-Kent is improving in its reputation, and more schools are taking it seriously. However, when competing with students from Northwestern and the University of Chicago, jobs are not coming to the students. Alumni networking is more of a recent thing—the school and the alums are trying to create networking sessions. The Student Bar Association started a Networking lunch this year that had great success. More are forthcoming next year.

Status: Current student, full-time
Dates of Enrollment: 8/2004-Submit Date
Survey Submitted: May 2006

"Chicago-Kent students know how to write." That has always been the buzz I've heard around students from our school—that our legal writing program is one of the best in the country when it comes to preparing students to research and write. In fact, the writing program was one of the biggest reasons why I choose Kent. Before law school, I worked with a large law firm on the East Coast. As I spoke with each of the attorneys, asking them what I should look for and what was most important, they all had the same first answer: writing. In the law, you learn things, and forget them, and relearn them, and reforget them. But I've always felt as if I have a leg up on job applicants from other schools because I know how to write, and the employer knows I can too.

I have been able to join several of the student organizations. Through these organizations, in combination with the career services office, I have been able to attend several networking events with local attorneys. I have been able to get excellent advice, I have been able to make valuable connections, and I have been able to gain a greater knowledge of how best to present myself to employers once I graduate.

Lastly, the career services office is fantastic. I have met with counselors on several occasions to discuss job options, to have them critique my resume and writing samples, and to gain general knowledge on how I can get a leg up on my peers when it comes to finding a job. I have been very pleased with the career services office, and the school in general, with how they have prepared me to be competitive in the job market.

Status: Current student, full-time
Dates of Enrollment: 8/2003-Submit Date
Survey Submitted: April 2006

Prestigious jobs: people in the top percent of the class or those who networked starting from their first day of school are the ones who get the prestigious jobs

Public Interest/Government:you have to volunteer to get a permanent position with these employers, but even that doesn't guarantee you will get a job. But you HAVE to volunteer.

Small/Mid-size: you have to look, career services will help with whatever you ask for, but you have to look for these jobs on your own and it is your own personal traits and attributes which will land you the job.

Read all of Vault's Law School Surveys at www.vault.com/lawschool — get complete surveys on top law schools, expert advice on applicaton essays, LSAT prep and more.

VAULT CAREER LIBRARY 203

Status: Current student, full-time
Dates of Enrollment: 8/2004-Submit Date
Survey Submitted: April 2006

On-campus interviews are offered. Mock interviews done by alumni are available. Job postings are great (I found my current clerking job though the school job board). Any attorney in Chicago knows about Chicago-Kent, and it is clearly the leader technology-wise.

Status: Alumnus/a, full-time
Dates of Enrollment: 8/2002-5/2005
Survey Submitted: March 2006

Employment prospects for the typical Chicago-Kent student are probably the weakest aspect of the school. Graduates do run the gamut, with some working as judicial clerks, some working in high-profile firms, some in smaller firms, and some solo practitioners. However, the jobs with the highest prestige are open to only a select few graduates, and the typical student will end up in a much more run-of-the-mill job. The prestige of the school just is not terribly high among employers (although this attitude is changing as recent graduates, prepared well thanks to the excellent legal writing program, prove themselves to be effective attorneys).

Status: Alumnus/a, full-time
Dates of Enrollment: 9/2001-5/2004
Survey Submitted: April 2005

Top 15 percent can expect a job at a top big firm if they have the chops to get through the interview. The top 30 to 40 percent can expect to find work in mid-sized firms who know the value of Kent's "in the trenches" approach to legal education. The remainder of the class will usually wind up in the public sector, or working for smaller boutique and sole practitioners until they get enough experience to move laterally into other positions.

Status: Alumnus/a, full-time
Dates of Enrollment: 8/1998-6/2001
Survey Submitted: March 2005

To get in to a BigLaw firm you have to be top of the class, but it seems that more and more students are breaking in every year.

Status: Alumnus/a, full-time
Dates of Enrollment: 8/2000-5/2003
Survey Submitted: September 2003

The career services office on campus is wonderful. Along with the traditional having employers come to campus and interview, there are job listings posted online and in the career services office. Additionally, the career services personnel offer programs throughout the school year on various topics relating to getting a job. There is also a second-year symposium that every second-year student is required to attend, which has speakers from various legal fields talking both about their field and their career path, as well as professionalism in general.

There were specific programs geared toward persons interested in intellectual property or litigation, which allowed students to determine whether the transactional side of law or the litigation side of law was more appealing to them. The career services office also has a reciprocity program, whereby a student at Chicago-Kent can make arrangements to use the career services office at another law school. The personnel in the office were always helpful and willing to look over a resume or cover letter or suggest places outside their office where students might find a job.

Status: Current student, full-time
Dates of Enrollment: 8/2003-Submit Date
Survey Submitted: January 2004

Kent has an incredible network in Chicago, and a great reputation nationwide among academics. Having said that, its rough if you're here and want to work there...(read: outside Chicago). Campus recruiting brings the usual suspects, and some smaller firms as well, but this is still a tier-two school, for the time being at least, and it shows. This is a tight legal market, and Chicago's loss of two behemoth firms is not going unnoticed here. Kent does make an effort on behalf of its students though, and it is obvious that they take career placement VERY seriously.

 **Quality of Life**

Status: Current student, full-time
Dates of Enrollment: 8/2003-Submit Date
Survey Submitted: May 2006

The downtown campus has much of a feel of a commuter campus. There is no a truly developed campus with multiple buildings. Therefore, there is no studen housing near the law school, and the neighborhood is generally busines oriented. Dining during the week is plentiful—restaurants that workers will eat Corner Bakery, fast food restaurants, etc. However, the weekends are harder, no many places are open.

The school is equipped with a cafeteria. The food receives mixed reviews Complaints about it are: (1) there are no healthy alternatives to eat there; (2 outside persons and workers from other offices will take up space and seating because of the inexpensive food; (3) replace the current model with commercia restaurants.

Status: Current student, full-time
Dates of Enrollment: 8/2004-Submit Date
Survey Submitted: May 2006

Chicago-Kent is in the West Loop area of Chicago, the third largest city in the country. The school is located in the downtown campus, and so there is [no direct campus affiliation with the main campus. There is, however, full acces to the main campus, and shuttles that run regularly to provide access. Severa friends and I play basketball down on the main campus at least twice a week. also have several friends who have chosen to live down on campus and commute to school on the shuttle.

However, Chicago-Kent has much more of a commuter-school feeling. Friends and co-students come from all over the Chicago area to attend. The campus is ideally located directly west of Union Station, making it extremely easy to get to school from most anywhere in the Chicago area. The school is, at most, a five minute walk, providing easy access to all the entertainment, dining, culture, and experience of Chicago.

Some students prefer a campus life; they prefer the all encompassing nature of what a campus provides. But with Chicago-Kent the city is our campus. Our dorms are our own apartments in Lincoln Park, Wicker Park, Bridgeport, Gold Coast, Museum Park, Greek Town, Edgewater, Bucktown, Naperville, and so forth. Our dining halls are the fine restaurants and dining facilities of the great city of Chicago. If a student wants a life like they had in undergrad, a place where your whole life is constricted to a few city blocks, then Chicago-Kent is not for you. But as for me, the city is my campus, and I wouldn't have it any other way.

Status: Current student, full-time
Dates of Enrollment: 8/2005-Submit Date
Survey Submitted: April 2006

Chicago is a fantastic city to go to law school in. It has all of the attributes of a metropolis: diversity, fine and performing arts, great restaurants, gorgeous parks, and nightlife. But, it also does not have many of the problems that most large cities share: it is unusually clean, not overcrowded, quite safe, and the cost of living is remarkably low.

The campus itself is located just west of the heart of downtown and is convenient to the bus, subway, and trains from the suburbs. There are restaurants at all price levels within short walking distance, as well as several bars including Dylans, the traditional Kent hangout. The campus is also close to banks, a post office, shopping districts, and basically all amenities of daily life. While it is downtown, the area is relatively safe and there are escorts available to students leaving the building late at night. These security guards/escorts will accompany students to their cars parked nearby or even to some nearby apartment complexes.

Status: Current student, full- and part-time
Dates of Enrollment: 8/2004-Submit Date
Survey Submitted: April 2006

Housing is plentiful throughout the city and beyond, but can be pricey closer to school, so many students live further out, north of the city or in the suburbs. Luckily, Chicago has an extensive mass transit system. The campus consists of one building so if you're looking for ivy covered walls, forget about it. On the other hand, the school is within walking distance of the various court houses, state/local administrative offices and many law firms, so it's downtown location is very convenient. The neighborhood is improving in terms of restaurants—it's only a few blocks away from Greektown and there are the usual chain restaurants in the area. Kent also houses a cafeteria—the food is fair and not terribly expensive. After eating there a lot first year you'll probably want to venture out. Crime doesn't appear to be a factor around school and the school offers a security escort and a shuttle to the main campus daily.

Status: Alumnus/a, full-time
Dates of Enrollment: 9/2001-5/2004
Survey Submitted: April 2005

You're in the middle of the best city on the country. What more is there to say? There is housing available for every budget. There is no campus, but the building itself is amazing, and it offers some of the most advanced technological resources available. Food is great and varied—again, you're in the middle of a city. Safety is great. Kent is in a very safe area and as long as you use your head, you're in no real danger. Remember, it's a city—see the theme here?

Status: Current student, full-time
Dates of Enrollment: 8/2003-Submit Date
Survey Submitted: January 2004

Competitive school. No doubt about it. But the environment is so amazing that the competition seems less hostile. This is a bright, cheery place. There's one building, operated like an office building. VERY modern looking, clean lines, efficient use of space. Network access and open computer terminals dominate open spaces. The library is incredible: bright, well designed and big enough to get lost in. The international collection is nothing less than extraordinary. Students seem to spend a great deal of time with each other in the cafeteria, and in study lounges. Housing nearby is very safe, but not that convenient to the rest of the city. Kent is downtown, and you can feel it.

Status: Alumnus/a, full-time
Dates of Enrollment: 8/2000-5/2003
Survey Submitted: September 2003

The College of Law at Chicago-Kent is in a very safe location, near Union Station in downtown Chicago. There are security guards at an information desk in the entryway and security guards who do rounds in the classroom building. Additionally, if a student wants an escort to a location in the area and feels unsafe, a guard will escort them. Chicago-Kent does provide some law school housing and has a bus to take students from the housing area to the law school, but I do not know very much about where it is or how nice it is, etc. Many students choose to rent apartments in a building several blocks from the law school, which has all the amenities anyone could want right in the building.

The facilities at Chicago-Kent are very modern and well kept. Almost every classroom has computer ports at every chair. The library has adequate computers for every student who chooses to use one at a given time and has several floors of reference material. It is certainly as adequate as the Cook County Law Library, and many attorneys in the area use Chicago-Kent's library for research purposes.

The cafeteria (or Spaketeria as it is called in honor of the donors) at Chicago-Kent is small, but there is always a salad bar, two hot entree choices, a sandwich bar and a grill along with two different kinds of soup and chili every day. Breakfast is also available and students have both hot and cold choices. The prices are reasonable and the food is very good.

 ## Social Life

Status: Current student, full-time
Dates of Enrollment: 8/2005-Submit Date
Survey Submitted: May 2006

The city of Chicago has so much to offer that you can have a great social life. Different clubs and organizations at Chicago-Kent hold social events as well throughout the year. These are great opportunities to meet students in other sections, or just to kick back and have a good time. They usually offer a discount cover and all you can drink (very cheap!). The socials are at popular bars around town such as Joe's on Weed St., Sauce, Moe's Cantina, Transit, City Saloon, etc.

Status: Current student, full-time
Dates of Enrollment: 8/2003-Submit Date
Survey Submitted: May 2006

The Student Bar Association works with area bars to have a Thursday bar party once a month. These socials are typically an open bar for all students for three hours on a Thursday night. Other social events include the black tie Barrister's Ball in April. Students like to attend Dylan's after class—it's a bar a block from the school. Other students party in their own neighborhoods (Old Town, Gold Coast, Lincoln Park, Wrigleyville, Lakeview, etc.)

Status: Current student, full-time
Dates of Enrollment: 8/2004-Submit Date
Survey Submitted: May 2006

Chicago-Kent spend more money, per student, on student organizations than most any other law school in the country. This means two things: first, we have school-wide social events several times a month. Our Student Bar Association will rent out entire bars for socials and they fund study breaks and special outings. Additionally, the SBA funds each individual student organization. The Jewish Law Society, the Corporate Law Society, the Black-American Law Society, the Asian-Pacific Law Student Association, the Gay/Lesbian Law Society. These organizations are numerous and active. Each individual organization will use their budgets to plan events and hold socials. The only person you can blame for not having a social life will be yourself.

Status: Current student, full-time
Dates of Enrollment: 8/2003-Submit Date
Survey Submitted: April 2006

Kent has the best social activities and quality of life outside of law school of any school this student knows. Between two and four times a semester the Kent Student Board hosts social gatherings at various bars and clubs throughout Chicago. Also, many students participate in Chicago intramural sports and in the spring semester a group of students have the opportunity to travel to Virginia to play in an all law school softball tournament with law schools from all over the country. The overall social life creates a very collegial atmosphere.

Status: Current student, full-time
Dates of Enrollment: 8/2004-Submit Date
Survey Submitted: April 2006

Chicago provides an unlimited outlet for social life, but Chicago-Kent does what it can to supplement it. Chicago-Kent has one of the highest levels of student funding levels in the country. Once a month, the Student Bar Association will rent out one of the best clubs in the city on a Thursday night and students can enjoy hanging out without the daily pressures of law school.

Status: Current student, part-time
Dates of Enrollment: 8/2005-Submit Date
Survey Submitted: April 2006

I had a boyfriend coming into law school so I'm not too sure about the dating scene firsthand. I do know that there are a lot of people that I've met who are engaged, married, or in serious relationships. But that might just come because many of the people in my class are older. I do think, for single people, there is pressure to find someone. The social life at Kent basically revolves around the Kent Socials they have at local bars where you pay five dollars for all you can drink. They are very well attended and a lot of fun, although there is some debauchery that takes place. Greektown is very close to school and students like to go out in all neighborhoods in Chicago: Lincoln Park, Bucktown, Wicker Park. Angelo's Cafe is next door and a lot of students go there for food during

Read all of Vault's Law School Surveys at www.vault.com/lawschool — get complete surveys on top law schools, expert advice on applicaton essays, LSAT prep and more.

VAULT CAREER LIBRARY 205

the week (also Prof's use Angelos in their hypotheticals which makes it kind of fun).

Status: Alumnus/a, full-time
Dates of Enrollment: 8/2002-5/2005
Survey Submitted: March 2006

The social life at Chicago-Kent varies considerably from student to student. Many students are older and/or working part time (or even full time), and even many younger students who do not work do commute from the suburbs or outlying neighborhoods. These students do not provide for a vibrant social life. However, there are abundant student organizations, and there are lots of events going on all the time, so students who wish to find a social life can find one.

Status: Alumnus/a, full-time
Dates of Enrollment: 9/2001-5/2004
Survey Submitted: April 2005

I often wondered how my colleagues found time to do their work. There is no dearth of parties, happy hours, receptions, banquets, dinners, gatherings, knitting circles, study groups, special-interest clubs, mixers, volunteer opportunities, and more The student body is keenly aware of the need to decompress, and the administration is a very cooperative partner. The school sponsors innumerable social events. Also, private firms and interest groups sponsor many more pizza parties and happy hours. The real problem is fitting everything in with the rest of your schedule.

Status: Alumnus/a, full-time
Dates of Enrollment: 8/2000-5/2003
Survey Submitted: September 2003

There are numerous non-social events sponsored by the school as well from volunteer opportunities to speakers on various issues. Most of the clubs are the ones who coordinate these events. Speaking of clubs, if a student has an interest there is a club, or they can start one of their own. While I was at Kent, students created an animal rights law club and succeeded in getting a professor to teach a class (for credit) on animal rights law.

No information on Chicago-Kent would be complete without mentioning the Conviser Bash. Several times a year, Professor Conviser, who also runs the Barbri bar review course, throws a party at a club in the area for all Chicago-Kent students and their friends. It usually runs from nine p.m. to midnight and is on a Thursday night (after the first year, most students don't have class on Fridays). Admission is free and so are beer, wine and well drinks. The other fun thing is that Professor Conviser is always there and in his classes for about the week previous he states that he will be taking notice of who is there and who is still there when it ends, stating that it is mandatory that all of his students are there.

All in all, while the academics are certainly important, there is an opportunity for students to become involved in any club that interests them as well as moot court or law review or the legal clinic program, but there is also ample time for social events and socializing, as well.

The School Says

Chicago-Kent College of Law, the law school of Illinois Institute of Technology, is located in downtown Chicago, the heart of the city's commercial and legal communities. The second oldest law school in Illinois, Chicago-Kent was founded in 1888 by two judges who believed that legal education should be available to working men and women. Today, Chicago-Kent students come from more than 40 states and several foreign countries, and from more than 260 colleges and universities.

Drawing on its distinctive affiliation with Illinois Institute of Technology, Chicago-Kent is at the vanguard of exploring new frontiers in the law raised by biotechnology, cyberspace, environmental regulation, intellectual property, international criminal law enforcement, and much more. Chicago-Kent's faculty engages in broad-ranging legal scholarship and research and is among the nation's most productive law faculties based on the number of scholarly books and articles they publish in leading academic presses, law reviews, and journals.

Chicago-Kent is committed to maintaining the diverse community that has been one of the law school's strengths since 1895, when the first women and minority students graduated. Each application is individually reviewed, and decisions are based on a range of factors, including quantitative and qualitative criteria. Although the GPA and LSAT are important criteria, consideration also is given to nonnumerical factors such as the nature and rigor of the undergraduate curriculum, writing ability, graduate work and professional experience, extracurricular activities, diversity, and the personal statement. Admission is highly selective and applicants are encouraged to submit their applications as early as possible in the admissions cycle.

Chicago-Kent has approximately 10,000 graduates living and practicing throughout the United States and in various countries. They are represented in every major firm in the city of Chicago and on the federal and state benches. Typically, 97 percent of recent graduates find professional employment within nine months of graduation.

For additional information about Chicago-Kent, please visit our Web site at www.kentlaw.edu or contact the Office of Admissions at (312) 906-5020 or admit@kentlaw.edu.

DePaul University College of Law

Admissions Office
25 East Jackson Boulevard
Chicago, IL 60604
Admissions phone: (312) 362-8300
Admissions e-mail: lawinfo@depaul.edu
Admissions URL: http://www.law.depaul.edu/applicants/

 Admissions

Status: Current student, full-time
Dates of Enrollment: 8/2005-Submit Date
Survey Submitted: May 2006

The admissions process was smooth. I suggest doing it online. It is easier and less time-consuming. Also, the admissions office was very nice and worked with me when I chose to defer for a year.

Status: Alumnus/a, full-time
Dates of Enrollment: 8/2003-5/2006
Survey Submitted: May 2006

I believe that over the past two years, the admissions process has been better organized and far more rigorous. The best advice I can give on getting in is to make yourself stand out. An admission essay should highlight what is unique about you and what you can contribute to the law school community. DePaul is a school that values diversity in ALL of its forms. In my essay I wrote about my home city and how it has shaped my understanding of the world. I also wrote about taking a big risk and how it changed my outlook on the world. I did not interview and DePaul did not interview at the time I applied.

Finally, a note about selectivity, DePaul is an underrated school at this point in time. Even though it recently jumped over 20 spots in the *U.S. News* rankings, it is still on the rise. Thus, selectivity is high, but not too high, and for anyone in the 160 to 165 LSAT range, DePaul is a school where you can both be challenged and excel. For those in the 154 to 160 range, if you can convince the admissions committee that you have something unique to contribute to the DePaul Law community, there is an excellent chance that you will be offered admission.

Status: Current student, part-time
Dates of Enrollment: 8/2005-Submit Date
Survey Submitted: May 2006

The admissions is consistent with most law schools. I did not interview for admissions, but the admissions office was readily available to answer all of my questions. I chose DePaul because of its International Human Rights Institute and related courses. I wrote my essay specifically about my interest in pursuing an international human rights career. I am unsure how much my specific interest affected my application.

Status: Current student, full-time
Dates of Enrollment: 8/2004-Submit Date
Survey Submitted: April 2006

I was a transfer student so I applied after I got my second semester 1L grades. I received a one-page letter of admission as a transfer and that was it. They did absolutely nothing to welcome me as a transfer and provided me with basically no information. I tried to set up a transfer program, but the administration was not interested.

> **The school says:** "For fall 2007, the College of Law created a special informational mailing for all admitted transfer students. All admitted transfer students are also required to meet personally with the Dean of Students to register for classes. Finally, all entering transfer students are invited to participate in the College of Law's New Student Orientation Program."

Status: Current student, full-time
Dates of Enrollment: 8/2004-Submit Date
Survey Submitted: April 2006

I applied very early, I believe by October. I knew that applying early could be the difference between me getting in or not. For my personal statement, I chose to focus on diversity and what makes me diverse. I find that schools really want to know what you can bring to their school that no one else can—what makes you unique.

Status: Current student, full-time
Dates of Enrollment: 8/2003-Submit Date
Survey Submitted: April 2006

The admission standards of the school have increased recently. But I think that based on the students in attendance, the law school looks for high undergraduate GPA greater than 3.0, good LSAT scores (158) and other achievements. For example, I know many students who worked before law school, or already have a higher-level educational degree. I believe the school wants well-rounded students, and therefore, participation in undergraduate activities is important. Most people I know were involved in many activities in undergrad. I think the school also looks at students who want to study specialized areas of law. The school accepts many patent law/health law students. I did not interview for this school. I remember the essay being very typical. I don't think there was a essay "topic." I believe the purpose of the essay was to assess the [applicant's] level of writing. I remember that DePaul was the first school I received a response from, so I believe that the school makes their decisions regarding admission quickly.

Status: Current student, part-time
Dates of Enrollment: 8/2005-Submit Date
Survey Submitted: April 2006

The admissions office was so helpful, definitely utilize this resource. Attend the open houses and speak with some of the professors and deans. DePaul is one of those schools that looks at the total package so it's great to give people the opportunity to put a face with the name on the application. DePaul is selective but the criteria for entrance is not solely GPA and LSAT.

Status: Current student, full-time
Dates of Enrollment: 8/2004-Submit Date
Survey Submitted: April 2006

Applying to DePaul was much like applying to any other law school. DePaul however, tends to be a school that focuses a lot of energy in giving back to the community. It may be the religious affiliation, or it just may be the mark of a good school. But, emphasizing strong commitment to diversity and ability to relate to the community around you in a very important aspect of being admitted to DePaul Law.

Status: Current student, part-time
Dates of Enrollment: 9/2004-Submit Date
Survey Submitted: April 2006

The admissions staff at DePaul was very helpful and assisted me in getting some issues I had with LSADS resolved. The school is getting more selective, and LSAT scores are going up by two points or so a year. All in all, I thought the admissions process was relatively easy. As with most schools, it is very important to show your talent in the essay.

Status: Current student, full-time
Dates of Enrollment: 8/2004-Submit Date
Survey Submitted: September 2005

Applying to DePaul was the same as any other school. Nothing out of the ordinary and there were no interviews. However, my admissions process required frequent communication with the school because I erroneously received a letter and e-mails reflecting incorrect changes in my admissions status. The most helpful advice and guidance I received from the admissions office came when I was able to talk to a student worker.

Read all of Vault's Law School Surveys at www.vault.com/lawschool — get complete surveys on top law schools, expert advice on applicaton essays, LSAT prep and more.

VAULT CAREER LIBRARY   207

Status: Current student, full-time
Dates of Enrollment: 8/2001-Submit Date
Survey Submitted: September 2003

Similar to all other law schools. The best thing to do is to get the application from law school data services and fill it out online. I heard back from them right away. No interview. Fairly selective.

 ## Academics

Status: Alumnus/a, full-time
Dates of Enrollment: 8/2003-5/2006
Survey Submitted: May 2006

Getting my JD at DePaul has been the most difficult task in my life. I found the class format, the Socratic Method, to be taxing on both my intellectual and emotional capacities. By that I mean that the professors would drill students with poignant questions about the material and expect prompt thorough replies. Although I thought the professors never pulled a punch, I NEVER saw a prof intentionally embarrass or humiliate a student. I found the profs to be engaging, encouraging and available at all times.

I feel that DePaul's greatest strength is the quality of its professors. Whether you want to talk about prior restraints during wartime with Shaman, the nuances of hearsay with Cavise, how to effectively word a statement of facts with Sowerby, the inherent political nature of judicial decisions with Cho, international politics with Coll or just life and how great it is to be alive with Kiely, these are just a few of the best law professors in Chicago as far as I am concerned, and DePaul has many more just like them. The range of classes is broad, but sometimes scheduling can be problematic. I never had a problem getting a class I wanted, but I never took "bar classes," so my experience is limited.

In addition, DePaul's Public Interest Certificate Program is well on its way to being the premier public interest program in the country.

The first-year workload is intense, just like every other law program. Teachers expect an average reading of 60 to 100 pages per week and they expect you to know the material and participate in class. I spent about 60 hours per week on schoolwork my first year and I ended up in the top 10 percent of my class.

Status: Current student, full-time
Dates of Enrollment: 8/2005-Submit Date
Survey Submitted: May 2006

The professors are all very friendly and not as intimidating as I expected. Because there are so few accredited law schools in the country, the quality of the professors and classes your first year at any law school will be substantially similar, especially since everyone takes the same classes. The difference at DePaul is how open the professors are and how friendly the students are. It makes for a much better learning experience than some of the ultra-competitive schools, while [you still receive] a top education. The workload is not bad. Most students can get their work done in between classes and by staying a couple hours before/after classes. Many people also hold part-time jobs even during their first year.

> **DePaul says:** "The College of Law strongly discourages students from holding jobs during the first year of law school."

Status: Current student, full-time
Dates of Enrollment: 8/2003-Submit Date
Survey Submitted: April 2006

Quality of classes were good. DePaul encourages students to take advantage of Trial Advocacy classes, where students learn how to be courtroom attorneys from actual practicing attorneys (classes are held in the Daley Center Courtrooms), and of two externship opportunities where students are given class credit for working in a meaningful law related position for 180 hours over the semester (12 hours a week for 15 weeks). The rest of the classes are probably what you would find at any other law school. DePaul has many classes taught by adjunct professors, all of whom have been very high quality and worth taking classes from, since they generally practice in whatever field they are teaching during the day and then come in to teach at night. Most DePaul full-time faculty

are very nice and helpful, occasionally you find one or two who do not like helping students out, but they are rare. I never had a problem getting into any of the classes I wanted, but I always registered at the first minute classes were open to me to register. Workload is what I think should be expected—it takes a bit of time, but was not overwhelming.

Status: Current student, full-time
Dates of Enrollment: 8/2003-Submit Date
Survey Submitted: April 2006

I don't believe the first-year law classes are set up properly. I think that contracts could be a one-semester course, while property and civil procedure should be taught in more depth. I think the legal writing classes are not at the level they should be. The program was recently changed from two semesters of legal writing to three, but now the appellate briefs are not written until the third semester. I believe that will hurt students that work after their first year, because most employers will expect them to have knowledge in brief-writing.

I also do not believe the university offers enough bar-prep courses. I believe that each major bar class (commercial paper, secured transactions, wills and trusts, sales and biz orgs) should be offered each semester, but that is never the case. Therefore, students take other classes that won't be on the bar to fulfill credit requirements. Also, because those classes aren't offered every semester, the spaces in the bar classes fill up very quickly during registration. I hear students complaining about this problem constantly. I do not think the problem at DePaul is getting into the "popular" classes, I think the problem is getting into the bar classes. Students like the "popular" classes, but I think most students realize that the bar classes are more important, and, although they enjoy the popular classes, they would rather take the prep classes.

I believe the grading scale at DePaul could be changed. I have been on interviews in Chicago where employers have asked how it is possible for my GPA and rank to coexist. DePaul does not give A-'s or B-'s, which other law schools in Chicago do; and therefore, it changes our GPA in relation to our rank when compared to other schools. I also think that less courses should be graded on a curve. This ultimately lowers the students GPAs because professors are required to give C's.

> **Regarding academics, the school says:** "After several exhaustive internal studies of how and what DePaul's students learn, and after review of the available current practices and scholarly literature on learning theory, DePaul did convert its two-semester curriculum in Legal Analysis, Research and Communication to a three-semester curriculum. The new three-semester curriculum provides far more depth and breadth than the former curriculum did, and the core skills of analysis and trial-level persuasion that students learn and practice in their first year far outweigh any advantages that might come from students' work on any particular type of document, specifically an appellate brief. In the spring semester of the first year, students write a thorough and detailed trial brief, which may be used as a writing sample. Summer jobs after the first year of law school do not typically concentrate on appellate work. Brand new summer associates or law clerks tend to concentrate on trial-level litigation, and DePaul's students are well-prepared for this work.
>
> "The grading curve at DePaul University College of Law is comparable, and often higher, than many other law schools. The lack of minus grades does not have an impact on the overall GPAs of our students."

Status: Current student, part-time
Dates of Enrollment: 7/2003-Submit Date
Survey Submitted: April 2006

I've learned that probably the most important thing in law school is having a good professor. It makes all the difference in the world, and could in fact steer you in the direction of your career. I guess that, generally, the better the school, the higher quality of faculty. I've found some really special professors at DePaul. Overall it's been great, but there have been a bad seed or two. I guess that's normal.

Status: Current student, full-time
Dates of Enrollment: 8/2004-Submit Date
Survey Submitted: April 2006

DePaul is wonderful—the professors are great and the staff is very friendly and caring. Because we have a good night program and many of our professors are practicing lawyers, there is some imbalance in the classes offered for 2Ls and 3Ls (too many night classes). We also have a smaller selection than some schools because of classroom constraints, but if you are interested in public interest law, this is the place for you.

Status: Current student, part-time
Dates of Enrollment: 9/2004-Submit Date
Survey Submitted: April 2006

The academic nature of the program is improving very quickly, as the school has taken active steps to move older faculty (who tend to be less academically rigorous) off the rolls. If you are selective about your professors, you will certainly be able to secure a full class schedule of EXCELLENT classes. The clinics are also terrific, but in demand.

The workload all depends on you! If you want to make law review as a part-timer, then be prepared for a heavy (but worthwhile) load, especially if you are working. If you want to make C's or are just going part-time for the hell of it, then you'll have more time for drinking. As a part-time student with a full-time job, I don't do ANYTHING at night or the weekend but study. But as a result, I've made very good grades, and I don't regret it for a second. I still get seven hours a sleep on most nights.

One last word about public interest: the school has a FABULOUS structure in place for those interested in public interest law. There are many opportunities to make a difference while in school and to get yourself positioned for an interesting career in public interest after you graduate.

 # Employment Prospects

Status: Current student, full-time
Dates of Enrollment: 8/2005-Submit Date
Survey Submitted: May 2006

The alumni network is amazing; in the Chicago area that are over 8,500 DePaul alumni. If you are in a particular area, like being a fellow of the Health Law Institute, then that opens even more doors. The Health Law Institute director can help you get employment at places like Children's Memorial Hospital, Blue Cross Blue Shield and even the American Medical Association the summer after your first year. While jobs are available all over the country and many students go abroad, if a student is interested in staying around Chicago the opportunities are endless.

Status: Alumnus/a, full-time
Dates of Enrollment: 8/2003-5/2006
Survey Submitted: May 2006

I know of many students who took positions at blue-chip law firms in Chicago and around the country. I also know of students who took government jobs. The largest percentage of people I know went to work at either the State Attorney or the Public Defender. I know of only one student who took a federal judicial clerkship and I can only assume it is because DePaul's career services won't get with it and submit judicial clerkship applications as a packet from the school as a whole—like the judges have requested. Every other school in Chicago does this.

I feel that the greatest weakness of DePaul is the career services office. On-campus interviewing is a laughing stock, where other schools have 75 to 100 employers, DePaul has 30. The externship program run by John Decker is a stellar operation and it places many students at federal agencies, in federal judicial externships and at nonprofits around Chicagoland.

The DePaul College of Law states: "For fall 2005, 68 employers participated in DePaul's interview program. In 2005, within nine months of graduation, 97 percent of DePaul law students were actively employed. Starting salaries for our graduates

have remained consistently high. For the graduating class of 2005, 55 percent joined law firms, 18 percent entered business, 11 percent entered government, 8 percent serve in public interest, 2 percent secured judicial clerkships, 1 percent entered academia and 4 percent are unspecified. Within the past five years, 11 out of 30 DePaul law students who secured judicial clerkship opportunities did so at the federal level. DePaul utilizes OSCAR, which is an online federal clerkship application process utilized by the majority of federal judges.

The Office of Law Career Services continues to reach out to numerous employers in the form of in-person visits as well as written correspondence, seeking to increase the number of employers interviewing at DePaul."

Status: Current student, full-time
Dates of Enrollment: 9/2003-Submit Date
Survey Submitted: May 2006

If you are able to distinguish yourself first-year—top 10 percent automatically make Law Review—your employment prospects are extremely high. The Chicago law firms seem to think highly of DePaul grads. But, if you're a middle-of-the-pack student, you might have problems finding a competitive job.

Status: Current student, part-time
Dates of Enrollment: 7/2003-Submit Date
Survey Submitted: April 2006

Currently working at a law firm. Most big firms don't interview at DePaul unless you are top 5 or 10 percent of the class. Kind of stinks, but it's life. You need to work hard and network while you are in school. DePaul has been moving up in the ranks though, so hopefully future classes will be given more opportunities through the school in the future (and the big firms will realize it's not all about the pedigree!)

The school says: "The Career Services Office has no control over the academic qualifications and criteria set forth by employers. We strongly encourage, and provide resources for, students to seek employment opportunities outside of the fall interviewing season as only 20 percent of students nationally secure employment through that process."

Status: Current student, full-time
Dates of Enrollment: 8/2004-Submit Date
Survey Submitted: April 2006

For the most part, DePaul students find their own jobs. There is some on-campus recruiting by big firms (who hire several of our students, especially IP students), but that honor is primarily reserved for law review/top 10 percent. The alumni network is great—most students find work through that system. DePaul is well-known and respected in the Chicago law community as a school of hardworking, practical, small to mid-size law firm lawyers.

Status: Alumnus/a, full-time
Dates of Enrollment: 9/1996-5/1999
Survey Submitted: March 2005

Locally, the prospects for law firm jobs and jobs in the public sector are very good. Clerkships generally go to graduates of more prestigious schools. Nationally it is more difficult to get interviews.

Status: Alumnus/a, full-time
Dates of Enrollment: 9/1996-12/1999
Survey Submitted: January 2005

If you want to work at a large law firm this is not the place to go. The school might not have the prestige necessary to get your foot in the door. School prestige matters most.

Read all of Vault's Law School Surveys at www.vault.com/lawschool — get complete surveys on top law schools, expert advice on applicaton essays, LSAT prep and more.

VAULT CAREER LIBRARY **209**

Quality of Life

Status: Alumnus/a, full-time
Dates of Enrollment: 8/2003-5/2006
Survey Submitted: May 2006

I found my quality of life to be very high at DePaul. The Loop campus is easy to access by public transit—the law school is literally a block or two away from every single L train line. There is also a Metra (regional train) stop within four blocks so anyone traveling from outside the city can get there easily. Apartments are plentiful and affordable in the Loop because most people don't actually live there. Moreover, there is plenty of housing available slightly farther away from the campus. I live about 30 minutes away by train, in a great neighborhood with a strong sense of community.

DePaul also has a great athletic center, "the Ray." It has a pool, racquetball courts, a track, four dance studios, physical therapy and massage, a sea of exercise machines and free weights, as well as a smoothie, coffee and snack bar.

Status: Current student, full-time
Dates of Enrollment: 8/2005-Submit Date
Survey Submitted: May 2006

The university has added some housing in the Loop campus as well as the Lincoln Park campus that some students find quite convenient. However, most students prefer to find an apartment around the city to live in a specific neighborhood or find the cheapest rent. The school buildings are very safe, especially for being in the city. The facilities are modern and wireless Internet is provided throughout. There are many fast-food and small restaurants around the school as well as a school cafeteria. And it is very easy to travel to and from school with a pass to ride the public transportation as much as you want with the U-Pass.

Status: Current student, full-time
Dates of Enrollment: 8/2003-Submit Date
Survey Submitted: April 2006

The building is old and the elevators are very slow. There are undergraduate classes on the floors above the law school, and we have to compete with those students to get to class. I have waited over 10 minutes for an elevator before. Generally, at 5:30 on any weekday there are over 40 students in the lobby waiting for an elevator. The lecture rooms are not set up well. There are large pillars in the middle of the rooms that act as visual obstructions so that students on one side of the room can't see students on the other side of the room. This makes it hard for class discussion.

I personally know more than one person that has had their laptop stolen at school. Therefore, I would not classify the campus as safe. No one checks IDs and it seems as if anyone who wants to come in the building is allowed in. I know that there have been several laptops stolen this semester. I believe this is a problem that needs to be addressed by the university. Security guards, especially on weekends, are normally on their cell phones and don't even seem to notice who is coming and going.

Status: Current student, part-time
Dates of Enrollment: 7/2003-Submit Date
Survey Submitted: April 2006

Campus is downtown. Very convenient for me because I found a law firm downtown to work at. Tough working full-time and doing the part-time program. I'm in my third year and am now taking a couple day classes because the last two and a half years have burnt me out. I've never had a crime/neighborhood issue with DePaul. I love living in the city and couldn't imagine going to school anywhere else.

Status: Current student, full-time
Dates of Enrollment: 8/2004-Submit Date
Survey Submitted: April 2006

First-years rejoice. DePaul recently built, in conjunction with some other area schools, the University Center of Chicago. It is, no matter what anyone tells you, a dorm. A dorm with some apartment-style rooms, but a dorm nonetheless. However, what this place lacks in actual apartment feel, it gains in location. Two blocks from school, a three-minute walk to class and an excellent cafeteria. If you don't know a thing about Chicago, this is the place to start. As for those who know Chicago, I recommend skipping the UCC and getting an apartment in Lincoln Park or Lakeview. Since DePaul includes a transit card with tuition, you can ride the elevated trains into the school for free.

Status: Current student, full-time
Dates of Enrollment: 8/2004-Submit Date
Survey Submitted: April 2006

DePaul is located in the southeast end of the Loop, which is good and bad. It's bad because it is a very small, old, urban campus. Therefore, we do not have our own dining hall and only limited housing options (most students live scattered throughout the city). On the other hand, it is wonderful to study and live in the middle of a dynamic neighborhood. We are steps away from the state and federal courthouses, U.S. Attorney's Offices, government agencies (EPA, Homeland Security) and dozens of law firms. If you work or intern, school is extremely convenient.

Social Life

Status: Current student, full-time
Dates of Enrollment: 8/2005-Submit Date
Survey Submitted: May 2006

The students are constantly putting together apartment parties or meeting at bars or doing other activities on weekends that make the environment much more friendly and open than it may be at other schools. There's even a bar almost in the basement of the law school that students meet at after classes. The student bar association and other organizations have many social events from dances and theater deals to BBQs. Some students don't take advantage of being in a great city like Chicago, but there really is always something fun to do.

Status: Alumnus/a, full-time
Dates of Enrollment: 8/2003-5/2006
Survey Submitted: May 2006

The first weekend after classes started in my 1L year, my entire section had a blowout party at one of the swankiest bar/lounges in Chicago. I found it easy to connect with lots of different people who all shared my commitment to intellectual exploration, but came from vastly different life backgrounds and were not afraid to be themselves. Law school is like high school in many ways, but the difference is that you know everything you learned in college. I felt that, although there were cliques, it was easy to move between them and to makes friends of great quality in each.

The Student Bar Association puts on great events where students and teachers can just "hang out" and have fun. Also, the Public Interest Law Association holds an auction every year that is consistently the most well-attended and fun event of the year. Various student groups are constantly holding one social event or another and it is easy to find a place to fit in. I cannot say enough about the depth and diversity of experiences that DePaul has to offer, you will just have to come and see for yourself.

Status: Current student, full-time
Dates of Enrollment: 8/2004-Submit Date
Survey Submitted: April 2006

Mondays. No, not the day of the week, the bar under the law school. OK, technically it's called the Demon Den, but really, no one calls it anything other than Mondays, the restaurant that sits above the bar. But, this is the best place to sit sometimes after class, meet classmates and even chat with a professor over a brew. If only the elevator went right down to this place could it get any better. As for other "social outings," you'd better hit the Brown Line and get yourself up to Lincoln Park because the places downtown tend to be over-priced and not filled with the most closely representative crowd; i.e., downtown usually attracts 40-somethings that are busy chatting about this or that stock. Find love and cheap beer elsewhere.

Status: Current student, full-time
Dates of Enrollment: 8/2004-Submit Date
Survey Submitted: April 2006

Social life? In law school? Surely you jest.

Status: Current student, part-time
Dates of Enrollment: 8/2005-Submit Date
Survey Submitted: April 2006

Based on the location, there are a lot of bars and restaurants around DePaul. The Greek burger and Aegean pizza at Exchequer are phenomenal and it is a block away from the school. I don't know anything about the Greek system. The school hosts a lot of events like human rights speakers or health law symposia etc. the more "social" events are usually the result of students just hanging out but the SBA does have a few events that were pretty fun.

The dating scene is out of my realm, because my boyfriend is not a DePaul student. The city of Chicago is basically your dating scene. You do not have to date someone from your own school when you can date someone from the city or date someone from another school (Loyola, Kent, Northwestern, Chicago, UIC, Roosevelt).

Status: Current student, full-time
Dates of Enrollment: 8/2005-Submit Date
Survey Submitted: April 2006

As a law student, you can join the international legal fraternity, Phi Alpha Delta. It is the largest legal fraternity in the world, and our chapter is one of the largest and most involved. Being in downtown Chicago provides access to many bars and restaurants. Trust me, you can do whatever you find fun.

Status: Alumnus/a, full-time
Dates of Enrollment: 9/1996-5/1999
Survey Submitted: March 2005

Great. The students are generally very down to earth and interesting. I had a great time in law school socially, and I still count some of my fellow DePaul grads among my closest friends.

Status: Current student, full-time
Dates of Enrollment: 8/2001-Submit Date
Survey Submitted: September 2003

Students are younger than at some schools, so they like to be social.

Read all of Vault's Law School Surveys at www.vault.com/lawschool — get complete surveys on top law schools, expert advice on applicaton essays, LSAT prep and more.

VAULT CAREER LIBRARY 211

The John Marshall Law School

General Office
315 S. Plymouth Court
Chicago, IL 60604
Admissions phone: (312) 987-1406
Admissions e-mail: admission@jmls.edu
Admissions URL: http://www.jmls.edu/admission/

 Admissions

Status: Current student, full-time
Dates of Enrollment: 8/2004-Submit Date
Survey Submitted: November 2005

The admissions process is similar to that of the other law schools I applied to. Important advice I have for students who want to get in to this school or any school, is to apply as a part-time student. Schools do not include part-time students in their statistics for GPA and LSAT reporting so they are more inclined to allow borderline applicants for part-time admission.

John Marshall is not very selective, however, a number of top students are attracted to John Marshall because a number of scholarships are awarded. There is a condition that recipients maintain a GPA that places the student in the top 20 percent of their class.

John Marshall boasts that they are committed to diversity in faculty and students. However, even though the incoming class has 25 percent minority students, it is the second lowest percentage in Illinois.

Status: Current student, full-time
Dates of Enrollment: 9/2004-Submit Date
Survey Submitted: September 2005

Compared to many other law schools it's not that hard to get in. From what I understand, it is getting to be much more selective than in the past, probably due to the increased number of applicants. There is no interview, and the higher your LSAT score and GPA, the quicker you will hear back about admissions and scholarships.

Status: Current student, full-time
Dates of Enrollment: 8/2003-Submit Date
Survey Submitted: March 2004

The admission process for the John Marshall Law School was rather standard, with no real surprises. Typical questions included: undergraduate honors and activities; any work experience; any extracurricular activities with established participation; and then the typical essay requirements.

I applied to quite a few schools, and John Marshall's application process was pretty painless. Also, the admissions office was exceptional. They were always professional and were able to update my status over the phone regularly. Some schools I had applied to were short and downright nasty, but not Marshall.

As far as advice on getting in, I just went to a Law Forum in Chicago and any questions I had for the admissions counselor were answered at that time.

Status: Alumnus/a, full-time
Dates of Enrollment: 1/2000-1/2004
Survey Submitted: March 2005

Admission paperwork was as easy to fill out as paperwork for most other schools. The process was pretty standard and it is easy to get in. JMLS also has a conditional acceptance program that gives college grads not with stellar records a "second chance." Very good scholarship opportunities are offered even without asking for it.

Status: Current student, full-time
Dates of Enrollment: 8/2001-Submit Date
Survey Submitted: March 2004

While some say that everyone gets in, the new dean is raising the standards considerably. It also has the most law students of any school in Illinois and is a very busy place. You should be aware that JMLS is very conscious of its bar passage rate and goes the extra mile to help its students pass the bar. The school offers its own bar review courses and helps subsidize a six-day PMBR program (multistate multiple choice portion of the bar). This is in addition to the regular PMBR courses you can sign up for (another six days and three days). While the school was plagued by not so excellent bar passage rates, the rate has dramatically improved with these new programs at the school.

> **The school says:** "The law school's Academic Achievement Program provides multiple bar preparation programs for students. Bar applicants can attend lectures on and practice taking multiple choice questions for the 200-question Multistate Bar Examination. They can also attend lectures on bar exam essay topics and practice writing actual bar examination essay questions. The program engages a nationally renowned expert on bar examinations who helps bar applicants become fully aware of the challenges the examination presents. Through a special arrangement, students may also take the PMBR Bar Review Program at a discounted rate."

Status: Current student, full-time
Dates of Enrollment: 1/2001-Submit Date
Survey Submitted: May 2004

I entered JMLS as a conditional student, and I think every law school should adopt this practice. The conditional program consisted of two classes, one is a 1L required course, and the other is agency law. This combination seems rather odd on the surface, however, being placed in an advanced class with no prior legal training is a great way for the student and the school to determine if a student is cut out for law school. This program allows students to test out the "waters" of law school. Because the program is only six hours, the transitional process from undergrad to career life to law school life is less traumatic. Furthermore, the students that do not make it through the program have invested or borrowed less money to find out that they are not cut out for the law school experience. Additionally, the professors encourage the conditional students to work together and help each other to succeed.

The grading curve is not used for this program so the pressures of competition between the students is removed. Students who earn at least a 2.5 GPA are accepted into the JD program for the following semester with six to nine hours (summer school) completed. The students may then choose to take 15-hour semesters and graduate in three years, or take a lighter load and graduate with the class in which they are officially designated. The best part of this program was the friends I made in my unofficial first semester, and with my "conditional experience," I was not a deer in headlights my first year. Looking back, my conditional admission to law school was the best thing for me.

Status: Alumnus/a, full-time
Dates of Enrollment: 8/2000-5/2003
Survey Submitted: September 2003

Everyone gets in!

Academics

Status: Current student, full-time
Dates of Enrollment: 8/2004-Submit Date
Survey Submitted: November 2005

The nature of the required classes at John Marshall are geared to litigation. John Marshall has a strong reputation in Chicago for producing trial lawyers and judges. In addition, there is a strong IP program that attracts a number of students from around the country.

The difficulty and workload of classes are difficult to assess, since I am unsure how other schools operate. The writing program at John Marshall is mandatory, intense and provides a valuable experience. The writing department is arguably the best department and has recently received national recognition.

The quality of professors is mixed. There are a number of professors, including very recently hired professors, that are extremely dedicated to their field and the students. Even though these professors are in high demand, it is relatively easy to get in their classes because the class sizes are too large. There are a number of professors, that are identified as great people, but terrible professors. In two semesters, I have encountered three professors that "borrowed" multiple choice questions directly from commercial outlines, a professor that started the exam late because he didn't finish writing it, and a course where 43 out of 50 (86 percent) multiple choice questions gave the student a D in the class. (I received a 47, which was a B). Generally, I would say students are more dissatisfied than satisfied with the quality of professors.

The academic program is frustrated by the administrations neglect toward minority students and professors. John Marshall has recently pushed for tenured minority faculty, however, the African-American Dean that promoted these efforts faced much opposition, and has now left John Marshall. In terms of diversity, there is little to positively distinguish John Marshall from other schools in Chicago. The lack of effort to recruit and retain minority students and faculty negatively affects all students, especially those who seek to work in Chicago, one of the most diverse cities in the country.

Status: Current student, full-time
Dates of Enrollment: 9/2004-Submit Date
Survey Submitted: September 2005

The quality of the classes is excellent. John Marshall has some really excellent professors that really try to encompass every aspect of legal practice in their lectures. Most professors, in addition to the Socratic Method, will work in some practical, interactive exercise into the program. The first year you have no choice about classes or professors, but after that, it is pretty easy to get the classes you want. Grading is on a set curve for most classes. The workload really depends on what professor you end up with and how efficiently you study.

Status: Current student, full-time
Dates of Enrollment: 8/2003-Submit Date
Survey Submitted: March 2004

As a 1L, most of my classes for the entire year have had over 50 students in them, but less then 100. All of the legal writing classes at John Marshall are 14 students or less, which leads to high levels of personal interaction.

The overall academic nature of the program in my opinion is one of practicality. There is not much theory tossed around in class, at least as a 1L. The school is incredibly focused on shaping us into "practitioners." The program is very meat and potatoes, with a large emphasis on the application of the legal principles we are learning within the profession. This is not a program that trains future theorists or educators—this program trains lawyers.

I personally think the quality of classes is topnotch. My professors have come from Yale, Northwestern, Harvard and the University of Chicago, mostly. One has come from Valpo. But my legal writing professors are practicing attorneys, not full-time faculty, so their background is unavailable.

I have never had a problem getting a class I wanted, but, then again, I am only a 1L. It doesn't seem like it would be a problem though. Many sections are usually available.

The university has implemented a grading curve which has caused some bitterness, particularly among the 2Ls and 3Ls. When it was introduced just last fall, the system was met with much scrutiny, but as a 1L it is all I have ever known; so personally, I don't have a problem with it. I have talked with other law students from different Chicago schools, and the new curve seems to be rather typical throughout local universities.

Workload varies from class to class, but overall I would say it is rather heavy. The professors work you at Marshall. Read, read, read and then read some more! Now write an appellate brief! Now sleep!

Status: Alumnus/a, full-time
Dates of Enrollment: 8/1994-6/1997
Survey Submitted: March 2005

Excellent choice of intellectual property classes. Good professors that teach not only theory but practical skills.

Status: Alumnus/a, full-time
Dates of Enrollment: 1/2000-1/2004
Survey Submitted: March 2005

While JMLS is one the lowest ranked schools in the state, I firmly believe that one can have the best education possible at this school. You make out of law school what you want to! It is (almost) entirely up to you! It is true that you may go through this law school without attending many of the classes and you can even manage to get decent grades without much studying. However, this school can actually prepare you for whatever the professional life may throw at you after graduation. They have an excellent writing program and advocacy skills courses. It is relatively easy to get involved in the moot court competitions and the coaching and training received in preparation for each competition is excellent. The competition between students is not very stiff and there is a feeling of general collegiality. Most of their professors are excellent and genuinely concerned about your educational well-being.

Status: Alumnus/a, full-time
Dates of Enrollment: 1/1993-1/1996
Survey Submitted: March 2005

Classes were great and very helpful. Professors were very good and very friendly. Did a great job of preparing me for bar exam.

Status: Current student, full-time
Dates of Enrollment: 8/2001-Submit Date
Survey Submitted: March 2004

The first year is pretty standard. Everyone is split into a section and writing courses. The writing instructors are phenomenal! My professor took a considerable amount of time to help me and this really helped train my mind to think like a lawyer and made the rest of my law school career easy. I really think the writing courses are the heart of the legal education and the school does a terrific job with this. In particular, the later writing courses are tailored toward your interests, so if your interests lean toward business transactions you can take a writing course that emphasizes those skills instead of some other topic like criminal law. This becomes very significant when you apply for internships and are asked to provide writing samples. The second year is part required courses, part electives. While first year is difficult because of the high learning curve, second year here can be life consuming especially if you pursue Law Review and moot court (you can do either, or both). Constitutional Law was taught by a Harvard/Emory grad (Olken) who is as entertaining as he is insightful. His love of sports, undergrad in history, and research into Supreme Court justices help provide a rich context in which to explore the numerous cases. Follow up Con Law with Criminal Procedure with O'Neil. He is the perfect professor. Taking him after or consecutively with Olken will make you feel like your're not at some lower-rated school (which I've concluded means nothing anyway) but rather entrenched within the halls of Harvard.

Take some substantive courses, but if you want to litigate get involved in every mock trial or advocacy class you can so that you can really develop these skills. Fortunately, JMLS is THE BEST school to become a litigator and gives you hundreds of opportunities to develop these skills. Also, the fair housing clinic allows you to get your 711 and teaches you excellent practice skills. JMLS also offers a government/court externship for credit throughout your time there, so take advantage of it. I would also consider studying abroad first semester of

Read all of Vault's Law School Surveys at www.vault.com/lawschool — get complete surveys on top law schools, expert advice on applicaton essays, LSAT prep and more.

VAULT CAREER LIBRARY   213

third year. The only significant disadvantage of JMLS is its lack of business courses. You can get the fundamental business courses like tax and corporations, but not M&A, start-up, finance, etc. However, it does offer excellent classes and LLM in employee benefits and executive compensation (if you want a job, the firms hire students with this specialty).

Status: Current student, full-time
Dates of Enrollment: 1/2001-Submit Date
Survey Submitted: May 2004

In my opinion, JMLS students receive a better overall education compared to other top-tier law schools in the Chicago area. Students CAN and DO fail out of JMLS.

The professors at JMLS are very dedicated to the students and to the law. As at every law school, there are some that aren't the greatest, but the majority of the faculty are alums from Ivy League and top-tier law schools. Most Importantly, their primary concern is NOT getting published, but teaching the law. The only negative part of JMLS is the new grading curve. As a 3L, I don't think that it is fair for the school to change the rules half way through the "game." However, the curve applies to core courses only, and if this new system will weed out students that aren't cut out for law school early on, it benefits those students by saving them time and money.

Status: Alumnus/a, full-time
Dates of Enrollment: 8/2000-5/2003
Survey Submitted: September 2003

Old school process. With the grading curve, fewer A's are given out, making students at other universities appear to have higher GPAs, which could get them hired faster and keep JMLS students at the bottom.

Employment Prospects

Status: Current student, full-time
Dates of Enrollment: 8/2004-Submit Date
Survey Submitted: November 2005

The employment prospects are somewhat limited. Most John Marshall graduates initially work in government roles. Chicago is highly competitive with Northwestern, University of Chicago, DePaul, Loyola, Kent and University of Illinois nearby. There were approximately 20 firms that came to John Marshall for on-campus recruiting.

The career services office and alumni offices are terrific. There are a number of programs that both offices offer every year, that encourage students to network and obtain employment. John Marshall has a strong reputation in Chicago and the alumni are very supportive of its students.

There are also valuable internship, externship, study abroad and clinical programs offered. There is an asylum, fair housing, criminal prosecution and criminal defense clinic, and possibly a couple others. There are opportunities to gain employment, however, it is more difficult and requires more effort than a top-tier school.

Status: Current student, full-time
Dates of Enrollment: 9/2004-Submit Date
Survey Submitted: September 2005

John Marshall alums are very friendly and usually very willing to help out the students. The employment prospects don't appear to be that different than for the other law schools not in the top tier if you do well in your first year. Most of the big firms have a few John Marshall alums. The employment prospects seem to be a little better for IP students.

Status: Current student, full-time
Dates of Enrollment: 8/2003-Submit Date
Survey Submitted: March 2004

This is a rough spot for John Marshall. Our bar passage rate was rather low in February of 2003. In July, it went up over 12 percent, but was still below the state's average. Let me say this about Marshall: the school cleaned house. We have a brand new dean, and she has hit the ground running. This school has a lot going for it: the Trial Advocacy Program is in the Top 10 within the nation; the Intellectual Property Program is in the Top 25; the Legal Writing Program is topnotch; the moot court at Marshall is consistently one of the best in the nation; and, most importantly, the school has a ton of money. Dean Mell has this program headed in the right direction rather quickly, and I think there is going to be nothing but consistent and steady improvement within this school.

That being said, the major reason I attended Marshall was because it offered me the most money. It was not my first choice, but in talking with numerous legal professionals throughout the city, I feel the choice will not hurt me. I don't understand why so many of our students are bitter or torn about being a Marshall student This program is one of the most established in the Chicago metropolitan area; for every one DePaul or Loyola graduate their are three Marshall grads. The networking in Chicago is endless!

Nationally, this school is not well-known. You have to work a little harder at Marshall because the school has stumbled recently, but the administration is now more committed then any I have ever experienced. Bottom line: if you are in the top 15 to 20 percent of your class at Marshall, you have got a shot at almost any firm you choose.

> **The school says:** "John Marshall alumni are employed at 29 of Chicago's 30 largest law firms, as well as a range of small and mid-sized law firms, federal, state and local government agencies, and public interest employers. The Career Services Office provides individual counseling to all John Marshall students to assist in their career development and hosts over 65 career-related workshops and programs each school year. The location of the law school in the Chicago Loop allows John Marshall students an incredible range of legal opportunities. Also, being located next to the Chicago Bar Association ensures students have easy access to networking opportunities and informational programming."

Status: Alumnus/a, full-time
Dates of Enrollment: 8/1994-6/1997
Survey Submitted: March 2005

Those who finish in the top of their class have very good prospects. The nationally recognized IP program helps those who want to practice IP law.

Status: Alumnus/a, full-time
Dates of Enrollment: 1/2000-1/2004
Survey Submitted: March 2005

If you want a job with a big firm, you need to be in the top 3 percent of your class. Big firms in Chicago will hire one or two people from each class. However, being number one in your class does not guarantee you a job. For students in the bottom half of the class, it is difficult to find a job, at least a well-paid one. Not impossible, just difficult.

Status: Current student, full-time
Dates of Enrollment: 8/2001-Submit Date
Survey Submitted: March 2004

Career services is helpful. If you want to litigate, you will have no problem finding a job. If you want another career (e.g., in corporate), go to another school unless you already have solid business credentials. Keep in mind that many students work while they go to school. My experience is that by third year, the"community" feel has evolved into a young professionals' circle where the real world has already become a significant reality of everyone's daily lives. While this somewhat trivializes the classes in the third year, it really supplements coursework with the real world and is a great transition. (Besides, third year is the bore year at all schools.)

John Marshall Law School says: "For the class of 2004, 20.9 percent of all students reporting their employment status were employed in the business sector. An additional 22.4 percent of the class was employed in the government, public interest, or academic sectors or as judicial clerks."

Quality of Life

Status: Current student, full-time
Dates of Enrollment: 8/2004-Submit Date
Survey Submitted: November 2005

The school is located in the center of Chicago and, as with all major cities, crime and safety is always a concern. Some students have had issues with crime, but none have been related to John Marshall or its students. In fact, students leave laptops and bags unattended in the library constantly, and I have never heard of any theft of any kind in the school. Outside the school, students must encounter the same elements they would in any major city.

The facilities at John Marshall are quite poor, but they suffice. John Marshal is a private institution and does not receive the funding, nor does it have the amenities of a public institution. The library is not open 24 hours, the classes lack an adequate amount of outlets (about 10 for 90 students), there are an insufficient amount of lockers for the students, and not enough library space. Again, the best is made out of a poor situation.

Status: Current student, full-time
Dates of Enrollment: 9/2004-Submit Date
Survey Submitted: September 2005

My favorite thing about John Marshall is the effort the administration makes to help students that have unique personal or family situations. Even though we have the largest law program in Chicago, it seems like almost everyone knows everyone. There isn't much to say about housing or campus, other than it's the city of Chicago. Most people live somewhere on the north side (Lincoln Park, Wrigleyville, etc). Chicago is a great city, but everything depends on where you live. The facilities at the school are pretty limited, because it isn't affiliated with any large university. The school itself is pretty safe and we have really tight security.

Status: Current student, full-time
Dates of Enrollment: 8/2003-Submit Date
Survey Submitted: March 2004

The quality of life is decent, but it is an urban school, so I don't really require much in terms of school provisions. For instance, it has a small cafe in it, but there are so many surrounding places to eat affordably, I just go out to eat. There are probably 20 places within walking distance—the school is in the heart of downtown Chicago, so I am never left wanting, so to speak. Again, as far as housing, I rent an apartment that I found in the newspaper. I take the subway to and from school, and I have never had a problem with safety (knock on wood). I feel extremely safe within the school at any time of day; ID is required to get past the main entrance of the school, and there are a ton of security cameras. Security has never been an area of concern, fortunately.

The campus is in downtown Chicago, what more could you want? As far as the building, it is an 11-floor single building attached to the Chicago Bar Association's headquarters, which is quite nice. The building is a bit old, but it is totally up to date: wireless connections in every room; one of the most comprehensive law libraries in the city; West Law and Lexis Accounts; numerous computer labs; a brand new student lounge; video games; free daily Chicago newspapers. I mean, it pretty much has everything you need.

Status: Alumnus/a, full-time
Dates of Enrollment: 8/1994-6/1997
Survey Submitted: March 2005

Downtown campus is convenient, safe and allows part-time employment at top Chicago firms.

Status: Alumnus/a, full-time
Dates of Enrollment: 1/2000-1/2004
Survey Submitted: March 2005

This is Chicago, you can have the quality of life your heart desires—even if you don't have a lot of money to spare. The school does not have a campus and many students prefer the surrounding restaurants to the cafeteria.

Status: Current student, full-time
Dates of Enrollment: 8/2001-Submit Date
Survey Submitted: March 2004

Chicago is a great city and whatever you want here you can find. Summers are heaven and winters can be dreary. The school itself offers an astonishing number of programs to students. There is free food at most of these events. There are also a ton of organizations to get involved in and the school is very helpful if you want to start your own. But you should know that JMLS has a considerable evening student program and plenty of commuters. So while there is a community feel, especially in your first year, that sense can quickly dissipate as your interests change from that of your friends and you find yourself in courses with very new faces. The night students are hard working and add beneficial real world experience to class, however because the school has to accommodate both day and night students, once you seek electives you may find the courses you want offered only at night, which usually means once a week for three hours.

Facilities include three buildings. The old building is early era charming with all the modern needs like outlets and wireless Internet. The newer building is 12 stories high and was converted from an old department store. The lounge is new, clean and bright. I love being right on the L (brown line and red line).

Status: Current student, full-time
Dates of Enrollment: 1/2001-Submit Date
Survey Submitted: May 2004

The school has recently implemented a new security staff. These proactive steps provide a safer environment for the students and staff.

Status: Alumnus/a, full-time
Dates of Enrollment: 8/2000-5/2003
Survey Submitted: September 2003

Good programs, but the school is old and outdated. Equipment constantly fails and the professors are hard to get a hold of because they do not use up-to-date technology.

Social Life

Status: Current student, full-time
Dates of Enrollment: 8/2004-Submit Date
Survey Submitted: November 2005

The social life in Chicago is wonderful. It's a first class city that has everything you could possibly want. The student organizations and student bar association are very active. There are a number of cultural and ethnic celebrations by the respective organization, panel discussions or debates every week on a variety of topics and after school social events almost every week. As a culinary capital, Chicago will provide you with all the restaurants you could ever need. The city is filled with everything from dive bars to clubs that stay open until the sun rises. There is something for everyone.

Status: Current student, full-time
Dates of Enrollment: 9/2004-Submit Date
Survey Submitted: September 2005

Law students at John Marshall love to drink. John Marshall is pretty close to a lot of the other Chicago law schools, and everyone seems to end up at Mondays a lot during the week. Weekends there is usually something going on near the north side. JMLS has something like 40 student organizations, and they usually sponsor some sort of event. We have a pretty active PAD chapter, and there are a couple other fraternities as well.

Read all of Vault's Law School Surveys at www.vault.com/lawschool — get complete surveys on top law schools, expert advice on applicaton essays, LSAT prep and more.

VAULT CAREER LIBRARY 215

Status: Current student, full-time
Dates of Enrollment: 8/2003-Submit Date
Survey Submitted: March 2004

Again, because this is a urban law school only, and not a university, the city is really your playground! We have a couple of law fraternities and a ton of associations, so there is always something to do.

Plus, the school or one of the organizations is always sponsoring something: Bulls games, Cubs games, Blackhawk games, casino nights, bar nights, cruises on the lake. You never feel like there is nothing to do.

There are probably at least two to three seminars a week sponsored by the career services office or some other department or academic organization. Again, there are too many options sometimes!

Overall, the quality of social and academic life are both quite high at the John Marshall Law School.

Status: Alumnus/a, full-time
Dates of Enrollment: 8/1994-6/1997
Survey Submitted: March 2005

Local bars are busy after afternoon classes; students get along well. Those who work hard at John Marshall play hard.

Status: Alumnus/a, full-time
Dates of Enrollment: 1/2000-1/2004
Survey Submitted: March 2005

Various student organizations coordinate regular outings at various bars, but I did not notice any student favorites.

Status: Alumnus/a, full-time
Dates of Enrollment: 1/1993-1/1996
Survey Submitted: March 2005

Social life was excellent.

Status: Current student, full-time
Dates of Enrollment: 8/2001-Submit Date
Survey Submitted: March 2004

The SBA does throw a lot of socials but also offers a lot of volunteer opportunities and other events. Clubs are abundant and always have meetings. There are some fun Back to School, Halloween and Christmas parties. Restaurants are everywhere, theater is close by, festivals in the summer are at your doorstep and the beach isn't far.

Status: Current student, full-time
Dates of Enrollment: 1/2001-Submit Date
Survey Submitted: May 2004

Chicago is a great city, bottom line! JMLS has many extracurricular programs, and the student body is made up of good, genuine and intelligent individuals.

Status: Alumnus/a, full-time
Dates of Enrollment: 8/2000-5/2003
Survey Submitted: September 2003

There are plenty of bars and parties to unwind at.

Loyola University Chicago School of Law

Office of Admission
Loyola University Chicago
School of Law
25 East Pearson Street, Suite 1440
Chicago, IL 60611
Admissions phone: (312) 915-7170
Admissions e-mail: law-admissions@luc.edu
Admissions URL: http://www.luc.edu/law/admission/jd/

 Admissions

Status: Current student, full-time
Dates of Enrollment: 8/2003-Submit Date
Survey Submitted: September 2005

Loyola Law places a great deal of emphasis on the personal statement, according to professors involved in the selection process. The GPA and LSAT scores are definitely used for an initial cut-off, but my understanding is that they also take into consideration a desire for diversity. In fact, almost all of my classes have been well over 50 percent women, with many more in the 60 to 70 percent range.

Status: Alumnus/a, full-time
Dates of Enrollment: 9/2000-5/2004
Survey Submitted: March 2005

Very straightforward, supportive with respect to financial aid and how to get loans from government; school has less financial aid than most I think.

Status: Current student, full-time
Dates of Enrollment: 9/2003-Submit Date
Survey Submitted: March 2004

The admissions process is quicker than at most other schools in Chicago. I also applied to Kent and DePaul, and I heard almost a month earlier from Loyola than from the other two schools. I can't remember the date, but I think it was late January or early February.

I highly recommend applying to the night program if you think you may not be able to get into the full-time program. It is easy to transfer and graduate in three years, all it requires are some summer classes, which are usually grade-boosters anyway. If you do this, you are still eligible for on-campus interviewing. Some employers seem to look down those who were part of the evening division, but it is still worth it if you really want to attend Loyola. The same professors are used for first-year part-time and full-time students; they just rotate year by year. It is also a break in tuition. Scholarships are given at entrance, I think these also might be easier to get if you apply to the night school. They are small, but still helpful.

Because it is a Jesuit school, applicants are well served if they include a desire to help others in their personal statement or if they have experience in some kind of philanthropic activity.

Status: Current student, full-time
Dates of Enrollment: 8/2001-Submit Date
Survey Submitted: January 2004

The admissions process was pretty straightforward and required a typical law school essay. Loyola is very much geared toward public interest and has a well-known child advocacy program. A lot of people write about their desire to serve the public interest in their admission essay, whether or not it is true.

Status: Current student, full-time
Dates of Enrollment: 8/2001-Submit Date
Survey Submitted: February 2004

I don't think the school is very selective. Routine admissions process. Personal statement, resume, LSAT, etc.

Status: Alumnus/a, part-time
Dates of Enrollment: 8/1995-12/1997
Survey Submitted: November 2003

The admissions process is straightforward: typical LSATs, transcripts and essays. Although traditionally viewed as a strong Midwestern litigator training ground, the school is pushing more to create specialties in health law and some corporate presence. It aims to grow more national recognition, so there might be some advantage to being from outside the Chicago area.

 Academics

Status: Current student, full-time
Dates of Enrollment: 8/2003-Submit Date
Survey Submitted: September 2005

For first-year students, there is no choice as to classes. You are assigned into one of three daytime sections of about 70 students each, and have the same group of students as classmates for all classes for the entire first year. Professors are assigned to a section number, so you have no choice here either. There is an additional, separate section for evening students, averaging about 50 to 70 students, with professors generally self-selecting into evening classes.

The school last year switched to a new online registration system, which comes with the traditional bugs of any new computer system. On your assigned day to register, if you are not online and ready to register, the best professors teaching the most popular classes are completely taken within a matter of minutes. And many people are blocked out from even accessing the system during this time due to the very limited capacity of the computers. So a certain amount of luck is involved.

Status: Current student, full-time
Dates of Enrollment: 9/2003-Submit Date
Survey Submitted: November 2003

Some professors are good. For the most part, they are easy to talk to about concerns or questions for class. When it comes to exam time, some are very helpful, hold review sessions, etc.; others seem to disappear. Most put practice exams on reserve in the library; this is helpful.

One good thing about Loyola is that there are academic tutors (2L or 3L) for each first-year class. Although students give mixed reviews of these tutors, it is nice to hear what exams are like from those who know. It also helps that many of the tutors had the teacher they are tutoring for class.

Getting classes is very hard. Unlike some schools there are still two required classes as a 2L (Federal Tax and Business Organization); somehow this makes getting classes you want really hard in the second semester of your second year. It is extremely frustrating to schedule classes. Also, they tend to schedule classes that all conflict. If you do transfer from part-time to full-time, you are still required to take some night classes second year, and that makes scheduling even harder.

The grading is competitive. It is on a 4.0 scale (curved), and, as at all law schools, people take it very seriously. I think 5 to 10 percent get A's, and it goes down from there. For some reason there are no minus grades (A-, B-, C-), but I'm not sure whether that helps or hurts compared to other schools.

There is a significant writing requirement during the first year and a half, but after that there is none, and no 3L thesis or paper is required. A positive for the

Read all of Vault's Law School Surveys at www.vault.com/lawschool — get complete surveys on top law schools, expert advice on applicaton essays, LSAT prep and more.

VAULT CAREER LIBRARY 217

law school is that it often has working lawyers teach classes for specific fields. Although the teaching is sometimes lacking, if you are really interested in the field it is good for contacts and learning what lawyers deem really important. Those who get the highest grade in any class are given the CALI award.

Status: Alumnus/a, full-time
Dates of Enrollment: 9/1999-6/2002
Survey Submitted: April 2005

There are many great classes from which to select; I never understand the students who do not like the variety. With the quarter system, you can take 24 to 30 different courses over your 2L to 3L years. That is a tremendous opportunity. The professors are generally outstanding.

Status: Current student, full-time
Dates of Enrollment: 8/2001-Submit Date
Survey Submitted: February 2004

I've never had a problem getting a class I want. I've pretty much loved every professor I've had. Grading seems fair; I don't have much to compare it too. As with all subjective grading systems, there is room for uncertainty. There have only been a few classes that I thought were sort of a waste of time.

Status: Alumnus/a, part-time
Dates of Enrollment: 8/1995-12/1997
Survey Submitted: November 2003

The program is a typical, straightforward, bar-preparation legal program. Though well known for its advocacy and litigation preparation, the school is growing into certain niche specialties such as health care law. There are not many law-and-economics types of classes like at other Chicago schools—or at least University of Chicago—but Loyola provides a solid foundation in the law, as evidenced by its high bar passage rates.

 Employment Prospects

Status: Current student, full-time
Dates of Enrollment: 8/2003-Submit Date
Survey Submitted: September 2005

While Loyola is seen as a good name in the legal environment, and respected as a good school, it must be remembered that here in Chicago there are two Top 20 schools: Chicago and Northwestern, so on-campus interviews and other preferred job selection methods are overwhelmingly monopolized by students from those schools. Loyola students generally can count on getting a job, just not with the BIG firms unless the student is in the top five (not top 5 percent, top five students!).

Status: Alumnus/a, part-time
Dates of Enrollment: 8/1995-12/1997
Survey Submitted: November 2003

Loyola provides strong ties to Chicago and Midwestern litigators and advocates. It is less strong in corporate placement, and weaker in extra-regional placement. However, hopefully that improves with time.

Status: Alumnus/a, full-time
Dates of Enrollment: 9/1999-6/2002
Survey Submitted: April 2005

Tons of law firms come to campus, and your options are endless. Good grades are key to the best firms, but that is true no matter where you go to law school.

Status: Current student, full-time
Dates of Enrollment: 9/2003-Submit Date
Survey Submitted: March 2004

On-campus interviewing—it seems as though only a small number of people got jobs through this, although the program appears to be relatively well run. I would suggest if you are thinking of going here that you really try to find out what percentage of students get jobs through on-campus interviewing, not just a national average, but actual Loyola students. This is kind of a mystery around the school. Other than OCI, I am not really aware of any services career resources offers that are helpful.

I guess the main concern is determining what lawyers in Chicago really think about Loyola and the education you get there. If thinking about going there, you may also want to consult lawyers in Chicago regarding the reputation. Also a concern: I don't think the school has a ton of alumni support. Some alumni seem to have negative feelings about the school, particularly those in their 40s (often hiring partners now). It seems as when they were in law school, the school was overcrowded and not popular with its students. Loyola alums also do not seem that involved in helping out current students.

Status: Current student, full-time
Dates of Enrollment: 8/2001-Submit Date
Survey Submitted: February 2004

Loyola is a regional school, so it has more prestige in Chicago than anywhere else. Career resources are focused on the traditional big firm jobs and placing those students in the top of the class.

Status: Current student, full-time
Dates of Enrollment: 8/2001-Submit Date
Survey Submitted: January 2004

The top 10 percent of the class will probably find the on-campus interviewing helpful, which attracts mainly Chicago firms. As for other options, especially in government and nonprofit, the services are not as good. The staff is very reactive and posts notices they receive, but don't look for them to be proactive.

 Quality of Life

Status: Alumnus/a, full-time
Dates of Enrollment: 9/1999-6/2002
Survey Submitted: April 2005

The students are wonderful; I have more close friends from law school than I did from college. This is a special environment. Hyde Park isn't the most hip place in the world, but it is very unique and a fine experience for three years. Law school has new facilities, too.

Status: Alumnus/a, full-time
Dates of Enrollment: 9/2000-5/2004
Survey Submitted: March 2005

Supportive environment, good quality of life.

Status: Current student, full-time
Dates of Enrollment: 8/2003-Submit Date
Survey Submitted: September 2005

Loyola-Chicago is three blocks from Water Tower and Michigan Avenue, which makes for excellent shopping opportunities, most of which are financially out of reach for students. There is no "campus" per se, merely a few buildings along the same block that house law, business and some undergrad classes. The school is not traditionally of much assistance with housing, but is currently building a new grad student housing building across the street.

Status: Current student, full-time
Dates of Enrollment: 8/2001-Submit Date
Survey Submitted: January 2004

The school provides no housing for law students, leaving students to rent apartments. Chicago is more affordable than other major cities. The law school is ideally located off Michigan Avenue near an L stop. The facilities are fine. Crime and safety concerns are pretty minimal.

The school says: "Housing will be available in fall 2006."

Status: Current student, full-time
Dates of Enrollment: 8/2001-Submit Date
Survey Submitted: February 2004

Quality of life is fine. Chicago is a great city, but if someone is looking for a tight-knit community, it is a little more difficult because you are not on a college campus. Students live all over the city.

Status: Current student, full-time
Dates of Enrollment: 9/2003-Submit Date
Survey Submitted: March 2004

The facilities of the law school are not great. Computers are slow, the building has poor heating and air conditioning, and the biggest classroom has few laptop outlets and no Internet connections. The student lounge is small and also quite old. Almost nothing is done online, and getting paper copies of important things (like registration information) is often very difficult.

The law library, in another building, is a more modern facility but still has a small computer lab with computers that don't run all that well. Housing is on your own somewhere in Chicago, which is really not a problem. The neighborhood the law school is in is probably the best thing about it. Michigan Avenue is nice, and there is a Starbucks and a bar across the street. Another note is that the law school has more women than men; many of the classes are almost all women.

> **The school says:** "We have moved to the same building as the library and are now wireless."

Status: Alumnus/a, part-time
Dates of Enrollment: 8/1995-12/1997
Survey Submitted: November 2003

The campus is conveniently located near the Water Tower and is in the midst of the Michigan Avenue Miracle Mile. It is a few subway stops to the Loop and a few stops south of Lincoln Park. There is no housing to speak of, and most students live in one of the Chicago neighborhoods, though in the night program there are many suburban commuters as well.

 ## Social Life

Status: Current student, full-time
Dates of Enrollment: 8/2003-Submit Date
Survey Submitted: September 2005

A quick review of any tourist information about Chicago will lead one to understand why this is a GREAT city to live in! The social opportunities are innumerable, whether you are interested in the bar scene on Rush Street, the great festivals, or enjoying the parks and lakeshore of Lake Michigan. The city of Chicago itself presents perhaps the best reason to attend Loyola!

Status: Alumnus/a, full-time
Dates of Enrollment: 9/1999-6/2002
Survey Submitted: April 2005

There are things to do in Chicago at all hours of every day; it's hard to imagine a better social scene.

Status: Alumnus/a, full-time
Dates of Enrollment: 9/2000-5/2004
Survey Submitted: March 2005

I was an older student and did not rely on social life; younger students seemed fine and found lots of good relationships; it is not an overly competitive place at the level of affecting your social life.

Status: Current student, full-time
Dates of Enrollment: 9/2003-Submit Date
Survey Submitted: March 2004

There is a student bar party every Thursday. Also, there is a bar across the street that is popular with students. The students can be very competitive and unhelpful if you miss class and need notes, etc. The night students are much less competitive and more friendly. Generally, students seem to have friends in the city outside of school; it seems like many of the students went to high school in Chicago and the suburbs. There are definitely some nice, fun people in the mix; you just have to work to find them.

There is a good number of student-run organizations, both academic (moot court, law reviews) and social (student bar association). One of the biggest organizations is the public interest law society, which provides stipends to students who do work in the public interest.

Status: Current student, full-time
Dates of Enrollment: 8/2001-Submit Date
Survey Submitted: February 2004

The school is not on a campus. But there is no shortage of things to do in the city. Anyone can find a niche in Chicago

Status: Current student, full-time
Dates of Enrollment: 8/2001-Submit Date
Survey Submitted: January 2004

You have infinite possibilities for social activity at Loyola. A lot of students hang out together and can cause an atmosphere a bit like high school.

Status: Alumnus/a, part-time
Dates of Enrollment: 8/1995-12/1997
Survey Submitted: November 2003

There is a fairly strong social life. I noticed a great deal of activity among the tight-knit night students, who hung out frequently after classes to discuss the issues facing those seeking a rigorous course of study while maintaining careers, families and outside lives (it is very difficult to do so). Given the cauldron that many night students found themselves in, there is a great deal of camaraderie.

Read all of Vault's Law School Surveys at www.vault.com/lawschool — get complete surveys on top law schools, expert advice on applicaton essays, LSAT prep and more.

VAULT CAREER LIBRARY 219

Northern Illinois University College of Law

Office of Admission & Financial Aid
Northern Illinois University
DeKalb, IL 60115-2890
Admissions phone: (815) 753-8595 and (800) 892-3050
Admissions fax: (815) 753-5680
Admissions e-mail: lawadm@niu.edu
URL: http://law.niu.edu/

 Admissions

Status: Alumnus/a, full-time
Dates of Enrollment: 8/2002-5/2005
Survey Submitted: April 2006

Although law school admissions have been on the rise and NIU Law had become more selective in their admissions, they have not given in to the numbers game. They evaluate each potential candidate for admission on an individual basis, taking into consideration each candidate's unique background. Take your time with your essay for admission for this school and they will take the time to actually read it. And if you are accepted, you will get a personal phone call from the admissions director extending NIU Law's congratulations.

The admissions process was part of the reason I chose NIU Law. After I was admitted, I received phone calls from current students offering their guidance and support to help me ease into my first year of law school. I was also invited to a visitor's day in the early spring to meet other admitted and current students, to sit in on a class, and to meet the professors. By the time I walked through the door in August as a 1L, I already felt comfortable with my new surroundings.

Status: Current student, full-time
Dates of Enrollment: 8/2004-Submit Date
Survey Submitted: April 2006

The admissions process was straightforward and uncomplicated. There was no interview, but an essay/statement of suitability for the practice of law was required. Honesty is always the best policy. However, as future advocates for clients a prospective student should practice advocating for her/himself at this stage. Many law schools, including NIU, are concerned with obtaining a diverse student body. As in law, what is perceived on the surface does not tell the entire tale. I, a white male, initially appeared not to be "diverse." I looked beyond those base characteristics to highlight those aspects that provide a different perspective or background that would indicate my contribution to diversity. What unusual activities, hobbies or jobs have you done? I was a police officer and I used that as my unusual perspective and contribution.

Status: Current student, full-time
Dates of Enrollment: 8/2003-Submit Date
Survey Submitted: April 2006

At the time I applied, there was a paper admission form that required completion. That form required a statement of personal goals. NIU also required letters of recommendation from two unrelated people, an official transcript from your undergrad school, and LSAT score.

When I initially inquired about attending NIU, I was encouraged to apply because I would bring diversity to the school, as a 50+ year old woman. I did not receive any other assistance and I do not know what criteria were used in selecting students. There were three of us over 50 in my class and we are all graduating. The average age of the students in my class is around 25 years of age. It appears to me that there was a real effort to boost the numbers of Hispanic students, however I felt the Black students were under-represented for the northern Illinois area.

Regarding diversity, the school says: "NIU Law has long recognized the value of having a student body that reflects the

diversity of our society. *U.S. News & World Report* ranks NIU Law among the top 20 percent of law schools for diversity. Typically, one-third of entering classes are students of color."

Status: Current student, full-time
Dates of Enrollment: 8/2003-Submit Date
Survey Submitted: April 2006

I came up to the school and had a tour on a Saturday and talked to a few of the current students about what they liked. I then sat in on the moot court finals and watched current students compete. Afterwards when refreshments were being served I was able to talk to the director of career services. I applied to several schools and thought about going to an out-of-state school. I even got several scholarships. In writing my essays for schools I pretty much used one and worked on that one for several months with one of my undergraduate communication's teacher. What was more grueling than anything was realizing how much I had spent on applying to law school.

Status: Alumnus/a, full-time
Dates of Enrollment: 8/1995-5/1998
Survey Submitted: April 2006

Northern is difficult to get in because of the high percentage of non-traditional students who apply. They seem to value life experience and volunteer work. It is particularly difficult to get in right out of college. If you have been away from school working this is the law school for you.

Status: Alumnus/a, full-time
Dates of Enrollment: 8/2002-6/2005
Survey Submitted: April 2006

I received the application, which was fairly self-explanatory and got right to work! I remember being so nervous as I typed my actual application. I spent a couple of weeks working on my entrance essay with my college advisor, and wrote an essay I was proud of. I was really disappointed when I got a rejection letter from another Illinois law school, but was ecstatic when Northern accepted me. They were so welcoming—I've even saved my original acceptance letter! During orientation, I realized what a diverse community I had become a part of. Finding out about my classmate's backgrounds was interesting, Spanish majors, nursing majors, political science majors. People who had studied abroad, people who working in criminal justice, and people who were older and had families.

Status: Current student, full-time
Dates of Enrollment: 8/2004-Submit Date
Survey Submitted: April 2006

The process required an applicant to take the LSAT, fill out an application, and submit an essay. The median range for the LSAT seems to be in the mid to high 150s and the median range for undergraduate GPA appears to be in the low 3.0s. An LSAT over 160 and a GPA of 3.0 should get you in.

Status: Current student, full-time
Dates of Enrollment: 8/2003-Submit Date
Survey Submitted: April 2005

The admissions process at NIU Law included a submission of an application by mail or online with LSAT scores and undergraduate GPA. Requirements are generally consistent with those of other third-tier schools—although, these are increasing with each newly admitted class. The school is also big on diversity (including race, geography, and experience prior to law school) and characteristics that make an applicant diverse are factored into the admissions process.

Status: Current student, full-time
Dates of Enrollment: 8/2002-Submit Date
Survey Submitted: April 2005

The admissions process is fair. They take into consideration not only the LSAT score and the grade point average, but also the personal statement, your involvement in extracurricular activities and more. The admissions committee usually selects a very diverse group of students. And by diverse I mean not only race, but also age and employment background and more.

Status: Current student, full-time
Dates of Enrollment: 8/2003-Submit Date
Survey Submitted: April 2005

The admissions process is pretty much like all other law schools. You can apply online or through hard-copy package. If you apply online sometimes the application fee is reduced or waived all together. The school does not do interviews. I did an essay that was about a trip I took abroad and how I related it to law school. I used the essay for all the law schools I applied to.

Academics

Status: Alumnus/a, full-time
Dates of Enrollment: 8/1998-5/2001
Survey Submitted: April 2006

The clinical courses are exceptional with several options offered, including participation in the law school's legal clinic. The academic atmosphere, while demanding, is not vicious or demeaning. Students are collegial toward each other and share resources and materials. Professors foster a learning environment, are extremely accessible, and willing to work with students.

Status: Alumnus/a, full-time
Dates of Enrollment: 8/2002-5/2005
Survey Submitted: April 2006

NIU Law is a community environment—a community where professors know their students and take time to invest in their education. I felt I was able to receive an incredible education at an incredible value. I received one-on-one instruction and guidance from my professors, and I was evaluated and graded fairly. At NIU Law the professors do not "pad" their grades. If you deserve an F, you get an F. If you deserve an A, you get an A. The workload is not easy, but it is fair. The professors expect you to work hard and they did not tolerate slacking. If you put in the time and the effort, the professors would give you the same time and effort in return. Classes were kept at a manageable size, but if it came down to letting one more student into a popular class, most professors would try to accommodate their students.

Status: Current student, full-time
Dates of Enrollment: 8/2003-Submit Date
Survey Submitted: April 2006

I had two truly outstanding teachers—one was always very positive and energetic and wrote on the blackboard, something that is very important to those of us who are visual learners. She has remained a source of inspiration and a counterweight to the oppression I've experienced from so many of the teachers. The other instructor was in legal writing. She, too, was very good at breaking down the important things we needed to know into small parts that made the assignments doable and meaningful.

NIU has a procedure for taking certain practical classes, like trial advocacy and the clinics. Students must apply ahead of registration for the slots for these classes and then are assigned. Because some of the courses require pre-requisites, students are blocked from taking these courses till their third year. Unfortunately, by their third year, many students have jobs and no longer have the time for clinics. Additionally the NIU clinics are all off campus. For example, in order to participate in the Zeke Giorgi clinic, one has to travel about an hour to Rockford. For many students, this adds too much travel to their day. Many students travel one or more hours each way to get to the campus, so this additional travel, out of their way, is a burden.

Many students choose their courses based on when the finals are assigned. The biggest burden by far has to do with the time between finals. It is really hard to take finals one day after another. So most of us avoid that by picking our courses by looking at the final schedule. Overall, my experience has been that the full-time instructors primarily are theorists, having very limited real-world experience as lawyers.

Status: Alumnus/a, full-time
Dates of Enrollment: 8/1995-5/1998
Survey Submitted: April 2006

The academics are challenging, but not overwhelming. All classes are small and the professors know who you are and what your interests are in law. The first-year classes are done in blocks so you have every class with the same 45 people. The school only accepts about 100 students each year. The upper-level classes are popular and because the school is small you have to be diligent in planning your schedule. I found it easy to get the classes I wanted if I planned ahead.

For a small school, Northern offers a wide variety of law classes. All upper-level classes have 20 to 30 people. The seminar classes have as few as six people and at most 14. There is a lot of emphasis on public interest law and a great deal of course offerings on criminal law and procedure. I found the quality of the instruction excellent and the grading fair, but not easy. Some classes have a greater workload than others, but because it is a small school your classmates can help you figure out what classes will meet your needs.

Status: Alumnus/a, full-time
Dates of Enrollment: 8/2002-6/2005
Survey Submitted: April 2006

My first year was tough. I was floored by the Socratic Method and the voluminous reading. But soon, I got the hang of it. I struggled with exams, mostly because there was so much information to remember, but writing has always been my strong-suit so after the first two semesters, I had those exams figured out!

Northern was typical of all other law schools; property, torts, crim law, civil procedure, con law, etc. for the first year, and then AWESOME elective courses for second and third year. I was able to take a wide variety of classes, including three practical courses—Lawyering Skills which taught me about the day-to-day activities of litigation lawyers, Trial Advocacy, which gave me "courtroom" practice and trial experience, and the Domestic Violence Clinic, which allowed me to work as a 711 with Prairie State Legal Services helping low-income individuals with orders of protection. Without those three classes, I would not have had the confidence to jump into litigation and motion practice with my present employer.

Our professors were incredibly friendly. I do not believe there was one professor at Northern that was "un-approachable." At anytime you could catch a professor at a local event, at the supermarket, or in their office, and they would take the time to chat. Not only were they friendly, but they were professional. Out of six semesters, there were probably only one or two classes I didn't really like. For some classes the reading was quite a lot, and for other classes, I could get away with "skimming." I found though, that it was always better to be prepared. Grading was fair, getting into classes was not too difficult (especially if you knew the professor), and overall, I received a GREAT education from Northern.

Status: Current student, full-time
Dates of Enrollment: 8/2003-Submit Date
Survey Submitted: April 2006

Northern Illinois University is a much more relaxed and enjoyable law school experience than I have heard from others. Part of this could be because students are in a sense forced to make new friends and hang out with everyone because Northern is in DeKalb, rather than Chicago or another major city. The classes are smaller and you are able to get more attention from professors. At the end of the semester usually students hang out with the professors in their office going over hypotheticals just to make sure they know what they are talking about. Getting the right class schedule at times can be difficult, but normally teachers will open up their class so that more students can get in.

Status: Current student, full-time
Dates of Enrollment: 8/2003-Submit Date
Survey Submitted: April 2005

The academic program is something that left a bad taste in the mouth of quite a few students as reflected by a recent Student Bar Association survey. The facilities are in need of a major overhaul, they're bad enough to affect our ABA accreditation.

Read all of Vault's Law School Surveys at www.vault.com/lawschool — get complete surveys on top law schools, expert advice on applicaton essays, LSAT prep and more.

VAULT CAREER LIBRARY 221

The administration (which is three people) has horrible communication with the students and the university at large. Many alumni have flat out told me they will not donate while certain administrators are present. The Dean is weak and ineffective and to top it all off is a poor teacher as well. The only upside to the school is a few true diamond teachers and great staff. however both of those are being slowly run off. The other plus is absolute dirt cheap law degree but that is starting to cut too close to the bone in getting what you pay for. It's possible to come out with less the $30,000 grand in debt after three years. This is due to finding research assistantships and graduate assistantships in the great university. Many students have GA's outside of the law school. A third great secret benefit is a dual law student/grad student degree. However you must being willing to fight the red tape both within and without the law school.

> **Regarding its facilities, the school says:** "NIU Law has made significant improvements to meet the ever-changing needs of its students, faculty and staff. Recently renovated 'smart' classrooms feature multimedia instruction tools and desks outfitted with power and wireless network access for laptop computers. Among NIU Law's most significant additions is the Kenneth C. Chessick Legal Skills Training Center, a state-of-the-art facility for educating students in the use of technology in the advocacy process; fewer than 5 percent of law schools across the nation have facilities of this type."

Status: Current student, full-time
Dates of Enrollment: 8/2003-Submit Date
Survey Submitted: April 2005

The academics at NIU Law are what you make them. There are more difficult classes and there are easier classes and it is up to the second- and third-year student what classes they want to take and whether or not they want to challenge themselves. The first-year curriculum is challenging but excellent professors allow 1L students to get the most out of the courses and all 1Ls have the opportunity to succeed. I would say the first-year workload was not too heavy. Additionally, the professors were accommodating to the first-year legal writing course. For example, when the appellate brief became due, the professors cut the 1Ls some slack in requirements for course participation. For the upper level courses, popular courses are entered by use of a balloting system. Students rank the courses and submit their ballot to the administration. Preference is then given to 3Ls, however, I have not had any problems getting into any of the courses I have attempted to ballot into. The faculty is great and due to the small size of the school they are able to make connections with the students. Many faculty members attend student-run events, so the interaction with faculty continues even outside of the classroom.

Status: Current student, full-time
Dates of Enrollment: 8/2002-Submit Date
Survey Submitted: April 2005

The academic nature of the program is also pretty fair. Normally, the upper level students have priority and therefore get more of the classes that they desire to take. However, with Northern being a pretty small law school not many classes are offered, especially if only a few students are interested in the class. In addition, the grading procedures are pretty fair because most of the professors grade on a curve. Aside from grades, the professors are wonderful. Northern Illinois University College of Law has some of the best professors. The professors are very helpful and they have an open-door policy. Professors will schedule time with outside of class and their regular office hours to meet with students. I love the professors here at Northern.

Status: Alumnus/a, full-time
Dates of Enrollment: 8/1991-5/1993
Survey Submitted: April 2005

The academic program was appropriately tailored for lawyers intending to practice law in the Chicago metropolitan area and the surrounding rural areas. Not too philisophical—not too nuts and bolts.

Employment Prospects

Status: Alumnus/a, full-time
Dates of Enrollment: 8/1998-5/2001
Survey Submitted: April 2006

NIU Law grads are employed in a variety of areas throughout the legal field. Northern is prominent in preparing students for positions in public interest law, including state's attorneys and public defenders. Numerous NIU alums are judges and judicial clerks. There are a variety of networking opportunities offered throughout the year in locations throughout the state. The career services office has a free online job list as well as a job bulletin obtained by subscription.

The career services office helps students obtain part-time work while in school, including 7-11 positions that allow students to appear in court under supervision. Career services also provides informal presentations by alums highlighting different legal positions. On-campus recruiters regularly visit campus.

> **Regarding job postings, the school says:** "All job postings are available online and do not require a subscription."

Status: Alumnus/a, full-time
Dates of Enrollment: 8/2002-5/2005
Survey Submitted: April 2006

When I first started at NIU Law, it was known as a public interest school, probably due to the fact that tuition is reasonable and students can afford to pursue jobs in the public sector without worrying about how to pay back enormous loans. However, when I graduated from NIU Law, my classmates and I got jobs in all different jobs: corporate, government, large firms, small firms, public interest, litigation, etc. There is no one mold. And because of NIU Law's close proximity to several large cities (Chicago, Rockford, Springfield), there are alumni just about everywhere you go.

Status: Current student, full-time
Dates of Enrollment: 8/2004-Submit Date
Survey Submitted: April 2006

Employment prospects are very good. The career services office works very hard to provide opportunities to network and interview (on and off campus). Although the distance from Chicago limits the familiarity of Chicago firms with the law school, employment is probable with effort and determination. Creative approaches to obtaining a position the summer after the first year can pay large dividends for the future. For example, I volunteered at a Chicago firm (90 attorneys). This led to being hired for the spring semester of the second year and for that summer. Although there is no guarantee of future employment upon graduation, I have gotten in the door and obtained the chance to show the quality of my work. This is just one approach; creativity and a focus on the career after graduation are a powerful combination.

Status: Alumnus/a, full-time
Dates of Enrollment: 8/2002-5/2005
Survey Submitted: April 2006

Alumni are still extremely active with the law school, and they return to campus frequently for various events. The career services office reaches out to students, even those that don't think that they need the help. The law school is still in its infancy stages, so those people that graduated when the law school first opened are just now making names for themselves as judges and lawyers. There is a huge emphasis on public interest employment.

Status: Current student, full-time
Dates of Enrollment: 8/2003-Submit Date
Survey Submitted: April 2006

I think NIU is geared toward producing lawyers who will do everyday general law. It is not a prestigious school and does not have connections with BigLaw firms. The location—far from the big cities, and without any public transportation to get to them—isolates the students from many opportunities to intern or work for many big firms in the large cities. I believe many graduates work locally, work for the government as assistant state's attorneys or public defenders. A few leave the state for jobs. I know of two who work in patent law, one of my classmates has a job and recently passed the patent bar.

At this point, one month away from graduation, I have not received any help from the alumni network for future employment. I do not know if there is even a system of referral, other than the web site that lists jobs. The on-campus recruiting is primarily for firms in Rockford, or other cities west or south of DeKalb. The location of NIU makes internships difficult for some of us who live at a distance from the school and even more remote from Chicago or the western and southern cities.

Status: Alumnus/a, full-time
Dates of Enrollment: 8/1995-5/1998
Survey Submitted: April 2006

Northern is small school with a great reputation in the public interest field. It really means something to graduate from NIU if you are interested in prosecuting or defending criminal cases. Unfortunately, if you are interested in larger firms then this may not be the firm for you. Most of the graduates get a job in the government or small firms. The alumni network is helpful and growing in stature. There are numerous opportunities for internships and clerkships because of the long history of government interest.

There are plenty of alumni who start their own practice and seem to make a go of it. There is a large network of NIU alumni in the surrounding area practicing law. Everyone who graduates gets a job pretty quickly, but few make it to the highest paid positions. Because of the large number of law students at NIU are older they seem to be attracted to the stability of government law.

Status: Alumnus/a, full-time
Dates of Enrollment: 8/2002-6/2005
Survey Submitted: April 2006

The two legal jobs that I held during law school were both "word-of-mouth" jobs. My second law-clerk job turned into an associate position. All of my close friends have associate positions, or law related positions, and I have come across very few people who remain jobless. The career services office provides a lot of help to soon-to-be grads looking for jobs, especially when they are looking outside of their home area. It's always reassuring when you find out that there is a Northern alum at the firm to which you are applying.

Status: Current student, full-time
Dates of Enrollment: 8/2002-Submit Date
Survey Submitted: April 2005

We also have very supportive alumni (which include lawyers and judges). We have a mentoring program, in which the school pairs students with an alumni. We also have several events in which alumni and current students associate. Most of the alumni are very helpful in providing information to current law students seeking employment. We also have a great Career Services Department here in the law school. This department keeps the students abreast of available job openings/opportunities. As a result of the resources that we have at Northern, most of our graduates obtain jobs after passing the bar. Although, several students obtain jobs before. However, most students have jobs or internships during the summer after completing their second year.

Quality of Life

Status: Alumnus/a, full-time
Dates of Enrollment: 8/1998-5/2001
Survey Submitted: April 2006

NIU Law is located in DeKalb, IL, which is approximately 65 miles west of Chicago. The county is rural although DeKalb has plenty of strip malls, restaurants and bars. The university, the main employer in the area, is surrounded by residential areas that are mixed students and permanent residents. The downtown is within walking distance from campus as are several drinking and eating establishments. The law school is located in a magnificent building on campus, with newly renovated classrooms, including a new "smart" courtroom that employs all the latest in technological wonders. The overall environment at the law school is very comfortable; students often hang out studying, visiting, sleeping. There is seemingly abundant housing, the procurement of which admissions will assist. Some law students opt to live on campus in the dorms.

Status: Alumnus/a, full-time
Dates of Enrollment: 8/2002-5/2005
Survey Submitted: April 2006

One word: balance. At NIU Law, you can balance your education with family, work, and other obligations. Although the curriculum is demanding, the faculty at NIU Law understands that your life is not just just within the walls of the law school. NIU Law provides a supportive community in which students can get an excellent education without having to give up their entire life. I had classmates that worked part time, had young children at home, had spouses living far away, were entering into their second career and those (like myself) that came straight from undergrad, bright eyed and completely clueless. The community at NIU Law catered to all of us and made it possible for each of us to have a unique experience that suited our lifestyle.

Status: Current student, full-time
Dates of Enrollment: 8/2004-Submit Date
Survey Submitted: April 2006

I live off campus (being a non-traditional student), so I have no information regarding housing. The campus is a good size: large enough not to feel limited, but not so large as to be lost. The administration has been repairing the law school for the last year or so, and there have been a lot of updates made. As with any campus town, there is crime. The DeKalb (city) Police Department and the DeKalb County Sheriff Department work well with the NIU Campus Police (not rent-a-cops, but actual police officers) to provide safety to students, residents and visitors. This is not to say that the neighborhood is bad or that there is a lot of crime, because there isn't. Being outside of Chicago dramatically reduces the incidence of crime.

Status: Alumnus/a, full-time
Dates of Enrollment: 8/2002-5/2005
Survey Submitted: April 2006

My best friends in law school are still my best friends post-graduation. Due to the small size of each class, it is possible to have some sort of interaction with each person in the class. The law school is very involved in intermural athletics on campus, the law students are Thursday night regulars at the local bars, and DeKalb is constantly expanding (a shopping mall is the next big future development). The campus is safe, and the cost of living is low. It is easy to find housing, even at the last minute.

Status: Alumnus/a, full-time
Dates of Enrollment: 8/1995-5/1998
Survey Submitted: April 2006

Quality of Life on campus is excellent. NIU is 60 minutes from downtown Chicago and some students even commute from the city. I would not recommend this as with traffic the commute can be much longer. There is plenty of housing off campus that caters to older students. NIU is considered somewhat of a commuter school so the campus tends to get very quiet on weekends. This is great for studying.

The university has over 25,000 students and has all the facilities associated with a large university. Some of the highlights include a great library, recreation center, support services and dining opportunities. The campus dining halls are large and varied. Food can be delivered 24 hours a day from off-campus restaurants.

Status: Current student, full-time
Dates of Enrollment: 8/2005-Submit Date
Survey Submitted: April 2006

I love DeKalb and Northern Illinois so this is a perfect fit for me. DeKalb is a small farm town with a university in it. As a result, it's small enough to be small, but still has decent shopping and restaurants. NIU is a great place to have a family; it's got small town feel but plenty of focus and tax dollars for things like decent libraries and elementary schools.

Status: Current student, full-time
Dates of Enrollment: 8/2004-Submit Date
Survey Submitted: April 2006

Quiet environment...ideal for a law student.

Read all of Vault's Law School Surveys at www.vault.com/lawschool — get complete surveys on top law schools, expert advice on applicaton essays, LSAT prep and more.

VAULT CAREER LIBRARY   223

Status: Current student, full-time
Dates of Enrollment: 8/2003-Submit Date
Survey Submitted: April 2005

The law school has undergone numerous upgrades, but is still in bad shape in many areas. Crime and safety are not bad, but when there have been incidents the law school has not done much to remedy them or make sure the [students are] aware of the incidents as far as further prevention goes.

Status: Current student, full-time
Dates of Enrollment: 8/2003-Submit Date
Survey Submitted: April 2005

The town is a very nice small town. There are not a lot of activities like theater or music available, but Chicago is only an hour away. The environment is conducive for studying because of the limited distractions. The housing is typical for a college town. There is limited crime. There isn't a lot of variety for dining but all of the basics are available.

Status: Current student, full-time
Dates of Enrollment: 8/2002-Submit Date
Survey Submitted: April 2005

DeKalb is a great place to attend school for several reasons. First, the neighborhoods are fairly quiet. Second, the cost of living is reasonable. Third, there is a fairly low crime rate. A majority of the houses and apartments are spacious and beautiful. There is always security patroling the neighborhoods. And the police are always right behind them.

Status: Current student, full-time
Dates of Enrollment: 8/2003-Submit Date
Survey Submitted: April 2005

DeKalb, IL is a college town so there is plenty of housing for law students near the school. Additionally, many students commute from the surrounding cities. Also NIU has university-owned apartments made specifically available for law students. DeKalb is growing as a city and as a result entertainment and dining choices in the area are increasing. The law school building is in the middle of campus near the student center and the financial aid and main campus registration offices. However, the law school has its own financial aid and registration office. DeKalb is a reasonably safe community.

 Social Life

Status: Alumnus/a, full-time
Dates of Enrollment: 8/2002-5/2005
Survey Submitted: April 2006

If you're looking to be social, you won't be dissapointed. There are a lot of clubs and activities to get involved with and there is always something going on. One favorite of students is the Friday Bar Review where the Student Bar Association provides beer and pizza at a local bar on Friday afternoon for students and faculty—a great way to get to know your professors and fellow classmates! Other favorites include the Dean's picnic in the fall, the annual Halloween party and the spring formal.

The international law society has a wine tasting that's always a hit, in addition to the lunches and dinners hosted by the Italian Law Students, Latino Law Students, and Black Law Students Societies. There are also law fraternity socials, and of course the Public Interest Law Society Auction where you get to have cocktails in the law school library and schmooze with alumni. The students at NIU Law work hard, but they also know how to relax and have fun. It's a great balance!

Status: Alumnus/a, full-time
Dates of Enrollment: 8/2002-5/2005
Survey Submitted: April 2006

The law fraternities are active in social and philanthropic events. There are opportunities for fraternity members to travel to national conferences, all-expenses paid. Alumni provide fraternity members with scholarships, and 2Ls and 3Ls offer study sessions for the 1Ls before exams. Outline banks are extensive in all the law fraternities. The bars are packed with law students, and there is live entertainment on the weekends that always draws a crowd.

Status: Alumnus/a, full-time
Dates of Enrollment: 8/2002-6/2005
Survey Submitted: April 2006

There are many local bars and restaurants in DeKalb that are frequented and serviced by NIU students. The law school holds many functions at Molly's, a local pub. There are different bands playing at all the bars every weekend—and one weekend, at a show, I met my current husband!

The law school itself provides a lot of different social opportunities. There are organizations such as the Public Interest Law Society (PILS), Delta Theta Phi, Amnesty International, and the Student Bar Association (SBA), etc. Most students joint PILS and the SBA, and one of the legal fraternities. There are also activities such as Law Review and moot court for students to participate in to gain notoriety for resume purposes.

I loved Northern and I loved DeKalb. My law school years were not just an extension of college, but an enjoyable addition to my 20s!

Status: Current student, full-time
Dates of Enrollment: 8/2003-Submit Date
Survey Submitted: April 2005

Half the students are older students, married with kids. If you're older, married with kids and want to commute then, hey this might be your school. Young, single, and looking for a nice atmosphere stick with U of I or Southern Illinois. Events are hard to really pull off when you have to be home to feed the kids. Nothing against non-traditional students, it's just reality at a small school.

Status: Current student, full-time
Dates of Enrollment: 8/2003-Submit Date
Survey Submitted: April 2005

DeKalb is a college town so there are numerous bars/clubs and restaurants. There are bars that are known to be for undergraduates and there are those that are favorites among the older/graduate student crowd. Additionally, the Greek system is very large at NIU and the law school has three legal fraternities. The bar that has been the choice of law students for the past couple of years has been Molly's. Most social events organized by student organizations are held there as well as the Student Bar Association (SBA) Bar Reviews. On any given night you can go to Molly's and find at least a few law students there. In my opinion law students seem to typically go out more during the week after classes and spend the weekends relaxing or doing homework.

Status: Current student, full-time
Dates of Enrollment: 8/2003-Submit Date
Survey Submitted: April 2005

The law school provides a number of social events for the students to get to know each other and the professors. The bars seem like frat bars or towny bars. There is little in between the two. The Greek system for the undergrads is very active and a few of the law students are in contact with the Greek houses that they were in during their undergrad (I am not involved in this and cannot give details). The social life at the school can be whatever a student wants. If a person wants to be social the opportunities are there, but if a person is not into that scene the town is peaceful and offers some alternatives.

 The School Says

As the only public law school in the greater Chicago area, the Northern Illinois University College of Law was founded on a core belief that a high quality, challenging legal education should not be cost prohibitive. NIU Law has built a proud tradition of graduating students not only skilled in legal knowledge and practice, but also imbued with a high degree of community responsibility, committed to serving the needs of a diverse and ever-changing society. In and out of the classroom, we seek to promote the formation of lifelong bonds among students, faculty, and administration.

Diversity

NIU Law is a place where a diverse society is valued and reflected in our student body, faculty, and administration. *U.S. News & World Report* ranks NIU Law among the top 20 percent of law schools for diversity. Approximately one-third of our students are minorities and one-half are female. NIU Law ranked Number Four in the nation for most diverse faculty in the 2006 *Princeton Review* rankings and Number Four in the nation as the most welcoming of older students in its 2005 rankings.

Academic Programs

The first year program emphasizes the development of analytical skills, legal reasoning, research, and writing. Second and third year students may choose from extensive elective offerings, essentially designing individualized curriculums. Students benefit from an extraordinary level of interaction and accessibility to faculty and administration. Small class sizes and low student-to-faculty ratio preserve an identity and intimacy for students far more typical of a private college than a law school associated with a major public university. Outside the classroom, NIU Law provides students with a variety of both theoretical and experiential educational opportunities through practical skills courses and Clinical and Externship programs. Students also have an opportunity to study abroad in Agen, France.

Facilities

NIU Law is housed in Swen Parson Hall, an impressive Gothic structure on the University's DeKalb campus. NIU Law offers students the latest in technology-based advocacy training through its state-of-the-art facility, the Kenneth C. Chessick Legal Skills Training Center; fewer than 5 percent of law schools across the nation have facilities of this type. Recently renovated "smart" classrooms feature multimedia instruction tools and desks outfitted with power and wireless network access for laptop computers. The Francis X. Riley Courtroom, which serves primarily as a classroom, also plays host to nationally known speakers and actual proceedings argued before the United States Court of Appeals and the Illinois Court of Appeals. Finally, the David C. Shapiro Memorial Law Library provides one of the best ratios of library resources to students.

Employment

Approximately 94 percent of the Class of 2005 obtained employment within nine months of graduation. Graduates work across the United States and in many other countries, including China, Lithuania, Spain, the Philippines, and Germany. Our graduates' debt load continues to be less than half of the national average, affording graduates the freedom of professional choice. Approximately 30 percent of graduates go into public sector/public interest jobs each year. More than 50 of our alumni serve as judges.

NIU Law provides a broad-based educational experience taught in an atmosphere of shared goals and achievements. Come discover the difference.

Read all of Vault's Law School Surveys at www.vault.com/lawschool — get complete surveys on top law schools, expert advice on applicaton essays, LSAT prep and more.

V∧ULT CAREER LIBRARY **225**

Northwestern University School of Law

357 East Chicago Avenue
Rubloff Building, Room 160
Chicago, IL 60611-3069
Admissions phone: (312) 503-8465
Admissions e-mail: admissions@law.northwestern.edu
Admissions URL:
http://www.law.northwestern.edu/admissions/

 ## Admissions

Status: Current student, full-time
Dates of Enrollment: 8/2003-Submit Date
Survey Submitted: April 2006

Smooth as butter. The interviews let you get your real-life personality out on the table, the traditional application gets your intellect and academics in full view. It's a nice, rounded picture, and the admissions staff values the full thing—all of you, not just your grades. So if you have a good persona, come show it off.

Status: Current student, full-time
Dates of Enrollment: 8/2004-Submit Date
Survey Submitted: April 2006

Northwestern likes to take well-rounded, social students. If you're coming straight from undergrad, you'd better be a superstar, or else they won't want you. Almost everyone here has at least a couple of years of work experience behind them, and it makes for an interesting, diverse class. As for the interview, request one early so that you can be sure to get one in your area, and just be yourself—Northwestern doesn't like cutthroat workaholics. Apply early—you have a better chance of getting in. And don't freak out if you get waitlisted—I know several people who are here because they got off the waitlist shortly before school started.

Status: Current student, full-time
Dates of Enrollment: 8/2004-Submit Date
Survey Submitted: April 2006

More than any other school I applied to, Northwestern consistently showed an interest in candidates as individuals. Clearly, they want students with good credentials (LSAT, undergraduate GPA) and writing skills, but they also communicated that they wanted a class of interesting individuals with diverse life experiences. My classmates certainly fulfill that requirement, and it makes for a much more interesting environment (in and out of the classroom).

Status: Current student, full-time
Dates of Enrollment: 8/2003-Submit Date
Survey Submitted: March 2006

The admissions office is looking for work experience, now accepting almost exclusively students with one year or more. This is not to say you can't get in without one, but the rest of your record will have to be impressive (or you'll have to have some special quality they are looking for to complete their incoming class). Northwestern still tries to interview all applicants. One friend recently told me that she believes it is the interview that got her in, where her application otherwise may have been rejected. However, I never had an interview and was admitted without any problems.

Status: Current student, full-time
Dates of Enrollment: 8/2004-Submit Date
Survey Submitted: March 2006

I really appreciated the effort that Northwestern Law made to interview applicants. It was certainly a marked difference from other law schools, where the message is, "Don't call us, we'll call you."

Status: Current student, full-time
Dates of Enrollment: 8/2004-Submit Date
Survey Submitted: March 2006

Application—there is one required essay and three optional ones. I did all four to show my commitment to the school. Our dean cares about maturity, work experience, and diversity. These attributes should come through. I devoted an entire essay to work experience exclusively.

In the interview, I think the admissions staff is looking for sincerity, commitment to social justice, maturity, work experience and personality. It lasts about 30 minutes—don't be too serious—it's OK to laugh. My interviewer went to my undergraduate school and worked for the school paper, *The Daily Illini*, so in my thank you note (via e-mail) I wrote in the subject line: "*DI* reporter brings hard-hitting questions." Just be yourself. They ask the standard questions—why do you want to come to law school, why do you want to come to Northwestern. Know something about the school that isn't on the web site. I think it's a good idea to visit the school or e-mail some students and try to talk to some people.

Status: Current student, full-time
Dates of Enrollment: 8/2005-Submit Date
Survey Submitted: March 2006

I applied as a transfer student, so I don't have much insight here. All I can say is that the interview actually seems to make a difference for Northwestern Law. In addition, the school really pays attention to the backgrounds of students and looks beyond numbers, in contrast to most law schools. They look for people with job experience: business background or other interesting things you have done prior to law school. You can compensate for lower LSAT scores or GPAs by having an interesting resume and having a personality at the interview.

Status: Current student, full-time
Dates of Enrollment: 8/2005-Submit Date
Survey Submitted: March 2006

Evidently extremely selective, however, in addition to grades/LSAT scores, Northwestern is becoming more of a national school, so they're accepting more people from California, Florida, Texas, etc. They put a huge emphasis on strong work experience and interpersonal skills. Get some experience, rock the LSAT, schedule an interview (it's a huge part of the process, unlike at other schools), and dress nice, be interesting. In your essay, if you like writing, emphasize that writing is what you spend an awful lot of time doing.

Status: Current student, full-time
Dates of Enrollment: 8/2005-Submit Date
Survey Submitted: March 2006

Northwestern has a separate essay about why you want to attend it specifically. This is a key essay—take the time and do research about the programs, faculty members, etc. I applied twice to the law school and had a horrible first interview and did not make much of my application, but the second year, my interviewer was terrific and told me about all of these specific programs that I would be interested in based on my work experience and I used those programs in the essay. Northwestern is hard on the LSATs but only looks at the best score so there is nothing to lose by taking the test again. They ended up rejecting me a second time before receiving my updated scores the second year, but I wrote to the admissions office and made my case, and they finally accepted me. Persistence pays off.

Status: Current student, full-time
Dates of Enrollment: 8/2005-Submit Date
Survey Submitted: March 2006

I received a letter from Northwestern inviting me to apply based on the information provided to them from LSAC. I scheduled a local interview (which I would encourage anyone interested in doing to do so EARLY, as it takes them a while to get back to you with the information) and had my application complete by the end of December. Before the end of January, I'd received my acceptance. I was very happy with their prompt response and the amount of information that the school provided upon acceptance. I also recommend the Admitted Students' Day—lots of helpful information and a great opportunity to really get a sense of what the school is all about.

Status: Current student, full-time
Dates of Enrollment: 9/2003-Submit Date
Survey Submitted: March 2006

Northwestern School of Law is very much focused on creating a student body that is collegial and that is diverse not only in race, gender, sexuality, religion, etc., but in interests as well. When writing an application essay, it is important that the student be him or herself and that the student express his/her interests and accomplishments that might set him/her apart. Northwestern does require an interview. So long as you are yourself during the interview and are not so business like that you lose your uniqueness, you should do well and the interview should play to your advantage. Northwestern is very selective. Each year, the average LSAT gets higher and the incoming class gets more accomplished. Those that have work experience and are older have a better chance of getting in.

Status: Current student, full-time
Dates of Enrollment: 9/2004-Submit Date
Survey Submitted: March 2005

The Northwestern Law admissions process is highly distinguishable from any other top law school because they are the only top law school to personally interview applicants. While one may often have a difficult time explaining certain aspects of her/his credentials within the confines of a short written statement, one's qualifications become imminently clearer when (s)he is able to look an interviewer in the eye and talk about them. Each day that I interact with my classmates, I become more convinced that the quality of student at Northwestern Law is significantly enhanced by the fact that most of my classmates were interviewed.

Status: Current student, full-time
Dates of Enrollment: 8/2002-Submit Date
Survey Submitted: March 2005

Northwestern takes a business school approach to admitting students and it pays off. Work experience is a must and you must be able to interview well which includes good grooming. Everyone is extremely qualified, but it is difficult to tell the "extras" other than work experience that the committee is looking for.

Status: Current student, full-time
Dates of Enrollment: 8/2003-Submit Date
Survey Submitted: March 2005

Candidates are well-selected. Everyone has a great background prior to coming to law school. Everyone I have had class with seems well-adjusted to school and work. Interviews are not required, but I think they only help you. The process went very quickly—acceptance following a month after I took the LSAT. Financial aid is generous, as many people I know have received grants.

Status: Current student, full-time
Dates of Enrollment: 8/2003-Submit Date
Survey Submitted: January 2004

Northwestern University is a great place to be. As a minority student, I felt that NU really, I mean really, tried hard to get me to come here. I gave up a full scholarship to another lower-tiered school because of NU's reputation and the sense of camaraderie I felt when I came for Admitted Students Weekend. Now on to real business. Dean Van Zandt's new law school strategy is to make it more like the Kellogg school's MBA program in that it is really looking for students that had two or more years of work experience. I didn't do the interview, but I hear that it is helpful in getting in.

Status: Current student, full-time JD/MBA program
Dates of Enrollment: 9/2001-Submit Date
Survey Submitted: January 2004

The JD/MBA program underwent significant changes in 2000. The application is comprised mostly of the Kellogg MBA application, along with an additional essay on "why a JD/MBA degree?" The admissions process is a challenging one, compared to law school admissions. While applicants fill out only one unified application (instead of the traditional two, one for each school), and are required to take the GMAT only (and not the LSAT, unlike almost all other

JD/MBA programs), the program admits only 15 to 20 students per year (although that number is said to increase by five or 10 within the next few years). Applications for the NU dual-degree has doubled since the program switched from a four-year to a three-year program, so the applicant must stand out in three ways: (1) outstanding record of significant work experience (since JD/MBAs are admitted to the business school, the work experience expectations are high, so you probably won't see many 22 to 24 year-olds in the program—sorry); (2) superior academic performance (including GMAT and LSAT, along with a strong GPA); and (3) outstanding communication skills as evidenced by the applicant interview and the essays. While law school applications basically require a personal statement, LSAT score, one letter of recommendation, and a transcript, the JD/MBA process is more attuned to the business school format: two or more letters of recommendation, transcript, GMAT and LSAT, [six or more letters of recommendation] and significant work experience.

The school states: "LSAT is not required for JD/MBA applicants."

Academics

Status: Current student, full-time
Dates of Enrollment: 8/2003-Submit Date
Survey Submitted: March 2006

I would say that Northwestern is not a particularly intellectual environment. By that I mean that the student population doesn't seem as interested in learning about the law as they are in learning how to make gobs of money with their shiny new JD degrees. I think this is partially because Northwestern largely admits people with years of work experience, so their main goal in attending law school seems to be to add to their capital as a worker-bee. I find this frustrating because I am kind of a nerd. That said, there are classes available that feed the intellectual curiosity of dorks like me. There are several extremely talented professors who really do push you to think about the law and society and what is right and wrong with the world.

In your second and third years you have the option of taking a class called International Team Project, where you travel to a country of your choice and do a comparative law research project. In your third year you can earn a lot of class credit by tailoring your own Senior Research project.

The Socratic Method is used by some professors but not most, and those who use it really do more of a modified Socratic thing. It's pretty rare that you get grilled by a prof (unless you have McGuiness) but it's also generally unacceptable to "pass" or give crappy answers. I'd say that as long as you engage the professor enough to let her know that you did the reading and thought about it a bit, you'll be OK. Also, since the school has wireless in every room you can send your friends the answers over IM and get them out of jams (plus you can make fun of the professors while they lecture and see which one of your friends laughs).

In general it was considered pretty uncool to be a gunner and look too prepared. If you raised your hand a lot or said the word "obviously" too much you were definitely the subject of instant messenger scorn. So overall, I'd say taking yourself too seriously and being overprepared was not a good idea.

Status: Current student, full-time
Dates of Enrollment: 8/2004-Submit Date
Survey Submitted: March 2006

First-year professors are not just smart, approachable and committed, but they are also funny. They basically have a 24-hour open-door policy in addition to ample office hours. My professors care about the subjects and they also care about the students. They stick around after class to talk to students, they know us personally within weeks of the semester starting. Some of them make it a practice to take their students out to lunch (and the professors pay.) Also, I find that the professors, in addition to being very smart, are humble. They are open to learning from student discussions. I have heard profs say "That's a great hypothetical. I'm going to use it in the next edition of the text." or "I've never thought of that problem before—it would make a good exam question."

Nature of the program—perfect mix between theoretical and practical Generally, exams have two or three fact based/issue spotting questions and one

Read all of Vault's Law School Surveys at www.vault.com/lawschool — get complete surveys on top law schools, expert advice on applicaton essays, LSAT prep and more.

VAULT CAREER LIBRARY 227

or two policy questions. It is a theoretical school—we study model rules and general federal case law (rather than the law of any specific jurisdiction) and we study the policies and rationales behind the law. On the other hand, working in the clinic, doing judicial externships or externships with federal prosecutors or defenders [can really supplement one's learning process].

Status: Current student, full-time
Dates of Enrollment: 8/2004-Submit Date
Survey Submitted: March 2006

The workload of the first year is brutal, due in large part to the writing program, which is undervalued in terms of the number of credit hours the school awards. The workload slackens dramatically after the first year, even for students who participate in Law Review and other extracurricular activities, like moot court competitions.

Status: Current student, full-time
Dates of Enrollment: 8/2005-Submit Date
Survey Submitted: March 2006

I had the most amazing professors. Almost all of my classes first semester had ungraded midterms so we could practice with such a different exam format before it actually counted. I did really badly on one, so the professor spent over half an hour doing exam strategies with me and then allowed me to take another one for practice which he spent a lot of time showing me what was better about than the first. The professors here want you to do well. They are also brilliant, I enjoy going to class to hear their perspectives on what we are studying.

Status: Current student, full-time
Dates of Enrollment: 8/2005-Submit Date
Survey Submitted: March 2006

There are four different sections and I think everyone in each section had a different experience depending on their section. The professors I had first semester were all excellent, some more than others, but the common thread between them was their approachability, understanding and patience for student frustrations and their assistance before final exams to make sure we were prepared. All of them had office hours and, with one exception, most were receptive to e-mail communications. I think that grading was very fair to my surprise. I believe I earned every grade I got and didn't feel disadvantaged.

One of the negatives of first semester was CLR, which is a very time-consuming course. Don't expect to have a lot of time to do reading and outlining for other classes when memos are due for this class. The grading for this class seemed arbitrary in some sections but my CLR professor was very helpful and fair.

Status: Current student, full-time
Dates of Enrollment: 9/2003-Submit Date
Survey Submitted: March 2006

The quality of the classes at Northwestern is excellent. The students make the real difference. Because students are older and come with varied backgrounds (from an ex-CEO of an Internet company to an engineer that invented a portable photo booth and started a company to a Pulitzer-prize winning journalist and a camera man for MTV), the students have much to bring to class discussions. Also, the increased age and maturity levels make it a friendly campus where you won't find the cutthroat competitiveness that makes other law schools so unendurable. People will offer to take notes when you are unable to make it to class and you can sit down with any group and be received in a friendly manner since people are more mature and cliques are rare.

Status: Current student, full-time JD/MBA
Dates of Enrollment: 8/2004-Submit Date
Survey Submitted: March 2006

The program is three years in duration instead of the normal four years, which is a tremendous advantage. The program is quite rigorous since school continues from the beginning of the first year (at the law school) through the summer of the first year and then through the second year (at Kellogg). There is no break, and to some extent, the summer is the most busy time due to the requirements of beginning work at Kellogg so soon after finishing over the summer.

The workload in law school is heavier than in business school in many ways, but it is very different. Law school is a very academic, reading/writing intensive, and individual exercise. Business school is extremely group-work oriented and

so just tends to involve a lot of time spent discussing issues and cases. Quality of classes is, for the most part, extremely good, though I would say I've had about 15 to 20 percent mediocre profs at both schools (relatively speaking). The exceptional professors make up for these weaker ones, however, since they are profs who can change your academic life. Grading is very structured at the law school with very strictly enforced grade distributions, which results in a more competitive environment. Kellogg has requirements as well but they are more diffused and it seems less strictly enforced. Kellogg is much more "what you want to get" from the experience, while the law school is "you will get X" from the experience.

Status: Current student, full-time
Dates of Enrollment: 8/2005-Submit Date
Survey Submitted: March 2006

First year of law school is tough no matter what, but Northwestern isn't as cutthroat as many other programs I've heard of. Students study together and share notes. Most of the professors are very nice and make time available for office hours. The faculty has such a wide range of expertise, there are all kinds of different programs and lectures happening all the time—something for everyone. Some of the popular electives can be hard to get into but again, persistence pays off—I was on the waitlist for two weeks but finally got into my top choice.

Status: Current student, full-time
Dates of Enrollment: 8/2005-Submit Date
Survey Submitted: March 2006

First-year classes have about 65 students in each class. The writing class has about 20 or 30 students. The smaller class size allows students to get to know their section better and have more interaction with the professor. In the second semester of 1L, students can actually choose a couple of electives, which cannot be done at most schools. Elective classes are done by electronic lottery. Most people can get into the classes that they want without too much of a problem. A couple of the more popular classes can be tough, but it becomes easier later since 2L and 3L students get priority in the lottery.

The workload is manageable. I treat it like a real job and usually I can get everything done between 7 a.m. and 6 p.m. Occasionally I have to read in the night to catch up, especially around timing of papers or exams, which is a little more hectic. Some people do less work than this and are fine. Some people are crazy and work all the time—ignore them, a lot of their time is just spinning their wheels.

Status: Current student, full-time
Dates of Enrollment: 8/2005-Submit Date
Survey Submitted: March 2006

The workload at Northwestern is very reasonable. Few students feel overwhelmed by academics. On the other hand, the faculty, for the most part, is outstanding. The law school has a tendency to rely on adjunct professors to teach some courses which can be a disadvantage since these professors do not have as much experience. But they have an excellent faculty over all and the professors here take teaching seriously.

The curriculum at NW sets itself apart in that in addition to the typical first-year schedule of contracts, torts, etc., the students take at least one bi-disciplinary class (e.g., education and the law). There is also a strong emphasis on legal writing the first year. Like most schools, you have more flexibility your second and third year. The trial advocacy program is first rate and very popular. The legal clinic is also very well run and respected. One thing that is also unique about Northwestern is that there are clinical-type classes for students interested in transactional work as well. I took a "start up" class where we learned the benefits of different entity types (LLC vs. corp., etc.), drafted an operating agreement, dealt with employment issues and other issues facing new companies.

Status: Current student, full-time
Dates of Enrollment: 8/2004-Submit Date
Survey Submitted: March 2005

The program is extremely challenging. And I feel the need to qualify this by saying that I have always been a hard worker and an avid reader, and I graduated from an Ivy League college with a GPA of 3.87. Still, my GPA after one semester here is about a 2.7. This is despite working well over 12 hours a day and consuming mass quantities of caffeine. I knew law school would be difficult. However, I was certainly not prepared for exactly how demanding this program would be, especially in light of the year I spent supporting my boyfriend through his first year at Harvard Law. There is no question that 1Ls at Northwestern have more work than their Harvard counterparts.

Status: Current student, full-time
Dates of Enrollment: 8/2002-Submit Date
Survey Submitted: October 2003

Northwestern Law School has grown 15 to 20 percent in the last two years alone. Students are bearing the consequences of the strategic decision to grow. There are more grade-curved classes and less slots for clinics, and it is more difficult to get into popular classes (Introduction to Trial Advocacy with Steve Lubet and Securities Regulation with David Ruder are two of those classes).

Northwestern has a renowned Clinical and Trial Advocacy Program. The efforts of the Center on Wrongful Convictions were largely responsible for then-Governor George Ryan's decision to commute the death sentence of all death-row inmates in Illinois in 2003. The trial advocacy program recruits top practitioners in Chicago to work with students on various facets of the trial process, providing individualized and in-depth critiques of students' performances in various trial-related exercises.

Status: Current student, full-time
Dates of Enrollment: 8/2003-Submit Date
Survey Submitted: January 2004

When you come here be prepared to work. NO, I DON'T THINK YOU HEARD ME. BE PREPARED TO WORK! I, for some reason, felt that law school was a wonderful place for the exchange of ideas and rhetoric. It is all of those things, but make no mistakes—the curve here is brutal. Everyone is smart. So, as I have come to learn by painful experience...THE UNDERGRAD CRAM SESSIONS ARE NOT ENOUGH TO GET AN A.

The people here are so collegial and genuinely fun, I seem to have forgotten about the curve. It's not that I didn't do well, but a lot of people did better! The professors are pretty topnotch. My Civ Pro and Contracts professors were right on target, but my Torts and Criminal Law professors taught more theory-based courses. They taught using law and economics and the MPC respectively. Not very practical Black Letter Law stuff, but interesting anyway, and L&E does seem to come up in other courses as well.

 Employment Prospects

Status: Current student, full-time
Dates of Enrollment: 8/2004-Submit Date
Survey Submitted: April 2006

Northwestern attracts very prestigious employers, from all over the country. Some students perceive this to be a very Midwestern school, and while it's true that a large percentage of alumni choose to stay in Chicago, I think that's more the result of their growing to love the city during their time here than anything else. I interviewed in two East Coast cities and felt that my access to employers in both locations was comparable to what my friends at East Coast law schools had.

Status: Current student, full-time
Dates of Enrollment: 8/2003-Submit Date
Survey Submitted: March 2006

I think that the best thing about Northwestern has been the ease I've had in getting a job for after graduation. The school has a great deal of prestige and thus can tell employers that they have to interview everyone at the school according to a blind lottery system. This is in comparison with other schools that only let the top 10 percent of the class participate in on-campus interviewing. There is no real OCI for 1Ls so you are on your own for that, but I didn't have a problem getting an unpaid job in sports law. I think getting a firm job was a bit trickier, but I'm not sure since I wasn't interested in that. For my second summer I worked at a firm that interviewed me through OCI. Because I ended up changing my mind about location and deciding to stay in Chicago I did OCI

again as a 3L, which is pretty rare. I was able to secure employment for after graduation this way. Most of my friends are going to be working at large- or medium-sized firms here in the city. A number of others will do clerkships first.

Status: Current student, full-time
Dates of Enrollment: 8/2004-Submit Date
Survey Submitted: March 2006

Public interest students have ample prospects too. Funding is great. Almost anyone who want to do public interest can get $5,000 for a summer job, regardless of what year. Post-graduation funding is good too. We have a career advisor who is solely dedicated to public interest, and the professors are good resources too.

Status: Current student, full-time
Dates of Enrollment: 8/2005-Submit Date
Survey Submitted: March 2006

Good employment prospects. Few students have trouble finding a job, and Northwestern has a considerable reach beyond the Midwest. It used to be a mainly regional school but today, lots of students find jobs outside the Midwest. Mainly California, D.C. and New York, but also Atlanta, Texas, the Northeast and, of course, major placements in Chicago and the Midwest.

Status: Current student, full-time
Dates of Enrollment: 8/2005-Submit Date
Survey Submitted: March 2006

At graduation, 95+ percent of graduates have jobs lined up. Most graduates have an average of two or three offers to choose from. This is important because at that point most people are choosing the best offer among good offers, rather than being forced to take the only offer they have whether they really like it or not.

Alumni mentors are available in the area and market that you are interested in. Unfortunately, there can be more students than mentors, so some people (like me) got left out on that opportunity. Still, a good opportunity to get solid advice and help with resumes and interviewing.

Status: Current student, full-time
Dates of Enrollment: 9/2003-Submit Date
Survey Submitted: March 2006

Northwestern School of Law is an asset when it comes to finding a job. Employers KNOW Northwestern whether you are interviewing on the East or West Coast (trust me, I did both). Getting a 3.2 or a 3.0 at Northwestern still makes you a great job candidate while at other lesser ranked schools, having a 3.2 could kill your chances of getting a job. TONS of employers come to NU to hire students and for those that don't, having NU on your resume makes you a job candidate that they want to interview. The career center does a great job of lining up networking events and the alumni network at Northwestern is always helpful. Internships during school are plentiful—with judges, firms, etc.—and can be taken for credit. Second and third year, you can work part time for pay at one of the many firms in Chicago.

Status: Current student, full-time JD/MBA
Dates of Enrollment: 8/2004-Submit Date
Survey Submitted: March 2006

To my knowledge, all of the persons in my class got almost exactly the job offers they wanted for the summer. This includes the Top 10 law firms in the country, the Top Three consulting firms in the world, and the top investment banks in the world. One person even got an internship with a major league baseball team. Frankly, firms and companies drool over hiring a JD-MBA from Northwestern, and it's even more powerful than I believed when I enrolled. To my experience, a JD-MBA can get away with having somewhat lower grades than a JD- or MBA-only student and still get an offer. Graduates from the program tend to split about 50-50 between law firms and business jobs (consulting and I-banking tend to dominate on this side). Alumni are very tight-knit and willing to help a ton with the job search.

Status: Alumnus/a, full-time
Dates of Enrollment: 9/1998-5/2001
Survey Submitted: March 2006

I can't think of a single top-tier law firm that does not come to on-campus interviews at Northwestern. The job prospects are very good if you do

Read all of Vault's Law School Surveys at www.vault.com/lawschool — get complete surveys on top law schools, expert advice on application essays, LSAT prep and more.

VAULT CAREER LIBRARY   229

reasonably well your first year. The on-campus interview program is run very well and I believe now it occurs before school begins in August so as not to interfere as much with classes. Many graduates also attain prestigious clerkships and government positions.

Status: Alumnus/a, full-time
Dates of Enrollment: 9/1998-5/2001
Survey Submitted: March 2006

You should be able to walk out of your second-year first semester with a good idea about your job at graduation. The alumni network is great—the on-campus interviewing for large- and mid-size firms as well as some government agencies is organized and efficient. The employers are topnotch. It is tough to be a C or low B student at NU because everyone is incredibly hard working and smart— but even the students with lower grades usually get a few offers.

Status: Alumnus/a, full-time LLM
Dates of Enrollment: 8/1996-6/1997
Survey Submitted: March 2006

Northwestern University School of Law is a Top 15 law school in the U.S., with a very impressive history and reputation. The only member of the U.S. Supreme Court who is not a graduate from Harvard is from Northwestern: he is Justice Stevens, the "doyen" of the Court. Graduates of the School of Law are welcome in all legal professions both in the U.S. and abroad. Also, Chicago is an excellent place for being a summer associate in the summer vacations with plenty of opportunities at federal and state government, courts, law firms, and other companies.

Status: Alumnus/a, full-time
Dates of Enrollment: 9/2002-6/2005
Survey Submitted: March 2006

Attending NU provided a door into every employer I wanted; I never felt that if I had gone to Yale/Harvard I would have had a better shot at a certain job. Everyone complains about the career placement people at schools but the ones at NU actually do a pretty good job.

Status: Current student, full-time
Dates of Enrollment: 9/2002-Submit Date
Survey Submitted: November 2003

This is an elite school that has a growing national reputation. Other than Wachtell, Covington and I think Gibson Dunn, every firm in the country worth mentioning comes to our on-campus interviewing season. Especially if you want to work in Chicago, a NU degree is gold, but even in other cities you can get really plum jobs (e.g., three or four people in my class are going to Cravath next summer). With the downturn in the economy the placement rate for 2Ls seems to be something less than 100 percent, but most people in my class seem to have good offers to choose from for next summer. The school's location in downtown Chicago makes for wonderful internship opportunities with judges, prosecutors'/public defenders' offices and all kinds of public interest placements. Many of these will give you course credit.

Status: Alumnus/a, full-time
Dates of Enrollment: 9/1997-5/2000
Survey Submitted: April 2004

100 percent of my graduating class was employed by graduation. The career services office is devoted to helping students find interesting jobs, and to guide them through the process of getting those jobs. They conduct "mock" interviews on campus to help students get a feel for interviewing, and they have a network of alumni who sign up to review students' resumes and provide them with job searching tips. The office is very well organized and extremely helpful. The prestige of the school makes it very easy for students to sell themselves to employers.

Quality of Life

Status: Current student, full-time
Dates of Enrollment: 8/2003-Submit Date
Survey Submitted: March 2006

My quality of life has been pretty great actually. I don't mean to suggest that law school isn't a lot of work, because it is a huge time commitment. Between classes, journal participation, looking for a job and other extracurricular activities it is easy to feel spread thin. But the flip side is that you are still living the student lifestyle which means getting up at noon and going out almost every night. My first year was great because I lived in the dorms (which are now condemned for being old and general crappiness) and got to meet a ton of other people who also enjoyed living like college students. Eating meals together and living close to campus made it very easy to make fast friends. I chose to stay close to campus for my second and third years because I don't like getting up any earlier than I have to. I think this area is pretty safe except a 1L got beat up pretty bad sort of near campus recently. But overall I feel safe walking home to my apartment at night. Campus police are very nice and fast-acting. However, the administration is pretty bureaucratic and at times deceitful when dealing with certain issues that have arisen.

Status: Current student, full-time JD/MBA
Dates of Enrollment: 8/2004-Submit Date
Survey Submitted: March 2006

I love the program and would not trade it for anything. The first year is the most intense, but pressures ease up after that. The food options at the law school are bad, especially in comparison with Kellogg, but there is a lot of external options within a short walking distance of the law school.

Status: Current student, full-time
Dates of Enrollment: 8/2005-Submit Date
Survey Submitted: March 2006

There is no on-campus housing, but the off-campus market is reasonable, especially compared to other big cities like NY, D.C., Boston, L.A., San Fran, etc. A lot of students live very close to school their first year but find that the neighborhoods a little further out are much more fun (and your commute is usually only 15 or 20 minutes to these places). The neighborhood the school is in is fine for school, working, and shopping, but it can be a bit boring and sterile to live there. The nearby neighborhoods like Wicker Park, Bucktown, Lincoln Park, Hyde Park, Lakeview, Wrigleyville, Andersonville, etc. are more residential and have a lot more fun things to do. You will have time to do some fun things while studying law here.

The campus is relatively safe considering the big city setting. The school is in a nice neighborhood downtown, right next to the "Magnificent Mile" shopping district where a lot of tourists and natives come to shop. The city cannot afford to tolerate a lot of crime in this area so the crimes tend to be small stuff like car break-ins and such. Some laptops have been stolen when people left them out in the open, but it's easy to get a lock for the laptop or just remember not to leave it out in the open unattended.

Dining at the university is virtually nonexistent but there are tons of places nearby where students can eat for cheap. There is a small cafe in the basement but it's not that good. There are fridges downstairs for people who want to bring a lunch. There are "lunch trucks" that stop by every day at noon — not necessarily healthy but you can get a good meal with drink and chips or side for $5. There are sandwich, barbeque, Indian and pasta options with the lunch trucks.

Status: Current student, full-time
Dates of Enrollment: 8/2005-Submit Date
Survey Submitted: March 2006

Most people live in the Streeterville or Lakeview. I lived in the North Loop. My best advice is to live downtown, at least in your first year, but make sure you are either right near school (there are a handful of apartment complexes and condos a few blocks from school) or find a place that is only one bus ride away from campus. I had the hassle of having to work with multiple buses to get to campus and it was a huge drain on my time. Downtown is pretty safe as long as you are no further south than the North Loop. There are tons of restaurants and shopping out groceries are difficult to get if you don't live near the new Dominick's in Streeterville.

Status: Current student, full-time
Dates of Enrollment: 9/2003-Submit Date
Survey Submitted: March 2006

The quality of life at Northwestern is unsurpassable. It truly is a community and people care about one another. Housing is plentiful—whether you choose to live on the Lakefront within walking distance to the school or in many of the downtown neighborhoods such as Lincoln Park, Lakeview or Rogers Park. If you want to live in a true suburb, you can live in Evanston since a free shuttle runs from the undergrad campus to the law school hourly. The campus is great—the buildings are centralized and located steps from the Magnificent Mile and Water Tower Place. Being in downtown Chicago, the courthouse, major law firms and other employment opportunities and observational opportunities for classwork are a train ride or cab ride away.

Status: Current student, full-time
Dates of Enrollment: 8/2005-Submit Date
Survey Submitted: March 2006

The school is in the heart of downtown and has pretty views of Lake Michigan from some of the classrooms. There's a nice little park across the street to take a breather (when it's not too cold). The classrooms are nicely maintained, there is a lot of seating in the atrium and the library (med students come to work because it's nicer than the med school) and there's pretty good wireless connection everywhere. The only downside is the gym, which is small and in the basement of a nearby building (unless you want to take the bus up to the beautiful gym on the Evanston campus). Housing is all off campus and people live all over the city. Transportation is convenient with numerous buses and the red line train nearby. I walk around the neighborhood late at night and have never had any safety concerns.

Status: Current student, full-time
Dates of Enrollment: 8/2004-Submit Date
Survey Submitted: March 2006

Northwestern has the best urban law school campus in the country (at least among the Top 20 law schools—but maybe among all law schools). Completely separate from the suburban undergrad campus up in Evanston (both an advantage and a disadvantage), the law school is located in arguably the most desirable real estate in Chicago. The library gives unobstructed views of Lake Michigan which cannot be beat. The campus is a few blocks from the famous Magnificent Mile of Michigan Avenue. The only drawback is that the area around the school doesn't have a neighborhood feel.

Status: Current student, full-time
Dates of Enrollment: 8/2005-Submit Date
Survey Submitted: March 2006

There are no longer student dorms, so everyone needs to find their own apartment. There is, however, a student organization (Student Space) which can help facilitate incoming students' apartment search. The campus is in a fantastic location, right downtown; my only complaint is that some of the classrooms have poor wireless access, but we've been told that the administration is working to fix that.

Status: Current student, full-time
Dates of Enrollment: 8/2003-Submit Date
Survey Submitted: October 2005

The school is located right downtown in a great location, but housing nearby is not the cheapest the city has to offer. Students do live in a few popular buildings right near school and also in various neighborhoods throughout the city. There is easy access to the L or buses and a UPass for this transit is provided to all students each semester. Parking passes are also available for those who live further from campus. Crime in the neighborhood is minimal, although being in a large city, there will always be some incidents.

Status: Current student, full-time
Dates of Enrollment: 8/2002-Submit Date
Survey Submitted: March 2005

I would bet that the quality of life at Northwestern rivals any law school in the country. The increased emphasis on group work and student interaction, and an admissions process that focuses more on personality and life experience than other law schools, leads to a friendlier, more mature, less cutthroat, and happier student body. I transferred from a lower ranked law school to Northwestern after my first year, and while students at my first school were scratching and clawing at each other to finish with a better GPA, most students at Northwestern are friendly, cooperative, and not interested in stabbing one another in the back to finish with a higher GPA. Sure, there are gunners, but I bet that there are less at Northwestern than almost anywhere else.

Status: Current student, full-time
Dates of Enrollment: 8/2003-Submit Date
Survey Submitted: March 2005

Northwestern is the kinder, gentler law school. Seriously. The people here are friendly, respectful, intelligent, and just plain nice to one another. I expected to attend a school which was similar to Scott Turow's Harvard in *1L*. Northwestern is the polar opposite. People here share notes and outlines, they will help you out with questions, and aren't selfish with resources. Mean and bitterly competitive people do not do well here, simply because no one will tolerate that sort of behavior.

One downside is that the law school's immediate neighborhood is very expensive, and unless you are a trust-fund baby you can forget buying a home in the neighborhood. Renting a one-bedroom apartment in the neighborhood will set you back between $900 and $1,500 a month, not including utilities. Parking is a pain and also very expensive. On the upside, the university is close to many different sources of public transportation. After this year, there will be no dorm facilities, but this is no huge loss. The costs of the dorms were very high for students, with a very limited cost-benefit analysis. More than 80 percent of students lived off campus their first year, with nearly all off campus by second year. Now the dorms won't be available, so if you come here, don't count on getting cheap housing through the university.

 **Social Life**

Status: Current student, full-time
Dates of Enrollment: 8/2004-Submit Date
Survey Submitted: April 2006

Great social life, but remember that this is an elite school, so socioeconomic background varies from "upper middle class" to "insanely rich with multiple mansions." However, because students tend to be a little older, the overall maturity and conversation levels are MUCH higher than at other law schools, even the top ones. People also tend to be more laid back, because they have more perspective—there are gunners, but not nearly as many as you would expect at a place like this. The dating scene is very good—opportunities abound for everything from random hookups to engagements. That said, married and engaged students are welcome out at the bars. Bar Review is on Thursdays, and is generally accompanied by crowds of drunk 3Ls and 2Ls who are amused by drunk 1Ls.

Status: Current student, full-time
Dates of Enrollment: 8/2004-Submit Date
Survey Submitted: April 2006

Awesome social life—the school is very committed to the social lives of its students. Timmy O' Toole's and Streeters are neighborhood favorites, but we like to try out different neighborhoods and different types of places (though crappy Irish pubs tend to dominate—with cheap beer specials, it's hard to say no. This past Bar Review was at a place in Lincoln Park with $1 beers. No joke. It was fantastic.) Restaurants around school are kind of lacking, but you've got the rest of the city at your disposal.

Status: Current student, full-time
Dates of Enrollment: 8/2004-Submit Date
Survey Submitted: March 2006

Post finals parties—last year was Cinco de Mayo and all the 1Ls went out for Mexican food and Margaritas. It was so fun. Then we met up with the rest of the school at Joe's, where we traditionally have the first and last Bar Review of the year. It's a huge place, big enough for the whole school, and a great dance floor.

Read all of Vault's Law School Surveys at www.vault.com/lawschool — get complete surveys on top law schools, expert advice on applicaton essays, LSAT prep and more.

VAULT CAREER LIBRARY   231

Status: Current student, full-time JD/MBA
Dates of Enrollment: 9/2005-Submit Date
Survey Submitted: March 2006

Students are more mature than those of other law schools (in terms of work and life experience), as Northwestern generally requires post-graduation experience for admission. As a result, work-life balance is good, and the wide variety of people make for many intimate sub-communities.

Status: Current student, full-time
Dates of Enrollment: 9/2005-Submit Date
Survey Submitted: March 2006

I'm married (and so are a lot of other Northwestern students), so I can't speak with great authority on the dating scene except to say that my single friends have seemed to have little trouble meeting people and going on dates—and they're not all dating people who go to Northwestern! There are bars and restaurants within walking distance of the campus, but every student also gets a free transit pass so going out in other neighborhoods is popular. Frankly, because Chicago is such a big city, with a large young professional population, students at Northwestern have a lot of fun just being in the city. The school definitely encourages that.

Status: Current student, full-time
Dates of Enrollment: 8/2005-Submit Date
Survey Submitted: March 2006

There are tons of school organizations to get involved with very early on. The main group I was involved in was the Asian Pacific Law Students Association (APALSA). There is a really tight-knit but sizeable and social Asian and Asian American community on campus. If you are interested in public interest, one of the perks at Northwestern is the Student Funded Public Interest Fellowship (SFPIF) group. If you volunteer with the group you can get up to a $5,000 grant to do public interest work during your 1L summer which is great especially since most of those jobs don't pay. There is also the annual Barrister's Ball to benefit SFPIF.

Status: Current student, full-time
Dates of Enrollment: 7/2005-Submit Date
Survey Submitted: March 2006

The SBA's Social Committee is extremely active and the weekly Bar Reviews are always well attended. Having a slightly older student body certainly doesn't mean that they don't like to go out. In fact, they know better how to balance work with fun. Any event can be celebrated with a beer down at Timmy O'Toole's and there are plenty of your classmates who will join you at the drop of a hat. The school even sponsors a "First Friday" with beer in the atrium each month.

Status: Current student, full-time
Dates of Enrollment: 9/2003-Submit Date
Survey Submitted: March 2006

There is an active social environment at the law school. There is a fair amount of dating between law school and much dating by law students outside the parameters of the law school. The law school has a social committee that plans Bar Review—a weekly night out at a different Chicago bar with drink specials as well as social events like Bulls Games, Bowling nights, etc. Clubs and Organizations have events at Chicago clubs, Salsa Dancing Bars, and even food tastings at five-star restaurants by the Epicurean Society (a food appreciation club). Chicago has TONS of dining options and many of them are renowned restaurants and bars. There are many clubs and organizations and Northwestern is very receptive to starting organizations so long as there is an interest. From Animal Rights Organizations to Hispanic, Black, Asian, Indian, etc., law student organizations, to Public Speaking clubs, and Scotch Appreciation Clubs, NU has a club from every taste. The social scene is unsurpassed!

Status: Current student, full-time
Dates of Enrollment: 8/2005-Submit Date
Survey Submitted: March 2006

The neighborhood right around the school is kind of dead in the evenings, but within a short walk from campus are a lot of restaurants, bars, and museums for entertainment. There are lots of student organizations, though most of them are co-curricular in nature. I'm personally dating another first-year student that I

met after coming here, so dating can happen, though I understand that a lot of students arrive with spouses or serious girl/boyfriends, which can make the dating pool a lot smaller.

Status: Current student, full-time
Dates of Enrollment: 8/2005-Submit Date
Survey Submitted: March 2006

Lots of cool bars and restaurants. Good theatre, from musicals like *Wicked* to cutting edge stuff at Steppenwolf (started by John Malkovich, Gary Sinese, and others). Also good improv comedy (Second City, Improv Olympic) and fantastic museums. Great sporting events—a Cubs game is fun even when they lose (and they usually do).

There are a lot of different clubs for different career and personal interests. They are not time consuming unless you want to have an office and really pour your time into it. The Federalist society is popular among the conservatives (one of the founders is a professor here). The "Wigmore Follies" puts on a play to spoof the law school once a year and that can be a laugh riot. Not recommended for your friends or non-law significant others as there are just too many inside jokes.

Status: Current student, full-time JD/MBA
Dates of Enrollment: 8/2004-Submit Date
Survey Submitted: March 2006

Social life is much stronger at Kellogg as one might expect. This is due to more people (500 in a class rather than 250 at law school) and just the nature of the program and people in the schools. Law school has a weekly Bar Review on Thursday nights which vary in attendance, but that can be about it sometimes. Kellogg almost always has something going on, and Tuesday, Thursday, and Friday/Saturdays tend to be very active, though less so in the Winter quarter. In Evanston, the Keg and Nevin's tend to be the hotspots. Clubs are extremely active at Kellogg also, and have incredible breadth and depth to them in most cases.

Status: Alumnus/a, full-time LLM
Dates of Enrollment: 8/1996-6/1997
Survey Submitted: March 2006

Social life is excellent. The School of Law and its nearby dormitories have bars and restaurants, as well as several clubs, including sports clubs. But if you leave the campus, you will also find yourself in the middle of the life of Chicago with its fabulous night life and culture, including its musical (blues, musicals, operas) life and its breath-taking architecture (high rise skyscrapers and the buildings of Frank Lloyd Wright). I just loved it better than New York although the latter is also a great fun. I highly recommend becoming one of the Northwestern "purple Wild Cats".

Status: Current student, full-time
Dates of Enrollment: 8/2004-Submit Date
Survey Submitted: March 2005

Greatest part of the social life at NU is that since we're in a big city, there are great opportunities to meet NON-law school students. It's important to have outlets outside of law school social life. Although I'm probably surrounded by law students 90 percent of my free time, it's nice to know there are non-law students living life around me. The actual neighborhood NU is in (Streeterville), doesn't have many great bars, but everything we may need is a cab ride or bus ride away. We get a free CTA pass, so transportation is usually free. Also, regardless of where I go, I've never paid more than $20 for a cab. As for events, there's always a speaker, conference, etc., but the reality is that as law students, our time for having social lives is limited.

Status: Current student, full-time
Dates of Enrollment: 8/2002-Submit Date
Survey Submitted: March 2005

Northwestern is replete with clubs focusing on matters both academic and fun. There are a number of ethnic organizations, an a cappella singing group, the Federalist Society, the ACLU, OUTLaw (supporting LGBT rights), several public service clubs, the Single Malt Scotch Society, many law area-specific organizations, and a ton of others. If Northwestern students don't get involved, it's not for lack of opportunity. Also, Northwestern has weekly Bar Reviews each at a different Chicago bar. Again, the school is in the heart of Chicago, so the entire city is at every student's finger tips.

The School Says

Consider this: any top law school will give you excellent legal education. Each will have esteemed scholars on the faculty, impressive library holdings, and an extensive curriculum. So, if the academic factors are relatively equal, how do you choose one law school over another? You choose not just a school, but a community.

While other top law schools may boast non-competitive environments and a strong sense of community, no other law school in the country comes close to taking the steps Northwestern has to instill and foster such an atmosphere. Our sense of community is ingrained in everything we do.

It is a major driving force of our strategic plan to set a new standard in legal education, and it binds together the five points of distinction we call the Northwestern Law Difference.

Our students are mature, experienced leaders with excellent communication and interpersonal skills in addition to excellent academic ability. We use interviews to access personal as well as academic ability. More than 90 percent of our students have at least one year of work experience and entering classes' median LSAT scores have risen to a median of 169 in recent years. Employers recognize that Northwestern enrolls and then trains students who will thrive in the changing legal and business world. Each year more than 700 employers recruit our students, and more than half of new graduates accept offers outside the Midwest.

Our professors are world-class scholars who comment daily on leading legal, academic, and public policy issues. In the past several years, we have aggressively recruited new faculty members in key areas. They are experts not only in law but also philosophy, political science, economics, and psychology. Our relatively small size and low-student faculty ratio (12:1) allow students to work closely with their professors.

Our curriculum provides a solid foundation in legal reasoning, analysis, and writing, and also focuses on communication and teamwork as well as cross-training in business and real-world experience. Teambuilding begins at orientation and continues throughout the curriculum. Many students take advantage of our close relationship with Northwestern's Kellogg School of Management to take cross-listed courses. Through our comprehensive clinical program students hone their professional skills in our top ranked trial advocacy and negotiation and mediation programs and by representing clients in one of our four Bluhm Legal Clinic centers.

Our close-knit community fosters collaborative learning and leads students to develop excellent leadership and organizational skills. Students play an important role in the life of the Law School. We rely on their input to make major decisions ranging from faculty appointments to technological improvements. More than 30 student organizations represent diverse political ideologies, career interests, public concerns, and ethnic, minority and religion affiliations.

Our superior facilities and resources integrate state-of-the-art technology and stately architecture in one of Chicago's most dynamic neighborhoods, near downtown law firms, trial and appellate courts, and government offices. The city provides an ideal setting for the study of law, and students take advantage of the location through visits to courts, law firms, and corporations

Read all of Vault's Law School Surveys at www.vault.com/lawschool — get complete surveys on top law schools, expert advice on applicaton essays, LSAT prep and more.

VAULT CAREER LIBRARY **233**

University of Chicago Law School

Admissions Office
1111 East 60th Street
Chicago, IL 60637
Admissions phone: (773) 702-9484
Admissions fax: (773) 834-0942
Admissions e-mail (JD Admissions):
admissions@law.uchicago.edu
Admissions e-mail (LLM Admissions):
llm-admissions@law.uchicago.edu
Admissions URL:
http://www.law.uchicago.edu/prospective/

 Admissions

Status: Alumnus/a, full-time
Dates of Enrollment: 9/2003-6/2005
Survey Submitted: April 2006

UChicago tries to have a very well-rounded class. Everyone meets the requisite grade and LSAT requirements, of course, but they also look for people with differing backgrounds, experiences and perspectives. For example, my class had a number of former military, an Olympic athlete, numerous entrepreneurs, some doctors, etc. The essay should explain why you'll make a positive contribution to the class—essentially, describe why you'll be an asset, rather than what you plan to take from the school.

Status: Current student, full-time
Dates of Enrollment: 8/2003-Submit Date
Survey Submitted: February 2006

The admissions process is fairly standard, with the only exception being interviews granted to approximately one-fourth of the applicants. I was not asked to interview, and therefore cannot report on what the interview entails. The admissions committee was extremely prompt when responding to questions and communicating with admitted students. The Admitted Students Weekend was excellent and very informative, while fun at the same time. As far as advice on getting in goes, the standards at U of C are obviously quite high, and getting higher by the year. A good LSAT score and GPA are a must, along with a creative personal statement that makes you stand out from the rest of the applicant pool.

Status: Alumnus/a, full-time
Dates of Enrollment: 9/2001-6/2004
Survey Submitted: January 2005

Although Chicago only admits very smart people and is obviously very selective, it seems like gaining admission may be easier than at other top schools. This could be a matter of self-selection: only very intelligent, intense people are willing to apply. I have heard that about a third of applicants must come in for an interview. I did not have to, so I don't have specific advice on that, besides be yourself.

> **Regarding interviews, UChicago Law School says:** "We offer interviews for certain candidates after their file has been reviewed. We also may request that applicants submit an additional writing sample as part of their application. Requests for interviews will not be granted."

Status: Current student, full-time
Dates of Enrollment: 9/2003-Submit Date
Survey Submitted: September 2004

The admissions process is rigorous. Undergraduate grades and LSAT score are weighted heavily. Interviews are granted infrequently and are completely at the discretion of the admissions office. The school is selective about who is admitted, and having a background in economics won't hurt you. The school claims to be taking more of an interest into recruiting women and minorities but the proof still remains to be seen. The admissions office is a small group, so I would advise students to have as much personal contact with the representatives in the office as possible. They definitely will remember who you are if you call or visit the campus. It's a good idea to contact student groups on campus too because they can forward your name onto the admissions office as a prospective student.

Status: Alumnus/a, full-time
Dates of Enrollment: 9/2000-6/2003
Survey Submitted: March 2005

You have to submit all the usual suspects (LSAT, grades, recommendations, essay). I think Chicago might weigh the LSAT a bit more heavily than other schools as a means of ensuring that similarly qualified people are offered admission, regardless of the grade inflation tendencies of a number of elite undergrad schools. As a result, you get a well-balanced class from a range of undergraduate institutions. I also have the impression that the essays are read carefully. Chicago is quite selective, although its numbers don't always suggest that. The applicant pool is smaller but, on the whole, more qualified than at many other elite schools.

Status: Alumnus/a, full-time
Dates of Enrollment: 9/1998-6/2001
Survey Submitted: March 2005

Chicago required the basics—a high LSAT, high GPA and an essay. I did not have an interview. When I attended Chicago, it was very important that you showed commitment, interest and drive in whatever you did. People in my class were experts in their fields of interest, and those fields varied. There were former psychiatrists, actors, musicians, professional athletes, teachers, etc. The worst thing a person could do on an application is try to show the school that they understand the law. You don't. You aren't expected to know the law. Chicago will teach you how to think about the law. Chicago wants to know that you are brilliant, driven and intellectually curious.

Status: Alumnus/a, full-time
Dates of Enrollment: 10/1998-6/2001
Survey Submitted: March 2005

Chicago is a highly-selective law school that attracts smart students who care about the development of the law. Strong grades and LSAT scores are required, but a personal statement that shows a spark of personality or an interest in the law for the law's sake will be beneficial.

Status: Alumnus/a, full-time
Dates of Enrollment: 9/1998-6/2001
Survey Submitted: March 2005

Chicago had a standard admissions process. I interviewed with then-Dean Badger. I was waitlisted. I wrote an optional additional essay, then stopped by Chicago while on my way to my second-choice law school for an impromptu interview and got in then and there!

Status: Alumnus/a, full-time
Dates of Enrollment: 9/2000-6/2003
Survey Submitted: January 2005

The admissions process was pretty much like everyone else's process. The advantage here is they gave a stipend to fly up and visit the school once I was admitted. That visit made all the difference. My essay was about my influences growing up, not some esoteric legal topic (I can't imagine those would do well).

Status: Current student, full-time
Dates of Enrollment: 9/2002-Submit Date
Survey Submitted: October 2003

The school is very selective. Most students agree that there is a very high value placed on LSAT scores in admissions (which is true of most schools). That said, they look beyond LSAT—the range of LSATs in last class was 155 to 180. If you are borderline, or the school has questions about you, they may ask you to do a supplementary essay or interview. If you are asked for the supplementary information, don't be discouraged. I know many people who submitted as much information as requested and are in the class.

Status: Alumnus/a, full-time
Dates of Enrollment: 9/1997-6/2000
Survey Submitted: April 2004

One of the few law schools that conduct interviews of applicants. The law school attracts and matriculates a diverse body of students, but because of the strong academic reputation and reputation for being a place in which students are required to attain business skills of presenting arguments cogently and publicly, the body of applicants may be smaller than at certain other top-tier law schools because of a self-selection process. I recommend that, during interviews and essays, the applicant state how she or he would contribute to the Law School environment.

 **Academics**

Status: Alumnus/a, full-time
Dates of Enrollment: 9/2003-6/2005
Survey Submitted: April 2006

The professors are the best. UC focuses on high-quality instructors. It's well known in the community, so requires no further discussion. The classes are your standard law school classes, at least in the first year. After that, there is a wide variety of classes, including several courses taught by well-known federal appellate judges, prominent practitioners in the Chicago area, and visiting professors from other top law schools. The smaller seminars can be difficult to get into due to space restrictions and the lottery system, but if you persevere, you can usually get into the one you want.

The academics are intense, as they should be. You must put in the hours to get the results you want from the classes. If you're going to law school just to slack through it by doing the minimum required, you're cheating yourself. The cost is too high in both time and money to waste this unique opportunity. While everyone knows practicing law is completely different and mostly unrelated to law school itself, you do learn some valuable skills, and the ability to think critically.

Status: Alumnus/a, full-time
Dates of Enrollment: 9/2002-6/2005
Survey Submitted: March 2006

The best thing about Chicago is how small the community is. This means that you end up making dinner, playing squash and discussing graphic novels with truly illustrious professors. Some popular classes fill up really quickly, but most professors respond to e-mails pleading your case for why you should get to take the course. In my three years there, I got to take everything I wanted.

Grading is weird at Chicago, and employers know it. In a way, it's good. People have no idea what a 77 (the mean) really means. On the other hand, it's hard to distinguish yourself from the pack when it appears that 80 percent of the class does about the same. Workload is hefty, and I've confirmed this having talked to other friends. But because the classes are consistently excellent thanks to the amazing professors, the work is always meaningful and not just busywork.

Status: Current student, full-time
Dates of Enrollment: 8/2003-Submit Date
Survey Submitted: February 2006

The small class setting here allows you to take pretty much any class that you want to before you graduate. I've never had trouble getting into a class yet. The grading system is intentionally obscure, designed so you have to explain it to employers who are new to U of C. The regular players understand the numerical

grading system and won't have to ask...although every few years U of C does something to change the system to keep it interesting (such as adding 100 points to every grade as they did a couple years ago). The academic program is rigorous, and you have to work hard to simply get median grades. There is no grade inflation here—everyone is intelligent and works hard. It takes a lot to receive an "A" (180 or greater on the U of C scale). The classroom is usually entertaining with the great variety of faculty on hand, and you will certainly get a great education.

Status: Current student, full-time
Dates of Enrollment: 9/2003-Submit Date
Survey Submitted: September 2004

The school does not inflate grades. Grading is competitive but generally accurate. Professors are easily accessible due to the small size of the Law School. Most students get to take the classes they want. One problem is that some courses are not offered every year so students must sign up for a class when it is offered if they are interested in taking it during law school. Classes are good but heavy on the Socratic Method system. The workload is overwhelming as a first-year student but tends to lighten up in upper level classes.

Some of the best professors in the country teach at the Law School. The best thing with going to school with such great professors is you can do independent studies on any topic you want with the professor's permission. Many of the judges on the Seventh Circuit Court of Appeals also teach at the Law School (Posner, Wood, Easterbrook, etc.)

Status: Alumnus/a, full-time
Dates of Enrollment: 9/2000-6/2003
Survey Submitted: March 2005

RIGOROUS! Grading is on a tightly regulated curve, and it is very difficult to get an A. Grading is on a 186 point scale, with 180 and up being an A (maybe 10 to 15 percent of each class), 174 to 179 a B (maybe 70 to 80 percent of each class) and 168 to 173 a C (the remaining portion of the class). Getting a C is bad. Getting below that is almost unheard of.

Workload is heavy, particularly in the first year. After that, you can tailor it as you wish, but the norm is to maintain a full load throughout school. There are certainly slackers, however, and they still almost always get good jobs—they just don't have quite the number of choices.

Professors are almost uniformly excellent All are highly accomplished researchers/writers, but what separates Chicago is that they are almost all very good teachers. The Socratic Method is the norm, which gives students a great reason to do their reading. A poor performance in class is embarrassing, but can't be held against your grade because in most classes grading is completely blind and based only on your final exam performance.

Status: Alumnus/a, full-time
Dates of Enrollment: 9/1998-6/2001
Survey Submitted: March 2005

The professors were almost universally brilliant. The program was extremely rigorous. Unlike most of the other top schools, students take three quarters per year. While this exposes students to a greater number of classes, it also tends to increase the workload (since coursework is completed over a shorter period of time). The lectures were the most intellectually stimulating experiences I've had. Most of my second- and third-year classes were seminars, which included approximately 15 students. I was able to enroll in every class I wanted. Grading generally is curved, but there is very little competition between students.

Status: Alumnus/a, full-time
Dates of Enrollment: 9/2000-6/2003
Survey Submitted: March 2005

The academics at the University of Chicago are probably the most respected of any law school in the country. Chicago, like the other top three to four schools, houses some of the country's most esteemed legal thinkers. What is truly remarkable about Chicago, however, is that almost every one of those individuals teaches a full course load (and seems to relish that opportunity). The courses were challenging in the best possible way: not needlessly so for the sake

Read all of Vault's Law School Surveys at www.vault.com/lawschool — get complete surveys on top law schools, expert advice on applicaton essays, LSAT prep and more.

VAULT CAREER LIBRARY   235

of creating grade-distinctions, but in the sense of actually forcing the students to truly think—a goal aided by the Socratic Method.

While slightly petrifying at first, the Socratic Method makes everyone be truly interactive. Instead of just accepting a lecture, students are forced to consider the issues and learn more from classmates' wrong answers (that they probably would have had as well) than they do from just hearing the right answers spouted monotonously. And in law, where "right answers" are rare, much is learned from the process of discovering how large the gray area is in each subject. Outside of the most popular seminars, everyone gets the courses they desire. And the lottery system for those popular seminars is eminently fair. Grading is weighted towards the middle, with only the truly exceptional in either direction falling far outside of the mean.

Status: Alumnus/a, full-time
Dates of Enrollment: 9/2000-6/2003
Survey Submitted: April 2004

The classes offered at Chicago are generally very rigorous (with the possible exception of the evening seminars), and all faculty are very involved in teaching, as opposed to principally writing. Particularly in the first year of law school, but even in the second and third years, the Socratic Method is still much utilized by professors unlike most law schools today. Regular classes are easy to get into—it is the seminars that allow limited enrollment (15 to 25 usually) that can sometimes present problems. A lottery system is used for admittance into popular seminars.

Status: Alumnus/a, full-time
Dates of Enrollment: 9/1999-5/2002
Survey Submitted: January 2004

Small classes, hands-on professors are easy to talk to outside of class if you make the effort. This is pure learning at the feet of the masters: Posner, Sunstein, Epstein, Case. Grades are based on a curve, and it is easy to get into popular classes if you're an older student because of the small student body and the wide variety of classes available. Huge workload, though, especially for first-years. Plan to study almost all your free time.

Status: Alumnus/a, full-time
Dates of Enrollment: 9/1998-6/2001
Survey Submitted: April 2004

The program is extremely rigorous, perhaps the most rigorous out of the top law schools. However, the environment is not particularly competitive, as for the most part, fellow students are cooperative and in the same boat. Grading is on a fairly strict (and unforgiving) curve, but employers are all well aware of the curve. Workload is high, but it is not necessary to complete 100 percent of the work to succeed. Professors are all extremely accessible and approachable, and, more than many other top schools, enjoy the daily interaction with students.

Professors seem to relish teaching, some perhaps more than they relish publishing. As the professors run the gamut of political views, the in-class discussions are even more rewarding than they might be at a school that is too conservative or too liberal. Note that if UChicago has a reputation of being conservative, it is only because: (i) they have top conservative scholars as well as top liberal scholars, unlike other schools that may have only top liberal scholars; and (ii) law students tend to be more liberal than the population at large (myself included) and therefore anything that is evenly balanced seems to be skewed to one side.

Status: Alumnus/a, full-time
Dates of Enrollment: 9/1997-6/2001
Survey Submitted: November 2003

The first year of law school is infamous. First year at Chicago is infamous times 20. The writing requirements (one full year of class and a greater workload than other schools) will prepare you for the real world, but will rob you of many, many hours of sleep. On top of a heavy courseload and a rigorous Socratic Method, the academics can at times be overwhelming. Just keep your eye on the prize—when you graduate, you'll run circles around your peers because you will have learned the law and how to argue it. The academics can be daunting, but know that they are also unparalleled.

Employment Prospects

Status: Alumnus/a, full-time
Dates of Enrollment: 9/2003-6/2005
Survey Submitted: April 2006

UC grads have their pick of jobs. There are a very large number of judicial clerks, mostly federal. The top firms recruit heavily. Others go on to government positions as staff attorneys or prosecutors. Some go directly into academics. The alumni network is very wide-spread, and because the U of Chicago "brand" is so highly valued in the market, alumni can be sure that students or other alumni who contact them for help have a certain level of intelligence and competence.

Status: Alumnus/a, full-time
Dates of Enrollment: 9/2002-6/2005
Survey Submitted: March 2006

Everyone I know got the jobs or clerkships that they wanted. About 20 percent of the class goes for clerkships, the rest are largely at firms. Firms look at Chicago as one of the most prestigious schools. It is definitely not a hindrance to have gone here, except perhaps with MoFo, which seems not to like us and doesn't even send recruiters to on-campus interviews.

A good number pursue public interest or other government jobs. In my class, a few went totally away from the law, becoming teachers and journalists. Since the school is small, there isn't much of an alumni network compared to the other top law schools, but the desire to help one another is strong and there are definitely good people in high places. On-campus recruiting works really well though, like everywhere else it is a major grind. At least, Chicago plans it so that it takes place before classes start.

Status: Current student, full-time
Dates of Enrollment: 8/2003-Submit Date
Survey Submitted: February 2006

There is no shortage of jobs coming out of this law school. Everyone I have spoken with in my class knows exactly what they are doing next year (I am a 3L currently), including the very bottom of the class. There are more employers coming to campus than students needing jobs, which is quite comforting. I was able to obtain numerous job offers at some of the most prestigious D.C. law firms and have my pick of where to go. Further, clerkship opportunities are many and anyone who wants a clerkship coming out will be able to find one.

Status: Alumnus/a, full-time
Dates of Enrollment: 9/2000-6/2003
Survey Submitted: March 2005

No problem getting a job anywhere, from my circuit court clerkship to my position with one of Chicago's finest law firms. People who graduated lower in my class also got very good jobs. Only the people who literally finished last in my class had trouble, and I believe all of them have also found decent jobs. Although Chicago may not have quite the impact with the man on the street, among legal employers it is widely recognized to be the most rigorous of the top law schools, and Chicago grads have virtual carte blanche in the legal market.

Status: Alumnus/a, full-time
Dates of Enrollment: 9/2000-6/2003
Survey Submitted: March 2005

Fantastic. Any city in the country respects U of C grads immensely, and desires to hire them. Of my fellow graduates, few had any trouble getting hired at the top firms in Chicago, New York, D.C. or on the West Coast. Five of my classmates clerked for the Supreme Court, and most everyone who wanted a clerkship was able to get an amazingly prestigious one. On-campus recruiting gets all of the top firms in the country, and the alumni networks are quite strong and very willing to help.

Status: Alumnus/a, full-time
Dates of Enrollment: 9/1997-6/2000
Survey Submitted: March 2005

From the employer standpoint, I know that my firm does try to attract U of C students. We compete with the other big law firms in town for the U of C grads who want to stay in Chicago. As an attorney, I've found that there are many opportunities for lateral moves because of my U of C degree (colleagues with degrees from less prestigious law schools have not been quite as lucky).

Status: Alumnus/a, full-time
Dates of Enrollment: 9/2000-6/2003
Survey Submitted: April 2004

As many lawyers feel that Chicago is arguably the most rigorous law school education a student can receive, regardless of its current overall ranking in various publications, it seemed to me that most employers tend to add unofficial points to U of C applicants in their selection process. Particularly, if interviewing outside of the Chicago area, where there is a dearth of Chicago candidates in the market generally (we only have about 180 graduate each year), I found the school's reputation to be the primary door-opener in getting a summer internship. Furthermore, just surviving in the middle of the pack at Chicago usually presents an opportunity at all but the most prestigious of firms in the few major markets. Thus, my friends and I have discussed that it often feels as though job offers are yours to lose (not earn) when you go into an interview, which is very reassuring.

Status: Current student, full-time
Dates of Enrollment: 9/2002-Submit Date
Survey Submitted: October 2003

WOW! Everyone I know in my class has an offer from some firm, if that is what they were looking for. This is amazing, especially with the shape of the economy. The Chicago name will get you a job anywhere in the country with a big, quality firm. That said, we have incredibly strong ties in Chicago and New York with alumni. Career services are very helpful, and give you a lot of attention in your job search. There are meetings and workshops for people who want them, but they are not required for those who don't.

Status: Alumnus/a, full-time
Dates of Enrollment: 9/1997-6/2001
Survey Submitted: November 2003

Lawyers from around the globe descend on Hyde Park every year to scoop up highly desired Chicago law students. Almost every major law firm known to man will talk to Chicago law students. A large proportion of students choose the corporate law life following graduation; however, the percentage of those seeking clerkships seems to be climbing. The most difficult aspect of recruiting is determining the geography of where you'd like to work.

Quality of Life

Status: Alumnus/a, full-time
Dates of Enrollment: 9/2003-6/2005
Survey Submitted: April 2006

Neighborhood and campus are not big draws to this school, as both leave much to be desired. The classroom facilities are newly renovated, however, and phenomenal. Dining options are limited within the Law School, but there are other cafeterias and restaurants within walking distance on the main campus of the university.

Status: Alumnus/a, full-time
Dates of Enrollment: 9/2002-6/2005
Survey Submitted: March 2006

There's a dorm and an International House that most of the LLMs and other homey sorts live in right down the street. Otherwise, most everyone lives around the city in their own apartments. Chicago has a great gym and a skating rink right in front of the Law School. While Hyde Park gets a bad rap, any problems that occur there happen when someone is walking around alone late at night.

Status: Current student, full-time
Dates of Enrollment: 8/2003-Submit Date
Survey Submitted: February 2006

Hyde Park is no Beverly Hills—the crime rate is quite high and you don't exactly feel safe walking around. It takes some getting used to, and I would recommend living "up north" in one of the Northside Chicago neighborhoods. The commute down Lakeshore Drive is not nearly bad enough to outweigh the increase in quality of life you'll experience. The law school was just renovated

with all new classrooms, and apparently the library will be renovated this summer. The new facilities are great, though the building itself is still pretty outdated.

Status: Alumnus/a, full-time
Dates of Enrollment: 9/2001-6/2004
Survey Submitted: January 2005

Housing is OK. Some people rented houses that were actually very nice. I lived in campus-owned apartments. The first one was like a small dorm room and I hated it. The second one was an actual apartment, with a parking space; there were six apartments in the building and it was nice.

You need to be careful where you live in Hyde Park. Do not live south of the Law School—that's a terrible neighborhood. Also, do not live more than 10 blocks north of the Law School. And not too far east or west, either. The neighborhood is bad enough that I wouldn't want my kids going there for undergrad. During undergrad you're supposed to be able to have fun, get drunk, do other stupid things, and not worry too much about your safety. That could not happen in Hyde Park. Also, the undergrad kids are extremely intense, I think too intense. However, at the graduate level, the area is OK as long as you keep your wits about you. The campus itself is beautiful. It looks like a typical Ivy League school.

Status: Alumnus/a, full-time
Dates of Enrollment: 9/1998-6/2001
Survey Submitted: March 2005

I loved Hyde Park. The intellectual community is stimulating. During warm weather, you can bike into the city. There are Thursday night beach concerts during the summer a few blocks south of the school. During the year, the Law School is isolated by cold from most other locations, but perhaps that adds to the collegiality of the school.

Status: Alumnus/a, full-time
Dates of Enrollment: 9/2000-6/2003
Survey Submitted: March 2005

Quality of life at the school is quite high. While Hyde Park is far from the ideal "college town," its shortcomings are lessened by several factors. While it gets a bad rap for being dangerous, Hyde Park is not dangerous if one does not stray too far from the campus—but it is boring. A recent renaissance of sorts has brought numerous new bars and night spots to the area, a night out will most likely involve a 15-minute trip to downtown—which is where many students live after their first years. The school makes up for this, however, ensuring a weekly wine-mess (Friday afternoon cocktail party) and coffee-mess (weekly morning opportunity to get free doughnuts, bagels and coffee and meet and chat with professors, the dean and fellow students.

Status: Alumnus/a, full-time
Dates of Enrollment: 10/1998-6/2001
Survey Submitted: March 2005

Reports of Hyde Park's dangerousness are greatly exaggerated. Chicago is located in an urban setting, but Hyde Park has long been a bastion of the middle and upper class, and its surrounding neighborhoods are rapidly gentrifying. Furnished dorm housing is available to 1Ls. Many students live in Hyde Park for the first year, then move to trendier Northside neighborhoods. Students with families, however, may prefer to stay in Hyde Park—an integrated community with excellent school options.

Status: Alumnus/a, full-time
Dates of Enrollment: 10/2000-6/2003
Survey Submitted: April 2004

Hyde Park has a bad reputation that is totally undeserved. The law school building is old but comfortable, and the school is working to improve it all the time. Crime and safety will not be a problem, no matter what you've heard. Public transportation is poor, however, so if you aren't going to live in Hyde Park be prepared to have a car. The campus is beautiful, and if you want a comfortable neighborhood that's a little laid-back and quiet with lots of trees, then you'll love Hyde Park. Plus, it just got a Borders.

Read all of Vault's Law School Surveys at www.vault.com/lawschool — get complete surveys on top law schools, expert advice on applicaton essays, LSAT prep and more.

VAULT CAREER LIBRARY   237

Status: Alumnus/a, full-time
Dates of Enrollment: 9/2000-6/2003
Survey Submitted: April 2004

The quality of life at Chicago is the most disappointing aspect of the school. As a person who valued her social life and a break from talking strictly academic and social policy concerns of the time, I found the Law School [social life] at best tolerable and at worst often depressing. A certain kind of person thrives in this environment; however, those who have myriad interests that do not always focus on academic and professional enlightenment, can often feel as though they must get a needed break from the Law School and all those who make it their entire life.

Status: Alumnus/a, full-time
Dates of Enrollment: 9/1997-6/2001
Survey Submitted: November 2003

Life can be tough at Chicago Law—particularly in your first year. Hyde Park doesn't do much to help the situation, but there's little that could. The law school is located across the "Midway" (a large, grassy area owned by the city of Chicago) from the rest of the University of Chicago, and can at times isolate the Law School from the vibrant campus (especially during Chicago winters when the Midway doubles as a wind tunnel).

Hyde Park itself can be beautiful and scary at the same time. The area immediately surrounding the campus is rife with restored brownstones and [exudes] old-age aristocracy. The area immediately south of the Law School can seem like run-down projects. The new part of the Law School is equipped with state-of-the-art classrooms where most students type notes in laptops. The original classrooms of the Law School are [being renovated this summer, and] there is some charm to knowing that you're sitting in the same [rooms as] some of the great legal minds of the 20th Century. Unfortunately, that charm is short-lived.

 ## Social Life

Status: Alumnus/a, full-time
Dates of Enrollment: 10/1994-6/1997
Survey Submitted: March 2006

There is an event called "Wine Mess" every Friday afternoon in the student lounge. The administration and professors sometimes attend. It's very relaxed and fun. The administration also hosts snacks for students around 10 p.m. every night around finals, which is great. There is something called Bar Review where students set up a bar for everyone to go to; those were fun sometimes, although the same small group tended to go every time. There are also fun extracurricular activities, such as the Law School Musical.

Status: Current student, full-time
Dates of Enrollment: 8/2003-Submit Date
Survey Submitted: February 2006

The social life at U of C is what you make of it. Everyone has their group, and because of the vast discrepancy in ages everyone finds their niche. I was surprised at how good of friends I made within the first six months, since U of C has such a bad reputation of being purely nerds.

Status: Alumnus/a, full-time
Dates of Enrollment: 9/2001-6/2004
Survey Submitted: January 2005

Chicago Law is sort of like a very nerdy high school, which I mean as a compliment (I liked high school). The classes are tightly knit. We study together a lot. We hang out in the Green Lounge, playing cards or talking. We eat out in Hyde Park and get coffee. There is less drinking at Chicago than most other places. A large percentage of the students are Mormon, for one thing. In addition, I know lots of people who just don't drink much. They're either married and therefore not going out to bars, or they're in the library.

There are tons of clubs and events. You can start any club you want, and get funding both from the Law School and from U of C general funds across the midway (most of the campus is north of Midway Plaisance, so the Law School is a little isolated). The best law school events are the daily free lunches where

professors talk about their current research, or whatever other topic the students ask them to discuss. There is always free lunch. While I was there, I didn't realize how rare it is to have so much access to professors and to interact with them at these lunches on a constant basis. It was very special.

Status: Current student, full-time
Dates of Enrollment: 9/2003-Submit Date
Survey Submitted: September 2004

Socializing is minimal. There are students who go out and organize activities, but for the most part the focus is on academics. The Law Students Association is good about planning activities and giving students social alternatives. For the most part, the workload at the Law School does not allow time for much partying. There are lots of relationships within the Law School.

Status: Alumnus/a, full-time
Dates of Enrollment: 9/2000-6/2003
Survey Submitted: March 2005

I had a great time in law school, although I also worked very hard. The bar scene in Hyde Park is LIMITED to say the least, but we always managed to have a good time. Many law students move up north their second or third year, and much of the social life centers around weekly Bar Review sessions at bars in Lincoln Park, Wrigleyville, or downtown.

The male-female ratio in my class was somewhat skewed, but a number of people met their spouses and my overall impression was that there was a fair amount of intraclass dating going on. In recent years the numbers have evened out, which I would guess is further helping things in that regard.

Status: Alumnus/a, full-time
Dates of Enrollment: 9/1998-6/2001
Survey Submitted: March 2005

The law school had a satirical musical every year, weekly wine mess, weekly Bar Review, and many intramural sports. We even had a Law School Band that played '80s cover songs for various events at the school and at venues in the city. I was never bored. What could be better than going to a bar with not one or two, but 15 really smart people who enjoyed debating? I loved my three years there.

Status: Alumnus/a, full-time
Dates of Enrollment: 10/1998-6/2001
Survey Submitted: March 2005

Like any small school, students at Chicago frequently know more than they'd like about everybody else's business. On the other hand, in a city of three million people, it's pretty easy to meet non-Chicago students at bars, the gym, sporting events, religious services, the grocery store, etc. Students do date (and marry) each other. There are a number of student groups based on ethnicity, political affiliation, sexual orientation, charitable activities, and the like. There is a weekly student-run wine mess at the school during which the students drink for cheap and the professors drink for free. There is also a weekly Bar Review event, usually in Lincoln Park or Lakeview.

Status: Alumnus/a, full-time
Dates of Enrollment: 9/1998-6/2001
Survey Submitted: April 2004

Small class size so everyone knows everyone and everything about everyone. Social life is focused around your classmates. Not too many bars right around the school, but restaurants are sufficient, though not plentiful. Dating is common among classmates—but word gets around, so be careful! The Pub, across the Midway where the rest of the university is located, is popular. Most of the city's entertainment is found outside of Hyde Park so having a car is extremely helpful.

The School Says

The University of Chicago Law School has been at the forefront of legal education for more than 100 years. Affiliated with a university that brings together students from dozens of disciplines on a lovely urban campus, 15 minutes from a vibrant city center, we are known for providing a rigorous intellectual environment with constant student-faculty interaction. We take pride in preparing our students for careers in private practice, public service, academia and government, and especially in our nearly unparalleled record in placing our students in judicial clerkships.

But Chicago is not a school content to rest on its laurels. We have been adding exciting clinical programs, including an urban housing program and an appellate advocacy clinic, so that we now have eight clinical projects in full bloom. We have long been known for our fantastic classroom teachers, and for our faculty's groundbreaking scholarship, but now we have expanded our focus to include the Chicago Public Initiatives. These initiatives bring together students, faculty, and alumni to study some of the most important issues facing our world today, such as the politics of judging, animal treatment, and adolescents who are wards of the court. Our goal is to develop novel solutions to important problems, and, as with so many things here, our students will be in the middle of it all.

Our alumni already select careers across the spectrum of legal work, but through our innovative Hormel Public Interest Program we are making it easier for students and alumni to choose diverse careers. This funding program is designed to assist recent graduates in relieving some of their debt when they choose careers in public service. It is one of the most generous programs in the country.

The law school building was designed to facilitate constant interaction between all students, as well as between students and faculty. Recent renovations will allow future generations of students to learn in a comfortable, high-tech, state-of-the-art environment. Our auditorium, courtroom, and entire classroom wing were fully updated in 2004, and the renovation of our library tower will be completed by the fall of 2007.

We invite you to visit the Law School, sit in on some classes, and talk with our students and faculty to determine if our student-friendly, intellectually stimulating environment is right for you.

Read all of Vault's Law School Surveys at www.vault.com/lawschool — get complete surveys on top law schools, expert advice on applicaton essays, LSAT prep and more.

VAULT CAREER LIBRARY **239**

University of Illinois College of Law

Admissions Office
504 East Pennsylvania Avenue
Champaign, IL 61820
Admissions phone: (217) 244-6415
Admissions fax: (217) 244-1478
Admissions e-mail: admissions@law.uiuc.edu
Admissions URL: http://www.law.uiuc.edu/prospective/

 ## Admissions

Status: Current student, full-time
Dates of Enrollment: 8/2004-Submit Date
Survey Submitted: April 2006

Fairly selective in that its median LSAT score is higher than that of similarly ranked schools. Still, the admissions team (headed by Paul Pless) does a great job of attracting well-rounded students from all over the country.

Status: Alumnus/a, full-time
Dates of Enrollment: 8/2002-5/2005
Survey Submitted: March 2006

Many prospective students may be familiar with the large undergraduate program at the University of Illinois and not understand the significant difference in admissions policies for the College of Law. The law program is a standard-sized program (200 students per year, although it has been recently announced that this is being reduced to 180). Regardless, "selectivity" varies widely. A wide-range of LSAT scores will be admitted. A low LSAT score can be balanced by caliber of undergraduate school and GPA there. The school also seems to have a goal of becoming more of a national school, so if you come from outside Illinois, play that up! The admissions essays simply aren't that important. If you have a low LSAT score or low undergrad GPA, use the essay to show you do have intelligence, but otherwise it isn't a big deal. You can write about any life experience, definitely don't make it a one-page bio.

Status: Alumnus/a, full-time
Dates of Enrollment: 8/1998-5/2001
Survey Submitted: March 2006

The admission process is largely numbers-oriented (grades, undergrad class rank, LSAT scores). Work experience and minority status are also factors. Interviews are difficult to schedule and recommended only in borderline cases. Letters/calls from alumni are considered.

Status: Alumnus/a, full-time
Dates of Enrollment: 8/1999-5/2002
Survey Submitted: March 2006

The admission process was very standard: take the LSAT, submit your transcripts and scores, complete the application and send in your money.

The school isn't especially selective, but it is becoming more selective over time. So, draft your essays carefully. Everyone who has a reasonable chance of being admitted will have good grades and LSAT scores. If you're on the bubble, an essay that says something unique and insightful may well be what the committee needs to go your way.

Status: Alumnus/a, full-time
Dates of Enrollment: 7/2002-5/2005
Survey Submitted: October 2005

I think the admissions process for most law schools is the same. Focus on the schools that fall withing your LSAT range, unless you have something unique that separates you from the crowd. Law schools are very focused on diversity: ethnic, academic, geographic, age, etc. So I would emphasize those things about you that stand out in your essay.

The College of Law is very selective, and getting more so by the day. However, don't let it daunt you from applying. While it is true that you should assess you chances by the published LSAT score, if you want it, roll the dice.

Status: Current student, full-time
Dates of Enrollment: 8/2004-Submit Date
Survey Submitted: January 2005

It's tough to get into a first-tier schools and this public law school is no different. Annually ranked in the Top 25 law schools in the nation, Illinois usually gets LSAT scores of 165+ with strong undergraduate records. This school does value diversity and it shows in the classroom with students from all over the country and the world.

Status: Alumnus/a, full-time
Dates of Enrollment: 8/2002-5/2004
Survey Submitted: November 2003

The College of Law is selective. The admissions process is run by the dean of admissions (who reads every single application—at least Maggie Austin did; I don't know much about the new dean of admissions). One nice touch is that the dean of admissions writes a short personal note on each letter of admission. It's nice and it lets you know that they actually read your application.

Status: Current student, full-time
Dates of Enrollment: 8/2001-Submit Date
Survey Submitted: October 2003

The school is highly selective. They want a strong undergraduate record and a high LSAT score. The school also values applicants with public or community service and work experience. There is no interview process so the personal statement is key. [You are asked to submit a resume,] along with any other information that you feel will assist the admissions committee in their decision to admit you.

Status: Current student, full-time
Dates of Enrollment: 8/2001-Submit Date
Survey Submitted: June 2004

I applied on the last possible day to Illinois. I got in promptly with a scholarship, but I do not recommend this path to others. I had good grades and an excellent LSAT score. It seems that GPA and LSAT can balance each other out. I have a friend here who had a 3.9 and only a 156 on the LSAT, and I have another friend who had about a 2.0 and an LSAT in the low 170s.

> **Regarding admissions, the school notes:** "We currently have over 3,000 applications for 185 seats in the class."

 ## Academics

Status: Current student, full-time
Dates of Enrollment: 8/2004-Submit Date
Survey Submitted: April 2006

Classes at Illinois strike the right balance between challenging students to think on their own and providing guidance on specific areas of the law. I have never had a problem getting into the courses I want, and preference is given to rising 3Ls, so you are basically guaranteed to get a class before you graduate. Grading is very fair, but competitive like at all law schools. Most professors are fantastic—they just have that WOW factor. They are leaders in their field, and really seem willing to sit down with willing students. There are some professors (e.g., Smith and Moore) for which you almost want to clap or cheer after every class—they are just that knowledgeable and entertaining. Illinois is repeatedly recognized for its faculty reputation, and it is only getting better with several recent key hires.

Status: Alumnus/a, full-time
Dates of Enrollment: 9/1975-5/1978
Survey Submitted: April 2006

It was very easy to get the classes you desired at the law school. During the first year, you were assigned to a section and had a set schedule that was with all the people in your section. The two following years it was easy to get whatever classes you wished. The quality of the professors varied but, in general, was very good. Grading was fair. As would be expected, the workload in law school was challenging. The goal of the law school was not to teach you about every law but to teach you how to think like a lawyer.

Status: Alumnus/a, full-time
Dates of Enrollment: 8/1979-5/1989
Survey Submitted: April 2006

Academic life at U of I was fabulous. The instructors were encouraging, tentative, patient and intellectual. Class book lists and assignments were posted outside the instructors doors well in advance of the first day of classes. My friends and I would get our book lists, shop for books and begin the process of reading two or three assignments ahead. In this way we were better prepared for the first day of class and beyond. The professors had students hours that they kept faithfully. Even as a minority on campus, I felt that they were vested in my future success at the university. I learned much that I find myself using now about life, how to think and process information, and how to develop and cultivate relationships. That's why I believe I have been successful in my legal career. I learned at the U of I how to be a quick study and how to accomplish my goals.

Status: Alumnus/a, full-time
Dates of Enrollment: 8/2001-5/2004
Survey Submitted: April 2006

The classes were very interesting. There is a waitlist to get in to some of the smaller classes, so you may have to wait until your third year to get in to some of the best classes. The professors, for the most part, are wonderful, easy to approach after class and at their offices, and the workload wasn't bad.

Status: Alumnus/a, full-time
Dates of Enrollment: 8/2002-5/2005
Survey Submitted: March 2006

For many years the University of Illinois College of Law was known as a research institution and offered primarily a theoretical education. A new dean is changing the face of the institution, including a movement away from the strictly-academic to a more balanced approach, bringing in high quality professors and more current practitioners on an adjunct basis. But the last couple years of transition—including significant state-funding cuts—have been very problematic. During these last few years, it has been very difficult to get desired classes and the number of classes offered has been significantly reduced (resulting in much larger class sizes). My understanding is that the class problem should be temporary, and in the 2004-2005 year it was already better than in 2003-2004. Ultimately, it should be significantly better, as better professors are being hired.

Status: Alumnus/a, full-time
Dates of Enrollment: 8/2002-5/2005
Survey Submitted: March 2006

After the mandatory first year classes, there are enough programs for almost any diverse academic interest. There are classes on everything from more academic pursuits to nuts and bolts clinics. If you're not satisfied with the course of your legal education, you can only blame yourself.

Status: Alumnus/a, full-time
Dates of Enrollment: 8/1999-5/2002
Survey Submitted: March 2006

For the most part the program was fairly standard as law schools go. However, first year students are permitted to select and "elective" in which they are taught the methods of statutory interpretation. The available electives vary from year to year. As a 1L we had to choose from courses on the ADA, Copyright Act, and Employment Discrimination (Title VII and the ADEA).

Never was I unable to get a course that I wanted, and for the most part I was very happy with the courses that I took. Professors are always going to be a bit hit or miss, but for the most part the professors at Illinois were hits. Moreover, the courses combined just the right amount of real world practicality with Ivory Tower omphaloskepsis.

Status: Alumnus/a, full-time
Dates of Enrollment: 7/2002-5/2005
Survey Submitted: October 2005

Illinois sticks to a strict 3.1 curve in its first-year courses, and the use of the curve is currently being foisted upon upper level courses as well. I knew a lot of people who attempted to avoid this problem after first year by taking mainly small classes where there was no mandatory curve. A bonus to that strategy was getting to know your professor much better—which can be a challenge in a class with over 50 people.

Your first year, the classes and professors are assigned to you. It seems that the "powers that be" try to mix less socially graceful professors with fantastic ones so that no one section is screwed. It's law school. Be prepared to work hard. And the dirty little secret is, for some of you, be prepared to work hard and get Bs. For a lot of my classmates this was the most challenging aspect. Working much harder than they did in undergrad, and receiving lower grades for their efforts.

Status: Current student, full-time
Dates of Enrollment: 8/2004-Submit Date
Survey Submitted: January 2005

Academics at Illinois are topshelf. It's hard work. There's certainly a no nonsense feel here. As a 1L, much like everywhere else, your courses and professors are selected for you. But there are so many quality professors at the College of Law that you won't be disappointed in that department. The best thing about the profs though is there accessibility. Every single one of my profs has an open-door policy and often stay after every class to answer questions.

Status: Alumnus/a, full-time
Dates of Enrollment: 8/2001-5/2004
Survey Submitted: June 2004

I loved more than half of my professors. They do a great job of assigning excellent professors to the first-year classes. About 80 percent of them are wonderful. It is fairly easy to get into the classes and professors of your choice. You just have to be patient and sometimes wait on lists. For the smallest classes, there is a bid system involving assigning points to classes, and giving priority to 3Ls over 2Ls. There is a curve for first-year classes and other large classes with an average of 3.2. Smaller classes can, and often do, have mostly As given out. There are no Ds or Fs. The professors are trying to help and retain the students, not fail anyone out.

Status: Current student, full-time
Dates of Enrollment: 8/2002-Submit Date
Survey Submitted: November 2003

The first year is rough, but no worse than what I hear from people at other schools. Students are placed in one of three sections (A, B or C). Each section has about 70 to 80 people. Competition is pretty low. If you start acting hyper-competitive, you will be shunned socially. The grading curve is about a 3.2. Cs happen, but Ds are rare. Quality of classes varies widely. There are some great profs (Reynolds, Kinports, Kaplan, etc.) and some not-so-great profs. Some profs are famous and very smart but very hard to communicate with. The good ones seem to have a genuine love of teaching.

Status: Current student, full-time
Dates of Enrollment: 8/2001-Submit Date
Survey Submitted: October 2003

The first year consists of required courses in a set schedule. You get no flexibility (except for one course in your second semester where you choose one course from a list of three). The second and third year are for electives. The popular courses run on a bid system, which favors 3Ls over 2Ls. Overall the system seems pretty fair. I personally have always been able to get the courses I wanted. The professors are accessible and generally nice, with a few exceptions. Grading in law schools generally is unfair, so you can expect a similar curve here. I think the middle of the first-year curve is between 3.0 and

Read all of Vault's Law School Surveys at www.vault.com/lawschool — get complete surveys on top law schools, expert advice on applicaton essays, LSAT prep and more.

VAULT CAREER LIBRARY 241

3.1 on a 4.0 scale. That is a little lower than many other schools in the Top 25. The workload is heavy but manageable.

Employment Prospects

Status: Current student, full-time
Dates of Enrollment: 8/2004-Submit Date
Survey Submitted: April 2006

Employment prospects at Illinois are great, with an obvious emphasis on Chicago. Every major Chicago firm, along with several mid-size and small firms, come down to interview here. Several students go to the top BigLaw firms every year. Like all law school programs, students at the top of their class are well-positioned for a wide range of opportunities. Some students also go on to clerk for judges right out of law school, including at the federal appellate level.

Status: Alumnus/a, full-time
Dates of Enrollment: 8/2002-5/2005
Survey Submitted: March 2006

Illinois is a top-tier school. If you are looking to practice law in the Midwest but outside Chicago, this is probably the best school for you. That said, the location in Champaign, IL is a hurdle to overcome if you want to practice in Chicago. There are six law schools in Chicago; employers there are not eager to travel to Champaign for on-campus interviews and, being so far away from Chicago, it's very difficult to network while in school. If you want to practice in Chicago, it's still bargain-priced, but know the downside with respect to employment prospects.

Status: Alumnus/a, full-time
Dates of Enrollment: 8/1999-5/2002
Survey Submitted: March 2006

A student at the top of the class will be able to get a position with just about any firm in any major market in the country. Students in the middle of the class will find it difficult to get jobs outside of the major cities nearby (i.e., Chicago, Indianapolis, and St. Louis), this is due in part to the fact that the school's ranking doesn't attract many schools to on-campus interviewing for positions outside of the Midwest. That being said, there are a ton of alumni in the Chicago area and most are only too happy to help out their fellow Illini.

Status: Alumnus/a, full-time
Dates of Enrollment: 7/2002-5/2005
Survey Submitted: October 2005

This is always a debate amongst the students. The top 25 percent of the class generally works for BigLaw in Chicago. The alumni network is out there, but you're going to have to find it yourself. Most of my classmates are employed. Be nice to everyone you meet, because unless you do really well first year, you are going to spend the rest of law school networking to find yourself a job after graduation.

Status: Current student, full-time
Dates of Enrollment: 8/2004-Submit Date
Survey Submitted: January 2005

At Illinois, it's often said that being in the top third of the class pretty much guarantees you big firm jobs in Chicago, St. Louis, and Indianapolis. Working outside of the Midwest though requires legwork. It is doable however, as more NY and California firms are coming to the school every year. In Chicago especially, the alumni network is unreal. There will be a good chance that the hiring partner came from Illinois Law.

Status: Alumnus/a, full-time
Dates of Enrollment: 8/2001-5/2004
Survey Submitted: June 2004

It is easy to get a great job in Chicago by graduating from Illinois. If you want to go somewhere else, it is substantially harder, and you'll have to do most of the work yourself. I recommend going to a school in the region where you want to practice. We have OCI (on-campus interviews) for several dozen firms in the fall and a couple dozen in the spring. The fall is mostly for 2Ls, and the spring is mostly for 1Ls. It is a great program to get a job, mostly with large firms and

mostly in Chicago. Unfortunately, fewer than 30 percent of us get jobs through this process. I got my job this way, so I don't know details of how to get a job otherwise, but it's a lot harder. You have to do a lot of calling and researching yourself, although career services tries to help. Nine months after graduation, 9 to 100 percent of graduates have jobs, but almost half my friends did not have jobs at graduation.

Status: Current student, full-time
Dates of Enrollment: 8/2002-Submit Date
Survey Submitted: November 2003

Large firms tend to hire people in the top 25 to 30 percent of the class. I am currently a 3L with a job lined up at a large firm. All of the large Chicago firms recruit and hire students from Illinois. Going out of state is more challenging (especially if you want to leave the Midwest—it's relatively easy to transition to other cities in the Midwest; e.g., St. Louis, Indy, Minneapolis, Detroit, Kansas City). You need to to a lot of your own legwork if you want to work on either coast.

Quality of Life

Status: Current student, full-time
Dates of Enrollment: 8/2004-Submit Date
Survey Submitted: April 2006

Champaign-Urbana is obviously smaller and more relaxed than big cities however, it has the appeal of a Big 10 campus. Life as a lawyer can be hectic, so I am enjoying the relaxed tempo of the Midwest right now.

Status: Alumnus/a, full-time
Dates of Enrollment: 9/1975-5/1978
Survey Submitted: April 2006

Urbana Champaign provides the quintessential college atmosphere. There are thousands of students with a multitude of opportunities both academically and socially. Housing of all types is readily available. The campus is sprawling, but flat with great bike paths. The Intramural Physical Education Facility provides many fitness and sports advantages. The campus is safe and well-lit.

Status: Alumnus/a, full-time
Dates of Enrollment: 8/2002-5/2005
Survey Submitted: March 2006

Champaign, IL is an easy place to live. Champaign is one of the "twin-cities" of Champaign and Urbana. Nothing is farther than 15 minutes away (by car), and there is a pretty decent public transportation system, especially for a city this size. The law facility itself was probably built in the 1960s and looks like it; nothing to write home about, but they are slowly renovating it. There is a meager cafeteria in the law building. The campus is HUGE. There is a huge undergraduate population, comprising "campustown" which has the usual cheap stores and bars of any Big 10 college town. The campus is basically in the middle of cornfields; there isn't too much charm, but it's cheap to live here and safe.

Status: Alumnus/a, full-time
Dates of Enrollment: 8/2002-5/2005
Survey Submitted: March 2006

Champaign is a college town and there are always plenty of apartments, cultural activities, bars, and restaurants. Big-name bands come through and there's always a basketball or football game to go to. It doesn't have all of the amenities of a large city, but then again it doesn't have the cost of living either. Besides, Chicago is only two hours away, which isn't much more than commuting downtown from the farther suburbs.

Status: Alumnus/a, full-time
Dates of Enrollment: 7/2002-5/2005
Survey Submitted: October 2005

Like a lot of universities, the law school got smacked around by 1960s and 70s architecture. The building is a bit harsh. The technology level is good, the whole place is wireless.

The town is also very safe. There is random theft (someone stole 10 bucks from my wallet once, but they also turned it into the lost and found with everything else still inside). But for the most part, as a woman, you can go anywhere, at any time, and feel perfectly safe.

Status: Current student, full-time
Dates of Enrollment: 8/2004-Submit Date
Survey Submitted: January 2005

Champaign-Urbana is no big city. But, as the flagship state university in Illinois, the campus is huge. The twin cities swell to over 100,000 when school is in session. Plus, Chicago is right up I-57. Housing is ridiculously cheap and crime is just not much of a problem, especially compared to Chicago and other big city campuses.

Status: Alumnus/a, full-time
Dates of Enrollment: 9/2000-5/2003
Survey Submitted: June 2004

Champaign may be better suited to an undergraduate experience than a grad experience. There is a bevvy of bars and social opportunities, but the undergrads tend to keep to themselves. The law campus is separated from the undergraduate campus and is relatively self-contained

Status: Current student, full-time
Dates of Enrollment: 8/2002-Submit Date
Survey Submitted: November 2003

Crime is pretty low. Champaign is a college town in the middle of nowhere. This is probably a plus for law school (especially the first year) because there are very few distractions in town. All of the basic amenities are here (chain restaurants—Fridays, Red Lobster, Outback; malls—Limited, Gap, Old Navy, movie theaters, bars, etc.). You're not going to get anything upscale around here, but hey, you're living on loans, and it's better to keep your money. Apartments are reasonable (one-bedrooms cost $400 to $600, and two-bedrooms $500 to $800). I must admit that the rumors are true. The stench of South Farms can be overpowering. Other than that the quality of life is pretty good.

Status: Current student, full-time
Dates of Enrollment: 8/2001-Submit Date
Survey Submitted: October 2003

Champaign is a college town. Housing is plentiful and cheap. Beer is also plentiful and cheap. Campus is large and diverse. The facilities are up to par overall, and crime is pretty low (typical campus-type crime). Overall it is large campus living at a pretty low cost. Drawbacks: the winters can be murder; and outside of campus the nightlife is pretty slow, but improving with new clubs in downtown Champaign.

 Social Life

Status: Current student, full-time
Dates of Enrollment: 8/2004-Submit Date
Survey Submitted: April 2006

All of the rumors about law school consuming your life do not apply at Illinois. I was surprised at how much time I had to pursue interests outside of school. Since Illinois is not in a large city, it escapes the drawbacks associated with "commuter" city schools. You meet a lot of new friends, and almost everyone gets involved in some aspect of the school. Law school at Illinois is like its only little community filled with some of the brightest professors and the most talented students. It simply does not have the fiercely competitive, unmanageable workload, and uninviting atmosphere that friends have told me they experience at other schools.

Status: Alumnus/a, full-time
Dates of Enrollment: 8/2002-5/2005
Survey Submitted: March 2006

The law school itself has plenty of clubs, etc. There are also multiple movie theaters, a mall, and both chain stores and restaurants and quaint downtown "main street" type establishments. Downtown Champaign has undergone major revival in the last five or so years, and now has a martini bar (Boltini), a sports bar (Guido's), and an Irish bar (Mike & Molly's) where grad students and other

young professionals congregate. There are a variety of bars and clubs along the downtown Champaign four-block area. There are additional bars in the Urbana downtown area, near the county and federal courthouses. The Office is a restaurant and bar that is popular, and also the location of the law school's Beer League Darts darts games on a weekly basis.

Status: Alumnus/a, full-time
Dates of Enrollment: 8/1998-5/2001
Survey Submitted: March 2006

School's social life is somewhat geared toward younger students, but the law school sponsors many social events with and without professors, that have appear to older students. Law students tend to avoid the campus bars as U of I bars are open to students 19 and older and many of the bars are filled with younger people. Many bars off campus are more popular with law students. Accessibility to good restaurants is surprisingly good for a town of the size. Art scene also is good. Dating can be limited for those over 30. Popular law school events include Beer League Darts (a weekly team dart league with several skill levels), Keg Ball (softball games with kegs), intramural soccer, softball, broomball (hockey without skates) and basketball leagues, and U of I sporting events/tailgating.

Status: Alumnus/a, full-time
Dates of Enrollment: 8/1999-5/2002
Survey Submitted: March 2006

Having come from an undergraduate school that was ranked the Number One party school in the country twice while I was there, I have very high expectations of a school's social life but U of I more than lived up to those expectations. A very good portion of the law students are laid back enough to participate in the school's "beer darts" league on Wednesdays, and it is very common to find large groups of law students out together at bars (e.g., Boltini and Jupiters) on Friday and Saturday evenings. Since this is a Big 10 campus, football and basketball seasons are particularly great and create welcome diversions from studying. The only drawback is that the law school students are somewhat isolated from the rest of campus (i.e., it's difficult to meet other grad/professional students). That being said, as difficult as law school is supposed to be, I would gladly go through another three year stint in Champaign at U of I (and this is coming from a person who grew up in Los Angeles and lived in Washington, D.C.).

Status: Alumnus/a, full-time
Dates of Enrollment: 7/2002-5/2005
Survey Submitted: October 2005

Many people in Champaign bemoan the middle-of-nowhereness of it all. I found it to be quite a blessing. Your peers aren't busy competing over who has the best, most prestigious job during the school year because there really aren't that many options. Instead, time is spent getting to know each in one of the area's numerous bars. It's small town America so everyone lives 10 minutes away from each other. There really is just a lot more time to make friends, and occasionally, a ruckus.

One's opinion of the dating scene correlated pretty closely to their success in navigating it. The biggest obstacle was that as a small school, it was very difficult to start dating someone casually without involving almost everyone in your class. Some people chose to keep their relationships and dalliances secret, others were far more comfortable in the spotlight. Regardless of the dating scene, law school prom was a blast. You could bring a date or go stag, it didn't really matter. Everyone was just out to let off some steam before finals really kicked up at the end of April.

Status: Current student, full-time
Dates of Enrollment: 8/2004-Submit Date
Survey Submitted: January 2005

With over 30,000 students, you better believe the weekends are for partying. Whatever you like to do, there are students doing it. And while graduate students tend to segregate themselves by going to bars a little further off-campus, you won't have a problem making friends.

Read all of Vault's Law School Surveys at www.vault.com/lawschool — get complete surveys on top law schools, expert advice on applicaton essays, LSAT prep and more.

VAULT CAREER LIBRARY 243

Status: Alumnus/a, full-time
Dates of Enrollment: 8/2001-5/2004
Survey Submitted: June 2004

There are plenty of restaurants, bars and movie theaters, and it's only two and a half hours from Chicago. First-year classes have a different happy hour every Friday. There is an [organization called] Beer League Darts, where most students go out together every Wednesday and socialize, and some people play darts. There is a nice gala and crazy prom every spring.

Status: Current student, full-time
Dates of Enrollment: 8/2001-Submit Date
Survey Submitted: October 2003

The law school is a very social place. There are "beer darts" every Wednesday, happy hour (with alcohol) every Thursday at 4 p.m. and something going on with a student group almost daily. In addition, the campus community as a whole provides many interesting and entertaining activities. The law students don't hang out at campus bars too much. We tend to hang in the downtown Champaign area with other graduate and professional students. The nightlife is OK for a smaller city but can in no way compare to Chicago.

Indiana University
School of Law—Bloomington

Admissions Office
School of Law—Bloomington
Indiana University
211 South Indiana Avenue
Bloomington, IN 47405
Admissions phone: (812) 855-4765
Admissions fax (812) 855-0555
Admissions e-mail: lawadmis@indiana.edu
Admissions URL:
http://www.law.indiana.edu/prospective/

 ## Admissions

Status: Current student, full-time
Dates of Enrollment: 8/2003-Submit Date
Survey Submitted: May 2006

I have three suggestions for students wishing to get into IUB. First, do a phenomenal job with your LSAT. If you get over a 170, you tend to get considered for bigger scholarships. People are also considerably more interested in you and will give you more individual attention. Also, definitely make an appointment to talk with someone on campus. Kevin Robling was their admissions director when I entered and he was frank, completely honest, and incredibly interesting and fun. Finally, do something interesting with your essay. I made mine into a brochure, for example. It was full-color with pictures and fun, shiny paper. I enjoyed making it and everyone to whom I applied spoke highly of my technique for gathering interest. I also attached some black and white copies on normal paper if people needed to make copies or just didn't want to look at the pictures.

Status: Current student, full-time
Dates of Enrollment: 8/2005-Submit Date
Survey Submitted: May 2006

Indiana University-Bloomington is a fairly selective law school. Being in the middle of the pack of the Top Tier attempting to become a "Top 20" law school program is a position IU shares with several other good programs. Typically, one will find with all of these programs one thing above all else matters: the LSAT score. Generally, it seems it is safe to say that if you want to get accepted into IU Law, you need to be at the 90th percentile with your LSAT score. If you have done this, little else will matter. You likely will become accepted. If you got a score below this, you will need to have a strong GPA to balance it out. Remember that law school admissions for all but the elite programs (where numbers are already satisfied), is going to be an almost pure numbers game.

There are some programs, (such as Washington in St. Louis and Northwestern) that are known to like non-traditional students that have had interesting experiences and have been out of school a number of years. IU is not one of those programs. With fairly strong numbers you will get in. However, one definite exception is that it seems our school is quite deferential to those with military experience. If you have a military background, I'd consider applying to IU. This seems to have been a good policy, because I know that many with military backgrounds are towards the top of the class.

The school says: "The quality of students applying to the School of Law increases every year. No LSAT score is sufficient alone to guarantee admission. Substantial weight is also placed on the undergraduate GPA, difficulty of major and courses taken, as well as demonstrated leadership and letters of recommendation reflecting skill at research and writing. The personal statement can make or break any applicant's chances

of admission. The School of Law actively seeks students with substantial postgraduate work experience or graduate study. In recent classes, approximately 40 percent of entering students had more than two years of experience after completion of the undergraduate degree. The School of Law's Strategic Plan sets a goal of increased postgraduate work experience among entering students."

Status: Current student, full-time
Dates of Enrollment: 8/2005-Submit Date
Survey Submitted: May 2006

I personally think that my school is at a crossroads. It has always touted itself as a school that is independent of the rankings game, and that the reason people come to this school is because of the quality of life, the people, the relaxed atmosphere, etc. But now I think the school is feeling the pressure that comes with the reality that the *U.S. News* rankings aren't going away anytime soon, and as a result, the admissions process is getting a lot more competitive and "numbers-based" than it was before.

Status: Current student, full-time
Dates of Enrollment: 8/2005-Submit Date
Survey Submitted: May 2006

I worked for the admissions' office and they really do read everything at Indiana, so if your scores are lacking in some areas, you can make up for in the essay and other areas of your file. Make no mistake, it is a competitive process, but they truly do value the person at Indiana not just the scores. Thus, unless you are at the very top in terms of GPA. and LSAT scores, take everything seriously. Also, I challenge you to find a more helpful and friendly admissions office in the country.

Status: Current student, full-time
Dates of Enrollment: 8/2005-Submit Date
Survey Submitted: May 2006

The most important part of your admissions package is the personal essay—even if your grades and LSAT score are above average. The school is relatively close-knit and the staff in the admissions office takes the make up of the class very seriously. If you have any questions, the staff is wonderful and will always take a moment to help you.

Status: Current student, full-time
Dates of Enrollment: 7/2005-Submit Date
Survey Submitted: May 2006

Although there was no interview process, when I called to schedule a visit just in general, they immediately set me up with an appointment with the assistant dean because the head dean wasn't in town the day I'd be visiting. I was impressed, but more impressed to find out later that most students who visited met with the actual dean and received personal letters from him. The admissions process was very easy and the fee was reasonable, in fact almost cheap compared to other schools. It was fantastic as well that they don't require a seat reservation fee in the spring as most other schools do for law programs.

Status: Current student, full-time
Dates of Enrollment: 8/2005-Submit Date
Survey Submitted: May 2006

The admissions process at IU Bloomington is really painless. Be candid. Don't take yourself too seriously, and put your best foot forward by writing thoughtfully and proofreading carefully. The essay questions are very similar at most law schools, and most applicants will have well-written responses. Earnestness can come across even on paper, so be true to yourself and tell the school honestly what you can bring to your class and to the profession. Call if you have questions, about the school or about the process, and take advantage of

Read all of Vault's Law School Surveys at www.vault.com/lawschool — get complete surveys on top law schools, expert advice on applicaton essays, LSAT prep and more.

VAULT CAREER LIBRARY **245**

open houses to understand the atmosphere at the school and what aspects of you will be most appreciated at different schools. IU has a very collegial and friendly atmosphere, but also topnotch students from topnotch schools. You don't need to be overly formal, but you do need to be organized and have a nice presentation (no spelling or grammar errors, formatting glitches, etc.).

Status: Current student, full-time
Dates of Enrollment: 8/2005-Submit Date
Survey Submitted: May 2006

I filled out an online application, along with the LSAC online application. I asked for a meeting with a member of the admissions' committee. For the personal statement, I wrote about how the experiences I have had would make me a unique law student. I only wanted to go to two schools; not much selection for me, so no comment on the "selectivity" area. I did receive two pieces of advice from one professor I met when I toured the school. (1) In the personal statement, write about real-life experiences; not about how playing high school sports taught you so much about life. (2) If you don't get accepted at the school you want, you let them know that you won't take no for an answer. That means if they have an opening on the first day of classes because someone didn't show up, and if you really want to go there, you let them know that you'll be there the first day if they need you to be.

Status: Current student, full-time
Dates of Enrollment: 8/2005-Submit Date
Survey Submitted: May 2006

The admissions process at IU is fairly straightforward, I think. You don't have to jump through any hoops that you're not already jumping through in the admissions process for other schools. I think the main thing is to concentrate on getting your best possible test scores and then write an essay that really shows how you have had experiences that will make you a good contribution to a student body. That doesn't mean you have to have gone out and saved the world, just that you are bringing something to the table. IU really seems proud of bringing together a student body with a wide range of world experiences.

Status: Alumnus/a, full-time
Dates of Enrollment: 8/1998-5/2001
Survey Submitted: April 2004

For Indiana residents, the admissions process is not too problematic. If you did reasonably well at your undergraduate institution (3.3+ GPA) and pulled down a decent LSAT score (top 25 to 30 percent), you have a great chance of getting admitted. The essays ask all the regular law school admission questions, nothing unusual. As far as I know, the school of law does not conduct interviews.

> **The school says:** "Indiana residents receive no advantage over nonresident applicants in the admissions process. For several years, the majority of entering students have come from outside Indiana. The two most recent entering classes have had a median LSAT score of 163 and a median undergraduate GPA of approximately 3.5."

Status: Current student, full-time LLM
Dates of Enrollment: 8/2003-Submit Date
Survey Submitted: June 2004

Applicants must have received a bachelor's degree in law or its recognized equivalent from a college or university in the United States or abroad. Applicants whose first language is not English must take the TOEFL. Most students who are admitted to the program have minimum scores of 560 (paper-based TOEFL) or 213 (computer-based TOEFL). Applicants with lower TOEFL scores but otherwise excellent qualifications will also be considered for admission. Besides that, you have to submit your resume, statement of purpose and letters of recommendation. No interview. I graduated from my university in June 2002. I prepared for application materials for half a year and entered IU School of Law in August 2003.

> **IU School of Law says:** "Applicants for the LLM program must have a JD degree from the United States or a bachelor's degree or equivalent degree from a foreign university that qualifies for engaging in the practice of law."

 **Academics**

Status: Alumnus/a, full-time
Dates of Enrollment: 8/2003-5/2006
Survey Submitted: May 2006

The first-year classes were taught by highly qualified professors, indeed, some of the best teachers at the school. The incoming class was split into two large sections taking four out of five classes together, with a small Research and Writing course with only about 15 students . Each incoming student was also assigned to a Peer Group Advising section that had five or six 1Ls and a 2L or 3L student helping with all of the odds and ends of law school like social functions, extracurriculars, outlining and briefing, etc. The upper level classes were varied and I do not recall anyone not getting into a class they wanted during either their 2L or 3L year. The classes are designed for a national law school (more out-of-state than in-state students and many leaving Indiana to practice), focusing on the way to learn law and comparative thinking over specific practice points local to the jurisdiction, like pleadings, etc. Some classes, such as trial advocacy and negotiations were hands-on, practical course. Some classes, like information law, were survey classes applicable to many different areas.

Status: Current student, full-time
Dates of Enrollment: 8/2005-Submit Date
Survey Submitted: May 2006

The school emphasizes class participation—not just knowing the material but actively engaging in discussion both with professors and other students. Legal writing class requires intensive research. The second-semester brief writing and oral argument require critical thinking and a real time commitment. My favorite parts about the first year were the conversations I had with other students about class materials. Other students encourage you to prepare simply by engaging you in active thinking—always pressing you to analyze and think seriously about your opinions.

Status: Current student, full-time
Dates of Enrollment: 8/2003-Submit Date
Survey Submitted: May 2006

The professors are very involved with the students and care a lot about helping us learn and do well on our exams. Making appointments with professors is very easy; they are accessible and friendly. I found the students in my classes to be a mixed bag. Some are really eager and love to answer questions and engage in discussions, while others are silent studiers—and still others dork around on the Internet instead of paying attention. Thus, it's pretty easy to find your niche in a classroom! Law classes at IU are like most other things: you get out of it what you put in. I've chosen to put my heart and soul into the program and really have learned a lot.

We have three law journals (two are excellent and one is merely good). I have learned a lot about leadership in my journal, as well as a lot about citation and legal research that I didn't learn in class. I highly, highly recommend getting involved in a journal. We also have three moot courts, at least one trial team, and four or five clinics. I plan to do a clinic during my last year of school, having heard such great things about how well the prepare you for practice and for dealing with clients.

Status: Alumnus/a, full-time
Dates of Enrollment: 8/2003-5/2006
Survey Submitted: May 2006

Of course, the first year we took required courses in core law classes. At the end of the first year, the dean of students was helpful in holding a meeting and giving us hand-outs to let us know what we could expect on the bar exam and made recommendations for what classes to take in order to do well. I was always able to get the classes I chose, except for one class, which I was able to take the next semester.

Status: Current student, full-time
Dates of Enrollment: 8/2005-Submit Date
Survey Submitted: May 2006

We sort of have a different system than other schools in that we aren't broken down into specific "sections." That is, the make-up of your classes varies from class to class. This can be good in that you get to meet different people, but somewhat bad in that some of your classmates for criminal law, for instance, will have a much easier load in torts, and thus, more time to spend competing against you. Again, there is a this clash between the "friendly" atmosphere the administration wants to create, and the increasingly competitive nature of the students.

Status: Current student, full-time
Dates of Enrollment: 8/2003-Submit Date
Survey Submitted: May 2006

Big core classes are easy to get into. Sometimes popular seminars will fill up, but if a student is proactive, even those are often accessible. For the most part, professors are pleased to meet with students for extra explanation or to suggest extra reading. A lot of classes stress a policy or theoretical approach in addition to Black Letter Law. The average grade in most classes is a B. Workload (and indeed, the entire experience) is what you make of it. If you decide to really get the material, you will have to put in a lot of time. If you decide that you don't mind a B-, you probably don't have to put in very much time. Though classes are obviously the centerpiece of the legal education at IU, I have to say that I learned just as much from participation in co-curriculars like moot court, journal, or clinic, which take up just as much time and provide practical experiences to complement the theory of class.

Status: Current student, full-time
Dates of Enrollment: 8/2005-Submit Date
Survey Submitted: May 2006

The quality of the classes at my school varies. I think that the first year of my program, which is set by administrators, isn't necessarily reflective of what the rest of my semesters will be like. As with any school, I had some professors that I really liked and some that I really disliked. The overall discussion for all of the classes was at a much higher level than I had previously experienced. I found this beneficial come test time, because some of those conversations stuck in my head and offered good illustration for exam questions. There definitely are a group of "popular" classes, some for which you even have to interview for. However, from what I can tell the school is committed to getting you enrolled in a later semester if it doesn't work out the first time around. The grading in law school is very arbitrary. This is the only aspect of law school that I dislike. It seems unfair that your grades do not necessarily reflect the amount of time you put into your studies, but that is just the name of the game. The competitiveness in grading is also very intense, so I notice that it puts a strain on friendships and such.

Status: Current student, full-time
Dates of Enrollment: 8/2005-Submit Date
Survey Submitted: May 2006

Simple things are not given to students (e.g., online student directory; online registration for classes). The drop/add period for classes is two days, which doesn't help if your class meets say, on a Wednesday, and you are required to either drop/add classes on Thurs. and Fri. because classes commenced for Fall semester on Thursday.

> **The school says:** "Student directories in online or hard-copy formats were discontinued in light of increasing privacy concerns expressed by students. To assist students in getting to know one another, however, a CD is produced and distributed each year with the names, photos, and video clips of students introducing themselves to classmates. A hard copy of this "face book" also is available at the check-out desk of the library.
>
> "Online registration is not currently available due to differences in the scheduling and registration priorities between the law school and greater university. Conversion to the University's registration system at this time would preclude flexibility in class scheduling that allows, among other things, a week-long fall break and two reading days prior to the exam period in the spring.
>
> "The drop/add period runs for a full week each semester— beginning two days prior to commencement of classes and providing time for students to attend at least one session of each class before finalizing their schedules."

Status: Alumnus/a, full-time
Dates of Enrollment: 8/2000-5/2003
Survey Submitted: April 2004

Academics at Indiana are topnotch. With only one exception, all of the professors I encountered were very bright, well-versed in the subjects they taught and genuinely interested in teaching—as opposed to only being interested in research. Prospective students should realize that the major difference in top-tier law schools is probably not the quality of professors, but rather the quality of students.

To the extent that one references rankings when making decisions about which schools to apply to, students will probably encounter only very slight differences in the quality of the faculty between a school ranked 10th and a school ranked 40th. There will probably be a greater difference in the quality of students admitted, simply because it's so much harder to get admitted to schools much higher up on the rankings totem pole. Even still, the vast majority of my classmates at Indiana were very bright people, which made for interesting, intellectually challenging classroom discussions.

Status: Alumnus/a, full-time
Dates of Enrollment: 8/2000-5/2003
Survey Submitted: November 2003

The school offers a wide variety of classes taught by an excellent faculty. The recently appointed dean has been steadily increasing the size of the faculty and therefore the number of classes taught. The curriculum was set out for first-years, and after that it was fairly easy to register for the classes I wanted. Registration was easy because we did not register through the university—the law school has its own recorder. The faculty has instituted a curve. Students must maintain their studies to do well, but the workload is not overwhelming. As are possible even with the curve

Status: Current student, full-time LLM
Dates of Enrollment: 8/2003-Submit Date
Survey Submitted: June 2004

There are various courses at IU-Bloomington. As an LLM student, I can choose whatever I want, such as Intellectual Property, International Law, or Commercial Law. It is not difficult to take popular courses here. Professors here treat LLM students very well. They like to help LLM students and converse with us. LLM students have to take a Legal Writing and Research course for two semesters. This is also a very useful course. I learned a lot from this course, especially how to do legal research and legal writing.

Students may choose a course of study to fit their specific interests and can select from courses covering U.S. domestic, comparative, foreign and international law. Some LLM students use this as an opportunity to become broadly acquainted with several areas of U.S. law. They can prepare for the New York bar exam. Others follow a more targeted approach, either crafting their own programs of specialization or focusing their courses in one of the areas of concentration that the school of law has identified.

 Employment Prospects

Status: Alumnus/a, full-time
Dates of Enrollment: 8/2003-5/2006
Survey Submitted: May 2006

On-campus recruiting was well used by students and helped many obtain jobs with Midwest, mid- to large-size corporate firms. The school seemed to be well-respected by employers in the Midwest and in many other pockets of the country where alumni have made an impact. The application process for clerkships, both federal and state, was good and many students pursued this path. A large recent donation from a faculty member and new student groups such as the Public Interest Law Forum and Loan Repayment Assistance Program and clinics such as the Tenants' Assistance Program and Inmates' Assistance Program seem to be making a difference. The hardest area for students to get a job placement is at medium or small firms outside of the Midwest.

Read all of Vault's Law School Surveys at www.vault.com/lawschool — get complete surveys on top law schools, expert advice on applicaton essays, LSAT prep and more.

VAULT CAREER LIBRARY 247

Status: Current student, full-time
Dates of Enrollment: 8/2005-Submit Date
Survey Submitted: May 2006

The career services office is incredibly active and works just as hard as the students here do. Employment with law school is scary, because frankly there is an incredible amount of competition to get the top jobs in the big markets. Additionally, the one downfall (that I see) of IU Law is that it is not in or near a big market. This, I feel, probably hurts efforts to get employers to interview here. The lack of proximity to a big legal market is probably IU's biggest barrier to being an elite law school.

Status: Alumnus/a, full-time
Dates of Enrollment: 8/2004-5/2006
Survey Submitted: May 2006

The vice dean personally helped me get a dream job with Arnold & Porter in Washington, D.C. He is well-connected and needed only to make a phone call on my behalf to personally vouch for me. I was given a job offer shortly after my second interview.

Status: Alumnus/a, full-time
Dates of Enrollment: 7/2003-5/2006
Survey Submitted: May 2006

I consider myself somewhat lucky in getting a job through on-campus recruiting at a prestigious law firm in New York. Most of my friends are employed. Because I'm pleased with how my situation panned out, I have a hard time complaining, but I found that there were very few opportunities for students who wanted to get a job outside of the Midwest. Granted, the majority of students at IU are from the Midwest, but I expected more from a nationally recognized school. Only four firms with a New York office interviewed on campus.

Status: Alumnus/a, full-time
Dates of Enrollment: 9/1998-5/2001
Survey Submitted: March 2005

Employment opportunities for top half are easily found in the Midwest. The bottom half is more restricted but there are still a decent amount of opportunities in Indiana and nearby states. Employment outside the Midwest is not easy.

> **The school says:** "60 percent of the School of Law's recent graduates secured employment outside the state of Indiana. Of that number, 25 percent took positions in other Midwestern states, and another 25 percent found positions in states along the Atlantic seaboard, from Florida to Massachusetts. A growing number of students (approximately 5 percent currently) are employed in the far west and along the Pacific coast. Acquiring positions outside the Midwest does require greater effort, but our students are aided by active and growing alumni communities, particularly in Washington D.C., New York, Texas, Florida, Arizona, and California. In addition, in 2004, the School of Law's Career Services Office hosted 91 employers that recruited for offices in 24 states and the District of Columbia.

Status: Alumnus/a, full-time
Dates of Enrollment: 8/2000-5/2003
Survey Submitted: April 2004

Indiana is in the process of beefing up its career services office. I'd estimate that, among my classmates, there was probably a 50-50 split with respect to whether students felt that career services was helpful. Among those who were of the opinion that the career services office was not helpful enough were a significant number of students who felt that it was the job of career services to get a job. That is emphatically not the case.

Status: Alumnus/a, full-time
Dates of Enrollment: 8/1998-5/2001
Survey Submitted: April 2004

The school of law has a strong on-campus interview process, but unfortunately it is most helpful only to those in the top third of the class. If you are fortunate enough to be in that position, you will have a good chance of landing a great job in places like Chicago, Indy, D.C. and Louisville. If you are interested in

working on the Coasts or further outside the region, the job search can be a bit tougher, and you can count on having to do most of the legwork yourself. For those in the bottom two-thirds of the class, the career services people will bend over backward to help you find something, and it seems like most people had suitable jobs lined up by the time graduation rolled around.

Status: Alumnus/a, full-time
Dates of Enrollment: 8/2000-5/2003
Survey Submitted: November 2003

The career services office worked diligently throughout the year to help students with summer and permanent employment placement. Major strategies were on-campus interviewing (employers from across the country routinely participated), alumni networking (again, alums work across the country and were always helpful) and faculty contacts. The school also guarantees a public interest internship for the summer following the first year of school. This is a wonderful opportunity to get hands-on experience and become more competitive for the second summer.

 Quality of Life

Status: Current student, full-time
Dates of Enrollment: 8/2003-Submit Date
Survey Submitted: May 2006

Law students benefit from all the resources of Indiana University, which are many. I also think Bloomington is a great place to spend a few years, no matter what you like to do. Lots of hiking and outdoor activity, but also biggish-name jazz and music acts come through on their ways to Chicago or because of Bloomington's world-renowned music school. Law students typically don't live in dorms on campus, but there's lots of rental housing within walking distance of campus. The biggest student complaint, a perennial in college towns, is parking for those who drive in.

Status: Current student, full-time
Dates of Enrollment: 7/2005-Submit Date
Survey Submitted: May 2006

Bloomington is a very safe area and I've never felt unsafe even walking to and from the library at midnight or in darkness. There is tons of housing at all income/quality levels in the area, although most students live in cheaper student housing near the campus. There are still many students that live in houses or in nicer apartments a bit of ways away from the school and drive. Parking is a problem for some of those students.

Status: Alumnus/a, full-time
Dates of Enrollment: 7/2003-5/2006
Survey Submitted: May 2006

The law school itself is beautiful in a classic way, but is in need of updates. The chairs are quite possibly the most uncomfortable on earth, and the classrooms are dated. (Although the addition of plugs for computers is a huge improvement.) They just can't keep up with the swivel chairs and fancy amenities of newer schools, like IUPUI. That said, the library is gorgeous and the lounge and TV room are great.

Status: Current student, full-time
Dates of Enrollment: 7/2004-Submit Date
Survey Submitted: May 2006

Facilities are OK. The library is great. The lecture classrooms all have wireless networks and an outlet for every seat, which is really nice. It's hard to get study rooms a lot of the time. Tip—the library front desk has nutshells and hornbooks for all the classes. No one tells you this, I don't know why. Read them BEFORE you start a class—it makes a HUGE difference.

The biggest quality of life thing for me is the lack of information. The school doesn't tell you what programs are available, there's almost no info about the clinics, I was here two years before I figured out that the Trial Competition is different from moot court, and I'm still mad about missing that opportunity.

> **The school says:** "The School endeavors to make students aware of its wide variety of programs and clinical offerings

through diverse means. The School web site has a page dedicated to providing details about its programs and centers that includes links to descriptive material about for-credit clinical offerings, other client service projects, and programs like the Trial Competition Team and the Sherman Minton Moot Court Competition. Each spring, schedule planning sessions and open houses are held in which students have an opportunity to hear about distinctive curricular and extra-curricular programs from administrators, faculty, and student participants. Additionally, detailed descriptions for all credit offerings are disseminated prior to registration each semester, and student representatives for client service projects periodically set up information tables and hold call-out meetings."

Status: Alumnus/a, full-time
Dates of Enrollment: 8/1996-5/1999
Survey Submitted: December 2005

Bloomington is a charming college town with much to offer. Besides a world-class university and its resources at your fingertips (world-class musical events, theatre, sports, employment, social, etc.), the town offers great dining and cultural experiences. Just how many small towns offer dozens of ethic dining choices (including Tibetan, Thai, French, Moroccan, Eritrean, African, etc.).

Status: Current student, full-time
Dates of Enrollment: 8/2004-Submit Date
Survey Submitted: September 2004

While the law school is small, it is cozy and comfortable and the law library has everything you would need. Facilities are great—a brand new gym has just been recently finished, and for dining there are plenty of places to eat; it is a college town. In terms of crime, Bloomington is safer than most college campuses I have been on, and everyone here is friendly so they look out for you.

> **The school says:** "The School of Law's Law Library was recognized in 2004 by the National Jurist magazine as the best law school library in the country (a two-way tie for first place)."

Status: Alumnus/a, full-time
Dates of Enrollment: 8/2000-5/2003
Survey Submitted: April 2004

Indiana is a great place to attend law school. The law school is on the same campus as a major state university. Consequently there is always something to do: museums, lectures, world class theater and opera, concerts, Big 10 athletics, etc. Restaurants are abundant. For a town its size, Bloomington has much to offer in this area, from Afghan to Thai cuisine, and the usual American suspects to boot. The facilities are becoming somewhat dated, though the law school is modernizing. Wireless Internet works throughout the building, even if the classrooms aren't well wired for technology.

> **The school says:** "Off-campus housing in the vicinity of the School of Law is plentiful, varied, and relatively inexpensive. More than 450 units have been built within 10 blocks of the school in the last 18 months. It is recommended that students start searching early for the most convenient and best-priced units. The School of Law has recently installed electrical power to every classroom seat for laptop users as well as Internet-linked multimedia presentation equipment in every classroom. Students may elect to take examinations using their laptops rather than writing by hand. Indiana University is recognized as one of the nation's most advanced universities in providing information technology support for students."

Status: Alumnus/a, full-time
Dates of Enrollment: 8/2000-5/2003
Survey Submitted: November 2003

The school is known for the community approach to law school, and it made my experience phenomenal. The faculty, staff, administrators and students mix every day. There are a variety of extracurricular activities including clubs, clinics, public outreach; in every setting the students and faculty work as a team. Most students live within walking distance of the school. The school is self-contained, so the physical building is a home away from home. The library is

open almost around the clock and welcomes food and drink. Everyone is friendly, and there is never a feeling of competition or nastiness among students.

 **Social Life**

Status: Current student, full-time
Dates of Enrollment: 8/2003-Submit Date
Survey Submitted: May 2006

More importantly, though, people at IU Law are very friendly. Most people here have a large group of friends who are willing and able to help them procrastinate around finals week (or any other time!). When I lived in Bloomington, I enjoyed camping and fishing around Monroe Lake. I also went kayaking and sailing on the lake. There is a make-your-own pottery place that I enjoyed, too. IU offers free exercise classes (deep water exercise, swim lessons, aerobics, strength training, etc.) that I enjoy a lot, too. Some of my friends like to go out to clubs, visit Indianapolis, see IU's excellent opera, and get involved in student groups. Student favorite hang-outs include: Nick's, the Video Saloon (not for the faint of heart—especially after dark), and Kilroy's.

Status: Current student, full-time
Dates of Enrollment: 8/2005-Submit Date
Survey Submitted: May 2006

The people are all generally nice to each other, but there's more competition below the surface than anyone wants to admit. The school just isn't what it was five years ago, when the law community was very happy in its collegial, rankings-hating mode. It still retains a good deal of this, but around finals and when grades come back, the competition is there. People are reading the message boards, and realize that if they don't get top grades, there is a distinct possibility that their geographic mobility will be limited. In fact, I even heard a rumor this year about one person who actually hid a book before finals—whenever I hear admissions tours in the hall, the student inevitably says "This isn't like other places where people hide books..." But it's still far from cutthroat—just changing a bit. Overall, in fact, I would still say that this school has retained its ability to command a lot of pride from it's students, and I think when it's all said and done, people are generally pretty happy to be here.

Status: Current student, full-time
Dates of Enrollment: 8/2002-Submit Date
Survey Submitted: May 2006

The dating scene is good for someone right out of undergrad or a few years thereafter. I suspect older single students might have more difficulty but there are efforts being made campus wide. There are graduate student mixer nights and older students normally focus on a couple bars. Plus, there is plenty of community involvement where you might meet someone.

Status: Current student, full-time
Dates of Enrollment: 8/2003-Submit Date
Survey Submitted: May 2006

Bloomington is home to a huge state university, so if you go looking, you can find someone interested in almost anything you're interested in. There are lots of bars (Nick's is the usual choice for law students) if that's your thing, but also lots of shows, opera, free music, plays, etc. through the university. Law students have access to IU outdoor equipment, and Southern Indiana is a beautiful place to hike and camp. Law students can also get student basketball and football tickets—if you're coming from out of state, you will learn that Indiana LOVES basketball. Get tickets. Watch the movie *Breaking Away* before you come and then attend the Little 500 bike race in April. The City of Bloomington has a good network of green space and parks and puts on a number of free events spring-fall. If you want to blend in with the locals and get some good produce, don't miss the farmer's market near City Hall April-November.

Status: Alumnus/a, full-time
Dates of Enrollment: 8/2000-5/2003
Survey Submitted: April 2006

The undergrads from the university tend to dominate the social scene (bars, etc.). The school and the students try hard to make their own social life by putting on events such as the Talent Show and the Public Interest Law Forum's annual Singing for Summer Salaries event as well as bringing in interesting lecturers

Read all of Vault's Law School Surveys at www.vault.com/lawschool — get complete surveys on top law schools, expert advice on applicaton essays, LSAT prep and more.

VAULT CAREER LIBRARY **249**

(Representative Lee Hamilton, part of the 9-11 committee, etc.). They try hard and often succeed.

Because the university is so big and is a cultural hub for the area, it also provides excellent cultural/entertainment events regularly. While in school I went to a few concerts (DJ Skribble, Wyclef John with The Black-eyed Peas, De La Sol and Nelly) a few operas, and even managed to hear Colin Powell speak. The travelling performances of *Rent* and *Showboat* came as did famous local and world renown violinist, Joshua Bell.

Status: Alumnus/a, full-time
Dates of Enrollment: 8/2000-5/2003
Survey Submitted: April 2004

The social scene is focused a bit heavily on bars, though there is plenty to do that does not involve drinking. Law students will be out in droves on any weekend night at Nick's and the Upstairs Pub. Don't bother heading out until 9 or 10 p.m., though, as most of the bars are fairly empty until that hour. Try the Bluebird for live music, Kilroys for a very fraternity-heavy crowd, or the Video Saloon for a much more "eclectic" crowd. If a dance club is what you seek, check out Axis. You can even find drag shows and a primarily gay crowd at Bullwinkle's. All these spots are populated by grad students as well as undergrads.

Crackdowns on drinking at fraternity parties in recent years (IU is a "dry campus") have resulted in more Greek types out at the bars, making things a bit more crowded than they used to be. A trip to Indianapolis is very easy—just one hour to the north. Indy offers dozens of great restaurants, world class shopping, theater, music, bars, the NBA Pacers, the NFL Colts, and the Triple-A Indians, which play at one of the finest minor league parks in the country, right in downtown Indy. Farther to the north, Chicago is still well within reach for a weekend trip at four hours by car. Louisville can be reached in two.

Status: Alumnus/a, full-time
Dates of Enrollment: 8/1998-5/2001
Survey Submitted: April 2004

Much of the cultural life in Bloomington centers around the university. It has a great auditorium and theaters that host both national and local shows. A surprising number of international restaurants thrive side by side with diner-type establishments; try Samira and the Uptown on the Square downtown. Like any university town, there is a wide range of drinking establishments to choose from. Bloomington has a strong liberal bent, so there are many political, environmental, animal rights, human rights and other groups to join and events to attend.

 The School Says

Established in 1842, the Indiana University School of Law—Bloomington teaches students to solve 21st Century problems with a solid grounding in legal skills and traditional professional values. First-year students follow a standard curriculum focused on the formation of basic lawyerly skills in reading, listening, writing, conducting research, and public speaking, and on the application of those skills to foundational courses in contracts, torts, civil procedure, property and constitutional law. Indiana's emphasis on writing and research continues into the second- and third-year curricula. Second- and third-year students can specialize in such fields as business and commercial law; intellectual property; taxation; civil and criminal litigation; environmental law; international business law; international public law; comparative law; and Internet, communications, and information law.

The School of Law is home to the Center for Constitutional Democracy in Plural Societies, which is currently working with constitutional reformers in Burma, Azerbaijan, Liberia, and Kazakhstan in developing draft constitutional provisions and essential supporting institutions to ensure the rule of law with respect for the rights of minorities. Students can participate in a wide variety of projects undertaken by the Center. The School of Law also offers programs in conjunction with the Center for Applied Cybersecurity Research; the Center for Law, Society, and Culture; and the Conservation Law Center.

Students can obtain practical experience in the profession of law by participating in the practices of the Community Legal Clinic, the Entrepreneurship Law Clinic, the Federal Courts Clinic, the Conservation Law Clinic, the Family and Children Mediation Clinic, The Elder Law Clinic, Indiana Legal Services, Student Legal Services, and the Tenant Assistance Project. Many students benefit from an Indiana law that permits them to appear in court and engage in the practice of law, either through the school's clinics or through working directly with prosecutors and other agencies.

The school offers eight formal joint-degree programs in the areas of business administration, accountancy, public affairs, environmental science, telecommunications, journalism, and library science. These programs offer a JD and a master's degree after four years of academic work. Students may also create individualized concurrent-degree programs leading to the award of the JD and any other master's degree regularly granted by Indiana University at its Bloomington campus. Most concurrent-degree programs extend for four years. Concurrent-degree programs have combined the JD with degrees in economics, history, Central Asian studies, music and psychology. Joint- and concurrent-degree programs are especially attractive to a growing number of law students who intend to apply their legal education to fields outside law.

The School of Law has recently opened an accelerated program which allows candidates to earn the JD and a Master of Business Administration degree in only three years.

Students edit three law journals, engage in intramural and external moot court and trial court competitions, and operate a wide range of student organizations. The Indiana University School of Law—Bloomington offers a collegial, supportive, small school environment in which students gain strong foundations for the practice of law and build lasting bonds with the faculty and their classmates.

University of Notre Dame Law School

Admissions Office
112 Law School
Notre Dame, IN 46556
Admissions phone: (574) 631-6626
Admissions fax: (574) 631-5474
Admissions e-mail: lawadmit@nd.edu
Admissions URL: http://law.nd.edu/prospective_students/

 Admissions

Status: Current student, full-time
Dates of Enrollment: 8/2003-Submit Date
Survey Submitted: January 2006

Community service experience is given a lot more weight at Notre Dame than at many other schools. I recall during orientation that the dean told my class that 100 percent of us had emphasized community service work on our applications. I am under the impression that indicating that you are a Roman Catholic will help your application.

Status: Alumnus/a, full-time
Dates of Enrollment: 9/2001-5/2004
Survey Submitted: March 2006

The application process was very similar to other schools I applied to. There was not an interview and the essay was your basic open-ended personal statement. I did meet with people in the admissions office to get an idea of selectivity and how the process worked. Notre Dame is a pretty selective school, and they really look at the entire package. Notre Dame prides itself on educating a "different type of lawyer" so they really look for well-rounded applicants. That is not to say that grades and LSAT do not matter, but it seems that they look for work experience and other unique experiences that sets one applicant apart from others.

Status: Alumnus/a, full-time
Dates of Enrollment: 8/1998-5/2001
Survey Submitted: March 2006

I was somewhat late in the process, and was surprisingly put on the waitlist. Continual follow-up worked wonders, it showed interest, and as spots opened up, I was one of the first people contacted. Admissions was very helpful and friendly in the process.

Status: Alumnus/a, full-time
Dates of Enrollment: 8/1991-5/1994
Survey Submitted: March 2006

Along with having a GPA and LSAT score in range of the mean, the school considers sincere desire to attend Notre Dame and commitment to its mission. They will also give considerable weight to work experience; at least they did in my case—far more than any other school I applied to.

Status: Alumnus/a, full-time
Dates of Enrollment: 8/2001-5/2004
Survey Submitted: March 2005

The application process can be done and is much more user friendly than most other law schools. Though the admission standards are quite high, the admissions staff is very good at selecting students with different types of talents (i.e., they aren't just looking at undergraduate GPA).

Status: Current student, full-time
Dates of Enrollment: 8/2003-Submit Date
Survey Submitted: March 2005

The admissions process was fairly simple. There was the usual application asking for your GPA, and LSAT score. There was also a personal essay required. There was no interview requirement.

Notre Dame law school was actually less competitive (compared to the public law schools I applied to) because fewer students applied for roughly the same number of spots.

Status: Alumnus/a, full-time
Dates of Enrollment: 8/2000-5/2003
Survey Submitted: January 2005

I had gone to Notre Dame for undergrad. ND law is one of the few law or graduate schools that actively LIKES former undergrads. We all had our theory as to why; maybe the university thinks former students are used to the South Bend weather, maybe they think these students are more likely to stick around for the full three years. At any rate, in my class and the surrounding classes, up to one out of every five or six law students had gone to ND for undergrad.

As for essays, the law school, like the other entities of the university, likes to hear about things like social activism or sympathy to social causes, whether championed by the Catholic church or not. Really, more than nuts and bolts of the admissions process, I do want to warn you—if you do not like football, if you have a dying need to be in an urban environment, if you need to be surrounded by diversity, think very seriously before applying. If you are accepted, you may be miserable. Most people either really like or really hate the school once they are there. I really liked it but my girlfriend really hated it. More people liked the law school than hated it, but be sure to make an informed choice before choosing this or ANY law school.

Status: Current student, full-time
Dates of Enrollment: 8/2001-Submit Date
Survey Submitted: April 2004

The admission process was pretty standard for law school. LSAT, resume, transcripts, essays. One huge benefit to Notre Dame is their generally lower concern about LSATs. I did not have great LSATs, but did have good undergrad grades (magna cum laude) and good work experience. For a lot of schools, my lower LSATs were a turnoff. And Notre Dame generally cares about the type of student they are getting. I was waitlisted and, at the time, I was given the opportunity to send additional information about myself and why I wanted to attend ND. It paid off for me and ND. I am graduating with honors and have secured a job at a BigLaw firm in Los Angeles.

Status: Alumnus/a, full-time
Dates of Enrollment: 9/2000-5/2003
Survey Submitted: June 2004

The application can be completed and submitted. Do not use "form" answers on the application, as each applicant is considered a whole person rather then the sum of scores and grades. Be sure that your answers reflect your personality and values. Be sure to read the guidelines regarding your personal statement and to add a few lines explaining why you want to receive your legal education at ND. Contact local alumni, they'll be more than happy to talk to about life at ND.

Status: Alumnus/a, full-time
Dates of Enrollment: 8/1997-5/2001
Survey Submitted: April 2004

I found the admissions process to be very user-friendly. The classes are small enough (about 180) that they can give each person a great deal of individualized attention. I'd recommend applying early; when I applied, admit letters seemed to go out on a rolling basis, and Notre Dame was the first school I was admitted to (in mid-January).

Read all of Vault's Law School Surveys at www.vault.com/lawschool — get complete surveys on top law schools, expert advice on applicaton essays, LSAT prep and more.

VAULT CAREER LIBRARY **251**

 **Academics**

Status: Current student, full-time
Dates of Enrollment: 8/2003-Submit Date
Survey Submitted: January 2006

Much more of a theory-based curriculum. Like a little Catholic Yale. Many professors chose to incorporate discussions of morality and philosophy into their courses. The Notre Dame Law Review is a fabulous opportunity for those who are invited to join. The Law Review is primarily "grade on" which means that the staff is composed of roughly the top 10 to 12 percent of your class, determined at the end of your 1L year. I think that is rare now. Most schools have a writing competition combined with grades to determine the law review staff.

Status: Alumnus/a, full-time
Dates of Enrollment: 9/2001-5/2004
Survey Submitted: March 2006

I think Notre Dame offers a very wide array of different types of and unique classes. The first-year curriculum is pretty standard, but the professors as a whole are very well qualified, good teachers, and approachable and available outside of class. What I found appealing about the ND curriculum was that beyond first year, there really was a lot of freedom to take classes that interested you. There were a few required classes (Tax, Business Associations, Jurisprudence), but for the most part you were free to pursue your interests. I never had a problem getting classes that I wanted. At the most, I had to wait a semester to get into a class, but it really was not a problem because the number of students is relatively small. The grading was very fair...if you worked hard, you were rewarded. The workload first year is manageable. It was slightly overwhelming at first, but you get used to it and it certainly isn't more than you can handle. After first year, the workload really tapers off and you have a lot more free time.

Status: Alumnus/a, full-time
Dates of Enrollment: 8/1998-5/2001
Survey Submitted: March 2006

Very strong core curriculum-oriented program with lots of requirements. Definitely more of a nuts and bolts program compared to many of my friends who attended NYU or more theoretical schools. Looking back, I think I was more soundly educated and prepared to practice law than many who went to comparative peer institutions.

Status: Current student, full-time
Dates of Enrollment: 8/2003-Submit Date
Survey Submitted: March 2005

The professors were (with one or two exceptions) very knowledgeable and seemed to care about the student's learning process. I think, however, that the expectations were often that the students should be learning the material on their own, and the professor was only there to provide a forum for discussion. Personally, I don't agree with this approach since I think that it ought to be the professor's job to help us learn by teaching us the fundamentals (e.g., Black Letter Law) and we shouldn't be forced to learn everything from simply reading a text book. If we are expected to learn most of the concepts on our own, then I start to question the value of attending class to begin with.

My other two criticisms are that the required and more popular classes were often too large (up to 80 students in one lecture hall) which I found to limit the quality of instruction that I got. Larger classes tended to create more distance between the professors and the students and generally hindered the learning process by limiting the interaction between teacher and student. Popular classes would go fast—2Ls were often out of luck, by the time they had enrolled the 3Ls had already filled up the classes they wanted—and there were a number of classes that were on the bar exam in virtually every state (such as Trusts and Estates and Constitutional Law II) which were often only one semester a year or not offered at all in some years.

Grading tended to vary wildly among professors—some were notoriously tough and others notoriously lenient graders—but the school did conveniently post the previous semester's grade distributions for each class, so at least most students were aware of what to expect from a given professor. Workload was crushing

the first year, and after that it really varied depending on the class—the required classes were all—other than ethics—tough and demanding, along with a number of others, including many of the subjects on the bar exam.

Status: Current student, full-time
Dates of Enrollment: 8/2003-Submit Date
Survey Submitted: March 2005

First-year classes are assigned. It can be difficult to get the classes you want in your second year—you're given a randomly drawn lottery number that determines when you may register. So if you get a later registration time, many of the good classes are already full by the time you can register. By third year, it's pretty easy to get the classes you want. First-year classes are curved to around a 3.0. 2L and 3L grades are curved more generously. A lot of it depends on the professor. Some have reputations for being particularly tough or lax graders. The professors are, for the most part, very approachable. The younger faculty, in particular, are topnotch and very popular. The workload seems pretty average compared to other law schools.

Status: Alumnus/a, full-time
Dates of Enrollment: 8/2000-5/2003
Survey Submitted: January 2005

The professors are, on the average, great teachers and human beings. The courseload is hard, just as at any other law school. There is not as much variety as at a larger school (only about 190 per class), and the emphasis is on learning how to think like a lawyer, so not only will you graduate without any practical knowledge of, say, New York or California law, unless you knock down the doors of the underfunded clinic to get in there, you may graduate with little if any practical lawyering skills. For example, I moved to a major East Coast city where I felt the new attorneys from the second tier regional schools had a step or two on me regarding certain legal terminology and procedures. The idea, of course, is that you have to teach yourself these things. Still, it was more than a little irritating to spin my wheels a little more in my first few months.

That being said, if you like philosophical-style classes, you would love Notre Dame. The law school still has a jurisprudence requirement, while I doubt many schools even offer such a class. As far as practical classes, the National Institute for Trial Advocacy is located on campus, or nearby, or somewhere. It's got an affiliation of some gleefully ambiguous sort with the law school, and many of its staff teach the Trial Advocacy class, but looking back on it, I'm not exactly sure of the connection. AND if you like federal criminal law, you'd love the almost endless parade of similarly-styled classes on that topic. There is also a professor at the law school who wrote the venerable RICO statute, which has such a key place in federal criminal law and increasingly in most major civil complex litigation.

Although some students complained that popular classes were difficult to get into, I never had that problem. It worked this way: register for whatever crappy classes are left if you had a late registration time, then during winter or summer break, check the registration every so often, and spots for most classes are sure to open. If all else failed, you could show up to a class on the first day and grab a spot in the class from the inevitable no-shows who were too lazy to drop the class in the meantime.

Status: Alumnus/a, full-time
Dates of Enrollment: 9/2000-5/2003
Survey Submitted: June 2004

All classes are taught by actual professors and are high quality (although some are more interesting than others). There are ample classes to choose from, including a number of small seminars that explore discrete areas of the law in depth and classes emphasizing practical skills like negotiating or taking depositions. Workload and exams vary in format, depending upon the professor. Grading also varies by professor but is relatively consistent and always fair. ND does not rank students, which can be a good or bad thing depending on where you would place, but in any event does reduce competition among students.

Status: Current student, full-time
Dates of Enrollment: 8/2001-Submit Date
Survey Submitted: April 2004

Classes and professors are good, but relatively old-school. ND focuses a lot on litigation and practical skills. Could use more transaction law-oriented courses.

Grade inflation does not exist. Average GPA at the end of the first year is near 3.0—really low for other Top 20 law schools.

Notre Dame wants students to have fun, but not too much fun. The school regularly schedules "mandatory" or popular classes (evidence, corporate law, etc.) on Friday mornings at 8 a.m. Professors are approachable outside of class, and students are not cutthroat. Everyone is competitive, but they want all to succeed.

Status: Alumnus/a, full-time
Dates of Enrollment: 8/1997-5/2001
Survey Submitted: April 2004

Notre Dame has eliminated a few of its upper-year requirements, but it still requires every student to take certain courses after first-year. In general, I found this to be very helpful. I never would have taken Federal Taxation or Corporations if they weren't required, and not only did I learn a lot from them, those courses have proven invaluable to me in practice.

Overall, there's very little grade inflation, compared to some schools. Some of the professors are excellent and tough; you can learn a great deal from them. Like anywhere, there are a few professors who have some cake courses, and everyone knows which ones they are. It's fairly easy to get whatever set of courses you want, whether challenging or easy.

 # Employment Prospects

Status: Current student, full-time
Dates of Enrollment: 8/2003-Submit Date
Survey Submitted: January 2006

I can only speak to my own experience. I worked at a top firm in D.C. during my 2L summer and have since clerked for a federal judge and moved to another top D.C. firm. For the top 10 percent or so, I don't think there are many limitations. I imagine that the bottom 50 percent are limited to a more regional market, namely Indianapolis, Detroit, Chicago. But for those who do well (good grades, law review, etc.), you can get a job in any market in the country.

Also, a little known fact, as of a few years ago, Notre Dame had more Supreme Court clerks than any school other than Harvard and Yale. I believe this is because there are so many conservative Justices who hold Notre Dame in high esteem because of its commitment to educating well-rounded moral practitioners of law. Former Chief Justice Rehnquist had a Notre Dame clerk about every other year. Scalia and Thomas also hire from Notre Dame. It's yet to be seen whether Roberts and Alito will, but I imagine they might. On that note, there are a lot of federal judges across the country that hire Notre Dame graduates. To name a few, Judge O'Scannlain (9th), Judge Emilio Garza (5th), Judge Wilson (11th), Judge McConnell (10th). Students who excel at Notre Dame Law School do very well.

Status: Alumnus/a, full-time
Dates of Enrollment: 9/2001-5/2004
Survey Submitted: March 2006

I think there is no other alumni network in the country that can compare to ND. ND alumni are known for helping each other out whenever they can. I have made several connections as a result of my attending Notre Dame. I had no problem finding a job when I graduated law school, and I would dare say that most people did not.

Status: Alumnus/a, full-time
Dates of Enrollment: 8/1998-5/2001
Survey Submitted: March 2006

The alumni network is incredible and very helpful. I was initially worried about "getting back" to NYC from a Chicago area school. Not a problem at all, especially because of enthusiastic alumni. Two things stand out: (1) alumni or not, Notre Dame is a "name"—you stand out everywhere you go in the world by identifying with the institution. (2) People believe in ND and what it stands for passionately—alumni and others connected to the school always go the extra mile because they have such intense feelings about the school.

Status: Alumnus/a, full-time
Dates of Enrollment: 8/2001-5/2004
Survey Submitted: March 2005

The Notre Dame network is unrivaled. Virtually any market in the country—and many throughout the world—will have an active alumni network in place and willing to help you find employment. Despite being ranked in the Top 20, the academic prestige of the law school is still somewhat undiscovered outside of the Midwest. But employers in Chicago, Detroit, Cleveland, and other Midwest cities are constantly on the look out for ND grads.

Status: Current student, full-time
Dates of Enrollment: 8/2003-Submit Date
Survey Submitted: March 2005

Notre Dame is a pretty impressive name to future employers. Everyone knows it's a top-tiered law school. Plus, just going to a school like Notre Dame gives you something to talk about because almost all employers have preconceived ideas about the school (or football team) that they want to ask you about. On-campus recruiting is good for larger firms. It's particularly good if you want to work in the Midwest, especially the Chicago area. Some interviewers come from CA and D.C., but the majority of employers who come to campus are from the Midwest. The majority of grads go on to work for firms. However, career services often encourages students to look into doing public interest work.

Status: Alumnus/a, full-time
Dates of Enrollment: 8/2000-5/2003
Survey Submitted: January 2005

As much as it hurts to say, this is where I and many in my class were sorely let down. Although Notre Dame has a nice reputation and looks good on a diploma, its reputation as a national school exceeds its reach in obtaining employment for its slightly above-average to poor students. Of course, my classmates and I learned this lesson the hard way, after spending most of our time there thinking that eventually a job would fall into our lap with the help of the career services office. Those students who did get the great federal clerkships and the lofty Manhattan jobs (and there were many, just not as many as in the "boom" years of the late 90s) mostly took it upon themselves to find these jobs. By third-year, only a handful of decent employers actually came to campus to interview third-year students; they all spoke to the second-years and left us out to dry. Who knows how things might have been if I had been in contact with a large firm from the end of first semester, first year onward. But I wasn't, and if you can't motivate yourself to write some cover letters and make some cold contacts, then you should probably go to a regional school with a good career services office or go to a Top 10 school and become editor-in-chief of the law review.

Status: Alumnus/a, full-time
Dates of Enrollment: 8/1997-5/2001
Survey Submitted: April 2004

Like everywhere, Notre Dame has an on-campus interview program for finding large firm jobs. Overall, I found the program quite good. There were numerous employers, especially given the relatively small size of each class. Plus, I found the faculty to be a tremendous career resource. Several faculty members used their personal contacts to get me in the door at firms that didn't interview on campus.

 # Quality of Life

Status: Current student, full-time
Dates of Enrollment: 8/2003-Submit Date
Survey Submitted: January 2006

Notre Dame has a great campus and great graduate student housing for those interested. I spent almost all of my three years on campus. South Bend is not a very vibrant town, but I understand that it is getting better. I recently heard that the university is trying to facilitate the growth of a main street area sort of like State Street in Ann Arbor.

Read all of Vault's Law School Surveys at www.vault.com/lawschool — get complete surveys on top law schools, expert advice on applicaton essays, LSAT prep and more.

VAULT CAREER LIBRARY 253

Status: Alumnus/a, full-time
Dates of Enrollment: 9/2001-5/2004
Survey Submitted: March 2006

Notre Dame has graduate housing which is great. It is walkable to campus, is furnished, and is very inexpensive. There are also a lot of apartment complexes very close to campus, so finding housing is no problem. The campus and its facilities are great. The campus is beautiful and is great for outdoor activities when the weather permits, and the on-campus workout facilities are great. Graduate students can obtain meal plans which permit them to eat in the dining halls on campus, one of which is a two-minute walk from the law school. The food at the dining halls is better than any other school I have been to. I have never feared for my safety on campus. There is a great campus security force and they will walk you to your car if you ever feel unsafe. I think ND is a great place.

Status: Alumnus/a, full-time
Dates of Enrollment: 8/1998-5/2001
Survey Submitted: March 2006

The best three years of my life, an incredible experience. What Notre Dame is about is spirit, passion and enthusiasm for everything related to the school athletics, your classmates, your personal and spiritual life. It was (and is) hard to encapsulate what the experience is like. And it's dirt cheap to live there, that helps.

Status: Alumnus/a, full-time
Dates of Enrollment: 8/1995-5/1998
Survey Submitted: March 2006

Great quality of life. Fantastic community—much less competitive than other law schools. Great campus, great students. Wonderful learning environment. South Bend isn't much, but the law school community more than makes up for it.

Status: Alumnus, full-time
Dates of Enrollment: 8/2001-5/2004
Survey Submitted: March 2005

There is no doubt that ND has the best quality of life for any school that is comparable in rankings. Though I am a non-Catholic Christian, the Catholic principles of the school create a higher quality of life for all students, whether religious or not.

Status: Current student, full-time
Dates of Enrollment: 8/2003-Submit Date
Survey Submitted: March 2005

Housing is pretty easy to find. The graduate housing is decent and very convenient. Grad housing isn't the cheapest in the area, but it's reasonable and you can't beat the convenience. The campus itself is very safe, but surrounding parts of South Bend are not as safe. The campus is very pretty. The law school building itself is rather new, but we are supposed to be getting a new building in the near future. The food on campus is not bad. There's a cafe in the law school and then there are several dining options elsewhere on campus. There's plenty of variety if you don't mind paying for it

Status: Alumnus/s, full-time
Dates of Enrollment: 8/2000-5/2003
Survey Submitted: January 2005

South Bend is relatively cheap, relatively safe, and will bore you to tears if you grew up in a major city. I grew up in a rural area/small city in a different university town, so I loved it. But I warn those who need too much stimulation that you may not want to live in South Bend for three years. The area restaurants, coffee shops, movie theatres, etc. are nice enough, but tourists generally only come to South Bend for the football.

Luckily, for those in need of a little urban flavor, there is a YEAR-LONG program in London for the entire second year. Yes, decades ago, the law school started a year-long program, and it is now grandfathered in as I think the ONLY year-long program allowed by the certification powers-that-be at the ABA. The classroom facilities in London are located just off Trafalgar Square in a great section of London. And classes are easier than those at the main campus. Two drawbacks, though to the London program: you miss a season of home football

games AND the cost of living in London, especially now with the weak dollar, will absolutely kill you unless you are a trust fund baby.

Neighborhood crime and safety is good, except for those that do live in the readily identifiable and easily avoidable bad areas of South Bend. These are generally far from the university, and I only knew of a few people who ended up living in bad areas. The university itself is almost entirely isolated from the surrounding town/city. It's virtually impossible to walk to the law school, unless you live in the grad student housing on campus. But the campus is absolutely beautiful—one of the best in the nation. Most students take advantage of the opportunity to be in shape, whether undergrads or grad students. The on-campus gyms are busy, and it is pretty rare to see anyone truly obese on campus. The grad students are very active in intramurals and sports leagues, for those who like organized sports. Like most dining plans, it is best to cook for yourself when you can. Although the dining halls are nice enough and serve all you can eat food, you just don't want to drop something like eight bucks on lunch every day.

Status: Alumnus/a, full-time
Dates of Enrollment: 8/1997-5/2001
Survey Submitted: April 2004

The overall quality of life is quite good. The law school family is far more cooperative than it is competitive. For example, Notre Dame does not rank its students, so that eliminates some of the competitive drive.

Notre Dame is a religious institution that takes its religious identity seriously. This means that a whole range of moral, social and spiritual issues can be freely discussed in ways that are impossible at secular schools. This does not mean anyone who isn't Catholic is an outsider; to the contrary, I'm not Catholic, and I felt nothing but welcome from the law school community. What it does mean is that a variety of points-of-view—secular and religious, Catholic, Protestant, Jewish, Muslim, etc.—are allowed to inform the discussion of legal issues of every kind, which is an unalloyed good.

 ## Social Life

Status: Current student, full-time
Dates of Enrollment: 8/2003-Submit Date
Survey Submitted: January 2006

Law school is like high school. Especially at a small school like Notre Dame. There is no limit to social opportunities, much to the detriment of the bottom half of my class. There is also no limit to the silly cliquish behavior, but, from what I have heard, that is the case at most law schools.

Status: Alumnus/a, full-time
Dates of Enrollment: 9/2001-5/2004
Survey Submitted: March 2006

The Notre Dame social life is interesting. As a graduate student, most people frequent bars around the area. The dating scene for graduate students is pretty good, though a lot of people hang out in groups. South Bend doesn't have as much character as other college towns. Most of the restaurants are chains, and the bars are few in number. It is growing and developing though, and it is made better by the fact that Chicago is so close by.

Status: Alumnus/a, full-time
Dates of Enrollment: 8/1998-5/2001
Survey Submitted: March 2006

Tailgates, football games, Irish bars. Not much in the way of things for the suave urban dwellers, but Chicago is an hour-plus away for that. January and February are the most brutal months if you're not heavily involved in something. But, oddly enough, those are the days that I miss the most.

Status: Alumnus/a, full-time
Dates of Enrollment: 8/2001-5/2004
Survey Submitted: March 2005

For those who are interested in having an active social life, and can balance their time effectively, the social life can be every bit as good as a major undergraduate university experience. University sports play a major role in the social life, as do intramural sports and weekly trips to house parties, local sports bars, and the Linebacker!

Status: Current student, full-time
Dates of Enrollment: 8/2003-Submit Date
Survey Submitted: March 2005

There isn't a whole lot to do in South Bend, IN. But Chicago isn't that far away and students often go there for the weekend. It's a cheap, short train ride away. There are plenty of bars in town and they get frequented very often by law students. The Backer is probably the most famous place in town; all the students go there. South Bend and nearby Mishawaka have almost every imaginable chain restaurant known to man. The law school has a fair number of clubs.

Status: Alumnus/a, full-time
Dates of Enrollment: 8/2000-5/2003
Survey Submitted: January 2005

While things are nice and safe, and the campus is beautiful, there are a percentage of students that are absolutely miserable because they need more urban-style stimulation. The good bars—depending on your tastes, Corby's, the Linebacker, CJs, Heartland, etc.—are smoky, packed, and repetitive. Heartland isn't a bad "club" considering where it's located. But that's like saying a random street performer spinning two plates on different sticks is anything like one of those big Cirque de Soliel shows. Luckily, Chicago is within striking distance for those willing to stay overnight after hitting the bars/clubs there.

The dating scene is much like high school or a smaller undergrad population. You find yourself in a 600-person law school for three years, what can I say? Of course, not many students date "townies," and not many students date the undergrads, although both things do happen. Generally, if you can't find someone to date within the law school, you'll be single for the duration, or until the next class of 1Ls shows up.

Luckily, for those easily entertained, like me, the student bar association puts on about one large social event per month, such as a Halloween party, Mardi Gras or St. Patrick's Day, a fall dance, a spring "ball," and the yearly "Father Mike Show," a skit show that usually ends up offending at least a few students every year while entertaining many more.

A mention of social life would not be complete without talking a little bit about the football games. For about six weeks every fall, Thursdays through Saturdays (into those Sunday morning headaches) center on home football games. If you like football, you'll love the atmosphere on campus and in the bars. If you don't like football, or like being around those who do, you might actively hate those weekends. So I've heard. But I absolutely loved these weekends. I encourage anyone with ready-made love for Notre Dame to apply.

Status: Alumnus/a, full-time
Dates of Enrollment: 9/2000-5/2003
Survey Submitted: June 2004

There are plenty of social activities arranged by the school, as well as informal gatherings at local bars and nightclubs. Football weekends are insane; there are food and merchandise stands set up all over campus and tailgating in the parking lots. Many students play on intramural teams, and often non-participants will attend games to cheer them on.

Status: Current student, full-time
Dates of Enrollment: 8/2001-Submit Date
Survey Submitted: April 2004

Notre Dame is a great place to attend law school. One downside is the relative lack of "cool" things to do in South Bend. Not surprising that Notre Dame events, especially sports, dominate. The most important thing to know—Notre Dame law students like to have fun. Parties and other social activities cover the calendar every week. Also if you are interested in international law, Notre Dame offers a year abroad program, run by ND, in London. I spent my second year in London, and it was fantastic.

Status: Alumnus/a, full-time
Dates of Enrollment: 8/1997-5/2001
Survey Submitted: April 2004

The law school is very social. Every Wednesday night, most of the class goes out to the same bar to socialize. Classes are so small that you'll get to know most of the people you go to school with. South Bend is a little sleepy, but it has decent bars and pretty good restaurants—certainly enough to support a fun social scene.

Read all of Vault's Law School Surveys at www.vault.com/lawschool — get complete surveys on top law schools, expert advice on applicaton essays, LSAT prep and more.

VAULT CAREER LIBRARY 255

University of Iowa College of Law

Admissions Office
276 Boyd Law Building
Melrose & Byington Streets
Iowa City, IA 52242-1113
Admissions phone: (319) 335-9095 or (800) 553-IOWA, ext. 9095
Admissions fax: (319) 335-9019
Admissions e-mail: law-admissions@uiowa.edu
Admissions URL: http://www.law.uiowa.edu/prospective/

 ## Admissions

Status: Alumnus/a, full-time
Dates of Enrollment: 9/1996-5/1999
Survey Submitted: March 2006

At the time, Iowa had one of the lowest application fees. It also had relatively poor materials relating to the school—materials that did not reflect the school's quality.

Status: Current student, full-time
Dates of Enrollment: 1/2003-Submit Date
Survey Submitted: October 2005

Admissions is relatively easy if you have good grades and came from a good school. If you are from Iowa, it may be a little more difficult as they are trying to maintain their national reputation.

Status: Alumnus/a, full-time
Dates of Enrollment: 5/1995-5/1998
Survey Submitted: January 2005

It is a very simple application process weighted mostly on grades and LSAT scores. The essays are not as demanding or as detailed as some of the Top 10 schools. If you are a racial minority, the school will look closely at you, especially if you have excellent undergraduate academics and/or an excellent LSAT score.

Status: Alumnus/a, full-time
Dates of Enrollment: 8/2001-5/2004
Survey Submitted: March 2005

The school is selective, especially for out-of-state applicants. They kept in contact with me throughout the process, and made decisions quickly.

Status: Alumnus/a, full-time
Dates of Enrollment: 8/1993-5/1996
Survey Submitted: February 2005

I found the admissions process at Iowa to be very smooth and straightforward. I did not experience any glitches. I took the LSAT in the fall of my senior year and submitted my application to Iowa in December. By early March, I had received my acceptance letter. I don't believe there was an "interview" component; if so, I didn't have to go through it.

From what I can tell, Iowa values well-rounded individuals, such that students should do their best to emphasize their "well-roundedness" in their application and essay. If one's grades and/or LSAT scores are sub-par, one should be sure to highlight a particularly outstanding achievement and/or accomplishment that would merit additional consideration. It's my understanding that Iowa has a formula for giving applicants an academic score, based on grades and LSATs, and I believe that grades are weighted slightly higher than LSAT scores. College students interested in law school should think twice before picking a major or taking a class that has a strong potential to drop their GPA. They shouldn't necessarily major in basket-weaving just to get a 4.0 GPA, but I don't think that Iowa or other law schools care much about your major was.

Status: Current student, full-time
Dates of Enrollment: 8/2001-Submit Date
Survey Submitted: February 2004

My understanding is that you don't need stellar LSAT scores to get into Iowa, and that Iowa may weigh your GPA more heavily than some other schools. Since Iowa is a state school, it's much harder for out-of-state students to be admitted. I know that the University of Iowa admissions staff does make a tour, and I think it would be important to meet with them and talk about your background. I think it's possible you can make an impression. If you do have a unique background, perseverance and keeping contact with the admissions office may help.

Status: Alumnus/a, full-time
Dates of Enrollment: 8/2000-5/2003
Survey Submitted: April 2004

The law school is selective. The personal statement counts. As with nearly every law school, LSAT and grades are the primary considerations.

Status: Alumnus/a, full-time
Dates of Enrollment: 8/1999-5/2002
Survey Submitted: April 2004

The admissions process includes all of the usual criteria, including the essay. Iowa is a Top 20 school, so grades and LSAT are very important. However, Iowa struggles with recruiting a diverse student body due to its geographical location. Therefore, they are very interested in how the prospective student can contribute to the diversity of the law school.

Status: Alumnus/a, full-time
Dates of Enrollment: 9/1998-5/2002
Survey Submitted: November 2003

I understand in the last two years admissions have become more selective as there are many more applicants than spaces. Iowa residents have an easier time getting in.

 ## Academics

Status: Alumnus/a, full-time
Dates of Enrollment: 9/1996-5/1999
Survey Submitted: March 2006

Iowa is to a large degree a "theory" school, as opposed to a practice school. Many of the professors went straight from clerkships or fellowships to teaching. As a result, the instruction tended toward the theoretical rather than the practical. That said, there are ample avenues for practical instruction available mock trial, legal clinics, etc. From a theory perspective, the instructors are topnotch. Many could have had jobs at more highly-ranked institutions, but had young children they wanted to raise in a safe environment with the best public schools in the nation.

Status: Current student, full-time
Dates of Enrollment: 1/2003-Submit Date
Survey Submitted: October 2005

Professors actually teach. It's a a miracle, really. Although you always have a few lesser ones in the bunch, for the most part the great thing about Iowa is its faculty.

Status: Current student, full-time
Dates of Enrollment: 1/2003-Submit Date
Survey Submitted: October 2005

This is the campus that pretends to be uncompetitive under an exceedingly friendly guise.

Status: Alumnus/a, full-time
Dates of Enrollment: 5/1995-5/1998
Survey Submitted: January 2005

The University of Iowa has an academically rigorous program really geared toward the basics during the first year (Property, Contracts, Torts and more) and in the remaining years, students mostly take the same corporate law oriented courses. I started in the accelerated summer programs which was also a smaller class. We had the option of decelerating and doing the regular three-year program or remaining accelerated and completing law school in two or two and a half years. In retrospect, I realize that I received an excellent law school education which had a great blend of the theoretical and practical. I never had a problem getting the courses I wanted and they also offered interesting, "progressive" classes such as Law and Sexuality, Critical Race Theory and others. These classes were also open to non-law students, which also made discussions interesting.

Status: Alumnus/a, full-time
Dates of Enrollment: 9/1996-5/2001
Survey Submitted: March 2005

Largely enjoyed classes and professors.

Status: Alumnus/a, full-time
Dates of Enrollment: 8/1997-5/2000
Survey Submitted: March 2005

I never had difficulty getting into classes, even popular ones. Iowa has great faculty and has more of a hands-on approach. All of the professors were easily accessible and most of them were very focused on the students.

Iowa is different from a number of other law schools that my colleagues attended because they actively try to keep their students and see that they graduate. Other schools are intent on cutting the bottom of the class to ensure that they have high bar-pass rates, but it was never like that at Iowa. If a student has difficulty, Iowa makes every attempt to address their need (even giving them time off) to prevent them from failing out of school.

Status: Alumnus/a, full-time
Dates of Enrollment: 8/2001-5/2004
Survey Submitted: March 2005

The faculty is wonderful. The administration uses a very fair system that enables almost every student the opportunity to take any course, including the most popular, they can fit into their schedule.

Status: Alumnus/a, full-time
Dates of Enrollment: 8/1993-5/1996
Survey Submitted: February 2005

I was thoroughly impressed throughout my three years at Iowa with their academics. I don't recall any disappointments about not getting into classes or getting the professors that I wanted. I think Iowa limits their class size enough so that the students aren't killing each other to get into classes. The professors varied tremendously in their teaching styles—everything from the strict Socratic Method to the kindest, gentlest teaching techniques. I enjoyed the variety and even for the Socratic Method professors, I think they all had the students' best interests at heart and did not seek to unnecessarily humiliate students. Iowa offered some great hands-on training and extracurricular activities with their moot court and mock trial programs, legal clinic experience, client counseling training and journal membership and writing. The law school valued these activities and allowed some academic credit for them. I understand that some schools don't offer any credit for these while others offer a tremendous amount. I think Iowa tends to fall in the middle. Every year the top four moot court advocates get to "perform" in front of the Iowa Supreme Court, and the Eighth Circuit frequently will hear oral arguments in real cases at the law school.

Status: Current student, full-time
Dates of Enrollment: 8/2001-Submit Date
Survey Submitted: February 2004

Like most law schools, the first-year courses are already determined by the school. Iowa has had difficulty in keeping its numbers down, which has lead to overcrowded classrooms and a limited curriculum (faculty members are pressured to teach first-year courses to handle the overload at the expense of 2Ls

and 3Ls). Recently, Iowa has made more of an effort to invite practitioners to teach more specialized courses and intersession classes.

I'm not under the impression that the workload is particularly heavy here. Iowa does have a greater writing requirement than many other schools. Iowa requires five writing credits to graduate, which translates into about 100 pages of writing. Many of the more interesting seminars have writing requirements, and so it's not unheard of that students write much more than that. The second year at Iowa is extremely busy, especially since they put second-years through a mandatory appellate advocacy (the time and effort far outweigh the credit). Since your entire moot court experience is limited to your second year (with the possibility of enrolling in a noncompetitive program in your third year) with the exception of regional and national competitions, the second year can be very busy and may limit your ability to take classes that you would like to take if it wasn't for the heavy load. The professors are generally very accessible. The professors here are not that smitten with the Socratic Method. There's more emphasis on lecturing or what we call "soft Socratic method," where the professor will ask one or two students a few questions and move on. Grading is on a 90-point scale, and there is a mandatory curve. It's very difficult to fail at Iowa.

Status: Alumnus/a, full-time
Dates of Enrollment: 8/2000-5/2003
Survey Submitted: April 2004

Excellent professors—personable and approachable. More interaction with professors than at any other school I've seen. The curriculum was demanding. Some old school (i.e., Socratic), some new school teaching techniques. A good balance. The grade scale is delineated by policy and very strictly followed. Getting an A is difficult; usually only two or three are given per class.

Status: Alumnus/a, full-time
Dates of Enrollment: 8/1999-5/2002
Survey Submitted: April 2004

The academic nature is excellent, yet laid-back. The professors are topnotch but they pride themselves on not creating an ultra-competitive environment. Professors are very easy to meet outside of class, and often have their classes over for dinner at their house. Class selection is done on a point system. If a student really wants to take a class, they can "spend" all of their points on that one class, and they will get into the class without a problem. The only way a student would be denied admission to a class is if they signed up for all of the popular classes. They may get their first two picks, but not the third.

Grading is done in a fair manner. First-year students are graded on a mandatory curve, while second- and third-year student grades are left to the discretion of the professor. Tests range from take-home essays to on-site multiple choice.

Status: Alumnus/a, full-time
Dates of Enrollment: 9/1998-5/2002
Survey Submitted: November 2003

Academically, Iowa is challenging, and grades are not inflated. Students are graded on a strict curve. If you were used to easily earning good grades in undergrad, first semester can be shock. Many of my classmates earned their first B in law school.

After their first year, students choose their own classes. There is a lottery and ranking system. For highly sought-after positions in the legal clinic, it will take more than one try to get in. There are many interesting electives and good variety of visiting professors who teach specialized classes.

Compared to the skills exhibited by East Coast law students during my clerkships, Iowa students have a leg up on the real practice of law. Other schools may give you more nuts and bolts training, but Iowa provides a good balance of theory and practice.

Read all of Vault's Law School Surveys at www.vault.com/lawschool — get complete surveys on top law schools, expert advice on applicaton essays, LSAT prep and more.

VAULT CAREER LIBRARY 257

Employment Prospects

Status: Alumnus/a, full-time
Dates of Enrollment: 9/1996-5/1999
Survey Submitted: March 2006

From my own experience, Iowa is not well-known in most parts of the country. Large firms in Minneapolis, Kansas City, St. Louis and Chicago provide most of the large firm employment opportunities. Even so, graduates land good jobs in D.C., New York and L.A. every year. Certainly prospects are better for those in the top 15 percent of the class, but this is always the case. I did not make use of the alumni network, and on-campus recruiting by firms in many parts of the country has declined since the hiring explosions of 1998-1999. This is in part a result of the fact that a majority of the school's students are from the Midwest and were not interested in relocating, and in part because travelling to Iowa City is very expensive, and there are no other schools around that firms can simultaneously recruit from.

Status: Current student, full-time
Dates of Enrollment: 1/2003-Submit Date
Survey Submitted: October 2005

Iowa has a great reputation in the Midwest. There are a lot of alumni that work in all the major metropolitan Midwestern cities like Chicago, Minneapolis, St. Louis and, for some reason, Arizona. Apart from the Midwest, however, its reputation is leaves something to be desired.

Status: Alumnus/a, full-time
Dates of Enrollment: 5/1995-5/1998
Survey Submitted: January 2005

A handful of firms from the major metropolitan areas came on campus from New York, D.C. and Chicago. Over the years, more students from Iowa have sought out those opportunities, although it seems most students end up staying in Iowa or the Midwest. Iowa does not have a big name outside of the Midwest but those Iowa alums who ventured out of Iowa especially into the major metropolitan areas are now associated with very prestigious firms and corporations.

Status: Alumnus/a, full-time
Dates of Enrollment: 9/1996-5/2001
Survey Submitted: March 2005

Well-received out of the state of Iowa. Statistics about grads are deceiving without the context that many stay in the state at small practices.

Status: Alumnus/a, full-time
Dates of Enrollment: 8/1997-5/2000
Survey Submitted: March 2005

Obviously, it is more difficult to get a job on the East or West Coast because Iowa is not as well-known as the local schools. It helps to remind potential employers of Iowa's repeated Top 25 status in the law school rankings. On the other hand, some firms with Iowa grads actually show preference toward hiring Iowa grads because they have had a positive experience in the past. I moved out to California without a job offer and landed at a Top 100 law firm because one of the partners there used to have a favorite associate who was an Iowa grad. A lot of it is timing and your own personality. Being from Iowa is a bit of a novelty out on the West Coast, and it definitely makes you more memorable.

Status: Alumnus/a, full-time
Dates of Enrollment: 8/2001-5/2004
Survey Submitted: March 2005

The placement services are great. The school has an excellent reputation regionally and nationally.

Status: Alumnus/a, full-time
Dates of Enrollment: 8/1993-5/1996
Survey Submitted: February 2005

Almost 10 years out of law school, I am still employed by the firm that I interviewed with during the fall of my second year for a "summer associate" position between my second and third years. Iowa recruits a wide variety of employers to campus every year. Particularly from the Kansas City, Chicago and Minneapolis markets, but there are many firms across the country with strong ties to Iowa law school who send attorneys back there to interview every year or at least collect resumes from interested students. Although Iowa is a top-tier law school, its reputation is not particularly well-known on the coasts, but I think that is changing every year. The placement office staff at Iowa are just fabulous. There is not enough time nor space to say all the good things about them that should be said. They are amazingly dedicated to finding jobs for every student—regardless of grades or interests or geographic preferences—and really go above and beyond to help students in any way they can. In my experience, most Iowa alumni are very proud of having graduated from Iowa and are very willing to help current students or other Iowa alums.

Status: Alumnus/a, full-time
Dates of Enrollment: 8/1996-5/1999
Survey Submitted: January 2005

In my experience, Iowa graduates are well-received. Iowa has a pretty extensive on-campus recruiting program with firms from all over the country coming for interviews. My classmates got jobs on both coasts and in larger Midwestern cities, such as Minneapolis and Chicago.

Status: Alumnus/a, full-time
Dates of Enrollment: 8/2000-5/2003
Survey Submitted: April 2004

Campus recruiting was great. Iowa grads are highly coveted.

Status: Alumnus/a, full-time
Dates of Enrollment: 8/1999-5/2002
Survey Submitted: April 2004

The career center at Iowa is the best I have ever seen. They offer several workshops on resumes, interviewing skills and summer associate skills. The office works hard to recruit firms to do on-campus interviews, and they have thousands of publications available for the students who want to interview at a firm that does not come on campus. My firm (800 lawyers) will always recruit at Iowa because the students are smart hardworking students who are team players.

Status: Current student, full-time
Dates of Enrollment: 8/2001-Submit Date
Survey Submitted: February 2004

Students who are looking beyond the Midwest may not want to consider Iowa as their top choice. Iowa has a great academic reputation among academic institutions, but its merit as an academic institution does not translate into a great reputation in the working world. Iowa does have a great reputation in the Midwest and will find plenty of resources. It's rare that firms from the East and West Coasts will take notice of Iowa, and so they don't come to on-campus interviews or post vacancies.

My impression is that the alumni network isn't very strong, but that may all change now that they are hiring a new dean. Since the law school is located in a small college town, there are not many opportunities for students looking for experience while in law school. There is only a handful of firms or organizations, and most will likely place a preference on those who are looking to stay in the area. The career services staff here are wonderful. They are helpful in offering suggestions and keeping the student body updated. They need to make a better transition into up-to-date technology (as does the rest of the school). If there seems to be a lack of resources regarding employment on the coasts, it's really because of the poor alumni network.

Status: Alumnus/a, full-time
Dates of Enrollment: 9/1998-5/2002
Survey Submitted: November 2003

The career placement office is excellent. They are in tune with the market. On-campus recruiting is a popular way to get interviews with firms from bigger markets. Many of the firms have been coming to Iowa for years with good results.

Iowa offers lifelong career advising. The office is great resource for alumni who are considering making changes.

Quality of Life

Status: Alumnus/a, full-time
Dates of Enrollment: 9/1996-5/1999
Survey Submitted: March 2006

Iowa City is one of the cleanest, most picturesque cities I've ever lived in. Given that university students, faculty and staff easily make up 40 percent of the town's population, the education level is extreme. If you have children, Iowa City has a fantastic public school system. The law school's building is quiet, functional and even attractive, depending on one's perspective. There are good restaurants, and overall the cost of living, including housing prices, is extremely low.

Status: Current student, full-time
Dates of Enrollment: 1/2003-Submit Date
Survey Submitted: October 2005

It's relatively inexpensive to live here. My rent is $550 a month and that's considered expensive!

Status: Alumnus/a, full-time
Dates of Enrollment: 5/1995-5/1998
Survey Submitted: January 2005

Iowa City really revolves around the university, and it is a very Midwestern and friendly community. It could certainly use more racial diversity. Considering that the Midwest is generally racially homogenous, the law school did a decent job of recruiting from outside the Midwest and trying to obtain racial and ethnic diversity.

Status: Alumnus/a, full-time
Dates of Enrollment: 9/1996-5/2001
Survey Submitted: March 2005

Iowa City is a fun town.

Status: Alumnus/a, full-time
Dates of Enrollment: 8/1997-5/2000
Survey Submitted: March 2005

Iowa City is great. It is a bit like Berkeley but without all the homeless people (unfortunately, there are cold winters). People are fairly open-minded, as evidenced by Iowa's liberal hiring policies. At the time I attended, we had one of the only lesbian couples who were both full professors at the law school.

I doubt you could find cheaper housing at other campuses. Although I am sure the price has gone up, my two-bedroom apartment was $400 a month (I didn't have a roommate). When I moved to California, my apartment cost $2,500 a month for virtually the same apartment. Food is also inexpensive; I remember "Flip Night" where you could win 25-cent beers, and pitchers for $5.

Because the city revolves around the university, the city is extremely supportive of the school. It is a fun, safe, nurturing place.

Status: Alumnus/a, full-time
Dates of Enrollment: 8/2001-5/2004
Survey Submitted: March 2005

Housing is easy to find, and the city is easy to get around. The campus is great and the facilities are new. It is a very safe community.

Status: Alumnus/a, full-time
Dates of Enrollment: 8/1993-5/1996
Survey Submitted: February 2005

Iowa City is truly the cultural oasis of Iowa, if not the Midwest in general. You have all the advantages and perks of living in a large metropolitan area without all of the crime, traffic and other disadvantages typically experienced in larger cities. It is a very safe city (I don't recall any "bad" areas that I felt I needed to avoid), not to mention beautiful. I have the fondest memories of jogging through City Park along the Iowa River on a crisp fall morning, a winter-wonderland day and a sunny spring afternoon. The university's "Cambus" system provides for very easy and free transportation. I didn't live particularly close to the law school but I was near a "Cambus" stop and found that to be very convenient. The law school building itself is relatively new and was very well designed—

aesthetic pleasing, comfortable and well-suited for the needs of various classes, groups and guest speakers.

Status: Alumnus/a, full-time
Dates of Enrollment: 8/1996-5/1999
Survey Submitted: January 2005

Iowa City has a small town feel to it, but there's a lot going on because of the presence of the university.

Status: Alumnus/a, full-time
Dates of Enrollment: 8/2000-5/2003
Survey Submitted: April 2004

Iowa City is not very urban and is secluded geographically. Flights are expensive out of the nearest airport. The city itself, however, is very livable. Low crime, nice people, very much a college town.

Status: Alumnus/a, full-time
Dates of Enrollment: 8/1999-5/2002
Survey Submitted: April 2004

Iowa City does not offer everything that a bigger city offers, but this is not always a bad thing. Housing is cheap, parking easy, the commute simple. Iowa City has all of the shopping malls, movie theaters, etc., a person could hope for.

Status: Current student, full-time
Dates of Enrollment: 8/2001-Submit Date
Survey Submitted: February 2004

Since the law school is located in a small town and inconveniently located away from downtown (restaurants and shopping), it's easy to become claustrophobic. There is plenty of housing located within walking distance of the law school, but parking is limited (which can be a major pain). Public transportation is inconvenient at best, but it's possible to strategically locate yourself next to a bus line (although its infrequency and the cold weather may make for an intolerable combination).

There is a large international community here, as the campus at large does attract foreign students. The law building itself is fairly comfortable and well maintained. However, it's reaching its capacity, which at peak times means crowded hallways and no place to sit to eat lunch. Student groups will find that they have no office space, and some of the faculty even share their offices.

The law building has two major flaws: it has a terrible heating system (which is tragic considering the winters here), and it is technologically challenged. The classrooms and buildings are poorly equipped with Internet connections and outlets, and students who prefer the use of laptops and PDAs find themselves fighting for outlets, carrying extra batteries or just out of luck. Not even considering the lack of dining options available in the town as a whole, the law school is poorly situated, forcing students to choose between eating at the dining commons at the undergraduate dorms, eating a poor selection of cafeteria-style food (with very limited hours—lunch only), or eating the unhealthy selection offered by four vending machines. You bring your lunch at your risk, as the single refrigerator available to students is often crammed with junk and molding food.

The library is excellent with a great, helpful staff and vast and well-kept resources. They have a dizzying array of law journals (though their maintenance of non-legal periodicals is not wonderful). They have great study carrels (equipped with outlets, Internet access and a place to store books), but these are for the most part limited to second- and third-years.

Regarding facilities, the school states: "In 2004, the College of Law equipped its general classroom space with electrical outlets to enable students to utilize laptop computers during class. The law library is fully computerized, both in its internal operations and in its public services. It provides 41 Gateway Pentium 4 desktops with flat panel monitors for general student use (including high-speed connection to the Internet and to the law library network printers), as well as individual study carrels for students that are hard wired for laptop network connections and provide high-speed Internet access."

Read all of Vault's Law School Surveys at www.vault.com/lawschool — get complete surveys on top law schools, expert advice on applicaton essays, LSAT prep and more.

VAULT CAREER LIBRARY 259

Status: Alumnus/a, full-time
Dates of Enrollment: 9/1998-5/2002
Survey Submitted: November 2003

Iowa City is great college town. It is much like the other Big 10 college towns, with a downtown nightclub scene and weekend tailgaters. Iowa City has thriving intellectual community and is near some larger metropolitan areas. Housing is pricey for Iowa but reasonable compared to urban campuses. Iowa City is a diverse community.

 ## Social Life

Status: Alumnus/a, full-time
Dates of Enrollment: 9/1996-5/1999
Survey Submitted: March 2006

Iowa City has a large bar scene, which is not to be confused with a club scene. In other words, there are lots of drunken college students staggering around downtown at night, yelling "Wooooooo!" Unless there have been drastic changes in the last few years, Iowa City has no real club scene. But, Chicago is a two-hour drive, and really you should be hitting the books.

Status: Current student, full-time
Dates of Enrollment: 1/2003-Submit Date
Survey Submitted: October 2005

It's Iowa, so not much going on but football and bars. Still, it is a nice college town, without the pressures or expenses of going to school in a big city.

Status: Alumnus/a, full-time
Dates of Enrollment: 5/1995-5/1998
Survey Submitted: January 2005

I hung out at The Airliner (now closed), Martinis, Yacht Club, Vito's and other bars in the "downtown" area. I generally dated within the law school community, which could be pretty gossipy, although I think more guys in law school dated undergraduates and outside the law school. Coralville also had nice restaurants. Every Wednesday, people would informally gather for "law night" at a local bar.

Status: Alumnus/a, full-time
Dates of Enrollment: 8/1997-5/2000
Survey Submitted: March 2005

Most of the law school would have nights to go out on the town. The nice thing about it was that because there were fewer places to go, you could always run into someone you knew, if you wanted to. Dating is probably a bit harder, unless you are partial to undergrads, although there are a number of other graduate schools with older students.

Quite a few students also hosted dinner parties and other house parties almost on a weekly basis. There was never a lack of something to do on the weekends (or even most week nights).

Iowa City also has decent cultural events at Hancher Auditorium.

Status: Alumnus/a, full-time
Dates of Enrollment: 8/2001-5/2004
Survey Submitted: March 2005

The law school sponsors many events for students to meet each other, especially in the first year. Various organizations host weekly social gatherings.

Status: Alumnus/a, full-time
Dates of Enrollment: 8/1993-5/1996
Survey Submitted: February 2005

The social life in Iowa City is a blast. The ped-mall in downtown Iowa City is quite the hot spot for restaurants, bars and clubs. Although largely dominated by undergrads, there are a number of bars that cater more to the graduate students. Student favorites when I was there included Joe's Place, Mickey's, the Sports Column and the Airliner. For dancing, there was the Union and One-Eyed Jake's. For the size of the community, there is an impressive number of good restaurants as well. The dating scene is as good as they come. The city is very

liberal—surprisingly so for being in the heart of the Midwest—and people from all racial, ethnic and socioeconomic backgrounds thrive in Iowa City.

Status: Current student, full-time
Dates of Enrollment: 8/2001-Submit Date
Survey Submitted: February 2004

Iowa City is very bar-oriented, so much of the law school activities are bar- and drinking-oriented. Iowa has two law fraternities (one with a more social agenda and the other more community service-oriented). Sports are also a big deal here, so tailgating before football games is a favorite fall pastime. The law students also engage in intramural sports (among themselves, though to a limited extent with other graduate students). It's difficult to meet other students (partly due to our location and partly because of the nature of our curriculum). There are quite a few student organizations, and the school often hosts speakers, discussions and food events (cultural food festival, chili cook-off, Saturday barbecues). Some students will also host house parties, some school-wide and others just among friends. Restaurants aren't a focal point of student life here.

Status: Alumnus/a, full-time
Dates of Enrollment: 8/1999-5/2002
Survey Submitted: April 2004

Downtown Iowa City provides an amazing social scene stocked with bars and coffeehouses. Restaurants are also very good. Most law students hang out at Quinton's or the Airliner, depending on the happy hour. The law school organizes a happy hour at a different bar every Wednesday that is very well attended. Usually 50 to 60 law students will attend the happy hours on Wednesdays.

Status: Alumnus/a, full-time
Dates of Enrollment: 9/1998-5/2002
Survey Submitted: November 2003

Law students at Iowa tend to stick together for social activities. There is always something going on. Law students' favorite bars seem to change each year depending on where or whether a classmate works at a particular bar. Younger graduate students tend to frequent places like Joe's Place, the Atlas and the Summit for cocktails and socializing. There are plenty of meat-market-type bars in town, too.

The fall semester is dominated by the UI football schedule. Non-alcohol weekend entertainment is sometimes a challenge during football season.

 ## The School Says

Since its founding in 1865, The University of Iowa College of Law has prepared generations of men and women to be professional and civic leaders through a challenging program that helps students develop their individual strengths amidst a friendly and comfortable environment. The college is located in Iowa City, a lively college town that is home to a dynamic teaching and research university with approximately 30,000 students.

The objective of formal legal education is to establish a solid foundation for a lifetime of professional growth. Iowa places equal emphasis on developing fundamental lawyer's skills and an appreciation of the roles of law and lawyers in society. Iowa offers a broad curriculum in an educational program that cultivates active student participation in the learning process and creates regular opportunities for individuals and small groups to confront teachers who are genuinely interested in each student's professional development. The first-year "small-section" program integrates legal research and writing instruction into substantive courses in classes that number approximately 30 students during the first semester and 20 students during the second semester. The upper-class elective curriculum features a diverse selection of mainstream doctrinal courses, challenging perspective courses, practical skills-training exercises and clinical opportunities. Iowa's intensive writing program with faculty-supervised writing projects is also an integral part of each student's legal education and training.

Beyond the classroom Iowa offers four student-edited law journals, several co-curricular programs including client counseling, moot court and trial advocacy, and over two dozen student organizations. Within a 20-mile radius there are thousands of acres of parks and other open recreational areas for walking, hiking, biking, swimming, boating, fishing, camping and cross-country skiing. Together with the university, Iowa City also offers a wealth of civic and cultural activities to satisfy every interest.

Iowa currently offers two entrance dates for the full-time program leading to a juris doctor (JD) degree: summer (May) and fall (August). Each year approximately 30 students enroll in the summer entering class and 180 to 190 students enroll in the fall entering class.

Read all of Vault's Law School Surveys at www.vault.com/lawschool — get complete surveys on top law schools, expert advice on applicaton essays, LSAT prep and more.

VAULT CAREER LIBRARY   261

University of Kansas School of Law

Admissions Office
205 Green Hall
1535 West 15th Street
Lawrence, KS 66045-7577
Admissions phone: (785) 864-4378 or
(866) 220-3654 (toll-free)
Admissions fax: (785) 864-5054
Admissions e-mail: admitlaw@ku.edu
Admissions URL: http://www.law.ku.edu/admissions/

 Admissions

Status: Current student, full-time
Dates of Enrollment: 5/2005-Submit Date
Survey Submitted: April 2006

The admissions process was easy because everyone in the admissions office was helpful, answering questions throughout the entire process. In addition, the law school student ambassadors were helpful in gaining insight from a student's perspective. I was surprised to be able to talk directly with the Director of Admissions whenever needed. The process was quick and painless. I received notice of my admission by phone and then was sent a packet.

Status: Current student, full-time
Dates of Enrollment: 8/2003-Submit Date
Survey Submitted: April 2006

The admissions process at KU was relatively painless. You can complete the application online and it doesn't require some of the detailed essays some schools require. The application fee is relatively cheap. All the general advice about getting in and writing essays applies.

Status: Current student, full-time
Dates of Enrollment: 8/2005-Submit Date
Survey Submitted: April 2006

The admissions process is similar to that of the other law schools I applied to. The application is fairly standard. I believe that the school is as selective as its ranking and reputation would suggest. I did not interview with the admissions staff, although I believe that option is available to those who would like to do so.

There is some good scholarship money available. My GPA and LSAT were at the 75 percent level of the entering class, and I received a nice scholarship as a non-resident.

Status: Current student, full-time
Dates of Enrollment: 8/2004-Submit Date
Survey Submitted: April 2006

The ease of the application process at KU was impressive compared to some of the other schools that I applied to or considered applying to. I was probably their worst nightmare as I constantly contacted the staff via both e-mail and phone with small technical questions. The staff was quick and cheerful in their responses, however, and very free with advice on how to best complete the application process. They provided me with updates on the status of my application and I was notified early in December of my admission decision. This prompt decision greatly helped my decision to attend KU.

Status: Current student, full-time
Dates of Enrollment: 8/2003-Submit Date
Survey Submitted: April 2006

KU's admissions staff is the friendliest you will find at any law school. They remembered my name from the moment I applied and they were always willing to answer any questions I asked.

KU looks for high quality applicants and the admissions staff does a good job of selecting students who have diverse life experiences.

Status: Current student, full-time
Dates of Enrollment: 8/2005-Submit Date
Survey Submitted: April 2006

The admissions process is very painless. The admissions staff answer the phone directly and kindly answer any questions you may have. I would suggest that you come visit the school and meet with the Director of Admissions, that way they can put a face with a name. Once you have met the admissions staff they will not forget who you are—which is very nice. KU is a very good school but has a lower amount of applications per year than comparable schools, which may give some people with borderline scores a chance. Don't hesitate to apply, they are very friendly.

Status: Current student, full-time
Dates of Enrollment: 12/2003-Submit Date
Survey Submitted: April 2006

I applied to 12 schools, and 11 of them had no real contact with me. The University of Kansas, on the other hand, had current students write me postcards letting me know where my application was in the selection process. Someone from the admission office even called me and asked if I had any questions about their program.

Status: Current student, full-time
Dates of Enrollment: 5/2004-Submit Date
Survey Submitted: April 2006

Fill out application, include personal statement, take a tour, attend open house, attend a class. Personal statement should reflect you, and should not just be a reiteration of your resume. Tell an interesting story about yourself, something they cannot get from the rest of your application. Keep it simple, keep it short. Good Luck!

Status: Current student, full-time
Dates of Enrollment: 8/2004-Submit Date
Survey Submitted: April 2006

Get your application in early! I did not have an interview, but did meet with the Admissions Director when I came to KU Law for my visit/tour. Getting a tour from a current student ambassador and sitting in on a class will really give you a feel for the relaxed nature of the school. In your essay, be sure to pinpoint anything about yourself that makes you unique and will make the program diverse.

Status: Alumnus/a, full-time
Dates of Enrollment: 8/2000-5/2004
Survey Submitted: April 2005

In order to be admitted to any law school you have to take the LSAT. Admission is based mostly on the combination of your LSAT score and your GPA. The baseline may change from year to year, but in 2000 you needed at least a 3.5 GPA and an LSAT score of 150. That year there were 750 applicants with 150 being accepted. When you write your essay for admission, be sure it is an organized, with proper paragraphs (umbrella sentences, etc.) They like to see someone eager to learn. Always be candid on your application, because it is included when you apply for the bar.

Status: Current student, full-time
Dates of Enrollment: 5/2002-Submit Date
Survey Submitted: September 2003

The admissions process used to be less selective. Many applicants who met certain baseline statistics were simply admitted by the director, without any review from a board of professors or administration. However, the class of 2005 ended up being a bit larger than expected, due to more individuals attending graduate school instead of fighting the job market. This has resulted in the school raising the bar on admissions. Not only was the 2006 class smaller, but according to many, students who saw KU as their back-up option didn't get in. Rumor has it that the administration is using the "over-admittance" in the 2005 class as an excuse to raise the quality and decrease the quantity of its entering classes.

Scholarships are pretty much nonexistent. In-state students have a much better chance of landing some measure of financial assistance. Compared to other schools, however, don't expect much in the way of financial incentives to attend. To increase your chances of a scholarship, apply as soon as possible. Otherwise, you will be put on a waiting list for a scholarship, and unless enough people decide not to attend law school, you're out of luck.

Status: Alumnus/a, full-time
Dates of Enrollment: 5/1997-5/2000
Survey Submitted: April 2004

KU looks at a variety of factors, including the usual criteria of grades and LSAT scores, as well as the applicant's background and prior work experience. Approximately 30 percent of every class come from states other than Kansas. A campus visit and meeting with the admissions staff can improve your chances of admission.

Status: Alumnus/a, full-time
Dates of Enrollment: 5/1995-5/1998
Survey Submitted: April 2004

An interview and on-site visit were not required, but I did both voluntarily. I think KU is interested in having a diverse student body and would be receptive to out-of-state, nontraditional and minority students.

Academics

Status: Current student, full-time
Dates of Enrollment: 5/2005-Submit Date
Survey Submitted: April 2006

The professors are absolutely outstanding. After reading horror stories of law school professors, I was pleased to find out that KU Law professors were quite the opposite. The professors are challenging, yet professional. I have found that most professors truly care about their students and are passionate about teaching.

Status: Current student, full-time
Dates of Enrollment: 8/2003-Submit Date
Survey Submitted: April 2006

All first-year classes are set for you, and they are all the core legal subjects (contracts, torts, property, civil procedure, etc.). Each 1L has one class that is his or her small section. It is a class of about 15 to 20 students. Students usually get to know their small section professor very well. Furthermore, all the students in your small section rotate through all of your other classes with you, so you always have someone to call about notes or questions.

The professors have a very easy-going style and are very approachable outside of class. There are only a few classes in the upper-level curriculum that are difficult to get into. Most students don't have a problem if they plan their classes ahead of time.

Classes are graded on a curve, as they are at most law schools. The workload is significant your first two years, as it probably is at any law school. However, most students manage the work and still have time for outside activities, families, etc.

Status: Current student, full-time
Dates of Enrollment: 8/2004-Submit Date
Survey Submitted: April 2006

Overall I have been impressed with the quality of the faculty at KU. In your 1L year you have little control over your schedule and primarily take basic required classes (Civ Pro, Contracts and Property) but I feel that this keeps the new students from overly burdening themselves and ensures a workable schedule.

They grade on a forced curve which is necessary due to the inability of a single professor to teach every 1L. To do otherwise would, in my opinion, potentially give half the class an advantage in class rank because there is simply no way that two professors can lecture, test and evaluate in exactly the same manner. There are plenty of sections and electives available after your first year but some of the smaller classes (Environmental Law in particular) are only offered on a biennial basis and your year of enrollment may make it difficult to enroll in all of the classes you wish to take.

Status: Current student, full-time
Dates of Enrollment: 8/2005-Submit Date
Survey Submitted: April 2006

I have been thoroughly impressed with the faculty at KU, and I have found them to be a real bright spot, among many, for the law school. They are extremely intelligent, have practical experience, and are down-to-earth. Further, the faculty are interested in the student's development and are always willing to meet one-on-one to discuss issues the student may have. There is a mandatory curve for each class and it varies between required courses and electives. All first-year required courses have a mandatory GPA range of 2.8 to 3.0. The grading distribution is usually a bell-curve scenario with most students gathering around the 3.0 (B) range. There are very few students who receive a D+ or worse, and F's are almost never given. Upper-level courses have a mandatory curve of 3.1 to 3.4. There is a wide variety of courses and designated programs (i.e., International Business, Tax, etc.). The Clinical Programs offer a great way for students to get hands-on experience to supplement classroom learning. There are 10 programs including Criminal Prosecution, Judicial Clerkship, Public Policy, Media Law, Elder Law, Tribal Law, and Criminal Defense.

Status: Current student, full-time
Dates of Enrollment: 8/2003-Submit Date
Survey Submitted: April 2006

The workload at any law school is going to be tough, and KU is no different. I worked incredibly hard my first year and sometimes I felt overwhelmed by all of the work. I will say that I always felt like my fellow 1Ls were supportive and helpful at all times. During my two years here, I have never felt that KU has the nasty competitive atmosphere that law schools are typically known for. People work hard but everyone is willing to help others if they need it.

I have never been shut out of a class that I wanted but I have heard of people being shut out of Trial Ad.

KU's professors are outstanding! They recognize their students in the hallways and they initiate conversation. They want to be involved with students and they welcome questions. I cannot say enough good things about them. They know their stuff and they want to help students succeed.

Status: Current student, full-time
Dates of Enrollment: 8/2005-Submit Date
Survey Submitted: April 2006

The workload is typical of any first-year law student. The legal writing program is a lot of work. Kansas boasts very credible professors, which is apparent in the class rooms. While each professor uses different methods during class, they are all available throughout the week to answer questions from students.

There are only one or two classes that are hard to get into. There are A LOT of clinics, most of which are easy to get into, but provide quality first-hand experience. If you want clinical experience KU is the place to be.

Grading for the first year is done on a 2.8 or 3.0 mandatory curve. All grading (with the exception of Legal Writing) is done by anonymous number.

Status: Current student, full-time
Dates of Enrollment: 5/2004-Submit Date
Survey Submitted: April 2006

The quality of classes is pretty subjective. Depending on your learning style, you will prefer some professors over others, and enjoy some classes more than others. Sometimes the classes with the most challenging subject matter are the easiest to excel in, whereas the classes with easier subject matter are harder because everyone else does well. All of the classes are graded on a curve, so your success depends largely on the composition of your class—and I am pretty sure this is the same at most ABA accredited law schools.

Getting into classes is pretty easy and the school is small enough (about 160/class) that exceptions are made without too much red tape. The workload

Read all of Vault's Law School Surveys at www.vault.com/lawschool — get complete surveys on top law schools, expert advice on applicaton essays, LSAT prep and more.

VAULT CAREER LIBRARY 263

seems hard your first year, however, it is probably because you spend most of your time just learning to read case law and spot issues. The workload your second year is much tougher, in part because you are joining clubs, law review, journal and participating in clinics, so out-of-class activities increase. I also started working for a firm part-time my second year (which many students do), and that can sometimes take precedence over classes. Overall, be ready to work hard if you want to do well.

Status: Current student, full-time
Dates of Enrollment: 8/2004-Submit Date
Survey Submitted: April 2006

All of my classes have exceeded my expectations. The quality of the classes is high. The atmosphere is competitive but friendly. For classes that have limited enrollment, there is a lottery process. Those classes are taught every semester though, so it is generally pretty easy to get in. Professors have an open-door policy and are very approachable. Grades are figured on a mandatory curve.

Status: Alumnus/a, full-time
Dates of Enrollment: 8/1998-5/2001
Survey Submitted: March 2005

I did not have any "bad" instructors while at KU. There was a good mix of seasoned faculty with young energetic professors—a great combination. I was thoroughly impressed with the faculty during my time at KU. There may be more variety in the classes offered now, but I think KU would be still be considered a traditional legal education. Very solid basic courses and instructors. The classes and the workload were tough, but I don't recall much trouble getting into classes, but then again, I took all the hard classes that most people tried to avoid.

Status: Current student, full-time
Dates of Enrollment: 5/2002-Submit Date
Survey Submitted: September 2003

Very solid academics. Kansas is known for the practical side of its legal education. Even in the first year, the legal research and writing courses concentrate on teaching skills applicable in summer internship programs and in practice after graduation.

It has not been a problem getting into popular classes, as it seems there is no universal opinion on which classes are popular. For every negative opinion on a class or professor, there are refuting opinions. Even the "scary" and "boring" professors of legend are, in the end, approachable and brilliant. Only one of my professors has not been a down-to-earth type of person.

During the first year, two of every student's classes meet in what are called "small sections." This allows for more intimate student-professor contact, as well as a chance for more socialization among students. Grading is A to F, with the mandatory curve being set at 2.9 for first-year students. All grading is anonymous.

Class participation is generally predictable: The professor starts at the end of a row and moves back and forth through the class. It is pretty simple to figure out what day you're going to have to be accountable for the reading. A few professors randomly call on anyone in the class. This isn't so bad, because it gives an incentive to be prepared. In general, the professors can be a little intimidating, but it's nothing worse than the scare you get at a good suspense movie. And if you've read what you were supposed to, you'll do fine. They don't try to crucify you in front of the entire class.

Status: Alumnus/a, full-time
Dates of Enrollment: 5/1997-5/2000
Survey Submitted: April 2004

Personal interaction with faculty was routine. The faculty are of exceptional quality and are the real strength of the law school. Courses in business, commercial and tax law are particularly strong. Grades are on a curve, but it is basically a C+/B curve. About 10 percent of each class receives either an A- or A. As at every law school, students work hard, especially if they participate in journals and clinics.

 Employment Prospects

Status: Current student, full-time
Dates of Enrollment: 8/2003-Submit Date
Survey Submitted: April 2006

KU offers an excellent Career Services office that works tirelessly to help each student find a summer or permanent position. The school hosts an on-campus interviewing process twice per school year, has frequent "brown-bag sessions" to teach students about various areas of law as well as how to craft the perfect resume, cover letter, etc. The Career Services Office has resources to help every law student, no matter what the situation. The student just needs to ask.

Status: Current student, full-time
Dates of Enrollment: 8/2005-Submit Date
Survey Submitted: April 2006

KU Law has a great reputation in the Midwest. All of the firms in Kansas City, Tulsa, Omaha, Wichita, and everywhere in between heavily recruit at the law school. Further, there are numerous opportunities for students who desire to head to either of the coasts. KU Law has alumni in New York, California, and everywhere in between. Several firms recruit 1L's on campus, and I was able to secure a great internship with an outstanding organization in Kansas City.

The Career Services Office is a great resource. The staff is friendly and knowledgeable. The people in the office seem to be genuinely concerned with each individual and his/her aspirations.

Status: Current student, full-time
Dates of Enrollment: 8/2004-Submit Date
Survey Submitted: April 2006

KU has an excellent reputation locally (basically the central portion of the country from Chicago to Kansas City to Dallas) and enough national clout that I have not felt at a disadvantage when discussing job opportunities with firms on either the East or West Coast. We're not Harvard, but I do feel that our reputation nationally is one that opens doors of opportunity wherever you go.

The career services staff at KU has recently expanded as well and they have proven to be extraordinarily helpful, even to those students pursuing a job outside of the legal profession. Our on-campus recruiting and internship activities have both recently been expanded (in direct relation to our expansion of staff) and new initiatives have been started to assist students in contacting and interacting with alumni of the law school. I feel that this increased alumni interaction has greatly increased the potential of our job placement services.

Status: Current student, full-time
Dates of Enrollment: 8/2005-Submit Date
Survey Submitted: April 2006

KU provides students with jobs at a lot of large firms in the Kansas City area. However, they have a strong alumni network throughout the country, including: Washington, D.C., Chicago, Phoenix, and Denver. There are A LOT of on-campus interviews each semester, and the Career Services Office has two full-time attorneys working with the students.

Each first year student is paired with a mentor attorney who practices in the area. That gives each student a chance to meet and network with a lot of different attorneys and firms.

Graduates obtain mostly private practice jobs, but there are many students in other types of work. KU is generally the most favored school in the state.

Status: Current student, full-time
Dates of Enrollment: 5/2004-Submit Date
Survey Submitted: April 2006

Our Career Services Office provides an enormous amount of help to students seeking jobs, including extensive on-campus interviews with local and national firms for 1Ls, 2Ls and 3Ls, resume help, world-wide alumni network, Legal Career Options Day (exposing students to jobs outside of the traditional law firm setting).

KU Law grads work in all of the big cities in the country, including Los Angeles, New York, Phoenix, Chicago, Washington, D.C., in law firms, government jobs, nd corporate counsel. I happen to work for an intellectual property boutique in Kansas City. If there is a job you want, you can get it with a law degree from KU Law.

Status: Alumnus/a, full-time
Dates of Enrollment: 8/1997-5/2000
Survey Submitted: January 2005

Strong in Midwest. If leaving the Midwest, you need a connection to the location where you are headed or strong academics (or both). Alumni are all over the country and were helpful to me when I looked away from Midwest

Status: Alumnus/a, full-time
Dates of Enrollment: 8/2000-5/2004
Survey Submitted: April 2005

KU is highly-ranked and respected not only locally, but also nationally. Many employers recruit on campus, but they almost always interview only the top of the class. Everyone else will have to find their own employment. Grades are critical in law school. The higher your grades, the easier time you'll have finding employment. A new person took over the career services office just prior to my graduation. They do post jobs on a bulletin board and on their web page. KU also offers several clinics (internship-type programs) to their students. These are excellent programs designed to give students "real life" experience under the supervision of licensed attorneys and/or professors.

Status: Current student, full-time
Dates of Enrollment: 5/2002-Submit Date
Survey Submitted: September 2003

There are wonderful administrators in the career services office at the law school. They are very helpful and generally encouraging. If you want to know your prospects based on grades, they will tell it to you straight.

The campus recruiting situation can be frustrating to those not in the top 25 percent of the class. The majority of interviewing firms require law review or law journal experience, as well as a GPA requirement. Generally, if a student does not fall within these preferences, he or she will not get an interview, unless someone in the firm recognizes the student's last name or the student has some other sort of connection. Basically, it helps to know people who can pull some strings for you. However, for a firm to recruit and interview on campus, they can only select 80 percent of the students they interview. The other 20 percent are drawn from a hat of those students who had an interest in the firm, but were not selected by the firm for an interview.

Kansas is the best law school in the Kansas City area if you look at the rankings. UMKC and Washburn students seem to be just as competitive in the KC area, although a Kansas degree would do better outside of the KC metro. Kansas has had a few U.S. Supreme Court clerks within the last decade, a fact which has helped elevate its degree's reputation.

Status: Alumnus/a, full-time
Dates of Enrollment: 5/1995-5/1998
Survey Submitted: April 2004

KU has a great clinical program and, essentially, everyone who wants to be in a clinic can do so. I was impressed with the quality of firms and employers that visited the campus, although the vast majority of employers were from the Kansas City, Topeka, Wichita, and surrounding areas. Students will need to take more initiative if they are seeking employment on, for example, one of the coasts.

Quality of Life

Status: Current student, full-time
Dates of Enrollment: 8/2003-Submit Date
Survey Submitted: April 2006

Lawrence is a wonderful community in which to live. It is close to a big city, Kansas City, if one prefers city living. Commuting is easy. It is also surrounded by several well-established suburban communities that offer wonderful schools and homes.

Lawrence itself is a wonderful city, offering KU basketball, great downtown shopping, unique restaurants, diverse cultural opportunities, and a rich history. There are plenty of apartments and homes to choose from for every taste and budget. Clinton Lake and surrounding areas provide plenty of fun outdoor activities. Lawrence is a safe community.

Status: Current student, full-time
Dates of Enrollment: 8/2004-Submit Date
Survey Submitted: April 2006

The majority of the students at KU Law live off campus, because to the age of the student body and their desire to separate themselves from the undergraduate population. Lucky for us, Lawrence is a growing, vibrant college town. A number of new apartment complexes have recently been completed and new houses are going up at a record rate.

The cost of living in Lawrence falls well below the national average and the crime rate is extraordinarily low. On top of that Lawrence is a college town in all the right ways with a great deal of school pride. The population is large enough to provide sufficient dining and entertainment opportunities, yet not so large that you encounter traffic or transportation issues.

Status: Current student, full-time
Dates of Enrollment: 8/2005-Submit Date
Survey Submitted: April 2006

Housing in the Midwest is extremely affordable when compared to other areas of the country. There are an abundance of housing options including apartments, condos, townhouses, and rental homes. The law school is located directly across the street from a student union which is convenient. Further, the law school is across the street from Allen Fieldhouse, a shrine to college basketball. Another nice feature of the law school is that it is self-contained. The law school has lounge areas, a kitchen, a bookstore, and all faculty offices. Essentially, everything a law student needs is contained in one building. The law school also underwent some very attractive interior renovations this year which include leather couches, plasma TV's, and more attractive decor.

Status: Current student, full-time
Dates of Enrollment: 8/2005-Submit Date
Survey Submitted: April 2006

The student commons were remodeled last years and so the law school isn't such a bad place to hang out.

Lawrence is an anomaly in Kansas. It's an amazing little college town with a vibrant art and music scene. There are some really wonderful bars and restaurants. You can get a really nice apartment for cheap. You can live like a king or queen in Kansas.

Status: Current student, full-time
Dates of Enrollment: 5/2004-Submit Date
Survey Submitted: April 2006

One of the great things about KU Law is our strict honor code. Students share study carrels/desk cubbies spread throughout the library, and most students leave their belongings including books, etc., at their carrel instead of lugging their books home every night. It is nice to not have to worry about stealing or vandalism.

The level of competition here is strong, but students are more interested in pushing themselves than undermining each other to get ahead. In my time there I've never heard of any stealing or moving books in the library, removing pages or otherwise preventing access to information. People widely share outlines, notes and help each other.

There is no formal housing for grad students. Most students live in apartments or houses nearby. Lawrence is a quintessential college town, crime is low, people are always out walking on campus, or in neighborhoods. The school has a state of the art gym open to students, great restaurants, and a beautiful campus. There are tons of restaurants in the area, and Kansas City is only 45 minutes away. Many students commute.

Read all of Vault's Law School Surveys at www.vault.com/lawschool — get complete surveys on top law schools, expert advice on applicaton essays, LSAT prep and more.

VAULT CAREER LIBRARY 265

Status: Current student, full-time
Dates of Enrollment: 5/2005-Submit Date
Survey Submitted: April 2006

You can't beat Lawrence. I lived in Madrid and Milwaukee for many years,and I visit Chicago often. You can get everything here that you could in a major city, from good restaurants down on Massachusetts Street to the many unique clothing stores that carry what's trendy. Plus, you support your local stores, which leads to a great sense of community. The music scene can't be beat if you like live music. Some say it's the best place to catch shows between Denver and Chicago, and I would agree.

Status: Current student, full-time
Dates of Enrollment: 5/2002-Submit Date
Survey Submitted: September 2003

Law students at Kansas are pretty spoiled. Across the street from the law school is a parking garage. All books for all classes are sold at the law school's own book store in the law school. No need to fight undergrads just to get your books. The book store also sells many items at a reduced cost, as it is nonprofit. Everything is still expensive, but they do what they can.

The majority of students live in Lawrence and, because it is a college town, finding a place to live off campus is not a problem. Crime is rare and never a concern. Many students actually live in the suburbs of Kansas City and commute to Lawrence every day.

Status: Alumnus/a, full-time
Dates of Enrollment: 5/1997-5/2000
Survey Submitted: April 2004

Lawrence is one of the best college towns in the country. Housing was very affordable, there are no long commutes and amenities such as music, art, drama and sporting events are plentiful. The only problem is finding time to enjoy those events. Law students receive priority in purchasing tickets to KU basketball games, if that's your passion. Lawrence also has several golf courses of excellent quality and moderate price.

 ## Social Life

Status: Current student, full-time
Dates of Enrollment: 5/2005-Submit Date
Survey Submitted: April 2006

If social life was the sole factor in deciding a college—KU would be the only option. The students are incredibly friendly...even in a highly competitive "cutthroat" program such as law school. The students help each other out. Many bars are located on Mass., the main street in Lawrence, which makes meeting new people extremely easy.

Status: Current student, full-time
Dates of Enrollment: 8/2003-Submit Date
Survey Submitted: April 2006

KU has a very active student bar association. They plan parties and events throughout the year, as well as weekly TGIT's at local bars. There is a formal party, Barrister's Ball, every spring, as well as a well-attended Pub Night talent competition and auction. Popular bars include The Wheel, The Hawk, Quinton's, The Red Lion and Louise's. There are many student groups and organizations. The Greek system is mainly limited to undergraduates.

Status: Current student, full-time
Dates of Enrollment: 8/2004-Submit Date
Survey Submitted: April 2006

With KU being a college of nearly 30,000 students, there are ample opportunities to interact socially. Downtown Lawrence (Massachusetts Street) has a vibrant live music scene, numerous bars within walking distance and a safe and friendly atmosphere at all times of the day and night. The most popular hangouts are closer to campus and include The Wheel (often referenced on SportsCenter), The Hawk and Louise's West.

From posh and upscale to shorts and flip-flops you can find an establishment that fits your personality in Lawrence. In addition, Lawrence prides itself on having

a local flavor and supporting small business, so while you will find the typical Chili's, On The Border, etc. the town also boasts dozens and dozens of small family owned restaurants. From Mexican food to Greek to tapas, you can find virtually every type of food locally.

Status: Current student, full-time
Dates of Enrollment: 8/2005-Submit Date
Survey Submitted: April 2006

There a quite a few law students who meet their sweetheart in law school. A surprising number of students are married and even have kids. There is a vibrant gay community in Lawrence.

Most of the clubs are a joke because the students are too busy studying.

Status: Current student, full-time
Dates of Enrollment: 5/2005-Submit Date
Survey Submitted: April 2006

The social scene is great if you can manage to get out (we're in law school after all). Every Thursday we have TGIT at one of the local bars sponsored by the SBA, and the Wheel is a KU Law stronghold. Every type of ethnic food is available in Lawrence and the student organizations are very active in having cultural activities. You'll always have a great time in Lawrence, guaranteed.

Status: Alumnus/a, full-time
Dates of Enrollment: 8/1997-5/2000
Survey Submitted: January 2005

Fine. Typical law school. Competition among students is not too bad, so the social life tends to be pretty good.

Status: Alumnus/a, full-time
Dates of Enrollment: 8/2000-5/2004
Survey Submitted: April 2005

There always seemed to be a party somewhere, even though I didn't attend many of them. There are also numerous organizations to join, like the Federalist Society and Women in Law. When these organizations have a meeting it's usually with free pizza if it's on campus or free beer and pizza if it's outside the school.

Also, when you start law school you are assigned to a small group section. The people in that group and that professor will likely become your best friends. It is designed to prevent students from getting lost in a sea of 150 new students. Most small sections also have get-togethers. Lawrence is dominated by KU, so there are numerous bars and restaurants.

Status: Current student, full-time
Dates of Enrollment: 5/2002-Submit Date
Survey Submitted: September 2003

Massachusetts Street is the main drag in Lawrence, just off campus. It has all the shopping and dining anyone could want. The law school student body takes advantage of this area regularly. Nearly every week there is a law-sponsored event at a bar for everyone to show up and relax for cheap. The student bar association has organized bus trips to Royals baseball games, as well as bus trips from bar to bar in Lawrence. The social scene is very healthy. It is hard to not have a friend after the first week of classes, and impossible not to know over half the class by the end of the first semester.

There are many student groups to join at the law school as well. Usually these are dominated by students motivated in the subject matter of the group, but if you want to get involved, it's simple, and you're very welcome. Many of these groups sponsor their own events throughout the year, including road trips to conferences.

 ## The School Says

The University of Kansas School of Law is located in Lawrence, Kansas which is the home of the University of Kansas. Lawrence is a diverse and multifaceted town unlike any other. It offers a rich history, a broad range of cultural experiences, and unique shopping and entertainment opportunities. With a population of just over 80,000 people, Lawrence has all the convenience and comforts of a small town community. With Lawrence's close proximity to Topeka (25 miles) and Kansas City (40 miles) there are many benefits and attractions found in large metropolitan areas.

Our curriculum is diverse and offers both breadth and depth. We have six certificate programs, 10 clinics and seven joint degree programs. Courses are offered in virtually all areas of the law from agriculture law to the law of cyberspace and upper level students have over 100 electives to choose from. Students may also participate in a rich array of moot court programs.

A unique benefit of KU Law is the relationship between students and faculty. With a student body of 500, students have the opportunity to establish strong relationships with faculty and administrators. Members of the faculty are open and accessible, committed to excellence in classroom teaching, and extremely loyal to KU Law.

The Office of Career Services provides assistance, counseling and employment resources to students and graduates seeking legal employment. The office maintains career-oriented materials, including legal directories, bar journals, books, bar exam information and monthly employment newsletters. The

Office of Career Services sponsors a variety of events throughout the year, including but not limited to the first year Mentor Program, Legal Career Options Day and a Brown Bag Lunch Series.

KU law students are highly sought after by employers throughout the state, region and nation. Law firms, government agencies, public interest groups, and other employers seeking summer interns and graduating students send representatives to interview at the law school each year or contact the school with information about openings. The school's approximately 6,000 alumni live and practice in all 50 states, the District of Columbia, Puerto Rico and 19 foreign countries.

We welcome and encourage applicants to visit the law school, sit in on a class, meet faculty and students, and tour the building. To learn more about our program, request a catalog or schedule a visit please call toll free (866) 220-3654 or visit us on-line at www.law.ku.edu.

Read all of Vault's Law School Surveys at www.vault.com/lawschool — get complete surveys on top law schools, expert advice on applicaton essays, LSAT prep and more.

VAULT CAREER LIBRARY 267

Washburn University School of Law

Admissions Office
1700 SW College Ave
Topeka, KS 66621
Admissions phone: (785) 670-1185
Admissions e-mail: admissions@washburnlaw.edu
Admissions URL: http://washburnlaw.edu/admissions/

 ## Admissions

Status: Current student, full-time
Dates of Enrollment: 8/2003-Submit Date
Survey Submitted: October 2005

The admissions process was incredibly smooth, and I received a quick response. The process included transcripts, letters of reference, a personal essay and an application.

Status: Alumnus/a, full-time
Dates of Enrollment: 8/1999-5/2002
Survey Submitted: January 2005

Take a LSAT preparation class (like Kaplan), register with LSDAS and find a Washburn application on the web site, www.washburnlaw.edu. Make sure your personal statement is just that. Make it personal, but don't get carried away with bragging about yourself—take it easy on analogies as well.

Status: Current student, full-time
Dates of Enrollment: 8/2003-Submit Date
Survey Submitted: December 2003

Washburn has a fairly simple admissions process. Essentially there is an application like all other school and a personal statement. Washburn tends to have a lot of "non-traditional" students—people starting their second or third careers and people with families. They really look at your experience and community involvement. The admissions staff is really helpful. And prompt—I received my acceptance less than a week after I sent in my application.

 ## Academics

Status: Current student, full-time
Dates of Enrollment: 8/2003-Submit Date
Survey Submitted: October 2005

The workload is significant, but hey, it's law school. Overall, the professors truly care about the students. I have always gotten the courses that I wanted. I only wish more course offerings were made.

Status: Alumnus/a, full-time
Dates of Enrollment: 8/1999-5/2002
Survey Submitted: January 2005

Law school should be tough. If it is easy for you, you are not working hard enough. You generally take 12 to 15 hours per semester for three years. On top of that you should participate in law journal, moot court or clinic. You get a lot of homework and you should do it all, all of the time. You should also spend several hours each week outlining what you learned so far. You don't have to do all of this—but if you don't, it will be reflected in your grades. It will also affect your employment prospects.

Status: Current student, full-time
Dates of Enrollment: 8/2003-Submit Date
Survey Submitted: December 2003

I am a 1L, so I'll I can speak to is the first year...They divide the 1Ls into two sections, and two subsections of those sections. Therefore, you have classes with the same people. It's really nice because you get to know the people who

you are in class with every day. Plus, it makes it much easier to set up study groups. The faculty really wants to see their students learn and succeed. The often go above and beyond to ensure the success of their students. Mos professors make themselves available to talk—whether it's about class, the stres of being a first-year law student, or a mutual obsession with a rock star. Beside being approachable, they are all very knowledgeable about the area of law the are teaching. The workload is probably comparable to other law schools—tough, but not impossible.

 ## Employment Prospects

Status: Current student, full-time
Dates of Enrollment: 8/2003-Submit Date
Survey Submitted: October 2005

The on-campus recruiting process is interesting. And, I earned a job from it,s that's always good.

Status: Alumnus/a, full-time
Dates of Enrollment: 8/1999-5/2002
Survey Submitted: January 2005

If you apply yourself and get good grades (top 5 percent) you will have n problem getting almost any job. Of course your personality will have som impact. You need to be in the top five following your first year to get jobs at th top Kansas City and Wichita firms. Top five grades after your first year will hel you get a clerkship (top one or two will increase your chances). Of course mos people are not in the top five. I think most people in my class got jobs that the were happy with. Some got whatever they could get and built up experience fo a couple years before looking for a "better" job. On-campus recruiting i focused on the top 10 in the class, but the career services office does provide jo postings for a multitude of legal jobs that students get during school and durin the summer. Graduates work in a wide variety of environments: large, mediun and small firms, solo practitioners, government, and non-law jobs.

Status: Current student, full-time
Dates of Enrollment: 8/2003-Submit Date
Survey Submitted: December 2003

Washburn has some areas of specialties, which make graduates mor marketable—including family law, business, and advocacy. Most recruitment i done by Kansas law firms, so if you want to practice elsewhere, it takes a littl more effort to get internships and jobs.

 ## Quality of Life

Status: Current student, full-time
Dates of Enrollment: 8/2003-Submit Date
Survey Submitted: October 2005

The facilities are fabulous. The school was updated recently, the campus adde a workout facility and the entire school has wireless Internet.

Status: Alumnus/a, full-time
Dates of Enrollment: 8/1999-5/2002
Survey Submitted: January 2005

The campus has recently expanded. It is a pretty setting with housing option and a new dining facility. Parking is free, but seems to be getting more limite as they build more dormitories. The neighborhood is fairly safe. If you ar looking for an apartment, ask the admissions office for advice—and stay awa from the east side of Topeka (generally, stay away from downtown and east o Burlingame).

Status: Current student, full-time
Dates of Enrollment: 8/2003-Submit Date
Survey Submitted: December 2003

Nobody lives on campus. There are some nice apartments in Topeka, though. All within 10 to 15 minutes of the campus.

Social Life

Status: Current student, full-time
Dates of Enrollment: 8/2003-Submit Date
Survey Submitted: October 2005

Plenty of restaurants, bars and women. But, the social life doesn't provide so much distraction that a person with a reasonable sense of duty can't finish their work.

Status: Alumnus/a, full-time
Dates of Enrollment: 8/1999-5/2002
Survey Submitted: January 2005

Topeka is not the most entertaining city. It is, however, a good place to go to law school because it doesn't have many distractions. It has a few restaurants, but nothing impressive (Kiku is good, the chains on Wanamaker are usually crowded). A lot of the single people drove to Lawrence of Kansas City for clubs. Topeka has a nice running trail (the Shunga), and you can buy a decent house for a reasonable price. The law school has a variety of social events and the students always find ways to have fun. My advice is to go easy on the social activities (moderation is key) and focus on school. Law school is easier if you are married, especially if you have a supportive spouse.

Status: Current student, full-time
Dates of Enrollment: 8/2003-Submit Date
Survey Submitted: December 2003

Many students are married and/or have families, so Washburn isn't a huge party school. For people who are interested in going out to bars and such there is a bar across the street that people frequent. And Topeka has quite a few bars.

The School Says

The essence of Washburn University School of Law is the commitment of the law school community at every level—from the dean's office to facilities staff—to the success of our students. In addition, the law school endeavors to impart to its students the values of treating others with respect, dignity, and a sense of caring.

For more than a century, Washburn University School of Law's student-centered approach to teaching has produced well-

prepared law professionals ready to engage in successful careers. Our worldwide network of more than 6,100 alumni located in all 50 states and many foreign countries includes nationally recognized lawyers, state and federal judges and justices, journalists, politicians, and senior executives of Fortune 500 companies.

With a 14.2:1 student/faculty ratio, Washburn exposes students to diverse perspectives of the law. Our 31 full-time faculty are graduates of 21 law schools. More than 40 percent of the full-time faculty members hold advanced degrees. More than 35 percent of the full-time faculty are women, and 24 percent are minorities.

In 1970, the Washburn Law Clinic was one of the first in-house clinics in the nation. From its inception the clinic has had tenure-track faculty, placing itself on the cutting edge of legal education.

Washburn Law's Writing Program sets the standard for writing programs across the country by employing only tenure-track professors of legal writing. Washburn Law's tradition of outstanding teaching is enhanced by its three Centers for Excellence-the Business and Transactional Law Center; the Center for Excellence in Advocacy; and the Children and Family Law Center. Students may add an element of concentration by participating in one of the school's seven certificate programs, a number of which are attached to the law school Centers. Washburn encourages students to understand different legal systems through its summer abroad program at Utrecht University and its semester abroad program at Maastricht University, both in the Netherlands.

Washburn Law offers all students access to innovative workshops, mock interviews, alumni mentoring opportunities, and individual and group career planning and job search skill development sessions. At nine months after graduation, 98.1 percent of our 2005 graduates were employed, seeking an advanced degree, or not seeking employment.

Washburn Law's prime location in the capital city of Kansas offers advantages only a state capital can provide with unique opportunities within the halls of justice. Topeka offers a variety of cultural and recreational activities for its metropolitan population of 150,000, yet the cost of living is well below that of major cities.

Please contact our Office of Admissions to schedule your personal tour at (800) 927-4529.

Read all of Vault's Law School Surveys at www.vault.com/lawschool — get complete surveys on top law schools, expert advice on applicaton essays, LSAT prep and more.

VAULT CAREER LIBRARY **269**

University of Kentucky College of Law

Office of Admissions
209 Law Building
Lexington, KY 40506-0048
Admissions phone: (859) 257-6770
Admissions e-mail: lawadmissions@email.uky.edu
Admissions URL:
http://www.uky.edu/Law/prospective_students/

 Admissions

Status: Current student, full-time
Dates of Enrollment: 8/2005-Submit Date
Survey Submitted: March 2006

The admissions process for UK is very easy to follow and they are pretty quick to get back to you. My main advice is that if you get put on a hold, send in as much extra helpful information that you can to push you over the top. I did this by sending in more letters of recommendation, my new spring transcript, projects I had taken part in since I had applied, etc. and received an acceptance about a week after I sent that new stuff in. Also, if you are a UK undergraduate, try to get letters of recommendation from various teachers in the history department that you know have a relationship with people on the board of admissions. I think this helped me greatly.

Status: Current student, full-time
Dates of Enrollment: 8/2003-Submit Date
Survey Submitted: March 2006

Compared to other law schools, UK Law serves as a model for how the admissions process is supposed to work. Correspondence is answered quickly, and the responses are more than canned snippets from a brochure. The admissions staff, particularly Dean of Admissions Drusilla (Drusy) Bakert, are friendly, efficient and punctual. I applied to a wide range of schools, from some of the "best" (Georgetown; UVA) to the mid-second tier, with UK Law somewhere in the middle. My experience with their admissions office was a big factor in choosing to attend here.

I applied fairly early in the process, and heard back from UK Law weeks before the next fastest school, and months before the more highly-ranked schools (even one I had applied to as a nearly admissions candidate). When I later interviewed for a scholarship, it was clear that my entire application had been considered, not just my GPA and LSAT score. They had read not just my personal statement and recommendations, but my senior thesis that had recently been published (and was NOT in my application packet). As far as selectivity goes, the *U.S. News & World Report* stats give only a bare snapshot. More highly-ranked schools definitely have students with better undergraduate GPAs and LSAT scores, but the quality of the students at UK Law is excellent.

Status: Current student, full-time
Dates of Enrollment: 8/2005-Submit Date
Survey Submitted: March 2006

My admissions process was pretty dry. I was not eligible for a scholarship so I did not have any interviews. I used the online law school entrance site (LSAC I think) to apply to all of the schools that I chose. I found the essay to be the hardest part simply because there weren't really any guidelines. Yes, there were topic choices but because the topic was ultimately "me" I found that it was difficult to slim it down and write in a manner that didn't sound like stream of consciousness/story of my life rambling. I am still not sure that I succeeded in that endeavor but as I am in school, I will try not to fret over it too much. I selected UK because I am from Lexington and it is ranked highly by all the law school reports. Also, in-state tuition is too good a deal to pass up.

Status: Current student, full-time
Dates of Enrollment: 8/2005-Submit Date
Survey Submitted: March 2006

I think going to the open house before sending in your application is very helpful. Dean Bakert explained a few things that you definitely do not want to do in your personal statement. I'm sure there were a few people out there who thought, "Whoops!" after her speech. It is competitive, but as students we don't have much of an idea as to how they pick the candidates, I just tried to do my best in school, on the LSAT, and on my personal statement.

Status: Current student, full-time
Dates of Enrollment: 8/2005-Submit Date
Survey Submitted: March 2006

I also went to the University of Kentucky for my undergraduate degree, but took two years off before beginning law school. In my junior year of undergrad I met and discussed my intentions to go to law school with the College of Law' Associate Dean for Admissions and with a former Dean of the College. I also had many discussions with my undergraduate advisor in the College of Agriculture, with parents (Dad is a lawyer and a UK Law alumni), and with several other attorneys working in varies legal fields. During the first of two years between undergrad and law, I worked in Washington, D.C. for the U.S. Department of Agriculture. There I worked with many young people my own age who were going through the same period of researching law schools and working on admissions. These friends and colleagues were from all different states and looking and many schools around the country, so we all researched a lot of these schools and compared notes. I did most of this research at least a year before I submitted any applications.

Once I had my LSAT scores, I waited about two months before beginning the rest of the application process. (I do not recommend delaying this process unless absolutely necessary.) THE APPLICATION PROCESS THEN TOOK ME ABOUT TWO MONTHS TO COMPLETE—concurrently writing personal statements, getting my letters of recommendations, and completing the admissions and financial aid applications. I was very late in beginning writing my personal statements for applications and securing letters of recommendation beginning in late December. To get comments and editing of my statements, I sent several drafts to my friends in and applying to law schools and to my undergraduate advisor. This took a lot of time as these people are all very busy but this was a valuable process and truly helped me see deficiencies in my initial drafts. I finished my personal statements in three to six weeks, focusing on the different deadlines of the schools to which I was applying; however, I chose to first complete my personal statement that I thought was the most generally applicable and that would serve as the basis of the others. This first completed statement was also for one of my top two choices for specific law schools.

Also, because I was turning in my applications close to the deadlines, and because I had such an improvement in my LSAT score, I SUBMITTED AN ADDENDUM to my applications to every school that permitted me to do so. This allowed me to explain the personal reasons for my delay and to explain why my original score was so much lower. I believe this helped me enormously with at least a third of the schools I applied to.

Of the four programs that accepted me, I again considered career preparation and comfort/location; however, I now began considering the out of pocket costs to attend. Of the four programs, I was now only interested in three, so I visited those three—Kentucky, Louisville, and UC Berkeley. MY FINAL DECISION WAS BASED ON: (1) COST; (2) CAREER; and (3) COMFORT/LOCATION. For me, the choice was easy, since Kentucky offered by the best option for all three considerations.

Status: Current student, full-time
Dates of Enrollment: 8/2004-Submit Date
Survey Submitted: March 2006

Prospective law school students are encouraged to apply to UK's early admission program. This is what I did. It involved registering for and sending other college transcripts to LSAC early, taking the LSAT early (I took it June, but you can also take the early fall test and apply for early admissions), obtaining two letters of recommendation, and writing a two-page personal statement. What I like about the personal statement is that UK leaves the topic choice wide-open, so you have a lot of latitude to express yourself and make yourself stand-out from the others.

Status: Current student, full-time
Dates of Enrollment: 8/2004-Submit Date
Survey Submitted: March 2006

The admissions process is simple. You submit your application with a personal statement/essay. You are automatically considered for most scholarships by simply submitted your application. The admissions staff is very friendly and helpful. When I was on the alternate list the first time I applied to UK, I asked the Dean of Admissions to meet with me to look over my application. She told me explicitly what looked good and what I needed to improve.

Status: Current student, full-time
Dates of Enrollment: 8/2004-Submit Date
Survey Submitted: March 2006

UK Law school looks for a well-rounded applicant with diverse interests. While a high GPA and LSAT score are important, the admissions committee also considers criteria such as work experience, extra-curricular activities, and of course the Admissions essay. Generally, when writing your essay try to make it stand out; don't write the "I want to go to law school because..." It just sounds so generalized. Make your essay uniquely you, with a funny story or anecdote about your life, and if possible somehow tied in to your qualifications as a law school applicant.

Status: Current student, full-time
Dates of Enrollment: 8/2004-Submit Date
Survey Submitted: March 2006

A committee made up of law school administration, faculty, and at least one student makes the admissions decisions. Three things must be submitted with the application: the application form, all academic transcripts (official from all degree programs), and the personal statement. The application form asks the applicant about basic information—current address, education completed, work history, etc. The transcripts are self-explanatory—just make sure they are official and sealed by the academic institution. The committee generally puts very little focus on the personal statement, and it will only be a factor if it is extremely well-written or if it is obvious that the applicant has absolutely no ability to express a coherent thought.

The main determining factors are undergraduate GPA and LSAT (Law School Admissions Test) scores. Both are taken into account for admissions, but the committee usually gives scholarships to incoming first-year students based on LSAT score. For example, I did not have a particularly high LSAT score (157), but I had an outstanding GPA (4.0). I was accepted into the law school, but I did not receive any scholarships. A person very close to me had a high LSAT score (163) and a pretty good GPA (around a 3.7). He got half his tuition paid. The school has average selectivity—it's not Yale, and it's not Thomas Cooley. If the applicant has both a good GPA (3.5 or better) and a decent LSAT score (154 or better), he or she will probably get into the law school.

> **Regarding admissions, the school says:** "Admission to the University of Kentucky College of Law is a competitive process. The admissions committee reads all admissions files in full and the full Committee (five faculty members, the Dean of Admissions and one student member) discusses and votes upon every application for admission. Writing skills, letters of recommendation, work history, extracurricular activities, leadership roles and diversity are considered as well as the candidates' undergraduate records and LSAT scores. For fall 2007, the Committee will be considering the highest of multiple LSAT scores in many cases. For the fall 2005 entering class,

the median LSAT and GPA were 160 / 3.57 respectively, with credentials at the 25th percentile of 157 and 3.30 and at the 75th percentile of 163 and 3.81. Entering classes at UK Law usually include 40 to 47 percent women, 9 to 11 percent minority students and 20 to 28 percent nonresidents of Kentucky."

Status: Current student, full-time
Dates of Enrollment: 8/2003-Submit Date
Survey Submitted: March 2006

The application process was very easy, since you could submit the application online. There is also no interview process. The admissions process seems to favor stronger LSAT scores as opposed to higher GPAs, especially lately, since the university as a whole is aiming to be a Top 20 university by 2015. This drive has put more pressure on the law school to be more selective. The admissions process also seems to favor Kentucky residents. UK also is attempting to recruit more minority students, so I am sure the admissions committee takes race into account as part of its consideration of candidates.

 ## Academics

Status: Current student, full-time
Dates of Enrollment: 8/2004-Submit Date
Survey Submitted: March 2006

In order to pick your classes, a name is drawn out of hat and that person gets to register for two classes of his or her choice. Then, the next person in the alphabet gets to choose and so on. After everyone in the class has chosen two courses, then the order is reversed and the person who went last gets to go first and choose up to four classes. It is totally antiquated. I was used to being able to register online, but the professors apparently don't know how to use the internet. Also, if you end up towards the end of the list, then it is almost a guarantee that you will end up with classes that no one wants. But you are still paying the same amount of tuition as those that get to choose first. Speaking of classes, none of the professors actually do any teaching with the exception of a few professors. Professors also tend to be very dishonest and try to trick students, for example, my property professor lied about the format of the exam. Grades are handed out arbitrarily. One professor said, "I cannot tell the difference between an A and a B and a B and a C exam." So if you just so happen to get a C, there is usually no explanation. The curve is 2.7 GPA (B-). Many schools have curves that are much higher. Employers will focus on grades and they usually like to see at least a 3.0 GPA so I would recommend going to a school that has at least a 3.0 curve.

> **Regarding academics, the school says:** "The faculty of the College of Law has been recognized for their dedication to good teaching. Nine members of the law faculty have been named among UK's Great Teachers, a university-wide award based on student nominations. Additionally, in 2005, the College of Law's faculty was ranked among the Top Five in the nation based on students' responses to a national survey."

Status: Current student, full-time
Dates of Enrollment: 8/2005-Submit Date
Survey Submitted: March 2006

The academic nature of the program is very good. The teachers are excellent and are very willing to answer questions or stay after class to clarify issues or points. The Legal Research and Writing class would probably work better if classes met more than once a week and if topics were covered in more than one assignment. Since this is a three-hour course, it should be taught three hours a week for a full semester (perhaps one hour of research and two hours of writing per week). The more intense program would definitely help to hone research and writing skills and having the two parts taught simultaneously would allow students to use what they are learning in Legal Research in their Legal Writing class while they are learning it. This should probably be done second semester to avoid overloading students who are already under considerable stress during the first semester.

Read all of Vault's Law School Surveys at www.vault.com/lawschool — get complete surveys on top law schools, expert advice on applicaton essays, LSAT prep and more.

VAULT CAREER LIBRARY 271

Status: Current student, full-time
Dates of Enrollment: 8/2003-Submit Date
Survey Submitted: March 2006

The academics at UK Law are second to none. While there are certainly a number of nationally respected professors in a number of disciplines, the school obviously places a greater emphasis on teaching ability than number of articles published. The professors are all experts in their respective fields, but more importantly they can impart their knowledge effectively. Classes are of course conducted in the Socratic Method (more so in the first year than in upper-level classes), but there is none of the "hide the ball" method I have heard of from friends at other schools. Many of the teachers also routinely use non-traditional methods to help students understand difficult concepts, from mock arguments to PowerPoint presentations.

There are really two kinds of "popular" classes: core classes (like Corporations or Con Law) and more narrow classes that deal with pressing legal issues (like Law and Religion, Intellectual Property, or Alternative Dispute Resolution). The "core" classes are taught in enough sections that I have never heard of a student wanting such a class and not getting it. The narrower classes are much smaller, but are frequently offered—some classes always fill up quickly, but my experience has been that the students who couldn't get in usually get in the next semester or next year. The workload is daunting at first, as it is for 1Ls across the country. In my first year, 50 hours of studying was a light week. In my second and third years, the law school workload has dropped only slightly, but much less of my time is devoted purely to classes, and much more to other pursuits within the law school (mostly moot court and law journal). I would estimate that 30 to 40 hours of coursework per week is average for upper-level classes.

Status: Current student, full-time
Dates of Enrollment: 8/2003-Submit Date
Survey Submitted: March 2006

The classes at UK tend to be taught in the traditional Socratic Method, although, with certain professors, the classes relax somewhat after the first year. The first-year curriculum is set by the university—there is no choice in classes at all. The first-year classes are the highest quality of the three years. After that, the classes seem to fall off and it is VERY difficult to get into popular courses in the second and third year. I have twice taken a schedule of classes that I have no interest in whatsoever because there was simply nothing else to take.

There is a required writing requirement in the curriculum, referred to by students as "seminar." My seminar was a fantastic experience—it was well taught, interesting, and I think it really developed my writing and analytical skills. From what I've heard from other students, though, the quality of the seminar depends on the professor who teaches it, and there doesn't seem to be any uniformity at all. Professors are somewhat accessible; it just takes time and persistence to develop any sort of personal relationship with them. The personal relationship is completely optional—no professor will try to get to know you personally unless you make the effort (which you should because it is critical in the employment process). The student body takes academics very seriously, but the competition remains friendly. We don't have any book theft or intentional sabotage of other's studying, and there is always a study group to join or someone willing to send you extra notes, etc. The workload is tedious and constant because each class builds to a single final exam (again, with a few exceptions). It is important to keep up with the material as you go along and to be prepared for each class (there is nothing more humiliating than being called on in one of these classes and not being able to follow the professor).

Status: Current student, full-time
Dates of Enrollment: 8/2005-Submit Date
Survey Submitted: March 2006

My first semester proved to be a humbling experience, receiving my first C ever and ranking somewhere in the middle of my class, a place I have also never been. I found my classes very interesting but I think I owe a lot of that to the professors. I know, for example, that Civil Procedure can be very dry (as my brother, a 1L at College of Charleston, can attest) but Professor Robert Schwemm presents the material in ways that make it interesting and, dare I say, fun. My other professors have also been great. I have yet to register for classes so I cannot speak to that topic but I have experienced the legendary law school workload and I believe it deserves its status as such. Although I believe that we

have more time than we think, I don't want people whose wedding showers have missed because "I have too much work to do" to know that I might not have been telling the entire truth. I think the key to the workload is time management, a task easier said that done. For me it was very important to have scheduled time set aside to go to the gym or play with my dog and I think everyone needs a life apart from law school. As to the grading, it's no secret how that works and UK is no different.

Status: Current student, full-time
Dates of Enrollment: 8/2004-Submit Date
Survey Submitted: March 2006

The quality of the program is excellent, in general the professors do a good job of conveying the information. There are some professors who are not great teachers, but even they are accessible and helpful. Friendliness and accessibility are the highlights of the faculty. The workload is generally manageable. The grading is anonymous and reasonable. The main problem is class selection. Since we have a small faculty sometimes it is very difficult to get certain popular classes...however, there is never any real trouble getting the important classes and this shouldn't detract from the overall academic experience which is great.

Status: Current student, full-time
Dates of Enrollment: 8/2005-Submit Date
Survey Submitted: March 2006

Our first year is completely planned for us. That means no registration, which is a relief since we have so many other things to worry about. For the first two weeks of law school, my head was spinning with all the tasks we were required to do. At times, it felt like there wouldn't be enough time in the day to finish it all and still have time to eat and sleep. However, once the initial "shock" of those first two weeks subsided, I adjusted. The professors are really fantastic here, they take what could be a dry subject and turn it into something that keeps you on your toes. The grading is tough, but you just give it your best shot and see where the chips fall.

Status: Current student, full-time
Dates of Enrollment: 8/2004-Submit Date
Survey Submitted: March 2006

The classes are very business oriented. If you are not interested in business law, this is not the school for you. You will see a variety of course offerings in the recruitment brochures, but you should not interpret this to mean that these may actually be offered. Class quality varies. Your fellow students will tell you which professors have been here so long they have stopped trying and which professors are impossible to understand. Those are the two main categories, though there is absolutely a minority population of excellent professors. Good luck getting those classes.

Recently the students had to stage a near revolt to get a bar class expanded so that the 3Ls who wanted it could have the opportunity to take it. Other popular classes don't fare so well. For example, ADR is taught every other semester by an adjunct and holds 20 or fewer students despite its incredible popularity. Grading seems harsh because of the forced curve. UK has an anti-grade inflation policy, which means that when compared to students from other schools, your grades will look a bit worse. Sure, some firms will notice your rank and discern the B- curve (which is what it is RAISED to after first year's roughly C+ curve) and not assume you less qualified, but I have no method of telling you how many are this astute. Also, it is routine for someone to get some form of a D. Good luck. This is not a school where the bulk of the competition is getting in. In spite of this curve, many professors do not adhere. Sometimes that is in your favor and sometimes not.

The school says: "Regarding the grading curve, the University of Kentucky College of Law has a faculty rule defining a range for the average (mean) grade for each course. For first-year courses, the mid-point of the range is a B-. For second- and third-year courses, the range extends from B to B-. The average grade rule may be viewed at the College's web site."

Status: Current student, full-time
Dates of Enrollment: 8/2004-Submit Date
Survey Submitted: March 2006

There are several core four-credit courses, as well as co-curricular activities such as Law Review or moot court, which carry three credits each. If you are selected for these activities, they will count toward your credit requirement. There are two law journals, which select among the top 30 percent of the freshman class at the end of the spring semester based on GPA. Moot court selects through direct competition. There is a substantial writing requirement each student must fulfill, which is normally done in one of several seminars offered at the law school. Every student is required to take Professional Responsibility (three credits) before they graduate.

Status: Current student, full-time
Dates of Enrollment: 8/2004-Submit Date
Survey Submitted: March 2006

The average class size is 70 students. The scheduling process is out-dated and silly, names are literally drawn from a hat and the process goes alphabetically from that lucky name. It is very hard to get popular classes like Criminal Procedure or Evidence. The courses offered are not as broad as the ones listed in the view book. One of the deans admitted to me that the view book lists every class that has ever been offered at UK, even if it was only offered once. There is a big focus on the criminal and business law areas. The professors are alright, but stick to the curve when grading.

Status: Current student, full-time
Dates of Enrollment: 7/2005-Submit Date
Survey Submitted: March 2006

The atmosphere at UK law is very friendly and open. It does not seem to be as competitive as many law schools are said to be. Everyone seems to help each other, whether it be by studying in groups or giving notes to a peer that missed class. The teachers on a whole are great. All of them make their subject interesting making all of the classes of high quality. The workload was about as expected, with about an hour of reading for each class.

Status: Current student, full-time
Dates of Enrollment: 8/2005-Submit Date
Survey Submitted: March 2006

It's law school, so the workload is a lot heavier than most people are used to from undergraduate school. I have an MBA and am several years older than most of the other first-year law students, so my perspective is a lot different. There is a lot of reading and it is really important to keep up in class. Unlike undergrad, you have to go to class in law school. The professors are extraordinary and care a lot about the students. The only grade you get is from the final exam. The final exams are three hours long, and although they are challenging and extremely comprehensive, they are straightforward (no trick questions). The tricky thing about your grade is that it not only matters how well you did, but also how well you did compared to everyone else.

 Employment Prospects

Status: Alumnus/a, full-time
Dates of Enrollment: 8/2000-5/2003
Survey Submitted: March 2005

To start with, our career services center does a great job in getting students ready for interviews by holding resume workshops and review as well as mock interviews. We have numerous law firms come to campus for an initial round of interviews. I had great success with this, but that would be true only if you are in the top third of your class. Otherwise, you will be left trying to find a job yourself (or so I have been told).

Status: Current student, full-time
Dates of Enrollment: 8/2003-Submit Date
Survey Submitted: March 2006

I think our career services office does its best to attract a number of employers, and basically every large firm in our region comes to campus for interviews. The problem is that large firms want to interview the top students, so the same

students benefit over and over from the activities of career services, while students who struggle academically struggle with employment. I do think that the career services office is supportive of students who aren't in the top of the class as long as they show initiative (send out resumes on their own, do their own networking, etc.). Employers in the region seem to like hiring UK graduates, and I'm honestly not sure how UK is viewed outside the region. It seems that most graduates go to work for firms, at least initially, and those firms range from 200 lawyers plus to working with solo practitioners.

> **The school says:** "UK Law students have the benefit of a large on-campus job interview program which usually includes law firms (large, medium and small), government agencies, judges, legal publishers, military branches and public interest employers. UK Law students also have the opportunity to participate in over 20 off-campus job fairs and interview programs in different areas of the country, including Atlanta, Washington, D.C., Chicago, and Nashville. In addition to campus interviews, assistance is provided to help students prepare for their job searches and research and obtain positions with public interest employers, judicial clerkships, firms which do not visit campus, and government opportunities."

Status: Current student, full-time
Dates of Enrollment: 8/2003-Submit Date
Survey Submitted: March 2006

UK is far and away the best law school in Kentucky (out of three). Unfortunately, there's a glut of lawyers in Kentucky right now, so if you want to work in a big Kentucky firm, you'll probably need to be in the top 10 percent to 20 percent of the class. Employment prospects improve with your willingness to travel. Other work is available in local and state government, for example. UK Law just got a big federal grant to help place graduates state-wide in prosecutors' offices and with the public defenders—including loan forgiveness of $10,000 a year.

Status: Current student, full-time
Dates of Enrollment: 8/2004-Submit Date
Survey Submitted: March 2006

Lexington, itself, is a flooded market for prospective students who want to practice civil, corporate litigation. For those students, doing very well the first two semesters is essential. After the first semester, interviews for the summer begin and a handful of jobs are given to the handful of students at the top of their class. However, other jobs and opportunities open up after the first semester, and most students have some type of summer employment. Even more receive summer employment for the summer after the second year of law school. These summer employment opportunities are intended as stepping stones into a permanent position after graduation. The law school provides a lot of assistance to students in obtaining public interest work, work with small firms, firms outside of Lexington, government work, etc. Professors can also help students make valuable connections. In addition, during the second and third year, students may work part-time at local firms or work for professors as research assistants.

Status: Current student, full-time
Dates of Enrollment: 8/2003-Submit Date
Survey Submitted: March 2006

I believe the school is regarded as the best in KY, so that's good. But right now, I'm a third-year and myself and most of my classmates are anxious because we don't have jobs. However, I have had two summer jobs that I found out about through the school, and I've had a few interviews for jobs. I'd also like to add that the school has good internship opportunities—such as a prosecution internship I'm taking now, which allows me chances to argue in court, etc.

Status: Current student, full-time
Dates of Enrollment: 8/2004-Submit Date
Survey Submitted: March 2006

UK College of Law is a regional school, one of the best in the region, and certainly the best in Kentucky. Private employers from Ohio, Tennessee, Indiana and West Virginia, as well as federal and state employers, recruit on campus. The majority of graduates usually work in the private sector. A number of students are able to secure internships (unpaid) and clerkships (paid) with

Read all of Vault's Law School Surveys at www.vault.com/lawschool — get complete surveys on top law schools, expert advice on applicaton essays, LSAT prep and more.

VAULT CAREER LIBRARY 273

employers through the on-campus recruiting process. The career services office at the law school is an invaluable resource. They have updated information on every employer who interviews on campus (and on many who do not). The CSO conducts a number of seminars to help you prepare for interviews and for your summer clerkships—take advantage of those seminars, as are they are very useful.

Status: Current student, full-time
Dates of Enrollment: 8/2004-Submit Date
Survey Submitted: March 2006

The prospects for UK Law graduates are extremely good. Career services works hard to make sure that everyone has a job when they leave, and the that work pays off. There is about a 99 percent placement rate for graduates. That's good by anyone's standards. I will say this, though: if you come to the University of Kentucky, you probably need to want to work in Kentucky. UK has a really good reputation in the state, and generally, firms would rather have UK grads than ones from any other state law school. But the people looking for out-of-state jobs have a more difficult time because so many applicants from better law schools in other states are fighting for those jobs too.

Also, I would tell out-of-state people applying to UK that it is more difficult to get jobs in Kentucky. Every single employer will ask you why you came to Kentucky, and even if you have the best reason in the world, they will probably not believe that you have any intention of staying. The people that are in my class from out of state have had the worst time finding jobs. One guy I know is in the top 10 percent of the class, but he is from out of state, and none of the employers can get over that. No attempt he has made to explain it away has been successful. Even with his incredible rank and his position in the editorial board of the school's Law Review, he remains one of the few people without a job. Watch out for this.

> **The school says:** Students at UK with high academic standing, no matter where they originated, tend to receive lucrative job placements within the state of Kentucky if they choose to remain local.

And now an overview of the process: there are lots of on-campus interviews. Probably about 50 firms and other programs (like KY's Legislative Research Commission, the Governor's Summer Associate Program, and KY Supreme Court Justice John Roach) have come on campus to interview UK students for jobs. Fall interviews are for second- and third-year students. They usually start a couple weeks after school has begun (early September) and last basically the entire semester—at least for people who don't get jobs right from the get-go. Spring interviews are on Saturdays. All the firms who want to interview come to campus on Saturdays, and people with interviews go basically all day long. They are better because you don't have to have interviews interrupting your class schedule or interfering with other things during the week. However, the downside is that they often start very early in the morning and can go until late afternoon; it's exhausting, and when you interview with a whole lot of firms in one day, it gets hard to keep them straight, and you end up talking about Lexington to a firm from Louisville (or something similar).

 ## Quality of Life

Status: Current student, full-time
Dates of Enrollment: 8/2003-Submit Date
Survey Submitted: March 2006

The campus itself is at the heart of the city, and you will find almost everything you need within walking distance of the law school. Lexington dining is something of a mixed bag. The majority of the restaurants are of the chain variety: some derivative of the classic dine-in burger joint with pointless Americana relics on the walls. However, if one is willing to drive a little further from downtown (home of the independent yet hopelessly overpriced fare favored by those who have already graduated from law school), one can find some incredible dining. Lexington is home to a large and thriving immigrant community, and the lesser-known restaurants reflect this. There are several excellent Chinese places (but stay away from anywhere that delivers to campus), some topnotch Japanese hibachi grills (where dinner is the show), a number of

high-quality Indian and Thai restaurants, the best BBQ I've found north of the Mason-Dixon line, and of course the ubiquitous Italian cuisine (a good rule of thumb for Italian restaurants is: the smaller, the better).

Status: Current student, full-time
Dates of Enrollment: 8/2003-Submit Date
Survey Submitted: March 2006

The law school itself is not in any way aesthetically pleasing, but it is functional. There is an office to buy snacks and keep up with student events, and the classrooms are generally adequate in terms of size. Most classrooms are now well-equipped technologically, and wireless internet access is available in most parts of the law school. I know there is a plan to build a new law school, so these comments are probably not very relevant.

Lexington is surrounded by horse farms, so there are beautiful drives available, and the town itself is a pretty place to be. It is, however, a large town—not a city at all. The campus is fine—there are not many dining choices close to the law school. I have never felt unsafe in the area, but we occasionally receive public safety e-mails alerting us that an assault has taken place. Parking is a problem with the current law school building—you have limited options and all of the good options are very expensive. I would recommend spending extra money to park in a private lot closer to the law school, especially if you plan to study at home often (the books get ridiculously heavy).

Status: Current student, full-time
Dates of Enrollment: 9/2004-Submit Date
Survey Submitted: March 2006

The campus is pretty, most people live off campus with lends to a very comfortable life style. Because UK is so small, everyone knows you and say hi. I am very happy to be around most of the people at school and over the summer I miss seeing them. Overall good quality of life and good balance of life.

Status: Current student, full-time
Dates of Enrollment: 8/2004-Submit Date
Survey Submitted: March 2006

The building of the law school is a bit old. The law school has received funding and is going to build a new one, however. Our law school library is one of the best, and best-staffed, in the region. Most of the librarians have law degrees. There is wireless internet throughout the entire building, and elsewhere on the university campus.

Status: Current student, full-time
Dates of Enrollment: 8/2004-Submit Date
Survey Submitted: March 2006

UK law students generally live off campus in nice neighborhoods (such as Chevy Chase) that are only a five-minute drive to school. The law school is located on the heart of campus, so there are tons of options for eating either on or off campus all around. Law students often frequent the Johnson Center, the new athletic complex on campus that has six basketball courts, free aerobic classes, and all kinds of weightlifting equipment. Of course, any UK student will spend an inordinate amount of time cheering on the CATS at Rupp Arena or Commonwealth Stadium! Generally, campus is quite safe and students can enjoy spending time outdoors studying when the weather turns warm.

Status: Current student, full-time
Dates of Enrollment: 8/2004-Submit Date
Survey Submitted: March 2006

Quality of life in Lexington is good. It is a very safe place to live. I wouldn't say that the "facilities" are very good. If I didn't know any better, I would rank UK's law building as one of the Top 10 worst in the country. It's old and dingy, and designed terribly. There is only one way in and out of the library, but there are three floors. If you study in the basement, you have to walk up to the first floor and go out that way. Also, there are no bathrooms in the library, which exacerbates the "one entrance" problem. You have to walk up to the first floor and go all the way around the building to get to a restroom. You're looking at taking 15 to 20 minutes out of your study time just to have a bathroom break. There isn't a cafeteria in the building, so everyone has to bring their lunch. There really isn't time to go home to get anything to eat. There are only a couple of restaurants close to the law school: Arby's, Dirty Phil's (the name explains it ll), Pizza Hut, a campus restaurant in the building next door (way too expensive for what you get), and a Bedminster coffee place that has wraps (good but also way too expensive).

If you are willing to walk, there are a few more restaurants down the strip (Jimmy John's, Pazzo's, McDonald's, Chipotle, Pita Pit, Subway), but this is a pretty good walk, and you probably don't have enough time considering your study schedule. There is also a student center that's fairly close with all the typical campus restaurants (the highlight is Chick-fil-A). There's also a Starbucks in there. The main problem with that one is that it's full of undergraduates, so it's crowded a lot of the time. Plus it's a bit of a walk too.

The best place to live is probably the Lexington Theological Seminary, which is directly across the street from the law school. The rent is cheap, the apartments are nice, and all you have to do is roll out of bed and walk two minutes to class. It's important to get in on these early, though, because a pretty big wait list builds up. There are also houses close to campus that some people live in, and big apartment complexes pretty close. I live in Merrick Place, which is a nice complex with a pool, and it's about a 15 minute drive to school. Not bad all in all. One more thing: MAKE SURE YOU GET A PARKING PERMIT THE DAY THEY GO ON SALE!!! I have failed to do that the past two years and have had to park a million miles away both times. Trust me, get on it, because they'll be gone the next day.

Social Life

Status: Current student, full-time
Dates of Enrollment: 8/2005-Submit Date
Survey Submitted: March 2006

The social life at UK's law school is outstanding. The SBA organizes several events for the law students to get together and mingle. The biggest events are the Law School Prom and the Halloween Party. In the fall everyone looks forward to football tailgates and in the spring everyone looks forward to Keeneland (the most beautiful horse racing track in the world) tailgates. There are numerous clubs to join and the UK campus has a wide variety of events planned every year for all students including Hoosier Daddy, the Gator Roast, and the Valentine's Gala. There are an immense amount of singles in the Lexington area of all ages so the dating scene is major here. If anything, you will never be bored. There is always something going on on and off campus in which you can take part.

Status: Current student, full-time
Dates of Enrollment: 8/2005-Submit Date
Survey Submitted: March 2006

The school is infinitely more homogeneous than the city itself. The city has tremendous opportunities beyond what my classmates suggested. The students are all about football (and bad football at that), but the town has a thriving agricultural/organic scene, numerous nature preserves, and more bars than anyone else in law school knows about. Also, the town in general is an infinitely better place for gay people than the school suggests. Dating seems...OK. The spouse-hunters are always able to find a victim. The rest of us have more time for school work.

Status: Current student, full-time
Dates of Enrollment: 8/2003-Submit Date
Survey Submitted: March 2006

If you enjoyed high school, you'll love UK Law because it is basically round two. The majority of the students are from Kentucky and most have known each other for years. Many still enjoy retelling old stories and most have maintained the same groups of friends for years. UK Law is overwhelmingly white, upper-middle class, conservative and not interested in mixing with anyone who isn't exactly like that. There is a small group of black students which tend to stick together but if you didn't know better you would think the school was segregated. Anyone considering themselves to be at all "diverse" economically, socially, ethnically, religiously, etc will likely have a hard time feeling like they fit in.

Status: Current student, full-time
Dates of Enrollment: 8/2005-Submit Date
Survey Submitted: March 2006

There is plenty to do as far as social life. The undergraduate students are more likely to be found at the bars closer to campus, while the grad students move downtown where more of the young-professional crowd congregates. Undergrad favorites include the World Famous Two Keys Tavern, Gambino's, and Avio (a huge bar with a dance club, karaoke bar, sports bar, etc.). Downtown features McCarthy's Irish bar, the Rosebud bar, Cheapside Bar and Grill, and a couple of joints for live music—The Dame, which brings in a surprising amount of good music, and Redmon's, a local scene with more country music.

With 250,000 plus living in the county, and 26,000 enrolled at the University total, there is plenty to do and plenty of people to meet. In the spring and fall, the Keeneland race course is an experience that must be seen. Regularly drawing crowds of close to 30,000 people, it's quite a party. UK football and basketball games also draw large crowds and provide a great social scene. Commonwealth Stadium is the place to be on a Saturday afternoon in Lexington, as 70,000 will turn out for a game and the tailgating.

Status: Current student, full-time
Dates of Enrollment: 8/2004-Submit Date
Survey Submitted: March 2006

The Student Bar Association organizes tailgates during football season, as well as a number of socials every year. If you like art and independent movies, you would love going to the Kentucky Theatre in downtown Lexington. This historic theatre is also the home of Woodsongs Oldtime Radio Hour and the Troubadour Concert Series, among others, which bring singer-songwriters and other interesting talent to Lexington. The University of Kentucky offers a number of concerts throughout the year, as do neighboring colleges such as Centre College in Danville, KY. If you like Japanese food, Lexington boasts the best sushi restaurant in the region, Seki's (for which you need a reservation—be very polite on the phone), and the best izakaya (the Japanese version of a tapas bar), Izakaya Yamaguchi.

If you have a chance to visit campus, you should, because then you will be able to experience the friendly atmosphere, and meet with students and professors. They are not putting on an act, they are just that friendly. Even though we are ranked and competing for employment with each other, competition is not as cutthroat as at other law schools.

Status: Current student, full-time
Dates of Enrollment: 8/2004-Submit Date
Survey Submitted: March 2006

The social life is one thing I can say is really awesome at UK. Everyone gets along SO well, and we have a lot of fun together. The admissions people do a really good job of choosing a class that will mesh well and can hang out all the time without much of a problem. And believe me, these people will become your best friends because it is like being in the trenches of war together. It's that kind of bond. The Student Bar Association (SBA) hosts several events throughout the year to help everyone get to know each other. The summer before school starts, there are some happy hours here and there at different bars that people can go to so they can meet a few people. At the end of orientation weekend, there is an orientation party. It's always really fun. I suggest that every incoming student attend these because you meet a lot of people and the SBA gives away some good prizes (free dinners, gift certificates, etc.).

In the middle of the year, there's the Halloween party. This is one of the best things ever. The drinks are free (or at least discounted), and everyone is dressed up in costumes. There is also a cash prize for best costume—and people really do go for this, so it's great to see what everyone has come up with. Last year it was at Two Keys Tavern, and this year it was at Avio's Bar. It was incredible both times.

And the highlight of every year: The Barrister's Ball (a.k.a., the "law school prom"). Both years this event has been held at the Radisson Hotel in downtown Lexington. You pay $25 a person for unlimited beer and wine all night long, and for an excellent meal. There is, of course, a DJ, and this year we had karaoke. It is awesome to see everyone dressed up and dancing and just having a good time in general. This is always the most fun weekend I have in my second

Read all of Vault's Law School Surveys at www.vault.com/lawschool — get complete surveys on top law schools, expert advice on applicaton essays, LSAT prep and more.

VAULT CAREER LIBRARY   275

semester of each year. Even if you think you wouldn't like doing prom all over again, you're wrong. It's the best time ever. As with job prospects, the social life is what you make it. There are TONS of really fun bars in Lexington (Rosebud's, Avio's, Two Keys, Cheapside, and Chinoe Pub, just to name a few), and definitely some good house parties thrown by law students. Whether you seize these opportunities or not is up to you.

 # The School Says

The University of Kentucky College of Law is a small, moderately priced, state-supported law school located on the main campus of the university in scenic Lexington, Kentucky, a city of approximately 250,000 in the center of the Bluegrass horse farm region. Founded in 1908, the college has been a member of the Association of American Law Schools since 1912 and has been accredited by the American Bar Association since 1925. The faculty has wide experience in law practice and government service, as well as teaching and research, with approximately 430 full-time students and a student-faculty ratio of 15 to one. UK Law has a strong tradition of faculty knowing their students and of faculty concern about their students' progress and success. The curriculum offers broad training in the law and legal methods, drawing upon sources from all jurisdictions. Accordingly, UK Law graduates are prepared to practice in any of the 50 states.

For the last 10 years, the College of Law's employment rate within nine months of graduation has been between 98 to 100 percent for those graduates seeking employment or pursuing advanced degrees. Although the majority of graduates obtain employment with law firms (large, medium and small) and judges (federal and state), graduates also elect to work in government, business and public interest. Each year between 15 and 30 percent of our graduates opt to work outside of Kentucky. We have an extensive alumni network; our graduates are located in 47 states and the District of Columbia.

The law school has several externship opportunities and a legal clinic where students can receive practical training. There is also a public interest summer fellowships grant program for students interested in public interest work. During the summer of 2006, the law school administered a grant where 51 students worked in funded positions with prosecutors, judges and public defenders.

UK Law graduates who were first-time takers of the Kentucky bar exam in July 2005 achieved an 88 percent pass rate. The pass rate for first-time takers from all law schools other than UK was 79 percent.

Please contact the Office of Admissions at lawadmissions@email.uky.edu or (859) 257-6770 with questions or if you would like to schedule a visit.

Tulane University Law School

Tulane Law School
Weinmann Hall
6329 Freret Street
New Orleans, LA 70118-6231
Admissions phone: (504) 865-5930
Admissions fax: (504) 865-6710
Admissions e-mail: admissions@law.tulane.edu
Admissions URL: http://www.law.tulane.edu/admissions/

 ## Admissions

Status: Current student, full-time
Dates of Enrollment: 8/2004-Submit Date
Survey Submitted: March 2006

The admissions process was less strenuous than other schools, fewer letters of recommendations required, etc. I would recommend submitting just as many materials as other schools require, however, as it can't hurt. Probably not as selective as higher tiered schools, but great scholarship opportunities for those whose admissions profiles are in the 75th percentile and higher.

Status: Current student, full-time
Dates of Enrollment: 9/2003-Submit Date
Survey Submitted: March 2006

Tulane law school relies heavily on LSAT scores. So, its important for students to study for the LSAT. It doesn't seem that they look at the difference of undergrad institutions, and whether applicants come from a more difficult school vs. an easier school.

Status: Alumnus/a, full-time
Dates of Enrollment: 8/2002-5/2005
Survey Submitted: March 2006

I applied to law school at Tulane University during my senior year at the University of Michigan. I filled out the application using a CD that I purchased for that purpose. In addition to the application, I submitted a resume and an essay. Tulane was highly selective with grades above a 3.0 and a solid LSAT score out of the University of Michigan, I was in the statistical bottom 25 percent of the class that Tulane admitted. When I was accepted, the law school preceded my acceptance letter with an e-mail informing me of the good news. I really appreciated that.

Status: Alumnus/a, full-time
Dates of Enrollment: 8/2001-5/2004
Survey Submitted: March 2006

Apply early! This has more to do with a better shot at getting some money, but since they don't wait until all of the applications are in to begin deciding, it can't hurt to be one of the first in the door. If you apply to a particular specialty program, like environmental law, the faculty that program will review your application so make sure to highlight why you want to participate in that program and what you can offer as well as receive.

Status: Current student, full-time
Dates of Enrollment: 8/2004-Submit Date
Survey Submitted: March 2006

Tulane was very effective in keeping prospective students informed. The admissions office arranged alumni to meet with me and answer my questions because I was unable to come visit the school. Furthermore, the current students were very receptive to answering questions by e-mail or meeting up for coffee.

Anyone who is interested in Maritime Law or Sports Law should express this interest since Tulane specializes in these areas.

Status: Current student, full-time
Dates of Enrollment: 8/2004-Submit Date
Survey Submitted: November 2005

Tulane is obviously a pretty selective institution given its top-tier law school ranking. However, from my experience, the admissions process is not as selective as many other comparatively ranked law schools. So, it may be that if your GPA and LSAT aren't spectacular, you still have a great chance of getting in. Also, it never hurts to know an alumnus or two who attended Tulane and can write a thorough recommendation on your behalf.

Status: Alumnus/a, full-time
Dates of Enrollment: 8/2000-5/2003
Survey Submitted: April 2006

The process is traditional, but smooth and professional. Questions of the admissions staff were responded to in a timely manner, and the school gave periodic updates on the process. The school seems to consider a wide range of applicant information, beyond GPA and LSAT, though both clearly are important. Anecdotally, Tulane will permit significant work or other experience and/or essays to bolster GPA with a good LSAT.

Status: Current student, full-time
Dates of Enrollment: 9/2003-Submit Date
Survey Submitted: April 2005

Tulane admits students from across the country with varied backgrounds. In addition to looking for great grades and LSAT scores, it also tries to guarantee that it will have students interested in its specialty programs, such as admiralty, public interest, environmental, comparative, and sports law. Showing through past experiences that you have a desire to work in these areas is a plus. If you aren't interested in these areas, don't be discouraged—probably 75 percent of Tulane students just take a general survey of lots of areas of law. I worked for several years before coming to law school, and discovered that it really helped my application—there is a big population of students who are not coming directly from undergrad at Tulane. While Tulane is selective, they are also generous with their scholarships—so definitely apply and see what sort of award you can get. I would definitely recommend one of the "visiting days" in the spring if you even remotely consider coming here. It's helpful in seeing how different we are.

Status: Alumnus/a, full-time
Dates of Enrollment: 8/1999-5/2002
Survey Submitted: November 2004

Tulane has rolling admissions. Apply early. Scholarship money is given out on a "first come, first serve" basis—if you are a pretty good candidate and apply in February, there might not be any money left for you. On the other hand, Tulane makes a very strong effort to bring in top students so there will likely be money for these students no matter when they apply. There is no interview. I think that it is all numbers driven. Undergrad GPA of 3.5 with LSAT of 162 will just about guarantee admission. They also like Ivy League undergrad degrees. They are trying to boost their rankings, so statistics count.

Status: Alumnus/a, full-time
Dates of Enrollment: 9/2001-5/2004
Survey Submitted: April 2005

After I started the Environmental Law Certificate program, I realized that I was essentially hand-selected by the environmental law faculty—I probably would not have been accepted otherwise. Apply early—a big factor in deciding who gets scholarship money is when the student applies. I applied late the first time and received nothing, but then deferred and re-applied early, which put me in position for a scholarship that I was able to maintain all three years.

Status: Alumnus/a, full-time
Dates of Enrollment: 8/1999-5/2002
Survey Submitted: April 2004

Read all of Vault's Law School Surveys at www.vault.com/lawschool — get complete surveys on top law schools, expert advice on applicaton essays, LSAT prep and more.

VAULT CAREER LIBRARY 277

I filled out an application, attached a resume and wrote a personal statement. The admissions committee looked at the first round of applications in December prior to the fall semester of admittance. I made sure that all of my information (LSAT scores, recommendation letters) had been submitted to LSAC by the time my application was completed. I made sure that my application was submitted before the admissions committee met for the first time in the beginning of December. Tulane receives at least 3,000 applications for around 300 spots in the first-year class. Tulane touts itself to be a public interest-oriented school. I made sure to mention my years of volunteer work in my personal statement. Also, I believe it was important to bring out information that made me stand out from the other applicants.

Academics

Status: Alumnus/a, full-time
Dates of Enrollment: 8/2002-5/2005
Survey Submitted: March 2006

Tulane has a strong academic program complemented by professors who are very accessible and extremely willing to help students navigate the material. There are interesting classes offered each semester—a student is never at a loss for interesting options after first year!

I was extremely happy with the academic experience at Tulane. It has prepared me well for my current position. I was always challenged by my professors and my fellow classmates. There is not a whole lot of competition. The student body is pretty laid-back. Everyone wants to do well but not at the expense of other people!! It makes for a very good learning environment. Professors do not rush out of the classroom after class, they linger for a few minutes to answer questions, address student concerns. Many have open-door policies for students to drop by with questions. Many host review sessions prior to exams and most have old practice exams (some with answers) available online—a great resource come exam time!

Status: Current student, full-time
Dates of Enrollment: 8/2004-Submit Date
Survey Submitted: March 2006

Despite the city's reputation as the Big Easy, Tulane is academically rigorous. Having had the opportunity to spend time at another school this semester, my entire class agrees that Tulane professors expect more out of their students, give more complex exams, and generally maintain a high level of academic rigor. I cannot say enough about how wonderful the faculty is at Tulane. The classes are comprehensive, the lectures are engaging, and the professors are always available outside the classroom to answer any additional questions, particularly around exam time. If you're lucky the professor might even throw an end of the semester cocktail party, which is always lots of fun. The workload is not more than one should expect, but definitely be prepared to be called on in class even as a second and third-year!

Status: Alumnus/a, full-time
Dates of Enrollment: 8/1995-5/1998
Survey Submitted: March 2006

Required classes were generally very good with a few professors who are more "egghead" and less teachers. I have been surprised by how much I learned from law school, even in required subject areas in which I didn't intend to practice. I pursued a certificate in Environmental Law and cannot begin to sufficiently praise the quality of that program. The professors, related research and projects happening on campus, the CLINIC, annual conference, journal, students and extracurriculars were outstanding. I think students were usually able to take whatever they wanted. The grading was very fair, almost always anonymous, in bigger classes, on a bell distribution. It seemed to work out pretty well. I am unaware of any grade inflation and don't think it existed. As to workload, there was always lots to do. No professor was "easy." All were very rigorous and demanding. Being a "kiss up" gets you nowhere in law school.

Status: Current student, full-time
Dates of Enrollment: 9/2003-Submit Date
Survey Submitted: March 2006

Tulane Law School has excellent professors. Using the Socratic Method, the law school professors draw the answers out of students by requiring them to be prepared in class and leading them to the correct conclusion. This method, for me, is more preferable than a professor merely stating the legal conclusion that the students should learn. The first-year classes are fairly large. However, the second- and third-year courses are smaller. I've had classes as big as 120, and as small as six or seven. One unique aspect of Tulane Law is the opportunity to study Civil Law, which is important for anyone seeking to practice in Louisiana or internationally.

Status: Current student, full-time
Dates of Enrollment: 8/2003-Submit Date
Survey Submitted: March 2006

Academic programs are all topnotch, particularly international law, environmental law, and maritime law. Has a nice mix of older and younger professors. All professors are very accessible and helpful in structuring your particular program of study. Getting popular classes is not a problem. Preference is often given to 3Ls so if you don't get what you want as a 2L, you will as a 3L. Grading is fair, but the curve is not as easy as some other top-tier institutions. The workload is considerable, but not unusually so. Tulane is a serious law school, but any decently organized individual should be able to find time for plenty of R&R.

Status: Alumnus/a, full-time
Dates of Enrollment: 8/2002-5/2005
Survey Submitted: March 2006

After speaking with friends at other law schools, I really began to appreciate the breadth of academic options at Tulane. Classes were pretty small with plenty of opportunities to take 15-student or smaller classes. Popular classes were very accessible at Tulane and if you really wanted to enroll, the school would almost always accommodate you. There is a reason why Tulane is consistently a tier-one law school—the faculty is outstanding. As a whole, the faculty is either Ivy League educated or representing the absolute best public and private universities. They have taught at other very highly regarded law schools, have taught around the world, have been involved at every level of government and demonstrate a commitment and zeal for their professorships that can stand alone as a mark of excellency.

Status: Alumnus/a, full-time
Dates of Enrollment: 8/2000-5/2003
Survey Submitted: April 2006

The program is competitive, but not cutthroat. There are few horror stories of overt attempts improve one's standing at the expense of other classmates. Students that arrive with an outwardly competitive nature are negatively reinforced to the point that at least such behavior is more tacit. This makes for a quietly competitive class, which makes the overall law school experience a little more bearable for most everyone. The professors (especially first-year) are of a very high quality, and most classes are accessible to interested students. Grading is, of course, anonymous, and but for a few professors, it is generally perceived as fair. The workload is intense but reasonable (again, for most professors).

Status: Current student, full-time
Dates of Enrollment: 9/2003-Submit Date
Survey Submitted: April 2005

Tulane is unique in that it offers students opportunities to study both civil and common law. While most students choose the common law track, many will take elective courses in civil law. The civil law is beneficial to those who plan to practice in Louisiana and in many European and international areas. It is a big attraction for foreign students and those interested in international and comparative law. Tulane also has lots of classes every semester in admiralty, environmental law, and tax. While browsing the list of course offerings recently, I thought to myself that the only thing that I could think of that was missing was a course in Native American law, which I remembered seeing in the admissions information of other schools, but it is being offered next fall. Some of the writing seminars can be a bit competitive and fill up quickly, but I have never heard students complain that they can't get a popular class. The grading is on a B curve, and even though the law school is located in the Big Easy, plan to work really hard—the competition is friendly but real.

Status: Alumnus/a, full-time
Dates of Enrollment: 8/2000-5/2003
Survey Submitted: September 2003

Tulane is an excellent school if you're interested in international or comparative law. As is it located in Louisiana, you benefit from living in the only jurisdiction in the continental U.S. that has a unique blend of common and civil law. Tulane has both Common and Civil Law Programs (most take common law). However, even if you choose the common curriculum, you can take civil law courses. Tulane offers a diverse range of classes—most people get their first choices. Also, Tulane offers certificate programs to complement your degree. A few of these programs are: European Legal Studies, Tax, Entertainment Law, Sports Law, Civil Law, etc.

Tulane is a highly academic school with a relaxed atmosphere. The professors are experts in their fields, and most are willing to help you and guide you both inside and outside the classroom. The workload is heavy but manageable. [For any class with more than 20 students, the curve is mandatory.] Tulane's clinics are one of its major attractions, particularly the environmental law clinic. In the environmental law clinic, students have the opportunity to represent clients against some high-profile clients (e.g., the U.S. EPA, Exxon, Orion).

> **The school says:** "There are only about a dozen courses (out of well over 100 offered each year) for which there is a common law-civil law distinction. Most courses are federally oriented, or statutory in nature. But for the few private law courses with the common law-civil law distinction, we always offer both. After the first year, students at Tulane take the courses they want to take. There are no requirements after the first year other than Legal Profession, an upperclass writing requirement and 20 hours of community service. No student is required to take a single civil law course. Also, we have five certificate programs: European Legal Studies, Sports Law, Environmental Law, Maritime Law and Civil Law. Beyond those official certificate programs, there are certainly opportunities to concentrate in other areas—intellectual property, business and corporate, and constitutional law come to mind—but the five listed are the only certificate programs."

Status: Current student, full-time
Dates of Enrollment: 8/2002-Submit Date
Survey Submitted: March 2005

The academic nature of the program very much depends on the professors you will have. It is possible to put together an extremely challenging class schedule by taking classes in subjects such as Comparative Law, Antitrust Law, International Trade and Finance, Public International Law, and other similar courses. That being said, it is also possible to stay on the practical side of the law in other subjects. The quality of instruction in all but two classes I took was excellent. The professors are engaging, the workload is manageable, and I always managed to get into the courses I wished to take. With regards to the two classes I did not like, it boiled down to a difference in style rather than in content.

Employment Prospects

Status: Alumnus/a, full-time
Dates of Enrollment: 8/2002-5/2005
Survey Submitted: March 2006

Tulane is a well-known school with a good reputation. That being said, at Tulane, students in the top 25 percent of their class will have an easier time obtaining positions through on-campus recruiting. Big firms from New York, Washington, D.C. and the West Coast regularly recruit at Tulane. Students interested in these positions who meet the class rank cut-off can simply submit their resumes through career development office's web site to be considered. Students interested in positions in Florida and Texas will find lots of options through on-campus recruiting including firms smaller in size.

Students who are not interested in big firm work may have more of a challenge with respect to obtaining work through on-campus recruiting. Utilize alumni—they are extremely helpful. Go to the programs offered by the Career Development Office (CDO). They will not hold your hand. You need to make an effort to let them know what you are interested in and they will work with you to make it happen.

Status: Alumnus/a, full-time
Dates of Enrollment: 8/1998-6/2001
Survey Submitted: March 2006

I had no problem getting interviews with BigLaw firms in New York and Washington, D.C., which I attribute to the fact that Tulane has a national reputation and that I had excellent grades. As someone who now does a lot of recruiting and interviewing for a major law firm, I know that the key to getting an interview with a BigLaw firm is excellent grades from a Top 50 law school or having a highly specialized educational background. Period.

Status: Alumnus/a, full-time
Dates of Enrollment: 8/1995-5/1998
Survey Submitted: March 2006

Tulane grads' employment runs the gamut from the biggest, most prestigious law firms to public interest careers. Tulane's name is held in high esteem throughout the country and I think it has even achieved a cache it didn't have previous to Katrina due to law schools around the country accepting Tulane students and seeing how well they performed. Further, Tulane has had an exceptional response to Katrina and I think that has impressed many. I have found that I keep in touch with fellow alums that I know but I haven't been involved in any official alumni events. When I meet a fellow alum however, there is certainly a great deal of camaraderie.

Status: Current student, full-time
Dates of Enrollment: 9/2003-Submit Date
Survey Submitted: March 2006

Employment prospects for a successful student at Tulane Law within the New Orleans area market are good. Hurricane Katrina has really spotlighted New Orleans and its educational institutions. For that, as well as many other reasons, law firms across the country have taken an interest in hiring students from Tulane. On-campus recruiting is fair. Certainly the Career Development Office could use some work. Jobs and internships are available, but its mainly up to the students to proactively seek them out, interview and gain employment on their own. Students with excellent grades have little trouble getting many good offers from reputable firms in New Orleans, and across the country. However, students with fair to low grades appear to have a good deal of difficulty finding employment. Obviously, this is in part due to their performance. However, it seems that the university's career development office could do more to help those students in finding job prospects either within the legal community or with non-legal business or public interest work.

Status: Alumnus/a, full-time
Dates of Enrollment: 8/2002-5/2005
Survey Submitted: March 2006

Simply stated, Tulane Law School places students at all of the major law firms around the country. With the majority of students taking the bar outside of Louisiana, many of my classmates have prestigious law firm jobs in New York, Washington, D.C., Philadelphia, Atlanta, Houston, Miami, Los Angeles, Phoenix, Dallas. Additionally, Tulane students fill the ranks of clerkships, government, and public interest law jobs. The law school alumni are very loyal and are happy to help you network and find your niche in a chosen market. Lastly, while I can't provide an exact number, many, many law firms, both big and small, interviewed on campus at Tulane, in addition to Tulane's participation in off-campus interview programs.

Status: Current student, full-time
Dates of Enrollment: 9/2003-Submit Date
Survey Submitted: April 2005

Because Tulane has great opportunities for students interested in public interest work, environmental work, and comparative and international work, professors and career specialists devote special energy to helping students find employment in these areas, as well. Currently, a grant program provides funds for students who do public interest work during the first-year and second-year summers, and

Read all of Vault's Law School Surveys at www.vault.com/lawschool — get complete surveys on top law schools, expert advice on application essays, LSAT prep and more.

VAULT CAREER LIBRARY 279

a program sponsored by the law school provides student-loan relief to those who work in these areas post-graduation. There is a counselor who works solely on judicial internship development, and many students seek opportunities on the federal and state level post-graduation. This focus really comes in handy for first-year students—nearly a third of the first-year class clerked for a judge during the summer last year.

Status: Current student, full-time
Dates of Enrollment: 8/2002-Submit Date
Survey Submitted: March 2005

The school offers great employment prospects along the Gulf Coast and the New York, Texas, and Southern California markets, as well as internationally—if you want to find a job in London, Frankfurt, Paris or Madrid, there is no better school for contacts. If you are interested in working in the Midwest however, you need to have your own network to fall back on. The alumni base there is too thin to be of much help. That being said, Tulane has great prestige with employers wherever a critical mass of Tulane lawyers has settled. As a general rule, if you are looking in markets where Tulane can help you, and if you are willing to do the legwork, you will be able to get the job you came to law school for. We have a great reputation with big firms, the public sector, and smaller firms alike.

Status: Alumnus/a, full-time
Dates of Enrollment: 8/2000-5/2003
Survey Submitted: October 2003

Those in the top 10 to 20 percent have tremendous opportunities, including jobs at the top firms in New York, D.C., Texas and California. The top 25 to 33 percent have good opportunities, too, especially in the Southwest and Southeast. Lower than that, students will find jobs, but it takes longer. Some employers are very open to Tulane; others are somewhat uninformed (i.e., many don't realize that Tulane provides a full common law program, and nearly 75 percent of students don't take the Louisiana bar exam). Clerkships are available for top students, including clerkships at federal circuit courts and district courts.

> **The school says:** "Although it's true that federal judicial clerkships are usually filled by students ranked near the top of the class, we certainly see exceptions to that. And students ranked throughout the class regularly receive state judicial clerkships. The Career Development Office, for the past three years, has put on a day-long program for incoming 1Ls to give them a better sense of the job search process, and what legitimate expectations they should have. Among the things discussed is the student's responsibility to attend career-related programs, engage in research and networking, and read his or her e-mail and regularly check the career development database for job opportunity postings. The career development office has had a significant infusion of resources in recent years. Employer development is a high priority, and a great deal of employer development has taken place in the last two years."

 ## Quality of Life

Status: Alumnus/a, full-time
Dates of Enrollment: 8/2002-5/2005
Survey Submitted: March 2006

Students in New Orleans have an excellent quality of life. The city is very affordable compared to big cities up North or on the West Coast. There are numerous opportunities or housing, including graduate student housing on campus, large scale apartment complexes, and private homes turned into apartments. Tulane provides a wonderful intranet site for admitted students. This site is a wonderful source of information for incoming students—providing information such as apartments for rents and fellow students interested in roommates. Restaurants and bars are affordable on a student budget as are most of the tourist opportunities the city presents.

New Orleans like any major U.S. city experiences crime to a certain extent. The school does a good job of letting students know the areas that should be avoided. The area in and around campus is very safe—it is very residential and populated by families and students. The tourist areas are also very safe, very populated.

There are some less-traveled areas where a student should use caution and common sense. It remains uncertain what safety will be like in New Orleans post-Katrina.

Tulane's campus is very nice. The law school sits right on the undergrad campus, which means amenities such as the wonderful student center (great exercise equipment) and outdoor pool are within walking distance! The law school is modern with great amenities—wireless Internet, two great courtyards. There is no cafeteria in the law school but there is one a few hundred yards away. Several student groups regularly sponsor bake sales and the Business Law Society sell discounted sandwiches during the school week.

Status: Current student, full-time
Dates of Enrollment: 8/2004-Submit Date
Survey Submitted: March 2006

The quality of life in New Orleans is second to none. Aside from the occasional hurricane that renders the city uninhabitable for months at a time, there is no reason not to go to school here. Apartments are beautiful and spacious and are extremely affordable. The Uptown area is an oasis of parks, trees, flowers, and wonderful atmosphere. The restaurants are world-class (which you can try when the parental units fly in for a visit), but even the cheapie dives that students subsist on are excellent: Juan's Flying Burrito, need I say more? I would hazard a guess that there are more coffee shops per capita here than anywhere else in the country—we have not one, but three local coffee chains that give Starbucks a run for their money and they make a great place to study. The campus building is great, tons of light, the library is absolutely amazing—one trip to the reading room and you'll be sold. The area around campus is one of the safest in the city though that is a relative statistic. The gym facilities are tops, if a little small. But why exercise indoors when Audobon park is at your doorstep? There's a levee bike path that stretches for miles along the Mississippi and there's a golf course with really low greens fees. Everybody loves to get outside and do things especially when the weather is nice (which is most of the time).

Status: Alumnus/a, full-time
Dates of Enrollment: 8/1998-6/2001
Survey Submitted: March 2006

Pre-Hurricane Katrina, New Orleans was an excellent back-drop for grad school. Cheap rent, great weather and the incomparable New Orleans lifestyle and culture. I've lived all over the country—New York, Philadelphia, D.C.—and I felt more safe in New Orleans although I was acutely aware that the city could be very dangerous in parts. Post-Katrina, it's my impression that the university has invested a great deal of money and planning in trying to return a sense of normalcy to the Uptown campus. It also appears that the neighborhoods surrounding the university were spared the complete destruction experience by other parts of New Orleans. In short, I'd say if you remain for the most part in and around the university the quality of life will be about as good as could be expected under the circumstances.

Status: Current student, full-time
Dates of Enrollment: 9/2003-Submit Date
Survey Submitted: March 2006

Some people get very involved in the Tulane Law School life and programs. Other people choose to immerse themselves in what New Orleans as a city has to offer. But the school does offer a host of legal and non-legal organizations, clubs and scholarly journals. The food on campus is OK. Tulane is in the process of building a new student center, so the food and facilities at Tulane will soon be drastically improving. The neighborhood around Tulane is very student oriented. Many undergraduates and graduate students live within blocks of the school. There is some crime in the area. This is mostly likely because petty thieves and criminals are aware that there are students stumbling around drunk on the streets at all hours of the night and are easy targets of crime. Since Hurricane Katrina, crime of all sorts has been drastically reduced. It has yet to be determined as to whether some of those criminal elements will be returning to the city.

Status: Current student, full-time
Dates of Enrollment: 8/2003-Submit Date
Survey Submitted: March 2006

New Orleans has been roughed up pretty good, but the "world" of the typical Tulane student has escaped relatively unscathed. Things will probably be a little dirtier than usual for a while, but everyone in town is working hard to make the place better than ever. For any civic-minded students, the city is perfect. There are so many opportunities to give back to the community and so many interesting political and legal developments unfolding.

Status: Alumnus/a, full-time
Dates of Enrollment: 8/2002-5/2005
Survey Submitted: March 2006

The quality of life at a law school could not be higher. New Orleans is a great place to live while in school. Laid-back atmosphere and great coffee shops to spend all day studying. Also, you don't feel that poor because the city doesn't have lots of young professionals throwing money around. Often times law students and med students are the only ones in the higher class bars. The students are great to one another. People are always sharing outlines and notes. Not a cutthroat atmosphere at all. People generally like each other.

Status: Current student, full-time
Dates of Enrollment: 8/2003-Submit Date
Survey Submitted: January 2005

Quality of life is great at Tulane. New Orleans is possibly the perfect place to go to law school. There is great weather, always something going on, and most of the students were very laid-back. There is a graduate dorm which is adequate, but most students lived off campus. The facilities are topnotch, as the school building is relatively new. Tulane also has a very racially diverse population. It has a strong Black Law Students Association, Asian Students Association, and Hispanic Association. It also has an active Gay and Lesbian Association.

Status: Current student, full-time
Dates of Enrollment: 8/2004-Submit Date
Survey Submitted: September 2004

Life is great here. If you like nightlife, you have it, if you like history and culture you definitely have it. It's a beautiful place to live and the most unique American city. While much of any law student's time is (and should be) occupied by attending classes and studying, Tulane Law students quickly realize that the Law School is a place where things are always happening, both inside and outside the classroom. There are over 35 student organizations, any of which may be holding business meetings or substantive programs on any given day. Eight different journals offer students writing and editing opportunities, and the moot court program oversees both intra-school competitions and as many as one dozen teams participating in inter-school competitions.

Status: Alumnus/a, full-time
Dates of Enrollment: 8/1999-5/2002
Survey Submitted: April 2004

Most law students, including myself, lived off campus. The university does provide assistance in finding off-campus housing. There is a Legal Assistance Program called TULAP that has a list of "slum lords" to avoid—they also give free assistance to law students with landlord issues. The law school itself is relatively new and a pretty nice facility. The surrounding neighborhoods can be a bit sketchy—but that is just New Orleans. The law school was very good about notifying students about any crime issues that were going on around campus.

 **Social Life**

Status: Alumnus/a, full-time
Dates of Enrollment: 8/2002-5/2005
Survey Submitted: March 2006

The law school student body at Tulane is very social—which is one of the reasons I chose Tulane. There is a "work hard, play hard" mentality, which isn't unexpected given the school's location in New Orleans. Students take their studies seriously, but they find time to enjoy New Orleans—the city provides wonderful opportunities for anyone interested in maintaining a social life while in law school. Various student organizations host Bar Reviews frequently—at least once a month. These Bar Reviews provide first-year students an opportunity to visit a variety of bars around New Orleans. Students from all three classes regularly attend. You'll frequently see law review members in attendance.

A favorite of students is the annual Bar Review hosted by the *International Law Journal*. This is the only Bar Review that charges a cover ($25). The rest are completely free for students! The *Journal* rents out the top floor and balcony of Tropical Isle, a bar right on Bourbon Street for the Thursday prior to Mardi Gras. Students from all classes gather on the balcony to toss beads and enjoy the craziness on the street below. The rest of the evenings of Carnival Season are spent on the parade routes with friends. Another favorite of students is the annual Crawfish Boil, where the school literally provides a truckload of crawfish, kegs of beer and fun local music for a fun March afternoon. Each law journal hosts a banquet in the Spring. Several professors regularly host students in their home. One Evidence professor orders appetizers and kegs and hosts an annual party at F&M's, a fun student bar! Several times a year the school provides lunch in the outdoor courtyard so students can take a break from work and enjoy the beautiful weather in New Orleans. Students often choose to spend their afternoons running in Audobon Park, playing golf in City Park, laying out on the makeshift beach at the "Fly," shopping on Magazine Street or sitting outside at one of the city's numerous coffee shops. There is never a loss of fun things to do as a break from the books!

Status: Current student, full-time
Dates of Enrollment: 8/2004-Submit Date
Survey Submitted: March 2006

Tulane students work hard and play hard. School clubs and organizations hold Bar Reviews once a month at a different bar that everyone attends: free pizza and beer all night. The school also organizes mid-week student-faculty mixers, law school "prom," a crawfish boil in the spring with a live zydeco band, and the annual auction run by the public interest group where students can bid on dinner and lunch outings with their favorite professors. The students at Tulane are really friendly and social, though if you want to stay in on a Saturday night to study nobody gives you a hard time because they probably will be doing the same the following week. Activities range from meeting up for coffee to group dinners at nice restaurants to all night bar-hopping ending with late-night cheese fries at F&Ms. Mardi Gras is always a great time of year. There are no classes and lots of students who live on the parade route throw big parties for friends and their out of town guests. In short, Tulane is just a lot of fun.

Status: Alumnus/a, full-time
Dates of Enrollment: 8/1995-5/1998
Survey Submitted: March 2006

There is such a vibrant nightlife in New Orleans and such tremendous cuisine. The city, even post Katrina, celebrates regularly with parades, drink and dancing. I personally love Le Bon Temps, Cafe Brasil, the Columns and Checkpoint Charlies for nighttime. Commander's Palace, The Palace Cafe and Franky and Johnny's are favorite restaurants. People in New Orleans are super colorful and there is never a shortage of adventure. It's a really fun place to go to school.

Status: Current student, full-time
Dates of Enrollment: 9/2003-Submit Date
Survey Submitted: March 2006

New Orleans is fantastic. There is so much to offer in terms of food, music and other entertainment. New Orleans is a very diverse town, with options for all tastes. Since the hurricane, people across the city have become extremely involved in volunteer work and community service, where they otherwise were not. Citizens are motivated to get involved with new organizations, whether political, social or volunteer. Hurricane Katrina brought New Orleans citizens together and people seem so much more energized and dedicated to the city and other citizens. While some establishments have yet to open, there are so many new options for entertainment and music.

New Orleans is most notably known for Mardi Gras and Jazz Fest. Mardi Gras is what you make of it. It can be wild and debaucherous, if you spend time on Bourbon Street. But it can also be a fun family event, if you view the parades from St. Charles Avenue in the Garden District. Jazz Fest always features well known and world renown musicians. However, Jazz Fest is traditionally during the two weeks of Law School exams, so most law school students do not get the opportunity to take advantage of Jazz Fest. The Law School puts on events throughout the year, including Bar Reviews almost every weekend. Once a year, the school hosts the Barrister's Ball, a law school "prom" like event that is always held at an upscale hotel with an excellent band. The school also hosts a Spring Fling Crawfish Boil.

Read all of Vault's Law School Surveys at www.vault.com/lawschool — get complete surveys on top law schools, expert advice on applicaton essays, LSAT prep and more.

VAULT CAREER LIBRARY   281

Status: Current student, full-time
Dates of Enrollment: 8/2004-Submit Date
Survey Submitted: November 2005

I would describe the law school as a very close-knit community where everyone either knows or knows of everyone else. This can be a great thing, but on the other hand many aspects remind me of high school where everyone is in everyone else's business and/or affairs. So, you make the decision whether this is right for you, but I assume this is the same as nearly every law school in the country.

Status: Alumnus/a, full-time
Dates of Enrollment: 8/1998-6/2001
Survey Submitted: March 2005

If socializing is important to you (and it is to most TLS students), then going to school where you can party on Bourbon Street every weekend is a dream come true! Although your first year is spent primarily studying and in the library, there are generally no classes on Friday at TLS, so you have pretty long weekends all three years. Going out in New Orleans is cheap and easy any night of the week, although most students go out Thursday, Friday, and Saturday nights only because of study demands. The allure of the French Quarter does wear off eventually and most law students migrate back to bars and clubs nearer the law school—of which there are many including the great Tipitina's Uptown for live music.

New Orleans also has a very vibrant and historic coffee house culture. It is definitely not the sanitized Starbuck's experience and is much closer to the European cafe culture. Many law students spend their entire days in the coffee houses drinking coffee, smoking cigarettes and studying with friends. Because of the great New Orleans weather, this means you can study outside on the patios almost year-round. Big favorites are Rud de La Course on Magazine Street and any outpost of PJ's. Mardi Gras, Jazzfest, and French Quarter Fest, are all great events that a Tulane student has the insider access to, but the everyday in New Orleans has the feeling of a festival.

Status: Alumnus/a, full-time
Dates of Enrollment: 8/2000-5/2003
Survey Submitted: March 2005

People are very happy at Tulane and have a positive attitude about the school and the town. New Orleans is a fabulous place to be a student—not too expensive and tons of fun things to do. People managed to have a very balanced life of studying, partying, going to the gym or playing sports. People also made close friendships that they have maintained since graduation.

 **The School Says**

As the 12th oldest law school in the United States, Tulane Law School is one of the most exciting places for a student to attain their law degree for a variety of reasons. New Orleans has always been a unique and seductive city, but now it is a city in which every student can make a difference just by being here. Tulane Law School was the first law school in the U.S. to require community service as a prerequisite for graduation. Now community service is more meaningful than ever, as every student has an opportunity to participate in the re-building and renewal of New Orleans.

The neighborhood in which Tulane Law School is located, and the neighborhoods in which most students live and play, were little affected by 2005's Hurricane Katrina. What is gratifying to see, however, is the involvement of Tulane students in recovery efforts in other parts of New Orleans. Students' involvement ranges from working on legal matters with individuals directly affected by the storm to physical labor in helping schools to re-open and helping families return to their homes.

Tulane is particularly well known for its strength in international and comparative law, environmental law and maritime law. It has a well-regarded Sports Law Program, as well as significant course offerings in such areas as business, corporate and commercial law, intellectual property law, and constitutional law, among others. Tulane's law clinics enable third-year students to represent clients in the criminal defense, civil litigation, domestic violence, juvenile litigation and environmental law areas. Both second- and third-year students can participate in the Administrative and Legislative Advocacy Clinic. Writing opportunities for Tulane Law students include seven journals, from the *Tulane Law Review* to specialty journals in maritime law, international and comparative law, environmental law, law and sexuality, sports law, and comparative and civil law.

Among the support services available to students are the Office of the Assistant Dean of Students and a Career Development Office with five professional career counselors who work with students on their job searches. The Career Development Office is pro-active in identifying employment opportunities for Tulane law students and in developing ongoing relationships with legal employers.

Tulane Law School is located in the center of Tulane University's uptown campus, enabling law students to participate fully in the life of the University. Students regularly interact with the School's full-time faculty and with dozens of lawyers who teach advanced and specialty courses at the law school. It is worth emphasizing that the full-time faculty is fully committed to teaching, and students consider the faculty a special strength of the school. Over 40 student organizations are available to law students, and not surprisingly, the diversity of those organizations reflects that of the student body.

University of Maine School of Law

Admissions Office
246 Deering Avenue
Portland, ME 04102
Admissions phone: (207) 780-4341
Admissions e-mail: mainelaw@usm.maine.edu
Admissions URL:
http://mainelaw.maine.edu/admissions.htm

 ## Admissions

Status: Current student, full-time
Dates of Enrollment: 8/2003-Submit Date
Survey Submitted: April 2006

Maine Law is moderately competitive. About 800 people apply for 80 to 90 seats. They've recently become tougher in terms of not caring if they fill all the seats if it means to do so they'll have to accept marginal applicants. However, the school is very white. Therefore, it searches for great Hispanic and African American applicants. The application process is the same as for all law schools. You have to use the hated LSAC.

Status: Current student, full-time
Dates of Enrollment: 9/2005-Submit Date
Survey Submitted: April 2006

I have experience both going through the admissions process and working for the admissions office during my first year here. I think the admissions process is very user-friendly and helpful. Since it is a small school, you can actually talk to the admissions director with questions you have. Also, I received calls from current students and faculty while I was making my decision after I was accepted, which helped me learn more about the school.

The admissions does not seem to have a "formula" for letting students in, but promotes a diverse and interesting class of students. Essays are looked at, and can add to the interest of a student's file. The selection is pretty competitive, and the sooner you get it in, the better, since it is on a rolling basis.

Status: Current student, full-time
Dates of Enrollment: 8/2005-Submit Date
Survey Submitted: April 2006

The admissions process is rolling, consisting of several rounds. Apply early. Maine Law's selectivity is consistent with other third-tier schools, but scholarships for first year students are limited and the scholarship application process is ambiguous. For the most part, the students who call and say that they have offers from other schools and ask for scholarship money (politely) are the students who receive the scholarships.

> **The school says:** "Maine Law offers merit scholarships targeting excellence, diversity and depth of experience."

Status: Current student, full-time
Dates of Enrollment: 8/2005-Submit Date
Survey Submitted: April 2006

The admissions office is incredibly helpful. I had to call frequently to get clarification of different items that were required as well as to report a delay in the delivery of transcripts. Each time I called, I was able to speak with the same person and did not have to repeat my previous conversations. The admissions office knew who I was, and what the follow-up call was about. It made the application process a breeze.

After I was admitted, I received detailed weekly e-mails from the admissions office inviting me to events taking place at the school as well as how to prepare myself for the upcoming year. These e-mails were a great way to stay in touch over the summer and put me in contact with others admitted to the school.

The school is highly selective and difficult to get into due to its desire to keep class sizes small. The best way to get in is to have a good standing in undergraduate school, prepare hard for the LSATs and write a meaningful essay. I wrote about why I wanted to go to school in Maine as well as why I wanted to practice a particular area of law. The essay was personal and reflected my desire to be a part of the Maine community.

Status: Current student, full-time
Dates of Enrollment: 8/2004-Submit Date
Survey Submitted: April 2006

Admissions process was through LSAC service. Interview was not necessary. I'm not sure how selective the school is. Many students are originally from Maine who went away for college/work and returned for the in-state tuition rates. Many students went to top undergraduate universities and colleges like Bates, Bowdoin, Williams, Tufts, Davidson, Yale, Colby, etc.

Status: Current student, full-time
Dates of Enrollment: 9/2004-Submit Date
Survey Submitted: April 2006

The Maine Law admissions process really is no different than any other school's program. LSAT and a general essay are required, as well as the normal info about one's previous schooling, employment history, etc. No interview needed, either.

If one measures selectivity in terms of LSAT, then the school is moderately selective: 150 is the average. However, the school does look for people with diverse backgrounds—this is not a school of all recent college graduates. Any questions one would have about the process can be directed to Elaine Borne, the admissions director, or to the Assistant Dean, Carol Vizzier. They are both extremely receptive to questions and comments, and will make time to meet with you personally as well.

> **The school says:** "The median LSAT for the Maine Law Classes of 2006, 2007 and 2008 is 156; the 25th to 75th percentile LSAT is 153 to 158."

Status: Current student, full-time
Dates of Enrollment: 8/2005-Submit Date
Survey Submitted: April 2006

I spoke with the director of admissions at an open house in the fall of my senior year of college and throughout the admissions process she sent me personalized letters. The admissions office is very small, so if you need to contact someone be sure to be polite, because they will know who you are. If you have the grades and the right attitude, Maine Law will want you. There are several current students who were admitted after being denied admission after their first application, so if you don't get in you should contact the director of admissions to figure out what you can do to have a better chance next year.

Status: Current student, full-time
Dates of Enrollment: 8/2005-Submit Date
Survey Submitted: April 2006

Transferring to this school can be quite difficult. Persistence is key. Was not admitted until 10 days before classes began. Having a recommendation from an alum was key. No interview required.

Status: Current student, full-time
Dates of Enrollment: 9/2002-Submit Date
Survey Submitted: April 2005

The admission process was simple. The application was straightforward and did not need explanation. The essay was open-ended enough to allow for creativity without being so open-ended as to inspire dread. The admissions staff was helpful and knew the answers to my questions. I did not interview. Maine Law is very focused on public interest law. Although I cannot speak to their motives directly, my guess is that having a background working with people in need of

Read all of Vault's Law School Surveys at www.vault.com/lawschool — get complete surveys on top law schools, expert advice on applicaton essays, LSAT prep and more.

VAULT CAREER LIBRARY 283

some services helps. Many of my classmates have worked in education, social work, and others.

Status: Current student, full-time
Dates of Enrollment: 9/2004-Submit Date
Survey Submitted: April 2005

The admissions staff is very helpful. I had hundreds of questions and I always received prompt, honest answers. My advice would be to visit the school and take an opportunity to talk to current students. I initially applied because I'm a Mainer but thought I wanted to go somewhere else. Speaking with current students helped me make the decision to come here and it was absolutely the right decision. As far as getting in, my only advice is to do well in school and on the LSAT. I spent a lot of time on my essay, too.

Status: Current student, full-time
Dates of Enrollment: 8/2003-Submit Date
Survey Submitted: April 2005

The admissions process is simple for Maine Law and they were really fast at getting back to me with my acceptance. Make sure you are able to get across what makes you unique as compared with all of the other high GPA, high LSAT score students applying. From my conversations with the professors on the admissions committee, they truly consider the entire package. If there is a gap in a resume or a grade in a course that is inconsistent, the admissions essay is the opportunity to explain.

 **Academics**

Status: Current student, full-time
Dates of Enrollment: 8/2003-Submit Date
Survey Submitted: April 2006

The classes in the first year are fabulous. They've scheduled the best professors for the 1L year. It becomes increasingly more difficult to get the courses you want in the last two years. The school is small, so they only offer limited courses. Then, they have a habit of scheduling both the business tracks and the litigation tracks opposite of each other. You almost have to choose one track in the beginning of your 2L year or you'll never get the prerequisites for advanced business classes, like bankruptcy, unless you start taking them immediately. Of course, what that means is you'll never get all the pre-requisites for Estate Planning because you were in business classes in the 2L year. So, it's tough to get everything you want, or need, for the bar exam.

Status: Current student, full-time
Dates of Enrollment: 8/2003-Submit Date
Survey Submitted: April 2006

The workload is comparable to other law schools in terms of the core courses that one needs to take for the bar exam and for general legal knowledge. It's basically a generalist program. A majority of the faculty did their undergraduate and graduate work at Ivy League or top tier schools. Many present scholarly papers and write texts.

Because of the student body and faculty size, the number of specialized courses are very limited because the offerings are tied to the number of interested students. Also, the faculty are not experts in many specialized areas.

The popular core course are always offered, but they often conflict in the schedule. In addition, some popular courses are offered every other year or only when a faculty member is willing to teach it.

Academic planning is key, but the tentativeness of the schedule makes it difficult. Grading runs the gambit. It really depends on who is teaching the class in a given year because there is no set criteria.

The school relies heavily on lawyers in Portland to teach core or specialized courses. During some years there may be a 1:1 ratio between full-time faculty to adjuncts. In the classroom, most professors do not use the Socratic Method.

Maine Law says: "The school utilizes adjuncts when they offer something positive to the pedagogic experience (i.e., trial practice taught by a U.S. Attorney and/or trial lawyer; patent

law taught by an attorney with an active patent practice). We do not use adjunct faculty to teach core of specialized courses. Most faculty utilize the Socratic approach in conjunction with the case or problem-study methods of teaching."

Status: Current student, full-time
Dates of Enrollment: 9/2005-Submit Date
Survey Submitted: April 2006

The workload here seems to be manageable with good time-management skills and commitment. The first-year curriculum is basically the same as at most schools. Sometimes it seems that some of the first-year professors do not really want to teach their classes, but have to to stay on faculty to teach the classes they are interested in. BUT more than half of the professors I have had so far seem super excited and happy to be teaching all of their courses here and are interesting.

Getting good grades falls a lot on exam-writing skills, and talking to older students who did well can certainly help you learn what each teacher is looking for. There are no official teacher assistants for classes, so seeking out "mentors" to talk to is really helpful.

Status: Current student, full-time
Dates of Enrollment: 8/2005-Submit Date
Survey Submitted: April 2006

The workload at Maine Law is manageable. Some of the professors are wonderful teachers and others are not. In terms of second- and third-year courses, the smaller seminar or clinical courses are determined by lottery, limited to 15 to 20 students, and can be very difficult to get into. Many of the second- and third-year professors are adjuncts who also practice law in Maine. I find these classes more practical and a refreshing change from academic courses that are often more theoretical and policy driven. Professor Petruccelli is fantastic and rated one of the top 10 litigators in the country!

Status: Current student, full-time
Dates of Enrollment: 8/2005-Submit Date
Survey Submitted: April 2006

I cannot compare the workload to other law schools as this is the only school I have been to, however I will say that it is a lot during the first year. You take the following classes your first year and they truly want to make sure you get a general understanding of the law: Criminal Law, Civil Procedure I and II, Constitutional Law, Torts, Contracts, Sale of Goods, Property, Legal Writing I and II. This is five classes a semester and they take a lot of your time.

There does not seem to be too much difficulty getting into the classes you want and need. First year, your schedule is determined for you but in the other years you are able to select your classes as you wish. The most popular classes are offered each semester and during the summer so if you do not get in the first time, you are likely to get in the second semester you apply.

Grading depends on the professor and is fair. Most spend a great deal of time with your work before giving it a grade and each has a particular style of writing or answer they wish to see.

The classes here are fantastic and it's not only because of the professors, but also because of the other students in your class. While there is an undertone of competition, it is never evident in the day to day life at the school. Everyone helps each other and we often work together in study groups to get through the material. However, it is not required and not everyone has a group with which they work.

Status: Current student, full-time
Dates of Enrollment: 8/2004-Submit Date
Survey Submitted: April 2006

The 1L program is standard. Most 2L and 3L classes are offered on an every-other-year basis so it is sometimes difficult to have flexibility in your schedule. Good clinic programs, have an externship program but without many options. Excellent 1L writing program and many opportunities to work with/meet with judges in the area.

Grading is not on par with other New England schools. Professors curve with the average at a C unlike most schools where the average is a B. Students who received all A's in undergrad with be humbled.

In regards to grading, the school says: "The law school does not have a mandatory grading standard or curve. We do, however, have a suggested grading curve. In a normal large enrollment course, the median grade is typically a B."

Status: Current student, full-time
Dates of Enrollment: 8/2005-Submit Date
Survey Submitted: April 2006

For the most part, the classes are pretty good. I've learned way more in one year than I did in four years of undergrad. The curriculum is pretty standard—Torts, Civil Procedure, Legal Writing, Con Law, Criminal Law, Contracts and Property in the first year and electives after that. Most classes are open enrollment and the ones that are not are filled by a lottery system.

The professors are generally nice and interested in making sure the students understand the material and are doing well both in school and personally. It is rare to see a professor leave a classroom without talking to students for several minutes after class. There are some professors who are only interested in scholarship and not students. There is a lot of work, but it can be balanced—many people try to keep an 8-to-5 schedule and enjoy their evenings and weekends.

Status: Current student, full-time
Dates of Enrollment: 9/2004-Submit Date
Survey Submitted: April 2006

The 1L academics follow the normally prescribed structure elsewhere: Torts, Property, Con Law, Civil Procedures, etc. The structure for 2L and 3L years is not prescribed, and there is a good mix of "Code" classes (Tax, Business Associations, Secured Transactions) and non-Code, including anything from Administrative Law to Insurance. There's a good mix of classes, and the school is making a big push to increase its depth within IP. The school is also exploring elder law and health law as areas to grow. There is also a commitment to environmental law (with a focus on marine law) at the school.

It's pretty easy to get the classes you sign up for, though there is a lottery system for Trial Practice, Clinic (there are three at the moment), and bridge courses, such as Depositions or Computer Crimes. The biggest detraction from the wealth of classes is scheduling—it's a small school with a small faculty, so some classes are only offered in the fall, and conflict with other popular classes. There is a possibility that students will have to forego a class simply because taking Tax or Business Associations (which are on the bar) conflicts with, say, International Trade Law.

Professors run the gamut from tedious to terrific. There are some faculty members who, without fail, will devote time, energy, and enthusiasm to any student who walks through their office doors (which are almost always open). There are also those who fail to see that they bore their students to tears, or who lecture rather than call on students, thus leading to a one-sided learning experience. Fortunately, some upper-level classes are taught twice a year by different teachers, so if you want to avoid someone while still taking the class, it is possible.

At Maine, it's basically impossible not to take part in a conversation in a class, to avoid getting called, or hide from being asked to participate in one way or another. Classes are active! There are no major lecture halls, and students are expected to be contributing members. If you want to avoid discussion, go to a larger school where you can get lost in the crowd.

Grading is not static at Maine Law. A major issue in students' minds is that first year GPAs are not weighted in favor of 1Ls, a practice that nearly all other New England schools do, and that puts a disadvantage upon 1L's with a mediocre GPA who may wish to practice outside of Maine. Moreover, there is no uniform system of grading; one professor's B could be another professor's C+ or A-. Although I think most professors place a premium on writing skills, and good work is rewarded, there is room for improvement.

Workload is not impossible, but it's certainly demanding. Besides the four core classes that students have to take each semester, there is also a Legal Writing Program where students are expected to turn out one, if not two, major writing products. You are kept busy! However, a social life is possible, and with it being such a small school with mostly approachable professors, getting an extension on something, or talking over your time managements skills with the dean, is certainly available to you.

Status: Alumnus/a, full-time
Dates of Enrollment: 8/1998-5/2001
Survey Submitted: March 2005

The professors are very approachable. By second semester first year, most will know your name and remember you from class. All of the professors abide by their office hours and will take the time to work with you through any issues you may be hung up on.

The grading varies somewhat from professor to professor. It does not take long to find out which professors are "hard." None of them are particularly easy. Maine Law is very proud of its rigorous academics.

A student can get into almost any class. Very few classes have limited enrollment. Being a small school keeps class size down for most classes. Some more popular (prerequisite) classes will be packed (tax, business associations), but everyone gets in. Those classes with limited enrollment are filled by lottery. If it is needed to graduate, 3L's are given preference.

Maine Law has an incredible clinical program. Cumberland Legal Aid Clinic provides student attorneys for people who could not otherwise afford a lawyer. Most of the cases are family law, with some criminal law. The student attorneys get sworn in and actually practice law while enrolled at the clinic. Faculty supervisors guide student attorneys through court dates, motions, mediations, and anything else that may come their way. The program provides real-life experience that really helps put the academics in perspective. While this is limited enrollment, very few 3-L's who want to get into the clinic are turned away. This is an incredible program with fabulous faculty and staff.

Status: Current student, full-time
Dates of Enrollment: 9/2004-Submit Date
Survey Submitted: April 2005

A unique aspect of the Maine Law experience is that for your first year you take all of your classes with your whole class (80 to 100 students) and sit in the same seat every day. At first this seems childish but you develop an appreciation for the situation quickly because it allows you to get to know everyone in your class. Most schools do not work as hard as Maine law does to help students build connections to each other. Also the professors are very approachable, always willing to make time for your individual questions, and well-prepared

Status: Current student, full-time
Dates of Enrollment: 8/2003-Submit Date
Survey Submitted: April 2005

The professors at the school are amazing. I went to an Ivy League for my undergraduate education, as did several other people in my class, and I think we all have found that the level of teaching is definitely equivalent. It is quite simple to get into a class. In addition, the administration makes it simple to petition for additional classes that are not on the syllabus or that are listed as offered every other year. If there is enough interest, then the class is offered. The workload is not what I had anticipated. I knew that law school was "hard" but I didn't quite realize just how much work would be involved. That said, I think it is a fair amount of work.

The best attribute of the school is the overall supportive environment—professors always have their doors open, students are always willing to explain esoteric rules of law to one another and reserve books do not mysteriously go missing. We just aren't that competitive with one another, which has also helped create an incredibly friendly bar in Maine.

Read all of Vault's Law School Surveys at www.vault.com/lawschool — get complete surveys on top law schools, expert advice on applicaton essays, LSAT prep and more.

VAULT CAREER LIBRARY **285**

Status: Current student, full-time
Dates of Enrollment: 8/2004-Submit Date
Survey Submitted: April 2005

The workload is rather heavy and the grading seems difficult. The classroom instruction is a great asset of this school. There are many professors that make an effort to be accessible.

Status: Alumnus/a, full-time
Dates of Enrollment: 8/1998-5/2001
Survey Submitted: March 2005

I found the academic program at Maine to be strong. I later went to the Washington office of an AmLaw 100 firm, and think that my preparation for practice was more solid than many of my peers who went to name-brand schools. In particular, there is an emphasis on the fundamentals, and in training in the law as an academic subject. There are fewer survey courses that cover eclectic non-legal subjects from a "legal" perspective (i.e., all those course with names that follow the pattern of "[Blank] and the Law"), and fewer courses that offer light training in "legal skills." The shift in many law schools toward these non-core courses is caused, I think, by their popularity, and the perception among prospective students that they somehow offer better preparation for practice than traditional, academically-oriented course work. This is unfortunate, because I think that these courses do not offer a solid foundation in the law. Maine Law's continued emphasis on traditional training is therefore admirable, although I think it has hurt its popularity among prospective students under the misapprehension that course like "Internet and the law" will better prepare them for practice in the modern world.

 Employment Prospects

Status: Current student, full-time
Dates of Enrollment: 8/2003-Submit Date
Survey Submitted: April 2006

Did I mention that they keep each class' GPA artificially set to 3.0? I'm sure I must have. OK, now try to compete for jobs with graduates who went to a shiny law school in Boston who have a nearly 4.0 GPA. You see the problem...

Status: Current student, full-time
Dates of Enrollment: 9/2005-Submit Date
Survey Submitted: April 2006

Since Maine Law is the only law school in Maine, within the state, employers have high esteem for Maine Law students, since many employers are alums or work with alums. Maine students get comparable jobs to out-of-state students coming into Maine looking for a job, but getting a job out of state takes a little more effort on your part just to do the research, make the contacts and get things going.

Career Services is really helpful, willing to help you write your resume and cover letter, network, and apply for jobs and even has an on-campus interviewing program for students to interview for jobs on campus after employers review resumes and select candidates to interview. This program brings a lot of Maine jobs as well as some national interests such as Navy JAG or other opportunities. The top people in the class certainly have an easier time finding a job, but everyone seems to end up finding something for summer jobs/experience by the middle of April or so.

Status: Current student, full-time
Dates of Enrollment: 8/2005-Submit Date
Survey Submitted: April 2006

If you are in the top 15 of the first-year class, your chances of being offered a summer job at a large Maine firm are fantastic. The career services office conducts a fall and spring on-campus interview program, and opportunities to network with practicing Maine attorneys are abundant. However, opportunities to network out of state are limited, but many students do take jobs in MA, NY, NH and D.C. The Women's Law Association runs a mentor/mentee program which will match law students with practicing Maine attorneys, and this is a wonderful networking opportunity.

Status: Current student, full-time
Dates of Enrollment: 8/2005-Submit Date
Survey Submitted: April 2006

There is a great career services department who works together with the alumni committee to get alumni together with students. You have the option of getting an alum as a mentor to help guide you through your class selections, help you determine the field you are interested in and tell you about their life after school.

Events throughout the year give you the ability to talk to various members of the local legal community, many of whom are graduates of the school. There is a very close relationship between the bench and bar and the school and this proves to be a great resource and provides for an enriching experience.

Status: Current student, full-time
Dates of Enrollment: 8/2005-Submit Date
Survey Submitted: April 2006

Most graduates stay in Maine (they go to Maine Law because they want to work in Maine). Many also get jobs in Massachusetts, New Hampshire and other states. Maine Law provides a lot of opportunities to meet alumni through mentoring programs, networking events, and fund raisers. Graduates work in both small and large firms. There are several public interest summer fellowships that are funded by the school.

Status: Current student, full-time
Dates of Enrollment: 9/2004-Submit Date
Survey Submitted: April 2006

Maine is an amazing place to live, for various reasons. However, southern Maine, with its bigger population and bigger paychecks, is saturated with lawyers. If you are not an excellent student with a strong resume, it may be difficult to secure a summer associate position or employment past graduation in this area. That is not to say it's impossible to get a job in Portland, you have to hit the pavement yourself and work outside of the career office to make connections and make it happen.

In addition, the top firms in Maine do hire Maine Law graduates, and work with the career office to set up on-site recruiting. The current 2L class (Class of 2007) had students that were hired by every single top-tier firm in the state, and successfully competed against students from out of state vying for the same positions. But large firms from Augusta and Bangor, as well as those in North Conway and Manchester, NH also interview.

Getting a job outside of Portland is certainly easier. Small firms tend to not do full-on recruiting efforts, but the career office will have information on who's out there for 1Ls to contact on their own. The career office also stresses opportunities outside of Maine, and alerts students to job fairs and government positions.

There are internships each summer open to 1Ls and 2Ls that range from working with bankruptcy, district court, or probate judges to working at nonprofits or having an externship with the Unites States Attorney for Maine.

The alumni network is plugged in—this is a small state, with only one law school—you're going to run into Maine Law alums. The school and its student groups foster relationships with alums through programs, events, receptions, you name it. Getting a question answered, or an interview passed to people is not difficult due to a strong and successful law school/alumni relationship. A fair number of students graduate with clerkships. The Maine Law court annually selects at least one or two students, for example, to clerk for specific judges. The large majority of students will join firms (of all sizes), and only a few intrepid souls hang out their own shingle. Those who enter business or nonprofits are also limited in number.

Status: Current student, full-time
Dates of Enrollment: 9/2002-Submit Date
Survey Submitted: April 2005

Getting a job has more to do with the student than anything else. Students who want a job and network, get jobs. Portland is not a big city and Maine is pretty rural, so it does not take long to get to know people. The school hosts many functions that allow students to meet alumni and non-alumni members of the Maine Bar. If a student chooses to spend all of their time locked in the library or at home, they will not make the connections necessary to find a job. There are ample opportunities for on-campus interviews. There are many internships/externships.

As far as prestige is concerned, nobody cares. Perhaps some of the bigger firms would rather hire an Ivy Leaguer, but most employers in Maine care more about the individual's ability to do their job. If you expect to get a job because of the school you go to, skip Maine Law. If you want to meet and get to know actual practitioners, get job offers based on your ability and personality, then Maine is the place for you.

Status: Alumnus/a, full-time
Dates of Enrollment: 8/1998-5/2001
Survey Submitted: March 2005

A degree from Maine Law makes one competitive for positions with legal employers in Maine and elsewhere in northern New England. Class standing will certainly be much more of a factor for more competitive employers than it would be for somebody from, say, Harvard. Getting a job outside of northern New England is more difficult. The school is not well-known [and does not] have a strong reputation. It is difficult and rare for a Maine Law graduate to land a position with one of the very top firms in a major metropolitan area, especially as one gets farther away from Maine. That being said, graduates of the top of each year's class are able to find jobs with well-known, reasonably high-powered national firms. Generally, however, obtaining a position like that requires high class standing (at least top 5 to 10 percent is probably really necessary depending on how competitive the market is that year). Also making it difficult to find employment outside of northern New England is that fact that few legal employers outside that area participate in on-campus recruiting.

 Quality of Life

Status: Current student, full-time
Dates of Enrollment: 8/2003-Submit Date
Survey Submitted: April 2006

Fabulous, fabulous, fabulous. For the most part, the professors are accessible. Portland is a blast. It's safe to live around the campus and there are tons of things to do, whether you like to party, ski, or get back to nature. It's all just outside the door.

The only negative I can think of is the school uses the University of Southern Maine (USM) for its administrative functions. It saves money apparently. Anyway, the financial aid office at USM is incredibly stingy. They have no idea of what it costs to get through law school, especially if you're a little older or have a spouse and God forbid a child.

Status: Current student, full-time
Dates of Enrollment: 8/2003-Submit Date
Survey Submitted: April 2006

Portland is a phenomenal small city with no shortage of things to do and see. The university does have a dorm in the heart of the city, but it's shared by undergraduate students. Unfortunately, housing costs are very high here in Portland, but deals can be found. The law school has its own building that houses a small library and canteen.

Status: Current student, full-time
Dates of Enrollment: 9/2005-Submit Date
Survey Submitted: April 2006

Portland is a fabulous place to live. There is only minimal dorm housing for law students, and it is mixed with undergrad housing and not very favorable. Most students rent or buy in the area or commute from a bit outside of Portland. The area is relatively safe, accessible, and a great place for young families or single students. There are lots of bars, restaurants, museums, and outdoor activities like hiking, climbing, kayaking etc. It is my favorite place I have ever lived, and also has a reasonable cost of living. Apparently *Men's Health* also proclaimed Portland one of the healthiest cities in the nation.

Status: Current student, full-time
Dates of Enrollment: 8/2005-Submit Date
Survey Submitted: April 2006

Portland and the surrounding areas are a great place to be. There are plenty of apartments available at various rents and no one seems to have a problem finding a place to live. The school does offer housing but it is on a first come, first serve basis.

Status: Current student, full-time
Dates of Enrollment: 8/2005-Submit Date
Survey Submitted: April 2006

Quality of life is the most important reason to come to Maine Law! If you love the outdoors, hiking, biking, healthy living, or kayaking Maine is the place for you. Crime is virtually nonexistent. Downtown Portland is beautiful, right on the water, and there are a surprising number of restaurants, theaters, and shops considering the small size of the city. Apartments are generally pretty easy to find. Many students live within walking distance of school. Rent for a nice two bedroom is generally around $800. The School just built a new parking garage so parking is never a problem.

The only complaint that can be lodged about Maine Law is the building. It is old, the heating system is terrible, and classrooms can sometimes be cramped. Rumor has it, that a new building is in the works. The law library is on the second and third floor of the law school building, and second and third year students are assigned study carols, which are wonderful if you like to study in the library.

Status: Current student, full-time
Dates of Enrollment: 9/2004-Submit Date
Survey Submitted: April 2006

Maine Law is a state school, loosely affiliated with the University of Maine system. Separated by a street from the University of Southern Maine's Portland campus, it takes one look at our round, cement building to know we're on our own. Hence, it's no surprise that there is no housing or any real "campus" for the School of Law. That said, Portland's numerous neighborhoods offer plenty of housing options.

The facilities are worn—I'd be lying if I said the school was anything other than old and slightly depressing. A new building is in the works, but not for another seven years or so. That said, we make do, our library, computer lab, cafe, moot court room, student lounge, etc., are fine. We are not going to win style awards any time soon, but this is a state school with a limited budget. Heck, to graduate without being saddled with $140K in debt from fancier schools is a sacrifice worth making.

The neighborhood is residential, but we're on a major intersection leading to the interstate and a major commercial street. Crime is rarely an issue, we're a very open and trusting school, and people leave laptops out and about, I think there's only been two thefts of anything in the two years I've been here. But, dude, look out for the parking ticket! There's a parking garage a good walk away, so if you utilize street parking, be vigilant! Tickets come fast and furious otherwise.

Status: Current student, full-time
Dates of Enrollment: 8/2005-Submit Date
Survey Submitted: April 2006

The students are very collegial and not competitive at all. Students will go out of their way to help other students. Most students live in apartments or houses in Portland. A few live in the dorm. Many also commute from nearby towns. Portland is a very safe, fun, small city. The campus housing is not near the law school, so I wouldn't recommend living there. If you rent an apartment, aim for downtown Portland rather than close to the school. The University of Southern Maine gym is horrible, so plan on getting a package at one of the local gyms (Planet Fitness, YMCA, or Bally's) if that is something you are interested in. The law school building itself is less than stellar, but the facilities are fine. The library is nice, and that is all that matters because you will be living there.

Read all of Vault's Law School Surveys at www.vault.com/lawschool — get complete surveys on top law schools, expert advice on applicaton essays, LSAT prep and more.

VAULT CAREER LIBRARY **287**

Status: Current student, full-time
Dates of Enrollment: 8/2003-Submit Date
Survey Submitted: April 2005

There is a dormitory located in downtown Portland, but the majority of the residents are undergraduate students. Most students rent apartments or houses near the school or in neighboring towns (the cheapest option). Be aware that the cost of housing in Portland is high. The facilities are adequate and the dining is decent, but rather expensive and fairly limited. The campus and surrounding neighborhood are very safe. Overall, Portland is a very safe, small city.

Status: Current student, full-time
Dates of Enrollment: 9/2003-Submit Date
Survey Submitted: April 2005

Life as a law student is probably sub-par to life prior to becoming a law student. However, as law school goes, Maine Law is not so bad. If you make sure to keep sleep and food a priority things will go smoothly. Maine Law is a branch of the University of Southern Maine. We use their financial aid, their dining services, their gym, and their computer facilities. The gym and computer labs are usually only crowded mid day. Financial aid is difficult to work with. They never tell you the same thing twice and they are usually less than eager to aid you. Housing is fairly readily available in Portland and cheaper than major metropolitan areas. (Most people pay $400 to $600 per month, depending on the neighborhood.) Crime exists, but you are in Maine so it is not that bad. There are plenty of good restaurants and pubs around and most parts of the city are within 10 minutes of school.

 Social Life

Status: Current student, full-time
Dates of Enrollment: 8/2003-Submit Date
Survey Submitted: April 2006

There are a number of bars, great restaurants (Standard American, plus Thai, Vietnamese, African, Japanese, Indian, etc.). The dating scene is a little limited because of the city's size. The school has small student groups that host events, lectures and lunches.

Status: Current student, full-time
Dates of Enrollment: 9/2005-Submit Date
Survey Submitted: April 2006

As mentioned above, the social life in Portland is great, with the state's semi-pro hockey and baseball teams right in town, hundreds of bars, lots of breweries and shops down near the water in the Old Port, and tons of restaurants of all kinds. There are great Thai, Indian and ethnic foods, markets, and organic grocers. There are clubs down in the Old Port that are hopping on the weekend with lots of undergrad students and also grad students and people travelling from outside Portland.

The school is very accessible to get to the airport, bus station, train station that travels to Boston, the largest mall in Maine, and both major highways. Most law students go out on Thursday nights to the same bar to meet older students and fraternize. Also, since the school is small, you get to know everyone and form good friendships and go out in groups for dinner or drinks a lot.

Status: Current student, full-time
Dates of Enrollment: 8/2005-Submit Date
Survey Submitted: April 2006

Each Thursday, the Men's Law Association hosts a get-together at one of the local bars. This is a great time for all to take a night off from reading and just have fun. There were annual picnics, some trips to Boston, and a formal at the end of the year. There is so much to do and see in Portland that one can never tire of the area.

Status: Current student, full-time
Dates of Enrollment: 8/2005-Submit Date
Survey Submitted: April 2006

Social life at Maine Law is what you make of it. The classes are small, about 75 to 85 students each, so if you make the effort you will know almost everyone by name. Every Thursday night is MLA night, a tradition at Maine Law, where

some secret group posts the name of a bar Thursday morning, and all the students go to that bar in the evening. It is really fun and a great way to blow off steam at the end of the week. Otherwise, opportunities to socialize abound and the workload is manageable enough that you can go out with friends on the weekends and have a good time.

Status: Current student, full-time
Dates of Enrollment: 8/2004-Submit Date
Survey Submitted: April 2006

Small, close-knit student population. Men's Law Association (MLA, open to everyone) chooses a bar for students to meet at Thursday evenings. It is the best way for 1L's to meet their classmates and the 2L and 3Ls.

Portland's Old Port has a lot of good bars, ranging from establishments for professionals to those frequented by the local fishermen. There are a variety of good restaurants with chefs from large cities who moved here for the more relaxed way of life. See *NYTimes* article "Two Portlands," fall 2005.

A lot of opportunities for outdoor activities.

Status: Current student, full-time
Dates of Enrollment: 9/2004-Submit Date
Survey Submitted: April 2006

Portland rocks. Although the school is located in a residential area, the Old Port section of the city is less than 10 minutes away. There is a plethora of music, bar, dining,and cultural options. The school itself has a bunch of student groups as well, and they are as loud and active as the students chose to make them.

The "Men's Law Association" is actually the weekly drinking/social event where the entire school is invited to a bar of choice. Not everyone comes, of course, but the evenings are a fun break from the daily grind. As for dating, it's a small school—dating is virtually nonexistent aside from those who pair up in first year and stick together.

The school does a good job of having speakers, panels, debates, and other activities on a regular basis. For example, we have one lecture series that draws a major figure each year, plus an annual nonprofit auction that raises money for students' salaries for summer intereships. Overall, Maine is an incredibly welcoming and comfortable place to attend law school. You've got three years to work your butt off, why not spend it at a school where people are not uber-intense, cutthroat, or super competitive. We simply don't work that way. Study groups turn into friendships, and outlines are shared, not stolen. While we work very hard and maintain some level of competition (mostly against our very own selves), we are supportive of one another. In addition, the administration and professors are accessible and there is no huge bureaucracy. State tuition + the ocean + a pleasant student body + talented faculty = three worthwhile years at Maine Law.

Status: Current student, full-time
Dates of Enrollment: 8/2005-Submit Date
Survey Submitted: April 2006

The classes are very small (the Class of 2008 is 73 people), so we all know each other very well. I am friends with almost everyone in my class—they are great people. There isn't a whole lot of interaction between different class years. Some people date classmates. Even though I grew up in the area and have friends around, I spend most of my time socializing with my law school friends. Every Thursday the Men's Law Association picks a bar to go to in town and 50 or so students go every week. I usually go out with my law school friends every weekend. Bull Feeneys is the bar for Maine Law, and Gritty's is a popular second.

There are tons of restaurants in Portland. The Great Lost Bear is a restaurant near school that is pretty popular—good food and beer, but over priced for what it is. After the last day of classes in the fall, the school buys kegs and the 1Ls put on a skit. In the spring their is a ball. There are picnics, golf tournaments, fund raisers, trips to Red Sox games...you name it. There are usually one or two lunchtime speakers every week as well. The school publishes the Maine Law Review and the *Ocean and Coastal Journal*, and also has a moot court team. There are many common interest associations as well as an active Student Bar Association.

Status: Current student, full-time
Dates of Enrollment: 8/2005-Submit Date
Survey Submitted: April 2006

There is very very little offered here for social life. Most students are from Maine and have family here. Therefore, there is less camaraderie of "we're all in this together" that I experienced at other law schools where students had moved to a new place specifically for law school. There is a weekly drink fest at a different Portland bar every Thursday which is jokingly referred to as "Men's Law Association." The clubs are good, considering that this is such a small school.

Status: Current student, full-time
Dates of Enrollment: 8/2003-Submit Date
Survey Submitted: April 2005

Portland is often called Boston's little brother. There are great standard American and ethnic restaurants. There's a range of bars from which to choose. Dating will be the last thing you'll be thinking about during the first year, but if you have the time, the dating scene is fairly casual.

Keep in mind that Portland is small (approximately 100k people). It's also important to note that Portland is the most progressive city in Maine and provides civil protections and offers some social options for gay men and women. There is no Greek system at the graduate level, and the undergraduate Greek system does not have a huge presence on campus. Law students are friendly and cordial, but small groups form quickly, so some will have to forge friendships and social connections outside of law school.

Status: Current student, full-time
Dates of Enrollment: 8/2004-Submit Date
Survey Submitted: April 2005

Students take school very seriously, but there are many student groups and a variety of near-by restaurants and bars in Portland. Every Thursday the Men's Law Association hosts gatherings at different downtown bars for all students. These events help students get to know members of other classes they may not otherwise have a lot of contact with. Other events include school-sponsored academic talks that are always interesting and include a reception. The school also puts on the "Barrister's Ball" each spring as well as an auction to raise money for public interest law fellowships. The Maine community is very active socially and academically.

Status: Current student, full-time
Dates of Enrollment: 8/2004-Submit Date
Survey Submitted: April 2005

The town of Portland consists of mostly young professionals and students. There is a great nightlife with many eclectic bars and pubs near the waterfront area. Gritty McDuff's (a.k.a., Gritty's) is a popular favorite in the local brewpub department. Most students keep an active social life, partially inspired by the weekly Men's Law Association Thursday night bar gatherings.

Status: Current student, full-time
Dates of Enrollment: 8/2003-Submit Date
Survey Submitted: April 2005

Social life? We're LAW students. That said, there are weekly trips to bars that are posted around the law school, of which many people partake. Also, people organize potluck dinners and other get-togethers if they are not as into the bar scene. We have a wide mix of students at the school from Maine and elsewhere and multiple age groups. We all get along really well.

Status: Alumnus/a, full-time
Dates of Enrollment: 8/1998-5/2001
Survey Submitted: April 2005

The school is small and the classes tend to be rather homogeneous in most respects other than age (there is a good mix of 23-year-olds fresh from undergrad, 30-year-olds who have worked for five years and are looking for a change, and 40, 50, and even a few 60-year-olds). Fortunately the people are relatively friendly and fun, but it helps to reach out to the general Portland social scene rather than relying entirely on the 80 other people in your class for all of your socializing needs.

 The School Says

Maine Law is a wonderful, distinctive place to study law. Students study law in a supportive and personalized environment and are prepared for success in today's global economy.

Maine Law holds a pivotal place in state and regional affairs and is a destination point for students, scholars and civic leaders from near and far. The state's only law school and one of the smallest in the nation, Maine Law fosters educational and scholarly excellence, professionalism and public service through a close community of faculty members and students. Our location in the vibrant coastal city of Portland, Maine—the largest city in the state and two hours north of Boston—allows students to benefit from a multitude of hands-on training opportunities offered through clinical programs, externships, community service projects and employment. We have a tradition of training remarkably distinguished graduates—governors, federal and state judges, prominent lawyers and civic leaders—who remain close to the law school. We are the law school of the University of Maine system and an administrative unit of the University of Southern Maine.

Read all of Vault's Law School Surveys at www.vault.com/lawschool — get complete surveys on top law schools, expert advice on applicaton essays, LSAT prep and more.

VAULT CAREER LIBRARY 289

University of Baltimore School of Law

Admissions Office
1420 North Charles Street
Baltimore, MD 21201-5779
Admissions phone: (410) 837-4459
Admissions fax: (410) 837-4450
Admissions e-mail: lwadmiss@ubalt.edu
Admissions URL: law.ubalt.edu/admissions/index.html

 ## Admissions

Status: Alumnus/a, part-time
Dates of Enrollment: 9/2000-12/2003
Survey Submitted: March 2006

The admissions process was smooth. I appreciate the returned phone calls from the admissions officer explaining in detail the part-time admissions process and the first-year class selection process.

Status: Alumnus/a, full-time
Dates of Enrollment: 8/2005-5/2006
Survey Submitted: May 2006

The admissions process was extremely straightforward; LSAC report, essay and transcript. If you had any further writing samples or activities you wanted the admission committee to know—you were encouraged to add an addendum. The Admissions Office also invited applicants to come to visit and have a one-on-one meeting with an admission counselor to go over and address questions and concerns about the program. Good grades and LSAT score will give you and edge, but don't count yourself out if either one are not the best. They do take a look at the whole application. Go talk to them face-to-face.

Status: Alumnus/a, full-time
Dates of Enrollment: 8/1991-5/1994
Survey Submitted: April 2005

When I applied to UB, there were only three requirements. We had to submit an application (which was surprisingly short), submit our LSAT scores (which, in most cases, had already been submitted because we selected prospective law schools when we took the test) and we had to submit official transcripts. It was an easy, user-friendly process, and the admissions office was responsive to all inquiries. The year I applied, UB had a lengthy waiting list and many students had to start as part-time or evening students. However, everyone I knew who started as a part-time or evening student was able to transition to a full-time day student by the second year.

Status: Current student, full-time
Dates of Enrollment: 8/2003-Submit Date
Survey Submitted: March 2004

The rolling admissions at UB are a fantastic way to increase your chances of being accepted. Four weeks after I sent in my completed application, I received my acceptance in the mail. I have since heard from faculty and admission staff that having a completed file (LSDAS file must be complete, too) in early is certainly a favorable situation. I believe the admissions department sponsors some social functions for applicants, and I strongly suggest attending them to increase your chances of being admitted by meeting some faculty members and showing interest in UB.

Status: Alumnus/a, full-time
Dates of Enrollment: 9/1999-5/2003
Survey Submitted: March 2005

The admissions process is fairly simple. There are no interviews involved. A personal statement, in addition to grades and LSAT score, however, is critical. If you have marginal grades and a fair LSAT score, you can make up for it by writing a superb personal statement. That's what I like so much about this school. It looks beyond grades and other academic success indicators and is willing to hear your story. This is not to say that a great personal statement will get you in even if you did poorly in college and on the LSAT, but at least you can be reassured that your personal story will be considered.

Status: Alumnus/a, full-time
Dates of Enrollment: 8/1972-5/1977
Survey Submitted: September 2003

The process includes submission of an application form, revealing prior education, degrees, GPA, honors, prior work experience and LSAT score. On my own, I also chose to speak with the head of the admissions office to discuss how their full-time evening program would mesh with my full-time day job in downtown D.C. and my three-way commute from Falls Church, VA.

Status: Alumnus/a, full-time
Dates of Enrollment: 9/1990-5/1993
Survey Submitted: September 2003

I'm afraid I can't help much here; I had a 3.8 GPA, strong LSATs and other activities on my resume but I don't know what the school valued more. Since 1990, it has been even tougher to get in. Don't think you can get in because it's a "state school." It's tough! One thing I would suggest to anyone considering a first year: take a bar review course NOW. It will prepare you for the subjects in first-year, and help confirm if you're ready for the stress of three more years.

 ## Academics

Status: Alumnus/a, part-time
Dates of Enrollment: 9/2000-12/2003
Survey Submitted: March 2006

Generally, your courses could be as challenging as you wanted them to be. There were certain professors to steer clear of if you didn't want to work hard or be challenged. I typically chose classes that prepared me for the bar exam regardless of the professor.

Status: Alumnus/a, full-time
Dates of Enrollment: 8/2005-5/2006
Survey Submitted: May 2006

Like any other JD program, your courseload is filled with the usual suspect courses: Civil Procedure, Torts, Property, Constitutional Law and Contracts. Also, there's a tremendous amount of reading. What makes the first year so incredibly hard for law students is not understanding how the game is played. You're not going to have a test until the end of the semester—what do you do 'til then? How do you know that you understand the material? During the semester, professors at UB are more than willing to go out of their way to make sure you get it—e-mail, office hours, appointments, phone...The trick is that you have to make the first move. You've got to stay on top of the information to KNOW you don't know it. Trying to talk to them during finals week isn't going to help you. They won't answer you anyway.

There is only going to be a small amount of A's because the curve for each course must be within 2.25 to 2.75 somewhere around there—so you've got to stay on top of the workload—even though it's immense. Get the book *Law School Confidential* and invest in *Law Preview*—something that gives you insight about what you're going to see and summaries of what to get out of each course because you're going to be moving, reading and writing too fast to really see the big picture. Get the big picture first, then fill in all the little details.

UB offers what they call Law Scholars for each subject. These are students who took the same course with the same professor and got the highest grade in the course. Some of them are average and some are fantastic—what this gives you is an opportunity to talk out your problems in the subject area and get feedback. It also forces you to stay on top of your work.

UB prides itself on its LARW program because they tell you that students from other schools graduate and can't even write a legal brief well. I don't know how true that is, but if UB's program is better—it can't be by much. The LARW program is taught by "writing professors" who are actual lawyers out in the field. The come in as adjunct to teach you how to research and write a brief, memo and other forms of legal writing. LARW is a three-part series, which means you get three different professors. The goal is to learn how to write in three different styles of writing. The goal fails because professor never REALLY tell you how to construct a brief or a memo. All of that is self-taught. You go into the first draft blind—praying you find a sample on the Internet—and after you get it back with a grade that brings you to tears or drives you to an alcoholic beverage—you correct what you did wrong. BUT that's not only it!!! You don't just correct what's wrong—you must go back to the guessing game to make sure that you've constructed the brief correctly.

Some writing professors are wonderful about teaching how to pull it together. And some...well, I have some serious doubts about whether they actually practice law outside UB! The first semester of LARW is a nightmare because it's a savenger hunt for an entire semester—you go to the library to look up stuff that a workbook gives you clues about...if you've ever been a paralegal before—take some Advil with you to the library—it's going to be a long weekend. If you have never been a paralegal—pray and become friends with the librarian.

The next two semesters in LARW are supposed to be a breeze if you can take one of them over the summer and get it out of the way. Remember that the first year at UB is graded on a curve. That might not seem like a problem, but when it comes time to get a job—employers only look at your first-year grades! Yeah the school will tell you that your second year counts, but if you want to get into a major firm—those first-year grades weigh a helluva lot more.

As far as getting into popular courses, UB has so many requirements (two upper-level writing requirements, advocacy and perspectives courses) on top of the ones that they suggest you take to pass the bar—it's hard to say. Where would you find the time unless you plan to graduate in seven years?!! You MUST make sure that you plan your concentration EARLY. Because UB is a small school, not all seminars and courses are offered every semester. So if you miss it the first time, you might have to wait out a semester.

Otherwise, the professors (outside of the LARW program) are what really make the program. They are highly educated, motivated and really know their subject matter. They offer every opportunity for you get to know them. I have heard that many people even get job contacts through them. You just have to initiate the relationship with them.

Status: Alumnus/a, full-time
Dates of Enrollment: 8/1991-5/1994
Survey Submitted: April 2005

As with anything, you get out of law school what you put into it. I applied myself as best I could and received a topnotch education. The professors were approachable, knowledgeable and reasonable. Each professor followed his or her syllabus closely, so students always knew what to expect. Most professors put former exams on reserve at the library so that students could see what to expect on exams. The larger classes had no more than 75 to 80 students, and the smaller classes often had no more than 20 to 25 students. Grading was reasonable. Generally, there was the typical breakdown of grades with there being mostly B's and C's and only a few A's and D's/F's. The workload was also reasonable, but it was up to each student to pace him/herself.

Professors didn't baby the students, but they were always available for giving extra support and time management advice. As a first-year selecting classes for my second year, it was difficult to get the classes I wanted. I took a three-credit elective the summer between my first and second years and that put me ahead of most of the other second-year students in number of credits. This enabled me to register for classes before the rest of the second years when I was registering for classes in my second year, second semester and thereafter. I was well-prepared for the Maryland Bar exam because UB professors spent a lot of time on Maryland law.

Status: Alumnus/a, full-time
Dates of Enrollment: 8/2001-5/2004
Survey Submitted: January 2005

My first year was extremely trying. We had a great deal of work to do. However, my classmates and professors made this time less harsh.

Status: Current student, full-time
Dates of Enrollment: 8/2003-Submit Date
Survey Submitted: March 2004

The academics are rigorous, as I assume they are everywhere. The first-year program is standard, and the first-year teachers are mostly excellent teachers, with a passion for the Socratic Method. Having been adequately prepared my first year, the second year has been a much more enjoyable experience, and I am in a position to learn as much as I can. UB offers very specific Maryland Bar exam classes, which focus on enhancing a students chance to pass the bar exam. I have had no problem getting popular classes, as there are typically several sections (usually at least one day section and one night section).

Having both day and night classes makes getting popular classes and teachers much easier. The workload for the day classes is noticeably heavier than that of night classes. The night classes tend to recognize that night students are at work full time, going to school at night and are less intense about reading assignments and overall workload. The seeming theory of night professors is that it is more important for the students to come to every session, than to miss class because they [didn't do the reading]. Night classes technically start as early at 4 p.m.— and many day students also take a few "night" classes.

Status: Alumnus/a, full-time
Dates of Enrollment: 9/1999-5/2003
Survey Submitted: March 2005

This is an awesome school. There is no horrible grade inflation policy in place. The professors are really awesome and they are reasonable and understanding when it comes to workload. My favorite thing about this school is the awesome Clinical Law Program, which allows law students to handle real cases. The program is excellent because it really forces law students to learn (in a hurry) the practice of law. It prepares law students for what will inevitably face them in their first law job out of law school.

Status: Alumnus/a, full-time
Dates of Enrollment: 8/1972-5/1977
Survey Submitted: September 2003

The academic program is strong and competitive. It features a sound basis in the fundamentals—contract law, criminal law and procedure, civil procedure, legal writing and research, and torts, among others. The coursework also regularly compares Maryland law with federal law. Grading was done in a fair manner— examination answers that recognized and dealt with all relevant issues tended to receive high scores, even if the ultimate conclusion differed from the one preferred by the professor. Popular classes were accessible. The faculty contained a mixture of full-timers and outstanding adjunct staff who were distinguished judges and practitioners (i.e., Ron Shapiro, former MD State Securities Commissioner and current well-known sports agent). The workload was substantial but not overwhelming.

Status: Alumnus/a, full-time
Dates of Enrollment: 9/1990-5/1993
Survey Submitted: September 2003

As with other law schools, group study is critical to honing your thinking. The education I received here surpasses anything I've experienced based on interactions with lawyers who went to other schools. Take advantage of the wonderful Clinical Law Program, and do whatever it takes to get on law review. This doesn't enjoy an Ivy League reputation yet, so you need to distinguish yourself.

Read all of Vault's Law School Surveys at www.vault.com/lawschool — get complete surveys on top law schools, expert advice on applicaton essays, LSAT prep and more.

VAULT CAREER LIBRARY 291

Employment Prospects

Status: Alumnus/a, part-time
Dates of Enrollment: 9/2000-12/2003
Survey Submitted: March 2006

UB is fine for employment in the local legal field in Maryland. However, if your goal is to work for a national firm, it's possible provided that: (1) you do very well academically; (2) you are active in law review/law journal; (3) you work as a summer associate at a good firm; and/or (4) clerk for a MD appellate-level or federal judge. UB is not well known outside of MD and not respected outside of MD.

Status: Alumnus/a, full-time
Dates of Enrollment: 8/2005-5/2006
Survey Submitted: May 2006

This is a fourth-tier school. Please don't forget that; whether we want to admit it or not employers look at those rankings to decide whether or not they'll hire from a particular school. If you want to work in a large Baltimore firm such as Venable and DLP Piper—then you might have a chance. That chance is still small even if you're graduating in the top third of the class.

If you want to work in the public sector—then this school is for you! Why? It's cheap and many judges, prosecutors and public defenders have graduated from this school. In the state arena this school is big news. Also, the school has programs that offer a free year of tuition if you go into public sector and commit to a few years of working there.

However, if your dream is to work for one of the large, magnificent firms in D.C. or New York—forget it. This school just doesn't have prestige with the larger, more prominent firms in the area.

I applied to the same firm I was a legal assistant with in D.C. as a summer clerk and my old boss literally laughed! He wasn't trying to be mean, but when firms in the area have Georgetown, GW, American, Catholic and Maryland, which are all Top 50 schools, why would they go to a fourth-tier? A lot of graduates go into self-employment and state government. Only a small number get that golden salary of $125,000 a year starting out after graduation. The alumni network is small—most of them you will meet as your writing professor for LARW.

The career center at UB is great—extremely helpful staff to 1Ls, 2Ls and 3Ls. The staff will do whatever they can to help you find your dream job. But they are not a job agency. You have to do a good amount of leg work yourself. Make sure you send out your letters and resumes during your second semester first year and first semester of your second year.

The other great thing about UB is that if you've never held a legal job at all then the school offers judicial and attorney practice internships that are only open to 1Ls—called the EXPLOR program. This is to get your feet wet and add something credible to your resume. They do offer on-campus recruiting but the opportunities are small.

Status: Alumnus/a, full-time
Dates of Enrollment: 8/1991-5/1994
Survey Submitted: April 2005

UB is well-respected among the Baltimore law firms and judges. The judge I clerked for was a UB graduate, and he is still active in the UB community. I believe graduating from UB made me a more attractive candidate because UB is known for turning out quality attorneys. Graduates usually end up at Baltimore law firms, in clerkships or at the state's attorney or public defender's office. The alumni network is very strong. UB alumni maintain contacts at the career counseling office, so there are always doors that are already open for UB graduates. Internships are widely available and have proven to be great methods of networking for students. UB's internships and mentoring program are the most impressive things UB has to offer its students.

Status: Alumnus/a, full-time
Dates of Enrollment: 8/2001-5/2004
Survey Submitted: January 2005

My friends and I typically found jobs at law firms.

Status: Current student, full-time
Dates of Enrollment: 8/2003-Submit Date
Survey Submitted: March 2004

There are so many career opportunities at UB. First, the e-attorney web site is boasted by the career center to be the best way to find a job, and I agree. I found a job on e-attorney, which is a great site as you can see the description, requirements and salary all in one little blurb. Also, having a posted date lets you know if the position is likely already filled. Second, the EXPLOR program for summer internships is a great way to land a job and start making contacts (to one day lead to a paying job). My only problem with this program is that it requires students to sign up early in the school year, and commit to volunteering all summer when the UB faculty member finds the student a job. Third, the Legal Writing Program uses local lawyers and judges as writing professors, which affords a student a great way to make some legal contacts. I know several students who used their writing professors to get interviews, and eventually jobs. Better still, there is a new writing professor for each of the three required semesters of legal writing, so you have a good chance to meet several different contacts. Finally, as a participant in the client counseling competition this year, I can confidently say that school activities often offer students networking opportunities. At the reception after the competition, local lawyers (who were the competition judges) were mingling with the competition participants and often offering summer job advice.

Status: Alumnus/a, full-time
Dates of Enrollment: 9/1999-9/2003
Survey Submitted: March 2005

If you remain on the East Coast after graduating from this law school, your chances of finding a law job are pretty good, especially if you graduated in the top third of your class. This school is known for its clinical law program and if you participate in that, it will help you find a job. This is one of two law schools in Maryland and is the better one of the two law schools, so if you are staying in Maryland after law school you are pretty much guaranteed a job.

Status: Alumnus/a, full-time
Dates of Enrollment: 8/1972-5/1977
Survey Submitted: September 2003

In the 1970s, the best job prospects for UB Law grads were in MD firms, state agencies and corporations located within the state. Now, UB law grads are more readily employed by the better firms in D.C. and elsewhere, and federal agencies. The prestige of the program has definitely grown. A few years ago, the new physical facilities (including greatly expanded library space) were completed, and in recognition of one of its great benefactors, the school is now known as the Peter Angelos School of Law.

Quality of Life

Status: Alumnus/a, part-time
Dates of Enrollment: 9/2000-12/2003
Survey Submitted: March 2006

Good neighborhood location of campus. Housing is limited. I've heard that the student facilities have improved greatly as a new student center has opened.

> **The school says:** "In the spring 2006 semester, the University of Baltimore hosted the grand opening of its new Student Center. This modern building features comfortable study space, food and coffee service, function rooms, meeting space, a game room and a large student organization workroom."

Status: Alumnus/a, full-time
Dates of Enrollment: 8/2005-5/2006
Survey Submitted: May 2006

Baltimore has gotten better in the last two years. Crime is still prevalent, but the area around UB has improved. Housing in Baltimore is relatively cheap in comparison to other areas, such as D.C. You can still find a nice apartment for $700 to $850 a month. The campus is pretty small and the law school is located right off the Highway 83 and a few blocks from I-95, which allows students to commute from other areas. Entertainment can be found within walking distance from the school. There are nice restaurants and the Opera House has concerts by well-known artists.

During the winter months you can't sit outside—it can be depressing if all you do is hang out in the law school. The business center and the new student center offer law students an air of reprieve and loads of light. They also serve as places to get away from anyone who wants to talk about school, quiet rooms, food service, a coffee bar and lots of seating near windows.

As far as places to eat—the cheapest places are Subway and Blimpie. You may get sick of sandwiches, but it's a good way to save money. Otherwise bring lunch.

The law library...well...you can use other area law libraries at least.

Status: Alumnus/a, full-time
Dates of Enrollment: 8/1991-5/1994
Survey Submitted: April 2005

To my knowledge, there is no housing available, but there are many affordable options for students in the area. The campus is small but it is truly spectacular—always neat, well-maintained, landscaped and appealing. There aren't a lot of facilities, but what they have certainly meets the needs of the student population. There is a very nice dining hall and a couple of delis in the area that have late hours to accommodate the law students. The neighborhood is one of the better neighborhoods in Baltimore. I would guess that its crime rate is very low, but I don't know that for sure. Campus police are always visible, and it's rare to see a stranger on campus. As a single mother going to law school full time, I was impressed with my overall quality of life. UB was a school where I could learn a great deal while still having a life outside of school.

Status: Alumnus/a, full-time
Dates of Enrollment: 8/2001-5/2004
Survey Submitted: January 2005

Because the campus is located in the city, there were a few incidents of crime. However, there were more than enough social activities.

Status: Current student, full-time
Dates of Enrollment: 8/2003-Submit Date
Survey Submitted: March 2004

To be honest, the facilities at UB leave much to be desired. The buildings are old, there is no wireless Internet in the classrooms or in the law library and even the elevators in the law school building are old and slow. There are several computer labs around campus but they require a log-in and password, which are only valid for a semester. I have not checked my UB e-mail account in over a year since it is difficult to use and the password changes constantly. Not a very user-friendly style of e-mail. The Prometheus web site (where some classes have portals) is sometimes helpful, and there are old exams available on Prometheus. The neighborhood is kind of seedy, but it is turning around. Businesses are opening in the immediate neighborhood, houses are being redone and the crime is lessening.

> **The school says:** "The entire school building, including the Law Library, is wireless capable and Internet connections are available in the Library."

Status: Alumnus/a, full-time
Dates of Enrollment: 9/1999-5/2003
Survey Submitted: March 2005

Quality of life issues are one downfall of this school. The school, itself is absolutely beautiful. It was just built and is absolutely gorgeous. However, the surroundings of the school are not so gorgeous or beautiful.

> **The school says:** "The law school building was not recently built. However many parts have undergone renovation in an ongoing attempt to improve our facility."

Status: Alumnus/a, full-time
Dates of Enrollment: 8/1972-5/1977
Survey Submitted: September 2003

Many of the students commute from the Greater Baltimore area. The attractiveness of Baltimore has been greatly enhanced by the development of the Inner Harbor and the Camden Yards baseball (Orioles) and football (Ravens) facilities, which are but 15 minutes away from campus. Baltimore, like all big cities, has some better areas and some less desirable areas. The school seems to be safe and is accessible (within 30 to 45 minutes) to all areas of greater Baltimore.

Status: Alumnus/a, full-time
Dates of Enrollment: 9/1990-5/1993
Survey Submitted: September 2003

Baltimore has become a fabulous mid-size city!

 ## Social Life

Status: Alumnus/a, part-time
Dates of Enrollment: 9/2000-12/2003
Survey Submitted: March 2006

Lots of good restaurants and bars in the downtown area a short cab ride away. The school is mostly a commuter school, so not many evening activities.

Status: Alumnus/a, full-time
Dates of Enrollment: 8/2005-5/2006
Survey Submitted: May 2006

What social life? You're a law student—erase the idea social life from your SOUL! You have two choices: do mediocre in law school and have a great social life or do excellent in law school and have a thread of a social life. While your debating the answer, remind yourself that this is a fourth-tier school and you NEED a job after school!

There are many, many organizations on campus. Some of them have job information sessions and speakers that come during the afternoon when you need to be in the law scholar review session. Or they'll have some riveting meeting when you have to work on your LARW memo. Time will be your enemy in about everything you want to get involved in.

UB does not help with making certain that activities are held when students can make them. They try to hold events either in the morning or evening, but that's it. The professors are usually the ones that step in and make sure they aren't assigning something when you have a memo or brief due for LARW or overlapping a review when you have a law scholar. Professors even remind you of some of the events they think you should be involved in if you're interested in a particular field.

Like a number of law schools around the nation, social activites after hours involve alcohol. It's usually a block party with beer, happy hour, real estate club happy hour, PAD happy hour, family law happy hour...you get the picture. There are athletic events that many students participate in, such as the basketball tournament or flag football.

No, there isn't any hiding books in the library here. Like any law school there are cliques—some are more trustworthy than others. The curve that is imposed on the first-year class just creates this environment of "I've got to be better than everyone to get ahead." It does make it a little hard to relax among people who may not have your best interest at heart.

Status: Alumnus/a, full-time
Dates of Enrollment: 8/1991-5/1994
Survey Submitted: April 2005

The social life of UB students does not center around UB other than to the extent students gather at local delis to hang out. Generally, students' social lives center around the Baltimore social life, which includes Fell's Point (a popular area for young professionals with lots of bars and places to dance) and Canton (an area becoming increasingly popular among young professionals with lots of restaurants and bars). It seemed like there were a lot of law students dating and

Read all of Vault's Law School Surveys at www.vault.com/lawschool — get complete surveys on top law schools, expert advice on applicaton essays, LSAT prep and more.

VAULT CAREER LIBRARY   293

marrying each other. To a large degree, it was as if we lived in our own little world at UB. Most of our socializing occurred off campus in Fell's Point, in Canton or at someone's house or apartment.

Status: Current student, full-time
Dates of Enrollment: 8/2003-Submit Date
Survey Submitted: March 2004

There are a number of bars and restaurants within walking distance of the law school that are often filled with students on Friday nights or during NCAA tournament times. A few times a year there are carnivals in front of the law school where there are attractions, beer trucks and food. Also, the school sponsors a Barrister's Ball formal dance at an upscale venue in the city—definitely a student favorite. There is a basketball league that plays at the school gym which is a student favorite, also. There are several teams, made up with students of all years at UB, who like the competition, exercise and friendly rivalries.

Status: Alumnus/a, full-time
Dates of Enrollment: 9/1999-5/2003
Survey Submitted: March 2005

This law school provides a great social experience. You will meet people from every cultural, regional and ethnic background. The law school has plenty of bars and restaurants in the vicinity and these bars and restaurants have lots of character! The law student body is a very closely knit group here.

Status: Alumnus/a, full-time
Dates of Enrollment: 8/1972-5/1977
Survey Submitted: September 2003

Because I commuted from Falls Church, VA to a full-time day job in D.C. and then to the full-time evening program at UB, the social life aspects were not of major importance to me. But, the school is within 15 minutes of the Inner Harbor, Little Italy and other prime social spots.

Status: Alumnus/a, full-time
Dates of Enrollment: 9/1990-5/1993
Survey Submitted: September 2003

Not much; does any law school have social life? Fells Point is fun!

University of Maryland School of Law

Admissions Office
500 West Baltimore Street, Room 130
Baltimore, MD 21201-1786
Admissions phone: (410) 706-3492
Admissions e-mail: admissions@law.umaryland.edu
Admissions URL:
www.law.umaryland.edu/prospective.asp

 Admissions

Status: Current student, full-time
Dates of Enrollment: 8/2005-Submit Date
Survey Submitted: June 2006

Maryland's process appears very similar to other schools from the student end. I applied online through LSAC in November. By applying relatively early, I heard back from Maryland quickly—they sent me an acceptance within five or six weeks. I have since had the opportunity to discuss the admissions process with some faculty and staff members. The consensus was that while Maryland does not look for any special combination (other than the usual strong grades and LSAT scores), they do favor students: (1) with a public service background or who intend to seek a career in public service law; and (2) who have some time out of school in a challenging job. As a career-changer, I am gratified to discover that a significant portion of the students at Maryland applied after one to four years in the workforce.

Maryland also seems to have built a significant merit scholarship program in recent years. I was one of more than 55 recipients of such a scholarship in a full-time day student class of just over 200. Maryland invited prospective merit scholars to interview for the program in April. Though a little late in the decision-making process, the interview day sold me completely on the school and made the prospect of attending Maryland, in general and as a merit scholar, extremely exciting.

Status: Alumnus/a, full-time
Dates of Enrollment: 1/2000-1/2003
Survey Submitted: June 2006

Standard admissions process. Know the strengths of the school (business law journal, environmental law is huge, healthcare law certificate). Have a good story to tell in addition to a good LSAT and grades. Be diverse (not necessarily in ethnicity). In your personal statement, explain why your background (i.e., ice cream entrepreneur) has prepared you to take on law school and WHY you want to be a lawyer. Be careful about buzz words ("blind justice") as the readers are astute and will call your bluff. Be sincere and don't be a know-it-all, just be yourself.

Status: Current student, full-time
Dates of Enrollment: 8/2004-Submit Date
Survey Submitted: June 2006

The school is focusing on climbing the rankings, which means that the raw scores (GPA/LSAT) are getting an increased focus. There is less chance of a good recommendation bumping you up the list. However, since the school competes with the D.C. schools for top students, those on the waitlist tend to get offers of admission during the summer as students decline Maryland to attend Georgetown or George Washington.

Status: Current student, full-time
Dates of Enrollment: 8/2005-Submit Date
Survey Submitted: May 2006

The faculty and staff were very friendly during the admissions process. I became well acquainted with various deans and helpful members of the admissions staff. I was asked to visit the campus for scholarship interviews and they flew me in from the small town where I was going to undergrad, paid for a hotel and set up a lovely dinner with various deans and other scholarship candidates. No other school went to such great lengths.

Status: Current student, full-time
Dates of Enrollment: 8/2004-Submit Date
Survey Submitted: May 2006

The admissions process was good. I took a tour of the school before I made my decision and the admissions officer who gave the tour was very helpful. The application process was average. Personal statement, GPA and far too much emphasis on the LSAT. Unfortunately the LSAT issue pervades all law school admission processes.

Status: Current student, full-time
Dates of Enrollment: 9/2005-Submit Date
Survey Submitted: May 2006

The admissions process seems to put a lot of emphasis on diversity, which may in fact be hurting its rankings. They seem to eat up essays that have any sort of liberal slant. The school is trying to be more selective, but if you get waitlisted, don't worry, chances are you will get in. Most of the students I have talked to were taken off the waitlist. I was actually really surprised by the number of students from the Ivies and other prestigious undergrad programs.

Status: Current student, full-time
Dates of Enrollment: 9/2004-Submit Date
Survey Submitted: May 2006

Maryland is committed to diversity of all kinds—race, class, gender, previous employment, returning students, different majors. The admissions committee seems committed to ensuring that the incoming class is well-balanced and interesting. As far as I know, there are no interviews given. Maryland can be quite selective, more so than some of the higher-ranked schools.

Status: Alumnus/a, full-time
Dates of Enrollment: 8/2003-5/2006
Survey Submitted: May 2006

I thought the admissions process was stringent. I was unable to get an interview however others told me that I had a good chance of getting in with my scores. The admissions staff was friendly and helpful whenever I had any questions about the application or the school. I suggest taking a tour of the school.

Status: Alumnus/a, full-time
Dates of Enrollment: 8/1998-5/2001
Survey Submitted: March 2006

The admissions process includes an application, an essay and the LSAT. The admissions office clearly gives great weight to the essay, or the "personal statement," regarding why a student wishes to attend law school. A well-written, thoughtful personal statement can make the difference between acceptance and denial for those students who are "borderline" based on their previous undergrad grades and LSAT scores. As proof they read the statements, my acceptance letter came with a personal, hand-written note from the dean commenting on my statement! Maryland also looks for students who have "done something" with their lives and are not just going to law school straight out of college for lack of direction or a better idea.

Status: Current student, full-time
Dates of Enrollment: 8/2003-Submit Date
Survey Submitted: May 2004

They say getting in is the hardest part of law school at UMD. It's become a really popular school both for quality and for price. I would venture to say that your essay is equally important, if not more than your LSAT scores. Most people applying will have LSAT scores in the same general area—so make sure your essay sets you apart. The admissions team really seems to look for people that will add something to a class.

Read all of Vault's Law School Surveys at www.vault.com/lawschool — get complete surveys on top law schools, expert advice on applicaton essays, LSAT prep and more.

VAULT CAREER LIBRARY 295

Status: Current student, full-time
Dates of Enrollment: 8/2001-Submit Date
Survey Submitted: September 2003

Apply early to law school. I applied late and got lucky. I think out-of-school experience and high LSATs compensate for low undergraduate GPA.

 ## Academics

Status: Current student, full-time
Dates of Enrollment: 8/2005-Submit Date
Survey Submitted: June 2006

The workload for a first-year at Maryland equals or exceeds that of other first-year law programs. Each semester of first-year, students are assigned to sections of four "substantive law" classes (one of the four in second semester is an elective). First-years take an intensive writing class both semesters and an intensive eight-week research class in second semester. In the first semester, the writing class is paired with a substantive law class, so students also receive a kind of practical application of what they are learning through writing memos. Requirements beyond the first year include a third semester of writing, a second research class, a second semester of Con Law (semester one is in first-year) and a legal ethics and professionalism class. Maryland also requires that all students complete an experiential-learning class, basically a clinic, where they work on real cases and/or for real clients.

First-year classes are excellent. The core faculty are, for the most part, great teachers of the foundational classes. Maryland is a "state school" but has the feel of a small liberal arts college. Professors have an open-door policy and are very available to meet with students, clarify confusing points of law and doctrine and suggest methods for further study. Almost all of my first-year classes included intensive (optional) study sessions prior to the exam conducted by the professors. And most of the professors made themselves available to students through phone, e-mail and personal meetings in the days prior to exams to address last-minute questions and concerns. The overall atmosphere at Maryland is respect for the students and a commitment to their learning and success.

Status: Current student, full-time
Dates of Enrollment: 8/2005-Submit Date
Survey Submitted: June 2006

It was my expectation that the law school would dramatically expand my horizons and enhance my analytical ability much in the way college did, but, inconceivably, the opposite seems to have happened as a result of the unimaginative teaching method. Originality is discouraged. Socratic Method is used scarcely, if ever. Grading can be subjective and/or inaccurate (multiple-choice grades were changed on several occasions due to coding mistakes, who knows how many went undetected?). Worse of all, the school strives to differentiate itself by being exceedingly patronizing: there are numerous "how to study" sessions worthy of a community college, the students are continuously being reassured that "it's going to be ok," deadlines for papers get pushed back if there is enough whining and the pace of the first-semester classes is downright embarrassing (slow). This may be well and nice, but it is simply not a way to prepare future lawyers!

Status: Alumnus/a, full-time
Dates of Enrollment: 1/2000-1/2003
Survey Submitted: June 2006

Grading is tough and you will see a lot of students working very hard in the end of the semester. Good grades are not impossible if the work is put in. The quality of the classes is high, as most professors are very distinguished in their fields. Many take a Maryland angle for their classes, so if you are looking to practice outside the state some quirks in the law may not apply. Getting classes is competitive the first year and a half, but eases up dramatically as seniority in the school puts you ahead of others in picking classes. The student association provides an anonymous feedback system on classes and professors that you can read and that are very helpful in determining which class to take. In general, seminars are nice breaks from the "tough" classes, but should not be taken too lightly as a paper with significant research is normally required.

Status: Alumnus/a, full-time
Dates of Enrollment: 8/2003-5/2006
Survey Submitted: June 2006

The academics were overall outstanding here, especially the options in the clinical law program. The workload is consistent with any other top law school in the nation, but is definitely manageable and becomes easier as the years go on. I never had a problem getting into a class I wanted. The professors were very competent, a bit arrogant, yet very experienced in their fields and good teachers. A few went above and beyond the call of duty and became great mentors and friends.

Status: Current student, full-time
Dates of Enrollment: 9/2005-Submit Date
Survey Submitted: May 2006

The courseload is exhausting. You start off taking a mandatory 16 credits your first semester. Expect to do at least 60 hours of work a week. The second semester you must take 13 credits of assigned classes and a mandatory two- or three-credit elective. Your second and third year you choose your classes but you must take certain classes in order to graduate. The school reserves most bar-classes (Business Associations and Evidence) for second-year students, so you are more likely to get those classes if you apply your second year. As well, you get a wild card that allows to walk into any class that you need.

Status: Alumnus/a, full-time
Dates of Enrollment: 8/2003-5/2006
Survey Submitted: May 2006

Naturally there is a little dead wood, but on the whole the professors are good and quite a few are outstanding. Classes are mostly practice-oriented, not incredibly theoretical, but still conducted on a pretty high intellectual level. Through course selection, your experience can be not-all-that-demanding or really very challenging. I had little trouble getting classes with popular professors.

Status: Current student, full-time
Dates of Enrollment: 9/2004-Submit Date
Survey Submitted: May 2006

Professors at Maryland are enthusiastic and very knowledgeable about their subject matter. Getting the most popular classes is generally pretty easy—everyone can pretty much take what they want before graduating, but you may not get your ideal schedule every semester. Maryland does abide by a pretty tough (comparatively to other schools) B- curve. The workload is as to be expected, but only during finals do you feel like you can't get anything done.

Status: Current student, full-time
Dates of Enrollment: 8/2004-Submit Date
Survey Submitted: May 2006

The faculty at the University of Maryland School of Law far surpassed my expectations. Of the eight full-time faculty members I had my first year, six were Harvard Law graduates. (The other two attended Yale and Duke law schools.) Going into my third year, I have had no difficulty getting into the classes I selected. The workload is typical for law school; e.g., 500+ pages of reading a week. The grading is on a B- curve for the first year, but seems to be on a B/B+ curve the second year. *The Maryland Law Review* is an excellent journal and a terrific academic experience.

Status: Current student, full-time
Dates of Enrollment: 8/2004-Submit Date
Survey Submitted: May 2006

Getting into classes at Maryland is difficult because they insist on only offering one section of each bar course. My approach to law school was to take classes that applied to the bar exam yet each semester they insist on only offering one section of each and it often meets at night, which I did not like. They offer a wide range of seminars, which is great but not as useful as the bar courses.

Status: Alumnus/a, full-time
Dates of Enrollment: 8/1998-5/2001
Survey Submitted: March 2005

The academic program was probably comparable to many other programs, except that when studying for the bar, I discovered that Maryland focused a lot on the "details" of the law, while the people I met from Ivy schools focused more on theory. Therefore, I knew a lot more of what I needed to know when it came to passing the bar than they did!! All first-years are broken down into 25-person, "small sections." You have one class with just your small section. Other classes might combine two or three small sections. You take all your classes your first year with your "small section." These classmates generally become your closest friends and confidants and you all help each other through the first year. Maryland is not a "cutthroat" kind of school, everyone helps everyone get through it. Classes are not huge, the most people I ever had in any class was about 75. Normally there were 25 to 50 in a class.

A "fall back" plan is to take classes at the "other" Baltimore law school. The great thing about classes at the "other" school is that the credit transfers, but the grade does not! It was a relaxing way to take some upper-level courses and not have to fret about the final grade—a C was required for credit. The "other" school also offered some classes that we did not, which was a good way to try new things. The "other" school did not require additional fees as the schools are part of the same system.

Maryland recently revamped their writing program for the better. More writing classes are required and you can fulfill the requirement a number of different ways. The writing programs are generally in your "small section" classes your first year and you get a lot of attention. Professors are accessible for help in improving your writing. The workload is tough your first year. If you don't have to work, then don't. I treated law school as my job, and worked every day from 9 a.m. to 5 p.m. regardless of how few classes I might have that day. I spent time between classes in the library rather than socializing (well, sometimes I couldn't help myself). It worked well for me; I didn't feel pushed in the last two weeks to try to learn the entire semester.

Status: Alumnus/a, JD/MBA
Dates of Enrollment: 8/2000-5/2003
Survey Submitted: April 2004

Classes were easy to enroll in and challenging all around. If you wanted to, you could very easily create a customized course of study. I, for example, did a JD/MBA and focused studies on corporate law. I even taught a small section of an elective "Basic Business Law Concepts" for first-years.

> **Regarding academics, the school says:** "UM Law School's writing program has been revised: for information contact Professor Susan Hankin at shankin@law.umaryland.edu"

Employment Prospects

Status: Alumnus/a, full-time
Dates of Enrollment: 8/2003-5/2006
Survey Submitted: May 2006

A good fraction of my class got jobs with large firms through on-campus recruiting, and many people had jobs by graduation, though certainly not everyone. UMD is without question the best place to go to law school if you want to practice in Baltimore—you'd be crazy to go anywhere else. It seems like about half the practicing attorneys in this town are alumni. If you are involved in an activity like Law Review or moot court, you have an instant connection with alumni who were involved in that, too. The school has great internship opportunities in judges' chambers and legislative internships in Annapolis and D.C. If you want one, they will get you one, even if you are not a star student.

Status: Current student, full-time
Dates of Enrollment: 8/2004-Submit Date
Survey Submitted: May 2006

If you are at the top of the class, this is the right time to go to Maryland (especially if you're getting the bargain in-state price). The top of the 2L class landed some summer associate positions at all but the most prestigious firms in D.C., e.g., Arnold & Porter, Covington & Burling and Wilmer Hale. That said, be in the very top of the class (probably 10 percent) and on Law Review to land those jobs. Otherwise, you may very well be stuck practicing in Baltimore or elsewhere in the state of Maryland. Maryland is absolutely rising in the minds

of employers; this year is our first to have interviewing sites in NYC, Boston and Chicago. The brass ring is absolutely there for the taking, but you must beat the top of the class to get it.

Status: Alumnus/a, full-time
Dates of Enrollment: 8/2000-5/2003
Survey Submitted: November 2003

I did all my interviewing on campus and got my offers for summer programs and full-time employment from it. Career services is a great resource for information and suggestions.

Status: Alumnus/a, full-time
Dates of Enrollment: 8/1998-5/2001
Survey Submitted: March 2005

Most everyone at Maryland graduates with a job. Top jobs at prestigious firms are available to the top 5 percent of the class, and great jobs at excellent firms are available to the top 25 percent of the class, maybe even to the top 50 percent. Lots of firms come to campus and the campus recruiting program is well run by the career services center. The career center does a great job in keeping in touch with alumni and has often gone the extra mile for the graduate looking for something special or different. There are also many many internships available, particularly with the judiciary. Maryland judges "take care of their own" and welcome Maryland students for internships.

Getting clerkships after graduation is much more difficult than getting an internship or getting a job. I discovered how hard it was to compete against the large Washington, D.C. law schools when I interviewed all over D.C. and seemed to be edged out over and over by the "big schools." I talked to some of the people I was up against and discovered that their career center completely handled the application process for them. Meanwhile I was doing my own research, getting my own letters of recommendation, filing my own applications. I landed a clerkship, but it was a tough road.

Quality of Life

Status: Current student, full-time
Dates of Enrollment: 8/2005-Submit Date
Survey Submitted: June 2006

Maryland is not a school to attend for its fabulous campus. Though the law building is great, Maryland positions itself as a professional campus for the law, medical and nursing schools. The facilities are excellent academically but offer nothing much beyond that. No fancy gym and no fancy student center.

Status: Alumnus/a, full-time
Dates of Enrollment: 1/2000-1/2003
Survey Submitted: June 2006

Students live scattered throughout the Baltimore-metro area. Most find fellow law school roommates and share an apartment. Pick your neighborhoods well as there are some very dangerous areas where crime is high. There are, however, some great places to live and the school makes every safety accommodation possible going to and from the school (you'll see state and city police everywhere). The gym is adequate (it is at the top of a parking garage with basketball courts, weights and fitness equipment). Dining is great and you'll immediately catch on to the "law" bars and the good places to take your family and friends.

Status: Current student, full-time
Dates of Enrollment: 8/2004-Submit Date
Survey Submitted: May 2006

The area immediately around the campus is on the up-and-up. Baltimore is in the process of implementing its "West Side Revitalization" that thus far has brought many new businesses and restaurants, as well as hotels and luxury apartment buildings within a couple of blocks from the law school. The law school's buildings are the best I saw when I was looking at law schools (far superior to Georgetown, GW, Baltimore and American). Each room has Internet-access and cutting-edge technology..

Read all of Vault's Law School Surveys at www.vault.com/lawschool — get complete surveys on top law schools, expert advice on applicaton essays, LSAT prep and more.

VAULT CAREER LIBRARY   297

Status: Current student, full-time
Dates of Enrollment: 8/2004-Submit Date
Survey Submitted: May 2006

The new student housing (called the University Suites) is really nice and located so close. However the neighborhood is only so-so because of Lexington Market being nearby. They have a police escort service if you have to come back from classes late and the on-campus housing has 24-hour security.

Status: Alumnus/a, part-time
Dates of Enrollment: 8/2002-12/2005
Survey Submitted: May 2006

Other than traveling to/from from the law school building, specifically, I never utilized the other facilities. I was working full time and an evening student. Never had an issue with crime though I utilized the campus parking garage exclusively. $4 after 5 p.m. was worth the risk of parking on the street. A security guard was always present near the entrance of the school and the garage was across the street.

The law school is in the city, three blocks from the Camden Yards ballpark. The school is on the same campus as the other professional programs of UMD (e.g., medical, dental and nursing). Not an enclosed campus but buildings among other commercial buildings in the city.

Status: Current student, full-time
Dates of Enrollment: 8/2005-Submit Date
Survey Submitted: May 2006

The neighborhood the school is in is a rough section of Baltimore. The school does offer a lot of security, and there are police cars almost on every other corner so we usually always feel safe. The school is also located in a cluster with other UMaryland graduate programs so there are a lot of students everywhere. There isn't a great deal of affordable housing in the area. The University Suites are apartments affiliated with the university but are over priced and the management is terrible. A lot of students live in other parts of Baltimore and just commute. There is a lot of available parking but it can be expensive. There also aren't many food options in the neighborhood, but the city is revitalizing the area and a few large food chains have moved in to make the area a little bit more convenient.

Status: Alumnus/a, full-time
Dates of Enrollment: 8/1998-5/2001
Survey Submitted: March 2005

The law school is in brand new digs and is like a palace. I cannot imagine how nice it must be to attend school there! We went in the basement and had classes in a bomb shelter! I can't comment on the new system, the new food or the new facility. I know housing was pretty good; I didn't need school housing, but my friends who did managed to find affordable housing that met their needs. The neighborhood is rough. Don't go out alone at night and campus police will escort you anywhere. I had my car broken into once, right in front of one of the campus police stations! And I had a car alarm! But I never had any other crime issues, nor did I know anyone who did. One of the greatest "quality of life" offerings at Maryland is their Peer Advisor program: a group (three or four) of second-year students are assigned to each "small section." They are there for advice, for help with outlines and teacher tips, for socialization, for class selection and for coping. The peer advisors meet with the small sections a few times during orientation, then throughout the first year. We went bowling, had parties, had bag lunches in the park and did random things together. The peers were always available for a question, knew you by name and were very helpful. They helped you believe you could "make it."

Status: Alumnus/a, full-time
Dates of Enrollment: 8/2000-5/2003
Survey Submitted: November 2003

Baltimore's cost of living is much lower than other cities. It is also experiencing a renaissance as the Inner Harbor takes off. The campus is located so close to the baseball stadium and the Inner Harbor; it is like two different worlds coexisting. I enjoyed hanging out at the Harbor on weekends I was in town or driving 45 minutes into D.C. or 30 minutes to Annapolis. A blue collar town with white collar elements; a thriving but small art community that was at the

crossroads between the North and South during the Civil War. Interesting and eclectic!

Social Life

Status: Current student, full-time
Dates of Enrollment: 8/2005-Submit Date
Survey Submitted: June 2006

Baltimore has a decent selection of bars, restaurants and things to do. Though the city is struggling, it is undergoing a mini-economic expansion that has benefitted the area around the law school significantly. The baseball and football stadiums are also just a few blocks from the school, as well as some great cultural landmarks.

Status: Current student, full-time
Dates of Enrollment: 8/2004-Submit Date
Survey Submitted: June 2006

The social scene is great and is furthered by the fact that the school is located at a campus for graduate programs only. There are none of the problems that stem from undergraduate binge drinkers on our campus. The local bars, stadiums (Oriole Park at Camden Yards lets students in for $5 on Friday games) and proximity of student housing makes for a lot of opportunities to go out and have fun with your classmates.

Status: Current student, full-time
Dates of Enrollment: 8/2005-Submit Date
Survey Submitted: June 2006

Sliders always goes over well as a convenient place to grab a drink whether after studying or before a game at Camden Yards (just a few blocks down from school). Another favorite newcomer is Maggie Moores, a faux Irish bar that just opened a block from our building.

Status: Current student, full-time
Dates of Enrollment: 9/2005-Submit Date
Survey Submitted: May 2006

There are many bars and restaurants. The different student organizations have many different social events (bar crawls, Octoberfest, wine tastings). Because we are right next to the other professional schools (UM Med and UMD Dental) there are a lot of activities going on every week. The different schools throw dating events. There are also two major legal fraternities. The school is also very close to Camden Yards (home of the baltimore Orioles) and the Ravens stadium.

Status: Current student, full-time
Dates of Enrollment: 8/2004-Submit Date
Survey Submitted: May 2006

Very little social life outside of law school. I was lucky I already had a network of friends in the area. The minimal social life revolves around the same bars day in and day out. Not many people go out; everyone is more interested in studying.

Status: Current student, full-time
Dates of Enrollment: 8/2004-Submit Date
Survey Submitted: May 2006

We are a little dorky and reserved but there are plenty of socialization opportunities if you want to partake. Common hangouts are the bars by the baseball stadium where the owners are super-receptive to students who make up much of their clientele during the off season.

Status: Current student, full-time
Dates of Enrollment: 9/2004-Submit Date
Survey Submitted: May 2006

Law students are notoriously social bar flies on the weekends and Maryland is no exception. There are a lot of great restaurants in Baltimore, a few clubs and a lot of bars. Students are friendly, especially in the beginning, and law students tend to congregate at one or two places so it's easy to meet people.

Status: Current student, full-time
Dates of Enrollment: 8/2004-Submit Date
Survey Submitted: May 2006

For being law school, the people are very friendly. I attended a highly-ranked top-tier undergraduate institution where the student body was very intellectual but socially awkward. Maryland is not like that at all. The students are largely type-A, well-rounded people.

Status: Alumnus/a, full-time
Dates of Enrollment: 8/1998-5/2001
Survey Submitted: March 2005

There are lots and lots of things to do at Maryland. Many clubs, social activities and local hangouts. There are volleyball and basketball leagues. All students get to belong to the local gym and many take part in that. Lots of young students means lots of dating! Even though I was "married with children" the "kids" included me in their outings. We often met after our long, boring library class (required first year) and played pool and ate dinner together at a local restaurant. My third year, a bunch of students discovered a local bar that offered free swing dancing lessons if you came early, then they'd stay well into the night swing dancing together. Many of the local bars had special happy hours for the students.

Status: Current student, full-time
Dates of Enrollment: 8/2003-Submit Date
Survey Submitted: May 2004

There are a ton of clubs, all of which sponsor multiple happy hours and other get-togethers. People date each other and it gets a bit incestuous at times, but generally people act as they should in a professional environment. They know how to have a good time within reasonable boundaries.

Read all of Vault's Law School Surveys at www.vault.com/lawschool — get complete surveys on top law schools, expert advice on applicaton essays, LSAT prep and more.

VAULT CAREER LIBRARY   299

Boston College Law School

Admissions Office
885 Centre Street
Newton, MA 02459
Admissions phone: (617) 552-4351
Financial aid phone: (617) 552-4243
Admissions fax: (617) 552-2917
Admissions e-mail: bclawadm@bc.edu
Admissions URL: www.bc.edu/schools/law/admission/

 Admissions

Status: Current student, full-time
Dates of Enrollment: 9/2005-Submit Date
Survey Submitted: April 2006

As in most things, BC Law makes the admissions process fairly painless. The office staff is helpful in answering questions on the phone and over e-mail. It's hard to get a sense of the school without visiting—people are incredibly friendly in a genuine way. Professors are truly excited about student participation, think *Dead Poet's Society.*

The school does not do a great job of making the financial aid process transparent. Whether you qualify for aid (beyond being allowed to borrow $50,000/year) is based on some criteria that no one can describe. I think that BC is worth the price you'll pay—but don't be surprised if you're a great student who is completely independent and you don't get any aid.

> **The school says:** "Applicants' financial aid awards are prepared after a careful review of the financial aid materials submitted. Eligibility for all sources of aid is calculated based on this self-reported data. BC Law applies the federal need analysis formula to evaluate eligibility for federal assistance; eligibility for Boston College aid is based upon institutional methodology, availability of funding and timeliness of your application."

Status: Current student, full-time
Dates of Enrollment: 9/2004-Submit Date
Survey Submitted: April 2006

BC Law is highly selective. In order to get in you must not only have good grades and LSAT scores, but also a great life story. Most of my classmates have done really neat things before law school—worked in Africa, worked as a VP of accounting firm, etc. So I think that BC is definitely looking for a well-rounded student.

Status: Current student, full-time
Dates of Enrollment: 9/2003-Submit Date
Survey Submitted: April 2006

The admissions process at BC was very smooth. They were very timely with letting you know your status and very helpful any time you needed to call for a financial aid question. BC is able to maintain such a friendly and down-to-earth student body because they really rely on the essay to figure out the kind of person you are. The more personal and insightful the essay is, the better.

Status: Current student, full-time
Dates of Enrollment: 8/2004-Submit Date
Survey Submitted: April 2006

The application to BCLS is nicely streamlined, and candidates can be sure that their files are read carefully by actual faculty members. Demonstrating familiarity with what BC offers is important; an identification with BC's Jesuit Catholic identity can also help. Most students are from the top colleges and universities in the Northeast, but the school is actively engaged in trying to recruit students from outside the Northeast and such students will have a slightly easier time getting in. Given the large number of students coming from the top northeastern institutions, the admissions office places a greater emphasis on grades than LSAT scores.

> **The school says:** "Every year there is significant representation in our entering class from universities outside the Northeast, e.g., UC Berkeley, the University of Notre Dame, Stanford and Duke Universities. Outside the Northeast, the permanent states of residence most represented in our last entering class were California, followed by Texas, Virginia, Washington, Ohio, Florida, and the District of Columbia.
>
> "While both academic record and LSAT scores are important in the application review process, all information submitted in support of an application is carefully considered."

Status: Alumnus/a, full-time
Dates of Enrollment: 8/2002-5/2005
Survey Submitted: March 2006

As with most law schools, BC has a "yes box," "no box" and "maybe box" for the applications it receives. BC, however, appears to have a bigger "maybe box" than most top-tier law schools. This means they give greater attention to things like resumes, personal statements and recommendations than a lot of comparable schools do so it is worth putting in the extra effort to make those components shine for BC.

Status: Current student, full-time
Dates of Enrollment: 8/2005-Submit Date
Survey Submitted: September 2005

This year, the average student that decided to attend BC Law had a 164 LSAT and a 3.61 GPA. In the application process, BC looks for people that stand out. This seems to be more important than raw numbers, which is rare in the law school admissions process these days. Your personal statement and experience outside of school are therefore very important. BC asks for the usual two-page personal statement, in which applicants should focus on describing facets of their personality, value-forming experiences and other things that make one stand out in a pool of highly-qualified prospective law students.

Status: Current student, full-time
Dates of Enrollment: 9/2004-Submit Date
Survey Submitted: February 2005

Send as many letters as you can from BC alumni. It is pretty selective and they place a large amount of people who apply early on the waitlist. Do not despair if you are placed on it—send them more info about yourself.

Status: Current student, full-time
Dates of Enrollment: 8/2003-Submit Date
Survey Submitted: November 2004

The admissions process at BC Law is extremely typical. LSATs and GPA will get you in or keep you out. There is no "secret" to getting accepted.

That being said, I think that BCLS places a greater emphasis on public service work than other schools. Several applicants a year that are committed to doing public service work upon graduation receive full three-year scholarships (if you receive the scholarship and wind up working in the private sector you are obligated to pay it back). I also get the impression that students with a strong community service background are probably at a slight advantage in the admissions process.

BCLS is getting much, much tougher to get into. In recent years, an extremely high percentage of accepted applicants have wound up matriculating so the admissions department has had to decrease the acceptance rate each year as a result. Like every other top-tier law school as of late, getting in to BCLS is probably not a "safe bet" even for top students.

Status: Current student, full-time
Dates of Enrollment: 9/2001-Submit Date
Survey Submitted: February 2004

I believe that the admissions process is very personal at BC Law. My law school advisor from college was in contact with the admissions staff to check on my status. I had an LSAT score of about 173 and GPA of about 3.7, and received a scholarship from BC Law. Also, the school loves to consider diversity and gives individual attention to all applicants. From my past experience, anyone applying who has ties to BC Law should use them. I wrote a letter on behalf of a friend who was on the waiting list. Surprise, surprise...he got in!

Status: Current student, full-time
Dates of Enrollment: 8/2001-Submit Date
Survey Submitted: September 2003

I received a 165 LSAT and my undergrad GPA was something like 3.04. But I was able to explain my low GPA by submitting a chart that demonstrated how my grades went up every semester and was able to explain my terrible freshman college grades away. I did not have any previous work experience but I wrote my essay on studying abroad and the characteristics. I related what I needed to survive overseas to the skills you need to do well in law school.

Status: Alumnus/a, full-time
Dates of Enrollment: 8/2000-5/2003
Survey Submitted: September 2003

BC looks first at grades and LSAT scores. They publish a chart on your likelihood of getting in based on the numbers. If an applicant meets the criteria, they are likely to be let in, pending a cursory look at the essay and writing sample and assuming space allows. To that extent, get applications in EARLY! Once the class is full, even a 4.0 Harvard grad will be on the waitlist. If an applicant does not make the grade/LSAT cut, the application goes to current 3Ls who volunteer to be on the Student admissions committee. They read the entire application, including extracurriculars, change in GPA over the college years and work experience (things that are ignored in the initial process). If the reader thinks the applicant deserves a second look, the application goes back to the admissions committee (administrators and professors) for a final decision.

Applicants must pay attention to their LSAT and writing sample. First, law school exams are taken under pressure so people should be able to work under similar conditions. Second, if the essay is much better than the writing sample it sends out warning signals that the essay may have been professionally written. Applicants should also be sure to state why they want to go to law school. It is not important to know exactly what one wants to do, but even the best application can be denied if the reader gets no sense that the applicant really wants to go to law school.

Academics

Status: Current student, full-time
Dates of Enrollment: 9/2003-Submit Date
Survey Submitted: April 2006

The professors here are wonderful. They take their teaching seriously and are very approachable. I've been able to walk into professor's office almost at any time to ask them questions.

Status: Current student, full-time
Dates of Enrollment: 9/2005-Submit Date
Survey Submitted: April 2006

BC Law is challenging and demanding—but it's humane. Professors, especially 1L professors, are aware of what you're doing in your other classes and do a pretty good job of helping you to keep a constant workload. In addition, every professor I have had has been intellectually curious, dedicated to teaching and available for students. Grades are done on a strict curve, but employers know that so it's OK (I'm told) that half of the class gets all B's.

Status: Alumnus/a, full-time
Dates of Enrollment: 8/1985-5/1988
Survey Submitted: April 2006

I focused in the area of public interest, and thus did a number of clinical programs. The school offered a a number of programs that allowed me to participate in different government jobs, which gave me that ability to determine what I wanted to do after law school. The programs were well run.

Status: Current student, full-time
Dates of Enrollment: 9/2003-Submit Date
Survey Submitted: April 2006

I've rarely been unable to take a class I wanted. I did have a very unfortunate experience, however, when a class that was widely advertised in the admissions information ended up getting canceled and was never replaced. When I expressed my concern over this to two different administrators, I wasn't taken seriously and my input was tossed aside as not important.

The curve at BC is very tough. Though it eases up a little in second- and third-year smaller classes, it's still a force to be reckoned with. BC offers a good variety of classes—lectures, seminars, clinicals. In your second and third years, it's very easy to find a good balance of classes.

The workload at BC is surprisingly manageable. It is what you make of it. Some people like to spend all day in the library. I prefer to become over-involved in extracurricular activities, yet I've always been able to manage my workload and get decent grades.

Status: Current student, full-time
Dates of Enrollment: 8/2004-Submit Date
Survey Submitted: April 2006

The 1L curriculum will be overhauled for the 06-07 academic year, introducing Criminal Law. An intensive writing program is a major component of the 1L curriculum at BC, and is very valuable. Classes are occasionally poorly scheduled. I.e., too many corporate law classes scheduled in the spring, with too few scheduled in the fall. The faculty at BC is generally very good, but there are several older faculty members who would clearly never get hired today because hiring standards at BC have improved in the last 10 years or so. There is some mediocrity and laziness in the faculty that does not comport with how BC likes to view itself as the equal of any school outside the Top 14.

Another serious problem with the faculty here, though, is the extreme lack of conservative and even moderate voices. The faculty is overwhelmingly liberal and this can occasionally skew class instruction. Even though the students here are generally liberal, they are often puzzled by the seeming lack of willingness of many faculty to credit alternative viewpoints, philosophies and value systems. Our peer schools, like Boston University, have far more ideological balance in their faculties, as do far more elite institutions like Harvard; when you consider that BU and Harvard are generally viewed as liberal, you realize just how truly liberal BC really is. Nevertheless, the current Dean is doing an outstanding job of trying to re-center the law school without offending too many. BC is trying to figure out how to rededicate itself to its Catholic Jesuit mission while remaining open and inclusive to all (this is part of broader trend in Catholic higher education).

I imagine that on the whole the workload and grading system here is comparable to other similar law schools. BC deserves credit for developing some innovative classes and clinical offerings that do not exist at other schools such as the semester-long internship at the War Crimes Tribunal in the Hague; this semester BC became the first law school in the country to offer a class on Hedge Funds. BC also makes excellent use of the enormous depth of talent in the legal community in Boston by bringing many outstanding adjunct faculty members to teach classes.

Status: Alumnus/a, full-time
Dates of Enrollment: 8/1999-5/2002
Survey Submitted: March 2006

BC Law professors are tops. They are approachable and the school definitely has a small school, "touchy-feely" sort of style to it. The classes were all good—I only wish I had taken more. There is a real emphasis on societal impact that I found really important in order to keep perspective. Popular classes are

Read all of Vault's Law School Surveys at www.vault.com/lawschool — get complete surveys on top law schools, expert advice on applicaton essays, LSAT prep and more.

VAULT CAREER LIBRARY   301

accessible. I don't remember ever being shut out of a class I wanted to take. Grading was fair to heavy on the B's (like most law schools). Workload was manageable—they try very hard NOT to foster a super-competitive environment.

Status: Alumnus/a, full-time
Dates of Enrollment: 8/2002-5/2005
Survey Submitted: March 2006

BC Law has a 1L program designed to reduce the stress of that year. Students take a practice exam in December and get feedback that will help when it comes to the real final/mid-term in February. The second semester is shorter. BC also has a strong writing program required for 1Ls. It is a year long class weighted more heavily than others. All around, BC Law does well to try and keep students' stress down and spirits up. It is a great place to learn without a lot of the cutthroat behavior law students sometimes hear about elsewhere.

> **The school says:** "BC Law's first-year curriculum has changed. Students are now on a regular semester system."

Status: Current student, full-time
Dates of Enrollment: 8/2003-Submit Date
Survey Submitted: November 2004

First-year students at BCLS are required to take the standard 1L classes—torts, property, contracts, constitutional law, civil procedure, a year-long writing class and an ethics class (ILPR). Where BC differs from other law schools is that it does not require criminal law your first year (or any other year) and makes property a year-long class. Additionally, every first-year student is placed into a section where they will stay the entire year. The first-year curriculum is rigorous but not ridiculous. In fact, I think that BCLS does a much better job of easing the stress of first year than other law schools. The first semester for 1Ls is "extended," meaning that it lasts from September to February rather than from September to December. As a result, first semester finals for 1Ls are in February rather than before Christmas, giving them a much greater time to settle in and make the "law school transition" before being held accountable for information. I think this works really well. I was definitely much less stressed out my first year than my friends at other law schools.

> **The school says:** "BC Law now requires Criminal Law as part of the first-year curriculum and is on a regular semester schedule."

After first-year there are a wide range of classes to take and few requirements (Con Law II, a writing requirement and a professional responsibility requirement). Generally speaking, classes are pretty easy to get into. The professors that I have had so far have been amazing and among the best that I have ever had. They tend to be extremely effective in the classroom and extremely accessible outside of class. While, like at any other school, there are exceptions to this rule, there are so many classes to take that you can avoid the bad apples and stick with the superstars. I would say that the grading and workload at BCLS are standard for law schools.

Status: Alumnus/a, full-time
Dates of Enrollment: 8/2000-5/2003
Survey Submitted: September 2003

The variety of electives can be limited, especially in business law, but the school has recently made an effort to hire IP and business professors (hiring about five or six in the last two years). I have never had a problem getting into a class, regardless of how late I registered. BC grades on a strict B curve, which can be a pain when grades matter so much during the hiring season. The nice thing about BC is that they have diagnostic exams halfway through the first semester that do not count against your grades. Thus, you can determine what you need to work on before the finals. The large majority of professors are both great academics and teachers. Most of them genuinely care about their students, and most are very accessible to the students for questions.

Status: Alumnus/a, full-time
Dates of Enrollment: 8/2000-5/2003
Survey Submitted: September 2003

Unlike most law schools, BC does not require Criminal Law. The first year consists of Torts, Contracts, Property, Constitutional Law, Civil Procedure and Legal Writing. Students must also take a second semester of Constitutional Law

and complete an advanced writing requirement (Law Review or moot cou suffices). I never had a problem getting the classes I wanted. It is true that som are small and get closed out, but professors are often willing to override th limit. Third-year students get priority in the registration process. The va majority of professors are wonderful. Upperclassmen are only too happy recommend specific professors and classes. Besides class, the professors kee their doors open for everything from class help to chats about the law to care advice. Most have deep rolodexes that they will gladly share with any studen who needs a contact. Most professors give out the final grade based on on exam or paper. This is a law school standard and takes some getting used to afte college, but the way to succeed is to prepare early and talk to the professors there are any problems.

The workload can be tough, but it really depends on the specific mix of classe each person takes. The work is especially tough the first semester of secon year, when students typically take a heavy courseload and have to interview fo jobs. Most students, however, prefer this because they can stock up on credi and then take the minimum during their last semester third year. A good optio for third-year students is independent study. It allows a student to work wit his/her favorite professor on a topic that interests him/her, and perhaps get th result published. It has been especially popular with third-years who have othe obligations, as they do not have to spend as much time on the campus physicall but can still do valuable work.

Employment Prospects

Status: Alumnus/a, full-time
Dates of Enrollment: 9/1984-5/1987
Survey Submitted: May 2006

I am from the West Coast and had no difficulty getting offers for employment In fact, I found that receiving an education at BC set me apart from other Wes Coast lawyers when interviewing for positions. BC has strong name recognitio and has a large alumni presence on the West Coast. The alumni are active i assisting with employment opportunities and networking for busines development.

Status: Current student, full-time
Dates of Enrollment: 9/2005-Submit Date
Survey Submitted: April 2006

If you're interested in working in Boston, especially at a medium- or large-size firm, BC Law is perfect for you. Alumni are frequently tripping over themselve to help you network. The career services office is helpful if you approach then but won't go out of their way. It's important to have a sense of what lifestyl you want going into law school so that you don't get sucked down the large firr vortex unwillingly.

Status: Alumnus/a, full-time
Dates of Enrollment: 8/1985-5/1988
Survey Submitted: April 2006

As a result of my working in a clinical program, I was able to get a job at the District Attorney's Office that I worked at in law school right when I graduate and passed the bar.

Status: Alumnus/a, full-time
Dates of Enrollment: 8/1989-5/1992
Survey Submitted: April 2006

BC has an excellent reputation. As an alumnus, I have always gotten positive feedback from potential employers about the quality of my BC degree. In one case, my employer told me that they look for BC grads because they view us as smart, but also as well-rounded and practical.

Status: Current student, full-time
Dates of Enrollment: 9/2004-Submit Date
Survey Submitted: April 2006

The Boston firms that recruit are all of the same firms that recruit at Harvard However, to get a job with the very top firms you have to be in the top 10 to 15 percent of your class. There are many opportunities for those interested in non-firm jobs. Anyone who wants to get a job is able to get one.

The career center is absolutely wonderful. The people who work at the career center are willing to go above and beyond for any of the students. They organize many meet-and-greet events for employers and students. They try to connect students with BC alumni working at the local firms and have them give the students first-hand accounts of what the firms are actually like. They are by far the best career center in Boston!!

Status: Alumnus/a, full-time
Dates of Enrollment: 8/1999-5/2002
Survey Submitted: March 2006

If you had good grades, getting a top job was easy. Otherwise it was a little more challenging. (I think this is true of everywhere.) Boston employers are VERY impressed by BC Law...NY employers are impressed, but not as impressed. There is definitely an emphasis on going to a large firm—smaller firm jobs were much tougher to get. The alumni network was a great asset. On-campus recruiting is in full force.

Status: Alumnus/a, full-time
Dates of Enrollment: 8/2002-5/2005
Survey Submitted: March 2006

BC clearly guides its students more toward large- to mid-sized corporate law firms than any other employment. For this, it puts most of its efforts into the OCI system of electronic bidding and interview schedules for 2L summer associatships. As competition has grown among schools in recent years, it seems that fewer BC Law students find placement this way and the career services office has yet to compensate for this with other avenues toward employment. Many students end up calling alumni and networking on their own, but they eventually seem to find satisfactory employment. A few go into the public/nonprofit sector, but financial aid for this is tough to come by, though BC talks a good game about ethics and public service.

> **The school says:** "During the last academic year, 401 employers interviewed our students through our on-campus and off-campus recruitment programs. At least 96 of these employers were from the Government and Public Interest Sector. In fact, in conjunction with the other Massachusetts law schools, BC Law coordinates two Government/Public Interest interview programs each year.
>
> "In addition, over 150 other employers collected batches of resumes of BC Law students and another 900 employers (947) posted student employment notices on our job bank."

Status: Alumnus/a, full-time
Dates of Enrollment: 8/2000-5/2003
Survey Submitted: March 2005

I graduated in a lean time. Prospects were not that great and the Career Center offered limited help. Alumni connections are great, but the school is tied mostly to the Boston area. It does not really seek to expand beyond Boston to say, New York and D.C. The school needs to think about taking high quality students who will most likely NOT stay in Boston—otherwise, it will stay a regional school.

> **The school says:** "Last year we placed over 20 percent of our students in the NY/NJ area. Overall, approximately 50 percent of our students stay in the New England area; the other 50 percent are scattered across the country."

Status: Alumnus/a, full-time
Dates of Enrollment: 8/2000-5/2003
Survey Submitted: September 2003

One thing I wish I had known is that the first semester for first-years at BC ends in February, a good two months after the other law schools. This means that when you are looking for a job for your first-year summer, you have no grades to give to employers, and that WILL limit some of your choices. During recruiting of my second year, I received offers from firms in each city I interviewed with (New York, San Francisco, Seattle and Boston). BC is strongest in Boston, but you can get jobs in other markets. I note, however, that I was in the top 10 percent of my class and on Law Review, which matters. Boston law firms are very supportive of the law school and think very highly of BC Law grads, with alumni at all the major firms. Career Services tends to do

a poor job helping students who are not top 10 percent get work. In fact, some students I know have complained about being openly discouraged by Career Services from looking for particular kinds of work because of their grades. Some may call this a reality check, but they really need to work on their bedside manner. In addition, the students who do receive help from them (this in the top 10 percent), really do not need help from them to get a job.

Status: Alumnus/a, full-time
Dates of Enrollment: 8/2000-5/2003
Survey Submitted: September 2003

Generally, BC students are in a great position to get good jobs. Aside from Harvard, BC is the highest-ranked school in the area. Employers come from everywhere to recruit. The past two years have been very difficult because of the economy, but still nearly every student has a job by Christmas after graduation. BC offers a stipend to students after their first year to work in government or public interest. It is funded by grants, a huge auction and a program called work-a-day, where students at high paying jobs give a day's pay to the stipend fund. Campus recruiting is very intense. I had upwards of six interviews every week on campus. Bidding is done over the Internet, so that students simply click on the employers they want to interview with and then career services sends off the resumes. There is also a lottery process, so at least one or two interview spots go to a randomly chosen student. Career services is fantastic for students who want to go to big firms, but they are lacking somewhat for the rest of us. The bottom line is that unless a student wants to work at a big firm, he/she should count on doing a LOT of legwork alone. The last few years have seen a lot of controversy about military recruiting. The school follows the ABA non-discrimination policy that excludes the military since it discriminates in employment, but BC (the entire school, not just law) could lose funding if it does not allow military recruiters on campus. Thus, for the moment they are allowed on, but that is subject to change.

 ## Quality of Life

Status: Alumnus/a, full-time
Dates of Enrollment: 9/1984-5/1987
Survey Submitted: May 2006

BC's law school campus in located in scenic Newton, MA, which is a bedroom community of Boston. Being slightly outside of Boston, I was provided with the quiet needed for study while also being close to the exciting Boston scene. There is no better place to spend your college years than Boston, with its rich historic and academic traditions. The BC Law campus is also modern, aesthetically pleasing and comfortable. The other students were very friendly and there are numerous student organizations to become involved with. Weekly social functions at the school also helped build a sense of community.

Status: Current student, full-time
Dates of Enrollment: 9/2005-Submit Date
Survey Submitted: April 2006

The law school is in a safe residential neighborhood about a mile from a town center. It's also a mile from the Mass Pike—so it's pretty easy to get there by car no matter what. Students without cars aren't that happy about public transportation options—but they do exist. They're just starting to have graduate housing next year, but there are copious apartments in the area and lots of students end up living together. There's a dining hall on campus that has decent food; although the menu doesn't change that much. There are also plenty of nearby places to run out to during the day.

> **The school says:** "BC Law now has a limited number of graduate housing units available."

Status: Current student, full-time
Dates of Enrollment: 8/2004-Submit Date
Survey Submitted: April 2006

The number one most important thing to be said about BC is that the students here are overwhelmingly good, decent, giving, fair, non-competitive, collegial, friendly, smart, fun-loving, sociable, curious people who get along very well with one another and enjoy one another's company. I think this is very special and remarkable, and I know for a fact it isn't like this everywhere. Some will

Read all of Vault's Law School Surveys at www.vault.com/lawschool — get complete surveys on top law schools, expert advice on applicaton essays, LSAT prep and more.

VAULT CAREER LIBRARY 303

see this school as too touchy-feely, which it may be in its poorest application of this spirit, but at its best it creates a truly enjoyable atmosphere for being a law student. A hiring rep. of a top D.C. law firm once said that his favorite hires were graduates of BC and UVA for precisely this reason, so I think there is definitely a perception in the wider world, as well, that this is a friendly place. Attention gunners, self-promoters and back-stabbers: please do not come here and spoil this place!

Status: Current student, full-time
Dates of Enrollment: 9/2003-Submit Date
Survey Submitted: April 2006

The biggest problem with the Newton Campus is that it's not T-assessable and you must use a shuttle to get from the main campus to the law school. You share the dining hall and snack bar with the freshmen who live in the dorms on the Newton Campus, but they're not too bad. The dining hall is way overpriced, so a lot of students bring their meals. The library is really nice—offers a lot of windows and nice common spaces and smaller meeting rooms. Parking is a bear. There are entirely too many parking spaces reserved for faculty/staff and so most mornings there are few student spaces but tons of empty faculty/staff parks you can't park in.

Status: Current student, full-time
Dates of Enrollment: 8/2005-Submit Date
Survey Submitted: September 2005

Life at BC Law school is great. Newton, just outside of Boston, has a reputation of being the safest city per-capita in the United States. The students are extraordinarily congenial; sharing outlines and notes is the norm. While all of the students at BC are of exceptional intelligence and ability, they do not compete with each other to the point of detriment. It is more of a friendly competition. Since everyone knows they are going to get a great job regardless of where they place, fiercely competing is rendered pointless. The facilities at the law school are exemplary. The law library was just built and the brand new East Wing, home of the classrooms and offices, is technologically superior. The grounds are beautiful and clean and the main campus is just down the street for those times students need to deal with administrative matters. Transportation is exceedingly convenient, with shuttle busses running between the main campus, the law campus and the city of Boston.

Status: Current student, full-time
Dates of Enrollment: 9/2004-Submit Date
Survey Submitted: February 2005

The dining center is overpriced, but it serves pretty good food. The cafeteria is shared with BC freshmen, but it is really not a big deal at all. BC has wireless throughout the law school and it is awesome. Most of the first-year sections consist of five to six student cliques—which is kind of weird, but it seems that it is like that at most law schools. There isn't that much diversity at BC, but I heard that other schools are even worse. There are only two black students in my class even though the school claims it has a much higher "diversity" rate.

Status: Current student, full-time
Dates of Enrollment: 8/2003-Submit Date
Survey Submitted: February 2005

Newton, where the law school is located, is considered one of the safest towns in the country. I have not heard of any major issues from law students in this area. The only crime I heard was of persons who took a couple of unattended laptops in the library. But no stolen cars or violent acts. This safety does come at a cost. I am paying about $1,300 for a two bedroom and that is about par for the area. This city is expensive and the community a pain if you live in Brighton or Allston for lack of parking. Parking on campus is available for a cost. Personally, I am a big fan of Boston because of the history of the place and the amount of cultural opportunities. A down side is that the people here are rude and there tends to be too much racial segregation in the city. However, having lived in Chicago, this is no worse.

The facilities in the school are great in terms of the classrooms being wired and all up to date. The cafeteria on campus is expensive and the food options get rather repetitive. The library is well-stocked and a great place to study, if that is your style. I would complain about the gym, which is on the main campus; that needs to be updated. Finally, you need to take a bus from main campus to the

law school if you do not have a car. It is just inconvenient and makes you feel like you are wasting your time. The bus ride is only five minutes.

Status: Current student, full-time
Dates of Enrollment: 8/2003-Submit Date
Survey Submitted: November 2004

I continue to be amazed by my quality of life at BCLS. There is a mytholog built up around law school and I entered thinking that it would be the mos hellish and trying three years of my life. Instead, I have been very pleasantl surprised by how enjoyable it has been. Yes, I am working harder than I hav ever had to work before. Yes, it's much, much harder to get A's here than at an other school I've been to. Yes, I don't have much time to do non-law schoo things. But, on a day-to-day basis I have to say that I am happy and satisfie with my life at BCLS. BCLS is not a back-biting kind of law school.

Students here are competitive but don't get out of hand. While I think a lot o your experience here is dictated by the section you wind up in your first year (had a fantastic one), I have been genuinely surprised by how friendly and kind everyone is here. I have absolutely no trouble getting notes from (numerous people when I miss class and people do not engage in the ripping-pages-out-of library-books behavior that goes on at other schools.

In general, I would say that BCLS students are pretty low-key. I would also say that there is a palpable sense of community at the law school. When we have social events at the law school a large number of students, faculty members administrators and staff show up and mingle happily. There are people socializing at all hours of the day. Yes, there are downsides to the school—ou cafeteria is expensive and often overrun with undergraduates, our bookstore i basically a dungeon and living in Boston can be pricey—but they do no overshadow all of the positive things about it. We have a beautiful library, ar exceptional wireless network throughout the entire law school and a beautiful campus. While the school is not located in the heart of the city and lacks fur surroundings (it's in a very ritzy suburban neighborhood), I question whether this should be a salient issue for people. I, like most other people, am at school most of the time, so the campus surroundings are not really an issue.

Status: Alumnus/a, JD/MBA
Dates of Enrollment: 8/1996-5/2000
Survey Submitted: October 2003

No on-campus housing at all. They don't even have enough for the undergrads and force them to live off campus at least one year. It is Boston, so it is expensive. But BC is pretty good about listing off-campus stuff, and there are tons of leasing agents around, most of whom work with students, and are relatively reputable and reasonably priced. The law school is on its own campus, with just it and a bunch of freshman dorms, so that's kind of a weird dynamic. It has ample parking, provided you buy a sticker (which is pretty reasonably priced, considering it's Boston). The other option is public transportation, which is prevalent. BC's main campus is at the end of the B Green Line, BC shuttles run from the end of the B line to the law school campus (maybe one or two miles away) and make a couple of other convenient stops too. The B line runs along Comm Ave, which is mostly residential, and mostly students/young professionals, so the vast majority of students have a very straightforward commute. Both the business and law schools have VERY new (less than five years old) buildings, which are GORGEOUS with laptop/Internet hook-ups at almost every seat in every classroom, amazing libraries and are VERY, VERY nice. The campuses are pretty safe, very nicely maintained and just pleasant to be on.

The neighborhood is a mix of student housing/dining/laundromat kind of things and VERY upscale homes, so there is some tension there, but it's not the dangerous kind. It is maybe 30 to 45 minutes on the B line to downtown Boston, but only about 15 by cab. Cleveland Circle, Brookline and Newton Center are all student neighborhoods where you can get to either campus in 15 minutes by public transportation and all are full of nice, but affordable, housing, Starbucks, Thai restaurants, Irish bars, upscale microbreweries...pretty much anything you want! Being a grad student, the undergrads can get a little wearing, but it still is nice to be able to go to BC football games, which are very "rah rah," and have that campus life but be near enough a city that you can have a real internship or go clubbing when the mood strikes. One thing that is not cool on campus is that the undergrad dining facilities are pretty bad (gloopy pizza, dreary tables, 18-

year-olds screaming and throwing food at each other), and getting off campus to a restaurant and back between classes is pretty tight. Most grads bring food in during the day.

Status: Alumnus/a, full-time
Dates of Enrollment: 8/2000-5/2003
Survey Submitted: September 2003

Those from out of town must be aware that BC is not in Boston!!! Every year first-years from outside Massachusetts end up in Cambridge or Boston and have a ridiculous commute. The benefit of being in the suburbs is a beautiful campus. There is plenty of grassy space to eat lunch, play frisbee or occasionally have class outside. Clubs also hold picnics and other events outdoors, and if the weather is nice graduation is outdoors as well. BC is divided into two campuses, and the law school is about one mile west of the main campus. The only other people on the law campus are freshmen from the undergraduate school. Thus, the law campus has a very overpriced (though not too horrible) cafeteria, a very small gym and a closet-sized bookstore. But for most services, the main campus will serve students better. The gym is $250/year (spouses may join for the same price) and offers free personal training, numerous classes and full aerobic and weight rooms. The cafeterias are much better on the main campus and the book store is huge. It does not stock course books, but it has more school supplies and BC clothing.

The law school neighborhood is beautiful, but the main campus area is more dangerous. There are at least two to three reports a year of armed robberies on the streets. Anyone with a car should consider living in a safer area and students should always walk in groups at night. The BC police are very responsive, however, and look out for the students. The dining halls are getting more and more conducive to vegetarians, now offering tofu scrambles in addition to eggs and vegetarian soups. But the pricing is based on freshman undergraduates whose parents pay for points on their dining cards, so many law students will want to bring their own lunches or go out to local restaurants (which are plentiful, cheap and good!).

Social Life

Status: Alumnus/a, full-time
Dates of Enrollment: 9/1984-5/1987
Survey Submitted: May 2006

There are many student organizations on campus to become involved with. There is no lack of opportunities to network with fellow students. We would frequently have campus BBQs, dances and open bar events. There was also a law school drama event where students paraded student life. Boston has a fantastic night life with numerous bars, pubs and discos The sports scene is also fantastic. Apart from the campus teams which do well in football, basketball and hockey, the Red Sox and Patriots give any sports fan something to cheer about.

Status: Alumnus/a, full-time
Dates of Enrollment: 8/1989-5/1992
Survey Submitted: April 2006

The law school is extremely friendly. We used to call it the Disneyland or the "warm and fuzzy" law school. The administration instills in students from day one, that we are to treat each other with mutual respect. Least you be mislead, the students are smart and savvy—but not cutthroat. The social scene is very good for law school. A number of my classmates met at BC and are happily married. It was a wonderful place to spend three years...if you have to go to law school

Status: Current student, full-time
Dates of Enrollment: 9/2003-Submit Date
Survey Submitted: April 2006

Newton is a family city. Most eating places close pretty early—like nine during the week and 11 on the weekend. There are a couple of fun bars/restaurants that students frequent. Most of the time students hang out in the Brighton area or go downtown. Boston has a great nightlife and has great public transportation. The only problem is that the T shuts down at 12:30 a.m., so cab rides home can get expensive.

BC plans a lot of social events throughout the year. We have a Harbor Cruise and Halloween party in the fall, Bar Reviews every month, a prom in the spring, intramural sports (mainly softball in the fall), trivia in the snack bar. There are also lots of great events going on at the law school year round, as well. Speakers, attorneys, authors, scholars—a lot of really noteworthy people come to BC every year.

Status: Alumnus/a, full-time
Dates of Enrollment: 9/1991-5/1994
Survey Submitted: April 2006

When I was at BCLS, we prided ourselves in being the "Disneyland" of law schools. The atmosphere was competitive, but not cutthroat. I had a large circle of friends. We would often attend school-sponsored social functions (weekly happy hours and Halloween party) and also would go out at least once a weekend most weekends to a bar or night club, either locally or in downtown Boston. Boston is not a cheap city, especially on a student's budget, but we managed to have a good time. Although I did not have personal experience with the dating scene (I was in an exclusive relationship throughout law school), it seemed to be a pretty good scene, considering that several of my friends married their BCLS classmates.

Status: Alumnus/a, full-time
Dates of Enrollment: 8/2002-5/2005
Survey Submitted: March 2006

The social life at the law school is fairly insular. The age range of the law students range from early 20s to 40s so many people are married or in serious relationships. Dating among the students certainly happens, but law students are busy. Really busy. The law school periodically organizes events like Bar Reviews on campus or at local pubs where students and sometimes faculty can mingle and drink. There are clubs, but most are academically oriented. 1Ls tend to be more sociable, especially within their section (BC has three sections of about 90 for 1Ls) because they are on the same schedules. Once separate classes and journal/law review responsibilities set in for 2Ls and 3Ls, people socialize on their own time in smaller groups. Newton has a couple of bars, but most people go downtown where the bar scene is big and crowded.

Status: Current student, full-time
Dates of Enrollment: 8/2005-Submit Date
Survey Submitted: September 2005

Students immediately form strong friendships when they get to campus, regardless of age, race, religion or even political views. Excursions to Boston bars, house parties and various receptions and events spice up the life of a law student. Whether the students are looking for intellectual activities such as lectures and symposiums, fun at bars and clubs or cultural activities like theater, art or music, law students can find it around campus at BC.

Status: Current student, full-time
Dates of Enrollment: 8/2003-Submit Date
Survey Submitted: February 2005

I think that BC does a good job of mixing up the types of students. There were many married and engaged students and I think that has to do with the age of the students. Most students here are social and there is a good community atmosphere. There are many bars in the Fenway area where people go. A favorite spot is An Tua Nua. Also in Newton is the Union Bar and Grill, which has half-price burgers on Thursday. Personally, I am not much to hang out with the law students in general because of other social commitments I have. However, there are things to do here because you are in the city and many of the students live by a T so that they can do something. No Greek system. Dating your law school classmates is just a messy business all around.

Status: Current student, full-time
Dates of Enrollment: 8/2003-Submit Date
Survey Submitted: November 2004

Social life at BCLS is good but not exceptional. Everyone is friendly but the school can be sort of cliquish. I was disappointed that social life here is pretty much like it was when I was an undergraduate—a lot of going out to bars and getting drunk.

There are a fair number of older students. Many people come to BCLS after getting PhDs and masters degrees and a lot of people arrive at BCLS already

Read all of Vault's Law School Surveys at www.vault.com/lawschool — get complete surveys on top law schools, expert advice on applicaton essays, LSAT prep and more.

VAULT CAREER LIBRARY 305

married. The school is large enough, I think, for everyone to find a crowd that they like.

Status: Alumnus/a, full-time
Dates of Enrollment: 8/2000-5/2003
Survey Submitted: September 2003

There is no Greek system at BC. The law school has a chapter of PAD, the legal fraternity (co-ed), but it costs to join. The law school hosts tons of events. There are speakers nearly every week—during my years I saw Mr. Korematsu, from the Japanese internment case, Ken Starr and three Holocaust survivors. Each of the law reviews hosts symposiums during the year that bring together a number of speakers on diverse topics. The school also has a Law Students Association (LSA), which plans social and charitable events. Every few weeks we had a Bar Review, which was a night out at a local bar. The LSA also hosts a Halloween party and a few on-campus barbecues, as well as an annual semiformal gala. Students can also take part in an LSA-sponsored charity race and a number of work days at local schools and Boys and Girls Club-type places.

Students usually go out on their own on weekends. Boston is a great city to be near for students, and since BC ID's don't distinguish between undergrad and grad students, they will get law students into movies, theater and other events at student prices! Many students go out to lunch if they have time or dinner if they're studying late (an unfortunate reality!). Johnny's and Cabots are popular local diners, with tons of healthy and vegetarian options and ice cream. JP Licks is also a good ice cream place. Newton and Boston are also known for ethnic food. Newton has Coconut Cafe for Thai, Cafe Sol Azteca for Mexican, Sapporo for Japanese, Sabra for Middle Eastern, and India Palace for Indian. Boston has everything from Cambodian to Ethiopian. Newton has one popular bar, Union Street, a popular place for lunch and dinner, drinks and weekend brunch. BC gives out a discount card that, among other things, gives 15 percent off food at Union Street.

The School Says

The school offers the following student testimonial:

From the admissions process to graduation, BC Law has been the perfect place for me! The law school seems to always include the full picture in everything it does. The admissions office remembered my application essay the first day I walked in the door. I was more than just an LSAT score and a GPA. As I began studying the law, professors did not merely ask us to repeat what the law says. They made us question if it was right. The law is not just something you find in books. Learning the law includes joining a clinical program and finding yourself in front of a real judge arguing motions for a real client. What's more, the school's commitment to the students does not stop at the classroom door. As president of the student government association, I can attest to the personal attention the dean for students office gives to students facing personal, family or other challenges while attending school. And finally, BC follows you all the way to your job after graduation. I will be working at a law firm in my hometown of Nashville, Tennessee due to BC's good national name and career services' wise guidance. I have had a great experience with the career services office. They do a great job working with many different kinds of people. If you are choosing among top law schools, you will forever be grateful for making BC Law your path to the legal profession.

Sincerely,

Kenny Byrd, former LSA President

byrdk@bc.edu

Boston University School of Law

Admissions Office
765 Commonwealth Avenue
Boston, MA 02215
Admissions phone: (617) 353-3100
Admissions e-mail: bulawadm@bu.edu
Admissions URL:
http://www.bu.edu/law/prospective/apply/

Note: The school has chosen not to comment on the student surveys submitted.

 Admissions

Status: Alumnus/a, full-time
Dates of Enrollment: 8/2001-5/2004
Survey Submitted: April 2006

BUSL does seem to look for people who have interesting and diverse backgrounds and not just in a racial sense; people who have worked a couple years after undergrad before law school doing unique volunteer work, working abroad in public-interest type jobs or working in the government for a year or two.

Status: Alumnus/a, full-time
Dates of Enrollment: 8/1995-5/1998
Survey Submitted: April 2006

In my case, I felt that having an undergraduate degree in a field that was so different from most law school applicants helped make my application stand out. I was a Phys Ed major.) As far as the essays go, in my experience, it helps to write essays that explain your motivation for wanting to go to law school. It certainly can't hurt to tug at the heart strings as well. I wrote an essay about an abused little boy I met during student teaching to show why I wanted to become a lawyer and work on children's defense issues.

Status: Alumnus/a, full-time
Dates of Enrollment: 8/1998-5/2001
Survey Submitted: March 2006

BUSL has a competitive admissions process and draws a strong group of academic candidates. Current students call prospectives and give them advice and information regarding the process, which is helpful and makes the experience more personal. The admissions office is also helpful. The financial aid office is less helpful and responsive.

Status: Alumnus/a, full-time
Dates of Enrollment: 8/2001-5/2003
Survey Submitted: March 2005

Boston University has a highly competitive admissions process. Many people want to go to graduate school in Boston, and rightfully so, as it is a terrific place to study. Therefore, most people apply to BU and BC and make their decision based on preference.

Status: Alumnus/a, full-time
Dates of Enrollment: 8/1999-5/2002
Survey Submitted: March 2005

As with all schools, get in there and meet them face-to-face and tell them why they should admit you. Of course, write well and make sure your references (preferably at least one judge) are air-tight. Also, meet with financial aid people because they will be more likely to award you more money if you've got a personal relationship with them or at least they at least can put a face to your name.

Status: Alumnus/a, full-time
Dates of Enrollment: 8/1996-5/1999
Survey Submitted: March 2005

BUSL is a very selective institution. More than others, they seem to value diversity of experiences in candidates. My prior professional experience seemed to have been valued more at BUSL than at other schools to which I applied. I applaud them in this regard because I think that diverse pre-law school experiences make for a better learning environment.

Status: Current student, full-time
Dates of Enrollment: 9/2002-Submit Date
Survey Submitted: October 2003

The admissions office is very responsive during the whole process. BU's admissions office conducts itself with an extremely personal touch. They called me to tell me about my acceptance before they sent a letter. With increasing selectivity, the school has also seen an amazing surge in applications. The mean LSAT score jumped from about 160 to somewhere between 163 and 165. They seem to like diverse and untraditional students. Most of the students here took some time off before coming to school, something that I highly recommend.

Status: Alumnus/a, full-time
Dates of Enrollment: 9/2000-0/2003
Survey Submitted: October 2003

The essay is really important in the admissions process. The admissions office has staff read them, and often other professors will read and comment on them as well. It is very important to identify why you want to pursue a legal career and how you think BUSL will get you there. BU has gotten really competitive in the numbers since I was there (partly due to the economy, I'm sure). There is a real interest in attracting people from different fields (especially folks with non-legal careers).

Status: Alumnus/a, full-time
Dates of Enrollment: 8/1999-5/2002
Survey Submitted: April 2004

I applied for Early Admission and was accepted. I had no interview. My essay focused on a personal situation, how I handled it and how I grew because of it. My undergrad GPA from a small school was 3.71 and my LSAT was 162, and despite early acceptance at BU I was waitlisted at Boston College. I suspect the difference was I had a letter of recommendation from a BU alum.

Status: Alumnus/a, full-time
Dates of Enrollment: 9/1999-1/2001
Survey Submitted: November 2003

The administrative staff was readily available to answer questions and address concerns; they returned all my phone calls immediately. Although there was no interview process, I spoke to the admissions director several times on the phone and she was very insightful. She gave me a clear idea of the admissions criteria and the high standards for admission.

Status: Current student, full-time
Dates of Enrollment: 9/2003-Submit Date
Survey Submitted: November 2003

Getting more selective in the past two years due to high number of applicants. Essentially numbers-oriented. If you meet the required LSAT and GPA cutoffs you will probably be admitted. Not a lot of weight given to job experience, extracurriculars or recommendations. Being a minority helps a little; being from California or other non-East Coast states also helps a little.

Status: Alumnus/a, full-time
Dates of Enrollment: 8/1999-5/2003
Survey Submitted: April 2004

Admissions process is set forth in detail on BUSL's web site. Score 160 or higher on your LSAT and carry at least a 3.6 GPA from a Top 100 undergraduate university. BUSL is more selective than not, but unlike some law schools, a

Read all of Vault's Law School Surveys at www.vault.com/lawschool — get complete surveys on top law schools, expert advice on applicaton essays, LSAT prep and more.

VAULT CAREER LIBRARY 307

lower LSAT can be offset by a higher undergraduate GPA, depending on the university and curriculum. There were no interviews when I applied. If BUSL does conduct application interviews now, then they will probably be less impressed with a demonstration of your IQ and more impressed with your ability to carry a conversation. Regarding essays—content is probably less important than style and format.

 ## Academics

Status: Alumnus/a, full-time
Dates of Enrollment: 8/2001-5/2004
Survey Submitted: April 2006

First year, your grades somewhat depend on how lucky you are in getting into a section with nicer, more generous professors. My section had the hardest professors so our 1L curve for that section was a B- while the other two sections had curves around a regular B/B+. This wasn't fair to our section when all sections were lumped together as a 2L class.

Status: Alumnus/a, full-time
Dates of Enrollment: 8/1995-5/1998
Survey Submitted: April 2006

The faculty at BUSL is generally excellent. Professors Petit, Maclin and Volk are topnotch, as are many others. They are the types of professors you will remember long after leaving law school. Grading is tough at BUSL. If you are used to getting excellent grades, it can be a shock at first. The workload is tolerable, although things seem to hit all at once because mid-semester and end-of-semester deadlines are quite common. You will get good at managing your time while you're in law school at BUSL. Professors generally do not take into consideration obligations other professors have put on students, so keep that in mind.

Status: Alumnus/a, full-time
Dates of Enrollment: 8/1998-5/2001
Survey Submitted: March 2006

Most of the students in my first-year section, including myself, were Ivy League grads and many, regardless of undergrad, had graduated with honors and/or had very diverse backgrounds and brought a good deal to the table. The professors were excellent; without exception a topnotch faculty. Workload was heavy but manageable.

Status: Alumnus/a, full-time
Dates of Enrollment: 8/2000-5/2003
Survey Submitted: April 2005

I can't say enough about the professors. They all love teaching and take the time to make sure you understand what they are trying to teach. Very accessible office hours and seem to care about the students as whole, not just as a seat in their class. Grading varied, though the school runs on a B+ curve. Workload was significant but manageable—no busywork. Excellent clinical programs, too.

Status: Alumnus/a, full-time
Dates of Enrollment: 8/2001-5/2003
Survey Submitted: March 2005

In a word, excellent. Even years later, I am amazed at the terrific education BU Law gave me. Grading is on a B+ mandatory curve for classes of 25 people or more. You can always get into classes—often, talking to the professor directly helps. It just is not an issue. The course selection is gigantic and diverse. The professors are amazing. I still correspond with two professors and there were countless trips to the Pub with professors after final exams. It is a great community of academics; the law school is a closely-knit community in the big city.

Status: Alumnus/a, full-time
Dates of Enrollment: 8/1998-5/2001
Survey Submitted: March 2005

The professors at BUSL are outstanding—recognized scholars in their areas of work, but always available to take time to meet with students after and outside of class. They offered a wide range of classes and first-years were allowed to

take an elective second semester. I was never shut out of a class I wanted to take. The writing program is excellent, with small classes with hands-on teaching assistants.

Status: Alumnus/a, full-time
Dates of Enrollment: 8/1999-5/2002
Survey Submitted: April 2004

My second year, the school added a second session of a UCC course taught by the popular Professor Miller after more than 150 students signed up. The tough classes to get are the seminars; they are very specialized and generally have only 10 to 30 students each (I think the limit was 30). Seminars fill up fast because most have no final exam, only a paper due at the end of the semester. They are sought-after classes, particularly any IP seminars. I took a number of IP courses including IP General, Copyright and Trademark.

BU is known as a top IP school for good reason: the IP professors are topnotch. Professor Muerer teaches IP and Patent. He grades very fairly and practically hands out his entire outline of the course to you in the form of slides.

Status: Alumnus/a, full-time
Dates of Enrollment: 8/1999-5/2002
Survey Submitted: April 2004

The classes vary a lot depending on the professor. Almost all are Socratic during the first year. I occasionally did not get the classes I wanted during registration, but I was always able to get in by showing up on the first day.

There are a lot of seminars taught by adjunct professors who are lawyers in the community. Those were some of the best classes I took because they were completely real-world-oriented (a law school rarity). The workload is not overwhelming, although it might seem that way to someone who went straight from undergrad. I worked for four years before matriculating and found law school to be much less time-consuming than my former job.

Status: Current student, full-time
Dates of Enrollment: 9/2002-Submit Date
Survey Submitted: October 2003

They take a lot of pride in the faculty and for the most part this pride is well-founded. The professors are leading experts in their areas of expertise, not only in New England but also in the country and the world. An interviewer at a prestigious Chicago firm told me that one of my professors basically created the business of alternative dispute resolution. Another professor regularly writes Supreme Court Amicus briefs on criminal procedure issues. A few years ago, the school went on a recruiting rampage and got many professors from very elite law schools. Most people are surprised that a lot of the professors are not teaching at Harvard or Yale. Despite their obvious brilliance, most professors are extremely accessible outside of class.

First year, you are put in sections so you do not have any control over your curriculum or professors. In later years, students select their courses through a somewhat elusive lottery system. Although people do not always get every class they want, the system seems to be fair and third-year students definitely have priority. The school also offers numerous clinical programs and study abroad opportunities. Given the school's ties with the Boston legal market, a lot of people get amazing positions through the clinical and externship programs.

Status: Alumnus/a, full-time.
Dates of Enrollment: 8/2000-5/2003
Survey Submitted: October 2003

Professors are amazing and highly approachable. They are challenging yet friendly. Grades are curved on a B/B- scale. Criminal Clinic professors were the best. They were by far my favorites to learn from and work with. Workload is intense in the first year as at all law schools, but by the third year, it's great.

Status: Current student, full-time
Dates of Enrollment: 8/2003-Submit Date
Survey Submitted: February 2004

Professors are the pride and joy of BU. The school makes sure to provide a wide range of professor-types to each section during the first-year program, and all but one were absolutely great: motivated, experienced, energetic and they actually teach you things.

Status: Alumnus/a, full-time LLM
Dates of Enrollment: 8/2001-5/2002
Survey Submitted: January 2004

The one-year program gives you great freedom in selecting your courses and concentrating in the areas that interest you. As an LLM student, you are pretty much certain to have access to all the classes that you desire. A few exceptions may apply to the seminars and clinics. The grading curve also only applies to LLM students if there is a certain number of LLM students registered for the class, and generally the LLMs are judged on the same level as the JDs. The workload entirely depends on your habits, goals and English abilities. The quality of classes depends on the professor. BU has some excellent professors in IP, Taxation, Health and Dispute Resolution.

Status: Alumnus/a, full-time
Dates of Enrollment: 9/2000-6/2003
Survey Submitted: October 2003

The clinical programs (civil or criminal) are fantastic. The professors in those programs know what they are doing. They are a great bunch of folks. Because you spend so much time at the clinic office with your fellow classmates and professors, you get to know them really well. It's a great bonding experience. I would definitely recommend the clinical programs at BU.

 Employment Prospects

Status: Alumnus/a, full-time
Dates of Enrollment: 8/2001-5/2004
Survey Submitted: April 2006

In 2004, the legal job market was quite tough, especially for anyone who wasn't in the top 25 percent of the class and who was looking for jobs outside of Boston, New York and D.C. Getting a job at a big firm through OCI shouldn't be a problem if you're in the top 20 percent of the class and not socially inept. There are also good public-interest opportunities, but dismal loan repayment assistance. Career services does not think outside the box, and isn't that helpful if you're not in the top 20 or 30 percent.

Status: Alumnus/a, full-time
Dates of Enrollment: 8/1995-5/1998
Survey Submitted: April 2006

I have found that employers are very impressed when they hear I graduated from BUSL. I did not use the career center as much as I should have. I assumed that since I was not a top percent student, they would not have jobs for me. That was not a correct assumption. The career center was very helpful when my second-year summer job fell through—that situation actually landed me a job that led to a full-time attorney position after graduation. Whenever I have needed anything, the career center has been very responsive.

Status: Alumnus/a, full-time
Dates of Enrollment: 8/1998-5/2001
Survey Submitted: March 2005

If you want to work in the Boston area, the prestige of BU is great. If you want to work in another state, only the top, top firms seem to recruit on campus. So if you're in the middle of the class and looking for an out-of-state job, you must work a lot on your own. I know the school has an alumni network but, again, most alumni are located on the East Coast and they are not very helpful if you plan to go elsewhere after graduation. If you want to stay on the East Coast, there's lots of recruiting and alumni networking available.

Status: Current student, full-time
Dates of Enrollment: 8/2003-Submit Date
Survey Submitted: November 2004

Once you get out of the top third, it gets more difficult to get on-campus interviews/jobs, but not impossible. I know a person in the middle third who recently received offers from two big Boston firms. This seems to be more of an exception than the rule, but it shows that it can be done. Also, the career services office is helpful, but you have to go to them; they will not come to you.

Status: Alumnus/a, full-time
Dates of Enrollment: 8/1999-5/2002
Survey Submitted: April 2004

BU has a national reputation, and I interviewed with employers all over the country, eventually choosing a West Coast firm. That said, the majority of employers who come to campus are East Coast firms. The school does set up off-campus job fairs around the country. It is your responsibility to pay to get yourself to those, but I got several job offers from them, so it is probably a good deal. It doesn't seem that clerkships are highly emphasized, although that seems to be changing. It seems to me that those below the top third had a tough time in the job search during second year. About a year after graduation, I have a few friends who still don't have jobs, but those tend to be people who didn't do very well and have specific and inflexible demands.

Status: Alumnus/a, full-time
Dates of Enrollment: 8/2000-5/2003
Survey Submitted: April 2004

The career development office is helpful with job placement. With the assistance of the CDO, I found my summer job after my first year of law school from the CDO and obtained my summer associate position with my current firm. I am now a full-time associate at the firm where I summered.

Status: Alumnus/a, full-time
Dates of Enrollment: 8/2000-5/2003
Survey Submitted: April 2004

Decent career services, although they are unwilling to spend too much time with first-year students. They seem to have pretty good contacts, and most of the prestigious firms interview on campus. However, you are somewhat on your own if applying for jobs outside the Northeast Corridor.

Status: Alumnus/a, full time
Dates of Enrollment: 9/1999-1/2001
Survey Submitted: November 2003

BU has an excellent reputation among employers, especially on the East Coast. There is a large network of alumni all over the nation, and the alumni association is constantly hosting receptions in most large cities to facilitate networking. Their on-campus recruiting was extensive and resulted in most students receiving offers. Many of my classmates moved out of Massachusetts.

Status: Current student, full-time
Dates of Enrollment: 9/2002-Submit Date
Survey Submitted: October 2003

The career development office is geared towards big firm jobs. Even in a tough market, people at the top of the class get interviews with top firms all over the country. You probably need to be in the top 30 percent to get those though. There is also an emphasis on clerkships, although the programs they have set up are not too helpful. As for government opportunities, that is a weak part of BU's CDO.

Status: Alumnus/a, full-time
Dates of Enrollment: 9/2000-6/2003
Survey Submitted: October 2003

Yes, there is a career development office, but you have to learn how to use their resources. First, they will not land you a job. The CDO is great in telling you where to go, giving you the resources and giving you feedback. I found a great person there that I talked to for three years through the ups and downs. Yes, the top whatever percent will have jobs thrown at them (at least a few years ago they did). The rest of us have to find jobs through networking, shaking hands, collecting business cards and going to bar association meetings. The administration has tried to improve the CDO (for instance, by having someone at the front desk who knows your name). They do listen to the consumers (the students) and try to improve their services.

Status: Alumnus/a, full-time
Dates of Enrollment: 8/1999-5/2002
Survey Submitted: April 2004

All the big firms from Boston interviewed on campus. In addition, the school was part of job fairs in NY, D.C., Miami, Chicago, L.A. and even Manchester, NH for smaller firms from VT, NH and ME. I did not hear of many people who

Read all of Vault's Law School Surveys at www.vault.com/lawschool — get complete surveys on top law schools, expert advice on applicaton essays, LSAT prep and more.

VAULT CAREER LIBRARY   309

could not find a second-year internship, and the staff in the career development office was very helpful.

Quality of Life

Status: Alumnus/a, full-time
Dates of Enrollment: 8/2001-5/2004
Survey Submitted: April 2006

Neighborhood is awesome, it's right by Kenmore Square, on the Charles River. The law building is unattractive but has awesome views of Boston and the Charles. And it's located right on the central BU campus near the great student center with decent food options and a nice grassy quad area. It's also right on the T (subway) line in Boston proper.

Status: Alumnus/a, full-time
Dates of Enrollment: 8/1995-5/1998
Survey Submitted: April 2006

BU is a great place to go to school. The campus is not the most beautiful you'll ever see, but it is safe, active and full of energy. The union has a large food court that is quite nice. On-campus housing for law students is minimal, but there is plenty of off-campus housing that is often nicer and more affordable that the BU on-campus apartments. The off-campus housing office will help students to find roommates. BU has a brand-new sporting facility and student village.

Status: Alumnus/a, full-time
Dates of Enrollment: 8/2000-5/2003
Survey Submitted: April 2005

Facilities are old and dated—most people don't care that they attend "the tallest law school in the nation." Currently, there is a capital campaign in progress to fund a badly needed new building. Campus is urban, right in the middle of Boston; which is either good or bad depending on what you prefer. You certainly have access to a wide variety of housing and dining options, but crime can also be an issue (like in any big city).

Status: Alumnus/a, full-time
Dates of Enrollment: 8/1998-5/2001
Survey Submitted: March 2005

Housing in Boston is AWFUL, in terms of getting a place. Make sure to look for an apartment before the summer. As a law student, you have access to the undergrad student union and activities. BUSL has a great student government that always had something going on, from inviting speakers to organizing an annual ski trip and monthly socials on the 12th floor of the school.

Status: Alumnus/a, full-time
Dates of Enrollment: 8/2000-5/2003
Survey Submitted: April 2004

The facilities at Boston University School of Law are long due for renovations. The recent addition of a cafeteria and lounges is nice and the first-year classrooms are great but all other rooms need work. The acoustics and comfort (or rather lack thereof) of the chairs can be problematic sometimes.

Nice neighborhood. Beautiful view of the Charles River and "BU Beach." There aren't enough dining selections around the school—more often than not, if you don't have a car you'll have to settle for the food served at the student union.

Status: Alumnus/a, full-time
Dates of Enrollment: 8/1999-5/2002
Survey Submitted: April 2004

Boston is a great town but it's expensive. There is no on-campus housing for law students (at least there wasn't when I was there; although who would want to live in a dorm with a bunch of other stressed-out law students anyway?). My two-bedroom seemed ridiculous at $1,400 per month when I started school, but was an absolute bargain three years later when I left. You can live farther away for cheaper, but I would advise against it. Most students live in the Brookline, Allston or Brighton areas, so there is always a lot going on and it's easy to take the T to school. As far as crime goes, it is a city but the area around BU is quite safe. I always felt safe there.

Status: Current student, full-time
Dates of Enrollment: 9/2002-Submit Date
Survey Submitted: October 2003

The student body is extremely high strung. This is almost certainly a product of BU's ranking—good, bordering on excellent. A lot of people did not get into the school of their choice so they have something to prove. Also, the strict curve and obvious benefits of being at the top of the class add to the competitiveness. For the most part, people are nice and genuine (just really intense and academic).

The campus is undergoing massive change. BU is in the process of building a new student gym, new hockey arena and a new basketball stadium. The Law Tower is definitely BUSL's biggest drawback—it's ugly, the elevator system is inefficient, and the temperature is rarely comfortable. The classrooms are nice, however, and there are plugs and wireless Internet all over the building. The school is addressing the facilities issue and they plan on starting the construction of a brand-new, state-of-the-art facility within the next few years.

Since BU is an urban campus, security is something of a concern. The new building will probably make security better. Aside from the petty thefts, the urban location of BU has a lot of benefits. It is about three blocks from Fenway Park and it definitely makes Boston more accessible to BU students.

Housing is EXPENSIVE; there really is no way around that. Even though the Boston housing market is rough, BU helps incoming law students get in touch with each other with access to message boards and realtors. Although the school does not have on-campus housing for law students, the neighborhoods surrounding the school provide a wide range—in quality and price—of living options for students. Also, Boston's size and public transportation system means that students do not need of cars. In Boston, cars are expensive and a major pain, so spare yourself the trouble unless you have other concerns such as family nearby, children or a spouse.

Social Life

Status: Alumnus/a, full-time
Dates of Enrollment: 8/2001-5/2004
Survey Submitted: April 2006

Great social life. SBA had lots of fun events and subsidizes most of them with drink tickets and discounted drinks. Tons of bars and restaurants in the area and in Boston to go to with friends. Lots of dating amongst students. Good size, too—about 260 per class, so you end up knowing a lot of people by 3L year but not feel sick of them.

Status: Alumnus/a, full-time
Dates of Enrollment: 8/1995-5/1998
Survey Submitted: April 2006

A lot of drinking goes on at BUSL. School-sponsored social events have alcohol and law students at BUSL take them up on that offer and then some. Being located in Boston right near Kenmore Square, there are plenty of restaurants, bars, concerts and events to participate in or attend.

Status: Alumnus/a, full-time
Dates of Enrollment: 8/2000-5/2003
Survey Submitted: April 2005

Pretty active social scene, both school-sponsored and otherwise. The average law student is fairly young—I think it was 23 when I was there—so lots of parties and late-night bar stops. People also got together to go to Sox games and hang out. Plenty of options in the city for whatever it is you like to do for fun.

Status: Current student, full-time
Dates of Enrollment: 8/2003-Submit Date
Survey Submitted: November 2004

You really can't beat Boston as a college town. There are great student bars near where most students live and plenty more downtown. Great Italian restaurants in the North End (something like 85 in a four-block radius) and, obviously, excellent seafood all over the place. Also, if you are sports fan, forget about it!

Status: Alumnus/a, full-time LLM
Dates of Enrollment: 8/2001-5/2002
Survey Submitted: January 2004

LLMs and JDs mixed a lot; there was a ton of partying. Boston also has a huge number of bars and clubs that are very accessible. However, you should know that everything closes at 2 a.m. Some of the most popular clubs are the three clubs near Fenway Park on Landsdowne Street, and [Gypsy] downtown (excellent Latino nights on Wednesdays). There are also bars on Commonwealth Avenue that are popular with the students, and BU has its own place called "The Castle," which is nice. In Allston, Brighton Avenue offers sports bars and partying like nowhere else. If you live off campus, Allston is definitely the place to be, especially if you can find a house to share with some other students. I did it, and it was the best year ever!

Status: Alumnus/a, full time
Dates of Enrollment: 9/1999-1/2001
Survey Submitted: November 2003

Dating scene was very good according to my single friends. The student body is very diverse and open. There are many foreign students and the social groups are very exciting. There are so many bars and restaurants that there did not seem to be any one popular joint. There is a good-sized Chinatown with excellent restaurants that are fairly affordable for all. Newbury Street is very posh and populated by the chic and savvy. BU is very close to Fenway Park, which is loaded with sports bars and dance clubs. The city is also peppered with numerous gyms that are frequented by all the local schools (Harvard, New England School of Law, Northwestern, Boston College). And for those interested, there are excellent martial arts schools in various convenient locations. Excellent city.

Status: Alumnus/a, full-time
Dates of Enrollment: 8/1999-5/2002
Survey Submitted: April 2004

There is a lot of going out in large groups during the first year, less so in the second and third years as people hang out with their closer friends. The Pub (it's down some stairs by the BU central T stop, across Comm Ave from the law school) is a total dive and a big favorite after finals. They actually keep the law school finals schedule posted on the wall (so they know when to take your beer away and send you back over to the Tower?).

Status: Current student, full-time
Dates of Enrollment: 9/2002-Submit Date
Survey Submitted: October 2003

Students generally live in the Kenmore/Fenway/Brookline areas, which are smack dab in between BU and BC. Tons of students live in and around Coolidge Corner, and rightfully so because it is a great place to live with great restaurants (Zaftigs is the ultimate brunch place) and you have access to everything you need for everyday life (great grocery store on Comm Ave, Gap at Coolidge Corner). This area also provides easy access to the T ($2 per ride) so downtown Boston is barely a 20-minute ride away.

Some students also live in the area around Fenway Park (which is also popular with the BU undergrads so it is a bit more social and gets crazy during baseball season), which is also great because it is two T stops from Back Bay/Newbury Street (chic shopping, great people watching, good places to eat), and close to the Landmark Center, which provides things like Best Buy, REI, Boston Sports Club, Bed Bath and Beyond, movie theaters and so on. Also, the reading room at the Boston Public Library (Copley Square) offers a great place to study (complete with free Internet access) if you want to get away from the stress of the Law Tower.

Read all of Vault's Law School Surveys at www.vault.com/lawschool — get complete surveys on top law schools, expert advice on applicaton essays, LSAT prep and more.

VAULT CAREER LIBRARY 311

Use the Internet's
MOST TARGETED
job search tools.

Vault Job Board

Target your search by industry, function, and experience level, and find the job openings that you want.

VaultMatch Resume Database

Vault takes match-making to the next level: post your resume and customize your search by industry, function, experience and more. We'll match job listings with your interests and criteria and e-mail them directly to your in-box.

Harvard Law School

JD Admissions Office
Harvard Law School
1563 Massachusetts Avenue
Cambridge, MA 02138
Admissions phone: (617) 495-3109
Admissions e-mail: jdadmiss@law.harvard.edu
Admissions URL: www.law.harvard.edu/admissions/

Note: The school has chosen not to comment on the student surveys submitted.

 ## Admissions

Status: Current student, full-time
Dates of Enrollment: 9/2004-Submit Date
Survey Submitted: October 2005

People in the admissions department were very friendly, but I did have a sense through the entire process that if you had a certain LSAT score, you were virtually guaranteed a spot in the 1L class. I don't know what that score is, and I assume if everything else about you were terrible, you wouldn't get a spot. Or if you had a lousy LSAT score, but you were otherwise incredible, you might get a spot. But IN GENERAL, it seems that most of my classmates had very high scores (in the mid to upper 170s). I didn't have an interview at all, and I'm not sure it would have helped my chances if I had. I barely remember my essay, but I remember saying how enthusiastic I was about law school—how original, right?? I had been in another grad program before law school, so I thought it was important to explain why I was making the shift.

Status: Alumnus/a, full-time
Dates of Enrollment: 9/2001-5/2004
Survey Submitted: March 2006

I don't really know how I got in. The good grades and a good LSAT score (I would suggest taking a course like Kaplan) of course helped, but I believe I got into HLS because my resume from college was amazing. I had great references including a few Dean's from my college and, most importantly I studied abroad. I really believe that studying or living abroad will help your chances of getting into Harvard.

Status: Alumnus/a, full-time
Dates of Enrollment: 9/1998-5/2001
Survey Submitted: March 2006

Admissions here are difficult, but perhaps not as difficult as at the absolute most selective schools because HLS brings a bigger class through the door. I actually found this large class size to be a great benefit—selectivity may improve the school's *U.S. News* ranking, but I was constantly amazed by the diversity and the depth of experience of the people in my class.

Status: Current student, full-time
Dates of Enrollment: 9/2005-Submit Date
Survey Submitted: March 2006

LSATs and grades are key, but a good essay and extracurriculars are also necessary. The numbers can probably only hurt you rather than help you—a high score/GPA doesn't guarantee you'll get in, but they won't even look at your application if you're not near the range. The admissions committee clearly has their pick of who they want to take, and they're looking for a range of interests and activities so that when people graduate and go off to do important and exciting things, they get to boast about diverse alumni. Sadly, this means that for some people, it can just be good/bad luck of whether someone with very similar credentials is applying in the same year. For example, the admissions committee may not need more than one Hispanic woman who studied art history

and speaks Russian per year. Regardless, pointing out what makes you a unique and indispensible candidate for admission is important.

Status: Current student, full-time
Dates of Enrollment: 9/2005-Submit Date
Survey Submitted: November 2005

While grades and LSAT scores are very important, the school does look at other things. Just make sure your overall application is strong. If you have superior grades and LSAT scores and were in a lot of activities in undergrad your app should be fine (but no guarantees). But there are many students here, like me, who have been out of undergrad for two or more years, which is a great time to beef up your resume, if your grades and LSAT scores are in HLS's bottom 25 percent.

Status: Alumnus/a, full-time
Dates of Enrollment: 8/1998-5/2003
Survey Submitted: April 2005

Highly selective admissions process that is guided far more by GPA and LSAT scores than the admissions process office would want to admit. With a class of around 550, it is only natural that Harvard is less quirky in its admissions process than say, Stanford or Yale, simply because of the larger numbers it has to fill. Students have no input into the actual process so it hard to say how much the 500-word essay matters.

Status: Alumnus/a, full-time
Dates of Enrollment: 10/1999-5/2002
Survey Submitted: March 2005

No interviews, standard paper application with essays, highly selective but don't let that discourage you. Because of the size of the classes and Harvard's conscious efforts at building an interesting and diverse class, lots of folks who thought they'd never get in did because of some unique attribute or life experience. Obviously, you need high undergrad grades and a pretty darn good LSAT, but if not within those parameters, don't conclude that you are out.

Status: Alumnus/a, full-time
Dates of Enrollment: 9/1999-6/2002
Survey Submitted: March 2005

The admissions process is grueling. Aside from the academic qualifications, the possibility of being placed on hold (and then subsequently waitlisted) means a long wait for a final decision in some cases. But take heart, quite a few of my friends stuck out the process and were admitted off of the waitlist.

Status: Alumnus/a, full-time
Dates of Enrollment: 9/2001-5/2004
Survey Submitted: March 2005

Harvard is basically a numbers game. They tell you that they look for interesting people in the application, but my property professor was on the admissions committee and he told our section quite candidly that he only "occasionally" even reads an essay. Unlike some law schools, Harvard puts little to no weight on work experience prior to law school. The class is basically made up of really, really smart type-A personalities, with no real life experience. Unless your GPA and LSAT numbers fit into the *USNWR* "grid," acceptance is a long-shot no matter how interesting your background is.

Status: Alumnus/a, full-time
Dates of Enrollment: 9/2000-6/2003
Survey Submitted: April 2004

HLS is highly selective. The school tends to take significant numbers of applicants from the Ivies, particularly Harvard and Yale, and equivalent schools, such as Duke and Stanford. HLS appears to take at least one student from every other major college and university in the country (you'll need to be a 4.0 student or otherwise stand out). The application process is no different than that found at other major law schools. Be aware that HLS has, in addition to accept, decline and the waitlist, a fourth response category for applicants known as "hold."

Read all of Vault's Law School Surveys at www.vault.com/lawschool — get complete surveys on top law schools, expert advice on applicaton essays, LSAT prep and more.

VAULT CAREER LIBRARY 313

Think of hold as an early waitlist (with better odds than the general waitlist). HLS notifies hold applicants of their status by the end of May (note that you may be accepted, declined or placed on the waitlist at that time).

HLS does not conduct interviews. There are no secrets for getting in—you need a solid GPA (preferably from a top undergrad program), a coherent, well-written essay and a solid LSAT score. The school also looks for outstanding or unique qualities (HLS regularly brags each year about the former astronauts and world-renowned pianists that matriculate in the incoming class).

Status: Alumnus/a, full-time
Dates of Enrollment: 9/1997-6/2000
Survey Submitted: April 2004

I was waitlisted, despite a 3.7 from an Ivy League and a 178 LSAT. I wrote a letter reaffirming my interest and included the information that I had made Phi Beta Kappa and that I had been featured in a *New York Times* article. I got in in July.

Status: Alumnus/a, full-time law
Dates of Enrollment: 9/1995-6/1998
Survey Submitted: July 2004

Like most law school admissions processes, HLS remains a "black box"—you need good grades, a good LSAT score and "that extra something" that comes through via the combination of your paper credentials and essays. If you're borderline on scores/grades, it probably makes sense to focus on "marketing yourself" to stand out. The trick is to do so in a way that is genuine (they're not stupid people), and positions you as someone who would add a unique voice to the chorus of bickering that is an HLS classroom.

 ## Academics

Status: Current student, full-time
Dates of Enrollment: 9/2004-Submit Date
Survey Submitted: October 2005

I'm a 2L now, so I'm just starting to pick my own classes. So far, it seems that most people are able to get most of the classes that they want. The professors are usually willing to open classes (other than seminars) to pretty much everyone who wants to take them. My 1L classes (all required with sections and profs assigned before the year starts) were half VERY good and half mediocre. They seem to distribute the good professors throughout the seven sections, and then fill the rest of the teaching with not-as-good professors. But from what I heard everyone had a pretty decent balance. The other students are incredibly smart and motivated, which makes for a lively and interesting discussion in every class. I found the grading standards pretty harsh (maybe because I did less well than I had hoped). There is a strict curve, so that means in EVERY 1L class (I don't know as much about upper-level classes) some students will get B-'s. And since the average is supposed to be between a B and a B+, as many students will get below that as will get above it. And this is in a group of people who have been used to getting the highest grades for the entire academic careers. When fall semester grades come out in early February a pall strikes the campus.

Status: Current student, full-time
Dates of Enrollment: 9/2003-Submit Date
Survey Submitted: October 2005

Harvard is much less intense than its reputation would lead people to believe. The quality of the classes and professors is extremely high, and due to the size of the school, there are classes offered in every subject imaginable. Grading seems fair; most people I know end up in the middle of the curve. The workload also seems normal; no more or less work than my friends are doing at other law schools.

Status: Current student, full-time
Dates of Enrollment: 9/2005-Submit Date
Survey Submitted: March 2006

We work hard and play hard. It's Harvard Law School, after all. On the one hand, everyone here is used to being an overachiever and is somewhat competitive. On the other, we're all pretty much guaranteed jobs at this point so there is a lot less incentive to do TOO much work. Those who want Supreme

Court clerkships still have to worry about grades, but the majority of students who will be fine starting with six figures at law firms are pretty much set. Professors are all across the spectrum—they're all brilliant, no doubt, but some are better lecturers than others and some will give you a lot harder time in the Socratic Method. In the first year, most of your classes are set, and you'll get many of the famous/popular professors even still. Grading is stressful in that everything rides on the one final exam, but good in the sense that you get to spend the whole semester not worrying about it.

Status: Current student, full-time
Dates of Enrollment: 9/2005-Submit Date
Survey Submitted: November 2005

The classes and professors are great. For those of you who have heard all the negatives surrounding HLS, they are no longer present. Thanks to the arrival of our new dean, Dean Kagan, the atmosphere of the school had completely changed. When I came to HLS for admit weekend, 3Ls all confirmed the drastic improvement due to the arrival of the new dean. In terms of the academic environment, the class is now split in to seven sections of 80 students. These are the students you spend your entire 1L year with. The professors are very accessible and there is a mandatory HLS sponsored lunch that the professors have with the students (in groups of five). The school is now heavily public-interest focused and provides guaranteed funding to any student who is interested. While I am interested in M&A it is nice to know that people with other interests are drawn to the school.

There is plenty of time to involve yourself in extracurricular activity with leadership roles. I, myself am involved in four groups on campus with a leadership role, and one that is purely social. I have heard that there can be competition for popular classes, but then I have also heard that some of the most famous professors are not the best teachers. Basic idea in terms of academics is it is what you make of it. Everyone here will get a job. If you are interested in the top 20 firms, then you want to focus heavily on the grades and law review. If you do not necessarily care about that you can spend more of your time with extracurriculars.

Status: Alumnus/a, full-time
Dates of Enrollment: 9/2001-6/2004
Survey Submitted: April 2005

The quality of some classes is high and others is low. Pick your classes based on the professor and past student comments on the class. It really makes a difference in your own grades whether you like the professor or not. Seminars can be particularly bad unless you have a very good professor. I got into every class I ever wanted to. If it's popular and oversubscribed, just keep trying or tell the registrar's office or the professor that you really want to take the class. The workload is heavy, but the same people know how to set limits on what they do and don't do.

Status: Alumnus/a, full-time
Dates of Enrollment: 9/1999-6/2002
Survey Submitted: March 2005

Academics are fantastic. I had some of the best professors of my life there, but the real point is learning from the other students. I'll always be glad to have had the opportunity to meet and work with so many sharp, articulate, well-informed people who disagreed with me. What a luxury! That being said, contrary to myth, many of the profs, even the superstars, are both excellent teachers and really nice people who are accessible to students. The workload is not bad at all unless you CHOOSE to kill yourself studying. Most people coast with B's and do very little work (an hour or two a day outside of class) because they know they'll still get great jobs. It is NOT a dog-eat-dog competitive environment. Everyone shares notes and outlines.

Status: Alumnus/a, full-time
Dates of Enrollment: 9/2001-5/2004
Survey Submitted: March 2005

Harvard is improving on this front. They implemented smaller 1L sections in 2001 and are trying to make classes more personal. Also, Dean Kagan (who just took over) is AWESOME and is doing much to try to whip the Law School into better shape. Unfortunately, a lot of the professors are still of the opinion that they are far superior intellectually to their students, so it is difficult to really build a relationship with some professors. (There are exceptions to this, but it is rare.) Arrogant professors aside, one nice thing about HLS is the fact that due to the school's large size, we have a plethora of interesting courses to take. I never had trouble getting into a course that I wanted to take. The workload is not that heavy either—it is very true that the hardest part about Harvard Law is getting accepted. As for grades, unless you are one of the few in the class who are truly brilliant, the grades will seem random. Not that it really matters though, because nobody ever gets below a B in anything.

Status: Alumnus/a, full-time
Dates of Enrollment: 9/2000-6/2003
Survey Submitted: April 2004

HLS is rigorous, perhaps more so than peer school Yale Law. You will likely find HLS to be much more demanding than college. Course quality varies and can be both pleasantly surprising or maddeningly frustrating. Professors are hired based on academic credentials, not teaching skills. It can almost be guaranteed that whoever you have as a professor will be brilliant; whether or not that person can teach well is another story. If you read course reviews and plan accordingly, you can generally do all right picking professors (except in the 1L year, when your course schedule is set for you).

The workload is heavy, but bearable. People generally only become overwhelmed if they try to combine school with an excessive extracurricular schedule (e.g., law review students often miss classes) or outside work. Note that the amount of work involved with any given class bears little relationship to the number of course credits assigned (course credits are based strictly on classroom hours per week). Again, read course evaluations and reviews to steer clear of two-credit classes with more work than most five-credit classes.

HLS offers more courses than most law schools. It can do so because of the large size of the student body. A perk of HLS is that you can take classes on some rather obscure areas of law (areas not covered at other law schools). HLS has worked recently to reduce class size. 1Ls formerly attended 140-person lectures. Now, most 1L courses are 75 to 80 students per class, a major improvement. The school is actively recruiting more faculty to further reduce the student-to-faculty ratio. Most students are able to enroll in any course they choose. Only the most popular courses present difficulties for admission. HLS has an innovative course selection system that allows students to rank their preferences and then uses a series of complicated formulas to ensure that everyone is treated more or less fairly and gets most of their top choices.

The academic program is just that, academic. HLS considers itself above a professional school. You will learn a lot of theory here, mainly from a litigation perspective (even in business law classes). HLS is concerned with what the law could or should be, with much less emphasis on practical matters concerning what the law is. If you enjoy the law for the law's sake, this is a wonderful thing. If you are looking at law school like the legal equivalent to business school (more hands-on and practical), you will be disappointed.

Status: Alumnus/a, full-time
Dates of Enrollment: 9/1997-6/2000
Survey Submitted: April 2004

I loved most of my second- and third-year classes (when I got to choose). There were no distribution requirements and I got to take civil rights and negotiation classes to my heart's content. It's not too hard to get into the most popular classes, but it is hard to take too many seminars because of credit-hour requirements. It's also hard to fit cross-registering with other Harvard schools into your schedule.

 Employment Prospects

Status: Current student, full-time
Dates of Enrollment: 9/2003-Submit Date
Survey Submitted: October 2005

Every law firm in America (and abroad) is trying to hire Harvard students. I don't know a single student who didn't have multiple job offers. Students at Harvard basically have their pick of any market and law firm in the country. The ease of finding a job makes students pretty laid back and noncompetitive.

Status: Current student, full-time
Dates of Enrollment: 9/2005-Submit Date
Survey Submitted: March 2006

Very highly recruited here; no doubt everyone will get a job. Every night a different firm comes to wine and dine us to tell us how great they are and that they hope we'll interview with them in the fall. Second-year students participate in on-campus interviewing and then have a week off to fly out for callbacks in the fall. The office of career services and the public interest office are amazing at helping students find good jobs. Very few students here are stressed about a place to work come the third year.

Status: Current student, full-time
Dates of Enrollment: 9/2005-Submit Date
Survey Submitted: November 2005

Everyone here gets a job. Period. People bicker over whether they are at the top firms (like one to 40) or at the middle of the top. This is only because everyone gets a job so they find something else to stress over. The reality is many of the people here in the bottom of the class will get jobs that many people would not get at the top of other law schools. Fortunately or unfortunately many top firms still care about prestige. For those people who could care less about firms, HLS is excellent for people who are interested in academia, politics and non-legal careers such as business, journalism and public interest. HLS guarantees summer public funding for those interested in public interest and OPIA (the career services version for public interest) will help you get a job. Furthermore, if you want to permanently work in public interest HLS will pay off your loans up to 100 percent (depending on how little you make). This means that if you are in public interest for 10 years you have the potential to not have to pay anything back. The alumni network at HLS is huge and almost incestuous, and every major firm comes to the on-campus recruiting.

Status: Alumnus/a, full-time
Dates of Enrollment: 9/2000-5/2003
Survey Submitted: April 2005

Harvard is the place to be for jobs. Though jobs were scarce in the legal world in general, we were largely insulated from this bleak reality. On-campus interviewing was great—firms threw cocktail parties, wined and dined us and I received so many callbacks I cancelled my last week of interviews. I knew people at other less prestigious, though still very quality, law schools who were having a horrible time getting a job.

Status: Alumnus/a, full-time
Dates of Enrollment: 9/2001-6/2004
Survey Submitted: March 2005

800 employers come to Harvard to offer jobs to its 550 graduates each year. It's almost difficult to avoid getting a job offer. The best firms fight to hire Harvard grads. The best judges want Harvard clerks. The best employers in the public sector do everything they can to entice Harvard students to join their ranks. It's pretty nice to feel so wanted.

Status: Alumnus/a, full-time
Dates of Enrollment: 9/2001-6/2004
Survey Submitted: March 2005

Everyone gets a job. If you want to make a six-figure salary and live in a large city, there is nothing easier once you're at HLS. If you want to clerk and/or teach, Yale is the place to go. Alumni network is huge. So big in fact, that it sometimes loses any meaning.

Status: Alumnus/a, full-time
Dates of Enrollment: 9/1999-6/2002
Survey Submitted: March 2005

Employment prospects are, not surprisingly, fabulous. Even near the bottom of the class, you pretty much have to run screaming in the other direction to avoid having a $125k job in the city of your choice fall into your lap. Even federal clerkships aren't hard to come by.

Read all of Vault's Law School Surveys at www.vault.com/lawschool — get complete surveys on top law schools, expert advice on application essays, LSAT prep and more.

VAULT CAREER LIBRARY 315

Status: Alumnus/a, full-time
Dates of Enrollment: 9/1995-6/1998
Survey Submitted: July 2004

If you're not a mutant and want to practice law, you'll have a lot more difficult a time figuring out what you want to do than actually getting a job (save two or three uber-selective firms). If you want to go the non-law financial route (e.g., banking, PE), be prepared for a marginally tougher road—they will concede that you are smart but insist on seeing an applied interest in the field that you are applying for.

Status: Alumnus/a, full-time
Dates of Enrollment: 8/1999-5/2002
Survey Submitted: September 2003

The job prospects are unparalleled. I was living overseas when I applied to law school and chose Harvard because of its name recognition in other countries. If you do well at Harvard, all doors are open to you.

Quality of Life

Status: Current student, full-time
Dates of Enrollment: 9/2004-Submit Date
Survey Submitted: October 2005

There is on-campus housing, which many 1Ls use, but as an older student, I wasn't interested. Cambridge and Somerville are great places to live, but are unbelievably expensive. The HLS campus is very nice, and is improving each semester since Dean Kagan is committed to improving QOL for us—we just got a brand-new student center and a brand new gym, both state of the art.

Status: Current student, full-time
Dates of Enrollment: 9/2003-Submit Date
Survey Submitted: October 2005

I think the quality of life at HLS is great. The on-campus housing tends to be pretty awful, but you don't have to live there (I didn't). There are plenty of apartments near campus that rent to students. Cambridge can be fairly expensive, but not any worse than any other major city. The administration has done a lot over the past few years to increase quality of life. They redid the Law School gym, provide free coffee in the mornings and put up an ice skating rink in the winter.

Status: Alumnus/a, full-time
Dates of Enrollment: 9/1997-5/2000
Survey Submitted: March 2006

For some unexplainable reason, Harvard students are generally not happy. As far as I can tell, there is no rational reason for this. Quality of life compared to other law schools is excellent. Because of the good job prospects, there is no reason for competition among students.

Status: Alumnus/a, full-time
Dates of Enrollment: 9/2001-5/2004
Survey Submitted: March 2006

HLS is not as hard as everyone thinks it is. I had plenty of time for socializing, studying, dating and I even held a part-time job. I lived on campus for the convenience, but honestly, on-campus living is really overpriced. The dormitories and suites are old and in need of serious updating. Only one of the dorms on campus comes with a private bathroom (North Hall). In all other dormitories one must share a bathroom with anywhere between one and 20 people. I lived in Wyeth Hall, it has three-person "suites," or rather three different sized rooms centered around one bathroom. It worked nicely for me because two of my friends signed up to be in my suite and there is a kitchen on every floor. It felt like a big apartment to me. The worst dorms are those in the Gropius Complex; these dorms remind me of my freshman year of college—they are small, old and there is one bathroom (either male or female) on each floor, thus dozens of people share the same bathroom. The restaurants and neighborhoods surrounding HLS are great. I always felt safe walking around.

Status: Current student, full-time
Dates of Enrollment: 9/2005-Submit Date
Survey Submitted: March 2006

It's not as bad as you think it could be, it's not as good as you wish it were. Harvard is a gorgeous campus, the winters are rough but the university is great. Dorm housing is actually not terrible, aside from the fact that they're dorms. For the cost and convenience, most students think it's well worth it, at least for the first year. Harvard Square has decent bars to go to and pretty good food options, but no chain restaurants, so if you like fast food, you might not be so happy. Also, crime in Cambridge is more prevalent than you think; walking alone at night is not recommended.

Status: Current student, full-time
Dates of Enrollment: 9/2005-Submit Date
Survey Submitted: November 2005

Most people end up having to live in an HLS dorm, which can be daunting if you are used to living in an apartment. Most of the dorms are single occupancy, but you have to share a bathroom. It is not impossible to find an apartment, but the school pretty much leaves you on your own to do it. The claim that they will help you is pretty much a bogus. Furthermore, Harvard offers subsidized apartments, which are on a lottery system and very hard to get as a 1L. The HLS dining facility is quality but over priced. Luckily, there are great restaurants in the area and little grocery markets everywhere. Plus there are a lot of places to shop (clothes and electronics) in the Square. Almost everything else you can get to by subway or taxi.

Status: Alumnus/a, full-time
Dates of Enrollment: 9/1999-6/2002
Survey Submitted: March 2005

Cambridge and Boston have a lot to offer. Unfortunately, the Law School does its best to ensure that one doesn't have time to enjoy any of it, though this is great preparation for working in a major law firm. The public interest office is wonderful; lots of staff with diverse real-world experience to provide advising and assistance to those who are looking to work in the public sector (not to mention the loan repayment program which can pay off some or all you student loans if you go into public interest). The school really cares that some of its students do something other than private firms and provides a lot of financial and institutional support for those endeavors.

Status: Alumnus/a, full-time
Dates of Enrollment: 9/2001-5/2004
Survey Submitted: March 2005

The campus is kind of dingy (especially the dorms, campus center and the gym) but Dean Kagan is improving things. Part of the reason for the rundown was the fact that President Summers was considering moving the Law School across the river to be closer to the business school. That plan was voted down by the faculty, so now there are plans in the works to renovate the campus. (Plus Dean Kagan builds us an ice-skating rink on the yard every winter. How many law school deans do that?)

Status: Alumnus/a, full-time
Dates of Enrollment: 1/2003-Submit Date
Survey Submitted: April 2005

The housing and campus facilities are great—all first-year students manage to get on-campus housing. The health club is of excellent quality; it has a gym, a pool, tennis courts and basketball courts. Neighborhood crime is at a minimum, except for the occasional stray dog! Great food is available in the cafeteria and a variety of other cuisines are available near the school. Rates for on-campus food are reasonable.

Social Life

Status: Current student, full-time
Dates of Enrollment: 9/2003-Submit Date
Survey Submitted: October 2005

Harvard is much more social than people would expect. Most of the social events are organized by a student-run business called HL Central. They run social events pretty much every week, including Bar Reviews, parties at clubs and outings to cultural events. There is definitely something for everyone at HLS.

Status: Alumnus/a, full-time
Dates of Enrollment: 9/1997-5/2000
Survey Submitted: March 2006

Harvard is in Cambridge, which has lots of bars, restaurants, nightclubs and all the amenities of nearby Boston: shops, the aquarium and historical sites. There is no shortage of things to do for any interest.

Status: Alumnus/a, full-time
Dates of Enrollment: 9/2001-5/2004
Survey Submitted: March 2006

Cambridge is a great place to have fun on a student budget. There are a number of bars, restaurants and lounges in the area that will satisfy everybody's tastes. Some of my favorites (near the campus) are Redline and the Hong Kong. Boston has some fun clubs also, but I found that going out in Boston was really expensive and I didn't seem to have as much fun.

Status: Current student, full-time
Dates of Enrollment: 9/2005-Submit Date
Survey Submitted: November 2005

The option for a social life here is surprisingly huge. There are Bar Reviews at least three times a week. HLS has plenty of restaurants and a lot of organizations. For example, I am in five groups in which I personal participate heavily. Some interesting one's are RAP (the Recording Artist Project) in which we represent a local recording artist pro bono. In Vino Veritas, which is a wine tasting group in which we fly different wine companies in to taste their wine, and learn about wine and food parings. I am also chair of the Corporate Law Firm Panel, for which I bring partners in from major corporations to talk at conferences. The groups are endless. There is also Lincoln's Inn, which is basically the co-ed Frat of HLS. HLS also often rents out bars with other Harvard graduate schools and throws parties. The only complaint I would have about social life is that there is so much to do socially and academically you hardly get a chance to leave Cambridge. This can be quite annoying for someone who likes big cities. While parties are thrown in Boston at least once a week, the students seem to mostly stay in Cambridge. If this bothers you, you have to make an effort to leave.

Status: Alumnus/a, full-time
Dates of Enrollment: 8/1998-5/2003
Survey Submitted: April 2005

Lots of bars in and around Boston, and the restaurants in Cambridge are good, but expensive. Don't bring a car, it will only be a nightmare to park. The dating scene at Harvard is pretty weak, but what do you expect from 550 uber-competitive people?

Status: Alumnus/a, full-time
Dates of Enrollment: 9/2001-6/2004
Survey Submitted: April 2005

The dating scene and bars are also much like being back in high school. You can follow the romantic intrigues of all your classmates all through three years of law school, and they will gossip about you, too. For gay and lesbian students (especially lesbian students) the situation is particularly bad. The law school GLBT association is OK, but the school isn't very progressive and neither are most of the students. Try to find a fun and interesting group of friends who don't talk about law school on Friday night and things will be much happier all through school. I knew a lot of miserable people there who were mostly unhappy because they surrounded themselves by mean or super-competitive friends who were not fun or supportive.

Status: Alumnus/a, full-time
Dates of Enrollment: 9/2000-6/2003
Survey Submitted: April 2004

Cambridge and Boston boast an excellent social scene. Lots of restaurants, theater, sporting events, concerts and clubs. HLS offers a limited number of social opportunities on campus. Bar review is popular among students. HLS is definitely a scene for young, single types. If you're older and/or married, you may not fit in particularly well (most social events are not family-friendly). There is a couples association, but its budget is minimal and activities are few. Cambridge has an excellent geographic location. Cape Cod offers wonderful beaches, while Vermont, New Hampshire and Maine offer mountains for hiking and skiing. Casinos are close by in Connecticut. You are only a few hours from New York. There are any number of excellent weekend destinations within easy driving distance.

Read all of Vault's Law School Surveys at www.vault.com/lawschool — get complete surveys on top law schools, expert advice on applicaton essays, LSAT prep and more.

VAULT CAREER LIBRARY **317**

New England School of Law

The Admissions Office
New England School of Law
154 Stuart Street
Boston, MA 02116
Admissions phone: (617) 422-7235
Admissions e-mail: admit@admin.nesl.edu
Admissions URL: www.nesl.edu/admissions/

 ## Admissions

Status: Alumnus/a, full-time
Dates of Enrollment: 8/2002-5/2005
Survey Submitted: March 2006

From the applicant's end, the admission process is typical for a law school. Students are admitted based on their undergraduate GPA and their LSAT score. New England School of Law (NESL) seems willing to look beyond these two main metrics and weigh other factors, such as an applicant's work experiences or demonstrated commitment to law, in making offers.

To improve your chance of getting in (or getting a scholarship), your personal statement should evince more than a passing interest in law. It is helpful to point to particular interests you have within the law, and more helpful still to tie those interests to something you have done in the past. The more specific you can be, the better. (Decent: "I have a strong interest in criminal law." Better: "I have a strong interest in criminal law. I developed this interest in my years working for the Las Vegas police department." Best: "I have a strong interest in criminal law, particularly in protecting the Constitutional rights of indigent defendants. I developed this interest in my years working for the Las Vegas police department. I find Professor X's work in this field to be intriguing, and I would love an opportunity to take classes from him in this area.")

Status: Alumnus/a, full-time
Dates of Enrollment: 8/2002-5/2005
Survey Submitted: September 2005

Standard process consisting of: application, essays and LSAT scores. The *U.S. News* law school ranking does no justice to the dramatic increase in NESL's LSAT range and undergraduate GPA range from 2002 to present.

Status: Alumnus/a, full-time
Dates of Enrollment: 8/2001-5/2004
Survey Submitted: June 2004

Admission depends heavily on experience, GPA and LSAT scores. This is very apparent in the wide diversity in each year's incoming class and the average age of day division students (around 25 to 26). The admissions standards have risen dramatically each year, with the LSAT and GPA requirements pushing higher and higher than in years past. This is only beneficial because the caliber of students that pass through the school are excellent and many are placed on the waitlist. Their current acceptance rate is less than 7 percent of total applicants. You need to know exactly why you want to come to law school.

Status: Alumnus/a, full-time
Dates of Enrollment: 9/1999-5/2002
Survey Submitted: March 2005

The admissions process was fairly straightforward, consisting of an application and an essay. LSAT scores, college transcripts and SAT scores were also required.

> **The school says:** "A complete application consists of an application, personal statement, LSDAS report (includes LSAT scores and transcripts) and two recommendations."

Status: Alumnus/a, full-time
Dates of Enrollment: 9/2000-5/2004
Survey Submitted: December 2004

Business resume and work experience, C or better GPA at a minimum, decent LSAT scores and a good essay are all required. The admissions committee is comprised of faculty and the head of admissions. You should be able to prove academic achievement and exhibit superb communication skills.

> **The school says:** "The admissions committee balances the applicant's undergraduate record and LSAT score with recommendations, proven achievements and apparent motivation to study law. Applicants who have not achieved at least a C (2.0) cumulative average in undergraduate work should not apply. For the full-time fall 2005 entering class, the median LSAT was 151 and the median GPA was 3.32."

Status: Alumnus/a, full-time
Dates of Enrollment: 8/1997-5/2000
Survey Submitted: September 2003

I don't remember much. I just remember that there was a rather lengthy application to fill out and an essay that had to be written along with it. Of course, one needed their transcripts and references in order, as well. I don't recall having to interview.

> **The school says:** "Although the law school does not interview candidates for admission, applicants are encouraged to visit the school, tour the facilities, attend classes and talk with students and staff. A representative of the Office of Admissions, current student or alumnus/a is available to take prospective candidates around the school by appointment."

 ## Academics

Status: Alumnus/a, full-time
Dates of Enrollment: 8/2002-5/2005
Survey Submitted: March 2006

The quality of the instruction is typically very good. The professors are, for the most part, interested in helping their students master the subject matter. (As opposed to writing their own research papers.) Note, however, that in an effort to earn credibility, the school does not inflate its grades. Expect to earn one or two C's at NESL even if you are a bright and hard-working student.

There is a good balance of students to professors. This means that generally you can take whatever class you're interested in. Sometimes this requires careful planning: you can expect to be waitlisted at least once if you're taking only popular courses.

The most popular courses are the subjects that are tested on the bar exam. Thus, if you have a desired speciality (e.g., criminal law, intellectual property, real estate, taxation or environmental law) then it is unlikely you'll be waitlisted for specialized courses in this area.

Status: Alumnus/a, full-time
Dates of Enrollment: 8/2002-5/2005
Survey Submitted: September 2005

The professors are esteemed scholars as well as industry bests. Plus, with the medium class size and professor dedication, a student's personal pursuit to improve his or her understanding is easy. Additionally, the adjunct professors are judges and attorneys practicing in Massachusetts who offer incredible insight to the practice of law. The school offers three Journals that students, after their first year, can join based on high grades and a writing hypothetical posed by the Journals.

The workload depends on the person. Do you want to be top 10 percent or just graduate? Also, do you want to be on a Journal, do a clinic, moot court or other extracurriculars? The books are the same books that every other law school uses and the teachers use Socratic Method (for the most part, particularly in the first year). The teachers teach theory, but teach practicality more. NESL also requires two years (totalling three semesters) of legal research and writing. From talking with other law students, which I have interned with, I have learned that the two years of LRW have significantly helped my writing skills, as well as how to start writing. I find that I hit the ground running, whereas, the others have to incessantly ask questions. (i.e., deciding what the headings should be on a memo should not take a full day of work.)

Status: Alumnus/a, full-time
Dates of Enrollment: 8/2001-5/2004
Survey Submitted: June 2004

One cannot say enough about the academics at this school. Rated nationally as having one of the Top 10 faculties, it is clear that this school is a teaching school first, scholarly endeavors second. What that means is that as a student the professors are more interested in making sure you learn, understand and can apply all and any concept taught. Professors are sensitive to student workloads, but consistently challenge students in the classroom and outside of the classroom. Access to individual professors is never a problem.

Students who come away from this school are far more equipped to enter the legal community and practice. Moreover, due to the high focus on bar passage, academically, students are some of the best educated for the bar exam.

Status: Alumnus/a, full-time
Dates of Enrollment: 9/1999-5/2002
Survey Submitted: March 2005

The focus of New England School of Law (NESL) is very much about passing the bar exam. The school encourages all students to take courses that are heavily tested on the bar and provides a bar review course for all third-year day and fourth-year evening students. The school is fairly small and I never had a problem getting classes I wanted. Most professors are very fair graders, but NESL as a rule has no grade inflation. The faculty is outstanding; they are, for the most part, very dedicated to teaching and very accessible.

Status: Alumnus/a, full-time
Dates of Enrollment: 9/2000-5/2004
Survey Submitted: December 2004

NESL has a no-scale grading policy. The clinical studies can quickly fill up. They have a waiting list. There is a diverse range of courses. The full-time faculty are generally approachable and good instructors. There are guaranteed seats in the first-year program. There is a lottery system in use so that the more senior students can get a seat in a full course. The first-year students have an extra help program available. To graduate, students must complete some elective courses in different areas from a pre-approved list: i.e., either two practical and simulation or clinical courses, two public law courses (which includes administrative law, family law and others) and a seminar course.

Status: Alumnus/a, full-time
Dates of Enrollment: 8/1997-5/2000
Survey Submitted: September 2003

New England has a great faculty. It is usually ranked as one of the best law school faculties in the nation. I think the professors focus on teaching what practical knowledge they can and also focus on preparing students for the bar exam. The classes in most of my experience were very valuable. For the most part, I found that is was not too difficult to get the classes that I desired. The school also has a first-rate library with great resources and a very helpful reference staff.

 # Employment Prospects

Status: Alumnus/a, full-time
Dates of Enrollment: 8/2002-5/2005
Survey Submitted: March 2006

NESL does not carry a great deal of prestige with local employers, particularly large law firms. However, there is a growing recognition that graduates from "brand-name" law schools are poorly trained in the practicalities of the daily practice of law. (In my large law firm, I heard at least one description of someone as "another useless [high-ranked law school] grad.")

Graduates generally work very hard to obtain permanent employment. Such employment is typically at a small- or medium-size law firm or in government. I get the impression that NESL's name has relatively more clout in criminal law and real estate law circles.

Status: Alumnus/a, full-time
Dates of Enrollment: 8/2002-5/2005
Survey Submitted: September 2005

Many graduates pursue state judicial clerkships. The prospects are good for those who are aggressive. Graduating when there is an economic downturn (so bad it actually affects attorney jobs) is not fun. My class did not get many second-year summer associate offers, however, that same hiring season, many programs were cut in half or cut completely. Also difficult considering our city has many top tier schools versus somewhere like Missouri that has two schools and many law firms. However, the class below me had many summer associate offers.

Status: Alumnus/a, full-time
Dates of Enrollment: 8/2001-5/2004
Survey Submitted: June 2004

New England can boast that they have the most number of graduates sitting as judges than any of the Boston area law schools for a reason. As practitioners, graduates of the school in general don't have problems delving into their career choices. The career services office, clerkship office, and other within school resources provide ample opportunities for students to develop their careers, provided that they take the opportunity to do so themselves. With any CSO, they aren't handing over anything to anyone on a silver platter. But, if you are willing to work for what you want, then they are incredible resource. Only critique is that there is not enough on-campus recruitment with firms, but that has been changing dramatically within the last two years. Should you wish to work for the state or federal government, to become an Assistant District Attorney, or enter the public service field, this school surpasses all other area law schools not only in opportunity, but percentage of hired by these agencies.

Status: Alumnus/a, full-time
Dates of Enrollment: 9/1999-5/2002
Survey Submitted: March 2005

The career services office does a great job of getting prospective employers to come on campus to interview, and providing information on local job fairs for students. Boston is a tough market for law students since there are three very good schools in the area. As such, it is extremely competitive to get a job with a large law firm. That being said, many NESL students succeed in getting state government jobs including with local district attorneys' offices. The alumni network is extremely helpful, as well. Many alumni provide mentoring advice to law students including conducting mock interviews, as well as answering general questions about the school and employment.

    The school says: There are six law schools in the Metropolitan area.

Status: Alumnus/a, full-time
Dates of Enrollment: 9/2000-5/2004
Survey Submitted: December 2004

E-attorney is used as the recruiting seminar. Career services has some resources as in resume writing, and alumni contacts. The number of students selected to interview is limited to only a few slots.

Read all of Vault's Law School Surveys at www.vault.com/lawschool — get complete surveys on top law schools, expert advice on applicaton essays, LSAT prep and more.

VAULT CAREER LIBRARY 319

The school says: "The Career Services Office maintains an active and highly competitive on-campus interview program. Symplicity (replaced E-attorney) is the recruitment tool used to collect student applications and to schedule interviews for this program; it gives students considerable flexibility and convenience by allowing them to apply for interviews via the web. The CSO also has an extensive office library and maintains more than 30 career-related Web pages linked to the law school's web site. The CSO also runs numerous career development programs, workshops and panels throughout the school year."

Status: Alumnus/a, full-time
Dates of Enrollment: 8/1997-5/2000
Survey Submitted: September 2003

Well, when one goes to law school, one usually plans on practicing law, so there really is no problem figuring out what one will do. However, especially in Boston, jobs and internships are very competitive and hard to come by it seems. There are about eight or so law schools all located within Boston or within a close radius.

Quality of Life

Status: Alumnus/a, full-time
Dates of Enrollment: 8/2002-5/2005
Survey Submitted: March 2006

Housing for any Boston area school will be tough. NESL is no exception. However, NESL is fairly centrally located for public transportation, which gives students a great deal of flexibility in choosing where they live. The campus consists essentially of one building located in the theater district. (Administrative offices are in a nearby separate building). The school's location straddles trendy spots for tourists and locals on the west and Chinatown on the East. One block west and you can buy Prada and Gucci. The more sketchy elements tend to keep to themselves. If you go to NESL, you will get hit up for change, but it's unlikely anything more serious will happen if you don't seek it out.

Status: Alumnus/a, full-time
Dates of Enrollment: 8/2001-5/2004
Survey Submitted: June 2004

Being in Boston, your own individual, private quality of life is your own. But, as a student, there is no school experience like New England. The students here are known (and rightly so) as a body of students interested in helping each other accomplish all of their goals, not step on them. It is clear that every single student who enters the halls of the school understands that they are all colleagues and will be colleagues when they graduate. What that creates is a strong sense of community and a need for everyone to succeed. As one student has remarked, they were happy that they went to New England more than any of the other area law schools simply because of the "human" factor of each student. This school is competitive, but not to the point of misery.

Status: Alumnus/a, full-time
Dates of Enrollment: 9/1999-5/2002
Survey Submitted: March 2005

NESL is located in theater district which has pros and cons. The area is generally safe but late night can be a little sketchy. Most students live in Brighton or Brookline and commute by T (subway). There is no real campus and, therefore, no housing or dining facilities. The area has many restaurants and is within walking distance of Chinatown which provides a lot of options.

Status: Alumnus/a, full-time
Dates of Enrollment: 9/2000-5/2004
Survey Submitted: December 2004

No on-campus housing. Many students are able to share rooms with each other. The school has a bulletin board to post available apartments. School has security personnel at the front desk and main entrance. Generally, it is a safe area but occasionally there are homeless people that hang out at the corner of Tremont and Stuart by the 7-11. Some students, particularly in the evening division, are off-duty policemen, which adds to the security. Parking is available in the area

Status: Alumnus/a, full-time
Dates of Enrollment: 8/1997-5/2000
Survey Submitted: September 2003

OK, if you like the city. There is no on-campus housing at New England School of Law, so that means you have to find an apartment. Finding an apartment in Boston is not fun (can take weeks), there is usually a 1 percent vacancy rate and the rents are ridiculously outrageous. One bonus is that public transportation goes just about anywhere one would need or want to go. The subway trains are usually packed and always fun to ride.

Social Life

Status: Alumnus/a, full-time
Dates of Enrollment: 8/2002-5/2005
Survey Submitted: March 2006

NESL is a small school crammed into a small building. By the time you graduate, you will know most of the people in your graduating class, if only in passing. The school has regular general social events and more particularized clubs. The school's location near several bars and restaurants makes after-class get-togethers easy to spontaneously orchestrate.

Status: Alumnus/a, full-time
Dates of Enrollment: 8/2002-5/2005
Survey Submitted: September 2005

It is Boston. If you can't find a bar, you should seek medical treatment because law school has made you prematurely senile.

Status: Alumnus/a, full-time
Dates of Enrollment: 8/2001-5/2004
Survey Submitted: June 2004

The Student Bar Association, which is the governing body of the students, not only provides the student with a strong governing council, but is imperative to the social life development of each student. Every opportunity is taken to ensure that every student feels like they have a social network. Having said that, being in downtown Boston, ample opportunities to exist to go out with friends and to make friends. A city of 20-somethings, you'll never feel alone and lack human connection.

Status: Alumnus/a, full-time
Dates of Enrollment: 9/1999-5/2002
Survey Submitted: March 2005

There are many bars and clubs in the immediate area. There is no Greek system, but depending on the student body there can be private parties. Most students go to bars after class. The student body tends to be a little older so many students are married and don't party as much.

Status: Alumnus/a, full-time
Dates of Enrollment: 9/2000-5/2004
Survey Submitted: December 2004

Located centrally in the Theater district and a short walk to Boston Common. Public transportation is readily available. There are numerous shows such as Shear Madness or Blue Man Group on. In addition, there are many restaurants such as Dominic's (excellent Pizza), Subway, P.F. Chang's, Legal Seafood, McCormick and Schmick's, Bennigan's and a food court in the transportation building. There are many more options. The Alley behind the transportation building has some bars where students congregate. The entire city is easily accessible. Boston is a great student city.

Status: Alumnus/a, full-time
Dates of Enrollment: 8/1997-5/2000
Survey Submitted: September 2003

It's Boston. Need I say more?

The School Says

New England School of Law is an educational community characterized by substantive instruction with a strong foundation in ethics. Founded in 1908 as Portia Law School, the only law school established exclusively to educate women, the school has been coeducational since 1938. It was renamed New England School of Law in 1969. ABA-accredited and a member of the Association of American Law Schools, it offers options for full-time and part-time study, including day and evening part-time programs, as well as a flexible part-time program for parents with primary childrearing responsibilities.

The law school's location in downtown Boston provides students with convenient access to the Massachusetts legal community. The school is within walking distance of the State House; state and federal courthouses, administrative and legal offices; and many law firms. This proximity provides extensive opportunities for clinical placements, clerkships and part-time employment. The school's location also allows it to draw on prominent and experienced attorneys and judges for its adjunct faculty and for guest lectures.

Many of the school's full-time faculty are top graduates of the nation's best law schools and most have had practice experience in their areas of expertise. They are readily accessible to students and are committed to teaching, scholarship and professional activities in their fields.

The academic program emphasizes extensive preparation in practical skills and a focus on ethics. Three semesters of Legal Research and Writing are required, more than at most law schools, and most students also write a major paper in a seminar. Ethical issues are addressed in a required course, the Law and Ethics of Lawyering, and faculty are also expected to integrate ethical discussions into their courses. To graduate, students must take at least two professional skills courses, two public law courses and a seminar.

The law school's clinical program offers 16 clinics in a variety of fields of law and students enrolled in a clinic take a related substantive course as well. About two-thirds of New England students take at least one clinic.

New England School of Law is home to three academic centers—the Center for International Law and Policy, the Center for Law and Social Responsibility and the Center for Business Law—all of which sponsor conferences and symposia and support faculty and student research. Students publish three scholarly journals and participate in six advocacy teams that engage in regional and national competition. A wide range of student organizations is active at the school.

New England sponsors a summer abroad program in Galway, Ireland, and a semester exchange program at the University of Paris X-Nanterre. With three other independent law schools—California Western School of Law, South Texas College of Law and William Mitchell College of Law—the school is a founding member of the Consortium for Innovative Legal Education, which sponsors summer abroad programs in London/Edinburgh, Malta and Prague; a summer program about NAFTA; and semester abroad programs in The Netherlands and Denmark. Students may also visit for a semester at any of the member schools.

Read all of Vault's Law School Surveys at www.vault.com/lawschool — get complete surveys on top law schools, expert advice on applicaton essays, LSAT prep and more.

V/\ULT CAREER LIBRARY   **321**

Northeastern University School of Law

Admissions Office
P.O. Box 728
Boston, MA 02117-0728
Admissions phone: (617) 373-2395
Admissions fax: (617) 373-8865
Admissions e-mail: lawadmissions@neu.edu
Admissions URL: http://www.slaw.neu.edu/admiss/

 Admissions

Status: Current student, full-time
Dates of Enrollment: 8/2004-Submit Date
Survey Submitted: April 2006

My impression is that Northeastern is sort of mid-range in terms of selectivity. In all honesty, I applied because the school waived my application fee, I assume based on my LSAT score. I don't know the inner workings of the admissions process, but I know based on ABA stats that the school's GPA and LSAT scores are lower than "highly competitive" schools.

But as a student, my impression of the other students around me is that there is a huge range—there are some really smart people who turned down Ivy League schools to come here, and there are some people I'm not so impressed with. There's a big range. I went to a really academically rigorous undergraduate school where everyone was really academic and just really smart. Here, I feel like a bit like a bigger fish in a very different pond.

Status: Current student, full-time
Dates of Enrollment: 9/2004-Submit Date
Survey Submitted: April 2006

Northeastern did a fantastic job during the admissions process. I felt like I was in constant contact with the school after I applied and was accepted; they really made an effort to answer my questions. The open house for admitted students was the reason I decided to attend NUSL. Nearly the entire faculty showed up and shared why they love teaching at the school. I remember getting goosebumps.

Status: Current student, full-time
Dates of Enrollment: 8/2004-Submit Date
Survey Submitted: April 2006

I'm on the admissions committee so I know a bit about this! The applications are pre-screened by admissions staff, who pull out the presumptive admits and denies (based on the target cutoffs for GPA and LSAT). If you're below the cutoff for one or the other, or in the right range but not a shoo-in, your file goes to a student reader who fills out a sheet commenting on personal statement, optional essays, work experience, whether you fit the character of the school, GPA and LSAT, recommendations and diversity. (Diversity isn't just race; it's age, LGBT and geography, anything that makes you really stand out and potentially contribute something unique to the class.) The student recommends admit, deny or hold—hold is when you really like someone but their numbers suck, or if the numbers are good but you hate them, or if they're right on the edge but seem immature or something like that, lots of files get holds.

Whatever the student recommends, it goes to a faculty/staff reader who reads the student's comments in addition to the file. If the second reader agrees with the student's assessment, that's pretty much the fate of the application but admissions staff signs off on it. (the Holds are set aside for admissions staff to deal with later, could be waitlist, could be admit or deny depending on how the applicant pool looks later on). If the second reader doesn't agree, the admissions staff makes the decision.

Advice on getting in: they really prefer you to have some work experience—coming straight from college, especially if your first semester senior grades

aren't in the file, is a disadvantage. Since the school has a public-interest focus, experience or interest in that area is a plus.

Status: Current student, full-time
Dates of Enrollment: 9/2004-Submit Date
Survey Submitted: April 2006

The admission process is relatively straightforward. They application can be submitted using the common form through LSAC. Essay question is the usual and not out of the ordinary. I submitted my application along with 19 others via LSAC, using the same essay and common form. There was no interview.

I believe I got accepted due to my non-traditional pre-law school undergraduate majors. I hold a BS in Computer Science and BA in Mathematics. My LSAT score was 160. I believe a combination of undergrad majors and my LSAT score got me admitted. After you are accepted, they invite you to an admitted student reception. This is their opportunity to woo you to come to their school. They offer a one- to two-day program of talks, discussion panels by professors, tours, free food and drinks and other such things. After you accept, you won't see those goodies for the three years you're there, so take advantage of it while they care.

Status: Current student, full-time
Dates of Enrollment: 8/2003-Submit Date
Survey Submitted: April 2006

The admissions process is like most law schools—you have to do well on your LSATs, have good undergrad grades, provide a well-written essay and provide a few good recommendations. An awful LSAT score will not kill your chances, but in the past few years more emphasis has been put on the "numbers" aspect of admissions.

Definitely do one of the extra essays and do not try to pander to the admissions committee. It's transparent (I know, I sat on the admissions committee for two years). The most annoying attribute I've seen on incoming applications is a prospective student's insisting they've overcome some sort of adversity. If you have, great, but don't go on and on for three pages about how you really turned your life around after not getting into your first choice of sorority your freshman year in undergrad. That's not overcoming adversity.

Northeastern looks for well-rounded, mature individuals. It's very hard to gain admission if you are still in undergrad, you have to have some pretty spectacular numbers to overcome that obstacle. The student body is much older and more mature than a lot of the other Boston area law schools and it is a direct result of the extensive admissions process (at least three people read your application and make comments—usually one student, one faculty or staff and the head of admissions). If you don't get in the first time, take a year off, really do something with your life, and try again. Show the committee you are really working on becoming a mature, thoughtful and interesting person.

Status: Current student, full-time
Dates of Enrollment: 8/2003-Submit Date
Survey Submitted: April 2006

I applied for early admission because Northeastern was my first choice. Our school doesn't have interviews, so I didn't have to worry about that. There is a main essay you are required to write and two to three optional essays. I know people that didn't write any of the optional essays and still got in. Since I really wanted to go to this school, I answered all of the personal essays. In the essays, I think it is important to demonstrate that you have actually researched the school and that the essay reflects why you would be a good match. In terms of references, I would recommend getting people that actually know you instead of people that just sound impressive on paper.

Status: Current student, full-time
Dates of Enrollment: 8/2003-Submit Date
Survey Submitted: January 2005

Northeastern is getting more selective, but the class size is getting bigger. Most students come here either for the co-op program (how can you beat four internships?) or the public interest aspect of the school. An interest in public interest work is considered a huge plus. LSAT scores don't need to be stellar, but don't count on getting in if you can't even make the national average (about 150). The writing sample is particularly key. Please proofread and don't accidentally leave references to another law school in your standard writing sample. That will get you an automatic denial.

> **The school states:** "Our class size is not getting bigger. Our class size remains at approximately 210 students. Our LSAT range is highly competitive, with a median of 161 for the Class of 2008."

Status: Current student, full-time
Dates of Enrollment: 9/2002-Submit Date
Survey Submitted: October 2003

Northeastern is not very hard to get into compared to other Boston-area law schools. It is getting better and harder, though. If you've done the Peace Corps or the like, you'll probably get in, no problem; they care more about that than grades, it seems. In terms of the co-op program, it helps in getting your first one if you've had experience prior to going to law school, although I didn't and I got a good co-op.

> **The school states:** "While we believe a wide range of experiences, such as Peace Corps service, is important, such activities in no way guarantee admission. We do indeed care about grades, among other criteria assessed by the admissions committee. The median GPA for the class of 2009 is 3.41."

 ## Academics

Status: Current student, full-time
Dates of Enrollment: 8/2004-Submit Date
Survey Submitted: April 2006

Northeastern is a professional school that trains you to be a practicing attorney; it doesn't train you to be a legal academic. There is no law review journal, which is significant. There are intense academic offerings, involving a lot of research and theory and writing a very long paper, for those who are so inclined.

The heart of the program is "Co-op"—every student completes four three-month full-time (40 hours/week) internships with various legal employers. These quarters alternate with full-time academic quarters. You can choose to do these so they coincide with summer associate or other recruiting programs, or you can do them other times of year, when you get to see what that legal office is really like away from the summer recruiting wining and dining. It's sort of an apprenticeship idea. You learn how to be a lawyer by working with lawyers, doing what they do, watching and listening and asking questions.

Status: Current student, full-time
Dates of Enrollment: 8/2003-Submit Date
Survey Submitted: April 2006

Northeastern's academic program is odd, to say the least. We don't have grades, we don't rank, and we don't have law review. And if you don't like it, go somewhere else.

However, despite not having these things, Northeastern's academic program is extremely rigorous. Professors expect a lot out of their students, and, in turn, we expect a lot out of them. The first-year exams are done on a semester basis. Whether an exam is open book is at the discretion of the professor, but there has been a recent movement to make more exams closed-book.

Professors then write individual evaluations. The exams are anonymous, but the professor has the opportunity to provide feedback on in-class performance and other aspects of a student's worth after the initial grading. Most professors use "buzzwords." These aren't set in stone, but if you get an "outstanding" you are doing extremely well. A "marginal pass" is miserable (you didn't fail, but you might as well have). And then there is a slew of other options: "excellent," "very good," "good," "fair," and "poor" are seen most often.

After the first year, the students move on to a quarter-based system with one quarter spent in academic classes and the next spent on "co-op" (an internship). The first-year class is split into two rotations, half the students will be in class while the other half are out in the real world applying what they've learned.

You end your law school career with four academic quarters and four co-op quarters. Unfortunately, class selection can be spotty. And you don't always get into the classes you want. Scheduling can be a pain. But we have wide variety of classes and clinics that are available. The clinical programs at Northeastern are excellent and provide unique opportunities to provide legal services. The professors are, for the most part, awesome. They are a fun, welcoming group. But they also know their stuff. Most professors have an open-door policy and are always willing to meet with students.

Status: Current student, full-time
Dates of Enrollment: 9/2004-Submit Date
Survey Submitted: April 2006

The first year of law school is composed of two semesters, just like any law school. Second and third years are broken up into quarters (four per year), of three months each. Every other quarter you're in classes. The quarters you're not in class, you're on co-op (internship) full time. Half the class will be on co-op at any one time, and you can choose which quarter you want to go on co-op and which to stay in school. I chose to be on co-op during the spring and fall, figuring that I wouldn't have to compete with other law school students for internships during the summer since that's when I'll be in classes.

Northeastern doesn't use the traditional grading system. In fact, they claim they don't have grades. That is a half truth. Instead of grades, they use "evaluations." It is true that you get neither a number nor letter grade. It is also true that there are no class rankings, so competition among students is greatly diminished. The evaluations consist of the professor writing about your performance at "length" at the end of the quarter or semester. The length of the evaluations depends on the individual professor. Some are a sentence long, some are a paragraph, and some are a couple of pages. What's consistent among all professors and evaluations are the "buzz words" they use. This is where the half truth of grades come in. There are "buzz words" to indicate in one word how you did each semester. The students aren't given a list of the buzz words and are not suppose to know which words are better then others. However, students have mostly figured it out and employers all know since they are given a list.

Classes in general are not bad. They are however, short and condensed since each quarter is only three months long. Professors try to teach all the materials that other law schools offer in a full length course, and sometimes they succeed, and sometimes they don't. Most times, if time runs out in the quarter, there are only a couple of classes not covered. Classes are not hard to get into, even the limited enrollment ones. And the workload is not bad at all. If you can get past the first year, you will graduate. The first year is the tricky part since that's when you'll take the bulk of your classes (half of all needed credits to graduate), get adjusted to law school and freak out.

Status: Current student, full-time
Dates of Enrollment: 8/2004-Submit Date
Survey Submitted: April 2006

My experience has been that the profs are AWESOME! I haven't had anyone I didn't like. They're not the typical law school profs who pick on you in class—some will call on you randomly, but many will assign certain people to be on call so you know ahead of time that you need to prepare extra well. Northeastern is unique in that there are no letter grades—you get a written evaluations that range from very short to quite detailed, depending on the prof. As with any school, some profs have reputations as hard graders. The evals are fodder for student moaning and groaning, but I think it's better than competing with everyone for the three As or whatever.

Status: Alumnus/a, full-time
Dates of Enrollment: 9/2000-5/2003
Survey Submitted: April 2006

Northeastern uses a pass/fail grading system with written feedback from instructors. It's not for everyone, but I liked it. And I think it gives us an advantage in hiring, because our transcripts cannot be reduced to a GPA;

Read all of Vault's Law School Surveys at www.vault.com/lawschool — get complete surveys on top law schools, expert advice on applicaton essays, LSAT prep and more.

VAULT CAREER LIBRARY 323

someone actually has to read them. That's a double-edged sword in some cases, but overall it seems like an advantage to me.

I found the academic program to be strong, particularly in classes taught by regular faculty or adjunct faculty who have regular teaching experience. The quality of the first-year Legal Research and Writing program is also excellent. Every student finds it challenging in various ways, but for those students who are able to put aside their preconceptions and allow themselves to be trained in the conventions of legal writing, the program can quickly bring them to a high level of proficiency. And while it is not strictly-speaking "academic," the co-op program is an essential part of the educational program. When I was a summer associate (at the firm I eventually joined after graduation), I felt that having two co-ops under my belt helped me differentiate myself from other summer associates from more "prestigious" schools, because I could demonstrate an ability to do real work right away.

One issue, which I believe the school has been working on, is the quality of teaching offered by practitioners—judges and lawyers—serving as adjunct faculty. While they often bring a useful hands-on perspective to the classroom, sometimes they are too busy or too inexperienced in teaching to do a good job. It is worth exploring what the school is doing to ensure these courses are taught at a high level of quality.

Status: Current student, full-time
Dates of Enrollment: 8/2003-Submit Date
Survey Submitted: January 2005

The first year is like any other: grueling, boring, but necessary. Most of the first-year professors are fabulous and all are approachable. Many professors have an open-door policy and are more than willing to help. The second and third years are even better. Small classes and professors with a true enthusiasm for the types of law they teach. There aren't any easy classes at Northeastern. Just because we don't have grades doesn't mean you can slack off. Because of the small class size the professors notice your participation and often have ways of boosting your evaluation even if you bombed the final. Most of the professors are fair evaluators and if you are unhappy with a grade, they will explain their reasoning. A few professors are notoriously difficult, but they push you and want you to perform at an even higher level.

Status: Current student, full-time
Dates of Enrollment: 9/2002-Submit Date
Survey Submitted: October 2003

There are no letter grades, but there are written evaluations which include "buzz words" that are basically grades (in fact, many law firms convert them into grades for hiring purposes). Although they claim to be noncompetitive here, it is actually quite competitive, because they post the names of everyone who gets interviews and offers for co-op jobs.

It is not competitive in that there is no rank, which only helps the students who would be ranked lower. Many of the professors are very good, but all think exactly alike (liberal) and some are hired simply because they worked for the ACLU and not because they would necessarily be the best choice.

Status: Current student, full-time
Dates of Enrollment: 8/2001-Submit Date
Survey Submitted: September 2003

We have no grades. That's right. We are evaluated at the end of the semester or quarter by our professor. They give a detailed synopsis of how you did in class, the final and where you need improvement. It is very hard to get used to, but it helps to foster the noncompetitive atmosphere that we have here.

Employment Prospects

Status: Current student, full-time
Dates of Enrollment: 8/2004-Submit Date
Survey Submitted: April 2006

Excellent—in Boston. Employers love Northeastern students because we're better prepared to do legal work than students from other schools who haven't had the legal experience we get on co-op jobs. However, most Northeastern

students stay in Boston, so the reputation stays here too. There are, however, some alumni all over the country, primarily in cities like New York and San Francisco, but they are also everywhere from Anchorage to Miami. Most grad tend towards public interest, a lot go into criminal defense, and plenty go into high-paying firm positions and the like.

Status: Current student, full-time
Dates of Enrollment: 8/2003-Submit Date
Survey Submitted: April 2006

Northeastern's co-op program and career services department is outstanding. Most students end up getting jobs through the co-op program. We are essentially out in the legal work force in our second year. This gives us an advantage over schools that have a traditional program, if they are lucky they get two summer internships. We automatically get four. You can end up working for judges, legal services, the government, small firms or the big gigantic law machines (and not just in Boston, we co-op all over the world).

We have real experience before we graduate, which is a huge plus for most employers (I've heard more than once that employers love Northeastern students and I personally got an internship, beating out numerous other applicants from other area schools, because I was a Northeastern student). 98 percent of students have a job within six months of graduation, and a great deal have positions before they even graduate.

Status: Current student, full-time
Dates of Enrollment: 9/2004-Submit Date
Survey Submitted: April 2006

Students go on co-op starting their second year and continue in their third year. You go on co-op during the quarters that you are not in school. Northeastern is the only ABA accredited law school to offer such a co-op program. They help you in picking out employers to work for through their extensive contact list (approx. 8000).

What's also exceptional is that there are many judges and large law firms that hire Northeastern students on co-ops. Working for a judge is very prestigious and will help garner you future co-ops. Some places even pay when you're on co-op. Those are generally the small to large firms. Most government and public interest co-ops don't pay.

What Northeastern lacks in academics, they certainly make up for in their co-op program. You learn so much more by "doing" than by sitting and listening to a lecture. NU is very geared towards public interest post-graduate employment but due to the wide variety of co-ops that students take, the possibilities are limitless.

Status: Alumnus/a, full-time
Dates of Enrollment: 9/2000-5/2003
Survey Submitted: April 2006

Northeastern grads' employment prospects are best with employers who are already familiar with the school's co-op and evaluation systems. They are concentrated in the Northeast, Northern California and Alaska (an alum is/was on the Alaska Supreme Court). And if an employer takes co-op students, they are very likely to seriously consider grads for employment.

Many grads, such as me, take jobs with co-op employers (a summer associate position is a co-op). But, I think that employers anywhere can be educated to value the uniquely practical training of Northeastern grads. One of the best things about the school is that students have a wide variety of career goals. There are people who want to follow virtually every path—from firms, public interest, nonprofits and government, to the private sector and other places. It makes the student experience richer than I imagine it to be at other more uniform schools.

Status: Current student, full-time
Dates of Enrollment: 8/2003-Submit Date
Survey Submitted: January 2005

The co-op program at NUSL is the school's most unique program and provides students with hands-on training and the ability to make contacts outside of law school. Most attorneys I've talked to and interviewed with say they always love their NUSL interns. They work harder and have a better understanding of the nuts and bolts of law. The program arms you with practical law—not just theory.

Most third-years have a job waiting for them when they graduate. Although a good portion of the graduates go into clerkships or public interest work, there are many who end up with firms (large, medium and small), in-house counsel positions or into government positions. Most, if not all, of the big firms in Boston have a Northeastern grad partner. And the alums are always willing to help you out.

Status: Alumnus/a, full-time
Dates of Enrollment: 9/1999-5/2002
Survey Submitted: April 2004

Given that NUSL is not a top-tier law school, it is definitely more challenging to secure a position at a large law firm outside of Boston. If you are in the top of your class, you should be in a good position as far as large Boston law firms are concerned. The evaluations given, instead of grades, are not always welcomed by non-Boston firms. That said, NUSL is a public interest oriented law school and affords many career opportunities in the nonprofit and public sectors.

Status: Alumnus/a, full-time
Dates of Enrollment: 9/1998-5/2001
Survey Submitted: April 2004

Northeastern has a good reputation locally. I had a couple of interviews from out-of-state firms where I spent most of the interview explaining why I didn't have a class rank or GPA. Thankfully I wanted to stay local. All local big firms have interviews on campus, but the number of students from Northeastern at any given law firm is small in comparison to numbers from other local law schools. This may be because many of Northeastern's students enter the public interest sector.

Quality of Life

Status: Current student, full-time
Dates of Enrollment: 8/2004-Submit Date
Survey Submitted: April 2006

I think the main reason I decided to come here was that when I visited, the Northeastern students seemed happier than the students I met at other schools. Northeastern students are involved in a lot more than school—they are organizing activism campaigns and volunteering and doing all kinds of activities—so school is not the only thing in their lives, and they aren't stressed out about grades and class rank.

As a Northeastern student, you study because you need to know the rules of evidence to be a lawyer, not to get a particular grade on the evidence exam. We don't have grades or class rank, which means students don't compete against each other, which makes everyone much nicer to each other. Everyone is willing to share notes and help each other out. It's a very collaborative school in a lot of ways and much more collegial than most law schools.

Status: Current student, full-time
Dates of Enrollment: 9/2004-Submit Date
Survey Submitted: April 2006

Northeastern is located in the Back Bay/Fenway area. It's located right on the Green E line and Orange line. It's very convenient to get to and from campus. Located in the middle of Boston, it is ideally situated blocks from the Prudential Center, Copley, Newbury and Fenway Park. Good restaurants and great shopping are just blocks away. A short T ride will get you to Faneuil Hall, Downtown Crossings, South End and North End. Great food and shopping all around.

The neighborhood around campus is very safe. It's surrounded by dorms that are patrolled by police. Next to campus is also Wentworth Institute of Technology (WIT) and Simmons College. It's very collegial and safe. I live in private housing, about a 10-minute walk from campus. I have a studio apartment that costs $950/month.

Status: Current student, full-time
Dates of Enrollment: 1/2005-Submit Date
Survey Submitted: April 2006

The campus is pretty intimate. Most of the law school is housed in three buildings. While the facilities aren't the best (small library and few places to study), it's a great reason why so many NEU students bond so heavily—we go off campus to study. NEU does share a campus with undergrads, which isn't the most exciting, but it does lead to a great number of businesses being in and around campus.

Status: Current student, full-time
Dates of Enrollment: 8/2003-Submit Date
Survey Submitted: April 2006

Northeastern is located very centrally in the heart of Boston. The campus isn't much to look at, but it gets the job done. Nearly all students live off campus in the surrounding areas (the South End, Jamaica Plain, Fenway), which are much prettier to look at. There is some graduate level on-campus housing available, but it isn't recommended.

Boston is wicked expensive, so plan on having a roommate or two. And, like any big city, Boston does have a crime rate, but as long as you aren't a dimwit the city is relatively safe. Northeastern often gets dinged when it comes to the facilities—it's true, we aren't state-of-the-art. Other schools spend their money on first-class facilities, we spend it on first-class professors and helping our graduates with things like loan forgiveness. Luckily we have some other facilities available to us, like the university's two awesome gyms. You'll always find students and professors alike working out or playing hoops in the Marino Center (just avoid the afternoon rush when the undergrad meat market goes on sale).

Status: Current student, full-time
Dates of Enrollment: 9/2003-Submit Date
Survey Submitted: April 2006

The school facilities are lacking and we need a new building. However, I think the feeling at the school makes up for it. All the students are interesting and unique, and in school for different reasons. Almost all of them are committed to improving the world. The school is close to some awesome things in Boston and has a great location.

Status: Current student, full-time
Dates of Enrollment: 8/2003-Submit Date
Survey Submitted: January 2005

The NUSL campus is ok, nothing spectacular. Don't expect to be coddled and provided with on-campus housing. Nearly all the students live off campus in the various surrounding neighborhoods: the South End, Jamaica Plain, Mission Hill, Back Bay. Boston is not cheap. Be prepared to have a roommate. The law school building is right across from the state-of-the-art gym (best to go during mid-day or early morning when the undergrads have most of their classes). The law library is pretty good and the staff is great. The law school recently installed wi-fi, so bring a laptop.

Status: Current student, full-time
Dates of Enrollment: 8/2001-Submit Date
Survey Submitted: September 2003

Housing is limited because for one, we are in Boston, the mecca of higher education. The second part is that the law school gets housing through the main university, which is a pain at times. However, students are very helpful to one another and we are always subletting to one another, so it tends to work out great that way. The law school does not have much campus, but the university is huge, and we can use all of their stuff: the state-of-the-art gym, the pool, the ice-skating rink, the cafeteria, the ATM and more. Food is never a problem in Boston—you just have to make the choice of where and what you want that night.

Crime and safety—when the 1Ls come in, there is always a rash of laptop and book thefts. So don't have a cheap lock on your locker and don't put your laptop in your locker! Oh! And if you leave your laptop unguarded it may get swiped! Other than that (which happens to at most five people a year), no real crime here. The university police watch over us, too.

Read all of Vault's Law School Surveys at www.vault.com/lawschool — get complete surveys on top law schools, expert advice on applicaton essays, LSAT prep and more.

VAULT CAREER LIBRARY 325

Social Life

Status: Current student, full-time
Dates of Enrollment: 8/2004-Submit Date
Survey Submitted: April 2006

Boston is quintessentially a college town. There is a lot of everything—but it's Massachusetts, so the bars close early and public transportation stops running early. If you're coming from anywhere except New York, it won't bother you.

Status: Current student, full-time
Dates of Enrollment: 9/2004-Submit Date
Survey Submitted: April 2006

NUSL is a school that you tend to get out socially what you put in. If you make an effort it's easy to find other students who are interested in socializing. The dating scene is spotty if you are straight, we are known as the "gayest law school in America" for a reason. Luckily, there is not a shortage of grad students in Boston.

Status: Current student, full-time
Dates of Enrollment: 9/2003-Submit Date
Survey Submitted: April 2006

Your social life will depend on what groups you will get involved with, if any. Some students show up for classes and go home at the end of the day. Others form tight-knit cliques around the clubs/societies that they are involved in. Still others hang out casually and maintain friendships both within and outside of the school.

Status: Current student, full-time
Dates of Enrollment: 8/2003-Submit Date
Survey Submitted: April 2006

Northeastern students know how to have a good time. You can almost always find a get-together or party to go to. Weekly Bar Reviews are held throughout the city. And, nine times out of 10 you can find a law student or two at Punters, our local bar. We sometimes venture over to Our House East, but that's considered an undergrad hang-out.

House parties are a favorite and anyone from school is always invited. It can be cliquey, but there are relatively few loners. Everyone finds a group eventually. There are tons of clubs and groups—everything from the local National Lawyer's Guild Chapter to a newly formed law fraternity. You have to try pretty hard not to have a good time while going to Northeastern. We are a laid back group.

Status: Current student, full-time
Dates of Enrollment: 9/2003-Submit Date
Survey Submitted: April 2006

Students go out together all the time, especially to the nearby dive bar, Punter's. Boston is the ultimate college town, so there's tons of nightlife. Most law students spend time out of school working on community service projects, too.

Status: Alumnus/a, full-time
Dates of Enrollment: 8/1996-5/1999
Survey Submitted: March 2006

Being a student in Boston, you get free memberships to all museums in the city. There are great restaurants and bars. However, it can be a hard city to be young, poor and married in.

Status: Current student, full-time
Dates of Enrollment: 1/2005-Submit Date
Survey Submitted: April 2006

Social life during law school? Yeah right.

Status: Current student, full-time
Dates of Enrollment: 8/2003-Submit Date
Survey Submitted: February 2005

Ok bars and restaurants directly in the vicinity of the school. Easy subway ride into better downtown spots. Not too many large-scale events for the law school, but enough programming to make you happy and give you good breaks from studying. There is a "No-Talent" show every year that is a hoot—even professors join the fray.

Status: Current student, full-time
Dates of Enrollment: 8/2003-Submit Date
Survey Submitted: January 2005

The biggest difference between NUSL students and other law students in Boston is the amount of fun we have. Because there isn't law review or grades NUSL is a bit more laid back. None of the competitive cutthroat stuff you see at other schools. This allows you to actually make friends and have fun. Nearly everyone is willing to share notes or outlines. The law students often hang out at Punter's, the local watering hole, and complain about their current classes and gossip. If you are female, don't count on finding a husband. The women outnumber the men two-fold. And most of the men are either married or gay (our nickname is the "queerest law school in the nation").

Status: Current student, full-time
Dates of Enrollment: 8/2001-Submit Date
Survey Submitted: September 2003

Punter's Pub and Our House are NUSL favorites. There is so much to do in Boston that you could never be bored. Tons of clubs, art exhibits and cultural affairs. Most people don't wear Greek paraphernalia in law school, but if you need to connect with your old frat or sorority, you'll find them here in Beantown. We have too many students for you not to find at least one person. The school is always giving away free food, so a lot of us hang out here, too.

The School Says

Northeastern University School of Law offers the nation's only Cooperative Legal Education Program. This innovative approach provides all students with a full year of hands-on legal experience gained through four, three-month internships in law offices, judges, chambers and other organizations throughout the world. By participating in co-op placements with four different legal employers, students have an extraordinary opportunity to experience the actual practice of law and to integrate practical experience with an excellent theoretical foundation of in-depth classroom study.

Northeastern students customize their education, choosing not only among diverse co-ops, but also from a wide range of classroom and clinical courses. The faculty play the central role in making the law school an exciting, provocative and supportive learning environment. These highly productive scholars and teachers not only develop new ideas, but also put them into practice. They are also a diverse group: 50 percent are women and 24 percent are people of color.

The School of Law is nationally recognized for its emphasis on public interest aspirations. On average, 84 percent of students complete a public interest co-op, and many students participate in the school's clinics and institutes, which are dedicated to challenging existing boundaries of law in pursuit of economic and social justice. On average, graduates of the School of Law enter public interest careers at a rate five times the national average for all law school graduates.

The School of Law's placement statistic is impressive: 97 percent of the class of 2004 obtained employment within six months of graduation. The co-op program significantly contributes to students' career success: on average, 40 percent of Northeastern law students accept post-graduate employment with one of their former co-op employers. In addition to playing leadership roles in the public interest sector, Northeastern law graduates are highly successful in securing coveted judicial clerkships and positions with major law firms. 37 percent of the class of 2004 began their legal careers in law firms; 34 percent of this group joined firms with 100 or more attorneys.

Suffolk University Law School

General Office
120 Tremont Street
Boston, MA 02108-4977
Admissions phone: (617) 573-8144
Admissions e-mail: lawadm@suffolk.edu.
Admissions URL: http://www.law.suffolk.edu/admissions/

Admissions

Status: Current student, part-time
Dates of Enrollment: 5/2003-Submit Date
Survey Submitted: January 2006

The admissions process was very simple. After taking the LSAT, a complete package of all of the necessary paperwork and admissions requirements were sent. I recall that the application itself was very simple and easy to complete. An interview was not necessary in my case. I believe there are certain circumstances when interviews are required. The essay was a broad topic, asking us to explain why we want to attend Suffolk Law School and what our career objectives are.

I do not have an opinion as to the selectivity. I can only speak to that they have particular standards that are publicized in their brochures and I believe I met those qualifications and was therefore accepted.

Status: Alumnus/a, part-time
Dates of Enrollment: 9/2000-5/2004
Survey Submitted: May 2006

Streamlined, quick and easy. Informational interviews offered to those who request them.

Status: Alumnus/a, part-time
Dates of Enrollment: 9/1999-1/2003
Survey Submitted: March 2005

Suffolk Law's admission process is similar to any [law school] admissions process including providing a college transcript, LSAT scores and filling out a standard appplication. The evening program appears to consider work experience and professional development as an important criteria for admission (more so than LSAT scores).

Status: Alumnus/a, full-time
Dates of Enrollment: 8/2001-5/2004
Survey Submitted: March 2005

The selectivity was not particularly high because the school is not highly-ranked. I was called in for an interview since I was local. When visiting the school, I was impressed both by the facilities and the attitudes of the people I met and saw.

Status: Alumnus/a, full-time
Dates of Enrollment: 9/2000-5/2003
Survey Submitted: December 2003

You have to submit your standardized test scores and undergraduate transcripts. The essays are typical questions of why study law, why at Suffolk and where you see yourself.

Academics

Status: Current student, part-time
Dates of Enrollment: 5/2003-Submit Date
Survey Submitted: January 2006

This is a law program. I have attended a few classes that did not meet my expectations, but overall I have enjoyed all of my classes and find them to be informative, challenging and practical. I am in my last year of the program and so far, I have only had two professors that I did not find to be particularly good. Otherwise, I think there is an excellent balance of professors with academia backgrounds and firm experience. I have found grading, in general, to be very fair. The examinations include the information that the professors have taught and specified that would be on the exam. The workload is hefty, but it is not any different than what was advertised when I signed up for going to law school at night (while I am still working full-time).

Status: Alumnus/a, part-time
Dates of Enrollment: 9/2000-5/2004
Survey Submitted: May 2006

Quality of classes is excellent. Some world-class professors, but also some amazing adjunct faculty. Certain very popular classes are difficult to get into but professors/instructors are usually cooperative. Grade competition is high in early years, but gives way to collegial atmosphere as you progress. Workload, especially in first year, is heavy.

Status: Alumnus/a, part-time
Dates of Enrollment: 9/1999-1/2003
Survey Submitted: March 2005

Classrooms are modern and comfortable with Internet access at every seat. Many professors are full-time attorneys working at the top firms in Boston, providing excellent real-world instruction. The IP program includes complimentary theoretical and practical courses (e.g., Patent Application Drafting), which appear to be competitive with other IP programs.

Status: Alumnus/a, full-time
Dates of Enrollment: 8/2001-5/2004
Survey Submitted: March 2005

The classes are extremely well taught, for the most part, especially the first-year courses. It is sometimes difficult to get a popular class if you are late in signing up, but professors often make exception to the limits for students who wouldn't have another chance.

Status: Alumnus/a, full-time
Dates of Enrollment: 9/2000-5/2003
Survey Submitted: December 2003

Quality of education was superior for the practical preparation for the practice of law. The quality and variety of classes depended on the semester, with many classes available to fit your schedule and your curriculum.

Employment Prospects

Status: Current student, part-time
Dates of Enrollment: 5/2003-Submit Date
Survey Submitted: January 2006

I already have a job that intend to stay at when I graduate. I have been with my employer for five years so I am not up to date on the job searching process. I do know that Suffolk has an extensive career services program. There are numerous resources available to the students. There are job fairs and on-campus recruiting. We receive weekly e-mails regarding opportunities or any changes that are being made.

Read all of Vault's Law School Surveys at www.vault.com/lawschool — get complete surveys on top law schools, expert advice on applicaton essays, LSAT prep and more.

VAULT CAREER LIBRARY   327

Within the Boston market, I believe that the Suffolk name is very prestigious. I do not believe that the school carries the name carries the same weight in other parts of the country, given the proximity and prestige of Harvard, Boston College and Boston University.

Status: Alumnus/a, part-time
Dates of Enrollment: 9/2000-5/2004
Survey Submitted: May 2006

Excellent within the Boston market, especially for litigation. Big firms are starting to take notice as school rises in rankings.

Status: Alumnus/a, part-time
Dates of Enrollment: 9/1999-1/2003
Survey Submitted: March 2005

As an electrical engineer specializing in patent law, I was hired at arguably the top firm in Boston with a Suffolk Law degree.

Status: Alumnus/a, full-time
Dates of Enrollment: 8/2001-5/2004
Survey Submitted: March 2005

Few Suffolk students get top jobs. Most big firms outside of D.C. just aren't looking at Suffolk. There are exceptions made, however, for students going into patent law.

Status: Alumnus/a, full-time
Dates of Enrollment: 9/2000-5/2003
Survey Submitted: December 2003

The career network in New England is strong and in the spectacular city of Boston. Jobs are offered and obtained based upon the normal criteria of ability and personality.

 **Quality of Life**

Status: Current student, part-time
Dates of Enrollment: 5/2003-Submit Date
Survey Submitted: January 2006

The college is generally a "commuter school." There are some housing facilities, but I have never visited or used. The campus is directly across the street from public transportation and the Boston Common and close to local shops and pubs. There are several restaurants nearby and the school has a cafeteria in the building. The area is very safe and there always campus police officers patrolling the school and surrounding areas.

The classrooms and Law School building are fantastic. There are internet connections and plugs for your laptop in every classroom, the library, in the cafeteria and common areas. The library contains a number of useful resources and is perfect for studying. There are great views of Boston Common and other landmarks from the library.

Status: Alumnus/a, part-time
Dates of Enrollment: 9/2000-5/2004
Survey Submitted: May 2006

Being an evening student certain conveniences were missing, like professors or administrators being around when you are in class. Overall, the school is well run, in a top-of-the-line building and caters to the needs of commuter students.

Status: Alumnus/a, part-time
Dates of Enrollment: 9/1999-1/2003
Survey Submitted: March 2005

The evening program is challenging. Typically three days per week for four years. I also took classes in the summer to eliminate a semester; I completed my degree in three-and-a-half years.

Status: Alumnus/a, full-time
Dates of Enrollment: 8/2001-5/2004
Survey Submitted: March 2005

Great, safe location. I have heard of thefts in the building but have never experienced any myself. I always felt safe, even late at night. Beautiful new building with the latest high-tech equipment and Internet connections at every seat. Friendly people and helpful professors.

Status: Alumnus/a, full-time
Dates of Enrollment: 9/2000-5/2003
Survey Submitted: December 2003

Quality of life is what you make of it. Diverse ages and occupations create a more professional environment. There is no housing on campus for law students, yet there is plenty of available housing within a short trip. The classroom and actual educational facilities are far and above more technologically advanced than 99 percent of law schools.

 Social Life

Status: Current student, part-time
Dates of Enrollment: 5/2003-Submit Date
Survey Submitted: January 2006

Law school is so demanding and it is easy to have close relationships with others in the same shoes as you. I have made a number of people that I know I will be friends with for a very long time. Our favorite local hang out is the Beantown Pub. It is only two doors from school and it is a place for everyone to go, play pool, drink and just hang out.

There are a number of clubs and school-sponsored events. These are advertised often via e-mail and postings at school. I can't speak to the dating scene; I am married.

Status: Alumnus/a, part-time
Dates of Enrollment: 9/2000-5/2004
Survey Submitted: May 2006

Excellent opportunity for social life. Right in downtown Boston with clubs, bars and shopping all around. Student organizations are well-run and provide ample socializing opportunities.

Status: Alumnus/a, part-time
Dates of Enrollment: 9/1999-1/2003
Survey Submitted: March 2005

Excellent location in the center of Boston across from Boston Common, walking distance to the Theatre District, North End and Fleet Center.

Status: Alumnus/a, full-time
Dates of Enrollment: 8/2001-5/2004
Survey Submitted: March 2005

Not much social life. Many evening students have families or jobs.

Status: Alumnus/a, full-time
Dates of Enrollment: 9/2000-5/2003
Survey Submitted: December 2003

Boston is literally at the footstep of Suffolk's Law School. And as many visitors and locals can testify, the city of Boston plays second chair to no other U.S. city. Restaurants, theatre and local pubs make Boston a mature place to party.

Western New England College School of Law

Office of Admissions
1215 Wilbraham Road
Springfield, MA 01119-2684
Admissions phone: (800) 782-6665 or (413) 782-1406
Admissions fax: (413)796-2067
Admissions e-mail: admissions@law.wnec.edu
Admissions URL: http://www1.law.wnec.edu/prospective/

 ## Admissions

Status: Current student, full-time
Dates of Enrollment: 8/2004-Submit Date
Survey Submitted: May 2006

It was a smooth process. I strongly suggest having a well-written personal statement. In addition, if you can attend an open house, do so. This will give you an indication of what the culture of the law school is truly like. Western New England College School of Law is very student focussed and it lacks the 'cutthroat' student culture I sensed at other open houses.

Status: Current student, full-time
Dates of Enrollment: 8/2005-Submit Date
Survey Submitted: May 2006

The admissions process is fairly simple. The application is available online and only takes a short time to fill in. Once I sent the application in I received e-mails and phone calls to let me know that my application was being processed. Once I was accepted I received a phone call from the dean of admissions to let me know that I was accepted and also that I was being awarded a scholarship. Once I was accepted the office was very easy to work with. They answered any and all of my questions. Once I decided I was going to attend, the office did everything they could to ensure that I would have an easy transition and that I was up to date on what was going on. It is the personal touches that make the admissions office to friendly and easy to work with.

Status: Current student, full-time
Dates of Enrollment: 8/2005-Submit Date
Survey Submitted: May 2006

Admissions process was great. I appreciated that they let me know so quickly that I had been accepted. Class size was a factor for me. The big determining factor for me was Dean Johnson calling me personally inviting me to join the law school in the fall. Other than that, all I had to go on was what I read about the law school on the LSAC web site.

Status: Current student, part-time
Dates of Enrollment: 8/2005-Submit Date
Survey Submitted: April 2006

The admissions office was very helpful. I wasn't able to come up and visit the school during the open houses (I moved from Florida), but when I stopped in during the summer the head of admissions was not only excited to give us an unexpected tour, he really made us feel welcomed. I just couldn't get over how friendly he was.

Status: Alumnus/a, full-time
Dates of Enrollment: 8/2002-5/2005
Survey Submitted: April 2006

The admissions process was fairly simple and hassle-free. I completed an application, mailed it in and received a telephone call from the Direction of Admissions shortly thereafter offering me admission and a scholarship. I was living some distance away from the school at the time of application and did not interview. I'm not sure that the essay is all that important in getting admitted. Schools are looking at scores and the essay is there to make sure you can form some coherent thoughts. I wrote about how I became interested in law and why

I wanted to go to law school. It was a somewhat generic topic, but it seemed appropriate. As far as selectivity, it was not the most difficult school to get into, it was not the easiest school to get into and I had above average scores which gave me a slight advantage in obtaining the scholarship.

Status: Current student, full-time
Dates of Enrollment: 8/2003-Submit Date
Survey Submitted: April 2006

The application process to Western New England was similar to that of the other schools I applied to for law school. There were three things that set it apart. First, though I couldn't attend their admitted student open house because I was traveling from the Southeast, they still bent over backwards to accommodate my schedule, had me meet with students and faculty, and answered my endless questions throughout the process. Second, the admissions committee reads every file, cover to cover, regardless of your LSAT score or GPA. While other schools discard you based solely on your numbers, Western New England seeks to learn about the whole student, not just the student's numerical value.

Finally, the Director of Admissions called me to tell me I had been admitted. While I received form letters from every other school notifying me of my acceptance, the Director at Western New England took the time to call and let me know not only that I had been accepted, but also that they were offering me a scholarship. I appreciated the personal attention in the admissions process, and I'm pleased to say that individual attention carried into the academic arena.

Status: Current student, part-time
Dates of Enrollment: 8/2005-Submit Date
Survey Submitted: April 2006

I am not sure how selective the evening program process really is because several fellow classmates were admitted the week before classes started. I was interested in either full- or part-time and was asked if I would take part-time when at an open house. The application was easy to follow and equitable with other applications. I did not have a formal interview with an admissions dean. I did have discussions with several professors at the open houses. You could see them mentally taking notes on prospects. I thought that was a good thing. The essay portion of the application was good for me as it gave me an opportunity to express to the school my experiences and differences from the typical first year student. Selectivity seems more ridged in the full time day program. I believe most of my classmates are as qualified to be in the program as I, but wonder about the ability to apply a month prior to start of classes and get a spot in the evening program.

Status: Current student, full-time
Dates of Enrollment: 8/2004-Submit Date
Survey Submitted: April 2006

The admissions process was simple and user-friendly. Any questions I had were quickly answered by the admissions office and they were more than willing to take time from their day to help me. I believe the essay portion of the application was truly considered by the committee—more so than at other law schools. The committee seemed to consider all areas—not just LSAT scores and GPA—and that consideration showed in the diversity of the class.

Status: Current student, full-time
Dates of Enrollment: 9/2004-Submit Date
Survey Submitted: January 2006

WNEC is becoming much more selective each year. This selectivity is well deserved, given the high quality professors that the school is recruiting. I think that people should take WNEC seriously, especially because it is constantly trying to get better and more selective. This makes this school special in a way that some more highly rated schools of law are not. While I was applying to schools, I got into more selective schools that are considered to be better. However, I choose WNEC not only because of the wonderful financial package that they offered me, but also because the school is truly dedicated to being the best it can be. Other schools that I visited were content to be in the rank that they

Read all of Vault's Law School Surveys at www.vault.com/lawschool — get complete surveys on top law schools, expert advice on applicaton essays, LSAT prep and more.

VAULT CAREER LIBRARY 329

were. This made them less impressive to me. Specifically, these schools did not have the type of commitment to stellar professors and students that WNEC has. I think that this is the biggest thing that WNEC has to offer.

The essay was general and allowed me to elaborate on my personal attributes. As for advice getting in, I would say that even if your LSAT score is not the best, you have a good chance at getting into WNEC if you have other things to offer the school. I think that LSAT scores are important to the school, but unique personalities and passion for the law and society are also very important at WNEC. For this reason, personal essays are often embraced at WNEC. Other schools may not want this type of emphasis in the admissions essay, but WNEC really does seem to respond well to it.

Another important thing WNEC offers is scholarship packages. These can be quite generous. A large percentage of the top-achieving students have some scholarship money. I have heard that this is because the school is actively recruiting top students to come to the school. These attractive packages are the reason that many of the students at the top of the classes came to WNEC instead of to the higher-ranked schools that they also got into. Having this scholarship on your resume can be impressive to prospective employers, and shows that the school really wants to have top students.

 # Academics

Status: Current student, full-time
Dates of Enrollment: 8/2004-Submit Date
Survey Submitted: May 2006

Classes are very well-rounded with a lot of co-curricular options. Professors are fantastic and extremely intelligent. Workload is manageable.

Status: Current student, full-time
Dates of Enrollment: 8/2005-Submit Date
Survey Submitted: May 2006

The classes are great. The smaller class size makes it easy to excel. The professors know who you are and take in interest in the students. They are very easy to get in touch with when there is a question. They are also very willing to help you understand the materials. The overall quality of the classes is excellent. The grading is generally very fair and the professors are always willing to discuss how they grade and what they are or were looking for in an assignment/exam. The process for getting into classes is fairly simple. It is all online and it can be done at any time of the day or night during the sign-up period. Generally getting the classes you want is easy. They do have a seniority preference, though, so that the upperclass students are able to get the classes they need or want before they leave. The workload is overall manageable. It is all about knowing your study habits and working around them.

Status: Alumnus/a, full-time
Dates of Enrollment: 8/2002-5/2005
Survey Submitted: April 2006

Western New England has an excellent faculty. Many of the professors are not only extremely knowledgeable in their field, but also have that unique ability to present the sometimes complicated subject matter—break it down to a level that is easier to comprehend for students. The grading system is fair. You have a chance to know what each professor expects for work product and what kind of work will get you a good grade. For papers and non-exam work, most professors are willing to look at your work before it's due to point out what can be done better.

Workload was a bit of a surprise to me. It's the same kind of workload you will get at other law schools, but it's definitely not college. That was my one mistake going into law school. At first, I viewed it as an extension of college. It's not that. There's a lot more material to absorb and getting behind in work is not an option. As far as popular classes, I never had trouble getting into a class I wanted to take. Anything I ever signed up for was put on my schedule.

Status: Current student, full-time
Dates of Enrollment: 8/2003-Submit Date
Survey Submitted: April 2006

I find the quality of the education I am receiving here to be excellent. I enjoy the variety of classes offered (Trusts and Estates to Islamic Law) and the accessibility of the professors is unparalleled at any school I visited. The Socratic Method is the preferred method of teaching, but the faculty assists you through the process and allow you to ease into it your first year. Their expectations are high, but the expectations of your peers are even higher. The difference about the community here is that it encompasses the academic, professional and personal realms of the students' lives. Here, you're a name, not a number. You may specialize in a program if you so choose (we have especially strong tax, health law and public interest courses) or you can take a broader approach. I appreciated having the option to go in depth with a subject while still broadening the scope of my coursework.

Status: Current student, full-time
Dates of Enrollment: 8/2005-Submit Date
Survey Submitted: April 2006

The classes are smaller in the first year (about 50 students) so it provides more camaraderie amongst the students as well as the professors. The professors are very accessible, as well as encouraging. Some professors have a much more intense workload than others and some are historically harder graders. However it all works out in the wash, especially during the first year when every class is graded on a bell curve.

Status: Current student, part-time
Dates of Enrollment: 8/2005-Submit Date
Survey Submitted: April 2006

The professors to date have been excellent. They are not just interested in teaching their subject but about the law in today's society as well. These professors are also well aware of the different lives most evening part-time students have as compared to the day students. They don't make accommodations but they do have a bit more latitude in the coursework. Coursework for evening is spread over three evenings from six to 10 p.m. It makes a manageable workload for those with jobs, families and other responsibilities other than just school.

Status: Current student, full-time
Dates of Enrollment: 8/2004-Submit Date
Survey Submitted: April 2006

There is no hidden agenda. The work is hard but, with proper organization, able to be managed. All of the classes are easy to get except some of the qualified writing courses (those courses are capped to keep the class size small). The professors are phenomenal and literally have an open-door policy—they expect you to visit and go to them with problems or concerns.

Status: Current student, full-time
Dates of Enrollment: 8/2004-Submit Date
Survey Submitted: April 2006

The degree program offers a well-developed selection of required courses, as well as many elective options. As a 1L, the workload at the beginning is structured so students are eased into the experience and then is increased as they become more familiar with the requirements and the material. While the more popular professors and/or courses are in high demand, the administration does everything it can to allow class sizes to grow (within reason obviously) in order to avoid students being bumped from classes. There are a number of externship and clinical opportunities that offer real-world experience. The grading is fair and the suggested curves in required classes are pretty much adhered to by professors.

Status: Current student, full-time
Dates of Enrollment: 9/2004-Submit Date
Survey Submitted: January 2006

The academic demands of the school are great, as is to be expected in law school. The school has a very demanding curve, which makes it less of a possibility to grade into a higher score. Specifically, the grades are not inflated in any manner, as they are at other schools. The courses are on par with a higher-ranked school. The professors are all very good. This is not just because they are accessible, which they are, but it is also because they all have very marketable backgrounds. The fact that WNEC has the ability to get these professors to teach at the school is another outstanding attribute of the college. The school has been able to recruit some of the best names in the field to teach at the school. This includes Jennifer Levi, who was an attorney for the couples that won the right to legal marriage in Massachusetts. As of now, MA is the only state to have done this and she was behind that effort. To have her teach at the school is really to be at the cusp of the legal world. Many of the professors are still practicing, which makes for very interesting class discussions and real life opportunities. Additionally, a large number of the professors have graduated from top-ranked schools—especially from Harvard Law School. The professors are all brilliant—there really are not any lack-luster ones. Therefore, it isn't difficult to get into classes because they are all good. Even the courses for the first-year students are taught by top professors.

Status: Alumnus/a, full- and part-time
Dates of Enrollment: 8/2000-5/2004
Survey Submitted: March 2005

The full-time professors at the school are, for the most part, pretty fantastic! They remain at the school because they genuinely want to teach. They are very, very, accessible, and I attribute my academic success in law school in large part to their teaching ability and accessibility. The quality of classes in usually excellent, although some of the adjunct professors are not always great, however, some are terrific. One drawback is, because of the size of the school, there aren't always lots of choices of classes to take. Usually you can get the classes you want unless it is limited to 20 or 24 students and is a very popular class. Another strength is that the school has a number of clinics, although with the increasing classes, it will prove more difficult to get into the clinics. I was in the antidiscrimination clinic and I won settlements for two clients. The school has a curve where classes are supposed to have a mean grade between 78 and 82, but it is for all mandatory classes only. Some professors use it for all classes, it does not apply if the class has less than 20 people. Professors are allowed to give up to three points for participation, but they don't have to. The school has an excellent academic program and you will get a well-rounded legal education there. The workload is hard, but doable. As an added bonus, the bar exam is given at WNEC twice a year, if you are going to be taking the MA bar.

 ## Employment Prospects

Status: Alumnus/a, full-time
Dates of Enrollment: 8/2002-5/2005
Survey Submitted: April 2006

The career services department does an excellent job creating the resources you need to find a job. Although I feel a lot of the on-campus recruiting was geared toward students at the top of their class (very GPA oriented), the alumni network was a valuable tool to many students. Coming from Vermont, there were not a lot of job postings around for the area I wanted to practice in, but there was a great collection of contacts in my area that had graduated from WNEC or were interested in hearing from law students. The job I ended up with was a result of my own job search once I returned to Vermont, but there are definitely opportunities and resources available at the school for students who want to start their job search earlier.

Status: Current student, full-time
Dates of Enrollment: 8/2004-Submit Date
Survey Submitted: April 2006

Many WNEC graduates stay in the Springfield, MA area where they are respected and hold various positions from business law to public interest to judicial positions.

Status: Current student, full-time
Dates of Enrollment: 8/2003-Submit Date
Survey Submitted: April 2006

I believe that networking is essential to securing a job, particularly when you attend a lesser known law school. My experiential learning opportunities have bolstered my resume and I am pleased about my job prospects as a graduating student. I have secured interviews for each job I've applied for and I have utilized the network I have built here to seek employment.

Status: Current student, full-time
Dates of Enrollment: 8/2005-Submit Date
Survey Submitted: April 2006

I came upon a paid internship after my first year relatively easily. The career services office does a great job in keeping students in touch with employment opportunities, and is more than willing to help a student search in a region other than New England. They could truly improve the on-campus recruiting, as many of the career fairs occur at schools in Boston, but if you're willing to travel, it provides a nice getaway for a night.

Status: Current student, full-time
Dates of Enrollment: 8/2004-Submit Date
Survey Submitted: April 2006

If I want to get a job in New England, I know my school can get me far. In terms of big city jobs—they are harder to get, but our school does not really produce the type of student that wants one. We are all about the small- to medium-sized firms and those jobs are definitely out there for us. Also, the career services and alumni relations offices work with you personally to get a job, both during and after school.

Status: Current student, full-time
Dates of Enrollment: 8/2004-Submit Date
Survey Submitted: April 2006

While the law school is smaller in comparison to other regional schools, the career services office works with employers and other law schools to ensure students have as many opportunities as possible to seek employment and make contacts. It would easier if more recruiting occurred on campus, rather than students traveling to Boston, NY or D.C. Graduates obtain jobs in a number of areas—public interest, prosecution, defense, all size firms and private practice. The alumni network is a work in progress, but definitely on the right track and the alumni locator service is open to all students/alumni.

Status: Alumnus/a, full- and part-time
Dates of Enrollment: 8/2000-5/2004
Survey Submitted: March 2005

The biggest program that WNEC grads face is that most people have never heard of our school. Most people don't even know that there is an accredited law school outside of the Boston area. Despite this, a number of our grads have gone on to very good jobs, but mostly here in MA or in CT. There is a fair bit of on-campus recruiting, but most of it centers on the law review students. There are a wide variety of internships available, including one with the federal district judge in Springfield, who usually takes one each semester. The alumni tend to be pretty helpful. The career services department is marvelous in helping students with anything they need in their job search!

Status: Alumnus/a, full-time
Dates of Enrollment: 9/1997-5/2000
Survey Submitted: September 2003

As the only law school in Western Massachusetts, it definitely has an edge in that area in terms of career prospects. Although not yet recognized as a national school, it has earned a solid reputation in the New England region and its graduates have no difficulty securing jobs in that area. Lots of internship opportunities (legal clinics and externships) during law school, which often lead to full-time positions. Lots of firms, mostly from CT and MA, participate in the OCI.

 ## Quality of Life

Status: Current student, full-time
Dates of Enrollment: 8/2005-Submit Date
Survey Submitted: May 2006

Quality of life for me was excellent. I was fortunate to find a nice house in a nice, quiet neighborhood not too far from the school. Campus facilities like the gym and field were readily available for work-outs. Dining could stand a little improvement but no big complaint there except for the hours (too short or not enough). Relatively crime free and the campus police and security personnel always there to help.

Read all of Vault's Law School Surveys at www.vault.com/lawschool — get complete surveys on top law schools, expert advice on applicaton essays, LSAT prep and more.

VAULT CAREER LIBRARY   331

Status: Current student, full-time
Dates of Enrollment: 8/2005-Submit Date
Survey Submitted: May 2006

There is a housing coordinator that contacts the students regularly to ensure that everyone has housing. The campus is very small and easy to work in; the law school itself only has one building. There is a dining facility inside the law school. The school has many areas to study in, including plenty of room in the library. There are several computer labs in the library and there is even a laptop printing station so that you can print directly from your laptop while at school. Every classroom has wireless internet access, as does the library and the rest of the building. The neighborhood is overall very safe. The campus police are always doing patrols to ensure that the students are safe and when something does happen they are right at work to solve any problems. There are also security guards in the school building itself and campus safety will escort you to your car if you feel the need. They are always looking out for the students safety in every respect.

Status: Current student, part-time
Dates of Enrollment: 8/2005-Submit Date
Survey Submitted: April 2006

I moved off campus and purchased a home in a neighboring town. I live approximately 20 minutes away from school in Enfield, CT. To be honest the area surrounding the campus isn't the safest. Downtown Springfield needs work, however the law school keeps the building and the parking lots well monitored and the guards are always willing to walk you to your car if you are there late at night. I would suggest to an incoming student to check out the surrounding cities or on-campus residences for housing.

Status: Alumnus/a, full-time
Dates of Enrollment: 8/2002-5/2005
Survey Submitted: April 2006

Springfield was not my favorite city in which to live. Coming from Vermont and low crime rates, Springfield was a different experience. There are definitely the good and bad areas. I found decent housing at affordable prices throughout my three years there. In that time, I did have one break-in at my house and had my laptop stolen. My advice—make sure you have renter's insurance. Aside from the actual city, the campus is a beautiful place and in a nicer area of the city. There are a couple dining choices if you want to get a meal while at school and some great restaurants. Law students can take advantage of all facilities offered to the undergrad students and the gym is probably a favorite to many. If you have a couple hours break in between classes, it's a great time to walk up to the gym for your workout, to play some basketball or use the indoor track. Overall, quality of life is good.

Status: Current student, full-time
Dates of Enrollment: 8/2003-Submit Date
Survey Submitted: April 2006

As I mentioned earlier, the community at Western New England is one of the unique characteristics about it. From the time you are admitted until you matriculate, there is a full-time housing coordinator to assist you in finding area housing. The Orientation Committee also assists students in learning the area for groceries, shopping and movie theaters. The staff at the school is always willing to offer recommendations about dentists and doctors, and the faculty care about student wellbeing. As for our facilities, the school was built in 1974, but has updated technology and a revamped food court. The plans for reconstruction look amazing, and I am looking forward to returning as an alumnus to visit the new building.

Status: Current student, full-time
Dates of Enrollment: 8/2005-Submit Date
Survey Submitted: April 2006

There is no on-campus housing, but there is an exhaustive list of housing opportunities in the area. Springfield, though not the prettiest city in the Northeast, certainly is not the worst place on the map. The undergraduate campus is beautiful, and the law school is set apart geographically. The law school is due for some renovations in the next couple years, and it will certainly improve not only the already good facilities, but also the aesthetic look of the school. There is a myriad of restaurants in the Springfield area, and the cultural

capitals of Northampton and Amherst are only a quick 20- to 30-minute ride away.

Status: Current student, full-time
Dates of Enrollment: 8/2004-Submit Date
Survey Submitted: April 2006

Springfield is definitely an urban setting and while many students live in the downtown area, others live in surrounding communities which are a little more "tame." The city is in the process of trying to remake itself and attract corporate investment. The law school shares a campus with the undergraduate college which offers some unique opportunities—more choices for dining, large indoor pool/gym/workout facilities, intramural sports and additional library options. Housing varies between apartments (which is what most people choose), private homes and a couple of houses on campus.

Status: Alumnus/a, full- and part-time
Dates of Enrollment: 8/2000-5/2004
Survey Submitted: March 2005

I was happy living in Springfield, but a lot of my classmates did not find it lively enough. It certainly is not as exciting a town as Boston, but there usually is some neat stuff going on in Northampton, and it is a lot cheaper than Boston. There isn't much on-campus housing, but there is a lot of off-campus housing. However, there is very little housing that accepts dogs, cats seem to be ok, but no one wants dogs at all. Parking was an issue, but the law school added an additional parking lot after I graduated!! Crime can be an issue depending on which neighborhood you live in, but it is usually OK by the school. Campus facilities are ok, but not outstanding. The librarians will bend over backwards to help you, and they keep updating the computer lab. Some of the classrooms are pretty dated, but they do keep adding technology. Don't expect gourmet dining in Springfield! The food is good to very good, with better food in Northampton but nothing like NYC!!

Social Life

Status: Current student, full-time
Dates of Enrollment: 8/2005-Submit Date
Survey Submitted: May 2006

The school is centrally located. Many of the students live near the bars and restaurants. The school is close to the highway and that makes it easy to access all that the area has to offer. The school itself also offers many clubs and activities. Students can join any of the many clubs and associations and they can also start their own. There is also opportunities to participate in the undergraduate programs and activities as well.

Status: Current student, full-time
Dates of Enrollment: 8/2005-Submit Date
Survey Submitted: May 2006

I am a 1L. For me, forget about a dating scene. Social life was decent though. Couple of bars and restaurants near or not too far from school. School hosted interesting events and the clubs had great guest speakers. There were enough activities hosted by the school that would have kept it interesting by themselves. I thought it was a great year. Great school and wonderful people willing to help you. I did not meet one unkind soul my first year here.

Status: Current student, part-time
Dates of Enrollment: 8/2005-Submit Date
Survey Submitted: April 2006

Every Thursday night many of the law students gather across the street from the campus at Sophia's for karaoke night, cheep beer, good bar food and pool. Just about every other weekend we go downtown where there is a strip of bars and clubs on Worthington Street all on the same block within walking distance of each other. Enfield, CT (about 15 to 20 minutes from campus) has the widest restaurant selection. There is an Outback, Olive Garden, Friday's, Panera Bread, Ruby Tuesday's, Red Robin, 99 and the ever college student favorite, Denny's (open 24 hours of course) all in the same mile radius.

The School Says

Status: Current student, full-time
Dates of Enrollment: 8/2003-Submit Date
Survey Submitted: April 2006

The social opportunities at Western New England College School of Law are numerous. If you're into a party scene, Worthington Street in downtown Springfield provides plenty of bars and nightclubs. If you just want to grab a beer and some pizza, Sophia's is right across the street. If you're looking for cultural events, Northampton has a plethora of concerts that come to town, plays and fine dining for students to take advantage of on the weekends. Internal to the school is our Social Committee which plans casino trips, a semi-formal, a Halloween party and nights out on the town. We're also about an hour and 15 minutes from Boston and two hours from NYC, so trips into larger cities are doable. Hartford, CT is just 30 minutes away as well, so for a change of nightlife scenery students can head down there. There are also plenty of opportunities for mingling with law students at UConn and at the six schools in Boston, so if you tire of your classmates, you can expand your horizons.

Status: Current student, part-time
Dates of Enrollment: 8/2005-Submit Date
Survey Submitted: April 2006

The school has many different social events geared for the law students specifically. An active Student Bar Association, legal fraternity and many other law-related organizations offer activities ranging from social evenings at local pubs to formal balls. Sporting events are also available.

Status: Current student, full-time
Dates of Enrollment: 8/2004-Submit Date
Survey Submitted: April 2006

Tons of bars and restaurants. Dating scene stinks. It's all what you make of it.

Status: Current student, full-time
Dates of Enrollment: 9/2004-Submit Date
Survey Submitted: January 2006

The school is not as competitive as some other law schools. Although there are those who try to make it like that, most students are happy to help each other out with notes, study groups and even jointly create outlines for final exams. The upper-class students are also very nice to the incoming first-years. There are many activities planned at the beginning of the year to facilitate this bonding. Most importantly, the way that the first-year class is divided up makes for an environment where students can bond easily with others in their section. This is helpful when trying to make study groups and new friends. This is another positive about the school—there are many different types of students, especially for such a small school, that there are many opportunities to find a similar mind. The school sponsors a number of events throughout the year that are widely attended. Most of the students go to events at the school and a large number also attend events off campus. They are a good way to meet people and left off steam. Around exams the law school puts on a lot of coffee-related events in the building so you can feel like you are taking a break even though you really aren't!

The student law groups are also good at WNEC. There is a group for basically whatever you might be interested in, from environmental law to gay-straight alliance to minority law groups to an international law society to a women's law society. These groups have high attendance rates. There is also a law review and several moot court teams. Although there is only one law review for the school, it is good for building morale and for limiting decisions. This also helps the retention rate, as hardly anyone leaves the Review for the two years that they are on it. The Review is very close and plan many events together. They seem to be closer than the moot court teams, although the Negotiation team is close, and have many events to attend together. I would recommend being part of something—whether it be the newspaper or a focused law group in your first year—or becoming a leader in your second year or joining a moot court team—or making it on law review. These groups foster a sense of community that is really nice to have when you are at the library all the time studying! There are a lot of clubs, bars and restaurants in Springfield that many students visit, especially at the beginning of each year.

Western New England College School of Law is located in Springfield, Massachusetts, in the heart of the Pioneer Valley. Springfield is the third largest city in the Commonwealth, and home to a lively cultural scene. Founded in 1919, the School of Law was originally part of Northeastern University and merged with Western New England College which itself was founded in 1951. The School of Law has been accredited by the ABA since 1974 and is a member of the Association of American Law Schools.

Western New England College School of Law offers many ways to earn a law degree. In addition to our three-year, fulltime program, the School of Law also offers four-year, part-time evening and part-time day programs. Students may also combine their law degree with three other programs. These programs include the JD/MBA (Masters in Business Administration) with Western New England College, the JD/MRP (Masters in Regional Planning) with the University of Massachusetts, and the JD/MSW (Masters in Social Work) with Springfield College.

Western New England College School of Law affords students the opportunity to merge theory with practice. Students take advantage of clinical coursework, a wide variety of simulation courses, and participation on a number of moot court teams in order to hone their lawyering skills. The students enjoy the small class sizes where the close-knit environment and continual interaction with faculty and peers make the law school experience a rewarding one. First-year, full-time students are grouped in three sections of 50 students. The small class size promotes a collegial learning environment in which students are challenged to actively participate in their legal education.

Please contact the Office of Admissions at admissions@law.wnec.edu or (800) 782-6665 or (413) 782-1406 should you have any questions regarding Western New England College School of Law. We encourage you to visit our web site at www.law.wnec.edu.

Read all of Vault's Law School Surveys at www.vault.com/lawschool — get complete surveys on top law schools, expert advice on applicaton essays, LSAT prep and more.

VAULT CAREER LIBRARY **333**

Michigan State University College of Law

230 Law College Building
East Lansing, MI 48824-1300
Admissions phone: (517) 432-0222
Application request line: (517) 432-0222
Admissions fax: (517) 432-0098
Admissions e-mail: law@law.msu.edu
Admissions URL: http://www.law.msu.edu/admissions/

 ## Admissions

Status: Current student, full-time
Dates of Enrollment: 8/2004-Submit Date
Survey Submitted: March 2006

The admissions staff was wonderful. They welcomed personal meetings and provided answers to all the questions from the hopeful candidate. I believe that applying early does help one's chance of admission and furthermore, the office makes prompt admissions decisions and so you will not be stuck waiting around for months on end to find out the status of your application. The essays were not overly complicated and demand honest responses. The school is becoming increasingly more selective as the applicant pool continues to increase.

Status: Current student, full-time
Dates of Enrollment: 8/2005-Submit Date
Survey Submitted: March 2006

Since most law schools use the Law School Admissions Council (LSAC) to expedite the admissions process, the admissions process was similar to the 12 other law programs I applied to. I applied to public schools, private schools (Michigan State is a private law school), large schools, small schools, Tier I (*U.S. News* rankings) and Tier II schools. Using the LSAC was an easy way to research where an applicant's GPA and LSAT score relate to the current first year class.

Michigan State University College of Law does not include an interview as part of the admissions process. According to my research when I was applying to law school, Northwestern was the only ABA law school that was doing interviews as part of the admissions process. Almost all schools require a personal essay, some require two or maybe even three. Michigan State University College of Law required one personal statement that included goals, personal history and uniqueness.

I also included—and would advise others to include—a resume. MSU College of Law is becoming more selective each year as applications continue to grow. My advice would be first, obviously, to work hard on a good GPA during undergrad education, as well as try to achieve a good score on the LSAT. Second, I would try to apply as early as possible. Michigan State University College of Law uses rolling admissions. Therefore, it is an advantage to apply early. Lastly, I would advise that when writing one's personal statement try to focus on anything that is unusual about him or her. MSU College of Law, like other law schools, loves diversity: religious, geographic, racial, odd hobbies, records, anything. I have noticed that the law school loves anything that one can offer to that diversity.

Status: Current student, full-time
Dates of Enrollment: 8/2005-Submit Date
Survey Submitted: March 2006

My admissions process was different than most. I was recruited to MSU from a Native American Pre-Law program. I had a brief "interview" (more like question and answer) with an admissions personnel and a student. After the question and answer if you were interested in the college you were encouraged to apply. I applied and soon found out I was accepted through a phone call (approximately two weeks after). I was then sent an acceptance letter and sent in the required information within a day or two of receiving it.

Status: Current student, full-time
Dates of Enrollment: 8/2004-Submit Date
Survey Submitted: March 2006

Worked with a liaison to admissions. Filled out the application and ordered transcripts. The whole process was quite easy. Most difficult part was filling out the essay on the admission application. I applied in February of 2004 and received notice of admission quickly due to strong undergrad GPA and high LSAT scores. Received merit scholarship (75 percent tuition) shortly after informing admissions that I would be unable to attend without financial aid.

Status: Current student, full-time
Dates of Enrollment: 8/2003-Submit Date
Survey Submitted: March 2006

While researching schools in Michigan, I originally only found information on MSU's law college in a huge book listing all the schools in the country; none of the smaller books had any detailed information on MSU or what life as a law student here was like. I attended the LSDAS Los Angeles Forum and was enthusiastically greeted by one of the recruiters there, who convinced me to apply at MSU through her description of the school's history, academic concentration availability and student body composition, as well as her general Midwestern charm. The application had several short-answer questions, and the essay was simply a "personal statement," which is required by most schools. I had pretty good LSAT scores but a decent GPA, so I was originally placed in the evening/part-time program, but switched to full time the second semester as the inevitable first semester withdrawals took place.

Status: Current student, full-time
Dates of Enrollment: 8/2001-Submit Date
Survey Submitted: November 2003

MSU has a very friendly and helpful admissions staff. They were always very warm and cordial on the telephone whenever I called with questions about the admissions process. The law college is starting to become very selective as the school continues to rise in prestige, so make sure that you really try to make yourself stand out in the essay portion of the application. I would recommend asking for an interview if you can get one. The scholarship opportunities are amazing at MSU Law, so if you feel that you are up to par in getting one, I would highly recommend going after one. The admissions office is able to answer any questions you may have regarding that.

Status: Current student, part-time
Dates of Enrollment: 8/2002-Submit Date
Survey Submitted: October 2003

The school is very helpful throughout the process. I was always able to reach a school representative to answer all of my questions. My phone calls were always returned promptly. I never once experienced or heard of an admissions error resulting in late or missing documents. For all admissions questions and concerns, it is best to ask. There is always a way for someone to help you out; you just have to ask. Application forms were easy and concise (no interview required). The whole process was relatively quick.

MSU Law was one of the first schools I was accepted into. I received information from the school and various organizations shortly after acceptance. Admissions standards at MSU Law are on the rise. If you are a solid student with solid, well-rounded experience, you will get in. This school is very interested in making a legal education possible for all students. If your grades or scores are low, talk to someone and explain it in your essay. Overall my experience was positive. I would give the whole process an A!

Academics

Status: Current student, full-time
Dates of Enrollment: 7/2003-Submit Date
Survey Submitted: March 2006

Our Legal Research and Writing program is quite excellent; I've heard favorable comparisons to other regional schools' programs several times while in the workplace. We then have some upper-level required classes, Constitutional Law (individual liberties), Business Enterprises, Professional Responsibility, Evidence and an upper-level writing requirement.

Status: Current student, full-time
Dates of Enrollment: 8/2003-Submit Date
Survey Submitted: March 2006

Quality of classes—superior. While there are always the boring courses, the professors really make an effort to excite students. I found the strong suit of classes at MSU is an effort to connect the concepts to current law topics, with practice tips and tips for the bar exam. The classes are taught by many professors and prepare students for practice or the bar exam, as opposed to just learning the material for the class exam.

Some of the popular classes are too small; for example, Torts II and Business Enterprises, with a favorite professor, were difficult for me to get into. However, with priority enrollment and a long enrollment period, you can usually keep checking and get into your choice of classes perhaps the week that classes start. Overrides are easy to get. The only problem was contacting adjunct faculty to get an override—the office needs to work on getting out to students better contact information for adjunct faculty during enrollment.

One thing I like about MSU is that the curve is different depending on the size/type of class. Thus, if you are in a seminar, it is proportionally easier to get an A or a B, as opposed to only one student getting an A if the curve for large classes was used. The curve also gets easier after the 1L year. Professors are fair about grades, make it clear what they are looking for and are approachable after the grades come out to discuss exams.

The professors are second to none. MSU seems to be hiding all of the really great profs in the state. I would describe the majority of the professors as extremely bright and enthusiastic. It doesn't matter how prestigious or published a professor is if I am falling asleep in class, and that point is well-taken at MSU. Our professors are experts in their fields, are accomplished authors and have impressive CVs. However, they remain approachable, friendly and enthusiastic. The professors appear to truly love what they do, and are able to get students excited about what otherwise would be a boring concept. I have found great mentors in the faculty, and would not trade my experience with them for any big-name school or professor.

Status: Current student, full-time
Dates of Enrollment: 8/2003-Submit Date
Survey Submitted: March 2006

MSU Law appears to be gaining momentum as far as attracting top law scholars as professors. Almost all of my classes have been taught by top scholars from top schools. Many of them have multiple degrees (such as two MD/JDs, several JD/LLMs, several JD/PhDs and several JD/MAs). The Intellectual Property program is ranked in the Top 20 in the nation. Although it is tempting to brand the school a "boutique" IP school, this would be a mistake considering the numerous and excellent certification and specialty programs that the school runs. I personally am pursuing a concentration in public and administrative law, to which the location of the school, three miles from the seat of the state government, is very conducive.

As far as classes, law school is law school. If it isn't difficult, even overwhelming, then the faculty is not doing its job. This is not an environment that tolerates slacking and the tough, fixed grade curve gives pretty much every student nightmares from time to time. Also be warned that, since MSU Law is so generous with scholarships, it attracts a number of excellent students. These are the students with which everyone must compete. It does appear at times that there is a race to each end of the curve; there are those who just wish to get through, and those who are driven to excel. It is fairly easy to know who is who

in a given classroom from what is displayed on a student's laptop screen (games = not that serious).

Status: Current student, full-time
Dates of Enrollment: 8/2003-Submit Date
Survey Submitted: March 2006

The program is certainly on the rise with many excellent faculty members, both young and old, bringing invaluable experience and enthusiasm to the classroom, as well as their stewardship of the non-class programs such as the student journals, academic symposia and extracurricular activities. There is an emphasis on intellectual property law here, as well as indigenous peoples' law and policy, business law, environmental law and several other concentrations where students can also pursue a dual degree with associated MSU grad programs (JD/MBAs are common). There are active clinical programs that offer students academic credit while gaining unparalleled experience in the practice of law, as well as strong moot court and arbitration programs that provide additional skills-based training.

The school's academic journals are also quite strong and getting stronger. *The Michigan State Law Review* has recently been ranked as tied for the No. 12 spot nationally for most-cited journals, including a couple of recent Supreme Court citations. The *Law Review* has also recently adapted its publication agreement in a way that garnered national attention from the likes of Lawrence Lessig and other intellectual property experts, and while it has continued to garner strong articles from some of the brightest academic legal minds in the U.S. and abroad, the *Law Review* also continues to host timely symposia on some of the most compelling legal topics of the day.

Beyond the first-year hysteria, most law students here also continue to work hard through their second and third years, although there is usually more emphasis on journal/moot court/clinic/internship experience at that time, so courseloads can be managed efficiently if a student is capable of doing both.

Status: Current student, full-time
Dates of Enrollment: 8/2005-Submit Date
Survey Submitted: March 2006

I am impressed with the program. It is well organized. We students are kept well updated with a daily e-mail of announcements, as well as individual updates and announcements. The MSU College of Law faculty and staff tries very hard to guide us. I am a first-year student, and that is very important to me. The MSU College of Law has some very capable professors. More importantly, however, are the attitudes of the professors themselves. I am so impressed with how willing the professors are to meet with students, even outside of class or through e-mail. Some even have provided phone numbers for emergencies.

Status: Current student, full-time
Dates of Enrollment: 8/2004-Submit Date
Survey Submitted: March 2006

After speaking with friends at other institutions, I realized our curriculum is almost identical to most other schools. One thing I do not like is the fact that our school grades the Research Writing and Advocacy (RWA) class, where as some schools treat it on the pass/fail basis. Due to the competitive nature of our law school, the two-credit RWA class ends up consuming a huge amount of time but is only worth half as much as a class like Property.

Status: Current student, full-time
Dates of Enrollment: 8/2004-Submit Date
Survey Submitted: March 2006

Class quality is good. The professors are topnotch and the grading for the most part is fair. Tenured professors have somewhat more freedom with their grades so I would suggest taking tenured professors as opposed to visiting professors (my worst grades are from the visiting profs). I've only had problems getting into one or two classes. I asked for a specific class to be offered because the firm I work for is hiring in that area and the dean went out and found a professor to teach it and got it on the schedule the next semester for me!! I can't say enough good things about their willingness to accommodate students needs.

Read all of Vault's Law School Surveys at www.vault.com/lawschool — get complete surveys on top law schools, expert advice on applicaton essays, LSAT prep and more.

VAULT CAREER LIBRARY   335

Status: Alumnus/a, full-time
Dates of Enrollment: 8/2001-5/2004
Survey Submitted: April 2005

There are many concentrations offered. I was enrolled in the Corporate Law Concentration Program, which had some excellent courses. I believe that this concentration helped me get my job out of law school, and also has helped with my work in the corporate environment. Many of the subjects that I deal with on a day-to-day basis were touched on in the classes and have made me perform much better in my first year as a corporate attorney.

Status: Alumnus/a, full-time
Dates of Enrollment: 8/2000-5/2003
Survey Submitted: April 2005

The quality of classes is great. You are required to take certain classes your first year, so no selection in that year. However, if you want to "concentrate" in a specific area of law, you can tailor your schedule your second and third years. Of course, there are also required courses that you have to fit into your schedule, but the flexibility in making your schedule is great. I never had a problem and didn't have Friday classes my second and third years.

The workload is heavy (it's law school so expect it) and the professors are wonderful. Visit them during their office hours and utilize all of your resources. The study rooms are great and so are the librarians. Also, everyone has Internet access at every seat in the lecture halls—very nice when looking up cases. Law school is what you make it. Get involved. Do extracurricular activities in the law field. It's tough, but hey, people survive. You have to be dedicated. Make sure law is what you want to do before you go. It's sad to see some of the people you grow closest to either fail out for non-dedication or leave for disinterest. It costs a lot of money to figure out you don't want to go to law school.

Status: Alumnus/a, full-time
Dates of Enrollment: 8/1997-12/2001
Survey Submitted: April 2005

All classes relate to the law. Outside of the "required" courses, there is a good selection of elective subject matter, as well. There are also several "specialty" curricula available (e.g., tax law, litigation and real estate). Required courses (and many elective courses) are not state specific—they are federal or common law. However, there are several elective courses which offer state specific material. Generally, required courses seem to have a higher difficulty level than elective courses. They may be due, in part, to the size of the class. Many elective courses offer a smaller class setting.

Law school requires an excessive amount of reading. It is not uncommon to have hundreds of pages assigned for reading before the next class. Multiply that by the number of classes you are taking and the results can be staggering. In addition, several courses require "papers" (more like short novels) as part or all of the grade. The student must be organized, committed and have some structure to their life to succeed in law school. What does make the experience more enjoyable is the connectedness and camaraderie amongst the class members. There is a willingness to assist classmates (share insight/info regarding classes and instructors). I believe this is a huge benefit as I have spoken to many who have attend schools where it is a dog-eat-dog atmosphere and everyone is viewed as future competition.

 Employment Prospects

Status: Current student, part-time
Dates of Enrollment: 8/2002-Submit Date
Survey Submitted: March 2006

It really depends on what your goals are. If you want to get job outside of Michigan or upper Midwest, it may be difficult unless you have a connection. If you want to work in a big Michigan firm, you have to get good grades and should be on moot court and/or Law Review. That part can be difficult for part-time students. The other difficulty for part-time students is if you are trying to change careers, as opposed to furthering your existing career, because you have to work a legal summer job to get a decent legal job after school. MSU Law's rankings are going up and in time, the recognition of the law school will increase

enough to where getting a job after school will be easier, but for now, you really have to know what you want to do.

Status: Current student, full-time
Dates of Enrollment: 8/2003-Submit Date
Survey Submitted: March 2006

I have a job at a Top Five firm in the state. The firm hired four MSU students this year (and none from U of M or Wayne). MSU has a reputation for hard working and down-to-earth students that employers like. While it might be difficult to get a big firm job out of state, Michigan is a wide-open market for MSU grads because the students before us have set such a great standard.

I experienced success with the on-campus recruiting process. The career center was organized, and did their best to get employers here. The training, lecture and support they provided was great. Most students complain about career services because they expect the office to come to them and take care of them. Any student who takes the initiative to use their services will be very pleased. That being said, one thing the office could do better is use the information students give them to help others; for example, maintain files on different firms with opinions and notes from students who worked there.

Status: Current student, full-time
Dates of Enrollment: 8/2004-Submit Date
Survey Submitted: March 2006

The student body is shifting closer to half out-of-state. It is difficult to compete in the job market in Michigan right now for a couple of reasons. First, the economy is poor, even assistant prosecutors are being laid off. Second, it's difficult to compete against University of Michigan for summer associate positions. However, the law firms that do come to campus to interview, and those that are primarily in-state firms do seem to respect the candidates from MSU. Some firms have stated a preference for MSU graduates in their interviews.

The career services office works hard to help the students find work or internships. The alumni and upperclassman students have been a useful information network for me. I was able to contact several people that worked for the firm that hired me for summer associate. This made me feel prepared for my second interview.

Status: Current student, full-time
Dates of Enrollment: 8/2005-Submit Date
Survey Submitted: March 2006

As I approach the end of my first year, I must say I am most impressed with the career services office at the law college more than almost anything else! A career advisor who personally has a law degree has a mandatory personal meeting with each 1L student and revises the student's resume, inquires what the student's interests are, gives the student practical advice and instructs the student on the process for finding a summer job.

The office also offers a lot of VERY helpful free literature on job searching, resume building, writing cover letters and other related topics. Most impressive, however, is the office's job network. MSUCL is a member of eAttorney.com which lists literally thousands of vacant positions for all law students (1L, 2Ls, 3Ls and graduates). The office has an ongoing relationship with many of the employers and assists the students in initiating contact with the employers.

As a first-year law student, the office is ensuring that we all have some sort of practical legal experience over the summer. The office goes over all cover letters and resumes and makes sure all materials are accurate before a student submits their application to any employer. The office also ensures that every student, no matter how poor their grades, will find some sort of summer opportunity with their assistance. In addition to all of this, the center frequently puts on career-building seminars and workshops on various topics, and gives required and non-required presentations for first-year students. The student's interaction with the career services office at the law school is at least 100 times more interactive and useful than the general undergraduate career services experience. If all career services offices were this personal, interactive and guaranteed results like MSUCL's, no law school graduate would be unemployed at graduation. It is comforting to me to know that the office will not let me graduate without having a job lined up.

Status: Alumnus/a, full-time
Dates of Enrollment: 8/1987-6/1990
Survey Submitted: March 2006

The career services office found me my first job. They received a call from a firm in my hometown that was looking for an entry-level attorney. They called me and asked if I was interested. I went for an interview, was hired and ended up working there for a year and a half.

Status: Alumnus/a, full-time
Dates of Enrollment: 8/2001-5/2004
Survey Submitted: April 2005

I was hired right out of law school and offered a job from my first interview. No matter what school you go to, you can't expect others to do the work of finding a job for you, you need to go out and find it. I thought that the school was good at giving people leads, but you need to realize that everyone at your school applies for almost every job that comes through there. That is the problem that most people had when working with the career center. You need to develop your own contacts and do your own networking if you really hope to be employed when you graduate. The professors were very helpful in me getting my job because they offered wonderful recommendations, which my employer later told me really impressed them. As far as the prestige with employers, mine were impressed in my interview when I described all of the education and experience that I received, and when I talk with other attorneys at other companies, they always have a high regard for the school. It also helps to go to a well known school because when you say you are from MSU, they recognize it because it has such a presence in so many different national academic and sporting areas.

Status: Alumnus/a, full-time
Dates of Enrollment: 8/2000-5/2003
Survey Submitted: April 2005

Employment prospects are good. Use career services. They will help place you somewhere. They will help find you a job. They will look over your resume, suggest things and are an important part of the program. Of course, you will be looking for a law job (probably an attorney position) so this is what is most available. Almost all graduates obtain a job in the legal field. The alumni network is great. On-campus recruiting is ok, but is getting better. Make sure to use all of your resources. They are there, just ask!

Status: Alumnus/a, full-time
Dates of Enrollment: 8/1997-12/2001
Survey Submitted: April 2005

I believe employment prospects are very good. Many large firms are seeking graduates within the top third of the class. However, whether or not you have that status at graduation, I do believe that employability is very high. I was able to acquire the job I desired just prior to graduation. In fact, I was hired by a MSU/DCL graduate. There are a wide range of employment opportunities. Not all graduates go on to hold law related positions as the JD can be used in many fields. Law related employment ranges from law firm associate to Judge and every conceivable position in between. There is frequent on-campus recruiting, as well as a great alumni network for referrals.

Status: Alumnus/a, full-time
Dates of Enrollment: 8/1996-6/1999
Survey Submitted: April 2005

My classmates are all over the place! We are in the military, private practice, academia and government work—but I don't know if anyone is a judge yet! Some of my classmates returned to their original occupations, but with a better understanding of the law and are doing much better in their field as a result. I am an exception to the rule; my current employer called me and offered me this job. I never sent out a single resume. I recall there were constant on-campus opportunities for job interviewing practice and recruitment. so I suppose [the career services office] is adept at meeting that need.

Quality of Life

Status: Current student, full-time
Dates of Enrollment: 8/2004-Submit Date
Survey Submitted: March 2006

The campus is GREAT. Of course, Michigan State University is a Big 10 school with an exciting and beautiful campus. On the weekends in the fall there are great football tailgates. MSU offers a full-service graduate dormitory nearly across the street from the law school. The maid service provides room cleaning, new towels and changes the sheets on the bed once per week for no additional charge. This is a great service to the busy law student. Furthermore, if dorm life is not for you, the East Lansing area provides hundreds of apartment and home rental choices that will suit the needs of just about any lifestyle.

Status: Current student, full-time
Dates of Enrollment: 8/2005-Submit Date
Survey Submitted: March 2006

Must like snow!

Status: Current student, full-time
Dates of Enrollment: 8/2003-Submit Date
Survey Submitted: March 2006

There is a TON of housing around the campus, in East Lansing, in Lansing and in Okemos. The leasing companies all have excellent web sites and the MSU newspaper maintains housing ads on their web site. Many law students live in graduate housing, which consists of fairly small dorm rooms; but it's a three-minute walk to the law building. I lived in a studio apartment about 30-minute walk from the building, five-minute drive. I paid $380/month. Other friends paid $400 to $700 for their own apartments. The trick is to look early and look in locations farther away from the "main drag" of East Lansing.

The campus is beautiful. It's great for walking and even reading outside on a sunny day. People complain about the parking, but the law college is lucky, we have a parking garage connected to our building. It's a bit expensive, but there is cheaper parking across the street at the Wharton Center. If you buy a semester pass there for $50 or so, you get half-price at that parking garage.

The Sparty's cafe has coffees and drinks, soups, sandwiches, all the breakfast items you'd want, and now they have paninis and Middle Eastern food from our local Woody's restaurant. I've been happy with this cafe, even though I don't often use it. There are microwaves on each of the floors to cook meals from home.

Great restaurants and shops downtown; however, if you are looking for shopping, you'll need to go north about 10 minutes to the East Towne Center or east 20 minutes to the Meridian Mall. If you come from a bigger city, you might feel more at home driving to Ann Arbor or the Detroit area for entertainment.

East Lansing is a college town and there are lots of friendly and responsible people. Everyone takes care of each other. There is a problem sometimes with alcohol, this being a Big 10 campus. Law students normally stay out of the fray, we are studying too hard to riot! The closer you live to downtown East Lansing, however, the closer you may be to some rowdy behavior.

Status: Current student, full-time
Dates of Enrollment: 8/2004-Submit Date
Survey Submitted: March 2006

Michigan State is East Lansing. It is a complete college town with the regular student apartments near the school. If you need on-campus housing, the school will offer you a graduate dorm room in Owen Hall (the smallest room on earth) or an apartment in the University Apartments ([they are not very nice]). If you have a car, there is an apartment complex called the Village. The apartments are very nice, but the management is awful. Good news for 1Ls is that the school will give a housing tour in May to show you available residences to live. You can also check out (www.allmsu.com) for housing reviews and help.

Food is what you typically find in a college town. There are a dozen pizza places, the wing places, Chinese food joints and the list goes on. Check out (www.gogreenmenus.com) for delivery options. Crime was not an issue. You

Read all of Vault's Law School Surveys at www.vault.com/lawschool — get complete surveys on top law schools, expert advice on applicaton essays, LSAT prep and more.

VAULT CAREER LIBRARY   337

will, of course, have the usual knucklehead undergraduates that drink excessively and cause trouble, but that's college. No major crimes.

Status: Current student, full-time
Dates of Enrollment: 8/2005-Submit Date
Survey Submitted: March 2006

There is no time for your own "life issues." If you get sick, have a hard time or are over-tired, you cannot fit it into your schedule. You begin to put your life on the back burner along with your health and think to yourself you can sleep on the weekend and do homework now. Housing on campus is decent for a one-bedroom apartment. The graduate dorms are very small, a prisoner has more room in his cell than a grad student here in the dorm. Dining for the law students is OK but only if you know where you can go to eat. Most students don't know about it because they get on campus and as soon as class is up they leave. Crime is bad because of the undergraduates. You have the larceny, fights and child-like drama because there are so many undergrads on campus, as well.

Status: Current student, full-time
Dates of Enrollment: 8/2005-Submit Date
Survey Submitted: March 2006

MSU College of Law is located on the MSU campus. The entire university has an enrollment of about 47,000 (all undergrad and grad students). The nice thing is that the campus is not broken up; it is in one area. It has a great campus feel. All the facilities that one could imagine at a large university are available for us law students. Everything we need for law school, including the law library and research facility, is in one building—our law college building—which is very convenient. However, we law students are MSU students and have access to all MSU facilities. I am able to walk right over to one of the on-campus fitness centers (for students only) to work out during the day. We can take a break from research to go to the union or to one of the many food courts around campus. Or, we might go study at another MSU library to get away from all the scary law books. (I can't lie. We go there to check out girls) I have not had problems or heard of any other law students who have had problems with safety. I am pleased with my experience thus far.

Status: Current student, full-time
Dates of Enrollment: 8/2005-Submit Date
Survey Submitted: March 2006

MSUCL is a part of one of the largest research universities in the country, which is a major benefit. There are unbelievable opportunities for employment, housing, shopping, dining, recreation and entertainment. The university offers major college sporting events and a beautiful campus. The university also offers three free medical visits to the on-campus health center per semester, which is an amazing benefit! The city of East Lansing is beautiful and extremely safe, and is only 10 minutes away from the state capital and downtown Lansing (where the main court buildings of the state of Michigan are located, a benefit that the other law schools in the state do not offer!). Also, Lake Lansing is within a short distance and offers beaches and other recreation. There are so many things to do in this area of Michigan, they are impossible to list! There is something for everyone.

Status: Alumnus/a, full-time
Dates of Enrollment: 8/1995-5/1998
Survey Submitted: April 2005

The campus is beautiful and the building is very high tech. The administration and staff was very helpful with anything a student needed. It was the policy of the professors that "tuition was good for a lifetime." Even after graduation, the professors are experts who can be turned to for advice. At the time of the bar exam, the professors were available to talk to the examinees who were very stressed out. The professors were there to give the students a pat on the back and to be empathetic because they knew that the bar exam was like.

Status: Alumnus/a, full-time
Dates of Enrollment: 8/1994-1/1998
Survey Submitted: April 2005

The program is very rigorous yet very rewarding. One of the best things about being on a large campus is the social and educational diversity. Interaction among the different colleges of the university provide incredible opportunities for cross-discipline studies. Very few programs can offer this type of interaction.

Cost of living is relatively low in East Lansing. The people are typical friend Midwesterners. I don't think anyone at any top tier law school would say t quality of life during law school is leisurely. However, I believe MSU la provides its students with a rigorous yet balanced approach to learning the la Housing is incredibly convenient; dining is topnotch. Crime is very low.

 Social Life

Status: Current student, full-time
Dates of Enrollment: 1/2004-Submit Date
Survey Submitted: March 2006

The students here like to visit Harpers or Crunchies. I would say that any bar restaurant within three miles is fair game. People like to go to Detroit for th games and for the food. The dating seen can be great depending on what yo want. For me, it was not that great because I am used to a diverse crowd th this city lacks. Therefore, I just dream of the day when this is all over and I ca go back to my melting pot and pick up with my social life.

Status: Current student, full-time
Dates of Enrollment: 8/2004-Submit Date
Survey Submitted: March 2006

The bar and club scene in East Lansing is well above average. There are dozen of great bars which provide tons of entertainment options just about any night the week. The restaurant options are also plentiful and will suit just abou anyone's tastes. There is a large variety of ethnic restaurants in the East Lansin area which seem popular to the young crowd. The Greek life is strong amon the undergraduate students where just about every Greek organization represented. The law school has two legal greek organizations which seem t maintain a small but steady membership. The law school is home to hundred of legal and non-legal clubs for the interested student, which are easy to join an a great way to make friends with common interests.

Status: Current student, full-time
Dates of Enrollment: 8/2005-Submit Date
Survey Submitted: March 2006

There is a wide variety of bars catering to undergraduates. The general "scene reflects the generic 20-something crowd. There are some bars in the Eas Lansing and Lansing community that host a more mature crowd—The Templ Club (good music venue) and Beggars' Banquet. Moderate local music scen exists off campus.

Status: Current student, full-time
Dates of Enrollment: 8/2005-Submit Date
Survey Submitted: March 2006

This is where MSU College of Law shines. I am a single male in my mid-20s Don't get me wrong, I like to work hard. But I like to play hard, too. MSU College of Law's location on the MSU East Lansing campus makes that easy There are plenty of different bars and restaurants that cater to students. Ou Student Bar Association makes sure there are plenty of events planned so we ge to know each other as law students. We have become friends and sometimes we get together to take a night off from studying to have a good time.

Another bonus: MSU is a Big 10 University, which means awesome sports. I tailgated and sat in the student section for football games. I pray to get seats i the student section for basketball games; the "Izzone," as our student basketbal section is called, is the most impressive in the nation. As far as dating, there are over 20,000 female students on this campus. If I can't find a date, then I know the problem is with me. I have only been at this law school, and in this state fo that matter, for about six months, but I am very comfortable here, and have n desire to drop-out or leave anytime before graduation.

Status: Current student, full-time
Dates of Enrollment: 8/2004-Submit Date
Survey Submitted: March 2006

At first I felt that the social life at MSU was terrible. I think that every kid was so competitive their first year that they were stand-offishwhen you tried to approach them. Many were afraid you were trying to work an angle. After my first year, everyone knew where they fell in the law school hierarchy and mos ecame much more outgoing. This was never a real problem for me because ince MSU is a Big 10 campus, there is always a lot going on throughout ampus.

The bars are a lot of fun. If you like the frat scene go to Rick's; if you like the unaffiliated type bars, the Riv is a lot of fun. If you are looking for more grad chool-type bars go to the Peanut Barrel or Beggar's Banquet. You also have the ption of going tailgating or even hitting up Lansing bars if you just want to mingle with non-MSU students. If you want a social life you can find one easily here.

Status: Current student, full-time
Dates of Enrollment: 8/2003-Submit Date
Survey Submitted: March 2006

There are a lot of bars in East Lansing. Wednesday night it is half-off drinks at at least three bars. Wednesday through Saturday the downtown is "hopping," and you'll always run into a few groups of law students. There can be lines sometimes, especially at some of the wilder bars, but most law students gravitate towards the more "chill bars" such as Beggars' Banquet, Crunchy's and the Peanut Barrel. Downtown Lansing offers a more "adult" nightlife, with classier points such as the Exchange and 621.

There is great Thai and Mexican downtown. The highest-grossing BW3 in the nation resides in East Lansing. Favorite restaurants include Lou & Harry's, Beggars Banquet, Noodles & Company, Jimmy Johns and Giorgio's, our local giant slice pizza joint, which is open until 4 a.m. many nights. When your parents or family visit, there are a lot of nicer restaurants to take them to: All Seasons' Bistro, Dusty's Cellar, Villegas, the Red Cedar Grill, and in Lansing, Troppo and Majority. I haven't run out of favorites in seven years in East Lansing.

East Lansing hosts art festivals, jazz festivals, movie festivals and folk festivals. Part of what I love about living in a college town is there is always something cool going on, especially in the warmer months. Breslin Center hosts, aside from MSU basketball games, some great concerts. There is also a great gallery scene in Old Town in Lansing. As with any college, you get your share of nationally known speakers and concerts.

Status: Current student, full-time
Dates of Enrollment: 9/2004-Submit Date
Survey Submitted: March 2006

Many, many, many of the local bars are infested with underdressed, anti-intellectual undergraduates, so if that's your thing, you're all set. If not, avoid Rick's, the Riv, Harper's and P.T. O'Malley's. Lansing bars offer more variety. Stoeber's and Moriarty's are laid-back small pubs, and 621 and the Exchange offer a more typical nightclub atmosphere for the 25-and-older set. The Peanut Barrel in downtown East Lansing has been a favorite of graduate students (and sometimes professors) for decades, and they make the best Long Island Ice Teas in town (but you can only have two...). There are some decent clubs in Oldtown, notably Spiral (also a gay bar) and the Temple Club. Sadly, Lansing lacks a decent art museum, although there are some nice galleries in Oldtown Lansing. Restaurants are OK.

Status: Current student, full-time
Dates of Enrollment: 8/2005-Submit Date
Survey Submitted: March 2006

There is always a lot to do at MSU. There are great bars and wonderful sporting events to attend as MSU is a Division One Big 10 school. I love MSU basketball!

Status: Alumnus/a, full-time
Dates of Enrollment: 8/2000-5/2003
Survey Submitted: April 2005

MSU has a great social life and is known as a party school. The law school does things as well and is very socially involved, such as getting together hockey teams or providing options to go on trips. Also, you will do a lot of extra things through extracurricular activities like travel and compete. The bars are fun (the law school rents out a bar at the end of each semester and provides free drinks—it's all your colleagues and quite relaxing after stressful exams!) The dating scene is great; there are a lot of prospects in law school. There is always

something going on whether it be a speaker, a lecture, a football game. Like I mentioned, there are law clubs and even legal fraternities that you can get involved with. I recommend it. Mine was Phi Alpa Delta. It was fun and I networked. That's what's important. I was also on the *Journal of International Law* and did some moot court competitions. If you want to do it, it's there to do. My colleague argued in Italy for a international moot court competition. If you like to get involved, MSU-DCL is where it's at!

Status: Current student, full-time
Dates of Enrollment: 8/2001-Submit Date
Survey Submitted: November 2003

Being that Michigan State is a Big 10 school, sporting events are a favorite pastime for any student. You can choose from football, basketball or hockey. Many student organizations host tailgates before and after the football games on Saturdays. Furthermore, the law college has their own intramural ice hockey team that competes with other MSU intramural teams and the University of Michigan Law School team as well. Being that East Lansing is a college town, there are plenty of bars and restaurants. Furthermore, with the state capital less than 10 minutes away, there is also a decent night scene downtown as well.

The school says: "The law college has a basketball team and a rugby team as well."

 ## The School Says

MSU College of Law is fully integrated with Michigan State University, a Big 10 school and one of the top research universities in the world. While we remain a private, financially independent law school, MSU College of Law is a constituent college within MSU and is located in the center of the university's East Lansing campus.

The association with a major university means that you will benefit from our distinctive interdisciplinary programs. MSU Law offers substantive integration with other disciplines and programs, through dual degrees and certificate programs with other colleges, collaborative clinical and externship experiences, team-teaching and cross-teaching opportunities between law and other MSU faculty and joint sponsorship of national and international symposia.

What does this integration mean to you, as an MSU Law student? Law is a significant force in our society, but it is not practiced in isolation. By offering the best in interdisciplinary legal education, MSU Law trains lawyers with a wide range of capabilities. You will be prepared to practice in the vibrant and dynamic legal profession as it adapts to new issues as they arise. You also will be ready for a variety of exciting career opportunities.

Another aspect to integrated learning is MSU College of Law's approach to its curriculum, which connects theory with practice. The law college teaches both knowledge- and skill-based competencies so that you are ready to practice law upon graduation and have the theoretical base for lifelong learning. In addition to an abundance of hands-on learning opportunities through clinics, externships and internships, your law classes teach important skills in research, writing and oral advocacy. Your classes and experiential learning experiences also will provide you with the opportunity to make a real contribution to your own legal education. Faculty and supervising attorneys actively encourage students' individual ideas and thoughts.

Student Testimonial

"As the 2003-2004 President of the MSU College of Law Student Bar Association, I welcome your interest in joining our community at the Law College. Choosing a law school is a daunting experience, and I am glad that you have decided to

Read all of Vault's Law School Surveys at www.vault.com/lawschool — get complete surveys on top law schools, expert advice on applicaton essays, LSAT prep and more.

VAULT CAREER LIBRARY 339

consider Michigan State University College of Law. Located on the beautiful MSU campus, our Law College is a dynamic school with a proud reputation for excellence, both in the academic and non-academic environments. The faculty and staff strive to ensure that all students are provided the tools with which to succeed in the legal environment, allowing students the opportunity to grow both personally and professionally. The Law College also places great emphasis on personalizing the experience through clinical opportunities, student organizations, study-abroad initiatives and joint-degree programs, such as the Joint JD/LLB program in which I am a participant as a Canadian student. I am very proud to be a member of the MSU College of Law community, and I encourage you to come and visit us in East Lansing to see for yourself what we are all about!"

Kate McNeill, 2003-04 Student Bar Association President

The Thomas M. Cooley Law School

Admissions Office
The Thomas M. Cooley Law School
PO Box 13038
Lansing, MI 48901
Admissions phone: (517) 371-5140 ext. 2241
Admissions fax: (517) 334-5718
Admissions e-mail: admissions@cooley.edu
Admissions URL:
http://www.cooley.edu/admissions/introduction.htm

 ## Admissions

Status: Alumnus/a, full-time
Dates of Enrollment: 8/1993-5/1996
Survey Submitted: April 2006

Admission process at Cooley is very simple. The school does a calculation based on your LSAT score and undergraduate GPA. I couldn't have asked for a more user-friendly process. I appreciated that the school did not require all the standard formalities—interview, essay or letters of recommendation. The useless red-tape is eliminated.

Status: Alumnus/a, full-time
Dates of Enrollment: 9/1997-12/2000
Survey Submitted: April 2006

I was required to take the LSAT and submit a completed application with references. Prior to doing so, I took a tour of the school. It was a one-on-one tour with a current student. She also explained to me some of the course requirements and performance expectations.

Status: Alumnus/a, part-time
Dates of Enrollment: 1/1986-8/1990
Survey Submitted: April 2006

The admission process was easy. I obtained a copy of the application, filled it out and sent it in. I had several meetings with the admissions director to review the status of my application. The admissions director was friendly and helpful. I was assured that I met the qualifications required to get in and just had to wait on the Law School Admissions Council to forward all of my information to the school.

Status: Alumnus/a, full-time
Dates of Enrollment: 9/2002-1/2005
Survey Submitted: April 2006

Cooley's admissions process has got to be one of the easiest out there. There was an extremely simple online application and essays were not necessary. The school admits people based on an "index." The index is based on your undergrad GPA and your LSAT score. You will get in if you have a decent LSAT score and poor GPA, decent GPA but poor LSAT score, or mediocre GPA and LSAT score. What's more, the school offers scholarships based on these scores—if you have an index or LSAT score above a certain number, you'll get a scholarship of up to full tuition. No questions asked.

> **The school says:** "Meeting the minimum index or LSAT score determines academic eligibility for admission and scholarships, but the Faculty admissions committee may deny admission to candidates who lack the requisite character and fitness to study the law. All applicants must complete an official Thomas M. Cooley Law School application and must answer every question, including disclosure questions, completely and forthrightly. Failure to disclose information may result in denial of admission or revocation of admission."

Status: Alumnus/a, full-time
Dates of Enrollment: 5/2000-8/2004
Survey Submitted: April 2006

The admissions process and the information requested was an indication of how professional the institution is and the emphasis that the law school puts on ethics. Although at the time I apply the school was not as selective as it is now, each applicant had to complete a detailed application form, a personal statement and recommendation letters.

> **The school says:** "No personal statement or letters of recommendation are required."

The telephone interview with a faculty member was very informative and professional. The admissions approach that the school follows is very unique and fair. As long as the applicant meets the minimum admission requirements set by an index formula, the applicant should not have a problem admitted to the program unless he or she does not meet the guidelines of the character and fitness. A low amount for a deposit to secure a seat and a confirmation form are the only things required after the acceptance letter. The most difficult thing of all application materials was to prepare for the LSAT test and register for the test. Although other law schools offered interviews and gave many promises during the admissions process, Cooley really provided what it offered!

Status: Current student, full-time
Dates of Enrollment: 1/2004-Submit Date
Survey Submitted: September 2004

Cooley has an open admission policy. Basically anyone can get in. There is no selectivity requirements, no interviews—all you need is an application and a bachelors degree and you are in.

> **The school says:** "Applicants must possess a minimum Cooley Admission Index score with a minimum LSAT score (established annually) to be considered for admission to the school. The Admission Index formula utilizes both the applicants LSAT score and cumulative undergraduate grade point average as determined by the Law School Data Assembly Service (LSDAS). In addition, all candidates must submit character and fitness disclosures. Proof of the Bachelor's Degree is required."

Status: Alumnus/a, full-time
Dates of Enrollment: 9/1999-12/2002
Survey Submitted: May 2004

The school is known for its liberal admissions process, but this is rapidly changing. In fact, the average LSAT score is almost 15 points higher than three years ago. I was accepted elsewhere (two top-tier schools), but the liberal nature of admissions is what swayed me. The school philosophy appealed to me because it believes everyone should have the choice to go to law school. The process was created to allow people who worked or had a "previous life" to come back to law school—a trait that many other law schools see as a detriment.

> **According to the school:** "The average LSAT for students entering in the fall of 2005 was 148."

Status: Alumnus/a, full-time
Dates of Enrollment: 9/2000-5/2003
Survey Submitted: September 2003

Getting into this school is very easy. You only need a minimal standard and it is not very selective. You need to write an essay and submit your information. Don't get me wrong—not everyone gets in but relatively speaking it is much easier than other law schools.

> **The school says:** "No essay is required for students who meet the minimum Admissions Index (184 for 2005-06). Other applications will be forwarded to the Faculty admissions

Read all of Vault's Law School Surveys at www.vault.com/lawschool — get complete surveys on top law schools, expert advice on applicaton essays, LSAT prep and more.

VAULT CAREER LIBRARY 341

committee for a review of the LSAT Writing Sample for consideration for a qualifying program."

Status: Alumnus/a, full-time
Dates of Enrollment: 7/1996-5/1999
Survey Submitted: September 2003

TMCLS is very easy to get into. The difficult part is STAYING IN. Students can get booted out right up until the last semester if they do not maintain the required cumulative GPA.

> **The school says:** "To be in good academic standing, a student must maintain a cumulative grade point average of 2.0 in required courses as well as an overall cumulative grade point average of 2.0 in all courses. Whenever an enrolled student has a cumulative grade point average below 2.0, the student is on academic probation. Students enrolled in the part-time program, or full-time students beyond the first year, must raise their GPA to 2.0 or higher in the next two enrolled terms or be academically dismissed."

 **Academics**

Status: Alumnus/a, full-time
Dates of Enrollment: 9/1997-12/2000
Survey Submitted: April 2006

Quality of classes was excellent! Every professor had clinical experience and brought real-life experiences and situations to the classroom. During the first year of classes it was difficult to vary from the prescribed program (such as mixing day and evening classes) but that changed in years two and three. As a commuter (I live an hour and 45 minutes from Lansing), I wanted to make the best use of my time. Workload was typical for law school, I am told. The reading assignments varied from 100 to 150 pages per week and the grading was, for the most part, very fair. Except for electives, we had only one exam in each class and that was completed the last week of class. The system requires that the student use numbered blue books absent the student's name to keep the procedure anonymous and unbiased. In the elective classes we were assigned papers and may or may not have had a final exam. With the required courseload at Cooley, there was not a lot of opportunity for electives. I believe I took most of my electives in my last year of school.

> **The school says:** "With 90 credits required for graduation, students have the ability to enroll in 10 to 13 elective courses depending on their chosen concentration."

Status: Alumnus/a, part-time
Dates of Enrollment: 1/1986-8/1990
Survey Submitted: April 2006

The academic program was excellent. The faculty is outstanding. All faculty were knowledgeable in the subjects they taught. This was especially true of the elective classes as those are taught by adjunct professors practicing in those fields. While I understand that the workload is a bit heavier than other law schools, it is excellent preparation for real life practice and provides a more in depth knowledge of law than may be received at other law schools. I never had difficulty getting the classes that I wanted and needed. However there is a tendency to professor shop, and the school's registration process makes it difficult to do a lot of professor shopping—so I did not always get the professor that I wanted for a particular class. Grading was fair and reflective of my knowledge and understanding of the material. The library has an excellent collection and is well-staffed. The librarians were knowledgeable and helpful in assisting me with my research needs.

Status: Alumnus/a, full- and part-time
Dates of Enrollment: 5/1988-5/1991
Survey Submitted: April 2006

Cooley requires quite a few courses: more than other law schools I've heard about. But that helped me tremendously in practice. First, I clerked for a Justice on the Michigan Supreme Court. My exposure to courses like Evidence and Appellate Practice helped tremendously. Then I worked for an insurance

defense firm. We represented credit unions, and when a member fraudulently filed for bankruptcy, I went to the bankruptcy court to represent the client because nobody else in our office had ever read bankruptcy law. That was a required class when I attended Cooley.

Cooley's professors really care. They are among the most accessible profs of any law school. Of course, students should try to find the answer before they resort to asking the prof. They are going to be lawyers one day, after all. And part of lawyering is doing legal research. Many profs have an open-door policy, and others are readily available by appointment. In addition, many of the profs function as faculty advisors to student organizations. If you want to get to know a prof, you can easily accomplish that. (Brown nosing, however, is readily discovered.) Workload averages about three hours of preparation time for every credit hour of class. Cooley prepares you to hit the ground running as an attorney. Part of that is preparing you for the work time some firms expect from new associates. If you have a work ethic, you should have no problem completing the work and doing well. If, however, you expect to skate through law school, this is not the place for you.

Cooley also has an active skills program. For example, a student who chooses a litigation concentration must take Moot Court, Trial Skills, Pretrial Skills and Alternative Dispute Resolution. These classes take students through the nuts and bolts of their respective practice skills. Students don't just sit in class and listen to lectures—they're actually on their feet practicing the skills they're learning. That includes, for example in the Pretrial Skills class, writing complaints and answers, taking depositions and arguing a summary judgment motion before one of Michigan's sitting circuit court judges.

Status: Alumnus/a, full-time
Dates of Enrollment: 9/2002-12/2004
Survey Submitted: April 2006

Cooley had a very rigorous curriculum and a "tough" grading schedule. Although it was somewhat easy to get admitted, it was quite difficult to pass and remain a student in good standing. Because of the required courses in the first two to three semesters, 1L's schedules are completed for them. Once you begin taking elective courses in your second year, some classes and certain professors are difficult to get. But overall, scheduling was not too bad. As for the workload, because of the intensity of law school, Cooley was very intense and workload was quite heavy. However, it was not unmanageable as long as you were committed to your studies. Those who remained committed were often rewarded in their final grades. Grading is anonymous, which prevents any display of favoritism by professors. Most professors were Cooley alumni who were committed to carrying on Cooley's reputation through their teaching.

Status: Alumnus/a, full-time
Dates of Enrollment: 9/2002-1/2005
Survey Submitted: April 2006

Law school course material is virtually the same wherever you go. The difference comes in the manner in which the course is taught. With the exception of a couple of professors, professors at Cooley are there because they actually want to teach. I was actually taught the law—not just given cases to read and regurgitate. Again, with the exception of a couple of professors, Cooley professors actually care that students do well in their classes—they are there because they want to teach, not just write journal articles.

Grading at Cooley is not easy. It may be easy to get admitted to Cooley, but it's certainly not easy to stay. Because the professors actually teach, it's almost as if there are "no excuses" for doing poorly in a class. Unlike other schools, there is no grade inflation—the grade you receive is the grade you earned.

If you are interested in litigation, Cooley is a great place to go to school. There are state-of-the-art courtroom facilities and you are taught by professors who have spent plenty of time in the courtroom. I have often heard practitioners say that Cooley grads are the most prepared new grads entering the courtroom.

Status: Alumnus/a, full-time
Dates of Enrollment: 9/1998-8/2001
Survey Submitted: April 2006

Although being admitted is easy—the workload is difficult. There is not grade inflation—the average is a C, not a B like other schools. Also, there are many more requirements that go into your second, and maybe even your third year.

Most schools only have one year worth of requirements and these requirements may miss important subjects like Real Property!!! I had enough knowledge to pass two different state bars on the first try. I now teach (part time) for the bars and it does make quite a difference if you are just learning the subject for the first time or relearning it for the bar.

Status: Current student, full-time
Dates of Enrollment: 9/2003-Submit Date
Survey Submitted: November 2004

Cooley has the highest attrition rate in the U.S. for law school. Cooley also has a dual GPA requirement. You have a required GPA and an elective GPA. You cannot use the elective GPA to keep you off academic probation. If you have a 1.95 GPA in your required courses, you cannot take an elective to pull your GPA up to a 2.0 GPA. The school policy is that you have to take another required to pull your GPA up for academic probation purposes. No other school in the country does this. Cooley also has a C to B- curve. Most student have a 2.0 to 2.4 GPA.

> **The school says:** "The Thomas M. Cooley Law School grading policy is demanding, but fair. In most courses, grades are based on written final examinations, administered and graded under a system that assures student anonymity. Professors adhere to established grade definitions.
>
> "Grades at Cooley are known for being hard-earned and truly indicative of a student's grasp of the subject matter. The law school does not practice grade inflation. The grade definitions are closely associated with how students are expected to perform on the bar examination and in the legal profession."

Status: Current student, full-time
Dates of Enrollment: 1/2004-Submit Date
Survey Submitted: September 2004

With the exception of one professor, all have been very informative and have made themselves available out of class to answer any questions. The first-year classes are large—about 80 to 100 students per class. But the professors are very good at trying to answer all questions. First-year classes are chosen for you so I have not had the opportunity of having to go through the electives classes yet. The professors do grade pretty harshly though. I would say that some of the B exams at this school would be A exams at other schools. The workload is extensive but doable if you don't have a job.

Status: Alumnus/a, full-time
Dates of Enrollment: 9/1999-12/2002
Survey Submitted: May 2004

Cooley is nothing but tough, but the experience is unparalleled. I took five exams a week through law school. Painful? Maybe. Beneficial? It put me in a better place for the Bar Exam and "real world" than the schools of my colleagues. I went to take the Bar in California after I graduated, which is known for its grueling three-day mental marathon. It was nothing compared to the rigorous schedule I'd been following for three years! The classes at Cooley require attendance (yes, even electives—some of the hardest classes I took!), and require a knowledge of all those subjects you need to know for almost any Bar Exam. You work for your grades—there are no curves or easy passes. This provides a foundation for an unsurpassed work ethic.

> **Regarding academics, the school says:** "Typically, Cooley only dismisses between 4 and 7 percent of its student population each semester. To be in good academic standing, a student must maintain a cumulative grade point average of 2.0 in required courses as well as an overall cumulative grade point average of 2.0 in all courses. Whenever an enrolled student has a cumulative grade point average below 2.0, the student is on academic probation. First-year students who are enrolled in, and remain in, the full-time program must raise their cumulative GPA to 2.0 or higher in the next term or be academically dismissed. Students enrolled in the part-time program, or full-time students beyond the first year, must raise their GPA to 2.0 or higher in the next two enrolled terms or be academically dismissed. No enrolled student shall be permitted to continue to be enrolled if the student's required courses GPA or cumulative GPA has been below 2.0 for three consecutive terms.
>
> "Entering classes at Cooley are comprised of full-time and part-time students. Thus, although students enter the institution as part of one class, the class they graduate with will vary depending on the pace of degree completion."

Employment Prospects

Status: Alumnus/a, full-time
Dates of Enrollment: 8/1993-5/1996
Survey Submitted: April 2006

I would like to see Cooley have a better alumni network for students. I have signed up a few times to be a contact/mentor and I have never received a response from the school or any student. I saw very little on-campus recruiting. More internships would be a benefit to the school. The school needs better access to alumni directories and more alumni involvement.

> **The school says:** "Each year Cooley conducts its Fall On-Campus Interview Season (FOCIS) and its Spring Term Associate Recruitment Season (STARS). In 2006, over 140 employers participated in recruitment activities coordinated by the Career and Professional Development Office. Every student also has the opportunity to conduct an externship at one of over 1,000 sites located around the country specifically designed for Cooley students. This list of sites is continually being revised and expanded."

Status: Alumnus/a, full-time
Dates of Enrollment: 9/1997-12/2000
Survey Submitted: April 2006

The school provided many, many opportunities for externships and internships in in-house programs (Elder Law Clinic, Estate Planning Clinic, and Innocence Project). I found a position within two months of graduation in a federal/state funded program. Because I was an "older" student, I had no desire to work for a large firm and so never investigated the opportunities. Several of my classmates did take positions with well-known firms in Michigan. There was support from the school with the job hunting and job prospects, and I did take advantage of the offer to assist me in updating my resume. The alumni association is growing and reaching out to alumni as well as current students in an effort to grow the association and support the students. We have a mentoring program as well where new grads are matched up with alumni in their area to help them make the transition from student to lawyer.

Status: Alumnus/a, full- and part-time
Dates of Enrollment: 5/1988-5/1991
Survey Submitted: April 2006

Almost all of Michigan's top firms hire Cooley grads who have the academic and personal qualities they're looking for. Many firms have said they want to hire Cooley grads because Cooley grads are prepared to practice law. I had the awesome opportunity to work as a judicial law clerk to one of Michigan's Supreme Court Justices. And I'm not alone. Many Cooley grads have had clerkships with various state and federal appellate and trial court judges.

Cooley's alumni network is becoming more helpful. The school's alumni relations department now routinely organizes networking opportunities across the country to introduce recent grads to established grads in their area. Established grads function as mentors to these students.

Cooley has an extensive externship program. Every student must participate in a three-credit "clinical" experience before he or she graduates. Most students do that as an externship in the area of the country in which they want to practice law. Externship sites are pre-screened and the students do everything the lawyer does (except of course hold themselves out as lawyers in those states where they cannot do that until they've passed the bar). Many states, however, will let students appear in court on a client's behalf if they're working with a prosecutor's office, a public defender's office, or a legal aid agency. This

Read all of Vault's Law School Surveys at www.vault.com/lawschool — get complete surveys on top law schools, expert advice on applicaton essays, LSAT prep and more.

VAULT CAREER LIBRARY **343**

program is one of the most valuable parts of a student's education. It allows the student to grow both personally and professionally.

Status: Alumnus/a, full-time
Dates of Enrollment: 1/2003-9/2005
Survey Submitted: April 2006

Employment prospects are many for Cooley grads. There is a large contingent of Cooley grads in all corners of the Earth. All seem willing to lend a hand to recent grads, from reviewing and advising on one's resume to actively assisting the job search to providing employment with their own practices. I've been on several interviews and have been told that Cooley grads work hard, but one particular interviewer told me "Cooley grads work harder than any other law school grad [he's] seen."

Status: Alumnus/a, full-time
Dates of Enrollment: 1/1998-9/2000
Survey Submitted: April 2006

Looking around MI for a job I found that Cooley was not viewed as highly as other MI schools, often looked down upon. When I started looking in Chicago and my native New York, I found Cooley had a very good reputation. Out east any attorneys I have met, when I tell them I went to Cooley, always had positive things to say about it and the people they have known that attended Cooley.

Status: Current student, full-time
Dates of Enrollment: 1/2004-Submit Date
Survey Submitted: September 2004

It's a small town and if you graduate from here I think it will be very difficult to get a job in another city. The school has a career services office which always has announcement for clerks.

> **Regarding employment prospects, the school says:** "The Lansing metropolitan area has a population of over 400,000. Cooley Law School's main campus is less than one block from the State Capitol (all three branches of government), the State Supreme Court, a State Appellate Court, a Federal Court, the Michigan State Library and Historical Center, to name a few attributes. Cooley alumni are employed in every state in the nation, and worldwide. Members of the 2004 graduating classes found employment in areas of private practice, public interest, academe, government, business, or judicial clerkship in 14 states."

Status: Alumnus/a, full-time
Dates of Enrollment: 9/1999-12/2002
Survey Submitted: May 2004

The opportunities are limitless. The school has a wonderful career services office (CSO) that not only keeps rooms and rooms of employer contacts and openings, but the information is kept up-to-date weekly. The CSO sends out weekly and monthly job openings and articles, and during the on-campus interview process, will pretty much take care of everything for you, eliminating repetitive time while you're trying to take exams! Give them one copy of everything, give them a list of employers you're interested in and they do the rest!

Likewise, you will leave Cooley with at least some kind of experience. Besides an Elder Law Clinic, the Innocence Project, a Public Defender Clinic and a newly developing Appellate Clinic on campus, Cooley students are required to do a one-term internship. You can do it at one of the clinics, or you can go to the school's list of approved internships or you can go wherever you want and create your own (even internationally!). Although not being a top-tier school factors in, once you find a job, you are one of the most valuable assets an employer could ever hope for!

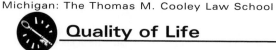 ## Quality of Life

Status: Alumnus/a, full-time
Dates of Enrollment: 9/1975-9/1978
Survey Submitted: April 2006

The quality of life in Lansing for my family and me has been excellent. We have lived in the city for 33 years, sent our children to the Lansing School District, participated in community activities and enjoyed an active social life.

Status: Alumnus/a, full-time
Dates of Enrollment: 9/2002-1/2005
Survey Submitted: April 2006

Cooley has the best scheduling options for non-traditional students—you can take classes seven days a week at all times of the day. If you're a traditional day student, be prepared to take some night classes, as Cooley only offers some classes at night to accommodate the non-traditional students. Cooley's "campus" is not really a campus. It is three buildings in downtown Lansing, Michigan. The buildings are fine, but if you're expecting a traditional campus you should go somewhere else.

> **The school says:** "The school offers students the option of taking classes during the day, the evening and on weekends. All classes are available during each time offering. Students do not have to deviate from their preferred time schedule but may do so if they choose. Cooley has three campuses in Michigan. One in Lansing, one block from the state capitol, one in Rochester on the 1,441-acre campus of Oakland University, a Division I institution, and one in downtown Grand Rapids, the state's third largest city."

Status: Alumnus/a, full- and part-time
Dates of Enrollment: 5/1988-5/1991
Survey Submitted: April 2006

Cooley's campus is in downtown Lansing and consists of several buildings within a two-square-block area. Its classrooms have the latest and greatest technologies, including wireless internet access. Because Lansing is Michigan's capital city, students have access to part-time employment in all of the state's agencies. The down side is that the downtown does tend to roll up the sidewalk at 5:00. The up side is that students have access to tons of small eateries and bistros right behind the school building. Washington St. for three or four blocks is lined with small restaurants and shops. The immediate campus area is relatively safe, as are the blocks surrounding the campus. As in any city, petty crime occurs. But I'm not aware of any student injuries due to crime.

Status: Alumnus/a, full-time
Dates of Enrollment: 5/2000-8/2004
Survey Submitted: April 2006

The main campus of the law school is in the downtown of the capital of Michigan. The environment is ideal for the study of law. The school is located around governmental buildings, near the capitol building and within very short distance from a very large community college and one of the largest universities in the USA, Michigan State University. The law schools facilities are very new, couple of years old, very modern, technologically advanced—state-of-the-art. The housing is very good off campus, and there is just about no crime in the downtown area of the city. The downtown area and the surrounding areas provide very good dining and other entertainment.

Status: Alumnus/a, full-time
Dates of Enrollment: 9/1989-5/1992
Survey Submitted: April 2006

The Lansing classroom building and law library was more than serviceable when I attended, but the school has since constructed a new library and the new "Cooley Center." These are state-of-the-art facilities—very functional and very attractive. The Cooley Center boasts a large appellate courtroom and a number of "trial" courtrooms in various sizes.

Status: Alumnus/a, full-time
Dates of Enrollment: 9/1998-8/2001
Survey Submitted: April 2006

The campus is beautiful and the library is outstanding. I have seen other law school libraries and there is no comparison. Housing is available nearby—but expect to rent; there are not any dorms. The biggest issue was parking while I was there. You will have to pay downtown parking rates; the school did not have parking available for the students. But, most schools would require you to pay if you parked on campus, so that is a toss up. Because of the ethical code, crime was minimal on campus—although items were occasionally stolen.

Status: Current student, full-time
Dates of Enrollment: 1/2004-Submit Date
Survey Submitted: September 2004

Housing is affordable. Rent ranges from $500 to $600 for a one-bedroom apartment. The neighborhood is very quiet and peaceful. Excellent for studying, I think. The campus is divided into three separate buildings, the classroom building, the office and book store building across the street and the library two blocks away. Dining could be better. The best restaurant in town is Friday's. There is hardly any crime, except every once in a while people walk up to my front door asking me for money.

Status: Alumnus/a, full-time
Dates of Enrollment: 9/1999-12/2002
Survey Submitted: May 2004

I loved every moment at Cooley, but it's true that it was not because of the location! Lansing is the Trivial Pursuit answer to "the capital city with the most cloudy days per year." Really. But Lansing is affordable and the crime rate is not too bad (very few incidents affecting students). And because it's across the street from the Capitol, it is a prime location for networking and getting involved. It is a "small" town, but there are plenty of things to do. The offices at the school (financial aid and the business office) do everything they can to make your life easier.

Status: Alumnus/a, full-time
Dates of Enrollment: 8/1998-5/2001
Survey Submitted: November 2003

As far as housing or part-time jobs, the school provided very little assistance, if any. Downtown Lansing was not that bad of an area as far as crime goes. I walked all over town during all hours and was only asked for money maybe five or six times during my three years. The winters can be very raunchy.

 Social Life

Status: Alumnus/a, full-time
Dates of Enrollment: 8/1993-5/1996
Survey Submitted: April 2006

The welcome back parties, held at the beginning of each new term, were always fun and well-organized. The school also has a formal dance every year, which is affordable and well-attended by both students and faculty. Lansing has a lot to offer socially and there are numerous bars with a good student atmosphere in large part because of the enormous Michigan State University campus in East Lansing. Cooley offers the best of both worlds—school located downtown by capitol and government offices, with a very professional feel and an easily accessible college-style atmosphere with one of the biggest college campuses in the country located nearby. While I attended, Cooley had a rugby team; however, I never felt that the school provided enough notice of games. I am sure the team would have appreciated more student interest. The campus is so close to the courts—trial, appellate and supreme. Students were always welcome to stop in and watch proceedings—this type of location provides countless opportunities to see all types of cases and proceedings at every level. One of my electives was held in the professor's courtroom.

Status: Alumnus/a, part-time
Dates of Enrollment: 1/1986-8/1990
Survey Submitted: April 2006

While not exactly bursting with nightlife, there are several venus available for the student to find relaxing things to do in their limited amount of free time. East Lansing is home to Michigan State University, so there is a wide variety of activities associated with Michigan State University—Spartan sports, Wharton Theater. There are also many clubs and bars in the East Lansing area. Lansing supports a variety of museums, local theater (including a professional theater), malls, several movie theaters and excellent riverwalk, with many biking/hiking trails.

There are several restaurants downtown near the Cooley campus that provide reasonably priced lunches/dinners for students. My personal favorite is Clara's. A restaurant with everything from pizza to steak on the largest menu (with the most choices I have ever seen). Clara's is in a renovated train station and provides a nice relaxing atmosphere. A favorite student hangout is Kelly's Bar about a block from campus. Student organizations are very active on campus and provide many activities for students to participate in as well as build community on campus.

Status: Alumnus/a, full- and part-time
Dates of Enrollment: 5/1988-5/1991
Survey Submitted: April 2006

Lansing and its surrounding suburbs have plenty of night life and cultural events to offer. East Lansing, home of Michigan State University, provides even more. Some bars are located behind the school and Kelly's seems to be especially popular with students. Other popular bars within a mile or two from the school include The Green Door (a faculty band plays there regularly), Rum Runners and the Nut House (across from Oldsmobile Park home to the Lansing Lugnuts minor league baseball team). The greater Lansing area is also home to quite a few festivals every summer including a blues festival and Common Ground—a festival that draws "name" acts from across the country. The surrounding area is also home to almost any chain restaurant one can imagine.

Cooley also has quite a few student organizations. Among the most popular are the Black Law Students' Association, the Moot Court Board and the Mock Trial Board. Cooley also has many national legal fraternities. All of the student organizations also participate in community service work. And Cooley's students are quite civic minded. For example, Cooley students managed to raise 25,000.00 for victims of Hurricane Katrina who attended Cooley. That was an entirely student-led effort. One of Cooley's missions is to instill a sense of public service in its students (and faculty), and that carries over into the student organizations. Student organizations frequently sponsor events where students can meet and socialize.

Status: Alumnus/a, full-time
Dates of Enrollment: 9/1998-8/2001
Survey Submitted: April 2006

The first-year moot court competition is very popular and I recommend trying it, even if you never plan to step foot in court. It is a great learning experience (and you still may have to go to court, even if you never thought you would!).

There are bars nearby; if that is your scene—get a Guiness at Kelly's. Just remember, you are there (and are paying a lot of money) to study and learn the law. So don't party every night! Remember what you will get out of your experience at Cooley is what you put into it. For me, it was a tough but wonderful experience. I wouldn't have gone to any other law school (my husband started at Cooley and then transferred because we moved—he said in comparison to his tier-one law school, Cooley has their act more together and he would have rather stayed there).

Status: Alumnus/a, full-time
Dates of Enrollment: 9/1999-12/2002
Survey Submitted: May 2004

OK, small town, but it doesn't mean there's nothing to do. There are local favorites (like The Exchange and Kelly's), and East Lansing is rapidly expanding with a new mall (huge!) with wonderful dining and authentic cuisine. One added benefit is the opportunity to interact with professors at school and non-school related gatherings. For example, one professor has been playing in

Read all of Vault's Law School Surveys at www.vault.com/lawschool — get complete surveys on top law schools, expert advice on applicaton essays, LSAT prep and more.

VAULT CAREER LIBRARY 345

a classic rock band every Wednesday night at The Exchange for years. Both students and professors go and law is almost always off topic! It is within walking distance of the school, as are many other restaurants and quick eateries (fast food, Greek, Blimpie's.). The school is right next door to Beaner's (the Michigan version of Starbucks that is much better than Starbucks!), so you are close to caffeine any time you need it. And you will surely find other students parked there, books in hand, chatting about their last class, how hard the law is and how funny the teacher had been.

Status: Alumnus/a, full-time
Dates of Enrollment: 8/1998-5/2001
Survey Submitted: November 2003

There are lots of little Mom-and-Pop type restaurants and bars within walking distance. I was married when I went to Cooley, but it seemed like all the male students talked about how there were no good women at the school and all the female students talked about how there were no good men at the school. I never did figure out what that was all about. There were many clubs, and Cooley seemed to be very liberal about allowing new clubs to open and older ones to die off.

The University of Michigan Law School

Admissions Office
726 Oakland Avenue
Ann Arbor, MI 48104
Admissions phone: (734) 764-0537
Admissions fax: (734) 647-3218
Admissions e-mail: law.jd.admissions@umich.edu
Admissions URL:
www.law.umich.edu/prospectivestudents/welcome/dean.htm

Admissions

Status: Current student, full-time
Dates of Enrollment: 5/2005-Submit Date
Survey Submitted: April 2006

Michigan grants its applicants a great service by placing emphasis on the whole package a student brings to the table, and not a mere secret calculation of LSATs and GPA scores. To this end, the admissions staff provides applicants ample opportunity to show what is special about them with two "optional essays" and an invitation to supplement the application with any important materials. The admissions staff is incredibly dedicated and spends great time, care and attention to not just accepting qualified candidates, but accepting the best class of students.

An applicant with lower numbers, but with significant achievements in a previous career, particular undergraduate program or strong writing skills is advised to take advantage of the optional essays in addition to the personal statement, and should craft an application package that helps the admissions staff readers best get to know him/her—the applicant—as a person. Michigan has the benefit of being able to reject each year hundreds of candidates with numbers strong enough for admission. This selectivity allows the admissions staff to really focus on getting the best people to Michigan. (And by best, I don't mean having the best grades and scores—I mean being the best for the Michigan Law academic and social community.) There is no interview requirement for admission, however, a student with questions about Michigan should be advised to call or e-mail the admissions office, whereby questions can be best answered and the staff might get a better sense of the applicant. Word to the wise, however—don't be annoying! The staff is very busy and doesn't have time do deal with those who pester them and call every day. Several well-informed questions posed to a staff member will have good results, while annoying everyday phone calls and e-mails might be looked upon more unfavorably!

When addressing the essays, students would be wise to craft each of the three essays to highlight different aspects of their personality. The admissions staff is certainly interested in why you are coming to law school, but three essays entirely on the topic is ill-advised. Far more effective is showing the admissions officers why they should choose you from the thousands of applications, why you are different, why you are special, what you bring to the table. Frequently this means that the "why I want to go to law school" question is simply an afterthought or can be incorporated through other means. The most important thing that you can do in your essays is to write well. Good writing is perhaps one of the most important aspects of a good lawyer, and well-written essays can do as much to get you in to Michigan Law as a perfect LSAT score.

Finally, edit your application and make it presentable. There are a number of applicants each year who from the application alone it is easy to tell that they are uninterested in Michigan or that they weren't interested enough to take that extra two-minute step to make sure that words are spelled right, the application is actually the one for Michigan Law and that you are presented well by the organization of your materials. This step is often forgotten, but is vital for a successful applicant. It takes very little time to re-read everything and edit it, but can make a lot of difference!

Status: Current student, full-time
Dates of Enrollment: 9/2005-Submit Date
Survey Submitted: April 2006

Michigan is very selective, but the admissions staff make going through the admissions process very pleasant. Michigan's admissions staff—especially Dean Zearfoss—is the best I encountered at any school to which I applied—very responsive, lively, helpful, encouraging, straightforward, even fun.

Based on my classmates, I'd guess that Michigan puts a higher priority on admitting students who have had work experience than other schools. Folks who have either work or school experience in technical fields are particularly well-represented. I think the essay question that asks you to talk about overcoming an obstacle is a tricky one; it's potentially very powerful but has to be handled in a manner that suggests you neither diminish nor overstate what you've faced. A sense of perspective is important.

Recommendation letters are important. The admissions office really reads them and even sent a thank you letter to my recommenders.

Status: Current student, full-time
Dates of Enrollment: 9/2005-Submit Date
Survey Submitted: April 2006

Michigan wants the "Michigan student." They read the personal statement to look for signs that you're outgoing, collegial and driven, without being overly competitive. It's important to the law school and to the alumni that students be proud of Michigan and fit in well with the school community. You should avoid the temptation to brag in your personal statement, and you should instead concentrate on your interactions with other colleagues. The admissions office wants to know that you'll contribute to the collegial atmosphere and not detract from it.

Get your application in early. It's a selective school with rolling admissions. One application reader told me that she sees the best applications first. Waiting will probably hurt your chances. And find professors to write letters of recommendation which actually say something unique about you, and more than just that you had a class together.

Status: Current student, full-time
Dates of Enrollment: 6/2005-Submit Date
Survey Submitted: February 2006

I would recommend writing two of the optionals essays that each applicant feels would help them convey the most about themselves. I didn't graduate from a very impressive undergraduate institution and my LSAT score was below the median, but I think that Michigan looks beyond numbers and at the character of the applicant. I tried to focus on unique aspects of my personality that would contribute to the diversity of the law school. Someone from the admissions office called me to ask some questions and 15 minutes later the Dean called to let me know that I had been accepted. The admissions staff is extremely friendly and helpful, so applicants should feel free to contact them during the admissions process with any questions or concerns. I also HIGHLY recommend starting in the summer, you get three extra credits, an opportunity to enjoy Ann Arbor in warm weather and you will be much closer to your classmates than the fall sections.

Status: Current student, full-time
Dates of Enrollment: 9/2005-Submit Date
Survey Submitted: November 2005

The admissions office uses students to the best of their ability in the effort to recruit. Students call you. Students e-mail you. Students send you mail about organizations. The school sends a package with info in it just about weekly. The mailings bugged a lot of people, but I loved it. It made me feel like Michigan really cared about getting me to come. Also, the mailings were very informative. The more you learn about Michigan, the more you want to come. If the mailings on their professors, interdisciplinary approach, clinics, career opportunities,

Read all of Vault's Law School Surveys at www.vault.com/lawschool — get complete surveys on top law schools, expert advice on applicaton essays, LSAT prep and more.

VAULT CAREER LIBRARY 347

housing, food, activities and the calls from students don't hook you, coming to the Preview Weekend will. Most people who come to the Preview Weekend end up coming to Michigan for school. People love the Preview Weekend. The students, whether they call you or speak with you in person, seem to be pretty honest about the school and they are more genuine than any students I spoke with about any school. The admissions office is really great and helpful.

Status: Current student, full-time
Dates of Enrollment: 9/2002-Submit Date
Survey Submitted: April 2005

Before I decided to apply to law school, I e-mailed a professor at the University of Michigan Law School and asked her to go for coffee because I wanted advice on whether law school was for me. At the time I was in graduate school working on a PhD in ecology. She graciously spent an hour with me going through the pros and cons of law school given what career path I wanted to take. This professor did not know me, but was very helpful and giving with her time. I decided to apply to law school. I applied to six law schools and got into all of them. I couldn't attend the admitted students preview weekend at Michigan, but I arranged with the admissions office to come at another time. They were great! They arranged for a half hour meeting with the dean of admissions to discuss academics and student life at Michigan and gave me a personal tour of the law school. I was very impressed with the admissions staff's friendliness and willingness to answer questions. To this day, four years after I first met the dean of admissions, she still remembers me, knows me by name and chats with me whenever we see each other.

Status: Alumnus/a, full-time
Dates of Enrollment: 9/1999-5/2002
Survey Submitted: May 2004

The admissions process is standard for a top law school. The one thing I remember that was different was that Michigan asked for three essays. Most law schools only require one. Michigan is slightly less selective than the other Top 10 law schools in part because it apparently must take a certain quota of Michigan residents. I recall that when I was admitted, I received a personal call from the dean of the law school who was very friendly and remembered one of my essays. I had intended the essay to be humorous and she seemed to have found it amusing so perhaps that is a sign that a slightly off-kilter, non-traditional essay might make your application stand out.

> **The law school says:** "Michigan requires only one essay, in the form of a personal statement. We provide applicants with an opportunity to write up to two optional essays. While we do have an in-state goal of 25 percent, our Michigan residents are in fact numerically of the same calibre as non-residents. More generally, we would observe that according to our admissions policy we give many factors weight in the admissions process; we attempt to resist the various pressures to make the LSAT the centerpiece of the decision making."

 **Academics**

Status: Current student, full-time
Dates of Enrollment: 5/2005-Submit Date
Survey Submitted: April 2006

Michigan Law is endowed with first-rate professors and an academically inquisitive and accomplished student body. Students are from all over the world and professors are leaders in the legal field nationally and worldwide. Each student seems to be motivated to be there and do well, not because you have to do well at Michigan to be successful, but because they want to be the best student that they can be. Classroom dynamics depend on the professor, but are generally pretty laid back and discussion between classmates on issues at hand is strongly encouraged. Some professors employ the Socratic Method more than others, but no one is ever ridiculed or punished for their inability to adequately answer a posed question. In my experience, classroom discussions are dynamic and involved, and frequently nearly half the class will get involved.

Grading at the law school is done on a curve—and Michigan's curve is notoriously on the low side. Students' grades are generally based on a final

examination alone, though some first-year professors have begun to introduce a mid-term and most seminars require a final paper. In my experience, grading is extremely fair and balanced. Professors are generally good about providing practice exams and holding review sessions and office hours, and nearly all will provide time after grades come back for students to discuss their specific exam and their grade. This can help a great deal first year when it is frequently systematic mistakes that students are making on law school exams.

> **According to the school:** "The law school's grading guidelines set out a 3.13 to 3.25 target mean GPA range for all classes of 40 students or more. The mean GPA for most of these classes falls in the upper part of that range. Faculty who teach smaller classes are not bound by that range, and in these classes, the mean GPA is frequently far above the range."

Finally, the academic environment at Michigan is very accepting of all types and is very community orientated, wherein the school, students, professors and administration realize that you can learn in so many other venues than the traditional classroom. This is vital to the schools' creation of a community of scholars. Furthermore, the students on a whole are not competitive, yet each wants to do his/her best. The school is not cutthroat and people are very willing to help, share notes and outlines, and answer questions if confusion persists outside class.

Status: Current student, full-time
Dates of Enrollment: 9/2005-Submit Date
Survey Submitted: April 2006

The workload in the first year is very tough. Come prepared to spend more time than you expected reading every day. My first-year classes all were good. I had a particularly good Con Law professor. He didn't dumb down the material, but he did explain difficult concepts very clearly. Legal Practice covers two semesters, and it takes quite a bit of time, too. The legal writing experience is essential, and you don't get that in other first-year courses. I ended up not doing all my Legal Practice reading, but that was a mistake because some of the research and writing tips are useful in summer jobs.

Enterprise Organization (Corporations) is not required, but they have several really good professors teaching it, so it's worth taking no matter what you plan to do. There are great co-taught classes, particularly folks doing Intellectual Property and related subjects. There seems to be a nucleus of professors interested in health law developing, which is exciting because of the connection to health research in other areas of the university. The Public Interest Fellows program is a new program to bring practitioners in to both teach classes and mentor students; it adds to the diversity of course offerings and helps with employment prospects, too.

Status: Current student, full-time
Dates of Enrollment: 9/2005-Submit Date
Survey Submitted: April 2006

There are some amazing professors here, both young and old, who are leaders in their field and who are committed to teaching. I haven't had a professor yet that I felt wasn't interested in the success of their students and willing to go out of their way to help. They want to get to know you and are willing to be accessible, but you also have to seek them out. The first-year classes are relatively big and they are unlikely to know you well unless you make that extra effort (which I encourage—not enough people do that!). It can be hard to get some of the core courses for your 2L year, like Evidence and Enterprise Organizations (Michigan's version of Corporations), but I think they are trying to remedy that by adding more sections in the fall.

Michigan's commitment to public interest is also evidenced through it's public service faculty fellow program. The faculty they have brought in through this program to teach public interest courses is amazing—they have great experience, are passionate about their work and eager to help students. One of them even flies in every week from the ACLU of Southern California to teach courses. And the most recent addition to the faculty in criminal law is also amazing. The only area where I think the faculty is lacking is in the field of labor and employment law. I thought that those courses would be offered regularly but have been disappointed by the lack of offerings.

Status: Current student, full-time
Dates of Enrollment: 8/2004-Submit Date
Survey Submitted: April 2006

Law school is not about the classes you take but the people you take classes with. My classmates have provided me with as much knowledge as my professors have. Classroom discussion is lively and centered not only around the topics of a particularly subject matter, but also reaching to the important questions that shape our communities and thus our public policies. Along with student contribution, my professors are the best I have had at any level. They are both brilliant and down to earth, and they are constantly challenging their students to reach a new level of understanding. Outside of the classroom I have been invited to professors' homes for wine and cheese, to socialize or for study groups. For the most part, professors really care about building real relationships with their students.

However, for those interested in transactional work (e.g., business and real estate) the school is sorely lacking in this area. So much so that you will see the same professors for many of these classes. There has been an initiative put forward by the students and supported by the law school to strengthen the school in this area, but it should be at least a year or two before that happens. In the meantime the law school offers the opportunity to take classes in all other graduate schools and there are a multitude of classes in the business school that are extremely applicable to law students.

> **The school says:** "The Law School has expanded its offerings in recent years. Please visit cgi2.www.law.umich.edu/CurriculumInterestAreas/home.axp."

Status: Current student, full-time
Dates of Enrollment: 9/2005-Submit Date
Survey Submitted: April 2006

First-year classes, as with any school, are chosen for you (except for one elective your second semester). All of the first-year courses are taught by the best faculty though. They're the tops of their fields nationally. The Legal Practice course is taught by full-time faculty. While it's beneficial to learn to draft briefs and memos, it can be dull (relative to your other first year courses).

Second and third years offer a lot of flexibility. You can take one seminar and one clinic or practice simulation each term, in addition to you regular upper-level courses. You can also do externships or outside graduate work. I haven't had problems getting whatever course I want. The courses are offered frequently enough that there aren't many courses with waitlists. The professors also work to get you into their courses if they know you have a particular interest.

Status: Current student, full-time
Dates of Enrollment: 9/2004-Submit Date
Survey Submitted: October 2005

If you put in the effort watching the class registration web site, you will get the classes you want. Also, people here are remarkably friendly. This year, when I hadn't gotten into one of the classes I wanted, three people contacted me and let me know when spaces became available on the registration web site. Intensely nice people; everyone is looking out for everyone else.

Grades are harsher than some other schools, but most employers know that. Also, students from those schools have often told me that they don't think they learned anything significant—rather they've learned how to think. You'll certainly learn how to think at Michigan, but you're going to learn a lot more than that too. At my job this summer, I regularly found myself more knowledgeable and better prepared than other interns. Particularly at writing legal memoranda and briefs, but also in my grasp of legal doctrines, research and other material. I wish I could attribute it to my own intelligence, but Michigan deserves all the credit.

Status: Current student, full-time
Dates of Enrollment: 9/2004-Submit Date
Survey Submitted: April 2005

The workload for the first year really isn't that bad. The classes for first-year students are spread out during the day, and a lot of students do the reading for classes in the one to two hours before the class. Many students do a nine to five type schedule and rarely take work home. The main exception is legal practice

writing assignments that can take up a good part of a weekend. The hours also kick up around two to three weeks before finals start. Each student has two "priorities" that they can use during class registration to make it easier to get popular classes. The priorities can be used anytime in the student's law school career, but I've heard that most 3L students get the classes they want without them.

 Employment Prospects

Status: Current student, full-time
Dates of Enrollment: 5/2005-Submit Date
Survey Submitted: April 2006

In my experience, Michigan Law has a fantastic reputation in every corner of the world. For a state school, only 16 percent of the graduates stay in the state of Michigan, which means that Michigan Law graduates are spread all over the U.S. and the world. These alumni represent some of the greatest legal minds of the time, and are nearly 100 percent supportive of their fellow graduates. It basically doesn't matter where you want to end up, there are likely several Michigan Law grads in practice there. This is an incredible boon for current Michigan students. Not only does it essentially open up the entirety of the U.S. (and world) to Michigan students, it also provides students with a distinguished and dispersed alumni network that is, in general, ready and willing to help other Michigan Law graduates.

While, like many other Top 10 programs, the majority of graduates choose to seek a career in the firm world, Michigan does a great deal to support and encourage graduates who are interested in practicing in other venues. Nearly a quarter of our class chooses to pursue a career in the public interest and we send one of the largest numbers of graduates into federal judicial clerkships. To this end, the school has an office of public interest which works in tandem with the career services office to make sure public interest issues are discussed on campus and to help mentor those interested in public service law. Additionally, the career services office has a staff member entirely devoted to counseling students on their judicial clerkship applications.

Status: Current student, full-time
Dates of Enrollment: 9/2005-Submit Date
Survey Submitted: April 2006

There are so many employers that come to campus, it's amazing! Over 700 in the fall for only about 360 second-year students. And they come from all over. I think that if you have great grades at Michigan, your choices are unlimited, and even with a mediocre GPA, you still have some pretty amazing options. The office of public interest also does a good job of supporting those students who don't want to interview with firms by providing some funding for public interest career fairs and such.

For 1Ls, it can be hard to find a firm job unless you are going to a smaller market and have ties to the area. The Student Funded Fellowship program is great, however—they give $3,000 grants to about 70 students who want to work in government or public interest. A lot of people also end up clerking for judges their first summer, which is unpaid.

Status: Current student, full-time
Dates of Enrollment: 8/2004-Submit Date
Survey Submitted: April 2006

Without question, one of Michigan Law School's greatest strengths is its ability to place students in their desired market in the positions they want. An example of this is my own experience: as a 1L I wanted to place in New York so that I could be near my girlfriend of four years for the summer. I knew that a firm job was necessary so that I could help pay for school and because I know that I am a firm person. Through alumni connections and through the name Michigan I was able to get an unprecedented five interviews at Top 20 law firms. I ended up taking an offer from a well-known New York firm where I took the only spot reserved for a first-year law student not through a scholarship or city- or state-run program.

Read all of Vault's Law School Surveys at www.vault.com/lawschool — get complete surveys on top law schools, expert advice on applicaton essays, LSAT prep and more.

VAULT CAREER LIBRARY 349

Status: Alumnus/a, full-time
Dates of Enrollment: 9/2002-5/2005
Survey Submitted: October 2005

Michigan alums are CRAZY about Michigan, so there is a very strong, active network of potential mentors and contacts across the country and around the world. Most students get placed in large firms through Michigan's on-campus interviewing program. The program is very well attended by large firms and the career services office does a nice job coordinating the event.

The Michigan name goes a long way, but in tough job markets, perhaps not long enough for those in the bottom quarter of the class (who, again, can be plagued by what appear to be unimpressive transcripts when compared to their similarly situated peers at schools that elect more lenient grading policies).

Status: Alumnus/a, full-time
Dates of Enrollment: 8/1999-5/2002
Survey Submitted: April 2006

A Michigan graduate can get a job most anywhere. Michigan sends more students to the East Coast than any West Coast schools and vice versa. So it's particularly great if you don't know which side of the country you may want to end up on. On-campus recruiting has improved; it is now in a larger space at an off-campus hotel instead of in cramped cubicles in Hutchins Hall. Soon, they will hopefully find a large venue on campus for the interviews. Many, many employers show up so it is quite easy to get a job if you have been keeping up with your studies.

Status: Current student, full-time
Dates of Enrollment: 9/2005-Submit Date
Survey Submitted: November 2005

You're not allowed to deal with career services or contact anyone about jobs until November. In November, you can contact career services, and they and student organizations start having career panels and resume-help services. In December, you can mail resumes to firms and other places of employment. 2Ls and 3Ls spend the first weeks of class interviewing and doing callbacks. They all seem pleased with the opportunities they are receiving.

It seems like it's so easy to network yourself into opportunities here. We have all kinds of prominent speakers in just about every area of law come here, and our student organizations help so much with passing along job opportunities and handing out contact info in the area of law you're interested in (for example, the entertainment law organization has contacts to employers for jobs in that area...so does the public interest organization and GLBT organization). As long as you want a job and are not being too picky, you will leave here with something every single summer and after you graduate.

Status: Current student, full-time
Dates of Enrollment: 9/2004-Submit Date
Survey Submitted: April 2005

The office of career services at UM is always on top of things. Every fall, they run an on-campus interview program that has something like 800 employers. Students who participate usually will have interviews with around 25 employers. Nearly every week outside attorneys come to the law school to give presentations about their jobs. They feature pretty much every type of attorney imaginable: academics, nonprofits, firms and non-traditional jobs for JDs. Panels of 3Ls are also arranged frequently to give job-hunting advice. The presentations are usually at lunch time so it's not hard to find time to go.

Status: Alumnus/a, full-time
Dates of Enrollment: 6/2001-12/2003
Survey Submitted: February 2004

While I talk to people at other law schools across the country who don't have jobs, I am really, extremely, terribly grateful I decided to go to Michigan, even though it cost more than I was intending to pay for law school. Practically everyone graduated with a job that I know of, and almost everyone who had aspirations other than "to work at a BigLaw firm" is doing precisely what they want to do.

For instance, I have a friend who didn't graduate with us because he's got a Fulbright Scholarship to study Islamic law in Rabat, Morocco. Another friend of mine got a post-graduate "Prettyman"—some sort of special fellowship award

for those who want to do public defense. Personally, I spent a semester doing an internship at the ACLU of Southern California with some of the best civil rights attorneys in the country. Every year that I know of, two Michigan grads get "Skaddens"—a prestigious fellowship sponsored by a huge New York law firm.

Quality of Life

Status: Current student, full-time
Dates of Enrollment: 6/2004-Submit Date
Survey Submitted: April 2006

Housing is wonderful—I live five minutes off campus and I'm able to have a yard and a one-bedroom apartment for less than a studio in most cities. There are trees everywhere, parks, rivers, amazing restaurants and a lot of fun concerts and theaters. I'd love to live in this environment when I graduate if there was any way to get a job here. I feel very safe, and I have enough space from school—although considering how gorgeous the law quad is I don't mind heading in to campus.

Status: Current student, full-time
Dates of Enrollment: 5/2005-Submit Date
Survey Submitted: April 2006

Michigan Law students tend to live at a fairly high quality of life compared to other law students, mostly because it is relatively cheaper to live in Ann Arbor, Michigan than many of the large metropolitan centers other law schools call home. Ann Arbor is a great college town, but just that—a college town. It is very safe and relatively inexpensive. There are nearly unlimited options of social environments for anyone in school—as the town basically caters to a university crowd. There is a separate downtown area which is a short walk from campus, and then a campus hub. In these close-to-campus areas, students can find all different types of restaurants, shops, eateries, clothing stores and bars.

Many students, like myself, choose not to live in the Lawyers Club and for us, Ann Arbor has a rich housing market which spans the gamut of quality and price ranges. Many students live a short walk away from campus, while others choose to live on the outskirts of town to get more space for less money and take the free bus service or commute to campus. A student who lives off campus can buy or rent, and has a choice of nearly every sort of housing arrangement imaginable. The law school's iconic Gothic buildings are beautiful, but they were built in the 1920s and sometimes lack some of the flare of the new technologically advanced classrooms at other law schools. However, Michigan is in the process of renovating each classroom, adding outlets, carpeting, paint and other modern touches to make the classrooms state-of-the-art. Additionally, the school will soon break ground on a new classroom building that promises the best of everything!

The current classroom and legal research buildings are very intimate, and reflect the close knit quality of the student body. The Reading Room is most similar to the great hall of Hogwarts described by J.K. Rowling in her *Harry Potter* novels. It is a beautiful room and it provides students and faculty alike a quiet space to study. If the open spaces of the reading room aren't the space you prefer to study, the underground library is one of the most well-lit (from natural light!) places on campus and provides students with tables and carrels and a study room for all study styles. The library itself is one of the most extensive law libraries in the country and as it is non-circulating, every book is available to students at all times. The library staffs five librarians, all of whom have a JD and a Library Science degree. In my experience, they are very helpful and enjoy the opportunity to help students.

Status: Current student, full-time
Dates of Enrollment: 8/2004-Submit Date
Survey Submitted: April 2006

I like to start with technology because I believe that its the most important thing in your graduate school career. The law school is one of the leaders in technology among law schools. That said, we are blocked from using the internet in the classrooms per the professors request. However, students have had lengthy discourse with the administration about this issue, and I expect that it will be allowed again within the next year.

Housing is just like it is in any university town. If you want to live on top of the law school you can, if you want to get as far away from the law school as you can at night then you can also do that. There are traditional apartments, apartments in houses, condos, dorm rooms, and anything else your heart can desire. The closer you live to school the less you need a car. That said, parking on campus is a challenge. The business school and the law school are very close in proximity as well as a new public policy building, therefore there is a high demand for parking. The only parking in the area for students is meter parking and to say this in easiest way to understand...Ann Arbor makes more money off giving people tickets than any other city activity.

Status: Current student, full-time
Dates of Enrollment: 9/2005-Submit Date
Survey Submitted: November 2005

We have pretty excellent dorms. I have lived on three campuses prior to living on Michigan's campus, and these are the nicest dorms I've ever been in. My room is huge (it's a single suite); it's like an apartment. I think even if you end up in a double, you get your own room—those are set up kind of like apartments, as well. Whenever there's a problem with your room, you call maintenance and they come right away...which is also something different from most other schools I've lived at. The one problem I had was there was no air conditioning. It's really hot here during the summer, and it's hard to work out in the gym with no air conditioning in the summer. The gym is very nice, by the way, and they seem to have everything you could want in a gym. Actually, there are, I think, three gyms. Another problem I have with the dorms is you can hear more noise than you might like from the hallways and, somewhat, other rooms. A lot of people live off campus, though, and there seems to be a lot of housing options in walking distance.

Status: Alumnus/a, full-time
Dates of Enrollment: 6/1999-5/2003
Survey Submitted: March 2004

U of M Law School is housed in a set of beautiful old buildings in the heart of Ann Arbor, Michigan. The setting is idyllic with its hand-carved stone and tree-shaded expanse of lawn in the quad. Most of the classrooms have been recently renovated to show off the intricate woodwork and stained glass. Classrooms are equipped with up-to-date technology including wireless Internet, adequate outlets, video confrencing rooms, computer labs and a first-rate law library.

Students can choose to live in the law dorm, known as the Lawyers Club, which forms one side of the law quad. Students living in the Lawyers Club can purchase a meal plan so they may eat all or some of their meals in the Lawyers Club dining room, a standard university cafeteria. Students living off campus can purchase meal tickets to join friends for a meal in the Lawyers Club dining room as frequently as they would like. Students living off-campus can choose to rent apartments or even houses sprinkled throughout the city and the suburbs. Some students even choose to purchase a house or condo while at U of M. Commuting is feasible from as far away as Detroit or even Lansing. Generally, the closer one lives to campus the more expensive the housing is.

 **Social Life**

Status: Current student, full-time
Dates of Enrollment: 5/2005-Submit Date
Survey Submitted: April 2006

Michigan's social life revolves a great deal around the school. There are few outside distractions in Ann Arbor, so students tend to look to the law school and their law school friends for social outlets. Much of the student body is involved in student organizations who run everything from speakers, to symposiums, to movie nights to bar nights. The law school has over 50 student organizations so students can almost always find something to get involved in that peaks their interest. Also the student senate runs bar nights and dances for the entire school, which are generally well attended.

Ann Arbor has pretty much every kind of nightlife you can ask for—from sports bars to brew pubs to martini lounges to outdoor cafes and dance clubs. Student favorites are Rick's American Cafe—a dance club/bar, Dominick's—an outdoor cafe with killer sangria, Leopold Bros—a brewpub with board games and picnic

tables, Ashley's—a bar with some 35 beers on tap, Buffalo Wild Wings—pool, cheap beer and more TVs than you can imagine playing all the big games.

The dating scene in Ann Arbor is not exactly what you would call hot. (Mostly because students in the law school are generally entirely too busy to date!) However, there are plenty of opportunities to meet people if you have time. Each section has its share of couples and so it is definitely possible. However, there is plenty to do where you can meet people and some extra time too, if you find someone you want to date.

Status: Current student, full-time
Dates of Enrollment: 9/2005-Submit Date
Survey Submitted: April 2006

Student clubs make for a lot of the social life. There are lots of clubs of all sorts, from the Outlaws GLBT group to the Federalist Society to the American Constitution Society to National Lawyers' Guild to Black Students Association to Labor Law Roundtable to Refugee/Asylum Law Club to the Business Law Association (and on and on). These groups and the law school student senate arrange bar nights or social events. Ann Arbor has a wide range of clubs and restaurants. Because Ann Arbor has a lot of medical and high-tech industry, it is a fairly high-income town. That means there are cheap dives for student budgets and fine dining for special occasions and everything in between. There are a number of decent Middle Eastern, Latino and Indian restaurants around town, too. The town has a nice ethnic mix, which means that there are churches, synagogues, temples to fit every need.

Status: Current student, full-time
Dates of Enrollment: 9/2005-Submit Date
Survey Submitted: April 2006

Michigan students are smart and interesting, but they're also friendly! There is really no sense of competition or back-biting—everyone wants to have an good experience and enhance the learning environment around them! There are a lot of student groups that are active in the law school and the surrounding community. Bar night—the Law School Student Senate sponsors a bar night once a month at a different establishment, except in February when bar nights are once a week.

As for restaurants, here's the low down: Dominick's is a popular choice for students for their food and their amazing sangria. The outdoor patio makes it a great spot for relaxing on the beautiful fall and spring days, and it's right across the street from the law school. Many student groups hold happy hours and informational meetings at Dominick's and so do some of the firms when they come to campus to recruit. There are coffee places all over; not one specific favorite, but you can usually find a professor getting his caffeine at his Espresso Royale in the mornings. Ricks is a cheesy undergrad bar that a lot of people go to. But I'm married and too old for that! A lot of the older students head for the Main Street establishments like Good Night Gracie's or Live at PJs (both martini bars) or Conor O'Neills Irish Pub and Leopold Brothers Brewing Co. for a more mature atmosphere.

Best food in town can be found at the same place as the best beer in town—Grizzly Peak Brewing Co. on Washington. Casey's is also a townie bar and grill place where many undergrads don't frequent—they have amazing burgers. The most famous burger joint around, Blimpy Burger, is only a couple of blocks from the law school—an Ann Arbor tradition for many many years, but be careful, it's greasy.

Status: Current student, full-time
Dates of Enrollment: 8/2004-Submit Date
Survey Submitted: April 2006

Yeah, this is law school, that said Michigan Law School can be a fun place to be and you will never be short on social activities. Ann Arbor has a plethora of bars where not only law students, but graduate students as a whole hang out and socialize. The law school has a monthly bar night where many of the students come out and dance and drink together. We also have large school events like Date Auctions, SFF Auction, numerous scholarship balls and the LSSS Prom.

You will oftentimes find yourself out at Rick's on a Thursday night, which is akin to parting in your parents' basement, but continues to be entertaining somehow anyway. In addition, there are nicer places like Studio 4, OZ and Bab's Underground where you can sit at nice tables and drink nice drinks. Then

Read all of Vault's Law School Surveys at www.vault.com/lawschool — get complete surveys on top law schools, expert advice on applicaton essays, LSAT prep and more.

VAULT CAREER LIBRARY 351

you end your night eating pretty good food at Pizza House because it stays open until 4 a.m. or some other crazy hour.

Status: Current student, full-time
Dates of Enrollment: 9/2005-Submit Date
Survey Submitted: April 2006

The social life is very community-focused. Every night revolves around student group events and bar nights organized by the school. Most students participate and look forward to large group events. The student groups are a big deal. Most students are involved in various legal and non-legal groups. It's the best way to take your mind off classes and get to know people who aren't in your section.

Status: Current student, full-time
Dates of Enrollment: 9/2004-Submit Date
Survey Submitted: October 2005

Best social life ever. Whether you're a younger student interested in the pounding and dark dance floor at Rick's, or a more mature older student looking for the camaraderie and socializing around big oak tables at bars like Ashley's or Leopolds, Ann Arbor and Michigan have a scene for you. The football fans turned me from uninterested into a huge fan, and they are great fun (though you don't have to go). Dominick's and its sangria is a great place to spend a lazy Friday, and last year we all went every Thursday before the last class of the day, which was very, very fun.

The gay scene is small but remarkably welcoming. If you need the sophistication and snobbery of New York, don't come here. If you want to meet a lot of nice and friendly people who will help you out, this is the place to be.

Status: Current student, full-time
Dates of Enrollment: 9/2002-Submit Date
Survey Submitted: March 2005

Ann Arbor is definitely a college town. All the undergrads look so young. Much of law school life (and possibly the legal profession—firm wise) centers around alcohol so the bar scene is fairly big. There are, however, two independent theaters and plenty of other things to do in the larger Ann Arbor community if someone seeks them out. I haven't had much time to take part in that, which is probably a matter of laziness. Regarding meeting people from other grad programs: students complain about not meeting other people in other schools and there are mixer events, but they don't really take off. I think it depends on your personality. I, unfortunately, have not ventured out much either. Dating leaves much to be desired, but people find a way to come together. The school held a Terms of Art event where law students were invited to display their various pieces of art in the law school basement. Very nice. There are a lot of restaurants in a wide variety of price ranges that students like to frequent. Afternoon Delight is a great brunch spot and Big 10 Burrito gives you more than your money's worth. Downtown Main Street is a upscale with nice restaurants and boutiques and a Mongolian BBQ!

Status: Alumnus/a, full-time
Dates of Enrollment: 6/2001-12/2003
Survey Submitted: February 2004

From my perspective, Michigan has one of the best social lives of all the Top 10 law schools. It's in a college town, so some of the bars can be on the "undergrad" side, but for some law students (you can guess which gender), that can be seen as a good thing. The dating scene is good in general, but the club scene can be a bummer for people coming from a place like NYC or L.A Detroit is about 45 minutes away, and there's not all that much going on there besides the casinos. Many people prefer the Canadian casinos in Windsor anyway, because they are right across the border in Canada, and the exchange rate makes it like playing with "Monopoly money."

Wayne State University Law School

Admissions Office
471 W. Palmer
Detroit, MI 48202
Admissions phone: (313) 577-3937
Admissions e-mail: lawinquire@wayne.edu
Admissions URL: http://www.law.wayne.edu/prospective/

 ## Admissions

Status: Alumnus/a, full-time
Dates of Enrollment: 8/2002-5/2005
Survey Submitted: May 2006

The admission process is pretty straightforward and resembles admissions at any other law school. The only advice I can give would be to make sure you stand out in your personal statement, either through a personal experience or story that will reflect positively on yourself, while leaving an impression on the admissions committee.

Status: Current student, part-time
Dates of Enrollment: 8/2003-Submit Date
Survey Submitted: May 2006

Application process is similar to all law schools: sign up on the LSAC site, take the LSAT, get references to submit to LSAC, send transcripts to LSAC. Once you've done this, submit your application to Wayne State Law. They will get your scores and references from the LSAC site, but you may choose to have additional references sent directly to the school instead of the general reference. This is never a bad idea. They admit on a rolling basis, so it's best to get your application in early. WSU Law is fairly selective, so make sure that if there is an issue with your undergrad grades or your LSAT school that you address this in your essay. Not everyone is required to interview prior to admission, but if you are, be prepared to explain why you are a good candidate for this school. If there are red flags on your record, don't assume that it's a deal-breaker—it isn't necessarily. But make sure that you are ready to discuss the issues candidly.

> **Wayne State says:** "In fact, personal interviews are not part of the normal admissions process at Wayne State. Occasionally, a student may be contacted and asked for further information if the admissions committee has a question after reading the application."

Status: Current student, full-time
Dates of Enrollment: 8/2005-Submit Date
Survey Submitted: May 2006

START EARLY! Make sure that you explain any difficulties reflected in your grades in your personal statement. Wayne State Law School has a great program.

Status: Current student, full-time
Dates of Enrollment: 8/2004-Submit Date
Survey Submitted: May 2006

In comparison to many schools, Wayne State had a very straightforward admissions process. The application was easy to fill out, only one essay was needed and two recommendation letters were required. I also applied to several big name schools, and their applications were overly long, complicated and intrusive. Wayne was a refreshing change for such a highly accredited school.

I felt that Wayne was fairly selective—the median GPA coming in with my class was around a 3.4 to 3.5. The class was well rounded with a number of older students, night students, students who were pursuing law as a second career and many people who were fresh out of college.

Also, the admissions office was extremely helpful in answering all of my questions about applying, getting accepted and financial aid. And the best part, partial and full scholarships are readily available for students who have high undergraduate GPAs and high LSAT scores.

When I applied to law school, I applied to Wayne and several larger schools. I was accepted to the University of Michigan Law School, but I was really happy that I decided to go to Wayne. It is a great school with low tuition (for a graduate program), I received a partial scholarship (which would have never happened at a larger school), I made a lot of great friends and I have a summer job with a great firm in Detroit. I could not be happier.

> **The school says:** "Actually, the median GPA for the class than entered in fall 2005 was 3.52."

Status: Current student, full-time
Dates of Enrollment: 8/2004-Submit Date
Survey Submitted: May 2006

The admissions process includes an application (and a fee, of course!) and personal statement. Wayne State has become increasingly more selective in the last few years. While your LSAT score is important, for the vast majority of prospective students the single most important submission is the personal statement—it is your opportunity to shine. The faculty and admissions staff give great weight to people who have unique backgrounds socially, economically and professionally, and how such backgrounds will add to the quality of class discussions; with the exception of some first-year classes, almost all courses are theory based, placing distinct analytical skills at a premium.

Of course, apply early. Wayne State is a rolling admissions school.

Status: Alumnus/a, full-time
Dates of Enrollment: 8/2001-5/2004
Survey Submitted: March 2006

WSU is getting more selective, as evidenced by the profiles of its entering class. I did not participate in an interview, but was required to write an essay. Further, the admissions department sponsored extremely informative sessions to help prospective students assess the school, its program, personnel and atmosphere. The scholarship programs are also very competitive.

Status: Current student, full-time
Dates of Enrollment: 8/2004-Submit Date
Survey Submitted: March 2006

After being accepted to the law school, I called to set up a tour. I had already been on a tour of one other law school (Michigan State) where the assistant dean of admissions conducted the tour for my parents and I, and made us feel very welcome. When arriving at Wayne State, we were greeted and led around by a student that worked in the admissions office. I was at first put off by that as I had received such a warm welcome at my previous tour. But in the end, our tour guide was extremely knowledgeable and a law student himself, so it was very nice to see a familiar face when I began. I didn't have to go through any type of interview process and submitted the same personal statement that I used for all other applications. The school gave me an extremely nice financial aid package and in my opinion has been generous in giving out financial aid to other students as well. I was pleasantly surprised when my financial aid package was increased after a tuition increase, even though the school was under no obligation to do so.

Read all of Vault's Law School Surveys at www.vault.com/lawschool — get complete surveys on top law schools, expert advice on applicaton essays, LSAT prep and more.

VAULT CAREER LIBRARY   353

Academics

Status: Alumnus/a, full-time
Dates of Enrollment: 8/2002-5/2005
Survey Submitted: May 2006

The quality and availability of classes are exceptional, with very reputable faculty members. Popular classes are not difficult to get into, as the more popular classes are larger. Grading is straightforward with a standard law school curve. Workload depends on the professor teaching the class.

Status: Current student, part-time
Dates of Enrollment: 8/2003-Submit Date
Survey Submitted: May 2006

The classes at Wayne are generally quite good, though, as in any school, some professors are better teachers than others. The education is good and students learn a lot in the classes (contributing to the school's high bar passage rate). Getting into some of the smaller sized classes can be difficult; you have to play a game of registration Russian Roulette sometimes, but they are worth the agony. Grading for first year is on a curve; there are a limited number of A's available, but this is ABA-mandated. After the required classes, it's completely on your merit. In my experience, the grading has been fair (and I am not one of the top-tier students, by any means, so I think I'm being as unbiased as possible). The workload is law school caliber—be prepared to study like you've never studied before.

Status: Current student, full-time
Dates of Enrollment: 8/2005-Submit Date
Survey Submitted: May 2006

I have had a very good academic experience. All of my professors were very knowledgeable and had practical experience in the field. I learned a great deal, and though it was difficult, professors were willing to help you through.

Status: Current student, full-time
Dates of Enrollment: 8/2004-Submit Date
Survey Submitted: May 2006

I feel the classes are difficult but fair. Almost every professor that I have had has been exceptional. We have professors from all around the country who graduated from Yale, Harvard, etc. Wayne is also very good about having their own alumni, who are currently practicing, teach classes in their field. I prefer those professors since they have more insight into the law because they are actually practicing in that field.

Most of the professors explain things clearly, are happy to answer questions, and have office hours readily available. Most classes at Wayne are taught using the Socratic Method, but the teachers are usually very fair about it, and there is nothing terrifying (like you see in movies) where you don't know the answer and the professor embarrasses you in front of the class.

Grading is tough usually. First year and all required classes are taught on a curve. Upper-level classes are also curved, but the teachers will hand out a few more A's. The workload really depends on each class. Three credit courses with a tough professor can be even more work than a four credit hour class. The amount of reading is very dependent on the teacher. For one professor, the reading amount may be very small because you will supplement your reading with a great lecture. For another professor, you may get a lot of reading, supplements and problems assigned, and you will need to be ready to discuss all of it in class.

I have never had a problem getting into any of the popular classes here at Wayne. We have several popular professors whose classes will fill up quickly, but you simply have to get up early to register for those classes. I am a 3L now and I have never missed out on a class that I have wanted or needed to join a waitlist.

Status: Current student, full-time
Dates of Enrollment: 8/2003-Submit Date
Survey Submitted: May 2006

The professors took their jobs very seriously. Many of them were available after class or during office hours. Sometimes, the most popular classes filled up too quickly, but I imagine that happens in other programs, too. The workload was

typical for law school, as well. Overall, it was manageable and a very worthwhile experience.

Status: Current student, full-time
Dates of Enrollment: 8/2004-Submit Date
Survey Submitted: May 2006

Wayne State (WSU) has an excellent academic program that is augmented by the University of Michigan's (UM) law faculty. We are dual enrolled at both institutions; we can take UM classes at WSU prices. The only downside is that we do not receive a UM diploma at graduation!

> **The school says:** "It's not accurate to say that WSU Law students are 'dual enrolled' at both institutions. Wayne State law students may take courses at UM Law School on a pass/fail basis, while paying WSU's lower tuition rate, with the permission of both schools."

As with any school, there are the teachers to avoid at all costs and there are the teachers that you would sacrifice a limb to learn from them. Thankfully, the latter outnumber the former! The ease of getting into their classes is a different story. WSU has finally caught up to the digital age and conducts class registration online. Unfortunately, however, registration currently begins at 7:00 a.m. Consequently, if you do not have a high-speed Internet connection (and DSL doesn't cut it!), then you likely will not receive the class you want—popular classes (such as for Professor Moran) fill up in the first 10 or 12 minutes.

Generally, the professors are fair graders. We have a few bad apples. The Student Bar Association does a pretty good job of publishing a yearly list of professors to take, which is the back-handed way of telling you which professors to avoid.

For a tier-three school, our professors are remarkably pedigreed. Almost all of them come from Ivy League schools. WSU also supplements its faculty with exceptional adjuncts who are powerhouse practitioners in their fields (e.g., local defense bar legend Kenneth Mogill and Federal District Judge Gerald Rosen).

Workload is not too bad. Most professors keep the reading under 40 pages per class and most classes meet two or three times per week. I've never experienced the horror stories of 150 pages each night. No, law school books don't have the nice pictures that undergrad books have, but the typeface is much larger (especially books published by Foundation Press)!

Status: Current student, full-time
Dates of Enrollment: 8/2004-Submit Date
Survey Submitted: May 2006

Good course offerings. Grading is inconsistent so really depends on the professor. Workload seems average for law school.

Status: Current student, part-time
Dates of Enrollment: 8/2003-Submit Date
Survey Submitted: May 2006

Most professors I have had have been great, with a few exceptions. Some classes are popular enough to only be offered to graduating students, which is a pain because your last term is very late to find out if you want to work in ADR or litigation. Evening class selection tends to be somewhat slim. Most classes are offered at some point for evening students, but maybe every other term or year, which is annoying.

Status: Alumnus/a, full-time
Dates of Enrollment: 8/2001-5/2004
Survey Submitted: March 2006

I found the classes to be appropriately challenging. It was rare that I was not able to enroll in a popular class I wanted to take. The workload was heavy but not unreasonable. The professors were extremely accessible during and outside of class, and encouraged active participation. WSU also offers flexibility in its law program offering both a traditional full-time day program, an evening program, and a combined day/evening program that allows students to attend law school while attending to other obligations (e.g., career, family).

Status: Current student, full-time
Dates of Enrollment: 8/2004-Submit Date
Survey Submitted: March 2006

have been pleased with the quality of academics. I don't feel as if I am getting any less of an education as compared to students at top schools. In fact, my first-year Criminal Law professor was concurrently teaching the same class at University of Michigan. The only difference was that we knew which day we would be called on and it was completely Socratic at U of M. While I do know that people have been shut out of popular classes, I personally have never had a problem yet. And the professors seem to allow more students in the class than originally slotted for in order to accommodate more students.

Employment Prospects

Status: Alumnus/a, full-time
Dates of Enrollment: 8/2002-5/2005
Survey Submitted: May 2006

Wayne grads are highly recruited and respected within Southeastern Michigan and in the state. However, it is more difficult to pursue a legal career outside of Michigan, though by no means impossible. It just takes more time and determination. Graduates obtain jobs from Federal Circuit and District Court clerkships through political positions. Almost every type of career is available to you as a graduate. The alumni network is particularly strong in Michigan, as well as in the Washington, D.C. area. There is some on-campus recruitment. Many internships are available, especially with the Federal Court system.

Status: Current student, full-time
Dates of Enrollment: 8/2005-Submit Date
Survey Submitted: May 2006

On-campus interviews are great. Many employers in Detroit actively seek Wayne State students/alumni for employment. Big firms such as Honigman, Miller-Canfield, Butzel-Long and Dykema recruit at our school

Status: Current student, full-time
Dates of Enrollment: 8/2004-Submit Date
Survey Submitted: May 2006

Employment prospects are very good. The on-campus interview season is excellent, and we have many prestigious Detroit firms participate and extend offers to students. Many government agencies (Michigan Association of Prosecuting Attorneys, Court of Appeals) also recruit from Wayne.

Like at many schools, on-campus interviewing tends to cater to the students with high GPAs. For the rest of us, career services office (CSO) does keep a very active collection of job postings, and every week the CSO sends out an e-mail with five "hot jobs" for which students can submit applications. These "hot jobs" include law clerk positions at firms and clerking positions with judges.

Post graduation employment levels are very high at Wayne. Wayne is a really well-known and well-respected law school in the Detroit area, so many doors just open for you because of your degree. Also, a ton of judges and partners at major firms are Wayne graduates, and thus they are seeking out the Wayne students to work for them.

Status: Current student, full-time
Dates of Enrollment: 8/2003-Submit Date
Survey Submitted: May 2006

Many, if not most, of the judges and lawyers in and around Detroit have a direct affiliation with Wayne State. So, the employment prospects are apparent with such strong ties to the community.

Status: Current student, full-time
Dates of Enrollment: 8/2004-Submit Date
Survey Submitted: May 2006

WSU is in the heart of Michigan's legal community: Detroit. WSU is a regional powerhouse. While someone from California or Texas probably will not have heard of it, you'll probably find a great number of people from Chicago to Pittsburgh who have, not to mention anyone living in the Sixth Circuit.

Our graduates generally do not have problems getting jobs. Unfortunately, at the time of graduation, approximately 50 percent do not have a job lined up. However, six months out, approximately 85 or 90 percent are employed. However, this is not to say that our CSO isn't great. On a shoe-string budget, they have managed to put on numerous networking events, set up luncheons with law firms, increase the number of on-campus interviewing firms, provide mock interviews and conduct resume checks. They do a phenomenal job.

Status: Current student, full-time
Dates of Enrollment: 8/2004-Submit Date
Survey Submitted: May 2006

Great clinical opportunities on campus. Many people have found jobs through school and personal contacts in the Detroit area.

Status: Alumnus/a, full-time
Dates of Enrollment: 8/2001-5/2004
Survey Submitted: March 2006

I did not participate in the on-campus interview process, but it is my understanding that all of the major Detroit firms, as well as a number of firms from other states, recruit heavily at Wayne. Many graduates from my class are working as associates in the top five firms in Michigan. Wayne graduates have a reputation of being prepared to practice law in the real, as opposed to theoretical, world.

Status: Current student, full-time
Dates of Enrollment: 8/2004-Submit Date
Survey Submitted: March 2006

I went through the on-campus recruiting program in the fall of my second year. I found that entire program extremely helpful and secured a summer clerkship at one of the top firms in Detroit. All the firms in Detroit seem to view Wayne State as a top school and hire many students from here. It seems that the Detroit-based firms mainly recruit from Wayne State and U of M. I do not know how Wayne's perception is at out-of-state firms. After my first year, I replied to a flyer in the career services office and received an internship with a federal District Court judge. That was an easy process and she was an alumna who looked at Wayne State's Law School very favorably. However, I do know that many students who are not in the top 10 percent are frustrated with the job-seeking process..

Quality of Life

Status: Alumnus/a, full-time
Dates of Enrollment: 8/2002-5/2005
Survey Submitted: May 2006

Wayne has the only evening student program in the state and understands that, for some students, family is more important. Quality of life is great, as Wayne is not too competitive of an institution as compared to tier-one schools. On-campus housing is available in new dorms and specific floors are reserved for law students. The campus is large with many dining facilities, a great rec center and very diverse. The campus is very safe, with the surrounding neighborhoods as safe as any neighborhoods surrounding an inner-city university.

Status: Current student, part-time
Dates of Enrollment: 8/2003-Submit Date
Survey Submitted: May 2006

As an evening student who works full-time during the day, I've not had the opportunity for exposure to most of this. The campus is very attractive, but there are issues with the availability of food and beverage service after 6:00 p.m. There is very little service for the evening students. Crime and safety issues are about average for an urban campus; there are occasional vehicle breakins and petty thefts; this calls for common sense precautions, but is not a blot on the school.

Status: Current student, full-time
Dates of Enrollment: 8/2005-Submit Date
Survey Submitted: May 2006

The university provides student housing although I lived off campus. Parking is conveniently across from the school.

Read all of Vault's Law School Surveys at www.vault.com/lawschool — get complete surveys on top law schools, expert advice on applicaton essays, LSAT prep and more.

VAULT CAREER LIBRARY   355

Status: Current student, full-time
Dates of Enrollment: 8/2004-Submit Date
Survey Submitted: May 2006

Wayne is mostly a commuter school, but the university has just established student housing, which seems very nice and affordable.

The area around the law school is very nice. There are many places to eat or grab a cup of coffee within walking distance. We also have a bar across the street where many of the law students hang out and relax.

The school is in the middle of Detroit, which is a large urban area that does have crime. The school and surrounding areas are very safe. The Wayne State Police are always driving around and cruising through the parking structures. The parking garage for the law school is directly across the street from the classroom building and library. I have personally never had a problem, but it is always important to be street smart.

Status: Current student, full-time
Dates of Enrollment: 8/2004-Submit Date
Survey Submitted: May 2006

The campus is currently in the process of adding great amenities. The first residence hall has opened, and there is a wonderful gym to work out in. There is ample parking so it is easy to live in the suburbs and commute to the Wayne State campus, which is just minutes from downtown Detroit.

Status: Current student, full-time
Dates of Enrollment: 8/2004-Submit Date
Survey Submitted: May 2006

Quality of Life: here is where WSU ranks lowest. The faculty, as great as they are as professors, have a real problem with responding to student concerns. We have a very active Student Bar Association that advocates changes to improve student quality of life issues; unfortunately, the standard response is: "That infringes upon our academic freedom." Apparently, the faculty are under the impression that students do not have any academic freedom of our own. Heck, we have even been told that certain areas of the law school (e.g., the main courtroom) were not designed for students! Sometimes the words "audacious" or "oblivious" appropriately describe a large segment of our faculty.

WSU is making great strides with on-campus housing. While we are traditionally a commuter school, the university president and our dean have created a residential community for law students on campus in the new dorms. If you are tired of dorm living, then there are plenty of apartments, lofts and condos within walking distance not only of the school, but the Detroit Institute of Arts, the Detroit Public Library, and Orchestra Hall.

Campus is about one square mile. Some of the buildings look like they are straight out of the 60s and 70s (I especially like the upside down pyramid building across from the law school). However, the university has spent 10s of millions in the last few years to make capital improvements, and they are continuing to raise money today.

Facilities are a little slow on technology. There are not enough plugs (or ampage) for student to operate a computer. The classrooms do not have wireless Internet. Final exams are still done by hand or by typewriter (which you have to supply!). Some incredibly smart person green-lit the law school buildings to be built to capacity, so finding space to hold meetings, parties or just for students to hang out is a challenge.

On-campus-dining is something to be desired. The university just snagged a Jimmy Johns, a Starbucks and an Einstein Bagels. Other than that, eat off campus!

WSUPD are real police and provide better police protection to the campus than some suburban police departments. They are always very courteous and helpful and work well with students in planning outdoor events that may impact traffic. We are in Detroit, so we do have crime. Auto-theft and larceny are the biggest problems. If you don't leave your things unattended and if you don't have the most likely stolen car in America, then you'll probably be fine. There are emergency kiosks (a.k.a., "the blue lights") that provide direct communication to WSUPD if you are ever concerned someone may attack you. I've only call the police once (because I locked my keys in my car) and they responded in under

three minutes. I've heard of under two minute response times in emergency situations. Of course, be smart, safety in numbers. While it may be sexist and should go without saying, ladies should not walk to their cars alone at night; but that's just common sense, whether you're in Detroit parking deck or in "Pleasantville."

> **Wayne State says:** "The Law School is installing wireless Internet in the classroom building in the summer of 2006. Students will be able to take laptop final examinations in 2006-2007."

Status: Current student, full-time
Dates of Enrollment: 8/2003-Submit Date
Survey Submitted: May 2006

For the most part, it was a comfortable environment. However, there were some safety concerns since the campus is close to some unsafe areas in the city and parking safety was always an issue, especially if you didn't park in any of the lighted structures.

Status: Current student, part-time
Dates of Enrollment: 8/2003-Submit Date
Survey Submitted: May 2006

Campus is very safe. There are campus cops patrolling. Parking is expensive, unless you park on the street, but that's hard to find. Most students are commuters, but there are dorms and apartments.

Status: Alumnus/a, full-time
Dates of Enrollment: 8/2001-5/2004
Survey Submitted: March 2006

WSU is located in downtown Detroit. Despite its location, Wayne is a safe campus with a visible presence of public safety officers. I never felt unsafe walking across campus. The student union offers a number of dining choices, and the law school has its own small cafe in the building. I did not live on or near campus, so have no knowledge of housing facilities. The law school facility itself is beautiful, and much of it is new construction.

Status: Current student, full-time
Dates of Enrollment: 8/2004-Submit Date
Survey Submitted: March 2006

I have felt surprisingly safe walking to school, parking and spending late hours at the school. Since the school is in Detroit, there seems to be a higher crime rate and students do need to be aware of their surroundings at all times when coming and going. But, I have never felt the need to be any extra cautious while inside the school. There is a wide array of food choices in the Student Union. The rec center is nice, but I don't feel that the locker rooms are clean enough to shower.

 Social Life

Status: Alumnus/a, full-time
Dates of Enrollment: 8/2002-5/2005
Survey Submitted: May 2006

Plenty of bars and restaurants in the immediate and surrounding area for law students to blow off steam. Check out Circa!

Status: Current student, full-time
Dates of Enrollment: 8/2005-Submit Date
Survey Submitted: May 2006

There are many organizations and almost every day there is a lunch event. I don't really go out clubbing, but when I was younger, Detroit clubs used to be that deal. The law school has its own de facto bar across the street as well; it is the hangout spot. I am a slight introvert so I don't really go out socially that much.

Status: Current student, full-time
Dates of Enrollment: 8/2003-Submit Date
Survey Submitted: May 2006

The students were friendly and always up for socializing after classes or on the weekends. Student organizations did a good job putting on many events throughout the year, especially ones dedicated to helping charities. Dating-wise, a lot of students were either already in committed relationships or too committed to studies to date.

Status: Current student, full-time
Dates of Enrollment: 8/2004-Submit Date
Survey Submitted: May 2006

Law students don't have that much free time to have a social life. But, I really enjoy the atmosphere at Wayne. Everyone is very friendly and willing to help each other out. Unlike a lot of other law schools, there is not a ton of competition where people are tearing pages out of books or stealing notes.

Also, Wayne Law has a ton of clubs and extracurricular activities to join. Whether it is student government or a club devoted to just one area of law (like public interest, international law, environmental law), there is something for everyone. Also, Law Review, moot court and international moot court are great ways to make friends.

Finally, because we have such a wide range of students here, everyone really fits in. There are lots of students who are married, single and everything in between. That makes the social atmosphere lively and diverse. Wayne State is a really great law school, and I love it. It is a lot of hard work and effort, but it is worth it in the end.

Status: Current student, full-time
Dates of Enrollment: 8/2004-Submit Date
Survey Submitted: May 2006

As fun as you make it! Detroit and the surrounding suburbs offer a variety of options for a great night out on the town.

Status: Current student, full-time
Dates of Enrollment: 8/2004-Submit Date
Survey Submitted: May 2006

Detroit and the first ring suburbs have great restaurants. You could easily through all three years of law school and never eat at the same place twice. Unfortunately, you have to drive or take the bus to most of them! There are some good eateries on Cass Avenue or Woodward Avenue around campus, but the best are down around Greektown, Mexicantown, Campus Martius and the Entertainment District (e.g., Comerica Park, Ford Field, the Opera House).

There's a decent dating scene in Detroit in the warmer months. In the colder months, most of the action is in the suburbs. Why this is, I couldn't tell you.

Student favorites: skipping class on the Tigers' home opener, Byblos Cafe, Circa 1890 Saloon, Campus Coney, La Pita restaurant.

Unfortunately, the law school is not very supportive of social life. The school barely gives any money to students who form sports teams to play against other law schools. Almost all the money for students to do anything comes from the Student Bar Association, which is economically self-sufficient.

Status: Current student, part-time
Dates of Enrollment: 8/2003-Submit Date
Survey Submitted: May 2006

I only know about law school hang outs like Circa and Honest John's, which are nice little dives. Because it's a commuter school, social life is pretty spread out.

Status: Current student, full-time
Dates of Enrollment: 8/2004-Submit Date
Survey Submitted: March 2006

The school's social life is very alive. There are numerous bars, restaurants and clubs around school. Detroit is a big city and there are many things to do around here. Also, there is nice shopping in the suburbs, within 20 minutes of the city. One thing to be aware of is that Detroit is unlike other major cities in that everyone has an automobile. I have lived in a Detroit suburb my entire life and never used the public transportation system. Everyone drives, even when going out to bars and clubs in the downtown area.

Read all of Vault's Law School Surveys at www.vault.com/lawschool — get complete surveys on top law schools, expert advice on applicaton essays, LSAT prep and more.

VAULT CAREER LIBRARY 357

University of Minnesota Law School

Admissions Office
290 Walter F. Mondale Hall
229 19th Avenue South
Minneapolis, MN 55455
Admissions phone: (612) 625-3487
Admissions e-mail: umnlsadm@umn.edu
Admissions URL: http://www.law.umn.edu/prospective/

 Admissions

Status: Current student, full-time
Dates of Enrollment: 9/2005-Submit Date
Survey Submitted: March 2006

The admissions process was highly formalized and impersonal, and after a delay I received a letter. In short, the decision-making processes of the university were, and to some extent remain, unclear. One thing of note about the student body, which indicates something about the admissions process: maturity and professional/non-academic experience seem to be given some weight during the admissions slog. While most students come directly from their undergrad or graduate work, fresh with student loans, there is a substantial chunk of the student body that comes from professional and even seasonal work.

Status: Alumnus/a, full-time
Dates of Enrollment: 8/2002-5/2005
Survey Submitted: March 2006

Admission was straightforward. About two-thirds of students come from MN/WI/ND/SD. The rest are mostly from the Midwest and Mountain West. I don't think that there is any preference for any geographic area, though. That's just the application pool that gets drawn from.

Status: Alumnus/a, full-time
Dates of Enrollment: 9/1998-5/2001
Survey Submitted: March 2006

The admissions process was straightforward with no interview. A personal statement is required. The school is highly selective, but very friendly throughout the process. With, or shortly following, the admission letter, I received other congratulatory letters from senior administration, some with handwritten notes. Financial aid information was provided promptly after notification of admission.

Status: Alumnus/a, full-time
Dates of Enrollment: 9/2001-5/2004
Survey Submitted: March 2006

The admissions process was fairly simple and included an application with essays. (I did not do any interviewing, but others did.) As the law school is one of the Top 20 in the country, high grades and LSAT score were a must, but I also think diversity of experience played a key role in my acceptance. Not only did I have work experience in a variety of fields, but I had international living and working experience that added to my resume.

Minnesota's admission staff is excellent, in fact, that is one of the main reasons I chose to attend that school. Once I was accepted, I received some sort of communication from the school on a weekly basis. Whether it was a call from an admissions counselor or an alum, a letter signed by the dean or a t-shirt, I felt welcomed and desired as a student. (Many other schools just tell you that you are accepted but don't give the student the impression that the school actually cares if they attend.) The law school really made me feel like they wanted me to join the program and be part of their school.

Status: Alumnus/a, full-time
Dates of Enrollment: 9/1997-5/2000
Survey Submitted: April 2005

I made several calls to the admissions staff, who were always prompt and helpful in their responses. I received at least one call from a current student who answered my questions about the academic and community climate of the law school. Generally, the admissions process was very smooth.

Status: Current student, full-time
Dates of Enrollment: 8/2002-Submit Date
Survey Submitted: March 2005

It is my impression that the admissions process is relatively standard as far as law schools go. One thing that I was impressed with was the fact that Minnesota has a program for people who have been admitted and want visit the school—if you visit and then decide to attend, they reimburse your travel costs. That was a very nice perk. The one other thing that I felt truly distinguished Minnesota was the fact that the law school was very proactive and responsive, compared to other schools where it was difficult to get information and where you felt like people didn't really care whether you came or not.

I did not do an interview but I did speak with the dean in charge of admissions at one of the law school fairs that I attended. I heard later that this particular dean was also in charge of scholarships. I received a small scholarship from Minnesota and it was the only school among the several to which I was admitted to offer me money.

Status: Current student, full-time
Dates of Enrollment: 9/2002-Submit Date
Survey Submitted: March 2005

As I remember it, the admissions process was not onerous. I believe I sent my file from LSDAS with my recommendations and a personal statement. I did not interview. That may be because I sent my application on the last date it was permitted to be postmarked. I remember that once I was admitted, the University of Minnesota was exceptionally good at communicating with me over the next several weeks to encourage me to attend. Once I accepted my offer, the communication remained strong throughout the summer.

Status: Alumnus/a, full-time
Dates of Enrollment: 9/2001-5/2004
Survey Submitted: April 2005

Professors made personal calls and wrote notes while I was deciding whether to attend the "U." One professor was even willing to suggest school districts for my wife, a teacher, to apply to—a big help for people who had never been to the state.

Status: Current student, full-time
Dates of Enrollment: 8/2003-Submit Date
Survey Submitted: April 2004

The admission process is extremely straightforward and they will be diligent in giving you a decision well before the deadline. One of the greatest aspects of the process was the non-binding early decision option—just get your application in before the stated date and the school will give you a decision very early in the game. Unfortunately, the school seems to err on the side of caution, meaning if they are unsure, they will defer you into the regular batch. This happened to me and I ended up getting an academic scholarship, so don't be discouraged. But if you do get a deferral, definitely send a follow-up letter stating that you are still very interested in the school.

Status: Current student, full-time
Dates of Enrollment: 8/2003-Submit Date
Survey Submitted: February 2004

The University of Minnesota is a Top 20 law school and is, therefore, one of the more difficult law schools as far as admittance goes. A high undergraduate GPA and high LSAT scores are important in the admissions process. However, U of

Minn has a policy of reviewing in entirety each application and does not exclude any application solely on the basis of numbers.

The law school does not conduct interviews but does offer several information sessions for admitted students and/or students seeking admission. I attended one of these sessions and found it extremely informative, not only insofar as information about the school, but also for information about the admissions process and what is looked for in an application for admittance.

Status: Current student, full-time
Dates of Enrollment: 8/2002-Submit Date
Survey Submitted: October 2003

The admissions process is fairly standard in the law school realm. Like all of the other law schools in the country, the school is caught in a catch-22 with the *U.S. News & World Report* rankings. It says publicly that it doesn't like them, but it is just as obsessed as everyone else with ensuring they at least maintain their ranking. This means that for students, LSAT scores and GPAs are the key. If you are a minority, particularly an African-American (a small population in the school), then you will be given strong plus factors in the admissions process. The school is making an effort to broaden its geographic base, so it seeks to attract students from further and further away from Minnesota roots. If you are from New York or California, expect the school to want you just a little bit more. The school sees this as a way of ensuring that the school will be seen as a national law school, as they expect that a lot of people from those areas will go back after graduation. If the benefit in admission alone is negligible, expect a better shot at scholarship money.

Academics

Status: Current student, full-time
Dates of Enrollment: 9/2005-Submit Date
Survey Submitted: March 2006

The curriculum at the University of Minnesota presses hard on the theoretical currents and controversies during the first year. (In this respect, it seems to be on par with most law schools.) In subsequent years, however, extensive practical training is available. There are enough journals and moot courts for every student to have a place on one—and, indeed, just to flaunt these resources, the school requires every student to participate in at least one journal or moot court. The "practical skills" approach of the later curriculum mixes peculiarly with the academic rigor of the faculty, who are more interested in, say, reinventing the notion of cognitive awareness than in examining the jurisdictional rules governing "good faith."

Status: Alumnus/a, full-time
Dates of Enrollment: 9/2001-5/2004
Survey Submitted: March 2006

Academics at the U of M Law School are rigorous. It's a top-tier school and the academics demand as much. Exams require detail and much preparation, and classes are most often taught with the Socratic Method, which demands daily preparation. However, the professors make themselves available after class and in office hours to address student concerns. I never had an instance where I couldn't get an answer to a question. The professors go out of their way to talk to students, and encourage class participation and conversation after class. Some professors will give students a heads up if they will be called on the next day, which is a wonderful way to put already-nervous law students at ease. The professors' contribution has continued since graduation as well. I have corresponded with a couple of my professors since graduation on issues in my own practice. They always welcomed my questions and got back to me very quickly. It's great to have that expertise available to students in school and alumni who have begun working as well.

The grading is difficult. Any high grades at the U of M are actually earned and are not due to grade inflation. Few people get the best grades, and students work hard to get them. The workload is challenging, but a balance between studies and life is manageable if the student is disciplined. Having professors (and great librarians) available for questions helps with this balance.

Status: Alumnus/a, full-time
Dates of Enrollment: 9/1998-5/2001
Survey Submitted: March 2006

Students take only required courses in the first year and can begin selecting their own courses in the second year. There is a lottery system through which 2Ls and 3Ls sign up for classes, and it is sometimes difficult to get a popular class or instructor.

Grading is now done on a four-point scale, which I understand to be an improvement over the 16-point system that was in place when I was a student. Every teacher grades on a curve and there is no such thing as grade inflation. The professors are excellent and always happy to talk to students before class, after class, during office hours and outside of office hours They all seem to love teaching.

The workload is not bad. As with any school, there can be a lot of reading and students sometimes may need to choose not to read every word of every assignment. Since exams come only once—at the end of the semester—there is plenty of time to catch up. Law journals, moot courts and clinics tend to be more demanding day-to-day than course work.

Three years of legal writing are required. A course in legal research and writing fulfills the first year requirement. In the second and third years, students participate in either a moot court or a law journal. There are quite a number of law journals (including, among others, *The Minnesota Law Review, Law and Inequality, The Minnesota Journal of Global Trade* and *The Minnesota Intellectual Property Review*) and moot courts to choose from. The school also has a really solid clinical education program, which currently offers 16 clinics. These offer invaluable hands-on experience and real-life lawyering lessons.

Status: Current student, full-time
Dates of Enrollment: 8/2002-Submit Date
Survey Submitted: March 2005

I have been very impressed with the quality of the faculty, and their general concern for student learning. While there has been a lot of turnover in the law school faculty recently, I don't feel that those who have left have been the best teachers, just the biggest names. On the other hand, some of the new faculty that have been recently hired are excellent teachers. I have felt that grading was consistently fair and unbiased and that the professors, for the most part, work hard to ensure that they grade objectively. Classes are generally easily accessible—you may initially be placed on a waiting list, but are very likely to get into the class within the first week. The one exception is the clinics, which are consistently very difficult to access.

The workload definitely is a full-time job, particularly in the first and second years for many students. It is highly variable depending on the classes that you choose, however. During the first year, many students were frustrated that the law school organizes classes in such a way that it is almost impossible to also have a job. The school does this intentionally however and discourages first-year students from working.

Status: Current student, full-time
Dates of Enrollment: 9/2002-Submit Date
Survey Submitted: March 2005

I have found all of my professors to be extraordinarily talented teachers. The courses are rigorous and challenging, but intellectually rewarding. I find the workload to be very heavy if you actually complete it all, but in the second- and third-year students learn how to prioritize their most important work and eliminate anything unnecessary. We register for classes using the lottery system, where students can preference the classes they most wish to take. I have never had a problem getting into a class that I wanted to take. If I didn't get assigned a spot by the lottery, I signed up on a waitlist and contacted the professor personally for permission to join his or her class. The grading system used to be a number system, on a 16-point scale. That was confusing for out-of-state employers. The school has switched to a standard A through F scale now—a welcome change. Additionally, the grading curve used to be harsh compared to other law schools, with the curve set at the equivalent of a B-. The curve has been set higher now to be more in line with other law schools. This way our students aren't disadvantaged when their grades are compared to students at other comparable law schools.

Read all of Vault's Law School Surveys at www.vault.com/lawschool — get complete surveys on top law schools, expert advice on applicaton essays, LSAT prep and more.

VAULT CAREER LIBRARY   359

Status: Current student, full-time
Dates of Enrollment: 8/2003-Submit Date
Survey Submitted: February 2004

As a first-year law student, the curriculum is set so I have not had any experience with attempting to get into popular classes. The U of Minnesota is set on a small section system, where all incoming students are placed in one of five sections of around 60 students. Each class is then comprised of your section and one other section, with one or two classes being comprised of solely one small section.

Legal Writing is conducted in even smaller 12 to 15-student sections. Students all have the same classes but professors vary based on section. The quality of professors, in general, is very high. All professors have a distinct background and most have a particular interest or interests that they have demonstrated a passion in. Most classes are matched so that professors are teaching a topic that they are particularly interested and well versed in. The teaching styles of professors vary somewhat, allowing most students to have at least one, if not many, professors that they identify with.

Grading is on a 16-point scale with all first-year classes on a strict curve so that grades depend on the relative performance of all students in the class. This creates an atmosphere in which students tend to work together and encourage each other to gain an understanding of the material. Each student may have a different view and understanding, so the more that students work together, the more likely that each student will have a full and complete understanding. The workload is heavier than any undergraduate program that I have encountered but is reasonable. Students spend a great deal of time at school and with other students so studying becomes natural and the workload does not seem unmanageable.

Status: Current student, full-time
Dates of Enrollment: 8/2002-Submit Date
Survey Submitted: October 2003

There are some truly amazing scholars here, some people that are truly amazing teachers and some people that are filling up a slot. The teaching quality is actually pretty good. The school has lost some important scholars in recent years, and budget troubles don't make keeping and adding scholars any easier. Still, the school is going to provide you with some great access. If you are interested in constitutional issues, then this is a great area for the school.

Most of the 1L classes are pretty standard fare, although you won't get the yearlong exposure that some of your friends in other law schools will get. Some contracts professors merely discard talking about the UCC because they don't have time in one semester to get it all in. Some property professors will focus on one or two issues that they like (such as future interests) and hammer them home, merely giving brief summaries of other issues. Criminal Law is a broader course because it eschews procedure altogether. You'll simply learn the broad strokes of criminal law. On the other hand, you get a year of Civil Procedure, and while some professors take a leisurely pace, you'll face nearly every major issue. Because Civil Procedure is the only class currently graded as one grade for the whole year, it can be a grade-maker or grade-killer. It is one-fifth of your total 1L grade. You will get two semesters of Con Law, although they are contemplating either cutting it down to one or grading it as a year-long course. Some professors take an encyclopedic approach to Con Law, having you work through so many cases and issues in a year that your head spins. Others get caught up in pet issues and simply decide that a year isn't long enough to get past judicial review, the commerce clause, due process and equal protection. As for Torts, expect this to be the class that demands the most in-class participation.

One thing not to overlook when thinking about Minnesota is its amazing clinical program. Some 60 percent of students leave Minnesota with clinical experience. Just about any clinic you could want is available. They are extremely popular, but for good reason. You can be in court trying cases as a 2L. You will have clients. You will be practicing, within parameters, in some pretty amazing areas. There are business clinics, civil practice clinics, family law, tax, bankruptcy and so on. Just about anything you can imagine. (American Indian law clinic, anyone?) One clinic allows you to work with the U.S. Attorney's office doing criminal prosecution work. The clinical program is probably the best thing going for the school.

 ## Employment Prospects

Status: Current student, full-time
Dates of Enrollment: 9/2005-Submit Date
Survey Submitted: March 2006

Much depends on locality. For someone comfortable with life in Minnesota, the university maintains firm connections with practitioners in the community. For someone looking beyond—in particular, towards the Coasts—the school's name is disproportionately underwhelming in relation to its rankings. Many firms don't interview in Minnesota. One large Chicago firm, when asked how their firm viewed Minnesota graduates, said that "it doesn't matter which school you come from, we think good students come from all schools."

Status: Alumnus/a, full-time
Dates of Enrollment: 8/2002-5/2005
Survey Submitted: March 2006

Great prospects. Decent alumni network across the country, and it's exceptional in the upper Midwest. In the Cities, there is serious competition for jobs between William Mitchell and the U of M. However, beyond the Twin Cities, Minneapolis is the top school until you get to Chicago. Very well respected. The on-campus program is well run. However, it has limited impact. I found that even though there were 100 firms or more interviewing (each with, say 10 to 20 interviews), it was the same 50 to 75 students that were getting all the interviews (roughly the top quarter of the class). Career services does some work to make sure that the firms interview more than just the top students, but I got the feeling that the lower-ranked students who got the interviews felt like they didn't really have a chance. Like it was just a pity interview.

Status: Alumnus/a, full-time
Dates of Enrollment: 9/1998-5/2001
Survey Submitted: March 2006

Excellent. University of Minnesota Law School grads practice in every discipline in every major U.S. market, and in many international markets. Classmates of mine went on to the SEC, the DOJ, the most prestigious firms in New York, Chicago, Minneapolis and Los Angeles (among other cities), federal clerkships, state clerkships, in-house positions, prosecutors' offices, politics and so on. The school is very well regarded and should be an asset no matter what kind of work one wants to do. While many employers do not come to the law school to do on-campus interviews, many do. For those that do not come to Minneapolis, the candidate can always visit the employer. The alumni network is good and consistently provides me with reliable advice and tips, and I in turn try to help other alumni whenever possible.

Status: Alumnus/a, full-time
Dates of Enrollment: 9/2001-5/2004
Survey Submitted: March 2006

The U of M does on-campus interviewing and employment fairs. OCI brings in all the major firms in the area and in the nation. As a top school in the country, many students got jobs at the best and largest firms in the country. With the U of M's concentration on social justice as well, there are considerable opportunities for students seeking public interest jobs. The post-graduation employment rate is exceptionally high, and I had no difficulty finding a job for any of my in-school summers and after graduation.

While the career services can always be improved, I found that if students needed individual help with job placement, help was provided. Not only did they help find me a job, but I given contact information for alumni in the field in which I was seeking a job, and even contact info for people working at the particular firms where I was looking.

Status: Current student, full-time
Dates of Enrollment: 8/2003-Submit Date
Survey Submitted: February 2004

U of Minn has a career services office with two full-time career counselors ready to help student with career decisions and the process of applying to jobs and internships. There are a great number of internships and clerkships advertised and available to students. As it is a Top 20 law school, students at the U of Minn have an advantage in the national market in that the school has a great deal of name recognition, allowing students to get a foot in the door at various big-name irms and judicial clerkships. Through additional classes and clinics specifically directed towards particular fields of law, students are able to gain a step up in the market place by individualizing their education.

Status: Current student, full-time
Dates of Enrollment: 8/2002-Submit Date
Survey Submitted: October 2003

The school is really more prestigious with employers than you might think, and there are some firms out there with great Minnesota grads carrying the flag, but don't expect a free ride into a high paying job. The Minneapolis legal market is a good one, but it is second-tier nationally. It isn't a market like Chicago and the school has a lot of work to do in attracting Chicago firms on campus (this is probably the career program's weakest point).

Many of the best Minneapolis firms also expect to (and do) get the best students from here. Don't expect to slack off and just "settle" for a job with Dorsey or Faegre (the top two Minnesota firms). They will laugh in your face. You slack off and you'll be mourning your career prospects. Now, all of that said, relax a little. This is a well-respected school, and you will get a job. But don't expect the career services office (CSO) to get one for you. They are understaffed, with really just two people serving some 800 students. In all honesty, they are going to have a grade cutoff, too. If you have bad grades, a lot is going to depend on your connections, hustle and outside work. If you are in the third quartile, what is the CSO going to do for you? They can't call a top firm and tell them to hire you. In other words, the more work you do getting good grades and on law review, the less you will have to do in trying to hustle a job.

Quality of Life

Status: Current student, full-time
Dates of Enrollment: 9/2005-Submit Date
Survey Submitted: March 2006

Minneapolis has some definite perks. It is astonishingly safe, and (even more astonishing) the people are used to it. Families bring their kids to play in Loring Park after sundown. Minneapolis has a good arts scene, certainly more than a full-time law student could hope to experience. All in all, Minneapolis is good, with qualifications. The saving grace of life in Minneapolis while attending law school is that, as a student, one's urban needs are greatly reduced. Of course, one pays more in bigger cities for the larges of one's experiences, and in this respect the smaller cost of living is proportional to the lesser thrill of being here. Don't expect the spontaneous and unavoidable diversions of life in a bigger city; rather, Minneapolis provides a world of entertainment that is easily planned and delegated to that dwindling realm of your life that only infrequently gets indulged. At least in Minneapolis, it won't grow obsolete.

Status: Alumnus/a, full-time
Dates of Enrollment: 8/2002-5/2005
Survey Submitted: March 2006

Minneapolis is a great place to live. As to the weather, it's not that the winters are cold. January is bitterly cold. The rest of the winter is no worse than other places I've lived: Detroit, Pittsburgh, Cleveland, Salt Lake City. It ain't L.A., but it's not that bad. Plus Minneapolis is aware that it is a northern city. It is built to be not-that-bad during winter. All of downtown is connected by tunnels. You never need to step outside. Plus there are tons of arts, sports and other indoor entertainment.

Status: Alumnus/a, full-time
Dates of Enrollment: 9/2001-5/2004
Survey Submitted: March 2006

Housing is not provided by the school for law school students. However, the law school is located very near downtown and near the undergrad campus where there are a multitude of apartments. I lived right across the street from the law school and didn't need to own a car as a result. It was very convenient because I could go to the library at any hour, yet I was just a short bus ride away from my job downtown.

The law school facilities were also very accommodating. There are lots of private carrels and desks throughout the huge library, so students did not need to

fight for study space. The library and law school also had a wireless network throughout, so studying and surfing the Web between classes was easy. Students without wireless cards could check them out as well. There are a number of lounges with couches and comfortable lounging chairs, plus a small cafeteria for between class snacks and meals.

The law school is very well-located as well. There are many restaurants within a very short walk from the school, and the entire undergraduate community and buildings are just a quick walk over the river bridge. There are biking and walking trails just below the law school and law students may participate in some undergrad sports as well. The law students also have access to the large fitness center.

Status: Alumnus/a, full-time
Dates of Enrollment: 9/1997-5/2000
Survey Submitted: April 2005

The quality of people at the law school, from staff to faculty to students, was impressive. It was easy to find people to relate to, and to forge friendships with people of different backgrounds and goals. There was much more camaraderie than competition among students.

Status: Current student, full-time
Dates of Enrollment: 8/2002-Submit Date
Survey Submitted: March 2005

The Twin Cities is a great place to live and many people do not realize it. While it is certainly cold during the winter, if you like winter sports it is a great place to be. There is a lot to do, from theater to sports teams to great restaurants and clubs. Nice rental housing is not difficult to find. It is very helpful to have a car, because while there are buses, there is not a Metro system. The Twin Cities are a very safe place to live. The university facilities are pretty average from what I have seen at other law schools.

Status: Current student, full-time
Dates of Enrollment: 9/2002-Submit Date
Survey Submitted: March 2005

The quality of life at Minneapolis is always rated as among the best, if not first, in the country. The city is safe, clean and cosmopolitan for one of its size. Housing is affordable. A lot of students live in Uptown or St. Paul or downtown Minneapolis. The bus system for students is great. You can get a bus pass for $50 a semester that will take you anywhere you need to go. The city runs special express bus lines from the university to neighborhoods where most students live. It is really convenient. Parking can be obtained for about $60 a month at the structure across the street or $3 a day in various lots. There are a few restaurants across the street from the law school (Chipotle, Noodles, Quiznos and a few local restaurant bars) and many more on the East Bank of campus. The law school facilities are good. We have an outstanding library. Last I heard, it was eighth largest in the country. Our law librarians are geniuses and extremely helpful. They also teach the most informative and useful classes that we take in law school on research. The classrooms are all wireless. The whole building has wireless access and each desk has a power outlet for laptop use.

Status: Current student, full-time
Dates of Enrollment: 8/2003-Submit Date
Survey Submitted: February 2004

The law school is on the West Bank of campus, separated from the East Bank by the Mississippi river. The West Bank is comprised of the law school and other graduate school buildings. The East Bank is the main part of campus, comprised of undergraduate classrooms and dorms, as well as athletic facilities. There are both advantages and disadvantages to this setup. On the positive side, students are in their own environment, away from the undergraduate life of the college and able to focus on studies while associating with mostly other students of the same experience and mindset.

Status: Current student, full-time
Dates of Enrollment: 8/2002-Submit Date
Survey Submitted: October 2003

You will spend almost all of your time at the law school, and will be cut off from general campus life. The law school's facilities are ok, but not great. The architecture leaves much to be desired, and you hardly feel like you are surrounded by splendor, but the place works. You will have wireless access

Read all of Vault's Law School Surveys at www.vault.com/lawschool — get complete surveys on top law schools, expert advice on application essays, LSAT prep and more.

VAULT CAREER LIBRARY   361

anywhere you go in the school. Pretty much only 2Ls and 3Ls get study carrels, so you'll have to stake out space at one of the tables in the library. Generally only an issue for a couple hours in the middle of the day. The school has a cafe, but the selection is limited. Across the street there are several restaurants which are of mediocre quality, but they are popular.

 Social Life

Status: Alumnus/a, full-time
Dates of Enrollment: 9/1998-5/2001
Survey Submitted: March 2006

First-year social life seems to center around a weekly Bar Review event at a local bar. There is a law fraternity, and there are frequent events at the school itself. Lots of dating happens. The Twin Cities have lots of theater, book stores, sporting events and museums and a variety of music (including jazz, classical, rock to offer. People generally have a very good time.

Status: Alumnus/a, full-time
Dates of Enrollment: 9/2001-5/2004
Survey Submitted: March 2006

Most law students go to Bar Review every Thursday night. One person from the "B" section becomes the Bar Review guy and he selects a bar each week and puts out flyers for all to attend. He also publishes a bi-monthly newsletter on the social happenings of Bar Review and law school gossip.

The school also does a yearly musical production, put on by "TORTS." They involve students and professors and do auditions for players and support teams. There is one law school fraternity called the Gamma House. Many of the law school parties happen at this frat, and they are always very well-attended by all student levels.

Status: Alumnus/a, full-time
Dates of Enrollment: 9/1997-5/2000
Survey Submitted: April 2005

There were lots of opportunities to go out with law school friends, with up to 10 bars and restaurants just blocks away. I was active in many student groups, and found this a great avenue to making friends and professional contacts with alumni. Town Hall, Sargeant Preston's and Grandma's were favorite local establishments.

Status: Current student, full-time
Dates of Enrollment: 8/2002-Submit Date
Survey Submitted: March 2005

As a married student, I don't have as much information about this as some other people might, but there are a large number of student organizations at the law school, including a "fraternity," which has a house where students can apply to live for a very reasonable price. There is a very well-attended weekly social scene at Bar Review. The law school also has an annual musical, which has become a huge success in recent years and is a good way for students to get to know each other in a totally social setting.

Status: Current student, full-time
Dates of Enrollment: 9/2002-Submit Date
Survey Submitted: March 2005

As for social life, probably like every law school we have the weekly Bar Review. Bar review is at a rotating venue (always a bar) for a weekly get together. Mostly first-year law students go to Bar Review to get to know each other. The law school also sponsors events that are fun. I managed to avoid dating other law students, but it happens. Minneapolis has a lot of great bars, ethnic restaurants and a hip music scene. Students are sociable and friendly. A particular highlight of the year is the Law School Musical!

Status: Current student, full-time
Dates of Enrollment: 8/2003-Submit Date
Survey Submitted: February 2004

Many of the first-year law students tend to spend the majority of their social time with other law students. Each Thursday night a first-year law student, termed Bar Review man, picks a different bar in the Minneapolis area and a large portion of the students attend Bar Review. This offers a chance to socialize with other students in a relaxed atmosphere while also allowing students that are new to the area to discover many of the hot spots around town. Popular areas include downtown and uptown, which has a more small town privately owned feel than the typical big city downtown feel. Sergeant Preston's, Grandma's and Town Hall Brewery are all within walking distance of the law school and popular places for students to go to lunch or relax after class.

There are also a large number of student organizations, both at the law school and at other graduate and professional schools that offer students a more traditional way to meet other students, while also pursuing common interests. Other events include intramural sporting events with other local law schools, group trips to U of Minn sporting events and a student-written and produced play (generally a parody involving poking fun at the law school experience) each year.

Status: Current student, full-time
Dates of Enrollment: 8/2002-Submit Date
Survey Submitted: October 2003

The Thursday evening Bar Review is a big deal for 1Ls. Don't miss the first few Bar Reviews. Also, be sure to show up for the Halloween Party at the Gamma House, which is the law school fraternity house. The "fraternity" isn't much, but the first couple parties they throw are well attended. There is limited interaction between upper-level students and 1Ls.

Some students will have families or be married to their books, but a number of students are very social. Most sections organize as smaller social groups. Expect most of your friends to come from the section in which you are placed. People are pretty laid-back here, and competition is fairly muted. People want to win, but they want to win "Minnesota nice." The only time things get a little rough is during interviewing season in the fall. People who are succeeding tend to feel good, while people who are not tend to be a little bitter. It isn't a major issue, however.

The restaurant scene here is mediocre. Vegans and vegetarians will have few options unless they cook for themselves. (Ecopolitan is a raw food restaurant, but it is not very good. Good Earth is more organic than vegetarian, but it is about as good as you will get. There are some other co-op places, but quality is mixed.) There are few truly great upscale restaurants, but that should rarely be a concern for poor law students. As for lunch spots in between classes, walking-distance options are extremely limited. If you want a quick bite, and you eat meat, Chipotle is a hugely popular choice. The burritos are pretty good and you will see the Chipotle brown bag as a staple around the school. The Winery is one option if you don't care about health codes. Another popular option is trying to pick up free pizza from the myriad of extracurricular activities during the lunch hour. Don't worry about feeling guilty, they openly use the pizza to ramp up attendance.

 The School Says

One of the elite public law schools, the University of Minnesota Law School's location in the midst of a thriving, cosmopolitan area provides a host of unique benefits. Students enjoy access to a world-class research university and to the Twin Cities, one of the most progressive and livable metropolitan communities in the country. Following are tidbits of information. Please contact the admissions office or our web site for more!

Faculty members are prolific and influential scholars, having published over 160 books and 1,400 articles. Members of the faculty include the recent chair of the United Nations Sub-Commission on the Promotion and Protection of Human Rights (the first U.S. citizen to chair the commission since Eleanor Roosevelt), a State Department Counselor on International Law and members of the Brookings Institution. But while scholarship has earned the faculty national acclaim, their equally energetic passion for teaching and mentoring, along with a 13:1 student-faculty ratio, have earned them the respect and appreciation of their students.

With 257 students in the entering class, the student body is large enough to enjoy the benefits of diverse backgrounds, perspectives, and interests, while remaining small enough to foster the kind of collegial and supportive community that is a hallmark of Minnesota life. Although the atmosphere and camaraderie reflect distinctly Minnesotan values, 28 states, five countries and 120 undergraduate institutions are represented in the current JD class.

The award-winning Walter F. Mondale Hall offers wireless Internet access for students and houses the entire law school community, including faculty offices, research institutes, classrooms, auditorium, cafeteria, bookstore, the law clinic, student organization offices, student lockers, lounge areas and computer lab. Mondale Hall also houses the law library, which is the eighth largest in the United States, and is unique in that it offers students 24-hour access.

With 19 clinics, Minnesota has one of the country's largest clinical programs. Students represent real clients under the tutelage of clinic faculty. Over 60 percent of the second- and third-year students participate in a clinic prior to graduation, compared to the national participation average of 25 percent. Clinic students provide 18,000 hours of pro bono legal services every year.

Minnesota hosts international exchange programs in France, Germany, Ireland, Holland, Spain and Sweden. A newly-created summer program now exists in China.

Minnesota sponsors four student-edited law journals, eight moot court programs and an extensive legal writing program. More than 40 student organizations in addition to numerous intramural sports groups provide an active learning environment.

Read all of Vault's Law School Surveys at www.vault.com/lawschool — get complete surveys on top law schools, expert advice on applicaton essays, LSAT prep and more.

VAULT CAREER LIBRARY **363**

Mississippi College School of Law

Admissions Office
Mississippi College School of Law
151 E. Griffith Street
Jackson, MS 39201
Admissions phone: (601) 925-7150 or (800) 738-1236
Admissions e-mail: Pat Evans, pevans@mc.edu
Admissions URL: http://www.law.mc.edu/admissions/

 ## Admissions

Status: Current student, full-time
Dates of Enrollment: 8/2005-Submit Date
Survey Submitted: May 2006

The admissions process consists of filling out a basic application and writing an essay on a provided topic. Recommendation letters were not required although they were highly suggested. I did not have to go through an interview process. I mailed them my application, essay, application fee and sent a letter of recommendation. The school responded within a couple of weeks telling me that they had received my application and were considering it. About six weeks later, I received my acceptance letter.

Status: Alumnus/a, full-time
Dates of Enrollment: 8/2003-5/2006
Survey Submitted: May 2006

I enjoyed the admissions process at MCSOL. The first experience I had with the school was at their Preview Day and it was encouraging to see all they had to offer. The application process was not difficult and the admissions office was very helpful if I had any questions.

Status: Current student, full-time
Dates of Enrollment: 8/2003-Submit Date
Survey Submitted: May 2006

Very traditional admissions process. Combination of LSAT and undergrad GPA considered, along with additional information (extracurricular activities, community involvement). Dean Evans of the admissions office is extremely helpful and informative. Recent trend is that there are many more applications than usual, so the school is becoming a little more selective. Overall, the school is growing in size, as well as in quality of applications. As a result, the average LSAT/GPA combination has been rising.

Status: Current student, full-time
Dates of Enrollment: 8/2004-Submit Date
Survey Submitted: May 2006

The interview process is very thorough but fair and not complicated. The school does a good job at judging the whole person as opposed to simply viewing candidate's scores. The admissions office was very helpful the entire way through and very personal. If I called the office to ask a question, they would actually know who I was by name.

Status: Current student, full-time
Dates of Enrollment: 8/2003-Submit Date
Survey Submitted: May 2006

The admissions personnel at MCSOL are great. They are easy to get in touch with and always willing to answer questions. Although MCSOL weighs GPA and LSAT scores, the admissions selection is also based on activities, community service and recommendations. Advice on getting in: have at least a 3.0 from undergrad and at least a 150 on LSAT. The lower your GPA, the higher your LSAT should be; and the lower the LSAT, the higher the GPA should be. I was admitted with a 3.3 GPA and a 155 on the LSAT.

Status: Current student, full-time
Dates of Enrollment: 8/2004-Submit Date
Survey Submitted: May 2006

The admissions department was very helpful and was always eager to help. In addition to the school's admission staff/faculty, the school also has STAR students who help recruit and introduce new students into the world of law school. I found the STAR program, in conjunction with the typical admissions staff, to be very effective. There was always someone who could answer a question, be it when the application deadline was or where students new to the area should live/shop.

Another aspect that I really liked was the fact that the dean sent a personal note to me after I was accepted. That is certainly one of the many advantages to attending a smaller school. You are more than a number and you feel that from the moment you are accepted.

Also, I cannot remember the exact topic we were to write on for our admissions essay. However, I do remember the fact that I was pleased with the fact that the question was rather open-ended. If gave me a chance to really express what I thought was key information about myself and why I should be accepted. Had the topic been narrow, I do not think that I would have been as pleased.

As for selectivity, I think that the school is competitive in the caliber of students it accepts. MCSOL has come a LONG way in the past 10 years and I think that the school can finally afford to be a little more selective. However, this is at odds with the school's desire to grow. I enjoy the small classes and the intimate quality of the school as a whole. I hope that the admissions board does not decide to accept more than 200 incoming 1Ls at any point.

Status: Current student, full-time
Dates of Enrollment: 8/2003-Submit Date
Survey Submitted: May 2006

I cannot say enough concerning the admissions process and the individual focus on prospective students. MSCOL's admission procedures are not solely "numbers" based. Their goal is to have a diverse student body with life experiences that bring different perspectives and knowledge to that class. While maintaining the highest academic standards and achievements as a starting point for consideration of admission, the interest is much broader in what each individual can bring to enhance the law school program. Each applicant is asked to submit a "personal essay," which I know for certain that the admissions committee reads and evaluates. I am a non-traditional student, a mother of three and a grandmother of six. I know when reviewing my application the committee did not just see numbers from an LSAT score and GPA, but they saw me as a person with value and insight from my life experiences. I am grateful for the willingness to step out of the box of numbers and explore the resources and assets that such a diverse student body can bring to the law school journey.

Status: Current student, full-time JD/MBA
Dates of Enrollment: 8/2004-Submit Date
Survey Submitted: May 2006

MC was not previously renown for its selectivity. But after the addition of our new dean, the quality of the students selected to attend MC has be elevated such that there are numerous locals who are now rejected in order to admit students from other regions with higher qualifications. As for me, I was impressed with the direct attention MC provides to its applicants. They kept in constant contact with me throughout the process and when I was accepted, the dean of the law school called me on a Saturday to congratulate me. I was overwhelmed. Also, when I arrived on the first day of school, many of the professors already knew my name. MC is an amazingly familial school.

Academics

Status: Current student, full-time
Dates of Enrollment: 8/2005-Submit Date
Survey Submitted: May 2006

I really enjoy the program at MC. The classes are very challenging and there are some really good professors. Of course, as with any school, there are some not so great professors. All in all though, the faculty is very knowledgeable and they take a considerable interest in student development and making sure students understand the material. Classes are assigned your first year, and after that you register on the Internet. To get into popular classes, you have to participate in a random lottery selection and if you are chosen, you can register for the class.

The school has a blind grading policy. Each student is assigned an exam number to put on the tests instead of his or her name. The professors do not find out the name of the person until they have submitted the grades. At that point, the professor has the discretion to adjust the grade up or down by half a point based on things like attendance, participation and preparedness for class. Grading is on a four-point scale and is divided into A, B+, B, C+, C, etc. The workload is pretty heavy, which is typical of law schools in general, but it is manageable.

Status: Alumnus/a, full-time
Dates of Enrollment: 8/2003-5/2006
Survey Submitted: May 2006

Overall, I believe the academics at MCSOL are really good. The classes, like any school, are what you make of them. Meaning that you can select a stressful courseload or take easier classes outside of the required courses. I have friends at other law schools and from their experiences, I believe that MCSOL has a more stringent grading scale than others.

Status: Current student, full-time
Dates of Enrollment: 8/2003-Submit Date
Survey Submitted: May 2006

The first year is a prescribed courseload (Civ Pro, Property, Torts, Contracts, Criminal Law). Second year begins the freedom to choose courses. Only courses required after the first year are Appellate Advocacy and Ethics. There are several VERY good professors who are highly sought after during class registration. The quality of instruction is outstanding in most cases. There will always be a few class/professor combinations that do not work well. But by and large, the quality of the courses at MCSOL is exemplary. The grading is mostly the traditional competitive curve procedure. The workload is normal for law school, heavy during the first year and manageable after that.

Status: Current student, full-time
Dates of Enrollment: 8/2004-Submit Date
Survey Submitted: May 2006

The academics at Mississippi College are wonderful. It is a very thorough program focused on helping the students become successful lawyers. On the whole, the classes are great and fairly easy to get into. The professors are very fair and the workload is manageable. I have a small child and it has been easy for me to go to school without sacrificing all of my time with her.

Status: Current student, full-time
Dates of Enrollment: 8/2003-Submit Date
Survey Submitted: May 2006

The law school curriculum is exhausting. The first-year classes are geared to allow each student to gain a definite base for understanding and interpreting the law. The workload that first year is a little overwhelming and can be daunting. The result is that if you survive the "baptism by fire" you will be able to achieve graduation. More importantly, there is a major emphasis on ensuring that all students prepare themselves adequately for the Bar. The professors are extremely interested in each student as individuals and in their progress. For the most part there is a great deal of accommodation provided for each student's needs and schedule after that first year. The grading is quite difficult in that MCSOL curves to a C so anything above that is harder to achieve, yet worth the effort.

Status: Current student, full-time JD/MBA
Dates of Enrollment: 8/2004-Submit Date

Survey Submitted: May 2006

MC robustly utilizes the Socratic Method, even in upper-level classes. They are very concerned with substance of the courses and that each student is actually learning the law and not merely receiving a grade. The professors are often comical but caring and they are very assessable. Grading is blind and fair. The classes are designed to prepare student for the bar and the classes rarely close to ensure that each student who wants to take a particular class is granted that opportunity. The workload is not overbearing but is enough to keep the average student busy.

Status: Current student, full-time
Dates of Enrollment: 8/2004-Submit Date
Survey Submitted: May 2006

Of course, there are a few things that I would change. For instance, at least some of the classes (a VERY small percentage) are not worth the time it takes to come to class. Students learn little, if anything, from these classes. They are very popular classes though because students need "fillers" in their schedules.

There are some problems with the registration process. However, this is a new process and I understand that the school has not worked all of the kinks out just yet. The new system has caused a bit of a headache when trying to get popular classes. To the school's credit, it has tried to increase the size and quantity of many of the popular classes. For instance, in the coming spring semester, another Ethics class was added and the most popular Ethics class (with a particular professor) was increased to hold 100 students.

Smaller classes are still hard to get into, but I think that will always be the case. I am not sure that MCSOL (or any school) will ever be able to make a schedule of classes that will allow everyone to take exactly what they want when they want it.

I would say that the majority of the professors are WONDERFUL. Most of them take the time to really know the students and are actually interested in what the students have to say and in student progress.

The workload is what I would consider typical for law schools in the region. However, there are some two-hour classes that require more work and preparation than many three- or four-hour classes. I think that the school should address this by allowing more than two credit hours for courses with a larger work-load OR by putting a maximum limit on what the professors in a two-hour class can require.

Grading is fair. I especially like the fact that there is not a strict curve in place. Teachers are not required to give a certain number of A's, B's and C's. (Some students swear this is not true though.) I do wish that final grades would be made available a little sooner. It takes some professors almost a month to get grades posted.

Status: Current student, full-time
Dates of Enrollment: 7/2003-Submit Date
Survey Submitted: May 2006

The professors at MC have been great. The procedure classes (Civ Pro, Fed Juris) certainly excel to the top. MC has done an excellent job of recruiting new professors the last few years and I have very few complaints about the quality education I received. Basic legal analysis is the overall focus and we have truly learned to "think like a lawyer." A perfect example of this is the fact that I competed in the national bankruptcy competition in New York without ever having taken bankruptcy. My partner and I advanced the final argument and won the best brief overall, competing against schools such as Northwestern, Miami, Emory, Hofstra, Connecticut, Kansas, Tennessee, Alabama and Gonzaga.

Status: Current student, full-time
Dates of Enrollment: 8/2003-Submit Date
Survey Submitted: May 2006

MCSOL follows the typical first-year program (Torts, Contracts, Criminal Law, Property, Civil Procedure and Legal Analysis). The class sizes during the first year consist of about 60 to 80 people per section. I think the sections are larger now, however. The professors are wonderful. All have different personalities. After your first year you can take what you want, but you must take Evidence, Constitutional Law and Ethics.

Read all of Vault's Law School Surveys at www.vault.com/lawschool — get complete surveys on top law schools, expert advice on applicaton essays, LSAT prep and more.

VAULT CAREER LIBRARY 365

Employment Prospects

Status: Current student, full-time
Dates of Enrollment: 8/2005-Submit Date
Survey Submitted: May 2006

The law school is located in the heart of downtown Jackson, near many of the larger firms (including several regional firms). A large number of firms conduct on-campus interviews for summer associate positions. Graduates are employed in most of the larger firms and several smaller firms. There are also several graduates with their own practice. The school has an employment director who is very helpful and does a good job of finding employment prospects and passing the information on to the students.

Status: Alumnus/a, full-time
Dates of Enrollment: 8/2003-5/2006
Survey Submitted: May 2006

Speaking from my personal experience, MCSOL has a very good reputation among practicing attorneys in central Mississippi. I believe that the prestige associated with MCSOL is definitely on the rise!

Status: Current student, full-time
Dates of Enrollment: 8/2003-Submit Date
Survey Submitted: May 2006

MCSOL has a short history in the state and has been working very hard to reach its current position in the legal community in MS. Within the last few years, employers in the state have become much more interested in the students from MCSOL. In the interest of full disclosure, the legal job market in MS has been tightening up recently. As a result, fewer firms are hiring ANYONE. But when firms do hire, MCSOL stands on equal footing with students from any other comparable schools. The professors and administration at MCSOL have done a great job in improving the quality of the school, and that is paying dividends in the job search. From my limited perspective, I can report that fellow members of the Law Review here at MCSOL have received jobs in private practice, government service and state and federal clerkships. At least two graduates this year have received federal appellate clerkships with Circuit Courts, and several more students have received District Court clerkships and state-level clerkships.

The career services office is very helpful in arranging a large number of on-campus interviews, ranging from small to large firms, to government and military organizations. In addition, the career services office also keeps students notified of many internships and study abroad programs. Finally, the alumni association is only just now beginning to grow large enough to have an impact on the school's growth and job prospects. The school is only 30-something years old, and it has taken some time for the alumni to become active and strong enough to really help the school. Having said that, in the last two or three years, the alumni have become very involved in placement and recruiting, and I expect that this will only continue to increase in the future.

Status: Current student, full-time
Dates of Enrollment: 8/2003-Submit Date
Survey Submitted: May 2006

I believe that because MCSOL is in Jackson, the capital city, we have a great relationship with the legal community and lots of firms in this area hire from this school. The market seems to be tight right now so some don't have jobs, but I know last year all but one person was placed in legal employment. On-campus recruiting is good too.

Status: Current student, full-time
Dates of Enrollment: 8/2004-Submit Date
Survey Submitted: May 2006

First of all, I would like to say that the recruiting department at our school is wonderful. On-campus interviews are scheduled for all grade levels (1L, 2L and 3L). The firms who participate in the on-campus process are quite selective. However, they are some of the most prestigious firms in the Jackson-metro area.

 # Quality of Life

Status: Current student, full-time
Dates of Enrollment: 8/2005-Submit Date
Survey Submitted: May 2006

There is an apartment complex right across the street from the law school where several students live, and there are also several apartment complexes within 10 minutes of the law school. The school also provides students with the option of on-campus housing located on the main campus in Clinton, about 20 minutes away. The law school recently opened up a new student center with a food counter offering sandwiches, salads, muffins, bagels, smoothies and Starbucks coffee. The school provides on-campus security. The downtown area is safe during the day with many restaurants within walking distance of the school. At night, the back parking lot remains open and security is on hand. It is safe around the school and the parking lot, but I wouldn't go walking around downtown by myself at night. The city is currently trying to lower the crime in downtown, so it could become safer at night.

Status: Alumnus/a, full-time
Dates of Enrollment: 8/2003-5/2006
Survey Submitted: May 2006

The campus at MCSOL is topnotch. The college has made great strides in the quality of facilities over the past five years. Most notably being the two new buildings being added to the campus and the renovation of the "old" building. With MCSOL be in an urban environment, the administration is aware of the dangers associated with this and provides security for the buildings and grounds.

Status: Current student, full-time
Dates of Enrollment: 8/2003-Submit Date
Survey Submitted: May 2006

Housing is virtually nonexistent. The school is located in the heart of downtown Jackson, MS. Students are expected to find their own housing, which increases the cost of the education. However, the school has a distinct advantage in that it is in Jackson and is a center of activity for the legal community in MS—CLE classes, seminars, speaking events. Job opportunities are more common as a result, helping to offset these additional expenses.

There have been some cases where students have acquired housing at the main campus, about 20 minutes away from the law school in Clinton, MS. However this is not advisable, particularly for the first year. There is an older no-frills apartment complex across the street from the law school with relatively low rent and is fairly well-maintained and secured (Sterling Towers). As I recall, the rent is approximately $500 per month including all utilities, except cable and Internet. The apartments are one-bedrooms with a separate living room/kitchenette area. Not glamorous, but manageable. The school's facilities are comprised of three buildings: the old classroom and faculty building; the new classroom building; and the student center with snacks/coffee, bookstore and auditorium. The school has "round the clock" private security guards, and the guards have a reputation in the downtown area for being extremely protective. As a result, the less desirable elements of downtown stay away from the block which contains the school and Sterling Towers. In addition, the area nearest to the school has been under a new urban renewal project that has been greatly improving the immediate vicinity. Overall, the quality of life is good, with a low cost of living (notwithstanding the additional housing expenses), combined with a relatively slow pace of life. Add all this together, and the experience at the school is a fairly relaxed one.

Status: Current student, full-time
Dates of Enrollment: 8/2003-Submit Date
Survey Submitted: May 2006

Quality of Life at MCSOL is OK. The campus is not like a typical college campus in that it is located down town business district of Jackson, MS and not on the main campus of Mississippi College. Although crime in Jackson is an issue, the campus is safe. It is gated and there are some wonderful security guards who really look out for you. Overall, I have never felt like my safety was at issue.

Status: Current student, full-time
Dates of Enrollment: 7/2003-Submit Date
Survey Submitted: May 2006

The campus at MC is almost brand new. We have two new buildings with the old building having been renovated last summer. The facilities are second to none. All buildings have wireless Internet access and laptop capabilities.

Status: Current student, full-time
Dates of Enrollment: 8/2004-Submit Date
Survey Submitted: May 2006

The Jackson, MS area is not the most "happening" place to live. However, there are many safe places to live (safety is a key for most female students like myself). Most important to me is the campus security. We have two full-time security guards on campus. All of the students know these guards by name. I can personally say that since the school is downtown, it was key for me to know that I would be watched over and protected while I was walking from my car at 10 p.m. after leaving the library. The guards really are great and take the time to get the know the students.

While there is no on-campus housing for the law school, there are apartments across the street from the campus. Additionally, at orientation all new students are given an information packet with a list of places to shop, eat and live in the area.

Status: Current student, full-time
Dates of Enrollment: 8/2003-Submit Date
Survey Submitted: May 2006

Now, this is an area of concern. The school is located in downtown Jackson. The facility is amazing and drastic improvements have been made in the past two years to the physical facility. However, the area of town is less than desirable as far as living conditions. In any event, the school's effort to maintain a safe, secure environment is beyond reproach. There is always security and they are amazing men, who truly know each student by name. While the area concerns me, I personally felt safe once on the campus.

Status: Current student, full-time JD/MBA
Dates of Enrollment: 8/2004-Submit Date
Survey Submitted: May 2006

Across the street from the law school is a housing unit that is, at most, habitable. In addition, because of the school's central location, many students choose housing that is a 15 to 20 minute commute from the school. The neighborhood around the school is less than ideal, but it is for the most part safe. Our school has recently undergone renovations that have rendered the school more comfortable and visually pleasing.

The school schedule affords students the opportunity to maintain non-law school friendships and romantic relationships. I am married and my spouse and I have dinner together every night while my grades remain in the top of the class.

 Social Life

Status: Current student, full-time
Dates of Enrollment: 8/2005-Submit Date
Survey Submitted: May 2006

Students at the school have active social lives. The Student Bar Association (the school's version of SGA) plans several activities throughout the year, including back-to-school parties, a Halloween party, BBQs, a fish fry, a crawfish boil and softball tournament and a golf tournament to name a few. The Jackson area has a large number of bars and restaurants to choose from. Student favorites include Hal & Mal's, Old Venice, The Sportsmen's Lodge and Fenian's. There are also three malls and five movie theaters.

Status: Current student, full-time
Dates of Enrollment: 8/2003-Submit Date
Survey Submitted: May 2006

Since the law school is detached from the main campus, there is no real dorm or Greek life. However, the school is in downtown Jackson, which has access to many clubs and restaurante. Several local landmarks are worth the attention of

students: Stamp's Superburgers, Schimmel's, La Cazuela and others. Mississippi is not an overly exciting and hip place, but one can find plenty to do if he or she does not have unreasonable expectations.

Status: Current student, full-time
Dates of Enrollment: 8/2003-Submit Date
Survey Submitted: May 2006

Once again, this area is a little out of my personal experience range. However, for all those people who enjoy socializing with classmates outside the educational experience, there seems to be a "family" spirit at the school. While I personally do not have many occasions to be a part of that experience, even I am always included and invited to be a part of the school. I had a terrible accident my first year and was incapacitated for almost seven months. The support I received from my classmates was unbelievable. I probably would not have been able to continue my education without that support. MSCOL student life is fun and enjoyable, even though the stress and demands of law school are great. People seem to truly enjoy each other and socializing as a student body. There are always activities that involve not just the students, but their families and they are geared for everyone to be able to participate if they desire.

Status: Current student, full-time JD/MBA
Dates of Enrollment: 8/2004-Submit Date
Survey Submitted: May 2006

Mississippi College has a variety of law related organizations on campus such as Phi Alpha Delta, Phi Delta Phi, Mississippi Trial lawyers Association and Christian Legal Society, as well as organizations that are specific to our school such as STAR (Students Teaching, Assisting and Recruiting). To gain members, these organizations (excluding Christian Legal and STAR) often have social events at local bars and pubs.

Status: Current student, full-time
Dates of Enrollment: 8/2004-Submit Date
Survey Submitted: May 2006

Again, Jackson, MS is not the most "happening" place to live. However, there are numerous restaurants in the area—everything from hamburgers to sushi.

Most of the social events are hosted or put on by the Law Student Bar Association. These events are great because it allows all of the students to get together and really get to know each other. Among the annual LSBA events are the Halloween Party (lots of fun costumes!!), the Crawfish Boil/Softball Tournament, Flag Football Tournament, Summer Picnic, Barristers' Ball (kinda like law school prom) and other parties throughout the school year (i.e., this year we had a back to school party and an 80's Party)

The Jackson, MS area is also home to the Mississippi Braves (an Atlanta Braves farm team). Law students are often seen at these games during the week nights.

I can't really comment on the dating scene because I am married. Actually, I would say that a large number of the law school population is either married or engaged.

Status: Current student, full-time
Dates of Enrollment: 8/2003-Submit Date
Survey Submitted: May 2006

Jackson, although the largest city in the State of Mississippi, is relatively small in comparison to other U.S. cities. If you come to Jackson and you are from a large city out of state, be prepared to have less to do. The restaurants, shopping and bars are average, some better than others. There is a good theater here and a wonderful ballet. Remember, however, that you are in law school and the less distraction the better!!

 The School Says

Mississippi College School of Law is a mid-size law school with the feel of a smaller school. The law school offers a collegial atmosphere, a capital city setting, and a geographical diverse student body. The curriculum features courses that provide a thorough theoretical examination of a broad array of legal principles as well as courses that offer skill training and practical

Read all of Vault's Law School Surveys at www.vault.com/lawschool — get complete surveys on top law schools, expert advice on applicaton essays, LSAT prep and more.

VAULT CAREER LIBRARY   367

application. The distinguished faculty take a personal interest in student learning.

Law students have an opportunity to interact with the local legal community of judges and lawyers. There are opportunities for networking and service, which include a new Legal Aid Office that uses volunteer lawyers and students to provide legal services to the underserved. A respected group of judges and practitioners serve as adjuncts and teach skill courses such as Trial Practice and Alternative Disputes Resolution.

The law school campus is a modern one that provides a comfortable environment for classes and study. A library renovation project in the summer of 2007 will complete the building program for the school. All classrooms and seminar rooms are equipped with an audio-visual package, and wireless connections to the Internet are available throughout the campus. A new bookstore and food court are recent additions to the campus.

The Law School has increased the opportunities to participate in regional and national trial and appellate moot court competitions. This past year one of the teams placed second nationally in the Duberstein Bankruptcy Competition in New York and won the award for best brief. Another team advanced to the quarterfinals in the Pace Environmental Law Competition in New York. Yet another team won the regional competition in the Frederick Douglass Moot Court Competition.

The Law School uses a rolling admissions process and encourages applicants to apply early. The admission deadline of June 1 permits consideration of some outstanding applicants who take the February LSAT or who decide later in the year to apply to the Law School. The admissions committee evaluates applicants using a "whole person" concept and seeks applicants who demonstrate drive, academic achievement, character, leadership and service. Merit scholarships are awarded as part of the application process and also after the first and second year to recognize academic achievement.

Tuition is "locked in" and will remain the same for all three, continuous years of law school. This helps students plan and budget.

Applicants are invited to review information about the Law School at www.law.mc.edu and to visit the school. The Admissions Office will be pleased to meet with you individually and to arrange for a tour of the school and a classroom visit.

Saint Louis University School of Law

Office of Admissions
3700 Lindell Blvd
St. Louis, MO 63108
Admissions phone: (314)-977-2800
Admissions e-mail: admissions@law.slu.edu
Admissions URL: http://law.slu.edu/admissions/

 ## Admissions

Status: Alumnus/a, full-time
Dates of Enrollment: 8/1997-5/2000
Survey Submitted: March 2006

Admissions was standard as with all other major law schools; LSAT scores were considered along with an application and personal statement. Weight was given equally among LSAT scores and essays. There was an "orientation" before orientation that allowed potential students the opportunity to come in and sit and listen to professors and students talk about SLU and what life is like as a law student there, which was really helpful and made the school seem like a very open and warm environment—more so than other law schools I visited.

Status: Alumnus/a, full-time
Dates of Enrollment: 8/1998-5/2001
Survey Submitted: April 2005

The admissions process was fair and highly selective. I would emphasize obtaining a high LSAT score. As far as I'm concerned, you either get in or you don't, and if you do—don't ask why!

Status: Alumnus/a, full-time
Dates of Enrollment: 8/1998-5/2001
Survey Submitted: April 2005

The admissions process was fairly smooth. No hang ups, no interviews. I sent what they asked for, they sent some materials for me to review while I was waiting for a decision and then I received my acceptance letter. After that there was some, but not an extensive effort, to convince me to attend that it was the right place for me.

Status: Alumnus/a, full-time
Dates of Enrollment: 8/2000-5/2003
Survey Submitted: April 2005

Very personal; competitive.

Status: Current student, full-time
Dates of Enrollment: 8/2005-Submit Date
Survey Submitted: August 2005

The admissions process was straightforward and like many other ABA approved law schools. I wrote an essay describing my interest in law and answered basic questions that covered my undergraduate qualifications.

Status: Alumnus/a, full-time
Dates of Enrollment: 8/2001-5/2004
Survey Submitted: March 2005

Saint Louis University has a rolling admissions process. Applications are accepted starting September first for the following academic year and decisions are made in the late fall. The law school is selective and the competition for scholarships is very competitive. Therefore, it is advised that applications be submitted in the early fall if interested in scholarships. Admissions acceptance and scholarship awards are made concurrently, and generally all scholarships are awarded by February first.

 ## Academics

Status: Alumnus/a, full-time
Dates of Enrollment: 8/1997-5/2000
Survey Submitted: March 2006

First year, the class is split into two sections and all classes for the entire year (both semesters) are pre-set with all the traditional 1L bar related courses. I thought the quality of professors was very high. Grading was more or less on a curve; it was competitive. The workload was manageable and not overly demanding. Most classes were some form of the traditional Socratic Method. 2L and 3L students could pick from an array of classes and there was no set plan. Grades were distributed online and for the most part, professors were timely. I never had a problem getting into a class I wanted.

Status: Current Student, full-time
Dates of Enrollment: 8/2004-Submit Date
Survey Submitted: April 2005

The classes are definitely good. Although some of the professors should not be teaching what they teach, the overall quality is good. Some of the more popular classes are harder to get into than I would appreciate, but I haven't had too much trouble to date.

Status: Alumnus/a, full-time
Dates of Enrollment: 8/1998-5/2001
Survey Submitted: April 2005

As with all law schools, the workload was high, yet manageable, and the instructors were well-qualified, with many being leaders in their fields—corporate white collar crime, UCC, securities, corporations, immigration and intellectual property. The school puts a strong emphasis on legal theory and the Socratic Method, which I feel is very helpful in getting students to interact and think on their feet. The quality of classes I took was high, with the exception of two classes. Those two professors are no longer with the university.

I had no problem getting into popular classes, even if they were filled. Generally, enough people switched around at the beginning of the semester that you could get into even the most popular classes through the waitlist. Grading was tough. I believe the forced median was 83, which wound up being around 85 at the end of three years. I wound up at about 84. It takes a lot of work to get an A, but that's how law school should be. I chose my courses according to professor, not by course, and have not regretted it. For example, though I had no interest in practicing tax, my favorite course was Federal Income Tax because of the professor. As with anywhere, there were a few instructors whom I didn't care for. To my knowledge, none are with the university anymore.

Status: Alumnus/a, full-time
Dates of Enrollment: 9/1997-5/2000
Survey Submitted: April 2005

Overall, I thought the quality of the academic program was high. With few exceptions, very talented professors teach the core courses. I also understand that the school has taken important steps (after my graduation) to improve the Research and Writing course that first-year students take. I truly like and admire many (though certainly not all) of the professors I studied with. The clinical program is especially strong and worth becoming involved in. I never had a problem getting into the classes or clinics that I wanted.

Status: Alumnus/a, full-time
Dates of Enrollment: 8/2001-5/2004
Survey Submitted: March 2005

The academic nature of the program focuses on teaching students how to "think like lawyers." Compared to other schools, there is not a lot of "spoon feeding" of the material and therefore some students seem to struggle in areas outside their "comfort zone." For my particular area of focus (health law), I found the quality of classes to be outstanding. The classes taught by the adjunct

Read all of Vault's Law School Surveys at www.vault.com/lawschool — get complete surveys on top law schools, expert advice on applicaton essays, LSAT prep and more.

VAULT CAREER LIBRARY 369

professors, in particular, gave the students a real world understanding of current issues in health law and gave the students a solid foundation for the first years of practice. Registration is done online which means that classes with the popular professors tend to fill up immediately; however, there are circumstances where a student may talk to a professor and explain their circumstances and still get into the class, but this is generally on a case-by-case basis.

Grading is pretty tough, especially in the first year. The mean GPA for the first year is around a 2.7 with only 5 to 10 percent of students in each class receiving A's. In the second and third years, the mean is around a 2.9 with 5 to 15 percent of students eligible for A's, in smaller classes and seminars the means and number of A's that can be awarded are higher. As a result, it is sometimes difficult to compete with students from other law schools, especially in markets where employers are unfamiliar with the "deflated" grading system at St. Louis University. I found that most of the professors were genuinely interested in the students and were fairly accessible. The workload depends on the class. Generally, the average is about two and a half hours for each hour of class.

 Employment Prospects

Status: Alumnus/a, full-time
Dates of Enrollment: 8/1997-5/2000
Survey Submitted: March 2006

On campus interviews were conducted and I found the school employment center to be helpful. Finding prestigious jobs is a little tough if you are not in the top 20 percent or so of the class because you are also competing with law students from Washington Univ. for all the top jobs in St. Louis and Wash U is ranked higher than SLU. I believe somewhere around 85 percent of the students in my class had jobs secured by the time they graduated, maybe more. Most everyone I know had a job at a law firm by they time they graduated. I did not find the alumni network to be helpful, though other SLU grads in St. Louis are very positive about hiring new SLU grads; and there are a lot of them.

Status: Alumnus/a, full-time
Dates of Enrollment: 9/2000-5/2003
Survey Submitted: April 2005

A great school to choose if you want to practice in Chicago, D.C., St. Louis or anywhere in the Midwest.

Status: Alumnus/a, full-time
Dates of Enrollment: 8/2001-5/2004
Survey Submitted: March 2005

Saint Louis University has a strong regional reputation. However, once out of the St. Louis metropolitan area, its reputation fades. Also, because grades tend to be deflated compared to other law schools, students sometimes find it difficult to get jobs outside the St. Louis market. However, the Health Law Program has a strong national reputation, and alumni from the Health Law Program can be found all over the country. On-campus recruiting is great if you want to stay in St. Louis and you are in the top 10 percent of the class. Unfortunately, there are only a handful of employers from outside the St. Louis area who do on-campus interviews. If you want to go outside the St. Louis market, you are left to your own resources. However, the professors at the law school have a lot of connections, so it is imperative to develop strong relationships with them. The professors are great with helping students find jobs, especially outside St. Louis.

 Quality of Life

Status: Alumnus/a, full-time
Dates of Enrollment: 8/1997-5/2000
Survey Submitted: March 2006

The neighborhood around the campus can be dangerous, as is true with any city school, but campus itself is beautiful, well-lit, patrolled and has beautiful architecture. The school did a major addition building out a nice library with lots of windows and study areas.

SLU is a little bit of a commuter school, no one really lives on campus at the graduate level. Rental housing is plentiful in hip areas such as the West End or Clayton, although can be expensive. St. Louis is a wonderful city to live in and a lot of fun nightlife things to do. Because of the two major universities, it is more cultural and diverse than most midwestern cities.

Status: Alumnus/a, full-time
Dates of Enrollment: 8/1998-5/2001
Survey Submitted: April 2005

There is both on-campus and off-campus housing that is all fairly safe. There are some less safe areas a little ways from campus, but just stay west of the school and you will do fine. Pretty cheap living, especially if you are coming from the East Coast. You can ride bike to school if you want. Plenty of things to do to distract you from school if you are looking for that. Never once did I feel I needed to get out because the quality of life was poor.

Status: Current student, full-time
Dates of Enrollment: 8/2003-Submit Date
Survey Submitted: April 2005

I love my neighborhood and it's less than 20 minutes from the school. The campus is BEAUTIFUL and it is nice to have all the classes in one building. Housing is one of those things where you need to be picky and talk to other people about neighborhoods first. The school puts out a survey of which neighborhoods the students most enjoy and which landlords are sketchy.

Status: Alumnus/a, full-time
Dates of Enrollment: 8/2001-5/2004
Survey Submitted: March 2005

There is no on-campus housing for law students. St. Louis University is an urban campus, but the university has done a remarkable job with trying to create a bonafide campus. Probably the biggest problem with the campus is the location—it is located in a "not so good" part of town, and, as a result, there are issues with crime and safety, ranging from petty theft to stolen cars. However, the public safety department does an admirable job trying to keep students apprised of crime and safety issues. As far as car theft goes, it generally occurs on the side streets near the university; students who park in the parking garage generally have no problems with car theft.

 Social Life

Status: Alumnus/a, full-time
Dates of Enrollment: 8/1997-5/2000
Survey Submitted: March 2006

I had a great social life at SLU. I found the law school to be very collegial and less competitive—not to say that competition wasn't there, but the people were for the most part very friendly and very well adjusted. The professors were extremely "open-door" and really valued the academic nature of law school.

There is/was one bar on campus that we all hung out at for 1 cent pitchers (that doesn't sound so good these days!) and generally the law school held social functions at least two to three times a month for one group or another. I made some of the best and strongest friends at SLU. I never wanted for a social life,;the city has so many wonderful things to do: baseball, hockey, Forest Park, great trendy restaurants and bars in Clayton, golf courses, the Galleria, the Fox Theater and the museums.

Party in Park every second Thursday of the summer months (a huge street party—500 or so people) in Clayton is where all the young (and old) professionals come out of there offices or in from down town and just hang out and drink, the restaurants all serve food and beverages on the street and it's a great environment to relax after work and meet people. St. Louis is a great mix of young singles and people who are married and starting families; it didn't feel like a slow Midwestern town.

Status: Alumnus/a, full-time
Dates of Enrollment: 8/1998-5/2001
Survey Submitted: April 2005

The social life at the law school was very enjoyable. I'm one of those strange people who loved law school as a whole, and this included the social life, which I found to be as memorable as in college. The St. Louis area has numerous wonderful restaurants, including several off-the-track hole in the walls. The law school has a free happy hour in the student commons every Friday (your tuition does not pay for the beer), which is a good way to meet up with people and make plans for the weekend.

Status: Alumnus/a, full-time
Dates of Enrollment: 8/1998-5/2001
Survey Submitted: April 2005

There were a lot of opportunities in the area, both inexpensive and not, both near to campus and not. There were plenty of bars and places to eat, but not the huge variety of quality places to eat like in bigger cities. But, if you spend a little time exploring and investigating, some very fine places to eat can be found. There are many school-sponsored activities and social opportunities with fellow students and community members at-large.

Status: Alumnus/a, full-time
Dates of Enrollment: 8/2000-5/2003
Survey Submitted: April 2005

The social life was as good as a social life can be in law school. There are many areas in St. Louis with culture, fun places to go and things to see.

Status: Alumnus/a, full-time
Dates of Enrollment: 8/2001-5/2004
Survey Submitted: March 2005

The social life is adequate for law school. As many of the law students are in the mid to late 20s, there are not as many social activities as in the undergraduate program. However, there is a softball league on Fridays during the spring and fall; Barristers Ball (Law Prom), auction, Halloween party and other events.

 The School Says

Located in midtown St. Louis, Saint Louis University School of Law is perfectly positioned to provide students with unparalleled exposure to law firms, corporate offices and governmental agencies. Local, state and federal courthouses are just minutes from campus, including the Thomas F. Eagleton Courthouse, the largest federal courthouse in the United States. Additionally, many of the city's colorful, eclectic and culturally diverse neighborhoods are in close proximity to the School, offering an array of dining, entertainment and artistic options for those times when a break is necessary. St. Louis also boasts one of the largest urban parks in the nation, which houses the St. Louis Zoo, the Muny Opera, the Missouri Historical Society, the St. Louis Science Center and the St. Louis Art Museum.

The School features one of the premier Health Law Studies programs in the nation, along with specialized Centers in Employment Law and International and Comparative Law, and offers concentrations in Business Transactional Law, Civil Litigation Skills, Criminal Litigation Skills, Taxation and Urban Development, Land Use and Environmental Law. The School also offers intensive dual-degree programs in cooperation with other University schools: the JD/MBA, JD/MHA, JD/MA in Public Administration, JD/MA in Urban Affairs, JD/MPH and a JD/PhD in Law and Health Care Ethics.

First-year full-time law students benefit from the school's unique small section program where two of five classes average 35 students. This allows for individualized instruction and focused student interaction, and builds a sense of community among classmates. The remaining classes combine different small sections, allowing students to get to know their entire class.

For those who work full time and are unable to attend classes during the day, the school offers a Part-Time Evening Program, the only program of its kind in the state of Missouri. Through the program, students can earn their law degree in four years with summer attendance or five years without summer attendance.

The graduating classes within the past five years have averaged over a 90 percent employment rate within six months of graduation, and graduates work in 49 states.

Please contact the Office of Admissions at admissions@law.slu.edu or (314) 977-2800 with questions or to schedule a visit.

Read all of Vault's Law School Surveys at www.vault.com/lawschool — get complete surveys on top law schools, expert advice on applicaton essays, LSAT prep and more.

VAULT CAREER LIBRARY 371

University of Missouri-Columbia
School of Law

MU School of Law
Admissions Office
103 Hulston Hall
Columbia, MO 65211-4300
Admissions phone: (573) 882-6042 or (888) MULAW4U
Admissions fax: (573)882-9625
Admissions e-mail: umclawadmissions@missouri.edu
Admissions URL: http://law.missouri.edu/prospective/

 ## Admissions

Status: Alumnus/a, full-time
Dates of Enrollment: 8/1999-5/2002
Survey Submitted: April 2006

When I applied, I applied early to gain status as a Roberts Scholar. At that time, if you applied by a certain date (I think November) before completing 75 undergraduate hours, with an ACT score above 30 and a GPA of (I think) 3.5 or higher, you were guaranteed acceptance, regardless of your LSAT score, along with a $1,000 scholarship.

I was admitted as a Roberts Scholar and invited to visit the campus. I personally sat in on a couple of classes and the Domestic Violence Clinic debriefing. I don't remember ever being interviewed, but I did write an essay as part of my application about why I wanted to attend law school.

Advice on getting in: have a high GPA or a decent LSAT, or vice versa. Getting the review book and taking practice LSATs worked really well for me. Visiting a campus is a great opportunity to determine what kind of learning environment you will be facing, and Mizzou is one of the most cooperative law school environments I've heard of.

> **The school says:** "The Roberts Scholars Program (a program for undergraduate students) has changed over the years and will change again for the fall 2006. Please contact the Admissions Office or visit our web site for the most current information on the program."

Status: Current student, full-time
Dates of Enrollment: 8/2003-Submit Date
Survey Submitted: April 2006

Need around mid-160s LSAT and 3.0 GPA—obviously the higher the GPA, the LSAT can probably dip as low as high 150s.

Fair selective—getting more and more selective last three years.

Admissions process not that rigorous, pretty standard—recommendations, essay, application and applcation fee.

Status: Alumnus/a, full-time
Dates of Enrollment: 8/1999-5/2002
Survey Submitted: April 2006

Admissions process was very straightforward with an emphasis on LSAT scores and undergraduate GPA. Looking for a cross-section of undergraduate backgrounds, varying from engineering to music to the traditional liberal arts background. Very selective process admitting only approximately 10 percent of applicants.

> **The school says:** "We admit about 30 percent of our applicants, with 150 being our target entering class size."

Status: Current student, full-time
Dates of Enrollment: 1/2003-Submit Date
Survey Submitted: April 2006

The admissions process was relatively straightforward and the admissions office was very good about communicating with prospective students about the requirements and how to turn them in, as well as what admission was based on. They were very timely in replying to applications and gave ample time to make seat deposits, as well as helped students with moving to Columbia.

Status: Current student, full-time
Dates of Enrollment: 8/2005-Submit Date
Survey Submitted: April 2006

School admissions staff provided plenty of opportunities to tour the school, ask questions, and were both candid and helpful in their answers. The school provided fast updates on the status of my application. The school seems to be more selective than the other schools to which I applied, but I knew this from the onset.

Status: Current student, full-time
Dates of Enrollment: 8/2003-Submit Date
Survey Submitted: April 2006

The admissions office at MU makes the entire process fairly painless. Of course, you still have to jump through some hoops with the LSAT folks and register with the LSDAS, but that is a requirement no matter where you apply. MU has gotten increasingly selective over the last 10 years, and the major focus is on your LSAT and GPA; however, there is a personal essay in which you detail the information that tests and GPAs don't provide—work and experience.

All in all, I found the process fairly easy and the admissions staff was incredibly supportive and helpful. I believe the application fee was about $50.

Status: Alumnus/a, full-time
Dates of Enrollment: 8/2000-5/2003
Survey Submitted: April 2006

I applied to several different law schools—both in and out of state, expensive and moderate, and public and private. I really didn't know what direction I wanted to take and felt more comfortable having options. My recommendation is to not have one school as the one "acceptable" one in your mind. Be open to the benefits that different schools have to offer.

Another suggestion: study for the LSAT. It sounds obvious, but being people who have done well academically I think there is a tendency by those wanting to attend law school to underestimate the difficulty of the test. Familiarize yourself with the types of questions.

Status: Alumnus/a, full-time
Dates of Enrollment: 9/1999-5/2002
Survey Submitted: April 2006

As the school's solid reputation spreads to markets like Chicago, Missouri is becoming a more competitive law school.

Status: Alumnus/a, full-time
Dates of Enrollment: 8/1989-5/1992
Survey Submitted: April 2006

The admission process was straightforward and not complicated. It involved a simple form, application fee and forwarded transcripts. Published averages for undergraduate GPA and LSAT scores were very helpful in making the application decision.

> **The school says:** "Items that are required for application have changed. Please contact the Admissions Office or visit our web

site for the most current information on applying to the School of Law."

Status: Alumnus/a, full-time
Dates of Enrollment: 9/1997-5/2000
Survey Submitted: January 2005

The admissions process is very selective and the essay is more important than at most schools. The selection process is tempered, somewhat, by the relatively small applicant pool compared with national schools. Undergraduate accomplishment in a rigorous field of study is slightly more important than LSAT scores in the admission process. The admissions board looks very favorably at students who attend out-of-state undergraduate programs. There is no interview.

> **The school says**: "The admissions process at MU is competitive. The LSAT and undergraduate GPA are the two most significant factors in the process, however, to create a dynamic learning environment, each file is fully reviewed by the admissions committee for unique individual qualities such as (but not limited to) work or military experience, community involvement, personal achievements, disadvantaged status and overcoming adversity. The Committee does not give specific preference to any applicant (such as in-/out-of-state residency or for attending MU as an undergraduate). The admissions committee admits on a rolling basis, beginning in November. It is to the applicant's advantage to complete the application process as early as possible for admission consideration and scholarship awards."

Academics

Status: Alumnus/a, full-time
Dates of Enrollment: 8/1999-5/2002
Survey Submitted: April 2006

I really enjoyed my time at Mizzou. I can honestly say that there was only one class that felt like a waste of time. The rest were great.

In all my years of education, my time at Mizzou exposed me to some of the best professors/teachers I've encountered. The vast majority of the faculty is very approachable outside of class and they really want you to succeed both academically and personally. It seems that the administration is aware of which classes are popular and does its best to accommodate the popularity and give everyone the option of taking the class at some point.

As far as grading and workload, there's not much to say that would be different from other law schools. Law school is hard, plain and simple. I definitely had to get used to not being the straight-A student I had always been before.

Status: Current student, full-time
Dates of Enrollment: 8/2003-Submit Date
Survey Submitted: April 2006

Professors are wonderful—many are experts in their field. Alternative Dispute Resolution Program is top-tier, always Number One or Two in the country. Grading is fair even though 77 is the bell curve for 1L classes (lower than some schools' curves).

Real lack of transactional classes; they're trying to improve but it's frustrating for those students interested in M&A and Securities Regulation.

Status: Alumnus/a, full-time
Dates of Enrollment: 8/1999-5/2002
Survey Submitted: April 2006

Outstanding academics with an emphasis on maintaining small to medium class sizes. Professors are renowned for their open-door policies and actually being available to students. Very welcoming academic environment that encourages success for every student.

Status: Alumnus/a, full-time
Dates of Enrollment: 8/2000-5/2003
Survey Submitted: April 2006

Professor quality suffered. There were too few good teachers to keep students interested. We needed a better array of available classes. Best teachers should be involved in the core classes like Con Law.

Status: Current student, full-time
Dates of Enrollment: 1/2003-Submit Date
Survey Submitted: April 2006

The first-year classes give a basic intro into the study of law with Contracts, Torts, Property, Criminal Law, Civil Procedure and Legal Writing. The grading is on a strict curve. Most classes are very good, however there are classes that other students will advise you to take or avoid.

In selecting courses, you may not always get every class you wish, but the process is fair and students will rarely miss opportunities to take most of the courses they desire. Popular professors, while harder to get, are not too difficult.

Status: Current student, full-time
Dates of Enrollment: 8/2005-Submit Date
Survey Submitted: April 2006

I have not had any problems getting the classes I want, and the school offers what appears to me to be a broad variety of classes. There is a good mix of procedure, substantive, policy and practical experience courses.

As for the quality of professors—one of my instructors is quite easily the best instructor I have had at any school at any level. He makes highly technical or complex material easy to digest with his clear, organized and entertaining approach.

Status: Current student, full-time
Dates of Enrollment: 8/2003-Submit Date
Survey Submitted: April 2006

MU is ranked the second best ADR (alternative dispute resolution) school and you can definitely see that when you get here. The ADR classes are amazing and fun—and not just "fun law school." The clinical programs are also very good, and the clinical staff is committed, not just to the cause, but to expanding your understanding of practical skills.

The "regular" professors—Torts, Contracts, Civ Pro—are also amazing. We have one professor who wrote President Bush's Faith Based Initiative (not my side of politics but brilliant), the state's Solicitor General teaches State Con Law, our Business Organization/Finance guy has an engineering degree from MIT and our Environmental Law guru worked for one of the biggest law firms in the country. Harvard, Standford, Chicago, you name it, we have a professor who was educated there.

Because MU has reduced 1L class sizes and increased admission standards, it is fairly easy to get into any class you like. Workload is hard, there is no doubt about that, but the faculty and staff are always there to help you with emergencies and any problems you may have.

Status: Alumnus/a, full-time LLM
Dates of Enrollment: 8/2001-5/2004
Survey Submitted: April 2006

MU follows what I consider to be a traditional state law school curriculum. It is highly competitive, relies on the Socratic Method for the majority of classes, has an historical bell curve grading system around the score of 78 and highlights those courses needed to prepare for bar admissions in the majority of states. MU is also consistently ranked in the Top Five ADR schools in the country (often ranked Number One), and back in 2001 MU touted their incorporation of ADR into their first-year courses. I did not find this be accurate. However, I was afforded the opportunity to take LLM courses in ADR that met my needs.

The LLM classes were amazing. The JD courses prepared me for the bar, which I took nine months after graduating and only studied for a total of two weeks. That shows how spectacular of a base education I received. Most of the professors are easy to approach and do all that they can to assist their students. There is diversity in perspective, although not in race.

Read all of Vault's Law School Surveys at www.vault.com/lawschool — get complete surveys on top law schools, expert advice on applicaton essays, LSAT prep and more.

VAULT CAREER LIBRARY 373

The school says: "ADR is now integrated into the first-year curriculum through a required course entitled 'Lawyering.'"

Status: Alumnus/a, full-time
Dates of Enrollment: 8/2000-5/2003
Survey Submitted: April 2006

I felt that I received a solid education at MU. Overall, I felt that most of my professors were thorough, helpful outside of the classroom, and knowledgeable in their areas. I really appreciated the professors who were willing to help when a subject area was tough to understand. At the same time, I can't say that about 100 percent of my professors. I would say my overall satisfaction rate with professors was 70 percent. The other 30 percent did not convey ideas well, were disorganized, or frankly, just not approachable or understandable.

The first year was definitely overwhelming and the hours of studying (particularly the month before finals) were significant. But as I got used to school and learned what was necessary to spend time on, I became more time efficient and did not feel overwhelmed constantly. I never had a class that I really wanted that I was not able to get into.

As far as grading goes, it usually felt fair, although there was the occasion when it seemed like the professor threw the papers in the air and picked piles as different categories of grades (which was to my benefit and detriment). Generally though, I can say that my level of effort and enthusiasm was reflected in my grade for the class.

Status: Alumnus/a, full-time law
Dates of Enrollment: 8/1999-5/2002
Survey Submitted: April 2006

Classes included the basic law classes—first-year program and required modules throughout. Also a number of excellent electives, including skills classes.

Status: Alumnus/a, full-time
Dates of Enrollment: 9/1999-5/2002
Survey Submitted: April 2006

The school program is rigorous. Like most law schools, there is a heavy emphasis on litigation. Professors are generally nationally known—choosing to work in Columbia for the great quality of life. There are some easier classes available for credit through the undergraduate program, but hey, everybody needs a break! Popular classes were generally pretty easy to get into. However, they are not always offered each semester, so you have to plan carefully.

> **Regarding class credit, the school says:** "The law school does not give credit toward graduation for undergraduate coursework. A limited number of undergraduate courses (three to six hours) are permitted with prior approval."

Status: Alumnus/a, full-time
Dates of Enrollment: 9/1997-5/2000
Survey Submitted: January 2005

Academics are rigorous and competitive. If you're not prepared to work hard, don't expect superior grades. The grading system, especially in the first year, is intended to distinguish both the best and worst students. The effect of first-year grades may either establish a student as an excellent candidate for prestigious judicial clerkships and law firm associate positions, or weed out those students who will not be competitive in the legal industry. Most of all, it's essential to perform well during your first year. The grading curve is re-graduated during the second and third year, making it more difficult to distinguish yourself from other students.

 Employment Prospects

Status: Alumnus/a, full-time
Dates of Enrollment: 8/1999-5/2002
Survey Submitted: April 2006

Being a graduate of Mizzou law school definitely opens doors to legal employment in Missouri. I find it nearly impossible to attend a gathering of Missouri attorneys without finding several Mizzou grads in the crowd. Graduates of Mizzou Law find work in private firms, large and small,

government work, judicial clerkships, the military and other secondary educational institutions.

Mizzou has two time periods a year where firms and public employers come to campus for interviews. The job I currently hold was acquired during an on-campus interview. I think that some of the best preparation for future employment is through the clinical programs. Not only are they great experience, but employers love to see them on your resume.

Status: Current student, full-time
Dates of Enrollment: 8/2003-Submit Date
Survey Submitted: April 2006

Strong footholds in St. Louis and Kansas City. Also, a growing network with Chicago firms. Pretty much anywhere in Missouri, MU is a good law school to get a job. Outside Missouri, percentages drop off. OCI has all the big St. Louis and KC firms and some from Chicago, but not a lot of other big cities. Public Interest jobs are also not in big supply. Good opportunities for internships with Missouri Legislature nearby as well.

Status: Alumnus/a, full-time
Dates of Enrollment: 8/2001-5/2004
Survey Submitted: April 2006

MU has a national reputation for their work in ADR, but has no national recognition outside of that. It made finding a job outside of Missouri difficult.

Status: Alumnus/a, full-time
Dates of Enrollment: 8/2000-5/2003
Survey Submitted: April 2006

This is a difficult area for me to assess because I did not want to go into private practice. That being said, although I was in the top 20 percent, I did not attempt to interview with large firms that are more focused on prestige. Going to MU did open doors, though because there are so many alumni across the state.

I am currently a lawyer in the state legislature. However, I have friends that are in all kinds of jobs—state jobs, sole practitioners and big firms so I definitely think that all of those avenues are open to MU's graduates. If you are wanting a more "non-traditional" job, be ready to creatively and persistently find it.

Status: Alumnus/a, full-time
Dates of Enrollment: 9/1999-5/2002
Survey Submitted: April 2006

On-campus recruiting is THE place to obtain jobs. Most students take jobs in St. Louis or Kansas City, but there is a growing cadre of students migrating to Chicago's larger legal market place. The University of Missouri at Columbia is the flagship of the university system and produces graduates as capable (and ultimately as successful) as any produced by the more well-known private schools in St. Louis. Not to mention that the cost of an education at Missouri is much, much more affordable.

Status: Alumnus/a, full-time
Dates of Enrollment: 9/1997-5/2000
Survey Submitted: January 2005

If you perform well, your employment prospects for any legal position in the Midwest, including Chicago, are excellent. Federal and state judicial clerkships, as well as associate positions at large firms in Kansas City and St. Louis, are filled with MU graduates. The alumni network is a powerful employment tool, as many law firms are populated with partners who attended MU. MU graduates have a stellar reputation among legal employers and are among the leaders of many of the most prestigious law firms in the Midwest.

 **Quality of Life**

Status: Alumnus/a, full-time
Dates of Enrollment: 8/1999-5/2002
Survey Submitted: April 2006

Columbia is a fantastic town to live in. It's small enough that it's not big city-like, but it has all of the big city amenities, such as shopping, bars, clubs, coffee houses and a very active (and beautiful) downtown. The Mizzou campus is also really beautiful. The recreation center was recently renovated and is awesome.

There are lots of campus activities to be involved in (in case school doesn't keep you busy enough), and there's a bowling alley just down from the law school (a great study break). I can't speak to housing because I lived with my parents the first two years and then in a small nearby town my third year with my husband. I honestly never felt unsafe during my three years even when I would stay late at night studying. The law school locks after hours and only law students have access.

Status: Current student, full-time
Dates of Enrollment: 8/2003-Submit Date
Survey Submitted: April 2006

Columbia is a great town. Low crime and near St. Louis and Kansas City (two hours each way). Columbia is perennially a Top 10 city in the U.S. Plenty of housing close to campus. Good restaurant and bar selection.

Status: Alumnus/a, full-time
Dates of Enrollment: 8/1999-5/2002
Survey Submitted: April 2006

Outstanding quality of life. The school is located in Columbia, Missouri, which is a thriving and diverse community that always has something to offer—the quintessential college town. The school's facilities are also pretty good as it is one of the newer buildings on campus. No problem with crime or safety at all.

Status: Alumnus/a, full-time
Dates of Enrollment: 8/2001-5/2004
Survey Submitted: April 2006

Columbia, Missouri is a very easy city/town to live in. It helped keep my student loans to a minimum. The town is not very diverse, however, and so was difficult for some students.

Status: Current student, full-time
Dates of Enrollment: 8/2005-Submit Date
Survey Submitted: April 2006

Columbia is a great "college town" with a strong undergraduate feel.

Status: Current student, full-time
Dates of Enrollment: 1/2003-Submit Date
Survey Submitted: April 2006

Crime is low, safety is good, cost of living is very reasonable, there is ample housing near campus, facilities are nice and the overall environment is very inviting.

Status: Current student, full-time
Dates of Enrollment: 8/2003-Submit Date
Survey Submitted: April 2006

Columbia is a fantastic college town. Housing is inexpensive and fairly nice, the parks and recreation department is amazing; biking/running trails, tennis courts, a multi-million dollar community rec center, dog park, you name it. Crime is virtually nonexistent on campus and off.

Status: Alumnus/a, full-time
Dates of Enrollment: 8/2000-5/2003
Survey Submitted: April 2006

I lived in an apartment five minutes from campus. It was nice to be close to school. It was also nice to have the law school close to downtown so that you could walk with friends to lunch and have a break from everyone at school. I thought the law school was a nice building and had comfortable spots to study and hang out, which was important considering how much we were in the building.

Status: Alumnus/a, full-time
Dates of Enrollment: 9/1999-5/2002
Survey Submitted: April 2006

Columbia Missouri is a fabulous place to attend law school. The college town has all of the academic and social endeavors one could ask for as well as close proximity to Kansas City, St. Louis, Chicago and Memphis for employment

opportunities. The nearby state capital, Jefferson City, offers a great training ground for young law student clerks.

Status: Alumnus/a, full-time
Dates of Enrollment: 9/1997-5/2000
Survey Submitted: January 2005

Quality of life is excellent. There is collegial atmosphere among students and close, "first-name" working relationships with professors. However, MU is located in Columbia, Missouri, a collegetown of approximately 125,000, including students. If you're looking for a large, cosmopolitan area in which to live during law school, look elsewhere.

 ## Social Life

Status: Alumnus/a, full-time
Dates of Enrollment: 8/1999-5/2002
Survey Submitted: April 2006

Mizzou has a Student Bar Association that typically organizes social activities such as happy hours, tailgates, the Barrister's Ball (law prom) and Halloween parties. However, there are numerous organizations within the law school that offer volunteer activities, speakers, forums and other outings. Because Columbia houses three colleges/universities, there are lots of bars and restaurants filled with the 20-something crowd.

Status: Current student, full-time
Dates of Enrollment: 8/2003-Submit Date
Survey Submitted: April 2006

Again, this is a college town. There are more bars and restaurants than you can shake a stick at! It is amazing. Sushi, Thai, Italian, American, French, Pakistani, you can find it here. The Student Bar Association puts on football tailgates at every home game, the student organizations have happy hours, pizza stops and the occasional coffee bar for all to enjoy.

Status: Alumnus/a, full-time
Dates of Enrollment: 8/2001-5/2004
Survey Submitted: April 2006

Columbia, Missouri has plenty of social activities for students. With a large undergraduate university in town, the entire town caters to students. I spent the majority of my time in downtown Columbia—Lakota Coffeehouse, Snappers Bar, Flatbranch, Teller's and the small film house on Ninth St.

Status: Current student, full-time
Dates of Enrollment: 8/2005-Submit Date
Survey Submitted: April 2006

Living in a "college town" you definitely get all of the social advantages. However, because Columbia is a small city, you don't have the opportunity for some of the higher-end restaurants, bars and attractions that would find in the larger cities.

Status: Current student, full-time
Dates of Enrollment: 1/2003-Submit Date
Survey Submitted: April 2006

Many good bars and restaurants in walking distance from the law school. There tend to be activities for a variety of interests. Dating scene is not bad, but as I am in a serious relationship I am not the best to answer that question.

Status: Alumnus/a, full-time
Dates of Enrollment: 8/2000-5/2003
Survey Submitted: April 2006

My social life was so much better than I anticipated. I came to school thinking my life was over and that I would never go out again. After a semester, though, I was able to find people that I clicked with and am still friends with today.

Columbia is a classic "college town"—plenty of bars and restaurants, considering its size. There is also a good level of acceptance, diversity and tolerance in Columbia. Also, you can find a little culture too (symphony, concerts).

Read all of Vault's Law School Surveys at www.vault.com/lawschool — get complete surveys on top law schools, expert advice on application essays, LSAT prep and more.

VAULT CAREER LIBRARY   375

Status: Alumnus/a, full-time
Dates of Enrollment: 9/1999-5/2002
Survey Submitted: April 2006

Bars, restaurants, dating is all great in Columbia. The town's large undergraduate population, great athletic teams and wonderful biking and running trail network make living in "C-Mo" a pleasure!

Status: Alumnus/a, full-time
Dates of Enrollment: 8/1989-5/1992
Survey Submitted: April 2006

Social life during law school is somewhat of a limited experience. However, the law school's programs helped foster a family of fellow law students. The Student Bar Association held regular happy hours, especially during football season, that were always well attended. The Heidelburg was a favorite watering hole and it seemed like there was always time to play basketball at Brewer Field House with law school friends or play other intramural sports.

Status: Alumnus/a, full-time
Dates of Enrollment: 9/1997-5/2000
Survey Submitted: January 2005

The social life at MU law school is second to none. MU is a great place to meet people and is located in a great town that caters to students. It's important not to allow too much social life to interfere with your studies (especially during the first year). I've seen good students fail in the competitive atmosphere of MU law school because they spent too much time socializing and not enough time studying.

 **The School Says**

The University of Missouri - Columbia School of Law is a vibrant and collegial community. Founded in 1839, MU is the first state university west of the Mississippi. The School of Law was established in 1872 and has had an enviable history of service to the state and nation.

The student body of the law school is composed of students from numerous states and several foreign countries. This diverse group provides a wealth of experiences and fosters a stimulating learning environment.

Located in Columbia, Missouri, MU is 35 miles from Jefferson City, the state capital. Our location provides students with easy access to the legislature, the Supreme Court, and various offices of state. In addition to living and studying in one of America's most livable cities, students are within two hours of the cultural, athletic and entertainment centers of St. Louis and Kansas City. Columbia combines a small town feel with the diversity and opportunities often found only in large cities.

University of Missouri-Kansas City
School of Law

Admissions Office
5100 Rockhill Road
Kansas City, MO 64110-2499
Admissions phone: (816) 235-1644
Admissions fax: (816) 235-5276
Admissions e-mail: law@umkc.edu
Admissions URL: http://www1.law.umkc.edu/admissions/

 ## Admissions

Status: Current student, full-time
Dates of Enrollment: 8/2003-Submit Date
Survey Submitted: April 2005

I submitted my LSAT scores and a mandatory essay. There was no mandatory interview, but I scheduled a tour of the school and spoke to professors and students before applying. Both the professors and the students were very accessible and helpful in answering my admissions questions.

Status: Current student, full-time
Dates of Enrollment: 8/2002-Submit Date
Survey Submitted: April 2005

I gained a lot of knowledge when deciding whether to apply to UMKC from the web site; it was very helpful and provided all the answers to the questions I had. I had an undergraduate pre-law advisor who helped so I never needed to contact the school itself, but I have had contact with the admissions staff in my attendance at the school and I think very highly of all of them and know that they would help anyone they could. The application and essay were not to difficult of a process and I was not selected for an interview. I have been told that a lot more students are applying than can be accepted so I am sure admissions are selective.

Status: Current student, full-time
Dates of Enrollment: 8/2004-Submit Date
Survey Submitted: April 2005

The admissions process at UMKC involves filling out an application that is standard to most law school applications. Applicants write an essay on why they want to go to law school or on any other topic they may choose. Additionally, applicants submit letters of reference.

UMKC Law School considers factors such as one's LSAT score, undergrad GPA, job experiences, life experiences and other factors when admitting applicants. The school takes a holistic approach when considering individual applicants. This has allowed the UMKC law school to be comprised of strong students with diverse backgrounds.

Status: Current student, full-time
Dates of Enrollment: 8/2004-Submit Date
Survey Submitted: April 2005

Compared to other law schools, the admissions process is extremely friendly. I was sent confirmation letters for every step along the way and was assigned a personal student ambassador. I was also automatically considered for some scholarships.

Status: Current student, full-time
Dates of Enrollment: 8/2002-Submit Date
Survey Submitted: April 2005

The Emissary Group is a good organization of students. Needs diversity. Often times, UMKC forgets that not everyone who goes to UMKC is from Kansas City and/or wants to stay in Kansas City. It's not good when almost every student that spoke to me about why they came to UMKC said, "because it was close to home and it was cheap."

Status: Current student, full-time
Dates of Enrollment: 8/2004-Submit Date
Survey Submitted: April 2005

Admissions seems pretty streamlined; I was a late-admit, and applied with little information regarding the school. Admission requirements seemed reasonable, and the school was very quick in getting back to me with a response.

Status: Current student, full-time
Dates of Enrollment: 8/2002-Submit Date
Survey Submitted: April 2005

I had no contact with the school regarding my admissions. I simply filled out the application, and submitted my essay and three letters of recommendation. I had a fairly decent LSAT score and GPA, and I believe those two, combined with my recommendations, are what made my acceptance quite easy. I applied in the summer and was accepted in November 2001, nearly a year before classes started.

> **Regarding admissions, UMKC says:** "No one is admitted until the file is complete (application, LSDAS report and letters of recommendation). The school is on a rolling admission cycle; therefore, those who apply early with strong credentials will receive an early response."

 ## Academics

Status: Current student, full-time
Dates of Enrollment: 8/2003-Submit Date
Survey Submitted: October 2005

This school curves all 1L classes to a 2.8, meaning 20 percent of the class has to get a C- or below, which is failing. This artificial curve puts UMKC at a disadvantage as the GPAs are artificially low compared to other schools in the region. 1L classes are fixed and divided into sections. The section stays together and the professors change. The teaching quality is above average, but varies greatly by professor. Ask around and make sure you know which ones to avoid. I never had trouble getting into the classes I wanted. Make sure to rank your preferences accordingly.

> **The school says:** "The percentage of grades below C is a recommendation and is not mandatory. Only an F is a failing grade."

Status: Alumnus/a, full-time
Dates of Enrollment: 8/2000-5/2003
Survey Submitted: March 2006

The classes, for the most part, are of excellent quality. Much better than top schools in the sense of learning useful things to the practice of law. They live up to the billing of being a practitioner's school.

A good thing is that they require you take classes many top law students never take, and UMKC grads are better off because of that. A bad thing is that they have such a small selection of classes, and interests in electives do not vary. The school attempted in 2002 to offer an antitrust course. I signed up and the class was cancelled because only two people signed up. That is beyond pathetic. I had to take tax classes when I needed units in my senior, or be subject to everyone's favorite classes: Juvenile Law and Children and the Law.

Read all of Vault's Law School Surveys at www.vault.com/lawschool — get complete surveys on top law schools, expert advice on applicaton essays, LSAT prep and more.

VAULT CAREER LIBRARY 377

Status: Current student, full-time
Dates of Enrollment: 8/2003-Submit Date
Survey Submitted: April 2005

The quality of classes is first-rate. I found the grading extremely competitive in the first year, and the difficulty of getting popular classes in the second year was minimal.

Status: Current student, full-time
Dates of Enrollment: 8/2004-Submit Date
Survey Submitted: April 2005

UMKC law school has exceptional academics and its students are very pleased with the program. The classes are of a very high quality and the professors take a genuine interest in their students. The school offers a wide variety of classes and works hard to ensure that students can take the classes they want at convenient times. While many students dislike that grading is done on a curve, the grading system is fair and is similar to other grading systems.

Status: Current student, full-time
Dates of Enrollment: 8/2004-Submit Date
Survey Submitted: April 2005

The professors at our school are amazing! It constantly blows me away when I think of the accomplishments of our faculty. I have had nothing but positive things to say about my interaction with professors and their willingness to help students. There is a serious focus on academics—our curve is significantly lower than other schools, which makes us work that much harder! Workload is intense, and there is a strong focus on legal writing and researching.

Status: Current student, full-time
Dates of Enrollment: 8/2004-Submit Date
Survey Submitted: April 2005

The professors are well-known and respected nationally. Many write nationally published textbooks and their law review articles are cited in precedent-setting cases. The professors are difficult, but sympathetic to student needs and eager to provide clarification.

Status: Current student, full-time
Dates of Enrollment: 9/2002-Submit Date
Survey Submitted: April 2005

What's the reason why everyone should ignore all the magazine ratings crap and beg to be let into this school? THE PROFESSORS, THE PROFESSORS, THE PROFESSORS! Sure, it is easy to go to this school's web site, look up the biographies of its faculty, and discover that this school has recruited and held onto venerable professors with very impressive resumes, in a variety of areas of practice, from all over the United States.

But if anything should compel a candidate to seriously consider this school— especially foreign students looking for professors very willing and able to help them—it is that this school, above all else, is characterized by what is most important to a student once he or she takes the actual plunge and the doors of law school slam behind them: the professors virtually without exception care deeply about the students! They beg students to ask them for help outside the classroom and practically do everything but study for you. The professors themselves even conduct programs to show students how to study. To prepare students for the Bar, professors give one-on-one assistance to prepare students for the essay portion, the most weighted portion of the Bar.

Additionally, the professors achieve all this friendliness and approachability while not pulling any punches as far as hammering home to students what real-world lawyering involves. They break things down and tell it like it is. Depending on the professor, the Socratic Method is still used, and those who do use it, use it to instruct and keep students on their toes, not to embarrass anyone. Students are plenty capable of embarrassing themselves without any help!

The school has a long list of professor-sponsored, hands-on clinic programs where students get real-life lawyering type experience. UMKC's professors love to teach and crank out students truly as ready as they can be for the real world. This will continue to be the tradition of this school as long as the dean stays at the school. She's been serving students tirelessly at this school for many years and she exemplifies the kind of "true" professor this school consciously seeks out and attracts. Finally, the good-natured, engaging atmosphere is handed down

through its students. Students are often pleasantly surprised by how fellow students go beyond the call to help one another. There's not so much "one upmanship" here. The professors know how to pile on the workload, too!

Status: Current student, full-time
Dates of Enrollment: 8/2002-Submit Date
Survey Submitted: April 2005

I think the workload is an adequate challenge and indication of the stress in the legal profession. I do not however feel that many of my classes actually provided me with any information that I will use in my career or to study for the bar. I can count on one hand the number of classes I actually feel have taught me anything and even fewer professors who have educated me about the real legal profession and the law as it stands today.

Status: Current student, full-time
Dates of Enrollment: 8/2003-Submit Date
Survey Submitted: April 2005

It is fairly easy to get the classes you need and to get into the more popular ones. Grading is fair, but sometimes is highly arbitrary. For example, I got a C plus in two first-year classes first semester and two A minuses for the same class in the second semester. Grading seems to depend on the professors' moods. Teachers are hit-or-miss with some being really good and some mediocre to fair. However, the teachers are really approachable and willing to help.

Status: Alumnus/a, full-time
Dates of Enrollment: 8/2001-5/2004
Survey Submitted: February 2005

The academic environment was great. Although my first-year classes were relatively large (around 50 people), this was small enough to get to know the professor and my classmates. In the second and third years my classes were much smaller, usually between 15 and 25 people. I was always able to get into the classes I wanted, although I wish there would have been more course selection in some areas. The classes and professors were generally VERY good. My professors were always approachable and very willing to help.

 Employment Prospects

Status: Current student, full-time
Dates of Enrollment: 8/2003-Submit Date
Survey Submitted: October 2005

Local law firms are exceptionally receptive to UMKC grads and students. I've been clerking since my first summer and have never had a problem finding work. If you want to clerk, there are plenty of places that will take you, including the courthouse. Our administration has made it a point to help us pass the bar. We're now the best in the state.

Status: Alumnus/a, full-time
Dates of Enrollment: 8/2000-5/2003
Survey Submitted: March 2006

Most UMKC grads either are at small firms or work in government (public defenders). There is OCI, but only a handful of KC-based firms interview (the big ones in KC). Firms based in St. Louis with no KC office don't even bother to do OCI. Small firms use OCI, but they are all in KC, some in Springfield. You can forget about going to a national firm unless you are number one in your class.

There are a few internships, but you need good grades and have to be in a special crowd to get them. Alumni network stinks OUTSIDE KC, so don't think that lone UMKC grad in NYC, D.C., Chicago or SF can help you out (but they try, they are nice).

Status: Current student, full-time
Dates of Enrollment: 8/2003-Submit Date
Survey Submitted: April 2005

Strong employment prospects in the city and generally throughout the region. This is a very competitive program that doesn't stop after the last test is taken. You have to take the initiative and find a job yourself, but the law school employment office is always willing to help. Several firms come to the school for interviews but few get jobs out of that.

Status: Current student, full-time
Dates of Enrollment: 8/2004-Submit Date
Survey Submitted: April 2005

The school is in a big Midwestern city, so it gives us an advantage of having several large firms, as well as many smaller ones. We also have a federal courthouse and the county courthouse nearby. The largest law firms in KC hire a majority of their new associates from our school, and we have an excellent relationship with the firms in the city.

Status: Current student, full-time
Dates of Enrollment: 8/2004-Submit Date
Survey Submitted: April 2005

On-campus recruiting happens throughout the year. As a first-year law student, it is better to rely on opportunities other than on-campus recruiting because it is extremely competitive. Nearly 100 percent of graduates are employed after graduation and the bar passage rate is the highest in the state. Alumni are very eager to help.

Status: Current student, full-time
Dates of Enrollment: 9/2002-Submit Date
Survey Submitted: April 2005

Kansas City is no small town, but it's small enough that the school has a very close and long history with all the major firms and employers. The career center at the school has a great program with dedicated staff that methodically connects employers and students.

Status: Current student, full-time
Dates of Enrollment: 9/2002-Submit Date
Survey Submitted: April 2005

We have an above-average rate of hiring from on-campus interviews. But the networking with local professionals is WAY beyond great. We have social and professional gatherings going on all the time. And our proximity to the primary job market in the area means we have tons of internship opportunities that lead to the best possible jobs after graduation.

 **Quality of Life**

Status: Current student, full-time
Dates of Enrollment: 8/2003-Submit Date
Survey Submitted: October 2005

The neighborhood is a bit sketchy since it's an urban campus. Crime is sporadic, but still a factor. Some cars are broken into, but nothing out of the ordinary. Parking is a constant problem, but I think that's on par with any college campus, as they derive revenue from parking lots and parking tickets.

Status: Alumnus/a, full-time
Dates of Enrollment: 8/2000-5/2003
Survey Submitted: March 2006

KC is the last place you want to live in if you want to live in a major metropolitan area. Weather stinks, people are racist and uneducated and there is a lot of crime. I personally had my house burglarized and my wife's car was stolen.

The campus at UMKC is not so bad, except parking is horrible. In the years I was there, they kept taking away more and more student parking close to the law school to the point where you have walk a mile from where you park to the school.

Status: Current student, full-time
Dates of Enrollment: 8/2003-Submit Date
Survey Submitted: April 2005

Most law students live in apartments nearby, and the neighborhood is safe and respectable.

Status: Current student, full-time
Dates of Enrollment: 8/2004-Submit Date
Survey Submitted: April 2005

It is relatively easy to find a place to live near UMKC, as there are many surrounding neighborhoods and apartment complexes. Also, for people who do not wish to live near the city, there are many of surrounding suburbs that require only a short commute. UMKC's campus is localized and well-maintained. The law building itself has many good features, including a very nice student lounge, a large computer lab and offices for upper-level students. However, the building is older and could use some renovating and some new furniture.

Crime and safety are not an issue. You rarely hear about any crimes that have occurred on or near the campus.

Status: Current student, full-time
Dates of Enrollment: 8/2004-Submit Date
Survey Submitted: April 2005

Although I have nothing to compare it to, UMKC is a great environment to be in law school. The school is in a beautiful part of town and safety is never of concern. The people are really what make the school so special, though. It is such a huge commitment and takes up so much of one's life, that it would be downright unbearable to spend the next three years with people I don't like! The students at UMKC are down to earth, unpretentious and generally great to be around!

Status: Current student, full-time
Dates of Enrollment: 9/2002-Submit Date
Survey Submitted: April 2005

Kansas City is big enough to get everything you need, and small enough that you won't get lost in the shuffle. It's very neighborhood oriented, so that it's easy to live walking-distance to hangouts. And parking is abundant and free, if you do have to drive somewhere.

Housing is pretty cheap. The one downside is that the urban core is a little drab, but that's changing, and has made great strides in the five years I've lived here.

Status: Current student, full-time
Dates of Enrollment: 8/2002-Submit Date
Survey Submitted: April 2005

You will need to be comfortable living with very little money, and with very little free time. Especially in your first year, an average week will consist of 15 in-class hours and at least 30 out-of-class hours of work for adequate preparation. If you want the grades, you better make it 45 hours out of class.

Status: Current student, full-time
Dates of Enrollment: 8/2004-Submit Date
Survey Submitted: April 2005

The neighborhood is full of beautiful, turn-of-the-century houses. It is very safe and very close to wonderful shopping on the Plaza. There are many nice apartments in the area for relatively low rent.

Status: Current student, full-time
Dates of Enrollment: 8/2003-Submit Date
Survey Submitted: April 2005

The neighborhood is really nice and the campus is safe. The school is on the Southwestern side of the campus and is across the street from homes and churches. Facilities could use an upgrade, however, as most don't seem to have been touched since the building opened (early 1970s). This school tends to be more of a commuter campus.

Status: Alumnus/a, full-time
Dates of Enrollment: 8/2001-5/2004
Survey Submitted: February 2005

The campus is very much a commuter campus, especially in the graduate schools. I spent most of my time in the law school building and therefore, cannot comment on the "college life" in general. The gym facilities are very good. I always felt safe and the dining options around the law school are very good.

Read all of Vault's Law School Surveys at www.vault.com/lawschool — get complete surveys on top law schools, expert advice on applicaton essays, LSAT prep and more.

VAULT CAREER LIBRARY **379**

Social Life

Status: Current student, full-time
Dates of Enrollment: 8/2003-Submit Date
Survey Submitted: October 2005

The student life is great, lots of competition, but lots of camaraderie as well. The male-female ratio is almost even, so dating isn't a problem. Overall, we're an attractive student body. There are many places to eat and drink near campus. The Plaza, Brookside and downtown all offer many watering holes. We have seasonal parties to let loose, get drunk and have fun. I don't like Kin Lin, but most people do. Chipotle and Subway are close.

>   **The school says:** "The aforementioned activities are sponsored by student organizations, not the law school."

Status: Current student, full-time
Dates of Enrollment: 8/2003-Submit Date
Survey Submitted: April 2005

The law school is only minutes away from the Plaza, where some of Kansas City's best bars, restaurants and shopping boutiques are located.

Status: Current student, full-time
Dates of Enrollment: 8/2002-Submit Date
Survey Submitted: April 2005

There is a social life for any type of person coming to this school. There are lots of happy hours and there are also family events. We are so close to many bars, including the hot spot of Kansas City. The Country Club Plaza has great restaurants and bars. There are also tons of other things to do in Kansas City including sporting and local cultural events. The law school has three Greek organizations that are very active and tons of student organizations to get involved in. I would say the best part of being a student at UMKC is the social life since there is so much to choose from.

Status: Current student, full-time
Dates of Enrollment: 8/2003-Submit Date
Survey Submitted: April 2005

Again, it's in the middle of a big city so there is always plenty to do. Its really up to the individual to make the best out of it.

Status: Current student, full-time
Dates of Enrollment: 8/2003-Submit Date
Survey Submitted: April 2005

The people are laid-back and nice. Brookside and the Plaza are hot spots.

Status: Current student, full-time
Dates of Enrollment: 8/2004-Submit Date
Survey Submitted: April 2005

Kansas City is a wonderful place to live as far as social life is concerned. There are multiple areas, including the Plaza, Westport and downtown to enjoy. There are more restaurants, bars and shopping opportunities than any one person could take advantage of while attending school. Also, UMKC puts a lot of effort into providing social opportunities for its students. SBA is constantly planning events, such as softball games, "Law School Idol," happy hours and $1.98 Law Review night. In addition to SBA events, many other clubs plan and host events throughout the year.

Status: Current student, full-time
Dates of Enrollment: 8/2004-Submit Date
Survey Submitted: April 2005

Our Student Bar Association (SBA) does a great job of putting on really fun programs for students to get together, such as a fall softball tournament, a spring kickball tournament, a karaoke competition, casino night, variety show and lots of happy hours. Since the school is in a metropolitan area, there are tons of great bars and club; plus, it is within walking distance to the Plaza, the city's major shopping and eating district.

Status: Current student, full-time
Dates of Enrollment: 8/2004-Submit Date
Survey Submitted: April 2005

The law school organizes regular happy hours. There are traditional law school social events including an alumni picnic, Halloween party, softball tournament, formal party, casino night and a theatrical review of law school.

Status: Current student, full-time
Dates of Enrollment: 9/2002-Submit Date
Survey Submitted: April 2005

The law school has "$1.98 Law Review," where students compete by doing performances—comedy, impersonations of professors, singing, anything. Students also have organizations like the Black Law Student Association, Hispanic Law Student Association, Asian Pacific Islander Law Student Association and others that routinely draw speakers and contribute to charities, including an ongoing effort to raise funds for the family of a deceased but beloved law student. The school has heart and fun!

Status: Current student, full-time
Dates of Enrollment: 8/2002-Submit Date
Survey Submitted: April 2005

The social life at the law school is very active. Just make sure you take the time to enjoy it. All that work and no play makes for a very burned out law student. Make the balance work.

The School Says

UMKC School of Law is the urban public law school with the small liberal arts feel. The school provides academic and professional training to students seeking careers in law. We are committed to providing a high quality legal education in a professional and supportive environment, concentrating always on the foundations of good lawyering: respect for people, respect for knowledge and ideas, and respect for justice.

An engaged faculty and student body

Our faculty are outstanding scholars who have extensive practice experience. Faculty at UMKC are actively engaged with students both inside and outside the classroom. Our classes are relatively small (by law school standards) and many of our substantive courses incorporate simulations and service learning opportunities. Our faculty and students are collegial and the school provides many opportunities for interaction and development of close personal relationships that will last throughout one's career.

Working in the best traditions of the profession

We teach students to become lawyers in the best tradition of the profession, introducing them to the opportunities and obligations of the legal profession and its role in the greater community. We appreciate the work of lawyers and their many contributions, which include educating people and institutions about their rights, helping to design prosperous business and community ventures, and working towards the effective and efficient resolution of disputes. We maintain a faculty devoted both to professional service and to advancing knowledge through the production of excellent academic scholarship.

To produce outstanding lawyers and community leaders

As a Law School, we build on a strong tradition of advocacy, civic engagement, and academic excellence. Our program has not only produced some of the region's best lawyers and judges, but has also trained a U.S. Supreme Court Justice (Charles Whittaker) and an American President (Harry Truman). We embrace and foster a collegial, collaborative model of professional education and maintain an intellectual and cultural environment that fosters broad thinking, local and global awareness, and creative problem solving.

We offer special emphasis areas in which students can integrate scholarship, classroom instruction and skills training to develop the skills needed for cutting-edge practice. Emphasis is available in the following areas:

- Litigation

- Child and Family Law

- Business and Entrepreneurial Law, including our unique programs with a special focus on solo and small firm practice

- Urban, Land Use and Environmental Law

If you are looking for a school where everyone knows your name, a school that values practical skills and community involvement and a school that fosters intellectual excitement, then UMKC is the school for you.

Read all of Vault's Law School Surveys at www.vault.com/lawschool — get complete surveys on top law schools, expert advice on applicaton essays, LSAT prep and more.

VAULT CAREER LIBRARY 381

Washington University in St. Louis School of Law

Admissions Office
Campus Box 1120
One Brookings Drive
St. Louis, MO 63130-4899
Admissions phone: (314) 935-4525.
Admissions e-mail: admiss@wulaw.wustl.edu
Admissions URL: http://law.wustl.edu/Admissions/

 ## Admissions

Status: Current student, full-time
Dates of Enrollment: 8/2005-Submit Date
Survey Submitted: May 2006

The admissions staff is absolutely wonderful. The employees are polite, professional, down to earth, knowledgeable and extremely helpful. During the admissions process I was pleasantly surprised with the direct one-on-one contact I had with the people in the admissions office. I was not at all familiar with the school, nor did I know a person in St. Louis, but the admissions staff made me feel right at home.

Status: Alumnus/a, full-time
Dates of Enrollment: 8/2002-5/2005
Survey Submitted: November 2005

The school conducts interviews for those applicants who request them. It is hardly necessary, however, to interview with the school in order to be accepted. The school is highly selective, so an applicant's undergraduate grade point average and LSAT scores are very important. Admissions essays should be interesting and well-written. The essayist should focus less on trying to impress the school with "lawyer-like writing" and more about the applicant's personality and vision.

Status: Current student, full-time
Dates of Enrollment: 8/2003-Submit Date
Survey Submitted: October 2005

The admissions process was relatively painless. It's very important to find out all the scholarships you might be eligible for and be sure to find out what separate application process is required for these scholarships. I did not have to go for an interview, but I believe I wrote an excellent personal statement/essay. The admissions office is very proactive about contacting students, and they have a personal touch—my admissions letter had a handwritten note on it from the admissions office asst director, and I got an e-mail from the director when I got my scholarship. They were not overly pushy, but they definitely let me know that they would be delighted to have me at the school. I was able to go for a tour of the school, and it had the most welcoming atmosphere compared to the other law schools I visited.

If possible, be sure to go for a tour and assess the school for yourself. Selectivity is very competitive, so be sure to study hard for the LSAT and have a good GPA—otherwise make sure your personal statement is a fantastic one that highlights your best features and makes you stand out of the crowd because the school does consider other factors apart from grades.

Status: Alumnus/a full-time
Dates of Enrollment: 9/1998-5/2001
Survey Submitted: March 2006

Washington University is one of the top schools in the country where they look at the ENTIRE candidate. While good grades and LSAT scores will definitely help you get in, a great personal essay can also be the deciding factor. My understanding is that at several top law schools, a personal essay will either help

in a tie-breaker, or if poorly written, overshadow good grades and LSAT scores. At WashU, however, it can mean a whole lot more. I recall one day visiting the admissions office and hearing the Dean of Admissions comment about a phenomenal essay she had just read, stating, "This person does not have the best grades or LSAT score, but we HAVE to get him in. His experiences would add so much to the school." It was at that time that I knew that WashU was not just interested in getting in the best candidates—they were interested in creating an environment comprised of individuals that will contribute to the overall learning experience.

Status: Alumnus/a, full-time
Dates of Enrollment: 8/2000-5/2003
Survey Submitted: April 2005

The admissions process at Washington University becomes more selective each year. But, I believe that the school seriously considers factors other than grades and LSAT scores. The school seeks and appreciates students with diverse backgrounds and interests. I thus highly recommend focusing on unique experiences and personal attributes in the admission essay. Most of all, the essay should be sincere and legitimately reflect the writer's goals and interests. Though Washington University has no formal interview process, I do recommend visiting the school and setting up an informal informational interview with someone in the admissions office, preferably after submitting a written application. This enables the admissions office to put a face and personality with the application and gives the applicant an opportunity to gain valuable information about the school.

Status: Alumnus/a, full-time
Dates of Enrollment: 9/2000-5/2003
Survey Submitted: March 2005

I found the admissions process to be very organized and applicant-friendly. The admissions office staff at Washington University was extremely helpful. While I was still making my decision regarding which law school to attend, the admissions office put me in touch with a current student at the law school so we could exchange e-mails. The student shared a similar background to mine and we had many common interests. She provided me with insight into the "real world of law school." No sugar-coating involved. Our conversations played an integral role in my decision to attend Washington U. When I came down for a weekend and went for a tour of the campus, the admissions staff greeted me by name before I introduced myself and treated me like an old friend throughout my stay.

Status: Current student, full-time
Dates of Enrollment: 8/2002-Submit Date
Survey Submitted: March 2005

Working with WashU's admissions office was one of the many factors that influenced my decision to select this school. At the time, I was unsure of where to enroll and even if I should go at all. The patience, advice, flexibility and encouragement I received from WashU led me to defer admission for a year and eagerly anticipate starting the following fall. I believe that the office looks not only to good grades for potential candidates, but also to other experience and contributions you may make to the incoming class. In writing essays for admission, be candid about your experiences and what you hope to achieve from an education at WashU Law.

Status: Alumnus/a, full-time
Dates of Enrollment: 8/2002-5/2004
Survey Submitted: October 2004

I was a transfer student and I found the admission process outstanding for a Top 20 law school. I called Mark Smith, who was then the dean of career services, as he was in charge of transfer students and asked him what my chances were of being accepted. He asked for my grades and rank and he then told me that I was admitted, to fill out the application online and he would have an acceptance letter in the mail that day. Within two days I had a letter in hand! Compared to other schools that I applied to transfer to, this was the best by far with the fastest turn around. However, although the process is very easy, the selection in transfer students is strict. You must be in the top 10 percent of your class, although they do make exceptions occasionally. If you're in between picking Notre Dame or a school that is ranked close to WashU—you'll be happy you picked WashU as the school is really all about serving the student and not making the money! They really cater to your every need in every department there. If you need money, financial aid finds it for you.

Status: Current student, full-time
Dates of Enrollment: 8/2002-Submit Date
Survey Submitted: December 2003

The school is not shy about paying people with high grades and test scores to come to the school. There is a myriad of merit scholarships. You don't need to apply for the scholarship; they just send you a letter saying you got one. Approximately two-thirds of the student body receives scholarships, with the average around $12,000 per year (I think). Admissions personnel gets back to students relatively quickly to inform of acceptance; informing of scholarships comes later on.

Status: Current student, full-time
Dates of Enrollment: 8/2002-Submit Date
Survey Submitted: February 2004

The admissions process is fairly similar to those at other Top [20] schools. Washington University requires that you use LSAC and that you submit records through that service. WashU is a hands-on school with an active faculty and conscientious admissions staff. I would visit the school and make appointments with admissions counselors. They usually will meet with students to discuss the admissions process, but it is also a good way for them to get to know you, and for you to show what a great candidate you are. Stay in constant contact with the office. They like students who seem excited about WashU and who are not applying to the school as a safety.

 **Academics**

Status: Alumnus/a, full-time
Dates of Enrollment: 8/2002-5/2005
Survey Submitted: November 2005

Washington University School of Law has an excellent academic program. The professors are top quality. It seems as if the majority of them either wrote or co-wrote a major work (i.e., treatise or casebook) in the area in which they practice. Additionally, the credentials of the professors are impeccable. The majority of the classes are driven by theory and not simply by Black Letter Law. An applicant who is solely concerned with passing the bar exam should not apply. Almost every student has the opportunity to take any class he/she wants. It may not always be that there is room in the class in the particular semester the student wants, but before he/she leaves the law school, there will be room in the class. As for grading, the school works on a mandatory mean. All student grades are distributed based on the mean. The workload is relaxed at times and intense at times. Because the majority of classes base grades upon one examination at the end of the semester, this time of the year is particularly exhausting. Otherwise, applicants should expect two to four hours a night of studying throughout the semester and 10 to 12 hours of studying in the final three to four weeks of the semester.

Status: Current student, full-time
Dates of Enrollment: 8/2003-Submit Date
Survey Submitted: October 2005

The program is challenging and exciting. The classes are taught by excellent professors who are leaders and recognized in their fields. Professors are the best part of my school as far as I'm concerned—they are so student-oriented. My professors are always willing to help me be it in my classes or a personal problem they can help with. It's not too hard to get into popular classes as the waiting list moves pretty quickly. Grading can be depressing sometimes due to the curve, but my professors make it clear that grades are not always the best indicator of my ability to succeed as an attorney. The workload is pretty

manageable, but with extracurricular activities and interviews, things can get hectic. Overall, I'm satisfied with the academic nature of my school.

Status: Current student, full-time
Dates of Enrollment: 8/2004-Submit Date
Survey Submitted: September 2005

There are a number of classes with attendance requirements. My advice to you is that you pay close attention to these attendance requirements and make sure that your attendance complies with the requirements. If you fail to comply with the requirements, it is highly likely that your grade in the course will be penalized for failure to comply with the requirements stated by the professor in the course attendance policy.

Status: Alumnus/a full-time
Dates of Enrollment: 8/2000-5/2003
Survey Submitted: March 2006

Quality of classes is high; professors are sometimes amazing, sometimes average. Workload seems normal. The distinguishing feature of the academics is the congenial nature of the student body—this is not the hypercompetitive atmosphere you read about occurring in law schools.

Status: Alumnus/a full-time
Dates of Enrollment: 9/1998-5/2001
Survey Submitted: March 2006

My academic experience at WashU was topnotch. WashU has gone out of its way to provide students with small class sizes with some of the most gifted professors available. Indeed, in my first year, I had three of the brightest and most senior professors teaching my Property, Contracts and Torts classes. Each professor bends over backwards to provide any additional help you need, and office hours are not limited solely to their "posted" times. WashU's main strength comes from its faculty. Each is cherry-picked from among the best in the country. In fact, it was a well-known fact that Top 10 law schools regularly "stole" WashU professors because of their teaching ability and academic acumen and credentials.

Getting into popular classes was never an issue for me. In fact, I was able to take two of the most popular clinic courses available, a judicial internship with a federal district court judge and an internship with the Public Defender. At both internships, I was given hands-on experience, either drafting orders and observing trials, or conducting intake interviews, arguing preliminary hearings and drafting motions.

The workload, obviously, is what you make it. Personally, I took no chances with my first-year grades, studied from six in the morning to 11:00 at night, indulging in only WashU's weekly happy hour (six kegs in the courtyard every Friday) and late night work-outs. It most assuredly paid off.

Status: Alumnus/a, full-time
Dates of Enrollment: 8/2000-5/2003
Survey Submitted: April 2005

WU's professors are collectively one of the school's greatest assets. WU claims its share of internationally renowned legal scholars representing a variety of different fields and interests. More impressive, in my opinion, however is that the professors are truly accessible resources who care about the success of their students and the quality of the education they provide. WU is very proud of its open-door policy and, in my experience, the vast majority of professors abide by that policy. Students are encouraged to go to professors' offices to ask questions or to simply discuss cases. Students commonly approach professors for assistance with law review articles and research topics and even for career advice. I also had no difficulty finding professors who were willing to provide recommendations or to help with writing samples. I was very happy with the quality of the academic courses I took, and, in particular, I believe WU's clinical program is outstanding. The workload is rigorous, but, I believe, on par with comparable law schools.

Status: Alumnus/a, full-time
Dates of Enrollment: 8/2000-5/2003
Survey Submitted: April 2005

The academics at WashU School of Law are excellent. They provide an excellent variety of classes that thoroughly cover the subject matter, and the

Read all of Vault's Law School Surveys at www.vault.com/lawschool — get complete surveys on top law schools, expert advice on applicaton essays, LSAT prep and more.

VAULT CAREER LIBRARY 383

classes range from topics that all law students should learn to some very interesting non-traditional classes that allow you to round out your schedule with something a little more fun. Almost all of my professors were very gifted and really knew what they were talking about and how to explain the concepts. There were a few who didn't quite reach this level, but you can't expect them all to be perfect. I don't think that I was ever shut out of a class that I wanted, even if I had to go on the waiting list a few times.

The workload is tough, but it is law school. And after your first semester you can figure out how much you want to work, and that will be directly related to how well you do in classes. Grading is all on a curve, so get used to it. At first I didn't like that system, but it actually works very well and probably does provide more fair results, most of the time. Overall, I had a really great experience there and I am glad that I chose this school.

Status: Current student, full-time
Dates of Enrollment: 8/2003-Submit Date
Survey Submitted: April 2005

WashU is an exceptional law environment in that it is very rigorous, yet also very friendly, open and easy-going. I'm not a fan of all of the professors, but have managed to take every class I want with fantastic faculty and have easily avoided the handful that I don't like. Many of the faculty are particularly noted in their specializations and provide opportunities to work with some of the best in the world. Most professors are easily approachable and virtually all have gotten to know me on a first-name basis. While the workload is heavy, it's manageable and there is an expectation that you will have a life other than just law school. Some students treat school as a nine to six job outside of the finals period and seem to do just fine.

Status: Alumnus/a, full-time
Dates of Enrollment: 9/1997-5/2000
Survey Submitted: March 2005

It's rough. You are truly expected to work very hard on a full-time basis. The library is wonderful. The professors are available, I mean really available; I had a Trust and Estates professor who met with me and two other students on a Sunday afternoon because of her travel schedule. Professors answer e-mails and all of them were willing and available to give Q&A sessions after classes ended and before exams started. The Legal Research and Writing professors are awesome. They will work with you until you get it right. That was one of my most valuable courses and everyone who intends to practice law should take the Advanced Legal Research and Writing. There are some professors of course, who put on this persona of grandeur and pretend to be untouchable, but honestly, if you just put your pride aside, you'll be surprised at how human they are and how much they really want you to succeed. Grading is very competitive of course; the early bird gets into the best classes, but that's life. You must attend class. I cannot stress this enough. Unless you have a dire emergency, GO TO CLASS, DO NOT SKIP CLASSES, you lose so much more than you can ever get back.

Status: Alumnus/a, full-time
Dates of Enrollment: 8/1999-5/2002
Survey Submitted: March 2005

I thought my academic experience at WashU was exhilarating. One of my favorite aspects of the offerings that is unique to WashU is their emphasis on interdisciplinary classes. Each year I attended, there was a different focus, from Norms and the Law (where various guest lecturers spoke at the school and students in the class go to meet with the lecturers in more intimate settings to discuss their papers and ideas too) to Ethics and the Human Genome Project. My favorite professor specializes in the Supreme Court and in addition to being a law professor was a member of the faculty of the political science department. She would bring to her classes the perspective of "political science style testing" to general ideas and concepts.

 # Employment Prospects

Status: Alumnus/a, full-time
Dates of Enrollment: 8/2002-5/2005
Survey Submitted: November 2005

The employment prospects leaving Washington University are better than most law schools. Recruiters from large firms throughout the country visit the school every semester and conduct days of interviews with students. Outside of large firms, however, other firms from the coasts are not as apt to visit Washington University. On the coasts, the prestige of the law school is less recognized. In the Midwest, however, the law school is recognizably as prestigious as any major law school in the nation. Graduates obtain jobs in all different areas: public interest, government, small firms, large firms, corporate. A number of students accept federal and state clerkships each year.

Status: Alumnus/a full-time
Dates of Enrollment: 9/1998-5/2001
Survey Submitted: March 2006

Wash. U is a fantastic feeder school for the Midwestern market, especially Chicago and St. Louis. Most, if not all, of Chicago's major law firms interview on campus. Wash. U also has been establishing significant ties with major New York, Washington D.C., and other East Coast law firms. West Coast ties, however, were not as strong as Wash. U's other geographic ties.

Wash. U is one of the top schools in the country, and that prestige has followed me to every interview. On-campus recruiting—so long as you are at or near the top of the class—is extremely helpful.

Status: Alumnus/a, full-time
Dates of Enrollment: 8/2000-5/2003
Survey Submitted: April 2005

WU has very high job placement numbers, and I believe the employment prospects are very good for students graduating from WU Law. A large number of large, prestigious firms recruit on-campus at WU. Though a majority of the firms that come on-campus are from Chicago or St. Louis, WU has done a great deal to expand its geographical reach. More and more firms from NY and D.C., as well as other cities of interest, are recruiting WU students each year. Students in my graduating class are now working in a variety of different cities, including Houston, NY, D.C. and Atlanta. In addition to jobs with large firms, many students successfully obtained positions with various government agencies, smaller boutique firms and nonprofit agencies, as well as judicial clerkships (both state and federal). WU's clinics provide a particularly useful tool for finding jobs. The D.C. clinic, which enables students to spend their last semester of law school interning on the Hill or working with other agencies in D.C., is a wonderful way to make contacts and secure offers for employment.

Status: Alumnus/a, full-time
Dates of Enrollment: 8/1999-5/2002
Survey Submitted: March 2005

My affiliation with the school helped me obtain two summer internships— as well as a job post-graduation. Overall, the school is beginning to emphasize career resources and expanding their networking and branding to the coasts and outside their predominant base of St. Louis, Chicago and Kansas City. Alumni always seemed willing to talk and would pass along information about opportunities they were aware of. In the last three years since graduation, I have begun to notice that WashU is becoming more and more well-known in these areas, albeit partly based on its undergraduate programs.

Status: Alumnus/a, full-time
Dates of Enrollment: 8/1999-5/2002
Survey Submitted: March 2004

To begin, Washington University School of Law is the best law school in the city and state. I am speaking of rankings and recognition, NOT personal opinion. Career services is very well staffed and knowledgeable. However, they do focus on the most qualified students. This means you should plan on doing more of your own legwork if you are not in the top 25 percent of your class. Career services is a huge resource with a ton of information. Also, this law school is focused on law firms and a bit on government agencies.

One caveat: WashU has moved up quite a bit, with Dean Seligman joining the team in 1999. WashU has traditionally been a very prestigious regional law school. In the past few years, students have begun to go to both East Coast and West Coast large national and international law firms, especially the big names in New York. This began as more the impetus of the law students pounding down the doors than career services being well connected. Academically the school is very well thought of, and this law school is now nationally known rather than primarily Midwestern in reputation. This makes internships very easy to get locally.

Status: Current student, full-time
Dates of Enrollment: 8/2002-Submit Date
Survey Submitted: December 2003

The career center will work closely with students, if students put in the effort to work with the career center. There are numerous on-campus interviewing opportunities, but as the job search goes, more interviews are given to students at the top of the grade pile. Those below the 50-percent mark have a harder time. There are approximately [five] lottery slots per interviewer, though, so if you aren't chosen to interview based on your academic credentials, your pure luck might get you through the door. WashU has a strong name within St. Louis and the Midwest and is somewhat strong on the East Coast. The school is working on getting alumni and support base in the West Coast, but they "aren't there yet."

> **The school says:** "In addition to a growing on-campus interview program, the Career Services Office (CSO) provides the opportunity for students to interview off campus in programs held in New York, D.C., Atlanta and Boston, and on the West Coast (which includes employers from the Los Angeles area and the Bay area). Participating employers include law firms, government agencies and public interest organizations. In addition to formal interviewing programs, the CSO assists students with numerous programs and individual counseling to help students formulate a job search strategy. Extensive funding is available for summer public interest internships, as well as a loan repayment assistance program to assist graduates working in public service careers."

 ## Quality of Life

Status: Alumnus/a, full-time
Dates of Enrollment: 8/2002-5/2005
Survey Submitted: November 2005

St. Louis is a nice city in which to attend law school. The housing situation is very diverse. Within 10 miles of the law school, there is housing for those that like a more suburban feel and those who want to live in the city, those who want a house and those who want an apartment or a hotel, those who want a "young" neighborhood or an "artsy" neighborhood, and those who want specific amenities as opposed to others. In most places parking is free. Naturally, crime increases as you move closer to the city, but those who want to stay free from high-crime areas should have no problem doing so.

The campus is beautiful. Look at a picture, you'll see. Campus has extracurricular opportunities for every student, both graduate and undergraduate. The law school is relatively new. The architecture of the building is stunning, the library is expansive, and the entire building has wireless Internet. It is a very safe campus. If there is a drawback to the campus, it is the workout facilities. The gym is a bit of a rathole.

Status: Current student, full-time
Dates of Enrollment: 8/2003-Submit Date
Survey Submitted: October 2005

Quality of life is excellent—although law students are not allowed to live on campus, there is an extensive network of off-campus housing. Facilities are excellent—wireless network in the entire law school, 24/hour access to the law school with card access. The law school neighborhood is pretty safe especially with the on-campus police. Dining can be improved upon, but the law school cafe is pretty good.

Status: Alumnus/a full-time
Dates of Enrollment: 8/1998-5/2001
Survey Submitted: April 2006

WashU's law school moved into handsome new facilities a few years ago, and the law school is fairly well integrated into the campus community. WashU is located on the western-most edge of St. Louis, blending into two suburbs, University City to the north and Clayton (a business hub) to the southwest. Housing, dining and entertainment options within a short walk to the law school are plentiful. The campus front onto Forest Park, one of the largest and loveliest urban parks in the country, featuring the St. Louis Museum of Art, the St. Louis Zoo and a variety of cultural and sports facilities.

Status: Alumnus/a full-time
Dates of Enrollment: 9/1998-5/2001
Survey Submitted: March 2006

St. Louis is an extremely friendly city to live in. Local restaurants, bars and other social venues are all close-by campus, parking is abundant and housing is affordably priced. If a candidate is looking for a sprawling metropolis, St. Louis may not be for you. If you are looking to focus on great law school academics and blow off steam at great local eateries and bars, then St. Louis is a fantastic option. Personally, I relished the fact that St. Louis did not provide too many social options, as it allowed me to focus more on my academics.

Status: Alumnus/a, full-time
Dates of Enrollment: 8/2000-5/2003
Survey Submitted: April 2005

The biggest contributor to the quality of life at WU is the school's remarkably laid-back atmosphere. Though students are personally driven, there is not a lot of competition—by law school standards. Overall WU offers a very supportive environment. Students share class notes, work in study groups and genuinely work to help each other. After years of hearing law school horror stories about ultra-competitive students, I was extremely pleased to find such a welcoming student body. WU does not offer on-campus housing for graduate students, but there are plenty of apartments within walking distance or short drive from the school. WU offers a housing tour each summer before school begins to familiarize students with the various neighborhoods and facilitate lease-signings. They also help interested students find roommates. The campus is beautiful, as is the relatively new law school building. WU prides itself on its technological capabilities. Laptops are widely used among students, both in class and for final exams, but are not required. The law school has its own cafeteria and students have access to all of the main campus dining options. The school is located in one of the nicest neighborhoods in St. Louis and, while incidents do occur, the overall crime rate is very low. The relatively low cost of living is also a plus.

Status: Current student, full-time
Dates of Enrollment: 9/2004-Submit Date
Survey Submitted: April 2005

St. Louis is a good place to be. It is a manageable city with lots to do, and the people are overwhelmingly nice. Housing is affordable and right now gas prices are among the lowest in the country. Most students live in the University City/Loop area or in the Central West End. Both are nice and cheap, however, you would be more likely to have your car broken into or stolen, and one student was mugged there a couple years ago. I live in Brentwood, which is in the middle of St. Louis county, and only four miles from school. That is a very nice, central location, isn't too expensive, especially if you can get a roommate, and is safe. Campus is pretty, and is walkable. There are on-campus cafeterias and restaurants nearby that are good and preferable to the law school cafeteria. I've been to the gym a few times, and it is pretty standard. There's a Bally's close to campus, though, if you are interested in that.

Status: Alumnus/a, full-time
Dates of Enrollment: 8/1999-5/2002
Survey Submitted: March 2004

Quality of life here is fantastic. St. Louis has dramatically evolved in the past 10 years. There is plenty of action in this Midwestern town. WashU is very well located in a safe and clean area of St. Louis suburbs. Although there is no on-campus housing, there are plenty of apartments to rent at reasonable prices. From the WashU Medical School Campus in the West End runs a bus to take students to the main campus where the law school is located. Campus facilities

Read all of Vault's Law School Surveys at www.vault.com/lawschool — get complete surveys on top law schools, expert advice on applicaton essays, LSAT prep and more.

VAULT CAREER LIBRARY 385

are full-service, and the law school building has its own cafeteria. Note: WashU has a new law school that was built less than 10 years ago. Crime and safety are the lowest if you live in the Clayton area apartments.

Social Life

Status: Alumnus/a, full-time
Dates of Enrollment: 8/2002-5/2005
Survey Submitted: November 2005

Social life at Washington University is what you make of it. As a major city, St. Louis has a good amount of nightlife. At the law school, there is a happy hour every Friday evening in the courtyard. There are campus-wide parties every semester in which major musical acts perform. St. Louis has a good, not great, restaurant scene. It is an exceptional scene for those who love Italian food; it is a disastrous scene for those who love Mexican food. For those who enjoy American, Middle Eastern, Thai, Vietnamese and Chinese, the selection in St. Louis is comparable to the selection in most major cities. All in all, there is something for everyone.

Status: Current student, full-time
Dates of Enrollment: 8/2003-Submit Date
Survey Submitted: October 2005

Social life is unbelievable—we have happy hour every Friday with free beer and food—this is definitely a student favorite! There is a good variety of clubs in St. Louis ranging from Salsa Clubs to clubs that play traditional West African music. The dating scene is sort of weird as there's a lot of intra-law school dating, and personally that's a no-no, but overall the social life is pretty good.

Status: Alumnus/a, full-time
Dates of Enrollment: 8/2000-5/2003
Survey Submitted: April 2005

The law school hosts a happy hour every Friday, which is sponsored and organized by a different student group each week. And St. Louis offers a wide variety of restaurants, clubs, and bars, as well. Among the most popular areas is "The Loop," located within walking distance of the school. The Loop contains a St. Louis and WU favorite, Blueberry Hill, as well as unique clothes and jewelry boutiques, eclectic restaurants and shops and a couple of great shoe stores. Also popular is the Central West End, which similarly houses a number of stores, restaurants and bars. Wonderful restaurants abound (for Italian food, you can't beat any of the restaurants in "the Hill"). Wine bars, jazz and blues clubs and traditional dance clubs are also located in close proximity to the school. And, the many great coffee shops provide a great alternative to the library for studying.

Status: Current student, full-time
Dates of Enrollment: 9/2004-Submit Date
Survey Submitted: April 2005

The school can get a little clique-ish, but people can either rise above that or fall into it; it is your choice. There are tons of student organizations for you to join, and they sponsor lots of events like guest lectures, panel discussions and how-to sessions. I came into school engaged, so I don't know what the dating scene is like here.

There are several bars in the University City/Loop area, which is only a few blocks north of the school, and particular favorites there include Blueberry Hill (good Thursday night karaoke) and Pin-up Bowl. We've also gone out in the Central West End a few times, as well, and there are several places to choose from down there. I like to go to the hotel bars at the Ritz-Carlton in Clayton and the Chase Park Plaza in the Central West End. Clayton has some nice, trendy, somewhat more upscale places to go out and be seen, if you are into that, too. People frequent the clubs at the Landing, downtown near the river, then gamble on the casino boats. Those are more of a meat-market scene and it can get a little rough there. There are tons of places to eat everywhere, with a wide variety of cuisines. I've been a little disappointed in the Thai places I've tried, though.

Status: Alumnus/a, full-time
Dates of Enrollment: 9/1997-5/2000
Survey Submitted: March 2005

The school of law puts on a full calendar of activities and really brings in lots of famous people. The university is huge, the graduate school of business is close by and they really party or so I hear. I'm a bit older than the average student, so I wasn't as involved in the social scene and that is one of the high points of WashU, the law students are married, they have children, they're single, divorced, in their 20s, in their 30s plus, there are joint degree candidates, there are students with lots of work experience and some with none (which really puts you at a disadvantage in my opinion). The Symphony is great. The downtown life is really developing, with lots of affordable loft housing. Shopping is excellent, from huge, popular malls, to stand-alone shops in nearby Maplewood and Dogtown. There's something for everyone. Come!

Status: Alumnus/a, full-time
Dates of Enrollment: 8/2001-5/2004
Survey Submitted: March 2005

It is no secret that the law facility is Anheuser-Busch Hall. It is also no secret that you will find law students tapping kegs (provided by the various student groups) all afternoon and early evening on Fridays. It is also no secret professors and even the former Dean like to stop by for a schmooze and cold one (let alone celeb appearances from a few St. Louis Rams in 2001). These law students like their weekends, embodying the work hard, play hard mantra of the institution. St. Louis has traditionally been a city of few great restaurants, but recently has added major chains to make up for the culinary quagmire. Local haunts such as Blueberry Hill remain law student staples for the beer, burgers and Berry (Chuck Berry, who performs there monthly). Other St. Louis institutions include toasted ravioli, frozen custard and anything associated with the Cardinals.

The School Says

For more than 135 years, Washington University School of Law in St. Louis has offered a strong legal foundation on which our students have built their futures. Take a few moments to consider what distinguishes us from other law schools:

- The Center for Interdisciplinary Studies, which supports interdisciplinary legal research and scholarship by sponsoring annual programs and activities that focus on cutting-edge legal issues and that require expertise, exploration, and discussion from other disciplines.

- The Whitney R. Harris Institute for Global Legal Studies, which functions as a center for instruction and research in international and comparative law.

- An expanding Intellectual Property and Technology Law program, including a new Center for Research on Innovation and Entrepreneurship and a new Intellectual Property and Business Formation Legal Clinic.

- First-year class sizes among the smallest of the top law schools with half of first-year courses having about 40 students or less.

- A clinical guarantee which allows every student the opportunity to participate in our Clinical Education Program, ranked third among law schools by *U.S. News & World Report*.

- Through the Congressional and Administrative Law Clinic, Washington University is one of very few law schools with the ability to offer a significant number of students the chance to work as full-time interns on Capitol Hill.

- Scholarship awards represent guaranteed three-year commitments. Our students have the security of knowing they will continue to receive their scholarships regardless of their class rank.

- A longstanding commitment to public service demonstrated by our Clinical Education Program, Webster Society Scholarships, summer public interest stipends, Public Service Project, Mel Brown Family Loan Repayment Assistance Program, and other related initiatives.

- A nationally ranked Trial and Advocacy Program.

For more information about these and other exciting initiatives, visit our web site at http://law.wustl.edu/

Read all of Vault's Law School Surveys at www.vault.com/lawschool — get complete surveys on top law schools, expert advice on applicaton essays, LSAT prep and more.

V/\ULT CAREER LIBRARY   **387**

University of Nevada, Las Vegas

William S. Boyd School of Law
Admissions Office
4505 Maryland Parkway
Box 451003
Las Vegas, NV 89154-1003
Admissions phone: (702) 895-2440
Admissions fax: (702) 895-2414
Admissions e-mail: request@law.unlv.edu
Admissions URL: www.law.unlv.edu/admissions.html

 Admissions

Status: Current student, part-time
Dates of Enrollment: 8/2006-Submit Date
Survey Submitted: April 2006

Although the admission's committee considers an LSAT of 154 to 160 and GPA of around 3.2 to 3.6 competitive, they also consider soft factors very highly. However, they are still highly selective and only admit about 10 to 11 percent of applicants. In addition, the admissions committee seems to go easier on Nevada residents and part-time applicants. Decisions are usually announced by April, but most acceptances go out in March, rejections in April and waitlists in late April to May. Boyd law school is very helpful and approachable in answering questions from prospective students.

Status: Alumnus/a, full-time
Dates of Enrollment: 8/1998-5/2001
Survey Submitted: January 2005

I was a member of the charter class of this relatively new law school in 1998. While the competition was stiff, given the school's prompt ABA accreditation, new facility and additional illustrious faculty, it is considerably tougher now. The school places great weight on community involvement and civic activities, credit is given for work experience and the school strives to admit a diverse student body.

Status: Alumnus/a, full-time
Dates of Enrollment: 8/1999-5/2002
Survey Submitted: April 2004

Admissions are very selective in that a large number of people apply for a very few seats. However, the reality is that, since the school only recently gained full accreditation, the quality of the applicant pool has not been the best, so an applicant with an above-average LSAT score and GPA can usually expect to be one of the chosen few. That will likely change as the school has gained accreditation and has been ranked in the Top 100 by *U.S. News & World Report*. The admissions process for me was exceptionally painless. There was no interview involved, the application did not require any overly burdensome attachments and I received an acceptance letter, along with a scholarship offer, within a very short period of time after submitting my application.

Status: Current student, full-time
Dates of Enrollment: 9/2003-Submit Date
Survey Submitted: June 2004

The admissions process included the standard law school steps: LSAT, application and essay. The director of admissions is dedicated to helping each applicant. There are very informative open houses. I attended the one for admitted students and it was very helpful in my decision and offered the opportunity to talk to many current students.

Status: Alumnus/a, full-time
Dates of Enrollment: 8/2000-5/2003
Survey Submitted: May 2004

It was a very lengthy admission process. The application required two letters of recommendation, one personal and the other related to employment experience. In addition, potential students were required to submit employment history, educational history, including proof of undergraduate degree and three references. Lastly, potential students were required to submit proof of a passing score on the LSAT and a personal statement. Overall acceptance was based upon an average LSAT score of 153 and GPA of 3.5. At the time that I was admitted, the law school was only starting its second year and it was not accredited. However, prior to my graduation, the law school received full accreditation. There was no entrance interview.

 Academics

Status: Alumnus/a, full-time
Dates of Enrollment: 8/1998-5/2001
Survey Submitted: January 2005

The faculty is topnotch. Grading seems fair and, for the most part, reflects a student's efforts. The workload the first year is tough (as it should be) especially when combined with the mandatory community service requirement. The school's clinical opportunities have grown tremendously in the past few years.

Status: Alumnus/a, full-time
Dates of Enrollment: 8/2000-5/2003
Survey Submitted: May 2004

Due to the relative infancy of the law school, I have a high regard for the administration in securing top professors from other highly accredited law schools. Our professors were highly qualified and extremely knowledgeable. The size of our classes was fairly small and fairly easy to get into.

The workload was similar to other law schools, however, I do not feel that I was forced to participate in the overall classroom experience. As such, several students, myself included, spent four years reading, going to class (or not), and taking finals, without any fear of being called on. There were minimal group activities and written work during the semester, with the exception of a Legal Writing class. We were only graded on our final at the end of the semester. Overall, I would say this law school is typical with regard to workload, but atypical with regard to class participation. The scenes from *The Paper Chase* did not play out at this law school.

Status: Alumnus/a, full-time
Dates of Enrollment: 8/1999-5/2002
Survey Submitted: April 2004

From the first day that the school opened its doors, its faculty has been topnotch; and one of the advantages of UNLV is that the class sizes are small enough that each student can get personal attention from the professors. UNLV now has a good variety of classes and scheduling is usually no hassle. The workload was moderate to heavy, and the grade curve set a median grade of B-. Very few D's or F's are given.

Status: Current student, full-time
Dates of Enrollment: 9/2003-Submit Date
Survey Submitted: June 2004

The quality of the first-year classes is very high. The majority of the professors are excellent. Grading is done on a strict B- curve. The workload is tough, but it's law school.

Employment Prospects

Status: Alumnus/a, full-time
Dates of Enrollment: 8/1998-5/2001
Survey Submitted: January 2005

The top law firms in this market heavily recruit from the top third of the class Don't let anyone tell you differently—grades matter—even several years post-graduation. Involvement in the Law Journal and/or moot court is also extremely important to potential employers. The school also provides on-campus interviews with numerous local firms for summer associateships.

Status: Alumnus/a, full-time
Dates of Enrollment: 8/2000-5/2003
Survey Submitted: May 2004

Our career services program was very good. Because of the infancy of the law school and because this is Nevada's only law school, the community was very active and receptive to our students. Not only were the law firms willing to recruit and hire our students, so was the bench. Coupled with the legal community's willingness to hire our students, was a willingness to contribute money and time to the education of our students. This came in the form of internships, externships, career fairs, lectures, forums, literary scholarships and academic scholarships. I certainly feel this was a very unique opportunity, and certainly not the general reception that law students feel during law school and immediately thereafter.

Status: Alumnus/a, full-time
Dates of Enrollment: 8/1999-5/2002
Survey Submitted: April 2004

If there were only one reason to attend UNLV, it would be the opportunities for employment that are available to graduates. The local bar, and particularly the local judiciary, has been very supportive of the school. A high percentage of graduates obtain coveted judicial clerkships with the federal district court and the Ninth Circuit Court of Appeals, as well as the Nevada Supreme Court. Las Vegas has a very good economy, and there is much more legal work in Las Vegas than there are lawyers to do the work, so firms are always hiring, and they love to hire UNLV graduates.

Status: Current student, full-time
Dates of Enrollment: 9/2003-Submit Date
Survey Submitted: June 2004

Career prospects out of UNLV Boyd Law are good. The employment statistics are very high. Boyd has a great externship program. I am currently working with a judge for the summer. However, there are also congressional and public law extern programs. I don't have personal experience yet with the campus recruiting program so will refrain from commenting. Boyd has very good community support and local employers recognize that it is a quality law school. The prestige factor may be more limited the farther you get from the Southwest; however, now that the school is ranked (and should continue to rise in the rankings) the prestige should continue to rise.

Quality of Life

Status: Alumnus/a, full-time
Dates of Enrollment: 8/1998-5/2001
Survey Submitted: January 2005

The new facility is on the main campus of UNLV and is beautiful. The law library is becoming highly-regarded and invaluable to this community.

Status: Current student, full time
Dates of Enrollment: 9/2003-Submit Date
Survey Submitted: June 2004

Quality of life is good. There are many student clubs that encompass and support many different issues affecting student quality of life. There is no on-campus housing for law students; however, housing in Las Vegas is plentiful and there are many options. The cost of housing is increasing very quickly so that may impact the quality of life for future classes. The campus is large and spread out and students generally stay close to the law building. The library is very good, especially for such a new school, and resources continue to grow.

The dining options on campus near the law school consist of a small "cafe" with prepared salads and sandwiches, a Burger King and a Pizza Hut. The student union offers a wrap counter, burger counter and Mexican counter. Off campus but near enough for lunch are an In n' Out, Chipotle and other fast-food places. The school is not in a "neighborhood," so to speak, and there is limited housing immediately surrounding the campus. Law students reside in all areas of the Valley. The campus seems fairly safe and I know of no one who has had any problems. Las Vegas in general is probably similar to any rapidly growing city with regard to crime.

Status: Alumnus/a, full-time
Dates of Enrollment: 8/2000-5/2003
Survey Submitted: May 2004

The first and second year that I was enrolled in the law school, we were forced to attend classes in an old elementary school off campus while the old library was being converted into the law school. Clearly, this was not optimal. However, by the beginning of my last year, we were attending classes in an extraordinary law center. Each of our classrooms had individual Internet connections and extensive audio/visual equipment. With regards to housing, most of the students, if not all, lived off campus. However, I do believe that our students would have qualified for dorm housing, if necessary.

Status: Alumnus/a, full-time
Dates of Enrollment: 8/1999-5/2002
Survey Submitted: April 2004

The school moved into a new facility in the fall of 2002. The new facility has well-designed classrooms with state-of-the-art technology and a large library, as well as a moot court room and a large and comfortable student lounge. The school is located in the heart of the main campus. Las Vegas is a rapidly growing city, but it is still relatively small, and the campus is within a 30-minute commute of most places in the Las Vegas valley.

Social Life

Status: Alumnus/a, full-time
Dates of Enrollment: 8/1998-5/2001
Survey Submitted: January 2005

The school has a very diverse array of associations for its students. Since this is Nevada's only law school, the community is very supportive.

Status: Current student, full-time
Dates of Enrollment: 9/2003-Submit Date
Survey Submitted: June 2004

The social life is up to each individual. There are many Vegas locals at the school who know where to eat, drink and dance. There are many student clubs, with more being organized all the time.

Status: Alumnus/a, full-time
Dates of Enrollment: 8/2000-5/2003
Survey Submitted: May 2004

This area, due to the extensive workload of a law student, was extremely limited. We did have a tremendous number of events and clubs centered around the academic experience and the law, however, law school is definitely different than undergraduate school. In this regard, our campus is very similar to others but we have the unique opportunity to be attending school in the tourist capital of the world, Las Vegas. As the university is situated in Las Vegas, one need not go very far to find shows, gambling, drinking, nightclubs and restaurants—24 hours a day. All in all, it could be very distracting for students who are not committed to their studies.

Status: Alumnus/a, full-time
Dates of Enrollment: 8/1999-5/2002
Survey Submitted: April 2004

The campus is located just East of the Las Vegas Strip, with some of the world's best restaurants and nightclubs just minutes away. I won't belabor this point because, come on, it's Vegas. If you want social life, this is as social as it gets.

Read all of Vault's Law School Surveys at www.vault.com/lawschool — get complete surveys on top law schools, expert advice on applicaton essays, LSAT prep and more.

VAULT CAREER LIBRARY 389

Franklin Pierce Law Center

Admission Office
2 White Street
Concord, NH 03301
Admissions phone: (603) 228-9217
Admissions e-mail: admissions@piercelaw.edu
Admissions URL: www.piercelaw.edu/admissions.htm

Note: The school has chosen not to comment on the student surveys submitted.

 ## Admissions

Status: Current student, full-time
Dates of Enrollment: 8/2001-Submit Date
Survey Submitted: February 2004

The admissions process is straightforward and simple to complete. Online form and an essay. Complete and submit materials early as acceptances are offered on a rolling basis. The school is getting more selective with its entering class, but they look for real-world experience to determine success in law school. No interview is needed; however, you can sign up to come to an open house and sit in on a class.

Status: Alumnus/a, full-time
Dates of Enrollment: 8/2002-5/2004
Survey Submitted: March 2005

I transferred from California. Easy, basic application. They requested LSDAS, letters of recommendation and writing samples.

Status: Alumnus/a, full-time
Dates of Enrollment: 8/1996-5/1999
Survey Submitted: April 2004

Admissions follows the same process as at other schools. Grades, LSAT score, references and essay are considered. Because the school is so small, however, each application gets a full review. Because the school is heavily invested in IP law, technical degrees are given weight and are considered in reviewing grades. The essay may get more weight than at other schools because each application is reviewed. A visit to the campus is unnecessary, and probably has no effect on the admissions decision.

Status: Alumnus/a, full-time
Dates of Enrollment: 8/2000-5/2003
Survey Submitted: April 2004

Unlike most law schools, Franklin Pierce does not solely focus on GPA and LSAT score. Franklin Pierce considers an applicant's community service, employment history and any other factors that make the applicant unique.

Status: Current student, full-time
Dates of Enrollment: 8/2003-5/2005
Survey Submitted: September 2003

I had to take the LSAT examination and apply with the LSAC, which is a central hub that distributes your transcripts, LSAT scores and letters of recommendation. There are no interviews for law school. The school also takes into consideration your personal statement, which is a plus.

 ## Academics

Status: Current student, full-time
Dates of Enrollment: 8/2001-Submit Date
Survey Submitted: February 2004

The program focuses on both practical and policy skills. The classes are excellent. The Socratic Method is used by some but not prevalent. Most classes are lectures and seminars and use the case method (similar to a business school). The professors do not embarrass you with the Socratic Method, but are genuinely interested in teaching. Grading is done on a B- mean, with smaller classes (under 15) not having to conform. Other than scheduling conflicts, popular classes are very easy to get into. Rarely is anyone denied entry. Workload is manageable. The program goes to great lengths not to overburden one with mindless work. Reading material and length of assignments are very manageable. Focus is on the quality of work not quantity. I know my professors by their first names. I was assigned a professor as an advisor. I treat law school as a job (8 a.m. to 5 p.m., five days a week) and do not need more than that to handle the workload.

Status: Alumnus/a, full-time
Dates of Enrollment: 8/2002-5/2004
Survey Submitted: March 2005

Helpful and caring professors. The atmosphere is that of a family. You are there to learn, but the professors care.

Status: Alumnus/a, full-time
Dates of Enrollment: 8/1996-5/1999
Survey Submitted: April 2004

The first year is identical to that at any law school. All the basic courses are covered. The 1L schedule has one opening for an elective. The second and third years offer a wide range of opportunities. There are on-campus legal clinics and externships with local attorneys and courts are plentiful. FPLC is the only law school in NH and has a strong relationship with the Court of Appeals for the Federal Circuit. In addition, a summer institute for intellectual property is offered. I was able to graduate in three years with a JD and a Master's in Intellectual Property.

Many (if not all) of the professors have actual experience as practicing attorneys and bring real-world perspective to the classroom. Unlike many of my contemporaries, I had drafted complaints, motions, patent applications and other patent related papers before I graduated. The classes tend to skew to the practical rather than the theoretical. Because the school is so small, students are seldom locked out of classes.

The workload is heavy but very manageable. The first year in particular is specifically designed to avoid projects being due on the same date, but the next due date is never more than three days away. This requires a good deal of planning and attention to one's schedule.

Status: Alumni, full-time
Dates of Enrollment: 8/2000-5/2003
Survey Submitted: April 2004

The classes are small and professors typically know students by names. Very few professors conduct their classes in the Socratic Method. The Legal Research and Writing Program is among the best in the nation, as is the Intellectual Property program. Students typically are able to enroll in all classes selected.

Status: Current student, full-time
Dates of Enrollment: 8/2003-5/2005
Survey Submitted: September 2003

The workload is equivalent to all other law school programs. The program here is ranked third in the nation in Intellectual Property Law. The courses are highly ranked and we offer over 50 specialized IP courses, where other law schools generally have significantly fewer.

Employment Prospects

Status: Current student, full-time
Dates of Enrollment: 8/2001-Submit Date
Survey Submitted: February 2004

Career prospects very good if you're patent eligible and willing to do patent litigation or prosecution. If you want to work locally (New Hampshire), many firms will hire. It's easy to get a local internship since the school is located in the capital city. Probably around a quarter to a half of the of class externs over the course of the 2L/3L years. Prestige of school is related to intellectual property expertise and locale. It may be difficult to get a job outside of New Hampshire with poor grades. The career placement office is helpful and always available.

Status: Alumnus/a, full-time
Dates of Enrollment: 8/2002-5/2004
Survey Submitted: March 2005

The best patent firms come to Pierce to interview. Very good on-campus opportunities for Northeast located firms. Opportunities for life beyond NYC and Boston.

Status: Alumnus/a, full-time
Dates of Enrollment: 8/1996-5/1999
Survey Submitted: April 2004

FPLC is well-regarded with employers in the IP field. Less so in other fields. The program in IP is excellent and consistently ranks in the Top 10 in the country.

Many employers conducted on-campus interviews and collected resumes. However, those students outside the top 10 percent of the class will have a hard time getting noticed.

Career services is excellent and always willing to help in any way possible. Generally, there is no problem walking in for advice. Again, the small size of the school is a plus. The career placement office and faculty have many contacts in firms and industry and are ready to help find a placement for a deserving student.

I landed my job in the conventional manner—on-campus interview, call back, summer associate position 2L summer, full-time offer by fall of my 3L year. My roommate, however, did not have stellar grades and was able to land an externship with a Fortune 500 company, which turned into an offer for a full-time position. He eventually landed a second offer from a Fortune 500 company with the help of the dean. He accepted this offer.

Very few of my classmates failed to have offers by the time we graduated. As a caveat, I should note that we graduated in the middle of the last hiring boom in the spring of 1999.

Status: Alumnus/a, full-time
Dates of Enrollment: 8/2000-5/2003
Survey Submitted: April 2004

Many firms whose practice areas include intellectual property interview on campus. Many students clerk for the Court of Appeals for the Federal Circuit, which hears mostly intellectual property appeals.

Status: Current student, full-time
Dates of Enrollment: 8/2003-5/2005
Survey Submitted: September 2003

Campus recruiting is strong. FPLC is highly-respected in the IP realm on the East Coast. Currently, we are moving into the West Coast IP market and showing large firms what we are capable of. We only graduate 120 students each year, since the 70s.

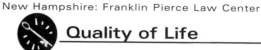 # Quality of Life

Status: Current student, full-time
Dates of Enrollment: 8/2001-Submit Date
Survey Submitted: February 2004

Quality of life is good. Lots of outdoor activities in summer and winter. Housing can be tough to find. It can get expensive for what you get. The school has very limited housing of its own. Virtually no crime—very safe. Neighborhood is charming. Good for families.

Status: Alumnus/a, full-time
Dates of Enrollment: 8/2002-5/2004
Survey Submitted: March 2005

Small town feeling, but close to mountains, beach and Boston. Little traffic and great locals.

Status: Alumnus/a, full-time
Dates of Enrollment: 8/1996-5/1999
Survey Submitted: April 2004

The quality of life at FPLC is excellent. There is a real sense of community (again because of the size). The joke is that Frank is the "little law school that cares." It is nearly impossible to fall through the cracks. Absences are noticed by classmates and faculty.

Unlike the stories I have heard about other schools, students are generally willing to help fellow students and I know of no incident of sabotage (stolen reference tools or intentionally erroneous outlines) during my time at FPLC, although every one of my contemporaries from other schools have such stories.

FPLC offers very little housing and what is offered are school owned houses for rent. However, the cost of living is very reasonable and rental space is plentiful.

The school has few facilities beyond the classrooms, library and a small dining area. It is, however, walking distance to downtown Concord, and any amenity is readily available.

Concord is a small town with few crime problems. The school is located in a quiet residential neighborhood. Next to the school is a park with a small pond that is perfect for studying outside on spring and summer days.

Status: Alumnus/a, full-time
Dates of Enrollment: 8/2000-5/2003
Survey Submitted: April 2004

Housing can be hard to secure if the incoming student waits until the last minute to look. Franklin Pierce does not have any dorms, so all housing is off campus. Because Franklin Pierce is located in a residential neighborhood, many students are able to secure housing within walking distance to the school.

Status: Current student, full-time
Dates of Enrollment: 8/2003-5/2005
Survey Submitted: September 2003

Crime is low. The living expenses are cheap. The snow and cold weather take some adjustment if you are from Huntington Beach, CA. The campus is close to stores and housing. Most students live within walking distance.

 # Social Life

Status: Current student, full-time
Dates of Enrollment: 8/2001-Submit Date
Survey Submitted: February 2004

No Greek system. Independent law school. Social life can be limited. Concord is a small town and it does not particularly cater to its law students. A few bars and restaurants locally. Many of the chain restaurants. Quite a few clubs for the school's size. Very easy to start your own. Hourly buses from downtown Concord to Boston. Only one hour to the sea coast and less to the mountains.

Read all of Vault's Law School Surveys at www.vault.com/lawschool — get complete surveys on top law schools, expert advice on applicaton essays, LSAT prep and more.

VAULT CAREER LIBRARY 391

Status: Alumnus/a, full-time
Dates of Enrollment: 8/2002-5/2004
Survey Submitted: March 2005

Not many bars in Concord, but you have Boston and Portsmouth less than an hour away. No Greek system; this is law school! Small school feeling, but great opportunities after law school.

Status: Alumnus/a, full-time
Dates of Enrollment: 8/1996-5/1999
Survey Submitted: April 2004

The social life at FPLC tends to revolve around the school and classmates. Concord is not a hot bed of activity and weekend house parties are regular. I found it strange how often faculty members show up at these parties.

As for drinking holes, Forefather's and Tio Juan's are favorites for after-class or after-exam drinks and dinners. The dining in Concord leaves something to be desired.

There are three yearly events of note: an alumni/reunion weekend featuring an inter-class football tournament; an auction to support the school's public interest clinic; and a talent show featuring students, staff and faculty (always good for many laughs).

The only drawback to being so tightly knit is that there is sometimes a cliquey, high school feel to the relationships between the classes and among groups within the classes. Some groups are "cool" and others not. It was, at times, marginally childish.

Status: Alumnus/a, full-time
Dates of Enrollment: 8/2000-5/2003
Survey Submitted: April 2004

There is no Greek system at Franklin Pierce other than the nationwide legal fraternity (I don't know the name of it). There are not that many social opportunities in Concord, but Boston is about an hour and a half away. To me, attending law school in a small city was a benefit because I didn't have the distractions in front of me. But, if I wanted a big city experience, Boston was less than two hours away.

Status: Current student, full-time
Dates of Enrollment: 8/2003-5/2005
Survey Submitted: September 2003

Main Street Concord is popular. We are approximately an hour outside of Boston. The seafood is cheap and delicious. We have the only law school chapter of the Licensing Executives Society at FPLC. Many students are members of the Student Intellectual Property Law Association.

Rutgers University School of Law—Camden

Admissions Office
406 Penn Street, 3rd floor
Camden, NJ 08102
Admissions phone: (856) 225-6102 or (800) 466-7561
Admissions e-mail: admissions@camlaw.rutgers.edu
Admissions URL: http://camlaw.rutgers.edu/site/admissions/

 ## Admissions

Status: Current student, part-time
Dates of Enrollment: 5/2003-Submit Date
Survey Submitted: July 2005

Send your application early because the school employs a rolling admission process. I sent my application in late February or early March, but the class was already full. I called the dean of admissions to let her know that Rutgers was my top choice, and she was able to squeeze me in. So if you find yourself in my position contact the admissions office. They are very nice people and are extremely helpful.

Status: Current student, full-time
Dates of Enrollment: 8/2004-Submit Date
Survey Submitted: August 2005

As with all law schools, it helps to have a good GPA and LSAT score (approximately 3.6 and 162). Good schools make a big impact as well. Rutgers tends to look fondly on students from powerhouses such as Princeton, UPenn, Notre Dame and Stanford. That being said, Rutgers' commitment to providing a diverse student body is represented in the classroom, and not just as boilerplate language in admissions guides. Interesting students with varying backgrounds will be viewed as such by the admissions office, and will actually have a better chance at being admitted. A great essay will give prospective students a good chance at admission even if grades and test scores aren't above the 80th percentile.

Status: Alumnus/a, full-time
Dates of Enrollment: 8/1995-5/1998
Survey Submitted: March 2005

The admissions process was fairly simple and easy—there were no interviews; I just sent in application.

Status: Alumnus/a, full-time
Dates of Enrollment: 8/1997-5/2000
Survey Submitted: March 2005

Relatively selective the year I got in and very quick to get back to you. The selectivity has increased two-fold since I was admitted!

Status: Alumnus/a, full-time
Dates of Enrollment: 8/1999-5/2002
Survey Submitted: February 2004

It is now pretty difficult to get in. I did well on my LSATs, graduated from a Top 10 school with honors and had great letters of recommendation. I was impressed when I got here and realized that my classmates were all extremely impressive candidates from every background. The competition to get in has become much harder!

Status: Current student, full-time
Dates of Enrollment: 8/2001-Submit Date
Survey Submitted: February 2004

Dean Andrews is in charge of admissions, and she couldn't be more helpful or friendly; in fact, she goes out of her way to help students both before and after admissions. It goes without saying that it is important to have very good numbers and a clean essay—be confident in your ability to succeed, but do not cross the line into arrogance or it will kill you. Rutgers is very selective due to the large number of applications it receives. In fact, its acceptance rate is nearly as low as at some Top 10 schools.

They love out-of-state students. As an out-of-state student, they went out of their way to help me transition to Rutgers, even going to look at apartments for me while I was still in Ohio. I have heard that Rutgers will interview borderline cases, but I don't know much about this. Rutgers also is one of the few schools who participate in an ABA study to test the correlation of GMAT scores with law school success. If you haven't taken the LSAT and have a very good GMAT, you may want to ask them about the possibility of accepting that score.

Status: Alumnus/a, full-time
Dates of Enrollment: 8/1998-11/2002
Survey Submitted: September 2003

My LSAT score was nominal at best. The way to get in is a nice letter and good references. The competition to get in is not as tough as they want you to think.

 ## Academics

Status: Current student, part-time
Dates of Enrollment: 5/2003-Submit Date
Survey Submitted: July 2005

Rutgers offers both a full-time and a part-time program. I am a part-time student. A typical part-time student takes four years to graduate, however you can take summer classes and graduate in three and a half years. I actually went full-time during my first year, and part-time for the rest of my time here and along with summer classes I will graduate in three years along with the full-time people. So even part-time students can graduate early.

For the most part the level of instruction is excellent. Professor evaluations and past student grades are available to all students. Avoid professors who are new and do not have evaluations and grades on file. I made the mistake of taking one such professor and absolutely hated the class. On the other hand, I had one professor who was teaching for his first time and was one of my favorite instructors. So I guess when you go for a new faculty member it could go either way.

As far as course selection, even evening students have plenty of classes to pick from whatever your interests. They rotate the classes offered at night so that over your time here you will have a chance to take whatever classes you are interested in. Also, part-time students are not limited to evening classes. So, if you are able to get to campus by 4:30 p.m., you will be able to take classes that start at 4:30 instead of 6:20. This significantly increases your course selection in any given semester.

Status: Current student, full-time
Dates of Enrollment: 8/2004-Submit Date
Survey Submitted: August 2005

The first year is intense, but not as scary as they say. The faculty and staff are very nurturing and patient. Rutgers doesn't waste students' time with intro to law classes that fade in importance mid-way through the semester. Instead, the curriculum is made up of three major classes of four credits each and a two-credit writing class. While this doesn't cut down on the amount of time, it does cut down on the amount of work and subjects for which students are responsible and reduces the stress. The environment is not that competitive as far as law schools are concerned, but it is still way more intense than college. The good news is that the professors are great, they don't play favorites and most are willing to meet with students whenever necessary. Class selection for second-year classes can definitely be improved. Many of the class times conflicted with each other, precluding students from choosing more than two classes that really interested them. Other classes, such as Alternate Dispute Resolution, were only available through a lottery.

Read all of Vault's Law School Surveys at www.vault.com/lawschool — get complete surveys on top law schools, expert advice on applicaton essays, LSAT prep and more.

VAULT CAREER LIBRARY 393

Status: Alumnus/a, full-time
Dates of Enrollment: 8/1995-5/1998
Survey Submitted: March 2005

In general, I found the quality of classes to be good. I went to Rutgers because of their International Law Certificate Program, which they discontinued my first year and was a big disappointment. However, they still continued to offer a good selection of international law classes.

As a prospective law student, I was dismayed at having to spend the first year taking required classes, but once I was there, I saw the importance of having to take them and even surprised myself that I actually ended up liking Contracts and UCC classes. When I started law school, I wanted to take every international law class offered, however when I attended an international law meeting in Washington, D.C., I met a partner from a large firm whom I asked what classes he would recommend taking to prepare me for a position in international law, to which he replied: "You still have to pass the bar before you can become an attorney, so take classes that will help you accomplish that." Rutgers is good in that it does offer a lot of bar classes like Secured Transactions and Sales. Additionally, in the International Business Law class I took, which were some of the best classes I ever took, we actually drafted our own contracts and presented those contracts and business proposals in front of the class.

While some of the general first-year classes were large, I never felt that I didn't get enough attention. Also, Rutgers offers smaller classes, such as some of the seminars, which are fantastic.

If Rutgers doesn't offer a class you're interested in, Rutgers gives you the opportunity to register through them for elective classes at Temple law school in Philly, so you're not just limited to what Rutgers offers.

If you're interested in a class that isn't being offered, sometimes you can get them to offer the class. I approached a professor about teaching an Indian Law class and he agreed to it. The course was offered, but I guess I was the only one who signed up for it and the class never happened. But I think if there had been two more people interested, they would have kept the class that semester.

Status: Current student, full-time
Dates of Enrollment: 8/2001-Submit Date
Survey Submitted: February 2004

Professors are topnotch. Many of the professors you encounter are leading academics in their field and frequently have written the textbook you will be using. Use of the Socratic Method is varied. Some professors do not call on any students and will lecture and field questions. Others ask for volunteers. I would say a majority will either tell you that your row will be on call next class or will simply travel up and down the rows.

Grading is fair, and students always have the ability to see a professor's grade distributions for previous courses as well as the previous exams. The workload is challenging but very manageable. There is not much of a sense of intense competition between students. Rutgers students are not ranked, because it is felt rankings do not reflect how close students really are. This is something you will find out at Rutgers and most other law schools. While competition for getting into some limited enrollment course is intense, you can frequently simply seek out the professor's permission the first day of class and get in.

Status: Alumnus/a, full-time
Dates of Enrollment: 8/1999-5/2002
Survey Submitted: February 2004

First-year classes were tough. There is definitely no grade inflation to help you out. The median is set below a B. The quality of many of the classes left something to be desired. Upper-level courses have a higher level of quality, and the professors are impressive. Many classes are difficult to get into unless you are a third-year student. Professors will often fit you in if you have a strong interest in the course.

Status: Alumnus/a, full-time
Dates of Enrollment: 8/1997-5/2000
Survey Submitted: March 2005

Excellent classes. First-year grading is difficult with about half the class generally getting a C plus or below. Workload is relatively light, but it all depends on how much you study!

 Employment Prospects

Status: Current student, part-time
Dates of Enrollment: 5/2003-Submit Date
Survey Submitted: July 2005

All the top firms in the Philly area and throughout New Jersey recruit at Rutgers. Also, Rutgers Camden is among the top schools for landing judicial clerkships. I believe that last year or the year before we were Number One, surpassing even Yale and Harvard. Many students end up clerking at the federal court house in Camden.

Status: Current student, full-time
Dates of Enrollment: 8/2004-Submit Date
Survey Submitted: August 2005

The employment prospects are great if you're looking to practice in the Northeast or Mid-Atlantic regions. As one of three law schools in New Jersey, the market is substantially better than in other regions. Plus, income levels are some of the best in the country. Obtaining summer internships and clerkships with judges is relatively easy for Rutgers students. The only challenges as far as employment is concerned seem to be for students who are looking for work in the Deep South or the West. Rutgers is second in clerkships only to Yale, but many other students work for big law firms in Philadelphia, New York, Wilmington (DE) and New Jersey. Rutgers' prestige is rising as well because it is such a great value for New Jersey's brightest students who don't want to pay private school tuition. The alumni network could be better, but the law school is relatively new. On-campus recruiting seems to be strong, but there also seems tobe a lack of New York firms, which might concern some students.

Status: Alumnus/a, full-time
Dates of Enrollment: 8/1995-5/1998
Survey Submitted: March 2005

Rutgers is a good school to come from for the South Jersey and Philly area, although in the New York area, you are fighting to get noticed with the flood of Ivy League schools in the area. Outside of New York, Rutgers has a better reputation. If you want to be considered for a large firm coming from Rutgers, you must be on Law Journal and have impeccable grades.

While I did do some on-campus interviews set up by the school, it's generally not worth your time unless you're on Law Journal (which I wasn't). I'm not plugged into the alumni network, especially since I'm not in the South Jersey or Philly area, so I can't speak as to how helpful the alumni network is.

As an alumni now working at a big firm in New York, I have been contacted by law students trying to work the alumni angle and was surprised that the law students didn't take the time to introduce themselves—that they blindly send resumes to me without even including a cover letter. While I think the alumni angle can be useful, it's still important to remember that you are still presenting yourself to a total stranger—even if it is an alumnus/a—so don't expect that you have to do less in presenting yourself as a potential candidate just because you went to the same law school.

Status: Alumnus/a, full-time
Dates of Enrollment: 8/1997-5/2000
Survey Submitted: March 2005

All large Philadelphia firms, which is a huge legal market, interview at Rutgers. Not to mention many large NJ firms, as well.

Quality of Life

Status: Current student, part-time
Dates of Enrollment: 5/2003-Submit Date
Survey Submitted: July 2005

The city of Camden is run-down. The law school is in the downtown area of the city, which is largely taken up by educational institutions and government buildings, including a federal court house. The downtown area is well patrolled and students feel safe. However, there is little to do there and I highly recommend living off campus. Many students chose to live in Philly or in neighboring towns such as Collingswood.

Status: Current student, full-time
Dates of Enrollment: 8/2004-Submit Date
Survey Submitted: August 2005

Rutgers-Camden is located in Camden, which was recently ranked as the most violent city in America. Camden is also a very poor city, which raises concerns as well. Thus, it is hard to get anyone outside the community to believe that the campus is fine and safe. Personally, after all I heard about Camden, I was shocked at how nice the campus was. It is definitely not a tree-lined, ivy campus, but it is not nearly as bad as people make it out to be. Many students take the subway into town and walk a few blocks to the school. This is not as harrowing as it sounds because the area around the law school is pretty nice and there is a pretty decent security presence. My advice for anyone interested in Rutgers-Camden because of its academics is just to visit the campus, and not be dissuaded by rumors about Camden. The facilities are currently a bit run-down, but a new law school is being built in 2007, which will raise Rutgers to the top of the facilities lists. One of the perks is the federal courthouse across the street from the law school, which is a great place to learn and get a summer clerkship. Camden also provides a lot of opportunities for students interested in urban policy and pro bono work. The law school is very involved with the city.

Status: Alumnus/a, full-time
Dates of Enrollment: 8/1995-5/1998
Survey Submitted: March 2005

Security is very tight on campus and in the surrounding area. I lived two blocks off campus in the "nicer" section of Camden and our apartment was broken into while we were on spring break and my car was broken into at least once. A lot of students lived on campus at least their first year in the dorms, which lends itself to living in a fishbowl. In one sense, it's nice that you get to know everyone and there is quite a sense of community within the law school, but on the flip side, you also know everybody's business and they know yours.

Food options weren't so great; there's a sandwich truck outside the school that almost everyone got lunch from. The cafeteria options were minimal and there few decent restaurants around the area with the exception of one pizza joint a block off campus. There are no grocery stores in the area, you have to drive out to Cherry Hill to find one, unless you go to the dismal neighborhood corner store, where you probably want to check the expiration dates on food and milk.

Status: Alumnus/a, full-time
Dates of Enrollment: 8/1997-5/2000
Survey Submitted: March 2005

You must travel to Philly (only 10 minutes away) or Cherry Hill to do any shopping. Campus life was pretty much nonexistent.

Social Life

Status: Current student, part-time
Dates of Enrollment: 5/2003-Submit Date
Survey Submitted: July 2005

The Student Bar Association plans numerous events throughout the semester. Most of the events are in Philly and the school provides bus transportation to Camden free of charge.

Status: Current student, full-time
Dates of Enrollment: 8/2004-Submit Date
Survey Submitted: August 2005

Rutgers is a commuter school and some students are married, so the social scene is not what you would expect out of a college. However, the students who are around know how to have a good time. Hank's is the local watering hole where students can enjoy Camden's best happy hour. The nightlife usually centers on Philadelphia, which is an eight-minute train ride away. During the day, there are always interesting speakers and events. Plus, students can visit the famous Camden Aquarium and the U.S.S. New Jersey. In addition, there are countless numbers of historic sites in Philadelphia.

Status: Alumnus/a, full-time
Dates of Enrollment: 8/1995-5/1998
Survey Submitted: March 2005

Rutgers has a very active social life, which was great. The law clubs are very active and there is always some kind of social event going on. Also, a lot of the students end up going out to the same places across the river in Philly.

As compared to what I've heard about other law schools, the student body at Rutgers Law-Camden is very social, down-to-earth, friendly and cooperative. I never had any cut-throat experiences like I've heard from some of my colleagues. I really enjoyed my time at Rutgers. There was always a good balance of being able to hunker down and get your work done, while at the same time being able to blow off steam and go out when you wanted to, especially after every final exam.

There are basically two bars about a block or two off campus that students go to—the rest of the time people generally go into Philly. Some of the places in Philly that I remember are McGillan's ($5 pitchers of Yuengling), Sugarmom's and Warm Daddy's. McGillan's is nice old Irish pub down an alley that has been in operation since the 1860s. Sugarmom's is a microbrewery pub in a basement that is a little bit of a challenge to find. It has a bit of a laid-back alternative crowd with pool tables and foozball games. Warm Daddy's is a blues bar that has live music almost all the time.

Then there is always Delaware Avenue, right along the Delaware River, that has all the big cheesy clubs where the cocktail waitresses are wearing bikinis right next to the dance floor, selling beers out of big tubs of ice. Although there is one place, Rock Lobster, on Delaware Avenue that is more relaxed and open when the weather is nice.

Status: Alumnus/a, full-time
Dates of Enrollment: 8/1997-5/2000
Survey Submitted: March 2005

One bar, Hank's, is a little dive down the street. That is it. Do not attend Rutgers-Camden for a social life, although I did have a great time there! Go there to get a good education and job after you graduate.

Read all of Vault's Law School Surveys at www.vault.com/lawschool — get complete surveys on top law schools, expert advice on applicaton essays, LSAT prep and more.

VAULT CAREER LIBRARY   395

Rutgers University School of Law—Newark

Office of Admissions
Center for Law and Justice
123 Washington Street
Newark, NJ 07102
Admissions phone: (973) 353-5557
Admissions e-mail: geddis@andromeda.rutgers.edu
Admissions URL:
http://law.newark.rutgers.edu/admissions.html

 Admissions

Status: Current student, full-time
Dates of Enrollment: 8/2004-Submit Date
Survey Submitted: April 2006

The admissions process was very straightforward. The application was online and all other documents were submitted through the LSAC. The admissions committee appears to focus on diversity, which is also a focus of the law school. This means that the entering class will be varied, with a mixture of young and older students from various backgrounds and with a variety of experiences. An applicant's essay should highlight what she/he would offer to the school that sets her/him apart—standard for most essays, I guess. However, Rutgers admission committee members actually seems to read the essays as I'm sure my essay was the only reason I was accepted.

Status: Current student, full-time
Dates of Enrollment: 8/2004-Submit Date
Survey Submitted: April 2006

The admissions process is fairly straightforward. My advice is to really spend time on your essay...specifically WHY you want to be a law student, and NOT "I have always wanted to be a law student." This program is selective, but one of the highlights of the program here is its diversity; the age range is wonderful, so that everyone feels welcome here, instead of out of place.

Status: Current student, full-time
Dates of Enrollment: 8/2004-Submit Date
Survey Submitted: April 2006

The student population largely believes that admission selectivity is strictly dependent on your background. There is an alternate admissions policy, in which the school emphasizes experience, rather than LSAT scores and GPA. Most believe that this "alternate" process is used to facilitate candidates for Rutgers' Minority Student Program (MSP). If you do not qualify for the MSP program admissions is very selective. Almost all non-MSP students have also received acceptance letters from schools ranked in the first and second tier.

> **The school says:** "The Minority Student Program is a *post-admissions* program and selection for the program is separate from and subsequent to admissions to the law school. All matriculated students, regardless of race or ethnic origin, who can demonstrate disadvantage through a history of socio-economic, educational, cultural or other disadvantage, are eligible for consideration for the MSP."

Status: Current student, full-time
Dates of Enrollment: 8/2004-Submit Date
Survey Submitted: April 2006

Rutgers is unusual and, in my mind, innovative in that there is an option on the application to request that you be evaluated with emphasis on your essays, life experience and other qualifications rather than on grades and LSAT. This is not to say that you can get in as a slouch, it is only to say that the admission process is perhaps less rigidly mechanical than at other schools. The interesting, even eclectic, student body is no doubt in part a result of this approach. There are people here from all socioeconomic, ethnic and overall experience backgrounds,

and a fair number of older students with previous careers under their belts. The admission process is nevertheless like all reputable law schools, highly competitive and very selective. The school does not grant interviews as far as I know.

Status: Current student, full-time
Dates of Enrollment: 8/2003-Submit Date
Survey Submitted: October 2005

As long as you submit the basic requirements though LSAC, you should be fine. The application does offer a choice: you can have your application evaluated mostly on scores (GPA and LSAT) or on other factors (such as job experience). I think people who have taken more than a couple years off before going to law school take the second option more often.

Status: Current student, full-time
Dates of Enrollment: 8/2002-Submit Date
Survey Submitted: April 2005

I did it all on my own and it worked out well. Once I got in, I did set up an appointment with the financial aid office to discuss my options, but other than that I did not do much but fill out the application. In fact, it was kind of nice to know that you can get into law school without spending an entire year interviewing and meeting with people. I think that type of grueling process deters many from even applying to law school. My admission process was pain free!

Status: Current student, full-time
Dates of Enrollment: 9/2003-Submit Date
Survey Submitted: April 2005

Good process. The school held open house meetings for prospective students with an opportunity to sit in on a first-year class to see what it was like. The school provided an online link to your admission status so you could check regularly and find out if you were admitted as soon as the decision was made.

Status: Current student, full-time
Dates of Enrollment: 8/2003-Submit Date
Survey Submitted: April 2005

Rutgers Law-Newark's admissions process is incredible for its focus not only on students with outstanding numbers/scores (there are many) but for its explicit goal of compiling a diverse class. In today's PC world it's easy to claim "diversity" based on a handful of students that break the white, privileged law-school mold. That is not the case at RU-Law. Each class consistently features students of myriad different ages, races, religions, ethnicities and classes. There are doctors, engineers, recent college grads, social workers, activists, business people, accountants, glass blowers and Peace Corps alumni—the list is endless. The process is selective in the best possible way—seeking those who are most likely to contribute positively to the unique culture of our truly diverse law school.

Status: Current student, full-time
Dates of Enrollment: 9/2003-Submit Date
Survey Submitted: April 2005

The admissions process was fairly similar to those at the other schools I applied to because I opted to use the standard application. The one place where Rutgers stood out was my campus visit. People went out of their way to talk to me, the admissions office had a student employee take me on a tour even though I was unannounced, I sat in on a class, my tour guide introduced me to a professor and the three of us talked for about 10 minutes. As far as selectivity, I am thoroughly impressed by my fellow students; they come from a variety of educational backgrounds including the Ivy League, state colleges and PhD programs, among others. Rutgers' bar is clearly not low.

Status: Current student, full-time
Dates of Enrollment: 8/2003-Submit Date
Survey Submitted: April 2005

The admissions process at Rutgers-Newark is probably different than the process at other law schools. Although you do have to fill out the same kind of applications and write essays, Rutgers-Newark is looking for different kinds of candidates. The school takes a lot of pride in its diversity and that obviously starts during admissions. This is not the kind of school that is going to look at your LSAT and GPA exclusively, although those numbers should be as good as you can possibly get them. However, this school is also looking for people with various life experiences, people of various ages, cultures and backgrounds. For instance, my LSAT and GPA were pretty good and my background was nothing terribly unique, except that I went to a state school in New Jersey (not Rutgers), so I was coming from a different place than many other applicants. I think that really helped me.

Status: Current student, full-time
Dates of Enrollment: 9/2003-Submit Date
Survey Submitted: October 2004

The law school allows students to choose whether the admission decision will be based on either numerical factors (GPA and LSAT) or other factors (life experience, disadvantaged background). Students have a better shot at getting admitted if they choose the non-numerical option, even if they have good grades and test scores, because the school will end up looking at both anyway. This option just gives you more of an opportunity to sell yourself.

Status: Current student, part-time
Dates of Enrollment: 9/2002-Submit Date
Survey Submitted: April 2004

I attended open houses, sat in on classes and met with admissions before I submitted a very reasonable application with short essays. I heard back about six weeks later (March, I think). I did hear that some others were admitted as late as summer.

Academics

Status: Current student, full-time
Dates of Enrollment: 8/2004-Submit Date
Survey Submitted: April 2006

The first-year classes are rigorous and the faculty/administration has a "hide the ball" mentality. This forces you to learn how to learn on your own, discover what you need and get it and research everything. In moderate doses, this is a good thing. However, when carried to an extreme like it is at Rutgers, you feel used and abused, and frequently feel as if the 1L year is an endurance contest rather than a learning experience. A plus, though, is that this "boot camp" mentality helps to build relationships within the class as you are forced to cooperate with and support your classmates in order to survive. I saw little evidence of the backbiting and ruthlessness that characterizes other law schools.

Status: Current student, full-time
Dates of Enrollment: 8/2004-Submit Date
Survey Submitted: April 2006

Now reaching the end of my second year as a full-time student, I have had exceptional professors, many of them intimidatingly intelligent and knowledgeable in their respective areas of specialty. Several of my professors were clerks to United States Supreme Court justices. Several of them have had extensive experience outside of the Academy and several are actively and intensively involved in advocacy of various sorts. I've developed friendly personal rapports with almost all of my professors; the mood is certainly not Ivory Tower-ish at Rutgers. My classes have been demanding, universally so, and the workload always heavy, but I have not yet taken a class that was not well-organized or genuinely informative and useful. It has not been easy, but nor does one feel there is a hazing thing going on here; the "hide the ball" prototypical pompous law professor is the exception here—thankfully. I've not been closed out of any class I wanted to take yet and have only observed that one or two classes were lotteried each of the semesters I've been here.

Status: Current student, full-time
Dates of Enrollment: 8/2004-Submit Date
Survey Submitted: April 2006

The classes are great...not too big. There are certain guidelines for the "popular" classes, students graduating or 1Ls may have preference for some electives. That is to ensure that 3Ls have what they need to graduate and 1Ls have a selection, since they have so very few electives open to them. The grading is relatively fair, although more than one student has been unpleasantly surprised by the grade they received on an exam they thought they did very well on. The professors have an open-door policy, both through the semester and after exams have been submitted, so you can discuss your concerns and your performance on exams. The workload for a 1L is predetermined and can be completed. For upperclassmen, the workload is designed by the student. The frustration may be that you do not have enough credits to take all the courses you want to take.

Status: Current student, full-time
Dates of Enrollment: 8/2004-Submit Date
Survey Submitted: April 2006

Academics here are a mixed bag. Some professors are fantastic educators, while others clearly need to retire. The school operates on a "B" curve for its first-year students and the curve can work against you. The school really needs to raise this curve in line with other universities. Workload is particularly heavy in the first year like other law schools. In particular, Rutgers has a very intensive and demanding first-year legal research and writing program. While this LRW program makes first year even more difficult, it's worth it. Rutgers students know how to write. Also of note are Rutgers numerous clinics—they provide not only invaluable hands-on experience, but are a source of mentoring from the professors that oversee them.

Status: Alumnus/a, full-time
Dates of Enrollment: 9/2000-5/2003
Survey Submitted: October 2005

If you are a minority, the minority program is exceptional, giving you a lot of extra help and tutoring during your first year. If you are not in the program, you are left to fend for yourself in preparing for exams and writing outlines. The minority student program also has a program in the summer before the school year starts to prepare for law school. So when the other students come to the classes, the individuals in the program already have begun getting to know the school and uppercalssmen and have begun making friends. There was definitely a catch up time that needed to happen during that first year for the people outside of the program to keep up. Plus, the program members get old exams and practice tests to prepare for taking the actual tests at exam time. However, as long as you are a self-starter and self-motivated, someone outside the program can certainly compete. Overall, the members of the minority student program did not do considerably better than the people that were not in the program.

> **The school says:** "The law school has developed an academic support program for all first-year students to assist them in outlining and exam preparation."

Status: Current student, full-time
Dates of Enrollment: 9/2003-Submit Date
Survey Submitted: April 2005

First year you're required to take Torts, Contracts, Property, Criminal Law, Constitutional Law, Civil Procedure, Legal Research and Writing, and one elective. After that, you're on your own to pick classes. The quality of classes varies by the professor, with some professors standing out as truly exceptional. Getting into popular classes isn't a problem over the long run, but about two classes a semester tend to have waitlists, along with the clinics. 3Ls get priority, and I haven't heard of a 3L getting completely shut out of a class. The workload varies by professor, but generally, you can expect to read about 20 pages per class session unless the class meets once a week. If that's the case, all bets are off and over 100 pages per class can be required (sometimes much more).

Read all of Vault's Law School Surveys at www.vault.com/lawschool — get complete surveys on top law schools, expert advice on applicaton essays, LSAT prep and more.

VAULT CAREER LIBRARY 397

Status: Current student, full-time
Dates of Enrollment: 8/2003-Submit Date
Survey Submitted: April 2005

The professors are amazing. They all have incredibly impressive backgrounds—have worked on ground breaking cases, at top firms and organizations and clerked for the Supreme Court. The professors are really accessible and I would suggest taking the time to build relationships with them. All of my professors have been willing to talk after class or meet in their offices. Some have even provided the class with their home phone number to call with questions. The workload is definitely rigorous, but if you work hard, it can also be rewarding. Socratic Method is, of course, popular during the first year. It can be intimidating, but after a few weeks, most people get used to it.

Status: Current student, full-time
Dates of Enrollment: 8/2003-Submit Date
Survey Submitted: April 2005

The academics at Rutgers Law vary like I imagine they do at other schools. I've had great classes and I've had boring classes. Some professors have inspired me, and some have not, but I have to say that every professor I've had was really trying to do their best and was committed to what they were doing. I have not had a professor that acts like he/she did not want to be in the classroom, which is nice. Fortunately, there have been many more good classes than bad classes. Some of my classes have been absolutely outstanding and I feel they could go head-to-head with any class at any school. There seems to be a pretty wide selection of classes, including typically popular classes. The grading is fair except that it takes forever to get turned in and they only post them at the school, which is inconvenient for people who live far away. The workload is just that—a load of work. That being said, after your first year, it's pretty easy to find shortcuts and get away with minimal work, but most people don't seem to do that. It's not going to do you any good in the future because lawyers work hard. You might as well get used to it.

> The school says: "Since spring 2005, grades have been posted online within several days of their submission by the faculty member."

Status: Current student, part-time
Dates of Enrollment: 8/2002-Submit Date
Survey Submitted: October 2004

A vast majority of upperclass electives for the part-time evening program is taught by professionals as adjunct professors. This makes the evening program vastly different from the academic experience of my full-time counterparts, whose day classes are taught mainly by full-time professors.

I believe that my evening program offers an education that combines both educational/theoretical discourse and pragmatic/professional representation of the subject matter. The adjunct professors present not only the "textbook" analysis of the subject matter, but also present how they themselves practice it in the field. Some are even eager to point out which concepts are actually not practiced, though the text may argue otherwise. Altogether, I am exposed to more than the full-time students. One complaint about the part-time program is the relative paucity of class selection as compared to the full-time program. Though all of the first- and second-year customary courses are offered, many electives that are offered during the day are not offered in the evening. Sometimes, the students have no other option but to take a class in which they show absolutely no interest other than to fulfill the credit requirements for the semester.

Status: Alumnus/a, full-time
Dates of Enrollment: 8/1999-5/2002
Survey Submitted: April 2005

Academics were rigorous. Class selection was probably the only easy part of it—I do not remember being denied entry into any class for which I registered. First-year is the most difficult, as students who do not "get it," in terms of thinking like a lawyer, will fail. By fail, I mean getting a C. There is a B curve, but only the bottom 10 percent or so of the class ends up with a C average. The key to success is wedging your way past the B plus stage into the elite A minus and A range. The professors are impeccable, but their credentials often exceed their innate teaching abilities. My first year I had several professors who had clerked for Supreme Court justices and all were preeminent in their fields. All professors are accessible, offering office hours which I would encourage students to use more than I did.

Employment Prospects

Status: Alumnus/a, full-time
Dates of Enrollment: 9/1974-5/1977
Survey Submitted: April 2006

Excellent then and excellent now. I routinely recruit at the law school and am very impressed with the caliber and knowledge of interviewing applicants. On-campus recruiting procedures are easy and effective

Status: Current student, full-time
Dates of Enrollment: 8/2004-Submit Date
Survey Submitted: April 2006

I think that employment prospects are good here. Mainly because there are a number of meet-and-greet events, as well as law firm mixers and job fairs to attend. In addition, the student organizations are a great way to network to meet other professionals. Internships and externships are excellent opportunities to meet people in your field of interest, and those are definitely supported by the school, as are the clinics. A large number of students participate in both internships and clerkships, so they have a number of opportunities to network for jobs. In addition, the Rutgers Alumni Network is awesome! Our alumni are always willing to serve as mentors and help students traverse the perils of law school.

Status: Alumnus/a, full-time
Dates of Enrollment: 9/2000-5/2003
Survey Submitted: October 2005

You need to get solid grades—a B+ or better—to keep your prospects high. With good grades, you can go almost anywhere in the New York/New Jersey region. If you don't have great grades, there are plenty of opportunities for public interest and clerking. I knew of only a handful of people that didn't have jobs after graduation. The downside to the employment prospects is that there are a lot of other law firms in the New York/New Jersey area to compete with for spots in all legal positions in the area. Most of the people from the local law schools are looking for local jobs, so the competition is fierce. The opportunities through on-campus recruiting are limited. My year, about 6 percent of the people recruiting for summer positions found them through on-campus recruiting. Networking early on in the beginning of law school could also be beneficial, as there are a lot of opportunities to become involved in the legal community, which has resulted in job opportunities as well. Furthermore, if you are in the minority student program, you have a lot more resources at your disposal. There are even a number of law firms that takes students in their first summer after their first year of law school to be a summer associate if the student is in the minority student program.

> The school says: "Typically, 25 to 30 percent of students from each class obtain jobs through on-campus recruiting. Many others obtain positions through out web-based job posting system. Consistently, 94 percent or more of graduates obtain employment within six months of graduation."

Status: Current student, full-time
Dates of Enrollment: 9/2003-Submit Date
Survey Submitted: April 2005

If you are in the top 10 percent of the class, the doors to a number of top New York law firms are open for you. If you are a little lower in the class, you can still find a top position at regional and in-state (New Jersey) firms. The bottom half of the class has a harder time finding jobs and often must try for state trial court clerkships or small firm practice.

> The school says: "The law school does not rank students, and firms from both New York and New Jersey look at a diverse group of candidates."

Status: Current student, full-time
Dates of Enrollment: 8/2003-Submit Date
Survey Submitted: April 2005

Our students have access to some of the most prestigious firms and public interest organizations in existence. The on-campus interviewing process regularly places top students with firms known worldwide. Our proximity to Manhattan means that employment opportunities are endless and career services maintains strong ties with large New Jersey firms, as well. Internships abound at Rutgers Law-Newark. During semesters and summers our students intern everywhere from federal courts in Newark and Prudential Insurance here in Newark, to the ACLU, the Center for Reproductive Rights, the Army JAG, American Friends (immigration assistance), Legal Services and much more.

Status: Alumnus/a, full-time
Dates of Enrollment: 9/1998-5/2001
Survey Submitted: July 2004

There is a good campus recruiting process, but is limited to firms in the geographic areas of NY and NJ. The reputation of Rutgers in NJ firms is enhanced by the major numbers of alumni. Career placement is hit or miss. There is a good connection to state clerkship opportunities, less of a connection to the NY firms.

> **The school says:** "The Office of Career Services works with students interested in any geographic location, including all regions of the U.S. and abroad. In 2005, 40 percent of employers participating in the on-campus interview program were from New York, 40 percent from New Jersey and 20 percent from outside the NY/NJ region."

 ## Quality of Life

Status: Current student, full-time
Dates of Enrollment: 8/2004-Submit Date
Survey Submitted: May 2006

The quality of life in Newark is fair. Newark is in the process of rebuilding its infrastructure with a newly elected mayor, major renovations to its streets and public transportation system in conjunction with the New Jersey Performing Arts Center (NJPAC), as well as the construction of the brand new New Jersey Devils stadium on Broad Street. The city is seeing massive redevelopment that will transform downtown, bringing new hotels, condominium developments and refurbished lofts. Many of the students stay at a new nearby housing community, Society Hill, which features around the clock security, tennis courts, pool and other amenities.

Status: Current student, full-time
Dates of Enrollment: 8/2004-Submit Date
Survey Submitted: April 2006

Housing is available both in the dorm and in graduate student housing. In addition, the university provides a listing of available housing. Of course students are the best resource for housing...for example, I live in an apartment complex with about nine of my classmates, which is great for socializing and studying. The gym is directly across the street and totally accessible, and there are places to eat in the area. Parking may be an issue, even if you buy a parking pass, as the school (and most places) tends to oversell their available spaces. The general neighborhood is not really too safe at night, but the main street is safe, as is the area around and on campus.

Status: Current student, full-time
Dates of Enrollment: 9/2004-Submit Date
Survey Submitted: April 2006

The school is basically brand new—it's a beautiful building. All the classes are in one building—with lockers, the whole deal. It's really convenient, and fosters a real sense of community in the law school. It's like high school all over again. But minus the braces and with more textbooks.

Status: Current student, full-time
Dates of Enrollment: 8/2003-Submit Date
Survey Submitted: April 2005

The neighborhood is completely safe during the day while students and business people populate the area. At night, the climate is different and sometimes intimidating. The result is that students work together to ensure that no one walks alone to the parking deck, and the university provides an escort service to complement. Our location in an economically depressed city with a unique history of racial strife is challenging, but our students rise to the challenge by serving the community which we inhabit through clinical work, volunteer

opportunities and direct advocacy. For example, our Domestic Violence Advocacy Project sends students to the Essex County Superior Court to assist victims of domestic violence (a majority of them Newark residents) seeking restraining orders.

Status: Current student, full-time
Dates of Enrollment: 9/2003-Submit Date
Survey Submitted: April 2005

Newark isn't exactly a thrilling place to be, but the Rutgers campus is a highlight of the area. We have full access to the gym, and the campus itself is well-manicured. There's a cafe in the basement of the law school, and there are restaurants on the edge of the campus (across the street from school) and within walking distance in Newark. I don't live on campus, and I commute as often as possible by train (which is a huge bonus—the school is walking distance from two major train stations). I avoid walking by myself when it's dark out (even around campus), but after evening events at school, there are always people to walk with.

Status: Current student, full-time
Dates of Enrollment: 8/2003-Submit Date
Survey Submitted: April 2005

As far as the neighborhood goes, it's Newark. Everyone knows the stories of Newark, but honestly it's not that bad. I personally like downtown Newark. We are a block away from the Newark Museum, which is an often overlooked treasure, and a block away from the Newark Library. Downtown also offers plenty of opportunity with firms, politicians, public interest organizations and government agencies. Plus a few blocks away are the state courts, and a little further is the Federal Court and the Federal Building.

Status: Alumnus/a, full-time
Dates of Enrollment: 9/1998-5/2001
Survey Submitted: July 2004

It is what you make of it. Life in Newark, both night and day, has improved of late, but it is a long way from being a social hotspot. The school has new facilities that are a vast improvement over the previous building, but is a bit cramped as enrollment increases. Housing is below average in quality and amenities but is close to the school. Crime is not rampant, but is present. Safety and precautions are the responsibility of the residents and students.

Status: Current student, full-time
Dates of Enrollment: 9/2003-Submit Date
Survey Submitted: April 2005

Rutgers-Newark has an amazing law school facility. The law school building features an open atrium that spans four flights, so it is hard not to see anyone you are looking for at the school. It is one of the most diverse law schools and somehow manages to maintain a fairly unified community. Newark is an up and coming area.

 ## Social Life

Status: Current student, full-time
Dates of Enrollment: 8/2004-Submit Date
Survey Submitted: May 2006

The student body at Rutgers School of Law—Newark is extremely active. The Student Bar Association funds 31 student organizations, as well as the five accredited journals for the school. There is hardly a week that passes where a major event, speaker or social gathering is not taking place.

Status: Current student, full-time
Dates of Enrollment: 8/2004-Submit Date
Survey Submitted: April 2006

Again, as a married commuter from Manhattan, I've not been terribly involved socially, except for the Intellectual Property Law Students Association and a Journal. There are myriad on-campus organizations and events. Recent speakers I particularly enjoyed hearing were a former International Court of Justice (in the Hague) Judge speaking about that court's Nuclear Weapons Advisory Opinion (for which he wrote a dissenting opinion), the Chief Legal Counsel to the International Monetary Fund and a professor who is also a

Read all of Vault's Law School Surveys at www.vault.com/lawschool — get complete surveys on top law schools, expert advice on applicaton essays, LSAT prep and more.

VAULT CAREER LIBRARY 399

Director for Amnesty USA speaking about a recent human rights fact-finding investigation to Afghanistan.

Status: Current student, full-time
Dates of Enrollment: 8/2003-Submit Date
Survey Submitted: October 2005

Students usually hang out at McGovern's, the small dive bar across the street from the law school. There are some nice restaurants in the Ironbound area of Newark, but students don't really venture out there during the day. There are organizations at school for just about every legal interest and every culture. There are also journals—the Law Review and five or six other legal journals—and moot court.

Status: Current student, full-time
Dates of Enrollment: 9/2003-Submit Date
Survey Submitted: April 2005

Social life here revolves around a few big parties every year that are hosted by student groups and two local bars (Hamilton's and McGovern's). People tend to go into New York City and Hoboken as well. As for dating, there are some student couples, but it's not a huge deal. Student clubs abound, ranging from the Public Interest Law Foundation to a Republican Club to the National Lawyers Guild to the Irish Law Students Association. There are more groups than I can count, and they tend to keep things interesting around the building with speakers and other events.

Status: Current student, full-time
Dates of Enrollment: 8/2003-Submit Date
Survey Submitted: April 2005

The student organizations throw great parties. There are more parties, speakers, workshops and panels that anyone could ever actually attend. The Public Interest Law Foundation (PILF) holds a live auction every year, which has been nicknamed "The Biggest Party of the Year." They raise money to provide funding to students working in unpaid public interest summer jobs by auctioning great items such as dinner with professors, tickets to sporting events, gift certificates and weekend getaways. It is a wonderful event and everyone has a great time.

Status: Current student, full-time
Dates of Enrollment: 9/2003-Submit Date
Survey Submitted: April 2005

One student favorites is McGovern's, an Irish pub directly across the street from the law school. Student groups host events with food and drinks all the time. There are tons of student groups to choose from. Rutgers has a growing LGBT student group that is lacking at a lot of other law schools.

Status: Current student, full-time
Dates of Enrollment: 9/2003-Submit Date
Survey Submitted: October 2004

Students are very friendly and come from diverse backgrounds. There are several bars in the area where students meet after classes, the most popular being McGovern's, an Irish tavern across the street. There are many on-campus groups for all sorts of activities and interests, and there are so many events that it would be impossible to attend them all. There are surprisingly few restaurants in the area and the school's cafeteria has an inadequate, overpriced menu. Most students bring their own lunches or go to one of the local pizza parlors, the best being Robert's, which is directly across the street from the school.

Status: Alumnus/a, full-time
Dates of Enrollment: 9/1998-5/2001
Survey Submitted: July 2004

Bars and restaurants: two bars of note, Hamilton Pub and McGovern's. McGoo's is an institution, but has been changing to keep up with the times. Sadly they have even added TV and karaoke. Hamilton is newer and shiny, and attempts to offer an upscale feel. Both places are frequented by the law school community and the Essex legal community as well, including lawyers, judges, prosecutors and cops.

The School Says

Rutgers School of Law—Newark is a leading center for the study of the theory and practice of law, the advancement of law reform, and the application of the law to promote equality and social justice. Four core principles shape the work of our faculty and students: academic excellence, scholarship, public service and equal opportunity. Through a unique combination of traditional doctrinal courses and clinical education, we prepare our students to become highly skilled, ethical lawyers who will assume influential roles in the law and other disciplines.

Our internationally recognized faculty regularly contribute to the development of legal theory and produce scholarship that addresses significant social issues from interdisciplinary perspectives. Faculty members engage students through teaching styles that range from the traditional Socratic Method to interactive problem solving, from required courses to research seminars and clinical practice. Through our pioneering clinical program and pro bono activities, faculty and students serve the public by giving the principles of justice and equality under the law a practical significance.

The law school seeks and attracts a student body with breadth of experience and depth of talent, and provides unparalleled opportunity for women, minorities and others who historically have been excluded from the legal profession. Our highly selective admissions process enrolls students of extraordinary academic and professional promise, who enrich the classroom with their intellectual strength as well as significant life and work experience. Many already have earned one or more advanced degrees and have achieved considerable success in business, the arts, social work, medicine or government before entering the law school. Others have studied or lived abroad, adding a global perspective to the classroom discourse.

Our minority student program, established in 1968, ensures that disadvantage will not be a barrier to success. In each entering class, between 30 and 40 percent of our students are people of color. Typically, the class is equally divided between men and women. Moreover, all regions of the nation and two dozen or more foreign countries are represented.

The Rutgers experience is enhanced by our home in the Center for Law and Justice, one of the most attractive and technologically advanced law school buildings in the country. Numerous features in the five-story building facilitate creative teaching and generate a strong sense of community. The building opens onto a pedestrian plaza and a garden terrace that are favorite gathering spots for students.

The School of Law is located on the Newark campus of Rutgers, The State University of New Jersey. Fully 20 percent of our full-time law students live in on-campus graduate apartments, located just minutes from the Center for Law and Justice. The campus is situated in the heart of Newark's cultural center. New York City is 20 minutes away by mass transit, and Philadelphia is just a one-hour train ride. Newark and the surrounding area are home to many of the state's and nation's leading law firms, as well as numerous government offices, corporations, entrepreneurial ventures and public interest groups that represent a wealth of employment opportunities.

Seton Hall University School of Law

Admissions Office
Seton Hall Law School
One Newark Center
Newark, NJ 07102-5210
Admissions phone: (973) 642-8747 or (888) 415-7271
Admissions fax: (973) 642-8876
Admissions e-mail: admitme@shu.edu
Admissions URL:
http://law.shu.edu/administration/admissions/

 Admissions

Status: Alumnus/a, full-time
Dates of Enrollment: 8/2000-6/2003
Survey Submitted: March 2006

Seton Hall has grown increasingly selective over the last five or so years. While long the gold standard in New Jersey, Seton Hall's reputation has grown dramatically in recent years. As a consequence there of, candidates for admission have increased greatly in number and ability.

With that said, I believe the professors and admission staff continue to seek candidates who are genuinely interested in the law and its function, as opposed to merely the highest scores and greatest resumes.

Status: Current student, full-time
Dates of Enrollment: 8/2003-Submit Date
Survey Submitted: October 2004

Getting in to Seton Hall was not that difficult. The application was not nearly as involved as other schools to complete. It was the last application I sent, and I received an acceptance letter only a couple of weeks later. There was no interview or follow up from my application—just the acceptance letter.

Status: Current student, full-time
Dates of Enrollment: 8/2003-Submit Date
Survey Submitted: March 2005

Admissions have become more difficult than in the past. The admissions department over-admitted the last few classes causing severe overcrowding in the school. Because of this, they have been tweaking with their admissions formula and have increased the level of their acceptable criteria. The school doesn't usually conduct interviews, although I believe they do upon special request.

Status: Alumnus/a, full-time JD/MBA
Dates of Enrollment: 8/1997-12/2000
Survey Submitted: March 2005

LSAT, LSAT, LSAT! Although not one of the top-tier schools, SHU is still selective in choosing its students. Once admitted into the law school, it is a bit easier to get into the MBA program but the GMAT is still required.

Status: Alumnus/a, part-time
Dates of Enrollment: 8/1997-6/2001
Survey Submitted: January 2005

Gaining admission to law school is not an easy process and it is not for the faint of heart. Due to the constraints of my job at the time, as well as my living and family situation, there were only two law schools I could realistically hope to attend. Seton Hall was at the top of my list. The law school application was fairly standard and comprehensive. Seton Hall's application did include a section for the applicant to submit an essay. I used the essay to try and set forth the specific reasons why I thought I was a good fit for the law school, not vice versa. As a non-traditional applicant (I was in my mid-30s, had a solid work history in a non-legal field and had an MBA), I felt that my job in the application process was to showcase my individuality, highlight the different perspective I

could bring to the classroom and express what attributes I felt would make me a successful law student and ultimately a successful lawyer.

Seton Hall probably wasn't the most selective law school at the time, however, as only one of three law schools in the state of New Jersey, two of which I could attend, it was crucial for me to make a very strong impression as an applicant. Interviews were not included as part of the admissions process, however I did want to meet with the admissions staff to try and get a feel for what the school administration was like, and to let them know, face-to-face, how much I wanted to attend law school. I would strongly advise anyone seeking to gain admission to a law school to take the time to make a visit to the school to meet with current students, professors, sit in on a class if possible and meet the administration. If you go at night, these are the people you will be spending a lot of time dealing with over the next four years. You should feel confident that these individuals are people with whom you can interact comfortably. I was impressed by every person with whom I met, and felt very confident that should I gain admission, my time spent at Seton Hall would be fruitful.

Status: Current student, full-time
Dates of Enrollment: 8/2002-Submit Date
Survey Submitted: September 2003

First, I took the LSATs. The score gave me an indication of which schools I could target (I applied to two reach schools, two target schools and two safety schools). During this process (after LSATs, but before I got the scores back—it takes about three weeks), I contacted my undergraduate school to have them send the LSAC my transcript, I also contacted professors and employers to write me letters of recommendation. That way, by the time my LSAT score was in, my file was complete. The next step was to fill out all of the law school applications. I had some from a law school fair I went to the previous year, but they are also accessible online. I typed all of my applications using a typewriter (looks more professional than handwritten applications), and I also wrote a personal essay (why I wanted to go to law school) and submitted a resume.

Status: Alumnus/a, full-time
Dates of Enrollment: 9/1996-6/1999
Survey Submitted: July 2004

Admissions are not particularly selective, and SHLS offers a lot of scholarship incentives to decent candidates.

Status: Alumnus/a, full-time
Dates of Enrollment: 9/1999-5/2002
Survey Submitted: April 2004

Admission seems to concentrate on LSAT scores especially when giving out scholarships. More likely to give full scholarships to out-of-state students because they want to diversify the student body.

Status: Alumnus/a, full-time
Dates of Enrollment: 8/1997-6/2000
Survey Submitted: April 2004

As with every law school, numbers are key (LSAT and GPA from undergrad). Seton Hall has scholarships they offer prospective students who fit in a certain area in their LSAT and GPA grid. I asked whether my "outstanding essay" made the difference in my admission and the offer of a scholarship. The response was: not really. It's all based on the numbers.

Read all of Vault's Law School Surveys at www.vault.com/lawschool — get complete surveys on top law schools, expert advice on applicaton essays, LSAT prep and more.

VAULT CAREER LIBRARY 401

 **Academics**

Status: Alumnus/a, full-time
Dates of Enrollment: 8/2002-5/2005
Survey Submitted: November 2005

Popular classes can be difficult to get into. Grading system is changing this year, so I can't speak to it. Professors are excellent. For me there was a bit too much focus on health law and IP law, and my interests are elsewhere.

Status: Alumnus/a, full-time
Dates of Enrollment: 8/2000-6/2003
Survey Submitted: March 2006

Overall the one thing that stands out about Seton Hall, and that I continue to rave about to those who ask about my experience there, is the quality of the professors there. Almost every professor I had at Seton Hall was a wonderful educator, who was there to because they loved to teach. Every professor was there to teach, not to write their books or articles, but to teach. I think that separates Seton Hall from the majority of law schools out there.

Status: Current student, full-time
Dates of Enrollment: 8/2003-Submit Date
Survey Submitted: October 2004

The professors and quality of the classes are excellent. Each professor seems to really care about what he/she does and wants to help you as much as they can. The workload is heavy, but as far as I can tell, it is right on par with other law schools. It is not easy to get popular classes and professors. In the first year, you are assigned professors for each class. You have no choice whatsoever. For the second and third years, you are put into a sort of hierarchy of registration. Each student is put into a group: group A, B, C or D. Group A gets to register first, then Group B, and so on. The groups rotate each semester to allow a new groups to register first in an attempt to be fair. However, you have to take certain classes in certain semesters, and therefore really only have the opportunity to pick the popular professor or class if you happen to be in the first group to register.

The grading at Seton Hall is tough. The grading system at Seton Hall is no doubt the biggest flaw of the school. The mandatory curve for mandatory classes is based on a C plus. Other schools in the area have curves of B or B plus. As such, during the interview process, when grades are very important to prospective firms looking to hire you, Seton Hall students come across as less accomplished than other law students, and have a tougher time getting jobs. Seton Hall is looking to change the curve to be more in line with other schools, but that has not yet been rolled out. If I could do it over again, I would have chosen to go to a different school just because of the problems that result from the curve.

> **Regarding the curve, the school says,** "Seton Hall Law requires a minimum of 50 percent of grades to be a B plus or better."

Status: Current student, full-time
Dates of Enrollment: 8/2003-Submit Date
Survey Submitted: March 2005

The grading curve at Seton Hall is tough. A C plus curve at best. However, the large majority of the classes are terrific. The professors are UNBELIEVABLE talents. Some of the most talented and brilliant people I have come across. Most professors hail from Harvard or other top ranked schools and have clerked at the federal circuit level and some at the Supreme Court. I can't say enough about the quality of the faculty, they are truly impressive. Registration for popular classes has been difficult because of overcrowding. However, as the school gets that issue under control, registration is becoming a little easier.

The workload is manageable. Depending upon how you juggle your own classes. A common complaint is the amount of work given in two-credit courses. Most often, the only difference between a two and a three credit course is the tenure (or lack thereof) of the faculty. Usually the workload for a two credit class is the same, if not sometimes more than that assigned for a three credit course. For a three credit course, reading assignments are usually about 30 or 40 pages per class (twice a week). For two credit classes, reading assignments range from 50 to 85 pages per class (meets once a week).

Status: Alumnus/a, full-time
Dates of Enrollment: 8/1997-12/2000
Survey Submitted: March 2005

The classes at the law school, especially the upper level classes, were excellent. Professors know who you are and frequently cold call on students to discuss issues and cases. The upper level classes all have practical aspects to them to expose students to the real world of practicing law. As a corporate attorney, I found the drafting and negotiating classes to be especially useful (a scarcity in most law schools). Grading was fair and not always based upon the "mandatory" curve. Workload was significant but manageable.

Status: Alumnus/a, part-time
Dates of Enrollment: 8/1997-6/2001
Survey Submitted: January 2005

Again—law school is not for the faint of heart. During the first year students are immersed into a new way of thinking, a new way of speaking, a new way of participating in the classroom dialogue and a strange new way of studying. The professors at Seton Hall were all extremely gifted educators. I was especially impressed that during my first year, over 75 percent of my classes were taught by full-time professors—not adjuncts and not "associate" professors. Since the first year of law school is THE critical year, this was important. Class quality was consistently high throughout my four years at Seton Hall. Grading on curve was the modus operandi for the first two years or so. This forced ranking leaves some students feeling short-changed, but it is probably the only way to create realistic class-ranking.

The workload is intense for the first two years. It takes that long to really come to grips with how one needs to study in law school. With only one examination at the end of each semester for each class, you have to cultivate strong self-discipline, and be very adept at managing your time. It is very easy to get three quarters of the way through the semester and then realize that you don't understand one critical element that is impeding your overall understanding of the course material. As with any college or graduate program, the popular classes fill up quickly. In addition, as an evening student, I was limited in terms of which classes I could take simply by virtue of the fact that I could not get to school during the day. However, having said that, there was only one occasion during my entire four years at Seton Hall when I could not sign up for a class that I really wanted to take.

Status: Alumnus/a, full-time
Dates of Enrollment: 8/2001-5/2004
Survey Submitted: January 2005

For the most part, I enjoyed the academic programs at Seton Hall. Unlike some other schools where professors teach theoretical and esoteric concepts, Seton Hall professors taught the nuts and bolts of lawyering. I feel that such a focus on the practical elements of lawyering has helped me hit the ground running as a first-year associate.

The first-year courses, like those in any school, were very large. However, the Seton Hall professors did a great job of making the classes seem smaller and more intimate. The rigor of the classes and the quality of the instruction were for the most part, challenging and interesting. Again, for the most part, the workload was manageable.

Some negatives: some classes were nearly impossible to get into, which was frustrating for many students. Also, there are more required courses at Seton Hall than most other schools. Furthermore, many classes were only offered at nights because they were taught by practicing lawyers. Although it was beneficial learning the practical elements of certain subjects from adjuncts, it created scheduling problems. Finally, some niche courses were only offered once every other year, so if you got shut out one year, you might not have the opportunity to register again.

I did not work too hard, and I achieved very high grades. I strongly believe the workload and the grading were both fair. There is a mandatory curve for all first-year classes, which then becomes discretionary for classes in future years.

Status: Current student, full-time
Dates of Enrollment: 8/2002-Submit Date
Survey Submitted: September 2003

The first-year curriculum of most U.S. law schools is the same. Usually students take Constitutional Law, Civil Procedure (my favorite class), Contracts, Torts, Criminal Law, Property (my least favorite!), Legal Research and Writing.

During the second year in most schools, one can begin taking electives. However, Seton Hall has required second-year classes. One must take Business Associations, Federal Income Taxation, Professional Responsibility, Evidence and Appellate Advocacy. This is to ensure that all students get familiar with these commonly bar-tested subjects.

Status: Alumnus/a, full-time
Dates of Enrollment: 8/1997-6/2000
Survey Submitted: April 2004

The workload is tough, and the curve is based on a C+ (whereas most law schools have a B curve). You must be prepared to work hard. The professors are the best I have had anywhere. Seton Hall has an outstanding faculty that really cares about its students, in my experience. You can visit with professors and discuss issues or questions, and they are always available to discuss exam grades. It is not a competitive atmosphere, which I found nice. The facility is outstanding. Getting into popular classes can be difficult; priority is based on a lottery.

 Employment Prospects

Status: Alumnus/a, full-time
Dates of Enrollment: 8/2000-6/2003
Survey Submitted: March 2006

I had several offers upon graduation, but chose to spurn them all and head to Boston. I took the Massachusetts bar exam and had a job shortly thereafter. I am now at Morgan Lewis & Bockius in Philadelphia and have spoken at length about my experience at Seton Hall in every interview I've had. The internships available through Seton Hall are amazing. Specifically, there are opportunities to intern with the U.S. Attorney's Office, the Federal Public Defenders Office, any number of pro bono programs, the State Legislature and Judiciary and the Federal District and Circuit Courts. Personally I participated in the Federal Public Defenders office and with a Federal District Court Judge. Both experiences were tremendous and shaped my approach to law.

Status: Alumnus/a, full-time
Dates of Enrollment: 8/1997-12/2000
Survey Submitted: March 2005

The law school has an extensive alumni network with both top firms and judges in New Jersey. It is a bit more difficult to get into Manhattan positions. Career services offers extensive opportunities for on-campus recruiting but was not that helpful in considering careers outside of public or private practice. I did not use career services on the main campus.

Status: Alumnus/a, part-time
Dates of Enrollment: 8/1997-6/2001
Survey Submitted: January 2005

Seton Hall is highly regarded among the most prestigious law firms in New Jersey. Employment prospects are generally very good for all Seton Hall law graduates. Those who graduate in the top 30 percent of the law school class will typically gain employment at New Jersey's best and largest law firms. On-campus recruiting is a major event at Seton Hall, and it is this process which usually results in the best job offers. A word to the wise: as an evening student it is easy to miss the importance of the on-campus interview process.

Status: Alumnus/a, full-time
Dates of Enrollment: 8/2001-5/2004
Survey Submitted: January 2005

I know that problems has been rectified, and the process is operating much more efficiently. When I was there, I found the on-campus recruiting was very strong for New Jersey firms and New Jersey clerkships, but weak with respect to New York firms and judges. I got many offers from New Jersey firms and one from

a New York firm (which I secured myself outside the OCR process). Seton Hall is very respected in New Jersey and has excellent placement rates in the state. Seton Hall is noted for placing judicial clerks.

Negatives: the alumni network seemed weak while I was there, and the school was not particularly helpful placing students after their first-year of education.

Status: Current student, full-time
Dates of Enrollment: 8/2002-Submit Date
Survey Submitted: September 2003

First-year—if you do really well, getting a judicial internship with a federal district court judge (or State Supreme Court judge) during the summer is best. You don't get paid, but some schools give credit for this internship. If you do really well, you can also try working at a good firm. Some (but not all) accept first-year students. For either job, send out a cover letter, resume, transcript (and writing sample, if asked) as soon as possible after your first-semester grades come out.

Second year is the meat of the hiring process. Most big firms participate in OCI (on-campus interview). What happens is that during the summer, all interested students submit a resume and bid for employers (just check off which employers they are interested in). The school's career services center then sends out all of the resumes. The employer picks anywhere from 10 to 30 students, and then gives them a 20-minute on-campus interview. If you make a good impression, you are invited to a second round of interviews in the office. These are generally three hours. Then, if you again make a good impression, you may be offered a summer associate position for the following summer. Many first-year associates get their permanent jobs from these summer associate positions.

Status: Alumnus/a, full-time
Dates of Enrollment: 8/2000-6/2003
Survey Submitted: April 2004

This school is mainly a feeder into New Jersey's vast clerkship program. As there are only two law schools in New Jersey and many courts, most students are able to find a clerkship, and the school will push you to take this route. In better years this probably was not a bad process; unfortunately, many of my friends are having a hard time finding employment after this process with the way that the legal market is these days.

The best way to avoid this system is to make the top 10 percent of the class your first year and then get onto Law Review. Even if you don't accomplish this, hold out for a smaller firm and don't buy into the administration's clerkship program. As far as watching my friends, this is basically a waste of your time unless you get a federal clerkship, and again, this is only offered to the top 5 to 10 percent of the class (and one guy whose father got him in).

Status: Alumnus/a, full-time
Dates of Enrollment: 9/1996-6/1999
Survey Submitted: July 2004

If you are thinking of working at a big firm in New York, getting a job means being a summer associate first, usually. This entails being at the very top of the class (we're talking top 5 percent maybe), being on Law Review and interning for a federal judge in your first year or something equally impressive. Do not spend your first-year summer working as a lifeguard. Most firms in New York City have a real aversion to New Jersey. They don't come on campus to interview. You will need some kind of connection even to get an interview generally. If, instead, you are thinking of working in New Jersey, SHLS will be fine. Again, being at the top of the class will mean all the big New Jersey firms will be recruiting you.

 **Quality of Life**

Status: Alumnus/a, full-time
Dates of Enrollment: 8/2002-5/2005
Survey Submitted: November 2005

Immediate neighborhood is lame. Downtown Newark doesn't have a lot going on, but it is a bit of a commuter school with lots of people living in Hoboken and

Read all of Vault's Law School Surveys at www.vault.com/lawschool — get complete surveys on top law schools, expert advice on applicaton essays, LSAT prep and more.

VAULT CAREER LIBRARY 403

NYC, which are both very close and have ample opportunities. School is collegial and people go out a lot together.

Status: Alumnus/a, full-time
Dates of Enrollment: 8/2000-6/2003
Survey Submitted: March 2006

It is Newark. And unfortunately maintains some of the gritty side that has become infamous. Not to mention being the fertile ground of the *Sopranos*, which is much more a positive then a negative. You see them shooting in an around the city every now and again. Not a reason to go to law school there, but fun nonetheless.

Newark has a great Portuguese and Italian heritage that comes to light in a number of fantastic restaurants in the immediate vicinity of the school. Many students live in Hoboken and make the short 15 minute commute to school. Hoboken consists of a large number of bars and restaurants and maintains both a young professional and blue collar immigrant populations. And New York City is right there.

Status: Current student, full-time
Dates of Enrollment: 8/2003-Submit Date
Survey Submitted: October 2004

The school is just a couple of blocks away from Newark Penn Station, which makes it convenient to everything. There is no on-campus housing, so if you are not living with parents, you need to find a place nearby to live. This is comprised mostly of city environments—Hoboken, Jersey City, Newark, and the school itself is in a city environment. Like any city, you need to be careful, but I don't feel unsafe when traveling to and from school. The cafeteria is not much to speak of, but there are several places near the school to go out to eat if you feel like getting some air.

Status: Alumnus/a, part-time
Dates of Enrollment: 8/1997-6/2001
Survey Submitted: January 2005

As an evening student, my experience with quality of life issues was obviously very different from the experiences of a traditional day student. Seton Hall Law is located in Newark—specifically in a section of the city that is undergoing an on going revitalization. Housing is available nearby, but I did not have to take advantage of this. The facilities at the Law School are remarkable. It is a bright, open and technologically advanced facility. Security is good. The library is huge, and conducive to effective study. It is difficult to really assess the quality of life, since there is nothing upon which to base a comparison. However, the physical facility is outstanding, and certainly helped make four difficult years easier to handle. There is a small snack bar and cafeteria which served extremely good strong coffee, pizza, fruit, and so on. On a slightly different note, the professors definitely did adhere to an open-door policy, and in my experience were always available to discuss any problems or areas of concern. This certainly enhanced the quality of life at the school.

Status: Current student, full-time
Dates of Enrollment: 8/2002-Submit Date
Survey Submitted: September 2003

SHU is in Newark, and there are no dorms. However, it is very close to the PATH, so many students live in New York City or Hoboken. Newark is not the safest city, but the school provides a shuttle service for students free of charge.

SHU's quality of life is typical of many law schools; most students spend a lot of time in the library. The campus is just one building. There are great things about this building: its design lets in a lot of sunlight, it's the kind of building that you can't hide in, and it is attached to the Legal Center, where many of the big New Jersey firms are.

Status: Alumnus/a, full-time
Dates of Enrollment: 9/1999-5/2002
Survey Submitted: April 2004

The building and facilities are new and state-of-the-art. There is a terrific library and plenty of computers in the computer labs. There is no on-campus housing—the law school campus is at a different location than the main campus, which has housing. There is no formal housing for law students. Most live in suburbs of Newark and commute. Despite its reputation, Newark is a safe and enjoyable

place to go to school. The campus is steps from New Jersey PAC and some of the state's most prestigious law firms. It is also close to various courthouses and government offices.

Status: Alumnus/a, full-time
Dates of Enrollment: 8/2000-6/2003
Survey Submitted: April 2004

There isn't a campus unless you count a few park benches on a cement patio. Crime is a problem in Newark and the surrounding neighborhoods. Students' cars were often stolen if not parked in the lots, which are very expensive. If you do not drive, you can take public transportation.

 Social Life

Status: Current student, full-time
Dates of Enrollment: 8/2003-Submit Date
Survey Submitted: October 2004

The social life tends to be created by friendly students. Students will organize happy hours for their classmates or a flag football game and things of the like, but you kind of have to make your own fun. A few students have become couples over the first and second year, but the dating scene is not that hopping. Everyone is too busy studying, I guess.

Status: Current student, full-time
Dates of Enrollment: 8/2003-Submit Date
Survey Submitted: March 2005

Seton Hall has a VERY active social life. There are constantly open bar events and people going out during the week and on weekends, in Hoboken and in NYC. A good majority of the school seems to focus more on social life than on academics. I would classify this law school as a party school. There are usually kegs present at orientation events for first-years.

Status: Alumnus/a, full-time
Dates of Enrollment: 8/1997-12/2000
Survey Submitted: March 2005

There were numerous organized student events but largely students got together on a more informal basis.

Status: Alumnus/a, part-time
Dates of Enrollment: 8/1997-6/2001
Survey Submitted: January 2005

I cannot comment on the social life at Seton Hall. I would typically arrive at school at six o'clock, and proceed immediately to the first of two classes. The 15 minute break between class was generally sufficient time to get coffee at the school's snack bar. After class (usually ten o'clock or later), I would leave for the hour drive home. This is not intended as a criticism at all. I know that some of my fellow night students would make arrangements to go out for dinner or drinks after class. There are a number of very good restaurants and bars in the school's vicinity.

Status: Alumnus/a, full-time
Dates of Enrollment: 8/2001-5/2004
Survey Submitted: January 2005

I really enjoyed my first-year experience. The school does a great job of integrating new students and setting up social activities for our first year. There are many programs that the school offers, including parties, functions, and speaking engagements, that make things fun and interesting. Orientation was run very well and really started my experience in a positive light. There are many academic and social clubs that students can join to meet new people and further their practical experience. The school's clinic offers students a great opportunity to work on real cases with real clients. Finally, there are several journals, which are run, for the most part, very well. There are many bars, pubs, and restaurants that the students go to, and there really is a positive atmosphere among the students, unlike some schools that breed competition and resentment. Overall, I enjoyed my social life at Seton Hall.

Status: Current student, full-time
Dates of Enrollment: 8/2002-Submit Date
Survey Submitted: September 2003

SHU has many activities: every Thursday is "thirsty Thursday," where there is beer and wine free of charge. There are many other social events—we have a holiday party and a formal every year, which many of the students and professors attend.

Status: Alumnus/a, full-time
Dates of Enrollment: 8/2000-6/2003
Survey Submitted: April 2004

The social life is great, if you live in Hoboken. Many students lived there and had a great time every weekend. Do not live anywhere in Newark, as there is absolutely nothing there to do except go to the Ironbound for some good food.

Status: Alumnus/a, full-time
Dates of Enrollment: 9/1999-5/2002
Survey Submitted: April 2004

There are formal and informal gatherings of students throughout the school year. Full-time day students are the most frequent attendees of such events. Students often go out socially in nearby Hoboken and sometimes go to bars and restaurants in Newark, including the nearby Don Pepe, a Spanish restaurant. There is a semiformal ball at a nearby hotel at the end of the year, and there is also a holiday party.

Status: Alumnus/a, full-time
Dates of Enrollment: 8/1997-6/2000
Survey Submitted: April 2004

There are some bars in the Ironbound district and in Newark—plenty to occupy the law school in my opinion. But the school even had a great social scene, with the Irish Law Students Association hosting weekly parties on Thursday. There was a lot of dating among students. The student body is very attractive, as a whole, compared to almost any other law school you can find.

 ## The School Says

At Seton Hall University School of Law, you'll find a school that stands apart through the success of our graduates, the strength of our faculty and the range of professional opportunities provided to our students. At Seton Hall Law, you'll be taught by professors nationally respected as leaders in their fields, who truly value the art of teaching. Seton Hall Law professors bring life, energy and real-world relevance to the law school experience, both in the classroom and, as importantly, in their availability when you need assistance. Their teaching style ranges from the traditional Socratic style to guitar-strummed explanations on current doctrine, exemplifying the commitment to enhancing student learning that typifies Seton Hall Law.

We're also one of the leading law schools in the New York-New Jersey metropolitan when it comes to bar passage rates and job placement. In 2005, 89 percent of first-time exam takers passed the New York bar, while 85 percent passed the New Jersey bar. A total of 96 percent of our 2005 graduating class was employed within nine months after graduation. You'll find our graduates not only in the top-tier New Jersey firms, but in firms from Washington, D.C. to Philadelphia and New York, who all recruit heavily on campus. Over the last three years, the number of top 100 New York firms taking part in our fall recruiting program has doubled, as recent graduates have obtained positions with such top-named firms as Skadden Arps Slate, Meagher & Flom; Cahill Gordon & Reindel; Dewey Ballantine; Jones Day; and Weil, Gotshal & Manges, to name just a few.

When it comes to a social life, Seton Hall Law's location provides plenty to explore. Located in Newark, Seton Hall Law is proud to be part of a community rich in history and culture. Whatever your interest, you'll find it here—the performing and visual arts, sports, great food are all within easy reach. Just blocks from the law school, you'll also find Newark's famed Ironbound district, a vibrant Portuguese, Brazilian and Spanish community with quaint and affordable restaurants and paella as it truly is meant to be eaten and experienced. Plus, we're within surprisingly easy access—by train, bus or car—of New York City and the Jersey shore—just a few of the region's many popular student destinations. Living opportunities abound both near the campus and the surrounding area. One favorite of Seton Hall Law students is Hoboken, which has become a mecca for young professionals.

To find out more, please visit our web site at http://law.shu.edu, or call the Admissions Office with any questions you may have or to schedule a personal visit, (973) 642-8747.

Read all of Vault's Law School Surveys at www.vault.com/lawschool — get complete surveys on top law schools, expert advice on applicaton essays, LSAT prep and more.

VAULT CAREER LIBRARY 405

The University of New Mexico School of Law

UNM School of Law
MSC11 6070
1 University of New Mexico
Albuquerque, NM 87131-0001
Admissions phone: (505) 277-0958
Admissions fax: (505) 277-9958
Admissions e-mail: admissions@law.unm.edu
Admissions URL: http://lawschool.unm.edu/admissions/

 Admissions

Status: Current student, full-time
Dates of Enrollment: 8/2005-Submit Date
Survey Submitted: May 2006

First step was taking the LSAT, which went to LSAC along with official transcript and letter of recommendation. Release of this information to the law school accompanied completion of the application, along with a personal statement. The personal statement is the key component; most applicants have high test scores and grades, but the personal statement is where you set yourself apart from every other applicant.

Status: Current student, full-time
Dates of Enrollment: 8/2005-Submit Date
Survey Submitted: May 2006

The personal statement weighs heavily in the admissions process, which is one of the reasons I chose this school. I like that they're just as interested in a person's personal history as they are in the student's academic achievement. There's no interview, but they give you ample opportunity to describe yourself in your personal statement (it's one of the longest statements accepted that I've seen). UNM is one of the smaller schools, but it's still very competitive, so don't blow it off. As the only law school in NM, significant preference is given to NM residents, but there are still a sufficient number of out-of-state students in the class. A current student is involved in the selection process (although I'm not sure how involved this person is), so that's also another unique feature to consider when writing your statement.

> **UNM says:** "The five-member admissions committee is composed of three faculty members, one third-year law student and the Assistant Dean for Admissions. All committee members read the application files separately and meet once a week during the admissions season to make decisions. The law student is a full member of the committee, and his/her input is given the same weight as that of the other members."

Status: Current student, full-time
Dates of Enrollment: 8/2003-Submit Date
Survey Submitted: May 2006

In addition to the standard process of submitting your LSDAS materials (transcripts, letters of recommendation), it is important to convey your particular interest in the University of New Mexico and in the state of New Mexico in general. UNM is the only law school in the state and is therefore a precious resource for New Mexicans. If you have a connection to New Mexico or a compelling reason why you want to come to UNM, you should definitely include that information in your personal statement.

Status: Current student, full-time
Dates of Enrollment: 8/2004-Submit Date
Survey Submitted: May 2006

I appreciated the process as it was very simple, no interview or anything elaborate. The selectivity is pretty high, hard to get in, but the admissions board pays a lot of attention to diversity (e.g., age, race, family status) and background (e.g., undergraduate university, work history), which plays an important role in

a student integrating comfortably into the law school community. Also, after acceptance, there is the Accepted Applicants Program which is a great opportunity to meet current students, professors and staff, and to solidify decision to attend or not.

Status: Current student, full-time
Dates of Enrollment: 8/2004-Submit Date
Survey Submitted: May 2006

Representatives were very helpful. I was offered an opportunity to have a personal tour of the school. That was fun, informative and helpful in making my decision about where to attend. I was able to sit in on a class during this tour which was helpful to see classroom atmosphere. Requirements for admission are high, while still affording minorities the encouragement to apply.

Status: Current student, full-time
Dates of Enrollment: 8/2003-Submit Date
Survey Submitted: May 2006

The admissions process was fairly straightforward—LSAT, statement and application form. I was completing a master's degree on the same campus while I applied to the law school, so I was fortunate enough to be able to approach the admissions staff personally. They were all very approachable and helpful, and I have no reason to think that would be different for applicants that could not meet with them personally.

Also, the admissions staff organizes several events throughout the year for both prospective applicants and for accepted applicants. These "open house" events or dinners combine presentations from staff, faculty and current students, and the law school provides a dinner for everyone afterwards. Overall, these events generate a lot of informal contacts and learning, making the application process more transparent and less intimidating.

> **The school says:** "The law school offers several Open House events each year for prospective applicants. At the Open Houses, prospective applicants learn more about admissions, financial aid and career opportunities. They also have the chance to speak with a panel of current law students. Light refreshments are provided. In addition, admitted applicants are invited to an Accepted Applicants' Program to meet faculty, staff, and current students and attend a catered dinner."

Status: Alumnus/a, full-time
Dates of Enrollment: 8/2001-5/2004
Survey Submitted: July 2006

My understanding has always been that UNM is looking for a very diverse group of students so as to enrich the learning experience both in and out of the classroom. While there's no magic formula for getting in to UNM, I would recommend that potential students be as genuine as possible in their essays as to why they want to be in law school and what they want to do with a law degree when they get out. No matter what the essay is about, if the person is genuine in what's written that will do nothing but help.

Status: Current student, full-time
Dates of Enrollment: 8/2003-Submit Date
Survey Submitted: April 2006

UNM LAW has a massive in-state preference built in to the admissions policy, as a state government-funded law school, and as the one and only law school in the whole state (public or private), UNM has to take care of local residents seeking admission, first and foremost. Only a few, outstandingly qualified out-of-state residents are admitted as students each year. 80 to 90 percent of the seats in each class of students are officially reserved in the UNM law school admissions policy for New Mexico residents or former NM residents who wish to return (they graduated from a NM high school and went to college out of state and want to return to their home state).

The school says: "While UNM, as a state-funded institution, does give a strong admissions preference to New Mexico residents, each year approximately 20 percent of the incoming students are non-residents. The law school values geographical diversity in the classroom and believes that it enhances the educational experience for all students."

UNM law school does not conduct formal interviews as part of the admissions process. However, Mrs. Susan Mitchell, Associate Dean of Admissions, who reads all of the applications, does do community open house events. At the admissions Open Houses for Prospective Students (three or so per year, two in the fall semester, one in January), prospective students can come to group sessions, introduce themselves to the admissions director, meet other members of the admissions committee and thus do an informal interview.

If you go to the Open House two or three times, and ask questions during the interactive information sessions, the staff will learn your name and see that you really are committed to attending UNM, if admitted. Telling the admissions committee, both in person and in your personal statement (application essay) that UNM law school is your top choice helps as well, since it shows real commitment to accepting any offer of admission, if they decide to let you in.

UNM Law says: "The Open Houses are designed to provide information to prospective students. Most speakers are staff members at the law school, including the Assistant Dean for Admissions and Financial Aid, Susan Mitchell. Other members of the admissions committee do not attend the Open House events. Interviews are not offered as part of the admissions process at the UNM School of Law. All Open Houses in a given academic year offer the same program, and we recommend that prospective students attend no more than one Open House.""

Status: Current student, full-time
Dates of Enrollment: 8/2003-Submit Date
Survey Submitted: April 2006

UNM really looks at the whole candidate, including interests and character. The admissions committee spends a lot of time with applications. I encourage applicants to make connections (even over e-mail) with professors that share their interests. The administration, staff and professors are really interested in cultivating those interests and helping to foster lawyers who excel at their craft with integrity.

Status: Current student, full-time
Dates of Enrollment: 8/2005-Submit Date
Survey Submitted: April 2006

The admission process also assures that the "diversity" factor is not artificial. For example, the nearly 40 percent of the class that comprises minorities is not largely upper middle class Asians. Instead, the number reliably represents the population of the state: Native Americans from various tribes, African-Americans, Hispanics and a few foreign students.

The downside to this is that few LSAT/GPA combinations will guarantee admission. Several people with numbers well above the averages find themselves being waitlisted or right out rejected. This is not fully explained by yield protection. UNM only has 100 to 120 seats in each class, and it easily fills them with people who strongly desire to practice and live in the land of enchantment.

Regarding diversity, UNM says: "During the 2005-2006 academic year, minority students represented 41 percent of the total student body. African-Americans constituted 4 percent, Native Americans 11 percent, Hispanics 24 percent and Asians 2 percent."

 **Academics**

Status: Current student, full-time
Dates of Enrollment: 8/2005-Submit Date
Survey Submitted: May 2006

The best part of UNM in many departments is the faculty—the law school has awesome, topshelf faculty. It's hard even to choose who is really the most brilliant/renowned Harvard-decorated of them. New Mexico attracts a certain type of intellectual/urban refugee. Very close contact with faculty—small school, too small sometimes. No problem getting into most classes.

UNM is a poor underfunded state school in a poor state. There is incompetence and hostility at every level, however the law school is a little better in this regard. However, the law school is not free of a frustrating lack of interest in things that impact students directly. It can be frustrating to attend UNM—until you are in the classroom and then you feel very lucky because you are often getting the best instruction that exists at half the price.

Status: Current student, full-time
Dates of Enrollment: 8/2004-Submit Date
Survey Submitted: May 2006

There is a wide variety of classes offered at UNMSOL, and most classes are "small" in comparison to other schools. The largest first-year (required) classes probably consist of 50 to 60 students at the very most. There are also many seminar classes offered each semester, with a maximum of 12 students allowed, which really gives everyone a chance to participate and get to know the professors.

One of the best things about UNMSOL is that it's a small enough community that you can really get to know your professors, and they (and much of the staff) know you by name—and it's nice to be a name rather than a number. Grading seems fair, and the workload seems to be comparable to other programs—LOTS of reading! Also, our clinical program (a requirement) has consistently been rated among the top in the country.

Status: Alumnus/a, full-time
Dates of Enrollment: 8/2001-5/2004
Survey Submitted: July 2006

The student-faculty ratio at UNM is outstanding and the faculty is second to none. Most of the very popular classes have an open enrollment so it wasn't difficult to get in. There are a few classes with limited enrollment that are challenging to get into—like the basic Mediation Training Program—but the courses are offered so frequently that over the course of three years a student can find a way to make it work.

After the first year, the workload depends on the type of experience a student wants to have. If you take the challenging courses and push yourself then your workload will be tough. One of the great things about UNM is that a student can take the basic courses to master the fundamentals of being a competent attorney, but there is ample opportunity to explore fields that may only be on interest to a small group of students or just that student. The school encourages students to pursue the areas of law and policy that excites them.

Status: Current student, full-time
Dates of Enrollment: 8/2004-Submit Date
Survey Submitted: May 2006

As the student body is very small, almost all of the important and good classes are unlimited. A friend of mine at the University of Houston couldn't get into a class necessary for the bar and I was surprised because I've really never had that problem. The teachers are brilliant and extremely approachable; I've had the opportunity to help one of my professors write a book! Also, there is no competitive tension, at least not very salient. If you want to be you can, but there's no pressure at all.

Status: Current student, full-time
Dates of Enrollment: 8/2003-Submit Date
Survey Submitted: May 2006

The academics at UNM School of Law are very demanding. Similar to other law schools, the first year is the most stressful and demanding, but the second and

Read all of Vault's Law School Surveys at www.vault.com/lawschool — get complete surveys on top law schools, expert advice on applicaton essays, LSAT prep and more.

VAULT CAREER LIBRARY 407

third years bring their own challenges. Personally, I do not feel like my second and third years were any less demanding than the first, since I continued to pursue the classes I wanted to take but also participated in a Law Review and in moot court competitions.

One of the strengths of UNM's law school, is the ease with which individual students can meet with professors. We have one of the lowest student-faculty ratios in the country, and though this didn't mean much to me before I arrived at the law school, I quickly realized how meaningful a one-on-one conversation with a professor can be. Throughout law school, I have had multiple individual meetings with professors in the form of lunches, dinners at their homes and impromptu conversations after class. I would not have had this kind of access to my professors at a larger law school. Finally, our professors here at UNM match up against the best professors in the country.

Status: Current student, full-time
Dates of Enrollment: 8/2003-Submit Date
Survey Submitted: May 2006

The academics at UNM are incredible. My first-year classes were stellar, the professors topnotch. I felt like my particular section got the best professors at the school, who were kind to the students, and known state and nation wide for their academic contributions to their respective areas of scholarship. I have only had trouble getting into one class during my three years at UNM. The student-teacher ratio has always been favorable, with my largest class being no more than 50 students. All of our professors are willing to work with us outside of class, and some go beyond even that. For example, this semester, my Remedies professor offered to meet with any study group for as long as needed until the night before our final exam. I am thoroughly impressed by the dedication to learning that my professors have shown.

Status: Current student, full-time
Dates of Enrollment: 8/2005-Submit Date
Survey Submitted: May 2006

Classes in the first year are larger than I would like, but size drops significantly after the first year. Of course, quality of classes is dependent upon the professor you have (many are absolutely incredible), but even if you're in a section with a professor or class tutor you're not particularly compatible with, students are welcome to seek outside help or utilize the tutors from any other section. In fact, most tutors open their reviews to the entire first-year class, rather than just their own section. Grading is based on the final exam and grades are curved, but the teachers get together to try and make the curves as fair as possible among sections. The workload is heavy. Don't expect to have a real life your first year, and there's a chance your vision may be affected. This is probably true for any law school though.

Status: Current student, full-time
Dates of Enrollment: 8/2005-Submit Date
Survey Submitted: April 2006

The academics are rigorous and demanding. I graduated in the top 2 percent of the Number One liberal arts school in the country, and the quality of the education at UNM School of Law is easily comparable. The workload is heavy, but not unmanageable. The professors are incredible and really care about the students. They come from the top schools in the country, and they're always willing to meet with students and study groups.

Grading follows typical law school patterns—most classes are curved at a B-, and most grades are based on either a single final exam or a paper (a few professors also count class participation, but it's the exception, not the rule).

The school has excellent Indian law and Natural Resources law certificate programs, including the opportunity to work on the prestigious *Natural Resources Journal*.

Status: Current student, full-time
Dates of Enrollment: 8/2003-Submit Date
Survey Submitted: April 2006

I found the classes to be very challenging my first year, and the workload huge but manageable. My second and third years the workload leveled off at 12 or 15 credits a semester, since I did three credits of summer school one year and six credits the next year. By spreading my classes out, law school became much

more fun and I could get a part-time job to reduce the amount of loan money I had to borrow. Plus, my grades went up when I cut back from 16 credits my first semester to 12 credits each semester my second year.

You can easily get into most classes, since most of them do not have an enrollment cap. There is very little need for an enrollment cap when there are only 120 student per grade level and 360 students in the whole school. The only exception is the Mediation Training Program, since basic and advanced mediation classes are offered as a short intensive seminar taught once a semester. The seminar consists of three day weekend, three long days of class, plus writing a reflection paper, for an easy three credit hours. That course has an enrollment cap of 30 students and fills during the first 120 seconds of enrollment online. The dean is going to fund an additional section to relieve crowding.

So, other than the mediation program, you can get into any full semester-length class you want. All students must take one semester of Clinical Law in their second or third year of law school to graduate. This has been a requirement since the 1970s. There are multiple clinic classes offered every semester (fall, spring and summer) and students usually get there first or second choice of topic and/or semester time preference, but technically a lottery is used to make assignments if demand exceeds supply for a specific clinic course.

All classes at UNM law school are taught by faculty, not teaching assistants or tutors (except for a few supplemental exam review sessions right before final exams, after the professor has already given a full course review lecture). Most classes are taught by full-time, tenured faculty. For trial advocacy, the tenured professor divides the class of 60 people into groups of 10 and brings in adjunct instructors who are full-time courtroom litigators to work of specific skills (cross-examination, closing arguments) with small groups of 10 students in separate night classes.

Status: Current student, full-time
Dates of Enrollment: 8/2005-Submit Date
Survey Submitted: April 2006

The classes usually have a fair balance of black letter and theory, while some professors tend to lean more one way than the other. The upper level course offerings are good, considering the fact that we are a small school. There is definitely a leaning towards environmental/natural resources and Indian law. The school has actively sought to cultivate those emphases because of the location of the school.

For students interested in corporate law, we have some offerings, but probably not as broad as what some other schools might offer. We also have courses in Entertainment, Sports Law, Trademarks, Patents, Copyrights, Health Law and Bioethics, International Law, Immigration and some others. It is not always possible to pursue full-fledged specialties in any of these areas, but at least there are basic offerings. We also have a few truly theoretical/academic courses on jurisprudential matters, critical theory, and race and gender issues. In fact, we have faculty that specialize academically in gender and race issues. They offer several very interesting courses.

 Employment Prospects

Status: Current student, full-time
Dates of Enrollment: 8/2004-Submit Date
Survey Submitted: May 2006

In all honesty, prestige is probably highest among New Mexico employers. It's not so much that UNMSOL isn't prestigious, but that it's just not very well known. There is an on-campus recruiting program in the fall for 2Ls looking for summer jobs and 3Ls looking for permanent jobs. Lots of employers come, and it's a great opportunity. There is also a new judicial clerkship workshop offered through the career services office, which helps explain the requirements of clerkships. Also, the career services office will help put together student application packets, which is a tremendous undertaking!

Status: Alumnus/a, full-time
Dates of Enrollment: 8/2001-5/2004
Survey Submitted: July 2006

Going to law school at UNM is a huge advantage when looking for a job, particularly in New Mexico. The faculty have strong relationships with the vast majority of the legal community including the most prominent judges, lawyers and elected officials. Many UNM graduates end up in various government positions—judicial clerkships, DA/PD, that sort of thing—but my classmates took jobs in every area of the legal field including the biggest private law firms and the smallest nonprofit groups.

On-campus recruiting doesn't play a huge role in finding a job for most students but that's mainly because many students get job offers from their summer clerkships and other externships. If a graduating UNM Law student wants to get a job, and makes even a lazy effort, there are plenty of good jobs available.

Status: Current student, full-time
Dates of Enrollment: 8/2003-Submit Date
Survey Submitted: May 2006

Employment prospects are high. UNM's law school is the only law school in the state, so prospective employers look to the law school for the vast majority of their hires. Employment opportunities include clerkships (state and federal), entry-level positions with small and large firms, public interest jobs and public sector jobs. For example, several of my classmates are clerking for the state Supreme Court next year, as well as for the state Court of Appeals and a 10th Circuit District Court. Others are going to be working for the state legislative or executive branch, the public defender's offices and district attorney's offices across the state, while many more are entering any number of private firms across the state. Others received funding for research after school, and plan on future academic positions.

Status: Current student, full-time
Dates of Enrollment: 8/2003-Submit Date
Survey Submitted: May 2006

We are lucky at UNM. Being the only law school in the state, we have the extraordinary opportunity to network with partners of firms, as well as state supreme court justices. Most of my friends have argued in front of our state Supreme Court justices for mock trial and other activities. All of my fellow graduates have work before taking the bar.

For those leaving the state, I have noticed that they have been able to compete on a national level for competitive positions. One of my friends, for example, got a fantastic job with the Department of Justice in Natural Resources in D.C. Most of my fellow graduates have been granted associate positions, with a few others doing contract clerking to decide what area to go into. The best thing about practicing law in this state, is that networking is as easy as attending one meeting. I myself, having done a small pro bono project in a remote part of the state while in school, found that doing that small project had the unintended, but fantastic result of putting my name out in the community. My friends on various boards passed on to me that my name had been mentioned in various state-wide meetings. However, the down side to this small state, is that you have to be very careful what you do in law school, as it will be with you as long as you are in the state.

Status: Current student, full-time
Dates of Enrollment: 8/2003-Submit Date
Survey Submitted: April 2006

If you want to work in New Mexico, there is no other place to go. The law school shares space with the Court of Appeals, the Judicial Selection Committee/Institute for Public Law. State and national politicians frequent the place, so it is largely at the center of the New Mexico universe. If you want to leave the state, UNM sounds exotic. Professors have great connections in international humanitarian law and other specializations, such as Indian and Water Law. On the flip side, if you want a big-time firm job outside New Mexico, UNM may not be the place for you.

UNM says: "Although most UNM law school graduates choose to work in the state (which contains no law firms meeting the ABA definition of 'large' firms), or in the surrounding states, those graduates who have chosen to practice outside the

Southwest have been successful in finding work at large firms in major metropolitan areas."

Status: Current student, full-time
Dates of Enrollment: 8/2005-Submit Date
Survey Submitted: April 2006

We do not send an inordinate amount of graduates into large law firms. This is partly because New Mexico has no large law firms, and most graduates want to remain in-state. Students who do wish to leave and practice in law firms do have the opportunity, though they should have a strong law school record with journal experience. Our school does not create a national buzz, and the graduate seeking a position at a prestigious firm will probably have to be very proactive in getting an interview and a job. After all, they will be competing in places that have their own law schools that are more familiar to them. That said, it can and does happen.

Last year, 14 of of 100 graduates had judicial clerkships upon graduation. These ranged from federal to state. Mainly, these clerkships went to the top students who had journal experience. Overall, UNMSOL has had a respectable clerkship representation, as graduates from UNMSOL have clerked for the Supreme Court of the United States, U.S. Court of Appeals and U.S. district courts. It is obviously more difficult for UNM grads to get the more coveted clerkships, but it does happen.

 Quality of Life

Status: Current student, full-time
Dates of Enrollment: 8/2005-Submit Date
Survey Submitted: May 2006

It is not hard to find a very nice place to live here—rents are still relatively low, but rising. Most students live in one/two/three-bedroom houses near the school. There are some good neighborhoods for going out, bars are not that far away. Not everyone has a car (I don't) but most people do and can't imagine living here without one. A car is advised. The university area is a large, dense section of the city.

Status: Current student, full-time
Dates of Enrollment: 8/2003-Submit Date
Survey Submitted: May 2006

If you like sunny weather, outdoor activities and delicious New Mexican food, then you will like UNM. The law school is situated on UNM's north campus, which is close to the restaurants and bars of Nob Hill, but is also surrounded by a nice residential area in which students can rent apartments or homes. While crime is a concern anywhere, the law school is located in a tranquil part of town. Additionally, UNM's North Golf Course is adjacent to the law school and many students and faculty can be seen jogging or walking their dogs around its perimeter.

Status: Current student, full-time
Dates of Enrollment: 8/2004-Submit Date
Survey Submitted: May 2006

Crime in Abq. is pretty high, but I've never had any problems with it personally, just hear stories. I didn't like Abq. at first, having moved from Dallas, but it has grown on me. Housing is very cheap (as is the school) and it was easy to find my one-bedroom duplex with a backyard for $450 a month. Although the law school is small, the entire campus is very big and easily accessible. I go to the gym on main campus and the $2.00 movie theater often.

Status: Current student, full-time
Dates of Enrollment: 8/2004-Submit Date
Survey Submitted: May 2006

Quality of life in Albuquerque is good, especially if you like the outdoors. Among other things, UNM is close to great golf courses, hiking trails and exceptional skiing. There's plenty of sunshine and lots of nice weather. Dining is great if you like green chili on your food, but it is a little lacking in other areas. There are a couple great steak houses and a few really good Italian restaurants, but it's hard to find good Chinese or Tex Mex. Crime is an issue in Albuquerque, but it's mostly car theft. The housing around UNM is pretty safe.

Read all of Vault's Law School Surveys at www.vault.com/lawschool — get complete surveys on top law schools, expert advice on applicaton essays, LSAT prep and more.

VAULT CAREER LIBRARY 409

Status: Current student, full-time
Dates of Enrollment: 8/2005-Submit Date
Survey Submitted: May 2006

Housing is OK, depending on where you want to live or how much you're willing to spend. The areas around UNM main campus tend to be sketchy, but the areas closer to the law school are much nicer. These also cost a little more. If you're willing to fight traffic, you can live in even nicer areas of town.

The law school is located right next to the med school, and both are pretty much secluded from the rest of main campus, because of geographical location. However, you will never have to leave the law school for anything other than financial aid. The only problem is there's not much selection as far as food goes. Main campus facilities are fine and the student rec center and gym are actually really nice in comparison to other schools I've seen. Lots of law students use the student gym, so it seems convenient and sufficient.

> **The school says:** "The law school has its own Registrar's Office, Financial Aid Office and Career and Student Services Office located in the building."

Status: Current student, full-time
Dates of Enrollment: 8/2005-Submit Date
Survey Submitted: April 2006

UNM has the best quality of life of any law school that I've heard of. Friends at other law schools tell me their experiences are that the schools are inhumane to say the least. UNM, on the other hand, has been an absolute pleasure to attend, and I'm not the only student who feels that way. The school focuses on building community rather than competition. The students work very cooperatively, and are always willing to help each other out. I've been awed by how supportive this school has been in every way. The school does its best to accommodate parents and students with outside family responsibilities, although students in the first semester are not allowed to work.

> **UNM says:** "Pursuant to a pilot project due for review in 2009, first-year law students may work up to 15 hours per week. Second- and third-year law students may work up to 20 hours per week."

The neighborhood of the law school is lovely. It's separated off from the sprawling main campus of UNM in its own separate building with great facilities, abutting a golf course with a really nice walking trail around it. It's very safe, and there are a number of rentals close enough to walk to the campus. The school has two computer labs for student use, an excellent library with carrels (many with fantastic views of the Sandias) for all. The NM Court of Appeals is right across the street, and sometimes uses the school's moot court room for actual oral arguments. The school has an amazing clinic (participation is a graduation requirement, so all students leave with hands-on practice) that is as well-equipped as any law firm. It's also all wireless Internet connected.

Status: Alumnus/a, full-time
Dates of Enrollment: 8/2001-5/2004
Survey Submitted: July 2006

UNM is an institution that values balance in life. Students definitely need to keep up with their school work, but there is a strong consensus that students need to keep a good balance with the schoolwork—still spend time with family and loved ones, go the gym, get outdoors, whatever it is that keeps a student sane and able to keep learning.

Status: Current student, full-time
Dates of Enrollment: 8/2005-Submit Date
Survey Submitted: April 2006

The facilities are excellent. the library has a large collection and more study area than there are students at the law school. The entire school is fully equipped for wireless Internet access, there are two computer labs with great printing services, and classrooms are modern, Internet-equipped and comfortable.

 ## Social Life

Status: Current student, full-time
Dates of Enrollment: 8/2005-Submit Date
Survey Submitted: May 2006

Albuquerque, especially the UNM community, feels like a small village. It is not hard to meet people here but, personally, I find Westerners in these parts a little aloof. There are a lot of people not from New Mexico who live here and go to UNM too. Social life is generally good, but limited. This describes life here and UNM-SOL in general. Good, but limited. People either love it here or hate it.

Status: Current student, full-time
Dates of Enrollment: 8/2004-Submit Date
Survey Submitted: May 2006

Social life can be good if that's what you're looking for. There are often parties on the back patio of the law school, which is great (the weather is usually fantastic here so it's nice to get outside and hang out). We have an annual Halloween party thrown by the law school Student Bar Association for the law school and med school, usually at a bar downtown, with lots of drinking and dancing. There are several bars and tons of good restaurants in Nob Hill and downtown Albuquerque in particular, and of course there's other stuff all over the city.

Status: Current student, full-time
Dates of Enrollment: 8/2003-Submit Date
Survey Submitted: May 2006

Albuquerque is a large and growing city of about 500,000 people, and the larger metropolitan area approaches one million, so there is a wide variety of bars, restaurants and nightclubs. I don't go out as much as I used to, but the Anodyne downtown is still one of my favorites, as well as Gecko's. If you're in the mood for something a little more upscale, I've had a good time at Seasons and Zinc.

For good New Mexican food in a quite, modest setting, I recommend El Patio at Harvard and Silver, or Perea's at Central and Alvarado. If you can handle a little grease and are not a vegetarian, breakfast at Perea's can't be beat (try anything with carne adovada or chorizo). If you don't mind sacrificing some flavor for a little more ambience, check out Sadie's or El Pinto in the northern part of the city.

In addition to these spirits and food, there are countless other activities in town. UNM houses a first-class performing arts center, as well as recreational activities for all seasons. There are several small theater groups in town, and one of them sponsors the annual Revolutions Theater Festival, which brings different groups from around the world. The Latin American Studies program also sponsors the annual Sin Fronteras Film Festival, which keeps getting better and better. At the law school itself, student groups often sponsor social events, and individual students often throw parties to which the entire school gets invited.

Status: Current student, full-time
Dates of Enrollment: 8/2003-Submit Date
Survey Submitted: April 2006

I was the chapter president of the local cheaper of Phi Alpha Delta Law Fraternity at UNM and I loved it. It has about 15 active members. We meet monthly and lead the organization and operation of two major social events at UNM: the Fall Children's Halloween Carnival (trick or treat at offices, cake walk) and the Spring Carnival (Easter egg hunt on golf course, games). These are the two big annual family events at the law school. The Student Bar Association organizes the annual Halloween Costume dance party for adults at the El Rey Theatre in downtown Albuquerque.

The Mexican American Law Student Association (MALSA) has a Mexican-style manzana (BBQ) each fall at the law school, a fundraiser golf tournament in September and the Fighting For Justice (FFJ) award banquet each spring. The Association for Public Interest Law (APIL) hosts a fundraiser event called "Casino Night" every April, where students gather to eat, socialize and play casino games (not with real money, just worthless chips) at the Doubletree Hotel, downtown. The money raised pays for summer fellowships to do free legal aid work.

Status: Current student, full-time
Dates of Enrollment: 8/2003-Submit Date
Survey Submitted: April 2006

UNM, because of its size, has a very familial vibe. There will always be people to go out with, fellow new mothers with whom to trade babysitting, biking buddies, study groups, fellow hip hop dancers and everything in between. If you socialize with law school crowds, you will find yourself sitting at dinner with liberals, conservatives, libertarians, progressives, anarchists, Christians and the gamut. There is a general attitude of respect and a refreshing sentiment of "why can't we all just get along" (at least outside of a political arena and the courtroom).

Status: Current student, full-time
Dates of Enrollment: 8/2005-Submit Date
Survey Submitted: April 2006

The atmosphere is less cutthroat than a lot of other law schools—it's not because people don't work hard, but because they have a somewhat better perspective. Students also make sure they have fun on weekends and whatnot, and the school is close enough to ski areas that a lot of students go skiing on weekends in the winter. There are also a decent number of students with families, and they tend to do well here.

Status: Current student, full-time
Dates of Enrollment: 8/2005-Submit Date
Survey Submitted: April 2006

The UNM School of Law is isolated from the main campus, so its students do not often participate in activities with the undergraduates. In fact, the school can be some what insular. Nonetheless, many organizations in the law school put on parties, BBQs, coffee breaks, musical jams, intramural sports teams, internal tournaments and political activities. These provide plenty of extracurricular activities, especially considering the fact that law school students don't have an overwhelming amount of free time.

Dating in our insular community inevitably happens. But, someone who dates in a law school with 300 students accepts the consequences if things don't work out. This goes for the gay and the straight community, too.

 The School Says

With its 11:1 student-faculty ratio, diverse and supportive educational environment, and accessible faculty members, the University of New Mexico School of Law has a lot to offer its students. Kept small by design (approximately 350 total students), UNM prides itself on providing both a solid grounding in legal theory and an opportunity for practical application of this knowledge. In fact, the clinical program at UNM law school is consistently recognized as one of the best in the country. All students are required to complete six credit hours of clinic work, enhancing their legal training while gaining valuable experience dealing with real cases.

In addition to their required coursework, second- and third-year students are invited to choose from a wide variety of elective courses. Students who wish to specialize may earn certificates in Indian Law or Natural Resources. International study programs are also available, including the Guanajuato Summer Law Institute, in which students travel to Mexico to learn more about the country and its legal system. Students interested in pursuing a dual degree may combine their JD with an MBA, a Master's Degree in Public Administration or Latin American Studies or other graduate degrees.

Law students at UNM play active roles in the community, taking part in a variety of student organizations, competing in moot court and mock trial competitions, and working with law journals. The law school is located on the Albuquerque campus of the University of New Mexico. With a population of approximately 700,000, the greater Albuquerque area is both the geographic and demographic center of the state, and in their spare time, law students enjoy all the advantages of living in one of the major cultural centers of the Southwest.

After graduation, the UNM School of Law works with alumni to help them find their place in a competitive legal market. Graduates are recruited for work in law firms, businesses, government agencies and public interest organizations throughout the Southwest, the rest of the country, and the world. UNM law school's alumni are represented on all New Mexico state courts, including the New Mexico Supreme Court; are partners in major law firms in Albuquerque, Washington, D.C. and other large cities; are leaders in the state legislature and the executive branch; and hold positions throughout the legal academy.

Students are accepted for the three-year Juris Doctorate program on a full-time basis only, with courses starting in the fall semester. The application deadline for first-year students is February 15. Supporting documents (LSAT scores, LSDAS report, personal statement, resume and letters of recommendation) must be submitted no later than March 16. All applicants are considered for merit-based scholarships on the basis of their application files. Students who wish to apply for federal financial aid should file the Free Application for Federal Student Aid (FAFSA). Those seeking grant funding should also complete the Need Access application. Further information about the UNM School of Law, including the application form and checklist, may be found on the law school's web site at http://lawschool.unm.edu/.

Read all of Vault's Law School Surveys at www.vault.com/lawschool — get complete surveys on top law schools, expert advice on applicaton essays, LSAT prep and more.

VAULT CAREER LIBRARY   411

Brooklyn Law School

Admissions Office
250 Joralemon Street
Brooklyn, NY 11201
Admissions phone: (718) 780-7906
Admissions fax: (718) 780-0395
Admissions e-mail: admitq@brooklaw.edu
Admissions URL: http://www.brooklaw.edu/admissions/

 Admissions

Status: Alumnus/a, full-time
Dates of Enrollment: 8/1998-5/2001
Survey Submitted: April 2006

BLS is an excellent law school with a long history and tradition. Although the admissions board is selective, a good LSAT score is helpful.

Status: Alumnus/a, part-time
Dates of Enrollment: 9/1987-5/1991
Survey Submitted: April 2006

I was awarded a scholarship that covered half my tuition each year. It was based on my grades and potential, I suppose. Write an essay that will allow the school to get a glimpse of who you are and how well you write.

Status: Current student, full-time
Dates of Enrollment: 8/2005-Submit Date
Survey Submitted: April 2006

The Admissions Office was very receptive to questions and understanding of my worries. I was waitlisted, so I spent a lot of time asking what more I could do to bolster my application.

Status: Alumnus/a, part-time
Dates of Enrollment: 6/1997-5/2001
Survey Submitted: April 2006

The admissions process includes a financial aid workshop, open to students applying to law school, whether or not they plan to go to BLS. Also included was a tour of the school and the neighborhood and participation in a mock class led by a faculty member. The response to the application was a matter of a few weeks, after which an alum of the school called to handle any questions I had to prepare for attendance.

Status: Alumnus/a, full-time
Dates of Enrollment: 8/1993-6/1996
Survey Submitted: April 2006

Brooklyn has a very high caliber of students applying for admission. They have a large alumni base in private practice, yet still maintain one of the best legal programs for pro bono and nonprofit/government attorneys.

Since Brooklyn has such high expectations for its placement status both writing skills and oral advocacy are essential to getting in. As a result, you must not only draft excellent essays, you must also interview extremely well. Brooklyn will not be impressed by the fluff often submitted for multiple applications. It must be specific to the question asked and not the generic answer you have already prepared for other schools. It was well worth all of the effort to get in!

Status: Current student, full-time
Dates of Enrollment: 8/2005-Submit Date
Survey Submitted: April 2006

BLS, like most law schools, uses a "rolling admissions" process, so get your applications in early. I don't believe the school grants interviews.

If you are a public-interest-minded applicant, be sure to apply for the Edward V. Sparer Public Interest Fellowship when you submit your application. You can use an abbreviated version of your personal statement for the requisite essay (the BLS admissions committee members do not sit on the Sparer committee), and the Sparer is a good reason to come to BLS.

Though there are other opportunities to apply for the fellowship once you matriculate, I find those of us who entered as Sparers benefitted from having a good community of faculty and other students immediately upon arriving.

Status: Alumnus/a, full-time
Dates of Enrollment: 8/2002-6/2005
Survey Submitted: October 2005

The marketing material from Brooklyn was the best that I received, which led me to believe that they were a great school. The essay was standard. It has become very selective over the past few years. If I were to apply now, I would not have gotten in based upon my LSAT scores.

Status: Alumnus/a, full-time
Dates of Enrollment: 8/2001-5/2004
Survey Submitted: March 2005

My impression is that BLS evaluates a candidate's entire profile, taking into account work experience and factors that make out a "well-rounded" applicant, in addition to the hardcore qualifiers of LSAT and GPA. In my time at BLS, the average test scores and GPAs dramatically improved and, with the addition of a much needed dormitory for incoming students in the fall of '05, BLS seems to be "on the rise."

Status: Alumnus/a, full-time
Dates of Enrollment: 8/1998-6/2001
Survey Submitted: April 2005

The admissions process is pretty straightforward. I would add that it is very much numbers-based, with your GPA and LSAT being extremely determinative. I was initially waitlisted at BLS, considering my LSAT was atrocious (<150) but my GPA from a top state school was pretty solid.

I received a pending letter from the admissions office in late January and then was placed on the official waitlist in early March. At the time, Brooklyn had two waitlists—a primary and a secondary list. I was placed on primary and made several phone calls throughout the next few months expressing my interest in the school. I was then removed from the waitlist at the end of the summer.

Status: Current student, full-time
Dates of Enrollment: 8/2002-Submit Date
Survey Submitted: February 2004

The admissions process at Brooklyn is very clear-cut and relatively easy. Even with that, I managed to forget to sign one page, and they called me about two days after submitting my application and had me correct the mistake. I was impressed with their diligence, to say the least. As the months went by, Brooklyn was amazing at providing tons of information sessions and activities to get to know the law school atmosphere. I found the process to be easy and well structured.

Status: Alumnus/a, full-time
Dates of Enrollment: 8/2000-6/2003
Survey Submitted: September 2003

Brooklyn Law School's application packet immediately impressed me. It seemed to be a school that was willing to invest in their students and that was appealing. They provided a few opportunities to visit the school after I was offered admission and prior to my acceptance of their offer. These programs included an Admitted Students Day and a neighborhood tour. The former was a day when the prospective students could attend some "classes" of their choosing taught specifically for them by professors from the school. During those classes, law was discussed and the professors offered their advice and talked to the students about their jobs and interests. There were also tours of the school and the library that were very impressive as the school was renovated pretty recently.

The neighborhood tour was a historical walking tour of Brooklyn Heights, which is located just across the Brooklyn Bridge from lower Manhattan. The dean of admissions, who guided the tour, had some very interesting factoids to share about the neighborhood which has a very rich and colorful history. Needless to say, I enjoyed this very much and I think that it had a lot to do with my final decision.

There is no interview process, but everyone I met in the admissions office (as I approached them with endless questions), was very informative and pleasant. From what I gathered by talking to newer students, Brooklyn Law School has gotten much more selective in recent years. This is probably due, in part, to Dean Wexler's work in improving the school. There is a dorm being constructed which should have a profound effect on the composition of future classes. Historically, BLS has been very much a "commuter" school, but this changed substantially when the school acquired several brownstones and apartment space to use as student housing. Now, with the addition of a full-fledged residence hall and the school's pervasive New York City reputation and alumni base, Brooklyn Law School has no way but to go up.

 Academics

Status: Alumnus/a, full-time
Dates of Enrollment: 8/1983-5/1986
Survey Submitted: April 2006

The classes were great. The professors were provocative, cutting edge and knew how to teach. The workload was pretty rough first and second years, especially with Law Review thrown in, but lightened up the third year.

Professors were very approachable. Grading was almost exclusively dependent on a single final examination, a lengthy hypothetical intended to draw out all the issues covered in the class.

Status: Alumnus/a, full-time
Dates of Enrollment: 8/1998-5/2001
Survey Submitted: April 2006

BLS provides an excellent atmosphere for success in law school. There are many different classes to choose from and the professors are helpful and interesting. The one caveat is that too much emphasis is placed on your first-year grade in legal writing.

Status: Alumnus/a, part-time
Dates of Enrollment: 9/1972-6/1976
Survey Submitted: April 2006

The quality of the classes was greatly influenced by the fact that almost 100 percent of the class were people with professional day jobs. We had the benefit of expertise from law enforcers, accountants, academics and scientists. Evening classes were taught by the same professors as the day classes and the professors were generally excellent.

Scheduling could be a challenge for courses with limited enrollments but we all knew that was a fact of life in a school with a limited number of classrooms where sections could be held. We did not evaluate professors or courses; that is something that came after my time and is a excellent idea.

Status: Alumnus/a, full-time
Dates of Enrollment: 8/1993-6/1996
Survey Submitted: April 2006

Brooklyn is very good at ensuring that there are multiple sections for the popular classes. I never had a problem getting a class that I registered for. They may have switched me into a different section, but it never prevented me from getting into other classes on my schedule.

The staff is truly amazing. The school draws such a wonderful group of faculty. All of my professors for New York Civil Practice, Torts, Criminal Procedure, Criminal Law and Constitutional Law wrote the leading publications and statutes/law for their respective topics. I am sure that there were others that I can't remember, but that is obviously representative of the caliber of the staff.

If you are looking for an easy ride, this is not the school for you. Their grading is tough and no one gets a free ride. Getting in is not enough; you must perform. The workload is at times unbearable. I don't think that is unique to Brooklyn, but they don't disappoint in that department either. If you work hard you are guaranteed to come out an excellent attorney.

The best part of Brooklyn was my participation in the trial lawyers moot court program. It made me completely at ease when I finally went out into a real courtroom!

Status: Current student, full-time
Dates of Enrollment: 8/2005-Submit Date
Survey Submitted: April 2006

First-year classes are hit and miss. I have had world-class faculty and not-so-great faculty, which I believe happens at any law school. Most schools' first-year programs are the same in terms of workload and grading.

I do credit our professors, however, for engaging sometimes huge classes of people, and encouraging all students to share their points of view.

Status: Alumnus/a, part-time
Dates of Enrollment: 6/1997-5/2001
Survey Submitted: April 2006

The professors are highly recognized in their respective specialities, including some who have written widely used texts. The classes mostly featured two-way discussion between professors and students. After the initial semesters, the elective classes tended to be of manageable size. My smallest class was 12 students.

The "curve" method of grading is sometimes a problem, as it can penalize as well as help students, but this type of grading seems to be widely used in law schools. The workload was challenging but exciting. Popular classes filled almost immediately and often took more than one term to get into.

Status: Alumnus/a, full-time
Dates of Enrollment: 8/1998-5/2002
Survey Submitted: April 2006

Brooklyn Law has a strong academic program. They offer a great variety of substantive classes. They also have a lot of hands-on, practical seminar classes. The professors are fabulous and very accessible.

Status: Current student, full-time
Dates of Enrollment: 9/2003-Submit Date
Survey Submitted: April 2006

The professors, for the most part, are incredible. Very smart, great teachers. They're not just there because they're famous and doing research. They love to teach, they love students, and they love their topics. BLS is unique in that professors have an open-door policy to students.

Status: Alumnus/a, full-time
Dates of Enrollment: 8/2002-6/2005
Survey Submitted: October 2005

The clinics were amazing! I actually practiced as a lawyer as a Workers' Rights Clinic intern, arguing cases before an administrative law judge. Like any law school, the workload is immense and the competition is high. I was rarely closed out of classes that I wanted, but there were a few that are difficult to get, like Negotiations Seminar.

The professors are very good, highly knowledgeable, and usually welcoming to questions. The emphasis on practical legal experience is high (as opposed to mostly theory). This is what sets Brooklyn apart from the NY tier-one schools that emphasize policy and theory. Most of Brooklyn's professors have practiced law before teaching it.

Read all of Vault's Law School Surveys at www.vault.com/lawschool — get complete surveys on top law schools, expert advice on applicaton essays, LSAT prep and more.

VAULT CAREER LIBRARY **413**

Status: Alumnus/a, full-time
Dates of Enrollment: 8/2001-5/2004
Survey Submitted: March 2005

I had an absolutely fantastic experience with the professors—always available and effective. For me, the best thing I can say about BLS is the quality of professors. I never had a problem getting into a class, and as far as grading and workload, it seemed to be the same as other law schools. The clinical programs are great.

By virtue of its size, BLS classes can be large and the grading gets competitive. I don't think that is any different elsewhere, but the size of the student body can compound the sometimes apparent ambiguity of law school grades.

Status: Alumnus/a, full-time
Dates of Enrollment: 8/1998-6/2001
Survey Submitted: April 2005

The professors are a wealth of knowledge if you know how to use them. Their office hours are a good time to get to know them, see what their proclivities for exam scenarios may be like, and great if you want a reference letter. I particularly love professors who do an excellent job of teaching students to UNDERSTAND the concepts and not just memorize. Classes were entertaining and enjoyable, and I felt extremely prepared for whatever I would encounter in my legal practice.

I would be wary of a few of the adjunct professors. I had one professor for real Estate Practice, who really did little for the class. He did talk about his experiences as a real estate developer, but theoretically—everything followed the casebook.

Like any law school, you will have a few good and bad apples. I definitely think that the first-year law professors are tops in their fields—and seeing your professor on CNN can be intimidating.

Status: Alumnus/a, full-time
Dates of Enrollment: 8/2000-6/2003
Survey Submitted: September 2003

As for Brooklyn Law School's academics, they are first-rate. Dean Wexler has (even during my short time as a student there) been very attentive not only to the academic excellence and qualifications of the professors and adjuncts, but also to their teaching ability, which is of the UTMOST importance in anyone's ability to succeed in law school.

The ability to get into popular classes is pretty good. There are a few classes that are so popular (usually because of the professor's reputation), that students just accept that they won't be able to take the class until their last year and, ultimately are able to graduate without having taken that coveted class. One semester, there was only one Corporations class offered, and because it is a prerequisite for so many other classes, it was packed. The school had to move the class to the auditorium. It was difficult for the professor and for the students in the beginning, but it seemed that the professor and the school worked together to make the best of a bad situation for students, and the semester turned out fine. The best part about it was that the school actually learned from its mistake and didn't let that happen again. I think there is something to be said for that, because my undergrad college never seemed to catch onto that sort of thing.

In most law schools, there is a curve that professors must abide by, and in the elite schools, it is definitely more lax and higher (because their admissions requirements are so high, and they want all their students to have at least a B average to put on their resumes). BLS is in a position where, although it knows the caliber of its students is very comparable to other schools' students, it must weed out the best of the best to present to employers to gain credibility (for lack of a better word). Therefore, the curve at Brooklyn is a little lower...like a B curve instead of a B+ curve, which makes things a little more competitive. The workload is rough during the first year, but that's the case at any law school. After that, it gets MUCH, MUCH more manageable.

Status: Alumnus/a, full-time
Dates of Enrollment: 8/1996-6/1999
Survey Submitted: April 2004

Brooklyn divided the class into sections, and then there is a small section within the large section. Major classes like Torts and Contracts were taught with your large section, and the seminar class with your small section was Civil Procedure. All classes relied on the Socratic Method, more so in the small section. Some professors called on students in alphabetical order, and others were random.

All of the professors I had were excellent and very accessible. I had very few, if any, bad experiences. I also never had any trouble getting into popular classes, although I know preference was given to third-years for elective classes. The workload was heavy, but I think that would be true at any law school. Professors definitely tested more on what they taught in class, rather than what was assigned to read, so I always felt like the exams tested fairly on what was presented in class. Of course this meant that attendance was essential, and taking detailed notes. Grading was done by exam number (i.e., anonymously) and the curve was based on a "B" when I was there. Exam grades could be accessed through the Internet, which was very handy. A couple of times I felt that professors were delinquent with their grades, but overall grades came out in a timely manner.

 Employment Prospects

Status: Alumnus/a, full-time
Dates of Enrollment: 8/1983-5/1986
Survey Submitted: April 2006

The intership opportunities really make Brooklyn unique. I interned for three federal judges in the southern and eastern districts of New York while I was in school. This helped me tremendously in getting a full-time post-graduate clerkship on the third circuit court of appeals. All the BigLaw firms recruit on campus. When I attended, the top 10 percent of the class had more job offers than they knew what to do with. The next 25 to 40 percent had decent offers. I am not sure about the lower half of the class.

Status: Current student, full-time
Dates of Enrollment: 8/2005-Submit Date
Survey Submitted: April 2006

I haven't had a lot of experience with the employment prospects. Our Career Services Center is amazing—we get a dedicated counselor for all three years, and they're in constant contact with students. Also, despite being vastly understaffed, the public service career counselor is amazing. She's absolutely a lifesaver.

Status: Alumnus/a, full-time
Dates of Enrollment: 8/1993-6/1996
Survey Submitted: April 2006

As far as I know Brooklyn has virtually 100 percent placement for its graduates. I find that those who are not employed at graduation are either lazy and not pursuing employment actively, or are waiting on multiple offers. When I graduated I had four job offers before finals.

There was a wonderful mentoring program that I participated in getting off the ground. The alumni response to our request for help was overwhelming. I had more mentors than students at the beginning. There was on-campus interviewing for private and public sector employment. I met with almost all of my employer prospects on campus.

Status: Alumnus/a, part-time
Dates of Enrollment: 6/1997-5/2001
Survey Submitted: April 2006

Many area judges are graduates of BLS, and many BLS alums work as clerks and as Assistant District Attorneys in the area. BLS alums in private practice are very supportive of grads in their placement and in networking. The range of jobs is from human rights, as many international agencies have offices in NYC, to corporate to public services. There is almost no area of law one can imagine that is not available to BLS students.

Status: Current student, full-time
Dates of Enrollment: 9/2003-Submit Date
Survey Submitted: April 2006

I am a public interest student. Every time I tell anyone in the New York nonprofit world I go to BLS, they say "Oh, I've heard they have a great public interest program." I think that carries well.

I think employers know that BLS students are smart and will work hard. True, we may not automatically get the most prestigious positions simply because our school is not the top of the top, but I think we do very well.

Every fancy firm comes to the school, and if you have good grades, you can get a good position. Also, Brooklyn Law School has been around for more than 100 years, so there is a good alumni base that reaches out and gives the students jobs.

Status: Alumnus/a, full-time
Dates of Enrollment: 8/1998-6/2001
Survey Submitted: April 2005

The employment prospects are EXCELLENT. I had the option of attending a higher ranked school outside NYC, but I knew the experience of interning at the local law firms and government agencies within NYC would be invaluable. I was ranked near the bottom of my class at graduation, but sent out about 50 resumes in the spring of 3L, and received an offer of employment in early August. Most of the employers didn't care about my grades and were impressed by my activities with two law school clinics (including a federal clerkship internship in 1L summer) and law school activities.

Apart from OCI, where big firms come to campus and hire the top of the class, the REAL activity for the rest of the graduating class doesn't come until early to mid-3L. A few friends who did not fare well in OCI secured 2L summer law firm positions and later were invited to return as permanent first-year associates. This is how most graduates secure jobs, through part-time and summer "law clerk" positions. Nothing beats having close access to all the NYC courts!

Status: Alumnus/a, full-time
Dates of Enrollment: 8/2000-6/2003
Survey Submitted: September 2003

The career center is helpful, but for all but the top 5 percent, it requires substantial work on the part of the student to really derive the full benefit of what the center offers. They have an extensive on-campus interview program where the career counselors get legal recruiters from firms to come to the school and interview people based on submitted resumes. They also have an online job database where employers list available positions, which is also very helpful. Regarding their reputation, Brooklyn Law School is very well regarded among the legal community in NYC and its surroundings. If you end up looking for a job elsewhere in the country, it might be harder to find a job, but that would be because of few connections, certainly not because of reputation.

Status: Alumnus/a, full-time
Dates of Enrollment: 8/1996-6/1999
Survey Submitted: April 2004

BLS does a much better job helping the people at the top of the class (top 25 percent or better) than the students just below, who really need the most help getting jobs. When it comes time for on-campus interviewing, there is no maximum number of interviews. So, all of the top students get lots and lots of interviews, and can take only one job, so the others tend to get left out altogether. I know this was frustrating for students who were in the middle of the pack. BLS is very well known by the firms and the courts, so judicial externships and big-firm exposure were never a problem. Especially in New York, BLS has a great reputation and was always regarded highly during my interview experience. BLS is considered a "New York school" and a place where students are likely to pass the bar. I think both of those aspects give BLS an added advantage.

Status: Current student, full-time
Dates of Enrollment: 8/2002-Submit Date
Survey Submitted: February 2004

The clinical program at Brooklyn is excellent and provides students with resume-building jobs and practical experience in a number of fields. But the career center is a total nightmare. I have gone in to have my resume reviewed and been told that it was "perfect." That's great, but I know that I am not the

foremost expert on resume writing, and I would have enjoyed a little input. When trying to find a job, their advice is to talk to people we know as lawyers and see if they can get us a job. Again, networking is important and can help in getting contacts, but it does not lead to jobs, especially in a still difficult economy. Additionally, Brooklyn has been around for a long time and has many prestigious graduates, and yet there is no alumni career network.

Status: Alumnus/a, full-time
Dates of Enrollment: 8/1995-6/1997
Survey Submitted: October 2003

The school has a decent career office, and I have always been able to access their counselors on the phone or by appointment at the last minute. I still occasionally use the career office (questions on the phone or a brief meeting). Someone is always accessible on a moment's notice. With that being said, you are really on your own looking for a job if you are not in the top 10 percent. However, I think BLS has EXCELLENT internship opportunities, especially with the courts being so close by.

> **Regarding career opportunities, Brooklyn Law School says:**
> "With seven full-time attorney-counselors and a full-time job development associate, the Career Center has been very successful in helping all students obtain satisfying employment both during school and after graduation. The record speaks for itself. Within nine months of graduation, 98 percent of the Class of 2005 were working or pursuing graduate degrees. The average nine-month employment rate for Brooklyn Law School graduates for the last three years is 98 percent."

 ## Quality of Life

Status: Current student, full-time
Dates of Enrollment: 8/2005-Submit Date
Survey Submitted: April 2006

Brooklyn is the best! I love Brooklyn, it just feels so much more like a neighborhood than Manhattan. The new housing at Feil is opulent, and makes me jealous that I already have a great apartment in the area. Seriously, the Feil apartments are a great bargain and are fabulous, even if they tend to make for a more dorm-ish atmosphere.

Cobble Hill, the neighborhood just beyond Atlantic Avenue, is fabulous, with great restaurants and bars along Smith Street, and the Promenande a short walk away for amazing views of Manhattan.

Status: Current student, full-time
Dates of Enrollment: 9/2003-Submit Date
Survey Submitted: April 2006

Huge new dorm. Beautiful library. Only two buildings, so not quite a "campus." But I like the environment. Brand new computers in the lab. Just a few blocks away from Brooklyn Heights, which is beautiful, and lots of cool neighborhoods to live in while you're in school.

Status: Alumnus/a, full-time
Dates of Enrollment: 8/1993-6/1996
Survey Submitted: April 2006

The school's one draw back was the cost of living in NYC. I had to take out significant loans to cover my expenses. I have heard that the school has now built some school housing facilities. I am not aware of the cost of those facilities. It should be a big help.

Brooklyn is a commuter school. Many people that go there reside at home or outside the city. As a result there was not a true campus when I got there. They were doing major construction through most of my time there. I have been back and it is amazing. I believe that they have created a little world within the walls of the school very supportive of socializing, dining, studying and other activities.

I never felt unsafe in Brooklyn Heights. It is one of the nicest parts of the city outside the city. It is very difficult to have a car there so don't bother. The public transportation system is amazing (although slow at times from delays). I would move back to the Heights if I could.

Read all of Vault's Law School Surveys at www.vault.com/lawschool — get complete surveys on top law schools, expert advice on applicaton essays, LSAT prep and more.

VAULT CAREER LIBRARY 415

Status: Current student, full-time
Dates of Enrollment: 8/2005-Submit Date
Survey Submitted: April 2006

We have tons of new housing in one of the coolest parts of New York City, Brooklyn Heights. The building is gorgeous, the library is spacious and new, and though we house about 1,500 law students, the school's community is tight-knit.

The neighborhood is safe but, as with in any city environment, all people should take precautions.

We are blocks away from all the courts, state and federal, which is a huge draw.

The school has tons and tons of excellent programming, complete with great food and frequent beer and wine. It is often difficult to juggle all the events I want to attend with my school work, but both aspects are important to a legal education.

Status: Alumnus/a, full-time
Dates of Enrollment: 8/2002-6/2005
Survey Submitted: October 2005

Brooklyn just opened new apartment-style dorms in downtown Brooklyn, which were not available while I was enrolled. I believe this will be huge in getting Brooklyn a more national status, elevating it in the rankings.

The downtown Brooklyn area is great. It is right next to Brooklyn Heights, which is a very safe, yuppy neighborhood that is one subway stop away from Wall Street. The school is also located directly across the street from State and Federal courthouses, which allows for internship possibilities and an easy commute. Almost every subway line stops near Bourough Hall.

Status: Current student, full-time
Dates of Enrollment: 8/2002-Submit Date
Survey Submitted: February 2004

There is limited housing at the moment, but the new dorms that they are building are sure to change that. It would be nice if they would put a gym in the dorm, but I am not sure whether that is in the plans.

The neighborhood is easily accessible and has many options in terms of eating and shopping. The building is great, and the library is excellent. The cafeteria is small and crappy, but the food in the neighborhood makes up for that.

Status: Alumnus/a, full-time
Dates of Enrollment: 8/1998-6/2001
Survey Submitted: April 2005

I think the residential life at Brooklyn is very tightly knit. Although I commuted to the school by subway every day (I lived at home), I wish I'd opted for the student housing. The fact that students are only a hop, skip and a jump away from the dorms makes living in Brooklyn Heights a real delight. Even though I commuted, I visited friends in their dorm rooms and participated in student activities. Anyone who says: "Brooklyn is a commuter school" is wrong!

Status: Alumnus/a, full-time
Dates of Enrollment: 8/1996-6/1999
Survey Submitted: January 2004

When I was at BLS, housing was a real problem, but I know that has changed tremendously in the five years since I graduated. The housing that is offered is very nice, affordable and close to campus. BLS was also working on its computing facilities, which weren't quite up to par when I left, but had improved a lot since first year.

The library is beautiful, with lots of quiet places to study in addition to group study rooms. The cafeteria was adequate and reasonably priced, but nothing to write home about!

The campus is in Brooklyn Heights, and it doesn't get much better than that. All major subways converge at the law school, the EDNY is right down the street, in addition to many other court houses and municipal buildings. Brooklyn Heights offers great restaurants, shopping and amazing views of the city. I never felt unsafe on or near the campus.

Status: Alumnus/a, full-time
Dates of Enrollment: 9/1998-6/2001
Survey Submitted: September 2003

BLS is building a brand new housing complex for students and owns other apartments in the neighborhood. The neighborhood is very "law-oriented." Court Street is around the corner; it is home to many small law offices and borders state, city and federal courts. BLS also borders Brooklyn Heights, which is both residential and home to great restaurants, shops and nightlife.

> **Regarding quality of life, the school says:** We own and operate nine student residences, including Feil Hall, a magnificent new high-rise building that opened in August 2005, which provides housing for an additional 360 students. The school is proud to be able to offer housing to one-third of our student body, and to guarantee housing to all of our first-year students. With the opening of a new, modern YMCA in the Summer of 2005 one block from our new residence hall, students now have yet another physical recreation option. The Y offers generous discounts to our students.

 Social Life

Status: Alumnus/a, full-time
Dates of Enrollment: 8/1983-5/1986
Survey Submitted: April 2006

Lots of informal get-togethers of friends for drinks, dinner, going out to clubs. A few school-sponsored social events, which were lots of fun. I met the best friends of my life at this school.

Status: Current student, full-time
Dates of Enrollment: 8/2005-Submit Date
Survey Submitted: April 2006

The school works hard to provide students with plenty of opportunities for an active social life. The Student Affairs Office is always receptive to new ideas for activities and clubs. Great bars in the area guarantee that students have ample opportunities to complain about class over a quality beer. Floyd's NY is a favorite with boccie ball tournaments.

Status: Alumnus/a, full-time
Dates of Enrollment: 8/1993-6/1996
Survey Submitted: April 2006

There are tons of bars and restaurants in the area. It is noteworthy that BLS is only two subway stops from Wall Street and within 30 minutes from almost anywhere in Manhattan. I had the best time of my school years at Brooklyn. I would recommend the school to anyone!

Status: Alumnus/a, part-time
Dates of Enrollment: 6/1997-5/2001
Survey Submitted: April 2006

Organizations are coordinated through the Student Affairs office and represent many interests and ethnic groups. Lots of restaurants and bars, active neighborhood in Brooklyn, as far as events. Transportation to Manhattan and other areas in and around NYC starts either right under the school or subways and buses located within a block of the gates of the school. School is located blocks from the Brooklyn Bridge.

Status: Current student, full-time
Dates of Enrollment: 9/2003-Submit Date
Survey Submitted: April 2006

Lots of school-wide activities. I think people generally like each other and hang out. I think there is less of a competitive atmosphere. I find people to be really down to earth and friendly. There is less snootiness than I've seen when I've visited other schools.

Status: Alumnus/a, full-time
Dates of Enrollment: 8/2002-6/2005
Survey Submitted: October 2005

There aren't many bars near the school, but the proximity to Manhattan allows for a wonderful social life! The best way to meet people is to join clubs and organizations. Being an active law student is the best way to create a social life on campus.

Status: Alumnus/a, full-time
Dates of Enrollment: 8/1998-6/2001
Survey Submitted: April 2005

There is a bar close to the school called O'Keefe's, where students usually meet after class or professors meet with students. There are numerous eateries on Montague Street and Court Street.

Status: Alumnus/a, full-time
Dates of Enrollment: 8/1996-6/1999
Survey Submitted: April 2004

BLS had as much or as little social life as you wanted. For those who lived in Brooklyn close to the school, I think the social life was better than it was for those who commuted from Manhattan or Long Island. There were so many fun bars and restaurants right by the school that there were many informal happy hours, especially after exams, or law school competitions. There wasn't that much of a "dating scene," but I made several lifelong friends there.

As an independent law school, there is no chance to plug into a larger university setting or a Greek system, but I think staying focused is an advantage. Plus, at most universities, the law school is separated geographically anyway. There were several fun social events to look forward to every year, including the Brooklyn Law Students for the Public Interest auction. Faculty donated great prizes (like dinner at their homes or canoe trips), and there were other great prizes. It was always a fun event. The law school also hosted great events in the city that were well attended. And the party at Tavern on the Green when we graduated was very nice. Graduating at Lincoln Center was also a nice bonus!

Status: Current student, full-time
Dates of Enrollment: 8/2002-Submit Date
Survey Submitted: February 2004

There are many student events at Brooklyn organized by the very active student groups. In addition, there are many bars in the area and students frequently go have a drink to unwind after sitting in the library for hours. As I said before, there are good places to grab food, but mainly lunch, as dinner options are few and far between.

Read all of Vault's Law School Surveys at www.vault.com/lawschool — get complete surveys on top law schools, expert advice on applicaton essays, LSAT prep and more.

VAULT CAREER LIBRARY 417

Columbia Law School

Admissions Office
435 West 116th Street
Mail Code 4004
New York, NY 10027-7297
Admissions phone: (212) 854-2670
Admissions fax: (212) 854-1109
Admissions e-mail: admissions@law.columbia.edu
URL: http://www.law.columbia.edu

 Admissions

Status: Current student, full-time JD/MBA
Dates of Enrollment: 9/2003-Submit Date
Survey Submitted: February 2006

In order to get into the JD/MBA, applicants need to apply to the two programs individually. Since I was coming straight from undergrad, I applied to law schools first. When I got my law school acceptance, I applied early the business school. In order to get up on the first day and say that the class is very diversified, they seem to let in a few select candidates that have non-traditional backgrounds (in my class we had an opera singer, a priest). The minority make-up of the law school does not appear to try and mimic the population at large, which leads me to believe that they don't really use affirmative action programs in their application process. Also, I should mention that the people from different backgrounds are some of the smartest people in the class. As far as an application essay for law school goes, I'm still not clear how much it really counts. I wrote mine about a team at school and that worked for me.

Law school is all about the LSAT and grades and it wouldn't surprise me if most schools used a calculator to determine most of their classes. Columbia Law is fourth in the nation and (I think) the best located of the top four schools. Business school is less clear to me. They are looking for a certain "je ne sais quoi," which means that you get people with a range of backgrounds and talents. Columbia has recently stated that its goal is to get the future leaders of the world, and so they accept people from everywhere and anywhere (undergrad GPA and institution are much less important). Having past leadership seems to be the key (or the golden goose), but not essential if you have enough things which point to you being a future leader. Also, way easier if you're already in the law school since it's a higher ranked program at the school and the business school seems to take most people who apply for the joint.

Status: Alumnus/a, full-time
Dates of Enrollment: 9/1999-5/2002
Survey Submitted: March 2006

I think that grades, LSAT and college made the biggest difference in my class composition. While some students had varied life experience, and had certainly done interesting things, about half the students came from the Ivy League. Perhaps the test-takers keep moving up the ranks, but I believe that there were certain spots left open for certain schools.

Status: Alumnus/a, full-time
Dates of Enrollment: 8/2001-5/2004
Survey Submitted: March 2006

The admissions process is very simple. It consists of a short application, two letters of recommendation, an essay and your LSAT scores. It doesn't get any easier than that. There was no interview required. My decision came in the mail very soon after I applied (I applied Early Decision). When you call the admission office, they are very nice and helpful. Getting them on the phone is hard during critical times.

To get in, you must be an all-around great student. This is a top law school and it admits only the best candidates of the country and the world. You must have high LSAT scores—I would say a 163 as a bare minimum. It is a very selective

school in terms of grades. Students who graduated straight A's (or pretty close) from college are the norm rather than the exception. Columbia looks for students who are well-rounded, who in addition to their good grades have a good extracurricular portfolio of activities, who have some international experience, who have done worthy things for society and who demonstrate a passion for excellence. It is a very diverse law school.

Your essay can't be a typical, run-of-the-mill, cookie-cutter law school essay about how when you were 12 you saw some injustice being committed in the street and that motivated you to be a lawyer. That's just like asking for a denial. You need to be honest about who you are, and then write it in a clever, creative way. You need to catch the attention of the reader. Good writing is emphasized at CLS, so people who can write will be regarded as superior candidates.

Status: Current student, full-time LLM
Dates of Enrollment: 6/2005-Submit Date
Survey Submitted: January 2006

The admissions process at Columbia was fairly straightforward, and its online application system worked well. Columbia looks for students from a diverse group of nations with a diverse group of legal interests, so if you are a banking lawyer but have an interest in Human Rights, mention that in you application essay.

Status: Alumnus/a, full-time
Dates of Enrollment: 8/1999-5/2001
Survey Submitted: April 2005

I originally applied to Columbia Law School in the fall of 1997. From what I understood, students who are admitted have had very strong undergraduate grades and stellar LSAT scores. Many successful applicants who have been out of college for several years have attended graduate school or have advanced degrees. I was waitlisted and was not admitted; however, after attending another prestigious law school for one year, I applied as a transfer student and was admitted. Columbia does admit a fairly large number of transfer students; often they are students who did very well academically in their first years at respected law schools and who were involved in significant extracurricular activities.

Status: Alumnus/a, full-time
Dates of Enrollment: 8/2000-5/2003
Survey Submitted: April 2004

Columbia is highly selective ([8,500] apply for 350 spots), but students such as myself could be admitted even without a stellar undergraduate career if they have something else to offer. For me, it was an LSAT score in the 99th percentile and a number of years working abroad.

If Columbia is your first choice, apply through the [Early Decision Program]. This means the applicant has to submit the application [by November 15]. The applicant will find out very early whether or not she is admitted, but she also has to promise that if accepted she will attend Columbia. Although the applicant limits her options in this way, she also may stand a better chance of being accepted than if she waits until the spring to apply. [Columbia accepts 20 percent of its class] each year from the early admissions application process. These students compete with far fewer other applicants for the same number of spaces as do students who wait to apply until spring. But among the students applying in the spring are those who [were] accepted to Harvard or Yale, who have outstanding academic records from the top schools and fantastic LSAT scores and life experiences. It's much tougher to get accepted to Columbia when competing with these folks.

I would recommend focusing a lot of effort on the written application and essay. Bring up any relevant awards and experience. Show the ways in which the applicant is unique and has an interesting perspective. Really put the time into it; it's important that the applicant stand out from the crowd in a very positive way. Look at the web site to see what Columbia is proud of among its students and graduates—the applicant should try to present herself in a similarly impressive light.

Status: Alumnus/a, full-time
Dates of Enrollment: 9/1999-5/2002
Survey Submitted: April 2004

I think grades, LSATs and extracurriculars in college are the top three criteria for getting in. Though there are plenty of people with high college GPAs and LSATs, I found that that was not universal, as Columbia tries to ensure a diverse class by admitting people with interesting, if not "bookwormish," backgrounds. Columbia also has a lot of older students who have worked or been in PhD programs for several years after college.

Status: Alumnus/a, full-time
Dates of Enrollment: 8/1998-5/2002
Survey Submitted: April 2004

I was accepted into the joint degree program between Columbia Law School and the University de la Sorbonne from the French side of the admission process. I sent an application containing a resume, motivation letter, grades since high school and documents attesting that I was proficient in English. My application was selected, and I was invited for a round of interviews with Columbia Law School professors. Each year, Columbia selects two French applicants for the joint degree program. I was lucky enough to be selected for this extraordinary academic and human experience.

 # Academics

Status: Current student, full-time JD/MBA
Dates of Enrollment: 9/2003-Submit Date
Survey Submitted: February 2006

First-year classes are basically totally determined for you, so no big worries there. I didn't have the second semester elective when I went through so not sure how well it works out, although I've heard it's fairly easy to get what you want. Second year can be really tough to get the right classes with the right professors (my year was especially so since we had a larger than normal class and a larger than normal transfer set). The thing to know (and use) is that most of those classes are doable if you just show up to the first day and tell the professor how much you admire him/her and how much you'd like to take the class. Yes, it's gaming the system, but eight out of 10 times it probably works. By third year, life is a lot better since you end up much higher on the scales.

Status: Alumnus/a, full-time
Dates of Enrollment: 8/1998-5/2002
Survey Submitted: May 2006

Classes were generally high quality. CLS solicits student reviews of their professors, which are made available to students in binders. I looked at these before selecting courses, and tried to choose professors who students rated highly, in courses that students rated as not being overly difficult.

Status: Alumnus/a, full-time
Dates of Enrollment: 8/2001-5/2004
Survey Submitted: March 2006

I'm told the program is changing. When I was there, classes were a mixed bag. As with any school, the key is seeking out the best professors, regardless of subject matter. There are certainly plenty of excellent teachers at Columbia. The only classes I didn't enjoy were those I took out of obligation irrespective of who was lecturing. Popular classes are easy to get into if you make a little extra effort to lobby the instructor. The variety of offerings at Columbia is impressive, especially the various clinics, seminars and externships.

Status: Alumnus/a, full-time
Dates of Enrollment: 8/2001-5/2004
Survey Submitted: March 2006

Academics were great. There were a lot of good professors who were at the top of their fields. We had experienced professors even in the first year. There were a great deal of interesting classes, especially in international law. Also, some giants in the human rights/civil rights field. On the other hand, it seemed to be luck of the draw in the first year as far as who you got. Some professors were just not organized and were doing a lot of catch up at the end. Others gave these exams with questions that just seemed like they were from the moon. Still,

overall, the professors were very committed and wanted to be there. Workload was not bad, as long as you did your reading every night you would not be avalanched. Grading was as frustrating as most of the top schools—hard to get a B-, even harder to get an A. B+ to A- seemed to be the only realistic range, so it was hard to set yourself apart from fellow students. The best thing the school has to offer is the small seminars. The worst thing is that we don't get as much practical, get you ready for the bar or for the practice of law classes as some of the lower-tier schools. A little more practical knowledge would have been nice.

The best part of the classes are the students in them. Granted, some are very annoying because they feel like they have to show how smart they are, but all of them are very bright people. It is an extremely intellectually stimulating environment. The debates unfold at high intellectual levels, and the students educate each other just by expressing their point of view or reading of a case or situation.

Status: Alumnus/a, full-time
Dates of Enrollment: 8/2001-5/2004
Survey Submitted: March 2006

First year is excellent. The classes are fantastically interesting, you have at least one class each semester that is taught in a "small section" of about 25 students, there is a three-week introductory seminar that gets you acquainted with law school methods, there are additional programs (writing classes and moot court) that are extremely interesting, a great program all around. Professors are generally very good. There are a few who can be boring, but generally the professors are well-respected in their field and very passionate about what they do.

Your workload is whatever you make of it. You can stack your classes so you have tons of work, or you can take classes outside of the law school, do "independent study," work as a TA and do other things so that you can basically sit around eating pizza and watching *The Simpsons* all day. Even though it's possible, I wouldn't recommend the latter The biggest academic problem at Columbia may be the students. Columbia Law School is a professional school, not an academic school. People are there to get their degrees and work at law firms, not to debate the finer points of legal philosophy or societal justice. I found this VERY disappointing.

Status: Current student, full-time LLM
Dates of Enrollment: 8/2004-Submit Date
Survey Submitted: January 2005

LLM students generally take upperclass (2L and 3L) courses. They can also get permission to take the foundation (1L) courses and many opt to do this as those courses give a more basic and general understanding of U.S. law and may also be helpful bar exam preparation. Many students also take courses at other Columbia departments, particularly the business school, and at NYU.

There are some excellent clinics which provide practical experience. These tend to be among the most popular courses. There are also a large number of extracurricular and pro bono activities to get involved in, both at Columbia and in New York City generally. It is easy to find out what the most popular classes are by looking at students' comments from previous years. (These are available online on the law school's internal network.) Students are incentivized with prizes and pizza parties to fill out the course evaluations each term, so there is a lot of information available. Many professors also seem to take these comments on board (!) so the quality of the classes is generally quite high.

Status: Alumnus/a, full-time
Dates of Enrollment: 8/2003-Submit Date
Survey Submitted: September 2004

It is a first-rate institution with a very competitive atmosphere. The professors are accessible. Grades do matter, and they are usually only based on a final exam—so it becomes the worst of both worlds. They have outstanding scholarship in international law, human rights law and corporate law. There are a number of scholarly journals edited by students, the best among this group are the *Columbia Law Review*, the *Columbia Journal of Transnational Law* and the *Columbia Journal of Law and Social Problems*.

Read all of Vault's Law School Surveys at www.vault.com/lawschool — get complete surveys on top law schools, expert advice on applicaton essays, LSAT prep and more.

VAULT CAREER LIBRARY **419**

Status: Alumnus/a, full-time
Dates of Enrollment: 8/2001-5/2004
Survey Submitted: April 2005

The first-year curriculum is required, as well as one class (property) the first semester of second year. Otherwise, people are free to take any class they want. Other than required classes, which are assigned, people are usually able to get into classes they are interested in with professors they prefer if they are persistent (attend class until enough people drop out to open up a spot). However, often students are unable to take all their first choice classes because of scheduling conflicts. A few classes with popular professors are almost impossible to take as a second-year because third-year students and LLMs have priority.

Status: Alumnus/a, full-time
Dates of Enrollment: 9/1999-1/2003
Survey Submitted: March 2005

Columbia has what I would call a suggested curve. No mandatory curve exists, but most professors still grade around a B/B+ average. I never had an issue getting into the classes I wanted, although I do remember some people complaining that the most popular classes were somewhat difficult to get into. The course selection process is quite strange, instead of merely listing the courses you want in a preferred order, you also provide an alternate for each course—so that if your first choice is not available when they get to you, rather than moving to choice number two, they search for your first alternate. Only in the second round of course selection do they look at your second choice class. The professors are a mixed bag; some are excellent teachers, whereas others were clearly hired for their academic research prowess.

Status: Alumnus/a, full-time
Dates of Enrollment: 9/1999-5/2002
Survey Submitted: April 2004

There is a wide variety of course offerings, but don't be misled by the course catalogue—many classes are not offered every year because professors are away or busy teaching some other class. It can be tough getting into some seminars or smaller classes initially, but the administration is very accommodating, and with a little persistence you can usually squeeze in. The main issue with getting into classes comes from overlapping schedules—many of what I thought were the most interesting seminars were offered at the same time as popular lecture classes. There definitely were more classes that I wanted to take than I had time for.

Status: Current student, full-time
Dates of Enrollment: 9/2002-Submit Date
Survey Submitted: October 2003

Classes are amazing. The professors are intelligent, clear, organized, knowledgeable and all-around good people. The material is stimulating, and most everyone is prepared. Classmates are engaged in the environment, making the classroom a good place for debates. Workload is heavy, but what do you expect from an Ivy League school? You really get to learn the material like the back of your hand. Popular classes are usually closed, but some professors open more spots, and you might get into the class. All together, I couldn't be happier with the quality of academics here at Columbia.

Status: Alumnus/a, full-time
Dates of Enrollment: 8/2000-5/2003
Survey Submitted: April 2004

The quality of teaching is outstanding. Nearly all the professors are well known and well respected in their fields. Unlike many other "regional" law schools, which focus primarily on New York State law, Columbia gives a broad overview with little to no emphasis on local law. The teaching is more theoretical and the training is focused on making you "think like a lawyer." Many popular classes tend to have long waiting lists, but with a few exceptions students can almost always get into any class they wish to take.

 # Employment Prospects

Status: Current student, full-time JD/MBA
Dates of Enrollment: 9/2003-Submit Date
Survey Submitted: February 2006

If you want to be a big firm lawyer, Columbia's recruitment could not be better (at least in the second year). In the first year, you'll still be sending out the mass array of resumes and cover letters to the 150 firms closest to where you want to be for the summer. I got my job through a Columbia alum, most of whom are pretty devoted to the school. All of the major firms that have 1L programs (Sullivan & Cromwell, Wachtell) look to the top performers at Columbia to supply them. The career services office is not all that helpful, but that's the way it goes. Second year, however, jobs are basically laid out on a silver platter. The school rents out an entire hotel in Midtown and for five days all of the second-years get out their navy blue or black suits and go from suite to suite interviewing. Firms are required to interview whoever the school sends to them so any student can get an interview with any firm. Clerking can be a bit harder since Columbia is not typically seen as a clerking school, but most people who want one manage to find one.

Status: Alumnus/a, full-time
Dates of Enrollment: 8/2001-5/2004
Survey Submitted: March 2006

This is the creme de la creme. 98 percent of graduates have employment before they graduate. This is one of the favorite spots to recruit for the top law firms of New York and the country. It is also a good place for government recruiters. The career center and Public Interest center have career fairs where several employers participate. The alumni networks are also helpful. But with a degree from CLS, you're most certain to find a job (or, more likely, plenty, since you'll be sought after).

Status: Alumnus/a, full-time
Dates of Enrollment: 8/2002-5/2005
Survey Submitted: March 2006

The $150,000 price tag is justified by the phenomenal employment possibilities. Columbia students would have to try hard to avoid getting hired into a job that promises $160,000 in the first year. Of course, competition remains high for the very top firms, clerkships and fellowships. Students from Columbia battle with their peers at Yale, Harvard, Chicago, Stanford and NYU for the most selective legal jobs in the country.

Status: Alumnus/a, full-time
Dates of Enrollment: 8/2001-5/2004
Survey Submitted: March 2006

You have to differentiate among (1) clerkships, (2) public interest jobs, (3) academic jobs and (4) law firm jobs. Clerkships: Columbia has an excellent program with a team of professors that are dedicated to helping students get clerkships. This is a very active program and I think students are generally pretty happy with the support they get. There are complaints, but these complaints have to do with the clerkship process, not with Columbia's support or support network.

Public interest jobs: Columbia has an undeservedly bad reputation when it comes to public interest jobs, but it is true that there is room for improvement. Overall, however, I think Columbia's public interest program is one that many schools would be envious of. If you want a public interest job, you will get one, you just have to work harder at it than you do for a firm job, but that comes with the territory. Academic jobs: after neglecting this area for quite a while, Columbia has begun to focus on academic jobs and is pouring resources into creating a program to train students for academic jobs and to help them find them. If you are looking to enter the academic world, I believe you will get a LOT of individual attention and support from a large number of professors, who will also involve you in their own internal research and paper review processes.

Law firm jobs: like shooting fish in a barrel.

Status: Alumnus/a, full-time
Dates of Enrollment: 8/2003-Submit Date
Survey Submitted: September 2004

Most people find a job that they are excited about after graduation. Not everyone is fortunate, though. There are people who cannot get jobs after graduation, and it can be a very lonely experience because they are isolated from their peers during the third year of law school. Most people opt for working in big New York City law firms, but there are a few who do judicial clerkships and work for governmental agencies or public interest legal organizations.

Status: Alumnus/a, full-time
Dates of Enrollment: 8/2001-5/2004
Survey Submitted: April 2005

Columbia sends several people each year to all of the most prestigious firms in New York, a few to those in L.A. and many others scattered around the country. The school seems to have an excellent reputation with employers as a source of students who are smart and practical. For those who are interested in academia, Columbia is among the few law schools that produces many professors. Columbia also sends many of its graduates into public interest organizations.

Note that although the funding for people pursuing public interest positions is decent and improves every year, many people are still financially compelled to choose to work for corporate firms in order to pay off their loans and support themselves in New York.

Status: Alumnus/a, full-time
Dates of Enrollment: 8/2000-5/2003
Survey Submitted: April 2004

Career prospects for students from Columbia are very good. There is a lot of competition for summer jobs following the first year, but career resources provides plenty of opportunities to train for the job searching and interview process. At the start of the second year of law school, a student can line up her summer job for the end of that school year. The summer job in most cases leads to an offer of full-time employment. This means that before the start of the third year of law school, a student could have full-time employment lined up a full year in advance of the start date, nine months before graduating from law school. That firm will pay the costs of moving from the dorm to an apartment and for the bar exam expenses, and will give students a salary advance to help them live while preparing for the bar exam.

Status: Alumnus/a, full-time
Dates of Enrollment: 8/2000-5/2003
Survey Submitted: April 2004

For students interested in public interest law, there is a whole division in the law school dedicated to public interest jobs. A certain number of living stipends are provided to students who take public interest jobs during their 1L or 2L summers. Job opportunities are also circulated on an almost daily basis, for both part-time and full-time employment. These include private-sector, government and public interest jobs. Some part-time positions can be taken on for credit.

Status: Alumnus/a, full-time
Dates of Enrollment: 8/1998-5/2002
Survey Submitted: April 2004

I was amazed by the career opportunities. Columbia has fabulous prestige with employers. The on-campus interviews at the end of the first summer of law school are extremely well organized and guarantee almost every student a high paying and challenging job. I had 15 callbacks at 15 major New York law firms. I spent a summer at the law firm Shearman & Sterling, got an offer, then spent the next summer at the law firm Debevoise & Plimpton, which I eventually chose over Shearman. I am now a third-year associate at Debevoise in the corporate department.

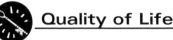

Quality of Life

Status: Current student, full-time JD/MBA
Dates of Enrollment: 9/2003-Submit Date
Survey Submitted: February 2006

Living in New York is awesome. There are a million and one things to do and when you're at one of the premier institutions in the city, you have just tons of interesting speakers passing through the doors. It's impossible to keep up with everything. Law school is law school and I think the quality of life is about the same as it is everywhere. Of course, that is a personal choice. The law school guarantees housing, which is a pretty big deal. The quality of it varies significantly and while some people have awesome deals on huge rooms or one bedrooms or whatever, other people have crappy deals on small places. There are ways to game that system too though.

Status: Alumnus/a, full-time
Dates of Enrollment: 8/1998-5/2002
Survey Submitted: May 2006

Housing is excellent. I liked that for a school in the middle of NYC, it does have an actual campus, with a quad and places where students gather. The gates/walls help demarcate the school from the surrounding neighborhood, although much of the surrounding neighborhood is still the school (other campus buildings, student housing, etc.). I thought facilities were pretty good; law library is excellent, student lounges and cafeteria were fine, gym was decent. I thought it was pretty safe when I was there.

Status: Alumnus/a, full-time
Dates of Enrollment: 8/2001-5/2004
Survey Submitted: March 2006

Housing is available, though some students choose (as I did) to live nearby off campus. New York lives up to its reputation as the most expensive apartment market in the country. The campus facilities are first rate for the most part. Few law students participate in any kind of dining plan; everyone has kitchens available to them and the dining-out alternatives on the Upper West Side are so plentiful and cheap that a meal plan would be pointless for all but a few. Morningside Heights is a terrific, vibrant neighborhood; and of course all of NYC is your backyard.

Status: Alumnus/a, full-time
Dates of Enrollment: 8/2001-5/2004
Survey Submitted: March 2006

Very high. Columbia is renovating the classrooms. The law school housing is of high quality, even if some students are slobs and don't make the most of it. Generally, students get large apartments withing two blocks of the law school. While expensive, housing at Columbia is still considerably cheaper than at NYU. The Columbia campus is beautiful. It is really astonishing to be in the middle of New York on a beautiful college campus.

Columbia is VERY safe, no matter what anyone else tells you. Yes, Harlem is just north of the campus, but Harlem isn't a teaming mass of murderers, it's just Harlem. As an added benefit, there are a number of reasonably priced restaurants in the neighborhood that are actually quite good. On-campus dining is bad, but it's bad at every university. Finally, the law school is in the middle of New York City. That is probably the biggest draw and it raises quality of life to an unbelievable level. TIP: take advantage of student tickets to the opera, ballet and Philharmonic at Lincoln Center. You will never get to see performances this good, this cheap, this often.

Status: Alumnus/a, full-time
Dates of Enrollment: 8/2001-5/2004
Survey Submitted: March 2006

The school was fine. The buildings were nice, the campus is far safer than you'd expect in New york City. Housing was also the best deal in town. Low priced big apartments. Student groups were friendly and didn't tend to be a big time commitment. That being said, the school really lacked school spirit. Not much feeling of community.

Read all of Vault's Law School Surveys at www.vault.com/lawschool — get complete surveys on top law schools, expert advice on applicaton essays, LSAT prep and more.

VAULT CAREER LIBRARY   421

Status: Current student, full-time LLM
Dates of Enrollment: 6/2005-Submit Date
Survey Submitted: January 2006

The quality of life is excellent. Housing provided by the law school is perfectly adequate and reasonably priced for New York (very expensive for anyone not used to NY prices). Unfortunately there isn't enough for all incoming LLMs and the organization that allocates housing (University Apartment Housing), is a Byzantine nightmare. If you don't get an initial housing offer, you may be able to get a housing offer a month or two later, as there are always some students that drop out and leave empty rooms.

Status: Alumnus/a, full-time
Dates of Enrollment: 8/2001-5/2004
Survey Submitted: April 2005

The neighborhood is pretty safe and getting nicer and safer every year. Campus is beautiful and provides access and a sense of belonging to an incredible university community. Facilities are good. Administration can be cumbersome and frustrating.

Status: Alumnus/a, full-time
Dates of Enrollment: 9/1999-1/2003
Survey Submitted: March 2005

The Columbia campus is rapidly changing, much of it for the better. It seems that money is constantly being spent on both expanding and upgrading the resources that are available to the law school. The campus is somewhat splintered, with buildings being spread out over about five or six blocks, but for the most part, I never had any issues with the infrastructure or safety.

Status: Alumnus/a, full-time
Dates of Enrollment: 8/2000-5/2003
Survey Submitted: April 2004

The campus is beautiful; old, with gorgeous buildings and lawns. The law school is across the street from the main campus—it's less impressive architecturally, but has been renovated recently to bring the classrooms into the 21st Century.

Housing near the school is not that great. Most apartments and dorms are old and small with no central air or heat. Even with the subsidy provided by the school, most tiny one-bedroom apartments are around $1,000 per month or more. The neighborhood is pretty enjoyable with lots of restaurants and shops. There was the occasional mugging reported, but most potential problems could be avoided with common sense. The school would post campus security guards on streets and near buildings that had been the site of any recent incidents.

Status: Current student, full-time
Dates of Enrollment: 9/2002-Submit Date
Survey Submitted: October 2003

Housing is guaranteed on campus and is incredible! For New York, I couldn't be getting a better value. Although Morningside Heights leaves one wanting a little more activity, the area has a "campus" feel. Columbia has the best resources in legal materials, computers, dining—everything is state-of-the-art. Students are encouraged to embrace the "university" by taking classes in various departments. I am taking a business school class that helps ease the workload but also helps to give me a different perspective.

 Social Life

Status: Current student, full-time JD/MBA
Dates of Enrollment: 9/2003-Submit Date
Survey Submitted: February 2006

Well, social life is one of those things that not all law students put a premium on. For those that do, there is Bar Review on Thursday night where "bar czars" negotiate cheap drink specials for people with Columbia Law IDs. It's more of a 1L scene than anything else, but it's a great place to identify the other people in the class that recognize life is more than torts and contracts. Depending upon the night (weeknights were often bars around campus, Am Cafe, Radio Perfecto, 1020, Lionshead; weekends are often either farther down the West Side—George Keeleys, Time Out, Prohibition, 420, Bourbon St. or all the way

downtown; the Lower East Side is a favorite), fun law students go just about everywhere in the city. For sports, Blondies is a perennial favorite. For beirut, Time Out or West End on Wednesday nights.

Really the 80s and Amsterdam area becomes the normal destination spot, but there's variety when people want to stay closer to home or head farther out. Note that most law students live near campus at least their first year, which determines a bit more where they go. After first year most people have their group of friends that they hang out with and they stop attending law school events (with the exception of Barristers Ball, which is always a night full of debauchery and completes the illusion that one really has regressed to high school). As far as dating, well, relationships only seem to work when they're keep on the DL and so most people keep them a secret for as long as possible. There definitely is in-school dating, hook-ups, but the school is small enough that most stuff becomes common knowledge eventually. We did have a marriage this past year and there are some long-term couples that are heading that way, but I think most people would agree that law school is not exactly where one goes for love.

Status: Alumnus/a, full-time
Dates of Enrollment: 8/2001-5/2004
Survey Submitted: March 2006

Lacking. I made five or six very close friends, and that was about it. And I think I was on the lucky side. I think it's a combination of overly intense people and the fact that the campus clears out at 5:00. I went to a competitive Ivy for undergrad and the difference between the social life at Columbia and there was like night and day. Nobody came to school events, and many people were just downright annoying. You found a lot of great diamonds by third year, but in general we had to deal with show-offy, socially awkward people in class daily. It was a relief to find that law firm life was better socially than law school.

Status: Current student, full-time LLM
Dates of Enrollment: 6/2005-Submit Date
Survey Submitted: January 2006

Social life is pretty good for the LLMs. There are regular friday drinks organized by the law school and LLMs can join in in the functions organized by the Student Senate for the JDs. The LLM class is pretty collegial and tends to socialize within itself, but that depends on individuals.

Most social life is organized by the students themselves. It's New York. If you can't find amazing bars, clubs, shows, places to go, there is something wrong with you!

Status: Alumnus/a, full-time
Dates of Enrollment: 8/2003-Submit Date
Survey Submitted: September 2004

The law school senate does a good job of trying to improve the social life of the law school. There are numerous clubs that allow each student to pursue his or her individual interest. Again, the problem is that most students see Columbia as a high-end trade school, and thus there are loathe to take advantage of the the many social activities offered on campus. The highlight of the social calendar are the Rights of Spring Party held by the Law School Senate and the Columbia Law Revue.

Status: Alumnus/a, full-time
Dates of Enrollment: 9/1999-1/2003
Survey Submitted: March 2005

I found that Columbia law students were excellent actors—on the surface, everyone seemed friendly and civil, but dig down just a little bit, and there was an immense amount of competition and one-upmanship going on. Although I am sure that some people can thrive in such an atmosphere, I was not one of them. I ended up taking a short leave of absence to pursue other things and to give me a chance to "recharge."

Status: Alumnus/a, full-time
Dates of Enrollment: 8/1998-5/2001
Survey Submitted: April 2004

The social life is awesome, thanks to an active (and fun) student senate. Students should take advantage of all the campus has to offer by participating in as many fun activities (such as the Law Revue and Cabaret Show or Di Vinimus) as possible. I have many more fond memories of extracurricular activities than I do of classroom experiences (as is true for most of my colleagues). There are plenty of great restaurants around the campus, but for bars, you have to travel downtown.

Status: Alumnus/a, full-time
Dates of Enrollment: 8/2000-5/2003
Survey Submitted: September 2003

There are tons of organizations, journals, activities and other goings-on, both at the law school and on campus. It usually felt like there were too many that sounded interesting, but not enough time. So many public figures, artists, activists show up to speak, perform and otherwise interact on the Columbia campus that it really feels like the center of the world sometimes. You shouldn't miss the 1L welcome dinner, which takes place in the beautiful atrium of Low Library.

The food in the law school cafeteria is pretty decent. But if you walk over next door to the buffet at Faculty House, the price for food is similar for more variety and better quality.

Status: Current student, full-time
Dates of Enrollment: 8/2003-Submit Date
Survey Submitted: July 2004

As far as more specifically CLS-related social activities, there is a seemingly endless list of clubs and organizations both within the law school and within the broader Columbia University, most of which are presented to you in a pamphlet when you are admitted to CLS, and all of which regularly advertise on the campus premises. Whatever you're in to, I think you'll find it somewhere at Columbia. It's that cosmopolitan.

Read all of Vault's Law School Surveys at www.vault.com/lawschool — get complete surveys on top law schools, expert advice on applicaton essays, LSAT prep and more.

VAULT CAREER LIBRARY   423

Cornell Law School

Admissions
Myron Taylor Hall
Ithaca, NY 14853-4901
Admissions phone: (607) 255-5141
Admissions e-mail: lawadmit@postoffice.law.cornell.edu
Admissions URL:
http://www.lawschool.cornell.edu/admissions/

 Admissions

Status: Current student, full-time
Dates of Enrollment: 8/2005-Submit Date
Survey Submitted: October 2005

Cornell looks for diversity and a well-rounded class. When applying, make sure to write an essay on something unique to you. Like all other top law schools, admission to Cornell requires a top LSAT score and GPA. However, if you are lacking in one of those areas, make sure to lift it up with great letters of recommendation, a personal statement and extracurricular activities. Again, uniqueness is key. One does not have to have legal related jobs on there resume or major in liberal arts. For example, some of the jobs people held in my first year class before attending law school were a horse trainer, seal trainer, sitcom writer and bartender, to name a few. It is also a myth that one should take time off before attending law school. If you want to attend law school now apply! 45 percent of my class came straight from undergrad.

Status: Alumnus/a, full-time
Dates of Enrollment: 8/2001-6/2004
Survey Submitted: March 2006

Grades, grades, grades. And hit a 164 or above on the LSAT. Cornell goes for a diverse class, not just based on race or sex but also on backgrounds and individuality. If you did something interesting or overcame something challenging, get it in front of them.

Status: Alumnus/a, full-time
Dates of Enrollment: 8/2002-5/2005
Survey Submitted: March 2006

The admissions process is similar to most law schools I applied to. There is a standard form, they require at least one essay and they do not conduct interviews. They have become increasingly more selective, I think because the number of highly qualified applicants has increased in recent years while the number of available spots at top schools has remained about the same. The best advice I can offer is to include in your essay explanations of why you are choosing the law and why you think Cornell and/or Ithaca would be a good fit. Be specific!

Status: Current student, full-time
Dates of Enrollment: 8/2003-Submit Date
Survey Submitted: October 2004

Apply early! Cornell Law does process applications quickly; I heard from them earlier than any other school. If you look at the *U.S. News & World Report* LSAT info, it is misleading; you can get into Cornell with a lower LSAT and good grades (lower, of course, relative to schools like Columbia or Stanford). High LSAT/low grades does not work as well.

Status: Alumnus/a, full-time
Dates of Enrollment: 8/2001-5/2004
Survey Submitted: April 2005

Admissions is competitive. One thing that helped my application stand out, I believe, was the fact that I had two older cousins who attended Cornell as undergraduates and I mentioned this on my admission application. Be sure to mention anyone you know who goes there or has gone there. In addition, a friend of mine helped himself get off the waitlist and get admitted by having a friend of his who was a current law student write a letter of recommendation on his behalf to the admissions committee while he was on the waitlist.

Status: Alumnus/a, full-time
Dates of Enrollment: 8/2001-5/2004
Survey Submitted: March 2005

I applied for normal admission, and got in. I've heard the waiting list is essentially like being rejected, since so few students are admitted after being waitlisted.

> **The school says:** "The dynamics of the summer waitlist change every admissions year. The number of students that are admitted from the summer waitlist varies greatly each year."

Status: Alumnus/a, full-time
Dates of Enrollment: 9/2001-5/2004
Survey Submitted: March 2005

The one unique thing I know about CLS's admission process is that I have heard that they only consider your top LSAT score, as opposed to all other schools, which average all of your scores on the LSAT.

> **The school says:** "We will consider taking the higher of multiple LSAT scores, if the applicant provides us with an explanation regarding the difference in the scores and the scores differ by more than three points."

Status: Alumnus/a, full-time
Dates of Enrollment: 8/1997-5/2000
Survey Submitted: March 2005

I think Cornell must be seeking more well-rounded individuals, because of my graduating class from Denison about eight of us applied to all of the major schools and we each were different in our own way and we each got into certain schools quickly. I think it helped that I had many extracurricular activities where I demonstrated leadership—president of a fraternity; class co-governor; treasurer of the community association; and more. I also think that my writing sample was a little more creative and therefore may have put off some of the old line schools, but I think Cornell liked it. I say this because Cornell accepted me before my safe school, Ohio State. The only other thing I would say is that the professors I had write my reference letters were very good professors, professors I had a good personal and "professional" relationship with and who I knew would give me high marks. That probably helped put me over the top as well, and I truly think that those reference letters can put you into the "accepted" category.

Status: Current student, full-time
Dates of Enrollment: 8/2001-Submit Date
Survey Submitted: January 2004

Obviously, grades and LSATs are the most important. If you have significant work experience or graduate degrees, your chances improve. The class is not very diverse in terms of race or socioeconomic status. If you can make yourself appear more interesting than the average Greek undergraduate whose parents are lawyers, you will have an advantage. It seems like more than half the class is second-generation lawyers or former presidents of their fraternity or spent a year as a paralegal. If this describes you, I wouldn't emphasize that aspect in your application. Try to find something, anything that makes you seem different.

Cornell likes to emphasize its international law curriculum. The Paris Summer Program is very popular and focuses on international law. If you can demonstrate your interest in things international, you might have an advantage over someone else with similar grades and test scores without such an interest.

> **The school says:** "Our law school class is quite diverse. We have included a profile of our most recent class in the 'School Says' section at the end of the profile."

Status: Alumnus/a, full-time
Dates of Enrollment: 9/2000-5/2003
Survey Submitted: April 2004

Typical process: essays and scores. No interview for the law school. Definitely know the feel of the school before you apply and reference that in your essays. They seem to like knowing people have a personal interest in the school and are not just applying to add it to their list because it is ranked in the Top 10 (or 15 some years). They really seem to read the essays, including the diversity one. It is rather selective, but I think they have long been committed to looking at the whole applicant, so do not be discouraged from applying if you are interested and fall outside their typical admission range.

> **The school says:** "We interview applicants upon the law school's request."

Status: Current student, full-time
Dates of Enrollment: 9/2003-Submit Date
Survey Submitted: July 2004

Cornell, like any of the top 14 law schools, puts a large emphasis on grades and LSAT scores. But they do try to attract a very diverse class in terms of the different schools people are from. If you are coming straight out of undergrad you should probably have mid-160s LSAT and a GPA over 3.5. Obviously, if someone is from a lesser-known school, they need a higher GPA. Cornell, like most schools, does not interview. Essays were pretty standard. I personally think Cornell cares more about activities that one did as an undergrad than other law schools, so emphasize those. Community service is good, and leadership positions in undergrad organizations always help.

> **The school says:** "We individually review each application. We do not have different academic standards for applicants directly from undergraduate school and those with work experience. There are no set GPA admissions standards at any school or university."

Status: Current student, full-time
Dates of Enrollment: 9/2002-Submit Date
Survey Submitted: October 2003

Very competitive, especially after September 11. Schools Cornell really likes: Stanford, U of Chicago, U Penn, CUNY, Princeton, Cornell, Berkeley, Bucknell, Yale. Otherwise, the applicant had better be a truly outstanding student in his/her college class.

 **Academics**

Status: Current student, full-time
Dates of Enrollment: 8/2005-Submit Date
Survey Submitted: October 2005

Since I am a first-year student, I cannot comment on the ease of getting popular classes and grading. However, the classes are high quality at Cornell. Unlike schools in major cities, the professor are dedicated to teaching and make themselves available to the students. You do not run into the frequent problem of professors being inaccessible do to other engagements. Since Cornell is a small school (550 students) a student can potentially meet with all of their professors every day if they have trouble getting through course material. The workload is not too heavy at first. The professors do a great job of starting of light to emphasize reasoning and then making the workload heavier.

Status: Current student, full-time
Dates of Enrollment: 8/2004-Submit Date
Survey Submitted: November 2005

It's great to have professors who wrote your casebooks or are cited a lot in them. Like other schools, I'm sure, there's more of these in some subjects than others. Grading is on a B+ curve, the majority of students in each class getting a B+, some room for A- and A's, but they're sparse because they have to average each grade above a B+ out with one below. Haven't had any trouble getting the classes I wanted. Professors are approachable, perhaps more so because of the rural location, they're not running out after class to be expert witnesses or do any

side work for a firm. First-year workload is pretty heavy, not sure if more than other school, but eases up a lot 2L and 3L.

Status: Current student, full-time
Dates of Enrollment: 8/2004-Submit Date
Survey Submitted: November 2005

It's law school, so it's no walk in the park. However, I appreciate the quality of education I receive here. Cornell has great professors and most of our casebooks were written by the professors here. There seems to be more of a focus on traditional Socratic Method teaching than other law schools during 1L year, but I feel that it really helped prepare me for practice and handling difficult judges and tough questions from partners. Our Lawyering/Legal Methods class is excellent. It is more of a practical class where we learn how to handle the daily assignments given to young associates at a law firm. Unlike some other schools, this class is taken seriously with substantive assignments and a letter grade. We are really forced to learn how to do the research and legal writing required, but also how to handle various situations such as tough partners or reviews and client meetings. 2L and 3L year are not as Socratic and classes are very small. Four of my five classes this semester had fewer than 20 students! This is good in that you are not some anonymous face in the crowd, you get your questions answered and learn from your colleagues' individual experiences. The small class size at Cornell is bad in that there are fewer course offerings than larger schools. I found, however, enough diversity and all the main bar-related topics offered almost every semester.

Status: Alumnus/a, full-time
Dates of Enrollment: 8/2002-5/2005
Survey Submitted: March 2006

Workload is tough, especially during the first year. No matter how hard you work, there is always something more you could do. Most of the professors are well known in the field, often extensively published and very knowledgeable of their subjects. (Word to the wise: visiting professors are a gamble. Sometimes they're excellent, sometimes really not.) Grading is on a strict curve where the average grade for each class must be a B+ or lower. It can be tough to get into popular seminars, but the selection system is as fair as possible. Two classes NOT TO BE MISSED: Trial Advocacy with Galbreath and Lawyers & Clients with Kysar.

Status: Current student, full-time
Dates of Enrollment: 8/2003-Submit Date
Survey Submitted: October 2004

The quality of classes is fairly high, although not uniformly so. A big selling point of the school is its low student/faculty ratio, but you really shouldn't decide to go to Cornell for that. Because of the curve, which is enforced in all but the tiniest of classes, you can't take small classes unless you don't care about your grades or are really, really confident. So you end up taking the big classes. Because Cornell is small, the class selection is not the greatest. Lots of things listed in the catalog are not offered regularly.

> **The school says:** "The course listing includes courses that are taught in the current or next academic year."

Status: Alumnus/a, full-time
Dates of Enrollment: 8/2001-5/2004
Survey Submitted: April 2005

Cornell Law is a conservative law school. Most classes are Socratic, even in the second and third years. My experience has been that most professors are tough in the classroom but friendly out of the classroom. In addition, my classmates, I think, would agree that grading was fair overall. I had only one grade that I disagreed with in my time there, and it wasn't that far off from what I probably deserved (a B when I should have gotten a B+ or A-).

Overall, the academics are quite intense but the professors are very, very good. Classes are pretty small because the total class size is small. Getting the classes you want is not very difficult, and Cornell has a very equitable system for choosing classes in your second and third years (with points and weights). Bottom line: this is as good a legal education as you can get anywhere in the country.

Read all of Vault's Law School Surveys at www.vault.com/lawschool — get complete surveys on top law schools, expert advice on applicaton essays, LSAT prep and more.

VAULT CAREER LIBRARY 425

Status: Current student, full-time
Dates of Enrollment: 9/2003-Submit Date
Survey Submitted: April 2004

Cornell has great professors. It may be one of the hardest working law schools in the country. Expect to spend most of your first year working. Around finals, like every law school, the amount of studying becomes extreme. I hear it's better after the first year though. All first-year courses are required. First semester you will be assigned one small class with the rest of your section (there are six or seven sections) which will only have 30 students. This is to get you used to law school. Your other three classes will have a lot of students, as will your other classes second semester.

Note that Cornell requires 1Ls to take Lawyering-Legal Writing, and this class is relatively small as well. So the first-year schedule includes for first semester: Contracts, Torts, Civil Procedure, Constitutional Law and Lawyering. Second semester: Contracts, Civil Procedure, Property, Criminal Law and Lawyering. Note the Lawyering class only has 30 students each semester, as does one other of your first-semester courses.

Status: Alumnus/a, full-time
Dates of Enrollment: 8/1997-5/2000
Survey Submitted: April 2004

Cornell is a rigorous academic institution, and that includes the law school—it oozes intelligence and hard work. The professors are fantastic, the grading is on a curve that is more than fair and the workload is what you should expect: heavy. You should expect that everyone at the law school is going to work very hard and is exceptionally bright. Upperclassman law school students are good for helping out the younger folks with different classes, though, so seek that help and get to know 2Ls and 3Ls (they may be the difference between an B and an A-).

As far as ease of getting popular classes, it is probably the same as anywhere else—3Ls get first dibs and then so on and so forth. If you are specializing in a field (i.e., international studies), you'll get into those classes.

I almost forgot a very good and interesting part, and that is the partnership of the law school with the business school. If you are interested in a transactional practice, take advantage of those JD/MBA classes, because MBA students offer fascinating insights, and those are probably the folks you'll be working with in your career.

Last thing: because Cornell is in Ithaca, there are not many distractions. This is a curse (employers moan about coming out to Ithaca; it does get quite gray at times) and a blessing (law school is not about fun and games, and studying and getting to know your professors and other students should be your main focus).

Status: Alumnus/a, full-time
Dates of Enrollment: 8/2000-5/2003
Survey Submitted: April 2004

The classes are generally fantastic! The classes are taught by renowned treatise authors, restatement reporters, nationally known lecturers, former U.S. Supreme Court clerks and respected practitioners in every field of law. The concentrations help one achieve a focus in one's studies without becoming mired in a field too early.

Status: Alumnus/a, full-time
Dates of Enrollment: 8/2000-5/2003
Survey Submitted: November 2003

The number of credits assigned for your first year is on the high side for the other Top 10 New York law schools. Cornell requires 16 credits per semester your first year, and all of the credits—including the writing class—are graded. Currently the law school is functioning under an unofficial B+ curve (with the mandatory curve being found unconstitutional by Cornell University). The class size is on the small side and some of the professors try to remember the students—at least enough to recognize them in the hallway.

Status: Current student, full-time
Dates of Enrollment: 9/2002-Submit Date
Survey Submitted: October 2003

Amazingly friendly, approachable professors. You will run into them at the supermarket, and they will talk to you, sometimes about reality TV shows or, as

is more likely the case, civil procedure. Most professors use casebooks they have written, so they often provide insight beyond the text. The drawback is that the workload is sort of insane; requires deep thought, more than can be done in a few hours the night before. But hey, it's Cornell.

 Employment Prospects

Status: Current student, full-time
Dates of Enrollment: 8/2005-Submit Date
Survey Submitted: October 2005

Once at Cornell, your foot is in the door. It is up to you to put in the work to get the good grades required to work for a prestigious law firm. With that said, 99 percent of the class has a job by graduation. Thus, one should not worry about getting employed. Most graduates work with a private firm in New York upon graduation, but by attending Cornell you can go anywhere nationwide. During second-year interviews, students interview in New York, Washington, D.C. Chicago and Los Angeles. This wide reach of interview opportunities makes the offers one receives exponential. The alumni have a vested interest in seeing Cornell graduates succeed. Whether by talking with the alumni office or contacting the alumni directly from an online search, the alumni will be more than willing help where they can.

Status: Current student, full-time
Dates of Enrollment: 8/2004-Submit Date
Survey Submitted: November 2005

Coming from Cornell Law School equals your choice of a large firm job in the city you want, regardless of your grades. All the big players from the major legal markets come to Cornell and recruit. There are also regional job fairs where Cornell sets a day or two in a specific city and a range of law firms from the city interview us. I think it is very advantageous to come from Cornell. If you want to work in New York, Cornell has ties to all the firms and a good reputation. But even outside of New York, Cornell students are heavily recruited because there are so few of us. This is another example of why our small class size makes a difference—the employers want a diversity of law schools represented in their summer associate class, and since there are so few of us to go around, we seem to be sought after. Everyone I know had their choice of where to work—no one struggled to get a job, only struggled with which offer to accept! If you are looking at public interest, there is a great loan forgiveness program and a counselor who concentrates solely on those types of jobs, and a group set up for those who have such interests. But most of the class goes to the large prestigious NYC firms that start at $125,000 salaries. I did not have ties to New York or Boston, but received offers from almost every firm to which I applied. Going to Cornell Law is no risk that the tuition dollars will go to waste—it means you will have options to do what you want afterwards.

Status: Alumnus/a, full-time
Dates of Enrollment: 8/2002-5/2005
Survey Submitted: March 2006

Cornell Law School's career office is one of the most competent and dedicated groups of professionals I've ever seen. They are the school's best asset. They host numerous job fairs around the country, meet with students one-on-one in preparation for interview season, and make themselves available around-the-clock when the pressure to accept or decline offers starts to mount. Although it's fair to say that big firms are a focus point, they are also helpful with clerkship applications, pro-bono opportunities and all kinds of interesting internships.

Status: Current student, full-time
Dates of Enrollment: 8/2003-Submit Date
Survey Submitted: October 2004

If you are in the top 10 percent you will be absolutely fine—members of my class went to all of the most prestigious firms in NYC. However, the rest of the class does have to settle for less prestigious firms, and a few people each year don't get jobs. If you want to work in California, don't go to Cornell; we have a hard time getting jobs there. Cornellians are close however, so when you do have a contact, it is a good one.

The school says: "Cornell Law School students enjoy a strong record of legal placement after graduation. Usually nine months after graduation, 99 or 98 percent of all law students have secured employment, often at highly selective employers. Outside of the East Coast, the State of California represents the biggest employment market for Cornell Law Students. Employers from the State of California interview Cornell Law Students at our August, Los Angeles and San Francisco off-campus job fairs and during the on-campus interview process."

Status: Alumnus/a, full-time
Dates of Enrollment: 8/1997-5/2000
Survey Submitted: March 2005

Employment prospects are obviously great—this is an Ivy League school with a good reputation. I think most of the students coming from Cornell go into BigLaw firms in NYC or other big markets, and all of those firms generally come to Ithaca or set up at one of the job fairs, which are great. I was looking at D.C. and Atlanta and Cornell had in job fairs at both which was great for exposure.

If you are interested in NYC, the NYC job fair is a must and also excellent. I think alumni networking is very strong, but I did not take great advantage of it. Call it pride, but I wanted to go where Cornellians had not been before (yes, that's pride). On-campus recruiting was actually very good for being in Ithaca, but if you are looking at more "exotic" destinations, you may have to work on getting there. I had no problem getting an internship in any year, and again, it's the Cornell name.

Status: Alumnus/a, full-time
Dates of Enrollment: 9/2000-5/2003
Survey Submitted: April 2004

Most folks go to large law firms after their second year and after school. All the big firms recruit on campus, no shortage of firm opportunities. Other career options are less represented. Some local nonprofits recruit on campus, and the school facilitates students going to regional job fairs and the NALP conference. Career office is friendly. First summer can be a bit of a struggle, but most find rewarding (if unpaid) work for nonprofits. Also, PIF grants are available to provide some funding during the first summer.

Status: Current student, full-time
Dates of Enrollment: 8/2001-Submit Date
Survey Submitted: January 2004

Cornell holds a three-day job fair in New York City in early August. Every firm in New York is there, as well as most of the national firms. If you are in the top half of the class, you will get several callbacks from this process. Cornell has a good reputation among employers. Obviously, there are hundreds of Cornell grads working in all of the major law firms in New York City. Cornell has a good reputation there.

I think that the Cornell advantage might be even stronger in the Midwest and West. The reputation is strong in these areas, but there are so few Cornell law grads practicing outside the I-95 area, that you are something of a prize. So law firms can add another top law school to their office roster. The career placement office does a pretty good job of bringing in law firms to Ithaca to recruit. There are also several symposia offered to help match nonprofit organizations with students.

Status: Alumnus/a, full-time
Dates of Enrollment: 8/2000-5/2003
Survey Submitted: April 2004

The career office is terrific! The professionals who work there know each student by name and character. They know what each student's academic and professional interests are and do all they can to speak to those needs. I could not have survived recruiting without them.

Quality of Life

Status: Current student, full-time
Dates of Enrollment: 8/2005-Submit Date
Survey Submitted: October 2005

Cornell has graduate housing, so if you need housing it is made available. There is also a lot of off-campus housing. Some individuals come a couple of days before school starts and are still able to secure housing. With the best Hotel Administration School on campus and several dining halls, one does not have to go far to find a good meal. Although the prices can be high at times, there is a plethora of options to choose from. Neighborhood crime is the last thing to worry about when coming to Cornell. Whether walking during the day or at 3 a.m., most students do not have any issues with safety. This is attributed to the both Cornell and Ithaca police patrolling the area 24 hours a day.

Status: Current student, full-time
Dates of Enrollment: 8/2004-Submit Date
Survey Submitted: November 2005

Cornell and Ithaca gets an undeserved bad reputation. Sure, we are not in a bustling city, but I found that to be a good thing. Cornell Law School has a real sense of community. The entering class is around 190 students, and sections are around 30 students. This results in you getting to know your professors and colleagues. It seems that people at other law schools feel isolated, lost in the crowd and do not have friends. Here I can say that I know most people in my class, everyone's face if not their name as well, and will walk away will friends that I will keep in contact with for the rest of my life. This is complemented by being in a smaller town. When I was stressed out and sleep deprived, it helped to go to the local pizza shop and they knew my name and my order, or to be walking down the street and have people say hello. Being away from a large city results in my not having to worry about walking alone at night or my car getting stolen and I had less distraction and could concentrate on law school. There is a dorm for entering law students, your choice of apartments a five-minute walk away that are SO much cheaper than anywhere else I have lived, and lots of food places near the law school. Coming from a large undergraduate institution, I appreciate not being just a number here.

Status: Current student, full-time
Dates of Enrollment: 8/2004-Submit Date
Survey Submitted: November 2005

Ithaca is beautiful, but it gets cold and snows a lot in the winter. However, it's great first year cause there're fewer distractions. Even though it's in the middle of nowhere, because there's a huge university here, Ithaca itself is pretty lively, except that by law bars close at 1 a.m. Safety is a non-issue, I leave my laptop on a table in the library for eight hours and no one's touched it when I get back. Some dorms (attached to the law school) are available to 1Ls but they recently converted some of the old dorms into new offices. There's graduate housing off campus as well as ample off-campus private apartments.

Status: Current student, full-time
Dates of Enrollment: 8/2003-Submit Date
Survey Submitted: October 2004

Ithaca is cold and snowy. Lots of snow. Like 110" of snow in one winter. The fact that you are stuck in a frigid wasteland is hard to get around. Ithaca is also extremely liberal—Democrats are considered conservative. Lots of vegetarian options for a town so small. Housing is expensive, because Cornell University has over 20,000 students, and Ithaca isn't really big enough for them all. You can pay $1,300 for a small one-bedroom within walking distance of the law school. If you don't know how to drive on snow, make sure you don't live on top of the hill (Cornell is on one of the slopes of Cayuga Lake, and the hill is very very steep, and occasionally impossible to get up or down in the winter). Lots of parks, and of course, the gorges, as in "Ithaca is Gorges," the local slogan. Say it out loud to understand.

The school says: "For the last 15 years, the average snowfall in Ithaca has been about 67.3 inches."

Status: Alumnus/a, full-time
Dates of Enrollment: 8/2001-5/2004
Survey Submitted: April 2005

The best part was because of Cornell's many international study abroad opportunities, I was able to spend the fall semester of my third year in Sydney, Australia. About one third of each class leaves Ithaca in their second or third year for a semester (either studying abroad or working in an externship). Housing in Ithaca is pretty cheap. For 1Ls, they can apply to live in Hughes Hall—a law school dorm that is literally connected to the law school. I

Read all of Vault's Law School Surveys at www.vault.com/lawschool — get complete surveys on top law schools, expert advice on applicaton essays, LSAT prep and more.

VAULT CAREER LIBRARY 427

recommend this. Hughes Hall is nice and being able to walk to class without going outdoors in the first year is a big plus. Also, living there is a great way to meet and become friends with classmates. In general, campus facilities are excellent and plentiful, and law students can use all undergraduate facilities.

Status: Alumnus/a, full-time
Dates of Enrollment: 8/1997-5/2000
Survey Submitted: March 2005

The campus is beautiful and Ithaca is "gorges," as the bumper sticker reads. There is a lot of value to having a smaller law school in a larger university—the resources at your disposal are that much larger because Cornell is such a large university. Also, the MBA school works very closely with the law school and that joint cooperation is very good for those looking to go into corporate law. Housing is decent from what is provided—you can live in the law school (well, next to it) as a first-year, and Cornell has other options for grad students. However, many folks choose to live in Collegetown, which is a walk away from the law school, and Ithaca provides plenty of apartment/house/room choices. Also, Ithaca is one of the cleanest towns and is fairly safe. Besides Cornell, you have Ithaca College, so Ithaca truly is a college town.

Status: Current student, full-time
Dates of Enrollment: 8/2003-Submit Date
Survey Submitted: June 2004

Housing is very expensive near the law school (an area known as Collegetown) but no more so than housing in a major city. Housing farther away is much less expensive as you would expect in a small community so you can save a lot on housing compared to the cost of going to school in New York City, D.C. or similar places. Don't be deceived by looking at a map of Ithaca, though. Downtown looks close to the law school, but the downtown to law school walk is a fairly steep upward slope the whole way—not something you want to do carrying a laptop and a bunch of books, especially in the winter. Fortunately, bus service between downtown and campus is pretty good, and full-year bus passes are very cheap for students, as Cornell subsidizes them.

Status: Alumnus/a, full-time
Dates of Enrollment: 8/1997-5/2000
Survey Submitted: April 2004

I think Ithaca is a great town; when I was there it was voted the best small city in the country. The law school and Cornell in general offer several housing choices for students, from dorms and suites to apartment-style housing. The bus system is great in Ithaca, too. Plus, there are tons of apartments and houses that can be rented anywhere in the Ithaca and surrounding areas. Cornell is a huge institution with a beautiful campus and a lot to do—there's a bowling alley on campus, a couple of different workout facilities and basketball courts, several libraries and eating halls, and lots of niches for everyone's taste. Ithaca is the same way, with waterfalls and nature parks, wineries and pubs, and local shopping at the Commons and in other places and Wegmans (the greatest grocery store ever, I still miss it).

I always felt safe, and even though the weather can be cold, can be snowy and can get you down at times, I got lucky because I had the mildest winters they had seen two out of three years. I did get married between my first and second year, and my wife had a lot of issues with Cornell's use/treatment of trailing spouses as workers (it really hurt her when we moved back to Atlanta to explain that).

Social Life

Status: Current student, full-time
Dates of Enrollment: 8/2005-Submit Date
Survey Submitted: October 2005

I must say, there is nothing to do in Ithaca. There is one strip of bars in Collegetown, but nothing more. However, that makes students more friendly. Since the bar and club scene is so small, everyone gets to know one another. Some of the favorite hangout spots are Stellas, Palms and Johnny O's. If you go out to a bar make sure you go late. Most people do not start going out until 11:30 p.m. and the bars close at 1 a.m.

The school says: "For a busy law school student, there are certainly a bevy of things to do in Ithaca and on the Cornell campus. In fact, for most students the issue is finding the time do all the things that are available to do."

Status: Current student, full-time
Dates of Enrollment: 8/2004-Submit Date
Survey Submitted: November 2005

It's like high school and because it's small, everyone knows everything about everyone. Also, because there are only about five bars around, you can expect to see law students wherever you go, which can be good or bad depending whether you're trying to get away from it. There are many active clubs, social, religious and political. Dating within the law school is pretty frequent, but messy when it ends, again because of the size. Some law students date undergrads (there are so many more of them) but there seems to be a stigma attached to that, like it's cheating or just too easy.

Status: Current student, full-time
Dates of Enrollment: 8/2004-Submit Date
Survey Submitted: November 2005

If you have to go to the best restaurants and out to clubs every night, Ithaca is not for you. But if you are serious about your legal education and can be away from that for three years, if you want a supportive and friendly academic environment, then Cornell is the place. I have lived in large cities my entire life and will admit I would never live here after law school, but during law school found the class size and close-knit community more important than it being the most bustling city in the country. If you want to have a fun exciting social life, you should be seriously reconsidering law school anyways! You don't have time for that stuff! But don't get me wrong, there are bars aplenty here that we all head to after a memo is due or finals are over. It is always a fun time to go out to the little alcohol shack with people that you really like.

Status: Alumnus/a, full-time
Dates of Enrollment: 8/2002-5/2005
Survey Submitted: March 2006

Depends what you're looking for. It's a little clique-y for my taste, but I made some great friends. Favorite hangouts: Chapter House is low-key if you want to grab a beer and listen to live music, Stella's has a more urban feel, law students seem to love Dino's (though I'll never know why).

Status: Alumnus/a, full-time
Dates of Enrollment: 8/1995-5/1997
Survey Submitted: November 2004

It's not a major city. No institution can substitute the resources (restaurants, people, events) of a major U.S. city (especially New York). Still, I thought that Ithaca would have two stoplights and a cow before I went there, and that was not true, either. There are a number of restaurants. You are still in this town with 20,000 other students who also came to the same place for an education. And there are enough events (talks, films) to keep you busy, given what free time you will have. And in fact, I stayed on the East Coast, in part, because of the relationships I made up there.

Status: Current student, full-time
Dates of Enrollment: 8/2003-Submit Date
Survey Submitted: October 2004

Because Cornell is so remote, the student body is pretty close. There is not a lot to do. The bars and restaurants that most law students end up at are all in Collegetown, just below the law school. College Town Bagels is a staple of law school existence, although Stella's has better coffee. Aladdin's has excellent pasta. Smoothie Hut, although appealing, takes longer than you would believe possible. Wegman's grocery store, is awesome. Incredible selection.

Status: Alumnus/s, full-time
Dates of Enrollment: 8/2001-5/2004s
Survey Submitted: April 2005

There is a limited number of bars around campus and they get old after a while. Yet despite all this, I enjoyed myself in law school. I liked hanging out with my classmates and there were plenty of house/apartment parties thrown. Also, New York City was just a drive away. It is common for classmates to hook-up frequently, largely because of the small law school environment and the upstate ocation. Also, dating and interaction with undergraduates is common. The estaurant scene is limited, but there are some great places there. If you're a city erson, Ithaca will be an adjustment—but even so, it was a nice place to go to chool before coming to work in NYC.

Status: Current student, full-time
Dates of Enrollment: 8/2001-Submit Date
Survey Submitted: January 2004

n those few spare hours you do have, most people go to one of three places: the movies, the restaurant or the bar. Ithaca has plenty of all three of these. There re three movie theaters—one Hollywood-dominated chain, one artsy ndependent chain and one that straddles the line between the two extremes. There are dozens of bars in Collegetown and several more downtown. There are dozens of restaurants; most of the ones actually worth eating at require you to go half a mile down the hill to downtown Ithaca or driving in your car.

For the nontraditional types, there are several alternative sources of entertainment. Cornell hockey is very popular, but requires camping in line for eason tickets two days in advance of purchase. If you aren't that dedicated, you an buy single-game tickets for all games except against arch-rival Harvard. If you like blues, jazz, folk or other non-Top 40 types of music, there are many opportunities to attend concerts with national acts in Ithaca.

The School Says

Cornell Law School is a major research center and a leader in legal education. Its primary purpose is to prepare lawyers who will render the highest quality of professional service to their clients, who will further legal progress and reform and who can fulfill the vital role of the lawyer as a community leader and a protector of ordered liberty.

For the recent class of the law school, the Class of 2008, we enrolled 193 students:

- 25 percent of students identified themselves as racial or ethnic minorities.

- 6 percent of these students identified themselves as African American.

- Most represented undergraduate institutions: Cornell, Georgetown, Dartmouth, Columbia, Harvard and SUNY-Binghamton.

- They attended 102 different undergraduate institutions.

- They majored in over 45 different undergraduate subjects.

Cornell Law School's placement statistics over the past 20 years indicate that our students have an excellent chance of landing a job before they graduate. In the past five years, 94 percent of each graduating class received job offers before graduation; nine months after graduation, approximately 99 percent of respondents were employed in the legal field.

Read all of Vault's Law School Surveys at www.vault.com/lawschool — get complete surveys on top law schools, expert advice on applicaton essays, LSAT prep and more.

VAULT CAREER LIBRARY **429**

Fordham University School of Law

Admissions Office
33 West 60th Street, 2nd Floor
New York, NY 10023
Admissions phone: (212) 636-6810
Admissions fax: (212) 636-7984
Admissions e-mail: lawadmissions@law.fordham.edu
URL: http://law.fordham.edu/

 Admissions

Status: Current student, part-time
Dates of Enrollment: 8/2003-Submit Date
Survey Submitted: December 2005

I filled out a rather brief application. Sent one recommendation letter (I don't remember if it was mandatory). I also sent in one general essay. There was no topic requirement for the essay. I just wrote about whatever I wanted and sent that in. I was given a personal call once admitted, which was nice. I have been told by others that the admission process is not as smooth if you apply later than November. I applied early and got in before the end of the year. But others who applied in January and after had a much longer wait and often were not kept up to date about the application process. Fordham is known to respond/admit people only after the deadlines for other schools have passed.

Status: Current student, full-time
Dates of Enrollment: 8/2000-Submit Date
Survey Submitted: April 2005

You must fill out an application that includes a personal essay, letters of recommendation and take the LSAT. They are very selective, high LSAT scores are important. I had to take the LSAT several times before getting a score high enough to be accepted and even then I had the help of a faculty member to get in. I was initially admitted to the evening program which is a little easier to get into (if you have low LSAT scores) then I transferred to the day program after my first year. I would recommend highly that you write and rewrite your personal essay and have several people look at it before you turn it in. Also, you need strong letters of recommendation from your professors or employers.

Status: Alumnus/a, full-time
Dates of Enrollment: 8/1998-5/2005
Survey Submitted: April 2005

Fordham, as of late, has become very competitive. Excellent GPAs and LSATs have become the norm for the entering students. Having said this, Fordham is still interested in a diverse student body. I took eight years off between undergrad and law school. I found Fordham's admissions office was as interested in that experience as it was in my grades and LSATs. Make sure to explain why you as an individual are unique and how your participation in the Fordham community will help to enhance and strengthen Fordham. The admissions office is very human and are willing to assist in any way they can.

Status: Current student, full-time
Dates of Enrollment: 8/2003-Submit Date
Survey Submitted: April 2005

Fordham Law School is extremely selective. Although I applied early, the volume of applications was such that I didn't learn that I was accepted until very late in the decision game. I found this to be extremely stressful as I ended up having to put a deposit (which I lost) on another school in case I was not accepted. The essays and application itself were very reasonable. Once accepted, Fordham was extremely out-reaching in providing information and supporting the beginning process.

Status: Current student, full-time
Dates of Enrollment: 8/2002-Submit Date
Survey Submitted: April 2005

Overall, the admissions process was pretty smooth and easy, especially because you can do most of it online. I applied pretty early and found out quickly, which was nice. It seems like it's getting more and more selective every year, too. I think the median LSAT has gone up about two or three points. I have to say that I don't think they take the essays very seriously, but I'm not sure any law school really does. Another thing they do that is good is that if you only get in for the evening program, you can transfer to day after your first year (maybe even first semester) and that's a great way to move to full-time if you want to finish in only three years. There is no interview process, but if you want to go see the school there are tours and lots of opportunities to talk to different students.

Status: Alumnus/a, full-time
Dates of Enrollment: 8/2000-5/2003
Survey Submitted: September 2003

[For my personal statement,] I wrote about how my interest in music led me to the dream of becoming an entertainment lawyer. Fordham is very selective: it's a top-tier school, with many, if not most, students hailing from Ivy League schools. I didn't go to one, though, and I still got in with their "average" statistics—a 3.7 GPA, 164 LSAT and lots of leadership in extracurriculars (164 is the average LSAT, and the average GPA is about 3.3 to 3.6). Fordham, with its Jesuit background, is a very service-oriented school. Many students have held leadership positions in community service organizations in the past (and many of them still do). Volunteer work in college in programs like Habitat for Humanity or children's aid programs could add a boost to a lower LSAT score or GPA. Extra points probably go to those who did similar work internationally. The best thing about the Fordham admissions process? It was the only school out of seven that I got into that actually called me on the phone to tell me I got in. That extra attention to detail is always a plus.

Status: Current student, full-time
Dates of Enrollment: 8/2003-Submit Date
Survey Submitted: June 2004

Fordham's admissions process is later than most other schools, so you may have to commit to another school before hearing anything from Fordham. Otherwise it is similar to most schools. Once admitted, there seemed to be a problem getting all the necessary information to actually start school. You cannot even submit financial aid applications until admitted, which means that you may not hear back about your package until pretty late.

Status: Current student, full-time
Dates of Enrollment: 8/2002-Submit Date
Survey Submitted: September 2003

The process is standard fare for prospective law students. You submit your materials and send them the LSAC forms. An added nicety of the Fordham admissions program is the ability to apply to the full-time and/or evening program. The evening program is slightly easier to get into; however the quality of students and teachers does not falter. After the first year, evening students may transfer into the full-time program. In addition, those students who applied only to the day program and got waitlisted may be offered the opportunity to expand their application to the night program. This is an intelligent means of getting qualified students in when full-time spots are short.

Status: Current student, full-time
Dates of Enrollment: 8/2002-Submit Date
Survey Submitted: February 2004

Fordham has one of the most selective admissions processes in the country. It's the Number Three school in New York (behind good company in NYU and Columbia), and New York is one of the most desirable places to go to law school because of both the city itself and the job opportunities following graduation. I remember Fordham had some additional questions on its application for admission that were not on other schools' applications (although I don't remember specifically what they were). I did not interview and am unsure of whether interviews are offered.

My advice on getting in would be to apply as early as possible. Most, if not all, law schools have rolling admissions. As the class fills up, the schools can afford to be pickier. Thus, applying early gives you better odds at getting in. This may also help in getting scholarships.

 Academics

Status: Current student, full-time
Dates of Enrollment: 9/2004-Submit Date
Survey Submitted: September 2005

The day program students tend to be more competitive (not necessarily smarter) than the evening program. The evening professors also seem nicer, and more forgiving than day profs. 1L, like any other school, is challenging. I don't have experience at any other law school. So it's hard to compare. In general, I actually felt 1L was not as bad as they made it out to be.

Status: Current student, part-time
Dates of Enrollment: 8/2003-Submit Date
Survey Submitted: December 2005

The classes are good. Classes related to corporate law are plentiful. There are decent IP-related classes as well. The program is definitely tilted towards day students, making life a little more difficult for evening students. But all in all, not too much to complain about (aside from the schedule of classes available for evening students—sometimes they position a core class in such a manner that it conflicts with many other classes).

Status: Alumnus/a, part-time
Dates of Enrollment: 8/2001-12/2004
Survey Submitted: April 2005

The evening program often gets the short-shift at Fordham. While day and evening classes are often the same quality, I found the selection much more limited. Furthermore, there is nothing to prevent day students from taking evening classes (and vice versa); so while this is a boon for non-working evening students or day students who did not want to take classes during the day, it was very difficult to schedule classes around a job. Good classes filled up early, even in the evening.

That being said about scheduling difficulties, the quality of classes and professors are excellent. Many of the professors will make an effort to get to know their students and one adjunct even took the entire class (35 people) out to dinner on his own tab at an upscale restaurant in an effort to have people get to know each other better. Furthermore, now that I have graduated, I have called on various professors and deans for help and advice in my job and there has never been a failure to return my call, even professors whose class I did not take. While securities law classes are considered excellent and very popular, it was a subject in which I had no interest. That being said, there was a wide selection of classes focused on other topics and when I could not find a class to exactly match my interest, the school was helpful in guiding me through an independent study.

Status: Current student, full-time
Dates of Enrollment: 8/2002-Submit Date
Survey Submitted: April 2005

The first-year curriculum is pretty much the typical 1L law school curriculum. All the 1L and many of the upper-level courses are graded on a curve. After the first-year requirements, the only other required classes are corporations and professional responsibility. Fordham has a good variety of upper-level classes, whether you want to focus on anti-discrimination law and community economic development or corporate finance and securities regulation, Fordham's faculty and course offerings are generally quite strong.

The clinical program is also excellent and it appeals to a lot of students, meaning that for much of the day the clinic is noisy and difficult to work in. Getting into popular classes is generally not too difficult, with the exception of one or two popular seminars. The workload is generally very heavy across the board—

although a few students try to take classes with professors with reputations for being easier, most students are motivated and take classes relevant to their future careers. The cafeteria sells a whole lot of coffee and you see a whole lot of overtired people in November and December and April and May.

Status: Current student, full-time
Dates of Enrollment: 8/2003-Submit Date
Survey Submitted: July 2004

Academics are, of course, central to the Fordham experience. Although an occasional professor seems an odd fit for the course or the material, most are experts in their fields. Some classes are also taught by adjunct professors, so students get working knowledge based on actual New York practice. Grading is similar to that at other top-tier schools; most students get B's, some get A's, a handful get C's, and no one gets below a C unless they try. Upperclassmen get to register first, and registration is done both online and by phone, so popular classes go fast. But Fordham features a waitlist that gives you some chance of getting into a class even if it is full should someone else drop out. (I can't say how useful that is; I got all my requested courseload this year.) The workload is extreme, but that's what law school is all about.

Status: Current student, full-time
Dates of Enrollment: 8/2003-Submit Date
Survey Submitted: June 2004

The faculty is really great. Professors are, for the most part, very welcoming and helpful in the first year. There are certainly a few bad eggs, but largely most professors are eager to help you. It is not hard to get face time with professors in the first year. Most first-year classes have 80 students, and all first-years have one class with only 40 students. Registration for the second year was not a problem for me, although rumor has it that some extremely popular classes can be difficult to get into.

Status: Current student, full-time
Dates of Enrollment: 8/2002-Submit Date
Survey Submitted: February 2004

The classes and professors at Fordham are fantastic. Popular classes are not necessarily easy to get. Fordham's registration system is slow and frustrating. Registration starts at 7 a.m. and can either be done over the phone (busy signal) or online (web page error). Although both systems are usually fine, during the morning of registration they are not. Classes close out quickly. I'm two-for-two on getting into classes on the waitlist though. Grading is like at any other law school. The majority of classes are curved, so it's anyone's guess how good you'll do. The workload is tough first year. Every time you get a grip on things, they seem to up the ante. As bad as it is though, it's very manageable. You just have to be willing to put in lots of time. The upper-level classes have varied work. A few are very intense, but most of them don't require a ton of work.

Status: Alumnus/a, full-time
Dates of Enrollment: 9/1999-5/2002
Survey Submitted: September 2003

I thought the quality of teaching at Fordham spans the full spectrum from excellent to pathetic. Some professors (mostly practicing attorneys) are true experts in their field, but others may be Ivy League law school grads who opted for the academic life and really don't know all that much about any particular field. The curve has gotten up to par with Ivy law schools recently to combat the job market crunch. Popular classes are not hard to get into once you're willing to wait a semester or two.

Status: Current student, full-time
Dates of Enrollment: 2/2001-Submit Date
Survey Submitted: September 2003

The Fordham faculty is very strong. I'm in my third year. I've had two or three duds, but 14 or 15 terrific teachers. We have a new dean, a former Supreme Court clerk and member of the faculty who is young and dynamic, and a new academic dean who is deeply committed to public interest law and as personable and smart as they come. Several of our professors have written leading casebooks and hornbooks.

The first-year program is standardized in American law schools and at Fordham: Torts, Contracts, Property, Criminal Law, Constitutional Law and Legal Writing. As at other law schools, there are very few requirements after first year.

Read all of Vault's Law School Surveys at www.vault.com/lawschool — get complete surveys on top law schools, expert advice on applicaton essays, LSAT prep and more.

VAULT CAREER LIBRARY 431

Fordham requires students to take Corporate Law and strongly encourages Evidence. We have an outstanding Evidence professor, a national authority and the author of one of the leading evidence casebooks, who is as entertaining and knowledgeable as a lecturer can be. One of my professors is a sitting federal judge.

In addition to the regular academic program, Fordham has an outstanding clinic program. I say this from firsthand experience. I spent a semester as a student in our Criminal Law clinic (there are also clinics for Immigration, Family, Tax, Bankruptcy and so on). The three professors supervising the Criminal clinics are terrific lawyers, so the level of practice in the clinic is very high. It provides a great experience for a young lawyer's first exposure to practice.

Grading at Fordham is very tough. The grades are governed by a strict curve. Before grades can be entered, professors have to send their grades to the registrar so that he can make sure the grades conform to the curve. Until this year the middle of our curve was a B, while other schools in New York City, including Columbia and NYU set the middle at B+. This year, Fordham shifted the curve up so that the mid-grade is a B+. In terms of taking popular classes, third-years get first choice. I have been able to take all of my first-choice classes, though I had to wait a year to get into the Evidence class.

 # Employment Prospects

Status: Current student, part-time
Dates of Enrollment: 8/2003-Submit Date
Survey Submitted: December 2005

Great prospects for employment in the New York area. Especially if you are interested in corporate law, the jobs are plentiful. The same is true for IP law and SEC. Fordham is not as well regarded by firms as NYU, Columbia or Cornell in the New York area, but it is not far behind. The location is definitely a major plus in terms of looking for a job. The career placement office is adequate, and there are many programs geared towards helping individuals find jobs. I had no problems finding employment, and the statistics for bar pass-rates for Fordham are also good.

Status: Current student, full-time
Dates of Enrollment: 8/2000-Submit Date
Survey Submitted: April 2005

Fordham has a very strong alumni base that is very active in helping students get post-graduate jobs, as well as internships while in school. The Fordham alumni are very active and helpful with Fordham-sponsored events (job searches, career panels, mock interviewing, recommendation giving and mentoring). They are always very eager to help and also accessible to Fordham students. Graduates from Fordham Law get placed in very prestigious firms, governmental positions and nonprofit organizations, and similarly obtain prestigious and highly coveted federal clerkships and fellowships. I obtained both my internships and my post-graduate job through Fordham alumni. Most of my classmates have post-graduate jobs or offers and also benefitted from tapping into the alumni resources at Fordham. The strong alumni base at the offices where I interviewed was integral in getting the position. Fordham has an extended on-campus interviewing and recruiting program every fall and spring in which all of the big, small and medium sized firms, as well as government employers attend. They also have public interest job and career fairs which they hold every spring, and the Fordham faculty also hold seminars for students interested in clerkships and fellowships. There are also several internship programs that help to place students in the internships of their choice during the summers and throughout the school year both for credit and for pay. Fordham is very much committed to the employability of their students, as well as their academic enrichment.

Status: Current student, full-time
Dates of Enrollment: 8/2002-Submit Date
Survey Submitted: April 2005

This is an area where Fordham really is much better than the *U.S. News* ranking would indicate. We are interviewed and recruited right up there with the Top Five schools because we are in NYC and have a great reputation at all the big firms and many of the public interest organizations in the city. The alumni network is also great and quite involved. Also, one of the best things about Fordham is that you can get credit for doing an externship. I got to work for a district court judge for a semester, and plenty of people I know did similar types of work. It's an amazing opportunity to meet people and see what you want to do.

The big problem, though, is that typically only about half or two-thirds of the class graduates with jobs. It's really easy if you're in the top 25 percent but otherwise it's much harder, and the career services department seems to work hard at trying, but it just doesn't always work. Also, Fordham has just recently stepped up its clerkship advising and that has made a huge difference in increasing the number of people that got clerkships this year.

Status: Current student, full-time
Dates of Enrollment: 8/2002-Submit Date
Survey Submitted: April 2005

Fordham is known as a BigLaw law school. Many people do go to BigLaw firms and make the big bucks. But there's also a good public interest program—the Stein Scholar Program—and a good international human rights program—the Crowley Program. I'm clerking for a federal district court judge next year, as are a number of my colleagues. If you know what you want to do, there are a ton of Fordham alumni in the city who are willing to help you get there.

Status: Alumnus/a, full time
Dates of Enrollment: 8/1998-5/2001
Survey Submitted: April 2004

The dedication of Fordham alumni is striking, and the reputation of the school as producing hardworking, less than arrogant (and perhaps less than brilliant) associates carries over to the work world and is borne out there. After all, the practice of law is less rocket science than dedicated hard work and much of it teamwork, all of which I think was fostered by a good sense of school spirit. Clerkships are certainly possible, and alums make up a healthy percentage of NY area clerks.

Status: Alumnus/a, full-time
Dates of Enrollment: 9/1999-5/2002
Survey Submitted: April 2004

The school does seem to have a strong placement record with big firms that have New York offices. It seems that students in the top half to top third land jobs with the big firms. Students in the bottom half can have a much harder time. Internship opportunities are fairly strong due to Fordham's strong base in the New York City area. Most firms seem to appreciate Fordham graduates, although the school is still considered a local law school that is not particularly prestigious, even compared to schools like Penn or Georgetown. Fordham is considered on par with BU, BYU, Vanderbilt and other "higher ranked" schools that are below the Top 14. Many Fordham graduates have made partner at large firms in recent years, which will further aid the school's recruiting efforts. With respect to large firm recruiting, the school is very much a well-oiled machine. The career services people know what they are doing in this area, and the process runs smoothly from start to finish.

 # Quality of Life

Status: Current student, part-time
Dates of Enrollment: 8/2003-Submit Date
Survey Submitted: December 2005

The building at Columbus Circle has a perfect location, but is not the nicest (i.e., not maintained very well). The area is great, but housing is very expensive because the school is located in the heart of Manhattan. I am not sure about on-campus living, but living in a regular apartment nearby costs a small fortune, adding to the already large cost of attending school. The subway obviously makes commuting easy, as is the case with most places in NYC. The building itself is not kept as clean as I would like. The cafeterias are adequate, but not great. I don't know much about the outside facilities because I didn't venture outside too much. There is not much land, given the location (Columbus Circle). There is some nice shrubbery surrounding the buildings however. The computer facilities are adequate. You must pre-pay about $75 per year in computer fees and you get that credited towards printing out documents at five cents a page.

Status: Current student, full-time
Dates of Enrollment: 9/2004-Submit Date
Survey Submitted: September 2005

Like every school, there are cliques. Some people hang out a lot with their classmates, and others aren't in law school to make friends. You can pretty much tell the first day of school who fits into which category. Facilities, comparatively, are not as nice as other NYC schools. But not horrible either. Location is the best thing about Fordham.

Status: Current student, full-time
Dates of Enrollment: 8/2002-Submit Date
Survey Submitted: April 2005

Fordham's law school campus is small, as Fordham's main campus is in the Bronx and the law school is in midtown Manhattan. The campus is right next to Lincoln Center, about as wealthy and safe a neighborhood as you will find in the city. The campus is small, which may be a good thing; the law school takes up about half of the campus and you recognize people walking around school, unlike a law school that is situated among 20,000-plus other students. It has a nice courtyard for when the weather is warm. However, in general, the facilities at Fordham are mediocre, at best. The library is good and features very comfortable chairs (important, as you could be sitting in them for hours) and the school is trying to improve its technology with more outlets for laptops and improved wireless access. But the school has too few computers available for student use, a number of small classrooms without windows, ugly 1970s concrete architecture, tiny, cramped offices for journals and student groups and a lousy cafeteria (although there are lots of restaurants nearby).

Status: Current student, full-time
Dates of Enrollment: 8/2002-Submit Date
Survey Submitted: April 2005

There's a dorm that's relatively inexpensive (for being in the heart of NYC), where you live in suites with a couple of other students. Fordham is located in probably the safest and one of the nicest parts of Manhattan. I walk around at all hours and take the subway from here at all hours and feel completely safe doing so. The law school cafeteria is horrendous, but there's a better cafeteria in the undergrad/business building next door. There are restaurants nearby, including a great Whole Foods at Columbus Circle. The law school building itself is dingy; the temperature is out of control and there's not enough light anywhere, but there's a huge revamping that's going to happen over the next 25 years (maybe you'll see it!). The library is really nice but very crowded.

Status: Current student, full-time
Dates of Enrollment: 8/2003-Submit Date
Survey Submitted: April 2005

The quality of life at Fordham is very positive: there is a lot of outreach to students and interest in well-being. I have heard others who have had particularly rough times, but for the most part, I have been happy. I find the administration to be responsive to student concerns and very available.

Status: Current student, full-time
Dates of Enrollment: 8/2004-Submit Date
Survey Submitted: September 2004

The facilities are very good, and improvements are underway. The law school has wireless Internet access, and there are electrical outlets at every seat in the classrooms. Most students bring a laptop to class every day. The professors and students are friendly and always ready to help out whenever you need them. Many professors even give you their home phone numbers so that you can get a hold of them more easily and more often.

Status: Current student, full-time
Dates of Enrollment: 8/2002-Submit Date
Survey Submitted: February 2004

The campus is in the middle of Manhattan. It doesn't get any better. The dorms are relatively inexpensive for New York and look like, well, dorms. The housing is mostly only available for people from outside of the metropolitan area. It's very easy to find an apartment nearby though. The campus is small (it's in New York City), but nice. It's right next to Lincoln Center and also has an amazing quad outside of the public view (although the public can enter, they usually don't). The law school building is good but not great. It reminds me of high

school. Some of the classrooms are renovated and nice, with ethernet terminals at every desk. But some others are older, uncomfortable and have bad acoustics. Every classroom has outlets for each chair, but not necessarily ethernet terminals. There's a new wireless network, too. The campus is very safe and I know of no crime. From walking near the campus after midnight to leaving stuff unwatched in the library. I've never had a problem and know of no one who has.

Status: Alumnus/a, full-time
Dates of Enrollment: 8/2001-5/2003
Survey Submitted: September 2003

There are dorms connected by an underground corridor to the building where classes are held. The dorms are nice and quite large. They are somewhat expensive, but a great deal compared to New York City living in general. First-year law students are guaranteed a spot, but upperclassman students must go through a lottery. The campus also houses the graduate social work and business schools, as well as some undergraduate programs (acting, arts). There are also many many restaurants and bars. There is a large dining hall on the campus. To get to it from the law school you need to walk through an underground corridor. The dining hall has many different selections, such as frozen yogurt, hot dishes that change daily, a salad bar, pizza, hamburgers, wraps. There are meal plans or you can pay a la carte. There is also a small snack bar right near the law portion of the campus that has sushi, pizza, sandwiches, cereal, yogurt.

Social Life

Status: Current student, part-time
Dates of Enrollment: 8/2003-Submit Date
Survey Submitted: December 2005

A lot of bars in the area. I think that, as with any NYC school, the opportunities for engaging in a plentiful social life are there. It depends on the people. As an evening law student, the social life was less critical, and it shows in the evening student body. There isn't as much socializing as with day students I believe, but that is largely due to the fact that many evening students hold full-time jobs and often have families. There is also less tension in the evening students with regard to grades as far as I could tell, perhaps because many people already have jobs and the people are not competing for Law Review as much as day students.

Status: Current student, full-time
Dates of Enrollment: 9/2004-Submit Date
Survey Submitted: September 2005

The school, and many of the journals and clubs have a lot of social events. Most of the events are held close to school, so it's convenient, and a significant amount of the events are either free or a very small cover for an open bar.

Status: Alumnus/a, part-time
Dates of Enrollment: 8/2001-12/2004
Survey Submitted: April 2005

Fordham students have an active social life. There are get-togethers hosted by the student association at local bars, tons of clubs and activities and bi-weekly pizza nights for the evening students. Day student life seems very different from evening student life and I can only speak to the latter. Day students seem to always be hanging out and socializing, but evening students tend to have families and jobs and see school as another commitment in their schedules. This does not mean you are not going to make friends as an evening student. I met my best friend as a fellow evening student at Fordham. In fact, there was almost no competition between evening students and people shared notes and outlines constantly. Since evening students had so many other commitments, they were more than understanding when a fellow student missed class and always helped out. Evening students also grab the occasional drink after class and on the weekends but law school was only one thing on our plates and often took a back seat when it came to making social plans.

Status: Alumnus/a, full-time
Dates of Enrollment: 8/1998-5/2005
Survey Submitted: April 2005

There are many social organizations in the school. The interests range from social to religious, from ethical to academic. There is rarely a week night that the organizations isn't holding a gathering. Symposia, talks and general student

Read all of Vault's Law School Surveys at www.vault.com/lawschool — get complete surveys on top law schools, expert advice on applicaton essays, LSAT prep and more.

VAULT CAREER LIBRARY   433

meetings abound. There are plenty of possibilities for social outreach. These range from teaching, to legal training, to domestic violence outreach and everything in between.

Status: Current student, full-time
Dates of Enrollment: 8/2002-Submit Date
Survey Submitted: February 2004

Fordham has a great social life. My section during first year went out all the time. There are bars and restaurants within a few blocks of school. The most common hang-out is probably Lincoln Park. It's hard to walk in and not find a law student. The best part about Fordham students is they work hard and play hard. Students know when it's time to sit in the library and to go out whenever they can. The students are also very friendly. Although law school is very competitive by nature, everyone there is very supportive of each other and really just trying to get by on their own merits without trying to bring other students down. Because of this, there's a more comfortable social life, no one's out to get anyone. There're also lots of events with free food and open bars. It's rare to find a week without them.

Status: Alumnus/a, full-time
Dates of Enrollment: 8/2000-5/2003
Survey Submitted: September 2003

If you think you're going to make up for being a nerd in college, forget it. While there are weekly bar nights, you'll be lucky in your first year if you can go out any more than one night a week. It gets a little easier in the second and third years, especially if you've already gotten a job through the on-campus program after your first year. You make friends initially with those in your "section," which you're assigned to your first year. People also bond with others in their journal or moot court group. Fordham tends to be a bit cliquish, but there are also quite a few down-to-earth people who are neither snobby nor obsessive. The school-sponsored events tend to be at dive bars about a mile north of campus. They're fun if you don't mind the crowds and the bad beer. There is no room for house parties, so most of the partying is done out.

Hofstra University School of Law

Admissions Office
121 Hofstra University
Hempstead, NY 11549
Admissions phone: (516) 463-5916
Admissions e-mail: lawadmissions@hofstra.edu
Admissions URL:
http://www.hofstra.edu/Academics/Law/law_admissions.cfm

 Admissions

Status: Current student, full-time
Dates of Enrollment: 8/2004-Submit Date
Survey Submitted: October 2005

The admissions process was similar to that of other accredited law schools. It does appear that Hofstra focuses on more than just high LSATs and strong undergraduate GPAs, although these are obviously very important. Hofstra seems to attract a student body that is diverse in terms of background and the average age of entering students is 24, which is young, but most students have some work experience. This shows that the school sees a benefit in students who have demonstrated that they are strong not only academically, but also in the workplace.

The school places particularly strong emphasis on community involvement and public service, more so than most other law schools, and especially in the New York area. Therefore, those applying should consider their experience with this area and include it in their applications. The essay question was a basic "why do you want to go to law school"-type question. A strong essay would probably go a long way, as it appears that the administration cares about the people who apply rather than just the statistics. I did not go on an interview for the school, and I do not know anyone who did such an interview; however, the school was more than willing to meet students interested and I myself took this opportunity to meet members of the faculty. In terms of selectivity, on a scale of one to 10, with 10 being most competitive and one being least competitive, I would probably put Hofstra at seven-and-a-half.

Status: Alumnus/a, full-time
Dates of Enrollment: 8/2000-5/2003
Survey Submitted: March 2006

The process isn't that different from applying to college—type your application so that it's neat, write an essay on the subject of your choice and have your LSAT scores sent in. There were no interviews.

My feeling is that the school is moderately selective. Clearly, it's not top tier, but it's not like the doors are wide open. For a NYC-area school, it's fairly easy to get in.

Status: Alumnus/a, full-time
Dates of Enrollment: 8/2001-5/2004
Survey Submitted: March 2005

The admissions process is similar to any other school of comparable rank (lower end of Top 100). The school has become more selective recently, but that is a product of more applications because of the slow economy not because of the school having a more stringent admissions policy.

Status: Current student, full-time
Dates of Enrollment: 8/2003-Submit Date
Survey Submitted: November 2004

There was no interview process. The school offers a free application if you apply online, which was nice. I heard back from the admissions department within two weeks and they offered me a scholarship. I've even heard that if they don't let you into the full-time program, some people have gotten into the part-

time or night school with a scholarship and you can then try to transfer to full-time after the first year.

Status: Current student, full-time
Dates of Enrollment: 8/2004-Submit Date
Survey Submitted: October 2004

The admissions process was terrible. I didn't get in the first time I applied but transferred into the school for my second year of law school. I was very involved as an undergraduate in the same school and they did not take anything into consideration except for a standardized exam. When I reapplied, the application process went quickly but only after I personally brought my application material to the school (since they lost everything). The only thing you need to get in is a good LSAT score. It doesn't matter how well you do in undergrad or how many activities you are involved in. There is no interview process and the only thing you have to write is a personal statement if you are entering as a first-year, or a transfer letter if you are entering as a transfer. It seems that as a transfer as long as you were in the top third of your class you were automatically accepted. There are about 20 transfers.

Status: Current student, full-time
Dates of Enrollment: 8/2003-Submit Date
Survey Submitted: January 2004

Hofstra is located about 30 minutes east of NYC. From what I hear, it is getting more competitive. Student body is very diverse, ranging from professionals to fresh-out-of-college students. Hofstra has students from around the world in the JD and LLM programs.

 Academics

Status: Current student, full-time
Dates of Enrollment: 8/2004-Submit Date
Survey Submitted: October 2005

The academic program at Hofstra is stronger than the school gets credit for. The professors at Hofstra are, on the whole, excellent at conveying the material, and most are quite good at keeping students interested. What I have found most refreshing about the professors has been their accessibility and their basically uniform willingness to meet with students by appointment or during office hours to answer questions about the course, about career planning or even just to discuss current events. On the whole, professors at Hofstra are engaging and receptive to the students. They are also quite involved in their respective practice areas and publish frequently on average. The classes are often very interactive. About half of the professors from my experience and from hearing about others' experiences, employ the Socratic Method, with others using a more voluntary system of participation. Generally class participation does not count, even though some professors say that it does (of course there are exceptions to this rule).

The grading varies widely, which is a downside. Your GPA at the end of the first year may be highly dependent on the professors you have gotten rather than the classes you have taken, which tends to be frustrating considering the importance of first-year grades. There needs to be a more structured system of grading because although there is a "curve," some professors do not follow it. Similarly, the workload can vary depending on the professor. In my Property class, I had around 50 pages of reading per class. Other students I know had markedly less—as low as five pages per class! Generally though most professors during my first year assigned around 30 to 40 pages per class, which was very manageable.

In terms of getting the classes one wants, most everyone gets all the classes they want by third year, although sometimes they may have to wait until third year to take some seminars, which are generally much smaller and sometimes require students to show an interest in the area. This is both a positive and negative; positive because students are more likely to participate and contribute to

Read all of Vault's Law School Surveys at www.vault.com/lawschool — get complete surveys on top law schools, expert advice on applicaton essays, LSAT prep and more.

VAULT CAREER LIBRARY   435

interesting classroom discussion (or online discussion, which most classes employ through message boards). But also negative because the student diversity in the class may be compromised. On the whole, though, I have found that classes are diverse. Hofstra has an exceptionally strong family law program, and for those interested in family law, I would venture to say that it is the best program in the country, with professors who are revolutionary and well-known in the field. Likewise, the school has a strong real estate program. The journals are extremely competitive, with the *Labor and Employment Law Journal* being in the top 20 of labor law journals. There is a healthy choice among clinics, with clinics being added, it seems, by the year, and the administration is quite willing to listen to suggestions.

Status: Alumnus/a, full-time
Dates of Enrollment: 8/2000-5/2003
Survey Submitted: March 2006

The professors are first-rate. The classes offered are typical to that of other law institutions. There isn't a huge focus on clinics, though they are available.

Status: Alumnus/a, full-time
Dates of Enrollment: 8/2001-5/2004
Survey Submitted: March 2005

The shining light at Hofstra is the faculty. Great professors who, for the most part, are accessible and welcoming of interaction with students. However, professors become frustrated with the bottom-end, unqualified students who not only can't handle law school studies, but don't even try (are constantly unprepared for class and don't care) and are only at Hofstra because they can afford the tuition and don't feel like getting a job.

Status: Current student, full-time
Dates of Enrollment: 8/2003-Submit Date
Survey Submitted: November 2004

The professors, for the most part, are outstanding. I had great professors for my first year. There is a large selection of classes but trying to get into some is hard. There is also not a great selection of class times. You may have a seven hour gap in between two classes. The workload is to be expected and the grades are on a B curve. The first year, it was rumored that most of the scholarship students were put into one section, which had harder professors than the other section so that the scholarship students were competing against one another.

Status: Current student, full-time
Dates of Enrollment: 8/2004-Submit Date
Survey Submitted: October 2004

The workload is ridiculous, as is any law school's. It is a theory-based school so you don't learn statutes but instead the theory and history behind the law. The professors are excellent and many classes of interest are offered. I have not yet experienced the grading but I have a take home exam, which did not happen in my previous law school. Getting popular courses is almost impossible unless you know someone on the staff who will help you.

Status: Alumnus/a, full-time
Dates of Enrollment: 9/1997-5/2000
Survey Submitted: April 2004

The professors were topnotch, with some exceptions. Grading was consistent with one exception (students would get an asterisk next to the grade given by this professor on their transcript to help explain why it was so much lower). The old dean was excellent (now president of the university).

The top 20 percent of the students can compete with any school in the country; the bottom 25 percent are not great and that affects the classroom. Although the students are competitive, the overwhelming majority are not cutthroat. Students help each other where and when they can, which makes the overall experience much more enjoyable.

Status: Current student, full-time
Dates of Enrollment: 8/2003-Submit Date
Survey Submitted: January 2004

In my opinion, professors are among the best nationwide. Many of them wrote textbooks and supplements that are used nationwide and are graduates from top law schools. Students can easily talk to professors and get individual help. Workload is quite heavy and challenging, but that also means being more

competitive than most schools. From what I observe, tuition at Hofstra is fairly high, but that translates into higher-quality education with topnotch professors.

 Employment Prospects

Status: Current student, full-time
Dates of Enrollment: 8/2004-Submit Date
Survey Submitted: October 2005

The employment prospects at Hofstra are fairly strong, if students are interested in working in the tri-state area. The top 10 percent of the student body after the first year will generally get interviews with the top corporate firms. At the same time, the networking at Hofstra is pretty good, especially if students join certain clubs like the International Law Fraternity or cultural groups. The journals also help students in the job search. As such, the average graduate of Hofstra will find herself or himself in a good position, averaging around $70,000 or more the first year out of law school (keep in mind that this includes those who do clerkships, which generally pay less). Graduates obtain jobs that run the gamut from public service (legal aid, government jobs) to corporate law. There are many opportunities for internships during the semester, with judges, government agencies, bar associations and law firms in Long Island. A student interested in working during second or third year will find many opportunities are available to do so.

Overall, I would say that students not in the top of the class should try to take advantage of these opportunities, or through clubs or journals, for networking purposes, because the career services is somewhat lacking in helping students interested in corporate law who do not have the grades. This is not the case for students interested in family law or public service, where the school is exceptionally strong in exposing students to such opportunities.

Status: Alumnus/a, full-time
Dates of Enrollment: 8/2000-5/2003
Survey Submitted: March 2006

To participate in on-campus recruiting and actually get a job, you really need two things: (1) a GPA in the top 10 percent; and (2) to be on Law Review. Without either of those two credentials, your chance of getting a job in a big NYC law firm is really slim.

It was my impression that for those students who are not on any journal and who are not near the top of the class, the school's recruiting OCR office was of very little help. Really, the focus is on that small segment of the student population that can compete for big firm jobs.

Status: Alumnus/a, full-time
Dates of Enrollment: 8/2001-5/2004
Survey Submitted: March 2005

Depends on what you want to do. If you want to work in a big Manhattan law firm that pays top dollar you had better be on Law Review AND be well in the top 10 percent. If you do not have those numbers, you had better know someone at one of these firms. If you have neither of these, you have no chance of landing one of these jobs. Even the top three Long Island firms that pay the best on Long Island require top grades. If you want to work at other Long Island or smaller Manhattan firms (meaning starting salary of $40k) then you have a good shot but still need to finish with a respectable rank.

Status: Current student, full-time
Dates of Enrollment: 8/2003-Submit Date
Survey Submitted: November 2004

The employers (private firms) that come to campus are outstanding. With the exception of two or three firms, they are all in the Vault 100. There are only about 30 that come to campus, as compared to other schools, that have 100 to 200 firms. However, only students in the top 10 percent of the class will even be looked at. It's the same 20 or so students who get all of the interviews. Even students in the top 10 percent struggle to find a job with one of these firms. If you are not in the top 10 percent, you will have to be pretty much on your own for the job search. I was in the top 10 percent and fortunately did get a job with one of the big firms, but I still sent out over 100 resumes just to be safe.

Status: Current student, full-time
Dates of Enrollment: 8/2004-Submit Date
Survey Submitted: October 2004

There is excellent on-campus recruiting but they are looking only for the top of the class. The school has an excellent reputation, however, top paying jobs only seek the top students.

Status: Alumnus/a, full-time
Dates of Enrollment: 9/1997-5/2000
Survey Submitted: April 2004

Campus recruiting is good, due to proximity to NYC. Career services tends to focus on the top 10 percent of the class.

Status: Current student, full-time
Dates of Enrollment: 8/2003-Submit Date
Survey Submitted: January 2004

From what I saw, virtually all top students have offers from big firms. Firms from NYC and Long Island continue to recruit. Career office is very friendly and accessible.

 # Quality of Life

Status: Current student, full-time
Dates of Enrollment: 8/2004-Submit Date
Survey Submitted: October 2005

The housing at Hofstra is decent; there is a new dorm for graduate and law students, which keeps life interesting because the residents are diverse. At the same time, the apartments, while close to campus, could use updating. The campus is very attractive, with gardens and trees, and the facilities at the law school are technologically current and always improving. There is wireless Internet throughout the classroom; the library is fairly extensive and subscribes to multiple databases useful for research purposes. There are two computer labs also, and there is rarely a time (in fact this has never happened to me) when a student would not have access to a computer and a printer. The surrounding neighborhood is in Hempstead and Uniondale, NY. The school is located next to an elementary school, so at least during the day, it is safe to walk around without fear of crime. After dark, the neighborhood is a little more dangerous from what I hear, although I know of no one who has had any problems. Most students commute, and usually there are not a whole lot of cars at the school late at night. The safety is good on the whole—public safety paroles the campus 24/7.

Status: Alumnus/a, full-time
Dates of Enrollment: 8/2000-5/2003
Survey Submitted: March 2006

Hofstra is basically a commuter school, which most of its students living back home with their parents. The dorms are not particularly comfortable and the immediate neighboring area is not exactly safe. However, the school is a quick commute to cities like Long Beach, which is a great city for young people.

Status: Alumnus/a, full-time
Dates of Enrollment: 8/2001-5/2004
Survey Submitted: March 2005

Quality of life is OK at Hofstra. Facilities are good both in the law school and the larger undergraduate campus. Parking is a nightmare and that's an understatement. I'd rather have a root canal with sedation than have to go through that disaster again. Dining is surprisingly good. Neighborhood is not too bad during the day but dangerous at night (not uncommon to read about violent crime in the area or towards Hofstra students).

Status: Current student, full-time
Dates of Enrollment: 8/2003-Submit Date
Survey Submitted: November 2004

The program is fine. I wouldn't say great. Most of the people are nice and not overly competitive, although there are a few bad apples. The problem is that its a commuter school so often people have friends or family nearby and don't want

to socialize much at school. Also, a lot of people live far distances and want to get home to avoid traffic.

The housing is also OK. There is New Complex that houses mostly law students and a few graduate students. The dorm is fairly new with large bedrooms and a small common room between two rooms. There are study rooms and a large parking lot.

Speaking of parking, parking is horrendous and the school really should provide a lot exclusively for the law students. If you don't get to school by 8 a.m., especially now with night school, forget ever getting a spot in any lot. You will have to park on side streets or walk long distances from the lots on the other side of campus.

The law school building itself looks like its been frozen in the 70s. But they are slowly remodeling the classrooms. Those that have been done are really nice and modern. There are a few of the large lecture halls that have yet to be touched but I've noticed some progress over the months. The library just added much needed study rooms. About eight were added to the existing five. Plus, they added a large study area which was also needed. The resources in the library and the library staff are outstanding.

The dining areas could use better food caterers and it wouldn't hurt to get some name brand chains like Subway or McDonald's. Sbarro is the only one you will find.

Status: Current student, full-time
Dates of Enrollment: 8/2004-Submit Date
Survey Submitted: October 2004

The campus is beautiful, however, once it gets dark it is not safe at all. It is located in a horrible neighborhood and there is no security in the academic side of campus at night so anyone is welcome to go in. The classrooms are beautiful, with an outlet for every seat and the wireless services are excellent in all the classrooms.

Status: Alumnus/a, full-time
Dates of Enrollment: 9/1997-5/2000
Survey Submitted: April 2004

The campus is beautiful. Housing is relatively new. Overall the neighborhood is safe with some petty crimes such as car break-ins. The dining halls are fair and expensive.

Status: Current student, full-time
Dates of Enrollment: 8/2003-Submit Date
Survey Submitted: January 2004

Hofstra is probably the best place in Long Island—a suburban setting where you can easily go to NYC and also enjoy a quiet atmosphere. Compared to NYC, I think living standard is definitely better. The campus is really nice with a national botanical garden. Food is much better than most other colleges. Outside of the campus, Hempstead is kind of dangerous. The school has public safety patrolling.

 # Social Life

Status: Current student, full-time
Dates of Enrollment: 8/2004-Submit Date
Survey Submitted: October 2005

The social life at the school is very good considering it's law school! There are two school dances during the year that are very well attended by the student body (one in the fall and one in the spring). Happy hours are commonly held by various groups and organizations, at local bars (there are several around, although there are not many that are within walking distance; it's pretty much assumed that students either have their own transportation or have easy access to it). There is a plethora of restaurants in Long Island, from the very cheap to the very expensive, and many close to the school, including a great mall (Roosevelt Field). There are various lectures held that have been interesting, as well as a few debates. The students are especially participatory in Student Bar Association events, which have included intramural sports such as volleyball, softball and flag football. Free food is often available from various

Read all of Vault's Law School Surveys at www.vault.com/lawschool — get complete surveys on top law schools, expert advice on applicaton essays, LSAT prep and more.

VAULT CAREER LIBRARY 437

organizations—always popular with the law students! The Hofstra Law community is warm, tight-knit, and extremely cooperative.

Status: Alumnus/a, full-time
Dates of Enrollment: 8/2000-5/2003
Survey Submitted: March 2006

Because it is a commuter school, people tend to go home after school. That being said, you can usually find a group of law students at a nearby bar drinking on Thursday nights.

Status: Alumnus/a, full-time
Dates of Enrollment: 8/2001-5/2004
Survey Submitted: March 2005

Whether you like the social scene or not depends on where you are in life and what you are at law school for. If your parents are footing the bill, you're 22 years old, don't want to get a job and you don't care how you do, then Club Hofstra can be a three-year Mardi Gras because there are plenty of bars in the area and there is always Manhattan.

Status: Current student, full-time
Dates of Enrollment: 8/2004-Submit Date
Survey Submitted: October 2004

There is no such thing except for the random happy hours on Thursdays for the law school.

Status: Alumnus/a, full-time
Dates of Enrollment: 9/1997-5/2000
Survey Submitted: April 2004

Bogart's is great and offers law school happy hours every Thursday, usually sponsored by one of the law school clubs. The club will get a couple bucks at the door and then there's a cash bar at happy hour rates. Athletics are really good also. Football is 1-AA but the team is usually nationally ranked. Men's lacrosse is 1-A and also nationally ranked. Women's lacrosse and basketball and men's basketball are competitive. Both the stadium and the arena are close enough to the law school to be an excellent "study break," especially on sunny days in the fall or spring.

Status: Current student, full-time
Dates of Enrollment: 8/2003-Submit Date
Survey Submitted: January 2004

There are many bars near the school. The giant Roosevelt Field Mall is right next to the school (about less than a mile). Many law school student organizations as well.

New York Law School

Admissions Office
57 Worth Street
New York, NY 10013
Admissions phone: (212) 431-2888 or (877) YES-NYLS
Admissions fax: (212) 966-1522
Admissions e-mail: admissions@nyls.edu
URL: http://nyls.edu/

Note: The school has chosen not to comment on the student surveys submitted.

 Admissions

Status: Current student, full-time
Dates of Enrollment: 8/2004-Submit Date
Survey Submitted: March 2006

New York Law School looks for the best in every applicant. Whether it is an applicant's dedication to community service, success in the workplace, commitment to extracurricular activities or strong personal statement, we rely on more than LSAT scores and undergraduate grades to build our community. New York Law School seeks new colleagues who will thrive in innovative, yet rigorous, academic programs.

Status: Alumnus/a, full-time
Dates of Enrollment: 9/2002-5/2005
Survey Submitted: September 2005

A significant rise in the number of law school applicants has forced most law schools to raise their academic standards. Therefore New York Law School, like all other schools pays particular attention to grades and LSAT scores. At one point New York Law School was considered a "safety school." However, that is no longer the case. The caliber of each entering class has improved tremendously and the school has become more selective about applicants.

Status: Alumnus/a, part-time
Dates of Enrollment: 9/1992-6/1997
Survey Submitted: March 2006

I had to complete the application, including an essay, and provide LSAT score, copies of transcripts from universities I had attended and a letter of recommendation. My suggestion is to write an essay that shows your passion for something, particularly something that you think should be improved and you would like to help improve.

Status: Current student, full-time
Dates of Enrollment: 8/2003-Submit Date
Survey Submitted: October 2004

When I applied, I think that it was easier to get in, mainly because it was the only school I got into. It was supposedly the hardest year on record for admissions though, so I didn't let it get to me. The school has become much more selective, though, and it's starting to show with our move up to the second tier.

Status: Alumnus/a, part-time
Dates of Enrollment: 8/1997-6/2001
Survey Submitted: October 2004

Acceptance was easy having applied from the West Coast. All the Eastern schools want to look like they get students from all over the country. When it comes to apply to NYC schools, if you are from outside the tri-state area, think twice about going outside Manhattan. The Manhattan schools are in nice areas, but outside they can be a little iffy.

Status: Current student, full-time
Dates of Enrollment: 1/2003-Submit Date
Survey Submitted: October 2003

With 6,000 applications for 470 positions, the school is selective. I had a 159 and 3.3 and was admitted.

Status: Alumnus/a, part-time
Dates of Enrollment: 8/1998-6/2002
Survey Submitted: September 2003

First I had to take the LSATs. The application process is quite simple. I had to complete a paper application, which can now be done online, and submit a personal essay along with two recommendations, which I got from my employer and a former professor. Then I had to secure my undergraduate transcripts. Other than that, there was a fee for filing the application; I believe it was $100 at that time. Then it was all a matter of waiting.

Status: Alumnus/a, full-time
Dates of Enrollment: 8/1997-6/1990
Survey Submitted: April 2004

Admission is based upon application only; i.e., no in-person interviews. Grades are important, but a high LSAT will compensate for a lower GPA. The school also looks for students with various interests and experiences, and is a good school for those who are seeking a "second career."

Status: Alumnus/a, full-time
Dates of Enrollment: 8/1998-6/2001
Survey Submitted: October 2003

Intense interviewing, essay-writing and background research.

Status: Alumnus/a, full-time
Dates of Enrollment: 8/1998-6/2001
Survey Submitted: September 2003

The admissions process was quite easy. Of course you had to fill out the application and write a personal statement, which is pretty standard among the law schools. There was no interview required, but I did visit the school on my own accord.

 Academics

Status: Current student, full-time
Dates of Enrollment: 8/2004-Submit Date
Survey Submitted: March 2006

The full-time faculty and instructional staff of 70 teach all the required courses and most of the elective courses. They have broad experience in law practice, public as well as private, and are actively engaged in legal scholarship. The law school also enjoys the contributions of more than 175 adjunct faculty members, consisting of attorneys, judges and other public officials who offer many elective courses each year in the fields of their expertise.

Students choose from two primary course sequences: the full-time day program and the part-time evening program. Full-time students usually complete the 86 credits required for the Juris Doctor in three years; part-time students in four years. The required courses include: Applied Analysis; Civil Procedure; Contracts I and II, Constitutional Law I and II, Criminal Law, Evidence, Property, Torts, and The Legal Profession. Students also complete two courses emphasizing the development of professional legal skills: a two-semester course on Legal Reasoning, Writing and Research, and a one-semester course on lawyering.

Read all of Vault's Law School Surveys at www.vault.com/lawschool — get complete surveys on top law schools, expert advice on applicaton essays, LSAT prep and more.

VAULT CAREER LIBRARY **439**

Status: Alumnus/a, full-time
Dates of Enrollment: 9/2002-5/2005
Survey Submitted: September 2005

Classes are rigorous and professors expect the most from their students. There is very little hand-holding, which forces students to quickly learn and develop skills required of attorneys. The online registration system allows students to plan out their schedules one semester in advance. Most students do get their first choice.

Grading (anonymous) is based on a curve and for the most part is fair. Students who work hard see the results. Professors are well-established in their particular area of expertise and most come from top-tier law schools. They are also very accessible and have a vested interest in seeing their students excel in the legal field. The workload is what is expected; there is a lot of work but with good time-management skills, most students will be able to balance school work, extracurricular activities and personal lives.

Status: Alumnus/a, part-time
Dates of Enrollment: 9/1992-6/1997
Survey Submitted: March 2006

The courses are very practitioner-oriented. I had no difficulty getting into courses that were in demand. Grading, professors and workload were demanding, for the most part. Some professors piled on reading assignments and others placed more emphasis on interactive exercises and writing.

Status: Current student, full-time
Dates of Enrollment: 8/2003-Submit Date
Survey Submitted: October 2004

I think that the academics are the same as any other school. The testing is what I hate (that might be just me personally, though). In one of my first-year classes, I ended up getting a C on the final but when we were given the breakdown, it was a matter of one question per grade. It just really bothered me that it was a matter of just a few questions on an extensive test that caused me to drop that far down the grading scale. I haven't been locked out of a class in three years, personally I think that the upper-level corporate and securities classes are second to none.

Status: Alumnus/a, part-time
Dates of Enrollment: 8/1997-6/2001
Survey Submitted: October 2004

The number of classes is amazing. You can take anything from Municipal Finance to International Finance. The evening program is heavy on corporate, finance, securities and real estate classes. Very few classes have limited size. However, this also means the B- curve still applies if class has over 18 students.

NYLS is the only NYC school on the B- curve, all others are on a B+ curve. This means that when you graduate the average student at NYLS has a 2.67 GPA, whereas every other law school alum in NYC will have a 3.33. If you are offered an academic scholarship based on maintaining a 3.2 GPA, figure on it being a one-year scholarship. The student body is very competitive, and most that get that offer lose it. A 3.2 will get you almost always on Law Review. At other NYC schools, you will not even get on a secondary journal with that low of a GPA, because of there grade inflation with B+ curves. With that curve, if you don't put in the effort, they will flunk you out. Bottom of the class is gone before graduation.

Professors are excellent. You will discover that students get very upset when professors from NYLS are cited in newspapers and on TV as being from NYU. There is a feeling that NYLS's ranking suffer because many voters are giving NYLS professors accomplishments to NYU's rankings. Outstanding group to learn from.

Status: Alumnus/a, full-time
Dates of Enrollment: 8/1998-6/2001
Survey Submitted: September 2003

NYLS is one of the only schools in the area that offers a part-time night program, which is great. Also great about the academics of the school is that many professors are also practicing attorneys. We study practical learning and aren't caught up in the theoretical B.S. that "better" schools focus on. For example, our Corporations class did more than just read the hundreds of boring cases on

reasons to pierce the corporate veil; we did an incorporation exercise. We had many judicial externship opportunities and classes like Trial Advocacy, where we would put on a mock trial so that we could learn by doing and not reading.

Another noteworthy class was New York Practice (Civil Procedure), where our textbook was not the casebooks but the hornbook of the GOD of civil procedure, Siegel. The professor, realizing that after the first semester of law school we all knew how to read a case, had us learn the rules of civil procedure from the hornbook.

One thing that's ironic about NYLS is that our grade point average curve was a lot stricter then at the "better" schools, so obtaining an A at a "better" school was like obtaining a B at NYLS. But because we didn't have Harvard or NYU in front of our JD we were assumed to be less worthy by prospective employers. However, like at every school you have your crackpot professors and ones that are so wrapped up in themselves, they almost break their arms patting themselves on the back. Workload was tolerable, but I worked and was on the Law Journal, so I can't really be a good judge of a good or bad workload. There was plenty of work and reading to do, and since I only went to NYLS, I can't compare it to other schools, but I don't see it as being any lighter or heavier than the others.

Status: Alumnus/a, full-time
Dates of Enrollment: 8/1997-6/1990
Survey Submitted: April 2004

The courses are challenging and demanding. The professors are generally excellent and do not teach through fear. Professors assign a lot of reading, but the workload is manageable once you learn how to separate the wheat from the chaffe. I've never been shut out of a class I wanted, and I do not know of anyone else who has either.

Status: Alumnus/a, full-time
Dates of Enrollment: 8/1998-6/2001
Survey Submitted: October 2003

Professors all well established in their respective fields of study and published.

Status: Alumnus/a, part-time
Dates of Enrollment: 8/1998-6/2002
Survey Submitted: September 2003

The evening law program was wonderful! They catered to full-time working adults who already had a lot on their plates. The first year, first semester was the toughest, as it was a very brand-new environment, you're not used to the workload and you're just exhausted! The professors are also great. Many of them graduated from Ivy League schools and really are scholars who teach law with passion and commitment. Law school is tough and very expensive; if you are not sure this is what you want to do, then don't commit. It's not a lot of fun and glamour, it's grueling nights of reading, analyzing, making sense of arcane practices and regulations. Thus, it must be something you, yourself are passionate about; it is only sheer will and absolute determination that will enable you to succeed in such a competitive program while working full-time.

 Employment Prospects

Status: Alumnus/a, full-time
Dates of Enrollment: 9/2002-5/2005
Survey Submitted: September 2005

The top students often find placements in top law firms. 90 percent of NYLS students find jobs within one year of graduation, ranging from the private sector to the public sector. The NYLS alumni network is far reaching and ever-expanding. NYLS alumni are always eager to answer questions and provide helpful advice to fellow NYLS students and alumni. Many law firms, companies and government agencies participate in on-campus recruiting at NYLS. Most students will be able to find internships during their first two years.

Status: Alumnus/a, part-time
Dates of Enrollment: 9/1992-6/1997
Survey Submitted: March 2006

If you want to work in the field of financial services, this is an excellent school because it is tied in with the Wall Street network.

Status: Current student, full-time
Dates of Enrollment: 8/2003-Submit Date
Survey Submitted: October 2004

We always see flyers and presentations of alumni in prominent positions, so I guess it isn't a matter of the school putting out quality applicants, it just takes them longer to get there. I think the best thing to do is take advantage of the externship program. You don't get paid, but you get credit and if you are able to get a good one, can make seriously valuable connections. Even though I needed the money, I thought that it would be more valuable in the long run to have a major financial or investment institution on my resume than a small firm that I was just pushing papers for.

Status: Alumnus/a, part-time
Dates of Enrollment: 8/1997-6/2001
Survey Submitted: October 2004

Top of the class goes into big firms in the city. Can be a little more difficult as you go down in ranking. The B- curve is a killer. You can end up with a 2.67 at NYLS at the same rank as a student from Brooklyn or Fordham who has a 3.33. Placing that on a resume right out, guess who gets the interview. I am four years out, and just had someone ask me my GPA. Thankfully, my resume and background make up for being middle of the pack and a B- school. But, not everyone else can make up for the B- curve.

The evening program is full of Wall Streets with good prospects to stay on the Street. Many already have other advanced degrees, like MBAs or PhDs. Law degree means an advance to an already impressive career. Day students tend to be right out of undergrad, with little work experience and parents that make them go to grad school.

The alumni network is impressive but the school needs to use it a little better. Many of the biggest firms were started by NYLS grads, but nowadays you have to look into the Wall Street companies to see a lot.

On-campus recruiting needs to be improved. Basically geared to the top 20 percent of the class. Everyone else is pretty much on their own.

The internship program could be so much better. Location is great for many big companies, federal court, state court, government agencies and some big firms. If you get an internship on your own, don't expect to get credit for it. Also, the direction is very much geared toward public interest or big firms. The opportunities of Wall Street are so vast and untapped by the school, but you can get them on your own.

Status: Alumnus/a, part-time
Dates of Enrollment: 8/1998-6/2002
Survey Submitted: September 2003

NY Law School does offer good career placement resources. Although the job market is currently in a horrid state, the school attempts to place you in various internships and on-campus employment. Graduates are also given advance notice of on-campus recruitment fairs, which are great opportunities for top-grade students. As the job market is so competitive and saturated with law graduates and non-experienced attorneys, the more you stand out, the better your chances are. For instance, experience as a paralegal while in school, life experience in other professional positions, writing awards and top grades can help you stand out.

Status: Alumnus/a, full-time
Dates of Enrollment: 8/1997-6/1990
Survey Submitted: April 2004

The school is not high on the prestige list with employers. However, top firms do recruit at the school. If you are top 10 percent and get on a Law Journal, you will be able to land a job with those firms. Also, the school offers many clinics and internships, both of which go a long way toward building a strong resume and developing future contacts and relationships.

Status: Alumnus/a, full-time
Dates of Enrollment: 8/1998-6/2001
Survey Submitted: October 2003

Modest campus recruiting. Fair resources for New York residents. Good internship opportunities.

 **Quality of Life**

Status: Alumnus/a, full-time
Dates of Enrollment: 9/2002-5/2005
Survey Submitted: September 2005

NYLS does not have an official campus. There is one main facility where most of the classes are held. All of the computer labs have state-of-the art technology. The food in the student cafeteria is not five-star quality but does suffice for students on the go. NYLS is located near SoHo and Chinatown, which allows students to venture out for a bite to eat. NYLS is located in a safe area. It would be safe to walk to the subways late at night, located just three or four blocks from the school.

Status: Alumnus/a, part-time
Dates of Enrollment: 9/1992-6/1997
Survey Submitted: March 2006

As far as I know, there is still no campus housing. The campus is contained in one building at a busy intersection in lower Manhattan. The upside to this is that it is very urbane and close to the courthouses, Wall Street and very much a part of the fabric of New York City. The downside is that there is little room to find solitude and quiet, except for the library.

Status: Current student, full-time
Dates of Enrollment: 8/2003-Submit Date
Survey Submitted: October 2004

I love the area—right in the heart of Tribeca—two blocks from Canal Street and tons of surrounding bars. I lived in Park Slope (in Brooklyn) and it was about a 20-minute subway ride to school each day (subways are three to four blocks in every direction). The most frustrating thing to deal with is the aging elevators if you are in a hurry or late for class.

Status: Alumnus/a, part-time
Dates of Enrollment: 8/1997-6/2001
Survey Submitted: October 2004

Quality of life is second to none. Tribeca is awesome. Housing is limited, but Brooklyn Heights is one great neighborhood. Around the school can be pricey, but it is lower Manhattan. Between the school's location and school housing's location, crime is probably the lowest for any law school in NYC. School is a group of buildings in lower Manhattan. They are updated, clean and very convenient to Wall Street. Most of the evening students are working on Wall Street during the day.

Status: Alumnus/a, part-time
Dates of Enrollment: 8/1998-6/2002
Survey Submitted: September 2003

NY Law School is right in the heart of downtown New York. Six blocks away from the former World Trade Center (Twin Towers), the school has history and attitude. Convenient to many trains and buses. I was an evening student, living in the Bronx. I would get home approximately at midnight. The surrounding area was always well-lit, and you will always find a student or two traveling your way. Safety is not really an issue. The school has a cafeteria, and there are many shops that are open, although not very late at night. Most students would grab a bite from the cafeteria, especially in the winter, when it's too cold to go out. They also have many local, inexpensive bars for those of you who actually have a life!

Status: Alumnus/a, full-time
Dates of Enrollment: 8/1997-6/1990
Survey Submitted: April 2004

The school is located in the heart of Tribeca, so there is no shortage of restaurants. Most students tend to commute, although there is some housing. As a school in New York City, there is no campus per se.

Read all of Vault's Law School Surveys at www.vault.com/lawschool — get complete surveys on top law schools, expert advice on applicaton essays, LSAT prep and more.

VAULT CAREER LIBRARY   441

 **Social Life**

Status: Alumnus/a, full-time
Dates of Enrollment: 9/2002-5/2005
Survey Submitted: September 2005

There are quite a few restaurants and a few bars located near the school in case students need to unwind. There are over 50 student organizations ranging from the Asian American Law Students Association to the New York Law School Public Interest group. The school often hosts an annual Barristers Ball at one of New York's finest restaurants where students are able to dress in their finest and enjoy a night of dining and dancing. Every year there is an annual multicultural fair where all of the different cultural organizations bring food for the students to sample. New York Law School also participates in the AIDS Walk and has always held fundraisers for various charitable causes.

Status: Alumnus/a, part-time
Dates of Enrollment: 9/1992-6/1997
Survey Submitted: March 2006

Because this is a city school, it has everything that New York City has to offer.

Status: Current student, full-time
Dates of Enrollment: 8/2003-Submit Date
Survey Submitted: October 2004

We always found a way to go out. Usually for 1Ls (like everyone else) it is Thursday nights since there are no classes on Fridays (unless you are really unlucky). If you are looking to date, I would look outside of school. I couldn't imagine dating someone going through the same thing—classes, being moody and stressed, the exact same experiences—I mean, what would you even have to talk about, really?

Status: Alumnus/a, part-time
Dates of Enrollment: 8/1997-6/2001
Survey Submitted: October 2004

Social life is pretty good. You can do just about anything in NYC. Day students have more of a thing happening. Night students are professionals that go home to families after class, and off to work in the morning. Thursday nights are like at another law school that I know of. Everyone heads out for a few, but not that big of a group in the night program, and not for all night either.

The dating scene is very good.

Status: Alumnus/a, full-time
Dates of Enrollment: 8/1997-6/1990
Survey Submitted: April 2004

The school is surrounded by trendy bars and restaurants. The school also has the usual assortment of clubs, newspapers, as well as a few fraternities.

Status: Alumnus/a, part-time
Dates of Enrollment: 8/1998-6/2002
Survey Submitted: September 2003

The school is surrounded by many local, inexpensive bars for those of you who actually have a life! The school's student body is very diverse, and there are many different school groups including Jewish, Latino and African-American groups. There are also school get-togethers and fundraisers. Overall, I think NYLS is a great school.

Status: Alumnus/a, full-time
Dates of Enrollment: 8/1998-6/2001
Survey Submitted: September 2003

We are in Tribeca, so we had some nice places for dining, but there really wasn't anything else to do around there. There was a local hangout called Reade Street Pub, but that was a hole in the wall.

New York University School of Law

110 West Third Street
New York, NY 10012
Admissions phone: (212) 998-6060
Admissions e-mail (JD): law.jdadmissions@nyu.edu
Admissions e-mail (LLM and JSD):
law.llmadmissions@nyu.edu
Admissions URL: http://www.law.nyu.edu/prospective/

 ## Admissions

Status: Current student, full-time
Dates of Enrollment: 8/2004-Submit Date
Survey Submitted: May 2006

I began preparing my application for NYU Law almost four months in advance. This was helpful because NYU offers the opportunity to write a diversity essay, in addition to the standard personal statement. There are also a number of scholarship opportunities that require fairly extensive essays and interviews. One of the biggest things admissions counselors look for is consistency within the entire application. If a personal statement claims an interest in public service, the student resume should show volunteer experience and social justice courses. When crafting an application, it is important to identify weaknesses and try to make up for them. For example, if an applicant is applying straight out of undergrad and has little work experience, they should point out all of the skills they acquired through involvement in extracurriculars, clubs and activities. NYU in particular, has a big commitment to forming a well-rounded student body. The majority of students seem to have tremendous amounts of world experience such as traveling, studying abroad, working for NGOs. Applicants need to use their personal statement and resume to point out what unique contributions they can make to the student body. For example, I went to a local state college for undergraduate so I discussed in my essay how this made me diverse/unique because so many current students are from Ivy League schools.

Statistically, NYU is pretty selective, but students don't really compare their scores once they get there, so I don't exactly know how hard it is to get in. It is of course, better to apply early in the application process so that there are more spots open. NYU does not have an interview process for regular admissions, so again, the student must make sure they have a thorough application. I decided to attach an addendum to my application explaining a low grade in one of my undergraduate courses. If there is a glaring weakness or inconsistency, it is better to address it up front, instead of hoping the admissions committee accidentally overlooks it.

Status: Alumnus/a, full-time
Dates of Enrollment: 8/2000-5/2003
Survey Submitted: March 2006

The admissions process is exhaustive. I know the people in that office review the applications very carefully so I would focus on the essay...it's really the only element within the applicant's control since their grades and LSATs will be determined by that time. I think they look for a well-rounded class but it is selective and grades and LSAT scores play a significant role in the determinations.

Status: Alumnus/a, full-time
Dates of Enrollment: 8/2001-5/2004
Survey Submitted: April 2005

NYU looks for students who are well-rounded and have demonstrated care for and interaction with the world around them. It's not enough to have great grades and a high LSAT score—NYU looks for students who have experiences and are able to work well with others.

Status: Alumnus/a, full-time
Dates of Enrollment: 8/2001-5/2004
Survey Submitted: March 2005

The admissions process at NYU is no different than most other schools. Requirements include LSAT scores, college transcript, references, resume and admissions essay. I believe that NYU places a higher emphasis on LSAT scores than other comparable schools (e.g., Harvard, Columbia, Virginia). I, for example, had very high LSAT scores, but a lower college GPA than NYU's average. Friends who did very well in college, but not as well on their LSATs did not gain admission. For those who didn't do as well on their LSATs, but have solid grades and other credentials, there does seem to be a back door to NYU. NYU takes a high number of transfer students, many of whom were denied admission on the first attempt due to lower LSAT scores, but did well at another school. Many speculate that because the *U.S. News* rankings factor the median LSAT scores of first year students, but not all students, NYU has a pro-LSAT bias for first-year admission that does not manifest for transfer admission candidates. Therefore, for those who want to go to NYU above all else and have good grades, it makes sense to go to a less competitive school for your first year.

Status: Current student, full-time
Dates of Enrollment: 9/2002-Submit Date
Survey Submitted: January 2005

I applied using the CD version of the general form to all law schools in late January. There was no interview, and I don't believe there were any additional essays. Keep your statement limited to two pages, single-spaced, and be sure to highlight that is special about you and why law school is a necessary next step in your professional development. Keep it entertaining. NYU has a number of scholarships which applicants should definitely consider. I applied at the same time for a Root-Tilden-Kern Public Interest Scholarship and had to submit an additional statement for that. NYU is selective but there is no absolute cut off point in terms of combined GPA and LSAT. NYU is especially committed to ethnic and racial diversity and no one should self-select themselves out of the process. I received an acceptance from NYU probably in early March. At that time, I was also offered the opportunity to apply for a Dean's Merit Scholarship. You should definitely apply if offered that opportunity

Status: Alumnus/a, full-time
Dates of Enrollment: 8/1999-5/2002
Survey Submitted: March 2005

The admissions process is the same as any other law school. There is a form application and one essay required. An additional essay may be submitted to be considered for certain scholarships. NYU places a strong emphasis on public service, on being a global law school and on clinical experience. A good essay should mention how you intend to use your degree for the benefit of the public, and why you think NYU's dedication to public service, international population and clinical programs make it the ideal school.

Status: Current student, full-time
Dates of Enrollment: 8/2003-Submit Date
Survey Submitted: October 2004

NYU's admission decision is made on a rolling basis, so it is to one's advantage to apply early—especially considering the fact that the school usually responds with a decision quickly. For those interested in applying for the prestigious scholarships open to incoming students, it is necessary to note the earlier deadlines as one will not be considered for these opportunities if the application fails to meet these deadlines. The school prides itself on its commitment to public interest, so internships and other pursuits, especially those relating to public interest are a plus. But the competition for a spot in NYU is keen, so it is worth investing your time on every part of the application—GPA and LSAT, as well as the personal statement.

Read all of Vault's Law School Surveys at www.vault.com/lawschool — get complete surveys on top law schools, expert advice on applicaton essays, LSAT prep and more.

VAULT CAREER LIBRARY **443**

Status: Current student, full-time
Dates of Enrollment: 8/2003-Submit Date
Survey Submitted: November 2004

NYU is highly selective but does have a good diversity of undergraduate institutions represented. It appears to place more emphasis on undergrad grades than LSAT scores. There is a great diversity of geography and a decent amount of ethnic diversity. The admissions process was no nonsense and efficient. NYU was the first school to release their application, the first to respond. The volume of mail is not overwhelming. Their Early Action plan is an excellent option if NYU is a top choice. I knew by December, which took the pressure off. There are also admitted student days. The only thing to not hold your breath about is a good financial aid package.

Status: Current student, full-time
Dates of Enrollment: 8/2003-Submit Date
Survey Submitted: January 2004

NYU Law is a very competitive school and greatly values GPAs and LSAT scores (it's very numbers-oriented). If coming straight from college, expect to have competitive figures. However, the school also highly values outside experiences (there are a number of students here with other degrees and/or years of experience in the work force). I think that the waitlist is utilized a lot in the admissions process. Therefore, if waitlisted, be sure to communicate your continued interest in attending NYU!

Status: Current student, full-time
Dates of Enrollment: 4/2001-Submit Date
Survey Submitted: January 2004

NYU is certainly a hard school to get into—and has gotten more competitive since I started. Two friends and I were teaching assistants for a first-year class, and we joked (sort of) that the new batch of students was way smarter than us. Like all top law schools, I think NYU is looking for high LSAT scores and good grades. Taking some time off in between undergrad and law school doesn't hurt. If you get on the waitlist, be persistent, send letters, make phone calls. Some of my friends who got in off the waitlist turned out to be some of the best students. Like most law schools, there is no formal interview process, but you can make an appointment to speak with someone in admissions, and if NYU is your top choice, it couldn't hurt to show your face and express just how interested you are. An additional piece of info: everyone I know at NYU also got into Columbia.

 **Academics**

Status: Current student, full-time
Dates of Enrollment: 8/2004-Submit Date
Survey Submitted: May 2006

Academics at NYU are taken very seriously and the teachers are all high quality. For the most part, I found the professors to be very accessible. NYU Law actually funds each professor to take every student to lunch one time per semester. This is a great way to get some additionally insight into the professor's interests. Further, NYU has teacher rankings and class statistics available so it is possible to avoid taking "bad" professors.

The workload is what you make of it. There are no graded assignments throughout the semester, so it is up to the individual to be disciplined and keep up with the reading. Luckily, NYU has a B curve which means that almost 80 percent of students will get a B. NYU does not require professors to even give out Cs so unless someone blows of the final exam, there is pretty much no way of failing. NYU also pays for tutoring if a student is struggling in a particular class.

Some of the courses are harder to get into than others. This is especially true of certain clinics. NYU has an amazing clinical program and there is simply not enough slots to go around. By the end of three years, however, most people will be able to get into at least one clinic and take the majority of classes they desire.

Status: Alumnus/a, full-time
Dates of Enrollment: 8/2000-5/2003
Survey Submitted: March 2006

Classes were my favorite part of law school. They were rigorous and interesting. I never had a professor I didn't like. I think the faculty is outstanding at NYU. They're all at the top of their field and many are very well-known. Yet they are interested in teaching and all devoted substantive time outside the classroom to office hours. 99 percent of the classes are open to anyone so it isn't hard to get the class you want. Grading is tough. It's a strict curve. The workload was much more demanding than I anticipated, but it was so challenging and interesting that I never dreaded it.

Status: Alumnus/a, full-time
Dates of Enrollment: 9/2001-5/2003
Survey Submitted: March 2006

The course selection is amazing. I took classes on Chinese Law, South Asian Law, Globalization, Domestic Violence Law and many others that I didn't even expect to find here. I was constantly rubbing elbows with notoriously brilliant people—from judges to renowned prosecutors, to intellectual giants. It isn't easy to earn an A as NYU Law grades on a curve with only about 5 percent of the class getting an A. But the workload and expectations are fair.

Status: Current student, full-time
Dates of Enrollment: 8/2002-Submit Date
Survey Submitted: July 2005

The clinical programs at NYU are superior. There are too many to list, so anyone interested should just look them up. Because it is located in New York, there are many professors who are judges, city officials. Getting into popular classes depends on a lottery system to an extent and some classes are limited to graduating students. But one can always count on someone dropping the popular class, so watch the class space list and get in when you see an opening. Like any school there are laid back professors and obsessive professors. That can be good or bad. It can be an unbearable workload, but if you do the work, you can learn the subject inside out. On the flip side, you can be overwhelmed and lose the important points.

Status: Alumnus/a, full-time
Dates of Enrollment: 8/2000-5/2004
Survey Submitted: March 2005

The professors are great. There's not much left of the old Socratic teaching style at NYU—even first-year, I pretty much knew when I was going to get called on. The professors are extremely smart and accomplished, but are more approachable. I would guess more than regular law school professors. It isn't hard to get into popular classes, and when it is difficult you can usually wait to take them the next year.

Status: Alumnus/a, full-time
Dates of Enrollment: 9/2001-5/2004
Survey Submitted: March 2005

Lecture style classes generally require daily reading of cases out of a casebook and culminate in one test that determines the student's grade. Seminar classes are smaller and more interactive, and will often require reading articles, researching, writing articles or mock legal briefs, and preparing for presentations. Clinics typically combine seminar work with real-life legal research. NYU has an outstanding clinical program with newly updated facilities and a phenomenal faculty. As a corollary, you will generally have no problems getting into lectures that you want, though you may have to be a bit strategic with respect to popular clinics or seminars.

Status: Alumnus/a, full-time
Dates of Enrollment: 9/2000-5/2003
Survey Submitted: November 2003

NYU academics are extremely strong. First-year sections are among the largest (along with Harvard) in the country. Recent changes to the grading policy have resulted in gross grade inflation. The credit system at NYU is such that seminars—providing the only real opportunity to learn other than by Socratic humiliation—are only two credits, making it extremely difficult to avoid taking lots and lots of lectures. Professors are highly accessible for those of us with high grades and good jobs, and who are "interesting" to them.

Status: Alumnus/a, full-time
Dates of Enrollment: 8/2000-5/2003
Survey Submitted: April 2004

The classes were fantastic. Getting a class is rarely a problem. Most of the professors are well regarded, and the atmosphere in the classroom is amazing—very open and collegial. I loved all of my classes all three years. The grading is so tough and can feel arbitrary; it's the worst part by far. The workload is steady but manageable if you're disciplined with your time.

Status: Alumnus/a, full-time
Dates of Enrollment: 9/1997-5/2000
Survey Submitted: April 2004

Topnotch academics. Great professors, a challenging workload, but we still had time to balance a social life (you're in a fabulous city, after all). Great after-class discussions with professors and TAs, on material covered in the course and otherwise. Not too hard to get the popular classes—it's a diverse student body. Clinics are hard to get into, but they are pretty challenging—they make sure the good students find a spot.

Status: Alumnus/a, full-time
Dates of Enrollment: 8/1998-5/2001
Survey Submitted: April 2004

The grading curve is strictly adhered to, with As very difficult to come by. However, the level of competition among students is surprisingly low, the competition being to get into the school in the first place. Professors are world-class and engaging, with a great variety of subjects to pick from in second and third year. The workload is as heavy as one would expect from a top-quality law school.

Status: Current student, full-time
Dates of Enrollment: 8/2003-Submit Date
Survey Submitted: January 2004

School is tough, no lies! The reading assignments are tedious. But, with a disciplined schedule, it's not impossible...in fact, it's quite possible. I've learned that the way of life here really is "work hard, play hard." The students put in their work. But, come Thursday or Friday, it's time to have a bit of fun! The classes are very theoretical (and Socratic). And the caliber of the students enables the discussions to be enormously enlightening and interesting. The professors are very qualified...but expect to wait a while before getting any grades!

Status: Current student, full-time
Dates of Enrollment: 8/2001-Submit Date
Survey Submitted: January 2004

The professors are the best professors I have been around. They are willing to help inside and out of the classroom. On numerous occasions I have received help from professors from classes that I am not even enrolled in. I have not had any problems getting my class preferences. The first-year workload is very hard; however, it eases in the later years.

Employment Prospects

Status: Current student, full-time
Dates of Enrollment: 8/2004-Submit Date
Survey Submitted: May 2006

The Office of Career Services (OCS) is absolutely fabulous for both firm-seekers and public interest students. OCS takes the time to help each student with their resumes and interview prep, which gives us an advantage when applying to jobs. Every student I know has been able to find work over the summer. NYU does not even offer summer school because virtually every student gets a summer internship. OCS actually has the goal of 100 percent employment for 100 percent of students. In August of each year, NYU brings in all of the major firms for on-campus interviews which makes things very convenient. There are NYU alum at all of the major firms, and NYU's reputation is improving every year.

NYU is also one of the only top law schools with a Dean of Public Interest. There is a big public interest symposium every year for public interest employers and student job-seekers. NYU offers funding for all students who want to do a summer internship at public interest offices. Many students take advantage of this opportunity and find it very rewarding.

Status: Alumnus/a, full-time
Dates of Enrollment: 8/2002-5/2005
Survey Submitted: March 2006

Career services were excellent. They really help you out in your search for employment. They provide individual guidance, and they also help out the student body in general with information sessions and on-campus interview set-ups and the like. The reputation of the school naturally helps students get the kinds of employment opportunities they seek.

Status: Alumnus/a, full-time
Dates of Enrollment: 9/2001-5/2003
Survey Submitted: March 2006

I felt that the career office was dedicated to placing each student and that they had the clout to place its students anywhere. Being an alumnus from NYU Law is truly an asset as I can find mentors anywhere on account of the institutional affiliation.

Status: Alumnus/a, full-time
Dates of Enrollment: 8/2000-5/2003
Survey Submitted: March 2006

An NYU grad can get any job they want. The career services office will spend a ton of time helping students get the jobs they want. Most every large private and public employer comes to campus for recruiting. Getting a good job, so long as the job market is decent, will not be a problem.

Status: Current student, full-time
Dates of Enrollment: 8/2002-Submit Date
Survey Submitted: July 2005

The clinical programs at NYU are superior. There are too many to list, so anyone interested should just look them up. Because it is located in New York, there are many professors who are judges, city officials. The sky was the limit. I had about 15 job offers for the summer before third year, and I got a job offer from the firm I summered with. On-campus recruiting is great—all of the employers just come to you. The career services department is also great about preparing students for interviews by helping with resumes, holding mock interviews.

Status: Alumnus/a, full-time
Dates of Enrollment: 9/2001-5/2004
Survey Submitted: March 2005

Come here if you want a firm job at one of the most prestigious firms in the country. Three-quarters of the class end up at firms, most of them large and prestigious. The remaining quarter splits between clerkships, government service and "public interest" jobs (though arguably government jobs are in the public interest, "public interest" jobs usually refers to nonprofit legal services and/or public defender-type jobs). These remaining jobs are tougher to get because there are fewer of them, but with an NYU degree you will be in as good as a position as any other law graduate in the country. The NYU network is particularly strong in New York City.

Status: Alumnus/a, full-time
Dates of Enrollment: 8/2001-5/2004
Survey Submitted: March 2005

NYU has an outstanding career services department. They hold every student's hand through the process—from resume writing to firm selection, interview preparation and post-interview analysis. All of the top firms recruit and recruit heavily at NYU. Only those in the very bottom of the class have a difficult time with employment, and that is relative—it only means they may not get a job with a Vault 100 firm. They will get a good job, however. Being in New York is a huge advantage for those wishing to work after school in New York.

Read all of Vault's Law School Surveys at www.vault.com/lawschool — get complete surveys on top law schools, expert advice on applicaton essays, LSAT prep and more.

VAULT CAREER LIBRARY   445

Status: Alumnus/a, full-time
Dates of Enrollment: 8/1998-5/2001
Survey Submitted: April 2004

Career placement is outstanding for students interested in law firms, with campus recruiting from every big firm imaginable. Graduates are highly sought after by most, if not all, firms on the East Coast, and many firms in big Midwestern cities like Chicago. There is a presence on the West Coast, but the school's reputation is probably lacking due to the lack of graduates practicing out West—it is recognized as an excellent school, but not necessarily one of the Top Five.

 Quality of Life

Status: Current student, full-time
Dates of Enrollment: 8/2004-Submit Date
Survey Submitted: May 2006

I cannot imagine any law school with a higher quality of life than NYU. I loved my law school apartment. The housing is right in the heart of Greenwich Village and there are literally hundreds of restaurants withing walking distance. I felt safe in the neighborhood at all hours of the day and night, even when walking alone.

NYU's campus is absolutely state of the art with the most modern technology. A new building was recently constructed to house all of the clinical programs and is gorgeous. There is also catering every day for breakfast and lunch.

Status: Alumnus/a, full-time
Dates of Enrollment: 8/2002-5/2005
Survey Submitted: March 2006

New York city is obviously very expensive, especially housing. NYU housing was quite acceptable, though, if you don't want to find your own place. The law campus space more than doubled a couple years ago with the opening of a new building. The facilities were nice beforehand and with the added space they're excellent. The Village is a great neighborhood to go to school in. This is one of the main advantages of NYU over its uptown rival. Anecdotes also suggest that "the other" school has less friendly atmosphere—i.e., more spiteful competition. NYU is academically rigorous but generally laid back and not overly competitive.

Status: Alumnus/a, full-time
Dates of Enrollment: 9/2001-5/2003
Survey Submitted: March 2006

The village is a thriving, dynamic neighborhood—it is perhaps one of the most exciting places on earth to live! There is no shortage of excellent nearby restaurants, with a number of affordable options as well. Being in New York means that almost any dietary restrictions can be accommodated without much trouble. Safety in the city has improved greatly over the last dozen years or so, although housing is still very expensive. I was able to find affordable day care nearby for my toddler son.

Status: Alumnus/a, full-time
Dates of Enrollment: 8/1999-5/2002
Survey Submitted: March 2005

The housing in D'Agostino is awful—tiny and cramped, and on an extremely loud corner (always filled with drunk people leaving the many area bars or heading for the park). Mercer is huge and very nice housing—still tiny kitchens, but nice rooms. The rooms facing Broadway get a lot of traffic noise, and the rooms facing Mercer get a lot of wind noise—the U-shape of the building creates a sort of wind-tunnel. The housing is absurdly expensive, but it saves you a broker's fee, and it's an amazing location. Right smack in the middle of the Village, walking distance to 8th Street, SoHo, Little Italy, Chinatown, the East Village, the West Village, Tribeca—everything!

No real meal plan to speak of, at least when I was there, but there are so many great cheap restaurants in the area that you don't need one and wouldn't want one. The area is safe from about 7 a.m. to about 4 a.m., because the streets are always full of people. Try catching a cab at 5 or 6 a.m., though, and you might want to have the security guard come out with you. I also never liked to walk

through the park alone after dark. Really, I can't say enough about how amazing it is to be living in Greenwich Village. Incredible. Everyone should spend three years there.

Status: Current student, full-time
Dates of Enrollment: 9/2002-Submit Date
Survey Submitted: January 2005

The NYU facilities are excellent—the classrooms and library are newly renovated. There is ample study space and public computers for student use. I've heard the student housing is on the pricey side. I would recommend living off campus anyway, just for general maintenance of sanity and a life apart from school. Being in the city is not as dangerous as one might think. General street smarts will keep you out of harm's way.

Status: Current student, full-time
Dates of Enrollment: 8/2003-Submit Date
Survey Submitted: January 2004

NYU provides housing for all of its law students (if desired). However, the downside is the high cost. A number of students end up living off campus to absorb some of the costs. On the upside, there is no place like New York...it's exciting and there's always something to do (in your limited free time). If you're interested in eventually practicing law in New York City, there is no better school than NYU!

Status: Current student, full-time
Dates of Enrollment: 8/2001-Submit Date
Survey Submitted: January 2004

New York is the greatest city in the world, and for my money NYU is the greatest law school in the city. I was accepted at both Columbia and NYU and chose NYU due to the students and the great location. With the addition of the new building on the law school campus (this winter), the decision should be even easier.

Status: Alumnus/a, full-time
Dates of Enrollment: 8/2000-5/2003
Survey Submitted: April 2004

If you love New York City, this is the school for you. The dorms are classic New York City—small but functional. It's in a busy part of the city, so it can feel very hectic, but it's a great place to live. The campus community is strong. I absolutely loved living in the Village and within a block of school. It's not a dangerous neighborhood for the city.

Status: Alumnus/a, full time
Dates of Enrollment: 9/2000-5/2003
Survey Submitted: November 2003

NYU is in Greenwich Village. The cost of living is extremely high. NYU students are well advised to look off campus. Good options include the better neighborhoods of Brooklyn—they are safe, cheaper and, in some cases, as little as twenty minutes from campus. NYU generally takes student safety very seriously—this is NOT a reason anyone would opt not to attend. The new building is very beautiful.

 Social Life

Status: Current student, full-time
Dates of Enrollment: 8/2004-Submit Date
Survey Submitted: May 2006

Many students choose NYU because the students tend to be really down-to-earth and non-elitist. Whenever I missed class people would e-mail me their notes before I even asked anyone. The school sponsors keg parties/bar nights almost every week and also has a dance every semester. There are 50 bars within a few blocks of the law school, which is super fun, but can be dangerous to one's studies. Some of the most popular are the Fat Black Pussy Cat, Town Tavern, B-Bar, 1849, Down the Hatch and Bleecker Street Bar.

Every day of the week the law school has activities ranging from documentaries on human rights, to beer and pizza parties, to ethnic club meetings to helping homeless people with legal issues.

NYU law students are incredibly innovative and as such, there are a wide variety of clubs. Some examples are Law Students for Human Rights, National Lawyers Guild, Law Students Against the Death Penalty, Black Allied Law Students Association, Latino Law Students Association, Research, Advocacy and Education to Combat Homelessness (Reach) and the Prisoner's Rights and Education Project (PREP).

Status: Alumnus/a, full-time
Dates of Enrollment: 8/2002-5/2005
Survey Submitted: March 2006

Being an international city and school, there are a lot of LLMs from out of the country about, who don't necessarily have their own social networks outside school. And domestically, people come from all over the country and many are new to the city. So the Student Bar Association has lots of organized social events for law students, including plenty of free drinking. If you join a journal or moot court your second and third years, there's plenty of socializing there, too. So social opportunities abound, but I wouldn't say there's pressure to join in. Plenty of people have families or have their own social networks and just show up for class and go home.

Status: Alumnus/a, full-time
Dates of Enrollment: 9/2001-5/2003
Survey Submitted: March 2006

It is easy to make friends at NYU law as it is a large enough student-body that anyone can find like-minded people with whom to grab a coffee after class. The student-body is nothing if not diverse—politically, socially and economically. There are many events at the school worth attending, and certainly not enough time to have your fill. If you seek out what interests you, you will naturally meet plenty of people who share your interests.

Status: Current student, full-time
Dates of Enrollment: 8/2002-Submit Date
Survey Submitted: July 2005

I hang out in exclusive nightclubs because I am a native New Yorker and have been clubbing since I was 15. For the rest of the students, I guess they hang out at bars located around the school. To be quite honest, my lifestyle prevented me from making any friends at school. I am not nakedly ambitious and I travel in different social circles. I get the impression that the other students liked each other and hung out with each other.

Status: Alumnus/a, full-time
Dates of Enrollment: 9/2001-5/2004
Survey Submitted: March 2005

Law school is a blast. Though the weeks around finals are typically stressful, you will find people to socialize with at all other times of the year. Since the law school is located in Greenwich Village, you will have the country's most extensive selection of bars, restaurants, dating opportunities and events at your fingertips. The law school tries to help you out in any event. There are weekly law school parties sponsored by the Student Bar Association, as well as a plethora of student groups where you can meet like-minded students. In addition, you will find your first-year section will contain its share of friendly types, and will probably make lasting friendships with brilliant and interesting people from day one.

Status: Alumnus/a, full-time
Dates of Enrollment: 8/2000-5/2004
Survey Submitted: March 2005

Honestly, I had more fun in law school than in college. Within the first week, I was going out every night with my roommates, neighbors and people in my section. I think it's the social life that distinguishes NYU. Most people I work with and know hated law school because they never got to be good friends with the other students (many of whom they may have hated). Because of the way housing is, because the school funds a lot of social activities and because there just seem to be a lot of nice people that choose to go to NYU, I think most people come out with really close friends. In a profession where connections are everything, that's really important.

Status: Current student, full-time
Dates of Enrollment: 8/2003-Submit Date
Survey Submitted: January 2004

I'm sure this sounds so biased...but, I can almost claim for a fact that NYU Law's social life is one of the best of all the law schools. The school is constantly throwing happy hours and parties...the students are always throwing parties, and we're located right in Soho! One of the student favorites is the Student Bar Association's weekly drinking party EVERY THURSDAY NIGHT! For those who don't drink, there are still bunches of clubs, activities and free meals every day (literally).

 **The School Says**

The New York University School of Law is one of the oldest law schools in the United States. It offers a comprehensive first professional program leading to the degree of Juris Doctor and a graduate curriculum leading to the degrees of Masters of Laws and Doctor of Juridical Science. The law school is a leader in providing scholarships to promising students, recruiting top faculty and improving tuition subsidies and loan forgiveness programs. The School of Law regularly posts recent graduates to the U.S. Supreme Court for the highly-coveted clerkships. The Root-Tilden-Kern scholarship program has produced more than 800 of the finest public service leaders in the country. Each year, some of the world's top foreign lawyers visit to teach at the Hauser Global Law School, founded in 1995. An extraordinarily wide-range of course offerings, research centers, colloquia and special programs is made available to students. Policy-makers and practitioners regularly converge on Washington Square South to explore critical issues in the law.

Read all of Vault's Law School Surveys at www.vault.com/lawschool — get complete surveys on top law schools, expert advice on applicaton essays, LSAT prep and more.

VAULT CAREER LIBRARY **447**

Pace University School of Law

Pace Law School
Admissions Office
78 North Broadway
White Plains, NY 10603
Admissions phone: (914) 422-4210
Admissions fax: (914) 989-8714
Admissions e-mail: admissions@law.pace.edu
Admissions URL: http://www.law.pace.edu/adm/

 Admissions

Status: Current student, full-time
Dates of Enrollment: 8/2005-Submit Date
Survey Submitted: April 2006

A stressful process all around when applying to law schools in general. The admissions process was simple with easily understandable instructions, clearly written essay questions and a staff willing to help in any aspect of the process along the way. Interviews are an option, and beneficial for visiting the school and feeling out the staff.

Status: Current student, full-time
Dates of Enrollment: 8/2004-Submit Date
Survey Submitted: April 2006

After applying on time and being accepted, everyone in admissions was very open, friendly, and informative. They answered all my questions, offered tours, and connected me with students to talk to with additional questions.

Status: Current student, full-time
Dates of Enrollment: 8/2003-Submit Date
Survey Submitted: March 2006

Pace has a fairly standard admissions process, with LSATs and grades carrying the most weight. Based on our student body, I do think the school has a preference for students with interesting pre-law school experiences, so I would suggest keeping that in mind in writing essays. Although we do have our share of fresh-out-of-college students, we also have plenty of students in their 30s, 40s, and even 50s and 60s. And, of course, there's a lot of cultural and ethnic diversity.

Admitted students may come in to "interview the school." Students who have been waitlisted or might otherwise be border-line applicants may also be granted interviews. When I applied to Pace three years ago, the school admitted roughly 25 percent of all applicants. I'm not sure whether this figure has changed since then.

Status: Current student, full- and part-time
Dates of Enrollment: 8/2003-Submit Date
Survey Submitted: March 2006

Visit the school—Pace or any other. Meet some of the professors and students and get a feel for the place. It could be a long time to be in school if you are not happy with the environment.

Status: Current student, full- and part-time JD/LLM
Dates of Enrollment: 8/2002-Submit Date
Survey Submitted: March 2006

As a part-time evening student who must work for a living, I applied only to those JD programs within commuting distance from my home (Albany, Fordham, Pace—I live in Poughkeepsie, NY). Pace Law School was not only the only school of the three that had a dedicated evening program, they were excited and proud of it. Moreover, the professional, courteous and helpful admissions and administrative staff made all the difference in my choice.

Status: Current student, full-time
Dates of Enrollment: 9/2004-Submit Date
Survey Submitted: March 2006

Pace Law School uniquely offers prospective students the opportunity to interview on campus as part of the admissions process. I strongly encourage any student to take advantage. You will interview with one of the law school professors and it's a great chance to ask any questions you have as well as strengthen your application with an in-person appearance. I decided to attend Pace because my interview experience was so positive. One should also consider the early notification option to see if it's right for them. In general, the earlier you apply, the better off you are. Touring the school is also a great idea since it will provide you with more information upon which to base your decision and you can get a feel for the school.

Status: Current student, part-time
Dates of Enrollment: 9/2005-Submit Date
Survey Submitted: March 2006

I submitted an application along with my LSAT scores and went in for an interview, which was optional. I wanted to speak directly with a professor since I would be attending the evening program and had some questions about how that was run. I liked the professor very much but the specifics about the program were slim. Then I attended admitted students day where we got to visit different classrooms for lectures about programs at the schools and we even had materials sent to us ahead of time for a mock class. That was what put me over. I knew that day that Pace was where I wanted to study.

Status: Current student, full-time
Dates of Enrollment: 9/2004-Submit Date
Survey Submitted: March 2006

I was admitted from the waitlist. My undergrad grades were low, but my LSATs were high. Once I was waitlisted, I called the admissions office weekly and got to know the people in the office. I believe my persistence is why I was offered a spot. I've done well there and will be on a full merit scholarship for my third year.

Status: Current student, full-time
Dates of Enrollment: 8/2005-Submit Date
Survey Submitted: March 2006

Admissions office was very helpful, and kept in touch with me regarding the status of my application. Director of Admissions found out about my interests and referred me to a professor who e-mailed me several times about the programs offered and internship/externship opportunities. One of the few schools that offered an interview with an alumnus in the city I was living in (Washington, D.C.) as well as on campus.

Status: Current student, full-time
Dates of Enrollment: 8/2005-Submit Date
Survey Submitted: March 2006

Law school admissions is pretty standardized with LSAC.org. Pace doesn't add much to your application load except for the opportunity to present some personalized material to give a better picture of yourself (e.g., personal statement with a pretty open topic, resume). I also included an addendum and if memory serves me, a short explanation of some of my undergrad activities on my resume. All in all, short, sweet, pretty middle ground as far as the applications go. I did not have a chance to interview as I missed that deadline. If you apply earlier, you have the opportunity for an admissions interview. I bet that would be an advantage due to the small size of Pace—personal evaluation. Law school admission is a numbers game. I believe I managed to land a spot at Pace due to a little personality (in my personal statement) and some prior work experience in law.

Status: Current student, full-time
Dates of Enrollment: 8/2004-Submit Date
Survey Submitted: March 2006

The administrators and students at the school are more than helpful in providing prospective students with useful information. I was sold on the school when I attended the admitted students reception where active students, administrators and professors were very forthcoming and spoke highly of the institution.

Status: Current student, full-time
Dates of Enrollment: 9/2004-Submit Date
Survey Submitted: April 2005

This is among the best admissions staff that I encountered among the five schools I applied to and visited. The staff was extremely friendly and helpful in answering questions, not only about the school, but about other people in similar situations as mine. I felt like I mattered to them, and that made a difference in my decision.

Status: Current student, full-time
Dates of Enrollment: 9/2003-Submit Date
Survey Submitted: April 2005

The admissions process is similar to other law schools (LSAT scores, GPA, application). Pace does offer a personal interview, which I feel is an important element that sets Pace's admission process apart from other law schools. I attended undergraduate in the Westchester area, so I was familiar with the success of Pace's Environmental Program. Undergraduate professors encouraged me to apply to Pace's Environmental Law Program. Pace continues to become more and more competitive and selective each year.

Status: Current student, full-time
Dates of Enrollment: 1/2003-Submit Date
Survey Submitted: April 2005

The Pace Law School admissions process is extremely supportive and welcoming. Actually, it is one of the primary reasons I decided to attend Pace Law. Not only are the admissions people very friendly and helpful, but they will send you personalized e-mails with reasons to attend the law school and happenings at the law school that would be of interest to you. I do not believe it is very hard to be admitted to Pace Law, especially if you have an interest in the environment or are a minority. Pace is desperate to increase minority enrollment. I did not have a personalized interview and applied through the LSAC system.

Status: Current student, full-time
Dates of Enrollment: 8/2003-Submit Date
Survey Submitted: March 2005

I applied to over 15 law schools and, as I'm sure you are aware, the application process is NOT fun. However, with law school you have LSAC to help out and that makes everything run a little bit more smoothly. There was no interviewing process and it was actually a pretty simple application. They not only accepted me, but also gave me about $11,000 in grants and scholarships. From the other people that I have talked to at this school—they were very liberal with the handing out of scholarships to first-year law students in order to attract them to the school. All in all, a pretty simple and smooth admissions process.

 **Academics**

Status: Current student, full-time
Dates of Enrollment: 8/2003-Submit Date
Survey Submitted: March 2006

Overall, we have a solid academic program, with a good balance between theory and clinical and/or externship practice. Pace has a B- curve for first-year and other required courses; but for most second- and third-year courses, professors have more discretion in grade distribution.

Personally, I'm at Pace for the environmental program and have been uniformly pleased with the quality of the classes, the instructors and the opportunities. I'm taking Hazardous Waste with a professor who helped write the original CERCLA and RCRA regulations at EPA. My environmental skills professor was senior counsel in one of the key cases every environmental law student in

the country reads and knows. And right now, I'm learning environmental litigation from Robert F. Kennedy, Jr. and Karl Coplan. (And yes, Bobby really is *that* good-looking. Oh, and smart and dedicated, too, of course.) In fact, just yesterday, I made my first appearance in front of an adjudicatory body in a dispute over a Clean Water Act permit. Overall, being an environmental law student at Pace is very exciting—and very rigorous.

Status: Current student, part-time
Dates of Enrollment: 8/2002-Submit Date
Survey Submitted: March 2006

Pace tries to give evening students a wide array of classes to choose from. In addition, they also indicate when and how often a class will be offered so students can plan their schedules. We have some very good professors and practitioners at Pace. There is also a variety of very good simulations courses including Trial Advocacy, Pre-Civil Litigation and others that provide a different experience than traditional law school classes. We also have the Land Use Center and Women's Justice Center where students can get hands on experience.

Status: Current student, full-time
Dates of Enrollment: 9/2004-Submit Date
Survey Submitted: March 2006

Academics at Pace are very challenging. One can definitely survive the first year, yet the next year will continue to challenge you. I'm sure all law schools are like that though. What is truly important when academic rigors challenge you, though, is a supportive and positive environment. My highest praise goes to the student body. The students here are very supportive of one another and there are no real issues of competitiveness or rudeness. You can ask people you don't even know for the notes to a class. Also, upper-class students are a valuable resource and give great advice on what classes to take and how to thrive at the Law School.

Status: Current student, full-time
Dates of Enrollment: 8/2005-Submit Date
Survey Submitted: March 2006

There is a variety of teaching styles—but there is the use of the Socratic Method for the first year, predominantly. Classes don't get "closed out" too much. The student body is sympathetic and congenial. Students really help one another, as much as permitted, and there is not that harsh, competitive feeling among the student body. The workload is probably like in any first-year law school program—a lot of reading! Grading is on the traditional curve, also—typical of any law school—and based almost entirely on the final exam.

Status: Current student, full-time
Dates of Enrollment: 8/2002-Submit Date
Survey Submitted: March 2006

The workload at Pace is fair to moderate. It is manageable if you keep up on your work but if you fall behind, it is difficult to catch up. The quality and variety of the classes are great. The only negative part of the course selection is the fact that Pace is Number Three in the country in Environmental Law and as such many of the classes are geared towards environmental students. This has thus taken away a lot of opportunities for non-environmental law students. The school though, at the same time, makes every effort to make classes available to students and allow for students to take a wide variety of classes. Class selection is done on a lottery basis which allows for upper-level students to take the classes they want prior to graduation. In the case that a class is closed out, the first- and second-years have the opportunity to take the classes when they become last year students. Grading is sporadic depending on the teacher and the type of examination. I have found that take home exams and paper classes grade much more favorably than classes with in-class exams. Furthermore, as with any school, grading depends to a certain degree on the teacher and their expectations.

Status: Current student, full-time
Dates of Enrollment: 8/2006-Submit Date
Survey Submitted: March 2006

I was pleasantly surprised by the academics at Pace. Coming from a small liberal arts college, I was used to classes of no more than 10 students and one-on-one work with professors; I expected a culture shock coming to law school, but found anything but. True, classes are larger, but I speak to other friends in law school and classes here are a third the size and the professors are always

Read all of Vault's Law School Surveys at www.vault.com/lawschool — get complete surveys on top law schools, expert advice on applicaton essays, LSAT prep and more.

VAULT CAREER LIBRARY 449

available. You work hard, you work long, and you reap the benefits of the caring professors and intelligent faculty and staff. I couldn't ask for more.

Status: Current student, full-time
Dates of Enrollment: 8/2004-Submit Date
Survey Submitted: March 2006

Pace has excellent faculty members who do everything they can to ensure that you succeed in your studies. They have review sessions with students who previously did well in the classes for first-year and mandatory second-year classes along with an excellent academic support department. If a class is full they do everything they can do either let you in or add another section.

Status: Alumnus/a, full-time
Dates of Enrollment: 9/2001-5/2004
Survey Submitted: March 2006

The student to teacher ratio is good. The average class size is roughly 180. You can always get into popular classes, if not one semester then the next. The professors are very hands-on and welcome students to visit their offices for questions or help. Most professors have prior exams on file to study from. The workload varies, but most classes require a fair amount of work and preparation. It is law school. Grading for required courses follows a mandatory curve. Other classes do not. The professors also are topnotch. Most of them graduated from NYU, Columbia, Harvard and Yale.

Status: Current student, full-time JD/MBA
Dates of Enrollment: 8/2004-Submit Date
Survey Submitted: March 2006

Because it is a small school, it is easy to talk to the administration if you have a problem getting into a class. The first-year courses are pretty much the same as any school. The negatives are that criminal law and legal writing are combined in one course, which they definitely should not be. Also there is a disparity in the quality of professors that teach this course. The other negative is that tax is a required course, which it is not at other schools, but this may change soon. I think the education I am getting here is good, and a lot of students are smart and have meaningful input.

Status: Current student, full-time
Dates of Enrollment: 8/2005-Submit Date
Survey Submitted: March 2006

Professors know the names of everyone in the class, and are readily available for questions/discussions out of class. All have an open-door policy and are quick to respond to e-mails, even late at night. Workload is heavy, but never skipped over. Coming prepared to class is an absolute must. Professors give interesting background on the cases, and pay specific attention to certain points of the dissent and concurrence as to garner an all around understanding of the case, and why it was ruled in a certain way. Three of my professors have been current or former deans. (e.g., one dean of academic curriculum, two deans of the law school)

Status: Current student, full-time
Dates of Enrollment: 8/2005-Submit Date
Survey Submitted: March 2006

Great Environmental Law Program. There is an environmental Law Review as well as an international Law Review. The also have a great land use internship for those who are interested in environmental, land use or real estate law. Great faculty; professors' doors are always open and most are very willing to help.

Status: Current student, full-time
Dates of Enrollment: 9/2002-Submit Date
Survey Submitted: April 2005

The workload at Pace is reasonable for the character of the program. The first year is somewhat of an eye-opener with regard to required class preparation. The classes are demanding, as they should be—this is law school. If it were easy, everyone would be attending. As challenging as some of the classes can be, there are opportunities to take less intense classes that provide a breather from the heavy workload. Grading is relatively consistent during the first year of school. Each professor is obviously looking for different results from his/her individual students. For the most part, first-year professors set a kind of standard by which a student may gauge his/her future efforts and achievement. Before I started law school, former students would tell me, "The first year is the hardest.

Get through that and the rest is easy." I have to say that I have now adopted tha mantra when I speak with prospective law students. The first year is the mos difficult for a variety of reasons, and these vary with each individual studen Once that first year has passed, and students get through that first summer, the return to school with an entirely optimistic perspective.

By the time they are in their third- or fourth-year, students are thinking far les about the challenges of law school and more about the challenges that com post-graduation. Pace provides challenging study for its students throughou their entire course of study. There is no way that I've seen to "skate" throug law school. By a student's final year here, the challenges have changed fro dealing with a significant workload and an entirely new subject matter to seeing real results from his or her work and efforts.

Status: Current student, full-time
Dates of Enrollment: 8/2003-Submit Date
Survey Submitted: March 2005

The classes at Pace are excellent. Of course, it is a smaller school so there ar fewer classes in total, but you will find ALL of the classes you need to pass various bar exams. The professors are, for the most part, fantastic. There are professors here from the top law schools and most of them have actually worked in the field so they are not just academics teaching you the theory of law. Rather, you learn how a certain case would turn out in the real world. Because it is such a small school, it is so simple to get the classes that you want. I have never tried to register for a class and had it be full. The grading at the school is anonymous, which is nice because those kids who are the typical "brown-nosers" will receive nothing in return for their antics. The workload is heavy, but I think that you'l find that in any law school. There is a lot of reading and writing.

Status: Current student, full-time
Dates of Enrollment: 9/2003-Submit Date
Survey Submitted: March 2005

The grading is fair. The academic rigor of the classes is taken very seriously. The professors are hit or miss. Some are amazing and their classes always get filled to over capacity, while other professors can't fill a class. The Environmental Law Certificate Program is pushed on everyone, even if you came to Pace for another focus area. The program doesn't have much flexibility and only focuses on federal environmental law. I plan to practice environmental law, but I am not going to go for the magic "certificate."

 Employment Prospects

Status: Current student, full-time
Dates of Enrollment: 8/2004-Submit Date
Survey Submitted: April 2006

If interested in prosecuting, as I am, get an internship during your enrolled years at the Westchester DA's office; you will receive top priority if you want to apply after graduation.

Status: Current student, full-time
Dates of Enrollment: 8/2003-Submit Date
Survey Submitted: March 2006

Environmental students command immediate respect across the board with employers looking for environmental lawyers. EPA and DOJ actively recruit from Pace, as do firms with environmental and land use practices. Personally, I was interviewed for about 80 percent of the jobs to which I applied, and ultimately found the exact job I came to law school hoping to do.

Because Pace isn't as well know in other areas, the job hunt for non-environmental students can be more challenging, particularly given that we're competing against students from NYU, Columbia, Yale, Seton Hall, Rutgers and Cardozo, all of which are in the same general geographic area. Fortunately, the school has recently revamped its career development center, which really does work for everyone and the staff is extremely helpful. Plus, Pace alumni are always eager to help current students. At this point, just about everyone I know whose actively sought help and put some time into their job search has found good work. Plenty of students go on to work at big NYC firms, but most seem to find work at small- and mid-size firms or with government employers.

Status: Current student, full-time
Dates of Enrollment: 9/2004-Submit Date
Survey Submitted: March 2006

Pace Law School has completely revamped its career development center. It's located in a brand new space and the law school has hired a new, highly qualified and high energy Dean of Career Development. I have worked with a couple of Pace Law School alumni and have been very impressed with how much they want to help students, as well as how connected they still are to Pace Law. I have my own mentor and he gave me advice that led me to apply to a summer position. Since professors are happy to write letters of recommendation and are very responsive, my application went smoothly and I've secured the summer position I wanted.

Status: Current student, full-time
Dates of Enrollment: 8/2003-Submit Date
Survey Submitted: March 2006

Pace Law students have a great market of job opportunities in Westchester County since Pace is the only law school in the area. Students have successfully broken into the New York City market, but such opportunities are reliant on alumni connections or past positive experiences with Pace students. The Environmental Program at Pace has a strong reputation and environmental students usually have many options for job opportunities. Pace recently reorganized its career counseling department, which has been a very positive change. The current career counseling staff is very proactive and dedicated to helping each and every student get a job. This is important since Pace students are competing against well-known, top-tier law schools' students for jobs in Manhattan.

Status: Current student, full-time
Dates of Enrollment: 8/2002-Submit Date
Survey Submitted: March 2006

Employment prospects for Pace Law graduates are good. While there was a low placement rate a few years ago, the law school has committed itself to increasing its placement rate by hiring placement professionals, having more on-campus interviews, and having an online service that provides students with recent job opportunities that they can apply to either through the system or independently. In terms of summer internships, the school is unfortunately not as helpful. Many students, myself included, had to find these opportunities on our own through past work experiences or networking. One of the benefits of attending Pace is that it is the only law school located between New York City and Albany. As such, students looking for jobs in the Westchester area have a lot of opportunities they can apply to and by virtue of its location, there are a lot of alumni in the Westchester area willing to hire Pace students for either summer employment or permanent positions upon graduation. The key to job placement success is securing an internship in your first or second year and maintaining the relationship throughout the duration of your time at law school so that it may turn into a job upon graduation.

Status: Current student, full-time
Dates of Enrollment: 8/2004-Submit Date
Survey Submitted: March 2006

Pace just updated their career department. We have an online career center with listings where you can upload your resume and apply, along with weekly e-mails that go out with new job postings. They have career counselors who help you with your resume. They have summer programs that get you internships in the local courts and at local nonprofit organizations. The New York Judicial Institute is in the same building as the law school and frequently holds events along with training all the judges for New York State.

Status: Alumnus/a, full-time
Dates of Enrollment: 9/2001-5/2004
Survey Submitted: March 2006

The best firms have on-campus interviews at Pace. If you want to get a job at a big firm in New York City, you need to be in the top 10 percent of your class, but that is pretty much the case for all schools, except for the elites. But good students will find plenty of opportunities at smaller firms, nonprofit organizations, and state jobs, such as working for the court system or a district attorney's office. The career services office at Pace is very good and does everything possible to help students secure employment.

Status: Current student, full-time
Dates of Enrollment: 8/2004-Submit Date
Survey Submitted: March 2006

We have an alumni development office that works hard to make sure that we stay connected to Pace alumni. In addition, the career services office is very hands-on with the students and will help us prepare application packages. They also work to enhance the students' professional skills. Also, prospective employers in interviews have told me that good students tend to come from Pace Law School. With that, I would say that we have a pretty good reputation.

Status: Alumnus/a, full-time
Dates of Enrollment: 9/1997-5/2000
Survey Submitted: July 2004

While Pace does not carry the prestige of some of the other NY law schools it has a better reputation than some—though I still think the reputation is undeservedly low. I'm not sure of the current tier rankings, but Pace certainly has a better regional reputation than a national one. Because of that regional reputation, however, graduates must often plan to remain in the tri-state region after graduation. There were a good number of law firms that interviewed at fall OCI, but the competition for positions was very tight. Thus, students considering attending Pace must be near the top of the class to have the most opportunities. While I have been successful in my career, I know that others who graduated with lower grades and fewer relevant activities have had a harder time. No matter how well you do, you will have to often justify your decision to attend Pace (while interviewing) and you will also encounter prejudice from a few lawyers and firms that can't get past certain names.

Quality of Life

Status: Current student, full-time
Dates of Enrollment: 8/2005-Submit Date
Survey Submitted: April 2006

The campus is small with affordable housing and state-of-the-art facilities. The buildings are all computerized with wireless access. Housing around campus is very easy to obtain with a supportive neighborhood always willing to help and participate with Pace law students.

Status: Current student, full-time
Dates of Enrollment: 8/2003-Submit Date
Survey Submitted: March 2006

Living in White Plains is expensive. Shockingly so. I mean, if you have the money, you can certainly find nice housing, and very near campus, too. I can't say much (at least, not much nice) about White Plains, except that it's a 36-minute train ride from Midtown, Manhattan. And that's pretty cool. But even if you're stuck in White Plains (news flash: if you go to law school, it really doesn't matter where you live, because you're not going to see much of it anyway), you can still find better-than-decent sushi, and there are a plethora of not-very-good, but certainly adequate, bars and restaurants.

As for the school itself, it's fine. Our library is getting a major overhaul this summer; hopefully that will eliminate at least some of its truly horrific 1970s Brutalistic ambiance. The main building where classes are held, however, is really lovely.

I've never felt "unsafe" around campus, and frequently walk the mile back to my house after midnight.

Status: Current student, full-time
Dates of Enrollment: 8/2005-Submit Date
Survey Submitted: March 2006

It's quite safe here—and the students are friendly and pretty social on Friday and Saturday nights. White Plains is tough on parking violations, and there are police at every corner waiting for people to run yellow-turning-red lights. One has to be very careful to abide by every little law here. Parking in White Plains is always metered and the police give more tickets here per capita than anywhere I've ever been! Rent is not cheap around here, either! And the dorms are pricey! But overall, it's easier than living in NYC, for example, although much less cultural.

Read all of Vault's Law School Surveys at www.vault.com/lawschool — get complete surveys on top law schools, expert advice on applicaton essays, LSAT prep and more.

VAULT CAREER LIBRARY **451**

Status: Current student, full-time
Dates of Enrollment: 9/2004-Submit Date
Survey Submitted: March 2006

Living and going to school in White Plains is a lot better than I actually thought it would be. When I was looking at schools, White Plains seemed like a random location, but in reality it's ideally situated close enough to NYC so one can just hop on a train and be there in 30 minutes. White Plains has lots of parks and quiet spots, as well all of the amenities a student would need, like convenient shopping and quick access to all the highways if you want to travel.

Status: Current student, part-time
Dates of Enrollment: 8/2005-Submit Date
Survey Submitted: March 2006

I am a commuting student so my response is naturally limited. What I can say is that when I arrive on campus, it does lend itself to an "oasis" type feeling (since I am driving in from NYC). The peace and quiet of campus is definitely a plus.

Status: Current student, full-time
Dates of Enrollment: 8/2002-Submit Date
Survey Submitted: March 2006

As opposed to many of the New York City area schools, Pace is one of the few schools with a campus. This is possibly one of the biggest draws to Pace. Since it is situated in White Plains, but has a campus of its own, students get the benefits of both a city and country environment. This allows for peace and tranquility while on campus and bars, restaurants and malls right outside of campus. White Plains is a generally safe city and many students live off campus within a few blocks away. There exists the same crime as in any small city but Pace security surveils the area and the campus 24 hours a day to secure the safety of its students, faculty and administrators.

On-campus housing is also available to students and is pretty easy to come by due to the fact that Pace is largely a commuter school. This convenience comes at a price though: Pace on-campus housing is approximately $1,100 a month, much more than apartments in the area. Although, included in that $1,100 is cable, a cleaning staff who maintains the bathrooms and common areas and all utilities such as heat, electric, internet and cable television, including premium channels like HBO.

Status: Current student, full-time
Dates of Enrollment: 9/2005-Submit Date
Survey Submitted: March 2006

Amazing. Law school is tough. You don't want to go through it with competitive students who hope you fail. Most New York law schools are cut throat. Pace is the exception. Largely because the campus is so pretty it's downright soothing, and because environmental law students and professors tend to hope that everyone does the best.

The housing around White Plains can get a bit pricey, especially for a suburb, but there are cheap places that are less nice but still livable. White Plains is a great small city but really, you won't be worrying about that since there's so much work. The good thing to know is that a lot of restaurants deliver to the library and it's safe to walk around the campus by yourself at night.

Status: Current student, full-time JD/MBA
Dates of Enrollment: 8/2004-Submit Date
Survey Submitted: March 2006

This is a great neighborhood—I factored this into my decision to come here. The school shares a driveway with a Catholic high school, but other than that the grounds are nice. There is free parking although sometimes a hike. The reason I like this campus is because it is only the law school, so you are not mixed in with undergraduates.

Status: Current student, full-time
Dates of Enrollment: 8/2004-Submit Date
Survey Submitted: April 2005

The school is in a very nice area, which means that rent is a little pricey. There are lots of restaurants. The school is on the same grounds as a Catholic private school, so there are old and new buildings. I was attracted to this school because the law school is a separate campus from the undergraduate and this is a big plus. I was truly afraid of school and thought that you just don't make friends in law school, but everyone is pretty friendly. The upperclassmen are willing to share their opinions on what classes to take and professors, and other information even when they're not asked. Every school is competitive but you're not directly competing against anyone, so there are no crazy stories of stealing books that I've heard.

Status: Current student, full-time
Dates of Enrollment: 9/2002-Submit Date
Survey Submitted: April 2005

On-campus housing is limited to the dorms. Most students opt for off-campus rentals. There are plenty of multi-family houses in close proximity to the school that traditionally rent to students and are very affordable for Westchester. With the "revitalization" of the White Plains downtown area there is also plenty of higher end housing. The facilities have incorporated the old with the new seamlessly. The main administrative, granite block and stone building has been joined by a new classroom building and is now attached to the judicial institute, which is a state-of-the-art facility available to student organizations, speakers and classes. The library is also undergoing a major renovation. White Plains, and the surrounding neighborhoods are extremely safe, and women do not have to fear walking home late at night from social events on campus or in the White Plains downtown area.

 Social Life

Status: Current student, part-time
Dates of Enrollment: 8/2004-Submit Date
Survey Submitted: March 2006

Social life for young, full-time day students appears to be good. Social events for part-time, older students is lacking.

Status: Current student, full-time
Dates of Enrollment: 8/2003-Submit Date
Survey Submitted: March 2006

Pace is definitely a great place to make friends. There are dozens of clubs and there's always something going on. The Environmental Law Society sponsors hikes, river clean-ups, dart tournaments and a great Earth Day Celebration. The Pace Law School Democrats play political jeopardy on occasion, in addition to bringing in local politicos. The Lawyers Guild puts on good debates. Basically, if you want to find something to do with your classmates, you really don't have to look that hard.

Status: Current student, part-time
Dates of Enrollment: 8/2005-Submit Date
Survey Submitted: March 2006

This is something that I can say is totally different from undergrad—with the exception of those who simply cannot due to family or other reasons—the ENTIRE night class goes out after the last class on Thursday and unwinds together at one of the local watering holes. This is amazing...the camaraderie noteworthy. Everyone talks to everyone even if its only for a short time until the "groups" form. If there is one thing that prevents me from transferring to another school—it's the relationships that have formed in such a short time. Pace Law is definitely a good place to be.

Status: Current student, full-time
Dates of Enrollment: 8/2003-Submit Date
Survey Submitted: March 2006

The student organizations at Pace provide an academic discourse for current legal issues, but they also organize social events that are well attended. For example, each year students look forward to the Earth Day celebrations sponsored by the Environmental Law Society. Essentially each Thursday night a different student organization sponsors a fund-raising event at a local pub that draws many students out to relax and socialize together off campus. Students frequent Patrick's Pub—it is off beaten path and the bartenders know us all by name.

Status: Current student, full-time
Dates of Enrollment: 8/2002-Submit Date
Survey Submitted: March 2006

Being situated in White Plains provides a great social life for students. Campus organizations regularly hold functions both on campus and off campus, providing "specials" to students. The sense of community is strong and many students are involved in at least one organization. These range from the Womens Association of Law Students, to the Jewish Law Students Association, to the Latin American Law Students Association, and include such other groups such as the American Federalist Society, a club whose focus is on strict construction of the constitution. Pace's faculty plays a role in the clubs and there is a real camaraderie when students and faculty come together, something that is not readily available at a school without a campus, such as many of the New York law schools. Thursday night is the biggest night for Pace students with many going to local bars and restaurants and congregating as a group.

The four or five times you go out a month the first half of each semester are great. The bars, like all bars, are only as fun as the students you go with. There is a group that goes out regularly if that's your priority in White Plains and not a weekend goes by that a club isn't sponsoring a drink special for students at a local pub. There are too many amazing events to attend all of them. Pace does a great job of getting speakers and panelists. Dating occurs quite a bit, as well.

Status: Current student, full-time
Dates of Enrollment: 8/2005-Submit Date
Survey Submitted: March 2006

The dating scene is not great. A lot of people are married or have serious boyfriends/girlfriends. I made a lot of great friends so far. Every one is really nice and friendly. This is a not a cutthroat, competitive-feeling atmosphere. Everyone tries to help everyone else out. The bars around here aren't bad—and the City is really close so a lot of people go out in NYC also.

Status: Current student, full-time
Dates of Enrollment: 8/2004-Submit Date
Survey Submitted: March 2006

Law school students don't have a lot of time. However, there are frequent get-togethers both on and off campus. There are over 20 different school organizations that have meetings along with social gatherings. They have pizza parties with professors, BBQ's on the quad and even a dodgeball competition coming up. Pace has a superb cafeteria with made-to-order and to-go food along with a large student lounge. To know what's going on all you have to do is look on the sides of the white boards in each classroom and they have daily updates of all the activities.

Status: Current student, full-time
Dates of Enrollment: 9/2002-Submit Date
Survey Submitted: April 2005

Pace Law School is within walking distance of downtown White Plains, which is an ever-growing mini-metropolis. Life outside of law school is in no way wanting for things to do. There are bars, restaurants, movie theaters, bookstores,

big malls, little malls, gyms and churches all down the block from the law school campus. There is literally something for everyone in this neighborhood. Bars become a favorite place to blow off steam and relieve some stress. There are a few more popular than others, but that has to do simply with the bar's desire to solicit business from the students. Several very good restaurants are in the area, and there are new ones opening all the time. It's a great place to go to school!

 The School Says

Located on a sprawling 13-acre campus just 25 miles from New York City, Pace University School of Law combines the beauty of open spaces and classic buildings with the convenience of technology and the amenities of a small, vibrant urban community. Law firms are abundant in White Plains, the federal and district courthouses are close by, and a new City Center has recently just been built.

The law school is home to the New York State Judicial Institute, an innovative center for judicial education and the only center of its kind in the United States.

Students are attracted nationally and from abroad for our congenial atmosphere, diverse population and our award winning Centers. Extensive opportunities exist through our clinics, externships and internships for students to learn practical lawyering skills and to become litigators. Leveraging our premier location in suburban White Plains, Pace Law School students enjoy enhanced internship opportunities with the local Westchester and Connecticut headquarters of major corporations. The Center for Career Development has fostered strong relationships with major corporations which provide summer and academic-year internship opportunities for Pace Law students. Corporate employers through our program have included The Dannon Company, Direct Energy, Fortis Capital Corp., Heineken USA, IBM, International Paper, Morgan Stanley, Pepsi Bottling Group, Pernod Ricard, USA and Pfizer, Inc.

Pace Law School has a history of student-centered growth and innovation built on a foundation of deep mutual respect between faculty and students. Students from diverse backgrounds come together to learn lawyering skills, gain vital professional experience and contribute to the creation of a more just society.

Read all of Vault's Law School Surveys at www.vault.com/lawschool — get complete surveys on top law schools, expert advice on applicaton essays, LSAT prep and more.

VAULT CAREER LIBRARY   453

St. John's University School of Law

Admissions Office
8000 Utopia Parkway
Queens, NY 11439
Admissions phone: (718) 994-6474
Admissions e-mail: lawinfo@stjohns.edu
Admissions URL:
http://www.stjohns.edu/academics/graduate/law/prospective

 Admissions

Status: Current student, full-time
Dates of Enrollment: 8/2003-Submit Date
Survey Submitted: April 2006

Admissions is the easiest, but least quantifiable, aspect of the process. On some level, having strong grades and a decent LSAT score would appear to give an applicant a greater chance of admission, but I've personally seen it vary. St. John's strives to accept individuals with a diverse set of experiences, so if an applicant is less competitive academically (in a relative sense), they can be more competitive in other areas.

Status: Alumnus/a, part-time
Dates of Enrollment: 8/2005-12/2005
Survey Submitted: February 2006

I was fortunate enough to work as an assistant for a large law firm that recruited from St. John's and my letters of recommendation came from both St John's alumni and contacts within the firm. It definitely gave me an advantage as my grades were not considerably impressive in comparison to the applicant pool. The school is considerably selective in the number of applicants they let in, so my advice would be to do your homework on who you ask for recommendation letters. It may fall down on who you know and not necessarily what you know.

Status: Alumnus/a, full-time
Dates of Enrollment: 8/2001-6/2004
Survey Submitted: April 2005

Typical of other schools; the on-campus open house was nice. There was no essay.

Status: Alumnus/a, part-time
Dates of Enrollment: 9/1995-6/1999
Survey Submitted: March 2005

It is fairly competitive and requires your undergrad transcript, your LSAT score and an essay discussing why you would be an asset to the university. At the time I applied, they had a rolling admissions policy, so the sooner you submitted your application, the more likely it was that you got admitted.

Status: Current student, full-time
Dates of Enrollment: 8/2001-Submit Date
Survey Submitted: October 2003

The admissions standard has improved each year that I have attended (I am currently 3L). I believe the average LSAT score this year was 160. The application process was standard—I don't remember anything standing out, other than finding out almost immediately about getting in. It's a rolling admission operation. I attended several open house events at New York law schools, and St. John's stood out because it felt the most natural.

The students all said wonderful things about the school. I could tell they were very sincere. Also, the faculty members were very approachable and helped with all my questions. The woman in charge of admissions was fabulous. She answered every question honestly and had all the facts at her fingertips. I would also say that SJU is VERY generous with its financial aid packages. The majority of my friends have substantial scholarships—average being about half-tuition. I believe they do this to attract high-caliber law students, and it

definitely works. Many classmates were accepted to the very best law school as well as SJU and chose SJU because of their scholarships. It is also very easy to retain your scholarship as well. At many schools you must be in a ridiculous percentile of your class, but at SJU it's only top 50 percent.

Status: Current student, full-time
Dates of Enrollment: 8/2002-Submit Date
Survey Submitted: February 2004

St. John's was the quickest school to respond to my application. This was a big plus because it automatically gave me an option to attend law school. Many schools drag out their admissions process, which is extremely burdensome on the applying student who is waiting day after day for responses. By responding quickly, St. John's really helps the student with the processes of making his or her decision. More schools should be on top of their admissions processes and response times, like St. John's has managed to be.

Status: Alumnus/a, full-time
Dates of Enrollment: 8/1998-6/2001
Survey Submitted: April 2004

The admissions process was very similar to most law schools. The application was submitted in late winter (February), and responses were received by May. For purposes of admission, it was helpful to be in the mid to high 150's on the LSAT at least. Grade point average appeared to be slightly less important than LSAT score, but undergraduate academic reputation may play a significant role where GPA is concerned.

Status: Current student, full-time
Dates of Enrollment: 8/2001-Submit Date
Survey Submitted: March 2004

The application included LSAT scores and an undergrad transcript. St. John's highly prizes above-average scores in both, but LSATs seem to be more important.

Status: Alumnus/a, full-time
Dates of Enrollment: 8/2000-5/2003
Survey Submitted: November 2003

LSAT, LSAT, LSAT, grades, LSAT.

Status: Current student, full-time
Dates of Enrollment: 1/2003-Submit Date
Survey Submitted: January 2004

The admissions process included taking the LSAT (in preparation, I took the Kaplan test prep course), personal statement, letters of recommendation (which I got from college professors and my employer) and completion of the standard application. Major tip: complete and submit your application as early as possible!

Status: Current student, full-time
Dates of Enrollment: 1/2003-Submit Date
Survey Submitted: January 2004

The admissions process was standard by comparison to other schools. It involved an application form, reference letters and an essay on why I wanted to go to law school. There was no interview. The school offered open houses and pre-decision orientations. In terms of selectivity, it seems the school is most selective when it comes to giving out scholarships to its top students and prospective students.

Status: Current student, full-time
Dates of Enrollment: 8/2001-Submit Date
Survey Submitted: January 2004

St. John's is in the "middle tier" of selectivity of the NY schools. Its statistics for the entering class go up by leaps and bounds each fall. The school also has a January admissions program and an evening students program. The consensus is it's a little easier to get into the evening (four-year) program than the three-year day program.

The school says: "As of February 2005, St. John's University School of Law's mid-year entering program has been discontinued. Applications are now accepted for full-time day, part-time day or part-time evening beginning only in the fall of each year."

Status: Alumnus/a, part-time
Dates of Enrollment: 9/1995-6/2002
Survey Submitted: April 2004

The process consisted of an application, LSAT score and essay. There was no interview. The school is fairly competitive to get into, so it's important to do well on the LSATs and to have a good undergraduate GPA. My GPA was not so good; however, I had a diverse work background and was applying to the evening section—so most of my fellow classmates had also been out of school for a number of years as well.

 ## Academics

Status: Current student, full-time
Dates of Enrollment: 8/2003-Submit Date
Survey Submitted: April 2006

The quality of the classes is largely dependent on what one seeks to gain from class. If a student wants to achieve a practical understanding of the law as a whole, and be in an advantageous position when taking the bar, the quality at St. John's is rather high. However, if one views quality from the perspective of gaining a strong understanding of the theoretical underpinnings of legal concepts, there are few classes that provide that experience. Popular classes are difficult to get into, although I've been advised that the system will change for the fall 2006 class. The professors are all excellent (or mostly excellent). The workload is a law school workload. I don't think it really varies from school to school. The grading is a huge problem. We have one of the lowest curves for law schools of our tier in the tri-state area, which puts students at a disadvantage as compared to graduates from competing schools.

Status: Alumnus/a, full-time
Dates of Enrollment: 1/2003-5/2005
Survey Submitted: April 2006

The academic program is very much geared towards the NY State Bar Exam, as well as practicing in NY. Classes are generally available, however, enrollment is prioritized by class seniority. There is a wide spectrum of professors, some of whom are very good and others who are poor. Grading tends to be harsh. A curve is used, and therefore, only a small percentage of students will achieve an A-range grade. Therefore, a student's GPA is highly impacted by the curve.

Status: Alumnus/a, full-time
Dates of Enrollment: 8/1995-5/1998
Survey Submitted: March 2006

St. John's is a very competitive school. As you are constantly competing against students at Cornell, NYU, Columbia, Fordham, Brooklyn and Cardozo for top law firm jobs; you must have a solid GPA and make it on to either the Law Review or be successful in the moot court competitions. The professors are topnotch and most teach by the Socratic Method. The professors will help you transform into a solid law practitioner; at least that is the reputation St. John's law graduates have in New York City. The grading is on a bell curve, so high grades are tough to come by since, again, a majority of the students are so competitive in vying for a top law firm position. The workload is heavy, but that's the case for any law school.

Status: Alumnus/a, part-time
Dates of Enrollment: 8/2005-12/2005
Survey Submitted: February 2006

First semester workload was heavy but manageable if you don't mind spending your weekends reading and doing briefs. I lost touch with much of my family and friends and seldom did anything outside of schoolwork. St. John's has some extraordinary professors and my experiences with them were mostly positive.

Status: Alumnus/a, full-time
Dates of Enrollment: 8/2001-6/2004
Survey Submitted: April 2005

It is easy to get the classes you need. It was hard, but not too hard. St. John's students, generally, are not as competitive as other schools.

Status: Alumnus/a, part-time
Dates of Enrollment: 9/1995-6/1999
Survey Submitted: March 2005

The majority of the professors were very good and had some practical information to impart, as well as theory. St. John's does a great job preparing law school graduates for the bar exam because of the number of required courses. Many other schools allow more electives, which results in students taking "easy classes" or off-the-beaten path classes that do not help you get ready for the bar. Conversely, St. John's has a really good core curriculum of required courses so that when you take the bar preparation classes after graduation those classes end up being mostly a review.

Status: Alumnus/a, part-time
Dates of Enrollment: 9/1995-5/1999
Survey Submitted: January 2005

I went to the evening program but took some day classes, too. Evening classes had the same professors as the day classes and the competition was slightly more difficult at night.

Status: Current student, full-time
Dates of Enrollment: 8/2002-Submit Date
Survey Submitted: February 2004

While getting into certain classes of your choice is sometimes difficult, the teaching quality and overall academic value at St. John's are extremely high. Teachers are enthusiastic and genuinely enjoy the subject matter. This translates into interesting class discussions as well as a learning environment that is also enjoyable for the students. Teachers are approachable and have convenient office hours for students to contact them.

Registration for classes is another matter. Most of the popular classes close out quickly, and unless you plan on waking up before 7 a.m. the morning of registration to make sure to register first in your class, you may not be guaranteed a spot in classes you wish to take, including electives. That said, the phone and online registration programs are easy to use.

Status: Current student, full-time
Dates of Enrollment: 1/2003-Submit Date
Survey Submitted: January 2004

The workload is about the same as any other law program. There are a few excellent professors, and unfortunately some poor professors. Some of the most popular classes, Sports Law, for example, have very limited enrollment, approximately 20-student maximums. These classes are impossible to get into. But the majority of classes are relatively easy to enroll in. Grading varies depending on the professor. There is a curve at the school (approximately 15 percent of the class gets an A, 40 percent gets a B), [but it does not apply to classes of 20 or fewer]. This means, as I've personally experienced, the highest grade in the class is a B+. Another grading issue is the wide disparity among the B-range grades. Someone may be on the cusp for a B+ and another on the cusp for a B-, and wind up with the same grade.

Status: Alumnus/a, full-time
Dates of Enrollment: 8/1999-5/2002
Survey Submitted: April 2004

Classes cater to general practice in New York. A specialty in bankruptcy exists. Constitutional Law has gone through many course changes.

Status: Alumnus/a, full-time
Dates of Enrollment: 8/1998-6/2001
Survey Submitted: April 2004

The program is divided into three full-time day sections, one evening section and one February admission (accelerated) section. Your first-year curriculum will be determined by section, so you will have the same classmates in every class for the duration of your first year. Based on St. John's grading curve ([B] average),

Read all of Vault's Law School Surveys at www.vault.com/lawschool — get complete surveys on top law schools, expert advice on applicaton essays, LSAT prep and more.

VAULT CAREER LIBRARY   **455**

 **Employment Prospects**

this can either help you (if you land in a less competitive section) or hurt you (if your section is more competitive).

Like most law schools, the quality and personality of professors run the spectrum. First year, your schedule is predetermined, so you have no control over the professors and courses. However, some of second and nearly all of third year, you have the freedom to choose electives, and I would recommend speaking with 3L students who know professors' styles and personalities. Most professors are very nice and quite approachable.

> **The school says:** "As of February 2005, St. John's University School of Law's mid-year entering program has been discontinued. Applications are now accepted for full-time day, part-time day or part-time evening beginning only in the fall of each year."

Status: Current student, full-time
Dates of Enrollment: 8/2001-Submit Date
Survey Submitted: March 2004

First-year is two semesters each of the core courses of Torts, Contracts and Property. Others like Civil Procedure, Criminal Law and Legal Writing are one-semester courses. It might be changed somewhat now for first-years.

> **St. John's University Law School says:** "The upper-class curriculum is now almost entirely elective, with students required to pick five core electives from a group of 10."

Status: Current student, full-time
Dates of Enrollment: 8/2001-Submit Date
Survey Submitted: January 2004

St. John's has just changed its core curriculum for entering students. All the basic classes are still required first year, but there is more flexibility second year. It's easy to get classes. The professors are highly ranked. Workload is greatest in the second year, when students are also competing for journals, Law Review and moot court.

Status: Current student, full-time
Dates of Enrollment: 8/2001-Submit Date
Survey Submitted: October 2003

The professors are excellent. Most abide by the Socratic Method, but not all of them. The class sizes for 1Ls are about 80, but upper-level classes are much smaller. There is a B curve, and I would categorize the school as competitive with respect to student environment. Workload is evenly distributed. While as a 1L it feels like you have a ton of work, it's mostly because it's new and you don't know what you're doing. As a 2L you are doing coursework and extracurricular things (journal, moot court) and also attempting to find a job.

Status: Alumnus/a, part-time
Dates of Enrollment: 9/1995-6/2002
Survey Submitted: October 2003

The academic program is terrific for preparing law school grads to take the New York Bar Exam—and passing that exam is the ultimate goal of the majority of grads. The curriculum is tough, but balanced, fair and useful. If you are in the evening section, there is only one session for each class in the evening, so there is no issue about "getting into" a specific professor's class.

The majority of the professors are great, with only a few that don't cut the mustard. The school doesn't offer many "fluff" classes, and the overall quality of the program is very good to great. The workload is quite large—but then again, it's law school, so it is expected to be large. But it is manageable, and the grading is pretty fair. Unlike a lot of other law schools that give inflated bell curve grades, St. John's is tougher on its students but remains fair.

Status: Current student, full-time
Dates of Enrollment: 8/2003-Submit Date
Survey Submitted: April 2006

St. John's is highly beneficial if one wishes to engage in criminal law, whether as a criminal defense attorney or as an assistant district attorney. The alumni network is helpful, but under-utilized. On-campus recruiting is an area that needs further improvement and development. Although the school offers an education that is above-average, and the students are capable of achieving in a number of fields, the school is somewhat underestimated by the broader legal community. Unfortunately, the school is viewed as one for attorneys who are litigators or practice criminal law. There is a growing recognition for those who want to practice real estate or bankruptcy law, but there is still a long way to go. These stereotypes of students and graduates of the school serve to limit the job opportunities of those who want to accomplish something different. Without a serious background in securities law (before law school), it is very different to gain employment in that field. The same holds true for a variety of other fields. As a result, if one does not want to practice in the above mentioned fields, the path to one's goals is far more arduous.

Status: Alumnus/a, full-time
Dates of Enrollment: 1/2003-5/2005
Survey Submitted: April 2006

As far as top-level large firms are concerned, some do recruit at St. John's however, they look for a very specific candidate and tend to hire one or maybe two students only. One thing that makes it difficult to find a competitive job from St. John's is the fact that you're competing with students from schools with better reputations, and most of the other schools do not use grading curves, therefore making those students' GPAs inflated compared to someone from St. John's. St. John's does have strong connections with judicial clerkships, particularly in the Second Circuit.

Status: Alumnus/a, full-time
Dates of Enrollment: 8/1995-5/1998
Survey Submitted: March 2006

On-campus recruiting is solid, but you have to be at the top of your class and/or on Law Review (or one of the other top journals) or moot court to get an interview slot. Most of the interviews are given by recruiters to the same students, so if you are not within this category, you must be persistent and send out mass mailings to St. John's alumni (I sent out letters to alumni who had the same background as me, i.e., St. John's and my undergraduate college, and actually landed a few interviews this way!).

Internships are plentiful in the career services binder so try and secure the best one early. Internships at the courts can get you academic credit during the semester so look into this option; this is a great way to bolster your resume and be a few credits closer to graduating.

Status: Alumnus/a, part-time
Dates of Enrollment: 9/1995-6/1999
Survey Submitted: March 2005

If you are going to work in NY, then St. John's will provide you as good an opportunity to land a good job as any other local law school. It has a great alumni base that takes pride in being St. John's grads and is loyal to the school. Of course, you still need to be in the top 15 percent of the class to have the best and most diverse employment options.

Status: Alumnus/a, full-time
Dates of Enrollment: 8/1998-6/2001
Survey Submitted: April 2004

If you perform well during your first year, you will have a very good chance of landing a summer associate position with a large reputable New York City firm. The difficulty lies in the grading curve and your luck in the section assignment process. Although St. John's has a strong presence in the large New York City firms, the majority of those persons were in the top 10 to 15 percent of their first-year class and then received a summer associate offer after their first year based entirely on their first-year grades. Most firms offer associate positions to 90 percent or more of their summer associate class. Your best shot at landing a position with a prestigious Manhattan firm is to have a very strong first year, because during the on-campus interviewing process, the visiting interviewers are comparing you to your peers at St. John's and not to students at other law schools. Given the harsh grading curve, you will be at a disadvantage when interviewing against students at other law schools unless the interviewer is familiar with the grading curve.

The school says: "Over 97 percent of St. John's graduates have obtained jobs as of nine months after graduation."

Status: Current student, full-time
Dates of Enrollment: 8/2001-Submit Date
Survey Submitted: March 2004

On-campus interviewing encompasses a lot of New York City firms and public interest work. The career services center has a lot of information about clerkships and other work. They do not hold your hand; you must hustle to get opportunities.

Status: Alumnus/a, part-time
Dates of Enrollment: 9/1995-6/2002
Survey Submitted: April 2004

St. John's is a great school to go to if you plan on practicing law in New York. The alumni base is huge, influential and loyal. Grads from St. John's practice law in so many different areas that the door is open (if you do well). Career prospects are directly related to your grades and whether you made it onto a journal. The profession is very competitive, so you need to do well regardless of what school you attend. St. John's grads do get more respect in the job marketplace than a lot of other area law schools.

Status: Current student, full-time
Dates of Enrollment: 8/2001-Submit Date
Survey Submitted: October 2003

BigLaw is definitely a possibility, but it's a probability if you are top 10 percent. There is also a pretty good externship program and several clinics to get involved in. SJU is very prestigious with NY law firms—probably not so great if you are not planning to stay in NY. Several students have secured clerkships for after law school.

 ## Quality of Life

Status: Current student, full-time
Dates of Enrollment: 8/2003-Submit Date
Survey Submitted: April 2006

The school has no serious housing program for its students in the law program. The campus is in a nice area of Queens, and one doesn't have to worry about safety too often. The facilities are great, especially if a potential student wants to hit the gym on a regular basis. Due to the past successes of the school's basketball team, the gym is well funded.

Status: Alumnus/a, full-time
Dates of Enrollment: 1/2003-5/2005
Survey Submitted: April 2006

The campus is gloomy and located in an environment that is not very student-friendly and is also inconvenient for students who live in Manhattan. It is very much a commuter school. Many undergrads live on campus and there is a wide disparity between the undergrads and law school students. There have been incidents of crime on campus, mostly related to harassment and theft. In particular, several cars have been stolen and damaged in the campus parking lot.

Status: Alumnus/a, full-time
Dates of Enrollment: 8/1995-5/1998
Survey Submitted: March 2006

St. John's is for the most part a commuter law school. There are a few students that reside in the dorms that were recently built, and many others either go to school from "home" or rent an apartment near the school. The law school facilities are excellent, especially the state-of-the-art moot court room that was recently built and the law school library, which has plenty of space to accommodate all those who like to study in the library. The cafeteria has good

food and the area outside of campus has a few diners and restaurants that work as well.

Status: Alumnus/a, part-time
Dates of Enrollment: 8/2005-12/2005
Survey Submitted: February 2006

I rented a one-bedroom apartment with a parking spot off campus about 10 minutes from campus for roughly $1,100.00 a month. Off-campus housing was very much available for the typical Queens area. I would suggest searching Craigslist for other students attending St. John's who would like to share an apartment to keep costs down. I knew several students who were very successful in finding another first-year law student. Otherwise, using a broker (although pricey) is very helpful.

Status: Alumnus/a, part-time
Dates of Enrollment: 9/1995-6/1999
Survey Submitted: March 2005

The cafeteria in the law school is decent and there are plenty of places to eat around the school. Parking can sometimes be an issue but the school was very safe. I didn't live on campus but I know the school has limited housing.

Status: Alumnus/a, full-time
Dates of Enrollment: 8/1998-6/2001
Survey Submitted: April 2004

Housing is often a difficult situation, because of the school's location in Queens. However, by comparison to Manhattan, rental rates are quite reasonable. St. John's has recently erected on-campus housing facilities that may also serve to relieve some of the housing problems as well.

The campus is nice and it's in a fairly nice area. I felt comfortable walking home from school every day (about six to eight blocks). Parking on campus can be a bit of a challenge; however, I understand that a new parking structure has been built to alleviate some of that problem as well. The dining facilities are adequate, and the cafeteria has an atrium that is a nice place to study or even watch television on the big screen.

The principal complaints that I have with my experience while at St. John's include the fact that the law school building is located on the edge of the undergraduate campus. However, students at St. John's, whether graduate or undergraduate, have unrestricted access to the law school facilities (except the library). This does pose something of a security risk.

Status: Current student, full-time
Dates of Enrollment: 8/2001-Submit Date
Survey Submitted: March 2004

The immediate neighborhood is nice. The school has concocted the most ridiculous security system to keep the bad element out, but mostly it makes for a traffic jam. There are OK places to eat immediately around the school, and the school's food is edible but incredibly high-priced.

Status: Current student, full-time
Dates of Enrollment: 8/2001-Submit Date
Survey Submitted: January 2004

The law school is great, but the undergraduate campus can mar the experience. I lived in the dorm my first semester of law school, and it was a miserable experience. You cannot drink alcohol in the dorm, even if you are over 21 and in a grad program. There are undergraduates running all over the place at night, loud and drunk. It was not conducive to learning.

Status: Current student, full-time
Dates of Enrollment: 8/2002-Submit Date
Survey Submitted: February 2004

The neighborhood is nice and has a lot of available restaurants, stores and so on. There is obviously New York City just 20 minutes away. St. John's usually has a competitive sports program, though they have some problems now.

Read all of Vault's Law School Surveys at www.vault.com/lawschool — get complete surveys on top law schools, expert advice on applicaton essays, LSAT prep and more.

VAULT CAREER LIBRARY   457

Status: Current student, full-time
Dates of Enrollment: 8/2001-Submit Date
Survey Submitted: October 2003

The cafeteria food stinks, but the technology at the school is great, and the library is gorgeous and comfortable for studying. Some of the classrooms are a bit outdated, but there is a phenomenal moot court room. SJU is set in a safe neighborhood, and it is easily accessible by public transportation.

 Social Life

Status: Current student, full-time
Dates of Enrollment: 8/2003-Submit Date
Survey Submitted: April 2006

There's not really too much of a social scene at the school. There are two bars near the school, the Last Call and the Sly Fox, both of which are refreshingly average. Outside of that, there's not too much there. Additionally, the school has strong Irish, Catholic and Jewish communities, all of which have social events that are really good.

Status: Alumnus/a, full-time
Dates of Enrollment: 8/1995-5/1998
Survey Submitted: March 2006

Again, as St. John's is, for the most part, a commuter law school; many students just go to class and either leave campus or go to the library and study. Some students go to the local watering holes right off of Utopia Parkway for a few drinks, or gather in the cafeteria to catch up and mingle. There's an atrium next to the cafeteria where people hang out and can watch a little TV, but, for the most part, the social scene is pretty limited.

Status: Current student, full-time
Dates of Enrollment: 8/2001-Submit Date
Survey Submitted: January 2004

Law students go out on Thursday nights. The two big bars are the Sly Fox and Iguana's. The Sly Fox is a little stodgy (a lot of older men hitting on the law school girls). It's a good place to go for bar food and a beer, though. There's also a sit-down restaurant, but overpriced. Iguana's is better, in my opinion. It has a Mexican theme, a big tequila selection. There's great music on the jukebox.

Status: Current student, full-time
Dates of Enrollment: 8/2001-Submit Date
Survey Submitted: October 2003

Thursday nights are spent at the local bars. The social environment there is great. There is a bunch of school-sponsored events that are amazing! Softball

games, barbecues, St. Patrick's Day Party (where professors and the dean sing Irish songs). There are also over 30 student-run organizations and clubs to become a part of.

Status: Current student, full-time
Dates of Enrollment: 1/2003-Submit Date
Survey Submitted: January 2004

Social life is practically nonexistent. Once in a while people all get together for a party at some bar, but most of the students are pretty independent, and the fact that it is a commuter school does not lend itself to being a very social campus. Besides, the campus is in Jamaica, NY (Queens), not exactly the crucible of the party life.

Status: Alumnus/a, full-time
Dates of Enrollment: 8/1998-6/2001
Survey Submitted: April 2004

There are a few local bars that law students frequent near the campus. All in all I found my experience at St. John's to be very rewarding. I made some wonderful friends, learned a great deal from some amazing professors and had an otherwise great time learning and living with other people who shared my love of the law. While I did feel that our needs as law students were not always adequately met, I felt that the education and the experience that I gained from my years at St. John's gave me a strong foundation for the practice of law and a solid grounding in the ethical considerations essential for a well-rounded career.

Status: Current student, full-time
Dates of Enrollment: 8/2001-Submit Date
Survey Submitted: March 2004

The bar scene first year consisted of walking to the three bars on Union Turnpike: Gantry's, The Sly Fox and Iguana's. Last year, Gantry's lost its liquor license and was shut down. Since then my class seems to go out intermittently, but the first-years can always be found there.

Status: Alumnus/a, full-time
Dates of Enrollment: 8/2000-5/2003
Survey Submitted: November 2003

Drinking, more drinking and gossiping.

Syracuse University College of Law

Office of Admissions and Financial Aid
Suite 340
Syracuse, NY 13244-1030
Admissions phone: (315) 443-1962
Admissions fax: (315) 443-9568
Admissions e-mail: admissions@law.syr.edu
Admissions URL: http://www.law.syr.edu/admissions/

 Admissions

Status: Current student, full-time
Dates of Enrollment: 8/2004-Submit Date
Survey Submitted: May 2006

Syracuse has an admissions program where students may visit the school, attend a class, meet other students, talk to financial aid officers, and attend a luncheon with other students and teachers.

Status: Current student, full-time
Dates of Enrollment: 8/2005-Submit Date
Survey Submitted: May 2006

I applied in September and was admitted off the waitlist two weeks prior to the first day of orientation. I stayed in monthly contact with the admissions office, and then more frequently once May hit. I found the school highly selective with regards to LSAT scores.

Status: Current student, full-time
Dates of Enrollment: 9/2003-Submit Date
Survey Submitted: October 2005

The admissions process at Syracuse is identical to those of other law schools and the median LSAT score for the school for last year's incoming 1L class was 155.

The admissions office at the school itself is one of the college's most organized and enthusiastic departments. They were very active in sending out materials to accepted students and facilitating campus tours.

Status: Alumnus/a, full-time
Dates of Enrollment: 8/2002-5/2005
Survey Submitted: October 2005

Syracuse University's admissions process is pretty fair. Most students go here because, despite the high tuition (which increased every year I attended by at least 5 percent), they offer enough money (more than most other schools) to make it worth your while to attend school here. They advertise the ease of getting a joint degree at SUCOL, but in reality this is frowned upon by both the law school and the other schools (business, Maxwell, Newhouse). This is because all three of those schools rank very highly.

Status: Current student, full-time JD/MBA
Dates of Enrollment: 8/2004-Submit Date
Survey Submitted: October 2005

The admissions process was friendly and personal. Since I was a law student, I went to the School of Management and discussed what the process would entail and whether I was a good candidate. I got to know quite a few of the admin staff even before starting business school. The process took a while including the essays and resume and interview (those without enough work experience are required to interview), but it was all worth it.

Status: Current student, full-time
Dates of Enrollment: 8/2004-Submit Date
Survey Submitted: May 2005

The admissions process was relatively easy—it required the same components as other law schools. Syracuse has a later deadline than most other law schools (April 1st), which is part of the reason I applied. Like most other law schools,

there is no interview and the essay is a basic personal statement. I do not know much about the selectivity of the admissions process. I applied on March 31st (sent my application overnight) and found out within a few weeks that I was admitted (and also received a partial scholarship—one thing Syracuse is known for is giving out a lot of financial aid in the form of merit scholarships—if you apply early enough and have above average scores, either LSAT or GPA.)

Status: Current student, full-time
Dates of Enrollment: 8/2004-Submit Date
Survey Submitted: October 2004

Admissions seems to have really made the effort to examine whether or not a candidate would make a competent attorney by thoroughly reviewing his/her application, as opposed to making a decision wholly based on the candidate's LSAT score and/or GPA as most schools do, despite their claims of doing otherwise.

Status: Alumnus/a, full-time
Dates of Enrollment: 9/2000-5/2003
Survey Submitted: April 2004

SU has a great admissions process and team. The school awards a number of scholarships. It also has a great Visitor's Day Program for students considering the school (who have been admitted, but have not yet accepted). There is no interview, as is typical for law school. The application itself is standard and includes an essay.

Status: Alumnus/a, full-time
Dates of Enrollment: 9/1998-5/2001
Survey Submitted: April 2004

The admissions process for law school was pretty standard, although I was interested in obtaining a joint degree (MPA) with the Maxwell School, and the law school admissions office was not very knowledgeable on the most efficient way of applying for admission to the joint degree program. If you are interested in a joint degree program, make sure you talk to the admissions office at the other school to make sure you are ensured admission. If I had taken the law school's advice, I would have been competing with over 50 law students for eight slots in the joint degree JD/MPA program. Instead, I applied with all the other MPA students for 100 slots, was accepted, and then deferred enrollment for a year. Much easier on the nerves.

> **Syracuse University College of Law says:** "The College of Law Admissions Office always refers prospective students who are interested in pursuing a joint degree to the individual admissions offices of the graduate programs they are interested in. We can help with the process somewhat, but because students must apply, and be admitted to, both programs separately, we tell them to ask those graduate programs for specific details on admissions criteria. Each graduate program's admission requirements are different. The College of Law has added a new Department of Student Life and will include an academic advisor who will assist students with joint degree interests."

Status: Alumnus/a, full-time
Dates of Enrollment: 8/1999-5/2002
Survey Submitted: October 2003

If you did well (or reasonably well) on the LSAT, getting into Syracuse is easy. I received a 159 on the LSAT, and Syracuse did its utmost to recruit me, including giving me well over half my tuition in grants. However, after you are admitted, the process gets a bit tricky. It is very hard to contact someone by telephone as a new admit.

> **The school says:** "It is inaccurate that it is 'easy' to get admitted to Syracuse College of Law if you 'did well on the LSAT.' Each year we deny many students with very high LSAT scores. We base admission decisions on a variety of factors, and the LSAT is only one of them. We have three types of merit

Read all of Vault's Law School Surveys at www.vault.com/lawschool — get complete surveys on top law schools, expert advice on applicaton essays, LSAT prep and more.

VAULT CAREER LIBRARY 459

scholarships for incoming students, and these are awarded primarily based on a student's LSAT and GPA, but many other factors are looked at as well. Grant money is awarded by the Financial Aid office based on a student's financial need. It is not difficult to contact someone in the Admissions or Financial Aid offices once you're a new admit. Both offices always try to be very accessible to students whether they are prospective, current, or alumni. We have many types of communications that go out to newly admitted students through the mail, on our admitted student web site and through an admitted student listserv."

 ## Academics

Status: Current student, full-time
Dates of Enrollment: 8/2004-Submit Date
Survey Submitted: May 2006

Academically I believe Syracuse is average. Like every school, there are good and bad teachers. Gripes that many students here have are the fact that our curve is based on a B, while other schools have it on a B+; or the fact that the administration takes a long time before responding to a professor complaint. Getting into classes has been fairly easy, despite popularity. Again, depending on the teacher, the workload varies.

Status: Current student, full-time
Dates of Enrollment: 8/2005-Submit Date
Survey Submitted: May 2006

The professors are exceptional. They are well qualified to teach. That being said, the apathy of the students is astounding. I think it deters some of the professors from teaching as well as they could. The registrar's office could use some help in scheduling classes. It is very hard to get into the required courses. It's a computerized system that is basically first come, first served. If the registrar's office went to a bidding process with points like other schools, it would be a better system. Workload is workload. Law school is hard. Get used to it.

Status: Current student, full-time
Dates of Enrollment: 8/2005-Submit Date
Survey Submitted: May 2006

First-year program is pre-determined, with the exception of one elective. I had no problem getting into this elective. Grading is a curve—odious—but common to all law schools (and equally odious to all). Professors are either SU grads or Harvard and Yale—enormously talented and very approachable. Workload—difficult but not impossible. Requires the commitment of a serious student, which is good.

> **The school says:** "The Syracuse University College of Law faculty includes graduates of JD advanced law, and other advanced degree programs from institutions including Yale, Harvard, Stanford, Penn, Cornell, NYU, Columbia, Temple and Georgetown among others."

Status: Current student, full-time
Dates of Enrollment: 8/2004-Submit Date
Survey Submitted: May 2006

The academic program is geared toward the students being practictioners, i.e., it's a practical education without much abstract legal theory. Many of the professors are the highest caliber educators I have ever encountered—there are the occasional sub-par performers however. The classes are generally quite interesting, but some (of the better) professors take more basic approaches to presenting the subject matter to the students, which is due to the intellectual limitations of a few students. There is virtually no problem getting any class regardless of whether it is a popular or has limited enrollment. One giant plus is the ability to take graduate classes outside of the law school and get joint degrees in conjunction with your JD. The Maxwell School of Citizenship and Public Affairs (rated the Number One school in public policy I believe) has professors at the forefronts of their fields and offers law students the opportunity to get joint degree with either a Masters in Public Affairs or a Masters in International

Relations. Numerous law students choose to get a joint JD/MBA degree at the Whitman School of Business. Furthermore, the Newhouse School of Communications, widely recognized as one of the leading communication schools in the country, offers law students the opportunity to get as Masters in Communications. The brilliant thing about these joint degrees is that most of them don't require students to be at the school any longer than is necessary to complete a law degree (with the exception of one summer during law school must be spent taking classes).

> **The school says:** "The College of Law offers a curriculum designed to meet a broad range of needs in the legal profession. Courses typically include elements of theory and practice. Many courses offer opportunities for interdiciplinary study and research."

Status: Current student, full-time
Dates of Enrollment: 9/2003-Submit Date
Survey Submitted: October 2005

The College of Law has great course selection for students who want to pursue careers in litigation, however there is little selection for the many students who want to do corporate or transactional work. The school and the students would definitely benefit by adding classes on negotiating and drafting.

> **The school says:** "The College of Law offers a newly designed Center on Property, Citizenship, and Social Entrepreneurism (PCSE). This Center includes two certified program options; Advanced Property Studies and Corporate Counsel. The Center on PCSE offers students an opportunity to learn about market activities that reach across the intersections of property, commercial law, and community development."

For the most part, the associate and full-time professors at the College of Law are intelligent, engaging and easily accessible. However, classes taught by adjunct faculty are a sham. The adjunct faculty do not cover the material, do not provide adequate examinations, and often fail to show up to class altogether.

Status: Alumnus/a, full-time
Dates of Enrollment: 8/2002-5/2005
Survey Submitted: October 2005

Class quality is adequate. Ease of getting popular classes is low. Grading is tough. The school puts pressure on professors to keep to a strict bell curve, even for 2Ls and 3Ls. Professors are decent, nothing extraordinary. Workload is average. SUCOL is strictly middle of the road in terms of its academic enrichment. There is NO support from the administration for students not in the top 10 percent. If you are a joint degree student (the reason I chose SUCOL) you will NOT be permitted to accept a graduate assistantship from the other college you are getting a degree from (since you are paying tuition to the law school and the graduate assistantship reduces the amount of this tuition for work done for another college within Syracuse University). The opportunities to do a research assistantship have been severely limited in recent years, and the pay has been seriously decreased.

> **The school says:** "There are work opportunities and financial resources that cover a broad range of students. We have Career Service support, leadership training, leadership scholarships and a significant number of Law Research Assistant positions that are available to all students, without have to be in the top 10 percent."

Status: Current student, full-time
Dates of Enrollment: 8/2004-Submit Date
Survey Submitted: October 2004

There is a large, growing interest in the international law field at Syracuse, and the administration is making great efforts to expand the opportunities available to students by including more courses, professors and practical experience in conjunction with the top-rated Maxwell School. Syracuse is also renowned for their trial advocacy, high tech and national security programs that are gaining respect and solid reputations in their respective fields.

Status: Alumnus/a, full-time
Dates of Enrollment: 9/2000-5/2003
Survey Submitted: April 2004

SU provides a good education and solid foundation to help its students practice law. The Clinical Legal Education Program—which includes a variety of clinics and externships as well as the Law Technology and Management Program—is great. SU's required courses are the same as what the ABA demands. The quality of professors does vary a bit, but there are some fantastic professors. Most professors have an open-door policy and are very willing to meet with students. It is tougher to get into popular classes if you have a late registration time. There are a number of terrific electives that are challenging and rewarding. The best example is Law and Literature, which focuses on great oration as well as ethical issues in the law.

Status: Current student, full-time
Dates of Enrollment: 8/2001-Submit Date
Survey Submitted: June 2004

Currently the grading curve has just shifted so that there is a new mandatory curve for upper-class courses. Also, the grades from dual degree programs no longer are added into your "law" GPA. I think this is great for future students because there were a rash of students pumping up their GPA by getting a dual degree in "public policy" at SU's acclaimed Maxwell School—you would have to work pretty hard to get below an A- in that school. It was unfair for those of us who actually studied law and had to compete for graduation honors or jobs.

Status: Alumnus/a, full-time
Dates of Enrollment: 9/1998-5/2001
Survey Submitted: April 2004

Academics were good. They need to be more challenging for SU to become a higher-ranked school. Very good Trial Advocacy Program, sometimes to the detriment of other areas. First-year writing program is very good (now has dedicated writing professors), but good upper-level writing courses were hard to find. Also, as at most schools, the academic and theoretical focus very often outweighs the practical application of the law. I'm a strong advocate for law schools focusing more on the practical. Syracuse does a fine job (especially in trial advocacy), but could do better.

Status: Alumnus/a, full-time
Dates of Enrollment: 8/1999-5/2002
Survey Submitted: January 2004

Past the first-year, classes fill very quickly, and 3L students get the first pick. However, even when given a "good" registering time, students are often in class and have to register online later in day and lose seniority. In terms of classes, there is a wide range of difficulty and competence among the faculty. Often, faculty do not cover basic elements of law (Black Letter Law), and information can be different for the same class depending on the professor.

Status: Alumnus/a, full-time
Dates of Enrollment: 8/1999-5/2002
Survey Submitted: October 2003

Certain programs at SUCOL are topnotch, and accordingly, they are difficult to get into. Some professors are at the top of their game, specifically in newly important areas of public law, such as National Security and Constitutional Law. The private law courses, including criminal defense, corporate and business transactions, are decent but not spectacular.

Getting onto moot court helps you get the really good trial and appellate advocacy courses (which often are the first to fill up).

Employment Prospects

Status: Alumnus/a, full-time
Dates of Enrollment: 9/2002-5/2005
Survey Submitted: April 2006

Established alumni are very helpful. Top of the class graduates can get the same jobs as graduates of Ivy League schools. Some graduates with lower grades, as with any school I imagine, have more difficulty finding jobs after graduation.

Status: Current student, full-time
Dates of Enrollment: 8/2005-Submit Date
Survey Submitted: May 2006

I do not rely on the school to get me a job. Other students intend to rely on the school to help them get a job. I understand that I am the key factor in getting a job. Career services is adequate for providing basic information. I found my 1L internship myself. I got a little help in redoing my resume (I have previous work experience) to the law school format and someone in the career services office reviewed a cover letter. I found two summer internships. One was with a U.S. Attorney's Office. One of the professors hooked me up with an alumnus who worked in that office. That was immensely helpful, so the alumni network is good.

That being said, in applying for other internships, I contacted about 10 other alumni, only one had the grace to respond. Either they don't like the school or they don't think it's important to maintain a network with the school. Whatever the reason, that was disheartening. Other schools that I have attended, or my friends have attend, have very aggressive and helpful alumni associations. An important factor in the *U.S. News and World Report* ranking is getting JOBS. And passing the bar. Six months after graduation, only something like 70 percent of the Class of 2005 had jobs. Nine months after graduation, only 81 percent passed the bar.

> **The school says:** "Syracuse University just had its highest *U.S. News* employment percentage ranking in a decade. Syracuse University has just added an ABA-approved for-credit New York State Bar preparation course to its curriculum."

Status: Current student, full-time
Dates of Enrollment: 8/2004-Submit Date
Survey Submitted: October 2004

Many large firms are becoming increasingly present for on-campus interviews, as they have indicated their appreciation for the Syracuse student's comparably better writing and research skills than most of their peers. Other opportunities to practice law in the public sector or at corporate organizations are also becoming more prevalent among the employers who are hiring Syracuse students.

Status: Alumnus/a, full-time
Dates of Enrollment: 9/1998-5/2001
Survey Submitted: April 2004

Career services at Syracuse is good but has its shortcomings. One common complaint was that CS focused more on the top percent of the class at the expense of all others. Initially this is true, mostly because students in the top of the class are sometimes easier to place earlier in the process. Complaints also focused on the lack of information regarding government positions that were not "mainstream," such as administrative law judge positions. Information on alternative career opportunities was also scarce.

Status: Alumnus/a, full-time
Dates of Enrollment: 9/2000-5/2003
Survey Submitted: April 2004

SU has a solid career services office. It also has a national reputation, which is helpful to students who don't know where they want to be upon graduation or a few years down the road. The career services office is always working to increase campus recruiting and network for more career placement options. Like any school that isn't in the Top 20 of law schools, SU fights hard for the top jobs and does place students at large law firms and in clerkships.

Status: Current student, full-time
Dates of Enrollment: 8/2001-Submit Date
Survey Submitted: June 2004

Despite the school's claims to the contrary, SU is not a national law school. This means that if you want to work for White and Case, Cadwalder or some other huge firm you better be in the top 10 in your class at the end of first year or else give up on that dream now. Also, if you don't want to work in the Northeast, meaning upstate NY, you will have find a lot of your own opportunities. SU does not have great connections in Boston. The cities you would have the best chance of getting a job in are: Syracuse, Rochester, Buffalo, NYC, Philadelphia and maybe Albany.

Read all of Vault's Law School Surveys at www.vault.com/lawschool — get complete surveys on top law schools, expert advice on applicaton essays, LSAT prep and more.

VAULT CAREER LIBRARY 461

Quality of Life

Status: Current student, full-time
Dates of Enrollment: 8/2004-Submit Date
Survey Submitted: May 2006

The qualify of life in Syracuse is fine—for those that like outdoor activities, Syracuse is a perfect place. There's cross-country skiing, snowboarding, skiing, snowshoeing in the winter time. During the summer time, there are plenty of golf facilities available. In addition, graduate and undergraduate students are allowed to play golf for free at a Syracuse owned facility.

Status: Current student, full-time
Dates of Enrollment: 8/2005-Submit Date
Survey Submitted: May 2006

Administration recently hired a dean of student resources to improve quality of life. Dean serves as a liaison between students and administration, and works with student organizations in implementing various activities. As I type this, they are setting up a "midnight" student breakfast as an exam study break. Facilities are older, but well-kept. There is one off-campus housing option available for law students; otherwise, most live off campus.

Status: Current student, full-time
Dates of Enrollment: 8/2005-Submit Date
Survey Submitted: May 2006

I commute, so know nothing about housing or dining. I do know there are great ethnic restaurants two blocks from campus—Middle Eastern, Mexican, Chinese. This is the FRIENDLIEST law school of all time—students here network very well; it's like a large family.

Status: Current student, full time law program
Dates of Enrollment: 8/2005-Submit Date
Survey Submitted: May 2006

In terms of the location, Syracuse is much like New Haven. It is crime ridden; at one point in time, there were weekly crime reports of muggings, attacks, both physical and sexual, and petty theft. As a female, this is disturbing. Syracuse University did respond by increasing the number of patrols around the campus area, offered rides to cars and rides home. There are blue light emergency stations scattered around campus. Syracuse is doing the best they can in spite of the city. Maybe in cooperation with the city they could increase city police patrols and chase off beggars and vagrants from the area.

> **The school says:** "Syracuse faces all of the challenges of any metropolitan area, however the University through the Department of Public Safety, working in collaboration with the local law enforcement and government, works hard to develop a safe environment for all members of the Syracuse University community."

Status: Alumnus/a, full-time
Dates of Enrollment: 8/1999-5/2002
Survey Submitted: October 2003

For being in the Northeast Rust Belt, Syracuse is actually somewhat underrated. The rent around campus is inflated, but if you take some time you can find some really good deals (like a big three-bedroom house for $600 per month). SUCOL recently went through a remodel (1998-1999), so the facilities are decent.

The immediate area around school is all right, but it turns a bit unsafe in some areas. Crime is average for other Northeast schools, but there are definitely more auto break-ins.

Status: Alumnus/a, full-time
Dates of Enrollment: 9/2000-5/2003
Survey Submitted: April 2004

The entire SU campus is pretty, with a variety of architectural styles. There are always concerts, speakers and various other activities brought to campus by the university (or through undergraduate/graduate organizations). Marshall Street is a short walk away and provides casual, fun lunch options as well as a Starbucks and a small off-campus shopping area with a non-university book store, two shoe stores, some clothing stores, a copy center and a post office.

Status: Current student, full-time
Dates of Enrollment: 8/2004-Submit Date
Survey Submitted: May 2005

Syracuse is REALLY cheap—you can get a great apartment for about $500 (two bedrooms, for yourself!), if you share it's even less. The campus is really nice but surrounded by some sketchy neighborhoods. If you love sports, especially college basketball, than you are in luck, because this city LOVES SU sports and students get great discounts—Carrier Dome is the largest dome in the country (on a college campus), basketball games see 30,000 fans per game. Syracuse is small city with very friendly people, but that said, it's more family-oriented than young people (in their 20s and 30s) oriented. Don't expect a ton of bars. There's one major "downtown" area which is fun, but that's it. Syracuse does have great places to hike, run and downhill ski and snowboard (five mountains within an hour's drive, closest is 25 minutes) if you make the effort. BRING A CAR. This is a city where you need one. Also, the best grocery store in the entire world is here: Wegman's (based in Rochester). If you've never been, you're in for a treat.

If you are coming from CA or FL, please give serious consideration to the weather. Granted you will be inside most of the time anyway, but it will make you miserable if you are not accustomed to the Northeast. This is the worst winter in the Northeast, you will need to buy snow tires for your car, you will need a heavy coat and boots which you will wear for four months of the year. If you can deal with that, then you are fine.

Social Life

Status: Current student, full-time
Dates of Enrollment: 8/2004-Submit Date
Survey Submitted: May 2006

Syracuse has an abundance of student groups—APALSA, BLSA, LALSA. Each group organizes Bar Nights to fundraise their activities which most law students attend to relax and meet up with friends.

> **The school says:** "Student organizations sponsor symposia on a wide variety of legal issues, are involved in regional and national advocacy and trial competitions, provide and promote community and engagement through community service and pro-bono activities, and support a strong academic environment through their work and activities."

Status: Current student, full-time
Dates of Enrollment: 8/2004-Submit Date
Survey Submitted: May 2006

The law school students, despite the law school being located on the main campus, do not mix much with non-law school students. The law students genrally break up into small groups. These groups can get a little cliquish, but not in an exclusive sense. Law students tend to go to downtown area of Syracuse (Armory Square, Clinton Square, Franklin Square, Little Italy) where the undergraduates tend not to be. Downtown offers some bustling nightlife, but it involves mostly going from one bar to another. There are several live music oriented bars, which are fast gaining popularity.

Status: Alumnus/a, full-time
Dates of Enrollment: 8/2002-5/2005
Survey Submitted: October 2005

The downtown of Syracuse is pretty and nice, but it closes at 4 pm, and is deserted afterward. There are some blocks that are pretty shady (government subsidized housing surrounds it). The town is planning on building a sewage treatment plant near smelling distance of downtown. If you want Mexican food you will be told to go to Taco Bell. If you want Italian, you will be told to go to Olive Garden. If this does not bother you, then choose SUCOL. There is a bar night every week at the law school. The bars are OK for a city Syracuse's size

Status: Current student, full-time JD/MBA
Dates of Enrollment: 8/2004-Submit Date
Survey Submitted: October 2005

There is the Syracuse Stage and downtown (Armory Square) for entertainment on the weekends if you have time. There are plenty of places close by for weekend trips, such as Buffalo or Albany or Niagara Falls—all awesome. Students seem to LOVE the Wine Tours—I have never been, so I can't say, but it seems to be the best thing since sliced bread.

Status: Current student, full-time
Dates of Enrollment: 8/2004-Submit Date
Survey Submitted: May 2005

Law school doesn't have much of a social life and SU is no exception. Law students organize a bar night or two every week. The school does try to offer other social events, but people don't usually go—they usually work. Syracuse itself does have stuff to do (a few bars, restaurants, theater, movies, the usual) but I promise you, you'll be studying most of the time. Lots of parties happen in the on-campus housing (Slocum) and living there is a good way to make friends if you are new to the area.

Status: Current student, full-time
Dates of Enrollment: 8/2004-Submit Date
Survey Submitted: October 2004

The law school's social atmosphere is more cohesive than competitive. Bar nights are popular, as are other functions sponsored by law school organizations such as dinners, trivia nights, community volunteer opportunities, comedy presentations and even a dance.

Status: Alumnus/a, full-time
Dates of Enrollment: 8/1999-5/2002
Survey Submitted: October 2003

Social life at SU is decent, but don't get sucked into every Bar Night (a tradition among SUCOL 1-3Ls). You might find love (and at least lust) among your fellow classmates, but hook-ups beware. SUCOL is an extension of high school for most of the underaged (the 22- to 25-year-olds), and rumors are rampant. Better to date outside of the law school.

Some places to go out: Faegans (good pub grub and beer, close to campus); the Stoop (good food, good drinks and good people); Velvet Underground (as close as Syracuse gets to being happening); Blue Tusk's Wine Bar; (good wine, but the people sometimes are annoying); Empire (good food and on-site brewery); and PJ Dorsey's (meat market, but usually lively).

Status: Alumnus/a, full-time
Dates of Enrollment: 9/1998-5/2001
Survey Submitted: April 2004

I was married and had three children during school, so I did not have the opportunity to get actively involved in the social scene. Bar Nights are frequent occurrences, as are informal gatherings of students.

Read all of Vault's Law School Surveys at www.vault.com/lawschool — get complete surveys on top law schools, expert advice on applicaton essays, LSAT prep and more.

VAULT CAREER LIBRARY **463**

Touro College

Jacob D. Fuchsberg Law Center
225 Eastview Drive
Central Islip, NY 11722
Admissions phone: (631) 761-7010
Admissions fax: (631) 421-2675
Admissions e-mail: admissions@tourolaw.edu
Admissions URL:
http://www.tourolaw.edu/admissions_and_financial_aid/

 ## Admissions

Status: Alumnus/a, full-time
Dates of Enrollment: 9/2003-5/2006
Survey Submitted: June 2006

The process has become more and more difficult through the years. The average LSAT and GPA criteria has been getting higher and higher, especially after the economic downturn from 9/11. The procedure was quite standard, including an essay on why the applicant wanted to go to law school.

Status: Alumnus/a, full- and part-time
Dates of Enrollment: 8/1992-5/1995
Survey Submitted: June 2006

I submitted an application, essay, LSAT scores, graduate and undergraduate school transcripts, and was admitted to the full-time division.

Status: Alumnus/a, full-time
Dates of Enrollment: 8/2003-5/2006
Survey Submitted: June 2006

According to the Touro Law Center web site, admissions are at about 30 percent and seem to be getting more selective. It's not easy to get into any law school. The school seems to take a whole application into account in assessing the individual and for older students their work experience seems to be important. I was looking at the commencement listing of where students received their undergrad degrees and saw a lot of Stony Brook, Hofstra, LIU, St. John's and SUNYs.

Status: Current student, full-time
Dates of Enrollment: 8/2004-Submit Date
Survey Submitted: May 2005

Obviously, Touro isn't the most difficult law school to get into. I'd use this school as a safety school. If you're a minority, and you've done well, you'll most likely get a sizeable scholarship. Not difficult to get into at all. There is no interview and it isn't very selective.

Status: Alumnus/a, full-time
Dates of Enrollment: 8/1998-5/2001
Survey Submitted: August 2004

Easy online application with fee waiver was a breeze!

 ## Academics

Status: Alumnus/a, full-time
Dates of Enrollment: 9/2003-5/2006
Survey Submitted: June 2006

The professors, in general, are excellent. In addition to regular class, I went on two study abroad programs through Touro Law Center (China and India). The India program is the only law school program of its kind offered in the U.S. Both programs were remarkable. On both programs, I was able to interact with people from other schools and I felt equally knowledgeable, if not more, than the students from supposedly "better schools."

The grading system is much tougher than other schools because the grade curve is not as lenient and there is little to no grade inflation. For this, I believe Touro students really have to be on the ball to receive good grades. Going on these programs allowed me to switch to part-time halfway through the law program, which proved to be more cost-beneficial.

Status: Alumnus/a, full- and part-time
Dates of Enrollment: 8/1992-5/1995
Survey Submitted: June 2006

Because Touro is a relative newcomer to the New York law school market, which has more than 10 schools in New York State alone, Touro's academic policies are rather rigorous compared with other local and national law schools. The faculty and administration make every effort to afford the students the most up-to-date information and innovative courses to prepare them to be more than competent attorneys.

Status: Alumnus/a, full-time
Dates of Enrollment: 8/2003-5/2006
Survey Submitted: June 2006

The grading is on a curve and seems to be a good indicator of which students will pass the bar or not. If you finish in the top half, your odds are very good. Professors are very easy to find as the classrooms are right near the offices. Many professors are on a first-name basis with students. They mostly have very good academic credentials having graduated from the best law schools. The adjuncts usually come from the real world and I'm more a student who likes war stories more than theory, so I mixed up which professors I chose. My grades were pretty good, so no serious complaints! But if you're not ready for law school and somehow got in, you will be revealed really quickly.

Status: Current student, full-time
Dates of Enrollment: 8/2004-Submit Date
Survey Submitted: May 2005

Much of the faculty is quite distinguished, but there are some I wish I had never come across. Honestly, the workload is hefty. If you're lucky enough to get Judge Lazer for Torts, you'll be laughing at his out-of-nowhere jokes but he makes you work. We completed the book straight from intentional torts all the way through to Civil RICO and beyond. Hopefully, you won't get the useless professors who are more interested in talking about their personal issues than teaching the law. TAs are helpful if you actually go.

Status: Alumnus/a, full-time
Dates of Enrollment: 8/1998-5/2001
Survey Submitted: August 2004

Make no mistake, classes at Touro are rigorous! Professors don't hand you your A's on a silver platter. In fact, the grading curve is below the norm, which means that your B is probably the equivalent of an A elsewhere. Touro faculty rocks! You'll work harder than you ever have academically, but when you graduate, you're grateful, especially when you meet Harvard grads who can't recall their seminal cases.

 ## Employment Prospects

Status: Alumnus/a, full-time
Dates of Enrollment: 9/2003-5/2006
Survey Submitted: June 2006

Because our school is relatively new, we don't have a solid alumni base. The base is strong in Long Island, especially in the Suffolk court system, but students get overlooked in New York City. Unfortunately, our students get short-changed when it comes to salaries, which really is a shame because we are just as prepared, if not more so, as students from other law schools.

Status: Alumnus/a, full- and part-time
Dates of Enrollment: 8/1992-5/1995
Survey Submitted: June 2006

Alumni networking is key for students. Many obtain jobs through alumni. Further, each year the top students place at prestigious law firms including, Skadden, Arps and Sullivan & Cromwell. I was employed by a boutique commercial litigation firm of 45 lawyers upon graduation in 1995.

Status: Alumnus/a, full-time
Dates of Enrollment: 8/2003-5/2006
Survey Submitted: June 2006

Touro is a pretty young law school so most alumni are rather young and still working their way up the ladder. I did find the alumni web site very useful. There were interesting firms recruiting on campus and I'm considering working for one that is recruiting me, after the bar! Touro Law Center is well known in the New York region and if you get decent grades you'll be fine in looking for a job.

Status: Alumnus/a, full-time
Dates of Enrollment: 8/1998-5/2001
Survey Submitted: August 2004

Unfortunately, since many employers still subscribe to the process by which law schools are ranked, Touro suffers because of its newcomer status. In addition, employers who recruit at the campus tend to be local Long Island firms, not the NYC firms. The CPO is excellent in alerting students to opportunities out there. But the best thing you can do to ensure you have access to a great job after graduation is knock those grades out of the ballpark.

Status: Current student, full-time
Dates of Enrollment: 8/2001-Submit Date
Survey Submitted: October 2003

We participate in the Minority Bar Fellowship Program through the Association of the Bar of the City of New York. It allows minority first-years to be placed with large firms in NY. It is only through this program and prior work experience that I have heard Touro students being placed at top-tier firms right after graduation. However, usually after the bar results are published, you will find that the majority of Touro grads are very employable.

In the Suffolk County area, we have a great reputation. Firms are eager to work with our students and judges are familiar with our school and credentials. However, our reputation does not extend much farther than that. You will find that a great deal of the larger firms will not look at Touro students. This is largely due to the fact that partners in firms are the ones who decide where recruitment efforts will be invested. They usually concentrate on their own alma maters and the Ivy League schools. Touro is rarely, if ever, the institution from which these partners came. However, in its defense, Touro is the youngest school in New York and most of its graduates are only now at the level in their professional careers to be partner. In addition, many of our faculty members have practiced in a lot of the more prestigious firms but that resource is not tapped. Basically, you have to get your own job. You must be extremely aggressive and persistent in order to do so. You are not "riding" on the name recognition of your school here, we have to work hard to get those interviews.

Quality of Life

Status: Alumnus/a, full-time
Dates of Enrollment: 9/2003-5/2006
Survey Submitted: June 2006

The school [has moved] to Central Islip, which will prove very beneficial because it is on the same property as the state and federal court houses.

Status: Alumnus/a, full- and part-time
Dates of Enrollment: 8/1992-5/1995
Survey Submitted: June 2006

Touro will be moving the school to a state-of-the-art facility being built in Central Islip, New York in the fall. It would be unfair to comment upon the current facilities. The new building will have all the amenities one would expect from a new facility and is easily accessible from New York City via the Long Island Railroad.

Status: Alumnus/a, full-time
Dates of Enrollment: 8/1998-5/2001
Survey Submitted: August 2004

The environment at Touro is supportive and collegial. Don't get me wrong, folks are competitive academically speaking, but it's more in the nature of good sportsmanship than it is backbiting.

> **Regarding campus life, Touro Law Center says:** Starting in fall 2006, Touro Law Center is located on a new campus in Central Islip. Please see the *School Says* narrative below to read more about our new location.

Social Life

Status: Alumnus/a, full-time
Dates of Enrollment: 9/2003-5/2006
Survey Submitted: June 2006

The social life is very good at Touro. Practically every Thursday night there is a social activity planned and they are always a lot of fun (either a bar outing, a themed party or even a talent show to raise money for charity). The students are friendly and much more willing to help than I thought they would be. Although the students do have to fight for their grades more so than in a school with greater grade inflation, the students are friendly. The faculty are also friendly and very easy to get a hold of, which is a great help.

Status: Alumnus/a, full- and part-time
Dates of Enrollment: 8/1992-5/1995
Survey Submitted: June 2006

We had a blast in law school. While we took our studies seriously we took partying equally as seriously. My best friends currently are those I made in law school.

Status: Alumnus/a, full-time
Dates of Enrollment: 8/2003-5/2006
Survey Submitted: June 2006

There's not much student life in any law school. Study, study, study! But the graduation ceremony at Lincoln Center was very nice. There are a lot of opportunities to join student groups, run for offices, work on publications and the like. Finding the time is the hard part. Many students do go to a local bar to unwind. The new campus in Central Islip should offer many more opportunities to network.

Status: Current student, full-time
Dates of Enrollment: 8/2001-Submit Date
Survey Submitted: October 2003

Now this is law school ladies and gents, which means all work and little play. However, you'll find a decent amount of Touro events to give a nice break from the library monotony.

Every Thursday night there are specialty drinks offered to Touro students at a local bar called Finley's. There is plenty of music and good company because a lot of students make it a weekly "must do" to kill some stress.

In addition, the various clubs on campus offer annual dances, fright night for Halloween and a host of lectures and forums of interest. Karaoke night is becoming a favorite and occurs about once a semester. The Student Bar Association tries to "spice" thing up with things like an 80s party or sports night. These are usually very well attended as people are always looking for a reason to go out.

Read all of Vault's Law School Surveys at www.vault.com/lawschool — get complete surveys on top law schools, expert advice on applicaton essays, LSAT prep and more.

VAULT CAREER LIBRARY 465

Manhattan is a one-hour train ride away but this is not heavily exercised; who has the time?

A lot of Touro "couples" but the dating scene is limited. A large percentage of the student population is older students who tend to be already married or engaged, sorry!

Clubs include the Black Law Students Association, Latin American Students Association, Christian Legal Society, Jewish Law Students Association, Student Bar Association and Gay and Lesbian Society. These are the most active. Then we have a series of "one hit wonders" like the Entertainment and Sports Law Society and International Law Society.

 **The School Says**

Touro Law Center Offers New Location, New Curriculum

In the fall 2006 semester, Touro Law Center transformed itself with a move to a new campus in Central Islip, NY, adjacent to and working with state and federal courthouses. This modern, 180,000-square-foot law campus is the first of its kind anywhere and hopes to become a national model, merging the teaching of law with its practice.

Touro is a law school on the rise with new energy, a cutting-edge academic plan and, with the move, a setting that offers students a competitive advantage and an unparalleled law school experience.

Touro has created a Court Observation Program for its new, innovative curriculum that meshes the courtroom and the classroom. The program coordinates regular class field studies in the state and federal courts adjacent to the new campus, and then facilitates subsequent campus visits by the judges and lawyers whose cases students witnessed first-hand. This gives students a unique behind-the-scenes view of how cases are prepared and decided.

Touro's new building provides, rent-free, facilities for approximately a dozen area nonprofit advocacy groups, giving them a central Long Island location and access to Touro's law students. This creative partnership helps the advocacy groups obtain legal assistance while also providing students with invaluable experience working with real clients on real cases.

The new campus is completely wireless and interactive. U-shaped classrooms foster debate, complemented by smart-technology podiums, closed-circuit video-conferencing and digital overhead displays. While Touro is well-known for its accessible and accomplished faculty, the design of the new building allows for even more student-teacher camaraderie.

The campus also has two trial classrooms, a moot court room that seats 500 and a rathskeller that encourages interaction between students and area judges and lawyers.

The library is four-stories high and 40,000 square feet—an amazing resource not only for students but also the Long Island legal community. Convenient residency options and easy access to New York City complement Touro's growth as an institution of national acclaim.

Touro Law Center, known for its expert faculty and high-quality programs, was established in 1980 as part of Touro College, which has campuses in New York, California, Nevada, Florida and Germany, Israel and Russia. The Law Center is fully accredited by the American Bar Association and is a member of the Association of American Law Schools. Touro Law Center offers the degrees of Juris Doctor (JD), Master of Laws (LLM) and Master of Laws (LLM.) in U.S. Legal Studies for foreign law graduates. Also, students may combine the JD degree with a Master of Business Administration (MBA), a Master of Public Administration (MPA) in Health Care, and a Master of Social Work (MSW).

Touro Law Center's ongoing $35 million strategic plan helps provide a learning experience like no other for students, and the new setting serves as an integral part of the New York legal community.

Touro Law Center, with a student body of over 750, welcomes excellent entering classes. Selectivity and test scores for the 26-year-old institution have significantly improved in recent years, surpassing national and regional trends for law schools.

University at Buffalo Law School

Office of Admissions
University at Buffalo Law School, SUNY
309 O'Brian Hall
Buffalo, NY 14260-1100
Admissions phone: (716) 645-2907
Admissions fax: (716) 645-6676
Admissions e-mail: law-admission@buffalo.edu
Admissions URL: http://law.buffalo.edu/Admissions/

 Admissions

Status: Current student, full-time
Dates of Enrollment: 8/2003-Submit Date
Survey Submitted: May 2006

The admissions process was a very fair one. It consisted of all of the standard elements of submitting an application: taking the LSAT, preparing a personal statement and making sure the application was submitted on time. I was placed on the waiting list to get into the school, but I requested an interview, and that, I believe, was one of the best things I could have done. I was able to explain in detail and in person why I wanted to attend UB Law and the various perspectives that I expressed in my personal statement. I definitely think that requesting an interview is a good idea.

Status: Current student, full-time
Dates of Enrollment: 8/2003-Submit Date
Survey Submitted: May 2006

The admissions process was similar to most law schools. The applicant fills out the application, supplies a personal essay, transcripts and LSAT scores. There is no interview requirement but the school is extremely accommodating to the student that shows interest in learning about the school, the professors and the UB Law experience.

During the year I applied, we were required to write an essay on something we were currently reading. I thought that was a particularly good question merely because law school reading is like nothing a student encounters in their lifetime. Therefore, it would follow that if you were an avid reader of some substance you just might have what it takes to complete three years of legal study. The UB Law admissions process is very efficient, I had my acceptance letter fairly quickly compared to the length of time it took to hear back from other schools and once I was accepted, I found the administration to be exceedingly helpful with financial and course information.

Status: Current student, full-time
Dates of Enrollment: 9/2003-Submit Date
Survey Submitted: May 2006

I found the admission process to be relatively smooth. Definitely follow up with calls to the admissions office; my acceptance arrived later than expected and it made the decision a little more difficult. The staff is very friendly and I would recommend meeting with professors and taking a tour.

Status: Current student, full-time
Dates of Enrollment: 8/2004-Submit Date
Survey Submitted: May 2006

Well, I applied for my first year and was waitlisted. I then applied as a transfer student and was admitted. It was a very short and quick process to be admitted. I had no interview. I had to write essays, including a creative story essay. My grades as a transfer were very good (ranked top 19th percentile).

Status: Current student, full-time
Dates of Enrollment: 8/2003-Submit Date
Survey Submitted: May 2006

If I remember correctly, UB does not conduct interviews. I also remember that there were two essays, one that was a standard essay and then one that asked you to discuss the last two books you read. UB is not super-selective, but it is pretty competitive, because it is so cheap. It is the only state school for law school in NY, so there are students here that went to Ivy League schools. The nice thing is that, even though UB is a state school, there are still students from all over. I have friends from California, Wisconsin, Oregon and many other places.

Status: Current student, full-time
Dates of Enrollment: 9/2003-Submit Date
Survey Submitted: May 2006

Buffalo is getting quite selective because of the soaring tuition of law schools. Therefore, you will find graduates from some of the country's best undergraduate schools. But UB selects students for varying reasons, i.e., the LSAT alone will not get you in or keep you out. If you're a solid academic student and a well-rounded person, you have a good shot.

I actually turned down Buffalo because they requested an early decision, but then when it turned out I could not attend the law school of my choice, I called Buffalo less than a month before classes started. I asked if I could still attend, and they said of course. I thought that was amazing.

Status: Current student, full-time
Dates of Enrollment: 8/2003-Submit Date
Survey Submitted: May 2006

UB likes people with diverse backgrounds and it is actually known for exceeding other schools in the number of enrolled students that are older than the prevailing average. I thought my GPA mattered but the LSAT was less of a factor. Focus on the essay and on making yourself stand out.

Status: Current student, full-time
Dates of Enrollment: 8/2004-Submit Date
Survey Submitted: April 2005

UB was very careful in selecting a broad range of people with diverse backgrounds, ethnicities and experiences. All of my classmates are capable students with a really remarkable degree of individual intelligence and proactivity. The pre-entry tours and optional interviews were excellent, as UB provided both current students, alumni and leading professionals from the Buffalo area to answer questions. I can't emphasize enough the clear professionalism and student-friendly atmosphere here at UB and in UB admissions, in particular.

Status: Current student, full-time
Dates of Enrollment: 9/2002-Submit Date
Survey Submitted: June 2004

A very face-friendly school. Take the time to visit and meet with the dean of admissions, although there is no formal interview requirement. Two essays: the first is your pretty standard law school essay; the second wants you to discuss two books you have read that were not assigned reading. I thought this showed they really wanted to get to know me as a person beyond my LSAT and GPA. In terms of selectivity, I think we have a great mix of intelligent students from very different backgrounds, some who are approaching law school as a second career and others who are coming straight from undergrad.

Status: Alumnus/a, full-time
Dates of Enrollment: 9/2000-5/2003
Survey Submitted: June 2004

UB Law is increasingly selective, but seems to value eclecticism in its student body, welcoming students with unusual life and work experiences. Law school admissions processes are so standardized today that one can expect little variation from the norm—LSATs, three essays, a personal statement. My advice

Read all of Vault's Law School Surveys at www.vault.com/lawschool — get complete surveys on top law schools, expert advice on applicaton essays, LSAT prep and more.

VAULT CAREER LIBRARY 467

is to be honest, sincere and straightforward. Buffalo is a down-to-earth town, and nobody here likes pompous bullshit or puffery. Emphasize those things that make you genuinely unique. UB specializes in brilliant oddballs, good humor and humility. Show 'em that you're smart, then chill out.

Status: Alumnus/a, full-time
Dates of Enrollment: 8/1999-5/2002
Survey Submitted: September 2003

I thought the admissions process was typical. The fee was a bit high for a state school. I did not have to have an interview.

> **The school says:** "The in-state tuition for 2004-2005 is $12,170 per year, making UB Law comparable and more affordable than other state schools. The non-resident tuition is $18,270 with the added benefit of gaining in-state residency after the first year of law school. The application fee is $35 when applying online or $50 when applying with a paper application."

 # Academics

Status: Current student, full-time
Dates of Enrollment: 8/2003-Submit Date
Survey Submitted: May 2006

UB Law is an amazing school because it offers students the opportunity to concentrate in areas of law where they may have a specific interest. I personally chose the International Law concentration, but I know of other students who found their calling in the Criminal Law, Health Law and Labor Law concentrations. The professors at UB are truly quality. My only criticism of UB Law as well as law school in general is that I don't see the utility of a refusing to give exams throughout the semesters, gradually testing students' knowledge of legal concepts and materials. I think if intermediate exams were given throughout the year, final exams wouldn't be as intense as they are and students would actually walk away from their courses with a much deeper and much more cultivated understanding of the subjects.

Status: Current student, full-time
Dates of Enrollment: 8/2003-Submit Date
Survey Submitted: May 2006

There are a lot of good professors here. Most of the professors are very good at responding to questions. Upperclassmen have priority in getting in popular classes. You can add/drop classes freely at the first week of semester. I worked hard and I received very good grades. There are always hard graders and lenient graders in law school. You can talk to fellow law students and upperclassmen about the professors before choosing classes.

The school is responsive to student requests about the programs. I am interested in corporate finance and security law. The school used to have a security law professor, but he left one year before I enrolled. I mentioned to two of my professors teaching Corporate Law and International Finance that I want to take securities law. The next year we had a securities regulation course. I am not sure if that's because of my complaint but we do have the class now.

In addition, the school set up a 12-credit international finance course in New York City. Students could take the course and stay in NYC for one semester, taking courses and working with international investment banks and large firms. Compared to my friends in other law schools, the workload here is OK. Besides, the school takes care to make sure that you don't have all your finals crammed in the same week.

Status: Current student, full-time
Dates of Enrollment: 8/2003-Submit Date
Survey Submitted: May 2006

The workload at UB Law is no heavier than it would be anywhere else. However, the school year runs on a trimester basis so you have the opportunity to take bridge classes during the winter semester in order to lighten your courseload during the fall or spring semester. The bridge courses are also fantastic ways to get exposure to an area of law you may be interested in that you

haven't quite committed yourself to. For example, if you are interested in environmental law but you haven't decided you want to take a full survey course in the subject you can take a one-credit bridge course in the area during the winter to familiarize yourself with the area and see if the study of environmental law is something you would enjoy.

I have never been unable to get into a class I wanted at UB Law School and the professors are extremely approachable and willing to spend extra time working with students individually.

Status: Current student, full-time
Dates of Enrollment: 9/2003-Submit Date
Survey Submitted: May 2006

Simply stated: you cannot get a better education for the price you pay at UB Law. The professors have been topnotch, engaging and lively lecturers. Practical education is emphasized along with learning Black Letter Law. The combination of the two have provided me with applicable job skills.

There were very few times that I had a problem getting into popular classes, because the school usually just expands (or creates another section) the class size to allow students in. The biggest problem I encountered was when the school canceled Anti-Trust and never offered it again that year.

Status: Alumnus/a, full-time
Dates of Enrollment: 8/1995-5/1998
Survey Submitted: May 2006

The classes were intensive but enjoyable. I did not encounter the Socratic Method in any classes. The law school had wonderful mini-classes known as bridge courses which in most cases were taught by practicing attorneys and which provided a lot of insight into the real-world practice of law. I did not have much trouble getting into the classes of my choice; though occasionally I needed to wait a semester or two for a spot to free up.

Professors were bright, friendly and generally engaging. I took three tax classes not because I am particularly fond of tax law but because the professor was fabulous! After exams I often met with the professors to review my test and grade to gain a better understanding of how I could have done better, and I found these meetings to be insightful and laid back.

Status: Current student, full-time
Dates of Enrollment: 8/2003-Submit Date
Survey Submitted: May 2006

UB Law School rules. It is easy to get good grades because all of the professors are accessible and will communicate with you to work with you. After you take the core classes, you get to pick your classes for subsequent two years of law school. This flexibility allowed me to take the law classes that I found interesting enough to want to learn about. The workload is totally manageable.

Status: Current student, full-time
Dates of Enrollment: 8/2002-Submit Date
Survey Submitted: April 2005

The quality of classes was great; there was a wide variety to choose from. I was also set up with practical experience including an internship with a local district attorneys office and a clerkship with the appellate division. All the professors were easily accessible and willing to help. Getting into popular classes was a problem my second year. I was, however, able to get into them in my third year. Classes that are full at registration are usually available for add once the semester starts.

Status: Current student, full-time
Dates of Enrollment: 8/2004-Submit Date
Survey Submitted: April 2005

Classes are very good with the added bonus that professors care! You are not just a number. Class sizes are decent. Property One gets consistently great reviews from students. Even Civil Procedure, which can be dry, is taught by dynamic professors.

Grading is fair. What you put in is what you get out, but that also means learning what style of exam your professors use. There is an exam bank at the library to help you prepare. That is especially helpful.

Status: Current student, full-time
Dates of Enrollment: 9/2002-Submit Date
Survey Submitted: June 2004

The quality of classes overall is really good. If you do not get into a class you want initially, as long as you put your name on the waiting list you have a very good chance of getting in. We do not have a forced curve or GPA or rank, so you are graded based on your performance, which definitely pushes you to do the best you can. With regards to workload, it's law school, so there is a lot of work. But if you can manage your time, you will do well.

Status: Alumnus/a, full-time
Dates of Enrollment: 9/2001-5/2004
Survey Submitted: June 2004

Throughout my time at UB, the law school consistently has brought absolutely outstanding faculty on board. Every year that I have been here, the faculty has increased in excellence, and I expect that trend to continue. Buffalo's reputation for plainness and pragmatism seems to rub off on the faculty, who are very accessible and willing to keep pace with ambitious students. Adjuncts, particularly elderly civic leaders who remain involved in the school, lend experience and authenticity to UB's programs that can't be found anywhere else.

I have never had difficulty enrolling in popular classes—just schmooze. If you can convince a professor at UB that you are sharp and engaged in the subject matter, the prof will let you in, no doubt about it. Sharp elbows won't help you here; competence will.

Status: Current student, full-time
Dates of Enrollment: 8/2002-Submit Date
Survey Submitted: April 2004

The classes are what you would expect of a top-tier law school. They are demanding, and most students endure an adjustment period. We have some fantastic professors who really care about their students. I think the faculty and classroom experience at UB is reflective of the school as a whole. It's surprisingly warm and receptive for a law school. Most of the professors are extremely helpful and regularly available. In fact, many professors host parties at the end of each semester for their students! In contrast, there certainly are a few professors who aren't necessarily the best teachers, but UB keeps them here because of their expertise and prominence in their field. I guess it's a necessary evil. However, most professors here are not only extremely bright, well-known professionals, but genuinely caring about their students.

> **The school says:** "Faculty are not required to grade on an established curve and there is no individualized class ranking."

 Employment Prospects

Status: Alumnus/a, full-time
Dates of Enrollment: 8/2002-5/2005
Survey Submitted: May 2006

Overall, UB Law graduates may have the best employment prospects of any law school in the country. This is not hyperbole. Consider the fact that UB Law is a highly ranked tier-two school and tuition is a fraction of what it would be at most any other law school. The result is that students with good grades can work at large New York City and Chicago Law firms, but smaller firms are also an option because there is no pressure from large debt payments.

Status: Alumnus/a, full-time
Dates of Enrollment: 8/1980-5/1983
Survey Submitted: May 2006

As a member of the alumni board, I am aware that UB graduates are now located in many far-flung places in the U.S. and abroad. While many graduates opt to stay in the Buffalo area, many settle elsewhere and there are large pockets of graduates throughout the East Coast (including New York City and Washington) and in Chicago. Most graduates go into private practice after graduation. There is a very active on-campus recruiting program.

Status: Alumnus/a, full-time
Dates of Enrollment: 8/1995-5/1998
Survey Submitted: May 2006

All of my classmates found jobs quite easily either during law school or after the bar exam. As with all law schools, the best and the brightest nailed high paying jobs at the BigLaw firms. I stayed in Buffalo and found the alumni network to be robust and especially helpful. As an average student, my job prospects were limited initially but as I got to know more people around town I found myself with plenty of offers, and still do to this day. On campus, there were many job postings and opportunities to connect with employers and I had a certain amount of confidence that the law school would not let its graduates fall through the cracks.

Status: Current student, full-time
Dates of Enrollment: 8/2004-Submit Date
Survey Submitted: April 2005

UB has a wonderful mentor program in which they pair you with alumni. Additionally, they hold events that many alumni attend, so you are constantly exposed to the alumni network. The are law firms hold events and are always willing to speak with UB students who have any questions about a particular area, law in general, or their law school experience.

Status: Current student, full-time
Dates of Enrollment: 8/2002-Submit Date
Survey Submitted: April 2004

My strongest criticism of UB's CSO is its focus on upstate New York firms and clerkships. If you want to practice law in any of the upstate New York cities (e.g., Buffalo, Rochester, Syracuse and Albany), you will have no trouble finding employment. Unfortunately, UB doesn't place as much emphasis on recruitment in New York City and Washington, D.C. We do send a fair number of students to these areas, but it isn't our specialty.

Typically only Law Review students land jobs with major New York City firms, in large part, I believe, because of CSO's limited efforts to expose our school to these locations. I think employment opportunities are somewhat limited to a regional area with a UB degree. However, I do have friends with jobs in New York City, Florida, D.C., California and so on.

> **The school says:** "UB Law continues a long tradition of strong placements in New York City. Recent graduates work in large firms, district attorneys offices, small firms and public interest organizations in and around New York City. Typically, approximately one-fifth of each class finds employment outside New York state. Since 2000, our graduating classes have landed in 38 states, six foreign countries and Washington, D.C. Our widespread and diverse alumni are instrumental in working with the Career Services Office to provide contacts in all areas of the country."

Status: Alumnus/a, full-time
Dates of Enrollment: 9/2000-5/2001
Survey Submitted: June 2004

One note of caution: you will have to do all of the career legwork yourself. Students have luck working directly through UB's extraordinarily helpful faculty members and the many members of the regional legal community who are actively involved in the law school. UB Law enjoys an excellent reputation among people in the know. UB steadfastly refuses to rank its students. This makes for a much more collegial law school environment than might otherwise be the case, but sometimes confuses far-away employers who expect a class rank and are suspicious when they don't see one.

> **The school says:** "UB Law does not officially rank its students and thereby achieves its goal of a collegial and constructive learning environment. However, for job-search purposes, students are allowed to estimate their rank within two tiers: top 15 percent and top 25 percent. These unofficial rankings can be calculated by individual students based on a given formula. Employers accept these unofficial estimates."

Read all of Vault's Law School Surveys at www.vault.com/lawschool — get complete surveys on top law schools, expert advice on applicaton essays, LSAT prep and more.

VAULT CAREER LIBRARY **469**

Quality of Life

Status: Current student, full-time
Dates of Enrollment: 8/2003-Submit Date
Survey Submitted: May 2006

UB is located primarily in a suburban setting. If a student is accustomed to city life, UB will definitely take some getting used to. However, the atmosphere at UB is a veritable non-competitive one, which makes for a rather calm experience. The staff and the students are non-threatening and there are a lot of activities on campus in which to become involved. On-campus housing is nice, but expensive. Living off campus is not as convenient, but saves a great deal of money.

Status: Current student, full-time
Dates of Enrollment: 8/2003-Submit Date
Survey Submitted: May 2006

By what I know, it is pretty safe here. There are on- and off-campus housing. Shuttles are frequent during school time. The school has a online program so you can pay tuition, add/drop classes and check your grades online by 11 p.m. every day, seven days a week. I really like that.

On-campus housing costs around $600 a month. For off-campus ones, you can rent a room for as low as $120. I am paying $125 for a room in a four-room apartment. It's within walking distance to south campus.

Status: Current student, full-time
Dates of Enrollment: 8/2003-Submit Date
Survey Submitted: May 2006

Housing is fantastic at UB Law. The on-campus apartments for graduate students are beautiful, spacious and located in relaxing settings. The shuttle busses from the on-campus apartments are convenient and frequent. There is also a bus that runs between the north and south campuses of UB that is available to students who want to get off campus and explore the city. The UB shuttle that connects the two campuses connects students to a main bus terminal and subway station that enables students to traverse the whole city of Buffalo at an extremely low cost. The shuttle buses are all free and the city buses or train are a mere $1.50 per trip.

Status: Current student, full-time
Dates of Enrollment: 8/2003-Submit Date
Survey Submitted: May 2006

I have never lived in the campus housing, but a lot of my friends have, and it is great. They just built it about three years ago and it is very new and clean and high tech. If you choose to live off campus, the nice thing about Buffalo is that it is tremendously inexpensive. I live in a three-bedroom downtown with two other law students and we pay $750 total for our apartment, which is actually a really nice apartment.

Warning, however: the cost of heat in the winter is outrageous, so if you can find somewhere that includes heat in the rent price, take it.

Status: Current student, full-time
Dates of Enrollment: 9/2002-Submit Date
Survey Submitted: April 2005

Amherst, the town where the school is located, was ranked the safest town in the U.S. three years in a row, and this year was Number Three. To live anywhere off campus in the Amherst area (or in another surrounding town) is considered very safe and affordable; Buffalo is known for its low cost of living. Although there isn't a great public transit system, so you will probably need a car, you don't have to drive far to be where you need to be (grocery store, drug store, Target/Walmart, a mall).

Living downtown is another option for students, and just like any big city you need to be careful where you choose to live. However, there are five colleges in Buffalo and the areas where most students choose to live in the downtown area are relatively safe and very fun, popular areas, near bars and other social and art events. School housing for graduate students is affordable and washers and dryers are in each apartment. Apartments can also come furnished for out-of-

state or students from far distances. They are right on or near campus, within walking distance.

Status: Alumnus/a, full-time
Dates of Enrollment: 9/2000-5/2003
Survey Submitted: June 2004

The law school has asserted itself and generally enjoys better technology and physical plant services than the larger university, but non-law campus buildings and facilities, like the graduate library, are poorly maintained. If you were hoping to find a good place on campus to eat with friends, think again. Excellent for weight loss, though. In warm months, the university enjoys close access to scenic running trails, tennis courts, affordable public golf courses and the many civic activities that make Buffalo a fun town to live in. If you don't have a car, you'd better come equipped with a friend who does.

Status: Current student, full-time
Dates of Enrollment: 8/2002-Submit Date
Survey Submitted: April 2004

I'll start with campus housing. In short, it's outstanding! UB has two primary locations on campus for law students. First, there is Flint Village. This is where most law students live. These apartments were built solely for law students. They are only a couple of years old (constructed in 2000, I believe). The exterior is very aesthetically pleasing, consisting of a traditional brick exterior with well-maintained lawns, a basketball court, track and a small football stadium just outside. It's located directly across the street from the law school. However, if you are lazy or it is snowing, a shuttle bus comes directly to each building and drops you off at the law school.

The second option on campus is Creekside Village. I lived here during my first year. Creekside is unique because other graduate students live in these townhouses. Your roommates are law students unless you request otherwise. Typically, they do put all law students in the same group of townhouses (a sort of cul-de-sac). These townhouses were opened in 2002 and are beautiful! Fully furnished with all appliances, even a washer and dryer in each unit. It's a great quality of life. These townhouses are located further from the law school, but a shuttle runs every 15 minutes that takes you directly to the law school.

UB is a very large university, so dining on campus is phenomenal. Nearly anything you could imagine is available in cafes and restaurants throughout. Plus the law school has its own food lounge. As for the law school's facilities, they are good and rapidly improving. Honestly, we have a few classrooms that need remodeling. On the positive side, a new courtroom was just constructed on campus, and it is amazing! Our dean has recently engaged in a massive fundraising event that has firms sponsoring classrooms throughout the school. It's great because the firm gets to put its name in front of each classroom.

Social Life

Status: Current student, full-time
Dates of Enrollment: 8/2003-Submit Date
Survey Submitted: May 2006

Every week there are about three bar nights advertised during the regular semester, as well as "decompression" parties after final exams. The students that come to UB usually party fairly hard to complement the diligent lifestyle of study that accompanies attending the law school. A lot of the bars are located on the city's Chippewa strip as well as within the Elmwood neighborhood.

Status: Current student, full-time
Dates of Enrollment: 9/2003-Submit Date
Survey Submitted: May 2006

Law school organizes countless "bar" nights for all students. Great places to meet students and others. "Barristers Ball" (a.k.a., law school prom) each year is funded by the school, with a formal dinner and dance, it's well subsidized. Law school deans are very willing to spend money on our activities. Free pig roast for 3Ls. The list of law school funded events goes on and on.

Status: Current student, full-time
Dates of Enrollment: 9/2003-Submit Date
Survey Submitted: May 2006

People in Buffalo do two things well: eat and drink. The culture of Buffalo is heavily influenced by the bar scene. There are other things to do, such as go see plays, the symphony, the art museum, go to a coffee house, but many people just prefer to drink. That has been disappointing to me. The bars are fun, but it gets old after a while.

The restaurants in Buffalo are great! They aren't that expensive and the food is amazing. There are all types of venues and cuisines. This has definitely been most impressive. My favorite restaurant is Toro!, a tapas bar. The atmosphere and the food are to DIE for! Probably the best are to explore is Elmwood Avenue. There are all these cute little shops: Delish, Everything Elmwood, Spot Coffee, New World Record. They all have their own little charm and it's just such a great neighborhood to people watch.

Status: Current student, full-time
Dates of Enrollment: 8/2004-Submit Date
Survey Submitted: April 2005

The Student Bar Association at UB is really dynamic and active. Dining in Buffalo is wonderfully diverse with excellent restaurants to be found for almost any ethnic food imaginable—and there are the famous "Buffalo" style chicken wings! The winters might be on the cold side, but the people are warm and friendly.

Status: Current student, full-time
Dates of Enrollment: 9/2002-Submit Date
Survey Submitted: April 2005

Presba is currently one of the most trendy bars if you want to run into other law students. Fat Bob's a must if your're looking for cheap beer and BBQ pork. Most of the other favorites are located on Elmwood Ave and Allen Street. The Chippewa area is also always packed and has a wealth of undergraduate-style dance clubs.

Buffalo also has a number of fantastic places to dine. The Buffalo Chop House has some of the best steak on the East Coast. When you go, just make sure to bring mom and dad's credit card, and don't expect to leave with a bill under $100 for two people. Left Bank is a phenomenal date place with a great wine list. Toro is one of the areas best tapas-style restaurants.

Status: Current student, full-time
Dates of Enrollment: 8/2002-Submit Date
Survey Submitted: April 2004

There are various social events regularly held, such as the annual Barristers Ball held at the Hyatt in downtown Buffalo. Different student organizations sponsor events such as Buffalo Sabres and Bills games. I've never had one week in two years here when there hasn't been at least a couple of events to chose from each week.

Outside of law school, Buffalo has the most students per capita, second only to Boston. As a result, downtown Buffalo and Main Street near UB's south campus are fantastic for social life. In particular, Chippewa, Buffalo's main club/bar street, is typically off the charts. The nice part about UB is that our campus is nestled in Amherst, one of the safest suburbs in the country. Yet we have shuttles that take us to UB's south campus (a five- to 10-minute ride) where we can catch the subway (locally called the "metro") to downtown for a night of fun. Also, there are always law students throwing parties both on and off campus.

Status: Current student, full-time
Dates of Enrollment: 9/2002-Submit Date
Survey Submitted: June 2004

There is definitely enough of a social life. There are tons of student groups at the law school and with the other schools of the university. In the law school there is typically a Bar Night every week. Most of the Bar Nights are held at SOHO. The Latin American, Asian and Black Law Students Associations also throw events like food sales and parties, as well as an annual party to introduce some diversity into the school. If you want something to do you will not have to look hard to find it. And if you get bored with Buffalo, Toronto is only an hour and a half away.

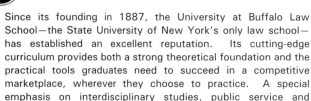

The School Says

Since its founding in 1887, the University at Buffalo Law School—the State University of New York's only law school—has established an excellent reputation. Its cutting-edge curriculum provides both a strong theoretical foundation and the practical tools graduates need to succeed in a competitive marketplace, wherever they choose to practice. A special emphasis on interdisciplinary studies, public service and opportunities for hands-on clinical education makes UB Law unique among the nation's premier public law schools.

During the first year, students are gradually introduced to the rigors of law school by a caring and supportive faculty. (Even the Dean teaches a first year class). Our students hail from some of the best undergraduate schools in the nation. The size of the first year class falls between 235 and 247 students and the faculty to student ratio after the first year is 1 to 14. The law school offers a vast array of classes—over 300 courses—and students appreciate the flexibility to customize the curriculum. Our nationally renowned clinics, some of which were the first of their kind in the nation, are an added benefit. The law school also has a working courtroom in which federal, state and local trials and judicial proceedings are held. Our Advocacy Program is outstanding! In 2006 our teams won both the Trial competition and the Mediation Competition for the entire Northeast Region. Nationally, our teams finished second and fifth respectively out of more than 180 eligible schools.

There is no class rank and we do not grade on a curve. Our students discover that in such a supportive and collegial environment, they are able to master the material without the added stress of competition.

Our Career Services office takes a very personal approach in assisting students with their career search. The Associate Dean meets with all of the first year class to discuss their long-range goals. Our employment rate nine months after graduation is 97 percent. Our students are employed across the country and work with all sectors of public and private practice. Our bas passage rate for New York state is 80 percent as compared the state average of 72 percent. Our reasonable tuition cost for 2005-2006—$12,170 for in-state and $18,270 for out-of-state students make UB Law a very attractive choice.

Please contact the Admission Office at law-admissions@buffalo.edu or (716) 645-2907 to schedule an appointment or talk with an admission staff member.

Read all of Vault's Law School Surveys at www.vault.com/lawschool — get complete surveys on top law schools, expert advice on applicaton essays, LSAT prep and more.

VAULT CAREER LIBRARY 471

Yeshiva University

Benjamin N. Cardozo School of Law
Admissions Office
Brookdale Center
55 Fifth Avenue (at 12th Street)
New York, NY 10003
Admissions phone: (212) 790-0200
Admissions e-mail: lawinfo@ymail.yu.edu
Admissions URL: http://www.cardozo.yu.edu/admissions/

 Admissions

Status: Current student, full-time
Dates of Enrollment: 8/2005-Submit Date
Survey Submitted: April 2006

I applied to Cardozo in late December of 2004. As I had a 3.6 GPA from an Ivy League college and a 167 LSAT score, I didn't think I'd have difficulty getting in. I was right; the school let me know that I had been accepted (first via e-mail, then via letter) in early March of 2005. I got a lot of personal attention from the admissions office (e-mails, letters, phone calls from current students, invitations to campus events), and the school offered me a substantial merit scholarship. I was very impressed by the incredible effort the staff at Cardozo put into making me feel wanted by this school, and I know that's part of the reason I chose it over schools that are considered to be more selective.

Status: Alumnus/a, full-time
Dates of Enrollment: 8/2002-6/2005
Survey Submitted: March 2006

The application process is comparable to other law schools, but Cardozo is willing to give generous scholarships to highly qualified students. They also seem very interested in increasing the diversity of the student body—in terms of race, religion, geographic area, background and interests. So differentiating yourself from the masses of other applicants is particularly important. Cardozo's recruiting is truly fabulous. The admissions office does a great job reaching out to admitted students, putting them in touch with current students and alums, and giving them a sense of the school.

Status: Current student, full-time
Dates of Enrollment: 8/2004-Submit Date
Survey Submitted: March 2006

There was an application much like any other school, but the process seemed way more personalized with Cardozo. The dean literally calls you on your cell phone to congratulate you that you have been admitted. Then there is a follow-up call from a student, and a really nice reception where a ton of professors and deans show up to talk about the school. Most other schools send you a "congrats" letter and are not the slightest bit helpful when you call with questions. It made the difference for me, obviously.

Status: Current student, full-time
Dates of Enrollment: 8/2004-Submit Date
Survey Submitted: March 2006

I heard from Cardozo very soon after I sent out my admissions material. I loved the way I found out about my acceptance—a personal phone call from the Dean of Admissions—which is the way all students are initially told of their acceptance. It immediately made me feel the school was more of a community. In addition, in order to attract students with high LSATs (something I do think Cardozo does put a lot of emphasis on), they provide a lot of scholarships. That is another reason that got me to Cardozo. The school is definitely working to move up a tier, and they want the best students they can get in order to do that. So, the money was a big incentive for me to go there, especially since I was funding my own law school education.

Status: Alumnus/a, full-time
Dates of Enrollment: 5/2002-5/2005
Survey Submitted: March 2006

Cardozo is clearly becoming more selective as its reputation grows. When I was applying to Cardozo, I knew I wanted to do IP Law and it's reputation for IP is excellent. I knew that my LSAT scores were not that great, so I made myself a part of the community during the admissions process. I went to as many IP events at the school as possible and met with various professors who were happy to talk with me about the school. I believe if you truly want to go there and make the effort to familiarize yourself with the school you will be able to give yourself a better chance of admission if you have low LSAT scores. I ended up in the top 15 percent my first year, so, I think they recognize that one could do well at Cardozo without having the LSAT scores.

Status: Current student, full-time
Dates of Enrollment: 8/2004-Submit Date
Survey Submitted: April 2005

Cardozo admissions is very organized, very receptive to questions, and once you get in, they are even better than that. I got copious help with finding housing, and I got a same-day response from the director of admissions every time I e-mailed him. He was very familiar with my application, which showed me that they put a lot of time and effort into the selection process.

Also, many law schools will not take a graduate degree or a graduate transcript into account at all. Others, like Cardozo, value graduate degrees very highly. This is something that an older student should take into account when applying.

Status: Current student, full-time
Dates of Enrollment: 5/2002-5/2005
Survey Submitted: April 2005

Cardozo has become increasingly more selective. The number of applicants has steadily increased since 2002. The median LSAT score and the GPA of the admitted students has risen quite a bit. One of the aspects of the admissions process that I enjoyed was that they opened up the law school to prospective students. I was able to attend many functions including Symposia and Lectures at Cardozo, while I was still in the application process. I believe that making yourself a part of the Cardozo community beforehand and truly showing an interest in the school are factors that the admissions people really look to in making their decision.

Status: Current student, full-time
Dates of Enrollment: 8/2002-Submit Date
Survey Submitted: March 2005

The admissions process was very straightforward. The application was included in the information booklet, complete with essay questions regarding a variety of topics. While there are no individual or group interviews for admission, students are encouraged to visit the law school for a tour and/or to speak with the admissions counselors regarding any questions they may have. Throughout the admissions process prospective students/applicants will receive an abundance of information related to various programs, organizations and activities available for all students. Overall, it was an in-depth and inviting process.

> **The school says:** "Only one personal statement is required in the application."

Status: Alumnus/a, full-time
Dates of Enrollment: 8/1999-6/2001
Survey Submitted: May 2004

Cardozo, part of New York City's Yeshiva University, is gunning to be one of the most prestigious schools nationwide. It highly values numbers, perhaps more than other second-tier schools, even if it has to accept fewer students (and less cash therefore). Practice your standardized testing, and keep your GPA high. If you are edged out of the top-tier schools, you are very likely to be accepted to Cardozo, which will probably achieve prestigious status within the next 10 years.

Status: Current student, full-time
Dates of Enrollment: 9/2001-Submit Date
Survey Submitted: September 2003

The admissions process at this school is much like with any other law school: although some care is taken into looking at the overall applicant, a combination of the LSAT and GPA is the deciding factor for admission. However, Cardozo clearly does seem to take efforts to find out about the student—interviews are done—which is more than can be said for most schools, who effectively decide to reject or admit based solely on the numbers. Of course, this is all surmised from anecdotal evidence.

 ## Academics

Status: Alumnus/a, full-time
Dates of Enrollment: 9/2001-6/2004
Survey Submitted: May 2006

In my view the highlight of the Cardozo experience is the Cardozo faculty. Obviously the professors control the classroom environment but the Cardozo faculty is able to create an interactive and stimulating environment without dominating and repressing student interests. The Cardozo professors are stellar and in many cases unmatched in their respective fields but they are also down to earth both in and outside the classroom (I recall many casual lunches with professors). I am not aware of any professor whose expertise is limited to a single field of law. Most have considerable multidisciplanary expertise which means that in their classes the law has a vitality that is not otherwise evident, say in reading textbooks or other class materials. A fact that I've noticed is not known to applicants is that the Cardozo faculty ranks world class in matters of legal theory, again with a multidisciplinary and often critical focus. In my experience and the experiences of my fellow alumni, this overlooked fact has enriched and enriches the average Cardozo student experience—there has rarely been a month in recent years without a seminar and the student journals, particularly the Law Review, publish the products of some of these seminars and thereby have the opportunity to collaborate closely with the faculty and other distinguished experts.

Status: Current student, full-time
Dates of Enrollment: 8/2005-Submit Date
Survey Submitted: April 2006

As I'm in my first year, all of my classes are required, so I haven't yet encountered the process of choosing classes. Everyone says first year of law school is a lot of work, and that's true, but I don't find it overwhelming. I put a lot of time into reading, briefing cases, and reviewing notes before each class, and I always feel like I'm among the most prepared of my classmates. Two of my professors are really terrific—brilliant scholars in their fields and engaging, organized teachers of the material. Two others are clearly very knowledgeable, and I like them both, but I think the students find them a bit disorganized and hard to follow. One is definitely teaching outside her field, and the school shouldn't have her teach this course again. We have very few grades at this point—we've completed only six credits of the 32 total that we take first year, as three of our courses (Property, Contracts and Civil Procedure) are year-long. This scheduling system makes May seem rather daunting. But the school has set the average for each course at 3.2, so I think it would be hard to do too poorly

> **The school says:** "As of fall 2005, Cardozo has a new curve. The mean grade in all first-year courses other than legal writing falls between 3.10 and 3.20. The mean grade in legal writing and all upper-class courses with 25 or more enrolled JD students falls between 3.10 and 3.33. The mean grade in upper-class courses with fewer than 25 enrolled JD students falls between 3.00 and 3.50."

Status: Alumnus/a, full-time
Dates of Enrollment: 8/2002-6/2005
Survey Submitted: March 2006

Classes are difficult—in fact, I think Cardozo may be more difficult than other (higher ranked) law schools. Because Cardozo is a relatively young school, they feel that they need to send their students out into the market knowing more than students from better-known schools. The result is a difficult, vigorous and practically-oriented curriculum that prepares students incredibly well for both the Bar Exam and the real world. I never had a problem getting into a class that I wanted. You will never have a problem getting a class that you need. Additionally, there are a lot of clinical opportunities and journals to participate in. Due to the sheer number of these programs, almost all interested students get a chance to participate. Cardozo (like all law schools) grades all first-year classes on a strict curve. Most upper class classes are graded on a curve as well. Because of the curve, whenever a student gets a particularly high grade, someone else needs to get a low grade. Different professors handle this differently. Some will give mainly B's and very few A's so that they don't have to give many C's. Others are more willing to give out high/low grades. Which professors fall into which camp is easy to find out, and students can choose to take more classes with professors that fall into the camp they prefer.

Status: Alumnus/a, full-time
Dates of Enrollment: 5/2002-5/2005
Survey Submitted: March 2006

The academics offered a great balance between the theoretical and the practical. I was quite lucky in that during my first year when you do not get a chance to choose your professors, I had wonderful professors save for one. Even our Civil Procedure Professor made the usually dry subject interesting. The first year is quite rigorous, and there is a great legal writing, legal research, moot court program for the first year students. This program helped immeasurably when looking for summer clerkships as you had a writing sample to show the judges. In the upper level courses, there were some basic distribution requirements, professional responsibility requirements as well as advanced legal writing and research requirements.

In addition to the upper level courses, Cardozo offers a wonderful variety of clinical programs like its Innocence Project with Barry Scheck, the Mediation Clinic, as well as externships and fellowships at law firms and Federal Judges Chambers. For the most part, getting classes you wanted was very good. I never missed an opportunity to take a class I wanted.

The workload first year is like any other law school—heavy. However, there is a part-time program beginning in May where you do your first year over the course of three semesters as opposed to two. This spaces out your work just that little bit more, so as to ease the burden slightly. Because the summer session is shorter, you only take two substantive course, and so you are only taking one fewer course than the rest of the fall full-time students. But it makes all the difference in the world. There is no separation and no stigma attached. No one even knows that you are part-time, because you're in all but one class with everyone else.

Status: Current student, full-time
Dates of Enrollment: 8/2004-Submit Date
Survey Submitted: November 2005

There is a lot of cutthroat competition first year. 1L at Cardozo is a hellish experience. On average, most students work a lot harder at Cardozo than most students at similarly situated schools.

Status: Current student, full-time
Dates of Enrollment: 8/2002-Submit Date
Survey Submitted: March 2005

While the workload is substantial, particularly the first year of school, I believe it is comparable to most New York law schools. The opportunity to take classes in various fields is tremendous during the second and third years of school. While Cardozo certainly specializes in intellectual property and ADR classes, students may take seminars and lectures for topics ranging from securities to environmental law to criminal defense. The professors are extraordinarily accessible, and some were even students here not too long ago, which makes the connection that much easier. Grading is based on a curve set forth by the administration, with the exception of smaller seminars that have no curve at all. During the first year of law school, students can expect anywhere from two to five hours of work per day outside of the classroom. As you take fewer credits during the second and third years, that time diminishes significantly. Upper-level classes may have papers instead of final exams, and some tests are given as take-home exams. Overall, professors are very popular with the students.

Read all of Vault's Law School Surveys at www.vault.com/lawschool — get complete surveys on top law schools, expert advice on applicaton essays, LSAT prep and more.

VAULT CAREER LIBRARY 473

Status: Current student, full-time
Dates of Enrollment: 5/2004-Submit Date
Survey Submitted: February 2005

Great professors—nasty curve though. I have enjoyed all of my classes, but the grading curve is depressing, especially coming from a top public college with a 3.73. This might account for my ambivalence about Cardozo's grading policy that says you cannot contest your grade after it has been given. Professors are always available and most seem genuinely interested in the students.

Status: Alumnus/a, full-time
Dates of Enrollment: 8/1998-5/2001
Survey Submitted: September 2003

The first year of classes at ABA-approved law schools are very similar. At Cardozo, the second- and third-year curricula consist of a combination of classes that are completely elective, a distribution requirement in three areas and an upper-level writing requirement. The writing requirement is fulfilled either by membership on a journal or by a class that is designated as satisfying the requirement. Grading is curved. The professors advise you at the outset that you are competing against everyone else in your class.

Professors are fairly formal. Everyone is addressed by his or her surname. First-year classes are conducted according to the "Socratic Method," otherwise known as interrogation. This is more or less eases off in upper-level classes, although some professors believe the process is beneficial and refuse to be weaned off it. Some professors take this "Socratic Method" to the extreme. The workload is mainly reading, with as many as 500 pages per week during the first year.

 Employment Prospects

Status: Alumnus/a, full-time
Dates of Enrollment: 8/2002-6/2005
Survey Submitted: March 2006

Students who do well at Cardozo have as many (if not more) job opportunities that students from the county's highest-ranked law schools. Almost all of the big New York firms interview on campus at Cardozo...but many will only interview students in the top of the class. This means that students who do well can expect many interviews, and many offers. Students in the bottom of the class have a harder time finding employment, but the Office of Career Services sponsors many networking events, seminars on applying for small-firm jobs and other similar programs.

Status: Alumnus/a, full-time
Dates of Enrollment: 5/2002-5/2005
Survey Submitted: March 2006

Again, I think that Cardozo's continued growth in its reputation has significantly helped its students land good jobs. Now, the reality of the situation is that many major law firms that come on campus have a cut-off GPA that they will look at from Cardozo. Most of the top firms look to the top 10 percent or top 15 percent of the first year class. However the law firm where I work, told me that they are increasing the number of Cardozo students that they are looking at because the students they had already taken have done such a good job. One of the reasons they say is that Cardozo students work harder because they don't have that top-tier law school sense of entitlement. So, I believe more and more major law firms are looking at Cardozo. I was able to land a summer clerkship for a federal judge in the EDNY, and a summer associate position at the law firm where I currently work. Cardozo's on-campus interviewing has grown since I started there. Cardozo's reputation in New York is excellent, and it is beginning to extend outward as well.

The school says: "The nation's major law firms are, in fact, looking more deeply into the class at Cardozo than every before. Half of the students selected to work at large firms for summer 2006 were below the top 10 percent of the class and, in some instances, were below the top 50 percent."

Status: Current student, full-time
Dates of Enrollment: 8/2002-Submit Date
Survey Submitted: March 2005

The counselors in the Office of Career Services are all available to meet with students, review resumes, and help students to meet their career goals. In addition, there are a number of programs run and opportunities available through the office. For example, some programs include mentor/mentee program in which alumni meet with students, practice profile lunch series and summer institute program. In addition, the school's on-campus interview program is very successful and includes very prestigious employers. The new Public Service Center in the office is also very impressive. In general, the dean of career services and the other counselors are always enhancing the school's recruiting efforts.

The school says: "Cardozo graduates experience great success in the job market, with an impressive 98.3 percent employment rate for 2005 graduates within nine months of graduation. The Office of Career Services has implemented a number of new programs to maximize employment opportunities for all students, regardless of their class standing. For example, in response to the Office's outreach programs, the nation's most prestigious firms are now looking more deeply into the class than ever before. Most of those firms hire nearly exclusively through their Fall Recruitment programs, under which they seek students to serve as summer associates following their second year of law school.

"In the 2005 Fall Recruitment program alone, more than half of all second-year students were granted interviews on campus and others were invited directly to the firms' offices. Students who seek opportunities outside of large firms can take advantage of Cardozo's relatively new and expanding Spring Recruitment program, which complements the Fall Program by targeting small and medium-sized firms, as well as governmental agencies and public interest organizations. In addition, the Office of Career Services hosts many programs throughout the year geared toward networking with attorneys in a broad variety of practice areas and obtaining practical hands-on legal experience throughout law school."

Status: Current student, full-time
Dates of Enrollment: 8/2002-Submit Date
Survey Submitted: March 2005

While the majority of students end up in the private sector, many students work for judges and government agencies immediately following graduation. The average salary of students eight months after graduation is around $80,000. Since Cardozo is a relatively young school, the alumni base is not as large as compared to other New York City schools. However, the school does provide some networking through mentor programs, on-site events and outreach events. Many students obtain internships during the semester through the Office of Career Services in order to obtain some academic credit, while still others work part time on their own for law firms both for experience or for some pay. Approximately 60 percent of students will obtain their jobs through on-campus interviewing, and that includes a combination of summer internships, as well as post-graduate positions.

Status: Alumnus/a, full-time
Dates of Enrollment: 8/1998-6/2001
Survey Submitted: April 2005

Cardozo's prestige is growing with each year. Many top firms hire Cardozo graduates. Prime NYC locations help not only with on-campus recruiting, but also with interviewing in the NYC area and working part time during school. Strong clinics and externship programs and good job prospects for graduates.

Quality of Life

Status: Alumnus/a, full-time
Dates of Enrollment: 8/2002-6/2005
Survey Submitted: March 2006

One great thing about Cardozo is that it is very centrally located, so you can get there easily from just about anywhere. Many students commuted from various places in Manhattan, outer boroughs and even NJ. It is near multiple subway lines, and there are almost always taxis around. Additionally, the neighborhood is great! There are tons of restaurants, stores and bars within blocks of the school. Whole Foods is right around the corner, Strand Bookstore and Barnes and Noble are within a few blocks. There is a great farmers market in Union Square just a few blocks away. Because of the popularity of the neighborhood, there are always people around, so the neighborhood is very safe. Even the subways are completely safe and full of people until late into the night.

Status: Current student, full-time
Dates of Enrollment: 8/2004-Submit Date
Survey Submitted: March 2006

The school is in Greenwich Village—one of the best areas of New York City. It is also easily accessible from other parts of the city. It can be difficult to live by the school because it is an expensive neighborhood, so the fact that it is by so many subway lines is a huge plus. The school itself is nice, with improvements coming every year. The library and moot court room are brand new, with more improvements to the student lounge and cafeteria on the way. The classrooms all have outlets for laptops, but are not wired for Internet (rumor has it that professors have stopped this from happening because they don't want the students online while class is going on).

> **The school says:** "Over the course of the past several years, Cardozo has undergone a multimillion dollar capital improvement plan. It has included the addition of a residence hall, several thousand square feet for a larger and improved library, new offices and clinic spaces, as well as a new and larger lobby, moot court room and new ground-floor seminar room. In addition, older classrooms have been renovated with new desks and chairs and outlets for laptop use. During the summer of 2006, Cardozo will install a new, $5 million student lounge and cafe on the third floor with windows looking out on downtown New York and stairway access to the second and fourth floors where most of the classrooms are located."

Status: Alumnus/a, full-time
Dates of Enrollment: 8/2002-5/2005
Survey Submitted: April 2006

I found the housing and social atmosphere to be one of the best elements of Cardozo. The school felt like a real community, with the nearby housing providing instant connections and relations beyond the classroom. The facilities were very new and improved during my tenure, with the final improvements being completed soon after my graduation. It was a very safe environment, both inside and outside the school, with endless choices for restaurants and cafes in the Union Square area of New York City.

Status: Current student, full-time
Dates of Enrollment: 8/2004-Submit Date
Survey Submitted: April 2005

This is a city school, and like many others, there is very little "campus life." There is a dorm that is totally adequate, and very handy for those students who are coming in from out of state to attend Cardozo and need to secure housing from a far. The facility at the school is very adequate. Of course, they still intend to add more bells and whistles to the student lounge and to the library, which are likely unnecessary, but will be appreciated.

For first-years that are not used to such things, the fact that the facility is closed on Saturday is an enormous pain. In hindsight, it was likely a good thing, because even in the throes of first year, the shut-down forced me to take most of Saturday off from studying. In the end, this was a huge benefit. The students that do the best in law school are those that manage to keep some perspective.

Status: Current student, full-time
Dates of Enrollment: 5/2002-5/2005
Survey Submitted: April 2005

Cardozo is in the greatest neighborhood in New York. Located on Fifth Avenue and 12th street, it is near NYU, the New School and Parsons, giving the area a great student feel and also student friendly (discounts at stores in the area) It is also centrally located with respect to mass transit and so it is easy to get to from uptown, downtown, Brooklyn or Queens. There is housing available, but as you can imagine, being in New York, the space is limited.

> **The school says:** "For the last several years, every incoming student who has wanted to live in Cardozo housing has been able to do so."

There are plenty of restaurants in the neighborhood, as well as local and gourmet grocery stores and delis to buy great food. There is not much on campus, but then again, who needs it when there is so much just outside. The building has gone through a remarkable renovation and the library is completely redone. All of the classrooms have also been renovated, and there is a great new moot court room which was inaugurated by the Second Circuit who heard oral arguments to open the room. It was the first time the Second Circuit had heard oral arguments at a law school.

Social Life

Status: Current student, full-time
Dates of Enrollment: 8/2005-Submit Date
Survey Submitted: April 2006

There are many bars nearby, and the Student Bar Association (SBA) hosts about four or five "bar nights" per semester, which generally include $3 beers for a few hours. Some of the favorite bars are Fiddlesticks, Finnerty's, Bar None and Reservoir. There's one formal event per semester: Fall Bash was in October and the Barristers Ball is next week. This week we had "Law Revue," a student-written comedy and cabaret show, which was great fun since three people from my section were involved, and almost 20 of us went as a group so we could laugh at—I mean, cheer for—them. My section has 48 people, about half of whom are in law school only part-time, which means that they are taking only three and a half classes, while the rest of us take six. About 60 percent are married or in serious relationships, and there's been no intra-section dating at all, which I think is surprising (and I hear is unique to our section among the five first-year sections). I think there are a number of clubs at school; I'm involved in the Media Law Society and the Federalist Society.

Status: Alumnus/a, full-time
Dates of Enrollment: 8/2002-6/2005
Survey Submitted: March 2006

There are too many clubs and organizations to even begin listing them. The Student Bar Association, and the various other groups host frequent social events including bar nights, culturally themed dinners, lectures and other special events. One popular favorite is the Law Revue Show—a student written and performed show featuring skits about the school. Although the professors are frequently a target of the humor, some will roll up their sleeves and perform in it. Hearing your Property professor sing is a truly unique experience. Additionally, there are two larger events, the Spring Fling and the Barristers Ball, which gives you the chance to see your classmates (who are usually shuffling around in sweatpants) get dressed up in fancy clothes. Even though Cardozo is affiliated with Yeshiva University, it is really a secular law school within a religious university. You would never know that you were in a "Jewish School" except for the fact that they order kosher pizza for school sponsored events. There is nothing particularly Jewish about the school, the curriculum or the environment.

Status: Alumnus/a, full-time
Dates of Enrollment: 5/2002-5/2005
Survey Submitted: March 2006

You can't beat the location of Cardozo. Located on 12th street and 5th avenue, it is close to some of the best new york restaurants and bars. There is a great sandwich shop around the corner on 13th Street called Te Adore...great place for lunch. At Cardozo, there are many clubs to join, both legal societies (like the IP

Read all of Vault's Law School Surveys at www.vault.com/lawschool — get complete surveys on top law schools, expert advice on applicaton essays, LSAT prep and more.

VAULT CAREER LIBRARY   475

Law Society) and social groups (like the Wine Tasting Club). I found the people there very friendly, and certainly very intelligent. There are plenty of activities to mix and mingle with people. I enjoyed my time there and would highly recommend Cardozo.

Status: Current student, full-time
Dates of Enrollment: 8/2002-Submit Date
Survey Submitted: July 2004

The racial diversity is good, though a large segment of the population is Jewish (both Orthodox and not). The ethnic student groups are very active and their presence in the school prevalent. Just try to avoid discussing the conflict in the Middle East in the student lounge too loudly.

The students are friendly and some do date within the school. Average age of students is about 24 or so, but there is a decent group of "older" students in their early 30s to late 70s. Lots of great restaurants in the immediate vicinity—school is near Greenwich Village, and Union Square has a great farmers' market on Mondays, Wednesdays and Saturdays to get local organic produce, fresh bread, cheese. Student clubs are active in bringing in speakers, putting on events, shows, outings. SBA sponsors bar nights regularly, and the school offers some discounts to the area's gyms. And the SBA offers $7 movie passes to its students (a nice deal). Most people meet their friends during the first year or through the student groups.

> **The school says:** "The average age of students is 25. Approximately 32 percent of the class comes straight from college, 50 percent of students have been out of college for one to four years, and 18 percent have been out of college for more than five years."

Status: Alumnus/a, full-time
Dates of Enrollment: 8/1999-6/2001
Survey Submitted: May 2004

Although it is under Jewish auspices and closes for all the holidays (even ones most New York Jews have never heard of) and Fridays after sundown until Sunday morning, Cardozo is rather mixed. When I was attending, there was a strong Orthodox group there that had regularly printed words in the school newspaper against the gay and lesbian student organization. But this merely led to the development of a strong diversity coalition movement that gained the ear of the Cardozo administration and printed more speeches against anti-hate expressions in the Cardozo newspaper.

Status: Current student, full-time
Dates of Enrollment: 9/2001-Submit Date
Survey Submitted: September 2003

As a grad school, and a law school at that, the social scene is not nearly as well developed as at an undergraduate institution. However, the students at Cardozo are a relatively fun-loving bunch. There are frequent bar nights on Thursdays where open bars (although for only a small duration) exist. A few professors have even trekked out to such events. In the spring of each year is the annual Barristers Ball, a rough equivalent of the prom, only without the staunch requirement of a date, and with alcohol readily available. A specific favorite of the students is a local bar called the Reservoir, where students traditionally go after first-year exams to engage in copious drinking. Second- and third-years continue to go there, as well.

Status: Alumnus/a, full-time
Dates of Enrollment: 8/1998-5/2001
Survey Submitted: September 2003

The school schedules many events centered around a speaker of national prominence, or around a panel of prominent jurists. Alumni panels are also featured from time to time. When I was in attendance, then-President Clinton was one such speaker. Alumni receive invitations to these events, as well as alumni networking events.

Duke Law School

Duke University School of Law
Office of Admissions
Science Drive & Towerview Road
Box 90393
Durham, NC 27708-0393
Admissions phone: (919) 613-7020
Admissions fax: (919) 613-7257
Admissions e-mail: admissions@law.duke.edu
Admissions URL: http://law.duke.edu/admis/

 ## Admissions

Status: Current student, full-time
Dates of Enrollment: 8/2004-Submit Date
Survey Submitted: May 2006

The program is obviously a selective one and, unfortunately, you aren't given an opportunity to interview with the admissions personnel. Like other top-tier law schools, Duke has minimum GPA and LSAT requirements that students must achieve in order to be considered. Although the requirements are on the high side, it doesn't seem as though your scores conclusively knock you out of the running if your LSAT or GPA is slightly lower than the benchmark score. There is an essay requirement in the application process, which provides students with the opportunity to talk about personal life experiences or anything else the applicant thinks the admissions committee should know about him/her. Because there are no formal interviews, the essay is really the only chance for students to show who they are.

Status: Current student, full-time
Dates of Enrollment: 8/2003-Submit Date
Survey Submitted: May 2006

I was significantly below the median GPA and I think Duke took a chance on me. While numbers are important, they also look at other things. I wrote the optional essay on an issue that I am very passionate about and I believe that that made the difference for me.

Status: Current student, full-time
Dates of Enrollment: 8/2003-Submit Date
Survey Submitted: April 2006

Duke stood out to me when I applied for a number of reasons. First of all, I have a disability so I get sick a lot. Most law schools don't ask or seem to consider that factor in the application process. However, in the Duke Law application, there is an optional essay for students with disabilities. The fact that Duke had an extra essay for those who are disabled signaled to me how accommodating the institution was. Duke is a Top 10 law school and no other law school of its caliber seemed to care about disabilities in the application process.

For those students that are waitlisted, Mark Hill [director of admissions] and the admissions office truly work with the students to figure out what is in their best interests. For example, last semester a number of students from Tulane and Loyola law schools were "visiting students" at Duke. However, because of university policy, they had to return to their respective law schools this semester. The law school admissions office worked with the students, to see if they could be placed on the waitlist and then admitted in the fall 2006—just last week one of my Loyola friends was admitted—a dream come true for her!

Additionally, for those students who are waitlisted, they have the option to meet with students or request interviews. Admitted students also have the option of attending an Admitted Students Weekend and/or interview to gather a sense of what Duke Law is like. Admitted Students Weekend is definitely a weekend of fun. This year it happened to be during March Madness, so there was a law school basketball party that all admitted students attended. This gave them a feel for how sports truly are an integral part of the social life at Duke. The following day there was a panel discussion of life at Duke, a luncheon and then a party at everyone's favorite pizza/bar, Satisfactions.

Finally, another aspect of the Duke admission process that truly amazes me is how organized it is. The school still has a copy of my application! (Which I oddly needed to submit to the Illinois Bar Exam!) It is a good thing Duke Law saved it!

Status: Current student, full-time
Dates of Enrollment: 8/2004-Submit Date
Survey Submitted: April 2006

I think you really want to point out how you want to help society. Everyone here is going to be a great lawyer, but the law school seems to make an effort to attract "scholar-citizens" people who are going to give back to the community and the world. Also, tell the law school what you will bring to the law school (previous work experience, diversity), because the law school is not solely focused on grades and LSAT scores.

Status: Current student, full-time
Dates of Enrollment: 6/2005-Submit Date
Survey Submitted: April 2006

Duke Law is unique among its peer law schools in that the school, like the university at large, looks at students holistically, so grades and LSAT scores aren't an end all, be all. This goes beyond just minority candidates. Thus, honors and awards, extracurricular activities and even a compelling essay matter to Duke Law more than other schools. Having said that, Duke Law has recently aimed for a 169 LSAT range, and is forced to join its peer schools in the upward trajectory of LSAT scores that seem to inch closer and closer to 180 each year.

Status: Current student, full-time
Dates of Enrollment: 6/2005-Submit Date
Survey Submitted: April 2006

To apply for admission, students must submit an application, complete a personal statement and submit at least one additional essay. There is no interview process. Students who are placed on a waitlist have had success getting admitted by submitting additional letters of recommendation. The law school also commonly allows students to defer if needed. Duke Law School is interested in creating a diverse student body from a variety of backgrounds. While a student's GPA and LSAT score receive significant attention, important life experiences and work background also go a long way towards helping a student get admitted.

Status: Current student, full-time
Dates of Enrollment: 8/2004-Submit Date
Survey Submitted: October 2005

Duke is fairly selective in terms of admissions. Generous with financial aid packages, the school appeals mostly to students who are looking for a community experience with law school. Both faculty and students are typically drawn to Duke because of how collaborative and open everyone is. Interviews are not required, but certainly it would not hurt a candidate's chances to make the trip to Duke, go on a tour of the law school through the admissions office and meet with an admissions counselor.

Status: Current student, full-time
Dates of Enrollment: 8/2003-Submit Date
Survey Submitted: May 2005

Like all top schools, Duke is very selective and the admissions process is very competitive. LSATs and GPA are important. But one of the things that distinguishes Duke (in my opinion) is that Duke seems to take other factors into consideration a little bit more than other schools. Granted, the LSAT and GPA are huge, but if I remember correctly, Duke is the only top school that I applied to that asked for an additional essay (besides Yale) and I think that made a difference in my acceptance and scholarship offer (which was different from other schools').

Read all of Vault's Law School Surveys at www.vault.com/lawschool — get complete surveys on top law schools, expert advice on applicaton essays, LSAT prep and more.

VAULT CAREER LIBRARY 477

Status: Current student, full-time
Dates of Enrollment: 8/2004-Submit Date
Survey Submitted: May 2005

While there's no clear way to ensure admission to any prestigious school, several things seem to be especially important: study for the LSAT—whether through a formal course or self-disciplined study, it is essential to practice. The LSAT tests particular skills that must be learned and are not just intuitive to the intelligent individual. Use the personal statement and essay as an opportunity to be yourself and show that you are more than just a high LSAT number. Diversity of perspectives makes for a healthy, vibrant learning environment. Show that you have initiative and challenge yourself. Choose the individuals who will write your recommendations not by their prestige but by how thorough a letter they will write. Everyone has glowing recommendations. The ones that stand out are those that show how well the writer knows and respects you as an individual.

 Academics

Status: Current student, full-time
Dates of Enrollment: 8/2003-Submit Date
Survey Submitted: May 2006

Like an law program, the first year is very difficult. But the professors are amazingly friendly here. I have been invited to professors' homes on numerous occasions. Professors come out to play pool, go bowling and just relax with students. And, of course, they always welcome you to drop by their office. I would say that the quality of the instruction combined with the obvious effort that they put into developing relationships with students have made my time here incredible.

Status: Current student, full-time
Dates of Enrollment: 8/2003-Submit Date
Survey Submitted: April 2006

Before I begin to describe the academic environment at Duke Law, it is important to understand the Duke Bar Association (DBA) mentor program. Basically, from the time you are a 1L, you are set up with a mentor. This mentor is your social/academic advisor. She is the key to your success. Because my mentor and I hit it off, she sent me outlines for all of my first-year classes—huge advantage. However, something about Duke that is extremely unique is that EVERYONE shares outlines. For example, I was looking for an outline for my bankruptcy course. I asked two fellow classmates. In the past week, three 2Ls and four LLMs have e-mailed me outlines! There is no competitive academic atmosphere at Duke whatsoever!

One of the reasons that I chose to go to Duke is because I am interested in practicing sports law after graduation. Duke Law is one of the only schools across the nation that offers a sports law curriculum. Over the course of the past three years, I have taken Sports Law, Comparative Sports Law and Sports Ethics. I have also done two independent sports law research projects. This past semester, my Sports Law professor and Poverty Law professors worked together to find me an internship—I spent the semester being a research assistant for a sports professor at Indiana Law—dream come true.

Another key aspect of Duke is that students have the opportunity to take one class outside of the law school. I chose a sports-related class. This is a unique opportunity that I think other law schools should offer. Often, students take a business class in the Fuqua Business School as their outside class. Another advantage of the Duke academics is that some Duke Law classes are cross-listed with the business school classes. For example, one of my classes, entitled Corporate Restructuring, was a business school class offered to law students. It gave law students a perspective about the financial aspects of LBOs, divestitures and valuations. Such a course is extremely useful for someone who plans on practicing corporate law after Duke. I'm not sure if many other Top 10 law schools offer students the chance to take: (1) business school classes; or (2) classes outside of the graduate school systems (e.g., my Sports Ethics class).

Another aspect of the Duke academics that I especially like is that many of our clubs are extensions of classes. For example, there is a Sports and Entertainment Law Society that brings in speakers for the Sports Law class. The class and club work together to foster an interest in sports law among the students.

Status: Current student, full-time
Dates of Enrollment: 8/2004-Submit Date
Survey Submitted: April 2006

Duke is, of course, an exceptional school with great professors. What makes Duke different from the other highly ranked schools is that our professors teach us about the policy of law as well as the practice of law. Many top-ranked schools focus solely on policy, so when you have to go to work you have to be trained on exactly how to do what your clients need you to do. Here at Duke, our professors make sure we discuss and gain an appreciation for the policy behind the law, but they also make sure we understand how the law works in everyday situations. Therefore Duke graduates are very successful in the job market earlier than our counterparts.

The Socratic Method is very light at Duke and after the first year almost nonexistent. Our professors do not like to embarrass students, so their questions are usually simple and more conversation provoking than fear provoking.

Status: Current student, full-time
Dates of Enrollment: 6/2005-Submit Date
Survey Submitted: April 2006

First-year classes typically hold 50 to 70 students. The registration process is simple and straightforward and popular classes are repeated frequently enough to allow students to access to the courses they want. All courses are blind-graded, meaning the professor sees only a nondescript student number when grading a test. Grades and GPAs are not published in any format, allowing students to keep their grades confidential and eliminating competitive posturing. The atmosphere at the law school is very collegial and friendly. Professors are talented, bright and friendly. They are also very accessible. Many professors actively encourage students to go to lunch with them by allowing small groups of students to sign up for lunch appointments in groups. The workload is demanding but manageable. The student affairs office works hard to teach students about courses offered, courses needed to graduate and other details of academic life. Duke Law is a very supportive environment. There are also many conferences and symposia to help students learn about various fields of law and potential careers.

Status: Current student, full-time
Dates of Enrollment: 8/2004-Submit Date
Survey Submitted: October 2005

The first year of law school is broken down into three substantive classes each semester and a yearlong, graded Legal Writing class. The Writing class wraps up just past halfway each semester (just after fall break and just before spring break) so as not to be a burden come exam time. Popular classes are doled out in as egalitarian a way as possible—first come, first serve during online registration. Outside of the typically small classes offered jointly with the business school (e.g., Real Estate Entrepeneurship), most classes are readily available to all.

Status: Current student, full-time
Dates of Enrollment: 6/2004-Submit Date
Survey Submitted: May 2005

My professors have been universally brilliant, although each had a distinctive style. They are all quite committed to teaching while at the same time exceedingly accomplished in their field. Twice last semester, my Constitutional Law professor apologized to our class for having to cancel because he was going to argue before the Supreme Court. Professors are also quite accessible. I was working on a project this year that necessitated background information on legal issues in the War on Terrorism. I was able to schedule an appointment with an expert on national security law and talk about my areas of interest with him, even though I had never had a class with him. Having access to such a widely accomplished faculty is one of the great draws of Duke.

Status: Current student, full-time
Dates of Enrollment: 8/2004-Submit Date
Survey Submitted: May 2005

Classes are stimulating and class discussion is robust. Students have a lot to say but class conversation never degenerates into personal attacks or boring political ping-pong discussions. Professors are beyond accessible; I expressed interest in a related topic with one professor and he invited me to join a group that was discussing it that evening, at his house. I had instructions in hand five minutes later. The faculty wants students to succeed not only academically, but personally and professionally.

Status: Alumnus/a, full-time
Dates of Enrollment: 8/2000-5/2003
Survey Submitted: May 2005

Law school is intrinsically split between theory and practice. Law school can be as high-minded as the study of classical philosophy; or as practical as accounting or finance. Academics at Duke Law represent a particularly good mix of scholarship and real-world application. Almost no professor ignores the realities of practice; after all, important social change usually must be accomplished through the constraints of bureaucracy. At the same time, the most thoughtful of students will feel stimulated by the level of scholarship and discussion.

Employment Prospects

Status: Current student, full-time
Dates of Enrollment: 8/2003-Submit Date
Survey Submitted: April 2006

Like the DBA mentorship program, there is also a mentoring program involving job searches at Duke. Students not only have mentors, but also the ability to attend panels and workshops on etiquette and recruiting skills. Some of my friends actually went to school-sponsored etiquette dinners. (I passed because I was at Cameron Indoor for a basketball game.)

Duke Law is definitely held with much prestige by employers. Not only do the top firms from all the major cities come to Duke (e.g., NYC, Chicago, Atlanta, D.C., Los Angeles), but firms from foreign cities even come to Duke. One of my friends will be working in London after graduation. Another is working at the embassy in South Africa.

Besides the alumni network, I have many Duke people to thank for obtaining my summer job. First, for those students who have an ideal firm that does not come to Duke, that is where the office of student services comes in. My summer before 2L year, the dean of student services probably e-mailed me every day. She helped me draft and revise my cover letter so the firms I was targeting would not throw my resume solicitation in the garbage. Luckily for me, the plan worked and I got my dream job in Chicago.

Status: Current student, full-time
Dates of Enrollment: 8/2004-Submit Date
Survey Submitted: April 2006

There are also practical reasons for why Duke is so successful in the job market. First, Duke does not rank its students, so employers cannot discern where you are in the class, and it is impossible for them to request the "top 20 percent" because that does not exist at Duke. Second, Duke is a national school with a national student body, so we all want to go to different parts of the country. Unlike some schools, we are not all competing to go into one job market. For example, when 20 firms from Atlanta, GA come to interview the 15 students who want to go to Atlanta, those students have an excellent chance of getting a job. Third, our class size is small but the number of employers coming to campus is not. We continually have at least 350 employers and law firms coming to interview 200 students. The chances of you finding and employer in that mix is nearly guaranteed!

Status: Current student, full-time
Dates of Enrollment: 8/2004-Submit Date
Survey Submitted: October 2005

Duke's alumni love Duke; I mean LOVE Duke. They go out of their way to hire current students as summer associates and judicial clerks. Duke does especially well with on-campus recruiting, particularly because we send graduates everywhere, so employers from everywhere want to come to Durham to interview. Consequently, there are a variety of options and opportunities for students.

Status: Alumnus/a, full-time
Dates of Enrollment: 8/2001-5/2004
Survey Submitted: April 2006

Duke is universally recognized as a good school, and it shows at recruiting time. I was able to pick up and move to a new city, not one of the bigger legal markets in the country, and get a job lined up within a couple weeks. The alumni network, alumni office and career services office were all instrumental in helping me with the interview and job placement process. The people Duke hires for each of these offices know their stuff, and it shows!

Status: Alumnus/a, full-time
Dates of Enrollment: 8/1998-5/2001
Survey Submitted: March 2006

Duke students typically have little trouble getting jobs at prestigious firms nationwide. Duke grads do not cluster in one city, and tend to go to many places, the most popular of which are New York, Washington, D.C., California, Texas and Boston. The career services office is pretty organized. Some grads go into government or public service. I would guess about 30 percent of students do federal clerkships. Top students tend to do federal appellate clerkships.

Status: Alumnus/a, full-time
Dates of Enrollment: 6/2000-12/2002
Survey Submitted: March 2006

Everyone I know from my graduating class got exactly the job they wanted. On-campus recruiting is extensive, and the career services office coordinates everything for you—it takes almost no effort on the part of the students to get jobs, whether they are with firms or in the public sector.

Status: Alumnus/a, full-time
Dates of Enrollment: 8/2001-5/2004
Survey Submitted: March 2006

Most of my class (by choice) went on to large firms, many by way of prestigious clerkships. Some continue to work in the judiciary branch; others found jobs with nonprofits, legal service providers (e.g., jury consultants) or in academia. Geographically, we really spread out, though concentrations of graduates are in D.C., New York and Atlanta. On-campus recruiting was efficient; I was surprised by the number of employers who came to Durham to interview such a small pool of applicants.

Status: Current student, full-time
Dates of Enrollment: 8/2004-Submit Date
Survey Submitted: May 2005

Career services, despite high turnover in the past few years, provides excellent help to students. Aside from on-campus interviews (about 40 to 50 for 1Ls, 300 to 400 for 2Ls), there are numerous panels on topics ranging from cover letter writing to interview skills (there are also mock interviews done with alumni for all interested parties), to dining etiquette and resume writing workshops. Also, they organize "brown bag" lunches to pester current 2Ls and 3Ls about different job markets. Also, OCI is run a bit differently than at other schools; employers don't select the students, students select the employers. Students bid on employers based on their interest level and from there, the interview schedule is set. That way, all students can ensure that they have a chance at an interview, even if their first year didn't go as well as they had planned.

Status: Alumnus/a, full-time
Dates of Enrollment: 8/1999-5/2002
Survey Submitted: June 2004

The placement office is focused like a laser beam on BigLaw. Accordingly, job prospects and on-campus recruitment are solid, if not exceptional. Every moderately capable student will get offers from big firms in big cities with big salaries, no exception. Most students go to New York or D.C., but many end up in Los Angeles, San Francisco, Florida and even overseas as a result of on-campus interviews. The office is less interested in helping students interested in alternate paths, but not inept.

Read all of Vault's Law School Surveys at www.vault.com/lawschool — get complete surveys on top law schools, expert advice on applicaton essays, LSAT prep and more.

VAULT CAREER LIBRARY   **479**

Quality of Life

Status: Current student, full-time
Dates of Enrollment: 8/2003-Submit Date
Survey Submitted: April 2006

Another factor that makes living in Duke extremely safe is the access to good, quality medical care. As a student with a disability, this was a factor that motivated me to come to Duke. As long as you are a Duke student you can attend parts of the well-known medical center for certain student rates, I believe. Also, students can obtain free medication at the school health center. This was extremely nice when I had bronchitis in December and got free medications!

Finally, the facilities are state-of-the-art. Duke Law just built a few new wings this year for clinics and journals. Sometimes I feel as if that part of the building looks nicer than an actual law firm. Regardless, everything at Duke is modern. The beautiful courtyard is especially nice when it is sunny out and you want to do some work outside. The classrooms all have access to wireless, state-of-the-art technology. The seminars tend to be in the newer, smaller classrooms.

Status: Current student, full-time
Dates of Enrollment: 8/2004-Submit Date
Survey Submitted: October 2005

The quality of life has been great in Durham. It's a city that's changing in a lot of ways for the better for people at the university. There are many more bars, restaurants and apartments in locations that would have been unthinkable five or 10 years ago. Though there is still a vestige of the 80s depression (when tobacco moved out of Durham), generally the area is very clean and safe. Chapel Hill is just down the road, too, which adds a second city—or more precisely a college town—to hang out at when needed. Believe it or not, UNC and Duke students are very civil to each other, except when it comes to sports. Yes, you can even wear a Duke hat out to the bars, just don't expect to pick up many UNC undergrads! Everything in Durham is also very inexpensive compared to other school locations. Two- and three-bedroom townhouses can be bought for less than $100,000, and the upkeep is less than $500 a month. One-bedroom apartments cost around $600 a month, and they have more room than anything in D.C. for three times that much! Your dollar definitely goes a lot farther down here.

Status: Alumnus/a, full-time
Dates of Enrollment: 6/2000-12/2002
Survey Submitted: March 2006

The quality of life in Durham, NC is amazing. I lived in a large house, two miles from school, with a yard, decks, etc., for $400 a month. There is no traffic, nothing is expensive, people are calm and relaxed. I can't think of a better place to go to law school. The weather is gorgeous all year round, the law school sponsors softball tournaments and outdoor events, and students can almost always be found lounging around on the lawn studying (as opposed to in the library). The law school is brand new and state-of-the-art, and the Durham/Chapel Hill are provides great restaurants, bars and cultural options.

Status: Alumnus/a, full-time
Dates of Enrollment: 9/2002-5/2005
Survey Submitted: March 2006

Housing in Durham, however, stinks. There is an extremely limited number of on-campus apartments, and I think they are stuck in undergrad dorms—be prepared to nanny. Almost everyone lives off campus in a house or apartment. The trouble is that Durham has some pretty sketchy neighborhoods, and they are occasionally next door to gorgeous areas. Worse, the patchwork changes constantly as old areas are gentrified and others deteriorate. Get started on your housing search as soon as you are admitted and make sure to use all of the resources available to you, including the ample resources provided by the law school, the university and the Graduate and Professional Student Council. You really need to use local resources like that, because you cannot know until you've lived there whether a particular place is going to be a good place to live.

The only huge quality of life issue is crime. All of this is getting much better; the university has significantly beefed up security on campus, and the law school is doing a better job of monitoring (there are security cameras strategically placed, for instance). Also, Durham itself is stepping up, and the crime rate in the city is dropping. As Durham's economy picks up a bit, expect the crime rate to drop off even more. In any event, all of the crime that effected students while I was there was preventable. Take warnings and suggestions seriously, and be smart.

Status: Current student, full-time
Dates of Enrollment: 8/2004-Submit Date
Survey Submitted: May 2005

The neighborhoods in the Raleigh-Durham-Chapel Hill Triangle are great. You will need a car but parking is not a problem. The area around campus is dominated by the university. The law school is undergoing a major renovation—a new wing is being added for fall 2005, which will offer office space for all of the journals and new clinic space.

Duke's facilities generally are nice. They just renovated the Wilson Center—adding some plasma screen TVs in front of the cardio machines—and there are plenty of on-campus eateries around the Bryan Center.

Status: Current student, full-time
Dates of Enrollment: 8/2004-Submit Date
Survey Submitted: May 2005

Durham is incredibly affordable, safe and friendly and offers surprisingly good food. Its character as an old tobacco manufacturing town makes it stand out among the cookie-cutter college towns around. The graduate, professional and undergraduate schools are well-integrated and the services on campus (gyms, chapel, music productions) add greatly to the quality of life in a small Southern town.

Status: Current student, full-time
Dates of Enrollment: 5/2003-Submit Date
Survey Submitted: May 2005

Durham is great. However, a lot of my classmates who were coming from big cities had a bit of a culture shock moving here last year. It is one of those places with a lot of hidden treasures. Unfortunately, the public transportation system is not one of them; you need to have a car if you live here. Durham is less expensive than the areas surrounding other top law schools, and there are tons of outdoor activities in North Carolina. Plus, the basketball team is great.

Status: Alumnus/a, full-time
Dates of Enrollment: 8/1998-5/2003
Survey Submitted: September 2003

Living in Durham with student debt is a better quality of life than many will find once they start working (especially if it's in a major metropolitan city). The weather is great. The apartments are like living in a country club: new, beautiful, often with pools, tennis courts and great service. North Carolina has beautiful trees and is just a wonderful place to relax and read law for three years. The IT facilities and level of support at Duke law are far better than most law firms or investment banks! The school should really be proud of itself for this.

Social Life

Status: Current student, full-time
Dates of Enrollment: 8/2003-Submit Date
Survey Submitted: May 2006

I cannot believe my luck in the friends that I made here. I have met the most amazing people and I always say that I cannot wait to see what they are doing with their lives in 10 to 15 years. They are brilliant, thoughtful, considerate and devoted to the same progressive causes that I care about. They are truly inspiring to be around and they are fun to hang out with. I have met some of my best friends here and I will have them for life.

Status: Current student, full-time
Dates of Enrollment: 8/2005-Submit Date
Survey Submitted: April 2006

This law school is very much like college. Since it is small you will know everyone, but in a good way. The school feels like a community. Because the school is relatively small, many people seem to participate in the school sponsored activities. The general scene is pretty young. There is a divide etween the married students and single students in terms of the social scene. There is not a lot of interaction with the outside community, but if you are looking for more of a "scene" Raleigh is about a 20-minute drive. For late night food, Cosmic Cantina, a local burrito place, is a favorite and one of the few things open until 3 or 4 a.m.

Status: Current student, full-time
Dates of Enrollment: 8/2003-Submit Date
Survey Submitted: April 2006

Every Monday, students tend to get together to watch *24* or Monday Night Football. When basketball was still in season there are basketball parties. Monday and Sunday are probably the two low-key nights when students may get their work done. Every Tuesday students go to Bubs for trivia night. Winners get free drinks, but the catch is that you can't use your phones if you play trivia. If you do, you're eliminated!

Every Wednesday is Duke Law Bowling League. 9 to 11 p.m., get ready for some fun. Bring your appetite, your love for beer and whatever bowling skills you have to AMF Lanes in Durham. There are typically three bowling commissioners and a bowling league photographer. There are two bowling seasons, fall and spring. At the end of each season, the playoff season begins where students compete for the Bar Bri Cup. Typically, after bowling ends at 11 p.m., bowlers head off to the local bars for more drinks and fun.

Every Thursday the student-run DBA coordinates a Bar Review, when the DBA rents out a bar in Chapel Hill or Durham and gets students drinking specials. Bar Review is definitely the biggest night all week (well, besides bowling night described above). Bar Review is a place for 1Ls and 3Ls to interact and for relationships to form. Favorites for Bar Review depend on what type of person you are: some Bar Reviews feature clubs and others are more of lounge-type bars. All in all, Bar Review is definitely one of the top two nights all week.

Friday and Saturday is spent at Durham or Chapel Hill bars. Typically students will pre-game at someone's house firt or there will be a party. There are typically one to four house parties per weekend.

Status: Current student, full-time
Dates of Enrollment: 8/2004-Submit Date
Survey Submitted: October 2005

At around 200 people a class, it's possible to recognize everyone who goes out on a Thursday or weekend night. My small section was about 30 people and nearly 15 of us have stayed remarkably close. I have lunch with between three and seven sectionmates every day, and we have done fall break and post-1L trips together. The small size, on the other hand, can give the place a middle school-like feel—clicks, gossip and jealousy are everywhere! I guess your expectations for being with "normal" people should be lowered if you choose to attend law school. But it can be frustrating when everyone knows who you are dating and how long it's been going on before you even know you ARE dating.

Status: Alumnus/a, full-time
Dates of Enrollment: 8/2001-5/2004
Survey Submitted: April 2006

Despite not being located in one of the country's larger metropolitan areas, Duke has a plethora of social options. Durham, nearby Chapel Hill and the Triangle have a lot to offer, including world-class cultural events, sports and the outdoors. There are plenty of great restaurants and pubs around, and the students at Duke Law are a very collegial bunch, taking advantage of all these social outlets. Road trips are popular as well, with the Outer Banks, Wilmington, Washington, the Smoky Mountains, Myrtle Beach and Charleston all within easy road-tripping distance.

Status: Alumnus/a, full-time
Dates of Enrollment: 9/2002-5/2005
Survey Submitted: March 2006

For many law students at Duke, "social life" means drinking, and there are plenty of opportunities. The James Joyce ("the Joyce") and Satisfaction's Pizza ("Sati's") downtown are favorites. A lot of folks wind up down in Chapel Hill; Franklin Street is basically paved with beer slop and lined with bars. More sedate Dukies still find plenty to do: eat out at Four Square, Vin Rouge or one of the excellent restaurants in Chapel Hill, catch a movie (forget the theater on MLK, the only good one is at the Streets at Southpoint Mall), or almost anything else your heart fancies. The law school has (anyway, had) a very active softball league, and a bowling league. Both competed against other law schools, as well as within Duke.

Sports, of course, are close to the heart of all Duke Law students. Obviously basketball is central to many conversations. Student tickets are available to law students by lottery. In order to enter the lottery, you have to attend "camp out," which is a three-day riotous party. Everyone gets ripped, beer flows like water and music pumps constantly. Tons of fun if you're into that sort of thing.

Status: Current student, full-time
Dates of Enrollment: 5/2003-Submit Date
Survey Submitted: May 2005

I find that many law students do not get to know anyone outside the law school network; a big mistake in my opinion. The school can feel stifling if all your social activities happen with the same folks you attend class with. There are options to meet people outside the law school and the Triangle (Raleigh, Durham and Chapel Hill) has about a million people, lots of them young and smart. Bars are better in Chapel Hill, though there is a great new place on Main Street called the Federal. In addition, for its size, Durham has a vibrant food scene with a number of great places such as Magnolia Grill (expensive) to Cosmic Cantina (super cheap, and open until 3 a.m.).

Status: Current student, full-time
Dates of Enrollment: 8/2004-Submit Date
Survey Submitted: May 2005

Duke students are fun. The undergraduate motto, "work hard, play hard," applies to law students too. An undercurrent of competitiveness crops up only around grades time and is quickly gone. The law school is smaller, though not suffocatingly so, which means that it is pretty easy to get to know anyone you want. Everyone loves basketball and other Duke sports, and there is a lot of good-natured ribbing around NCAA tourney time.

Read all of Vault's Law School Surveys at www.vault.com/lawschool — get complete surveys on top law schools, expert advice on applicaton essays, LSAT prep and more.

VAULT CAREER LIBRARY 481

North Carolina Central University School of Law

Office of Admissions
1512 S. Alston Avenue
Durham, NC 27707
Admissions phone: (919) 530-7173
Admissions e-mail: recruiter@nccu.edu
Admissions URL: http://www.nccu.edu/law/admissions/

 Admissions

Status: Current student, full-time
Dates of Enrollment: 8/2003-Submit Date
Survey Submitted: April 2006

The staff was wonderful. Ms. Van Hook walked me through the application process; my interview with Dean Douglas was informative; and the students greeted me graciously.

Status: Alumnus/a, part-time
Dates of Enrollment: 8/2000-5/2004
Survey Submitted: April 2006

Admission to the evening program is very competitive. It is the ONLY evening law program in North Carolina and attracts many top professionals who are seeking a law degree. High LSAT scores are important. However, because applicants are generally professionals in other fields, work experience and leadership are also factors that enhance your application.

Status: Alumnus/a, full-time
Dates of Enrollment: 8/2001-5/2004
Survey Submitted: March 2006

The admissions process appeared to be very similar to other law schools. Though the average LSAT score for the student body is not very competitive, the acceptance rate for admissions is quite low. The school does an excellent job of selecting a very diverse pool of students. NCCU has got to be one of the most diverse law schools with the highest percentage of female students and female professors in the country.

Status: Current student, full-time
Dates of Enrollment: 8/2005-Submit Date
Survey Submitted: March 2006

I filled out an application and wrote a personal statement about why I wanted to attend law school.

Status: Current student, full- and part-time
Dates of Enrollment: 8/2004-Submit Date
Survey Submitted: March 2006

Straightforward application, reasonable application fees. School is becoming more selective as the applicant pool expands.

Status: Alumnus/a, part-time
Dates of Enrollment: 8/1994-5/1998
Survey Submitted: April 2004

Admissions to the evening program followed the standard practices of the full-time program. Some professors said that the selection process for the evening program was a little more rigorous.

> **Regarding Admissions, the school says:** "We have a very competitive admissions process. Last year, we received over 2,000 applications for 170 day and 30 evening slots. The median LSAT and GPA scores for the entering evening students are generally higher than for the day students."

 Academics

Status: Current student, full-time
Dates of Enrollment: 8/2003-Submit Date
Survey Submitted: April 2006

Although majority of the professors are great teachers, many don't prepare exams that are practical or bar-like to ready the students for life after law school. We prepare for exams in a manner completing opposite of the writing style required by the bar. Additionally, the faculty assesses the students on a C grading curve. The bell has a negative impact on the students.

> **Regarding Academics, the school says:** "North Carolina Central University School of Law follows a rigorous 4.00 scale and encourages its faculty to adhere to C grade expectation curve (a C representing average work). Students who do not maintain a 2.0 at the end of their first or second year are academically dismissed. The law school has an intense Legal Writing Program with required courses for students each year."

Status: Alumnus/a, part-time
Dates of Enrollment: 8/2000-5/2004
Survey Submitted: April 2006

The evening program academic expectations are the same as for the day program. In fact, many evening and day classes have the exact same syllabus, text and final exam. With that in mind, being a part-time student adds a much higher level of difficulty than for the full-time student. The evening student has high academic expectations while also managing the same expectations at their employment. Additionally, many evening students have families and those expectations remain regardless!

The evening program does not offer a lot of selection for electives. Because the program is designed with a structured time frame (to accommodate students who have daytime commitments and ABA requirements) there is not a lot of room for flexibility. However, this does not impact the quality of the curriculum. I learned the same general subjects as every other law student in the country—just not a lot of exotic/impractical topics.

The quality of classes was generally good. Of course, there are always a few duds—no academic experience is complete without them! Many of the professors are quite helpful and pride themselves on ensuring the students' success. When I was a student, it was more difficult for evening students to integrate themselves into the law school extracurriculars. I believe this may be a problem for evening students in general. However, I found that this was often frustrating and evening students sometimes felt left out. It was possible to overcome—it simply required extra effort (on top of all the effort already) to get involved. At the time of my graduation I was a part of the moot court team and the Law Review along with several other evening students. I sensed that the tides were shifting and I certainly hope that has continued.

Status: Alumnus/a, full-time
Dates of Enrollment: 8/2001-5/2004
Survey Submitted: March 2006

The small size of each graduating class offers a much more intimate interaction with professors and law school staff. The quality of classes varied and the best classes seemed to be the clinics and classes taught by the more senior professors. There is very little, if any, difficulty when enrolling in the more popular classes.

Overall, I believe that I received an excellent legal education. Having attended a much larger undergraduate university, I found the level of support and personal interest in my future from professors to far exceed my undergraduate experience.

Like any law school, the workload is very heavy. Unlike other law schools, NCCU has a very strict C curve, which can be discouraging for first-year students. Despite the strict C curve, most students support each other and are not overly competitive.

Status: Current student, full-time
Dates of Enrollment: 8/2005-Submit Date
Survey Submitted: March 2006

This is the hardest academic work that I've ever done. It is extremely difficult and one must spend hours reading and preparing for class to be successful. The classes for the first year of law school are arranged for you. The quality of the professors is topnotch.

Status: Current student, full- and part-time
Dates of Enrollment: 8/2004-Submit Date
Survey Submitted: March 2006

Program is VERY rigorous with more required course than many other schools. Program is somewhat unique: first-year classes have midterm exams, and grading is VERY difficult, as there is little to no traditional grade curving in first-year classes. Grade inflation is NOT a concern at this school right now, so be prepared for potential GPA shock! Required writing and research courses are terrible—bad instructors, worse assignments. However, other professors and most other course offerings are tremendous. Lots of dynamic and respected teachers. The criminal-, civil rights- and tax-related courses are particularly strong.

Employment Prospects

Status: Alumnus/a, part-time
Dates of Enrollment: 8/2000-5/2004
Survey Submitted: April 2006

It is my experience, in talking with with others in the legal community, that the evening program at NCCU has a particularly high regard. Other professionals are aware of the highly competitive admission process. Beyond that, they are aware of the expectations on the student and the great motivation and hard work it takes to balance school with employment and family. I believe this reputation helped me overcome some of the barriers presented by the school's lower-tier ranking and lack of prestige compared to other NC law schools.

Status: Alumnus/a, full-time
Dates of Enrollment: 8/2001-5/2004
Survey Submitted: March 2006

NCCU is a competitive school for local or NC-based jobs, especially because a lot of NCCU alums work in NC. I don't think the school racks up a compeative reputation outside of NC. However, any student with a strong academic record who pursues meaningful summer internships can be competitive in the legal job market.

Status: Current student, full- and part-time
Dates of Enrollment: 8/2004-Submit Date
Survey Submitted: March 2006

Prospects slim compared to other state schools, and focus has been mainly on public interest work. However, this area is focus for improvement and strides have been made. I expect growth of opportunities and continued improvements.

Status: Current student, full-time
Dates of Enrollment: 8/2005-Submit Date
Survey Submitted: March 2006

The only experience that I have had with the employment aspect is trying to get an internship after my first year. I received a job as a clerk for a North Carolina Supreme Court Justice. This is a prestigious position and I am excited about it.

Status: Alumnus/a, part-time
Dates of Enrollment: 8/1994-5/1998
Survey Submitted: April 2004

Many of the courses retained a national perspective, but approximately two-thirds of the curriculum was geared to North Carolina-specific law (e.g., decedents' estates and family law). This factor was especially helpful to those preparing for the NC bar exam. Some of the bigger-name law schools in the

state did not focus on NC-specific law and those grads taking the NC bar exam had familiarize themselves quickly during the bar review courses following graduation.

Status: Alumnus/a, part-time
Dates of Enrollment: 8/1994-5/1998
Survey Submitted: April 2004

The full-time program enjoyed the typical career opportunities of internships; however, the year-round nature of an evening program precluded such opportunities.

Quality of Life

Status: Current student, full-time
Dates of Enrollment: 8/2003-Submit Date
Survey Submitted: April 2006

The rigorous pace of academics at NCCU School of Law hinders the quality of life. We are given so many practical experiences to ensure we are able to move from the class to the courtroom that students are burdened when it comes to participating in law journals and moot court competitions. Our facilities are wonderful but the disconnect with main campus causes a burden when dealing with issues such as financial aid and registration.

Parking is ridiculous. I don't understand why the administration continues to build new structures and recruit more students but fail to provide adequate parking arrangements.

> **Regarding Quality of Life, the school says:** "North Carolina Central University has doubled its student body in the last few years to approximately 10,000 students, and the size of the campus has increased dramatically with several new buildings. Parking for students, faculty and visitors has been a problem during this time of growth. The university continues to work on parking alternatives and long-term parking solutions. The law school moved back into the Turner Law Building in July 2005 after a two-year intensive renovation of the existing building, and the construction of an addition to the building. The law building is now state-of-the-art, with technology in every classroom, wireless capability throughout the building, and other technological features."

Status: Alumnus/a, full-time
Dates of Enrollment: 8/2001-5/2004
Survey Submitted: March 2006

The best aspect of the quality of life at the law school is the diverse student body. The more serious drawbacks are the limited and aging facilities, which are being upgraded. The campus, which is located in an urban setting, has little open space, few healthy food options and no quiet outdoor areas to study or contemplate your navel.

The heart and spirit of the professors left a lasting imprint on me and far outweigh any of the drawbacks I experienced while attending NCCU law school.

Status: Current student, full-time
Dates of Enrollment: 8/2005-Submit Date
Survey Submitted: March 2006

My quality of life is the law. I eat, sleep and drink the law. There is no time for other things if one wants to be in the top of the class.

Status: Current student, full- and part-time
Dates of Enrollment: 8/2004-Submit Date
Survey Submitted: March 2006

Great overall for area. UNC-Chapel Hill and NC State within short drives. Durham has many bright spots and activities, although crime in city and near the campus is an issue that's being addressed. NC is end-to-end fantastic for the young and old, single and married, kids and no kids.

Read all of Vault's Law School Surveys at www.vault.com/lawschool — get complete surveys on top law schools, expert advice on applicaton essays, LSAT prep and more.

VAULT CAREER LIBRARY   483

Status: Alumnus/a, part-time
Dates of Enrollment: 8/1994-5/1998
Survey Submitted: April 2004

Facilities were adequate (at the time) and have become much more impressive since my graduation (i.e., several capital improvement initiatives are underway).

 # Social Life

Status: Current student, full-time
Dates of Enrollment: 8/2003-Submit Date
Survey Submitted: April 2006

NCCU has a wonderful social atmosphere. We have plenty of student leaders eager to plan activities and each club opens events to the entire school. It is a great place to make lifelong connections.

Status: Alumnus/a, full-time
Dates of Enrollment: 8/2001-5/2004
Survey Submitted: March 2006

As an older student who lived half an hour away, I did not socialize much in Durham, NC. The social life is definitely geared towards younger students (less than 30 years old).

Status: Current student, full-time
Dates of Enrollment: 8/2005-Submit Date
Survey Submitted: March 2006

I "live" at the law school.

Status: Current student, full- and part-time
Dates of Enrollment: 8/2004-Submit Date
Survey Submitted: March 2006

Socialization seems to be a very strong trait of NCCU Law.

Status: Alumnus/a, part-time
Dates of Enrollment: 8/1994-5/1998
Survey Submitted: April 2004

Very friendly atmosphere with a spirit of students helping one another (instead of a competitive environment).

University of North Carolina School of Law

UNC School of Law
Admissions Office
Campus Box 3380
Chapel Hill, NC 27599-3380
Admissions phone: (919) 962-5109
Admissions e-mail: law_admission@unc.edu
Admissions URL: http://www.law.unc.edu/PAStudents/

 ## Admissions

Status: Alumnus/a, full-time
Dates of Enrollment: 8/1998-5/2001
Survey Submitted: March 2005

Highly selective, but with an interest in a diverse student body. Be creative with your essays and show how you can bring a unique viewpoint to the school and how you contribute to the law school community. UNC is very focused on its role as a public institution and it wants students who will give back to the community, as well as make the student body representative of different cultures, views and backgrounds.

Status: Alumnus/a, full-time
Dates of Enrollment: 8/1998-5/2001
Survey Submitted: January 2005

At the time of my application, UNC valued non-academic experience and exposure to diversity-related issues. UNC also takes pride in its reputation as one of the law schools for public interest law. Applicants would be well-served by expressing their willingness to get involved with/volunteer in the school's public interest programs.

Status: Current student, full-time
Dates of Enrollment: 8/2004-Submit Date
Survey Submitted: November 2004

Obviously, scores and grades are important. What sets UNC apart, I think, is that more than any other top-ranked public law school, UNC embraces its public mission. Unlike many other schools in its class, it's not striving to be a private institution. It wants to be relevant to the needs of the people of North Carolina. UNC does this by pulling from all parts of the state—rural, urban, East, West—and taking a much smaller percentage from out-of-state. The students at Carolina—much more so than most other Top 25 law schools—not only take part in public service-oriented activities, but actually pursue these careers at a much higher rate than other schools. Most students desire to live and work in North Carolina after graduation.

Status: Alumnus/a, full-time
Dates of Enrollment: 8/2000-5/2003
Survey Submitted: May 2004

The admissions process was relatively simple and run-of-the-mill in that LSATs and undergraduate GPA are the most important factors. I believe the application also included the standard personal statement as the essay requirement. Interviews are not part of the process. I'd recommend applying as early as possible so as to be considered for the best scholarships, including the Chancellors Scholarship Program (full tuition and living expenses for top candidates).

> **The school says:** "The Chancellors' Scholarship award is $10,000 annually and is our highest award. UNC School of Law offers no full-tuition scholarships at this time."

Also, because this is a state institution, I would recommend that if you are currently not a resident of NC, you should move to NC for one year and attain residency (it only takes one year). Additionally, if you get in from out-of-state and are interested in becoming a resident for tuition purposes or otherwise, definitely try (i.e., pay NC state taxes, get an NC driver's license and NC vehicle registration and register to vote in NC), because it is possible, and you can wind up saving a lot of money (and you become a resident of one of the most gorgeous, wonderful states in the country).

Status: Alumnus/a, full-time
Dates of Enrollment: 8/1999-5/2002
Survey Submitted: March 2005

There is definitely a different standard between in-state and out-of-state. Out-of-state students need better scores, and grades but this should not discourage out-of-state applicants applying.

Status: Alumnus/a, full-time
Dates of Enrollment: 8/1998-5/2001
Survey Submitted: April 2004

Highly selective school, but they value diversity. I think they put great weight on the essays and any proven commitment to public service. The law school is proud to be a public institution and focuses on public service. For an out-of-state applicant, the process is more difficult, but they are not focused only on numbers.

Status: Alumnus/a, full-time
Dates of Enrollment: 8/2000-5/2003
Survey Submitted: April 2004

An admissions officer once told me that Carolina Law seeks students that demonstrate the intelligence, integrity and motivation to use their juris doctorate to go out into the world and do good with it. As with undergraduate admissions, applying as an in-state student helps tremendously.

Status: Current student, full-time
Dates of Enrollment: 8/2002-Submit Date
Survey Submitted: September 2003

The admissions process involves an application that included, among other things, an essay about yourself and why you want to attend law school. There is no interview process, although applicants are invited to visit the law school. The law school selects about 235 students out of an applicant pool of 3,600 for the Class of 2006. The median GPA of the incoming class was 3.65, and the median LSAT score was 162.

 ## Academics

Status: Alumnus/a, full-time
Dates of Enrollment: 9/2000-5/2003
Survey Submitted: April 2005

Professors are amazing—they could teach anywhere and probably make sizeable raises at other institutions but stay in Chapel Hill because they love to teach. They are amazingly accessible, the workload is fair and the atmosphere is very cooperative.

Status: Alumnus/a, full-time
Dates of Enrollment: 9/2001-5/2004
Survey Submitted: April 2005

The academic curriculum is strong, with a heavy emphasis on public service-oriented classes. For instance, in 2003-04 the school offered about four courses related to corporate legal work, while they offered around eight or 10 that dealt exclusively with niche topics of the First Amendment. Carolina suffers (in my opinion) from the stigma that if you want to be a corporate lawyer, go to Duke; if you want to practice public services law, go to Carolina. That said, I practice corporate litigation for an AmLaw Top 10 firm, and I'm very pleased with the quality of education I received at Carolina. Moreover, I've never once regretted not going to Duke (which I had the option to do), especially given the astronomical difference in price.

Read all of Vault's Law School Surveys at www.vault.com/lawschool — get complete surveys on top law schools, expert advice on applicaton essays, LSAT prep and more.

VAULT CAREER LIBRARY **485**

As for the faculty, by and large it is excellent. Like all law schools, Carolina has a number of nationally-recognized scholars and a number of faculty deadweights that should have retired 30 years ago. The current dean, Gene Nichol, is terrific, but unfortunately (for Carolina) he has been chosen as the next president of William and Mary, so it remains to be seen how the next dean will do. The Legal Writing Department is, in both my opinion and many others, the highlight of Carolina's curriculum. Not only is it given great attention in the first-year curriculum, but it is taught by tremendously devoted faculty who know what they're doing. I would put the Writing Program up against any other school's in the country.

Status: Alumnus/a, full-time
Dates of Enrollment: 8/1998-5/2001
Survey Submitted: March 2005

UNC was very flexible about adding courses based on student demand. My class circulated a petition to get a Sexuality and the Law class added and it was done by the next year and is still being taught. The first year is the basics—Contract Law, Property—then the last two years are electives. Many great professors to chose from—not too difficult to get the classes you want except for some of the smaller writing sections with the most popular professors.

Status: Alumnus/a, full-time
Dates of Enrollment: 8/1998-5/2001
Survey Submitted: January 2005

Like most quality law schools, UNC strives to create create well-rounded lawyers that are well-grounded in the fundamental principles of law. UNC professors, for good reason, are not overly concerned with preparing students for any state's Bar exam. The school does a good job of making the most popular classes (Trial Advocacy and anything with Professor Hornstein) available to most students. Grading generally follows the traditional law school format, particularly in the first-year classes—based on subjective analysis of one final exam containing three to five essays. UNC generally will not allow students to attend part-time, in light of the workload and extracurricular involvement expected.

Status: Current student, full-time
Dates of Enrollment: 8/2004-Submit Date
Survey Submitted: November 2004

The professors are extremely down-to-earth. They all seem to realize how lucky they are to be (1) teaching and (2) living in a vibrant but relaxed town. For the first couple of weeks, the 80-person classes made me feel like a number, but after a couple of months in, the professors basically know who you are, and the school offers small sections of 40 people in a couple of 1L courses.

The only downside, I would say, is that you don't have classmates from diverse places. But if you confine diversity to North Carolina, I'd say there's a great deal. And there's a great deal of economic diversity, which is not something the private schools like to discuss. You may find people from all over the world at other schools, but you may find they have a lot more in common with each other than people who grew up with completely different economic opportunities.

> The school says: "There were students from 27 states and Washington, D.C. in the Class of 2005."

Status: Current student, full-time
Dates of Enrollment: 8/2002-Submit Date
Survey Submitted: September 2003

The first year of law school consists of a standard set of classes for all students. Your schedule is given to you. Your class of 235 is divided into three colleges, and you take all your classes with the students in your college. Grading is on a strict curve, and the workload is heavy. In your second and third years you select your own classes, and it is not difficult to get the classes you're interested in. I have had some fantastic professors and only one really terrible professor.

Status: Alumnus/a, full-time
Dates of Enrollment: 8/2000-5/2003
Survey Submitted: May 2004

I would say that the academic program is excellent. The professors are very approachable on the whole, and the classes are interesting. Like any law school of its caliber, the coursework is challenging and popular classes may be difficult to get into. However, professors are generally accommodating, and if you don't get into a class on your first try, you should be able to get in the next semester.

The best opportunities are found in programs outside the classroom, like the university's excellent clinical programs, Pro Bono Program, Holderness Moot Xourt, Public Interest Law Program and a variety of journals. The workload is what you make of it. The busier you make yourself, the more you'll get out of the education.

Status: Alumnus/a, full-time
Dates of Enrollment: 8/1998-5/2001
Survey Submitted: April 2004

A very cooperative learning environment. Top-level faculty. Grading is on a curve—more difficult the first year, then becomes a less steep curve. Great selection of classes; a wide variety, including Public Interest Law, Sexuality and the Law, Banking, Family Law and so on. I cannot compare the workload to that of other law schools.

Status: Alumnus/a, full-time
Dates of Enrollment: 8/2000-5/2003
Survey Submitted: April 2004

Carolina Law, like the rest of the entire university, embodies our mission statement that our ultimate purpose is, through academic pursuit, to serve our state, our country and the broader global community. We are a public school with a range of students and professors from many different social and economic backgrounds. Those who understand and believe in this approach to higher education will love every second they spend at Carolina.

 Employment Prospects

Status: Alumnus/a, full-time
Dates of Enrollment: 9/2000-5/2003
Survey Submitted: April 2005

EXCELLENT. The CSO has gotten abundantly better in the last few years. From Chapel Hill you can go anywhere and to any firm.

Status: Alumnus/a, full-time
Dates of Enrollment: 9/2001-5/2004
Survey Submitted: April 2005

On the one hand, I think the career services office has a devoted staff who genuinely strive to help graduates gain employment. The big firms' on-campus interview processes clearly dominate the bulk of the office's efforts, but that's the case at every tier-one law school. The office makes efforts to participate in minority job fairs and other alternative means of gaining employment. Regarding judicial clerkships, there has been a recent movement by the tremendous devotion of one faculty member to assist students with obtaining clerkships. This faculty member deserves great recognition for her efforts, which I think will pay off (if they haven't already).

While Carolina likes to tout that approximately 70 percent of its graduates enter the private law sector, I think that number is somewhat skewed because a substantial portion of graduates enter small- to medium-sized firms throughout the state. There is a fairly strong employment pipeline from Carolina to Atlanta, Charlotte, D.C. and New York, but if you want to work in some other market, you're largely left on your own. A large number of graduates seem to end up taking jobs in the public sector. As for Carolina's prestige among employers, that's difficult to determine. Notably, Carolina's Law Review is highly regarded among employers (meaning that it has a better reputation than the school itself).

Status: Alumnus/a, full-time
Dates of Enrollment: 8/1999-5/2002
Survey Submitted: March 2005

I had no problem getting a job outside of North Carolina (Atlanta, Richmond and D.C. markets.) The competition for jobs in North Carolina was intense. It is a great place to go if you have no NC ties and know you want to live elsewhere on the East Coast or if you have NC ties and want to stay in NC.

Status: Alumnus/a, full-time
Dates of Enrollment: 8/1998-5/2001
Survey Submitted: March 2005

UNC grads are a favorite of my law firm. Atlanta is a big market and the UNC Law reputation is strong nationwide. My friends all went on to work at top firms in D.C., Atlanta, NYC and even California. I enjoy working side-by-side with law grads who paid a lot more for their education and have the same job as me. UNC grads enter private practice, government work, as well as public interest fields. I have friends from law school who are working in all of these sectors. Huge alumni network; many on-campus interviews with firms from all over the country.

Status: Alumnus/a, full-time
Dates of Enrollment: 8/1998-5/2001
Survey Submitted: January 2005

Job prospects are significant for students wishing to remain in North Carolina. Prospects are improving for jobs outside North Carolina. UNC is considerably more well-known and therefore more well-respected in the Southeast than other parts of the U.S., but its reputation is improving in large metropolitan centers. The dean has made efforts to strengthen the alumni network in New York City, for example.

Status: Alumnus/a, full-time
Dates of Enrollment: 8/2000-5/2003
Survey Submitted: May 2004

Campus recruiting is excellent if you are at the top of the class. If not, it can be very frustrating and regionally limited. Although career services works hard to help out, their connections are limited.

Internships and externships during the year are another story—the program is phenomenal, and the professors involved make sure you are placed with quality employers and mentors and that you get the most out of your experience. Careers pursued by graduates are all over the spectrum. Because the tuition is relatively low compared to that of other schools of its rank, UNC grads have the option of pursuing careers in the public interest and public sectors, unlike many graduates from private schools. All the same, many of my classmates are now doing very well in private practice.

Status: Alumnus/a, full-time
Dates of Enrollment: 8/1998-5/2001
Survey Submitted: April 2004

Great career placement department. Frequent seminars on interviewing skills. Top firms interview on campus, especially Southeastern firms, but that seems to be expanding to a nationwide class of great firms. Also good for public interest jobs—the school is active in public interest job fairs. After graduation, alumni can still use an online job posting service, and they keep in contact to notify you of potential jobs of interests. My law firm recently called to see if they had anyone interested in a lateral position we had opening, and my recruiting person came and told me what a great job UNC's career placement services does, because the main guy called her back, spoke to her and helped her find an applicant.

Status: Alumnus/a, full-time
Dates of Enrollment: 8/2000-5/2003
Survey Submitted: April 2004

In what has always seemed contrary to the overarching mission of the school, the career services office focuses primarily on helping students get jobs at large- and medium-sized private law firms. It is good at what it does.

Quality of Life

Status: Alumnus/a, full-time
Dates of Enrollment: 9/2001-5/2004
Survey Submitted: April 2005

Chapel Hill is gorgeous. Few college campuses are more picturesque and offer a better quality of life. There are abundant activities to pursue both on campus and off, and the nightlife is a lot of fun. The law school campus, while not geographically isolated from the rest of the university, is effectively self-

contained. Thus a law student, somewhat sadly, would never have an academic reason to visit other parts of the university's campus. The law school facilities are nice but not luxurious; there is a noticeable difference between additions completed in the mid-90s and older parts of the school. I believe that housing is available, especially for married students, but I don't know of anyone who lived in university-provided housing. Most students rent apartments in Chapel Hill or nearby Durham. Rent is typically around $700 or $800 per month for a two-bedroom apartment.

Status: Alumnus/a, full-time
Dates of Enrollment: 8/1998-5/2001
Survey Submitted: March 2005

Chapel Hill is an excellent college town. Safe, fun, beautiful—not too crowded, not too small. Also, you are near Duke and NC State so the Research Triangle is full of smart people and stimulating conversations. UNC's law school is in a new building (completed in 2000) and you have access to the main campus perks such as the cafeteria, recreational facility and intramural sports teams. You are also walking distance to the bars and restaurants of Franklin Street. You can live on campus or in Chapel Hill, Durham or Carrboro. It is a great area.

Status: Alumnus/a, full-time
Dates of Enrollment: 8/1998-5/2001
Survey Submitted: January 2005

UNC is unrivaled for affordability of a quality law school education. It has a long way to go before tuition catches up to institutions of comparable quality. UNC Law students enjoy the opportunity to integrate into general campus life at UNC more so than at other universities. The town of Chapel Hill offers an excellent quality of life at less expense than most urban law schools. The trade-off is that students have few local internships and summer job opportunities. Students are generally forced to relocate in the summers to get quality summer legal experience.

Status: Current student, full-time
Dates of Enrollment: 8/2004-Submit Date
Survey Submitted: November 2004

I can't imagine a better place to be a student than Chapel Hill. There's practically no traffic to deal with. Crime is a non-issue. The cost of living is incredibly low and there's plenty of housing. There are always events happening—speakers and films. In fact, if you're interested in documentary film, the largest documentary film festival in North and South America happens in Durham, NC every year (only 20 minutes away).

Status: Alumnus/a, full-time
Dates of Enrollment: 8/2000-5/2003
Survey Submitted: May 2004

Quality of life is probably the best in the country. Seriously, the three years I spent in Chapel Hill were three of the best of my life! The town is incredible and very friendly and safe. The law school is truly a part of the university, such that law students can enjoy football and basketball games and feel connected with the university. Housing is relatively inexpensive, plentiful and new. The area has great bars and great venues for live music as well. The mountains are about a four-hour drive, the beach takes about two hours, D.C. is a four-hour drive and New York and Atlanta are about eight-hour drives. It doesn't get any better than this!

Status: Alumnus/a, full-time
Dates of Enrollment: 8/2000-5/2003
Survey Submitted: April 2004

Both the town and campus of Chapel Hill are gorgeous. Housing is plentiful. Crime and safety are of no concern. Dining on the law school campus, however, could be improved.

Status: Current student, full-time
Dates of Enrollment: 8/2002-Submit Date
Survey Submitted: September 2003

There is minimal graduate student housing available to UNC Law. There are some married student on-campus apartments, but most people live off campus.

Read all of Vault's Law School Surveys at www.vault.com/lawschool — get complete surveys on top law schools, expert advice on applicaton essays, LSAT prep and more.

VAULT CAREER LIBRARY   487

Status: Alumnus/a, full-time
Dates of Enrollment: 8/1998-5/2001
Survey Submitted: April 2004

At UNC Law, you are part of the larger campus life, but with the benefit of a small graduate school. The law school recently moved into a new building— very nice. You are also located an easy drive to the beach or mountains. Chapel Hill is very safe, Durham is not bad either. Cheaper to live in Durham or Carborro. The town is so great, people never want to leave!

 ## Social Life

Status: Alumnus/a, full-time
Dates of Enrollment: 9/2000-5/2003
Survey Submitted: April 2005

Franklin Street—enough said.

Status: Alumnus/a, full-time
Dates of Enrollment: 9/2001-5/2004
Survey Submitted: April 2005

Franklin Street, the main street running through campus, is well-known for its nightlife. Bars are abundant, and although most are tailored to the undergraduate crowd, there are some more upscale places as well. The same is true for restaurants.

Status: Alumnus/a, full-time
Dates of Enrollment: 8/1999-5/2002
Survey Submitted: March 2005

Chapel Hill is truly a college town with lots going on and tons of things to do. Also, Raleigh and Durham are close by—also college towns with a fair amount to do.

Status: Alumnus/a, full-time
Dates of Enrollment: 8/1998-5/2001
Survey Submitted: March 2005

Again, you are near two other major universities with lots of students, including grad students. Many cool bars and restaurants. Chapel Hill has Top of the Hill, an upscale bar owned by a law school grad with views of Franklin Street, and other bars. No shortage. Greek system is not relevant in the law school world.

Status: Alumnus/a, full-time
Dates of Enrollment: 8/1998-5/2001
Survey Submitted: January 2005

The law school is generally very social. There are numerous school-sponsored and unsponsored activities. Chapel Hill, mostly because of the many bars and restaurants on Franklin Street, is consistently ranked among the best college towns in the U.S. Carolina basketball plays a pivotal role in the social life of the school and town during the winter and early spring. Unless you went to Duke, you will eventually find yourself pulling for the Heels.

Status: Current student, full-time
Dates of Enrollment: 8/2004-Submit Date
Survey Submitted: November 2004

There's no shortage of places to go. But don't focus too much on your social life as a 1L. Your grades in the first year will matter more than any other grades you've had to date. You won't have a problem finding ways to amuse yourself (especially if you're a college basketball fan), but I wouldn't choose a law school based on the social life or lack thereof.

Status: Alumnus/a, full-time
Dates of Enrollment: 8/2000-5/2003
Survey Submitted: May 2004

As a Northerner I thought I might have some trouble getting used to the South. Nope! I loved it! The town is great—fun bars (including a good variety: Top of the Hill, Lucy's, the Dead Mule and BW3s), great music scene and some of the best college sports in the country—Duke is a 15-minute car ride away, and beating them in anything just feels SO good!

The social life is excellent. Most people are not originally from Chapel Hill and don't know many people when they move there, so people are very willing and eager to meet new friends and go out at night. By the same token, there are many native North Carolinians that went to undergrad at Duke or UNC, and many married folks that also add to the social scene. Basically, people are really friendly and lots of fun—which is NOT typical of most law schools. I actually liked most of the people I graduated with, as well as the people in the years around me. Again, for social life, Carolina is as good as it gets when it comes to law school!

Status: Alumnus/a, full-time
Dates of Enrollment: 8/1998-5/2001
Survey Submitted: April 2004

Chapel Hill is a great college town, full of students from several universities (Duke, NC State). Good bars and restaurants. The undergrad scene has a lot of women and a few men, so the undergrad bars tend to be a bit much. But there are more laid-back, graduate school hangouts that are fun. The yuppie crowd like Top of the Hill (started by a UNC Law alumnus) or the wine bar; for cheap drinks and an undergrad scene, Bud's is the place. Also, everyone likes the outdoor bar known as He's Not Here, where you can get the famous "blue cup" of beer. A favorite post-exam hangout.

Status: Alumnus/a, full-time
Dates of Enrollment: 8/2000-5/2003
Survey Submitted: April 2004

The student leadership at Carolina Law provides many opportunities for law students to hang out together. The weekly Bar Review every Thursday is an easy favorite of many students. The social center of the law school campus, the Rotunda, also makes for easy socializing during lunch and in between classes.

Status: Current student, full-time
Dates of Enrollment: 8/2002-Submit Date
Survey Submitted: September 2003

Franklin Street is hopping with all the social activities a student would want. The law school has a weekly Bar Review where law students meet at a certain bar and enjoy each other's company.

Wake Forest University School of Law

Admissions Office
Suite 2305, Worrell Professional Center
P.O. Box 7206
Winston-Salem, NC 27109
Admissions phone: (336) 758-5437
Admissions fax: (336) 758-3930
Admissions e-mail: admissions@law.wfu.edu
URL: http://law.wfu.edu/

Admissions

Status: Current student, full-time
Dates of Enrollment: 8/2005-Submit Date
Survey Submitted: April 2006

The admissions process was very straightforward and did not require much additional work. The essay topic was a generic topic, so a separate essay did not have to be written just for WFU. The people in the admissions office are all very helpful and willing to answer any questions you may have during the process. I was impressed with how quickly I was notified of acceptance as well. There is an admitted students open house in early April, which is very well done and helped solidify my decision to attend WFU.

Status: Current student, full-time
Dates of Enrollment: 8/2005-Submit Date
Survey Submitted: April 2006

There was no interview involved and I did have to write one essay, my personal statement. I got a 165 on the LSAT so I thought I had a good shot. Once I applied in December, I heard nothing back until about a month before their decision date (April 15). I learned I had gotten in and was ecstatic. In retrospect, I think my essay was very important to my admission to Wake Forest. Wake Forest prides itself on creating ethical lawyers and my essay was related to that topic. Also, as far as I can tell it is a selective school. All the students are bright and many come from unique backgrounds. Really a diverse group.

Status: Current student, full-time
Dates of Enrollment: 8/2004-Submit Date
Survey Submitted: April 2006

The admissions office did a great job of keeping me informed throughout the whole process and appeared to be very organized. I would strongly recommend requesting an interview—I feel it can help your chances for a scholarship. I bluntly requested an interview to discuss financial aid options and left the meeting assured I would receive some type of scholarship. About two weeks later I got a letter offering me a full scholarship. I definitely think taking the time to visit and express my sincere interest had a sizable hand in my good fortune.

Also, while everyone here is obviously bright and used to doing well, those with not-quite-perfect records should still apply. The admissions office appears to put great weight on students who are unique and bring an entirely different perspective. If you can differentiate yourself, that will probably help your chances.

Status: Current student, full-time
Dates of Enrollment: 8/2005-Submit Date
Survey Submitted: April 2006

The admissions staff was available very early on in the process. I was able to contact them the summer before I applied. They were very willing to help me learn about the school even though they were dealing with the admission of the class that fall. The admission form was reasonable—I believe that it was five pages in length. It was more detailed than some of the other forms though.

Wake required an applicant to submit ALL charges INCLUDING traffic tickets as well as short-answer essays on all activities that were important to the applicant. The personal statement was pretty standard. Nothing specific was required and I don't remember there being a page limit.

As far as selectivity goes, they seemed to match the selectivity I found on the LSAC web site. From talking to students, that grid was pretty representative. I think that my best piece of advice is to utilize the admissions staff, be VERY honest on your application about any discrepancies, and take the time to write a thoughtful personal statement because they actually do read it. The head of admissions knew who I was and mentioned things from my personal statement the first time I met her after being accepted.

Status: Current student, full-time
Dates of Enrollment: 8/2003-Submit Date
Survey Submitted: April 2006

This was the most personalized interview process of all my applications; in the end it's what brought me to Wake Law. Wake was just wonderful. Their admissions counselor came to my hometown (Chicago) and was such a good presenter that I decided to apply to Wake Law, even though I had not considered living in Winston-Salem before. She gave me detailed admissions and financial aid info, answered all my questions, responded to every e-mail in person in a timely manner and made the application process normal (not excruciating and pointless like some other law schools that seem to enjoy drowning you with paperwork).

If you're applying to Wake, PLEASE go to the April Open House and the June House Hunt, because it will totally open you up to all the greatness of Wake, and give you a head start on housing, classes, professors, friends, the neighborhood and, of course, North Carolina BBQ.

As far as selectivity goes, Wake wasn't easy to get into—none of the schools I applied to were—but you can just tell, from the way the admissions office talks and from the diversity of the student body, that they sincerely look at each essay and application to evaluate the whole candidate. Numbers are important, but Wake is more than just a numbers game.

Status: Current student, full-time
Dates of Enrollment: 8/2005-Submit Date
Survey Submitted: April 2006

Visit, Visit, Visit. Wake Forest is a beautiful school in a beautiful setting. The law school is located on the campus and is a truly first-class facility. Wake Law likes good people, not stuffy jerks. Admission Director Melanie Nutt is awesome.

Status: Current student, full-time
Dates of Enrollment: 8/2005-Submit Date
Survey Submitted: April 2006

My LSAT score was decent, but not great (161). However, I had a very good undergrad GPA from Tennessee (3.97). I was notified in March, I believe, that I was on the waiting list at Wake. I did not have an interview. For my admissions essay, I discussed my work experiences and why that guided me to choose law as a profession. For the essay, I would advise people to try to highlight any unique experiences. Personally, I discussed the two months I spent in Nicaragua for Peace Corps training and volunteering as a guardian ad litem.

Wake Forest is selective—there are a lot of people here who are extremely intelligent and did extremely well in undergrad; however, Wake considers more than just academics when making their admissions decisions.

Status: Current student, full-time
Dates of Enrollment: 5/2003-Submit Date
Survey Submitted: April 2006

Application is easy, typical. They do not have interviews, however, they do have "alumni events," which are little cocktail parties across the country, so if you are interested in attending one, call the school and see if there is going to be one close to you.

Read all of Vault's Law School Surveys at www.vault.com/lawschool — get complete surveys on top law schools, expert advice on applicaton essays, LSAT prep and more.

VAULT CAREER LIBRARY   **489**

Status: Current student, full-time
Dates of Enrollment: 8/2004-Submit Date
Survey Submitted: April 2006

The admissions process is pretty standard; earlier is better. It gets significantly harder to get in the later that you apply. The school is primarily concerned with LSAT scores. It is much more important to the school than undergrad GPA and other activities, though these factors can help a borderline candidate. The school is becoming more and more selective each year. When I applied in 2004, the mid-50 percent LSAT range was 160 to 163, and it has risen to 162 to 166 for the current first-year class.

Status: Current student, full-time
Dates of Enrollment: 1/2003-Submit Date
Survey Submitted: March 2005

The admissions process is fairly typical, and quite straightforward. With very few exceptions, everyone receives an on-campus interview. (They will accept phone interviews if traveling to campus is simply not feasible.) I strongly recommend a campus visit, because you simply cannot grasp the feel of the campus and the warmth of the people without visiting. In addition to the standard LSAT scores and application forms, you'll need to write a couple of essays detailing why you're looking for an JD and why Wake Forest. You cannot spend too much time on these essays; you will find that the self-examination they entail will really help you have a sense of direction when you start.

While one might suspect that a small university in the South would be dreadfully conservative, it simply isn't true. The student body is very diverse, with a fair number of very competent international students (whose perspective is invaluable) and a good mix of gender, race and age. (Our incoming class has students from ranging from a 21-year-old young woman from Russia to a 62-year-old retired MD with entrepreneurial aspirations.) As a gay man of 40 who spent the last 15 years living and working in San Francisco, moved here with my partner, and we have been warmly welcomed at every turn. He's originally from North Carolina and I'm originally from the Midwest, so it was actually refreshing to slow things down a bit.

Status: Alumnus/a, full-time
Dates of Enrollment: 8/2000-5/2003
Survey Submitted: June 2004

Wake Forest is one of the schools that, I believe, uses an admissions index. Everybody I knew in my class was in the same range of GPAs and LSAT scores. In 2000, everybody was high 150s and low 160s. Now, because of the economy, it's more competitive.

I toured the campus and sat in on a class. Wake was one of 13 schools I visited (I only applied to four). Its campus and vibe closed the deal for me over William and Mary and Washington & Lee.

 **Academics**

Status: Current student, full-time
Dates of Enrollment: 8/2004-Submit Date
Survey Submitted: April 2006

Classes are pretty small, professors are approachable and friendly. There's a little bit of every type of class available. Wake has three really spectacular summer abroad programs that teach courses you can't take at the law school. I highly recommend studying abroad after your first year.

Workload is usually the worst when it's time to turn in a LRW paper. It's like the straw that breaks the camel's back. Grading at Wake is kind of odd. You get an actual number instead of a GPA, so your average is 85 instead of 3.0. I don't know if employers really understand that. I also hear that we are one of the only schools that gives the top 50 percent of the class individual rankings, as opposed to percentages. So you can be ranked Number One or Number Two in your class instead of just being in the top 5 percent. I don't think it's very hard to get most of the popular classes. They do make you wait until the summer to sign up for classes, which can be a real pain if you're trying to plan ahead. I strongly recommend taking a clinical program if you can, it's so worth it.

Status: Current student, full-time
Dates of Enrollment: 8/2003-Submit Date
Survey Submitted: April 2006

Going to law school is never going to be a walk in the park, and Wake is no different. However, it provides a friendly, welcoming atmosphere—a definite benefit. The other students are nice and cooperative; in general, backstabbing and other cattiness is foreign. We do have our fair share of gunners, but even gunners will share their notes.

The Law Review has a free outline site open to everyone. For the most part, the professors care about their students, both inside and outside the classroom. You should definitely take up professors on their offer to take you out to lunch. The classes by Wake professors are usually outstanding; the classes by adjunct and visiting professors range from excellent to poor. The practical classes, such as Clinic and Trial Practice, provide invaluable experience. You can generally get into the classes you want by using the waitlist and asking the professor to add you to the roster. You can take even the most popular classes—National Security Law, Dispute Resolution, and the Elder Law Clinic—if you have the patience to wait until your 3L year (or maybe even your 2L year). Grading is all right; it's the same standard curve.

Status: Current student, full-time
Dates of Enrollment: 8/2005-Submit Date
Survey Submitted: April 2006

The first year of law school has entirely mandatory classes: Legal Research and Writing (two semesters), Civil Procedure (two semesters), Contracts (two semesters), Torts, Property, Criminal Law. After that, there are a few mandatory classes (Legal Research and Writing III, Professional Responsibility among others). I have not yet had to register for new classes, but supposedly it is no difficult, as long as you are prepared the minute you can register. Registration opens at the same time for all students from a particular year.

Classes are great because they are so small and the professors are really helpful. They are usually not typical "hide-the-ball" teachers and actually want the students to learn. The work is hard and varies from teacher to teacher on how much is given. But, it is a topnotch law school and you are expected to work and be prepared. However, they are understanding and sometimes you just can't be ready for all classes. As long as you are not consistently unprepared, there is no problem.

Status: Current student, full-time
Dates of Enrollment: 8/2004-Submit Date
Survey Submitted: April 2006

YES, the work is both confusing and PLENTIFUL. If you find yourself saying you're done with all your work, then you're not doing it right. Thankfully, none of my professors have used the traditional Socratic Method, but they certainly don't shy away from putting you on the spot at a moment's notice.

Your classes are assigned to you the entire first year, but I can report that I had no problems getting exactly the schedule I wanted for my second year. So no complaints here. However, the administration is woefully lacking because we don't get class schedules to look at and plan with until mid-July. Then, two weeks later, we must register for the entire next year. Besides the uncertainty of waiting this long to register, it is highly inconvenient to register in July when many people are at internships or travelling abroad with no Internet access.

Status: Current student, full-time
Dates of Enrollment: 8/2004-Submit Date
Survey Submitted: April 2006

The first year at Wake, like at all schools, is very demanding. Wake has eased the load by making two 1L classes into one-semester classes instead of two semester classes. That translates to one fewer exam to take your first fall and spring. The small class size (40) also eases the academic difficulties that come with taking class with other very bright students. You feel that you can ask anyone in your class for notes or help. To show how tight sections bond, there are quite a few students who refer to their section numbers and sectionmates when they need help or to plan parties.

Wake also has the dreaded curve. The curve has been moved to an 85, which was greatly appreciated by all the students! Professors tend to grade close to the curve so you don't have anyone failing a class just so someone else can have an A. Professors have an excellent open-door policy which means you can walk in any time. I have never looked at a professor's office hours because I know I can always poke my head in if I have a question. They are also genuinely interested in how the students are doing. The professors are supportive of the Academic Success Program, created so students help 1L students succeed in classes and hone study skills by offering practice exams, problems and being available for questions.

The small size of Wake, besides creating a supportive environment, also allows students the opportunity to take every class they want at some point during their last two years. Classes such as Litigation Clinic and Elder Law Clinic are guaranteed to any student who wants to take them (you might have to wait until 3L depending on the number of opportunities available your 2L year). Wake has also worked diligently on hiring new faculty to decrease class size. I have never been in a class with over 60 to 70 people, and that was one of the most popular classes. The really popular classes are usually the smaller classes taught by professors that specialize in that area of law. Again, you can always get into those classes at some point during your 2L or 3L years.

Status: Current student, full-time
Dates of Enrollment: 8/2003-Submit Date
Survey Submitted: April 2006

Wake follows a STRICT curve. The class sizes are small. In the first year the entire class is split in four. All of your classes are with your assigned group. Each group has around 30 to 40, depending on the number of students enrolling.

The workload is very tough. Plan on working six to seven days a week if you want to do well. The teachers are all very knowledgeable. First-year is heavy on the Socratic Method. On the whole, the teachers are rough on first-year students. Upper years it is a collegial environment between students and teachers.

Status: Current student, full-time
Dates of Enrollment: 8/2005-Submit Date
Survey Submitted: April 2006

The workload is heavy, but as with anything, it is what you put into it. Some students stay at school 15 hours a day, every day of the semester. Some students do very little. On average, most students start their work at nine in the morning and usually finish up between eight and 10 in the evening. Most people start studying for final exams between a month and a month and a half before the first exam.

Status: Current student, full-time
Dates of Enrollment: 8/2005-Submit Date
Survey Submitted: April 2006

Professors are great. They have a mostly open-door policy, meaning you can walk by their offices and just pop in. The majority are really just willing to help you learn. While the Socratic Method is employed, particularly your first semester, it's not nearly as daunting as *The Paper Chase* makes it out to be (in most cases).

The classes are excellent quality and most of the time you learn a lot. The workload is what you would expect for law school—it's a lot. Don't expect the same life you had in undergrad. You can't get away with not studying here. You are in a group of people who ALL got away with that in their undergrad careers and it's just not going to cut it anymore. There can be some competitiveness, but it's mostly w/in the section and nothing really serious I'd say.

Status: Current student, full-time
Dates of Enrollment: 8/2003-Submit Date
Survey Submitted: April 2006

The students are wonderful. At Wake, we don't spend time hiding books from each other or making other students fail, instead students are very willing to share notes and helpful hints. In fact, we store outlines on the school's network so they are available to everyone!

Furthermore, not only are the classes at Wake becoming more diverse and interesting every semester, they are also pretty easy to get into. Although you may have to sit on a waitlist for the first week or two of class, it is a rare occasion you won't get into the class eventually. I have always been able to get into the classes I wanted. As for grading, Wake, like most law schools, is graded on a curve. Thus, it's tough because you can't just be smart to do well, you have to be smarter.

Status: Alumnus/a, full-time
Dates of Enrollment: 8/1999-5/2002
Survey Submitted: April 2004

Wake is great because the school has remained small, even when the number of applicants has risen. It is great that the first-year sections have stayed at about 40 people, and the writing courses have only 20 students. It gives students more opportunity for one-on-one interaction with professors and fellow students.

I felt like the workload varied from class to class and from professor to professor. Some professors felt that it was more important to focus on one legal decision, which may only require a student to read a few pages for a class period while other professors liked to work through a number of legal decisions in one class period. However, rarely did I feel overloaded with work, and most professors were receptive to when students felt like the workload was too overwhelming.

 Employment Prospects

Status: Current student, full-time
Dates of Enrollment: 8/2004-Submit Date
Survey Submitted: April 2006

I've found that alumni are a huge help here. Not only do they hire you, but they'll give you great recommendations to take to other alumni. Many alumni ACTUALLY KNOW each other, so the recommendations have a weight to them. It's definitely a benefit of being at a smaller school; because the class sizes are smaller, everyone knows most everyone else. If you can get the interviews through on-campus recruiting, it's definitely worth the effort—and don't opt not to apply just because you don't meet their stated criteria. I have two jobs lined up for the coming summer and I didn't meet the initial criteria for either. You get points for having the nerve to apply DESPITE their guidelines, and once you get that interview you can win the job. It's really just about getting the interview.

A wide range of employers come to the school—from well-known, very large firms to single-attorney firms. Many people complain that not enough employers from out of the region recruit here, but that's something you can expect from any law school. There are PLENTY of law schools—employers don't need to travel across the country to find qualified people, so why would they? You should go to law school close to where you hope to practice. Plus, it's easier if you're living in the state where you plan to take the bar.

Status: Current student, full-time
Dates of Enrollment: 8/2004-Submit Date
Survey Submitted: April 2006

The alumni network at Wake Forest University gives students an "in" all over the country. Students from my class are going everywhere from California to NY, to D.C., Atlanta and Cincinnati and all points in between! The career services office helps by putting us in touch with alums in those areas and organizing networking events. One staff member is dedicated to job fairs. She makes sure we know about the job fairs and get to them!

The 2L class has two staff members. All students talk to all the staff members, though, again, it's the open-door environment that makes it work. On-campus interviewing (OCI) is a busy time for all students and starts as soon as you get back to school from the summer (2Ls and 3Ls) or Christmas (1Ls). OCI employers come from all over, with the majority coming from the East Coast. There are also resume collections for employers who cannot send someone to interview but who want to hire a Wake student. Wake Forest is also lucky enough to host an Inns of Court that students can participate in. It's a great opportunity to meet and network with practicing attorneys in the area. These often lead to mentoring relationships.

Most students leave Wake Forest for a job with a law firm. This year, there are 10 or so students taking judicial clerkships right after graduation. The judicial clerkships range from the Superior Court in NJ to the NC Supreme Court. All of these students have already offered any help they could give at a career

Read all of Vault's Law School Surveys at www.vault.com/lawschool — get complete surveys on top law schools, expert advice on applicaton essays, LSAT prep and more.

VAULT CAREER LIBRARY 491

services program focusing on judicial clerkships. The loan forgiveness program at Wake helps those students who go into public service. Law school is not cheap, but Wake works to help students with their loans when they take a public interest position.

Status: Current student, full-time
Dates of Enrollment: 8/2003-Submit Date
Survey Submitted: April 2006

Top students (top 25 to 33 percent) will have several employers actively seeking them out, and will obtain jobs (many very high paying: $85k to $145k) with little effort. Other students will have to take a more active role in seeking out employment, but career services has many good connections in the local community and other major metropolitan areas (Charlotte, New York, D.C.)

Status: Alumnus/a, full-time
Dates of Enrollment: 8/1999-5/2002
Survey Submitted: April 2004

Getting a job out of Wake Law is particularly promising if you plan to remain in North Carolina or within the general region, because the school has an extremely good reputation there, due to its strong emphasis on developing students' writing skills and its practical courses. However, it is a little more challenging if you choose to leave the NC area after law school.

The recruiting department is getting better, but it has not gotten to the point where students can rely on it primarily to produce the types of job opportunities that they might desire. I did not get any of my summer associate jobs through the campus recruiting. Although they tried to help when I was looking for a job post-graduation, I still felt that I did much of it on my own. But Wake's name and the quality education that I received were good selling points in becoming employed out of school.

 Quality of Life

Status: Current student, full-time
Dates of Enrollment: 8/2004-Submit Date
Survey Submitted: April 2006

Campus is pretty. As a law student you can use the gym and join intramural teams. The law school building is all right, but since all the classes are 50 minutes they all let out at the same time and the hallways get REALLY crowded. People call the law school "Worrel High." We actually have bells that ring to let you know that class is over and we have lockers. The lockers are nice when you have to carry 30 pounds of books and a laptop to class . 1Ls get their own carrels in the library; 2Ls and 3Ls mostly share carrels. The library is pretty safe, you can leave your stuff there and it won't get stolen.

Status: Current student, full-time
Dates of Enrollment: 8/2005-Submit Date
Survey Submitted: April 2006

Housing is really easy to find and really cheap compared to other places I've lived. There is an abundance of housing so the different complexes are forced to keep their rates low in order to attract new renters. If one is looking for a house, there is also a large housing market and usually they can be relatively inexpensive as well.

The campus is gorgeous. The problem is, if you are a law student you are primarily stuck to one building that is about a five- to 10-minute walk from the rest of campus. But, it really is a beautiful place to look at. There is a dining center with a variety of fast-food places on campus. However, this is also a small lunch place behind campus in the Information Services building. This is also where the law school bookstore. It is independent of the school's general bookstore.

I've never felt unsafe living here. I do know that there were a few car break-ins in the complexes. We are also warned not to keep our windows or doors open when we are not at home. While it is always best to err on the side of caution, I've never felt overly threatened or heard of anyone who was threatened.

Status: Current student, full-time
Dates of Enrollment: 8/2005-Submit Date
Survey Submitted: April 2006

There are no specific graduate dorms. I believe that the grad students may apply for the on-campus apartments, though. The other way to get on campus is to apply for the Graduate Hall Director position. The position gives the student free housing, a meal plan and a stipend. It is work, but it is an incredible deal.

Everyone else lives off campus. There is a condo complex two blocks from campus. About 10 to 15 students from every class live in that complex. The complex is primarily MBA students, law students and families Next to the condo complex is a road of houses. Nearly all of the houses are rentals and several groups of law students live there. That street is mostly undergrads with a few groups of grad students and law students. Most students live about a mile from campus. There are four apartment complexes and one condo complex on the same road. These are high-quality abodes and house the most students.

Finally, there is a decent number of students that live about five miles from campus. The apartments over there are the same quality but less expensive. They aren't paying the premium for being so close to campus. Crime is generally pretty low.

Dining is pretty easy on campus. There is a full-service deli and grill behind the professional school. There is also the normal dining hall on the main/undergrad campus. Unlike most schools, though, there is no street full of shops and eateries. If you want to eat off campus, you have to drive. There is really no where to walk off campus and eat.

Status: Current student, full-time
Dates of Enrollment: 8/2003-Submit Date
Survey Submitted: April 2006

There is no on-campus housing, which is fine. Most people live nearby and drive a few minutes to school. Like any campus, there are parking issues from time to time, but you will never walk more than five to seven minutes from the parking lot to class. We mostly fight over the spots that are six yards from the entrance.

I think if you enjoy the outdoors, you will have an excellent quality of life. If you are looking to go clubbing and get drunk, then you should not be applying to law school in the first place. As for crime and safety, I have never had a problem, day or night...and there have been some late nights.

Status: Current student, full-time
Dates of Enrollment: 8/2005-Submit Date
Survey Submitted: April 2006

The campus is beautiful with lots of landscaping. Wait Chapel looks very pretty especially lit up at night, and you get a nice view of it as you leave school. The Worrell Professional Center is where the law school is located and is shared with the MBA school. Law has the right half of the building. The law library is pretty and a nice place to work. Sharing the building with the business school is usually mutually beneficial, since we get to share interview rooms and the library. However, occasionally the business school people get annoyed with us law students when we encroach on their study rooms during finals. That is the one thing I would add if I could—more study rooms for law students for group study sessions.

Next door to Worrell is the IS building, which has a little cafe. The food is overpriced, but it is very convenient, and there is a BB&T ATM there. On the main campus, there is a bigger selection in the Benson University Center, including Chick-fil-A, and it is a nice break to walk over and have some time away from the law building.

Status: Current student, full-time
Dates of Enrollment: 8/2004-Submit Date
Survey Submitted: April 2006

The food is really good! There are several places to eat on campus, but the restaurants around town are excellent. There is Reynolda Village near the campus with several topnotch restaurants, plus a coffee shop with wireless Internet. The coffee shop on campus is good, too and there is wireless all over the campus. The workout center is across the street from the law school along ith an intramural field, tennis courts and the track. All of these are open for ny student to use. There are also cross-country trails for the students.

Status: Current student, full-time
Dates of Enrollment: 1/2003-Submit Date
Survey Submitted: March 2005

ousing is easy to come by, and though it's probably not practical for most in a vo-year program, the real estate market favors buying (especially if you're oming from elsewhere—having sold a house, it's pretty easy to park some of our equity here); with a four-year stint ahead of me, I decided to buy, in part ecause I may stay after graduation. The cost of living index is right at the ational average, meaning that it's a great deal for a college town, and an xcellent value for an excellent school. As a student told me last year before I ot here, "Brace yourself; you're going to wonder why they're giving the food way." Coming from San Francisco, it's nice to know you can eat out without aving to leave stock certificates with the maitre d'! As a graduate student, I on't spend much time on the main campus; B-school, law school (together in ne facility) and the Worrell Professional Center (designed by famed architect aesar Pelli) are on the periphery. Technology and facilities on campus are reat, and are pretty much on par with what I saw when visiting Duke. While a ouple incidents have occurred on campus this year, the campus security staff ave been very active (and proactive) to do all they can to ensure these problems on't recur.

Social Life

Status: Current student, full-time
Dates of Enrollment: 8/2004-Submit Date
Survey Submitted: April 2006

o be fair, there are a few little shops and restaurants "downtown," if you can eally call it that. This town is NOT for singles either. It's more family-oriented. here aren't many young single professionals here. People get to law school and tart dating each other, and soon realize that was a bad idea. Then, due to the ack of singles in this town, a lot of law students revert back to dating someone ney knew in their hometown before they came here. The school is so small, veryone knows everyone and knows everything about you (or at least think they o).

t's nearly impossible to go out to a bar and not run into a group of law students. he Opera House is the most popular law school bar; it's also the smokiest and erves the strongest drinks. The wine bar is nicer and Foothills is a popular angout. There are no real dance clubs in this town. If you want to dance, you an check out Red Rooster but that's primarily country music. The law school ries to create social events for the students. Bar Review every Thursday, lalloween party in the fall and we used to have a Barristers Ball in the spring. t's fun to go to these things every once in a while, but easy to get sick of seeing he same people you see all the time. It's a small school in a small town.

Status: Current student, full-time
Dates of Enrollment: 8/2005-Submit Date
Survey Submitted: April 2006

ocial life is a difficult thing to digest. There are bars here, but I have not found ny of them entirely appealing. There are a few near the school that are typical ollege bars (Freddie B's and Cobalt's) and a nice place called Ziggy's that gets ome decent bands.

Vinston-Salem has a lot of artsy things as well. There are constantly plays, pecialty movies and gallery hops downtown. There are also bowling alleys, nini golf courses and a couple of movie theaters. If you like golf, there are ourses aplenty. Also, college athletics is important and even more so because he only "major league" team is a single-A baseball team, the Winston-Salem Varthogs.

Status: Current student, full-time
Dates of Enrollment: 8/2005-Submit Date
Survey Submitted: April 2006

he law school hosts several functions annually. There is the summer Housing lunt that allows 1Ls to meet each other before school and find housing. There

is a monthly 1L meeting to encourage all the 1Ls to meet each other (and get free lunch). The SBA also hosts a weekly Bar Review. Every week, the SBA goes around to local bars and requests specials. If the bar gives them a decent special, they announce to the school, "Bar Review will be at X bar with Y special" and everyone interested in going attends. This is a great way to meet the upperclassmen and find mentors. I think the student favorite is Ziggy's. The law school also hosts several networking events with local lawyers and a formal dance in the spring at a local venue.

The dating scene is somewhat limited. About a third to half of the students are either married/engaged or previously attached. Most students find it easier to date the business school students (who are located in the same building). They attend some functions with us including weekly presentations. The Greek system in the law school is limited. There is the honor fraternity but social fraternities are not very prevalent. Many of the students in the law school came from a Greek background, but no one I know is extremely active on campus here. The undergrad campus is fairly active in the Greek system, though.

Status: Current student, full-time
Dates of Enrollment: 8/2005-Submit Date
Survey Submitted: April 2006

WFU Law's administrators, and to some extent professors, want you to have a life. They stress taking time for yourself and pursuing your interests while keeping up with your work as well. There is a program for the 1Ls every first Thursday of the month in order to stress professionalism and keeping your quality of life up, with free lunch!! Free lunch is a staple at WFU, and on Wednesday and Thursday, don't even think about leaving campus between the 12 to 1 p.m. activity hour because there will be Papa John's Pizza somewhere!

Status: Current student, full-time
Dates of Enrollment: 8/2005-Submit Date
Survey Submitted: April 2006

E-mails are sent out to all the law students about social activities going on at Wake or in the community in general. There are a lot of clubs at the law school, including ones based on interest in an area of the law (SELA, Sports and Entertainment Law; IPLA, Intellectual Property; DVAC, Domestic Violence Advocacy), based on political affiliation (Federalist Society, ATLA), and based on other groups (Women, African Americans, Asians, Latinos, Gay/Lesbian). If you can't find a club at Wake that you want to join, then you aren't looking— there are tons of things you can do, no matter what you are interested in.

Status: Current student, full-time
Dates of Enrollment: 8/2004-Submit Date
Survey Submitted: April 2006

The Winston-Salem community embraces Wake Forest University so there is no weird town/school tension. Winston-Salem also houses the NC School for the Arts, which brings in lots of art programs such as gallery openings, dance performances and recitals. The bar and club scenes are not hopping. There is never lack of parties. Law students tend to stick together at places like Burke Street, Freddie B's, and 6th and Vine.

Also, the SBA organizes Bar Review every Thursday night. Bar Review consists of all the law students going to the same bar to hang out on Thursday nights. Bar Review has also included minor league baseball games and Mellow Mushroom (pizza joint). Additionally, Kegs in the Courtyard has become a mainstay through the fall. The MBA and law schools get together to socialize in the courtyard several times through the fall sharing beer and snacks. The B-school also puts on an international food evening in the fall that law students attend. Imagine tons of food from all over the country for free outside! Good times!

Status: Current student, full-time
Dates of Enrollment: 8/2005-Submit Date
Survey Submitted: April 2006

Wake Law is also known as Worrell Junior High. We have lockers. We have bells. We have gossip. Law students who come in without significant others usually end up dating other law students. Most of our friends are law students. You have to actively look for non-law schoolers as friends if you want them. However, we're all also very close, and become more of a family than anything else.

Read all of Vault's Law School Surveys at www.vault.com/lawschool — get complete surveys on top law schools, expert advice on applicaton essays, LSAT prep and more.

VAULT CAREER LIBRARY   493

Winston Salem is NOT a college town. There is no strip of bars, instead they are scattered all over the city and cabs are almost impossible to come by. Fortunately, anywhere in all of Winston is only 10 minutes from anywhere else, so the cab situation doesn't really impair anything too much. Some of the favorite bars are Foothills, West End Opera House and Burke Street.

Status: Current student, full-time
Dates of Enrollment: 1/2003-Submit Date
Survey Submitted: March 2005

Social activity among students is abundant and frequent. With social gatherings nearly every week, casual parties and meetings, fundraising events and intramural sports, if you want to meet people and be active, you can't blame the environment. For those of us with spouses or partners, there is a partners organization that organizes all sorts of social activities and provides an outlet for those we love, but nonetheless neglect for two years as we immerse ourselves in the challenges of law school.

Though Winston-Salem is a relatively small town by New York, Chicago, L.A or San Francisco standards—it's no backwater. There is a nightlife, and a vibran community if you want it. W-S has a symphony, plus all that comes with th North Carolina School of the Arts, and is only an hour or so away from Raleigh Durham, Greensboro, Charlotte and the Research Triangle Park area. Activitie with students from Duke or UNC Chapel Hill occasionally crop up throug student clubs and other special interest groups.

Case Western Reserve University School of Law

Case School of Law
Case Western Reserve University
11075 East Boulevard
Cleveland, OH 44106
Admissions phone: (800) 756-0036
Admissions fax: (216) 368-1042
Admissions e-mail: lawadmissions@case.edu
Admissions URL: http://lawwww.cwru.edu/admissions/

Admissions

Status: Current student, full-time JD/MBA
Dates of Enrollment: 8/2005-Submit Date
Survey Submitted: April 2006

Admissions is as friendly as law admissions can get. Come for a visit, they do a great job explaining their unique CaseArc system, which provides practical lawyering skills for all three years. They make it really easy to apply for a joint degree with other Case grad programs after you come, so don't worry about that yet if you just want to focus on getting into law school first.

I'm going to be getting a JD/MBA from Case Law and Case's business school, Weatherhead (Top 10-ish entrepreneurship program). Plus, they combine scholarship money towards the cost of the first school you attend. If you have an undergrad business major, you can earn a JD/MBA in just three years.

I do think Case needs to up their admissions and get better-testing students just for the rankings. Case is seriously under-ranked, especially for how good the programs are, how much you can do here and what a legal community Cleveland is. But I'd rather go to an under-ranked school now and have the ranking go up as it will, than vice versa. If Case is on your short list but you're looking at higher-ranked schools, all I can say is I was too and I'm glad I came. I got into a school ranked much higher, but passed it up because I would have been just another number there. Here, I get scholarship money, great teachers, great job prospects, low cost of living and great community.

I recommend you check Case out by visiting. You will be impressed with the programs and the area. Sure, many kids move to NY or Chicago for the flashy jobs after they graduate, but I couldn't imagine being a poor student in those high-cost towns.

Status: Current student, full-time
Dates of Enrollment: 8/2005-Submit Date
Survey Submitted: April 2006

Apply as early as humanly possible. Definitely come for a tour and a class if possible. I came during the summer to visit, and I don't think I got a good enough picture of the school. Talk to current students about their feelings on the school and LISTEN TO THEM.

Status: Current student, full-time
Dates of Enrollment: 8/2004-Submit Date
Survey Submitted: April 2006

Standard personal statement, LSAT scores and GPA from undergraduate university. I had done quite a bit of work abroad and I believe that this helped me in securing a spot. In addition, I worked with a couple of firms prior to applying and was certain that I wanted to practice law. My undergraduate GPA and LSAT scores were fair but not necessarily strong. I truly believe that the activities I was involved in, legal and abroad experience and writing abilities played an important role.

Status: Current student, full-time
Dates of Enrollment: 8/2005-Submit Date
Survey Submitted: April 2006

My situation is unique because I did not get in when I first applied. However, after a successful year at another law school, I was able to transfer to Case Western. The biggest piece of advice I would give to an applicant is to be genuine in the application process. Certainly, one should put his or her best foot forward, so to speak, but it is important that the admissions committee see who you really are.

After being admitted, I worked some with our director of admissions and discussed the process. Obviously, grades are important and LSAT score is important. But the key question he will ask is, "Will this person succeed at Case?" In drafting your essay, I would focus on practical reasons why you are qualified and why you want to go to Case. With a substantial pool of qualified applicants, this is crucial. Don't just talk about law school generally, talk about Case. Don't just talk about your qualifications generally, get specific: scholarly writing projects, voluminous reading. The admissions committee needs to know you have the skills and, most importantly, the endurance, to go through law school.

If your LSAT is particularly low, don't be afraid to address it. Generally, higher LSAT scores perform better and vice versa. However, the admissions committee knows this is not a fixed rule. My LSAT was around the national average. After proving myself for a year at another school, I convinced Case that I could succeed here. Admissions committees realize you are not defined by your score—feel free to remind them why the score does not reflect your best work or why you work hard enough to make up for it.

Status: Alumnus/a, full-time
Dates of Enrollment: 9/1999-5/2002
Survey Submitted: May 2005

The admissions office at Case was extremely helpful throughout the admissions process. They answered all my questions, and I had a lot of them. On very short notice, they set up a tour of the school and arranged for me to attend classes and meet with current students. As I was living in another state, they also helped me get in touch with alumni in my area who were more than willing to answer questions about Case. Case really seemed to welcome diversity of all kinds, and we had students of all different ages, backgrounds, races, ethnicity and more.

Take advantage of the admissions staff. They are there to answer questions and it can't hurt to have them get to know you. They will be more invested in you and want to help. It worked for me.

Status: Current student, full-time
Dates of Enrollment: 8/2004-Submit Date
Survey Submitted: April 2005

After I applied for admission to Case, I was contacted by the admissions committee in six days. I sent in my application in late December and was extremely impressed with the efficiency and promptness of this institution. The essays that I submitted for Case were the standard personal statement essays that most schools request. There is an option if you would like to submit additional essays but it's not necessary. There is no interview process but it is highly encouraged that you come and visit.

There are tour guides, who are actual students themselves, who give daily tours around the law school. When you visit the law school, they have a little plaque outside that lists all the visitors for the day. It's a nice personal touch that makes people feel welcome.

I was personally contacted about my admission through e-mail. A letter of congratulations followed in the mail a few days later. Of all the schools I applied

Read all of Vault's Law School Surveys at www.vault.com/lawschool — get complete surveys on top law schools, expert advice on applicaton essays, LSAT prep and more.

VAULT CAREER LIBRARY 495

to, Case's admission staff put in the most effort trying to recruit me. This was one huge factor in why I decided to attend. I received a daily e-mail from different individuals at Case I also received very helpful information in the mail at least twice a week, such as housing information and even a law school t-shirt. When I visited the law school, the admission officers and many current students were there to answer all my questions. I was taken on a trolley ride around town and even got to sit in on a class.

Status: Current student, full-time
Dates of Enrollment: 8/2001-Submit Date
Survey Submitted: January 2004

If done online, there is no admissions fee, which can be a big plus. The school did not offer interviews when I applied. I got in off a waitlist because my undergrad GPA was 3.0 and my LSAT was a 153, so I guess I was borderline. The essays are generic, and the admissions office places great emphasis on these because they look at them as a way to get to know the applicants. Selectivity is probably a little higher than medium, although I understand that now the competition is much greater, so higher LSATs and GPAs are needed. The school does seem to favor people who already hold advanced degrees.

> **The school says:** "For the 2006 entering class, the median LSAT was 159; the median GPA was 3.38. Fewer than 27 percent of our applicants were admitted, compared to a selectivity rate of 55 percent in 2001."

 ## Academics

Status: Alumnus/a, full-time JD/MBA
Dates of Enrollment: 9/1999-5/2003
Survey Submitted: May 2006

The quality of classes was excellent due to the experience and aptitude of the professors and program depth with regard to real-world application. The wide diversity that Weatherhead offers with students from around the world contributed world-class experience with different cultures, circumstances and backgrounds that added to the classroom learning. Students in the joint degree programs, such as myself, had no problem getting into popular classes because we held priority to maintain high classloads to graduate on time. The workload is very high, which is indicative of any graduate-level program to prepare students for real-world responsibility and multi-tasking.

Status: Current student, full-time
Dates of Enrollment: 8/2006-Submit Date
Survey Submitted: April 2006

I found the breadth of classes and the classroom experience to be very diverse. I think in terms of International Law, I was very impressed with the caliber of courses, faculty and students. Case recently revamped their LLM program bringing in many students from all over the world. This aspect greatly enhanced the learning experience with practical examples and different views.

Status: Current student, full-time JD/MBA
Dates of Enrollment: 8/2005-Submit Date
Survey Submitted: April 2006

Case Law provides the perfect blend of the traditional, doctrinal education (think *Paper Chase*) with practical lawyering skills. In the past, the best schools only focused on how to think like a lawyer and practical skills were considered the province of lower-end schools. Progressive schools like Case realize that you must not only have a trained legal mind, but also know how to apply that mind to actual legal work. Case grads are known for being brilliant and effective, and firms like to hire Case grads because they don't have to spend the first year teaching them how to write a brief.

As a first-semester 1L, I had three doctrinal courses and a practical legal writing course. All my first-semester tests were open-book, which took some pressure off. You have two additional courses second semester and closed-book exams. Law school is fun but not easy, so just get used to the idea of working really hard.

I LOVED my writing course, both because the adjunct professor teaching it was an amazing associate from Squire Sanders who provided real-world advice (and

helped me get a great summer job), and also because you really learn how to write, negotiate and argue persuasively before a judge in oral argument (like appellate work). The best part was that we took our hypothetical problem/issue through from meeting and interviewing the client to negotiating a settlement and it was based on what we were learning in our doctrinal courses. This mean that we weren't trying to keep learning new hypos or new law, and could focu on the actual skills. Second semester we took a law suit from filing through arguing motions for summary judgment before a judge. The other class and ou teacher taught took the opposing side, and we argued against each other using the motions we had written ourselves for a writing assignment. No dumb busywork, just becoming effective lawyers.

Faculty is impressive; we have three major law journals, mock trial and moot court. Case has a great Health Law Program, International Law Program (with Nobel Prize nominee Michael Scharf), IP Program and Litigation Programs (trial tactics). Case also has practical courses for writers, oral argument and public service work. You can even create a specialty or take other graduate programs as part of a specialty (like media law). With the Browns, the Indians and the Cavs in town, plenty of opportunities to get into sports law as well.

Status: Current student, full-time
Dates of Enrollment: 8/2005-Submit Date
Survey Submitted: April 2006

Good overall; the registrar is a disaster, and there's no structured academic advising whatsoever—you have to seek out advice from professors and upperclassmen yourself. 1Ls aren't given any guidance as to course plans for 2L and 3L years.

> **The school says:** "Our Academic Advising program has been revamped. Each new 1L is now formally assigned a faculty advisor."

Status: Current student, full-time
Dates of Enrollment: 8/2005-Submit Date
Survey Submitted: April 2006

To some extent, law schools are probably comparable in terms of what goes on in the classroom. Bar preparation is one of the chief objectives for legal education, so this is understandable.

Case provides a diverse course offering and I think students are generally satisfied with the professors. The workload is manageable. Law school will be difficult no matter where you go, but I do not think Case is particularly burdensome.

To be quite honest, the writing program, CaseArc, does leave something to be desired as it stands currently. To some extent this is unavoidable because it is in a transition phase. This is probably the most significant source of student complaints. I doubt, however, that this is unique to Case—legal writing programs are very difficult to implement effectively and fairly. I do think students can get a lot out of the courses if they apply themselves, though. CaseArc attempts to combine traditional writing with more practical skills. This results in students drafting legal memos and contracts while also participating in mock client interviews and oral arguments.

Status: Alumnus/a, full-time
Dates of Enrollment: 9/1996-5/1999
Survey Submitted: October 2005

The Socratic Method was alive and well during my tenure at Case. But the in-class persona of the professors was just that, in class. During office hours, at mixers or just around town, the professors were helpful, friendly and really committed to the success of the student body. All of the professors were readily accessible. The Case community is big enough to hide if you want to but small enough that you really get to know your classmates and professors.

The workload could be overwhelming at times but so goes the practice of law. I truly believe Case is under-rated academically. The quality of the professors and the real-world experiences they bring to the classroom translate into better prepared lawyers not academics. The law clinics and the opportunities to participate in varied pro bono work around the city of Cleveland is topnotch. Getting popular classes such as Scientific Evidence is almost impossible but once you learn the system there is always a way to "work it." If you have any interest in health law, this is the place to be. *The Health Matrix* (Law Review) is at your disposal, as well as the resources at the Cleveland Clinic and University Hospitals.

Status: Current student, full-time
Dates of Enrollment: 8/2004-Submit Date
Survey Submitted: April 2005

Case has a very unique legal writing program known as CORE. This program is distinguished from other law schools because it has actual faculty members teaching it as well as a section called Simulation. In these Simulation sections, students are required to give actual interviews to live witnesses and clients, who are portrayed by actors. One of my favorite assignments was the appellate brief argument, in which we argued in front of local judges. This was the best experience of my first-year writing course. The workload from the other main classes is very similar to that of any other law school. However, Case not only requires you to take standard Civil Procedure, Torts, Contracts, Crim Law and Property, but we also take Constitutional Law and one elective class as a first-year student. This elective class is a nice segway to see how upper division classes are. The workload is extremely challenging and there is a lot of reading.

Like many other law schools, the grading system is plagued by the curve. There are the usual complaints of those who don't feel like the scoring system has given them justice. Case participates in a program called CALI. Professors are required to submit the name of the individual who scores the highest in their class for the semester. That individual receives an award for his/her accomplishments. I think this is a great program that makes you work that much harder to try and get the top grade.

Status: Alumnus/a, full-time
Dates of Enrollment: 8/2000-5/2002
Survey Submitted: September 2003

Case is a much better school than the *U.S. News & World Report* rankings show. The academics are particularly strenuous. The first-year curriculum is standard, with the exception of one elective. The electives change, but are usually more interesting than the core classes. The faculty is like faculty anywhere. Case has recently been beefing up the faculty with younger, more energetic professors. Some of the old [professors] are priceless, though. I liked some of my professors more than others. The core curriculum professors are rounded out by adjunct attorney faculty. These adjunct professors typically teach more skills-based classes (like Lawyering Process). I thought the adjuncts were particularly good.

There is a concentration program where you can choose from a concentration in: [Law, Technology and the Arts (Law and Technology or Law and the Arts); International Law; Business Organizations; Litigation; Health Law; Public Law (Individual Rights and Social Reform or Public and Regulatory Institutions); and Criminal Law]. They may have added additional classes. The concentrations allow students interested in certain areas a means to show their additional interest to perspective employers. The workload is pretty strenuous the first year. There is one first-year writing professor who is notorious. She is an excellent professor, but her students experience an unequal workload compared with the rest of students who have another writing teacher. Her demanding requirements are tempered by her good nature and the fact that she is just a class-A professor.

All of the professors are demanding, and some exams are harder than others. My experience was that most of my grades were based on closed-book exams. Students are allowed to handwrite or type their exams. Very few of my classes allowed papers in lieu of exams. Grading depends on teachers, like any school.

 Employment Prospects

Status: Current student, full-time
Dates of Enrollment: 8/2004-Submit Date
Survey Submitted: April 2006

The alumni that I have contacted have been very helpful in providing information and contacts. At Case Law, the employment prospects tend toward the Midwest, Northeast and Mid-Atlantic. If international justice and/or human rights is your goal, Case Law is the only school with students working on every

international tribune, the WTO and the International Bar Association. Several students return to the West Coast each year, so the alumni network there continues to grow. If the Midwest is your destination, practically every large firm and countless medium and small firms visit Case every year.

Status: Current student, full-time
Dates of Enrollment: 8/2005-Submit Date
Survey Submitted: April 2006

I'm a 1L and did pretty well on grades (not perfect at all), and I'll be working a $6K/month medium-sized firm gig this summer. Most places you go, you work for free your first summer just because firms don't hire 1Ls. Not in Cleveland. Here, you get a job and you get paid well!

Many of the firms located in Cleveland have NY, Chicago and CA. branches (Squire and Jones Day have international offices as well), so you're interviewing for national jobs without leaving the city. The career services office has a comprehensive program that includes on-campus interviews as well as out-of-city interviews. There's also a great judicial externship program that puts students in federal judge's offices for the summer or part-time during the school year. I can't even list all the other opportunities career services provides, from public-interest to government. JAG and the FBI recruit at Case.

There are common-pleas, state courts and federal courts downtown, the capital of Ohio (Columbus) only a couple hours away and plenty going on in between. The area has other great law schools (Cleveland-Marshall and Akron) that have good in-state reps, but Case is the top-dog when it comes to reputation. When I interviewed, most of the interviewers were either from Case or Akron but impressed by the fact that I was from Case. I asked one of my adjunct professors (who teaches part-time out of the goodness of his heart, since he's so successful) whether his firm hires Case grads, and he responded, "We ONLY hire Case grads." For employers, they know they're getting top students.

Status: Alumnus/a, full-time JD/MBA
Dates of Enrollment: 9/1996-5/1999
Survey Submitted: October 2005

Outside of Cleveland, the Case name may not do you much good. However, if you are willing to work at making contacts outside of the Cleveland Area on your own, your job prospects will be much better. As for on-campus interviews, the story is the same: make Law Review, be in the top 10 percent, and the world is your oyster. The school does sponsor a lot of informal interview functions with potential employers, take advantage of them.

The recruiting department was helpful during non-peak times to assist student who want to leave the area after law school or don't fit the traditional on-campus interview mold. Case is a great school for older students, students for whom law is a second career or students seeking a dual degree. The JD/MBA program has enough structure to make sure you know the basics, but the flexibility to keep it interesting for the student. The same holds true for JD/MSW and JD/Engineering. If you let your advisors know what your objectives are with the dual degree program they will work with you to achieve those goals within your degree requirements.

Status: Alumnus/a, full-time
Dates of Enrollment: 9/1999-5/2002
Survey Submitted: May 2005

The career services office played a huge part in getting me a job with the third largest law firm in the country in their New York office. Through Case's off-campus interview program, I was able to interview with top law firms in New York, D.C., Chicago and Atlanta. I received multiple offers and took a job with my top choice in New York City. I had friends who went on to all types of jobs from big firms to small firms, military JAG, clerkships, nonprofits and more. The career service office has been continually expanding its on-campus interview program. They help students set up mock interviews with attorneys in the community and will look at your resume and cover letter as many times as you want to show it to them. I know that without the career services office at Case, I would not have had such a wonderful job waiting for me at graduation.

Read all of Vault's Law School Surveys at www.vault.com/lawschool — get complete surveys on top law schools, expert advice on applicaton essays, LSAT prep and more.

VAULT CAREER LIBRARY 497

Status: Alumnus/a, full-time
Dates of Enrollment: 8/1999-5/2002
Survey Submitted: March 2005

Case is the premiere school between New York and Chicago, so job prospects are good particularly in the Midwest, but also in New York, Chicago, Washington and to some extent California. My impression is that most Case students go on to law firm jobs, not government or public service jobs. The one weak spot is that career services at the law school focuses on getting students jobs in big law firms, which is the one place students don't need help. The alumni network is pretty vibrant, though, and Case lawyers work all over the U.S.

Status: Alumnus/a, full-time
Dates of Enrollment: 8/2000-5/2003
Survey Submitted: October 2003

If you are in the top 10 percent of the class and on Law Review, you can pretty much go anywhere. Even most of those between the top 10 and 20 percent ended up with jobs relatively soon after graduation. After that, the rate of those finding jobs (i.e., jobs they went to law school to get) drops precipitously. Also, the school is stronger in the local region. Of my class, about five went to New York (all in the top 10 percent and on the executive board of the Law Review), several went to D.C. or Chicago, but most, particularly those below the top of the class, stayed in Ohio. At this point, five months after graduation, I have five or six friends, all in the top 25 percent of the class, without jobs or prospects.

> **The school says:** "98.6 percent of the Class of 2005 was employed within nine months of graduation, compared with a national rate of 91.8 percent. 52.7 percent of Case Law grads obtained their job through a Career Services Office program, compared with a national average of 38.4 percent. And 47.8 percent obtained a job outside of Ohio, compared with the national average of 33.3 percent placement outside of the law school's state."

 ## Quality of Life

Status: Current student, full-time
Dates of Enrollment: 8/2006-Submit Date
Survey Submitted: April 2006

The Cleveland area is underrated as a large city I had my apprehensions moving into the area, but I've been very happy exploring the different districts of this city. The University Circle area is full of cultural havens and walking distance to wonderful art museums, restaurants and a world-class orchestra. I found housing two blocks away from the school for a really reasonable price; the housing around the area is old, but many new renovations are occurring. The undergrad campus was just renovated last year.

Status: Current student, full-time
Dates of Enrollment: 8/2005-Submit Date
Survey Submitted: April 2006

Although Cleveland gets a little cold in the winter, it's beautiful and warm in the spring, summer and fall. I even like the winter because the snow is fun and there's sledding. Case is in the heart of the beautiful University Circle area, which includes one of the best art museums in the world, one of the best orchestras in the world, multiple schools and universities and generally great living.

There are plenty of medium-cost apartments near the campus, which is a bit of an oasis in the city. Plus, Little Italy is just up the hill from the school (literally just blocks away), which has more housing, bars, restaurants, art galleries, high-end cigar shops, coffee shops and bakeries. Truly, my only complaint is the lack of grocery stores in walking distance, but if you have a car, no problem.

Transportation is easy, lots of great stuff in walking distance and the light-rail system (called the RTA, or Rapid) goes right downtown (for those summer firm jobs) and to the airport (for those summer vacations).

The security is fine, with both Case security (armed cars, bikes), and a special University Circle division of the Cleveland PD. Both groups work together to keep everyone safe, and I've never been hassled by anyone (crook or cop). Occasionally a car gets broken into or someone gets into trouble, but they actually catch people around here for crimes, which is reassuring.

It is an ideal mix of big city and college town: University Circle is technically in Cleveland but is very green, very clean and very safe. If you want to be in the heart of everything, get a place on Hessler St. at the Triangle or an apartment on campus. All super close (I walk two minutes to school in the morning). A lot of students and couples rent apartments in Cleveland Heights, which is relatively low-cost and gives a little more buffer from school than living right next door.

For families, you have Cleveland Heights and Shaker Heights within five minutes drive of campus, which both offer great homes and great schools (Shaker has some of the best public schools in the country). Plus, the Rapid runs two lines into Shaker, both of which go downtown and to the airport. The downtown station is Tower City, which is a great mall right in the heart of the city, converted from an old-style train station a la Grand Central.

Status: Current student, full-time
Dates of Enrollment: 8/2004-Submit Date
Survey Submitted: April 2006

There is no graduate student housing on campus, but most of us live in Cleveland Heights. It's quaint, there are a lot of bars that you can walk to and it's priced really reasonably. Dining in Cleveland in general is sort of lacking; there are a few really nice, good restaurants but they are expensive. Other than that, lots and lots of chain restaurants. Little Italy is nearby and it's nice, but the novelty sort of wears off after first-year.

Status: Alumnus/a, full-time
Dates of Enrollment: 9/1999-5/2002
Survey Submitted: May 2005

Most law students live in off-campus housing. There are lots of apartments available in nearby neighborhoods. Many students live the nearby eclectic Coventry area with restaurants and bars in walking distance from where you live. The law school provides information about various apartment buildings in the area. The Cleveland area as a whole has a lot of great restaurants. There are a bunch of options near the law school. You can walk across the street and grab lunch at the Cleveland Art Museum (free admission) and enjoy a break from classes. There is a lunch stand in the law school with great Middle Eastern food and a school cafeteria is only a short walk away. There are several coffee shops nearby that offer light meals. Crime isn't a big problem in the area of the law school, and there is safe, well-lit parking nearby.

Status: Current student, full-time
Dates of Enrollment: 8/2004-Submit Date
Survey Submitted: April 2005

There is one word to explain living in Cleveland: affordable. This city has the most reasonable housing prices, if not downright cheap. I live in a 1,000 square foot one-bedroom apartment less than a block from the law school and my rent at $800 a month is considered very expensive. However, most apartments are at least driving distance from campus and the equivalent to my apartment runs closer to $600 farther away. Cleveland is like any big city, just with fewer clubs, fewer restaurants and fewer places to go out. Despite the notion that this is the Midwest, it's more diverse than most people would realize.

However, it almost doesn't matter what city you live in if you are going to law school. The truth is most people study eight hours a day, are in class for six hours and catching up on sanity the rest of the time. There are safety issues that are less than desirable. Cleveland has a very high crime rate, even around the campus area. The school has a lot of security guards but you still have to be careful and not walk alone at night.

Status: Current student, full-time
Dates of Enrollment: 8/2002-Submit Date
Survey Submitted: April 2005

The law school is truly a community. There is no overwhelming sense of competition. Students are friendly and as helpful as they can be (within the realms of the honor code). Everyone wants everyone to do as well as they can.

The administration is generally receptive of students' concerns, and tries to work with the student body to address them. The support staff at the school is incredible, and students often have as good relationships with them as they do with the faculty. The library staff is extremely helpful and we are fortunate to have them.

The neighborhood is safe. At night, one has to be alert, but that is true of any campus in an urban setting. Affordable housing can be found close to campus and I hate the idea of giving up my apartment when I graduate. The law school is in one building, and I like that all of our classes are in one place. It makes it a lot easier to plan what you are taking to school for the day.

 ## Social Life

Status: Current student, full-time
Dates of Enrollment: 8/2006-Submit Date
Survey Submitted: April 2006

The Student Bar Association at Case is extremely active in providing opportunities for students socially. Whether it's sports tournaments or interactions with the faculty, there is always something going on at this school. Over 40 special interest groups and clubs bring in speakers each week during lunch hours to speak on various topics. This part of law school has been a great experience and deviates from traditional book-and-teacher method. I've learned a lot and I think students bring a lot to the table.

Status: Current student, full-time
Dates of Enrollment: 8/2005-Submit Date
Survey Submitted: April 2006

The school is relatively self-contained with a small cafe inside, a nice lounge and plenty of study space. It is located next door to the business school (Weatherhead) and the Mandel School of Social Sciences, both topnotch options for dual degrees. There's a great atmosphere of cooperation among the students, although everyone gets a little tense around finals (which is true anywhere you go).

The overall campus is open and fun. There's a student bar/restaurant where they do open mic, a patio-bar that has live music every night and lets people bring their dogs (the Barking Spider), and the art museum with its beautiful lagoon park and a number of other parks across the street. There's plenty of Greek stuff, but not oppressively so. Downtown is close, with plenty of bars and the Flats. The near West Side is lots of fun too. Great music scene, Rock and Roll Hall of Fame, amazing orchestra, theatre and other cultural events. Plenty of networking opportunities, both business and legal in nature.

Status: Current student, full-time
Dates of Enrollment: 8/2004-Submit Date
Survey Submitted: April 2006

Social life is good. Bar Review is popular on Thursday nights (bars you drink at, not the bar you study for). Since law school is sort of like high school, lots of people are dating each other. There are some great clubs, including Phi Delta Phi and the Multicultural Irish Council.

Status: Current student, full-time
Dates of Enrollment: 8/2005-Submit Date
Survey Submitted: April 2006

The social life is there if you want it. I think you need to make a choice when you come to law school and decide what you want to get out of it. That varies from person to person, but I think there is something for everyone. The Student Bar Association organizes weekly outings at bars around Cleveland. Other people go out in small groups and organize parties. There is also a variety of campus groups with which one can become involved. This is a good way to meet people with similar interests and career goals.

Status: Current student, full-time
Dates of Enrollment: 9/2003-Submit Date
Survey Submitted: April 2006

Students range dramatically in ages and interests, but there is always something to do when its time for a break. Every Thursday night the student government

sponsors Bar Review at a local bar that is willing to provide drink specials. Events like the Student Public Interest Law Forum's annual auction, where the students bid on various donated items (many of which involve professors giving legal tours of Cleveland or preparing dinners at their homes), always draw big crowds.

Status: Current student, full-time
Dates of Enrollment: 8/2004-Submit Date
Survey Submitted: April 2005

Within the law school, there is an organization for everybody. This past year, I was a senator in the Student Bar Association and recently was elected into an executive officer position. As an integral part of the student organizations at school, I take pride in knowing that Case has one of the most diverse groups of student organizations. Every day there are at least five events going on and you can always find free lunch at one, if not all, of these events. There is so much going on here, you cannot but be involved.

Status: Current student, full-time
Dates of Enrollment: 8/2004-Submit Date
Survey Submitted: April 2005

I feel sorry for the undergrads, but our social life is great. Everyone is pretty friendly; we go out almost every week and we play basketball together. There's a softball league and the student organizations organize lots of events, so it's all good.

Thursday night Bar Review is a popular event, and it might seem sad to admit, but we all became better friends after we saw each other inebriated. Case has worked out well for me because it is challenging but not cutthroat. People have shared their notes and outlines with me; professors have given me extensions when I was sick; the administration always has an open door and I've made some really good friends. It is a totally different experience than what I was used to in California, especially because I never knew so many conservatives before (and they're wonderful people). It has definitely broadened my viewpoint and helped me to grow as a person and a professional.

Status: Alumnus/a, full-time
Dates of Enrollment: 8/2000-5/2002
Survey Submitted: September 2003

Most students hang out in Coventry, the Flats or the Warehouse District. Coventry offers several restaurants, bars and live music venues. It's near where students live, allowing students to stumble home after a happy hour. The school has weekly Bar Reviews where they pick a different bar for a social event. Students tend to hang out together and party at each other's houses. The students don't interact with students from other schools that often. Mostly students hang out at school or in Coventry. Overall, Cleveland is lacking in restaurants. There is no place to get a good margarita. Alternatively, pierogi are prevalent.

 ## The School Says

At Case School of Law, we pride ourselves on blending the best of classical legal education with leading-edge innovations. We are facing head-on fundamental changes in the world and in the legal profession. The expansion and growing complexity of the law, the effects of globalization on virtually every segment of our economic, social and political lives, and the quest for a fair and effective legal system have altered the responsibilities of lawyers and the skills and learning that our graduates need. Our goal is to ensure that our graduates will be prepared to understand their clients' enterprises and the economic, social and political contexts in which they operate.

Innovation is the key to achieving this goal. Over the past seven years we have introduced over 150 new courses, seven concentrations, two additional dual degree programs, two new Centers of Excellence and our ground-breaking CaseArc Integrated Lawyering Skills programs.

Read all of Vault's Law School Surveys at www.vault.com/lawschool — get complete surveys on top law schools, expert advice on applicaton essays, LSAT prep and more.

VAULT CAREER LIBRARY 499

The opportunity for experiential learning is truly unique. Here are just a few examples:

- Over 250 spaces in skills courses alone

- Phenomenal opportunities for work abroad, including stipends. Placements have included: Medicins San Frontieres (Burma); International Criminal Tribunal (Yugoslavia); Appeals Chamber (The Hague); UNDP Hanoi (Vietnam); Special Court for Sierra Leone, Prosecutor's Office (Sierra Leone); International Trade Centre (Switzerland); Council for Legal Aid (India); International Criminal Tribunal for Rwanda (Rwanda)

- Intellectual Property Entrepreneurship Clinic

- Counterterrorism Lab

- Health Law Clinic

- Federal Judicial Externship Program

- War Crimes Lab

- Immigration Clinic

- Constitutional Law II Lab

- Judicial Reform Lab

- Regulatory Policy Research Lab

The most recent placement statistics (for the Class of 2005) demonstrate the strength of the Career Services Office as well as the employment opportunities nationally for Case Law graduates:

- 406 employers participated in our interview programs in the 2005-06 academic year.

- The median starting salary was $72,000, compared with a national average of $60,000.

- 98.6 percent of the Class of 2005 was employed or in a post-JD degree program after graduation.

- 53.6 percent of graduates were employed in law firms; 17.9 percent in business and industry; 6.3 percent in public interest; 3.4 percent in judicial clerkships and 3.4 percent in academics.

Cleveland State University

Cleveland-Marshall College of Law
Office of Law Admissions
2121 Euclid Avenue, LB 138
Cleveland, OH 44115
Admissions phone: (216) 687-2287 or (866) 687-2304
(toll-free)
Admissions e-mail: admissions@law.csuohio.edu
Admissions URL:
http://www.law.csuohio.edu/admissions/index.html

 ## Admissions

Status: Current student, full-time
Dates of Enrollment: 8/2004-Submit Date
Survey Submitted: May 2005

To gain admittance, one has to submit a resume and answer various essay questions, in addition to the usual law school requirements. I applied in late March and still was fortunate enough to be accepted. My recommendation would be to apply as early as possible.

> **The school says:** "A resume is not required but may be submitted in lieu of answering some questions on the application."

Status: Current student, full-time
Dates of Enrollment: 8/2003-Submit Date
Survey Submitted: April 2005

The admissions process for C-M is very user-friendly. All information is available both online and in the admissions office. Our admissions director is an extremely knowledgeable and friendly individual who is more than willing to work with prospective students and take them step-by-step through the admissions process. In addition to the general information forms, there is a personal statement that allows each applicant to detail his/her reasons both for choosing to go to law school and, more specifically, for choosing C-M.

Status: Current student, full-time
Dates of Enrollment: 8/2003-Submit Date
Survey Submitted: April 2005

The admissions process was comparable to other law school applications since I used the LSAC general computerized application that many law schools accept. I found the admissions staff efficient, I received a response quickly and was chosen for a scholarship. Cleveland-Marshall is not the most selective school, which I didn't mind since it helped me obtain the scholarship, but it's getting a reputation for being more selective.

> **The Cleveland-Marshall College of Law says:** "In 2003, the law school's selectivity rate was 38 percent. In the past two years, the rate was 29 and 30 percent."

Status: Current student, full-time
Dates of Enrollment: 8/2003-Submit Date
Survey Submitted: April 2005

The admissions process included the submission of LSAT scores, undergrad transcripts, letters of recommendation, essays and informal interviews with admissions staff.

Status: Current student, full-time
Dates of Enrollment: 8/2001-Submit Date
Survey Submitted: April 2005

I only applied to Cleveland-Marshall, so I was not seeking the kind of detailed information that one does if one is considering numerous schools. What I can say is that I believe the admissions staff is excellent, I even helped them with a

prospective student orientation. When I first applied, the office did not conduct face-to-face interviews. I believe the admission is much more selective now than when I first started at C-M.

> **The school says:** "Interviews are not conducted in the admission process."

Status: Current student, full-time
Dates of Enrollment: 8/2003-Submit Date
Survey Submitted: April 2005

I applied to Cleveland-Marshall online. I was committed to going to law school in the Cleveland area, which limited my choice of law schools to three—Cleveland-Marshall, Case Western Reserve University and University of Akron. I did not interview with admissions staff at Cleveland-Marshall. I did write an essay, although I can't remember the details of it. I knew quite a bit about Cleveland-Marshall prior to applying. I had two close friends who graduated from the school a year before I applied. I also worked with a couple of faculty members on some community projects prior to coming to law school.

Status: Current student, full-time
Dates of Enrollment: 8/2002-Submit Date
Survey Submitted: April 2005

The admissions process required an essay, completion of application form, three letters of recommendation and transcripts from an undergraduate college. My best advice is to work hard in preparation for the LSAT. I should have worked harder and was fortunate to gain admission with a score that was below what I could have gotten.

Status: Current student, full-time
Dates of Enrollment: 8/2004-Submit Date
Survey Submitted: April 2005

I submitted my application early and would recommend doing that. I was notified of acceptance in early to mid-March. I had to fill out an application and complete a personal statement, pretty typical for all law schools. There was no interview for admission. My advice is to get all your things in early. I know that the LSAT is a big factor, but GPA is also a factor. I didn't have a great LSAT score but was admitted with a high GPA.

Status: Current student, full-time
Dates of Enrollment: 8/2004-Submit Date
Survey Submitted: April 2005

The admissions process was a little nerve-wracking, but in the end it was obviously well worth it. The application process was painless, the most difficult part was writing a personal statement. Everything else was that same standard procedure: gathering recommendations, submitting transcripts and filling out an application. Cleveland-Marshall's admissions process was a lot easier in comparison to the other school that I applied to. C-M responded to my application in about one month, which relieved the pressure of finding out whether I was going to law school or not. Two more months rolled by before I received any type of response from the other institution.

 ## Academics

Status: Current student, full-time
Dates of Enrollment: 8/2004-Submit Date
Survey Submitted: May 2005

I have really enjoyed my first year. The professors are amazing and could not be more helpful in preparing you to succeed.

It was a little difficult trying to register for third-semester classes. The university assigns you a random registration time, and it is all the luck of the draw. I was stuck with a late time and could not register for three of the classes I wanted to take.

Read all of Vault's Law School Surveys at www.vault.com/lawschool — get complete surveys on top law schools, expert advice on applicaton essays, LSAT prep and more.

VAULT CAREER LIBRARY 501

The school says: "Course registration times are assigned on the basis of credit hours earned through the last completed term."

Status: Current student, full-time
Dates of Enrollment: 8/2003-Submit Date
Survey Submitted: April 2005

C-M has been an amazing fit for me—when I was first accepted and began here as a 1L, I was planning to stay for only one year and then transfer back to New York to a law school there. However, after only a few months at C-M, I knew that there was no way that I was going to leave.

The faculty here is fantastic; they are a very diverse group of individuals with a wide variety of experiences, which brings an interesting dynamic to the classroom. In my opinion, one of the biggest assets with the faculty here is their accessibility both in and out of the classroom. I have gotten to know several of my professors very well and had the opportunity to do research for several as well. Although they remain active outside the law school, their first priority is to the students.

The grading scale here is on a C curve, and it's tough, but you can do very well if you do the work. The workload is manageable as long as law school is your top priority (which is what it needs to be if you're truly going to get the most out of your time at law school). There is a wide variety of classes offered, and I personally have not had trouble getting into any classes I've been interested in. I have been on a few waiting lists, but they have always found a spot for me.

> **The school says:** "There is no mandatory grading curve at Cleveland-Marshall. The law school has two sets of grading guidelines that apply to first-year and upper-division courses, respectively. The first-year guidelines allow grades of B and better to up to 52 percent of the class. For upper division classes, up to 70 percent of B and better grades are permitted."

Status: Current student, part-time
Dates of Enrollment: 7/2004-Submit Date
Survey Submitted: April 2005

Law school is tough! The professors that I have encountered are brilliant in the subjects that they teach. They are receptive to questions, provide feedback and encourage students to think and not just memorize materials. Cleveland-Marshall prides itself on training effective advocates and resists becoming a "bar school," i.e., just teaching students to pass the bar exam. The workload is heavy, and there is no differentiation between the day and evening programs.

Status: Current student, full-time
Dates of Enrollment: 8/2004-Submit Date
Survey Submitted: April 2005

I experienced a vast array of teaching styles during my first semester. All of my professors were very knowledgeable about the subject matter and struck me as being very intelligent people. The classes were thoroughly demanding but there was nothing that a student could not handle as long as he/she did not fall behind. It is difficult to get popular classes, no matter what school or level of education. C-M allows students to select classes for the second and third year based on credit hours. If the student takes at least 13 to 15 hours per semester, it shouldn't be difficult to get into classes (spread over the next two years) but the student should be prepared to have alternative choices as well. C-M is on a C curve (the majority of students will receive C's); so it just makes students work harder to place in the top of the class to receive the highest grades. I see it as more incentive to work hard rather than something negative.

Status: Current student, full-time
Dates of Enrollment: 8/2003-Submit Date
Survey Submitted: April 2005

The academic nature of our school's program can best be described in one word: intense. I say that because at Marshall, a B is really a B, unlike most schools that grade on B curves, here, we earn our grades every day. Classes are very challenging and, in most classes, there is an unmistakable component of application to "real work."

Status: Current student, full-time
Dates of Enrollment: 8/2001-Submit Date
Survey Submitted: April 2005

One of the criticisms I had as a first-year student was that there was no orientation about when to take what classes second year and beyond. This has since been rectified and now first-years have a number of ways they can be assisted in selecting courses. I had two semesters when I was disappointed about the course offerings, and I know a number of my fellow students felt similarly.

Overall, I feel the professors at C-M are first-rate. My strongest professors taught in the areas of criminal law, labor law and constitutional law. I never had a problem getting into a course. The grading varied a lot depending on the professor. Sometimes my grade was only based on a final exam, and other times there were bi-weekly quizzes that accounted for a large percentage of the final grade. Most professors took into account class participation to one degree or another. The workload seemed pretty standard as far as law schools go.

Status: Current student, full-time
Dates of Enrollment: 9/2003-Submit Date
Survey Submitted: April 2005

Scheduling is relatively painless. I have only once been shut out of my ideal class, but I scheduled it for another time. The professors are fantastic—very experienced, knowledgeable, approachable, personable and understanding. The majority of them really want you to understand the material. Almost all professors will provide you with whatever extra help you need and ask for. The workload is challenging but fair. You will work hard, but you won't get frustrated to the point where you feel like you cannot handle it.

Status: Current student, full-time
Dates of Enrollment: 8/2003-Submit Date
Survey Submitted: April 2005

I have been wholeheartedly impressed with the program at Cleveland Marshall. With one exception, all of the faculty has been outstanding, both in their scholarship and their willingness to work with students. The workload is heavy but that was to be expected. By no means is the workload impossible. Careful time management and a strong committment to my education have aided my success in school. The professors, for the most part, stick to the syllabus distributed on the first day of class. This, of course, is very helpful with planning the semester.

Cleveland-Marshall grades on a C curve, which makes the program far more competitive than other schools. A lot of students complain about the grading structure, but I think it is important because it makes C-M students far more competitive when we are job hunting. A and B students are true A and B students, although I think the school could do more to communicate this to prospective employers.

I have had no problems getting the classes and professors I want. The school seems to work hard to accommodate the students' needs but is also fair in the process. The administration is also very helpful in working with students who have tough exam schedules (meaning one exam right after another). I met with Dean Lifter this week about my schedule and she was great in helping me to shift some exam times around so that I could get a good night sleep in between two heavy exams.

> **Cleveland-Marshall says:** "The Office of Career Planning sends letters to employers from the dean of the law school explaining our grading system, including the fact that C-M does not tolerate grade inflation."

Status: Current student, full-time
Dates of Enrollment: 8/2004-Submit Date
Survey Submitted: April 2005

During your first year, you are not able to select any classes. All of your classes, teachers and schedules are selected for you. Classes are a mix of lecture and the Socratic Method. Most professors are very knowledgeable in their areas and make class interesting. The nature of the program is demanding. It requires a lot of discipline, dedication and hard work outside of class. The workload is heavy with a lot of reading. Research and writing assignments add a lot of extra work and time. The atmosphere is pretty competitive. However, students seem o compete more with themselves than with each other. Most students are willing to help and are not cutthroat. I have not scheduled yet for next year to see availability of classes.

Regarding academics, the school says: "Cleveland-Marshall's law library is one of the 15 largest academic law libraries in the country. The superior research facility is 85,000 net square feet and houses over 500,000 volumes. Students study and do research in the four-story light-filled atrium where there are over 200 student carrels with built-in power and network ports for laptops. They have access to online research services, a computer lab, group study rooms, a bibliographic instruction room and a media center. There is cutting-edge technology in classrooms and in our moot court room. A state-of-the-art wireless network allows use of personal computers throughout the campus. In 2005, Cleveland-Marshall was recognized by *The National Jurist* magazine and the American Association of Law Libraries for its use and support of technology.

"In addition to coursework, students have invaluable learning opportunities outside of the classroom through our legal clinics, externships and participating in extracurricular and co-curricular student organizations. For example, this year, *The Gavel*, our student newspaper, once again received the Student Newspaper Award of Excellence from the American Bar Association, Law Student Division. And our moot court teams have earned a national reputation for excellence based on their consistent outstanding performances in regional, national and international appellate advocacy competitions. Our teams have won numerous first place awards for brief writing, oral arguments and overall team performance."

 Employment Prospects

Status: Current student, full-time
Dates of Enrollment: 8/2004-Submit Date
Survey Submitted: May 2005

The Office of Career Planning helped me out immensely. After talking to the director, she helped me obtain an externship with a federal judge. While some of my fellow first-years are struggling to find law-related work, I will have the opportunity to get both great experience and law school credit.

Status: Current student, full-time
Dates of Enrollment: 8/2003-Submit Date
Survey Submitted: April 2005

There are a variety of options available for interviewing here, and I got a job through our fall interview program, when most of the mid-size and big firms come to campus to interview. There is also a spring interview program for smaller firms, and with E-Attorney, you can always go online and see what jobs are currently available in the area. I have not dealt much with the alumni as far as networking goes, and I think that's an area that could be improved. However, I could not be happier with the position that I received through the interview process. Our Office of Career Planning does help out along the way, but the onus is really on the student to be informed and get out there to interview. If you take advantage of the opportunities you have, you'll be happy with the results.

The school says: "Opportunities exist for networking with alumni through a program where we bring in alumni from various practice areas to talk with students. We also have a strong mentor program with alumni, established during orientation. There are many opportunities throughout the year to meet alumni and networking connections with out-of-town alumni are available through the Office of Career Planning."

Status: Current student, part-time
Dates of Enrollment: 7/2004-Submit Date
Survey Submitted: April 2005

Cleveland-Marshall networks with both solo practitioners and large firms in the area, and there are numerous opportunities to gain practical work experience. There are many chances given to meet with alumni and a mentoring program is available to those choose to participate. The college's moot court team and Law Review are the pride of the area, and are highly regarded both locally and nationally.

Status: Current student, full-time
Dates of Enrollment: 8/2001-Submit Date
Survey Submitted: April 2005

As I got to know the Office of Career Planning (OCP) staff better, I found that they were of immeasurable help in comparing offers and securing a job. I think that employers in Cleveland recognize the accomplishments of students at C-M, but that the school does not enjoy a national reputation of any kind. I had several contacts with alumni about jobs and found them to be very helpful. When I first started at C-M, I found it difficult to know where to look for jobs that were in the public interest sector, but now I feel the OCP is much more proactive in finding the sources for these types of jobs.

The school says: "In addition to increasing public interest opportunities for students, C-M has established a Loan Repayment Assistance Program (LRAP) for graduates choosing to work in the public interest sector."

Status: Current student, full-time
Dates of Enrollment: 8/2002-Submit Date
Survey Submitted: April 2005

It has been my experience that Cleveland-Marshall is a regional school. Most of the employers who are familiar with the school practice in Northeast Ohio (specifically Cleveland) and maybe a little beyond (but even then, usually within Ohio). A lot of the prestigious and large firms in the area employ a number of Cleveland-Marshall grads. During the school's fall interview program, I had on-campus interviews will all 11 of the firms that I wanted to interview with. I received seven call-back interviews and accepted a job with one of those firms. (I will be working there after I take the bar this summer.)

During my second year of school I had an externship with a judge on the U.S. Sixth Circuit Court of Appeals, which was an invaluable experience and a great supplement to my class work.

Status: Current student, full-time
Dates of Enrollment: 9/2003-Submit Date
Survey Submitted: April 2005

C-M Law uses E-Attorney to post job listings. I have twice found jobs through this listing. It makes it easy when you are job hunting to go online periodically and see all of the postings. The fall interview program is well-organized but too late in the year. Most other schools interview in August and we do not begin until late September, which, I think, really puts us a step behind other schools. We also do not have a good feedback channel after the program to express crticisims and suggest improvements. Our school has good placement for clerkships, clinics and externships. We have a very large alumni presence in Cleveland, which is helpful but not fully utilized. An alumni network database with contact information would be helpful.

Cleveland-Marshall says: "While some schools, mostly on the East Coast, are holding their interview season during the summer months, most are still having their interview season in the fall. The hiring statistics show that C-M is not at a disadvantage in holding its program at the beginning of September and many employers are relieved that we have not pushed it into August."

Read all of Vault's Law School Surveys at www.vault.com/lawschool — get complete surveys on top law schools, expert advice on applicaton essays, LSAT prep and more.

VAULT CAREER LIBRARY **503**

Quality of Life

Status: Current student, full-time
Dates of Enrollment: 8/2003-Submit Date
Survey Submitted: April 2005

There is on-campus housing available; however, most students commute to school from around the Cleveland area. There are a good number of out-of-town students that do take advantage of campus housing and, from what I've heard, the apartment-style living accommodations are more than adequate. We're attached to CSU, so the athletic facilities are also available to the law students, which is nice. The neighborhood, for the most part, is safe; but this is the city, so you need to be careful and aware, especially when you're out at night by yourself. Our campus police force is great, though, and they are always visible around campus.

> **The school says:** "As part of the university's Master Plan, mid-rise apartments and townhouses are currently being built and a new $29 million student recreation center will open in the fall of 2006."

Status: Current student, full-time
Dates of Enrollment: 8/2004-Submit Date
Survey Submitted: April 2005

I live in a great loft across the street and the school is in the heart of the city, so there is a lot of downtown housing available. The school is also developing graduate housing that should be complete by fall 2006. Furthermore, urban communities always have an element of crime but I have never felt unsafe. Lastly, there is on-campus dining all over the campus and many restaurants within walking distance. C-M is downtown, so everything you need is right here and safety has never been a issue for me.

Status: Current student, full-time
Dates of Enrollment: 8/2003-Submit Date
Survey Submitted: April 2005

More than 90 percent of students live off campus. Cleveland is a good market for housing; you can get a nice place for very decent rent. The campus is downtown. I've had no safety worries during the day; at night there are safety escorts for those students who would like them. There are lots of little diners and restaurants in the neighborhood around the law school and in other university buildings, including a snack bar located inside the law school.

Status: Current student, full-time
Dates of Enrollment: 8/2001-Submit Date
Survey Submitted: April 2005

Housing is extremely limited and most students live off campus. The facilities are in desperate need of a face-lift. I never found much to eat at the snack bar in the law building, and although the main campus has better choices, it is quite far to walk. Public transportation is good, as the school ID gets you on the bus and train for free. The campus is not secure after hours because of its downtown location, and most students feel wary walking to their cars in the evening. Fortunately, the library now has a security guard at the entrance.

Status: Current student, full-time
Dates of Enrollment: 8/2002-Submit Date
Survey Submitted: April 2005

The greater Cleveland area is a great place to live. The school is in downtown Cleveland, but I live in the suburbs. I have under a half-hour commute each way. The school has food services (cafeteria) and there are restaurants close by. It is an urban campus, but the school has adequate security and an indoor garage, so even if you are working late in the law library, it doesn't seem to be a safety problem.

The school's downtown location puts it close to a lot of legal employers and the courts. And because traffic is usually not bad, you can easily live in the suburbs and commute to school. Public transportation, though, is not great.

Status: Current student, full-time
Dates of Enrollment: 8/2002-Submit Date
Survey Submitted: April 2005

My perspective is limited because I lived off campus for the entire three years, as did most of my classmates. Food service is available at the main Cleveland State student union, and is decent. A lesser service is offered in the law school basement, and there is ample room to sit and eat in comfort. Marshall is located in downtown Cleveland, so crime is always at least a background issue, but there were no incidents of a serious nature during my time at the law school. Downtown Cleveland also offers ample dining and entertainment options, although I didn't take the opportunity to get out and socialize much. Marshall also does a nice job of bringing in national, regional and local speakers and lecturers who present on an interesting breadth of legal topics.

Social Life

Status: Current student, full-time
Dates of Enrollment: 8/2003-Submit Date
Survey Submitted: April 2005

There are usually a variety of different social activities available—for the most part, you see people out at different socials hosted by our Student Bar Association or various other law school organizations. Those are probably my favorite. We have a couple of bars, including Becky's, The Clevelander, Bottom's Up and Velvet Dog that are within 10 minutes walking from school, and a lot of the socials are held at these establishments. Since we're right downtown, there's a variety of different options available: all sorts of restaurants, the theatre district and a bunch of different bars. Personally, I enjoy going down to the Warehouse District—there are a couple of great restaurants there, including the Chophouse and Johnny's Downtown, and a bunch of great bars, including Liquid, Fusion, Blind Pig and the Dive Bar. There's no lack of things to do, that's for sure!

Status: Current student, part-time
Dates of Enrollment: 8/2004-Submit Date
Survey Submitted: April 2005

Law school has its share of parties and social organizations. As stated there are many organizations, all of which provide social interaction. Cleveland is a city that parties. The Flats are down the street from the campus. If nightlife is what you want, Cleveland has it.

Status: Current student, full-time
Dates of Enrollment: 8/2003-Submit Date
Survey Submitted: April 2005

C-M has a decent social life. Much of it focuses around socials that different student organizations host at bars and clubs. Favorite student dive bar, Becky's, is right down the street. Becky's has cheap beer and good food. Many students also go out to the Warehouse District on the weekends.

Status: Current student, full-time
Dates of Enrollment: 8/2001-Submit Date
Survey Submitted: April 2005

There are many groups and organizations that sponsor any number of social events, and they are a great way to meet other students as well as faculty and staff. I met a lot of people doing volunteer activities with the Student Public Interest Law Organization. Downtown Cleveland is home to many bars and restaurants for those looking to escape the school to have some fun.

Status: Current student, full-time
Dates of Enrollment: 9/2003-Submit Date
Survey Submitted: April 2005

The law school hangout is Becky's, mostly because it is cheap and very close to campus. Rascal House Pizza is another favorite. On the weekends, many students go out in Lakewood (about 12 minutes from school) or the Warehouse District (five minutes from school). The nightlife in Cleveland is very good. There is a wide range of great restaurants. C-M Law puts on many great events during the year and hosts concerts and a Jazz festival. The law school has a wide variety of clubs and student groups with about five or six of them being very large and very active organizations.

C-M has an exhaustive list of activities and clubs students can participate in. The organizations do a lot of great things but don't require very high-level commitment. Since most students are focused on their studies, clubs and organizations tend to take a back seat.

Status: Current student, full-time
Dates of Enrollment: 8/2004-Submit Date
Survey Submitted: April 2005

And then there's Becky's! It seems like this is the watering hole for most law students, located just behind the school. Great place! There are many student-run organizations at the school and all of them are constantly having functions and events—you name it!

Status: Current student, full-time
Dates of Enrollment: 8/2003-Submit Date
Survey Submitted: April 2005

The school is located in downtown Cleveland—the good part! The school is located just 10 minutes walking from Jacob's Field, Browns' Stadium and all the restaurants and bars you could imagine. Many different law school groups hold socials and different bars in the city where students can relax and socialize without spending any money; how great is that?! Moreover, the different bar associations often host events where C-M students are exclusively invited to participate.

Status: Current student, full-time
Dates of Enrollment: 6/2003-Submit Date
Survey Submitted: April 2005

What social life? This is law school, right?

Read all of Vault's Law School Surveys at www.vault.com/lawschool — get complete surveys on top law schools, expert advice on applicaton essays, LSAT prep and more.

V∧ULT CAREER LIBRARY 505

The Ohio State University

Michael E. Moritz College of Law
Admissions Office
55 West 12th Avenue
Columbus, OH 43210-1391
Admissions phone: (614) 292-8810
Admissions e-mail: lawadmit@osu.edu
Admissions URL: http://moritzlaw.osu.edu/admissions/

 ## Admissions

Status: Current student, full-time
Dates of Enrollment: 8/2003-Submit Date
Survey Submitted: October 2005

Ohio State takes the admission process seriously. They really do try to select a diverse and talented student body. While numbers are important, they are not the sole consideration.

Status: Alumnus/a, full-time
Dates of Enrollment: 8/1999-5/2002
Survey Submitted: March 2005

Wonderful scholarships available for students who show an early interest in Moritz, including full tuition and living allowance.

Status: Alumnus/a, full-time
Dates of Enrollment: 8/1996-5/1999
Survey Submitted: January 2005

Good undergraduate credentials and a good LSAT score are essential. I recommend taking a prep class for the LSAT because it is emphasized by most law schools.

Status: Alumnus/a, full-time
Dates of Enrollment: 8/2001-5/2004
Survey Submitted: January 2005

Admission requirements get higher every year as the school is flooded with more and more applications. OSU does not favor in-state residents, so out-of-state students have just as good a chance for admission. I applied as a resident of Missouri, and I had a 162 LSAT (88 percent) and 3.87 GPA. One of the reasons I applied was because OSU is really good about giving out-of-state residents in-state tuition after the first year.

If you are married (as I was), you get AUTOMATIC in-state residency beginning with your first year of law school if your spouse works full-time while you attend school. So I received in-state tuition immediately, even though I was from Missouri.

OSU has a rolling admissions policy. The Early Admission deadline is October 15th, which will usually result in a decision by December 20th. That is how I was admitted. I believe the normal application deadline is either February or March 15th. Anyway, for the application, I had to submit my GPA, LSAT, application form, personal statement and two letters of recommendation. The personal statement could be "generic," rather than written especially to explain why you want to attend OSU as opposed to another law school. I know from working with admissions personnel that all applications are sorted into three piles: definite admission, definite denials, and in-between applicants. Those who are in-between go to the full admissions committee.

Once you are admitted, OSU sends out letters of scholarship awards in late January. Since Moritz's $30 million donation, 10 students a year receive a full ride, as well as a $5,000 stipend for living expenses. Other students receive substantial scholarships. I had my first and second year of law school paid for by OSU scholarships.

Once you receive a scholarship award letter, the school will actually invite all scholarship recipients to attend scholarship weekend, which is always held in late February. It is a three-day event when the law school puts you up in a nice hotel, feeds you, provides activities and social functions, and works very hard to give you a feeling for what it's like to be a law student at OSU. I attended this weekend, and it definitely sold me on OSU. I now help out with the program every year to help attract the best students. Beyond scholarships, the admissions office works very hard to attract the best and brightest students. We call every single admitted applicant in the spring to congratulate them personally on their admission and to answer any questions they might have about OSU or law school in general. I received this phone call after I was admitted, and I have helped call other admittees ever since.

Overall, the admission experience is VERY valuable at OSU. The admissions office bends over backwards to answer all your questions and make sure you feel comfortable with the school you choose. In addition to scholarship weekend, the admissions office hosts several open houses throughout the year for interested applicants to see what law school is all about. You can sit in on classes or even shadow a student for the day. This is particularly helpful for applicants who are admitted but do not receive scholarships—it allows them to get an idea of what the school is like.

> **The school says:** The admissions office does host several open houses every year.

Status: Current student, full-time
Dates of Enrollment: 8/2003-Submit Date
Survey Submitted: March 2005

Moritz gets tougher to get into every year; it's a school on the rise. The best part of the application process is how easy it is to also apply for the tremendous number of scholarship and financial aid opportunities at the same time. The admitted students weekends look pretty interesting, too.

Status: Alumnus/a, full-time
Dates of Enrollment: 8/2001-5/2004
Survey Submitted: October 2004

Ohio State's application process is in all ways similar to those of most other law schools. Applicants must complete an application form with their background information. Applicants also have to submit three reference letters, a personal statement detailing why they want to attend law school, another short essay and scores for the LSAT test. There is no interview in the application process. Ohio State is a fairly selective law school with entering class sizes of around 175 people.

> **The school says:** "Entering class sizes are around 220 people."

Status: Alumnus/a, full-time
Dates of Enrollment: 8/1995-5/1998
Survey Submitted: April 2004

I simply requested an application, submitted it and was accepted. I believe I wrote a brief essay as part of the admissions process, although I do not believe it was heavily weighted.

 ## Academics

Status: Current student, full-time
Dates of Enrollment: 8/2003-Submit Date
Survey Submitted: October 2005

Quality of the educational experience is exceptional. Many of the professors co-authored the text from which they lecture. Workload is strenuous but manageable. Strengths—ADR, Criminal Law, Transactional Law. Weakness—Environmental Law.

Status: Alumnus/a, full-time
Dates of Enrollment: 8/1999-5/2002
Survey Submitted: March 2005

Extremely challenging with some of the finest faculty in the nation. Able to get the classes I wanted.

Status: Alumnus/a, full-time
Dates of Enrollment: 8/1996-5/1999
Survey Submitted: January 2005

The academics and professors were excellent. I felt very confident that I had a firm understanding of the major areas of the law when I graduated.

Status: Alumnus/a, full-time
Dates of Enrollment: 8/2001-5/2004
Survey Submitted: January 2005

As with all law schools, OSU is competitive—but definitely not cutthroat. The first year is the worst because you don't know what to expect. There is always a lot of pressure to join Law Review after the first year, but students should not feel pressured to do this if they are not interested. The academic programs are great! The first year is very general, but the school offers a Legislation course that teaches students to apply interpretive rules to determine legislative intent behind statutory law. This was one of the most boring classes I took at the time, but it probably one of the most useful classes in practice.

The professors are very approachable—they all have an open-door policy even after their "official" office hours are over. Many classes are hands on, like Trial Advocacy. And there are a ton of clinics: Criminal Defense Clinic, the Prosecution Clinic, the Student Housing Legal Clinic, the Justice for Children Practicum, the Legislation Clinic, and the Judicial Externship. The only class that was difficult to get into was commercial law, which was a yearlong class taught by Professor Doug Whaley, who is a renowned professor in the field.

> **The school says:** "Professor Whaley has retired, but is continuing to teach. This fall, he will teach Commercial Law as an emeriti professor."

The professors are extremely distinguished—OSU can BUY the very best professors on the market thanks to Moritz's $30 million! The workload is what you make of it. I will give you my guidelines, and I graduated with honors. But everyone works differently, so some people may not need to work this hard and others may need to work harder, depending on the way you learn. First-year, you should expect to spend about five to six hours per night on homework—that is after the first month when you will freak out on everything and spend 12 hours on a single case! Second-year, you will be very busy with Appellate Advocacy, journal or moot court, as the case may be.

Homework will probably only take two or three hours of reading cases because you will be faster by then. But you will have additional work to make up for it. Expect to spend six or seven hours a day outside of class for both reading and extra stuff. Third-year can be really busy or really not, depending on how you plan it. If you are managing a journal or on a moot court team, chances are that you will be almost as busy as you were second year—sometimes. Third-year has its slow times and its busy times.

Status: Current student, full-time
Dates of Enrollment: 8/2003-Submit Date
Survey Submitted: March 2005

The professors are absolutely topnotch. The perfect combination of well-known academics and student-centered teachers. For example: in 2005, the U.S. Supreme Court will hear a case argued by Moritz professors on both sides, with students contributing a great deal of research and other work to the case. 2004's Election Central was another example: students worked closely with faculty to make Moritz the headquarters for election experts all over the national media in the time leading up to Election Day 2004 and all through that long night. The courses are comparable to any top law school, the classes are a very comfortable size (not so big that you don't get attention, but not so small that you get called on more often than you want to be), and the teaching method is mostly a flexible Socratic Method that uses more volunteers than random picks by profs. A good variety of courses.

Status: Alumnus/a, full-time
Dates of Enrollment: 8/2001-5/2004
Survey Submitted: October 2004

The quality of classes at Ohio State's law school is generally high, and the school is known for its high-quality programs in alternative dispute resolution, criminal law, and business law. If you're interested in health care law, admiralty or some other specialty, then Ohio State is probably not for you. Professors at Ohio State tend to be very personable and approachable and the quality of the teaching varies, but is generally very good. There are ample opportunities for students to obtain paid research positions with professors they are interested in working with.

The first-year grading process is mandatorily set so that approx 25 percent will get A's in a class, 50 percent will get B's and 25 percent will get C's. After the first year, the grading curve is not so strict, and professors have more leeway to award the grades they think students deserve. Grading is blind, so professors do not know which student's exam they are grading as they grade it. It is generally easy to get into desired classes, although some of the most popular classes do close and some students end up shut out. The scheduling process allows each student to preference one class per year and be practically guaranteed to get into it. Even if a student gets closed out of a class, there is a waitlist system, and, if they go and speak to the professor, the professor might allow them into the class anyway. Overall, I had no difficulty scheduling the classes I wanted to take while I was there.

> **The school says:** "A new grading policy is in effect for first-year students: the first-year curve is approximately 25 percent A's, 55 percent B's and 20 percent C's."

Status: Alumnus/a, full-time
Dates of Enrollment: 9/1995-5/1998
Survey Submitted: October 2003

I really loved OSU Law. People aren't supposed to like law school and coming back to school as a second career, I was skeptical, but Ohio State won me over. At orientation, we were told that the school cared about teaching and it's true. The average quality of instruction is excellent. The best is simply superb. Out of 30-odd classes, I had two that were sub-standard and over a dozen that were as good as any classes I have ever had, despite having had lots of good education at "more prestigious" institutions.

Ohio State is seriously underrated by the *U.S. News & World Report* rankings. The professors are excellent and accessible. The best of them were in the neighborhood of the smartest—and nicest—people I have ever met. The education is practical rather than theoretical. One is taught a lot of law and relatively little theory about the law. The other students were bright, friendly and noncompetitive. The facilities are OK—a newish building melded on to an old one, but basically rather blah. Still, I turned down half the Top 10 to go to OSU Law (financial reasons), and I don't regret it one whit.

Status: Alumnus/a, full-time
Dates of Enrollment: 8/1993-5/1996
Survey Submitted: May 2004

The program was very academic—the classes were challenging and taught by exceptional faculty who were very interested in the students. The workload was heavy but not overwhelming, especially after the first year.

Status: Alumnus/a, full-time
Dates of Enrollment: 8/1995-5/1998
Survey Submitted: April 2004

The academic level was excellent. The professors were outstanding and extraordinarily knowledgeable in their fields, sometimes beyond. The workload was significant, but not beyond what one anticipates upon entering law school.

Read all of Vault's Law School Surveys at www.vault.com/lawschool — get complete surveys on top law schools, expert advice on applicaton essays, LSAT prep and more.

VAULT CAREER LIBRARY 507

Employment Prospects

Status: Current student, full-time
Dates of Enrollment: 8/2003-Submit Date
Survey Submitted: October 2005

Ohio State has a massive alumni network. If you are in the top half of your class, and you are personable, you will have no problem obtaining a great job. Furthermore, if you are in the top 10 percent, you will be competitive for almost any federal clerkship.

Status: Alumnus/a, full-time
Dates of Enrollment: 8/1999-5/2002
Survey Submitted: March 2005

Graduating high in the class provides an endless list of opportunities.

Status: Alumnus/a, full-time
Dates of Enrollment: 8/2001-5/2004
Survey Submitted: January 2005

Let me qualify my answer first by saying that the entire legal market is experiencing difficulty with the economy. Period. So employers are hiring fewer law school graduates. That said, OSU has an EXCELLENT reputation across the country—if they don't know your law school, they will at least know the football team! But the law school is also ranked among the Top 30 or so in the country, and its ranking will likely rise as the $30 million is spent on amazing improvements.

Most of my class went into private practice, and several went into government or public service work as well. Others went to work for companies and still more decided they didn't want to practice law. The on-campus interview process is helpful, but students shouldn't put all their eggs in one basket. No matter how awesome the office of professional development is, not everyone can get a job from on-campus interviewing when there just aren't enough jobs to go around because of the economy.

Students sometimes get bitter about OCI (on-campus interviewing), but that is usually because they took no proactive efforts to network and explore all their opportunities. OCI is great, but the fact is that most students don't get their jobs from OCI. That's not a flaw with OSU, it's just a fact of EVERY law school. Only the best and the brightest are snatched up right away on campus. The others have to work a little harder to find their dream job. But everyone ends up happy.

Status: Current student, full-time
Dates of Enrollment: 8/2003-Submit Date
Survey Submitted: March 2005

D.C., Chicago and New York employers come by in spare numbers, but Columbus, Cleveland and other Ohio cities are the major recruitment markets. Which is fine, considering how huge those legal markets are. Columbus has over 700 law firms, including some really big ones with offices all over the country (and world). I've never met someone who wanted to work in another city (such as D.C., Chicago, and NY) that wasn't able to get work there. Students who want to work there put in the extra legwork to paper the towns with their resumes and visit the different cities for interviews, and it tends to pay off pretty well (especially if the student has good grades, of course).

> **The school says:** "In 2006, Moritz Law is hosting job fairs in Chicago and New York. In 2007, a New York job fair will be added."

Status: Alumnus/a, full-time
Dates of Enrollment: 8/2001-5/2004
Survey Submitted: October 2004

Ohio State's law school is well-regarded in Ohio, which is where my job search has been centered. For the most part, graduates end up taking law firm jobs after graduation, but students also take jobs in government, public interest or non-legal fields. The year I graduated, I think around 60 percent of grads had jobs as of graduation, and it was a poor year because the job market was very tight. The college's placement office works to keep an active alumni registry so that students can network with alumni who work in their fields or geographical

locations of interest. The college's placement office also oversees a pretty good on-campus interview program in both the fall and the spring. Most of the employers that participate are law firms, so if you are interested in government or alternate careers, the on-campus program will probably not be enough for you. However, the placement office does allow students access to a number of databases where legal job postings can be found and it also offers reciprocity whereby students who are looking for jobs in other states can receive job postings posted through other law schools. Ohio State also has several class offerings that have practical components that include internships. There is a Prosecution clinic where students are able to work with a nearby county prosecutor's office. Personally, I enrolled in the Legislation clinic and was placed in an internship with the Ohio Department of Insurance.

> **The school says:** "In 2006, 83 percent of Moritz Law graduates were employed as of graduation. For the Class of 2005, 98.9 percent of the graduates were employed nine months following graduation. An average of 130 firms interview on campus most years.
>
> "The college now hosts an on-site job fair in February for government and public interest employers. In 2005, the college created the position of director of public service and public interest within the career services office. This individual focuses on advising students who are interested in public interest and government sector jobs, honors programs, and fellowships. She also coordinates the judicial clerkship and the Public Service Fellows programs and serves as the LRAP coordinator."

Status: Alumnus/a, full-time
Dates of Enrollment: 9/1995-5/1998
Survey Submitted: October 2003

Almost all OSU Law graduates pass the bar and are working in legal careers within a year of graduation. It's regarded as the best law school in the state and has a good regional reputation (in the eastern Midwest—from Illinois through western Pennsylvania and West Virginia), but lacks the national clout of more prestigious schools. Still, people get jobs at top law firms in other cities and receive prestigious federal clerkships if they are at or near the top of their class. In my class, several people got federal appellate clerkships, another several federal district court clerkships. People who want to stay in Ohio couldn't do better.

Status: Alumnus/a, full-time
Dates of Enrollment: 8/1993-5/1996
Survey Submitted: May 2004

I had several interviews. The career placement coordinator at the time was only interested in placing candidates with large law firms, one of which is where I work. However, I believe that has changed.

Status: Alumnus/a, full-time
Dates of Enrollment: 8/1995-5/1998
Survey Submitted: April 2004

Almost all large law firms in the state interviewed on campus, and a number of prestigious law firms from New York and Chicago interviewed on campus as well. The school seemed to be held in high regard by most firms.

Quality of Life

Status: Current student, full-time
Dates of Enrollment: 8/2003-Submit Date
Survey Submitted: October 2005

The area surrounding the law campus has recently been renovated to prevent students from seeing the surrounding downtown poverty. Students have access to the new RPAC rec center, which is an awesome workout facility.

Status: Alumnus/a, full-time
Dates of Enrollment: 9/2000-5/2003
Survey Submitted: May 2005

Housing was no problem; I was married after my first year. Campus was an easy walk and there were no fears arising from crime in those times.

Status: Alumnus/a, full-time
Dates of Enrollment: 8/1999-5/2002
Survey Submitted: March 2005

Great city and a great school. Not all about the classes—fun and interesting classmates.

Status: Alumnus/a, full-time
Dates of Enrollment: 8/1996-5/1999
Survey Submitted: January 2005

Great program. Great college town.

Status: Alumnus/a, full-time
Dates of Enrollment: 8/2001-5/2004
Survey Submitted: January 2005

There is ample housing and the law school is actually in the process of constructing The Gateway Project, which will be very nice apartment buildings across from the law school. They will be for only law and graduate students, so there will only be serious students there.

The law school has a brand new cafe in the building that serves soup, salad, sandwiches nd espresso. It has a very nice dining room. There is also another lounge in the law school with a refrigerator, microwave, big-screen TV and a pool table. In case you want something else, the law school is right across from the student union, which houses about 15 restaurants. The law school is located on the edge of campus on one of the busiest streets in town, so there are a lot of people out there. There are some safety issues if you are walking alone late at night or if you leave your laptop someplace unattended, but that is going to be the case in all big cities. I moved there from a small town in Missouri, and I never felt unsafe or uncomfortable.

> **The school says:** "The Gateway Project opened in the fall of 2005 with 190 apartments available for law students. The project combines apartments, shops and offices along the 'Main Street' of the University District and creates a dynamic urban neighborhood. Among the project's anchor tenants are an eight-screen movie complex, restaurants such as Panera Bread, and a Barnes and Noble Bookstore. In addition, there are plans for 35 to 40 more restaurants, clubs, stores and banks and other personal service venues to locate in the Gateway."

Status: Current student, full-time
Dates of Enrollment: 8/2003-Submit Date
Survey Submitted: March 2005

It's not that competitive here, and people tend to work together a lot. Professors here are flexible, which is nice, and very accessible to discuss things when you get confused—that definitely improves the quality of life. The people here are generally very friendly, and the school tends to look out for its students pretty well, I think. Plus, you get some of the perks of being at the best law school in a state with some incredible opportunities (e.g., law firm open houses, opportunities to get credit clerking for judges and state legislators).

Status: Alumnus/a, full-time
Dates of Enrollment: 8/2001-5/2004
Survey Submitted: October 2004

Ohio State's law school has a very collegial atmosphere. It is competitive, but students tend to get along very well and I never heard any horror stories about books disappearing from the library or anything like that. The law school's student body was pretty diverse, with about an equal mix of men and women, a large number of African American students, as well as students of other races and ethnicities. Also, there were a decent number of non-traditional students, such as older students working on a second career.

Ohio State has a huge campus that will be difficult for somebody who is unfamiliar with it to get used to finding his/her way around. The good thing is the law school is contained in one building.

Parking at Ohio State is both scarce and expensive. I recommend purchasing a pass for one of the nearby parking garages to avoid having to arrive really early in the morning to get surface lot parking. The garage passes will run you close to $500 per year, though. Overall, parking is probably the most frustrating thing about Ohio State. An alternative is to use the Columbus City bus system, which has a stop right outside the law school. There is also a campus shuttle system in case you find that you have to park far away from the law school.

Most students at Ohio State's law school rent housing off campus, but there is some on-campus housing for grad students. I lived about 20 minutes away in an apartment. I found that this worked out well. Especially since I had another law student for a roommate and could split the cost of rent and bills. I personally would not recommend living close to campus because there is a bit of a crime problem near campus. Ohio State has really nice facilities. I frequently used the gyms there, and there is a rec center about a three-minute walk from the law school. Also, Ohio State just added a brand new state-of-the-art rec center in another location that is just gorgeous.

Status: Alumnus/a, full-time
Dates of Enrollment: 8/1993-5/1996
Survey Submitted: May 2004

The campus area is nice, generally safe. There is plenty of on-campus and off-campus housing at reasonable prices.

Status: Alumnus/a, full-time
Dates of Enrollment: 8/1995-5/1998
Survey Submitted: April 2004

Housing immediately surrounding the campus is not the best, but nice housing exists just a few miles away. Columbus, Ohio is generally a nice place to live and offers an entertaining nightlife.

Status: Alumnus/a, full-time
Dates of Enrollment: 9/1995-5/1998
Survey Submitted: October 2003

Columbus is a fairly decent place to live. It's cheap and has most of what one might want in a city of one million, including lots of eateries ranging from cheap to expensive. Decent student housing within walking or biking distance is affordable. (I biked from two miles away). The campus area is rather run-down and tawdry-looking, and is being reconstructed. The area around the law school has been almost entirely torn down. It was fairly sleazy when I was there, and women were somewhat nervous about walking alone, but that may have changed with the deconstruction of the area. I never knew or heard of anyone in law school who was actually a victim of street crime. The OSU campus is huge, but law students rarely get far away from the law school itself, which is merely a tolerable place to spend time. The law library is large and excellent, but windowless.

 Social Life

Status: Current student, full-time
Dates of Enrollment: 8/2003-Submit Date
Survey Submitted: October 2005

Like any major university, there are a host of activities and organizations to get involved with. Buckeye sporting events are taken pretty seriously. Like almost any major campus, the degree of your involvement is up to you, but the potential is almost infinite.

Status: Current student, full-time
Dates of Enrollment: 8/2002-Submit Date
Survey Submitted: May 2005

If you like to drink, then OSU is right for you. Most of the school events revolve around going out to the bar and so forth. Social life outside of the law school is good.

Read all of Vault's Law School Surveys at www.vault.com/lawschool — get complete surveys on top law schools, expert advice on applicaton essays, LSAT prep and more.

VAULT CAREER LIBRARY **509**

Status: Alumnus/a, full-time
Dates of Enrollment: 9/2003-Submit Date
Survey Submitted: May 2005

There was no problem with restaurants, except earning enough money to pay! Plenty of activities, particularly the law journal and the legal fraternity.

Status: Alumnus/a, full-time
Dates of Enrollment: 8/1999-5/2002
Survey Submitted: March 2005

A great amount of fun. Big 10 football—nothing finer than a Saturday game.

Status: Alumnus/a, full-time
Dates of Enrollment: 8/2001-5/2004
Survey Submitted: January 2005

There are TONS of single law students. And there are a TON of opportunities to do social activities. The law school has over 40 organizations, which include a co-ed social fraternity. The members seem to have a lot of fun. The law school also organizes a bowling league, a rugby team, and a soccer team every year. The best bars in the area (according to my single friends) is Brothers. There is a TON of great dining; if you like exotic cuisines, then Columbus is the place for you! The Ethiopian cuisine (The Blue Nile) and the Indian cuisine (Taj Mahal) are campus favorites.

Status: Current student, full-time
Dates of Enrollment: 8/2003-Submit Date
Survey Submitted: March 2005

There's something here for everyone, really. Columbus is a surprisingly incredible town with A LOT to do. There will always be groups of students who like to go out to bars and clubs a lot, and a group that prefers to do more low-key things most of the time. Everyone will feel compelled to spend a few weekend nights devoted to studying, of course, but really with Columbus's huge and varied social scene, OSU's campus social scene and the events that the law school puts on from time to time, there is always something to do—and students do them.

Status: Alumnus/a, full-time
Dates of Enrollment: 8/2001-5/2004
Survey Submitted: October 2004

Ohio State's law school has plenty of social opportunities. You tend to develop a group of friends pretty quickly at the beginning of your first year. I recommend attending some of the orientation activities because this is when a lot of people meet each other. Ohio State is located in Columbus, the state capital. Columbus is a very nice city with lots of restaurants of every conceivable type, as well as bars, clubs, museums, concerts and professional sporting events.

The popular hang out spots for law students include bars like B. Hampton's, the Varsity Club and Four Kegs, which are all near to campus. I always liked to go to a bar called Char Bar, which is downtown, because it tends to be more low key than campus area bars. One of the greatest things about Columbus is the shopping, especially at the Easton Towne Center outdoor mall.

I didn't really date when I was in law school, but I know plenty of people who did. There have been several couples I know who met while we were in law school and who are now married or engaged to be married. Overall, I think it was not difficult for singles to meet people at Ohio State or elsewhere in the Columbus community.

Status: Alumnus/a, full-time
Dates of Enrollment: 9/1995-5/1998
Survey Submitted: October 2003

Law students don't have a social life. There are bars and restaurants within walking distance; the law school is at the south end of campus on High Street, the main drag through town. Last time I was in town, I saw that a lot of the places we used to go to are now out of business, partly due, I think, to the deconstruction of the immediate area.

Status: Alumnus/a, full-time
Dates of Enrollment: 8/1993-5/1996
Survey Submitted: May 2004

There were several social things to do in and out of law school.

Status: Alumnus/a, full-time
Dates of Enrollment: 8/1995-5/1998
Survey Submitted: April 2004

Bars and restaurants are abundant.

 **The School Says**

Students at the Moritz College of Law at the Ohio State University have a variety of ways to learn more about the law and to become involved in the legal community.

In the 2005-06, Mentoring and More @ Moritz kicked off with more than 200 students and mentors. One of the first of its kind in the nation, the program serves as a bridge between the theory and the practice of law. Students join with faculty and mentors who are practicing lawyers at a series of luncheons to hear a prominent speaker address pressing issues and current trends in the law. The presentations are followed by discussions between mentors, students, faculty and guests and serve as a springboard for encouraging continued, informal contact between participants.

Through the Distinguished Practitioners in Residence Program in Business Law, Moritz Law students have the opportunity to learn from and exchange ideas with extraordinarily accomplished and prominent practitioners. The practitioners live in the law student apartment building near the law school and participate in college activities during their visit, in addition to teaching a concentrated, one-credit course.

Distinguished Practitioners for 2006-2007 include: Scott V. Simpson, partner, Skadden, Arps, Slate, Meagher & Flom (London); Roger E. Warin, partner, Steptoe & Johnson (Washington, D.C.); Gail Block Harris, of counsel, Simpson Thatcher & Bartlett (New York); Dan D. Sandman '73, chief legal and administrative officer, general counsel and secretary, U.S. Steel (Pittsburg); and William B. Chandler, chancellor, Delaware Court of Chancery.

Moritz Law students may enroll in summer programs in Oxford and Washington, D.C. in addition to a new semester-long program in Oxford. The programs are all approved by the American Bar Association.

Students who study at Oxford during the summer are part of a five-week program that is housed at St. Anne's College, one of the 40 schools that make up the University of Oxford. Law faculty from Ohio State teach in tandem with British professors.

The Semester Program, began in 2005, is a joint venture between the Moritz College of Law and the University of Georgia School of Law. Students take four courses and receive 12 semester hours of credit toward the juris doctor degree. Three of the four courses address comparative law subjects and are taught in a traditional group classroom setting. The fourth course is a supervised research tutorial, in which each student writes a lengthy research paper on a comparative or international law topic of his/her choosing.

The Washington Program is directed by Professor Peter Swire, a prolific scholar and successful teacher on privacy, the law of cyberspace, legal ethics and other subjects. (From 1999 to early 2001, while on leave from the Moritz College of Law, he served as the Clinton Administration's Chief Counsel for

Privacy.) Students in the program have the opportunity to engage in externships in the nation's capital accompanied by a high-quality academic program.

The opportunities at the Moritz College extend far beyond these special programs and the challenges of its classrooms. Look at the Moritz College of Law (http://moritzlaw.osu.edu/index.php) to learn more about the five academic journals, 16 moot court teams, more than 60 student organizations and an array of other opportunities that allow aspiring lawyers and leaders to develop skills that will help them make a difference in the lives of others.

Read all of Vault's Law School Surveys at www.vault.com/lawschool — get complete surveys on top law schools, expert advice on applicaton essays, LSAT prep and more.

VAULT CAREER LIBRARY 511

University of Cincinnati College of Law

Admissions & Financial Aid Office
College of Law
University of Cincinnati
P.O. Box 210040
Cincinnati, OH 45332
Admissions phone: (513) 556-0078 or (513) 556-6805
Admissions fax: (513) 556-2391
Admissions e-mail: admissions@law.uc.edu
Admissions URL: http://www.law.uc.edu/admissions/

 ## Admissions

Status: Alumnus/a, full-time
Dates of Enrollment: 8/2001-5/2004
Survey Submitted: March 2006

There was an interview; the school looks at academics and LSATs, usually requiring the 85th percentile in each. Other factors also come into play, such as real-world experience. The school is not the most selective in the country, but has its pick of top qualified students regionally and is selective.

> **The school says:** "Interviews are not a part of the admissions process at UC. However, students are strongly encouraged to visit the campus either through individual appointments or an open house program. The University of Cincinnati College of Law does a full file review for each student and asks each applicant to submit the following: a completed application for admission, two letters of recommendation through the LSAC Letter of Recommendation Service, application fee, personal statement and the supplemental information questionnaire (optional)."

Status: Alumnus/a, full-time
Dates of Enrollment: 8/1996-5/1999
Survey Submitted: March 2006

UC likes people that really want to be UC students. If you are on the bubble, visit the campus and ask for a tour. They will respond.

Status: Current student, full-time
Dates of Enrollment: 8/2003-Submit Date
Survey Submitted: February 2004

Regular law school admission process—application, single essay and the usual LSDAS info. The school strives for diversity so don't be shy about what might be different about you: living overseas, military experience, first in family to attend law school or college, non-traditional student.

> **The school says:** "Admission to the College of Law is based upon a careful evaluation of each individual's application file. Although the admissions committee, composed of faculty, students and administrators, relies heavily on the undergraduate grade point average and the Law School Admission Test (LSAT) score to determine the applicant's academic potential, other non-quantitative factors believed to be relevant to success in law school are considered. These factors include the quality of the applicant's previous education, trend of academic performance, participation in community service or significant extracurricular activities, employment experience, graduate work and thoughtful letters of recommendation.

> "University of Cincinnati College of Law begins accepting applications on September 1. Students who apply by December 1 through the Early Decision Program will be notified of their status by January 15. Regular Admissions decisions will be

made on a rolling basis. The admissions committee continues to evaluate application files until late spring. Every applicant will receive a decision letter (accept, waitlist, deny) within four to six weeks of being notified that his/her file is complete."

 ## Academics

Status: Alumnus/a, full-time
Dates of Enrollment: 8/2001-5/2004
Survey Submitted: March 2006

The courseload is somewhat heavy and the academic program is topnotch Grading the first year is on a curve. Thereafter, grades are on a B average. Some classes are difficult to get into. The academic program was excellent for preparation for the bar and the practice of law.

Status: Alumnus/a, full-time
Dates of Enrollment: 8/1996-5/1999
Survey Submitted: March 2006

The professors and classes were excellent. The first year, the grading is a rigorous curve system and the competition is tight. The second and third years were a little better. The workload is entirely self-driven and results-oriented. Some people worked constantly and received the highest marks. Other people did the bare minimum and barely passed. If you want to be high in the class, you need to work hard. The good news is you can still have fun as long as you know how to schedule your plans.

Status: Alumnus/a, full-time
Dates of Enrollment: 9/1970-0/1973
Survey Submitted: April 2004

This school has some of the best law school professors in the nation. Many are graduates of some of the Top 10 law schools for their particular areas of expertise.

> **The school says:** "Recently, three new faculty have joined the College of Law. Barbara Black joined the faculty as director of the Corporate Law Center. She is a graduate of the Columbia University Law School and Barnard College. Jacob Cogan joins the faculty to teach in the area of international law. He is a graduate of the University of Pennsylvania, Princeton University (masters and PhD in history), and Yale Law School. Timothy Armstrong joins the faculty to teach in the area of intellectual property law. Prior to joining the college, he worked as an assistant director for the Berkman Center for Internet and Society at Harvard Law School."

Status: Current student, full-time
Dates of Enrollment: 8/2003-Submit Date
Survey Submitted: February 2004

Grading is curved at a B and the workload is challenging, but it should be expected—this is law school.

Status: Current student, full-time PhD
Dates of Enrollment: 9/1999-Submit Date
Survey Submitted: September 2003

Mid- to high-quality facility, as to be expected there is always a crank or two. Courses limited due to small number of students.

> **The school says:** "The University Of Cincinnati College Of Law will offer over 100 upper-level courses for the 2006-2007 academic year. This number does not include important credit-earning opportunities such as law reviews, other journals and moot court. For reference, a typical law student will take between 22 and 28 courses during their second and third years,

depending on interest and co-curricular opportunities for earning credit."

 Employment Prospects

Status: Alumnus/a, full-time
Dates of Enrollment: 8/2001-5/2004
Survey Submitted: March 2006

Job placement depends on performance at the school. It is relatively difficult for those in the bottom 10 percent of the class to find employment. Regionally, the college does a good job of placing its graduates, particularly those in the top 50 percent of the class, with large firms. Several graduates each year obtain federal clerkships. The school is respected by law firms, particularly those located in Ohio.

> **The school says:** "The University of Cincinnati's employment statistics routinely exceed national figures. Most recently, 97 percent of the Class of 2005 was either employed or enrolled in a full-time degree program within nine months of graduation, compared to a national average of 89.6 percent. Graduates are also employed throughout the country, evidenced by the Class of 2005 securing jobs in 17 different states and the District of Columbia. Collectively, the Center for Professional Development staff has some 20 years of practical experience and is committed to helping all students, regardless of class rank or GPA, to get where they want to go."

Status: Alumnus/a, full-time
Dates of Enrollment: 8/1996-5/1999
Survey Submitted: March 2006

The employment prospects from UC are mostly in Ohio, Kentucky and Indiana. Unless you are in the top 10 percent of the class it is very difficult to get a great job outside of a three-hour radius.

Status: Alumnus/a, full-time
Dates of Enrollment: 9/1970-0/1973
Survey Submitted: April 2004

Almost 100 percent of the students find good jobs in law within four months of graduation. Some of the more financial successful grads are in the $2M bracket.

Status: Current student, full-time
Dates of Enrollment: 8/2003-Submit Date
Survey Submitted: February 2004

Plenty of internship opportunities. OCI appears to be getting better. The Center for Professional Development now has three full-time attorneys working their magic.

Status: Current student, full-time PhD
Dates of Enrollment: 9/1999-Submit Date
Survey Submitted: September 2003

University is generous with research and assistantship stipends.

 Quality of Life

Status: Alumnus/a, full-time
Dates of Enrollment: 8/2001-5/2004
Survey Submitted: March 2006

Housing is sub-par in the immediate area—but the university is in the process of constructing additional housing, which should vastly improve the housing situation. The campus itself has undergone significant renovations in the past several years, making it superior in terms of facilities. Crime on campus is nonexistent. Off-campus crime can be an issue once you begin to move several blocks away.

Status: Alumnus/a, full-time
Dates of Enrollment: 8/1996-5/1999
Survey Submitted: March 2006

Cincinnati is a great city. You can get anywhere in town within 15 minutes. The campus is improving all the time. The cost of living is low and you can live in a nice area like the Gaslight District and still only be three minutes from campus.

Status: Alumnus/a, full-time
Dates of Enrollment: 9/1970-0/1973
Survey Submitted: April 2004

I loved the Clifton area; Graeter's Ice Cream and Skyline Chili are favorites of all the locals. I also believe this the Cincinnati location to be one of the most affordable.

Status: Current student, full-time
Dates of Enrollment: 8/2003-Submit Date
Survey Submitted: February 2004

The school borders a bit of a depressed area, but there is a LOT of ongoing construction so there is hope that things are of improving. There are plenty of housing and dining possibilities. Crime and safety are about what you'd expect in an urban environment, but the police presence is noticeable.

> **The school says:** "Cincinnati is a progressive three-state region that offers world-class arts and culture, hospitality, major league sports and recreation. *Fortune* magazine called Greater Cincinnati one of the Top 10 Places to Live and Work. Cincinnati's live music scene has earned us a place on *Esquire* magazine's 'Top 10 Cities that Rock' list. The city is an important business and legal center for the region. It is the seat of the United States Court of Appeals for the Sixth Circuit and the U.S. District Court for the Southern District of Ohio. In addition, 10 Fortune 500 companies, more than 300 foreign-owned companies and over 685 law firms are located in the tri-state area."

 Social Life

Status: Alumnus/a, full-time
Dates of Enrollment: 8/2001-5/2004
Survey Submitted: March 2006

The social opportunities at the College of Law are superior. The law school is close-knit, averaging class sizes around 120 per year, and provides a great opportunity to get to know your classmates. Woodies, across the street, is a frequent haunt of college of law students.

> **The school says:** "At the University of Cincinnati College of Law, our first-year class is limited to 135 students. The total enrollment for the College of Law is limited to 385 students. Together with our 12:1 student-faculty ratio, our enrollment helps students build rewarding relationships with professors and a close-knit, intellectually adventurous community with their peers."

Status: Alumnus/a, full-time
Dates of Enrollment: 9/1970-0/1973
Survey Submitted: April 2004

Everything is close, so you don't need a car. People are friendly, they have 3.2 beer, the Red's and Bengals; what more could you ask for? You won't have much free time anyway if you plan to graduate in three years.

Status: Current student, full-time
Dates of Enrollment: 8/2003-Submit Date
Survey Submitted: February 2004

Plenty of bars and restaurants, but we're just too busy to really enjoy them.

Read all of Vault's Law School Surveys at www.vault.com/lawschool — get complete surveys on top law schools, expert advice on applicaton essays, LSAT prep and more.

VAULT CAREER LIBRARY 513

Get the BUZZ on Top Schools

Read what STUDENTS and ALUMNI have to say about:

- Admissions
- Academics
- Career Opportunities
- Quality of Life
- Social Life

Surveys on thousands of top programs
College • MBA • Law School • Grad School

The University of Toledo College of Law

Office of Admissions
College of Law
The University of Toledo
Toledo, OH 43606-3390
Admissions phone: (419) 530-4131
Admissions e-mail: law.admissions@utoledo.edu
Admissions URL: http://law.utoledo.edu/admissions/

Admissions

Status: Current student, part-time
Dates of Enrollment: 8/2004-Submit Date
Survey Submitted: May 2006

Everyone in the admissions office is very easy to approach and quite helpful. In my case, I was a transfer student from another law school. Unfortunately my LSAT scores were not strong enough to get in on my first attempt, so I enrolled at another law school and worked hard to maintain a sufficient GPA in order to transfer to UT Law.

Status: Current student, full-time
Dates of Enrollment: 8/2005-Submit Date
Survey Submitted: May 2006

I found the admissions process easy. The essays were fairly straightforward, there was no interview and the web site walked applicants through the whole process easily. I heard back from them before Christmas.

Status: Current student, full-time
Dates of Enrollment: 8/2005-Submit Date
Survey Submitted: May 2006

I was recommended to go to UT Law, which I had never heard of by a very close professor of mine from undergrad. I appreciate his advice because the law school and I are a great fit. It is important to listen to what others have to say when trying to decide what school to attend, particularly for law school, it is difficult to transfer so it is likely you will stay at the institution you first attend. Visiting the campus and meeting other students that will be in your incoming class is also important in order to get a feel for whether the campus is the right place for you. The admissions process is quite tedious and one must be willing to fill out everything completely, even though it might take a long time. Apply to several schools and do not bet on getting into a particular law school because each school is looking for something different. One might not get into a not-so-great school but get into an excellent school even though all the information sent was the same. Make sure to get all the required materials in as soon as possible because generally you will receive an answer that much sooner.

Status: Alumnus/a, full-time
Dates of Enrollment: 9/2002-5/2005
Survey Submitted: April 2006

The application process was easy—the application is online and can be submitted online. Despite being a tier-two school, it awards an incredibly large number of full-tuition scholarships to incoming students.

> **The school says:** "The University of Toledo College of Law was ranked in the Top 100 Law Schools by the 2006 edition of *U.S. News & World Report*. It gave out $1.5 million in scholarships for the 2005-06 academic year."

When a student is in the process of selecting a school, the student visits the school and meets with professors and can sit in on classes. This was the only school I visited where the professors took the time to speak with me. There is no interview but students applying for admission are required to submit an essay.

> **The school says:** "The submission of a personal statement is optional."

Status: Current student, full-time
Dates of Enrollment: 8/2003-Submit Date
Survey Submitted: April 2006

The best part is that UT has a free online application (essay was optional!!). After I found out I was accepted, the letter was quickly followed up with notice that I had received a full tuition scholarship, renewable for all three years as long as I kept a 3.6 GPA. All this with just a 157 LSAT. I believe the school looks at resumes and undergrad transcripts as much as LSAT scores to get a good mix of students with diverse backgrounds. The scholarship program attracts a great group of high caliber students, many who got accepted to higher-ranked schools but are wary of loads of student loan debt so go to UT.

> **The school says:** "A grade point average of 3.6 is not required for students to renew full tuition scholarships. Students can renew full-tuition scholarships for all three years of their legal education as long as they maintain a 3.3 grade point average."

Status: Alumnus/a, full-time
Dates of Enrollment: 8/2002-5/2005
Survey Submitted: April 2006

The selections process at the University of Toledo College of Law was as simple and straightforward as they come. The application is available online at www.utlaw.edu. The application was neither lengthy nor arduous and did not require any essays. The school was exceedingly prompt with an acceptance response, which was very helpful in allowing me to start planning for the future.

Status: Alumnus/a, full-time
Dates of Enrollment: 8/2002-5/2005
Survey Submitted: April 2006

The University of Toledo College of Law has one of the friendliest faculty and staff I have met in my academic years. The admissions office does what it takes to help you in making a decision. Personally, I did not have the funds to go to law school. An admissions officer personally met with me and patiently listened to what I had to say. The financial aid office at the College of Law is independent from the rest of the university. They work with you to ensure a competitive interest rate. The College of Law and the faculty made sure that finances did not stand in the way of a quality education for me. The online application process makes applying for admission free. I also recall that the admissions fee was waived if the application was done online.

> **The school says:** "On July 1, 2006, The University of Toledo merged with the Medical University of Ohio, creating a university that now offers a great range of programs. In fact, the new University of Toledo is one of only 17 public universities in the country to possess colleges of business, education, engineering, law, medicine and pharmacy. The merger also gives UT a research budget of more than $56 million, positioning the university as a future medical and technical powerhouse. The new University ranks third in the state in extramural research funding and is the third largest public university in Ohio. For law students, the merger adds to already existing opportunities for cross-disciplinary study on campus."

Status: Current student, full-time
Dates of Enrollment: 8/2005-Submit Date
Survey Submitted: April 2006

Campus visits and tour; law preview day in NYC; online free application; immediate offer of scholarship prior to application and scholarship recipient dinner.

Read all of Vault's Law School Surveys at www.vault.com/lawschool — get complete surveys on top law schools, expert advice on applicaton essays, LSAT prep and more.

VAULT CAREER LIBRARY 515

The school says: "The College of Law admissions committee considers many factors in deciding whether to offer a spot in each year's class. Committee members do look at the traditional indicators, such as LSAT scores and grades, but they also look closely at the applicant's transcript to determine the type and degree of difficulty of courses taken during the applicant's undergraduate studies. Essays are also read and taken into consideration."

Status: Current student, full-time
Dates of Enrollment: 8/2004-Submit Date
Survey Submitted: April 2006

The application process was really simple—you can just apply online with no application fee. (I'm sure there's an application process for mailing in hard-copies that is equally simple, but I only used the online process.) The personal statement is optional, but I would recommend it. There is no interview. The school is becoming more selective, but they still offer full scholarships to about one-third of the incoming class just based on the online application. With such a user-friendly process (no fee, easy application, good shot at a scholarship), there's no drawback to applying.

Status: Alumnus/a, part-time
Dates of Enrollment: 8/1992-12/1995
Survey Submitted: March 2006

I had excellent undergraduate and graduate grades and 98th percentile LSAT score, so admission was not an issue. In fact, I was offered a scholarship to attend full-time, but preferred part-time attendance so I could work.

Status: Alumnus/a, full-time
Dates of Enrollment: 8/1991-5/1994
Survey Submitted: January 2004

The admission process is pretty straightforward. No tricks. No gimmicks. No problems.

Academics

Status: Current student, part-time
Dates of Enrollment: 8/2004-Submit Date
Survey Submitted: May 2006

Each of my professors has been an excellent mentor in his/her particular field. I have been thoroughly impressed at the depth of their knowledge and skills.

Status: Current student, full-time
Dates of Enrollment: 8/2005-Submit Date
Survey Submitted: May 2006

I cannot imagine having better professors for 90 percent of my classes, they were extremely thorough, clear, and made even dry subjects interesting. The professors are personable, make an effort to learn student's names and are ALWAYS available for any questions and help outside of class. I had no trouble scheduling the classes I wanted for next year. There is a heavy workload for the first year, but the professors coordinated so that when things were really hectic for one class, they other classes had shorter, smaller assignments.

Status: Current student, full-time
Dates of Enrollment: 8/2005-Submit Date
Survey Submitted: May 2006

All the professors are incredibly intelligent and know their topics extremely well. They are more than willing to meet with you outside of class to answer questions or even to talk about non-academic things. Everyone learns a lot from the classes, even if their grade is not that high. One should expect to not always be the best student in the class because, unlike undergrad, everyone in the class is fairly intelligent and understands the material. Law school is very competitive in the sense that in order to be at the top of the class, one must know practically everything about the course since everyone else will know almost everything as well. There is not a great deal of work in regards to writing out homework or writing papers, but law students spend hours upon hours reading and writing outlines. The earlier one can start an outline, the better because there is a lot of information covered in a semester. It is easy to get far behind.

Status: Alumnus/a, full-time
Dates of Enrollment: 9/2002-5/2005
Survey Submitted: April 2006

The best thing about UT is the professors. There is not a single one who is no willing to take time out of his or her schedule to meet with students. For th most part, the professors are also excellent in the classroom—each has a uniqu teaching style and it's clear that so many of them love their jobs. The first-yea grading scale is difficult because it is on a C curve, but for second and thir years, it is on a B curve. During the first year, the classes are assigned and eac student takes the same classes (except for those starting out part-time). Durin the second and third years, students work to complete their required courses, bu are also able to select other classes in which they're interested. Those classe are first come, first serve, but I never had a problem getting the classes that wanted. The workload is heavy, but I think it's comparable to the workload a any law school.

Status: Current student, full-time
Dates of Enrollment: 8/2003-Submit Date
Survey Submitted: April 2006

First, UT's professors are very accessible and have all been extremel personable and open to student interaction. All the profs offices are located i the same building as classes, so students run into them in the hallways, at lunc time and at speakers. I found the classes to be challenging and my professors t have brought a lot of their personal experience into the classroom via stories tha brought lectures to life. Grading is on a curve, which was a bit concerning a first but I realized that if you keep apace with your classmates (study group were abundant and very helpful) it all works out in the end. UT offers lots o two-credit electives, many in the IP area, many in assorted other areas. UT als offers weekend one-credit "flex" courses in other select areas that are grea overviews of other areas of law (I took a class on international human rights an one on international terrorism). Workload was extremely manageable—eve during my Law Review semester. Professors are easy to talk to and you ca always check in with them if you feel overwhelmed.

UT also has a very active speaker series bringing in speakers on various contemporary law issues sometimes two times a week. I've heard both Sandra Day O'Connor and Ruth Bader Ginsburg in my three years here. I understand Scalia is already signed up to visit next year. Other speakers in the past have included Erwin Chemerinsky on con law issues, Joshua Dressler on criminal law issues, a Day After series for speakers who have recently argued in front of the Supreme Court and many area politicians including U.S. Representatives Marcy Kapture and John Conyers.

Status: Alumnus/a, full-time
Dates of Enrollment: 8/2002-5/2005
Survey Submitted: April 2006

The law program at UT is exceptional. The teachers are always available for assistance outside, attentive, helpful while in class, and open to suggestions and student feedback throughout the semester. Classes are not difficult to get into. The first year of classes is selected and assigned by the administration. The second- and third-year classes are selected entirely by the student. With a number of "certificates of concentration," the classes and available areas of focus are vast. On the rare occasion that a class is full, the administration has been exceedingly helpful and responsive to expanding the class to meet student needs. The grading is done anonymously and fairly by the professors. Once the grades are completed after final exams the professor gets a list of the grades with student names to allow for adjustment in the case of exceptional participation and effort by a student that is "on the border" between grades. The workload is comparable to any law school. Each class meets two or three times a week and has nightly reading assignments of varying length based on subject matter. All professors are required to provide a syllabus at the beginning of the semester, and through three years every professor I had kept to the syllabus precisely. Professors are also very attentive to other exams, midterms and projects in other classes and will often adjust their own syllabus and workload to accommodate students.

Status: Alumnus/a, full-time
Dates of Enrollment: 8/2002-5/2005
Survey Submitted: April 2006

believe that the faculty of the College of Law is not well publicized. The college boasts some of the best and the brightest in the country. It's the University of Toledo label that is bringing the excellent roster of legal scholars down. Some of the classes such as Evidence and Criminal Procedure are really hard to get into. But that is because the professors are really, really good at teaching those courses and are very knowledgeable in the area. The University of Toledo has a hard grading curve. Unlike other universities that have started inflating the grades, University of Toledo grading is hard but generally fair. The workload was manageable, although you have to work hard every day. Law school is tough, so studying only during the exams (as in undergrad) is only going to end up in disaster. The UT faculty and staff work with you even during the exams to accommodate personal problems and conflicts.

Status: Current student, full-time
Dates of Enrollment: 8/2005-Submit Date
Survey Submitted: April 2006

Very strong faculty and high quality of core first-year curriculum. No problems getting classes—set schedule for first year. Workload at times is heavy.

Status: Current student, full-time
Dates of Enrollment: 8/2005-Submit Date
Survey Submitted: April 2006

Great professors, great workload. I could not be happier.

Status: Current student, full-time
Dates of Enrollment: 8/2004-Submit Date
Survey Submitted: April 2006

Classes depend in large part on the professors teaching them. There seems to be a high turnover rate among the faculty lately, and some of my professors had never taught before or were pretty new. That said, professors are really accessible. They are generally around the building or in their offices with the doors open, available for students' questions. Grading is done on a curve for almost every class. Popular classes generally don't fill up immediately; I've been able to get every class I wanted with no difficulty. I think the workload is standard—a bit terrifying at first, but you get used to it and understand how much work you need to do throughout the semester to be prepared for the exam at the end.

Status: Alumnus/a, part-time
Dates of Enrollment: 8/1992-12/1995
Survey Submitted: March 2006

The professors are topnotch. The workload is typical, grading is fair and classroom interaction is enlightening.

Status: Alumnus/a, part-time
Dates of Enrollment: 8/1996-5/2000
Survey Submitted: September 2003

Bell curve is lower than most other schools. Weeding out process the first year.

The school says: "The University of Toledo College of Law admits students with the idea and expectation that they will succeed in their law school studies and in their legal careers. Faculty members and administrators have traditionally had open door policies for students who would like assistance outside of class. A great degree of camaraderie exists among the student body, and students often form study groups to help one another with the material. The coursework is demanding. During the first year of law school, many students find there's a period of adjustment to the rigors of legal study. However, there are many opportunities and support systems available for students to seek help throughout their law school careers."

Employment Prospects

Status: Current student, full-time
Dates of Enrollment: 8/2005-Submit Date
Survey Submitted: May 2006

Career services is extremely helpful! They offer constant e-mail postings of jobs, mock interviews, resume help, seminars and are always available to help one on one. It is so busy during classes, it's nice to know they are going to alert us of deadlines, options and decisions that need to be made.

Status: Current student, full-time
Dates of Enrollment: 8/2005-Submit Date
Survey Submitted: May 2006

The alumni network at UT Law is outstanding, particularly in the area of Toledo. Because of this, during the school year it is very easy to get in contact with alumni who are willing to help you through your law career. The alumni range from working in small firms to large firms and from local government to federal government. Thus, for whatever law topic a student is interested in, there is a UT Law alum who can be in contact with the student to help through law school and give advice. Getting involved in groups at school is one of the best ways to get involved particularly by getting a mentor (or two). Even lawyers who are not alumni are willing to help law students throughout their law school career.

Status: Alumnus/a, full-time
Dates of Enrollment: 9/2002-5/2005
Survey Submitted: April 2006

UT is becoming better known throughout the legal community. While the name is still not well known, it is becoming more recognizable as there are more grads moving away from Ohio. Career services is not as helpful as it could be (most certainly due to understaffing) and unfortunately tends to focus on those students with the best employment prospects. A student who is self-motivated, however, will be able to schedule interviews and meetings on his/her own. The school tries to connect alumni with students interested in a certain geographical area, and from what I understand, this has become more successful due to the former dean's encouraging alumni to sign up for mentor programs through the web site. The school does provide for some on-campus recruiting, but most of those firms are based in Ohio. UT also has an internship program and some clinics that provide varying experiences for first- and second-year students. Judicial clerkships are encouraged, but there is not a system in place for informing students about the application process or assisting those students who would like to apply.

The school says: "In the last academic year, The University of Toledo College of Law Career Services office has increased staffing. This enables career services staff to give even more one-on-one individual attention to students as they navigate through the multiple career paths available to them in the legal field. Career services staff coordinates a healthy on-campus recruiting season every year. Staff members also coordinate a large number of group resume collections requested by hiring partners in firms across the country, including firms in Arizona, California, Florida, Georgia and New York."

Status: Current student, full-time
Dates of Enrollment: 8/2003-Submit Date
Survey Submitted: April 2006

As a small school, UT's on-campus recruiting opportunities are few. And Toledo firms are generally small so local firms may do interviews on campus but offer few jobs. I understand the alumni network is being updated and revamped so it should be much more helpful in coming years. For me, I mostly did self-guided public interest career searches but had access to Equal Justice Works Career Fair and other conferences. In the area of immigration law, I found great experience with Toledo's legal aid organization and the legal clinic on campus is a great way to get experience. Although they don't normally do immigration work in the legal clinic, the professor is very flexible and open to new things so I was able to partner with the local legal aid org. and do an asylum case for credit! Two other 3Ls and I were able to obtain federal clerkships, many other students local and state clerkships. The school has an externship program to place students with local judges (including the federal court and state appeals court) for credit

Read all of Vault's Law School Surveys at www.vault.com/lawschool — get complete surveys on top law schools, expert advice on applicaton essays, LSAT prep and more.

VAULT CAREER LIBRARY   517

during school. This is a great opportunity to do career searching/preparation while still in school. UT is working gradually on its prestige in the community and it is ever-growing. We're in the Top 100 this year and many local firms have commented that the quality of student is getting better and better. The top 20 students of each class have the opportunity to participate in Univ. of Michigan's on-campus recruiting every fall as well.

The school says: "The University of Toledo College of Law's national alumni network is extensive and growing. The career services staff coordinate with alumni affairs staff to make countless contacts with alumni from across the country. As a result of these contacts, numerous alumni have offered to give career guidance to UT Law students. Also, students are encouraged to attend alumni receptions in geographic areas in which they have an interest in practicing. The career services office also supports many events throughout the year that connect alumni practicing in particular areas of law with students who are interested in that area of law. Overall, UT Law's career services and alumni affairs staff have focused their energies in recent years in facilitating even more of these contacts between students and alumni.

"All students are provided with the same information about on-campus interviewing opportunities at the University of Michigan in Ann Arbor, about 45 minutes away from Toledo. Participation is not limited to the top 20 in each class."

Status: Alumnus/a, full-time
Dates of Enrollment: 8/2002-5/2005
Survey Submitted: April 2006

Employment prospects are good, but not great. The UT College of Law has a good reputation that continues to improve every year. Within the Toledo and surrounding communities UT alumni have great prospects. Outside of Northwest Ohio the prospects diminish significantly. Jobs are certainly available and prevalent, but the jobs are provided based on individual merits with little to no "help" based on the reputation of the school. The alumni of UT are always exceptionally helpful and willing to extend a helping hand to a fellow UT alum. This alumni network significantly helps ease the tension of job and internship searches.

The school says: "The University of Toledo College of Law is increasingly gaining a positive national reputation. This is, in part, due to UT Law's exceptional base of alumni who are federal judges, state supreme court justices, high-ranking public officials, CEOs, general counsel in Fortune 500 companies, partners in some of the largest law firms in the country, key players in public interest work, international law practitioners, professors and administrators at law schools across the country, in addition to more non-traditional career paths such as sports management and communications. The national alumni network includes representation from people practicing in states all over the country and from some foreign countries as well, including England, Belgium and Nigeria. As UT Law alumni continue to achieve, opportunities for students continually expand. Recent efforts to capitalize on the College of Law's national alumni base are focused on giving students more opportunities to connect with alumni who are in a position to lend guidance to students seeking to begin their careers in various regions of the country. These mentor relationships can help guide students in decisions such as where to live, which firms to contact and what to expect in terms of quality of life."

Status: Current student, full-time
Dates of Enrollment: 8/2005-Submit Date
Survey Submitted: April 2006

No problem with local placements in the Ohio-Michigan area—extensive alumni network and well-placed. Very successful externship program for summer placements, including federal and state clerkships. Alumni are helpful as are local firms. Internships are readily available.

Status: Current student, full-time
Dates of Enrollment: 8/2004-Submit Date
Survey Submitted: April 2006

Jobs and help are available through the alumni network. Alumni are really grea with helping students and giving tips and a foot in the door, especially wit geographical areas outside of Northwest Ohio. I think the prestige of the schoo with employers is unjustifiably low, the alumni know it, and therefore the alumn are more motivated to help students get their foot in the door with firms. I regard to internships, any student who wants a public service internship with court or government program can get one through the school. The internshi director is great.

 ## Quality of Life

Status: Current student, full-time
Dates of Enrollment: 8/2005-Submit Date
Survey Submitted: May 2006

UT is in a nice neighborhood, the campus is extremely safe and the law schoo in particular has a very low theft rate. There are nice lounge areas for student to meet, the classrooms are comfortable and the library staff is very helpful.

Status: Current student, full-time
Dates of Enrollment: 8/2005-Submit Date
Survey Submitted: May 2006

The campus is very nice and fairly small (I came from a large undergraduat university more than twice the size of UT). I prefer to have the smaller campus for a graduate program because there is a strong connection among all th students and we are all very friendly towards one another. There is quite a bit o off-campus housing, but generally people live farther from the school to ge away from the undergraduate housing. The neighborhood is generally safe an there are several activities to do nearby.

Status: Alumnus/a, full-time
Dates of Enrollment: 9/2002-5/2005
Survey Submitted: April 2006

UT does not provide housing for law students. However, UT has severa surrounding neighborhoods, which are beautiful, safe and very affordable. The law school does have a cafe, but most students go off campus to eat. There are many restaurants and coffeeshops located nearby. If you wanted to eat free lunch every day, however, you likely could because there is a speaker or even almost every day and the school provides pizza for these events. The law school is in a safe area (all of UT is a safe campus) and students can park right outside the law school, which makes it safe to leave the building at night. The City o Toledo is a great place to be for law school—it does not have a ton of things to do, but does have its hidden treasures. One of the best things about Toledo is its surprisingly amazing parks system.

The school says: "Housing is provided on-campus for graduate students."

Status: Current student, full-time
Dates of Enrollment: 8/2003-Submit Date
Survey Submitted: April 2006

Toledo is a great bargain—cost of living, especially housing, is extremely affordable and there are great historical neighborhoods for those interested. I have lived 10 minutes from campus for three years in a shared house for $300/month and no problems with crime/safety. As with any city, there are area to avoid, but that easy to do here. All of the law school is contained in one building but the student union with food/coffee is a short walk away. Other fast-food restaurants are a short drive away. The larger campus is connected via a bike path to a major park and Toledo has lots of parks for biking, frisbee golf and ultimate. From campus, most everything in the city is a 10 or 20 minute drive including downtown law firms, courthouses and entertainment.

Status: Alumnus/a, full-time
Dates of Enrollment: 8/2002-5/2005
Survey Submitted: April 2006

The UT campus offers a state-of-the-art recreation center with a vast weight room, large array of cardiovascular machinery, four basketball courts, an indoor soccer court, climbing wall and other great amenities. The dining halls and bookstores are all readily accessible from anywhere on campus. Law students typically live off campus and there is no short supply of apartments or rental homes within five minutes of the campus. The housing ranges from cheap and cramped to country club living. Finding a location to live is no concern at all.

Status: Current student, full-time
Dates of Enrollment: 8/2004-Submit Date
Survey Submitted: April 2006

There isn't much assistance with housing, but I don't think any is really necessary—there is a picnic a couple months before the 1Ls start classes so that they can meet and maybe pick roommates. The law school has its own building with a couple big lounge areas but no hot food available, just vending machines and a little deli area with sandwiches/wraps/salads that's open during lunch hours. The neighborhood around campus is pretty nice, there are a lot of little restaurants and some decent bars. In terms of crime, there have been some problems with people stealing students' backpacks when the students leave their stuff unattended, but no crimes against people that I've heard of at all. The law building has wireless Internet, a computer lab, a four-story library, an auditorium, a legal clinic, a mock court room, its own career services and financial aid office, plus routine things like admission and administration.

> The school says: "Toledo is home to many amenities. A world-class art museum, nationally recognized libraries, minor league baseball team with a new baseball stadium, hockey team, science center, nationally ranked zoo, scenic river byways, an extensive metro park system, and beautiful residential neighborhoods are just some of the highlights. In fact, the UT campus itself has been named one of '100 most beautifully landscaped places in the country,' according to the *American Society of Landscape Architects*. Only 22 college campuses are on the list."

Status: Current student, full-time
Dates of Enrollment: 8/2005-Submit Date
Survey Submitted: April 2006

Very affordable area—low rent, low cost of living. Toledo has more to offer than is typically advertised—outdoor recreation, parks, lake, Toledo Museum of Art (nationally recognized and free), Toledo Zoo, theater and many restaurants, movie theatres and bars. Active region in sports—Detroit is one hour away. Locally—Mud Hens and much sports.

Social Life

Status: Current student, part-time
Dates of Enrollment: 8/2004-Submit Date
Survey Submitted: May 2006

UT Law offers several clubs and organizations. Furthermore, Toledo is home to many lively restaurants and first class attractions. The Toledo Zoo and the Toledo Museum of Art are both world-class.

Status: Current student, full-time
Dates of Enrollment: 8/2005-Submit Date
Survey Submitted: May 2006

The Student Bar Association hosts get-togethers at different bars almost every Friday night with discounted drinks, no cover charge and free wings. There are many organizations to be a part of and always something to do. Everyone in my class is friendly, there is a sense of community, and we try to help each other out.

Status: Current student, full-time
Dates of Enrollment: 8/2005-Submit Date
Survey Submitted: May 2006

There is an incredible social life with the other law students because of Bar Review (where students meet at a new bar each week). After first semester, we are all friends and there really is not the typical hostile competition between students that law schools often find. There is a medical school nearby so some law school and medical students date but there are also relationships between the law students. There are numerous events and activities the law school puts on that most students attend as well as activities put on by the different law clubs/groups, which are very beneficial as well.

Status: Alumnus/a, full-time
Dates of Enrollment: 9/2002-5/2005
Survey Submitted: April 2006

The social life at UT is what you make of it. Some students choose not to participate in the social life at all and others choose to participate in the varying activities the school and community provide. There are two Greek organizations for law students and those groups organize several social events throughout the year. Every Thursday night there is a Bar Review and the Student Bar Association chooses a bar where all the law students meet. The school also holds a Barristers Ball each year, which is like a law school prom. There are several other things to do in Toledo, including dining at the Docks, going to Mud Hens games or enjoying the fabulous Greek food the area has to offer. My favorite place is the Bronze Boar located in downtown Toledo.

Status: Current student, full-time
Dates of Enrollment: 8/2003-Submit Date
Survey Submitted: April 2006

UT Law has lots and lots of student organizations with a very active Student Bar Association. The SBA hosts a Bar Review at a selected local bar every week and hosts various other social activities throughout the year including a pig roast, Barristers Ball, fundraising 5K, and Grad Bash. Toledo has lots of bars, including lots of sports bars, and a growing downtown scene thanks to our minor league ball team, the Toledo Mud Hens. The Women's Law Student Association is especially active with a partnership with the local Toledo Women's Bar Assoc. for a mentoring program.

Status: Alumnus/a, full-time
Dates of Enrollment: 8/2002-5/2005
Survey Submitted: April 2006

The law school social scene is entirely different, but not necessarily separate, from the UT undergraduate scene. The law school has numerous student associations (sports law, women's law, black law students) that provide numerous outlets for involvement and entertainment. Each organization has a signature event or fundraiser each year that provides ample opportunities for students to socialize amongst themselves and with the faculty and administration. There are the typical fast-food restaurants within walking distance of the UT Law campus. A world-class mall and restaurants are all within a 10-minute drive. Restaurants in the area range from well-known chains (Outback, Hooters) to locally owned and controlled hidden gems (Charlie's, Coney Island, Tony Packo's). Downtown Toledo is a mere 10 to 15 minute drive from the law school campus. The revitalized downtown features renovated historic buildings with loft-style apartments and townhomes, restaurants, bars and clubs of all varities and for all ages. The downtown also features Fifth-Third Field, a state-of-the-art minor league baseball facility and home to the AAA Baseball Toledo Mudhens. When it's Hens season, the downtown area is quite the scene. In short, Toledo is a medium-sized city with all the advantages and scenes of a big city, but with none of the drawbacks.

Status: Current student, full-time
Dates of Enrollment: 8/2005-Submit Date
Survey Submitted: April 2006

Restaurants and bars are plentiful. School sponsors many speakers (with lunch provided). There are a variety of student groups—academic and special interest. I enjoyed most the speaker series and more socially, the Chili Goof-Off sponsored by the Environmental Law Group.

Read all of Vault's Law School Surveys at www.vault.com/lawschool — get complete surveys on top law schools, expert advice on applicaton essays, LSAT prep and more.

VAULT CAREER LIBRARY 519

Status: Current student, full-time
Dates of Enrollment: 8/2004-Submit Date
Survey Submitted: April 2006

There are a lot of student clubs, some better managed than others. The Student Bar Association is pretty active in planning 5K runs, weekly social events at bars, a lot of other student social activities (for example, we have an Ice Cream Day every semester), and public service things like blood drives and canned food drives. Another big thing at the school is the lecture series—the school brings in people (Congresspeople, judges, people who have argued before the Supreme Court, authors) to speak on different topics in the auditorium during lunch. The school doesn't schedule classes for anyone between 11:40 a.m. and 1 p.m., so people have time to go to lunch together, go to club meetings, or attend the speaker series. I don't know much about the dating scene—maybe about a quarter of all the students (including the evening part-time students) are married or in a serious relationship.

Status: Alumnus/a, part-time
Dates of Enrollment: 8/1992-12/1995
Survey Submitted: March 2006

There are always plenty of bars near campus. My favorites were the Pub and Charlie's Blind Pig. There are several good restaurants in the Toledo area, including J. Alexander's, Olga's, Ciao and the Olive Garden. When I lived on campus, there were always plenty of activities and parties. I'm not very familiar with the Greek system because I chose not to participate in it.

 The School Says

The University of Toledo College of Law offers a rich curriculum with plenty of electives, as well as the option to specialize in particular areas of the law. The college offers five certificate programs: Intellectual Property Law, Homeland Security Law, Environmental Law, International Law and Labor and Employment Law. The curriculum boasts a broad range of courses taught by full-time faculty as well as esteemed practitioners and scholars from around the world recruited to teach specialty courses.

Faculty members are prolific writers and respected experts in their field, but remain accessible and friendly to students. Their offices are located in a central area of the law school building, making them easy to find, and their doors are often open.

UT Law also boasts a widely respected speaker series. The College of Law brings in people of national prominence in their fields for noontime public talks that are enjoyed by students, faculty, staff, as well as members from the University and greater Toledo communities. Recent visitors include three U.S. Supreme Court Justices and four labor union presidents. The annual Day After series sponsors a talk from an attorney who is fresh from arguing a case in the U.S. Supreme Court. The annual Great Lakes symposium addresses the hottest environmental topics related to preserving the Great Lakes. Through the speaker series, students have a continuous stream of opportunities to interact with leaders in the law.

The College of Law building is completely wired. Students can access the internet from anywhere in the building. All classrooms are equipped with SmartBoards™ and the library offers plenty of computer workstations. Various areas in the law school are currently undergoing renovations to better serve students.

The college offers many opportunities for refining skills needed in the workplace. The College of Law Legal Clinic serves low-income clients on a wide variety of civil matters. Students also participate in the Domestic Violence Clinic, which enlists their help in prosecuting domestic violence crimes, and the Dispute Resolution Clinic, which has allowed law students to mediate hundreds of cases in the community.

Students who participate in the Public Service Externship Clinic often work in the chambers of federal and state judges, researching legal issues and drafting opinions. Students are also placed with a wide variety of public agencies where they are put to work on legal issues. The Reinberger Honors Program in Prosecution places students with prosecutors offices throughout the country during the summer.

Outside of class, students are active and friendly with a wide array of student groups. Students take advantage of the many amenities of Toledo and coordinate many charitable events. At UT Law, students don't have to choose between the excitement of intellectual challenge and the comforts of community. Here, they have both.

For more information, go to www.utlaw.edu. To contact the law admissions office, call (419) 530-4131 or send an e-mail to law.admissions@utoledo.edu.

University of Oklahoma College of Law

Admissions Office
300 Timberdell Road
Norman, OK 73019-5081
Admissions phone:(888) 298-0891 (toll-free); (405) 325-4728 (in Oklahoma)
Admissions fax: (405) 325-0502
Admissions URL: http://www.law.ou.edu/prospective/

Note: The school has chosen not to comment on the student surveys submitted.

Admissions

Status: Alumnus/a, full-time
Dates of Enrollment: 8/2000-5/2004
Survey Submitted: March 2006

Admission is fairly difficult, but that's to be expected, as it's a great education for a bargain price. High LSAT scores and undergrad grades are helpful. However, students with low LSAT scores and/or low grades may apply for a special program that allows them to start earlier than the rest of their class.

Status: Alumnus/a, full-time
Dates of Enrollment: 9/1999-5/2002
Survey Submitted: February 2005

I was a late applicant. The admissions office was very accommodating, allowing me to submit a "late" application. However, I was not considered for scholarships my first semester due to my late application. There was no interview.

Status: Alumnus/a, full-time
Dates of Enrollment: 8/2000-5/2003
Survey Submitted: September 2003

The admissions process at OU can be interesting. Apply early and commit early to have the best chance at receiving scholarships. OU has a full tuition scholarship based on undergraduate grades and LSAT score that when combined with the low cost of living, results in little or no debt at graduation.

Get to know the people in the admissions office. If you are from out of state, a visit will show you are serious and get you face time with the dean. Personal relationships can still play a big role for getting admitted in Oklahoma, especially for in-state students. Interviews are not required and I am not sure how much importance was placed on the essay.

I think they are simply trying to raise their rank through LSAT scores. When I arrived at OU, they began raising their standards in order to compete on a regional and national basis. The average LSAT score rose so quickly that half of the third-years when I was a first wouldn't have gotten into my class and the same could be said of my class with last year's 1Ls. As the class size shrinks, LSAT score requirements go up, so do the number of applications. Selectivity at OU could be at an all-time high.

Status: Alumnus/a, full-time
Dates of Enrollment: 8/2000-5/2003
Survey Submitted: April 2004

The school has become much more competitive over the past several years. The academic quality of the students has vastly improved as well as the number of applicants. A solid LSAT score, strong undergraduate performance and extracurricular activities are all heavily considered.

Academics

Status: Alumnus/a, full-time
Dates of Enrollment: 8/2000-5/2004
Survey Submitted: March 2006

Almost all of the classes and professors are very good. Due to various sized classrooms, popular classes can be larger. Therefore, it is usually fairly easy to get into the best classes. Enrollment is based on seniority, so students eventually get to take the classes they want.

Status: Alumnus/a, full-time
Dates of Enrollment: 9/1999-5/2002
Survey Submitted: February 2005

Classes were enjoyable overall. I had no problem enrolling in any classes that I wanted to take, and you are granted preference in your second and third years.

The grading is fair. The professors were good overall. There are a few outstanding professors and a few terrible ones. The workload is very manageable.

Status: Alumnus/a, full-time
Dates of Enrollment: 8/2000-5/2003
Survey Submitted: April 2004

The first-year program is topnotch. It is extremely challenging and a great value for the money. However, there is a lack of depth in the elective courses that you can take over the second and third year. This creates some scheduling issues since everyone wants to take the same courses.

Ultimately, the lack of a vast array of elective courses doesn't seem to matter that much in practice because all of the fundamental courses are offered. You never learn what you need to know to be able to completely practice an area of law from a course, anyway. But what you do walk away with from OU is the ability to learn the law in whatever field you desire, which is the ultimate goal of law school.

Status: Alumnus/a, full-time
Dates of Enrollment: 8/2000-5/2003
Survey Submitted: September 2003

OU has some excellent professors and some that are not so good. The class size keeps shrinking, so the availability of classes was never really a problem. Grading does vary from professor to professor but the grading is generally either disclosed or passed on from year to year. The workload is what you make of it. The professors are highly capable and are, as a whole, extremely available to students. I got to know many of them as people instead of merely as torturers. They are accomplished in their fields. Although the faculty does not compete with the credentials of Top 10 schools, they are extremely bright, motivated, excellent teachers as well as researchers.

In order to be competitive you will be required to commit your life to studying. There are plenty of opportunities to augment curricular studies with extras such as journals, mock trial, moot court and an exceptional clinical program.

Employment Prospects

Status: Alumnus/a, full-time
Dates of Enrollment: 8/2000-5/2004
Survey Submitted: March 2006

As long as students don't just count on the campus placement office, there are plenty of employers looking for OU graduates.

Read all of Vault's Law School Surveys at www.vault.com/lawschool — get complete surveys on top law schools, expert advice on applicaton essays, LSAT prep and more.

VAULT CAREER LIBRARY   521

Status: Alumnus/a, full-time
Dates of Enrollment: 9/1999-5/2002
Survey Submitted: February 2005

If you want to work in this region (e.g., Oklahoma, Kansas, Texas), I think our reputation is very good and employment should not be a problem. On-campus recruiting and internships are available for the better students.

Status: Alumnus/a, full-time
Dates of Enrollment: 8/2000-5/2003
Survey Submitted: April 2004

There are very prestigious employers that do recruit. The only problem is that there isn't the depth of employers as there is with top-tier schools. I think this is the main difference between OU and the top of the spectrum schools. OU simply does not have the national recognition as other big name schools to draw a large pool of employers, but this seems to be changing.

Status: Alumnus/a, full-time
Dates of Enrollment: 8/2000-5/2003
Survey Submitted: September 2003

Career prospects from OU are nationally competitive as long as you want to practice in Texas and are in the top 10 percent. After that, the market in Oklahoma is great if you were in top 25 percent and are happy with $45,000 to $75,000. If not, not a pretty picture.

The career services office is very responsive and does the best that it can do [in the current situation]. OU is rapidly gaining prestige with employers because, as they have raised their standards and attracted better students, employers are beginning to notice the change and are dipping down a little further into each class. Campus recruiting is good with a broad range of firms interviewing. Everyone from large national firms to sole practitioners interviews on campus for jobs and internships. My post-grad job came from an interview on campus at the end of my second year.

 ## Quality of Life

Status: Alumnus/a, full-time
Dates of Enrollment: 8/2000-5/2004
Survey Submitted: March 2006

Norman is a beautiful, low crime community. It's close enough to Oklahoma City to enjoy the advantages, but far enough away to avoid the negatives. Housing is very affordable.

Status: Alumnus/a, full-time
Dates of Enrollment: 9/1999-5/2002
Survey Submitted: February 2005

Very high. The law school was social, people were fairly laid-back, and my class had little competition. The cost of living in Norman is very low, and social life revolves around parties, OU football and other local traditions.

Crime was not much of an issue, although there are issues to be aware of.

Status: Alumnus/a, full-time
Dates of Enrollment: 8/2000-5/2003
Survey Submitted: April 2004

Excellent quality of life. Norman is a great place to live. Very low crime, friendly people and, most important, football-crazy. It's the kind of place where you can still leave your doors unlocked.

Status: Alumnus/a, full-time
Dates of Enrollment: 8/2000-5/2003
Survey Submitted: September 2003

Quality of life is great!!! Housing is plentiful, affordable and safe. Facilities underwent a complete overhaul and are brand new and beautiful. Norman, as a college town, has experienced a lot of growth recently and is now 100,000 strong. Most campus-area apartment complexes are mainly student occupied, making it easy to meet people and find things to do. Condos and houses are cheap to rent, and there are some very nice properties that are very close to campus. Crime is low, and safety is high. OU has its own police officers, and they patrol the law school parking lots and grounds regularly.

 ## Social Life

Status: Alumnus/a, full-time
Dates of Enrollment: 8/2000-5/2004
Survey Submitted: March 2006

The main campus has a club for every possible interest, and the law school has dozens (if not more) of clubs of particular interest to law students. Many students married people they met during law school, as law school affords little time for outside dating, particularly in the first year.

Status: Alumnus/a, full-time
Dates of Enrollment: 9/1999-5/2002
Survey Submitted: February 2005

While at OU, law school students frequently had parties. Social life also revolved around OU football, and frequent hangouts included The Library (a bar not the actual library), Bison Witches and Othello's. Live music was popular.

Status: Alumnus/a, full-time
Dates of Enrollment: 8/2000-5/2003
Survey Submitted: September 2003

Social life in Norman is not social life in NYC, or even Dallas. It is a fun town with quick access to Oklahoma City. Oklahoma City has undergone a complete renovation of their downtown area called "Bricktown." It is a fun place to party but the drive home can be perilous. Norman's scene is mainly bars with beer specials that cater to the 21 to 23 crowd.

First-year law students at OU are grouped into sections that have all of their classes together and form a ready-made group to go out with on Thursday or Friday nights, or Saturday, or sometimes on Sunday through Wednesday nights. There are a lot of fun beer bars, the staff are all young and friendly and there are always cheap drink specials to be found. Restaurants are OK; very few in Norman outside of national and regional chains. Oklahoma City has some excellent dining opportunities, as do surrounding communities.

Status: Alumnus/a, full-time
Dates of Enrollment: 8/2000-5/2003
Survey Submitted: April 2004

There are numerous bars and places to meet people. It's a beautiful campus with beautiful people. Go and have fun.

Lewis & Clark Law School

Office of Admissions
0015 S.W. Terwilliger Blvd.
Portland, OR 97219-7799
Admissions e-mail: lawadmss@lclark.edu
Admissions phone: (800) 303-4860
Admissions URL: http://law.lclark.edu/dept/lawadmss/

Admissions

Status: Alumnus/a, full-time
Dates of Enrollment: 8/2000-5/2003
Survey Submitted: December 2005

There are no interviews offered, but admissions officers definitely read your essays. They are looking for unique individuals from all over the country, and want to have a diverse group of students.

Status: Current student, full-time
Dates of Enrollment: 6/2004-Submit Date
Survey Submitted: January 2005

The admission process was simple and fast—your LSAT score is an important factor and if your GPA is above 3.0, you are fine.

> **The school says:** "Lewis & Clark does not have any GPA or LSAT cut-offs. Admission is not automatically granted based on a test score or grade point average. The admissions committee uses a holistic approach to reviewing files, meaning all required items are evaluated and considered thoroughly. Application requirements can be found at http://law.lclark.edu/dept/lawadmss/requirements.html. Questions about the application process should be directed to the Admissions Office."

Status: Alumnus/a, full-time
Dates of Enrollment: 9/1997-6/2000
Survey Submitted: April 2005

I applied and received my acceptance letter in the fall of 1997. At the time, I was working as a paralegal in New York City. Two professors from the law school reached out to me and talked me through the decision process. I was very impressed with both of the professors and really learned a lot about the school from them. They were very influential in my decision to accept at L&C.

Status: Alumnus/a, full-time
Dates of Enrollment: 8/1999-5/2002
Survey Submitted: March 2005

Admission requires submitting an application that includes short answers, a personal statement (essay), transcripts, letters of recommendation and your LSAT score. Although most students receive some scholarship aid, a high LSAT score (above 165) is very helpful in securing a substantial scholarship. As for advice, practice the LSAT, take a class if your scores are low and draft your essay well in advance of the deadline so you have time to get it proofread by a reliable person (hopefully, a former professor). Once you get admitted and receive a scholarship offer, call or write the dean and ask for more money. In my experience, the school usually increases the offer by at least a couple thousand dollars for students who request more, but you have to make the request BEFORE you accept the admissions offer, and it helps to be able to say you are entertaining other offers.

> **The school says:** "The application does not include any short answers. We require an application form, transcripts, LSAT score, personal statement, resume and two letters of recommendation.

"Scholarships are awarded based on the merit of one's application, with academic indicators given the heaviest consideration. No LSAT or GPA formulas or cutoffs are used when making awards. Approximately 40 percent of our incoming students receive a scholarship. Students may, at their discretion, contact the Admissions Office to request scholarship reconsideration. These are considered on a case-by-case basis; however, most requests are denied.

"It is best to complete an application for admission early in the process in order to be considered for scholarship. We recommend that you contact the Admissions Office directly with any questions about the application or scholarship process so that you receive the most accurate information."

Academics

Status: Alumnus/a, full-time
Dates of Enrollment: 8/2000-5/2003
Survey Submitted: December 2005

Some of the brightest minds teach at Lewis and Clark. They recently built a new library, study center and classrooms that are technologically state of the art. They incorporated nature and technology into the classrooms, and they are amazing.

Status: Current student, full-time
Dates of Enrollment: 6/2004-Submit Date
Survey Submitted: January 2005

Workload is a killer—you will read so much your eyeballs will nearly pop out. But the students are friendly and there is no cutthroat competition here. The upper-division students will usually help you if you are nice. The professors are kind and helpful. Some are very tough in class, but some are kind of easy later on. The quality of teaching is good as they are well-qualified professors from top schools and some have published books or are top prosecutors.

Status: Alumnus/a, full-time
Dates of Enrollment: 9/1997-6/2000
Survey Submitted: April 2005

Grading was tough and the curve has since been revised for the benefit of current students. I found the classes academically challenging, yet accessible. It was possible to schedule the "best professors" and the registrar was very accommodating in making your academic life work for you, especially since a lot of students work part time in the third year. The workload was fair, however I do not care for a system with one final per semester as the only source of your grade. Seminars with papers were challenging but very interesting.

Status: Alumnus/a, full-time
Dates of Enrollment: 8/1999-5/2002
Survey Submitted: March 2005

The professors are accessible (lots of one-on-one office time, if desired), talented and friendly. Small seminar classes leave a lot to be desired, though. They are student run and many students put in the minimum amount of prep and it shows. Grading is tough. Most classes are graded on a hard B- curve. Workload is also tough, but probably the same as most law schools. The school offers a part-time night program (it's a four-year program). The program is unique and commendable in that the classes are of the exact same quality and difficulty as day-student classes (they're taught by the same professors).

Read all of Vault's Law School Surveys at www.vault.com/lawschool — get complete surveys on top law schools, expert advice on applicaton essays, LSAT prep and more.

VAULT CAREER LIBRARY **523**

Employment Prospects

Status: Alumnus/a, full-time
Dates of Enrollment: 8/2000-5/2003
Survey Submitted: December 2005

Employers have a lot of respect for Lewis and Clark. They have the best environmental law program in the nation, and their IP and business law programs are highly regarded by employers.

Status: Current student, full-time
Dates of Enrollment: 6/2004-Submit Date
Survey Submitted: January 2005

Oregon, Washington and California are where 90 percent of all employment and environmental law students get national placement. Getting a first-year job is tough and if you want out-of-state, you should have contacts in that state. We have some people from Hawaii also and one student from Guam. There is a small international student population but there is no international placement. The career services are good and helpful; you may schedule and appointment and they will take you step-by-step into the process of getting a job. The maxim wait I have ever seen is two days so it is very good. They have good quality resume paper and a printer that students may use for free. They even have a conference room that you can book for an interview with an employer. Fax service is free for job-related faxes.

> **Regarding employment prospects, the school says:** "Lewis & Clark Law School alumni can be found in all 50 states, D.C. and several U.S. territories, as well as over 35 countries. The Career Services Office has a number of programs for students who wish to practice out of the region including mentor programs, networking opportunities through our alumni network, workshops on relocating, individual advising, externship programs, etc. Please refer to our Career Services web site for the most up-to-date information about placement and services (http://law.lclark.edu/dept/lscs)."

Status: Alumnus/a, full-time
Dates of Enrollment: 9/1997-6/2000
Survey Submitted: April 2005

In the Pacific Northwest, especially Portland and Seattle, the school's reputation is very good. Once you leave the Pacific NW, the fewer people know the school, except for its reputation as the top environmental law school. However, I think the students are incredibly bright and talented and succeed wherever they end up practicing.

Status: Alumnus/a, full-time
Dates of Enrollment: 8/1999-5/2002
Survey Submitted: March 2005

The degree has regional prestige, especially in the Portland area. But, the top local firms typically only hire recent graduates from the top 10 percent of the class. Top graduates can easily get judicial clerkships with the Oregon Court of Appeals, Oregon Supreme Court and U.S. District Courts. It's unusual, though, for graduates (even top ones) to get judicial clerkships with U.S. Courts of Appeals.

Quality of Life

Status: Alumnus/a, full-time
Dates of Enrollment: 8/2000-5/2003
Survey Submitted: December 2005

Quality of life is great. We had class outside on beautiful days. Dogs were allowed in class and in the library. First-year students get to participate in "Dean for a Day" where the dean will personally come to your class with a keg of beer and serve it to students. The professors are amazing and always available. It's a very familial environment.

Status: Current student, full-time
Dates of Enrollment: 6/2004-Submit Date
Survey Submitted: January 2005

Life? You're in law school. This is a small campus so not much life; you ha~ to look outside.

> **The school says:** "While law school is quite demanding, we recognize that how much time one spends studying truly depends on the individual. We encourage students to maintain a balance between law school, family and friends, and outside activities."

Status: Alumnus/a, full-time
Dates of Enrollment: 9/1997-6/2000
Survey Submitted: April 2005

Very safe and beautiful campus on the outskirts of Portland. It is a beautiful ci~ and great area to attend graduate school. Housing is plentiful and reasonable.

Status: Alumnus/a, full-time
Dates of Enrollment: 8/1999-5/2002
Survey Submitted: March 2005

For law school, the quality of life is great. Students are not overly competiti~ with one another—there's no book stealing or hiding. Students study in grou~ and help each other out. The school has a new library that is very nice.

Social Life

Status: Alumnus/a, full-time
Dates of Enrollment: 8/2000-5/2003
Survey Submitted: December 2005

Portland's great. There are tons of great restaurants and bars. You can par~ downtown for 99 cents an hour. It is safe. The entire city comes out for even~ whether it's a ball game in the stadium downtown or concerts by the river. It~ not a commercial city, so most places are unique. It's modern and progressive~

There is a restaurant called Portland City Grill that is on the 30th floor of~ building and has panoramic views of the city. It's an upscale restaurant, but aft~ 10 p.m. is happy hour when many of the appetizers are two or three dollars an~ underground parking is free. Tons of young people are there, especially o~ Thursday nights.

If you want to get out of the city, you can go hiking, camping, skiing or even t~ the coast. Most outdoor adventures are an hour to two hours away. Portland ha~ no sales tax, and if you have an Oregon identification card, many shoppin~ establishments in Seattle, Washington will also honor Oregon's no tax polic~ when shopping there.

Status: Current student, full-time
Dates of Enrollment: 6/2004-Submit Date
Survey Submitted: January 2005

You are in the Northwest, so if you are an outdoor person you'll love i~ Classmates are friendly but dating them is not a good idea. The area around th~ law school is beautiful. Hiking and skiing are both great activities to do. Durin~ summer, the coast is the place to be. You will love the beaches. Hiking into th~ hills for the weekend is also a great idea

Status: Alumnus/a, full-time
Dates of Enrollment: 9/1997-6/2000
Survey Submitted: April 2005

Very social student body. Lots of marriages from our class—in fact, I met m~ husband at school.

Status: Alumnus/a, full-time
Dates of Enrollment: 8/1999-5/2002
Survey Submitted: March 2005

Going to school at Lewis and Clark is more like going to work than going bac~ to undergraduate college. There's not much of a scene and definitely no Gree~ system. As a result, the school attracts more mature (older) students. This is a~

lus. The social scene is less cliquish and the students are typically friendly, teresting people with some life experience. Still, students do hang out together t local bars, especially across the river in Sellwood.

The School Says

Lewis & Clark Law School is fortunate to have one of the most beautiful law facilities in the nation—a campus adjacent to forested Tryon Creek State Park, a 645-acre wilderness preserve—while being only minutes from downtown Portland. Lewis & Clark believes in a balanced approach to legal education, assuring a solid theoretical foundation along with hands-on experience through clinics, internships, externships and pro bono opportunities. Students choose between a three-year day program and a four-year evening program. After the first year, students may select courses from either division. Our diverse student body enjoys a vast curriculum and our alumni practice all types of law. Lewis & Clark has special certificate programs in business and commercial law, intellectual property law, criminal law, tax law and enjoys a reputation for offering the nation's finest program in environmental and natural resources law. Student satisfaction at Lewis & Clark is high, largely due to the accessibility of the faculty, flexibility and number of program offerings, beautiful location and supportive atmosphere.

Lewis & Clark Law School enrolls 220 to 230 students from approximately 2,300 applications each year. The student body reflects a spectrum of ages, experiences and priorities. Close to 50 percent of the students are women. More than half of the entering class come from outside the region. About 18 percent of our students are members of minority groups. Three of every 10 students are married. Most students are full-time day students, but about 25 percent opt for the part-time or evening program.

Our students cite many reasons for choosing Lewis & Clark Law School. Probably the most important reason is the quality and attitude of the people on campus, primarily the sense of shared effort and mutual support among faculty, staff and students. Here a student finds all the hard work, long hours and intellectual challenge customarily associated with law school. However, students also discover that they are regarded as individuals by their fellow students, by their professors and by the staff. Both faculty and staff take special pride in seeing students progress and succeed.

Our bar passage and placement rates are high and our graduates take jobs throughout the nation. Today, our alumni practice everywhere from New York City and Washington, D.C.; from as far away as Alaska and Hawaii; and from Florida to California, and points in between. They can be found in every part of the United States and in several foreign countries, using their legal training in a diverse range of specialties.

To learn more about Lewis & Clark Law School, contact the admissions office at (800) 303-4860, lawadmss@lclark.edu or visit our web site at http://law.lclark.edu.

Read all of Vault's Law School Surveys at www.vault.com/lawschool — get complete surveys on top law schools, expert advice on applicaton essays, LSAT prep and more.

VAULT CAREER LIBRARY   525

University of Oregon School of Law

Office of Admissions
School of Law
1221 University of Oregon
Eugene, OR 97403-1221
Admissions phone: (541) 346-3846
Admissions fax: (541) 346-3984
Admissions e-mail: admissions@law.uoregon.edu
Admissions URL:
http://www.law.uoregon.edu/prospective/

 ## Admissions

Status: Alumnus/a, full-time
Dates of Enrollment: 9/2000-9/2003
Survey Submitted: November 2005

The school is selective. They give preference to in-state applicants. Pay attention to your application. Do a reasonable job on your essays and don't have typos.

Status: Alumnus/a, full-time
Dates of Enrollment: 8/2001-6/2004
Survey Submitted: October 2005

The school is focused on racial diversity right now. It is also having a problem recruiting women candidates. It took a long time for the school to respond to applications, but even at a seemingly late date, dean's scholarships were available. Bargaining for more scholarship dollars is possible, particularly if the candidate has another school and can get into a bidding war between the two. The top professors review candidate applications, and getting in has become tougher and tougher the last 10 years or so.

Focus on diversity, a broad range of experience (e.g., work, former career, family), devotion to pro bono if that is true for you (the school has won the state pro bono challenge the last few years in a row with over 10,000 hours posted by students each year). Finally, keep calling the admissions director. Also, if you can, do a pre-application interview with the admissions director and anyone else who will meet with you. That way, you can reference your meeting in your application cover letter.

Status: Alumnus/a, full-time
Dates of Enrollment: 8/2002-5/2005
Survey Submitted: September 2005

Much more competitive now, but still attainable if you are looking for a relatively affordable state school environment in the PAC NW. They really look to create a well-rounded, diverse student body, so the more you can do to distinguish yourself, the better. There is a good mix of non-traditionals and those fresh out of undergrad. All the basic advice applies—get good letters of recommendation, median LSAT score and show them you're interested. Visiting is also a great idea.

Status: Alumnus/a, full-time
Dates of Enrollment: 8/2000-5/2003
Survey Submitted: April 2004

Visited school first. Faced [with the choice] between the Univ. of Washington and Univ. of Oregon. Chose UofO because the faculty/staff remembered my name, knew who I was and seemed generally interested in me as a law student and as a person.

Even though UW was ranked higher, I chose UofO and have no regrets. I ended up visiting UW for my third year for personal reasons. Being a UW "visiting" 3L confirmed for me that Uof O was the better school.

Status: Alumnus/a, full-time
Dates of Enrollment: 8/1994-5/1997
Survey Submitted: March 2005

The admissions process when I applied was a little more loose than it became after I enrolled. I went to visit the school and met with a number of faculty and the director of admissions. I think my visit made a difference as to whether I was accepted.

> **Regarding admissions, the school says:** "Since 2001, we have experienced a 46 percent increase in applications. In 2006, the first-year class of 178 was drawn from 2,015 applications.
>
> "Beyond a competitive test score, our admissions committee expects a strong and consistent academic record, references that give insight into your intellect, and a clear and precise personal statement. You may include a one-page addendum to explain specifically why you wish to attend Oregon.
>
> "The school's leaders are committed to its women students, currently 42 percent of the first-year class. Of 13 law professors hired since 2000, 54 percent are women. Overall, women are 43 percent of faculty and 63 percent of administration, including the dean.
>
> "Our students of color flourish. Many are involved in the larger community and some serve on boards of national organizations. In addition to the Minority Law Students Association, there are four other active multicultural groups (Asian Pacific, Black, Latino/Latina and Native American). In the first-year class, 20 percent are students of color. There is also a Middle Eastern Law Student Association.
>
> "Students and faculty are active in public interest, public service and pro bono projects—and they often work together. We look for students who share this commitment. Our students enjoy an intellectually challenging curriculum without the excesses that an overly competitive environment breeds."

 ## Academics

Status: Alumnus/a, full-time
Dates of Enrollment: 9/2000-9/2003
Survey Submitted: November 2005

The professors are topnotch. You can generally get in to every class that you want. The classwork is tough and the caliber of students is high. You may have been in the top of your class in college and end up in the bottom half of your class at UofO.

If you want to do environmental law, the school is excellent. Each year the students organize the Annual Public Interest Environmental Law Conference. This is attended by over 3,000 people from all across the globe. The student environmental law group Land Air Water is a sting and active group. The new building is fantastic and state of the art.

Status: Alumnus/a, full-time
Dates of Enrollment: 8/2001-6/2004
Survey Submitted: October 2005

The school is great if you want environmental law, family law or anything to do with pro bono. However, for those of us interested in corporate and business law, until recently it was a real struggle to get decent classes.

However, now the school has a small business clinic run by a former law school dean, securities and fiduciary duties expert and a practicing sole practitioner who is outstanding as a supervisor. The Law and Entrepreneurship Center is run by he former and both are funded in part and supported by the Chambers family very influential business family). The Center works hard to help students mix n business MBA courses, and helps sponsor a summer technology program that llows law and business students to pair up and work with a premier patent esearch facility. Those teams have been winning U.S. and international usiness competitions for the last two or three years. The school hosts a business ompetition in Portland annually, and it is pulling the top business planning eams from around the country. So, it is now possible to get a great foundation or business at this school.

The school also has a unique multi-disciplinary mediation program and several rbitration and mediation classes and extracurricular training. The professors are ome of the top in their fields, some in the world (such as family law), and they re at this school because they want to live in Eugene—a great small town with n abundance of outdoor and cultural activities.

The school says: "The greatest growth in the curriculum in recent years has been in business, financial and commercial law. The Center for Law and Entrepreneurship engages students through our Small Business Clinic and Technology Entrepreneurship Program. Our Portland Externship Program expands summer opportunities in our largest city.

"Because we are part of a major university, we can offer concurrent degrees in business administration, conflict and dispute resolution, international studies, and environmental studies."

Status: Alumnus/a, full-time
Dates of Enrollment: 8/2000-5/2003
Survey Submitted: April 2004

Grading in most classes made things competitive. Grades were earned. Sometimes the students weren't as involved as I'd hoped in classes.

Status: Alumnus/a, full-time
Dates of Enrollment: 8/2002-5/2005
Survey Submitted: September 2005

First year is tough and the curve is strictly enforced by all professors. Some professors continue to curve grades through 2L and 3L year, while others are an "easy A"—ask around if you want to know who's who and what's what. That being said, the challenging classes are generally worth taking and suffering the slightly lower grade, as they better prepare you for the bar exam and challenge your critical thinking skills, which are often crucial in practice.

UO is probably as non-competitive as a law school can be. Of course, people still care about grades and making Law Review and such but, overall, the students are friendly and helpful to one another. There are very few "soft" classes—I had friends at other law schools in the Pacific NW who took classes such as "Law of Film," where they simply watched legal movies and critiqued/responded to the films. You won't find softies like that at UO, but you will find excellent professors and challenging and innovative courses in all kinds of areas—business law, environmental law and alternative dispute resolution, to name a few.

Status: Alumnus/a, full-time
Dates of Enrollment: 8/1994-5/1997
Survey Submitted: March 2005

First-year program is very good. There is a forced curve and the faculty stick to it. I learned a great deal in this year. Second- and third-year elective courses are more of a mixed bag. Some were great, while others were a joke. Certain professors were known as easy graders and students flocked to their classes and seminars regardless of the subject area. My absolute, hands-down, worst class was evidence. Given that I am a litigator, this is a hole I am still trying to fill. I was very disappointed by that class, the teaching, and the content.

The professors are fully accessible and willing to meet and talk with students. While I was at UofO, I only had one faculty member who did not give out his home phone number. Everyone else did and was happy to be available to their students.

Regarding academics, the school says: "We are the only law school in the state with membership in Order of the Coif, which recognizes outstanding legal scholarship. Only 80 of the 193 ABA-approved law schools in the country are Coif members. The law school consistently ranks among the Top 50 in reputation among scholars and lawyers.

"In 2005, the law school became the home of a new master's program in conflict and dispute resolution. In 2007, it welcomes its inaugural LLM class in Environmental and Natural Resources Law.

"Skills training is key to many doctrinal courses. We offer seven clinics. Our Legal Research and Writing Program was recognized as the best among public law schools in the West and is ranked 26th in the nation."

 Employment Prospects

Status: Alumnus/a, full-time
Dates of Enrollment: 9/2000-9/2003
Survey Submitted: November 2005

I have had a number of good jobs. If you do well at UofO, you should be able to get a good job. This is particularly true if you want a job in the Pacific Northwest. The career services office is a bit under staffed. There are UofO grads doing all sorts of interesting careers out there. Alumni will be helpful if you contact them.

Status: Alumnus/a, full-time
Dates of Enrollment: 8/2001-6/2004
Survey Submitted: October 2005

The last few years, since 2001, has been tough for getting jobs from this school. All the top students (top 15 percent) found jobs fairly quickly (all but one prior to graduation). However, for those lower in the class rankings, getting jobs was more difficult unless they had pre-law school connections of some sort. Many went to less prestigious judicial clerkships (magistrates) or to LLM programs. They then ended up with good jobs.

Finding state or lower paid jobs was not so difficult as jobs with private firms. The firms in Eugene typically hire very few new associates, though they almost always hire from this school. To get a local job, a student almost has to do a 2L clerkship in town. Several of the very top students transferred to "name" schools (Top 10) after first year, and their job search was much easier.

Top students who remained were picked up generally by whatever firm they wanted to work for, including O'Melvany and Meyers in California. The reach of the school is pretty much restricted to Washington, Oregon and California. Folks getting jobs further afield did so because of judicial clerkships in a different area or pre-law connections. On-campus recruiting focuses on local and big West Coast firms, most from Portland. The Ducks football team is generally the best talking point to employers outside Oregon.

The school says: "Most of our graduates find careers in Oregon (56 percent of the Class of 2005.) Career Services helps students who plan to work outside the state with individual counseling and workshops, a large jobs database and with referrals and networking with alumni.

"Our helpful and involved alumni work in 49 out of 50 states and internationally—including many in California and Washington D.C., the West, the upper Midwest and the East Coast.

"60 percent of our 2005 graduates found jobs in private practice and business immediately following graduation. They work in large and small law firms primarily in Portland, Seattle and California but also in Washington, D.C., New York and throughout the U.S."

Read all of Vault's Law School Surveys at www.vault.com/lawschool — get complete surveys on top law schools, expert advice on applicaton essays, LSAT prep and more.

VAULT CAREER LIBRARY   527

Status: Alumnus/a, full-time
Dates of Enrollment: 8/2002-5/2005
Survey Submitted: September 2005

If you want to work in Oregon, UofO is a GREAT choice. Most alumni end up in Oregon—Portland or Salem. Eugene itself is not a great town to find legal work, but opportunities in Salem and Portland are plentiful. Oregon is a well-respected school in the West and you will also find good employment opportunities in CA, AK, ID, WA. However, if you are looking to be in the Midwest/South/East, you may struggle to find work without personal connections and/or topnotch credentials. I decided I wanted to work in WA after law school and, while I was lucky enough to gain experience with a WA firm, my options were more limited than those of my classmates seeking work in OR.

Most UofO grads, myself included, go into public service and the school has an EXCELLENT reputation in that area. One big piece of advice—apply for a 1L summer clerkship at the OR Dept. of Justice. It is one of the few paying summer opportunities for 1Ls and opens a lot of doors for work during 2L summer and after graduation, especially if you want to remain in OR.

> The school says: "As a public law school, we pride ourselves on having a significant number of graduates (40 percent in 2005) go into government, public service and public interest jobs.""

Status: Alumnus/a, full-time
Dates of Enrollment: 8/1994-5/1997
Survey Submitted: March 2005

UofO is mostly a regional school. Employment prospects are good in the Pacific Northwest, particularly in Portland, Oregon. It can be very hard to get an USAO position or local prosecutor position unless you are politically connected. For the USAO positions, a UofO credential really does not cut it. Employment prospects away from Oregon are more limited and must be sought out by students on their own initiative as on-campus recruiting is largely limited to Pacific Northwest firms.

> The school says: "U.S. Attorney offices are U.S. Department of Justice field offices. Most do not hire recent graduates. Entry level positions are offered through the Honors Attorney Program. Two of our 2005 graduates were selected for these positions in New York and Washington, D.C. In 2006, our students worked with the DOJ in paid and volunteer summer positions in Eugene, Washington, D.C. and Miami. "

Status: Alumnus/a, full-time
Dates of Enrollment: 8/2000-5/2003
Survey Submitted: April 2004

UofO is usually attended by public interest types. I wanted to work in a firm, which made UofO seem like an odd choice. In some ways it lessened the competition at OCI because many students didn't want to work at a firm. EXCELLENT place to go if you want to clerk for a federal judge following law school. UofO has a "clerkship committee" whose goal is to get anyone a clerkship that wants one. They usually meet this goal, too.

 **Quality of Life**

Status: Alumnus/a, full-time
Dates of Enrollment: 9/2000-9/2003
Survey Submitted: November 2005

Some of the best years of my life were when I was in law school at the UofO. Eugene is a lovely university town with lots to do. If you are coming from a big city, you might be bored, unless you like the outdoors. My classmates were wonderful and I keep in touch with many of them.

You will generally have to rent an apartment—I don't think there is on-campus housing available. You can find a decent place to live near the school and the city is on the whole safe. There are some problems with property theft, but crimes against people are few and far between. If you like to hike there are plenty of trails nearby. If you like to bike, the city is full of great bike lanes and

bike paths. If you like to ski, there are options nearby. If you need to see the ocean Eugene is only 45 minutes from the coast.

Status: Alumnus/a, full-time
Dates of Enrollment: 8/2001-6/2004
Survey Submitted: October 2005

Most law students live off campus in apartments, which are inexpensive. The bus system is very good, and there are several very nice neighborhoods within walking or biking distance. Eugene has a well-developed walking/biking trail that generally follows the river. People are laid back and there is a lot of diversity, though the university area (which is separated somewhat from the law school area) can be riotious at times, and undergraduates obnoxious.

The law school is excellent—a brand new building that is a real delight to be in. Excellent technology, including wireless Internet. Seems to be low crime. Inexpensive dining all around campus. In a nice and quiet neighborhood. Law school has its own parking, which is a big deal as parking generally on campus is very, very bad.

Status: Alumnus/a, full-time
Dates of Enrollment: 8/2002-5/2005
Survey Submitted: September 2005

If you looked up "college town" in the dictionary, there would be a picture of Eugene, Oregon. The town really revolves around the university. When there is a Duck football home game, stores are empty. The city really lives and breathes the UofO! Eugene is very friendly and safe, and you'll find plenty of excellent housing opportunities. However, housing can be competitive because of all the students seeking clean living near campus.

Law students do have an edge here, as UofO Law both starts and ends its academic year [before the undergrads,] and most landlords prefer to rent to grad students. UofO has a great newer recreation center as well, and you can use it free of charge (included in tuition). Overall, it has all the amenities of a big state school in a friendly mid-sized city.

Status: Alumnus/a, full-time
Dates of Enrollment: 8/1994-5/1997
Survey Submitted: March 2005

Eugene is a fabulous place to go to school. Housing is plentiful and pleasant. Utilities can be expensive (we couldn't afford to heat our house in my third year). The law school facilities are new (since I graduated) and quite spectacular. The university has a good library collection, both in the university proper and the law school, and very helpful and friendly research librarian assistance.

Crime was never an issue, although there were a number of "homeless" students begging around campus. It is very easy to get around Eugene by bus or bike and even by car, though parking can be a bit of a challenge near campus.

UofO also has great medical health facilities for its students. Eugene is not a great place to be if you need to work while in school, there is limited work in the area. In a full-time law program, the ABA discourages work, but some students must do so anyway to support themselves and their families.

Be prepared for a lot of rain and fabulous springs, filled with rhododendrons blooming in incredible ranges of colors all over town.

Status: Alumnus/a, full-time
Dates of Enrollment: 8/2000-5/2003
Survey Submitted: April 2004

Very fun. Worked hard as an undergrad and never had fun. UofO folks made law school fun...weird eh?

Social Life

Status: Alumnus/a, full-time
Dates of Enrollment: 9/2000-9/2003
Survey Submitted: November 2005

Students socialize with each other regularly. There are many law school-sponsored events as well. There is a regular Public Interest Law Association Auction where students and faculty contribute interesting things and opportunities. You can win at auction a dinner at the dean's house or a raft trip with your Property Law professor.

If you are a member of Land Air Water, the student environmental law group, there is an annual raft trip weekend that is NOT to be missed. You will never be at a loss for something to do. There is a lot of intra-law school dating. Many of my classmates are married to other former classmates.

Status: Alumnus/a, full-time
Dates of Enrollment: 8/2001-6/2004
Survey Submitted: October 2005

Lots of groups at the school and activities going on in town. Student groups for just about any interest. Some are stronger than others. Some students party and socialize a lot, the serious students didn't. Typical law school.

Status: Alumnus/a, full-time
Dates of Enrollment: 8/2002-5/2005
Survey Submitted: September 2005

Social life at UofO Law can't be beat. The law school hosts parties in the school building itself, where you can drink wine and beer and eat snacks while socializing and dancing My friends at other law schools were always amazed when I told them about these parties—I don't know of any other school that offers this.

There are upscale events, such as the wine and art show and a charity benefit auction. There are also more collegial events, such as a Halloween party and a Disco dance, complete with all-you-can-drink beer. These events are by no means mandatory, but if you enjoy having a beverage and hanging out with your colleagues, they are a lot of fun.

There are also numerous groups and events for non-traditional students and families. Overall, UofO offers a great mix of mature, refined and raucous social

activities. UofO Law students organize intermural teams for most every sport and hold tailgaters for UofO football games—whatever you're into, there's a good chance you can take part at UofO.

Don't date your classmates. That's really all there is to it. True, it has worked for some people. But the number of people that is hasn't worked out for is MUCH larger.

There are plenty of college bars (Taylor's, Rennie's), hipster bars (Indigo District, Horsehead), an authentic pub that inspired Moe's on *The Simpsons* (Max's), plus a fair number of good restaurants and music venues. Portland is just two hours away and Seattle just five, so you can always escape to the big city for major league sports, upscale shopping and dining, and more varied nightlife.

Status: Alumnus/a, full-time
Dates of Enrollment: 8/1994-5/1997
Survey Submitted: March 2005

Our class was very close knit. People socialized with each other a lot, both in and out of school. There are a lot of student organizations active in the law school and some way for everyone to participate in activities.

Status: Alumnus/a, full-time
Dates of Enrollment: 8/2000-5/2003
Survey Submitted: April 2004

Very nice people. Rennie's and Taylor's were regular.

The School Says

Though we are a small law school and the city in which we are situated is medium-sized, there is enormous vitality here. Eugene, Oregon is recognized nationally for its quality of life and the natural wonders nearby.

The law school community exudes the values of the West: informal, friendly and open.

Read all of Vault's Law School Surveys at www.vault.com/lawschool — get complete surveys on top law schools, expert advice on applicaton essays, LSAT prep and more.

VAULT CAREER LIBRARY **529**

Willamette University College of Law

Admission Office
245 Winter Street SE
Salem, OR 97301
Admission phone: (503) 370-6282
Admission fax: (503) 370-6087
Admission e-mail: law-admission@willamette.edu
Admission URL:
http://www.willamette.edu/wucl/admission/

 ## Admissions

Status: Alumnus/a, full-time
Dates of Enrollment: 8/1991-5/1994
Survey Submitted: March 2006

15 years ago, the admissions process was fairly simple. Application, including essay, was required. Information from undergraduate and/or other graduate schools similarly required. Process is fairly selective, depending on class size and number of applicants. Usually approximately 120 to 170 students are accepted each year as first-year students. Some "lateral" students are accepted from other law schools as second and third year students. Selectivity is good, but could be better. Middle-rung law school.

Status: Alumnus/a, full-time
Dates of Enrollment: 8/2001-5/2004
Survey Submitted: April 2005

Willamette's admissions process has become more selective every year since I applied. Although its acceptance rate is fairly high, Willamette is certainly "selective." Good grades from a recognized undergraduate institution, especially a liberal arts school, can help those applicants who have less than desirable LSATs (of course with higher LSAT scores one has better chances for scholarships).

Willamette tends to select quite diverse classes—students straight out of undergrad, as well as people in their late 40s who want to make a career change. Past work experience, especially abroad, is highly regarded. Willamette also likes to accept students from different regions of the country—not just the NW or West Coast.

As for personal essays—make yourself come alive—tell your story and how your acceptance will make Willamette a more diverse place to learn the law. If you are accepted, be sure to go to the "preview" weekend. It is a great time to meet current students and faculty; it sold me on the school when I applied.

Status: Alumnus/a, full-time
Dates of Enrollment: 8/2003-5/2004
Survey Submitted: July 2004

The admissions process is standard of most law schools. It consists of their basic application and sending the LSDAS report. Over 65 percent of the applicants are accepted each year. Willamette doesn't conduct any interviews, the entire admission decision is based upon your LSAT score, GPA and essay with the application. The essay is straightforward, mainly consisting of the questions about why law school and why Willamette.

In your essay, be very specific about why you want to attend Willamette. Be honest, but let them know you will attend if accepted. Be excited about studying law at Willamette. If you have a low GPA or LSAT score be sure to briefly touch on this in your essay. Don't make excuses, but do offer a genuine explanation such as you were working part-time, you had added responsibilities above and beyond your typical college student.

Scholarships are awarded based on your LSAT score first, GPA second. Many do receive a scholarship, usually around $6,000 or less. It is guaranteed for the first year; but to keep it, your first-year GPA must be above a 2.9.

> **The school says:** "Because of our modest size, admission to Willamette University College of Law is highly selective. Willamette emphasizes small enrollment, which fosters an intellectual intimacy unmatched by most law schools. We hold applicants to the highest standards and have been increasingly more competitive in attaining the most qualified students each year. For the academic year 2003, Willamette University College of Law's acceptance rate was 53 percent. That number dropped to 39 percent in 2004. Both years saw major increases in the number of applicants as well.

> "In addition to LSAT score and GPA, admission to Willamette is based on letters of recommendation and the applicant's essay. All of these items also are considered when we make any scholarship determinations, though LSAT is not weighed more heavily than GPA in this decision. The average scholarship awarded in the 2004-2005 school year was $10,000."

Status: Alumnus/a, full-time
Dates of Enrollment: 8/2000-12/2002
Survey Submitted: September 2003

As with all law schools, you must take the LSAT. Willamette is not the most selective law school, but you should still have at least a 150 score on your LSAT and a 3.0 GPA. A majority of students enrolled receive some scholarship from the trustees. I had a 160 LSAT and a 3.78 undergraduate GPA and received nearly a full scholarship. There is no interview involved in the admissions process—only an application with a section for a personal statement. The admissions office is very helpful, as is student services. You are not just another number to them.

Prior to law school, I thought I would need to go to a Top 25 school, and I did get accepted to one of those schools. It wasn't until the very last minute that I changed my mind (it was the end of May 2000). I contacted Willamette to say that I made a mistake and did want to accept the offer of admission. They went out of their way to help me and I was still able to keep my scholarship.

Scholarships are important. I think I made a good choice going to a lesser-known school and receiving a full-scholarship. I have much less debt than I would have had I gone to a more prestigious school and not received a scholarship.

> **The school says:** "Willamette University College of Law does not adhere to a strict cut-off for GPAs or LSAT scores when evaluating students for admission. Rather, the admission committee examines the overall strength of each candidate. In addition to previous academic achievement and performance on the Law School Admission Test, the candidate's maturity, leadership skills and character also are examined."

 ## Academics

Status: Alumnus/a, full-time
Dates of Enrollment: 8/1991-5/1994
Survey Submitted: March 2006

During the time period from 1991 to 1994, each law school level (one to three years) was divided into six small sections of 20 or 30 students. Some courses are limited to one small section, others combine as many as four. Workload is heavy, as is typical for law school, and it is fairly easy to find out reputations of professors to get a sense ahead of time regarding style of instruction and what to watch for in exams. Classes are of moderate to high quality. Students generally know who to "watch out" for. Contracts, Civil Procedure, Property, commercial code classes all are of high repute.

Status: Alumnus/a, full-time
Dates of Enrollment: 8/2001-5/2004
Survey Submitted: April 2005

There is a good mix of curriculum, although in the past students have complained about conflicts in scheduling—making it hard to get ALL the classes you want. It is pretty easy to get into popular classes. Some classes have limited enrollment (limited to fewer than 20 students), which are often done by lottery (so you actually have a chance, even without a good registration time.) Classes are generally high quality (with a few exceptions.) The professors at Willamette are most often practitioners with years of experience, who have chosen to teach after having made their money when they practiced. Professors, therefore, love to speak with students and work with them closely. Professors do a fine job of mixing theory and real life application. Some still hold out for the Socratic Method, but fewer professors use it—and all respect those students who aren't into speaking during class.

The workload at Willamette is reasonable. Some professors are sticklers for getting your reading done—and if they sense that you haven't read—you'll feel it as they continue to ask questions. As for grading, Willamette is rather tough, with its newly implemented curve for classes of more than 20 students. Professors are required to give a certain number of grades below a C- in those courses, which can be frustrating when you know you've done better than your grade and the professor tells you that they "had to give the C minus to someone." Professors, generally, are fair graders and many try to avoid the curve as much as possible—sometimes appealing to the administration or by limiting classes to fewer than 20 students.

> **Willamette says:** "Willamette University College of Law maintains uniform grading standards for all students. This is in conformity with other law schools in the United States. In a recent study by the American Association of Law Schools, 70 percent of U.S. law schools reported that they utilize a curve. In contrast to the negative depiction of a curve provided above, the curve helps equalize sections of students because it provides norms and prevents discrepancies among professors' grading practices. Additionally, after implementation of the uniform grading standards at Willamette, on average, students' GPAs increased, rather than decreased."

Status: Alumnus/a, full-time
Dates of Enrollment: 8/2003-5/2004
Survey Submitted: July 2004

Your first semester is assigned to you; you won't have any choices among your classes. You will be assigned with a group of people, and the majority of your classes will be with the same people. Your Legal Research and Writing class will be with a small group, generally around 20. They also try and have your Civil Procedure class be roughly the same size, although this is not guaranteed. Second semester you will be able to pick one elective course: Intro to Business; International Law; Lawmaking Process or Dispute Resolution. Relax, unless you care about earning a certificate in one of the above areas, it doesn't really matter what you take.

Grading is on a forced curve. The median grades for a first-year class are around 2.9. That doesn't leave very many As for the class. You will be disappointed in your law school grades. Not everyone can be at the top of the class. Most professors adequately prep you for their exam. Pay attention to what each professor is looking for and tailor your exam to that professor.

The quality of the classes is generally very good. I only had one class where I was disappointed with the teaching of the professor. The professors are available after class to answer any questions. Law school is like drinking through a fire hose—be prepared to struggle with the material.

The workload is tough, but very doable. The saying in law school is "long days, fast months." Be prepared to study when you go to school. Days of relaxing like in undergrad are over. Take good notes, attend every class, keep up with the reading and you will do fine. Remember, everyone is learning the same material

from the same teacher. The ones who do well are those that take the time to wrestle with the text.

Status: Alumnus/a, full-time
Dates of Enrollment: 8/2000-12/2002
Survey Submitted: September 2003

Despite its ranking (Willamette recently dropped to the fourth-tier), Willamette has an excellent academic program. It has renowned professors in areas like Contracts, International Law and Estate Planning. Very rarely were the popular classes closed, and the administration would frequently add additional sections to the very popular classes. The upperclassmen receive priority in registration, and if you really want a class before graduation, the registrar's office staff will go out of their way to see you get it. If it is a requirement for graduation, you can be guaranteed to get it.

Willamette has an excellent Dispute Resolution Program, in which students can receive a certificate of specialization. They have also recently added an LLM program in international law. There are many intern and externship opportunities, as well as a legal clinic.

All of the professors have open-door policies and are very helpful. The Socratic Method is still used, but no professors at Willamette use that as a way to degrade or embarrass students. I found the workload reasonable. How hard you have to work depends on you. Typically, it is two to four hours of homework for every hour in class.

Grading is fair, but tough. The one difficulty (although people hesitate to talk about this occurring in American law schools) is grade inflation. There is no grade inflation at Willamette. You can have a 2.7 GPA and still be in the top 50 percent. This makes it difficult to compete for a job after graduation, as some schools are known for grade inflation. So, while students from different schools may be ranked the same, students from Willamette may have a lower GPA.

To graduate, students must complete a thesis paper in conjunction with some class or independent study. They must be supervised by a professor, but there is no requirement to present the paper, unless the class you chose has that requirement (it's rare).

There are many moot court opportunities in a variety of areas, including environmental law, torts, business, arbitration and criminal law. There is a first-year moot court requirement. Beginning your first semester, you will take Legal Research and Writing. Your particular section will focus on another first-year course, like civil procedure or torts. You will do lots of practice memos and briefs. During the second semester, you will spend the entire time preparing a brief for your first moot court competition. You are required to do one practice round and one competition round, but after your first competition round, you do not have to continue the competition if you don't want to. You can opt out.

> **The school states:** "Willamette University College of Law is solidly positioned among the top of the third-tier law schools in the U.S. and anticipates moving to the second-tier in the near future.
>
> "Relative to specialization opportunities, the college currently offers four distinct certificate programs: International and Comparative Law Certificate, Dispute Resolution Certificate, Law and Government Certificate, and Law and Business Certificate. In addition, the college offers a joint JD/ MBA and a LLM in Transnational Law.
>
> "The College of Law utilizes a letter grading system that includes minuses and pluses for letter grades, which range from A+ (4.3) to F (0.0). This system was designed to ensure Willamette graduates successfully compete with students attending schools with a maximum 4.0 grading scale."

Read all of Vault's Law School Surveys at www.vault.com/lawschool — get complete surveys on top law schools, expert advice on applicaton essays, LSAT prep and more.

VAULT CAREER LIBRARY 531

Employment Prospects

Status: Alumnus/a, full-time
Dates of Enrollment: 8/1991-5/1994
Survey Submitted: March 2006

Graduates at the top of the class (10 percent and up) can usually obtain prestigious positions at local law firms in Washington, Oregon and Idaho. May be more difficult to get top paying jobs on the East Coast or Southern California due to the fact that the law school is not well-known. Always helpful to have Law Review, moot court and other activities on the resume. Some professors and alumni are well-connected. On-campus interviews are popular and well-attended on both sides, by students and prospective employers. A good way to get your foot in the door.

Status: Alumnus/a, full-time
Dates of Enrollment: 8/2001-5/2004
Survey Submitted: April 2005

Oregon's legal economy is not the best. That being said, Willamette has a strong reputation throughout the state, especially since Willamette has dramatically improved its bar passage rate (quite a bit higher than the state average.) Willamette is well respected in Oregon with two or three Oregon Supreme Court justices being alumni. Students obtain a variety of jobs, from the big Portland firms (quite a few people obtained these jobs from the class of '04) to positions at the DOJ, various DA's offices, as well as smaller firms throughout Portland, Salem and Eugene. Students who go out of state get the same variety of job options as well.

The alumni network is quite strong—a great way to get informational interviews during your first year—to develop a network for 2L summer associate positions. Mostly NW law firms visit the campus. People do get jobs through on-campus interviews, but it is limited, like everywhere else. Internships are readily available, as well as externships with various local private sector and public sector employers—where you can also earn academic credit during the semester. A big opportunity for internships is just across the street at the Oregon Legislature, Court of Appeals and Supreme Court.

Status: Alumnus/a, full-time
Dates of Enrollment: 8/2003-5/2004
Survey Submitted: July 2004

Willamette has a decent reputation in Oregon. If you don't plan on practicing in Oregon or Washington, I would think twice about attending here. The Salem economy is depressed right now, and they aren't exactly hurting for attorneys.

The director of career services was excellent, but she left. Career prospects are decent if you finish in the top 33 percent. I don't know how the recent graduates are doing, but about 60 percent are employed currently. Clerkships are hard to come by, but keep networking!

> **The school says:** "In a survey of the class of 2004, 91 percent of graduates had jobs at the nine-month survey mark. These jobs were located in 14 states and the District of Columbia. Of those graduates who secured employment in Oregon, 40 percent were in Portland, 36 percent were in Salem and 24 percent were in various other locations throughout the state.
>
> "Most graduates, regardless of their class rank, are highly successful in finding meaningful employment—thanks to the many job-placement and networking opportunities available to students and alumni."

Status: Alumnus/a, full-time
Dates of Enrollment: 8/2000-12/2002
Survey Submitted: September 2003

Career services is very helpful, offering seminars on resume and cover letter writing, interviewing, legal specializations, among others. Willamette operates a mentorship program, which matches first-year law students with attorneys in the area. The programs does its best to match students and lawyers with similar interests. It is an excellent way to start networking. The mentorship program continues as long as the student wants, and many students stay in touch with their mentors throughout law school and after.

On-campus interviews begin in the fall. Not as many firms interview on campus as at the "big" schools, but I recall at least 30 or so while I was there. There are many more firms that interview off campus, but use the career services office to collect the resumes.

Willamette has a good reputation in the Northwest, but if you plan to move very far out of the area, going to Willamette will probably not help job prospects. But I think that is true for many schools. Firms are looking for people with community ties, so prospective students should consider that when making their school choice.

Career services continues to assist students after graduation, for however long is necessary. They have a web site with job openings and information on events related to career planning.

Also, many of the professors take on research assistants. This is a great opportunity to improve your research and writing skills, while gaining an additional reference for your resume. It helped me a lot in my job search after graduation.

One secret to Willamette: during first-year orientation, run down to the law library at put your name on the waiting list to be a library clerk. It's a peach of a job. It only pays $7 per hour, but it's at night. Each student hired is assigned a particular day of the week. Weekdays you would work from four p.m. until midnight, and on weekends there are two shifts—one from eight a.m. to four p.m. and one from four p.m. to midnight. All you have to do is check books in and out and answer phones. It's usually really quiet, and is a great opportunity to get paid while you study. Plus, it's just one more thing you can put on your resume. If you put your name on the waiting list, you may not get a call to come to work until the end of your second year, or beginning of your third year, but it's worth it!

Quality of Life

Status: Alumnus/a, full-time
Dates of Enrollment: 8/1991-5/1994
Survey Submitted: March 2006

Salem is a small town and is the seat of government for the state of Oregon. Excellent place to be for future politicians or those who desire to go into public practice. Nearly all law students live off campus. The school itself has one of the best endowments of all universities on the West Coast. Pretty school, boring town. Great places to go running and biking. Oregon is a super place to go if you are an active person that enjoys the outdoors.

Status: Alumnus/a, full-time
Dates of Enrollment: 8/2001-5/2004
Survey Submitted: April 2005

Salem is a good town for law school. It's a somewhat sleepy town—not much to do late at night—but that's great for studying. Salem is easy to get around—pretty good housing options throughout town. The university does provide some graduate housing, which is pretty popular, but you can certainly find a number of apartments/houses for rent of varying quality and cost. The law school is in a safe part of town—practically downtown, close to the state legislature, with many different places to eat.

The campus is beautiful, lush, green, and has many inexpensive and great places to eat. The law school is a rather new building, equipped with a wireless network and laptop friendly class rooms. Law students have 24-hour access to the building, the law library and work stations. There are a number of computers for students to use, as well as printing privileges. Work stations are secure, but students do need to take precautions during winter and summer months when not as many students are around. Salem is about an hour from Portland and the airport. The coast is a little over an hour away, as well as skiing in the mountains. Quality of life is above average to excellent, when you consider the surrounding areas and close proximity to Portland and its varied nightlife.

Status: Alumnus/a, full-time
Dates of Enrollment: 8/2003-5/2004
Survey Submitted: July 2004

Everyone pretty much lives off campus. My advice is to live in South Salem; DO NOT live north of the law school. Stay west of I-5 and you will be fine. Many of the nicer apartments are in South Salem located off of Commercial Street. For a typical two bedroom, expect to spend between $575 to $650 per month.

The campus was recently renovated and it is very nice. The law school has wireless Internet in the entire building. The facilities are first rate.

Crime in Salem is a problem; many students have had their cars broken into at their apartments. Remember, live south of the law school! Their are many great places to eat in Salem, but everyone ate the undergrad campus or brought a lunch with them.

Status: Alumnus/a, full-time
Dates of Enrollment: 8/2000-12/2002
Survey Submitted: September 2003

I loved living in Salem. It is a small town, but close to the big city (Portland, OR is only 45 minutes away by car). Cost of living is much less compared to living in the city. The university operates two apartment complexes for graduate students. I stayed in one of those apartments during my last year there. It was great! The law school was across the parking lot. There was air conditioning, free Internet access, free local phone calls. There is also an optional meal plan at the cafeteria.

During my first year and a half, I lived in my own apartment without roommates. It was within walking distance to school. It was a two bedroom, one-and-a-half bath townhouse with two stories and a deck. I paid only $510 per month—not something that can be found in most cities.

Law students have access to all facilities at the main university, including the sports complex (swimming pool, gym). In particular, law students have 24-hour key card access to the law school and law library, which is a big plus that many other schools don't have. If you are stressing about a big test, you can head over to the law school at 2 a.m. and study. Each student is assigned a carrel in the library (you share with one other person). It's a great place for peace and quiet. On the first floor of the law school, there is a locker room (everybody gets their own), a pool table with TV, a kitchen with two refrigerators, four microwaves, dishes and silverware and vending machines. With the key card access, you can practically live there without going home. There is even a "sick" room with a bed in it, although very few truly sick people use it.

There is not much crime in Salem. It mostly amounted to car stereos being stolen. But I think that kind of thing can be expected anywhere. Campus security offers escorts for students on campus.

In addition to the cafeteria on campus, there on many restaurants close by, including a sports bar across the street from the main campus (it's quite popular). I am vegetarian, so I was afraid living in a smaller town would limit my options, but I found a great little organic store that had lots of vegetarian and vegan options. Plus, there are many vegetarian restaurants and shops in Portland.

The Amtrak station is walking distance to campus via a pedestrian bridge. Great if you want to go to Portland, Seattle or California. My family lives in Washington, so I would frequently take the train to Olympia. If you buy your ticket in advance, it's only about $19 one-way (cheaper if you buy a round-trip ticket).

Social Life

Status: Alumnus/a, full-time
Dates of Enrollment: 8/1991-5/1994
Survey Submitted: March 2006

It's been such a long time since I was a student. Local hang-outs have probably changed. Seems that there were several bars that the law students frequented. Brew pubs are a top choice. Options to go to Portland, 40 miles to the north. Good skiing over the mountains and the Oregon coast is only a couple of hours' drive. For undergraduates, there is a small Greek system.

Status: Alumnus/a, full-time
Dates of Enrollment: 8/2001-5/2004
Survey Submitted: April 2005

Social life is pretty good. The Student Bar Association plans a number of events throughout the year, including BBQs. Other student organizations have get-togethers, Halloween and other parties. The law school is a tightly-knit community and often students have get-togethers at their own homes. Salem has a variety of restaurants, a few nightclubs (nothing too exciting). The law school, depending on each class, has a varied dating scene. Lots of opportunities to make new law school friends on Thursday at the Bar Review (a local bar is selected each week for drinks.) Law students also have free admission to Willamette sport events, such as football and baseball—not a bad way to get away from the library during the weekend.

Status: Alumnus/a, full-time
Dates of Enrollment: 8/2003-5/2004
Survey Submitted: July 2004

SBA does a lot of events that involve the students. Most students didn't find the time to attend first year. Generally you will be busy studying. If you aren't, then you are doing something wrong.

Status: Alumnus/a, full-time
Dates of Enrollment: 8/2000-12/2002
Survey Submitted: September 2003

The Student Bar Association plans many events for the law students like dances, picnics and softball. "Law Revue" is similar to a prom, but for law students, and includes an award ceremony for the professor voted most popular. Another big event is the Halloween party.

There are also many on-campus clubs, including Law Partners, which brings law students and their families together for fun events (bowling, barbeques). The Willamette University Public Interest Law Project (WUPILP) has a major auction in the spring. This is a very popular event. It includes both an oral and a silent auction. Professors get very involved and submit various things to bid on, including dinners with law professors, golf games, a stay in one of their vacation homes and other prizes. In the past, dinners at the professors' homes have gone for as much as $900 for a dinner for eight. The auction includes wine tasting from local wineries, kegs and appetizers.

The Ram is a popular sports bar close to campus. Magoo's, another bar, is also a popular bar for students to meet and has a shuffleboard! I was a big fan of the Newport restaurant's happy hour; $2 for an entree like fish and chips, hamburgers or pasta.

Read all of Vault's Law School Surveys at www.vault.com/lawschool — get complete surveys on top law schools, expert advice on applicaton essays, LSAT prep and more.

VAULT CAREER LIBRARY 533

Duquesne University School of Law

Admissions Office
Hanley Hall
Duquesne University
600 Forbes Avenue
Pittsburgh, PA 15282
Admissions phone: (412) 396-6300
Admissions URL:
http://www.law.duq.edu/Admissions/Admissions.html

Note: The school has chosen not to comment on the student surveys submitted.

 ## Admissions

Status: Alumnus/a, full-time
Dates of Enrollment: 8/2000-5/2003
Survey Submitted: November 2004

Have to take the LSATs and have those scores submitted to the law school. Fill out your applications. For higher tier schools it helps to have some letters of recomendation from former teachers, employers. Make sure you visit all schools you are considering at least once. Duquesne encourages visitors, and will allow you to take a guided tour of the school and even sit in on a class if you wish. I believe that Duquesne accepts around 70 percent of the applicants, which makes it less selective than most law schools.

Status: Alumnus/a, part-time
Dates of Enrollment: 8/1999-5/2003
Survey Submitted: April 2004

The admission process begins with an accpetable LSAT score in the range of 140 to 160 or higher. A written essay accompanying the application is required. The essay included an explanation of ones interest in law and future career goals. Selectivity was highly weighted on LSAT score and undergraduate GPA, and knowing alumni as a reference was a plus.

Status: Alumnus/a, full-time
Dates of Enrollment: 9/2001-6/2004
Survey Submitted: October 2005

Standard process, increasing selectivity. LSAT 155 or higher, recommendations, essays required. Interview optional. Set yourself apart—almost all apps are from Pittsburgh area with middle class background—they are desperate for a more diverse (economically or racially) class. The school takes many Duquesne undergrads into the law school, which immediatey divides students into set social groups.

 ## Academics

Status: Alumnus/a, full-time
Dates of Enrollment: 8/2000-5/2003
Survey Submitted: November 2004

Very good JD program. Spend most of the first year studying. A good rule of thumb is to treat law school like a full-time job and spend 40 or more hours a week in class and in the library. Law school will change your way of thinking rapidly. In your first year, your classes are all pre-determined, but in subsequent years you have a lot of freedom in choosing your classes and classes are easy. Your grades are based entirely on one exam, which can have brutal consequences. A bad afternoon in an exam can result in a grade that is not indicative of the time and effort you have spent.

Status: Alumnus/a, part-time
Dates of Enrollment: 8/1999-5/2003
Survey Submitted: April 2004

Academics ranged between the evening program and day program. I attended the evening program and found the quality of classes highly sensitive to which professor was teaching the subject. Duquesne has only a few topnotch professors whose classes quickly fill up. Grading at Duquesne, usually essay testing, is anonymous (or so they say). I don't believe grading was actually anonymous because the professors ended up placing the grades in the end. Workload for first-year law students was high but as expected. The workload diminished as you progressed through the program.

Status: Alumnus/a, full-time
Dates of Enrollment: 9/2001-6/2004
Survey Submitted: October 2005

Rigorous academics, pressurized environment. School is very competitive and students who don't perform well cannot return. Only a select few "quality" professors; usually no trouble getting into desired classes. Workload first year is immense, second year tolerable and third year nonexistant. Unique mandatory grading policy—20 percent can receive an A—which hurts many borderline students.

 ## Employment Prospects

Status: Alumnus/a, part-time
Dates of Enrollment: 8/1999-5/2003
Survey Submitted: April 2004

Of the students in the evening program, most were already employed and looking to switch careers. The career services office was located in a different building than the law school. On-campus recruiting is highly seasonal and a student must pay attention to the schedule or entirely miss the boat on internships and clerkships. Duquesne's prestige is most notably limited to the city of Pittsburgh and surrounding area. Its reputation (not ranking) surpasses the University of Pittsburgh within the city. Outside the city however, Pitt's higher ranking carries more weight in the legal community than Duquesne.

Status: Alumnus/a, full-time
Dates of Enrollment: 8/2000-5/2003
Survey Submitted: November 2004

Jobs for attorneys are very limited right now, but this is a cyclical thing and in no way indicative of the law school's success. The career services office is very useful and will provide you with job leads, a resume service, on-campus interviews and access to an alumni network. Duquesne is not the most prestigious law school, but their willingness to aid your job search certainly compensates for this.

Status: Alumnus/a, full-time
Dates of Enrollment: 9/2001-6/2004
Survey Submitted: October 2005

Pittsburgh is saturated with attorneys and thus not many jobs are available. Big firms downtown hire from top-tier schools, Duquesne grads usually end up in smaller firms and often have difficulty finding employment. Moving is an option; I had no trouble finding a job in another state.

Quality of Life

Status: Alumnus/a, full-time
Dates of Enrollment: 8/2000-5/2003
Survey Submitted: November 2004

School is in the middle of downtown Pittsburgh, but is extremely safe. Campus is pleasant. Housing is adequate. Law school students can live on campus in a wing of the dorm reserved specifically for them. It makes the morning commute much easier and it helps having roommates who share your trials and to bounce ideas off of. Most facilities you need are located on campus. Parking is a nightmare but this is part of the Pittsburgh tradition, I suppose. The law school library is rated as being something less than outstanding, but I never understood why. There is access to dozens of computers with high-speed Internet, a friendly and often life-saving staff and of course, plenty of books. Their treatise and periodical sections need a little beefing up, but the majority of this work can always be done on the computer. Eating at Duquesne is about average. A meal plan can be purchased to eat on campus or you can always grab lunch downtown. That can get a bit pricey, though.

Status: Alumnus/a, part-time
Dates of Enrollment: 8/1999-5/2003
Survey Submitted: April 2004

This question is nearly inapplicable to Duquesne's law school. In my four years, I never met an individual who actually lived on campus. Located in the city, most students housed in the nearby Southside of town. Duquesne's law library recently experienced a great library renovation with additional computer equipment, labs and more study space. Much needed and it looks great. The parking at Duquesne is terrible and overpriced. Even if you have a parking pass, you're likely to be tagged for some ridiculous oddity by the end of the semester.

Status: Alumnus/a, full-time
Dates of Enrollment: 9/2001-6/2004
Survey Submitted: October 2005

Duquesne borders the Hill District, the most dangerous area of Pittsburgh. Most people commute to the law school and live outside of town, which works out fine (aside from the outrageous cost of parking!). The dining halls on campus are fine, there is a small cafe in the law school that suffices. Overall, the campus is small and pretty, and convenient to walk to downtown internships/jobs after class.

 # Social Life

Status: Alumnus/a, full-time
Dates of Enrollment: 8/2000-5/2003
Survey Submitted: November 2004

Law school hosts many parties and events, and in downtown Pittsburgh you are only a short walk away from a bar or restaurant. The law school has its own fraternity and several clubs. You can always join these if you have any free time left after studying. Which is doubtful. Duquesne is located on the bus line and is close to Station Square, Southside and the Strip, where there are hundreds of bars and restaurants.

Status: Alumnus/a, part-time
Dates of Enrollment: 8/1999-5/2003
Survey Submitted: April 2004

Duquesne law school's social life has lessened. On- and off-campus planned events were virtually all abandoned after a few unfavorable undergraduate experiences with alcohol that eventually affected graduate school social functions. Duquesne's location, however, lends itself to nearby hot-spots like the Southside, downtown and the Strip District. The dating scene was terrible in law school.

Status: Alumnus/a, full-time
Dates of Enrollment: 9/2001-6/2004
Survey Submitted: October 2005

Social events are largely unattended, most students are commuters and don't return at night for events. There is one bar in walking distance that becomes the hangout after finals, it's no big prize. Most bars in Pittsburgh are in the Southside or Strip District, so you have to drive from the school.

Read all of Vault's Law School Surveys at www.vault.com/lawschool — get complete surveys on top law schools, expert advice on applicaton essays, LSAT prep and more.

VAULT CAREER LIBRARY **535**

Pennsylvania State University

The Dickinson School of Law of
The Pennsylvania State University
Admissions Office
1170 Harrisburg Pike
Carlisle, PA 17013-1617
Admissions phone: (717) 240-5207 or (800) 840-1122
Admissions fax: (717) 241-3503
Admissions e-mail: dsladmit@psu.edu
Admissions URL: http://www.dsl.psu.edu/admissions/

 ## Admissions

Status: Alumnus/a, full-time
Dates of Enrollment: 8/2001-5/2004
Survey Submitted: September 2004

During the application process I was looking for a school on the East Coast that had a reputable name that would be transferable to the West Coast when I moved back upon graduation. Penn State was exactly the name and reputation that I and my future employers were looking for.

With regard to the application process Penn State is pretty standard. I wrote a personal statement, submitted letters of recommendation as well as filled out an application with my academic qualifications. Although the application process was standard the acceptance process was not. During the waiting period, I was able to contact the school to make sure that they had received all of my information, and just as importantly the school took the time to send me letters and updates on my application and my opportunities for acceptance into PSU. Upon getting accepted, I was offered season tickets to the football games and, to be honest, that sealed the deal for me.

Status: Current student, full-time
Dates of Enrollment: 8/2002-Submit Date
Survey Submitted: May 2004

The admissions process was wonderful. When calling in, everyone was helpful and kind. Most other law schools were not as together, and were rude on the phone. They are rather selective—and place emphasis on characteristics outside of the traditional LSAT and GPA scores.

Status: Current student, full-time
Dates of Enrollment: 8/2003-Submit Date
Survey Submitted: September 2005

Score high on the LSAT. Have above a 3.3 GPA. Minority students have an advantage. You have to focus your strength on your essays. If you have international experience, make sure you emphasize that, because the school is putting a lot of focus on international law. It is not very selective if you have above a 3.3 GPA and a 155 LSAT. If you score over 160 on the LSAT, you are likely to receive some form of scholarship. They take around 200 students per class with a little more than 2,500 applications.

Status: Alumnus/a, full-time
Dates of Enrollment: 8/1997-5/2000
Survey Submitted: January 2005

Admissions is a fairly personal process, as there is a relatively small group that reviews all applications. Applicants can distinguish themselves by drawing attention to accomplishments that demonstrate a clear record of success and accomplishment. An interview really helps, as it can put a face on a name. Essays are important, but are evaluated in the context of the entire application. The school is fairly selective, but, unfortunately, not a top-tier school so your chances at Dickinson are better than at many other schools.

> **The school says:** "Penn State's Dickinson School of Law's ranking in the 2007 *U.S. News & World Report* ranking of all

ABA-approved law schools remained in the Top 100 and improved from 90 to 87. Additionally, the law school was named one of 'The Most Diverse Law Schools' in the United States, and our Dispute Resolution Program retained its ranking as one of the Top 10 in the United States."

Status: Current student, full-time
Dates of Enrollment: 8/2002-Submit Date
Survey Submitted: April 2005

The admissions process was great. Each time I called the admission office I was nicely greeted and recognized. The admissions officers were organized, knowledgeable and very friendly.

 ## Academics

Status: Current student, full-time
Dates of Enrollment: 8/2003-Submit Date
Survey Submitted: September 2005

Professors are great. Workload is pretty tough. Professors will give students grades below 70 [i.e., a grade of D or lower] if they aren't competitive. Students are very nice and supportive. The Dispute Resolution Program is one of the best in the country. We have several good professors in the program. International law is also very strong. We recently hired two of the most prominent International Law professors in the country. The LLM program is also strong. We have about 20 LLM students. There are three different kind of study abroad programs, so if you want to study abroad after a first year, there's a lot of opportunity. Credit transfer from other summer abroad program is also very lenient.

DSL is also building new facilities. One is renovating the current Carlisle campus, the second is building a new building in University Park [the location of the University's main campus]. They will be completed in 2008.

> **The school says:** "In addition to offering two European summer abroad programs and a summer program at the McGill University Faculty of Law in Montréal, Québec, Canada, we are able to accommodate students' desires to pursue semester or year-abroad programs virtually anywhere in the world. For example, we recently entered agreements that will allow for student exchange programs with the University of Maastrict Faculty of Law in the Netherlands and Yeditepe University in Turkey.
>
> The law school is moving forward with plans for new, completely interconnected facilities in Carlisle and University Park, PA. The original portion of Trickett Hall in Carlisle will undergo extensive renovations. In University Park, a new facility will be constructed on Park Avenue in close proximity to the new Smeal College of Business Administration building and School of Forestry Resources building. Expected occupancy of the new facilities is the 2008-2009 academic year."

Status: Current student, full-time
Dates of Enrollment: 8/2002-Submit Date
Survey Submitted: April 2005

The quality of the classes is first-rate. I have learned so much during law school that my friends at other law schools have not learned. The open-door policy at the school is great. I can easily walk to my professors' offices each day and speak with them. Grading is competitive, like all law schools, but very fair. The workload is very reasonable. Since after my first year I have been able to maintain employment (approximately 22 hours a week).

Status: Alumnus/a, full-time
Dates of Enrollment: 8/2001-5/2004
Survey Submitted: September 2004

The PSU-DSL experience is unlike most law schools in the nation. I had many other friends at other institutions and when we compared stories or they came to visit me they all remarked how different my experience was from their's—how friendly the environment was, not only between the faculty and students, but between the students and other students. The environment at Penn State was so nurturing that it allowed students to flourish in a very challenging, grueling and competitive atmosphere. Even my father, a graduate of Stanford, agreed that my experience was second to none.

In regards to the classes and the professors, I was never denied the opportunity to take a class that I wanted to or denied the opportunity to be instructed by any professor. Grading was relatively fair. However, I am still a little uncertain as to how the curve works, but the grading was fair and if a student ever questioned the grading they were encouraged to speak with the professors about their decisions. As far as workload is concerned, it's law school. You would not be there if you could not handle it, but again its law school, so be ready.

Status: Current student, full-time
Dates of Enrollment: 8/2002-Submit Date
Survey Submitted: May 2004

The quality is astounding. Classes are easy to find, and professors are VERY approachable. Most law schools say that they have an open-door policy—but this school actually has it. I have developed great relationship with nearly every one of my professors. The workload is traditional for law school—it is tough, but the staff and faculty are always there to provide support!

Status: Alumnus/a, full-time
Dates of Enrollment: 8/1997-5/2000
Survey Submitted: January 2005

Dickinson has many very good professors who do an excellent job of preparing students to actually practice as lawyers. Most teachers have a good balance of legal theory and the practical aspects of practice. Unfortunately, there are a significant number of professors who appear to be showing up at the school merely to collect a pay check—they are hiding behind tenure and sliding by with barely acceptable competence. Generally there is a small ratio of students to teachers, so classes are personal and students can interact with professors. Grading is generally fair, although there are teachers who are notoriously easy and can be counted on for a high grade. Workloads is not difficult.

Employment Prospects

Status: Current student, full-time
Dates of Enrollment: 8/2002-Submit Date
Survey Submitted: April 2005

Great prospects! Many of my friends, including myself, will be working in Center City Philadelphia after graduation. The Career Service Department is topnotch!

> **The school says:** "The Office of Career Services reports that the law school consistently enjoys a percentage of graduates employed or pursuing advanced degrees that exceeds 90 percent."

Status: Alumnus/a, full-time
Dates of Enrollment: 8/2001-5/2004
Survey Submitted: September 2004

Because I attended Penn State I was able to find jobs on both coasts. I spent my first summer working for a large Los Angeles based law firm and my second summer working for a start-up firm in New York City. The Penn State name carried so much weight.

> **Penn State says:** "Roughly 200 employers participate in the school's fall recruitment program each year and offer employment in approximately 30 states. The Office of Career Services reported in its last employment statistics that the Class

of 2005 secured employment in 21 states, the District of Columbia, and internationally."

Status: Current student, full-time
Dates of Enrollment: 8/2002-5/2005
Survey Submitted: May 2004

I have great career prospects. Most of my friends will be working in Center City Philadelphia this summer—and I will as well. Many students also participate in externships during school in Harrisburg and the surrounding areas in Federal Clerkships, DAs offices, PDs offices, clerkships and law firms. On-campus recruiting was topnotch—that is where I met my summer employer!

Status: Current student, full-time
Dates of Enrollment: 8/2003-Submit Date
Survey Submitted: September 2005

Rank high (top 10 percent) then you will not have any problem getting employed. Otherwise, you can work in the government. Moved to second tier in *U.S. News* last year. Employment prospects should be pretty good.

Status: Alumnus/a, full-time
Dates of Enrollment: 8/1997-5/2000
Survey Submitted: January 2005

Employment prospects are excellent. Dickinson is well respected in Pennsylvania, especially in central Pennsylvania where it holds a near monopoly on lawyers. While the alumni network is fairly loosely organized, there is generally a strong bond among alumni and a real willingness to help students and recent alumni. This allegiance, however, may be eroding as Dickinson is being taken over by Penn State. Many alumni feel that Penn State has betrayed the law school and that students, by attending, are siding with Penn State. Many do not hold this view, but until relationships between Penn State and the "old school" Dickinson grads are mended, students looking for jobs may suffer.

Status: Alumnus/a, full-time
Dates of Enrollment: 9/1994-5/1997
Survey Submitted: April 2004

DSL has an excellent reputation locally (Harrisburg, PA and Central PA generally). The school's proximity to the state capital provides students with excellent opportunities for internships in government and private practice and public service. I had internships at the Attorney General's office, Legal Services and Pepper Hamilton. Many firms come to campus to interview candidates, and there are many DSL graduates in all the major Harrisburg firms, and in state government.

> **The school says:** "This year, the law school introduced the Washington, D.C. semester externship program to provide third-year students accepted to the program with increased exposure to the D.C. area. The program offers semester-long externships with legislative committees and executive and independent agencies."

Quality of Life

Status: Current student, full-time
Dates of Enrollment: 8/2003-Submit Date
Survey Submitted: September 2005

Very cheap to live. On weekends, students gather at one of the three bars in the town. Very supportive atmosphere. There is a lot to do in the town. Running, going to gym are very popular. Very calm weather. Plenty of opportunity to do an externship in the city.

Status: Current student, full-time
Dates of Enrollment: 8/2002-Submit Date
Survey Submitted: April 2005

The cost of living in Carlisle is unbelievable! I have saved so much money here! The neighborhood is nice as well. Carlisle is a nice little town, but very close to New York, D.C. and Philadelphia.

Read all of Vault's Law School Surveys at www.vault.com/lawschool — get complete surveys on top law schools, expert advice on applicaton essays, LSAT prep and more.

VAULT CAREER LIBRARY   537

Status: Alumnus/a, full-time
Dates of Enrollment: 8/2001-5/2004
Survey Submitted: September 2004

The quality of life was great. I came from Los Angeles and yet still found the small town atmosphere quite refreshing. The law school is located between many large metropolitan hubs. The campus is two hours from Washington D.C., Philadelphia, Pittsburgh and Baltimore and only three hours from New York City. If you want the opportunity to work anywhere on the East Coast without being pigeonholed in one region because the law school is located in a specific city, then Penn State is a great place to be.

Status: Current student, full-time
Dates of Enrollment: 8/2002-Submit Date
Survey Submitted: May 2004

The quality of life in Carlisle is unique. It has a small town feel, with the resources of the capital just 20 minutes away. Housing is cheap—some of my friends pay $300/ month! And there is little crime.

Status: Alumnus/a, full-time
Dates of Enrollment: 8/1997-5/2000
Survey Submitted: January 2005

Dickinson is in a charming suburb of Harrisburg (PA state capital), so this is not the place for people looking for an urban setting. Parking is atrocious—the school doesn't really have a parking area and the street parking is managed by the Borough of Carlisle to maximize parking ticket revenue. The school has no real housing or dining facilities, although there are plenty of high quality accommodations in the community. Crime is almost nonexistent, and safety is not really an issue because of the setting. The facility is nice, but needs improvements.

> **The school says:** "Penn State is investing $110 million in new law school facilities and programs in Carlisle and University Park, PA. During the construction phase of our facilities, the law school will operate in a stately, four-story office building with ample parking in Carlisle and in the Beam Building, former home to the Smeal College of Business, in University Park."

 ## Social Life

Status: Current student, full-time
Dates of Enrollment: 8/2003-Submit Date
Survey Submitted: September 2005

D.C. and Philly are only two hours away. Baltimore is one and a half hours away. You can also go to NYC in four hours. You can always find things to do in the area. There are three popular bars in the town. G-man is the most popular. $5 a pitcher. Students gather around and relax on weekends. A lot of house parties. Harrisburg is 20 minutes away. You can find good restaurants in the area.

Status: Current student, full-time
Dates of Enrollment: 8/2002-Submit Date
Survey Submitted: April 2005

Not as many bars and restaurants as you may see in NY or Philly, but perfect considering this is law school!

Status: Alumnus/a, full-time
Dates of Enrollment: 8/2001-5/2004
Survey Submitted: September 2004

Honestly, we partied so much in law school, it was unbelievable.

Status: Current student, full-time
Dates of Enrollment: 8/2002-Submit Date
Survey Submitted: May 2004

There are a few bars in Carlisle and quite the nightlife in Harrisburg. The clubs and activities on campus are extensive—I do not think it would be possible to even attend all of them!

Status: Alumnus/a, full-time
Dates of Enrollment: 8/1997-5/2000
Survey Submitted: January 2005

The student body has an excellent social life, largely because they are their own group in a relatively small community. Plenty of bars and restaurants in Carlisle all of which cater to Dickinson students. No real Greek scene because the law school is separated from Penn State.

Status: Alumnus/a, full-time
Dates of Enrollment: 9/1994-5/1997
Survey Submitted: April 2004

A handful of bars and restaurants are available for students. There is far less of a social scene for students that would be available at a large city campus or major college town. Dickinson College is right next door, and this provides opportunities for events like concerts and lectures. However, Dickinson is a small college that is not associated with the law school, so the offerings are few and far between. I was married before law school and I did not participate much in the nightlife and not at all in the dating scene. Those issues are beyond what I know.

> **Penn State says:** "The law school will begin admitting students for its inaugural class in University Park, Penn State's largest campus, in fall 2006. Our presence in University Park will allow us to tap into the extensive programmatic and intellectual resources of a major research university and to deliver those resources to all students in both Carlisle and University Park."

 ## The School Says

The future of Penn State's Dickinson School of Law is exceptionally bright. During the past few years, applications for admission to the law school have increased almost 100 percent, the diversity of our student body has more than tripled, and the average academic credentials of our students continue to improve dramatically. Additionally, the University is investing approximately $110 million in programs and new law school facilities, designed by world renowned Polshek Partnership Architects, in Carlisle and University Park, PA (expected occupancy 2008-2009 academic year). Each facility will contain state-of-the-art courtrooms, classrooms, conferencing facilities, reading rooms, indoor and outdoor gathering spaces and an auditorium designed for law school as well as public use. Advanced audiovisual and telecommunications capabilities in each building will allow for the real-time delivery to each campus the classes and programs of the other. All students will have access to the same curriculum, programmatic resources and student groups, regardless of location.

Our recent faculty appointments include several of the world's top scholars in their respective fields. William Butler, the world's preeminent authority on the law of Russia and CIS nations, joined us from the University of London, as did Takis Tridimas, a leading financial institutions scholar who served recently as counsel to the presidency of the European Union. This year we also will welcome Professor Ellen Dannin, an experienced and internationally prominent labor law and civil procedure scholar; Professor Jeffrey Kahn a tax scholar and co-author of two of the nation's leading tax textbooks; Professor Kit Kinports, one of the nation's leading scholars of feminist jurisprudence, criminal law and federalism; Professor John Lopatka, one of the nation's top antitrust scholars and a former senior official of the Federal Trade Commission; Professor Marie Reilly, a prominent bankruptcy and commercial law scholar; and Professor Stephen Ross, one of the nation's leading sports law, antitrust, and comparative Canadian law scholars.

The diversified interests of our faculty, our increasing integration with Penn State's top graduate departments and our physical presence on the University's flagship campus enables us to tap into a wealth of academic resources, joint degree programs and externship opportunities that will enhance our already dynamic educational program.

We have recently established a semester-long Washington, D.C. externship program, a Child Advocacy Clinic, an Asylum Clinic, and the Penn State Institute of Arbitration Law and Practice.

Students can also take advantage of hands-on learning through our Disability Law Clinic, Elder Law and Consumer Protection Clinic, Family Law Clinic, the Miller Center for Public Interest Advocacy, and the Agricultural Law Resource and Reference Center, or participate in one of our scholarly journals or moot court teams. Specialized training and programs are available in areas such as dispute resolution and advocacy, environmental and natural resources law, international and comparative law, public interest and sports law.

Read all of Vault's Law School Surveys at www.vault.com/lawschool — get complete surveys on top law schools, expert advice on applicaton essays, LSAT prep and more.

VAULT CAREER LIBRARY **539**

Temple University

James E. Beasley School of Law
Admissions Office
1719 North Broad Street
Philadelphia, PA 19122
Admissions phone: (215) 2040-5949
Admissions e-mail: lawadmis@temple.edu
URL: http://www.law.temple.edu/

 Admissions

Status: Alumnus/a, full-time
Dates of Enrollment: 9/2002-5/2005
Survey Submitted: April 2006

Very selective; average median LSAT 161 to 164. Strong GPA needed as well. Easier to get into the night division than the day division.

Many scholarhips awarded.

Status: Alumnus/a, full-time
Dates of Enrollment: 9/2000-5/2003
Survey Submitted: March 2006

Temple has gradually gotten more and more competitive, due in part to tuition. Temple is very affordable, even for out-of-state residents, compared to other Philadelphia-region schools.

Status: Current student, full-time
Dates of Enrollment: 9/2002-Submit Date
Survey Submitted: September 2004

Temple admissions is getting more competitive, which can be viewed as a good thing or as a bad thing depending on your position. Temple has always been a school where non-traditional students are welcome. Temple does try to put more emphasis than a lot of schools on life experience and diversity of background so in your application for a seat you should definitely discuss the parts of your life that make you different.

Status: Alumnus/a, full-time
Dates of Enrollment: 9/1999-5/2002
Survey Submitted: April 2005

There was no interview process for Temple. It was governed by the association that standardizes admissions for law school. I remember there was a general essay, and I received scholarship money without requesting it—not only in my first year but throughout. The process is getting more and more selective, I've heard.

Status: Alumnus/a, full-time
Dates of Enrollment: 9/1999-5/2002
Survey Submitted: March 2005

Temple tries to select a diverse student body, but over the past few years, they have been attracting stronger academic candidates. There seems to be less of a focus on the LSAT. Life experience and post-grad degrees also seem to be a plus. You probably get farther at Temple showing you are a well-rounded candidate than trying to get by purely on grades and the LSAT. Let's face it, if you have a 4.0 and a 175, you're probably going to Harvard, so try to show that you are an interesting person dedicated to the sort of diverse learning experience Temple provides.

Status: Alumnus/a, full-time
Dates of Enrollment: 8/1993-5/1996
Survey Submitted: March 2005

Students come from truly diverse backgrounds. I recommend emphasizing whatever unique qualities or experience an applicant has. Judging from the breadth of people in my class, it appears that the admissions officers are fully aware of the benefits students from non-traditional paths can bring.

Status: Alumnus/a, full-time
Dates of Enrollment: 8/2001-5/2004
Survey Submitted: January 2005

I think that Temple is getting increasingly difficult to get into, but I think that they are still looking for a diverse, interesting student body.

Status: Alumnus/a, full-time
Dates of Enrollment: 9/1983-5/1986
Survey Submitted: August 2004

I remember the admissions process as being fairly routine. There was an application including essay and an interview but the bulk of the decision appeared to rest on the results of the LSAT test.

 Academics

Status: Alumnus/a, full-time
Dates of Enrollment: 9/2002-5/2005
Survey Submitted: April 2006

Number Two Trial Advocacy Program in the country. Number Two Integrated Writing Program in the country.

Easy to get your choice of classes and professors. Grading is curved for first-years.

Workload is a lot but manageable with a social life. Professors' doors are always open and encourage students to meet with them outside of class. Encourage active classroom participation—hardly ever lecture.

Status: Alumnus/a, full-time
Dates of Enrollment: 9/2000-5/2003
Survey Submitted: March 2006

Temple has a strict curve, about 2.78 when I attended. This is frustrating to the middle and lower portions of classes because it means many students have sub-B averages from a non-top 25 school. That being said, being at the top of the curve is more of an accomplishment because A's are much tougher to come by than at more prestigious institutions that embrace grade inflation.

Status: Current student, full-time
Dates of Enrollment: 9/2002-Submit Date
Survey Submitted: September 2004

By far the best thing about Temple is the incredible faculty. Faculty qualifications are universally impressive but the real perk here is the open-door policy for students. I have yet to meet a professor that didn't love to sit down with a student at any hour of the day and have a conversation about job search, classroom issues or advice about other academic or life choices. Because of the quality of the faculty, I have enjoyed most of my classes immensely. We are on a lottery system for getting classes, which sometimes results in disappointment but I've been able to get into most classes I didn't get in the lottery by paying attention to openings during the drop and add period. The work is hard and the legal research and writing program is serious. There is a mandatory curve in most classes.

Status: Alumnus/a, full-time
Dates of Enrollment: 9/1999-5/2002
Survey Submitted: April 2005

I have only great things to say about Temple's academics. The professors are accessible and the student body was highly motivated without being competitive. I think it was a more diverse and perhaps more liberal group than at some other schools. Some classes are scheduled for evening hours only, so you may be required to stay in North Philly after dark to get into what you want, but there is usually a big group around during the evening hours, so it did not feel at all unsafe. Grading is anonymous, but from what I understand, subject to a strict curve, so there have to be a range of grades. The workload was heavy, but not insurmountable, and it gets easier as you go along. The Trial Advocacy Program is nationally recognized.

Status: Alumnus/a, full-time
Dates of Enrollment: 9/1999-5/2002
Survey Submitted: March 2005

The quality of the classes is probably underrated, but a lot depends on the classmates you end up with. I had a great class, so classes were good. In the second and third years, it becomes very competitive to get into good classes and programs. Class selection is done by a lottery system. Get a bad number, and you will either end up taking a lot of classes at night or at eight a.m., or you'll end up not getting anything you want. The Integrated Trial Advocacy Program can be tough. Seminar classes with particular professors, like David Sonenshein, fill up every semester they are offered. Good classes with good teachers tend to fill up, but the school tries to make room for everyone, and you can usually get good stuff.

Status: Alumnus/a, full-time
Dates of Enrollment: 8/1993-5/1996
Survey Submitted: March 2005

The academic quality was outstanding. The faculty is, for the most part, talented and very accessible. In practice, I have found that my education at Temple is equivalent to, and in the case of practical courses such as writing and trial advocacy, far superior to schools ranked in the Top Five.

Status: Alumnus/a, full-time
Dates of Enrollment: 8/2001-5/2004
Survey Submitted: January 2005

LOVED IT! Especially the Trial Advocacy Program, which I believe is second to none.

Status: Alumnus/a, full-time
Dates of Enrollment: 9/1983-5/1986
Survey Submitted: August 2004

The workload was tough and the school had a good reputation in the community. Some of the professors were well known in their fields, and published authors. I had no problems getting the courses that I wanted. Grading always seemed fair and impartial.

Employment Prospects

Status: Alumnus/a, full-time
Dates of Enrollment: 9/2002-5/2005
Survey Submitted: April 2006

Temple is extremely respected in Mid-Atlantic region. Philadelphia/New Jersey/Wilmington/New York/Pittsburgh big firms love Temple students.

Besides big firms, Temple students work in public sector as prosecutors, defenders, governmentt positions, mid-size and small firms, public interest and corporate positions.

Fall and spring on-campus recruiting is very well organized and helps lots of students get jobs while still in school.

Status: Alumnus/a, full-time
Dates of Enrollment: 9/2000-5/2003
Survey Submitted: March 2006

The top echelon will do very well, but even they will find that a Temple degree is less marketable the farther you go away from the Philadelphia region.

Status: Current student, full-time
Dates of Enrollment: 9/2002-Submit Date
Survey Submitted: September 2004

Area employers pay a lot of attention to Temple. The Trial Advocacy Program gets us a lot of press and the regional alumni network is great. If you want to

work elsewhere though, it can be a struggle to find someone who is familiar with Temple. Career services is helpful.

Status: Alumnus/a, full-time
Dates of Enrollment: 9/1999-5/2002
Survey Submitted: April 2005

My thought is that if you want to practice in Philadelphia, there is no better place to be than Temple. The alumni network is extensive and the biggest firms hire more Temple has a strong focus on nonprofit work too, although the big firm recruitment is definitely the emphasis of career development. If you think you might want to go into academics or across state lines, you might want to shoot for more Ivy League schools.

Status: Alumnus/a, full-time
Dates of Enrollment: 9/1999-5/2002
Survey Submitted: March 2005

The career development department is helpful, if you want to work in Philadelphia, Temple is probably the place to go. Temple still places more students in law firms in Philadelphia than any other school. The mayor and many in city government are Temple alumni, so city jobs are plentiful. The top 10 to 15 percent of the class will get offers for large firm jobs through on-campus recruiting. Below that rank, people can typically find jobs in mid-size or smaller firms, government jobs or elsewhere. It sometimes took people a little longer to find work, but most of my classmates are either in firms, or they are DAs or PDs. Alumni are fairly active, and do a lot behind the scenes to bring more Temple grads into their respective workplaces.

Status: Alumnus/a, full-time
Dates of Enrollment: 8/1993-5/1996
Survey Submitted: March 2005

Temple graduates have impressed the employers who have hired them. Temple has a strong reputation and a very large alumni network.

Status: Alumnus/a, full-time
Dates of Enrollment: 8/2001-5/2004
Survey Submitted: January 2005

I think most grads find employment pretty quickly, but to get the high dollar jobs you have to be in the top 20 percent of the class.

Status: Alumnus/a, full-time
Dates of Enrollment: 9/1983-5/1986
Survey Submitted: August 2004

I think that a JD with Temple Law School is highly respected in the Philadelphia and surrounding areas, but I am not sure how it perceived outside of that area.

Quality of Life

Status: Alumnus/a, full-time
Dates of Enrollment: 9/2002-5/2005
Survey Submitted: April 2006

Law buildings were newly renovated; new library, state-of-the-art classrooms and computers.

Temple's gym is amazing, with tons of classes, a pool and indoor and outdoor tracks. Various shops and restuarants to eat at.

Cops patrol campus 24 hours a day and have several security stations in and outside of every building.

Status: Alumnus/a, full-time
Dates of Enrollment: 9/2000-5/2003
Survey Submitted: March 2006

The campus is very urban, but is constantly being upgraded. An perk is that it is a very short ride away from the excitement of center city Philadelphia, where many students live and recreate.

Read all of Vault's Law School Surveys at www.vault.com/lawschool — get complete surveys on top law schools, expert advice on applicaton essays, LSAT prep and more.

VAULT CAREER LIBRARY 541

Status: Current student, full-time
Dates of Enrollment: 9/2002-Submit Date
Survey Submitted: September 2004

Temple has a reputation for being in a dangerous part of the city but I've never had a problem. Our campus security is great and if you feel the need, which I generally don't, you can get a police escort at any hour of the day or night. Temple is a city campus so don't expect rolling hills and picnic areas but they have done a great job of improving the look of the buildings and the surrounding areas lately and the technology available to students (wireless Internet, online class structures) is definitely getting better.

Status: Alumnus/a, full-time
Dates of Enrollment: 9/1999-5/2002
Survey Submitted: April 2005

Temple is primarily a commuter campus. I would not recommend living on campus, as almost anywhere in Philly is better than North Broad Street and public transportation is pretty easy (if you are anywhere near the subway you can get to Temple no problem). There is also a student parking lot right across from the law school.

I did feel that the class bonded together pretty quickly despite the fact that most did not live on campus, and it was a very congenial atmosphere. If you really want to get to know people better, Temple has amazing summer programs abroad and strong friendships are often built then.

Status: Alumnus/a, full-time
Dates of Enrollment: 9/1999-5/2002
Survey Submitted: March 2005

When I started, the law school was housed in an old, ugly building. Since then, they have extensively renovated the old building and added a new building, so the classrooms and related areas are now very comfortable. There are also new facilities added to that part of campus, including a couple new restaurants, so you might actually have somewhere to eat now. The campus is in a less than desirable part of town, but the campus itself is very safe and extraordinarily well-lit—in the middle of the night, it looks like noon-time. There is not a dark alley or shadowy corner to be found anywhere on-campus. Most law students live off campus and commute. There is safe, well-lit parking less than a block from the law school and the subway stop is a few hundred feet from the steps of the law school. The school's reputation as being unsafe is undeserved. For an urban campus, it is incredibly safe.

Status: Alumnus/a, full-time
Dates of Enrollment: 8/1993-5/1996
Survey Submitted: March 2005

Live in Center City and take the subway—a 10-minute ride to campus. Center City has fantastic dining, great museums, good shopping and good nightlife. There are lots of good grungy bars for broke law students. Housing prices vary dramatically in Center City. You can get a really good deal if you really look. Much cheaper than New York, Washington or Boston.

Status: Alumnus/a, full-time
Dates of Enrollment: 8/2001-5/2004
Survey Submitted: January 2005

Improving—North Philly is no main line, but it is getting much nicer.

Status: Alumnus/a, full-time
Dates of Enrollment: 9/1983-5/1986
Survey Submitted: August 2004

I cannot say since I was an off-campus student. Certainly being located in North Philadelphia has its disadvantages but Temple seemed to provide everything within reach that on-campus students needed.

Social Life

Status: Alumnus/a, full-time
Dates of Enrollment: 9/2002-5/2005
Survey Submitted: April 2006

Dowtown Philly is five minutes away, with lots of bars, clubs, events, museums and stadiums. Everything and anything you could want within a 15-minute radius. Old City, Rittenhouse, art museum, University City are all within three or four miles of each other. Don't need a car to live in city and get to Temple. Subways/trains/trolleys/buses can take you anywhere.

Manayunk, a young urban neighborhood, is 10 minutes away

Status: Alumnus/a, full-time
Dates of Enrollment: 9/2000-5/2003
Survey Submitted: March 2006

There is the usual assortment of clubs, organizations, happy hours and campus restaurants.

Status: Current student, full-time
Dates of Enrollment: 9/2002-Submit Date
Survey Submitted: September 2004

There isn't a ton of social life on campus at Temple since most people live off campus. The Draught Horse, the campus bar, is a sorry piece of baggage indeed. The good news is that the city location means you have unlimited choices for where to go and what to do. The SBA does a great job of organizing mid-semester happy hours and open bar nights at area clubs.

Status: Alumnus/a, full-time
Dates of Enrollment: 9/1999-5/2002
Survey Submitted: April 2005

There are a large number of clubs and the student body is pretty active. Most of the clubs sponsor happy hours in the city. There is also a bar right next to the book store. Most of the "restaurants" are food carts in true Philly style, so people eat in the lounge or outside. As for dating, I met my soon-to-be-husband there, so I have a pretty high opinion of it. The scene can be as intense or as low key as you want it, because more students at Temple are part-time than at some other campuses, and have families or jobs that they are focused on when not on campus, although the party scene was definitely available.

Status: Alumnus/a, full-time
Dates of Enrollment: 9/1999-5/2002
Survey Submitted: March 2005

Because most law students live off campus, they are absolutely not limited to campus social life. There is a bar, the Draught Horse, around the corner from the law school, but except for a couple of happy hours beers, it's not a place you'd spend a lot of time. There are several bars and clubs in the city that are frequented by graduate and professional students. Philadelphia has some of the best restaurants in the country. Students also go to Temple basketball games and play intramural sports, among other things.

Status: Alumnus/a, full-time
Dates of Enrollment: 8/1993-5/1996
Survey Submitted: March 2005

The school is large, and hardly anyone lives on campus. That said, the first-year sections are comprised of about 75 students each who become the student's social circle. There are also first-year outings at various city bars, usually the ones with the cheapest pitchers. The school also has a good mentoring program allowing first-years to meet upperclassmen. There also is a student organization for virtually every group or interest.

Status: Alumnus/a, full-time
Dates of Enrollment: 9/1983-5/1986
Survey Submitted: August 2004

There was not much of a social life outside of school other than study groups. The curriculum was intensive and we were serious about our pursuits.

University of Pennsylvania Law School

Office of Admissions
3400 Chestnut Street
Philadelphia, PA 19104-6204
Admissions phone: (215) 898-7400
Admissions fax: (215) 573-2025
Admissions e-mail: Admissions@law.upenn.edu
Admissions URL: http://www.law.upenn.edu/prospective/

 ## Admissions

Status: Current student, full-time
Dates of Enrollment: 8/2003-Submit Date
Survey Submitted: May 2006

Penn Law admissions process was very seamless. Everyone was very helpful any time I called to check on the status of my application or to ask specific questions. Penn also organizes admitted students days and encourages current students to participate. Students are usually more than willing to provide their contact information because everyone is usually very enthusiastic and eager to talk about their life at Penn Law.

Status: Current student, full-time
Dates of Enrollment: 8/2004-Submit Date
Survey Submitted: May 2006

The Penn admissions process is fairly standard for law schools—with a twist. The law school asks for undergraduate transcript, LSATs and an essay, but it also asks for an additional essay explaining why you chose to apply to Penn in particular. I found that this extra steps helps winnow the pool of applicants, separating those who just apply to a laundry list of schools from those who have a particular interest in Penn.

Status: Current student, full-time
Dates of Enrollment: 8/2005-Submit Date
Survey Submitted: May 2006

The admissions process is rigorous regardless of where you apply. Penn is a selective school, and getting in involves strong performance across the board. My best advice would be to be honest and accurately portray who you are and what you want out of law school—if you convince a law school you are someone you aren't, you're hurting yourself because you aren't making sure the school is a good fit for the real you. Penn received my materials and, early in the cycle, I received an acceptance phone call from the Dean of Students, Derek Meeker. I was impressed that not only was he making the phone calls but he also seemed familiar with my personal statement and even asked a few questions about me based on my application. I was pleased to have such one-on-one contact early in my decision process. I later visited the school, which convinced me that Penn was the right place for me.

> The school says: "Derek Meeker was the Dean of Admissions."

Status: Current student, full-time
Dates of Enrollment: 9/2004-Submit Date
Survey Submitted: May 2006

Penn is a great school and can afford to be very selective in its admission process, high numbers are a must (GPA and LSAT), but everyone needs something more. There are no interviews, but the personal statement is very important to demonstrate that an applicant's personality, ambition, and attitude are the right fit for Penn. Also, visiting the school and meeting with students and deans helps.

Status: Current student, full-time
Dates of Enrollment: 8/2005-Submit Date
Survey Submitted: May 2006

The application process is pretty standard. My sense in talking to my classmates is that the selection process was very numbers focused, especially focusing on the LSAT. The conventional wisdom is that the "why Penn" optional essay is a difference maker, but I never sent it in and I was a fairly marginal candidate (on the other hand, I wasn't accepted until May, so draw your own conclusions). Penn also seems to be very focused on diversity, not only in the racial/ethnic sense, but also in the lifestyle/experience sense. After I was admitted, the admissions director told me that some of my experiences before law school were the difference maker for me. Bottom line: it is tough to get into Penn, and you should think about how you want to distinguish yourself from the pack in ways other than numbers.

Status: Current student, full-time
Dates of Enrollment: 9/2005-Submit Date
Survey Submitted: May 2006

It is certainly no cake-walk getting into Penn and it has been getting more competitive. The application is pretty much the same as any other school. People who are public interest oriented should strongly consider coming. The school loves people with that background, but gets few since most Penn students plan on being big-firm New York lawyers.

Status: Current student, full-time
Dates of Enrollment: 8/2004-Submit Date
Survey Submitted: May 2006

At Penn Law an impressive LSAT score and a strong undergraduate transcript are necessary, but not sufficient, for admission. That said, the selection committee is known to take every application seriously, because Penn Law prefers non-traditional students or students with interesting backgrounds. The committee especially values progressive politics, evidenced by the refreshingly liberal student body. Penn Law's gay and lesbian population surpasses that of any other Ivy League law school.

Status: Current student, full-time
Dates of Enrollment: 9/2005-Submit Date
Survey Submitted: May 2006

I thought admissions was already extremely selective, but from looking at the incoming class, it's getting even more selective. You definitely need a top LSAT score and GPA for this Ivy League gem. The admissions office truly does value diversity, whether ethnic, socioeconomic and/or intellectual. Each person in the class has a different aspect to highlight. To make your application shine, choose one interesting aspect (e.g., a life story, a thesis you wrote, your intellectual interests) and make it your own. They are not looking for generic "I want to be a lawyer to achieve social justice" essays UNLESS you can support that with something concrete and personal to you.

Status: Current student, full-time
Dates of Enrollment: 9/2005-Submit Date
Survey Submitted: May 2006

Penn Law's application can be done online, which saves a lot of time and hassle. There are a few optional essays which you should probably do it you're serious about getting in. The admission staff seemed very proud of the fact that the Class of '08 had such diverse background, so applicants should make sure they play up what makes them unique and leave their academic achievements to their resume. Be sure to stay in touch and let them know you're still interested.

Status: Current student, full-time
Dates of Enrollment: 9/2004-Submit Date
Survey Submitted: April 2006

Penn is highly selective when it comes to the standard criteria, but I think you need more than great LSATs and grades to have a good chance to get in. I would definitely advise prospective students to visit Penn before deciding for or against attending here. It is an urban campus; I think that's a really good thing, especially since when you have so little free time you want to have as many opportunities as possible to maximize it. That will be easier to do in Philly than in some smaller communities. I also think you would benefit from meeting current students and administrators. Everyone here seems to be pretty happy

Read all of Vault's Law School Surveys at www.vault.com/lawschool — get complete surveys on top law schools, expert advice on applicaton essays, LSAT prep and more.

VAULT CAREER LIBRARY   543

with their choice, and that enthusiasm sort of radiates throughout the law building.

Status: Current student, full-time
Dates of Enrollment: 8/2003-Submit Date
Survey Submitted: April 2006

As a waitlist student the year that Penn Law had over-admitted its incoming class, I had to submit letters and supplemental information. When I called, the admissions staff was helpful and seemed to personally know about my application. However, my LSAT score was lower than their average. The LSAT score is a very important and determinative factor in admissions, especially because so many applicants have tremendous credentials.

Status: Alumnus/a, full-time
Dates of Enrollment: 8/2000-5/2003
Survey Submitted: March 2005

I do not believe that they conduct interviews—I think that the admissions process is based solely on the GPA/LSAT grid. One thing to be careful of is that Penn often offers substantially higher financial aid and scholarships to first-years than to first- and second-years. For example, my financial aid in my second year was reduced substantially from my first year based on my summer earnings, even though all I earned was $5,000 through Penn's work study program, which did not even cover my apartment in San Francisco for my 1L summer. My worst experience with Penn was related to financial aid—my financial aid was reduced for my second semester of my third year, long after I had applied for loans and made my budget for the school year. And I ended up in a huge bind because I did not have the money to pay for that semester and pay for my living expenses (I ended up paying the extra amount with the bar loan that I received from my firm).

> **The school says:** "Beginning with the Class of 2008, Penn Law awards financial aid on a three-year basis. Students apply once for financial aid, and it is not adjusted from the initial evaluation."

Status: Alumnus/a, full-time
Dates of Enrollment: 8/2002-5/2005
Survey Submitted: April 2005

Penn Law has an early notification application process, and I was lucky enough to benefit from it. I received word that I had been admitted to Penn Law on December 24th, a wonderfully exciting gift during the holiday season! I also received Penn's Public Interest Scholarship, which was not awarded until late-March/early-April.

Status: Alumnus/a, full-time
Dates of Enrollment: 8/2001-5/2004
Survey Submitted: April 2005

There's no formal interview, but admissions officers are hugely helpful and spend a lot of time talking to students and answering questions. Further, prospects with specific interests will be directed to current students with similar interests. This individual focus is one of Penn Law's hallmarks—and it begins with the admissions process. Once students are admitted, Penn runs numerous formal and informal programs to help students learn more about the law school and Philadelphia.

Academics

Status: Current student, full-time
Dates of Enrollment: 8/2003-Submit Date
Survey Submitted: May 2006

Penn offers a variety of classes preparing students for practicing in all areas of law. Professors teaching these classes are leaders in their respective areas. Getting into most popular classes is usually not a problem—the waitlist system is well organized, as well. Additionally, Penn offers a great number of truly unique classes and seminars that encourage one's thinking and expose one to nontraditional legal issues. These classes, including Law and the Holocaust, Religion, Law and Lawyering and Animal Law, truly encourage one to think "outside the box."

Status: Current student, full-time
Dates of Enrollment: 8/2005-Submit Date
Survey Submitted: May 2006

Penn is very rigorous, and the nature of law school is competitive. However although all students are competing for grades and various jobs, people ar respectful of one another and the students have such diverse interests (from wha they want to do after law school to what city they are looking for a job to which journal they'd want to write for), the sense of competitiveness is prett diffused—you never really get the sense of being in direct competition with al those around you. The professors are bright and engaging and there is a good variety of teaching styles. I haven't had any problems getting the classes I've wanted, the grades seem fair, and the workload is comparable to what you would find at any top law school (based on discussions I've had with friends at other schools).

Status: Current student, full-time
Dates of Enrollment: 8/2004-Submit Date
Survey Submitted: May 2006

I've liked all but one of my professors at Penn and have been particularly impressed with my peers—both by the quality of their work and the extent to which they are willing and able to collaborate. I don't think the scheduling of classes is a very strong point of the school's—there seem to be multiple classes in the same general interest area that meet at the same time making it tough to find classes fit that happens to be your interest. The newly renovated classrooms make attending class a dramatically more pleasant experience. Finally, I have taken full advantage of Penn's liberal attitude towards allowing students to take classes at other graduate schools and as a result, believe I am getting a more well-rounded education and a meeting people and resources outside of the law school.

Status: Current student, full-time
Dates of Enrollment: 8/2005-Submit Date
Survey Submitted: May 2006

I've had some of the best professors here that I've ever had. Half of my professors this semester were Supreme Court Clerks and offered great insight into the Alito nomination. There is a wide range of classes and clinics offered. Penn is one of the few law schools that allows its students to take electives its first year. Penn is also unique in that its students are allowed to take classes and earn certificates from other schools in the university. One of the principle reasons I came to Penn was because I can take classes with the MBAs at Wharton and earn a certificate in Business and Public Policy from that school. Penn also has a relatively small class size (only 250 students/year). This allows every student to have lunch or coffee with their professors at least once throughout the year. The law school strongly encourages professors to get to know each student on an individual level.

> **UPenn notes:** "250 students per year is an approximate number."

Status: Current student, full-time
Dates of Enrollment: 8/2003-Submit Date
Survey Submitted: May 2006

Penn probably doesn't offer the same breadth of classes that other top schools do. But the quality of the classes is very high. Professors are as committed to teaching as they are to being academics, and virtually all professors are more than happy to spend time outside of class talking with students. It is a Penn tradition to go out to lunch, in groups of two or three, with all your first-year professors. Penn is extremely strong in the corporate law arena, but could use some work in public interest law.

Status: Current student, full-time
Dates of Enrollment: 8/2004-Submit Date
Survey Submitted: May 2006

The academic opportunities at Penn Law are as broad as the students are curious. Since I prefer to learn in a small class setting, I took mostly seminars in my second and third years, and had no trouble whatsoever in the enrollment process. In addition, the curriculum at Penn can be highly customized based on the student's academic interests. This semester I was enrolled in an advanced seminar along with one other student who was interested in the subject matter.

The professor met with the two of us weekly for a two-hour discussion of the the week's course material, which was selected based on input from the two students. I was also enrolled in a year-long independent research project where, under the guidance of a professor, I authored a full-length legal article that is now pending submission to law journals for publication. The academic opportunities at Penn Law are flexible and can be uniquely tailored to the particular interests of the student.

Status: Current student, full-time
Dates of Enrollment: 9/2005-Submit Date
Survey Submitted: May 2006

Classes aren't exceptionally interesting. The lecture style is a bit cold, especially if you're used to a more intimate classroom setting. The best professors are masters of the Socratic Method, and the way they tie people's minds in a knot is a beautiful thing. But generally, class discussion is limited. Professors are generally approachable, and are almost always willing to grab lunch with a couple of students. The nicest part of Penn's first-year program is the electives that are offered in the spring semester. The elective courses give students a chance to explore areas of personal interest in their 1L year, take a class with a prof they've heard is amazing or just get to know new 1Ls.

Status: Current student, full-time
Dates of Enrollment: 8/2003-Submit Date
Survey Submitted: May 2006

The best thing about classes at Penn are the sizes of the classes. Your 1L section is going to be at most 80 or 90 students thus ensuring you won't be totally lost in a huge mix. After that, most classes will be small, 15 or 25 students and allow for great interaction with the professors. However, when a class is particularly popular and fills up quickly the school is very susceptible to moving it to a larger room and professors are great at allowing students off the waitlist into the class.

Status: Current student, full-time
Dates of Enrollment: 8/2004-Submit Date
Survey Submitted: April 2006

Classes are rigorous, and 1Ls take more classes than at some peer schools (four per semester) with the bonus of having two electives as a 1L. Many students take classes outside the Law School, a good minority get the Wharton certificate, and some are in dual degree programs. 1Ls have a mandatory B+ curve and you have to work really hard to get either an A (about seven or eight per class) or a C (about zero or two per class).

Status: Alumnus/a, full-time
Dates of Enrollment: 8/2002-5/2005
Survey Submitted: March 2006

Good grades can help you make Law Review, but because Penn places lots of emphasis on a writing competition for journal applicants given at the end of the first year, you can make Law Review (or another journal of your choice) even without very good grades, and vice versa; i.e., top grades do not guarantee you a Law Review spot. Professors are topnotch, many world-renowned experts in their fields.

The workload can also be quite varied in the second and third years—it isn't all regular class work, you can also have pro bono work, journal work, summer recruiting work, clinical work, moot court work, interdisciplinary work and other extracurricular, campus and community activities. The workload in the first year is almost exclusively regular course work (going to class, reading to prepare for class, studying for final exams at the end of the semester). But in the second and third years, the workload is very diversified, which makes it exciting and challenging. In general, though, the workload tends to be most heavy towards the end of the semester because there are NO midterms or other exams throughout the semester, just one big final at the end. Some second- and third-year classes have a paper in lieu of a final, but that is also due at the end of the semester. Thus, it can be easy to slack-off and keep your schedule pretty work-free throughout the semester, if you want, but the end of the semester is always a killer. The more you stay on top of your work throughout, the less stress you will have at the end. But it is up to you to manage that, you won't have professors breathing down your neck in Sept. and Oct., making sure that you're ready for exams in Dec.

Status: Alumnus/a, full-time
Dates of Enrollment: 8/2002-5/2005
Survey Submitted: April 2005

UPenn law is simply amazing. In my three years here, I have never had a bad professor. In fact, three of my professors here were the best professors I have ever had. UPenn's faculty is incredible. Every professor is a national expert in their field. Another great aspect to a Penn education is that it can be interdisciplinary. Future lawyers can take classes in the other graduate schools of Penn, including the Wharton school. There is no other school with the depth and breadth of quality graduate school, except maybe Harvard. At Penn, this entire range of schools is open to the prospective law student. I highly recommend both Fels government school and Annenberg communications school. Wharton speaks for itself. Penn was also the first of the major national law schools to develop a clinical program. The clinics are great and can include everything from trying a civil case in Philadelphia municipal court to working in a U.S. Senator's office in D.C. once a week. Law students can actually practice law while in law school (under the supervision of an attorney).

Status: Alumnus/a, full-time
Dates of Enrollment: 8/2002-5/2005
Survey Submitted: April 2005

Penn Law is like most other law schools when it comes to grading; there is a mandatory curve to which professors must adhere. That said, Penn is unique as a law school insofar as you are not told your class rank until graduation! I will be graduating next month, and still do not know where I stand relative to my classmates. This helps foster at Penn Law a truly supportive and non-competitive atmosphere compared with other law schools. I have been largely successful in gaining admission to classes of my choosing, but once was closed out of a popular class due to space limitations.

> **The school says:** "The mandatory curve is for the first year and for large courses."

Status: Current student, full-time
Dates of Enrollment: 8/2004-Submit Date
Survey Submitted: March 2005

Unlike many law schools, first-years get to choose two electives in the spring from a short list of choices. Setting Penn apart from other law schools is the ability to take classes in Penn's other excellent grad schools. In general, you can take approximately four classes in schools outside of the law school. Penn was one of the first law schools to institute a pro bono requirement and presents plenty of opportunities to obtain these hours through established clinics or doing your own thing. All classes are taught by faculty who are renowned in their field. It is not at all uncommon for your professor to have written your casebook here. Additionally, you will find references to professors and their work all over their place.

 Employment Prospects

Status: Current student, full-time
Dates of Enrollment: 8/2005-Submit Date
Survey Submitted: May 2006

For those who would like to pursue a career other than the law, there is a very interesting program at Penn called the Dean's Rountable Series. Dean Fitts invites prominent alumni who are working in a field other than the law to come to the school. Penn Law students meet with the dean and the alumni over breakfast or lunch and hear the alumni speak about what he does on a day to day basis, how he ended up where he is, and how his JD has (or hasn't) helped him to get there. The meetings are kept to be very small (maybe 10 or 12 people) and the students have the chance to ask the alumni questions and pick his or her brain. I've had breakfast or lunch with two CEOs this semester alone!

Status: Current student, full-time
Dates of Enrollment: 8/2004-Submit Date
Survey Submitted: May 2006

The federal judiciary's perception of the caliber of Penn grads appears to have been rising as well, and a significant fraction of my classmates have obtained

Read all of Vault's Law School Surveys at www.vault.com/lawschool — get complete surveys on top law schools, expert advice on applicaton essays, LSAT prep and more.

VAULT CAREER LIBRARY **545**

clerkships at both the district and circuit levels. Although Penn grads are concentrated in the Northeast, I found the alumni network to be a valuable and effective resource across the country and around the world (e.g., the school connected me to an LLM program graduate in Italy with whom I had lunch during a visit there last summer).

Status: Alumnus/a, full-time
Dates of Enrollment: 8/2002-5/2005
Survey Submitted: March 2006

Employment prospects for graduates of Penn Law are excellent. Everyone I know of had a job at graduation. Most graduates seem to go into private practice at large law firms in major northeastern cities (NYC, Philadelphia, Washington). But lots of graduates go into other areas of law (e.g., public interest or government, assisted by Penn's loan forgiveness programs) or business, academia. Judicial clerkships are also a popular route upon graduation. The types of jobs graduates obtain vary widely, according to graduates' varied interests, but everyone seems to be able to find the work they want. Employers seem to view Penn as a prestigious institution, which is reflected both informally, in conversation with recruiters, and more substantively in the requirements for employment; i.e., firms will hire Penn students with lower grades or lack of journal experience because of the school's prestige, while they may require higher grades or journal experience of applicants from other, less prestigious schools.

The alumni network is very helpful, but more in terms of researching potential employers and giving general career advice than in actually getting jobs. But it is not really necessary to rely on alumni to get jobs because the on-campus recruiting (OCR) program is so successful. OCR takes place at the beginning of your second year, and most people get summer associate jobs (which lead to post-graduation employment) through that program. There is no pre-screening of resumes or transcripts, so anyone can sign up to interview with any firm (which is not always the case at other schools). Interviews are scheduled randomly, but there is such a wide selection of firms participating in OCR that people can usually get all their top choices. And if you don't get randomly assigned to interview with a firm you like, you can always try to be added to that firm's interview schedule later on. Penn's career development staff can be very helpful, but you do have to seek out their assistance, especially if you don't want to work in a law firm.

Status: Alumnus/a, full-time
Dates of Enrollment: 8/2002-5/2005
Survey Submitted: April 2005

While it is unsurprising that students at a Top 10 law school would obtain law firm jobs with relative ease, I have been impressed with the number of students who have obtained even more prestigious jobs. I obtained my number one job choice each of my summers during law school, and will be clerking next year on a federal court of appeals. Penn Law students can definitely compete with the likes of Yale, Harvard and others.

Status: Alumnus/a, full-time
Dates of Enrollment: 8/2002-5/2005
Survey Submitted: March 2005

Employers come to Penn from all over the country to recruit, and Penn runs regional recruiting programs during the summer all over the U.S. Employers love Penn law students. OCI is via lottery, students bid for interviews with employers and interview are assigned by a specially designed software package. But even if you don't get an interview with a particular employer, as long as you bid the employer gets a copy of your resume and is free to contact you off-grid. Most post-grad BigLaw employment is via firms' 2L summer program, but even students who choose to spend their summers doing public interest work are able to find BigLaw employment post-grad, with a fair amount of 3L hustling. A fair number of students clerk for a year after graduation, most on the federal level, deferring their firm jobs for a year.

Status: Alumnus/a, full-time
Dates of Enrollment: 8/2001-5/2004
Survey Submitted: June 2004

The career planning office was a tremendous help during my time at Penn. found them reaching out to us early in our first year, to give us a feel for what things we should be aware of and what types of things we should do to prepare for both summer jobs, as well as jobs after graduation. There was a tremendous amount of guidance, in the form of meetings, seminars, guest speakers and ample literature, about any possible legal, or relevant non-legal career path. I was made very clear from the beginning that as long as students stuck to the office's suggested timeliness, we would have no difficulty finding opportunities of interest. Second-year recruiting was particularly well organized, as our priorities were sorted by computer and our scheduled interviews were easily changed as necessary as we progressed through the process. The mock interview program, where Penn brought attorneys from several firms all over the country was particularly helpful in terms of practice and constructive feedback to employ in the actual interview process. The office also did a great job in helping us understand what things about ourselves we most wanted to emphasize to employers, as well as what to expect at call-back interviews.

> **Penn Law says:** "Career Planning and Placement provides individual counseling, research resources and application support. Individualized applications are required for small firms, businesses and other industries since they do not hire on an annual basis, nor do they typically hire right after law school."

 ## Quality of Life

Status: Current student, full-time
Dates of Enrollment: 8/2004-Submit Date
Survey Submitted: May 2006

Penn is just a chill place to go to school. It's a law school, sure, but it's about as laid-back as a law school can (realistically) be. There's not that undercurrent of unhealthy competition that pervades a lot of peer schools, and the relatively small size means that everyone has to get along. The facilities are great, now that four dismal classrooms have been gutted and rehabbed. University City is a vibrant neighborhood; because the law school is on the edge of Penn's campus, it has access to everything the greater university offers, but is not smack in the middle.

Status: Current student, full-time
Dates of Enrollment: 8/2005-Submit Date
Survey Submitted: May 2006

Philadelphia is an affordable northeastern city—a dying breed. It is affordable to live downtown, and the entire downtown area is small enough to be navigable on foot or bike, and public transportation is clean and safe. University City, where the law school is located, is where lots of undergrads and some professional students live because of the proximity to campus and because it is cheaper than living downtown. However, cheap housing can also be had in Center City, especially if you look for an apartment somewhere other than at the high rise apartment complexes. I walk to and from school every day (about a 20-minute walk) and haven't felt unsafe—though I try not to walk home alone late at night.

Status: Current student, full-time
Dates of Enrollment: 9/2004-Submit Date
Survey Submitted: May 2006

Penn Law School is a noncompetitive, progressive environment. Students share notes and outlines, there are clubs and leadership opportunities for every interest, and the law school dorms are right across the street. Off-campus housing is coordinated through the housing office, and Philadelphia is very affordable compared to most cities. The security force is a constant presence, and extends several blocks beyond campus to keep watch over the off-campus housing.

Status: Current student, full-time
Dates of Enrollment: 8/2003-Submit Date
Survey Submitted: May 2006

On-campus housing at Penn should be avoided if at all possible. It's not comfortable and is more expensive than just finding an apartment. Apartments are plentiful and not expensive for a city. I have never felt unsafe in the area near Penn nor in much of Philadelphia. There are many dining opportunities near Penn and in the city in general. The facilities at Penn Law are first rate.

Status: Current student, full-time
Dates of Enrollment: 9/2005-Submit Date
Survey Submitted: May 2006

The school is extremely accessible, even if you are living off campus. Penn Law's campus is OK. About half the class buildings have been refurbished in recent years, and one wing is completely new and state-of-the-art. Many people swear by the library, but be forewarned, it's a bright modern space bearing no resemblance to the law library in the movie *Philadelphia*! The Courtyard at the center of the law school block is absolutely lovely, especially in the fall and spring—it's like having a private park to study and relax in. There is a passable cafe, which is slated for closure this year, to be replaced by vending machines. The law school is slightly on the periphery of Penn's campus, but feels very safe.

Status: Alumnus/a, full-time
Dates of Enrollment: 8/2002-5/2005
Survey Submitted: March 2006

There are tons of interesting academic, cultural, social and political events every day. The campus is extremely diverse and dynamic and really adds to the law school experience. There is a great new gym with a terrific pool, in addition to the older gym (also with pool), indoor and outdoor tennis courts, ice skating rink and every other athletic amenity one would expect to find on a major college campus. There are dozens of dining halls on campus, including one at the law school itself. Students can sign up for a wide variety of meal plans to suit their individual needs. Kosher options are available, as are a variety of other ethnic cuisines. But it is not necessary to have a campus meal plan if you don't want one. There are plenty of other dining options on and near campus. The neighborhood is not known for its safety, and unfortunately, crime is not rare. The most common crime is bike theft, but more serious crimes like muggings and even shootings have occurred in the vicinity. But these do not usually involve students, and Penn has its own very competent police force that works with the local Philadelphia police to keep students safe.

Status: Alumnus/a, full-time
Dates of Enrollment: 8/2002-5/2005
Survey Submitted: April 2005

Penn provides an excellent environment for study. The physical structure of the institution—with a large grass courtyard with tables in the center—is wonderfully conducive to a nurturing social climate. Philadelphia is a great place to live for school, particularly if you live in Center City. In moving here from New York, I found Philadelphia quite reasonably priced, very cute, quaint and manageable. The proximity of the law school to the main campus (one block) is a great asset—you have both the vibrancy and excitement of the undergraduate community, and the resources of the other graduate and professional schools at your fingertips. I have found this enriching in social and academic ways—from the grad-student Spanish conversation group that I attend weekly, to the Child Advocacy Clinic that combines the efforts of law, medical and social work students in providing comprehensive services to children in need.

Status: Alumnus/a, full-time
Dates of Enrollment: 8/2002-5/2005
Survey Submitted: March 2005

The campus keeps getting nicer and nicer. In seven years at Penn, it has changed a lot and it just keeps getting better. I have no love for the student housing options, but there is tons of off-campus living. Dining could use some improvements, but there are a wealth of food trucks around the school that are very cheap and quite delicious and the restaurants right across the street from the law school are all terrific. The neighborhood is quite nice and crime is what you might expect from a large city, although Penn does a good job with its own police force.

 ## Social Life

Status: Current student, full-time
Dates of Enrollment: 8/2003-Submit Date
Survey Submitted: May 2006

The advantage of being located in Philadelphia is that restaurants, bars and theaters are abundant. Philadelphia has a great restaurant scene, from high-end restaurants owned by celebrity chefs (e.g., Morimoto's) to the Philadelphia cheesesteak rivals Geno's and Pat's. In addition to this, Penn Law often sponsors various social events, including formals, BBQs and happy hours.

Status: Current student, full-time
Dates of Enrollment: 8/2005-Submit Date
Survey Submitted: May 2006

Philadelphia is known as the home of the BYOB; it is filled with small restaurants that allow patrons to bring in their own alcohol, from Mexican restaurants with BYOTequila who sell various margarita mixes to the standard Italian restaurant allowing you to bring your own wine; this niche is certainly unique to Philly. There are plenty of extracurricular activities sponsored by the law school and students who find none of them speak to their particular interests are often proactive enough to start their own club or organization. Stephen Starr has a handful of amazing restaurants here—each one matching in ambiance what it also offers in taste, from Buddakan (Morrocan) to Continental (upscale diner chic) to Jones (comfort food) to Morimoto (Iron Chef sushi restaurant) each is an experience unto itself. There are also great bars in every area from University City to Old City (where the Real World Philadelphia was taped) to South Street (Philly's version of Greenwich Village) to Rittenhouse Square (the posh area of downtown) to the Italian Market area (with the best cheeses!), there is something for you no matter what your taste.

Status: Current student, full-time
Dates of Enrollment: 8/2005-Submit Date
Survey Submitted: May 2006

The social life is as active as you want it to be. Most people seem to take 1L first semester rather seriously. Students will choose one or two activities to get involved in, and hang out a couple of nights a week. Being a student is a full-time job, so, if you want to be prepared every day, you really don't have that much spare time. That being said, there is usually a happy hour a couple days a week and people do grab lunch with each other between classes. There were a few parties that I attended but they resembled college frat parties, which is not my thing. However, a good-sized group would get together to have pot-lucks on the weekends. We also would plan restaurant nights and going to events, like the Art Museum, running 5K and 10K races and seeing a Phllies game. A lot of my social life revolved around going to yoga or for runs. As for the dating situation, I have a serious boyfriend from grad school, so I can't speak first-hand, but some of my friends started dating. Again, most people focus on school the first year, so I imagine that social life will change next year.

Status: Current student, full-time
Dates of Enrollment: 8/2003-Submit Date
Survey Submitted: May 2006

The school itself has a variety of student groups, including many that offer students the opportunity to blow off a little steam throughout the semester. Particularly popular are the flag football and basketball intramurals. Perhaps the most popular, however, is the Penn Law Bowling League, which meets every Wednesday throughout both semesters. The league is designed with a handicap system, which allows even the most inexperienced team to have a shot at winning the league title each semester, so everyone has a good time. The bowling alley also employs a BYO policy, and teams generally pick up a case of beer for the evening from the beer distributor across the street.

Status: Current student, full-time
Dates of Enrollment: 9/2005-Submit Date
Survey Submitted: May 2006

There is an organization called Graduate and Professional Student Association, which organizes social events among the different schools. It's a great opportunity to interact and build connections with medical, Wharton and engineering students. The bars right on campus and in Center City are great—different styles and atmospheres depending on your mood. Philadelphia people

Read all of Vault's Law School Surveys at www.vault.com/lawschool — get complete surveys on top law schools, expert advice on applicaton essays, LSAT prep and more.

VAULT CAREER LIBRARY 547

are extremely friendly and it's often that we go to bars and make friends with the locals. At the risk of being cliche, at Penn we work hard and we play hard.

Status: Current student, full-time
Dates of Enrollment: 9/2004-Submit Date
Survey Submitted: April 2006

Penn Law has many many social clubs, some based on activities (like intramural football or wine appreciation), some based on political ideology (American Constitution Society, Equal Justice Foundation, Lambda, Federalist Society), some on ethnic origin (Black Law Students Association, Asian-Pacific Law Students Association, many Jewish groups). Each of these clubs provides a lot of opportunities for socializing and interaction, and many require very small dues, or no dues at all. There are also a lot of journal-run activities for the various journals' members (we have four official journals and several other student-run journals).

Status: Current student, full-time
Dates of Enrollment: 8/2004-Submit Date
Survey Submitted: April 2006

Penn has a well-deserved reputation for being a collegial place. If you want to you could party with law students every night of the week, or never leave the library once. I wouldn't recommend either course. Most students strike a balance between the two while working hard and having a really good time doing it. I think friendly easy-going students self-select Penn over peer schools by the vibe they get at new admit day. I've never even heard of a problem with "being cutthroat," in fact I've never heard of anyone being denied when asking for class notes or an outline. One time first year a girl in my section had he laptop stolen two months into school. She e-mailed the class asking for note and her inbox crashed because 60 out of 80 students in the section sent her wha they had immediately. She got up in front of class the next day and started to cr when thanking everyone. It's a competitive place because you need to b competitive to get in here, but you never feel like you are directly competing with your peers.

Status: Alumnus/a, full-time
Dates of Enrollment: 8/2002-5/2005
Survey Submitted: April 2005

Penn Law is a surprisingly social law school, particularly early in the term From moment one at "pre-orientation," the multitude of social events i staggering. Not all students partake of the social scene (some prefer to treat law school as a professional experience only), but those who do find it a lot of fun Penn Law has a bowling league that meets every Wednesday. Imagine this: 5(law students in teams of four with handicaps (!), drinking beer and hitting the lanes. Needless to say, most of us aren't noticed by the Professional Bowler Association for our bowling talent, but everyone enjoys this Wednesday nigh relief. Penn Law is social internally and externally—within the Penn Law community, with other students at the med school, Wharton and others, and in the greater Philadelphia community. I have been extremely pleased with my experience at Penn Law that has allowed me to live a well-rounded life during law school.

University of Pittsburgh School of Law

Office of Admission and Financial Aid
3900 Forbes Avenue
Pittsburgh, PA 15260
Admissions phone: (412) 648-1400
Admissions fax: (412) 648-1318
Admissions e-mail: admissions@law.pitt.edu
Admissions URL: http://www.law.pitt.edu/admissions/

 Admissions

Status: Current student, full-time
Dates of Enrollment: 9/2003-Submit Date
Survey Submitted: April 2006

I found the interview process to be fairly straightforward. No special essay questions or anything like that. Merit scholarships are awarded automatically on the strength of your entire application; no one invites you to fill out a separate application for this or that scholarship. This is nice in that you can get a scholarship offer along with your acceptance letter, but maybe not so nice if you don't get chosen for a scholarship and would have been willing to put together an additional application.

> **The school says:** "Students admitted prior to April 15th earning an average LSAT score of 161 or better and an undergraduate cumulative grade point average of 3.4 (on a 4.0 scale) are guaranteed the Dean's Scholarship. However, all admitted students are reviewed for consideration for a merit scholarship. Students awarded merit scholarships will be notified in writing within three weeks of receiving their admit letter. The minimum award amount starts at $10,000 per academic year with two equal payments of $5,000 per term."

Status: Current student, full-time
Dates of Enrollment: 8/2004-Submit Date
Survey Submitted: April 2006

The admissions process was fantastic, mainly because the admissions group at Pitt is head and shoulders above any other school I applied to (I had seven applications out there). The office is genuinely interested in each prospective student and is overly helpful and kind. If you call, you're not an annoyance, but a happy surprise. The forms are the usual forms that everyone wants, including the recommendations and the essay, everything else is through LSAC. Make sure you point out your unique personality, and that will help.

Status: Current student, full-time
Dates of Enrollment: 9/2005-Submit Date
Survey Submitted: April 2006

Once you get in, the school makes a strong effort to sell the school. You get e-mails from faculty and admissions with a description of the school. There is an accepted student open house. It's nice, because you feel like they really want you to attend.

Status: Current student, full-time
Dates of Enrollment: 8/2005-Submit Date
Survey Submitted: April 2006

The admissions process was pretty easy. I highly recommend submitting materials early because they do seem to adhere to the "rolling" admissions process. I applied in October and was accepted in December. The staff is really helpful and answer questions quickly. I am not sure how selective they are, but I felt they took into account all of my information. My admissions letter even included a hand-written note from one of the members of the selection committee.

Status: Current student, full-time
Dates of Enrollment: 8/2005-Submit Date
Survey Submitted: April 2006

The admissions process was pretty fast—Pitt seems to have a good turn around on applications. I believe that personal statements are key, whether you have stellar numbers or lower numbers. When I look at the composition of my class, I can see that the ad-com really does take a look at the person as a whole. We have people from a wide variety of backgrounds—people straight from college, young parents, post-military, post-graduate and many people who took one to four years off to work between college and law school. Additionally, the students are from a variety of states, not just from PA. Many come from the Mid-Atlantic area, and also come from as far away as TX, FL, CA and WA. I think that using the essay to truly sell yourself and your experiences can make a big impact on your application. Don't worry so much about saying what you think "the ad-com wants to hear"—just be honest and direct about your goals, and show what you have to offer to the program and how this program can help you further your goals.

Status: Current student, full-time
Dates of Enrollment: 8/2004-Submit Date
Survey Submitted: April 2006

I actually transferred into Pitt Law right before my second year. At this stage in the admissions process the staff was extremely helpful and attentive. They actually called me on the telephone to tell me that I was admitted prior to sending an acceptance letter. They immediately set up meetings for me with admissions, financial aid and a professor to help schedule my courses. The year that I was admitted as a transfer I believe that there were only one or two others admitted as transfers also. Although I have no idea how many applied to be a transfer student I would guess that it was a highly selective process based upon comments provided to me by the admissions office.

Status: Current student, full-time
Dates of Enrollment: 8/2004-Submit Date
Survey Submitted: October 2005

Same as for other law schools. HOWEVER, if you have LSAT scores above their 25th percentile (which is currently around 163 or 164, I think), you WILL get a significant partial scholarship. Once you factor in the scholarship, my law school education is only costing me about $8,000 a year—this compares VERY favorably with the $34,000 a year every other law school I got into wants (Michigan, UPenn and waitlisted at Columbia)!

Status: Current student, full-time
Dates of Enrollment: 8/2004-Submit Date
Survey Submitted: February 2006

The process is similar to all the other schools that take the common application, which is what I submitted, which seems to have worked. I do recommend tailoring an essay to one of Pitt's certificate programs (IP, Health, Litigation, Environment or International); some are still getting off the ground and need participants.

> **Pitt Law says:** "One way to prepare for law practice in a society facing information overload and increasingly complex legal issues is to concentrate your academic study in a particular field of law. Pitt Law students who choose this route have the advantage of taking any of five certificate programs, each of which offers students the opportunity to take sharply-focused courses leading to a certificate verifying completion of a concentrated course of study. All of these certificate programs have been established since before 2003. You can begin to participate in the certificate programs after your first year of law school and you do not need to know at the point of admissions if you plan on entering one of our certificate programs."

Read all of Vault's Law School Surveys at www.vault.com/lawschool — get complete surveys on top law schools, expert advice on applicaton essays, LSAT prep and more.

VAULT CAREER LIBRARY 549

Status: Current student, full-time
Dates of Enrollment: 8/2004-Submit Date
Survey Submitted: April 2005

The admissions process at Pitt Law is fairly typical of most law schools. The school requires a strong academic background and increasingly high GPAs and test scores though it seeks candidates with diverse backgrounds. For example, many of my classmates worked for several years and/or already have graduate degrees and come from all over the country. Most students are thrilled to be at Pitt Law, which is increasingly students' first choice. I would advice interested candidates to take the admissions process VERY seriously as the school's increased status has prompted more and more applicants, and each year the profile of the accepted student is more competitive. Sell yourself on why you are different and what your classmates will gain from you as a peer. Pitt is looking for smart, professionally-minded candidates who will contribute to the student body. I believe my proven commitment to school and past success in the work force helped my admission. Show Pitt that you have leadership potential.

> **The school says:** "Pitt Law is highly competitive and decisions are based upon several factors with the GPA and LSAT being the most important. When evaluating an undergraduate degree, the committee pays careful attention to the strength of the major field of study, as evidenced by the courses listed on the undergraduate transcript. The school is looking for applicants who have demonstrated the discipline and ability to handle a rigorous and demanding program. The same assessment is made of graduate and professional work."

Status: Current student, full-time
Dates of Enrollment: 8/2004-Submit Date
Survey Submitted: December 2004

Pitt weighs the LSAT very heavily. I know many students with sub-par grades and good LSATs who are here. I had a horrendous undergrad GPA (2.6) and had been placed on academic probation as a freshman, but Pitt was very aggressive in recruiting me. In contrast, I was rejected by several lower-ranked schools, including some where my LSAT was 10+ points above their 75 percent threshold. I didn't interview and didn't receive any feedback from my essay, but most everyone I know who has a scholarship is a member of an ethnic or religious minority group, so I assume that had something to do with my scholarship and admittance.

> **The school says:** "Approximately 43 percent of the student body receives scholarship funds from the School of Law in the form of merit and need-based scholarship awards. There is no application necessary for merit scholarships. Admitted students are automatically considered for these funds on the basis of past academic performance and will be notified in writing within three weeks of receiving their admit letter of any scholarship award. Applications must be submitted, however, for need-based scholarships. In determining these awards, we consider undergraduate debt, student income, other resources such as savings and property and parents' ability to contribute funding."

Status: Alumnus/a, full-time
Dates of Enrollment: 8/2000-5/2003
Survey Submitted: January 2004

The admission process was easy. Pitt does extensive on-campus recruiting, which is how I became interested. The dean of admissions was extremely open and very helpful. I then completed the online application and supplied the standard information (LSAT scores, undergrad transcripts), and waited. I received an e-mail acceptance before the fat envelope in the mail. I think that Pitt is looking for people who are from different disciplines. I can't think of 10 people who have the same interests in law. It makes for an interesting student experience. The applications have increased immensely in the last two years, so be clear and dynamic in your essays.

Academics

Status: Current student, full-time
Dates of Enrollment: 9/2003-Submit Date
Survey Submitted: April 2006

I found first year very challenging here (a surprise since I went to an Ivy League undergrad and came in something of a snob). If you choose your classes carefully—that is, by talking to other people about what classes and professors are good—you can put together a good schedule. If I couldn't get a class one semester, I could usually get it by trying again a different semester.

Professors are absolutely terrific—my favorite thing about Pitt Law. They are all very well credentialed, bright and hard-working academics. They take teaching seriously and are very accessible to students for any kind of help or advice at all. I've never had a professor behave as if they were anything other than delighted that I stopped by their office and asked for their help. The physical layout of the building helps—their offices form a ring around the perimeter of the library, and it's easy to stop by and knock on their door without worrying about figuring out when office hours are.

Status: Current student, full-time
Dates of Enrollment: 8/2004-Submit Date
Survey Submitted: April 2006

The jewel of Pitt Law is the certificate programs. Whether you're interested in Intellectual Property, Health Law, International Law or Litigation, you will learn from some of the best in their fields. I have never been unable to get into a class I wanted. Pitt was in a flux due to some professors passing, but the professors that are here are excellent. The workload is heavy, but if you want to be a lawyer, that's part of the career.

Status: Current student, full-time
Dates of Enrollment: 9/2005-Submit Date
Survey Submitted: April 2006

During my first semester I had the same classes as all my other classmates: Criminal Law, Contracts, Legal Process, Torts and Legal Writing. Second semester, students take Criminal Procedure, Constitutional Law, Property, Legal Writing and Civil Procedure. The first-year class is divided into three sections (A, B and C), which are subdivided again into smaller sections. Each section has about 70 students and each small section has about 25 students. You have two classes that consist of only your small section (one of which is Legal Writing) and the other three consist of your larger sections.

Every law school has a similar teaching style (the Socratic Method and reading of casebooks) and grading system (based on a strict curve), but what makes Pitt better is the academic atmosphere. I found my section to be friendly and not overly competitive. Students share information with each other and take part in study groups. The professors are very approachable and are available after class or during their office hours. My friends at other schools complain that their professors are not friendly and are unapproachable, and this is not the case at Pitt.

Status: Current student, full-time
Dates of Enrollment: 8/2004-Submit Date
Survey Submitted: April 2006

I believe that the quality of legal education provided at Pitt Law is extremely high and challenging. Also, professors do not attempt to foster a competitive atmosphere in their classrooms and despite a Socratic Method are very respectful to their students. Since I attended a different law school my first year I can tell you that in comparing the two schools Pitt Law is superior by far!

Status: Current student, full-time
Dates of Enrollment: 8/2005-Submit Date
Survey Submitted: April 2006

The law program was even better than I expected. There are many nationally renowned faculty members, and I am very satisfied with all that I have learned here so far. The classroom experience has been stimulating and challenging, and professors are always accessible after class. The workload is a lot, but still doable. Our curriculum tends to approach law from a national perspective, which I like a lot more than other schools that take a more "state-specific" approach. We've had many opportunities to compare issues by looking at the case law from a variety of states, while also learning about case law within PA. I have greatly enjoyed studying law with this broad view approach. There are also some unique certificate programs that give students a chance to focus on one area of the law and become certified on the particular topic (such as Health Law, Intellectual Property, check the web site for more info). Upperclassmen have said that the certificates have really worked to their benefit, and many potential employers have been quite impressed with their pursuits within the academic program.

Status: Alumnus/a, full-time
Dates of Enrollment: 9/2002-5/2005
Survey Submitted: April 2006

The academics are challenging yet the professors are friendly and accessible. You are certainly expected to be prepared for class on a daily basis and anyone planning to only show up for finals should consider a different school (or perhaps a different career plan!). The workload first year is the most challenging because of the exam anxiety and complexity of the study of law, but all professors are cognizant of this and are generally willing to cut students some slack who are occasionally unprepared.

The second and third years are more dependent upon the curriculum a student chooses, as some courses are much easier and less time consuming than others. The interviewing process, journals, moot court and writing competitions make these years more of time-management issue than first year, but also more rewarding. Overall, I think Pitt offers a wonderful academic program for most specialities and the professors are gifted, professional and helpful.

Status: Current student, full-time
Dates of Enrollment: 8/2004-Submit Date
Survey Submitted: February 2006

The professors were even better than I expected. As in all places, there are a few duds, but most are informed, congenial and published leaders in their fields. The professors and administrators are very accessible—they answer e-mails quickly and are always available after class. They take an interest in student activities and don't shy from participating in forums. There's definitely a personal touch, and it doesn't feel like you're being pushed through a meat-grinder. It's not as competitive as I've heard other schools are. The students cooperate and share notes, and I've never heard of someone hiding a book. If you need a competitive environment to perform, I'd look elsewhere. That's not to say students don't work hard, but you better self-motivate. Even first-year classes are rarely Socratic, so time-management skills are key.

The new library is great and there are more than enough computers in the labs. The lack of a consistent wi-fi signal outside the library is annoying and merely pushes the bored students to Solitaire. Not having consistently wired desks in the classrooms is a minus, although there are a number of flat-panel plasmas that display when and where student groups are meeting.

Status: Current student, full-time
Dates of Enrollment: 8/2003-Submit Date
Survey Submitted: May 2005

Pitt operates on a strict curve for first-year classes and large upper-level classes. It is not hard to get the favored professors who are very good, but if you don't get them, the second choice professor is usually pretty poor. The workload is reasonable, but Pitt requires a LOT of credits to graduate.

> **The school says:** "It takes 88 credits and three years of full-time study at two semesters per year to earn the JD degree. Grading guidelines adopted by the faculty encourage, but do not require, faculty members to assign certain percentages of students in the class grades in a specified range. Professors teaching first-year and large upper-level courses are encouraged to assign 20 percent of students grades in the A range, and either 20 percent (for first-year courses) or 10 to 15 percent (for large upper-level courses) of students grades in the C or below range."

Status: Current student, full-time
Dates of Enrollment: 8/2004-Submit Date
Survey Submitted: April 2005

I have been very happy with my first-year professors. It has been an interesting mix. Some professors have been teaching a long time while some are new. Some regularly call on people, willing or not; one had a pre-set schedule for who was going to be called on. The diversity in approaches has been refreshing: each class is different. I thought the school as a whole, and some professors in particular, were very supportive about preparing for first-year exams. There were countless review sessions, info. sessions with upperclassmen, exam preparation workshops, sample exams on reserve and so forth. There was plenty of information about what was expected and how to prepare for exams. This support alleviated somewhat of the stress of the unknown, since there was so much preparation for what was ahead.

Status: Current student, full-time
Dates of Enrollment: 8/2004-Submit Date
Survey Submitted: April 2005

Pitt Law is VERY hard, but an incredible academic experience. This is not the school for someone looking to hit auto-pilot for three years. You will not pass if you are not prepared and do not take your education seriously. Professors grade on a very traditional curve and the pressure can be overwhelming. My friends who have graduated and are in practice believe that Pitt's rigorous education enabled them to pass up peers from other law schools. The school's intense curriculum prepares you to be a legal professional. Every professor and classroom experience I have been a part of has been overwhelmingly positive.

It's important to note that Pitt Law has a new attendance policy which is a bit "big brother." You have to attend at least 80 percent of classes or you fail the course. Overall, students see the point but think as adults it's unnecessary and very junior high. If professors can't get students to attend their classes because of their capabilities to engage students and teach content relevant to exams and practicing law, that's an indication of something other than students' tendency to sleep in and the remedy is not forcing attendance. More than anything, it sends a strange message to the students. Hopefully this will change.

> **The school says:** "The American Bar Association, which accredits law schools, requires that each accredited school require regular class attendance and adopt and enforce policies relating to class attendance."

 Employment Prospects

Status: Current student, full-time
Dates of Enrollment: 8/2004-Submit Date
Survey Submitted: April 2006

As a second-year, there is a myriad of opportunities through Pitt Law. I will be working for a large firm considered the best in its field in the country this summer. My friends are in every spectrum of the rainbow of the job market: from research positions for those interested in becoming professors to nonprofit organizations to public service to small, medium and large firms. Contrary to what you might think, about half of us won't even be in Pennsylvania this summer, let alone the 'Burgh. But if you want to work in Pittsburgh, Pitt's the law school to go to.

Status: Current student, full-time
Dates of Enrollment: 9/2005-Submit Date
Survey Submitted: April 2006

I think career services does a great job of trying to help students find jobs. There is a job opportunities web site that is updated frequently and e-mails are sent out to students about these opportunities and strategies/tips for job hunting. You have a meeting with someone from career services as early as your first semester to review your resume and to outline your goals. There are also other meetings throughout the second semester to provide job advice. For example, career services set-up mock interviews to help students develop better interviewing skills and they also set up several networking events with attorneys from the Pittsburgh community.

Read all of Vault's Law School Surveys at www.vault.com/lawschool — get complete surveys on top law schools, expert advice on applicaton essays, LSAT prep and more.

VAULT CAREER LIBRARY 551

Status: Alumnus/a, full-time
Dates of Enrollment: 9/2002-5/2005
Survey Submitted: April 2006

Employment prospects are generally what the student makes of them. Obviously, if you are in the top 10 percent, on-campus interviewers will seek you out and you will find a position at a large firm rather easily. If you are the large majority of students (the other 90 percent), you must take advantage of postings by the career services for openings, look for judicial positions, and basically find your own job. Surprisingly, there are many students unwilling to do this and expect the jobs to find them. This rarely works. If a student is diligent and explores all options, employment will follow, no matter the grades.

Status: Alumnus/a, full-time
Dates of Enrollment: 8/2001-5/2004
Survey Submitted: April 2006

Since I was a mean of the bell curve, on-campus interviews were nonexistent for me. Nobody wanted to interview me because of my grades despite having an impressive resume, Moot Court Chair, Health Law Moot Court Team, previous work experience and many externships. I found this disappointing.

I attempted to move across country after graduating, and I found the alumni network was helpful. They were all willing to meet with me and discuss the local economy. Although none led to a job, I found I was better prepared for the move. In the end, I changed my mind and stayed in the Pittsburgh area.

I was disappointed by the preparation I was given by the school for searching for job. Most of the energy from the career services was given to OCI. However, any of the career staff were available whenever I need something. And, in the end, they did get me a job. I kept my resume in their resume bank and they supplied my resume to my current employer.

> The school says: "We provide as much one on one attention as students require until they find either a job of their choice or a job that will eventually lead to career satisfaction. On-campus interviewing may be perceived as the program that utilizes most of the CSO's energy, but the reality is that the majority of students find employment outside of the OCI process. We therefore expend significant time and energy through an extensive array pf services, including professional development and networking opportunities, individual counseling, educational programming, interviewing opportunities, written and online resources, job posting databases and a substantial alumni network, in order to educate students and graduates for a lifetime of successful career management."

Status: Current student, full-time
Dates of Enrollment: 8/2005-Submit Date
Survey Submitted: April 2006

There are many externships and research assistant positions available for students. Pitt is well connected in the city, and the law school has a strong reputation. Even if you don't plan to stay in the area, there are many opportunities here that can serve as stepping stones towards other prospects out of the state. A large number of grads go to D.C., NY, MD and VA if they are not staying within the state. However, I have also met other soon-to-be grads who are planning to work in the South and West Coast regions as well. On-campus interviews take place every year, and the career services does their best to help students with everything from resume writing to career decisions.

Status: Current student, full-time
Dates of Enrollment: 8/2004-Submit Date
Survey Submitted: October 2005

Fantastic. Pittsburgh is a great market, everything from tiny nonprofits to huge international law firms, and every level of government work: city, county, state (the state Supreme Court sits here), and federal (district and circuit courts for Third Circuit; U.S. Attorney's Office; bankruptcy court). In addition to being in a great market, this is the best law school for 300 miles in any direction—and the two higher-ranked law schools that are a little over 300 miles away (Michigan and Penn) send most of their graduates to the East Coast, the West Coast or Chicago, so we don't have a lot of competition anywhere in the area. The career services office is fantastic; helpful, nice, well-connected people. The

firms pay almost as much here as they do in New York (for example, big firms pay $105k to $115k, versus $110k to $125k in New York), but the cost of living is so absurdly low that you can live like a king (you can buy a pretty nice house for $70,000 and a gorgeous one for $150,000). That being said, some people I know have gotten big-firm or government jobs in very competitive markets, like New York City and D.C. You don't have to stay in Pittsburgh if you don't want to, though obviously it's easier to get your foot in the door here than in New York.

Status: Current student, full-time
Dates of Enrollment: 8/2004-Submit Date
Survey Submitted: April 2005

I think that Pitt's rise in the rankings and efforts to help students access other markets means that the degree is certainly valuable outside this market as well. For example, the school organizes trips to D.C. every fall. (Here, I would argue that the value of a Pitt law education needs to be measured more holistically, it is SO much cheaper to go here than some other places, in part because the cost of living is so much lower, so that you're getting more for your money by going to a place like Pitt where you can take that degree elsewhere with less debt.)

I have reached out this year about career issues to professors, administrators, alumni, upper-level students—ALL of them have been helpful. They have taken time out to talk to me about career goals, strategies, etc. I have been pleased with how willing they have been to talk to me and advise me.

Status: Alumnus/a, full-time
Dates of Enrollment: 8/1997-5/2000
Survey Submitted: February 2005

I live and work in Washington state. Pitt is a relatively unknown school here. It has (I believe) the disadvantage of people believing it is a private school, rather than a public school. As public schools go, it is better than average. But since there are literally hundreds of private schools, I fear it tends to be lumped in with the mediocre private schools rather than the better half. Of course, I'm over 2,500 miles away from where I went to school. Speaking positively, after four years working in a government job, I made the leap to a top private firm without difficulty; a degree from Pitt may not have been an enormous help, but it certainly was not an impediment.

On-campus recruiting was strong for people interested in the Pittsburgh market. For those interested in other markets, however, OCI was lacking. At least two classmates of mine got federal judicial clerkships, and several went to excellent firms in New York City, D.C. and Philadelphia. Most, of course, stayed in Pittsburgh. Each of the top firms in Pittsburgh hired one or more Pitt grads, I think, the year I graduated.

Quality of Life

Status: Current student, full-time
Dates of Enrollment: 9/2003-Submit Date
Survey Submitted: April 2006

Pittsburgh is a cheap place to live with lots of entertainment and culture for a city its size. I think the quality of life is very high. There are special programs for grad students that allow you to get ridiculously cheap, or even free, tickets to plays, concerts, opera, hockey and baseball. Most students live in Shadyside or Squirrel Hill, which are very pleasant and accessible to Oakland, where the school is. If you want to go off the beaten path, you can live in Bloomfield, Friendship or Regent Square, where the rents are lower but the accessibility to Oakland is still quite good.

Status: Current student, full-time
Dates of Enrollment: 9/2005-Submit Date
Survey Submitted: April 2006

Pittsburgh is a nice city. Some areas are course are safer than others. The cost of living is cheap and the people are very friendly. There is no on-campus housing, but admissions helps students find places, by sending out a list of apartments that students live, which also includes a review of those places.

The law school consists of one building. The area around the school has various restaurants, cafes and is usually bustling with students. If you get sick of studying in the law school library, you can study in the undergraduate or graduate libraries, which all have wireless Internet.

Status: Alumnus/a, full-time
Dates of Enrollment: 9/2002-5/2005
Survey Submitted: April 2006

Quality of life in Pittsburgh is close to ideal from my perspective. You can get a nice apartment close to the campus for around $600 a month (about $450 with roommates), take the bus for free to class, and live in an environment of young professionals drawn to the city's numerous graduate programs at Pitt, Carnegie Mellon and Duquesne. A student's budget can go pretty far here and the friendly atmosphere of the city is incomparable. The revitalization efforts downtown are sure to bring even more young people into the urban area and the suburbs have great safe communities. Oh, did I mention Super Bowl Champions?

Status: Current student, full-time
Dates of Enrollment: 8/2004-Submit Date
Survey Submitted: October 2005

The student body and teachers are very collegial. No *Paper Chase* or Scott Turow *1L*-type stories here; it's not cutthroat at all, it's a genuinely friendly atmosphere. The student body is also racially well integrated. There are several ethnicity-based groups (Black/Asian/Hispanic Law Students Associations), but no race-based cliques that I've noticed. Most of the professors are very willing to talk or offer reasonable amounts of help outside of class. A further quality of life detail is that we have a Starbucks in the law library—nice!

Status: Current student, full-time
Dates of Enrollment: 8/2004-Submit Date
Survey Submitted: September 2005

The main advantage here, aside from a convenient location (good area with plenty of amenities, within a couple blocks of the biz school and med school in case you want to take outside classes), is the social life. I don't mean parties (there's plenty of that, if you want your grades to suck), but the overall atmosphere. It's surprisingly collegial. Everyone helps each other! Amazing! It's nothing like Scott Turow's *1L*. The professors are much kinder and more accessible than in *1L*, too.

Facilities are also quite good. In addition to the law library (which was completely updated/renovated within the past year, and has a Starbucks in it), all the university's other libraries (main, medical) and the enormous Carnegie public library are within two to five minutes' walk.

Status: Current student, full-time
Dates of Enrollment: 8/2004-Submit Date
Survey Submitted: February 2006

Pittsburgh is eminently affordable, and a mortgage is probably cheaper than rent. It feels like more people are moving back into the city, and I couldn't pick a better city to be in during the last Super Bowl. Churches and bars dot the streets in equal number and there are a ton of great places to eat. Pennsylvania has yet to join CA and NY, so everyone smells like an ashtray after going out, but there are some good bars.

People in Pittsburgh are unbelievably friendly, and in the spring there are a multitude of great parks. They just turned a parking lot across from the Cathedral into green-space, so there's a commitment to rejuvenating the city. The Pitt ID gets you into museums and onto city buses free, and the city has events like the gallery crawl that show off the local arts scene. People from here leave here, but they all seem to come back.

Status: Current student, full-time
Dates of Enrollment: 8/2004-Submit Date
Survey Submitted: April 2005

I love Pittsburgh (and I'm not from here originally, so I'm not biased.) It's relatively cheap, so you can live close to campus and have a better quality of life (less commuting) and still live in some great communities. I have a family, so that influences my perspective. It's a great place for kids. There are tons of family-friendly activities here that are really accessible—easy to get to, fairly inexpensive and varied (theater, zoo, museums). The weather is pretty dismal

much of the time, but when it is nice out, there are fabulous parks—right near campus—so you can actually go enjoy the outdoors. In the meantime, you can always go to the absolutely amazing Phipps Conservatory to see some real flowers.

Status: Alumnus/a, full-time
Dates of Enrollment: 8/2000-5/2003
Survey Submitted: April 2004

Pitt is an urban law school in a semi-urban environment. Yes, the Oakland section of Pittsburgh is urban. But just a mile away are beautiful brownstone houses in Shadyside. The rent is fairly cheap. The public transportation is free to students. The university facilities, available to every student, are fantastic. Why would someone want to live in a law school dorm anyway?

The only downside to attending an urban law school: no parking. This makes interviewing season a little uncomfortable.

Status: Alumnus/a, full-time
Dates of Enrollment: 8/2000-5/2003
Survey Submitted: January 2004

The law school building has wireless Internet access in the student lounge and library. Several of the classrooms have ethernet access. The computer labs (two) have more than enough computers. There was never any time in three years that I had to wait for a computer. Free printing of 900 sheets per semester is available at a nearby computer lab.

There are extensive food choices within several blocks, from hot trucks with Indian and Asian food to pizza joints to homemade ice cream to great Mexican and American fare. Feel free to sue any or all of them if you gain weight. Even though the area is quite urban, it is quite safe for anyone taking reasonable care. There are campus police parked outside the law school almost all the time.

 ## Social Life

Status: Current student, full-time
Dates of Enrollment: 9/2003-Submit Date
Survey Submitted: April 2006

A certain group of people really gets into Thursday night "Bar Review," but by and large this is a nine-to-five kind of school.

Student groups are a little bit of a weak point—they are relatively few and not terribly active. The Public Interest Organization is generally well run and active in its mission to raise summer grants for students who get unpaid public interest jobs. The Black Students' Association is pretty active. Beyond that, it's hit or miss.

> **Pitt Law says:** "Numerous organizations at the law school also provide support and opportunities for learning beyond the classroom. Please visit our web site for a listing of all the organizations that are active under 'Student Resources.' Organizations participation varies from year to year based on student interest but there are always plenty to choose from in any given year."

Status: Current student, full-time
Dates of Enrollment: 8/2004-Submit Date
Survey Submitted: April 2006

As a married person, I'm not so into the singles' scene, but I know a good chunk of the students attend Bar Review sponsored by the Student Bar Association every week. There are more student organizations than you can shake a stick at, and Pittsburgh's many grad schools in the area (three universities within three miles of each other) make it a lot easier to find people with common interests, whatever they are. For those with children, as well, Pittsburgh offers a lot to young families, and the law school even has an organization for parents within the school.

Status: Alumnus/a, full-time
Dates of Enrollment: 9/2002-5/2005
Survey Submitted: April 2006

Read all of Vault's Law School Surveys at www.vault.com/lawschool — get complete surveys on top law schools, expert advice on applicaton essays, LSAT prep and more.

VAULT CAREER LIBRARY 553

Most students live in Shadyside where there are posh shops, dining and bars all within walking distance. It is a vibrant young professional scene that is ever-changing and growing. The law school itself provides many great organizations for social outings, most notably PLISF, the Pitt Legal Income Sharing Fund, which raises money for student who wish to pursue unpaid nonprofit jobs in the summer. They organize numerous fun events to raise money, the largest of which is the auction. You can bid on everything from dinner cooked by your favorite professor to a trip for spring break. All in all, Pittsburgh and Pitt Law are what you make of it. The options are there to pursue almost anything you can think of. Those who fail to take advantage of these opportunities are likely the ones sitting bored at their desk right now wishing they were back in law school again.

Status: Current student, full-time
Dates of Enrollment: 8/2005-Submit Date
Survey Submitted: April 2006

I love that most places in the city are close together, so you don't have to worry about driving from place to place. You can walk to local bars or take the bus or cab down to another part of town. I'm from a larger city and will admit there is not as much going on when compared to more populated areas, but there are still plenty of fun things to do. There are good concert venues and fun bars throughout the city. There are a variety of places to eat, and lots of coffee shops that are very student-friendly. On the whole, school will keep you VERY busy, so I doubt you will be bored here. You'll be thankful for the free time you have to do something besides reading casebooks!

Status: Current student, full-time
Dates of Enrollment: 8/2004-Submit Date
Survey Submitted: February 2006

There's Bar Review Thursday nights, but there's not a law school social scene like some other schools; there's no kegger in a courtyard with students and faculty drinking together on Friday afternoons. However, there are a few events at the school, such as an auction to aid students who take public service internships, that bring faculty and students together. There's some dating, but most people are married or re-living high school.

Status: Current student, full-time
Dates of Enrollment: 8/2004-Submit Date
Survey Submitted: April 2005

Since I have a family, I don't attend many of the organized social functions at school and don't go to bars. There have been some great school-sponsored activities; for example, the Asian Law Students Association had a Diwali festival with food, music and dancing. I brought my kids and they loved it.

There is a substantial group of "non-traditional" students here, so it's a welcoming environment for those of us who aren't going to law school straight from college. One of the great parts of this year for me has been meeting with a Pitt Law Moms Group—it has been really wonderful to talk about the similar issues we face.

There are lots of clubs here. Every Thursday from 12 to 2 p.m. is reserved for student group meetings and career services presentations, so there are no class conflicts; but often there is so much going on that I often have conflicts between two different things that I want to attend. Clubs are a great way of exploring areas of the law, especially when you're a first-year and you're not sure what you want to do. I went to Health Law Society meetings even though I don't know if that's what I want to do. I joined a new group this year and really enjoyed getting to know people through it and helping to organize a forum (and getting the chance to meet with the speakers because of that, another good opportunity for networking and learning from practicing lawyers in the community). I especially like how the clubs and forums connect the law school with the outside world.

Status: Current student, full-time
Dates of Enrollment: 8/2003-Submit Date
Survey Submitted: April 2005

The SBA organizes numerous events. Typically, weekly Bar Review sessions, as well as annual Golden Gavel Olympics (various sports and arts competitions) with Duquesne School of Law. Bars are plentiful. The campus is adjacent to Carngie Mellon University, so there are plenty of opportunities to socialize.

Status: Alumnus/a, full-time
Dates of Enrollment: 8/2000-5/2003
Survey Submitted: January 2004

Pitt Law students are collegial. No one hides books in the library. Pitt Law students are competitive, but I think most are driven by internal pressures, no by "beating" other people. This doesn't mean that during a moot cour competition people won't posture; they should. But when all is said and done Pitt Law is a great place to find what you want in the vast field of law. I shoul mention that careers outside the law are encouraged, too.

Status: Alumnus/a, full-time
Dates of Enrollment: 9/2000-5/2003
Survey Submitted: April 2004

The students are very social, with a weekly gathering at local bars. If you're single and looking to meet your soulmate at school, this is not the place for you While a few rare students will marry a classmate, most dating is casual an transient.

 The School Says

The University of Pittsburgh is in one of America's great urban settings, a place of extraordinary educational and professional opportunity where students enjoy every lifestyle amenity. Because the area is a technological, industrial and cultural center, students are able to immerse themselves in a broad interdisciplinary education. One way to practice in an interdependent world is to develop particularized expertise. Pitt students seize that advantage through certificate programs, which allow them to specialize in the following areas: Civil Litigation, Environmental Law, Science and Policy, Health Law, Intellectual Property and Technology Law and International and Comparative Law. Certificate programs are taught both within and outside the law school by full-time faculty who are acknowledged experts in their fields, as well as by leading practitioners, professionals and executives in associated industries.

The faculty includes a number of renowned researchers who are quoted regularly in such national print publications as *The New York Times*, *Washington Post* and *Los Angeles Times*. In addition, they are distinguished teachers, eminently approachable human beings who like nothing better than helping students to learn. Indeed, nearly one-third of the law faculty has received the Chancellor's Distinguished Teaching Award, established by Pitt in 1984. Ask our students about these teachers and mentors and they will speak in superlatives.

During the past five years, the Barco Law Building has undergone extensive renovation. The law library has been completely revamped and now provides students with access to a wireless network, two large computer labs, new study carrels, tables for group study and an outstanding coffee bar that encourages students to unwind. All classrooms have state-of-the-art technology that enhances the learning environment. The Teplitz Moot Courtroom, for instance, has been upgraded so students are able to utilize wireless access while presenting law cases and a sophisticated videotaping package that will store students' presentations to be used for critiquing purposes. In the near future, the courtroom will be equipped with distance learning capabilities. Faculty will take advantage of this technology for teaching classes to be viewed here and abroad.

The career services office plays a central role in the life of the law school. The three professionals on staff meet with students throughout year and employ our extensive alumni network to help open many doors. Pitt law grads are currently practicing in 50 states and over 30 foreign countries worldwide.

For further information, contact the Pitt Law School at (412) 648-1413 or admissions@law.pitt.edu or visit its web site at www.law.pitt.edu.

Villanova University School of Law

Admissions Office
Villanova University School of Law
Garey Hall
299 North Spring Mill Road
Villanova, PA 19085
Admissions phone: (610) 519-7010
Admissions fax: (610) 519-6291
Admissions e-mail: admissions@law.villanova.edu
Admissions URL:
http://www.law.villanova.edu/admissions/

Admissions

Status: Current student, full-time
Dates of Enrollment: 8/2004-Submit Date
Survey Submitted: October 2005

When applying to Villanova, I was required to take the LSAT entrance exam. Because applying to law school was extremely competitive, grades and undergraduate GPAs were also of great importance. When applying to Villanova, there was no interview requirement for acceptance.

An entrance essay was required to accompany the initial application. The essay was in regards to why the applicant wanted to practice law, and why he/she believed he/she would be a good attorney. After being accepted, I feel that great weight was placed on the entrance exam scores over anything else, most likely do to the increased pool of applicants. I feel the law school class is much more diverse, with many students having prior work experience before coming to law school.

Status: Current student, full-time
Dates of Enrollment: 8/2004-Submit Date
Survey Submitted: August 2005

Villanova Law has a pretty simple admissions process with a standard application and essay. No special essay was required of me. However, when I applied in 2004 Villanova was not participating in the LSAC online application, which required me to fill out my application by hand. I believe you can now fill out the application on Villanova's web site.

There is no interview for the law school. I believe Villanova is pretty selective. We were told that our class last year was the most competitive yet.

Status: Current student, full-time
Dates of Enrollment: 8/2003-Submit Date
Survey Submitted: April 2004

Every type of college is represented here, from the Ivies to dinky Pennsylvania schools. The school is more selective than those guidebooks say, because I only got in off the waitlist in late July, yet my LSAT was at the top of the published range and I graduated from an Ivy League college with a B+ GPA. Having ties to Pennsylvania is a near-must to get in here (I had none whatsoever), but the NY and NJ student demographic is huge as well. I suggest that you stress a devotion to Pennsylvania in your essay.

Status: Alumnus/a, full-time
Dates of Enrollment: 5/1994-5/1997
Survey Submitted: October 2003

My understanding is that, overall, it is not very difficult to get admitted. Strangely though, the average GPA/LSAT scores are relatively high. My own conclusion is if you have a decent GPA (3.3 +) and LSAT (155+) your chances are pretty good (one in three, last time I checked).

The faculty have all got heart, so if you are really interested in empowering yourself to help the underprivileged, make a difference in the world, contribute to your society, then Villanova is more likely to give you a shot (as opposed to a law school looking to improve their rankings by accepting only the top 5 percent of the applicant pool).

Academics

Status: Current student, full-time
Dates of Enrollment: 8/2004-Submit Date
Survey Submitted: October 2005

The first year of law school is extremely intense, no matter what the program. The structured curriculum at Villanova includes a full first year of the core law courses including: Property, Contracts, Criminal Procedure and Law, Civil Procedure, Torts, Legal Writing and Legal Research.

The classes also typify use of the Socratic Method. Students are called on at random to recite the assignment for the day, and must be prepared to avoid embarrassment. The workload is what each student makes of it. By managing time, it is not as burdensome come the end of the semester, because there will be less cramming. Poor time management and balancing of schedules results in a highly pressured environment come exam time.

Status: Current student, full-time
Dates of Enrollment: 8/2004-Submit Date
Survey Submitted: August 2005

Villanova seems to have a great program. The first year is broken up into 11 credits in the fall and then 17 credits in the spring. This gives students some time to adjust to the law school way of life. Even though spring semester is really tough, I think that this system is very positive.

The professors have all been pretty good, with exception of maybe one (and that professor was a visiting).

Getting classes seems to be pretty easy so long as you register on time, which I didn't, but still was able to get everything I wanted. Registration is done online.

Status: Current student, full-time
Dates of Enrollment: 8/2003-Submit Date
Survey Submitted: April 2004

Awesome profs! I love them all, and will be working for one this summer (1L summer). Villanova students tend to be reticent and insecure in class, but that just makes it easier for those students who thrive on active learning to make the most of each class. The profs do a great job adapting their material to the pace of their particular students. As a consequence, if you're a top achiever, the pressure's off and you can spend the time learning the details that interest you most, knowing all the while that you'll easily stay on top of the material on the exam.

This school is really offering me the opportunities I would have probably missed out on had I gotten into a big-name school, where competition would have been just as fierce as it was for me as an undergrad. I'm getting access to the A's, the one-on-one time with fascinating profs, the coveted spots in the legal clinics and maybe even a Law Review editorship. I put 100 percent of my energy into the school work every day, however, so the access is earned. It's really been a fun ride so far!

Status: Alumnus/a, full-time
Dates of Enrollment: 5/1994-5/1997
Survey Submitted: October 2003

All JD programs are pretty much the same. Not much of the traditional stuff actually helps you when you get out into the real world. The study of principles, theories, and philosophy of law are fantastic for academic and personal growth, so while you are in law school be sure to get all you can from the great faculty.

Read all of Vault's Law School Surveys at www.vault.com/lawschool — get complete surveys on top law schools, expert advice on applicaton essays, LSAT prep and more.

VAULT CAREER LIBRARY 555

Villanova also offers a number of excellent elective classes that are taught by attorneys actually working in the field, so there is plenty of "practical" learning available for those who are interested.

 # Employment Prospects

Status: Current student, full-time
Dates of Enrollment: 8/2004-Submit Date
Survey Submitted: October 2005

As a Philadelphia law school, top employers from the Philadelphia region recruit early second year. Law school alumni typically conduct the initial screening interviews for those selected on campus. Career Strategy, the on-campus recruiting source, is ideal for students in the top 15 percent of the class. Otherwise, it is extremely difficult to attain the best jobs with the largest, most prestigious firms in the city.

As far as blindly applying to firms for possible employment goes, your chances of anything coming to fruition are slim. Employers typically throw out cold applications received in the mail before giving the applicant a chance, and thus, without a contact, the student best not waste the envelope and stamp.

Status: Current student, full-time
Dates of Enrollment: 8/2004-Submit Date
Survey Submitted: August 2005

There are a lot of educational programs to help students pick what kind of practice they might be interested in. There are mock interviews conducted by alumni from Philadelphia area firms. Additionally, there are many OCIs, even for first-year students in the spring.

Status: Current student, full-time
Dates of Enrollment: 8/2003-Submit Date
Survey Submitted: April 2004

Alumni all easily get jobs in Philly, NJ and NYC. With the Career Strategy Program, attorneys hold your hand throughout the entire recruiting process. They are really pushing jobs in the public sector and public interest arenas right now, because apparently Villanova alums are notoriously drawn to the money in private practice firms.

Status: Alumnus/a, full-time
Dates of Enrollment: 5/1994-5/1997
Survey Submitted: October 2003

I moved to California right after graduation, so I cannot comment on career prospects in the Northeast. But my understanding is that Villanova is strongest in the Philadelphia area, and has a good number of alumni throughout the Northeast region (NY, NJ, DE, MD, D.C., MD).

Out West, there are some alumni that have done well. I got a great job at a large law firm paying a six-figure salary. After your first job, it doesn't matter as much (where you went to school).

 # Quality of Life

Status: Current student, full-time
Dates of Enrollment: 8/2004-Submit Date
Survey Submitted: October 2005

The quality of life around Villanova is ideal. The location is in the beautiful suburbs of Philadelphia; close enough to have fun and enjoy the social activities and culture that the city has to offer, but far enough that the crime rates remain very low. Because the cost of living in the area is high, housing is extremely pricey and the schools do not provide a very good network to attain any discounted rates.

Status: Current student, full-time
Dates of Enrollment: 8/2004-Submit Date
Survey Submitted: August 2005

Villanova undergrad campus is very beautiful, but the law school building is no so great. It looks like a 1950s high school. However, Villanova is set to build new building which seems to be much improved.

There is no on-campus housing, but there are many area apartment buildings fo students to live in. Many of which are sort of like dorms anyway.

The library is fine and there is wireless Internet throughout.

The law school cafeteria is not so bad, but it is only open until 7 p.m. Howeve you can go to an undergrad cafeteria/take out place to get late-night food.

The campus is very suburban and safe.

Status: Current student, full-time
Dates of Enrollment: 8/2003-Submit Date
Survey Submitted: April 2004

The Main Line area outside of Philly is a great place for study. There ar colleges and private schools on every block. The undergrad scene is huge, s police make their presence known often as an effective way to curb th craziness.

Status: Alumnus/a, full-time
Dates of Enrollment: 5/1994-5/1997
Survey Submitted: October 2003

Villanova is a quiet and safe neighborhood. You are close to great restaurant and bars all along the Main Line, and about a 30-minute drive into Philadelphi (great clubs, great food, lots to do and see). You're 90 minutes to Atlantic City two hours to NYC and three-and-a-half hours to D.C. Day trip destination abound (when you're not studying).

Although all the facilities of the university (track, basketball, tennis courts, gym are available, the law school is basically its own world. Most students neve leave the law school building, which has its own classrooms, offices, library cafeteria, lounges and so on. There are several affordable golf courses nearby Quality of life was great for me.

 # Social Life

Status: Current student, full-time
Dates of Enrollment: 8/2004-Submit Date
Survey Submitted: October 2005

There are several options on campus available to law students including th SBA, Law Review and moot court, pro bono societies and other clubs to mee individuals and network. Local bars include Brownies and Maloney's Pub which are very near campus and host happy hour events for students to mingle Going into either Center City for fabulous meals or Old City for the dancing nightlife are also options available.

Status: Current student, full-time
Dates of Enrollment: 8/2004-Submit Date
Survey Submitted: August 2005

There are a few law school hang-outs such as the Wild Onion and Kelly's. Thes bars are within walking distance of the school and most of the area apartmen buildings.

Status: Current student, full-time
Dates of Enrollment: 8/2003-Submit Date
Survey Submitted: April 2004

Thursday nights are bar nights. The student organizations are always throwing afternoon lectures, discussion panels and career-planning get-togethers. The big pleasers are the events that provide free alcohol. The law student population a Villanova is very young and slightly stuck in undergrad mode. I am not a big participant in random Thursday night binging, but I have enjoyed attending fun organized events like a neat annual auction that provides funding for studen ellowships for the summer, as well as charity events at local bars where profs o crazy things like bartend or sing karaoke with the students.

Status: Alumnus/a, full-time
Dates of Enrollment: 5/1994-5/1997
Survey Submitted: October 2003

When I was there, Villanova was really a close-knit family. Students were all pretty relaxed and friendly. We worked hard but also enjoyed our time at VLS. Once a month there would be a social event with food and beer (often times catered). I spent a lot of time there, so pizza and beer was much appreciated. There are also an endless series of events put on by the numerous student organizations—guest speakers, seminars, presentations, debates and so on—that's when you get top-shelf drinks and jumbo cocktail shrimp.

Read all of Vault's Law School Surveys at www.vault.com/lawschool — get complete surveys on top law schools, expert advice on applicaton essays, LSAT prep and more.

VAULT CAREER LIBRARY 557

Roger Williams University

Ralph R. Papitto School of Law
Roger Williams University School of Law
Office of Admissions
10 Metacom Avenue
Bristol, RI 02809
Admissions phone: (401) 254-4555 or (800)633-2727
Admissions fax: (401) 254-4516
Admissions e-mail: admissions@rwu.edu
Admissions URL: http://law.rwu.edu/sites/admission/

 Admissions

Status: Current student, full-time
Dates of Enrollment: 8/2006-Submit Date
Survey Submitted: March 2006

The admissions process at Roger Williams seemed slow to me at first but in the end I realized that it was worth the wait. The dean of admissions took the extra time to evaluate each candidate in the attempt to identify the most qualified candidates and to offer academic scholarships and financial assistance to as many students as possible.

Status: Current student, full-time
Dates of Enrollment: 8/2005-Submit Date
Survey Submitted: March 2006

The Honors Program is available by invitation. Your LSAT score and [undergrad] GPA are taken into consideration, and then your tuition is reduced at least 50 percent, and sometimes 100 percent. People applying to tier-one and tier-two schools should be able to make the requirements for the Honors Program at RWU.

> **The school says:** "The Honors Program is an academic enrichment program designed for very strong applicants. For 2006 the median LSAT is 161 and the median GPA is 3.4. Besides scholarship money, the Honors Program consists of a series of seminars in the first year on hot button legal issues and one credit perspectives classes in subsequent years. All applicants are considered for the Honors Program. Students may also be invited into the program at the end of first year. This invitation is based on first year grade performance."

Status: Current student, full-time
Dates of Enrollment: 8/2004-Submit Date
Survey Submitted: March 2006

The school is trying hard to get a stronger class every year and I think they are succeeding. It is a new school so it is not extremely selective, but it is getting better. The admissions staff is great and extremely helpful so definitely use them if you have any questions or go to the school and take a tour or ask questions on the chat rooms they offer online. This is definitely a school that people who have LSATs in the 160s should consider. Because they are attempting to raise the bar, they try really hard to attract better students by offering half and full scholarships and entry into the Honors Program. Not having to pay tuition or only half of it is HUGE. Imagine coming out of law school not $100,000 in debt. The Honors Program also offers some unique opportunities.

Status: Current student, full-time
Dates of Enrollment: 8/2004-Submit Date
Survey Submitted: March 2006

I first learned about Roger Williams Law at a law school forum in Boston. I met with the Director of Admissions, Michael Boylen, and he showed enthusiasm and great knowledge about the law school, programs, student activities, and the town of Bristol. I was provided with a great deal of information at the forum—

and not just the basics. I received information about new professors, the summer study abroad program and the area that Roger Williams Law is located in.

The application process was straightforward, and I heard back from Roger Williams well over a month before I heard from any other school. First received a phone call from the admissions team, and then received the official acceptance letter and information packet in the mail. The phone call was just the beginning of the individual attention that I received throughout the process. also received a phone call after I accepted the invitation to attend Roger Williams, from a professor, who knew (through my personal statement) of specific area of law that I was interested in. We talked on the phone at great length about the different ways I could pursue my interests at Roger Williams Law.

Status: Current student, full-time
Dates of Enrollment: 9/2005-Submit Date
Survey Submitted: March 2006

Admissions process was fairly straightforward, and typical of procedures encountered at other law schools during my application process. Because Roger Williams was on my "top five" list of schools which I wanted to attend, I opted for early admission. As I recall, my application, essay and supporting documents were sent and received by RWU Law by the end of September. Because of my disappointing LSAT score, I felt that it was important to showcase my strengths and experiences in my essay, which I accomplished by contrasting my "blue collar" work experience as a waitress with my professional experience as a legal assistant for a Vermont law firm. Needless to say, I think that the admission office was impressed because in mid-January I happily received a fat envelope from RWU containing not only an acknowledgment of acceptance, but a scholarship award as well.

My advice to prospective applicants is this: even if you don't have an unfavorable LSAT score or GPA, try to take advantage of the essay as an opportunity to tell a story about yourself in a way that ideally sets you apart from other applicants. In sum, try to make it memorable.

Status: Current student, full-time
Dates of Enrollment: 8/2005-Submit Date
Survey Submitted: March 2006

Roger Williams sent me an e-mail asking me to apply and waiving my application fee last April. I had not looked to schools in southern New England but their e-mail prompted be to look up the school's web site. Their application was very straightforward and simple to complete. After I was accepted I went on a tour which was very informational. I met with the Dean of Admissions and he spent over an hour showing me the building and answering my questions. He encouraged me to come to the school and even referenced my application essay during the tour. At the end of the tour I felt like the school was truly interested in me attending and succeeding there and that my application was not just a piece of paper.

Status: Current student, full-time
Dates of Enrollment: 9/2003-Submit Date
Survey Submitted: February 2006

While the admissions process at any school always remains a bit of a mystery to its current students, it is possible to pass on a few pointers. Roger Williams is a relatively new program which is quickly making its way out of the abyss of obscurity. The school needs to work on its diversity, not just of ethnic background, but of life experience. To this end, an application essay should focus on those things that make the applicant unique. Do not fear putting off the admissions office by appearing to operate outside the mainstream, as it is those very qualities that give you something additional to offer the law school community. Work experience, volunteer activities and even interesting hobbies will do a great deal to supplement an applicant's undergraduate grade point average and LSAT scores. These things are obviously important, and the mean scores of Roger Williams students have been steadily rising since the program's nception, but it is very important to remember that a little personality goes a long way.

Status: Current student, full-time
Dates of Enrollment: 8/2004-Submit Date
Survey Submitted: February 2006

first became aware of Roger Williams at a law school fair hosted by my undergraduate college. There was a huge view of university campus on a small peninsula that was simply breathtaking. I researched the school and found that the law school was a new addition to a top-rated undergraduate university in Bristol, Rhode Island. It has the unique position of being the only law school in Rhode Island and being located perfectly between Boston and New York. I applied and was accepted to the program.

believe I got into the school for a very particularly tailored application and because of a somewhat interesting background. A full year after being admitted the Dean of Admissions remembered a portion of my essay. Roger Williams really does give every applicant a thorough, comprehensive analysis to see what you would have to offer at the school. Roger Williams has a tremendous amount of momentum. Being the only law school in the state offers students lots of opportunities to get involved and great access to larger cities. I recommend applying early, visiting the beautiful campus and living in either Providence or Newport.

Status: Current student, full-time
Dates of Enrollment: 8/2004-Submit Date
Survey Submitted: April 2005

This is a young school (about 12 years) that is striving to establish a reputation as first-class law school. There is a dynamic energy among the faculty, staff and students. The dean is finishing his second year at the school and is committed to attracting and retaining the best quality students possible. The admissions staff is extremely responsive. Of the seven schools I applied to, this was the first acceptance I received, only about a week after submission. It was later followed by a personal letter from the Dean of the Law School, who had obviously read my application essay because he referred me to a marine affairs joint-degree program run by the law school and the University of Rhode Island that suited my back-ground in the Coast Guard and as a marine science under-graduate. I felt like they wanted ME here, rather than just my money, like I felt about some of the other schools.

Status: Current student, full-time
Dates of Enrollment: 8/2002-Submit Date
Survey Submitted: April 2005

The admissions process has become more competitive every year. Applications are up 125 percent since 2000. It is very important to maintain above average undergraduate grades as well as to achieve an above average LSAT score. RWU selects students who have been very active at the undergraduate level. RWU looks for people who have unique skills and personality to add to the school environment. A common misconception is that RWU recruits mainly students from RI. Actually, RWU represents over 40 states and several foreign countries. RWU does provide private tours and interviews for those interested in the school.

Academics

Status: Current student, full-time
Dates of Enrollment: 8/2006-Submit Date
Survey Submitted: March 2006

Roger Williams separates its first-year students into smaller sections so that everyone has the opportunity to interact and participate in their classes. The professors do follow the Socratic Method but they often allow students to volunteer answers as well as to discuss their thoughts with each other. Entering students are graded on a curve. Students are required to read approximately two hours outside of class for each class meeting. Research and writing add an additional 20 to 40 hours to the student's workload per semester. All of the professors are dynamic and genuinely want the students to achieve their personal best. They push students to succeed by encouraging participation and interactive learning.

Status: Current student, full-time
Dates of Enrollment: 8/2004-Submit Date
Survey Submitted: March 2006

I think most classes would be like classes at any other law school. We have no concentrations available, so there are a broad range of classes instead of only a few in a specialized areas, although they do have a large number of classes in marine affairs. There is an attendance policy where you cannot miss more than 20 percent of scheduled meetings. I haven't found it to be that difficult to get into popular classes. Trial Advocacy is one of the very popular classes but it is offered every semester with several sections. Obviously third-years get first preference for classes, so it is easier to get into choice classes then.

Grading can be somewhat of a pain. There is a mandatory grading scale that professors must adhere to for required classes, so how you do depends on how everyone else in your class does. For first-years, the median score for each class must fall between a 2.33 and a 2.67. For second-year required classes, it has to be between a 2.5 and 3.0. So when employers are comparing grades to other schools it might seem you didn't do well, but that isn't necessarily the case. After first year, a little above a 3.0 was in the top 20 percent of the class.

Like all schools we have a wide array of professors—some are great, some not so much. Most professors use the Socratic Method to call on people, so you have to be prepared every day to be called on. All the professors I have had have offered officer hours and extra times to help you if needed and/or offer exam sessions to go over past exams they give you or go over what you should know for the exam. This is extremely helpful hearing what we should know from the person who is making the exam. We have a lot of professors who were in practice for many years so it is great getting real life experience stories. Also, a lot of professors have taught at more prestigious schools and have chosen to come to RWU, which shows something for the school. The professors seem to really want to help the school succeed and get up in the rankings.

Status: Current student, full-time
Dates of Enrollment: 8/2004-Submit Date
Survey Submitted: March 2006

The professors here are amazing! You will get professors currently working in the field, widely published and highly qualified. The professors are very accessible. Classes can be difficult to get into your second year because third-years get first priority. The class variety seems wide in the fall and somewhat limited in the spring, however it depends of the semester, your interests and what professors at the time are willing to teach. I know students who asked professors to offer more business classes and they gladly agreed—so you can get what you want if you ask. The workload is well, law school—what can you say? It is difficult first year with legal methods, second and third years are a little better depending how much you load on your plate—you can take easier or harder classes depending on your goals. Law is challenging so it is never easy, but doable and you learn a lot.

Status: Current student, full-time
Dates of Enrollment: 9/2005-Submit Date
Survey Submitted: March 2006

I am extremely impressed with the knowledge, professionalism and energy of all of my professors at RWU. Here, the Socratic Method rules. If you don't show up for class prepared you run the risk of embarrassing yourself in front your classmates and your professor. Also, shrinking violets take note—professors at RWU like students who contribute to the classroom dialogue by offering insightful, intelligent comments and questions.

Status: Current student, full-time
Dates of Enrollment: 8/2003-Submit Date
Survey Submitted: March 2006

Roger Williams has rigorous academic standards, period. It is one of the few law schools with a mandatory grade curve for professors to abide by. This was a bit shocking for some of my classmates, but less shocking for myself because I came from an undergrad institution with a similar grade curve. While the grade curve helps keep grades from suffering from the inflation that runs wild at other graduate institutions, if you are on the lower end of the curve, it may be tougher to get jobs or clerkships. Even though the curve may be disadvantageous when compared to a student at another institution who may be able to do less work and get higher grades due to inflation, RWU is in the business of producing

Read all of Vault's Law School Surveys at www.vault.com/lawschool — get complete surveys on top law schools, expert advice on applicaton essays, LSAT prep and more.

VAULT CAREER LIBRARY 559

competent and skilled legal minds and lawyers. I came to law school in order to serve the public as an attorney, if to be a better attorney I have to work harder than students at other institutions, that is a sacrifice I have willingly made. My future clients and myself, will benefit from my decision.

> **The school says:** "Roger Williams, like most law schools, has a grade normalization policy. Our mandatory median grade is similar to many U.S. law schools. Students should research each law school's grading policy. Most legal employers focus heavily on class rank as opposed to GPA because of the various grading policies at U.S. law schools."

RWU has an extensive Marine Affairs program, which is something that I have no interest in at all. There are many students that attend this school specifically because of that program, but as someone with no interest in it, I sometimes was disappointed at the number of those classes offered at the expense of possibly offering other classes I would be interested in.

For a fairly young law school, the faculty here is fantastic. Most important to me, they are highly available. I can always find or get in touch with a professor if I need to. I have also noticed that many of the professors have left prestigious institutions and jobs to come to RWU. One example is the dean who left his tenured job at Wake Forest Law to come here. The faculty and staff CARE about the school. They want to see the students and the school succeed. Everyone has a vested interest, and as a student I benefit from the sheer desire to will the school to greatness.

Law school in general is a lot of work. The true amount of work that one does varies depending upon the individual. I am someone who does more work than most of my classmates. I definitely do work seven days a week. As a 3L, the type of work has changed at I have had the opportunity to work for a Judge on the RI Superior Court and am now involved in the RWU Criminal Defense Clinic.

Status: Alumnus/a, full-time
Dates of Enrollment: 1/2001-6/2004
Survey Submitted: April 2005

This school doesn't save its best professors for upper-level classes. We had some of the top professors teach ALL of our first-year classes. This made the experience much more amazing. While just being in law school is a dream come true for most of us, being able to learn from professors who are active globally and learning what is currently going on, coupled with learning from professors who actually were there when major cases were decided, really assists in making the law come alive.

We had a lottery system for course selection. This meant that each semester we would be assigned a number and then our course selections would be filled based up on what our number was. This system isn't as bad as it may at first seem. If you had a low number and registered "first" one semester, most likely you had a high number [the next semester] so that there was a rotation and everyone had the ability to get their first pick at some point. In addition, Student Services, is AMAZING and was able to handle any/all problems that arose in a timely manner.

This school is amazing. Have an issue? Bring it up to the administration, faculty, admissions, student services. All of them listen. All of them have a very flexible open-door policy. And dropping in to speak about your issue is NOT like talking into a black hole. They do something about issues and problems. Issues and problems ARE resolved. This school is VERY student oriented and cares sincerely about the welfare of the students it selects.

Status: Current student, full-time
Dates of Enrollment: 8/2003-Submit Date
Survey Submitted: April 2005

Well as with all law schools the first year kept me busy. The professors, who come from top-tier schools and are well-published and challenge you from the first day that you sit in class. In the first semester you take four main core courses and a legal methods class. The second semester, one core class is added and Legal Methods remains a requirement. Based on this workload a student does not have much time for socialization, but most of the students are good natured and make time to go out in town.

The classes are graded in a way that the average grades have to fall between certain GPAs. I think that the professors grade fairly and there is anonymous grading, so there is little opportunity for the professors to grade based on the "likability" of one student. The only downfall to the classes is the availability of the popular classes prior to your third year. But the new dean is aware of this problem and he has added more sections of the more popular classes. This is especially an issue with the required upper-level Legal Methods classes, but this is just because of the small nature of the classes and the lack of faculty to teach. But the administration is working on hiring the most qualified individuals to be professors.

The school also has two additional unique features. One is a full-time writing specialist who is willing to work with not only first-year law students on improving their legal writing, but also with many other second- and third-year students who "didn't get it" in their first year. Also, the school has a full-time employee (who is a Harvard graduate) whose only job is to prepare third-year students to take the bar exam. This means that a majority of graduate pass the bar on the first time.

Status: Current student, full-time
Dates of Enrollment: 8/2002-Submit Date
Survey Submitted: April 2005

The best part of RWU academics is that it offers a free bar training class to graduating students to take for the two semesters of their final year. RWU also has a deep commitment to public service—each student must perform 20 hours to graduate. Many students go above and beyond this requirement. RWU has offered and continues to offer a variety of unique classes and seminars including Law of the Sea, Aviation Law, Sexual Orientation and Criminal Sentencing. The professors make themselves available and are more than willing to give each student a generous amount of their time. The workload is demanding and rigorous but no more than was anticipated.

 Employment Prospects

Status: Current student, full-time
Dates of Enrollment: 8/2006-Submit Date
Survey Submitted: March 2006

The career services department at Roger Williams Law School is one of the top in the country. The dean makes a point to know EACH student by their FIRST name and holds several events including a career options day that make internships and job offers obtainable.

Status: Current student, full-time
Dates of Enrollment: 8/2004-Submit Date
Survey Submitted: March 2006

Career Services has gotten so much better since before I came. We have on-campus recruiting with Providence and Boston firms coming to our school to do on-campus interviews. We had two students that I know of from the second-year class get jobs with really prestigious law firms for the summer that are usually reserved for more prestigious law schools such as Harvard.

I have had difficulty finding a summer job for the summer following my second-year and have mostly been looking on my own, although I did visit career services and did have a few on-campus interviews. They also offer career fairs where law firms and other areas that graduates might go into come in and talk. I have met many alumni who are still involved in the school and really want to see it succeed so they help out where they can. Although RWU is well known in RI and has great access to state jobs, when we compete against Boston schools for those jobs in Boston, we don't necessarily fare so well. It seems like people value the schools in Boston more, despite having higher grades or better qualifications. Like I said before though, this seems to be getting better. It just seems unfair, because from what others have told me, we work harder than law schools who are ranked higher

Status: Current student, full-time
Dates of Enrollment: 8/2004-Submit Date
Survey Submitted: March 2006

The school is young, but growing. This year more and more students obtained summer associate positions with top law firms in Providence and Boston. These positions are difficult to get without a top law school name. However, the school is becoming more recognized, and alumni are demonstrating the quality work produced by Roger Williams. There is an amazing opportunity for public interest work as well. Each year the Feinstein Institute grants $2000 stipends to around 30 students who choose to work in public interest over the summer. The on-campus interview network is growing as well. The Annual Legal Career Options day is a great way for students to get an idea of what's out there, and network with top employers.

> **The school says:** "The Office of Career Services has placed increased emphasis on the Boston market since the arrival of the new Dean of Career Services in 2004. He spends significant time in Boston meeting with hiring partners at various Boston firms. As a result, Boston firms recruiting on campus in 2006 include Brown Rudnick Berlack Israels LLP, Edwards and Angel Palmer & Dodge LLP, Burns & Levinson LLP, and PricewaterhouseCoopers LLP."

Status: Current student, full-time
Dates of Enrollment: 8/2003-Submit Date
Survey Submitted: March 2006

Another reason I was sold on RWU is that it is the only show in town. Roger Williams is the ONLY law school in RI. (Most people think Brown has a law school, but it does not). This benefits RWU students for many reasons. First, RI employers look to RWU for students and graduates to work for them. Further, not many schools can say that the Supreme Court of their state sits in judgment of the school's moot court competition. I am from Massachussetts and even though I go to school in RI, I was able to find employment in Mass. for the summers after my first and second years of law school. I have found that going to school in RI and then applying to Mass. employers has helped because it makes me a bit more diverse from the applicants who all attended school in Boston. RI is a small state, RWU is a small school, and the entire legal community is RI is small. Alumni, judges, lawyers in RI all view RUW as THEIR school and readily offer advice and job prospects to students. In the last two years, the career services office has improved exponentially. The new staff in nationally recognized and have improved the morale on campus. They have begun annual job fairs (public and private sector) and have dramatically increased and improved the on-campus interviewing program.

They offer frequent workshops and personalized attention even offering after hours appointments. Through the assistance of career services I now have a tight resume, cover letter and writing sample. As a young school, RWU does not have an extensive network of alumni. However, the 10 plus years of alumni are very amenable to assisting current students in finding employment or at least pointing students in the correct direction. Current students, faculty, staff, and alums are all concerned with helping RWU grow in prestige.

Status: Alumnus/a, full-time
Dates of Enrollment: 8/2001-5/2004
Survey Submitted: May 2005

In Rhode Island, RWU is well regarded, although it wasn't like that in years past. From what I understand, RWU students are gaining employment in a wide variety of legal sectors including state clerkships, corporate field and government work. From my own personal experience the alumni experience has been extremely helpful in the interview process. Career services was lacking for a few years, but now with a new dean of career services the future looks better for RWU students in gaining employment.

Status: Current student, full-time
Dates of Enrollment: 8/2004-Submit Date
Survey Submitted: April 2005

As the only law school in Rhode Island, the interaction with the local legal community is outstanding. The Justices of the Rhode Island Supreme Court judge the annual moot court competition, and the U.S. First Circuit Court of Appeals and the Federal District Court for the District of Rhode Island have both

held open court sessions at the school this year. The dean of career services is new and has brought energy, vitality and an impressive collection of contacts to the school. The job opportunities, as good as they already are, will continue to improve, not just within Rhode Island, but throughout the rest of the country. The school has a robust internship and clerkship program, and has summer study abroad programs in London, England and Lisbon, Portugal (a classmate of mine will be attending both programs this summer).

Status: Alumnus/a, full-time
Dates of Enrollment: 8/1994-5/1997
Survey Submitted: April 2005

The law school prepares you well for employment. The types of jobs one can obtain are unlimited. RWU graduates have clerked for the judiciary, are in traditional small and large law firms, have opened their own law firms, teach, are involved in politics, and have also used their JD degrees for other non-traditional legal careers, such as medicine and business. The alumni are very involved with the law school and helpful in networking. As for on-campus recruiting, the new dean of career services is incredible. Last year, he organized an on-campus recruit that took place on a Friday night, had about 50 or 60 employers and literally half the students in the law school attend. The event was so successful that a larger space is needed next year. As for internships, because RWU is the only law school in Rhode Island, many meaningful internships are available. Students may represent real clients in court, intern for the state or federal judiciary, or work at many different law firms, including those within government, Attorney General or Public Defender.

 ## Quality of Life

Status: Current student, full-time
Dates of Enrollment: 8/2004-Submit Date
Survey Submitted: March 2006

You can live in RWU apartments, but they aren't on campus and it is extremely easy to find apartments in Bristol/Warren or nearby towns that are cheaper. RWU is located in Bristol which is absolutely beautiful and right near a huge park that is great in the spring and fall to go study at, or just to take a break and play some games at. The neighborhoods are very nice in Bristol and Warren and there are low crime rates. It is a very quaint town.

All the chain stores and restaurants are about 20 minutes away—so pretty close and easy to get to. Providence is probably about 25 minutes away, which is great because it has lots of cultural events, malls and city life. The law school cafeteria has the usual—chicken fingers, salads, sandwiches, but also offers some sushi and other foods that a lot of people seem to like. The gym is right across from the law school, which is perfect. It is gorgeous and new and all the cardio machines are lined along the floor to ceiling windows that overlook the bay.

Status: Current student, full-time
Dates of Enrollment: 8/2005-Submit Date
Survey Submitted: March 2006

I have not met one person at Roger Williams who has a complaint about where we live and study. Bristol is a beautiful, quaint New England town. I have described Bristol as "Pleasantville." The people are kind and friendly, the homes and parks are beautiful, the ocean and beaches are everywhere—visible from the law school itself. The East Bay, as this area of RI is called, has a plethora of outdoor activities—from a long bike trail to kayaking to rock-climbing—an array of good food and small-town bars, and it is a perfect place to relax and study. If one is looking for a more fast-paced and metropolitan feel, Providence is only 30 minutes away, and Boston is a little over an hour away. There are three wineries within 40 minutes of the law school, and Newport, a popular beach and summer resort, is only 20 minutes south of the school. There is a little bit of everything for everyone in this area of the country. While I will admit that Bristol is a sometimes quiet town, with places closing early in the evening, it is the perfect atmosphere for serious study with options for "getaways." Like I said, I have yet to meet a person who isn't in love with where we live.

Read all of Vault's Law School Surveys at www.vault.com/lawschool — get complete surveys on top law schools, expert advice on applicaton essays, LSAT prep and more.

VAULT CAREER LIBRARY 561

Status: Current student, full-time
Dates of Enrollment: 8/2003-Submit Date
Survey Submitted: March 2006

Bristol, RI is a small old town style community. We are directly on the water here on campus and down in the center of the historic part of town. In addition to the historical attractions, the other part of Bristol houses commercial establishments including stores, shops, supermarkets, restaurants and more. The location of all this in Bristol makes it convenient for the law student who does not have much time for travel. Further, for a night out on the town, one can go to the restaurants and bars of Bristol, Providence, Newport, or even Boston. None of which are a far distance.

RWU does offer campus housing which I lived in for two years. The housing I lived in was about three minutes from campus. Recently, the student housing has changed to a location which is about 20 minutes from campus, so for my final semester I moved out of student housing and found an apartment in Bristol. While my time in student housing was satisfactory, it was the undergrad campus and not the law school that controlled housing and therefore the housing department was not always cognizant of the needs of law students. My apartment in Bristol is decent. I have one roommate and between us the rent is approximately $950.00 per month and in addition we pay our electric (electric heat) and Internet bill. There is plenty of housing available in Bristol, but students also live in the surrounding towns including Providence, Warren, Newport, Portsmouth and Barrington. While there is plenty to do for recreation in the area, one must realize that Bristol is not a big city and if you are looking for big city action, Providence or Boston are probably the best option.

Status: Current student, full-time
Dates of Enrollment: 7/2005-Submit Date
Survey Submitted: February 2006

The campus is in a period of transition right now, as a new dining complex is being built right next door to the school. So for the next few months, there is one eating area in the school with a short order kitchen and various grab and go sandwiches, sushi, coffee. At the start of next year however, the campus will feature a Quiznos, pizza shops, specialty coffee shops, a southwestern grill and many other new eating options. This is a college town, and there is plenty of affordable housing in the immediate area, most within 10 minutes of the school. This is a town where people can leave their cars unlocked at night, on a small campus that is being organized to be intimate like the center of Anytown, USA.

Status: Current student, full-time
Dates of Enrollment: 8/2004-Submit Date
Survey Submitted: April 2005

The campus is located in the quaint New England town of Bristol, RI—which considers itself the most patriotic city in America and hosts a month-long Independence Day celebration. The worst crime you're likely to see is jay-walking as people peruse the historic downtown area. Most law student live off campus, and there is a fairly abundant supply of rental properties within a reasonable distance. Providence is only a short, 30-minute drive from the school, and Boston is about an hour. Both cities offer all the amenities of city life—malls, restaurants, theaters and TWO world-champion sports teams, the Boston Red Sox and the New England Patriots are a short drive away. The law school itself is a new building, about 12 years old, and the Campus Recreation Center (gym) is even newer, only about three to four years old.

Status: Alumnus/a, full-time
Dates of Enrollment: 8/1994-5/1997
Survey Submitted: April 2005

Quality of life is great. Rhode Island is a beautiful state. I was from out of state when I came to RWU and never intended to stay here—many years later I'm still in Rhode Island and never want to leave. If you are thinking about RWU, you definitely should see the school because once you do, you'll never want to leave. RWU is located in Bristol, Rhode Island, I've never felt that my safety was in jeopardy and would have no problem walking the streets alone at two in the morning. Housing is affordable and Rhode Island is a small state so everything is close to the campus.

Social Life

Status: Current student, full-time
Dates of Enrollment: 8/2005-Submit Date
Survey Submitted: March 2006

Some of my friends in other law schools complain that the other students ar overly competitive, but I really don't get that sense here. Everyone works har and wants to do well, but the atmosphere somehow stays quite friendly an supportive (for law school).

Aside from the other students, whom for the most part I really like, another thing I appreciate on a day to day basis here is the campus, which is right on the ocea and beautiful by any standard. It's nice to smell the salt air and hear seagull when I get out of my car in the morning. Also, there is a band new gym righ next to the law school, which a lot of students use to work off stress.

Bristol is also a scenic little coastal town and if you have any free time, which haven't so far, Providence and Newport are not far away.

Status: Current student, full-time
Dates of Enrollment: 8/2004-Submit Date
Survey Submitted: March 2006

There are a variety of local pubs and restaurants that are always law schoo favorites. Whenever we have needed a change we will go to Newport o Providence where there are a plethora of similar and different options. There ar lots of nightclubs and five star restaurants and there is always some sort o festival.

I am also a part of Phi Alpha Delta legal fraternity which has been very fun PAD throws lots of parties but also has many opportunities to share outlines learn how to take a test or take notes and all of it is run by the students. It is always nice to get advice and information from peers and not from the school.

Status: Current student, full-time
Dates of Enrollment: 8/2004-Submit Date
Survey Submitted: March 2006

The immediate area is not your typical "college town" with a plethora of bars and clubs. There are a few small town bars in Bristol but Providence offers the clubs and bars for the night owls. The restaurants are amazing. Great seafood in Bristol. Federal Hill in Providence offers authentic Italian. My personal favorites: Roberto's in Bristol, De Wolf's in Bristol, The Restaurant and Cafe in Warren, Liberty Cafe in Bristol, Coffee Depot in Warren. You can catch your favorite chain restaurants as well in Seekonk and Providence. Did I mention the shopping? Wrentham outlet mall less than 30 minutes away!

Status: Current student, full-time
Dates of Enrollment: 8/2005-Submit Date
Survey Submitted: March 2006

The social life at RWU is very close-knit. Everyone knows almost everyone and yet it lacks petty cliques and standoffish groups of people. The school fraternities hold bar nights a few times each semester, where any law student, member or not, can drink unlimited draft beer for $5 for a few hours. What a great deal! There are bars that are known as the law students' favorites, and each night of the week has the bar of choice. The bartenders at Aiden's Irish Pub know many of us by name. Topside's on Wednesday draws a big crowd with its $4 pitchers. In the fall and spring, Goff's has a roof patio over looking the water where we enjoy the ocean breeze and smells of salt water.

While there are not that many bars in Bristol, the types of places range from relaxing Irish pubs, to three story bars with live bands and pool tables, to dance floors. Dance clubs are a many in Providence, 20 minutes away. The seafood here is perhaps the best in the country, as RWU is right on the water, and restaurants range from pizza places to sushi bars, and from affordable to expensive.

Status: Current student, full-time
Dates of Enrollment: 8/2003-Submit Date
Survey Submitted: March 2006

The school has many different clubs and opportunities outside of school to socialize. Recently, the dean of students has made it a priority to offer more extracurricular activities for married students and student with significant others.

Status: Current student, full-time
Dates of Enrollment: 8/2004-Submit Date
Survey Submitted: March 2006

The school has two frats that host many events. I don't drink so I can't tell you about the bars, but there are several in town that students frequent. Plus, Boston and Providence are so close and they offer great nightlife and restaurants. The school has a number of organizations that offer lots of activities. SBA hosts the Barristers Ball that is like a law school prom, which is a blast with dancing, drinking and dinner. Dating is like it is anywhere you meet people, but this is law school, so it is hard to find time to date.

Status: Current student, full-time
Dates of Enrollment: 9/2005-Submit Date
Survey Submitted: March 2006

Admittedly, first-year law students don't have much time for socializing outside of school. However, on the rare occasion that I do make it out Bristol and nearby Newport and Providence provide an array of activities. Our favorite bar in town is the Topside, which overlooks Bristol Harbor and offers student-friendly prices, such a $4 beer pitchers and $.20 wings on Wednesdays. It's also popular with undergrads and locals. For something more eclectic and upscale my friends and I will venture into Newport. I love to run, and Rhode Island plays host to numerous races of varying distances year round. In fact, I think that my favorite race this year was the Bristol "Hangover Classic" which takes place in Colt State Park on January 1st.

Status: Current student, full-time
Dates of Enrollment: 9/2003-Submit Date
Survey Submitted: February 2006

Students at Roger Williams work very hard. When they let off steam, they do it with the same determination that they display in the classroom and the courtroom. The Student Bar Association is particularly active in supplying opportunities for students to get together and socialize, from the very popular annual Barrister's Ball, a black tie event that brings the entire law school community together, to semi-weekly gatherings at local pubs and restaurants. The law school fraternity also sponsors frequent gatherings, usually at bars. Students often leave Bristol as well, and venture into the nearby city of Providence, which offers a great deal in terms of restaurants, bars, clubs and music venues. There are also a great number of cultural events in Providence that take place throughout the year, a number of which offer free or low cost admission prices to students.

Roger Williams really is a community. It is a relatively small school and the students here tend to get along with each other quite well. The stories I have heard of competitiveness at other schools are not told here. We care about each other here, and we care about everybody doing well. Of course, everybody wants to do their personal best, and they want it to be number one, but I feel I can also honestly say that they want it to not be at the expense of another student's success. We are all in it together here. We work together, study together, play together—each of us, I think, have a real sense of having been part of something very, very special.

Status: Former Student, full-time
Dates of Enrollment: 8/2003-5/2004
Survey Submitted: July 2004

Social life at Roger Williams Law School completely depends upon the type of student. For those students that seek an active party life, there is one to be found, even in the small town of Bristol. Because the law school is small, the students all know each other and go out in small groups frequently. Students tend to know those in their section the best, and by the end of the year, very well.

Read all of Vault's Law School Surveys at www.vault.com/lawschool — get complete surveys on top law schools, expert advice on applicaton essays, LSAT prep and more.

VAULT CAREER LIBRARY **563**

University of Memphis

Cecil C. Humphreys School of Law
Admissions Office
3715 Central Avenue
Memphis, TN 38152
Admissions phone: (901) 678-5403
Admissions e-mail: lawadmissions@mail.law.memphis.edu
Admissions URL: http://law.memphis.edu/admissions/

 Admissions

Status: Current student, full-time
Dates of Enrollment: 8/2005-Submit Date
Survey Submitted: April 2006

The school's online application is very easy to follow and submit. Since the school does require interviews, you can request one if you would like to meet with someone face to face. If you can't make it in for an interview the admissions staff at the school are more than happy to talk to you on the phone. The essay required for admission is your chance to stand out from the crowd, so don't use the same essay you used for all other schools, because chances are they have probably read that before.

Status: Alumnus/a, part-time
Dates of Enrollment: 9/1995-5/2000
Survey Submitted: April 2006

It is becoming increasingly selective. However, the admissions people do a good job having a nice mix of traditional and non-traditional students to insure that the students reflect our society.

Status: Alumnus/a, full-time
Dates of Enrollment: 8/2003-12/2005
Survey Submitted: April 2006

They did not interview me. Admission was based on LSAT scores and undergraduate GPA. I went to the law school and talked with the dean of admissions several times, and she was very helpful in explaining deadlines and everything that was required.

Status: Alumnus/a, full-time
Dates of Enrollment: 8/1998-5/2001
Survey Submitted: April 2006

Score as high as possible on the LSAT. School seems to be seeking diversity. Recent immigrant minorities should be encouraged. Being black in Memphis is not a minority. Get application and supporting documents in as early as possible. Recommendations giving some unique perspective from lawyers and judges are helpful.

Status: Current student, full-time
Dates of Enrollment: 8/2004-Submit Date
Survey Submitted: April 2005

In order to get into the University of Memphis School of Law, you must fill out the standard application form (which can be done online) as well as register for the LSAC so that your information is readily available to prospective law schools. The university requires that each prospective student send in all former transcripts and obtain at least two letters of recommendation.

Status: Current student, full-time
Dates of Enrollment: 8/2003-Submit Date
Survey Submitted: April 2005

The admissions process for the law school is equivalent to any other law program. You must have taken the LSAT in order to apply. You must have your LSAT score sent to the university. Then you must submit the following (all forms are available online under "admissions" at www.law.memphis.edu). (1) An application form (filled out of course!) accompanied by an application fee of $25.00 (they'll accept checks and money orders). (2) A personal statement that states your reasons for seeking a law degree, including your personal goals and professional expectations. You should also include any relevant information in explanation of a low undergraduate GPA or LSAT score. Your personal statement may also describe any important or unique personality traits, characteristics or circumstances not otherwise apparent from your application.

(3) A Dean's Certification Form must be submitted from the academic institution from which you earned or will earn a baccalaureate degree. (4) (OPTIONAL) A letter of recommendation is not required for an application to be considered complete and evaluated by the admissions committee. However, I strongly encourage you to submit the maximum amount (three) because this will increase your chances of admission. You should get recommendation letters from former professors, instructors or other professionals who can give relevant information on your intellectual ability, academic performance and potential for success in law school (much better than letters from personal or family friends or social acquaintances who can only provide minimal information on your abilities and won't be considered helpful).

Status: Current student, full-time
Dates of Enrollment: 8/2004-Submit Date
Survey Submitted: March 2005

I found the application process to be quite similar to the process at other law schools. The admission staff was helpful, and the biggest influence they had on me was that the dean of admissions gave my wife and I an unscheduled tour of the law school. The selection of students seems fairly rigorous. I have noticed that most of the 1Ls in my class are extremely intelligent.

Status: Current student, full-time
Dates of Enrollment: 8/2004-Submit Date
Survey Submitted: March 2005

The admissions process was comparable to most state-run law schools. It was four to five pages long and not too difficult to fill out. The essay was the general one found on all law school admissions forms. No interview is required, though I did meet with the dean of admissions and she was extremely helpful in answering my questions. This school of law is one of the less selective ones in the South.

Status: Current student, full-time
Dates of Enrollment: 8/2002-Submit Date
Survey Submitted: January 2004

The University of Memphis, like every graduate school program, has benefited from the sluggish economy and made admission more difficult due to the influx of applicants. This fact, coupled with their desire to boost their ratings in the magazine polls, has allowed them to become more selective. When I entered, their median LSAT was a 153, whereas now it's a 156. Other than the LSAT, and one two-page essay, there are very few extra hoops they make you jump through. Being a Tennessee resident never hurts.

Status: Alumnus/a, full-time
Dates of Enrollment: 9/1999-5/2002
Survey Submitted: May 2004

The admissions office is very helpful. Be sure to understand the admissions process, admissions LSAT/GPA formula and the timelines before you get started. I do not recall that there were any interviews, but the admissions office will still be happy to talk with you. Your essay, of course, is important, but I believe your LSAT score and undergraduate GPA will play a more prominent role in the selection process. The school has become very selective lately because the current facility has limited space and because more people than ever are trying to get into law school.

Academics

Status: Current student, full-time
Dates of Enrollment: 8/2005-Submit Date
Survey Submitted: April 2006

The first-year curriculum is planned out for you and your schedule is given to you. The first-year classes are an excellent introduction to the basics of law. First-year students take Property, Torts, Criminal Law, Civil Procedure, Contracts and Legal Methods. The Legal Methods class is split into lecture with the entire first-year class and then you are also split into small groups of 10 students with a local attorney teaching writing skills. The small groups are great for getting one-on-one time in more of a relaxed setting than the typical class. The workload for each class is typically around two hours a night to prepare fully.

Status: Alumnus/a, part-time
Dates of Enrollment: 9/1995-5/2000
Survey Submitted: April 2006

A structured curriculum (many core courses) leaves little wiggle room in scheduling for those in a part-time program, but the faculty and staff bent over backwards to make it work. The faculty is unfailingly accessible and professional in their interactions with the students. They will go out of their way to get you the material you need, not only to pass their course, but to become a better attorney. The entire program is infused with the practical aspects of lawyering—that is, how to anticipate, identify and solve problems for your clients. The grading scale is tough—not everyone gets A's and B's. The GPA comparison can be a double whammy to graduates competing against others from more "prestigious" schools that are more generous in their grades.

Status: Alumnus/a, full-time
Dates of Enrollment: 8/2003-12/2005
Survey Submitted: April 2006

Overall, I feel that the law school has quality classes and professors. The Civil Procedure professors helped write the Tennessee Rules of Civil Procedure. Getting into popular classes proved to be more difficult. Certain classes would become booked within three minutes from the time online registration began. Another problem was the scheduling of classes. A lot of classes were scheduled at the same times, so often I would have to pick one over the other. Also, mandatory classes would be scheduled at the same time as an elective, so I would miss out on important electives that I wanted to take. There were at least three classes that I really wanted to take but could not because of the conflict in times.

Status: Alumnus/a, full-time
Dates of Enrollment: 8/1998-5/2001
Survey Submitted: April 2006

Core curriculum is geared towards passing the bar exam. U of M is consistently scoring highest amongst Tennessee law schools on the TN Bar Exam.

Status: Current student, full-time
Dates of Enrollment: 8/2004-Submit Date
Survey Submitted: April 2005

Availability of first-year classes is not a problem, because the first-year students have required core classes and are assigned to these classes. The classes I've taken thus far are interesting and challenging, and the workload is moderate. The only complaint I have with the school currently is the building in which our classes are held, but from my understanding, future students will have the benefit of a new and much improved building.

Status: Current student, full-time
Dates of Enrollment: 8/2003-Submit Date
Survey Submitted: April 2005

The law school offers a rigorous curriculum that provides students with a solid foundation in diverse areas of law and an ample opportunity to gain practical experience and to specialize in areas of interest. It is usually not a problem to get the classes that you want, especially if you are on the ball. Some seminars you may not get on the first try, but you shouldn't have a problem getting at some point during your second or third year.

The quality of classes at the university is fantastic. The U of M Law School is quickly gaining a reputation of preparing its students well for work after law school. The professors try to add a more practical approach to the study of law. Not only is the quality of classes excellent, but the professors are of equally high caliber. The professors are always well-prepared and are always willing to sit down with a student who has questions.

The law school is also known for having a tough grading system, in that unlike many other law programs, we tend to have lower GPAs because our grades are not inflated. However, this is good incentive to work hard so that when you do get great grades, you know that you earned it because you knew the material.

The workload is typical for any law school. Basically, be prepared to do some work. But don't worry, it will pay off and be worth it! It is NOT busy work.

Status: Current student, full-time
Dates of Enrollment: 8/2003-Submit Date
Survey Submitted: March 2005

The classes are challenging and full of work, but they are rewarding and, many times, full of fun. The first year, your professors are chosen for you, but after that it is pretty easy to get the classes and professors that you want. I have never gone to another law school, but I feel like we have some of the best professors that know the law and who are great at teaching. There is great interaction, but it is not too intimidating.

Status: Alumnus/a, full-time
Dates of Enrollment: 9/1999-5/2002
Survey Submitted: May 2004

The professors care about your academic success. There is no "weed out" program. Most of the professors are very approachable. The instruction is very high quality in nature. The U of M requires you to take many prerequisite courses. While [the program] constricts your freedom with regard to what classes you may take, it will ultimately assist you when you take the bar examination, and it will prevent you from pigeonholing your legal education too much in any one direction.

Status: Current student, full-time
Dates of Enrollment: 8/2002-Submit Date
Survey Submitted: January 2004

The university is very strict and allows very little leeway in what it allows students to take within their first three semesters. Students about to graduate are given priority in the registration process so getting courses you need for the bar is never a problem. If you're looking for a school that offers a number of diverse courses that have no relevance to the bar, Memphis is not your place. The focus here is on courses that will prepare and increase students' likelihood of bar passage.

Employment Prospects

Status: Current student, full-time
Dates of Enrollment: 8/2005-Submit Date
Survey Submitted: April 2006

The career services department at the law school does a wonderful job of having a number of opportunities for on-campus interviews. They also are constantly updating their bulletin board daily with job announcements. There is a broad range of employers who recruit at the school, some very prestigious while others are individual attorneys that are not well known.

Status: Alumnus/a, part-time
Dates of Enrollment: 9/1995-5/2000
Survey Submitted: April 2006

The career services office does an outstanding job of providing interview opportunities for the students. The growing alumni network and their stellar job performance, including the ability to "hit the ground running" with little of the hand-holding required for those from other, less practice-oriented institutions, means that CCH grads are being snapped up.

Read all of Vault's Law School Surveys at www.vault.com/lawschool — get complete surveys on top law schools, expert advice on applicaton essays, LSAT prep and more.

VAULT CAREER LIBRARY 565

Status: Alumnus/a, full-time
Dates of Enrollment: 8/2003-12/2005
Survey Submitted: April 2006

The law school has a pretty high esteem in Memphis because our bar passage rate is higher than Vanderbilt. A lot of graduates go to large firms, but usually they have interned at those firms over the summers while they were in law school. The career services office is a very helpful resource. It has a book with the names of alumni all over the United States with the firms that they work for. The office also has on-site interviews with certain firms for summer interns as well as associate positions. It also has a web site with job postings as well as helpful links to other law related web sites. The dean of career services is very helpful. He always made time to talk to me about my career dilemmas, advice on salary and what to do in certain situations. That office is a very valuable resource, but the student has to choose to use it.

Status: Current student, full-time
Dates of Enrollment: 8/2003-Submit Date
Survey Submitted: April 2005

The law school has a career services center which receives listings of job opportunities for students to apply for. They also obtain requests from firms from Memphis, Nashville, Chattanooga and other places to come and do on-campus interviews. These are also posted, and students submit a resume, and then the firm chooses when they want to interview. The range of jobs that graduates take is widely varied. In the past, graduates have received jobs from such places as the DA, U.S. Postal Service Legal Department, FedEx, local firms, Judicial Clerkships, large nationwide firms and non-traditional legal jobs, such as working for companies like WestLaw, Lexis Nexis, PMBR and Barbri.

The U of M law school consistently has the [one of] the highest job placement rates after graduation among the law schools in the state of Tennessee. From year to year, the placement rate usually hovers somewhere around 95 percent, with the lowest in the past 11 years being 11 years ago at 90.4 percent and the highest percentages being in the most recent years at 98.5 percent. U of M law school grads are known for their skills and abilities and always do well after graduation. Hey, a graduate from our law school made it into the top five of Donald Trump's *The Apprentice*. The alumni network is strong, and students have many opportunities to meet and work with alumni, through city organizations that have student chapters, internships and legal clinics. There are many opportunities for a student to work during the summers and even during the school year.

Status: Current student, full-time
Dates of Enrollment: 8/2004-Submit Date
Survey Submitted: March 2005

Within the state of Tennessee, Memphis probably gets overlooked in the job market, coming behind Vanderbilt and the University of Tennessee; however, around Memphis and the surrounding area, there is a plethora of firms willing to hire from this school. In the end, if one wants to work in the state, especially the western end, then Memphis is comparable to others; however a degree from this university probably does not carry as much weight if one wants to work in another state. As a first-year law student, there is not much opportunity for paid clerkships, but there are several volunteer opportunities and jobs after the first year are a lot more abundant.

Status: Alumnus/a, full-time
Dates of Enrollment: 9/1999-5/2002
Survey Submitted: May 2004

The career services office is exceptional. The director of career placement has a very healthy relationship with local firms and other organizations. Most large firms in town come to campus for interviews.

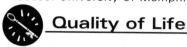 **Quality of Life**

Status: Current student, full-time
Dates of Enrollment: 8/2005-Submit Date
Survey Submitted: April 2006

The facilities are not in the best of shape right now. The law school is in the process of moving to a larger building in downtown Memphis so the current building does not receive much attention and it shows. The facilities, especially the library are very run-down. The current issue at the law school is the use of laptops in the classroom. Some of the professors are not allowing students to use laptops to take notes anymore because they believe students are "playing" on the Internet during class. Crime in Memphis is high but the area campus is located in is not that bad. There are plenty of great safe places to live in Memphis; on popular spot is Mud Island, where a lot of young people live.

Status: Alumnus/a, part-time
Dates of Enrollment: 9/1995-5/2000
Survey Submitted: April 2006

University of Memphis is a commuter school. Most live off campus, and there is a wide variety of affordable housing to choose from. Facilities are crowded and outdated, but the upcoming move of the campus to downtown Memphis will provide a state-of-the-art physical plant that honors the past and is prepared for the future

Status: Alumnus/a, full-time
Dates of Enrollment: 8/2003-12/2005
Survey Submitted: April 2006

The campus at the University of Memphis is not ideal. The law school is situated on a very busy street. The parking is atrocious. There are often not enough spots, too few entrances and exits, which causes backup in traffic, and they love to write tickets and put holds on the students' accounts. The dining is acceptable. In the campus dining area they have a wide variety of foods—meat and veggies, a grill, Subway, Chick-fil-A, even packaged sushi. In certain buildings, they have a Starbucks area that also sells light foods such as sandwiches, yogurt and fruit.

Status: Current student, full-time
Dates of Enrollment: 8/2003-Submit Date
Survey Submitted: April 2005

The campus offers a wide variety of services that law students have full access to, such as a bookstore, several dining places, several cafes, a health center and disability services. The university is also in a very convenient location with respect to the rest of the city of Memphis. It is only 15 minutes from the main part of downtown, 15 minutes from the airport and just a few minutes from many excellent restaurants, bars and a large mall.

Status: Current student, full-time
Dates of Enrollment: 8/2002-Submit Date
Survey Submitted: January 2004

Most students live in surrounding areas near the campus or out east in Cordova. You'll get little help from the admissions committee in finding a roommate when first moving here but your best bet is to post an ad on the bulletin board before school starts. The school does offer campus housing.

Status: Current student, full-time
Dates of Enrollment: 8/2004-Submit Date
Survey Submitted: April 2005

The library, although it has all of the necessary books, is definitely lacking in space, appearance, number of outlets, number of desks, bathroom facilities and the building in general is in need of renovation. The neighborhood is nice and has plenty of affordable student housing, and many students, like myself, commute to school each day. Parking is a problem, as it is with every school. The campus is relatively safe and the school has an excellent safety program.

Status: Current student, full-time
Dates of Enrollment: 8/2004-Submit Date
Survey Submitted: March 2005

Quality of life is the most glaring problem with this school. The surrounding area if full of culture and life, but the housing and rental market for students is not all that great. Living in Memphis does mean having to deal with a greater likelihood of crime, and the school building itself is past its prime. The building problem should be remedied in the next five years, but that is little comfort for the present students. There are other buildings on campus that provide a nice learning atmosphere, but the law school building is not one of them.

Social Life

Status: Current student, full-time
Dates of Enrollment: 8/2005-Submit Date
Survey Submitted: April 2006

The Student Bar Association does a great job of planning a number of social events. Every week on Thursday nights there is a Bar Review at a local bar where students can gather and socialize. There are also golf tournaments and cookouts. Memphis is full of great places to eat and hang out. There are a number of sporting events such as the Memphis Grizzlies (NBA), Memphis Redbirds Baseball, and of course The University of Memphis sports teams! World Famous barbecue is found in Memphis at Rendezvous BBQ. Of course there is Beale Street, a popular nightlife destination. Bottom line is there is never a lack of extracurricular activities to be found in Memphis.

Status: Alumnus/a, part-time
Dates of Enrollment: 9/1995-5/2000
Survey Submitted: April 2006

A vibrant and growing community means lots of places to hang out. Downtown is a magnet for great eating establishments, eclectic pubs and the best people watching this side of the *Star Wars* bar!

Status: Alumnus/a, full-time
Dates of Enrollment: 8/2003-12/2005
Survey Submitted: April 2006

There are about four bars and plenty of restaurants in the surrounding area. The law school had maybe 20 different clubs that students could join. However, when I went through orientation, hardly any of the clubs were represented. They would advertise by taping a piece of paper to the wall, and I never felt interested enough to join any. Every Thursday night the Student Body Association for the law school would have a "Bar Review," which usually consisted of people going to a certain bar and getting drunk. The SBA would have specific events every year, such as a student auction to raise money for graduation, a golf tournament, one big party and "Flaw Review" when each class would put on a skit making fun of school and professors.

Status: Alumnus/a, full-time
Dates of Enrollment: 8/1998-5/2001
Survey Submitted: April 2006

Religious student organizations cover the whole spectrum. There are also several other student-led social clubs. I think far to many, as it can distract from the educational work.

Status: Current student, full-time
Dates of Enrollment: 8/2003-Submit Date
Survey Submitted: April 2005

The school has a very active social life. There are many law school clubs to choose from such as the Association for Women Attorneys, Christian Legal Society, Black Students of America, Environmental Society, American Trial Lawyers Association and the Federalist Society. There is also a law fraternity that is a favorite with the student body, Pi Alpha Delta (P.A.D.), that hosts many social events, provides an outline bank for students and gets involved in the community. The SBA puts together many activities such as a Golf Classic, a Student Auction, Flaw Review (end of year activity where students perform skits making fun of professors and professors perform a rebuttal skit making fun of students), and "Law"-lapalooza (a big end of the year party and auction event where the professors offer things such as a day of golf and dinner for the students to bid on to raise money for graduation). Probably the most popular event put on by SBA is the weekly "Bar Review," which is held at a different local bar every Thursday night.

Status: Current student, full-time
Dates of Enrollment: 8/2002-Submit Date
Survey Submitted: January 2004

The law school is surrounded by a number of cool bars and restaurants. Memphis has Grizzlies basketball, Peabody rooftop parties in the summer and Beale Street. The law school has Bar Review every Thursday night and a number of student organizations ranging from the Black Student Society to a revived presence of legal fraternities on campus. Most students hail from Tennessee and there is a fairly good cross-section of age ranges and minorities on campus, which gives the classroom a relaxed feel and an interesting perspective.

Read all of Vault's Law School Surveys at www.vault.com/lawschool — get complete surveys on top law schools, expert advice on applicaton essays, LSAT prep and more.

VAULT CAREER LIBRARY **567**

University of Tennessee College of Law

Office of Admission and Financial Aid
1505 W. Cumberland Ave.
Suite 161
Knoxville, TN 37996-1801
Admissions phone: (865) 974-4131
Admissions fax: (865) 974-1572
Admissions e-mail: lawadmit@libra.law.utk.edu
Admissions URL:
http://www.law.utk.edu/departments/admiss/admissmain.htm

 ## Admissions

Status: Alumnus/a, full-time
Dates of Enrollment: 8/1996-5/1999
Survey Submitted: May 2006

I was fortunate to work closely with the admissions process as a third-year student. Honest, well-written essays are a must. Often, applicants think the admissions readers are looking for an awe-inspiring story when in reality, we just want one that is intelligently written and uses words that you would expect to hear in normal, everyday writing. In other words, put down the thesaurus and slowly walk away.

For reference letters, the applicant should always select someone who knows them well and can offer a substantive glimpse of the applicant. While a letter from a senator might sound impressive in theory, it offers very little to an admissions reader when it's obvious that the connection is nothing more than superficial.

UT has experienced a run of record-high applications for probably close to 10 years. I understand that applications are somewhat lower this year, but I believe the average is still something in the neighborhood of 1,200 applications for 150 seats. About half of those come from within the state. If you are an undergraduate alum of UT, you do not have any better shot of getting in; in fact, that can sometimes work against you as the college strives to create a diverse student population.

> **The school says:** "UT received almost 1,400 applications for admission for the fall 2006 entering class. Approximately 800 of those applicants were from states other than Tennessee—approximately 600 were from residents of Tennessee. The University of Tennessee, Knoxville is traditionally the largest feeder school; at press time, approximately one-third of the entering class members were graduates of UTK."

Status: Current student, full-time
Dates of Enrollment: 8/2005-Submit Date
Survey Submitted: May 2006

The admissions process was a relatively unfrightening experience. Given what I have heard about other institutions, UT takes every step possible to make the admissions process open, accessible and informative to those that apply. This includes allowing students to submit their Admissions application via the Internet, providing detailed information to potential applicants about the curriculum, concentrations and opportunities UT can offer them on their web site and being highly accessible by telephone, Internet and in person for questions and consultations.

In terms of actually applying, the admissions committee is looking for candor and honesty in an applicant's personal statement and the essay on an applicant's most significant learning experience. In addition, the committee looks at the ephemeral factors of a candidate beyond the numbers of the LSAT score and the GPA, such as motivation, military service, career experience and other significant talents or life experiences.

In terms of "advice on getting in" to UT, my suggestion would be to simply be yourself. UT is a school that like people that are hard working and ready to contribute to both the law and to the public good. They are selective in picking their students; however, the College of Law has a "knack" for recognizing good people that have great potential in Law. Thus, be yourself and be dedicated in the admissions process. I would also encourage potential students to apply early since UT is considered a top-tier law school and is currently in high demand by those seeking to attend here.

> **The school says:** "In recent years, the College of Law has admitted 19 to 16 percent of its applicants to fill the entering class."

Status: Current student, full-time
Dates of Enrollment: 8/2004-Submit Date
Survey Submitted: May 2006

UT Law seems to be very interested in diversity both in experiences and in demographics. The admissions people are especially knowledgeable and helpful. They suggest including essentially ALL of past experiences that might be relevant in admissions decisions.

Status: Current student, full-time
Dates of Enrollment: 8/2004-Submit Date
Survey Submitted: May 2006

The admissions office at UT was amazing. When I wanted to take a year off in between college and law school, they worked with me every step of the way in getting a deferral of my acceptance. I was also impressed with the selectivity of the College of Law. We are a relatively small law school with only 450 students and I know of several individuals from UT undergrad who just did not make the cut. It is clear that Tennessee is looking for students who attended big-name undergraduate schools.

> **The school says:** "One of several factors that the admissions committee can consider is the difficulty of the undergraduate school attended. UTK has traditionally been the largest feeder school; approximately one-third of entering class members are graduates of UTK."

Status: Current student, full-time
Dates of Enrollment: 8/2005-Submit Date
Survey Submitted: May 2006

I would advise people to send in their applications as soon as possible. UT is very good at getting back to people, and they responded to my application very promptly. The later you wait to apply, however, the longer it will take you to find out if you got accepted. You do not want to be the candidate who in April still does not know if they got in to law school.

Status: Alumnus/a, full-time
Dates of Enrollment: 8/2000-5/2003
Survey Submitted: April 2005

The University of Tennessee College of Law places great emphasis on a combination of your LSAT score and your undergraduate GPA. That being said, the university looks for well-rounded students who demonstrate a likelihood of post-graduate success in a law-related field. If a prospective student has a question about the admissions process, I found the admissions staff to be very approachable and eager to assist you.

Status: Alumnus/a, full-time
Dates of Enrollment: 8/1996-5/1999
Survey Submitted: April 2005

I was fortunate to participate in the admissions process as a 3L. I can tell you from the number of essays I was forced to read that being honest and candid is a must. It was very easy to pick out the canned essays. When I was reading the essay, I wanted to come away with some sense of who the applicant was. The more personalized (the more the essay talked to me), the more I felt that the application didn't belong to a faceless applicant, but an individual. Flowery phrases and vocabulary-word-a-day words only made the essay more difficult to read and made the process more frustrating for me and the other students on the admissions committee.

The school says: "The admissions committee has faculty and student voting members."

Status: Alumnus/a, full-time
Dates of Enrollment: 8/1999-5/2002
Survey Submitted: April 2004

The process is not difficult and it does not require an interview. While LSAT scores and undergraduate grades are considered, EVERY application is read. That means that the essays are very important.

Status: Current student, full-time
Dates of Enrollment: 8/2002-Submit Date
Survey Submitted: March 2005

As an applicant, my experience with admissions was great. All staff members were very helpful in applying to the law school. I could call with any question and they would answer to the best of their ability. I had begun to get nervous about whether I would be accepted or not, so I called the school and they told me they were deciding that day. As soon as they had a decision, they called me to let me know that I had been admitted.

The process was fairly painless, all you have to do is fill out the application and write a personal statement. As a current student, I have more insight into the actual process. Both faculty and staff read the applications and vote on whether they believe the student will be an asset to the school. They look at the whole student—college, grades, LSAT, personal life and outside extracurriculars.

The school says: "There are additional steps in the application process. Candidates should rely only on the most current application instructions and use only the most recent application forms."

Academics

Status: Alumnus/a, full-time
Dates of Enrollment: 8/2000-5/2003
Survey Submitted: May 2006

The academic program at UT College of Law is stimulating. The professors want you to learn how to think like a lawyer, write like a lawyer, and act like a lawyer (however that may be!). They want to prepare you to practice law successfully instead of focusing on theoretical applications. The academic environment is very challenging, but it's not "cutthroat" as you often hear about law schools. Students often work together in groups to produce outlines during exam preparation.

Status: Alumnus/a, full-time
Dates of Enrollment: 8/1996-5/1999
Survey Submitted: May 2006

The core curriculum allows for plenty of opportunities to explore areas of interest or lesser known areas of the law. UT is one of the few colleges in the country that offers two concentrations: Advocacy and Transactional. If you select one of those tracks (and you're not required to do so), you find your schedule does not allow for as many electives as if you do the general JD.

Grading is anonymous for every class that has an exam. Some seminars do not have exams and instead rely upon papers and class participation or class projects. The seminars are more intimate settings (usually a maximum of 12 students) and give you the chance to really get into a particular subject. For the most part, those classes in the advocacy track have a reputation for being GPA padders, while those of a transactional nature are seen as more difficult.

Status: Current student, full-time
Dates of Enrollment: 8/2005-Submit Date
Survey Submitted: May 2006

The academics at UT College of Law are summed up by saying that they are focused on the practical education of the law student. The professors at UT mix both theoretical legal concepts with practical real-world application in every subject, whether it is Torts or the Business Law Clinic. The classes are topnotch and engaging because of the mix of lively and highly analytical students and professors that not only emphasize teaching the material, but also emphasize learning and applying the material too.

In terms of getting classes, all students are required to bid on classes each term through a bidding system. Each student is given a set amount of points and then the student can bid on the classes they want. This is a fairly easy process, but takes some strategy. Thus, all students are treated fairly in the quest for the classes they want or for the "popular" classes.

The professors are always accessible for student consultation and make every attempt to make sure the student understands the material being taught. The professors are also a friend to those that know them well and make an effort to get to know them. The class sizes are small enough to allow for a more in-depth interaction between the professor and the students. Grading is done based on a mixture of the score on the final exam and attendance/class participation, depending on the professor.

The workload is manageable, even as a first year student. Typically, a class might require three to five hours of outside reading per week, with the first semester having five classes for a total of 15 credit hours. The classroom time passes quickly; however, the professor do require the students to be prepared in the subject matter for the day's assignment, since most of the professors employ the Socratic Method of teaching to some extent. Otherwise, the workload is manageable throughout the semester, even during final exams.

Status: Current student, full-time
Dates of Enrollment: 8/2005-Submit Date
Survey Submitted: May 2006

Professors have been topnotch. There is an emphasis on teaching and the professors appear to enjoy their work and the classes. There is a bid process so a student can prioritize and hopefully get the classes and professors they want. It works well. Workload is a lot but that is law school.

Status: Current student, full-time
Dates of Enrollment: 8/2004-Submit Date
Survey Submitted: May 2006

The thing that bothers me the most about UT Law is that we are billed as a "well kept secret." The quality of the program here should not be a secret any longer. The legal education is first rate and this school prepares us for the real world. There is an emphasis on the practitioner. Most of the professors are not career professors, but judges who have sat on the Tennessee Supreme Court and lawyers who have argued high profile cases themselves—even before the U.S. Supreme Court. Many of the professors carry on regular pro bono work to stay in tune with the true practice of law. While in some ways I am glad that Tennessee is a well-kept secret, others should know how great this law school is.

Status: Current student, full-time
Dates of Enrollment: 8/2005-Submit Date
Survey Submitted: May 2006

As any first-year student may say, the first year of law school is the worst year. However, that is only true if you do not take use of the help that is provided. At UT, the faculty members all have an open-door policy and if you need the extra assistance then that will be given. The grading can be intimidating, however, if you put your mind into your work you will prevail. Remember that all your colleagues are all smart or they would not be here so that makes it even more competitive. The professors are fair when it comes to grading because all work is graded on an anonymous bases. The workload can become heavy but stay on top of your work and if you get behind the take advantage of the open-door policy.

Read all of Vault's Law School Surveys at www.vault.com/lawschool — get complete surveys on top law schools, expert advice on applicaton essays, LSAT prep and more.

VAULT CAREER LIBRARY 569

Status: Current student, full-time
Dates of Enrollment: 8/2005-Submit Date
Survey Submitted: May 2006

The academic workload is tough, of course, because it is law school. The professors, however, are great. All of them are experts in their fields and can give both a theoretical and practical understanding of the course. Moreover, all of my professors stay after class to answer students' questions. In order to register for classes after your first year, you have to bid points, which can be a bit tricky. In order to get the most popular classes, you will have to bid a lot of points. The bidding system isn't that bad though, and most of the people I know get all the classes on which they bid.

Status: Alumnus/a, full-time
Dates of Enrollment: 8/2000-5/2003
Survey Submitted: April 2005

The professors at UT College of Law have an interest in insuring that students practically learn the law. The professors are engaging and approachable. Each professor was willing to spend time away from class answering questions and helping students grasp sometimes foreign subjects. The workload is demanding, but that will be the case at any law school. Law school is what you make of it and you have to be willing to sacrifice time—including weekends and late nights—to achieve success in law school. The expectations are high, and the grading is rigid.

Status: Alumnus/a, full-time
Dates of Enrollment: 8/2000-5/2003
Survey Submitted: April 2005

Class quality was excellent, grading is fair and workload was entirely manageable (even with two small children at home). I particularly appreciated the availability of professors outside of the classroom. Faculty doors were always open, which welcomed students and encouraged a deeper learning than can be obtained from classroom and group instruction.

Status: Alumnus/a, full-time
Dates of Enrollment: 8/2000-5/2003
Survey Submitted: April 2005

The instructors were world-class but also very grounded, approachable, helpful, and accessible. 90 percent of the time, classes were very challenging. Only 10 percent or so of the time did I find the class content to be "easy." Class selection and offerings could have been a little better, but the administration worked with us to help us if we had a special scheduling or substantive need. Grading was very tough, but I liked that about UT—Getting an A was a special event and something that motivated me. There were times when no one in the class received an A. Usually only one or two people out of 30 got an A. Basically, an A really meant something.

Status: Alumnus/a, full-time
Dates of Enrollment: 8/1996-5/1999

UT had some banner classes and some that I would rather not remember. The most highly sought-after classes were generally available; sometimes it involved talking directly to the professor, but that was only a minor hurdle. If you really wanted or needed the class, there was a way to get on the roll.

When bar review and bar exam rolled around, I felt very prepared. At UT, you can do the Advocacy Concentration, Business Transactions Concentration, or general degree. I chose the general track because of the freedom it allowed me in choosing the classes. The course requirements for the concentrations did not leave much time for electives, and there were too many seminars I was interested in taking to give up that freedom (Space Law, Health Care in Society, Labor Arbitration).

Status: Alumnus/a, full-time
Dates of Enrollment: 8/1999-5/2002
Survey Submitted: April 2004

Challenging classes with some great professors! Workload varies, but it is not a school you can "skate" through. As well as general law school opportunities, Tennessee has a concentration in Business Transactions as well as a Litigation track. As an alum of the business track, I recommend it highly. The college has professors who have real practice experience who strive to truly prepare students for their future job responsibilities.

Status: Current student, full-time
Dates of Enrollment: 8/2002-Submit Date
Survey Submitted: March 2005

First-year courses are set for you so that you get all of the basic classes. You get a wide variety of teaching styles so that you become familiar with them in the first year. First-year workload is relatively mild. After that, you determine what your workload will be. All professors are very knowledgeable in their fields and have open-door policies. They are always willing to talk to you about anything at any time. There are also a wide assortment of clinical programs that make what you learn in class come to life as you work at the DAs office or the public defender's office. Grading is fair overall.

 Employment Prospects

Status: Alumnus/a, full-time
Dates of Enrollment: 8/1996-5/1999
Survey Submitted: May 2006

There is a very active summer associate program at the law school, and students seeking jobs during their summers of school have a lot of information available to them both through the career services office as well as through the Tennessee Bar Association's TBA Job Link web site.

Status: Current student, full-time
Dates of Enrollment: 8/2005-Submit Date
Survey Submitted: May 2006

In terms of internships and on-campus interviews, UT makes as many opportunities available to its students as possible. Usually, career services will schedule two rounds of on-campus interviews, one for the Fall Term and one for the Spring Term. These include employers of most every field of legal work, including government and private practice. Furthermore, career services offers periodic workshops on how to prepare for these interviews and other employment topics, from resume and cover letter preparation to interviewing skills.

Status: Current student, full-time
Dates of Enrollment: 8/2004-Submit Date
Survey Submitted: May 2006

Most law students I know are working in law positions rather than other employment. The career services staff does a great job at listening to your desires and helping you figure out the best "fit" with employers. They also work with older students and provide great suggestions on second career types of folks.

Status: Current student, full-time
Dates of Enrollment: 8/2005-Submit Date
Survey Submitted: May 2006

Employment prospects range at the College of Law. The college provides an outstanding career service center that helps with resumes and posts or sends e-mails letting the students know when prospective law firms are considering taking one of the students from the law school. E-attorney is also available, which is a program where students can post their resumes so attorneys can pull them and have on-campus interviews. If all that the career services provides does not help, students have the opportunity to take advantage of the Knoxville Bar Association for networking opportunities.

Status: Current student, full-time
Dates of Enrollment: 8/2005-Submit Date
Survey Submitted: May 2006

Many of the firms that recruit from UT have UT alumni, so it is advantageous to have a UT connection. People who do not want to work in the South or who do not want the traditional legal job also find the career services department very helpful. Career services will put you into contact with UT Law alumni all over the country and/or help you find employers that offer jobs in different types of areas.

Status: Alumnus/a, full-time
Dates of Enrollment: 8/2000-5/2003
Survey Submitted: April 2005

Out of my close group of friends—about 14 people—12 of us had jobs at the time of graduation, and 100 percent of us were employed within three months of graduation. The university is well respected in the Southeast. The on-campus recruiting program is growing and becoming stronger. The university is seeking to enhance its reputation in other geographical regions and I think this will help recruit employers to interview. Many students go into private practice—civil and criminal—and some go to work for government agencies, and some go to work in other public sectors.

> **The school says:** "UT students have many different career objectives and interests, which the College seeks to inform and cultivate through formal and informal learning experiences. Many UT students seek employment with firms of fewer than 50 attorneys in smaller markets and with government and public interest employers. The hiring timetable for most of these employers is often after graduation and bar passage, unlike the largest law firms in major markets."

Status: Alumnus/a, full-time
Dates of Enrollment: 8/1996-5/1999
Survey Submitted: April 2005

Paid summer clerkships were difficult to obtain. I'm on the recruiting committee for my present employer, and we make it a practice of not hiring 1Ls. I found a lot of firms were like that when I was in school. My first year, I obtained one of my paid clerkships through the career services office at UT; the other one I obtained through an alumni contact at a firm. I clerked with my present employer during my second-year summer and was offered a job early fall of my third year. I had opportunities to interview at other firms and for other positions (such as judicial clerkships), so I felt that my career path was something I got to choose, not something I HAD to choose.

Government agencies, the judiciary, you name it came on campus to recruit. The geographic options seemed pretty decent as well; it wasn't only Tennessee firms that came to UT. Firms from Florida, Georgia, Virginia, North Carolina, Kentucky, Alabama were on campus during both fall and spring recruiting seasons. Career services also keeps a list of employers who may not come to campus but are still interested in receiving resumes.

Status: Alumnus/a, full-time
Dates of Enrollment: 8/1996-5/1999
Survey Submitted: April 2005

Those at the top they can do anything they want. For those in the middle of the class, it's relatively easy to get a job in the local market. For those in the bottom of the class, I think life is pretty tough.

> **The school says:** "All law schools measure employment nine months from graduation. The national average for the past three years has been just at 90 percent employment nationwide. UT graduates have averaged 97 percent employed nine months from graduation over this same time period."

Status: Current student, full-time
Dates of Enrollment: 8/2002-Submit Date

If you wish to work in the public sector or legal aid sector there are not quite as many on-campus opportunities. They do bring in many federal agencies but those are very specific jobs. Networking is great though. Many adjunct faculty members and other alumni help with networking. There are also many clinical opportunities that allow those wishing to work in the public sector to find jobs.

> **The school says:** "Public sector employers hire through on-campus interview channels less frequently than private law firms, which often ask students to apply directly to them through formal application processes they prefer."

 **Quality of Life**

Status: Alumnus/a, full-time
Dates of Enrollment: 8/1996-5/1999
Survey Submitted: May 2006

Knoxville is a great college town. Housing is easy to find, including that within walking distance of campus. If you want something more upscale, those housing complexes are also plentiful. For students wanting to be more frugal with the housing budget, campus-provided housing (some on, some off campus) is also available. UT's facilities are great as well. The work-out facilities eliminate any need for a gym membership. The law school itself is wonderful—although the present building was opened in 1997, it still looks new.

Status: Current student, full-time
Dates of Enrollment: 8/2005-Submit Date
Survey Submitted: May 2006

UT College of Law is located in Knoxville, TN and is just west of the downtown area, in the midst of the nationally known University of Tennessee campus. The law school is a extremely well-run facility, including an expansive five-floor law library, wireless Internet throughout the building and classroom that are both technologically advanced and easily accessible. The building, while a truly a modern facility, stills maintains the aura and atmosphere of a close-knit and tradition based law school, where the students are the driving energy behind the school.

The law school is readily accessible to the city of Knoxville via a free trolley system and a low cost public bus system. In addition, the law school is within walking distance of the downtown area and to many local dining and nightlife venues that are part of the UT Knoxville "college town" atmosphere. In addition, Knoxville is a large and diverse city that offers a low crime rate and may different choices for living, dining and recreation to suit most every personalized taste.

Status: Current student, full-time
Dates of Enrollment: 8/2004-Submit Date
Survey Submitted: May 2006

EXCELLENT. UT Law manages to feed just about everyone sometime during the week, no kidding. The school is very "community" oriented. The town is a great place to live (with or without a family). Safe place to live, you can live in walking distance to law school. Only issue in commuting is PARKING but it is not terrible. Many law students go on and pay for a set parking space so they can come and go faster. Others park on street for free but arrive early. Lots of options. Good ethnic foods all over town...but you have to search a little harder than in large cities. Lots of opportunities on campus for entertainment.

Status: Current student, full-time
Dates of Enrollment: 8/2005-Submit Date
Survey Submitted: May 2006

Safety and crime are not issues. After hours, students must use their ID that will give them access to the law school. The location is excellent. The college is located in the heart of University of Tennessee Knoxville, so one can take advantage of the undergrad life and football games to escape the walls of the law school. Housing, although not provided through the college of law, is convenient. There are apartments all around the campus. The college of law has boards posted by the mailboxes which at times have listings of apartments that are available in the surrounding area. Because the school is located in the heart of campus, fast food restaurants, coffee shops and grocery stores are all within walking distance.

Status: Alumnus/a, full-time
Dates of Enrollment: 8/2000-5/2003
Survey Submitted: April 2005

UT is a newly renovated law school and is a comfortable place to learn and study. It has a comprehensive library, modern classrooms and a cafeteria and dining area on-site. Beyond the law school itself, Knoxville is a great town with plenty to offer, but not so many distractions that it becomes difficult to focus.

Read all of Vault's Law School Surveys at www.vault.com/lawschool — get complete surveys on top law schools, expert advice on applicaton essays, LSAT prep and more.

VAULT CAREER LIBRARY 571

Status: Alumnus/a, full-time
Dates of Enrollment: 8/2000-5/2003
Survey Submitted: April 2005

Knoxville is a beautiful area in which to live. I moved to Knoxville from the beaches of Florida, which I thought I'd desperately miss, but in the end I decided to make Knoxville home even after graduation. The mountains are very accessible, there are plenty of freshwater lakes for boating (which is my favorite pastime), and you can't beat football season at the University of Tennessee.

Status: Alumnus/a, full-time
Dates of Enrollment: 8/1996-5/1999
Survey Submitted: April 2005

The computer lab is in the basement of the library, and I never had to wait for a computer. Additionally, when I was a student, law students had priority to those computers over undergrads or other graduate students. The library also has a ton of study carrels that can be reserved at the beginning of the semester. Up to three people can reserve one carrel; I never had an issue with someone being in my carrel when I needed to use it. There are also study rooms on each floor of the library that are made for study groups. These, too, can be reserved, and generally were pretty accessible. There would be times during the exam period when they would be full, but that was more of the exception instead of the rule.

The law school has a small cafe where you can find lots of snacks, salads, soups, sandwiches, and just about every kind of drink. If you can't find anything at the cafe that suits your fancy, the university center is just across the street, and it has a food court that includes many major fast food restaurants, as well as a cafeteria that has more traditional, home-cooked meals.

> **The school says:** "The College of Law Building is now wireless."

Status: Current student, full-time
Dates of Enrollment: 8/2002-Submit Date
Survey Submitted: March 2005

The College of Law is located in the midst of it all. There are plenty of off-campus housing opportunities within walking distance. And since it is located near the interstate, many students live away from school but have easy access and get there in little time. There are also many restaurants withing walking distance, as well as banks, bookstores and coffee shops within walking distance. The school is also very near to downtown where there are more restaurants, museums and night spots, and these are all within walking distance, as well. I live near campus and walk and do not feel threatened or unsafe. The actual building that houses the law school is new and great. It is an all inclusive building housing class rooms, the library, a small snack bar, faculty offices and study rooms, as well as offices for all school organizations. The building is very up-to-date and gives us a sense of home.

Social Life

Status: Current student, full-time
Dates of Enrollment: 8/2004-Submit Date
Survey Submitted: May 2006

People don't expect much of a social life in Knoxville, especially for those who are in law school. But they couldn't be farther from the mark. Of course, football season is amazing. All of the law students turn out in force for the games as the entire law school gets preferred block seating for most games. Thursday night "Rump Court" is a weekly trip to a new bar and the turnout is tremendous. The social life at Tennessee really keeps our community close. I went to one of the biggest party schools in the country for undergrad...and I couldn't be happier at Tennessee.

> **The school says:** "Preferred block seating for the entire law school? We wish! Students can obtain as many as 12 tickets with one student ID and each year selected games are available for block seating."

Status: Current student, full-time
Dates of Enrollment: 8/2005-Submit Date
Survey Submitted: May 2006

The UT College of Law provides a lively social life outside of the classroom, including many different ways to get involved in public service in Knoxville such as Habitat for Humanity, Tennessee Innocence Project and Saturday Bar for the UT Pro Bono Legal Group. The school has a charted chapter of Phi Alpha Delta legal fraternity and the school's law women chapter is active in community philanthropy and school service as well. In addition, the Student Bar Association has several social events every semester to provide students a chance for recreation and friendship. The College of Law is located in the midst of the UT Knoxville main campus and is readily accessible to all the events and opportunities that are afforded to the students on campus.

Status: Current student, full-time
Dates of Enrollment: 8/2004-Submit Date
Survey Submitted: May 2006

The law school has a strong social network but is also located relatively close to downtown with Old City, great bars and restaurants. School has active organizations, like Law Women, that put on parties and/or fund-raisers. Most/all students build friendships within the first week of orientation because of the school's emphasis on getting to know classmates. Strong network amongst the law students...both in law school and after. Law grads often return, sometimes to teach a single class, and are generally very supportive.

Status: Current student, full-time
Dates of Enrollment: 8/2005-Submit Date
Survey Submitted: May 2006

Social life is what you make it. The college provides a multitude of clubs for every type of interest that one may like (e.g., Black Law Student Association, Student Bar Association, Pro Bono, Human Rights, Women in the Law, Criminal Law Society, Sports and Entertainment Society). In the midst of all the law-related activities, the students all gather for a social outing every Thursday at one of the local restaurants. If time permits, then one may take advantage of getting to know other colleagues on an more intimate bases.

Status: Current student, full-time
Dates of Enrollment: 8/2005-Submit Date
Survey Submitted: May 2006

In the fall, the big law school event is the Halloween Costume Ball called "Chilla." The big event for spring is the formal Mardi Gras Ball put on by the Black Law Students Association. Football season is huge here, and law students tailgate every home game. Basketball is starting to get big here as well, so sports provides a much needed break from studying. Knoxville is small, but it is a college town, so there are an array of bars and clubs. There are also many different types of restaurants in the city for those who like to dine out a lot.

Status: Alumnus/a, full-time
Dates of Enrollment: 8/2000-5/2003
Survey Submitted: April 2005

There are few experiences that compare to a football game at the University of Tennessee. Game days in the fall are always "events." Rump Court, which is held every Thursday evening at a local bar—is a great way to get to know your classmates in a non-academic setting. A favorite among my classmates was Toddy's—I think we held more Rump Courts there than at all the other bars combined.

Status: Alumnus/a, full-time
Dates of Enrollment: 8/2000-5/2003
Survey Submitted: April 2005

No Greek system. But, there are lots of bars and restaurants near the school. The SBA organizes a couple of annual big events; students have parties almost monthly (and students are very good about including EVERYONE—putting up flyers saying that everyone is invited); and there are weekly "rump court" sessions where the SBA regulars go en masse to a local bar on Thursday nights.

> **The school says:** "UT has an extensive Greek system. Law students who were members of fraternities or sororities as undergraduates can become involved with their local chapter or alumni group."

Status: Alumnus/a, full-time
Dates of Enrollment: 8/1996-5/1999
Survey Submitted: April 2005

UT is known as a party school, and hardly two blocks west of the law school is where most of that takes place. The school is located on the lower end of what is known as "The Strip," where many students hang out in bars and clubs. OCI, or Old College Inn, is a hallmark of Knoxville; if you're a UT student, you have to make at least one foray into OCI. It's packed on football weekends. Another favorite is Charlie Pepper's, which is a restaurant that features an outdoor patio On Thursdays and Saturdays, they have disco on the deck, and the place gets packed to the gills.

Knoxville also has a great cultural scene. Starting in April, downtown features concerts as part of the "sundown in the city" program. This is an outdoor venue that features bands and singers like Robinella and the CC String Band, Steve Winwood, The Neville Brothers, Cross Canadian Ragweed, and the like (the web site is www.sundowninthecity.com). You can also catch some of the more mainstream acts at Thompson-Boling Arena on campus. The Tennessee Theatre can put up quite the marquee as well, such as Robert Earl Keen, Pat Greene, and Allison Kraus.

Labor Day weekend Knoxville features a fireworks show known as Boomsday. Boats line up along the river to watch the show from the water. People also come down to Calhoun's (a restaurant known for its barbecue) and watch from its docks, or Riverside Tavern. It's quite the gathering.

Status: Current student, full-time
Dates of Enrollment: 8/2002-Submit Date
Survey Submitted: March 2005

The law school is like a big family. There are always things to do. Within the school there are clubs for every kind of law, pro bono and other student activities. If we do not have a club you want, you can start it yourself. There are also bowling leagues, softball leagues, flag football and other sports that students can join in. Each week, the entire school is invited to a specific bar to mingle and de-stress for the week. Near campus there are many bars and dance clubs and the students tend to move from place to place since they are all so close together.

The dating scene is somewhat limited but we have had a few couples meet at school and either have married or are planning to marry soon. I have attended many of the Thursday night bar outings and found that it allows me to get to meet many students. I might not otherwise and also get to check out a new bar each week. I personally love a few of the places such as Toddy's Tavern, and 4620—a jazz and martini bar. One of my favorite restaurants withing walking distance is the Downtown Brewery and Grill. It has great food, live music and locally brewed beer and is in the middle of downtown nightlife. Another great place is McCleod's—if you like beer and karaoke.

 **The School Says**

The University of Tennessee College of Law has a productive, collegial, and engaged faculty and student body; low student faculty ratios; a modern technologically advanced facility; and an integration of substantive legal theory, practical law, and skills across its curriculum. It is an intellectually stimulating environment where people can learn to be excellent lawyers." This is a statement of the core strengths of the UT College of Law.

Most sound decisions in life are made after comparing the pros and cons of the available choices. Here are some factors that current Tennessee Law students cite and which candidates might want to consider as they weigh their options.

- Nationally recognized professors are focused on teaching. In addition to contributing to academic through scholarly works, they are primarily committed to ensuring their students' readiness—with skills, substance and ethics—to begin successfully practicing law after graduation.

- UT offers one of the lowest student-to-faculty ratios of any top-ranked law school. First-year sections are no larger than 55 students. Upper division classes averaged 22 students per class in the Spring Semester 2006, and special interest seminars were conducted with one faculty member and as few as five students.

- With fewer than 500 students, the College of Law could be smaller than a high school, but the services, programs, activities, and amenities of a comprehensive research university are right across the street.

- The living and learning climate at UT is supportive. Students remark about the exceedingly friendly, open, warm, and helpful atmosphere that is pervasive at the College of Law.

- Thanks to reasonable tuition and the low cost of living in Knoxville, students get a top rate education without oppressive financial burdens. The average indebtedness of UT Law graduates is below the current national average for public law schools.

- The nation's oldest continuously operating law school clinical program is at UT, along with a newer Business Clinic. These programs, along with the Concentrations in Advocacy and Dispute Resolution and the Concentration in Business Transactions, provide students with practical, applied lawyering skills in addition to exposure to a core of substantive and theoretical legal doctrine.

- Knoxville is a great place to live and study. The Great Smokey Mountains, the Ocoee River, and area lakes offer recreational opportunities in abundance. Knoxville is home to numerous cultural attractions that appeal to a variety of tastes. If a larger city beckons, Knoxville is an easy three-hour drive from Nashville and Atlanta—prime employment markets for UT law students and graduates. Knoxville blurs the line between small town and big city, and many UT law students find that characteristic appealing.

Read all of Vault's Law School Surveys at www.vault.com/lawschool — get complete surveys on top law schools, expert advice on applicaton essays, LSAT prep and more.

VAULT CAREER LIBRARY   573

Vanderbilt University Law School

Office of Admissions
131 21st Avenue South
Nashville, TN 37203
Admissions phone: (615) 322-6452
Admissions e-mail: admissions@law.vanderbilt.edu
Admissions URL: http://www.law.vanderbilt.edu/admiss/

 Admissions

Status: Current student, full-time
Dates of Enrollment: 8/2005-Submit Date
Survey Submitted: March 2006

Vanderbilt Law admissions has a fast turn-around for applicants and gives out merit-based aid quickly, as well. Students are well served by applying as early as possible. Because Vanderbilt is trying to move up in the USNWR rankings, high LSAT scores and/or high GPAs get a lot of personal attention and monetary aid. There is no interview requirement, although students are encouraged to come to one of two organized visitation days or simply visit campus at their convenience. Vanderbilt greatly values distinguishing personal characteristics. Admissions staff reads closely every personal statement on student application. The school places great importance on having students from all over the country and from varying types of undergraduate institutions in their entering classes. Class size is usually 200. The school will put a lot of students on the waitlist to ensure that an entering class is not too big. The average age of the class of 2008 was 23 years old.

Status: Current student, full-time
Dates of Enrollment: 8/2004-Submit Date
Survey Submitted: October 2005

From what I can recall, the admissions process was fairly standard: the same essay was required as with every law school. The standard law school form was acceptable. You do have to turn in a listing of all your prior traffic offenses, including speeding tickets, which was annoying, but that is about it.

> **The school says:** "Like most law schools, Vanderbilt inquires about the applicants' criminal and disciplinary records. However, we do not require a listing of all traffic offenses."

There is no interview requirement. Vanderbilt likes to see the typical well-rounded student. The average GPA is around 3.6, and the average LSAT around 165. There are certainly a number of students above and below both. Most students had serious and prolonged involvement in an activity in undergrad. Students come from almost every state and every major university. There are quite a few students from relatively small liberal arts colleges, also.

One of the nicest things about Vanderbilt's admissions process is that they get back to you within about a month. If you have not heard within that time, you are probably on the waiting list.

Status: Alumnus/a, full-time
Dates of Enrollment: 8/2002-5/2005
Survey Submitted: March 2006

Admissions group was very nice but had to call to keep updated. Though I applied late in May, I had good LSAT scores so was "recruited" even though it was after official deadline for application. Essay was typical. Selectivity was a mix—has a strong "diversity" commitment.

Status: Current student, full-time
Dates of Enrollment: 8/2002-Submit Date
Survey Submitted: April 2005

It is pretty much your customary law school application process. I think Vandy's median LSAT is around 164, but those who are "borderline" will definitely have

their entire application reviewed, so it is possible to overcome a lower LSAT with great grades and essays. The earlier you apply, the more scholarship money you're likely to get.

> **The school says:** "For the entering class in 2005, the median LSAT was 165."

Status: Current student, full-time
Dates of Enrollment: 8/2004-Submit Date
Survey Submitted: April 2005

The admissions process was very smooth. Vanderbilt does not do individual interviews, but students are encouraged to visit campus, sit-in on classes, meet faculty members and students, and tour the facilities. I felt very welcomed on my initial visit to campus. The admissions office was very friendly and helpful. I also met several students who came to be great future resources. I highly recommend visiting the law school and meeting the admissions staff. Although it doesn't reflect the same way as a formal interview would on the admissions process, it always helps if members of the faculty and staff have a face (and personality) to put with the application and essay. This year's class was very competitive and my best advice for admissions would be to apply early!

Status: Current student, full-time
Dates of Enrollment: 8/2002-Submit Date
Survey Submitted: April 2005

Let's face it, nobody likes the admissions process unless they get in. Once in, everything's rosy. Everyone's a doll.

The bottom line on admissions at Vanderbilt is that they are decent people forced to disappoint many other decent individuals. That's the nature of the game. The flip side is that hundreds of other folks receive the hoped-for "big envelope" and go merrily on their way. In either case, Vanderbilt's admissions staff is professional and first-class.

Status: Alumnus/a, full-time
Dates of Enrollment: 8/2001-5/2004
Survey Submitted: March 2005

Vanderbilt is extremely selective and tends to choose students based on the numbers and the reputation of their undergraduate institution. It has a strong commitment to diversity and is active in its recruitment of minority students. The school does not generally give interviews.

Status: Alumnus/a, full-time
Dates of Enrollment: 8/1999-5/2002
Survey Submitted: January 2004

The people in charge of admissions have changed focus in just the few years since I was admitted. Previously, the dean of admissions focused on numbers, but also emphasized unique personal attributes. Now, they are all about the numbers—about the only thing that is considered outside the numbers is race (which can be a plus or a minus, depending). The best bet for admission: have at least a little bit higher than the median reported numbers for GPA and LSAT.

> **The school says:** "The admission process has become more selective and competitive in recent years. However, many factors are considered beyond numbers and ethnicity/race. In the admission process, diversity is viewed broadly, and every applicant has the opportunity to include diverse and unique characteristics that they can bring to the VULS community."

Academics

Status: Current student, full-time
Dates of Enrollment: 8/2005-Submit Date
Survey Submitted: March 2006

1L professors are mostly very good classroom instructors—as well as accomplished scholars. Grading in large classes (including all 1L classes) is on a strict curve: 10 percent receive A+/A; 15 percent receive A-; 25 percent receive B+; 30 percent receive B; 20 percent receive B-/below. The entering classes are divided into two 100-person sections. The workload, while challenging, is not impossible. Most students feel hightened stress only within one week of Legal Writing assignments being due or within a few weeks of finals.

Status: Current student, full-time
Dates of Enrollment: 8/2004-Submit Date
Survey Submitted: October 2005

Vanderbilt is a wonderful place to attend law school. The school is really becoming national in its student base, with a lot of draw from out west. With the introduction of Dean Rubin from UPenn, there is a renewed draw from the Northeast. As always, there is also a strong Southeastern base. Most students are straight out of college, but a significant portion spent one or two years working before coming to law school. A significant minority of students are also over 35.

The students here are extremely hard-working, smart and talented. Many turned down Top 10 schools to come to Vanderbilt. While the student population is extremely gifted, it is also not overly arrogant. Of course you have a few gunners in each class, but they are few and far between. There is a general good-naturedness to the students here, and it is easy to get notes from fellow students when you miss class. Students are also willing to join study groups, and generally help one another out. Upper class students are always willing to hand down their old class outlines, and the Vanderbilt Bar Association maintains an outline bank online.

The quality of teaching here is excellent. Most of the professors here are actually good teachers, which can be unfortunately rare in the world of academia. Of course you do have a few bad apples, but on the whole, the professors here are very good. They are all extremely approachable outside of class. Those that are the most demanding in class are often times the gentlest and most helpful individuals outside of the classroom. The professors here seem very interested in your education and career, and are open to answer questions, help with journal notes, and offer career advice.

One of the downsides is that there are one or two really popular classes each semester that overbook. The school does one of two things in this situation: it either anticipates the overbooking and offers two sections of the same class, or it resorts to the lottery system. The lottery basically guarantees third-year students spots in these classes, and then randomly selects second years who have signed up for the class for enrollment. This semester, the overbooked classes were Evidence, Corporations, Constitutional Law II and Administrative Law. The school offered two sections for Con Law II and Corporations that accommodated everyone, and then held lotteries for Evidence and Administrative Law. There is not a whole lot of variety in the classes offered from semester to semester, but you do have lots of options in the classes that are regularly offered.

The workload is entirely manageable. Most people have time to pursue quite a few extracurriculars, spend times with friends or family, and socialize on the weekends. In the first semester of the first year, you only take four classes (about 15 hours), which helps you adjust to the whole law school thing. Second semester, you pick up an additional class and take 16 hours of classes. After that, you need to take about 15 hours each semester to stay on track for graduation. 88 credit hours are required for graduation.

For every four-hour class, you probably have about 10 hours of reading a week. For every three-hour class, six to eight. For every two hour-class, about four to six hours. First-year legal writing has ebbs and flows. There will be weeks when you have no work, and then two weeks before an assignment is due, you will probably work about 20 hours. Exams are almost always the standard three-

hour essay exams. There is no reading period, which is unfortunate, but as long as you start studying about two weeks before exams start, you will be fine.

There are lots of opportunities to get involved with extracurriculars. Vanderbilt Ambassadors host prospective students and help with recruiting efforts. The Legal Aid Society works with the community and, along with the clinic programs, offers pro bono legal services for indigent persons. In the first year, the school holds a mock trial tournament. At the end of that year, there is a write-on competition for journals. Finally, in the fall of the second year, there is a moot court tournament. In addition, there are numerous opportunities to get involved in student government, and various special interest and political organizations.

Status: Alumnus/a, full-time
Dates of Enrollment: 8/2002-5/2005
Survey Submitted: March 2006

Very good professors for the most part; very strong Constitutional Law professors. Popular classes are usually available to get at least once you are a 3L (except maybe a small/popular class). Grading is all blind (except for seminars) and seems pretty consistent with the established curve except for very small classes. Workload varies per professor—first-year classes are generally all heavy.

Status: Current student, full-time
Dates of Enrollment: 8/2003-Submit Date
Survey Submitted: April 2005

The professors are amazingly accessible inside and outside of the classroom. It's not uncommon to see professor participate in activities outside the classroom in order to support student organizations. The registrar seems to distribute the more popular professors amongst the first-year sections. I have never heard anyone complain about any of the 1L property professors. I would like to see more public interest. I assume the workload is similar to any other Top 20 law school. However, it's bearable at Vandy because my fellow students and law professors do not foster a cutthroat environment.

Status: Current student, full-time
Dates of Enrollment: 8/2002-Submit Date
Survey Submitted: April 2005

The first year is, like most schools, a set program and all 1Ls take the same classes. The workload first year is rough, but bearable. After that, it depends a lot on which classes you take, whether you are on a journal. 3Ls get priority in the selection process, and there is a lottery system for popular classes. I have gotten into every class I've applied for, but there are some waiting lists for popular seminars. The school is good about opening up spots or re-offering popular classes upon the requests of students. B+ is the average grade. Professors run the gamut. Some are just incredible and some are clearly more research-oriented and could use a teaching lesson.

Status: Current student, full-time
Dates of Enrollment: 8/2004-Submit Date
Survey Submitted: April 2005

I have found the quality of classes to be outstanding. All first-year students take the same required courses. I felt like the workload was very appropriate for the first semester and picked up a bit second semester after everyone had a chance to get their feet wet. The grading scale seemed very fair. Honestly, I haven't had a single professor that I have disliked so far. I think most students would agree that the legal writing courses have a few kinks to be worked out and they require a tremendous amount of work for the few credits that you receive, but I think this is an issue common to most law schools. Overall, I have been thoroughly satisfied with the academic program.

Status: Current student, full-time
Dates of Enrollment: 1/2003-Submit Date
Survey Submitted: April 2005

Academically, Vanderbilt is very difficult. To be honest, the school kicked my ass. I have not had any difficulty getting into even popular classes. The professors are great for the most part, but given the research focus of the school, some of them are well-published old folks with no social skills.

Read all of Vault's Law School Surveys at www.vault.com/lawschool — get complete surveys on top law schools, expert advice on applicaton essays, LSAT prep and more.

VAULT CAREER LIBRARY 575

Status: Alumnus/a, full-time
Dates of Enrollment: 8/2000-5/2003
Survey Submitted: April 2004

The faculty is excellent. Students get to learn from and interact with professors who are leaders in their field. The classes are small, and the professors are very accessible and genuinely care about their students. The staff is also excellent, and the school is very well run. The school offers a good variety of courses; however, it favors business and corporate law. It prepares you well for practice in large law firms. It is easy to get the classes you want. Grading is usually based on a final, and the school allows much flexibility in setting times for finals.

Status: Alumnus/a, full-time
Dates of Enrollment: 8/1999-5/2002
Survey Submitted: January 2004

Dean Syverud has focused the hiring on more "name" types, who focus more on publishing but might not be classroom all-stars. Still, there are a lot of good professors overall—just pray you don't get stuck with a visiting professor as a 1L—that amounts to the school experimenting with your future. Anyway, the workload is OK—higher if you're the anal, Law Review type. Still, it is not unmanageable or all-consuming (like a big firm workload...just wait...heh).

> The school says: "Visiting professors at VULS are nationally known scholars. Numerous visiting professors have won teaching awards. For example, Visiting Professor Tracey George received the outstanding teaching award voted on by the first-year class in 2004. Prof. George has now joined the VULS Faculty full time."

 Employment Prospects

Status: Current student, full-time
Dates of Enrollment: 8/2005-Submit Date
Survey Submitted: March 2006

Vanderbilt really is a "national law school." Over 550 employers come to campus for OCI for only 200 students. The only major markets that don't send their absolute top firms are Boston, New York and the Northwest (although Vandy is targeting more West Coast students to change this trend). Every major law firm from D.C. and Chicago comes to campus. Vandy even has a smaller version of OCI for 1Ls, hosting employers from markets including Atlanta, Houston, Dallas and Charlotte. Vandy also brings in countless speakers from firms regarding interview tactics, how to choose the right firm, how to build a resume. Most graduates go to law firms, with only 50 percent remaining in the Southeast United States. Roughly 1/4 graduates go to the Northeast. Vanderbilt alumni—on the whole—are very helpful if students contact them. Many come back to Nashville to host cocktail receptions for students each year. Students in the top third can go to virtually any legal market they want upon graduation. Students in the top 10 percent can get virtually any job they want, outside of the top four or five firms in New York.

Status: Current student, full-time
Dates of Enrollment: 8/2004-Submit Date
Survey Submitted: October 2005

The two largest markets represented at on-campus interviewing are D.C. and Atlanta. New York City and Chicago also have a good showing. Each year, more and more employers from NYC are showing up at Vandy. Particularly as the economy is improving, law firms are showing a greater and greater interest in Vanderbilt. I am not sure exactly how many firms came on campus this year, but there were probably around 300. All of the "top" law firms interview at Vanderbilt. Quite a number of small- and mid-sized firms come also, which offers students a nice variety. In D.C., Nashville and Atlanta, the name "Vanderbilt" goes a long way.

The career services office is to die for. Career services is there for you, no matter where you stand in the class. Their doors are always open, and they work very hard to make sure everyone has a job that they are happy with. If things don't work out, they are there to help you with Plan B. They are also very good about giving you a realistic view of your options.

> The school says: "During the fall semester of 2005, employers representing 550 law offices in 39 states, D.C., and London, Beijing, Shanghai and Tokyo came to Vanderbilt Law to recruit students. 51 represented D.C. employers, 39 represented California employers, and 36 represented New York employers."

Status: Alumnus/a, full-time
Dates of Enrollment: 8/2002-5/2005
Survey Submitted: March 2006

Based heavily on grades, Law Review, then other journals or diversity—after the middle of the class, it's hard to tell, many I knew did not have jobs until fall (but they were near bottom half). Those near top—no problem to go anywhere (as long as socially adept).

> The school says: "For the classes graduating in 2004 through 2006, 89 to 92 percent of the class had obtained employment prior to graduation. Typically, 99 percent of graduates are employed nine months after graduation."

Status: Current student, full-time
Dates of Enrollment: 8/2003-Submit Date
Survey Submitted: April 2005

Vandy alumni are very willing to put an extra foot forward to help current Vandy students. I am happy with my experience during OCI. However, Vandy's reputation hasn't spread all the way to the West Coast as much as I would like. Vandy students have become more geographically diverse and I think that's also reflected in where students are getting job offers.

Status: Current student, full-time
Dates of Enrollment: 8/2002-Submit Date
Survey Submitted: April 2005

Recruiting as VULS is pretty decent. Everyone doesn't get jobs, but most everyone does. A student's success during recruiting season is directly correlated to their GPA. Pretty much everyone ends up OK except for the few unfortunate souls at the bottom of the class. Most students gets jobs at private, Top 200 law firms, though. Oddly enough, most VULS students seem perfectly content living in Atlanta or somewhere. I would imagine that no Top 20 law school is as married to the South as Vanderbilt. I don't know if that's a good or bad thing. But there is also a good hodge podge of other legal work that some students venture into within the public sector, as well.

> The school says: "Vanderbilt Law alumni can be found in 18 countries, 49 states, the District of Columbia, Puerto Rico and the U.S. Virgin Islands."

Status: Alumnus/a, full-time
Dates of Enrollment: 8/1999-5/2002
Survey Submitted: March 2005

Career services does a good job in markets that are traditionally strong for Vandy (D.C., Atlanta, Texas, Tennessee, Alabama, New York). If you want to go somewhere like Chicago, California or Boston, you'll likely have to do more of your own legwork irrespective of how you're doing academically, but career services does an excellent job with them as well. If you want public service, government, or smaller markets far geographically removed, you will be doing most of the work yourself.

Status: Alumnus/a, full-time
Dates of Enrollment: 8/1993-5/1996
Survey Submitted: April 2004

I felt the Vanderbilt Law School prestige, while not nationally and immediately recognized, was very helpful in searching for a job. Vanderbilt has a career placement office that exceeds the school's actual ranking. The career placement office is helpful, patient and very friendly. I believe that the focus of such a group tends to be to find for the students large national-firm positions, primarily in the Southeast, Southwest, Northeast and mid-Atlantic and West Coast regions, in that order. As a result, finding careers in the judiciary, public interest or in-house or non-legal positions tends to be less of their focus.

> The school says: "Since 1999, Vanderbilt has placed graduates in all but one of the U.S. Courts of Appeals and three graduates

have clerked for the Supreme Court of the United States. Typically, 10 to 20 percent of the graduating class takes clerkships."

Quality of Life

Status: Current student, full-time
Dates of Enrollment: 8/2005-Submit Date
Survey Submitted: March 2006

Quality of life at Vanderbilt Law is above average. Nashville has the advantages of being a city—with plenty to do—but not too large and stressful. The campus is within 15 blocks of the heart of downtown. Most students live within a five- to eight-minute drive to the law school, and there is plenty of parking available right across the street. The campus is beautiful, although law students don't spend a great deal of time in areas not directly surrounding the Law School. The good news is that because each class contains students from all over the country, there is not a great deal of competition for the same few jobs. This helps the law school culture to be somewhat laid-back and certainly not cutthroat.

Status: Current student, full-time
Dates of Enrollment: 8/2004-Submit Date
Survey Submitted: October 2005

Housing is very affordable. For a single bedroom, top of the line apartment, you only pay about $1,000 a month rent. You can find decent single bedroom apartments for as low as $500 per month rent. There are lots of suburbs around the city to choose from, though most students live in town. The commute is not bad. If you live in the 'burbs, you usually spend about 20 or 30 minutes commuting. If you live in the city, you usually only have about a five to 10 minute commute. There are several popular apartment complexes within walking distance from the law school: one is even right across the street!

The law school is confined to a single building. It was built recently, and has a very new and open feel, with lots of sitting and study areas. There is a nice courtyard in the middle of the building dubbed "Blackacre," with tables and chairs. The library has two levels, and then a nice "loft" area for studying, with long tables. There is a cafe in the Law School, and another cafe in the business school right next door. The Law School is on the edge of the undergraduate campus, but is a two-minute walk from the student center and main library. A very pretty campus, with lots of grassy areas and magnolia trees.

Status: Current student, full-time
Dates of Enrollment: 9/2001-Submit Date
Survey Submitted: June 2004

Most people live off campus (I would not recommend living in the graduate school dorms if these are even still available). It's better to live close to the school, because Nashville can actually have really bad traffic (growing town that wasn't expecting it). It is slightly cheaper to live farther away from the campus. The law school is on the corner of the campus, next to the business school, and was renovated my first year. There are wireless connections available in most parts of the school (except for most of the classrooms). Everyone gets a locker, although you will be stuck in the basement for the first two years. People on journals, research assistants and moot court members can get assigned carrels in the library, but there are always open carrels for those who don't get an assigned one. I never really took advantage of the undergraduate campus, but it was very pretty, and the gym was pretty good (although all the way across campus from the law school).

> **The school says:** "Carrels are reserved on an individual, first-come, first serve basis. In order to make sure any law student can use most of our carrels, we reserve a select number of study carrels that are assigned to second- and third-year students with a demonstrated need to maintain a workspace and to shelve non-circulating library materials."

Status: Current student, full-time
Dates of Enrollment: 8/2001-Submit Date
Survey Submitted: June 2004

The law school building is the best part of coming to Vanderbilt, as it has been completely remodeled and is brand new. The classrooms are large with plenty of room and outlets for laptops. They wasted a lot of money putting Internet ports everywhere that they now cannot afford to activate, but wireless connections can be found outside the classrooms. People can pay a bit more to live closer to the campus, or less to live farther out and drive to the campus. The area around the campus is fine—people who complain about homeless people near the law school obviously haven't lived in cities before (there are only about two to three of them and all they do is ask for money). I have never had a problem with crime or safety concerns.

> **The school says:** "In order to not interfere with classroom dynamics and to optimize learning for all students, the VULS Faculty have requested that Internet access not be made available in classrooms. However, wireless access is available in the Law Library, other parts of the law school, and across the street at some local restaurants."

Status: Current student, full-time
Dates of Enrollment: 8/2002-Submit Date
Survey Submitted: April 2005

Nashville couldn't be a better place to live. Cost of living is low, the area around downtown (where Vandy is) is fun but not dangerous. There is always a ton of stuff going on in town—whether it is live music, theater, museums, or just hanging out at a cool bar. The area around campus is great for jogging, and people in the area are super friendly. My only complaint is that the school needs to get more outlets in the library and more comfy sofas in the the lobby and sitting areas. The law school cafe is really good with lots of different sandwiches, soups. (Although some complain it is a bit pricey.) Overall, it's the best experience I could imagine as far as quality of life goes.

Status: Current student, full-time
Dates of Enrollment: 8/2002-Submit Date
Survey Submitted: April 2005

I've had more fun during law school than I did in college, and believe me, I enjoyed the hell out of college. Vanderbilt is blessed with a remarkable student body. People here are able to grasp (post-1L) that elusive equilibrium of work and play. We know when to study and when to party. Luckily, opportunities for the latter are plentiful. Nashville is, in many ways, the ideal city in which to do law school. It's fun and lively, with an infinite array of musical outlets, yet also relatively inexpensive and quiet. It's no sleepy Southern town, of that you can be rest assured. At the same time, the citizens maintain a certain genteel politeness, whereby any happenstance stranger is afforded the benefit of the doubt. Local coffee shops are plentiful, as are cool bars of nearly every variety. Typically, we law kids haunt the same areas as other 20-somethings, though experimental jaunts to the non-preppy side of town are not infrequent.

Status: Current student, full-time
Dates of Enrollment: 8/2002-Submit Date
Survey Submitted: April 2005

The law school facilities are excellent. Almost everything is newly remodeled. Classrooms are beautiful. There is a small cafe in the school for easy dining and within a short walking distance there are a variety of food options and a pharmacy. The Vanderbilt campus itself is beautiful with lots of greenery. The campus feels very safe and there are very few instances of crime. In the law school itself, I never feel uncomfortable leaving my belongings at a table or desk for a few minutes. Students are generally very respectful of each other in that way.

Social Life

Status: Current student, full-time
Dates of Enrollment: 8/2005-Submit Date
Survey Submitted: March 2006

Nashville has a surprising number of great restaurants, with new ones popping up throughout the year. The law school (or a firm or organization) hosts free beer/wine and food every other Friday afternoon for students to relax and socialize in the school itself. Students go out to Bar Review every Thursday night, although attendance wanes as finals encroach. Nashville has a bar for

Read all of Vault's Law School Surveys at www.vault.com/lawschool — get complete surveys on top law schools, expert advice on applicaton essays, LSAT prep and more.

VAULT CAREER LIBRARY   577

everyone—from honky tonks to sports bars to trendy New York style bars. Student favorites include Cabana, The Stage, Tin Roof and Dan McGuinness.

Status: Current student, full-time
Dates of Enrollment: 8/2004-Submit Date
Survey Submitted: October 2005

Excellent social life: the students here are definitely capable of cutting loose and having a good time. As with most law schools, Thursday night Bar Reviews are a staple. On most Fridays, the law school also has "Blackacres," which are sponsored by various student organizations or law firms. These Blackacres have kegs, wine and food from about 4 to 6 p.m. on Friday afternoons. Every fall, we have a Halloween party, and every winter, a Barrister's Ball formal. In the spring, we also have a public interest auction, at which there is ample drinking and opportunity to bid on fun items, including dinner with the dean, lunch with 6th Circuit justices, and basketball with professors (to name a few). Students frequently go out to lunch and dinner during the week, and genuinely enjoy hanging out with each other. Definitely a fun, sociable place to be!

Status: Alumnus/a, full-time
Dates of Enrollment: 8/2002-5/2005
Survey Submitted: March 2006

Bar Reviews are hosted at school almost weekly. Lots of nightlife nearby as located near downtown and near village area. Smaller class size, so if you date other law students, everyone else knows (sort of gossipy—but that's mostly the younger students straight out of undergrad).

Status: Current student, full-time
Dates of Enrollment: 8/2003-Submit Date
Survey Submitted: April 2005

Vandy can sometimes seem like a fraternity party. However, that's not to say that those who would rather not play beer pong every weekend can't find alternative means for fun. Nashville is "Music City, U.S.A.," so there are a lot of fun things going on throughout the year. And it's not called "Music City, U.S.A." for nothing—you can see national acts in intimate settings—I saw Wilco perform for $10! So, there's definitely more than just country music going on in Nashville. East Nashville is the new up and coming place to be. In general, more diversity would be better. Everyone seems to be blonde. This is the most conservative school I've been too. If I see another "popped" collar on a pastel Lacoste shirt, I may vomit.

Status: Current student, full-time
Dates of Enrollment: 8/2004-Submit Date
Survey Submitted: February 2005

While people do date here, and amazingly maintain functional relationships inside a law school setting, the more common thing is just to hook-up at a Bar Review. But remember—if you don't want anyone to know whom you're dating or sleeping with, then I strongly suggest not dating or sleeping with anyone inside the law school. The student body is generally friendly, and you'll often see people socializing in the lobbies and near the lockers—yes lockers, we're in middle school again. There aren't too many of those weird people who hide books, but there have been incidences of stolen notes this year. Vanderbilt operates on an honor code, which most people are good about sticking to. However, don't let anyone convince you that a friendly student body means that they aren't competitive. Students care very much how they do on finals, and most have been at the tops of their undergraduate universities. That being said, you'll never have trouble finding a study group, finding people to send you notes if you miss a class, or finding people to help explain a concept to you. Competitive—yes. Cutthroat—not so much

Status: Current student, law school
Dates of Enrollment: 9/2001-Submit Date
Survey Submitted: June 2004

There are several bars in the proximity of the school—South Street is a favorite and only one block away. Plenty of restaurants as well. The school hosts events and there are plenty of clubs, but in comparison to other law schools, students don't appear to be as active in the school or as intellectually engaged. With the exception of the very big organizations, like Business Law Society and VBA, getting people to participate in clubs is like pulling teeth. People date within the law school, although it is pretty small for that, but more people date other graduate school students (dating business students is popular). Many people come with long-distance significant others and there are a significant number of married students. You can have a really active social life here if you want.

> **The school says:** "VULS has over 40 active student organizations, and in some years, the level of participation may vary depending on the leadership and membership of the organization."

Status: Current student, full-time
Dates of Enrollment: 8/2001-Submit Date
Survey Submitted: June 2004

Social life here is what you make of it. There are law school-sponsored events, such as Blackacres on Friday afternoons, and places to go out. The law school is somewhat confined for dating—rumors spread quickly—but people do date within the school. If you've been in a lot of areas of the country, you will recognize that this is not as Southern a town as Memphis or Knoxville, but I have noticed that people from outside the South do have a cultural shock adjustment when they come down here. The atmosphere is different from schools in NYC and D.C.—there is not as much an intellectual or urban atmosphere here, and there are definitely elements that are fraternity/sorority in nature.

Baylor Law School

Baylor University School of Law
Admissions Office
Sheila and Walter Umphrey Law Center
1114 South University Parks Drive
One Bear Place #97288
Waco, TX 76798
Admissions URL:
http://law.baylor.edu/ProspectiveStudents/PS_Admissions.html

 Admissions

Status: Alumnus/a, full-time
Dates of Enrollment: 8/1998-4/2001
Survey Submitted: March 2006

Application process includes essay. No interview at the time that I applied. Very selective school, in that enrollment is limited to around 400 or so students. Good undergraduate record and LSAT score prerequisites for admission.

Status: Alumnus/a, full-time
Dates of Enrollment: 8/1995-5/1998
Survey Submitted: March 2006

Admissions is weighted fairly evenly between GPA/undergrad and LSAT, as I recall. I had a very average LSAT (I think it was 155) and a 3.99 college GPA, so they evened out. I graduated third in my class in law school, so, anecdotally, I'd say LSAT is not a great predictor of success.

Status: Current student, full-time
Dates of Enrollment: 5/2004-Submit Date
Survey Submitted: March 2006

Don't sweat if you did not get in in the fall and have competitive scores: an LSAT of high 150s and GPA 3.5+ you'll get in the summer or spring

Status: Alumnus/a, full-time
Dates of Enrollment: 9/2003-4/2004
Survey Submitted: September 2004

The admissions process was very positive. I applied online and was e-mailed immediately to confirm reception of my application. The admissions director was very helpful and kept me informed. There is an online page that lets you know the status of your application which is updated often. Baylor is very concerned with LSAT score and GPA, as are all law schools, but you can get a scholarship if your index is at least a 196. This is your GPA multiplied by ten and then added to your LSAT score. They are very selective for the fall class and not as much for the spring and summer starters. They really do read your personal statements, so make sure you are letting them know who you are when you write it.

Status: Alumnus/a, full-time
Dates of Enrollment: 2/1998-6/2000
Survey Submitted: April 2005

The admissions process is relatively exhaustive, but Baylor is prompt in providing information and responses to applicant inquiries. Although the average LSAT scores and undergraduate GPA requirements have risen some in the last few years at Baylor, I do believe that Baylor looks for well-rounded individuals to fill its law school. A positive and forward-looking essay is useful—be descriptive and include your goals, personally as well as professionally; if at all possible, a separate visit with Dean Tobin, will work a long way in the consideration of an application and admittance. Baylor has become more selective over the past five years, considering the new facilities and the increased number of applicants.

Status: Alumnus/a, full-time
Dates of Enrollment: 8/1999-5/2002
Survey Submitted: April 2005

Baylor is looking at the total person—not just academics, although that is important. Baylor is not a graduate school of law—it is a professional school, training people to be practicing lawyers.

Status: Current student, full-time
Dates of Enrollment: 8/2003-Submit Date
Survey Submitted: January 2005

It requires a high LSAT and GPA, which has been increasing yearly. There is a personal statement, but there was no interview.

Status: Current student, full-time
Dates of Enrollment: 1/2002-Submit Date
Survey Submitted: April 2004

Baylor Law is very selective. Their goal is to keep the classroom size down in order to provide more one-on-one contact between professors and students. In order to get in, one must have solid LSAT scores, a solid GPA and a well-rounded, non-scholastic background.

Status: Current student, full-time
Dates of Enrollment: 8/2001-Submit Date
Survey Submitted: March 2004

Baylor is a very "oral advocacy" driven school. As a result, resumes that reflect success in debate—especially in college—will receive extra attention. College debaters can even receive generous scholarships in addition to an increased likelihood of admission.

Of course, having as high a GPA and LSAT score as possible are always beneficial. In the last two to three years, the LSAT and GPA averages have been going up for Baylor's entering classes. Even so, a 3.5 GPA and a mid-150s LSAT score should be enough to get you in. If you are concerned about your numbers, consider applying for one of Baylor's more unusual entering classes. Baylor is on a quarter system and has entering classes in the summer [early to mid-May], fall (August) and spring (February) quarters. The summer and spring entering classes have slightly lower numbers and make it more likely that applicants can gain admission. In addition, entering students who begin in summer or spring will have smaller classes for their first quarter or two. These entering students will have less competition from the more credentialed students for the highest grades in their classes.

Interviews are rare and are usually scheduled for the purpose of doling out scholarships. Essays are important and most of them seem to come in two categories—hard luck/life experience stories and significant accomplishment stories.

Status: Alumnus/a, full-time
Dates of Enrollment: 2/2000-5/2003
Survey Submitted: January 2004

The application process is pretty typical. They require LSAT scores. My score was 153, this is about the median score needed to be accepted. I also needed to fill out the application, which can now be done online. I did not interview, but I have heard that it can be very helpful to go for a tour and let them match a name to a face. It has become very competitive to get into Baylor Law, but there seem to be a few things that help. It helps to have some experience beyond college. I had gone to grad school. Many of my classmates had previous careers—in accounting, marketing and police work. Make sure your essay to include how this can help you succeed at Baylor. Baylor is a very practical school. It prepares you to be a lawyer, not just think like one. So, practical experience is good to show you can succeed at Baylor. Also, you can apply to start in May or February, because there is a quarter system. It is a bit easier to get accepted to start in February because there is less competition.

Read all of Vault's Law School Surveys at www.vault.com/lawschool — get complete surveys on top law schools, expert advice on applicaton essays, LSAT prep and more.

VAULT CAREER LIBRARY 579

Regarding admissions, **Baylor Law** states: "While an applicant's LSAT score and undergraduate GPA remain important parts of the admissions process, we are committed to a complete review of all the applications we receive. Your application will be reviewed by members of the admissions committee, who are faculty members of Baylor law school. Baylor has no set cut-off as to the LSAT score or undergraduate GPA; each file is individually reviewed in its entirety. The medians of our last three entering classes were 158, 157 and 161. Committee members consider carefully all facets of your application, including socioeconomic disadvantage, bilingual language skills, work experience, community involvement, leadership roles, and communications skills. Our goal is to enroll a student body of competent individuals coming to Baylor with varied perspectives and life experiences."

 # Academics

Status: Alumnus/a, full-time
Dates of Enrollment: 8/1998-4/2001
Survey Submitted: March 2006

Baylor Law School has a comprehensive program that prepares its students for the practice of law. The curriculum is challenging. Professors challenge the students and assist in providing a practical education.

Status: Alumnus/a, full-time
Dates of Enrollment: 8/1995-5/1998
Survey Submitted: March 2006

Baylor is a very unique law school because of its third-year Practice Court ("PC") program. (Think boot camp). At Baylor, the third year is twice as rigorous as first year, and first year is just as difficult as any other law school. Only go to Baylor if you want to become a litigator. You will graduate about two years ahead of your peers when it comes to Texas litigation practice, and employers know that. The professors are dedicated and smart, and you get a lot of attention. The focus at Baylor is less philosophical and more practical.

The quarter system also makes the entire three-year program more demanding than other law schools. You will complete your exams on a Friday and have 10 hours worth of reading for your new classes the following Monday—no Christmas break in between. Grading is tough—a handful of people usually fail PC and don't graduate with the rest of the class because they have to retake it. Baylor won't graduate you unless you're ready to become a lawyer. This all might sound daunting but I LOVED IT!!!! I would do it all again in a heartbeat and, if your interested in a Texas litigation practice, apply.

Status: Alumnus/a, full-time
Dates of Enrollment: 9/2003-4/2004
Survey Submitted: September 2004

Baylor is known as the boot camp of law schools—this name was given them by USNWR—and it is well-deserved. The amount of homework my first year was astounding. I studied a minimum of six hours a day and even more on the weekends. The classes were well-taught and very thorough. The professors are very committed to making sure they are graduating competent lawyers. It is very easy to get classes, as the student body is small. The grading curve is extremely harsh—they even give you a letter to send to employers explaining the curve. There is no A plus; there is no B plus. An A minus is a 3.5. In my Contracts class, out of 127 students, four A's and two A-'s were awarded. Terribly harsh. People are flunked in every class with quite a few getting D's. The usual "curve" was the B minus. The professors are generally very good. The Torts professor is excellent, as well as the Legal Research and Analysis professor. The Contracts professor has been there a long time and tends to be overly harsh. The Crim Law professor is very long-winded and does not respect the students' time (keeping us over sometimes 20 minutes when he knows there is no class after ours). The Civ Pro professor is very enthusiastic and intelligent. The Property professor is first-class.

Status: Alumnus/a, full-time
Dates of Enrollment: 2/1998-6/2000
Survey Submitted: April 2005

Baylor law school is different than all other schools in the country, in that the last year of law school is more rigorous than the previous two. Baylor requires its students to take PC I and PC II in their last year, and each are offered only once a quarter to one class of students in their last year—with Evidence and Professional Responsibility required to be completed at the same time. On average, 5 to 10 percent of the Practice Court class will NOT pass PC I or II, and will have to retake the course to graduate law school—regardless of your passing or failing the bar exam. People have flunked PC and had to decline job offers to retake the class. You run the full gamut of a trial in PC I and II, from filing the complaint to jury instruction. It is extremely rigorous. Most Baylor grads take the bar exam concurrently with either PC or their last quarter classes. Most complete their last set of finals and the bar exam within a week or two of each other.

Status: Current student, full-time
Dates of Enrollment: 8/2003-Submit Date
Survey Submitted: January 2005

The professors are amazing at Baylor. They actually care about your becoming a great lawyer, not about being a good law student. They really stress the practical side of the profession and the practice court program is nationally-ranked and well-known. It is the toughest and most competitive school in the nation, so do not apply if you are not ready for an extreme challenge.

Status: Current student, full-time
Dates of Enrollment: 8/2001-Submit Date
Survey Submitted: March 2004

Make no mistake about it—Baylor is hard.

Once you are past the first year, the difficulty gap between Baylor and other law schools really opens up. Baylor maintains and even increases the intensity in your second and third years. Baylor continues to do things that other schools only did during the first year. For example, Baylor students still must stand when called upon and analyze cases even in the second and third years. Baylor also has a large number of required courses in the last two years. The most significant of these classes comes in the third year. All students are required to go through the "Practice Court" program where students are taught a two quarter long intensive course of study in Evidence, State Civil Procedure and Trial Advocacy. Students routinely fail these courses even in the third year of law school. The classes are grueling—many days will last from 8 a.m. to 8 p.m.

Now for the benefits: all of this work really does pay off. Baylor's bar passage rate is always 95 percent plus. Even the top-tier University of Texas at Austin with its very smart students does not come close. Baylor has led the state in bar passage rate for about the last 10 years. In addition, Baylor performs extremely well in moot court and mock trial competitions. We routinely win. Baylor also turns you—without question—into a capable trial lawyer. You are more ready to try lawsuits upon graduation than you will be at ANY OTHER LAW SCHOOL. Once you have survived the Practice Court program, you will not be afraid of courtrooms, judges or juries.

Other academic benefits of Baylor stem from the fact that Baylor is small. There are about 400 total students and a couple dozen regular faculty members. I have always found that professors have time for me to ask questions and clarify the material. In addition, I have been able to get almost all of the classes I wanted.

The quality of the classes is high. The professors are all geared toward practical knowledge rather than theory. The classes are full of Black Letter Law and application thereof. If you want to become a politician, go somewhere else. In addition, if you want to be something other than an oral advocate—trial lawyer or appellate advocate—then you should strongly consider going to school somewhere else. Those who are uncomfortable with public speaking or who are sure they NEVER EVER want to step in a court room will enjoy Baylor less than those who are sure they want to be trial lawyers. However, if you want a program that will cure you of your shyness or force you to become a good speaker, Baylor is perfect.

Status: Alumnus/a, full-time
Dates of Enrollment: 2/2000-5/2003
Survey Submitted: January 2004

The professors at Baylor practice law, they don't just write about it as is the case at other schools. This means that you get the benefit of someone who is out doing what you want to do. It makes classes more relevant, because you get to hear stories about what is going on now. It also means the professors push you harder. They want to make sure you can do what they do by the time you graduate. This will make you a better lawyer, but often this is not appreciated by people you interview with because Baylor is still ranked as a second-tier school. If you want to practice litigation—go to Baylor. If you want to do transactional work, Baylor's emphasis on oral presentations (moot court and practice court are both required, time consuming and tough) can be a bit overwhelming.

I learned from all of my classes. Even the "easy" ones were insightful and worth the time and money. I never had a problem getting into a class. There is always room. Part of this is because Baylor has so many required classes. It has a reputation of "teaching to the bar." Sometimes I wished for more flexibility because I did not have room in my schedule to take some of the classes I wanted. But I, and 95 percent of my classmates, passed the bar the first time. In addition, the classes that are required are bar classes, but the information is tested on the bar because it is important and useful to know in practice. So, the classes are all worth it.

The professors are all tough, the workload (especially your first and third years) is heavy. I had to give up everything else. Do not plan on working anytime except your second year when you have the most flexibility in your schedule. The first year curriculum is the basic Contracts, Procedure, Criminal Law, but there is always homework, and always something you can be doing, even if you are done with what has to get done. The third year is Practice Court. This class takes up 24 hours a day. It makes things tough at a time when you would rather be relaxing, looking for a job, studying for the bar. But it is also a class worth its weight in gold. The best class to prepare you to be a lawyer anywhere in the country.

Status: Alumnus/a, full-time
Dates of Enrollment: 2/2000-5/2003
Survey Submitted: October 2003

The school is on a quarter system. The classes are at an accelerated pace. Taking an exam every 10 weeks. After you attend three quarters you can take any quarter off. The focus of classes and exams is application of the law and very little theory. The grading system is very tough. The average student's GPA is a 2.7. Professors will fail you. Showing up to class does not guarantee you will pass the class. There are only 400 students, so getting into the classes of your choice is not a problem. Professors are very accessible and have an open-door policy. Focus is on Texas law, and most classes are taught with the Texas code for that particular area.

Status: Current student, full-time
Dates of Enrollment: 1/2002-Submit Date
Survey Submitted: April 2004

The program is tough, but worth it. Baylor students leave the Law School able to walk into any courtroom in the country and be successful. Any elective class you want to take is available because of the small size of the school. Baylor professors' sole responsibility is to the students and their classroom preparedness, which creates a high quality of classroom instruction. Grading at Baylor is deflated rather than inflated, but what employers focus on is class ranking, so deflation rather than inflation is not a significant thing.

> **Baylor Law says:** "While rankings are not our primary concern, we are proud of being recognized as a top-tier school in 2004.
>
> "Baylor's program is designed to prepare students for the practice of law, whether that is in the courtroom or the boardroom. To achieve that end, students are required to take a broad range of courses to give all of our graduates a solid foundation in both substance and procedure. In addition to the core classes, students can designate one of six concentrations where electives can be tailored to work toward a specific

interest. The areas of concentration include Criminal Practice, General Civil Litigation, Business Transactions, Business Litigation, Estate Planning and Administrative Practice. Because our professors understand the significance of the work our students will be doing once they graduate, they have high expectations for their students—but they also work to mentor the students so that each student is able to succeed. We see the benefits of our rigorous program in our exceptional bar passage rate, high employment rate, and the satisfaction of our alumni."

Employment Prospects

Status: Alumnus/a, full-time
Dates of Enrollment: 8/1998-4/2001
Survey Submitted: March 2006

Given Baylor's reputation, especially throughout Texas, as preparing students for the practice of law, Baylor Law grads are sought after by employers, especially graduates in the top of class. Moot court and mock trial experience is favorable. On-campus interviews are key to getting access to top legal firms in Texas. Baylor Law grads typically are able to find work in a variety of places: big firms, small firms, clerkships and government jobs.

Status: Alumnus/a, full-time
Dates of Enrollment: 8/1995-5/1998
Survey Submitted: March 2006

Baylor is very well respected regionally. At the top-tier Texas firms (BB, VE, Fulbright, Haynes & Boone, TK), which is where I am, I'd say you generally have to be in the top 20 to 25 percent to get an interview. It's harder for me to speak on smaller firm placement, but I'd say most students end up in Dallas, Houston, Austin, Fort Worth or smaller towns in East Texas or the like. And most litigate. There is an exceptional amount of loyalty among Baylor Law graduates (partially because they all went through the same boot camp experience) and I always love recruiting at Baylor because we get excellent summer associates from there.

Status: Alumnus/a, full-time
Dates of Enrollment: 9/2003-4/2004
Survey Submitted: September 2004

The CSO at Baylor is fantastic. Very helpful, very friendly, very efficient. They have binders full of job opportunities. There is an extensive Baylor alumni presence in Texas which helps in job placement greatly. There is a fall OCI and a spring OCI, as well as job fairs. Baylor is known for producing excellent litigators.

Status: Alumnus/a, full-time
Dates of Enrollment: 2/1998-6/2000
Survey Submitted: April 2005

Employment in Texas, Oklahoma, Louisiana and many of the other Southern states is almost guaranteed after graduation from Baylor, but employment opportunities on the East Coast are much more difficult to obtain. The alumni network is extremely helpful, and the law school counselor is wonderful. Very prestigious Texas firms with strong litigation practices seem to prefer Baylor law grads to others, such as Texas and SMU.

Status: Current student, full-time
Dates of Enrollment: 8/2003-Submit Date
Survey Submitted: January 2005

I have had no problems getting a job. I'm in the top quarter of my class and I have two top summer associate jobs lined up for this summer. Others in my class are having problems. Part of it is personality, and part of it is lack of good grades. I mean if you aren't in the top 25 percent, you really are not going to even get an interview with the top firms. Also, if you do not want to practice in Texas, your chances for employment are fewer.

Read all of Vault's Law School Surveys at www.vault.com/lawschool — get complete surveys on top law schools, expert advice on applicaton essays, LSAT prep and more.

VAULT CAREER LIBRARY 581

Status: Current student, full-time
Dates of Enrollment: 1/2002-Submit Date
Survey Submitted: April 2004

Baylor's reputation in Texas for litigation is prestigious. We have the best firms in Texas and elsewhere recruiting on campus for future litigators and transactional attorneys. Our Career Services Office is run by a wonderful staff who care for the students, know them all by name, and help everyone (no matter what their ranking) try to find a job. Almost every student is employed within six months of graduation from Baylor. The unique part of Baylor is that you can take the time to work for a firm or do an internship, but can also decide to go straight through school in 27 months. It is nice, for someone who does not want to do a clerkship or did not find one they wanted, to have another option rather than wasting three months of their time. Most of the students here go into civil practice, although there are many looking into criminal law, government work and academics.

Status: Current student, full-time
Dates of Enrollment: 8/2001-Submit Date
Survey Submitted: March 2004

The campus recruiting scene is great—if you are at the top of the class. The Career Services Office is very enthusiastic and well meaning, but they are small and overworked. They will try hard to get you a job, but Baylor is not considered a top-tier school by employers. Very few employers interview students finishing their first year for clerkships. I think this is a reflection that Baylor does not have the academic reputation it should have.

Now, on the upside: Baylor is very small and tight-knit. The few firms that are out there with Baylor lawyers in them will do everything they can to take care of you. There really is a feeling that you belong to something when you are at Baylor. It is small enough that you really get to know your classmates. And Baylor grads will help you any way they can. It really is a network. There are even a small number of firms concentrating on trial work that realize Baylor lawyers can be plugged in and start trying cases immediately. So it is not all bleak.

Status: Alumnus/a, full-time
Dates of Enrollment: 2/2000-5/2003
Survey Submitted: January 2004

Do a summer internship!! Baylor advertises that you can complete the program in 27 months, but if you do not take a summer off to do an internship, you do not get a chance to make the contacts you will need to find a job at graduation. Texas employers know how great the Baylor program is. Baylor does have some national recognition, but you have to sell yourself more.

> **On the subject of career services, Baylor Law remarks:** "An advantage to being a small school is that the faculty, staff, and administration have the opportunity to get to know the students on a personal level. This is true of our Career Services Office where our Director and her assistant know virtually every student at the Law School. While many large firms limit their recruiting to the top of the class, a variety of employers—firms, agencies and businesses—interview on campus or solicit resumes from Baylor students. The Career Services Office also maintains a job-posting bulletin, which is regularly updated and available to all Baylor students and graduates. The Career Services director works with students individually to help them present themselves professionally both in writing in their resumes and cover letters, and in person in their interviews. In addition to the work the Career Services Office does, many faculty contact former colleagues and Baylor graduates on behalf of students to assist them in their job search."

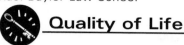 **Quality of Life**

Status: Alumnus/a, full-time
Dates of Enrollment: 8/1998-4/2001
Survey Submitted: March 2006

Waco is a good town for being in law school. Off-campus housing options are available close to the law school. The campus recreation facility is a great resource.

Status: Alumnus/a, full-time
Dates of Enrollment: 8/1995-5/1998
Survey Submitted: March 2006

I graduated before Baylor built its new facility (darn!), but have gone back for fall interviews. The new facilities are beautiful; the library overlooks the river. I also like the fact that it is now across the street from the main Baylor campus so parking is much easier.

Status: Current student, full-time
Dates of Enrollment: 8/2003-Submit Date
Survey Submitted: January 2005

Housing is excellent. There is an abundance of apartments within about one mile of the school. The school itself is located on the banks of the Brazos River, providing a beautiful location. The building is only three years old and the facilities are amazing.

The only complaint is the library is not open 24 hours during finals, which it needs to be. Also, technology resources are abundant, but the technical staff there is crap and breakdowns are routinely ignored.

Status: Current students, full-time
Dates of Enrollment: 8/2001-Submit Date
Survey Submitted: March 2004

Housing is cheap. This is Waco, TX. It is a fairly small city with about 200K people if you include the surrounding suburbs. The economy is not great, so things in general are cheap. The good news is that Waco is about halfway between Austin and Dallas, which are each about an hour and a half away. Therefore, it is easy to get to either city for summer employment or recreation. Overall, my cost of living has been far less than it would have been in other cities. That is a factor you must consider when thinking economics. For example, UT Austin is about half the tuition cost of Baylor, but the cost of living makes the two almost the same overall cost.

The campus itself is AMAZING. The law school is brand new having been built in 2001 at a cost of over $30 million. You will not find better accommodations. Each classroom is set up with semi-circular rows of stadium-style seating, so you always have a clear line of sight to the professor. Each seat is a plush office-style chair that is adjustable for height and reclining. Each seat also has electrical connections for your laptop and an Internet connection. The [second] floor has four full courtrooms with all the latest technology for trying cases. The library has a fully outfitted computer lab with all the latest machines and high-speed printers.

For such a small school, we have a significant number of handicapped students. At any time we have four or five students in wheelchairs. Since the school was recently built, the access for wheelchairs is really very good. The only thing Baylor could improve upon is parking. Baylor built a new parking lot with the new law school. However, they miscalculated how many students would be on campus at any given time and miscalculated the space needed for the number of parking slots they wanted. So, sometimes, you have to park across the street in a parking garage and walk across the street. This is a pretty minor complaint, because the parking situation is better than almost any school out there.

Crime downtown near the school is moderate. I know of a few students whose apartments have been broken into. The downtown area near the school is not very high-class. That makes housing very cheap. Even so, I know of many women living alone just blocks from the law school. In addition, I have never heard of any violent crime against students at either the law school or the nearby undergrad. Many live in suburbs about 10 minutes away that are quiet, even cheaper, and have even less crime.

Status: Current student, full-time
Dates of Enrollment: 1/2002-Submit Date
Survey Submitted: April 2004

Waco is a small town with big-town benefits. It was great studying law here. The temptation to go out is not great, since there is not a ton to do, and that is nice in a program that requires time and attention. However, when you do have free time, there is enough to do that will entertain you. From movies and malls to golf courses and horseback riding, Waco has enough to hold your attention for three years. The housing is very affordable and cute, and the community next to Baylor is a nice one, full of college students and younger residents. Waco does not have the crime rate of a big city like Dallas or Houston.

Status: Alumnus/a, full-time
Dates of Enrollment: 2/2000-5/2003
Survey Submitted: January 2004

Waco is small-town Texas. Some good places to eat. Some places to live in every price range, and everything pretty close to campus (although parking at the law school can be tough at times). There is some crime, but the campus is safe, and there are always people to walk you to your car if you request it. No student housing through the school but there are lots of cheap apartments within walking distance if you like the campus life. Or there are some nicer places if you want to be a little farther away and want to spend a bit more money. Can easily find a nice place for $500 a month. The gym at the school is great, but law students have to pay an extra fee to use it. The campus food is good, but there are plenty of places right around campus to eat.

Status: Alumnus/a, full-time
Dates of Enrollment: 2/2000-5/2003
Survey Submitted: October 2003

Our law school is beautiful and sits on the banks of the Brazos River. Waco is a good city to study in, because there is not much to do except for going out to dinner and the movies. There is a lack of diversity, especially for the African-American student. The school is working on increasing diversity more aggressively in the wake of the Michigan affirmative action cases.

 ## Social Life

Status: Alumnus/a, full-time
Dates of Enrollment: 8/1995-5/1998
Survey Submitted: March 2006

Waco isn't well known for its great bars and restaurants. Law school students usually hang out at George's, a dive, or at people's houses. Law students do not tend to be very competitive—the people in my "study group" are my best friends today—they were in my wedding, and we've all had kids around the same time.

Status: Current student, full-time
Dates of Enrollment: 5/2004-Submit Date
Survey Submitted: March 2006

I drink and most Wednesdays I sing at a bar. I can have a good time anywhere. I can have a good time alone. Beers are cheap, women believe in Jesus: small town fun. Most people have lost their social sense somewhere in the books, that's to be expected.

Status: Alumnus/a, full-time
Dates of Enrollment: 2/1998-6/2000
Survey Submitted: April 2005

Waco does suffer some with regard to social life for those in late 20s and 30s. Most of the social functions are for undergraduates, and there are few "clubs" which are not "cheesy." Most entertainment, as far as clubs and bars go, is geared more to a very casual, sporting crowd. George's, for instance, is an old restaurant which becomes a full bar late at night, with a jukebox and bar food, and cowboys and old football heros. There are a few very late night spots, however, and are open well past 1 a.m. Unique, four-star restaurants are few and far between, but you are at no loss for great Mexican dive restaurants, cheap and wonderful food. Several community events, including balloon rides, river and lake front events—plus, Waco is home to the second largest city park in the nation (second only to New York's Central Park) and is incredible for mountain biking and trail running. We go back to do exactly that. Summers are very warm, but you are not far from Galvaston Beach.

Status: Alumnus/a, full-time
Dates of Enrollment: 8/1999-5/2002
Survey Submitted: April 2005

The small class size allows everyone to know everyone, which contributes to a connected alumni base. With the Baylor Ballpark within walking distance of the law school, it's easy to sneak away for a break. A great student rec center too!

Status: Current student, full-time
Dates of Enrollment: 1/2002-Submit Date
Survey Submitted: April 2004

There are many restaurants, bars and danceclubs. Because Baylor Law is small in size, everyone knows each other and are friends. It isn't uncommon for a group of 15 students to hit some Tex Mex and then go dancing at Gram's dance hall. Of course, the dance hall comes complete with an electronic bull!

Status: Current student, full-time
Dates of Enrollment: 8/2001-Submit Date
Survey Submitted: March 2004

There are three or four little local bars a few blocks from the school that are the hang-out spots. I am an older married student, so I have not hit either the social or dating scene while I have been here. However, I am aware of the basics. The most popular hangouts are bars called "George's" and "Crickets." Both are fun with cheap drinks.

One thing to be aware of: Baylor is a Baptist school. The student body is very conservative, white and upper middle class. Minorities are few and far between. My experience has been that they are not uncomfortable—just rare. The professors are pretty liberal, just like at any law school. The religious nature of the University does not become apparent at the law school too much. However, there are strict rules against premarital cohabitation and the like. If you are looking for gay student groups or significant minority representation, Baylor is not the school.

Status: Alumnus/a, full-time
Dates of Enrollment: 2/2000-5/2003
Survey Submitted: January 2004

Several bars round town to relax in. Everyone found time to date. The law school holds several events each year (a Christmas party, alumni weekend events and so on). And the Law School Student Life Group is great at providing food during finals, a masseuse during finals, a pool table in the law school building, and a large screen TV. So there are ways to relax. The law school building is brand new so everything is up to date in the library and there is wireless Internet around the building. Each desk area in the classroom has a spot for you to plug in your laptop and connect to the internet. Some good restaurants include Charlie's, Rudy's, Willie's and some great smaller Mexican restaurants. It is small town but there is plenty to do. A good mixture of a college town plus a country town.

Read all of Vault's Law School Surveys at www.vault.com/lawschool — get complete surveys on top law schools, expert advice on applicaton essays, LSAT prep and more.

VAULT CAREER LIBRARY 583

South Texas College of Law

General Office
1303 San Jacinto Street
Houston, TX 77002
Admission phone: (713) 659-1810
Admission e-mail: admissions@stcl.edu
Admission URL: http://www.stcl.edu/admissions/

 Admissions

Status: Current student, full-time
Dates of Enrollment: 9/2003-Submit Date
Survey Submitted: April 2006

(1) Take the LSAT and do well; (2) complete the application for admission; (3) submit a resume of employment; (4) submit a three-page personal statement; and (5) submit two letters of recommendation—they'll accept a third, so I'd suggest that as well (one or two from a professor; one from work; maybe one from someone you know through community involvement).

Status: Current student, full-time
Dates of Enrollment: 8/2003-Submit Date
Survey Submitted: March 2006

Admissions process works well, but if you submit your application during the "normal" admissions period, the financial aid deadline might come up before you even find out if you've been accepted. I had to complete my financial aid application for the school before I even knew I was in.

Status: Current student, full- and part-time
Dates of Enrollment: 8/2003-Submit Date
Survey Submitted: March 2006

The admissions process is typical of any law school—references, LSAT, essay. They do participate with LSAC which makes everything easier and they recently started letting you submit applications online—they are getting on board with technology.

As far as essays go, I find that the more personal the better. They are impressed by stories of survival and learning and why you chose to go to law school. STCL aims for a good mix of students so your typical cookie cutter essay likely won't cut it.

I didn't interview, but I know they are offered. STCL is becoming a bit more competitive as the caliber of our students go up. But it also strives to be everyone's law school and give everyone the opportunity to come.

Status: Current student, full-time
Dates of Enrollment: 8/2003-Submit Date
Survey Submitted: March 2006

The interesting thing about STCL is that the admissions office focuses on slightly different criteria than do most other law schools I was accepted into. They focus on real-world experience instead of solely relying on undergraduate grades and standardized test performance. The school tries to provide an environment where many students can better themselves, and draws a wide and diverse range of students accordingly.

Status: Current student, full- and part-time
Dates of Enrollment: 8/2004-Submit Date
Survey Submitted: March 2006

The admissions process for South Texas is very straightforward. It's a standard law school application: resume, short form and a personal statement. The turnaround time is very quick. I applied in November and knew by the end of January that I had gotten in.

Status: Current student, full-time
Dates of Enrollment: 8/2003-Submit Date
Survey Submitted: March 2006

The admissions process is standard (LSAT score, undergrad GPA, transcripts, fee, application). They have a great group of people who take you around the campus on tours in case you visit before applying. The admissions office has never given me a hard time with anything, and I am A very "tenacious" questioner. I probably called 20 times before I applied and they were more than gracious!

Status: Current student, full-time
Dates of Enrollment: 8/2003-Submit Date
Survey Submitted: November 2004

The school runs full-time and part-time programs and admits students for admission beginning in both the fall and the spring. Although the school is not incredibly difficult to get into (the average GPAs and LSAT scores are low), admission is certainly not guaranteed, particularly with the boom of potential law students applying over the past few years. Solid personal statements and references are essential, and the school truly looks for well-rounded people who show promise of becoming good attorneys.

Additionally, the school is private. Its tuition is up there (around $20k per year), but is very reasonable for a private institution. Loans are easy to get, and the wonderfully helpful and the always cheerful folks in the financial aid office are glad to assist you. For instance, I had never filled out loan applications before, so I had lots of questions. They were a really great help to me and so patient with my questions!

You can visit the campus anytime and get a tour with a student or admissions office staffer. You can also sit in on a class of your choice if you like. The school hosts an orientation for its admitted students where you will hear from some of its professors and deans. Immediately before your first semester, you will attend the required orientation and get the "low-down" on classes, parking, security, grades, writing, organizations and everything else under the sun.

> **The school says:** "The median LSAT score for admission is currently a 154 and the median GPA is a 3.26."

Status: Alumnus/a, full-time
Dates of Enrollment: 8/1998-5/2001
Survey Submitted: April 2005

Admission is relatively easy compared to other schools. South Texas lets a lot of people in only to weed them out throughout the year

> **The school says:** "The retention rate for students at South Texas College of Law is currently 93.4 percent."

Status: Alumnus/a, full-time
Dates of Enrollment: 9/1997-5/2000
Survey Submitted: March 2005

No interviews. Good second-chance school. School's heritage is one of non-traditional students with diverse backgrounds, e.g., prior careers. Median age of first-year was 29 in 1997. While some students went straight from high school to undergraduate to South Texas, easily 40 percent of the students had done something before law school. Emphasize what you bring to the school by way of a diverse background, keeping in mind that a slight majority of incoming students are "traditional" students. It is also helpful if you have community service that you can emphasize, such as Big Brothers and Sisters, working for a charity and the like. Grades and LSATs are important, but not controlling.

Status: Alumnus/a, full-time
Dates of Enrollment: 8/1999-12/2002
Survey Submitted: September 2003

The admissions office was very helpful in applying to South Texas. They held an open house so that we could gain insight into the school and what they were ooking for. Once accepted, they had another open house to help us determine f the school was right for us. South Texas encourages second career students nd is supportive of the part-time program. They are not as selective in the dmissions process as some schools because they focus more on the whole pplication. They review your resume as well as your grades and LSAT scores. he like well-rounded people who have other interests besides law. It doesn't eally matter what your undergrad is in—I had everyone from a biochemist to a oroner to an elementary teacher in my night classes, plus had those "just out of ndergrad" in my day time classes. The age range is 22 to 72. It's very diverse, o there is no one "typical" STCL student.

Academics

Status: Current student, full-time
Dates of Enrollment: 9/2003-Submit Date
Survey Submitted: April 2006

Being a law school, the academic side of our education is fairly rigorous. The courses are always taught by experienced and good professors—the substantive courses are more intellectually focused, while the practical or skills courses are bviously more focused on honing your skills to make you the best advocate you an be. Classes are fairly easy to get into—most can accommodate a little over 00 students and there is always a waitlist. Grading is primarily done on a curve, ut the advanced courses and often skills courses either (1) don't have a curve r (2) have a very high curve. STCL has an open-door policy and the majority f the professors (probably about 90 percent) abide by that—their doors are ften open and they are always approachable; be it about a class or just life in eneral.

Status: Current student, full-time
Dates of Enrollment: 8/2003-Submit Date
Survey Submitted: March 2006

t is difficult to get into popular classes unless they are big classes or you have a ot of hours because of the enrollment process. It doesn't matter how quickly ou enroll in a class, because someone with more hours than you can register at he last minute and take your seat away from you. The workload is fine if you re dedicated. You can get by with doing the bare minimum and have time to arty, or you can do more and you will be rewarded with better grades. It's up o you.

Status: Current student, full- and part-time
Dates of Enrollment: 8/2004-Submit Date
Survey Submitted: March 2006

Most of the classes at South Texas are very good. The majority of professors are very knowledgeable about the topics they are teaching, as most of them practiced aw before moving into academia. It's very helpful to have a former plaintiff's ttorney teach you about products liability, or a former in-house counsel to a najor corporation teach you about corporations and business organizations.

Generally speaking, classes are reasonably easy to get into. There are some classes that are more popular than others, and those can fill up, but the school is very good about recognizing that and adding new sections of popular and mportant classes to accommodate need.

Grading is on the standard law school curve. The workload is heavy, but it is at any law school. However, one thing that South Texas offers to counter that workload is a very generous open-door policy for professors. Professors here are very willing to talk to students, and help them with anything. In fact, professors re willing to help out with subjects that they don't even teach!

Status: Current student, full-time
Dates of Enrollment: 8/2003-Submit Date
Survey Submitted: March 2006

The first year is ridiculously hard. Our school is accessible and has relatively ow admissions requirements for acceptance, but once accepted, staying in is very hard. Roughly 10 percent of the newly-admitted students each semester eave after the first round of final exams. However, although students might not be able to continue in the second semester, those who are eliminated are allowed to sit out for the semester and re-enter in the following fall with a clean GPA.

This allows students to reconsider if they really want to study law and reflect on the reasons their first semester was not as successful as possible. The professors are wonderfully helpful, and have open doors all around, but they also teach at a higher rate than students are used to from undergrad, and they are trying to give a comprehensive account of each subject. Since so many of the subjects have no real "beginning" it is difficult for students to understand topics as they arise, since they don't necessarily flow from the precious ones. The open-door policy of the faculty makes this challenge approachable, however.

Status: Current student, full-time
Dates of Enrollment: 8/2003-Submit Date
Survey Submitted: March 2006

The best part of the school is the Advocacy Program, particularly Mock Trial Litigation. This class is taught by practicing attorneys who teach the art of advocacy with a hands-on approach. The class culminates in a tournament at the end of the semester where you compete against your classmates and are judged and critiqued by successful attorneys from the Houston legal community. My finals round was judged by Justice Medina of the Texas Supreme Court and a number of Judges from the Houston Appeals Courts.

Status: Alumnus/a, full-time
Dates of Enrollment: 8/1995-5/1998
Survey Submitted: March 2006

South Texas College of Law has a very flexible program offering day, night and Saturday classes. Many of the professors are graduates from top-tier law schools and/or lawyers with real-world experience. The focus of the school is on the development of litigation skills so if you know you don't want to be a litigator this is not the school for you. There is an expectation that students will participate in moot court or mock trial—both of which are offered intramurally or as part of nationwide competitions (must be invited following a try-out). STCL is the Number One ranked law school in trial advocacy—having won more competitions than any other school.

Status: Current student, full-time
Dates of Enrollment: 8/2003-Submit Date
Survey Submitted: November 2004

First-year students should take advantage of the school's Langdell Scholar Program available for all required classes. Students can sign up for this program and attend Saturday supplementary classes with upper-level students who did very well in each class. For instance, a first-year student can attend a Saturday Torts Langdell class taught by a 3L who made an A plus in the same class taught by the same Torts professor. The scholars help students prepare for finals usually by collaboratively outlining the class and having students complete practice final exams. The program is extremely helpful and also provides newbies with an opportunity to get the perspective of an upper-level student on that course and professor, as well as on pretty much anything else. A good friend of mine is teaching a Langdell course as a 2L this semester, and I know that she has talked with many other students about their problems during their first year, both personal and school-related. In short, the scholars are great.

As a side note, the school also runs a summer abroad program with classes in Italy, England, Ireland, Mexico and Turkey. Students can also get credit during any semester through externships overseas at the Hague or can participate in full semesters abroad in the Netherlands or Denmark. One strong recommendation of mine for any student is to take full advantage of local externships for credit through the school. These give you hands-on experience and come complete with a required practical class in which you practice arbitration, negotiation and client counseling, among other things.

One more thing I must add—the school's library is amazing—one of the most beautiful and well-stocked I have ever seen. The staff is wonderful and you really never have problems finding a quiet place to study (though sometimes you have to boot out students from other local law schools who prefer to study at our library!).

According to the school, "South Texas College of Law currently operates and/or sponsors summer study abroad programs in Malta, Prague (Czech Republic), London (England), Galway (Ireland), Cuernavaca (Mexico), Durham (England) and Istanbul (Turkey)."

Read all of Vault's Law School Surveys at www.vault.com/lawschool — get complete surveys on top law schools, expert advice on applicaton essays, LSAT prep and more.

VAULT CAREER LIBRARY   585

Status: Alumnus/a, full-time
Dates of Enrollment: 8/1998-5/2001
Survey Submitted: April 2005

I believe the quality of education at South Texas is excellent provided that you want to pursue a career as a litigator. This is not the type of school that focuses on the theory and development of the law. It is a nuts and bolts of suing and being sued type of law school. Grading is very difficult; I believe that South Texas has a quota for how many students it will fail the first year. The workload is heavy the first year, but I was able to work part-time and take full loads my second and third year without any drop in my GPA. Generally, the professors are current or past practitioners, so they provide quite a bit of "real world" experience into the lessons.

Status: Alumnus/a, full-time
Dates of Enrollment: 9/1997-5/2000
Survey Submitted: March 2005

Excellent. STCL emphasizes "hands-on" or participatory learning. For instance, in evidence, rather than just listening to a lecture from the professor about hearsay and its exceptions, the professor gives the class the lesson, then calls on students to play lawyers, one side of which tries to get some piece of evidence in, and the other who opposes it.

> **The school says:** "South Texas College of Law provides ample opportunities to learn both litigation and transactional legal skills through the school's renown Advocacy Program, the Frank Evans Alternative Dispute Resolution Center, the Corporate Compliance Center and the Transactional Skills Center that are all designed to enhance the curriculum offered and extracurricular activities available."

Status: Alumnus/a, full-time
Dates of Enrollment: 8/1999-12/2002
Survey Submitted: September 2003

The professors are the best. I studied with well-respected professors. They were approachable and willing to help you do your best. The Bar classes are offered during the day and evening every semester. Being a part-time night student for most of my law school career, it was important to me to have access to the courses I wanted to take, especially since some friends at other schools found the classes they needed were only offered during the day. The upper-level elective classes were generally small, and you really got a chance to participate in discussion.

If you really needed a class and it was full, the registrar did her best to get you into it. STCL is also helpful should you have to defer an exam due to illness, etc. Many of my friends had to do so because of deaths in the family, illness or pregnancy. STCL made it as easy as possible for them to make up the exam the next semester.

 Employment Prospects

Status: Current student, full-time
Dates of Enrollment: 9/2003-Submit Date
Survey Submitted: April 2006

On-campus recruiting, for me, was the best way to find a job—I got two summer clerkships and my permanent employer through the CRC (Career Resources Office). The CRC often puts on different programs and workshops on how to obtain the job that best suits you and provides students with many networking opportunities. South Texas is a fairly tight-knit community; so often at social functions, alumni will attend and interact.

Status: Alumnus/a, full-time
Dates of Enrollment: 8/1995-5/1998
Survey Submitted: March 2006

Prospects are good if you plan to stay in Texas for several years after graduating. Many city judges in the State of Texas are graduates of South Texas College of Law. Honestly, after three or four years of solid practice, it really does not matter where you went to school. I work for a top-tier law firm and am being considered for partnership.

Status: Current student, full-time
Dates of Enrollment: 8/2003-Submit Date
Survey Submitted: November 2004

Facing the blunt truth of it, not many people outside of Houston are familiar with this school, so job prospects outside Texas can be grim. However, getting a job in Houston is relatively easy if you make good use of your resources. The alumni base in Houston and in many cities in Texas is extraordinary, and the legal community respects the practical approach to legal education used at our school. As was said by the federal judge for whom I interned the summer of 2004, "I can always tell what school an attorney did NOT go to when they come into my courtroom. If they are scared, seem unprepared, and don't have the first clue about what to do, I know they did NOT go to South Texas."

Our grads can get jobs with the big firms here but not without some serious work. The standard rules apply—great grades, Law Review, mock trial, moot court and journals are the keys to getting those coveted positions (and knowing someone never hurts). However, for those wishing to practice outside of Texas, there are really two viable options that I know of: work here for a while and transfer or—get involved in moot court or mock trial national teams. I have heard talk of many students receiving job offers during their competitions elsewhere. And with the school attending and winning so many competitions, you can theoretically get face time with many senior partners and even judges from federal circuits when you travel with the teams.

As far as types of employment, our grads go everywhere: private practice, government (our grads tend to do very well in getting positions with the District Attorney's office as they are aware we are prepared with practical knowledge), corporate (particularly oil and gas and energy in the Houston area), JAG, and others. The school's career resources center puts on several job fairs and encourages students to attend many conducted off our campus.

> **The school says:** "South Texas graduates, now more than 10,000, are present in all 50 states and seven foreign countries, the largest concentrations in Texas and Florida."

Status: Alumnus/a, full-time
Dates of Enrollment: 8/1998-5/2001
Survey Submitted: April 2005

It is difficult to rate employment prospects out of South Texas because there was a severe legal downturn in Houston when I graduated. Very few students go to the top firms. Most go to mid-level firms that want somebody who feels comfortable handling their own case load a few months out of law school.

Status: Alumnus/a, full-time
Dates of Enrollment: 9/1997-5/2000
Survey Submitted: March 2005

Top students (top 25 percent or so) can go wherever they like. The problem is not that STCL alumni don't look out for their own, but don't go far from Houston. As the concentric circles go out farther and farther from Houston, the job opportunities diminish precipitously. This speaks only to large law firms, as I have no experience with whether this is also true for government employers, smaller law firms or corporate employers, such as in-house counsel.

Status: Alumnus/a, full-time
Dates of Enrollment: 8/1999-12/2002
Survey Submitted: September 2003

Even after graduation, the Career Services Office has been supportive in helping me with my job search but only because I have asked for help and made myself known to the employees in the office. The recruiting programs are generally geared towards the very top of the class, so you have to be very proactive. If you interact with the career services associates and follow up, they will help you. I got several of my job leads because the employees in the career services office contacted me specifically to tell me about them, and they only did so because I made myself visible and known in their office.

Quality of Life

Status: Current student, full-time
Dates of Enrollment: 9/2003-Submit Date
Survey Submitted: April 2006

Because we are not affiliated with an undergraduate program and are merely a free-standing law school in downtown Houston, the housing is not exactly optimal. However, the growth of Midtown (an area about five minutes south of school) has helped create a nice neighborhood that is close to school, safe, reasonably priced and full of different activities. The campus itself has ample classrooms, study areas, a large library, a lounge and a small diner (Grisby's). However, because we are located in downtown, there are plenty of dining options within walking distance.

Status: Current student, full- and part-time
Dates of Enrollment: 8/2003-Submit Date
Survey Submitted: March 2006

The campus is downtown which is both awesome and annoying. We're in the same building as a Texas Court of appeals and blocks from Federal courts—this makes for an exciting law life. We are also close to most law firms. The bad part is parking and that downtown is a ghost town at night. But STCL has made efforts in both areas by providing limited student parking and offering escorts at night.

Status: Current student, full-time
Dates of Enrollment: 8/2003-Submit Date
Survey Submitted: March 2006

Housing is interesting in downtown Houston. Most students choose to live close by, in places like midtown which are young and vibrant (but also expensive) and Montrose (bohemian). Apartments run the gamut from $550 a month to as much as $1500 a month for a one-bedroom. The best part about going to school downtown is that you are inevitably close to your job, as most law firms in Houston are located in downtown or in the galleria, neither of which are very far from school.

Status: Current student, full-time
Dates of Enrollment: 8/2003-Submit Date
Survey Submitted: March 2006

The facilities are great!!! We have the newest courtroom in Texas. We also have the newest law library in Texas, with six floors of private study carols, and hundreds of computers and printers free to each student. We also have introduced wireless network to virtually the entire campus now, as well as electrical outlets at each seat in classrooms. The student lounge provides a great place to mingle as does the sixth floor balcony, which overlooks downtown Houston and has great views of the Toyota Center, Minute Maid Park and the courthouses. Each function we have is catered appropriately, and there is always a plethora of refreshments and food. Also, the CLEs we have here on a monthly basis (minimum) provide an environment where attorneys come into contact with students on a regular basis.

Status: Current student, full-time
Dates of Enrollment: 8/2003-Submit Date
Survey Submitted: November 2004

Because the school is downtown, safety is always a concern. However, Houston's downtown is being revamped, and the school's extremely close proximity to the new baseball and basketball stadiums provides better security due to the added police for events. The stadiums, I dare say, are also a serious temptation to students—I have seen many a student skip class to see the Astros or Rockets on opening day!

Status: Alumnus/a, full-time
Dates of Enrollment: 9/1997-5/2000
Survey Submitted: March 2005

STCL is located in the Central Business District of Houston. There is no on-campus housing, but there are many nearby neighborhoods that provide affordable, convenient housing for students, like Montrose and the Heights. There is also a rail line that runs along Main Street, which is about two blocks from the school, that takes you to the Medical Center, which has a number of affordable apartments, particularly if you room with someone. STCL has a

brand new, state-of-the-art court room that the school uses for its moot court program, but the Houston courts of appeal and even the Texas Supreme Court has also held court there. It also has a brand new law library with a contemporary design that is also state of the art.

Status: Alumnus/a, full-time
Dates of Enrollment: 8/1999-12/2002
Survey Submitted: September 2003

STCL is a stand alone law school with no housing. The student affairs office does help prospective students with housing issues, though. It is located in the heart of downtown Houston, so there's a lot of housing near it, but those complexes are generally expensive. Better to move outside of downtown and commute, unless you don't have a car. You pretty much need a car in Houston, though—I lived without one for several years, but it's very difficult to get around.

The campus can be a place just to go to class or can be a home away from home. There's a small lounge area to meet and eat lunch. There's a diner-style food counter where you can get sandwiches, burgers and daily special for cheap. The vending machines are often barren by the end of the week, especially when it comes to water—it goes fast. The neighborhood is mixed. There's a park a couple of blocks away where a lot of homeless people hang out. But, crime isn't too bad in that area considering it's in downtown. It should lessen even more when the Toyota Arena opens. One thing that's really nice is the school provides police officers to escort you to your car if you ask. Since the STCL building also hosts two appellate courts, security is a little better than other places. It helps too that there's only one entrance to the school.

Social Life

Status: Current student, full-time
Dates of Enrollment: 9/2003-Submit Date
Survey Submitted: April 2006

South Texas is a very social school. Whatever you are into—there's probably a group for you. Again, because we're downtown and next to Midtown; it's very common for students to go grab a beer after class or sit outside on the patio on a sunny afternoon (especially to the Front Porch).

Status: Current student, full-time
Dates of Enrollment: 8/2003-Submit Date
Survey Submitted: March 2006

The Office of Student Organizations is the hub of all the groups on campus. It is run by one of the most amazing women in the world. Everyone calls her "Amy K"—she works tirelessly to provide fun and imaginative events each semester. She helps coordinate the end of the semester parties, the Graduation Barrister's Ball, the Softball and Basketball Intermural Leagues, as well as clothing and canned food drives, Music Fest and Hurricane/Tsunami Relief efforts. Virtually all of their functions benefit a worthy cause in some way, while providing a social atmosphere for students to connect and unwind.

Status: Current student, full- and part-time
Dates of Enrollment: 8/2004-Submit Date
Survey Submitted: March 2006

The Student Bar Association is constantly offering social hours on the weekends and events like softball tournaments with other area law schools and area law firms. Additionally, student organizations are always coming up with new things to do with the student body, like speakers (Sen. John Edwards came to speak to the school last year), Astros game-watching parties during the World Series and other fun activities.

Status: Current student, full-time
Dates of Enrollment: 8/2003-Submit Date
Survey Submitted: March 2006

Tailgate is also a student favorite, mostly for its dollar beers and absolutely spectacular bar food. On a quieter note, Dog House Tavers is usually a nice place to have a conversation or even study. As far as I know, the club scene isn't huge with the law school set, who generally prefer cold beers to martinis. If you

Read all of Vault's Law School Surveys at www.vault.com/lawschool — get complete surveys on top law schools, expert advice on applicaton essays, LSAT prep and more.

VAULT CAREER LIBRARY 587

prefer something a little more upscale, students hang out at Pub Fiction which generally has loud music and beautiful people, especially on the weekends.

Status: Current student, full-time
Dates of Enrollment: 8/2003-Submit Date
Survey Submitted: November 2004

Following is a VERY brief list of the organizations available to join: Law Review; Board of Advocates (including mock trial and moot court); Corporate Counsel Review; Student Democratic and Republican Societies; Student Bar Association; Phi Alpha Delta and Phi Delta Phi Legal Fraternities; Animal Law Society; AMICUS (the school's gay & lesbian organization); Christian Legal Society; Black Law Students' Association; Houston Young Lawyer's Association—Law Student Division; and MANY more. The school has regular student-organized activities such as football and softball charity tournaments with local law firms, a Halloween carnival, parties after final exams and much more.

One thing worth mentioning here is the diversity of the school. Because the school began as a part-time institution geared towards second-career students, the school continues to love its second-career folks. Many scholarships are available just for such students. But the point here is that the school's student body runs the spectrum of the rainbow and ages range from 22 to 72, so the "typical" South Texas student doesn't really exist. Overall, I LOVE this school and wouldn't have chosen anywhere else!

> **The school says:** "South Texas has more than 30 student organizations, which include a newspaper, three legal journals and undergraduate affinity groups."

Status: Alumnus/a, full-time
Dates of Enrollment: 8/1999-12/2002
Survey Submitted: September 2003

There several options for lunch around the school, as many of the office buildings have food courts and restaurants. Fast food is just a couple block walk to the Park Mall, which has a nice food court, Bennigan's and Nina's for great Mexican food. The most popular haunt though has to be Josephine's across the street for Italian. Being downtown, there is easy access to lots of bars and restaurants via the downtown trolleys (which are free). In addition, the rail line opening later this year will pick up students two blocks over and can take them to the bars on the other end of town or be used as transportation to class if you live in the medical center. Downtown is the hot place to be, so you'll be close to the action. The Student Bar Association hosts socials in the atrium with beer, wine, soda and pizza. There's a chili cook off each fall and a Halloween carnival that a lot of students bring their kids to. There are also beginning and end of the semester socials at local bars. There are no Greek fraternities since it's a stand alone school, but there are legal fraternities to join. As far as bars go, the favorite happy hour place has to be (hands down) Cabo. They have killer margaritas and you can get great fish tacos to help sober you up. Sambuca Jazz Cafe is great too for happy hour and a nice dinner with a live band. There are so many places to go downtown that it would be hard to list them!

Southern Methodist University

SMU Dedman School of Law
Office of Admissions
PO Box 750110
Dallas, TX 75275-0110
Admissions phone: (214) 768-2550
Admissions fax: (214) 768-2549
Admissions e-mail: lawadmit@smu.edu
Admissions URL: http://admissions.law.smu.edu/

Admissions

Status: Alumnus/a, full-time
Dates of Enrollment: 8/2002-5/2005
Survey Submitted: September 2005

The admissions process is pretty much like other law schools; you have to take the LSAT and then fill out their application for entry into law school. There are also all these other requirements such as getting recommendations in order to gain admission. There is also an essay that students have to complete about one's life experiences in order to get in. There was no formal interview. SMU Law is deemed to be one of the most selective schools in the state of Texas.

> **The school says:** As SMU policy, no interviews are granted to applicants. Interviews are only conducted for third-party scholarships.

Status: Alumnus/a, full-time
Dates of Enrollment: 8/1997-6/2000
Survey Submitted: March 2005

Very responsive and accessible. I was thoroughly informed of the various stages of progress.

Status: Current student, full-time
Dates of Enrollment: 8/2002-Submit Date
Survey Submitted: December 2004

The admissions process at this school is highly selective, but reasonable. If you are serious about your education and you want a good private school education, then you will enjoy this school. The best advice for getting into this school is to work really hard on essays and personal statements. Take any opportunity that you can in order to show the admissions personnel who you are. The hard work that you invest on these statements will definitely pay off in terms of admission and financial aid, if that is a concern.

Status: Alumnus/a, full-time
Dates of Enrollment: 8/1998-5/2001
Survey Submitted: April 2004

Class size has been cut by one third, so SMU has become much more selective. No interviews except for 20 finalists for the full scholarship Hatton Sumners scholarship program. Admissions office is very friendly and very personalized—call them and they will know your name.

Status: Alumnus/a, full-time
Dates of Enrollment: 8/1994-5/1997
Survey Submitted: April 2004

It was relatively simple. I applied to SMU before the advent of online applications; I imagine that today's application process is even easier.

Status: Alumnus/a, full-time
Dates of Enrollment: 9/1994-5/1997
Survey Submitted: April 2004

The admissions process for SMU was the same as all other law schools, although I recall hearing from SMU very early.

Academics

Status: Alumnus/a, full-time
Dates of Enrollment: 8/2002-5/2005
Survey Submitted: September 2005

Workload—extremely tough. You've got to read hundreds upon hundreds of law cases. The first year is the worst and then the next two years you just begin to get used to it and I guess I didn't notice it as much.

Quality of Classes—I was thoroughly disappointed. I did not learn anything in those classes except what I taught myself. I do not think this is singular to SMU, but it is characteristic of law school itself. Though still somewhat stimulating; the required readings in the classes did cause you to think and they did expand your understanding of a subject

Grading was terrible. The teachers are highly subjective in how they grade; there is an utter lack of objectivity and many times they are unable to justify a grade to you if you confront them about it

Professors are highly educated but oftentimes they were unable to teach. They may have all been good lawyers or good students in law school but 99 percent of the teachers at SMU are dreadful when it comes to teaching.

Ease of getting classes—often difficult; when a class was closed it was often very difficult to get in to that class.

> **Regarding the ease of getting classes, SMU says:** Classes are scheduled on a semester basis. Students should be able to take most classes in another semester if not immediately.

Status: Alumnus/a, full-time
Dates of Enrollment: 8/1997-6/2000
Survey Submitted: March 2005

Very rigorous and the profs were accessible and supportive.

Status: Current student, full-time
Dates of Enrollment: 8/2002-Submit Date
Survey Submitted: December 2004

The JD program is very competitive. The undergraduate program is competitive, as well. I had the ability to get an undergraduate degree from this institution and I am now in the law program.

SMU has a very well-respected name in Dallas, and in the entire state of Texas, and the law school's prestige is growing by the year. Professors are caring and encouraging, but they also want you to learn—they will ensure that you are challenged intellectually, and many will have you on the edge of your seat wanting to know what comes next. The workload at SMU is moderate to high—after all, the degree is well-respected, and anything in life worth having requires hard work.

Status: Alumnus/a, full-time
Dates of Enrollment: 9/1994-5/1997
Survey Submitted: April 2004

SMU's curriculum is directed toward bar passage and legal practice, as opposed to esoteric legal theories. I never had a problem getting into the classes I wanted. The best professors at SMU focus on corporate and transactional (securities, corporations).

The workload is the same that can be expected at any law school. Most of the professors take volunteers as opposed to calling on people pursuant to the Socratic Method, so people that don't prepare for class can generally get away with it.

Read all of Vault's Law School Surveys at www.vault.com/lawschool — get complete surveys on top law schools, expert advice on applicaton essays, LSAT prep and more.

VAULT CAREER LIBRARY 589

The school says: First-year classes take the Socratic Method seriously. First-year students who do not prepare for their classes will not, in most classes, 'get away with it.'

Status: Alumnus/a, full-time
Dates of Enrollment: 8/1998-5/2001
Survey Submitted: April 2004

Quality academic program with cordial, easy to approach professors. Has some big-name law professors. Popular classes fill up quick, but there are a lot of offerings, and, worst case, you would just have to wait until next semester to get the class and prof you want.

Status: Alumnus/a, full-time
Dates of Enrollment: 8/1994-5/1997
Survey Submitted: April 2004

The workload was large but manageable if one was organized. The professors were both topnotch and approachable. Grading was tough the first year but eased up in years two and three. I don't recall having difficulty in getting into classes.

 ## Employment Prospects

Status: Alumnus/a, full-time
Dates of Enrollment: 8/1997-6/2000
Survey Submitted: March 2005

Finding a job is easy if you're in the top 25 percent.

Status: Alumnus/a, full-time
Dates of Enrollment: 8/2003-Submit Date
Survey Submitted: March 2005

SMU is well regarded in the Dallas/Fort Worth area—and in most of Texas. But if you are headed out of state, the price tag isn't worth it. SMU is clearly well down the food chain compared to the University of Texas.

Status: Alumnus/a, full-time
Dates of Enrollment: 8/1998-5/2001
Survey Submitted: April 2004

Every significant firm (and many smaller ones, too) with an office in Texas, actively recruits at SMU. In Dallas, SMU grads compete with every school in the country (every top Dallas firm has high-level SMU grads).

Status: Alumnus/a, full-time
Dates of Enrollment: 9/1994-5/1997
Survey Submitted: April 2004

The reason I went to SMU is that SMU is the only law school in Dallas. Dallas has a very strong legal market so I figured that my prospects of getting a job were better than if I attended a school in Los Angeles. That proved true; I got a job at the highest paying firm in Dallas when I graduated, even though I was only in the top 50 percent of my class. I had hoped to get back to L.A. at some point down the road, and I did. I'm now at a top firm, and I do not view the fact that I went to a regional school as a barrier to getting a job at a top NY based firm.

Status: Alumnus/a, full-time
Dates of Enrollment: 8/1994-5/1997
Survey Submitted: April 2004

The SMU JD is a great entry into the Texas law scene. I have no idea how it is viewed outside of the state of Texas.

 ## Quality of Life

Status: Current student, full-time
Dates of Enrollment: 8/2002-Submit Date
Survey Submitted: December 2004

Campus housing is wonderful. It is very convenient, and well-maintained. It is well worth the price. The campus is pretty, with trees everywhere and lots of squirrels and birds for you to enjoy as you walk to class. Some of the students are wealthy, and you can tell by the cars that they drive and the way that they dress. Other students are regular people who commute daily for classes and campus activities. Campus dining is OK—there is a Subway, a Chick-fil-A and another specialty sandwich shop on campus. Dining hall food is pretty good, but can be expensive. But what the actual campus lacks can be found in the shopping centers surrounding the school and within a five mile radius accessible by public transportation. The school is situated in the middle of one of the wealthiest neighborhoods in the city—crime rates are fairly low, but crime is not totally prevented. Theft is probably the most common crime on campus—but this is to be expected anywhere. I haven't had any problems, but I have friends that have had bicycles and purses stolen.

Status: Alumnus/a, full-time
Dates of Enrollment: 8/1998-5/2001
Survey Submitted: April 2004

Remodeled classrooms are very nice and very up to date. Campus is located in University Park, one of the Park Cities, the nicest neighborhood in Dallas. Very collegial environment at school.

Status: Alumnus/a, full-time
Dates of Enrollment: 8/1994-5/1997
Survey Submitted: April 2004

Great neighborhood; very safe.

Status: Alumnus/a, full-time
Dates of Enrollment: 9/1994-5/1997
Survey Submitted: April 2004

Housing was amazing—I lived in a 450-square foot apartment, right off campus and paid $239 per month! There is no crime in the area; SMU is situated in one of the most prestigious areas in Dallas. Quality of life is very good there. The campus is beautiful.

 ## Social Life

Status: Alumnus/a, full-time
Dates of Enrollment: 8/2002-5/2005
Survey Submitted: September 2005

Very few establishments for black students and other non-white students. The environment is very cliquish especially at the undergraduate level but also some in law school as well. Once you start knowing some people though you'll find they are relatively friendly regardless of their color.

> **The school says:** "Dallas has extensive nightlife and social activities. SMU has BLSA, HLSA and AALSA for minority law students. Students also have the opportunity to join external organizations for minorities such as certain sections of the Dallas Bar Associations."

The bars and night spots that are around the campus are on East Mockingbird or they are on Greenville Avenue. It doesn't matter though because once you start law school you are not going to have any kind of social life. Dating girls, forget about it at SMU—there's too much work to be done!!

Status: Alumnus/a, full-time
Dates of Enrollment: 8/1998-5/2001
Survey Submitted: April 2004

Lots of Student Bar Association happy hours.

Status: Alumnus/a, full-time
Dates of Enrollment: 8/1994-5/1997
Survey Submitted: April 2004

You won't party with anyone who isn't a law student.

Status: Alumnus/a, full-time
Dates of Enrollment: 9/1994-5/1997
Survey Submitted: April 2004

The social scene was very good, although as time went on (particularly after grades were released and on-campus interviews began) the environment became competitive. The Student Bar Association arranged happy hours every Friday at various different bars around town. Generally speaking the law school student body is comprised of good looking, "cool" people that are reasonably intelligent but a bit insecure.

 # The School Says

At Dedman, you are not a number. You are an individual with the potential to make a significant contribution to the field of law, and we treat you as such.

You will find that the campus culture is distinctly student-oriented. Our faculty's open-door policy encourages students to meet individually and often with faculty members. Thus, your learning continues outside the classroom, under the guidance of involved, supportive professors. In addition, you will be assigned a faculty advisor to help you get the most from your legal education.

In fact, you can craft your degree with as much depth, breadth and specialization as you desire. Once you have completed your first-year core curriculum, you will discover a broad range of upper-level courses, giving you the flexibility to tailor an individual course of study.

You will also discover that our academic community, while competitive, is also refreshingly collegial. Our small class size means that you will likely get to know most of your classmates on a first-name basis. Our first-year class is divided into three sections (two full-time day sections and one part-time evening section) of about 85 students each. One half of our upper-class courses have fewer than 25 students; three fourth have fewer than 50 students. And our favorable teacher-student ratio promotes interaction between students and the faculty both in and out of the classroom.

The individual attention for which SMU Dedman School of Law is known begins with the admissions process. We read and consider every application individually, not deciding on numbers alone, but looking for well-rounded students with solid academic backgrounds and the qualities that will enrich our educational community.

We seek students from a wide range of backgrounds, experiences and viewpoints in order to create an interesting class. We select students who will benefit from the educational opportunity at SMU, add to their classmates' learning experience and contribute to society both while at law school and after graduation. We also seek students of character and ability, with a record of commitment to rigorous work.

When you become part of the SMU Dedman School of Law community, you become part of a select group united by a common passion: to be outstanding practitioners of law.

Both day and evening programs are available. You are encouraged to visit the SMU Dedman School of Law campus to talk with professors, students and staff.

Read all of Vault's Law School Surveys at www.vault.com/lawschool — get complete surveys on top law schools, expert advice on applicaton essays, LSAT prep and more.

VAULT CAREER LIBRARY **591**

Texas Southern University

Thurgood Marshall School of Law
Office of Admissions
3100 Cleburne Street
Houston, TX 77004
Admissions phone: (713) 313-7114 or (713) 313-7115
Admissions e-mail: lawadmit@tsulaw.edu
Admissions URL:
http://www.tsu.edu/academics/law/admissions/

Note: The school has chosen not to comment on the student surveys submitted.

 Admissions

Status: Alumnus/a, full-time
Dates of Enrollment: 8/1999-5/2002
Survey Submitted: September 2004

The admissions process was fairly easy compared to most schools. If you have a fair GPA and LSAT, you are guaranteed entrance. The "open admissions" policy makes the school a good "back up" in case you choose another school as first choice. The administration will provide little assistance through the process. As long as you provide all of the information requested and send your packet via certified mail (so they cannot deny that they received it), you will be fine.

Status: Alumnus/a, full-time
Dates of Enrollment: 8/2001-5/2004
Survey Submitted: March 2005

In 2000, I completed an application and provided a writing sample detailing my reasons for desiring to attend law school. The process was fairly easy.

Status: Alumnus/a, full-time
Dates of Enrollment: 8/1999-5/2002
Survey Submitted: May 2004

The admissions process was straightforward. The school also offered a program known as LEAP, which provided an opportunity for those candidates with a lower LSAT score or GPA to matriculate to law school after successfully completing this program.

Status: Alumnus/a, full-time
Dates of Enrollment: 8/1999-5/2002
Survey Submitted: October 2003

The admission process is easy, although you may have trouble getting your financial aid on time, if at all. There is no interview process and the requirements to get in are not that difficult.

Status: Alumnus/a, full-time
Dates of Enrollment: 8/2002-6/2003
Survey Submitted: December 2004

The admission process was fairly simple, with a LSAT of 151 and a GPA of 3.0, I got a full academic scholarship.

 Academics

Status: Alumnus/a, full-time
Dates of Enrollment: 8/1999-5/2002
Survey Submitted: September 2004

At TSU, there are more required courses than at other schools. You can expect to have nothing but required courses through to your second year.

Unfortunately, certain required courses at other schools are taught over the course of an entire year while at TSU, they are only a semester. An example of this is Contracts, which is a foundation course encompassing vast amounts of information. I think a more solid foundation should be built for students, so these courses should be taught throughout the whole year.

Courses become more interesting in your second year. Courses are challenging and if you stay away from study groups with people who are not serious in their coursework, you will have time to prepare and study productively. Expect to read and brief between 150 and 200 pages a night. The good news is that the school provides midterm exams and therefore, you don't base 100 percent of your grade on one final exam. This can also be fatal if you are not prepared.

The best way to try to understand the grading curve is to understand that for every A given, there is an F given. Therefore, most grades will be in the B- to C range. This allows for the 50 percent attrition rate from first year onward.

Don't expect to get the popular classes. There is no rhyme or reason to scheduling and in many cases, a third-year cannot even get a class that they would like. The second-year students may have filled the class because they were allowed to register first. It is a crapshoot and expect to be frustrated every semester at registration time. My suggestion: become good friends with the professor of the course who can waive your entrance into the class without anyone knowing.

Status: Alumnus/a, full-time
Dates of Enrollment: 8/2001-5/2004
Survey Submitted: March 2005

The academics at the school were up to par. I participated in a 1L summer clerkship program at a medium-large sized Texas based firm in Houston with 2Ls and felt very prepared to compete with them. People were shocked that I was a 1L. I was able to attend the classes most desirable to me and I fulfilled my requirements on time. I occasionally questioned the the grading process which sometimes seemed arbitrary. However, overall I was pleased with how I was evaluated and the appeal process was an alternative for those who had more profound grievances. Generally, the professors were professional and knowledgeable. Although, many of them have been at the school for so long that they've become lackadaisical. The workload was sometimes overwhelming, but I don't believe it was terribly cumbersome or completely out of the norm. Time management is crucial at any law school.

Status: Alumnus/a, full-time
Dates of Enrollment: 8/1999-5/2002
Survey Submitted: May 2004

The atmosphere was competitive in nature. The school is known for its deadly curve, which wipes out approximately 45 to 48 percent of the first-year class. The professors are well versed and provide a rigorous yet educational class atmosphere.

Status: Alumnus/a, full-time
Dates of Enrollment: 8/1999-5/2002
Survey Submitted: October 2003

The law is the law is the law—it doesn't change based on the ranking of the school. You learn the same information at TSU as you would anywhere else. The grading curve, in my opinion, is harsh. However, there are some topnotch professors there with various academic pedigree.

Status: Alumnus/a, full-time
Dates of Enrollment: 8/2002-6/2003
Survey Submitted: December 2004

I think the classes were basic law school courses. Depending on the teacher, you could be exposed to the Socratic Method. I found that in the first year, my teachers were pretty lenient on calling on students.

Employment Prospects

Status: Alumnus/a, full-time
Dates of Enrollment: 8/1999-5/2002
Survey Submitted: September 2004

Large firms do come to on-campus interviews and will take an occasional student from the top of the class—but be forewarned: they are looking to enhance their firm's "diversity" element.

Status: Alumnus/a, full-time
Dates of Enrollment: 8/2001-5/2004
Survey Submitted: March 2005

I have been fortunate, so my experience is the exception not the norm. If you work hard and purposefully and strategically position yourself at the onset, the outcome can be very rewarding. Top grades and Law Review are the key to success for students coming from Thurgood. You must place yourself apart from the rest by getting published in a Law Review or being an executive officer on Law Review.

Status: Alumnus/a, full-time
Dates of Enrollment: 8/1999-5/2002
Survey Submitted: May 2004

The campus recruiting is great for those few who score in the top percent. However, many students were still able to obtain jobs by various job fairs and postings.

Status: Alumnus/a, full-time
Dates of Enrollment: 8/1999-5/2002
Survey Submitted: October 2003

It is difficult to get a job in Texas because of our school's ranking, but if you leave Texas and pass the Bar, you can get a job almost anywhere.

Quality of Life

Status: Alumnus/a, full-time
Dates of Enrollment: 8/1999-5/2002
Survey Submitted: September 2004

Campus facilities are currently being remodeled. Most students do not live near campus.

Status: Alumnus/a, full-time
Dates of Enrollment: 8/2001-5/2004
Survey Submitted: March 2005

Thurgood Marshall is located in the heart of "Third Ward," which is an area not particularly known for its affluence. You have to keep your eye on the prize and not be sidetracked by the environment. Since my arrival at the school, campus housing has greatly improved. There are also many apartments for rent in the area.

The law school has recently been renovated and from all accounts, I hear it is pretty magnificent. Even though the area is somewhat depressed economically, I never felt threatened during the three years I lived in Third Ward. Overall, the people were helpful and friendly.

Status: Alumnus/a, full-time
Dates of Enrollment: 8/1999-5/2002
Survey Submitted: May 2004

The school suffered from a flood in the summer of 2001. However, renovations are expected to be be completed soon.

Status: Alumnus/a, full-time
Dates of Enrollment: 8/1999-5/2002
Survey Submitted: October 2003

Housing is cheaper and more adequate in other areas of town. The facilities are currently being expanded so most classes are held in classrooms across the campus. There are mostly fast food places around the school and very few restaurants

Social Life

Status: Alumnus/a, full-time
Dates of Enrollment: 8/1999-5/2002
Survey Submitted: September 2004

Happy hour on the patio is the highlight of the week. Usually a student organization will sponsor a keg there on Fridays. It is a nice atmosphere that the professors actually get involved in.

It is easy to make friends if you aren't a grade bragger. Many people tend to get together in the evenings for dinner and dancing. Just don't avoid your studies. The village area around Rice University is a popular hang out area for the students. It has a casual atmosphere and cheap beer.

Status: Alumnus/a, full-time
Dates of Enrollment: 8/2001-5/2004
Survey Submitted: March 2005

The school is centrally located and there are lots of goings-on. Bars and restaurants are plentiful. Downtown is five minutes away and the major thoroughfares are easily accessible.

Status: Alumnus/a, full-time
Dates of Enrollment: 8/1999-5/2002
Survey Submitted: May 2004

Social life was great after my first year. The school is very much tied into the surrounding communities in the City of Houston, which is a wonderful place to attend school. The cost of living is reasonable as well as the variety of bars and restaurants. Another plus is that the legal community is sort of like a tightly knit family. The opportunities to network with other lawyers, law students, medical students, entertainers and other professionals are tremendous.

Status: Alumnus/a, full-time
Dates of Enrollment: 8/1999-5/2002
Survey Submitted: October 2003

Social life is fine, if you want to associate with your classmates. The City of Houston has great places for social life outside of school.

Status: Alumnus/a, full-time
Dates of Enrollment: 8/2002-6/2003
Survey Submitted: December 2004

I found the students unnecessarily competitive. Even though the student body was nicely diverse. The social and study groups seemed racially divided.

Read all of Vault's Law School Surveys at www.vault.com/lawschool — get complete surveys on top law schools, expert advice on applicaton essays, LSAT prep and more.

VAULT CAREER LIBRARY   593

Texas Tech University School of Law

Admissions Office
School of Law
Texas Tech University
1802 Hartford Avenue
Lubbock, TX 79409-0004
Admissions phone: (806) 742-3990, ext. 273
Admissions fax: (806) 742-4617
Admissions e-mail: lawadmissions@ttu.edu
Admissions URL:
http://www.law.ttu.edu/lawWeb/prospective/

 ## Admissions

Status: Current student, full-time
Dates of Enrollment: 8/2005-Submit Date
Survey Submitted: April 2006

Tech Law's admissions have shot up to record levels in the last three years despite admissions being down at other law schools this year. Over 50 percent of students that are accepted receive scholarships but it is very important to apply as early as possible to give yourself the best chance. If you apply late, the overwhelmed admissions office will take a long time to get back to you.

I talked to the chair of the admissions committee (who I had for Torts) about what they look for in the admission essays and he said the most important thing they are looking for is students who can succeed academically. The ability to succeed in law school is more important than community activities and other things unless you can show how those experiences will give you a foundation to succeed.

Status: Alumnus/a full-time
Dates of Enrollment: 8/2001-5/2004
Survey Submitted: September 2005

Texas Tech offers an early admissions process. I was notified in late January of my acceptance. The school requires a deposit to retain your seat sometime in early spring and then an additional fee for those noncommittal still later. Tech also awards whatever scholarships you would be awarded with your acceptance letter, which also reduces anxiety.

Status: Alumnus/a full-time
Dates of Enrollment: 8/1999-5/2002
Survey Submitted: September 2003

As with all law schools, grades and LSAT scores are paramount, particularly if you are hoping for a scholarship. However, the admissions committee gives a great amount of weight to essays in situations where two applicants are on the cusp, so it is important to show why you should be chosen.

Although Texas Tech is not anywhere as close to as selective as the University of Texas, it is still somewhat difficult to get in and is becoming more difficult with each passing year. In addition, scuttlebutt is that the school plans on decreasing the size of the next couple of incoming classes. This will make competition even more fierce. (As a side note, the reason classes have been so large lately is that the school began giving admissions decisions sooner than in the past. As a result of that change and the improving reputation of the school, more people accepted the invitation to attend Tech Law than the admissions committee expected. Quite a nice problem to have, overall.)

 ## Academics

Status: Current student, full-time
Dates of Enrollment: 8/2005-Submit Date
Survey Submitted: April 2006

Tech is unique because it emphasizes teaching in the classroom and has an open door policy that allows you to get help from your professors outside of class. My first-year professors have been more than willing to visit with me outside of class and have been far superior in the classroom to any I experienced in undergrad. Many of the professors are well known in their fields and are often quoted by the Supreme Court. Tech usually has the highest or second highest bar passage rates in the state. Students also win all kinds of moot court and negotiation competitions.

Your first year you will take 15 hours during the first semester and 14 during the second. Legal Practice is six hours taught over your first two semesters. There are also a variety of joint degree programs that allow you to add a master's and still graduate within three years. For example I will be getting a Masters in Personal Financial Planning and will only give up one summer to do it. Overall I couldn't be happier with the quality of education I am receiving at one of the most affordable law schools in the country.

Status: Alumnus/a full-time
Dates of Enrollment: 8/2001-5/2004
Survey Submitted: September 2005

Texas Tech, unlike many other law schools, has mandatory upper-level classes, these classes are traditional bar subjects: Business Entities (Associations), Commercial Law, Wills and Trusts, Taxation, Family Law, Evidence, Criminal Procedures and Professional Responsibility. This actually becomes a benefit as most firms and government offices are aware of this and "know the product." Texas Tech usually scores high in the bar passage rate for Texas (a difficult three-day bar) and out-of-state bars; the latest bar, February 2005 Texas Bar, Tech had the highest bar passage rate in the state of Texas from the nine law schools.

> **Regarding required courses, the school says:** "Although Family Law is a popular course with Tech Law students, and it is a topic covered by the Texas Bar Examination, it has never been an advanced required course."

Classes are doled according to seniority, so consequently, third-year law students usually have first choice for courses, but with the upper-level requirements, with some planning, you can get the classes you want. If a class is full, there is a published waitlist. I was only waitlisted once, but so many people had signed up (Taxation, if you can imagine that!) that the school opened another class.

Grading is done with a curve, but usually the lowest grades are C for upper-level courses. Tech does not give a minus grade, which is a down side, since for example, if you received a 3.6, you would receive a B+ rather than an A-. There is no grade inflation, which is another down side, but law firms within the region are well aware of this and weigh this when considering a Texas Tech student in comparison with a University of Texas student (which is known for grade inflation), this often results in a Tech student with a lower GPA getting hired over a UT applicant.

Texas Tech's faculty show a diversity in views, cultures and backgrounds. Most of the faculty have JD and LLM from Ivy League schools or have life experience credentials that are incredibly impressive. All faculty at Tech have an open-door policy and make themselves available after school and on weekends. Most of the professors sponsor a law school organization. Like many law schools, it is publish or die, which allows for many legal research opportunities.

The workload is continuous because of the mandatory classes, but most students plan accordingly. Many students ski in Colorado or visit the South Padre Islands during breaks. Those involved in law journals typically have assignments due over extended breaks.

Texas Tech has many national competition teams that have been recognized. For example, the the 2004 John Marshal Moot Court Team was the national Champion in Chicago; the 2004 ABA Moot Court team ranked fifth in the nation and was undefeated through the Western Regionals in San Francisco; the 2005 ABA Negotiation Team ranked second in the nation and went to Dublin, Ireland representing the United States as one of two teams in the International Competition; the 2005 Texas Young Lawyer's Mock Trial Competition was won by Texas Tech; the Tech was second in the nation at the 2004 William Daniel Mock Trial in Atlanta.

> **Texas Tech says:** In Dublin, the 2005 ABA Negotiation Team defeated 15 teams from 13 countries to capture the international championship.

The 2004 Outstanding Law Student in the nation, named by *Who's Who Among American Law Students*, came from Texas Tech and the highest score on the Texas Bar in 2003 came from Texas Tech.

> **The school says:** "We did it again! Brandon Barnett, a December 2005 graduate posted the highest score on the February 2006 Texas Bar Examination. Justin Ferguson is the alumnus that achieved this honor on the July 2003 bar examination."

Status: Alumnus/a full-time
Dates of Enrollment: 1/1997-1/2000
Survey Submitted: August 2004

First year of law school students are grouped into very large size classes mandatory curriculum in contracts, torts, const law, civil procedure. 2Ls and 3Ls are required to take a boring three-hour federal income tax course within the 90 hours required. There is very little clinical experience allowed in Lubbock, TX; the professors in charge of the clinical program think they run your entire life during a clinical experience.

Status: Alumnus/a full-time
Dates of Enrollment: 8/1999-5/2002
Survey Submitted: September 2003

Academics are rigorous at Texas Tech's law school. Expect to work hard, but also expect professors who will give you their all. I had only one professor at Texas Tech that I did not adore, and he has since retired.

All in all, this was the best academic experience of my life. My fellow students were intelligent, kind (apparently an odd trait among law school students) and entertaining. There were very few students who did not prepare for classes diligently.

Because the last few entering classes at Texas Tech have been quite large, popular classes are a little difficult to get. This might change if the next classes are decreased in size, as has been promised.

 Employment Prospects

Status: Current student, full-time
Dates of Enrollment: 8/2005-Submit Date
Survey Submitted: April 2006

98 percent of Tech graduates are employed six months after graduation. You can only assume the other two percent are sick or don't want jobs. I've heard many attorneys say they would rather hire a Tech Law grad than a UT grad because Tech students are better trained to actually practice the law. (Just remember UT still has more prestige than Tech).

The average first-year salary of a Tech graduate is around $80,000. People who choose to stay in Lubbock usually make less and people who go to the larger cities typically make a lot more. Your first summer, it will be easy to get an unpaid internship or externship, but very difficult to get a paid internship. My

2L friends have easily gotten high-paying internships during their second summers but most are not in Lubbock. On-campus recruiting goes on during the beginning of your 2L year, but less than 25 percent receive jobs so quickly.

Status: Alumnus/a full-time
Dates of Enrollment: 8/2001-5/2004
Survey Submitted: September 2005

Texas Tech is one of the top 10 law schools for hiring of corporate attorneys to the Dallas-Fort Worth (DFW) Area.

Tech, while considered by many a "regional school" because of its unique location in the Texas Panhandle, enjoys a region that includes the entire states of Texas, New Mexico, Oklahoma, Louisiana, Colorado and New Mexico. There is also a strong alumni base in the Washington, D.C. area, with many attorneys within the legislation and government areas hailing from this school.

Status: Alumnus/a full-time
Dates of Enrollment: 1/1997-1/2000
Survey Submitted: August 2004

The top 20 students out of a class of 200 usually get good federal or state clerkships, or good jobs with major law firms where they work like rodents for 20 hours a day for the next seven years until the firm downsizes in this competitive legal environment, or they make partner and only have to work 72 hours a week. The other 180 students scramble to find jobs, sending out resumes to every law firm in Texas and the surrounding states trying to get a job to get some real world experience, or they finally accept an entry level job with the government for $15.00 an hour.

Texas Tech Law is a young school, has among the fewest number of law alumni in Texas, therefore the alumni network with the heavyweight law firms is almost nonexistent. The law firms refuse to fly out to the West Texas desert in Lubbock on turbo-prop planes. (No jet service to the booming metropolis of Lubbock, TX.)

Status: Alumnus/a full-time
Dates of Enrollment: 8/1999-5/2002
Survey Submitted: September 2003

There is a great internship program at Texas Tech. Among the possibilities for placement are several judges' chambers, the U.S. Attorney's office, and the District Attorney's office.

Campus recruiting is about the same at every Texas law school. Pretty much the same law firms go to every school, although schools in major cities probably have more small to medium sized firms from their own towns. Upon graduation, I had multiple offers from which to choose, as did many of my classmates.

 Quality of Life

Status: Current student, full-time
Dates of Enrollment: 8/2005-Submit Date
Survey Submitted: April 2006

Lubbock is an isolated city of just over 200,000. It has a very low cost of living and it is very easy to find affordable housing. Crime is not bad and the law students have access to the high quality facilities at the main campus. Tech Law recently received 12 million dollars to add a state-of-the-art court room to the already high tech law school facilities.

My wife and I love it here. I would say our biggest complaint is traffic. Traffic is not very congested and you can get anywhere in 15 minutes, but there are a lot of bad drivers (students and people from surrounding small communities).

Status: Alumnus/a full-time
Dates of Enrollment: 8/2001-5/2004
Survey Submitted: September 2005

Texas Tech Law School is located in the southwest corner of the Great Plains. It is at a slightly higher elevation than much of Texas. Its climate is semi-arid, but water is plentiful from a great underwater water system, called the Ogalala Aquifer. Summers are hot, but with dry heat, usually up into the low 90s. Winters are usually in the 40s with one or two snowfalls in the dead of winter.

Read all of Vault's Law School Surveys at www.vault.com/lawschool — get complete surveys on top law schools, expert advice on applicaton essays, LSAT prep and more.

VAULT CAREER LIBRARY 595

 **Social Life**

Because of the location, students can travel into Colorado for skiing, into the Rocky Mountains, down to Mexico through El Paso, or head to Dallas, Austin or San Antonio, which are well within driving distance.

Texas Tech's facilities are outstanding. The law school was built in the early '70s, making it, for law schools, relatively new, but it reflects some of the Spanish design of the university, which was created in the 1920s. The IT department at Tech is strong and the school has a laptop policy that allows students to use part of their tuition to purchase laptops. The school also uses wireless Internet technology with in the school.

The law school is located directly across from "Spirit Arena" where the Red Raider's men and women basketball teams play: with Bobby Knight and Martha Sharp as head coaches, this is an excellent perk for the nationally known teams. The sports and fitness complex is co-located near the law school and while I was there, I would walk over and get a workout between classes. The complex was built in 2000 and is a state-of-the-art facility with aerobics, nautilus equipment, free weights, three basketball courts, 10 racquetball courts, an indoor running track and an Olympic pool that is open during certain hours for lap swimming and swimming classes.

> **Texas Tech says:** "The United Spirit Arena, or USA, hosts Big XII basketball action"

A unique feature of Tech are the student carrels. All law students receive a "carrel," which are located throughout the law school's library. These are small personal study rooms, with a desktop computer and overhead book shelves, that are shared by two students.

There is some on-campus housing for law students, but I am unfamiliar with it.

Lubbock Texas has the most dining locations per capita in Texas. There is no shortage of restaurants serving steaks, ethnic foods, buffets or popular franchises. Lubbock's economy allows money to go further than would occur in some larger metropolitan complexes, but Lubbock also serves as a focal point for many of the surrounding communities and is dubbed, "The Hub City."

The campus for Texas Tech is centrally located in this college town. Therefore, any apartment or house rented is within 10 to 15 minutes of the campus. The town enjoys a small town feel but has around a quarter million residents. Crime is very low and safety is high, although because of the extra-wide streets and young, college drivers mixing with local residents there are numerous traffic accidents. There is no violent crime on campus.

Status: Alumnus/a full-time
Dates of Enrollment: 1/1997-1/2000
Survey Submitted: August 2004

The law school physical plant gets passing marks but aging. (Built in 1972.) The computer network is slow and needs to be upgraded. No dining facility. Large 20 oz. soft drinks are $1.00 in the vending machine. Lockers are assigned to hold heavy law books so as not to have to lug around campus. Moderate size library but few current periodicals as they are expensive.

Status: Alumnus/a full-time
Dates of Enrollment: 8/1999-5/2002
Survey Submitted: September 2003

I can't imagine a better place to attend law school than Texas Tech as far as quality of life goes. Law school's pace is hectic. If you live in a big city, the pace of city life is equally hectic. Lubbock, Texas, forces you to slow down and breathe. No matter how crazy your schedule is at school, you always know that the checker at the grocery store is going to talk to you for 10 minutes before he or she will let you go home with your macaroni and cheese. I really think I would have had a much less successful law school experience if I had stayed in a large city like where I grew up.

In addition, Texas Tech has a lovely campus (it's a dead ringer for Stanford, even if it is in the middle of west Texas). The fact is, the university is the center of life for Lubbock. All the best restaurants are near campus, housing is comparatively cheap (I rented a four-bedroom house in a great neighborhood for $800 a month), and Lubbock is a very safe community.

Status: Current student, full-time
Dates of Enrollment: 8/2005-Submit Date
Survey Submitted: April 2006

There are dozens of organizations at the law school and plenty of opportunities for a social life outside the law school. There is also an organization (Law Partners) for spouses and significant others. The Hispanic Law Society is the biggest organization on campus and has all kinds of activities throughout the year.

Status: Alumnus/a full-time
Dates of Enrollment: 8/2001-5/2004
Survey Submitted: September 2005

Texas Tech Law students enjoy a rich social life through the many activities, clubs and facilities. Texas Tech is one of the few universities that has a co-located medical and law school. Somehow, barring the massive study, relationships form between the law and medical students. Texas Tech has a large undergraduate campus that has been well-developed in the ensuing 90 years of existence. Bars, microbreweries and eateries are available.

The Greek system is well-developed and all fraternities and sororities are represented in large numbers, with more than 140 student organizations (both graduate and undergraduate) listed on the Texas Tech Web. Within the law school, there are more than 24 student organizations, including the three main legal fraternities. I really enjoyed being part of Phi Alpha Delta, the largest fraternity within the law school and within the state of Texas with more than 100 members.

Status: Alumnus/a full-time
Dates of Enrollment: 1/1997-1/2000
Survey Submitted: August 2004

Most social life centers around Law Review and the Board of Barristers Trial Advocacy program, and the two law fraternities. Any drinking is in association with these activities or on competitions between law schools. 1Ls have no social life until grades are posted and a social pecking order is established as to who is in and who's not.

There is some dating but not much.

Status: Alumnus/a full-time
Dates of Enrollment: 8/1999-5/2002
Survey Submitted: September 2003

Social life at Tech Law is fabulous. In fact, my first year there, a class sold t-shirts that said, "Tech Law: We don't just pass the Bar, we practically live there." The law students play just as hard as they work. In addition, there was a traditional "Med-Mal weekend," where the law students and medical students got together for a picnic and party. This was popular with the law students, in part because the med school picked up the tab. Another popular event is the "100 days party," where graduating students have a huge party exactly 100 days before graduation. Also, what other law school can boast an annual chili cook-off? This usually coincides with Accepted Students Day, and it cemented my decision to attend Tech over other law schools in Texas.

There is a club for just about everything at Tech Law, from people who want to support the Second Amendment to a gay and lesbian group. If you have an interest, chances are, there's a club that will help you advance the interest.

Lubbock, by the way, has the cheapest alcohol I have ever seen. Bars cater to students, which means you can find a drink special every night of the week, and "two-penny pitchers" are common. Restaurants are equally plentiful, and Lubbock has surprisingly good fare. Not a lot of variety, but a lot of places to get good food at a great price.

Also, Texas Tech is a Big 12 school, which means great sporting events. Tickets for students are included in their tuition. Currently, all students taking at least four hours, including law and med students, pay $50 a semester, which gives them access to all sporting events on campus.

The School Says

Texas Tech University School of Law is a public institution located in Lubbock, Texas, on the main campus of Texas Tech University. The student body consisting of about 700 students enjoys full access to the amenities of a Big XII research institution. The program of study equips students to practice law as advocates, counselors, judges or law teachers, and the school recognizes that legal education is also a stepping-stone to careers in government, politics, or business. The required curriculum, coupled with a nationally recognized Legal Practice Program, provide a broad-based legal education to ensure success wherever our alumni decide to work. The Law and Science Certificate Program, eight joint degree programs and elective courses afford students the opportunity to create an area of concentration suited for their professional goals.

Housed within a newly-remodeled facility are five legal clinics allowing law students to represent clients in mediation proceedings as well as state and federal courts. Soon to arrive is the Mark and Becky Lanier Professional Development Center. The 34,000+ square foot addition will house a state-of-the-art courtroom, 300-seat auditorium, student organization and faculty offices and conference rooms. The facility will permit the law school to continue hosting legal education programs and visiting dignitaries such as Supreme Court Justice Clarence Thomas and Karen Tandy, Class of '77, Administrator of the Drug Enforcement Agency. It will also serve as the training ground for a nationally recognized advocacy program.

Students will find a cooperative spirit exists among their peers. With well over three dozen student organizations, the range of activities and events are just as diverse as the student body. The low student-to-faculty ratio (16.6:1) permits faculty to embrace a true "open-door" policy, enabling students to engage in continuing dialogue beyond formal class hours. A comprehensive academic support program exists to assist all students in achieving their highest potential. An expanded career services office, and new development and alumni relations office will pave the way to locating placement upon graduation through national job fairs and on campus interviewing events. Moreover, innovative programs such as regional interviewing events allows students to travel to major Texas cities to interview with small-to-medium sized law firms that typically do not make campus visits. Such efforts have led to a 98 percent employment rate (within six months of graduation) in recent years. Those results are not surprising given the consistent high bar passage rate.

A 2005 survey conducted by Coldwell Banker named Lubbock the most affordable college town. With a tuition rate of $12,929 for residents and $20,319 for out-of-state students, it is easy to see why the law school is considered by many to be the best "bang for your buck" within the State of Texas. Out-of-state students need not worry because the law school's Out-of-State Tuition Waiver Program will allow qualifying individuals to receive the significantly lower tuition rates enjoyed by residents.

Students interested in learning more about Texas Tech University School of Law may contact the Admissions Office at lawadmissions@ttu.edu or (806) 742-3990, ext. 273.

Read all of Vault's Law School Surveys at www.vault.com/lawschool — get complete surveys on top law schools, expert advice on applicaton essays, LSAT prep and more.

VAULT CAREER LIBRARY **597**

Texas Wesleyan University School of Law

Office of Admissions
1515 Commerce Street
Fort Worth, TX 76102
Admissions phone (817) 212-4040
Admissions e-mail: lawadmissions@law.txwes.edu
URL: http://law.txwes.edu/

 Admissions

Status: Current student, full-time
Dates of Enrollment: 8/2004-Submit Date
Survey Submitted: March 2006

Paper applications can be requested online or applicants can submit applications on the law school's web site. The Wesleyan Law application requires individuals to provide basic background information, and it also requires a personal statement. Because scholarships are given out on a rolling basis, those applying to Wesleyan should send in their applications early so as to procure the greatest possible scholarship amount.

Although not as selective as some other Texas law schools, Wesleyan Law maintains high academic standards, and it places a large emphasis on undergraduate transcripts. LSAT scores are also considered, and the median score has continued to rise since the school's inception.

Status: Current student, full-time
Dates of Enrollment: 8/2002-Submit Date
Survey Submitted: August 2004

A potential student can apply online by clicking on a link from the law school's web site. The admissions standards are becoming increasingly higher, as applications are reaching an all time high (over 2,000 for around 250 spots). Like many law schools, the admissions committee balances a candidate's LSAT score, undergraduate school and GPA, and life experiences (as demonstrated through the applicant's personal statement). The school also likes two letters of recommendation.

There is no formal interview; however, potential students are encouraged to visit the law school and sit in on a class if possible. The current application fee is $55.

Status: Current student, full-time
Dates of Enrollment: 8/2004-Submit Date
Survey Submitted: January 2005

The good thing is that the admissions office is small and easy to deal with—thanks to the staff. The university is timely as to getting back to you on whether you have been accepted—particularly compared to other schools. Competition is average to medium—I don't think the median LSAT exceeds 153.

> **Texas Wesleyan says:** "The median LSAT is now 154."

Status: Alumnus/a, full-time
Dates of Enrollment: 9/2000-5/2003
Survey Submitted: January 2005

The admissions process was similar to that of other law schools in Texas. Wesleyan requires a completed application, essay and LSAT score before making a decision. The key to getting in is to make sure that your application and essay reflect something unique about you and demonstrates, not only your potential for success, but also that you have the determination to succeed.

The school is selective and recent GPAs and LSAT scores have increased. The school does not interview per se, but they offer several admissions open house programs and orientation programs that allow you to meet the faculty and see how the school operates. The one thing that helped Texas Wesleyan to stand out from all other schools is that the dean of the school personally called to welcome

me upon my acceptance to the school and offered his home phone number if I had any questions in regard to making my decision.

 Academics

Status: Current student, full-time
Dates of Enrollment: 8/2004-Submit Date
Survey Submitted: March 2006

The academic program at Wesleyan Law is quite rigorous, and the professors are all exceptional. The professors are enthusiastic about the law, and their experience and knowledge is effectively conveyed to students. The professors are also easily accessible outside of class.

Generally speaking, the workload is intense. During the 1L year, a new student can expect to spend upwards of two hours per class per night. The workload during the subsequent two years of law school is less daunting, but the expectations of the professors remain high. Additionally, due to the number of extracurricular activities offered by the law school, 2L and 3L students can expect to spend an increasing amount of time on law school classes and activities during their last two years on campus.

In regards to obtaining desired classes, Wesleyan Law is very accommodating to students, and the school allows students to design their own schedules after 1L year. During the 1L year students will take a pre-determined schedule of core classes including Contracts, Torts, Property, Criminal Law, Legal Writing and Research and Civil Procedure. Constitutional Law is required during the first semester of 2L year. Beginning with 2L year, students can create their own class schedules, though there are still a number of required courses that must be fit into the student's law school career. These courses include Estates and Trusts, Evidence, Business Associations, Criminal Procedure and Professional Responsibility. Although some of these classes may fill up quickly, students can add their names to a waitlist or opt to complete the course during a different semester. A number of other recommend courses and elective options round out the law school curriculum, and the school helps students to design a course schedule that provides the broadest possible coverage in preparation for the bar exam.

Status: Current student, full-time
Dates of Enrollment: 8/2002-Submit Date
Survey Submitted: August 2004

The law school offers a variety of courses; however, not all are offered every semester. Most 1L classes (and some upper-division classes) are taught primarily through the use of the Socratic Method. Most upper-division classes, while still implementing the Socratic Method, begin to focus more on teaching students the practical aspects behind the material. Some popular classes can be difficult to get, primarily due to the school's expansion project that limits the space currently available. However, the project will be complete in 2005, and I expect that more classrooms, coupled with the increase in faculty, will mean that popular classes will be easier to get into.

> **The school says:** "The renovation was completed in fall 2005."

Every professor I have had has been outstanding. The school's faculty is diverse, and most hold degrees from Ivy League schools. One noticeable difference is that Wesleyan's professors know how to teach. Wesleyan's professors were ranked Number One in Texas for quality of classroom instruction by *The Texas Lawyer* last year.

Grading, of course, can be quite subjective, as almost all exams are purely essay based. There is only one exam per class, so exam time can be a crunch. While grading is subjective depending on the nature of the exams, the professors seem to be very fair (of course, all grading is purely anonymous).

The workload, like at any law school, can be very time consuming. Usually, one is expected to read the material prior to class, be prepared to flesh it out in class, organize it into an outline after class, and then memorize it for the exam. Some of my personal outlines have ranged from 200 to 300 pages per class, but each student approaches study techniques differently. I learned my first year that if I treated it like a 50 hour a week job and kept set hours, I was always on top of everything, and I could go into the finals time by extending these "set hours," and focusing purely on studying, as there was no new material to cover.

Status: Alumnus/a, full-time
Dates of Enrollment: 9/2000-5/2003
Survey Submitted: January 2005

The academic program was quite rigorous and intense. The first-year classes were mostly required courses so there was not much latitude in the types of classes a first-year could take, however, the school did what it could to accommodate students that had scheduling conflicts, such as small children or an ill parent. It was fairly easy to get the classes you wanted in the second and third years and you were allowed to take up to the maximum number of credits if you wanted to finish the program early. A full-time program usually requires about 16 hours of class time and 30 hours of study time outside of class per week. The grading is scaled, therefore, only a certain percentage of students will get A's, B's, C's. The professors are highly knowledgeable in their respective subject areas, and almost all have an open-door policy with respect to students.

Status: Current student, full-time
Dates of Enrollment: 8/2004-Submit Date
Survey Submitted: January 2005

The professors were, in general, OK. Most employ the Socratic Method and particularly for Civil Procedure, it is expected that you be prepared for class. The exams were mainly essay. The curve is not particularly pretty, especially in Legal Analysis, Research and Writing. Forget everything you know about style, vocabulary and lyrical sounds. Just be concise and organized. Don't expect your grades to come in quickly. We're still waiting on ours, and it's the week before second semester starts.

Employment Prospects

Status: Current student, full-time
Dates of Enrollment: 8/2004-Submit Date
Survey Submitted: March 2006

Employment opportunities are abundant at Wesleyan, especially for those who rank in the top of their class. A number of my colleagues have received job offers from major Texas and national law firms. Others have opted to pursue careers and internship opportunities with a variety of public interest groups. A large faction of Wesleyan students also pursue opportunities with the Dallas public defenders office and with the Tarrant County and Dallas D.A. Wesleyan Law students are quite successful in private practice as well.

The career services office keeps an updated list of job postings on the law school web site, and it offers opportunities for on-campus interviews. On-campus interviews are especially popular for those seeking jobs with large law firms and the government. Postings about career fairs are mailed out to students frequently, so there is ample opportunity for law students to find employment in the field of their choice.

Status: Current student, full-time
Dates of Enrollment: 8/2002-Submit Date
Survey Submitted: August 2004

The school has an externship program, that can be a good opportunity for student's to gain some practical experience, and perhaps open doors for a career with the firm with whom they extern. Campus recruiting has traditionally been lower than what was expected and hoped for, but it is improving.

Employers treat the school differently than others, most likely due in part to the fact that the school is so new in comparison to others. This means that students may have to do some ground work on their own, and educate some employers about the program. However, there have been many successful students in my

class, seeking out and obtaining positions with topnotch law firms in the DFW area, and out of state.

The career services department is working hard, and relationships with employers are improving drastically. Once an employer hires a Wesleyan student, they quickly seem to learn that they can compete with anyone else from anywhere else. Student's are just now getting that opportunity, which will likely open the door for future students.

The school notes: "The school is 17 years old."

Status: Alumnus/a, full-time
Dates of Enrollment: 9/2000-5/2003
Survey Submitted: January 2005

Many of the students have gone on to work for some of the area's top law firms, the attorney general's office and the district attorney's office, the military JAG programs, as well as in private practice for themselves. The career services department has made significant progress in bringing top name firms and great opportunities to the students through on-campus interviewing and internships or externships.

Status: Current student, full-time
Dates of Enrollment: 8/2004-Submit Date
Survey Submitted: January 2005

The 2Ls have been surprisingly helpful.

Quality of Life

Status: Current student, full-time
Dates of Enrollment: 8/2004-Submit Date
Survey Submitted: March 2006

The law school campus is located in downtown Fort Worth, across from the Convention Center and Water Gardens. There is no housing on the law school campus, itself, but Wesleyan (undergraduate university campus) offers housing to law students who are interested. While the undergraduate campus is not situated in the safest area of Fort Worth, I have not had any safety concerns as a law student at the downtown campus.

The campus itself is small, but exceptional. The entire law school campus has wireless Internet access. There are two computer labs, but the school is also very laptop friendly (outlets near every classroom seat). The library is newly renovated, and it houses a large quantity of legal texts and information. There are two courtrooms (one trial and one appellate) designed for use by moot court and trial advocacy groups. Finally, there are a number of offices for student organizations and campus groups.

Because of its downtown location, there are a number of dining options nearby (short driving distance). There is also a hotel restaurant next door to the law school that offers a lunch time buffet.

Status: Current student, full-time
Dates of Enrollment: 8/2002-Submit Date
Survey Submitted: August 2004

The law school is located in downtown Fort Worth, away from the main campus. Most students, including myself, have never even visited the main campus. There is no school housing; however, there are many, many nice and affordable housing opportunities (from apartments, to townhouses, houses and rentals) available within a 15-minute drive.

Fort Worth is a great environment. It has a large, growing, diverse, but tight legal community. It is a big city with a true small town feel (less traffic, Sundance Square, incredible theater, an arts and cultural district, fine dining, shopping for all budgets, and it is home to many large companies, including Pier One and Radio Shack).

The school, located directly across from the new Tarrant County Convention Center and Water Gardens, is in the process of a total renovation. The library will soon occupy the entire basement, more than tripling the shelf space; larger, more technologically savvy classrooms are being built on the main and second

Read all of Vault's Law School Surveys at www.vault.com/lawschool — get complete surveys on top law schools, expert advice on applicaton essays, LSAT prep and more.

VAULT CAREER LIBRARY   599

floor. Student organizations will be officed along the same hallway, and a new student lounge promises to be relaxing.

The school says: "The renovation was completed in fall 2005."

Status: Alumnus/a, full-time
Dates of Enrollment: 9/2000-5/2003
Survey Submitted: January 2005

The school is located at the east end of downtown Fort Worth across from the convention center. The school is contained within its own building and has several parking lots for student and faculty parking. It is accessible to Bass Hall Performance center, several theaters and restaurants and the nightlife of Sundance Square. I lived away off campus in my own home so I cannot comment on campus housing or neighborhood issues.

Status: Current student, full-time
Dates of Enrollment: 8/2004-Submit Date
Survey Submitted: January 2005

The school is hardly scenic; it's in the middle of downtown and at present, there's one building (that's the whole law school). If you like compact and efficient, you won't mind. One of the best points of the school is that it allows students to attend part-time and offers a night-class schedule.

Social Life

Status: Current student, full-time
Dates of Enrollment: 8/2004-Submit Date
Survey Submitted: March 2006

Wesleyan Law students LOVE Malone's, a bar across the street from the law school campus. You can find students at Malone's after class, in the evenings and on weekends. If Malone's is open, there are probably law students present.

Overall, the social scene at Wesleyan is quite active. The students aren't overly competitive in class, so everyone seems to get along well outside of the law school environment. A number of students are known to host frat-like parties at their homes, so if you are looking for a good time in law school, you can definitely find it at Wesleyan.

Status: Current student, full-time
Dates of Enrollment: 8/2002-Submit Date
Survey Submitted: August 2004

The school is located so close to Sundance Square that students can walk a short distance to be in the heart of downtown and have every kind of bar, restaurant and shopping experience the city has to offer. Some favorite student spots include The Library (a bar), 8.0's (a bar and dance club), the Flying Saucer (a bar), Barnes & Noble and Bass Performance Hall (a theater). If a closer walk is sought, Malone's (a bar) is across the street and down one block.

Student organizations range from political to academic, to social, to charitable to niche practice groups.

The student body participates in many Tarrant County Younger Lawyer's events, and many Tarrant and Dallas County Bar events.

Status: Alumnus/a, full-time
Dates of Enrollment: 9/2000-5/2003
Survey Submitted: January 2005

As a married student with children, I did not have much of a social life in law school. That said, there were group events sponsored by the various student clubs, such as parking lot barbecues before exam week, soup kitchen luncheons to raise funds for the local women's shelter and regular happy hours at Malone's (bar), which was everyone's favorite. The school also has several law fraternities, such as Phila Alpha Delta, and other law-related organizations such as the Women's Law Student Association, Black Law Students Association, Hispanic Law Students Association, Christian Law Students Association and Jewish Law Students Association, to name a few.

Status: Current student, full-time
Dates of Enrollment: 8/2004-Submit Date
Survey Submitted: January 2005

Bars...

The School Says

In its short 17-year history, Texas Wesleyan School of Law has provided excellence in legal education to traditional day-time students, as well as nontraditional night-time students. The increasing success in Texas Wesleyan's bar passage rate is a reflection of our continued effort to emphasize service to a diverse student body, the profession and the community. The February 2006 bar passage performance ranked the law school fourth among Texas' nine law schools. Only Baylor, Southern Methodist University and the University of Texas turned in better performances.

Over the last three years, the school has also seen a rise in the quantity and quality of students. Applications have doubled, median LSAT scores have risen from 149 to 154 and median undergraduate GPAs have risen from 3.0 to 3.19. Last year alone, there were approximately 2,000 applicants vying for one of the 240 open seats, a true testament to the increasing quality of education at Texas Wesleyan law school.

Students are now enjoying the increased technology and comfort of the recent $6 million renovation to the law school. The additional library study space, as well as new classrooms, multiple students areas and a new auditorium has enhanced all aspects of the academic program. Along with the school's downtown location, Texas Wesleyan allows students to study law in an exciting atmosphere.

If you've been considering a career in law, we encourage you to explore your possibilities at Texas Wesleyan. Call (817) 429-8050 for an application and portfolio, or visit our web site at law.txwes.edu and apply online.

University of Houston Law Center

Office of Admissions
100 Law Center
Houston, TX 77204-6060
Admissions phone: (713) 743-2280
Admissions e-mail: lawadmissions@uh.edu.
Admissions URL: http://www.law.uh.edu/admissions/

 Admissions

Status: Current student, full-time
Dates of Enrollment: 8/2004-Submit Date
Survey Submitted: September 2005

U of H is not too difficult to get into. However, the professors and student body are sharp. I think that as with most schools the LSAT and GPA are key, which can be irritating as an applicant, but it is basically the same system to find a legal job. Firms look at your GPA and class rank to determine whether you are qualified. Therefore, the admission process mirrors the job search process. I did not realize this until I started law school.

Status: Current student, part-time
Dates of Enrollment: 5/2002-Submit Date
Survey Submitted: April 2005

The admissions process was easy for me but that was because the school admitted almost 400 students that year. It was also the year after tropical storm Allison, so the school was still a mess and construction was going on. The cynical view is that the school admitted more students to pay for it. The more realistic view is that admissions numbers were up all over the country and no one expected as many people to accept and attend as did.

I provided two statements plus the other required transcripts and documentation. I used the same essay that I had used for the other three schools that I applied to. My GPA was in the top 75 percent for the incoming class and my LSAT was between the 25th and 50th percentile (3.72 and 155). I had no trouble getting in. However, since that time the admissions process was tightened up. According to the latest *U.S. News & World Report*, we had an overall acceptance rate of 22 percent.

My admissions process was also somewhat unique because I was applying for the part-time program which is especially popular among engineers interested in the school's intellectual property program and the acceptance rate has always been lower than that of the full-time program.

Status: Alumnus/a, full-time
Dates of Enrollment: 8/1999-8/2003
Survey Submitted: April 2006

East to get into, for a law school. LSAT scores do not have to be particularly high; neither do undergrad grades. It is very cheap, too, for a law school. Of course, if you have the grades and LSAT scores, I believe UT Law costs the same. I did not have to interview, although I'm sure people can if they choose. I don't recall the essay process, although a friend of mine assures me that one was required. The year I was admitted was immediately following a major flood here in Houston, so the school admitted about 100 extra students to help make some extra money. It was also shortly after the Enron disaster, so applications were way up.

> **The school says:** "The UH Law Center does not offer interviews as part of the admissions process."

Status: Alumnus/a, full- and part-time
Dates of Enrollment: 5/2001-5/2005
Survey Submitted: March 2006

Application, LSAT scores, essay required. Takes average scores or above.

Status: Alumnus/a, full-time
Dates of Enrollment: 8/2001-5/2004
Survey Submitted: April 2005

Pretty easy—no interviews, just standard admissions. Your LSAT score is the most important thing.

> **Regarding admissions requirements, UH Law Center says:**
> "Every applicant to the UH Law Center receives a full-file review, and no single factor in the review process is determinative of an admissions decision. LSAT and GPA are important, but the admissions committee also places emphasis on the personal statement."

Status: Alumnus/a, full-time
Dates of Enrollment: 5/2000-12/2003
Survey Submitted: March 2005

Like many law schools, the University of Houston focuses mainly on the GPA and LSAT index. No interview exists. Thus, the essays are the only opportunity to communicate information outside of the application information.

Status: Alumnus/a, full-time
Dates of Enrollment: 8/2000-5/2003
Survey Submitted: March 2005

As a candidate admitted to Top 10 ranked schools, I was awarded a full scholarship based on prior academic credentials and experience. The admissions office was friendly and easy to deal with.

Status: Alumnus/a, full-time
Dates of Enrollment: 8/1992-5/1995
Survey Submitted: March 2005

Typical entrance application, with essay. Moderately selective, used LSAT scores substantially, but they do look at post-college experience.

Status: Alumnus/a, full-time
Dates of Enrollment: 9/2000-5/2003
Survey Submitted: March 2005

It's difficult to get in—this is the best school in the city, but not the state.

Status: Alumnus/a, full-time
Dates of Enrollment: 9/2001-5/2004
Survey Submitted: April 2005

Selectivity has increased since the increase in applications following the downturn of the economy. Admissions seems hit or miss as some "less qualified" applicants win out over those that have better undergraduate grades and LSAT scores. Diversity recruiting is (evidently) nonexistent.

Status: Alumnus/a, full-time
Dates of Enrollment: 9/1990-5/1993
Survey Submitted: April 2004

The admissions process was fairly thorough, yet fair. A many-page application was filled out, which included an essay on "why I want to go to law school." The whole selection process was based on your college grades and your LSAT score. The application and essay helped the university to decide where they should place you in their curriculum. I'm sure the essay also decided any tie-breakers. The people selected for my first-year class were very diverse. We had newly graduated college students that were single, married people deciding on a new career for more money and those that just wanted a change of occupation.

Read all of Vault's Law School Surveys at www.vault.com/lawschool — get complete surveys on top law schools, expert advice on applicaton essays, LSAT prep and more.

V∧ULT CAREER LIBRARY   **601**

Academics

Status: Current student, full-time
Dates of Enrollment: 8/2004-Submit Date
Survey Submitted: September 2005

The first year is like other schools—you're divided into sections and have all classes with the same students. Therefore there is no ability to choose professors or subjects. I enjoyed most of my first-year courses, particularly Constitutional Law and Torts. Registering after your first year is an interesting system that depends on the last four digits of your social security number. If it begins with a nine, every other semester you may register first and every other you register last. A five always registers in the middle. Popular classes do fill up quickly, so this system does not work for everybody.

The workload at UH is like any other quality law school. There's a lot of it. At the same time, it does not have to be all-consuming. I was able to have fun my first year. Whoever said that the first year is the worst though has misled many students, as the first semester of the second year has been much more chaotic—with interviews and journal work in addition to classes.

Status: Alumnus/a, full-time
Dates of Enrollment: 8/1999-8/2003
Survey Submitted: April 2006

Overall, U of H Law is a good value. It is an inexpensive program, and there is a strong focus on practical education. The more popular classes are often difficult to get into; however, many of the classes are prioritized for certain students. Grading seemed as fair as any other grading process. Those who can write well will do better in probably any law program. Workload is manageable, especially if you can read quickly. I have a family and attended full-time, commuting in from the Houston suburbs. Because I read quickly, I had no real trouble keeping up with my classes.

Status: Alumnus/a, full- and part-time
Dates of Enrollment: 5/2001-5/2005
Survey Submitted: March 2006

Highly regarded for Health Law and Intellectual Property programs (Top Five nationally). Diverse evening offerings (especially IP) for part-time students. Excellent professors, little problem getting classes desired. Grading is typical law curve-type grading.

Status: Alumnus/a, full-time
Dates of Enrollment: 5/2000-12/2003
Survey Submitted: March 2005

The professors are the best part of University of Houston law school. For the most part, they teach well and care about the students.

Status: Alumnus/a, full-time
Dates of Enrollment: 8/1992-5/1995
Survey Submitted: March 2005

I never had a problem getting into any class I wanted to attend. Most professors were quite good, and several were exceptional. First year was on a fixed schedule and section, thereafter it was more like college. You picked the classes you wanted and just had to get enough credits to graduate. Professors were extremely accessible and willing to assist.

Status: Alumnus/a, full-time
Dates of Enrollment: 5/2000-5/2002
Survey Submitted: March 2005

Excellent programs in intellectual property law. Topnotch IP professors who are willing to go the extra mile in their teaching.

Status: Alumnus/a, full-time
Dates of Enrollment: 8/2000-5/2003
Survey Submitted: March 2005

The quality is generally very good—particularly in contracts, intellectual property and immigration law. A few of the professors were duds—but not many. Now that I'm practicing law, I still see (and am on speaking terms with) a handful of my former professors. To do well, the workload is heavy—

particularly if you have a responsible journal editing position (which, in hindsight, is well worth the effort!).

Status: Alumnus/a, full-time
Dates of Enrollment: 9/2001-5/2004
Survey Submitted: April 2005

First-year classes are more difficult than second- and third-year classes, as would be expected. U of H has MANY adjunct professors and TOO MANY evening classes. Even being a full-time student, you will find it difficult to fill a schedule that doesn't have you going late in the evening at least two nights a week. U of H does this to accommodate its part-time program.

Registration fills quickly for the most popular professors on "core" classes, but otherwise, it's relatively easy to get in. U of H's curve is more competitive with UT than it used to be—the curve is a 3.0 to 3.2 now.

Status: Alumnus/a, full-time
Dates of Enrollment: 9/2000-5/2003
Survey Submitted: March 2005

Middle of the road, a few stellar professors, especially the first year. Generally, the professors care.

Status: Alumnus/a, full-time
Dates of Enrollment: 9/1990-5/1993
Survey Submitted: April 2004

I believe the University of Houston law school is one of the best programs in Texas. The quality of the classes was superb. Due to the size of the law school, it was easy to get the classes you wanted, (except for summer school classes—the best teachers tended to fill quickly) and the quality of most, if not all, of my classes was excellent.

Grading was difficult. As everyone at the law school was smart, the grading was tough. However, the majority of my class pulled through and all have careers at this time. The workload was heavy but that is to be expected in a law school curriculum.

Status: Current student, part-time
Dates of Enrollment: 5/2002-Submit Date
Survey Submitted: April 2005

I personally have not found U of H to be that tough. However, that is coming from someone who made Law Review based on grades alone. I stopped talking to professors about how they graded after the second exam because it made little sense. However, I would urge any student to pay close attention to what the professors say they want because they mean it. I know of one student who didn't receive credit for information she wrote because it was beyond the space provided.

Popular classes can be difficult to get into. Also, when I say "popular," I do not necessarily mean a particular class but rather a particular professor. Classes like Professional Responsibility, Evidence and Business Organizations will often have three sections all offered at the same time. Students will all try to get in one section. My advice is to be careful about selecting the class based on the professor. Some of the professors at U of H have very different styles of exams.

I feel that the workload at U of H is perfectly manageable with the exception of one or two professors who do not seem to realize that you cannot read an entire book in one or two nights. If you are going to enter the part-time program, be prepared to read about 70 to 90 pages every night for your first class (Civil Procedure). However, the good news is that it will be the most brutal class you will ever have to take.

Employment Prospects

Status: Current student, full-time
Dates of Enrollment: 8/2004-Submit Date
Survey Submitted: September 2005

Houston firms hire from UH. Other cities—not quite as much. UH, of course, does not have the same prestige as does UT. Therefore, in order to be an attractive potential for a firm, it is important to make good grades here. Some firms might look at the top 20 percent at a more competitive private school, but only the top 10 percent from UH. Many of my friends who have done well here have gotten offers with large, competitive firms. You just have to study hard while in law school and do well. This is true anywhere.

Status: Alumnus/a, full-time
Dates of Enrollment: 8/1999-8/2003
Survey Submitted: April 2006

If you're looking for a job in Houston, you'll be able to find one with a law degree from U of H. I would expect it would be much harder to find a job outside of Houston, but I haven't looked. Because we aren't one of the top-tiered schools (and continue to drop in the rankings), it is probably difficult to find an employer in another large city, particularly one with a good local law school. Alumni are supportive, and there are many employed throughout Texas. On-campus recruiting did not work well for me, but I have several friends who had success through it.

Status: Alumnus/a, full- and part-time
Dates of Enrollment: 5/2001-5/2005
Survey Submitted: March 2006

Due to prestige in IP/health law, it helps those in IP or health law. Otherwise, only local firms will recruit graduates. Tough for those wanting to leave the state unless in those two programs or rank in top 10 percent. On-campus recruiting is typically Texas firms, and they typically only recruit the top 25 percent.

Status: Alumnus/a, full-time
Dates of Enrollment: 5/2000-12/2003
Survey Submitted: March 2005

Someone graduating with good grades from the University of Houston can work at any law firm. I had no problem getting job offers from the same firms that hired Harvard and Yale graduates (as was the case for many of my classmates in the top 10 percent of our class).

Status: Alumnus/a, full-time
Dates of Enrollment: 8/2000-5/2003
Survey Submitted: March 2005

Houston is a great legal market, and U of H offers a vast legal network of former students currently associated with prestigious firms here. On-campus interviewing and BigLaw jobs generally are reserved for the top 10 to 20 percent—working hard as a 1L pays off! These graduates have a choice of positions. As for the rest—I don't know of a single classmate who did not find a legal job within a few months of graduation (who wanted one).

Status: Current student, part-time
Dates of Enrollment: 5/2002-Submit Date
Survey Submitted: April 2005

If you don't make Law Review or the *International Law Journal*, watch out. You had better do as many other things as you can, such as moot court, mock trial, negotiations competition and whatever else you can. Most of the employment opportunities for U of H students come from the local community, so don't think you can go to U of H and end up just anywhere. I know of only a handful of students with out-of-state clerkships and they are going to big cities, like NY, L.A. and Atlanta.

Status: Alumnus/a, full-time
Dates of Enrollment: 5/2000-5/2002
Survey Submitted: March 2005

I received several offers from topnotch firms as a patent litigation associate.

Status: Alumnus/a, full-time
Dates of Enrollment: 8/1992-5/1995
Survey Submitted: March 2005

I think UH is highly esteemed in the Houston area—perhaps the second behind UT for Texas schools.

Status: Alumnus/a, full-time
Dates of Enrollment: 8/2001-5/2004
Survey Submitted: April 2005

As far as getting a job in Houston, you are OK.

Status: Alumnus/a, full-time
Dates of Enrollment: 9/1990-5/1993
Survey Submitted: April 2004

The University of Houston law school is considered an excellent starting place. I applied to be an assistant district attorney upon graduation from law school but before passing the bar. I was hired temporarily as a "precommit." Only 10 precommits were hired, seven of which were from the University of Houston. Upon my approval of being hired as an official assistant district attorney, over half were from the University of Houston.

Quality of Life

Status: Current student, full-time
Dates of Enrollment: 8/2004-Submit Date
Survey Submitted: September 2005

Quality of life is fair—the neighborhood is awful and the facilities are pretty dismal too. Very few people brave the on-campus living, and I could not be paid to live there. Although I have not heard of many problems with crime. The building has a dungeon-like feel to it and has few (any?) windows. It's dark, and a lot of it is underground.

Status: Alumnus/a, full-time
Dates of Enrollment: 8/1999-8/2003
Survey Submitted: April 2006

The Law Center is located in the armpit of the University of Houston campus. U of H is not in a particularly nice part of town. However, there are some really pretty parts to the campus; just not near the Law Center. If you get a chance, head over to the Fine Arts/Music school—much prettier than the area immediately surrounding the law school. Also, parking SUCKS. It is very difficult to get a convenient spot and you need to plan to arrive at least 20 minutes before class to even have a chance of scoring one of the few available spots. Be careful when heading off campus. Like most state schools that I'm familiar with, the university is not located in prime real estate.

Status: Alumnus/a, full- and part-time
Dates of Enrollment: 5/2001-5/2005
Survey Submitted: March 2006

Facilities are dated. Due for a new building. Parking is hard during the day with the MBA school next door.

Status: Alumnus/a, full-time
Dates of Enrollment: 8/1992-5/1995
Survey Submitted: March 2005

There are several, well-respected bar journals. The area of town is not the best. Most options are in Central and West Houston.

Status: Alumnus/a, full-time
Dates of Enrollment: 9/2001-5/2004
Survey Submitted: April 2005

From what I have heard, U of H has noticeably less competitive atmosphere. There is no on-campus housing for law students. Therefore, all of the students are commuters. When I attended, this caused some problems with parking. And unless you like to eat Subway everyday, there is no food to speak of.

Status: Alumnus/a, full-time
Dates of Enrollment: 5/2000-12/2003
Survey Submitted: March 2005

The University of Houston is planning on building a brand-new law center building on account of the damage that was caused by tropical storm Allison in 2001.

Status: Alumnus/a, full-time
Dates of Enrollment: 5/2000-5/2002
Survey Submitted: March 2005

Low cost of living, great in-state tuition. The school itself was flooded while I was there so there was a large amount of construction taking place.

Status: Alumnus/a, full-time

Read all of Vault's Law School Surveys at www.vault.com/lawschool — get complete surveys on top law schools, expert advice on applicaton essays, LSAT prep and more.

VAULT CAREER LIBRARY **603**

Dates of Enrollment: 8/2000-5/2003
Survey Submitted: March 2005

University of Houston Law School is an excellent commuter school—many who enter already have had another career. Some students enter right out of undergrad or grad school, but many others have some life experience, as well. While on-campus life probably is lacking, if that's what you're looking for, there are many convenient and safe places to stay in Houston from which you can commute.

Status: Alumnus/a, full-time
Dates of Enrollment: 8/1992-5/1995
Survey Submitted: March 2005

No on-campus housing to speak of, but there are lots of options in Houston. Campus life is good. First-year sections stick together, then other groups, bar journals and others provide good relationship opportunities with students. Every other week they have "arbitration" on the patio with free beer and many professors attend.

Status: Alumnus/a, full-time
Dates of Enrollment: 9/2000-5/2003
Survey Submitted: March 2005

Good. Although the dean has curtailed student drinking on campus, there is still good interaction. There is a good mix of ages and experiences.

Status: Alumnus/a, full-time
Dates of Enrollment: 9/1990-5/1993
Survey Submitted: April 2004

The University of Houston provided a very safe campus. I never felt ill at ease or afraid there and often would have to walk the law school campus out to my car at late hours. No one from the law school lived on campus but the facilities to accommodate us during our long days at school were good. We had several lounge areas, a very nice cafeteria with plenty of choices and private cubicles where we could study.

Status: Current student, full-time
Dates of Enrollment: 5/2002-Submit Date
Survey Submitted: April 2005

The wide expanse of [still insufficient] parking and its location in Houston's Third Ward makes U of H a wonderful target for car thieves and robbers. This problem is exacerbated because of the lack of parking in reasonable proximity to the law center. Many students end up parking near the business or architecture schools if they arrive after 9:30 a.m.

Social Life

Status: Current student, full-time
Dates of Enrollment: 8/2004-Submit Date
Survey Submitted: September 2005

Socially I enjoy UH. The other students are friendly and fun. We have happy hours regularly. Hot spots include the Flying Saucer downtown, the Marquee over on Bissonnet, and bars in the Village (Gingerman, Brian O'Neills). Additionally there are occasional tournaments—softball and football—that are really fun. The Student Bar Association puts these on and brings kegs, which are included in the registration fee. I've been surprised by how many students meet and date here. I am actually one of them. It's nice to be with somebody who understands the need to study and is willing to stay at home and do so on a Friday or Saturday night if necessary.

Status: Alumnus/a, full- and part-time
Dates of Enrollment: 5/2001-5/2005
Survey Submitted: March 2006

Minimal (especially for part-timers).

Status: Alumnus/a, full-time
Dates of Enrollment: 9/1990-5/1993
Survey Submitted: April 2004

There was always something to do as a law student at the University of Houston. One of our favorite events was on Thursdays. There was an "arbitration" on campus where the students chipped in to buy kegs of beer and everyone got to relax, mingle and meet students from other sections of their class, as well as older or younger students. This was a great time to meet new friends or mentors. Also many social groups were defined or expanded during this time.

Status: Current student, part-time
Dates of Enrollment: 5/2002-Submit Date
Survey Submitted: April 2005

The Student Bar Association (SBA) hosts "arbitrations" (that's legalese for a keg party) for students about once a month, generally on Thursday evenings (students are scarce on Fridays). If you are a full-time student, the social life is good. Houston has plenty of bars and restaurants. Downtown Houston (Flying Saucer, Mercury Room) and the Rice Village (O'Neills, Two Rows) are popular hangouts.

Status: Alumnus/a, full-time
Dates of Enrollment: 8/2001-5/2004
Survey Submitted: April 2005

None—unless the students instigate it because there are no neighborhood bars that are safe or desirable to go to around the school.

Status: Alumnus/a, full-time
Dates of Enrollment: 9/2001-5/2004
Survey Submitted: April 2005

Because it is a commuter school, social events are off campus and scheduled through organizations or your first-year section. There are plenty of opportunities to socialize, if you really want to be around those same people for any longer!

Status: Alumnus/a, full-time
Dates of Enrollment: 5/2000-12/2003
Survey Submitted: March 2005

The University of Houston is located in the fourth most populated city in the U.S. As such, there is no shortage of activities and venues for any interest.

Status: Alumnus/a, full-time
Dates of Enrollment: 5/2000-5/2002
Survey Submitted: March 2005

Many opportunities to socialize with your peers at sports events, bars, restaurants, clubs and parties.

The School Says

Let's get right to the heart of the matter. You're looking for a respected law school that can provide you with a great education, rewarding student experiences and a high-value education that will launch your career as a skilled professional without bankrupting you.

The UH Law Center is that school. Here's why.

It starts with our faculty. Our professors are leaders in their fields of expertise, and they blend groundbreaking scholarship with an innate love of teaching. You will learn from the best, and you will be challenged in every one of your courses. That's what great law school do: they ask you to work hard as they transform you into the best lawyer you can be.

What will define your "student experience" at law school? We have a diverse student body, a vibrant extracurricular environment and alumni who take an active role in our school. Our campus is geared to help you grow not only as a student, but also as aa person. We are the leading law school in the nation's fourth largest city, and you will benefit from an unmatched set of education, profession and social experiences while you pursue your degree.

The final consideration is our cost, or more accurately, our value. Thanks to reasonable tuition and fees and Houston's low cost of living, a top-quality education from the UH Law Center is recognized as one of the best values in legal education in the country.

We encourage you to learn about all of our advantages— everything from our national prominence in health law and intellectual property, to our leadership in advocacy and consumer law. We think you will agree that the UH Law Center is a great place to launch your career in law.

Read all of Vault's Law School Surveys at www.vault.com/lawschool — get complete surveys on top law schools, expert advice on applicaton essays, LSAT prep and more.

V/\ULT CAREER LIBRARY **605**

University of Texas School of Law

Admissions Office
The University of Texas School of Law
727 E. Dean Keeton Street
Austin, TX 78705
Admissions phone: (512) 232-1200
Admissions fax: (512) 471-2765
Admissions e-mail: admissions@mail.law.utexas.edu
Admissions URL:
http://www.utexas.edu/law/depts/admissions/

 Admissions

Status: Current student, full-time
Dates of Enrollment: 8/2005-Submit Date
Survey Submitted: April 2006

No doubt about it—the admissions process at UT is very competitive. Great numbers obviously are key. However, you can really get the attention of the admissions people if you've had some meaningful life experiences that you can write about in your personal statement. Really, the most undervalued parts of your application packet are your letters of recommendation. Don't get them from big names—get them from professors that know you really well, from your character to your academic capabilities. That is what will get the attention of the people reading your application.

Status: Current student, full-time
Dates of Enrollment: 8/2004-Submit Date
Survey Submitted: April 2006

The admissions process at UT Law was competitive, but manageable. It was made clear to me that the review process was a holistic review but a slight emphasis would be placed on the LSAT and GPA. I was surprised the law school did not require recommendation letters (although they would be considered if received). I spoke with an admissions counselor only one prior to being admitted and actually obtained most of my advice about the admissions process from the pre-law advisor at my undergraduate institution. She reviewed my resume and essay prior to my completion of the application process. The response was quick and the recruitment after the acceptance was frequent and very helpful in giving me an accurate impression of UT Law. Overall, I found the admissions process to be a pleasant experience (so much so, that I now participate in student recruitment).

Status: Current student, full-time
Dates of Enrollment: 8/2005-Submit Date
Survey Submitted: April 2006

While UT is definitely tough to get in, we are always looking for ways to have a more diverse student body. The best advice I can give is to distinguish yourself from all the other applicants you are competing with. Our admissions staff is definitely concerned with GPAs and LSAT scores but they honestly try to look at the whole candidate not just numbers. Tell us about your accomplishments and goals, what you've had to overcome to get where you are, anything you've done in your community. We are trying to find students that will really succeed and having the best grades isn't necessarily what determines your success as a lawyer.

Status: Current student, full-time
Dates of Enrollment: 8/2004-Submit Date
Survey Submitted: October 2005

Getting into UT is a bit mystifying. The administration has recently reduced the required percentage of the class that must be in-state from 80 percent in hopes of increasing the school's rank. The school works very hard to attract minority students (especially Hispanic and African-American students). Most students that get in have the mean GPA and LSAT scores, with lots of leadership, work

experience and/or excellent recommendations. The big "in" to getting accepted is connections, i.e., get a letter of recommendation from someone well-known in the legal community. But connections alone will not get you in—it may just tip the scales in your favor if you already have the requisite qualifications. I know many very qualified students who are not accepted. Most students do not get accepted as an "early decision" admit. Most are deferred and then later accepted after the regular decision deadline. The law school will also offer opportunities to interview to some.

Status: Alumnus/a, full-time
Dates of Enrollment: 8/2001-5/2004
Survey Submitted: March 2006

The law school admissions office is very selective, but not just a ranker of numbers. While LSAT scores and GPAs are important, so are your personal statements. Take your personal statement seriously, and don't just tell how you want to save the world; be honest without being cheesy. Also, when I was going through the admissions process, and when I was attending UT Law and working in the admissions office, interviews were optional, had to be requested, and could only hurt you. If interviews are still optional do not ask for one. If you call the admissions office they will give you up-to-date information on median LSAT scores and GPAs, but keep in mind that they do not completely determine your fate. They also used to have a book of sample personal statements in the office to look through.

Status: Alumnus/a, full-time
Dates of Enrollment: 8/1998-5/2001
Survey Submitted: April 2005

Besides simply drawing on numbers, UT places a high priority on selecting a diverse bunch of students for its law school. Not just ethnic diversity, but a diversity of backgrounds. Any information about what makes you unique and how that trait will impact the law school community will give you an edge. Essays on that topic are therefore very important. Also, be sure to choose letters of recommendation from people who KNOW you and can really provide insight into you as a person. Finally, don't forget that if you are an out-of-state resident, the Texas legislature severely limits the number of those students who are admitted, so your scores and grades need to be off the charts.

Status: Current Student, full-time
Dates of Enrollment: 8/2001-5/2007
Survey Submitted: April 2005

The law school is becoming increasingly selective as it tries to compete with the Ivies and their equivalents for students. Consequently, strong LSAT scores are a must, and a "real" undergraduate record (i.e., no perfect GPAs via classes like Pottery) is desirable. Texas residency remains a huge plus—living in the state for a year before applying generates admission advantages, as well as substantially lower enrollment costs.

Status: Alumnus/a, full-time
Dates of Enrollment: 8/2001-5/2004
Survey Submitted: September 2004

Although I was admitted to other schools, I decided to stay in Texas. My GPA was low, but that was because I was in engineering (you get a bonus for certain "harder" disciplines to equate it with "softer" disciplines). My LSAT was 160, which is slightly below average. Compared to my classmates, though, I had monster experience. That, I believe, helped off-set the lower numbers. I added diversity in that regard—most are straight out of school

Status: Alumnus/a, full-time
Dates of Enrollment: 8/2000-5/2003
Survey Submitted: April 2004

After speaking with professors on the admissions committee, I have found that they are highly selective. Grades and LSAT scores get you in the pile to be looked at. Once you are there, they are looking for something that will distinguish you from the rest. Look at your extracurriculars or highlight something that gives you a unique perspective because of your experience.

Status: Alumnus/a, full-time
Dates of Enrollment: 8/1996-5/1999
Survey Submitted: November 2003

The admissions process, as far as application requirements go, was like that of similar schools; however, the admissions staff at UT was outstanding. They assisted in all aspects necessary for the applicant to submit a complete application. After I was accepted, I lined up a place to live. Due to an emergency with my would-be roommate, I found myself without a place to live just two weeks before the first day of class. Even though it was not required of them, the admissions staff assisted in locating a place to live, since I was unfamiliar with Austin.

Academics

Status: Current student, full-time
Dates of Enrollment: 8/2005-Submit Date
Survey Submitted: April 2006

The professors here are amazing. UT places an absolute premium on profs who can TEACH, and who love teaching. You won't find any professors here who care more about their scholarship than their students, because UT won't hire them. All the classes I've had so far have been good, there is a lot of variety in teaching styles (Socratic vs. lecture), and again, the profs are more than welcoming. They genuinely want you to come talk to them and develop relationships with them.

Status: Current student, full-time
Dates of Enrollment: 8/2004-Submit Date
Survey Submitted: April 2006

The academic program at UT Law is excellent. We have some of the leading scholars in the country as professors. My Wills and Estates professor, for example, is the author of the book and many of the study aides on the subject. I have had only one negative experience with a professor, and have found that the majority of the professors enjoy teaching and are legitimately interested in the progress of their students. The mandated curve can be a bit frustrating at times and it is clear that professors do not always agree. I feel that if every student in the class deserves an A, then every student should receive an A and the professor should be able to distribute grades at his own discretion rather than being required to adhere to a specific class average. I've had no trouble scheduling popular classes and the overall class quality is fantastic. The workload is average for any top-tier law school (heavy, but manageable).

Status: Current student, full-time
Dates of Enrollment: 8/2003-Submit Date
Survey Submitted: April 2006

Professors are topnotch. Classes are often theoretical, not practical. There are some practical classes, but you have to make it your objective to take them. The school does not babysit you in class selection. There are very few class requirement. An individual has the autonomy to shape their legal education.

Status: Current student, full-time
Dates of Enrollment: 8/2005-Submit Date
Survey Submitted: April 2006

One of the great things about your first year at UT is that you really ease into law school. The first semester you are only taking four classes, while most other schools require you to take five. Honestly, this is a huge help because law school requires a new way of thinking, reading and expressing yourself. I have had wonderful professors who are always willing to help. They not only try to help you academically but also want to develop a personal relationship with by inviting you to lunches. This is great because you are always needing references for jobs, and a professor who knows you will really help.

Status: Current student, full-time
Dates of Enrollment: 8/2004-Submit Date
Survey Submitted: October 2005

All of the most popular professors frequently teach their area of expertise. It is not difficult to get into a class if you really want to take it. The Constitutional Law, Torts and Trial Advocacy faculty can't be beat and are the experts in their respective field—many of the professors have written their own textbooks. The curve is 30 percent of the class receive an A-, A orA+, 60 percent receive a B-, B, or B+, and the rest will receive a C+ or lower (there is no mandatory "fail" rate—that is up to the discretion of the professor). Some of the upper-level courses are Pass/Fail. You can also opt to take classes in the LBJ School of Public Affairs or business school (which is a popular option) or in other graduate schools on campus. The law school has recently been bringing in young and energetic law and economic scholars, who foster a much more easy-going atmosphere in class. There are few *Paper Chase*-esque professors left. My only complaint is that the 1L section-wide classes and more popular bar classes like Evidence and Business Associations can be as large as 130 students.

Status: Alumnus/a, full-time
Dates of Enrollment: 8/2002-5/2005
Survey Submitted: March 2006

The curriculum is very flexible. The first-year curriculum is entirely mandatory, except for one elective. After that, the only mandatory classes are a topic-specific Constitutional Law, Professional Responsibility and a seminar of your choosing. The course selection method isn't great—you rank about 10 classes and then a computer system spits out a schedule, which you then have to add-drop to get a schedule that actually works. However, if you're persistent you can usually get into the more popular classes. The school has a very fixed curve (actually a mean grade target), which has resulted in the curve tightening up a lot—not as many high grades, because many profs are worried about giving out the low grades that would be required to balance it out. The upside is that when they reset the curve, they moved it up. UT used to have one of the lowest curves in the Top 25, and we aren't allowed to say our class rank to employers, so it was tough to get Judges to realize that you were at the top of the class.

Status: Alumnus/a, full-time
Dates of Enrollment: 8/1998-5/2001
Survey Submitted: April 2005

Quality ranged greatly, depending on professor. Like many law schools, first-year classes often were not as helpful as others—an attorney and former Marine told me that first year at law school was more like boot camp than an educational program. UT wasn't quite as bad as *1-L* or *The Paper Chase*, but there was some of that. After the first year, the majority of my classes were very, very good. Most profs, even in larger classes, encouraged (and expected) participation. Exams, of course, varied from prof to prof. Overall, I was very pleased with the academic quality of the program.

Status: Alumnus/a, full-time
Dates of Enrollment: 9/1999-5/2003
Survey Submitted: April 2005

My biggest peeve is that they won't tell you your class rank, which is absurd. UT is a very large law school, so I still don't know most of the people I went to school with, but they have a great TQ system for 1Ls (you're with the same group of 15 students for the entire first year), which I think makes a big difference. The workload is decent (law school ended up being much easier than I thought, and I graduated with a 3.91), but I know a lot of kids who were in the library constantly.

Status: Alumnus/a, full-time
Dates of Enrollment: 8/1998-5/2001
Survey Submitted: April 2005

Most people immediately comment on the size of Texas Law—generally ranked the third largest law school behind Harvard and Michigan. However, that size provides for an incredible depth and breadth of classes, a relative ease of getting in to the classes you want, and the ability to hire topnotch professors. Texas recently changed its grading curve to be more in line with the approach taken by Top 10 law schools (much to the chagrin of alum—they didn't bump up our GPAs!), so the grade stress isn't there like it was in the past. Texas has a robust advocacy department and clinical education program, so the ability to receive a

Read all of Vault's Law School Surveys at www.vault.com/lawschool — get complete surveys on top law schools, expert advice on applicaton essays, LSAT prep and more.

VAULT CAREER LIBRARY **607**

"practical" legal education exists along with a first rate "theoretical" legal education. There are quite a number of Law Reviews and journals (at least 12), so there is a better-than-average opportunity to edit and publish.

Status: Alumnus/a, full-time
Dates of Enrollment: 8/2000-5/2003
Survey Submitted: April 2004

UT Law is especially well known for its Constitutional, Intellectual Property (including patent), Property, and Oil and Gas Law courses. First-year seminars are large (100+), but at least one required course is taught in seminar format, with about 20 students. Upper-level courses tend to be smaller, from 10 to 50 students, but some very popular classes have more. The workload is relatively heavy, but not backbreaking; likewise, competition among students can be intense, but the atmosphere is generally laid back, and students don't back stab each other like they do at East Coast schools. Teaching performance is highly valued at UT, and professors take pride in their courses. Most courses are very well taught.

Status: Alumnus/a, full-time
Dates of Enrollment: 8/1998-5/2001
Survey Submitted: April 2004

Academics varied from professor to professor. Every class demanded work, some more than others. More importantly, the quality of teaching ranged tremendously. I can say that all of my professors were very intelligent and knew their subject matter. A few were excellent teachers, approachable, interacted well with the students, encouraged discussion in class and out, and so on. Some professors were very tough on people in class, but only one went too far. Most of the content was taught relatively well, with only one or two classes that seemed as if nothing was learned.

It can be difficult getting into popular classes as a 2L, but is much easier as a 3L. Workload varied greatly, but students can plan accordingly by talking to other students ahead of them and coordinating their classes so as not to take too many with heavier workloads in the same semester.

Status: Alumnus/a, full-time
Dates of Enrollment: 8/1999-5/2003
Survey Submitted: April 2004

UT is not an easy program, but it does not weed students out like other law schools. Once you're in, UT will do everything it can to help you graduate. The majority of the professors are excellent. Getting certain classes can be difficult, but UT has set up registration in a way that everyone should be able to take all the classes he wants by the time he graduates (with the exception of certain seminars).

 Employment Prospects

Status: Alumnus/a, full-time
Dates of Enrollment: 8/2001-5/2004
Survey Submitted: March 2006

Employment prospects for UT graduates are good. Judicial clerkships and jobs at large firms are common. Public interest is also common and a focus of the career services office. The career services office has great programs on all areas of law practice, but individual counselors vary widely on helpfulness. The degree is especially helpful in getting a job in Texas, but is useful in a national job search, especially if there is someone at the firm went to UT. Mentors are good, and a lot are involved in helping current students and helping with student organizations. However, no one is going to find you a job, they just offer resources, including books, advice, and on-campus interviewing for firms and public interest jobs.

Status: Current student, full-time
Dates of Enrollment: 8/2004-Submit Date
Survey Submitted: March 2006

The employment prospects are not as good as you would think. The value of on-campus interviews (OCI) is overstated. I know many many students who left OCI empty-handed and are still looking for jobs. This is ESPECIALLY true for out-of-state students, of which I am one. Texas firms tend to be a bit Texas-

centric. So if you want to stay in Texas, they'll look upon you as an outsider and will take a native Houstonian with worse grades over an out-of-state student nin times out of 10. If you want to go back to wherever you came from, those firm will also be wary of you since you left (not to mention your inability to work i those cities during the school year). You basically get stuck between a rock an a hard place. DO NOT underestimate the importance of staying close to home to study if that's where you want to work after you graduate.

Status: Alumnus/a, full-time
Dates of Enrollment: 8/2002-5/2005
Survey Submitted: April 2006

I had no trouble getting a job out of law school—if you pay attention to you grades, a job is not going to be a problem. I went through the on-campus recruiting process—interviewed with eight firms from the city I wished to work in during the fall of my 2L year, had six clerkship offers for the summer; chose two and got offers from both firms at the start of my 3L year. Others whose grades weren't as good complained of more problems finding a job, but I think almost everyone has a job shortly after graduation.

Status: Alumnus/a, full-time
Dates of Enrollment: 8/2002-5/2005
Survey Submitted: March 2006

Employment prospects are great. It is the top school in Texas and you can get into any firm in the state if you have a decent resume. A UT degree also travels well outside of Texas, especially if you have ties to the other area (I had no trouble getting interviews with all the top firms in Chicago, and I had judicial clerkship interviews all over the country). On-campus recruiting includes a wide range of Texas employers and most of the big firms from other states/cities. The only downside is that the recruiting is very firm-centric, although the school has been working to increase opportunities for public service jobs. The school does have a large fellowship program that provides funding for summer public service opportunities, and more than 50 students take advantage of it most years.

Status: Alumnus/a, full-time
Dates of Enrollment: 8/2000-5/2003
Survey Submitted: April 2004

The career services program at UT Law is highly-funded and well-run. Approximately 400 employers interview students for on-campus interviews during the spring and fall. Many off-campus recruiting events are also offered around the country for students interested in particular areas of the law. Internship opportunities abound, including jobs with state and federal court judges, for credit. The nation's largest law firms recruit heavily at UT for their Dallas, Houston and New York offices. Local firms make a strong showing as well. Loyalty to UT runs strong and deep among UT alumni, and because it is a big law school, there are many alumni. This may help your chances if you are competing for a job with a student from another school.

Regarding Employment Prospects, UT Law says: "The career services office offers UT Law students the opportunity to participate in on-campus interviews (OCI) held each fall and spring. Nearly 60 percent of employers who participated in the Fall 2003 OCI were from out of state and included law firms of all sizes, government agencies and public service employers. Each year, the CSO also participates in 15 job fairs to provide recruitment opportunities nationwide in cities such as Atlanta, Boston, Chicago, Dallas, Los Angeles, Miami, New York, San Francisco and Washington, D.C. Furthermore, UT Law graduates hold or have held the hiring partner positions at such elite firms as Cravath, Swain, & Moore (New York), Williams & Connally (D.C.), and many other highly selective firms across the U.S. For more information, see the most recent Admissions Bulletin found at www.utexas.edu/law."

Quality of Life

Status: Current student, full-time
Dates of Enrollment: 8/2004-Submit Date
Survey Submitted: April 2006

The quality of life at UT is fantastic. The school fosters a laid-back environment which reduces the general stress of law school and improves life for its students. The facilities are great and are being continuously updated to meet with advancements in technology and accommodate the needs of students. Local housing is nice and affordable and the majority of Austin neighborhoods are very safe. The neighborhood around the law school is extremely safe and many students walk to and from campus. The law school is currently without dining facilities which has created a problem this year, but a new dining area is under construction.

Status: Current student, full-time
Dates of Enrollment: 8/2004-Submit Date
Survey Submitted: October 2005

The campus is relatively safe. The large classrooms have recently been renovated, there is a relatively new wing with a courtroom and classrooms, and the old dining area is currently being renovated to make room for a "cafe" type dining area. However, most of the law school retains its original 70's interior design and can be a bit on the ugly side. There are lots of places to hang out with groups of people in between classes and after school, as well as places to study alone. There is no on-campus housing. Housing around the law school tends to be expensive for what you get. Many students who can't afford to live around campus or downtown have about a 20-minute commute to school and have to pay a hefty parking garage fee to park near the law school. Those who decide to live on one of the UT Shuttle routes often choose to use that mode of transportation, but have about a 45-minute commute.

Status: Alumnus/a, full-time
Dates of Enrollment: 8/2001-5/2004
Survey Submitted: March 2006

Austin is great. It is mostly safe—there are shady parts of town, but even these are not that bad. Housing is expensive for Texas, but not when compared to the Coasts. The bus system is really good for UT students, even if you have a car. Parking is a huge hassle at the law school. Good neighborhoods are Far West, the Arboretum and Hyde Park. Riverside is less expensive, but a little shady. South Austin is great as a whole, but can be pricey for the quality of housing. Living within walking distance of the law school will probably leave you in a very pricey, but shabby, apartment. The law school is kind of by itself, and there aren't a lot of places to eat in close walking distance to the law school. But the bookstore branch for the law school (UT really only has one) and an annex to the UT gym are nearby.

Status: Current student, full-time
Dates of Enrollment: 8/2004-Submit Date
Survey Submitted: March 2006

The law school's building itself is getting quite old, but they just finished renovating the major lecture rooms and they're much better now. Austin is an awesome city and provides a very high quality of life. The school's new society program also does a good job in cultivating a friendly atmosphere within the school.

Status: Alumnus/a, full-time
Dates of Enrollment: 9/1999-5/2003
Survey Submitted: April 2005

Housing is a challenge, because UT in general is so big and Austin is relatively small. UT has a great campus, but the law school itself is not an architectural marvel. This is a fantastic town, with lots of beautiful outdoor areas and activities and a mentality that encourages a positive quality of life. You better like Tex-Mex if you're coming to Austin, but there is decent sushi, Asian food and American cuisine. And, of course, being a bit of a liberal hippie town, there are always good vegetarian options. In a small city, crime is not a major issue, although there are always minor problems at any large university.

Status: Alumnus, full-time
Dates of Enrollment: 8/2001-5/2004
Survey Submitted: September 2004

Well, Austin is an awesome town. If you want to have a good time, you can have a great time. If you want to get yourself in trouble, you can do that, too. There is not a lot to eat around the school except for vending machines and running across the street to some ghetto looking food places next to Kinko's, but if you hop into the car and drive for one to three minutes you can be at some great restaurants (Hoover's, Mueller's, Texadelphia). They do set you up in these artificial groups your first year. Of the 15 others, I still keep in touch with about four of them. The others parted ways well before my first year was over.

Status: Alumnus/a, full-time
Dates of Enrollment: 8/1998-5/2001
Survey Submitted: April 2004

The law school corner of the campus is easily accessible, safe and in a great location with respect to book stores, restaurants. Best of all, UT has a great shuttle system that goes all over town. And students get to ride free on city buses as well. Austin also offers unbeatable and many options for outdoor activities. Quality of life in Austin is just fantastic—which is why so many alumni want to stay here!

Status: Alumnus/a, full-time
Dates of Enrollment: 8/1999-5/2003
Survey Submitted: April 2004

Austin is an amazing place to live! There are so many fabulous restaurants, and lots of them are very affordable. The campus is in a very safe neighborhood, and there is lots of housing nearby, although it can be a pricey area. The school does not do much to help with housing for grad students, but it's not too hard to connect with a local realtor and find a place. The law school's facilities are always being improved. The library is amazing, and the classrooms are going wireless.

Social Life

Status: Current student, full-time
Dates of Enrollment: 8/2005-Submit Date
Survey Submitted: April 2006

Lots of social opportunities. Almost every Thursday there is Bar Review—drink specials for law students at a different bar every week. Very popular. Also, one major social event each semester—in the Fall, it's the Halloween party and in the Spring, it's Casino Night. Austin also has a nightlife of its own, but it's pretty dominated by undergraduates.

Status: Current student, full-time
Dates of Enrollment: 8/2005-Submit Date
Survey Submitted: April 2006

Not being from the South, I was so surprised by how great Austin is. There are so many activities going on in the city, and the law school is right at the heart of it all. There are amazing music venues, restaurants, bars, outdoor activities and so much more. Every Thursday the law school hosts Bar Review at a different local bar, which gets a great turn out from all the classes. The mentor and society programs are great ways to meet people. The law school has IM sport teams for a different sport every season and those are a lot of fun. There are always receptions and happy hours through the law school, which are also great ways to meet people.

Status: Current student, full-time
Dates of Enrollment: 8/2004-Submit Date
Survey Submitted: October 2005

The law school has a mentor group and society system in place for incoming 1Ls that began with the entering class of 2007. There are four Sections (125 students) which have two societies (about 60 or so students) a piece, which have two mentor groups (about 30 students) a piece. In your first year, all of the people you know are generally people in your mentor group or society or section, because those are the people you have all of your classes with. The mentor groups compete in a mentor Intramural sports tournament year round,

Read all of Vault's Law School Surveys at www.vault.com/lawschool — get complete surveys on top law schools, expert advice on applicaton essays, LSAT prep and more.

VAULT CAREER LIBRARY   609

and there are tons of social activities and academic enrichment activities for individual mentor groups and societies (booze cruises, outlining sessions, community service, poker tournaments, 2004 presidential election parties). Austin has a great downtown club and restaurant scene (Sixth and Fourth Streets) and no shortage of restaurants. Every Thursday the Student Bar Association holds a Bar Review at a bar or club downtown, and everyone pretty much attends. The biggest events in the Fall are the annual Halloween Party (Ex Parte) and Texas Law Fellowship Auction; the biggest event in the Spring is Casino Night. A lot of people take advantage of the drinking establishments downtown and around the city. Many students tailgate and attend the UT football games, as well.

Status: Alumnus/a, full-time
Dates of Enrollment: 8/1998-5/2001
Survey Submitted: March 2006

The biggest "official" school events are a massive Halloween party in the fall (Austin takes Halloween VERY seriously) and a student-produced musical in the spring. In between, there is simply too much Austin and UT have to offer to put in one review. Austin was recently named by *Forbes* as the Best City for Singles in America. The nightlife is legendary. If you like live music, spend your spring break in Austin for the SXSW music festival and check out over 1,300 bands over four days. Or the Austin City Limits music festival in the fall, with over 100 bands in a weekend. If you like sports, we're the reigning national champions in football and baseball (and currently in the Sweet 16 of basketball), and you get great, cheap seats as a student (especially as a grad student—the tickets are disbursed in order of seniority). The only bad thing I can say about Austin is...nope. Nothing.

Status: Alumnus/a, full-time
Dates of Enrollment: 9/1999-5/2003
Survey Submitted: April 2005

I spent most of my first year at Crown & Anchor, a local bar that is a big favorite of law students. There's also Trudy's, a very popular Tex-Mex restaurant that all of the UT students go to. Many students go to Mozart's (on the lake) for coffee, and the new Whole Foods is the place to go at the moment for much more than just groceries. Austin is a very social town, with lots of live music options (many of which are outdoors), restaurants and bars—and UT students take full advantage of all of them.

Status: Alumnus/a, full-time
Dates of Enrollment: 8/1998-5/2001
Survey Submitted: April 2005

Austin was recently ranked the top city in the U.S. for singles. While law school is going to be intense no matter where you go, you might as well do it in a city that will enable you to blow off steam when you need to. The infamous Sixth Street and the expanding Warehouse District are two entirely distinct nightlife areas within blocks of each other and less than 10 minutes from the law school. Posse East and Crown & Anchor are great college bars within a five minute walk. Austin has literally hundreds of extremely cool bars and restaurants sprinkled all over—if you come here, find someone who went to UT for undergrad and tag along to their favorite spots. And while UT Law is big enough at 1,500 students to provide ample opportunities to meet people to date, the university itself at over 50,000 provides limitless potential.

Status: Alumnus/a, full-time
Dates of Enrollment: 8/1999-5/2003
Survey Submitted: April 2004

Most people at UT Law are very friendly. They are high achievers and driven, but it is not a cutthroat program. People are willing to help others. The school divides 1Ls into small groups of 12 to 14 students, and this allows you to meet people. Your best friends in law school will probably come from your 1L section, since these are the people you spend most of your time with. Austin has fabulous restaurants. Law students hang out on Fourth Street a lot. You can always find people going out on any night of the week, especially after your first year.

Brigham Young University

J. Reuben Clark Law School
Admissions Office
341 JRCB
Provo, UT 84602
Admissions phone: (801) 422-4277
Admissions e-mail: admissions@lawgate.byu.edu
Admissions URL: http://www.law2.byu.edu/AdmissionsNew/

 ## Admissions

Status: Alumnus/a, full-time
Dates of Enrollment: 9/1998-5/2001
Survey Submitted: March 2006

If you are a white LDS (Mormon) male, you will not be admitted unless you have top grades and LSAT scores as well as evidence of significant leadership ability. Admission standards are lower (and scholarships are more plentiful) for minorities, especially blacks. Women also enjoy more relaxed standards because they still make up significantly less than half of the entering class. There does not seem to be any preference for LDS over non-LDS students. In fact non-LDS students may enjoy a slight advantage because there are perceived as diverse. The school does not conduct interviews, but the admission staff will meet with interested students. For those that are "on the bubble," requesting a meeting and school tour can end up being a big positive provided the student is normal and expresses a strong interest in the school. Also of note is the fact that BYU does not give preference to children of its alumni.

Status: Alumnus/a, full-time
Dates of Enrollment: 8/1996-4/1999
Survey Submitted: March 2006

BYU makes a concerted effort to recruit top students and many publications put them in the very top tier in terms of selectivity. Most applicants are Mormon; for diversity the school makes an extra special effort to recruit those who are not. In considering student applications, they give greater weight to GPA and less to LSAT than other schools. Tuition is very reasonable, as a result, the school uses more small scholarships to sweeten the deal for a greater percentage of the entering class than other schools, especially directed at women and minority students.

Status: Alumnus/a, full-time
Dates of Enrollment: 8/1998-5/2001
Survey Submitted: March 2005

Admission is fairly selective and depends primarily on GPA and LSAT. However, the school also appears to be actively recruiting diverse candidates. Consequently, your essay should highlight anything that would make the school consider you diverse, including coming from a geographic area other than Utah, Idaho or California.

Status: Alumnus/a, full-time
Dates of Enrollment: 8/2001-4/2004
Survey Submitted: April 2005

Very selective. It helps to have had an academically rigorous background and have unique characteristics. The admissions committee also seems to value strong moral character.

Status: Alumnus/a, full-time
Dates of Enrollment: 1/1999-12/2001
Survey Submitted: April 2005

I actually transferred from American University where I was in the top 10 percent of my class. I had to fill out a transfer application and I met informally with the dean of students and admissions. Everyone involved in the process was helpful and thoughtful.

Status: Alumnus/a, full-time
Dates of Enrollment: 8/2000-4/2003
Survey Submitted: March 2005

The admissions process is fairly standard—a few essays, LSAT score and references. The school is highly selective and therefore, anything you can do to make your application look unique and diverse is helpful. The average LSAT seems to rise every year, but a 160+ is almost mandatory unless you are a minority candidate who falls into the diversity category.

A combined GPA and LSAT score of 3.7 or higher or 164 or higher will get you in almost automatically. For those falling below this threshold, the essays (creativity and accuracy) become more important. They generally do not conduct interviews when determining admission

Status: Alumnus/a, full-time
Dates of Enrollment: 8/2000-4/2003
Survey Submitted: April 2004

My best advice is to do well in your undergrad coursework and study hard for the LSAT. BYU has very competitive admission standards, as well as many highly qualified applicants each year.

BYU has a rolling admissions process, so they admit people as they apply. Get your applications in very early, as class size is generally limited to [150] students per year. Students with good enough credentials to get in may be left out in the cold if they apply late, due to lack of space.

You will only have an interview if the school is considering you for a merit scholarship. In that interview do not spend time discussing what they already know about you (grades). Focus on what sets you apart from others. The school has a bad, and only slightly true, reputation as "non-diverse" and they are trying to change that by giving scholarships to "diverse" students. I do not mean race or color when I say "diverse," more along the lines of interesting past experiences.

Status: Current student, full-time
Dates of Enrollment: 8/2002-Submit Date
Survey Submitted: October 2003

High GPA is a must! Solid LSAT (94th percentile or higher would also be helpful). Personal statements take on extra significance as they are looking for more than just good scores. Life experience is a helpful boost.

Status: Alumnus/a, full-time
Dates of Enrollment: 8/2000-4/2003
Survey Submitted: October 2003

BYU's law school is competitive, even more so in the last few years. This makes personal statements increasingly important for those with less than stellar GPAs and LSAT scores. The school seeks to diversify the student body, so anything you can do to set yourself apart from the bulk of applicants will help. Scholarship money is generous for the upper third of the incoming class and, combined with ridiculously low tuition for a private school, BYU's financial aid makes the school one of the best buys in all of legal education.

Status: Alumnus/a, full-time
Dates of Enrollment: 8/1999-4/2002
Survey Submitted: October 2003

BYU's admissions are surprisingly competitive. The low tuition and high caliber of the faculty and facilities make it a highly desirable school, which inevitably means it is tough to get in. BYU routinely has higher median LSAT scores and GPAs than higher "ranked" schools. However, the admissions staff is very approachable and works hard to accommodate and consider individual circumstances. Their primary objectives are not only to accept a highly talented student body, but also one that is highly diverse.

Read all of Vault's Law School Surveys at www.vault.com/lawschool — get complete surveys on top law schools, expert advice on applicaton essays, LSAT prep and more.

VAULT CAREER LIBRARY **611**

Academics

Status: Alumnus/a, full-time
Dates of Enrollment: 9/1998-5/2001
Survey Submitted: March 2006

First-year classes are assigned. Students are divided into "small sections" of somewhere between 30 and 40. You get one small section class a semester. The rest of the classes are taken with the rest of the students in you class—something like 120. You are also assigned to a smaller class of 20 or so students for a class that teaches legal writing and oral advocacy. After first year, you are free to pick your classes and the size of the classes is usually smaller. However, standard bar classes like Evidence and Professional Responsibility are large. I was not ever aware of a student to being able to take the class he or she wanted because the section was full. Sometimes scheduling forces students to chose between two classes that they really like. Because not all classes are offered every year, this can be disappointing.

The workload for most classes is significant. I believe this is due mostly to the hyper-competitive student body rather than unreasonable professors. All classes are graded on a curve with usually only one or two 4.0 grades given per class. This means that the bulk of the class is bunched around the middle of the curve and students are pushing to distinguish themselves. On the other hand, BYU's median is higher than some other schools, and thus makes all students look better. The school has discontinued the practice of giving each student his exact numeric rank in the class. However, the students are given an idea about where they fall.

Status: Alumnus/a, full-time
Dates of Enrollment: 8/1996-4/1999
Survey Submitted: March 2006

BYU Law School was founded in 1973 by Univ. of Chicago alumnus Rex Lee, and many have observed that he built the school and curriculum on the old Chicago model. Though Lee died in the mid-1990s, his legacy manifests itself in many respects: (1) The faculty is more conservative than other schools (roughly a 50-50 conservative/liberal split). (2) The school stresses constitutional law and teaches a curriculum that places greater emphasis on the structural constitution (the originalism and textualism schools of thought) and less emphasis on the rights-based constitution (living constitution school of thought) that other top schools teach. (3) The curriculum generally favors legal theory over practical legal applications; and (4) Professors work very hard to help students get judicial clerkships.

Status: Alumnus/a, full-time
Dates of Enrollment: 8/2001-4/2004
Survey Submitted: April 2005

Excellent programs, with the exception of the first-year Advocacy Program that is generally a little above average; the flaw is mostly in the curriculum rather than the teaching. Excellent professors who are approachable and take time with the students, generally speaking. Given the small entering class each year, getting the best professors for a given class is generally not difficult.

Status: Alumnus/a, full-time
Dates of Enrollment: 8/2000-4/2003
Survey Submitted: March 2005

The law school has arguably one of the best writing programs in the country. It is rigorous, demanding and improves everyone's writing skills. The research section of the writing program is also unique because for the first semester, students are not allowed to use electronic research so that they become familiar with the West Reporters and Sheppard's system of citation. This makes BYU law grads some of the best researchers in the country.

While there is a variety of classes, there are not as many as other largers schools. The core classes are all offered and the electives cover almost every area of the law. Students usually, however, only have one chance in their 2L or 3L year to take certain electives so advanced planning and layout of your schedule is really required. Students generally can get in to almost any class they want.

Professors are some of the best teachers in the country. While a few also have outstanding research work, they are typically not as prolific publishers as

professors at some high-ranked schools. However, their teaching is generally fa[r] superior. Students leave the class with a firm understanding of the law and how to understand the law. Lofty policy discussions, while still part of th[e] curriculum, and not the sole topic as they are at many Top 10 schools.

Workload is substantial. The students are competitive and very focuse[d.] Because the vast majority of the students are Mormon, there is very littl[e] partying and lots of work. Despite the competition, the environment is ver[y] collegial.

Status: Alumnus/a, full-time
Dates of Enrollment: 8/1999-4/2002
Survey Submitted: October 2003

The size of the school makes for a great academic experience. The faculty i[s] exceptional and approachable. The academic environment is serious, but no[t] overly competitive. Despite the relatively small size of the school (about 15[0] students per class) the school offers a wide range of classes, some of them wit[h] only 10 students. This provides for an availability of focused study an[d] mentoring in a wide variety of subjects. Grading is done on a four-point scale with a forced median. This eliminates grade inflation and leads to some healthy yet not necessarily overt, competition. In other words, students are pressured t[o] learn the material well in order to do well, but do not generally feel over[ly] competition with their fellow students.

Status: Current student, full-time
Dates of Enrollment: 8/2002-Submit Date
Survey Submitted: October 2003

Not too hard to get the classes you want although the small size of the schoo[l] effectively limits the course offerings. Students are pretty serious and work hard[.] Nonetheless, most are quite friendly, helpful and cooperative. I have yet to hea[r] of anyone, in my class or past classes, pulling dirty tricks to get ahead or being unwilling to help out. A lot of the kids at the top of the class spend a good dea[l] of time helping the new 1Ls and their classmates.

Status: Alumnus/a, full-time
Dates of Enrollment: 8/2000-4/2003
Survey Submitted: October 2003

BYU is without question a conservative school, yet opposing viewpoints ar[e] welcomed by professors and by MOST students. Instruction is generally topnotch with a few exceptions, and after the first year, many classes will hav[e] fewer than 40 students enrolled making for excellent experiences (rarely i[s] getting into a desirable class impossible). Grading is based upon a mandatory median format (which was recently altered slightly, so my numbers may be slightly off). Basically, half of the class must receive a 3.3 or lower. High grades (3.8 and up) are awarded sparingly. To rank in the top 10 percent, a 3.6 or clos[e] to it will be required; coursework is rigorous and the students are bright and competitive (but rarely cutthroat). The Advocacy Program is demanding bu[t] worthwhile, producing many, many good writers each year. That may be a function of its structure—each advocacy section has only about 28 students and generally has three teaching assistants assigned per section.

Status: Alumnus/a, full-time
Dates of Enrollment: 8/2000-4/2003
Survey Submitted: April 2004

Professors are outstanding. All are very knowledgeable and love to teach. The atmosphere is very friendly, teachers care about the students and take the time to get to know them. The classes generally do not fill up; you can basically get into any class you want. Grading is very competitive, based on a curve and the student body make-up is very bright.

Employment Prospects

Status: Alumnus/a, full-time
Dates of Enrollment: 9/1998-5/2001
Survey Submitted: March 2006

The law school career services staff is very helpful and dedicated to helping students find employment. They review resumes, conduct mock job interviews and even call you when they have openings that they think would fit your interests and qualifications. I believe that everyone from my class had a job before graduation (or at least very shortly thereafter). Plus, career services is ready and willing to help job searches for lateral attorneys. The only weakness in BYU's placement is in academic jobs. The school offers little assistance or guidance to those interested in teaching law. Perhaps the faculty believes that a BYU degree does not yet carry enough weight for their top students to compete in the academic market.

Status: Alumnus/a, full-time
Dates of Enrollment: 8/1996-4/1999
Survey Submitted: March 2006

BYU has a very active alumni network, strongest in Southern California, Washington, D.C., Arizona and Utah. The network is present but less visible in other big markets like Chicago and New York City, where I started following a clerkship. As mentioned, the school places a great deal of emphasis on judicial clerkships and it has a surprisingly good track record placing Supreme Court clerks. With prestigious big firms, it can be hit or miss as some tend to see the school as an insular Mormon operation. In New York City, the school has had a fair amount of success placing students with firms like Cravath, Davis Polk and Sullivan & Cromwell. In Chicago, Kirkland & Ellis and Sidley Austin. In Washington, D.C., Sidley again and Covington & Burling. In Los Angeles, very good success at Latham and Gibson Dunn. Those firms and others usually, but not always, limit their recruitment to the top 10 percent or those with clerkships lined up.

Status: Alumnus/a, full-time
Dates of Enrollment: 8/2001-4/2004
Survey Submitted: March 2006

There is a great alumni network and my classmates placed at law firms all across the country. Salt Lake City was difficult to place in because of the demand, but people generally got positions in the other cities where they wanted to go.

Status: Alumnus/a, full-time
Dates of Enrollment: 8/2000-4/2003
Survey Submitted: March 2005

Graduates obtain jobs in law firms, government, legislature, business and in-house counsel—pretty much anything. The alumni network is fabulous and actually extends beyond graduates of BYU Law School to alumni of any school who choose to be a member of the J. Reuben Clark Law Society (typically Mormons who graduated from other law schools).

Status: Alumnus/a, full-time
Dates of Enrollment: 8/2000-4/2003
Survey Submitted: October 2003

In discussions with so many other students at other schools, I have come to appreciate the efforts of the Career Services Office. BYU attracts recruiters from the nation's best firms. The unfortunate reality is, however, that the top firms generally will interview only the top 10 percent. In fact, perhaps more than half of all employers want to interview only the top third of the class. Having said that, BYU grads (up until 2002-2003, when the economy went south) are usually employed by graduation. For students who are willing to seek employment outside of the Rocky Mountain region, ample opportunities exist. Moreover, because the average BYU grad has such little debt as compared to most new lawyers, employment options are broader. For those who do not have their hearts set on working at a mega-firm, it is ideal. Grads are able to accept government positions and less demanding firm jobs. For someone who only wants to work at the biggest NYC firms, however, a higher ranked school will dramatically improve those odds. Of course, it may be frustrating to take such a route only to find yourself clerking over the summer with top BYU students who will land the same job and do so with a third of the school debt.

Status: Alumnus/a, full-time
Dates of Enrollment: 7/2001-12/2003
Survey Submitted: April 2004

Internship opportunities are great—I spent my first summer working in the city of Surfer's Paradise in Australia. Other international internships ranged from London to Korea and Hong Kong.

Status: Alumnus/a, full-time
Dates of Enrollment: 8/1999-4/2002
Survey Submitted: October 2003

The career placement program is fantastic. The school has an internship program that essentially provides every first-year student—and interested second-years—with an internship for their first summer. These internships span the public and private sectors, including many international positions. Career placement is also very good, and the school maintains a high placement rate. With the built-in network of the school's sponsoring church (LDS Church), there are alumni and other affiliated lawyers and business people around the world that aid in the recruiting process.

Status: Alumnus/a, full-time
Dates of Enrollment: 7/1997-5/2000
Survey Submitted: September 2003

Many firms come to recruit students at BYU from all over the country. The Career Services Office is at the top of its field and really does a good job of inviting firms to recruit on campus and even has job fairs on the East Coast. The CSO also encourages students from their first year to begin networking and contacting the alumni network. Many jobs and internships are constantly being posted on the boards.

 ## Quality of Life

Status: Alumnus/a, full-time
Dates of Enrollment: 9/1998-5/2001
Survey Submitted: March 2006

No single law students live on campus. They typically live off campus in "BYU approved" housing where the landlord matches you with other BYU students for roommates. Some of these apartments are large and very social. Others are dumps. There is great married-student housing on campus. The waiting list for these apartments is long, so put your request in early. (Many BYU undergrads stay in their on-campus married housing while attending law school, so if you went somewhere else for undergrad, you may not get a spot.) There is very little crime and very little traffic.

There is a small lunchroom in the law school where you can heat your leftover casserole or soup. The cafeteria across the street serves various fast foods. The town has many, many restaurants that provide good food to students on a budget.

Status: Alumnus/a, full-time
Dates of Enrollment: 8/1996-4/1999
Survey Submitted: March 2006

Provo is a pleasant college town, too pleasant at times. The best part is living in the mountains: lots of outdoor opportunities, hiking, fishing, skiing/snowboarding and a lake for water-skiing. If you're not Mormon it can be unnerving to live in Provo, and the experience generally varies on an individual basis. For some, it's a net-net positive experience. For others, they're only too happy to finally leave. For what it's worth, the non-Mormon faculty tend to live in Salt Lake City, Sundance or nearby Springville/Mapleton.

Status: Alumnus/a, full-time
Dates of Enrollment: 8/1998-5/2001
Survey Submitted: March 2005

Provo is a very safe community with a generally low cost of living. Off-campus housing is widely available. On-campus married housing is nice and very affordable, but usually has a relatively long waiting list. The facilities at the law school are very good. Each student is assigned a desk with locking shelves and drawers. The desks have electrical and high-speed Internet connections. The building also has wireless Internet access. Parking is conveniently located next to the law school and is never a problem as long as you buy the reasonably priced graduate student parking pass that allows you to park the entire academic year.

Status: Alumnus/a, full-time
Dates of Enrollment: 8/2000-4/2003
Survey Submitted: March 2005

The quality of life is fantastic. Provo is a gorgeous city at the base of the Utah Mountains. Housing is fairly expensive, but law students are not required to live

Read all of Vault's Law School Surveys at www.vault.com/lawschool — get complete surveys on top law schools, expert advice on applicaton essays, LSAT prep and more.

VAULT CAREER LIBRARY 613

in BYU-approved housing. Campus is large, but law classes are limited to the law school. Each student is given his or her own individual carrel to study at, where they can lock up their books, hook up to the Internet and do almost anything. The school has a wireless network, so students can connect anywhere. Students with children also may watch class live in a separate study room on days where circumstances require them to take their children to school with them. This has enabled many single mothers or parents who have a sick child to still attend class.

Crime is low and the neighborhoods are very student-oriented. Dining is eclectic, with almost any cuisine you could want. The community is often perceived as very insular, but the law school is less so. There is a diverse law school student body with varying opinions and views.

Status: Alumnus/a, full-time
Dates of Enrollment: 8/2000-4/2003
Survey Submitted: October 2003

BYU is what you make it. There is an honor code and its requirements are no secret. So long as you understand the honor code beforehand and agree to abide by it, you simply need to keep your word. If you recognize that the honor code will be difficult or impossible for you to live by, then perhaps consider enrolling elsewhere. Housing options are plentiful, and Provo is a beautiful place to live during school, despite its homogenous population. Crime is very low, and the city is fairly clean. BYU's main campus is beautiful, and the law school facilities are excellent. A tour of the law school and library are worthwhile.

Status: Alumnus/a, full-time
Dates of Enrollment: 8/1999-4/2002
Survey Submitted: October 2003

The quality of life at BYU is excellent. The school is located in a beautiful part of the country. For those interested in the outdoors, it is particularly nice. Utah has more national parks than any other state, so between hiking, mountain biking and skiing, there is plenty to do. It is also one of the safest places to go to school. Housing is very affordable, both on and off campus (including married-student housing).

 ## Social Life

Status: Alumnus/a, full-time
Dates of Enrollment: 9/1998-5/2001
Survey Submitted: March 2006

The school has a great social atmosphere if you are married with two kids and don't drink. There will be couples dinners and kids playdates galore. But if you are looking for a bar, a fraternity or any type of club, you will be disappointed. The dating scene is very competitive and stressful. If you are single and moving to Provo, I suggest you take up snowboarding to give you something to do in your free time.

Status: Alumnus/a, full-time
Dates of Enrollment: 8/1996-4/1999
Survey Submitted: March 2006

As mentioned, Provo can be an uncomfortable social situation for a typical single law student. The student population generally marries early, leaving a smaller population of singles overall. If you did not go to BYU as an undergrad, the pool of potential friends is even smaller. That situation may be changing somewhat as the enrollment in the nearby Utah Valley State College has ramped up.

Status: Alumnus/a, full-time
Dates of Enrollment: 8/1998-5/2001
Survey Submitted: March 2005

Many of the law students are married. The school has a club for spouses (generally wives) of law students. There is also a group for single students that holds activities jointly with single students from the MBA programs. There is also a plethora of activities planned for undergraduate students which law students are free to attend. Because all BYU students must agree not to drink alcohol, there aren't many bars. My personal favorite thing on campus was Outdoors Unlimited, which rents outdoor equipment to students for next to nothing—kayaks, skis, snowboards, tents, outdoor clothing, snowshoes and rock

climbing gear. They also organized trips where you could meet others wit similar interests.

Status: Alumnus/a, full-time
Dates of Enrollment: 8/2000-4/2003
Survey Submitted: March 2005

Social life varies. Most students are Mormon, so the social scene does no involve bars or drinking. There is a split contingency—half of the law studen are married. So typically the non-married students have a more active socia scene. There are no fraternities. Some of the favorite student hang-outs are Caf Rio, Brick Oven, Los Hermanos and many others.

Status: Alumnus/a, full-time
Dates of Enrollment: 8/2001-4/2004
Survey Submitted: April 2005

No fraternities. Very low-key town, but great dating scene. If you like to reall party, this probably isn't the place for you. Excellent outdoor opportunities a around, including skiing, snowboarding and hiking. Zion's National Park i close enough for a weekend trip, and you can ski and be back in the same day.

Status: Alumnus/a, full-time
Dates of Enrollment: 8/1992-4/1996
Survey Submitted: April 2004

Most students are members of the sponsoring church, the LDS Church, an many are married. BYU also has an honor code based on the beliefs of th sponsoring church. All of this together means students are fairly focused and no usually partiers. As mentioned, Provo is also a small college town so not muc goes on, with an exception or two for a bar or dance club. Salt Lake City, 3 minutes to the north, offers more social and cosmopolitan opportunities.

Status: Alumnus/a, full-time
Dates of Enrollment: 8/2000-4/2003
Survey Submitted: April 2004

I was married and spent time with my family. Great atmosphere for "famil fun." People are really nice. Not many bars.

Status: Current student, full-time
Dates of Enrollment: 8/2002-Submit Date
Survey Submitted: October 2003

Not much on the bar, club or Greek scene; more in Salt Lake City (about an hou away). Dating is very active in Provo. Lots and lots of restaurants. Good tie with undergraduate institution. Plenty of good sports to watch (except fo football this year).

Status: Alumnus/a, full-time
Dates of Enrollment: 8/2000-4/2003
Survey Submitted: October 2003

So long as you can appreciate that BYU offers a Christian overlay to a topnotc legal education, you will not be disappointed in the social life. Let's face it, few law students have extraordinary amounts of free time. Students are friendly, and being part of a small class is great. There are student organizations that sponso activities, including one club for law student spouses. BYU is not a party school but it is first-rate otherwise. No better bang for the buck, especially if you'r serious about your law school education.

 ## The School Says

BYU's Law School is unique: affiliated with one of the largest private universities in the country, our student body is kept at 450 in an inviting, collaborative environment for developing intellect, faith and character. Our tuition is a bargain—no comparably ranked private law school even approaches BYU's low cost. Two-thirds of our students come from outside the intermountain area with many having lived or studied abroad. Our setting is unique: we're only a short drive away from canyons and the ski resorts that played host to the 2002 Winter Olympics.

University of Utah

S.J. Quinney College of Law
Office of Admission
332 S. 1400 East, Room 101
Salt Lake City, UT 84112-0730
Admissions phone: (801) 581-7479
Admissions e-mail: admissions@law.utah.edu
Admissions URL: http://www.law.utah.edu/prospective/

Admissions

Status: Current student, full-time
Dates of Enrollment: 8/2003-Submit Date
Survey Submitted: October 2003

Utah was actually something of an afterthought for me. After looking at the school's location, reputation and low tuition, I decided to send in an application. The admissions office was incredible. I received a phone call from the associate dean of admissions informing me of my acceptance a mere three weeks after the school received my completed application. Given my numbers and the promptness of my acceptance, I think it is very safe to say that the U is extremely LSAT heavy. (I'm in the lower 10 percent of GPAs and the upper 10 percent of LSAT scores.) I'd like to think that my essay helped, but after speaking to some of my classmates and hearing their (far more interesting) stories, I feel pretty confident that my admission was all about the numbers.

Status: Alumnus/a, full-time
Dates of Enrollment: 8/1998-5/2001
Survey Submitted: June 2004

S.J. Quinney College of Law (the "College") has a great personalized approach to the admissions process. There is no entrance interview. However, an admissions counselor was available both by phone and in person and prompt to return the calls. All of my admissions jitters were addressed in a most straightforward manner with statistics quoted and my personal background taken into consideration. I also got great pointers on essay writing with references to other resources available at the college library and in the bookstore.

The most valuable part of the admissions process was the availability and willingness of the alumni to talk to the prospective students about the admissions considerations and about their experiences as students. The school is very selective and, I believe, places great emphasis on diversity and on public service commitment. Apart from LSAT and GPA, a track record of community involvement, public service experience and commitment to the public good receive highest consideration.

Academics

Status: Alumnus/a, full-time
Dates of Enrollment: 8/2000-5/2002
Survey Submitted: April 2006

Great school. Most of the professors are very interested in the students and are willing to go the extra mile to help students not just with understanding class, but in helping them get a job and providing letters of recommendation.

The workload is very doable. Professors are not overly critical if you didn't read the day's cases. Grading is typical law school grading. Some professors are very fair and some seem to throw the papers down the stairs and grade based on where the papers land. The school does not rank students, which takes some of the pressure off of law school.

Status: Alumnus/a, full-time
Dates of Enrollment: 8/1998-5/2001
Survey Submitted: June 2004

The school has an amazingly intense and effective Legal Research and Writing Program with three full-time professors per 120-student class. It truly is a gift that keeps on giving; now three years in practice, I continue to reap the benefits of that 1L class. The school has a very powerful academic support program for 1Ls that you should definitely try and quality for. The grading curve is strictly enforced and very few alums can say they had a 4.0 after their first year. In the interests of fairness to all, there is very little interaction with professors outside of the classroom during the first year.

After the first year, professors make themselves very available for consultations and discussions. Second- and third-years are abundant in electives, including small group seminars, drafting workshops and practitioner's clinics. Also, great moot court and Law Review programs. 3Ls get preferences in signing up for small group classes. Core classes are offered every year. Popular, over-enrolled classes are usually repeated the following year.

Status: Current student, full-time
Dates of Enrollment: 8/2003-Submit Date
Survey Submitted: October 2003

1Ls at the U all have the same curriculum and are assigned professors. That said, the school is very careful to ensure that there is an equitable mix of abilities (as measured by LSAT and GPA) for each prof. Furthermore, between 13 percent and 33 percent of the students in each section must score above a B+, and all of the profs put their grades together so that the entire curve is consistent among all sections. The class sizes are incredible. The school staggers sections so that every 1L is in one small section (about 20 students), one medium section (about 40 students) and two large sections (about 60 students). All in all, the Class of 2006 has only 120 students, and the overall student/teacher ratio is 13:1.

Employment Prospects

Status: Alumnus/a, full-time
Dates of Enrollment: 8/2000-5/2002
Survey Submitted: April 2006

I think the U of U has a high percentage of graduates getting job within a year of graduation, at least 90 percent. The employers may not be top firms but you can easily get a job with a second- or third-tier law firm. Jobs obtained after graduation varied from in-house counsel and positions at large and small firms to city, county and federal prosecutors and defenders.

On-campus recruiting is helpful if you want to remain in the state. Not many out-of-state firms interview at the U of U. The alumni network for out-of-state prospects is not overly helpful. Generally, people are willing to talk to you but don't have much guidance or input. The school palcement office is terrible for helping with out-of-state placement.

Status: Alumnus/a, full time
Dates of Enrollment: 8/1998-5/2001
Survey Submitted: June 2004

The college is highly regarded in the community, and most local law firms are very committed to recruiting from its student ranks. A good number of recruiters also come from Nevada and California. The career center is very active and very well organized with a personalized approach to student placement. I recommend talking to the career counselor early to get help during the earlier years. For students who are committed to a certain career path, the career center goes the extra mile arranging for school-year internships leading up to summer jobs and postgraduate jobs.

Read all of Vault's Law School Surveys at www.vault.com/lawschool — get complete surveys on top law schools, expert advice on applicaton essays, LSAT prep and more.

VAULT CAREER LIBRARY 615

In addition to traditional summer job opportunities, the career center also develops several internships and diversity programs to increase the number of opportunities available to 1Ls and 2Ls. And the pro bono program is the true pride of the career center.

Status: Current student, full-time
Dates of Enrollment: 8/2003-Submit Date
Survey Submitted: October 2003

As a 1L [in my fall semester], I was not able to participate in OCIs [on-campus interviews]. However, in observing the process, I was pleasantly surprised by the number of firms on campus. Utah has a great deal of prestige locally, and that carries throughout the Mountain West. There are literally dozens of firms in the greater Salt Lake area, with perhaps 15 to 20 numbering 25 lawyers or more. Outside of the region, the school doesn't place as well (but a strong GPA/class rank may still get you in the door).

 ## Quality of Life

Status: Alumnus/a, full-time
Dates of Enrollment: 8/2000-5/2002
Survey Submitted: April 2006

Quality of life was great. There were tons of intramural sports teams and lots of local restaurants within walking distance or a quick ride on the light rail. Very safe area. Facilities are pretty nice and are currently expanding. Housing is affordable since it is Utah.

Status: Current student, full-time
Dates of Enrollment: 8/2003-Submit Date
Survey Submitted: October 2003

Housing in SLC is plentiful and (relatively) inexpensive. A two-bedroom house with a sizable yard can be rented for under $900/month. Be aware that this is an older city, and many of the rental properties are 80 or more years old. The campus is pretty sizable, as could be expected of any school with a 40,000 or more person-strong student body. The law school is not terribly impressive looking, but it is reassuring to know that the school is spending its cash on profs rather than impressive buildings.

The school recently obtained a $[26] million [endowment gift] and, rumor has it, is looking to move into a new building at some point in the future. Restaurants are plentiful, and range in quality from fast food to fine dining. If the dining in SLC doesn't strike your fancy, there is an even wider variety (albeit pricier) just over the hill in Park City. Crime and safety are two of the biggest reasons to move here. While not crime-free, SLC is substantially safer than many other metropolitan areas of comparable size. The overall atmosphere is just that much friendlier.

Status: Alumnus/a, full-time
Dates of Enrollment: 8/1998-5/2001
Survey Submitted: June 2004

The college has a desk and a storage locker for every 1L; the quieter law library has a desk and a locker for every second- and third-year law student. Plan to spend 10 to 12 hours a day between your desk and the classrooms. Most librarians are attorneys; keep that in mind when the legal writing program throws you a curveball. The college receives generous private donations from the thankful community, and I see a new improvement every time I go there. Your tuition dollars stretch a long way here, and you will get a top-tier legal education with very little financial burden.

Very few law students live in the dorms because the university has a great roommate matching program and there are a lot of affordable student rentals close to the campus. To make things better, the city has great public transportation. The university also offers discounts to the local water park and to the skiing slopes. Crime is extremely low, and the city has an overall perfect balance: there are high-end country clubs and low-end housing, but hardly any unsafe neighborhoods in the whole state.

 ## Social Life

Status: Alumnus/a, full-time
Dates of Enrollment: 8/2000-5/2002
Survey Submitted: April 2006

Social life is lacking a little. The only professional sports teams are basketball and soccer. There are lots of bars and pubs, but not many dance clubs worth going to. Dating is interesting with half the population being Mormon. There are some fun events, like the Brew Fest, that happen yearly. You just have to keep an eye out. If you want a great martini, try Kristoph's.

Status: Current student, full-time
Dates of Enrollment: 8/2003-Submit Date
Survey Submitted: October 2003

There are more misconceptions in this area than in any other. There are different types of bars: clubs serve beer, wine and liquor; taverns do 3.2 beer. Regardless, there are many of both all over the place. Regular attendance of Bar Review will assure that you visit many of them. I'm married, so the dating scene isn't an issue for me, but I've got friends who have already started dating. The law school and Student Bar Association put on all kinds of events (including Bar Review).

Status: Alumnus/a, full-time
Dates of Enrollment: 8/1998-5/2001
Survey Submitted: June 2004

Lunch dives are abundant around the college campus and very popular with the law students who tend to stay and study until late. Brumby's and Einstein Bros Bagels are all-time favorites. Every year, the college gets together with the medical school for the Halloween Party. They also do several public service events.

But if you are going to study law in Utah, do not count on a lot of nightlife. The city as a whole turns its lights out early. And "1Ls nightlife" is an oxymoron at best; at worst, it equals a night of outlining. So, if you are in for the nightlife, try another venue and do not pick law school.

 ## The School Says

S.J. Quinney College of Law

Supportive, Respectful, Collegial

The University of Utah S.J. Quinney College of Law, like many other fine law schools, offers a talented and accomplished faculty, a challenging and stimulating curriculum, and a diverse student body with high academic achievement and promise. What distinguishes our law school from others cannot easily be measured, but can and should be experienced: a collegial and supportive learning environment that seeks to develop each student's potential.

The administration of the University of Utah's S.J. Quinney College of Law believes students deserve not only excellence in their academic programs, but also a personalized and respectful experience. That is why the student/faculty ratio and class size are kept small, an open-door policy is fostered, and collaboration is encouraged.

This collegial and supportive environment sets the S.J. Quinney College of Law apart from other excellent law schools. It is an environment that seeks to develop each student's full potential. The most important element of the academic experience at the law school is the outstanding teaching. Not only have the professors at S.J. Quinney College of Law been officially recognized for quality teaching by their peers and the university, they are also accessible, and they welcome opportunities to work with students. The administrative and library staff regards service to students as their primary mission.

The College also seeks to instill students with a sense of responsibility to use their legal education to provide service to others. Professors and administrators emphasize that being a professional means making a true commitment to others. The pro bono initiative introduces law students to public service experiences.

The Wallace Stegner Center for Land, Resources and the Environment has become a leading academic center for environmental and natural resources law; it is an invaluable resource nationwide. The newly established Utah Criminal Justice Center is a unique interdisciplinary partnership between the University of Utah and state government. The center's objectives include conducting research that assists the government on issues of criminal and juvenile justice, creating an interdisciplinary curriculum in criminal and juvenile justice taught by faculty from across the university, and training and placement of students in the justice system.

The quality and reputation of the S.J. Quinney College of Law continues to grow. Our students continue to perform at the highest level in intercollegiate advocacy and dispute resolution competitions. Our students' bar passage rates rank among the highest nationally, and the many diverse contributions and accomplishments of the College's alumni throughout the nation is also a key indicator of the quality of the education.

Read all of Vault's Law School Surveys at www.vault.com/lawschool — get complete surveys on top law schools, expert advice on applicaton essays, LSAT prep and more.

VAULT CAREER LIBRARY 617

Vermont Law School

Admissions Office
Chelsea Street
South Royalton, VT 05068-0096
Admissions phone: (802) 831-1239 or (888) 277-5985
(toll free)
Admissions e-mail: admiss@vermontlaw.edu
Admissions URL: http://www.vermontlaw.edu/admissions/

 Admissions

Status: Current student, full-time
Dates of Enrollment: 8/2003-Submit Date
Survey Submitted: March 2006

The admissions process seems very standard for law schools. There are no mandatory interviews. I believe the average LSAT school has gone up significantly, but when I applied my LSAT was in the lower range for the school and my GPA was significantly higher, so I am not entirely sure what the deciding factor was, although I would guess it was my essays.

The people at Vermont are very interested in community-minded individuals: caring, thoughtful and concerned with local and global issues. Write candidly and be REAL—they want to see the person behind the words, not just some great written work. Also, I would HIGHLY recommend visiting the campus before even considering coming to school here. It is in a very rural (and beautiful) setting, but make sure that you understand what that entails (not many restaurants, little entertainment and lots of snow) before signing up.

Status: Current student, full-time JD/MSEL
Dates of Enrollment: 8/2003-Submit Date
Survey Submitted: March 2006

The admissions process was quick and painless—but I didn't do things the traditional way. All information in the application packet is available online. Take advantage of the online application; it allows you to easily type your application, which is nice on the eyes of the administrator reviewing your application. I didn't decide that I wanted to do the "law school thing" until really late in the process so I was put on the waiting list. I found out in the end of July that a spot was mine so I had about two weeks to find a place to live and get ready for the biggest change of my life. The admissions office was great during that whole process. They were in contact frequently, encouraged me to meet with professors and tour the school, and even met with me personally. For anyone on the waiting list, I encourage you to e-mail/call the school often and VISIT. Meet with the dean in particular and let her know how much you want to come to VLS.

Status: Current student, full-time
Dates of Enrollment: 8/2003-Submit Date
Survey Submitted: March 2006

First off, the school offers prospective students the chance to talk with a current student on a regular basis about what life is like, what school in general is like, and even offers a mentoring program for first-years to be linked with upperclassmen so that they may have a more experienced point-of-view on what life is like outside of law school.

Status: Current student, full-time
Dates of Enrollment: 8/2004-Submit Date
Survey Submitted: March 2006

I think the most important thing to know about VLS in terms of admissions is that the school is more interested in who the applicant is as a person than the scores and averages that most law schools base their decisions on. VLS wants individuals who are passionate about something and will bring that passion to the campus. Additionally, some sort of wacky or out-of-the-ordinary resume is also helpful. Most people here have done some pretty cool things before law

school took over their lives. Also, people with fine arts degrees do not be dissuaded: VLS thinks B.F.A.'s are rad.

Status: Current student, full-time
Dates of Enrollment: 1/2003-Submit Date
Survey Submitted: March 2006

Do you best on your LSATs, but know that they are looking carefully at other parts of your application, especially recommendations and your essay. Make sure your recommendations are really good and complete. The folks at financial aid and admissions are really accessible to talk to, not just about your questions but about how you plan to pay for your law career based on your individual situation. It is definitely worth asking questions because the people in those offices really care about students.

Status: Current student, full-time
Dates of Enrollment: 9/2005-Submit Date
Survey Submitted: March 2006

My undergraduate grades and LSAT score were not great but my essay rocked and got me in. My advice regarding the admission process is to highlight your "crunchiness" in your essay, i.e., anything on your resume that shows that you care about the world. Good examples of "crunchiness" (i.e., granola loving, peace child) are: Peace Corps service, volunteer work and work at nonprofits. Definitely get your application in no later than January 1st!

Status: Current student, full-time
Dates of Enrollment: 8/2005-Submit Date
Survey Submitted: March 2006

Admissions staff at VLS is courteous and helpful, and really starts to show the "small-town" feel of the school from the start. The admissions process was lightening fast. A great deal of weight is placed on non-traditional experience and the "total package," rather than grades and numbers alone, like many other schools. A campus visit is a must, as the magnitude of "small town" may be quite a shock to perspective students coming from city schools.

Status: Current student, full-time
Dates of Enrollment: 8/2005-Submit Date
Survey Submitted: March 2006

The admissions process was fairly straightforward—the typical essay submissions, letters of recommendation and transcripts. I applied early, which is highly recommended by most schools; you want to get your materials in front of the admissions staff before they begin to pile up. VLS, however, provided an extra touch of class, responding quickly once my packet had been received and later sending a holiday greeting card. When I wished to tour campus before making a commitment, VLS covered my entire trip, airfare, hotel, meals and car rental. Very impressive.

Status: Current student, full-time
Dates of Enrollment: 9/2004-Submit Date
Survey Submitted: March 2006

Kathy Hartman, the Dean of Admissions, is very helpful, honest and down to earth. They seem to accept a lot of students who have travelled abroad and who have shown they care about social justice issues. I think they make a good effort and succeed at creating a student body that is racially diverse. Very gay-friendly.

Status: Current student, full-time
Dates of Enrollment: 9/2004-Submit Date
Survey Submitted: March 2006

This school is known for its environmental programs and public interest. There were three essays that were required for admissions and a very lengthy application. These essays were used to identify the reasons for attending law school, the future thoughts of the applicant on current environmental topics and the unique characteristics that the applicant had. This school is selective only in that the applicant must be both passionate and serious about their dedication to either an environmental or public interest topic. The school is extremely friendly, loves diverse applicants and was the most helpful law school that I applied to. They were willing to talk to me on the phone for as long as it took, unlike many other top environmental law schools that I applied to. They made me feel welcome and important.

Academics

Status: Current student, full-time JD/MSEL
Dates of Enrollment: 8/2003-Submit Date
Survey Submitted: March 2006

VLS isn't like other law schools. We're not the competitive, eat your neighbor's heart out type of school. At VLS your fellow classmates might be your competition, but they are also your best friends. Everyone is always willing to help another student out, share notes, study together and join you for a beer at the local bar. The atmosphere is still slightly competitive and we take academics seriously most days, but first and foremost we're friends!

Status: Current student, full-time
Dates of Enrollment: 8/2004-Submit Date
Survey Submitted: March 2006

It is pretty much a given that law school is hard. During the first year, classes are selected for students, which I do not agree with. Then, for the remaining two years there are problems that arise. Core classes and bar classes are often scheduled at the same time, which means that one can only take one of those classes. Grading is crazy because law students compete for grades against one another. In addition, grading is based on the curve. The Socratic Method of teaching is used, where the professor students question instead of lecturing. This is not an easy way to learn. In a sense, in law school students teach themselves.

Status: Current student, full-time JD/MSEL
Dates of Enrollment: 8/2004-Submit Date
Survey Submitted: March 2006

The quality of education at VLS is excellent. The best measure thus far outside of VLS is from job experiences over the summer. The caliber of writing compared with other first-year law students is higher, evident by the feedback employers provided. The writing program at VLS stretches three semesters, firmly grounding students with a strong foundation to build upon. Additionally, enrolling in Appellate Advocacy the second year of law school allows students to better appreciate the class and gain much more from the experience.

The classes offered are varied, with a focus on environmental law. However, there are many professors that specialize in other areas and are fantastic.

As for workload, the classes are very demanding and VLS is designed only for serious students. You do not attend this school "just to go to law school." The students who choose to attend VLS are relocating from major cities across the country, and for a reason. They share the desire and mission of the law school: to provide law for the community and the world. Thus, you not only have topnotch professors, but also classmates that enhance the learning environment. Finally, the ease of getting into classes for me has been perfect. I have not experienced any issues with getting the classes I request and class sizes are ideal.

Status: Current student, full-time
Dates of Enrollment: 9/2005-Submit Date
Survey Submitted: March 2006

The academic program is challenging but not overwhelming. VLS does a great job of easing you into the swim of law school. I would definitely recommend taking advantage of their great Academic Success Program (which helps with studying and exam writing techniques) to help calm those 1L jitters. Ms. Ellen Swain, the head of the Academic Success Program and a VLS alumna, is very helpful and has a lot of knowledge to share with students. The grading is fair, and you really have to be screwing around not to get over a B-. Most students find it easy to get into the classes they want. Since we only have around 189 students per class it's also easy to get into see professors. In addition, Dean Jefferson, who is the dean of student affairs and a VLS alumnus, is very approachable and has done a lot to make minority and all students comfortable at VLS.

Status: Current student, full-time
Dates of Enrollment: 1/2003-Submit Date
Survey Submitted: March 2006

The professors at Vermont Law are some of the most amazing professors I've ever had. They really care about the students and about their subject matter. It is not unusual to go out to pizza with your professor and a group of students to talk about a recent Supreme Court case. For the most part, they are very accessible and willing to help, not just with legal questions, but also career ones, as well.

Though Vermont Law follows the traditional law curriculum, there are amazing classes in environmental and public service areas, particularly energy and land use law, as well as nonprofit management. You can usually get into the classes that you want.

Also, the externship program is amazing. If you are interested in spending a semester working for a nonprofit, the government or a judge, VLS will help you do that and you can get credit. This is a great way to make inroads at a future job and the VLS externship program is one of the best in the country. I loved my externship with a federal judge. It was one of the highlights of my law school experience.

Status: Current student, full-time
Dates of Enrollment: 8/2003-Submit Date
Survey Submitted: March 2006

VLS does not fit the traditional law school mold because professors place a great deal of emphasis on administering classes that facilitate thoughtful discussion rather than staying strict to the Socratic Method. At the same time, the reading load is demanding and grades are competitive. Most professors stay strict to a B- or B curve. Popular courses are not difficult to get, however popular courses with popular professors can be more of a challenge.

Status: Current student, full-time MSEL
Dates of Enrollment: 8/2004-Submit Date
Survey Submitted: March 2006

The classes are of high quality with great professors. This is especially true of the summer curriculum with visiting professors from real professions that you may want to be involved in. The workload at times can be a lot, but it is the responsibility of the student to look carefully at courses and choose the appropriate number of credits they can handle. Grading is mostly letter grades with a curve, though some first-year classes and such are pass/fail. Classes are offered frequently and in many sections so that there is relative ease in getting popular classes.

Status: Current student, full-time
Dates of Enrollment: 9/2004-Submit Date
Survey Submitted: March 2006

I think the professors do well in the classroom for the most part. Outside of the classroom, I often felt like they were not as accessible as advertised, although by second-year I realized they were accessible—you just need to be confident and plan ahead/make an appointment.

I think many of the profs would rather not give grades, and as a result, pretend they're not an issue. This can be frustrating, as I sometimes felt like there was no information given on how we could best prepare; but maybe that's just law school. People didn't seem to fail classes much...then again, people don't talk about their grades much either.

Academic program has your basic general practice stuff, plus LOTS of environmental law classes. Also classes on global human rights. First-semester Legal Writing is taught by third-year students—an inexpensive option for the school, but low quality learning experience, I think, for the students.

Classes have approx. 75 people per class; seminar classes have 12 to 20. First-year classes are large, with the exception of Legal Research and Writing (20 people). I enjoyed class. Professors varied styles quite a bit—some drilled the same person for 20 minutes, others rarely called on non-volunteers. Classroom environment was not as intimidating as I expected.

Workload: ugh. I found it impossible to get it all done.

Read all of Vault's Law School Surveys at www.vault.com/lawschool — get complete surveys on top law schools, expert advice on applicaton essays, LSAT prep and more.

VAULT CAREER LIBRARY 619

Status: Current student, full-time
Dates of Enrollment: 8/2005-Submit Date
Survey Submitted: March 2006

The first-year classes offered at VLS are the standard 1L fare. Constitutional Law and Civil Procedure are spread across two semesters while courses like Contracts, Torts, Property and Criminal Law are covered in either the fall or the spring semester. The professors are very competent and occasionally tough, but less emphasis is placed on the Socratic Method. Some professors retain a penchant for grilling students, but a cooperative and collaborative approach is generally encouraged.

VLS has recently turned up its writing program a notch, providing intense and in-depth legal writing courses from the get-go. Students are given the nuts and bolts in the first semester culminating in a legal memorandum. Students get to pick from a variety of topics in the second semester covering criminal law and ADR. Memorandums, motions and pleabargains are variously covered and projects are due every few weeks. VLS specializes in appellate advocacy, which also sets it apart from many schools.

The overall workload can be overwhelming, but this is to be expected from any law school. Bottom line: if you work consistently on a day-to-day basis, you will be fine. Professors are very approachable and have an open-door policy—all encourage students with questions to visit during office hours.

Status: Current student, full-time
Dates of Enrollment: 8/2004-Submit Date
Survey Submitted: March 2006

I think that Vermont Law School is one of the most under-rated institutions I have experienced. (I am very familiar with colleges and higher education, their reputations and who generally attends them.) While Vermont Law School continually ranks as one of the top environmental law schools, it receives little credit elsewhere. However, as a result of being a top environmental law school, VLS is able to attract very bright individuals who are not only very good at environmental law, but excel in all areas of law. The students' ability to excel is furthered by an excellent faculty, who on the whole are very accessible. Many of the professors have open doors and are more than willing to spend the time with students to help them understand and gain a strong handle on the material.

Additionally, VLS has a very strong writing program. From my understanding, students go through a much more extensive and rigorous writing program than at most other law schools, and this is particularly important given the amount of writing, and not test taking, one does in the real world. In addition to a faculty that appears to be unusually accessible and involved in school activities, the students are a huge asset to this school. Perhaps because of VLS's lower ranking and emphasis on the environment, though I think this is beginning to broaden, the law school is able to attract a relatively uncompetitive group of students. I am not aware of many schools, at least ones where friends attend, where the students work so collectively and in a friendly manner. This is not to say that everyone does not work very hard and there is no competition, but it is not so in your face. The friendlier nature of the student body as a whole enhances one's experience because there is so much to be learned from others through study groups or general discussion of law school material.

Status: Current student, full-time
Dates of Enrollment: 9/2003-Submit Date
Survey Submitted: March 2006

Vermont Law School provides the ideal environment for three years of legal study. The school is not, however, for those who need a city in order to survive. You'll find a quiet existence at Vermont Law School. Vermont Law School also offers a wonderfully supportive environment, free from the stress that permeates the halls in the more cutthroat schools to the south. This is not to say that VLS students don't excel or work extremely hard. The point is rather that three years of law school happen in altogether more relaxed environment.

As for quality of classes, it's quite high. Profs love living in rural Vermont just as much as many of the students do. It's a welcome escape from suburbia, which is why the faculty is so excellent. It is not very difficult to get the classes that one wants. In the past three years, I've never been closed out of a class that I wanted to take.

Workload is your typical law school workload. You can skate by without doing much, but if that's your approach, you'll have a JD but you'll struggle to get a job. The people who are successful are the people who work hard, are smart and create opportunities for themselves. A student should not come to Vermont Law and expect job offers to come out of thin air upon graduation. However, if one is at the top of the class, on Law Review and active on campus, the interviews and job offers are out there for the taking.

Status: Current student, full-time
Dates of Enrollment: 8/2005-Submit Date
Survey Submitted: March 2006

I think the quality of the classes and academics is superb. My only complaint is that there is not one Republican or conservative faculty member on the entire campus. The debate about issues is limited because of that fact. Based on my conversations with friends at other law schools, the workload at Vermont Law School is equal. The difference is that the faculty here is much more accessible to the students than at other schools.

Status: Alumnus/a, full-time
Dates of Enrollment: 8/2001-5/2004
Survey Submitted: March 2006

The Environmental Law Program is broadening its scope to cover a wide range of environmental topics. The program is a quick and intensive submersion in specific environmental topics which can be very helpful if you put in the time and effort. I would suggest taking advantage of the ever-expanding environmental clinical and institutional opportunities that are being offered because there will be some very unique environmental opportunities available to you that you would not have elsewhere.

Workload is what you make of it at VLS and the professors are strict but reasonable. We were not able to take advantage of the professors, but they were not looking to break us down either. I never had a problem getting into a class that I wanted and some professors were even willing to make exceptions to allow students who showed serious interest in the class in over capacity.

 Employment Prospects

Status: Current student, full-time
Dates of Enrollment: 8/2004-Submit Date
Survey Submitted: March 2006

Many graduates of VLS take the less popular jobs for environmental, non-government agencies and public defender's offices. As is such, the average salary of a VLS graduate is not very high, but the people that go to this law school are willing, and in many cases, eager to take the lower paying job because they want to make a difference. As VLS is an independent law school (not attached to a college or university), we do not have the same volume of on-campus recruitment as other schools may. However, our reputation in the environmental law field does bring some of the preeminent environmental law firms and agencies to campus.

Status: Current student, full-time JD/MSEL
Dates of Enrollment: 8/2003-Submit Date
Survey Submitted: March 2006

Maybe I shouldn't be this blunt, but here's the scoop on VLS and employment. VLS has an incredible reputation as an environmental law school. If you want to do environmental law, then a degree from VLS will help you get a job. If you want to do corporate law, then there are better schools out there for you. VLS is known among the environmental community for providing well-educated, passionate students dedicated to furthering the cause. Graduates go on to work for firms, nonprofits, for Congressmen and even a few for corporations. The school has wonderful internships that provide invaluable opportunities to network and meet potential employers. On the downside, I don't feel like the school does all that much to help students get jobs. It's all in who you know and how willing you are to put yourself out there. I'm not even sure the school has an alumni database and on-campus recruiting is a joke.

Status: Current student, full-time
Dates of Enrollment: 8/2003-Submit Date
Survey Submitted: March 2006

The majority of graduate students obtain public interest jobs, while a minority go to work for private firms and the government. The alumni network is ever-present throughout your law school career, offering opportunities for internships as well as jobs when you graduate. There is little on-campus recruiting, possibly because of the small size of the school.

However, we are not far from major cities such as Boston. We also have a very good Semester in Practice, as well as the Environmental Semester in Washington, D.C. Both of these allow you to work with a variety of groups in a variety of subject areas, from criminal to environmental. Many students work at the Department of Justice or at other nonprofit firms like the National Wildlife Federation. I can say from experience that the Semester in Practice is an extremely rewarding experience.

Status: Current student, full-time
Dates of Enrollment: 8/2005-Submit Date
Survey Submitted: March 2006

Career services is VERY hands-on. I don't know exact employment statistics, but VLS graduates seem to do very well in the workforce. The career services staff is constantly sending out information about upcoming application deadlines or internships, and they have a variety of seminars to really get every student prepared for life after the bar.

Status: Current student, full-time JD/MSEL
Dates of Enrollment: 8/2004-Submit Date
Survey Submitted: March 2006

My current class at VLS is working for an array of employers. Law firms all over the country, big and small; government jobs, federal and state; and clerkships, ranging from the D.C. Circuit to the Vermont State Supreme Court. As for me, my one desire was to become a Judge Advocate General with the U.S. Military. I received an offer, therefore employment possibilities at VLS were great for me since I earned the position I was looking for.

Status: Current student, full-time JD/MSEL
Dates of Enrollment: 8/2004-Submit Date
Survey Submitted: March 2006

Coming from VLS with a JD/MSEL makes you very valuable in the work field, especially in the environmental context. Students from the school work in every area imaginable, public and private. Alumni of the school frequently come to talk to students about how to get jobs and are always willing to help students get jobs or internships. There are many opportunities when employers come to campus to have interviews with students.

Status: Current student, full-time
Dates of Enrollment: 9/2004-Submit Date
Survey Submitted: March 2006

I think a lot of people do not end up becoming traditional lawyers, per se, but get a JD for other reasons. Abby Armstrong, our career services director, is awesome. I don't think VLS has particular prestige unless you're going into environmental law. Although, in Northern New England (VT, ME, NH) there are few law schools, so if you plan on being in New England it's a good place to come. There is on-campus recruiting for local jobs/internships (VT/NH) but not much other stuff. Career services sends weekly e-mails listing jobs, and has many programs where a variety of graduates speak about their current work. I have found these very helpful.

Status: Current student, full-time
Dates of Enrollment: 9/2005-Submit Date
Survey Submitted: March 2006

VLS is a fairly new law school (founded in 1972), so its name recognition in general circles is not as good as, say, Harvard's. However, VLS is well-recognized for producing excellent environmental attorneys.

I have heard one VLS professor describe having a VLS degree as a "wild card" on your resume: it can be helpful or not so helpful depending on what you want to do. The VLS Career Services Office has good connections and works hard to place students in interesting internships and jobs. Since it's the only law school

in VT and is only 40 minutes from the state capital, opportunities to learn about state government abound. I'm just now finishing my first year and have already obtained interviews with the Vermont Supreme Court and Sen. Leahy's office.

Status: Alumnus/a full-time
Dates of Enrollment: 8/2001-5/2004
Survey Submitted: March 2006

As a Tier III school, a VLS student needs to distinguish him/herself from other law school graduates. Many people find rewarding environmental jobs using VLS's reputation and curriculum, although the majority are in the environmental or governmental fields rather than the private sector.

The Career Services Office is there to help you if you need it, but they also do not seek you out or hold your hand. You need to have a plan when you approach them and then they can help you.

The school has a great reputation in Vermont and the New England area, as well as D.C. Also, almost anyone who works in the environmental field knows about Vermont Law School and looks highly on a graduate. On a nationwide scale, the school has contacts in most states, but the alumni network is still relatively small because the school is only 30 years old.

 ## Quality of Life

Status: Current student, full-time
Dates of Enrollment: 8/2003-Submit Date
Survey Submitted: March 2006

Excellent, as long as you don't mind lots of quiet time and tranquility. In my view, a perfect place to study because there are minimal distractions compared to living in a city. Housing stock is quite old, but often quite rustic and fun! Facilities are getting better, but they still have old Vermont charm, which does include power outages and frozen walkways. A perfect New England town, but don't expect to be able to go out to dinner after 9 p.m.!!

Status: Current student, full-time JD/MSEL
Dates of Enrollment: 8/2003-Submit Date
Survey Submitted: March 2006

VLS offers students the highest quality of life possible for a law student...seriously. The school does everything it can to keep students stress-free and happy. Debevois Hall recently underwent renovations and is now fabulous! I wish I could have a class in there! VLS is a green campus complete with composting toilets (you get used to them after a while). Wireless access throughout and definitely well kept.

Status: Current student, full-time
Dates of Enrollment: 8/2003-Submit Date
Survey Submitted: March 2006

The quality of life here in Vermont is good, but simple. With little exception, housing is high quality and affordable. The campus is constantly expanding its facilities and we have a brand-new classroom and office building. Crime is extremely low and very often, people leave their doors unlocked every night. People are friendly and it is easy to become part of the community around here, as people are very accepting.

Status: Current student, full-time
Dates of Enrollment: 8/2005-Submit Date
Survey Submitted: March 2006

VLS is in a VERY small town, which has its ups and downs. On the plus side, the small-town atmosphere makes you always feel at home, and there aren't as many distractions to take you away from studying. You definitely have to get used to driving to the grocery store, because while there are a few small shops in town, but most things are a good 20 minutes away by car. With a little effort, there's always something to keep the average law student entertained—and there are always plenty of people around who will join you on any excursion. All in all, the community is incredibly supportive, and it's a great place to live. Rent is a little high for the few amenities we have, but crime is virtually nonexistent in this quaint New England town.

Read all of Vault's Law School Surveys at www.vault.com/lawschool — get complete surveys on top law schools, expert advice on applicaton essays, LSAT prep and more.

VAULT CAREER LIBRARY 621

Status: Current student, full-time
Dates of Enrollment: 9/2005-Submit Date
Survey Submitted: March 2006

Vermont is beautiful, affordable, cold, quiet, extremely safe and sometimes boring! But all in all it's a great place to go to school for three years. Everyone is nice and pretty friendly. As a new student and a new driver, my neighbor down the road even helped me pick out my first car!

As a single woman who lives in a house by myself I feel pretty safe in Vermont. While there is no on-campus housing, VLS's housing office posts listings for apartments and houses in the area. You can find a cheap apartment for one person for around $600. If you have dog(s) expect to maybe pay a little more but it is definitely doable! (I have one crazy huge dog and another mellow dog and was able to find something, so owners of crazy dogs don't despair!) Definitely have something nailed down BEFORE Memorial Day Weekend if possible. Also ask to speak to the former tenant and/or to see a copy of the previous year's heating bills, which can be as high as $200/month in addition to your rent!

The town of South Royalton has a nice food co-op, a deli, a pizza parlor and two small restaurants that are all good in a flash. For more selection and big box stores, students travel to West Lebanon, NH (no tax!!) to do most of their shopping. Regardless of what the admissions office tells you, definitely get a car as soon as you are able to! Car insurance is pretty cheap (around $600 per year) in Vermont. You DON'T need to buy a big four-wheel drive vehicle. Buy a used Subaru with AWD, get snow tires, drive carefully and you will be fine! My Subaru has been great to me and has always started, even on VERY COLD mornings. The major bad thing about VLS is its horrible, little gym. While most students use this pathetic, tiny gym that is about the size of a trailer, some students pay to use Dartmouth's gym or join some private ones about 20 minutes away.

Status: Current student, full-time
Dates of Enrollment: 8/2003-Submit Date
Survey Submitted: March 2006

Excellent, except that there is very little culture beyond microbreweries and organic farming. The air is crisp, the food local and pesticide free. But housing is expensive if you want to live in town. However, many students rent fabulous old farmhouses a few miles away for very little money. As a former city person, I find it almost absurd how safe it is here, but keep in mind that it is totally rural.

Status: Current student, full-time
Dates of Enrollment: 8/2005-Submit Date
Survey Submitted: March 2006

VLS and South Royalton are the quintessential pictures of rural Vermont. Very appealing if you enjoy country scenery, easy access to parks, hiking trails, skiing and touring your motorcycle in the summer and fall. Farmers markets are abundant, but 24-hour cafes and restaurants with predictable hours are nonexistent. Of course, Montpelier and Burlington aren't far and offer more of a typical urban experience. Boston is only a couple of hours away.

The campus itself is very modern. Wi-Fi has been installed everywhere. Computer labs provide plenty of connectivity. There are many places to study, both private and communal, and all very comfortable. There is a well-maintained gym for students provided for a minimal fee.

Status: Current student, full-time
Dates of Enrollment: 8/2004-Submit Date
Survey Submitted: March 2006

Vermont Law School is in a very little town in Vermont. The surroundings are beautiful, but there is certainly no city life. Crime is pretty low, rent is certainly low and the outdoors are very accessible. When it is warm, you can find students outside on lawn chairs on the grass studying surrounded by beautiful green hills on almost all sides. The school itself has a brand-new wing with three classrooms fully wired with every type of electronic device one could think to put in a classroom or courtroom. The rest of the school is pretty modern and in very good shape.

While the rural setting of VLS initially might be a major turn off to some students who think that there is no way to get your hands wet with exposure to

the practice of law like you would be in a big city, this is not the case. Further the concern that there is nothing to do is also not true. While Vermont and New Hampshire do not have the big-name law firms, there are plenty of smaller la firms who are happy to have law student interns. And what is great about thes smaller places is that you actually get real experience because they need yo help. There are also all of the government employers and courts too.

Status: Current student, full-time
Dates of Enrollment: 9/2005-Submit Date
Survey Submitted: March 2006

The library is small, but contains many useful books (including a whole floor c environmental texts); and books not in the library's collection are availabl through interlibrary loan. Many students do the bulk of their research online, s it is entirely possible to avoid the library to some extent.

There is a cafe on campus, but no "dining hall" like students at residentia undergraduate institutions might expect. Food options include a few restauran in town, the cafe on campus and making your own (there is a co-op in town an supermarkets in surrounding towns). The neighborhood is quite nice for thos who like rural living. The two-person constable's office just became an offici town police department, and safety is not a huge concern. The community close-knit, and VLS students and staff look after each other. If you leave you car lights on or forget your laptop in the library, expect an all-campus e-mail t let you know!

 ## Social Life

Status: Current student, full-time
Dates of Enrollment: 8/2003-Submit Date
Survey Submitted: March 2006

The school provides ample social activities. You will become very close to you classmates. You have no choice unless you plan on leaving town every weekend This is an EXTREMELY community-oriented school, very liberal (althoug generally open to minority views) and very progressive (composting toilets! Don't be afraid if you're not "green," but realize that you might be when yo leave.

Status: Current student, full-time JD/MSEL
Dates of Enrollment: 8/2003-Submit Date
Survey Submitted: March 2006

You have to see South Royalton and experience it to truly appreciate it. It's rura Vermont living at its finest! Local bar, local restaurant, local co-op...it's all yo need! The school does a great job of providing social events. I highly encourag getting involved with the on-campus organizations to get the most out of th social opportunities. Join rugby (or better yet, just date a player) and you're sur to hit the hottest parties. Nearby towns offer an escape if that's what you' looking for and Burlington and Montreal aren't that far away. Great skiing within an hour's drive in any direction. There's tubing down the White River i the summer and PLENTY of great day hikes for all of the nature lovers out ther

Status: Current student, full-time
Dates of Enrollment: 8/2003-Submit Date
Survey Submitted: March 2006

There are two bars in town, as well as four restaurants. It's small pickings as fa as dating goes, because you either date someone at school or you don't reall date. It is a town of only about 700 people, and most of them are marrie Events are usually school-sponsored, such as the Snow Ball, or Lawyer Prom a we call it, town dances and numerous speaker events.

The favorite student pastime is going to the largest bar in town, Crossroads During our first year in law school, we were at the bar to hang out as soon a they opened as well as every weekend. It's a great place to talk and meet othe people from the area. Another student favorite is the Tunbridge World's Fai where you can go to see the pig races, farm animal judging, and go on variou rides. It is a good buzz to spend time out of town.

Lastly, the school hosts a one week-long event every semester. In the fall, w have Oktoberfest, where we have a week of team games and small schoo parties. There is a similar event in the spring with Wynterfoest, which culminates with the Snow Ball at the end of the week.

Status: Current student, full-time
Dates of Enrollment: 8/2005-Submit Date
Survey Submitted: March 2006

If you come to Vermont Law School, just be prepared to have to think creatively when it comes to having a social life. With only one bar in town and a few restaurants, students sometimes have to think outside the box to have a good time. All in all, there's always something to do—you just have to be willing to jump in the car and head to Hanover, NH (for the Dartmouth College activities) or just get a group of friends together during the winter to go skating on the town green. The law school's student activities board and all of the student groups do a pretty good job of planning events for the students, so despite our small size, there's usually something interesting going on. This definitely isn't city life, but even small town kids know how to have a good time!

Status: Current student, full-time
Dates of Enrollment: 8/2003-Submit Date
Survey Submitted: March 2006

Since Vermont Law School is located in a quaint farm town, there are not many areas that one can go hang out. There is basically one bar in town (Crossroads) and one restaurant (Five Olde Tavern). In my opinion, the restaurant is not that good. However, the community is very tight-knit and there are a lot of other things to do such as skiing, snowshoeing and just hanging out with other people.

Also, one can go to Burlington (75-minute drive) or Hanover (25-minute drive) if they really want to visit more restaurants, bars, or see more shows. These would also be the cities to visit in order to find any clubs. The dating scene is basically limited to the law school community and is very limited because of this. Not a great school to attend if you are a single person looking to find someone, but people have been able to find people to date here so it is not impossible by any means.

Status: Current student, full-time
Dates of Enrollment: 8/2003-Submit Date
Survey Submitted: March 2006

Ummm. Beer and skiing. House parties. Kind of like high school/boarding school. People are extremely laid back and friendly. There are lots of places to explore in Vermont. Montreal is not that far away. It is very necessary to have a car here.

Status: Current student, full-time
Dates of Enrollment: 8/2004-Submit Date
Survey Submitted: March 2006

The nice thing about Vermont is that there aren't too many distractions but if you need to be distracted you can usually manage it. There are two bars in South Royalton but we are only a short drive from Hanover, NH, which is a pretty big town. For longer trips, Boston is two and a half hours away.

As far as dating goes, you are pretty much limited to your classmates. Who needs to date in law school anyway? The activities committee on campus organizes a lot of events for students so there are usually things going on for those who are looking for something to do. Every year we have Oktoberfest and Wynterfoest, which are basically comprised of ridiculous team sports and drinking.

Status: Current student, full-time
Dates of Enrollment: 9/2005-Submit Date
Survey Submitted: March 2006

There are more than 40 active campus groups and motivated students can always create new groups. Students can also work on the *Vermont Journal of Environmental Law* or the *Vermont Law Review*. There is no greek system. Overall, social life at VLS is what you make of it. Many students choose to leave campus on the weekends to visit such metropolises as Burlington, Montpelier, West Lebanon or the Dartmouth College region. For those that remain on campus, there is more than enough to distract them from their studies.

The School Says

Five features distinguish legal education at Vermont Law School—a core JD curriculum that emphasizes the broader social context of the law in addition to focusing on legal doctrine and analysis; clinical/experiential programs that complement traditional classroom instruction; the internationally recognized Master of Studies in Environmental Law and LLM in Environmental Law programs; the informal atmosphere of a beautiful rural setting; and a real sense of community and commitment to public service.

Situated in a National Register Historic District along Vermont's scenic White River, the school's 13 acre campus is an integrated complex of renovated turn-of-the-century buildings, a new computer center, a modern library and community center. A 25,000 square foot classroom building was completed in summer 1998 and the original classroom building, Deveboise Hall, was completely renovated in 2005.

The student body is comprised of approximately 635 students. The entering JD class of about 200 students represents over 40 states and several countries, is 50 percent female, 20 percent students of color and has an average age of 26. Classes are small and students have ample opportunities to get to know their professors outside the classroom. The student-faculty ratio of 12.4:1 is one of the 10 lowest of all ABA approved law schools.

Our top ranked Environmental programs offer ten areas of specialization. The curriculum also focuses on Public Interest Law; General Practice, which has classes structured to operate as a law firm with professors in the role of senior partners; and International Law, with programs in Canada, France and Italy. Our wide range of experiential offerings provide students the opportunity to gain practical skills in settings that range from the South Royalton Legal Clinic on campus to Semester in Practice settings all over the U.S. and the world.

The joint JD/MSEL program can be completed in three years. The joint JD/MEM program, in collaboration with the Yale University School of Forestry and Environmental Studies, is a four-year program. The JD/French Masters II dual degree program allows participants to earn in four years both a JD degree from Vermont Law School and an advanced level Master's Degree in Business Organization Law from the University of Cergy-Pointoise. Graduates may sit for the bar examination in each country, according to each country's requirements. Because of European Union reciprocity rules, successful bar candidates in France may practice in all member states of the European Union.

Read all of Vault's Law School Surveys at www.vault.com/lawschool — get complete surveys on top law schools, expert advice on applicaton essays, LSAT prep and more.

VAULT CAREER LIBRARY   623

George Mason University School of Law

Law School Admissions
3301 Fairfax Drive
Arlington, VA 2220
Admissions phone: (703) 993-8010
Admissions fax: (703) 993-8088
Admissions URL: http://www.law.gmu.edu/admission/

 Admission

Status: Current student, full-time
Dates of Enrollment: 8/2003-Submit Date
Survey Submitted: October 2005

I believe, as with most law schools, the decision is made mostly upon your prior grades and LSAT score; however, as I had extensive work experience between undergrad and law school, this probably did help me somewhat. I had poor undergrad grades, a great LSAT score, good work experience and I still got in. I'm now in the top 20 percent because I've worked very hard.

Status: Alumnus/a, part-time
Dates of Enrollment: 8/2001-5/2005
Survey Submitted: April 2006

The admissions process was a typical one involving forms, transcripts and recommendations. The admissions staff is extremely friendly and accommodating. Since Mason broke into the top tier of law schools, it has been very difficult to be accepted, but the process itself is easy. What particularly impressed me was the way I was notified. Before I received a letter, I received a very nice call from Dean Richards. She congratulated me and expressed her hope I would choose Mason. I was not the only one—I believe most students received calls. I was very impressed with the personal touch.

Status: Alumnus/a, full-time
Dates of Enrollment: 8/2002-5/2005
Survey Submitted: March 2006

The admissions office is friendly and responsive. They have a discussion board on their web site now and the director will respond personally to e-mails or calls. The director called me personally to invite me. I applied early (October) and was accepted within three weeks. The school is becoming increasingly selective and, as a result, must focus on the "numbers" as do most top schools; however, GMU has a student body with a wide range of experience, so additional work experience can also help.

Status: Alumnus/a, full-time
Dates of Enrollment: 9/2001-5/2004
Survey Submitted: March 2006

The admissions process was routine but the acceptance process was magnificent. The dean of admissions contacts every admittee personally to invite them to join the entering class. It is an extremely welcoming experience. George Mason is a difficult school to get into. It is located two miles from Washington, D.C. (It takes me 17 minutes at rush hour to drive from my office in downtown D.C. to the campus.) The proximity to D.C. combined with state-school tuition makes it very popular—but that is not all that makes it a first choice for students. It is a top-tier school that is still on the rise. It is small enough to allow for a cohesive student body and great professor-student ratio.

Status: Current student, full-time
Dates of Enrollment: 8/2003-Submit Date
Survey Submitted: September 2004

GMU is all about the numbers—GPA and LSAT. The admissions office is well-organized, helpful and willing to help applicants, but in the end your numbers will make or break you. My undergraduate GPA was not particularly outstanding, so despite a masters degree (with a 3.93 GPA), seven years of work experience, and 167 on my LSATs, I was waitlisted. I was accepted to the evening program and then transferred to the day program with no difficulty.

Status: Alumnus/a, full-time
Dates of Enrollment: 8/2000-5/2003
Survey Submitted: March 2005

GMU is a highly competitive school when it comes to admissions. Each year, the LSAT average goes up. Similarly, each year GMU's ranking also goes up. When I started, we were a second-tier school and now we are ranked in the first tier, in the 30s. From my experience, while high LSAT scores make admissions easier, it is not the only focus. I believe that the admissions staff, which is excellent, is really looking for well-rounded candidates that are mature, sincerely interested in attending GMUSL and eager to begin law school. If you are sincerely interested in GMUSL, show your interest to the admissions staff. Also, write a good essay, try to meet the staff in person and take a tour. Personalizing the process can work to your advantage.

Status: Alumnus/a, full-time
Dates of Enrollment: 8/1997-5/2001
Survey Submitted: March 2005

Good undergraduate grades and high LSAT scores are a must. In addition, particularly for the evening program, the school seeks out students with diverse backgrounds and careers. Because of the school's focus on law and economics, financial or economic backgrounds are particularly useful.

Status: Alumnus/a, part-time
Dates of Enrollment: 8/2001-12/2004
Survey Submitted: April 2005

Admission to George Mason is highly competitive. My personal experience involves being waitlisted. I took the February LSAT and applied shortly thereafter. I was placed on the waitlist in early April. My impression is that in order to keep the ratio of admission offers to actual matriculation high, only those they believe will attend are admitted from the waitlist. In addition to mailing in my acceptance of the invitation to be on the waitlist, I wrote a letter to Anne Richard, the dean of admissions, emphasizing that Mason was my first choice and that I would definitely attend if admitted. I followed this up with additional letters of recommendation, and by using every opportunity possible to show up on campus (e.g., by sitting in on a class).

After admission, I strongly felt that Mason places a heavy premium on the factors that weigh heavily in the *U.S. News* rankings. Thus, high LSAT scores and a high GPA are important. That said, I was told by an admissions staff person that those whose strongest qualities are non-quantifiable—work experience, hardship—are most likely to be admitted early in the admissions process during the fall. Early in the admissions cycle, the admissions committee is fresh and has the time to review applications carefully. Late in the game (like in March), if you don't have the test scores or grades, your application is unlikely to be reviewed carefully.

Status: Current student, full-time
Dates of Enrollment: 8/2003-Submit Date
Survey Submitted: June 2004

Apply early, as soon after the initial deadline as possible. Have some economics background. George Mason is very selective for a school of its ranking, mostly because it is small and cheap. If you are worried about getting in, apply to the evening program. You can transfer to the day program if you want to after the first semester.

> **George Mason Law states:** "Our admissions standards are the same for the day and evening programs, although there is much greater demand for the day program. Students may switch from the evening program to the day program after the first year."

Status: Current student, full-time
Dates of Enrollment: 9/2003-Submit Date
Survey Submitted: April 2004

George Mason University School of Law is very selective. Last year fewer than
9 percent of applicants were accepted. The median LSAT score was a 164 and
the median GPA was a little below a 3.6. The admissions office is very helpful
and is willing to help in whatever way possible. I would encourage interested
applicants to take a tour of the school.

Status: Current student, full-time
Dates of Enrollment: 8/2002-Submit Date
Survey Submitted: December 2003

The admissions process is highly competitive. The admissions department is
very helpful, and the dean of admissions runs a discussion board on the school's
web site. The school does not conduct interviews. They place a word limit on
the essay. The school is in love with the law and economics, so an economics
background is a plus.

Academics

Status: Current student, full-time
Dates of Enrollment: 8/2003-Submit Date
Survey Submitted: October 2005

The program is very difficult. Much of the philosophy of professors here is
based on economics, so students are required to take at least a semester of
economics in their first year. Most of the best students don't seem to have real
study groups, because they all do all of the reading on their own and make their
own outlines. That said, even the best students do share their outlines and help
each other out in explaining sticky points. The atmosphere in that sense is very
congenial, and there's more self-competition than competition between students.
Being based in economics, the school is very conservative compared to other law
schools, which I like.

Every class with over 15 students is curved to a strict 2.9 grade point average.
This means that in some classes, it can be very difficult to get an A, and getting
an A means going the extra mile—including sometimes reading outside the
assignments. Professors, especially full-time professors, are extremely helpful.
They always have predictable designated office hours, and often will spend
plenty of time discussing issues with students. That doesn't mean they always
give you the answers though—often it means more hints and prompting for you
to go back and find the answer yourself. The Socratic Method is used
extensively by some professors here.

The writing program requires four semesters of standard writing classes,
including Legal Research and Writing I and II, Appellate Writing and Legal
Drafting. I think one could substitute other writing courses for the Legal
Drafting course, but at any rate, there's quite a lot of writing required. It's great
to get that much training in legal writing, but as the papers are graded by upper-
class students serving as "writing fellows," sometimes the grading can be
idiosyncratic and frustrating. At any rate, compared to most other schools, you
get a ton of training in writing well.

With a memo due every couple of weeks for the writing classes and tons of
reading for the other classes, the workload is heavy. Students really have to
manage their time extremely well in order to cope. Some people seem to do fine
with it, while other top students sleep very little the first couple of years. But
that's what you expect from law school, right?

Status: Alumnus/a, part-time
Dates of Enrollment: 8/2001-5/2005
Survey Submitted: April 2006

The program is primarily geared toward the practice of law. Where some
programs are more theoretical and geared toward producing professors, most of
Mason's curriculum is geared toward practical application and passing the bar
exam. The only exception is the school's requirement that all incoming students
take one Law and Economics class. The class is useful only in a theoretical
sense. It's a fun intellectual exercise, but other than that, it is fairly useless.

As with any school, the quality of classes depends on the teachers, so some
classes are better than others. Although there are some bad teachers at Mason,
they are few and far between (indeed, most of them left by the time I graduated).
Most of the classes are excellent. Some are taught by academics, and many are
taught by practitioners. There are many judges on the faculty and a Nobel Prize
winner.

Perhaps Mason's strongest attribute is its commitment to legal writing. It is an
excellent program. It is painful while you are in school, but the benefits are
tremendous. Employers need attorneys who can write, and the additional
research required for writing classes helps hone research skills. It is a
tremendous program, and the director of the program does a spectacular job.

Status: Alumnus/a, full-time
Dates of Enrollment: 8/2002-5/2005
Survey Submitted: March 2006

It's easy to get any class you want. Occasionally classes are cancelled for lack
of interest. There are not as many options for classes as there are at larger
schools because of the size of Mason's faculty. However, there are plenty of
specialized courses in IP and economics. We have some of the best IP and
economics faculty in the country. The professors are, for the most part,
extremely responsive and available to students. Because the school is fairly
small (200 to 300 per year) the classes are generally small and it's easy to get
individual attention and form close relationships with the professors.

Status: Alumnus/a, full-time
Dates of Enrollment: 9/2001-5/2004
Survey Submitted: March 2006

George Mason has highly experienced and well-published full-time faculty. In
addition, its proximity to D.C. attracts phenomenal adjunct professors. It was
such a privilege, for example, to study First Amendment Law under the
Honorable Raymond Randolph of the Court of Appeals for the D.C. Circuit.
When Judge Randolph talked about the Pentagon Papers, he spoke not just from
a legal perspective and an historical perspective but from his own personal
experience. I studied Administrative Law under a partner from Williams and
Connolly who was not only funny, warm and fabulous, but he brought such
experience and gravitas to his teaching. He made me fall in love with
Administrative Law, which was then a required course, and as a result, the very
first case I worked on was before an administrative law judge and I won! George
Mason is also a law and economics law school.

To be honest, I only applied to one law school and was completely unaware of
the economics angle at Mason. For the record, the required economics course in
my first year was my lowest grade in law school, so while I did not have an
economics bent personally, I still graduated magna cum laude. The fact that
George Mason has a law and economics focus should not put anyone off from
applying there.

Status: Current student, full-time
Dates of Enrollment: 8/2003-Submit Date
Survey Submitted: September 2004

The professors are outstanding. I have never had a problem getting the classes
I wanted. The grading is on a 2.9 curve, so lots of B's are given out. GMU offers
several different specialty tracks and sequences (like majors and minors in
college), with the Intellectual Property Track being the most popular. The
workload is very manageable, but it's still law school. Some professors assign
more reading than others. I never felt that I had too much work my first year; I
never felt overwhelmed.

Status: Alumnus/a, full-time
Dates of Enrollment: 8/2000-5/2003
Survey Submitted: March 2005

GMUSL does not have the course selection that you will see at some bigger
schools. On the other hand, most classes are relatively small, and most
professors are great. The most impressive thing about GMU is the professors.
Our professors are exciting, enthusiastic and smart. GMU recently ranked
seventh in the country, even above Yale Law, for its faculty research. I
particularly enjoyed three professors and was able to take two plus classes with
each professor. While GMU may not have the number of courses a larger school
may have, GMUs course selections are well thought out; there is no fluff.

Read all of Vault's Law School Surveys at www.vault.com/lawschool — get complete surveys on top law schools,
expert advice on applicaton essays, LSAT prep and more.

VAULT CAREER LIBRARY   625

Additionally, GMU offers the best opportunities of any school to learn litigation skills. There are many great legal clinics, several Trial Advocacy classes, Expert Evidence courses, Scientific Evidence courses and others. If you are interested in litigation, GMU is the right place to be. Furthermore, the Trial Ad courses are taught by outstanding local practitioners and judges. My Trial Ad course was conducted by Judge Sheridan in his courtroom. This was an amazing experience. It seems obvious, but to me the best person to learn trial techniques from is a judge.

Status: Alumnus/a, full-time
Dates of Enrollment: 8/1997-5/2001
Survey Submitted: March 2005

In my opinion, one of the best things about the evening program at GMUSL is that they require the full professors to teach both a day and an evening section. This means that the evening students receive the same instruction as the day students for the basic introductory courses while still enjoying the benefits of the wonderful adjuncts the school attracts for the upper-level elective classes. I discovered that this is not necessarily the case with the evening programs at other local law schools where the evening students pay the same tuition as the day students but often have sub-par professors for the key introductory courses.

Status: Alumnus/a, part-time
Dates of Enrollment: 8/2001-12/2004
Survey Submitted: April 2005

I never had trouble getting into a popular class so long as I didn't wait until the last minute. Students are graded on a strict curve—no one fails unless they really deserve it, but most students get a B or B+ in any given class. Be warned—getting grades back takes months sometimes, particularly in large classes. Fall grades in March or spring grades in August is not uncommon.

One thing I loved about Mason was that the part-time program is equivalent to the full-time program. The professors are the same—often you can opt to sit in on a class at a different time of day if it's more convenient for you. Mason also ensures that evening students have the same journal, moot court and other extra curricular opportunities as the day students.

Status: Current student, full-time
Dates of Enrollment: 8/2003-Submit Date
Survey Submitted: June 2004

There is a required economics course the first semester, which scares some people. If you have any sort of math background, though, it's almost a relief to have one "traditional" class your first semester of law school instead of having all case classes.

Status: Alumnus/a, full-time
Dates of Enrollment: 8/2000-5/2003
Survey Submitted: April 2004

GMU has an amazing faculty, and to me this was by far the best part of going to GMU. I never had trouble getting the classes I wanted to take. A great deal of GMU's faculty is relatively young (which is great, I think), and everyone is enthusiastic, not to mention incredibly intelligent and dedicated.

Status: Current student, full-time
Dates of Enrollment: 8/2001-Submit Date
Survey Submitted: September 2003

The faculty is very responsive to the needs of the students. Students do not struggle excessively to get into desired classes, and class sizes are reasonable. Grading is on a curve, as is typical for law school—which tends to create a somewhat competitive work environment (but that is not unique to this school). More seasoned professors tend to have more to offer in the classroom environment, though some of my favorite professors have been young.

Employment Prospects

Status: Current student, full-time
Dates of Enrollment: 8/2003-Submit Date
Survey Submitted: October 2005

Employment prospects for Intellectual Property students are incredible. W have access to alumni and adjunct professors from many of the top patent firm in D.C. If you want to get a part-time law clerk job at a top patent firm, ofte just asking at the right time can be enough. Many students in the top third of th class studying IP get summer associate jobs at these firms for both first- an second-year summers. This is an incredible place to learn IP—you will hav access to many of the best minds and prominent figures in the field, judges fro the Federal Circuit, alumni and adjuncts from the major firms in D.C., and man former patent examiners in the part-time program.

Many firms only interview students in the top 10 percent of the class. Th means that your first-year grades are extremely important. The top firm interview only the top 25, 20 or 10 percent of students, and the tip-top firm really want to see Law Review or moot court board on your resume. If you don get on a journal or moot court, you need to get real work experience distinguish yourself. Again, the students in the lower two-thirds of the class sti eventually find jobs, but have to solicit lots of firms and network to do it— won't come easily through the on-campus interview process.

Status: Alumnus/a, part-time
Dates of Enrollment: 8/2001-5/2005
Survey Submitted: April 2006

All my friends went on to BigLaw firms and I know BigLaw firms lik recruiting at Mason. In fact, my law firm currently has four Mason graduates i the litigation department alone. I don't have experience with the alumn network, but on-campus recruiting was a great experience.

The firm where I would eventually work was conducting fall interviews o campus. My GPA was just slightly below their minimum. One of the placemen office staff called my firm, and told them they had to meet with me despite th fact I did not meet their minimum. They met with me as a result, I got the ca back interview, did the summer associate program and now I work i commercial litigation there. The point of this is that the Career Planning an Placement Office work very hard for the students. They helped me apply t firms not recruiting at Mason, such as those out of state. They did a great job.

Status: Alumnus/a, full-time
Dates of Enrollment: 8/2002-5/2005
Survey Submitted: March 2006

GMU is a young school and therefore has fewer alumni out there to help However, most alumni are extremely loyal to GMU and participate in career related events, such as mock interviews, moot court, OCI and internships. Ther are some great ties to the government via the faculty. The career center is helpfu and pays attention to individual requests, but can only do so much. The OC process does not seem to be as automated as that at better-funded schools (e.g we have to copy all of our own resumes, letters and application packets). Th career center does coordinate the clerkship recommendation process, but doe not have much inside information about clerkships.

Status: Alumnus/a, full-time
Dates of Enrollment: 9/2001-5/2004
Survey Submitted: March 2006

I work at a fabulous top-tier law firm. As George Mason continues building i reputation and continues placing students in a wide variety of post-graduate jobs opportunities across all interest areas will continue expanding. There is a ver active career services office, the school conducts on-campus fall recruiting fo second-year students and a slightly smaller spring recruiting program targeted a the same category (others can participate, but the employers choose the student in which they have an interest). Career services is also spending more tim focusing on opportunities for students who are interested in non-traditional jobs i.e., who are more interested in public interest law than in working at a law firm

Status: Current student, full-time
Dates of Enrollment: 8/2003-Submit Date
Survey Submitted: September 2004

Most of the firms that recruit on campus are from D.C. or Northern Virginia. If you want to practice in these locations, GMU is a great choice. A few firms from NY, Boston and PA come to campus as well. I have received interest from firms in NY and NJ that did not come to campus; I contacted them via unsolicited mailings and have been invited in for interviews. So although GMU doesn't provide easy access to firms outside of D.C., finding a job outside of D.C. is do-able.

Status: Alumnus/a, part-time
Dates of Enrollment: 8/2001-12/2004
Survey Submitted: April 2005

I worked for an employer through school that can't provide me a legal position now that I've graduated. I don't have a job and I am not having a lot of luck at the moment. I am told job prospects will improve dramatically once the bar exam results are out (assuming I pass!). Many students also get clerkships. The Fairfax County judges are very supportive of Mason students—countless students work and clerk for judges every year.

Status: Current student, full-time
Dates of Enrollment: 8/2003-Submit Date
Survey Submitted: June 2004

There is a GREAT internship program with a local judge who places students with judges and public defenders Everyone gets law-related jobs their first summer if they want them—although most are unpaid. Washington, D.C. has lots of jobs even during bad economic times because of the government, and there is no city with more diverse options for lawyers.

Status: Current student, full-time
Dates of Enrollment: 8/2002-Submit Date
Survey Submitted: December 2003

Career services works overtime trying to help each student. Finding a paying job as a first-year is not hard, but it takes work. Second-year jobs are plentiful, and there are ample on-campus interviews for those in the top 33 percent of the class. The students in the bottom 67 percent need to work a bit harder at finding jobs, but they still get a lot of responses, just no on-campus interviews. The school's reputation is very strong in Virginia, D.C. and Maryland. Its national reputation is also rising with each passing year. The school is highly regarded by employers as a "school on the rise." The school does have a reputation for being more conservative than most law schools and for being economics driven.

Quality of Life

Status: Current student, full-time
Dates of Enrollment: 8/2003-Submit Date
Survey Submitted: October 2005

Housing in Arlington is expensive, but it's a cool area. There's really little crime to speak of, as opposed to D.C. or Maryland. The law school building is very new and has great facilities, including power outlets and network jacks at each seat, as well as wireless networking and printing now. There's free printing of cases through Lexis or Westlaw. Everyone has access to both Lexis and Westlaw, although you have to be doing something at school to continue using them during the summer.

Status: Alumnus/a, part-time
Dates of Enrollment: 8/2001-5/2005
Survey Submitted: April 2006

There is no housing for law students provided by the school. The campus is in a great location, just three blocks from the Metro. It is just a few blocks from several bars, restaurants and coffee shops (all essential for surviving law school). The building is state-of-the-art. It was built six or seven years ago. It is a sharp-looking building, wired for Internet in the classrooms and it has Wi-Fi, as well. The library is great and the library staff is very helpful. The neighborhood is great and crime is at a minimum. However, many students have had laptops stolen from the library, so all computers must be locked down in the library.

Status: Alumnus/a, full-time
Dates of Enrollment: 8/2002-5/2005
Survey Submitted: March 2006

One of the best parts of GMU is that the campus is in the heart of Arlington. It's extremely safe but close to many shops, restaurants and businesses. Also only about 10 minutes out of D.C. by Metro or car. There is no on-campus housing. There is a cafeteria that serves lunch, dinner and occasionally breakfast, with plenty of seating. Several vending machines and local places to eat nearby. Most students commute from various areas of Northern VA or D.C.

Status: Alumnus/a, full-time
Dates of Enrollment: 9/2001-5/2004
Survey Submitted: March 2006

George Mason is a commuter school. It is not located at the main campus of the undergraduate institution. Rather, it is located in a bustling part of Arlington, Virginia very, very close to the District of Columbia. The campus continues to expand, with new buildings going up even as I write this. Parking is always something of a problem but the school seeks creative solutions, including valet parking.

Status: Current student, full-time
Dates of Enrollment: 8/2003-Submit Date
Survey Submitted: September 2004

The neighborhood is clean and safe, with easy Metro access. Parking is a problem, so I just take the Metro. The facility is only four or five years old. There is no real campus. The law school is in Arlington and the undergraduate school is in Fairfax, so the building is the only campus to speak of. No housing is provided by the school.

Status: Alumnus/a, full-time
Dates of Enrollment: 8/2000-5/2003
Survey Submitted: March 2005

Another perk about GMU is the community you join when you begin your first year. You will not start class with cutthroat students jockeying for positions. You will start with classmates all eager to learn and to enjoy their law school experience. The facilities at GMU are topnotch. Most students live nearby, as there are several neighborhoods with moderate rental prices close to campus. GMU is also located three blocks from Virginia Square Metro, so you can Metro to school. GMU offers a great evening student program. I began this way and then switched to the full-time program. Each class is about 50/50 evening to day students. The evening program allows you to work full-time and to graduate in four years. You will have the option of transferring to the day program if space exists, and you just have to make up a few credits in the summer.

The summer program is great and offers fun courses with some of GMU's best faculty members. In my summer classes, there were several visiting students who came just to have a class with a specific professor on a specific topic. This speaks highly of the quality of the faculty. Summer is also a chance to earn extra credits and hopefully boost your GPA.

Status: Current student, full-time
Dates of Enrollment: 8/2003-Submit Date
Survey Submitted: June 2004t

No on-campus housing—housing in the area is expensive. One very small cafeteria, but lots of great restaurants nearby. Very near to D.C. and right off the Metro so people live all over the place. If you are a Virginia resident, you can't beat the price of tuition for a law school of GMU's reputation. Every student can get a parking pass, but there are not enough spaces so if you arrive in the afternoon, plan on leaving the key with the parking attendant and being stack parked—more parking is being constructed now about a half block away, I think.

Status: Alumnus/a, full-time
Dates of Enrollment: 8/2000-5/2003
Survey Submitted: April 2004

GMU's campus is excellent and the law school building is only a few years old. It is in a great neighborhood, Virginia Square/Clarendon. You can walk from school to lots of nice restaurants and bars and the area is very safe. Regarding quality of life, I highly recommend GMU. One reason I chose the area is because I could work part-time at a law firm to get some practical experience, be

Read all of Vault's Law School Surveys at www.vault.com/lawschool — get complete surveys on top law schools, expert advice on applicaton essays, LSAT prep and more.

VAULT CAREER LIBRARY   627

very close to D.C. and afford the tuition. I believe GMU is by far the best value school in the country.

Status: Current student, full-time
Dates of Enrollment: 8/2001-Submit Date
Survey Submitted: January 2004

GMUSL is located in Arlington, VA and is removed from the main campus of the university, which is in Fairfax, VA. Students tend to live in the surrounding areas, though there is no campus housing. The law school is located in one building, though there are plans to expand the Arlington campus in coming years.

 ## Social Life

Status: Alumnus/a, full-time
Dates of Enrollment: 8/2002-5/2005
Survey Submitted: April 2006

Mason students and faculty are like family. There are regular social events, both formal and informal.

Status: Alumnus/a, part-time
Dates of Enrollment: 8/2001-5/2005
Survey Submitted: April 2006

I went to school at night, so my perspective of the school's social life may be a bit off. I saw a decent social life. There are many bars and restaurants in the neighborhood and we would go out after class one or two nights a week. Dating is difficult when you work during the day and go to school at night, but I have friends who dated classmates, and two of them are getting married this spring. There are great Mason-led activities including Las Vegas nights, pool tournaments and happy hours.

The best bar is definitely Carpool. Most of us still hang out there several nights a week. Jay's is a bit of a dive, but it is cheap. Molly Malone's is good, but it is small. Molly's is the bar closest to the school. There is a Peruvian chicken place that is very popular with Mason students about a block and a half away.

Status: Alumnus/a, full-time
Dates of Enrollment: 8/2002-5/2005
Survey Submitted: March 2006

Because GMU is so small, you will leave knowing almost all of your classmates—a great networking bonus that GW and Georgetown students cannot claim! There are lots of local bars and restaurants where people gather. Several student-run events every month and social events. It seemed as if more GMU students were married than at other local schools (because the median age is higher, probably), so the dating scene is not too exciting.

Status: Current student, full-time
Dates of Enrollment: 8/2003-Submit Date
Survey Submitted: September 2004

The school doesn't have a campus per se, so students find their own social life. I am an older student, so I don't really go out to bars anymore. However, Arlington is a very cool city, with many excellent restaurants and fun things to do. D.C. is just across the river, and is home to many museums, monuments, bars, clubs, restaurants, places of historic interest, theaters and more. D.C. is a major city and Arlington is a very urban suburb.

Status: Alumnus/a, full-time
Dates of Enrollment: 8/2000-5/2003
Survey Submitted: March 2005

GMU boasts a great social life for students who are looking for one. I was mainly focused on academics, studying and what not. However, there are great outlets for socialites. There was at least one happy hour a month in the atrium hosted by the Student Bar Association with drinks and pretty good food. There are also other events throughout the year hosted by various student groups and the Alumni Association. Students hang out together, not only at school but outside of school. There are always student parties during the holidays. The school does an excellent job of encouraging students to have fun and get to know each other, rather than just encouraging competition.

Status: Alumnus/a, full-time
Dates of Enrollment: 8/1997-5/2001
Survey Submitted: March 2005

The school has many events and organizations geared towards encouraging socialization among the law students. The part of Arlington where the school is located has undergone a transformation over the last five to seven years and there are now many restaurants, bars and coffee shops within walking distance of the school.

Status: Alumnus/a, part-time
Dates of Enrollment: 8/2001-12/2004
Survey Submitted: April 2005

Arlington is a 15 minute metro ride to D.C. The social opportunities in a city this size are endless. Near campus, there are lots of bars and restaurants frequented by students—Clarendon Grill, Clarendon Ballroom, Carpool, Whitlows and Jays are all favorites.

Status: Current student, full-time
Dates of Enrollment: 8/2003-Submit Date
Survey Submitted: June 2004

The school is very small with only a few hundred students, many are older and married, but there is dating and lots of activities for those who aren't. Also, there are lots of law students in the area since there are so many law schools.

Status: Alumnus/a, full-time
Dates of Enrollment: 8/2000-5/2003
Survey Submitted: April 2004

The social scene is nice at GMU, very laid back. In general, the students are very easygoing, not cutthroat competitive as at some schools. Students socialize frequently at SBA happy hours and also at local bars, as GMUSL is within walking distance of many restaurants and bars.

Status: Current student, full-time
Dates of Enrollment: 8/2001-Submit Date
Survey Submitted: September 2003

The school sponsors happy hours and various other social events (through the Student Bar Association) to develop a positive social environment at the school. Law students certainly need social outlets, as the studying and academic rigors can be very intense.

Regent University School of Law

Office of Admissions & Financial Aid
Roberston Hall — 239
1000 Regent University Drive
Virginia Beach, VA 23464
Admissions phone: (757) 226-4584 or
(877) 267-5072 (toll free)
Admissions e-mail: lawschool@regent.edu
Admissions URL: http://law.regent.edu/admissions/home.cfm

Note: The school has chosen not to comment on the student surveys submitted.

 ## Admissions

Status: Alumnus/a, full-time
Dates of Enrollment: 8/1998-5/2001
Survey Submitted: April 2005

My admissions process was fairly unique—I applied just three weeks before the start of the school year. After a brief phone interview, during which I was told that I was eligible for significant financial aid based on my test scores and public service, I drove down to Virginia Beach to see the school and meet the admissions director. After a formal interview, I was accepted on the spot. Unfortunately, I don't consider the school to be particularly selective, given the fact that they don't maintain a high standard in terms of admissions test scores and qualifications. I do believe that the top 25 percent at Regent could compete with any law school, however it is the bottom 50 percent of each class that continually drag Regent down in the ranking.

Status: Alumnus/a, full-time
Dates of Enrollment: 8/2001-5/2004
Survey Submitted: April 2005

From the time of my first contact with the admissions office, the staff was very helpful. I had lots of questions and they took their time and answered each one in depth. The application process, while detailed, was outlined well in the application packet. A bit of advice: start early. All law school applications are long and require some work and thought. In addition to the typical questions though, such as undergraduate school, major and GPA, Regent Law also inquires into your spiritual life. All applicants must submit a reference from their pastor, and include where they are on their spiritual walk. Writing my essay regarding my faith took me a while, since I was a relatively new Christian, but I was honest about where I had been in the past and where God seemed to be directing me at that time. With this added dimension, applying to Regent is a little different, which is appropriate because Regent is like no other law school I have seen. The admissions staff was always available while I was completing my application to answer last minute questions.

Once admitted, the admissions office threw a welcoming reception at the Nautilus Museum in Norfolk, Virginia, so that all the new students could meet each other outside of the academic environment. I look back on that night now and remember my first meeting with people who are now so integral in my life. I just felt that this extra step on the part of the admissions office was important and set the tone for my entire Regent experience—going above and beyond.

Additionally, there are preview weekends that a prospective student can attend prior to applying, so that the student and his or her family can determine if Regent is right for them. The admissions staff goes to great lengths to insure that all questions are answered and that prospective students have an opportunity to meet with alumni, current students, faculty and the dean.

Status: Alumnus/a, full-time
Dates of Enrollment: 8/2001-5/2004
Survey Submitted: April 2005

I think that the admissions process at Regent might have changed a little bit since I applied. There was a fairly lengthy, standard law school application, and, of course, I provided them with my LSAT report. Regent did not require an interview at that time.

Status: Alumnus/a, full-time
Dates of Enrollment: 8/2000-5/2004
Survey Submitted: April 2005

The admission process is rather easy. The only problem was that I was applying as a joint-degree candidate and the two schools, law and government, did not seem to share any information or recognize that I was in the other program. For the essay, I recommend writing something from your heart. The field of law is a calling, and the people at Regent want to know that you feel called to practice law (or at least learn it).

Status: Alumnus/a, full-time
Dates of Enrollment: 8/1990-5/1993
Survey Submitted: April 2005

My experience with admissions is unique in that I graduated college with a 2.09 GPA. I applied to Regent because I wanted a Christian law school. I also applied to Cumberland. I was accepted at both. My LSAT score was high enough that I was offered an academic scholarship, but told I would be on academic probation. Both did occur. I did submit a writing sample and during my interview, was told that my writing skills were lacking. I was asked how I planned on handling the shortcomings, to which I replied, "I was hoping that you would be able to teach me."

Status: Alumnus/a, full-time
Dates of Enrollment: 4/1992-0/1995
Survey Submitted: April 2005

The admission process was rigorous in that it entailed a lengthy application process with essays regarding goals and life philosophy, as well as the normal GPA, LSAT scores and on-site interviews. While academics were important, other life issues were equally important in the admissions process.

Status: Alumnus/a, full-time
Dates of Enrollment: 8/1998-5/2001
Survey Submitted: April 2005

The admissions office at Regent was extremely personable—much more than any other school to which I applied. They work to treat the student with individual attention and less like a number. The application was a bit more cumbersome than the average law school application because Regent requires essays relating to its mission. Additionally, it took a bit of effort to acquire the clergy reference, a required part of the application. When I was admitted, Regent was not as selective in its admissions process, although I understand that this has changed quite a bit since I graduated. When I visited during the Spring Preview Weekend for admitted students, I received much more information and personal attention than any other law school visitation day that I attended.

Status: Alumnus/a, full-time
Dates of Enrollment: 8/1998-5/2001
Survey Submitted: September 2003

Took a while to complete the application as the application was not online at the time. My interview was rather interesting. Since Regent is a Christian school, considerable time was spent on theology with a particular focus on Christianity. The process was easy and focused, which was good.

Read all of Vault's Law School Surveys at www.vault.com/lawschool — get complete surveys on top law schools, expert advice on applicaton essays, LSAT prep and more.

VAULT CAREER LIBRARY 629

Academics

Status: Alumnus/a, full-time
Dates of Enrollment: 8/1998-5/2001
Survey Submitted: April 2005

The academic nature of the program was outstanding far beyond what you might expect at a fouth-tier school. The teachers were generally engaging, accessible and very knowledgeable. The workload seemed consistent with that of any other law school—not harder, but certainly not easier. There is a major focus on preparing students to pass the bar exam, and I think that Regent does this very well by offering classes designed to teach with an eye towards the bar. Grading was equitable, however there was no grade inflation or B curve that you might hear about at Regent. The school maintains its academic integrity by refusing to guarantee the bulk of students a B average. You have to work for it, and it is there for those who make the effort. Popular classes were accessible, even if you had to wait a semester to make sure you got in to a particular class. Regent also has first-rate Trial Advocacy and Appellate Advocacy Programs, and my participation here has been a key component of my post-grad success.

Status: Alumnus/a, full-time
Dates of Enrollment: 8/2001-5/2004
Survey Submitted: April 2005

The classes are Regent Law are quite rigorous and most challenging. Regent is a fourth-tier law school, which is unfortunate as I think it causes people to assume it is an easy school to get into, that the classes are easy and that the students are not of the caliber of those in first-, second- or third-tier schools. None of this could be further from the truth. I was challenged in all of my classes, challenged to think outside the lines, challenged to assimilate and process information in different ways and challenged to come up with solutions to problems that appeared to have no solutions.

The first-year program consisted of Torts, Contracts, Property, Legal Research and Writing, Civil Procedure and Common Law. It was an intense year, one I think was designed to weed out those not cut out for law school. One thing I was surprised by was that, with the exception of Legal Research and Writing, there was only one exam for each class at the end of the semester. Your entire grade for the class rode on that one exam. (This is true for all law schools, not just Regent.) This was especially intimidating during the first semester because you are being taught a new way to think and then being tested on it without having any practice runs. The stress level during exams is very high!

During my first year, I found the professors that pushed me the hardest ended up becoming my favorites and I would take their classes whenever I could. Unfortunately, since Regent Law is still growing, I did not get to study under my first-year teachers too often again. Regent Law employs many adjunct faculty who are practitioners or judges but teach in the evening or at night. While this allows them to bring a great deal of experience to the classroom, it also means that to get the classes you want as an upperclassman you have to take classes at night. This is my one complaint, but I also understand it is a growing pain of a younger institution. As the school continues to grow this may become a non-issue, but it is something to consider. If you are quitting a full-time job to become a law student and you have a family, it can be frustrating to be in class until 10:00 p.m. This is not to say that all adjunct professor's classes are at night—I had one at 8:00 a.m. and one at 10:00 a.m.

As for getting the popular classes, while I was at Regent the registrar's office split the student body into four groups and assigned each group a letter, A through D. When the time came to register for classes, registration was staggered by letter, A first, B second, etc. Then the next semester B was first and A was last, the next semester C was first and B was last, and so on. This way you always had a shot at being first. Of course, this system starts your second year as your first year curriculum is set for you. Of course, if you were a 3L, and needed a class to graduate then you would be given special deference.

The workload is overwhelming most of the time. You will never read as much as you will during your law school career. If you are single or married with no children, the workload is little more manageable, but if you have kids you will have to monitor your time closely and stick to your schedule. I have a family and lived 30 minutes away from school. I spent many nights studying until 12 or 1 a.m. and then got up at 4 a.m. to study some more. Sleep is not your well-worn friend during your first year especially. Law school is competitive by nature and usually the people who attend are used to being top in their class. Well, when everyone is used to being tops you have to work twice or three times as hard to distinguish yourself. Your first year, you just want to have all the facts of the cases down, and while you may not get the whole analysis, your professors understand that you are green. When you get to upper-level classes you have to read more in depth to understand the analysis because that is what is expected of you. You will sacrifice many nights, weekends and holidays to succeed in law school. Your family needs to know this.

Status: Alumnus/a, full-time
Dates of Enrollment: 8/2001-5/2004
Survey Submitted: April 2005

The professors were always available. Grading depended upon the professor. Heavy workload (but I did Law Review, so my opinion may be a bit skewed). It was tough to get popular classes your first try.

Status: Alumnus/a, full-time
Dates of Enrollment: 8/1990-5/1993
Survey Submitted: April 2005

Regent prepared me well. The academic nature of the program is intensive and progressive. I was consistent and graduated with a 2.3. However, I am one that never did well at the exams in either college or law school, but I did learn. The program was open to the idea that some students may not be the academic giants on paper, but are truly giants in their talents and abilities. I believe that the establishment of a successful law practice and thousands of satisfied clients are evidence that the academic grading system is not fool proof.

Status: Alumnus/a, full-time
Dates of Enrollment: 4/1992-0/1995
Survey Submitted: April 2005

The academics were rigorous in that competition was among students from top-tier colleges. Class quality was excellent. When I was studying for the bar exam in Florida, I was assisting students from Harvard and other top-tier schools to understand basic legal principles we had covered in classes, but that their schools had not. Professors were always accessible to students and were interested in their lives as well as their academic performance. Popular classes were fairly easy to get into. Grading was fair with a few exceptions. When students complained about one particular professor whose grading seemed unfair, the situation was resolved the following year. The workload was large, but seemed consistent with a law school program.

Because the facilities were new, all classrooms had the latest technology for professors to use. Even in 1992, all classrooms were wired for computer use. There were a great many opportunities for professional programs such as Law Review, moot court and mediation, which included trips for competition with other law schools. Regent teams were very successful in such inter-scholastic competitions. There were also intra-scholastic competitions for students, as well as various student groups and clubs organized by interest areas.

Status: Alumnus/a, full-time
Dates of Enrollment: 8/2000-5/2004
Survey Submitted: April 2005

I started law school at the age of 40. I thought I could approach law school as an eight-to-six job. However, I spent significantly more time than that reading, outlining and meeting with my study group. Many very intelligent people attend Regent's law school, but the students are not negatively competitive. I graduated third in my class and regularly studied with others in the top 10. We actually encouraged each other. The competition was healthy. The quality of the classes is just as good as one would get anywhere. One summer I interned with law students from Harvard, Michigan, Virginia and other top schools. I knew as much as they did and knew more regarding the moral foundations of the law.

Status: Alumnus/a, full-time
Dates of Enrollment: 8/1998-5/2001
Survey Submitted: April 2005

As a newer law school, one of my fears was the quality of faculty. However, a quick review of the faculty biographies gave me some confidence in their ability. But after sitting in classes for three years, I can confirm that the quality of education was quite high. The full-time faculty is tremendous, very personable, quite gifted in the classroom and has the credentials necessary to teach. My one criticism about the faculty would be the difference in quality between some of the full-time faculty and the adjuncts. However, when I graduated from Regent and began practicing, I realized during the bar exam preparation that my education was equal or superior to others who attended school elsewhere.

Status: Alumnus/a, full-time
Dates of Enrollment: 8/2001-5/2004
Survey Submitted: April 2005

I know it sounds crazy, but I really enjoyed the academic aspect of law school. I found it challenging and invigorating. The vast majority of my professors were fabulous, brilliant people, who not only had wide-ranging professional experience and strong academic credentials, but were also very approachable, caring people. Furthermore, since Regent is a smaller school, I had opportunity to be involved with Law Review, moot court and work as a graduate assistant to a couple of my favorite professors, something that really paid off when I needed references for my job applications at graduation.

Status: Alumnus/a, full-time
Dates of Enrollment: 8/1998-5/2001
Survey Submitted: September 2003

Loved my professors and classmates. The work was challenging, as I expected it would be. However, the profs made what could have been a horrible experience a good experience. I believe that the level of communication at Regent between profs and students to be unique. Many profs and students attend the same churches and students are frequently guests in the homes of the profs, which lends itself to a better teacher/student relationship. Plus, the weekly prayer service is attended by both students and profs and that too creates a better environment.

Employment Prospects

Status: Alumnus/a, full-time
Dates of Enrollment: 8/1998-5/2001
Survey Submitted: April 2005

I applied to and was accepted into the Navy JAG program. Therefore I didn't have to deal with the civilian private practice job market. After I was accepted during my 2L year to be a JAG, I didn't really pay attention much, sorry! I did all of my internships and job searching on my own so I don't have any experience with career services.

Status: Alumnus/a, full-time
Dates of Enrollment: 8/2001-5/2004
Survey Submitted: April 2005

The employment prospects for Regent grads are terrific. Regent Law School and graduates have done so much to impress employers that finding a job is not difficult. I am clerking for a federal judge, and these clerkships are difficult to obtain. I have several friends clerking for the Supreme Court of Virginia and other federal judges. There are Regent grads working with the most prestigious law firms in the area and D.C., such as Williams Mullen, Kaufman and Canoles, and Hunton and Williams.

The office of career and alumni services has much improved with the addition of its new director. He and his staff have done much to network and provide opportunities for Regent students and alumni. That office is working diligently to constantly improve the communication between alumni and students. I personally have not had to utilize the alumni network for connections or employment so it is difficult for me to assess its effectiveness.

The on-campus recruiting is improving. The big firms are starting to come to Regent's campus and Mr. Morrell is working to insure that happens. I interviewed with several of the large firms during on-campus interview season. As Regent's legacy grows I feel confident that all of the top firms from Virginia and D.C. will be interviewing at Regent. This is, yet again, another growing pain of a school that is still relatively young.

Status: Alumnus/a, full-time JD/MA
Dates of Enrollment: 8/1994-5/1998
Survey Submitted: April 2005

Regent is a young school and still developing its alumni network. I work at a 100+ firm in a large Midwestern city and we just hired another Regent grad who clerked with us for the summer. The alumni network is very helpful.

Status: Alumnus/a, full-time
Dates of Enrollment: 4/1992-0/1995
Survey Submitted: April 2005

Employment options become easier for Regent grads as other alumni get out into the legal field. Regent is a fairly new school and so has had to build a reputation in the legal world. Regent grads have now built a very good reputation for excellent work and law firms tend to become more interested in them after having a Regent graduate work for them or serve in an intern program. Also, Regent grads tend to want to hire other Regent grads, so as more and more alumni attorneys are looking for associates, other Regent grads get considered first. The alumni office is very helpful with online employment tips and contacts. Internships also become easier as Regent grads get a foot in the door and perform well and as other Regent grads begin to hire interns. Regent grads tend to be known as honest, hard-working employees. The alumni network also functions very well and is all computerized and online for easy employment searches. When I was at the school, students had options to take seminars in dressing for interviews and interviewing skills, which were very helpful.

Status: Alumnus/a, full-time
Dates of Enrollment: 8/2000-5/2004
Survey Submitted: April 2005

Before graduation, I received an offer from the U.S. Department of Justice in its Honors Program. This is the only way that the DOJ hires new law graduates. It was an honor to be selected to get one of six positions for which about 2,500 people applied. I am convinced that attending Regent University's School of Law helped me get the job at the DOJ.

Status: Alumnus/a, full-time
Dates of Enrollment: 8/1998-5/2001
Survey Submitted: April 2005

Regent seems to be very successful at placing graduates in governmental positions, small firms and in public interest firms. Its one area of needed growth would be with the larger firms. Again, this seems to be improving as the reputation of the school has grown. Students who graduate near the top of the class seem to have opportunities to work in judicial clerkships and larger firms. However, students in the bottom half of the class sometimes had a struggle to find employment. The alumni network is quite strong for a school with less than 2,000 alumni. In fact, many of my friends obtained jobs through an alumnus/a. There are several alumni gatherings a year that allow networking opportunities.

Status: Alumnus/a, full-time
Dates of Enrollment: 8/2001-5/2004
Survey Submitted: April 2005

Regent is still building its reputation with a lot of employers, but the institution as a whole is working very hard on that reputation. I am currently serving as a judicial clerk, and my court (which is located near enough to Regent to be familiar with it) was very open to hiring a Regent grad, even though I was the first that they had hired. I know people from my class who are clerking in state courts, (some state supreme courts), clerking in federal courts and working in large and mid-size firms. Several people are in public interest, but pretty much everyone has a job doing more or less what they wanted to do (as far as I know).

Read all of Vault's Law School Surveys at www.vault.com/lawschool — get complete surveys on top law schools, expert advice on applicaton essays, LSAT prep and more.

VAULT CAREER LIBRARY 631

Quality of Life

Status: Alumnus/a, full-time
Dates of Enrollment: 8/1998-5/2001
Survey Submitted: April 2005

Quality of life is high—there is no doubt that the first year of law school can be incredibly stressful. However, Regent does an excellent job of looking out for its students, and providing resources to care for the students and help them make it through. The camaraderie is high amongst the students, and I think this lends itself to good quality of life. As for housing, I lived in an off-campus house that I found myself through a local realtor.

Status: Alumnus/a, full-time
Dates of Enrollment: 8/2001-5/2004
Survey Submitted: April 2005

Regent Law is different from any other law school. While all law schools are very competitive, Regent's atmosphere is different from other schools. My experience from visiting other schools and having friends and family who attended other law schools is that students are always looking over their shoulders. The students at other schools seem willing to do whatever it takes to push others down in an effort to advance themselves. This stab-in-the-back mentality is not found at Regent, which I found to greatly impact the students quality of life. Law school is stressful enough without having to worry whether someone is trying to sabotage your efforts by hiding books or ripping out pages that you need to complete an assignment. At Regent, students are happy for other students when they perform well, they encourage each other during periods of struggle, and often pray for each other to persevere and overcome obstacles. There is a family environment, not just among the students, but with the faculty and staff as well. I still maintain contact with my dean and other faculty and staff. They are interested in your life and really care about you, both personally and academically.

As for housing, there is no on-campus housing, but some almost-on-campus housing called Regent Village. The rent is cheap and the apartments quite spacious. There is a park and the apartments have balconies. There are numerous other apartment and townhouse complexes within minutes of Regent and Student Services will set you up with a roommate to conserve on expenses.

The campus in general and the law school itself are absolutely gorgeous. Any time students visited for competitions they always remarked about how beautiful everything was. The facilities are amazing; there are screens, projectors, computers (for the professor) and overheads all built into a smart podium in every classroom. The library is beautiful and well-appointed. There is also a new student union center, which has fantastic food, a pool table, a large screen TV, computer labs and the bookstore.

The neighborhood is safe with low levels of crime. At Regent, you can leave your things, such as purse, laptop and books, sitting just about anywhere and no one will touch it. I tell you, it is different! I often have to remind myself I am not at Regent anymore and take my purse with me. Because the area is suburban and you have to drive to get most places. There is usually not anyone on campus who is not a student, faculty or staff member or guest speaker.

Status: Alumnus/a, full-time
Dates of Enrollment: 8/2001-5/2004
Survey Submitted: April 2005

I lived off campus. There are several nice, affordable apartment complexes near Regent. There is also an university-owned apartment complex that has cheaper rent, but it is mostly families and not all that great—decent and safe, but the apartments are kind of dark and older.

The campus itself is beautiful in a postcard, movie-about-law-school kind of way. Everything is Colonial-style red brick; there is gorgeous landscaping, lots of trees, fountains, lovely classrooms and libraries. Good technology (I think everything is wired now) and plentiful computer labs.

Status: Alumnus/a, full-time
Dates of Enrollment: 8/1990-5/1993
Survey Submitted: April 2005

I have always found the best in life. The Virginia Beach area provided grea work possibilities such as waiting tables. I worked all through law school, an must say I enjoyed every year. I was there to learn, work and survive. All thre were accomplished well.

Status: Alumnus/a, full-time
Dates of Enrollment: 4/1992-0/1995
Survey Submitted: April 2005

The quality of life at Regent was excellent. Because most students when I wa there were dedicated Christians, there was no need to worry about cheating o about losing material in library stalls or elsewhere. The most impressive thing for me was that a female student could leave a purse at a student desk in th library and be absolutely certain that it would be there untouched when sh returned.

The quality of life in the campus housing was excellent because there was n drinking or drugs and people tended to really care for one another. There was food pantry for students with limited financial resources that was run by othe students or student spouses. There were always student wives ready to babysi or care for children of other working spouses. Spouses of male students tende to become fast friends and to help one another out. Marriages stayed bette because spouses had friends to talk with about their situation.

Study groups were competitive but helpful; not cutthroat like at some other law schools. Students wanted to receive top grades but were also willing to help others with academics. The facilities were all new and very beautiful. Since the students took good care of their environment, it was a very pleasant place to be.

Status: Alumnus/a, full-time
Dates of Enrollment: 8/1998-5/2001
Survey Submitted: April 2005

Quality of life is the principle reason I selected Regent Law School over more established schools. I was not disappointed. My classmates were generally very kind people, willing to offer their help and eager for each other to succeed. Housing near campus offered a convenient option, although plenty of other loca housing is available for a fairly reasonable price. The location of Virginia Beac (20 minutes east), Norfolk (15 minutes north) and North Carolina (one hour south) provides a lot of options for recreation and weekend activities. The facilities on campus are outstanding—much more beautiful than any other school I attended or visited. Students and visitors respect the beauty of the campus and treat it with respect. Campus security is always visible and crime is nonexistent. The Kempsville area location is prime real estate in Virginia Beach so the neighborhoods feel safe and provide ample venues to eat and shop.

Status: Alumnus/a, full-time
Dates of Enrollment: 8/2002-5/2005
Survey Submitted: April 2006

Very good QOL with the exception of no sex, drugs, rock 'n roll or free speech.

Social Life

Status: Alumnus/a, full-time
Dates of Enrollment: 8/1998-5/2001
Survey Submitted: April 2005

Regent isn't known for having a rollicking social life since, it is, after all, a religion-affiliated school. However, Virginia Beach has its moments and stress relief can be easy with the beach such a short drive away. If you're looking to go to Regent to party, don't; it's just not that sort of school. But, if you want a competitively solid legal education that is based in religious principles, Regent is the school for you.

Status: Alumnus/a, full-time
Dates of Enrollment: 8/2001-5/2004
Survey Submitted: April 2005

Regent has just really gotten its degree completion program and online undergraduate degree program going, which means this is mainly a postgraduate education institution. Therefore, you will not find your typical college atmosphere. There is no Greek system. There are clubs and organizations to participate in, such as Student Bar Association (student government), Law Review (two of them but you must apply and be accepted), moot court (must apply and be accepted), Entertainment and Sports Legal Society, BALSA (Black Law Students Association), PILAR (Public Interest Law organization), Negotiations Board and many other organizations. Most of these are ways to build skills and develop interests that will impress prospective employers. There is usually something going on on campus to do such as a luncheon or a guest speaker.

Regent is a fantastic place, and for students focused on their studies, developing friendships and deepening their relationship with God, it is a great fit.

Status: Alumnus/a, full-time JD/MA
Dates of Enrollment: 8/1994-5/1998
Survey Submitted: April 2005

I met my wife in law school. 'Nuff said. The beach is nearby and there are plenty of great places to eat and drink on the beach or in nearby Norfolk/Ghent.

Status: Alumnus/a, full-time
Dates of Enrollment: 4/1992-0/1995
Survey Submitted: April 2005

I was an older married student living in a house off campus, so I was not involved closely in the social scene. However, from observation, students made close friends, dated each other and seemed happy. No one went to bars and the atmosphere was wholesome. Parties tended to be in private homes and students had Bible study groups for a lot of their social lives. Students also attended local churches and found wider social outlets there. Students tended not to be cliquish, but tried to include everyone and make everyone feel welcome and loved. That actually did tend to be the general environment. Even as an off-campus student and an older student, I never felt left out. Everyone tried to be friendly and helpful to others, including students, professors and other university support staff. The university sponsored events for students including plays, other cultural events from the fine arts school, chapel services and service projects to get involved in. It was a very caring and excellent environment.

Status: Alumnus/a, full-time
Dates of Enrollment: 8/2000-5/2004
Survey Submitted: April 2005

The social life is not the most exciting because Regent is primarily a graduate school. The new student center did open in 2003, which provides extra facilities and activities. Even though life at Regent is generally quiet, I met and became close friends with some amazing people.

Status: Alumnus/a, full-time
Dates of Enrollment: 8/1998-5/2001
Survey Submitted: April 2005

Because Regent operates only as a graduate school (it does not have an on-campus undergraduate program), many of the traditional collegiate activities are not available. Social life is typically in the community or at the beach. The dating scene seemed strong when I was a student, as many of my classmates paired up and were married before they graduated. Favorite beach spot for students: Sandbridge Beach (about 40 minutes from campus). Favorite place to watch Sunday football: Baker Street Grill.

Status: Alumnus/a, full-time
Dates of Enrollment: 8/2001-5/2004
Survey Submitted: April 2005

I worked and studied ALL of the time, so I can't help you a lot here. Other people seemed to be having fun though. The Hampton Roads area in general has a lot to do. Beaches, nice nightlife (I guess) in Downtown Norfolk and Portsmouth (both nearby), and there is the Virginia Beach waterfront as well.

Status: Alumnus/a, full-time
Dates of Enrollment: 8/1998-5/2001
Survey Submitted: September 2003

Well, with this topic, social life, you have a diverse crowd to deal with. For instance, at Regent there are those that do not approve of alcohol, so you will not see them at any event where there is alcohol. Then there are those that choose not to drink but go to events where alcohol is served and then there is yet a third group, my group, that consumes alcohol. So there are different dynamics at work at Regent that you do not see at other law schools. That being said, the majority of my class would gather on a regular basis for service and social events.

When it comes to social life at Regent, you get out of it what you put into it.

Read all of Vault's Law School Surveys at www.vault.com/lawschool — get complete surveys on top law schools, expert advice on applicaton essays, LSAT prep and more.

VAULT CAREER LIBRARY 633

University of Richmond School of Law

28 Westhampton Way
University of Richmond, VA 223173
Admissions phone: (804) 289-8189
Admissions e-mail: lawadmissions@richmond.edu
Admissions URL: http://law.richmond.edu/admissions/

 Admissions

Status: Current student, full-time
Dates of Enrollment: 6/2005-Submit Date
Survey Submitted: December 2005

Getting into law school is at least 90 percent GPA and LSAT score. Studying for and taking a prep class is most of the application process. Then, the common application online on LSAT.org is the best way to go. They compile your transcript(s), score(s), essay(s) and recommendations.

It's important to do a good job on the essays and to get good recommendations just so you don't hurt your chances rather than help them. It is how they get to know the applicant, since no interviews are offered, and it can help match them with the diversity of personalities and goals they are looking for. Rarely does either the essay or recommendation make the difference when the GPA or LSAT scores are below the school's target range.

A well-known individual, like a senator or big donating alumnus, might increase your chances significantly only if it is a very personal letter on how you have impressed them. I was privileged to see an accepted application of a student with a low GPA from a state school into a Top 10 law school during an information session. He had a recommendation by the actor Ben Affleck, but they stressed that this only helped because the student had worked with Ben personally for his entire acting career even before he was famous. It was very detailed about the specific skills of the student. Similarly, I also saw a student that would have gotten into a different Top 10 law school get denied because of his conceited essay.

Status: Current student, full-time
Dates of Enrollment: 9/2004-Submit Date
Survey Submitted: September 2005

The admissions process was fairly easy; it did not require anything more than my other applications. I heard later, however, that they are interested in people from outside of Virginia and people who are interested in practicing in other areas because they want to help their reputation as a national law school.

Status: Alumnus/a, full-time
Dates of Enrollment: 9/2001-5/2002
Survey Submitted: November 2004

The admissions process was hard for me. I took the LSATs three times to receive a competitive score. My family was friendly with a professor who agreed to speak on my behalf when they reviewed my application. I also sent in a follow-up letter in addition to my application.

My application was a standard form. It had at least two essay questions, one of which was why do you want to come to the University of Richmond School of Law. I did not have a personal interview. I believe it was the [professor's recommendation] and my follow-up letter that expressed the many reasons why I wanted to go to their law school [that got me in]. I told of how I would give back to their educational community after I was an alumnus, and that got me off of the waitlist.

> **Regarding recommendations, the school says:** We would like to point out that any recommendations, by Richmond Law professors or otherwise, are considered in conjunction with all other application materials, including LSAT, GPA, work experience, extracurriculars and essay. The power this alumnus

believes the Richmond Law professor exercised in his acceptance is only speculation.

 **Academics**

Status: Current student, full-time
Dates of Enrollment: 6/2005-Submit Date
Survey Submitted: December 2005

University of Richmond School of Law has a comparable workload to that of a variety of other law schools where I have friends. The law school stands out in two ways. It has a very laid-back atmosphere compared to other law schools with respect to both its competition between students and to the treatment of students in class. This is one law school that the famous book *1L* by Scott Turrow would not apply to. There is no cutthroat atmosphere. Everyone studies hard, remains friends and what happens, happens.

The professors vary on how they will react to a student that is not prepared (each with a different definition of the word) but nothing goes beyond temporary embarrassment. My friends at other law schools have been or have seen students yelled at or kicked out of the class in front of 90 peers. Besides the laid-back atmosphere, Richmond differs by focusing on much of the "how," as well as the "why" of law. Employers are pleasantly surprised when recent graduates do not need to be shown how to "be a lawyer." Most other law schools go through a rigorous process of teaching a student to think like a lawyer ("why" the law is). Richmond's four required semesters of Law Skills give the student experience with the day-to-day activities of meeting with clients and applying their knowledge to meet their clients' needs in the proper, professional way (memos, forms). Like all other law schools that I know of, first-year classes are predetermined and class grades are curved around a 3.0 scale.

Status: Current student, full-time
Dates of Enrollment: 9/2004-Submit Date
Survey Submitted: September 2005

I love my classes. Most of the professors are very nice and have an open-door policy. The workload is not too much even in first-year although there are a few busy seasons like moot court time and finals time. The grading is on a B curve so your grade will depend on how well you do in relation to other students. Nonetheless, this does not create the hyper-competitive environment that is found in many schools. Getting into popular classes is not very difficult as long as you pick which classes you want before registration opens and you register soon after it opens.

Status: Alumnus/a, full-time
Dates of Enrollment: 9/2001-5/2002
Survey Submitted: November 2004

The first-year law school class was divided into sections A and B and the administration picked all of your classes. It was nice because we were guaranteed to get all the classes we needed the first year. The teaching method was Socratic and that is nerve racking. The quality was good. Professors were eager to help.

> **The University of Richmond School of Law says:** "We balance our sections according to many factors, one of which is credentials."

Grading was done on a scaled method compared to class performance. This was bad for me because being from the waitlist, I was on the low end of the totem pole as far as academic ability compared to the rest of my class and unfortunately that is how they grade. So if your exam essay was not on par or above the class average, you got a low grade. The exams were all writing and we had code numbers to keep our names and identities from being exposed so the professors could not be biased. The reading was hard but not too bad. Preparing for exams was the hardest because all of the readings piled up and you never knew what the questions or laws pertaining to it would be.

Status: Current student, full-time
Dates of Enrollment: 8/2003-Submit Date
Survey Submitted: November 2003

The professors are excellent. Many of them are renowned scholars, but their real strength is that most are excellent teachers and they invoke strong preparation and create excitement about learning the law.

 # Employment Prospects

Status: Current student, full-time
Dates of Enrollment: 9/2004-Submit Date
Survey Submitted: September 2005

Within Virginia, the school is well-regarded. Outside of Virginia it becomes a little more difficult to get your foot in the door but not impossible. There are on-campus interviews but most people do not find jobs through these means. The people at the top of the class get most of the interviews and out of this small pool a few people get multiple offers. However, the Career Services Office is very friendly and helpful and people seem pretty happy with the jobs they get. There is also an active clinical program that places people in local government agencies, judicial clerkships, nonprofit organizations, firms and in-house council offices for corporations. Most people seem happy with the jobs they get.

> The school says: "Our graduates go throughout the country, although many choose to stay in the D.C. area."

Status: Alumnus/a, full-time
Dates of Enrollment: 9/2001-5/2002
Survey Submitted: November 2004

Internships as well as the most prestigious jobs go to the top of the law class. You pretty much should be above the top 25 percent of your class or have a major connection to the law firm of your dreams.

> **Regarding Employment Prospects, the University of Richmond says:** "Our students have had a 97 to 100 percent employment rate every year for many years."

 # Quality of Life

Status: Alumnus/a, full-time
Dates of Enrollment: 8/2002-5/2005
Survey Submitted: November 2005

Richmond is a great city. The university is located in the very safe, well-to-do, if somewhat boring, West End. But the Fan and downtown are only 10 minutes away—lots to do there.

Status: Current student, full-time
Dates of Enrollment: 6/2005-Submit Date
Survey Submitted: December 2005

The University of Richmond is in a great part of Richmond, Henrico County. The vast majority of law students live off campus and there are plenty of nearby housing options and other ones about 15-minutes away in the popular Fan district downtown. Students and staff are all very friendly and understanding.

Status: Current student, full-time
Dates of Enrollment: 9/2004-Submit Date
Survey Submitted: September 2005

The quality of life is very good. The university is located in the West End of Richmond, about 15 minutes away from downtown. The West End is a pretty safe area, and while Richmond is a high-crime city, UR students are fairly insulated from this. There is limited on-campus housing for law students but there are affordable housing options close by or downtown. The campus is beautiful and serene and has wireless Internet access throughout.

Status: Alumnus/a, full-time
Dates of Enrollment: 9/2001-5/2002
Survey Submitted: November 2004

There [is one housing option] the university offers for law students. It is close to the law school and the campus is a beautiful place to be. Most people live in Richmond so they have local residencies or if they are from out of town they stay in a nearby apartment complex. The campus and surrounding area are beautiful and pretty safe; there are restaurants and shopping nearby.

 # Social Life

Status: Current student, full-time
Dates of Enrollment: 6/2005-Submit Date
Survey Submitted: December 2005

The social scene is about one-third meeting up at bars/restaurants (like Three Monkeys or Sine's in the Fan district), one-third getting together at a student's house (students are good about inviting the entire class to a kegger, pooling together a few students' birthdays to celebrate every couple weekends), and one-third of some event sponsored by the Student Bar Association (most law students and faculty attend these and it's a relaxed way to have a conversation outside the classroom).

Status: Current student, full-time
Dates of Enrollment: 9/2004-Submit Date
Survey Submitted: September 2005

The social life in the law school is not as active as an undergrad program would be. People work hard and play hard. There is an active bar scene in the Fan District of Richmond as well as clubs in Shockoe Bottom. Additionally, the Student Bar Association hosts social events for the law school a couple of times a semester. The dating scene is a little sparse; a few people date within the law school but many people prefer not to date law students as it is a small school and gossip travels fast. As far as restaurants in Richmond go, there are some gems located throughout the city but it is heavily dominated by chain restaurants.

Status: Alumnus/a, full-time
Dates of Enrollment: 9/2001-5/2002
Survey Submitted: November 2004

The school has a pub called the Cellar where you can grab a beer after classes. It is not open late-night but it will do for a quick social gathering. The law school holds social gatherings on Fridays called "down unders." The Fan and downtown Richmond are close to the campus and there are several bars, restaurants and clubs to go to. Uof R is also a short distance from the suburban side of Richmond with new shopping malls and restaurants.

Read all of Vault's Law School Surveys at www.vault.com/lawschool — get complete surveys on top law schools, expert advice on applicaton essays, LSAT prep and more.

VAULT CAREER LIBRARY 635

University of Virginia School of Law

Office of Admissions
580 Massie Road
Charlottesville, VA 22903-1789
Admissions phone: (434) 924-7351
Admissions fax: (434) 982-2128
Admissions e-mail: lawadmit@virginia.edu
Admissions URL: http://www.law.virginia.edu/admissions

 Admissions

Status: Current student, full-time
Dates of Enrollment: 8/2005-Submit Date
Survey Submitted: April 2006

Don't freak out if you didn't apply in October. I applied a couple hours AFTER the deadline of January 15. Despite this flaw, UVA was among the first of the top-tier schools I applied to to send an acceptance, which came only a couple months later. A week or two after that came an offer for $13,000 a year in scholarship funds.

Time off is good. Most of the members of my section didn't go "straight through." We nearly all took at least a couple years to work. My friend, who also took five years off, was offered even more scholarship money from UVA. She and I both had 3.5 undergrad GPAs, but great LSATs (173, 176).

Status: Current student, full-time
Dates of Enrollment: 8/2005-Submit Date
Survey Submitted: April 2006

UVA wants the best, and they only take the best. I know students with around 170 LSAT scores who were Phi Beta Kappa in undergrad who were rejected here. So test scores and GPA are very important, but they aren't enough. Although there's no interview, UVA wants its students to be well-rounded and interesting, so getting amazing recommendations is key as well as providing a well-written personal statement. Of course, a resume that makes you stand out from the crowd is also an essential—playing a varsity sport in college, starting an organization, doing interesting research or working in some awesome job all help. However, if your GPA is less than stellar, you still may get in if you went to an Ivy League school and have great LSAT scores and recommendations to make up for it, or if you are a number of years out of college and have spent those years doing something really amazing. Additionally, UVA is a state school, which means that it's even harder for out-of-state students to be admitted.

Status: Current student, full-time
Dates of Enrollment: 8/2005-Submit Date
Survey Submitted: April 2006

Being one of the top law schools, it is admittedly difficult to get into UVA Law, especially if your GPA or LSAT is not phenomenally high. But UVA does pride itself on selecting extraordinary students, so your personal statement can really make a difference if it makes you stand out. Although my LSAT score was pretty high, my GPA did not put me even in the top half of my class. However, I also worked 60 hours a week to support myself on top of taking a full load of biomedical science curriculum. I explained my struggles and how much stronger and more determined this made me, and now, here I am at UVA Law.

Status: Current student, full-time
Dates of Enrollment: 8/2004-Submit Date
Survey Submitted: April 2006

Admission rigor varies with the number of applicants of course, but it has been tough and remains tough to get in here, but it is well worth it! Having an astronomical LSAT score and stellar grades are of course, quite helpful, but I think they pay particular attention to building an interesting and diverse class. While I am in school with some of the cleverest people I know, what surprises me is the range of experiences they have had—I go to school with a former Broadway actress, a stand-up comedian, a CPA and the future chief strategist for a stock exchange.

My recommendation for getting in is first, be interesting and second, be articulate. Make every effort of course, not to be pretentious, and honestly share why you think you're a good fit. The essay is particularly important. The community of trust based on our strict Honor Code is a part of daily life and I know that the admissions office wants to preserve and reinforce that.

The best way to know whether this is your dream school is to visit—the admissions office hosts tours and panels, and the professors and random students in the hallway are happy to stay and chat, too.

Status: Current student, full-time
Dates of Enrollment: 8/2005-Submit Date
Survey Submitted: April 2006

The application for UVA Law is pretty standard, but you may want to be aware that all applications are automatically considered for merit scholarships. So it might be worth it to spend a little extra time if that's important to you. Many students seem to receive a "Dean's Scholarship" (mine was $5,000 per year), and there are a number of full-tuition scholarships, including ones with an additional stipend.

What struck me first was how welcoming and hospitable everyone was. The receptionist, the student volunteers, admissions staff, everyone was so friendly and seemed laid-back and cheerful (qualities you don't always associate with a law school!). There were several activities in which professors came out to meet and greet, which I was surprised about; they were really friendly and easy to talk to and actually looked like they enjoyed meeting prospective students. The students so clearly loved their law school that I even thought it was sort of weird at first. There were also social events, including the school's "Libel Show," which is their annual satirical show that happened to fall on the same weekend that admitted students were there. Mainly, I was struck by how eager all the students seemed to meet the admits and to answer our questions. I kind of wondered when they had time to study.

During my visit, I went to visit a professor who I'd heard was interested in some similar things as me. I just sort of showed up at her office, so I was nervous and feeling intimidated. She basically stopped what she was doing and took me out for a coffee, and we had a nice talk about my college thesis (in comparative lit) and the kinds of research I liked. I was rather astonished at how genuinely interested she seemed in teaching and working closely with students. Her own research interests were a bit unorthodox, which I took to mean UVA wasn't as "conservative" institutionally as I thought it might be.

Status: Current student, full-time
Dates of Enrollment: 8/2005-Submit Date
Survey Submitted: April 2006

Application was typical for law school. Register through LSAC, then send the school's form, a personal statement and transcript. I applied early and was deferred. I wrote a letter stating all the reasons why UVA was my first choice. I'm not sure whether it made a difference, but I was admitted about 10 days after I sent that letter.

Status: Current student, full-time
Dates of Enrollment: 8/2005-Submit Date
Survey Submitted: May 2006

Applying early is recommended (pre-winter) but I took the October LSAT and completed applications in early January and was admitted in less than 30 days. There was no interview, only the LSAT, single essay, transcripts and recommendations. LSAT is the most important component particularly to getting merit aid; my GPA was not good from undergrad and I still received some aid. There is a box to check if you are a Virginia resident, although you do not have to prove residency until after you are admitted through tax returns.

 **Academics**

The school says: "Any applicant who checks the 'Virginia resident' box, but who fails to submit the required Application for Virginia In-State Educational Privileges will not have his or her application reviewed until the form is received or the applicant notifies us that he or she no longer seeks resident status. This is a state regulation and is not waivable by the admissions office."

Status: Current student, full-time
Dates of Enrollment: 8/2004-Submit Date
Survey Submitted: July 2005

UVA Law is highly selective, and only getting more selective as more people apply to law schools around the country. I applied using the LSAC electronic application and did not write the optional statement. My application was complete in late January, and I received notification of acceptance and a scholarship award in late March. I think for any application, it's important to demonstrate personal balance and in a personal statement, to highlight who you are without sounding self-important. Law applicants will learn that humility is a rare and precious commodity. If you have it, use it. Virginia residents have an advantage over out-of-state residents, but only slightly. The legislature and the university have given the law school a level of autonomy that's rare among public institutions. As a result, you're seeing higher tuition rates and fewer in-state residents. Also, a lot of the in-state students come from Northern Virginia, where they lived only a couple of years while commuting to D.C.

UVA Law says: "There is one—and only one—required personal statement that can be about any subject, in any format, and of any length the applicant chooses."

Status: Current student, full-time
Dates of Enrollment: 8/2004-Submit Date
Survey Submitted: July 2005

The admissions process is the same as at other schools, I think. UVA is a highly selective law school, placing great attention first and foremost on LSAT and GPA. UVA does value diversity, but does not recruit for diversity as aggressively as at other Top 10 schools. Looking at the numbers, it seems easier to get in if you are in state, however almost all of the in-state students I've met are also exceptional students who would have gotten in anyway.

Status: Alumnus/a, full-time
Dates of Enrollment: 8/2000-5/2003
Survey Submitted: March 2005

You've got to have great grades, great LSAT scores and a compelling story for why you want to attend law school. Virginia seems forgiving for people who take the LSAT more than once, and, unlike other top schools, will consider only the high score if a reasonable explanation is provided as to why they should do so. Virginia accepts approximately a third of its students from in state, so it's harder for out-of-state candidates to be admitted. A large portion of the in-state students are not Virginia natives, however. If you live and work in the D.C. area for two plus years, you qualify for in-state status.

The school says: "The University of Virginia accepts closer to 20 percent of its students from in state. So far this year about 18 percent of the accepted students are from in state."

Status: Alumnus/a, full-time
Dates of Enrollment: 8/1996-5/1999
Survey Submitted: January 2005

Reference guides identify the statistical likelihood of acceptance for in-state and out-of-state students, based on undergraduate GPA and LSAT score. I found this information to be accurate. Admission is obviously a bit easier for residents of Virginia, but the majority of "residents" at UVA were students who spent a year (or more) before law school working in Washington, D.C. and living in Virginia.

Status: Current student, full-time
Dates of Enrollment: 8/2005-Submit Date
Survey Submitted: April 2006

Teachers will call on students, but most of them try not to be sadists about it. Students circulate lists describing how professors operate their on-call systems so you can pick classes based on that. Five classes your first semester, for a total of 16 credits, makes a pretty rough load. If you try to do all your reading and take notes you will go insane, so the best method (and one it takes some 1Ls a whole year to figure out) is to carefully read the first 20 pages of the assignment, skim the rest and only take notes on what the professor talks about in class. Take notes in the book while reading, then fill them in during dead time in class, like when someone is stammering through his hour of glory on-call. This saves time later, when you will have to condense your 60 pages of notes into an outline for exams.

Status: Current student, full-time
Dates of Enrollment: 8/2005-Submit Date
Survey Submitted: April 2006

The first semester of your 1L year you take four classes and a one-credit, pass/fail Legal Research and Writing class. Second semester you have Legal Research and Writing again, as well as two required classes, but you have two electives. Everything is graded to a B+ mean, which means the worst you'll get is a C. No one fails here. Depending on how tight the professor's curve is, it can be extremely difficult to get anything other than a B+, or they might have a looser curve allowing more of a range of grades. Most classes your 1L year have a final exam, although a number of classes you take as an upperclassman have a final paper or weekly papers instead.

When you get here, you are divided into a number of first-year sections of 30 students each. You take all your classes the first semester with your section. Legal Research and Writing and one other class are made up of just your section, and the other three classes have from one to three other sections, so they are larger. You really get to know your section well, and there are six upperclassmen assigned to each section as peer advisors to help out with all sorts of things: class scheduling, how to brief, how to outline, how to take exams, what professors to take, what to do on the weekend, what organizations are fun to join.

Status: Current student, full-time
Dates of Enrollment: 8/2003-Submit Date
Survey Submitted: April 2006

Academics at UVA are topnotch; some of the best professors in the country teach at UVA Law, LOVE teaching here and, more importantly, love working with and meeting students. The Student Bar Association funds a "Take a Professor to Lunch" program and professors are THRILLED to spend their lunch hours with students talking about the law or life in general. Professors are super-accessible, and always able to answer any questions you may have.

Status: Current student, full-time
Dates of Enrollment: 8/2005-Submit Date
Survey Submitted: April 2006

Surprisingly (to me anyway), UVA was probably the most "academic" law school I visited, which I really liked. The university as a whole has a really strong sense of tradition, focused on Thomas Jefferson's idea of the "academical village" (and any UVA student will quickly tell you). At first, I was a little suspicious of this, but actually it makes things very pleasant; there truly is a sense of being a community and wanting to learn together.

To give you a sense of UVA's philosophy on class size, there is currently construction going on to convert a lecture room (that seated 120, I think, which is the biggest size) into a small classroom, a seminar room and a couple faculty offices. This is because there were more lecture rooms in the school than we needed and not enough small classrooms.

The community also prides itself on being really supportive, rather than competitive. The times that I've missed class, several people in my section have volunteered their notes. There isn't much formal "study group" activity (people tend to study more on their own, and spend a lot of time with each other

Read all of Vault's Law School Surveys at www.vault.com/lawschool — get complete surveys on top law schools, expert advice on applicaton essays, LSAT prep and more.

VAULT CAREER LIBRARY 637

socially), but I have never felt "alone." I hear stories from other law schools in the region of people hiding books in the library or trying to one-up each other with job offers, but that kind of thing seems preposterous here.

One more thing, the Army JAG school is next door, which I find to be a terrific and unusual resource. They co-sponsor a lot of events with the law school, especially the law school's Human Rights Program. If you have any interest in national security law, UVA is definitely the place to go. The discipline was invented here in the 1970s and some of the most well-established scholars are here. We've also had panels and speakers from the JAG school on very timely issues (torture, detention, terrorism) that are fascinating.

Status: Current student, full-time
Dates of Enrollment: 8/2005-Submit Date
Survey Submitted: April 2006

Academically, it's what I expected of law school. The reading load is huge, but overall it's manageable. UVA has an outstanding teaching faculty, and my professors have been energetic and engaging. Classes are assigned on a lottery system, so everyone has an equal chance at getting the popular classes. There are so many great professors here that you're pretty much guaranteed most, if not all, of your classes will be great, whether you get your top choices or not. The school has a [3.3] mean, so people don't generally stress much about grades.

Status: Current student, full-time
Dates of Enrollment: 8/2005-Submit Date
Survey Submitted: March 2006

The school really emphasizes learning to think in a different way rather than memorization. It's a wonderful, beautiful and relaxed environment in which to study and interact with high-caliber students and professors. I had a full range of classes—one 120-person, purely Socratic Method class and one small section, participation-encouraged class. I've found that the majority of the classes do count class participation in some way, which is good because it encourages students to keep up with the reading, to be engaged in class and to really think about the reading.

Status: Alumnus/a, full-time
Dates of Enrollment: 8/1997-5/2000
Survey Submitted: May 2006

Academics are rigorous, but not unduly so. The professors also were friendly and easy to get to know. The student newspaper, by the way, carries a feature each week of faculty quotes, which demonstrates that the professors have a great sense of humor and are not afraid of poking fun at themselves.

The workload is fairly typical. I found the rule-of-thumb of two hours out-of-class for each hour in class to be a good measure for first-year. That equates to about a 40 or 50 hour week—a normal work week for those who've worked before law school—and I was able to be very successful with that amount of work.

UVA has something like eight or nine journals. If you want to work on a journal, the chances are you'll be able to. Varying levels of prestige, of course—Law Review, *International Law Journal* and *Tax Review* at the top. Law Review invites about 45 from each year—25 for grades, 15 from the writing competition, and up to five from a diversity plan. (You can also be invited to join Law Review if you submit a note that is chosen for publication.) There is a unified journal tryout in the spring of first year (or right before classes start, for transfer 2Ls), which is jointly administered by and used for selections by all the journals. Moot court draws probably a third or more of the students for the two-year competition starting in the 2L fall.

Status: Alumnus/a, full-time
Dates of Enrollment: 8/2002-5/2004
Survey Submitted: March 2005

Quality of classes is strong across the board, but for some very popular classes there may be difficulty getting in before the third year. More and more is done to create areas of concentration, such as the Law and Business Program. Antitrust is very strong, as are all business classes, a few of the criminal law offerings and most of the classes with an international focus. A few classes really stand out as outstanding, and UVA had a good mix of more senior, accomplished scholars and energetic, young "rising stars."

Status: Alumnus/a, full-time
Dates of Enrollment: 8/1996-5/1999
Survey Submitted: January 2005

Students at UVA work hard, but the academic and social atmosphere is strikingly different from any other Top 10 law school (and most likely all the rest, too). Students at UVA are extremely competitive—on the softball field. There is no unhealthy academic competition among the students. Study groups, sharing course outlines to prepare for finals, and otherwise assisting each other are very common. School is not cutthroat; there is no back-stabbing or underhandedness. Instead, students work hard and play hard, and develop wonderful friendships in the process. I can honestly say that law school provided three of the best years of my life. I have maintained friendships with several of my former professors, and I don't think that is common at other schools. The workload was what I expected (and what anyone should expect) for law school—classes were often exciting, sometimes dull and finals exhausting. But the camaraderie, friendships and fun made the UVA law school experience unlike any other.

Employment Prospects

Status: Current student, full-time
Dates of Enrollment: 8/2003-Submit Date
Survey Submitted: April 2006

UVA sets up its graduates with jobs better than almost any school in the country. Career services is really topnotch, and a UVA Law degree is respected everywhere in the country—I found a job at a top firm in Chicago, while other friends are working in Los Angeles, Boston, New York, D.C., Seattle and Dallas. Clerkships are very common, too, with many current Supreme Court clerks being UVA alumni. In the legal job market, UVA students are prized, because for whatever reason, UVA students graduate with a healthy perspective on the law-life balance and end up being amazing employees.

Status: Current student, full-time
Dates of Enrollment: 8/2005-Submit Date
Survey Submitted: April 2006

There is an enormous and very helpful alumni network. (UVA has one of the highest alumni giving rates in the country.) It is quite easy to find alumni contacts at major firms and in courts (state and federal judges). At a recent public service conference (a big annual event) I signed up for a "mentoring session" with an alumnus who now works in the Hague on nuclear non-proliferation. He was very friendly and generous with advice.

I have heard complaints from students interested in human rights or nonprofit work that there isn't enough assistance finding jobs in those areas. The major advice I've heard for that is to take a firm job your second summer, even if that's not what you want to do after graduation, since it makes you more marketable. And, of course, first-year grades are important (though much more so for firms than for public service jobs).

Regarding clerkships, the school provides a good deal of guidance for applying for those. It comes in the form of info meetings, a schedule of "deadlines" for applying, lots of advice and harassing e-mails from the career center so that you don't forget to do necessary stuff. It's effective judging by the number of people who are offered clerkships. Also, there are a LOT of UVA alumni judges, which helps.

Status: Current student, full-time
Dates of Enrollment: 8/2005-Submit Date
Survey Submitted: May 2006

Top third of the class is likely to place in a Vault 100 firm. Middle third is about a 50/50 shot at it and the bottom third has little to no chance. Employers pre-screen resumes and transcripts although there are some lottery spots available for most employers. Prestige among employers is high particularly in D.C., Richmond and Atlanta. Alumni exist in all 50 states, however the name does not carry well overseas. On-campus interviewing occurs before classes and again later during classes for 2Ls and 3Ls. Most students go into private sector, although there are a high number that go into government work. There are generous loan repayment plans for public service work.

Status: Current student, full-time
Dates of Enrollment: 9/2004-Submit Date
Survey Submitted: September 2005

Unless your heart is set on Wachtell and only Wachtell, a UVA degree will allow you to go where ever you want. The top D.C., NYC, S.F., L.A., Chicago and Atlanta firms all come here for on-campus interviews as do smaller firms, and people from well into the heart of the class (i.e., not just Law Review) get callbacks from them. The on-campus interview has both a lottery and an employee prescreening component, which is probably a good balance; no employer prescreening will only result in a lot of frustration for both students and firms.

The UVA Law esprit de corps extends to the alumni network—once you get the callback, alumni in the firm will be your advocates in the hiring process. About a third go to D.C. ("D.C.?" said the admissions dean. "We *own* D.C."), and about third go to NYC, where we actually seem to have a slight comparative advantage. The others are distributed throughout the South and West Coast.

Status: Alumnus/a, full-time
Dates of Enrollment: 9/2001-5/2004
Survey Submitted: April 2006

I think that UVA grads really like UVA students—and UVA students will be happy to know that UVA grads are everywhere. I believe that UVA attracts interviewers looking to fill more positions of employment than UVA has job seekers. As a result, most of the people who are interested in finding a job through on-campus recruiting are able to do so. UVA also has generous programs in place to help interested students find public interest work.

Status: Alumnus/a, full-time
Dates of Enrollment: 9/1996-5/1999
Survey Submitted: April 2006

Tied only with Harvard, it has the best placement nationally and internationally of any school in the country. Alumni actively seek to employ new alumni. Most folks do land in large firms, however, if you are interested in doing something that doesn't pay that well the school has been developing a number of post-graduation financial aid opportunities.

Status: Alumnus/a, full-time
Dates of Enrollment: 8/1999-5/2002
Survey Submitted: March 2006

I think UVA Law alumni are generally well-respected in the legal market, particularly in the Mid-Atlantic (including Washington, D.C.). Despite its perennial ranking in the Top 10, however, I don't think it quite has the same panache as other Top 10 schools. Interestingly, despite the fact that it always outranks other D.C.-area law schools, it is not uncommon for there to be a subtle preference for Georgetown alumni in Washington.

Status: Alumnus/a, full-time
Dates of Enrollment: 8/2001-5/2004
Survey Submitted: March 2006

I received multiple callback interviews in every market I was interested in. I had more callbacks than I could handle and ended up cancelling several. UVA students have an excellent reputation as smart, good lawyers, but most importantly, as normal people. All of my friends had similar experiences.

Status: Alumnus/a, full-time
Dates of Enrollment: 8/2003-Submit Date
Survey Submitted: March 2005

In general, students at Virginia want corporate jobs, not government or public service jobs. The school is trying to change this attitude and strike a more reasonable balance. They have created a public service careers office and a student loan relief program for students who decide to pursue public service careers. One hiring partner at a large firm said that when hired, a Harvard student wants to know when she can take time off to pursue pro bono work, a Yale student wants to know when she can take time off to finish her screenplay, and a Virginia student wants to know how many hours can she bill the firm for and how much money can she make in bonuses!

Status: Alumnus/a, full-time
Dates of Enrollment: 9/1995-5/1998
Survey Submitted: April 2005

Employers in NYC, Washington, D.C. and most Southern cities are lining up to take graduates from the law school. West Coast employment is a little more challenging, but certainly doable. I relied extensively on the alumni network in California to get my job and it worked like a charm. On-campus recruiting is VERY heavy and digs pretty deep into the class. Guerrilla interview tactics are tolerated and even encouraged by the Career Services Office.

 ## Quality of Life

Status: Current student, full-time
Dates of Enrollment: 8/2005-Submit Date
Survey Submitted: April 2006

Parking is a disaster. You can expect to lug your incredibly heavy books about a quarter of a mile to and from the parking lot your entire first year unless you either do all your studying at school or else live somewhere right by campus. There is a dorm for student housing but it's not just for law students. The real "dorm" is Ivy Apartments, where most law students live.

There's a gym with weights and workout machines right by the law school, but the nice gym with the pool is much farther away—you have to drive or bike to get to it and the inconvenience means less exercise for stressed-out law students. This is a BIG deal. Candy is everywhere in the law school, like that's going to fix your stress.

Status: Current student, full-time
Dates of Enrollment: 8/2005-Submit Date
Survey Submitted: April 2006

Charlottesville has been consistently rated as the best place to live in America, and it is! Although the law school is somewhat separate from the main grounds of UVA, it's not too far away and we get the benefit of having great sports teams to watch, as well as other perks of going to a top university. The law school and business school have a gym right near them, and there are also fancier ones down on the main grounds.

The grounds of the law school are GORGEOUS. My parents look forward to visiting me just so they can walk around and be amazed. The building of the law school is quite new and really beautiful. It is built around a courtyard, with lots of big windows and lovely wood. I still actually look forward to going to classes each day because they are in such a great setting. The library is huge and full of great places to study, including traditional tables, carrels, nooks with just one desk and big comfy leather armchairs.

There is a cafeteria in the school, which actually serves good food such as fresh sandwiches, sushi, pizza and hot entrees. There is also a fancier faculty dinning room that students can use if they make reservations. There are quite a few places fairly near school to grab pizza, sandwiches or other food if you are tired of the cafeteria. Additionally, Charlottesville has a TON of great restaurants, on the Corner, on the downtown mall and along Route 29. There's always a fun option for going out to eat!

Status: Current student, full-time
Dates of Enrollment: 8/2005-Submit Date
Survey Submitted: April 2006

A couple years ago C-ville was ranked the Number One Best City to Live In by *Frommer's*, and it is growing pretty quickly. There's a very pleasant downtown area that is being developed as a walkable city center, with a pedestrian mall at its center and historic buildings all over. The city seems to be a magnet for young, well-off professional families—sometimes it seems like there are babies and toddlers everywhere! I'm not sure where they all come from, but many are transplants.

There are definitely a lot of shops and restaurants here, but I've always thought it was a weird selection. For both shopping and eating out, your options are mostly either "really cheap and unremarkable" or "great but really expensive." People complain a lot that there aren't many in-between places that are both fun

Read all of Vault's Law School Surveys at www.vault.com/lawschool — get complete surveys on top law schools, expert advice on applicaton essays, LSAT prep and more.

VAULT CAREER LIBRARY 639

and affordable for students. For me, one of the hardest things about living here is adjusting to the lack of diversity in cuisines.

Status: Current student, full-time
Dates of Enrollment: 8/2004-Submit Date
Survey Submitted: April 2006

UVA students are said to be self-selective in that they prefer a certain, relaxed atmosphere. The clang of baseball bats, the flow from the Thursday kegs and the infamous month of nightly theme parties in February keep students in check with their more chilled sides. Charlottesville is an extremely easy city to live in, offering amenities like restaurants and shopping uncomparable to cities of its size. It is also a great place to raise a family and despite the "fratty" atmosphere of the law school at times, students do build a real sense of community inclusive of all persons.

Status: Alumnus/a, full-time
Dates of Enrollment: 8/2001-5/2004
Survey Submitted: March 2006

Charlottesville is the ideal place to study the law. It isn't a commuter school so everyone lives near the grounds. This increases participation in all of the activities at the law school. At the same time, it is close enough to Washington, D.C. and Richmond that you can get away for a little urban entertainment. Also, the proximity to Washington, D.C. makes it easy for the school to attract high-end speakers at events and for trips to visit with Supreme Court Justices and other high government officials.

Status: Current student, full-time
Dates of Enrollment: 8/2005-Submit Date
Survey Submitted: June 2005

Virginia Law has some downsides like anywhere else, but the quality of life isn't one of them. The dominant mode of discourse is definitely talking about how happy you are to be at UVA (which, truth be told, gets a little creepy sometimes—but people really do love it). The downside is that although many people are very political, it's considered something of a social no-no to wear your politics (or really any sort of activism) on your sleeve outside of formal settings or the classroom. People will certainly respect and engage you in a forum or a debate, but at a party, nobody wants to hear what you think if it's going to add tension to the situation. Live and let live.

Status: Current student, full-time
Dates of Enrollment: 8/2003-Submit Date
Survey Submitted: September 2004

It can be difficult to not get sucked into spending your entire life at the law school but beyond that Charlottesville is a great town. The grounds are absolutely beautiful. The architecture of the entire university is fantastic and the law school facilities are no exception. Housing can be tight as there are a lot of undergraduate students, but a lot of areas will only accept young professionals and graduate students so you should be able to find housing without a tremendous amount of trouble. The school will also help you if you ask.

 **Social Life**

Status: Current student, full-time
Dates of Enrollment: 8/2004-Submit Date
Survey Submitted: April 2006

You will probably either love or hate the UVA social scene. There is a lot of emphasis on going out and drinking, which is great if that is your thing. If not, there are still a lot of good options in town to have a more low-key evening. Some law students hang out at "The Corner," which is overrun with undergrads. I prefer the Downtown Mall, which draws a more mature crowd. People at UVA are pretty friendly and there are a lot of opportunities to go out and meet people.

Status: Current student, full-time
Dates of Enrollment: 8/2005-Submit Date
Survey Submitted: April 2006

The best way to succeed at UVA is to like beer and softball. Not just any beer—weak, cheap beers that taste like water will be everywhere, and you better drink it. Be good at softball or just be enthusiastic, but, if you want lots of friends, you

pretty much have to play. There's almost no out gay presence, and homophobi is allowed to run wild and free. A lot of girls wear high heels and makeup ever single day or stiletto boots if it's winter, so there's a vibrant culture o stereotypical femininity going on as well.

Status: Current student, full-time
Dates of Enrollment: 8/2004-Submit Date
Survey Submitted: April 2006

You could probably stay entertained without ever leaving the law schoo grounds—we do play a good bit of softball when the weather is nice, but pursuit are certainly not limited to that. There are lots of visiting lecturers and panels i you've got an academic bent, and plenty of pro bono, service oriented project if you want to give back to the community (Rape Crisis Prevention Center host a pizza hour every Tuesday to get research and small projects done.)

Each first-year section is divided into smaller sections of 30, and five or six pee advisors are assigned to each. Everybody and their dog wants to be a Pee Advisor and introduce the 1Ls to the law school experience (that is a bit like high school, complete with lockers). They host BBQs and potlucks to get everybody acquainted and groups often form to study, watch *Lost*, go bowling or play golf

Status: Current student, full-time
Dates of Enrollment: 8/2005-Submit Date
Survey Submitted: April 2006

Work hard, play hard; that old cliche is true here at UVA. I haven't had so much fun in school since, well, never! We actually get a social calendar at orientation! There are a ton of clubs and organizations here, from the Public Interest Law Association (they host a semi-formal auction each year, complete with open bar) to Virginia Law Women (free golf lessons for members) to the Libel Show (they put on an AMAZING show each spring). There are groups for different religions, different political views, different ethnic groups, different sports interests, different legal interests, groups for married students and families, groups for singers, groups for moot court people. There's even a law school band! I have never been this involved in school!

Status: Current student, full-time
Dates of Enrollment: 8/2003-Submit Date
Survey Submitted: April 2006

How many ways can I count that UVA is social? There is a weekly Thursday keg in the law school courtyard for all students. Every Thursday night the Student Bar Association host a Bar Review at a different bar in Charlottesville. The month of February is "Feb Club" at the law school, when there is a different themed party (e.g., "Wedding Crashers," "Viva Las Vegas," "Edward 40 oz. Hands") every single night for a month (and many students make it to every party). The Libel Show, where students put on an amazing sketch comedy/musical/dance show making fun of the law school, impersonate professors and joke about the legal profession, and where professors participate by making funny videos for the show and singing a Faculty Response making fun of the students is an annual tradition. Other events inlcude the Barrister's Ball, which is the law school's prom; the Dandelion Parade, the official kick-off to softball season where first-year student sections build floats, dress in themed costumes and make drinks based on their section "letter," and which ends up being a huge street party on the steps of the law school; and section potlucks and barbecues enjoying the beautiful outdoors of Charlottesville. Birdwood Golf Course has super-cheap rates for students to play 18 holes of championship caliber golf. Foxfields is the huge, fancy horse race that happens twice a year in Charlottesville, complete with women in sundresses and hats, and men in pastels and seersucker. Family Field Day is when married law students with children and local community children come to the law school for games, cotton candy, snow cones, face painting and a dunk booth.

Status: Current student, full-time
Dates of Enrollment: 8/2005-Submit Date
Survey Submitted: April 2006

The student body is very young, with a majority of 1Ls coming straight from undergrad or just one year out. I think as a consequence, there's a lot of energy on campus, but there's also a lot of college-style drinking parties. Be prepared to play beer pong if you go out with your sectionmates much. I think UVA has an image of being very preppy, with lots of white, middle-class, former sorority/fraternity members. This is true. I do wish there were more ethnic/racial minorities. That said, it was a trade-off. I could choose a more diverse law school in a big city, but all my options would have been more stressful and competitive. I realized that I would pick preppy over competitive/high-strung classmates any day! The school is also more conservative politically than I am used to, but there is a surprising amount of political diversity among the faculty. The school has an openly gay dean, which surprised me (since UVA is sometimes thought of as a "good old boy" school), but the ethic seems to be to respect everyone. I have not found any hostility between opposing political groups on campus.

Status: Current student, full-time
Dates of Enrollment: 8/2005-Submit Date
Survey Submitted: May 2006

Buddhist Biker Bar is a popular law and grad student hangout because they are tougher on IDs than other bars on the Corner. There is an active casual dating scene, particularly because the class is young (average age is 24) and majority male (60/40). There is also a large family population and LDS population that staged a recent protest to increase their presence on campus.

Status: Current student, full-time
Dates of Enrollment: 9/2004-Submit Date
Survey Submitted: September 2005

Everyone knows someone in NYC, so when they move there, that's who they hang out with. Who knows anyone in Charlottesville? As a result, law students hang out with other law students. I think this is a good thing, but some can find it claustrophobic. The physical remove of Charlottesville from the rest of civilization, and the physical remove of the law school from the main grounds tends to reinforce this. But not necessarily; this is still a college town every night of the week.

Status: Current student, full-time
Dates of Enrollment: 8/2004-Submit Date
Survey Submitted: July 2005

It's a supportive atmosphere, but can be a little clubby. There is a set of students who are overly concerned with their place in the social pecking order, but even though it can feel like high school, people are cordial and were without question the nicest I encountered during my law school visits. The Corner is a bar area a few hundred yards from UVA's central grounds (main campus).

Status: Alumnus/a, full-time
Dates of Enrollment: 8/1998-5/2001
Survey Submitted: April 2004

Social life is HUGE at UVA. UVA is known for being the "beer and softball" law school. The majority of the students play softball through the North Grounds Softball League (NGSL). The NGSL even has commissioners who are supposedly the best softball players and also usually popular students. In that respect, going to UVA is a lot like going back to high school! As a 1L, you are assigned to a 30-student section, with which you have all your classes. You get to know your sectionmates very well, and it's a great social bonding experience during your first year.

Read all of Vault's Law School Surveys at www.vault.com/lawschool — get complete surveys on top law schools, expert advice on applicaton essays, LSAT prep and more.

VAULT CAREER LIBRARY **641**

Washington and Lee University School of Law

Office of Admissions
Sydney Lewis Hall
Room 508
Lexington, VA 24450
Admissions phone: (540) 458-8503
Admissions e-mail: lawadm@wlu.edu
Admissions URL: http://law.wlu.edu/admissions/

 Admissions

Status: Alumnus/a, full-time
Dates of Enrollment: 9/2002-5/2005
Survey Submitted: May 2006

W&L requires an essay along with a detailed application. As it is in the Top 25 law schools in the country, and is [one of] the smallest school in the Top 25, getting in is extremely competitive. You need a high LSAT score and a strong undergraduate GPA. Having a major other than political science or being a minority can also be a strong point in your favor. The admissions staff is friendly and accessible.

Status: Current student, full-time
Dates of Enrollment: 8/2003-Submit Date
Survey Submitted: May 2006

Go for an interview. Character truly counts in W&L admissions.

Status: Alumnus/a, full-time
Dates of Enrollment: 8/2002-5/2005
Survey Submitted: May 2006

W&L stresses finding law students that are well-rounded and can contribute to the small community within the law school. Advice on getting in: make your personality shine off the page of your resume. Once admitted, I strongly recommend attending one of the admitted students open houses, as that easily sold me on the school.

Status: Current student, full-time
Dates of Enrollment: 8/2005-Submit Date
Survey Submitted: April 2006

To get accepted at Washington and Lee you will need to have either a very high GPA or a very high LSAT score. The LSAT score has more weight than the GPA, so you should put a lot of energy into the LSAT. In fact, if you have a really high LSAT score, and a not-so-hot GPA, you should still get in. On the other hand, if you have a pretty good LSAT score—low 160s, with a very high GPA, you should still get in. Make sure your personal statement (essay) is not convoluted and vague. The admissions office wants to get to know who you are. W&L prides itself on the diversity of its students.

Status: Alumnus/a, full-time
Dates of Enrollment: 8/1996-5/1999
Survey Submitted: May 2006

W&L is one of the few law schools that will conduct personal interviews. This is something that really helped me get in. My grades in undergrad were below average overall, but good in my major and I did well on the LSAT. So, the interview was an opportunity for me to explain face-to-face why my GPA was low and let them know I was serious about law school and about attending W&L. W&L is very selective but uses a more individualized and personal selection process. It is not just number crunching. They evaluate each individual and are willing to overlook a less than stellar grade here and there.

Status: Alumnus/a, full-time
Dates of Enrollment: 8/2001-5/2004
Survey Submitted: March 2005

The admissions process at W&L focuses on many of the same things as other top schools—good grades and test scores. However, because the classes are so small, other parts of the application process really set students apart from the other very bright, talented applicants. Visiting campus and meeting professors and admissions personnel, writing essays that reflect your personality and commitment to the study of law and understanding what the benefits are of a small school in a small town; all of these things can help you figure out why you're a good match with the school and communicate that effectively to those reviewing your application.

Status: Alumnus/a, full-time
Dates of Enrollment: 8/1999-5/2002
Survey Submitted: March 2005

Fairly competitive—the school tends to place a slightly higher emphasis on LSAT than on grades. The admissions staff is very friendly and will usually take time to meet any prospective student who has questions or requests an interview (even though the interview is not usually a considered factor in admission). The admissions committee will occasionally select students who have weaker academic credentials but who have demonstrated their uniqueness in other ways, such as through volunteer projects or social justice-type jobs. (This usually requires demonstration of a significant commitment to these projects or jobs—not just something you can do for a few hours and put on your resume.) Depending on the number of applicants, waitlisted individuals may have success in gaining admission if they appear very interested and are persistent with the school. The school will take people off the waitlist as late as the first week of August, in some cases.

Status: Current student, full-time
Dates of Enrollment: 8/2002-Submit Date
Survey Submitted: May 2005

The selection process is much like other law schools in several aspects. The admissions team will consider LSAT scores and GPAs along with your personal statement. Washington and Lee is different from other law schools because of its unique Honor Code system. Law school exams are not proctored and students have the decision of when to take the exam and where to take the exam. This means professors and fellow students trust even one another to take a closed book exam in their own room, for example, and not open the book or resort to unallowed information. This honor system works because the students swear to follow it. I think the admissions team considers this system when they consider students for acceptance. Information about a student's background that indicates trustworthiness and honor may be particularly important at Washington and Lee.

Status: Current student, full-time
Dates of Enrollment: 9/2002-Submit Date
Survey Submitted: December 2003

In addition to a real push for racial diversity, the law school looks very favorably on geographic diversity. W&L aims to be a truly national law school, so candidates who live outside of the state of Virginia and the South, in general, can look forward to better chances of admission and scholarships. The rest of the admissions regime is unexceptional with its focus on LSAT/GPA. The school is incredibly generous with scholarship money, however, with the vast majority of students receiving grant money. Considering the already cheap costs here, it's a very good value.

Status: Alumnus/a, full-time
Dates of Enrollment: 8/1999-5/2002
Survey Submitted: May 2004

I liked having the ability to come visit the law school at a time of my choosing and having the opportunity to meet with the director of admissions individually. We talked casually for over half an hour discussing my background and things unrelated to the law. I think it was a good opportunity for me to learn about the school, and an even better one for the director to evaluate my interest in the school and to explore the depth of my interest and motivation for the study of law. This was especially important because my grades in undergrad were significantly below those of the average applicants, yet my LSAT was above the school's median. I think the personal interaction between the school and me during my visit convinced them that taking a chance on me was a good bet. (I graduated with honors, so they were right!)

 ## Academics

Status: Alumnus/a, full-time
Dates of Enrollment: 9/2002-5/2005
Survey Submitted: May 2006

The classes at W&L are topnotch, as are the professors. Registration is done by lottery numbers, although they rotate by semester, so if your number was last one semester, it will toward the front the next semester. Popular classes fill quickly. Professors have an open-door policy and are easily accessible. Most enjoy speaking one-on-one with their students; all are willing to help, even if they seem intimidating. Grading is tough as there are many great students from many great schools—if you were used to being at the top of your class in undergrad, so was everyone else and you may find yourself toward the middle of the pack, regardless of your intelligence and success in undergrad. It is a fairly tight curve.

Status: Current student, full-time
Dates of Enrollment: 8/2004-Submit Date
Survey Submitted: May 2006

Unbelievable student-faculty interaction. You have a personal relationship with EVERY professor. It is wonderful. As for course selection, I would like to see a greater variety. There are, however, plenty of good classes to choose from. Moreover, being such a small school, you never have to worry about not getting a class that you want.

Status: Current student, full-time
Dates of Enrollment: 8/2005-Submit Date
Survey Submitted: April 2006

We have one of the only professor-taught, first-year Legal Writing Programs in the nation. The quality of W&L's Research and Writing classes is topnotch. We also have the best professors in the country consistently rated Number One in the *Princeton Review*. Our professors have an open-door policy and are friendly, congenial, genuine and excited to discuss legal issues and questions from class. Above all, our professors are at the forefront of their respective fields of study in American jurisprudence.

Status: Current student, full-time
Dates of Enrollment: 8/2003-Submit Date
Survey Submitted: April 2006

Professors are excellent and very accessible. Just last night, one of my professors took me for a ride in his airplane. The classes are smaller than at most law schools. First year is tough but I always hear from employers that W&L students really know how to write. Our Legal Writing and Research Program is excellent.

Status: Current student, full-time
Dates of Enrollment: 5/2005-Submit Date
Survey Submitted: April 2006

Course selection just occurred; you are assigned a random number and the number is reversed accordingly the next semester, so you always have a shot a picking classes earlier the next time around. Only four classes closed and all have waitlists. Seminars can be hard to get, but you're almost guaranteed them as a 3L. Grading is about a 3.33 curve for first semester; 3.8+ will be top 5 percent; and 3.6+ will be top 15 percent. Curve is rough for first year, but that's how most first years are. Much more laid back after that; average GPA for grads was about 3.5, I think.

Status: Current student, full-time
Dates of Enrollment: 8/2005-Submit Date
Survey Submitted: April 2006

Washington and Lee is known for its honor system. As a result, students leave their belongings, including laptops, sitting unguarded on desks and tables around the building. Nothing is locked, nothing is stolen and students tend to get along well. Classes range from just a few students to about 70 students, but even with the larger classes, the professors take the time to get to know their students. There are fewer courses to choose from than I would have liked, but there are enough classes in my area of interest to keep me happy. Popular classes are offered every term, so you'll get to take them eventually. There's a strict curve, so grading is tough, especially in your first year. The professors are great, but they definitely expect a lot of us, which is reflected by a heavy workload.

Status: Alumnus/a, full-time
Dates of Enrollment: 8/1996-5/1999
Survey Submitted: May 2006

Academics at W&L are excellent. The professors are all extremely approachable. Whether students like it or not, they WILL get to know their professors. I have been out for seven years and when I go back to W&L (which is as often as I can) I still go and chat with professors and they remember me and my family. By third year you will find yourself drinking with professors, hunting with professors or spending time at their houses. It is truly a unique experience in that respect. Plus, the professors are largely good teachers and all are outstanding scholars. Grading is fair. First year is a hard 3.0 curve. For upper level courses the curve depends on the professor.

Status: Current student, full-time
Dates of Enrollment: 8/2004-Submit Date
Survey Submitted: April 2005

Small classes and lots of contact with tenured professors. The open-door policy isn't just something they say to prospective students—doors on the faculty floor are almost always open. Also, legal writing is taught by tenured profs, not 3Ls or special writing faculty. The quality of teaching in the classes seems to be very high—this is not a place that has academic superstars who can't teach their way out of a paper bag. But that doesn't mean the faculty isn't accomplished— they're as good as any outside of the Top 14, in my opinion. It's just that unlike most law professors, they actually enjoy teaching and they do it well. They don't just look at law students as something they have to deal with before they can get back to their research.

Status: Alumnus/a, full-time
Dates of Enrollment: 8/2001-5/2004
Survey Submitted: March 2005

The faculty at W&L is its finest feature. Most professors could be teaching anywhere they want, and they choose this environment because of their relationships with students and with each other. They know your name, and they are willing to help you figure out your academic career, your legal career and any other issues that you find yourself struggling with along the way.

Grading is firm but fair—if you work hard and you're bright, you'll be rewarded. A few popular classes fill up in your second year, but you'll have a good chance of getting almost all the classes you want in either your first or second semester as a 3L. All of the classes are of high quality and challenging—even the ones on topics you aren't sure you're really interested in like tax or accounting for lawyers.

Status: Current student, full-time
Dates of Enrollment: 8/2002-Submit Date
Survey Submitted: May 2005

Washington and Lee Law is one of the smallest top-tier law schools in the country. The positive side of this is the excellence of the teaching staff and the accessibility of professors to students. Professors have an open-door policy, which means they are available any time—this includes by phone or in their office. It is common for students to meet professors socially to discuss class or personal life.

The downside of the small nature of Washington and Lee is the class offerings. Depending on how specific your interest is when coming to law school, you may find W&L to have fewer classes specializing in that area. For example, fields

Read all of Vault's Law School Surveys at www.vault.com/lawschool — get complete surveys on top law schools, expert advice on applicaton essays, LSAT prep and more.

VAULT CAREER LIBRARY 643

like sports and entertainment law or international law will not have as many classes as larger schools will. However, the professors or lecturers that instruct in those areas are experts in their field and are a wealth of knowledge.

The one good thing about the grading at W&L is really the nature of the student body and the response to the competitive nature of the curve. Students all want to do well in their courses and obtain top grades, and unfortunately not all can end up at the top of the class. However, the competitiveness never leads to unfriendliness or the types of stories you hear from top schools where students hide books or sources of advantage from other students to gain a competitive edge. In my experience, students have gone out of their way to be helpful, including sharing outlines and links to information that I may not have found on my own.

Status: Alumnus/a, full-time
Dates of Enrollment: 8/2000-5/2003
Survey Submitted: April 2004

The classes are good and professors are excellent. You truly get one-on-one attention from professors who know (and care) what your name is. Work is demanding and the curve is hard because EVERYONE is so smart. But the learning atmosphere is amazing. Students really collaborate and help each other—there is no ripping pages out of books in the library here! It's pretty uncompetitive among the students, and most seem to truly like learning the law. 2Ls and 3Ls can schedule their own exams. Many are take-home or can be taken outside the appointed classroom; most are unproctored.

Status: Alumnus/a, full-time
Dates of Enrollment: 8/2000-5/2003
Survey Submitted: April 2004

School was awesome. Small classes and a true open-door policy with all professors. Due to size of the school (and surrounding town), people went out of their way to be helpful, polite and uncompetitive. In a place this small, you can't afford to be a jerk! That is, if you want to have any friends here. There is no sense of competition—a little of the usual first-year stuff, but nothing like I've heard at other schools. And after first year, any sense of competitiveness is totally nonexistent. People genuinely want their peers to do well, and there is a lot of sharing and inclusive study groups set up. A GREAT law school experience.

 Employment Prospects

Status: Alumnus/a, full-time
Dates of Enrollment: 9/2002-5/2005
Survey Submitted: May 2006

W&L is favored highly with law firms in the Southeast region. You may have to do a little more legwork to find a job on the West Coast or in New England, but lawyers generally recognize the caliber of W&L law students. Most people end up in law firm jobs, although public interest/government jobs are popular due to our proximity to D.C. There is a lot of on-campus recruiting, although most firms are from the Southeast: Atlanta, Charlotte, Birmingham, most cities in Virginia. The school participates in several off-campus job fairs. The alumni network is extremely strong and extremely loyal. Making friends with an alumnus in the type of law or area where you want to practice would be a great way to gain employment.

Status: Current student, full-time
Dates of Enrollment: 8/2003-Submit Date
Survey Submitted: May 2006

The alumni network is crazy-loyal. They love talking to current students. Moreover, the collegial, "helping" environment that exists at the school itself follows the alumni out into the workforce such that they are happy to help current students.

Status: Alumnus/a, full-time
Dates of Enrollment: 8/2002-5/2005
Survey Submitted: May 2006

On-campus recruiting is solid, especially to Washington and anywhere in the Southeast all the way to Texas. The school's participation in job fairs puts

students interested in New York/Boston/L.A./Chicago in touch with the best employers from those areas. Many students from my class started in the biggest firms in the biggest cities in the nation, and many others chose to begin with the government or in the public-service sector. In my opinion, the school's ties with private employers are better than contacts for high-profile public-service jobs.

Status: Alumnus/a, full-time
Dates of Enrollment: 8/1996-5/1999
Survey Submitted: May 2006

W&L has a growing national reputation as a topnotch law school. More people in my graduating class went to work for firms in California than for firms in nearby North Carolina. Many of my classmates went to top-tier firms in L.A., NY, Chicago, D.C., Atlanta, New Orleans, Dallas, Houston, Phoenix, San Diego, Seattle, Charlotte, Richmond and Birmingham.

Status: Alumnus/a, full-time
Dates of Enrollment: 8/2001-5/2004
Survey Submitted: March 2005

W&L alumni are always willing to help out current students, but you will have more trouble if you are trying to work on the West Coast at a firm with no alumni from the school. The school has great connections with many D.C., Virginia and Deep South firms. The prestige level is on the rise. There are many firms that recruit on campus, which is impressive since it can be quite a drive! Graduates work everywhere from big firms, to clerkships and government offices (local and state or federal). The alumni network is very active and they do a great job raising LOTS of money for the school.

Status: Alumnus/a, full-time
Dates of Enrollment: 8/1999-5/2002
Survey Submitted: March 2005

Employment prospects are very good for the East Coast, if you're in the top third of the class. If you're lower in the class, it may be more difficult to find a big NY/D.C. law firm job, but I knew very few people in my class who at graduation didn't have a job or clerkship, and everyone was really excited about the job or clerkship they had received.

Status: Alumnus/a, full-time
Dates of Enrollment: 8/2000-5/2003
Survey Submitted: April 2004

Professors are more than willing to act as career advisors for people interested in clerkships or a certain area of law or public interest. On-campus interviewing is strong if you are interesting in going to a good-name firm in the South. Off-campus interview job fairs are increasing W&L's presence in job markets in New York City, Boston and Chicago, and many students are now being hired in these geographic areas as well. Students complain that those not eligible grade-wise for large firms are left behind by the career placement office, so be prepared to be your own advocate if that's you. There are amazing opportunities for students to get experience in clinic settings, which looks good to employers. There are several journals available other than Law Review. Law Review reserves some spots for pure write-on talent even if those people don't meet the grade requirements.

Status: Alumnus/a, full-time
Dates of Enrollment: 8/1999-5/2002
Survey Submitted: April 2004

Lexington is in the middle of nowhere, and this presents somewhat of a challenge for getting good firms to participate in on-campus interviews. Although W&L is an excellent school, people outside of Virginia and the surrounding area are not as familiar with the school as other schools that are not ranked as well. The career placement office was working on getting additional employers to participate in on-campus hiring while I was at W&L, but it is not the best choice if you are hoping to go to New York City, Boston, Chicago or L.A. Only those who place in the top of the class are likely to be able to get jobs in those cities without expending a lot of effort. If you hope to go to D.C., Charlotte, Atlanta or other large Southeastern cities, or even to Pennsylvania, you will have a lot of career options coming out of W&L.

The school says: "Career Services has begun a remote interviewing program in Charlottesville to attract interest from the national employers who visit the University of Virginia."

Quality of Life

Status: Alumnus/a, full-time
Dates of Enrollment: 9/2002-5/2005
Survey Submitted: May 2006

Lexington is a small town, so it has the perks of nice but cheap housing, little to no crime, and excellent quality of life. W&L is a well-funded school so the facilities and campus are nice (undergrad more so than law school, but law school is making major renovations this year). But, again, it is a small town, so the restaurants are few, the nightlife is limited to a couple of bars (but the social life is far from boring if you like house parties and football/kegs on the lawn every Friday in the fall and cocktail parties). In other words, the school and the students take care of the social life.

Lexington is definitely not for everyone and anyone who tells you it is, probably isn't being completely honest. But, I can honestly say there is nowhere else I would've wanted to spend my three years in law school. Law school is stressful and even if you lived in NYC, living on loans limits your financial freedom to engage in most activities there, so it was nice to be able to have a great time in a beautiful city and still be able to afford to do fun things.

Status: Current student, full-time
Dates of Enrollment: 5/2005-Submit Date
Survey Submitted: April 2006

The cops can be a pain because they have nothing better to do then harass law students walking home drunk (instead of driving, but that means nothing to them) and you can go stir crazy every once in a while, but it's nothing a weekend in D.C. or Charlottesville can't fix. Plenty of houses and apts available; the average rent for a really nice house in $550 and nice apts can be had for about $400.

Law school is getting a new moot court room, which should be nice as the last one was from the 70s. Having your own designated carrel to study in and keep your stuff at is great. The Honor Code is amazing, you can leave cash, laptops and books in the middle of the reading room and everything will still be there whether it be through a class or overnight. Library is open 24/7 every day of the year—many a good night spent there.

Status: Current student, full-time
Dates of Enrollment: 8/2005-Submit Date
Survey Submitted: April 2006

Lexington is a small town with a lot of history, but sometimes it can feel like you're in the middle of nowhere. The benefits: cheap rent, decent housing that's close to campus, free fitness center, good parking, almost no traffic and extremely safe. The drawback: there are only two bars and we're an hour away from any bigger cities (three hours away from Washington, D.C.). While this might sound unattractive, it's great not to have distractions or hassles to deal with and even better to live in an affordable area.

Status: Alumnus/a, full-time
Dates of Enrollment: 8/1996-5/1999
Survey Submitted: May 2006

As to crime and safety, Lexington is probably one of the safest places in the world. I did not even have a key to my house second year and, obviously, the door was never locked. People will leave the keys in the ignition of their car when they go to class. I left my laptop in my study carrel in the library for weeks on end. I never used my bike lock in the three years I was in Lex.

Status: Current student, full-time
Dates of Enrollment: 8/2004-Submit Date
Survey Submitted: April 2005

Very little competition between students. This place is too small to be able to get away with gunner-like behavior—you'll wind up spending your Saturday nights alone for three years if you try to pull that stuff around here. Housing is affordable and very nice. The town itself is very pretty in the fall and spring, although it gets sort of gray and depressing during the winter. The architecture around here is gorgeous, and there's lots of outdoorsy stuff to do in the spring, summer and fall.

Status: Current student, full-time

Dates of Enrollment: 8/2002-Submit Date
Survey Submitted: May 2005

The environment surrounding Washington and Lee University is small and picturesque; it's small town life. The housing market in Lexington, VA is extremely affordable and it is easy to get away with a real steal. The on-campus housing alternative is small and while convenient regarding both pricing and location (directly across from the law school), there are so many affordable housing options in town that there is no need to deal with the dorm environment of sharing with three other persons, tiny space and cinder block walls. The law school, undergrad campus and surrounding areas are all wireless Internet accessible. The majority of the town is also wireless enabled and you can access the Internet almost anywhere in town from your laptop.

Status: Current student, full-time
Dates of Enrollment: 9/2002-Submit Date
Survey Submitted: December 2003

Off-campus housing is cheap since it's Lexington, but not as cheap as it should be. Everyone is very friendly, however, so you can pass the time. If you bring a spouse, best of luck. As it is such a small town, there are VERY few opportunities for interesting or challenging work.

Status: Alumnus/a, full-time
Dates of Enrollment: 8/2001-5/2004
Survey Submitted: March 2005

Lexington is one of the greatest small towns in America. It is surrounded by mountains and unbelievable views—and not far from the Blue Ridge Parkway and unbelievable hiking and climbing, a river runs through it and so do several creeks. Good running trails wind all over town. Several good restaurants make their home there, and history buffs will find plenty of places to spark their interest. There's a ghost tour through the cemetery, the best chocolate shop in the country (so says the *Wall Street Journal* and anyone else who's stopped in for a taste), and a downtown with plenty of interesting boutique shops to explore on a sunny afternoon.

Social Life

Status: Alumnus/a, full-time
Dates of Enrollment: 8/2002-5/2005
Survey Submitted: May 2006

The Palms, cook-outs, board games, dinner parties, softball, touch football, hiking, antiquing and camp-outs are all favorites. If you're into clubbing, this is not the school for you. Lexington is excellent for those who like living a low-key, low-stress life in a gorgeous location.

Status: Alumnus/a, full-time
Dates of Enrollment: 9/2002-5/2005
Survey Submitted: May 2006

We also have a LOT of intramural sports, the highlight (for me) being the kegs on the lawn and two-hand, touch, co-ed football league games every Friday throughout the fall. In February, the students put on Feb Club, which involves a party at least four nights a week at a different home every night, and each party has its own theme. It's a fun way to break the winter boredom.

The dating scene is interesting. Lexington isn't easily accessible by planes, trains or any thing really other than cars. So, jokingly, students often say that Lexington is where relationships come to die. If you're in a long-term but long-distance relationship when you come to Lex, chances are you won't be in that by the time you graduate. But that also has to do with the stress of law school, particularly when your significant other is not also in law school and so has no idea what you're going through. It's sometimes easier to find someone at the school who you can sympathize with...and then date. Honestly, though, dating around isn't really done. It's a small school—we often called it Sydney Lewis Jr. High because at times the relationships felt very middle school (friendships and otherwise). But I cannot imagine that I would've had any more fun anywhere else. It's not for everyone, but if you're willing to hang out with your classmates and be social, you'll have a great time.

Read all of Vault's Law School Surveys at www.vault.com/lawschool — get complete surveys on top law schools, expert advice on applicaton essays, LSAT prep and more.

VAULT CAREER LIBRARY 645

Status: Alumnus/a, full-time
Dates of Enrollment: 8/2002-5/2005
Survey Submitted: May 2006

Social life is almost entirely created intra-law school. The competitive intramural program, run by appointed "Sports Czars," consists of approximately five sports and other special events. The school's tradition-rich Honor System creates a fabulous community to live in as everyone trusts everyone else. Although there are only a couple of bars in town, it never really was that big of a concern.

Status: Current student, full-time
Dates of Enrollment: 8/2004-Submit Date
Survey Submitted: April 2005

Look, we're in rural Virginia. There are two bars in town. Two. Social life tends to revolve around going to friends' houses and knocking back a case of beer. Very collegiate social life—older students (particular single ones) will find it downright depressing. Younger students enjoy it, though, and they also tend to mingle with the undergrads. Intramural sports are big here—every year, we send a few teams up to UVA to compete in the softball tournament. Also, the [Student Bar Association] provides kegs on the front lawn every Friday afternoon, which is really nice.

Status: Alumnus/a, full-time
Dates of Enrollment: 8/2001-5/2004
Survey Submitted: March 2005

W&L's undergrad campus has an active Greek life, so if you're looking to stay involved, you might find a chapter there. The performing arts are amazingly strong in Lexington and surrounding communities—from Shakespeare to the most current theater, classical music and local bands, not to mention the yearly wine and food festival (go early, buy a bottle and listen to the live music). And that's just the stuff outside the school. Plenty of cocktails and parties, intramural sports and lots of time getting to know the 300 or so other people who share your law school experience. Like any social scene, you get out what you put in.

Status: Current student, full-time
Dates of Enrollment: 8/2002-Submit Date
Survey Submitted: May 2005

The social life outside of the school consists of primarily two bars. This is a daunting prospect for many! In spite of the lack of culture in town, the school maintains a pretty lively social scene with school-funded events, parties concerts and the like. If you need something more, there are better bars and restaurants 45 minutes away. The restaurants are better than the bar scene, but still lack real diversity or culture. Lexington does now offer a sushi restaurant but the majority of them follow the American or Italian theme. The prices are affordable, however and the town people are friendly and welcoming.

Status: Alumnus/a, full-time
Dates of Enrollment: 8/2000-5/2003
Survey Submitted: April 2004

There are several bars, including The Mirage (formerly the Oasis) with legendary Thursday night karaoke. No nightclubs, but there is dancing at The Mirage. The Palms has been there forever and is a great watering hole. Live music at the Southern Inn, which is more upscale and has great food. Students often complain about the dating scene, but plenty of people met and dated during law school, and some have married. Outside the other law students, dating options are pretty much nil.

Much of the social life revolves around parties put on by the Student Bar Association, including many theme parties, kegs and whatever sport is in season every Friday afternoon. Intramural sports are big, from soccer to football to rugby to softball to basketball to indoor hockey to volleyball. There are a lot of clubs focused on particular legal interests, ethnic/racial backgrounds, religious interests, political interests and married couples.

William & Mary School of Law

Marshall-Wythe School of Law
Admission Office
P.O. Box 8795
Williamsburg, VA 23187-8795
Admissions phone: (757) 221-3785
Admissions fax: (757) 221-3261
Admissions e-mail: lawadm@wm.edu
Admissions URL:
http://www.wm.edu/law/prospective/admissions/

 ## Admissions

Status: Alumnus/a, full-time
Dates of Enrollment: 8/2002-5/2005
Survey Submitted: May 2006

The admissions process is typical—your grades, LSATs and other experiences and commitments are considered. William & Mary Law does have an outstanding Graduate Research Fellowship program for out-of-state students. It basically allows out-of-state students to pay in-state tuition and to receive a stipend, in exchange for doing minimal research for professors. It's a great experience and well worth the money you save!

Status: Current student, full-time
Dates of Enrollment: 8/2004-Submit Date
Survey Submitted: April 2006

W&M admissions process, just like many others, plays a large numbers game—to stay within the top tier you do need a high median GPA and LSAT score. However, W&M in line with the "citizen lawyer" ethos does take personal characteristics of applicants into consideration when putting together its class. Take time to put together a compelling personal statement to round off your admissions package. Once you get in, the administration begins sending a barrage of letters to ensure that all students know that they are welcome.

Status: Alumnus/a, full-time
Dates of Enrollment: 8/2002-5/2005
Survey Submitted: April 2006

The one thing that stands out is that William & Mary was the most helpful in the admission process than any of the other first-tier schools I was admitted to. Although William & Mary is selective, once admitted, they are very welcoming. Other schools followed their admission letter up with a lengthy form (and $75 form fee) expecting you to sit down with your parents and ask them detailed personal financial questions like: how much did they pay for their car, how much do they make, what do they have in savings. William & Mary followed up its admission letter with welcome letters from each department and an offer of in-state tuition.

Status: Alumnus/a, full-time
Dates of Enrollment: 1/2000-1/2003
Survey Submitted: April 2006

The W&M admissions office is professional and attentive. While not everyone can be accepted, the office strives to give every applicant a good impression of the school—the hope being that every applicant walks away with a good impression (whether accepted or not and whether an admitted student decided to come to the school or not). The office undergoes a full-file review and does not short-change applicants by trying to sum applicants up by using a couple of numbers. While scores and grades are important, they are only one aspect of a potential student and future lawyer. Recognizing this, W&M seeks interesting and accomplished students from all disciplines and walks of life. So, if you want to get in to W&M, you should do everything in your power to adopt the "citizen lawyer" model: don't just join organizations, lead them; don't cruise through

with fluff classes, challenge yourself; don't settle for a routine personal statement, express yourself.

Status: Current student, full-time
Dates of Enrollment: 8/2004-Submit Date
Survey Submitted: April 2006

The admissions process is largely centered around grades, LSAT and interest in William & Mary. The school provides a very informative admitted students weekend, which should be attended to get a feel for the school. The school has become more and more selective each year as the quality of the school and its other Virginia competitor schools has increased.

Status: Current student, full-time
Dates of Enrollment: 8/2004-Submit Date
Survey Submitted: April 2006

The staff seems to do a good job of looking for well-rounded candidates and taking into account various strengths of individual applicants, but in the end, raw numbers are still huge. The admissions process has gotten increasingly competitive over the past few years, with more and better candidates applying each year. My advice on getting in (especially for those with less than outstanding GPA/LSAT) is to let your application paint a picture of exactly what you could contribute to the law school community. Law schools are so much more than classes and exams—play upon your leadership ability, your special talents, and let your personality come through in your essays. Also, visit the school and let the admissions staff put a face and a personality with your file—it'll make you that much harder to turn down (and that much easier to accept).

Status: Current student, full-time
Dates of Enrollment: 8/2003-Submit Date
Survey Submitted: April 2006

It is a highly selective process, consistently resulting in a diverse class of individuals who understand and appreciate a law school environment that focuses less on the competitive struggles that are traditional in many law school environments and more on making the most of the legal education and social opportunities provided at William & Mary. Interviews are not required, though a personal essay and an exceptional academic record are necessary. I feel that William & Mary places a higher-than-normal emphasis on community involvement and leadership in the selection process as they are the hallmark of W&M's theory of legal education.

Status: Alumnus/a, full-time
Dates of Enrollment: 8/2000-5/2003
Survey Submitted: April 2005

Write a forthright essay that highlights what you have to offer the law school. The school is very selective, but likes to have a diverse and interesting class, so tell them what makes you different. No interview required, but I think it helps to visit the law school and schedule some time with Faye Shealy (if she's available). They love people who are excited about William & Mary's rich history as well as people who are interested in being actively involved in the school during their time as a student and as an alumnus/a.

> **The school says:** "The applicant review process evaluates the information contained in the application, including extracurricular activities, work experience, and community service, as well as the personal statement, an optional essay, if submitted, and the two letters of recommendation."

Status: Alumnus/a, full-time
Dates of Enrollment: 8/2002-5/2003
Survey Submitted: September 2004

The admission process is good and efficient. After submitting my application, the admission office kept close touch with me. Various methods of communication were used—e-mail, mail and phone. There was an orientation before classes began which gave me a lot of awareness about the situation and

Read all of Vault's Law School Surveys at www.vault.com/lawschool — get complete surveys on top law schools, expert advice on applicaton essays, LSAT prep and more.

VAULT CAREER LIBRARY **647**

environment. I visited the campus and checked the facilities and accommodations. I also had a chance to talk to the professors and current students in order to get more information. The orientation made me well-prepared and comfortable before I began to study there.

Status: Alumnus/a, full-time
Dates of Enrollment: 9/1995-5/1998
Survey Submitted: May 2004

When I applied to W&M, the application was fairly detailed and required several essays. W&M afforded applicants an informal interview process, but there was no formal interview requirement. Once students have been admitted, W&M does a "preview" program that allows prospective students to interact with current students, administration and faculty.

> **The school says:** "You may call the admission office to arrange an informational meeting with an admission dean, arrange to observe a class and/or schedule a student-guided tour on weekdays during the academic year. When school is not in session, self-guided, recorded tours are available from the admission office or law library circulation desk."

Status: Alumnus/a, full-time
Dates of Enrollment: 8/1991-5/1994
Survey Submitted: April 2004

The admissions process went smoothly, I thought. Their GPA and LSAT requirements are quite competitive, but my scores and GPA were very high. Also, they are big on diversity and recruiting from as many states and countries as possible, so being from outside Virginia (I was from Louisiana) was also helpful. They also look for well-rounded individuals, so prior work or volunteer experience (even part-time work during college) and any extracurricular activities are important. They also had an invitational open-house program in the spring to which they invited all persons to whom they had extended an offer for the following fall. The program was very informative and really made the difference for me. I really got a feel for what a great school and fantastic program it was, and felt right at home.

Academics

Status: Alumnus/a, full-time
Dates of Enrollment: 8/2002-5/2005
Survey Submitted: May 2006

The professors are very good. There are virtually no "stereotypical" law professors at William & Mary—those who use fear, intimidation and embarrassment in teaching. Instead, most professors come with solid experiences in actually practicing law and strong academic backgrounds that combine to create an intellectually challenging, and yet fun, academic program. Grading is as fair as it can come in law school, where everyone is graded on a curve—while you can achieve a B+ by attending class and studying hard, the A- and A are hard to come by. The workload is intense, especially when balanced with the extracurricular activities (student organizations, trial team, moot court, law journal and community service) that many law students take on. But William & Mary does a good job of creating a supportive and collegial environment that makes even the toughest of semesters enjoyable and worth the hard work. While I cannot say I didn't work my butt off, I can say that I could not have done it without the support of my professors and peers.

Status: Alumnus/a, full-time
Dates of Enrollment: 8/2002-5/2005
Survey Submitted: April 2006

Academic program was topnotch. Most of my professors were academically renown and excellent instructors. With few exceptions, most professors took great pride in the quality of their lectures and made themselves abundantly available to students outside of class—most were involved in extracurriculars and social activities. The library staff would bend over backwards to help in research projects.

Status: Alumnus/a, full-time
Dates of Enrollment: 1/2000-1/2003
Survey Submitted: April 2006

W&M is a fairly small school (about 200 per class) and is in a fairly small town. The professors at W&M could go to almost any school—just look at their credentials—but they choose to stay in Williamsburg at W&M because of the pleasant atmosphere, close-knit community and welcoming environment. This carries over to the student body and law school community in a number of ways. Students are competitive with themselves and challenge each other, but the competition is healthy and respectful. Horror stories about hidden books and back-stabbing students simply don't exist. Professors have students over for dinner and get to know everyone by name. While the faculty expects students to be prepared and ready for class, they are pleasant and welcoming during class discussion, even when it takes the Socratic Method form that makes many prospective students so anxious. The courses are many and varied and, as an alumni that passed the PA and NJ bars on the first attempt, do an excellent job to prepare students for the bar exam and for practice.

Status: Current student, full-time
Dates of Enrollment: 8/2004-Submit Date
Survey Submitted: April 2006

In the first year of school students are required to take Contracts, Torts, Civil Procedure, Property, Constitutional Law and Criminal Law. In the second and third years students are free to choose from a wide variety of traditional classes and smaller seminars. Additionally, William & Mary also has their famed Legal Skills Program, where students are placed in a mock law firm and complete assignments as if they were actual lawyers. In the first year of the Legal Skills Program students learn Legal Writing and Research. In the second year of the Program students actually take on mock clients, perform a trial and even go through the whole appellate process.

Status: Current student, full-time
Dates of Enrollment: 8/2004-Submit Date
Survey Submitted: April 2006

The academics here are very strong. The 1L program is fairly uniform with most law schools, with the exception being the Legal Skills Program. The Legal Skills Program, graded on a pass/fail basis, gives students the opportunity to practice and study the concrete aspects of being a practicing lawyer, including interviewing clients, researching and writing memos, negotiation, document drafting, trial advocacy and appellate procedure. Because the program is pass/fail, each student will get out of it what he or she puts in to it. Given proper effort, however, the Legal Skills Program can be immensely valuable, especially during firm work after the 1L year (one fellow summer associate from a higher-ranked law school asked me where I learned to write memos so well).

Scheduling classes during 2L year has been perhaps my greatest area of concern about the academic program. Classes fill up very quickly (3Ls get first pick) and popular classes are often offered in only one section per semester—or year. That said, the range of course offerings and the quality of the curricula are generally very good.

Status: Alumnus/a, full-time
Dates of Enrollment: 8/1991-5/1994
Survey Submitted: April 2004

The law school has topnotch professors and a great program called the Legal Skills Program where they put all first-years in a pretend law firm with a senior partner (a member of the faculty), a senior associate (a second- or third-year) and all the junior associates (all the first-years in the firm), where they immediately begin handling mock cases, from beginning to end. They have practice interviewing clients, researching, deposing clients, having a trial (jury and bench trial) and arguing an appeal. Great program—gets you some practical experience and also immediately helps you meet and interact with members of your class.

We had a great class of people and made numerous close friends, with whom we remain in contact with to this day. (I also met my husband there.) I credit the school with the wonderful, positive law school experience I had and the numerous close friends I made. The program is geared towards teaching, while fostering interaction among classmates and encouraging law students to get involved. The environment is excellent for learning and creating well-rounded awyers. The law school also has excellent summer programs overseas, including England, Spain and Australia. I went on the Spain program and loved it—one of the greatest experiences of my life. I also had several friends who went to England and Spain, and they all really enjoyed it and even years later talk about what a special, exciting experience it was. Professors are excellent and really seem to care about the students and the quality of what they teach. Grading is fair—if you put in the time and effort, you'll do fine. Workload is what I'd expect from law school—heavy (what law school workload isn't?) but manageable if you put in the time.

> The school says: There are no longer Supper Abroad programs to England and Australia. The current Summer Study Abroad Program is in Madrid, Spain. Participants include approximately 100 law students from law schools around the country and a limited number of Spanish law graduates. The Law Studies Abroad Program, inaugurated in 2005, offers 2Ls and 3Ls the opportunity to pursue advanced study of foreign legal systems, international and comparative law, and practice for one semester in institutions in Japan, New Zealand or Spain.

Status: Alumnus/a, full-time
Dates of Enrollment: 9/1999-5/2002
Survey Submitted: December 2003

The school is willing to balance "publisher" professors with "teacher" professors. As a result, we generally do not suffer through classes by professors who are brilliant academics without the ability to succeed in the classroom. The grading is fair. The workload is intense, but manageable. There was only one class in law school I wasn't able to get the professor I wanted—I got "the other section."

Status: Alumnus/a, full-time
Dates of Enrollment: 8/1998-5/2001
Survey Submitted: September 2003

The quality of the classes overall was very high. While first-year classes were relatively large for the school (70 or so for certain classes), most other classes were small and allowed for good discussion. Furthermore, the professors were very accessible. As for getting classes, you could usually get classes you were interested in.

Employment Prospects

Status: Alumnus/a, full-time
Dates of Enrollment: 8/2002-5/2005
Survey Submitted: April 2006

William & Mary has a very capable office of career services. I don't know of anyone who didn't have a summer internship. Their public service fund pays $300 per week for summer internships that benefit the public and which would otherwise be unpaid internships (e.g., legal aid, county attorney's office).

Status: Current student, full-time
Dates of Enrollment: 8/2004-Submit Date
Survey Submitted: April 2006

William & Mary is highly regarded with legal employers, resulting in the vast majority of students obtaining well-paying firm jobs. For those interested in the public sector or government employment, William & Mary's proximity to Washington, D.C. provides the perfect opportunity to connect with employers providing this type of employment. The majority of employers come from the D.C./Virginia/Mid-Atlantic region. William & Mary students, however, obtain employment anywhere in the country including New York, Chicago, Los Angeles and San Francisco.

Since our school is so small, William & Mary alumni look out for other William & Mary alumni and students by providing support for finding employment and developing contacts. Just send them an e-mail and they will take you out to lunch, provide employment advice and connect you with the best contacts for finding the type of job that you want.

Status: Current student, full-time
Dates of Enrollment: 8/2004-Submit Date
Survey Submitted: April 2006

Although I have only applied to Virginia firms, I have had no trouble getting interviews and summer offers. Particularly in the Northern Virginia, Richmond and Hampton Roads areas, the alumni network seems quite strong and the name of the school opens doors. Even for those who wish to practice elsewhere around the country, the alumni network and prestige of the William & Mary education have landed fellow students summer internships in California, New York, Texas, Boston, Philadelphia, Atlanta and Washington, D.C., among other places. Almost every student utilizes on-campus recruiting. The school has well-equipped interview rooms that are filled every fall and winter with law firms from around the country.

Status: Alumnus/a, full-time
Dates of Enrollment: 8/1999-5/2002
Survey Submitted: March 2005

If you want to work in D.C., you will have plenty of opportunities for on-campus interviews. This is also true to a lesser extent for NYC and Boston markets. However, if you want to go to the West Coast, you can forget an on-campus interview. Williamsburg is just too rural and W&M is too low ranked to make the effort of getting to campus worthwhile. I think we have a pretty good reputation and most of my classmates found jobs after graduation.

> The school says: "Students also participated in 27 off-campus interview programs in 2005, including events in Atlanta, Boston, Chicago, Dallas, Houston, Los Angeles, New York, Seattle and Washington, D.C..
>
> "As of February 2005, 98.9 percent of 2004 JD graduates who reported their status and who were seeking employment had secured jobs or were pursuing advanced degrees. Class of 2004 graduates are located in 25 states, D.C., and one other country."

Status: Alumnus/a, full-time
Dates of Enrollment: 9/1999-5/2002
Survey Submitted: December 2003

The law school students are as bright as any out there. William & Mary enjoys a national reputation—one can compete for top jobs in every market. The list of on-campus recruiters reads like a "who's who" of the Am Law 100 and 200. Additionally, a number of folks end up with great positions at places like DOJ, the SEC and NASA. Federal clerkships are fairly common as well—both district and appellate.

> The school says: "2004 JD graduates reported working for the following employer types: private practice (58 percent), government agencies (13 percent), judicial clerkships (11 percent), military justice (8 percent), public interest organizations (5 percent), business/industry (4 percent) and academia (1 percent).
>
> "The Office of Career Services offers individualized career planning support to all students. There are, in addition, information sessions designed to educate students about the job search process, talks and panels by guest speakers representing a broad range of employment settings, and a comprehensive OCS Resource Library of career planning publications and electronic resources."

Quality of Life

Status: Current student, full-time
Dates of Enrollment: 8/2004-Submit Date
Survey Submitted: April 2006

William & Mary law students are really relaxed and easy going. We are all type-A, so there is some competition. But the competition here is by no means cutthroat. We all trade notes, share outlines and study together. The law students

Read all of Vault's Law School Surveys at www.vault.com/lawschool — get complete surveys on top law schools, expert advice on applicaton essays, LSAT prep and more.

 **649**

very much have a "we're going to get through this together" type of mentality, which really helps take some of the stress out of law school. Most students live off campus because housing is plentiful. Off-campus housing runs from normal student housing to gated communities with pools and tennis courts. There are on-campus graduate apartments that are mostly inhabited by law students. They are close to the law school and comparable in cost to off-campus housing. Living in Williamsburg can be an adventure. The tourism means that the town offers more than it should considering its actual population size. The law school is divided. The old part is undergoing renovations, but you can definitely tell that part of the building is dated. The newer part is actually really nice. The library is undergoing and expansion and renovation. It will be a lot nicer when it's finished, but the construction can be pain at times. Williamsburg crime really amounts to retirees getting ticketed for driving too slow. Other than that, the city is pretty harmless.

Status: Alumnus/a, full-time
Dates of Enrollment: 8/2002-5/2005
Survey Submitted: April 2006

First, the law school is going up in the rankings and that has made a slight difference in the atmosphere at the law school. However, because the school is small compared to other top law schools, students all know each other. This is incredibly helpful when it comes to the job process and in preparing for classes. Students are not competitive and I imagine that almost every student will tell you that you can leave your laptop unattended without fear that someone will touch it.

The new library is being built and will give students a lot more space to study in! I think that may have been the only complaint I had while attending. But, the school is very open and it does not lock students out of classrooms on the weekends or keep them from using rooms when classes are not is session. I spent several nights studying for exams or preparing for moot court in the facility meeting room.

Status: Current student, full-time
Dates of Enrollment: 8/2004-Submit Date
Survey Submitted: April 2006

The law school is disconnected from the undergraduate campus, and although we are invited to utilize all of the resources and spaces available over there, anyone who tells you that is commonplace is lying. This law school, like most law schools, is a pretty insular community (which is both a good and a bad thing).

Status: Current student, full-time
Dates of Enrollment: 8/2004-Submit Date
Survey Submitted: April 2006

Williamsburg is a quiet town, but presents an ideal location for graduate school. Housing, taxes and groceries are all extremely affordable. The crime rate is extremely low. Many of my friends never lock their car doors and only lock up their house if they are going out of town. Virginia Beach and Richmond are both only an hour away, which provide additional opportunities for spouses and significant others to work.

Status: Current student, full-time
Dates of Enrollment: 8/2004-Submit Date
Survey Submitted: April 2006

William & Mary provides on-campus graduate houses that are located approximately 75 yards from the law school building. Additionally, there are a multitude of apartment and condo complexes nearby that offer housing at a range of prices. Crime is negligible in Williamsburg, and the town is absolutely beautiful. There are a variety of local attractions to take advantage of, such as Busch Gardens and Water Country U.S.A. theme parks, Colonial Williamsburg, Jamestown, Yorktown and Virginia Beach. The law school facilities are average, but steadily improving. A library expansion is nearing completion and several classrooms are in the process of being remodeled. Additionally, a new wing was added a couple of years ago that houses small- and medium-sized classrooms, interview rooms, meeting rooms and faculty offices.

> **The school says:** "The law library broke ground in spring 2005 for a new addition, which will be followed by a complete renovation of the existing library. The $16.8 million expansion

and renovation will result in a new library facility in 2007 nearly two-thirds larger than the current one."

Status: Alumnus/a, full-time
Dates of Enrollment: 9/1999-5/2002
Survey Submitted: December 2003

Williamsburg is a nice enough town and not terribly far from D.C. [The area i special] because of Colonial Williamsburg; it has a fair amount of tourist traffic But Richmond, VA is just up the road, and it is an honest-to-God real city wit nightlife, great restaurants and so on.

 Social Life

Status: Alumnus/a, full-time
Dates of Enrollment: 8/2002-5/2005
Survey Submitted: April 2006

I truly enjoyed my experience at William & Mary. First, Williamsburg is a smal town, but it is close to Norfolk, Richmond and D.C. My friends and I too shopping trips to Richmond, visited the Outer Banks from Williamsburg an enjoyed living in a small town. Secondly, we made life fun because we went ou in Norfolk, took trips to D.C., went to Virginia Beach or the Jamestown Beac and enjoyed the outlet malls. Third, the local bars know law school students— we tend to have our favorite places to visit.

Students and professors also interact to a greater degree than at most top law schools. Professors will have students meet for class in their homes and wil often introduce their families to their classes. Professors are oftentimes foun sitting in the lobby speaking with students, participating in student-organize events (such as bowling or happy hours), and are always available to talk wit students.

Status: Alumnus/a, full-time
Dates of Enrollment: 1/2000-1/2003
Survey Submitted: April 2006

W&M law school students enjoy a wealth of social activities, which is couple with the small-town charm of Colonial Williamsburg (only three blocks from th law school campus). For sure, no one is going to confuse Williamsburg for Ne York City, but what Williamsburg lacks in 4 a.m. clubs and restaurants, it make up in beautiful surroundings, wonderful people and charm. While there ar certainly student mainstays (the Green Leafe Cafe has about 30 beers on tap, th Fat Canary was named one of the best restaurants in Virginia and has an amazin wine list, the Cheese Shop has cheap and delicious sandwiches to go), man times students generate their own fun.

Status: Current student, full-time
Dates of Enrollment: 8/2004-Submit Date
Survey Submitted: April 2006

William & Mary students study hard and they play hard. I can honestly say have gone out more in law school than I did in undergrad. We have Bar Review every Thursday night. The Student Bar Association puts on a lot of differen events. There are a semi-formal and formal. During the fall there is a raftin trip, and in the spring there is a skiing trip. The Public Service Fund also put on events to raise money. They host a poker tournament, a Mr. Marshall-Wyth Competition and a date auction. Between PSF events and SBA events, there i generally a law school function every weekend.

Williamsburg offers few options in the way of bars. On weekends, most peopl have their favorite hang-out spot—whether it be a bar or person's house—an then we all eventually end up that the Green Leafe. Karaoke at the Hospitalit House is also another favorite. Students also go to surrounding cities on th weekends to do any number of things such as attending comedy clubs or squar dancing. Dating in Williamsburg is an interesting prospect. Some law student get together, but the end result is usually either marriage or disaster (no mutually exclusive). Most people do not enter serious relationships while in la school. The main campus offers a lot of different activities such as sportin events, concerts and cultural events. Law students have access to all thes events and attend them with some frequency.

Status: Alumnus/a, full-time
Dates of Enrollment: 8/2002-5/2005
Survey Submitted: September 2005

For those that go out it is the Leafe. On Thursdays there is Bar Review. If you are expecting to interact with the undergrads it is a tough one. You're best going to Paul's to get away from law students. As any place there is always dating within the law school but beware it is like high school—everyone will know what you did and with whom. There is fun to be had but it is usually at the same one or two bars. The good thing is at William & Mary the students are smart but will help each other. I gave my outlines away all the time and no one would ever steal books. In fact, most students leave their computer around and they are always safe.

Status: Alumnus/a, full-time
Dates of Enrollment: 9/1999-5/2002
Survey Submitted: March 2005

Students must make their own social life. Williamsburg is a tourist town, not a college town. There are few bars (The Green Leafe being the law school favorite), and almost no mixing with undergraduates. The law school classes tend to be very diverse with regard to age and marital status, so there appears to be a circle of friends for all.

Status: Alumnus/a, full-time
Dates of Enrollment: 8/1999-5/2002
Survey Submitted: March 2005

I can't put too fine a point on this. Williamsburg is a great place to visit, a horrible place to live. You are basically in the middle of nowhere, yet the freeway that takes you to Hampton Roads or Richmond is always packed and slow. There is nothing to do in Williamsburg. There are two old crappy movie theaters and three bars. The bars are packed every night. If you want to do anything other than study and hang out at your house for the next three years, go somewhere else.

> **The school says:** "A new multiplex theater opened within three miles of campus in 2005; a small art film theater is open within walking distance of the law school."

Status: Alumnus/a, full-time
Dates of Enrollment: 8/2002-5/2003
Survey Submitted: September 2004

Of course, as everybody knows, this school stands for its tradition and virtue of history. So, you should not expect modern life and fashionable entertainment from this school. There are no restaurants, bars or clubs located on campus. But there are some very famous places you should go, such as the Williamsburg Inn. Although you do not have a lot of choices for fun, there are still some places the students can celebrate, take a break or relax. They often go to some certain bars at certain days for social life, dating or special events. Anyway, if you are looking for fun, do not come here. If you are looking for quiet, this is the first choice.

 # The School Says

Established in 1779, William & Mary Law School is the nation's oldest. Emphasis is placed upon the students' intellectual development as well as the students' character and value development so that they become excellent lawyers who will constructively contribute to society. The Law School is small enough that students know one another by name, but large enough to form a critical mass for learning and scholarship. The faculty have compelling academic and clerkship credentials and are distinguished scholars, addressing the legal issues of the day in the classroom or in the corridor or in publications and in symposia and conferences. To the students, they are very accessible.

The curriculum prepares the students for the increasingly complex world confronting lawyers. One aspect of the curriculum is the innovative program called Legal Skills. In this two-year program, each student joins a 16- to 18-associate student law firm led by a senior partner drawn from the faculty and a junior partner selected from the third-year students. With both classroom instruction and simulated client representation, the student learns how to research, counsel, interview, draft documents and perform actual court work, all in the context of their firm's cases. The Law School's McGlothlin Courtroom is at the cutting edge of courtroom technology, research and application. In the courtroom, each student receives instruction in using the technologies to support and conduct litigation.

Beyond the classroom and courtroom, the academic experience at William & Mary is enhanced by additional opportunities. The Law School's Institute of Bill of Rights Law has established itself as one of the preeminent institutions in the United States engaged in the study of the Bill of Rights. The Institute sponsors a variety of lectures, conferences and publications that stimulate scholars from across the country to examine important, current constitutional issues. The Institute publishes the student-edited William & Mary Bill of Rights Journal, considered one of the nation's leading journals on constitutional law issues.

William & Mary also offers three other student-managed publications, namely the *William & Mary Law Review*, the *William & Mary Environmental Law and Policy Review* and the *William & Mary Journal of Women and the Law*, all being recognized as leading journals. With a highly competitive Moot Court Program and a National Trial Team, excellent opportunities are available for students to develop their legal research, legal writing and advocacy skills. These are further supplemented by an active Student Bar Association, with activities to further stimulate intellectual curiosity and divergent thinking and to permit the students to become better acquainted with their classmates, the faculty, the College and the Williamsburg community.

William & Mary recently instituted several new programs, including the Election Law Program, the Human Rights and National Security Law Program, the Property Rights Program, and the Therapeutic Jurisprudence Program. A new civic leadership program, the George Why the Society of Citizen Lawyers, also debuted in fall 2005.

The Law School's Career Services Program offers individualized assistance to each student to develop a job search strategy and to identify and asses employment opportunities, both national and international.

Read all of Vault's Law School Surveys at www.vault.com/lawschool — get complete surveys on top law schools, expert advice on applicaton essays, LSAT prep and more.

VAULT CAREER LIBRARY **651**

Seattle University School of Law

Office of Admission
Sullivan Hall, Second Floor
901 12th Avenue
P.O. Box 222000
Seattle, WA 98122
Admissions phone: (206) 398-4200
Admissions e-mail: lawadmis@seattleu.edu
Admissions URL: http://www.law.seattleu.edu/admission

Note: The school has chosen not to comment on the student surveys submitted.

 ## Admissions

Status: Current student, full-time
Dates of Enrollment: 8/2003-Submit Date
Survey Submitted: April 2006

This school is very concerned with social justice, equality and diversity. You may have a better chance of getting in here if you have experience in social justice organizations or have a past that shows perseverance through diversity. Once you are accepted you get a letter from the school, and if you're lucky, they may have chosen to give you a scholarship too. This helps because the school is a private school, and therefore more expensive than the University of Washington, but the scholarship may make it just as inexpensive. They will also send you letters from students and you will might even get a call from a student or staff member welcoming you to the school. I felt very welcomed and really enjoyed talking with current students when I was trying to decide what school to go to. It was tough, though, to access someone in the admissions office when I first came in during the summer, because they had students working at the desks who weren't very helpful, but when it was closer to the actual fall semester the office seemed to come alive and the staff was easier to talk with.

Status: Current student, full-time
Dates of Enrollment: 6/2005-Submit Date
Survey Submitted: April 2006

Seattle University was by far the friendliest school that I applied to. Other schools that I applied to would send a letter saying that they had received my material and that was it. Seattle U. sent that letter, sent invitations to prospective student events, sent holiday greeting cards and kept you up to date on the progress of your application. The application was much like those of other schools. There was no interview, but there was an essay. Seattle U. processed my application very quickly, which was really great because many schools take months to get back to you whether you got in or not. Seattle U. is getting much more selective because they are moving up the rankings quickly. They are investing a lot of resources into the program so if you are on the bubble right now I wouldn't wait another year because you probably won't make the cut in another couple years.

Status: Current student, full-time
Dates of Enrollment: 6/2005-Submit Date
Survey Submitted: April 2006

Do it early. Be ready for the experience. Speak from real experiences in your essays. Don't fill it in with "I really want to change the world" stuff. This is pointless and they have seen it a million times. Even though there is rolling admission, the early bird still gets the place in a good law school.

Status: Current student, full-time
Dates of Enrollment: 8/2005-Submit Date
Survey Submitted: April 2006

It was based basically on an application process, which included essays and college resume. The topic was quite broad, and allowed insight into why you felt you'd be a good fit for law school and what past experiences helped you reach this point.

I didn't have an interview, but found that the selection process was fair, and the student body has a good mix of diversity, regarding race, religion, gender, age and economic status.

Status: Current student, full-time
Dates of Enrollment: 8/2004-Submit Date
Survey Submitted: April 2006

The personal statement portion of the application should likely stress the applicant's interest in social justice, as social justice is the school's mission. For example, one reason I wanted to be an attorney was so that I could help the elderly obtain access to legal advise for complex matters, such as taxes, medical issues and housing. I think this was an important factor in my being accepted. The school also highly values diversity in age, experience, religion and ethnicity. Further, an applicant's fluency in another language would be important to point out, as the school is known for its Access to Justice Program that helps non-native English speakers obtain legal help.

Status: Current student, part-time
Dates of Enrollment: 6/2003-Submit Date
Survey Submitted: April 2006

I found the admissions process to be a more comfortable process than I expected, and I can't say that for every law school. The admissions office does a great job of reaching out to applicants and providing them with a variety of ways to get to know the school. If you're considering SU, ask to talk to students or faculty (especially if you have particular interests), attend the admissions receptions and sit in on a class or two. All of these steps will help you to see what a great place the school is.

Some tips: I think the admissions department really pays attention to what people write in their statements. They want to know what kind of student you are and what kind of contribution you may make to the school. There's certainly some interest in encouraging diversity of thought, so don't be afraid to be honest and express yourself.

The school has a real focus on social justice. If that's a priority for you, let them know.

Status: Current student, part-time
Dates of Enrollment: 8/2003-Submit Date
Survey Submitted: July 2004

Fairly simple. I applied online and was accepted. I made a rather late decision to attend law school. I did not apply until the beginning of January 2001 in an effort to start in the fall of that year. I had not taken the LSAT when I applied but took the February exam. With high marks (top 90 percent) I was accepted to SU. I thought it was neat when I received my acceptance letter and the dean had written me a personal note about the great possibilities with my prior career and law. He let me know that I would find many opportunities with my doctor of pharmacy and a law degree.

Status: Current student, full-time
Dates of Enrollment: 8/2003-Submit Date
Survey Submitted: January 2005

The best advice for applying to Seattle University is to apply early. The class sizes are strictly limited, and the admissions office is notorious for filling it with the first first few waves of applicants, leaving many of the better students whose materials just slid in past the deadline on the waitlist. The student body is comprised mostly of students from selective Washington colleges and students from out of state. Students who don't fit either of these categories would probably be best served by detailing in their essays why they want to stay in Seattle and why, specifically, Seattle U is the choice for them. Seattle U is one of three Washington law schools, so clearly making Seattle a defined choice is key.

Additionally, the school places a huge emphasis on diversity, so if there is any way that an applicant can fathom being diverse, this should certainly be highlighted. The technicalities of applying are on par with other law schools; they're very similar to the college application process, wherein all one must do is mail one packet and instruct LSAC to do the same. There is no interview process. Seattle is very good about keeping correspondence with all its applicants, making for a relatively smooth process.

Status: Alumnus/a, full-time
Dates of Enrollment: 6/2001-5/2004
Survey Submitted: January 2005

The admissions process was smooth. SU was good about staying in touch throughout the process and answering questions almost immediately in most cases. The director of admissions gave a wonderful tour and seemed interested in my background. She even remembered who I was at graduation. The overall admission process was excellent.

The only drawback was that orientation was a little disorganized in that there was no clear checklist of tasks one needed to complete before the first day of law school. In addition, the coordination between the law school and the rest of the campus was poor at the beginning (SU acquired the law school the year before). Nevertheless, the law school and SU worked out the communication issues by my second semester.

Academics

Status: Current student, full-time
Dates of Enrollment: 8/2003-Submit Date
Survey Submitted: April 2006

This school has the typical law school courses, and the first-year classes are the same ones you'll find at just about any school. But our school has a really great Legal Writing Program, and you are likely to have more practice with legal writing here than most schools (and if you're lucky you might get a class with the professor who wrote the legal writing textbook used at most law schools in the nation!).

Your second year you may not get the classes you really want at first because you will register after the 3L students, but if you get on the waiting list you are likely to get a couple of the ones you want after the semester starts. So go to them anyway just in case (or talk with the registrar because they will tell you how far down the list you are and what the chances are of you getting in on the waiting list).

Status: Current student, full-time
Dates of Enrollment: 6/2005-Submit Date
Survey Submitted: April 2006

The first year at SU is much like that of all law schools around the country with the core classes of Property, Contracts, Torts, Criminal Law and Civil Procedure. The one thing that makes SU stand out is the Legal Writing Program. Currently ranked first in the country, the program adds a rigorous component to the first year. It's tough but it makes us all better writers and that really helps when trying to break into the workforce. The core classes are a ton of reading and no feedback over the course of the semester. For each class, you take one big final at the end of the semester and that is your entire grade. It is the same way everywhere else that I've heard of though. The professors are great. SU does have some lame-duck professors that have been around a long time; however, the professors hired within the last five or six years are outstanding. SU is trying to improve its standing in the country among law schools and hiring star faculty is a big goal for them.

Grading is really tough here, as well. SU has a very strict curve that is a little different from other law schools. Just recently they eliminated the requirement

that professors fail at least two students a semester (so that is good), but they are still required to meet quotas at every grade level, including 20 percent [of students in each class receiving] C-'s! So the curve here is around a B- where at other schools it is around a B or maybe a little higher. I haven't tried to register for classes yet so I'm not sure how tough it is getting into the popular classes.

Status: Current student, part-time
Dates of Enrollment: 6/2003-Submit Date
Survey Submitted: April 2006

The academic program is certainly challenging. The school has done a great job of building a strong core curriculum (the required classes), and then offers a good variety of "bar subjects" and more focused, specialized seminars. While many professors use a modified Socratic Method in the first year, it's nothing like *The Paper Chase*. They can really challenge you in class, but they do it in a non-threatening sort of way. And most of them are willing to work with you if you're really scared about speaking in front of the group.

The amount of time you spend on school work outside of the classroom will change over time, but in the beginning of school, you can expect to spend two to three hours for each hour of class. You could slack off in some classes and not read, but you'd fall tremendously behind and REALLY regret it at the end of the semester.

The faculty is outstanding, and the dynamic between students and faculty really enhances the law school experience. Even though they are demanding, faculty really want you to succeed and are willing to help you outside of class. They take such an interest in the student body and are so approachable. And many of them are really leaders in their field.

Status: Current student, full-time
Dates of Enrollment: 8/2005-Submit Date
Survey Submitted: April 2006

The first year, we all have to take the same intro classes: Contracts, Civil Procedure, Property, Criminal Law, Torts and Legal Writing. The quality of the teachers has been high thus far. Next year, we get to choose, and it's based upon a ranking system (3Ls go first, then 2Ls). Certain classes can be hard to get based on your priority for scheduling. Plus, some classes are only offered rarely, due to it being a specialty of a specific visiting professor. Grading is hard, since it is curved; you can't really do more than your best work and hope that it's good enough. The curve is quite rough.

Status: Current student, full-time
Dates of Enrollment: 8/2004-Submit Date
Survey Submitted: April 2006

There is usually a large variety of courses to choose from; however, because a third of the students are evening part-time students, a lot of bar courses are often offered at night. In general, the topics range from typical subjects like Trusts and Estates, to ones like Washington State Constitutional Law Seminars.

SU has one of the most harsh curves in the nation. In a class of 100 students, only four people will receive an A. However, seminars and upper-level courses that are not held in multiple sections are graded according to the professor's individual preference, so it is theoretically possible for all students to earn an A.

I have been more than impressed with every teacher that I have had thus far. While there may be a professor or two that I do not care for personally, each has taught me the substantive law and has helped me to develop my legal analysis skills.

Status: Alumnus/a, full-time
Dates of Enrollment: 8/2000-5/2003
Survey Submitted: February 2006

First off, SU has one of the best Legal Writing Programs. The head of the program has been recruited by Harvard for years and has chosen to stay at SU. That definitely says something about the caliber of legal writing education you will get at this law school. A lawyer has no more powerful a tool than his skills with the pen and paper. The first-year curve at this school is more difficult than at other schools, in my opinion. While other schools practice grade inflation, SU does not. In your first year, A's and B's are much harder to come by than at other schools. Although this can be very rewarding if you get one of those grades, it can also be frustrating when competing for jobs in the second year. Especially

Read all of Vault's Law School Surveys at www.vault.com/lawschool — get complete surveys on top law schools, expert advice on applicaton essays, LSAT prep and more.

VAULT CAREER LIBRARY **653**

when another local school is rumored to grade inflate. However, the curve after the first year is on par with other schools or does not even really exist for some classes. It then really depends on the professor and the level of difficulty of the course. Overall, you will get an excellent legal education and the skill-set to successfully navigate any state's bar exam and the future employment that lies ahead.

Status: Current student, full-time
Dates of Enrollment: 8/2003-Submit Date
Survey Submitted: July 2004

The first-year curve is harsh, C or C+. But the professors are pretty good. The adjunct professors are even better because they bring real life experience to the classroom. The visiting professors (I have had three) have all been mediocre. They did not seem to care, and one guy from Alabama was actually verbally abusive. The overall feel of the program, though, is a great experience. I have had great classes, and classes where I thought I might actually die of boredom. The overriding problem with several of the classes is the political atmosphere brought by the professor. This really detracts from the class, because it becomes a forum to vent your political frustrations rather than learn the law. The school does a great job in getting quality adjunct professors. Many of them are better than the tenured professors; they are more personable and able to relate more practical law to the class.

Status: Current student, full-time
Dates of Enrollment: 8/2003-Submit Date
Survey Submitted: January 2005

For the 2004-2005 school year, the first-year grade curve was significantly softened, making for a much less stressful 1L year. The academic program at Seattle U is stringent, with required courses through the end of second year. The first-year program is intense, and affords year-long approaches to all courses (courses which, consequently, are only semesters long at most other law schools). This approach at once gives students a firm grounding in first-year subjects and tends to give them the sense of cramming everything into the last semesters that remain. While most schools require Con Law and Evidence in the first year, we take them second year, leaving less space for electives.

Seattle U's intensive three-semester writing program also eats away at elective time, making it difficult to concentrate on any area of law specifically. There just aren't enough openings in the semesters that remain to fit everything into your schedule. Balancing courses of interest with bar courses and required courses can prove challenging at Seattle U, but is a feat that can be accomplished—in theory, anyway.

The registration process is a nightmare, with waitlists regularly three times the length of the enrollment. Many popular and specialized classes are not offered regularly, and when they are, only a fraction of the people interested can get in. Because so many courses of interest have prerequisites that are nearly impossible to get into or that conflict in scheduling with required courses, students are forced to take whatever classes fit, rather than whatever classes interest them. The school claims to have myriad "focus groups," but in reality, no one in the past five years has been able to graduate with a completed focus group—membership does not elevate registration status, and the sad fact of it is, it's impossible to win registration for all the classes needed to complete any entire area.

Whatever class you end up in, though, you will likely find that the professor is approachable and helpful, both inside the classroom and out. In curved classes, the grading is tough, but this is a standard for law school. A lot of professor claim to factor participation into grades, too, so paying attention in class and being prepared for discussion is key to success here.

If the first-year workload scares you (and it is intense), the second-year load will knock you dead. In the second year, assignments are brutal and the amount of work actually to be done is staggering, no matter the courses you take. It is seriously ill-advised to skip even one day of class; and if you don't understand something, get yourself to the professor's office before you're completely run over by with the next barrage of assignments.

Status: Alumnus/a, full-time
Dates of Enrollment: 6/2001-5/2004
Survey Submitted: January 2005

SU's classes were good overall. Like any school, some professors are better tha others. Different students relate better with different professors. There were r bad professors. Moreover, I had the privilege of attending some very goc classes with topnotch professors.

SU emphasized practical learning environments such as Legal Writing classe and participation in moot court and mock trials. Because of this emphasis o practical skills, SU students held their own in competing against other schoo students in the Pacific Northwest.

 # Employment Prospects

Status: Current student, full-time
Dates of Enrollment: 8/2003-Submit Date
Survey Submitted: April 2006

Seattle University School of Law has a lot of prestige in the Northwest regior Many employers are graduates of our school (or from the school that was bough and turned into SU) and they have a lot of loyalty to hiring SU students. Mar of our students are employed by major firms across the region and across th nation, and students are encouraged to go into social justice positions in all size of firms with scholarships and fellowships that help make up for the differenc in salaries. We have on-campus interviews each year, internships ar encouraged and our Career Services Office advertises those through e-mail eac week.

Status: Current student, full-time
Dates of Enrollment: 8/2004-Submit Date
Survey Submitted: April 2006

SU has prestige with Washington-based law firms. The school is really not o the national radar. If anything, its good reputation is known in Washington an Oregon. It is a strong school in the Northwest region, but I would nc recommend this school for someone who wanted to work on the East Coast o California. Graduates go to private firms, both large, medium and small; the also go to federal and state agencies, the state attorney general's offic prosecutor's office, the U.S. Marshall's and few go directly in-house.

Of the few alumni I have met, they seem extremely willing to help in any wa that they can. The school helps to foster this by inviting alumni to event including them in things such as moot court competitions where they act a judges, hosting alumni dinners and having them speak about their areas o practice. All is very helpful for cultivating a relationship between the alumni an current students. Further, because SU is a regional school, the majority of it alumni are located in the greater Seattle area, so there are many local alumni fc a student to connect with.

Status: Current student, full-time
Dates of Enrollment: 6/2005-Submit Date
Survey Submitted: April 2006

I am a 1L and I already have a job for the summer and it is apparently prett prestigious. Be ready to talk to employers about how your other experience besides law school, help make you a great candidate for the job. Speak othe languages, have hobbies, have a life; it serves you in the end. There are a millio law people out there, have something more to offer.

Status: Current student, part-time
Dates of Enrollment: 6/2003-Submit Date
Survey Submitted: April 2006

Seattle University's reputation is primarily regional, although the school' national profile is rising. In the 70s, during the school's early days, it used t play second fiddle to the other law school in town, but I think that mos employers now realize that the school is a good school and focus on th individual applicants, rather than the school. I've never felt slighted, an because we have more recent graduates, I encounter more SU alumni out in th field. Plus, the school has a really strong reputation for its Legal Writin Program and its Trial Advocacy Program.

here are fewer Seattle firms that participate in the traditional on-campus recruiting activities (that you'd see on the East Coast). They say only 10 percent of students get jobs through that program, and I think it has more to do with the region. Many students find jobs through career services postings or by networking. The school schedules many speakers/events that give students a chance to network with employers from small- and mid-sized firms.

The school also has an active externship program, which is a way of getting real-world experience for credit, rather than pay.

Status: Alumnus/a, full-time
Dates of Enrollment: 8/2000-5/2003
Survey Submitted: February 2006

SU is making great strides in improving its national presence. It has made a big investment in raising the school's prestige in most major markets and so far has done so with great success. It is extremely well respected in Seattle and the surrounding Pacific Northwest states. Knowledge of the school deteriorates as you move east, but as more students begin to venture out east, knowledge and respect of the school will increase exponentially. The school is also very well represented in places like California, Hawaii and Alaska. The one weak point I have found with SU, though, has been in career services, but this is a weak point at many schools. With greater staff and more creativity, there should definitely be a noticeable improvement in this area. However, there was a general feeling among students that if you were not in the top 15 percent of your class, career services did not have much help for you. This frustrated many students and I am not sure really how much has changed. But exciting days could be ahead with a facelift to the career service department. On-campus recruiting included mostly Seattle-based law firms. You did not see major East Coast firms coming out to SU when I was there. That might be different now. As the national presence of the school increases, there could be a noticeable change in participation of firms from outside Seattle. Graduates from SU work in private large, medium and small firms. Graduates work in government, public interest and some even hang their own shingle. Graduates also enter into corporate and non-law fields.

Status: Current student, part-time
Dates of Enrollment: 8/2003-Submit Date
Survey Submitted: January 2005

Every fall, career services sponsors OCI, or on-campus interviewing (a seven week process of interviews with big Seattle firms). Most 2Ls participate, though less than 5 percent of them actually find jobs this way. Part of the problem with OCI is that it is so limited to the best-of-the-best firms—firms that can, and regularly do, recruit nationally. It's common knowledge that only the top 10 percent will get call backs, and of those hired, few, if any, will find their summer jobs developing into careers. Students say again and again that OCI was a big waste of time. Students usually find summer jobs and later work in smaller firms, which abound in the Seattle area, but which career services does nothing to bring to campus.

Status: Alumnus/a, part-time
Dates of Enrollment: 6/2001-5/2004
Survey Submitted: January 2005

The job market was tough for every school. SU placed top students at top firms. The good students like me have had to work hard to find jobs. Most us have found jobs after five to seven months following graduation, which is an acceptable timeframe considering the bar preparation, test, announced results and swearing in.

Quality of Life

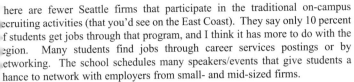

Status: Current student, full-time
Dates of Enrollment: 8/2003-Submit Date
Survey Submitted: April 2006

Seattle is a vibrant community with a lot of housing near the school and great shops, restaurants and access to Interstate 5, from where you can get to nearby communities quickly. The campus is really nice, and the law school is right in the middle of the campus, along with other graduate schools, so you aren't just surrounded by undergrad students. We have restaurants right on campus and across the street from campus, and have a nice school athletic facility down the street. There are dorms and apartments for rent right around here, but the price of living in the city can be expensive. There's not a lot of crime around this area, but like any big city we do have some criminal activity (like thefts) here so students need to stay vigilant.

Our school is working on being as family-friendly as possible, so students with families can feel welcome and respected here. We don't yet have a day care on campus, but there are day cares nearby and the school will help you find some if you need help finding it. We do have a room for students who have new babies to deal with breast feeding issues right in our law school building, and a night program for those students who need to attend school at alternative hours.

Status: Current student, full-time
Dates of Enrollment: 6/2005-Submit Date
Survey Submitted: April 2006

Some students choose to live nearby in one of Seattle's many neighborhoods, and some commute as much as four hours each day. Traffic is highly congested during rush hours, which makes commuting frustrating for some. The main campus is very beautiful and oasis-like, and the law school building is state-of-the-art, built only seven years ago. There are a few restaurants very close to campus and on campus there is limited dining available. There are many, many restaurants throughout the city, however. First Hill, the neighborhood where the campus resides, is diverse; there are several medical buildings and hospitals, luxury condo buildings and upscale restaurants, but there are also low-income housing buildings, incidences of crime and needle-exchange stations. However, overall, the neighborhood is very "hipster," with many young professionals, students and gays.

Status: Current student, full-time
Dates of Enrollment: 8/2005-Submit Date
Survey Submitted: April 2006

The campus is great. It is about eight years old, so everything is quite new. The building is nice and up to date. It is right on the Hill and downtown Seattle is about 15 minutes away on foot (or two if you drive). The campus housing, while limited, is suitable. All the law students live in one building. There is accessible laundry across the hall in another building. I've never had a problem with crime, although we occasionally get reports regarding criminal activity at early hours of the morning.

Status: Current student, full-time
Dates of Enrollment: 8/2004-Submit Date
Survey Submitted: April 2006

SU's campus is absolutely beautiful. There is perfect landscaping all year round, with flowers during the spring and summer everywhere. The law school is on the same campus as the undergraduate school, which is nice because there are students milling around outside, which makes the area feel even more safe.

The building that houses the law school is basically brand new, so all of the electronics, furniture and infrastructure are state-of-the-art. The library is comfortable, well-lit and open from 6 a.m. to midnight every day. The law school is 100 percent contained in one building. There is very interesting art located in the building, all donated of course, and one feels very important coming to such a beautiful facility. Each student is also provided a locker in which to keep their books and personal belongings, which is nice. There are a refrigerator, microwaves and free filtered water available for all students to use, too.

Read all of Vault's Law School Surveys at www.vault.com/lawschool — get complete surveys on top law schools, expert advice on application essays, LSAT prep and more.

VAULT CAREER LIBRARY   655

There are about five places to eat directly across the street from the law school. There are also apartments, a gas station, the school gym, soccer fields, tennis courts and houses very close by.

Status: Current student, part-time
Dates of Enrollment: 6/2003-Submit Date
Survey Submitted: April 2006

The neighborhood's a fun neighborhood, with quite a few places to eat within walking distance. It is an urban setting, and so it's important to take the normal safety precautions you'd take in such an area. The school offers a free escort service for people who don't want to walk around campus alone at night. The biggest problem is laptop theft. In those cases, though, the owners left their computers unattended. I've never heard of anyone having problems if they use a cable to lock up the laptop.

The law school building is topnotch. It's less than 10 years old and looks even newer than that. The entire campus has wireless Internet access and all of the classrooms are equipped with the necessary A/V equipment. The fourth floor of the library is an especially comfortable place. If you're going to spend the bulk of the next few years in one building, it's a good building to be in.

Status: Current student, part-time
Dates of Enrollment: 8/2003-Submit Date
Survey Submitted: July 2004

No big issues good or bad. I was able to live with my wife and kids and commute to school. There are apartments next to the school and nearby. The neighborhood is not the best but not the most hazardous place in the world. Prices in Seattle can be pretty high, so living with a roommate, or two, or living a bit farther away may be the best way to keep costs down. You can't beat the Seattle life, though. The mountains are 45 minutes away for very good ski slopes. The ocean is three hours; Canada is two hours. There are great clubs, bars and places for both families and singles to hang out and do things.

Status: Current student, full-time
Dates of Enrollment: 8/2003-Submit Date
Survey Submitted: January 2005

Seattle is a great place to live and go to school. Seattle U is located in Seattle's Capitol Hill neighborhood, which is a very liberal but kind of quaint area, marked by a lot of little shops, bars and restaurants. Activities are constant, and with the heart of downtown but a 10-minute drive away, we really have the city at our fingertips. The law school does not offer campus housing, but there is a plethora of cute, relatively inexpensive apartments in the surrounding areas. Parking can sometimes be a problem, as the garages are not all near the law building and are shared with all SU students in all programs. The law building itself, though, is beautiful and an excellent place to be and to study (which is good, as most law students practically live there anyway). As if a testament to the building's greatness, we constantly find ourself chasing undergrads out. The law building has a deli and coffee bar where the food is good and moderately priced. The building is, however, located just across the street from a Starbucks and multiple little restaurants, so a variety of dining options are readily available, even if time is of the essence.

 ## Social Life

Status: Current student, full-time
Dates of Enrollment: 8/2003-Submit Date
Survey Submitted: April 2006

There are a lot of clubs and restaurants near the school, and almost every week the law school student organizations sponsor social events either on or off campus. The Asian and Pacific Islanders Student Organization has a karaoke event and luau each year; the Student Bar Association has talent shows and school carnivals; there are Diversity Fairs each year; and there is a Public Interest Law Foundation auction to earn money for grants to students who choose to work in public interest law, among other fun events.

We also have a Barristers' Ball each year at a fancy place in Seattle when we get to dress up and pretend like we're back in high school going to prom, except the professors and many students' spouses go, so that keeps it professional. Students

here like to have a good time, but this is definitely not a "party school." People take their grades and their reputations as future lawyers seriously here, so the big, crazy events are off campus and rarely get out of hand.

Status: Current student, full-time
Dates of Enrollment: 6/2005-Submit Date
Survey Submitted: April 2006

Law school is a small, intimate affair and if you want it is very easy to make friends. There is no Greek system or anything but this is Seattle and the school is in the most lively part of town. There are unlimited opportunities to have fun in this town. If you like clubs, cozy bars, hiking, sailing, golfing or whatever you want, it is here. The Student Bar Association is always doing some kind of social event and at the end of every year there is a huge Barristers Ball, kind of like law school prom; very fun. SU is in a great place if you like to go out and Seattle has many nice getaways, as well, if you like to fly solo.

Status: Current student, full-time
Dates of Enrollment: 6/2004-Submit Date
Survey Submitted: April 2006

There is a strong social life supported by SBA functions at the school. On top of this Seattle has the highest percentage of college graduates of any major city so there is a vibrant social dynamic alive and well in the city. Favorites: The Chapel (bar), Kangaroo and Kiwi (bar), Nectar (bar), The Bad Juju lounge (bar), The War Room (bar), Bumpershoots (music festival), Bluegrass Festival, Solstice Festival.

Status: Current student, full-time
Dates of Enrollment: 8/2004-Submit Date
Survey Submitted: April 2006

The school really tries to get all 1Ls to be included socially so the first year there are constant mixers, both at local bars/clubs, as well as at the school. For example, there is an annual Halloween Party hosted by the school, where the school pays for drinks (sodas, waters, beer, wine), food and candy. There is also an annual karaoke bash used to raise money for certain clubs; the Public Interest Law Foundation Auction where professors donate things like a poker game or a dinner, and there are other items up for bidding; all of these activities try to get the students to mingle with each other so that they feel involved.

Seattle is full of awesome restaurants and bars. Captial Hill is the neighborhood where SU is located, and it is home to many bars, ranging from rock clubs where one can hear cutting edge rock and roll, to dance clubs, martini bars and wine bars. There is such a diversity of places to go, as each neighborhood in Seattle has a different feel and scene. Really, there is a place for everyone.

The school also sponsors outings to Mariners' (baseball) and Sonics' (basketball) sporting events. There are also community events that the school hosts, such as a speaker's event on the Japanese internment; further, the school has sponsored sessions of the WA State Supreme Court hearings at the school's own courtroom, and students were invited to watch. SU admissions does a great job of picking a diverse set of people who have enough in common to be friends, but who are also different enough to expand a student's social horizons. For example, prior to coming to SU I had never had a friend who was Jewish, or a friend who was born and raised in an African country, or a friend who was homosexual. I am so glad to be friends and colleagues with people who are different than me so that I have a better perspective of the world in general. Plus, everyone here is extremely friendly and there is not cutthroat competition.

Status: Current student, full-time
Dates of Enrollment: 8/2003-Submit Date
Survey Submitted: January 2005

Our Student Bar Association is extremely proactive in planning law school functions, both formal, seasonal and casual. The SBA strives to throw one free function per month, usually at a nearby bar, and the turnout for these events is usually high. Other organizations also step in and organize socials, with the result that one can find something fun to do with other law students almost every week.

Dating among law students is not common, but does happen. Because of the diversity of ages and groups represented, many students come to school already married or dating outside individuals. Seattle, while not itself a swinging singles cene, does provide a lot of lonely law students with opportunities to meet mates outside of the law building.

Status: Current student, part-time
Dates of Enrollment: 7/2003-Submit Date
Survey Submitted: December 2004

This is law school, who has time? Only the day students engage in regular activities—they are younger, have more energy and fewer responsibilities. But Seattle has pro teams in baseball, basketball, football, soccer, hockey and the WNBA, which provide year-round sports. There are Division II SU undergraduate sports, but they are very low profile. There is no Greek system. Elsewhere (and not very far away) are great nightclubs, bars and restaurants.

Read all of Vault's Law School Surveys at www.vault.com/lawschool — get complete surveys on top law schools, expert advice on applicaton essays, LSAT prep and more.

VAULT CAREER LIBRARY **657**

University of Washington School of Law

Admissions Office
William H. Gates Hall
Box 353020
Seattle, WA 98195-3020
Admissions phone: (206) 543-4078
Admissions fax: (206) 543-5671
Admissions e-mail: lawadm@u.washington.edu
Admissions URL:
http://www.law.washington.edu/Admissions/

 Admissions

Status: Alumnus/a, full-time
Dates of Enrollment: 9/1998-6/2001
Survey Submitted: March 2006

I had to take the LSAT and submit an application that included an essay. I also submitted three letters of recommendation, which I think were required.

UW Law school is fairly selective for out-of-state applicants and the statistical numbers for the average admittee were high (3.5+ undergrad GPA, 85 percent LSAT). But I do think the school gave a fair amount of consideration to extracurricular activities and post-undergrad employment. The average age of a first-year law student when I attended was 25, so a number of people took time off before starting law school.

Status: Current student, full-time
Dates of Enrollment: 7/2002-Submit Date
Survey Submitted: April 2005

The program has a two-tiered approach to admissions. First tier, if your LSATs and grades are high enough, you are in. Second tier, if your scores aren't high enough to get in "automatically," your application goes through a substantial process of being read and considered by several students and faculty. This law school is selective. Take the LSATs as many times as you need to to get onto the high 90s, percentile-wise.

Status: Current student, full-time
Dates of Enrollment: 9/2004-Submit Date
Survey Submitted: April 2005

I've never been the best standardized test-taker, so I've had to work hard at maintaining a respectable GPA. But I was very involved in college. In particular, I was a varsity athlete in college. I think that the University of Washington really takes into account the person, and not just the numbers (at least they did with me). I also think my admissions essay helped me get in, and it paid off to have it proofread over and over again.

Status: Current student, full-time
Dates of Enrollment: 9/2004-Submit Date
Survey Submitted: April 2005

This is a pretty tough school to get into (luckily for me, though, they don't mind the occasional preposition at the end of a sentence). I'd recommend being a resident. It's cheaper and they try to make incoming classes be 70 percent residents. It takes two years to establish residency, during which you can do something to make yourself more interesting.

A good story seems to be crucial. There are people in my class who are parents, who have worked for the Peace Corps, who have tried to make Olympic teams, who have been private investigators, who hold PhDs in other fields and who have done all sorts of other interesting things. The diversity of experience is key to the environment. Everyone brings something unique to the table.

Write a good story about yourself. Do you come from a single-parent home? Is English not your native tongue? Have you ever run for Congress? Ever write for a newspaper? Tell the school about it. Have a good (but not necessarily great) LSAT. Have a good (but not necessarily great) GPA.

Status: Current student, full-time
Dates of Enrollment: 9/2003-Submit Date
Survey Submitted: April 2005

UW requires what most schools require: an application, undergraduate transcript, letter of recommendation, LSAT and personal statement. Generally the school looks for an LSAT of at least 160 and a GPA of about 3.5. There are exceptions, of course, but that seems to be the low end of the scale. UW also has a goal of 70 percent enrollment by Washington residents. I'm not sure how firm that is.

Status: Current student, full-time
Dates of Enrollment: 10/2004-Submit Date
Survey Submitted: April 2005

The admission process was fairly straightforward; I sent in my LSAT scores, two letters of recommendation, my official transcript and an application fee. In mid-April I received a letter placing me on the waitlist. I received an e-mail in June letting me know I had been accepted. I wrote my essay about why I wanted to go to law school, and I have a fairly unique reason amongst my peers, so it was not overly cliche. There was no interview process.

Status: Alumnus/a, full-time
Dates of Enrollment: 10/2002-3/2005
Survey Submitted: April 2005

The admissions process is fairly straightforward: application, personal statement and LSAT score. Most of the people at UW Law come from the Pacific Northwest (WA, OR, MT, ID) so geographic diversity is something that the admissions people are actively looking for. In this regard, applicants from the Midwest and East Coast have a pretty good shot at getting in. Besides, if there's one thing that the Pacific NW needs badly, it's East Coast attitude.

Status: Current student, full-time
Dates of Enrollment: 9/2003-Submit Date
Survey Submitted: April 2005

UW Law is pretty selective. They were relatively quick with their admissions decision. They are looking for diversity in their applicants and seek people who have done interesting things in their lives. Financial aid packages aren't very generous. But if you get in-state tuition, you are getting one of the cheapest law school educations out there.

Status: Current student, full-time LLM
Dates of Enrollment: 9/2005-Submit Date
Survey Submitted: January 2006

The admissions process for the LLM in Taxation Program is very informal. I was notified within three weeks of my submission. The decisions are made solely by the director, Sam Donaldson. There were no required interviews, although I did visit the school myself. I would say if you were in the top 50 percent of your law school class, you are a shoo-in. My only advice for getting into the program is to perform well on your JD tax courses.

Status: Current student, full-time
Dates of Enrollment: 9/2004-Submit Date
Survey Submitted: April 2005

Write a good personal statement. Don't just summarize your resume. Anecdotes are better than life histories. If possible, tie in the anecdote to your reason for going to law school. Do not blow off the LSAT. If you're not a great standardized test taker, take an LSAT prep course.

Status: Current student, full-time
Dates of Enrollment: 9/2004-Submit Date
Survey Submitted: April 2005

I applied as a transfer student, so the process was a bit different. The application is due once your grades are available from your first-year school, and they let you know by mid to late July, which is a bit of a hassle since you then have to do some quick planning to get yourself ready for school to start. My only advice in getting in as a transfer is to do really well your first year. It's pretty competitive (they only took three my year), so you have to somehow make yourself stand out.

Status: Alumnus/a, full-time
Dates of Enrollment: 9/2000-6/2003
Survey Submitted: January 2005

I had an informational interview, and received the application materials, as well as additional information. UW Law really stresses diversity, but is sometimes hamstrung by I-200, a state law that prohibits affirmative action as it relates to race and gender. In terms of advice on admissions, I would advise the applicant to understand their strengths and weaknesses, and how the school matches up. The application process is essentially a sales job, showing how the school will benefit from the applicant.

Status: Current student, full-time
Dates of Enrollment: 8/2005-Submit Date
Survey Submitted: March 2005

The admissions process was fairly standard. There is a bit of a bias for hard scores, LSAT and GPA. I've met people who had fairly good numbers with outstanding work experience who were beat out by a younger person with slightly better LSAT or GPA. Despite what UW's literature says about diversity, there is not much of it in admissions. The key to getting into UW is high numbers and knowing someone at the school.

Academics

Status: Current student, full-time
Dates of Enrollment: 9/2003-Submit Date
Survey Submitted: October 2005

There are a lot of really bright students here who might have gone to higher ranking schools, but who chose this school because they want to live and work in Seattle. This creates an elevated intellectual atmosphere. The school also encourages cooperation among the students. This creates a unique non-competitive atmosphere that is very supportive. The administration puts a lot of trust in the students when it comes to test-taking, which reduces the stress during the exams. Because there are few professors here, they tend to teach classes that are not in their specialty, which can reduce the quality of the courses at times. However, they have a diverse faculty and do provide some good courses on interesting topics that can be difficult to find at other schools.

Status: Alumnus/a, full-time
Dates of Enrollment: 9/1998-6/2001
Survey Submitted: March 2006

I thought the quality of classes and professors was excellent. The faculty was incredibly accessible and professors really encouraged participation even in the largest classes. They had just adopted a new grading system when I was there, which imposed a fairly exacting curve. I think that has slacked a bit in the past few years as students and professors have had time to comment on the system. The workload is demanding, especially if you are on a journal or moot court, but most people find it manageable. I think it would be hard to maintain any employment in your first year and even a 50 percent job in your second.

Status: Current student, full-time
Dates of Enrollment: 9/2004-Submit Date
Survey Submitted: April 2005

I got lucky and ended up with three of the most well-regarded 1L professors, which made classes more enjoyable compared to the horror stories I've heard about 1L year. Because UW is on the quarter system, we have three, 11-week quarters. It's not fun having three sets of finals per year, but it's nice not having

as many exams at once like at semester schools. And the administration and professors really understand how overwhelming 1L year is, so they ease you into it to an extent, especially fall quarter. The workload is average.

Status: Current student, full-time
Dates of Enrollment: 9/2004-Submit Date
Survey Submitted: April 2005

The classload is solid, but probably in line with other top-tier law schools. The writing program is new (two years old), and they are still working out some kinks, but the problems are interesting and challenging. There is a new combined Contracts-Torts class (yes, we're calling it Contorts), which is taught by a misunderstood genius complete with a PhD in math. As a first-year student, I have been favorably impressed with all but one of my professors, and even she is good (I just don't like her).

The grading is tough. A's are given to no more than the top 15 percent of each section, so if you happen to be in a section of 29 people with more than four smarty-pants students, you won't get an A (unless you're one of them). On the other hand, the more smarty-pants students you have, the better your education will be. Opt for the latter. On the other end of the grading scale, things are much easier. Professors are only required to give grades as low as B (though they may give C's and D's), so if you are competent, you will get a 3.0.

Status: Current student, full-time
Dates of Enrollment: 9/2004-Submit Date
Survey Submitted: April 2005

I have the advantage of being able to compare UW to another law school, and would say I definitely prefer the more relaxed approach UW takes. You aren't ranked and never even find out your GPA (unless you want to compute it yourself). The built-in curve makes it so it's not as impossible to get an A, which is comforting. Also, the professors are all very good and very few of them focus on the Socratic Method, which makes classes less stressful and more focused on just learning the material. The workload is still intense, but what law school workload isn't?

Status: Current student, full-time
Dates of Enrollment: 9/2002-Submit Date
Survey Submitted: April 2005

Most UW school of law professors are top academics. The older professors are often the standard-setters in their respective fields and the younger professors are often energetic movers and shakers in their fields. Their teaching styles vary, but most seem to have gone beyond the Socratic Method. The workload is always heavy and competition among students intense, but grades are sometimes considered inflated as UW professors don't like to give grades below B's.

Status: Alumnus/a, full-time
Dates of Enrollment: 10/2002-3/2005
Survey Submitted: April 2005

The classes are fairly easy-going and are largely lecture-based. There is very little of the hard-core Socratic Method that you see at some schools. As a result, students and professors get along very well. The idea of students being afraid of professors is unheard of. The exam system is fairly standard: anonymous grading on a single end-of-term exam (although some classes do have minor midterm quizzes or are graded based on multiple hand-in assignments). The curve is fairly generous; pretty much everyone gets a B. You really have to work to get the A or distinguish yourself in a particularly bad way to get a C. The atmosphere is very friendly, helpful and cooperative. Backstabbing, cheating, ripping pages out of library books and things like this are virtually nonexistent. If you are one of those who thrives on cutthroat competition (generally referred to as "gunners" at UW) then UWLS is not the place for you. People like that are quickly singled out and politely ostracized. Seattle has a fairly tight-knit legal community where most lawyers in a given practice area know each other. Therefore, it is not a good idea to develop a bad reputation with your classmates in school because they could very likely end up being opposing counsel or judges on some case you work on years down the road.

Read all of Vault's Law School Surveys at www.vault.com/lawschool — get complete surveys on top law schools, expert advice on applicaton essays, LSAT prep and more.

VAULT CAREER LIBRARY 659

Status: Current student, full-time
Dates of Enrollment: 9/2002-Submit Date
Survey Submitted: April 2005

Overall, I've been pleased with my academic experience at UW. There have definitely been a few professors who have been terrible, but there have also been a few who were fantastic. I would say most are reasonably good teachers, well-intentioned and know their subjects well. 1L year, you have no choice in classes or professors, but after that you have almost complete freedom in choosing classes, so it's fairly easy to avoid bad professors, especially if you talk to 2Ls and 3Ls who are happy to provide advice informally and through formal peer-mentoring programs. I've only had one class that I couldn't get into, which was an extremely popular small seminar. One of the best things about UW is that it is a pretty friendly place. Most students are helpful, uncompetitive, and most professors want to help, not humiliate students.

Status: Current student, full-time
Dates of Enrollment: 8/2002-Submit Date
Survey Submitted: April 2005

Overall, the quality has been very high. Like all law schools, the workload is high, especially during the 1L year. But after that, I didn't have any trouble taking the classes that I wanted. Even if the smaller seminars fill up quickly, it is very easy to design your own seminar, and the professors are very amenable to this.

Status: Alumnus/a, full-time
Dates of Enrollment: 9/2000-6/2004
Survey Submitted: January 2005

The program has a wide variety of classes, perhaps some less traditional than other JD programs. It's highly-focused on social issues and lawyers as instigators of social change. The clinics are excellent. I never had a problem getting in a class I wanted, although some clinics are difficult to get into (lottery process). Grading is done using an A through D scale; but without an official GPA, which is a little difficult when you are looking for a job later. I advise putting an unofficial GPA (which you can calculate) on your resume.

Status: Current student, full-time
Dates of Enrollment: 8/2005-Submit Date
Survey Submitted: March 2005

Fairly standard first-year courses as required by the ABA. Great variety of courses for second- and third-year, but most are just fluff. Most students take courses required on the bar exam. Grading curve is ridiculous—up to 75 percent of the students can get a B or better. It's nearly to impossible to fail at UW and pretty easy to have a good GPA for graduation, which makes studying sort of pointless. But I guess the hard part is over once you get admitted. You can sit back and cruise the next three years.

 Employment Prospects

Status: Current student, full-time
Dates of Enrollment: 9/2003-Submit Date
Survey Submitted: May 2005

It's really good in the Northwest and the West Coast to an extent. Elsewhere, (I worked in a different part of the country during the summer) the school wasn't looked at as being very prestigious. The Career Services Office isn't very helpful at all and the staff, at times, can be incompetent. Alumni are generally supportive but the school has been hampered by the dean's poor relations with alumni. There are so many UW people in the area, though, that it's not especially advantageous to attend UW as opposed to other schools. There are good opportunities to intern (far more unpaid externship opportunities though).

Status: Current student, full-time
Dates of Enrollment: 9/2002-Submit Date
Survey Submitted: April 2005

The career services staff is doing a great job and I think the office will be great as they get more settled. My career counselor is wonderful and very helpful. Most students stay in Washington (by choice), and so this is where career services is most helpful. If you want to go elsewhere, you have to do a lot of

research on your own, though career services can provide some contacts and is working to develop this network further.

Status: Current student, full-time
Dates of Enrollment: 10/2004-Submit Date
Survey Submitted: April 2005

My 1L summer, I only applied for jobs in my hometown with local in-house firms and judges. The University of Washington was very highly-regarded with those with whom I spoke, and many still remembered when UW was in the Top 20 of law schools. Especially in the Pacific Northwest, UW is regarded favorably. Other people I know got firm jobs via the diversity programs or through mass-mailing. I have yet to participate in OCI.

Status: Current student, full-time
Dates of Enrollment: 9/2003-Submit Date
Survey Submitted: April 2005

UW is definitely the top school in the area, but there is still a lot of competition from Top 10 schools. It seems like everyone in the world wants to work in Seattle, so competition is really tough. That said, if you are attending school here, it at least shows a tie to the area. Students get jobs all over the place in firms, clerkships and public service. Career services, it seems, is a little weak at placing students outside the area. There are tons of opportunities for networking, which few students really take advantage of after their first year. Externships are promoted like crazy. If you want to work for free, UW will hook you up.

Status: Alumnus/a, full-time
Dates of Enrollment: 10/2002-3/2005
Survey Submitted: April 2005

The Washington legal market seems to be rather saturated at this time and so it can be tough to find that perfect law firm job or clerkship after graduation if you are looking exclusively in the Pacific NW. The alumni network is almost entirely in Washington, Oregon, Idaho and Montana. It can be tough if you are looking to work on the East Coast. Moreover, unless you are top of your class with straight A's and on Law Review, finding a job with a downtown firm will be tough because there are a lot of competing job applicants from Top 10 schools looking to return or relocate to Seattle. Recently, however, UWLS has overhauled its Career Services Office, so it's now a terrific source of contacts, resources and information. They particularly make the process of applying for clerkships a breeze as they have one full-time person designated to handle and send out all the clerkship applications for the students. If one is willing to cast his or her net wide and consider moving to other parts of the country, then employment prospects increase astronomically because UWLS generally enjoys a good reputation.

Status: Current student, full-time
Dates of Enrollment: 9/2004-Submit Date
Survey Submitted: April 2005

UW has a great reputation with employers and it appears as if most 3Ls have been getting jobs in the area that they want. The professors are excellent in helping you get a network in place for the area of practice you are interested in. The on-campus interview process was very good and a lot of employers participate in it.

Status: Current student, full-time LLM
Dates of Enrollment: 9/2005-Submit Date
Survey Submitted: January 2006

From word of mouth, I heard last year's LLM class was fully employed (quite a stat). At UW we have a recruiter assigned to the LLM student. She is available to give you consulting advice and give you names of alumni in your desired field. The top students are said to end up at some of the best Seattle firms, however, it is a tight market. I have talked to a couple of kids who are more interested in the accounting route. There is not much going on for campus recruiting in regards to LLM. Don't expect a job lined up when you get into the program. You are going to have to put your leg work in. Currently, I am balancing my schoolwork with networking opportunities in the community. I would love a job when I finish.

Status: Alumnus/a, full-time
Dates of Enrollment: 10/2001-6/2004
Survey Submitted: March 2005

It is a public service-focused school. That said, you can still get a job at the biggest of the NYC or L.A. firms if you want to pay off those student loans, which after the tuition increases might be more of a factor. The Seattle legal market is small and hard to break into. If you want a job in Seattle and aren't from the area, you need to go to UW or a Top 10 school.

Status: Alumnus/a, full-time
Dates of Enrollment: 9/2000-6/2003
Survey Submitted: January 2005

Most classmates appear to have found good-paying or good-fitting jobs prior to, or just after, graduation. Given the poor economy at the time [of my graduation,] some students and alumni believe that the two situations made it difficult for students to get jobs.

However, the local firms seem to have a positive view of the school and its alumni, and alumni seem very willing to help new graduates with advice and job offers. All in all, the alumni community seems to be doing well. However, there could be more cohesiveness to the alumni network so that students are able to turn to them for advice on particular firms and practice areas.

> **Regarding Career Services, the school says:** "We revamped Career Services in August of 2004. Our office has grown from one to six employees in the past couple of years. We now offer alumni receptions in other cities. In addition, the students have formed the William O. Douglas Society for those interested in leaving the state for jobs elsewhere. There is also a Career Coach for each student. Our placement rate post-graduation has been 99.4 percent. It is one of the best in the nation. We hired an Assistant Director for Public Service and an Assistant so the public service opportunities are plentiful."

Quality of Life

Status: Current student, full-time LLM
Dates of Enrollment: 9/2005-Submit Date
Survey Submitted: January 2006

The UW law building is amazing. It is a mix of brick with all-glass windows—very cosmopolitan. The building was donated by Bill Gates since his father is a graduate of UW School of Law. The whole building is wireless. It is in a great location at the end of the campus and next to University Avenue, where all the restaurants and bars are located. Also, as a UW law student you are able to use the fitness center. This is no ordinary fitness center. You have access to a gym (complimentary personal trainers), swimming pool, golf range, rock climbing facilities and many fitness classes. As for Seattle, it is a gorgeous and green city. For the record, it doesn't rain as much as people believe. The locals here say that to keep people out of the Evergreen State. All in all, the campus is topnotch.

Status: Current student, full-time
Dates of Enrollment: 9/2003-Submit Date
Survey Submitted: October 2005

Great place to live! Very cheap compared to other large cities such as S.F., L.A. or NY. There's a lot to do here. There are a lot of top companies in town and it's the biggest city in the region. It's also a wonderful area for those who like to get out into the outdoors and play. Lots of stuff to do here, both in the city as well as out. Wonderful environment.

Status: Alumnus/a, full-time
Dates of Enrollment: 9/1998-6/2001
Survey Submitted: March 2006

The law school is on the main campus of the UW in Seattle. I think Seattle is great, but UW's immediate area is very much tied to its undergrad community, which can be annoying as a grad student. That being said, it is easy to live in other parts of the city and just commute to school.

Status: Current student, full-time
Dates of Enrollment: 9/2002-Submit Date
Survey Submitted: April 2005

Seattle is great, but expensive. Parking around the law school is terrible and there is only good bus access from the neighborhoods immediately surrounding the law school. You either live in crappy, student houses and take the bus, or you live in a safe, stable neighborhood and pay too much money to park. I have kids and a family, so we had to have the safe, stable neighborhood, so we got stuck with the expensive parking.

Status: Alumnus/a, full-time
Dates of Enrollment: 9/2000-6/2004
Survey Submitted: January 2005

I don't know anyone who used on-campus or school-supported housing. There are lots of apartments in the UW area, although a good number of people live in Seattle proper, Leschi or Greenlake. The bus is the most popular mode of transportation for people who can because parking is scarce. It's worth your time to room with another law student and carpool because then you get on-campus parking. The law building has a little coffee shop with some food. The UW district itself has tons of restaurants. There are several grocery stores in the area, as well.

Social Life

Status: Current student, full-time
Dates of Enrollment: 9/2003-Submit Date
Survey Submitted: October 2005

Great. The school encourages a social and cooperative atmosphere, so it's really easy to make friends with other students. The school is also located just a block from major restaurants and bars, so it's very easy to find time to take a break off campus with friends or classmates.

Status: Alumnus/a, full-time
Dates of Enrollment: 9/1998-6/2001
Survey Submitted: March 2006

I think students are fairly collegial, but because it is an older community, I think they also have other lives besides school. I was married, so I did not see much of the dating scene, which I know existed based on the number of post-law school marriages.

Status: Current student, full-time
Dates of Enrollment: 9/2004-Submit Date
Survey Submitted: April 2005

The social life is all right, but I had a lot of fun with a great group of friends in college so it's hard to compare law school to that. I don't hang out with a lot of 1Ls, but there is a large group of 1Ls who like to go out and have a lot of house parties or go bar-hopping. There is a huge undergrad scene here, so there are tons of places to go out around here. Good food and good shopping are all I need.

Status: Current student, full-time LLM
Dates of Enrollment: 9/2005-Submit Date
Survey Submitted: January 2006

The social life in Seattle is mediocre. If you like eating at restaurants, then you will be in heaven. There is a restaurant in every corner of the town. The best thing about Seattle is that you are located about 130 miles south of Vancouver. Vancouver is an amazing city. If you attend UW, you must visit this city. All in all, I can't say too much about the social life, as I am married.

Status: Current student, full-time
Dates of Enrollment: 9/2004-Submit Date
Survey Submitted: April 2005

Seattle's time in the limelight may have passed with Kurt Cobain, but the live music scene has not. There are several clubs featuring local talent, and you never know when someone like Stone Gossard might show up and do a quick set. The UW district is quirky, like a lot of college areas, and it offers a wide variety of ethnic foods within a five-minute walk of the law school.

Read all of Vault's Law School Surveys at www.vault.com/lawschool — get complete surveys on top law schools, expert advice on applicaton essays, LSAT prep and more.

VAULT CAREER LIBRARY 661

UW is a major university complete with a Greek system and all that implies. If you are looking to party, you have plenty of options. If not, there is no shortage of other activities available. Everyone can find a niche on this campus.

As far as campus activities are concerned, the intramural activities center has a brand-new, world-class gym, a pool, an indoor track, fitness classes and row after row of cardio machines. There are intramural sports of every type (I have participated in swimming and Ultimate Frisbee). The campus sits between two lakes and there is a Waterfront Activities Center that rents canoes and rowboats, as well as a sailing club. There is a climbing wall, a driving range and a bike path that extends 20 miles to the north. The experimental college has classes in dance, fencing, pottery or any number of other areas of interest.

Not that there's any time for that sort of tomfoolery. Don't kid yourself. Most of your time is spent with your nose in a book. But the time that isn't spent studying can be spent doing something fun.

Status: Current student, full-time
Dates of Enrollment: 9/2004-Submit Date
Survey Submitted: April 2005

The law school's social life is great and there are organizations for every type of interest. Most groups meet once a week or so, and are involved in various ways through the community. Every Thursday there is a TGIT (Thank Goodness It's Thursday) in which one organization sponsors food and beverage for the whole school—it's a great time to relax and forget about the stress of law school.

Status: Current student, full-time
Dates of Enrollment: 9/2003-Submit Date
Survey Submitted: April 2005

This is a law school attended by a mix of just-out-of-college students and adults starting their second careers. Socializing is not orchestrated by the school. A person would be very lonely if he only socialized at TGITs or law school dances.

We're in a vibrant urban area, so there are dance clubs, sporting events and great restaurants. Seattle also is close to two mountain ranges and Puget Sound. There are plenty of hiking, biking, skiing, sailing and mountain climbing opportunities within a two-hour drive.

Status: Current student, full time
Dates of Enrollment: 9/2003-Submit Date
Survey Submitted: April 2005

There are regular TGIT (Thank God It's Thursday) kegs in the student lounge area. There are also several bars close by that law students hang out in occasionally. The reality is that law school is a lot of work and some people have very little time for a social life. A number of students are married with children and the school is deserted after hours except for people in night classes and those working on the journals. Journal membership is great for meeting people as are clinics. There are tons of clubs, again most with a social issue bend, that get like-minded people together. The SBA is very active and most of the clubs hold one social fundraiser every year like the auction, Halloween party or something similar.

West Virginia University College of Law

Admissions Office
P.O. Box 6130
Morgantown, WV 26506-6130
Admissions phone: (304) 293-5304
Admissions e-mail: wvulaw.admissions@mail.wvu.edu
Admissions URL: http://www.wvu.edu/~law/admission/

Note: The school has chosen not to comment on the student surveys submitted.

 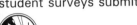

Admissions

Status: Alumnus/a, full-time
Dates of Enrollment: 8/2002-5/2005
Survey Submitted: October 2005

Admission to WVU Law is competitive, as is any law school. Preference is given to West Virginia residents. In order to get in, LSAT scores are important, but not as much as at Top 10 law schools. If you get a 155 or higher, you will have a good shot at getting in, provided your GPA, admission essay and all those items are in order. Applicants are not interviewed during the admissions process.

Status: Alumnus/a, full-time
Dates of Enrollment: 8/1993-5/1996
Survey Submitted: April 2004

The admission process is somewhat standard. There are no interviews (or there weren't when I was in the admissions process). Primarily, undergraduate and, if applicable, graduate transcripts, combined with the LSAT score and a brief essay are considered. I do not have any information with respect to selectivity. The law school is quite prompt is letting prospective students know about whether they are admitted, rejected or waitlisted.

Status: Alumnus/a, full-time
Dates of Enrollment: 8/1998-5/2001
Survey Submitted: February 2005

The admissions process is standard: LSAT, undergraduate transcripts, admissions essay. Although the typical statistics—LSAT scores—might suggest to some that this school is not very selective, the opposite is true. The students are predominantly West Virginia natives whose cultural/educational backgrounds often tend to skew LSAT median scores to the lower end of the scale.

Academics

Status: Alumnus/a, full-time
Dates of Enrollment: 8/2002-5/2005
Survey Submitted: October 2005

The classes at WVU Law are about the same as every other law school in the U.S. You will have the same first-year courses as every other 1L in America. Recently, the law school has made strides in the availability of a more diverse curriculum. There are many more courses offered now that were not offered just prior to my attending WVU. Popular classes fill up quickly, especially classes like Pre-Trial Litigation, Legislative Drafting Seminar and a few other classes that only alott about 20 seats. Most classes, however, allow 70 to 100 people in them.

Take caution: the grading scale at WVU Law sucks! In most schools, even Ivy League, once you are in, just do your best and you'll get an A or B. Not at WVU. This school doesn't grade on a B curve; it grades on a C curve. Only about 10 percent of students receive A's. Some professors even give D's and F's.

Status: Alumnus/a, full-time
Dates of Enrollment: 8/1993-5/1996
Survey Submitted: April 2004

West Virginia University College of Law probably is the most under-estimated law school in the country. The first year of law school is based on core courses: Con Law, Property, Contracts, Torts and Legal Research and Writing (yes, a full year of it). To me, the first-year focus on Legal Tesearch and Writing and then an additional semester of Appellate Advocacy in the second or third year creates new lawyers who write very well and persuasively. The approach at WVU is to actually prepare you to practice law, not to prepare you to teach some sort of legal philosophy class.

The quality of the core class instruction is outstanding. Additionally, the quality of the clinic program is outstanding. So much time, energy and all the resources possible are put into this program where 3Ls actually get to work with real clients, argue real cases (I argued one before the West Virginia Supreme Court as a third-year law student) and work closely with not only professors, but also practitioners. The experience was invaluable. As for getting into classes that are desired, that usually is not a problem. As for workload, it is commensurate with what I perceive is the workload at any of the top-tier law schools.

Status: Alumnus/a, full-time
Dates of Enrollment: 8/1998-5/2001
Survey Submitted: February 2005

This school provides a very good, but general legal education that is more focused on litigation. The curriculum reflects the fact that the vast majority of the school's graduates will practice law within the state's small towns where one will ultimately counsel clients on a range of legal topics.

Despite the limited choices among specialized courses (you won't go to school here if your ambition is practice securities law on Wall Street), the core curriculum is rigorous and demanding. However, I would not say I was over-worked, and had opportunities to participate in plenty of extracurricular activities.

Most of the professors are great teachers and are very accessible.

When I was a student, getting into popular classes was not very tough. For the most part, grading was fair.

Employment Prospects

Status: Alumnus/a, full-time
Dates of Enrollment: 8/2002-5/2005
Survey Submitted: October 2005

With the hiring of a new dean of career services, things are looking better. However, there's not much help getting work from the school or its alumni, unless you know some people. Even the bigger firms in WV are hiring out-of-state graduates and the school doesn't seem to care.

Status: Alumnus/a, full-time
Dates of Enrollment: 8/1993-5/1996
Survey Submitted: April 2004

Because most of the students at WVU are West Virginia residents, the career prospects are outstanding for practicing law in West Virginia. All of the top-ranked students get placed in excellent law firms primarily in Charleston, Huntington or Clarksburg. Additionally, as WVU students "spread their wings" they are finding out that they have the skills and abilities to compete with the best and brightest and, in doing so, have opportunities with national and international law firms. I, for instance, have practiced with the world's largest law firm and I am now practicing with one of the country's 15 largest law firms. Others from WVU has had success locating jobs out of law school at major firms in New York City, Phoenix, Atlanta and Pittsburgh, just to name a few.

Read all of Vault's Law School Surveys at www.vault.com/lawschool — get complete surveys on top law schools, expert advice on applicaton essays, LSAT prep and more.

VAULT CAREER LIBRARY   663

Status: Alumnus/a, full-time
Dates of Enrollment: 8/1998-5/2001
Survey Submitted: February 2005

If you want to remain in West Virginia, and the vast majority of students do, employment prospects are very good. At least 75 percent of West Virginia's practicing lawyers attended this law school (the state's only law school), and there is a close relationship between the bar and the law school.

Opportunities to find summer work are outstanding, even for students between their first and second years.

Finding employment outside of West Virginia is more problematic. Because most students tend to remain in the state, the school lacks both a network of out-of-state alumni and, as a result, a well-established reputation. However, past students have been able to find employment at top law firms.

 ## Quality of Life

Status: Alumnus/a, full-time
Dates of Enrollment: 8/2002-5/2005
Survey Submitted: October 2005

The quality of life at WVU is good. It's a small student body of about 500. However, some things like dining, lockers and the library are a little sub-standard. The law school sits alone atop a hill overlooking Mountaineer Field and WVU Hospitals. It's just the law school up there so parking isn't a problem like everywhere else.

Status: Alumnus/a, full-time
Dates of Enrollment: 8/1993-5/1996
Survey Submitted: April 2004

There are a number of reasonably-priced and close-to-the-law-school locations that law students have to choose from. And, the law school is right up the hill from the stadium, which makes it awesome on game days. As for quality of life, if you treat law school like a job at WVU, then you will have an excellent quality of life. Morgantown, the small city where the College of Law is located, is quaint, but certainly has the feel of a real collegetown. Although the cultural opportunities in Morgantown are not numerous, there is enough to do that you won't go crazy in "MoTown" during the time you're in law school there.

Status: Alumnus/a, full-time
Dates of Enrollment: 8/1998-5/2001
Survey Submitted: February 2005

There is plenty of quality modern housing within a close distance of the school. Moreover, housing is very affordable. Although small, the town has a number of amenities.

 ## Social Life

Status: Alumnus/a, full-time
Dates of Enrollment: 8/2002-5/2005
Survey Submitted: October 2005

Morgantown is a nice town. It's close to outdoor sports like mountain biking, skiing and whitewater rafting. Then, of course, there are the Mountaineers!

Status: Alumnus/a, full-time
Dates of Enrollment: 8/1993-5/1996
Survey Submitted: April 2004

Morgantown is a true collegetown with the reputation of being a "party" school. At the undergraduate level, that reputation may or may not be earned, but it certainly does not apply to the law school, which is on its own campus away from the undergraduate campus. The social life of law students is usually created from among your law school class. Frankly, the students who attend WVU are generally good natured, only somewhat competitive, and have a desire to excel in school without acting like their life depends on getting an A+ in every class.

Football games are always big (and fun) days. Restaurants aren't very diverse. But, hey, on a law school student's pocketbook, there's not much need for five-star dining. Additionally, the students who attend WVU are more diverse than an "outsider looking in" would expect. I was openly gay at the College of Law. Nevertheless, my experience was outstanding in every sense. Attending WVU paved the way for me to find excellent employment and, once employed, excel above my colleagues because I actually could "hit the ground running."

Status: Alumnus/a, full-time
Dates of Enrollment: 8/1998-5/2001
Survey Submitted: February 2005

Excellent.

Marquette University Law School

Office of Admissions
Sensenbrenner Hall, Room 116
P.O. Box 1881
Milwaukee, WI 53201-1881
Admissions phone: (414) 288-6767
Admissions fax: (414) 288-0676
Admissions e-mail: law.admission@marquette.edu
URL: http://law.marquette.edu/

 ## Admissions

Status: Current student, part-time
Dates of Enrollment: 8/2003-Submit Date
Survey Submitted: April 2006

The admission process is relatively painless. Aside from the LSAT, which by the way you can take more than once and they only consider your top score, the application includes the standard questions about why you want to attend law school, your job and school history, past "rap sheet" if any and the standard essay. No interviews are conducted. The selection committee seems to select as diverse a student body as they can and still admit high achievers. Since I'm not on the selection committee, I can only speculate as to the weight given each aspect of the application. Good grades from any undergraduate institution coupled with a 157 or higher LSAT score and a solid essay will get you admitted. Essays should be personal in nature and not just a life history.

> **The school says:** "The admissions committee reviews each application in its entirety, considering both qualitative and quantitative factors. While grades and test scores are very important, no combination of LSAT score and undergraduate GPA guarantees admission or denial."

Status: Current student, full-time
Dates of Enrollment: 8/2006-Submit Date
Survey Submitted: April 2006

The admissions process seems to like a very diverse student body. They seem to be very selective with students coming from Marquette. The biggest feeder school is Wisconsin and there are a lot of Notre Dame students as well.

Status: Current student, full-time
Dates of Enrollment: 8/2004-Submit Date
Survey Submitted: April 2006

I applied to Marquette primarily because of its location. It was close to home, so I wouldn't have to move or look for other part-time jobs than the ones I already had. I applied with a 164 LSAT score, a 3.4 undergraduate GPA and a BA in History. The essay didn't require anything different from any of the other schools I saw—the basic "why I applied to your school," "why I want to be in law" and "what I want to do later" theme. I included descriptions of my volunteer work and tried to show that I could be a good example of the type of alumnus that Marquette wants.

As far as selectivity, I was the only one I knew of applying to Marquette. They offered me a scholarship to attend that was less than the other schools that had accepted me, but I was sold on the location. Marquette has a very strong local reputation, so I would include it on a list of great-looking degrees for anyone intending to practice in Wisconsin (again, another great angle for the admissions essay).

Status: Current student, full-time
Dates of Enrollment: 8/2005-Submit Date
Survey Submitted: April 2006

The admission process is pretty standard: undergraduate transcripts, LSAT score, letters of recommendation and personal statements. Marquette seems to favor applicants that are unique in some aspect and that will contribute to the diversity of the law school. The admissions selection focuses on GPA and LSAT scores, but they also take into great consideration the other factors (e.g, personal statement, letters of rec).

Status: Current student, part-time
Dates of Enrollment: 8/2003-Submit Date
Survey Submitted: April 2006

No interview. Write a good essay to get in and preferably have decent undergrad grades (more important than the LSAT score). It is more difficult to get into the evening part-time program, but worth the while if you need to work during school. Take the opportunity to attend one of the information sessions.

Status: Current student, full-time
Dates of Enrollment: 8/2005-Submit Date
Survey Submitted: April 2006

Marquette requires the typical materials: law school application, personal statement, GPA, LSAT and letters of recommendation. There are no interviews. Admission or denial is decided by three or four members of the faculty. Being a minority has an advantage as the population here at the school is mostly Caucasian. Not many students receive scholarships from the school.

Status: Current student, full-time
Dates of Enrollment: 9/2005-Submit Date
Survey Submitted: February 2006

Marquette is somewhat selective, but certainly not terribly selective. The admission process was hassle-free. Marquette is a Jesuit institution known for pro bono activity. It is a non-competitive environment that tries to foster cohesion among the student body. In your essay, portray yourself as a person becoming of a Jesuit university.

Status: Current student, full-time
Dates of Enrollment: 8/2001-Submit Date
Survey Submitted: June 2004

The selectivity has increased over the past few years. LSAT scores and GPA requirements have increased steadily over the course of the last three years. Diversity is among the chief factors to be considered by the faculty committee in charge of selecting students.

 ## Academics

Status: Current student, part-time
Dates of Enrollment: 8/2003-Submit Date
Survey Submitted: April 2006

As a part-time student, I probably have a different take on this. I am thankful they offer a part-time program. They treat the part-time students wonderfully—possibly even better than the full-timers. They make an effort to offer a variety of evening classes to fit the needs of their part-time students, who mainly attend in the evenings. The classes have overall been super, with both full-time and adjunct faculty who are greatly respected in the Milwaukee legal community and beyond. I have had classes taught by faculty with a lifetime of practical legal experience, the state's U.S. attorney, and brilliant young faculty who bring a new perspectives. Professors are extremely approachable and accommodating to evening students and the summer classes are taught by the same professors that teach during the regular semesters.

Students are expected to work hard, keep up with their reading and attend class regularly. Overall, the workload has been manageable. I typically spend two to four hours preparing for each class and I tend to take as many as three or four classes. I have rarely had trouble getting into a course I wanted and there is a waiting system in place for courses that fill up for when spots become available. Personally, I have found my experience thus far to be a very positive one and I

Read all of Vault's Law School Surveys at www.vault.com/lawschool — get complete surveys on top law schools, expert advice on applicaton essays, LSAT prep and more.

VAULT CAREER LIBRARY 665

believe I am receiving a quality law school education part-time while holding down a full-time job.

Status: Current student, full-time
Dates of Enrollment: 8/2004-Submit Date
Survey Submitted: April 2006

Well-rounded curriculum with easy access to professors and staff. Admission to popular classes is usually not an issue. While classes are challenging, the focus on practical applications, ethics and writing pays dividends in our internships.

Status: Current student, part-time
Dates of Enrollment: 8/2004-Submit Date
Survey Submitted: April 2006

First year students (1Ls) are assigned classes by the dean so choice of professors is generally not allowed. The diploma privilege allows those students staying in Wisconsin to be admitted to the bar without having to take the bar exam.

Status: Current student, full-time
Dates of Enrollment: 8/2006-Submit Date
Survey Submitted: April 2006

The professors I have had in my first year are incredible. My Contracts and Constitutional Law professors have a great mix of practice experience and teaching and make going to class each day exciting. The professors all seem to be very accomplished and good.

Status: Current student, full-time
Dates of Enrollment: 8/2005-Submit Date
Survey Submitted: April 2006

This is law school; the workload is heavy. Marquette offers an immense selection of courses. The grading system is fair. Up to 30 percent of students in each class section will receive an honors grade (A or AB). All of the professors I've had thus far in my law school career have been extremely knowledgeable, helpful and enthusiastic about teaching.

Status: Current student, full-time
Dates of Enrollment: 8/2005-Submit Date
Survey Submitted: April 2006

It is important to understand that in law school, honors grades (A and AB) do not come easily, so most law students will get B's or C's. The grading is definitely difficult. Procrastination will not work in law school! You need to keep up with the reading, writing and outlining if you want to do well with the least amount of stress. Overall, the courses are very good and do well to prepare you for the real world. There are a few classes that are difficult to initially register for, but if you put your name on the waitlist, you will almost always get the course. The workload varies depending on the course. Marquette has a very good law school and I feel that I will be very prepared when I graduate.

Status: Current student, part-time
Dates of Enrollment: 8/2003-Submit Date
Survey Submitted: April 2006

The first year classes can be difficult because they force you to think like a lawyer and that can take time. By the second year, the classes get better. There are only three days for class sign-up and students are assigned one of those days to sign up for classes. Hopefully, you will get assigned the first day, or your chances of getting into popular classes is nill (as they are filled the first day). This was happening with mandatory classes, too, until students complained.

Status: Current student, full-time
Dates of Enrollment: 8/2005-Submit Date
Survey Submitted: April 2006

Lectures are taught by using the Socratic Method. Students are called on (usually at random) and must provide answers about the reading material. Most of the classes have been intellectually stimulating. A few of my professors have been questionable. Their lectures were cryptic and left us with more questions than answers when all was said and done. Overall, most of my professors have been very good. They are knowledgeable about the material provide us with an organized structure in which to study the material. The workload is large, but manageable if you schedule well. Grading is usually based on one exam at the end of the semester, which means there is little guidance throughout the semester

of how well you are grasping the material. However, the professors explain their exams and grading processes well, so there are usually no surprises.

Status: Current student, full-time
Dates of Enrollment: 8/2005-Submit Date
Survey Submitted: April 2006

The first-year courses are tough, but doable. The professors have a tendency to be harder on first-year students to discipline them and teach them to think quickly. Popular classes are difficult to get into. Registration is based on seniority, which means all the 3Ls get the best classes. The course streams have a wide range, which gives a good opportunity to take lots of different courses in many areas of law or a lot of courses in one specific area.

The professors individually are very helpful and responsive to student concerns. The Legal Writing classes are all taught by women. Sports Law is Marquette's biggest gimmick to recruit students, but beware, the program does not get everyone a job in sports law.

Status: Current student, full-time
Dates of Enrollment: 8/2004-Submit Date
Survey Submitted: April 2006

Marquette's law curriculum combines the rigors of studying the theory, policy and precedent of the law with a consideration of practical application and lawyer ethics. The faculty challenge the students in class but are always available and supportive of students throughout the law school endeavor! Beyond the fundamentals, MU has a range of course offerings that cover in-depth topics such as sports law, health law, intellectual property law and business law. There is also a good mix of class sizes available—ranging from large lecture halls (90+) to smaller workshops and seminars (10 to 20). During the first year, all classes are assigned to students; the second- and third-years students design their own class schedules (but have some additional core requirements that must be completed before graduation). Generally, it will be possible to enroll in all the classes that interest you at some point during your MULS career—but it may be more difficult early on to get more popular or smaller classes that tend to fill up quickly because priority of registration goes to students in order of their class status (3L, 2L, 1L).

Status: Current student, full-time
Dates of Enrollment: 8/2004-Submit Date
Survey Submitted: April 2006

I have been very pleased with the classes at Marquette. One of the emphasized areas is legal writing. There are a number of legal writing courses offered throughout the curriculum and I've found them very helpful. It's one of the skills that will make any lawyer better by tipping the scales in a close decision. In the first year, several professors expose students to the Socratic Method. It is somewhat intimidating, but helps you to learn to work under pressure.

Generally, the first-year classes have over 50 students (except the writing classes), but the professors are very approachable. The first-year classes are assigned to you. After that, getting into classes is fairly easy. In the last three registration periods, I was unable to get into only two or three classes I wanted.

As with any institution, the professors are pretty diverse. But, there are a number of professors that just "get it." These are the professors that do much more than stand up and talk about what they know. These professors are teachers first and lawyers second. To his credit, I think the dean is among them and it reflects on the institution as a whole.

Grading is always competitive at any law school. Marquette has a grading policy that varies on class size. In large classes, only one-third of the students may get honor grades. In smaller classes, there is no limit.

The workload varies from class to class and professor to professor. Generally, each class seems to give about 20 to 30 pages of reading per class period.

Status: Current student, part-time
Dates of Enrollment: 9/2004-Submit Date
Survey Submitted: April 2006

The academic opportunities for a part-time, evening student are wonderful. Having a full-time job makes the evening program doable. The dean of part-time students cares and helps with enrollment, orientation and questions. I find he classes to be well-taught and manageable. Professors work with each other o avoid overlapping assignments. Some classes are more difficult to get but hey are repeatedly offered. Some professors are more popular but that is a very ndividualistic consideration and often reflects the direction the student is pursuing.

Status: Current student, full-time
Dates of Enrollment: 8/2001-Submit Date
Survey Submitted: June 2004

Generally, the upper-level classes are smaller—some of mine had under 10 ndividuals. In these classes, you had access to faculty and support staff. Most of my professors I know on both a professional and personal basis. The faculty s wonderful at making contact with the students. I couldn't have asked for a better faculty! Obviously, the first-year classes were much more crowded; however, a class never had more than a total of 90 students.

Availability of classes was never a problem, although getting into some seminar and workshop classes was difficult. The process was random, which resulted in some 3Ls not being allowed in classes they wanted. Additionally, the class schedule is not conducive to some course streams. For example, many of the course schedules conflict, or their exams conflict with one another. The result is hat some of these students often have more than one exam per day at the end of he year. Unfortunately, it is also difficult to get permission to get an exam time earranged unless you have more than two scheduled for a single day.

> **The school says:** "Registration times are assigned based on credits earned and third-year students have priority in the registration process. The class schedule reflects a rich curriculum, which results in some class conflicts. Examinations are scheduled so that courses that meet at the same time have exams at the same time. Students are given the exam schedule prior to course registration so that the timing of exams can be factored into course selection."

Employment Prospects

Status: Current student, part-time
Dates of Enrollment: 8/2003-Submit Date
Survey Submitted: April 2006

Marquette University Law School is one of two law schools in the state of Wisconsin. Many extremely successful lawyers have graduated from Marquette, including Wisconsin Supreme Court justices and Seventh Circuit judges. If students plan to stay in the Milwaukee area, I believe job prospects are good. The Career Planning Center provides numerous networking, resume building and recruiting opportunities. Students who have recently graduated have taken obs at prestigious firms, clerked in the federal courts and started their own practices.

Status: Current student, full-time
Dates of Enrollment: 8/2004-Submit Date
Survey Submitted: April 2006

Marquette appears to have a strong regional presence, with most attorneys in Wisconsin, Chicago and Minneapolis recognizing the strength and quality of the school. An examination of the Wisconsin Bar web site indicates that most of the graduates from last year are currently employed as attorneys, and many of my fellow 2Ls are already "locked into" future employment. The types of jobs vary from large firms to small firms, clerkships to governmental agencies, traditional to non-traditional. The alumni I have spoken with have been more than willing to take time out of their busy schedules to assist me with my search for future employment, and there is an active OCI (on-campus interviewing) process.

Status: Current student, full-time
Dates of Enrollment: 8/2005-Submit Date
Survey Submitted: April 2006

Marquette is one of only two law schools in the entire state of Wisconsin, so employment is not a problem. Most people end up working for a law firm, but here is a wide variety of non-legal jobs. The big firms in the Milwaukee area look for Marquette grads, but there are opportunities for medium as well as small

firms. If you want to stay in Milwaukee or anywhere in Wisconsin, you do not have to take a bar exam, which everyone views as a huge advantage. It's hard as a 1L to get employment, but students make most of the opportunities for themselves. In the end, everyone gets a job.

Status: Current student, full-time
Dates of Enrollment: 8/2004-Submit Date
Survey Submitted: April 2006

There is a high likelihood that you will be able to obtain a job—Marquette prepares you well for success beyond its walls! Marquette has a particularly strong reputation and alumni network within the Milwaukee community and throughout the state of Wisconsin. The strength of the alumni network is strong throughout the Midwest and alumni are generally eager to assist students from their alma mater in finding job placements or in counseling them with advice about other career opportunities. The challenge is somewhat greater to find job placements in more distant geographic locations since the alumni network is less coordinated and employers tend not to recruit on campus or to be as aware of Marquette's program generally.

Status: Current student, full-time
Dates of Enrollment: 8/2003-Submit Date
Survey Submitted: October 2005

All I have to say about Marquette Law is this: if you are not in the top 10 percent of your class, or your dad/uncle is not an attorney/CEO, you will have problems finding a job after graduation. Seriously, 90 percent of the people I know who graduated in May 2005, are still unemployed/employed in non-law jobs. Some of them are waiting tables ("Hello, I'll be your waiter/lawyer this evening"), and with the prospect of student loans kicking in, they are seriously freaked out.

> **The school says:** "For the May 2005 graduating class, 94.3 percent of graduates reported that they were employed when surveyed at nine months after graduation."

Status: Current student, full-time
Dates of Enrollment: 9/2005-Submit Date
Survey Submitted: February 2006

Employment prospects are proportional to GPA. Receiving high grades dramatically increases your chances of employment. The Career Planning Center is helpful. Many employers come to campus in the fall and several employers come to campus in the spring. The most important advice I would recommend would be to do whatever possible to receive high grades—this will dramatically increase your job prospects. Marquette houses the National Sports Law Institute and offers an excellent program in Sports Law. Employment prospects in several areas are adequate as Milwaukee has eight big law firms and only one law school.

Status: Current student, full-time
Dates of Enrollment: 8/2003-Submit Date
Survey Submitted: June 2004

The Career Planning Center in our school has a great staff and will definitely provide help if you seek it. They point people to many different areas of law and sometimes outside of law if the need is there.

Status: Alumnus/a, full-time
Dates of Enrollment: 8/2001-4/2004
Survey Submitted: N/A

The career office does little to assist students not in the top 10 percent. Of these placements, most, if not all, are in the Milwaukee area.

> **Marquette Law says:** The school counters that the overwhelming majority of the efforts of the Career Planning Center (CPC) are devoted to assisting students outside the top 10 percent who commonly are least in need of assistance and often do not utilize the CPC services and resources. Virtually all programming, nearly every edition of the CPC newsletter, and individual student appointments are directed toward the majority. Furthermore, the CPC staff actively engages in alumni outreach on a local, regional and national level to gather information and gain insight to assist the majority as well as to enlist alumni to serve as networking and informational contacts

Read all of Vault's Law School Surveys at www.vault.com/lawschool — get complete surveys on top law schools, expert advice on applicaton essays, LSAT prep and more.

VAULT CAREER LIBRARY 667

for students. This has resulted in the creation of the Alumni Career Assistance Network, a large network of alumni in Wisconsin and throughout the nation who have agreed to serve as informational and networking contacts for students.

The school also points out that the percentage of members of a Marquette graduating class securing employment in Milwaukee reveals that the statement that "most, if not all" placement is in the Milwaukee is not accurate. For the Class of 2004, only 44.8 percent were employed in the Milwaukee area. Similarly, 42.1 percent of the Class of 2003, 43.6 for the Class of 2002 and 43.8 for the Class of 2001 were employed in the Milwaukee area.

Quality of Life

Status: Current student, full-time
Dates of Enrollment: 8/2005-Submit Date
Survey Submitted: April 2006

Marquette University has many new buildings. The aesthetic value of the campus has increased substantially over the past 10 years. I have found Milwaukee to be a great place to live. The current Law School building is a comfortable place to learn. In addition, plans are currently underway to build a brand-new building soon.

Status: Current student, full-time
Dates of Enrollment: 8/2004-Submit Date
Survey Submitted: April 2006

I have lived off campus for my entire law school career. I make a 30-minute commute. The school is located on the edge of the downtown area. Though the undergraduate portion of the school borders some deteriorating neighborhoods, the entire campus is well-patrolled. The Law School is probably in the safest, nicest and (after the freeway construction ends) cleanest area of the school. There are a number of major sports teams nearby (Brewers, Bucks, Admirals, Wave) covering almost the entire year. Within 15 minutes there are museums, a casino, an Olympic ice rink, a major brewery, a mall, several theaters and the lakefront.

Status: Current student, full-time
Dates of Enrollment: 8/2005-Submit Date
Survey Submitted: April 2006

The housing in the area if you want to live alone is from $400 to $900. There are many places that are very close to the law school and do not require a car on campus. There is an abundance of sandwich joints. The neighborhoods are relatively safe, but you should never walk alone any where at night and it is only the campus that is somewhat safe. About seven blocks from the law school are several dangerous areas and it's in your best interest to stay closer to campus. Public Safety Officers are Marquette rent-a-cops that constantly patrol the area and it makes the place a lot safer. If you want to go places at night on or around campus there is a Safe Shuttle service that will get you to and from.

There are two gyms, a Walgreens, small convenient stores and bookstores all on campus. A lot of people live on the East Side, but it's a lot more expensive to live out there. The bus system is pretty good and goes almost anywhere.

Status: Current student, full-time
Dates of Enrollment: 8/2005-Submit Date
Survey Submitted: April 2006

The school is small and kind of feels like a high school (not in a good way), the facilities are terrible, they need new everything. The housing is a plus though because there are nice nearby apartments that house many law students creating a dorm-like atmosphere.

Status: Current student, full-time
Dates of Enrollment: 8/2005-Submit Date
Survey Submitted: April 2006

Housing is somewhat higher-priced here than in other areas of the country, but it is by no means hard to find. There are many apartments, homes and duplexes

for rent. The law school's facilities are good. They have a student lounge with couches, a television, microwave and refrigerator. They also offer lockers to students who need them. The library has two computer labs, making computer access easy for students and there are several study areas in the library and the rest of the law school, generally. The law school is downtown, so crime and safety is an issue, but the university has hired its own Public Safety Officers and a student-led service offers free transportation; I have always felt safe on campus.

Status: Current student, full-time
Dates of Enrollment: 8/2004-Submit Date
Survey Submitted: April 2006

Marquette's motto (for both the university at-large and the law program) is *Cura Personalis* or "Care for the Whole Purpose." The Jesuit identity of the school shapes this concern for the well-being of the whole person and care for one another. No doubt, the challenges of law school are considerable and can be all consuming but the faculty, students and staff of the university are supportive and concerned about the success and well-being of one another.

Housing on campus is very limited for graduate students but there are housing opportunities in the surrounding area. Marquette's security force patrols campus and the surrounding area to ensure the safety of the students—but as with any campus nestled in the heart of a city, students need to mindful of their personal safety. There are pockets of students living all over the city and in all the surrounding suburbs.

Marquette is also undertaking efforts to improve Law School facilities with the addition of a new in-house coffee shop and increased technological connectivity throughout the building and classrooms (including more outlets for laptops and wireless connectivity). But beyond the Law School building, all of the dining and other campus amenities available to the undergraduate population are available for law student use, as well.

Status: Current student, full-time
Dates of Enrollment: 8/2005-Submit Date
Survey Submitted: April 2006

Live off campus. The Marquette campus area is not the nicest. There are plenty of other neighborhoods (like the East Side, Third Ward, downtown, Brady Street area, downtown) that are much nicer, not too expensive and closer to much more of the "fun stuff" in Milwaukee. Do not live in the suburbs, though. It might be cheaper, but you will feel very secluded and lonely!

Status: Current student, full-time
Dates of Enrollment: 8/2001-Submit Date
Survey Submitted: June 2004

Marquette is virtually in downtown Milwaukee. And though efforts have been made to keep the campus safe, incidents happen. Obviously, people need to be aware of their surroundings and just use basic common sense in this area.

As for the Law School facility, at this point, it is too small to house the amount of students it has. There are not enough computers or library space to accommodate all of the students. Most law students are forced into the undergraduate library or other colleges' libraries that are located nearby. Additionally, class space is at a premium, so there is not much room to spread out in classes either. This makes things difficult if you are using a laptop. Very few rooms are equipped to handle a computer for every desk. In every room but two, there are three plugs in the ENTIRE room. First come, first served.

> **The school says:** "Almost all classrooms in the Law School building, Sensenbrenner Hall, are now smart. Additionally, Sensenbrenner Hall is now wireless, allowing for easy access to the Internet from almost anywhere in the building, including all classrooms, study rooms and the Law Library."

Status: Current student, full-time
Dates of Enrollment: 8/2003-Submit Date
Survey Submitted: June 2004

The housing is affordable and you will be able to find a place to stay relatively close to the campus. It is hard to find parking and they ticket very aggressively on campus.

Social Life

Status: Current student, part-time
Dates of Enrollment: 8/2003-Submit Date
Survey Submitted: April 2006

I receive daily e-mails about events, seminars, guest speakers, trips, retreats, get-togethers, bar events and cocktail hours. There is always something to do and people to do it with. Again, as a part-time evening student I occasionally participate as my schedule allows.

Status: Current student, full-time
Dates of Enrollment: 8/2004-Submit Date
Survey Submitted: April 2006

The social life has been fun. The student body is pretty tightly knit. There are a number of nearby bars and there is an organized Bar Review every Thursday. A pretty common hangout is Haggerty's (a nice, one-block walk from the law school after any tough exams). And, about a mile away, Water Street has a number of bars and restaurants. I don't know enough about the dating scene to offer an opinion (I've been dating someone since before law school), but with three colleges in the area, I would imagine that it isn't bad at all.

Status: Current student, full-time
Dates of Enrollment: 8/2005-Submit Date
Survey Submitted: April 2006

Every Thursday the law school hosts a Bar Review. The student board picks a bar for everyone to get together at. The music at these places is annoying; there is never any hip-hop played. The school's social scene is very much like high school. Everyone gossips and knows who's dating whom and what not.

School takes up most of your time, but you still can be social if you manage properly. The Brewers and Bucks games are cheap and close by. There are TONS of different restaurants to eat at and the food is great because there are so many different ethnic types. This place is OK but if you've grown up in a big city your whole life (Chicago, NYC or L.A.) you won't like this blue collar, industrial town.

Status: Current student, part-time
Dates of Enrollment: 8/2003-Submit Date
Survey Submitted: April 2006

Plenty of bars in the area. The best ones are downtown or in the Third Ward, close to the school. Some cool bars include the Safe House (spy theme) and Club Havana (salsa dancing).

Status: Current student, full-time
Dates of Enrollment: 8/2005-Submit Date
Survey Submitted: April 2006

The school has MANY social groups, and one in particular devoted solely to sampling different venues in the city and providing students a chance to interact outside of school. You will never have trouble finding a bar in Brew City. The city itself has lots of restaurants, especially locally owned places, but there are only five or six near campus.

Status: Current student, full-time
Dates of Enrollment: 8/2004-Submit Date
Survey Submitted: April 2006

There is an active student social network at Marquette—including interest-area clubs and activities such as a weekly Bar Review (social gathering of law students at designated bar), Spring Follies, Malpractice Ball and Public Interest Law Society Auctions.

The Milwaukee community has a lot of cultural amenities such as the symphony, ballet and museums—but also continues to live up to its long history as a brew-city with an abundance of bars and breweries throughout the city, many of which are frequented by law students! One particular favorite activity in Milwaukee is the weekly five dollar tours at Lakefront Brewery, a deal that can't be beat since it includes not only a tour and pint glass but free beer as well.

Summertime in Milwaukee is also a welcome reward after the long winter, since the weather is not only beautiful but the city comes alive with an endless series of festivals and celebrations—most notably, Summerfest.

Status: Current student, full-time
Dates of Enrollment: 9/2005-Submit Date
Survey Submitted: February 2006

The social life is interesting. Milwaukee's most popular bars are within walking distance and the school has good promotions on local events, (sporting, concerts, movie tickets). The campus experience has been pleasant. The Law School has plenty of clubs to be a member of. Restaurants within walking distance in the area are decent, but there are excellent restaurants within driving distance of campus. Marquette is not a diverse community. It is one of the more racially segregated campuses I have been on with less than 5 percent minority students. Also, tuition is very high.

> **The schools says:** "In the Law School's fall 2005 first-year class 15 percent of entering students identified themselves as students of color. The Law School's 2005-2006 full-time tuition, $26,176, is in the bottom half of tuition prices among private ABA-accredited law schools in the United States."

 ## The School Says

What comes to mind when you envision law school? Do you expect large, impersonal lectures, cutthroat competition and nights of anxious, isolated study? At Marquette University Law School, you'll find a law school that belies the stereotype. We'll welcome you to our community and provide you with a values-based legal education that is markedly Marquette. At Marquette Law, we affirm our Jesuit heritage by following the principles and practice of *cura personalis*, or care for the whole person. We strive to meet each student's needs by offering a supportive, values-centered education. Marquette's founders were driven by a deep respect for all persons and a passion for social justice. Today, the law school retains their ideals and their commitment to expanding opportunities and serving the community. We develop lawyers who give back to society by helping people and organizations without the means to hire an attorney. We believe attorneys should be true counselors who help resolve conflict and restore harmony. We encourage our students to be not only good lawyers but also good human beings. Marquette Law prepares you to practice wherever you wish, including states that require bar exams. Moreover, graduates who meet course requirements and character and fitness standards are admitted without examination to the practice of law in Wisconsin, thus qualifying for admission as well to the federal courts and for reciprocity privileges in many other states.

Read all of Vault's Law School Surveys at www.vault.com/lawschool — get complete surveys on top law schools, expert advice on applicaton essays, LSAT prep and more.

VAULT CAREER LIBRARY **669**

University of Wisconsin Law School

Admissions Office
University of Wisconsin Law School
975 Bascom Mall
Madison, WI 53706-1399
Admissions phone: (608) 262-5914
Admissions e-mail: admissions@law.wisc.edu
Admissions URL: http://www.law.wisc.edu/prospective/

 ## Admissions

Status: Current student, full-time
Dates of Enrollment: 9/2004-Submit Date
Survey Submitted: October 2005

There is no interview process for admissions. It's much like any other admissions office at any other university. However, once you are accepted, the process becomes more personal. Wisconsin invites admitted students to a banquet they hold in the spring. It's awesome! It really makes the student feel like he's welcome. For a school that admits 275 students a year, it is very personal.

Status: Current student, full-time
Dates of Enrollment: 9/2003-Submit Date
Survey Submitted: September 2005

Wisconsin Law School looks at the applicant as a whole, rather than focusing solely on LSAT scores or grades. The admissions office consistently produces classes of diverse and interesting law students. The dean of admissions actually reads your essay and remembers it when you show up for orientation.

Status: Alumnus/a, full-time
Dates of Enrollment: 8/1998-5/2001
Survey Submitted: January 2005s

The admissions process is pretty standard with an application and essay. There is no interview (or at least there wasn't when I applied). Wisconsin is committed to recruiting and retaining a diverse student population, so including information in your application and essay that emphasizes diversity—be it race, gender, socioeconomic background or work experience—is a very good idea. The GPA/LSAT targets at Wisconsin are on the higher end; they seem to be pretty selective. Also, it is a fact that Wisconsin sets aside a certain percentage of its offers to in-state residents. My advice is, if you are serious about going to Wisconsin, become a resident! In-state tuition is ridiculous, literally a quarter of most law schools. I believe that taking a year or two to work between college and law school is a very good idea. If you do that, get a job in Wisconsin and take advantage of the great deal!

Status: Current student, full-time
Dates of Enrollment: 8/2003-Submit Date
Survey Submitted: October 2004

I found Wisconsin's application fairly tedious in comparison to some other law schools to which I applied. While it was annoying at the time, I think it reflects the fact that Wisconsin seriously considers factors beyond grades and LSAT scores. In terms of the essay, I think it is important to be yourself—that is, I don't think it is a good idea to tell the committee what you think it wants to hear. What they want to hear is what makes you unique. Wisconsin also makes a concerted effort to recruit racial and ethnic minorities.

Status: Current student, full-time
Dates of Enrollment: 9/2003-Submit Date
Survey Submitted: July 2004

The admissions process for the University of Wisconsin Law School is fairly standard. The application includes several essay-style questions. I don't recall there being a face-to-face interview. It is therefore important to try to impart who you are through your essay. I think that the UW is looking for students who are not just bright and have good grades but who also demonstrate commitment to interests outside the law, such as community activism or artistic endeavors.

Status: Current student, full-time
Dates of Enrollment: 9/2003-Submit Date
Survey Submitted: February 2004

The admissions process is basically the same as at every law school. Register with the LSDAS and take the LSAT, then apply. Since this is a state school, there is also an special section if you want to get in-state tuition. If you can qualify at all, definitely try applying as an in-state student. Not only are more WI residents accepted than non-residents, there is a significant savings. If you are designated "non-resident" you WILL NOT be able to change status in later semesters. So if you can get it, get it!

Admissions pays attention to essays and the personal statements (at least they did for me). Several of the admissions staff brought up items from these in our discussions during a campus visit. So, definitely spend some time on this; don't let it be just a "throwaway" part of the application. If it's exceptional (or in any way interesting) then it will get read, and that can't hurt!

Also, the admissions staff is very friendly during the application process, as are the students they have working for them. And once you are in and making your decision, they don't hype or oversell the school, but give you information and just let the school sell itself, which it does wonderfully.

Status: Alumnus/a, full-time
Dates of Enrollment: 8/1999-5/2002
Survey Submitted: April 2004

As with many law schools (or maybe most schools regardless of the academic discipline), good entry test scores are a plus. Although I do not remember much about the application process itself, I know that my general impression at the time—which was confirmed after I began my studies there—was that Wisconsin prided itself on creating a very diverse class of students each year from various backgrounds and walks of life. I can't say whether that differs greatly from other schools, but I can say that it made for a wonderful opportunity to get to know people who had a whole variety of experiences different from mine. So my advice on getting in? Good grades, good test scores, and above all, unique life experiences and interests that will make you stand out in the admissions process.

 ## Academics

Status: Current student, full-time
Dates of Enrollment: 9/2004-Submit Date
Survey Submitted: October 2005

In academics, Wisconsin is very competitive. It is very well regarded for its famous Law and Sociology Contracts professors and its Law in Action Program. This program allows professors to approach classes with a more practical approach that's more applicable to everyday lawyering. One example of this is Wisconsin's Criminal Law Program. It's one of the best and most practical classes at Wisconsin and it is a great example of how professors approach substantive law classes in Wisconsin.

Status: Current student, full-time
Dates of Enrollment: 8/2003-Submit Date
Survey Submitted: October 2004

Academically, I think Wisconsin is fantastic. The classes are fairly small, and the professors are more than willing to provide assistance outside of class, either through office hours or by e-mail. The first-semester classes are fairly Socratic but after that there is more focus on voluntary give and take. Grading is blind, so the only danger with Socratic Method is embarrassment (it will not affect your grade). The workload is overwhelming first semester (as it probably is at most top law schools), but by second semester you have the hang of it.

Status: Alumnus/a, full-time
Dates of Enrollment: 8/1998-5/2001
Survey Submitted: January 2005

The law program is rigorous, but not overly ambitious. The professors are, for the most part, topnotch and sincerely care about giving the students the best possible education. The grading is typically fair (though any system that relies on one grade from one inherently subjective essay exam is a little suspect). I never had a problem getting the classes I wanted. One thing that truly sets Wisconsin apart from other law schools is the incredible amount of clinical opportunities for law students to get hands-on, applicable experience before entering the work world. The Law Review and moot court are also some of the best in the country (in my opinion).

Aside from in-state tuition, the other best thing about going to Wisconsin is the ability to waive into the Wisconsin Bar upon graduation. No bar exam! This means a whole summer off prior to starting work in the fall, or the ability to start at an out-of-state firm already being admitted to practice in one jurisdiction. This is also great if you want to start your career somewhere else and eventually return to Wisconsin.

Status: Current student, full-time
Dates of Enrollment: 9/2003-Submit Date
Survey Submitted: July 2004

The UW has a very strong academic program. The professors are generally approachable, often top in their fields and are sometimes even funny. The classes are, I believe, fairly typical of most law schools in that the Socratic Method is the norm and most grades are based on a final essay exam. The school is fairly flexible in terms of workload. It is up to the student to determine what he/she can handle. It's necessary to get permission, however, before carrying a courseload that is less than full-time.

Status: Alumnus/a, full-time
Dates of Enrollment: 8/1992-5/1995
Survey Submitted: March 2005

The academic key is the "law in action" model—Wisconsin is famed for kind of a law and sociology approach. The core class for first-year students to learn about this approach is Contracts, which bears little relation to the class by that name taught at other schools. Unfortunately, many of the best-known professors have retired. Wisconsin does attract a number of up-and-coming young faculty members who call Madison home for a few years before taking a job in the Ivy League. The school used to have a hard time retaining faculty because it couldn't match salaries being offered by other schools. Workload is tough the first semester of the first year and then eases off afterwards. One class first semester of first year is a small section with about 20 people. The rest are lectures. Most professors used the soft Socratic Method, meaning you'd be called upon but often not at random.

> **The school says:** "Wisconsin has seen a normal pattern of retirement over the past 10 years; nevertheless many of the faculty members who have emeritus status still continue to teach and remain actively involved with students. In addition, new faculty members have been hired to continue both the outstanding scholarship and teaching for which Wisconsin is nationally recognized."

Status: Alumnus/a, full-time
Dates of Enrollment: 8/1999-5/2002
Survey Submitted: April 2004

The academic program was definitely challenging and, in my opinion, first-rate. The courses offered ranged from your standard fare (Torts, Contracts, Criminal Law and so on) to various clinical and seminar courses on a much wider array of topics.

Almost without exception, the professors were excellent and demonstrated a true interest in both the subject matter and the students. After your first year, there were some popular classes that were hard to get into, but usually you could manage to get into them at some point during your second or third year.

Grading was on a curve, so your ultimate grade was in part dependent upon the relative performance of your classmates. And not surprisingly, the workload was heavy, but learning how to balance all of it was part of the overall educational

process as well. In the end, I think the quality and diversity of both the classes and the professors made Wisconsin an excellent place to go to law school.

Status: Current student, full-time
Dates of Enrollment: 9/2003-Submit Date
Survey Submitted: February 2004

The academic program is exceptional. Being in the state capital, many of the professors are lawyers and judges who have experience in both the state and federal government. Indeed, several helped draft the laws they teach!

The first-year curriculum is set for you. First semester is the same for everyone—Torts, Civil Procedure, Substantive Criminal Law, Contracts I and Legal Research and Writing. The whole class is broken into small sections of about 20 to 25 students. One of those classes will be taught with just that section, and that same group is in each of the larger classes. Second semester the small sections are no longer the core, because you get one elective. In addition to Property, Criminal Procedure and Legal Research, you can choose from Constitutional Law I, Contracts II, Advanced Civil Procedure and Legal Process.

One big plus is that Wisconsin is the last state to retain the "diploma privilege" for passing the bar. If you graduate from an accredited school, you do not have to take a bar exam!

> **The school says:** "If you graduate from one of Wisconsin's two law schools, you do not have to take the Wisconsin Bar Exam."

 Employment Prospects

Status: Current student, full-time
Dates of Enrollment: 9/2004-Submit Date
Survey Submitted: October 2005

Wisconsin ranks among the best law schools in the country. Placing at a good firm or desired job should be easy. However, because of its location, students below the top 50 percent should expect to stay in Wisconsin or work at a smaller firm. This is not always true, though, if a student writes on Law Review or gets into moot court, the job hunting stress decreases exponentially.

Status: Alumnus/a, full-time
Dates of Enrollment: 8/1992-5/1995
Survey Submitted: March 2005

When I was there, it wasn't the greatest. The school has a national name but many employers don't make the trek to Madison to interview, meaning you needed to do a lot of work yourself. But all of my friends ended up getting the job they wanted, although it may have been their second job out of school rather than their first. The school is best known in the Midwest with pockets in New York, D.C., Arizona and Northern California, but it does have a national reputation and has graduates everywhere.

Status: Alumnus/a, full-time
Dates of Enrollment: 8/1998-5/2001
Survey Submitted: January 2005

Wisconsin graduates enjoy excellent job prospects upon graduation—if they graduate in the top half (or higher) of their class. The top 10 percent can pretty much go anywhere, including large, prestigious national (and international) firms. A degree from Wisconsin obviously doesn't have the prestige of an Ivy League education, but I have consistently found myself better-prepared and better-equipped than my Ivy League colleagues.

On-campus recruiting is fabulous if you want to stay in Wisconsin or the Midwest, and pretty good if you want to go to the Coasts. Unfortunately, though, in recent years, there have been fewer big firm participants in on-campus interviewing. Wisconsin students are invited to some out-of-state recruiting events, such as a New York recruiting fair where you can interview with firms that don't venture out to Wisconsin (provided the student foots the bill, however). I have not found the alumni network to be particularly effective or helpful, nor have I found the alumni job bank very useful—it's mainly full of ads posted by legal recruiters. But, when I decided to move back to Wisconsin from New York where I started my career at a big firm, the career services people were

Read all of Vault's Law School Surveys at www.vault.com/lawschool — get complete surveys on top law schools, expert advice on applicaton essays, LSAT prep and more.

VAULT CAREER LIBRARY   671

very helpful in passing along information on who was hiring and what the job market was like. They even offered to review my resume.

Status: Alumnus/a, full-time
Dates of Enrollment: 8/1999-5/2002
Survey Submitted: April 2004

Career prospects were arguably somewhat limited coming out of Wisconsin. Since Wisconsin is the only state that does not require a bar exam for admission to the bar (if you go to school at one of the two in-state law schools, take a required core set of course and pass the character and fitness evaluation), a large portion of the graduates stay in-state upon graduation.

The next two closest cities are Chicago and Minneapolis, where most students head to if they want to practice out-of-state. Beyond that, the remainder practice in the smaller communities in Wisconsin. Maybe this isn't as limiting in terms of choices as I perceived it to be, but if you were looking to go anywhere other than these areas, by and large you were on your own. The resources were made available to find law firms in other areas of the country, but Wisconsin usually was not on the list for firms that did not have an office either in-state or in Chicago or Minneapolis.

> **The school says:** "More than half of the students in a typical graduating class practice outside of Wisconsin, accepting jobs in approximately 30 other states each year. Graduates who choose to stay in Wisconsin generally remain in Milwaukee and Madison."

Status: Current student, full-time
Dates of Enrollment: 9/2003-Submit Date
Survey Submitted: July 2004

The Office of Career Services is the main source for job information and opportunities on campus. On-campus interviewing occurs in the fall semester of a student's second year. Most of the firms that come to Wisconsin are regional firms (Minneapolis, Madison/Milwaukee, Chicago) although there are occasionally a few from San Francisco and/or New York. It would be good to see career services expand their contacts for students who are not interested in pursuing work in law firms. Also, career services and professors should have more communication with the students about non-law firm work opportunities and judicial clerkships. The University of Wisconsin is highly regarded locally more than regionally. UW law students who plan to practice outside the Midwest and/or want to go into BigLaw should strive to rank high in their class and get involved in moot court and Law Review.

> **The school says:** "The UW Law School is highly regarded nationally and is considered one of the best public law schools in the country. Students interested in judicial clerkships work with an experienced judicial clerkship advisor. There is also a public interest law coordinator and extensive information for those who are interested in work outside of firms."

 **Quality of Life**

Status: Current student, full-time
Dates of Enrollment: 9/2004-Submit Date
Survey Submitted: October 2005

Mad Town is an awesome town to live in. It's the capital of Wisconsin, and although it's in the middle of the state, it has a very progressive culture. The town has great restaurants and a great party atmosphere. One downside is that the town is very homogenous. There is only a 7 percent minority population in the university as a whole. However, the law school has about a 30 percent minority population, which helps get a glimpse of what life is really like outside of Wisconsin.

Status: Current student, full-time
Dates of Enrollment: 9/2003-Submit Date
Survey Submitted: September 2005

The best place to go to law school. It's relaxing, challenging, and you get to run across the football field at Homecoming (long-standing tradition at UW where

third-year law students run across the field, throw a cane over the goal post, ar if you catch your cane you will win your first case).

Status: Alumnus/a, full-time
Dates of Enrollment: 8/1992-5/1995
Survey Submitted: March 2005

Madison is a great place to spend a few years. Housing is relatively cheap ar plentiful. The campus is beautiful. The Law School, however, isn't; it looks lik someone stuck a large aircraft hanger in the middle of the main quad. The la school is on the main quad rather than being stuck somewhere on the fringe of campus, so you're close to the union and other libraries, as well as downtow Madison.

Status: Alumnus/a, full-time
Dates of Enrollment: 8/1998-5/2001
Survey Submitted: January 2005

Madison has consistently been ranked one of the best places to live in th country for years. It is unbelievably safe and continues to be renovated an beautified (there are some neighborhoods that appear a bit run-down, but it getting better). The Law School was recently remodeled and the facilities ar excellent and centrally located. You have access to all of the trappings of a Bi 10 school—first-rate workout facilities and great sports teams. You also have al of the benefits of having a campus on a lake, with walking and biking path along the lakeshore, canoeing and sailing, and a student union right on the wate

Housing is plentiful, and mostly nice, including a bunch of brand-new apartmer buildings. Housing options are even better if you have a car, a bike or are willin to take public transportation to school (e.g., the bus), but parking is a bit of a issue, so bikes and buses are usually the way to go. Some choice parking lot have waiting lists that are literally years long, including the church across th street from the law school—but it's worth it if you want to drive. Get on the lis when you're a 1L.

Status: Current student, full-time
Dates of Enrollment: 9/2003-Submit Date
Survey Submitted: July 2004

The quality of life is excellent. It's where law school can actually be fun. Th Law School is contained in one building on a hill known as Bascom Hill. Th library has an entire wall of sheer glass. There is also a mural painted on one o the walls in a smaller section of the library. Also, the books smell old and goo In the underground section of the library, there are pictures of all the alumn going way back. I think you can find [Dept. of Health and Human Service Secretary and former Wisconsin Governor] Tommy Thompson in there.

Status: Alumnus/a, full-time
Dates of Enrollment: 8/1999-5/2002
Survey Submitted: April 2004

I found the quality of life to be great. Madison is a wonderful city, with th university campus, the state capital and three beautiful lakes, all of which draw people to the region. I lived off campus, but was able to utilize Madison' excellent public transportation to get to and from school. It is also a fairly sa place to live and inexpensive when compared to other major metropolitan areas

 Social Life

Status: Current student, full-time
Dates of Enrollment: 9/2004-Submit Date
Survey Submitted: October 2005

PARTY PARTY PARTY!!! Wisconsin hosts two of the biggest parties in th nation, Halloween on State Street and the Mifflin Street Block Party. All I hav to say is, I hope you get your reading done before these parties kick off!

> **Wisconsin Law says:** "You can choose to party or not to party. There are many social opportunities here and it is up to the individual student whether or not to participate."

Status: Alumnus/a, full-time
Dates of Enrollment: 8/1992-5/1995
Survey Submitted: March 2005

UW used to be a very social law school; I don't know if it still is. It was one of the few national schools where you could have fun for three years before going off to practice. Even during first-year, everyone went bar-hopping on Thursday nights. The Plaza was always a favorite, as was the Great Dane. You could also always find law students studying and drinking beer on the student union terrace in warm weather (cheap, local microbrew on tap).

Status: Alumnus/a, full-time
Dates of Enrollment: 8/1998-5/2001
Survey Submitted: January 2005

There is a wealth of great places to eat in Madison, with food of every origin and for every palate, from sushi to Nepali to Afgani to beer and bratwurst. There is a big music scene, being a collegetown, and more bars than you could reasonably visit in a semester. The fact that Madison is a collegetown with a medical, business, graduate and law school means that the dating pool is big and active. The annual Dean's Cup event pits the Law School against the medical school in such time-honored events as a pie-eating contest, arm-wrestling, tug-of-war, bar darts and bowling. There are also several cocktail hours held in the law school atrium/courtyard during the year sponsored by student organizations.

A favorite hangout of law students (and undergrads) is the terrace outside Memorial Union where you can sit by Lake Mendota, watch live music and drink beer. Law students also seem to like Luther's Blues, a great place for blues bands and State Street Brats—cheap beer and bratwurst with an outside patio. The Great Dane Brew Pub is also a local favorite, with pool tables inside and garden seating outside. The law school is on Bascom Hill, which is at the west end of State Street (the state capitol is at the east end), so all that State Street has to offer is right there. Nearly every restaurant has outdoor seating in the warmer months.

Status: Current student, full-time
Dates of Enrollment: 9/2003-Submit Date
Survey Submitted: July 2004

Excellent. The students are not snide and sneaky. They generally help one another. The law school has active clubs for non-traditional students and African-American students among other groups.

Status: Alumnus/a, full-time
Dates of Enrollment: 8/1999-5/2002
Survey Submitted: April 2004

When the weather is nice, there is simply no better place to be in Madison than sitting outside on the patio at the student union, overlooking Lake Mendota and having a beer from the Rathskeller (the bar in the Student Union). There are a number of good bars in the campus area (most are located on State Street), and quite a few good restaurants both on and off campus. And parties are always in abundant supply on the weekends.

The School Says

The University of Wisconsin Law School

Top students are drawn to the UW Law School because of its tradition of excellence, its beautiful setting in the heart of one of the world's leading research universities and its law-in-action philosophy—an approach that differentiates it from other law schools.

A commitment to diversity and community

A major indicator of the strength of any law school is its student body. The typical entering class of 270 students represents 30 states and 105 undergraduate institutions. 40 percent are from outside of Wisconsin; 46 percent are women; and 26 percent are students of color. The UW Law School's admissions policies enhance the diversity, vigor, social concern and academic ability of the student community. There is a special feeling of community in the school and an informal, supportive atmosphere.

The faculty: leading scholars and outstanding teachers

The UW Law School's nationally recognized faculty comes from a wide range of backgrounds and offers students strong role models and a variety of experiences. They are leading scholars who are also actively involved in the law. They are interesting lawyers doing interesting things, but first and foremost, they are excellent teachers, committed to their students. Eight professors devote their scholarship and teaching primarily to international or comparative law, and many others integrate analysis of foreign legal developments into their domestic law courses. A superb clinical faculty and an experienced adjunct faculty provide additional teaching resources.

The curriculum: law in action

Students at the UW Law School have many opportunities to explore the curriculum and to develop the lawyering skills they need. The UW Law School is a national law school that prepares students to practice wherever they choose. Students choose courses from an extraordinary breadth and depth of offerings.

Clinicals: hands-on learning

The UW Law School is committed to practical experience as a part of legal education. The Law School has been recognized in national rankings as having one of the best and largest clinical programs in the country. With spots for every student who wants to participate, the UW Law School offers a wide variety of hands-on lawyering experiences with real clients and excellent supervision.

Career opportunities

Leading law firms, government agencies, businesses and public interest organizations seek to hire UW Law School graduates. A broad range of legal employers from many major cities participates recruit Wisconsin students. The law school also participates in nine off-campus job fairs each year, in New York; Washington, D.C.; Los Angeles; Chicago and Minneapolis. Our students receive assistance from some of our more than 12,000 alumni throughout the country. In any given year, half of our graduates accept jobs in almost 30 different states, from New York to California.

Read all of Vault's Law School Surveys at www.vault.com/lawschool — get complete surveys on top law schools, expert advice on applicaton essays, LSAT prep and more.

VAULT CAREER LIBRARY **673**

About the Editor

Carolyn C. Wise is the Education Series Editor at Vault. Born and raised in Brooklyn, NY, she graduated from Princeton University with a degree in English Literature. Carolyn is a volunteer firefighter in Saltaire, NY.

About Vault

Vault is the leading media company for career information. *The Law School Buzz Book* is part of a series of books on educational programs based on surveys of students and alumni. Other titles in the series include *The Business School Buzz Book* and *The College Buzz Book*.

Our team of industry-focused editors takes a journalistic approach in covering news, employment trends and specific employers in their industries. We annually survey 10,000s of employees to bring readers the inside scoop on industries and specific employers. Our guides for law school students and attorneys include the *Vault Guide to the Top 100 Law Firms*, *Vault Guide to Corporate Law Careers*, *Vault Guide to Litigation Law Careers*, *Vault Guide to Labor & Employment Law Careers*, *Vault Guide to the Top New York Law Firms*, *Vault Guide to the Top Washington, DC Law Firms*, *Vault Guide to the Top Southern California Law Firms*, *Vault Guide to the Top Government and Nonprofit Legal Employers* and many more. To see a complete list of Vault's more than 100 career and education titles, go to www.vault.com.

Read all of Vault's law school surveys at **www.vault.com/lawschool** — get complete surveys on more than a hundred law schools, get expert advice on applicaton essays and LSAT prep and more.

V/\ULT CAREER LIBRARY 675